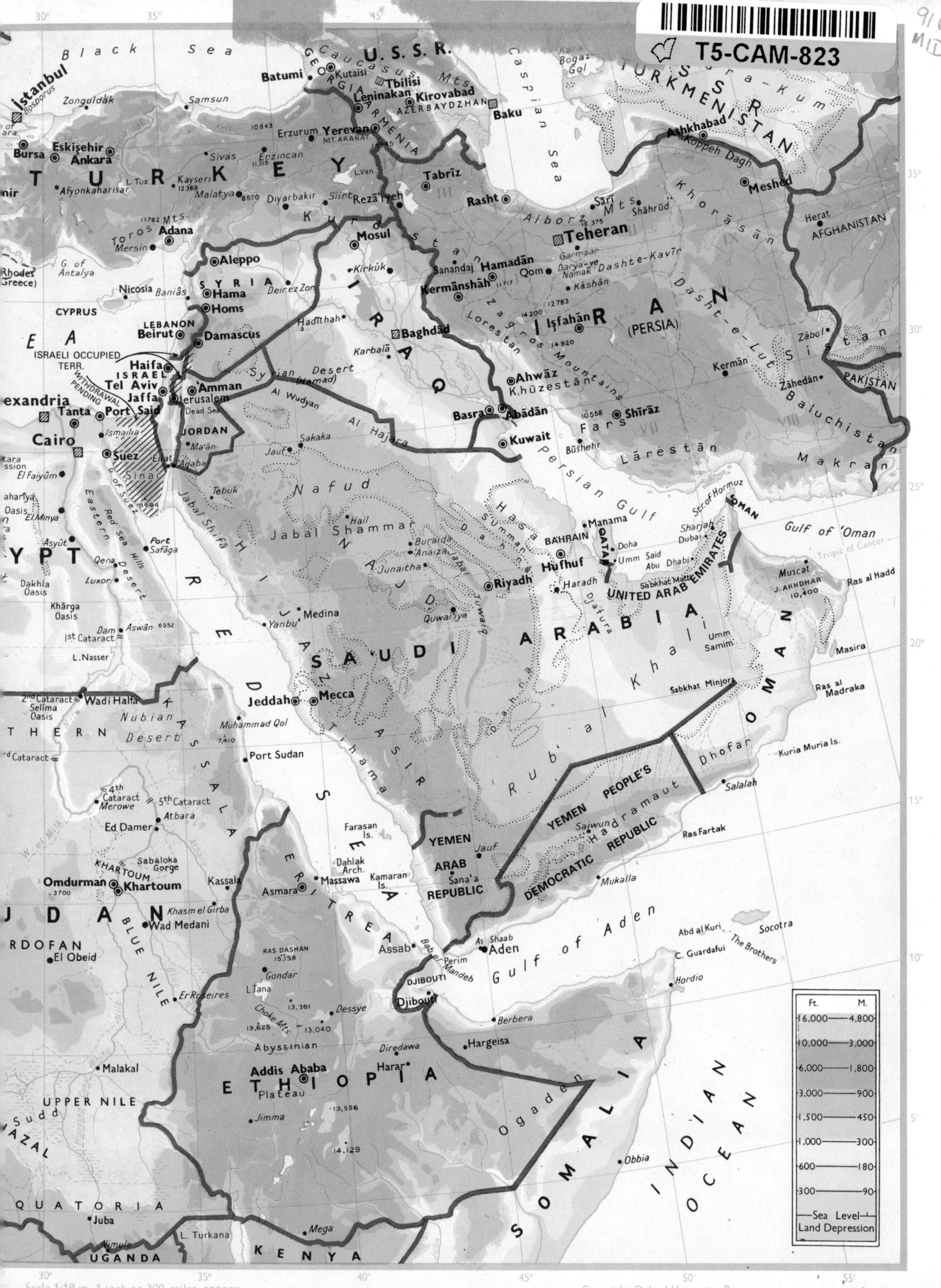

Scale 1:19 m. 1 inch to 300 miles approx.

THE MIDDLE EAST AND NORTH AFRICA

1979-1980

A survey and directory of Afghanistan, Algeria, Bahrain, Cyprus, Egypt, Iran, Iraq, Israel, Jordan, Kuwait, Lebanon, Libya, Morocco, Oman, Qatar, Saudi Arabia, Spanish North Africa, Sudan, Syria, Tunisia, Turkey, United Arab Emirates, Yemen Arab Republic and Yemen People's Democratic Republic.

THE MIDDLE EAST AND NORTH AFRICA

1979-80

TWENTY-SIXTH EDITION

EUROPA PUBLICATIONS LIMITED
18 BEDFORD SQUARE LONDON WC1B 3JN

26th Edition 1979

AUSTRALIA AND NEW ZEALAND
James Bennett (Collaroy) Pty. Ltd., Collaroy, N.S.W., Australia

INDIA
UBS Publishers' Distributors Pvt. Ltd., P.O.B 1882, 5 Ansari Road, Daryaganj, Delhi 6

JAPAN
Maruzen Co. Ltd., 6 Tori-Nichome, Nihonbashi, Tokyo 103

Library of Congress Catalog Card Number 48-3250

British Library Cataloguing in Publication Data
The Midlde East and North Africa 1979–80
1. Near East—Yearbooks 2. Africa, North—Yearbooks
956'. 04'05 DS41 48-3250
ISBN 0-905118-38-3
ISSN 0076-8502

Printed and bound in England by
Staples Printers Rochester Limited
at The Stanhope Press.

Foreword

As Professor W. B. Fisher has pointed out in his survey of the past year in the Middle East, two items have dominated the area since the appearance of the last edition of The Middle East and North Africa. The first was the revolution in Iran, which reached its climax in early 1979, and the second was the signing of the peace treaty between Egypt and Israel in March 1979. Both these events have had their repercussions on political alignments in other parts of the Middle East and upon the world energy situation. The relationship between Middle Eastern oil and the current world energy crisis is fully dealt with by Michael Field in his article on 'Oil in the Middle East and North Africa', which describes the position up to and including the OPEC meeting in Geneva and the Tokyo energy summit held by the seven major industrial democracies in late June 1979.

Once again we would like to thank the numerous individuals and organizations who have sent us both revised and new information for inclusion in this edition of The Middle East and North Africa. Without their assistance the book could not have become a recognized authority on the region.

August 1979.

Acknowledgements

We express our thanks for much help and information kindly supplied by many Foreign Ministries and National Statistical Offices and by the following embassies and other bodies.

Afghan Embassy, London
Algerian Embassy, London
Arab League
Arabian American Oil Company
Bahrain Embassy, London
Bank Markazi Iran
British Embassy, Kuwait
Central Bank of Yemen
Cyprus High Commission, London
French Embassy, London
Information Center on Eastern Arabia, Belgium
Institute of Petroleum Information Service, London
Iranian Embassy, London
Iraqi Embassy, London
Israel Embassy, London
Jordan Embassy, London
Kuwait Embassy, London
Kuwait Oil Company
Lebanese Embassy, London
Libyan Embassy, London
MEED Arab Report
Middle East Economic Digest
National Bank of Egypt, Cairo
National Iranian Oil Company
Moroccan Embassy, London
Oman Embassy, London
Organization of Arab Petroleum Exporting Countries (OAPEC)
Organization of Petroleum Exporting Countries (OPEC)
Palestine Liberation Organization, Beirut
Qatar Embassy, London
Regional Co-operation for Development
Saudi Arabian Embassy, London
Saudi Arabian Monetary Agency, Jeddah
Spanish Embassy, London
Sudanese Embassy, London
Syrian Embassy, London
Suez Canal Authority, Ismailia
Tunisian Embassy, London
Turkish Embassy, London
Embassy of the United Arab Emirates, London
United Nations Information Centre, London
United Nations Economic Commission for Africa
United Nations Economic Commission for Western Asia
United Nations Relief and Works Agency for Palestine Refugees in the Near East
Embassy of the Yemen Arab Republic, London
Embassy of the Yemen People's Democratic Republic, London

We also acknowledge with thanks the co-operation of the International Institute for Strategic Studies, 23 Tavistock Street, London, WC2E 7NQ, in permitting us to use data on defence manpower and finance from *The Military Balance 1978–1979*, and the Israel Embassy, London, for the use of two maps of the disengagement agreements between Israel and Egypt (1974) and Israel and Syria.

Contents

PART ONE
General Survey

PART TWO
Regional Organizations

PART THREE
Country Surveys

PART FOUR
Other Reference Material

Maps

Abbreviations

A .. .. Ambassador
AAHO .. Afro-Asian Housing Organization
AAPSO .. Afro-Asian People's Solidarity Organization
Acad. .. Academy
accred. .. accredited
AD .. .. Algerian Dinars
A.D.C. .. Aide-de-camp
Admin. .. Administrative; Administration; Administrator
Admin.-Gen. Administrator-General
ADMA .. Abu Dhabi Marine Areas
ADOCO .. Abu Dhabi Oil Company
ADPC .. Abu Dhabi Petroleum Company
AfDB .. African Development Bank
Afs... .. Afghanis
AIWO .. Agudath Israel World Organization
ALF .. Arab Liberation Front
ALN .. Armée de Libération Nationale (National Liberation Army of Algeria)
Amb. .. Ambassador
AMINOIL .. American Independent Oil Company
AMOSEAS .. American Overseas Petroleum Ltd.
AOC .. Arabian Oil Company
AOF .. Afrique Occidentale Française (French West Africa)
API .. .. American Petroleum Institute
approx. .. approximately
apptd. .. appointed
A.R. .. Arab Republic
Aramco .. Arabian-American Oil Company
A.R.E. .. Arab Republic of Egypt
ARGAS .. Arabian Geophysical Survey Company
ASFEC .. Regional Centre for Functional Literacy in Rural Areas for the Arab States
Ass... .. Assembly
Asscn. .. Association
Assoc. .. Associate
Asst. .. Assistant
ATAS .. Anatolian Refinery Company
ATUC .. African Trade Union Confederation
AUA .. Austrian Airlines
AUXERAP Société Auxiliaire de la Régie du Pétrole
Ave. .. Avenue

b. .. .. born
B.A. .. Bachelor of Arts
BADEA .. Banque Arabe de Développement Economique en Afrique (Arab Bank for Economic Development in Africa)
BAPCO .. The Bahrain Petroleum Company Ltd.
bbl(s). .. barrel(s)
BD .. .. Bahrain Dinars
Bd. .. .. Board
Bde. .. Brigade
B.Lit(t). .. Bachelor of Letters
Blvd. .. Boulevard
B.P. .. Boîte Postale (Post Office Box)
BP .. .. British Petroleum
BPC . .. Basrah Petroleum Company
br(s). .. branch(es)
B.Sc. .. Bachelor of Science
B.S.T. .. British Standard Time
BUSHCO .. Bushire Petroleum Company

CA .. .. Chargé d'Affaires
CAFRAD .. Centre Africain de Formation et de Recherches Administratives pour le Développement
CAMEL .. Compagnie Algérienne du Methane Liquid
cap... .. capital
Capt. .. Captain
CARE .. Co-operative for American Relief Everywhere
CENTO .. Central Treaty Organization
CEP .. Compagnie d'Exploration Pétrolière
CEPT .. Conférence Européenne des Administrations des Postes et des Télécommunications
CFP .. Compagnie Française des Pétroles
Chair. .. Chairman
Cie. .. Compagnie (Company)
c.i.f... .. cost, insurance, freight
C.-in-C. .. Commander-in-Chief
Co. .. .. Company
Comm. .. Commission
Commdr. .. Commander
Commdt. .. Commandant
Commr. .. Commissioner
Conf. .. Conference
Contrib. .. Contributor; Contribution
COPE .. Compagnie Orientale des Pétroles
COPEFA .. Compagnie des Pétroles France-Afrique
Corpn. .. Corporation
CPA .. Compagnie des Pétroles d'Algérie
CREPS .. Compagnie de Recherches et d'Exploration de Pétrole du Sahara
CRNA .. National Council of the Algerian Revolution
CRUA .. Revolutionary Council for Unity and Action (now FLN)
ČSA .. .. Československé Aerolinie
Cttee. .. Committee

Del. .. .. Delegate; Delegation
Dem. .. Democratic
D. en D. .. Docteur en Droit
dep... .. deposits
Dept. .. Department
Devt. .. Development
Dir... .. Director
Div... .. Division
DPA .. Deutsche Presse-Agentur
Dr. .. .. Doctor
DUP .. Democratic Unionist Party (Sudan)
d.w... .. dead weight

ECOSOC .. Economic and Social Council (UN)
ECWA .. Economic Commission for Western Asia
ed. .. .. Educated
Edn. .. Edition
Educ. .. Education
EEC .. European Economic Community
EFTA .. European Free Trade Association
EOKA .. National Organization of the Struggle for Freedom of Cyprus
ERAP .. Entreprise des Recherches et d'Activités Pétrolières
est. .. .. estimate(d)
excl. .. excluded; excluding
Exec. .. Executive
Extra. .. Extraordinary

f. .. .. founded
FAO .. Food and Agriculture Organization
FCM .. Federation of Muslim Councillors
Fed. .. Federation; Federal

FFS.. .. Socialist Forces Front
FIDES .. Fonds d'Investissement pour le Développement Economique et Sociale de la France d'Outre-Mer
FLN .. Front de Libération Nationale (National Liberation Front)
FLOSY .. Front for the Liberation of Occupied South Yemen
fmr... .. former
f.o.b. .. free on board
ft. .. feet; foot

gal. .. .. gallons
GDA .. Gas Distribution Administration
G.D.P. .. Gross Domestic Product
Gen. Man. .. General Manager
GFCM .. General Fisheries Council for the Mediterranean
G.H.Q. .. General Headquarters
G.M.T. .. Greenwich Mean Time
G.N.P. .. Gross National Product
G.O.C.-in-C. General Officer Commanding-in-Chief
Gov. .. Governor
Govt. .. Government
GPRA .. Gouvernement Provisoire de la République Algérienne (Provisional Government of the Republic of Algeria)
GUPCO .. Gulf of Suez Petroleum Company

ha. .. hectares
H.E. .. His Eminence; His Excellency
H.I.M. .. His Imperial Majesty
Hist. .. Historical
H.M. .. His (or Her) Majesty
Hon. .. Honourable; Honorary
HOPECO .. Hormoz Petroleum Company
H.Q. .. Headquarters

IAEA .. International Atomic Energy Authority
IATA .. International Air Transport Association
IBRD .. International Bank for Reconstruction and Development
ICAO .. International Civil Aviation Organization
ICATU .. International Conference of Arab Trade Unions
ICFTU—AFRO .. International Confederation of Free Trade Unions—African Regional Organization
ICOO .. Iraqi Company for Oil Operations
IDA .. International Development Association
IFC.. .. International Finance Corporation
ILO.. .. International Labour Organization
IMF .. International Monetary Fund
IMINOCO .. Iranian Marine International Oil Company
Inc... .. Incorporated
incl... .. included; including
Ind... .. Independent
INPECO .. Iran Nippon Petroleum Company
Insp. .. Inspector
Inst. .. Institute; Institution
Int... .. International
INOC .. Iraq National Oil Company
IOP.. .. Iranian Oil Participants
IPAC .. Iran-Pan American Oil Company
IPC.. .. Iraq Petroleum Company
IPO.. .. Iranian Plan Organization
IRCAN .. Iran Canada Oil Company
IROPCO .. Iranian Offshore Petroleum Company
ITU.. .. International Telecommunications Union

JAL .. Japan Airlines
JAT .. Jugoslovenski Aerotransport

kg. .. .. kilogram
KFAED .. Kuwait Fund for Arab Economic Development
kl. .. .. kilolitre
KLM .. Koninklijke Luchtvaart Maatschappij NV
km. .. .. kilometres
KNPC .. Kuwait National Petroleum Company
KOC .. Kuwait Oil Company
KSPC .. Kuwait Spanish Petroleum Company
kWh. .. kilowatt

L .. .. Legation
LAPCO .. Lavan Petroleum Company
lb. .. .. pounds (weight)
LINOCO .. Libyan National Oil Corporation
LL.B. .. Bachelor of Laws
LN .. .. League of Nations
LOT .. Polskie Linie Lotnicze
Ltd... .. Limited

M .. Minister
m. .. .. million
M.A. .. Master of Arts
Maj. .. Major
Maj.-Gen. .. Major-General
Malev .. Magyar Légyar Légiköz-lekedési Vállalat
Man. .. Manager; Managing
M.B.E. .. Member of the (Order of the) British Empire
M.D. .. Doctor of Medicine
MEA .. Middle Eastern Airlines
Mem(s). .. Member(s)
MEOC .. Middle East Oil Company
Mgr. .. Monseigneur; Monsignor
Mil. .. Military
Min. .. Minister; Ministry
MNA .. Mouvement Nationale Algérienne (Algerian National Movement)
M.P. .. Member of Parliament
MPC .. Mosul Petroleum Company
MRP .. Mouvement Républicain Populaire
M.Sc. .. Master of Science
MSS. .. Manuscripts
MTA .. Mineral Research and Exploration Institute of Turkey
MTLD .. Mouvement au Triomphe des Libertés Démocratiques (Movement for the Triumph of Democratic Liberties in Algeria)

n.a. .. not available
Nat. .. National
NATO .. North Atlantic Treaty Organization
NDRC .. National Defence Research Council
NECCCRW .. Near East Christian Council Committee for Refugee Work
n.e.s. .. not elsewhere specified
n.i.e. .. not included elsewhere
NIOC .. National Iranian Oil Company
NLF .. National Liberation Front (People's Democratic Republic of Yemen)
no. .. .. number
NUP .. National Unionist Party (Sudan)
N.Y. .. New York (City)

OAPEC .. Organization of Arab Petroleum Exporting Countries
OAS .. Secret Army Organization (Algeria)
OAU .. Organization for African Unity
O.B.E. .. Officer of the (Order of the) British Empire
OCAM .. Organisation Commune Africaine, Malgache et Mauricienne

OCRA .. Clandestine Organization of the Algerian Revolution
OECD .. Organisation for Economic Co-operation and Development
ORP .. Organisation de la Résistance Populaire (Organization of Popular Resistance in Algeria)
OPEC .. Organization of Petroleum Exporting Countries

Parl. .. Parliament; Parliamentary
PDFLP .. Popular Democratic Front for the Liberation of Palestine
PDO .. Petroleum Development Oman
PDP .. People's Democratic Party (Sudan)
PDR .. People's Democratic Republic
PEGUPCO .. Persian Gulf Petroleum Company
Perm. .. Permanent
Perm. Del. .. Permanent Delegate
Perm. Rep .. Permanent Representative
PFLO .. Popular Front for the Liberation of Oman
PFLP .. Popular Front for the Liberation of Palestine
Ph.D. .. Doctor of Philosophy
PIA .. Pakistan International Airlines
PLA .. Palestine Liberation Army
PLO .. Palestine Liberation Organization
P.O.B. .. Post Office Box
Pres. .. President
Prof. .. Professor
Prop. .. Proprietor
PSD .. Parti Socialiste Destourien (Tunisia)
PPA .. Parti des Peuples Algériennes (Party of the Algerian People)
P.R. .. People's Republic
p.u. .. .. paid up
Publ(s). .. Publication(s)

QPC .. Qatar Petroleum Company

R.A.F. .. Royal Air Force
RCC .. Revolutionary Command Council (Libya)
RCD .. Regional Co-operation for Development
Rd. .. Road
RDA .. Rassemblement Démocratique Africain
reg. .. .. registered
Rep. .. Representative; Represented
resgnd. .. resigned
retd. .. retired
R.P. .. Révérend Père (Reverend Father)
RPP .. Republican People's Party
Rt. Hon. .. Right Honourable
Rt. Rev. .. Right Reverend

SAS .. .. Scandinavian Airlines System
SCAP .. Supreme Command Allied Powers
SDF .. Sudan Defence Force
Sec. .. .. Secretary
Sec.-Gen. .. Secretary-General
SEHR .. Société d'Exploitation des Hydrocarbons de Hassi—R'Mel
SIRIP .. Société Irano-Italienne des Pétroles
SNPA .. Société Nationale des Pétroles d'Aquitaine
SNREPAL .. Société Nationale de Recherche et d'Exploitation des Pétroles en Algérie
Soc. .. .. Society; Société
SOFIRAN .. Société Française des Pétroles d'Iran

SONATRACH Société Nationale pour la Recherche, la Production, la Transformation et la Commercialisation des Hydrocarbures
SOPEG .. Société Pétrolière de Gérance
Sq. .. .. Square
St. .. .. Street

TAL .. Trans-Alpine Line
Tapline .. Trans-Arabian Pipeline Company
TAROM .. Transporturile Aeriene Române
THY .. Türk Hava Yollari
TMA .. Trans Mediterranean Airways
TPAO .. Turkish Petroleum Corporation
trans. .. translated; translation
TRAPES .. Société de Transport de Pétrole de l'Est Saharien
TRAPSA .. Compagnie de Transport par Pipe-line au Sahara
TWA .. Trans World Airlines

U.A.E. .. United Arab Emirates
U.A.R. .. United Arab Republic
UBAF .. Union des Banques Arabes et Françaises
UDMA .. Union Démocratique du Manifeste Algérienne (Democratic Union of the Algerian Manifesto)
UGTA .. Union Générale des Travailleurs Algériens (Algerian General Workers Union)
U.K. .. United Kingdom
UN .. .. United Nations
UNDOF .. United Nations Disengagement Observation Force
UNDP .. United Nations Development Programme
UNEA .. Union National des Etudiants Algériennes (National Union of Algerian Students)
UNEF .. United Nations Emergency Force
UNESCO .. United Nations Educational, Scientific and Cultural Organization
UNFICYP .. United Nations Peace-Keeping Force in Cyprus
UNFP .. Union National des Forces Populaires (National Union of Popular Forces in Morocco)
UNICEF .. United Nations International Children's Emergency Fund
UNIFIL .. United Nations Interim Force in Lebanon
Univ. .. University
UNMEM .. United Nations Middle East Mission
UNRWA .. United Nations Relief and Works Agency for Palestine Refugees in the Near East
UNTSO .. United Nations Truce Supervision Organization
UPAF .. Union Postale Africaine (African Postal Union)
U.P. .. University Press
UPI .. .. United Press International
U.S.A. (U.S.) United States of America (United States)
USIS .. United States Information Services
U.S.S.R. .. Union of Soviet Socialist Republics
UTA .. Union de Transports Aériens

vols. .. volumes
VSO .. Voluntary Service Overseas Limited

WEPCO .. Western Desert Petroleum Company
WFTU .. World Federation of Trade Unions
WHO .. World Health Organization

TRANSCRIPTION OF ARABIC NAMES

The Arabic language is used over a vast area. Though the written language and the script are standard throughout the Middle East, the spoken language and also the pronunciation of the written signs show wide variation from place to place. This is reflected, and even exaggerated, in the different transcriptions in use in different countries. The same words, names and even letters will be pronounced differently by an Egyptian, a Lebanese, or an Iraqi—they will be heard and transcribed differently by an Englishman, a Frenchman, or an Italian. There are several more or less scientific systems of transliteration in use, sponsored by learned societies and Middle Eastern governments, most of them requiring diacritical marks to indicate Arabic letters for which there are no Latin equivalents.

Arabic names occurring in the historical and geographical sections of this book have been rendered in the system most commonly used by British and American Orientalists, but with the omission of the diacritical signs. For the convenience of the reader, these are explained and annotated below. The system used is a transliteration—i.e. it is based on the writing, which is standard throughout the Arab world, and not on the pronunciation, which varies from place to place. In a few cases consistency has been sacrificed in order to avoid replacing a familiar and accepted form by another which, though more accurate, would be unrecognisable.

Consonants:

- d — represents two Arabic letters. The second, or emphatic *d*, is transliterated *ḍ*. It may also be represented, for some dialects, by *dh* and by *z*, e.g. Qāḍī, qadhi, qazi.
- dh — in literary Arabic and some dialects pronounced like English *th* in *this*. In many dialects pronounced *z* or *d*.
- gh — A strongly guttural *g*—sometimes written *g*, e.g. Baghdād, Bagdad.
- h — represents two Arabic letters. The second, more guttural *h*, is transliterated *ḥ*, e.g. Husain, Husein.
- j — as English *j* in *John*, also represented by *dj* and *g*. In Egypt this letter is pronounced as a hard *g*, and may be thus transcribed (with *u* before *e* and *i*), e.g. Najib, Nadjib, Nagib, Naguib, Neguib.
- kh — as *ch* in Scottish *loch*, also sometimes represented by *ch* and *h*, e.g. Khalīl, Chalil, Halil.
- q — A guttural *k*, pronounced farther back in the throat. Also transcribed *ḳ*, *k*, and, for some dialects, *g*, e.g. Waqf, Wakf, Wakf, Wagf.
- s — represents two Arabic letters. The second, emphatic *s*, is transliterated *ṣ*. It may also be represented by *ç*, e.g. Sāliḥ, Saleh, Çaleh.
- t — represents two Arabic letters. The second, emphatic *t*, is transliterated *ṭ*.
- th — in literary Arabic and some dialects pronounced as English *th* in *through*. In many dialects pronounced *t* or *s*, e.g. Thābit, Tabit, Sabit.
- w — as in English, but often represented by *ou* or *v*, e.g. Wādī, Vadi, Oued.
- z — represents two Arabic letters. The second, or emphatic *z*, is transliterated *ẓ*. It may also be represented, for some dialects, by *dh* or *d*, e.g. Hāfiẓ, Hafidh, Hafid.
- ' — A glottal stop, as in Cockney *'li'l bo'ls'*. May also represent the sound transliterated ', a deep guttural with no English equivalent.

Vowels

The Arabic script only indicates three short vowels, three long vowels, and two diphthongs, as follows:

- a — as in English *hat*, and often rendered *e*, e.g. balad, beled, emir, amir; with emphatics or gutturals usually pronounced as *u* in *but*, e.g. Khalīfa, Baghdād.
- i — as in English *bit*. Sometimes rendered *e*, e.g. jihād, jehād.
- u — as in English *good*. Often pronounced and written *o* e.g. Muḥammad, Mohammad.

In some Arabic dialects, particularly those of North Africa, unaccented short vowels are often omitted altogether, and long vowels shortened, e.g. Oued for Wādī, bled for balad, etc.

- ā — Long *a*, variously pronounced as in *sand*, *dart* and *hall*.
- ī — As *ee* in *feet*. In early books often rendered *ee*.
- ū — As *oo* in *boot*. The French transcription *ou* is often met in English books, e.g. Mahmūd, Mahmood, Mahmoud.
- ai — Pronounced in classical Arabic as English *i* in *hide*, in colloquial Arabic as *a* in *take*. Variously transcribed as *ai*, *ay*, *ei*, *ey* and *ê*, e.g. sheikh, shaikh, shaykh, etc.
- aw — Pronounced in classical Arabic as English *ow* in *town*, in colloquial Arabic as in *grow*. Variously rendered *aw*, *ew*, *au*, *ô*, *av*, *ev*, e.g. Tawfīq, Taufiq, Tevfik, etc.

TURKISH ORTHOGRAPHY AND PRONUNCIATION

Turkish has been written in Roman characters since 1928. The following pronunciations are invariable:

- c — hard *j*, as in *majority*, *jam*.
- ç — *ch*, as in *church*.
- g — hard *g*, as in *go*, *big*.
- ğ — not voiced, or pronounced *y*; Ereğli is pronounced *erayly*.
- ı — short vowel, as the second vowel of *'centre'*, or French *'le'*.
- i — *i* sound of *Iran*, *bitter* (NOT as in *bite*, *might*).
- o — *o*, as in *hot*, *boss*.
- ö — *i* sound of *'birth'*, or French *'oeuvre'*.
- u — as in *do*, *too*, German *'um'*.
- ü — as in *burette*, German *'Hütte'*.

The Year in the Middle East—June 1978-79

W. B. Fisher

Within a twelve-month more crowded than usual with serious events—even by Middle Eastern standards—two matters stand out as exceptional and dominant. These are the revolution in Iran, resulting in the withdrawal of the Shah and establishment of an Islamic Republic; and the signing of a peace treaty between Egypt and Israel. Besides these two highly remarkable developments, there have also been serious unrest throughout the year in Afghanistan, acute economic crisis in Turkey, the death of President Boumedienne of Algeria and significant shifts of policy involving Saudi Arabia, Iraq and Syria, Libya and Sudan. Unrest, intermittent civil strife and attacks by outsiders, particularly Israelis, continue in Lebanon, where the melancholy story of civil disturbance and irregular flare-ups of fighting between rival groups still continues.

A year ago, the present writer alluded to the "sustained challenge" to the authority of Shah Mohammad Reza Pahlavi of Iran. During July and August 1978 demonstrations continued, first in Mashad and Hamadan only, then at a greater intensity and more widely spread, leading early the following month to declaration of martial law in 12 Iranian cities. On August 14th there had been nearly 400 deaths when a cinema in Abadan was set on fire: by revolutionaries according to the Government, by *provocateurs* according to left-wing sources. On September 9th troops opened fire on a Teheran crowd that had refused to disperse, killing over 120 persons; the next day President Jimmy Carter announced United States support for the Shah, and the proposed sale of military equipment, including fighter aircraft. A devastating earthquake at Tabas on September 16th temporarily drew national attention away from the political scene, since some 16,000 to 20,000 deaths occurred; but recrimination developed over the speed and efficiency of rescue and rehabilitation attempts by the central government. Strike action began in September at the oil installations in Khuzestan, at first over pay and conditions, but gradually the strikers' aims took on a more directly political aspect. October 6th saw the move of a prominent, though as yet hardly dominant, opponent of the Shah—the Ayatollah Ruhollah Khomeini—from a 14-year exile in Najaf, Iraq, to a new location at Neauphle-le-Château, near Paris. Four days later President Carter reaffirmed U.S. support of the Shah.

By the end of the month the situation was extremely serious for the Iranian Government. Strike action had spread to most state organizations including Iran Air; and there were protest demonstrations in some 40 towns—some, however, in favour of the Shah's Government. Oil production was threatened with complete stoppage, and the essential services—utilities, communications, banking and administration—began to be severely curtailed. On October 31st President Carter once more affirmed his support of the Shah and the Iranian Government.

November saw a considerable change in governmental attitudes. The Minister of Higher Education and Science had resigned (October 17th) in protest over the government's inability to deal with now rapidly growing inflation; and during November several thousand demonstrators who had been imprisoned some weeks earlier were released, with amnesties also offered to dissidents abroad. Among those released from imprisonment was the Ayatollah Talleganji, a well-known but moderate opponent of the Shah. Dismissals of prominent officers of SAVAK (the security police) were also announced. This appearance of flinching and retreat on the part of the Government encouraged especially fierce rioting on November 8th and 9th. In Teheran several governmental buildings and part of the British Embassy were set on fire; whilst earlier El Al's Teheran office had been destroyed—a significant explosion of anti-Israeli feeling that was to develop further over the next few months—and the Shah responded by dismissing Jaafar Sharif-Emami's Government, in office only since August, and replacing it by a military Cabinet headed by Gen. Gholamreza Azhari. A former Prime Minister and Minister of the Court, Amir Abbas Hoveida, was arrested on unspecified charges, and the Shah agreed to open an investigation into the sources of wealth of the royal family—both as sops to public opinion. In the middle of the month yet more severe disturbances, accentuated by power cuts due to strikes, occurred in several towns; and while the new Prime Minister, Gen. Azhari, announced that he, not the Shah, was responsible for the conduct of affairs, the Shah himself spoke of remaining on the throne in order to avoid the disturbances that would follow any abdication. On November 26th a one-day general strike in opposition to the Shah brought most cities, including Teheran, to a virtual halt; and from Paris the Ayatollah Khomeini proclaimed a campaign of civil disobedience to begin on December 2nd, the start of the Islamic year. This act caused the French Foreign Minister to warn the Ayatollah not to undertake political activity whilst resident in France—a warning to be repeated with little or no effect several times in the next few weeks. Proclamation by the Iranian Government of a ban on processions, and imposition of a curfew, were increasingly ignored, with scores of deaths resulting from clashes in several cities between troops, police and demonstrators. On December 5th the Ayatollah advocated the use of arms directly against the Shah and his Government, and soon after began to threaten those Western nations which supported the Shah with future loss of oil supplies. By this time the difficulties of general living, shutdown of much production and rising xenophobia had led to a massive exodus by expatriate workers and their families. A government ban on all demonstrations by any group, and a military takeover of the oil installations (which temporarily raised production for a short time), were countered by a call by the Ayatollah Khomeini for another general strike on December 18th. During this strike, a section of the army in Tabriz mutinied and went over to the demonstrators—the first major identifiable defection of its kind.

Events were now coming to show some slight similarity to those in the Russia of early 1917. On January 4th, 1979, the Shah appointed as his fourth Prime Minister in five months, Dr. Shapour Bakhtiar, who immediately invited the Ayatollah Khomeini to return to Iran; not in a sealed train, but in fact, as did occur later, by special aircraft provided by Air France. After a further week of uncertainty and unrest, it became known that United States political leaders were advising the Shah to quit Iran. This he did on January 16th, leaving a Regency Council to oversee affairs. At the same time the Ayatollah Khomeini announced that he himself would soon return in order to set up a provisional government in replacement of that headed by Dr. Bakhtiar, despite an appeal by President Carter that he should co-operate with Dr. Bakhtiar. True to his word, the Ayatollah arrived in Teheran on February 1st with the acquiescence of the Bakhtiar Government that was now wholly uncertain about the loyalty of the armed forces. On February 5th a rival Republican government was announced under the Prime Ministership of Dr. Mehdi Bazargan. Dr. Bakhtiar at first refused to withdraw but, faced with street demonstrations in favour of the Ayatollah Khomeini's nominee, did so on February 11th, leaving the Ayatollah and Dr. Bazargan in joint control of a Republican Iran. By February 13th the United Kingdom, the U.S.S.R. and most Arab States had recognized this new government, followed by the U.S.A. on February 16th.

We may ask at this juncture: how could all this happen and so rapidly? The answer seems to be that the Shah pushed modernity and development too quickly and became insensitive and detached from almost all sections of society. His Government was not noticeably more corrupt or more cruel and overbearing than many others in Africa or Asia, though his system of rule was much more pervasive and, in many respects, efficient. There was a strong determination to achieve high political status and greatly improved economic levels, and a ruthless drive for objectives determined by the Shah himself rather than through any process of democratic consultation. These aims were often commendable and in the best interests of Iran, had they not been pushed too far too fast, with resulting inefficiency waste and unnecessary "prestige projects". There was no subversion or underground movement from leftist groups—which followed rather than influenced events, nor was there real scarcity or shortage of food. Such foreign intervention as occurred was merely inept; and the U.S.S.R. appears to have played little or no part in reacting to events with certainly no overt influence apparent.

Why did the Shah fall? Alienation, particularly of those groups who gained most from his policies: the new affluent middle class who did nothing in support of a system that had given them very much; the old landowners earlier affected by land reform remained aloof and apart. Second, there was a deep and rising tide of fundamentalist Islam, a factor that was of very recent growth but extremely important. Such fundamentalists were scandalized and repelled by the rapid and insensitive rush to Westernization, and by blatant displays of wealth and materialism. Then the ruthless control of opinion and, in late years, the operations of SAVAK further alienated most Iranians, who are very sensitive over the loss of self-expression. The country had become markedly richer, not poorer (though the new wealth was distributed unequally). Revulsion, rather than any economic and political difficulties, underlay the loss of power by the Shah.

Since February 1979 the new leaders of Iran have had to deal with four major problems, three of which have been serious separatist insurrectional movements. A Turkoman uprising occurred at Gonbad, in the Caspian area; and there have been Kurdish demands for some measure of autonomy, with armed Iraqi intervention on one or two occasions that have led to strained relations between the two governments. Most serious, however, is Arab separatism in the Khuzestan oilfields: here some two million people could be involved and the economic "leverage" is obviously very great. The other problem is a struggle for power within the new ruling groups. The Prime Minister, Dr. Bazargan, increasingly complains that he is far from being in charge of affairs since actions are frequently taken over which he has no control or even knowledge. There is also a fundamentalist-democratic split between the Ayatollah Khomeini and the more liberal intellectual, the Ayatollah Talleganji. Killings continue (some semi-legal as "executions" following summary trial by Islamic "revolutionary courts"); over 200 persons have been liquidated since the revolutionaries gained power.

EGYPT-ISRAEL

During the summer of 1978 the peace initiatives so dramatically started half a year earlier seemed to be bogged down—literally, in fact, over the Serbonian (Sinai) bog, as well as Gaza, the West Bank and Golan. Proposal and counter-proposal were put forward but quickly rejected, with exchange of acerbities between the leaders. Willy Brandt, former Chancellor of West Germany, and Dr. Bruno Kreisky, Chancellor of Austria, proposed a five-point peace plan during July, without success; and President Carter, who had expressed increasing disappointment over the way things had gone, called on August 8th for a summit meeting between Egypt, Israel and the U.S.A., to be held at Camp David, U.S.A. Both countries accepted but the rest of the Arab world showed itself either hostile or sceptical. A PLO attack on Israeli airline staff in London (July 20th) led to Israeli retaliation in the form of bomb attacks on the PLO camps around Damour, south of Beirut.

The Camp David talks duly began on September 6th but for the first nine days there was no agreement, with the Egyptian President, Anwar Sadat, and the

Israeli Prime Minister, Menachem Begin, both maintaining their earlier attitudes. President Carter eventually succeeded in bringing about a change; and on September 17th two Agreements were signed concerning the West Bank, Gaza, Sinai and associated problems of Israeli settlement. These were preliminary outlines rather than firm treaties. In the meantime an Arab "rejectionist movement" developed, with Syria and Iraq jointly taking leading roles. Cyrus Vance, the U.S. Secretary of State, visited various Arab countries in an effort to associate Jordan and Saudi Arabia, in particular, with the future Egyptian-Israeli peace talks—but without success.

Syrian and Iraqi *rapprochement*, once started after years of hostility, continued at a surprising pace. Reopening of the oil pipeline link from Iraq to Banias (Syria), closed for two years, was negotiated; and, after "reconciliation" visits to both capitals, a "Constitutional Union of Baathist Regimes" was proclaimed simultaneously on October 26th in Baghdad and Damascus.

During October and November the Arab rejectionist movement held various meetings, culminating in an "Arab Summit" in Baghdad on November 2nd–5th. The tone of the discussions was generally mild, with attempts to cajole Egypt into maintaining Arab solidarity rather than use of harder methods: Iraq went so far as to propose a substantial fund for this purpose. By December, however, the impetus of the earlier Camp David talks had clearly dissipated; and Mr. Vance once more undertook personal visits in order to try to restart negotiations. One continuing difficulty was the steady expansion of Israeli settlement in Arab occupied areas; and on December 14th the U.S.A. formally warned Israel that further settlements of this kind might prejudice United States aid to Israel. The award on December 10th of Nobel Peace Prizes to Mr. Begin and to President Sadat was further encouragement; though Mr. Sadat did not go personally to receive the Prize on the grounds that the projected Peace Treaty had not been signed. December 17th, the date originally envisaged in September for this signing, passed without action; and once again Mr. Vance resumed his journeys; this time to see the Foreign Ministers of Egypt and Israel in Brussels.

By mid-January 1979 U.S. concern had deepened. Israeli settlement in Arab areas continued, and progress towards resumption of talks seemed to have halted. Intensive activity from Mr. Carter, who had begun to view the Camp David discussions as a major personal issue in which his own prestige was increasingly involved, led to a restart of talks in late February, but between Ministers only: the principals were not willing to be involved. Early in March Mr. Carter himself travelled to Cairo with new proposals, and these were eventually successful. On March 26th a formal Peace Treaty was signed in Washington between Egypt and Israel. Previously, on the 16th, Mr. Carter had dispatched Zbigniew Brzezinski, his Assistant for National Security, to Riyadh and Amman in an attempt to enlist Saudi Arabian and Jordanian support, but without success. Instead, the Arab League states gathered in Baghdad to protest over the signing of the Treaty. The hard-liners (Syria, Libya and the PLO delegation) at first walked out of the meeting in protest over Saudi Arabia's refusal to impose immediate oil sanctions against the U.S.A., and also apply a total economic boycott of Egypt. On March 31st, however, Saudi Arabia shifted political ground more towards the "hard" stance; this left only Somalia, Sudan and Oman (none of whose representatives was present) as supporters of Egypt among the Arab states. The Arab League headquarters, it was decided by the meeting, would be moved from Cairo to Tunis, whereupon its Egyptian Secretary-General, Mahmoud Riyadh, resigned. Egyptian ambassadors were then (April 4th) recalled by President Sadat from all the Arab League states except the three non-participants in the March meeting. A referendum held in Egypt officially gave almost unanimous approval to President Sadat and the Peace Treaty, but some foreign observers commented that the actual turnout of voters appeared to be much below the "official" figures. However, it is clear that Mr. Sadat commands the fervent approbation of most Egyptians, particularly in rural areas. On April 27th the state of war that had existed between Egypt and Israel for 31 years formally came to an end with the ratification of the Peace Treaty by the Egyptian People's Assembly and the Israeli Knesset. During May frontier rectification in favour of Egypt took place, as a result of which El Arish returned to Egyptian possession—though not without some opposition by extremist Israeli settlers. In the same month the tenth Islamic Conference of Foreign Affairs Ministers, held at Fez (Morocco), barred Egypt from participating; and the Ayatollah Khomeini, in a letter to President Gaddafi of Libya, denounced President Sadat as a traitor to Islam.

During May and June various economic and political sanctions were applied against Egypt by the "rejectionist" Arab states. The Arab Organization for Industrialization, a $1,000 million armaments enterprise located in Cairo and funded by Saudi Arabia and other Gulf States, is to be shut down; a blockade of Egyptian air space by other Arab airlines will increasingly disrupt air travel; a Eurodollar loan to be floated for Egypt by Arab interests has been cancelled; and Kuwait has considered calling in nearly $1,000 million that it had deposited in Egypt. This has since had some effect on other loans and credits which are now under consideration in Europe and North America. Last, Sudan is now (June) possibly reconsidering its support of Mr. Sadat. Yet this could have many repercussions, particular for the Jonglei Canal project (now in progress) which is 50 per cent funded by Egypt. Perhaps this last fact is one reason why President Nimeri of Sudan sent a telegram of congratulation to President Sadat on the handing over of El Arish in early June.

What are the gains and losses over the Egyptian-Israeli Treaty? On the positive side, the ending of 30 years of bitter intermittent war, and the lifting of an intolerable burden to both countries; crushing debts—with, in some years, over 30 per cent of respective G.N.P. going into military expenditure—and the drain on manpower, especially severe for Israel. President Carter has striven to appear "even-handed", so, while the U.S.A. remains very obviously the patron and friend of Israel, Egypt now also has a new and valued supporter. In fact the Treaty was strongly lubricated by aid grants of $1,500 million to Egypt and over $2,000 million to Israel.

Arabs condemned the Treaty as a "non-Peace" and betrayal of the Palestinian Arab cause. In return for a pledge by an American President (whose political base at home is not strong) to "pursue a just settlement", Egypt has abandoned a clear undertaking previously given not to accept a separate peace unless Palestinian Arab rights were recognized and given substance. This has not occurred. As well, Arab unity, fragile at best, has been seriously disrupted. Countries supporting Sadat, though only three or four in number compared with the 17 other Arab states, include with Egypt half the Arab population of the Middle East. This split among Arabs has affected Saudi Arabia: during the spring months there were strong suggestions of uncertainty, even of dissension, among the ruling members of the Saudi royal house—though these appear now to have died down and been composed. Nevertheless, the bases of Saudi policy in the Middle East—support of Egypt and close relations with the U.S.A.—have been disturbed. Realism, therefore, after 30 years; or betrayal and destabilization, with peace only a temporary illusion?

TURKEY

Political uncertainty and economic difficulty intensified during the year. A "hung" political situation—with the Prime Minister, Bülent Ecevit, struggling to assert a positive line of action amid rapidly worsening monetary conditions, with Turkey at times actually short of currency to pay her representatives abroad and to buy sufficient petroleum for refining for home use—was compounded by Kurdish separatist movements and internal social unrest. By 1978 Turkey had a short-term external debt of over $6,000 million, and an annual trading deficit of $4,000 million. In an effort to improve Turkey's general political situation, Mr. Ecevit undertook a visit to the U.S.S.R. (June 21st–23rd), as a result of which plans were eventually agreed for joint collaboration in a range of projects—e.g. a petroleum refinery on the Black Sea, irrigation development in the provinces bordering the U.S.S.R., and co-ordination of certain trading activities. This slight leaning towards the U.S.S.R. may have had some influence in persuading the U.S. Congress to lift its arms embargo (August 1st), with the Senate adding the proviso that there should be some progress over the Cyprus issue. In return, Turkey agreed to reopen two U.S. air bases closed since 1975 (October). During July it was also announced in Delhi that Turkey wished for closer political links with India and other Asian countries in replacement of the CENTO commitment which was clearly failing in its objectives (events in Iran were soon to underline this situation).

Despite these very moderate gains, the internal situation grew steadily worse. On November 5th Mr. Ecevit announced measures to halt the rising level of sectarian and political violence which since January had claimed over 500 lives—more than twice as many as in the comparable period of the previous year. Certain universities were closed temporarily and martial law declared in a number of areas. Early in December NATO agreed to furnish more military and economic aid. Later in the same month (December 22nd–25th) severe disturbances broke out in the town of Karamanmaraş, near the borders of Syria and Iraq, with about 100 people killed and nearly 200 injured. Martial law was imposed throughout the 11 south-eastern provinces and also in Ankara and Istanbul, Mr. Ecevit announcing that troops would open fire on demonstrators. This led to the resignation of the Minister of the Interior.

By this time international concern over the position in Turkey had led to discussions involving the IMF. A phased scheme of loans was proposed early in 1979; but, for long, Turkey found much difficulty in accepting the stringent conditions—deflation, cut-backs and a considerable devaluation of the currency, so that while the earlier *tranches* of the loan were duly made there was deferment of later payment. Turkey has introduced an extremely involved scheme that in effect devalues the lira for tourists and Turkish workers abroad who send remittances home, whilst at first rejecting the IMF condition of a general 30 per cent devaluation (March-April) but then undertaking over 40 per cent devaluation in June. Further Cabinet resignations resulted, but these proved temporary, though the general indication of government weakness and indecision remained, to be underlined by the extension of martial law to six more provinces on April 25th. Disputes with Greece over demarcation of national territory in the Aegean; uncertainty arising from the Iranian revolution (at one time over 600 lorries were held up at the frontier); and the Kurdish issue are further complicating factors to the general economic and political difficulties.

Meanwhile there is some movement towards resolving the Cyprus issue. A UN plan sponsored by the U.S.A. and the United Kingdom was published in November 1978—to little effect—but in May there appeared some prospect of wider discussions involving the EEC, President Spyros Kyprianou, and Rauf Denktaş, leader of the Turkish Cypriots.

OTHER COUNTRIES

There was no real improvement over the 12 months in Lebanon. Although great efforts were made to restore the economy and infrastructures, these were negated by sporadic outbreaks of bombing, sniping and local violence. Several attempts to reconstruct Beirut and open its port were frustrated in this way. During July there was especially heavy fighting between Syrian troops and right-wing Christians. Uncertainties continued over the peace-keeping forces—the UN Interim Force in Lebanon (UNIFIL) especially found itself in increasing ambiguity, with its efforts often frustrated. The Secretary-General of the UN, Dr. Kurt Waldheim, repeated his complaints in November about the uncertain position of UNIFIL and drew attention to the restrictions on its activity increasingly imposed by what he termed "*de facto* forces" and by Israeli troops. This referred to the developments in South Lebanon relating to Christian Lebanese forces under Major Saad Haddad, whose troops were now fully collaborating with the Israelis and were supplied from Israeli sources. In effect, the territory controlled by the Haddad units had become a sort of protectorate dominated by Israel, with UNIFIL troops grouped uneasily to the north forming a screen between the Haddad forces and PLO groups immediately further north in refugee camps. During April Major Haddad did in fact declare a "free Lebanon of the south"; and conclusion of a Peace Treaty between Egypt and Israel has allowed Israel to divert more troops to this area and maintain reprisal activity against the PLO and other left-wingers in the rest of Lebanese territory. Lebanon thus remains a disputed "no man's land" fought over intermittently by rival armed bands, with occasional operational strikes from Israel, some of these amounting to heavy bombing.

Afghanistan, too, has reached the condition of near civil war. Opposition grew during the year to President Nur Mohammad Taraki from tribal elements opposed to his strongly left-wing policy, closely aligned to the U.S.S.R.; and there has been irregular fighting on an increasing scale with dissidents supported from Pakistan. On February 14th disturbances led to the death of the U.S. Ambassador and the resulting cut-off of U.S. aid. Guerrilla activity continues, with significant areas of the country now under dissident control, and strained political relations, not only with Pakistan but also with Iran.

Unrest has also characterized the Yemens. On June 24th Lt.-Col. Ahmed al-Ghashmi, the Yemen Arab Republic (North Yemen) Head of State, was assassinated under circumstances which led the Arab League formally to brand the leaders of the People's Democratic Republic of Yemen (South Yemen) as responsible. Two days after the assassination, Salem Rubayi Ali, Chairman of the Presidential Council of South Yemen, was deposed and executed on the grounds that he had attempted a *coup d'état* using Cuban troops. This last was later denied; but there was clearly a major shift of political influence further towards the Left, with the connivance and knowledge of the Soviet Union. Relations between the two Yemens continued poor during the winter months, with intermittent fighting across the common frontier. In early February the situation appeared rather more serious with fighting coming near the town of Ta'iz in North Yemen—enough for Saudi Arabia to express public disquiet. Then, like sunshine after a thunderstorm, came an agreement (late March) that political unity was highly desirable in order to improve relationships; and so, for the second time in a few years, political unity of the Yemens is now a declared objective.

Strains developed during the year among the members of the United Arab Emirates. Differences became apparent between two leading rulers, Sheikh Zayed of Abu Dhabi and Sheikh Rashid of Dubai, over interpretation of the "union", e.g. how far this transcended state rights and government; and in March the representatives of Dubai and Ras al-Khaimah were deliberately absent from a meeting held to discuss the general matter of Union policies. On April 25th the Council of Ministers resigned following these dissensions: an unprecedented situation.

In North Africa matters were relatively quiet. In Algeria a new group took over after the death of President Boumedienne and its members have maintained his policies; in particular, unostentatious but serious and active opposition to the Israeli-Egyptian Treaty, and organization of boycott measures. The Polisario dispute involving Algeria and Morocco continues—chronic rather than acute—and Morocco, as the less wealthy protagonist, is suffering more from the economic and political strains of maintaining a military force in the Western Sahara. Libya, after political flirtations with Malta and Turkey, is now occupied in retrieving the effects of a misjudged support of Idi Amin in Uganda, which has left some Libyans as prisoners-of-war there. For Sudan, with several highly unstable zones on her frontiers (in Ethiopia, Uganda, Zaire and the south-west), the year has involved much careful trimming and political balancing. Oil is not yet flowing; the Jonglei scheme has begun, but may need more finance than was previously envisaged; refugees are streaming in from the disturbed areas outside the country, finance for infrastructures is in very short supply; and, as noted earlier, there is the difficult decision as to which side to support in the Arab-Israeli issue.

LATE INFORMATION

MOROCCO

In August 1979 Mauritania signed a peace treaty with Polisario and renounced its own claim to the Saharan territory, Tiris el Gharbia, formally withdrawing from the capital, Dakhla, on August 15th. Morocco reaffirmed that it would not permit a hostile power to establish itself on the southern Moroccan border, and took over the administration of Dakhla as a prelude to the annexation of the whole territory. King Hassan announced that the whole of the former Spanish Sahara was to become Morocco's 37th province.

PLO

Maj.-Gen. MUHAMMAD AZZAM has succeeded ZUHAYR MUHSIN as Head of the Military Department of PLO. SAMI AL-ATTARI has succeeded ZUHAHR MUHSIN as Secretary-General of Saiqa.

PART ONE

General Survey

The Middle East and North Africa: An Introduction

W. B. Fisher

Definition of the Area

The term, "Middle East and North Africa" is a cumbersome, and, possibly to some, even a misleading description. Besides already embracing part of northern Africa, "Middle East" has the further objection of meaning different things to different people. Some would apply it to areas much farther east, and not to Africa at all—which is geographically more logical—but then Libya and Egypt would no longer be in the "Middle East", a nonsense for some others. Perhaps only when we come to consider alternatives do the merits, such as they are, of our present title begin to emerge. "Muslim World" is too extensive in that it could reach as far as Pakistan, Malaysia and Indonesia; whilst reference to "Arab" only would exclude Turkey, Iran, Cyprus (80 per cent Greek) and, logically to one way of thinking, the Berber areas of Tunisia, Algeria and Morocco.

We can trace popular use of "Middle East" back to the Second World War. It developed in a casual, almost haphazard, manner following the territorial expansion of a unified military command that was originally based on countries lying east of the Suez Canal. In this way, the British and American publics grew accustomed to the association of Jerusalem, Damascus, Cairo and then Benghazi and even Tripoli with the collective description "Middle East" (now increasingly shortened in America, to "Mid East"); and, in the writer's view, the expression has come to have a validity based on popular usage which it is now difficult to challenge. There are, however, numerous geographers and historians who are unwilling to abandon the older concept of southern Asia as divisible into a Near, Middle and Far East; and in 1946 the Royal Geographical Society protested against the British Government's continued official usage of "Middle East" to indicate Palestine, Egypt and countries further west. If we talk of a Middle East, the logical argument runs, there is also implied a Near East; and in fact this term was once in great vogue, as referring to the territories along the seaboard of the eastern Mediterranean. It was, moreover, a useful collective geographical description for the lands of the former Ottoman Empire.

However, usage of "Middle East" in the present volume may be justified on several grounds. (*a*) Few definitions of a Near East ever agreed—some authors extended it eastwards to include Afghanistan, others terminated it at the coastal ranges of Syria and Palestine; and some included Egypt, whilst others did not. (*b*) "Near East" is convenient to apply, in an historical sense only, to the now defunct Ottoman Empire. (*c*) Nowadays, for the English-speaking public at least, the term "Middle East" would have no validity if applied, in a strictly logical sense, to Afghanistan, Pakistan and India. (*d*) The term can be taken as denoting a single geographical area in which occur broadly similar features of physical environment and ways of life.

We thus arrive at the definition of the Middle East as given on the title-page of earlier editions of this volume—the highland countries of Turkey and Iran; Cyprus; the Arab-speaking states of the eastern Mediterranean seaboard; Israel; the Arabian peninsula; the valley of the Tigris-Euphrates (chiefly but not entirely comprising Iraq), the Nile Valley (Egypt, and also Sudan); and Libya. This, in no sense an ideal or unassailable solution, has at least considerable sanction in popular usage and technical utility. Subsequently, the addition of chapters on north-western Africa and on Afghanistan has extended the range of the present volume beyond many but by no means all of the numerous definitions of the "Middle East" which have been proposed. North-western Africa (Tunisia, Algeria and Morocco) spoken of by Arab geographers as "Jeziret al Maghreb" ("island of the west", or "setting sun"), or usually nowadays just "Maghreb" ("west"), surrounded as it is to the south by deserts and on its remaining sides by sea, may be looked on in many ways as linked to the Middle East both by environment and culture, whilst retaining something of the separateness indicated by the term "island".

Physical Background

STRUCTURE

Geologically speaking, the entire area can be regarded as deriving from two distinct provinces. The south consists largely of continental massifs (increasingly spoken of today as "plates") that would appear once to have been joined in one large mass, known as Gondwanaland. To the north of this mass there has been throughout most geological time a trough or geosyncline. This, a zone of crustal weakness, has mostly been occupied by deep seas of varying extent (at some periods more extensive than now) and in these seas lived the immense numbers of living creatures whose bodies after death decayed to form the oil deposits now so characteristic of the central Middle East. Alternate periods of quiescence and geological disturbance occurred. During quiescent phases, material eroded from the neighbouring continental masses accumulated in the oceanic deeps of the geosyncline, rapidly covering the fatty bodies of dead sea organisms to allow petroleum formation; then periods of contraction occurred, heaving up marine sediments in enormous flexures or fold-structures to produce mountain chains. Sometimes the flexures were relatively simple, like hogs' backs; in other instances they were much more intense, giving rise to tightly packed, highly distorted folds, with extremes where shearing and total deformation of the structures produced an overthrust ("nappe") rather than a recognizable fold.

From various parts of the geosyncline has emerged a great series of fold-mountain chains that are traceable from Western Europe and North-West Africa as far as Northern India. This is the so-called "Alpine" or Tertiary fold system, since it is the latest in geological time of three major mountain-building periods. The Pyrenees and Sierra Nevada of Spain, the Alps, Appennines, and Carpathians in Europe, and the massive Atlas Mountains of Africa are all part of this system. Further east many of the mountain chains of Asia Minor, the Caucasus, the Zagros and Elburz Ranges of Iran, and the complex of ridges that form the Afghan Pamir are all part of this "Alpine" system—geologically young in age, and relatively uneroded and therefore high in altitude.

This is by no means the whole story. Besides the actual fold ranges, simple and complex, there are often embedded between them portions of older, more resistant structures. Some of these are remnants of the first two mountain building phases: Palaeozoic (or Caledonian) and Mesozoic (Hercynian), the latter now being found extensively in central Europe. Parts of these remnant structures, certainly of Hercynian age and possibly also Caledonian, are found in western Morocco, the central Atlas, Asia Minor, the interior of Iran, and western Afghanistan. One cannot trace any simple pattern in the arrangement of the folds, which may occur in straight parallel ranks, or sinuous arcs and garlands that may alter trend abruptly.

North Africa is a good example of the complexity of conditions. Generally speaking, the entire highland zone consists of a series of parallel-fold mountain chains of Tertiary age running east-west or north-east/south-west, and separated by tablelands or narrow trough-like valleys. In the extreme west, however, areas of Palaeozoic and Mesozoic remnant structures are prominent. The whole mountain system is higher and wider in the west (Morocco) and diminishes considerably in width towards the east (Tunisia), as well as declining in height. Much discussion centres on how far the Tertiary Atlas fold structures can be regarded as continuations of the fold mountains of southern Spain and Italy: whether there is in fact an almost continuous ring of folds enclosing the entire western Mediterranean basin, and breached only by the Straits of Gibraltar and the narrows between Tunis, Sicily and Italy.

Somewhat different conditions obtain in Asia Minor, where much larger interior plateaux, often eroded into sumps or basins, are surrounded by Tertiary fold ranges. Of this kind are the Taurus and Anti-Taurus Ranges of the south, and the coastal ranges of the north, which continue into the Caucasus and Iranian mountains. Within Iran the interior basins (composed in part of Hercynian nuclei) are even more developed, so that, with minor variations, the whole country can be regarded as saucer-shaped, a rim of Tertiary fold mountains very clearly framing and defining a series of interior basins—which are hardly plains, since most are above 2,000 ft. in altitude.

Further east still, in Afghanistan, the Tertiary folds again develop into enormous dominating ridges that bunch together eastwards and northwards to form a formidable, though relatively narrow, mountain complex that presents a major barrier between central and southern Asia. The first portion of it is the Pamir "knot"—a "swag" or bunch of mountain ranges enclosing tenuous and restricted valleys. Intervening blocks or interior plateaux, present in the west on a small scale, disappear entirely towards the east, with topography passing unbroken into the main Himalaya.

The southern geological province of the Middle East contrasts markedly with that of the north as just described. It consists essentially of the platform (or basement) of extremely ancient rocks, some amongst the oldest known in the world (Precambrian and Archaean). These—chiefly granites, schists and quartzites—most likely once made up the enormous Gondwana continent, which included much of Australia, southern India, Arabia, most of Africa, and parts of South America. Whilst generally rigid and resistant to the pressures that rucked up the sediments of the geosyncline, this ancient mass was from time to time, especially on its northern fringe, overrun by shallow seas, which deposited thin, often horizontal layers of limestones and sandstones. In addition, wind- and water-eroded silts and sands from the surface became consolidated in similar thin, level strata. Thus the basement area of the south, whilst generally flat and fairly uniform in character, is not wholly so, since much of its surface is covered by these deposits, which erode differentially, the harder bands standing out as ridges and the less resistant as vales. The whole aspect of this southern basement/platform is one of a vast open plateau diversified here and there by small-scale hill-systems and shallow valleys. Much is occupied by sand deposits in the form of major dunes or as irregular shifting masses—the "sand-seas" of the Sahara and inner Arabia.

One major feature of considerable importance, now accepted as part in fact of a world-wide process, is the drift apart of the two major platforms of Arabia and Africa, which until relatively recent geological time (mid-Tertiary) formed a single larger continent. Further east was another relatively large platform, which appears to have drifted north from a location close to Mozambique and east Africa, and now forms the Deccan Plateau of India. Extensive fracturing in the area of the Red Sea, Gulf of Aden and east Africa led to the separation of Arabia from north-east Africa, and the tilting of the entire block of Arabia, uplifting the west (Red Sea coast) and downwarping the east (Persian/Arab Gulf) whilst the western side of the Red Sea has buckled and impacted to form the Red Sea hills of Egypt and the Sudan with the interior generally horizontal and much less disturbed.

Within the last 10-15 years, a new concept has been

[*continued on p.* 6

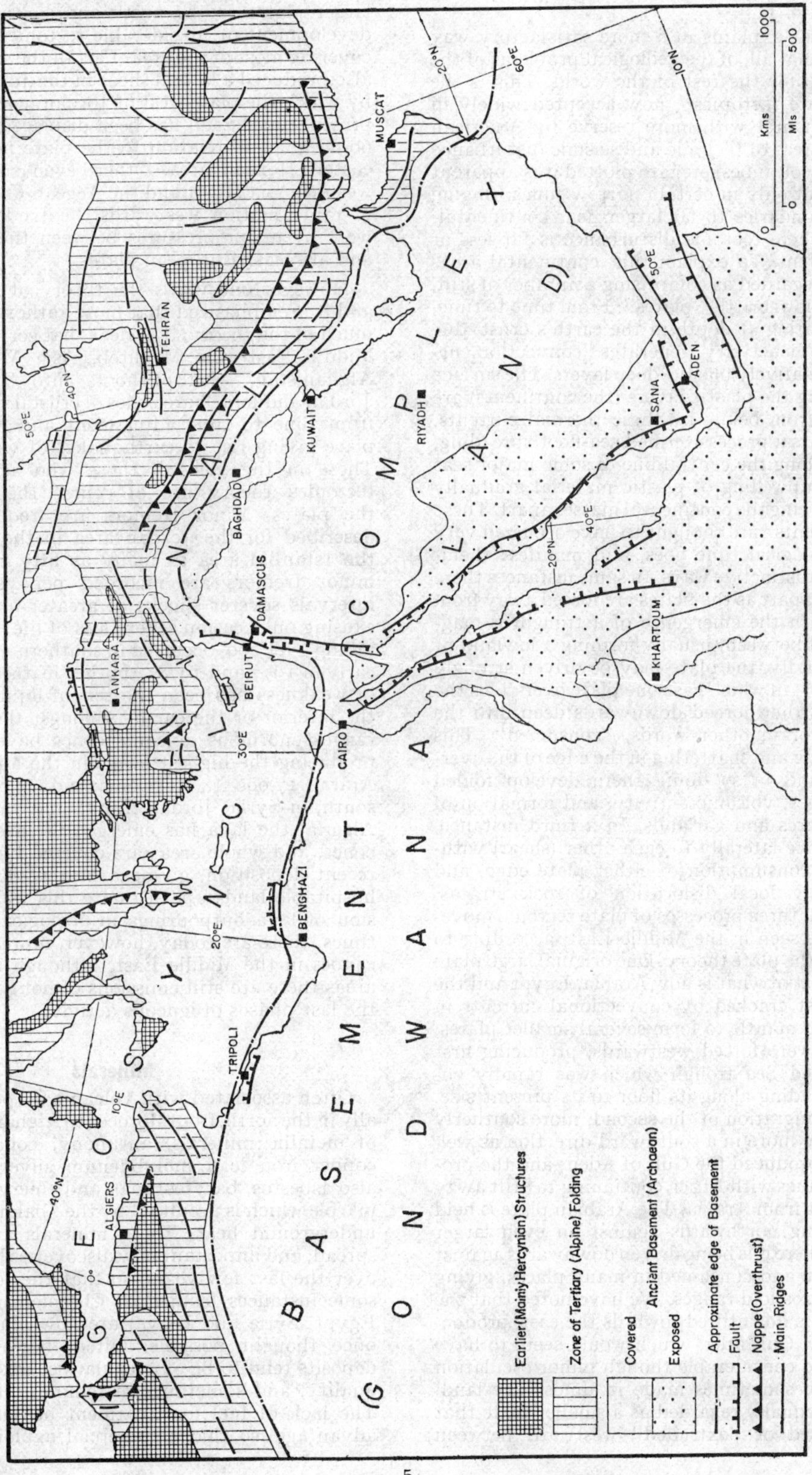

Sketch of structural elements.

continued from p. 4]
worked out that explains in a more satisfactory way many, though not all, of the geological problems of the area—and also for the rest of the world. This is the theory of "plate tectonics", now accepted widely in Britain, but at first with more reserve by American geologists. If areas of tectonic and seismic disturbance (earthquakes, volcanoes, etc) are plotted it is apparent that these occur only in certain narrow zones, ringing or forming boundaries to far larger near continental-size masses, where tectonic disturbance is far less or even non-existent. To explain this, continental areas generally are regarded as comprising a number of stiff, but rather shallow, brittle "plates". From time to time, differential heating at depth in the earth's crust, due to phases of radioactivity, generates "convection currents" in the relatively plastic, deep layers. The surface plates overlying the plastic layers (the continents) are then cracked from below by these thermal currents, and there occurs a process termed sea-floor spreading, where, often along the central line of some major seas or oceans, an upwelling of plastic material gradually takes place, forcing the continental masses apart. These "plate movements" are thought to have occurred very rapidly as geological time goes, and manifest themselves in three distinctive ways. In some instances there can be tearing apart as the plates are forced away from each other, with the emergence of a trough of magmatic material between, usually forming a lowland or sea floor. Secondly, the plate may be driven strongly against another; in which case one plate over-rides the other which is then forced downwards deep into the plastic layer, or in other words, "consumed". This leads to crushing and shattering in the edge of the over-riding plate and in so doing there develop folded mountain ranges, volcanic activity, and formation of mountainous arcs and garlands. In a third instance, plates may move laterally to each other (shear) without extensive consumption of either plate edge, and thus with only local dislocation of rock stratas. Examples of all three processes of plate tectonic movement are to be seen in the Middle East, according to proponents of the plate theory. One original large plate comprising most of what is now Arabia, Egypt and the Sudan was first cracked by convectional currents in the lower earth mantle to form several smaller plates. Two of these were forced westwards, producing first the narrow Red Sea trough which was rapidly enlarged by spreading along its floor to its present size. Then further migration of the second, more southerly plate, this time more in a southward direction as wel as westward, produced the Gulf of Aden; and the process still continues with Africa continuing to drift away south and west from Arabia. The Arabian plate is held to be impinging northwards against an even larger Asian plate, where it is being driven downwards against the Asian plate and consumed in many places, giving rise to the Zagros fold ranges. We have noted that the Arabian plate is downtilted towards the east, producing the shallow Gulf area, which would seem to have been subject to considerable though minor oscillation of level, which sometimes made it almost dry land. Asia Minor is equally regarded as a smaller plate that is being pushed or "extruded" westward between larger plates to the north and south west with the development of considerable tectonic weakness zones covering most of the area. Part of the same process has also produced a lateral shear in the Jordan Valley area by which the plate west of Jordan (comprising mainly present-day Israel) has been displaced southwards by 60-80 miles in relation to the plate now forming the eastern Jordan area. Other, even smaller plates in western Asia Minor and the Aegean-Crete area may be in rapid motion westwards, "extruded" again as it were by major pressures between the larger African and also east European plates.

However one views the theory of plate tectonics, and it is emphasized that most authorities now accept much of the theory, it is clear that certain areas of the Middle East (the Maghreb, Asia Minor, Iran and Afghanistan, with offshoots into Syria, Lebanon, Jordan and Israel) are zones of crustal weakness, where from time to time adjustment and movement take place giving rise to earthquakes of varying severity. These in the view of those who accept the plate tectonics theory are of course the boundaries of the plates. Minor tremors are frequent (they are described for the Jordan area in the Bible), and in the Istanbul area as many as fifty to one hundred minor tremors are recorded per year. At longer intervals severer shocks of greater amplitude occur, causing on occasion severe loss of life. The two latest, killing over 200, occurred in southern and eastern Iran early in 1977 and 1978. Another feature of these zones of weakness has been the rise of liquid magma from the interior or the earth. Amongst the northern fold ranges enormous volcanic cones have been formed, producing the highest peaks in the Middle East (Mt. Ararat, 17,000 ft., Mt. Demavend, 19,000 ft.). Farther south, in Syria, Jordan, Libya and parts of southern Algeria, the lava has emerged in sheets rather than cones, and whole areas are covered by basalt of very recent deposition, giving a barren, desolate, and inhospitable landscape. Despite this widespread extension of lava outpourings in geologically very recent times, there are today, however, no really active volcanoes in the Middle East, although in a number of areas there are still emissions of hot gases and mud—the last phases of igneous activity.

Minerals

Often associated with volcanic outpourings, especially in the north, from Morocco to Afghanistan, are veins of metallic minerals, antimony, cobalt, chromium, copper, iron, lead, molybdenum, silver and zinc—and also asbestos, barytes, coal, and emery, together with marble which is produced by the "baking" of strata by underground heat. These minerals are fairly widespread, and important new discoveries have been made over the last few years, so that the total reserves in some instances (copper at Chesmeh in Iran, iron in Egypt, Syria and Libya) are now much higher than once thought possible. Often, however, individual deposits tend to be of irregular occurrence, of varying quality, and sometimes in remote, difficult districts. The lack of fuel for treatment has also been a disadvantage, so that commercial exploitation has not always been possible. On the other hand, rises in world prices since 1940 and again in the 1970s have had a highly stimulating effect. World shortages, or threats of shortage, plus political attitudes (e.g., over Rhodesia and Chile) have led to increased interest in Middle Eastern minerals. Moreover, local governments will sometimes prefer to exploit national resources at higher cost rather than be dependent upon imports. Hence mineral exploitation has growing importance, with Turkey ranking second as a world producer of chromium and Cyprus a significant producer of asbestos, copper and iron ore. Egypt has recently begun to develop on an extensive scale the important iron deposits near Aswan, using hydro-electric power from the High Dam; and other iron deposits occur between the Nile Valley and the north-west coast of the Red Sea, and in the Behariya oasis due west of the Nile. Another important discovery of iron not yet producing is at Rajo, near Aleppo, in Syria, whilst it is now estimated that nearly four billion tons of mainly high-grade ore (some 5 per cent of world reserves) are located in the Wadi Shatty, in the Fezzan area of southern Libya. The region as a whole is now thought to have about 10 per cent of world reserves. North Africa is distinctly richer in minerals than most of the Middle East proper. Besides extensive deposits of phosphate (which make Morocco the second largest world producer), there are important deposits of iron ore, with smaller, but highly significant quantities of lead, zinc, antimony, cobalt, molybdenum and barytes.

Elsewhere in the Middle East, other mineral resources are found, but on a scale somewhat smaller than in North Africa: phosphate in Egypt, Israel, Jordan and Syria—all of these deposits are exploited commercially; manganese in the Sinai peninsula; and small deposits of copper and natural gas in Israel. There is increasing use of soluble salts found in such lakes as the Dead Sea and the Wadi Natrun west of Cairo, chiefly (in the case of the Dead Sea) as sources of bromine. Very small quantities of alluvial gold are still produced, mainly from Saudi Arabia. During 1977 it was announced that extensive coal deposits have been discovered in south-central Iran.

On the southern flanks of the fold mountains, rock strata are tilted into great domes, in which have accumulated the vast deposits of petroleum that now make the Middle East the leading oil province in the world with some 60 per cent of proven world reserves. The vast bulk of this—about half the world's oil and much natural gas—lies around and under the shores of the Persian/Arabian Gulf. More will be said later about these deposits, but it may here be noted that the occurrence of oil is closely dependent upon a certain kind of geological structure. There must be first an alternation of porous and impermeable strata, with the latter uppermost so as to act as a seal, and prevent the oil from running away; and there must also be a slight degree of disturbance enough to produce domes and traps in which the oil can collect, but not sufficient to produce cracks which will allow oil to escape. Such factors can explain why oil is restricted in occurrence to a few zones, and why its discovery is such a chancy affair, with many disappointments—for every boring that produces oil, at least nine others are made without success.

CLIMATE

One basic reason for the distinctive character of the Middle East and North Africa is the special and unusual climate. Most parts of the world experience their rainfall either mostly during summer (the warm season) or distributed throughout the year. Only in a very few areas is there a maximum in winter (the cold season). This is the so-called "Mediterranean" climate, giving a long intensely hot summer, and a relatively mild, rainy winter, with occasional cold spells. The distinction does not seem very important, but it "conditions" plant life to a remarkable degree, and thus also agriculture and general ways of life. Native plants "rest" in the hot season, not in the cold one, which is the opposite to what happens in cooler temperate climates. Some indigenous plants, such as cereals, mature quickly in order to complete a rapid growth cycle before the onset of hot weather; others, chiefly bulbs, flower in spring or autumn; whilst some, such as the citrus, bear fruit in winter. All this has a marked effect on agricultural routines and general living habits. One obvious result is the summer "siesta", which involves breaking the day into two rest periods, with a very early morning start, and continuance of work well into the evening.

Weather conditions are dominated by the long, hot and dry summer, which then quickly gives way to a relatively rainy winter that is mild near the coast but can be surprisingly cold inland. Autumn is warm and sunny, and spring changeable and liable to cold spells —both are short, merely intermediate, seasons. Because of the absence of cloud during summer (away from the coast there can be days without any cloud whatever) the sun beats down uninterruptedly, and the temperatures reached are far higher than those at the Equator. Day maxima of 100° to 115° F. are usual, and a figure of over 125° F. is known. Parts of the interior of Arabia, Algeria, Libya and Iran may experience the highest temperatures occurring in the world.

In winter, though frost is uncommon actually at sea level, the land interior can be cold, especially at higher altitudes. Snow can fall as far south as central Morocco and Algeria, Aswan, the Yemen A.R. and southern Iran, whilst the presence of high mountains has the effect of intensifying winter cold. The plateaux of Turkey and Iran in particular, and to a slightly lesser degree of the Atlas region, experience severe winters, with several months of frost, and up to 120 days of snow cover—a reminder of their geographical position adjacent respectively to Russia and to Spain, which is surprisingly cold in winter. Considerable seasonal change is thus the keynote of Middle Eastern climate, with 40° to 50° F. of temperature range between one part of the year and another (cf. the 26° F. range in London). Wide changes of temperature as between day and night are also characteristic of the interior, but not close to the coast.

[*continued on p.* 10

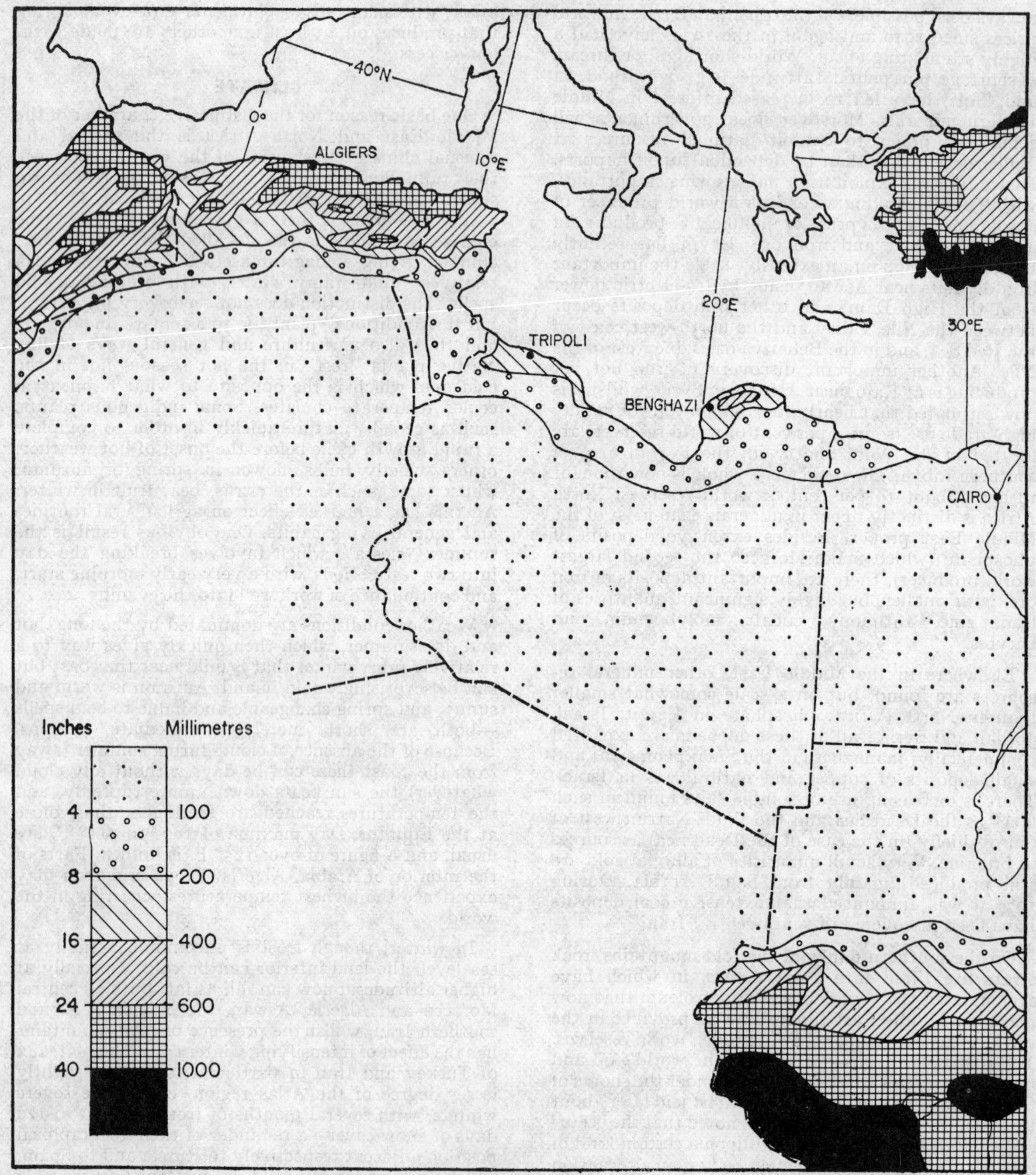

Annual rainfall: North Africa.

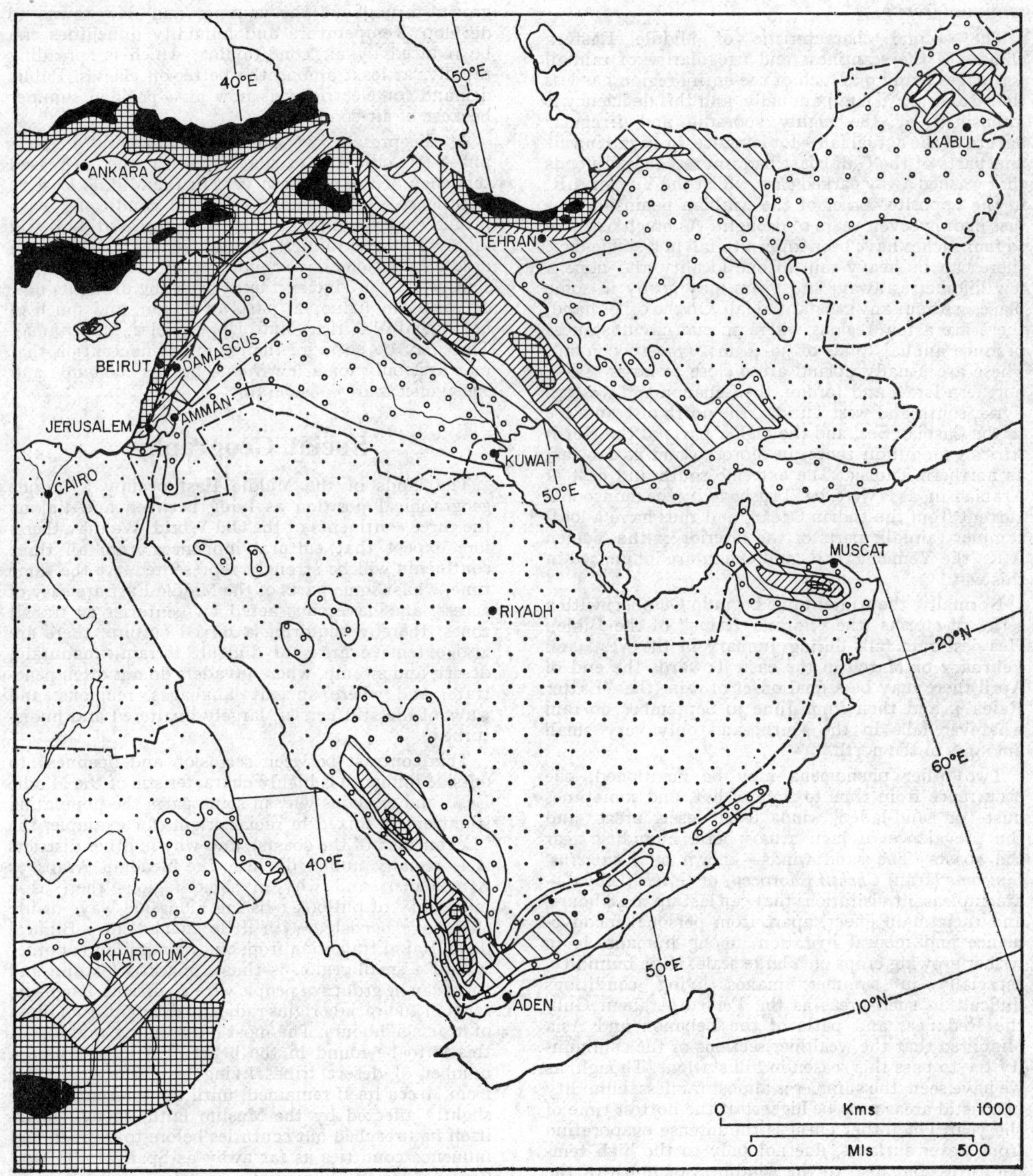

Annual rainfall: Middle East.

continued from p. 7]

The second characteristic of Middle Eastern climate is the scantiness and irregularity of rainfall (*see* pages 8 and 9). Much of the entire region has less than 10 ins. (250 mm.) annually, and this deficiency is intensified by the highly sporadic and irregular nature of the actual fall—for instance, in 1972 Kuwait and parts of the Gulf coast had unprecedented floods that washed away parked cars, whilst the Yemen A.R. in the opposite corner of the Arabian peninsula was just ending seven years of drought. As much as three to four inches have been known to fall in a single day; there can be heavy rain in one locality and none a few kilometres away; and years may go by in some places without any substantial fall. On the other hand, there are a few regions where special circumstances produce annual totals of 30-40 ins. (750-1000 mm.). These are usually upland areas close to large seas—northern Israel and Jordan, the Lebanon and western Syria, south and west Turkey, the north of Iran close to the Caspian Sea, and the higher parts of the North African mountain zones, in Morocco and as far east as northern Tunisia. The extreme south and east of Arabia can, as it were, be "brushed" by the monsoonal current from the Indian Ocean, and thus have a local summer rainfall: parts of the interior of the Yemen A.R., the Yemen P.D.R. and Oman are influenced in this way.

Normally, the winter rains begin in October, with a series of storms (the "Former Rains" of the Bible). Heaviest rain falls during January in the west, and February or March in the east. Towards the end of April there may be a final onset of rain (the "Latter Rains"), and then from June to September no rain whatever falls in the south, and only very small amounts in the north.

Two other phenomena may be mentioned: the occurrence from time to time of hot, and sometimes dust- or sand-laden, winds from desert areas, and the prevalence of high atmospheric humidity near the coasts. The sand winds—known as *Khamsins, Simooms* (Iran) *Chehili* (Morocco) or *Ghibli* (Libya)—are unpleasant visitations that can last up to 48 hours, and their main effect, apart from personal inconvenience and mental irritation among humans, is to wither growing crops on a large scale. High humidity, especially in summer, makes living conditions difficult in such areas as the Persian/Arabian Gulf, the Red Sea, and parts of the Lebanon and Asia Minor, so that the wealthier sections of the community try to pass this season in hill stations. Though, as we have seen, the summer is almost rainless, humidity in coastal areas may be highest at the hottest time of the year. One other effect is the intense evaporation from water surfaces, due not only to the high temperatures, but also to the windiness of much of the region, again more pronounced in summer.

Atmospheric pollution, with photo-synthesis of exhaust fumes to produce irritant "smog", is now becoming a feature of the larger cities.

The effects of climate are now increasingly mitigated by modern technology. Irrigation and, in a few places, large-scale distillation of sea water allows crops to be grown throughout the summer and new towns to develop. Temperature and humidity difficulties can be reduced by air conditioning, which is spreading rapidly, at least among the better-off classes. Public demand for electricity is now at a peak in summer because of air-conditioning.

At the present, we may be experiencing a minor phase of climatic oscillation, with the increased tendency of the northern part of the Middle East to experience slightly more unsettled conditions, with rather cooler temperatures, and increased but still highly sporadic rainfall. On the southern side, warm desert conditions have tended to intensify and creep southwards, producing the devastating droughts now occurring in Ethiopia, parts of Sudan, and much of north central Africa (Mali, Upper Volta, Mauritania). This may be no more than a minor fluctuation that may last only for a few years, but its economic and social effects are considerable.

Social Geography

The lands of the Middle East occupy a unique geographical position as lying between and linking the three continents of the Old World. We may therefore expect that cultural influences from all three continents will be strongly represented. At the same time, whilst some parts of the Middle East are easy of access, and have thus acted for centuries as transit zones, thereby acquiring a mixed culture, there are also extensive areas of difficult terrain—mountain, desert, and swamp, where invaders do not often penetrate, and where ancient languages, religions, and ways of life still persist, largely unaltered and undisturbed.

This contrast between seclusion and openness to outside influence is highly characteristic of the Middle East, and explains why in some parts the population is extremely mixed in racial origin (for example, the "Levantine" of the coasts), and why in other districts it is racially unmixed—(e.g. the Bedouin Arabs or Armenians); and why in some regions there is a modernity of outlook existing alongside ways of life that have persisted with little change since Biblical days. Rapid transition from one way of life to another within a small region is thus a marked feature, and there can be groups of people with traditions, language, religion and racial origins radically different from those of near neighbours. The most outstanding example of this is to be found in the heart of Arabia, where a number of desert tribes living less than 500 miles from Mecca itself remained, until quite recently, only slightly affected by the Muslim faith, though Islam itself had reached out centuries before to overrun and influence countries as far away as Spain, India, and Central Africa. Now, with greatly improved communications, isolation is rapidly declining, though not without some tensions.

RACIAL GROUPING

In recent years there has been a revaluation of ideas on racial questions. Previously the trend had been towards devising increasingly elaborate and subtle groupings based on finer and finer measurements of physical characteristics: bodily physique, hair and skin qualities, especially colour. But we are now aware that some, though not all of these, may be induced or modified by diet, upbringing as children, and social customs. At the same time, investigation of genetic differences, as partly evidenced by blood serum character, has demonstrated a whole new field of possible biological relationships that often bear little or no concordance with observed "racial" characters, but can be traceable in certain ways to geographical location and environment—for example, the perpetuation of certain physical traits and genetical characters through seclusion in a remote area with interbreeding, or the opposite in an "open" area subject to much human movement and interchange. Whilst it would be idle to deny that differences between various groups of the human race certainly exist—some are darker- or lighter-skinned, or with slight physical and anatomical differences—it would appear far less possible than was once thought to devise meaningful categories of racial groupings. Some authorities now speak only of a very few distinctive groups: "caucasoid" or white, "brown", "yellow" etc., and then distinguish minor variations as arising from the influences of genetical inheritance, geographical location, and cultural experience.

Thus, earlier typologies such as "Alpine", "Armenoid", or "Mediterranean" are increasingly abandoned in favour of a more detailed but in one sense restricted approach based on precisely measurable elements such as blood grouping or other genetic qualities, discarding what are now recognized as variable and partially subjective criteria such as bodily build.

The Middle East offers special difficulties partly because of its location, as just described, between major world zones, and partly owing to a dearth of information, for example, on blood groupings. At the present, given this unsatisfactory situation, it is perhaps best to limit our survey to noting that (a) there is, as might well be expected, evidence of considerable intermixture and variation, with African, Asian and other elements represented, alongside an indigenous "brown" racial type, from very dark to blond skin colour; and (b) there is evidence of persistence of special genetical factors (and hence of physical characters) in some groups, and much less in others. Variation of type is thus prominent.

LANGUAGE DISTRIBUTION

This is far clearer than the racial pattern. Arabic, the language of Muhammad, and of comparatively recent origin, was spread rapidly by the Islamic conquests of the seventh to ninth centuries A.D., and has now become universal in Egypt, the Sudan, Arabia, Jordan, Syria, Lebanon, and Iraq. There is a classical form, now understood with some difficulty and (as the language of the Koran) used for religious observance and broadcasting; and various regional dialects. Some of these latter are close to each other in syntax but differ in pronunciation (i.e. differences are of the order of those in English, spoken let us say, in London, Lancashire and Glasgow, or Massachusetts, Georgia and Nebraska). But in other instances the colloquial forms of Arabic can differ as widely, as say, French, Spanish or Italian, so that intercommunication is difficult.

Farther north, Turkish, a central Asiatic language brought in by the Turkish conquerors of the eleventh century A.D., is current over most of Asia Minor, with extensions into Iran and the U.S.S.R. Turkish was for many centuries written in Arabic characters, but as the sounds of Turkish are not easily adaptable to Arabic letters, Roman (i.e. European) characters were introduced by government decree in 1928. Persian is an Indo-Aryan language with affinities to some European forms of speech, but it is by no means universally spoken throughout Iran—probably by only one-half or at most two-thirds of the population. It is written in Arabic script. A variation known as Dari Persian is spoken in Afghanistan, as is the Pashtu language. The hill country from Asia Minor as far east as the Indian frontier is a mosiac of different dialects spoken by various tribal groups. Some of these dialects are remnants of ancient forms of speech that were once more widely current; some are of fairly recent origin; whilst some show relationships to languages of central and eastern Asia. Aramaic, the language of Palestine at the time of Christ, now persists in a modern and altered form only in a few villages near Damascus and Mosul; Kurdish, an Indo-Aryan language related to Persian (Farsi), has a fairly wide extension in the hills from central Turkey as far as south-west Iran; and Armenian, owing to the persecution and dispersal of Armenians from their homeland, is spoken in many large towns. Greek is the chief language of Cyprus. In Israel, Hebrew and Arabic are the two official languages, the former predominating. Berber is dominant in parts of the hill country and adjacent areas of Morocco, Algeria and Tunisia, with a few offshoots into Libya. Prior to invasion by the Arabs in the tenth and eleventh centuries, Berber was the major language in what is now Tripolitania, but it survives today in only a few towns—Aujila, Zuara and Garian.

Language and Educational Problems

Variation of language, as between written and spoken forms of the same dialect and as between families of languages, presents a serious problem at the present time, and is an important factor in the isolation and retarded economic level of several Middle Eastern states. In education, the problem is more complicated, because for a long time practically all modern scientific and technological works were written in English, French, German or Russian, with higher teaching often in the hands of foreigners. To the complication of having several indigenous languages within one country was thus added the difficulty of having higher instruction carried on by foreigners in their own tongue. Thus school and university teaching was frequently enmeshed in the toils of language, and timetables heavily weighted towards language teaching, as an essential preliminary to any other work. Because of the lack of contact, and the smallness of the potential market, which rarely made translation of serious works into Arabic, Turkish or Persian a commercial proposition, only a minority of standard texts from Europe or America could, until very recently, be read in the native languages of the Middle East. This has been a considerable, but not recognized, factor in the cultural and educational separation which has for long existed between the Middle East and other countries. Within the last few years certain governments, notably those of Egypt, Iran and Turkey, have tackled the problem, by sponsoring translation; and UNESCO has also been active in this connection. Another significant change is that with the expansion of general education, there is a greater flow of Middle Easterners abroad, and many of these have now returned as teachers, technicians and officials. In addition, locally trained Arabic-speaking personnel, chiefly Egyptian, but also Palestinian and Syrian Arab, have tended to take up appointments in less developed Arab countries. Thus there is much more specialist instruction in Arabic as compared with, say, twenty years ago. Nationalist feeling in itself, and the reduced openings for expatriates also foster this tendency. A few universities still use English as the main medium of instruction, but opinion is divided as to whether this should continue. To some it appears that fuller use of Arabic will allow more effective teaching; to others, that it will reduce the reading of textbooks (a number of which are available only in a foreign language) and limit yet further the possibility of employing expatriate staff. Radio and to a lesser extent television have been used with effect to overcome communication difficulties.

NOMADS

With much of the Middle East arid or semi-arid, animal rearing plays an important part in the life of the region, with numerous migratory tribes moving regularly in search of fresh pasture. Though the actual numbers of people who live as pastoral nomads are quite small and rapidly declining, their way of life, once of great significance but now less so, contrasts with that of the townspeople and peasant cultivators. The impact of desert life and ideas upon neighbouring peoples has from time to time been immense, through invasion and destruction, but also in more positive ways, often leading to cultural progress, particularly in the fields of religion and abstract thought. The Old Testament deals continually with the theme of desert against town; and we may also recall the words of T. E. Lawrence that the edge of the desert is littered with the relics of religions and ideas developed from the interaction of nomadic and sedentary ways of life. Many of these movements have perished, but a few have gained strength enough to affect the whole world.

The unit among nomads is the tribe—a group that ensures a certain advantage in numbers, yet is small enough to exist within the limits set by a hard environment. Tribal discipline is strong, and direction is in the hands of a leader whose right to rule is based partly on hereditary descent, and partly on personal merit This system of rule may to some extent explain the general importance of leaders and persons, rather than principles and party doctrines, in the general political life of the present-day Middle East.

The mobility of the nomads, their predilection for raiding and skirmishing, and their scanty material possessions for long made them difficult subjects for any national government that attempted to impose its rule. An unusually vigorous head of state, such as Reza Shah in Iran, could from time to time successfully break or limit the power of the tribes; but a better policy (followed by the Ottomans, and by several present-day governments) has been to let the nomads go their way, with a minimum of interference. This was the situation until very recently, but the exploitation of oil has been a powerful solvent of ancient custom. Thus many former nomads have found sedentary occupations within oilfields, or in towns, or as semi-settled cultivators using irrigation water paid for or supplied largely by oil revenues. Now, nomadism and tribalism are in rapid decline, and it is the policy, stated or implicit, of most governments to bring about sedentarization. Twenty years or so ago, about 10 per cent of the population of the Middle East and North Africa was in the main nomadic, now the figure is about 1–2 per cent: half a million in Saudi Arabia, 400,000 in the rest of the Arabian Peninsula, 350,000 in Turkey, 300,000 in Iran and also in Iraq, 200,000 in Syria; 70,000 in Jordan, 50,000 in Egypt, and in Libya; and 18,000 in Israel. There are also uncertain numbers of nomads in the Sudan who move relatively short distances to escape annual floods.

One important feature in the sedentarization of nomads has been land-reform schemes by which plots of agricultural land, sometimes even with houses, have been made over to former pastoral nomads, e.g. in parts of the Nile valley, northern Syria and in north-east Iran; for such schemes to be successful, education in cultivation methods, and the provision of facilities and agricultural credit schemes are essentials.

RELIGIOUS DIVERSITY

Religious divisions are still strong within the Middle East; and for many persons religious and sectarian fidelity even replaces nationality, so that it is frequently possible, on asking an Arab to what country he belongs, to receive the answer, "I am a follower of Islam". A remarkable feature of the area, possibly connected with its geographical function as a meeting-place of peoples and ideas, is that three great religions of the modern world—Judaism, Christianity and Islam—have arisen within its limits; and that others, notably Zoroastrianism (now confined almost entirely to the Parsees of Bombay), Manichaeism, and Mithraism (of great influence in the later Roman Empire) should also be associated with the Middle East. The most recent example is the rise of Baha'i. Until recently, it seemed that the general awareness of religion in the Middle East was declining, but over the past few years, and especially during 1977–78 there has been renewal of religious and sectarian awareness, both as affecting everyday life, and in relation to politics.

Judaism

All three of the modern religions have various branches or sects. Little need be mentioned concerning Judaism, except to note that one of the main social problems of the State of Israel is to absorb Jewish immigrants of widely differing backgrounds and religious traditions. Because of the dispersals of Jews in various continents, there have developed Hebrews of Oriental and African affinities, besides the two European groups of northern (Ashkenazim) and Southern (Sephardim) Jews. Since the establishment of the State of Israel divergence of view as to the part religion should play in everyday life, and its general relationship with politics have proved intractable questions in the Israel Parliament, and have led to several Cabinet crises. Because of greater levels of immigration and a generally higher birthrate Israelis of "Oriental" descent now outnumber those of "European" origin, and there are intense debates from time to time as to how everyday life in Israel should respond to the situation.

Christianity

Christianity in the Middle East is even more widely divided. Geographical separation and the development of regional feeling during and after the end of the Roman Empire resulted in the rise of many cults that varied greatly in dogma, ritual and opinion; and despite the efforts of the early Fathers of Christianity, it proved impossible to reconcile all conflicting views, and maintain the unity of Christian peoples. There arose the Greek (or Orthodox) Church; the Roman Catholic Church (called the Latin Church in the Middle East); the Nestorians, who were once widespread from Mesopotamia and Asia Minor as far as India and China; the Armenians (or Gregorians); Copts; Abyssinians; Jacobites (or Syrian followers of Jacob Baradeus); and the Maronites (adherents of St. John Maroun). All of these sects came in time to possess complete autonomy, but following the rise of Islam in the seventh century A.D. the fortunes of many of them declined. Numbers of Armenians, Copts, Greeks, Jacobites, Nestorians and others (and the entire Maronite Church) were driven to accept aid from Rome, but at the price of recognizing the Pope as their titular Head. Thus we have what are termed the Uniate Churches—Armenian, Coptic, Nestorian Catholics, etc.—which further reduced the strength of the older autonomous groups, most of which managed to continue, though no longer of great importance. At present, therefore, we have more than twenty separate Christian sects, some powerful and world wide, others purely local in allegiance. The appearance of Protestant missionaries in the nineteenth century and after has added further to the religious bodies represented, although the number of converts is small.

Islam

Division in Islam began on the death of Muhammad. As the prophet designated no successor, most followers agreed that leadership of Islam could pass from any individual to another, according to merit and circumstance. This group came to be known as the *Sunni*, or Orthodox, and numbers about 90 per cent of all Muslims. A minority supported the claims of the next male relative of Muhammad, and these Muslims took the name of *Shi'a*, or Party. Shi'a adherents are dominant in Iran and the Yemen Arab Republic; in southern Iraq, where they form a large majority of the inhabitants; and as minorities in Syria, the Lebanon, and Turkey. Many sub-sects of the Shi'a are known, representing different forms of belief; and one such group was for a time a warlike military order, with much power in Syria and Iran. Its head was finally forced to take refuge in India, where his direct descendant is today the Aga Khan. Groups of his followers still remain in Iran and Syria. Many Muslims believe that there will one day arise a Mahdi (Messiah) who will conquer the world for Islam, and this circumstance has led to the appearance at various times of leaders who have claimed to be the long-awaited incarnation—for example, the Mahdi in the Sudan in the late nineteenth century.

The revival during the present century of Wahhabi power may briefly be noticed. The Wahhabis, by reason of their dislike of ostentation in religious observance, and their desire to revive the earlier, simpler tenets of the Faith, have been termed the Puritans of Islam. Under the vigorous and skilled leadership of their late head, King Ibn Saud of Arabia, they rose from obscurity as a desert people to control of most of the Arabian peninsula, and hence domination of the holy cities of Mecca and Medina. One factor in the present Arab disunity is the division on general religious grounds between the Wahhabis, who tend to despise the Muslims of Egypt, Jordan and Syria as lax in observance, and as backsliders in the Faith, and who are in turn criticized as primitive reactionaries. There were also acute personal differences involving King Ibn Saud, who in conquering Mecca displaced the former ruler, Sharif Husain, a direct descendant of the Prophet. A descendant of the former Sharif rules in Jordan (as also until 1958 in Iraq), hence something of the animosity displayed between Saudi Arabia and its northern neighbours owed its origin to personal feuds. This particular issue has now declined; but other sharp issues with a religious basis have replaced them, notably in the Lebanon, but to some extent in Turkey, where there is the National Salvation political party, of extreme Islamic views, that has come to have a significant voice in national affairs.

Political Complications

There are other questions of a general political nature that stem from religious differences within the Middle East. The willingness of outside nations to support various religious groups in their struggle against each other has from time to time led to large-scale intervention. France has championed the cause of the Latin and Uniate Churches, basing many of her claims to influence and territory within Syria and the Lebanon on her long connection with the Uniates, who form the largest single sect in the latter country.

Russia, under Tsarist and Soviet rule alike, has maintained a link with the Orthodox Church, and from time to time Russian bishops visit Jerusalem, where the larger part of Christian shrines are owned by the Orthodox Church. Within the last few years Russia has strongly supported, by means of legal and diplomatic action, Orthodox claims to ownership of property and privileges; and whatever the position within the U.S.S.R., Soviet policy is firmly directed to maintaining the rights and position of the Orthodox Christians within the Middle East. Because of its territorial ownership within Old Jerusalem, Russia could in some respects make a good case for trusteeship of the Christian Holy Places. Britain, rather curiously, has at times supported Muslim groups—sometimes orthodox, sometimes dissident. American interest, though of long standing (as much as a century in one or two localities) has generally been much less direct, but over the last ten to fifteen years has greatly expanded. There are now within the Middle East a number of American educational institutions of great influence and standing (for example, the American University of Beirut and the American Colleges of Istanbul). Most of these were founded as Protestant missionary activities, but have since developed into secular institutions covering a wide range of subjects.

One other effect of religious differences may be noted. With the possibilities of appeal to outside assistance, and the internal vigorousness of religious feeling, it has happened that a political *modus vivendi* can be achieved only by a distribution of offices and appointments among the interested religious sects. This was for long particularly obvious in the Lebanon, where ever since independence the President of the Republic has been a Maronite Christian and the Prime Minister a Sunni Moslem—a precarious balance that in 1976 may well have ended for ever. Sunni Muslims have tended to have considerable influence in Iraq (especially up to 1958), though the majority of the population is Shi'a in adherence.

The last few years have however seen a remarkable change in the pattern of religious life in the Middle East. On the one hand there has been, usually among the better educated, a marked decline in religious beliefs—Christian, Moslem, and even Hebrew, with a parallel development of a growth in secular, materialist outlook that on occasion shows impatience over the prevailing close connection between religion and political and social life. But far more, there is an opposite tendency towards revival of a fundamentalism, most of all in Islam, though also recognisable (in a wholly different context) among extremist Jewish groups such as the *Gush Emunim*. Religious brotherhoods of an Islamic and extremist character have become prominent over the past few years, and a number of these—the *Ikhwan* of Egypt, *Fidaiyai* of Iran, and *Tijaniya* of Turkey—have demonstrably exerted growing and increasingly significant political influence. Moreover, there has been a general and rapid development of fundamentalist Islamic thinking throughout the Middle East and even beyond. The dramatic events of late 1978, when an exiled *Ayatollah* could bring down the Shah's Government are the most outstanding and compelling example of this new surge of fundamentalism; but it is by no means confined to the one state of Iran, and in slightly varied forms, but with a single clearly definable basic pattern, is clearly apparent in several countries, Sunni and Shi'a. President Sadat even felt it necessary in April 1979 to condemn this Islamic activism, saying that Islamic militancy was not desired in peaceful Egypt.

CITY LIFE IN THE MIDDLE EAST

From very early times, long before Plato commended the city-state as an ideal form of political organization, town life has exercised a predominant influence in lands of the Mediterranean; and this predominance, amounting to a marked disproportion, has been particularly characteristic of the Middle East. Here, towns stand out as islands of relative wealth, culture and progress in a poor and backward countryside; and it is significant that the two centres that dispute the title of the oldest continuously inhabited site in the world are Damascus and Aleppo, whilst the oldest undoubted port is Byblos (modern Jbeil, 20 miles north of Beirut), which from its trade in papyrus gave us the word Bible.

There have been several contributing factors in the precocious growth of Middle Eastern cities. Firstly, because of a wide variety in geographical environment—rich oasis or coastal plain, mountain, desert, steppe and forest—there soon arose a diversity of economic production, and hence a need for exchange and market centres. Then too, with frequent warfare and invasion, defence became a necessity, and strong points on mounds or peaks, commanding corridors, defiles and river passages soon developed and gathered around them a township. Examples of former simple tribal strongholds that have evolved into great cities are Aleppo, Ankara, Jerusalem, Mosul and Tabriz, the third city of Iran. Another feature of the Middle East is the number of "planted" towns—sites deliberately planned or designated to be important. Of this nature is Teheran, which before it was chosen as a new capital by the Qajar rulers in 1788 had few functions other than that of a wintering spot for pastoral nomads. Amman was largely uninhabited for several centuries previous to 1880, though the site (Philadelphia) had held importance in Roman times; and there are other towns whose origins can be clearly traced to planned development in early Arab, Roman or Classical Greek times. Alexander the Great, and especially his successors, fostered many new towns and extended others.

The City in Conquest

It is a feature of Middle Eastern history that, time and time again, small but energetic groups of people seized power, and for a limited period ruled a large territory. The Hyksos Kings of Egypt, the Medes, Assyrians, Macedonian Greeks, Romans, Arabs, and Ottomans can all be cited as examples; and for each conqueror there soon arose the acute problem of maintaining a hold on defeated but numerically superior subject races, and of spreading the language, religion and traditions of the minority ruling group.

Most conquerors found that it was usually easier to dominate the cities, partly for the reason that military operations could be undertaken with more success against the inhabitants of a closely packed town, rather than against the nomads or peasants of trackless steppes, deserts, or mountains; partly because the towns with their trade could easily be taxed to support military rule; and partly because the population of the cities, polyglot in origin and in touch with outside conditions, could be more often induced to accept a new idea, a new language, or even a new religion. It is no accident that the great evangelical religions of the modern world should have extended from towns—that men first called themselves Christians in Antioch, or that Muhammad could feel that his cause had succeeded when Mecca and Medina acknowledged his rule, or that Jewish ritual should include the phrase "Next year in Jerusalem". We also have the curious position that the towns of the Middle East may often be strikingly different in wealth, in outlook and even in language and religion, as compared with the immediately surrounding countryside. The most famous example may be cited from the New Testament, as when the inscription on the Cross of Christ indicated the presence of a Latin-speaking ruling class, a Greek-speaking town and professional class, and an Aramaic-speaking peasantry. Such contrasts are apparent even today, though, of course, involving different languages.

Economic and Political Dominance

Another feature of Middle Eastern cities is their economic dominance, amounting almost to a stranglehold, in the life of each country. Town merchants are in touch with world markets and can control or "corner" the produce of the rural areas in their own district, for which, owing to the difficulties of transport, they are the only outlet. The strength of the merchants is indicated by the fact that in many Middle Eastern countries there is relatively little, or even in a few instances no, direct taxation, most governmental revenue being raised by indirect imposts.

We also find that in many cities there are still, despite land reforms and nationalization, significant communities of wealthy absentee landlords. Unlike that of Europe the Middle Eastern countryside does not attract resident "landed gentry"—because it is an area of few amenities, and still characterized by poverty, discomfort and disease: for example, two-thirds or even three-quarters of Middle East doctors practise in the larger towns. Hence landlords tend to remain in the towns, with rents collected in cash or kind by agents. The same is true of religious bodies, Muslim and Christian, many of which may possess landed estates or control the exploitation of land by tenant farmers. This means that there is in general a net flow of money derived from the countryside towards towns, and this provides a living not only for the wealthy but for others: artisans, domestic servants and shopkeepers. Though land reform and nationalization have of late years diminished the importance and wealth of some absentee landlords, these have by no means disappeared, partly because a new group of landlords has arisen as the result of the reform. Also, with depreciation of currencies and share prices, the ownership of land still remains a useful (though not now "gilt-edged") outlet for capital gains.

Another feature of town life in the Middle East until recently was the absence, or relatively slight development, of traditions of civic government and responsibility. There was little to parallel the growth of the burgher class that became so prominent in parts of Europe, and hence less of a corporate pride and pattern of local, as distinct from provincial or national, interest in problems of rule. The situation is changing markedly in some localities; but the absence of a bourgeois outlook (in its best sense) is still a feature.

Lastly, it is interesting to observe that towns have long tended to dominate Middle Eastern political life. The lure of greater wealth attracts the energetic, dissatisfied, and sometimes turbulent elements from the countryside. Many such immigrants, together with the occupants of city slums who become periodically unemployed because of trade slumps, and also a third element, inexperienced secondary school and university students, form a very dangerous combination—the Middle Eastern city mob. Mob violence, awakened at first over a political matter, sometimes assumes a religious complexion directed against minorities and foreigners, and among the demonstrators are often groups with few political or religious convictions, but whose aim is to spread disorder so that shops can be broken open and looted. Most Middle Eastern shops in the cities carry iron shutters that can cover the whole of the shop-front at the slightest sign of trouble. A restless, underfed proletariat, excited by political and religious issues, and inflamed by student agitators, can be very menacing in close, narrow streets. Even politicians themselves may ultimately go in fear of the tide of disorder that they themselves have had a hand in provoking. Over and over again in Middle Eastern affairs, demonstrators in the streets have swayed or brought about a total change of government: and, as in 1951 (Egypt), 1956 and 1976 (the Lebanon), 1958 (Iraq), 1960 (Turkey), 1963 (Iraq, Syria and Jordan), 1977 (Egypt) and 1978 (Iran), the dilemma of Pontius Pilate—how far to give way to turbulence in the streets—arises in an acute form at unhappily frequent intervals. The swift explosion of anti-American and anti-British feeling, expressed through mob violence in centres as far apart as Kuwait, Benghazi and Tunis, was a feature of June 1967.

Urban Growth

A further considerable problem now arises from the exceedingly rapid physical growth of a few urban centres. Cairo, with a population of about 8 million, is not only the capital of Egypt but the largest town of the Mediterranean area and by far the largest city in Africa. "Greater" Teheran is now near 5 million, and Baghdad 2–2½ million in population. Beirut and Casablanca each (with their suburbs) have more than one million, Algiers about one million, and about one-fifth of the country's population live in Tunis.

This rapid and accelerating growth—placed at six to ten per cent per annum for many large towns—is leading to a concentration of economic power, political influence, and social prestige which poses acute problems of two kinds. Besides the difficulties of providing adequate amenities and methods of administration—the demand for electricity is doubling every five years in many large cities, with severe traffic congestion also—there is something of a retrogression of provincial life, with near stagnation in a few distant parts. As well, with the "drift" to the towns, shanty areas pose increasing problems: well over one half of all the inhabitants of Ankara, for instance, live in houses that are officially regarded as "illegal". Regeneration of regional centres is now being taken up as an urgent matter in those countries that have oil revenues to support expansion plans or programmes.

Economic Geography

By far the greater part of the land surface in the Middle East is either mountain, desert, or swamp, and cultivated areas are extremely small in extent, covering no more than 5 to $7\frac{1}{2}$ per cent of the total area. Nevertheless, agriculture is the main occupation of a large majority of the inhabitants; and a further proportion of the people is employed in processing the products of agriculture, as cotton and tobacco packers, fruit driers, or canners of fruit, vegetables, and olive oil. It is obvious, therefore, that the remaining activities in the Middle East are of relatively restricted extent. Pastoral nomadism is found in many districts, as the only possible way of life in an arid or mountainous environment; but few people are involved, and the nomads live mainly a self-sufficient existence, so that their contribution to general economic activity is on the whole small. Because of this relatively low level, we have the apparent paradox that, whilst in many (though not all) countries of the Middle East most of the inhabitants are engaged in agriculture or pastoralism, the total contribution of these two activities to Gross National Product is often well under 50 per cent and even in some countries declining—with oil and mineral exports and transit trading accounting for the larger share. For some countries, therefore, agricultural progress remains the least successful sector of current National Development Plans—Iran is a case in point.

AGRICULTURE

Cereals

The chief food crops grown in the Middle East are wheat, barley and rye in the north, and millet, maize and rice in the south. Wheat, the chief crop of Turkey, Syria, the Lebanon, Jordan, Israel, Algeria and Tunisia, is of the hard variety, planted in autumn, and harvested in late spring or early summer. The use of Mexican strains of high-yielding wheat has spread over the past few years, with good, sometimes dramatic, results. Barley is more important than wheat in Libya, Iraq, Morocco and parts of Iran, since it is hardier and more resistant to insects. Rye (with some oats) is restricted to the colder and hillier parts of Turkey and Iran, whilst rice though much prized as a luxury, and also for its very high yield per unit of farm land, needs much heat and abundant water, and is grown only in a few specially fertile and favoured localities—Lower Egypt, southern Iraq, the valleys of southern Turkey, Syria, and a few parts of North Africa, especially Morocco. In some countries, because of its demands on irrigation water, and its tendency to spread malaria (owing to the flooded ground), the cultivation of rice is limited by law. Maize is the chief cereal in Egypt, and its cultivation is also being greatly extended in Israel. Farther south, towards Arabia and the Sudan, millets of various species become of increasing importance.

Cotton and Tobacco

In addition to these food crops, which, with some notable exceptions, are not of the first quality and thus are retained for home consumption, there is increasing emphasis on cash crops, as communications develop and an export market can be found. Some of the finest cotton in the world is grown in Egypt, where about 20 per cent of the agricultural land is given over to its production, and four-fifths of the total exports are in the form of raw cotton. The same crop is also a chief export of the Sudan. Elsewhere, quality is much lower, but cultivation has spread, especially in the Seyhan plain of southern Turkey around Adana, in the Aleppo and Jezireh districts of Syria, and in parts of Iran and Iraq.

Production of tobacco, introduced into the Middle East during the sixteenth century, is considerable, mainly in the Black Sea and Aegean coastlands of Turkey, and in Cyprus. Pure Turkish tobacco is no longer in favour among British and American smokers, but most "Virginian" cigarette and pipe tobaccos contain a small admixture of Turkish leaf; and Central Europe still prefers the unmixed Turkish variety. Many Arab farmers grow small quantities for their own use, but here quality is generally low, except in the district of Latakia, from which there is some export.

Fruit

The Middle East has an extremely wide variety of fruit. Vines are found both wild and cultivated, and besides their use in Turkey and Cyprus for currants and sultanas, much local wine is made, the best probably coming from Cyprus, the Lebanon and Israel. North Africa is especially favourable for wine-growing, which immigrants from France did much to foster. As a result, quantities of *vin ordinaire* are sold abroad, to France especially, where the local product had to some extent been superseded by the cheaper Algerian wine, until pressure from domestic growers forced the government to reduce imports. The U.S.S.R. has recently become a large-scale importer.

Citrus fruits are of increasing importance along the north-eastern Mediterranean coast, whilst apricots, figs, peaches and plums are widespread. Olives form a very important part of Middle Eastern diet, since animal fats are scarce, and the poorer fraction of the oil also serves as a domestic illuminant and for soap-

[*continued on p.* 18

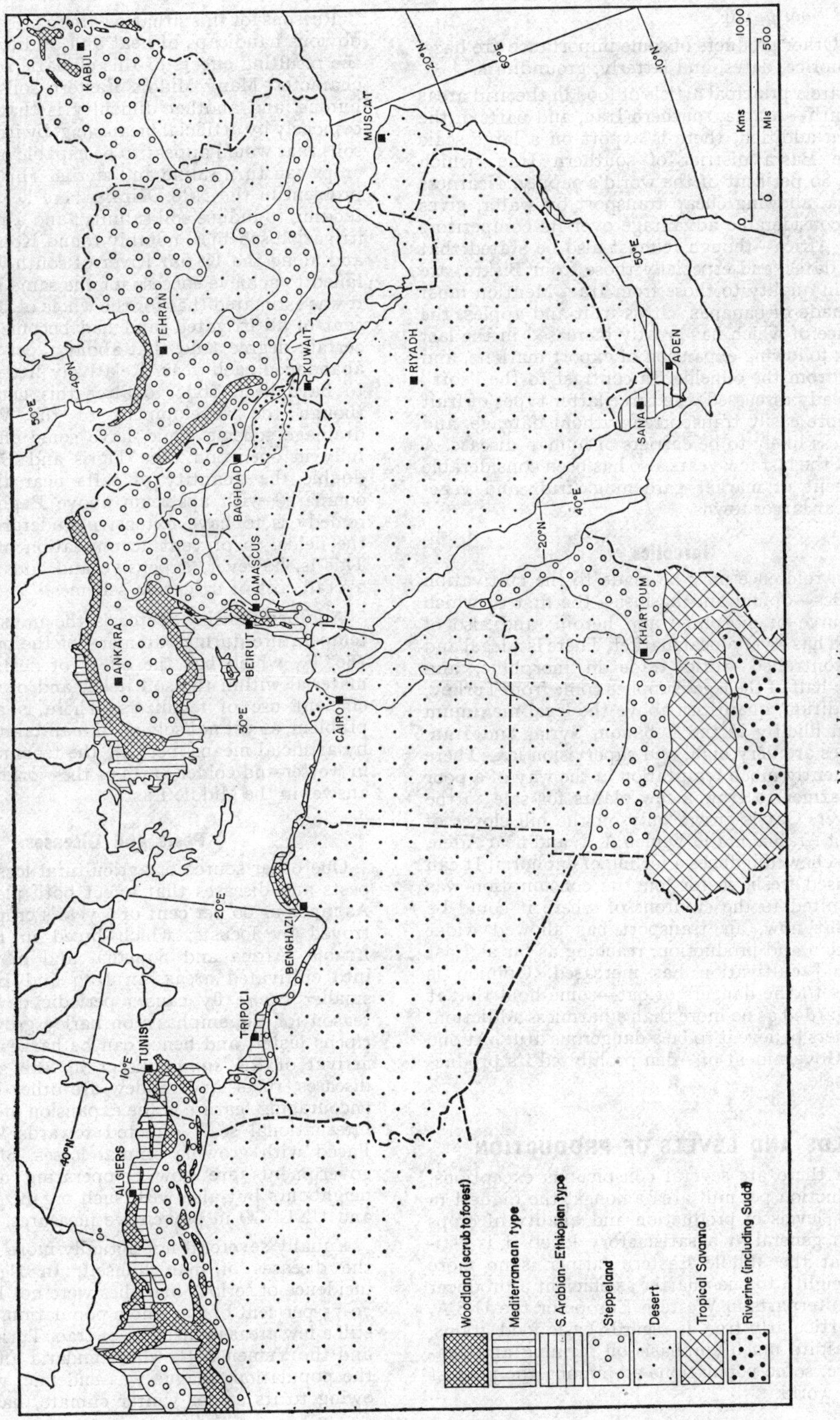

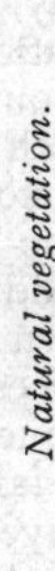

Natural vegetation.

continued from p. 16]

making. Other products of some importance are hazel nuts, liquorice, dates, and latterly, groundnuts.

Dates are a principal article of food in the arid areas of the south—Arabia, southern Iran, and parts of the Sudan. In addition, there is export on a large scale from the Basra district of southern Iraq, which produces 80 per cent of the world's supply. Nearness to the sea, allowing cheap transport by water, gives Basra a considerable advantage over its competitors in North Africa—though it must also be stated that Algerian dates, and especially those from Biskra, are superior in quality to those from Iraq. Mention must also be made of bananas, citrus fruit and apples, the importance of which has greatly increased in the last few years following expansion of export markets, and demands from the oilfields. In contrast to the "soft" fruits already discussed, the three latter types of fruit can be more easily transported without damage, and are also less likely to be carriers of human disease. A feature of the last few years also has been considerable development of market gardening (fruit and vegetables) near larger towns.

Narcotics

Finally, reference may be made to the cultivation of narcotics—opium and hashish—the first of which is the source of morphine and heroin; and also of qat, which has a very local market. There is a legal and strictly controlled world trade in morphine, and about one-half of the legal supplies come from Turkey; but in addition, quantities above the legal maximum are grown illicitly in the Lebanon, Syria, and Iran, since prices are very high, and supervision lax. There is consequently much temptation in the way of a poor peasant farmer to grow a few plants for sale to the illicit buyer. Qat is grown only on the hill slopes of south-west Arabia, in the Yemen A.R. and near Aden, and when chewed induces a feeling of euphoria. It can only be used fresh, so for long its consumption was closely limited to the environs of where it could be grown. But now, air transport has allowed wider consumption and production, reaching as far as East Africa, and cultivation has increased. Opinion is divided as to the dangers of qat—some hold that it can be regarded as no more than a harmless addiction, whilst others believe it to be a dangerous drug. At one time the Government of Aden prohibited its production and sale.

YIELDS AND LEVELS OF PRODUCTION

Though there are several conspicuous exceptions, with production per unit area amongst the highest in the world, levels of production and quality of crops are not in general at a satisfactory level: it is estimated that the Middle Eastern farmer is no more than one-eighth to one-quarter as efficient a producer as his counterparts in Western Europe or the U.S.A. This is particularly true as regards basic food grains, and so despite much emphasis on farming and self-subsistence, some populations are among the poorest fed in the world.

Reasons for this situation are to be sought first in the obvious handicaps of heat and aridity, together with the resulting effects of this climatic regime upon soil character. Many Middle Eastern soils are lacking in humus; and another difficulty is that when watered copiously by artificial means (e.g. by irrigation) certain soils that would appear to be capable of bearing heavy crops can turn saline and sterile. This is at present a problem in the Nile Delta, where heavy irrigation is tending to induce soil salinity; and a number of large irrigation schemes, notably round Konya in Anatolia, and along the Karun River of south-west Iran, have failed to achieve success for the same reason. In 1949 it was estimated that for the whole of Iraq some 60 per cent of all irrigated land had become salinated to a certain degree; and that about 1 per cent of area is abandoned each year. Relatively little would appear to have been done to alter this general situation; though the development of the Wadi Tharthar drainage scheme could have some effect when it is fully in operation. The Tigris and Euphrates carry double the quantity of salts near their mouth as compared with upstream above Baghdad. The best remedy is to have extensive underground drains in the fields, to prevent accumulation of excess water. This is, however, expensive and adds greatly to the overall cost of irrigation schemes.

Another limiting factor is the unusually high soil temperature during summer—of the order of 130° to 180° F., which has the effect of destroying organic material within the soil itself, and of preventing the efficient use of fertilizers. There is a fundamental problem, as yet not solved, of maintaining soil fertility by artificial means, because the techniques successful in wetter and colder parts of the world do not always answer in the Middle East.

Pests and Diseases

One other source of agricultural loss occurs in the pests and diseases that affect both plants and man. As much as 60 per cent of a year's crops may be destroyed by locusts, which breed in the deserts of Arabia, Africa and Somalia, and move as swarms into cultivated areas. In Iraq and Iran the much smaller *sunna* fly causes periodic devastation—one reason for the emphasis on barley growing is that it ripens faster, and hence can be harvested before the arrival of the *sunna* insect in late summer. Scale diseases, rusts, and mildew are other handicaps. An encouraging feature is the expansion of activity on an international scale directed towards locust control. Faced with growing annual losses, Middle Eastern governments are now co-operating not only with neighbours but also with such organizations as FAO and UNESCO in preventive measures.

Equally severe, if not actually more damaging, are the diseases of man himself. In Egypt, rates of incidence of serious maladies were not long ago up to 70-75 per cent of the whole population, and there are still a few areas in districts of Iraq, Turkey, the Sudan and the Yemen A.R. where malaria affects over half the population. Plague was endemic, whilst Turkey, owing to its colder winter climate, has long been a stronghold of tuberculosis. Eye diseases, chiefly trachoma, are rife, and in some areas produce blindness in up to 20 per cent of the population. Typhoid and venereal diseases are still prevalent, and from time to time there are outbreaks of cholera, sometimes minimized or "played down" by local governments. On the other hand, smallpox has been brought under control and eliminated in many parts. However, the Sudan has a particularly poor level of public health, especially in the south, where diseases are not only endemic but spread easily from tropical Africa. The riverine areas of Egypt and Iraq are particularly notorious for parasitic infections—ankylostomiasis, bilharzia and hookworm—which, most unfortunately, tend to spread with the expansion of irrigation. Dysentery (usually of a relatively mild form) is an almost ubiquitous feature, especially affecting newcomers. Despite this depressing list, it is also true to say that very considerable changes have been brought about in many areas by better public health measures, control of insect and animal disease vectors, provision of cleaner drinking water, and improved medical care. In a few regions (e.g. Kuwait and central Saudi Arabia) hospital services are among the best in the world. Thus incidence of many diseases, especially in towns, has shown a marked drop over the past decade.

The high incidence of disease was for long, and still remains in some areas, an important contributing factor to low agricultural efficiency: besides reducing physical capacity, mental alertness may also be reduced, thus retarding the introduction of new techniques. Until recently, one could speak of a "vicious circle"—the peasant was diseased and could not work hard, yields were thus precarious leading to malnutrition which in turn pre-disposed to disease. Malaria alone has in the recent past been cited as a major cause of backwardness, including also the decay of the earlier brilliant Arab civilization. Over the past twenty years malaria has successfully been eradicated in most, though not all parts of the Middle East: down to the 1950s, mosquito nets were found in the better hotels of most cities, now they are rarely to be seen. However, it would seem that in a few areas, species of mosquito more resistant to modern pesticides are now appearing, and strains of the disease itself also appear less susceptible to eradication by drugs: this is becoming something of a new problem in the southern areas of the Middle East.

Land Tenure

Yet more factors in agricultural backwardness are the methods of land holding and forms of tenancy. Full ownership, with the possibility of applying long-term methods of improvement, is not frequent among Middle Eastern farmers. Instead, there are various forms of share-cropping or tribal ownership, which collectively tend to perpetuate old, wasteful methods, to emphasize conservatism in outlook, and to make it extremely difficult for an individual to introduce any innovation. Holdings are often small and scattered, so that modern ploughs, tractors, or reaping machinery cannot easily be introduced; and owing to extremely high rents and dues, amounting in some instances to 65 per cent of the total yield of the holding, the peasant farmer is entirely lacking in capital for improvements, and remains dependent on his landlord for seed and even implements. Land-reform schemes now in progress in several countries, notably Iran, Iraq, Syria and Egypt, are altering this picture, but they do not affect all areas. When they do become more widespread there is a risk that production will decline initially, owing to the lack of capital and knowledge of new techniques of the new owners.

A further feature of Middle Eastern farming has been the existence of numerous absentee landlords, who invest money in land purely as a safe outlet for surplus capital, and have no real interest in farming itself. Such owners live mainly in the towns, and delegate control of their agricultural estates to overseers, being satisfied if the same level of production is maintained from one year to another. Such owners are not often willing to sink capital in new methods or machines, but are content to perpetuate existing methods. Because of the lack of outlet for investment in most Middle Eastern countries—movable property may be stolen, paper securities may be repudiated, and foreign currency, particularly the franc, lira, pound sterling and even the dollar have depreciated—real property represents a fairly safe long-term investment that cannot easily depreciate.

In recent years, many Middle Eastern governments have made attempts to improve the position by redistribution of holdings, and enactments limiting the total area of land held by one individual. This has had some good effect, but in some cases the laws have been loosely applied, or even remained a dead-letter; and ways of ignoring or circumventing them have further reduced their efficiency. Extensive handing over of Crown land to peasant ownership in Iran, followed by the redistribution to peasant ownership on a national scale of all large estates, and the organization of Liberation Province in Egypt, mainly from expropriated and irrigated land, are outstanding but by no means the only large-scale examples of reallocation of big estates, which has also been energetically pursued in Iraq. In Iran, the process has been so fully pursued as to invite the description "White Revolution": during the period 1962–72 some 700,000 peasant families received land for the first time as full owners. Reform schemes have, however, demonstrated that for success, it is necessary to do far more than merely make over land to peasants; agricultural education, credit and co-operative schemes, and handling of water rights are essentials too.

It is also necessary to state that despite all the handicaps noted above considerable progress has been achieved in certain areas of the Middle East. In parts of the Nile Valley, yields per acre of one or two crops are among the highest in the world; and in Israel a remarkable development of mixed farming, based on cereals, vegetables and animal husbandry, has transformed conditions in many areas. Much the same could be said of parts of Cyprus, Syria and Lebanon. The influence of French and Italian settlers in North Africa and Libya respectively was to demonstrate what might be done to improve yields and methods. Iran and Turkey, too, have experienced considerable agricultural development in certain directions over the last twenty to thirty years. Such ameliorations stand, however, in sharp contrast to conditions elsewhere in the Middle East. Overall, there is now growing realization that food production may be insufficient for population numbers, and that a crisis, identified by increasing shortages and high prices, may be at hand. For example, all the substantial agricultural progress realized in Egypt over the past 25 years may have done little more than keep an increased population at stationary levels of living.

INDUSTRIAL ACTIVITIES

In medieval times Middle Eastern industrial products had a high reputation. Steelwork, silverware, pottery, leather, and above all, textiles (from Damascus and Mosul, giving the words damask and muslin) found their way into many parts of Europe. At the present time, however, the scale of Middle Eastern industries is small; lack of fuel (particularly of coal and hydro-electric power), scarcity of mineral ores and some other raw materials, and the poverty of local markets being severe limiting factors. There is only one coalfield of any great importance—this is in north-west Turkey, at Ereğli (Heraclea), and production is only 4–5 million tons per annum; whilst very much smaller amounts are produced from fields in the region of Teheran. New discoveries in the Kirman area of Iran and in Egypt may well, however, transform the situation.

In recent years a significant degree of industrial development has, however, taken place in Egypt, Turkey, Israel and Iran, with some industry on a smaller scale in Iraq, the Lebanon and Syria. Some industrial activity, on a smaller scale, and related chiefly to production of building materials, processing of agricultural produce, or the limited treatment of mineral ores for export, has developed in North Africa. Textiles—chiefly cotton, but also silk, wool and mohair—are important, together with the transformation of agricultural products (sugar, tobacco, fruit processing and distilling) and the making of cement and bricks, for which there is a considerable local demand.

A further feature has been the growth of light consumer industries. Acute shortages during the Second World War impelled many Middle Eastern governments to try to develop local manufactures, even where local conditions were not outstandingly favourable; and over the last fifteen years there has been a marked growth of new power stations, factories and mills (detailed instances of which can be found in the economic surveys of the individual countries). Heavy capital goods such as machinery and vehicles are still imported on a large scale, though there are now assembly plants for motors and electrical machinery in Turkey, Iran, Israel and Egypt, with plans for similar plants, e.g. in the Lebanon, Syria and Iraq. Since 1960, however, there have been the beginnings of local manufacture of motors (in Egypt, Iran and Israel) and other machinery. Industrial expansion is marked in Egypt, Israel, Turkey and the Lebanon; and of late years particularly in Iran, Saudi Arabia and the Gulf States, where especially sophisticated industry based on petrochemicals and metals, with oil and natural gas as fuel and feedstocks, have recently developed. Restricted size of the potential market, competition of new nearby plant and of foreign produced goods are inhibiting factors, but the scale of actual and planned development (with the beginnings of exports in a few commodities such as fertilizers) is now impressive in a few countries.

The past few years have seen bold plans for raising steel production to some 15 million tons over the next decade, with possibilities even of 35 million. There are now 24 steel plants in the whole region, with a present capacity of about three million tons. Aluminium and copper smelting have also developed on a significant scale.

PETROLEUM RESOURCES

The general geological factors involved in the occurrence of petroleum have already been touched on; but it remains to add that there are a number of features special to the Middle East. Exploration has been retarded by the presence of what may be described as misleading surface structures—in some places, the possibility of finding oil was at first entirely discounted (as in Saudi Arabia); whilst in others, leakages of oil to the surface have given rise to optimism that has not always been justified. Moreover, the oilfields are often of extraordinarily large size, and the oil is held under considerable pressure, so that very few wells need be sunk to tap a large area, and the crude oil often rises of itself without much pumping—factors that allow an unusually low cost of production. The open nature of the country, as compared with the jungle of the East Indies, and the mangrove swamps of Venezuela, has been another favourable circumstance. Hence the cost of production of Middle Eastern oil is distinctly lower than that of oil from the U.S.A., the Caribbean, and from South-east Asia, both in terms of actual production costs and in terms of capital investment. Since 1974 we have seen Middle East producers, by virtue of their large levels of production and proved reserves, assume the dominant role in price-fixing for the world as a whole, with Iran leading a move towards high prices, and a slightly more "moderate" attitude pressed by Saudi Arabia. (Petroleum development is dealt with in more detail in a later chapter.)

One important factor in oilfield development has been the utility of pipelines. Broadly speaking, as compared with sea transport via the Cape, or, before 1967, the Suez Canal, a pipeline can move oil more cheaply from the Persian Gulf to the Mediterranean, and hence countries through which pipelines pass have been able to exact substantial royalties and other payments. Increasing demands of this nature (together with political troubles) have led to suggestions of developing alternative routes (e.g. through Turkey), events since 1956 having demonstrated the vulnerability of European consumers dependent on a single pipeline route. Use of larger tankers has, however, diminished the margin of profitability in using pipelines, and in 1972 the Iraq Petroleum Co. stated that it had become commercially cheaper to exploit fields closer to the Persian Gulf and export via the Cape, rather than move oil from the northern fields by pipeline to the Mediterranean. Nevertheless, Iraq has recently opened a new pipeline from Kirkuk to a Turkish Mediterranean terminal.

Present-Day Problems

In the context of a rapid survey, it is possible to do no more than hint at a few acute issues which exert a profound influence on current trends in the Middle East. These issues may be summarized as population pressure, the question of finding a reasonably equitable basis for the distribution of wealth between social classes, political leadership, and the cultural crisis within Islam.

POPULATION PRESSURE

The population problem arises as the result of a high birth-rate, together with a fairly high death-rate which is now in some parts declining rapidly, as the result of improvements in public health. There is, in consequence, an increasing number of survivors, producing a population growth of the order of 2.3 per cent (Egypt) to well over 3 per cent (Iran, Iraq, Jordan, Gulf States). For the larger States (Egypt, Iran, Turkey) there is now the situation of an annual increase in each state of about one million, with the general prospect of a doubling of numbers for the Middle East as a whole within about 30 years or less. It has been noted above that the agricultural gains made in Egypt have been negated by larger human numbers; and there are now clear signs of severe population pressure on natural resources. In parts of the Nile valley there are substantial groups living by agriculture and concentrated at densities of 3–5,000 per square mile; whilst as regards Turkey, FAO reported some years ago that despite improvements since the 1940s, the situation calls for "a truly heroic" agricultural and livestock programme. The need for food imports grows yearly: one estimate is that consumption is rising by 12.5 per cent per annum, and thus by 1980 some $6,000 million of food imports will be necessary within the Middle East.

EXTREMES OF WEALTH

A second group of problems arises from the social inequality that is a feature of many Middle Eastern countries. There is the large mass of the poor, and a small number of wealthy families, with few of a "middle" class. At present it is fair to say that the gap between the groups is widening rather than closing, as the standard of living of the poor remains the same, or even falls, and that of the rich rises rapidly, owing to profits from high world prices in cotton, tobacco, and, above all, in petroleum. Equally significantly, the appearance of western luxuries—large automobiles, radios, refrigerators, furs, and luxury hotels—tends to increase the visible gap between rich and poor. Until 1918, an Arab who lived ostentatiously risked the vigorous attentions of the Ottoman tax-collector; today, the wealthy Arab is himself often closely connected with the government, and can manipulate its fiscal policy closely to his advantage. We have noted that the larger proportion of the revenues of Middle Eastern states is usually derived from indirect taxation of necessities such as food and clothing—a system that bears heaviest on the poorer classes.

AUTHORITARIAN RULE

A third problem concerns the political organization in certain Middle East states. By temperament and experience, many Middle Easterners incline to personal and authoritarian forms of rule. Nomadic and pastoral ways of life tend to throw up individuals of much prestige and personal leadership; and even in religion—as indicated by the importance of prophetic revelation in Islam and Christianity—there is a tendency to respect the man equally with, if not more than, the principle. In consequence the idea of parliamentary democracy, introduced after 1920 partly in deference to the Western European views, has had a limited and uncertain extension. The average man has tended to be impatient of rule by general consent, as expressed through Western democratic methods, preferring to follow a single individual of superior appeal and ability. Where such a figure has not been forthcoming, there has been acquiescence in rule by a caucus or oligarchy. In this situation, the importance of armed services is very great. As the final repository of physical power—only artillery, tanks, and aircraft can really control a large dissident mob—the army leaders especially come often to be the final arbiters in a struggle for power. Moreover, as something of a meritocracy in which able officers can most easily rise from humble origins to positions of power, the armed forces in the Middle East have often come to a centre of evolved middle-class, or even radical, opinion essentially different from the bourgeois attitude of the merchant groups.

Saudi Arabia and the Gulf states are ruled by absolute monarchs. For the twenty years preceding 1940 Turkey and Iran were ruled by despots. In more recent times, there has been a partial rejection of democracy on the Western pattern in countries where parliaments existed, and the last few years have seen a tendency towards a recrudescence of personal rule, the outstanding instances being in Egypt and Iraq. Parliamentary government seemed fairly strongly developed in Turkey until about 1955, but later events have suggested a return to the now normal pattern within the Middle East. A few years ago, it was perhaps widely felt that, eventually, monarchy would be largely displaced by a rising tide of republicanism, as actually has happened in Egypt, Iraq and Libya. During the 1970s, however, partly due to increased oil revenues, the monarchial principle showed considerable leadership and resilience. Events in Iran during 1978–79 have however shown that this has been, for one area at least, merely a temporary phase.

MODERNIZING ISLAM

The widest problem of all concerns the cultural crisis within modern Islam. Until the end of the Middle Ages, Islamic culture was vigorous, and in many respects more advanced than that of Europe. Islamic thought greatly influenced the West, with a parallel superiority, or at least equality, in the political sphere. Since that time, however, there has been a considerable decline in power and intellectual strength: large-scale political penetration and domination from Europe began in the nineteenth century, and for several centuries material standards of life have no longer approximated to those of the West. There has, as a result, been much speculation in the Arab world upon the reasons for this decline. Three broad points of view can be discerned. There are those who see no good prospect in a continuance of Islamic traditions, and so wish to follow new ways of life—either Christian and western, or, less clearly, new materialistic doctrines, one ultimate expression of which may be Communism. At the opposite extreme are those, now more numerous, who suggest a return to a stricter form of Islam; and this policy is followed at the present time to a varying extent in Saudi Arabia, the Gulf States and Algeria. Then there is a third group of intermediates, whose position is perhaps the most difficult of all, since they wish to combine modernity with a maintenance of internal traditions. How far exactly can one go in this respect? And too often an attempt at combining widely diverse elements leads to superficiality, a rejection of fundamentals and a real understanding of neither aspect. We therefore have the phenomenon of the 'angry young Arab'—given more and more to rejection of existing ways and now actively critical of the failure of leadership over Palestine, and of inequalities in and lack of opportunity for economic advancement. He has an increasing sense of frustration which becomes more and more vocal with the spread of literacy. A further development, reflecting the special position of the Middle East between East and West, is the emergence of a specifically "Arab" socialism: neither Soviet nor Maoist communism, according to some Arab intellectuals, and certainly not "western" socialism, but reflecting the special social traditions of Islam. One aspect of this is the growth of Baathist ("Regeneration") movements of a socialist nature, in Syria and Iraq; the other, far wider in character, is, as we have seen, the rapid surge in fundamentalist Islam.

Summing Up

Having made a cursory survey of Middle Eastern lands and their resources, it is now possible to attempt a summary of conclusions. We may recall once again what was said concerning the geographical position of the Middle East as the land connexion between three continents; from this situation has arisen its main role in the world—as an intermediary between the nations of Europe, Asia, and Africa, both in the economic and cultural spheres. Sometimes this historic function has been discharged purely, so to speak, as an agent or middleman, without any indigenous contribution—as when, for example, silk, sugar, citrus fruit, paper, gunpowder, and the compass were introduced from Further Asia into Europe. At other times, a technique or an idea has been received or developed in the Middle East, expanded there into a great movement, and transmitted elsewhere. One may cite, for example, the system of garden irrigation brought by the Arabs to Spain, which is still a highly productive element in Spanish agriculture, or the religions of Christianity and Islam, or the scientific ideas of the Greeks and Hindus, which were preserved throughout the Dark Ages of Europe and later made available to the West through the works of Muslim commentators.

With the discovery of the sea route to India in the fifteenth century, the importance of the Middle East as a transit area greatly declined, but following the opening of the Suez Canal, and the later growth of air communications, the situation has once more altered. There has been a return to something of the ancient position, with air and sea routes now contributing again to outstanding prosperity, even though the Suez Canal, re-opened in 1975, cannot recapture all its former traffic unless it is enlarged.

Beirut early emerged as a world centre for air traffic—it was one of the first airports to be designed for jet aircraft—and because of its central geographical location, a climate that is exceptionally favourable for air navigation, and the topographical and political difficulties in regions further north and south, the Middle East has become a world nodal centre of air traffic. In a broader sense still there has very recently been a major shift of political and economic influence within the world. For several centuries, wealth and hence power were concentrated in north-western Europe; but since about 1900 the rise of America and Russia, the independence of India and black Africa, revival of China, and growing dependence of Europe on foodstuffs and primary materials imported from Australasia and Africa brought about an expansion of global relations. The Middle East, situated at the cross-roads of the world, has increasingly profited from what is now a central geographical position. Over and above this have been the dramatic effects first from the fact of having more than half the world's proven reserves of oil and natural gas, and in 1974 awakening by Middle East governments to the implications of this commanding geopolitical situation. In only a few weeks during 1974 the dominance of Middle Eastern oil suppliers was demonstrated, with effects that will last for decades. A question anxiously debated since the quadrupling of oil revenues in 1973–74 is how far the Middle East will play a much greater financial and hence political role in world affairs. Concern, even alarm, in early 1974 over whether the new revenues would overturn or disrupt world markets has subsided, as it becomes clearer that Middle Eastern oil states are now using the largest proportion of their revenues for internal development (including heavy emphasis on defence), and the remainder more or less equally split between outside loans (often to other Arab countries), and investment in world stock and property markets (mainly but not entirely American). The political effects of this new wealth are becoming apparent: a principal one is certainly the tendency of the U.S.A. to push Israel more strongly towards seeking political accommodation with its Arab neighbours.

Returning to more modest horizons, it is useful to notice one other feature of the Middle East, due in large part to its geography: potential as a tourist centre. It is probable that currently north-west Europe is experiencing a small climatic oscillation towards cooler, rainier summers; hence with "guaranteed" sunshine, excellent beaches, and considerable archaeological and human interest, certain parts of the Middle East have been able to develop a growing tourist attraction. New hotels, amenities and sports stadia are under construction; and given stable political conditions, this activity could well develop much further in the next few years, not merely for one season, but through a large proportion of the whole year.

POLITICAL OUTLINE

Similarly, there have been shifts in political fortune since the First World War. In 1916 the allocation of almost the entire Middle East as spheres of influence for European powers—Britain, France, Russia, Italy and Greece—had been agreed on. Treaties were actually in existence envisaging a territorial division which would have left only a fraction of Asia Minor under autonomous local rule.

From that apparent high water mark of Western influence, there has been a considerable decline; but the interest of external powers in the Middle East continues, fostered by the petroleum resources and strategic geographical location of the area.

At the same time there has been a parallel rise in nationalist feeling, helped on partly by differences among interested European powers and the skill with which these were exploited by Middle Eastern governments, and partly by the growth of internal wealth in the states themselves. This process became particularly vigorous after 1940, when from being a small marginal producer of in the main low-quality commodities, the Middle East became an important world supplier of petroleum, cotton, tobacco, wool and cereals.

The main element in the present-day politics of the Middle East is the existence of the state of Israel. To most Arabs, the creation first of a National Home for Jews and later of a Jewish State was a clear demonstration of hostility toward the Arab world on the part of Britain, France and the U.S.A.—a view which the events of 1956, and then of 1967, seemed only to confirm. As the Arabs see it, Western patronage of Zionism was a Machiavellian device to disrupt the Arab Middle East; and there can be no real friendship or understanding with the West until support for Zionism is disavowed. Moreover, uncertain of their own strength, Arab governments have increasingly turned to the U.S.S.R. for support against Zionism and its patrons. At times too it has been possible to take advantage of American divergence in policy from that of Britain and/or France (e.g. over oil concessions, Algeria, Cyprus and Suez). Moreover, the Middle East may offer a counterpoise to the forces balanced within the other southern extremity of Asia. Thus the present situation in many ways resembles that of the pre-1914 Balkans, with a number of small and antagonistic states manoeuvring between independence and "protection" from a great power in the background. But the Balkans never possessed more than half the world's oil.

ECONOMIC TRENDS

In the economic sphere, it is more difficult to present a clearly defined picture. There is the unique asset of petroleum, which has already transformed ways of life in areas where it is exploited, and brought unexpected wealth to port terminals such as Abadan, Bahrain, Tripoli (Lebanon), Baniyas, Sidon, Kuwait and Benghazi. A striking inequality has consequently developed between various countries. Those actually producing oil have substantial extra wealth, and can embark on schemes of improvement, with at some time the possibility of a relatively unfettered foreign policy. Next in order come the non-producers with locational advantages—pipelines, good harbours or oil refineries. These countries can profit in a minor way from petroleum exploitation, but a ceiling is set by the cost of alternative transport. If too much is demanded by way of transit dues, the oil traffic could be re-routed either via Suez (in relatively small tankers, or by the new SUMED pipeline), or the Cape of Good Hope, and by the alternative pipeline routes, such as that from Eilat on the Gulf of Aqaba to the Mediterranean, or from Iraq to the Mediterranean through Turkey.

The relationships of foreign exploiting companies have undergone dramatic changes since the 1920s and 30s, when approximately 16 per cent only of oil revenue was paid over to local governments, and companies enjoyed almost extra-territorial legal and fiscal rights. Although the volume of oil produced has increased enormously, the position of the foreign companies has been steadily reduced, until, in the mid-1970s, they have been entirely expropriated and reduced at most to the position of agents for a nationalized industry. The effect of a quintupling of revenue since 1973 has been enormous, both internally, where there is a leap forward in the commercial and industrial spheres, to be set against the corroding effect of sudden easy wealth on traditional outlook and ways of life. Externally, oil wealth is now being deployed with increasing vigour and sophistication as a political weapon: to create friends, extinguish enmities, and persuade countries such as the U.S.A. that Arabs, as well as Jews, may be entitled to a National Home in Israel/Palestine.

As regards agriculture, the position is less satisfactory. Though there are certainly richly endowed spots (especially parts of the Nile Valley), the Middle East is on the whole a poor area, condemned by aridity and scantiness of resources to a marginal place as a producer. Nevertheless, the last twenty years have seen highly significant increases, particularly in Egypt, Iran and Turkey, which are now undoubtedly in numbers if not wealth the leading states of the Middle East. But overall, as we have noted, it is now becoming apparent that, despite progress achieved, present levels of agriculture are becoming insufficient to support the population growth, and that imports of foodstuffs on an increasing scale are becoming necessary. The only area of the Middle East where there is still large potential for further sustained agricultural development may well be the Sudan.

Turkey

Though an agricultural country, Turkey in 1920 imported almost one-half of her foodstuffs: most of the few public utilities were foreign-owned; and modern industry could hardly be said to exist. Following several phases of development (the last of which from 1947 onwards amounting almost to an agricultural revolution) Turkey is almost self-sufficient in food, and in favourable years since 1950 has even exported wheat. Foreign ownership has been very greatly reduced, and a variety of light industry created. At first much of this activity was state-sponsored and owned, but since 1950 there has been a partial de-nationalization of industry. Over the past few years, however, there has been a fall-off in prosperity, with shortage of development capital and several devaluations of currency.

Egypt

Progress in Egypt has also been considerable. The careful use of river barrage systems has made the lower Nile valley one of the most productive agricultural areas in the world, with highest unit yields in maize and sugar, and highest quality in cotton. Intensity and quality of farming are unrivalled elsewhere in the Middle East, though there are ominous signs that future progress will be difficult—almost all the Nile water is now in use, and more and more fertilizers must be imported. Also, war periods greatly stimulated the growth of local industry, which, until the 1952 revolution, had always been on a capitalist, *laissez faire*, basis. Textiles are most important, but the increased wealth of the upper and middle classes has provided a market for light consumer goods that is now largely supplied within the country. An outstandingly important development is the full implementation of the Aswan High Dam project which, besides adding one-third to the present total of cultivated land in Egypt, provides electric power for heavy and light industry on a very considerable scale, at prices comparable with those of Europe. There are, however, certain criticisms now levelled against the Aswan concept, some of which are on technical grounds, some purely political. Egypt has massive debts, and her poor record over the last few decades has made outside investors cautious. In 1977, however, there was an attempt to improve the position by negotiating extensive outside loans for development and the re-scheduling of past debts. This would not so far appear to have had outstanding success; and the "open door" policy has not produced a massive inflow of capital. The rich may well be better off; but the poor are not noticeably so.

Israel

Israel had certain advantages when it began the desperate task of attempting to support relatively large numbers in a poor environment at high standards of life. There were the energy and skill of its European-trained population; an overriding determination to make a success from unpromising beginnings, much machinery imported from Europe (Hitler allowed refugees from Nazi Germany to take plant, but not capital), and financial support from outside, chiefly the U.S.A. The country is not richly endowed—though mineral deposits (oil, natural gas, copper and phosphates) on a relatively small scale have recently been discovered—and transport is difficult. Moreover, most of the south is arid, and good agricultural land is everywhere severely restricted. A further handicap has been the determination to maintain high levels of wages—a matter in which powerful trade unions are involved. The advances achieved both in agriculture and industry have been very great but some restriction of consumption of food and clothing is still necessary, and there is a severe adverse balance of trade with exports amounting to only one-half or in some recent years, one-quarter of imports. In consequence, despite stringent controls, and great efforts to expand production, loans from abroad are still vital to the Israel economy, and unemployment on a moderate scale had come to be a problem before the 1967 War. After that time, the Israeli economy experienced boom conditions until 1974, after which heavy defence costs began to affect economic life unfavourably, helped on by the world economic downturn.

Iran

Iran has a long tradition of craft industry, especially in wool; and there are varied mineral deposits, including coal. With the exception of petroleum, however, these deposits are scattered, small in amount, often of low grade. Within the last few years, however, there has been a considerable degree of industrial growth in Teheran City, which now has industrial quarters that produce a wide range of constructional and consumer products. Rapid development here of industrial capacity is now seen as excessive in that it is stultifying growth in other regions of Iran; and is in general too rapid a process for the installed capacity of electricity generation. Construction of a gas grid from the southern fields to Isfahan and northwards to the U.S.S.R. at Astara has been a great impetus to development, and a large steel-making plant has been constructed by Soviet technicians at Isfahan—this is already planned to be extended. Overall Iran has experienced considerable, at times spectacular development with annual growth-rates of between 15 and 24 per cent. Liquidity was a problem in 1976 and growth plans have in consequence since been trimmed, but Iran's industrial programme in absolute terms, and certainly in comparison with that of her neighbours, can only be described as impressive. However, the cutback in oil production that accompanied the change of government in 1978, together with frequent strikes and the withdrawal of most expatriate workers, has caused considerable fall-off both in levels of activity and expansion of new development projects.

Iraq

Until recently there was hardly any industry of any kind in Iraq, in distinct contrast to many of its neighbours. But since 1945 oil revenues have been allocated to a national Development Board, which has fostered the development of communications and agriculture, and begun to plan some industrial activity. Now, in addition to the processing of agricultural products, there is some textile manufacturing (chiefly cotton and rayon), a little light engineering, and a small chemical industry. Plans are in hand to expand these, especially the last. Agriculture is less developed than in Egypt, owing in part to the difficult nature of the two rivers, which have been more difficult to control and develop for irrigation. Since 1954, however, with the completion of Wadi Tharthar and other flood control and irrigation projects, the situation has changed, and large areas of good land which have hitherto remained unused can now be developed.

Syria, Lebanon, Jordan

At one time, Syria was the most industrialized province of the Ottoman Empire, with Aleppo second only to Constantinople in size. Loss of markets since 1918 has hampered but not destroyed the textile and metal manufactures of Aleppo and Damascus, and there are a small number of other industrial activities. Agriculturally, Syria has developed greatly since 1945. The irrigated "Fertile Crescent" has been expanded, and parts of the Euphrates valley brought back into cultivation for the first time in many centuries. Syria is self-sufficient in cereals, and exports these, together with raw cotton, to her less well-placed neighbours, the Lebanon and Jordan. The cotton is used both in the Middle East and in central Europe and Japan. The building of a dam across the Euphrates at Tabqa east of Aleppo, is only the largest factor in a general programme of Syrian development.

The Lebanon, like Israel, has severe natural handicaps. The rugged nature of the hills, which occupy most of the country, and aridity in the east greatly limit cultivation, and there are no mineral resources. Dependent on the import of foodstuffs, the country nevertheless has a considerable transit traffic, with the intelligence, adaptability and highly developed commercial sense of its people as the chief assets of the country. There is an international trade in gold, and Beirut (with four universities) has become a major cultural centre for the entire Middle East. Since 1975 civil war on an increasing scale has brought the country into a desperate position, but with the cessation of major warfare in 1977 and the formation of a Reconstruction and Development Council it is possible (given the resilience of Lebanese entrepreneurs) that some activities will re-develop.

Jordan, with almost no sea outlet, is in a very different situation. Most of the country is either arid or covered by bare sheets of lava—the only cultivable areas are west of the Jordan (Israeli-occupied since June 1967), in the Judaean uplands, and around Amman. Nomadic pastoralism is the only possible activity over much of the country—though the exploitation of substantial phosphate deposits provides a further source of occupation. An artificial territorial unit, with very few resources, Jordan is hardly viable, and has depended on outside subsidies, at present provided by Britain, the U.S.A. and, for varying periods since 1967, by Saudi Arabia, Kuwait and Libya. At present, there is a period of much improved conditions, partly due to fuller exploitation of mineral resources (chiefly phosphate), partly due to better political relations with Syria; and partly because of the shift of some commercial activity from the Lebanon, which has produced boom conditions, especially in Amman. Foreign loan and development capital has become available on a much more extensive scale.

Libya

A somewhat similar situation obtained in Libya until very recently where, despite the imposing size of territory, cultivated land is restricted to certain districts near or along the coast, together with a few inland oasis settlements. Now, discoveries of oil on a large scale are rapidly transforming the situation, and there is marked growth, especially in towns such as Benghazi and Tripoli.

Arabia

The Arabian peninsula is, so to speak, a stage beyond Libya. Before 1940 the territory was possibly the poorest in all the Middle East—only scattered oases with a largely nomadic population. Now the economic situation has been completely transformed; Saudi Arabia and Kuwait are, with the United Arab Emirates, among the largest oil producers of the Middle East. Qatar and Oman have also developed as significant contributors; and in all these countries schemes for infrastructures and industrial development are being pushed ahead. The immense oil revenues have financed lavish public works and welfare programmes, but the ease with which all imports needed for the small population can be paid for has reduced the incentive to develop the peninsula's other resources. Nevertheless, a major central industrial axis is rapidly developing across the country, based on Jeddah-Yanbo-Jubail in the west, and the oil complex around Dammam on the east.

Cyprus

Though small, Cyprus prior to the troubles of 1974 had a very sound agricultural system, with over 55 per cent of the total land area used—a figure far higher than in any other Middle Eastern country. There are also small but useful deposits of iron, copper and asbestos; with a growing tourist trade. Since 1974, however, agriculture has been disrupted by the exchange of populations, with crops in some areas untended. Despite all this, however, exports of fruit have picked up, from the south, and tourism has shown some signs of revival. The arrival of Lebanese Christian refugees (many with some capital) has proved a stimulus; and the speed of reconstruction in the southern (Greek) sector is now very remarkable.

The Maghreb

Lastly, North Africa is still suffering from the effects of colonial rule. The effects of prolonged and bitter warfare, the withdrawal of French "colons" who contributed in predominant measure to the more highly developed economic activities, and the resulting disequilibrium in an economy that until independence was strongly integrated with that of France—all these will take time to dissipate. Whilst over and above, there is the desperate need to provide for the rapidly growing numbers of inhabitants, with the concomitant problem of greater imbalance between urban and rural areas—a declining countryside, resulting in a fall-off in agricultural production, and congestion at declining levels of subsistence in the larger towns.

The most hopeful element is the presence of substantial mineral resources. Oil and gas could be used in part directly as fuel for industry; and revenues from exports might be directed to an expansion both of home manufacturing and improved agricultural techniques. Hydro-electricity is another possible source of energy, and this could foster *inter alia* more methodical exploitation and treatment of metallic mineral resources. At long term, the problem is also one of transferring the liability of an underemployed and growing population into the economic asset of a large pool of labour and consumer demand.

The Religions of the Middle East and North Africa

Islam

R. B. Serjeant

Islam is a major world religion and the faith predominating throughout the Middle East (with the exception of Lebanon the population of which is approximately half Muslim and half Christian) and North Africa. There are substantial Christian minorities in some countries and communities of oriental Jews and other faiths, for centuries integrated with the Muslim majority. Islam is not only a highly developed religious system but an established and distinctive culture embracing every aspect of human activity from theology, philosophy, literature to the visual arts and even man's routine daily conduct. Its characteristic intellectual manifestation therefore is in the field of Islamic law, the *Shari'ah*. Though in origin a Semitic Arabian faith, Islam was also the inheritor of the legacy of classical Greek and Roman civilization and, in its major phase of intellectual, social and cultural development after its emergence from its Arabian womb, it was affected by Christian, Jewish and Persian civilization. In turn, Greek scientific and philosophical writings—direct translations into Arabic or forming a principal element in the books of Arab scholars—began to enter medieval Europe in Latin renderings about the early 12th century from the brilliant intellectual circles of Islamic Spain, and formed a potent factor in the little Renaissance of western Europe.

Islamic civilization had, by about the 18th century, clearly lost its initiative to the ascendant West and has not since regained it.

HISTORY

The founder of the religion of Islam was the Prophet Muhammad b. 'Abdullah, born about A.D. 570, a member of the noble house of Hashim, belonging to the 'Abd Manaf clan, itself a part of the Quraish tribal confederation of Mecca. 'Abd Manaf may be described as semi-priestly since they had the privilege of certain functions during the annual pilgrimage to the Meccan Ka'bah, a cube-shaped temple set in the sacred enclave (*haram*). Quraish controlled this enclave which was maintained inviolate from war or killing, and they had established a pre-eminence and loose hegemony even over many Arabian tribes which they had induced to enter a trading alliance extending over the main Arabian land routes, north and south, east and west. With the powerful Quraish leaders in Mecca, temple guardians, chiefs, merchant adventurers, Muhammad clashed, when, aged about 40, he began to proclaim the worship of the one God, Allah, as against their multiplicity of gods. These Quraish leaders were contemptuous of his mission.

While his uncle Abu Talib, head of the house of Hashim, lived, he protected Muhammad from physical harm, but after his death Muhammad sought protection from tribes outside Mecca—they would not accept him even when he asked only to remain quietly without preaching—Thaqif of Taif drove him roughly away. Ultimately pilgrims of the Aws and Khazraj tribes of Yathrib (Medina), some 200 miles north of Mecca, agreed to protect him there, undertaking to associate no other god with Allah and accepting certain moral stipulations. Muhammad left Mecca with his Companion Abu Bakr in the year 622—this is the year of the *hijrah* or hegira.

Arriving in Yathrib, Muhammad formed a federation or community (*ummah*) of Aws and Khazraj, known as the "Supporters" (*Ansar*), followed by their Jewish client tribes, and the "Emigrants" (*Muhajirun*), his refugee Quraish adherents, with himself as the ultimate arbiter of the *ummah* as a whole, though there remained a local opposition covertly antagonistic to him, the *Munafiqun*, rendered as "Hypocrites". Two internal issues had now to be fought by Muhammad—the enforcement of his position as theocratic head of the federation, and the acquisition of revenue to maintain his position; externally he took an aggressive attitude to the Meccan Quraish.

In Yathrib his disposal of the Jewish tribes who made common cause with the "Hypocrites" improved his financial position. The Meccan Quraish he overcame more by skilful political manoeuvre than through the occasional armed clashes with them, and in year 8 he entered Mecca without fighting. Previously he had declared Yathrib a sacred enclave (*haram*), renaming it Medina, the City (of the Prophet)—the two cities known as al-Haraman have become the holy land of Islam. Muhammad was conciliatory to his defeated Quraish kinsmen, and after his success against Taif, south of Mecca, deputations came from the Arabian tribes to make terms with the new Prophet—the heritor of the influence of the Meccan Quraish.

Early Islam

The two main tenets of Islam are embodied in the formula of the creed, "There is no god but Allah and Muhammad is the Apostle of God." Unitarianism (*tawhid*), as opposed to polytheism (*shirk*) or making partners with God, is Islam's basic principle, coupled with Muhammad's authority conferred on him by God. Muhammad made little change to the ancient Arabian religion—he abolished idolatry but confirmed the pilgrimage to the Ka'bah; the Koran, the sacred Book in Arabic revealed to Muhammad for his people, lays down certain social and moral rules. Among these are the condemnation of usury or interest (*riba*) on loans and prohibition of wine (*khamr*)—both ordinances have always been difficult to enforce. On the whole the little change involved seems to have made it easy for Arabia to accept Islam. While there is incontrovertible evidence of Muhammad's contact with Judaism, and even with Christianity, and the Koran contains versions of narrative known to the sacred books of these faiths, yet these are used to point purely Arabian morals. The limited social law laid down by the Koran is supplemented by a body of law and precept derived from the *Hadith* or Tradition of Muhammad's practice (*Sunnah*) at Medina, and welded into the Islamic system, mainly in its second and third centuries.

Subsequent History

Immediately after Muhammad's death in 632, Abu Bakr, delegated by him to lead the prayer during his last indisposition, became his successor or Caliph. Some Medinan supporters had attempted a breakaway from Quraish overlordship but Abu Bakr adroitly persuaded them to accept himself to follow Muhammad. But office in Arabia, generally speaking, is hereditary within a family group, though elective within that group, and Abu Bakr's action had taken no account of the claims of 'Ali, the Prophet's cousin and son-in-law—the house of Hashim to which Muhammad and 'Ali belonged was plainly aggrieved that a member of a minor Quraish clan should have snatched supreme power. Muhammad's Arabian coalition also showed tendencies to dissolve, the tribes particularly objecting to paying taxes to Medina, but Abu Bakr's firm line held it together. The expansionist thrusts beyond Arabia during his Caliphate, continuing under his successor 'Umar and part of the reign of the third Caliph 'Uthman, diverted tribal energies to profitable warfare in Mesopotamia, Palestine-Syria, Egypt and Persia. Muslim armies were eventually to conquer North Africa, much of Spain, parts of France, and even besiege Rome, while in the east they later penetrated to Central Asia and India.

During 'Uthman's tenure of office the tide of conquest temporarily slackened and the turbulent tribes, now settled in southern Iraq and Egypt, began to dispute the Caliph's disposal of booty and revenue, maintaining that he unduly favoured members of his own house. A delegation of tribal malcontents from Egypt murdered 'Uthman in the holy city of Medina, and in the resultant confusion 'Ali, Muhammad's cousin, was elected Caliph with the support of the tribesmen responsible for murdering 'Uthman. This raised grave constitutional problems for the young Muslim state, and is regarded as the origin of the greatest schism in Islam.

If Legitimist arguments were the sole consideration 'Ali's claims to succession seem the best, but he had previously lost it to 'Uthman—whose father belonged to the Umaiyah clan which had opposed Muhammad, but whose mother was of Hashim. 'Uthman naturally appointed Umaiyah men loyal to him to commands in the Empire, notably Mu'awiyah as governor of Syria—the son of that very Abu Sufyan who headed Quraish opposition to Muhammad at Mecca—though later reconciled to him. Mu'awiyah demanded 'Uthman's murderers be brought to justice in accordance with the law, but 'Ali, unable to cope with the murderers, his supporters, was driven by events to take up arms against Mu'awiyah. When they clashed at Siffin in Syria 'Ali was forced, against his better judgement, to submit to the arbitration of the Koran and Sunnah, thus automatically losing the position of supreme arbiter, inherited by the Caliphs from Muhammad. Though history is silent as to what the arbiters actually judged it was most likely as to whether 'Ali had broken the law established by Muhammad, and that he was held to have sheltered unprovoked murderers. The arbiters deposed him from the Caliphial office though the historians allege trickery entered into their action.

'Ali shortly after was murdered by one of a group of his former supporters which had come out against the arbitration it had first urged upon him. This group, the Khawarij, is commonly held to be the forerunner of the Ibadis of Oman and elsewhere. Mu'awiyah became Caliph and founder of the Umaiyad dynasty with its capital at Damascus. The ambitions of the Hashim house were not however allayed, and when Umaiyad troops slew 'Ali's son Husain at Karbala' in south Iraq they created the greatest Shi'ah martyr.

The house of Hashim also included the descendants of 'Abbas the Prophet's uncle, a relative, in Arabian eyes, as close as 'Ali to him, but 'Abbas had opposed Muhammad till late in the day. The 'Abbasids made common cause with the 'Ali-id Shi'ah against the Umaiyads, but were evidently abler in the political field. In the Umaiyad empire the Arabian tribes formed a kind of military élite but were constantly at factious war with one another. The Hashimites rode to power on the back of a rebellion against the Umaiyads which broke out in Khurasan in east Persia, but it was the 'Abbasid branch of Hashim which assumed the Caliphate and ruled from the capital they founded at Baghdad.

The 'Abbasid Caliphate endured up to the destruction of Baghdad in 1258 by the devastating Mongol invaders of the eastern empire, but the Caliphs had long been mere puppets in the hands of Turkish and other mercenaries, and the unwieldy empire had fragmented into independent states which rose and fell, though they mostly conceded nominal allegiance to the 'Abbasid Caliphs.

The Mongol Ilkhanid sovereigns, now turned Muslim, were in turn displaced by the conquests of Tamberlane at the end of the 14th century. In fact the Islamic empire had largely been taken over by Turkic soldiery. The Mameluke or Slave rulers of medieval Egypt who followed the Aiyubid (Kurdish) dynasty of Saladin were mainly Turks or Circassians. It was they who checked the Mongol advance at 'Ain Jalut in Palestine (1260). The Ottoman Turks captured Constantinople in 1453, and took Egypt from the Mamelukes in 1516, following this up by occupying the Hejaz where the Ashraf, descendants of the Prophet, ruled in Mecca and Medina, under first Mameluke then Turkish suzerainty. In 1533 the Turks took Baghdad and Iraq became part of the Ottoman Empire. The Ottoman Sultans assumed the title of Caliph—though in Islamic constitutional theory it is not easy to justify this. The Ottoman Caliphs endured till the Caliphate was abolished by Mustafa Kamal in 1924. The Turks have always been characterized by their adherence to Sunni orthodoxy.

Throughout history the 'Ali-ids have constantly asserted their right to be the Imams or leaders of the Muslim community—this in the religious and political senses, since Islam is fundamentally theocratic. The Shi'ah or followers of 'Ali and his descendants were in constant rebellion against the 'Abbasids and came to form a distinct schismatic group of Legitimist sects—at one time the Fatimid Shi'ah rulers of Egypt were near to conquering the main part of the Islamic world. The main Shi'ah sects today are the Ithna-'asharis, the Isma'ilis, and the near-orthodox Zaidis of the Yemen. The Safavids who conquered Persia at the beginning of the 16th century brought it finally into the Shi'ah fold. Sunni Hashimite dynasties flourish today in Jordan and Morocco as they did till fairly recently in Iraq and Libya, and the Shi'ah Zaidi ruler of Yemen was only displaced in 1962. The main difference between Sunnis and Shi'ah is over the Imamate i.e. the temporal and spiritual leader of Islam, for whereas Sunnis, while they respect the Prophet's house, do not consider the Imam *must* be a member of it—the Shi'ah insist on an Imam of the descendants of 'Ali and Fatimah his wife, the Prophet's daughter.

It has been too readily assumed that, during the later Middle Ages and long Turkish domination, the Islamic Middle East was completely stagnant. The shift in economic patterns after the New World was discovered, and the Cape route to India, coupled with widening Western intellectual horizons and the development of science and technology did push European culture far ahead of the Muslim Middle East. It was confronted by a vigorous and hostile Christianity intent on proselytising in its very homelands. Muslims had to face the challenge of the ideas and attitudes of Christian missionaries. Muslim thinkers like Muhammad 'Abduh (1849–1905) of Egypt and his school asserted that Islam had become heavily overlaid with false notions—hence its decline; like earlier reformers they were convinced that present difficulties could be solved by reversion to an (idealized) pure primitive Islam. Sometimes, in effect, this meant re-interpreting religious literature to suit attitudes and ideas of modern times—as for instance when they saw the virtual prohibition of polygamy in the restrictions which hedge it about. Since the earlier modern days political leaders like Mustafa Kamal of Turkey have often taken drastic measures, secularizing the state itself even up to the sensitive field of education, and accusing the more conservative forms of Islam of blocking progress. Today the Islamic Middle East has regimes ranging from the strong supporters of traditional Islam—like Sa'udi Arabia and Libya—to the anti-religious Marxist group controlling Aden.

ISLAMIC LAW

Orthodox Sunni Islam finds its main expression in *Shari'ah* law which it regards with great veneration. The Sunnis have crystallized into four "schools" (*madhhab*) or "rites", all of which are recognized as valid. Though in practice the adherents of one school can sometimes be at loggerheads with another, in modern times it is claimed that the law of any one of the rites can be applied to a case. The schools, named after their founders, are the Hanbali, regarded as the strictest, with adherents mainly in Sa'udi Arabia, the Shafi'is, the widest in extent with adherents in Egypt, Syria-Palestine, Egypt, South Arabia, and the Far East, the moderate Hanafi school which was the official rite of the Ottoman Turkish empire and to which most Muslims in the Indian sub-continent belong, and the Malikis of the North African states, Nigeria, and the Sudan. The Shi'ite sects have developed their own law, and give prominence to *ijtihad*, the forming of independent judgement, whereas the Sunnis are more bound by *taqlid* or following ancient models. However as the law of Sunnis, the moderate Shi'ah, and the Ibadis is basically derived from the same sources the differences are generally more of emphasis than principle.

Civil Courts. In the modern states of the Islamic world there exists, side by side with the *Shari'ah* court (judging cases on personal status, marriage, divorce, etc.), the secular court which has a wide jurisdiction (based on Western codes of law) in civil and criminal matters. This court is competent to give judgment irrespective of the creed or race of the defendant.

Islamic Law as Applying to Minorities. In cases of minorities (Christian or Jewish) residing as a community in Muslim countries, spiritual councils are established where judgment is passed according to the law of the community, in matters concerning personal status, by the recognised head of that community.

Tribal Courts. In steppe and mountain areas of countries where a proportion of the population is still tribal, tribal courts administer law and justice in accordance with ancient custom and tribal procedure.

Awqaf. In Muslim countries the law of Awqaf is the law applied to religious and charitable endowments, trusts and settlements. This important Islamic institution, found in all Eastern countries, is administered by the *Shari'ah* courts. Awqaf, or endowments, are pious bequests made by Muslims for the upkeep of religious institutions, public benefits, etc.

SUFIS

As in other religions, many Muslims find their emotional needs are not satisfied by observing a code of law and morals alone, and turn to mysticism. From early times Islamic mystics existed, known as Sufis, allegedly from their wearing a woollen garment. They seek complete identification with the Supreme Being and annihilation of the self—the existence of which latter they call polytheism (*shirk*). The learned doctors of Islam often think ill of the Sufis, and indeed rogues and wandering mendicants found Sufism a convenient means of livelihood. Certain Sufi groups allowed themselves dispensations and as stimulants even used hashish and opium which are not sanctioned by the Islamic moral code. The Sufis became organized in what are loosely called brotherhoods (*tariqah*), and have to a large extent been incorporated into the structure of orthodox Islamic society. Some *tariqahs* induce ecstatic states by their performance of the *dhikr*, meaning, literally, the mentioning (of Allah). Today there is much disapproval of the more extravagant manifestations of the Sufis and in some places these have been banned entirely.

The completely Islamic state as the theorists envisage it, run in conformity with the rules of the *Shari'ah* has probably never been achieved, and people's practice is often at variance with some or other requirements of *Shari'ah*. The imprint of Islam is nevertheless unmistakably evident on every country in this volume.

BELIEF AND PRACTICE

"Islam" means the act of submitting or resigning oneself to God, and a Muslim is one who resigns or submits himself to God. Muslims disapprove of the term "Muhammadan" for the faith of Islam, since they worship Allah, and Muhammad is only the Apostle of Allah whose duty it was to convey revelation, though he is regarded as the "Best of Mankind". He is the Seal (*Khatam*) of the Prophets, i.e. the ultimate Prophet in a long series in which both Moses and Jesus figure. They are revered, but, like Muhammad the Prophet, they are not worshipped.

Nearly all Muslims agree on acceptance of six articles of the faith of Islam: (i) Belief in God; (ii) in His angels; (iii) in His revealed books; (iv) in His Apostles; (v) in the Resurrection and Day of Judgement; and (vi) in His predestination of good and evil.

Faith includes works, and certain practices are obligatory on the believing Muslim. These are five in number:

1. The recital of the creed (*Shahadah*)—"There is no god but God (Allah) and Muhammad is the Apostle of God." This formula is embodied in the call to prayer made by the muezzin (announcer) from the minaret of the mosque before each of the five daily prayers.

2. The performance of the Prayer (*Salat*) at the five appointed canonical times—in the early dawn before the sun has risen above the horizon, in the early afternoon when the sun has begun to decline, later when the sun is about midway in its course towards setting, immediately after sunset, in the evening between the disappearance of the red glow in the west and bedtime. In prayer Muslims face towards the Ka'bah in Mecca. They unroll prayer mats and pray in a mosque (place of prostration), at home, or wherever they may be, bowing and prostrating themselves before God and reciting set verses in Arabic from the Koran. On Fridays it is obligatory for men to attend congregational Prayer in the central mosque of the quarter in which one lives—women do not normally attend. On this occasion formal prayers are preceded by a sermon.

3. The payment of the legal alms (*Zakat*). In early times this contribution was collected by officials of the Islamic state, and devoted to the relief of the poor, debtors, aid to travellers and other charitable and state purposes. Nowadays the fulfilment of this religious obligation is left to the conscience of the individual believer.

4. The thirty days of the fast in the month of Ramadan, the ninth month in the lunar year. As the lunar calendar is shorter by 11 days than the solar calendar Ramadan moves from the hottest to the coldest seasons of the solar year. It is observed as a fast from dawn to sunset each day by all adults in normal health, during which time no food or drink may be taken. The sick, pregnant women, travellers and children are exempt; some states exempt students, soldiers and factory workers. The fast ends with one of the two major Muslim festivals, 'Id al-Fitr.

5. The pilgrimage (*Hajj*) to Mecca. Every Muslim is obliged, circumstances permitting, to perform this at least once in his lifetime, and when accomplished he may assume the title, *Hajji*. Over a million pilgrims go each year to Mecca, but the holy cities of Mecca and Medina are prohibited to non-Muslims.

Before entering the sacred area around Mecca by the seventh day of Dhu 'l-Hijjah, the twelfth month of the Muslim year, pilgrims must don the *ihram*, consisting of two unseamed lengths of white cloth, indicating that they are entering a state of consecration and casting off what is ritually impure. The pilgrims circumambulate the Ka'bah seven times, endeavouring to kiss the sacred Black Stone. Later they run seven times between the near-by twin hills of Safa and Marwa, thus recalling Hagar's desperate search for water for her child Ishmael (from whom the Arabs claim descent). On the eighth day of the month the pilgrims leave the city for Mina, a small town six miles to the east. Then before sunrise of the next day all make for the plain below Mount 'Arafat some twelve miles east of Mecca where they pass the day in prayers and recitation until sunset. This point is the climax of the pilgrimage when the whole gathering returns, first to Muzdalifah where it spends the night, then to Mina where pilgrims stone the devil represented by three heaps of stones (*jamrah*). The devil is said to have appeared to Abraham here and to have been driven away by Abraham throwing stones at him. This day, the 10th of Dhu'l-Hijjah, is 'Id al-Adha, the Feast of the Sacrifices, and the pilgrims sacrifice an animal, usually a sheep, and have their heads shaved by one of the barbers at Mina. They return to Mecca that evening.

The Holy War (*Jihad*) against the infidel was the means whereby Arab Muslim rule made its immense expansion in the first centuries of Islam, but despite pressures to do so, it has never been elevated to form a sixth Pillar of Islam. Today many theologians interpret *jihad* in a less literal sense as the combatting of evil.

The Koran (*Qur'an*, "recital", "reading") is for Muslims the very Word of God. The Koran consists of 114 chapters (*surah*) of uneven length, the longest coming first after the brief opening chapter called *al-Fatihah*. (The Koran is about as long as the New Testament). *Al-Fatihah* (The Opener) commences with the words, "*Bismillahi 'l-Rahmani 'l-Rahim*, In the name of God, the Compassionate, the Merciful", and forms part of the ritual five prayers (*salat*). Other special verses and chapters are also used on a variety of occasions, and of course Muslim children are taught to recite by heart a portion of the Koran or, preferably, the whole of it. The Koran has been the subject of vast written commentaries, but translation into other languages is not much approved by Muslims, though inter-linear translations (a line of Koran underneath which is a line of translation) are used, and a number of modern translations into English exist. The earlier (Meccan) chapters of the Koran speak of the unity of God and his wonders, of the Day of Judgement and Paradise, while the Medinan chapters tend to be occupied more with social legislation for marriage, divorce, personal and communal behaviour. The definitive redaction of the Koran was ordered by the Caliph 'Uthman (644–56).

HOLY PLACES

Mecca: Hijaz province of Sa'udi Arabia. Mecca is centred around the Ka'bah, the most venerated building in Islam, traditionally held to have been founded by Abraham, recognized by Islam also as a Prophet. It stands in the centre of the vast courtyard of the Great Mosque and has the form of a cube; its construction is of local grey stone and its walls are draped with a black curtain embroidered with a strip of writing containing Koran verses. In the eastern corner is set the famous Black Stone. The enlarging of the Great Mosque commenced under the second Caliph 'Umar. Both the Ka'bah and Great Mosque have undergone many renovations, notably recently since 1952. Mecca is the centre of the annual pilgrimage from all Muslim countries.

Medina (*The City*, i.e. of the Prophet): Hijaz province of Sa'udi Arabia. Medina, formerly called Yathrib, was created a sacred enclave (*haram*) by Muhammad who died there in the year 11 of the *hijrah* and was buried in the Mosque of the Prophet. Close to his tomb are those of Abu Bakr and 'Umar and a little further away that of his daughter Fatimah. Frequently damaged, restored and enlarged, the mosque building was extensively renovated by the Sa'udi Government in 1955.

Jerusalem (Arabic *al-Quds* or *Bait al-Maqdis, The Hallowed/Consecrated*): Jordan (currently annexed by Israel). Jerusalem is Islam's next most holy city after al-Haraman (Mecca and Medina), not only because it is associated with so many pre-Islamic prophets, but because Muhammad himself is popularly held to have made the "Night Journey" there. Jerusalem contains the magnificent Islamic shrine, the Dome of the Rock (688–91), built by the Caliph 'Abd al-Malik, and the famous al-Masjid al-Aqsa not long ago severely damaged by arson.

Hebron (Habrun): Israel-occupied Jordan. The Mosque of Abraham, called al-Khalil, the "Friend of God" is built over the tomb of Abraham, the Cave of Machpelah; it also contains the tombs of Sarah, Isaac, Rebecca, Jacob, and Leah. The shrine is revered by Muslims and Jews, and is also important to Christians.

Qairawan: Tunisia. The city is regarded as a holy place for Muslims, seven pilgrimages to the Great Mosque of Sidi 'Uqbah b. Nafi' (an early Muslim general who founded Qairawan as a base for the Muslim invaders of North Africa) being considered equivalent of one pilgrimage to Mecca.

Muley Idris: Morocco. The shrine at the burial-place of the founder of the Idrisid dynasty in the year 687, at Walili.

* * *

Every Middle Eastern country has a multitude of shrines and saints' tombs held in veneration, except Wahhabi states which consider saint cults to be polytheism (*shirk*). In Turkey, however, the policy of secularization led to Aya Sofya Mosque (St. Sophia) being turned into a museum.

The following shrines are associated with the Shi'ah or Legitimist sects of Islam.

Mashhad (Meshed): Iran. The city is famous for the shrine of Imam 'Ali al-Rida/Riza, the eighth Imam of the Ithna'ashari group, which attracts some hundred thousand pilgrims each year. The shrine is surrounded by buildings with religious or historical associations.

Qom: Iran. A Shi'ah centre, it is venerated as having the tomb of Fatimah the sister of Imam al-Rida/Riza and hundreds of saints and kings including Imams 'Ali b. Ja'far and Ibrahim, Shah Safi and Shah 'Abbas II. Since the Iranian revolution it has become the centre fovoured by Ayatollah Khomeini.

Najaf: Iraq. Mashhad 'Ali, reputed to be constructed over the place where 'Ali b. Abi Talib, the cousin and son-in-law of Muhammad is buried, is a most venerated Shi'ah shrine drawing many pilgrims.

Karbala': Iraq. The shrine of Husain b. 'Ali where, at Mashhad Husain, he was slain with most of his family, is today more venerated by the Shi'ah than the Mashhad 'Ali. 'Ashura Day (10th Muharram) when Husain was killed is commemorated by passion plays (*ta'ziyah*) and religious processions when the drama of his death is re-enacted with extravagant expressions of emotion.

Baghdad: Iraq. The Kazimain/Kadhimain Mosque is a celebrated Shi'ah shrine containing the tomb of Musa al-Kazim/Kadhim, the 7th Imam of the Ithna'asharis.

RELIGIOUS GROUPINGS

Sunnis

The great majority, probably over 80 per cent of Muslims, is Sunni, followers of the *Sunnah*, i.e. the way, course, rule or manner of conduct of the Prophet Muhammad; they are generally called "Orthodox". The Sunnis recognize the first four Caliphs (Abu Bakr, 'Umar, 'Uthman, 'Ali) as Rashidun, i.e. following the right course. They base their *Sunnah* upon the Koran and "Six Books" of Traditions, and are organized in four Orthodox schools or rites (*madhhab*), all of equal standing within the Orthodox fold. Many Muslims today prefer to avoid identification with any single school.

Wahhabis

The adherents of "Wahhabism" strongly disapprove of this title by which they are known outside their own group, for they call themselves Muwahhidun or Unitarians. In fact they belong to the strict Hanbali school following its noted exponent, the 13th/14th century Syrian reformer Ibn Taimiyah. The founder of "Wahhabism", Muhammad b. 'Abd al-Wahhab of Arabian Najd (1703–87), sought to return to the pristine purity of early Islam freed from all accretions and what he regarded as innovations contrary to its true spirit, such as saint worship, lax sexual practices, and superstition. His doctrine was accepted by the chief Muhammad b. Sa'ud of Dar'iyah (near al-Riyadh). Ibn Sa'ud and his son 'Abd al-'Aziz—who proved a capable general—conquered much of Arabia. Medina fell in 1804 and Mecca in 1806 to Sa'ud son of 'Abd al-'Aziz, but after his death in 1814 the Wahhabis were gradually broken by the armies of the Pasha of Egypt, Muhammad 'Ali acting nominally on behalf of the Ottoman Sultan of Turkey. After varying fortunes in the 19th century the Wahhabis emerged as an Arabian power in the opening years of the 20th century. By the close of 1925 they held the Holy Cities and Jeddah and are today the strongest power in the Arabian Peninsula. Though Wahhabism remains the strictest of the Orthodox groups, Sa'udi Arabia has made some accommodation to modern times.

The Tariqahs or Religious Orders

In many Middle Eastern countries the Religious Orders (*Tariqahs*) have important political cum religious roles in society. There are the widely spread Qadiriyah who with the Tijaniyah are found in North Africa, the Khatmiyah in the Sudan, the Rifa'iyah in Egypt and Syria to pick out a few at random. The West has no organizations exactly equivalent to these Sufi orders into which an individual has to be initiated, and in which, by dint of ascetic excercises and study he may attain degrees of mystical enlightenment—this can also bring moral influence over his fellow men. The Orders may be Sunni or Shi'ah; some few Orders are even so unconventional as to be hardly Islamic at all. It was the Orthodox reformist Sanusi Order that has played the most significant role in our time. The Grand Sanusi, Muhammad b. 'Ali, born at Mustaghanem in Algeria of a Sharif family, founded the first *zawiyah* or lodge of the Sanusis in 1837. The Sanusi *Tariqah* is distinguished for its exacting standards of personal morality. The Sanusis set up a network of lodges in Cyrenaica (Libya) and put up strong resistance to Italian colonization. The Grand Sanusi was recognized as King Idris of Libya in 1951, but lost his throne at the military revolt led by Colonel Gaddafi in 1969.

Shi'ah

The Legitimist Shi'ah pay allegiance to 'Ali as mentioned above. 'Ali's posterity which must number at least hundreds of thousands, scattered all over the Muslim world, are customarily called Sharifs if they trace descent to his son al-Hasan, and Saiyids if descended from al-Husain, but while the Sharifs and Saiyids, the religious aristocracy of Islam, traditionally are accorded certain privileges in Islamic society, not all are Shi'ah, many being Sunnis. By the 9th century many strange sects and even pagan beliefs had become associated with the original Shi'ah or Party of 'Ali, but these extremist sects called *ghulat* have mostly vanished except a few, often practising a sort of quietism or dissimulation (*taqiyah*) for fear of persecution. All Shi'ah accord 'Ali an exalted position, the extreme (and heretical) Shi'ah at one time even according him a sort of divinity. Shi'ite Islam does not in the main differ on fundamental issues from the Sunni Orthodox since they draw from the same ultimate sources, but Shi'ah *mujtahids* have, certainly in theory, greater freedom to alter the application of law since they are regarded as spokesmen of the Hidden Imam.

The Ithna'asharis (Twelvers)

The largest Shi'ah school or rite is the Ithna'ashariyah or Twelvers, acknowledging twelve Imams. From 1502 Shi'ism became the established school in Iran under the Safavid ruler Sultan Shah Isma'il who claimed descent from Musa al-Kazim (see below). There are also Ithna'ashariyah in southern Iraq, al-Hasa, Bahrain and the Indian sub-continent.

The last Shi'ah Imam, Muhammad al-Mahdi, disappeared in 878, but the Ithna'asharis believe he is still alive and will re-appear in the last days before the Day of Judgement as the Mahdi (Guided One)—a sort of Messiah—who will rule personally by divine right.

The twelve Imams recognized by the Twelver, Ithna'ashari Shi'ah are:

(1) 'Ali b. Abi Talib, cousin and son-in-law of the Prophet Muhammad.
(2) Al-Hasan, son of 'Ali.
(3) Al-Husain, second son of 'Ali.
(4) 'Ali Zain al-'Abidin, son of Husain.
(5) Muhammad al-Baqir, son of 'Ali Zain al-'Abidin.
(6) Ja'far al-Sadiq, son of Muhammad al-Baqir.
(7) Musa al-Kazim, son of Ja'far al-Sadiq.
(8) 'Ali al-Rida, son of Musa al-Kazim.
(9) Muhammad al-Taqi, son of 'Ali al-Rida.
(10) 'Ali al-Naqi, son of Muhammad al-Taqi.
(11) Al-Hasan al-Zaki, son of 'Ali al-Naqi, al-'Askari.
(12) Muhammad al-Mahdi, son of al-Hasan b. 'Ali, al-'Askari, known as al-Hujjah, the Proof.

Isma'ilis

This group of the Shi'ah does not recognize Musa al-Kazim as seventh Imam, but holds that the last Imam visible on earth was Isma'il, the other son of Ja'far al-Sadiq. For this reason they are also called the Sab'iyah or Seveners. There is however much disagreement among the Seveners as to whether they recognized Isma'il himself as seventh Imam, or one of his several sons, and the Fatimids of Egypt (10th–12th centuries) in fact recognized a son of Isma'il's son Muhammad. Schismatic off-shoots from the Fatimid-Isma'ili group are the Druzes, the Musta'lians first settled in the Yemen but now with their main centre in Bombay—where the Daudi section is known as Bohoras, but who are properly called the Fatimi Taiyibi Da'wah, and the Nizari Isma'ilis of whom the Aga Khan is the spiritual head. These sects have a secret literature embodying their esoteric philosophies. Small groups of Isma'ilis are to be found in north-west Syria, Iran, Afghanistan, East Africa and Zanzibar, and larger numbers in India and Pakistan.

'Alawis (Nusairis)

The 'Alawis believe Muhammad was a mere fore-runner of 'Ali and that the latter was an incarnation of Allah. This Shi'i extremist sect established in the ninth century has also adopted practices of both Christian and pagan origin. Most of its members today live in north-west Syria.

Druze

The Druze are heretics, an off-shoot of the Fatimid Isma'ilis (see above), established in Lebanon and Syria. Their name (Duruz) derives from al-Darazi, a missionary of Persian origin who brought about the conversion of these Syrian mountaineers to the belief of the divine origin of the Fatimid Caliph al-Hakim. The origins of this sect and its subsequent expansion are still obscure. Hamzah b. 'Ali, a Persian contemporary of al-Darazi is the author of several of the religious treatises of the Druze. This community acknowledges one God and believes that he has on many occasions become incarnate in man. His last appearance was in the person of the Fatimid Caliph al-Hakim (disappeared 1020). The Druze have played a distinctive role in the political and social life of their country and are renowned for their independence of character.

Zaidis

The Zaidis are a liberal and moderate sect of the Shi'ah close enough to the Sunnis to call themselves the "Fifth School" (*al-madhhab al-khamis*). Their name is derived from a grandson of al-Husain b. 'Ali called Zaid b. 'Ali whom they recognize as fifth Imam. They reject religious dissimulation (*taqiyah*) and are extremely warlike. Zaidism is the dominant school of Islam in the Yemen Arab Republic, but Shafi'is form roughly half the population.

Ibadis

The Ibadis are commonly held to have their origins in the Khawarij who disassociated themselves from 'Ali b. Abi Talib when he accepted arbitration in his quarrel with Mu'awiyah, but this is open to question. They broke off early from the main stream of Islam and are usually regarded as heretics though with little justification. Groups of the sect, which has often suffered persecution, are found in Oman where Ibadism is the state religion, Zanzibar, Libya and Algeria, mainly in the Mzab.

THE ISLAMIC REVIVAL

In a number of Muslim countries revivalist or reactionary Islamic movements are taking place. Islam makes no essential distinction between religion and politics so this affects not only the whole Muslim community but also those of other faiths residing in an Islamic state. In one sense it may be said that there is a common basis to the revival in all the Islamic states in that people believe that a reversion to an idealized Islamic community, or the substitution of the principles embodied in *shari'ah* law for the practice of a secular state, will resolve current problems and tensions. Each country however seems to differ as to against what it expects the Islamic revival to react.

Sa'udi Arabia, the heartland of Islam, has always maintained a strict formal adherence to traditional Islam. The late King Faisal, though tactfully curbing the extreme trends of Sa'udi Arabia's Mutawwa' "clergy", initiated and financed a policy of promoting Islam to counter President Nasser's alignment with socialist propaganda to subvert monarchic regimes elsewhere. King Faisal's initiative took the form of subsidising the building of mosques in Muslim countries, the publication of Islamic books and religious tracts, and the founding or support of such institutions as the Islamic Council of Europe. Links were made with groups like the Muslim Brothers, the well-established inter-state Islamic society which Nasser tried to crush.

In general the concept of a "permissive society" as promoted by certain Western elements, is rejected with distaste by all Muslim countries. Sa'udi Arabia's financial and moral strength has enabled it to take practical steps to pressure other Islamic states to conform, sometimes if they fear only to be out of line, to such Islamic prescriptions as the prohibition of liquor. On the other hand banks and insurance companies which depend on taking interest on loans, seem to be regarded as earning profit (*ribh*) which is lawful to a Muslim, not taking usury (*riba*) which is unlawful. To the West certain Islamic laws are repugnant, such as amputation of a hand for persistent theft, but the benefit in Sa'udi Arabia in compelling a high standard of honesty is undeniable—the penalty is probably not frequently inflicted. Stoning for adultery can rarely be imposed for in Islamic law this is next to impossible to prove at least as far as Sunnis are concerned.

In Iran the motivation of Islamic reaction as symbolized in the Ayatollah (a high religious office), Khomeini, is in part that of the conservative, even chauvinistic, provinces against a secular monarch who introduced foreigners bringing with them Western manners distasteful to Islamic society. This has found expression in the destruction of bars, cinemas, etc., and the attempt, by imposing the veil, to reverse the tide of female emancipation. Persecution of the in-offensive Baha'is puts the clock back to the late 19th century. To what extent the economic, as contrasted with the religious, factor, the concentration of great wealth in the hands of a very few families, motivated the revolution is as yet undetermined.

As the very existence of Pakistan lies in the conception of a "pure" Islamic community opposed to heathen Hindustan, this, coupled with its ever growing internal troubles, has encouraged the retreat into a more rigid Islamic state.

The Turkey of Mustafa Kemal Ataturk aimed at a complete separation of religion and state—in this secular state women were accorded equal rights with men. It is now clear that secularization did not penetrate deeply into the urban and particularly the rural population. Resentment of financial hardships after the Second World War against the Government was fanned by religious leaders, and ever-increasing religious freedom has had to be conceded within the secular state. Many women have, illegally, resumed the veil. The upper classes tend to favour a secular state, but religious feeling combined with chauvinism are behind the popular revival of Islam.

In no way is the interdependence of religion and politics in Islam better illustrated than in the condemnation of Egypt by forty Islamic states, over the Jerusalem question, a city sacred to Muslims from which the Prophet made his celebrated Night Ascent to Heaven.

Christianity

DEVELOPMENT IN THE MIDDLE EAST

Christianity was adopted as the official religion of the Roman empire in A.D. 313, and the Christian Church came to be based on the four leading cities, Rome, Constantinople (capital from A.D. 330), Alexandria and Antioch. From the divergent development of the four ecclesiastical provinces there soon emerged four separate churches: the Roman Catholic or Latin Church (from Rome), the Greek Orthodox Church (from Constantinople), the Syrian or Jacobite Church (from Antioch) and the Coptic Church (from Alexandria).

Later divisions resulted in the emergence of the Armenian (Gregorian) Church, which was founded in the fourth century, and the Nestorian Church, which grew up in the fifth century in Syria, Mesopotamia and Iran, following the teaching of Nestorius of Cilicia (d. 431). From the seventh century on followers of St. Maron began to establish themselves in northern Lebanon, laying the foundations of the Maronite Church.

Subsequently the Uniate Churches were brought into existence by the renunciation by formerly independent churches of doctrines regarded as heretical by the Roman Church and by the acknowledgement of Papal supremacy. These churches—the Armenian Catholic, the Chaldean (Nestorian) Catholic, Greek Catholic, the Coptic Catholic, the Syrian Catholic and the Maronite Church did, however, retain their Oriental customs and rites. The independent churches continued in existence alongside the Uniate Churches with the exception of the Maronites, all of whom reverted to Rome.

HOLY PLACES

Bethlehem: Israeli-occupied Jordan. The traditional birthplace of Jesus is enclosed in the Basilica of the Nativity, revered also by Muslims. Christmas is celebrated here by the Roman and Eastern Rite Churches on December 25th, by the Greek Orthodox, Coptic and Syrian Orthodox Churches on January 6th and 7th, by the Ethiopian Church on January 8th, and by the Armenian Church on January 19th. The tomb of Rachel, important to the three faiths, is just outside the town.

Jerusalem: Jordan (but annexed by Israel). The most holy city of Christianity has been a centre for pilgrims since the Middle Ages. It is the seat of the patriarchates of the Roman, Greek Orthodox and Armenian Churches, who share the custodianship of the Church of the Holy Sepulchre and who each own land and buildings in the neighbouring area.

The Church of the Holy Sepulchre stands on the hill of Golgotha in the higher north-western part of the Old City. In the central chamber of the church is the Byzantine Rotunda built by twelfth century crusaders, which shelters the small shrine on the traditional site of the tomb. Here the different patriarchates exercise their rights in turn. Close by is the Rock of Calvary, revered as the site of the Crucifixion.

Most pilgrims devoutly follow the Way of the Cross leading from the Roman Praetorium through several streets of the Old City to the Holy Sepulchre. Franciscan monks, commemorating the journey to the Crucifixion, follow the course of this traditional route each Friday; on Good Friday this procession marks a climax of the Easter celebrations of the Roman Church.

Outside the Old City stands the Mount of Olives, the scene of Jesus' Ascension. At the foot of its hill is the Garden of Gethsemane which is associated with the vigil on the eve of the Crucifixion. The Cenaculum or traditional room of the Last Supper is situated on Mount Zion in Israel.

Nazareth: Israel. This town, closely associated with the childhood of Jesus, has been a Christian centre since the fourth century A.D. The huge, domed Church of the Annunciation has recently been built on the site of numerous earlier churches to protect the underground Grotto of the Annunciation. Nearby the Church of St. Joseph marks the traditional site of Joseph's workshop.

Galilee: Israel. Many places by this lake are associated with the life of Jesus: Cana, scene of the miracle of water and wine, which is celebrated by an annual pilgrimage on the second Sunday after Epiphany; the Mount of Beatitudes; Tabgha, scene of the multiplication of the loaves and fish; and Capurneum, scene of the healing of the Centurion's servant.

Mount Tabor: Israel. The traditional site of the Transfiguration, which has drawn pilgrims since the fourth century, is commemorated by a Franciscan Monastery and a Greek Basilica, where the annual Festival of the Transfiguration is held.

Jericho: Israeli-occupied Jordan. The scene of the baptism of Jesus; nearby is the Greek Monastery of St. John the Baptist.

Nablus (*Samaria*): Israeli-occupied Jordan. This old town contains Jacob's Well, associated with Jesus, and the Tomb of Joseph.

Qubaibah (*Emmaus*): Israeli-occupied Jordan. It was near this town that two of the Disciples encountered Jesus after the Resurrection.

'Azariyyah (*Bethany*): Israeli-occupied Jordan. A town frequented by Jesus, the home of Mary and Martha, and the scene of the Raising of Lazarus.

Mount Carmel: Haifa, Israel. The Cave of Elijah draws many pilgrims, including Muslims and Druzes, who celebrate the Feast of Mar Elias on July 20th.

Ein Kerem: Israel. Traditional birthplace of John the Baptist, to whom a Franciscan church is dedicated; nearby is the Church of the Visitation.

Ephesus: Turkey. The city, formerly a great centre of pagan worship, where Paul founded the first of the seven Asian Churches. The recently restored Basilica, built by Justinian, is dedicated to John the Evangelist, who legend claims died here; a fourth century church on Aladag Mountain commemorating Mary's last years spent here now draws an annual pilgrimage in August.

Judaism

There are two main Jewish communities, the Ashkenazim and the Sephardim, the former from east, central and northern Europe, the latter from Spain, the Balkans, the Middle East and North Africa. The majority of immigrants into Israel were from the Ashkenazim, and their influence predominates there, though the Hebrew language follows Sephardim usage. There is no doctrinal difference between the two communities, but they observe distinct rituals.

HOLY PLACES

Wailing Wall: Jerusalem. This last remnant of the western part of the wall surrounding the courtyard of Herod's Temple, finally destroyed by the Romans in A.D. 70, is visited by devout Jews, particularly on the Fast Day of the 9th of Av, to grieve at the destruction of the First and Second Temples which had once stood on the same site.

Mount Zion: Israel. A hill south-west of the Old City of Jerusalem, venerated particularly for the tomb of David, acknowledged by Muslims as abi Dawud (The Jebuzite hill on which David founded his Holy City is now known as Mount Ophel, and is in Jordan, just to the east of the modern Mount Zion). Not far from the foot of the hill are the rock-cut tombs of the family of King Herod.

Cave of Machpelah: Hebron, Israeli-occupied Jordan. The grotto, over which was built a mosque, contains the tombs of Abraham and Sarah, Isaac and Rebecca, Jacob and Leah.

Bethlehem: Israeli-occupied Jordan. The traditional tomb of Rachel is in a small shrine outside the town, venerated also by Muslims and Christians.

Mount Carmel: Israel. The mountain is associated with Elijah, whose Cave in Haifa draws many pilgrims. (*See* Christianity section).

Safad: Israel. Centre of the medieval Cabbalist movement, this city contains several synagogues from the sixteenth century associated with these scholars, and many important tombs, notably that of Rabbi Isaac Louria.

Meiron: Israel. The town contains the tombs of Shimon bar Yohai, reputed founder in the second century of the medieval Cabbalist movement, and his son Eleazer. A yearly Hassidic pilgrimage is held to the tomb to celebrate Lag Ba'Omer with a night of traditional singing and dancing in which Muslims also participate.

Tiberias: Israel. An ancient city containing the tombs of Moses Maimonides and Rabbi Meir Baal Harness. Famous as an historical centre of Cabbalist scholarship, it is with Jerusalem, Safad and Hebron, one of the four sacred cities of Judaism, and once accommodated a university and the Sanhedrin.

Other Communities

ZOROASTRIANS

Zoroastrianism developed from the teaching of Zoroaster, or Zarathustra, who lived in Iran some time between 700 and 550 B.C. Later adopted as the official religion of the Persian empire, Zoroastrianism remained predominant in Iran until the rise of Islam. Many adherents were forced by persecution to emigrate, and the main centre of the faith is now Bombay, where they are known as Parsees. Technically a monotheistic faith, Zoroastrianism retained some elements of polytheism. It later became associated with fire-worship.

Yazd: Iran. This city was the ancient centre of the Zoroastrian religion, and was later used as a retreat during the Arab conquest. It contains five fire temples and still remains a centre for this faith, of which some 35,000 adherents live in Iran.

BAHA'IS

Baha'ism made its appearance in Persia during the middle of the nineteenth century. It was founded by Baha'ullah, who, after a revelation in Baghdad in 1863, declared himself to be the "Promised One". A member of the Persian nobility, he devoted his life to preaching against the corruption endemic in Persian society and as a result spent many years in exile; he died at Acre in Palestine in 1892. The Sect was administered by his descendants until 1957; the 56 national branches now elect the present governing body, the Universal House of Justice.

Baha'ism claims complete independence from all other faiths. Its followers believe that the basic principles of the great religions of the world are in complete harmony and that their aims and functions are complementary. Other tenets include belief in the brotherhood of man, the abolition of racial and colour discrimination, the equality of the sexes, progress towards world government and the use of an international language, monogamy, chastity and the encouragement of family life. There is no Baha'i priesthood, and asceticism and monasticism are discouraged. Most of the Middle Eastern adherents of the faith live in Iran or Israel.

Haifa: Israel. Shrine of the Bab and gardens, world centre of the Baha'i faith. Pilgrims visit this centre, and one in Acre where Baha'ullah was imprisoned, on the anniversaries of the birth and death of Bab and Baha'ullah.

SAMARITANS

Mount Gerazim: Jordan. The mountain is sacred to this small sect, who celebrate Passover here. The Samaritan High Priest lives at Nablus.

The Arab-Israeli Confrontation 1967-79

Michael Adams

Israel's decisive victory over the Arab states in the Six Day war of 1967 raised hopes that at last it would be possible to reach a definitive settlement of the Arab-Israeli conflict. Instead it soon became apparent that the conflict had merely been complicated by the occupation of further Arab territory, the displacement of still more refugees and the aggravation of the sense of grievance felt by the Palestinians and now shared more widely than ever in the rest of the Arab world.

The course of events after June 1967

As soon as a ceasefire had brought an end to the fighting in June 1967 a series of international consultations began with the aim of bringing to a final conclusion the nineteen year old conflict between Israel and her Arab neighbours.

Once the ceasefire was in operation, the Security Council's next step was to pass a resolution (No. 237, of June 14th, 1967), calling on Israel to facilitate the return of the new refugees who had fled (and were still fleeing) from the areas occupied by Israel during the war. The resolution also called on Israel to ensure the safety, welfare and security of the inhabitants of the "Occupied Areas".

An emergency meeting of the UN General Assembly reiterated on July 4th the Security Council's call for the return of the refugees and on the same day it declared "invalid" the Israeli decision to annex the Arab sector of Jerusalem; but the Assembly failed to produce an agreed resolution on the basis for a settlement. A plan put forward later in the month by President Tito of Yugoslavia, calling for an Israeli withdrawal to the pre-war frontiers and a guarantee of those frontiers by the international community, was rejected by Israel on the ground that to recreate the pre-war situation would endanger that country's security.

The deadlock became total when an Arab summit conference, held in Khartoum between August 29th and September 3rd, 1967, confirmed earlier decisions not to negotiate directly with Israel, not to accord her recognition and not to sign a peace treaty. The Israeli Government, for its part, announced its refusal to undertake any but direct negotiations; if no such negotiations developed, Israeli forces would maintain their occupation of the Arab territories conquered during the war.

RESOLUTION 242

It was against this background that the UN Security Council met in the autumn of 1967 to consider the situation. A number of draft resolutions were submitted but failed to gain approval, either because (in the eyes of the supporters of the Arabs) they condoned the acquisition or occupation of territory by military force, or because (in the eyes of the supporters of Israel) they contained no adequate guarantee for Israel's security.

Finally, on November 22nd, 1967, the Security Council unanimously adopted a resolution which was to remain the basis of all subsequent peace initiatives during the next five years.

This, the famous Resolution 242 of November 1967, (*see* Documents on Palestine, p. 67) precariously bridged the gap between the Arab and Israeli positions, which were also the positions adopted by their superpower supporters, the Soviet Union and the United States. By emphasizing the inadmissibility of the acquisition of territory by war, the resolution satisfied the demand of the Arabs and the Russians for an Israeli withdrawal. By being less than categorical about the extent of that withdrawal, it became acceptable to the Israelis and the Americans. All the subsequent arguments which developed centred around the question of whether the Israelis, in return for a definitive peace treaty, would have the right to retain parts of the Arab territories occupied during the war.

PALESTINIAN RESISTANCE

Even before these arguments developed, and during the interval of nearly six months which elapsed between the ceasefire and the adoption of the Security Council's resolution, events on the ground had hardened the positions of both sides. In the immediate aftermath of the fighting, despite the Israeli Prime Minister's declaration on the eve of the war that Israel had no intention of annexing "even one foot of Arab territory", the Israeli Knesset had legislated the "reunification" of Jerusalem,* which amounted in fact to the annexation of the Arab sector of the city. The Israelis had also destroyed a number of Arab villages, notably the three villages of Imwas, Beit Nuba and Yalu in the Latrun area, and had expelled their inhabitants. These actions, which appeared to confirm Arab accusations of Israeli expansionism, greatly encouraged the rise of a Palestinian resistance movement, already stimulated by the failure of the Arab governments and the humiliation which that failure had brought on the Arab world. When the Israelis began, as early as September 1967, to establish Jewish settlements in the occupied territories,† at a time when the stream of Arab refugees set in motion by the June war was still flowing eastward at the rate of several hundred a day, support for the resistance movement became

* For a discussion of the Jerusalem issue, *see* p. 55.

† Between June 1967 and June 1979 more than 100 of these settlements had been established by the Israelis in the occupied areas of the West Bank of Jordan, the Gaza Strip, the Golan Heights in south-west Syria, and Sinai.

widespread in the Arab world. It was strengthened when the Israelis, after agreeing in response to United Nations resolutions to allow the return of these new refugees, arbitrarily closed the border again after only 14,000 had been allowed to re-enter Palestine, out of 150,000 who had filed applications with the Red Cross to do so.

The situation, then, was deteriorating even before Dr. Gunnar Jarring, whom the Secretary-General had appointed as his Special Representative in accordance with Resolution 242, went to the Middle East to undertake his mission at the end of 1967. During the first half of 1968 there were increasingly frequent breaches of the ceasefire along the Suez Canal (which remained blocked to traffic), while Palestinian guerrilla raids led to heavy Israeli reprisal actions in the Jordan valley. After the first anniversary of the June war, and while Dr. Jarring was patiently pursuing his contacts with both sides, the trend towards violence accelerated. In July 1968 guerrillas of the Popular Front for the Liberation of Palestine carried out the first hijack operation in the Middle East, diverting an Israeli airliner to Algiers. President Nasser in the same month warned that another explosion in the area was inevitable if a stalemate which left Israel in occupation of territory belonging to three of its neighbours was allowed to continue indefinitely. In the course of artillery duels across the Canal the towns of Suez and Ismailia were virtually destroyed by the Israelis and their populations had to be evacuated into the interior of Egypt.

PHANTOMS FOR ISRAEL

The governments of Egypt and Jordan had accepted Resolution 242, while Syria rejected it. Israel, while not rejecting the resolution, said it could not be a substitute for specific agreements between the parties. When the UN General Assembly met in the autumn of 1968, Israel put forward a nine-point plan for a Middle East settlement which made no mention of withdrawal, speaking instead of "a boundary settlement compatible with the security of Israel and the honour of the Arab states". This produced no response from the Arab governments, which were shocked when President Johnson at the height of the American election campaign, announced that the United States was considering the sale of Phantom aircraft to Israel. A month later Richard Nixon was elected as President Johnson's successor and sent Governor William Scranton on a fact-finding mission to the Middle East. Mr. Scranton was reported as saying that the United States should adopt "a more even-handed policy in the Middle East", but the sale of fifty Phantoms to Israel was confirmed at the end of December and marked an important stage in the escalation of the arms race in the Middle East.

The day after the sale of Phantoms was announced, Israeli parachutists raided Beirut airport, in reprisal for an Arab guerrilla attack on an Israeli airliner in Athens, and destroyed thirteen aircraft. This incident, which for the first time directly involved the Lebanon in the Arab-Israeli confrontation, brought about renewed diplomatic activity to arrest the worsening situation. After the Security Council had unanimously condemned Israel for the Beirut raid, the Soviet Government took up an earlier French proposal that there should be Four-Power talks between the Soviet Union, the United States, Britain and France to obtain agreement between the major powers over the implementation of Resolution 242.

FOUR-POWER TALKS

Dr. Jarring withdrew from the scene while the "Big Four" tried to reconcile the conflicting interpretations of the Security Council resolution. At first the prospects seemed encouraging, with President Nixon eager to register an initial success in the field of foreign affairs and with general agreement that the drift to war in the Middle East threatened the peace of the world. At the beginning of February 1969, President Nasser declared his willingness to enter into direct negotiations once Israeli forces had withdrawn from Arab territory. Mr. Eshkol, the Prime Minister of Israel, stated his readiness to meet President Nasser and declared that Israel was prepared to be flexible about all the occupied territories except Jerusalem and the Golan Heights (captured from Syria in 1967). But as the year wore on, spasmodic fighting continued along both the Suez Canal and the Jordan fronts, until in July 1969 President Nasser publicly gave up hope of a peaceful settlement, forecasting that a long "war of attrition" would be necessary to dislodge Israel from the occupied territories. A month later a severe fire at Al Aqsa mosque in the Old City of Jerusalem, for which an Australian immigrant to Israel was later blamed, caused a further dangerous increase in tension.

THE ROGERS PLAN

The Four-Power talks were suspended while Soviet and American representatives engaged in bilateral contacts. There was a moment of optimism when it appeared likely that a formula had been found for "Rhodes-style" negotiations (on the pattern of the talks conducted in Rhodes which led to the armistice agreements between Israel and the Arab states in 1949), but the optimism faded when an Israeli suggestion that this would amount to direct negotiations led the Arabs to reject the formula. Instead the American Secretary of State, Mr. William Rogers, produced on December 9th, 1969, a set of proposals which came to be known as the Rogers Plan. The proposals represented an attempt to steer a middle course between the Arab view, that the Security Council resolution should be implemented *in toto* and did not call for negotiation, and the Israeli preference for direct negotiations which would decide where the new borders should be drawn. The most important aspect of the plan was that it made clear the American view that there should only be minor rectifications of the pre-June 1967 boundaries. This ensured Israeli hostility to the plan, since despite the insistence of the Israeli Foreign Minister, Abba Eban, that "everything is negotiable", it had now become clear that his cabinet colleagues were deeply divided on this crucial question.

President Nasser, impatient with what he saw as the hypocritical attitude of the American Government, also rejected the plan, which in any case was presently swept aside by a serious renewal of hostilities in January 1970, when the Israelis initiated a series of deep penetration bombing raids (using the new American Phantom aircraft) on targets inside Egypt. General Dayan announced at the beginning of February that the Israeli bombing attacks had three aims: to force the Egyptians (who had been sustaining heavy casualties along the Canal front) to respect the ceasefire, to prevent Egyptian preparations for a new war and to weaken the Egyptian regime. In practice, the raids (which caused heavy civilian casualties) had three results: they strengthened Egyptian support for President Nasser; they damaged Israel's image in the outside world; and they drew the Russians into providing further assistance to Egypt. In March 1970 the first reports appeared of the installation in Egypt of Soviet SAM-3 anti-aircraft missiles in the vicinity of Cairo, Alexandria and key targets in the Nile delta, while the number of Soviet military advisers in Egypt rose to an estimated 6,000.

International concern over these developments paved the way for a renewal of diplomatic efforts. In April 1970 the American Assistant Secretary of State, Joseph Sisco, visited the Middle East to explain the objectives of the Rogers Plan. Israeli requests for more Phantoms were not granted and it appeared that the immediate American objectives were to obtain a renewal of the ceasefire and to extract from the Israeli Government an undertaking to withdraw from the greater part of the occupied territories as part of an overall peace settlement. President Nasser, in a speech on May 1st said that "despite Phantoms and napalm" he was keeping the door open to the American initiative. The Israelis made no public commitment on withdrawal, but their response in private was sufficiently encouraging for Mr. Rogers to relaunch his proposals, with the backing of the four major powers. After a variety of bilateral contacts between the various parties, President Nasser announced in a speech on July 23rd, 1970, Egypt's acceptance of the American proposal for a renewal of the ceasefire, followed by negotiations through Dr. Jarring for the implementation of Resolution 242. A week later, the Israeli Government, after receiving assurances on the future supply of arms from the United States, also agreed to the American proposal, with the proviso that Israel would never return to the pre-war boundaries and that none of its troops would be withdrawn from the ceasefire lines until a binding peace agreement had been signed. Even so, the price of Israel's qualified acceptance of the Rogers proposals was a cabinet crisis which resulted in the resignation from Mrs. Golda Meir's cabinet of the right-wing Gahal party led by Mr. Menachem Begin.

The renewed ceasefire along the Suez Canal front came into operation on the night of August 7th/8th, with a duration of ninety days, during which the two sides were to engage in indirect negotiations under the auspices of Dr. Jarring. Two fresh developments, however, frustrated the movement towards an overall settlement. After a single meeting with Dr. Jarring in New York, the Israeli representative was recalled to Jerusalem and the Israeli Government protested that the ceasefire had been violated by the movement of Soviet missiles behind the Egyptian lines. The confused American reaction suggested that there had been a genuine misunderstanding about the conditions agreed to, but the negotiations in New York had not been renewed when a serious crisis in Jordan distracted the attention of all the parties concerned.

KING HUSSEIN AND THE PALESTINE GUERRILLAS

On September 6th, 1970, Palestine guerrillas of the Popular Front for the Liberation of Palestine hijacked two airliners and flew them to a desert airfield in Jordan. A third airliner was taken to Cairo and destroyed on the airfield there. Three days later a fourth aircraft was hijacked and joined the two in the desert near Zerqa, where the guerrillas, after releasing a number of passengers, held some three hundred others as hostages, demanding in exchange for them the release of a substantial number of Palestinians held prisoner in Israel.

This episode, which marked the high point of guerrilla activity, proved also the last straw as far as the Government of Jordan was concerned. During the previous two years, as the strength of the guerrilla movement increased, the Jordan Government had faced a dilemma. If it allowed the guerrillas freedom of movement in Jordan, it invited retaliation from Israel—and the retaliation had been heavy, in the form of ground and air raids which had depopulated the East Bank of the Jordan river and caused severe casualties in Irbid, Salt and other towns and villages of east Jordan. If the Government tried to control or suppress the activities of the guerrillas, it faced the possibility of civil war in Jordan.

The relationship between the Government and the guerrillas was linked to the question of a political settlement with Israel. The Palestine resistance movement, whose declared objective was the reconstitution in Palestine of a democratic state open to Jews and Arabs alike, opposed the idea of a political settlement with Israel, since this would involve the recognition and the perpetuation of a Zionist state. King Hussein had followed the lead of President Nasser in accepting the Rogers Plan and was thus committed to the principle of a political settlement involving the recognition of Israel. So long as a political settlement was not in prospect, it had been possible for the King and the guerrillas to pursue their diverse objectives without coming into open conflict, but as soon as such a settlement became a serious possibility the uneasy coexistence between them was threatened. On several previous occasions in 1969 and 1970 the Jordan Government and the guerrillas had come close to a confrontation and after the renewal of the ceasefire in August 1970 and the acceptance by the Jordan Government of the Rogers Plan, a clash became inevitable.

The multiple hijack operation by the PFLP, which explicitly challenged the authority of the Jordan Government, provided the spark and on September

16th King Hussein appointed a military government in Jordan which next day set about the liquidation of the resistance movement. After ten days of heavy fighting in Amman, mediation efforts by other Arab governments, and in particular by President Nasser, brought about a truce, which was signed in Cairo on September 27th, 1970. On the following day President Nasser suffered a heart attack and died almost immediately.

As far as a settlement between Israel and the Arabs was concerned, it looked as though the position so painstakingly established in August had been undermined. The ceasefire along the Suez Canal endured, though precariously; but the negotiations through Dr. Jarring were not renewed and until President Nasser's successor had had time to consolidate his position, it seemed unlikely that they would be. Jordan was faced with the task of overcoming the effects of an inconclusive civil war and only Israel, which had achieved its objective of a renewal of the ceasefire, had any reason to feel satisfied with the turn of events. Miraculously, all of the hostages held in Amman throughout the fighting were released unharmed (indeed, they praised their captors for the care they had taken to protect them), although the three airliners were blown up by the guerrillas.

PRESIDENT SADAT AND THE CEASEFIRE

There was both surprise and relief, therefore, when the new President of Egypt, Anwar Sadat, established himself without opposition and showed himself willing to take up the search for a settlement where it had been left by his predecessor. He agreed to renew the ceasefire for a further 90 days and, after intensive consultations between Israeli and American leaders and the extension to Israel of American credits worth $500 million, Israel agreed to return to the Jarring talks. Preliminary discussions took place in New York and in January 1971 Dr. Jarring visited Israel and Egypt, where both sides restated their positions to him on all the points at issue. When the ceasefire agreement was again coming to an end, on February 5th, 1971, President Sadat once more agreed to renew it, this time for 30 days, adding the proposal that Israel should begin to withdraw its forces from the east bank of the canal, in which case Egypt would be able to clear the canal for navigation.

On February 8th Dr. Jarring wrote to the Governments of Israel and Egypt, expressing his optimism about the desire of both parties for a settlement and inviting each of them to give firm commitments which would resolve the central deadlock. Israel, Dr. Jarring suggested, should agree on certain stated conditions (providing guarantees for security and freedom of navigation) to withdraw to the international boundary between Egypt and the Palestine of the British Mandate. Egypt should give a parallel undertaking to conclude a peace agreement explicitly ending the state of belligerency and recognizing Israel's right to exist in peace and security. In other words, both parties were asked formally to accept the principal obligations laid on them by Resolution 242.

The Egyptian reply gave the undertaking called for by Dr. Jarring, provided that Israel did the same and agreed to withdraw its forces to the international border. The Israeli reply stated firmly that, while Israel would be prepared to withdraw its forces to "secure, recognized and agreed boundaries to be established in the peace agreement", it would in no circumstances withdraw to the pre-June 1967 lines.

This official confirmation of Israel's insistence on territorial expansion as part of a peace settlement embarrassed the American Government, which had first withheld and then granted military and economic assistance to Israel, in the attempt to persuade the Israeli Government to accept only "minor rectifications" of the armistice lines. The Americans made one further attempt when Mr. Rogers, at a press conference on March 16th, 1971, urged the Israelis to accept international guarantees in place of territorial gains, adding that security did not "necessarily require additions of territory" and that in the American view "the 1967 boundary should be the boundary between Israel and Egypt".

PROPOSAL FOR A "PARTIAL SETTLEMENT"

When this too met with an Israeli refusal, the American Government took up instead President Sadat's suggestion of an Israeli withdrawal for some distance in Sinai to allow the reopening of the Suez Canal. But the opportunity had been lost and the new proposal for a partial settlement quickly became bogged down in arguments over the extent of the Israeli withdrawal and the question of whether it should be seen as the first step in a complete withdrawal or not. The arguments dragged on through most of 1971 until the proposal was finally dropped by the Americans on November 22nd—the fourth anniversary of the passage of Resolution 242.

In December the UN General Assembly, in a resolution reaffirming the "inadmissibility of the acquisition of territory by war" and calling for an Israeli withdrawal, also urged Israel to "respond favourably" to the proposals made by Dr. Jarring in February. Only seven states voted against the resolution (Israel and six Latin American states) and it was noted that the United States, which in the past had always voted in support of Israel on territorial questions, abstained, reflecting the American view that Israel should withdraw from all but insubstantial portions of the occupied territories. However, no action followed and the year ended with President Sadat in a dangerously weakened position. He had taken considerable risks in going so far in pursuit of a political settlement and had promised the Egyptian people that 1971 would be the "year of decision". He blamed the lack of progress on American "political manoeuvring", and when the American Government ushered in the new—election—year by promising Israel a further 42 Phantom and 90 Skyhawk aircraft, there was little likelihood that a fresh American suggestion of indirect talks between Israeli and Egyptian representatives in New York would come to anything.

In February 1972 the Israelis launched a large-scale incursion into the Lebanon, stating that its aim was the elimination of guerrilla bases near Israel's northern border. When there was a revival of guerrilla action in May and June, in the form of another hijacking and an attack by Japanese gunmen (acting for the PFLP) on Lydda airport, there was speculation about further Israeli action against the Lebanon (where the PFLP had established its headquarters after being driven out of Jordan). In June a further Israeli raid on the Lebanon was condemned by the Security Council after more than 70 civilians had been killed or wounded by what the Israeli Deputy Prime Minister described as an "error".

An unexpected development followed when President Sadat, in July 1972, called for the withdrawal from Egypt of the large contingent of Soviet advisers engaged on the reorganization of Egypt's defence system. This surprise move, which gravely damaged Egypt's defensive capability—to say nothing of its capacity to launch an attack against the forces of Israel—was interpreted as a final appeal to the American Government to bring pressure to bear on Israel to accept a settlement involving an Israeli withdrawal from Sinai. If this was its intention, the move was ill-timed, since the approach of the Presidential election made it virtually certain that no American politician would advocate a course of action so unwelcome to Zionist opinion in the United States. There was in fact no American response to President Sadat's gesture before the election in November; nor, after it, apart from generalized statements about the need for a new initiative to restore peace in the Middle East, was there any sign of a reappraisal of American policy towards the area.

In Europe, however, partly out of a feeling that an important opportunity was being allowed to slip and partly as a reflection of a sense of disillusionment with American leadership, a reappraisal of Middle Eastern policy was taking place. In preparation for Britain's entry into the European Community (which took place on January 1st, 1973) an attempt was being made to concert a European approach to important questions of foreign policy. The attempt found expression in the voting at the end of the annual Middle East debate in the General Assembly of the United Nations when, with the single exception of Denmark, all the members of the Community followed the lead of Britain and France in voting for a resolution strongly critical of Israel. (The United States again abstained.)

TERROR AND COUNTER-TERROR IN THE MIDDLE-EAST

The cease-fire along the Suez Canal was maintained, but along the northern borders of Israel and Israeli-held territory there was a renewal of violence in the second half of 1972, accompanied by a mounting series of terrorist attacks by both Israelis and Palestinians in various parts of the world. In July and August 1972, a number of Palestinian leaders were killed or seriously injured by explosive devices sent to them in Beirut. In September, during the Olympic Games in Munich, Palestinian guerrillas captured a number of Israeli athletes and held them hostage in an attempt to obtain the release of Palestinians held captive in Israel. The attempt failed when West German police, after promising the Palestinians safe conduct out of Germany, opened fire on them at Munich airport, whereupon the guerrillas killed the hostages and were themselves either killed or captured. (The three Palestinians who survived were later released when a West German airliner was hijacked and flown, with the guerrillas on board, to Libya.)

The Munich attack was followed by heavy Israeli ground and air raids into the Lebanon, which the Israeli Government held responsible for the activities of guerrillas whose bases (since their expulsion from Jordan in 1970 and 1971) were in the refugee camps of the Lebanon and in Beirut. The fact that many civilians were killed in these raids, among them women and children in the refugee camps, provoked a confused international response and a growing sense of alarm as the unsettled conflict in the Middle East sparked violence in countries far from the conflict itself. Letter bombs were posted to Israeli representatives in various countries—an attaché at the Israeli Embassy in London was killed by one in September 1972—and after the Israeli Prime Minister, Mrs. Meir, had announced that "we have no alternative but to strike at the terrorist organizations wherever we can locate them", representatives of the Palestine Liberation Organization were attacked by gunmen or with explosive devices in Rome, Stockholm, Paris and Nicosia.

For a brief period at the beginning of 1973 it looked as though an effort would be made to take the conflict out of the hands of the terrorists and return it to the political arena. In rapid succession Mr. Hafez Ismail (President Sadat's political adviser), King Hussein of Jordan and Mrs. Meir visited Washington for talks with President Nixon. But the frail hopes aroused by this diplomatic activity were dashed when, in February 1973, a heavy Israeli attack on guerrilla installations in a refugee camp in North Lebanon was followed immediately by the shooting down by Israeli fighters of a Libyan airliner whose French captain had strayed over occupied Sinai in a sandstorm. The two incidents caused the death of 150 people—almost all of them civilians—within twenty-four hours and provoked an unprecedented wave of criticism of the Israelis on the eve of Mrs. Meir's arrival in Washington. Before she left, however, Palestinian guerrillas had diverted international indignation onto themselves by attacking the Saudi Arabian Embassy in Khartoum, where they held hostage and eventually murdered the American Ambassador and two other diplomats, one American and the other Belgian. A month later, following an abortive Palestinian attack on the Israeli Embassy in Nicosia, Israeli commandos mounted a carefully planned and ruthlessly executed attack in Beirut, penetrating into a residential district in the heart of the Lebanese capital and killing, among a number of other people, three leading members of the PLO.

On May 7th, 1973, the twenty-fifth anniversary of the creation of the State of Israel was celebrated with a massive military parade in Jerusalem. The parade symbolized Israel's commanding military position but was widely criticized, both inside and outside Israel, as an indication of the Israeli Government's refusal to consider any compromise formula which might lead to peace with the Arabs. Public opinion polls in Israel, as well as the pronouncements of leading figures in the Israeli political and military establishment, indicated a significant hardening of Israeli attitudes over the crucial question of withdrawal from the territories occupied in 1967.

ENERGY CRISIS

A new factor which affected international attitudes towards the Arab-Israeli conflict began to make itself felt during the first half of 1973. This was the prospect of a serious energy crisis arising out of the rapidly increasing demand for oil products in Europe, the United States and Japan. In the United States in particular, the realization that industrial expansion in the following decade was likely to become much more dependent on imports of oil and natural gas from Middle Eastern producing countries caused serious concern at a time when America's support for Israel made the United States a particular target for criticism throughout the Arab world.

STALEMATE

In the autumn of 1973, the Arab-Israeli conflict appeared to be further than ever from solution. The Israelis, confident that their military supremacy over the Arabs had if anything increased, remained in control of all the territories they had occupied in 1967 and had established in these territories some fifty civilian and paramilitary settlements. The Egyptian and Jordanian Governments—though not yet the Syrian—had long since modified their earlier refusal to negotiate a settlement and had clearly indicated their willingness to recognize the State of Israel; but they still refused to envisage a peace settlement which did not provide for the return of all the occupied territories. The United Nations, despite the passage every year of resolutions calling for an Israeli withdrawal, found all its efforts to devise a settlement blocked by Israel's refusal to relinquish its 1967 conquests. A dangerous mood of frustration enveloped the Middle East, while for the outside world anxiety over a possible renewal of the conflict was compounded by apprehensions about the maintenance of vital oil supplies.

More than ever, the key to the situation rested in the hands of the United States, which found itself isolated in support of Israel and yet faced with the prospect of becoming increasingly dependent on Arab oil. America's allies, for whom dependence on Arab oil was already a fact, were growing increasingly impatient with the American Government's Middle East policy, which seemed to be aimed at maintaining Israel's overall supremacy without seeking in return any concessions from the Israeli government over the occupied territories or the other necessary ingredients of a peace settlement. The Watergate scandal in Washington appeared to make it even less likely than before that the Nixon administration would risk unpopularity with the Zionist lobby by proposing any fresh initiative to break the deadlock in the Middle East. The isolation of the United States was emphasized during the debate in the Security Council in the summer of 1973. After prolonged discussion, the Council considered a resolution put forward by eight non-aligned members which was strongly critical of Israel's continued occupation of Arab territory. The United States found it necessary to use its veto to prevent the passage of the resolution, which obtained the affirmative votes of all the other Council members except China, which abstained.

This American decision played its part in convincing the Arabs that only by a renewal of the war could they hope to break the stalemate in the Middle East and look forward to the recovery of their lost territories. They had no illusions about their ability to recover them by defeating Israel; but they judged that, unless the superpowers were brought face to face with the danger of a fresh round of fighting which would threaten their own interests, they would not exert themselves to obtain a settlement. They were influenced in forming this judgment by the American decision (announced in March, shortly after President Sadat's special envoy had visited President Nixon) to furnish another forty-eight jet fighters to Israel, and by the progress towards détente between the United States and the Soviet Union (symbolized by the meeting between President Nixon and Mr. Brezhnev in June). From both it appeared plain to the Arabs that the stalemate in the Middle East was to be preserved at their expense.

RENEWAL OF THE WAR

The attack which was launched on two fronts by the Egyptian and Syrian forces on October 6th took everyone by surprise. Unusual activity behind the lines had been observed by Israeli and American intelligence agencies west of the Suez Canal and east of the cease-fire line on the Golan Heights; but in each case its importance was discounted because of the Israeli conviction (shared by military experts elsewhere) that the Egyptian army was incapable of the elaborate operation required to cross the canal and breach the chain of Israeli fortifications known as the Bar-Lev line on the east bank. Their success in guarding the secret of the attack won for the Egyptian and Syrian forces on both fronts a substantial initial advantage, which was enhanced by the fact that October 6th was Yom Kippur, the Day of Atonement in the Jewish calendar, when all public services were suspended, which made it unusually difficult for the Israelis to mobilize their forces rapidly to meet the emergency. By midnight on the first day of the war, four hundred Egyptian tanks had crossed the canal, the Bar-Lev line had been outflanked and a massive Syrian tank attack beyond the Golan Heights had only been stemmed by a masterly rearguard action by greatly outnumbered Israeli armour, aided by costly air strikes.

During the fighting that followed and which continued for three weeks (despite a United Nations cease-fire on October 22nd) before all operations ceased, the Syrians were driven back beyond the old cease-fire line and Israeli forces counter-attacking on the Suez front effected a westward crossing of the canal, to establish a wide bridgehead on the edge of the Nile delta. At the end of the war, the military advantage lay with the Israelis, who had occupied a further area of Syrian territory and were threatening Damascus, while their units west of the canal had isolated an Egyptian army in Suez, cutting its communications with Cairo. Meanwhile, however, largely as a result of the intervention of the Arab oil-producing states, the political objectives of the Arabs had been achieved and the whole context of the confrontation with Israel had been decisively altered.

To begin with, the legend of Israeli invincibility had been shattered. Making unexpectedly efficient use of new weapons (especially portable anti-tank missiles) the Arab armies demonstrated that since 1967 they had significantly narrowed the technological gap between themselves and the Israelis. By doing so, they exposed the fallacy on which Israeli strategy had been based since the Six Day War: the fallacy that the control of wide buffer zones (in the shape of the territories occupied since 1967), together with the military supremacy of which they felt assured, rendered the Israelis immune to Arab attack. This assumption had encouraged in the Israeli leaders the dangerous conviction that since they were in no danger from the Arabs they could afford to disregard the mounting pressure of world opinion calling for an Israeli withdrawal as the essential condition for a negotiated settlement with the Arabs.

THE OIL WEAPON

Soon after the outbreak of the war, there were calls within the Arab world for measures to deny Middle East oil to the supporters of Israel. On October 17th a meeting in Kuwait of representatives of the Arab oil producers resulted in an agreement to reduce output; two days later Abu Dhabi took the lead in stopping altogether the export of oil to the United States. In adopting and presently intensifying these measures, the Arab oil-producing states showed an unexpectedly determined sense of solidarity. This had an evident effect on the Governments of Western Europe, conscious of their dependence on the free flow of oil from the Middle East. On November 6th the nine member states of the Common Market endorsed in Brussels a statement calling for an Israeli withdrawal from the territories occupied in 1967 and asserting that, while all states in the Middle East should enjoy the right to secure boundaries, the legitimate rights of the Palestinians should be taken into account in any settlement (*see* Documents on Palestine, page 65). This provoked accusations from the Israelis to the effect that the Europeans were giving in to Arab "blackmail", but these took too little account of the fact that for several years past (as shown by the yearly votes at the United Nations) the Europeans had been dissociating themselves from United States policy and registering their growing impatience with Israel's refusal to make any concession.

AMERICAN INITIATIVE

These developments underlined the central point which the Arabs had sought to make by their resort to war: the point that neither the Israelis nor those countries which were dependent on Middle East oil would be safe if they allowed a situation to continue in the Middle East which left large areas of Arab territory under Israeli occupation. The Americans, who alone possessed the influence that could induce the Israelis to withdraw—and who now found themselves inconvenienced much more by the oil embargo than they had anticipated—accepted the need to use their influence to bring about a settlement. The American Secretary of State, Dr. Kissinger, who had been active in obtaining Soviet co-operation over a cease-fire, now embarked on a dramatic series of visits to the capitals of the contestants in the Middle East, out of which there resulted disengagement agreements between Egypt and Israel (signed on January 18th 1974) and—after much more protracted and intricate exchanges—between Syria and Israel (signed on May 30th 1974). In the middle of June 1974 President Nixon, whose domestic position had become dangerously insecure on account of the protracted investigations into the Watergate scandal, embarked on a triumphant tour of the Middle East, forecasting a new era of co-operation between the United States and the Arab world, while reassuring the Israelis of continuing American support. Thanks largely to the personal success achieved by Dr. Kissinger with both Arab and Israeli leaders, this American initiative was generally well received, except by some Israelis who foresaw mounting pressure on Israel to make concessions inconsistent with her security, and by the extreme wing of the Palestinian resistance movement, which engaged in a series of terrorist attacks on targets in northern Israel in an effort to frustrate a settlement inconsistent with their aim of total liberation in Palestine. Otherwise, despite reservations about the future of President Nixon's administration and the continuity of American policy in the event of his resignation, Mr. Nixon's visit revealed a strong desire on the part of the Arab governments concerned to restore friendly relations between themselves and the United States. Diplomatic relations between Washington and Damascus were re-established and the embargo on the export of Arab oil to the United States was lifted in recognition of Dr. Kissinger's efforts to promote a satisfactory settlement in the Middle East.

CHANGE IN THE BALANCE OF POWER

This Arab-American reconciliation was one of the most striking results of the October war; it was a reminder of the greatly increased influence of the Arab states so long as they continued to act in concert. Conversely, Israel's international position had been much weakened by the failure of her pre-war policies and by the revelation of the extent to which the rest of the world was dependent on Arab goodwill. The Government headed by Mrs. Golda Meir, in which General Dayan had been the very influential defence minister, was widely blamed both for provoking the October war by its policy of "creeping annexation" and for being caught unawares when the war came. After winning a narrow victory in a general election at the end of 1973, Mrs. Meir finally abandoned the attempt to rebuild her coalition in April 1974. She was succeeded as leader of the Labour party and prime minister by General Itshak Rabin, who had been Chief of Staff at the time of the 1967 war and later Israeli ambassador in Washington. In the Arab world, the effect of the war was to strengthen the position of the regimes in Cairo and Damascus and to give new authority to King Faisal of Saudi Arabia, whose control of the greatest share of the oil reserves of the Middle East made him a dominant figure in Arab politics. The fact that the disengagement agreements arranged with the help of Dr. Kissinger involved small but significant Israeli withdrawals from Arab territory gave satisfaction throughout the Arab world; but the central problem of the future of the Palestinians remained unsolved. The difficulty of finding a solution to this problem which would prove acceptable both to the Israelis and to the Palestine Liberation Organization (which the Arab governments, meeting in Algiers in November 1973, had recognized as "the sole legitimate representative of the Palestinian people") posed a continuing threat to the stability of the disengagement agreements entered into in 1974.

Despite the general awareness of the new strength of the Arab world, the movement towards a settlement in the Middle East gradually lost momentum during the second half of 1974 and a mood of apprehension developed in which a further outbreak of war at times seemed imminent. The disengagement agreements were carried out and UN forces were inserted between the combatants in Sinai and on the Golan front, but mutual recriminations were exchanged between the Syrians and the Israelis over the ill-treatment of prisoners and the destruction of the Syrian town of Kuneitra, demolished by the Israelis on the eve of their withdrawal. The arms lost by both sides during the October war were rapidly replaced, although the Egyptians complained that the Soviet Government had restricted supplies to Egypt while making good all Syria's losses. During the year following the October war the United States Government committed $3,000 million of military aid to Israel, whose leaders claimed that the country was stronger at the end of 1974 than it had been before the Egyptians crossed the Suez Canal on October 6th, 1973.

While the optimism generated by the disengagement agreements was dissipated by the renewal of the stalemate between the Arab governments and Israel, the Palestinians saw their central role in the conflict strikingly endorsed. On September 21st, 1974, the UN General Assembly voted to include "the Palestine Question" on its agenda for the first time since the establishment of the state of Israel in 1948. (Only four governments opposed this decision: Israel, the United States, the Dominican Republic and Bolivia.) On October 14th the General Assembly invited the Palestine Liberation Organization to take part in the debate and a month later the Chairman of the PLO, Yasser Arafat, outlined to the Assembly the PLO's design for a "democratic, secular state" in Palestine in which Jews and Arabs would coexist on terms of equality, specifying that "all Jews now living in Palestine who choose to live with us there in peace and without discrimination" were included in this design. At the end of October a meeting of Arab Heads of State in Rabat confirmed that the PLO was the "sole legitimate representative of the Palestinian people", with the right to speak for the Palestinians at any future Middle East peace talks and to establish an independent national authority in any part of Palestine liberated from Israeli occupation.

These decisions greatly strengthened the hand of the Palestinians and of the PLO as their representative. However, they also deepened the impasse over movement towards a settlement because the Israeli Government adamantly refused to have any dealings with the PLO, dismissing it as a terrorist organization which Israel would meet, in Prime Minister Rabin's words, "only on the battlefield". The position of the PLO was also complicated by internal divisions over the objective which the organization should pursue. Although Yasser Arafat at the United Nations had spoken only of the PLO's goal of a unitary Palestine (whose achievement would mean the elimination of the state of Israel), he was under pressure from the Arab governments to accept the limited objective of a Palestinian state on the West Bank and the Gaza Strip, whose establishment could only be envisaged (if at all) in the context of a compromise settlement including the recognition of Israel within its pre-1967 borders. A majority within the PLO appeared at the end of 1974 to be moving towards acceptance of this formula, but the minority rejected any thought of compromising with the long-term goal of the total liberation of Palestine. This "rejection front", which had the backing of the governments of Iraq and Libya, made it difficult for the PLO openly to align itself with those Arab governments (notably the government of President Sadat in Egypt) which were prepared to exchange recognition of Israel for an Israeli withdrawal from the territories occupied in 1967, including Arab Jerusalem, and the creation of a Palestinian state on the West Bank.

This was in effect the pattern for a settlement which had been envisaged in the Security Council's resolution 242 in November 1967 and which had provided the basis for all the international initiatives undertaken, with diminishing prospects of success, between 1967 and 1973. These initiatives had failed because the Israelis, before October 1973, had felt confident of their ability to retain control of at least substantial parts of the occupied territories and to hold off any Arab attempt to recover them by force. The October war, by undermining this confidence, had made more evident the Israelis' total dependence on American support; and the initial efforts of Dr. Kissinger immediately after the war had encouraged the Arabs to believe that American influence would at last be used to promote a settlement based on an Israeli withdrawal. It was this belief which had brought about the restoration of diplomatic relations between Washington and both Cairo and Damascus and the lifting of the Arab oil embargo.

ARAB IMPATIENCE

The Arab-American reconciliation, in which President Sadat had taken the lead and to which he totally committed himself during 1974, had failed by the end of the year to produce any results beyond the initial disengagement agreements. Apart from the tiny areas of territory conceded by Israel under those agreements, the Israeli occupation was maintained in Sinai, the Golan Heights (including the plateau up to the outskirts of Kuneitra), the West Bank (including the Old City of Jerusalem) and the Gaza Strip, with no relaxation of the ban on political activity by the Arab population or of the repressive measures enforced against that population by the occupation authorities. None of the fifty-odd Jewish settlements established in the occupied territories before October 1973 had been given up; indeed, the Israeli Government, under pressure from the right-wing opposition and the religious parties in the Knesset, continued to announce plans to extend the pattern of Jewish settlement. In the wake of Yasser Arafat's appearance at the United Nations in November 1974 there were demonstrations on the West Bank in support of the PLO, to which the Israelis responded by widespread arrests of Palestinians and the deportation of a number of leading citizens, among them the President of Bir Zeit College, Dr. Hanna Nasir.

These developments caused growing impatience in the Arab world, symbolized by rioting in Cairo in January 1975, over the lack of progress towards a settlement. The tension was heightened by a series of widely advertised statements by American leaders, including Secretary of State Kissinger, hinting at the possibility of armed intervention by American forces in the event of a fresh oil embargo by the Arab oil-producing states. Although these statements were later discounted as somewhat heavy-handed propaganda, those Arab leaders, like President Sadat, who had pinned their faith to American sincerity in the search for a settlement and had nothing to show for it, found themselves under heavy pressure. It was in these circumstances that Dr. Kissinger announced his intention to use his own brand of personal diplomacy to carry the process of disengagement between Israel and Egypt a stage further. When he returned to the Middle East in March it was widely assumed that Dr. Kissinger had obtained prior assurances from both sides of their willingness to conclude a bargain; but after two weeks of intensive "shuttle diplomacy" he had to admit failure when the Israelis refused to withdraw from the Mitla and Giddi passes in Sinai and from the oilfield at Abu Rudeis without an explicit undertaking of future non-belligerency from President Sadat. The latter demand was clearly unrealistic, since to satisfy it would have confirmed Arab suspicions that the Egyptians were prepared to abandon their allies and envisage a separate peace with Israel. There was therefore little surprise when the American Secretary of State (and later President Ford) let it be known that they blamed Israeli obstinacy for the breakdown of the negotiations and announced that the United States would embark on a "reassessment" of its Middle East policy. This was held to mean that the latest Israeli request for increased military and economic aid from the United States would not be granted until the Israelis showed a more conciliatory attitude.

The breakdown of Dr. Kissinger's mission coincided with the assassination in Riyadh of King Faisal of Saudi Arabia, whose prestige and authority had been greatly strengthened as a result of his support for the Arab war effort during and after the October war. Together, the two events brought renewed anxiety about the stability of the Middle East; and this anxiety was increased by the simultaneous and abrupt collapse of American policy in Indochina, where the capitals of Cambodia and South Viet-Nam fell in rapid succession to communist forces.

Two practical steps were taken on the Arab side which helped to allay the anxieties aroused by the breakdown of the peace-making mission of Dr. Kissinger. In May the Syrian Government unexpectedly agreed to renew for a further six months the mandate of the UN force separating the two sides on the Golan front; and on June 5th the Egyptian Government reopened the Suez Canal, eight years to the day after the outbreak of the June war which led to its closure in 1967. Besides offering the Egyptians some hope of relief from their pressing economic problems, this step was taken to indicate President Sadat's continuing preference for a political settlement with Israel rather than a further round of war.

At the time of his failure in March, Dr. Kissinger's critics had pointed to two weaknesses in his "step-by-step" approach to peace-making in the Middle East. In concentrating on limited territorial issues, they said, he had ignored the real heart of the problem, which was the future relationship between Israel and the Palestinians. And by using his personal style of diplomacy, he had excluded the Soviet Government from participation in the negotiations for a settlement which they too would eventually be expected to accept and endorse. When his mission broke down, the Soviet and Egyptian governments at once called for the resumption of the Geneva peace conference, which had met briefly at the time of the Egyptian-Israeli disengagement agreement at the end of 1973 but had been in abeyance ever since. In the absence, however, of any real prospects for progress at Geneva until the gap between the positions of the two sides had been narrowed, none of the parties showed real enthusiasm for reconvening the conference and the Soviet Government tacitly agreed to let the Americans make one more effort to break the deadlock.

FURTHER DISENGAGEMENT IN SINAI

On August 21st Dr. Kissinger flew to Israel to renew his attempt to promote a second disengagement agreement between Israel and Egypt. His return provoked violent demonstrations in Tel Aviv and Jerusalem among Israelis who opposed the idea of further concessions; and while the American Secretary of State was well received in Egypt, the resumption of his mission aroused hostility in other parts of the Arab world. Disregarding the critics on both sides, Dr. Kissinger succeeded after two weeks of intensive negotiations in persuading the Egyptians and Israelis to accept an agreement which was signed in Geneva on September 4th, 1975.

The new agreement provided for an Israeli withdrawal from the strategic Mitla and Giddi passes and the return to the Egyptians of the Abu Rudais oilfields, on which the Israelis had been dependent for some 50 per cent of their oil supplies since they had captured them in 1967. As in the first disengagement agreement signed in January 1974, a UN buffer zone was established separating the Egyptian and Israeli forces and the most important new element was the provision for five electronic listening posts in this zone, of which one was to be manned by Egyptians, one by Israelis and the other three by a team of 200 American civilians who would monitor troop movements both east and west of the passes. Both sides undertook to respect the ceasefire and to resolve the conflict between them by peaceful means rather than by the use of force. Non-military cargoes in ships sailing to or from Israel were to be allowed through the Suez Canal and the agreement was to remain in force "until superseded by a new agreement".

The conclusion of this second disengagement agreement was considered a triumph for American diplomacy and it had significant effects both on Egypt's relations with its Arab allies and on the pattern of international relationships with the various parties to the Middle East conflict. Within the Arab world, where only Saudi Arabia, Sudan and (with reservations) Kuwait expressed approval, the agreement was criticized—most vehemently by the Syrians and the PLO—as a surrender to American and Israeli interests. In response to a strongly-worded statement issued by the Central Council of the PLO in Damascus condemning the agreement as "an isolated partial solution ignoring the Palestinian cause . . . and the pan-Arab nature of the struggle against Zionism", the Egyptian authorities assumed control of the *Voice of Palestine* radio station operated by the PLO in Cairo since 1968. The united Arab front created during the October War and precariously maintained during the two succeeding years was now disrupted.

On the international plane, the second disengagement agreement marked a further stage in the American-Egyptian rapprochement and the estrangement between Egypt and its former ally, the Soviet Union. In October 1975 President Sadat was well received on an official visit to Washington (and less well in New York, where he addressed the General Assembly of the United Nations and urged the necessity of bringing the PLO into any future negotiations for a Middle East settlement), but his repeated criticisms of the Soviet Union led to a steady deterioration of relations which culminated in Egypt's abrogation of the Soviet-Egyptian Treaty of Friendship in March 1976.

By refusing to follow the Egyptian example and agree to a further partial agreement with Israel, Syria now assumed the leadership of the Arab cause which Egypt appeared to have renounced. President Assad, who impressed foreign visitors (including Dr. Kissinger) as a skilful and determined politician, found his position in the Arab world greatly strengthened and even succeeded in restoring close relations with King Hussein of Jordan, with whom he established a joint Syrian-Jordanian Command Council. In October 1975 President Assad visited Moscow, where he had talks with President Podgorny and other leaders and gained a promise of further arms supplies to counter the very considerable deliveries reaching Israel from the United States. At the end of November Syria's already considerable prestige as the most consistent defender of the rights of the Palestinians was enhanced when President Assad agreed to renew the mandate of the UN Disengagement Observer Force (UNDOF) on the Golan Heights, extracting in return a promise that the Security Council would hold a special debate on the Palestine question in January with the PLO taking part.

PLO'S STANDING ENHANCED

This debate marked a further strengthening of the international position of the PLO. Already in November 1975 the UN General Assembly had adopted three resolutions concerning Palestine, of which the first had established a twenty-nation committee to work out plans for the implementation of the Palestinian right "to self-determination and national independence", the second invited the PLO to take part in all future UN debates on the Middle East, and the third denounced Zionism as "a form of racism and racial discrimination". (The last of these provoked an international storm of criticism in which the importance of the other two resolutions was widely overlooked.) A month later only an American veto saved Israel from censure by the Security Council for a series of severe air raids on targets in the Lebanon in which 75 people were killed and 150 wounded. When the Security Council, at Syria's request, debated the Palestine question in January 1976, the American delegate again found it necessary to use the veto to prevent the adoption of a resolution affirming the Palestinians' right to establish a state of their own and calling for an Israeli withdrawal from all the territories occupied since June 1967.

Despite America's continuing support for Israel, many Israelis were alarmed by indications that the attitude of the United States Government, despite the pressures of a presidential campaign, was moving in the direction of an acceptance of Palestinian rights as an essential ingredient in any Middle East settlement. In November 1975 the Ford administration had given wide publicity to the testimony given by Harold Saunders, deputy assistant Secretary of State, before a congressional sub-committee, in which Mr. Saunders had said that it was "obvious that thinking on the Palestinian aspects of the problem must evolve on all sides", adding that the American administration was "prepared to consider any reasonable proposal from any quarter and we will expect other parties to the negotiations to be equally open-minded". In January 1976 there had been reports in the Western press that American officials were already in secret contact with Palestinian representatives. The impression that a major change in American policy was in the making was reinforced in March when the UN Security Council debated the question of Israeli policies in the occupied territories. Although the American delegate again exercised the veto on Israel's behalf (for the third time in less than four months) to defeat a resolution which gained the affirmative votes of the other 14 members of the Security Council, he strongly condemned Israel's establishment of "illegal" settlements in Jerusalem and other occupied areas, emphasizing that "the presence of these settlements is seen by my Government as an obstacle to the success of the negotiations for a just and final peace between Israel and its neighbours".

The Israelis' persistence in establishing these settlements was a major factor in provoking serious rioting all over the occupied West Bank and in Gaza during the spring and summer of 1976. The riots, which found an echo inside Israel on March 30th (when a strike led to a confrontation with the Israeli security forces in which six Israeli Arabs were killed), had a decisive effect on the outcome of municipal elections organized by the Israeli occupation authorities on the West Bank in April. Instead of producing, as the Israelis had hoped, "moderate" Palestinian leaders who would be content with a measure of autonomy under a continuing Israeli occupation, the elections demonstrated the strength of Palestinian nationalism and the widespread support enjoyed by the PLO among the Palestinians living under occupation.

Confidence in Mr. Rabin's Government was undermined, both in Israel and in the outside world, by the failure to develop any clear policy for the future of the occupied territories. Extreme nationalists among the Israelis, who were represented in Mr. Rabin's coalition Government, pressed for more intensive Jewish settlement in the West Bank, as well as on the Golan Heights and in Sinai. Their opponents, including the Mapam element in the coalition, pointed to the dangers involved in this process of overt colonization, which stiffened Arab resistance and brought criticism from some of Israel's most steadfast friends abroad. Divided as it was over this crucial issue, the Government also faced growing discontent internally, where the rapidly rising cost of living (due in large part to very heavy defence expenditure), together with the fear of a renewal of war, provoked emigration from Israel on an unprecedented scale at a time when the figures for immigration had fallen to their lowest level since 1967. The loss of morale was reflected in the fact that in the course of 1975 the number of new immigrants was approximately balanced by the number of Israelis leaving the country to settle elsewhere. In 1976 the position worsened, with emigrants actually exceeding new immigrants by some 1,500.

CIVIL WAR IN LEBANON

At the same time the lack of unity within the Arab camp was highlighted by events in the Lebanon, where armed clashes between Palestinian guerrillas and Christian militiamen in April 1975 touched off a civil war which threatened to destroy the Lebanese state and came near to provoking yet another Arab-Israeli confrontation. Attempts at mediation by the Arab League and by French and American emissaries failed to reconcile the warring parties in the Lebanon, which in turn were supported by rival interests in a divided Arab world, while the Israelis kept a close watch on events whose outcome was bound to affect the security of Israel's northern border. After nine months of heavy fighting, in which Palestinian guerrillas were drawn into a leftist alliance against the defenders of the conservative Christian establishment, the Syrian Government in January 1976 used Syrian-based units of the Palestine Liberation Army to impose a ceasefire which was to be followed by a reform of the Lebanese political system. However, the ceasefire broke down in March, like more than a score of others before it, when Christian extremists supporting President Frangieh prevaricated over the implementation of the reform programme and the Druze leader of the leftist alliance tried to seize the opportunity to force the president's resignation.

Faced with the prospect of an outright victory for the leftists and their Palestinian allies, which in turn might provoke the Israelis into military intervention in southern Lebanon, the Syrian Government used all its influence to restrain the leftists, eventually sending Syrian troops across the border at the end of May 1976. This move was made with tacit American approval and at the same time President Assad renewed the mandate of the UN force on the Golan front for a further six months. He thus reassured his opponents in Israel but found himself virtually isolated in the Arab world and facing a confrontation with the PLO.

The disastrous situation in the Lebanon and the recriminations it caused in the Arab world provided the Israelis with a breathing-space, temporarily obscuring the weakness of their position. Together with the suspension of almost all political activity in the United States during the 1976 presidential election campaign, it relieved the Israeli Government of the necessity to take any initiative to resolve the conflict with its Arab neighbours and left it free to press ahead with the colonization of the occupied territories, where fresh settlements were established in the Golan Heights, in Sinai and on the West Bank. The Arabs, unable to set their own house in order, watched this process in angry frustration and saw the political advantage which they had gained in 1973 slipping from their grasp.

In the autumn of 1976, however, both of the factors which had prevented any movement towards an Arab-Israeli settlement were removed. After repeated failures on the part of the Arab League to play an effective mediating role in the Lebanon, determined efforts by the Saudi Arabian and Kuwaiti governments brought about a restricted Arab summit meeting in Riyadh in October, at which the leaders of Egypt, Syria, the Lebanon and the PLO agreed to the terms of a ceasefire. These were confirmed at a further meeting in Cairo on October 26th and provided for the creation of a substantial Arab peace-keeping force which within a month had put a stop to the savage fighting in Beirut, reopened the Beirut-Damascus road and occupied the main towns in the north and south of the country.

NEW ADMINISTRATION IN WASHINGTON

By this time the presidential election in the United States was over and the new President-elect, Jimmy Carter, had indicated his intention to take early action over the Middle East. Both from the Arabs, whose renewed solidarity was symbolized by a reconciliation between the presidents of Egypt and Syria, and from the Americans, freed at last from the handicap of a lame duck administration, the Israelis found themselves again under pressure. Even before the Carter administration formally took office in January, a new tone was discernible in the pronouncements coming out of Washington and a clearer American voice began to be heard at the United Nations. On November 11th, 1976, the American delegate joined in approving a unanimous "consensus statement" by the Security Council which "strongly deplored" Israel's actions in establishing settlements in the occupied territories and attempting to alter the demographic balance in Jerusalem. On November 19th the American Ambassador to Israel, speaking to the annual convention of B'nai B'rith in Jerusalem, said that "unless Israel's professed willingness to return occupied territory is seen as more than mere rhetoric, the vicious circle of mutual mistrust cannot be broken". On November 24th the United States joined 117 other nations in voting in the UN General Assembly (against the opposition of Israel and Costa Rica) to deplore Israel's refusal to allow the return of the Palestinian refugees who had left their homes in 1967.

In the occupied West Bank intermittent unrest continued throughout 1976. Demonstrations in Nablus, Ramallah and the Old City of Jerusalem in May and June, in which Palestinian schoolchildren played a leading part, were subdued by the Israeli security forces with exceptional violence. In October there were serious riots in Hebron over the respective rights of Jews and Arabs to pray in the mosque built over the Tombs of the Patriarchs. In December a hunger strike by Arabs detained in the Israeli prison at Ashkelon focused attention on the grievances of Arab political prisoners and the lack of any prospect of ending an occupation which had been in existence for nearly ten years. Israel's occupation policy was again condemned by the UN General Assembly on December 20th, following the publication of a report by the UN Special Committee for the Investigation of Israeli Practices in the Occupied Territories, and on February 15th, 1977, the UN Human Rights Commission expressed "grave concern" over the deteriorating situation in the occupied territories and unanimously called on the Government of Israel to adhere to the terms of the Fourth Geneva Convention in its treatment of civilians in "all the occupied territories, including Jerusalem".

Conscious of the growing tension in the Middle East and of the steadily increasing dependence of the Western world on supplies of oil from the Arab world, the new American administration which took office in January 1977 moved with unexpected swiftness to reactivate the machinery for an Arab-Israeli settlement. In February President Carter despatched his new Secretary of State, Cyrus Vance, on a tour of the Middle East (where he followed in the footsteps of the Secretary-General of the United Nations, Dr. Waldheim) and invited Israeli and Arab leaders to visit him in Washington. In the course of a visit by the Israeli Prime Minister, Yitzhak Rabin, in March 1977, President Carter surprised all parties by speaking frankly about the nature of the settlement he envisaged. He pleased his Israeli guest by a reference to Israel's need for "defensible borders", but disconcerted him by making plain that in the American view an ultimate settlement should involve a return to the 1967 borders with only "minor adjustments". During an interim period and as the prelude to the conclusion of a final peace agreement, the American President indicated that arrangements might be made to extend Israel's defence capability beyond its eventual legal frontiers. A week later, speaking in a small New England town, President Carter confirmed the broad lines of his thinking about an Arab-Israeli settlement and added, again unexpectedly, that the final element in such a settlement should be the creation of a "homeland" for the dispossessed Palestinians.

ISRAELI GOVERNMENT RESIGNS

The renewed emphasis on the Palestinian aspect of the problem, which had been highlighted by the unrest on the West Bank and reflected in the repeated decisions of the United Nations and which was now echoed by President Carter, was unwelcome to the Israelis. The governing coalition was already under considerable internal pressure as a result of the difficult economic situation and the failure to devise any constructive policy for achieving peace with the Arabs; in addition, it had been undermined by a series of scandals involving leading figures in the Labour Party which had dominated this and every preceding government since the creation of the state. The most crucial issue facing the Government concerned the occupied territories and in particular the extent to which it should allow—or could control—Jewish settlement on the West Bank. Mr. Rabin's cabinet, already under pressure from the right-wing Likud party (which opposed any withdrawal from the West Bank), was divided within itself on this issue and in

December 1976, following a dispute with one of his coalition partners, Mr. Rabin announced the Government's resignation. This necessitated a general election, which was fixed for May 17th, 1977. (The Israeli constitution required Mr. Rabin to stay in office as head of a caretaker government and it was in this capacity that he visited Washington in March).

ARAB GOVERNMENTS AND THE PLO

Once they had achieved a reconciliation between themselves and put an end to the war in the Lebanon in the autumn of 1976, the Arab Governments set about enlisting the help of the new American administration in working towards a peace settlement with Israel. Their common position was that the Geneva conference should be reconvened, with the Palestinians participating, and that an overall settlement should be negotiated on the basis of an Israeli withdrawal to the 1967 borders and the establishment of a Palestinian state on the West Bank and the Gaza Strip. Their efforts were complicated by the refusal of the PLO to agree explicitly to renounce its objective of the establishment of a unitary, "secular, democratic state" in the whole of Palestine (which would replace the existing state of Israel), although PLO spokesmen on a number of occasions did indicate their willingness to establish a state "on any part of Palestine" from which the Israelis would withdraw.

Since the Israelis refused either to entertain the idea of an independent Palestinian state or to negotiate under any circumstances with the PLO (whether or not the PLO agreed to recognize the state of Israel), no movement appeared possible unless the American Government brought pressure to bear on Israel. This the new administration in Washington was reluctant to do in the run-up to the Israeli general election, although the Israelis were uneasy over repeated indications that the Americans, like the Arab Governments, were in contact with the PLO in an effort to persuade the Palestinians to modify their attitude. There were hopes that a much-postponed meeting of the Palestine National Council, which was eventually held in Cairo in March 1977, would produce a more flexible stance; but in the event the Council meeting, while it reiterated the readiness of the Palestinians to establish a West Bank "mini-state" on any territory liberated from the Israelis, refused to modify the clause in the Palestinian National Charter which asserted the "secular democratic state" as the ultimate objective.

RIGHT-WING VICTORY IN ISRAEL

The prospects for a negotiated Arab-Israeli settlement received a severe setback in May, when the elections in Israel resulted in an unexpected victory for the right-wing Likud grouping at the expense of the Labour alignment. The elections were fought mainly over domestic issues and the defeat (for the first time in the history of the state) of the ruling Labour party was widely attributed to discontent over the failure to control the economic situation and over the series of scandals which had involved senior figures in the former administration. The result, largely unforeseen, was to put in power a party publicly committed to maintaining Israeli rule over the whole of the occupied West Bank, on the ground that it constituted part of Israel's divinely-ordained biblical inheritance, and led by the veteran politician, Mr. Menachem Begin, who had made his name in the pre-state period as the leader of the terrorist organization *Irgun Zvai Leumi*. This caused widespread apprehension in the Arab world and presented a challenge to President Carter, whose tentative ideas for a settlement presupposed an Israeli withdrawal from at least the greater part of the West Bank. It reduced still further the chances of reconvening the Geneva peace conference before the end of 1977.

Faced with this difficulty, President Carter invited the new prime minister of Israel to visit Washington and before his arrival took steps to restate his own view of the essentials for a peace settlement in the Middle East and to obtain the endorsement of this view by America's allies in Europe. A statement published at the end of June by the U.S. State Department reaffirmed American adherence to Security Council resolution 242 and stressed that a settlement must involve Israeli withdrawal "on all three fronts of the Middle East—that is, Sinai, Golan, West Bank and Gaza—with the exact border and security arrangements being agreed in the negotiations". The State Department spokesman added that a Middle East settlement which was to be durable would have to deal with the Palestinian issue and that "in this connection the President has spoken of the need for a homeland for the Palestinians, whose exact nature should be negotiated between the parties".

The theme of a Palestinian "homeland" was taken up two days later at a meeting of the Heads of Government of the European Community in London. In a Declaration published on June 29th, 1977, the leaders of the nine members of the European Community restated "their view that a peace settlement should be based on Security Council resolutions 242 and 338", adding that a solution to the Middle East conflict would be possible "only if the legitimate right of the Palestinian people to give expression to its national identity is translated into fact, which would take into account the need for a homeland for the Palestinians". The Declaration also said that representatives of "the Palestinian people" must be included among those taking part in negotiations to reach a peace agreement.

When Mr. Begin arrived in Washington in July 1977, he was warmly received by President Carter and achieved an unexpected success with the American public; but it was clear that no serious attempt had been made in the talks between the two leaders to examine the basic conditions for a peace settlement, on which there was an implicit divergence of views. In particular, the American administration was now intent on securing Palestinian participation in any peace negotiations, to which the Israeli Government was strenuously opposed. When the Secretary of State, Mr. Cyrus Vance, in the course of a tour of Middle East capitals in August, was told by the

Saudi Arabian Government that the PLO would accept resolution 242 if it were amended to include provision for Palestinian self-determination, there was a moment of optimism in which Mr. Carter spoke of the possibility that acceptance by the PLO of resolution 242 might open the way to PLO participation in a reconvened Geneva peace conference. But the Secretary of State's visit ended discouragingly in Israel, where Mr. Vance encountered a categorical refusal on the part of Mr. Begin's government to negotiate under any circumstances with the PLO or to consider the idea of a Palestinian homeland. In any case, the PLO, sceptical about the terms of the proposed bargain, finally refused to amend its stand over resolution 242 without firm assurances that it would receive in return something more substantial than a vague offer to talk to the Americans.

Within a few days of Mr. Vance's departure from Jerusalem, it was announced that Israeli social services in the fields of education, health and welfare were to be extended to the Arab population of the West Bank and the Gaza Strip, which was widely interpreted as a step towards the annexation of these areas; and the same intention seemed to be implicit in the Israeli Government's decision to authorize three new Jewish settlements on the West Bank. Both decisions caused an immediate hardening of the PLO attitude and complicated still further the task which the Americans had set themselves of bringing the Israelis and the Arabs—including, if possible, the Palestinians—to the negotiating table.

When the Israeli Foreign Minister, Mr. Moshe Dayan, went to Washington in September 1977, he took with him draft proposals for a territorial settlement which envisaged the maintenance of the Israeli occupation throughout the West Bank and the Gaza Strip. These proposals, approved by the Israeli cabinet, expressed the continuing resolve of Mr. Begin's government to agree to no step which in any conceivable circumstances could lead to the creation of an independent Palestinian state. The Americans, by contrast, were apprehensive that anything which appeared to extinguish all hope of that ill-defined Palestinian "homeland" to whose existence President Carter had committed himself would not merely ensure the continuation of Palestinian resistance but would also alienate those Arab governments on whose goodwill the United States was increasingly dependent.

The American dilemma was highlighted by the publication in September of a report by the Federal Energy Administration, which revealed that in the first half of 1977 the United States had imported 47 per cent of its oil supplies and was twice as dependent on the Arab producing countries as it had been before the oil embargo in 1973.

Towards the end of September there was a fresh outbreak of fighting in south Lebanon, with Israeli troops openly intervening across the border in support of right-wing forces and against the Palestinians. This helped to prompt an American initiative, reluctantly accepted by the Israeli Government under considerable pressure from Washington, to include Palestinian representatives in a joint Arab delegation to the peace conference when it should be resumed in Geneva. Mr. Moshe Dayan emphasized on behalf of the Israeli Government that this did not mean that Israel was ready to abandon its attitude towards the PLO or its rejection of the idea of a Palestinian state; but the conviction of the Israelis that they were being driven in that direction was strengthened by the publication on October 1st, 1977, of a joint Soviet-American statement calling for a Middle East settlement that would ensure "the legitimate rights of the Palestinians". The use for the first time of this phrase by the American Government (whose representatives had previously spoken only of Palestinian "interests") alarmed the Israelis and was taken by the Arabs as an indication that President Carter was prepared for the confrontation that had long been threatening with the Israeli Government and its powerful supporters in the United States.

As the controversy over this aspect of the Soviet-American statement died down, its true significance as a symbol of superpower co-operation in the Middle East became apparent. The Soviet Union and the United States had been the joint Chairmen of the Geneva Conference at its first and only meeting at the end of 1973. After that Dr. Kissinger's ostentatiously personal style of diplomacy had numbered among its disadvantages the fact that it excluded the Soviet Union from any useful role in Middle East peace-making. The prospect that the two superpowers were now prepared to collaborate again made a renewal of the Geneva Conference look less unlikely and encouraged a fresh outburst of diplomatic activity, with even the PLO expressing its qualified acceptance of the Soviet-American statement as the basis for a reconvened peace conference.

PRESIDENT SADAT'S VISIT TO JERUSALEM

Once again, however, the momentum was lost and as fresh procedural arguments developed which seemed likely to defer indefinitely the opening of serious negotiations, the Middle East settled back into an atmosphere of mistrust and intermittent violence. In October the Israeli Government announced its intention to establish six new settlements on the West Bank before the end of 1977 and on November 9th, in retaliation for a rocket attack by Palestinian guerrillas which killed three Israelis in a northern settlement, the Israeli air force attacked refugee camps in south Lebanon and completely destroyed the village of Azziye, killing more than 100 Lebanese civilians.

A few hours later, in the course of a speech to the Egyptian Parliament in which he expressed impatience with the endless debates over procedural questions, President Sadat said that he would be willing to go to Jerusalem and to the Knesset itself to negotiate a peace agreement with the Israelis. Despite widely expressed scepticism, the suggestion was immediately taken up by the Israeli Prime Minister and pursued through intermediaries in the American embassies in Cairo, Beirut and Jerusalem—and later through the CBS television network in the United States. Resisting a rising tide of Arab disapproval, and despite the last-minute resignation of his foreign minister and the minister's deputy, President Sadat flew to Jerusalem on November 19th, 1977, and the next day made a dramatic appeal for peace in the Knesset and before the television cameras of the world.

This altogether unexpected initiative took the world by storm. It was greeted with enthusiasm in the West, where it was regarded as a bold and constructive break with the sterile attitudes of the past, and with incredulous delight by the Israelis, who glimpsed the prospect of an end to their dangerous isolation. Among the Arabs, however, while there were scattered and mainly private expressions of approval and optimism, the general reaction of furious resentment left the Arab world in a state of unparalleled disunity, whose immediate effect was to make it harder than ever for the Arabs to achieve a common platform on which to negotiate a settlement with Israel.

Nor did the euphoria which surrounded President Sadat in Jerusalem long survive his return to Cairo after a series of meetings with Israeli political leaders. It soon became apparent that his Israeli hosts had assumed—like his Arab critics—that President Sadat had despaired of achieving an overall settlement between the Arabs and Israel and had set himself the more limited objective of an Egyptian-Israeli peace treaty. For this, the Israeli leaders were ready to withdraw from almost all Egyptian territory; they were not prepared to meet Mr. Sadat's other demands for a complete withdrawal from all Arab territory occupied in 1967 and recognition by the Israelis of the Palestinian right to self-determination.

In the conviction that his initiative must not be allowed to founder for lack of movement, President Sadat summoned a conference in Cairo to which he invited delegations from the United Nations, the two superpowers, Israel, the Arab confrontation states and the PLO. Of these, only Israel, the U.S.A. and the UN accepted the invitation, while the mutual recriminations between Egypt and the absentees widened still further the rift in the Arab world. Serious negotiations were postponed until December 25th, 1977, when Mr. Begin flew to Ismailia for a much-advertised "summit" meeting with President Sadat, at which the Israeli Prime Minister produced a set of proposals for the future of Sinai, the West Bank and the Gaza Strip. On the crucial question of the future of the Palestinians, Mr. Begin offered only a limited form of self-rule for the population of the West Bank and the Gaza Strip, with Israel remaining in control of "security and public order", and this was criticized in the Arab world as being merely a formula for the maintenance of the Israeli occupation.

President Sadat's position was made more difficult, not only by his failure to win a more constructive response from the Israelis, but also by a statement from President Carter apparently approving the Begin proposal for Palestinian "self-rule". When Mr. Carter, in an evident attempt to repair the damage, altered the schedule of a foreign tour in order to spend an hour and a half with Mr. Sadat at Aswan on January 4th, he took the opportunity to reiterate the need to recognize "the legitimate rights of the Palestinian people" and to enable the Palestinians "to participate in the determination of their own future". This did something to restore relations between the United States and Egypt, but elsewhere in the Arab world cynicism about the prospects for an overall Arab-Israeli settlement was deepened by mistrust of President Sadat's motives and by the apparent inconsistency of American policy, especially where the rights of the Palestinians were concerned.

The Ismailia summit meeting produced a decision to institute bilateral talks on political and military questions affecting a settlement. The military talks opened in Cairo on January 11th and were at once complicated by a dispute over Israeli settlements in Sinai, which had been criticized as illegal by the International Commission of Jurists in Geneva on January 5th. This criticism was echoed in unusually categorical terms by President Carter a week later and when the political talks opened in Jerusalem on January 16th they were interrupted after only twenty-four hours when President Sadat recalled the Egyptian delegation, saying that in view of Israel's insistence on retaining the settlements he saw no hope of reaching agreement on a declaration of principles which might form the basis for negotiations.

When President Sadat visited Washington at the beginning of February for talks with President Carter and leading members of both houses of Congress, his claim that the Israelis had made no constructive response to his Jerusalem initiative was sympathetically received. The Israeli Prime Minister at the same time was encountering an unprecedented wave of criticism from American politicians and editorial writers, who found his policies incomprehensibly rigid, especially on the issue of the settlements in the occupied territories. When Mr. Begin chose this moment to assert that UN resolution 242, in the Israeli Government's opinion, did not require an Israeli withdrawal from the West Bank, American impatience was redoubled. The Israeli prime minister was invited to visit Washington in the middle of March 1978 and it was widely assumed that President Carter would take the opportunity to exert serious pressure on the Israeli Government to alter policies which were clearly frustrating President Sadat's peace initiative and weakening the position of the moderates in the Arab world.

ISRAELI INVASION OF SOUTH LEBANON

In the event, Mr. Begin's journey to Washington was delayed for a week by a fresh crisis arising out of a terrorist raid near Tel Aviv by Palestinian guerrillas operating from south Lebanon, in which 36 Israelis were killed, including a number of women and children, and 76 wounded.

The Israeli response was to mount a major attack across the border into south Lebanon, whose original purpose was to wipe out Palestinian guerrilla bases and establish a security belt some six miles wide along the Lebanese side of the frontier. When the United States hurriedly introduced a resolution in the

UN Security Council calling for an Israeli withdrawal to be supervised by a UN force, the Israelis deepened their penetration and when a ceasefire finally came into effect on the evening of March 20th their forces were in occupation of the whole of south Lebanon as far as the Litani river, with the exception of the port of Tyre.

The terrorist raid by the PLO on March 11th had been very widely condemned; but the Israeli invasion, which was accompanied by heavy and indiscriminate land, sea and air bombardments in which most of the towns and villages of south Lebanon were destroyed, provoked even more severe denunciation, especially as it became clear that, while most of the guerrillas had escaped, an estimated 1,000 Lebanese civilians had been killed, in addition to some 200 guerrillas, and upwards of 200,000 refugees had been driven from their homes.

When Mr. Begin finally met President Carter on March 20th, the differences between them over the basic requirements of a Middle East peace settlement led to a confrontation which was barely masked by the niceties of diplomatic protocol. Relations between the United States and Israel had reached their lowest point since President Eisenhower ordered Mr. Ben Gurion to withdraw his forces from Sinai in 1957, and Mr. Begin returned from Washington to face a threat to his leadership in Israel, where there was dissension within the cabinet and a movement of ex-servicemen urged the prime minister not to press territorial claims at the cost of peace.

There was friction over the role of the UN Interim Force in Lebanon (UNIFIL), whose mandate was to supervise the withdrawal of the Israeli army from south Lebanon and to restore the authority of the Lebanese Government in the area. The Israelis carried out a partial withdrawal at the end of April but insisted that they would maintain an armed presence in Lebanon until the UN force could ensure the security of northern Israel against attacks by Palestinian guerrillas. The PLO, which was determined not to relinquish its last area of operations, promised to co-operate with UNIFIL but found it difficult to control the activities of some of its units in the area around Tyre, which remained in Palestinian hands. The tension was reflected in Beirut, where severe clashes between Syrian units of the Arab peace-keeping force and Christian militiamen led to the fall of the Lebanese Government (although subsequently re-appointed), on April 19th.

At the beginning of May 1978 Mr. Begin again visited Washington, where President Carter assured him that "we will never waver in our absolute commitment to Israel's security". However, two weeks later, as the Israelis were celebrating the thirtieth anniversary of the birth of their state, the US Senate authorized the sale of advanced fighter aircraft to Saudi Arabia. The Senate's decision, which was taken despite a sustained attempt by the pro-Israeli lobby in Washington to prevent it, was the first of its kind and clearly reflected American impatience with Mr. Begin's stand on peace negotiations with the Arabs, as well as the importance attached by the United States to retaining the friendship of Saudi Arabia, the leading oil producer in the Middle East.

When the Israelis withdrew the last of their forces from South Lebanon on June 13th, they refused to hand over their positions to UNIFIL but left them in the hands of Christian Lebanese militia units which had been collaborating with the Israelis against the Lebanese Government. This helped to cause a renewed crisis in Beirut at the beginning of July, when the Syrian-dominated Arab peace-keeping force attempted to impose its authority on the right-wing Christian militias.

The American Government, alarmed at the prospect of renewed Israeli intervention and of the final breakdown of the peace initiative launched by President Sadat in November 1977, exerted its influence to restrain both sides in the Lebanon and persuaded the Israeli and Egyptian Governments to send their foreign ministers to a meeting in England, which took place at Leeds Castle on July 18th. When this meeting failed to narrow the gap between the two sides, President Sadat announced that he would not engage in further negotiations with Israel unless the Israeli Government changed its position. Faced with a deteriorating situation, President Carter took the unexpected step of inviting the Egyptian and Israeli leaders to meet him in a final attempt to break the deadlock in the privacy of the presidential lodge at Camp David at the beginning of September 1978.

CAMP DAVID SUMMIT

There was little optimism in advance of the Camp David summit meeting, since the Egyptian and Israeli positions seemed to be as far apart as ever on the crucial questions of the future of the West Bank and Gaza. The atmosphere was worsened by continuing friction between the Israelis and UNIFIL in South Lebanon and by persistent though contradictory reports about the Israeli Government's intention to expand the number of Jewish settlements on the West Bank. On both issues the United States was critical of the Israeli stand and it was widely felt that President Sadat, by involving the Americans so closely in the search for a settlement, had put himself in an advantageous position for the approaching confrontation at the summit, especially since Mr. Begin continued to assert Israel's claim to sovereignty over the West Bank (and so, by implication, its refusal of Security Council resolution 242).

The Camp David meeting, which lasted for twelve days and appeared more than once to be on the point of breaking down, ended on September 17th when President Carter made a triumphant appearance on television to announce that Mr Begin and President Sadat had signed two documents which together provided a framework for peace in the Middle East. One of these dealt with the bilateral problems between Egypt and Israel, which the two leaders undertook to resolve by concluding within three months a peace treaty providing for an Israeli withdrawal from Sinai and the establishment of normal relations between the two countries. The other dealt with the wider question of the future of the West Bank and Gaza and provided for the election of a Palestinian self-governing authority to replace the existing Israeli military government; once the authority was in being, there should be a transitional period of not more than five years, during which the inhabitants of the West Bank and Gaza would exercise autonomy; and finally, "as soon as possible, but not later than the third year after the beginning of the transitional period", there should be negotiations to determine the final status of the West Bank and Gaza and to conclude a peace treaty between Israel and Jordan.

The Camp David agreements were greeted with a very mixed reception by the different participants. President Carter's own standing was greatly enhanced in the United States, where it was felt that his daring personal diplomacy had forced the Israeli and Egyptian leaders to make the concessions without which no positive outcome was possible. In Israel the agreements were greeted with more cautious approval, in the belief that Mr Begin had realized Israel's long-standing ambition to conclude a separate peace with Egypt without making any substantive concessions over Israel's right to maintain control of the West Bank and Gaza. In the Arab world, however, the agreements were seen as confirmation of the charge that President Sadat had abandoned the Palestinians and his Arab allies in order to satisfy purely Egyptian interests. In the chorus of protest that followed, even the government of Saudi Arabia contributed the unusually outspoken comment that the Camp David agreements constituted "an unacceptable formula for a definitive peace", while the resignation of the Egyptian foreign minister (who was at Camp David with President Sadat) showed that not even Egyptian opinion was wholeheartedly in favour of the Camp David formula.

The controversy within the Arab world centred around the question of whether or not the agreements gave any real promise of eventual self-determination for the Palestinians. The advocates of the Camp David "framework for peace" argued that if the Palestinians cooperated in the arrangements for a transitional period of self-rule they would set in motion a process which would be irreversible; that the end result of this process would be, sooner or later, an independent Palestinian state; and that, if the Palestinians refused to cooperate, they would provide Israel with an excuse to perpetuate its occupation of the West Bank and Gaza. Against this the critics argued that it was futile for Egypt to negotiate on behalf of the Palestinians over an issue on which the Palestinians themselves had not been consulted; that the arrangements for Palestinian autonomy outlined at Camp David were so imprecise as to be useless; that in any case the Israelis would hold a power of veto over their implementation and over the eventual future of the West Bank; and that the Israelis had no intention of ending their occupation or of allowing any development which might lead in the end to Palestinian independence.

The last of these arguments was much strengthened in the immediate aftermath of the Camp David meeting by the actions of Mr. Begin. Even before he left the United States, the Israeli prime minister declared that Israeli forces would remain on the West Bank (which he refused to refer to as anything but "Judea and Samaria") and publicly challenged President Carter's assertion that he had agreed not to establish any more settlements there during the five-year transitional period. As soon as he was back in Israel, he declared emphatically in the Knesset that Israel would not allow "under any conditions or in any circumstances" the establishment of an independent Palestinian state, and that Israel would continue to create new settlements on the West Bank and would expect to maintain an armed presence there even after the end of the transitional period.

ARAB OPPOSITION HARDENS

In the circumstances it was not surprising that the U.S. Secretary of State, Mr. Vance, whom President Carter dispatched to the Middle East with the special assignment of trying to enlist Arab support for the Camp David agreements, met with a frosty reception even in the capitals normally most friendly to the United States. The governments of Jordan, whose co-operation would be necessary if the provisions for the West Bank were to be put into effect, and of Saudi Arabia, whose influence was likely to be decisive in shaping the Arab attitude, both expressed serious reservations, while the more radical Arab governments, led by Syria acting in cooperation with the PLO, declared their total rejection of the agreements.

So strong were the feelings aroused in the Arab world that they led to a reconciliation between the rival Baathist governments of Iraq and Syria, which had been at loggerheads for a decade, and to a summit conference of all the Arab states (apart from Egypt) which met in Baghdad at the beginning of November 1978 to consider means of preventing the implementation of the Camp David agreements. After a fiery debate in which various proposals were aired for isolating Egypt and denying it all forms of economic aid, the Arab leaders agreed, at the insistence of Saudi Arabia, to delay the implementation of any such measures until Egypt should actually sign a peace treaty with Israel.

In this way the door was left open for President Sadat to reconsider a policy which would leave him totally dependent on the support of the United States. Together with further decisions by the Israelis to press ahead with the expansion of their settlements on the West Bank, this led President Sadat to press for a revision of the Camp David agreements in order to link the provisions concerning the future of the West Bank more closely to those for a bilateral peace treaty between Egypt and Israel. This question of "linkage", to which President Sadat added the demand that a specific timetable should be adopted for the introduction of autonomy on the West Bank, brought the peace-making process once again to a standstill. Despite another hurried visit to the Middle East by U.S. Secretary of State Vance, which was cut short after five hours of inconclusive discussions with Prime Minister Begin in Jerusalem, the target date of December 18th (by which the two sides had agreed at Camp David to sign a peace treaty) came and went with the outstanding issues still unresolved.

REVOLUTION IN IRAN

During the final weeks of 1978 a fresh complication arose with the disintegration of the Shah's regime in Iran. This had important repercussions throughout the Middle East. The inability of the United States to do anything to prevent the collapse of its principal ally in the area struck a damaging blow at American prestige. The suspension of oil exports from Iran, as a result of a strike in the oilfields, threatened to provoke an international energy crisis and cut off the most important source of Israel's oil supplies. It also became clear, even before the Shah went into exile on January 16th, 1979, that whatever government might succeed him would give strong backing to the Palestinians in their struggle to achieve independent statehood.

These developments gave added urgency to the American desire to achieve at least a partial Arab-Israeli settlement, but stiffened the attitudes of all the possible participants in any such settlement. The Israelis now insisted on including a clause in the draft peace treaty with Egypt guaranteeing them access to oil from Sinai after their evacuation of the peninsula. For President Sadat, who could ill afford to seem less fervent a protector of Arab rights in Palestine than the non-Arab rulers of revolutionary Iran, it became more necessary than ever to obtain some concession over the West Bank. Without such a concession it was even more unlikely that Saudi Arabia or Jordan—let alone the other Arab states—would moderate their opposition to the Camp David peace formula.

In these circumstances President Carter embarked in February on a series of foreign policy initiatives which were designed to demonstrate the continuing usefulness of the United States as an ally in the Middle East. The U.S. Defense Secretary, Mr. Harold Brown, was sent on a tour of Saudi Arabia, Jordan, Egypt and Israel with the twin assignments of reassuring both Arabs and Israelis of American backing and enlisting the support—or at least the acquiescence—of the conservative Arab states in a fresh attempt to get the Egypt-Israel peace treaty signed. Both Mr. Brown and the U.S. Energy Secretary, Mr. Arthur Schlesinger, referred publicly to the determination of the United States to protect its interests and those of its allies in the Middle East, if necessary by force; and when fighting broke out on the border between North and South Yemen, a consignment of American arms was rapidly dispatched to North Yemen in an attempt to allay the anxiety of its neighbour, Saudi Arabia, while at the beginning of March an American aircraft carrier was sent to cruise off the south Arabian coast.

PRESIDENT CARTER VISITS THE MIDDLE EAST

These moves did little to lessen the tension and when a further meeting in Washington between the Egyptians and Israelis at ministerial level failed to remove the remaining obstacles in the way of the peace treaty, President Carter again took matters into his own hands. On March 7th, 1979 he flew to the Middle East to exert his personal influence in a final effort to persuade the Egyptian and Israeli leaders to sign the long-deferred peace treaty.

After a week of alternating optimism and pessimism, Mr. Carter returned to Washington to announce that "we have now defined the major components of a peace treaty"; but before the treaty could be signed there were further acrimonious arguments about Israeli settlements on the West Bank (which were again condemned by the UN Security Council on March 22nd, in a resolution which called for the establishment of a special commission to examine the position regarding the settlements and to report back to the Security Council by July 1st, 1979), while opposition to the peace treaty on the part of even the most moderate Arab governments emphasized the isolation of Egypt within the Arab world. The reaction of America's European allies was also unenthusiastic, especially as it became plain that the United States expected them to share the high cost of the treaty and that Arab resentment was likely to find expression in higher oil prices.

ARAB BOYCOTT OF EGYPT

The attitude of Saudi Arabia was crucial and the euphoria in the United States over the signing of the peace treaty—which finally took place in Washington on March 26th—was sharply reduced when Saudi Arabia made plain its opposition to the treaty by attending a meeting of the Arab League in Baghdad at which a decision was taken to impose a political and economic boycott against Egypt. Arab ambassadors were withdrawn from Cairo, economic aid to Egypt was suspended and it was announced that the headquarters of the Arab League would be transferred from Cairo to Tunis. In agreeing to these measures and in subsequently breaking off diplomatic relations with Egypt, the Government of Saudi Arabia in effect chose to maintain solidarity with the rest of the Arab world at the expense of an open breach with the United States. The implications of this were ominous at a time when the United States was hoping to persuade Saudi Arabia to increase its output of oil in order to meet a growing world shortage.

The opposition to the peace treaty throughout the Arab world was due to the treaty's failure to make any clear provision for Palestinian self-determination. President Sadat maintained that the treaty was the first step towards a comprehensive settlement which would restore the rights of the Palestinians; but to the other Arabs it appeared to be a separate peace between Egypt and Israel which would restore Sinai to Egypt but would leave Israel in unfettered control of the rest of the occupied territories. That this was also the view of the Israeli Government seemed to be confirmed when Mr. Begin, in an outspoken broadcast on Israel's Independence Day on May 2nd, 1979, reiterated that no border would ever again be drawn through "the land of Israel" and that "We shall never withdraw from the Golan Heights". Such statements embarrassed the United States and strengthened the conviction of the Arabs that President Carter, despite his earlier support for "the legitimate rights of the Palestinians" and their need for a "homeland", had been deflected by the opposition of the Zionist lobby in the United States from his pursuit of a comprehensive settlement in the Middle East.

The Jerusalem Issue

Michael Adams

The Arab sector of Jerusalem, including the old walled city, was captured during the June War in 1967 by Israeli forces, which went on to occupy all the Jordanian territory lying west of the River Jordan. Theoretically, there was no difference in status between Jerusalem and the rest of the West Bank; both were occupied territory. In practice, the Israelis immediately removed the walls and barriers dividing the western (Israeli) and eastern (Arab) sectors of the city and at the end of June 1967 the Knesset passed legislation incorporating the Arab sector into a reunited Jerusalem under Israeli sovereignty. At the same time the boundaries of the municipal area of Jerusalem were greatly extended, reaching to near Bethlehem in the south and incorporating Kalandia airport (close to Ramallah) in the north.

Juridically speaking, the status of Jerusalem was already complicated. The plan for the partition of Palestine adopted by the General Assembly of the United Nations in 1947 had envisaged separate Arab and Jewish states, with the city and environs of Jerusalem constituting an international enclave. In the war of 1948, Israeli and Jordanian forces had fought for possession of Jerusalem and the armistice of April 1949 had left each in control of part of the divided city. The international community had never recognized this *de facto* arrangement, which endured for 18 years until the June War of 1967.

Faced with Israel's effective annexation of the Arab sector, the General Assembly on July 4th, 1967, ruled, by 99 votes to none, that the annexation was invalid and called on Israel not to take any measures to alter the status of the city. Ten days later the Assembly adopted a second resolution "reiterating" the earlier one and "deploring" Israel's failure to implement it.

Before the first of these resolutions was passed, the Israeli authorities had embarked on a series of structural alterations and demolitions in the Old City of Jerusalem, which aroused strong Arab protests and whose continuation was to lead to considerable international controversy. In clearing the area in front of the Western (Wailing) Wall, they expropriated 50 Arab families at very short notice and demolished their houses, while in the Jewish Quarter they dispossessed a further 200 Arab families. In all, and before the end of June 1967, some 4,000 Arabs in Jerusalem had lost their homes. In some cases, but not all, they were provided with alternative accommodation.

In November 1967 the UN Security Council passed its unanimous resolution number 242 setting out the basis for an overall settlement between Israel and its Arab neighbours. The resolution spoke of "withdrawal of Israeli armed forces from territories occupied in the recent conflict", but made no specific mention of Jerusalem, where the anxiety of the Arab population was increased by the growing signs of Israel's intention to exclude the city from the scope of any eventual negotiations. In January 1968 the Israeli authorities expropriated more than 800 acres of land in the Arab sector and announced plans for the construction of housing estates on the slopes of Mount Scopus, overlooking the Old City. A joint protest signed by fifty leading members of the Muslim and Jewish communities in Jerusalem had no result, beyond provoking the expulsion by the Israelis of the Mayor of Arab Jerusalem, but in May 1968, after the Israelis had held (in defiance of a unanimous resolution by the Security Council) a military parade in Jerusalem to commemorate the foundation of the State of Israel, the Security Council passed its first resolution dealing specifically with the Jerusalem issue.

The resolution (No. 252 of May 21st, 1968) deplored Israel's failure to comply with the two General Assembly resolutions of July 4th and 14th, 1967, confirmed that any measures taken by Israel to alter the status of Jerusalem were invalid and called on Israel to rescind all such measures and to refrain from similar action in the future. The effect was only to increase the haste with which the Israelis set about changing the face of the city. Bulldozers had been at work on Mount Scopus since February and soon the first of the new housing estates began to take shape beside the Nablus Road leading northwards out of Jerusalem. In the absence of any progress towards a peace settlement, it became clear that the Israeli Government intended to forestall, by establishing a physical presence in the Arab sector of Jerusalem, any future attempt to challenge their sovereignty over the whole of the municipal area.

Meeting again to consider the question in July 1969, the Security Council adopted, this time by a unanimous vote (in the previous year the United States had abstained from voting on the Jerusalem resolution), an even stronger resolution (No. 267 of July 3rd, 1969). Reaffirming its earlier stand and deploring "the failure of Israel to show any regard" for the previous resolutions both of the General Assembly and of the Security Council, the Council "censured in the strongest terms" all measures taken by Israel to change the status of Jerusalem, confirmed that all such measures were "invalid" and again called on Israel to desist from taking any further action of the same kind. The Israelis formally rejected the resolution and the Israeli Minister of Information stated in Jerusalem that it could not influence the "facts" which had been intentionally created by Israel "after due consideration of the political danger involved".

The situation in Jerusalem itself was further aggravated in August 1969 by a disastrous fire in Al Aqsa mosque, which at first sight appeared to confirm the fears of the Arabs for the safety of the Muslim and Christian shrines in the Old City. Israeli investigations showed that the fire had been caused by a deranged Australian religious fanatic and the Australian was later brought to trial; but from that moment the concern of Muslim communities throughout the world reinforced the Arab sense of grievance at the loss of the Holy city.

In the following year Christian concern also began to make itself felt, especially after the publication of an Israeli "master plan" for the future of Jerusalem. This plan envisaged the doubling of the Jewish population of the city by 1980 and an eventual total population of 900,000. An international conference of town planners, convoked by the Israeli municipal authorities at the end of 1970 to consider the plan, was almost unanimous in condemning its aesthetic implications. Early in 1971 a dispute also developed between the United Nations and the Israeli Government over the intention, announced in the master plan, to build another housing estate in the neighbourhood of Government House, the headquarters in Jerusalem of the United Nations. In March 1971 articles in the official Vatican newspaper *L'Osservatore Romano* and in the English Catholic weekly *The Tablet* revealed the strength of Catholic feeling over developments in the Holy City, and these feelings were strengthened when it became known that in the same month the Israelis had destroyed an Arab village on the hill of Nebi Samwil, north-west of Jerusalem, in preparation for the building on Arab land of yet another housing estate for immigrant Jews.

Israeli opinion was divided over the future of Jerusalem. Only a small minority of Israelis were in favour of relinquishing Israeli sovereignty over the Arab sector of the city, if negotiations for an overall settlement of the Arab-Israeli conflict should ever materialize. In the absence of any sign of such negotiations, the issue remained a hypothetical one and the Israeli Government made no secret of its determination to establish a hold on Jerusalem which would prove unbreakable. A further resolution by the Security Council (No. 298 of September 25th, 1971—*see* Documents on Palestine, p. 66) was rejected as brusquely as the previous ones and even the provision in the resolution that the Secretary-General, "using such instrumentalities as he may choose", should report to the Council within 60 days on the implementation of the resolution, failed to achieve any result since the Secretary-General had to report at the end of that period that he had been unable to execute his mission, for lack of co-operation from the Israeli authorities.

On purely aesthetic grounds, however, many Israelis were disturbed by the physical changes overtaking Jerusalem. Within five years of the June War of 1967 the construction of large housing estates had transformed the appearance of Mount Scopus, where the Old City (and the whole of the Arab sector) was dominated by a row of apartment blocks breaking the historic skyline. There were acute disagreements between the Mayor of Jerusalem and the Ministers of Housing and of Tourism over some of the implications of this building programme, but continuing uncertainty over the prospects for a political settlement with the Arabs gave encouragement to the "activists" in Israel, and the creation of "facts" continued, in Jerusalem as in the rest of the occupied erritories, throughout 1972 and up to the eve of the war in October 1973.

Anxiety over the future of Jerusalem and resentment at the Israelis' treatment both of the Arab population and of the physical fabric of the city played a part in provoking the Arab decision to resort to war in 1973. In particular, these feelings influenced King Faisal to throw Saudi Arabia's weight behind the attempt to enforce Israel's withdrawal from the occupied territories, including Arab Jerusalem. Henceforth the restoration to Arab sovereignty of the Old City became one of the principal conditions demanded by the Arabs for a comprehensive peace settlement with Israel.

Immediately after the October war political and economic conditions in Israel combined to slow down for a time the work of demolition and construction by which the face of the city was being transformed. In the course of 1974, however, the same general pattern as before was maintained, resulting in the steady eviction from the Old City of Arabs whose houses were demolished and replaced by dwellings for Jewish immigrants. Between 1967 and 1977 6,300 Arab residents of Jerusalem were evicted in this way from their homes in the Old City. Protests from the international community, stimulated by anxiety over the continuing exodus from Jerusalem of Christian Arabs, became more frequent and achieved some publicity, but no practical result.

Similar protests over excavations being conducted by the Israeli authorities in the vicinity of Muslim and Christian holy places in the Old City of Jerusalem brought to a head criticisms which had been voiced for more than five years within UNESCO. Recalling that urgent appeals previously addressed to the Israeli Government to suspend these excavations had been ignored, the Executive Board of UNESCO, in June 1974, voted "to condemn the persistent violation by Israel of the resolutions and decisions adopted by the General Conference and the Executive Board". In its turn the General Conference of UNESCO, meeting in November 1974, condemned Israel's attitude as "contradictory to the aims of the Organization as laid down in its Constitution" and resolved to withhold assistance in the fields of education, science and culture until Israel agreed to respect previous Conference resolutions in the matter.

The attitude previously expressed by both the Security Council and the General Assembly of the United Nations were reaffirmed in subsequent years, despite the failure to obtain the compliance of the Government of Israel with existing resolutions. In a unanimous "consensus statement" adopted on November 11th, 1976, the Security Council "strongly deplored" Israel's actions in the occupied territories, including Jerusalem, required Israel once more to "desist forthwith from any action which tends to alter the status of Jerusalem", and called on her to comply with the terms of the Geneva Convention on the Protection of Civilians in Wartime.

Documents on Palestine

DECLARATION OF FIRST WORLD ZIONIST CONGRESS

*The Congress, convened in Basle by Dr. Theodor Herzl in August 1897, adopted the following programme:**

The aim of Zionism is to create for the Jewish people a home in Palestine secured by public law.

The Congress contemplates the following means to the attainment of this end:

1. The promotion on suitable lines, of the settlement of Palestine by Jewish agriculturists, artisans and tradesmen.

2. The organization and binding together of the whole of Jewry by means of appropriate institutions, local and general, in accordance with the laws of each country.

3. The strengthening of Jewish sentiment and national consciousness.

4. Preparatory steps towards obtaining government consent as are necessary, for the attainment of the aim of Zionism.

McMAHON CORRESPONDENCE†

Ten letters passed between Sir Henry McMahon, British High Commissioner in Cairo, and Sherif Husain of Mecca from July 1915 to March 1916. Husain offered Arab help in the war against the Turks if Britain would support the principle of an independent Arab state. The most important letter is that of October 24th, 1915, from McMahon to Husain:

. . . I regret that you should have received from my last letter the impression that I regarded the question of limits and boundaries with coldness and hesitation; such was not the case, but it appeared to me that the time had not yet come when that question could be discussed in a conclusive manner.

I have realized, however, from your last letter that you regard this question as one of vital and urgent importance. I have, therefore, lost no time in informing the Government of Great Britain of the contents of your letter, and it is with great pleasure that I communicate to you on their behalf the following statement, which I am confident you will receive with satisfaction:

The two districts of Mersina and Alexandretta and portions of Syria lying to the west of the districts of Damascus, Homs, Hama and Aleppo cannot be said to be purely Arab, and should be excluded from the limits demanded.

With the above modification, and without prejudice to our existing treaties with Arab chiefs, we accept those limits.

As for those regions lying within those frontiers wherein Great Britain is free to act without detriment to the interests of her ally, France, I am empowered in the name of the Government of Great Britain to give the following assurances and make the following reply to your letter:

(1) Subject to the above modifications, Great Britain is prepared to recognize and support the independence of the Arabs in all the regions within the limits demanded by the Sherif of Mecca.

(2) Great Britain will guarantee the Holy Places against all external aggression and will recognize their inviolability.

(3) When the situation admits, Great Britain will give to the Arabs her advice and will assist them to establish what may appear to be the most suitable forms of government in those various territories.

(4) On the other hand, it is understood that the Arabs have decided to seek the advice and guidance of Great Britain only, and that such European advisers and officials as may be required for the formation of a sound form of administration will be British.

(5) With regard to the *vilayets* of Bagdad and Basra, the Arabs will recognize that the established position and interests of Great Britain necessitate special administrative arrangements in order to secure these territories from foreign aggression, to promote the welfare of the local populations and to safeguard our mutual economic interests.

I am convinced that this declaration will assure you beyond all possible doubt of the sympathy of Great Britain towards the aspirations of her friends the Arabs and will result in a firm and lasting alliance, the immediate results of which will be the expulsion of the Turks from the Arab countries and the freeing of the Arab peoples from the Turkish yoke, which for so many years has pressed heavily upon them. . . .

ANGLO-FRANCO-RUSSIAN AGREEMENT (SYKES—PICOT AGREEMENT)

April-May 1916

The allocation of portions of the Ottoman empire by the three powers was decided between them in an exchange of diplomatic notes. The Anglo-French agreement‡ dealing with Arab territories became known to Sherif Husain only after publication by the new Bolshevik government of Russia in 1917:

1. That France and Great Britain are prepared to recognize and protect an independent Arab State or a Confederation of Arab States in the areas (A) and (B)

* Text supplied by courtesy of Josef Fraenkel.

† British White Paper, Cmd. 5957, 1939.

‡ E. L. Woodward and Rohan Butler (Eds.). *Documents on British Foreign Policy 1919–1939*. First Series, Vol. IV, 1919. London, H.M.S.O., 1952.

marked on the annexed map, under the suzerainty of an Arab Chief. That in area (A) France, and in area (B) Great Britain shall have priority of right of enterprises and local loans. France in area (A) and Great Britain in area (B) shall alone supply foreign advisers or officials on the request of the Arab State or the Confederation of Arab States.

2. France in the Blue area and Great Britain in the Red area shall be at liberty to establish direct or indirect administration or control as they may desire or as they may deem fit to establish after agreement with the Arab State or Confederation of Arab States.

3. In the Brown area there shall be established an international administration of which the form will be decided upon after consultation with Russia, and after subsequent agreement with the other Allies and the representatives of the Sherif of Mecca.

4. That Great Britain be accorded

(*a*) The ports of Haifa and Acre;

(*b*) Guarantee of a given supply of water from the Tigris and the Euphrates in area (A) for area (B).

His Majesty's Government, on their part, undertake that they will at no time enter into negotiations for the cession of Cyprus to any third Power without the previous consent of the French Government.

5. Alexandretta shall be a free port as regards the trade of the British Empire and there shall be no discrimination in treatment with regard to port dues or the extension of special privileges affecting British shipping and commerce; there shall be freedom of transit for British goods through Alexandretta and over railways through the Blue area, whether such goods are going to or coming from the Red area, area (A) or area (B); and there shall be no differentiation in treatment, direct or indirect, at the expense of British goods on any railway or of British goods and shipping in any port serving the areas in question.

Haifa shall be a free port as regards the trade of France, her colonies and protectorates, and there shall be no differentiation in treatment or privilege with regard to port dues against French shipping and commerce. There shall be freedom of transit through Haifa and over British railways through the Brown area, whether such goods are coming from or going to the Blue area, area (A) or area (B), and there shall be no differentiation in treatment, direct or indirect, at the expense of French goods on any railway or of French goods and shipping in any port serving the areas in question.

6. In area (A), the Baghdad Railway shall not be extended southwards beyond Mosul, and in area (B), it shall not be extended northwards beyond Samarra, until a railway connecting Baghdad with Aleppo along the basin of the Euphrates will have been completed, and then only with the concurrence of the two Governments.

7. Great Britain shall have the right to build, administer and be the sole owner of the railway connecting Haifa with area (B). She shall have, in addition, the right in perpetuity and at all times of carrying troops on that line. It is understood by both Governments that this railway is intended to facilitate communication between Baghdad and Haifa, and it is further understood that, in the event of technical difficulties and expenditure incurred in the maintenance of this line in the Brown area rendering the execution of the project impracticable, the French Government will be prepared to consider plans for enabling the line in question to traverse the polygon formed by Banias-Umm Qais-Salkhad-Tall 'Osda-Mismieh before reaching area (B).

8. For a period of twenty years, the Turkish customs tariff shall remain in force throughout the Blue and Red areas as well as in areas (A) and (B), and no increase in the rates of duties and no alteration of *ad valorem* duties into specific duties shall be made without the consent of the two Powers.

There shall be no internal customs barriers between any of the areas mentioned above. The customs duties to be levied on goods destined for the interior shall be collected at the ports of entry and remitted to the Administration of the area of destination.

9. It is understood that the French Government will at no time initiate any negotiations for the cession of their rights and will not cede their prospective rights in the Blue area to any third Power other than the Arab State or Confederation of Arab States, without the previous consent of His Majesty's Government who, on their part, give the French Government a similar undertaking in respect of the Red area.

10. The British and French Governments shall agree to abstain from acquiring and to withold their consent to a third Power acquiring territorial possessions in the Arabian Peninsula; nor shall they consent to the construction by a third Power of a naval base in the islands on the eastern seaboard of the Red Sea. This, however, will not prevent such rectification of the Aden boundary as might be found necessary in view of the recent Turkish attack.

11. The negotiations with the Arabs concerning the frontiers of the Arab State or Confederation of Arab States shall be pursued through the same channel as heretofore in the name of the two Powers.

12. It is understood, moreover, that measures for controlling the importation of arms into the Arab territory will be considered by the two Governments.

BALFOUR DECLARATION

November 2nd, 1917

Balfour was British Foreign Secretary, Rothschild the British Zionist leader.

Dear Lord Rothschild,

I have much pleasure in conveying to you on behalf of His Majesty's Government the following declaration of sympathy with Jewish Zionist aspirations, which has been submitted to and approved by the Cabinet.

"His Majesty's Government view with favour the establishment in Palestine of a national home for the Jewish people, and will use their best endeavours to facilitate the achievement of this object, it being clearly understood that nothing shall be done which may prejudice the civil and religious rights of existing non-Jewish communities in Palestine, or the rights and political status enjoyed by Jews in any other country."

I should be grateful if you would bring this declaration to the knowledge of the Zionist Federation.

Yours sincerely,

Arthur James Balfour.

HOGARTH MESSAGE*

January 4th, 1918

The following is the text of a message which Commander D. G. Hogarth, C.M.G., R.N.V.R., of the Arab Bureau in Cairo, was instructed on January 4th, 1918, to deliver to King Husain of the Hejaz at Jeddah:

1. The *Entente* Powers are determined that the Arab race shall be given full opportunity of once again forming a nation in the world. This can only be achieved by the Arabs themselves uniting, and Great Britain and her Allies will pursue a policy with this ultimate unity in view.

2. So far as Palestine is concerned, we are determined that no people shall be subject to another, but—

(*a*) In view of the fact that there are in Palestine shrines, Wakfs and Holy places, sacred in some cases to Moslems alone, to Jews alone, to Christians alone, and in others to two or all three, and inasmuch as these places are of interest to vast masses of people outside Palestine and Arabia, there must be a special régime to deal with these places approved of by the world.

(*b*) As regards the Mosque of Omar, it shall be considered as a Moslem concern alone, and shall not be subjected directly or indirectly to any non-Moslem authority.

3. Since the Jewish opinion of the world is in favour of a return of Jews to Palestine, and inasmuch as this opinion must remain a constant factor, and, further, as His Majesty's Government view with favour the realization of this aspiration, His Majesty's Government are determined that in so far as is compatible with the freedom of the existing population, both economic and political, no obstacle should be put in the way of the realization of this ideal.

In this connection the friendship of world Jewry to the Arab cause is equivalent to support in all States where Jews have political influence. The leaders of the movement are determined to bring about the success of Zionism by friendship and co-operation with the Arabs, and such an offer is not one to be lightly thrown aside.

ANGLO-FRENCH DECLARATION†

November 7th, 1918

The object aimed at by France and Great Britain in prosecuting in the East the war let loose by the ambition of Germany is the complete and definite emancipation of the peoples so long oppressed by the Turks and the establishment of national Governments and Administrations deriving their authority from the initiative and free choice of the indigenous populations.

In order to carry out these intentions France and Great Britain are at one in encouraging and assisting the establishments of indigenous Governments and Administrations in Syria and Mesopotamia, now liberated by the Allies, and in the territories the liberation of which they are engaged in securing and recognizing these as soon as they are actually established.

Far from wishing to impose on the populations of these regions any particular institutions they are only concerned to ensure by their support and by adequate assistance the regular working of Governments and Administrations freely chosen by the populations themselves. To secure impartial and equal justice for all, to facilitate the economic development of the country by inspiring and encouraging local initiative, to favour the diffusion of education, to put an end to dissensions that have too long been taken advantage of by Turkish policy, such is the policy which the two Allied Governments uphold in the liberated territories.

RECOMMENDATIONS OF THE KING—CRANE COMMISSION‡

August 28th, 1919

The Commission was set up by President Wilson of the U.S.A. to determine which power should receive the Mandate for Palestine. The following are extracts from their recommendations on Syria:

1. We recommend, as most important of all, and in strict harmony with our Instructions, that whatever foreign administration (whether of one or more Powers) is brought into Syria, should come in, not at all as a colonising Power in the old sense of that term, but as a Mandatory under the League of Nations with the clear consciousness that 'the well-being and development', of the Syrian people form for it a 'sacred trust'.

2. We recommend, in the second place, that the unity of Syria be preserved, in accordance with the earnest petition of the great majority of the people of Syria.

3. We recommend, in the third place, that Syria be placed under one mandatory Power, as the natural way to secure real and efficient unity.

4. We recommend, in the fourth place, that Amir Faisal be made the head of the new united Syrian State.

5. We recommend, in the fifth place, serious modification of the extreme Zionist programme for Palestine of unlimited immigration of Jews, looking finally to making Palestine distinctly a Jewish State.

* British White Paper, Cmd. 5964, 1939.

† Report of a Committee set up to consider Certain Correspondence between Sir Henry McMahon and the Sherif of Mecca in 1915 and 1916, March 16th, 1939 (British White Paper, Cmd. 5974).

‡ U.S. Department of State. *Papers Relating to the Foreign Relations of the Untied States. The Paris Peace Conference 1919.* Vol. XII. Washington, 1947.

(1) The Commissioners began their study of Zionism with minds predisposed in its favor, but the actual facts in Palestine, coupled with the force of the general principles proclaimed by the Allies and accepted by the Syrians have driven them to the recommendation here made.

(2) The Commission was abundantly supplied with literature on the Zionist program by the Zionist Commission to Palestine; heard in conferences much concerning the Zionist colonies and their claims; and personally saw something of what had been accomplished. They found much to approve in the aspirations and plans of the Zionists, and had warm appreciation for the devotion of many of the colonists, and for their success, by modern methods in overcoming great, natural obstacles.

(3) The Commission recognised also that definite encouragement had been given to the Zionists by the Allies in Mr. Balfour's often-quoted statement, in its approval by other representatives of the Allies. If, however, the strict terms of the Balfour Statement are adhered to—favoring 'the establishment in Palestine of a national home for the Jewish people', 'it being clearly understood that nothing shall be done which may prejudice the civil and religious rights of existing non-Jewish communities in Palestine'—it can hardly be doubted that the extreme Zionist program must be greatly modified. For 'a national home for the Jewish people' is not equivalent to making Palestine into a Jewish State; nor can the erection of such a Jewish State be accomplished without the gravest trespass upon the 'civil and religious rights of existing non-Jewish communities in Palestine'. The fact came out repeatedly in the Commission's conference with Jewish representatives, that the Zionists looked forward to a practically complete dispossession of the present non-Jewish inhabitants of Palestine, by various forms of purchase.

In his address of July 4th, 1918, President Wilson laid down the following principle as one of the four great 'ends for which the associated peoples of the world were fighting': 'The settlement of every question, whether of territory, of sovereignty, of economic arrangement, or of political relationship upon the basis of the free acceptance of that settlement by the people immediately concerned, and not upon the basis of the material interest or advantage of any other nation or people which may desire a different settlement for the sake of its own exterior influence or mastery.' If that principle is to rule, and so the wishes of Palestine's population are to be decisive as to what is to be done with Palestine, then it is to be remembered that the non-Jewish population of Palestine—nearly nine-tenths of the whole—are emphatically against the entire Zionist program. The tables show that there was no one thing upon which the population of Palestine were more agreed than upon this. To subject a people so minded to unlimited Jewish immigration, and to steady financial and social pressure to surrender the land, would be a gross violation of the principle just quoted, and of the people's rights, though it kept within the forms of law.

It is to be noted also that the feeling against the Zionist program is not confined to Palestine, but shared very generally by the people throughout Syria, as our conferences clearly showed. More than 72 per cent—1,350 in all—of all the petitions in the whole of Syria were directed against the Zionist program. Only two requests—those for a united Syria and for independence—had a larger support. This general feeling was duly voiced by the General Syrian Congress in the seventh, eighth and tenth resolutions of their statement.

The Peace Conference should not shut its eyes to the fact that the anti-Zionist feeling in Palestine and Syria is intense and not lightly to be flouted. No British officer, consulted by the Commissioners, believed that the Zionist program could be carried out except by force of arms. The officers generally thought that a force of not less than 50,000 soldiers would be required even to initiate the program. That of itself is evidence of a strong sense of the injustice of the Zionist program, on the part of the non-Jewish populations of Palestine and Syria. Decisions requiring armies to carry out are sometimes necessary, but they are surely not gratuitously to be taken in the interests of serious injustice. For the initial claim, often submitted by Zionist representatives, that they have a 'right' to Palestine, based on an occupation of 2,000 years ago, can hardly be seriously considered.

There is a further consideration that cannot justly be ignored, if the world is to look forward to Palestine becoming a definitely Jewish State, however gradually that may take place. That consideration grows out of the fact that Palestine is the Holy Land for Jews, Christians, and Moslems alike. Millions of Christians and Moslems all over the world are quite as much concerned as the Jews with conditions in Palestine, especially with those conditions which touch upon religious feelings and rights. The relations in these matters in Palestine are most delicate and difficult. With the best possible intentions, it may be doubted whether the Jews could possibly seem to either Christians or Moslems proper guardians of the holy places, or custodians of the Holy Land as a whole.

The reason is this: The places which are most sacred to Christians—those having to do with Jesus—and which are also sacred to Moslems, are not only not sacred to Jews, but abhorrent to them. It is simply impossible, under those circumstances, for Moslems and Christians to feel satisfied to have these places in Jewish hands, or under the custody of Jews. There are still other places about which Moslems must have the same feeling. In fact, from this point of view, the Moslems, just because the sacred places of all three religions are sacred to them, have made very naturally much more satisfactory custodians of the holy places than the Jews could be. It must be believed that the precise meaning in this respect of the complete Jewish occupation of Palestine has not been fully sensed by those who urge the extreme Zionist program. For it would intensify, with a certainty like fate, the anti-Jewish feeling both in Palestine and in all other portions of the world which look to Palestine as the Holy Land.

In view of all these considerations, and with a deep sense of sympathy for the Jewish cause, the Commissioners feel bound to recommend that only a greatly reduced Zionist program be attempted by the Peace Conference, and even that, only very gradually initiated. This would have to mean that Jewish immigration should be definitely limited, and that the project for making Palestine distinctly a Jewish commonwealth should be given up.

There would then be no reason why Palestine could not be included in a united Syrian State, just as other portions of the country, the holy places being cared for by an international and inter-religious commission, somewhat as at present, under the oversight and approval of the Mandatory and of the League of Nations. The Jews, of course, would have representation upon this commission.

ARTICLE 22 OF THE COVENANT OF THE LEAGUE OF NATIONS

1. To those colonies and territories which as a consequence of the late War have ceased to be under the sovereignty of the States which formerly governed them and which are inhabited by peoples not yet able to stand by themselves under the strenuous conditions of the modern world, there should be applied the principle that the well-being and development of such peoples form a sacred trust of civilization and that securities for the performance of this trust should be embodied in this Covenant.

2. The best method of giving practical effect to this principle is that the tutelage of such peoples should be entrusted to advanced nations who by reason of their resources, their experience or their geographical position can best undertake this responsibility, and who are willing to accept it, and that this tutelage should be exercised by them as Mandatories on behalf of the League.

3. The character of the Mandate must differ according to the stage of the development of the people, the geographical situation of the territory, its economic conditions and other similar circumstances.

4. Certain communities formerly belonging to the Turkish Empire have reached a stage of development where their existence as independent nations can be provisionally recognized subject to the rendering of administrative advice and assistance by a Mandatory until such time as they are able to stand alone. The wishes of these communities must be a principal consideration in the selection of the Mandatory.

7. In every case of Mandate, the Mandatory shall render to the Council an annual report in reference to the territory committed to its charge.

8. The degree of authority, control, or administration to be exercised by the Mandatory shall, if not previously agreed upon by the Members of the League, be explicitly defined in each case by the Council.

9. A permanent Commission shall be constituted to receive and examine the annual reports of the Mandatories and to advise the Council on all matters relating to the observance of the Mandates.

MANDATE FOR PALESTINE*

July 24th, 1922

The Council of the League of Nations:

Whereas the Principal Allied Powers have agreed, for the purpose of giving effect to the provisions of Article 22 of the Covenant of the League of Nations to entrust to a Mandatory selected by the said Powers the administration of the territory of Palestine, which formerly belonged to the Turkish Empire, within such boundaries as may be fixed by them; and

Whereas the Principal Allied Powers have also agreed that the Mandatory should be responsible for putting into effect the declaration originally made on November 2nd, 1917, by the Government of His Britannic Majesty, and adopted by the said Powers, in favour of the establishment in Palestine of a National Home for the Jewish people, it being clearly understood that nothing should be done which might prejudice the civil and religious rights of existing non-Jewish communities in Palestine, or the rights and political status enjoyed by Jews in any other country; and

Whereas recognition has thereby been given to the historical connection of the Jewish people with Palestine and to the grounds for reconstituting their National Home in that country; and

Whereas the Principal Allied Powers have selected His Britannic Majesty as the Mandatory for Palestine; and

Whereas the Mandate in respect of Palestine has been formulated in the following terms and submitted to the Council of the League for approval; and

Whereas His Britannic Majesty has accepted the Mandate in respect of Palestine and undertaken to exercise it on behalf of the League of Nations in conformity with the following provisions; and

Whereas by the afore-mentioned Article 22 (paragraph 8), it is provided that the degree of authority, control or administration to be exercised by the Mandatory, not having been previously agreed upon by the Members of the League, shall be explicitly defined by the Council of the League of Nations;

Confirming the said Mandate, defines its terms as follows:

ARTICLE 1. The Mandatory shall have full powers of legislation and of administration, save as they may be limited by the terms of this Mandate.

ARTICLE 2. The Mandatory shall be responsible for placing the country under such political, administrative and economic conditions as will secure the establishment of the Jewish National Home, as laid down in the preamble, and the development of self-governing institutions, and also for safeguarding the civil and religious rights of all the inhabitants of Palestine, irrespective of race and religion.

ARTICLE 3. The Mandatory shall, so far as circumstances permit, encourage local autonomy.

* British White Paper, Cmd. 1785.

ARTICLE 4. An appropriate Jewish Agency shall be recognized as a public body for the purpose of advising and co-operating with the Administration of Palestine in such economic, social and other matters as may affect the establishment of the Jewish National Home and the interests of the Jewish population in Palestine, and, subject always to the control of the Administration, to assist and take part in the development of the country.

The Zionist organization, so long as its organization and constitution are in the opinion of the Mandatory appropriate, shall be recognized as such agency. It shall take steps in consultation with His Britannic Majesty's Government to secure the co-operation of all Jews who are willing to assist in the establishment of the Jewish National Home.

ARTICLE 5. The Mandatory shall be responsible for seeing that no Palestine territory shall be ceded or leased to, or in any way placed under the control of, the Government of any foreign Power.

ARTICLE 6. The Administration of Palestine, while ensuring that the rights and position of other sections of the population are not prejudiced, shall facilitate Jewish immigration under suitable conditions and shall encourage, in co-operation with the Jewish Agency referred to in Article 4, close settlement by Jews on the land, including State lands and waste lands not required for public purposes.

ARTICLE 7. The Administration of Palestine shall be responsible for enacting a nationality law. There shall be included in this law provisions framed so as to facilitate the acquisition of Palestinian citizenship by Jews who take up their permanent residence in Palestine.

ARTICLE 13. All responsibility in connection with the Holy Places and religious buildings or sites in Palestine, including that of preserving existing rights and of securing free access to the Holy Places, religious buildings and sites and the free exercise of worship, while ensuring the requirements of public order and decorum, is assumed by the Mandatory, who shall be responsible solely to the League of Nations in all matters connected herewith, provided that nothing in this Article shall prevent the Mandatory from entering into such arrangements as he may deem reasonable with the Administration for the purpose of carrying the provisions of this Article into effect; and provided also that nothing in this Mandate shall be construed as conferring upon the Mandatory authority to interfere with the fabric of the management of purely Moslem sacred shrines, the immunities of which are guaranteed.

ARTICLE 14. A special Commission shall be appointed by the Mandatory to study, define and determine the rights and claims in connection with the Holy Places and the rights and claims relating to the different religious communities in Palestine. The method of nomination, the composition and the functions of this Commission shall be submitted to the Council of the League for its approval, and the Commission shall not be appointed or enter upon its functions without the approval of the Council.

ARTICLE 28. In the event of the termination of the Mandate hereby conferred upon the Mandatory, the Council of the League of Nations shall make such arrangements as may be deemed necessary for safeguarding in perpetuity, under guarantee of the League, the rights secured by Articles 13 and 14, and shall use its influence for securing, under the guarantee of the League, that the Government of Palestine will fully honour the financial obligations legitimately incurred by the Administration of Palestine during the period of the Mandate, including the rights of public servants to pensions or gratuities.

CHURCHILL MEMORANDUM*

June 3rd, 1922

The Secretary of State for the Colonies has given renewed consideration to the existing political situation in Palestine, with a very earnest desire to arrive at a settlement of the outstanding questions which have given rise to uncertainty and unrest among certain sections of the population. After consultation with the High Commissioner for Palestine the following statement has been drawn up. It summarizes the essential parts of the correspondence that has already taken place between the Secretary of State and a Delegation from the Moslem Christian Society of Palestine, which has been for some time in England, and it states the further conclusions which have since been reached.

The tension which has prevailed from time to time in Palestine is mainly due to apprehensions, which are entertained both by sections of the Arab and by sections of the Jewish population. These apprehensions, so far as the Arabs are concerned, are partly based upon exaggerated interpretations of the meaning of the Declaration favouring the establishment of a Jewish National Home in Palestine, made on behalf of His Majesty's Government on November 2nd, 1917. Unauthorized statements have been made to the effect that the purpose in view is to create a wholly Jewish Palestine. Phrases have been used such as that Palestine is to become "as Jewish as England is English." His Majesty's Government regard any such expectation as impracticable and have no such aim in view. Nor have they at any time contemplated, as appears to be feared by the Arab Delegation, the disappearance or the subordination of the Arabic population, language or culture in Palestine. They would draw attention to the fact that the terms of the Declaration referred to do not contemplate that Palestine as a whole should be converted into a Jewish National Home, but that such a Home should be founded *in Palestine*. In this connection it has been observed with satisfaction that at the meeting of the Zionist Congress, the supreme governing body of the Zionist Organization, held at Carlsbad in September 1921, a resolution was passed expressing as the official statement of Zionist aims "the determination of the Jewish people to live with the Arab people on terms

* Palestine, Correspondence with the Palestine Arab Delegation and the Zionist Organization (British White Paper, Cmd. 1700), pp. 17–21.

of unity and mutual respect, and together with them to make the common home into a flourishing community, the upbuilding of which may assure to each of its peoples an undisturbed national development."

It is also necessary to point out that the Zionist Commission in Palestine, now termed the Palestine Zionist Executive, has not desired to possess, and does not possess, any share in the general administration of the country. Nor does the special position assigned to the Zionist Organization in Article IV of the Draft Mandate for Palestine imply any such functions. That special position relates to the measures to be taken in Palestine affecting the Jewish population, and contemplates that the Organization may assist in the general development of the country, but does not entitle it to share in any degree in its Government.

Further, it is contemplated that the status of all citizens of Palestine in the eyes of the law shall be Palestinian, and it has never been intended that they, or any section of them, should possess any other juridical status.

So far as the Jewish population of Palestine are concerned, it appears that some among them are apprehensive that His Majesty's Government may depart from the policy embodied in the Declaration of 1917. It is necessary, therefore, once more to affirm that these fears are unfounded, and that that Declaration, re-affirmed by the Conference of the Principal Allied Powers at San Remo and again in the Treaty of Sèvres, is not susceptible of change.

During the last two or three generations the Jews have recreated in Palestine a community, now numbering 80,000, of whom about one-fourth are farmers or workers upon the land. This community has its own political organs; and elected assembly for the direction of its domestic concerns; elected councils in the towns; and an organization for the control of its schools. It has its elected Chief Rabbinate and Rabbinical Council for the direction of its religious affairs. Its business is conducted in Hebrew as a vernacular language, and a Hebrew Press serves its needs. It has its distinctive intellectual life and displays considerable economic activity. This community, then, with its town and country population, its political, religious and social organizations, its own language, its own customs, its own life, has in fact "national" characteristics. When it is asked what is meant by the development of the Jewish National Home in Palestine, it may be answered that it is not the imposition of a Jewish nationality upon the inhabitants of Palestine as a whole, but the further development of the existing Jewish community, with the assistance of Jews in other parts of the world, in order that it may become a centre in which the Jewish people as a whole may take, on grounds of religion and race, an interest and a pride. But in order that this community should have the best prospect of free development and provide a full opportunity for the Jewish people to display its capacities, it is essential that it should know that it is in Palestine as of right and not on sufferance. That is the reason why it is necessary that the existence of a Jewish National Home in Palestine should be internationally guaranteed, and that it should be formally recognized to rest upon ancient historic connection.

This, then, is the interpretation which His Majesty's Government place upon the Declaration of 1917, and, so understood, the Secretary of State is of opinion that it does not contain or imply anything which need cause either alarm to the Arab population of Palestine or disappointment to the Jews.

For the fulfilment of this policy it is necessary that the Jewish community in Palestine should be able to increase its numbers by immigration. This immigration cannot be so great in volume as to exceed whatever may be the economic capacity of the country at the time to absorb new arrivals. It is essential to ensure that the immigrants should not be a burden upon the people of Palestine as a whole, and that they should not deprive any section of the present population of their employment. Hitherto the immigration has fulfilled these conditions. The number of immigrants since the British occupation has been about 25,000. . . .

REPORT OF PALESTINE ROYAL COMMISSION PEEL COMMISSION*

July 1937

The Commission under Lord Peel was appointed in 1936. The following are extracts from recommendations made in Ch. XXII:

Having reached the conclusion that there is no possibility of solving the Palestine problem under the existing Mandate (or even under a scheme of cantonization), the Commission recommend the termination of the present Mandate on the basis of Partition and put forward a definite scheme which they consider to be practicable, honourable and just. The scheme is as follows:

The Mandate for Palestine should terminate and be replaced by a Treaty System in accordance with the precedent set in Iraq and Syria.

Under Treaties to be negotiated by the Mandatory with the Government of Transjordan and representatives of the Arabs of Palestine on the one hand, and with the Zionist Organization on the other, it would be declared that two sovereign independent States would shortly be established—(1) an Arab State consisting of Transjordan united with that part of Palestine allotted to the Arabs, (2) a Jewish State consisting of that part of Palestine allotted to the Jews. The Mandatory would undertake to support any requests for admission to the League of Nations made by the Governments of the Arab and Jewish States. The Treaties would include strict guarantees for the protection of minorities. Military Conventions would be attached to the Treaties.

A new Mandate should be instituted to execute the trust of maintaining the sanctity of Jerusalem and Bethlehem and ensuring free and safe access to them

* *Palestine Royal Commission: Report,* 1937 (British Blue Book, Cmd. 5479).

for all the world. An enclave should be demarcated to which this Mandate should apply, extending from a point north of Jerusalem to a point south of Bethlehem, and access to the sea should be provided by a corridor extending from Jerusalem to Jaffa. The policy of the Balfour Declaration would not apply to the Mandated Area.

The Jewish State should pay a subvention to the Arab State. A Finance Commission should be appointed to advise as to its amount and as to the division of the public debt of Palestine and other financial questions.

In view of the backwardness of Transjordan, Parliament should be asked to make a grant of £2,000,000 to the Arab State.

WHITE PAPER*

May 1939

***The main recommendations are extracted below*:**

10. . . . His Majesty's Government make the following declaration of their intentions regarding the future government of Palestine:

(i) The objective of His Majesty's Government is the establishment within ten years of an independent Palestine State in such treaty relations with the United Kingdom as will provide satisfactorily for the commercial and strategic requirements of both countries in the future. This proposal for the establishment of the independent State would involve consultation with the Council of the League of Nations with a view to the termination of the Mandate.

(ii) The independent State should be one in which Arabs and Jews share in government in such a way as to ensure that the essential interests of each community are safeguarded.

(iii) The establishment of the independent State will be preceded by a transitional period throughout which His Majesty's Government will retain responsibility for the government of the country. During the transitional period the people of Palestine will be given an increasing part in the government of their country. Both sections of the population will have an opportunity to participate in the machinery of government, and the process will be carried on whether or not they both avail themselves of it.

(iv) As soon as peace and order have been sufficiently restored in Palestine steps will be taken to carry out this policy of giving the people of Palestine an increasing part in the government of their country, the objective being to place Palestinians in charge of all the Departments of Government, with the assistance of British advisers and subject to the control of the High Commissioner. With this object in view His Majesty's Government will be prepared immediately to arrange that Palestinians shall be placed in charge of certain Departments, with British advisers. The Palestinian heads of Departments will sit on the Executive Council, which advises the High Commissioner. Arab and Jewish representatives will be invited to serve as heads of Departments approximately in proportion to their respective populations. The number of Palestinians in charge of Departments will be increased as circumstances permit until all heads of Departments are Palestinians, exercising the administrative and advisory functions which are at present performed by British officials. When that stage is reached consideration will be given to the question of converting the Executive Council into a Council of Ministers with a consequential change in the status and functions of the Palestinian heads of Departments.

(v) His Majesty's Government make no proposals at this stage regarding the establishment of an elective legislature. Nevertheless they would regard this as an appropriate constitutional development, and, should public opinion in Palestine hereafter show itself in favour of such a development, they will be prepared, provided that local conditions permit, to establish the necessary machinery.

(vi) At the end of five years from the restoration of peace and order, an appropriate body representative of the people of Palestine and of His Majesty's Government will be set up to review the working of the constitutional arrangements during the transitional period and to consider and make recommendations regarding the Constitution of the independent Palestine State.

(vii) His Majesty's Government will require to be satisfied that in the treaty contemplated by sub-paragraph (i) or in the Constitution contemplated by sub-paragraph (vi) adequate provision has been made for:

(*a*) the security of, and freedom of access to, the Holy Places, and the protection of the interests and property of the various religious bodies;

(*b*) the protection of the different communities in Palestine in accordance with the obligations of His Majesty's Government to both Arabs and Jews and for the special position in Palestine of the Jewish National Home;

(*c*) such requirements to meet the strategic situation as may be regarded as necessary by His Majesty's Government in the light of the circumstances then existing.

His Majesty's Government will also require to be satisfied that the interests of certain foreign countries in Palestine, for the preservation of which they are at present responsible, are adequately safeguarded.

(viii) His Majesty's Government will do everything in their power to create conditions which will enable the independent Palestine State to come into being within ten years. If, at the end of ten years, it appears to His Majesty's Government that, contrary to their hope, circumstances require the postponement of the establishment of the independent State, they will consult with representatives

* British White Paper, Cmd. 6019.

of the people of Palestine, the Council of the League of Nations and the neighbouring Arab States before deciding on such a postponement. If His Majesty's Government come to the conclusion that postponement is unavoidable, they will invite the co-operation of these parties in framing plans for the future with a view to achieving the desired objective at the earliest possible date.

11. During the transitional period steps will be taken to increase the powers and responsibilities of municipal corporations and local councils.

14. . . . they believe that they will be acting consistently with their Mandatory obligations to both Arabs and Jews, and in the manner best calculated to serve the interests of the whole people of Palestine by adopting the following proposals regarding immigration:

(i) Jewish immigration during the next five years will be at a rate which, if economic absorptive capacity permits, will bring the Jewish population up to approximately one-third of the total population of the country. Taking into account the expected natural increase of the Arab and Jewish populations, and the number of illegal Jewish immigrants now in the country, this would allow of the admission, as from the beginning of April this year, of some 75,000 immigrants over the next five years. These immigrants would, subject to the criterion of economic absorptive capacity, be admitted as follows:

(*a*) For each of the next five years a quota of 10,000 Jewish immigrants will be allowed, on the understanding that a shortage in any one year may be added to the quotas for subsequent years, within the five-year period, if economic absorptive capacity permits.

(*b*) In addition, as a contribution towards the solution of the Jewish refugee problem, 25,000 refugees will be admitted as soon as the High Commissioner is satisfied that adequate provision for their maintenance is ensured, special consideration being given to refugee children and dependants.

(ii) The existing machinery for ascertaining economic absorptive capacity will be retained, and the High Commissioner will have the ultimate responsibility for deciding the limits of economic capacity. Before each periodic decision is taken, Jewish and Arab representatives will be consulted.

(iii) After the period of five years no further Jewish immigration will be permitted unless the Arabs of Palestine are prepared to acquiesce in it.

(iv) His Majesty's Government are determined to check illegal immigration, and further preventive measures are being adopted. The numbers of any Jewish illegal immigrants who, despite these measures, may succeed in coming into the country and cannot be deported will be deducted from the yearly quotas.

15. His Majesty's Government are satisfied that, when the immigration over five years which is now contemplated has taken place, they will not be justified in facilitating, nor will they be under any obligation to facilitate, the further development of the Jewish National Home by immigration regardless of the wishes of the Arab population.

16. The Administration of Palestine is required, under Article 6 of the Mandate, "while ensuring that the rights and position of other sections of the population are not prejudiced," to encourage "close settlement by Jews on the land," and no restriction has been imposed hitherto on the transfer of land from Arabs to Jews. The Reports of several expert Commissions have indicated that, owing to the natural growth of the Arab population and the steady sale in recent years of Arab land to Jews, there is now in certain areas no room for further transfers of Arab land, whilst in some other areas such transfers of land must be restricted if Arab cultivators are to maintain their existing standard of life and a considerable landless Arab population is not soon to be created. In these circumstances, the High Commissioner will be given general powers to prohibit and regulate transfers of land. These powers will date from the publication of this statement of Policy and the High Commissioner will retain them throughout the transitional period.

17. The policy of the Government will be directed towards the development of the land and the improvement, where possible, of methods of cultivation. In the light of such development it will be open to the High Commissioner, should he be satisfied that the "rights and position" of the Arab population will be duly preserved, to review and modify any orders passed relating to the prohibition or restriction of the transfer of land.

BILTMORE PROGRAMME*

May 11th, 1942

The following programme was approved by a Zionist Conference held in the Biltmore Hotel, New York City:

1. American Zionists assembled in this Extraordinary Conference reaffirm their unequivocal devotion to the cause of democratic freedom and international justice to which the people of the United States, allied with the other United Nations, have dedicated themselves, and give expression to their faith in the ultimate victory of humanity and justice over lawlessness and brute force.

2. This Conference offers a message of hope and encouragement to their fellow Jews in the Ghettos and concentration camps of Hitler-dominated Europe and prays that their hour of liberation may not be far distant.

3. The Conference sends its warmest greetings to the Jewish Agency Executive in Jerusalem, to the Va'ad Leumi, and to the whole Yishuv in Palestine, and expresses its profound admiration for their steadfastness and achievements in the face of peril

* Text supplied by courtesy of Josef Fraenkel.

and great difficulties. The Jewish men and women in field and factory, and the thousands of Jewish soldiers of Palestine in the Near East who have acquitted themselves with honour and distinction in Greece, Ethiopia, Syria, Libya and on other battlefields, have shown themselves worthy of their people and ready to assume the rights and responsibilities of nationhood.

4. In our generation, and in particular in the course of the past twenty years, the Jewish people have awakened and transformed their ancient homeland; from 50,000 at the end of the last war their numbers have increased to more than 500,000. They have made the waste places to bear fruit and the desert to blossom. Their pioneering achievements in agriculture and in industry, embodying new patterns of cooperative endeavour, have written a notable page in the history of colonization.

5. In the new values thus created, their Arab neighbours in Palestine have shared. The Jewish people in its own work of national redemption welcomes the economic, agricultural and national development of the Arab peoples and states. The Conference reaffirms the stand previously adopted at Congresses of the World Zionist Organization, expressing the readiness and the desire of the Jewish people for full cooperation with their Arab neighbours.

6. The Conference calls for the fulfilment of the original purpose of the Balfour Declaration and the Mandate which *"recognizing the historical connexion of the Jewish people with Palestine"* was to afford them the opportunity, as stated by President Wilson, to found there a Jewish Commonwealth.

The Conference affirms its unalterable rejection of the White Paper of May 1939 and denies its moral or legal validity. The White Paper seeks to limit, and in fact to nullify Jewish rights to immigration and settlement in Palestine, and, as stated by Mr. Winston Churchill in the House of Commons in May 1939, constitutes "a breach and repudiation of the Balfour Declaration". The policy of the White Paper is cruel and indefensible in its denial of sanctuary to Jews fleeing from Nazi persecution; and at a time when Palestine has become a focal point in the war front of the United Nations, and Palestine Jewry must provide all available manpower for farm and factory and camp, it is in direct conflict with the interests of the allied war effort.

7. In the struggle against the forces of aggression and tyranny, of which Jews were the earliest victims, and which now menace the Jewish National Home, recognition must be given to the right of the Jews of Palestine to play their full part in the war effort and in the defence of their country, through a Jewish military force fighting under its own flag and under the high command of the United Nations.

8. The Conference declares that the new world order that will follow victory cannot be established on foundations of peace, justice and equality, unless the problem of Jewish homelessness is finally solved.

The Conference urges that the gates of Palestine be opened; that the Jewish Agency be vested with control of immigration into Palestine and with the necessary authority for upbuilding the country, including the development of its unoccupied and uncultivated lands; and that Palestine be established as a Jewish Commonwealth integrated in the structure of the new democratic world.

Then and only then will the age old wrong to the Jewish people be righted.

UN GENERAL ASSEMBLY RESOLUTION ON THE FUTURE GOVERNMENT OF PALESTINE (PARTITION RESOLUTION)

November 29th, 1947

The General Assembly,

Having met in special session at the request of the mandatory Power to constitute and instruct a special committee to prepare for the consideration of the question of the future government of Palestine at the second regular session;

Having constituted a Special Committee and instructed it to investigate all questions and issues relevant to the problem of Palestine, and to prepare proposals for the solution of the problem, and

Having received and examined the report of the Special Committee (document A/364) including a number of unanimous recommendations and a plan of partition with economic union approved by the majority of the Special Committee,

Considers that the present situation in Palestine is one which is likely to impair the general welfare and friendly relations among nations;

Takes note of the declaration by the mandatory Power that it plans to complete its evacuation of Palestine by August 1st, 1948;

Recommends to the United Kingdom, as the mandatory Power for Palestine, and to all other Members of the United Nations the adoption and implementation, with regard to the future government of Palestine, of the Plan of Partition with Economic Union set out below;

Requests that

(*a*) The Security Council take the necessary measures as provided for in the plan for its implementation;

(*b*) The Security Council consider, if circumstances during the transitional period require such consideration, whether the situation in Palestine constitutes a threat to the peace. If it decides that such a threat exists, and in order to maintain international peace and security, the Security Council should supplement the authorization of the General Assembly by taking measures, under Articles 39 and 41 of the Charter, to empower the United Nations Commission, as provided in this resolution, to exercise in Palestine the functions which are assigned to it by this resolution;

(*c*) The Security Council determine as a threat to the peace, breach of the peace or act of aggression, in accordance with Article 39 of the Charter, any attempt to alter by force the settlement envisaged by this resolution;

(*d*) The Trusteeship Council be informed of the responsibilities envisaged for it in this plan;

Calls upon the inhabitants of Palestine to take such steps as may be necessary on their part to put this plan into effect;

Appeals to all Governments and all peoples to refrain from taking any action which might hamper or delay the carrying out of these recommendations, and

Authorizes the Secretary-General to reimburse travel and subsistence expenses of the members of the Commission referred to in Part 1, Section B, paragraph 1 below, on such basis and in such form as he may determine most appropriate in the circumstances, and to provide the Commission with the necessary staff to assist in carrying out the functions assigned to the Commission by the General Assembly.

Official Records of the second session of the General Assembly, Resolutions, p. 131.

UN GENERAL ASSEMBLY RESOLUTION 194 (III)

December 11th, 1948

The resolution's terms have been reaffirmed every year since 1948.

11. . . . the refugees wishing to return to their homes and live at peace with their neighbours should be permitted to do so at the earliest practicable date, and that compensation should be paid for the property of those choosing not to return and for the loss of or damage to property which, under principles of international law or in equity, should be made good by the Governments or authorities responsible;

Official Records of the third session of the General Assembly, Part 1, Resolutions, p. 21.

UN GENERAL ASSEMBLY RESOLUTION ON THE INTERNATIONALIZATION OF JERUSALEM

December 9th, 1949

The General Assembly,

Having regard to its resolution 181 (II) of November 29th, 1947 and 194 (III) of December 11th, 1948,

Having studied the reports of the United Nations Conciliation Commission for Palestine set up under the latter resolution,

I. Decides

In relation to Jerusalem,

Believing that the principles underlying its previous resolutions concerning this matter, and in particular its resolution of November 29th, 1947, represent a just and equitable settlement of the question,

1. To restate, therefore, its intention that Jerusalem should be placed under a permanent international regime, which should envisage appropriate guarantees for the protection of the Holy Places, both within and outside Jerusalem, and to confirm specifically the following provisions of General Assembly resolution 181 (II): (1) The City of Jerusalem shall be established as a *corpus separatum* under a special international regime and shall be administered by the United Nations; (2) The Trusteeship Council shall be designated to discharge the responsibilities of the Administering Authority . . .; and (3) The City of Jerusalem shall include the present municipality of Jerusalem plus the surrounding villages and towns, the most eastern of which shall be Abu Dis; the most southern, Bethlehem; the most western, Ein Karim (including also the built-up area of Motsa); and the most northern, Shu'fat, as indicated on the attached sketchmap; . . . [*map not reproduced*: *Ed.*]

Official Records of the fourth session of the General Assembly, Resolutions, p. 25.

TEXT OF UN SECURITY COUNCIL RESOLUTION 242

November 22nd, 1967

The Security Council,

Expressing its continued concern with the grave situation in the Middle East,

Emphasizing the inadmissibility of the acquisition of territory by war and the need to work for a just and lasting peace in which every state in the area can live in security,

Emphasizing further that all Member States in their acceptance of the Charter of the United Nations have undertaken a commitment to act in accordance with Article 2 of the Charter

1. *Affirms* that the fulfilment of Charter principles requires the establishment of a just and lasting peace in the Middle East which should include the application of both the following principles:

(i) Withdrawal of Israel armed forces from territories occupied in the recent conflict;

(ii) Termination of all claims or states of belligerency and respect for and acknowledgement of the sovereignty, territorial integrity and political independence of every State in the area and their right to live in peace within secure and recognized boundaries free from threats or acts of force.

2. *Affirms further* the necessity

(*a*) For guaranteeing freedom of navigation through international waterways in the area;

(*b*) For achieving a just settlement of the refugee problem;

(*c*) For guaranteeing the territorial inviolability and political independence of every State in the area, through measures including the establishment of demilitarized zones;

3. *Requests* the Secretary-General to designate a Special Representative to proceed to the Middle East

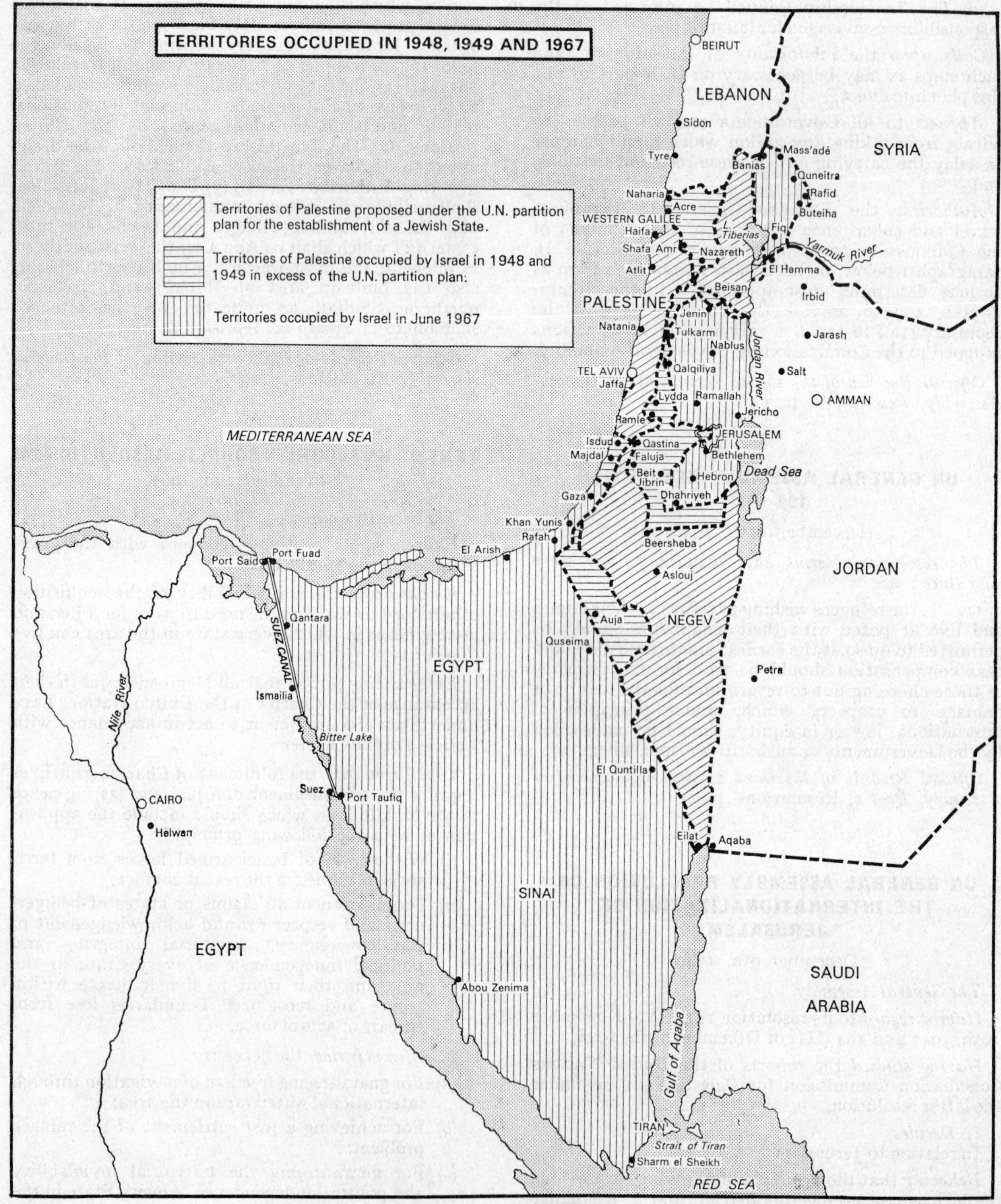

Territories occupied by Israel. See also the maps on pages 72, 74 and 80.

to establish and maintain contacts with the States concerned in order to promote agreement and assist efforts to achieve a peaceful and accepted settlement in accordance with the provisions and principles in this resolution;

4. *Requests* the Secretary-General to report to the Security Council on the progress of the efforts of the Special Representative as soon as possible.

Source: UN Document S/RES/242 (1967).

UN SECURITY COUNCIL RESOLUTION ON JERUSALEM

September 25th, 1971

The resolution, No. 298 (1971), was passed nem. con., *with the abstention of Syria.*

The Security Council,

Recalling its resolutions 252 (1968) of May 21st, 1968, and 267 (1969) of July 3rd, 1969, and the earlier General Assembly resolution 2253 (ES-V) and 2254 (ES-V) of July 4th and 14th, 1967, concerning measures and actions by Israel designed to change the status of the Israeli-occupied section of Jerusalem,

Having considered the letter of the Permanent Representative of Jordan on the situation in Jerusalem and the reports of the Secretary-General, and having heard the statements of the parties concerned in the question,

Recalling the principle that acquisition of territory by military conquest is inadmissible,

Noting with concern the non-compliance by Israel with the above-mentioned resolutions,

Noting with concern also that since the adoption of the above-mentioned resolutions Israel has taken further measures designed to change the status and character of the occupied section of Jerusalem.

1. *Reaffirms* its resolutions 252 (1968) and 267 (1969);

2. *Deplores* the failure of Israel to respect the previous resolutions adopted by the United Nations concerning measures and actions by Israel purporting to affect the status of the City of Jerusalem;

3. *Confirms* in the clearest possible terms that all legislative and administrative actions taken by Israel to change the status of the City of Jerusalem, including expropriation of land and properties, transfer of populations and legislation aimed at the incorporation of the occupied section, are totally invalid and cannot change that status;

4. *Urgently calls upon* Israel to rescind all previous measures and actions and to take no further steps in the occupied section of Jerusalem which may purport to change the status of the City, or which would prejudice the rights of the inhabitants and the interests of the international community, or a just and lasting peace;

5. *Requests* the Secretary-General, in consultation with the President of the Security Council and using such instrumentalities as he may choose, including a representative or a mission, to report to the Council as appropriate and in any event within 60 days on the implementation of the present resolution.

Source: UN Document S/RES/298 (1971).

UN SECURITY COUNCIL RESOLUTION 338

October 22nd, 1973

UN Resolutions between 1967 *and October* 1973 *reaffirmed Security Council Resolution* 242 (see above). *In an attempt to end the fourth Middle East war, which had broken out between the Arabs and Israel on October 6th,* 1973, *the UN Security Council passed the following Resolution:*

The Security Council,

1. *Calls upon* all parties to the present fighting to cease all firing and terminate all military activity immediately, not later than 12 hours after the moment of the adoption of the decision, in the positions they now occupy;

2. *Calls upon* the parties concerned to start immediately after the ceasefire the implementation of Security Council Resolution 242 (1967) in all of its parts;

3. *Decides that,* immediately and concurrently with the ceasefire negotiations start between the parties concerned under appropriate auspices aimed at establishing a just and durable peace in the Middle East.

Source: UN Document PR/73/29 (1973).

UN Security Council Resolution 339 called for the despatch of UN Observers to supervise the observance of the ceasefire.

UN SECURITY COUNCIL RESOLUTION 340

October 25th, 1973

The Security Council,

Recalling its Resolutions 338 (1973) of October 22nd, 1973 and 339 (1973) of October 23rd, 1973,

Noting with regret the reported repeated violations of the ceasefire in non-compliance with Resolutions 338 (1973) and 339 (1973),

Noting with concern from the Secretary-General's report that the UN military observers have not yet been enabled to place themselves on both sides of the ceasefire line,

1. *Demands* that an immediate and complete ceasefire be observed and that the parties withdraw to the positions occupied by them at 16.50 hours GMT on October 22nd, 1973;

2. *Requests* the Secretary-General as an immediate step to increase the number of UN military observers on both sides;

3. *Decides* to set up immediately under its authority a UN emergency force to be composed of personnel drawn from member states of the UN, except the permanent members of the Security Council, and

requests the Secretary-General to report within 24 hours on the steps taken to this effect; (*Details of the UN Emergency Force are given in the Chapter "United Nations in the Middle East and North Africa"—Editor*)

4. *Requests* the Secretary-General to report to the Council on an urgent and continuing basis on the state of implementation of this Resolution, as well as Resolutions 338 (1973) and 339 (1973);

5. *Requests* all member states to extend their full co-operation to the UN in the implementation of this Resolution, as well as Resolutions 338 (1973) and 339 (1973).

Source: UN Document PR/73/31 (1973).

DECLARATION OF EEC FOREIGN MINISTERS ON THE MIDDLE EAST SITUATION

November 6th, 1973

The Nine Governments of the European Community have exchanged views on the situation in the Middle East. While emphasizing that the views set out below are only a first contribution on their part to the search for a comprehensive solution to the problem, they have agreed on the following:

1. They strongly urge that the forces of both sides in the Middle East conflict should return immediately to the positions they occupied on October 22nd in accordance with Resolutions 339 and 340 of the Security Council. They believe that a return to these positions will facilitate a solution to other pressing problems concerning prisoners-of-war and the Egyptian Third Army.

2. They have the firm hope that, following the adoption by the Security Council of Resolution 338 of October 22nd, negotiations will at last begin for the restoration in the Middle East of a just and lasting peace through the application of Security Council Resolution 242 in all of its parts. They declare themselves ready to do all in their power to contribute to that peace. They believe that those negotiations must take place in the framework of the United Nations. They recall that the Charter has entrusted to the Security Council the principal responsibility for international peace and security. The Council and the Secretary-General have a special role to play in the making and keeping of peace through the application of Council Resolutions 242 and 338.

3. They consider that a peace agreement should be based particularly on the following points:

(i) the inadmissibility of the acquisition of territory by force;

(ii) the need for Israel to end the territorial occupation which it has maintained since the conflict of 1967;

(iii) respect for the sovereignty, territorial integrity and independence of every state in the area and their right to live in peace within secure and recognized boundaries;

(iv) recognition that in the establishment of a just and lasting peace account must be taken of the legitimate rights of the Palestinians.

Article 4 calls for the despatch of peace-keeping forces to the demilitarized zones.

Source: Bulletin of the European Communities Commission, No. 10, 1973, p. 106.

EGYPTIAN-ISRAELI AGREEMENT ON DISENGAGEMENT OF FORCES IN PURSUANCE OF THE GENEVA PEACE CONFERENCE

(signed by the Egyptian and Israeli Chiefs of Staff, January 18th, 1974)

This agreement was superseded by the second Egyptian-Israeli Disengagement Agreement signed in September 1975 (see p. 71 below) and then by the Peace Treaty between Egypt and Israel signed on March 26th, 1979 (see p. 77 below). A map showing the boundaries of the first agreement is reproduced in this edition (p. 72) and the terms can be found in the 1975–76 edition of The Middle East and North Africa *(p. 61). The 1979 Peace Treaty is reproduced in this edition on page 77.*

DISENGAGEMENT AGREEMENT BETWEEN SYRIAN AND ISRAELI FORCES AND PROTOCOL TO AGREEMENT ON UNITED NATIONS DISENGAGEMENT OBSERVER FORCE (UNDOF)

(signed in Geneva, Friday, May 31st, 1974)

(*Annex A*)

A. Israel and Syria will scrupulously observe the cease-fire on land, sea and air and will refrain from all military actions against each other, from time of signing this document in implementation of the United Nations Security Council Resolution 338 dated October 22nd, 1973.

B. The military forces of Israel and Syria will be separated in accordance with the following principles:

1. All Israeli military forces will be west of a line designated line A on the map attached hereto (*reproduced below*), except in Quneitra (Kuneitra) area, where they will be west of a line A-1.
2. All territory east of line A will be under Syrian administration and Syrian civilians will return to this territory.
3. The area between line A and the line designated as line B on the attached map will be an area of separation. In this area will be stationed UNDOF established in accordance with the accompanying Protocol.
4. All Syrian military forces will be east of a line designated as line B on the attached map.
5. There will be two equal areas of limitation in armament and forces, one west of line A and one east of line B as agreed upon.

C. In the area between line A and line A-1 on the attached map there shall be no military forces.

D. *Paragraph D. deals with practical details of signing and implementation.*

E. Provisions of paragraphs A, B and C shall be inspected by personnel of the United Nations comprising UNDOF under the Agreement.

F. Within 24 hours after the signing of this Agreement in Geneva all wounded prisoners of war which each side holds of the other, as certified by the International Committee of the Red Cross, will be repatriated. The morning after the completion of the task of the Military Working Group, all remaining prisoners of war will be repatriated.

G. The bodies of all dead soldiers held by either side will be returned for burial in their respective countries within ten days after the signing of this Agreement.

H. This Agreement is not a peace agreement. It is a step towards a just and durable peace on the basis of the Security Council Resolution 338 dated October 22nd, 1973.

A. Protocol to the Disengagement Agreement outlined the functions of the United Nations Disengagement Observer Force (UNDOF).

RESOLUTION OF CONFERENCE OF ARAB HEADS OF STATE

Rabat, October 28th, 1974

The Conference of the Arab Heads of State:

1. *Affirms* the right of the Palestinian people to return to their homeland and to self-determination.

2. *Affirms* the right of the Palestinian people to establish an independent national authority, under the leadership of the PLO in its capacity as the sole legitimate representative of the Palestine people, over all liberated territory. The Arab States are pledged to uphold this authority, when it is established, in all spheres and at all levels.

3. *Supports* the PLO in the exercise of its national and international responsibilities, within the context of the principle of Arab solidarity.

4. *Invites* the kingdom of Jordan, Syria and Egypt to formalize their relations in the light of these decisions and in order that they be implemented.

5. *Affirms* the obligation of all Arab States to preserve Palestinian unity and not to interfere in Palestinian internal affairs.

Sources: Le Monde; Problèmes Politiques et Sociaux, March 7th, 1975; *Arab Report and Record.*

UN GENERAL ASSEMBLY RESOLUTION 3236 (XXIX)

November 22nd, 1974

The General Assembly,

Having considered the question of Palestine,

Having heard the statement of the Palestine Liberation Organization, the representative of the Palestinian people,

Having also heard other statements made during the debate,

Deeply concerned that no just solution to the problem of Palestine has yet been achieved and recognizing that the problem of Palestine continues to endanger international peace and security,

Recognizing that the Palestinian people is entitled to self-determination in accordance with the Charter of the United Nations,

Expressing its grave concern that the Palestinian people has been prevented from enjoying its inalienable rights, in particular its right to self-determination,

Guided by the purposes and principles of the Charter,

Recalling its relevant resolutions which affirm the right of the Palestinian people to self-determination,

1. *Reaffirms* the inalienable rights of the Palestinian people in Palestine, including:
   (*a*) The right to self-determination without external interference;
   (*b*) The right to national independence and sovereignty;

2. *Reaffirms also* the inalienable right of the Palestinians to return to their homes and property from which they have been displaced and uprooted, and calls for their return;

3. *Emphasizes* that full respect for and the realization of these inalienable rights of the Palestinian people are indispensable for the solution of the question of Palestine;

4. *Recognizes* that the Palestinian people is a principal party in the establishment of a just and durable peace in the Middle East;

5. *Further Recognizes* the right of the Palestinian people to regain its rights by all means in accordance with the purposes and principles of the Charter of the United Nations;

6. *Appeals* to all States and international organizations to extend their support to the Palestinian people in its struggle to restore its rights, in accordance with the Charter;

7. *Requests* the Secretary-General to establish contacts with the Palestine Liberation Organization on all matters concerning the question of Palestine;

8. *Requests* the Secretary-General to report to the General Assembly at its thirtieth session on the implementation of the present resolution;

9. *Decides* to include the item "Question of Palestine" in the provisional agenda of its thirtieth session.

Source: UN Document BR/74/55 (1974).

SECOND INTERIM PEACE AGREEMENT BETWEEN EGYPT AND ISRAEL

(signed September 4th, 1975)

This agreement has now been superseded by the Peace Treaty between Egypt and Israel signed on March 26th,

[*continued on p.* 73.

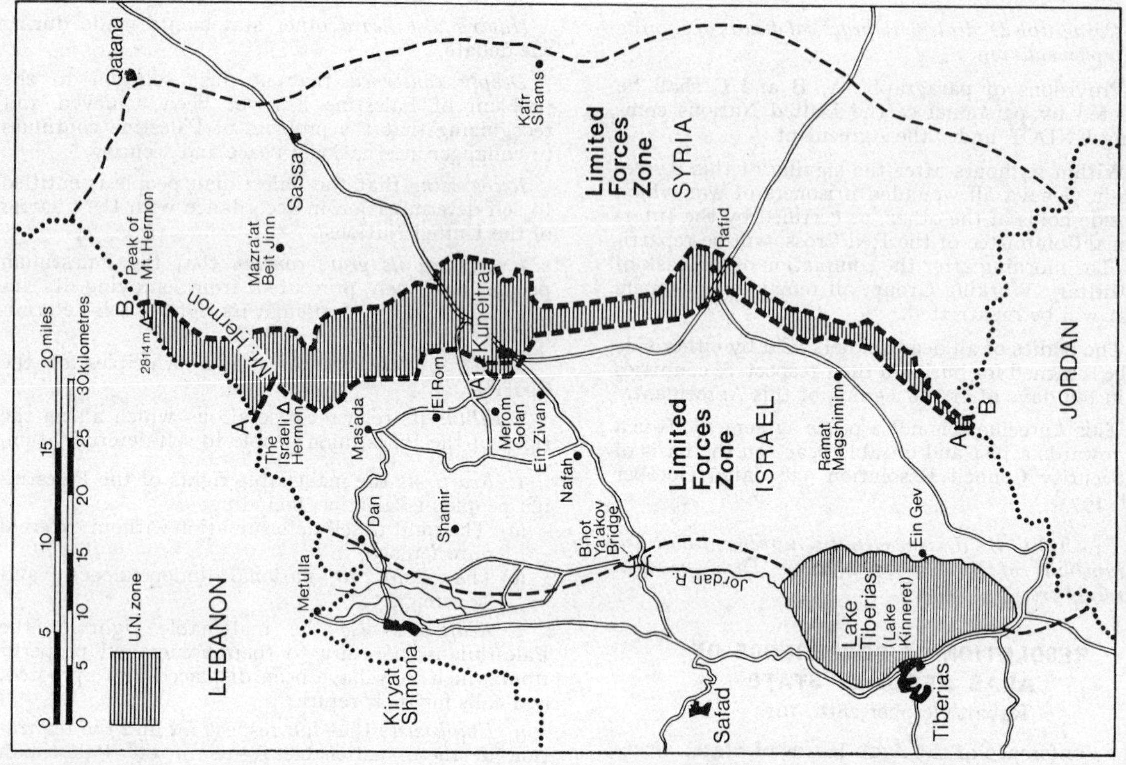

Disengagement Agreement of May 30th, 1974, between Israel and Syria.

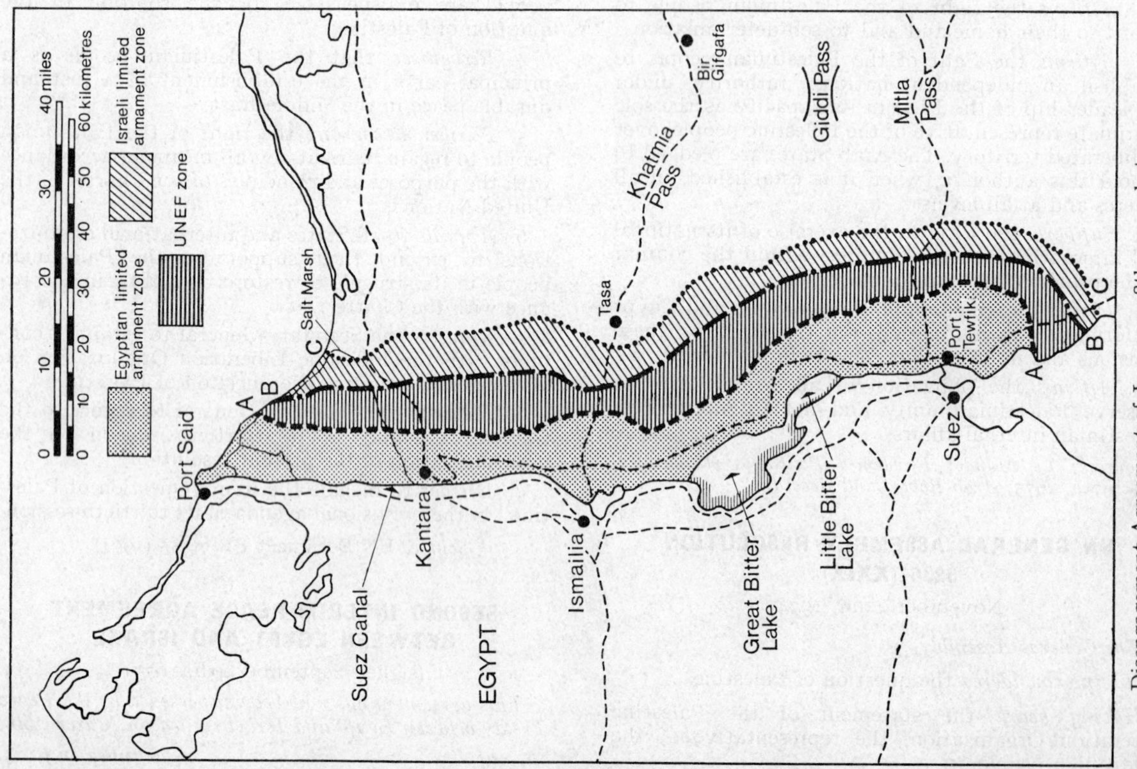

Disengagement Agreement of January 18th, 1974, between Israel and Egypt.

continued from p. 71]

1979 (see *p.* 77 *below*). *A map showing the boundaries of the Second Interim Peace Agreement is reproduced in this edition and the terms can be found in the 1978–79 edition of* The Middle East and North Africa (*p.* 70).

Article VI

The parties hereby establish a joint commission for the duration of this Agreement. It will function under the aegis of the chief co-ordinator of the United Nations peace-keeping missions in the Middle East in order to consider any problem arising from this Agreement and to assist the United Nations Emergency Force in the execution of its mandate. The joint commission shall function in accordance with procedures established in the Protocol.

Article VII

Non-military cargoes destined for or coming from Israel shall be permitted through the Suez Canal.

Article VIII

This Agreement is regarded by the parties as a significant step toward a just and lasting peace. It is not a final peace agreement.

The parties shall continue their efforts to negotiate a final peace agreement within the framework of the Geneva Peace Conference in accordance with Security Council resolution 338.

Article IX

This Agreement shall enter into force upon signature of the Protocol and remain in force until superseded by a new agreement.

Source: UN Document S/11818/Addendum 1 (1975).

DEVELOPMENTS 1975–78

At the 30th Meeting of the UN General Assembly in November 1975, General Assembly Resolution 3236 (XXIX) was reaffirmed and a 20-nation Committee (the Committee on Palestine Rights) was set up to report on the "Exercise of the Inalienable Rights of the Palestine People" by June 1st, 1976.

At the UN Security Council a draft resolution which would have affirmed the rights of the Palestinian people to self-determination, including the right to establish an independent state, was vetoed by the U.S.A. on January 26th, 1976. A Security Council draft resolution criticizing Israeli policies in East Jerusalem and on the West Bank of the Jordan was also vetoed by the U.S.A. on March 25th, 1976.

The Committee on Palestine Rights presented its report in June 1976 and recommended that Israel should withdraw from all occupied territories by June 1977. A resolution in the Security Council, stemming from the report, affirmed the "inalienable rights of the Palestinians" and called for the creation of a "Palestine entity" in the West Bank and Gaza. This resolution was vetoed by the U.S.A. on June 29th, 1976. The Committee on Palestine Rights then submitted its report to the UN General Assembly in November 1976 in the form of a resolution. The resolution (No. 20, of November 24th, 1976) was adopted by a vote of 90 to 16 (30 members abstained; 10 were absent). The U.S.A. and 10 other Western countries (including the U.K.) opposed the resolution.

Other General Assembly resolutions in December 1976 called for the reconvening of the Geneva Middle East peace conference by March 1977 and the participation in the negotiations of the PLO. Neither of these resolutions have been implemented. The policy of the Palestine Liberation Organization, as formulated in March 1977, is given in Palestine Organizations, pages 85–87.

After a meeting in London of the nine EEC heads of government at the end of June 1977, a statement was issued reaffirming earlier statements and stating that "The Nine have affirmed their belief that a solution to the conflict in the Middle East will be possible only if the legitimate rights of the Palestinian people to give effective expression to its national identity is translated into fact, which would take into account the need for a homeland for the Palestinian people. . . . In the context of an overall settlement Israel must be ready to recognize the legitimate rights of the Palestinian people; equally, the Arab side must be ready to recognize the right of Israel to live in peace within secure and recognized boundaries."

A UN General Assembly Resolution of November 25th, 1977 (32/30) "called anew" for the early convening of the Geneva Middle East peace conference.

A further UN General Assembly Resolution (33/29 of December 7th, 1978), repeated the call for the convening of the Geneva Middle East peace conference. The main focus of attention, however, had now moved away from the UN. President Sadat of Egypt visited Jerusalem in November 1977, and after protracted negotiations, the course of which can be found in 'The Arab-Israeli Confrontation 1967–1979', pages 50–54, President Sadat and Menachem Begin first of all signed two agreements at Camp David in the U.S.A. under the auspices of the U.S. President, Jimmy Carter, and subsequently signed a Peace Treaty in Washington on March 26th, 1979. The Arab League Council, angry at Egypt's unilateral action, met in Baghdad on March 27th and passed a series of resolutions aimed at isolating Egypt from the Arab world.

CAMP DAVID: THE FRAMEWORK OF PEACE IN THE MIDDLE EAST

Muhammad Anwar al-Sadat, President of the Arab Republic of Egypt, and Menachem Begin, Prime Minister of Israel, met with Jimmy Carter, President of the United States of America, at Camp David from September 5th to September 17th, 1978, and have agreed on the following framework for peace in the Middle East. They invite other parties to the Arab-Israeli conflict to adhere to it.

Preamble:

The search for peace in the Middle East must be guided by the following:

[*continued on p.* 75.

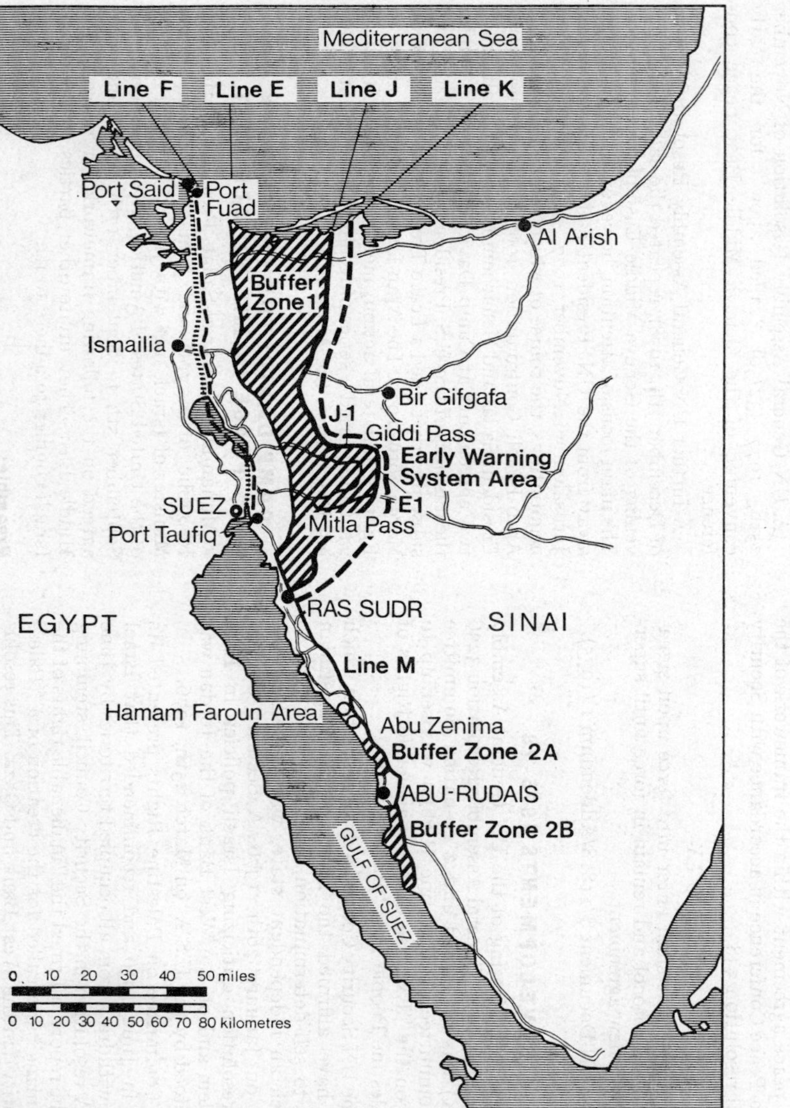

Second Egyptian-Israeli Disengagement Agreement, September 1975.

Line E: The Egyptian line.

Line J: The Israeli line.
The lines E and J will extend 12 nautical miles into the Mediterranean Sea perpendicular to the direction of the coast and the area between the lines will be UN buffer zone.

Line K: The limit of the Israeli area of limited forces and armaments.

Line F: The limit of the Egyptian area of limited forces and armaments.

Line M: The line separating the Israeli-controlled area from: the area south of line E and west of line M; and the areas of buffer zones 2A and 2B.

Buffer Zone 1: The buffer zone between lines E and J.

Buffer Zone 2A and Buffer Zone 2B: The buffer zone along the Gulf of Suez.

E1: Egyptian surveillance station.

J1: Israeli surveillance station.

○ UN Posts in the Hamam Faroun area.

continued from p. 73]

The agreed basis for a peaceful settlement of the conflict between Israel and its neighbours is UN Security Council resolution 242 in all its parts.

After four wars during 30 years, despite intensive humane efforts, the Middle East, which is the cradle of civilization and the birthplace of three great religions, does not yet enjoy the blessings of peace. The people of the Middle East yearn for peace, so that the vast human and natural resources of the region can be turned to the pursuits of peace and so that this area can become a model for coexistence and co-operation among nations.

The historic initiative by President Sadat in visiting Jerusalem and the reception accorded to him by the Parliament, Government and people of Israel, and the reciprocal visit of Prime Minister Begin to Ismailia, the peace proposals made by both leaders, as well as the warm reception of these missions by the peoples of both countries, have created an unprecedented opportunity for peace which must not be lost if this generation and future generations are to be spared the tragedies of war.

The provisions of the Charter of the UN and the other accepted norms of international law and legitimacy now provide accepted standards for the conduct of relations between all states.

To achieve a relationship of peace, in the spirit of article 2 of the UN Charter, future negotiations between Israel and any neighbour prepared to negotiate peace and security with it, are necessary for the purpose of carrying out all the provisions and principles of resolutions 242 and 338.

Peace requires respect for the sovereignty, territorial integrity and political independence of every state in the area and their right to live in peace within secure and recognized boundaries free from threats or acts of force. Progress toward that goal can accelerate movement toward a new era of reconciliation in the Middle East marked by co-operation in promoting economic development, in maintaining stability and in assuring security.

Security is enhanced by a relationship of peace and by co-operation between nations which enjoy normal relations. In addition, under the terms of peace treaties, the parties can, on the basis of reciprocity, agree to special arrangements such as demilitarized zones, limited armaments areas, early warning stations, the presence of international forces, liaison, agreed measures for monitoring, and other arrangements that they agree are useful.

Framework

Taking these factors into account, the parties are determined to reach a just, comprehensive and durable settlement of the Middle East conflict through the conclusion of peace treaties based on Security Council resolutions 242 and 338 in all their parts. Their purpose is to achieve peace and good neighbourly relations. They recognize that, for peace to endure, it must involve all those who have been most deeply affected by the conflict. They therefore agree that this framework as appropriate is intended by them to constitute a basis for peace not only between Egypt and Israel but also between Israel and each of its other neighbours which is prepared to negotiate peace with Israel on this basis. With that objective in mind, they have agreed to proceed as follows:

A. West Bank and Gaza:

1. Egypt, Israel, Jordan and the representatives of the Palestinian people should participate in negotiations on the resolution of the Palestinian problem in all its aspects to achieve that objective, negotiations relating to the West Bank and Gaza should proceed in three stages.

(A) Egypt and Israel agree that, in order to ensure a peaceful and orderly transfer of authority, and taking into account the security concerns of all the parties, there should be transitional arrangements for the West Bank and Gaza for a period not exceeding five years. In order to provide full autonomy to the inhabitants, under these arrangements the Israeli military government and its civilian administration will be withdrawn as soon as a self-governing authority has been freely elected by the inhabitants of these areas to replace the existing military government.

To negotiate the details of transitional arrangement, the Government of Jordan will be invited to join the negotiations on the basis of this framework. These new arrangements should give due consideration to both the principle of self-government by the inhabitants of these territories and to the legitimate security concerns of the parties involved.

(B) Egypt, Israel and Jordan will agree on the modalities for establishing the elected self-governing authority in the West Bank and Gaza. The delegations of Egypt and Jordan may include Palestinians from the West Bank and Gaza or other Palestinians as mutually agreed. The parties will negotiate an agreement which will define the powers and responsibilities of the self-governing authority to be exercised in the West Bank and Gaza. A withdrawal of Israeli armed forces will take place and there will be a redeployment of the remaining Israeli forces into specified security locations.

The negotiations shall be based on all the provisions and principles of UN Security Council resolution 242. The negotiations will resolve, among other matters, the location of the boundaries and the nature of the security arrangements. The solution from the negotiations must also recognize the legitimate rights of the Palestinian people and their just requirements. In this way, the Palestinians will participate in the determination of their own future through:

(i) The negotiations among Egypt, Israel, Jordan and the representatives of the inhabitants of the West Bank and Gaza to agree on the final status of the West Bank and Gaza and other outstanding issues by the end of the transitional period.

(ii) Submitting their agreement to a vote by the elected representatives of the inhabitants of the West Bank and Gaza.

(iii) Providing for the elected representatives of the inhabitants of the West Bank and Gaza to decide how they shall govern themselves consistent with the provisions of their agreement.

(iv) Participating as stated above in the work of the committee negotiating the peace treaty between Israel and Jordan.

The agreement will also include arrangements for assuring internal and external security and public order. A strong local police force will be established, which may include Jordanian citizens. In addition, Israeli and Jordanian forces will participate in joint patrols and in the manning of control posts to assure the security of the borders.

(C) When the self-governing authority (administrative council) in the West Bank and Gaza is established and inaugurated, the transitional period of five years will begin. As soon as possible, but not later than the third year after the beginning of the transitional period, negotiations will take place to determine the final status of the West Bank and Gaza and its relationship with its neighbours, and to conclude a peace treaty between Israel and Jordan by the end of the transitional period. These negotiations will be conducted among Egypt, Israel, Jordan and the elected representatives of the inhabitants of the West Bank and Gaza.

Two separate but related committees will be convened, one committee, consisting of representatives of the four parties which will negotiate and agree on the final status of the West Bank and Gaza, and its relationship with its neighbours, and the second committee, consisting of representatives of Israel and representatives of Jordan to be joined by the elected representatives of the inhabitants of the West Bank and Gaza, to negotiate the peace treaty between Israel and Jordan, taking into account the agreement reached on the final status of the West Bank and Gaza.

2. All necessary measures will be taken and provisions made to assure the security of Israel and its neighbours during the transitional period and beyond. To assist in providing such security, a strong local police force will be constituted by the self-governing authority. It will be composed of inhabitants of the West Bank and Gaza. The police will maintain continuing liaison on internal security matters with the designated Israeli, Jordanian and Egyptian officers.

3. During the transitional period, the representatives of Egypt, Israel, Jordan and the self-governing authority will constitute a continuing committee to decide by agreement on the modalities of admission of persons displaced from the West Bank and Gaza in 1967, together with necessary measures to prevent disruption and disorder. Other matters of common concern may also be dealt with by this committee.

4. Egypt and Israel will work with each other and with other interested parties to establish agreed procedures for a prompt, just and permanent implementation of the resolution of the refugee problem.

B. Egypt-Israel

1. Egypt and Israel undertake not to resort to the threat or the use of force to settle disputes. Any disputes shall be settled by peaceful means in accordance with the provisions of article 33 of the Charter of the UN.

2. In order to achieve peace between them, the parties agree to negotiate in good faith with a goal of concluding within three months from the signing of this framework a peace treaty between them, while inviting the other parties to the conflict to proceed simultaneously to negotiate and conclude similar peace treaties with a view to achieving a comprehensive peace in the area. The framework for the conclusion of a peace treaty between Egypt and Israel will govern the peace negotiations between them. The parties will agree on the modalities and the timetable for the implementation of their obligations under the treaty.

Associated principles

1. Egypt and Israel state that the principles and provisions described below should apply to peace treaties between Israel and each of its neighbours—Egypt, Jordan, Syria and Lebanon.

2. Signatories shall establish among themselves relationships normal to states at peace with one another. To this end, they should undertake to abide by all the provisions of the Charter of the UN. Steps to be taken in this respect include:

(a) Full recognition.

(b) Abolishing economic boycotts.

(c) Guaranteeing that under their jurisdiction the citizens of the other parties shall enjoy the protection of the due process of law.

3. Signatories should explore possibilities for economic development in the context of final peace treaties, with the objective of contributing to the atmosphere of peace, co-operation, and friendship which is their common goal.

4. Claims commissions may be established for the mutual settlement of all financial claims.

5. The United States shall be invited to participate in the talks on matters related to the modalities of the implementation of the agreements and working out the time-table for the carrying out of the obligation of the parties.

6. The UN Security Council shall be requested to endorse the peace treaties and ensure that their provisions shall not be violated. The permanent members of the Security Council shall be requested to underwrite the peace treaties and ensure respect for their provisions. They shall also be requested to conform their policies and actions with the undertakings contained in this framework.

The second agreement signed at Camp David was a framework for the conclusion of a peace treaty between Egypt and Israel. The actual Treaty was signed on March 26th, 1979, and is reproduced below.

THE PEACE TREATY BETWEEN EGYPT AND ISRAEL SIGNED IN WASHINGTON ON MARCH 26th, 1979

The Government of the Arab Republic of Egypt and the Government of the State of Israel:

Preamble

Convinced of the urgent necessity of the establishment of a just, comprehensive and lasting peace in the Middle East in accordance with Security Council Resolutions 242 and 338:

Reaffirming their adherence to the "Framework for Peace in the Middle East agreed at Camp David", dated September 17th, 1978:

Noting that the aforementioned framework as appropriate is intended to constitute a basis for peace not only between Egypt and Israel but also between Israel and each of the other Arab neighbours which is prepared to negotiate peace with it on this basis:

Desiring to bring to an end the state of war between them and to establish a peace in which every state in the area can live in security.

Convinced that the conclusion of a treaty of peace between Egypt and Israel is an important step in the search for comprehensive peace in the area and for the attainment of the settlement of the Arab-Israeli conflict in all its aspects.

Inviting the other Arab parties to this dispute to join the peace process with Israel guided by and based on the principles of the aforementioned framework.

Desiring as well to develop friendly relations and co-operation between themselves in accordance with the UN Charter and the principles of international law governing international relations in times of peace.

Agree to the following provisions in the free exercise of their sovereignty, in order to implement the "framework for the conclusion of a peace treaty between Egypt and Israel".

Article I

1. The state of war between the parties will be terminated and peace will be established between them upon the exchange of instruments of ratification of this treaty.

2. Israel will withdraw all its armed forces and civilians from the Sinai behind the international boundary between Egypt and Mandated Palestine, as provided in the annexed protocol (annexed), and Egypt will resume the exercise of its full sovereignty over the Sinai.

3. Upon completion of the interim withdrawal provided for in Annex 1, the parties will establish normal and friendly relations, in accordance with Article II (3).

Article II

The permanent boundary between Egypt and Israel is the recognized international boundary between Egypt and the former Mandated Territory of Palestine, as shown on the map at Annex 11, without prejudice to the issue of the status of the Gaza Strip. The parties recognize this boundary as inviolable. Each will respect the territorial integrity of the other, including their territorial waters and airspace.

Article III

1. The parties will apply between them the provisions of the Charter of the UN and the principles of international law governing relations among states in times of peace.

In particular:

A. They recognize and will respect each other's sovereignty, territorial integrity and political independence.

B. They recognize and will respect each other's right to live in peace within their secure and recognized boundaries.

C. They will refrain from the threat of use of force, directly or indirectly, against each other and will settle all disputes between them by peaceful means.

2. Each party undertakes to ensure that acts or threats of belligerency, hostility, or violence do not originate from and are not committed from within its territory, or by any forces subject to its control or by any other forces stationed on its territory, against the population, citizens or property of the other party. Each party also undertakes to refrain from organizing, instigating, inciting, assisting or participating in acts or threats of belligerency, hostility, subversion or violence against the other party, anywhere, and undertakes to ensure that perpetrators of such acts are brought to justice.

3. The parties agree that the normal relationship established between them will include full recognition, diplomatic, economic and cultural relations, termination of economic boycotts and discriminatory barriers to the free movement of people and goods, and will guarantee the mutual enjoyment by citizens of the due process of law. The process by which they undertake to achieve such a relationship parallel to the implementation of other provisions of this treaty is set out in the annexed protocol (Annex III).

Article IV

1. In order to provide maximum security for both parties on the basis of reciprocity, agreed security arrangement will be established including limited force zones in Egyptian and Israeli territory, and UN forces and observers, described in detail as to nature and timing in Annex 1, and other security arrangements the parties may agree upon.

2. The parties agree to the stationing of UN personnel in areas described in Annex 1, the parties agree not to request withdrawal of the UN personnel and that these personnel will not be removed unless such removal is approved by the Security Council of the UN, with the affirmative vote of the five members, unless the parties otherwise agree.

3. A joint commission will be established to facilitate the implementation of the treaty, as provided for in Annex 1.

4. The security arrangements provided for in paragraphs 1 and 2 of this article may at the request of either party be reviewed and amended by mutual agreement of the parties.

Article V

1. Ships of Israel, and cargoes destined for or coming from Israel, shall enjoy the right of free passage through the Suez Canal and its approaches through the Gulf of Suez and the Mediterranean Sea on the basis of the Constantinople Convention of 1888, applying to all nations. Israeli nationals, vessels and cargoes, as well as persons, vessels and cargoes destined for or coming from Israel, shall be accorded non-discriminatory treatment in all matters connected with usage of the canal.

2. The parties consider the Strait of Tiran and the Gulf of Aqaba to be international waterways open to all nations for unimpeded and non-suspendable freedom of navigation and overflight. The parties will respect each other's right to navigation and overflight for access to either country through the Strait of Tiran and the Gulf of Aqaba.

Article VI

1. This treaty does not affect and shall not be interpreted as affecting in any way the rights and obligations of the parties under the Charter of the UN.

2. The parties undertake to fulfil in good faith their obligations under this treaty, without regard to action or inaction of any other party and independently of any instrument external to this treaty.

3. They further undertake to take all the necessary measures for the application in their relations of the provisions of the multilateral conventions to which they are parties. Including the submission of appropriate notification to the Secretary-General of the UN and other depositories of such conventions.

4. The parties undertake not to enter into any obligation in conflict with this treaty.

5. Subject to Article 103 of the UN Charter, in the event of a conflict between the obligations of the parties under the present treaty and any of their other obligations, the obligations under this treaty will be binding and implemented.

Article VII

1. Disputes arising out of the application or interpretation of this treaty shall be resolved by negotiations.

2. Any such disputes which cannot be settled by negotiations shall be resolved by conciliation or submitted to arbitration.

Article VIII

The parties agree to establish a claims commission for the mutual settlement of all financial claims.

Article IX

1. This treaty shall enter into force upon exchange of instruments of ratification.

2. This treaty supersedes the agreement between Egypt and Israel of September 1975.

3. All protocols, annexes, and maps attached to this treaty shall be regarded as an integral part hereof.

4. The treaty shall be communicated to the Secretary-General of the UN for registration in accordance with the provisions of Article 102 of the Charter of the UN.

Annex 1—military and withdrawal arrangements: Israel will complete withdrawal of all its armed forces and civilians from Sinai within three years of the date of exchange of instruments of ratification of the treaty. The withdrawal will be accomplished in two phases, the first, within nine months, to a line east of Al Arish and Ras Muhammad; the second to behind the international boundary. During the three-year period, Egypt and Israel will maintain a specified military presence in four delineated security zones, (see map), and the UN will continue its observation and supervisory functions. Egypt will exercise full sovereignty over evacuated territories in Sinai upon Israeli withdrawal. A joint commission will supervise the withdrawal, and security arrangements can be reviewed when either side asks but any change must be by mutual agreement.

Annex 2—maps.

Annex 3—normalization of relations: Ambassadors will be exchanged upon completion of the interim withdrawal. All discriminatory barriers and economic boycotts will be lifted and, not later than six months after the completion of the interim withdrawal, negotiations for a trade and commerce agreement will begin. Free movement of each others nationals and transport will be allowed and both sides agree to promote "good neighbourly relations". Egypt will use the airfields left by Israel near Al Arish, Rafah, Ras an-Naqb and Sharm ash-Shaikh, only for civilian aircraft. Road, rail, postal, telephone, wireless and other forms of communications will be opened between the two countries on completion of interim withdrawal.

Exchange of letters:

Negotiations on the West Bank and Gaza—Negotiations on autonomy for the West Bank and Gaza will begin within one month of the exchange of the instruments of ratification. Jordan will be invited to participate and the Egyptian and Jordanian delegations may include Palestinians from the West Bank and Gaza, or other Palestinians as mutually agreed. If Jordan decides not to take part, the negotiations will be held by Egypt and Israel. The objective of the negotiations is the establishment of a self-governing authority in the West Bank and Gaza "in order to provide full autonomy to the inhabitants".

Egypt and Israel hope to complete negotiations within one year so that elections can be held as soon as possible. The self-governing authority elected will be inaugurated within one month of the elections at which point the five year transitional period will begin. The Israeli military government and its civilian administration will be withdrawn, Israeli armed forces withdrawn and the remaining forces redeployed "into specified security locations".

MAIN POINTS OF THE RESOLUTIONS PASSED BY THE ARAB LEAGUE COUNCIL IN BAGHDAD ON MARCH 27th, 1979

—To withdraw the ambassadors of the Arab states from Egypt immediately.

—To recommend the severance of political and diplomatic relations with the Egyptian Government. The Arab governments will adopt the necessary measures to apply this recommendation within a maximum period of one month from the date of the issue of this decision, in accordance with the constitutional measures in force in each country.

—To consider the suspension of the Egyptian Government's membership in the Arab League as operative from the date of the Egyptian Government's signing of the peace treaty with the Zionist enemy. This means depriving it of all rights resulting from that membership.

—To make the city of Tunis, capital of the Tunisian Republic, the temporary headquarters of the Arab League, its general secretariat, the competent ministerial councils and the permanent technical committees, as of the date of the signing of the treaty between the Egyptian Government and the Zionist enemy. This shall be communicated to all international and regional organizations and bodies. They will also be informed that dealings with the Arab League will be conducted with its secretariat in its new temporary headquarters.

—To condemn the policy that the United States is practising regarding its role in concluding the Camp David agreements and the Egyptian-Israeli treaty.

The Arab League Council, at the level of Arab Foreign and Economy Ministers, has also decided the following:

—To halt all bank loans, deposits, guarantees or facilities, as well as all financial or technical contributions and aid by Arab governments or their establishments to the Egyptian Government and its establishments as of the treaty-signing date.

—To ban the extension of economic aid by the Arab funds, banks and financial establishments within the framework of the Arab League and the joint Arab co-operation to the Egyptian Government and its establishments.

—The Arab governments and institutions shall refrain from purchasing the bonds, shares, postal orders and public credit loans that are issued by the Egyptian Government and its financial foundations.

—Following the suspension of the Egyptian Government's membership in the Arab League, its membership will also be suspended from the institutions, funds and organisations deriving from the Arab League.

—In view of the fact that the ill-omened Egyptian-Israeli treaty and its appendices have demonstrated Egypt's commitment to sell oil to Israel, the Arab states shall refrain from providing Egypt with oil and its derivatives.

—Trade exchanges with the Egyptian state and with private establishments that deal with the Zionist enemy shall be prohibited.

Source: MEED Arab Report, April 11th, 1979, p. 9.

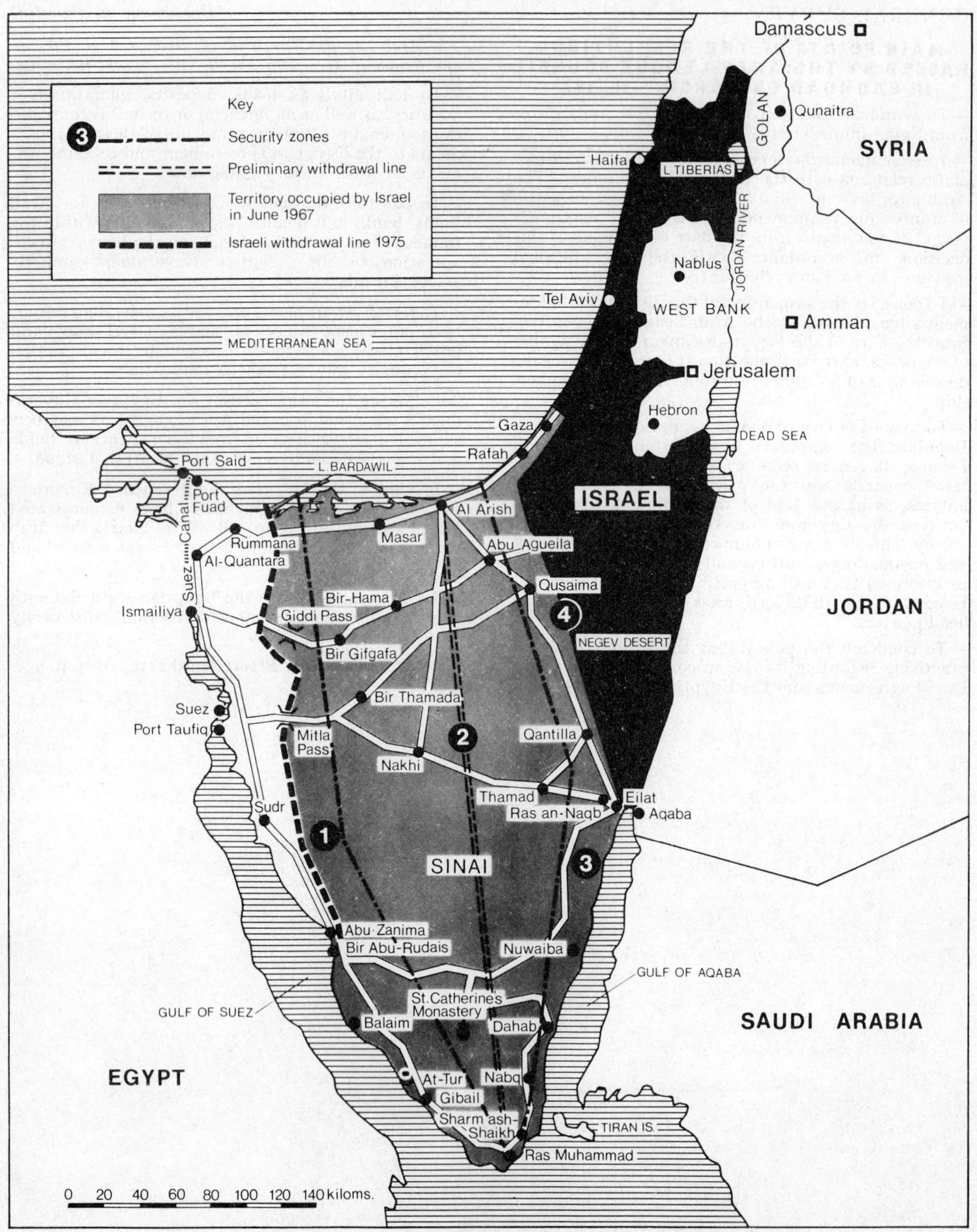

Map accompanying Egyptian – Israeli Peace Treaty, March 1979

Palestine Organizations

Palestine Liberation Organization (PLO)

The Palestine Liberation Organization was founded in 1964 at the first Arab Summit Meeting, and the Palestine Liberation Army was established in the same year. The supreme organ of the PLO is the Palestine National Council (*see* below), while the Palestine Executive Committee, consisting of 15 members, deals with the day-to-day business. Fatah (the Palestine National Liberation Movement) joined the Palestine National Council in 1968, and all the guerrilla organizations joined the Council in 1969. The Palestine Executive Committee controls the following eight departments, and a member of the Executive Committee is at the head of each department:

(i) Military Department, which includes Palestine Liberation Army
(ii) Cultural and Educational.
(iii) Political and International Relations.
(iv) Palestine National Fund.
(v) Social Affairs (includes Palestine Red Crescent).
(vi) Occupied Territories.
(vii) Information and National Guidance.
(viii) Popular Organizations (Trade Unions, Students, Workers, Women, etc.).

The PLO has offices and representatives in every Arab country, as well as in non-Arab states such as U.S.A., U.S.S.R., China, Cuba, Yugoslavia, Switzerland and Britain. The Rabat Arab Summit, in October 1974, affirmed the right of the Palestinian people to establish an independent national authority, under the leadership of the PLO in its capacity as the sole legitimate representative of the Palestine people, over all liberated territory (*see* Documents on Palestine, p. 71). In November 1974 Yasser Arafat addressed the UN General Assembly, and on November 22nd, 1974, the UN General Assembly passed a resolution acknowledging and reaffirming the PLO position (*see* Documents on Palestine, page 71. On the same day the PLO was granted permanent observer status at the General Assembly of the UN and at international conferences sponsored by the UN. A PLO Delegation was present at the Conference of the Inter-Parliamentary Union in London in September 1975, and also at the 30th Session of the UN General Assembly in November 1975. The PLO became a full member of the Arab League in September 1976.

The PLO condemned the Second Interim Egyptian-Israeli Disengagement Agreement as seriously weakening the united Arab effort to achieve the liberation of territories occupied by Israeli armed forces. In response Egypt closed the "Voice of Palestine" radio operating from Cairo. The general policy of the PLO was to remain aloof from the Lebanese civil war of 1975 and 1976, but after 1976 it became increasingly involved, particularly after the Syrian intervention. Although many guerrilla units suffered heavy losses the PLO has not moderated its official policy, and when an enlarged Palestine National Council met in Cairo in March 1977, no changes were made in the Palestine National Charter (*see* below), and a 15-point political programme (*see* below) was adopted which set out in a forthright fashion the aims and principles of the PLO. The PLO has condemned the Camp David agreements of September 1978 (*see* p. 73) and the Peace Treaty between Egypt and Israel of March 1979 (*see* p. 77).

Chairman: 1964-67 Ahmed Shukairi.
1967-68 Yahya Hammouda.
1968- Yasser Arafat.

Main Regional Offices with Representatives:

Abu Dhabi: Ribhi Awad.
Aden: Abbas Zaki
Addis Ababa:
Algiers: Ahmed Wafi.
Amman: Hazim al-Karzun
Beirut: Shafiq Hout.
Berlin: Nabil Qulaylat
Budapest: Abder-Rahin Abu-Jayab.
Damascus: Mahmoud Khalidi.
Dar es Salaam: Ndugu Fuad Baytar
Islamabad: Yousef Abu-Hatash
Khartoum: Abu Haitham.
Kuwait: Auni Battash
London: Nabil Ramlawi.
Luxembourg:
Maputo:
Moscow: Rebhi Halloum.
New York: Saa'dat Hasan.
Paris: Ibrahim Souss.
Peking: Tayeb Abder-Rahman.
Qatar: Yasin Sharif.
Rio de Janeiro: Salah Zawawi.
Riyadh: Rafiq Najshah.
Teheran: Hani al-Hassan.
Tokyo: Fathi Abdul Hamid.
Tripoli: Suleiman Shurafa.
Vienna: Dr. Ghazi Hussein.
Washington: Hatim Husseini.

Head of PLO Observer Mission at UN: Dr. Zehdi Terzi.

PALESTINE NATIONAL COUNCIL

It has 301 members and meets once a year. Cairo has been the normal venue, but the 14th session in January 1979 was held in Damascus. As well as the guerrilla organizations, the other PLO bodies, trade and student unions, etc. are represented. The Council also includes Palestinian representatives from Jordan, the West Bank, the Gulf States and other countries. At the 14th session in Damascus in January 1979 a unity plan to reconcile the various elements in the PLO was adopted, but the PFLP did not rejoin the Executive Committee

Chairman: KHALED FAHOUM.

Deputy Chairman: SALIM ZAANOUN ("ABU ADIB").

CENTRAL COUNCIL

It is appointed by the Palestine National Council; consists of the members of the Executive Committee, and other members, with a total possible membership of 55; acts as a steering group when the PNC is not in session. For details of affiliated organizations *see* page 83.

EXECUTIVE COMMITTEE

(elected March 1977 and re-elected January 1979)

This is elected by the Palestine National Council and is responsible for the running of the PLO in between meetings of the Council. In September 1974 the PFLP withdrew from the Executive Committee and Central Council of the PLO because it rejected PLO policies which recognized the existence of Israel. This "rejectionist front" was later joined by the PFLP—General Command, the Arab Liberation Front and the Front for the Popular Palestinian Struggle, and in practice their members ceased to serve on the Executive Committee and Central Council listed below, although they remained members of the Palestine National Council. At the March 1977 meeting of the Palestine National Council, however, only the PFLP continued to boycott the work of the Executive Committee.

Chairman: YASSER ARAFAT (also known as "ABU AMMAR"—Fatah); Political Adviser to YASSER ARAFAT: BASEL AQL.

Members: FAROUK KADDOUMI (also known as "ABU LUTF"—Fatah—Head of Political Dept.), (vacant) (Saiqa—Head of Military Dept.), YASSER ABD-RABOU (PDFLP—Head of Information Dept.), ABDER-RAHIM AHMED (ALF), TALAL NAJI (PFLP—General Command—Head of Higher Education Dept.), WALID KAMHAWEH (independent—Chairman of Palestine National Fund), AHMAD SIDQI AD-DAJANI (independent—Chairman of Palestine Research Centre), HABIB QAHWAJI (independent), MUHAMMAD ZUHAIR NASHASHIBI (independent—pro-Saiqa), ABDEL-JAWAD SALEH (PNF—Head of Occupied Areas Dept.), ABDEL-MUHSEN ABU-MAIZER (PNF—Official Spokesman), ALFRED TUBASI (independent), HAMED ABU-SITTA (independent), AHMAD MAJDI ABU-RAMADAN (independent—Head of Social Affairs Dept. and Central Bureau of Student Affairs in Egypt).

PALESTINE LIBERATION ARMY (PLA)

Commander-in-Chief: YASSER ARAFAT.

Commander: Col. MUSTAPHA SAADEDDIN.

Chief of Staff: Brig.-Gen. WALID JAMOUS.

PALESTINE NATIONAL FUND

The fund is financed by a contribution of between 3 and 6 per cent from the income of every Palestinian and also aid from Arab and friendly countries.

Chairman: Dr. WALID KAMHAWEH.

Director: DARWICHE ABYAD.

PALESTINE PLANNING CENTRE

Director: Dr. NABIL SHAATH.

PALESTINE RED CRESCENT

President: Dr. FATHI ARAFAT; operates 6 hospitals, 4 emergency centres and several clinics.

PALESTINE RESEARCH CENTRE

Chairman: AHMAD SIDQI AD-DAJANI.

PALESTINE MARTYRS' WORKS SOCIETY (SAMED)

P.O.B. 165024, Beirut; runs workshops making blankets, tents, uniforms, civilian clothes, toys, furniture, etc.

President: ABU ALA.

OTHER PLO BODIES

Palestine Labour Organization, General Union of Palestinian Women, Palestine Writers' Organization, Palestine Orphans' Trust, Palestine Youth Organization, General Union of Palestine Students, Palestine Medical Organization, Palestine Architects' Organization, Palestine Teachers' Organization, Palestine Artisans' Organization.

PRESS AND RADIO

Falastin Al-Thawra: Beirut; weekly newspaper of the Palestine Liberation Organization.

Al Hadaf: Beirut; organ of the Popular Front for the Liberation of Palestine; weekly; Editor BASSAM ABU SHERIF.

Voice of Palestine: official radio station of Palestine Liberation Organization; broadcasts from Baghdad and Algiers, and also from the Yemen Arab Republic.

Palestine News Agency (WAFA): Beirut; official PLO news agency; Editor ZIAD ABDEL FATTAH; Beirut Spokesman of PLO: MAHMOUD LABADI.

CENTRAL COUNCIL OF THE PALESTINE RESISTANCE MOVEMENT

It was created early in 1970 and represents all the guerrilla groups. The most important guerrilla organizations are:

Fatah (The Palestine National Liberation Movement): f. 1956; embraces a coalition of varying views from conservative to radical; leader YASSER ARAFAT; deputy leader SALAH KHALAF (also known as "ABU IYAD"); Commdr. of Fatah Forces (*Al Asifa*) KHALIL WAZIR (also known as ABU JIHAD). The "Fatah Revolutionary Council" is a split from Fatah and is led from Baghdad by NAJI ALLUSH, who is reported to have succeeded SABRI AL-BANNA (ABU NIDAL) in December 1978.

Popular Front for the Liberation of Palestine (PFLP): f. 1967; Marxist-Leninist; leader Dr. GEORGE HABASH; spokesman BASSAM ABU SHERIF.

Popular Front for the Liberation of Palestine—General Command: split from PFLP; pro-Syrian; leader AHMED JEBRIL.

Saiqa (Vanguard of the Popular Liberation War): f. 1967; Syrian-backed; leader SAMI AL-ATARI.

Democratic Front for the Liberation of Palestine (DFLP): split from PFLP in 1969; Marxist; leader NAIF HAWATMEH.

Arab Liberation Front (ALF): Iraqi-backed; leader Dr. ABDUL WAHHAB KAYYALI; Sec.-Gen. ABDER-RAHIM AHMED.

Popular Struggle Front (PSF): f. 1967; Sec.-Gen. SAMIR GHOUSHA.

Palestine Liberation Front (PLF): Pro-Iraqi; split from PFLP-GC in April 1977; Sec.-Gen. TALAAT YAQOUB.

"Black September" is a hard-core group which draws its support from a variety of organizations. "Black June" is the split from Fatah, the "Fatah Revolutionary Council" in Baghdad. The "Rejectionist Front" consists of those who reject any settlement which recognizes Israel (*see* under Executive Committee, p. 82). The "Palestine National Front" (PNF) emerged during 1974 as a political force among the Palestinians who had lived under Israeli occupation.

THE PALESTINIAN NATIONAL CHARTER

(Palestine Liberation Organization)*

1. Palestine is the homeland of the Palestinian Arab people; it is an indivisible part of the Arab homeland, and the Palestinian people are an integral part of the Arab nation.

2. Palestine, with the boundaries it had during the British mandate, is an indivisible territorial unit.

3. The Palestinian Arab people possess the legal right to their homeland and have the right to determine their destiny after achieving the liberation of their country in accordance with their wishes and entirely of their own accord and will.

4. The Palestinian identity is a genuine, essential and inherent characteristic; it is transmitted from parents to children. The Zionist occupation and the dispersal of the Palestinian Arab people, through the disasters which befell them, do not make them lose their Palestinian identity and their membership of the Palestinian community, nor do they negate them.

5. The Palestinians are those Arab nationals who, until 1947, normally resided in Palestine regardless of whether they were evicted from it or have stayed there. Anyone born, after that date, of a Palestinian father—whether inside Palestine or outside it—is also a Palestinian.

6. The Jews who had normally resided in Palestine until the beginning of the Zionist invasion will be considered Palestinians.

7. That there is a Palestinian community and that it has material, spiritual and historical connection with Palestine are indisputable facts. It is a national duty to bring up individual Palestinians in an Arab revolutionary manner. All means of information and education must be adopted in order to acquaint the Palestinian with his country in the most profound manner, both spiritual and material, that is possible. He must be prepared for the armed struggle and ready to sacrifice his wealth and his life in order to win back his homeland and bring about its liberation.

8. The phase in their history, through which the Palestinian people are now living, is that of national struggle for the liberation of Palestine. Thus the conflicts among the Palestinian national forces are secondary, and should be ended for the sake of the basic conflict that exists between the forces of Zionism and of imperialism on the one hand, and the Palestinian Arab people on the other. On this basis the Palestinian masses, regardless of whether they are residing in the national homeland or in diaspora, constitute—both their organizations and the individuals—one national front working for the retrieval of Palestine and its liberation through armed struggle.

9. Armed struggle is the only way to liberate Palestine. Thus it is the overall strategy, not merely a tactical phase. The Palestinian Arab people assert their absolute determination and firm resolution to continue their armed struggle and to work for an armed popular revolution for the liberation of their country and their return to it. They also assert their right to normal life in Palestine and to exercise their right to self-determination and sovereignty over it.

10. Commando action constitutes the nucleus of the Palestinian popular liberation war. This requires its escalation, comprehensiveness and the mobilization of all the Palestinian popular and educational efforts and their organization and involvement in the armed Palestinian revolution. It also requires the achieving of unity for the national struggle among the different

* Decisions of the National Congress of the Palestine Liberation Organization held in Cairo July 1st–17th, 1968.

groupings of the Palestinian people, and between the Palestinian people and the Arab masses so as to secure the continuation of the revolution, its escalation and victory.

11. The Palestinians will have three mottoes: national unity, national mobilization and liberation.

12. The Palestinian people believe in Arab unity. In order to contribute their share towards the attainment of that objective, however, they must, at the present stage of their struggle, safeguard their Palestinian identity and develop their consciousness of that identity, and oppose any plan that may dissolve or impair it.

13. Arab unity and the liberation of Palestine are two complementary objectives, the attainment of either of which facilitates the attainment of the other. Thus, Arab unity leads to the liberation of Palestine; the liberation of Palestine leads to Arab unity; and work towards the realization of one objective proceeds side by side with work towards the realization of the other.

14. The destiny of the Arab nation, and indeed Arab existence itself, depends upon the destiny of the Palestine cause. From this interdependence springs the Arab nation's pursuit of, and striving for, the liberation of Palestine. The people of Palestine play the role of the vanguard in the realization of this sacred national goal.

15. The liberation of Palestine, from an Arab viewpoint, is a national duty and it attempts to repel the Zionist and imperialist aggression against the Arab homeland, and aims at the elimination of Zionism in Palestine. Absolute responsibility for this falls upon the Arab nation—peoples and governments —with the Arab people of Palestine in the vanguard. Accordingly the Arab nation must mobilize all its military, human, moral and spiritual capabilities to participate actively with the Palestinian people in the liberation of Palestine. It must, particularly in the phase of the armed Palestinian revolution, offer and furnish the Palestinian people with all possible help, and material and human support, and make available to them the means and opportunities that will enable them to continue to carry out their leading role in the armed revolution, until they liberate their homeland.

16. The liberation of Palestine, from a spiritual point of view, will provide the Holy Land with an atmosphere of safety and tranquillity, which in turn will safeguard the country's religious sanctuaries and guarantee freedom of worship and of visit to all, without discrimination of race, color, language, or religion. Accordingly, the people of Palestine look to all spiritual forces in the world for support.

17. The liberation of Palestine, from a human point of view, will restore to the Palestinian individual his dignity, pride and freedom. Accordingly the Palestinian Arab people look forward to the support of all those who believe in the dignity of man and his freedom in the world.

18. The liberation of Palestine, from an international point of view, is a defensive action necessitated by the demands of self-defence. Accordingly, the Palestinian people, desirous as they are of the friendship of all people, look to freedom-loving, justice-loving and peace-loving states for support in order to restore their legitimate rights in Palestine, to re-establish peace and security in the country, and to enable its people to exercise national sovereignty and freedom.

19. The partition of Palestine in 1947 and the establishment of the state of Israel are entirely illegal, regardless of the passage of time, because they were contrary to the will of the Palestinian people and to their natural right in their homeland, and inconsistent with the principles embodied in the Charter of the United Nations, particularly the right to self-determination.

20. The Balfour Declaration, the mandate for Palestine and everything that has been based upon them, are deemed null and void. Claims of historical or religious ties of Jews with Palestine are incompatible with the facts of history and the true conception of what constitutes statehood. Judaism, being a religion, is not an independent nationality. Nor do Jews constitute a single nation with an identity of its own; they are citizens of the states to which they belong.

21. The Palestinian Arab people, expressing themselves by the armed Palestinian revolution, reject all solutions which are substitutes for the total liberation of Palestine and reject all proposals aiming at the liquidation of the Palestinian problem, or its internationalization.

22. Zionism is a political movement organically associated with international imperialism and antagonistic to all action for liberation and to progressive movements in the world. It is racist and fanatic in its nature, aggressive, expansionist and colonial in its aims, and fascist in its methods. Israel is the instrument of the Zionist movement, and a geographical base for world imperialism placed strategically in the midst of the Arab homeland to combat the hopes of the Arab nation for liberation, unity and progress. Israel is a constant source of threat *vis-à-vis* peace in the Middle East and the whole world. Since the liberation of Palestine will destroy the Zionist and imperialist presence and will contribute to the establishment of peace in the Middle East, the Palestinian people look for the support of all the progressive and peaceful forces and urge them all, irrespective of their affiliations and beliefs, to offer the Palestinian people all aid and support in their just struggle for the liberation of their homeland.

23. The demands of security and peace, as well as the demands of right and justice, require all states to consider Zionism an illegitimate movement, to outlaw its existence, and to ban its operations, in order that friendly relations among peoples may be preserved, and the loyalty of citizens to their respective homelands safeguarded.

24. The Palestinian people believe in the principles of justice, freedom, sovereignty, self-determination, human dignity, and in the right of all peoples to exercise them.

25. For the realization of the goals of this Charter and its principles, the Palestine Liberation Organization will perform its role in the liberation of Palestine in accordance with the Constitution of this Organization.

26. The Palestine Liberation Organization, representative of the Palestinian revolutionary forces, is responsible for the Palestinian Arab people's movement in its struggle—to retrieve its homeland, liberate and return to it and exercise the right to self-determination in it—in all military, political and financial fields and also for whatever may be required by the Palestine case on the inter-Arab and international levels.

27. The Palestine Liberation Organization shall cooperate with all Arab states, each according to its potentialities; and will adopt a neutral policy among them in the light of the requirements of the war of liberation; and on this basis it shall not interfere in the internal affairs of any Arab state.

28. The Palestinian Arab people assert the genuineness and independence of their national revolution and reject all forms of intervention, trusteeship and subordination.

29. The Palestinian people possess the fundamental and genuine legal right to liberate and retrieve their homeland. The Palestinian people determine their attitude towards all states and forces on the basis of the stands they adopt *vis-à-vis* the Palestinian case and the extent of the support they offer to the Palestinian revolution to fulfil the aims of the Palestinian people.

30. Fighters and carriers of arms in the war of liberation are the nucleus of the popular army which will be the protective force for the gains of the Palestinian Arab people.

31. The Organization shall have a flag, an oath of allegiance and an anthem. All this shall be decided upon in accordance with a special regulation.

32. Regulations, which shall be known as the Constitution of the Palestine Liberation Organization, shall be annexed to this Charter. It shall lay down the manner in which the Organization, and its organs and institutions, shall be constituted; the respective competence of each; and the requirements of its obligations under the Charter.

33. This Charter shall not be amended save by (vote of) a majority of two-thirds of the total membership of the National Council of the Palestine Liberation Organization (taken) at a special session convened for that purpose.

15-POINT POLITICAL PROGRAMME

(*adopted by the Palestine National Council, March 20th, 1977 and reaffirmed by the PLO Central Council, August 25th, 1977*)

Proceeding from the Palestine national charter and the previous national councils' resolutions; considering the decisions and political gains achieved by the PLO at the Arab and international levels during the period following the 12th session of the PNC; after studying and debating the latest developments in the Palestine issue; and stressing support for the Palestinian national struggle in the Arab and international forums, the PNC affirms the following:

1. The PNC affirms that the Palestine issue is the essence and the root of the Arab-Zionist conflict. Security Council Resolution 242 (*see* Documents on Palestine, p. 67) ignores the Palestinian people and their firm rights. The PNC therefore confirms its rejection of this Resolution, and rejects negotiations at the Arab and international levels based on this Resolution.

2. The PNC affirms the stand of the PLO in its determination to continue the armed struggle, and its concomitant forms of political and mass struggle, to achieve our inalienable national rights.

3. The PNC affirms that the struggle, in all its military, political and popular forms, in the occupied territory constitutes the central link in its programme of struggle. On this basis, the PLO will strive to escalate the armed struggle in the occupied territory, to escalate all other concomitant forms of struggle, and to give all kinds of moral support to the masses of our people in the occupied territory in order to escalate the struggle and to strengthen their steadfastness to defeat and liquidate the occupation.

4. The PNC affirms the PLO's stand which rejects all types of American capitulationist settlement and all liquidationist projects. The Council affirms the determination of the PLO to abort any settlement achieved at the expense of the firm national rights of our people. The PNC calls upon the Arab nation to shoulder its pan-Arab responsibilities and to pool all its energies to confront these imperialist and Zionist plans.

5. The Palestine National Council stresses the importance and necessity of national units, both political and military, among all the contingents of the Palestine Revolution within the framework of the PLO, because this is one of the basic conditions for victory. For this reason, it is necessary to co-ordinate national units at all levels and in all spheres on the basis of commitment to all these resolutions, and to draw up programmes which will ensure the implementation of this.

6. The Palestine National Council affirms the right of the Palestine Revolution to be present on the soil of fraternal Lebanon within the framework of the Cairo agreement and its appendices, concluded between the PLO and the Lebanese authorities. The Council also affirms adherence to the implementation of the Cairo agreement in letter and in spirit, including the preservation of the position of the

Revolution and the security of the camps. The Palestine National Council refuses to accept any interpretation of this agreement by one side only. Meanwhile, it affirms its eagerness for the maintenance of the sovereignty and security of Lebanon.

7. The Palestine National Council greets the heroic fraternal Lebanese people and affirms the eagerness of the PLO for the maintenance of the territorial integrity of Lebanon, the unity of its people and its security, independence, sovereignty and Arabism. The Palestine National Council affirms its pride in the support rendered by this heroic fraternal people to the PLO, which is struggling for our people to regain their national rights to their homeland and their right to return to this homeland. The PNC strongly affirms the need to deepen and consolidate cohesion between all Lebanese nationalist forces and the Palestine Revolution.

8. The Council affirms the need to strengthen the Arab front participating in the Palestine Revolution, and to deepen cohesion with all forces participating in it in all Arab countries, as well as to escalate the joint Arab struggle and to further strengthen the Palestine Revolution in order to contend with the imperialist and Zionist designs.

9. The Palestine National Council has decided to consolidate Arab struggle and solidarity on the basis of struggle against imperialism and Zionism, to work for the liberation of all the occupied Arab areas, and to adhere to the support for the Palestine Revolution in order to regain the constant national rights of the Palestinian Arab people without any conciliation or recognition.

10. The Palestine National Council affirms the right of the PLO to exercise its struggle responsibilities at the pan-Arab level and through any Arab land in the interest of liberating the occupied areas.

11. The Palestine National Council has decided to continue the struggle to regain the national rights of our people, in particular their rights of return, self-determination and establishing an independent national state on their national soil.

12. The Palestine National Council affirms the significance of co-operation and solidarity with socialist, non-aligned, Islamic and African countries, and with all the national liberation movements in the world.

13. The Palestine National Council hails the stands and struggles of all the democratic countries and forces against Zionism in its capacity as one form of racism, as well as against its aggressive practices.

14. The Palestine National Council affirms the significance of establishing relations and co-ordinating with the progressive and democratic Jewish forces inside and outside the occupied homeland, since these forces are struggling against Zionism as a doctrine and in practice. The Palestine National Council calls on all states and forces who love freedom, justice and peace in the world to end all forms of assistance to and co-operation with the racist Zionist regime, and to end contacts with it and its instruments.

15. Taking into consideration the important achievements in the Arab and international arenas since the conclusion of the PNC's 12th session, the Palestine National Council, which has reviewed the political report submitted by the PLO, has decided the following:

A. The Council confirms its wish for the PLO's right to participate independently and on an equal footing in all the conferences and international forums concerned with the Palestine issue and the Arab-Zionist conflict, with a view to achieving our inalienable national rights as approved by the United Nations General Assembly in 1974, namely in Resolution 3236 (*see* Documents on Palestine, page 71).

B. The Council declares that any settlement or agreement affecting the rights of our Palestinian people made in the absence of this people will be completely null and void.

Long live the Palestine Revolution. Long live Palestinian unity among the Revolution's contingents. Glory and immortality to our innocent martyrs. This Revolution will continue until victory.

RECOMMENDATIONS OF THE MILITARY COMMITTEE OF THE PALESTINE NATIONAL COUNCIL

(*approved by the Council, March 20th, 1977*)

1. Unification of the fighting forces of all the Palestinian revolutionary contingents, including the Palestinian armed struggle, the militia forces and the Palestine Liberation Army, in a united force to be named the army and the armed forces of the Palestine revolution that will be the military arm of the PLO.

2. The army and the armed forces of the Palestine revolution are to be composed of the following: (a) regular forces, to be named the Palestinian National Liberation Army, which will comprise all regular forces; (b) irregular forces; (c) the militia forces, including the youth and cubs organizations.

3. The Chairman of the PLO Executive Committee is the supreme commander of the army and the armed forces of the Palestine revolution; at the same time he will hold the position of general commander until someone is appointed to fill this post.

4. A supreme military council will be established under the leadership of the supreme commander, to include the military commanders of the organizations, the general commander and commanders of the three forces—the regular, irregular and militia forces. This council will pass the rules and regulations that are necessary to organize the army and the armed forces,

appointing the commanders, establishing the military units and laying down the plans, programme and budgets to guarantee the unification, the strengthening and development of the army and the armed forces.

5. The Palestine National Fund will undertake the task of meeting the financial needs of this army, in light of the regulations to be promulgated by the supreme military council. The organizations will pay in their commitments to the National Fund during the transitional period until financial unification is achieved.

6. All Palestinian military personnel who are not drafted into the army and the armed forces are to be considered members of the reserve, and the leadership retains the right to call them up for duty when it is deemed necessary.

7. National service is compulsory for all Palestinians in the Arab world. This will be carried out by co-ordinating with the Arab host countries, so that Palestinians serve in the Palestinian army and the armed forces.

8. Reconsideration of the military agreements that were reached between the PLO and the Arab countries in which Palestinian Liberation Army units are stationed, in order to reach new agreements that will enable the PLO's political leadership to control and command this army.

9. Confirmation of the need to step up the armed struggle in the occupied territories and to demand of the Arab confrontation states that they open their fronts for the Palestinian revolutionary forces to work against the Zionist enemy and guarantee the revolutionary forces the right to stay and operate in these countries.

10. Emphasizing of the right reserved for the Palestine struggle to retain all of its weapons in Lebanon, and its absolute right to defend the camps of our people.

11. That the Chairman of the PLO Executive Council, the general commander of the army and the armed forces of the Palestine revolution, be asked to carry out these resolutions, and that he be assisted by the supreme military council, on condition that this be done as soon as possible.

JANUARY 1979 PROGRAMME

On January 18th, 1979, the Palestine National Council adopted a "National Unity" Political and Organizational Programme which reaffirmed past policy, condemned the Camp David accords and proposed a reorganization of PLO departments.

Oil in the Middle East and North Africa

Michael Field

INTRODUCTION

A new oil crisis

In 1979 the world moved into an oil crisis that looked as if it might be every bit as severe as the crisis of 1973–4. The reduction in supply, caused by the revolution in Iran, was never as big as it was at the height of the Arab cutbacks and embargoes of late 1973; but it seemed likely to go on for longer.

Similarly the price rises that accompanied the drop in supplies were not as eyecatching in percentage terms as in 1973–4, but in actual dollar value in the January–July period of 1979 the rise was just as big. In the 15 months from October 1973 to December 1974 the cost of oil multiplied five times, rising by about $8 per barrel. In July 1979, when Saudi Arabia was holding its crudes several dollars below the levels being charged by other OPEC members, the weighted average price of Gulf crudes was $7–$8 per barrel, or 50 per cent, above 1978 levels. The OPEC secretariat calculated that this rise restored oil prices in real terms to the point they had reached at the end of 1973, though given the fall in the value of currencies, for the consumers the new rise implied less shock and a smaller transfer of wealth than the rise of 1973–4.

The crisis of 1979 began with the loss of all Iranian exports in January and February. In March production started again, but the new Iranian Government decided to run exports at less than two-thirds of the usual pre-revolution level and other OPEC states, which had raised their output during January and February, reverted to their normal levels.

Inevitably the effects of this reduction in supply took time to work their way down the pipeline to the consumers. In February the major companies who had marketed most of Iran's oil announced cutbacks in their crude oil deliveries to third parties and affiliates, making it known later that they would be phasing out third party sales altogether over the rest of the year. In the next two months the companies started "allocating" their product deliveries—rationing petrol stations and distributors to 100 per cent of 1978's supplies (not allowing for the growth in demand) or making cuts of up to 20 per cent below this level.

The first serious shortages at the pump showed up in early May in California and Ireland, where there happened to be particularly strong growth in demand for petrol in early 1979. In California Governor Jerry Brown announced a form of rationing involving cars with odd licence numbers being able to fill up on odd days and even licence numbers on even days. In Greece the Government introduced a system of allowing odd numbers to drive one weekend and even numbers to drive the next. It also lowered speed limits, banned late night advertising displays and announced that heating oil would be rationed in the winter. In Belgium the Government rationed oil to industry and stopped the illumination of public buildings and in Denmark speed limits were reduced and restrictions were put on display lighting and temperatures in public buildings.

Elsewhere it was left to the market to cut demand with price rises and local shortages. The members of the International Energy Agency, which was founded after the 1973–4 crisis to co-ordinate consumer policies and share supplies should there be a shortfall of more than 7 per cent, resolved in March to cut their demand by 5 per cent below the levels projected for 1979. In practice it was the shortfall in supply and the recessionary effect of the price rises, more than conservation measures, that did most to cut back consumption, especially in the U.S.A., which performed better than most other IEA members.

The IEA programme was backed up by the summit meeting of the leaders of the seven major industrial democracies in Tokyo at the end of June. The leaders agreed a series of target levels for each country's imports six years hence in 1985. At both this meeting, and at the IEA meetings every two months or so, there was some emphasis on not panicking the general public and on avoiding more than the minimum necessary curbs so as not to damage economic growth and employment. In all countries the worst fears were focused on stock levels. In the spring and summer, stocks were being run down throughout the industrialized world, and if they were not rebuilt sufficiently by the winter a shortage of heating oil would have much more severe economic consequences than a shortage of petrol in the summer.

It was also recognized by governments everywhere—if not by members of the public—that the Iranian revolution had only brought forward a crisis that had seemed bound to occur at some point in the 1980s.

Part of the problem was that since the end of the 1973–4 crisis no large new reserves of oil had been discovered, except in Mexico. One of the most recent disappointments has been in the Baltimore Canyon, off the coast of New Jersey, where over a dozen holes drilled between the start of operations in early 1978 and March 1979 yielded only one gas find. The oil industry's reassessment of this once promising area was reflected in the paltry bidding for new leases at an auction in February 1979.

Equally serious has been the poor performance of the consumer countries in diversifying into other sources of energy, though their failure has not been total. There has been some encouraging progress with solar power, though this is very much a marginal source, and some countries that are particularly dependent on imported oil have launched serious diversification programmes. Between 1972 and 1978 Denmark reduced its dependence on oil from 93 per cent of total energy needs to 78 per cent, while France has embarked on a major nuclear power programme. This programme is being pushed ahead despite the accident in early 1979 at the Three Mile Island in

Pennsylvania, which is increasing the public's anxieties about nuclear reactors elsewhere in the world.

More important for the world in the long term has been the difficulty consumers have had in cutting energy use over and above the cuts caused by recession in recent years. But here again the picture is not entirely black. In the United States fuel-efficient imported cars are commanding an ever-larger share of the market. On a broader scale it appears that there may have been a change in the relationship of energy to economic growth. Where energy demand grew at an average of around 1.1 to 1.2 per cent per annum for every 1 per cent growth in GNP in the period 1965–73, the rate has fallen to considerably less than 1 per cent in most countries since the crisis. Changes in technology and the gradual emergence of less energy intensive technologies as the engines of growth may be part of the explanation. At the same time it seems that consumers are at least more aware of energy costs.

It is the United States, whose citizens consume twice as much energy per head as the citizens of Western Europe or Japan, that is having most difficulty in changing its energy consumption habits. Indeed, opinion polls show that a large number of Americans simply do not believe that their country imports oil, while many more do not think that there is any crisis. These attitudes have been reinforced by distrust of the oil companies and government in Washington, and by the sudden West coast oil glut in 1978 caused by the arrival of Alaskan oil.

It was against this background that President Carter's first series of energy measures was mauled by Congress. These were introduced in April 1977 as "the moral equivalent of war", and passed into law in October 1978. The raising of the price of domestic crude oil, which had been one of its cornerstones, was removed from the bill altogether, while domestic natural gas, on which the President had intended to maintain reduced controls, is now eventually to become decontrolled entirely. At the same time the punitive clauses against "gas guzzling" cars and against the refusal of industry to convert to coal were both substantially watered down. Whereas the original intention was to cut imports by 4.5 million barrels a day (b/d) on projected levels by 1985, even on the most optimistic assumptions the October act was unlikely to reduce imports by more than 2.5 million b/d.

The President introduced a second series of proposals in April 1979, based around the decontrol of domestic oil prices between June 1979 and September 1981 and a windfall profits tax to claw back some of the extra revenues that would accrue to the oil companies. The decontrol plan, which did not affect Alaskan oil or oil from dying "stripper" wells both of which were already decontrolled, did not require Congressional approval, though the profit tax did. Both measures ran into immediate opposition from powerful Congressional lobbies which hoped to persuade the President to modify decontrol by withholding co-operation on other aspects of the package. A large body of Congressional opinion from the consumer states of the north-east, which have traditionally been distrustful of the major companies and the oil lobby of the southern states, felt that there was just not that much more oil to be discovered in the U.S.A., and that there was therefore little point in giving the companies more profits to finance intensified exploration.

Over the next three months, however, the public became increasingly frustrated, confused and angry about the energy problem, and Congressional attitudes towards electorally unpopular measures became less parochial. In response to the crisis, the severest challenge to his leadership that he had experienced during his presidency, Mr. Carter introduced a new series of proposals in mid-July. These aimed at cutting imports by 4.5 million b/d below what they were otherwise expected to be in 1990. The major proposals were for the creation of a $88,000 million Energy Security Corporation for the development of "synthetic" oils from coal, tar sands and shales, and the establishment of an Energy Mobilization Board to cut through red tape, including certain environmental restrictions, and speed oil exploration and the construction of new energy facilities. Given the new mood of Congress and the fact that several parts of the measures were already before Congress in one form or another, it was expected that much of the new package, plus the windfall profits tax, would pass into law fairly quickly.

At the same time as the Americans and the consumers in general have been having problems in cutting demand for OPEC oil, the exporters have been becoming more reluctant to increase supply. In mid-1979 there was a lot of OPEC capacity shut-in or not being developed; Saudi Arabia, Iran, Libya and Kuwait could all produce at least 1 million b/d more than they were producing .What is important, though, is that in other OPEC members, Venezuela and Algeria, production is already running down or about to begin running down. Meanwhile in the last few years Iran and Saudi Arabia, the two biggest OPEC producers, have realized that their maximum sustainable production will be substantially lower than they had earlier assumed.

This happened in Iran in 1975, when the Shah's Government realized that far from being able to install capacity of 8 million barrels a day it would have to make massive investments to achieve and sustain 6 million b/d.

In Saudi Arabia the limits of sustainable capacity have been recognized more gradually. In 1972 the Saudis were talking of producing 20 million b/d (if they were given the right incentives) but by 1977 it was understood that the Government was aiming at a capacity target of 16 million b/d by 1982. In the last two years this target too has been trimmed, mainly as a result of pressure problems and possible over-production of some of the biggest Saudi fields. Aramco has calculated, on the basis of probable Saudi reserves being about 180,000 million barrels, that a 16 million b/d production rate starting in 1990 could be sustained for only 2 to 7 years. Starting in the early 1980s a rate of 12 million b/d could be maintained for 15 to 20 years Equally alarming for the Saudis has been the calculation that capacity cannot be raised to 16 million b/d for less than $25,000 million.

At present Saudi Arabia has the capacity to *sustain* production (for six months or more) at 10 million b/d, and the government is working on a plan to raise this to 10.8 million b/d in 1983 and 11.2–12.0 million b/d in 1987. These figures would imply a "surge capacity" of about 1 million b/d higher.

The geological constraints on Iranian and Saudi production policy have been reinforced by conservationist political pressures. It is the policy of the new Government in Iran not to run output at more than 4 million b/d, while in Saudi Arabia the "normal" ceiling is 8.5 million b/d. These policies are based on the realization that the world is likely to be dependent on oil for much longer than was expected in 1974, while the producers are likely to be dependent on oil revenues for longer than expected.

Furthermore in Saudi Arabia, where there has always been a strong conservationist lobby in the royal family and in the Government outside the family, these considerations have recently been strengthened by observation of what has happened in Iran. One of the main lessons of the Iranian revolution for other Middle Eastern oil producers is that fast spending financed by high rates of oil production is socially destabilising. At the same time the Saudis are much less sympathetic to the United States's energy problems since President Carter pushed through the Egyptian-Israeli peace treaty. This treaty destroyed the foundation of Saudi Arabia's regional policy by making the continuation of the Riyadh-Cairo axis impossible, it increased the strength of the radicals in the Arab world (not least in bringing about a rapprochement between Syria and Iraq), and it pushed the Saudis uneasily into the radicals' camp. With the Kingdom's influence in the Arab world much impaired, and its confidence shaken by the Iranian revolution and communist encroachments on the borders of the region (in Afghanistan, Ethiopia and southern Yemen), the Saudi rulers no longer feel able to take a strong lead in OPEC.

For all of these reasons the Saudi oil minister, Shaikh Ahmed Zaki Yamani, explained early in 1979 that Saudi Arabia's power in the market was much diminished. In the past it seemed that the maintenance of spare Saudi capacity of 2 million b/d would be enough to undermine excessive price rises by other OPEC members. However, a reassessment of the engineering difficulties and the costs, both financial and political, of this policy, has now made it seem to the Saudis not worthwhile. And anyway there would never have been any chance of Saudi Arabia maintaining sufficient spare capacity to make up the size of shortfall that occurred when Iran stopped production entirely in early 1979.

It looks therefore as if the world faces a period of chronic marginal shortage of oil. This does not mean that the world is "running out of oil", but it does mean that there will be a pattern of periodic shortages of different products in different places. To avoid these shortages it would be necessary to maintain stocks of all products in all countries and regions at levels which will probably prove to be impossible. At the same time it will take smaller political disruptions than in the past to create new crises.

For the Western world the outlook is serious. In the medium and long term the ministers at an IEA meeting in Paris in May concluded that "if nothing is done to change present trends, available energy supplies will not be sufficient to support even moderate growth".

In the shorter term governments and oil companies are finding it difficult to make the public understand that although there is not a crisis in a dramatic sense, there is the prospect of a continuing slight imbalance in the market which will have serious long term consequences and which can only be corrected by taking real conservation measures. In explaining the problem there is no better parallel to be drawn than that of the stretched budget of Mr Micawber: "Annual income twenty pounds, annual expenditure nineteen pounds nineteen and six, result happiness. Annual income twenty pounds, annual expenditure twenty pounds nought and six, result misery."

OWNERSHIP OF THE INDUSTRY

Concessions

Until the end of 1972 the bulk of the Middle East's and North Africa's output was produced under the traditional concession agreements. The first of the concessions was granted in 1901 in Iran by Muzzaffareddin Shah to William Knox D'Arcy, a wealthy prospector who had made a fortune out of gold mining in Australia, in return for £20,000 in cash and the promise of a further £20,000 in shares. After a number of dry holes and an acute financial crisis, oil was finally discovered in 1908 at Masjid-i-Sulaiman, and just before the beginning of the First World War, the Anglo-Persian Oil Company which had been formed to take over the concession, began exports through the port of Abadan. (APOC was renamed the Anglo-Iranian Oil Company in 1935 and British Petroleum in 1954.)

During the 1920s and 1930s further concessions were granted in Iraq and in the states of the Arabian Peninsula—and in every case the concessionaire companies were made up chiefly by members of the seven major oil companies which have dominated the world oil business throughout this century. In approximate order of size these were: Standard Oil of New Jersey (which changed its name to Exxon in 1972 and markets its products in Europe under the name Esso), the Royal Dutch-Shell group, Texaco, Standard Oil of California (known as Socal and marketing as Chevron), Mobil, Gulf and British Petroleum. The only other company to participate in the early days was Compagnie Française des Pétroles (marketing as Total), which is considerably smaller than the big seven, but is often regarded as an eighth major company because of the world-wide spread of its operations.

Under the original terms of their concessions, these companies were given exclusive rights for drilling, production, sales, the ownership at the wellhead of all oil produced, and immunity from taxes and customs dues. The governments' receipts, apart from an initial downpayment and a rental, came either as a share of profits (which is how Iran's income was worked out until 1933, when Iran negotiated a fixed royalty plus share of company dividends formula) or as a fixed royalty of four gold shillings a ton (22 cents a barrel).

In view of the vast amounts of oil discovered during the 1930s and 1940s, and the extremely low cost of production, the Middle Eastern governments by the later 1940s no longer felt that the companies had been as generous as they had originally believed, and with the growing sophistication of the local populations in this period, all aspects of the concessions began to come under attack. The main complaints, apart from criticism of the financial terms, were that the concessions were too large in area and their duration too long, that they were run almost entirely by foreign nationals, that the companies had appropriated for themselves a quasi-colonial authority, and that the host governments had no control over the amount of drilling carried out nor the volume of exports. The strength of the producers' feelings was only reinforced when Kuwait in 1948 and Saudi Arabia in 1949 granted concessions in their respective halves of the Neutral Zone (now known as the Partitioned Zone) to American independent companies, Aminoil and Getty, on conditions which were very much more favourable than those obtained earlier from the Kuwait Oil Company (BP and Gulf) and Aramco (Exxon, Socal, Texaco and Mobil).

The major change in the financial terms of the concessions which followed did not, however, stem from events in the Middle East, but from Venezuela, where, after the first free elections in the country's history, the Acción Democrática party in November 1948 passed an income tax law giving the Government 50 per cent of the companies' profits. A year later the Venezuelans sent a delegation to the Gulf to explain the advantages of the new legislation, and the companies, realizing that such a revolutionary change could not be confined to one country, and that they would be able to deduct tax payments made abroad from tax paid in their home countries, promptly offered the same deal to the Middle Eastern governments. Under the new system, introduced in Saudi Arabia at the end of 1950 and in Iraq and Kuwait a few months later, the companies' "profits", arrived at by deducting the production cost per barrel from the posted price, were divided equally between the companies and the governments. Assuming that no special discounts off the posted price were given, this arrangement increased the producers' revenue per barrel from 22 cents to about 80 cents.

The only country not to receive the 50-50 profit split at this time was Iran. Despite various revisions in concession terms during the inter-war years, relations between Anglo-Iranian and the Government were bedevilled not only by financial disputes, but also by the Iranian population's view of the company as the symbol of their country's subjugation to foreign influence and of Britain's colonial power—which had involved Iran being invaded in 1941 (so that the allies could secure a supply route to the Soviet armies in the Caucasus) and Reza Shah being deported to Mauritius. In 1949, Anglo-Iranian and the Government resolved their differences in a Supplemental Agreement which gave Iran royalty and profit-sharing terms as good as those concluded in the Arab states a year and a half later. But the Iranian National Assembly was dissatisfied with the deal, and during the following months, Dr. Mohammed Mossadeq, an extreme nationalist demagogue and chairman of the Assembly's Oil Committee, managed to discredit the Agreement totally in the eyes of the Iranian people. In December 1950, the Government, which had hoped that it would be able to solve the issue peacefully by negotiating minor revisions, was forced to renounce the Agreement altogether. Anglo-Iranian immediately suggested further talks leading to a 50-50 settlement, while Mossadeq in February 1951 suggested nationalization, and, with Iran slipping into a state of internal chaos, the Shah on May 1st was forced to give his assent to the nationalization bill and appoint Mossadeq as Prime Minister.

Over the next two years, Mossadeq refused all compromise solutions offered to him, Iranian oil exports, embargoed by all the companies, came rapidly to a halt, and the economy collapsed. In July 1953, having tried to dismiss Mossadeq, the Shah was forced to flee to Rome; but within a few days, Mossadeq was overthrown by a *coup*, and the Shah returned in triumph. In the subsequent negotiations, the principle of nationalization was recognized, but the National Iranian Oil Company was forced to grant a lease (which was a concession in all but name) incorporating the 50-50 profit split to Iranian Oil Participants (known as "The Consortium") made up of BP, Shell, CFP and the five U.S. majors—who were later obliged by the U.S. Government to give a 5 per cent shareholding to a group of U.S. independents.

The Mossadeq debacle provided a reminder of the strength of the majors and although in 1961 the revolutionary government of General Kassem expropriated more than 99.5 per cent of the concession held by the Iraq Petroleum Company group (BP, Shell, CFP, Exxon, Mobil and Gulbenkian), on the grounds that this area was not being exploited by the companies, no Middle Eastern government again nationalized an important productive operation until 1971—when Algeria seized a majority share of the local operations of CFP and the French state company, ERAP.

Partnerships, contracts and production sharing

Although, at the time, the nationalization of AIOC was a disaster for Iran, the dispute did at least mark the end of the period in which Middle Eastern governments gave 75 or 95 year concessions, covering their whole country, to a single group. What new concessions were signed in the Arabian Peninsula states during the later 1950s and 1960s had a duration of 35 to 45 years, covered much smaller areas, and contained relatively tough terms, with bigger signature bonuses and provisions for the rapid relinquishment of acreage. Even in Libya, where the financial terms of the concessions let at the end of the 1950s were considerably more generous than those applying in the Gulf, the available acreage was divided among more than ten different groups.

From 1957 the concession concept itself began to be replaced by new arrangements giving the state a degree of direct participation, and placing heavier financial burdens and greater risks on the companies—which the producers discovered the American independents and the European national companies were prepared to accept for the sake of gaining a foothold in the Middle East. The first of the new arrangements was the partnership of Société Irano-Italienne des Pétroles (SIRIP) between the National Iranian Oil Company and the Italian state concern ENI, under which ENI's subsidiary, AGIP, agreed to bear the whole exploration cost (only to be repaid half if oil was found), and guaranteed to spend not less than $22 million on exploration. It was arranged that half of any oil produced would be owned by NIOC and sold by AGIP on the Iranians' behalf, while half would be owned by the Italian company and taxed at the normal 50 per cent rate—giving the Government a 75-25 profit split, together with valuable experience.

One year later the Iranians substantially improved their terms in a partnership with Amoco (a subsidiary of Standard Oil of Indiana), and during the early 1960s and early 1970s, they signed further partnerships containing cash bonuses, production bonuses, minimum exploration guarantees and minimum development expenditure guarantees. Four of these partnerships were in production in 1978.

With certain variations the Iranians' example was followed in the allocation of new acreage by Saudi Arabia and Kuwait in the Neutral Zone (where in 1957, a few months after the formation of SIRIP, the two countries obtained a stake of 10 per cent each when offshore acreage was let to a group of Japanese companies), by Kuwait on its own territory, by Algeria (where all acreage let since 1973 has been on a partnership basis), and by Egypt. In other countries, Saudi Arabia, Qatar, Abu Dhabi, Tunisia and Kuwait (with its offshore areas granted to Shell), the governments have concluded carried interest arrangements, where acreage has been let originally as a concession, with the proviso that the state has the right to negotiate a shareholding once oil is discovered. In few cases have these ventures been successful, so the carried interest charges have seldom come into operation. In all countries, the tax terms have been adjusted to reflect current OPEC rates.

In 1966 Iran led the way again by introducing the still more radical idea of service contracts when it let relinquished Consortium acreage to a French group, SOFIRAN. Like the foreign companies in partnership arrangements, SOFIRAN agreed to bear the whole cost of exploration; but if oil was struck it was to be refunded completely, and NIOC was also to provide all capital for development. NIOC was to be the sole owner of all oil produced, while the foreign contractor was to act as a broker for the national company on a commission of 2 per cent of the realized price, being paid by the guaranteed purchase of between 35 per cent and 45 per cent of production at cost plus 2 per cent. Fifty per cent of the difference between this sum and the realized price was to be payable as income tax—though when oil was brought on stream the financial terms were to be adjusted.

After 1966 Iran signed a further seven service contracts, the most recent (in 1974) allowing the foreign companies to purchase about half of production at discounts of up to 5 per cent, though only SOFIRAN brought oil on stream. Iraq signed three contracts, one of which, involving ERAP, brought the Buzurgan, Abu Ghrab and Fuka fields on stream. None of the other Middle Eastern or North African states has concluded contracts, but not dissimilar production sharing arrangements, on modified Indonesian lines, have been concluded by Egypt (which invited Western companies to bid for new acreage in 1973, following a period in which oil exploration had been given over to the Soviet Union), and by Libya in 1974. More recently Syria has signed a number of production sharing agreements, allowing Western companies into the country for the first time since 1964. There are considerable variations in this type of agreement, but in most cases the foreign company is compensated for its share of expenditure in cash or kind, or by favourable tax terms, while production is divided in a ratio of between 72-25 and 85-15 in favour of the state.

After the Iranian revolution, it was announced in May 1979 that the Government was thinking of ending its four successful partnerships—SIRIP, IPAC (with Amoco), LAPCO (with Arco, Murphy, Sun and Unocal) and IMINOCO (with AGIP, Phillips and the Indian Oil and Natural Gas Commission). No mention was made of SOFIRAN.

The drive for participation, and Algerian takeovers

Parallel with the development of partnerships and contracts on new acreage, the 1960s saw a growing desire on the part of the producer governments for participation in existing concessions. This idea was originally put by Saudi Arabia to Aramco in 1964, and in 1968 it was given formal voice in OPEC's Declaratory Statement of Petroleum Policy. Apart from being satisfactory on nationalist grounds, and giving the producers a more direct say in such matters as the relinquishment of acreage, the employment of nationals, production rates and investment in new capacity, the governments felt that participation would give them a foothold in the oil industry, which would later enable them to mount their own crude oil sales operations, or expand their national companies downstream into the tankering, refining and marketing business. The producers, however, did not feel strong enough to press their claim until after the appearance of a sellers market and their success in the Teheran price negotiations of February 1971; and so it was not until OPEC's Twenty-fifth Conference in Vienna in July 1971 that the members announced that they were going to call the companies to formal talks on participation.

By this time a precedent had already been set by Algeria. For political reasons Algeria had nationalized its American concessionaires and Shell in 1967, without causing itself economic harm. This left the French companies, CFP and ERAP, which were responsible

[*continued on p.* 94

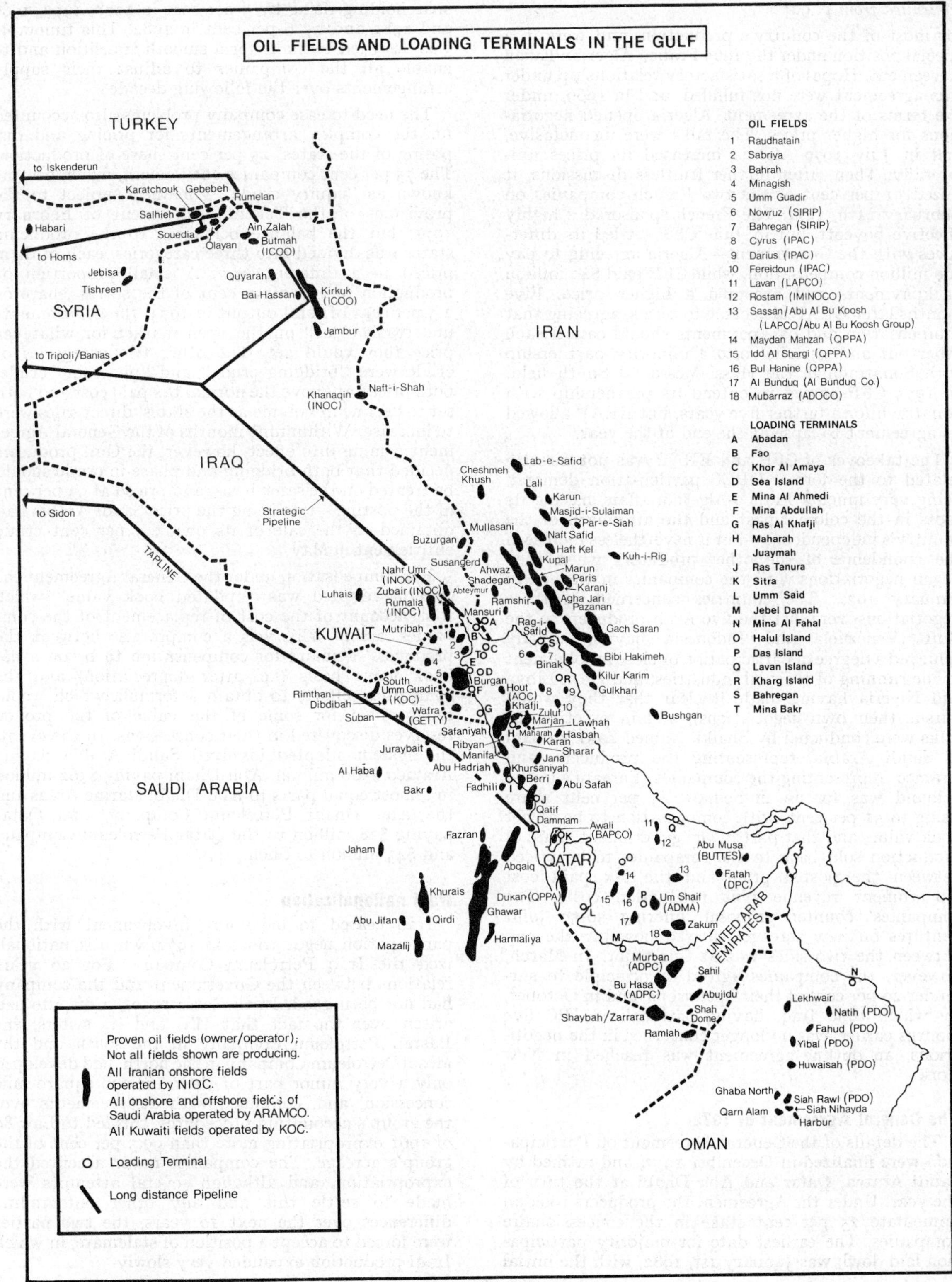
OIL FIELDS AND LOADING TERMINALS IN THE GULF
TURKEY
SYRIA
IRAQ
IRAN
KUWAIT
SAUDI ARABIA
QATAR
UNITED ARAB EMIRATES
OMAN
to Iskenderun
to Homs
to Tripoli/Banias
to Sidon
TAPLINE
Strategic Pipeline
Karatchouk
Gebebeh
Rumelan
Salhieh
Souedia
Olayan
Ain Zalah
Butmah (ICOO)
Habari
Jebisa
Tishreen
Quyarah
Bai Hassan
Kirkuk (ICOO)
Jambur
Naft-i-Shah
Khanaqin (INOC)
Cheshmeh Khush
Lab-e-Safid
Lali
Karun
Masjid-i-Sulaiman
Par-e-Siah
Mullasani
Naft Safid
Haft Kel
Buzurgan
Susangerd
Kuh-i-Rig
Kupal
Marun
Ahwaz
Paris
Karanj
Nahr Umr (INOC)
Shadegan
Zubair (INOC)
Abteymur
Ramshir
Agha Jari
Pazanan
Luhais
Rumalia (INOC)
Mansuri
Rag-i-Safid
Gach Saran
Mutribah
Bibi Hakimeh
Binak
Kilur Karim
Gulkhari
South
Umm Guadir (KOC)
Burgan
Hout (AOC)
Rimthan
Dibdibah
Khafji
Suban
Wafra (GETTY)
Zuluf
Marjan
Lawhah
Bushgan
Safaniyah
Maharah
Hasbah
Ribyan
Karan
Sharar
Juraybait
Manifa
Jana
Abu Hadriah
Khursaniyah
Al Haba
Berri
Abu Safah
Bakr
Fadhili
Qatif
Dammam
Awali (BAPCO)
Fazran
Abqaiq
Abu Musa (BUTTES)
Jaham
Fatah (DPC)
Khurais
Dukan (QPPA)
Um Shait (ADMA)
Ghawar
Zakum
Abu Jifan
Qirdi
Harmaliya
Mazalij
Murban (ADPC)
Sahil
Bu Hasa (ADPC)
Abujidu
Shah Dome
Shaybah/Zarrara
Ramlah
Lekhwair
Natih (PDO)
Fahud (PDO)
Yibal (PDO)
Huwaisah (PDO)
Ghaba North
Siah Rawl (PDO)
Qarn Alam
Siah Nihayda
Harbur
OIL FIELDS
1 Raudhatain
2 Sabriya
3 Bahrah
4 Minagish
5 Umm Guadir
6 Nowruz (SIRIP)
7 Bahregan (SIRIP)
8 Cyrus (IPAC)
9 Darius (IPAC)
10 Fereidoun (IPAC)
11 Lavan (LAPCO)
12 Rostam (IMINOCO)
13 Sassan/Abu Al Bu Koosh (LAPCO/Abu Al Bu Koosh Group)
14 Maydan Mahzan (QPPA)
15 Idd Al Shargi (QPPA)
16 Bul Hanine (QPPA)
17 Al Bunduq (Al Bunduq Co.)
18 Mubarraz (ADOCO)
LOADING TERMINALS
A Abadan
B Fao
C Khor Al Amaya
D Sea Island
E Mina Al Ahmedi
F Mina Abdullah
G Ras Al Khafji
H Maharah
I Juaymah
J Ras Tanura
K Sitra
L Umm Said
M Jebel Dannah
N Mina Al Fahal
O Halul Island
P Das Island
Q Lavan Island
R Kharg Island
S Bahregan
T Mina Bakr
Proven oil fields (owner/operator); Not all fields shown are producing.
All Iranian onshore fields operated by NIOC.
All onshore and offshore fields of Saudi Arabia operated by ARAMCO.
All Kuwaiti fields operated by KOC.
Loading Terminal
Long distance Pipeline

continued from p. 92]

for most of the country's production, and were in a special position under the 1965 Franco-Algerian Evian Agreement. Hopes of a satisfactory relationship under this agreement were not fulfilled, and in 1969, under the terms of the agreement, Algeria opened negotiations for higher prices. The talks were inconclusive, and in July 1970 Algeria increased its prices unilaterally. Then, after further fruitless discussions, it seized 51 per cent of the two French companies on February 24th, 1971. The French sponsored a highly effective boycott, but in June CFP settled its differences with the Government—Algeria agreeing to pay $60 million compensation, while CFP paid $40 million backpayments and accepted a higher price. Five months later ERAP also came to terms, agreeing that compensation and backpayments should cancel each other out and entering into a minority partnership with Sonatrach in the Hassi Messaoud South field. In 1975 CFP agreed to extend its partnership with Sonatrach for a further five years, but ERAP allowed its agreement to lapse at the end of the year.

The takeover of CFP and ERAP was not directly related to the formal OPEC participation demand, being very much a Franco-Algerian affair, having its roots in the colonial past and the aftermath of the country's independence—but it nevertheless increased the confidence of the other producers when they began negotiations with the companies in Geneva in January 1972. The countries concerned in these negotiations were just the five Arab producers in the Gulf (Venezuela and Indonesia having already achieved a degree of participation or close involvement in the running of their oil industries, and Iran, Libya and Nigeria having made it clear that they would pursue their own negotiations), and in practice the talks were conducted by Shaikh Ahmed Zaki Yamani of Saudi Arabia, representing the producers, and Aramco, representing the companies. Yamani's initial demand was for an immediate 25 per cent share rising to 51 per cent, with compensation to be at net book value, and that part of the government share of production sold back to the companies to be priced between the posted price and the tax paid cost (government revenue plus production cost). The companies' counter proposal, offering 50-50 joint ventures on new acreage, showed how big the gap between the two sides was at this point. In March, however, the companies agreed in principle to surrender 20 per cent of their operations, and in October, by which time Iraq, having nationalized IPC five months earlier, was no longer concerned in the negotiations, an outline agreement was reached in New York.

The General Agreement of 1972

The details of the General Agreement on Participation were finalized in December 1972, and ratified by Saudi Arabia, Qatar and Abu Dhabi at the turn of the year. Under the Agreement the producers took an immediate 25 per cent stake in the concessionaire companies. The earliest date for majority participation laid down was January 1st, 1982, with the initial shareholding rising by 5 per cent in 1978, 1979, 1980 and 1981 and by 6 per cent in 1982. This timetable was designed to make for a smooth transition and to enable all the companies to adjust their supply arrangements over the following decade.

The need to ease company problems also accounted for the complex arrangements for pricing and disposing of the states' 25 per cent share of production. The 75 per cent companies entitlement, which became known as "equity crude" remained subject to the provisions of the Teheran Agreement of February 1971, but the balance belonging to the producing states was divided into three categories, each of them priced in a different way. A small proportion of production (only 10 per cent of the states' share or 2.5 per cent of total output in 1973) the governments undertook to sell on the open market for whatever price they could get. The other two categories of crude were "bridging crude" and "phase in" crude, both priced at above the normal tax paid cost and both set to decline in volume as the states' direct sales were to increase. Within nine months of the General Agreement coming into effect, however, the Gulf producers decided that both bridging and phase-in crude should be treated on the same basis, and priced at 93 per cent of the posting—this being the price Saudi Arabia had obtained in the sale of its own 2.5 per cent crude entitlement in May.

For compensation under the General Agreement the criteria adopted was "updated book value" which took account of the cost of replacement of the companies' assets. This was a compromise between the producers' demand for compensation to be on a net book value basis (i.e. after depreciation) and the companies' efforts to obtain a formula which would repay them for some of the value of the proven reserves discovered in their concessions. In the event, the system adopted involved Saudi Arabia paying Aramco $500 million, Abu Dhabi paying $162 million in almost equal parts to Abu Dhabi Marine Areas and the Abu Dhabi Petroleum Company, and Qatar paying $28 million to the Qatar Petroleum Company and $43 million to Shell.

Iraqi nationalization

Iraq ceased to have any involvement with the participation negotiations in 1972, when it nationalized the Iraq Petroleum Company. For 20 years relations between the Government and the company had not been good. In the later 1950s, a dispute had arisen over the fact that IPC and its sisters, the Basrah Petroleum Company in the south and the Mosul Petroleum Company in the north, had developed only a very minor part of their 160,000 square mile concession, and, combined with disagreements over the group's accounting procedures, this led to Law 80 of 1961 expropriating more than 99.5 per cent of the group's acreage. The companies never accepted the expropriation, and although several attempts were made to settle this and any other outstanding differences over the next 10 years, the two parties were forced to accept a position of stalemate, in which Iraqi production expanded very slowly.

In June 1971, as part of the agreement on Iraqi Mediterranean crude prices which followed the Teheran pact in February, the IPC group gave commitments for increases in production, but in the following spring, the company found itself obliged to cut the throughput of its pipeline from Kirkuk to the Mediterranean terminals of Banias (Syria) and Tripoli (Lebanon). The company explained that in a period of low Gulf/Europe freight rates, the high prices negotiated for all Mediterranean crudes in the previous years made it uneconomic for its owners to run the pipe at more than half capacity. The Iraqi Government claimed that the cut-back was politically motivated, and presented IPC with alternatives: either the company was to restore Kirkuk production to normal levels and hand the extra production over to the Government, or it was to surrender the field entirely and concentrate production on BPC's acreage in the south. This conflict was further exacerbated by IPC's threats of legal action to prevent the sale of the Iraq National Oil Company's crude from North Rumaila (in expropriated BPC acreage), and by a number of old issues, including an Iraqi claim for royalty backpayments dating from 1964, which IPC had refused to pay until it received the compensation it was claiming for the acreage expropriated in 1971. On May 31st, IPC presented its answers to the Iraqi ultimatum. These did not satisfy the Government, and on the next day, IPC was nationalized. The affiliates, BPC and MPC, were not immediately affected.

In mid-July, negotiations got underway, with Nadim Pachachi, then Secretary-General of OPEC, and M. Jean Duroc-Danner of CFP, acting as mediators. IPC promptly announced that it would not pursue legal action against buyers of Kirkuk crude while mediation efforts were in progress, and the Iraqis were then able to sell substantial amounts of oil—including a deal in February 1973 under which CFP agreed to take 23.75 per cent of Kirkuk's output (equivalent to the company's stake in IPC) over ten years. On February 28th, 1973, IPC and the Government finally reached agreement. IPC accepted the expropriations of 1961 and the nationalization of the Kirkuk producing area, and at the same time handed over MPC and paid the Government $141 million of outstanding royalty backpayments. In return it was promised 15 million tons of oil in two batches in 1973 and 1974, and was given some assurance of the long-term security of its investment and growth of output from BPC's southern fields, where it agreed to more than double production from 640,000 b/d in 1972 to 1,626,000 b/d in 1976.

In the event, it was only seven months before BPC suffered the seizure, during the October war, of the holdings of Exxon and Mobil, and 60 per cent of Shell's share (a proportion relating to the Dutch-registered part of the group) as a political gesture against the U.S.A.'s and the Netherlands' association with Israel. Later the 5 per cent share of the Participations and Explorations Corporations (owned by the Gulbenkian family) was seized on the grounds that the company was registered in Portugal, which was pursuing racist policies in Africa. Thereafter the Government watched the progress of the takeover negotiations in Saudi Arabia and Kuwait, and a few days after a final agreement had been signed in Kuwait, it nationalized the remaining Western-owned share in BPC. It then held negotiations with the BPC partners over compensation and supply arrangements.

Iranian Sales and Purchase Agreement

Although it was clear from the beginning of the Saudi Arabian-Aramco negotiations in January 1972 that Iran was not interested in the type of participation envisaged by the Gulf states, the Shah did not decide exactly what Iran would demand instead until early 1973. On January 23rd the Shah gave the Consortium an ultimatum: under no circumstances would Iran extend its lease, and the companies could either continue under existing arrangements until the expiry of their lease in 1979 and then become ordinary buyers under contract, or they could negotiate an entirely new agency agreement immediately. The Consortium opted for the latter plan, and, under the Iranian Sales and Purchase Agreement signed in Tehran in May, NIOC took formal control of the management of the Consortium's entire production operation and the Abadan refinery. The agreement laid down that NIOC would provide 60 per cent of the capital for expanding production and that the companies would contribute 40 per cent of the funds needed in the first five years (then expected to be the period of greatest expansion) in return for a 22 cents discount on their liftings.

Under the Sales and Purchase Agreement, though NIOC became owner/manager, the Consortium members established a service company, the Oil Service Company of Iran (OSCO), to carry out operations for an initial period of five years, which could be renewed. NIOC undertook to raise total installed production capacity to 8 million b/d by October 1976. It was agreed that the national company would be entitled to take the oil needed for internal consumption and a "stated quantity" for export, which was to rise from 200,000 b/d in 1973 to 1.5 million b/d in 1981, and therefore, except in certain cases of *force majeure*, would remain in the same proportion to total crude available for export as 1.5 million b/d represented to oil available for export in 1981. The balance of crude production went to the Consortium members, which were guaranteed security of supply for 20 years.

Libya asserts 51 per cent control

It was only a matter of weeks after OPEC had made its formal call for participation in July 1971 that Libya, ever anxious to be first among the producers in militancy and to upstage any participation agreement negotiated by Saudi Arabia, let it be known that it would be interested in nothing less than an immediate 51 per cent share. Four months later, at the beginning of December 1971, Libya nationalized outright BP's half-share of the Sarir field, but this was a purely political gesture (against alleged British connivance in the Iranian invasion of the Tumbs Islands some 24 hours before Britain's withdrawal from the Gulf)—and for the next year the Libyan Government made no move while it awaited the outcome of the participation negotiations in the Gulf.

Talks on Libya's demand for majority control eventually began in early 1973, with the Government adopting its usual policy of negotiating on a company by company basis; but they made no progress. In June Libya nationalized outright the U.S. independent Nelson Bunker Hunt. This company had been BP's 50 per cent partner in the Sarir field, and the Government had chosen it for its first negotiations because it had no other source of oil outside the U.S. and seemed therefore to be especially vulnerable. Bunker Hunt, however, resisted hard. Being a private company it did not have shareholders to worry about and it was confident in the Libyan operators' secret agreement, under which the companies had promised to meet the supply commitments of any one of their number whose concession was expropriated. Colonel Gaddafi, the Libyan leader, correctly characterized the Bunker Hunt seizure as "a warning to the companies to respond to the demands of the Libyan Arab Republic". From circumstantial evidence it seems that Libya fully decided on nationalizing Bunker Hunt when it concluded that it would have no difficulty in selling the oil to markets apart from the East bloc. This followed the judgement of a local court in Sicily which dismissed a suit brought by BP against the importers and refiners of its expropriated Sarir oil.

Following its nationalization of Bunker Hunt, the Libyan Government proceeded in August to seize 51 per cent of Occidental's operations. Faced with the threat of having the rest of its assets seized and being deprived of its most vital source of oil outside the U.S., Occidental announced its "acquiescence" in the measure. For the other companies the significance of this "acquiescence" lay in the fiscal terms. The companies had in fact been prepared to offer Libya a nominal 51 per cent on the condition that the financial results gave parity with those deriving from the participation agreements with the Gulf producers and Nigeria—but this was not the case in the terms settled with Occidental. Compensation was agreed on at book value, rather than the updated book value formula used in the Gulf, and the buy-back price was set above the posting, rather than between the posting and the tax paid cost.

Five days after the Occidental seizure, three independent companies in the Oasis group, Continental, Marathon and Amerada Hess, accepted a majority takeover on similar terms, though Shell, the only major in Oasis, did not comply with the measure. Then in September the Government announced 51 per cent takeovers of all the other significant producing groups. Gelsenberg, a German concern in partnership with Mobil, and W. R. Grace, a small shareholder in the Esso Sirte venture, agreed to Libya's terms; but Atlantic Richfield (another partner in Esso Sirte) and the majors, Mobil, Esso (which held a concession on its own as well as the biggest share in Esso Sirte) and the Texaco-Socal company, Amoseas, joined Shell in resisting any sort of arrangement which might have undermined their participation agreements in the Gulf.

Libya's next move came in February 1974 when it seized all of the remaining assets of Texaco, Socal and Atlantic Richfield; and in the following month, Shell too was nationalized. Finally Mobil, in March, and Esso, in April, accepted the 51 per cent seizure of the previous September.

Gulf States achieve 60 per cent participation

The General Agreement on Participation concluded at the end of 1972 had satisfied the Kuwaiti Government, and had been signed by the Minister of Finance and Oil, Mr. Abdel-Rahman Atiqi, at the beginning of January 1973; but the Kuwait National Assembly refused its approval. The determination of the handful of radicals lending opposition to the measure was strengthened by Iraq's success in settling its dispute with IPC in February and by the signature of Iran's Sales and Purchase Agreement in May; and by the summer of 1973, it had become clear that the Government would not, as it had originally hoped, be able to rally sufficient support to get the General Agreement accepted. On June 13th, the Ruler formally requested a revision of the accord, and during the autumn, when Libya announced its series of 51 per cent takeovers, the other Gulf producers followed Kuwait's example. In November Sheikh Ahmed Zaki Yamani announced that Saudi Arabia would not be satisfied with a simple majority holding, and it was subsequently made clear early in 1974 that the Saudi Government would be negotiating a complete takeover of Aramco's operations.

Negotiations between the Kuwait Government and the Kuwait Oil Company shareholders, BP and Gulf, during the winter, resulted at the end of January in the state gaining a holding of 60 per cent, which, after several months of further wrangling in the National Assembly, was ratified on May 14th, 1974. The new agreement was made valid from January 1st, meaning that the companies had given way on the principle of retroactivity on which they had held so firm in the past, and was to last for six years—though in explaining the terms, Mr. Atiqi was insistent about the Government's right to call fresh negotiations at any point before the end of 1974. The compensation formula agreed was net book value (giving KOC $112 million) rather than updated book value, but there was no settlement of buy-back terms, with the volume and price of oil being left for more hard bargaining over the summer. In fact Kuwait did not conclude a buy-back deal with BP and Gulf until after it had rejected all bids put in for its 60 per cent crude share at an auction in July. For the third quarter of the year, the Government then sold rather over 55 per cent of its entitlement to the two companies at 94.8 per cent of the posted price; and for the last quarter, BP and Gulf bought two-thirds of the state's crude at 93 per cent of the posting.

Three months before the ratification of the Kuwaiti participation agreement, Qatar concluded a similar accord with its concessionaires (the Qatar Petroleum Company and Shell) in February, and in April it settled buy-back arrangements for the following six months. These involved the two companies purchasing 60 per cent of the state entitlement (about 36 per cent of total output) at 93 per cent of the posted price—the same level as that agreed in September 1973 in the original modification of the terms of the General Agreement. Then in June, after the Kuwaiti ratification, Saudi Arabia concluded an "interim" 60 per cent participation agreement with Aramco though no details emerged about the buy-back arrangements. Finally, in September, Abu Dhabi negotiated a 60 per cent share in the Abu Dhabi Petroleum Company and Abu Dhabi Marine Areas, which like all the other revised participation agreements of 1974 was backdated to the beginning of the year.

Aramco takeover negotiations

Although Saudi Arabia had decided that it would be asking for more than a simple majority stake in Aramco in November 1973, it was not until early 1974 that it finally became clear that the Government was seeking a complete takeover, linked to sales and contracting arrangements similar to those concluded between Iran and the Consortium in May 1973. Within a matter of weeks the two sides were reported to be close to clinching the deal, but over the next five years changing circumstances in the Middle East, in Saudi Arabia and in the world oil market continually postponed the conclusion of an agreement.

There was an initial breakthrough in November 1974 when Aramco conceded the principle of a complete takeover, and during the following 18 months in successive rounds of negotiations it was understood that general agreement was reached on all major practical issues. Indeed the two sides said as much in an announcement made after talks in Panama City, Florida, in March 1976. It was reported at this time: that compensation was to be a little more than $1,500 million for 75 per cent of Aramco's assets (which had expanded considerably since 1973) at net book value; that the companies would continue to take the bulk of Saudi production; that they would be paid a fee of 15 cents a barrel for production operations plus six cents a barrel for new reserves discovered; and that they would continue to put up part of the risk capital in exploration—only being refunded in the event of success.

Over the next three years there were further rounds of negotiations, but an almost complete lack of news as to the substance of the talks. In April 1979, however, it was reported that there was a disagreement between Aramco and the Saudi Government over the formula under which the company's fee would come out of a 75 cents per barrel margin allowed after deducting payments to the government and operating costs from the official selling price. This margin was supposed to cover exploration and the expansion of production capacity, including the sea water injection programme, and Aramco was clearly worried that these investment commitments would eat into its own fees.

Apparently there were also disagreements over Aramco's crude oil entitlements. The draft agreement as it stood until the summer of 1978 laid down a minimum of 6.5 million b/d. If the company failed to achieve that it would incur a penalty in the form of a lower maximum entitlement. The upper limit was set at 7.7 million b/d. In the summer of 1978, with slack market conditions and curbs on the production of the desirable Arabian Light, Aramco had difficulty in taking the minimum quota. (The restriction on liftings of Arabian Light was set at 65 per cent of total production—a ratio dictated by the Kingdom's reserves.) The maximum was subsequently cut to 7.2 million b/d before being raised to 8.1 million b/d in the first quarter of 1979, when the Saudi Government raised its output by 1 million b/d to offset part of the loss of output in Iran. However, in May 1979—when the crude oil market was exceptionally tight—the Government cut Aramco's liftings to 6.6 million b/d and was talking about a longer term entitlement of 7 million b/d or less. (These figures should be set against a Saudi production ceiling of 8.5 million b/d, and direct sales by Petromin rising from 190,000 b/d in 1973, the first year of participation, to about 600,000 b/d in 1978.)

While the negotiations with Aramco were in progress, for practical purposes the industry was run just as if Saudi Arabia already had complete control—in other words the Government made decisions but the day to day operations were run by Aramco as if it were a foreign contracting company. (Technically of course Aramco remains an entirely American company and its staff continue with much the same work as they have always done—the takeover process involves the Government's acquisition of the company's Saudi assets and its decision-making powers over exploration, development and the volume and allocation of output.)

The delay in Aramco and the Government finalizing their agreement stemmed in part from the Government's changing perceptions of what role Aramco might have in the Saudi economy in future. Some of the issues involved concerned purely oil matters: while the takeover remained incomplete nothing whatever was heard about the award of acreage, originally offered in 1973, west of unrelinquished Aramco areas, possibly because the Saudis were not sure whether they might not give all areas to Aramco under some new type of contracting arrangement. But at the same time it was clear that the Saudis had in mind a bigger role for Aramco. Apart from its commissioning Aramco to undertake a big expansion of production capacity and install a huge sea water injection system, the Government in 1975 and 1976 charged Aramco with supervising the construction of a gas gathering system (the biggest industrial project ever undertaken anywhere), a gas liquids pipeline across the peninsula to Yanbu, and a unified electric grid for the Eastern Province. In effect the philosophy of participation (or takeovers) was undergoing a process of change in Saudi Arabia.

For their own part the Aramco owners during this period must have been assessing and reassessing the opportunity cost involved in their channelling so much energy and manpower into Saudi Arabia rather than into operations elsewhere, and wondering what terms to ask for their co-operation.

Takeovers in Kuwait and Qatar

Over a year before Aramco and the Saudi Government reached even the general agreement in Panama City on the major issues of the takeover, the initiative in the movement towards complete ownership of oil producing operations in the Arabian Peninsula had been taken up by Kuwait, which announced on March 5th, 1975 that as of that date it had taken over all assets of the Kuwait Oil Company and would be beginning negotiations to settle the terms with BP and Gulf retroactively. The Kuwaitis made it clear that they wanted a continuing relationship with the KOC owners, but that they felt quite capable of running the production operations themselves. Given that geological and topographical conditions make Kuwaiti oil extremely cheap and easy to produce, and that the state has been fairly thoroughly explored and will not be requiring large-scale new exploration or development work, the continued presence of the major companies was very much less necessary for Kuwait than it was for Saudi Arabia and Abu Dhabi, where there are large potentially oil-bearing areas still to be opened up. For this reason it was felt at the time of the announcement that Kuwait might have decided on a complete takeover after consultation with the other Gulf producers—wanting to use Kuwait's negotiations to gauge what conditions the major companies might eventually be prepared to accept.

Successive rounds of negotiations, however, stuck on the problems of compensation, the service fee and credit terms, but at the beginning of December 1975 an agreement was announced. This involved: compensation of $66 million; a discount off the 93 per cent of postings third party selling price of 15 cents per barrel reflecting BP's and Gulf's continuing provision of technical services and technical personnel, the large size of their purchases and their undertakings to buy Kuwait's bunker fuel and use Kuwaiti tankers; and commitments by BP to take an average of 450,000 b/d between January 1st, 1976 and April 1st, 1980 and by Gulf to take 500,000 b/d over the same period. The two companies were given an option on a further 400,000 b/d. All of these quantities are subject to the normal plus or minus 12.5 per cent variations. Experience since 1975, the Kuwaitis say, has shown their major customers (including Shell and Exxon—former customers of BP and Gulf) to be better at sticking to these terms than KOC's smaller customers.

In February 1976 the Economic Affairs Committee of the Kuwait National Assembly concluded its review of the agreement by recommending that the Government should "endeavour to eliminate" the 15 cents discount—but this fee was strongly defended by the Oil Minister, and the agreement was finally ratified by the Assembly on March 6th, 1976.

The agreement in Kuwait opened the way for other producers to take 100 per cent of their former concessionaires. Within days of the announcement in December 1975 Iraq nationalized the Basrah Petroleum Company, and in February 1976 Kuwait began negotiations for the takeover of Aminoil in its half of the Partitioned Zone (while stating that it did not intend to change the status of the Arabian Oil Company's operation offshore). Negotiations did not go well—becoming involved in a lot of financial issues related to the technical problems of Aminoil's operations—and in September 1977 the Kuwaitis nationalized the company. For a few months a Kuwaiti Wafra Oil Company was established to run operations, until in April 1978 it was decided that KOC should take over the production operation and KNPC the Mina Abdullah refinery, which had processed Aminoil's entire output.

Starting in June 1976 Qatar negotiated the complete takeover of its two concessionaires, signing broadly similar agreements with QPC in September that year and, after a somewhat tougher series of talks, with Shell in February 1977. Compensation was calculated on the basis of net book value, involving the payment of $14 million for Shell's remaining assets and $18 million for QPC's; both companies established new contracting subsidiaries (Dukan Oil Services and Qatar Shell Service Company) to second personnel to run the industry for the Qatar Petroleum Producing Authority (a subsidiary of the national oil company, Qatar General Petroleum Corporation); and both companies accepted a fee of 15 cents per barrel of oil produced. This fee, which compared with the Kuwaiti terms of a 15 cents per barrel discount on just that part of production sold back to BP and Gulf, reflected the much bigger oil company presence retained in Qatar. (These fees, although invariably referred to as being 15 cents, were in fact tied to the official government selling prices, which meant that by the time the Shell deal was signing the fee had already risen to 16.7 cents.) Furthermore it was agreed that Shell should be paid an unspecified lump sum bonus as a condition of its undertaking further exploration (for gas) for QGPC on a contracting basis.

In Bahrain the Government announced the takeover of the production operations of BAPCO in April 1978, the arrangement being backdated to the beginning of January. The Sitra refinery, however, was left 100 per cent in the hands of BAPCO (owned by Caltex—50–50 Texaco and Socal).

In Abu Dhabi meanwhile the Government made it clear that it felt that its big potential for further discoveries and the technical problems involved in its offshore production made it very much in the state's interest for the companies to retain an equity participation and that the 60–40 agreement would be maintained. The same policy applied in Oman for a number of reasons: the small size of the country's oil industry, its shortage of financial resources, the complexity of Oman's oilfields and the Sultanate's acute lack of trained manpower, which made the Government reluctant to undertake any inessential commitments.

The end of the Iranian Consortium

In the true tradition of agreements of its type in the Middle East, it was not long before most of the Iranian Sales and Purchase Agreement became out of date. Whereas at one stage in 1973 the Shah had suggested that Iran's reserves might turn out to be more than 100,000 million barrels, in 1975 and 1976 it came to be realized quite suddenly that this was grossly over-optimistic. To add anything to the country's recoverable reserves beyond 65 billion barrels, or even to recover that volume of oil, the Iranians realized that they would have to invest huge sums in a gas re-injection secondary recovery system.

At the end of 1975 the Consortium stopped contributing the 40 per cent of development capital which it was supposed to invest under the Agreement, and in return NIOC reduced the Consortium's 22 cents a barrel discount to take account of interest accruing on the capital which NIOC saw itself as investing on the Consortium's behalf. Unsuccessful talks on a revision of the Agreement were held in late 1975 and early 1976. However, it was not until the beginning of 1978, after two years in which NIOC-Consortium relations had been further complicated by occasional big falls in Iranian production and by NIOC periodically lifting more than its share, that the two sides sat down to work out a complete replacement for the Agreement. After several rounds of difficult talks the negotiations were made irrelevant by the Iranian revolution of February 1979.

The disturbances of the autumn that preceeded the revolution had disrupted production (which normally ran at a bit below 6 million b/d) and in January and February 1979 exports stopped altogether. Production ran at only 235,000 b/d, not even enough to meet domestic demand of 700,000 b/d. At the end of February, soon after the Ayatollah Khomeini had appointed his Government, the NIOC Chairman, Hassan Nazih, announced that Iran was to have nothing to do with the Consortium ever again—though subsequently the company decided to employ directly (if it could) about 80 of OSCO's former 1,000 expatriate workers. It was reckoned that if Iran ran production at about two-thirds of its previous level, closing the more complex production areas and halting the development of its gas reinjection system, NIOC could carry out its work with minimal foreign assistance.

On March 5th exports started again, with production rising rapidly to over 4 million b/d, though this level was trimmed back by the beginning of May. It slowly emerged that government policy was not to allow production to exceed 4 million b/d, leaving about 3.3 million b/d for export.

Initial sales were on a spot basis, to test the market, but almost immediately NIOC began negotiating a series on nine month contracts involving a substantial surcharge on current OPEC prices and a clause enabling NIOC to make adjustments at will. An informal but apparently *de rigueur* requirement was that potential customers should purchase some Iranian crude at spot prices in order to be eligible for a longer term contract deal.

Inevitably early contracts were with former direct customers of NIOC and the Consortium and former Consortium members, though by mid-May NIOC was talking to a number of entirely new companies. In total the Consortium members, who had been lifting 3.3 million b/d before the revolution, got 1.1 million b/d, of which BP took 450,000 b/d and Shell 235,000 b/d. Up to 1.9 million b/d was allocated for about 50 other companies—some 30 of which had signed by mid-May—including among the biggest buyers old NIOC and Consortium customers such as the Japanese, Ashland, Petrofina (of Belgium), Amerada Hess and Marathon. All of these buyers signed for an average of 25 per cent less than was envisaged when negotiations began in March, and in June NIOC started negotiations for further cuts of about 15 per cent in all contract amounts, so as to make more crude available to new buyers.

THE DEVELOPMENT OF PRICES

The 1940s and 1950s

In the years before the introduction of the 50-50 profit split in 1950 and 1951, when most of the producers received their revenues on the basis of the fixed royalty arrangements (22 cents a barrel) the development of prices was of only academic interest to the Middle Eastern governments. For all of the 1930s, and the first half of the 1940s, the pricing formula applied was the "U.S. Gulf Plus" system, which was worked out by the chairmen of Shell, Standard of New Jersey and Anglo-Persian when they drew up their famous cartel agreement at Achnacarry House in 1928. The U.S. Gulf Plus system laid down that the price of oil in every export centre throughout the world should be the same as that obtaining in the Gulf of Mexico, but that the price at the point of delivery should be made up of the Gulf of Mexico price plus the cost of freight to that point from the Gulf of Mexico. It made no difference to the buyer where the oil actually came from. If a buyer in Bombay, for example, placed an order with a cartel company, the oil would probably be supplied from Persia, but he would still be charged the same freight cost as if the oil had been brought from the United States—and the saving, known as "phantom freight" would go to the cartel company. This system could also work in reverse. A shipment of Persian oil to London, which was nearer to the U.S. than to the Middle East, would still be priced at the Gulf of Mexico price plus freight from the Gulf of Mexico to London—leading to the company accepting an element of "freight absorption". The explanation for this peculiar system lay in the fact that the major companies, as a group, had their biggest and most valuable investments in the U.S., and therefore had an interest in maintaining the biggest possible market for American oil.

Given that all of the other major companies and most of the larger American independents joined the cartel, the U.S. Gulf Plus system continued to operate successfully until near the end of the Second World War, when the British Government objected to paying phantom freight for bunker fuel supplied to the navy in the Indian Ocean, and forced the companies to institute a Persian Gulf base. Under the new system, crudes f.o.b. the Persian Gulf were given the same price as similar crudes f.o.b. the Gulf of Mexico, and at the point of delivery only real freight was levied on top. This resulted in crude oils from the two producing areas finding their natural markets (which met in the Mediterranean near Italy)—though if Middle East oil was landed in north-west Europe, the company would, of course, still have to bear an element of freight absorption if its oil was to be competitive.

It was not long, however, before the Persian Gulf Base system itself began to come under attack from the governments of the importing countries. Immediately after the war, the U.S.A. swung rapidly round from being a big net exporter to being a small net importer (a position it maintained for the next 25 years), and as soon as domestic price controls were removed in 1946, prices in the Gulf of Mexico climbed fast. Persian Gulf prices followed automatically, and because the production cost of Middle Eastern oil was very much lower than that of Texan oil, the companies made enormous profits. Despite the freight disadvantage they were able to import Middle Eastern oil into the U.S. and undercut domestic oil as far inland as the mid-West. In 1948 the companies, influenced in part by criticism from the U.S. Government, lowered their Persian Gulf prices so that the delivered prices of Middle Eastern and Texan oil equalized at London; and in 1949 the U.S. Government forced a further cut in the Persian Gulf so that the delivered prices of Texan and Middle Eastern oil were made to equalize at New York. This reduction, of course, affected only the profits of the companies in their sales to third parties, and made no difference to the profits down their integrated chain of affiliates.

The large profits made by the companies in this period were a major factor behind the Middle Eastern governments' demands in the late 1940s for better financial terms—demands which were met in 1950 and 1951 by the introduction of the 50-50 profit split (*see* "Concessions" above). The new financial terms (which increased government revenues on Saudi Arabian Light from some $0.22 a barrel to about $0.80—depending on the fluctuations of prices in Texas) served to make the producers price conscious. In retrospect they did not fail to notice that the price adjustments of the later 1940s had been to their considerable disadvantage.

The producers also noticed soon after the introduction of 50-50 that the profit split was not quite as even as it seemed, because the companies were always able to press them into giving discounts off the posted price—like volume discounts and the marketing allowance (which was hardly justified when almost all production was sold to affiliates of the operator or to major companies under long-term contracts). In fact, Abdullah Tariki, the radical Saudi Oil Minister during the 1950s, calculated soon after 50-50 came into force that the effective split of profits was 32-68 in favour of the companies.

Worse still, in the early 1950s, the price discrepancies between Texan, Venezuelan and Gulf crudes continued to expand, destroying the principle of the three crudes equalizing at New York. This ushered in a new era in which the price of Gulf crudes was to be determined by the supply and demand situation in Europe rather than in America—which directly or indirectly had been the basis for all quotations for Gulf crudes since 1929. In these new circumstances, the growing availability of production capacity in the Middle East, and increasing competition in the European market, led the companies to start giving their own discounts off the posted price for sales to third parties. It was at this stage that posted (or tax reference) prices and f.o.b. (or market) prices in the Gulf began to part company. Given that the 50-50 profit split was still worked out on the basis of the posting, this meant that he producer government's effective share of profits began to climb back towards the 50 per cent it was always supposed to have been.

Then in 1957, after the closure of the Suez Canal, all prices went up—and although in the Middle East the increase was smaller than in Texas or Venezuela, the new price of $2.12 represented the highest posting for Saudi Arabian Light since 1948. These levels were maintained until February 1959, when there was a general reduction, in which Gulf crudes fell by more than the others. Two months later, the Venezuelan price was lowered again, and in August 1960, the Gulf price was reduced without any parallel reduction being made elsewhere. Thus the discrepancy between Arabian Light and Texan crude had expanded from zero in 1948 (when both crudes were priced at $2.68) to $1.20 in 1960—when Texan crude stood at $3.00 and the Saudi Arabian Light posting at $1.80.

From the point of view of the governments in the Middle Eastern capitals and Caracas, the price cuts of 1959 and 1960 (about which they were never consulted) were very damaging—affecting the size of their budgets and their development prospects. In April 1959, at the first Arab Petroleum Congress in Cairo (to which Iranian and Venezuelan representatives were invited as observers), the oil ministers of Saudi Arabia and Venezuela, Abdullah Tariki and Perez Alfonso, sponsored the formation of the Oil Consultation Commission. Then in September 1960, a month after the further reduction of Middle Eastern prices, the ministers of Iran, Iraq, Saudi Arabia, Kuwait and Venezuela met again in an atmosphere of crisis in Baghdad. The Oil Consultation Commission was already defunct, having run into opposition from Iran and Iraq who objected to the inclusion of Egypt, and the ministers decided to create a permanent and stronger institution. The body that emerged was OPEC—the Organization of Petroleum Exporting Countries.

Since OPEC's formation, the original five members have been joined by Qatar in 1961, Libya and Indonesia in 1962, Abu Dhabi in 1967, Algeria in 1969, Nigeria in 1971, Ecuador in 1973 and Gabon—as an associate member in 1973 and a full member in 1975.

OPEC in the 1960s

At first the major companies ignored OPEC. In accordance with a resolution passed at the Organization's fourth conference in June 1962, the members addressed protests to the companies against the price cuts of August 1960, and demanded that prices be restored to their previous level. But the companies refused to enter into any collective negotiations, and in their individual replies they argued that the development of prices did not depend on their own will, but was determined by economic factors over which they had no control.

OPEC realized that the only way to achieve a restoration of posted prices would be to force up market prices, and this the producers decided would best be done by limiting the annual growth in their output. So over two years (from mid-1965 to mid-1967) the members worked out a joint production programme. In both years they over-estimated the overall growth in demand for their oil, and at the same time certain members, notably Libya and Saudi Arabia, and, to a lesser extent, Iran, made no effort to keep within their quotas. The obvious conclusion was that in a period when prices were low enough to cause a tight budgeting condition in some states, those countries which were either new exporters and/or had big oil reserves and expensive development programmes, would not be willing to make a temporary sacrifice and await an improvement in the unit price of their oil, but would be tempted to increase revenues by maximizing the volume of their output.

However, OPEC did manage to increase its members' effective share of profits during the 1960s. First in 1963 the companies accepted a cut in the marketing allowance (which they were able to deduct as an expense before making the profit split) from some $0.01–0.02, depending on arrangements in different states, to a uniform half-cent throughout the Gulf. Secondly, and more important, the Organization negotiated two agreements on the expensing of royalties. These agreements the Middle Eastern members saw as removing an anomaly in their fiscal arrangements, and as bringing their taxes into line with the system prevailing in Venezuela. Although the producers' revenues since 1950 had nominally been made up of a royalty of 12.5 per cent of the posted price (as payment for the oil itself) and income tax (representing the 50 per cent tax on the profits from the sale of this oil), payments made under the heading of royalties had always been totally deducted from tax. The producers, referring to the normal internationally accepted arrangements, under which the royalty payer was entitled to deduct the royalty only from his gross income when computing his tax liability, wanted royalties to be treated as an expense in their own countries also—and in 1964 this was what was agreed. As part of a package deal the companies received various further discounts off the posted price in respect of "royalty expensing" and "gravity differential". These discounts were set to be reduced each year—this process being accelerated by a second agreement in 1968, which arranged for the complete disappearance of the royalty expensing discount in 1972 and of the gravity allowance in 1975. Under the new system the companies deducted their production cost, the 12.5 per cent royalty, and the applicable allowances and discounts from the posted price, then split the remainder 50-50, and then added the royalty on to the government's share. For Arabian Light, the royalty expensing agreements and the reduction of the marketing allowance increased government take from $0.84 at the end of 1960 to about $0.90 in 1968.

The Independents in Libya

It was not, however, OPEC's achievements in improving its members' share of profits that were to be of the greatest long-term significance for the oil industry in the 1960s. In 1957, oil had been found in Libya. Unlike the governments in the Gulf, Libya had not awarded all its acreage to a single group, and as the discoveries were brought on stream in the early 1960s, it became clear that some of the largest fields lay in concessions held by American independent companies. These companies had originally ventured out of the U.S. in the late 1940s with the intention of finding new supplies for their marketing operations at home, but when the U.S. Government imposed import controls in 1959, they were forced either to launch themselves downstream in Europe, as Occidental (marketing as VIP or Oxy) and Continental (marketing as Conoco or Jet) did, or to sell their crude to others, as Marathon and Amerada Hess did.

Libya proved to be an ideal source of crude for such operations. Its oil yielded a high proportion of high value products such as gasoline and heating oils, and had a low sulphur content. The country's position gave its crude a big freight advantage over Gulf crudes (an advantage only enhanced by the closure of the Suez Canal in 1967), concession terms were uniquely generous, and for the first half of the decade the profit split was made not on posted prices, but on the much lower realized prices. In the mid-1960s these advantages were somewhat reduced when Libya seized the occasion of the first royalty expensing agreement as an opportunity to renegotiate its profit split on the basis of postings. The majors in Libya, who did not favour the independents having access to crude on terms so much more generous than those applying to their own production in the Gulf, agreed to Libya's request in 1965, but the independents only gave in in 1966, after a bitter struggle in which the Government threatened to stop exports or nationalize their assets. Even with these new terms, Libyan crude was still very competitive with Gulf crudes in Europe, because its posted prices, while higher than those in the Gulf, only partially reflected its freight advantage.

Given the relatively low price, Libyan production expanded extremely fast—from 20,000 b/d in 1962 to 3.3 million b/d in 1970—and throughout the decade prices in Europe fell. The majors' response to the independents' sales and marketing operations was to seek economies of scale in building ever larger tankers, refineries and storage and distribution facilities; but because larger units become most attractive when operated at near full capacity, this led the majors themselves to look for the highest possible market share, and led to an acceleration of price cutting. Although this process was most apparent at the downstream end of the industry, there was also an erosion of market prices in the Gulf, and because the existence of OPEC prevented a lowering of postings, the majors' margins were squeezed. The net earnings per barrel on the seven majors' eastern hemisphere operations dropped from $0.60 in 1958 to $0.33 in 1970, while the effective profit split in the Gulf climbed to something in the region of 70/30 in favour of the governments.

Teheran and Tripoli Agreements

In 1970 the marginal surpluses which had been so strong a feature of the previous decade suddenly disappeared. A combination of higher than expected demand as the Western economies entered a period of upturn, a shortage of tankers and a growing tightness of European refinery capacity, led to an unusually tight supply situation, which left the oil industry with very little flexibility to deal with any disruption which might occur in the Middle East.

These conditions coincided with a series of negotiations in Libya, where in January the new revolutionary regime of Colonel Gaddafi had started pursuing a claim, originally formulated by King Idris' government in 1969, for higher prices which would reflect the true freight advantage enjoyed by Libyan crude since the closure of the Suez Canal, and would incorporate a premium for the oil's high quality. During the early months of 1970, the Government took a notably moderate stance, but negotiations made rather slow progress, and although it seemed that they might still be brought to a satisfactory conclusion, by the beginning of the summer the Government's position had hardened. In part the régime's determination stemmed from an agreement in the spring to co-ordinate its efforts with the Algerians, who were engaged in similar negotiations with their French concessionaires, but at the same time, the Libyans could see that their bargaining position as a short-haul supplier was being considerably strengthened by events in the tanker market. The economic upturn in Europe was resulting in a rapid rise in demand for industrial fuel oils of the type derived from the heavier Gulf crudes, and this additional pull on long-haul supplies increased the demand for tanker charters. The strain was only made worse by the loss of several of the new class of mammoth tankers in mysterious explosions early in the year; and in May the situation deteriorated further when a Syrian bulldozer broke Tapline, running from Saudi Arabia to the Mediterranean port of Sidon, and deprived the industry of 480,000 b/d of short-haul crude.

In the same month, the Libyans ordered Occidental, a particularly vulnerable independent which derived nearly a third of its earnings from its Libyan concession, to cut back its production. Whether this decision was made for conservation reasons, or because the Government realized what chaos a further reduction in the supply of short-haul crude would cause, remains unclear—but either way the Libyans soon appreciated the value of production cuts as a lever in their price negotiations, and they quickly imposed further reductions on Occidental and on the other companies. By the beginning of September, the industry had lost about one million b/d of Libyan production, and freight rates soared as extra supplies had to be brought in from the Gulf. One by one the companies surrendered—led, naturally, by Occidental and followed by the other independents in the Oasis group. The majors held out a bit longer, but finally Texaco and Socal broke ranks, and then Esso Mobil and, eventually, Shell gave in too. The Libyans achieved a price rise of $0.30, rising to $0.40 over the next five years, and their tax rate rose from 50 per cent to amounts varying from 54 to 58 per cent in payment for what the Government claimed should have been higher prices since 1965.

Although in theory these changes were made only to reflect the freight and quality advantages of Libyan crudes, the majors realized that they would be bound to result in higher prices in the Gulf, and they promptly decided to pay the Gulf producers a higher tax rate of 55 per cent and an extra $0.09 on heavier crudes (which although normally regarded as of lower quality, were in particularly high demand in 1970). Then in December 1970, at OPEC's Twenty-first Conference, in Caracas, the members decided that the Gulf countries should press for a further round of price increases.

The oil industry, with the support of the consumer governments, formed itself into a united front combining majors, independents and European national companies. When talks with the producers' representatives began in Teheran in January 1971, the companies agreed in principle to a price revision, but insisted that negotiations should cover all OPEC states, so as to avoid the leapfrogging of the past few months. The companies were forced to give in on this point and a parallel series of negotiations was begun in Libya. During the second half of January the gap between the Gulf producers and the companies was gradually narrowed, but on February 2nd the talks broke down. OPEC then held an extraordinary conference, and all members resolved to legislate a price increase if the companies did not respond to their minimum demands by February 15th. But none of the parties wanted a confrontation, and one day before the OPEC deadline, the companies gave in. The producers were given: an immediate $0.33 basic increase, $0.02 for freight disparities, half a cent for every degree API by which any crude fell below 40° API, the elimination of all remaining discounts and allowances, and provision for prices to increase by 2.5 per cent and $0.05 on June 1st, 1971, and January 1st, 1973, 1974 and 1975. This took 34° API Saudi Arabian Light from $1.80 to $2.18. In return, the companies were guaranteed that there would be no further claims until after December 31st, 1975, no more leapfrogging if the Mediterranean producers concluded better terms, and no embargoes.

Later, in March, negotiations were resumed in Libya, and on April 2nd an agreement was signed giving Libya $0.90, a uniform 55 per cent tax rate, and provision for annual price increases of 2.5 per cent and $0.07. Subsequent negotiations secured similar terms for Iraqi and Saudi crude arriving at Mediterranean terminals through the IPC pipe and Tapline.

The price explosion

It was hoped that the Teheran and Tripoli Agreements would give a full five years of price stability—but it was only a matter of months before they began to come under strain. In August 1971, President Nixon's decision to float the dollar (leading to a formal devaluation in December) produced OPEC claims for compensation—though in a notably moderate tone. The claim was settled on January 20th, 1972, when the companies agreed in Geneva to an immediate price rise of 8.49 per cent in the Gulf; and later, in May, after rather tougher negotiations, the same was agreed for Libya.

In February 1973, the dollar was devalued a second time by 10 per cent, and under the terms of the Geneva Agreement, prices were duly raised by 5.8 per cent on April 1st. The OPEC states were disappointed by the time the adjustment mechanism took to operate, and by the small size of their compensation, and, after a further series of discussions with the companies, on June 1st a second dollar compensation agreement was signed in Geneva. The producers obtained an 11.9 per cent increase (which included the 5.8 per cent increase in April plus compensation for the further slide in the dollar's parity during May) and it was agreed that prices would in future be adjusted monthly according to a weighted average movement of 11 major currencies against the dollar. This formula resulted in further rises in August and September and a reduction in October.

The companies presented the Geneva Agreements as supplementary to the Teheran Agreement—although they both involved a significant rise in revenues, and could equally be characterized as a breach of the five-year price programme. Similarly, the participation arrangement negotiated in 1972 meant a significant increment in government receipts and a modification of the fiscal structure; and a still more drastic alteration came in September 1973 when Saudi Arabia agreed with Aramco that both categories of buy-back crude should be priced at 93 per cent of postings—this being the price obtained by the Saudis in May at the first auction of their own direct crude entitlement.

In the summer of 1973, there were, however, much more fundamental forces undermining the Teheran Agreement. As production in the U.S.A. began to fall after 1970, the world's biggest consumer began to look to the Eastern Hemisphere not only to make up for its declining domestic output, but also for an annual increment in supplies that was nearly as big as the annual increase demanded by the whole of Western Europe. United States imports from the Arab countries and Iran grew from 0.6 million b/d in 1971, to 1.0 million b/d in 1972, and to 1.7 million b/d in 1973. It was in 1973 that U.S. demand became really noticeable in the Middle East, and prices on the open market began to move up accordingly.

The OPEC states profited from this situation in as much as they received bids close to postings for the small amounts of crude they were selling on the market themselves; but, with the fiscal terms applied to the bulk of their production still tied to modified 1971 prices, they were for the most part excluded from sharing in the boom, and the main benefit went to the companies. The producers calculated that the effective profit split had changed from about 80-20 in their favour at the time of the Teheran Agreement to about 64-36, [illegible] they suggested that the companies were making excessive profits, and that the whole set of prices negotiated two years earlier had become out of date. These arguments were backed up by the producers pointing out that the small annual increments agreed at Teheran were not keeping up with the rate of world inflation.

At the OPEC conference in Vienna on September 15th–16th, the members agreed to call the companies to negotiations in the following month, and to seek a sizeable lump increase in posted prices to bring them sufficiently above market realizations to permit them to resume their function as a realistic tax reference, while establishing a mechanism whereby the desired differential between posted and realized prices could be maintained in future. The six Gulf members of the Organization began meetings with a company delegation in Vienna on October 8th, two days after the beginning of the Arab-Israeli October war, but the two sides' positions were far apart. The producers demanded an increase of some 70 per cent and the companies offered only 20 per cent. At the end of the week, the companies requested a fortnight's adjournment. The producers immediately held a meeting of their own, and decided to hold a conference in Kuwait four days later on October 16th "to decide on a course of collective action to determine the true value of the oil they produced".

When the producers met again, they quickly abandoned the idea of holding any further consultations with the companies, and raised their posted prices by 70 per cent. For the Arabian light "marker" crude, the posting rose from $3.01 to $5.12, while government take went up by a slightly larger proportion from $1.77 to $3.05. Subsequently, Libya raised its price by 94 per cent from $4.60 to $8.92, thereby widening further the differential between Gulf and Mediterranean crudes. The new prices were designed to be 40 per cent above the market price for any given crude as determined by the direct sales of governments to third parties, and OPEC gave notice that the movement of prices would in future be determined for each quarter by actual market realizations. Both the size of the October increase and the fact that it was made unilaterally were unprecedented, and signalled the final complete transfer of control over the price system, which until 1971 had been in the hands of the companies, into the hands of the producers—after a transitional three and a half year period of negotiated prices.

The price increase of October 16th was an important milestone in oil politics, but immediately, for the world economy, the meeting of Arab producers in Kuwait on the following day was far more cataclysmic. Gathering under the aegis of the Organization of Arab Petroleum Exporting Countries, they decided to use the "oil weapon" in support of Egypt and Syria in their war with Israel. With Iraq opting out, the other nine members of OAPEC decided upon a policy of 5 per cent cumulative monthly cuts in production from the levels of September—to continue until the political objective of Israeli withdrawal from the territories occupied in 1967 and the "restoration of the rights of the Palestinians" had been achieved. The meeting was far from being an occasion of complete unanimity, and the decision on 5 per cent cuts was taken with a degree of hesitancy on the part of some members and amounted to something of a compromise. But once the cuts had started, they escalated rapidly. Within days all of the Arab producers (including Iraq) placed embargoes on the U.S.A. and the Netherlands and reduced their production by equivalent additional amounts, while Saudi Arabia and Kuwait also incorporated the 5 per cent reduction scheduled for November in their initial cutback. Irritated by the lack of response from the West, the Arab producers then decided at a further meeting in Kuwait on November 4th to reduce output across the board by 25 per cent of the September level, and gave notice of a further 5 per cent cut in December. But in practice, the cutback again turned out to be rather larger than it appeared to be on paper, and by the middle of November, output in the two biggest Arab producers, Saudi Arabia and Kuwait, was down by between 30 per cent and 40 per cent.

With winter setting in, the Arab cuts had a dramatic effect on the market. Cargoes of Algerian and Nigerian short-haul crude fetched as much as $16 a barrel, and in December the National Iranian Oil Company in an auction of its crude entitlement under the Sales and Purchase Agreement got the staggering price of $17.40. In these conditions, the OPEC Economic Commission's search for a market price on which could be based the quarterly revision of postings became impossible, and the views of company representatives, who suggested in November in a brief exchange in Vienna that no changes should be made until the market had become more stable, were brushed aside. When the Gulf producers met in Teheran on December 22nd, the new price level set was an arbitrary one dictated largely by the Shah of Iran, who intervened directly in the ministers' deliberations. The Shah suggested a price of $14, while Sheikh Ahmed Zaki Yamani, the Saudi Oil Minister, argued for a price of about $7.50—though he did not, perhaps, put his plea for restraint as strongly as King Faisal would have wished. The other ministers gave Yamani little backing, although they resented the way in which the Shah took control of the meeting, and it was eventually decided that the posted price should be increased by nearly 130 per cent from $5.12 to $11.65—taking the government revenue from $3.05 to $7.00. The Libyan price rise which followed was rather more modest in percentage terms—from $8.92 to $15.76.

1974—a dual pricing system

The OPEC conference at Geneva on January 17th–19th, 1974, revealed the full extent of Saudi Arabia's opposition to the price increase announced in the previous month—although in the conference chamber itself, Yamani did not raise a formal objection. As it was, members endorsed the new prices while deciding on a three-month freeze. This was extended for a further quarter, after a rather tougher argument, at the next meeting in March.

Coinciding with the OPEC conference in March, was another review by the Arabs of their embargo policy. In effect the cuts had come to an end in December, when the Arabs announced that they would not be imposing a further 5 per cent reduction in January, and reclassified most of the EEC and Japan as "favoured nations" for which they were prepared to run production as normal. But it was not until their meeting in March, by which time Dr. Kissinger had arranged the Egyptian-Israeli disengagement, that they lifted the embargo on the U.S. (with Libya and Iraq temporarily dissenting) and only in July was the embargo on the Netherlands lifted. The resumption of normal exports to the U.S. was accompanied by a decision to restore output to September 1973 levels, and Saudi Arabia, with an eye on the coming price battle within OPEC, which it saw would not be settled without reference to actual market realizations, let it be known that it would raise its output somewhat above September levels.

Inevitably, market prices weakened over the following months. After the failure of several participation crude auctions and price cuts of up to $3 by non-Gulf producers, in August, in the biggest single sale of 1974, the Kuwaitis failed to sell any of their 60 per cent of production at the 97 per cent of postings demanded. For the third quarter of the year they subsequently sold rather over 55 per cent of the oil on offer to BP and Gulf at 94.8 per cent of postings.

As the Saudis had hoped in March, the excess of supply assumed a critical importance in the struggle within OPEC over pricing policy. In June Yamani indicated the size of the reduction sought when he formally proposed that the marker crude posting should be lowered by $2.50. But when OPEC held its third meeting of the year at Quito in June, the other members argued for formulas which would have raised the cost of oil to the consumers by anything up to the region of $1.50. Saudi Arabia again threatened a unilateral lowering of prices, and a cheap auction of its participation crude entitlement, and the result was a stalemate in which it was decided (with the Saudis dissenting) to increase the royalty rate on the companies' 40 per cent crude entitlement (known as equity oil) from 12.5 to 14.5 per cent.

Although within OPEC in the summer of 1974 a major battle was being fought over the level of postings, there was at the same time a considerable (and unopposed) increase in government take (and therefore in the cost of oil to the consumers) coming about as a result of the 60 per cent participation agreements, concluded in the middle of the year but backdated to the beginning of 1974. In that the states' participation crude was either sold back to the companies at a level well above the governments' take on equity crude, or was sold on the open market at roughly similar prices, the average government revenue over their whole production was increased, even though on participation crude the governments had to bear the production cost themselves. In 1973, under the 25 per cent régime, the overall effect of participation was fairly small—increasing average government revenues by about $0.10 in the first nine months of the year and by $0.15/20 from September, when the 93 per cent of postings buy-back price came into force. But in mid-1974, under the 60 per cent participation régime, the weighted average revenue worked out, in theory, at some $2 above the government revenue on equity crude (which after the December 1973 increases was about $7.00). In practice, however, there were considerable variations between the different producers in the amount by which the weighted average revenue exceeded the take on equity crude, and in every case, the actual weighted average was lower than it appeared to be in theory. A relatively small factor in determining the variations between the states was the different percentages of postings (93 or 94.8 per cent) charged to the companies for buy-back crude. Much more important was that, following the failure of their auctions (or, in Saudi Arabia's case, in the event of their not holding an auction) the governments kept part of their crude entitlement in the ground, and thus lowered the proportion of participation crude in their overall output, and reduced their weighted average revenues. In Kuwait, for instance, during the third quarter of the year, the ratio of the two types of crude was 65 per cent equity and 35 per cent participation.

One of the consequences of this dual pricing system was that the companies got their crude on average at a price well below that demanded by governments for their direct sales, and the OPEC states realized that the companies' own sales of this relatively cheap crude to third parties were not only undercutting state prices and causing the failure of the auctions, but were also giving the companies large windfall profits. It was with these problems in mind that the producers met in Vienna for OPEC's fourth meeting of 1974 on September 12th–13th. The dispute between Saudi Arabia and the other members had mellowed considerably by this time, but the Saudis still argued that any increase in government take brought about by higher levies on the companies' equity crude should be offset by a reduction of postings, which would not only leave the average cost of oil to the consumers unchanged, but would also be the most effective way of narrowing the margin between the weighted average cost to the companies and the prices demanded at state sales. The Saudis did not accompany their arguments with threats as they had done at Quito, but they again dissented from the eventual OPEC decision, which was to effect a 3.5 per cent increase in average government take in the final quarter to offset the effects of inflation—calculated to be running at four times this level, or 14 per cent over the whole year. This was achieved by a further increase in the royalty rate on equity crude to 16.67 per cent, and by an increase in the tax rate on equity crude from 55 per cent to 65.65 per cent. Although OPEC did not mention the fact in its communique, the tax and royalty adjustments only had the effect of raising overall take by 3.5 per cent if it was assumed that the equity-participation crude ratio was in practice 40 : 60, and that the producers had previously been charging a buy-back price of 94.8 per cent of postings and would in future be charging 93 per cent. Shortly after the OPEC meeting Kuwait did indeed lower the buy-back paid by BP and Gulf to 93 per cent, but its equity-participation crude ratio had not previously been anything like 40 : 60, and because the Government simultaneously took steps to raise the ratio to 50 : 50 (selling two-thirds of its 60 per cent back to BP and Gulf in the fourth quarter of 1974), the overall increase in government revenue and the cost to the consumer of its oil as from October 1st, 1974, rose by considerably more than 3.5 per cent.

A single price system

During the late autumn of 1974, Saudi Arabia's determination to lower prices appeared to weaken further, and there emerged a marked discrepancy between the government's statements on the subject and its actions, which included the indefinite postponement of its long-promised auction, and its decision in October to call on Aramco for back-payments covering the royalty and tax rate adjustments agreed at Quito and Vienna. At the same time, the Saudis, along with the other producers, remained irritated by the "excessive" margin of profits made by the companies on sales of crude. To remedy this situation, Saudi Arabia, Abu Dhabi and Qatar held their own meeting at Abu Dhabi early in November, and agreed with effect from the beginning of that month to cut $0.40 off their postings while raising the royalty rate on equity crude to 20 per cent and the tax rate to 85 per cent.

When OPEC met in Vienna for its fifth and final conference of 1974, on December 13th–14th, the other members endorsed the new arrangements, and decided that from January 1st, 1975, (the date to which it was assumed the final takeover of Aramco would be back-dated) all of the Gulf states would apply the new weighted average cost to all of their production exported by their concessionaire companies, and that the new price levels should be frozen for nine months. The distinction between equity and participation crude, and the possibility of variations in the weighted average cost being caused by alterations in the ratio between the two crudes, therefore ceased to exist—even though the notion of a 40 : 60 split was still used to work out the new cost, known afterwards as the "acquisition price". The new single price system involved a big jump in government revenue, not only because it was based in part on the higher tax and royalty rates agreed at Abu Dhabi (which more than offset the drop in postings) but also because it was based on a 40 : 60 equity-participation crude ratio which had not existed before. The government revenue on the "marker" crude rose to $10.13, and the acquisition price for the companies to $10.25, reflecting the notional "marker" production cost of $0.12 (see note 3 in the prices table below). The gap between the acquisition price and the 93 per cent of postings, $10.46, which remained the official state sale price, was narrowed to $0.21.

Over the following years the acquisition price applied only in countries where the companies retained a 40 per cent equity stake—which soon meant just Abu Dhabi and Saudi Arabia among the bigger producers. In Kuwait and Qatar the former concessionaires got their crude at the government selling price (93 per cent of postings) less a discount. This gave the companies a smaller margin than in Abu Dhabi and Saudi Arabia, which reflected the fact that in Kuwait and Qatar the companies were no longer investing capital. In Iran, where until the end of 1975 the companies did continue to invest capital, the discount off the state selling price was bigger. In practice it was the state selling prices, in all countries, that became henceforth the important prices for OPEC.

Differentials—1975-78

December 1974 marked the end of the oil price explosion; in the space of 15 months government revenues and the cost of oil to the consumer had multiplied almost exactly five times. From then until January 1st, 1979 there were only two OPEC price rises. One was in Vienna in September 1975, when it was agreed that the state selling price should be raised by 10 per cent, and the other was in Doha, in December 1976, when the majority of OPEC members raised their prices by a further 10 per cent—causing a split with Saudi Arabia and the U.A.E.

During much of the four year period 1975–8, there was rather weak demand. There was something of a revival in the market in 1976, but in late 1977 and most of 1978 there was a serious glut caused by the new Mexican fields, Alaska and the North Sea, which began to make a significant impact on the world market at the same time. In these conditions the OPEC members' attention became focused mainly on differentials—the different margins between crudes of different qualities in different locations. This problem was an important theme (sometimes the only theme) in at least half a dozen OPEC meetings: at Vienna in September and December 1975 (it was on the latter occasion that the ministers were kidnapped by the terrorist gang of Carlos Illych Ramirez), Geneva in April 1976, Bali in May 1976, Stockholm in July 1977 and Caracas in December 1977.

Differentials seems like a matter of technicalities, but in practice it had caused some of the most bitter arguments within OPEC, because indirectly agreement on differentials would imply agreement on different producers' production levels. Sometimes when demand has been buoyant, the members have been able to agree systems of differentials (see note 2 underneath the prices table for the workings of the system in 1974). The difficulties occur at times of slack demand when producers are competing for market shares and output is dropping in states whose crude is marginally over-priced. In January 1976, when Iranian heavy crude was over-priced by just 10 cents relative to Kuwaiti crude, output fell dramatically to a point where the light/heavy export ratio changed from the normal 52/48 to 72/28.

Although ministers reached a flexible understanding on differential adjustments at the Bali meeting in May 1976, and periodically referred the matter to special committees (at Geneva in April 1976 and Stockholm in July 1977), the Organization was not able to agree on any comprehensive new system. Generally adjustments were made unilaterally, sometimes in accordance with guidelines laid down by one of the committees. More often they took place when a state experienced a particularly embarrassing fall in demand, or when a price rise (in October 1975 or January 1977) produced an opportunity for producers to adjust their own crudes by implementing a fractionally bigger or smaller rise than that announced for the marker crude.

Apart from the differentials issue, OPEC meetings in 1975–8 were marked by quite frequent battles over price rises. Iraq and Libya were always in the hawks' camp (often with Iran, Algeria and Nigeria), and Saudi Arabia generally stood as the single dove—though sometimes it had the support of the U.A.E., Qatar and occasionally Kuwait. Although the Saudis were forced to compromise in September 1975 and before Stockholm in July 1977, they succeeded in preventing rises at Bali, at Caracas in December 1977 and at Geneva in June 1978.

Other recurrent issues were production programming (the artificial limiting of output so as to influence the state of the market) and the protection of oil prices against the dollar's fluctuations. The Saudis invariably refused to entertain the idea of production programming, or even discuss the level of their own output, on which any programme would have hinged. On the matter of dollar compensation mechanisms, which was an issue in early 1975 (at Vienna and Libreville) and late 1977–early 1978, the Saudis were less adamant, but still doubtful of the value of any of the formulae put forward. These included the creation of a special OPEC dollar, the denomination of prices in terms of the IMF's Special Drawing Rights, and the introduction of OPEC's own basket of currencies formula. Apart from not wanting to undermine the dollar and damage the world economy, the Saudis were opposed to methods of compensation for reasons outlined by Sheikh Yamani in the summer of 1978: "These formulae are a two-way street. Either you stay with the dollar, you lose with it and you gain with it, or you go to a basket of currencies and when the dollar appreciates you immediately start to lose."

OPEC split and reconciliation—December 1976–December 1977

The major event in OPEC—and the major confrontation over prices—in 1975–8 occurred at Doha in December 1976. Saudi Arabia, with the support of the U.A.E., flatly refused to countenance the increases demanded by other OPEC members, ranging upwards from 10 per cent, though it emerged later that had compromise been possible it would have been prepared to accept 7 per cent. The outcome was that Saudi Arabia and the U.A.E. opted for an immediate 5 per cent increase for the whole of 1977, while the other members decided on 10 per cent for the first six months of the year with an additional 5 per cent to come into effect on July 1st.

In part the Saudi policy at Doha stemmed from a hard-headed realization that the health of the OPEC economies is linked to that of the Western economies, and that inflation caused by oil price rises rebounds on to the OPEC members; but at the same time there is no doubt that the Saudis felt a genuine sense of responsibility for the West's economic well-being.

After the Doha meeting the Saudis announced that they were raising their production ceiling from 8.5 million b/d to 10 million b/d, and immediately there were big drops in the production of some of the other states—in Iran output fell by 38 per cent in the first nine days of January. To some extent these falls were a normal reaction to the high level of liftings experienced in November and December, when the companies were trying to "beat the price rise", but the Iranians still became seriously worried that Saudi production increases would cause serious damage to their economy, and in one statement the Shah said that such a policy on the Saudis' part would be tantamount to an act of "aggression".

Yet for all the fuss there was no increase in Saudi production at the beginning of the year, indeed output in January and February fell from the record levels of late 1976 (9.2 million b/d in December) to only 8.2 million b/d and 8.7 b/d respectively. During the next four months, however, production picked up, reaching over 10 million b/d at one point. There was some mystery surrounding the reasons for this performance. On one hand it was suggested that the initial drop in output was caused either by the inevitable time lag that would elapse before the Saudis could sign up new customers or by the Saudis realizing that the expansion of production might be more effective as a threat than as something which had already come into operation. On the other hand, there was evidence that the Saudis had tried from the start to raise production to 10 million b/d but had been frustrated partly by bad weather preventing tankers loading, and partly by the realization that although they had rather over 10 million b/d of capacity installed in hardware terms and were planning on expanding this to some 12 million b/d by the end of the year, they did not have the personnel and management systems needed to maintain output at these levels. Certainly there was evidence in the frenetic activity visible in Dhahran early in the year that Aramco had been told to de-bottleneck its systems in a hurry.

Throughout the early months of 1977 there were attempts made to heal the rift in OPEC—notably by the President of Venezuela, Carlos Andrez Perez. At quite an early stage it became clear that the eleven upper tier countries would agree to a compromise involving Saudi Arabia and the U.A.E. raising their prices by 5 per cent in July and the rest at the same time forgoing their own scheduled 5 per cent increase, but it was not until sometime in June that it emerged that the Saudis would accept this formula. About a fortnight before the OPEC conference at Stockholm on July 12th, which it had been agreed should not be held unless a solution had been reached in advance, the two sides made their compromise public. The Stockholm meeting itself concentrated on the issue of differentials. At the later meeting in Caracas in December 1977 prices remained frozen, not because of a concensus, but because the Saudis managed to assemble behind them Iran, Kuwait, the U.A.E. and Qatar.

The second oil crisis—1979

Despite the oil glut of most of 1978, relations between OPEC members improved from the middle of the year. On May 6th and 7th the ministers held an informal exchange of ideas on long term strategy at the mountain resort of Taif in Saudi Arabia. Without the problems of decision-making or a fixed agenda, the meeting was relaxed and amicable, and one minister remarked that it was the most productive OPEC gathering he had attended. The good atmosphere was enhanced by the steps that Saudi Arabia was taking to cut its output. Late in 1977 it had reimposed its 8.5 million b/d ceiling, and in early 1978 it had decided to limit liftings of Arabian Light to not more than 65 per cent of total liftings (compared with 72–80 per cent in 1975–7). The market however was simply unable to absorb the extra amounts of heavy crude that this ratio implied at prevailing production rates, so for the first nine months of the year Saudi output fell sharply.

The broad drift of the ministers' discussions at Taif assumed that the glut would begin to come to an end in later 1978 or 1979, that there would then be a period of balance in the market—how long a period depending on the consumers' growth rates and their success or failure at developing alternatives and conserving energy—and that at some point in the 1980s the world would return to conditions of shortage. In these circumstances it was felt that the market itself would look after oil prices and that OPEC might possibly orientate itself to using its increased bargaining power for bringing about the new international economic order which had failed to emerge from the North-South dialogue in Paris. To study these questions the meeting established another ministerial committee composed of Saudi Arabia, Iran, Iraq, Kuwait, Venezuela (the five founders) and Algeria.

The turnaround in the market came much sooner than anyone had expected. At the end of October 1978 the strikes in Iran which were paralysing the Shah's regime began to affect oil production. During the next two months production fluctuated between its norm of about 5.8 million b/d and 1.2 million b/d, but at the end of December it fell to 235,000 b/d (insufficient to meet domestic demand), at which point it was to remain until March 1979.

Up to the end of the year the companies made up the shortfall by increasing liftings elsewhere; Saudi output in December ran at a record 10 million b/d—it being permissible for Aramco to exceed the 8.5 million b/d limit for a month or so as long as it kept within it over the whole year. The Iranian crisis had no effect on the spot market. Nor did the crisis give much added impetus to the OPEC meeting at Abu Dhabi on 16–17th December, when it was decided to raise prices for 1979 by 10 per cent. This was to be done in instalments of 5 per cent for the first quarter, 3.8 per cent for the second, 2.3 per cent for the third and 2.7 per cent for the fourth. These would bring the marker crude selling price from $12.70 in December 1978 to $14.54 in October 1979—a rise of 14.5 per cent over nine months but an average increase for the year 1979 of 10 per cent. What was remarkable was the storm of protest with which this rise was greeted by Western governments. In defence of their decision the OPEC leaders pointed out that their prices had remained frozen during two years of quite high inflation, that their increase over the course of 1979 would probably be half eaten away by inflation in that year, and that for the strong currency countries OPEC's increase had already been more than offset by the decline in the dollar's parity in 1978.

In the month that followed the OPEC meeting, however, spot market prices began to climb at a rate which was to destroy the price programme agreed at Abu Dhabi and, by mid-May, to cause the Western world to talk of a "second oil crisis". With Iranian exports halted the international oil industry was short of some 5 million b/d, which was only partially made up by Saudi Arabia raising its production ceiling from 8.5 million b/d to 9.5 million b/d (the extra 1 million b/d being charged at fourth quarter prices) and by smaller increases in Kuwait, Iraq and other producers. By the beginning of February the spot market, which handles only 1 or 2 per cent of the world oil trade, was charging a premium of more than $4 on the official government selling price for Arabian Light ($13.34) compared with a premium of just $1.40 at the beginning of January. By the middle of February, at which point OPEC announced an extraordinary meeting to be held in Geneva at the end of March, spot prices for light Gulf crudes had risen to $21 and higher, involving premiums of above $7.50.

On February 15th Abu Dhabi and Qatar imposed surcharges on their crudes of up to $1.02, promising an extra 18 cents at the beginning of April. A week later Libya followed with 68 cents and then Kuwait and Iraq with $1.20, Oman with $1.02, and the Soviet Union (for its Western customers) with $1.41.

On March 5th Iran resumed oil exports, building up over the next two months to a production level of some 4 million b/d (which meant exports of 1.5-2.0 million b/d less than before the revolution). This caused the spot premiums to fall from their end-February peak of $23, but the market pressure for a rise was still impossible for Saudi Arabia to resist when OPEC met at Geneva on March 26-27th. All producers agreed to bring forward their scheduled 1979 last quarter increase to the second quarter (raising the marker to $14.55), and it was decided that producers could impose whatever additional surcharges they deemed "justifiable in the light of their own circumstances". Saudi Arabia added no premiums to its Light, Medium and Heavy crudes, but $1.14 to its high quality Berri crude. All other Gulf producers maintained whatever surcharges they had imposed in February, on top of the new price levels, and during the course of the next two or three weeks Abu Dhabi, Qatar and Kuwait added additional surcharges (backdated to April 1st) of 60 cents, while Iran, which had not imposed any surcharge in February, imposed an additional $1.80–90. Meanwhile the African producers—Libya, Algeria and Nigeria, all selling exceptionally high quality crudes—raised their selling prices to the $17.50–18.50 range, a level not seen since the crisis of 1973–4.

In the middle of April it became known definitely that Saudi Arabia was not maintaining its extra one million b/d of output in the second quarter, partly because it argued that the resumption of Iranian exports made this unnecessary, and partly, it was thought, to show its displeasure with the United States over the Egypt–Israel peace treaty. Shortly after this the effects of the Iranian stoppage began finally to feed through to the market place, as oil companies cut back their deliveries and queues formed at petrol stations. Together these developments set off in May another jump in the spot market price for light crudes, taking the price back through the end-February level and then on to extraordinary levels in the region of $33 a barrel in mid-May.

At the beginning of May Iraq added 70 cents to its selling prices, but this was more a continuation of the April round of surcharge increases, which Iraq had not joined at the time. The new, May, round of increases was triggered by Iran, which at the end of the first week of the month levied an extra premium of 60 cents. Inevitably by the last week of the month Iran had been joined by Venezuela, Abu Dhabi and Kuwait. Algeria and Libya announced staggering rises of over $2, which took some of their prices above $21 a barrel.

At the beginning of June Iran led another round of price increases when it raised the price of its oil by $1.30, bringing its light crude to $18.47. Over the next two weeks this was followed by the imposition of further premiums by Indonesia and Ecuador, which set a new peak of $26.80 for contract prices. Iraq and Kuwait warned that they were considering putting into their contracts "most favoured seller" price clauses.

To try to alleviate some of the market pressures for higher prices, the Saudis let it be known before the OPEC meeting in Geneva on June 26th–28th that they were considering raising their output again. At the meeting the other members demanded further increases, which, if the Saudis had co-operated, would have raised the marker crude to at least $20. Meanwhile the Saudis, concerned at the recessionary influences that the oil price increases were having on the Western economies, sought to stabilize the price at a lower level of $17–$18. In the end the Organization reached an amicable compromise in which Saudi Arabia raised its marker price to $18 while the other members were allowed to impose surcharges up to $23.50. This figure was adopted for some of their crudes by Algeria, Libya, Nigeria and Venezuela. In the Gulf most of the producers opted for prices in the $19,50–$21.50 range, though Iran, when it announced its prices officially a week after the meeting, set its light crude at $22. This figure was dangerously out of line with the differentials applying to the other Gulf crudes and raised the possibility of further rounds of leapfrogging. Nobody at the meeting was entirely confident that the multi-tier price chaos of the preceding six months had really been ended.

The members collectively made it known that their policies on prices in the short term would be affected by the performance of the dollar, and in the longer term would be determined very much by the West's success or failure in cutting back its imports. For the coming months the Saudis decided to exert a stabilizing influence on the market by announcing early in July that they were raising production for the third quarter of 1979 by 1 million b/d to 9.5 million b/d.

Oil Statistics

(compiled by Michael Field)

CRUDE OIL PRODUCTION

(million barrels per day)

	1968	1976	1977	1978	1977/78 % change
Middle East OPEC:					
Saudi Arabia	2.830	8.525	9.200	8.270	−10.1
Kuwait	2.420	1.950	1.790	1.865	4.2
Partitioned Zone[1]	0.405	0.465	0.370	0.460	24.3
Iran	2.840	5.920	5.670	5.235	− 7.7
Iraq	1.505	2.280	2.210	2.600	17.6
U.A.E.—Abu Dhabi	0.495	1.595	1.660	1.450	− 7.2
U.A.E.—Dubai	—	0.315	0.320	0.360	12.5
U.A.E.—Sharjah	—	0.035	0.030	0.020	−33.3
Qatar	0.340	0.485	0.435	0.480	10.3
North Africa OPEC:					
Libya	2.605	1.930	2.080	1.975	− 5.0
Algeria	0.915	1.075	1.150	1.230	7.0
Other OPEC:					
Venezuela	3.645	2.375	2.235	2.235	—
Nigeria	0.145	2.065	2.100	1.920	−8.6
Indonesia	0.600	1.505	1.690	1.635	−3.3
Ecuador	0.005	0.185	0.180	0.205	13.9
Gabon	0.095	0.215	0.225	0.215	−4.4
Other Middle East and North Africa:					
Oman	0.240	0.365	0.340	0.315	−7.4
Bahrain	0.074	0.058	0.058	0.055	−5.2
Syria	0.019	0.180	0.180	0.170	−5.6
Egypt[2]	0.220	0.325	0.420	0.480	14.3
Tunisia	0.064	0.075	0.100	0.100	—
Turkey	0.060	0.050	0.055	0.055	—
Other producers:					
U.S.A.[5]	10.600	9.725	9.820	10.265	4.5
Canada	1.195	1.605	1.450	1.575	8.6
Mexico	0.440	0.820	0.985	1.330	35.0
Trinidad and Tobago	0.185	0.225	0.220	0.230	4.5
Colombia	0.175	0.145	0.140	0.130	−7.1
Argentina	0.345	0.390	0.430	0.455	5.8
Brazil	0.165	0.170	0.165	0.165	—
Brunei	0.120	0.205	0.220	0.205	−2.7
Australia	0.040	0.430	0.450	0.450	—
United Kingdom[4]	neg	0.235	0.770	1.095	42.2
Norway	—	0.280	0.280	0.350	25.0
U.S.S.R.	6.190	10.315	11.045	11.705	6.3
China	0.260	1.500	1.625	1.930	18.8
Eastern Europe	0.350	0.400	0.410	0.430	1.8
World Total	40.345	59.555	62.160	62.965	1.3
Free World Total	33.545	47.340	48.530	48.900	0.8
OPEC Total[3]	17.685	30.920	31.345	30.155	−3.8
OPEC % Free World Total[3]	52.7	65.3	64.6	61.7	−2.9
Middle East and North Africa Total	15.032	25.628	25.978	25.120	−3.3
Middle East and North Africa % Free World Total	44.8	54.1	53.5	51.4	−2.1

[1] Partitioned Zone production is shared equally by Kuwait and Saudi Arabia.
[2] Includes output of fields occupied by Israel from 1967.

[*Footnotes continued on next page*

CRUDE OIL PRODUCTION—*continued*]

[3] OPEC total production and OPEC percentage contribution to total Free World production is based only on the production of countries which were members of the Organisation in the years in question. In 1968 Algeria, Nigeria, Ecuador and Gabon were not members of OPEC. In 1974 Abu Dhabi asked that its membership of OPEC should be registered as United Arab Emirates, including Dubai and Sharjah.

[4] neg.=negligible—less than 5,000 b/d.

[5] Includes production of natural gas liquids in U.S. total.

Conversion factors based on world average crude oil gravity:

1 long ton=7.42 barrels — 1 short ton=6.63 barrels — 1 barrel=35 imperial gallons

1 metric ton=7.30 barrels — 1 barrel=42 U.S. gallons

To convert metric tons a year into b/d divide by 50.0 — To convert long tons a year into b/d divide by 49.2

PROVEN PUBLISHED WORLD CRUDE OIL RESERVES AS AT JANUARY 1st, 1979

('000 million barrels)

Middle East and North Africa	Reserves	Years of Production at 1978 Levels
Saudi Arabia	165.7	55
Kuwait	66.2	97
Partitioned Zone	6.5	48
Iran	59.0	31
Iraq	32.1	34
U.A.E.—Abu Dhabi	30.0	57
U.A.E.—Dubai	1.3	10
U.A.E.—Sharjah	0.02	3
Qatar	4.0	23
Bahrain	0.25	12
Oman	2.5	22
Syria	2.1	33
Algeria	6.3	14
Libya	24.3	34
Egypt	3.2	18
Tunisia	2.3	63
Middle East and North Africa Total	405.77	*

Other Leading Producers	Reserves	Years of Production at 1978 Levels
Other OPEC		
Venezuela	18.0	22
Nigeria	18.2	26
Indonesia	10.2	17
Ecuador	1.2	16
Gabon	2.0	25
Total OPEC	445.0	*
Rest of World:		
U.S.A.	27.8	7
Canada	6.0	16
Mexico	16.0	33
United Kingdom	16.0	40
Norway	5.9	46
U.S.S.R.	71.0	17
Eastern Europe	3.0	19
China	20.0	28
World Total	641.6	28

* Not applicable.

Source: Oil and Gas Journal.

Note: Reserve figures are subject to wide margins of error, and there are considerable differences between sources—including oil companies and governments. Proven reserves do not denote "total oil in place", but only that proportion of the oil in a field that drilling has shown for certain to be there and to be recoverable with current technology and at present prices. Normally recoverable reserves amount to about a third of the oil in place. Because the potential of fields is continually being reassessed in the light of production experience and because the production characteristics of a field can (and often do) change as it gets older, proven reserves figures may sometimes be revised upwards or downwards by quite dramatic amounts without any new discoveries being made. Price rises tend inevitably to increase reserves figures by making small fields or more complex recovery techniques economic.

In Mexico figures for proven reserves have jumped from 5,800 million barrels in 1974 to 20,000 million barrels according to the President in September 1978 and 40,000 million barrels according to Pemex, the national oil company, at the end of 1978. According to Pemex there are also probable reserves in Mexico of 45,000 million barrels and potential reserves of 200,000 million barrels, while in November 1978 the Director General of Pemex announced that an additional 100,000 million barrels are contained in the Chicontepec field, though these have not been added to the official proven figures.

Although there have been considerable discoveries in the past four years, part of the more extraordinarily large figures is accounted for by Pemex's unusual practice of lumping together oil and natural gas reserves converted into barrels of oil equivalent. In Mexican fields it seems that the oil/natural gas split is about 65/35. At the same time it appears that recent announcements have been politically motivated. In the past it was Mexico's policy to play down its reserves. Now it is anxious to play up the figures, partly to encourage international bankers to continue their lending, and partly to strengthen its bargaining position on a whole range of industrial, labour and energy matters on which it is negotiating with the United States.

RESERVES OF BIGGEST OIL FIELDS[1]

('000 million barrels)

	Year of Discovery	Cumulative Production to end-1977	Estimated Remaining Reserves Jan. 1st, 1978
Saudi Arabia			
Ghawar	1948	16.5	61.0
Safaniyah	1951	4.1	13.5
Abqaiq	1940	5.7	6.5
Kuwait:			
Burgan	1938	13.4	45.0
Iran:			
Agha Jari	1938	6.8	3.3
Gach Saran	1928	4.3	7.1
Marun	1964	3.7	7.0
Bibi Hakimeh	1961	1.4	6.8
Ahwaz	1958	2.5	6.7
Iraq:			
Kirkuk	1929	7.6	8.7
Rumaila	1953	2.9	10.9
Libya:			
Sarir	1961	1.1	7.2
Other OPEC producers:			
Venezuela:			
Bachaquero	1930	5.3	1.3
Lagunillas	1926	9.2	1.6
Indonesia:			
Minas	1944	2.2	5.0
Other producers:			
United States:[2]			
Wilmington (Cal)	1932	1.9	0.5
East Texas	1930	4.4	1.6
Prudhoe Bay (Alaska)	1968	0.1	10.0
Norway:			
Ekofisk	1970	0.3	1.2
Statfjord	1973	—	3.9
United Kingdom:			
Forties	1970	0.2	1.7
Brent	1972	—	2.1

[1] By normal international standards a big field is considered to be one with reserves of more than one thousand million barrels.

[2] Wilmington, East Texas and Prudhoe Bay are by far the biggest fields in the U.S.A. Few other U.S. fields have ever contained more than 300 million barrels.

* Rough estimate.

GOVERNMENT OIL REVENUES

(million U.S. dollars)

	1968	1969	1970	1971	1972	1973	1974	1975	1976	1977	1978
Iran	817	938	1,093	1,870	2,308	5,600	22,000	20,500	22,000	23,000	20,900
Saudi Arabia	966	1,008	1,200	2,160	3,107	7,200	29,000	27,000	33,500	38,000	36,700
Kuwait	766	812	895	1,395	1,657	2,800	8,000	7,500	8,500	8,500	9,500
Iraq	476	484	521	840	575	1,900	6,000	8,000	8,500	9,500	11,600
Abu Dhabi/ U.A.E.*	153	191	233	431	551	1,200	5,500	6,000	7,000	8,000	8,700
Qatar	110	115	122	198	255	600	1,650	1,700	2,000	1,900	2,200
Libya	952	1,132	1,295	1,766	1,598	3,000	6,000	6,000	7,500	9,400	9,300
Algeria	262	299	325	320	700	1,100	3,500	4,000	4,500	5,000	5,400

* Figures apply for Abu Dhabi from 1968 to 1973, and for U.A.E. from 1974 to 1978.

EVOLUTION OF PRICES AND GOVERNMENT REVENUES FOR THREE GULF CRUDE OILS

($ per barrel)

	Production Cost		API°	Percentage Sulphur Content	Pre-November 14th, 1970		January 1st, 1971		February 15th, 1971		June 1st, 1971		January 20th, 1972		January 1st, 1973		April 1st, 1973	
					p.p.	g.r.	p.p.	g.r.	p.p.	g.r.	p.p.	g.r.	p.p.	g.r.	p.p.	g.r.	p.p.	g.r.
Arabian Light	1970–71	0.11	34°	1.7	1.80	0.91	1.80	0.99	2.18	1.26	2.29	1.33	2.48	1.45	2.59	1.62	2.74	1.72
	1972–73	0.10																
	1974	0.16																
	1975	0.28																
Kuwait	1970–73	0.06	31°	2.5	1.59	0.83	1.68	0.96	2.09	1.23	2.19	1.29	2.37	1.41	2.48	1.57	2.63	1.67
	1974–75	0.07																
Abu Dhabi Murban	1970–73	0.15	39°	0.75	1.88	0.92	1.88	1.01	2.24	1.27	2.34	1.34	2.54	1.46	2.65	1.66	2.81	1.76
	1974	0.165																
	1975	0.20																

	June 1st, 1973		Sept 1st, 1973		Oct. 16th, 1973		Jan. 1st, 1974		July 1st, 1974		Oct. 1st 1974		Jan. 1st, 1975		Oct. 1st, 1975	Jan. 1st, 1977	July 1st, 1977	Jan 1st, 1979	Apr. 1st, 1979	July 1st, 1979
	p.p.	g.r.	p.p.	g.r.	p.p.	g.r.	p.p.	g.r.	p.p.	g.r.	p.p.	g.r.	p.p.	g.r.	g.s.p.	g.s.p.	g.s.p.	g.s.p.	g.s.p.	g.s.p.
Arabian Light	2.90	1.81	3.07	2.01	5.12	3.41	11.65	9.27	11.65	9.37	11.65	9.69	11.25	9.98	11.51	12.09	12.70	13.34	14.55	18.00
Kuwait	2.78	1.76	2.94	1.96	4.90	3.30	11.55	9.25	11.55	9.35	11.55	9.68	11.15	10.08	11.30	12.37	12.37	12.83	15.80	19.49
Abu Dhabi Murban	2.79	1.86	3.14	2.04	6.05	4.01	12.64	10.07	12.64	10.16	12.64	10.52	11.69	10.34	11.92	12.50	13.26	14.10	17.10	21.56

NOTES

p.p. = posted price; g.r. = government revenue; g.s.p. = government selling price.

1. **The government selling prices** of other major Gulf crudes at July 1st, 1979, were as follows:
   Arabian Berri 39° API, g.s.p. $21.32;
   Arabian Medium 31° API, 2.4 per cent sulphur, g.s.p. $17.54;
   Arabian Heavy 27° API, 2.85 per cent sulphur, g.s.p. $17.17;
   Iranian Light 34° API, 1.3 per cent sulphur, g.s.p. $22.00;
   Iranian Heavy 31° API, 1.6 per cent sulphur, g.s.p. $19.90;
   Abu Dhabi Marine (Umm Shaif) 37° API, 1.3 per cent sulphur, g.s.p. $21.36;
   Abu Dhabi Zakum 40° API, 0.95 per cent sulphur, g.s.p. $21.46;
   Iraq Basrah Light 34° API, 1.95 per cent sulphur, g.s.p. $19.96;
   Iraq Basrah Medium 30° API, g.s.p. $19.30;
   Iraq Basrah Heavy 24° API, g.s.p. $18.65;
   Iraq Kirkuk 36° API, g.s.p. $21.25;
   Qatar Dukan 40° API, 1.17 per cent sulphur, g.s.p. $21.42;
   Qatar Marine 36° API, 1.4 per cent sulphur, g.s.p. $21.23.

2. **Differentials:** Arabian Light has been designated the "Marker" crude, forming the basis of the prices of all other Gulf crudes. During 1974 other Gulf crudes were priced at the Marker plus or minus set amounts for: (*a*) API Gravity Differential—added to the price of crudes lighter than the Marker and subtracted from crudes heavier

continued from previous page]
than the Marker; (*b*) Sulphur Premium—for all crudes with a sulphur content lower than that of the Marker; and (*c*) Freight Differential—involving crudes loaded nearer the entrance of the Gulf (nearer the markets) being given a marginal price differential over those loaded at the top of the Gulf. Since the beginning of 1975, when the first unilateral adjustments to these set amounts were made, there has been no agreed system of differentials, and different producers have made their own adjustments on the occasions of price rises, or as and when they have felt that the prices of their crudes have got out of line with competing crudes. The result has been that during the last four and a half years there have been a number of significant anomalies in Gulf crudes' pricing.

3. **The dates in the table** denote changes in price and tax formulas (*see* text for details), excluding adjustments to differentials, as follows:

(*a*) Pre-November 14th, 1970: before price increase for heavy crudes (27° and 31° API) and introduction of 55 per cent tax rate. Revenue calculation: posted price, minus expensed 12.5 per cent royalty, production cost and appropriate discounts; taxed at 50 per cent with royalty added.

(*b*) January 1st, 1971: after November 1970 tax and price increases and scheduled reduction of price discounts and gravity adjustment discounts at beginning of year. Revenue calculation as in item (*a*) except for 55 per cent tax rate.

(*c*) February 15th, 1971: after Teheran Agreement price increases and elimination of all discounts. Revenue calculation as in item (*a*) except for absence of discounts and 55 per cent tax rate.

(*d*) June 1st, 1971: after first inflation and escalation increments of Teheran Agreement. Revenue calculation as in item (*c*).

(*e*) January 20th, 1972: after first Geneva Agreement for dollar compensation. Revenue calculation as in item (*c*).

(*f*) January 1st, 1973: after second inflation and escalation increments of Teheran Agreement and introduction of 25 per cent participation regime. Revenue calculation: Weighted average of revenue on: 75 per cent of production known as equity crude (calculated as in item (*c*)), 18.75 per cent of production known as buy-back bridging crude and 3.75 per cent of production known as buy-back phase-in crude—*see* text. Note: These calculations are somewhat notional because they do not take account of the remaining 2.5 per cent of production which the producers sold directly on the open market—at prices only a little below the postings.

(*g*) April 1st, 1973: after compensation for second dollar devaluation under terms of first Geneva Agreement. Revenue calculation as in item (*f*).

(*h*) June 1st, 1973: after additional compensation for second dollar devaluation under second Geneva Agreement. Revenue calculation as in item (*f*).

(*i*) September 1st, 1973: after introduction of 93 per cent of postings price for all buy-back crude under 25 per cent participation regime, and price adjustments under terms of second Geneva Agreement on July 1st and August 1st. Revenue calculation: weighted average of revenue on 75 per cent of production known as equity crude, calculated as in item (*c*), and 93 per cent of postings less production costs, on 22.5 per cent of production known as buy-back crude. See note at end item (*f*).

(*j*) October 16th, 1973: after first OPEC unilateral increase and price adjustment under terms of second Geneva Agreement on October 1st. Revenue calculation: as in item (*i*).

(*k*) January 1st, 1974: after second OPEC unilateral increase, introduction of 60 per cent participation regime (back-dated to January 1st) and previous adjustments under terms of second Geneva Agreement on November 1st and December 1st, 1973. Revenue calculation: weighted average of revenue on 40 per cent of production known as equity crude, calculated as in item (*c*), and 94 per cent of postings less production cost on 60 per cent of production known as buy-back crude. Note: in practice the weighted average figures for revenues in 1974 are notional—partly because during the year the division between equity and buy-back crude was often nearer 60–40 or 50–50 than 40–60, and partly because, up to October, there were variations at different times and in different states in the percentage of postings charged to the companies for buy-back crude. This percentage varied from 93 to 94.8 per cent of postings.

(*l*) July 1st, 1974: after royalty rate adjustment by OPEC at Quito. Revenue calculation: as in (*k*) except that royalty rate used in equity crude calculation is 14.5 per cent, and the percentage of postings charged for buy-back crude is 94.8 per cent.

(*m*) October 1st, 1974: after royalty and tax rate adjustments by OPEC at Vienna. Revenue calculation as in (*k*) except that in equity crude calculation royalty rate used is 16.67 per cent and tax rate is 65.65 per cent, and in the buy-back crude calculation the buy-back price is 93 per cent of postings.

(*n*) January 1st, 1975: after royalty and tax rate adjustment and posted price reduction agreed in Abu Dhabi in November, and introduction of single price structure in Vienna in December. Also after change in ratio used in calculating Abu Dhabi acquisition price from 40–60 to 50–50 made retroactive to January 1st, and introduction of 10 cents discount by Abu Dhabi on the 93 per cent of postings applied to the now notional buy-back crude. Revenue calculation: weighted average of posted price minus expensed 20 per cent royalty and production cost taxed at 85 per cent with royalty added for 40 per cent (or in Abu Dhabi's case 50 per cent) of production treated as equity crude, and 93 per cent of postings (less 10 cents in Abu Dhabi's case) less production cost for 60 per cent (or in Abu Dhabi's case 50 per cent) of production treated as buy-back crude. As from January 1st, 1975, this formula was applied to 100 per cent of production, so in practice the price distinction between equity and buy-back crude ceased to exist even if the notions of equity and buy-back crude were still used in working out the single price level. Note: In some cases figures in the table for government take in 1975 and selling prices in later years are notional because of unofficial discounts given by producers wanting to increase their output.

(*o*) October 1st, 1975: after 10 per cent increase announced by OPEC in Vienna. Revenue calculation: By October 1975 OPEC was talking in terms of official government selling prices to third parties (93 per cent of postings) rather than of posted prices. On this basis it is not possible to give a uniform formula for determining government revenues in later 1975, 1976 and 1977 because each country's situation was different. Variations would occur depending on whether a country had taken over its concessionaries entirely or whether the foreign companies still held a 40 per cent equity stake. In the first case crude sold back to the former concessionaries went at the selling price less varying amounts of discounts (15 cents per barrel *taken* by the foreign companies in the case of Kuwait and 15 cents per barrel *produced* in the case of Qatar) with further variations being caused by the different percentages of total production sold back to the concessionaires or sold to third parties. In the second case crude sold back to concessionaires had its price calculated as in item (*n*), while the remaining volume of crude went at the selling price. For these reasons the figures given in the table for October 1975 onwards are government selling prices, rather than posted prices and government revenues with production costs.

(*p*) January 1st, 1977: after the split in OPEC at Doha in December 1976. For revenue calculations *see* item (*o*).

(*q*) July 1st, 1977: after OPEC reconciliation. Revenue calculation as above.

(*r*) January 1st, 1979: after OPEC meeting in Abu Dhabi and adjustments to the differential affecting Kuwaiti crude in early 1978. Revenue calculation as above.

(*s*) April 1st, 1979: after OPEC meeting in Geneva in March which brought forward to the second quarter of 1979 the increase scheduled at Abu Dhabi for the last quarter. Also after surcharges in February and April, the latter being backdated to the beginning of the month.

(*t*) July 1st, 1979: after OPEC meeting in Geneva in June and surcharges of May and June.

REFINERY CAPACITY AND OWNERSHIP[1]

('000 barrels per day)

(on stream or due on stream in 1979)

State	Refinery	Capacity	State Total	Ownership
Iran	Abadan	630		National Iranian Oil Co.
	Esfahan	200		,, ,, ,, ,,
	Kermanshah	15		,, ,, ,, ,,
	Shiraz	80		,, ,, ,, ,,
	Tabriz	80		,, ,, ,, ,,
	Teheran	225	1,230	,, ,, ,, ,,
Iraq	Daurah	73		Government Oil Refineries Admin.
	Basra	140		,, ,, ,, ,,
	Kirkuk	18		,, ,, ,, ,,
	Alwand (Khanaqin)	12		,, ,, ,, ,,
	Haditha/K3	6		,, ,, ,, ,,
	Muftiah (Basra)	4		,, ,, ,, ,,
	Qaiyera (Mosul)	2	255	,, ,, ,, ,,
Kuwait	Shuaiba	180		Kuwait National Petroleum Co.
	Mina al Ahmedi	285		Kuwait Oil Co.
	Mina Abdullah	145	610	KNPC
Saudi Arabia	Ras Tanura	415		Aramco
	Riyadh	15		Petromin
	Jeddah	30	460	,,
Partitioned Zone	Mina Saud	50		Getty
	Ras al Khafji	27	77	Arabian Oil Co.
Bahrain	Sitra	250	250	Bahrain Petroleum Co.
Qatar	Umm Said	20	20	National Oil Distribution Co.
Abu Dhabi	Abu Dhabi	14	14	Abu Dhabi National Oil Co.
Yemen, P.D.R.	Aden	160	160	Government
Lebanon	Tripoli	30		Government
	Sidon	17	47	MEDRECO (Caltex & Mobil)
Jordan	Zerqa	60	60	Jordan Petroleum Refining Co.
Syria	Homs	100		General Petroleum Authority
	Banias	120	220	,, ,, ,,
Egypt	Mex-Alexandria	64		Alexandria Petroleum Co.
	Suez	100		Suez Oil Processing Co.
	Tanta (Nile Delta)	14		,, ,, ,, ,,
	Al Amiriyah (Alexandria)	36	214	El Nasr Petroleum Co.
Sudan	Port Sudan	22	22	British Petroleum & Shell
Libya	Marsa el Brega	8		Esso Sirte
	Zavia	60	68	Libyan Government
Algeria	Hassi Messaoud	2		SONATRACH
	Algiers	50		,,
	Arzew	53	105	,,
Tunisia	Bizerta	25	25	Soc. Tunisio-Italienne de Raffinage
Morocco	Sidi Kacem	15		Soc. Chérifienne des Pétroles
	Mohammedia	115	130	Marocaine-Italienne de Raffinage
M.E. and N.A. Total			3,992	

[*continued on next page*

REFINERY CAPACITY AND OWNERSHIP—*continued*]

STATE	REFINERY	CAPACITY	STATE TOTAL	OWNERSHIP
Venezuela			1,445	
U.S.A.			17,375	
United Kingdom			2,730	
Italy			4,270	
France			3,445	
Germany, Fed. Rep.			3,090	
Japan			5,450	

[1] Excludes topping plants.

Note: A major expansion of Middle Eastern refinery capacity is currently under way or planned. The main developments are taking place in Iran, Algeria, Libya, Egypt and the Arabian Peninsula producers. Saudi Arabia has three refineries (including a lube refinery) at an advanced planning stage; Kuwait is studying a major expansion of the Ahmedi refinery (an old plant, which has recently been running far below capacity); and Abu Dhabi has a big new refinery project on which work is starting in 1979. Algeria is building refineries at Skikda and Bajaia (both due on stream in 1979 or 1980) as well as expanding the Hassi Messaoud plant.

OIL CONSUMPTION

(million barrels per day)

	1977	1978	Oil as Percentage of Primary Energy Consumption in 1978
U.S.A.*	17.945	18.345	47
Canada	1.795	1.835	40
Total N. America	19.740	20.180	46
Belgium/Lux'bourg.	0.565	0.575	56
Netherlands	0.770	0.775	50
France	2.350	2.445	63
W. Germany	2.855	2.955	58
Italy	1.940	1.995	68
United Kingdom	1.895	1.930	44
Total W. Europe	14.235	14.600	58

	1977	1978	Oil as Percentage of Primary Energy Consumption in 1978
Latin America	3.985	4.190	66
Middle East	1.570	1.655	73
Africa	1.165	1.240	46
S. and S.E. Asia	2.590	2.875	49
Japan	5.200	5.420	72
U.S.S.R.	8.025	8.385	38
E. Europe	2.060	2.070	23
China	1.465	1.705	17
World Total	60.975	63.120	46
Free World Total	49.425	50.960	53

* U.S. Processing gain has been deducted from total domestic product demand.

Source: BP Statistical Review of the World Oil Industry.

OIL DEMAND PROJECTIONS

(million barrels per day)

	1973 Actuals	1973 Projections for 1980	1979 Projections for 1980	1973 Projections for 1985	1979 Projections for 1985	1979 Projections for 1990	1979 Projections for 1995	1979 Projections for 2000
N. America, inc. Mexico	19.1	24.4	21.5	28.8	20.6	20.7	20.8	20.8
Western Europe	15.2	21.8	15.0	28.5	15.9	17.1	18.1	18.6
Japan	5.5	9.0	6.5	12.0	7.2	7.9	8.2	8.2
World outside Communist areas (WOCA)	47.8	70.0	53.7	91.5	56.2	60.2	63.3	65.5

Note: This table illustrates the effects of the oil price rises and supply disruptions of the 1970s on projections of oil demand. The figures given for 1973 projections were at the lower end of the projections made in that year. The 1979 projections, dating from just before the price rises and oil shortages of May, assume slow growth in the consuming countries and a rather poor performance in diversification into other energy sources.

Principal Oil Groups Producing or Refining in the Gulf

This list accounts for well over 90 per cent of oil exploring, producing and refining operations in the Middle East. But it is not a complete list. There are a large number of small operators either exploring or producing oil in minor quantities. Further details of the national takeovers of these groups are given in the text which precedes the oil statistics.

NATIONAL IRANIAN OIL COMPANY

NIOC is responsible for all oil operations in Iran. At the end of February 1979 it was announced that the company would be taking over entirely the role of producing and marketing oil in the area of "the Consortium". The Consortium, officially Iranian Oil Participants, had originally been formed as a leasee following the settlement of the 1951–3 Mussadiq crisis in which the Anglo-Iranian Oil Company (BP) had been nationalized. Its members were BP with 40 per cent; Shell 14 per cent; Exxon, Mobil, Socal, Texaco and Gulf with 7 per cent each; CFP 6 per cent; and a group of U.S. independents with 5 per cent between them. In 1973 this group had surrendered administration of the oil fields to NIOC, but had remained as operating contractors, through the Oil Service Company of Iran (OSCO), and privileged buyers of Iranian crude. OSCO accounted for about 90 per cent of Iranian production and its owners took over half of this crude themselves—the rest being marketed by NIOC. Well before this agreement was terminated by NIOC in 1979 its terms were mainly inoperative following the failure of successive rounds of renegotiations. In March and April, as it restored production after the virtual shut-down of December 1978-February 1979, NIOC began concluding spot and medium-term sales contracts, initially with members of the former Consortium and former Consortium and NIOC crude oil customers. Later NIOC signed contracts with a number of new customers.

In addition to its production role in the former Consortium area, NIOC has for some years operated itself an oil field at Naft-i-Shah, and has entered into a number of partnerships and service contracts with foreign companies since 1959. Some of these in 1978 were exploring, others producing—the most successful involving ENI, Amoco, Atlantic Richfield and Elf-Aquitaine. In May 1979 it was announced that NIOC was considering terminating most—or all of these agreements.

NIOC owns all of Iran's refineries and the internal distribution business (Iran consumes some 700,000 barrels a day), as well as a growing tanker fleet and a number of overseas investments in refineries.

IRAQ NATIONAL OIL COMPANY

The Iraqi state oil company is responsible for foreign marketing operations for all Iraqi crude and runs or supervises various exploration and production operations in the south of the country. The biggest of these, centred on the Rumaila and Zubair fields, was taken over in stages from the Basrah Petroleum Company, which was part of the Iraq Petroleum Company group. (IPC was owned by BP, Shell, CFP and an Exxon-Mobil partnership with $23\frac{3}{4}$ per cent each, and Gulbenkian interests with 5 per cent). INOC accounts for rather over half of Iraq's production.

IRAQI COMPANY FOR OIL OPERATIONS (ICOO)

The state-owned ICOO was formed in June 1972 to take over the production operations of the nationalized Iraq Petroleum Company. ICOO manages production from the Kirkuk, Jambur and Bai Hassan fields on former IPC acreage, and from the Ain Zalah and Butmah fields on former acreage of the Mosul Petroleum Company, dissolved by the IPC group in early 1973. Marketing of production from the Kirkuk area is managed by INOC. Production from the former MPC fields is piped to the Daurah refinery near Baghdad.

KUWAIT OIL COMPANY

In March 1975 it was announced that the state had taken 100 per cent of the assets of KOC, which had originally been owned 50-50 by Gulf and BP. The state run KOC is now responsible for all producing operations in Kuwait proper and in the Kuwaiti part of the onshore Partitioned Zone. In this area it has taken over the assets of Aminoil, which was nationalized in the latter part of 1977. KOC operates the Ahmedi refinery and the LPG plants, but it is not responsible for marketing the products of either operation. All Kuwaiti refined products are marketed by KNPC. LPG and all crude oil exports are marketed by the Ministry of Oil.

KUWAIT NATIONAL PETROLEUM COMPANY

KNPC operates the Shuaiba and Mina Abdullah refineries (the latter recently taken over from Aminoil) and is responsible for sales of refined products from all Kuwaiti refineries, internally and externally. The company is building up a fleet of product carriers, although the state's crude oil tankers remain under the partially privately-owned Kuwait Oil Tankers Company.

ARAMCO

Aramco is responsible for all exploration, production and refining onshore and offshore in the Eastern Province. It accounts for all Saudi oil production except that coming from the Partitioned Zone. It has also recently been given charge of the construction of the government's gas gathering system, a natural gas liquids pipeline across the Kingdom to Yanbu and the unification of the Eastern Province electricity grid.

As of May 1979 only 60 per cent of Aramco's oil production and exploration operations were owned by the government, but it was intended that the government would soon take 100 per cent, negotiations having been under way for some years. Nonetheless, for practical purposes the government already had complete control of Aramco operations—making the company, in most respects, into a giant contractor working for the state. The only assets which remained entirely Aramco owned were the refinery and NGL plant at Ras Tanura, and Tapline.

Aramco itself remains an American company owned by Socal, Exxon and Texaco with 30 per cent each, and Mobil with 10 per cent—though the Mobil share is in the process of being raised to $12\frac{1}{2}$ per cent. The Aramco shareholders continue to market virtually all of the Kingdom's production.

PETROMIN

The Saudi state oil company is responsible for a small part of foreign crude sales (less than 10 per cent of production) and all internal distribution and refining. Petromin owns the small Riyadh and Jeddah refineries and will be the Saudi partner in the export refineries planned for Jubail and Yanbu. It will also be responsible for the Kingdom's NGL production and sales when the gas gathering system being built under Aramco supervision is finished.

QATAR PETROLEUM PRODUCING AUTHORITY (ONSHORE OPERATIONS)

In September 1976 the Qatar General Petroleum Corporation completed the takeover of the concession originally held by the Qatar Petroleum Company (part of the Iraq Petroleum Company group, *see* under INOC above). This operation, which accounts for all the state's onshore production, is now run by a QGPC subsidiary, QPPA (Onshore Operations) which has its personnel seconded by the Dukan Service Company owned by the Iraq Petroleum group.

QATAR PETROLEUM PRODUCING AUTHORITY (OFFSHORE OPERATIONS)

In February 1977 the Qatar General Petroleum Corporation completed the takeover of the concession originally held by Shell. The operation, which accounts for all of Qatar's offshore production except for a small field held jointly with Abu Dhabi, is now run by a QGPC subsidiary, QPPA (Offshore Operations) with personnel seconded by the Qatar Shell Service Company owned by Shell.

ABU DHABI PETROLEUM COMPANY (ADPC)

Originally a concession of seventy-five years from 1939, expiring 2014. Includes onshore acreage and a three-mile belt of territorial waters, minus areas relinquished. In 1973 the Government took a 25 per cent share in the operation, and in 1974 negotiated 60 per cent participation. No attempt is being made to complete the takeover of ADPC, although in 1978 all the shareholders established a locally incorporated operating company, Abu Dhabi Company for Onshore Operations, to run production on their behalf. The company accounts for all of Abu Dhabi's production onshore—over half of total output.

OWNERSHIP:

Abu Dhabi National Oil Company (ADNOC)		60%
Abu Dhabi Petroleum Company		40%
British Petroleum	9½%	
Royal Dutch/Shell	9½%	
Compagnie Française des Pétroles (CFP)	9½%	
Near East Development Corpn. (Exxon & Mobil)	9½%	
Participations and Explorations Corpn. (Gulbenkian)	2%	

ABU DHABI MARINE AREAS (ADMA)

Originally a concession held by BP (two-thirds) and CFP (one-third) running from 1953 to 2018, and covering areas of the continental shelf beyond the three-mile limit. In December 1972 BP sold part of its stake to a large group of Japanese industrial companies. In 1973 the government took a 25 per cent stake, and in 1974 negotiated a 60 per cent participation. No attempt is being made to complete the takeover of ADMA although early in 1979 all the shareholders established a locally incorporated operating company, ADMA-OPCO, to run production on their behalf. Under a separate agreement CFP is providing ADMA-OPCO with technical expertise. ADMA accounts for most of Abu Dhabi's offshore production, from the Umm Shaif and Zakum fields. Four other rather marginal fields are operated by foreign groups of mixed ownership, and on a bigger scale it has been agreed that a separate company will be formed to develop the upper part of the giant Zakum field. This company excludes BP and CFP among the ADMA shareholders, their shares being taken by ADNOC, although CFP will act for a fee as project manager.

OWNERSHIP:

Abu Dhabi National Oil Company (ADNOC)	60%
British Petroleum	14⅔%
Compagnie Française des Pétroles	13⅓%
Japan Oil Development Co. (JODCO)	12%

DUBAI PETROLEUM COMPANY (DPC)

In July 1975 Dubai announced that it had negotiated a 100 per cent takeover of the DPC group, though the terms of the takeover were very different from those applying anywhere else in the Middle East. Ownership of the DPC group's offshore concession, originally granted in 1952 for 60 years to BP and CFP as Dubai Marine Areas, had changed on a number of occasions before July 1976, but the Government had not previously taken a 25 or 60 per cent holding. Under the terms of the July agreement DPC itself (Conoco) remained as operator, and the DPC group continued to market Dubai's oil, take the risks, make the investment and bear the costs. The group was, however, paid back by the state all of its previous investment, and will in future be able to depreciate new investments over three years instead of ten, giving the Government ownership of the oil-producing assets. DPC accounts for all of Dubai's production.

OWNERSHIP:

Dubai Petroleum Company (Continental)	30%
Compagnie Française des Pétroles	50%
Deutsche Texaco	10%
Sun	5%
Wintershall	5%

PETROLEUM DEVELOPMENT OMAN (PDO)

Originally a concession of seventy-five years from 1937, expiring 2012. Onshore areas, originally covering northern provinces, now including Dhofar. Government took a 25 per cent share in 1973, and increased this to 60 per cent in 1974. PDO accounts for all of Oman's production.

OWNERSHIP:

Oman Government	60%
Royal Dutch/Shell	34%
Compagnie Française des Pétroles	4%
Participations and Explorations Corpn. (Gulbenkian)	2%

The Arms Trade with the Middle East and North Africa

Hanns Maull

The Middle East is today—judging by the percentage share of military expenditure in Gross Domestic Products—the most highly militarized area in the world. It is also one of the areas most plagued by military conflict and war.

The enormous oil wealth of the Middle East and North Africa gives the region a central strategic importance in East-West relations. At the same time, two geographical areas within the region have been sources of military and political conflict: Palestine and the Persian Gulf. In Palestine, the issue is the struggle between Jewish and Arab (Palestinian) nationalism over the same territory; in the Persian Gulf, there are various rivalries, conflicts and tensions which all appear at least connected with the main source of wealth in this zone: oil. Both areas have also seen an unparalleled military build-up in two major arms races: the Arab-Israeli arms race, dominated by Israel, Egypt and Syria, but also including other countries; and the arms race in the Persian Gulf in which Iran, Saudi Arabia and Iraq were the main participants. Here, as well, the arms race has shown a tendency to spill over to other countries in the area. There is also a certain link between the two zones: the financial, military and above all the political support (in the form of the oil weapon) which the Arab Gulf producers gave to the countries fighting against Israel is clear evidence of this now strongly established connection between the Persian Gulf and the Arab-Israeli zone. This connection has direct implications for the arms build-up in the Arab-Israeli conflict, since it provides Arab combatant States with a source of finance for their weapons procurement, and potentially widens the circle of countries directly involved in a potential future conflict.

The period 1974 to 1978 saw a distinct movement towards a peaceful management of conflict both in the Arab–Israeli zone and in the Persian Gulf. The disengagement agreements negotiated by Dr. Kissinger; the emphasis of the Carter administration on securing an overall solution to the Arab–Israeli conflict; its shift to direct and even-handed participation in the negotiating process; and finally President Sadat's peace initiative in late 1977—all this could be seen as part of a progression towards a satisfactory settlement of the conflict between Israel and the Arab world. The moderate Arab oil producers led by Saudi Arabia were during this period willing to support the search for an agreement, and to give the United States and Egypt the freedom of manoeuvre to do so. Their understanding was that such an agreement would have to be comprehensive, i.e. resolving all issues of contention between Israel and the Arab world, and notably the Palestinian question, in a way which would satisfy the majority of Arabs, as well as Palestinians. The meeting between Carter, Begin and Sadat at Camp David, however, seemed to confirm fears which had been aroused already by Sadat's visit to Jerusalem: that Israel and Egypt had embarked on the road to a separate peace agreement with at best tenuous links with other Arab–Israeli issues of contention.

During the same period 1974–78, the three major Gulf states Iraq, Iran and Saudi Arabia had managed to settle, at least temporarily, most issues under dispute between them (bilateral agreements were made between Iran and Iraq and Saudi Arabia and Iraq). Saudi Arabia and Iran had even developed a close partnership based on largely identical regional objectives. This helped to ensure stability in the Gulf and a predominance of moderate policies in the Middle East region as a whole.

In early 1979 three major events had fundamentally transformed the situation. First, the Egyptian–Israeli treaty had reduced the probability of a full-scale war between Israel and its neighbours very considerably, but it had also led to a polarization of the Arab world, with Egypt largely isolated: at the Baghdad meeting in late March 1979, a large majority of the Arab world agreed to ostracize Egypt through the severance of diplomatic and economic relations. Saudi Arabia and the other moderate oil producers reluctantly followed this course—from their point of view, the Egyptian–Israeli agreement did not make sufficient provisions for an overall settlement of the conflict and notably of the Palestinian problem. This left the Gulf producers vulnerable to pressures from the PLO and from radical regimes and groups in the Arab world, and gave them little choice but to align themselves with the mainstream of Arab reaction to the peace treaty.

The second major event—triggered off by the evolution of Israeli–Egyptian negotiations in the direction of a separate peace agreement—was the reconciliation between Syria and Iraq. This shifted the centre of gravity of Arab politics away from the Egyptian–Saudi axis; the moderate oil producers had to adjust their policies towards the new centre. One of the objectives of the Syrian–Iraqi alignment was to build up a credible military and political alternative to Egypt in the conflict with Israel; this implied closer co-operation with the U.S.S.R. at least with regard to arms purchases.

The third event was the revolution in Iran and the fall of the Shah. The new regime in Teheran was sympathetic to the PLO and thus gave a boost to radical forces in the Arab world; at the same time, the fall of the Shah meant that Saudi Arabia had lost a powerful conservative partner and therefore much of its ability to impose moderation on Arab politics. The precarious balance in the Gulf during the years 1974 to

1978 had thus been overthrown; the disintegration of Iran's military might created a vacuum with uncertain prospects for the resurgence of old and new conflicts such as the Kurdish fight for national independence or autonomy in Iraq and Iran, the Iraqi claim to the Arabic-speaking, oil-rich Iranian province of Khuzistan, and conflict between the Shi'ite majority and the Sunni rulers in Iraq. In the short term, the implication of Iran's revolution heightened concern about security in the conservative Arab Gulf states; in the longer term, the unclear domestic situation in Iran could produce a new regime with new foreign policy orientations of as yet uncertain character.

These two main centres of conflict in the region, however, are not the only sources of instability and tension: there are at least two epi-centres in North Africa, and at the Western coast of the Red Sea, where Middle Eastern and North African countries are directly or indirectly involved on opposite sides The former relates to the Moroccan/Mauritanian takeover of the Spanish Sahara, and the Algerian support for *Polisario*, the movement for independence of the Saharan Democratic Republic, which has mounted a guerrilla war against Moroccan and Mauritanian forces. The latter conflict, in the Horn of Africa, escalated considerably during 1977. The Ethiopian regime, weakened by internal differences within the ruling junta and an extremely bloody suppression of domestic opposition, found itself confronted with dramatic new advances by the liberation movements in Eritrea, and with what was *de facto* a major Somali offensive in Ogaden. The threats were successfully contained with the help of massive arms transfers from the Soviet Union and large troop contingents from Cuba. Soviet presence in the Horn of Africa is of obvious strategic importance and political significance for the Gulf region, and the possibility of a resurgence of conflict in the future with outside involvement from Gulf states and the U.S.S.R. cannot be excluded.

THE NATURE OF THE ARMS RACES

Arms races tend to develop quantitative and qualitative aspects, and both are strongly at work in the Middle Eastern arms races. The *quantitative* aspect is apparent in the rapid growth of the armed forces (in terms of manpower, tanks, aircraft, artillery etc.). In the 1967 war, Israel could muster some 1,050 tanks and 290 combat aircraft, while Egypt and Syria together had some 1,650 tanks and 550 aircraft. In 1977, two bitter and costly wars later, the military power of Israel stood at 2,765 tanks and 543 combat aircraft, while Egypt and Syria together possessed 4,375 tanks and 928 combat aircraft. The *qualitative* aspect is reflected by the rapid growth in destructive power of each weapon system and the deployment of totally new systems which replace old, outdated systems. This qualitative change means that less complex and sophisticated weapons are replaced by more sophisticated and therefore more expensive weapons. Impressive as the quantitative arms build-up in the Middle East may be, it is surpassed by the speed of qualitative changes. The gap between the arms technology of the Great Powers and the Middle Eastern countries has been gradually closed, with important thresholds being the deployment of supersonic jet fighters (between 1956 and 1967) and the large-scale introduction of missiles and electronic warfare (between 1970 and 1973). As far as conventional warfare is concerned, the main participants in the two Middle Eastern arms races now command weapon systems which are the most modern available for the Great Powers themselves; a development strongly underlined by U.S. deliveries of advanced aircraft and equipment (F–14 *Tomcat*, *Phoenix* air-to-air missiles, P–3F *Orion* anti-submarine surveillance planes; F–15 and F–16 fighter aircraft) to Iran, Israel and Saudi Arabia, and by the appearance of the most advanced Soviet fighter aircraft (MiG–23 and MiG–25) in Syria and Iraq. The rapid advance of the arms importers in technological terms is best reflected in the fact that some weapon systems are specifically developed or redesigned in accordance with the specifications of the buyers (e.g. the Iranian version of the U.K. *Chieftain* tank and *Rapier* missile, now both probably cancelled; the Saudi version of the *Maverick* missile), who also share development costs with the producer. The qualitative arms race also took a new turn in the past years in the area of surface-to-surface missiles: Israel received the American *Lance* missile (with a range of 70 miles), while both Egypt and Syria have been supplied by the Soviet Union with *Frog* (range: 30 miles) and *Scud* missiles (range: 185 miles). Both the *Lance* and the *Scud* are thought to be capable of delivering nuclear warheads, and this has once more focused attention on the last remaining qualitative difference between Middle Eastern and Superpower weapon systems: the nuclear threshold. While Israel certainly has had nuclear option for some years, and would be capable of assembling nuclear warheads within a relatively short period, should she desire to do so, the growing interest of other Middle Eastern countries in nuclear technology and reactors poses the question whether some of these countries might also eventually try to develop nuclear weapons. Nuclear reactors normally burn enriched uranium, and produce plutonium. Both can be used to manufacture nuclear warheads, provided a country has access to enrichment facilities geared to producing heavily enriched uranium, or reprocessing capacity. Countries to receive reactors and/or to develop some form of cooperation with nuclear powers or countries with considerable know-how and capabilities in nuclear technology (threshold powers such as Argentina or Germany) include at present Egypt, Iran, Iraq, Saudi Arabia and Libya. Of these countries, only Iran has signed, ratified and implemented the safeguards of the Non-Proliferation Treaty; Libya and Iraq have signed and ratified the treaty but are not yet subject to safeguards; Egypt has signed but not yet ratified the NPT, and Saudi Arabia has not even signed it yet.

Arms races of such dimensions in a third world area necessarily mean heavy reliance on imported weapons. True, some Middle Eastern countries have indigenous arms industries producing small arms and ammunition and four Arab countries have launched a new effort to develop an indigenous arms industry in a joint venture, using the oil revenues of Saudi Arabia, Qatar and the United Arab Emirates and the existing know-how in Egypt. In this connection Egypt reached an agreement to build British *Lynx* helicopters, *Hawk* and *Mirage* 2000 as well as the *Alpha Jet* aircraft under licence. But, so far, only Israel's arms industry is of military significance, and even she has to rely heavily on arms imports.* Table 1 shows the amount of arms imports by Middle Eastern countries and (by comparison with *total* expenditure on arms imports from 1961 to 1971) the financial implications of quantitatively and qualitatively rapidly expanding arms races.

THE MOTIVES FOR THE ARMS BUILD-UPS

Arms build-ups, and arms races (i.e. competitive build-ups) are predominantly fuelled by a feeling of insecurity and a (real or imagined) threat to vital foreign policy objectives among the participants. There are, however, other factors which make for higher military expenditures or facilitate military build-ups. Generally speaking, external objectives include not only the obvious one—military forces sufficient to guarantee the security of the state against a threat from outside. They may also include the intention to expand the influence of the state beyond its boundaries by the explicit or implicit threat and the application of force to achieve certain objectives. Military power also serves as a symbol of national independence and status. Prestige expenditure like Abu Dhabi's small airforce of Mirage 5 fighters (at present manned and serviced by Pakistani personnel) or Libya's air defence system hardly have any military function but serve mainly as showpieces in parades.

Another set of motives for increasing military strength is internal: some of the Middle Eastern and North African régimes are politically unstable and still have to enforce the central power of the Government against the return or threat of tribal and minority challenges. The guerilla war in the Dhofar province of Oman is a typical example here; the bloody civil war in the Lebanon no doubt also had strong roots in internal contradictions and conflicts, although outside interference and the presence of a large Palestinian refugee group linked the civil war to intra-Arab rivalries and the Israeli-Arab dispute. The internal violence in the Lebanon has led to a massive influx of arms from various sources through clandestine channels.

Many Middle Eastern and North African countries are ruled by military régimes or governments whose main source of support is the armed forces. Consequently, the armed forces form an influential pressure group, whose demands have to be taken into account. Since the rulers of these countries depend on the loyalty of the army they will try to keep this by dispensing various benefits and privileges. A good example here is Libya: in the last year of its existence, the monarchy embarked on a modernization programme for the armed forces in order to appease the growing discontent in the officer corps; after the coup, military expenditure rose dramatically, and it is difficult to say whether the Libyan interest in the Arab-Israeli conflict under the new leadership in fact caused this increase or was a justification for it.

These external and internal factors fuel the demand for higher military expenditure and consequently for increased arms imports. The various mechanisms of arms races (worst-case assumptions of defence planners and the trend towards over-insurance: Israel, for instance, will plan for a contingency of a large Arab coalition of armed forces and attempt to provide forces appropriate to it while Egypt might try to achieve parity with Israel by itself) actually cause these factors to interlock so that internally motivated arms purchases might induce the opponent to increase his force level as well.

Of crucial importance for the actual development of the arms race are factors of availability—the resources available for military expenditure, and the interest of Great Powers in particular countries or groups. High oil revenues enable the oil producers (and other Arab countries as well) to buy weapons, and the involvement of the United States and the Soviet Union in the Arab-Israeli zone and in the Persian Gulf allowed countries in the region to receive weapons even without the financial burden this would normally constitute (reduced or suspended payment, favourable conditions for repayment). Besides, Saudi Arabia has begun to use its importance as the principal oil producer in the Middle East, and its close relationship with the United States in oil price and production decisions, as a lever in its arms demands: the sale of F-15s to Riyadh was explicitly linked by Saudi Arabian officials to future price and production policies.

Let us now take a closer look at some countries. In the Arab-Israeli zone, one could draw a distinction between defensive and offensive objectives of a military build-up. Israel relies on military strength to deter any attack on its territory and to induce the Arabs to comply with its demands. Egypt and Syria, on the other hand, relied on an offensive military strategy to break the stalemate in the Arab-Israeli conflict. While Egypt seems to have renounced any military action against Israel in the peace treaty, it has nevertheless demanded substantial additional arms supplies to satisfy its security objectives in the region. Thus, Egypt will probably continue to import sub-

* Today, Israel produces two light transport airplanes, the *Arava* and the *Westwind*, and recently also started production of a new fighter, *Kfir* (based on French *Mirage* design and an American engine, the General Electric J-79) in addition to the *Barak*, another indigenous, less powerful Israeli version of the *Mirage* which had been already used in combat in 1973. The most recent major weapons system presented by the Israeli arms industry is a new battle tank, the *Merkava*. Israel also manufactures air-to-air missiles (*Shafir*) and ship-to-ship missiles (*Gabriel*) as well as missile boats and (under concession) the Sabra medium tank. The country has become an exporter of a considerable range of arms, from the UZI submachine gun to *Gabriel* and *Shafir* missiles, and has reportedly also offered the *Kfir* fighter for sale; according to the London-based IISS, Israel supplies military equipment to several Central and South American countries.

stantial quantities of modern weapon systems. And Syria is also likely to increase its efforts since the new configuration in the Arab–Israeli conflict means that the country can no longer count on Egyptian military support against Israel. Both defence requirements and the build-up of a military "option" against Israel will, therefore, tend to advocate higher levels of military power. Egypt and Syria, on the other hand, relied on an offensive military strategy to break the stalemate in the Arab-Israeli conflict.

THE PERSIAN GULF

While the Arab–Israeli conflict is essentially clear-cut, the Persian Gulf is characterized by a much more complex structure of varied, partly overlapping tensions. The crucial country in the past and present has been Iran, although for different reasons. Until the revolution, the country had been committed to a rapid build-up of military power, thereby providing a powerful stimulus for other Gulf states to expand their forces, too. After the revolution, the disintegration of the imperial army, the cancellation of arms deals worth several billions of dollars, and the uncertainty of the domestic situation in the aftermath of the Shah's departure, created a power vacuum in the Gulf, thus heightening concerns about security in the conservative Arab states and opening up new prospects for re-alignments and conflict.

Under the Shah, Iran's main concern had been the establishment of a dominant influence in the Gulf as a means to secure her vital trade routes. These trade routes were, in the eyes of Iran, potentially threatened by countries and forces hostile to Iran, and possibly through a Soviet co-ordination of these hostile forces. Iraq was viewed in Teheran as the main opponent to Persian hegemony in the Gulf; the two states were at loggerheads over a wide range of conflicting claims and issues such as the mutual support for dissident movements in Kurdistan (supplied by Iran), Khuzistan/Arabistan (which Iraw regarded as part of the Arab world and its own territory), off-shore demarcation lines, and the shipping rights in the Shatt al-Arab waterway. Iraq never fully accepted the Iranian bid for hegemony in the Gulf and tried to match growing Iranian military power through a parallel build-up. In March, 1975, the two states signed an agreement which settled the differences between them, and relations improved markedly; nevertheless, underlying suspicions lingered on, and the arms race between the two continued. In the case of Iraq, the military build-up drew further momentum from involvement in the Arab-Israeli region, and from the need to suppress the domestic challenge of Kurdish nationalism.

The Shah also saw the survival of conservative states and regimes on the other side of the Gulf as a vital security objective of Iran, and he tried to prevent the spreading of radical regimes, in the sheikhdoms through military support to the Sultan of Oman. This also enabled Iran to exert *de facto*-control over both sides of the Strait of Hormuz, strategically the most sensitive point in the Gulf. Ironically, the Shah also voiced concern over the stability of the Saudi monarchy, and tried to push Riyadh and other conservative Arab oil producers into domestic reforms to modernize their political systems in line with economic development.

Iran's rapidly evolving military power gave the country a clear superiority in the Gulf region, and an important role beyond it in the Indian Ocean. The Iraqi-Iranian agreement marked a reluctant and presumably tactical acceptance of this by Iraq, and other Gulf states also recognized the dominant position of Iran. Nevertheless, it was not only Baghdad which tried to challenge the Iranian military build-up by parallel measures of their own: Saudi Arabia also embarked on a massive programme of expansion and modernization of her armed forces. The external motivations for this were presumably a certain distrust of Iranian ambitions and a fear of the radical regime in Baghdad.

The revolution in Iran changed the situation in the Gulf fundamentally. The first aspect of this change was the erosion of Iranian power and dominance in Gulf affairs—a result of the rapid disintegration of the armed forces as the main pillar of support of the *ancien régime*, the cancellations of arms contracts with a total volume of more than $10,000 million, and the selling back of some modern Western weapon systems such as the F-14. This not only affected Iran's military capabilities, but even more so (although possibly only temporarily) other countries' perceptions of those capabilities. Secondly, the domestic situation in Iran remained undecided, and there were signs of disintegration and a splintering of the polity along ethnic and confessional lines, as well as a diffusion of power to power centres outside the control of the government. Thirdly, there were to be regional implications of the Iranian revolution in terms of its impact on other Gulf states, and on regional stability and co-operation, which had not yet become fully clear by mid-1979.

In Saudi Arabia, the fall of the Shah created a heightened feeling of insecurity. The loss of a powerful ally on the other shore of the Gulf, and the polarization in the Arab world resulting from the Egyptian/Israeli peace treaty reduced Saudi influence and leverage in the region. The U.S. role in the events leading to the fall of the Shah can also hardly have been comforting for the Saudi monarchy, although Washington publicly underlined through words and gestures its commitment to Saudi Arabian security.

One of the implications of the new situation in the aftermath of the fall of the Shah could well be additional momentum for the arms race in the Gulf. An example here is the U.S. attempt to stabilize the conflict between North and South Yemen by supplying substantial amounts of military hardware to the shaky regime in the North—a measure also meant to alleviate concern in Riyadh about the willingness and capability of Washington to act in defence of Saudi Arabian security interests. (*See* table 1). Another epicentre of the Gulf arms race is Kuwait: as a result of border skirmishes with Iraq, Kuwait has in recent years embarked on a massive rearmament programme. The

[*continued on p.* 124

Table 1

MAJOR REPORTED ARMS DEALS, MAY 1978–APRIL 1979

Recipient	Value of Total Arms Imports 1961–71 (million current U.S. $)	Supplier Approx. Date of Agreement	Name of System	Value of Contract (million $)	Approx. Quantity	Comments
Egypt	2,197	U.S.A., May 1978	F-5 E Fighter aircraft	400	42	Was to be paid by Saudi Arabia; now uncertain
			F-5 F Trainer aircraft		8	
		France, 1978	*Otomat* coastal defence mounted on *Berliet* trucks with Thompson CSF radar	293	1 system	
		France, 1978	SA 342 *Gazelle* helicopter	n.a.	20	
		U.K., 1978	42M Missile fast attack craft	n.a.	5	
Iran	1,091	U.S.A., Aug. 1978	155 m Self-propelled howitzer	192	214	
			203 m Self-propelled howitzer		84	
		U.S.A., n.a.	RF 4 E Reconnaissance aircraft	170	11	
		U.S.A., Aug. 1978	AIM-9H *Sidewinder* air-to-air missile	14.7	186	
		U.S.A., Aug. 1978	M-548 Cargo carrier	10.8	100	
		U.K., 1978	*Shir Iran* Chieftain battle tank with Rolls Royce engine	n.a.	200	now probably cancelled
		Germany, 1978	Type 209 Submarine	500	6	now probably cancelled
Iraq	760	Switzerland, Aug. 1978	AS 202/18 A *Bravo* training aircraft	n.a.	48	
		France, 1978	*Exolet* M 39 Missile	n.a.	n.a.	
		Japan, June 1978	Landing craft floating dock	25.7	1	
Israel	936	U.S.A., May 1978	F-15 Fighter aircraft	n.a.	15	delivery 1981–82
			F-16 Fighter aircraft	n.a.	75	delivery 1981–83
		U.S.A., 1978	Hughes 500 helicopter	n.a.	30–40	
		U.S.A., July 1978	*Walleye* I bombs	36.4	200	
		U.S.A., July 1978	*Sparrow* Air-to-air missile	24.2	170	
		U.S.A., Dec. 1978	*Hawk* Surface-to-air missile	n.a.	n.a.	
		U.S.A., 1979	AGM 45A-9/AGM 45A-10 Air-to-surface missiles	18.8	100+100	
Kuwait	46	Singapore, July 1978	17 m Fast Patrol Boat/ 32 m Supply craft	10	3+2	
Lebanon	70	France, Nov 1978	155 mm Gun, Missile Patrol Boats	250	3	
			AMX-13 Tank/AMX-30 Tank		100	
			Gazelle SA 342 helicopter		n.a.	
			Puma helicopter	35	n.a.	
			Milan launchers		18	
			Milan Anti-tank missiles		200	delivery Feb. 1979
Libya	210	Italy, 1978	G222 Transport aircraft	382	20	
		Italy, Jan. 1979	A 224 324 mm Torpedo	n.a.	240	
Morocco	125	U.S.A., 1978	Air defence system	200	1 system	
		Italy, July 1978	CH-47 C helicopter	n.a.	6	delivery 1979
		Spain, Jan. 1979	Frigate	n.a.	n.a.	
Saudi Arabia	322	U.S.A., May 1978	F-15 Fighter aircraft		45	delivery 1981–84
			TF-15 Training aircraft		15	
		U.S.A., May 1978	Mk 46 Med 2 Torpedo		52	
			V 150 Armoured car	15.8	94	
		U.S.A., Sept. 1978	F-5F Fighter aircraft		4	
		U.S.A., Sept. 1978	Antsq 73 Air Defence	1,500	1 system	

[*continued on p.* 123

continued from p. 122]

Recipient	Value of Total Arms Imports 1961–71 (million current U.S. $)	Supplier Approx. Date of Agreement	Name of System	Value of Contract (million $)	Approx. Quantity	Comments
Sudan	n.a.	U.S.A., Feb. 1979	F-5 Fighter aircraft	n.a.	12	probably all paid by Saudi Arabia
			M-60 Tank	n.a.	50	
			Armoured Personnel Carriers	n.a.	100	
			C-130 *Hercules* Transport aircraft	n.a.	2	
Tunisia	46	U.S.A., June 1978	M-113 Armoured personnel Carrier	23.3	60	
			Tow Anti-Tank Guided Missile		1,200	
U.A.E.	n.a.	Italy, n.a.	MB 326 KD+LD Counterinsurgency aircraft	n.a.	4	
Yemen Arab Republic	86	U.S.A., 1979	F-5 Fighter aircraft	n.a.	12	paid by Saudi Arabia. Delivery May 1979
			C-130 *Hercules* Transport aircraft	n.a.	2	
			M-60 Tank	n.a.	50	
			Armoured Personnel Carrier		100	

Source: International Institute for Strategic Studies, London.

Table 2

CUMULATIVE VALUE OF ARMS TRANSFERS TO THE MIDDLE EAST AND NORTH AFRICA BY MAJOR SUPPLIERS, 1967–76
(in current U.S. $ million)

	Total	United States	U.S.S.R.	France	U.K.	China People's Republic	Germany, Federal Republic	Other
Algeria . . .	445	5	315	5	—	—	120	5
Bahrain . . .	1	—	—	—	—	—	—	1
Egypt . . .	2,801	1	2,365	125	15	5	105	190
Iran . . .	5,271	3,835	611	15	270	—	275	267
Iraq . . .	2,451	—	1,795	95	5	5	35	515
Israel . . .	4,941	4,761	—	105	35	—	5	35
Jordan . . .	650	505	—	55	60	—	1	30
Kuwait . . .	181	31	—	—	71	—	20	61
Lebanon . . .	131	25	5	75	5	—	—	20
Libya . . .	1,835	65	1,005	325	55	—	15	370
Mauritania . . .	21	—	—	5	1	—	—	15
Morocco . . .	350	55	10	121	1	—	11	146
Oman . . .	71	5	—	—	21	—	—	46
Qatar . . .	5	—	—	5	—	—	—	—
Saudi Arabia . . .	1,440	671	—	225	451	—	11	80
Somalia . . .	185	—	181	—	—	—	5	1
Syria . . .	2,261	5	2,015	5	5	1	35	161
Tunisia . . .	65	40	—	15	—	5	5	1
U.A.E. . . .	105	—	—	50	31	—	—	25
Yemen Arab Rep. .	80	1	35	11	1	—	—	30
Yemen, People's Dem. Rep. . . .	165	—	151	—	1	—	—	30

Source: U.S. Arms Control and Disarmament Agency.

continued from p. 121]
smaller sheikhdoms have also stepped up their purchases of arms. The loss of implicit Iranian protection in the smaller Gulf states could well rekindle efforts to expand some military programmes which had appeared for the most part completed before the Iranian revolution. Equally uncertain is reaction to the U.S. proposal for a new defence organization for the moderate Arab states, which could also have implications for the Gulf arms build-up.

Finally, another arms race in the region has accelerated rapidly: the one between Algeria and Morocco. As a result of growing tensions between the two countries over the Sahara issue, Morocco has in recent years dramatically stepped up its imports of weapons to reduce its inferiority in military power to Algeria.

THE EFFECT OF INCREASED ARMS

The vast amount of highly sophisticated weapons flowing into the Middle East and North Africa often transcends the capacity of the armed forces to absorb these weapons. Highly skilled personnel are needed to man and to maintain them—but in most countries this is a valuable and desperately scarce resource. Long training periods will be needed to operate those weapons effectively, and training can to a large extent only be provided by foreigners. A country then has to send either a great number of soldiers abroad or alternatively provide for training teams. Already, foreign military advisers can be found in many Middle Eastern and North African countries (Americans in Saudi Arabia and Iran, Russians in Syria, Indians in Iraq, Pakistanis in Abu Dhabi and Libya).

These technical problems will prove a formidable and sometimes extremely difficult barrier on the way towards a highly effective military force. To overcome this barrier will mean a heavy drain on precious and scarce resources in terms of manpower and for the poor countries also in terms of capital. But the influx of modern weapons is also likely to have social and political consequences: it will strengthen the power of the military elites and increase their size. The officer classes in the Middle East and North Africa in many countries have proved themselves highly politicized, and their increased power could be accompanied by or lead to more involvement in politics.

THE ARMS SUPPLIERS

The international arms trade has become a competitive business; one could talk about a buyers' market. As table 1 shows, some countries have successfully attempted a degree of diversification in their sources of arms supply. The most important suppliers of arms to the Middle East and North Africa are the U.S.S.R., the United States, Great Britain and France. Other developed countries also export weapons into this region, but on a lower scale. Table 2 gives a survey of the main suppliers of arms to the Middle East and North Africa, and the volume of sales in the period 1967–1976.

Two distinct sets of objectives and motivations can be discerned which induce the industrialized countries to encourage and even actively promote arms exports into the area: political and economic. The political objectives in arms sales to the third world aim at gaining influence in the importing country and in the area. Arms exports can be used to strengthen a ruling group vis-à-vis external or internal threats, and if an exporting and importing country pursue similar foreign policy objectives in the area the latter can fulfill certain strategic functions which otherwise might require some form of military presence of the supplier himself. The supplier might also try to gain access to ports and receive naval and air facilities in exchange for arms sales. The leverage obtained by the exporting country consists basically of two factors: first, the buyer becomes dependent on a continuous flow of spares and the threat to cut this flow and thereby eventually reduce the military strength of the importing country might provide some influence on his behaviour. Second, and more important, sophisticated weapon systems require large-scale training and assistance by the exporting countrier which allows the seller to gain access to the offices corps and therefore to one very influential group within the political framework of most importing countries. Political objectives have been predominant in the arms supply policies of the Superpowers, the U.S. and the U.S.S.R., and also China, and often arms deals are concluded to pre-empt arms sales by the rival Superpower (this gives the importing country some leverage to press for new supplies). Such political motivations appear behind the U.S. intention to supply modern weapons to Egypt: these arms sales are an expression of support for Sadat's policy, and an attempt to reward the pro-Western course followed by Cairo. Similar motives are behind Chinese deliveries of MiG engines to the same country in an effort to counteract the Soviet embargo on spares to Egypt. Another example is the military assistance agreement with Saudi Arabia. U.S.-Saudi deals comprise not only considerable arms sales but also demonstrate the desire to back up the present regime by providing for arms deliveries and training for the National Guard, a military body which predominantly serves to protect the present regime against internal threats and to guard oil installations. It is on the National Guard the monarchy relies domestically, rather than on the army which in the past was considered to have only limited reliability. Attempts to gain political influence through arms sales, however, are not necessarily limited to states—as Soviet support for the PLO and the PFLO has demonstrated.

Unlike the Superpowers, the arms export policies of France and Britain and other suppliers are dominated by economic considerations—considerations which are of growing importance even for the U.S.A. and the Soviet Union (for the U.S.S.R., weapons can either be bartered for oil or—if sold—contribute welcome foreign exchange earnings). For Western countries, including the United States, the prevailing economic reason for arms exports is its positive impact on the balance of payments, which the recent oil price increases have worsened for almost all

Western industrialized countries. Arms sales help to offset the balance of payments deficits vis-à-vis oil exporting countries either directly (if oil producers and arms importers are identical) or indirectly (through increased export earnings).

Arms exports, however, are also vital for the economic viability of sophisticated arms industries in smaller industrialized countries such as France and Britain. Advanced weapon systems, with their enormous research and development costs, can hardly be produced on an economic scale on the basis of the comparatively small domestic military requirements of these countries: the costs would be prohibitive. Exports enable longer production runs, which reduce the cost per unit, and they can also make up for fluctuations in domestic demand which would otherwise have to be rescheduled according to economic rather than military requirements (this is done by Sweden, for example). Exports mean that labour and capital can be kept fully employed. It is not surprising, therefore, that the Governments of both Britain and France actively support and encourage arms exports by providing official sales' assistance and credit facilities and also design their own military requirements partly with the export potential of certain weapon systems in mind.

There is, however, also a restrictive side to arms exports, stemming in principle from the desire of exporting countries not to become unintentionally involved in local or international conflicts through their role as arms suppliers. All suppliers have some form of governmental say in the export decisions and licensing systems, and some of them have made exports conditional upon certain requisites, e.g. not to re-sell the weapons. There have also been repeated attempts to control the flow of arms in crisis areas by embargoes against certain countries or regions (such as the British embargo on combatant states in the Middle East war in 1973, which was lifted in January 1974). The most comprehensive attempt to control and limit the arms trade with the Middle East was the Tripartite Declaration of the U.S., France and Britain in 1950 which broke down with large-scale French sales to Israel and the appearance of the Soviet Union as arms supplier for Egypt in 1955. President Carter has attempted to arrive at an overall reduction of U.S. arms sales to Third World countries, and at negotiated constraints on such sales.

The Suez Canal

The Suez Canal joins the Mediterranean and Red Seas between Port Said and Suez, in Egypt. It was closed during the Arab-Israeli war of June 1967 and was not re-opened until June 5th, 1975. Between June 1967 and October 1973 the canal formed the demarcation line between Egypt and the Israeli-occupied Sinai peninsula. After 13 months of clearing the canal of obstacles, it was re-opened by President Sadat on June 5th, 1975. Transit rates were fixed at a level which represented an increase of more than 90 per cent on the rates before the closure in June 1967. After the Suez Canal reopened, the large container ship consortiums which were subject to a special surcharge of 10 per cent, effectively boycotted the canal. In January 1977 the surcharge was halved with a resulting increase in container traffic, although in June the Suez Canal Authority, with the consent of the main container shipowners, raised the surcharge to 7½ per cent. During the period from June 1975 to October 1978 a total of 60,553 vessels passed through the canal carrying 665,274 million tons of cargo and yielding a revenue of approximately E£970,000. At the same time the average of daily ship transits rose from 12.6 to 58.

PRINCIPAL FACTS

Length: 107 miles including approach fairways.

Maximum Depth: 50 ft.

Maximum Width: 660 ft.

Minimum Width: 600 ft.

Transit Time: Average transit time was fifteen hours in 1967.

ORGANIZATION

Suez Canal Authority (*Hay'at Canal Al-Suess*): Ismailia, Egypt; Chair. Mashhour Ahmed Mashhour; Dir.-Gen. Ezzat Adel; Chief Pilot Kamal Hamza. The Suez Canal Authority manages the Canal on behalf of the Government of Egypt.

CHRONOLOGY

1854 Ferdinand de Lesseps granted building concession.

1859 Excavation began.

1869 Canal opened.

1875 Ismail Pasha of Egypt sold his shares in the French Suez Canal Company (44% of total to the British Government for nearly £4m.).

1888 Convention of Constantinople declared Canal open to vessels of all nations.

1956 President Nasser of Egypt nationalized Canal. Canal closed following invasion of Egypt.

1957 Canal re-opened under the control of the Egyptian Suez Canal Authority (April).

1959 World Bank lend Authority U.S.$56.5m.

1961 UN surcharge of 3% on transit dues, levied in 1958 to pay for clearing the Canal, was lifted (March).

1964 Loan of £E9.8m. granted by Kuwait Fund for Arab Development for dredging and widening operations. Permissible draught increased to 38 ft.

1965 Transit rates increased 1%, July.

1966 Transit rates increased 1%, July.

1967 Canal closed (June) during war with Israel.

1975 Canal re-opened (June).

1979 First transit of Israeli ship (April).

IMPROVEMENT SCHEMES

In the years following the opening of the Canal the depth of the channel was 26.2 ft. (8 m.) and its breadth at the bottom 72.2 ft. (22 m.), with a wet cross-sectional area of 3,272 sq. ft. (304 sq. m.). The average gross tonnage of transiting vessels was then 1,700 tons and the highest authorized draught was 24.6 ft. (7.5 m.). Navigation speed was 6.21 miles (10 km.) per hour.

NASSER PROJECT

Seven programmes of improvement were executed between 1876 and 1954. The eighth programme had started before nationalization, was modified thereafter to achieve better results and is now called the Nasser Project. Under this scheme the Canal was widened and deepened to take large tankers. New navigational aids and dockyard facilities were built and tug and salvage services improved. A Research Centre has been founded at Ismailia.

Under the first stage, finished in 1961, the Canal was widened and deepened to take vessels of 37 ft. draught. Under the second stage, finished in 1964, the Canal was widened and deepened to take vessels of 38 ft. draught. The installation of two salvage stations and a system of direct radio between vessels and the traffic control station at Ismailia were finished during 1962.

SUEZ AREA REDEVELOPMENT

After the war of October 1973 Egypt announced a plan to re-open the Suez Canal and generally develop the canal area. The canal was re-opened in June 1975 with a permissible draught of 33 ft., increased to 38 ft. in July 1975. Under a widening and deepening plan it is hoped to increase the permissible draught to 53 ft. by 1978–79 (now thought to be 1980), thus allowing loaded passage of ships of 150,000 tons, and to 67 ft. by 1981–82, allowing passage of ships of 260,000 tons fully laden. Port Said and Suez harbours will be enlarged to accommodate the largest vessels and the dock facilities at Port Fuad and Port Tewfik will be modernized. Three tunnels, carrying railway tracks, motorways, electricity cables and water are to be built under the canal. One, the Ahmed Hamdi Tunnel, was started in September 1976 and is due to be operational by 1980.

STATISTICS

SUEZ CANAL TRAFFIC

Year	Ships		Merchandise ('000 tons)		Number of Passengers	Total Transit Receipts (E £'000)
	Number	Displacement ('000 net tons)	Northbound	Southbound		
1960	18,734	185,322	139,630	29,253	366,562	50,408
1961	18,148	187,059	139,599	32,795	322,842	51,088
1962	18,518	197,837	151,190	31,207	269,685	53,958
1963	19,146	210,498	159,482	34,050	297,955	71,294
1964	19,943	227,991	172,463	38,518	269,569	77,697
1965	20,289	246,817	183,441	42,001	291,085	85,792
1966	21,250	274,250	194,168	47,725	299,557	95,187
1976	16,806	187,729	71,957	45,633	n.a.	152,800
1977	19,703	220,477	72,636	56,063	n.a.	186,400
1978	21,266	248,260	69,597	79,683	n.a.	n.a.

NORTHBOUND GOODS TRAFFIC ('000 tons)

	1966	1977	1978
Cereals	1,787	1,592	1,139
Crude petroleum	154,092	23,913	20,997
Fabricated metals	n.a.	5,401	3,054
Fruits	941	331	259
Oil seeds	1,588	1,183	906
Oil seed cake	1,484	1,386	1,065
Ores and metals	6,490	7,302	7,203
Petroleum products	12,626	6,965	7,366
Rubber	1,387	925	681
Sugar	1,338	1,073	516
Tea	397	309	154
Textile fibres	1,838	644	476
Wood	891	2,176	2,046
Others	9,309	19,430	23,375
Total	194,168	72,630	69,597

SOUTHBOUND GOODS TRAFFIC ('000 tons)

	1966	1977	1978
Cement	1,407	6,035	11,226
Cereals	9,738	4,188	5,221
Chemical products	1,017	1,766	1,986
Crude petroleum	2,893	639	619
Fabricated metals	5,015	3,893	7,894
Fertilizers	6,748	6,197	9,025
Foodstuffs	n.a.	1,839	2,064
Lubricating oils	577	319	200
Machinery and parts	1,464	1,354	978
Ores and metals	925	1,341	1,581
Petroleum products	6,060	3,429	4,197
Sugar	1,231	801	1,672
Wood-pulp and paper	675	651	868
Others	9,563	23,611	32,651
Total	47,725	56,063	80,182

DISTRIBUTION OF NORTHBOUND PETROLEUM AND PRODUCTS ('000 tons)

Unloading Country	1977	1978
Egypt	3,934	3,852
France	966	981
Greece	2,778	1,322
Italy	7,544	8,920
Netherlands	580	642
Rumania	5,113	6,681
Turkey	3,275	1,778
U.K.	389	343
U.S.A.	1,076	417
Others	5,223	3,427
Total	30,878	28,363

FLAG DISTRIBUTION OF NET TONNAGE
('000 tons)

	1977		1978	
	Tankers	All Vessels	Tankers	All Vessels
China, People's Republic	361	3,873	725	4,826
Cyprus	85	3,385	89	3,922
Denmark	484	3,906	198	3,919
France	4,219	8,613	5,586	12,052
German Democratic Republic	838	2,742	615	2,400
Germany, Federal Republic	562	8,873	1,241	11,786
Greece	8,101	24,256	9,055	31,252
India	391	6,010	273	5,871
Italy	4,170	8,632	4,357	8,632
Japan	1,067	9,587	618	9,587
Kuwait	1,023	2,550	1,446	3,779
Liberia	16,663	27,947	17,227	31,624
Netherlands	563	5,003	443	6,333
Norway	4,779	13,235	3,948	13,978
Panama	2,976	8,568	2,832	11,193
Portugal	1,796	1,846	838	859
Romania	2,404	3,445	2,162	3,335
Singapore	1,698	4,705	1,291	5,604
Sweden	615	4,775	326	4,977
U.S.S.R.	2,547	11,630	3,109	13,781
United Kingdom	6,023	19,631	4,848	21,393
U.S.A.	1,537	7,519	582	4,950
Yugoslavia	1,147	3,845	1,173	4,028
Others	11,519	25,901	10,942	28,179
Total	75,568	220,477	73,924	248,260

GOODS TONNAGE IN BOTH DIRECTIONS BY REGIONS
('000 tons)

	1978
North of the Canal:	
N. and W. Europe and U.K. Ports	12,318
Baltic Sea Ports	2,000
N. Mediterranean Ports	9,623
E. and S.E. Mediterranean Ports	1,677
W. and S.W. Mediterranean Ports	5,688
Black Sea Ports	9,087
American Ports	5,209
Others	1,223
Total	46,825

	1978
South of the Canal:	
Red Sea Ports	7,360
E. African and Aden	1,531
India, Pakistan, Sri Lanka and Burma	12,183
Arabian Gulf Ports	10,627
S.E. Asia and Sunda Islands	4,267
Far East	8,562
Australia	2,272
Others	23
Total	46,825

PART TWO

Regional Organizations

The United Nations in the Middle East and North Africa

MEMBERS, CONTRIBUTIONS, YEAR OF ADMISSION

(assessments for percentage contributions to budget for financial years 1978 and 1979)

Country	Contribution	Year
Afghanistan	0.01	1946
Algeria	0.10	1962
Bahrain	0.01	1971
Cyprus	0.01	1960
Egypt	0.08	1945
Iran	0.40	1945
Iraq	0.08	1945
Israel	0.23	1949
Jordan	0.01	1955
Kuwait	0.15	1963
Lebanon	0.03	1945
Libya	0.16	1955
Morocco	0.05	1956
Oman	0.01	1971
Qatar	0.02	1971
Saudi Arabia	0.23	1945
Sudan	0.01	1955
Syria	0.01	1946
Tunisia	0.01	1956
Turkey	0.30	1945
United Arab Emirates	0.07	1971
Yemen Arab Republic	0.01	1947
Yemen, People's Democratic Republic	0.01	1967

PERMANENT MISSIONS TO THE UNITED NATIONS

(with Permanent Representatives)

Afghanistan: 866 United Nations Plaza, Suite 520, New York, N.Y. 10017; (vacant).

Algeria: 15 East 47th St., New York, N.Y. 10017; (vacant).

Bahrain: 747 Third Ave., 19th Floor, New York, N.Y. 10017; Dr. SALMAN MOHAMED AL SAFFAR.

Cyprus: 820 Second Ave., 12th Floor, New York, N.Y. 10017; ANDREAS V. MAVROMMATIS.

Egypt: 36 East 67th St., New York, N.Y. 10021; Dr. AHMED ESMAT ABDEL MEGUID.

Iran: 622 Third Ave., 34th Floor, New York, N.Y. 10017; (vacant).

Iraq: 14 East 79th St., New York, N.Y. 10021; SALAH OMAR AL-ALI.

Israel: 800 Second Ave., New York, N.Y. 10017; YEHOUDA Z. BLUM.

Jordan: 866 United Nations Plaza, Room 550–552, New York, N.Y. 10017; Dr. HAZEM NUSEIBEH.

Kuwait: 801 Second Ave., 5th Floor, New York, N.Y. 10017; ABDALLA YACCOUB BISHARA.

Lebanon: 866 United Nations Plaza, Room 533–535, New York, N.Y. 10017; GHASSAN TUÉNI.

Libya: 866 United Nations Plaza, New York, N.Y. 10017; MANSUR RASHID KIKHIA.

Morocco: 1 Dag Hammarskjöld Plaza, 245 East 47th St., 28th Floor, New York, N.Y. 10017; ABDELLATIF FILALI.

Oman: 866 United Nations Plaza, Suite 540, New York, N.Y. 10017; MAHMOUD ABOUL-NASR.

Qatar: 747 Third Ave., 22nd Floor, New York, N.Y. 10017; JASIM YOUSIF JAMAL.

Saudi Arabia: 6 East 43rd St., 26th Floor, New York, N.Y. 10017; (vacant).

Sudan: 747 Third Ave., 14th Floor, New York, N.Y. 10017; ALI AHMED SAHLOUL.

Syria: 150 East 58th St., Room 1500, New York, N.Y. 10022; HAMMOUD EL-CHOUFI.

Tunisia: 40 East 71st St., New York, N.Y. 10021; MAHMOUD MESTIRI.

Turkey: 821 United Nations Plaza, 11th Floor, New York, N.Y. 10017; ORHAN ERALP.

United Arab Emirates: 747 Third Ave., 36th Floor, New York, N.Y. 10017; Dr. ALI HUMAIDAN.

Yemen Arab Republic: 747 Third Ave., 8th Floor, New York, N.Y. 10017; AHMED ALI AL-HADDAD.

Yemen, People's Democratic Republic: 413 East 51st Street, New York, N.Y. 10022; ABDALLA SALEH ASHTAL.

OBSERVERS

League of Arab States: 747 Third Ave., 25th Floor, New York, N.Y. 10017; AMIN HELMY II.

Palestine Liberation Organization: 103 Park Ave., Room 701–702, New York, N.Y. 10017; ZEHDI LABIB TERZI.

UN INFORMATION CENTRES

Afghanistan: Shah Mahmoud Ghazi Watt, Kabul; P.O.B. 5.

Algeria: 19 Avenue Chahid el-Waly Mustapha Sayed, Algiers; P.O.B. 823.

Egypt: Sh. Osiris, Tagher Bldg., Garden City, Cairo; P.O.B. 262 (also covers Saudi Arabia and Yemen Arab Republic).

Iran: Off Takhte Jamshid, 12 Kh. Bandar Pahlavi, Teheran; P.O.B. 1555.

Iraq: House 167/1 Abu Nouwas St., Bataween, Baghdad; P.O.B. 2398, Alwiyah.

Jordan: Information Service, UN Economic Commission for Western Asia, P.O.B. 35099, Amman, Jordan (also covers Kuwait, Lebanon and Syria).

Morocco: "Casier ONU", Angle Charia Moulay Hassan et Zankat Assafi, Rabat.

Sudan: Plot No. 1 (9), Block 5D East, Nigumi St., Khartoum; P.O.B. 1992.

Tunisia: 61 Boulevard Bab Benat, Tunis; P.O.B. 863 (also covers Libya).

Turkey: 197 Ataturk Bulvari, Ankara; P.K. 407.

ECONOMIC COMMISSION FOR AFRICA—ECA

Africa Hall, P.O.B. 3001, Addis Ababa, Ethiopia

Telephone: 447200.

Initiates and takes part in measures for facilitating Africa's economic development. Member countries must be independent, be members of the UN and within the geographical scope of the African continent and the islands bordering it. ECA was founded in 1958 by a resolution of ECOSOC as the fourth UN regional economic commission and acts within the framework of the United Nations, being subject to the general supervision of ECOSOC. It is authorized to assist member states to deal, as appropriate, with the social aspects of economic development and the relationship of economic and social factors. The Commission may only act with the agreement of the Government of the country concerned and is also empowered to make recommendations on any matter within its competence directly to the Government of the member or associate member concerned, to Governments admitted in a consultative capacity, and to the UN Specialized Agencies. The Commission is required to submit for prior consideration by ECOSOC any of its proposals for actions that would be likely to have important effects on the international economy.

MEMBERS

Algeria	Equatorial Guinea	Madagascar	Sierra Leone
Angola	Ethiopia	Malawi	Somalia
Benin	Gabon	Mali	South Africa*
Botswana	The Gambia	Mauritania	Sudan
Burundi	Ghana	Mauritius	Swaziland
Cameroon	Guinea	Morocco	Tanzania
Cape Verde	Guinea-Bissau	Mozambique	Togo
Central African Empire	Ivory Coast	Niger	Tunisia
Chad	Kenya	Nigeria	Uganda
Comoros	Lesotho	Rwanda	Upper Volta
Congo	Liberia	São Tomé and Príncipe	Zaire
Djibouti	Libya	Senegal	Zambia
Egypt		Seychelles	

* Suspended since 1963.

ASSOCIATE MEMBERS

France Namibia (South West Africa) United Kingdom

ORGANIZATION

(as of May 1979)

THE CONFERENCE OF MINISTERS

The Conference of Ministers is the main deliberative body of the Commission. Originally, the Commission held general sessions, annually until 1965 and biennially thereafter. By a resolution adopted in 1969, the regular biennial sessions of the Commission were held at ministerial level and are now known as meetings of the Conference of Ministers. At the fourteenth session of the Commission and fifth meeting of the Conference of Ministers, held in Morocco in March 1979, it was decided to abolish the Executive Committee and the Technical Committee of Experts and that the Conference of Ministers should meet annually. The priorities and work programme of the Commission and the implementation of programmes and projects of other international bodies, along with issues of international significance, are to be considered at alternate meetings. A Technical Preparatory Committee representing all member states is to be established to deal with matters submitted for the consideration of the Conference.

The Commission's responsibility to promote concerted

action for the economic and social development of Africa is vested primarily in the Conference. It considers matters of general policy and the priorities to be assigned to the Commission's programmes, considers inter-African and international economic policy and makes recommendations to member states in connection with such matters. It reviews the course of programmes being implemented in the preceding two years and examines and approves the programmes proposed for the next.

The Conference is attended by Ministers responsible for economic or financial affairs, planning and development of governments of member states.

SECRETARIAT

The Secretariat provides the services necessary for the meeting of the Conference of Ministers and the meetings of the Commission's subsidiary bodies, carries out the resolutions and implements the programmes adopted there.

HEADQUARTERS

The Headquarters of the Secretariat is in Addis Ababa, Ethiopia. It comprises a Cabinet Office and ten Divisions.

Cabinet Office of the Executive Secretary:

Administration and Conference Services Division
Policy and Programme Co-ordination Office
Economic Co-operation Office
Office of the Secretary of the Commission
Technical Assistance Co-ordination and Operations Office
Information Services Unit

Divisions:

Socio-Economic Research and Planning
International Trade and Finance
Joint ECA/FAO Agriculture
Joint ECA/UNIDO Industry
Social Development
Natural Resources
Transport, Communications and Tourism
Public Administration, Management and Manpower
Statistics
Population

Executive Secretary: ADEBAYO ADEDEJI (Nigeria).

REGIONAL OPERATIONAL CENTRES

Multi-national Programming and Operational Centres (MULPOCs) act as "field agents" for the implementation of regional development programmes, replacing the former UN Multidisciplinary Development Advisory Teams (UNDATS). The Centres are located in Yaoundé, Cameroon (serving Central Africa), Gisenyi, Rwanda (Great Lakes Community), Lusaka, Zambia (East and Southern Africa), Niamey, Niger (West Africa) and Tangier, Morocco (North Africa). Each centre holds regular ministerial meetings.

SUBSIDIARY BODIES

INTERGOVERNMENTAL COMMITTEE OF EXPERTS FOR SCIENCE AND TECHNOLOGY DEVELOPMENT

Fourth meeting, Addis Ababa, Ethiopia, January 1978.

In March 1979 the Conference of Ministers decided that the existing Conferences of African Planners, of African Statisticians and of African Demographers should be combined into a single Conference to be known as the Joint Conference of African Planners, Statisticians and Demographers, which will be held every two years.

CO-OPERATION WITH OTHER ORGANIZATIONS

The ECA co-operates closely with the Organization of African Unity (the memberships of the two organizations are the same) and many other African bodies, notably the Economic Community of West African States (ECOWAS) and the African Development Bank, receiving delegations from these and other bodies in 1977–78.

It also participates in the work of many UN bodies in Africa and operates two divisions jointly with the FAO and UNIDO.

Relations with the Arab countries have improved of late and during 1977 the Executive Committee discussed the Declaration of Afro-Arab Economic and Financial Co-operation, adopted by the first Afro-Arab Summit Conference in March 1977.

PUBLICATIONS

STATISTICS

African Statistical Yearbook.

Foreign Trade Statistics for Africa series.

- *Series A: Direction of Trade* (quarterly).
- *Series B: Trade by Commodity* (twice yearly).
- *Series C: Summary Tables* (planned annual publication).

Statistical and Economic Information Bulletin for Africa (twice yearly).

Statistical Newsletter (quarterly).

ECONOMIC

African Economic Indicators (every two years).

Agricultural Economics Bulletin for Africa (twice yearly).

Economic Bulletin for Africa (twice yearly).

Investment Africa (quarterly).

Survey of Economic and Social Conditions in Africa (annual).

ECA LIBRARY SERIES

Series A: periodicals and serials, suspended.

Series B: New Acquisitions in the UN ECA Library (twice monthly).

Series C: subject bibliographies (irreg.).

Series D: directories, manuals, glossaries (irreg.).

Series E: Africa Index: Selected Articles on Socio-Economic Development (thrice yearly).

Series F: ECA Index: Bibliography of Selected ECA Documents (annual, issued since Dec. 1975).

PLANNING AND SOCIAL DEVELOPMENT

Planning Newsletter (twice monthly).

Rural Development Newsletter (quarterly).

Social Welfare Services in Africa (twice yearly).

POPULATION AND CENSUS

African Census Programme Newsletter (irreg.).

African Population Newsletter (quarterly).

African Population Studies Series (irreg.).

Demographic Handbook (irreg.).

TRADE

African Trade (quarterly).

See also *Statistics* above.

MAGAZINES

African Target (quarterly).

African Women, photo-spread poster folder (thrice yearly).

ECONOMIC COMMISSION FOR WESTERN ASIA—ECWA

P.O.B. 4656, Beirut, Lebanon

Established in 1974 by a resolution of ECOSOC to provide facilities of a wider scope for those countries previously served by the UN Economic and Social Office in Beirut (UNESOB).

MEMBERS

Bahrain	Lebanon	Saudi Arabia
Egypt	Oman	Syria
Iraq	Palestine Liberation Organization (PLO)	United Arab Emirates
Jordan	Qatar	Yemen Arab Republic
Kuwait		Yemen, People's Democratic Republic

ORGANIZATION

(as of May 1979)

COMMISSION

The sixth session of the Commission was held in April-May 1979 in Baghdad, Iraq.

The Commission approved its programme of work and priorities for 1980/81. It decided to reconsider a resolution adopted in 1977, by which Egypt was admitted as a full member of ECWA, and to recommend that ECOSOC suspend Egypt's membership of ECWA.

Chairman (Sixth Session): HASSAN ALI (Iraq).

SECRETARIAT

In September 1974 it was decided at a special session of ECWA that the headquarters should be at Beirut until 1979. During the hostilities in Lebanon in 1976 the Commission took up temporary offices in Amman, Jordan, moving back to Beirut in 1977. At its sixth session in 1979, the Commission decided to commence its move to permanent headquarters in Baghdad, Iraq, with effect from September 9th, 1979.

Executive Secretary: MOHAMMED SAID AL-ATTAR (Yemen Arab Republic).

WORK PROGRAMMES 1978-79

The region's pressing and growing needs in such important areas as agriculture, industry, development of natural resources, transport, trade and rural development have been accorded the required emphasis in the work programme of the Commission. Particular attention has been given to the provisions of General Assembly resolution 3442 (XXX) on Economic Co-operation among Developing Countries and the Economic and Social Council resolution 2043 (LXI) on Strengthening of the Regional Commissions for Regional and Inter-regional Co-operation in order to make effective use of complementary factors among the countries of the region and to promote co-operation at all levels. In this connection, the recommendations embodied in (*a*) the Manila Declaration and the Programme of Action adopted at the Third Ministerial Meeting of the Group of 77, (*b*) the Economic Declaration of the Fifth Conference of the Heads of State and Government of Non-Aligned Countries, (*c*) the report of the Conference on Economic Co-operation among Developing Countries at Mexico City, including the joint position paper presented to the Conference by the regional commissions, and (*d*) the Habitat Conference, have been taken into consideration in identifying and developing the sub-programmes and related individual programme elements. This includes the reorientation and inclusion of some of the projects envisaged under the 1976/77 Programme of Work and Priorities of the Commission which could not be implemented owing to the disruption in the work of the Secretariat of the Commission and the recruitment difficulties resulting from the civil strife in Lebanon between April 1975 and November 1976.

BUDGET

Budget approved by the General Assembly for the two-year period 1978–79: U.S. $10,566,000.

FOOD AND AGRICULTURE ORGANIZATION—FAO

Viale delle Terme di Caracalla, 00100 Rome, Italy

Telephone: 5797.

FAO, the first specialized agency of the UN to be founded after World War II, was established in Quebec in October 1945. The Organization fights malnutrition and hunger and serves as a co-ordinating agency for development programmes in the whole range of food and agriculture, including forestry and fisheries. It helps developing countries to promote educational and training facilities and institution-building.

SECRETARIAT

Director-General (1976–81): EDOUARD SAOUMA (Lebanon).

Deputy Director-General: RALPH W. PHILLIPS (U.S.A.).

REGIONAL OFFICES

FAO Regional Office for the Near East: Box 2223, General Co-operative Society for Agrarian Reform Bldg., 110 Kasr El Eini, Dokki, Cairo, Egypt; Regional Rep. SALAH JUM'A.

FAO Regional Office for Africa: UN Agency Bldg., North Maxwell Rd., P.O.B. 1628, Accra, Ghana; Regional Rep. S. C. SAR.

REGIONAL COUNCILS AND COMMISSIONS

Commission for Controlling the Desert Locust in the Near East: f. 1965 to carry out all possible measures to control desert locust plagues within the Middle East and to reduce crop damage.

Commission for Controlling the Desert Locust in North-West Africa: f. 1971 to promote research on control of the desert locust in N.W. Africa. Mems.: 4 countries.

FAO Commission on Horticultural Production in the Near East and North Africa: c/o FAO, P.O.B. 2223, Cairo, Egypt; f. 1964 to promote international collaboration in the study of technical problems and the establishment of a balanced programme of horticultural research at an inter-regional level.

General Fisheries Council for the Mediterranean—GFCM (*Conseil général des pêches pour la Méditerranée—CGPM*): Viale delle Terme di Caracalla, 00100 Rome, Italy; f. 1952 to formulate oceanographical and technical aspects of developing and utilizing aquatic resources, to encourage and co-ordinate research in the fishing and allied industries, to assemble and publish information, and to recommend the standardization of scientific equipment, techniques and nomenclature.

Near East Commission on Agricultural Planning: f. 1961 to review and exchange information and experience on agricultural plans and planning, and to make recommendations to members on means of improving their agricultural plans.

Near East Commission on Agricultural Statistics: c/o FAO, P.O.B. 2223, Cairo, Egypt; f. 1962 to review the state of food and agricultural statistics in the region and advise member countries on the development and standardization of agricultural statistics. Regular sessions are held every two years; technical subsidiary bodies include seminars and expert working groups.

Near East Forestry Commission: c/o FAO, P.O.B. 2223, Cairo, Egypt; first Session 1955; purpose to advise on formulation of forest policy and to review and co-ordinate its implementation at the regional level; to exchange information and, generally through subsidiary bodies, advise on suitable practices and action in respect of technical problems; and to make appropriate recommendations.

Near East Plant Protection Commission: c/o FAO, P.O.B. 2223, Cairo, Egypt; f. 1963 to advise member countries, through FAO Conference, on matters relating to the protection of plant resources in the region.

Animal Production and Health Commission in the Near East: c/o FAO, P.O.B. 2223, Cairo, Egypt; f. 1966 to provide a means of initiating and promoting agricultural development with special reference to the field of animal production and health.

Regional Commission on Land and Water Use in the Near East: c/o FAO, P.O.B. 2223, Cairo, Egypt; f. 1967 to study land and water use in the region; to identify the main problems concerning the development of land and water resources which require research and to consider related matters.

Regional Project on the Improvement and Production of Field Food Crops in the Near East and North Africa: c/o FAO, P.O.B. 2223, Cairo, Egypt; f. 1971 (replacing the Technical Committee on Cereal Improvement and Production in the Near East); aims to increase overall crop production (cereals, some food legumes and oil seed crops) through research, co-operative investigations and other forms of international action.

INTERNATIONAL BANK FOR RECONSTRUCTION AND DEVELOPMENT—IBRD (WORLD BANK)

1818 H Street, N.W., Washington, D.C. 20433, U.S.A.

The World Bank was established in 1945. It aims to assist the economic development of member nations by making loans, in cases where private capital is not available on reasonable terms, to finance productive investments. Loans are made either direct to governments, or to private enterprises with the guarantee of their governments.

LOANS TO COUNTRIES IN THE MIDDLE EAST AND NORTH AFRICA

TOTAL LOANS CUMULATIVE TO JUNE 1978 (U.S. $ million)

Country	Number	Amount
Algeria	18	803.0
Cyprus	14	111.6
Egypt	16	731.0
Iran	33	1,210.7
Iraq	6	156.2
Israel	11	284.5
Lebanon	4	116.6
Morocco	32	884.3
Oman	4	24.9
Sudan	8	166.0
Syria	10	417.1
Tunisia	31	479.9
Turkey	37	1,494.9

APPROVED LOANS JULY 1977—JUNE 1978 (U.S. $ million)

Country	Purpose	Amount
Algeria	Water supply and sewerage	82.0
	Education	90.0
Cyprus	Agriculture and rural development	10.0
Cyprus (Guarantor)	Transportation	8.5
Egypt	Transportation	100.0
(Guarantor)	Industrial development and finance	40.0
Lebanon	Reconstruction (nonproject)	50.0
Morocco	Water supply and sewerage	1.5
	Urban development	18.0
	Agriculture and rural development	65.0
Syria	Education	20.0
	Transportation	58.0
Syria (Guarantor)	Power	40.0

Source: World Bank/IDA 1978 Annual Report.

INTERNATIONAL DEVELOPMENT ASSOCIATION—IDA

1818 H Street, N.W., Washington, D.C. 20433, U.S.A.

The IDA began operations in 1960. An affiliate of the World Bank, it advances capital on more flexible terms to developing countries.

DEVELOPMENT CREDITS TO MIDDLE EASTERN AND NORTH AFRICAN COUNTRIES

TOTAL CREDITS CUMULATIVE TO JUNE 1978 (U.S. $ million)

Country	Number	Amount
Afghanistan	16	158.5
Egypt	16	434.1
Jordan	15	85.3
Morocco	3	50.8
Sudan	17	296.5
Syria	3	47.3
Tunisia	5	74.6
Turkey	10	178.5
Yemen Arab Republic	16	138.8
Yemen, People's Democratic Republic	10	49.8

APPROVED CREDITS JULY 1977–JUNE 1978 (U.S. $ million)

Country	Purpose	Amount
Afghanistan	Agriculture and rural development	40.0
Egypt	Water supply and sewerage	2.0
	Telecommunications	53.0
	Agriculture and rural development	32.0
	Urban development	14.0
Jordan	Water supply and sewerage	14.0
Sudan	Transportation	22.0
	Agriculture and rural development	56.0
Yemen Arab Republic	Transportation	11.5
	Agriculture and rural development	10.5
	Industry	7.0
Yemen, People's Democratic Rep.	Agriculture and rural development	5.2
	Power	5.0
	Water supply and sewerage	1.2

Source: World Bank/IDA 1978 Annual Report.

INTERNATIONAL FINANCE CORPORATION—IFC

1818 H Street, N.W., Washington, D.C. 20433, U.S.A.

Founded in 1956 as an affiliate of the World Bank to encourage the growth of productive private enterprise in its less-developed member countries.

Director of Investments, Africa and Middle East: GUNTER H. KREUTER (Federal Republic of Germany).

IFC COMMITMENTS IN MIDDLE EASTERN AND NORTH AFRICAN COUNTRIES
(up to June 30th, 1978—U.S. $'000)

	TYPE OF BUSINESS	ORIGINAL COMMITMENTS	INVESTMENTS HELD FOR THE CORPORATION
Cyprus	Cement and construction material	3,626	2,549
Egypt	Ceramics	5,652	4,151
	Food and food processing	23,000	17,000
	Ready-made garments	592	592
Iran	Pulp and paper products	14,193	8,194
	Chemicals and petrochemicals	3,553	2,127
Israel	Chemicals and petrochemicals	10,500	8,358
Jordan	Ceramics	1,826	1,576
	Fertilizers	76,494	26,493
Lebanon	Money and capital market	1,250	1,250
	Textiles and fibres	5,725	4,125
Morocco	Cement and construction material	8,519	8,519
	Development finance	2,695	1,544
	Food and food processing	1,388	399
Sudan	Textiles and fibres	20,266	18,458
	Food and food processing	12,382	7,361
Tunisia	Development finance	2,358	2,358
	Tourism	15,339	13,368
	Chemicals and petrochemicals	640	640
Turkey	Tourism	603	403
	Textiles and fibres	15,868	7,905
	Glass	11,583	6,813
	Iron and steel	27,622	26,157
	Cement and construction material	10,600	5,500
	Non-ferrous metal	9,946	5,379
	Chemicals and petrochemicals	15,000	4,886
	Development finance	63,321	16,249
	Pulp and paper products	3,169	2,388
Yemen Arab Republic	Food and food processing	3,150	2,400

Source: IFC 1978 Annual Report.

UNITED NATIONS DEVELOPMENT PROGRAMME—UNDP

One United Nations Plaza, New York, N.Y. 10017, U.S.A.

Established in 1965, through the merger of the Expanded Programme of Technical Assistance and the UN Special Fund, as the world's largest channel for international technical co-operation.

ORGANIZATION

GOVERNING COUNCIL

The policy-making body of UNDP. Also approves programmes submitted by individual countries outlining fields where UNDP assistance is needed, taking into account national development priorities and available aid from other sources.

President (1979): BERNARDO VUNIBOBO (Fiji).

Administrator: F. BRADFORD MORSE (U.S.A.).

REGIONAL BUREAUX

Four regional bureaux and an Office for Europe share responsibility for overall supervision of the programme with the UNDP's Administrator. Countries in the Middle East and North Africa are covered by the Regional Bureau for Arab States.

FIELD OFFICES

In countries receiving UNDP assistance there is a Field Office, headed by the UNDP resident representative, who co-ordinates all UN technical assistance, advises the Government on the formulation of programmes, monitors field activities and acts as the leader of the UN team of experts in the country.

There are eighteen such field offices in Arab States.

UNDP RESIDENT REPRESENTATIVES

Algeria: B.P. 823, Algiers.

Bahrain: P.O.B. 814, Manama.

Egypt: P.O.B. 982, Cairo.

Iraq: P.O.B. 2048 (Alwiyah), Baghdad.

Jordan: P.O.B. 565, Amman.

Kuwait: P.O.B. 2993, Kuwait City.

Lebanon: P.O.B. 3216, Beirut.

Libya: P.O.B. 358, Tripoli.

Morocco: Casier ONU, Rabat-Chellah, Rabat.

Oman: P.O.B. 5287, Muscat.

Qatar: Box 3233, Doha.

Saudi Arabia: P.O.B. 558, Riyadh.

Sudan: P.O.B. 913, Khartoum.

Syria: P.O.B. 2317, Damascus.

Tunisia: B.P. 863, Tunis.

United Arab Emirates: P.O.B. 3491, Abu Dhabi.

Yemen Arab Republic: P.O.B. 551, Sana'a.

Yemen, People's Democratic Republic: P.O.B. 1188, Tawahi, Aden.

ACTIVITIES 1978

At the end of 1978, UNDP was working with 18 Arab countries of the Middle East and North Africa to carry out 775 projects, at an estimated total cost of U.S. $1,148 million, 69.9 per cent of which is to be met by the governments concerned. Areas of particular concentration included those involving the availability of food, water, health care and low-cost housing; the provision of jobs and professional skills; the encouragement of science and technology; the improvement of rural conditions and the strengthening of planning and institutional infrastructure. Regional projects emphasized the exploitation of shared fishing resources, training for participation in multilateral trade negotiations, the promotion of industrial enterprises and planning for the investment of regional capital.

More specifically, the current sectoral distribution of UNDP assistance in the Arab States shows 33 per cent devoted to agriculture, forestry and fisheries, 13.2 per cent to industry, 15 per cent to transport and communication, 12.7 per cent to economic and social policy, 5.2 per cent to health, 5.9 per cent to science and technology, 6.0 per cent to education, and the remaining 9 per cent to labour management and employment; natural resources development; cultural, social and human sciences; relief activities; social security and other social services; and international trade.

PROCEDURES FOR UNDP ASSISTANCE

Support provided by UNDP is allocated in accordance with an Indicative Planning Figure (IPF) established by the Governing Council for each recipient country and for subregional and global activities as well. The IPF is a projection of the total financial resources the UNDP expects to be able to commit for technical assistance to each country over a five-year period. The five-year IPF programming cycle enables national development plans to be formulated with more certainty.

IPF ALLOCATIONS FOR ARAB STATES (1977–81)

(U.S. $'000)

Algeria	20,000
Bahrain	2,500
Djibouti	905
Egypt	31,500
Iraq	15,000
Jordan	15,000
Lebanon	10,000
Libya	5,000
Morocco	20,000
Oman	4,000
Saudi Arabia	10,000
Sudan	33,000
Syria	15,000
Tunisia	15,000
United Arab Emirates	1,000
Yemen Arab Republic	23,750
Yemen, People's Democratic Republic	14,500

Kuwait and Qatar have voluntarily relinquished further UNDP grant assistance, although they continue to participate in regional, inter-regional and global activities. They also continue to use the programme's services on a cost-reimbursement basis.

UNITED NATIONS RELIEF AND WORKS AGENCY FOR PALESTINE REFUGEES IN THE NEAR EAST—UNRWA

Headquarters (Vienna): Storchengasse 1, 1150 Vienna, Austria
Headquarters (Amman): P.O.B. 484, Amman, Jordan

Began operations in 1950 to provide relief, health, education and welfare services for Palestine refugees in the Near East.

REGIONAL OFFICES

Gaza Strip: UNRWA Field Office, P.O.B. 61, Gaza.
East Jordan: UNRWA Field Office, P.O.B. 484, Amman.
West Bank: UNRWA Field Office, P.O.B. 19149, Jerusalem.
Lebanon: UNRWA Field Office, P.O.B. 947, Beirut.
Syria: UNRWA Field Office, P.O.B. 4313, Damascus.
Egypt: UNRWA Liaison Office, 2 Dar el Shifa, Garden City, P.O.B. 277, Cairo.
United States: UNRWA Liaison Office, Room 1801, United Nations, New York, N.Y. 10017.

ORGANIZATION

Deputy Commissioner-General and Acting Commissioner-General a.i.: ALAN J. BROWN (United Kingdom).

UNRWA is a subsidiary organ of the United Nations General Assembly, and began operations in May 1950; it employs an international staff of 113 and 16,500 local staff, mainly Palestine refugees. The Commissioner-General is assisted by an Advisory Commission consisting of representatives of the governments of:

Belgium	Jordan	Turkey
Egypt	Lebanon	United Kingdom
France	Syria	U.S.A.
Japan		

ACTIVITIES

SERVICES FOR PALESTINE REFUGEES

Since 1950, UNRWA has provided relief (including food), health and education services for the needy among the Palestine refugees in Lebanon, Syria, east Jordan, the West Bank and the Gaza Strip. For UNRWA's purposes, a Palestine refugee is one whose normal residence was in Palestine for a minimum of two years before the 1948 conflict and who, as a result of the Arab-Israeli hostilities, lost his home and means of livelihood. To be eligible for assistance, a refugee must reside in one of the "host" countries in which UNRWA operates and be in need. A refugee's children and grandchildren who fulfil certain criteria are also eligible for UNRWA assistance. In April 1979, the registered refugee population numbered 1,790,013, including 634,068 registered in 61 refugee camps.

Whereas the vast majority (1.4 million) of the refugees are eligible for health services and, in the appropriate age-groups, for education, only 47 per cent receive rations. Over the years an effective community health service has been built up with technical guidance from WHO and there has never been a major epidemic among the refugees in UNRWA's care. An education system has been developed with technical guidance from UNESCO and in the 1978–79 school year there were 326,000 children in 622 elementary and preparatory schools operated by UNRWA. More than 27,000 refugees have already passed through UNRWA's eight vocational centres (capacity: 4,640 trainees) for training either as teachers or in a variety of industrial and semi-professional skills; UNRWA has become one of the most important channels for this type of technical assistance in the Middle East. Since 1950 UNRWA has also served more than 335 million meals to young children and distributed about 35,000 tons of clothing.

AID TO DISPLACED PERSONS

After the renewal of Arab-Israeli hostilities in the Middle East in June 1967, hundreds of thousands of people fled from the fighting and Israeli-occupied areas to east Jordan, Syria and Egypt. UNRWA provided emergency relief for displaced refugees and was additionally empowered by a UN General Assembly resolution to provide "humanitarian assistance, as far as practicable, on an emergency basis and as a temporary measure" for those persons other than Palestine refugees who were newly displaced and in urgent need. In practice, UNRWA has lacked the funds to aid the other displaced persons and the main burden of supporting them has fallen on the Arab governments concerned. The Agency, as requested by the Government of Jordan in 1967 and on that Government's behalf, distributes rations to displaced persons in east Jordan who are not registered refugees of 1948.

With the agreement of the Israeli Government, UNRWA has continued to provide assistance for registered refugees living in the Israeli-occupied territories of the West Bank and the Gaza Strip.

RECENT DISTURBANCES

Palestine refugees have been affected, and UNRWA's services disrupted, by continuing disturbances in Lebanon and the Israeli invasion of the south in March 1978, which caused the temporary evacuation of most of the 50,000 refugees living there and the flight of 17,000 refugees in other areas. With the assistance of governments and voluntary groups, UNRWA launched an emergency relief programme to provide food, clothing and blankets and temporary shelter in school buildings. Damage to UNRWA's property and installations, such as schools and clinics recently repaired in the wake of the civil war in Lebanon of 1975–76, was estimated at $450,000. While most of the refugees returned to their home towns and villages by the end of April, the devastated economy of the south left them in continued need of extra-budgetary relief supplies and services.

In the rest of Lebanon, UNRWA's services returned to pre-civil war levels.

FINANCE

BUDGET

As at April 1st, UNRWA's budget for 1979 was $162.7 million.

For the most part, UNRWA's income is made up of voluntary contributions, almost entirely from governments, the remainder being provided by voluntary agencies, business corporations and private sources. However, the cost of the Agency's 113 international staff is funded by the UN, WHO and UNESCO.

In recent years financial crises have posed serious threats of cuts in services, and in 1979 the Agency faced a budget deficit estimated to be $36 million. Devaluation of the dollar and incessant inflationary pressures, which have had an adverse effect on the price of supplies and the cost of living, seriously affected the Agency's ability to meet the higher cost of health, education and relief services with voluntary contributions. UNRWA's Commissioner-General appealed to non-contributing UN states, but without result. The Agency's ration distribution has been partially cut on an annual basis and the provision of preparatory education for 90,000 children, costing $10.5 million, is in doubt for the 1979–80 school year unless more funds are forthcoming. Cuts in, or suspension of, UNRWA's programmes are increasingly imminent.

STATISTICS

REFUGEES REGISTERED WITH UNRWA

(as at April 1st, 1979)

	In Camps	Not in Camps	Total
East Jordan	181,302	512,554	693,856
West Bank	80,669	235,027	315,696
Gaza	202,159	158,659	360,818
Lebanon	111,792	105,556	217,348
Syria	58,146	144,149	202,295
Total	634,068	1,155,945	1,790,013

DISPLACED PERSONS

Apart from the Palestine refugees of 1948 who are registered with UNRWA and who are UNRWA's main concern (*see* table at left), considerable numbers of people have, since 1967, been displaced within the UNRWA areas of operations, and others have had to leave these areas. According to government estimates there are 194,152 displaced persons in East Jordan and 125,000 in Syria.

NUMBER OF REFUGEE PUPILS RECEIVING EDUCATION IN UNRWA/UNESCO SCHOOLS

(October 1978)

Field	Number of Schools	Pupils in Elementary Classes			Pupils in Preparatory Classes			Total Number of Pupils
		Boys	Girls	Total	Boys	Girls	Total	
East Jordan	199	48,714	45,126	93,840	18,809	16,079	34,888	128,728
West Bank	99	13,003	14,343	27,346	5,294	5,100	10,394	37,740
Gaza Strip	132	28,269	25,096	53,365	12,011	9,900	21,911	75,276
Lebanon	81	14,599	13,660	28,259	5,725	5,672	11,397	39,656
Syria	111	16,578	15,168	31,746	7,140	5,901	13,041	44,787
Total	622	121,163	113,393	234,556	48,979	42,652	91,631	326,187

* An addition 78,171 refugee pupils in 1978–79 attended elementary, preparatory and secondary government and private schools in east Jordan, the West Bank, the Gaza Strip, Lebanon and Syria.

PUBLICATIONS

Annual Report of the Commissioner-General of UNRWA.

UNRWA—a survey of United Nations Assistance to Palestine Refugees (every 2 years).

Palestine Refugees Today—the UNRWA Newsletter (quarterly).

UNITED NATIONS PEACE-KEEPING MISSIONS IN THE MIDDLE EAST

Chief Co-ordinator of United Nations Peace-Keeping Missions in the Middle East: Lt.-Gen. ENSIO P. H. SIILASVUO (Finland).

UNITED NATIONS TRUCE SUPERVISION ORGANIZATION—UNTSO

Headquarters at Government House, Jerusalem

Set up in 1948 to supervise the truce called for by the Security Council in Palestine.

Chief of Staff (acting): Col. WILLIAM CALLAGHAN (Ireland).

COMPOSITION

As at May 1979 there were 296 Military Observers from the following countries:

Argentina, Australia, Austria, Belgium, Canada, Chile, Denmark, Finland, France, Ireland, Italy, Netherlands, New Zealand, Norway, Sweden, U.S.S.R., U.S.A.

FUNCTIONS

UNTSO was established initially to supervise the truce called by the Security Council in May 1948 and has assisted in the application of the 1949 Armistice Agreements. Its activities have changed over the years in response to the development of affairs in the Middle East and in accordance with the relevant resolutions of the Security Council.

UNTSO observers assist the three UN peace-keeping forces in the Middle East (see below), UNEF and UNIFIL as separate groups and UNDOF as an integral part of the force.

FINANCE

UNTSO expenditures are covered by the regular budget of the United Nations. For the biennial period 1978–79, a sum of U.S. $15,114,300 was appropriated by the General Assembly.

UNITED NATIONS EMERGENCY FORCE—UNEF

Headquarters at Ismailia, Egypt

Set up in October 1973 by Security Council resolution to supervise the ceasefire and troop withdrawals called for by the Council in the Egypt-Israel sector. The original mandate of the Force had effect for six months and has since been extended by Security Council resolutions until July 24th, 1979, but was thereafter not renewed.

Commander: Maj.-Gen. RAIS ABIN (Indonesia).

Deputy Commander, Chief of Staff: Brig.-Gen. STIG NIHLÉN (Sweden).

COMPOSITION OF FORCE

(April 1979)

Australia	46
Canada	834
Finland	487
Ghana	595
Indonesia	508
Poland	925
Sweden	646
TOTAL	4,041

ACTIVITIES

Following the conclusion of the agreement of January 18th, 1974, and later of the agreement of September 4th, 1975, UNEF supervised the redeployment of Egyptian and Israeli forces and established buffer zones as provided in those agreements.

The Force continues to supervise the ceasefire and to man, patrol and control the zone of disengagement and, with the assistance of 115 UNTSO Military Observers, it conducts regular and special inspections of the Israeli and Egyptian areas of limited armaments and forces, as well as inspections of other areas agreed by the parties.

FINANCE

In addition to previous expenditures totalling $443 million up to October 24th, 1978, inclusive, for UNEF and UNDOF, the General Assembly appropriated $58 million for UNEF for the period from October 25th, 1978, to July 24th, 1979, inclusive, and $12.1 million for UNDOF for the period from October 25th, 1978, to May 31st, 1979, inclusive. In addition to these appropriations, it authorized the Secretary-General to enter into commitments at a rate not to exceed $6 million a month for the period from July 25th to October 24th, 1979, inclusive, for UNEF and $1.6 million a month for the period from June 1st to October 24th, 1979, inclusive, for UNDOF, should the Council extend their mandates again.

UNITED NATIONS DISENGAGEMENT OBSERVER FORCE—UNDOF

Headquarters at Damascus, Syria

Established for an initial period of six months by a Security Council resolution on May 31st, 1974, following the signature in Geneva of a disengagement agreement between Syrian and Israeli forces. The mandate has since been extended by the Security Council until November 30th, 1979.

Officer-in-Charge: Col. GUENTHER G. GREINDL (Austria).

COMPOSITION OF FORCE

(May 1979)

Austria	523
Canada	171
Finland	148
Poland	98
UNDOF military observers (detailed from UNTSO)	88
	1,028

The average strength of UNDOF is about 1,250. The lower strength shown is due to the repatriation of the Iranian contingent and its partial and temporary replacement by part of the Finnish UNEF contingent.

ACTIVITIES

The initial task of the Force was to take over territory evacuated in stages by the Israeli troops, in accordance with the disengagement agreement, to hand over territory to Syrian troops, and to establish an area of separation.

UNDOF continues to man the area of separation, from which Syrian and Israeli forces are excluded; it carries out inspections of the areas of limited armaments and forces, and it uses its best efforts to maintain the ceasefire. The area of separation has been placed under Syrian civil administration.

FINANCE

UNDOF finances are treated in conjunction with those of UNEF (*see* above).

UNITED NATIONS INTERIM FORCE IN LEBANON—UNIFIL

Headquarters at Naqoura, Lebanon

Set up in March 1978 by Security Council resolution, for a six-month period, subsequently extended to December 19th, 1979.

Commander: Maj.-Gen. E. A. ERSKINE (Ghana).

Deputy Commander, Chief of Staff: Brig.-Gen. MARTIN VADSET (Norway).

COMPOSITION OF FORCE

(March 1979)

Country	
Fiji	656
France	611
Ireland	756
Nepal	596
Netherlands	756
Nigeria	777
Norway	884
Senegal	591
TOTAL	5,627

A group of 36 military observers of UNTSO assist UNIFIL in the performance of its tasks. They form the "Observer Group, Lebanon".

FUNCTIONS

The functions of the force are to confirm the withdrawal of Israeli forces, to restore international peace and security and to assist the Government of Lebanon in ensuring the return of its effective authority in southern Lebanon.

FINANCE

The operating cost of UNIFIL for the period from March 19th to September 18th, 1978, inclusive, was $60.9 million. At its 33rd regular session the General Assembly appropriated $44.5 million for UNIFIL for the period from September 19th, 1978 to January 18th, 1979, inclusive. It also authorized the Secretary-General to enter into commitments for UNIFIL at a rate not to exceed $11.1 million a month for the period from January 19th to October 31st, 1979, inclusive, should the Security Council extend the mandate of UNIFIL again.

UNITED NATIONS PEACE-KEEPING FORCE IN CYPRUS—UNFICYP

Headquarters at Nicosia, Cyprus

Set up in March 1964 by Security Council resolution, for a three-month period, subsequently extended to December 1979, by successive resolutions.

Special Representative of the Secretary-General: REINALDO GALINDO POHL (El Salvador).

Commander: Maj.-Gen. J. J. QUINN (Ireland).

COMPOSITION OF FORCE

(May 1979)

	Military	Police
Australia	—	20
Austria	330	—
Canada	515	—
Denmark	365	—
Finland	11	—
Ireland	6	—
Sweden	427	14
United Kingdom	817	—
TOTAL	2,471	34

FUNCTIONS

The purpose of the Force has been to keep the peace between the Greek and Turkish Cypriot communities pending a resolution of outstanding issues between them, to help maintain law and order, and to promote a return to normal conditions. UNFICYP now also performs functions in relation to the supervision of the ceasefire between the armed forces of Turkey and Cyprus, and in providing humanitarian assistance to refugees and to villages isolated behind military lines. The United Nations High Commissioner for Refugees acts as Co-ordinator of UN humanitarian assistance for Cyprus.

FINANCE

The estimated cost to the United Nations for maintaining the Force during the period from December 15th, 1978, to June 15th, 1979, was $11.8 million. The total costs from the beginning of the operation in March 1964 to December 15th, 1978, were estimated at $297.5 million, a sum covered entirely by voluntary contributions.

UNITED NATIONS HIGH COMMISSIONER FOR REFUGEES—UNHCR

Palais des Nations, Geneva, Switzerland

The Office of High Commissioner was established in 1950 to provide international protection for refugees and to seek permanent solutions to their problems. In 1977 the mandate of UNHCR was extended until the end of 1983.

ORGANIZATION

High Commissioner (1978–82): POUL HARTLING.

Deputy High Commissioner: DALE S. DE HAAN.

The High Commissioner is elected by the United Nations General Assembly on the nomination of the Secretary-General, and is responsible to the General Assembly and to ECOSOC.

EXECUTIVE COMMITTEE

The Executive Committee of the High Commissioner's Programme, established by ECOSOC, gives the High Commissioner directives in respect of material assistance programmes and advice at his request in the field of international protection. It meets once a year at Geneva. It includes representatives of thirty-one states, both members and non-members of the UN.

ADMINISTRATION

Headquarters includes the High Commissioner's Office, and the following divisions: External Affairs, Protection, Assistance, and Administration and Management. There are 11 Regional Offices, 29 Branch Offices and 12 Sub-Offices, 8 Chargés de Mission and 7 Honorary Representatives, Correspondents or Consultants, located in 56 countries. In the Middle East and North Africa UNHCR has one Regional Office, 2 Branch Offices and other representation located in a total of 8 countries.

ACTIVITIES IN THE MIDDLE EAST AND NORTH AFRICA, 1978

In the field of protection, UNHCR continued to encourage national practices and procedures benefiting refugees, and followed up the application of the provisions of the 1951 Convention and 1967 Protocol relating to the status of refugees, to which six States in the region are parties.

In North Africa UNHCR provided mainly individual assistance to some 3,000 aged refugees and refugee students in Algeria, Morocco and Tunisia, and assistance in various fields, including local settlement, education and supplementary assistance, to some 5,000 refugees in Egypt. In addition, UNHCR continued to co-ordinate humanitarian assistance for Sahrawis in the Tindouf area of Algeria.

The High Commissioner continued to act as Co-ordinator of United Nations Humanitarian Assistance for Cyprus, at the request of the Secretary-General of the United Nations. In accordance with the wishes of the Government of Cyprus, a total of U.S. $13.75 million was channelled through UNHCR in 1978 to finance the United Nations programme in the island. This programme included food and medical supplies for the displaced and needy, low-cost housing to replace temporary accommodation, and the continuation of existing efforts aimed at reactivating farms, small businesses and local crafts.

UNHCR was also called upon to contribute to the overall United Nations effort to help displaced persons in Lebanon. Funds were made available for emergency assistance and for a rehabilitation programme in rural areas. UNHCR also pursued its traditional activities on behalf of some 1,000 refugees in the country.

Elsewhere, in countries of Western Asia (Iran, Jordan, Kuwait, Saudi Arabia, Syria, the United Arab Emirates and the Yemen Arab Republic) UNHCR provided assistance for refugees who were primarily of African and Asian origin and who included arrivals from the Horn of Africa following events there in the first half of 1978, and from the People's Democratic Republic of Yemen (some 15,000 in 1978).

UNHCR's assistance activities in Turkey in 1978 were directed at some 1,000 refugees, either residing in the country or in transit to resettlement elsewhere. Those in the latter category included a small number of Vietnamese "boat people".

UNHCR's expenditures in the Middle East and North Africa in 1978, including those undertaken in the framework of the United Nations effort in Cyprus and Lebanon, amounted to over $18.6 million.

REGIONAL OFFICES OF OTHER UN BODIES

UNITED NATIONS CHILDREN FUND—UNICEF

New York, N.Y. 10017, U.S.A.

UNICEF Regional Office for the Eastern Mediterranean: P.O.B. 5902, Beirut, Lebanon (covers Cyprus, Israel, Jordan, Lebanon, Saudi Arabia and Syria).

Office of the Director for Europe and North Africa: Director, UNICEF Office for Europe, Palais des Nations, CH-1211 Geneva 10, Switzerland.

North Africa Area Office: UNICEF Representative, B.P. 660, Alger-Gare, Algeria.

WORLD HEALTH ORGANIZATION—WHO

Geneva, Switzerland

WHO Regional Office for the Eastern Mediterranean: The Director, P.O.B. 1517, Alexandria, Egypt.

WHO Regional Office for Africa: The Director, P.O.B. 6, Brazzaville, People's Republic of Congo.

INTERNATIONAL CIVIL AVIATION ORGANIZATION—ICAO

Montreal, Canada

ICAO Middle East and Eastern African Office: 16 Hassan Sabri, Zamalek, Cairo, Egypt.

ICAO African Office: P.O.B. 2356, 15 blvd. de la République, Dakar, Senegal.

INTERNATIONAL LABOUR ORGANIZATION—ILO

Geneva, Switzerland

ILO Regional Office for Africa: P.O.B. 2788, Addis Ababa, Ethiopia.

ILO Regional Office for the Middle East and Europe: 4 Route des Morillons, CH-1218, Grand Saconnex, Switzerland.

ILO Office in Algiers: B.P. 226, Algiers, Algeria.

ILO Office in Beirut: B.P. 105096, Beirut, Lebanon.

ILO Office in Cairo: 9 Dr. Taha Hussein St., Zamalek, Cairo, Egypt.

ILO Office in Kuwait: P.O.B. 20275 Safat, Kuwait, Kuwait.

ILO Office for Iran and Afghanistan: P.O.B. 1555, Teheran, Iran.

ILO Office in Ankara: P.K. 407, Ankara, Turkey.

ILO Office for the People's Democratic Republic of Yemen and the Yemen Arab Republic: c/o UNDP, P.O.B. 1188, Tawahi, Aden, People's Democratic Republic of Yemen.

UNITED NATIONS EDUCATIONAL, SCIENTIFIC AND CULTURAL ORGANIZATION—UNESCO

Paris, France

Africa Division.

Arab States Division.

Regional Centre for Functional Literacy in Rural Areas for the Arab States (ASFEC): Sirs-el-Layyan, Menoufia, Egypt; f. 1952 for the training of specialists, production of prototype educational materials, research in functional literacy and literacy teaching; advisory service to member states; exchange publications.

UNESCO Regional Office for Science and Technology in the Arab States: 8 Abdel Rahman Fahmy St., Garden City, Cairo, Egypt.

UNESCO Regional Office for Education in the Arab States: c/o UNESCO Regional Office for Science and Technology in the Arab States, 8 Abdel Rahman Fahmy St., Garden City, Cairo, Egypt; f. 1973; part of the Secretariat of Unesco, the Regional Office trains education personnel (especially planners and administrators), provides advisory services, information and documentation, and carries out studies and research.

Publs. *Review Education* (quarterly), *Bulletin du Liaison.*

Arab Bank for Economic Development in Africa—BADEA

Sharaa el Baladia, P.O.B. 2640, Khartoum, Sudan

Created by the Arab League at the Sixth Arab Summit Conference in Algiers, November 1973. Operations began in early 1975. The purpose of the Bank is to contribute to Africa's economic development by helping to finance development projects and by supplying technical assistance to African countries.

MEMBERS

Subscribing countries: all members of the Arab League (*see* page 149) except Djibouti, Somalia, the Yemen Arab Republic and the People's Democratic Republic of Yemen.

Recipient countries: all member countries of the Organization of African Unity except the member countries of the Arab League.

ORGANIZATION

BOARD OF GOVERNORS

Highest authority of the Bank; examines the Bank's activities in the past year and provides the resources required for the tasks assigned to it in the coming year.

Chairman: IBRAHIM ABDEL KARIM (Bahrain).

BOARD OF DIRECTORS

Makes recommendations concerning policy to the Board of Governors and supervises the implementation of their decisions; performs all the executive functions of the Bank.

President of the Bank and Chairman: DR. CHEDLY AYARI (Tunisia).

SUBSCRIPTIONS TO CAPITAL STOCK

(at December 31st, 1977)

	U.S. $ Million		U.S. $ Million
Algeria	30	Morocco	11
Bahrain	1.5	Oman	11
Egypt	1.5	Palestine	1.5
Iraq	105	Qatar	60
Jordan	1.5	Saudi Arabia	180
Kuwait	110	Sudan	1.5
Lebanon	5	Syria	1
Libya	120	Tunisia	6.25
Mauritania	1.5	United Arab Emirates	90
		TOTAL	738.25

SPECIAL ARAB ASSISTANCE FUND FOR AFRICA—SAAFA

Established by a resolution of a meeting of Arab Oil Ministers and the OAU Oil Committee in January 1974 under the title Arab Loan Fund for Africa. Objective: to provide urgent aid to African countries suffering from serious balance of payments deficits. Came to be referred to erroneously as the Oil Fund. Acts in response to emergency situations in Africa, such as natural disasters, as well as difficulties caused by the increase in petroleum prices since 1973. Assistance has also been provided to newly independent African countries.

The Fund was integrated with BADEA, and subscriptions to the capital stock of the two organizations were merged, in accordance with a resolution at an extraordinary session of the Board of Governors of BADEA in November 1976.

By the end of 1977 the Fund had disbursed aid to the total of U.S. $221.7 million to 33 African countries.

LOANS APPROVED BY BADEA AND SAAFA

(cumulative to December 31st, 1978)

	U.S. $ Million		U.S. $ Million		U.S. $ Million		U.S. $ Million
Angola	13.2	Congo	10.0	Liberia	10.7	Sierre Leone	8.6
Benin	15	Equatorial Guinea	0.5	Madagascar	21.7	Somalia	7.5
Botswana	7.6	Ethiopia	14.2	Mali	29.7	Swaziland	4.2
Burundi	12	Gambia	4.6	Mauritius	12.7	Tanzania	29.2
Cameroon	22.9	Ghana	22.7	Mozambique	27.0	Togo	3.3
Cape Verde	11.5	Guinea	5.9	Niger	18.6	Uganda	16.2
Central African Empire	2.4	Guinea-Bissau	1.4	Rwanda	13.0	Upper Volta	19.1
Chad	18.5	Ivory Coast	3.3	São Tomé and Príncipe	15.5	Zaire	26.8
Comoros	10.5	Kenya	8.6	Senegal	17.2	Zambia	22.7
		Lesotho	8.8				

Grants totalling U.S. $1.6 million were given for a PANAFTEL (Pan-African Telecommunication Union) Seminar and for a special programme to support three African pest-control organizations. A line of credit of U.S. $5 million was opened for the Banque des Etats de l'Afrique Centrale to help finance small and medium size industries in regional co-operation.

Arab Fund for Economic and Social Development

P.O.B. 21923, Kuwait City, Kuwait

Established in 1968, the Fund began its operations in 1972.

MEMBERSHIP

19 countries and the Palestine Liberation Organization (*see* table of subscriptions below)

FUNCTIONS

The Fund participates in the financing of economic and social development projects in the Arab states and countries by:

1. Financing economic projects of an investment character by means of loans granted on easy terms to governments, and to public or private organizations and institutions, giving preference to economic projects of interest specifically to Arab peoples, and to joint Arab projects.
2. Encouraging, directly or indirectly, the investment of public and private capital in such a manner as to ensure the development and growth of the Arab economy.
3. Providing technical expertise and assistance in the various fields of economic development.

ORGANIZATION

BOARD OF GOVERNORS

The Board of Governors consists of a Governor and an Alternate Governor appointed by each member of the Fund for a period of five years. The Board of Governors is considered as the General Assembly of the Fund, and has all powers.

Director-General and Chairman of the Board of Directors: Dr. Mohammad al-Amadi (Syria).

BOARD OF DIRECTORS

The Board of Directors is composed of six full-time Directors elected by the Board of Governors from among Arab citizens of recognized experience and competence. They are elected for a renewable term of two years.

The Board of Directors is charged with all the activities of the Fund in a general manner, and exercises the powers delegated to it by the Board of Governors.

FINANCIAL STRUCTURE

The authorized capital at commencement of operations in April 1973 was 100 million Kuwaiti dinars. In 1975 the capital was increased to KD 400 million (one Kuwaiti dinar being equal to 2.48828 grammes of gold). The capital is divided into 40,000 shares having a value of 10,000 Kuwaiti dinars each.

SUBSCRIPTIONS

	Million Kuwaiti Dinars
Algeria	30.0
Bahrain	1.0
Egypt*	40.5
Iraq	29.4
Jordan	8.0
Kuwait	75.0
Lebanon	2.0
Libya	47.7
Morocco	8.0
Oman	8.0
Palestine Liberation Organization	0.25
Qatar	4.0
Saudi Arabia	74.0
Somalia	0.2
Sudan	5.8
Syria	12.0
Tunisia	2.0
United Arab Emirates	20.0
Yemen Arab Republic	2.0
Yemen, People's Democratic Republic	0.04
Total	370.29

* In April 1979 all aid to and economic relations with Egypt were suspended, but finance for projects already in progress is continuing.

The Arab League

Khairaldin Basha Street, Tunis, Tunisia

The League of Arab States is a voluntary association of sovereign Arab states designed to strengthen the close ties linking them and to co-ordinate their policies and activities and direct them towards the common good of all the Arab countries. It was founded in March 1945.

MEMBERS

Algeria	Kuwait	Palestine (*see* below)	Tunisia
Bahrain	Lebanon	Qatar	United Arab Emirates
Djibouti	Libya	Saudi Arabia	Yemen Arab Republic
Egypt (*see* below)	Mauritania	Somalia	Yemen, People's Democratic Republic
Iraq	Morocco	Sudan	
Jordan	Oman	Syria	

MEMBERSHIP AND FUNCTIONS

While it is a prerequisite that members must be Arab states that are fully independent, the activities of the League also often include Arab countries which are not independent. Palestine is considered an independent state, as explained in the Charter Annex on Palestine, and therefore a full member of the League.

The status of Palestine as a full member of the League was confirmed at a meeting of the Arab League Council in September 1976.

In March 1979 Egypt's membership of the Arab League was suspended, and it was decided to make Tunis the temporary headquarters of the League, its Secretariat and its permanent committees.

The Arab League itself is an international body with its own independent statutory powers and general objectives.

ORGANIZATION

COUNCIL

The supreme organ of the Arab League. Meets in March and September. Consists of representatives of the twenty-one member states, each of which has one vote, and a representative for Palestine. Unanimous decisions of the Council shall be binding upon all member states of the League; majority decisions shall be binding only on those states which have accepted them.

The Council may, if necessary, hold an extraordinary session at the request of two member states. Invitations to all sessions are extended by the Secretary-General. The ordinary sessions are presided over by representatives of the member states in turn.

Sixteen committees are attached to the Council:

Political Committee: studies political questions and reports to the Council meetings concerned with them. All member states are members of the Committee. It represents the Council in dealing with critical political matters when the Council is meeting. Usually composed of the Foreign Ministers.

Cultural Committee: in charge of following up the activities of the Cultural Department and the cultural affairs within the scope of the secretariat; co-ordinates the activities of the general secretariat and the various cultural bodies in member states.

Economic Committee: complemented by the Economic Council since 1953.

Communications Committee: supervises land, sea and air communications, together with weather forecasts and postal matters.

Social Committee: supports co-operation in such matters as family and child welfare.

Legal Committee: an extension of the Nationality and Passports Committee abolished in 1947; studies and legally formulates draft agreements, bills, regulations and official documents.

Arab Oil Experts Committee: for study of oil affairs; also investigates methods to prevent the smuggling of Arab oil into Israel; and for co-ordination of oil policies in general.

Information Committee: studies information projects, suggests plans and carries out the policies decided by the Council of Information Ministers.

Health Committee: for co-operation in health affairs.

Human Rights Committee: studies subjects concerning human rights, particularly violations by Israel; collaborates with the Information and Cultural Committees.

Permanent Committee for Administrative and Financial Affairs.

Permanent Committee for Meteorology.

Committee of Arab Experts on Co-operation.

Arab Women's Committee.

Organization of Youth Welfare.

Conference of Liaison Officers: co-ordinates trade activities among commercial attachés of various Arab embassies abroad.

GENERAL SECRETARIAT

The administrative and financial offices of the League. The Secretariat carries out the decisions of the Council, and provides financial and administrative services for the personnel of the League. There are a number of departments: economic, political, legal, cultural, social and labour affairs, petroleum, finance, Palestine, health, information, communications, protocol. The most recently formed department deals with African affairs.

The Secretary-General is appointed by the League Council by a two-thirds majority of the member states. He appoints the Assistant Secretaries and principal officials, with the approval of the Council. He has the rank of Ambassador, and the Assistant Secretaries have the rank of Ministers Plenipotentiary.

Secretary-General: (vacant).

Assistant Secretaries-General: Dr. Ahmed el Saied Hamad (Sudan), Assaad el Assaad (Lebanon), Selim el Yafi (Syria), Dr. Mohammed el Farra (Jordan).

Assistant Secretary-General for Economic Affairs: Abd al-Muhsin Zalzalah.

Assistant Secretary-General for Military Affairs: Gen. Ahmad Badawi (Egypt).

DEFENCE AND ECONOMIC CO-OPERATION

Groups established under the Treaty of Joint Defence and Economic Co-operation, concluded in 1950 to complement the Charter of the League:

Arab Unified Military Command: Cairo; f. 1964 to co-ordinate military policies for the liberation of Palestine.

Arab Economic Unity Council: to compare and co-ordinate the economic policies of the member states; the Council is composed of Ministers of Economic Affairs or their deputies. Decisions are taken by majority vote. The first meeting was held in 1953.

Joint Defence Council: supervises implementation of those aspects of the treaty concerned with common defence. Composed of Foreign and Defence Ministers; decisions by a two-thirds majority vote of members are binding on all.

Military Advisory Organization.

Permanent Military Commission: Established 1950; composed of representatives of army General Staffs; main purpose: to draw up plans of joint defence for submission to the Joint Defence Council.

ARAB DETERRENT FORCE

Set up in June 1976 by the Arab League Council to supervise successive attempts to cease hostilities in Lebanon, and afterwards to maintain the peace. In March 1979 the Council renewed the mandate of the force for three months. The Arab League Summit Conference in October 1976 agreed that costs were to be paid in the following percentage contributions:

Saudi Arabia	20
Kuwait	20
United Arab Emirates	15
Qatar	10
Other Arab states	35
	100

Commanding Officer: Col. Ahmad al-Haj (Lebanon).

OTHER INSTITUTIONS OF THE COUNCIL

Other bodies established by resolutions adopted by the Council of the League:

Academy of Arab Music.

Administrative Tribunal of the Arab League: Cairo; f. 1964; began operations 1966.

Arab Authority for Exhibitions: f. 1964 to co-ordinate the planning and holding of international exhibitions and fairs in the member states of the League; has a Council of representatives appointed by the member states.

Arab Centre for Industrial Development: 22 Dr. Taha Hussein St., Zamalek, Cairo, Egypt; created in 1968 in compliance with a decision of the League Economic Council; the Arab states are represented at the Centre by an official representative and an alternate; the secretariat includes departments for technical and economic studies and aid for the promotion of industrial information; began operations in 1970.

Arab Institute of Forestry: Latakia, Syria.

Special Bureau for Boycotting Israel: Damascus.

SPECIALIZED AGENCIES

All member states of the Arab League are also members of the Specialized Agencies, which constitute an integral part of the Arab League.

Arab Centre for the Study of Dry Regions and Arid Territories: P.O.B. 2440, Damascus, Syria. Sixth session in April 1976, Tripoli, Libya.

Arab League Educational, Cultural and Scientific Organization (ALECSO): 109 Tahrir St., Dokki, Cairo, Egypt; f. 1964; aims: to promote intellectual unity of the Arab countries by means of education; to raise cultural standards; to enable the Arab countries to participate in technical development; to establish specialized institutes; to train experts for research in Arab civilization. Each member submits an annual report on progress in education, cultural matters and science. The Arab League has a Permanent Delegation at UNESCO which may act on behalf of Arab states that are not members of the world body. The first session of the General Conference was held in Cairo in 1970. Dir.-Gen. Mohieddin Saber (Sudan).

There are five institutions within the framework of the Arab League Educational, Cultural and Scientific Organization:

Institute for Arab Studies and Research Work: f. 1953 for specialization by graduates of Arab universities; provides for studies in contemporary Arab affairs, including national and international affairs, economics, social studies, history, geography, law, literature and linguistics. A special department of the Institute is devoted to Palestinian affairs, to research into the Arab cause; the Institute aims to develop the understanding of Arab nationalism.

Arab Literacy and Adult Education Organization: 1 Shehab St., Dokki, Cairo, Egypt; f. 1966 to assist in the establishment and development of national institutions for literacy and adult education; to assist in formulation of national plans in these respects; to hold regional training courses, seminars and conferences; to co-ordinate research work; to grant scholarships and provide technical assistance; and to provide information.

Institute of Arab Manuscripts.

Permanent Bureau for Arabization: Rabat, Morocco.

Museum of Arab Culture: Cairo, Egypt.

Arab Health Organization.

Arab Institute of Petroleum Research.

Arab Labour Organization: 7 Midan El Misaha, Dokki, Giza, Cairo, Egypt (in early 1979 the Organization announced its intention to transfer its headquarters to Baghdad); established in 1965 for co-operation between member states in labour problems; unification of labour legislation and general conditions of work wherever possible; research; technical assistance; social insurance; training, etc.; the organization has a tripartite structure: governments, employers and workers; Gen. Dir. Dr. Tayeb Lahdiri. Publs. *Bulletin* (monthly), *Arab Labour Review* (quarterly).

Arab Organization of Administrative Science: 8 Salah el Din St., Zamalek, Cairo, Egypt; set up with the approval of the League Council in 1961, commencing activity in 1969 soon after ratification of the agreement by four Arab states (Egypt, Iraq, Syria, Kuwait); to ensure co-operation in promoting administrative science, to improve the standard of administrative staff in the Arab states; Dir.-Gen. Kamal Nourallah. Publ. Research series in administrative science.

Arab Organization for Agricultural Development: 3 El-Jamea St., Khartoum, Sudan; proposed in 1969 by a decision of Arab Ministers of Agriculture, which was approved by the Economic Council in 1970 and ratified by the League Council; to contribute to co-operation in agricultural activities, and in the development of natural and human resources for agriculture.

Arab Organization for Standardization and Metrology: 25 Iraqi St. (off Shehab St.), Dokki, Giza, Cairo, Egypt; created 1965 after the Economic Council had approved an agreement for its creation by twenty Arab states as a specialized institution in the field of economic, commercial and industrial co-operation; began activity in 1968 to unify technical terms and standard specifications for products such as food, cloth, fertilizers, building materials, oil, minerals, electrical products; also deals with technical drawing and packaging; assists in the establishment of national bodies and collaborates with international standards activities; Sec.-Gen. Dr. Mahmoud Mohamad Salama (Egypt); publs. *Annual Report* (French and English), *Quarterly Bulletin* (Arabic and English), *Standard Specification* (Arabic, English and French) and information pamphlets.

Arab Postal Union: 28 Adli Street, Cairo, Egypt; f. 1954; aims: to establish more strict postal relations between the Arab countries than those laid down by the Universal Postal Union, to pursue the development and modernization of postal services in member countries. In 1979 the Union decided to suspend Egypt's membership and to move its headquarters to another Arab country. Sec.-Gen. Dr. Anouar Bakir. Publs. *Bulletin* (monthly), *Review* (quarterly), *News* (annual) and occasional studies.

Arab States Broadcasting Union (ASBU): 22a Taha Hussein St., Zamalek, Cairo; f. 1969 to promote Arab fraternity, to acquaint the world with the Arab nations, co-ordinate and study broadcasting subjects, to exchange expertise and technical co-operation in broadcasting. Mems.: 21 Arab radio and TV stations and four foreign associates. In April 1979 ASBU voted to boycott Egyptian TV and to move its headquarters to Tunis. Sec.-Gen. Saleh Abdel Kader. Publs. *Arab Broadcasts* (monthly, in Arabic), *ASBU Review* (quarterly, in English), *Broadcasting Studies and Researches* (irregular), *Broadcasting Reports* (irregular).

Arab Telecommunications Union: 83 Ramses Street, Cairo, Egypt; f. 1958; to co-ordinate and develop telecommunications between member countries; to exchange technical aid and encourage research. Sec.-Gen. Dr. Mahmoud Muhammad Riad. Publs. *Economic and Technical Studies; Arab Telecommunications Union Journal* (quarterly).

Civil Aviation Council of Arab States: Khalifa El-Mamoum St., Manshiet El-Bakri, Cairo, Egypt; created 1965, began operations 1967; aims to develop the principles, techniques and economics of air transport in the Arab World; to co-operate with the International Civil Aviation Organization and to attempt to standardize laws and technical terms; deals also with Arab air rates; Pres. M. S. el-Hakim. Publs. *Air Transport Activities in Arab Countries, Lexicon of Civil Aviation Terminology* (Arabic); *Unified Air Law for Arab States* (Arabic and English).

International Arab Organization for Social Defence against Crime: c/o League of Arab States, Khairaldin Basha St., Tunis, Tunisia; f. 1965 at League Headquarters by the League Council to study causes and remedies for crime and the treatment of criminals; Sec.-Gen. Dr. Abdel-Wahhab el-Aschmaoui; the organization consists of three bureaux:

International Arab Bureau for Narcotics: Tunis; Dir.-Gen. Ahmad Alhadiqah (Egypt).

International Arab Bureau for Prevention of Crime: Baghdad; Dir.-Gen. Amer Al-Mukhtar (Iraq).

International Arab Bureau of Criminal Police: Damascus; Dir.-Gen. Col. Ashdek Aldeiry (Syria).

Joint Arab Scientific Council for the Utilization of Atomic Energy.

EXTERNAL RELATIONS

Arab League Offices and Information Centres abroad.

Set up by the Arab League to co-ordinate work at all levels among Arab embassies abroad. The Arab League Office in New Delhi has been given full diplomatic status.

Argentina: Oficina de la Liga de los Estados Arabes, Calla o 1319, Buenos Aires.

Belgium: Bureau de la Ligue des Etats Arabes, 108 Ave. F. D. Roosevelt, Brussels 1050.

Brazil: Missão de Liga dos Estados Arabes, Sqs. 105, Bloco K, Apt. 201, 70000 Brasília, D.F.

Canada: Arab Information Centre, 170 Laurier Ave., West, Suite 709, Ottawa, Ontario.

Chile: Representación de la Liga de los Estados Arabes, Gallard 2175, Santiago de Chile.

France: Bureau de la Ligue des Etats Arabes, 138 blvd. Haussman, Paris 8.

Federal Republic of Germany: Delegation von der Liga der Arabischen Staaten, Friedrich Wilhelm Strasse 2A, Bonn 53.

India: League of Arab States Mission, 62 Golf Links, New Delhi.

Italy: Arab League Office, Piazzale Belle Arti no. 6, Rome.

Japan: Office of the League of Arab States, 1-1-12 Moto Azabu, Minato-ku 106, Tokyo.

Spain: Oficina de la Liga de los Estados Arabes, c/Alcala 89-20 Derecha, Madrid 9.

Switzerland: Délégation de la Ligue des Etats Arabes, 7 Ave. Kreig, Geneva.

United Kingdom: Arab Information Office, 52 Green St., London, W.1.

U.S.A.: Arab Information Center, 747 Third Ave., 25th Floor, New York, N.Y. 10017.

Arab Information Center, 18 South Michigan Ave., Chicago, Ill. 60603.

Arab Information Center, Suite 1302, Hartford Bldg., Dallas, Texas.

Arab Information Center, World Trade Center, Ferry Bldg., San Francisco, Calif. 94111.

Arab Information Center, 1875 Connecticut Ave., N.W., Suite 1110, Washington, D.C. 20009.

Arab League Representatives:

Kenya: Arab League Representative, c/o The Embassy of the Arab Republic of Egypt, Total Bldg., Koinange St., Nairobi.

Nigeria: Arab League Representative, Post Box 6916, 55 Ademola St., Ikoyi, Lagos.

Senegal: Arab League Representative, c/o L'Ambassade du Liban, 18 Ave. de la République, Dakar.

RECORD OF EVENTS

1945 Pact of the Arab League signed, March.

1946 Cultural Treaty signed.

1950 Joint Defence and Economic Co-operation Treaty.

1952 Agreements on extradition, writs and letters of request, nationality of Arabs outside their country of origin.

1953 Formation of Arab Telecommunications Union.
Agreements for facilitating trade between Arab countries.
Formation of Economic Council.
Convention on the privileges and immunities of the League.
First Conference of Arab Education Ministers, Cairo, December.

1954 Formation of Arab Postal Union.
Nationality Agreement.

1956 Agreement on the adoption of a Common Tariff Nomenclature.
Sudan joins Arab League.

1957 Agreement on the creation of Arab Financial Institution for Economic Development, June.
Cultural Agreement with UNESCO signed, November.

1958 Co-operation Agreement between the Arab League and the International Labour Organisation.

1959 First Arab Oil Congress, Cairo, April.

1960 Inauguration of new Arab League HQ at Midan Al Tahrir, Cairo, March.

1961 Kuwait joins League.
Syrian Arab Republic rejoins League as independent member.
Agreement on the establishment of the Arab Organization for Administrative Sciences.
Agreement with WHO on exchange of medical information, May.

1962 Arab Economic Unity Agreement.
U.A.R. announced intentions of leaving Arab League.

1963 U.A.R. resumes active membership of League, March.
Agreement on establishment of an Arab Organization for Social Defence against Crime.

1964 First Summit Conference of Arab Kings and Presidents, Cairo, January.
First session of the Council of Arab Information Ministers, Cairo, March.
First meeting of Economic Unity Council, June.
Arab Common Market approved by Arab Economic Unity Council, August.
Second Summit Conference welcomes establishment of Palestine Liberation Organization, September.
First Conference of Arab Ministers of Communications, Beirut, November.

1965 Arab Common Market established, January.
Third Summit Conference, May. Tunisia absent. Integrated plan approved to defend Palestine in the UN.
Agreement on Arab Co-operation for the Peaceful Uses of Atomic Energy.

1966 First session of Arab League Administrative Court, September.

1967 Meeting of Arab Foreign Ministers, Khartoum, August. Discussion of Arab oil embargo against the U.S.A. and the United Kingdom.
Fourth Summit Conference in Khartoum, August. Decision to resume oil supplies to the West. Syria absent.
Establishment of Civil Aviation Council of Arab States.
Agreement to establish an Arab Tanker Company, December.

1968 First Conference of Arab Tourist Ministers, Cairo, February.
Arab League approves Industrial Development Centre.
Economic Council approves establishment of Arab Fund for Economic and Social Development.

1969 Permanent Council of Co-operation Experts established to promote co-operative movement in Arab States, January.
First Session of the Arab States Broadcasting Union (ASBU), Khartoum, February.
Fifth summit Conference, Rabat. Call for mobilization of all Arab Nations against Israel.
Industrial Development Centre for the Arab States starts activities.
First Conference of Arab Health Ministers, Cairo.

1970 Establishment of the Arab Organization for Agricultural Development.
Establishment of the Arab Educational, Cultural and Scientific Organization.

1971 First meeting of Arab Labour Organization.
Bahrain, Qatar and Oman admitted to Arab League, September.

1972 First Arab Traffic Conference, May.
Mahmoud Riad succeeds Abdel Khalek Hassouna as Secretary-General, June.
Conference on Arab Women and National Development, Cairo, September.

1973 Treaty for Technical Co-operation between the Afro-Asian Rural Reconstruction Organization (AARRO) and the Arab League signed, May.
Declaration issued defining Arab demands for settlement of the Middle East conflict.
Sixth summit conference in Algiers, November; approval of three institutions to help Africa in the oil crisis: Arab Loan Fund for Africa, Arab Bank for Economic Development in Africa, and Arab Fund for Technical Assistance.
Mauritania admitted to Arab League, December.

1974 Arab oil ministers endow Arab Loan Fund for Africa with $200 million, January.
Somalia admitted to Arab League, February.
Agreement to establish a General Committee with the EEC to organize co-operation, July.
Joint Defence Council meeting, July. Decisions concerning political, financial and military assistance to ensure the defence of Lebanon.
Seventh summit conference in Rabat, October. Replenishes Arab Loan Fund for Africa with further $200 million.

1975 Arab Bank for Economic Development in Africa established.

1976 Mediation mission sent to Algeria, Mauritania and Morocco to seek a peaceful solution to the dispute in the Western Sahara, February.
Ministerial meeting in Dakar, Senegal in April as a preparatory meeting for the Afro-Arab Summit.
Arab peace-keeping force sent to Lebanon, June.
Summit conference attended by 16 member states to discuss the conflict in Lebanon, October.

1977 Afro-Arab Summit of member countries of the Arab League and the Organization of African Unity, Cairo, in March.
Djibouti admitted to membership, September.
Conference of Arab Foreign Ministers, November. No discussion of Lebanon or Western Sahara.
Tripoli Declaration, December. Decision of Algeria, Iraq, Libya and Yemen P.D.R. to boycott League meetings in Egypt in response to President Sadat's visit to Israel.

1978 24th session of Economic Council, February.
69th meeting of Arab League Council in Cairo, March, boycotted by "rejectionist" states. Resolutions calling for an emergency summit to settle differences within the League and for the establishment of an Arab Solidarity Committee to be chaired by President Nimeri of Sudan.
All members except Egypt were present at a Council meeting in Baghdad in November. A number of resolutions were adopted to be taken should Egypt sign peace treaty with Israel of which the three principal ones were: diplomatic rupture with Egypt, transfer of the League's headquarters from Cairo, and the economic boycott of Sadat's government.

1979 At a Council meeting in Baghdad ending on March 27th various resolutions were adopted of which the main points are: to withdraw Arab ambassadors from Egypt; to recommend severance of political and diplomatic relations with Egypt; to suspend Egypt's membership of the League on the date of the signing of the peace treaty with Israel; to make the city of Tunis the temporary HQ of the League, its Secretariat, ministerial councils and permanent technical committees; to condemn United States' policy regarding its role in concluding the Camp David agreements and the peace treaty; to halt all bank loans, deposits, guarantees or facilities, as well as all financial or technical contributions and aid to Egypt; to prohibit trade exchanges with the Egyptian state and with private establishments dealing with Israel. On March 27th Egypt declared that it had "frozen" its activities in the Arab League.

PUBLICATIONS

Information Department: *Information Bulletin* (Arabic and English); also bulletins of treaties and agreements concluded among the member states.

New York Office: *Arab World* (monthly), and *News and Views*.

Geneva Office: *Le Monde Arabe* (monthly), and *Nouvelles du Monde Arabe* (weekly).

Buenos Aires Office: *Arabia Review* (monthly).

Paris Office: *Actualités Arabes* (fortnightly).

Brasília Office: *Oriente Arabe* (monthly).

Rome Office: *Rassegna del Mondo Arabo* (monthly).

London Office: *The Arab* (monthly).

New Delhi Office: *Al Arab* (monthly).

Bonn Office: *Arabische Korrespondenz* (fortnightly).

Ottawa Office: *Spotlight on the Arab World* (fortnightly), *The Arab Case* (monthly).

THE PACT OF THE LEAGUE OF ARAB STATES

(March 22nd, 1945)

Article 1

The League of Arab States is composed of the independent Arab States which have signed this Pact.

Any independent Arab state has the right to become a member of the League. If it desires to do so, it shall submit a request which will be deposited with the Permanent Secretariat-General and submitted to the Council at the first meeting held after submission of the request.

Article 2

The League has as its purpose the strengthening of the relations between the member states; the co-ordination of their policies in order to achieve co-operation between them and to safeguard their independence and sovereignty; and a general concern with the affairs and interests of the Arab countries. It has also as its purpose the close co-operation of the member states, with due regard to the organization and circumstances of each state, on the following matters:

(*a*) Economic and financial affairs, including commercial relations, customs, currency, and questions of agriculture and industry.

(*b*) Communications: this includes railways, roads, aviation, navigation, telegraphs and posts.

(*c*) Cultural affairs.

(*d*) Nationality, passports, visas, execution of judgments, and extradition of criminals.

(*e*) Social affairs.

(*f*) Health problems.

Article 3

The League shall possess a Council composed of the representatives of the member states of the League; each state shall have a single vote, irrespective of the number of its representatives.

It shall be the task of the Council to achieve the realization of the objectives of the League and to supervise the execution of agreements which the member states have concluded on the questions enumerated in the preceding article, or on any other questions.

It likewise shall be the Council's task to decide upon the means by which the League is to co-operate with the international bodies to be created in the future in order to guarantee security and peace and regulate economic and social relations.

Article 4

For each of the questions listed in Article 2 there shall be set up a special committee in which the member states of the League shall be represented. These committees shall be charged with the task of laying down the principles and extent of co-operation. Such principles shall be formulated as draft agreements, to be presented to the Council for examination preparatory to their submission to the aforesaid states.

Representatives of the other Arab countries may take part in the work of the aforesaid committees. The Council shall determine the conditions under which these representatives may be permitted to participate and the rules governing such representation.

Article 5

Any resort to force in order to resolve disputes arising between two or more member states of the League is prohibited. If there should arise among them a difference which does not concern a state's independence, sovereignty, or territorial integrity, and if the parties to the dispute have recourse to the Council for the settlement of this difference, the decision of the Council shall then be enforceable and obligatory.

In such a case, the states between whom the difference has arisen shall not participate in the deliberations and decisions of the Council.

The Council shall mediate in all differences which threaten to lead to war between two member states, or a member state and a third state, with a view to bringing about their reconciliation.

Decisions of arbitration and mediation shall be taken by majority vote.

Article 6

In case of agression or threat of aggression by one state against a member state, the state which has been attacked or threatened with aggression may demand the immediate convocation of the Council.

The Council shall by unanimous decision determine the measures necessary to repulse the aggression. If the aggressor is a member state, his vote shall not be counted in determining unanimity.

If, as a result of the attack, the government of the State attacked finds itself unable to communicate with the Council, that state's representative in the Council shall have the right to request the convocation of the Council for the purpose indicated in the foregoing paragraph. In the event that this representative is unable to communicate with the Council, any member state of the League shall have the right to request the convocation of the Council.

Article 7

Unanimous decisions of the Council shall be binding upon all member states of the League; majority decisions shall be binding only upon those states which have accepted them.

In either case the decisions of the Council shall be enforced in each member state according to its respective basic laws.

Article 8

Each member state shall respect the systems of government established in the other member states and regard them as exclusive concerns of those states. Each shall pledge to abstain from any action calculated to change established systems of government.

Article 9

States of the League which desire to establish closer co-operation and stronger bonds than are provided by this Pact may conclude agreements to that end.

Treaties and agreements already concluded or to be concluded in the future between a member state and another state shall not be binding or restrictive upon other members.

Article 10

The permanent seat of the League of Arab States is established in Cairo. The Council may, however, assemble at any other place it may designate.

Article 11

The Council of the League shall convene in ordinary session twice a year, in March and in September. It shall convene in extraordinary session upon the request of two member states of the League whenever the need arises.

Article 12

The League shall have a permanent Secretariat-General which shall consist of a Secretary-General, Assistant Secretaries, and an appropriate number of officials.

The Council of the League shall appoint the Secretary-General by a majority of two-thirds of the states of the League. The Secretary-General, with the approval of the Council, shall appoint the Assistant Secretaries and the principal officials of the League.

The Council of the League shall establish an administrative regulation for the functions of the Secretariat-General and matters relating to the Staff.

The Secretary-General shall have the rank of Ambassador and the Assistant Secretaries that of Ministers Plenipotentiary.

The first Secretary-General of the League is named in an Annex to this Pact.

Article 13

The Secretary-General shall prepare the draft of the budget of the League and shall submit it to the Council for approval before the beginning of each fiscal year.

The Council shall fix the share of the expenses to be borne by each state of the League. This share may be reconsidered if necessary.

Article 14

The members of the Council of the League as well as the members of the committees and the officials who are to be designated in the administrative regulation shall enjoy diplomatic privileges and immunity when engaged in the exercise of their functions.

The building occupied by the organs of the League shall be inviolable.

Article 15

The first meeting of the Council shall be convened at the invitation of the head of the Egyptian Government. Thereafter it shall be convened at the invitation of the Secretary-General.

The representatives of the member states of the League shall alternately assume the presidency of the Council at each of its ordinary sessions.

Article 16

Except in cases specifically indicated in this Pact, a majority vote of the Council shall be sufficient to make enforceable decisions on the following matters:

(*a*) Matters relating to personnel.

(*b*) Adoption of the budget of the League.

(*c*) Establishment of the administrative regulations for the Council, the Committees, and the Secretariat-General.

(*d*) Decisions to adjourn the sessions.

Article 17

Each member state of the League shall deposit with the Secretariat-General one copy of every treaty or agreement concluded or to be concluded in the future between itself and another member state of the League or a third state.

Article 18

(deals with withdrawal)

Article 19

(deals with amendment)

Article 20

(deals with ratification)

Annex Regarding Palestine

Since the termination of the last great war the rule of the Ottoman Empire over the Arab countries, among them Palestine, which had become detached from that Empire, has come to an end. She has come to be autonomous, not subordinate to any other state.

The Treaty of Lausanne proclaimed that her future was to be settled by the parties concerned.

However, even though she was as yet unable to control her own affairs, the Covenant of the League (of Nations) in 1919 made provision for a regime based upon recognition of her independence.

Her international existence and independence in the legal sense cannot, therefore, be questioned, any more than could the independence of the other Arab countries.

Although the outward manifestations of this independence have remained obscured for reasons beyond her control, this should not be allowed to interfere with her participation in the work of the Council of the League.

The states signatory to the Pact of the Arab League are therefore of the opinion that, considering the special circumstances of Palestine and until that Country can effectively exercise its independence, the Council of the League should take charge of the selection of an Arab representative from Palestine to take part in its work.

Annex Regarding Co-operation with Countries which are not Members of the Council of the League

Whereas the member states of the League will have to deal in the Council as well as in the committees with matters which will benefit and affect the Arab world at large;

And whereas the Council has to take into account the aspirations of the Arab countries which are not members of the Council and has to work toward their realization;

Now therefore, it particularly behoves the states signatory to the Pact of the Arab League to enjoin the Council of the League, when considering the admission of those countries to participation in the committees referred to in the Pact, that it should do its utmost to co-operate with them, and furthermore, that it should spare no effort to learn their needs and understand their aspirations and hopes; and that it should work thenceforth for their best interests and the safeguarding of their future with all the political means at its disposal.

Arab Monetary Fund

P.O.B. 2818, Abu Dhabi, United Arab Emirates

The Agreement establishing the Arab Monetary Fund entered into force on February 2nd, 1977, following a meeting of the Council of Arab Economic Unity held in Rabat, Morocco, on April 27th, 1976.

MEMBERS

Algeria	Kuwait	Palestine Liberation Organization	Syria
Bahrain	Lebanon	Qatar	Tunisia
Egypt*	Libya	Saudi Arabia	United Arab Emirates
Iraq	Mauritania	Somalia	Yemen Arab Republic
Jordan	Morocco	Sudan	Yemen, People's Democratic Republic
	Oman		

* Egypt's membership was suspended in May 1979.

ORGANIZATION

BOARD OF GOVERNORS

The Board of Governors is the highest authority of the Arab Monetary Fund. It formulates policies on Arab economic integration and the liberalization of trade among member states. The Board of Governors is composed of a Governor and a Deputy Governor appointed by each member state for a term of five years. It meets at least once a year; meetings may also be convened at the request of half the members or of the Board of Executive Directors. Each member country has 75 votes regardless of the number of shares it holds and, in addition, one vote for each share held.

President (1977–82): Dr. Jawad Hashim (Iraq).

BOARD OF EXECUTIVE DIRECTORS

The Board of Executive Directors is responsible for the day-to-day operations of the Fund. It is composed of the President and eight resident Directors elected by the Board of Governors. Each Director holds office for three years and may be re-elected.

In 1979 the Board comprised representatives of Algeria, Bahrain, Egypt, Jordan, Mauritania, Saudi Arabia, Somalia and the United Arab Emirates.

THE PRESIDENT

The President of the Fund is appointed by the Board of Governors for a renewable five-year term. He serves as Chairman of the Board of Executive Directors.

He is to set up a Committee on Loans and a Committee on Investments to make recommendations on loan and investment policies to the Board of Executive Directors. He is required to submit an Annual Report to the Board of Governors.

FINANCE

The authorized capital of the Fund is 250 million Arab dinars. The Arab dinar (AD) is a unit of account equivalent to 3 IMF Special Drawing Rights (SDR 1 = U.S. $1.288 at June 22nd, 1979). The capital stock comprises 5,000 shares, each having the value of AD 50,000.

Each member deposited 5 per cent of the value of its shares at the time of its ratification of the Agreement and another 20 per cent when the Agreement entered into force. The second 25 per cent of the capital is to be subscribed by May 1979, when the paid-up capital will be U.S. $470 million. The Fund has undertaken to disburse half its paid-up capital by this date.

The Board of Governors, by a special majority and subject to prescribed conditions, may increase the capital of the Fund. The Articles of Agreement provide for the establishment of a general reserve fund and, if necessary, special reserve funds.

CAPITAL SUBSCRIPTIONS
(million Arab dinars; AD1 = SDR 3)

	Number of Shares	Value of Shares
Algeria	760	38.0
Bahrain	80	4.0
Egypt	500	25.0
Iraq	500	25.0
Jordan	80	4.0
Kuwait	500	25.0
Lebanon	100	5.0
Libya	186	9.3
Mauritania	80	4.0
Morocco	200	10.0
Oman	80	4.0
Palestine	34	1.7
Qatar	200	10.0
Saudi Arabia	760	38.0
Somalia	80	4.0
Sudan	200	10.0
Syria	80	4.0
Tunisia	100	5.0
United Arab Emirates	300	15.0
Yemen Arab Republic	100	5.0
Yemen, People's Democratic Republic	80	4.0
Total	5,000	250.0

AIMS AND LENDING POLICIES

The creation of the Arab Monetary Fund was seen as a step towards the goal of Arab economic integration. Like the IMF, it assists member states in balance of payments difficulties but it has a broader range of aims.

The Articles of Agreement define the Fund's aims as follows:

(*a*) to correct disequilibria in the balance of payments of member states;

(*b*) to promote the stability of exchange rates among Arab currencies, making them mutually convertible;

(*c*) to establish policies of monetary co-operation to speed up Arab economic integration and economic development in the member states;

(*d*) to tender advice on the investment of member states in foreign markets;

(*e*) to promote the development of Arab financial markets;

(*f*) to expand the use of the Arab dinar as a unit of account and to pave the way for the creation of a unified Arab currency; and

(*g*) to co-ordinate the dealings of member states with international monetary and economic problems.

The Arab Monetary Fund functions both as a fund and a bank. It is empowered:

(*a*) to provide short- and medium-term loans to finance balance of payments deficits of member states;

(*b*) to issue guarantees to member states to strengthen their borrowing capabilities;

(*c*) to act as intermediary in the issuance of loans from other sources;

(*d*) to co-ordinate the monetary policies of member states;

(*e*) to manage any funds placed under its charge by member states;

(*f*) to hold periodic consultations with member states on their economic conditions; and

(*g*) to provide technical assistance to monetary institutions in member states.

Loans are intended to finance an overall balance of payments deficit and members have the automatic right to draw up to 75 per cent of their paid-up subscriptions for this purpose. Such loans are to be granted unconditionally. Members may obtain loans in excess of this limit in support of a financial programme to be agreed with the Fund. In the case of a severe deficit in the balance of payments, the Fund will provide loans in accordance with a programme of economic reforms to be agreed between member state and the Fund. Loans can also be granted up to the full value of the member's paid-up subscription to meet a balance of payments crisis arising from a harvest failure.

Loans to an individual member in any one year may not exceed twice the amount of the member's paid-up subscription and a member's loans outstanding at any time may not normally exceed three times the amount. However, following a poor harvest, and with a three-quarters majority of the Board of Governors, loans may be granted up to four times the member's paid-up subscription. Loans are normally repayable within three years, although with some the period of repayment can be extended up to seven years, and are granted at concessionary and uniform rates of interest. In August 1978 the Fund made its first loan, of AD 4.7 million, to Egypt. By April 1979 a total of AD 9.9 million had been disbursed in loans.

Council of Arab Economic Unity

20 Sharia Aisha el Taymouria, Garden City, Cairo, Egypt*

MEMBERS

Egypt	Libya	Sudan	Yemen Arab Republic
Iraq	Mauritania	Syria	Yemen, People's Democratic Republic
Jordan	Palestine Liberation Organization	United Arab Emirates	
Kuwait	Somalia		

ORGANIZATION

GENERAL SECRETARIAT

Entrusted with the implementation and follow-up of the Council's decisions. It has a number of permanent committees.

Secretary-General: Dr. FAKHRY KADDOURY (Iraq).

COUNCIL

The first session was held in June 1964. Sessions are held twice a year.

*In March 1979 it was announced that the headquarters were to be moved to Amman.

ACTIVITIES

ARAB COMMON MARKET

Based on a resolution passed by the Council in August 1964; its implementation is supervised by the Council and does not constitute a separate organization. Customs duties and other taxes on trade between the four member countries were eliminated in annual stages, the process being completed in 1971. The second stage is to be the adoption of a full customs union, and ultimately all restrictions on trade between the member countries, including quotas and other administrative restrictions, are to be abolished. Mems.: Egypt, Iraq, Jordan, Libya, Sudan, Syria. Libya and Sudan joined in June 1977.

Investment and Movement of Capital: the Council approved five agreements facilitating capital movement, settlement of investment disputes, avoidance of double taxation and provision for a corporation to guarantee against non-commercial risks.

JOINT VENTURES

A number of multilateral organizations in industry and agriculture have been formed on the principle that faster development and economies of scale may be achieved by combining the efforts of member states. In industries that are new to the member countries, Arab Joint Companies are formed; existing industries are to be co-ordinated by the setting up of Arab Specialized Unions. The unions are for closer co-operation on problems of production and marketing, and to help companies deal as a group in international markets. The companies are intended to be self-supporting on a purely commercial basis; they may issue shares to citizens of the participating countries. The joint ventures are:

Arab Joint Companies (cap.=capital; figures in Kuwaiti dinars unless otherwise stated):

Arab Company for Mining, P.O.B. 20198, Amman, Jordan; cap. 120 million.

Arab Company for the Development of Animal Wealth: Damascus, Syria; cap. 66 million.

Arab Company for Pharmaceuticals and Medical Supplies: Cairo, Egypt: f. January 1976; cap. 50 million.

Arab Company for Industrial Investments: Baghdad, Iraq; cap. 150 million Iraqi dinars.

Arab Specialized Federations:

Arab Union of Producers of Fertilizers: Kuwait.

Arab Union of Textile Industries: Cairo, Egypt.

Arab Union for Engineering and Electrical Industries: Baghdad, Iraq.

Arab Union for Paper Industries: Cairo, Egypt.

Arab Union for Cement and Cement Products: Damascus, Syria.

Arab Union for Foodstuff Industries: Cairo, Egypt.

Arab Union for Iron and Steel: Algiers, Algeria.

Arab Union for Fisheries: Baghdad, Iraq.

Arab Union for Sugar: Khartoum, Sudan.

Arab Union for Maritime Ports: Alexandria, Egypt.

The European Economic Community and the Middle East and North Africa

THE MEDITERRANEAN POLICY OF THE EUROPEAN COMMUNITY

The Community's scheme to negotiate a series of parallel trade and co-operation agreements encompassing almost all of the non-member states on the coast of the Mediterranean, known as the global policy for the Mediterranean, was formulated in 1972. By April 1977 its most important elements had been realized.

Three Association agreements, with Greece, Turkey and Malta, had begun to operate, and the fourth of the series, with Cyprus, came into effect in June 1973. Simple trade agreements with Spain, Portugal and Yugoslavia were all effective by September 1973. The Commission then wished to set up a series of a new type of agreement, covering trade and economic co-operation, with the Arab Mediterranean countries and Israel, and to extend the scope of the agreement with Spain to fit in with this pattern.

The trade and co-operation agreements all have a similar structure, and have much in common with the main provisions of the Association agreements. The model on which both categories were based is in fact the older agreements between France and its former dependencies in North Africa.

All agreements establish free access to EEC markets for industrial products, either after a very short interim phase or else immediately. Access for agricultural products is facilitated, although some tariffs remain. For refined petroleum, cotton and phosphate fertilizers the Community imposes quotas for a transitional period on some of the Mediterranean countries.

The principle of reciprocity, or the granting of preferences in return, in this case by the Mediterranean countries, was not applied immediately in all of the co-operation agreements; in the Association agreements, and some others, there are provisions that it may be introduced in the medium- or long-term future, should the economic progress of the Mediterranean country concerned warrant this.

Many of the agreements are accompanied by financial protocols which state the amount of each category of aid which the Mediterranean country will receive. In April 1976 the EEC Council of Ministers announced that the total finance available for the Mediterranean countries up to the end of 1980 would be EUA 1,400 million (EUA 1 = approximately U.S. $1). This consists of various forms of aid from the EEC budget amounting to EUA 550-600 million, and EUA 800 million from the European Investment Bank in the form of loans, on terms similar to those of commercial banks.

Safeguards are provided: in the event of a disturbance in a particular sector, or a deterioration in the economic situation in a particular region, the contracting party concerned is entitled to take protective action. This applies also if a deterioration occurs or is threatened in the balance of payments of a country participating in the agreements.

Special organizations are instituted to supervise the implementation of the agreements. In most cases the organization is known as the Joint Committee, while Lebanon has a Co-operation Council with the EEC, and Turkey an Association Council.

The final objective of the EEC Mediterranean policy is thus a free-trade zone encompassing the Community and most of its southern neighbours, matching and complementing that which already exists between the EEC and EFTA countries.

One general problem arising in almost all the negotiations for the agreements concerned the agricultural exports of the Mediterranean countries. Certain features are bound to be common to the agriculture throughout the region, and this of course also includes two EEC member states which are Mediterranean countries—Italy and France. The items which the Mediterranean countries all wish to export to the Community, such as citrus fruits, olive oil and wine, are frequently in surplus in the Community already.

The Community has responded to this in recent years by offering concessions for these items as a form of aid to the Mediterranean countries, of comparable importance with the financial protocols themselves.

A further aspect of this problem is the difficulty of sharing out the concessions for exporting farm produce to the European markets among the various Mediterranean countries. Beginning with Turkey in 1963 the Community made modest concessions for agricultural produce, which were to improve on a slow timetable; and during 1973–76 it granted concessions which were clearly better to the Maghreb and Machrak countries.

THE MAGHREB COUNTRIES

Countries: Algeria, Morocco, Tunisia.

Signature: April 1976.

Date of coming into force: (trade provisions only) July 1976; full agreement signed January 1979.

Legal basis: Article 238 of the Treaty of Rome.

Industrial products were granted immediate duty free entry to the EEC, with the temporary exception of Algerian cork products. Customs exemption for refined petroleum products was subject to a ceiling of 1.1 million tonnes during 1976 for Algeria and 175,000 tonnes each for Morocco and Tunisia. These amounts were to be increased from 1977 to 1979, after which no quantitative restrictions apply at all.

For agricultural produce a wide range of customs reductions varies between products, from 30 to 80 per cent. Levies on olive oil are also partly reduced.

Duties on ordinary wines are reduced by 80 per cent, subject to compliance with EEC reference prices; table wines are imported duty free, within national quotas.

Conditions for migrant workers from the Maghreb countries are also slightly improved under the agreement. One innovation is the right to accumulate pension rights and other social benefits from periods of residence in different EEC countries; another is the right to continue to draw pensions and other allowances after returning to the country of origin.

Economic and technical co-operation is included, with special arrangements to assist Algeria in developing its energy programme. The financial protocols for 1976–81 amount to EUA 114 million for Algeria, EUA 130 million for Morocco and EUA 95 million for Tunisia.

THE MACHRAK COUNTRIES

Countries: Egypt, Jordan, Lebanon, Syria.

Signature: (Egypt, Jordan, Syria) January 1977; (Lebanon) April 1977.

Date of coming into force: (trade provisions) July 1977; (financial protocols) March 1977; the financial protocol with Lebanon was signed later in 1977; full agreement signed in September 1978 after ratification.

Legal basis: Egypt, Jordan, Syria: Article 113; Lebanon: Article 238, of the Treaty of Rome.

Industrial products were granted tariff reductions of 80 per cent until July 1977, and afterwards are exempted from tariffs by the EEC. Quantitative restrictions were removed as from January 1977. Annual quotas or ceilings for certain products were fixed for duty-free imports into the Community; these were to be raised by 5 per cent annually and abolished by the end of 1979.

A wide range of tariff reductions apply to agricultural produce, varying between products from 30 to 80 per cent. The EEC's internal scheme of preferences applies to Egyptian rice, within a quota of 32,000 tonnes per year. A small preference is given to Lebanon's olive oil.

The agreements with Egypt and Lebanon are intended to replace preferential trade agreements concluded in 1972, which entered into force in the case of Egypt only.

The financial means put at the disposal of the Machrak countries to further economic and technical co-operation and development from 1977 to 1981, amount to EUA 170 million for Egypt, EUA 60 million for Syria, EUA 40 million for Jordan and EUA 30 million for Lebanon.

CYPRUS

Signature: 1972.

Date of coming into force: June 1973.

Legal basis: Article 238 of the Treaty of Rome.

Immediate tariff reductions were made by the EEC of 70 per cent in the industrial sector, 40 per cent for citrus fruit and 100 per cent for carob beans.

Tariffs on imports into Cyprus from the EEC were generally reduced in annual stages, except in certain sectors, where the competition was felt to be harmful.

A preference in the EEC market was given for Cyprus sherry, which in effect was taken up only in the United Kingdom; this was intended only as part of the transitional arrangement for the United Kingdom's accession to the Community, up to 1977, but was subsequently extended.

A second stage of the agreement was to be negotiated during 1976 and 1977, but this was delayed as a result of the failure of intercommunal talks on the island. The EEC Council of Ministers instructed in May 1977 that the first stage of the agreement should continue to the end of 1979.

At the same time improvements were proposed in the existing trade arrangements, on condition that these could be made to apply to traders in both communities of Cyprus. Tariffs on industrial products were abolished from July 1977; however, no new concessions on agricultural produce could be offered, because of opposition from Italy. A quota of 140,000 hectolitres of sherry was given duty free access from July to December 1977, and various special preferences in the United Kingdom market for Cyprus agricultural produce were allowed to continue.

A financial protocol of EUA 30 million was proposed.

It was considered likely that these proposals would be accepted by the Cyprus Government.

TURKEY

Signature: September 1963.

Date of coming into force: December 1964.

Legal basis: Article 238 of the Treaty of Rome.

The preparatory phase lasted from 1964 to 1973, during which preferences were given on agricultural products accounting for 40 per cent of Turkey's exports to the EEC: unmanufactured tobacco, dried raisins and figs, and nuts. Financial assistance from the Community amounted to EUA 175 million between 1964 and 1969.

The transitional phase began in 1973, aiming to introduce a customs union by gradual stages over 12 to 22 years, depending on the product. The EEC granted immediate duty and quota free access for industrial products, but placed restrictions on refined petroleum products and three textile products. The EEC's financial assistance during 1970–81 was fixed at EUA 567 million.

The final phase, intended as a complete economic union of Turkey with the EEC, was thus projected to begin about 1995. However, the Community has since then found it necessary to abandon plans for economic and monetary union among its own members at any specific date, and the attainment of a customs union with Turkey is likely to be delayed for similar reasons.

The Community made new concessions in 1973 on imports of several agricultural products: tobacco, grapes, citrus fruits, fruit and vegetables, wines, other cereals, fish, certain categories of meat and olive oil.

Special new provisions for Turkish workers employed in the EEC concern: social security and the granting of "second priority" after EEC nationals for Turkish workers in the allocation of vacant jobs.

For the sake of protecting Turkey's developing industries, the EEC is prepared to accept a slowing down of the programme of Turkey's reductions in tariffs on imports from the EEC. By 1981, 45 per cent of imports will be free of quantitative restrictions and 80 per cent by 1991.

ISRAEL

Signature: May 1975.

Date of coming into force: (trade provisions) July 1975; (financial protocol) February 1977.

Legal basis: Article 113 of the Treaty of Rome.

In industrial sectors, tariffs and related obstacles to free trade are to be removed on both sides. This was to be achieved for Israel's exports to the EEC by July 1977, for 60 per cent of EEC exports to Israel by 1980 and for the remaining 40 per cent by 1985.

As regards agriculture, the EEC reduced its tariffs substantially for products accounting for 85 per cent of Israel's exports to the EEC; these include products which the community has traditionally imported from Israel, for example some vegetables and fruit juices.

Review meetings have been arranged, to be held in 1978 and 1983, at which possible improvements to the agreement might be discussed; if necessary, the dates might be postponed by up to two years for Israel's removal of tariffs on EEC industrial goods, which is to be completed by 1989 in the present arrangement.

A Joint Committee is to supervise the operation of the agreement and study the possibilities of economic co-operation. The objects of this are: to diversify the pattern of trade, assist the transfer of technology, encourage private investment and increase contacts between industries in Israel and the EEC, including scientific and technical co-operation.

An additional protocol on industrial, technical and financial co-operation, including aid of up to EUA 30 million, was signed in February 1977.

This agreement replaces one signed in June 1970, which thus ceased to apply.

Islamic Development Bank

P.O.B. 5925, Jeddah, Saudi Arabia

Established under the auspices of the Organization of the Islamic Conference (*see* page 166) in 1974, began operations in 1975.

MEMBERS

(*see* table of subscriptions below)

AIMS

To encourage economic development and social progress of member countries and Muslim communities; the Bank aims to raise living standards in accordance with the principles of the Islamic Shariah.

ORGANIZATION

(as of October 1978)

BOARD OF GOVERNORS

Each member country is represented by a Governor, usually its Finance Minister or his alternate. The Board of Governors is the Supreme Authority of the Bank. Meets annually; second meeting, Kuala Lumpur, Malaysia, March 1978.

President of the Bank and Chairman of the Board of Executive Directors: Dr. Ahmad Mohamed Ali (Saudi Arabia).

EXECUTIVE COUNCIL

Consists of 10 members, four of whom are appointed by the four largest subscribers to the capital stock of the Bank; the remaining six are elected by all Governors. Members of the Executive Council are elected for three-year terms. Responsible for the direction of the general operations of the Bank.

FINANCIAL STRUCTURE

The authorized capital of the Bank is 2,000 million Islamic Dinars divided into 200,000 shares having a value of 100,000 Islamic Dinars each. The Islamic Dinar is the Bank's unit of account and is equivalent to the value of one Special Drawing Right of the IMF.

The subscribed capital stood at 757.5 million Islamic Dinars in September 1978.

SUBSCRIPTIONS
(as at September 1978)

	Million Islamic Dinars		Million Islamic Dinars
Afghanistan	2.5	Morocco	5.0
Algeria	25.0	Niger	2.5
Bahrain	5.0	Oman	5.0
Bangladesh	10.0	Pakistan	25.0
Cameroon	2.5	Qatar	25.0
Chad	2.5	Saudi Arabia	200.0
Egypt	25.0	Senegal	2.5
Guinea	2.5	Somalia	2.5
Indonesia	25.0	Sudan	10.0
Jordan	4.0	Syria	2.5
Kuwait	100.0	Tunisia	2.5
Lebanon	2.5	Turkey	10.0
Libya	125.0	United Arab Emirates	110.0
Malaysia	16.0	Yemen Arab Republic	2.5
Mali	2.5		
Mauritania	2.5		

ACTIVITIES

During 1975/76, the Islamic Development Bank concentrated on setting up its organization and formulating its policies; financial operations began in 1976. The Bank, which adheres to the Koranic principle forbidding usury, does not grant loans or credits for interest, preferring to help development projects by taking up equity participation in them. By December 1977 it had taken up a direct participation of $53.6 million in various projects. The Bank also took an indirect participation of $5.7 million in the Malaysian Development Bank. Although the Koran forbids charging interest, the Bank lends at a nominal rate of "commission" and by December 1977 had extended $71 million in project loans. The Bank's third area of activity lies in financing foreign trade. During 1976/77 the Bank advanced $50.5 million to help countries buy necessary imports; in 1978 it extended further loans to Turkey, Algeria and Chad. Since commencing operations in 1976, the Bank has extended loans totalling $182 million.

The Maghreb Permanent Consultative Committee

(COMITÉ PERMANENT CONSULTATIF DU MAGHREB)

14 Rue Yahia Ibn Omar, Mutuelleville, Tunis, Tunisia

A permanent committee for economic co-ordination, established at Tunis in October 1964 by the Economic Ministers of the member countries. The permanent headquarters were opened in Tunis in February 1966.

MEMBERS

Algeria Mauritania Morocco Tunisia

Libya withdrew from all Maghreb institutions in 1970. Mauritania joined in 1975.

AIMS

The Maghreb Committee is a forum for inter-governmental consultation and the exchange of technical information. Its purpose is to investigate all problems relating to economic co-operation in the member countries. At the request of the Conference of Ministers of Economy or as part of the programme agreed by the Ministers, it proposes measures designed to reinforce co-operation and to bring into being a Maghreb Economic Community.

ORGANIZATION

(as at May 1979)

CONFERENCE OF MINISTERS OF ECONOMY

The highest authority of the organization. It is attended by Ministers of Economy with their delegations of senior officials.

PERMANENT COMMITTEE

The Committee consists of a President with the rank of Minister, and four delegates who represent the member states. It supervises the commissions and specialized groups, co-ordinating and directing their activities.

PRESIDENT

Each member state in turn appoints the President for a term of two years. He chairs the meetings of the Committee and is responsible for the implementation of projects given to the Committee by the Conference of Ministers of Economy. He also represents the Committee to the governments of the member states and to international organizations.

The Vice-President, who is the delegate from the country of the President, assumes some of his prerogatives in case of his absence.

SECRETARIAT

The Secretary is responsible for staff management, financial affairs of the Committee, and for the administration of the Secretariat. He provides secretarial services for the Conference of Ministers of Economy, the meetings of the Permanent Committee and for meetings of the specialized groups.

Secretary: (vacant).

SPECIALIZED GROUPS

Maghreb Centre for Industrial Studies: Tangier, Morocco; f. 1968.

Maghreb Committee for Tourism: Tunis, Tunisia; f. 1966.

Maghreb Committee for Co-ordination of Posts and Telecommunications: location varies; f. 1964.

Maghreb Commission for Transport and Communications: Tunis, Tunisia; f. 1965; has four subsidiary committees:

Maghreb Committee for Air Transport, Rabat, Morocco.

Committee for Maghreb Railways, Algiers, Algeria.

Maghreb Committee for Shipping.

Maghreb Committee for Road Transport.

Maghreb Committee for Co-ordination of National Accounts and Statistics: location varies; f. 1973.

Maghreb Committee for Administrative Studies and Research: f. 1970.

Maghreb Committee for Employment and Labour: Rabat, Morocco; f. 1970.

Maghreb Committee on Normalization: Tangier, Morocco; f. 1970.

Maghreb Committee for Insurance and Reinsurance: Rabat, Morocco; f. 1970.

Maghreb Committee for Electric Energy: Algiers, Algeria; f. 1974.

Maghreb Committee for Development of Stockbreeding: Rabat, Morocco; f. 1975.

Organization of Arab Petroleum Exporting Countries—OAPEC

P.O.B. 20501, Safat, Kuwait City, Kuwait

Established 1968 to safeguard the interests of members and determine ways and means for their co-operation in various forms of economic activity in the petroleum industry.

MEMBERS

Algeria	Kuwait	Saudi Arabia
Bahrain	Libya	Syria
Egypt*	Qatar	United Arab Emirates
Iraq		

* Egypt's membership was suspended as of April 17th, 1979.

ORGANIZATION

(as of May 1979)

COUNCIL

Supreme authority of the Organization, responsible for drawing up its general policy, directing its activities and laying down its governing rules. The Council consists normally of the Ministers of Petroleum of the member states. Meets twice yearly as a minimum requirement and may hold extraordinary sessions. Chairmanship on annual rotation basis.

Chairman (1979): Ezzedin Mabrouk (Libya).

BUREAU

Assists the Council to direct the management of the Organization, approves staff regulations, reviews the budget, and refers it to the Council, considers matters relating to the Organization's agreements and activities and draws up the agenda for the Council. The Bureau consists of senior officials from each member state. Chairmanship is by rotation. The Bureau convenes four times a year as a minimum requirement.

Budget (1979): 1,762,000 Kuwaiti dinars.

Chairman (1979): Salah Khawaja (Libya).

SECRETARIAT

Secretary-General: Dr. Ali Ahmad Attiga (Libya).

Assistant Secretaries-General: Abdul Aziz al-Wattari, Dr. Adnan Mustapha.

Besides the Office of the Secretary-General, which assists the Secretary-General in following up resolutions and recommendations of the Council, there are five departments: the Administration and Financial Department, the Legal Department, the Economic Department, the Information and Public Relations Department and the Petroleum Industries Department. There are also four Units: the Energy Unit, the Training Unit, the Library and Documentation Unit, and the Exploration and Production Unit.

JOINT UNDERTAKINGS

Arab Maritime Petroleum Transport Company (AMPTC): f. 1973 in Kuwait to undertake transport of crude oil, gas, refined products and petrochemicals, and thus to increase Arab participation in the tanker transport industry; capital authorized and subscribed $500 million. In January 1979 the Chairman requested that Arab states should demand that 20 per cent of their oil exports went in Arab ships; at that time about one-third of the AMPTC fleet was lying idle. Mems.: Algeria, Bahrain, Iraq, Kuwait, Libya, Qatar, Saudi Arabia, United Arab Emirates.

Chairman: Dr. Abdul Hadi Taher.

Managing Director: Abdul Rahman Sultan.

Arab Shipbuilding and Repair Yard Company: f. 1974 in Bahrain to undertake all activities related to repairs, service and eventually construction of vessels for the transport of hydrocarbons. In December 1977 the company opened a dry dock in Bahrain. Capital authorized and subscribed $340 million.

Chairman: Sheikh Khalifah Salman al-Khalifah.

General Manager: Antonio Machadolopes.

Arab Petroleum Investments Corporation: created 1975 in Dhahran, Saudi Arabia to finance petroleum investments in the Arab world. Authorized capital: $1,000 million; subscribed capital: $42 million.

Chairman: Jamal Jawa.

General Manager: Dr. Nureddin Farrag.

Arab Petroleum Services Company: established January 1977 at Tripoli, Libya. The company provides petroleum services through the establishment of one or more companies specializing in various activities. Also concerned with training of specialized personnel. Authorized capital: 100 million Libyan dinars; subscribed capital: 15 million Libyan dinars.

Chairman: Omar Muntasir.

General Manager: Hocine Malti.

Arab Petroleum Training Institute: f. 1979 in Baghdad.

General Manager: Burhan Eddin Daghestani.

RECORD OF EVENTS

1968

Sept. First meeting of the Council, Kuwait.

Dec. First meeting of the National Oil Companies, Riyadh, Saudi Arabia.

1970

May Extraordinary meeting of the Council, Kuwait, approved membership of Abu Dhabi, Algeria, Bahrain, Dubai, and Qatar.

1971

June Seventh meeting of Council, Kuwait.

Dec. Eighth meeting of Council in Abu Dhabi. Decided to alter constitution to allow membership of Egypt and Syria.

1972

June Second extraordinary meeting held in Beirut to assist Iraq and Syria in their dispute with the Iraq Petroleum Company.

1973

Jan. Council met in Kuwait as the constituent General Assembly of the Arab Maritime Petroleum Transport Company.

Sept. Third extraordinary meeting of the Council, Kuwait; Council expressed support for the partial nationalization of oil companies operating in Libya.

Oct. Gathering under the auspices of OAPEC, the Ministers of oil of Arab countries decided to reduce production of petroleum by at least 5 per cent progressively each month in support of Egypt and Syria.

1974

May Seminar on Arab-British co-operation, London.

Oct. Agreement with EEC Commission to have regular contacts and to exchange technical information.

Dec. Thirteenth Council Meeting held in Bahrain. The Constituent Assembly of the Arab Shipbuilding and Repair Yard Company declared the incorporation of the Company and appointed its Board of Directors.

1975

Nov. Creation of the Arab Petroleum Investments Corporation.

Seminar on Arab-French co-operation, Paris, France.

1976

May Sixteenth Council Meeting held in Baghdad, Iraq.

Decision taken formally to establish Arab Petroleum Services Company in January 1977.

Nov. Seminar on Arab-Japanese co-operation, Tokyo, Japan.

Seventeenth Council Meeting held in Kuwait. Proposal for the formation of an Arab Petroleum Training Institute.

1977

Jan. Council met in Libya as the Constituent General Assembly of the Arab Petroleum Services Company to declare the incorporation of the company.

May Eighteenth Council Meeting held in Kuwait. Decision taken to hold Arab Energy Conference in Abu Dhabi in March 1979.

Aug. Decision to set up Judicial Council to examine disputes arising within the organization involving member states.

Dec. Inauguration of Arab Shipbuilding and Repair Company's dry dock in Bahrain.

1978

May Twentieth Council Meeting held in Kuwait. Resolution to establish Arab Petroleum Training Institute; Protocol of OAPEC Judicial Board signed.

Sept. Seminar on Arab-Scandinavian co-operation, Oslo, Norway.

Dec. Twenty-first Council Meeting held in Abu Dhabi. Approval of proposal for feasibility study of establishment of a drydock in one of the Mediterranean littoral member countries.

1979

March First Arab Energy Conference held in Abu Dhabi, co-sponsored with the Arab Fund for Economic and Social Development.

April Fourth extraordinary meeting of the Council held in Kuwait. Suspension of the membership of Egypt and the joint-venture companies connected with it.

May Twenty-second Council meeting held in Kuwait. Board of Trustees approved Arab Petroleum Training Institute in Baghdad.

Organization of the Islamic Conference

Secretariat-General, Kilo 6, Mecca Rd., P.O.B. 178, Jeddah, Saudi Arabia

Formally established in May 1971 following a summit meeting of Moslem Heads of State at Rabat, Morocco, in September 1969, and the Islamic Foreign Ministers' Conference in Jeddah in March 1970, and in Karachi, Pakistan in December 1970.

MEMBERS

Afghanistan	Guinea	Morocco	Sudan
Algeria	Guinea-Bissau	Niger	Syria
Bahrain	Indonesia	Oman	Tunisia
Bangladesh	Iran	Pakistan	Turkey
Cameroon	Jordan	Palestine Liberation Organization	Turkish Federated State of Cyprus
Chad	Kuwait	Qatar	Uganda
The Comoros	Lebanon	Saudi Arabia	United Arab Emirates
Djibouti	Libya	Senegal	Upper Volta
Egypt*	Malaysia	Sierra Leone	Yemen Arab Republic
Gabon	Mali	Somalia	Yemen, People's Democratic Republic
The Gambia	Mauritania		

* Egypt's membership was suspended in May 1979.

ORGANIZATION

SECRETARIAT

Secretary-General: AMADOU KARIM GAYE (Senegal).

Deputy Secretaries-General:

Political affairs: DR. CIHAD FETHI TEVETOGLU (Turkey).
Cultural affairs: KACEM ZHIRI (Morocco).
Administration and finance: ZAFARUL ISLAM (Pakistan).

CONFERENCES OF FOREIGN MINISTERS

Ten Islamic Conferences of Foreign Ministers had been held by 1979, the first in March 1970 at Jeddah and the tenth in May 1979 at Fès, Morocco. Conferences have been held in the capitals and main cities of various Islamic countries. The eleventh Conference is to be held in Niger in 1981.

There have also been: Conference on Islamic Cultural Centres, in Rabat, 1971; and the first Islamic Economic Conference, in February 1976, at Mecca.

FINANCE

The Conference is financed by contributions and donations from member states.

AIMS AND ACTIVITIES

AIMS

1. To promote Islamic solidarity among member states;
2. To consolidate co-operation among member states in the economic, social, cultural, scientific and other vital fields, and to arrange consultations among member states belonging to international organizations;
3. To endeavour to eliminate racial segregation and discrimination and to eradicate colonialism in all its forms;
4. To take necessary measures to support international peace and security founded on justice;
5. To co-ordinate all efforts for the safeguard of the Holy Places and support of the struggle of the people of Palestine, and help them to regain their rights and liberate their land;
6. To strengthen the struggle of all Muslim people with a view to safeguarding their dignity, independence and national rights; and
7. To create a suitable atmosphere for the promotion of co-operation and understanding among member states and other countries.

ACTIVITIES

1. The International Islamic News Agency (IINA) was set up in December 1972.
2. The Islamic Development Bank was set up in Jeddah, Saudi Arabia, in 1974 (*see* p. 162).
3. Efforts to consolidate the activities of the Islamic Cultural Centres in non-Muslim countries.
4. Islamic States Broadcasting Organization set up in 1975.
5. Islamic Solidarity Fund set up in 1977.

PUBLICATIONS

News bulletin, issued three times a week by the International Islamic News Agency (IINA).

Organization of the Petroleum Exporting Countries—OPEC

Obere Donaustrasse 93, 1020 Vienna, Austria

Established 1960 to unify and co-ordinate members' petroleum policies and to safeguard their interests generally. The OPEC Special Fund is described on page 170.

MEMBERS

Algeria	Iraq	Qatar
Ecuador	Kuwait	Saudi Arabia
Gabon	Libya	United Arab Emirates
Indonesia	Nigeria	Venezuela
Iran		

ORGANIZATION

(as at May 1979)

THE CONFERENCE

Supreme authority of the Organization, responsible for the formulation of its general policy. It consists of representatives of member countries, decides upon reports and recommendations submitted by the Board of Governors. Meets at least twice a year. It approves the appointment of Governors from each country and elects the Chairman of the Board of Governors. It works on the unanimity principle.

THE BOARD OF GOVERNORS

Directs management of the Organization; implements resolutions of the Conference; draws up an annual Budget. It consists of one Governor for each member country, and meets at least twice a year.

Chairman (1979): ABDULLA ISMAIL (United Arab Emirates).

THE ECONOMIC COMMISSION

A specialized body operating within the framework of the Secretariat, with a view to assisting the Organization in promoting stability in international oil prices at equitable levels; consists of a Board, national representatives and a commission staff; the Board meets at least twice a year.

SECRETARIAT

Secretary-General: RENÉ G. ORTIZ (Ecuador).

Office of the Secretary-General: Provides him with executive assistance in carrying out contacts with governments, organizations and delegations, in matters of protocol and in the preparation for and co-ordination of meetings.

Research Division:

Energy Studies Department: Conducts a continuous programme for research in energy and related matters; monitors, forecasts and analyses developments in the energy and petrochemical industries; and the evaluation of hydrocarbons and products and their non-energy uses.

Economics and Finance Department: Analyses economic and financial issues of significant interest; in particular those related to international financial and monetary matters, and to the international petroleum industry.

Information Services Department:

Computer Section: Maintains and expands information services to support the research activities of the Secretariat and those of member countries.

Statistics Unit: Collects, collates and analyses statistical information from both primary and secondary sources.

Library: Provides information search and research assistance services to Secretariat staff and member countries, and has a stock of some 10,000 items and 350 current periodicals in the energy field.

Personnel and Administration Department: Responsible for all organization methods, provision of administrative services for all meetings, personnel matters, budgets, accounting and internal control.

Public Relations Department: Responsible for a central public relations programme; production and distribution of publications; and communication of OPEC objectives and decisions to the world at large.

Legal Affairs Unit: Undertakes special and other in-house legal studies and reports to ascertain where the best interests of the Organization and member countries lie.

ACTIVITIES

Technical and economic guidance for member countries and co-ordination of their petroleum policies.

RECORD OF EVENTS

1960 First OPEC conference held in Baghdad, September; meetings to be held twice yearly, secretariat to be formed.

1961 Second conference, Caracas, January. Qatar admitted to membership; Board of Governors formed and statutes agreed.

1962 Fourth conference, Geneva, April and June. Protests addressed to oil companies against price cuts introduced in August 1960. Indonesia and Libya admitted to membership.

1964 Seventh conference, Jakarta, November. Settlement of the royalties issue negotiated, giving producers an increased share of profits. OPEC Economic Commission established.

1965 Ninth conference, Tripoli, July. Agreement on a two-year joint production programme, implemented from 1965 to 1967, to limit annual growth in output in order to force up prices.

1967 Abu Dhabi admitted to membership.

1968 Fifteenth conference (extraordinary), Beirut, January. Accepted offer on elimination of discounts submitted by oil companies following negotiations in November 1967.

1969 Algeria admitted to membership.

1970 Twenty-first conference, Caracas, December. Tax on income of oil companies raised to 55 per cent.

1971 Negotiations between OPEC and oil companies on Gulf oil prices broke down, January; OPEC members prepared to legislate unilaterally to set posted prices and tax rates.
Twenty-second conference (extraordinary), Teheran, February. Five-year agreement between the six producing countries in the Gulf and 23 international oil companies (Teheran Agreement).
Twenty-fourth conference, Vienna, July. Nigeria admitted to membership.

1972 Meetings between OPEC and oil companies, Geneva, January. Companies agreed to adjust oil revenues of the largest producers after changes in currency exchange rates (Geneva Agreement).

1973 Meeting between OPEC and oil companies, Cairo, April, discussed OPEC's demand for compensation following 10 per cent devaluation of U.S. dollar in February.
Agreement with companies reached under which posted prices of crude oil were raised by 11.9 per cent and a mechanism installed to make monthly adjustments to prices in future (Second Geneva Agreement).
Thirty-fourth conference, Vienna, June. Ministerial Committee formed to review world energy situation.
Thirty-fifth conference (extraordinary), Vienna, September. Gulf states proposed negotiations with oil companies to revise the Teheran Agreement.
Negotiations broke down on October 12th. On 16th, the Gulf states held a meeting and, refusing to negotiate further with the companies, unilaterally declared 70 per cent increases in posted prices, from $3.01 to $5.11 per barrel.
Thirty-sixth conference, Teheran, December. Posted price increased by nearly 130 per cent from $5.11 to $11.65 per barrel from January 1st, 1974. Ecuador admitted to full membership, Gabon became an associate member.

1974 Thirty-seventh conference (extraordinary), Geneva, January. As a result of Saudi opposition to the December price increase, prices were held at current level for first quarter (and subsequently for the remainder of 1974). Abu Dhabi's membership transferred to United Arab Emirates.
Meeting, Quito, June, increased royalties charged to oil companies from 12.5 to 14.5 per cent in all member states except Saudi Arabia.
Meeting, Vienna, September, increased governmental take by about 3.5 per cent through further increases in royalties on equity crude to 16.67 per cent and in taxes to 65.65 per cent, except in Saudi Arabia.

1975 OPEC's first summit conference was held in Algiers in March. Gabon admitted to full membership.
Meeting in Gabon in June, Conference proposed that OPEC oil prices should be quoted in Special Drawing Rights (SDRs) of the IMF, instead of U.S. dollars. It was also proposed that prices should be indexed to world inflation rates.
A ministerial meeting in September agreed to raise prices by 10 per cent for the period until June 1976. It referred the question of pricing oil in SDRs to the committee of Finance Ministers, which had taken no further measures on this subject as of July 1978.
The year's second meeting of Conference, in Vienna in December, ended abruptly when a terrorist gang kidnapped some of the participants.

1976 The OPEC Special Fund was created in May.
Meeting in Bali, Indonesia, in May, Conference allowed the prices agreed in September 1975 to continue.
At the year's second meeting of Conference, in Doha, Qatar, December, a general 15 per cent rise in basic prices was proposed and supported by eleven member states. This was to take place in two stages: an immediate 10 per cent rise and a further 5 per cent rise in June 1977.
However, this was opposed by Saudi Arabia and the United Arab Emirates, who not only insisted on limiting their price increase to 5 per cent, but also proposed to increase their production and export capacity by up to 20 per cent, weakening demand for the higher-priced exports of the other 11 members.
The effect of this was that not all the 11 members observed the first stage of the price rise exactly as proposed.

1977 Forty-ninth conference, Saltsjøbaden, near Stockholm, Sweden, July.

Following an earlier waiver by 9 members of the 5 per cent second stage of the price rise agreed at Doha, Saudi Arabia and the United Arab Emirates announced that they would both raise their prices by 5 per cent. As a result, a single level of prices throughout the organization was restored.

Because of continued disagreements between the moderates, led by Saudi Arabia and Iran, and the radicals, led by Algeria, Libya and Iraq, the year's second conference at Caracas, December, was unable to settle on an increase in prices.

1978 Informal Consultative Conference, Taif, Saudi Arabia, May.

Ministerial Committee from six member states established to draw up long-term pricing and production strategy. Production ceilings of members lowered.

Fifty-first conference, Geneva, June. Price levels to remain stable until the end of 1978. Committee of Experts, chaired by Kuwait, met in July to consider ways of compensating for the effects of the depreciation of the U.S. dollar.

At the fifty-second Conference in December 1978 it was decided to raise prices by instalments of 5 per cent, 3.8 per cent, 2.3 per cent and 2.7 per cent. These would bring a rise of 14.5 per cent over nine months, but an average increase of 10 per cent for 1979.

1979 At an extraordinary meeting in Geneva at the end of March it was decided to raise prices by 9 per cent. Many members maintained surcharges they had imposed in February after Iranian exports were halted.

Fifty-third Conference, Geneva, June. For details, *see* chapter "Oil in the Middle East and North Africa".

FINANCE

1979 budget: 178 million Austrian schillings, contributed in equal parts by members.

OPEC Special Fund

P.O.B. 995, 1011 Vienna, Austria

Established by virtue of an agreement signed by all OPEC member countries in Paris on January 28th, 1976.

MEMBERS

Member countries of OPEC (*see* page 167)

AIMS

The Fund is established to provide financial assistance to developing countries (other than OPEC members) on concessional terms.

In particular, the Fund's resources may be utilized in the following operations:

(*a*) Providing loans to finance balance of payments deficits.

(*b*) Providing loans to finance development projects and programmes.

(*c*) Covering contributions which the Contributing Parties may make to international development agencies whose operations are directed to benefit developing countries.

ORGANIZATION

GOVERNING COMMITTEE

The Fund is administered by a Governing Committee composed of one representative of each Contributing Party to the Fund.

Chairman: Dr. MOHAMMED YEGANEH (Iran).

Director-General of the Fund: Dr. IBRAHIM SHIHATA (Kuwait).

Executing National Agencies

Each Contributing Party to the Agreement designates, by a written notice to the Governing Committee, its Executing National Agency (ENA). Each ENA establishes in its records a special account in the name of the Fund separate from its own accounts. The ENA disburses to Borrowers from such an account the amounts designated by the Governing Committee. Disbursements may also be effected through the Fund's central account.

FINANCIAL STRUCTURE

The U.S. dollar is the unit of account of the Fund and the means of payment of its loans. The initial resources of the Fund were set at $800 million. In October 1976, the OPEC Ministerial Committee on Monetary and Financial Matters recommended the donation by eight OPEC Member Countries of their profits in the IMF gold sales to the OPEC Special Fund. In August 1977 the Committee formally confirmed a resolution to increase the resources of the Fund by an additional $800 million, so that they now exceed $1,600 million.

Regional Cooperation for Development—RCD

5 Los Angeles Ave., Blvd. Elizabeth II, P.O.B. 3273, Teheran, Iran

Telephones: 658614, 656152, 658045.

Established in 1964 as a tripartite arrangement aiming at closer economic, technical and cultural co-operation and promoting the economic advancement and welfare of the people of the region.

MEMBERS

Iran Pakistan Turkey

ORGANIZATION

(as at May 1979)

MINISTERIAL COUNCIL

Established 1964 as the highest decision-making body of the RCD; composed of the Foreign Ministers of the three countries; considers and decides on measures for regional co-operation among the three countries.

REGIONAL PLANNING COUNCIL

Established 1964; composed of the Heads of the three Planning Organizations; makes recommendations to the Ministerial Council on measures for regional co-operation among the three countries.

Working Committees: Industry and Petroleum, Trade, Transport and Communications, Technical Co-operation and Public Administration, Culture, Information and Tourism, and Agriculture.

SECRETARIAT

Permanently established in Teheran in 1965; staff consists of Secretary-General, three Deputy Secretaries-General, six Directors and supporting staff, drawn from nationals of the member countries.

Secretary-General: MUKHTAR MASOOD (Pakistan).

ACTIVITIES

INDUSTRY AND STANDARDIZATION

In an agreement of November 1967 the three members agreed to collaborate in joint-purpose enterprises, and guidelines were laid down.

Materials, skills and, if possible, capital were to be pooled; national markets would be shared and industrial specialization encouraged; long-term agreements (off-take guarantees) were to be negotiated for the specific enterprises, ensuring that the partner countries provide a market for the products, and through fiscal arrangements the products would be protected against imports from outside the region.

About forty-three enterprises were identified of which ten were in production by April 1976. Three of these have equity participation by the member countries:

(a) Iranian Aluminium Company, Takht-e-Jamshid Avenue, Teheran.

(b) Bank note and Security Paper, Pakistan Security Printing Corporation Limited, Karachi.

(c) Ball Bearings Aizad Industries Limited, Palace Cinema Building, Civil Lines, Karachi.

Those without equity participation include the Ultramarine Blue Project and the Shock Absorbers Project in Pakistan, and the following Projects in Turkey: Tungsten Carbide, Borax and Boric Acid, Centrifugal and Special Filters for Chemical Industries, High Tension Insulators and Tetracycline.

In an attempt to streamline the portfolio of projects earmarked for industrial co-operation, a regional industrial survey was carried out. On the recommendation of the survey team, telecommunications, iron and steel and heavy engineering and diesel engine industries are to receive priority in future co-operation.

There is also provision for common RCD Standards, twenty-four of which have been so far established in the region.

PETROLEUM AND PETROCHEMICALS

Projects include the Glycerine Plant in Pakistan, which exports its products to Turkey, the Polystyrene project in Turkey and the Carbon Black Project in Iran.

Purchase of aviation fuel by the three national airlines, co-operation in the production and purchase of fertilizers and petrochemicals, and the exchange of trainees and experts are among other activities envisaged in this field.

TRADE

RCD hopes to introduce a system of regional trade preferences. The Ministers of Commerce met in April 1976 and laid down a schedule for the introduction of such a scheme, and in the same month the Heads of State and Government met in Izmir, agreeing to establish a free trade area within ten years.

Two agreements had already been signed, on RCD trade and on a multilateral payments arrangement.

Member countries participate in international fairs held within the region and have agreed to arrange separate exhibitions of the products of the three nations.

Ministers of Tourism of the RCD countries have agreed on measures to further tourism in the region, such as the issuing of group passports and joint publicity material.

It is also hoped to revive the traditional trade route from Europe to Asia through Trabzon in Turkey, which could substantially assist regional transit trade.

The RCD Chamber of Commerce and Industry has been in operation since 1966. Its secretarial work was taken over by the Secretariat in 1973.

INSURANCE

Five re-insurance pools have been created by RCD, for Accident, Engineering, Marine, Aviation and Fire. Forty-four companies had joined the Pools by 1973, with a total annual premium income of $1.5 to $2.0 million. Since the beginning of 1975, they have been merged into a single agency which is designed ultimately to form an RCD re-insurance company. An RCD International School of Insurance has also been active in Teheran since 1970.

The RCD Insurance Centre has its headquarters in Karachi; it undertakes research and disseminates information on insurance activities in the region.

TRANSPORT

RCD Shipping Services began operation in 1966, both within the region and to the United States. The organization has its office in Istanbul.

The RCD Highway is now nearing completion, linking the three member countries along a 5,180 km. route.

The rail link between Pakistan and Iran is to be completed by 1982. Iran and Turkey were linked by rail in 1971.

COMMUNICATIONS

Postal, telephone and telegraph rates within the region have been reduced and Operator Trunk Dialling has been introduced between Teheran, Ankara and Karachi.

TECHNICAL CO-OPERATION

Up to 1979, over 2,000 trainees, 1,250 students and 100 experts have visited the region under RCD programmes. In addition, 53 seminars and 11 joint courses on public administration have been held under tripartite arrangements.

An RCD Institute of Science and Technology, School of Economics, School of Hotel Management and a Science Foundation are to be established to strengthen regional co-operation in the technical field.

CULTURE AND INFORMATION

The RCD Cultural Institute in Teheran is engaged in research into the common historical and cultural heritage of the member countries. It has a library housing over 4,500 books. The Institute brings out a quarterly journal and has published 62 books, including original works and translations.

The RCD Cultural Exchange Programme includes exchange visits of artists, painters, eminent personalities, journalists and sportsmen. Four RCD Seminars of Journalists have been held, and a fifth is to take place in 1979.

The three national Radio/Television and News Agencies also co-operate under RCD programmes.

YOUTH

An RCD Youth Foundation is planned to increase contact amongst the youth of the three member countries.

RECORD OF EVENTS

1964 July — Meeting of Foreign Ministers of the three countries, Ankara. Agreement on collaboration outside the framework of CENTO.

Summit conference, Istanbul. Agreement on economic and cultural co-operation. Ministerial Council and Regional Planning Council established.

September — Meetings of Regional Planning Council and Ministerial Council, Teheran. Agreement to set up a joint international airline, a joint shipping company, joint petroleum organizations, and a regional cultural institute. Asphalt roads and rail links to be completed by 1968. Reduction planned of postal charges, insurance rates, and tariffs. Joint action to be taken to develop regional tourism. Secretariat established in Teheran. New committees on joint industrial ventures and technical co-operation set up.

1965 March — Meetings of Regional Planning Council and Ministerial Council, Islamabad, Pakistan. Agreement to set up a tripartite Shipping Conference. General agreement on technical co-operation. Joint industrial enterprises identified. Agreements on establishment of an RCD Chamber of Commerce, collaboration between news agencies.

July — Meetings of Regional Planning Council and Ministerial Council, Ankara. RCD Joint Chamber of Commerce and Industry established in Teheran. RCD Insurance Centre established in Karachi, Pakistan.

1966 May — RCD Shipping Services started operations on intra-regional routes.

August — Iran and Pakistan signed agreement providing for setting up a joint aluminium plant.

1967 January — Meetings of Regional Planning Council and Ministerial Council, Ankara. Agreement to set up a joint Bank Note Paper project in Pakistan. Decision to form a Payments Union among the three countries.

March — The following three Regional Reinsurance Pools started operations: *Accident*, managed by Iran; *Marine* (*Hull and Cargo*), managed by Pakistan; *Fire*, managed by Turkey.

April — Agreement providing for the RCD Union for Multilateral Payments Arrangements signed at Ankara, Turkey.

Second summit conference, Ramsar, Iran.

1968 April	Two more Regional Reinsurance Pools, *Aviation* and *Engineering*, started operations.
November	Agreement to establish joint Tungsten Carbide Plant in Turkey.
December	Third summit conference, Karachi, Pakistan.
1969 March	Agreement signed on the establishment of an Ultra-Marine Blue project in Pakistan.
July	Agreement signed between Iran Air and PIA for pooling traffic in Karachi-Teheran sector.
1971 September	First railway link between Iran and Turkey inaugurated.
1973 August	Experts Group meeting on the establishment of RCD trade showrooms in each member country, Karachi, Pakistan.
1974 November	Tour of the region by a team of experts on telecommunications and electronics.
1975 November	Tour of the region by an Industrial Survey team.
1976 January	Nineteenth session of Ministerial Council, Regional Planning Council and Co-ordination Committee, Lahore, Pakistan.
April	Fourth summit conference, Izmir, Turkey, preceded by special session of Ministerial Council.
1977 March	Signature of Treaty of Izmir (prepared following the Izmir summit), Teheran.
April	Signature of South and West Asia Postal Union Agreement, Teheran.
May	Twentieth session of the Ministerial Council, Regional Planning Council and Co-ordination Committee in Iran.
November	High-level meeting for the re-organization of the RCD Secretariat in Iran. Meetings of the Atomic Energy Organizations of the three countries in Teheran, Iran, the officials of the Central Banks in Pakistan, the Tourism Ministers in Turkey, the Shipping Services representatives in Iran and the representatives of the National Airlines in Iran.
December	Meetings of representatives of the three countries for the establishment of the RCD Investment and Development Bank, in Pakistan. Twenty-first session of the Committee on Technical Co-operation and Public Administration in Turkey.
1978 February	Meetings of the RCD Chamber of Commerce and Industry and the RCD Committees on Trade, Petroleum and Petrochemicals and Industry and Standardization in Pakistan.
May	Twenty-first session of the Ministerial Council, Regional Planning Council and Co-ordination Committee in Ankara, Turkey. Ministers agreed to establish a committee on Agriculture and to amalgamate the Committees on Industry and Petroleum and Petrochemicals.
June	Meeting of RCD Management Board.

PUBLICATIONS

The RCD Magazine (quarterly).
RCD Newsletter (monthly).
RCD Diary.
Economic Report.

Other Regional Organizations

These organizations are arranged under the following sub-headings:

Agriculture	Medicine
Defence	Planning and Administration
Development	Press, Radio and Telecommunications
Education and Arts	Religion and Welfare
Finance and Economics	Science and Technology
Industrial Relations	Tourism
International Relations	Trade and Industry
Law	Transport

AGRICULTURE

African Agricultural Credit Commission: Rabat, Morocco; f. 1966 to study agricultural finance problems. Mems.: Algeria, Ivory Coast, Libya, Morocco, Senegal, Tunisia, Upper Volta and Zaire.

Arab Authority for Development and Agricultural Investment (AADAI): Khartoum, Sudan; f. 1978 to carry out over 100 agricultural and infrastructural projects in Sudan to increase the Arab world's food supply. Cap. U.S. $500 million, provided by the Abu Dhabi Fund for Arab Economic Development (ADFAED) and the Arab Fund for Economic and Social Development.

Chair. Osman Badran (Egypt).

Arab Organization for Agricultural Development: 4 el-Gamaa St., P.O.B. 474, Khartoum, Sudan; f. 1970 by the Council of the Arab League; aims to develop natural and human resources in the agricultural sector; to improve methods on a scientific basis; to increase productive efficiency in order to achieve self-sufficiency; to achieve agricultural integration between Arab states; to encourage establishment of new enterprises and promote employment in agriculture and increase standards of living in rural communities.

Dir.-Gen. Kamal Ramzi Stino (Egypt).

International Olive Growers' Federation (*Fédération internationale d'oléiculture*): Agustina de Aragón 11, Madrid 6, Spain; f. 1934 to promote the interests of olive growers and to effect international co-ordination of efforts to improve methods of growing and manufacturing and to promote the use of olive oil. Mems.: organizations and government departments in Algeria, Argentina, France, Greece, Israel, Italy, Lebanon, Libya, Morocco, Portugal, Spain, Syria, Tunisia.

Pres. Pierre Bonnet (France). Publs. *Informations oléicoles internationales* (quarterly).

DEFENCE

Arab Joint Defence Council (*see* chapter *The Arab League*).

Arab Organization for Industrialization (AOI): Cairo, Egypt; f. 1977 by the Egyptian Government; initial capital U.S. $4,000 million subscribed by Saudi Arabia, Qatar, United Arab Emirates. In May 1979 it was announced that the Organization's official existence would terminate on July 1st, and that a committee of the four members was being set up to begin liquidation.

Arab Permanent Military Commission (*see* chapter *The Arab League*).

Central Treaty Organization—CENTO: f. as successor to the Baghdad Pact Organization after Iraq's withdrawal from the Pact in 1959 to provide mutual security and defence for member countries. Mems.: Iran, Pakistan, Turkey, United Kingdom. The organization became inactive after the withdrawals of Pakistan, Iran and Turkey in March 1979.

Islamic Institute of Defence Technology: 16 Grosvenor Crescent, London, S.W.1, England; f. 1978.

Pres. Salem Azzam (Saudi Arabia); Dir.-Gen. Group-Capt. Mukarram Ali (Pakistan).

DEVELOPMENT

African Institute for Economic Development and Planning: B.P. 3186, Dakar, Senegal; f. 1963 as autonomous organ within ECA.

Afro-Asian Housing Organization (AAHO): P.O.B. 523, 28 Ramses St., Cairo, Egypt; f. 1965 to promote co-operation between African and Asian countries in housing, reconstruction, physical planning and related matters.

Sec.-Gen. Hassan M. Hassan (Egypt).

Afro-Asian Organization for Economic Co-operation (AFRASEC): Special P.O. Bag, Chamber of Commerce Building, Midan al-Falaki, Bab el-Louk, Cairo, Egypt; f. 1958 to speed up industrialization and implement exchanges in commercial, financial and technical fields. Mems.: Central Chambers of Commerce in 45 countries.

Pres. Zakareya Tewfik. Publ. *Afro-Asian Economic Review*.

Afro-Asian Rural Reconstruction Organization (AARRO): C/117-118 Defence Colony, New Delhi 110024, India; f. 1962 to restructure the economy of the rural populations of Africa and Asia, and to explore collectively opportunities for co-ordination of efforts for promoting welfare and eradicating hunger, thirst, disease and poverty amongst the rural people; mem.s 12 African and 16 Asian countries including one national co-operative organization.

Pres. Egypt; Vice-Pres. Mauritius, Republic of Korea; Sec.-Gen. S. M. Osman (Egypt); Dir. M. R. Kaushal (India). Publ. *Rural Reconstruction* (half-yearly).

Near East Foundation: 54 East 64th St., New York, N.Y. 10021, U.S.A.; f. 1930. Aims: to conduct agricultural and educational programmes and demonstrations in order to improve standards of living in underdeveloped areas of the world, primarily the Near East, with technicians at work in Asia and Africa.

Pres. John M. Sutton; Comptroller N. T. Wallin. Publ. *Annual Report*.

EDUCATION AND ARTS

Afro-Asian Writers' Permanent Bureau: 104 Kasr el-Aini St., Cairo, Egypt; f. 1958 by Afro-Asian Peoples' Solidarity Organization; Mems.: 78 writers' organizations.

Sec.-Gen. Abder Rahman Sharqawi. Publs. *Lotus Magazine of Afro-Asian Writings* (quarterly in English, French and Arabic), *Afro-Asian Literature Series* (in English, French and Arabic).

Alliance Israélite Universelle: 45 rue La Bruyère, 75425 Paris Cedex 09, France; f. 1860 to work for the emancipation and moral progress of the Jews; maintains 42 schools in the Mediterranean area; library of 100,000 vols. Mems.: 12,000 in 25 countries; local committees in six countries.

Pres. JULES BRAUNSCHVIG; Sec.-Gen. EUGENE WEILL (France). Publs. *Cahiers de l'Alliance Israélite Universelle, The Alliance Review, Les Nouveaux Cahiers, La Revista de l'Alliance Israélite Universelle.*

Association of Arab Universities: Scientific Computation Centre, Tharwat St., Orman P.O.-Giza, Egypt; f. 1964. Mems.: 32 universities.

Sec.-Gen. Dr. M. MURSI AHMED. Publs. *Bulletin* (two a year), *Directory of Arab Universities, Directory of Teaching Staff of Arab Universities*, Proceedings of Seminars.

European Union of Arabic and Islamic Scholars (*Union Européenne d'Arabisants et d'Islamisants—U.E.A.I.*): Juan XXIII 5, Madrid 3, Spain; f. 1970 to organize a Congress of Arabic and Islamic Studies. Mems.: about 120.

Sec. Prof. F. M. PAREJA (Spain).

International Institute for Adult Literacy Methods: 52 Zartosht Ave., P.O.B. 1555, Teheran, Iran; f. 1968 by UNESCO and the Government of Iran; carries out comparative studies of the methods, media and techniques used in literacy programmes; maintains documentation service and library on literacy; arranges seminars.

Dir. Dr. JOHN W. RYAN. Publs. *Literacy Discussion* (quarterly in English and French, abstracts in French, English, Spanish and Arabic), *Literacy Work* (quarterly in English and French; abstracts in English, French, Spanish and Arabic), *Literacy Documentation* (3 times a year in English), *Literacy in Development* (monograph series, in English, French, Spanish and Arabic).

FINANCE AND ECONOMICS

Afro-Asian Organization for Economic Co-operation: AFRASEC Special P.O. Bag, Chamber of Commerce Bldg., Midan Al-Falaki, Bab el-Louk, Cairo, Egypt; f. 1958 to speed up industrialization and implement exchanges in commercial, financial and technical fields. Mems.: Central Chambers of Commerce in 45 countries.

Pres. ZAKAREYA TEWFIK. Publ. *Afro-Asian Economic Review.*

General Arab Insurance Federation: 8 Kasr El-Nil St., P.O.B. 611, Cairo, Egypt; f. 1964 to strengthen the bonds between Arab insurance companies by collection and preparation of data, co-ordination of legislation and Arabization of the insurance language. Mems.: 73 insurance and re-insurance companies in 17 states.

Sec.-Gen. ALI EL-SHAFEI. Publs. *Magazine* (two a year), *News Bulletin* (monthly).

International Centre for Research in Islamic Economics: P.O.B. 1540, King Abdulaziz University, Jeddah, Saudi Arabia; f. 1977 on recommendation of First International Conference of Islamic Economics held in 1976, to conduct, co-ordinate and support international research in Islamic economics.

Union de Banques Arabes et Françaises—UBAF (*Union of French and Arab Banks*): "Le France", 4 rue Ancelle, 92521 Neuilly/Seine Cédex, France; f. 1970 to group together 26 banks of 20 Arab countries (with 60 per cent of share capital), the Crédit Lyonnais of France (30 per cent share capital), the Banque Française du Commerce Extérieur (8 per cent share capital) and the Banque Générale du Phénix (2 per cent of share capital) with the aim of contributing primarily to the development of financial, commercial, industrial and economic relations between the Arab countries on the one hand and Europe, and in particular France, and the international financial markets on the other; cap. 250 million French francs, total deposits 12,900 million French francs.

Chair. MOHAMED MAHMOUD ABUSHADI; Gen. Man. GÉRARD GERVAIS. Publs. *Annual Report, Quarterly Economic Report.*

INDUSTRIAL RELATIONS

Arab Federation of Petroleum, Mining and Chemicals Workers (*Fédération arabe des travailleurs du pétrole, des mines et des industries chimiques*): 5 Zaki St., Cairo, Egypt; f. 1961 to establish proper industrial relations policies and procedures for the guidance of all affiliated unions; owns and manages the Arab Petroleum Institute for Labour Studies, Cairo; 18 affiliated unions in 12 countries.

Pres. GHAZI NASSEF (Syria); Sec.-Gen. ANWAR ASHMAWI MOHAMED (Egypt). Publs. *Arab Petroleum* (monthly); English, Arabic and French editions, specialized publications and statistics.

International Confederation of Arab Trade Unions (ICATU): Ramses Building, P.O.B. 1041, Cairo, Egypt; f. 1956; mems.: 15 unions in 13 countries.

Sec.-Gen. Dr. FAWZY EL SAYED (Egypt). Publs. *Arab Workers* (Arabic), *ICATU Review* (English), *La Revue de CISA* (French), *CISTA* (Spanish).

INTERNATIONAL RELATIONS

Afro-Asian Peoples' Solidarity Organization (AAPSO): 89 Abdel Aziz al Saoud St., Manial, Cairo, Egypt; f. 1957 as the Organization for Afro-Asian Peoples' Solidarity; acts as a permanent liaison body between the peoples of Africa and Asia and aims to ensure their economic, social and cultural development. The highest authority of the AAPSO is its Congress, headed by a Presidium. There is an annual meeting of Council. The Permanent Secretariat conducts the work of the organization between these meetings. The Congress elects 3 Deputy Secretaries General, one from Africa, one from Asia and one from the Arab countries, and 14 secretaries whose mandate ends at the following Congress. The Board of Secretaries is composed of 17 mems. from Algeria, Angola, Egypt, Guinea, India, Iraq, Japan, Palestine Liberation Organization, Somalia, South Africa (African National Congress), Tanzania, U.S.S.R., Viet-Nam, People's Democratic Republic of Yemen and Zambia. Mems.: 75 national committees and affiliated organizations.

Pres. and Sec.-Gen. ABDER RAHMAN SHARQAWI. Publs. *Solidarity* (monthly), *Afro-Asian Publications* (73 published).

EURABIA (European Co-ordinating Committee of Friendship Societies with the Arab World): 16 rue Augereau, 75007 Paris, France; f. April 1972 to achieve greater co-operation between European organizations working for friendship with the Arab world; sponsors meetings and seminars to improve understanding of political, social, economic and cultural aspects of the Arab world, including the need to recognize the national rights of the Palestinian people.

Chair. LUCIEN BITTERLIN (Association de Solidarité Franco-Arabe); Admin. Sec. ROBERT SWANN (U.K.). Publs. *Fortnightly Bulletin* (in French), pamphlets.

Federation of Arab Republics: Tripoli, Libya; f. 1972 to increase the political unity of Egypt, Libya and Syria; a Federal Nat. Assembly met twice per year until 1975, but since then the Federation has been in practice ineffective.

Jewish Agency for Israel: P.O.B. 92, Jerusalem, Israel; f. 1897 as an instrument through which world Jewry could build up a national home. Is now the executive arm of the World Zionist Organisation. Mems.: Zionist federations in 61 countries.

Chair. of Exec. LEON DULZIN; Chair. of Board of Govs. MAX M. FISHER. Dir.-Gen. SHMUEL LAHIS. Publs. *Israel Digest* (weekly), *Economic Horizons* (monthly in U.S.A.), *Folk and Zion* (monthly in Yiddish).

Parliamentary Association for Euro-Arab Co-operation: 16 rue Augereau, 75007 Paris, France; f. March 1974 as an association of more than 350 parliamentarians of the European Community to promote friendship and co-operation between Europe and the Arab world; Executive Committee has held joint meetings with Arab Parliamentary Union in Bonn, Paris, Dublin and Luxembourg; represented in Council of Europe, Western European Union and European Parliament; works for the progress of the European-Arab Dialogue and a settlement in the Middle East which takes into account the national rights of the Palestinian people.

Joint Chair. TIJL DECLERQ (Belgium), DENNIS WALTERS (U.K.); Gen. Sec. ROBERT SWANN (U.K.).

LAW

Arab Lawyers Union: 13 Tulumbat St., Garden City, Cairo, Egypt; f. 1956 to facilitate contacts between Arab lawyers, to safeguard and develop legislative and judicial language, to allow all Arab lawyers to take cases in any Arab country and to restore the study of Muslim law. Mems.: 15 Bar Asscns. in 12 countries.

Sec.-Gen. CHAFIK ARCHAIDAT. Publs. *Al Haak* (The Law), Documents and Studies.

Asian-African Legal Consultative Committee: 27 Ring Road, Lajpat Nagar-IV, New Delhi 24, India; f. 1956. Aims: to place the Committee's views on legal issues before the International Law Commission, to consider legal problems referred to it by member countries and to serve as a forum for Asian-African co-operation in international law. Mems.: 35 states.

Pres. Dr. A. H. AL-KATIFI (Iraq); Sec.-Gen. B. SEN (India).

MEDICINE

Middle East Neurosurgical Society: Neurosurgical Department, American University Medical Centre, Beirut, Lebanon; f. 1958; 212 mems. in Egypt, Greece, India, Iraq, Jordan, Lebanon, Pakistan, Syria and Turkey.

Pres. Prof. AHMAD BECHIR; Hon. Sec. Prof. FUAD S. HADDAD.

Society of Haematology and Blood-Transfusion of African and Near Eastern Countries: Tunis, Tunisia; f. 1965 for the promotion and co-ordination of scientific research in the field of haematology.

Pres. Dr. SY BABA (Ivory Coast); Vice-Pres. Dr. BENABADJY (Algeria); Sec.-Gen. Dr. ALI BOUJNAH (Tunisia).

PLANNING AND ADMINISTRATION

Centre Africain de Formation et de Recherches Administratives pour le Développement (CAFRAD) (*African Training and Research Centre in Administration for Development*): 19 rue Abou Alla El Maari, B.P. 310, Tangier, Morocco; f. 1964 by agreement between Morocco and UNESCO, final agreement signed by 31 African states; undertakes research into administrative problems in Africa, documentation of results, provision of a consultation service for governments and organizations; holds frequent seminars; aided by UNESCO and the UN Development Programme; library of 14,000 vols.

Pres. MOHAMED BIROUK; Dir.-Gen. J. E. KARIUKI. Publs. *Cahiers Africains d'Administration Publique* (twice a year), *African Administrative Abstracts* (quarterly, also in French), *Information Bulletin* (8 times a year, also in French), *CAFRAD News* (irregularly in English, French and Arabic).

International Planned Parenthood Federation: Middle East and North Africa Regional Office, 14 ave. Habib Bourguiba, (P.O.B. 18), Carthage, Tunisia; aims to advance education in family planning, to increase understanding of demographic problems, to stimulate scientific research and the formation of family planning associations, to organize the training of professional workers, and to attain a favourable balance between population and natural resources; Regional Office covers Algeria, Libya, Mauritania and Somalia (full mems.) and Afghanistan, Bahrain, Cyprus, Egypt, Iraq, Jordan, Lebanon, Morocco, Sudan, Syria, Tunisia, the Yemen Arab Republic and the People's Democratic Republic of Yemen (assoc. mems.).

Mediterranean Social Sciences Research Council: American University of Beirut, Beirut, Lebanon; f. 1960 to promote research on problems concerning the social and economic development of the land and peoples of the Mediterranean Basin. Mems.: Research Centres and individuals in 19 countries.

Chair. Prof. D. J. DELIVANIS (Greece); Sec.-Gen. Prof. N. ZIADEH (Lebanon).

PRESS, RADIO AND TELECOMMUNICATIONS

African Postal Union/AfPU (*Union postale Africaine—UPAF*): 5 26th July St., Cairo, Egypt; f. 1961 to improve postal services between member states, to secure collaboration between them and to create other useful services. Mems.: Burundi, Egypt, Ghana, Guinea, Guinea-Bissau, Liberia, Libya, Mali, Mauritania, Somalia, Sudan, Zaire.

Dir. DIARRA SIDIKI (Guinea). Publ. *African Postal Union Review* (quarterly).

Arab Postal Union (*see* chapter *The Arab League*).

Arab States Broadcasting Union (*see* chapter *The Arab League*).

Arab Telecommunications Union (*see* chapter *The Arab League*).

Federation of Arab News Agencies: Beirut; f. 1965. Pres. MUHAMMAD AL-MASHNOUQ; Gen. Sec. Dr. FARID AYYAR.

RELIGION AND WELFARE

Agudas Israel World Organisation (*Organisation mondiale agudas Israël*): Haheruth Sq., P.O.B. 326, Jerusalem, Israel; f. 1912 to help solve the problems facing Jewish people especially by promoting the co-ordination of effort between Jews in Eastern and Western Europe. Mems.: over 300,000 in 21 countries.

Chair. Rabbi I. M. LEWIN; Hon. Sec. M. R. SPRINGER (United Kingdom). Publs. *Hamodia* (Israel, daily newspaper), *Jewish Tribune* (London, fortnightly).

Bahá'i International Community: Office of UN Representative, 345 East 46th St., New York, N.Y. 10017, U.S.A.; f. 1844 in Persia to promote the teachings of the

Bahá'í religion; to promulgate the unity of the human race; to work for the elimination of all forms of prejudice and for equality of men and women; to establish basic education schools for children; to maintain adult programmes in basic literacy and community training. Mems. in 93,000 centres in 335 countries and territories. Governing body: The Universal House of Justice, Bahá'í World Centre, Haifa, Israel.

Rep. to UN Dr. VICTOR DE ARAUJO (U.S.A.); Alternate Dr. WILL. C. VAN DEN HOONAARD (Canada). Publs. *The Bahá'í World* (world survey), *La Pensée Bahá'íe* (quarterly), *World Order* (quarterly), *Maailman-Kansalainen* (quarterly), *Opinioni Bahá'í* (quarterly); national and local house organs; 18 Bahá'í Publishing Trusts in countries throughout the world; publications in over 600 languages and dialects.

International Council of Jewish Women: Rio Bamba 1020, Buenos Aires, Argentina; f. 1912 to promote friendly relations and understanding among Jewish women throughout the world. It exchanges information on community welfare activities, promotes volunteer leadership, sponsors field work in social welfare and fosters Jewish education. It has consultative status with UN, ECOSOC, UNICEF, UNESCO and the Council of Europe, with representatives to each of these bodies. Mems.: affiliates in 29 countries in all continents, grouping over a million individual members.

Pres. Dra. ROSA S. DE HERCZEG (Argentina); Sec. Dra. DEBORAH SCHLESINGER (Argentina). Publ. *Newsletter* (3 a year, English and Spanish).

International Hebrew Christian Alliance: P.O.B. 758, Palm Harbor, Fl. 33563, U.S.A.; f. 1925. Objects: to unite Hebrew Christians throughout the world, to maintain and extend the Christian faith among those of Hebrew birth and to help them and their families in need.

Pres. DANIEL FUCHS; Exec. Sec. and Treas. Rev. HARCOURT SAMUEL. Publs. *The Hebrew Christian* (quarterly), *Der Zeuge* (bi-annual).

International Muslim Union (*Union Musulmane Internationale*): Grande Mosquée de Paris, 2 *bis* Place du Puits de l'Ermite, Paris 5e, France; f. 1968. Objects: to assist the needy, defend the Muslim community, spread the knowledge of Islamic civilization and to organize Islamic worship wherever necessary.

Sec.-Gen. Dr. DALIL BOUBAKEUR. Publ. *Al Attihad* (weekly information bulletin).

Islamic Council of Europe: 16 Grosvenor Crescent, London S.W.1. England; f. 1973 as a co-ordinating body for Islamic centres and organizations in Europe; an autonomous Council collaborating with the Islamic Secretariat and other Islamic organizations; aims to develop a better understanding of Islam and Muslim culture in the West.

Sec.-Gen. SALEM AZZAM.

World Jewish Congress (*Congrès Juif Mondial*): 1 rue de Varembé, Geneva, Switzerland; f. 1936. It is a voluntary association of representative Jewish bodies, communities and organizations throughout the world. Aims: to foster the unity of the Jewish people, strive for the fulfilment of its aspirations and ensure the continuity and development of its religious, spiritual, cultural and social heritage. Mems.: Jewish communities in over 60 countries.

Pres. PHILIP M. KLUTZNICK; Sec.-Gen. Dr. GERHART M. RIEGNER. Publs. *Patterns of Prejudice* (bi-monthly, London), *L'Information Juive* (monthly, Paris), *Jewish Journal of Sociology* (bi-annual, London), *Gesher* (Hebrew quarterly, Israel), *Jewish Cultural News* (quarterly, Jerusalem, in English and Russian), *Boletin Informativo OJI* (twice monthly, Buenos Aires), *Folk, Velt un Medine* (monthly, Tel-Aviv, in Yiddish).

World Sephardi Federation: New House, 67-68 Hatton Garden, London, EC1N 8JY; f. 1951 to strengthen the unity of Jewry and Judaism among Sephardim, to defend and foster religious and cultural activities of all Sephardi Communities and preserve their spiritual heritage, to provide moral and material assistance where necessary and to co-operate with other similar organizations. Mems.: 50 communities and organizations in 30 countries.

Pres. NISSIM GAON.

World Union for Progressive Judaism (*Union mondiale pour le judaïsme libéral*): 13 King David St., Jerusalem, Israel; North American Board, 838 Fifth Ave., New York, N.Y. 10021, U.S.A.; European Board, 109 Whitfield St., London, W.1; f. 1926. Promotes and co-ordinates efforts of Reform, Liberal and Progressive congregations throughout the world; supports new congregations; assigns and employs rabbis; sponsors seminaries and schools; organizes international conferences; maintains a youth section. Mems.: organizations and individuals in 25 countries.

Pres. Dr. DAVID M. WICE (U.S.A.); Exec. Dir. Rabbi RICHARD G. HIRSCH (Israel). Publs. *AMMI* (quarterly), *Telem* (monthly in Hebrew), *International Conference Reports*, *European Judaism* (bi-annual).

SCIENCE AND TECHNOLOGY

Arab Engineering Union: 81 Ramses St., Cairo; a regional body of the World Federation of Engineering Organizations; co-operates with the Arab League, UNESCO and the other regional engineering federations. Holds a Pan-Arab conference on engineering studies every three years and annual symposia and seminars in different Arab countries. Mems.: 13 Arab countries.

International Meteorological Institute: Cairo; f. 1966 to carry out meteorological research and to provide training for Middle Eastern and African personnel engaged in meteorological work; set up by World Meteorological Organization (WMO).

Middle Eastern Regional Radioisotope Centre for the Arab Countries: Sh. Malaeb El Gamaa, Dokki, Cairo, Egypt; f. 1963; trains specialists in the applications of radioisotopes, particularly in the medical, agricultural and industrial fields; conducts research in hydrology, tropical and subtropical diseases, fertilizers and entomology; promotes the use of radioisotopes in the Arab countries.

TOURISM

Arab Tourism Union: P.O.B. 2354, Amman, Jordan; f. 1954. Mems.: Nat. Tourist orgs. of 21 Arab states, and 4 allied mems. in private sector; 9 members form the Executive Committee for a term of two years.

Sec.-Gen. ABU RABAH (Jordan). Publs. *Arab Tourism Magazine* (bi-monthly, Arabic), *Press Bulletin* (monthly, Arabic and English).

Arab Union of Automobile Clubs and Tourist Societies: 8 Kasr El Nil St., Cairo; f. 1965; Federation of 12 clubs in 10 Arab countries.

Federation of Arab Travel Agents' Associations (FATAA): Malab Salam St., Salam Bldg., P.O.B. 165035, Beirut,

Lebanon; f. 1970; sole Arab organization of travel agents; protects their interests and negotiates in their name with local, governmental and international tourist organizations; mems.: all Arab Travel Asscns. and over 250 Travel Agents; 6th Gen. Assembly, Beirut, May 78.

Pres. YASSER ABU SO'OUD (Jordan).

TRADE AND INDUSTRY

Arab Iron and Steel Union (AISU): B.P. 4, Cheraga, Algiers, Algeria; f. 1972 to develop commercial and technical aspects of Arab steel production by helping member associations to commercialize their production in Arab markets, guaranteeing them high quality materials and intermediary products, informing them of recent developments in the industry and organizing training sessions. Mems.: 54 producers, whose production is worth not less than £1 million per year, in 15 Arab countries.

Gen. Sec. MOHAMED LAÏD LACHGAR. Publs. *Arab Steel Review* (monthly), *Information Bulletin* (two a month), *Directory* (annual), *Descriptive Analytical Bulletin* (monthly).

General Union of Chambers of Commerce, Industry and Agriculture for Arab Countries (*Union générale des chambres de commerce, industrie et agriculture des pays arabes*): P.O.B. 11-2837, Beirut, Lebanon; f. 1951 to foster Arab economic collaboration, to increase and improve production and to facilitate the exchange of technical information in Arab countries. Mems.: 20 Chambers of Commerce in 20 countries.

Pres. ISMAIL ABUDAWOOD; Vice-Pres. ADNAN KASSAR; Gen. Sec. BURHAN DAJANI. Publ. *Arab Economic Report* (Arabic and English).

International Olive Oil Council: Juan Bravo 10–2°, Madrid, Spain; f. 1959; entrusted with the administration of the International Olive Oil Agreement, the objectives of which are as follows: to promote international co-operation in connection with world olive oil problems; to prevent the occurrence of any unfair competition in the world olive oil trade; to put into operation, or to facilitate the application of, measures designed to extend the production and consumption of, and international trade in, olive oil; to reduce the disadvantages due to fluctuations of supplies on the market; to examine the possibility of taking necessary action with regard to other products of the olive tree. Members of the Agreement as extended by protocols in 1967, 1969, 1973 and 1978: 10 mainly producing members, 10 mainly importing members and the EEC.

Dir. LUCIEN DENIS; Deputy Dir. Admin. and External Services Dept. LUIS F. DE RANERO; Deputy Dir. Tech. Services PASQUALE DI GREGORIO. Publs. *Survey of the International Olive Oil Council* (fortnightly, French and Spanish), *National Olive Oil Policies* (annual).

TRANSPORT

Arab Air Carriers' Organization (AACO): Arab Business Centre, Airport Blvd., Beirut, Lebanon; f. 1965 to co-ordinate and promote co-operation in the activities of Arab airline companies.

Sec.-Gen. SALIM A. SALAAM. Publs. Monthly statistical bulletins and research documents on aviation in the Arab world.

Arab Maritime Transport Academy: Gamal Abdel-Nasser St., P.O.B. 1029, Alexandria, Egypt; f. 1972; Gen. Dir. Dr. GAMAL MOUKHTAR; First Deputy Gen. Dir. EISA EL-MOKADDAMY. Publs. *Journal of Arab Maritime Transport Academy* (twice yearly), *News Bulletin* (monthly), *Arab Maritime Data* (annual), *Arab Maritime Directory* (annual).

Trans-Saharan Highway Committee: B.P. 8, Birmandreis, Algiers, Algeria; f. 1964 to study and build a Trans-Saharan Road and to obtain the necessary finance with UNDP backing. A feasibility study has been completed and a contract made with an international consortium for the design; estimated cost for the road, 4-7 metres wide and 2,800 km. in total length, is U.S. $86 million. In Algeria the section from El Golea to In Salah was completed in 1973, and the next section, as far as Tamanrasset, was expected to be completed by 1979. In Niger the Government began negotiations over finance and construction in 1977. The Tunisian section, from Nefta to Hazoua, was completed in 1976. Nigeria joined the Committee in June 1976. A new constitution for the Committee was drawn up in 1977, giving it full responsibility for implementing the project. Mems.: Algeria, Mali, Niger, Nigeria and Tunisia.

PART THREE

Country Surveys

Afghanistan

PHYSICAL AND SOCIAL GEOGRAPHY

W. B. Fisher

Occupying an area of approximately 250,000 square miles (estimates range between 240,000 and 270,000 square miles) Afghanistan has the shape of a very irregular oval with its major axis running N.E.-S.W. and extending over roughly 700 miles, and the minor axis at right angles to this, covering about 350 miles. The country is in the main a highland mass lying mostly at an altitude of 1,200 metres (4,000 ft.) or more, but it presents a highly variable pattern of extremely high and irregular mountain ridges, some of which exceed 6,000 metres (20,000 ft.); ravines and broader valleys, parts of which are very fertile; and an outer expanse of undulating plateau, wide river basins, and lake sumps.

Politically, Afghanistan has two frontiers of major length: one on the north with the Turkmen, Uzbek and Tadzhik Republics of the U.S.S.R., the other on the south and east with Pakistan.

This frontier follows what was once termed the Durand Line (after the representative of British India, Sir Mortimer Durand, who negotiated it in 1893 with the Ruler of Afghanistan). So long as the British occupied India, it was generally accepted as forming the Indo-Afghan frontier, but in 1947 with the recognition of Pakistan as a successor to the British, the Afghan government recalled that for much of the eighteenth century, Peshawar and other parts of the Indus Valley had formed part of a larger Afghan state, and were moreover occupied largely by Pashtuns, who are of closely similar ethnic character to many Afghans. Accordingly, the Durand Line frontier was denounced by Afghanistan, and claims were made that the territories as far as the line of the Indus, including Chitral, Swat, and Peshawar, and continuing as far as the Pashtun areas of the North-west Frontier Province and Baluchistan, ought to be recognized as an autonomous state, "Pashtunistan". This remains a topic of dispute between Afghanistan and Pakistan.

There are shorter but no less significant frontiers on the west with Iran, and on the north-east with Kashmir and with China. This last was fully agreed only in 1963, and the precise location of others in the south and west has not been fully delimited: an indication of the extreme difficulties of terrain, and an explanation of the uncertainty regarding the actual area of Afghanistan. It is noteworthy that, in order to erect a "buffer" between the then competing empires of Russia and India, under the Durand treaty of 1893 the Wakhan district, a narrow strip of land 200 miles long and under 10 miles wide in its narrowest part, was attached to Afghanistan. This strip controls the Baroghil pass over the Pamir, and avoids having a Soviet-Indian frontier.

PHYSICAL FEATURES

The main topographical feature of Afghanistan is a complex of irregular highlands that is relatively broad and low in the west, and very much higher and also narrower towards the east. In this eastern part the mountains form a group of well-defined chains that are known by the general name of the Hindu Kush (Hindu destroyer), and are linked further eastward first to the Pamirs and then to the main Himalaya system. The Eastern Hindu Kush ranges form the southern defining limit of the Wakhan strip whilst a short distance to the north and east, a small but high ridge, the Little Pamir, forms the topographic link between the Hindu Kush and the main Pamir. From maximum heights of 6,000–7,000 metres (20,000–24,000 ft.) the peaks decline in altitude westwards, attaining 4,500–6,000 metres (15,000–20,000 ft.) in the zone close to Kabul. Further west still, the ridges are no more than 3,500–4,500 metres (12,000–15,000 ft.) and in the extreme west they open out rather like the digits of a hand, with the much lower Parapamisus ridges (proto-Pamir) forming the last member of the mountain complex. The various ridges are distinguished by separate names. The Hindu Kush, which has a general altitude of about 4,500 metres, with peaks 2,000–3,000 metres (7,000–10,000 ft.) higher still, is, however, narrow and crossable by quite a number of passes, some of which are indirect and snow-bound for much of the year.

In geological structure, Afghanistan has close affinities both to Iran further west, and, as has just been stated, to the massive Himalayan system further east. Development of present-day land-forms has been greatly influenced by the existence of several large, stable masses of ancient rocks, which, by drifting northwards, have acted as cores or plates around which rock series of younger age first developed and were then closely wrapped as fold structures. Most important of these ancient massifs, or "plate" areas so far as Afghanistan is concerned, is the plateau of the Deccan, the effect of which was to "bunch" a series of tight folds in a double loop or garland on its northern side. In this way can be explained the existence of the "knot" or "bunch" of fold structures lying partly in Afghanistan, and comprising the Pamir which forms the eastern limb and the Hindu Kush that makes up the western segment of the "garland". The abrupt change of direction and swinging of the fold structures from an east-west to, in some places, a north-south direction are a direct result of the presence of the resistant mass of the Deccan. The fold ranges themselves are composed in part of sediments mainly laid down under water, and includes limestones with some sandstones, and are of Cretaceous and later age, Eocene especially. Extensive heat and pressure in some regions have metamorphosed original series into schists and gneiss; and there has been much shattering and cracking of the rock generally, with the consequent development of fault-lines and overthrust zones. A further feature in much of Afghanistan has been a good deal of differential earth movement, uptilting, downwarping and local adjustment which makes the region particularly susceptible to earth tremors, which occur frequently, usually on a small scale. Occasionally, however, a major disaster occurs, the latest being in the Uzbek Republic of the U.S.S.R., just north of Afghanistan, in 1976.

As a consequence of frequent crustal disturbance, the rise of magma from the earth's interior has produced lava-flows, and minor volcanos. Most of these are in a stage of old age—being merely fissures from which emanate gas, steam and mud flows; and the presence of soft volcanic debris adds considerably in places to soil fertility.

As far as river drainage is concerned, Afghanistan forms a major watershed, from which rivers flow outward. The Amu-Dar'ya (Oxus) rises on the north side of the Hindu Kush and flows northwestwards into the U.S.S.R. Here, away from the mountains the presence of loess (a yellowish soil of high fertility) in small pockets offers scope for agriculture. The Hari Rud rises a short distance only from the Amu-Dar'ya, but flows westward through Herat to terminate in a salt, closed basin on the Iranian frontier. From the south and west of the Hindu Kush flow a number of streams that become tributaries of the Indus; and in the extreme south-west the Helmand river flows through to end like the Hari Rud in a closed basin that is partly within Iranian territory. The Helmand basin is of interest in that because of a curious balance in water-level at its lowest part, the river here reverses its flow seasonally, and remains for much of its length non-brackish instead of becoming progressively more saline, as is normal when there is no outlet to the sea. The Helmand basin thus offers distinct potential for agricultural improvement, and in fact schemes for irrigation are in process of development. But political difficulties (part of the lower basin is Iranian territory) and remoteness have been inhibiting factors.

The lower-lying areas, which are in the main more densely peopled, occur either as a series of peripheral zones to north and south, or as a series of interior valleys and basins between the main mountain ridges of the centre. Largest of these areas is the piedmont lying on the northern flanks of the mountains, and dropping northwards in altitude to merge into the steppelands of Soviet Central Asia. This is Bactria, a region of, in places, light yellowish loessic soils. An interior situation, shut off from the sea by mountains, means that rainfall is deficient, and falls mainly over the mountains. Streams fed partly by mountain snow-melt straggle across the plain, to lose themselves in the sand, feed salt swamps, or in a few cases, join others to form larger rivers such as the Hari Rud. Much of Bactria thus consists of semi or full desert with sheets of sand and gravel in many places, with, nearer the mountains, outwash of larger, coarser scree. Given stable political conditions this area with its areas of highly fertile loess soils and moderate water supplies offers much scope for economic development. For long inhabited by pastoral nomads, and disputed politically between various claimants (Afghan, Iranian and Soviet), this northern zone is now developing rapidly with irrigated cotton growing as a main element. Links with the U.S.S.R. are considerable, and the two chief towns of Herat in the west and Mazar-i-Sharif in the north have grown considerably in size over the past few years.

On the south, towards the east, is the Kabul basin, which is a relatively flat zone hemmed in closely by steep mountain ridges. Some distance away to the north-west, and reachable through two major passes is the narrower Vale of Bamian; whilst south-east of Kabul occurs another fertile lowland zone around Jalalabad. Here lower elevation and southerly situation produce warmer conditions, especially in winter, as compared with most of the rest of Afghanistan.

In the south-west, extending through Ghazni as far as Kandahar, there is another series of cultivated zones; but the extent of this piedmont area is much smaller than the corresponding one we have just described as Bactria. To the west, aridity, the price of declining altitude, increases, so the lowland passes into the desert areas of Registan and the Dasht-i-Mayo. Registan has seasonal flushes of grass, which support relatively large numbers of pastoral nomads, who, however, are becoming increasingly settled following irrigation development on the Helmand and Arghandab rivers.

Two other regional units may be mentioned. South of the Parapamisus and Kuh-i-Baba mountain ranges are a number of parallel but lower massifs, with narrow valleys between. Here because of altitude there is relatively abundant rainfall, but owing to topography, the region is one of remoteness and difficulty. This is the Hazarat, so called from the name of the Hazara inhabitants; and it still remains despite a central position one of the least known and visited parts of the country. Another equally remote highland, this time located north-east of Kabul, is Nuristan, again high and mountainous, but well-wooded in places, and supporting a small population of cultivators and pastoralists who use the summer pastures of the high hills, and move to lower levels in winter.

CLIMATE

Climatically, Afghanistan demonstrates a very clear relationship with Iran and the Middle East, rather than with Monsoon Asia, in that it has an almost arid summer, a small amount of rainfall which is largely confined to the winter season, and considerable seasonal variation in temperature. The monsoonal condition of heavy summer rainfall does not occur, despite Afghanistan's nearness to India. Annual rainfall ranges from 100–150 mm. (4–6 in.) in the drier, lower areas of the west and north, to 250–400 mm. (10–15 in.) in the east; on the highest mountains there is more still. Kabul, with an average of 330 mm. (13 in.) per annum, is typical of conditions in the east, and Herat with 125 mm. typical of the west. Almost all this falls in the period December to April, though there can be a very occasional downpour at other times, even in summer, when a rare damp monsoonal current penetrates from the Indian lowlands. Temperatures are best described as extreme. In July, the lowlands experience temperatures of 43°C. (110°F.) with 49°C. not uncommon—this is true of Jalalabad on the edge of the Indus lowlands. But the effects of altitude are important, and Kabul, at an elevation of 1,800 m., does not often experience temperatures of over 38°C. (100°F.). Winter cold can be bitter, with minima of −22° to −26°C. (−10° to −15°F.) on the higher plateau areas, and as a result there are heavy blizzards in many mountain areas. The January mean at Kabul is −4°C. (25°F.). Generally speaking, a seasonal temperature range of 45–55°C. is characteristic of many areas (cf. 14°C. for London). A further difficulty is the prevalence of strong winds, especially in the west, where a persistent and regular wind blows almost daily from June to September and affects especially the Sistan area of the lower Helmand basin, where it is known as the *Wind of 120 Days*.

With highly varied topography and climate, Afghanistan has a wide range of plant life—a good deal of which is not yet fully recorded. Conditions range from Arctic and Alpine type flora on the highest parts to salt-tolerant arid zone species in the deserts. Woodland occurs in a few areas, but much has been used for fuel in a country that has cold winters.

PEOPLE AND ACTIVITIES

The considerable variation in the types of terrain, and the considerable obstacles imposed by high mountains and deserts, have given rise to marked ethnic and cultural differences, so that heterogeneity in human populations is most characteristic. The Pashtuns live mainly in the centre, south and east of the country, and are probably numerically the largest group. The Ghilzais, also of the areas adjacent to Pakistan, are thought to be of Turkish origin, like the Uzbeks who live in the north, mainly in the Amu-Dar'ya lowlands. Another important element are the Tadzhiks or Parziwans who are of Persian origin, and in the opinion of some represent the earliest inhabitants of the country. Other groups, such as the Hazara (who are reputed to have come in as followers of Genghis Khan) and the Chahar Aimak, may have Mongol ancestry, but they now speak Persian and the Hazara are Shi'a Muslims. In the north-east, the presence of fair-haired groups has suggested connection with Europe. Another possibly indigenous group of long-standing, is the Nuristani or Kafirs, now small in number. Most Afghans (the Hazara and Qizilbash of Kabul excepted) are Sunni.

For long a difficult topography, extreme climate with a generally deficient rainfall, and political instability inhibited economic progress. Small communities lived by cultivation where water and soil were available, and there were relatively numerous pastoralists, mostly nomads, who formed an important section of the community. Even today, it is estimated that about 15 per cent of the population is nomadic, and tribal organization is strong.

Two major handicaps, arising directly from its geography, have long been the fragmented nature of the settlement pattern and the difficulties of physical communications between the various communities. Scale of production and size of markets have consequently been very limited: local standards often prevail and the central government does not find it easy to develop full control. So inherently strong is this fact of regional subdivision and diversity that the improvement of infrastructure (roads, airfields, radio and telephonic communication), undertaken with vigour over the past few years, has largely resulted in the intensification of regionalism.

In common with other countries of south-west Asia, Afghanistan experienced severe drought between 1968–72. This is thought to have been due to a major cyclical climatic shift that is traceable over a very wide area of the Northern Hemisphere. The economic consequences of this drought have been considerable, though varied regionally within Afghanistan, not only for the 80 per cent or so of the population who still live directly by agriculture, but, as well, through restriction on water supplies for developing manufacturing and other activities.

Because of Afghanistan's former location as a buffer between Russia and British India, railways approached from various sides, but none actually penetrated the country, and so Afghanistan is one of the few parts of the world still to be totally without railways. During 1975 possibilities of constructing a railway with Indian assistance were discussed. The plan is to link Kabul, Kandahar, Herat and Islamqala (on the Iranian frontier) with a line that would be 1,810 km. in length, at a cost of probably more than U.S. $2,000 million. A possible extension from Kabul to Zahidan in Iran and the Pakistan border is also under consideration. The narrowness (despite the great height) of the mountain barrier as compared with the Himalayas, has made Afghanistan a traditional routeway between north and south, and at present, helped by various foreign agencies and governments, there is a programme for considerable road improvement and development. Given the difficulties of terrain, Afghanistan now possesses a reasonably good road system, with some very good sections. Air transport is also an increasingly important factor, though growth has not been as rapid as anticipated. Better accessibility has also resulted in the growth of a small, but far from insignificant tourist traffic. Recent political upheavals, with near civil war in some areas, have however been a major adverse factor.

HISTORY

Kevin Rafferty

Afghanistan was never a colony in the sense of being ruled by a Western colonial power, but its present-day boundaries were imposed upon it by the Great Powers of this and the last century. It is a historic land, variously described as the "crossroads of the world" or "cockpit of Asia", but sorting out that history offers difficulties.

There is the problem first of all of working out what is or was Afghanistan. That is a much more difficult task than to do a similar exercise for, say, Thailand. The word "Afghanistan" means "the country of the Afghans", that is Pathans or Pushtuns. But in its modern sense, the country has existed only since 1747, though the name "Afghanistan" first appears in the tenth century referring to a land to the east of the present country and bounded by the Indus. Much more rewarding is to consider Afghanistan as the country of the Hindu Kush. In that sense, it links the West with the east of both India and China; it offers a back door to the Soviet Union. Countless merchants and invaders have crossed Afghanistan throughout history using the Oxus River (now called Amu-Dar'ya) and going through the narrow Hindu Kush passes and defiles. The famous "Silk Route" passed through the Hindu Kush when the caravan trail was already old. Alexander the Great followed the trail, as did merchants with indigo and Chinese silk, the nomads from the Steppes, Buddhist monks, Moghuls, and the often hard-pressed armies of the British Raj.

EARLY HISTORY

Considering the great waves of human history that have flowed over what is known today as Afghanistan, it is surprising that they left so little permanent trace behind. This makes piecing together the rich history of the area a very difficult task. Persians, Greeks, Indians, Chinese, Huns, Mongols, Moghuls and finally Europeans, pagans, Buddhists, Hindus, Muslims and Christians, believers in the power of one God, of many, and of none, all swept over Afghanistan and conquered and finally fell to local tribes who were themselves migrants in the stream of history.

The first mention in history of the area now covered by Afghanistan comes in about the sixth century B.C. when Darius I was on the throne of Persia. Modern Afghanistan was probably divided into three or four Achaemenian Satraps. It is probable that Bactria included the plain of Oxus, that Arachosia included Kandahar and Aria, the valleys around Herat. Another area, Drangiana, possibly included parts of south-west Afghanistan, and the regions of Sindhu and Ghandara were almost certainly present day Sind and the North West Frontier Province (with possibly a part of the Punjab) of Pakistan. Confirmation of some of these facts comes from Herodotus.

However, modern archaeological finds have led experts to conjecture that some Afghan cities may have pre-dated even the Persians. These include Balkh, the centre of Bactria. Because of its position as a water source on good natural routes it may have been an important place as early as the third Millenium when the lapis lazuli trade to Mesopotamia was just starting.

Afghanistan remained in Persian hands until Darius III was defeated by Alexander in the fourth century B.C. Alexander spent some years pacifying Afghanistan and setting up five cities including Kandahar, then called Alexandria. Modern Kandahar derives its name from the Arabic form of Alexander, Iskander. When Alexander died, his empire was split. Seleucus, one of Alexander's generals, took the eastern Satraps including the greater part of Afghanistan but since his centre of power lay to the west, he could not prevent the eastern areas of Afghanistan coming under control of the empire of Chandragupta Maurya from India. Some confirmation of Indian sway is provided by discovery of two so-called Asoka edicts near Kandahar.

In the end, Asia swallowed the Greeks. Only in Bactria did they flourish until the middle of the second century B.C. when nomads defeated them. By that time internal quarrels and the rise of a strong Parthia had weakened Bactria. However, some Greek rulers clung on in the more accessible areas and Greek influences lingered till the Christian era.

By the middle of the second century, three barbarian nomadic groups appear, the Hsiung-nu Huns, the Yuëh-chi, and the Saka. The Hsiung-nu defeated the Yuëh-chi and forced them to flee to the Afghanistan area. The Sakai settled around the Hindu Kush towards India. The history at this point is uncertain but eventually the Kushans, the dominant tribe in the Yuëh-chi confederacy, established a kingdom which, at its height, stretched from Bactria to the frontiers of China and down to Mathura in India. Peshawar, present day capital of Pakistan's North West Frontier Province, was the centre of the Kushan Empire. They fostered the arts and Buddhism, and developed the famous silk route through to China. But the Kushan Empire did not survive long and began to decline in the middle of the third century. Once again, the cockpit of Asia was plunged into confusion.

There were Kushan princes still ruling in various provinces. There were Sassanids, or Sassanians, challenging from Iran. There was a threatening Turco-Mongol confederacy. One Mongol group called Hephatalites (or White Huns) dominated for about a century and were particularly punishing of Buddhism. Then the Turks, allied to the Sassanids, defeated the Hephatalites and took over the area until the Chinese arrived in A.D. 658. But Chinese rule was shortlived because Arab armies had already reached the borders of Afghanistan.

The Arabs already had possession of Herat and Balkh by the time the Chinese gained control of eastern Afghanistan. The Turks and the Chinese successively weakened each other so that there was no outside resistance to the Arabs. Even so it took a long time before the whole of Afghanistan to the Hindu Kush came under the sway of Islam. Parts of the east were not converted until the ninth century and the centre until the eleventh.

Again the area of Afghanistan went through a succession of changing dynasties as the Caliphate weakened and various men claiming nominal allegiance to the Caliph were able to carve out a kingdom for themselves. There were Tahirids followed by Safarids and Samanids. The next empire was that of Mahmud of Ghazni. He came to power in A.D. 998, brought all Afghanistan under his rule, conquered the Punjab as far as Multan, and conducted seventeen annual raids into India where he exacted vast treasures. His court was a glorious one and included such people as Firdausi the poet and Albiruni the polymath. But the Ghaznavid empire also proved the corrupting influence of power and the instability of dynastic rule. It had been founded by Mahmud's grandfather when he, a former Turkish slave, Alptigin, displaced the local ruler of Ghazni. The Ghaznavid empire crumbled because Mahmud's successors did not have his brilliance. The Ghaznavids themselves came under pressure of the Seljuks, a tribe of the Ghuzz who seized Khorassan. But it was another group, the Ghorids, who moved in and sacked Ghazni in 1152 under the leadership of Ala-ud-din Husayn.

The Ghorids came from the obscure hill country up the Hari Rud from Herat, an area which had remained isolated and extremely poor. Their empire was also shortlived and Ala-ud-din Husayn was driven out by the Seljuks. Then his nephews Mu'izzud-din (Mohammad of Ghor) and Ghiyas-ud-Din drove to Ghazni again and carved out a shortlived empire reaching from Herat to Ajmer in India. The Ghorids have extra importance because their general Qutub-ud-din Rybik became Sultan of Delhi when the Indian possession became cut off from those near the Hindu Kush. The Qutub-Minar in Delhi is named after him.

No sooner had Mohammad of Ghor died than the empire fell apart before the armies of Sultan Ala-ud-din Mohammad, known as the Khwarezm Shah. For a brief time his dynasty had an empire extending from Chinese Turkestan westward to the borders of Iraq. He was able to mount an invasion of Baghdad early in the thirteenth century. However, he had hardly reached his destination when he learnt that his dominion was being threatened by yet another invasion, this time from the Mongol Genghis Khan. Genghis Khan had consolidated his grip on Mongolia by 1206 and then started looking for fresh fields to conquer. By 1216, he had extended his rule to the Sinkiang Province of present day China, bordering on the Karakorams and the Hindu Kush mountains, and started to come south. Mohammad of Khwarezm had 400,000 cavalry under his command but did not consider this enough to face Genghis Khan's hordes who by this time had seized parts of Trans-Oxiana and were spreading destruction and death before them. He turned and retreated to the Caspian. Only his son, Jalal-ud-din, was prepared to face the Mongols and, using Ghazni as his headquarters, he managed to inflict two defeats on the Mongols before being defeated himself. Genghis Khan himself turned to give siege to Bamiyan (the historic Buddhist city which today has the largest Buddha in the world, a 175-ft. high statue carved out of the rock). In the siege Genghis Khan's grandson was killed and that so infuriated the Mongol that he laid Bamiyan utterly waste. By 1222 the whole of Afghanistan was in Genghis Khan's hands and was made to pay dreadfully for its resistance.

More than a century passed before a coherent administration was again established. When the legendary Kubilai Khan came to the throne, Afghanistan suffered once more because, although one of its local leaders supported Kubilai Khan, the other sided against him.

Genghis Khan's empire once more proved to be a personal one. It did not long survive his death in 1227 and fell quickly into a series of petty kingdoms. Timur the Lame (Tamurlane), however, reunited the country and its armies in the 14th century and continued on a violent course. However, his successors, the Timurites, based in Herat, brought an era of peace and stability and patronage of learning and the arts.

This rule, once more, was shortlived. War and warring was never far from the Hindu Kush. The Uzbecs, a Turkic people, entered Herat in 1507 and drove out Babur, a direct descendant of Genghis Khan and Timur. Babur fell back on Kabul from which he was to found the great Moghul empire. From his Kabul base, he took Kandahar before turning towards India. Having defeated the last of the Lodi Afghan kings of India at Panipat, north of Delhi, he transferred the capital to Agra. However, he did not forget Kabul and when he died in 1530, his body was returned there.

The shifting of Babur's base to Agra stretched Moghul rule in Afghanistan and they had to yield areas to the Safavids of Persia. Kandahar was disputed between the two. The early 18th century offered the Pathans their first taste of power. For a brief while, when Ghilzai Mir Wais revolted against the declining Safavids, they ruled even Persia itself. But then the Persians hit back. In 1736 Nadir Kuli Khan, a brigand, proclaimed himself as Nadir Shah, ruler of Persia. He extended his rule through Afghanistan and went on to sack Delhi and carry away the famous peacock throne and Koh-i-Noor diamond. But once again that empire did not survive its founder.

THE TRANSITION TO MODERN AFGHANISTAN

Nadir Shah was obviously impressed by the Pathans and placed them in high positions in his empire. This enabled them to seize power for themselves in the confusion following the assassination of Nadir Shah in 1747. An Afghan chief of the Sadozai clan, Ahmed Khan Abduli, took a contingent of some several thousand Afghans and was elected king in Kandahar with the title Dur-i-duran (pearl of the age) from which the dynastic name Durrani was derived. He built up his rule in the area now known as Afghanistan and was also able to exact tribute from the adjoining areas of Kashmir, Sind and Baluchistan. When he died, he was succeeded by his son Timur who moved the capital from Kandahar to Kabul. On Timur's death it seemed once again that another empire would break into fragments. He left 20 sons who squabbled for the throne, lost territory in the north to the Uzbecs, and other parts to other feuding families. The Sadozans sought alliance with the Barakzais (Mohammedzais), another powerful clan, betrayed them, and were driven to Herat by the Barakzais. At this point, Afghan rule really looked in disarray with Sikhs attacking from the east and signs of unrest from the Persians in the west.

In Ghazni, Dost Mohammad, the youngest of the Barakzai brothers had come to the fore. He went on to take Kabul, thus inviting the attention of the British who were inevitably concerned about Afghanistan which they regarded as the key to India. They distrusted Dost Mohammad, tried to replace him by the Sadozai, Shah Shuja, and involved themselves in the bitter first Afghan war. Only after the disastrous retreat from Kabul and massacre in 1842 did the British realize the error of their ways. They allowed Dost Mohammad to go back and take the throne, Shah Shuja having been killed by his own people as the British left.

Dost Mohammad ruled Afghanistan for 20 years and won the title of Amir-i-Kabir (the Great Amir). He named his third son Sher Ali to succeed him. Sher Ali spent the first few years establishing himself over his brothers. Then in the late 1870s he upset the British when he received a Russian mission in Kabul but refused to welcome a British one on the same terms. This led to the second British-Afghan War from 1878–81 in which the British captured Jalalabad and Kandahar. Sher Ali fled and died leaving his son as regent. Yaqub in 1879 agreed to receive a British embassy at Kabul and to conduct his foreign policy with the "wishes and advice of the British Government".

However, in September 1879, the British envoy and his companion were murdered in Kabul, so British forces again occupied Kabul, exiled Yaqub and in 1880 recognized a grandson of Dost Mohammad, Abdurrahman Khan, as Amir of Kabul. Just as they prepared to leave the capital, they learnt that a British force in Meilwand near Kandahar had been wiped out, so once again they returned with a vengeance and seized Kandahar. This intervention ceased in 1881, when a change of government in London led to the abandoning of the "forward policy". Abdurrahman remained on the throne where he organized the Government despotically, converted the Kafir areas by force, and renamed them Nuristan, and agreed to the Durand line effectively establishing the modern-day boundary between British India and Afghanistan. The British had taken the Khyber Pass as part of the spoils of the second Afghan war. In October 1901, Abdurrahman died and was succeeded by his eldest son Habibullah Khan.

MODERN AFGHANISTAN

It is worth considering what kind of country Emir Abdurrahman took over. His boundaries were fixed for him by the Great Powers of British India and Imperial Russia. The Afghanistan he tried to wield into shape was by no means a nation state in the European sense of the term. It contained large numbers of people who did not speak the same language. Most Afghans owed their first loyalties to their tribe which had its own much longer and more personal history. Moreover, tribal groupings often spilled over to the neighbouring countries. Even the majority Pathan tribes straddled Afghanistan and British India. There were Baluch in Afghanistan whose cousins and nearest kinfolk were in Iran or British India. There were Turkomen, Uzbecs, Tajiks, Kirghiz, the majority of whom were in Imperial Russian territory but who also had large numbers in modern Afghanistan.

In terms of language, Afghanistan was—and is—a living tower of Babel. Its Indo-European languages include Pushtu, Dari (the Afghan Farsi), the language of the Tajiks, Farsiwan, the Hezaras, Qizilbash and Aimaq, as well as Nuristani, Dardic and Pamir dialects. Also the Mongolian peoples speak Uralic-Altaic languages of which the subgroups include Kirghizi and the tongue of the Uzbecs. Moreover the Brahui tribes speak a totally different language, a Dravidian one which is akin to those of South India.

Although its external boundaries were fixed by outsiders who wanted Afghanistan as a buffer state, the internal power of the emir was by no means secure. The tribal leaders were conscious that they had established Afghanistan and the Durrani dynasty by electing the first ruler so as the better to protect their territory against outsiders. It was a difficult task for the emir to judge the extent of his powers.

Emir Abdurrahman solved all of these problems by a rough policy, a sort of imperialism from within. He built up a strong army led by Ghulam-Harda Charkhi and was not afraid to conduct more than a dozen major campaigns which he called "civil wars". He eliminated tribal leaders who opposed him, confiscated their weapons, levelled their forts, and, if necessary, held their sons hostage to prevent their fathers waging war again. He pushed the administration into rural areas and tried to make officials loyal to him.

He did not forget the influence of the religious leaders. He made the mullahs take tests in religious knowledge to prove their claims and the number of Islamic religious leaders dwindled. The emir did not live to have to face the repercussions of this brutal policy which, for example, produced a concentration of religious power in the hands of a smaller number of mullahs.

He also provided for his succession by naming his son Habibullah. The transition was smooth. There was no civil war and Habibullah began the arduous journey to the modern world by opening schools and factories, building roads and encouraging a weekly paper written in Persian. In foreign affairs Habibullah observed a careful neutrality. But there was evidence that Emir Abdurrahman had simply squashed the opposition but not extinguished it. This flared up when Habibullah was assassinated in 1919 near Jalalabad.

For a while there was turmoil in Afghanistan, which was settled when Habibullah's third son, Amanullah Khan, won himself the succession largely by seizing the treasury. He immediately declared Afghanistan to be completely independent in both internal and external affairs, a pronouncement which led to the third war between Afghanistan and Britain. The fighting was inconclusive but did lead to a peace in which the independence of Afghanistan was recognized and diplomatic relations opened with both Britain and the Soviet Union.

The new King Amanullah was an unusual man who persisted in his radicalism even when he had power. He tried to push through a series of reforms including the unveiling of women; the removal of parents' rights to betroth their children; the dismissal of government officials who wanted to have more than one wife; the curbing of the rights of the religious leaders and the introduction of secular laws in preference to the Islamic Shariah. In all this he showed a dashing sense of action and awareness of how to bring Afghanistan into the modern world; it was accompanied by an unmatched political naiveté in thinking that this was the way to do it. He learned that he could not ride roughshod over both vested tribal and Islamic chieftains. In the end the tribal and religious leaders joined forces against him and again Afghanistan was plunged into civil war. In January 1929 Kabul was seized by Baccha-i-Saqao, a brigand, and Amanullah abdicated. He tried to come back, failed, and left for exile in Italy. The Baccha held Kabul for a nine-month reign of terror before being driven off by Amanullah's cousin, Mohammad Nadir Khan, a former war minister, and his brothers. In the general assembly held soon afterwards, Nadir Khan was elected king as Nadir Shah. He tried to consolidate the country, but was assassinated in November 1933.

Surprisingly the changeover proved easy and Nadir's son, Mohammad Zahir, took over as king at the age of 19.

The long reign of Zahir Shah was marked throughout by its caution. For the first 20 years he was strongly under the influence of his three uncles, Hashim Khan, Shah Mahmud and Shah Wali Khan. They had shown remarkable forbearance in allowing Zahir to come to the throne in the first place. However, the arrangement not to squabble for the throne was helpful to them because with King Zahir there, he reigned while they ruled.

In 1953 Mohammad Daoud Khan, a cousin of the king, challenged the surviving and ageing uncles, Shah Mahmud and Shah Wali Khan, who allowed him to become Prime Minister although they were uneasy and distrusted his zeal. The main impact of the new prime minister was one of vigour in starting a series of five-year economic plans. The price, said critics, was in bringing the cold war in economic terms to Afghanistan. He did this by playing off the U.S.A. and the Soviet Union to obtain aid.

In 1956 Sardar Daoud obtained the approval of the Loya Jirga (tribal council) to accept military aid from the Soviet Union. He was able to do this only by claiming that Washington had refused a request for military assistance. The request had been made by the pre-Daoud Government and had included the proviso that Afghanistan must have a security guarantee of its border. Washington had pointed to the huge undefended frontier with the Soviet Union and said that such a guarantee would be meaningless, so Moscow furnished the military aid and came to provide the backbone of Afghanistan's forces.

Sardar Daoud also pressed the Pashtunistan issue against Pakistan, in this way raising the nationalistic spirit which made it easier to get the Soviet arms accepted. He also used military aid to modernize and strengthen the armed forces and thus tighten the grip of Kabul on the whole country. But there were fears that Sardar Daoud was taking too much power in his own hands and in 1963 the King forced his resignation.

For 10 years Sardar Daoud sat on the sidelines. The new man, Dr. Mohammed Yusuf, the first non-royal Prime Minister—and a non-Pathan, too—prepared a new constitution to bring democracy to Afghanistan, but it floundered on a rigid separation of powers, and Parliament became a battleground for the Government and the tribes. The King, autocratic and annoyed at the continual airing of grievances, refused to allow political parties. He had a succession of Prime Ministers, none of whom enjoyed independent power; this only made matters worse. The country remained backward, with 85 per cent of its people excluded from politics and modern life. But in Kabul there was a restless élite also excluded from power looking on at parliamentary squabbling and a corrupt, slow-moving bureaucracy.

POLITICAL CHANGES SINCE 1973

In 1973 an era of political change began and has proved quite as turbulent as any in the past. Not for the first time, Moscow entered the fray, but this time more powerfully than before. Events started bloodlessly enough. King Zahir, who was in Italy, learnt on July 17th, 1973, that he had been deposed in a *coup d'état*. His cousin and brother-in-law, Mohammad Daoud, was the best-known figure in the coup and took office as Head of State, also becoming Prime Minister, Foreign Minister and Minister of Defence. The new President Daoud abolished the monarchy and declared the country a Republic.

The coup of 1973 was clearly a "palace revolution". There is no doubt that there were many critics of the Government of King Zahir but these were probably irrelevant to events except in ensuring that there was not much opposition to the palace plotters. King Zahir's Government had become overwhelmed by its own hesitations and lack of decisiveness and this lack of progress made for acceptance of the new regime. Sardar Daoud was able to say at his first news conference, "I can safely say that this was in every sense of the word a bloodless coup. It not only enjoyed the co-operation of the army but also the support of all the people particularly the intellectuals and the youths".

For all the change of regime and its promised need for a new approach, changes were slow in coming. President Daoud seemed to be ultra-conscious of the need to take with him "the Afghan people and the Afghan nation" and to be more conservative than when he was Prime Minister under King Zahir.

When President Daoud took over, there were arguments as to whether the coup had been engineered by the Soviet Union or whether the Russians were merely the beneficiaries of President Daoud's return to power. But, despite this, as time wore on the new President showed that he was much more his own man.

In dealing with the Soviet Union, his powerful neighbour to the north, President Daoud showed great skill. When he came to power it was felt in some Western chancelleries that Afghanistan was in danger of becoming a Soviet satellite. But the President proved careful to put Afghan nationalism first, and diplomats from other developing countries expressed envy about how he managed to collect aid from both east and west without being beholden to either.

Early in 1977 President Daoud revealed the long-awaited framework for his new Republic, its constitution, which was adopted by the Loya Jirgah ("great tribal assembly"). The constitution was presidential in form, and Mohammad Daoud was acclaimed as the first President of the Republic. It aimed "to secure democracy based on social justice and the interests of the people, to respect human liberty and dignity and to eliminate all forms of torture and discrimination". The constitution provided for the establishment of a Meli Jirgah (National Assembly), the members of which would be nominated by the country's only political party, the *Hezbe Enqelabe Meli* (National Revolutionary Party), and then elected through "free, universal, secret and direct elections".

In many ways the new Republican constitution was not as far-reaching as the old constitution of 1964 which was not put into effect and was scrapped by the Republic. Recruitment of members for the political party began but was halted for a time in 1977 and after the 1978 coup the constitution became academic.

As his rule went on, President Daoud presented a public face of confidence. He visited Pakistan in early 1978 and there seemed to be hope of an end to the long-running border dispute between the two countries. Afghanistan had consistently refused to accept the British Durand line as its border with Pakistan (which inherited the western boundary of the old British Indian Empire). The Afghans remembered that they had Pathan brothers on the Pakistan side of the border and could not forget the days when the Afghan empire had a stronghold in Peshawar (capital of Pakistan's North West Frontier Province), not to speak of territories further east.

But at home, though he clearly did not realize it, the President's position was shaky. He had hardly returned from Pakistan when there were demonstrations that led to his downfall. The murder, by still unknown assailants, of Mir Akbar Khyber, a pro-Moscow trade union leader, brought thousands of people onto the streets outside the U.S. Embassy in Kabul shouting slogans against the CIA and SAVAK (the Iranian secret police). President Daoud, who had previously been tolerant of the Left (perhaps afraid of upsetting his Soviet neighbours), this time reacted with a series of anti-Communist swoops. He arrested some leaders, including Nur Mohammad Taraki of the banned People's Democratic Party. But the official intelligence net missed others and after 10 days, on April 27th, 1978, the opposition struck back and overthrew and killed Mohammad Daoud.

The Soviet-trained air force and sections of the army turned against President Daoud. Tanks rolled out and Soviet-built MiG aircraft strafed the Presidential palace. After a bloody 18-hour battle Air Force Col. (later Gen.) Abdul Qadir proclaimed that the Nadir Shah family had been liquidated and power transferred to "the people". The rebels brought Taraki out of prison and installed him as President and Prime Minister of a country with its name changed from the Republic of Afghanistan to the Democratic Republic of Afghanistan.

President Taraki claimed that only 72 or 73 people had been killed in the changeover—compared with a Western consensus of 2,000 to 3,000 dead, and initial exaggerated Press reports ranging as high as 10,000. To some extent he also tried to minimize the changes by declaring that Afghanistan wanted good relations with both East and West, though he added that "our friendship depends on the amount of support given to us".

First signs of sweeping changes soon appeared. The new regime conducted a thorough purge of important ministeries which included Daoud men and Mohammadzai clan members. The police, who had been loyal to the old regime, suffered in particular. Arrests ran to thousands, including the Muslim Rightists who had also been a target for President Daoud.

President Taraki delcared that Afghanistan would not become a Soviet satellite, but ties with Moscow grew stronger. The U.S.S.R. and its East European allies were the first to recognize the new rulers. Increasing numbers of Soviet advisers began to appear in Kabul. By the end of 1978 there was at least one in each ministry, and Soviet assistance to the armed forces was stepped up. Altogether there were more than 3,000 Soviet personnel in Kabul by 1979 and some shops in the Afghan capital put up signs in Russian script as well as in the local languages.

In spite of the popular disillusionment with the Daoud regime, the new rulers soon ran into their own difficulties, some of which were of their own making. Dissensions within the ruling People's Democratic Party ranks quickly appeared. Deputy Premier Babrak Karmal and five senior colleagues belonging to the Parcham wing were the first to be removed from the Government in mid-1978. Their subsequent whereabouts were a mystery: because of Babrak Karmal's reputation as a pro-Moscow hard-liner, some reports said that he was safely in Eastern Europe and might emerge if the Taraki Government met further problems. In August 1978, a plot against Taraki was discovered and Gen. Abdul Qadir, the Defence Minister, and his Army Chief were arrested and imprisoned. It was not clear whether the men had been pursuing a personal quarrel or whether, as a popular rumour in Kabul put it, they had spoken out too loudly against increasing Soviet influence in Afghanistan.

Taraki's Soviet connections were certainly causing him trouble. Numbers of influential mullahs denounced the "godlessness" of the Government and, as 1978 went on, a grumbling rebellion began to spread from the remoter tribal areas. By 1979 this was serious enough to be costing the time and lives of Afghan soldiers. The Government was able to control the towns, but then in February rebels managed to kidnap the U.S. Ambassador in the heart of Kabul. He and they were killed as Afghan security forces stormed the hotel where the envoy was held. In April the Government was further shaken by a rebellion in the army garrison at Herat. President Taraki attempted to blame Iran and Pakistan for the troubles in Afghanistan.

Government policies appeared to do little to relieve the pressure. Major land reforms, marriage reforms and debt relief decrees further inflamed the mullahs and defenders of the old order. Heavy-handed tactics in trying to put down the rebellion, including the use of artillery and bombs against villages harbouring opponents, stiffened the rebels' resistance. In the refugee camps just across the border in Pakistan former Afghan army officers were training new recruits to fight against the Taraki Government.

In April 1979 the rulers of Afghanistan made public admission of their difficulties by reconstituting the Government. Deputy Premier Hafezollah Amin took over as Prime Minister and a nine-member Supreme Defence Council was set up. The Kremlin also showed its alarm about murders of Soviet advisers by beginning the evacuation of women and children from Kabul back to the Soviet Union.

ECONOMIC SURVEY

Kevin Rafferty

The greatest problem of trying to present an accurate economic profile of Afghanistan is that it is a backward, underdeveloped country where correct information is hard to come by. Only 10 per cent of the people can read or write. (All figures must be subject to scepticism because there has never been a proper census of population.) Some economic statistics are published but they tend to be at best out of date and even then not very reliable. And since more than 80 per cent of the people of Afghanistan are rural or nomadic, scattered in remote villages dotted over the predominantly mountain and desert countryside, it is doubtful how much they are affected by government or anyone else's Western-style "guesstimates" of what is their economic performance.

Assessment of Gross National Product (G.N.P.), for example, illustrates the difficulties. In its seven-year economic and social development plan, published in 1976, the Government estimated G.N.P. for the Afghan year 1355* at Afs. 115,000 million. This is about U.S. $2,600 million. However, some non-Afghan economists would say that such G.N.P. estimates are too high. American sources, for example, think that U.S. $1,500 million would be a more reasonable estimate of G.N.P.

That is only the start of the problems of dealing with Afghanistan's statistics. There is the difficulty that no one really knows the size of the population, except that it is somewhere between 12 and 18 million (late 1970s). The Government's own figures would have surpassed 20 million by 1976 were it not for the fact that a substantial downward revision was made in mid-1976 to bring the estimated population to almost 17 million people, of whom 2.4 million were estimated to be nomads. Such a figure would give a per capita G.N.P. of about U.S. $160 by 1979. This was the figure used by such organizations as the World Bank. But it may be that the population is a good deal lower than 17 million. A UN study suggested 12 or 13 million in 1976, but that report has been withdrawn as the Afghans say that it was based on too small a sample and had other drawbacks. There is a problem, though, with all Afghanistan statistics and even such a figure has to be set alongside extensive and extreme poverty.

For much of the period since 1960 Afghanistan's economy has been stagnant. During the 1960s and early 1970s the rate of growth in real terms was below the rate of population increase. The years 1970 and 1971 marked the nadir as the serious droughts caused a 20 per cent drop in wheat production and killed livestock in large numbers. Since then economic performance has picked up. Better rains have pushed the annual wheat crop to about 3 million tons so that in

* This corresponds to the year 1976/77, since the Afghanistan year runs from March 21st to March 20th of the following year.

a normal year Afghanistan is self-sufficient in food production. Industrial performance has improved. Capital inflows pushed the foreign exchange reserves from U.S. $22 million at the end of 1974 to $259 million at the end of 1977 and led to an appreciation in the value of the afghani to 39 per U.S. dollar by late 1978, compared with 80.50 in 1972/73. By the late 1970s the time had come for a serious attempt to be made at planning Afghanistan's future economic development, taking into account all the disadvantages imaginable in a poor, land-locked country.

THE START OF ECONOMIC PLANNING

Prior to the 1930s Afghanistan was still in the Middle Ages as far as economic development was concerned. The great armies and trade caravans of ancient times had struggled over it, but modern development had ignored it because, with the coming of sea power from the fifteenth century onwards, there were less arduous ways to India and China than through Afghanistan and the cold, high, dangerous Hindu Kush passes. Even the railway age bypassed Afghanistan. Only in 1932 when the Banke Millie Afghan (National Bank) was established did modern economic development begin. Before that the only modern features were the Government's workshops in Kabul chiefly intended to attend to the needs of the army, and one small hydro-electric station. The formation of the bank gave an impetus to the foundation of private companies. These were mainly dealing in trade for karakul and lamb skins and wool, but textile and sugar companies were also set up. However, progress was slow and even at the end of the Second World War, internal trade was carried by caravan and inter-city roads were not paved. Only about 20,000 kilowatts of power was produced and few consumer goods were made locally.

In 1946, the new Prime Minister, Shah Mahmud Khan, began what he wanted to develop as an ambitious economic development programme using Afghanistan's agricultural exports as its base. But he failed for lack of finance. He hoped that the U.S. would provide the major part of the $100 million foreign component of the $450 million plan to develop industry, extend hydro-electricity and irrigation programmes and introduce better education and health care. After negotiations the U.S. Export-Import Bank was prepared to lend $21 million for three dams and followed it up by another $18.5 million loan for similar work.

The next attempt to start economic planning came when Mohammad Daoud took over as Prime Minister in 1953. Again, he ran into problems in finding foreign finance, and Washington refused to lend general support to the first five-year plan which got under way in 1957. It was ready only to provide money for individual projects. However, the Prime Minister, Daoud, neatly sidestepped that problem by improving relations with the Soviet Union and delicately playing off the U.S.S.R. and the U.S.A. so that the U.S.A. closely followed and almost matched Soviet aid to Afghanistan. Moscow was prepared to underwrite a general five-year exercise. In all, between 1957 and 1972 the Soviet Union offered more than $900 million to support these plans, that is nearly 60 per cent of foreign aid, although some Western experts say that the sums promised were larger than the money handed over. The U.S.A. provided the second largest amount of aid but it usually offered better terms.

The first three plans (from 1957 to 1961 for the first; 1962 to 1967 for the second; 1968 to 1972 for the third) cannot really be described as an attempt to control the whole economy, though the Government described the economy as its "guided economy" and later "mixed guided economy". The plans offered a series of projects basically to improve the infrastructure and bring Afghanistan at least closer to the twentieth century.

The first plan set the pattern by putting great emphasis on communications, particularly road building and the establishment of air links, both national and international. In addition, 32 industrial projects were due to begin, though not all were started. The achievements of the first plan were patchy. Its great merits were the attempt to establish planned economy development, to tap external sources of finance, and at the same time to realize the need for internal finance. The great drawback was that this daring in planning was not matched by daring or so much success in implementation.

By the time of the second plan, the difficulties of the planning were beginning to be apparent, at least to outsiders. Proper cost-benefit studies were neglected, and the impact of projects on income and job opportunities was virtually ignored. The second plan also attempted to expand the role of the public sector because private industry was not big enough to undertake developments in power, gas, supply and making of cement, chemicals, and other important capital intensive industry. One problem which was not properly examined beforehand was where to find competent operators and managers to run the plants.

At the start of the third plan, the Government reviewed the achievements and the lessons of the first two plans and emphasized the need to turn to more quickly yielding projects. However, in practice Afghanistan discovered that the ability to switch was more difficult than stating the intentions to switch.

For all this, 16 years of planning and public investment of Afs. 53,000 million produced an impressive list of achievements. Before planning started there were no paved roads in Afghanistan, few permanent bridges and air transport was almost non-existent. By the end of the third plan, in 1972, the country had 2,780 kilometres of paved roads and two international and 29 local airports. Dams and bridges were constructed. Registration of motor vehicles in Kabul went up from 16,000 in 1962 to 52,000 in 1971. In industry, production of cotton cloth quadrupled to 62 million metres, cement making and shoe manufacturing began, and output of the soap, sugar and coal industries increased by between 100 and 300 per cent. Electricity production rose almost nine-fold to 422.6

million kilowatt hours. Natural gas production was started and reached 2,635 million cubic metres annually, much of which is exported to the Soviet Union. There were big achievements in education where the number of schools rose from 804 to nearly 4,000, teachers from 4,000 to 20,000, and students from 125,000 to 700,000. Industrial employment rose from 18,000 in 1962 to nearly 27,000 in 1971. More than 60 private enterprise industries were set up employing nearly 5,000 people.

The fourth plan was published in 1973 and looked again to Soviet help as its mainstay but the planning procedure was disrupted by the coup and actual planning was on an annual basis. By 1976 an ambitious seven-year plan was announced, but before it had time to take effect President Daoud was overthrown in the April 1978 coup and the future of the plan became uncertain.

THE ECONOMY IN THE LATE 1970s

Agriculture

Agriculture is the most important contributor to Afghanistan's economy today, providing half the national income and four-fifths of the country's exports. Of the total land area of about 65 million hectares, 8 million hectares are considered to be arable, only half of which are cultivated every year. Experts estimate that a mere 2.6 million hectares of irrigated land provide 85 per cent of the crops. Irrigation is often primitive but ingenious. The impact of lack of water was shown sharply in 1971 when there was severe drought as a result of which the production of wheat, the main crop, dropped from nearly 2.5 million tons to below 2 million tons and millions of important livestock were slaughtered. It took two years for the crops to recover but production of wheat rose to 2,750,000 tons in 1974/75 and to 2,936,000 tons in 1976/77. Since then poorer weather has caused crop yields to fall again. Wheat production was 2,830,000 tons in 1978/79 and again doubts arise about Afghanistan's recovering its ability to feed itself.

Equally impressive was the rise in the output of seed cotton from 71,000 tons in 1968 to 159,000 tons in 1976. For cotton, too, 1976 was the high point. In 1977/78 production fell to 137,000 tons before rising to 153,000 tons the following year. Other crops also suffered after 1976/77. Fruit production dropped to 692,000 tons from 900,000 before recovering to 824,000 tons in 1978/79; barley was 325,000 tons in 1978/79 compared with the 1976/77 record of 400,000 tons; maize was 20,000 tons below the 800,000 tons reached in 1976/77; and paddy rice production was 428,000 tons, compared with 448,000 tons achieved in 1976/77. Of the industrial crops, sugar production was steady from 1976/77 to 1978/79, with beet output at almost 100,000 tons and cane at 64,000 tons. But oilseeds also fell victim to the weather and output was 35,000 tons in 1978/79, compared with 62,000 tons in 1976/77.

The severe drought of 1970 and 1971 is estimated to have cost between 30 per cent and 50 per cent of Afghanistan's livestock which in 1970 were estimated at 6.5 million karakul sheep, 15 million ordinary sheep, 3.7 million cattle, 3.2 million goats and 500,000 horses. By 1975 they were estimated to have increased to the 1970 levels.

Industry

Although its series of economic plans set up modern industry and took Afghanistan out of the handicraft age, the contribution of industry to the gross domestic product is small, less than 10 per cent. Handicrafts, especially carpet making and weaving, still contribute more to G.D.P. than modern industry. Industrial employment has hardly changed since 1971 when it was estimated that 27,000 people had paid jobs out of the total working population of about 4 million. Even the oldest established and largest industry, cotton textiles, is not able yet to produce enough cloth—output was 73.7 million metres in 1976/77—to satisfy domestic demand. Cement production fell to 125,000 tons in 1976/77 which was higher than the 1971 trough of 73,000 tons, but well below the 1966 peak of 174,000 tons. Changes in construction activity are responsible for these fluctuations. In 1972, owing to government concern to expand new industries, an Industrial Development Bank was established. The Daoud Government said that it was anxious to encourage private enterprise, but subject to government surveillance. There are only five private-sector industrial companies with more than 200 employees, the largest being a tannery and shoe factory of 500 workers.

Mining

Afghanistan has extensive mining resources of coal, salt, chrome, iron ore, silver, gold, fluorite, talc, mica, copper and lapis lazuli, but the country's problems of access and transport have posed questions about whether it is worth mining them. The most successful find has been of natural gas, most of which is piped to the Soviet Union in payment for imports and debts. Production may soon rise to 4,000 million cubic metres per year, compared with 2,546 million in 1976/77, a fall on the previous four years. However, unless new gas finds are made the existing fields may be exhausted some time before the turn of the century. Other minerals have been more disappointing. Coal production reached a peak of 164,000 tons in 1970/71 and lapis lazuli has varied between 5 and 10 tons per year. Chrome and salt are also mined.

Iron ore reserves at Hajigak in Bamiyan province, with 1,700 million tons of high-grade ore (62 per cent), are the most promising of recent discoveries. However, although the ore would fetch a good price, much of it is located at heights of 3,500 metres or more. Moreover, there would be high costs involved in exporting it from remote Afghanistan, which has no sea-port of its own, nor even rail lines. There are hopes that the iron and natural gas could be used to make steel, but this had not been realized by 1978. Another potentially important mineral is copper, with estimated reserves of 4.7 million tons of ore.

Trade

Afghanistan's trade is small although it shows a growing deficit, with exports valued at U.S. $330 million in 1978/79 and imports at $470 million. The balance of payments has shown a surplus, thanks to tourism and remittances from Afghans working abroad. The main export items are fresh fruit and vegetables to Pakistan and India, natural gas to the Soviet Union, karakul to the fur markets of Europe, and carpets and rugs, raw cotton and dried fruits and nuts, which are just beginning to make inroads into the developed country markets.

Imports include machinery, petroleum oil, pharmaceuticals, textiles and other consumer goods. Afghanistan is in the happy position, practically unique to the poor non-oil-producing countries, in that its oil-producing neighbours, Iran and the Soviet Union, have provided it with oil at low prices. Exports of natural gas mean that Afghanistan has a surplus of U.S. $20 million on its energy account.

Afghanistan's main trading partner is the Soviet Union, which in 1977/78 provided 26 per cent of imports and took 37 per cent of the country's exports. Japan increased its exports to Afghanistan to over U.S. $100 million in 1977/78, sixty times the value of Japan's imports, becoming the largest single exporter to Afghanistan. Afghanistan has been able to maintain large imports with the help of foreign aid, but this has recently begun to cause strains on foreign exchange because of heavy repayments and Kabul has had to ask for its debts to be rescheduled. In an attempt to resolve trade problems caused by Afghanistan's lack of a sea-port, a London firm began a weekly sea/rail/road container service to Kabul via the U.S.S.R. in 1976. This 40-day service is faster than the sea route via Karachi and less cumbersome than the overland route where customs have to be cleared at the border.

Money and Finance

The slow growth of the economy has created difficulties in raising the Government's internal revenues and the budget deficit has risen steadily. Half of the ordinary revenues come from indirect taxes. The next largest contributor is revenue from natural gas (almost 20 per cent). Only 10 per cent of the revenues comes from direct taxes. In 1978/79 domestic revenues were estimated at Afs. 15,684 million, leaving a huge deficit of Afs. 9,196 million, a rise of Afs. 2,400 million. Highest expenditure was on defence, accounting for almost 40 per cent. Social services were allocated 34 per cent of the budget.

In 1975 the Government decreed that all banks in Afghanistan had been nationalized in an attempt to bring about a more organized banking system. The move was directed at the Banke Millie Afghan, as the other banks were already under government control. The chief bank is the Da Afghanistan Bank, the central bank which also does commercial business.

Tourism

In recent years tourism has been an important contributor to Afghanistan's earnings, raising up to $10 million a year from visitors who numbered between 90,000 and 100,000 a year. The peak was 113,000 in 1971. At one time Afghanistan had the reputation of being a "hippy paradise" particularly because drugs could be obtained cheaply and are freely used locally. But this has been curbed and embassies will refuse to grant visas to people who look as if they cannot support themselves. But so far Afghanistan's location off the main air routes of the world and its poor hotel facilities (apart from two international hotels in Kabul) has meant that it has not been able to tap the lucrative Western package holiday market. Its main tourist visitors are travellers going overland to or from Pakistan and India. The development of tourism also suffered from the change of regime and internal unrest, which sharply curbed the number of visitors in 1978 and 1979.

The Seven-year Plan and After

In 1976 President Daoud inaugurated an ambitious Seven-year Economic and Social Development Plan intended to make major strides towards solving the problems of poverty and underdevelopment. The Plan is academic now because of the change of government. Given the political setbacks to the economy, its targets—to increase G.N.P. by more than 50 per cent by 1983, with annual growth rates of 6.3 per cent or double those of the past—also seem hopelessly optimistic.

Two things about the Plan are still worth noting. It aimed to bring Afghanistan into the railway age, through a U.S. $2,000 million project to build a 1,800-kilometres system linking with Iran in the west and with Pakistan, at Spin Boldak, in the east. Economically, it was a doubtful venture; politically, it is now dead because of the distrust of Afghanistan's neighbours.

The other factor was that Daoud saw the main thrust of development effort coming from the public sector and the main assistance coming from the U.S.S.R. The relationship of the State to private enterprise was rather paternal. The plan stated that: "The Republican State will encourage, protect, guide and control private investments and enterprises in the sphere of small and medium-level industries as well as handicrafts, and, in order to ensure harmonious and balanced growth of the national economy, will effect co-ordination and co-operation between the investments in the public and private sectors."

Western experts have pleaded that if Afghanistan wished to release the energies of the majority of its people it must be prepared to allow private enterprise to develop and not concentrate on expensive state-run capital-intensive projects. They advise also that there should be more emphasis on regional and rural development. Such changes might help the planners and decision-makers to appreciate that, in spite of truly impressive achievements in and around the main towns, the lives of 85 per cent of the country's population have been hardly changed.

The new Taraki Government quickly formulated plans to tackle the problems of this 85 per cent of the people. A Five-Year Plan started in 1979. Towards the end of 1978 it decreed important new measures: a major land reform limiting families to 15 irrigated acres each; a decreee remitting debts of peasants; and dowry rules outlawing payment of more than

Afs. 300 (about U.S. $8) in dowries and raising the minimum age for marriage to 16 years for women and 18 years for men. These measures caused head-on conflict with the powers of the old village and tribal order. The wisdom of such a direct attack could clearly be doubted. Given the distrust of officialdom it was not surprising that the reforms were ignored or circumvented.

The room for manoeuvre economically is likely to be reduced with the return of large numbers of Afghan workers from Iran. The remittances from these workers had allowed the country to run a growing trade deficit. Without this cushion of about U.S. $100 million each year Afghanistan will have to rely even more on foreign help to pursue its economic plans.

THE ECONOMY AND SOCIAL BENEFITS

Since planning in Afghanistan began nearly 20 years ago it has produced some splendid achievements. Schools have been built, factories opened, roads laid and they are there to see as impressive monuments to all the official zeal.

The achievements most obvious to the foreigner are probably the roads built with Soviet and American help. Before the planning started, it could take days along dirt tracks even to travel between the most important cities. Now it is possible to cross Afghanistan in about two days. The country has 2,500 km. of modern paved roads. The most magnificent is the highway between Kabul and Shir Khan on the Soviet border in the north which crosses the Hindu Kush through the 3 km. Salang tunnel and shortens the distance between Kabul and the rich north by 190 km. Another road links the capital with Peshawar (Pakistan) in the east, and stretches to Kandahar to the south and on to Herat near the border with Iran, so that the route which Alexander the Great took is now completely paved and open to use by buses and lorries. Airports have also been opened in Kabul and Kandahar for international travel. Afghanistan has its own airlines, Ariana for international flights and Bakhtar for domestic ones.

However, for all this, the question can still be asked as to whether the best use has been made of the plan money and the foreign aid. The major towns are Kabul, the capital, with 749,000 people (1975), Kandahar with 209,000 people in the main wool and fruit-producing area, and Herat with 157,000 people in the west. More than 30 per cent of the first three plan expenditures went to building the giant highways, but what use are such roads in helping the local people living in scattered rural areas to get their crops to market? Or to bring them in to modern life, especially when bus services are few and vehicles ancient? Although 85 per cent of the people of Afghanistan live in rural areas, and although their agriculture contributes 50 per cent to G.N.P. and 90 per cent of foreign exchange earnings, a much smaller proportion of the plan expenditure went to help agriculture or livestock and very little of the money going in those directions went to the smaller farmers. For example, of the Afs. 12,500 million spent on the agricultural sector, half went merely to two huge irrigation projects. More attention to feeder roads to the markets or to local irrigation might have reaped better benefits, raised foodgrain production higher than the 1.5 per cent annual increase in the ten years to 1962, and done much to bring the poorer people closer to the market economy.

Yet another problem has been the lack of ability to see a project through to its conclusion, a fact which was not helped by the long gestation period of many plan ventures. Even the schemes which have been finished under aid were often poorly assessed in advance, a fact which Afghanistan is finding out today. Kandahar airport, costing $15 million (an American project) has proved to be the whitest of white elephants as there is hardly enough international air traffic even for Kabul. The Balkh textile mill (French aid) was more costly than it should have been, and the Mazar-i-Sharif fertilizer factory (Soviet aid) was based on outdated technology. Factories in the public sector have generally operated below capacity because of inadequate supplies or poor machinery or the inability to plan maintenance.

In the last few years there have been some notable improvements. Agricultural production has increased, thanks to better weather, improved seeds and more application of fertilizer. Afghanistan has shown that it still offers plenty of grounds for hope and progress in agriculture. Its cotton has proved competitive in world markets. Its fresh fruit could be exported right round the Gulf area, and dried fruit like raisins could have world-wide markets.

In the industrial sphere the authorities have made determined efforts to promote new industries, particularly those based on local products and ones which will generate jobs quickly. This must have been occasioned by the fact that even the select Kabul élite were having difficulty finding jobs. However, there is a long way to go before enough jobs are created to absorb the net addition to the labour force; although in some areas, notably around Herat, there is a labour shortage.

Another problem is administration and training, a greatly neglected area of the Plan era. Without improvement, Afghanistan will continue to need foreign experts and advice even in the most basic areas, and the civil service machine will continue to be cumbersome, not to say bumbling—which only makes the development tasks further on the road slower and more difficult.

Beyond all these are the socio-economic questions. Afghanistan is largely tribal and in 1975 an estimated 2.4 million of its people were nomadic. The problem of development is made more difficult in such a society and in addition there are language barriers.

The pattern of society in Afghanistan is remarkably static. Though there is some marginal movement, the tendency is for a son, if he survives (since the child mortality rate up to the age of 5 is 50 per cent), to follow in his father's footsteps. Outside the cities, the chances are that he will not have any schooling and that he will not have any adolescence and hardly any childhood. As soon as he is big enough to walk and talk, a son can be usefully employed looking after sheep or other animals.

To make any breakthrough the authorities would have somehow to penetrate the traditional hostility to government. Officials are usually met by a "mud curtain" of the village because of the suspicion—justifiable in the past—that the officials have come to extract something from the village.

There is also the problem of the role of women. In 1959, Prime Minister Daoud passed a law saying that women no longer had to veil themselves. But the status of women has hardly changed. When a boy is born, he is greeted with bonfires and pistol shots signifying rejoicing that another man, a warrior, has entered the world. The father sees him as another defender of the family honour; the mother feels that her position is more secure in the family. But when a girl comes into the world, the reaction is more likely to be one of shame. Educational opportunities for girls have increased, although of the roll of 720,000 pupils in all educational institutions in 1970, only 96,000 were girls. In village schools, there were only 13,000 girls. Of an estimated 100,000 Afghan women who have finished some kind of schooling only about 5,000 are employed, mainly in the professions and the majority of these in teaching. There are hardly any women in industry—because of the high unemployment rate.

STATISTICAL SURVEY

AREA AND POPULATION

Area	Estimated Mid-Year Population					Density (per sq. km.)
	1973	1974	1975	1976	1977	1977
250,000 sq. miles*	15,924,000	16,290,000	16,665,000	17,050,000	17,447,000	26.9

* 647,497 sq. km.

PROVINCES*
(July 1st, 1975)

	Area (sq. km.)	Population	Density (per sq. km.)	Capital
Uruzgan	28,756	461,000	16	Tareenkoot (49,000)
Badghis	21,854	348,000	16	Qala-i-nau (70,000)
Bamian	17,411	332,000	19	Bamian (47,000)
Badakhshan	46,710	424,000	9	Faizabad (77,000)
Baghlan	17,106	565,000	33	Baghlan (85,000)
Balkh	11,833	428,000	36	Mazar-i-Sharif (97,000)
Parwan (incl. Kapisa)	11,269	1,152,000	102	Charikar (98,000)
Paktia	17,528	908,000	52	Gardiz (54,000)
Takhar	12,373	468,000	38	Taluqan (67,000)
Jawzjan	25,548	408,000	16	Shebergham (59,000)
Zabul	17,289	294,000	17	Qalat (37,000)
Samangan	16,220	301,000	19	Uiback (63,000)
Ghazni	32,902	1,010,000	31	Ghazni (48,000)
Ghour	38,658	339,000	9	Cheghcheran (82,000)
Fariab	22,274	493,000	22	Maimana (29,000)
Farah	58,834	364,000	6	Farah (47,000)
Kunduz	7,825	468,000	60	Kunduz (108,000)
Kandahar	49,430	803,000	16	Kandahar (209,000)
Kabul	4,583	1,463,000	319	Kabul (749,000)
Laghman	7,209	272,000	38	Meterlam (76,000)
Logar	4,411	314,000	71	Pulialam (88,000)
Nangarhar (incl. Kunar)	18,091	1,151,000	64	Jalalabad (58,000)
Neemroze	41,347	101,000	2	Zarunj (41,000)
Wardak	9,638	372,000	39	Maidan (37,000)
Herat	51,711	733,000	14	Herat (157,000)
Helmand	61,816	288,000	5	Bost (22,000)
Total	652,626†	14,260,000	22	

* Population figures refer to settled inhabitants only, excluding kuchies (nomads), estimated at 2,405,000 for the whole country.

† Other sources give the total area as 250,000 sq. miles (647,497 sq. km.).

Sources: Cartographic Institute and Central Statistics Office, Kabul.

PRINCIPAL CITIES

(estimated population at July 1st, 1975)

Kabul (capital)	749,000	Charikar	98,000
Kandahar	209,000	Mazar-i-Sharif	97,000
Herat	157,000	Pulialam	88,000
Kunduz	108,000	Baghlan	85,000

Births and Deaths: Average annual birth rate 49.8 per 1,000 in 1965–70, 49.2 per 1,000 in 1970–75; death rate 26.4 per 1,000 in 1965–70, 23.8 per 1,000 in 1970–75 (UN estimates).

EMPLOYMENT*

	1972/73	1973/74	1974/75	1975/76
Agriculture	3,130,000	3,210,000	4,022,000	4,022,000†
Manufacturing (incl. handicrafts)	280,000	290,000	310,000	350,000
Construction and mining	120,000	120,000	130,000	130,000
Transport and communications	30,000	40,000	40,000	80,000
Other production industries	80,000	90,000	90,000	n.a.
Education and health services	30,000	40,000	50,000	50,000
Government institutions	80,000	80,000	n.a.	90,000
Commerce	120,000	120,000	130,000	200,000
Other non-productive sectors	110,000	110,000	110,000	375,000
Unknown	670,000	670,000	n.a.	343,000
TOTAL LABOUR FORCE	4,650,000	4,770,000	n.a.	5,640,000

* Excluding kuchies (nomads). † Estimate.

AGRICULTURE

LAND USE

('000 hectares)

	1970	1975	1976
Arable land	7,870*	7,950*	7,980*
Land under permanent crops	300*	550*	555*
Permanent meadows and pastures	6,000*	5,950*	5,940*
Forest and woodland	1,900	1,900	1,900
Other land and inland water	48,680	48,400	48,375
TOTAL	64,750	64,750	64,750

* FAO estimate.

Source: FAO, *Production Yearbook.*

PRINCIPAL CROPS

(year ending March 20th)

	AREA ('000 hectares)			PRODUCTION ('000 metric tons)		
	1974/75	1975/76	1976/77	1974/75	1975/76	1976/77
Wheat	2,277.6	2,350	2,350	2,750	2,850	2,936
Maize	476.2	484	482	770	780	800
Rice (paddy)	210	210	210	420	435	448
Barley	340.2	320	310	380	384	400
Seed cotton	138	112	128	145	160	159
Sugar beet	4.5	5	4.8	66.6	108.5	91
Sugar cane	1.3	1.7	3.5	51.6	60	68.1
Vegetables	94.7	92	139	700	720	918.2
Fruits	140.8	140.3	140	865	880	900
Oil seeds	44.7	50	106.4	40	40	62

1977/78 (production in '000 metric tons): Wheat 2,652; Maize 760; Rice 400; Barley 300; Seed cotton 137; Fruits 692.

1978/79 (production in '000 metric tons): Wheat 2,830; Maize 780; Rice 428; Barley 325; Seed cotton 153; Fruits 824; Oil seeds 35.

LIVESTOCK

('000)

	1973/74*	1974/75	1975/76	1976/77*
Cattle	3,550	3,604	3,700	3,800
Sheep†	n.a.	20,417	21,200	22,000
Goats	2,300	3,000	3,000	3,000
Horses	370	370*	370*	370
Asses	1,250	1,250*	1,250*	1,250
Mules	27	27*	27*	26
Buffaloes	33	35*	35*	35
Camels	300	300*	290*	290
Poultry	7,500	8,000*	10,000*	10,500

* FAO estimate.

† Including Karakul sheep, numbering 6.0 million in 1974/75, and 6.2 million in 1975/76.

Sources: FAO, *Production Yearbook*, and Central Statistics Office, Kabul.

LIVESTOCK PRODUCTS

('000 metric tons)

	1975	1976	1977
Beef and veal	61	62	65
Mutton and lamb	69	92	93†
Goats' meat	25	25	25†
Poultry meat	7*	10*	10*
Cows' milk	584	600	627*
Sheep's milk	211†	216†	218†
Goats' milk	44†	45†	46†
Buffaloes' milk	3*	3*	3*
Butter	5.3*	5.3*	5.4*
Cheese	9.1	9.2	9.5*
Hen eggs	15.7*	16.0*	16.4*
Honey	3.3†	3.5†	3.7*
Wool: greasy	25	25.4	25.8†
clean	14*	14*	14*
Cattle and buffalo hides	10.3*	10.5*	10.8*
Sheep skins	11.9*	15.3*	15.5*
Goat skins	3.8*	3.8*	3.8*

* FAO estimate. † Unofficial figure.

Source: FAO, *Production Yearbook.*

FORESTRY

ROUNDWOOD REMOVALS

('000 cubic metres, excluding bark)

	CONIFEROUS (soft wood)			BROADLEAVED (hard wood)			TOTAL		
	1975	1976	1977*	1975	1976	1977*	1975	1976	1977*
Sawlogs, veneer logs and logs for sleepers	803	820	820	30	36	36	833	856	856
Other industrial wood	116*	119*	122	462*	475*	488	578*	594*	610
Fuel wood	1,735*	1,782*	1,830	4,049*	4,157*	4,269	5,784*	5,939*	6,099
TOTAL	2,654	2,721	2,772	4,541	4,668	4,793	7,195	7,389	7,565

* FAO estimate.

Source: FAO, *Yearbook of Forest Products.*

SAWNWOOD PRODUCTION

('000 cubic metres, including boxboards)

	1971	1972	1973	1974*	1975*	1976*
Coniferous	345	305	360*	360	310	380
Broadleaved	60	55	50	50	20	20
TOTAL	405	360	410	410	330	400

* FAO estimate.

1977: Production as in 1976 (FAO estimates).

Source: FAO, *Yearbook of Forest Products.*

Inland Fishing (1964–77): Total catch 1,500 metric tons each year (FAO estimate).

MINING

(Twelve months ending March 20th)

		1974/75	1975/76	1976/77	1977/78
Hard coal	'000 metric tons	115.0	149.7	159.9	172.7
Salt (unrefined)	,, ,, ,,	49.0	62.0	72.7	77.7
Natural gas	million cu. metres	2,946.0	2,959.2	2,546.0	2,581.9

INDUSTRY

SELECTED PRODUCTS

(Twelve months ending March 20th)

		1974/75	1975/76	1976/77	1977/78
Ginned Cotton	'000 metric tons	32.6	44.1	52.7	47.1
Cotton Fabrics	million metres	68.1	60.4	73.7	76.8
Woollen Fabrics	'000 metres	113.6	445.7	441.0	347.4
Rayon Fabrics	,, ,,	20,865.0	34,700.0	27,900.0	29,700.6
Cement	'000 metric tons	151.0	147.3	125.1	125.0
Electricity*	million kWh.	615.2	705.0	695.6	763.8
Wheat Flour	'000 metric tons	53.4	56.6	57.9	59.9
Raw Sugar	,, ,, ,,	8.9	13.6	11.1	11.2
Margarine	,, ,, ,,	10.2	10.6	10.1	13.0
Nitrogenous Fertilizers†	,, ,, ,,	18.7	65.5	55.1	99.6

* Production for public use, excluding industrial establishments generating electricity for their own use. Estimates of total electricity output (in million kWh.) are: 642 in 1974/75; 748 in 1975/76.

† Production in terms of nitrogen.

FINANCE

100 puls (puli) = 2 krans = 1 afghani.
Coins: 25 and 50 puls; 1, 2 and 5 afghanis.
Notes: 10, 20, 50, 100, 500 and 1,000 afghanis.
Exchange rates (June 1979): £1 sterling = 93.1 afghanis; U.S. $1 = 45.0 afghanis (official rates).
1,000 afghanis = £10.74 = $22.22.

Note: Multiple exchange rates were in operation before March 1963. Between 1956 and 1963 the official base rate was U.S. $1 = 20.00 afghanis. Since March 1963 there has been a single official rate of $1 = 45.00 afghanis. In terms of sterling, the official exchange rate was £1 = 108.00 afghanis from November 1967 to August 1971; and £1 = 117.26 afghanis from December 1971 to June 1972. Some trade takes place at the official rate; some at rates determined by discounts or premiums; and some at free market rates, which fluctuate widely. In March 1979 the free rate was $1 = 42.50 afghanis.

BUDGET

(million afghanis, twelve months ending September 21st)

Revenue	1974/75	1975/76*	1976/77
Direct Taxes	1,022	1,191	1,713
Indirect Taxes	6,036	5,630	6,159
Revenue from monopolies and other enterprises	447	945	887
Natural Gas Revenue	1,175	2,375	2,336
Revenue from other property and services	1,042	1,475	2,179
Other Revenue	530	408	676
Total Revenue	10,252	12,024	13,950

Expenditure	1974/75	1975/76	1976/77
Administration	757	1,078	1,485
Defence, Security	1,682	2,114	2,381
Social Services	1,430	1,866	2,254
Economic Services	491	584	957
Total Ministries	4,360	5,642	7,077
Foreign Debt Service	1,834	1,190	1,320
Subsidies (exchange, etc.)	1,144	2,856	2,771
Total Ordinary	7,338	9,688	11,168
Development Budget	2,373	3,319	5,060

* Estimates.

BANK OF AFGHANISTAN RESERVES

(U.S. $ million at December 31st)

	1973	1974	1975	1976	1977	1978
Gold	39.35	39.94	38.19	37.90	40.01	43.27
IMF Special Drawing Rights	5.16	5.45	6.23	5.95	6.90	7.01
Reserve Position in IMF	—	—	—	—	10.02	11.69
Foreign Exchange	16.45	22.19	80.32	124.97	258.90	371.86
Total	60.96	67.58	124.74	168.82	315.83	433.83

Source: IMF, *International Financial Statistics.*

MONEY SUPPLY

(million afghanis at March 21st)

	1975	1976	1977	1978
Currency outside banks	9,890	11,708	15,232	17,968
Private sector deposits at Bank of Afghanistan	2,298	2,357	3,412	5,179
Demand deposits at commercial banks	951	1,000	1,339	1,427
Total Money	13,139	15,065	19,983	24,574

Source: IMF, *International Financial Statistics.*

COST OF LIVING

(twelve months ending March 20th. Base: 1961/62=100)

	1970/71	1971/72	1972/73	1973/74	1974/75	1975/76
All Items	265	313	267	246	280	298
Cereals	318	401	307	233	278	309
Meat	223	204	245	311	356	369
Fruits	215	228	261	351	372	306
Vegetables	248	241	218	294	282	335
Other Food Articles	147	162	203	206	213	253
Non-Food Items	117	120	123	133	144	153

NATIONAL ACCOUNTS

(million afghanis, at 1965 market prices)

NET DOMESTIC PRODUCT BY ECONOMIC ACTIVITY

	1967	1968	1969
Agriculture, Forestry and Fishing	28,300	29,050	29,117
Mining	280	540	700
Manufacturing	5,707	5,777	6,200
Construction	860	900	990
Transportation, Communication, Utilities	1,481	1,630	1,820
Wholesale and Retail Trade*	7,122	7,350	7,650
Ownership of Dwellings	4,673	4,800	4,900
Public Administration and Defence	2,890	3,150	3,528
Other services	2,174	2,200	2,300
TOTAL	53,487	55,397	57,205

* Including storage, hotels and restaurants.

Source: United Nations, *Quarterly Bulletin of Statistics for Asia and the Pacific*, March 1974.

BALANCE OF PAYMENTS

(U.S. $ million, financial years)

	1971/72	1972/73	1973/74	1974/75	1975/76
Merchandise exports	104.2	121.4	159.4	208.6	225.0
Merchandise imports	−144.5	−161.3	−183.1	−223.7	−297.7
TRADE BALANCE	−40.3	−39.9	−23.7	−15.1	−72.7
Travel (net)	6.3	6.7	6.8	9.0	11.0
Service component of project aid	−6.0	−8.3	−7.5	−9.0	−14.0
Official loans and grants: project	29.8	41.6	37.4	45.2	70.0
other	34.6	31.8	32.5	17.0	21.0
External public debt service	−27.9	−31.0	−35.7	−45.0	−31.5
Other transactions (net)*	18.9	2.7	5.1	10.0	7.0
CHANGES IN RESERVES, etc.	15.4	−1.8	14.9	12.1	−9.2

*Including errors and omissions.

Source: Data Asia/Pacific 1978.

FOREIGN AID

(U.S. $ million, twelve months ending March 20th)

Source	1971/72	1972/73	1973/74
Import of commodities aid	22.9	—	32.5
Other grants	11.3	—	22.8
Foreign project and non-project loans	47.2	60.8	55.3
Total	81.4	60.8	110.6

EXTERNAL TRADE

(million afghanis, twelve months ending March 20th)

	1972/73	1973/74	1974/75	1975/76	1976/77	1977/78
Imports c.i.f.*	14,500	11,323	14,353	20,442	18,313	23,900
Exports f.o.b.	7,214	9,557	13,606	13,085	16,330	15,246

* Including imports under commodity loans and grants from foreign countries and international organizations.

PRINCIPAL COMMODITIES

(U.S. $ million)

Imports	1974/75	1975/76
Sugar	26.3	39.5
Tea	15.7	30.5
Vegetable oils	6.7	8.6
Tobacco	1.6	1.9
Medicines	6.4	6.7
Petroleum products	22.5	27.0
Other chemical products	2.0	2.7
Tyres and tubes	11.3	21.6
Cotton and rayon textiles	7.9	11.8
Chemical fertilizer	8.7	7.8
Soap	3.5	5.2
Rayon thread	10.9	7.9
Woollen and silk textiles	0.7	0.9
Footwear	2.2	2.9
Vehicles and machinery	7.0	11.1
Used clothes	4.2	4.1
Construction materials (iron)	3.5	3.9
Spare parts	4.6	5.8
Other goods	96.8	149.7
Total	242.5	349.6

Exports	1974/75	1975/76
Casings	1.9	1.3
Dry fruits	64.1	47.2
Fresh fruits	31.5	23.2
Oil seeds	4.1	8.3
Hides and skins	7.1	11.7
Karakuls	12.2	10.3
Wool	6.2	7.9
Cotton	34.7	32.5
Rugs and carpets	20.0	17.0
Natural gas	32.1	45.3
Cement	1.8	—
Medicinal herbs	8.9	10.4
Skin coats	1.0	—
Other goods	4.7	8.3
Total	230.5	223.4

PRINCIPAL TRADING PARTNERS

(U.S. $ million)

IMPORTS	1974/75	1975/76
Czechoslovakia	0.8	2.9
Germany, Fed. Republic	10.6	43.5
India	24.6	41.4
Japan	59.7	67.6
Pakistan	10.8	7.5
U.S.S.R.	73.3	83.4
United Kingdom	8.4	12.7
U.S.A.	10.5	22.8
TOTAL (incl. others)	242.5	349.6

EXPORTS	1974/75	1975/76
Czechoslovakia	3.1	2.1
Germany, Fed. Republic	5.7	22.3
India	37.7	26.8
Pakistan	26.2	29.0
Switzerland	8.4	5.9
U.S.S.R.	91.9	86.4
United Kingdom	23.0	15.1
U.S.A.	5.2	9.4
TOTAL (incl. others)	230.5	223.4

TOURISM

INTERNATIONAL TOURIST ARRIVALS BY COUNTRY

	1971	1972	1973	1974	1975
Australia	2,703	2,614	2,974	3,349	4,239
France	8,130	7,649	6,442	6,541	9,383
Germany, Federal Republic	7,524	7,020	7,516	7,157	8,577
India	1,533	2,769	3,619	4,608	8,393
Pakistan	51,792	49,161	28,470	26,864	15,013
United Kingdom	10,117	9,067	8,875	10,112	10,937
U.S.A.	11,965	11,630	12,769	10,369	9,317
Others	19,345	20,906	20,997	27,195	25,278
TOTAL	113,109	110,816	91,662	96,195	91,137

Receipts from Tourism: U.S. $4.3 million in 1969; $7.8 million in 1970; $11 million in 1971.

TRANSPORT

CIVIL AVIATION

(twelve months ending March 20th)

	1974/75	1975/76	1976/77	1977/78
Kilometres flown ('000)	3,871	3,900	3,850	4,514
Passengers carried	77,933	82,700	79,000	97,100
Passenger-km. ('000)	249,600	259,000	251,400	298,200
Freight ton-km. ('000)	35,529	34,100	36,200	40,300
Cargo	12,800	10,600	13,300	13,300
Mail	166	165	132	174

ROAD TRAFFIC

(motor vehicles in use)

	1973/74	1974/75	1975/76	1976/77	1977/78
Passenger cars	19,399	22,261	24,468	28,098	25,993
Commercial vehicles	11,955	14,518	16,934	19,298	26,692

COMMUNICATIONS MEDIA

Telephones in use: 23,200 in 1977/78.

Radio sets in use: 906,037 in 1976.

Television sets in use: 20,000 in mid-1978.

Daily newspapers: 18 in 1970 (total circulation: 101,000).

EDUCATION

(1975/76)

	Institutions	Pupils
Primary Schools	1,517	546,236
Village Schools	1,912	148,004
Middle Schools	512	112,616
Lycées	197	59,647
Commercial, Agricultural and Technical Schools, etc.	17	5,851
Teacher Training Colleges	10	4,033
Religious Schools	19	3,749
Universities and Higher Institutes	14	8,366

Note: Teachers in all institutions totalled 12,399 in 1975/76.

Source (unless otherwise specified): Central Statistics Office, Kabul.

THE CONSTITUTION

Immediately after the coup of April 27th, 1978, the 1977 Constitution was abolished. A special commission of the Revolutionary Council has started preparations for drafting the first constitution of the Democratic Republic of Afghanistan. Meanwhile the Revolutionary Council, as the supreme governmental power of the country, rules by decrees and directives. The Government of the Democratic Republic of Afghanistan is elected by the Revolutionary Council and is responsible to it.

THE GOVERNMENT

HEAD OF STATE

President of the Revolutionary Council: Nur Mohammad Taraki (took office April 30th, 1978).

SUPREME DEFENCE COUNCIL

President: Nur Mohammad Taraki.

Vice-President: Hafezollah Amin.

Members:

Dr. Shah Wali.
Col. Sher Jan Mazdooryar.
Maj. Aslam Watanjar.
Assadullah Akbar.
Maj. Yaqoub.
Col. Ghulam Sakhi.
Col. Nazar Mohammad.

COUNCIL OF MINISTERS

(*July* 1979)

President of the Revolutionary Council and Supreme Commander of the Armed Forces: Nur Mohammad Taraki.

Prime Minister and Minister of Defence: Hafezollah Amni.

Deputy Prime Minister and Minister of Foreign Affairs: Dr. Shah Wali.

Minister of Frontier Affairs: Col. Sher Jan Mazdooryar.

Minister of the Interior: Maj. Aslam Watanjar.

Minister of Communications: Faiz Mohammed Golabzoi.

Minister of Education: Dr. Abdulrashid Jalili.

Minister of Planning: Eng. Sediq Alemyar.

Minister of Agriculture, Land Reform and Public Health: Dr. Saleh Mohammad Ziray.

Minister of Finance: Abdolqadir Misaq.

Minister of Information and Culture: Malek Katawazi.

Minister of Justice and Attorney-General: Abdolkarim Shara'i.

Minister of Trade: Abdolqoddus Ghorbandi.

Minister of Mines and Industries: Eng. Mohammad Esma'il Danesh.

Minister of Transport: Mohammad Hasan Bareq Shafa'i.

Minister of Public Works: Ghulam Dastagir Panjshiri.

Minister of Water and Power: Mohammad Mansur Hashemi.

Minister of Higher Education: Prof. Mahmud Suma.

Minister of Border Affairs: Sahib Jan Sahrayee.

POLITICAL PARTY

People's Democratic Party: Kabul; f. 1965, later split; re-founded 1976, when the Khalq (Masses) Party and its splinter Parcham (Flag) Party re-united and annexed the Musawat Party; Left-wing; Gen.-Sec. Nur Mohammad Taraki; Sec. Hafezollah Amin; publ. *Khalq*.

No other political parties are allowed to function. The following parties are based in Pakistan and have joined forces to fight against the Government in Afghanistan: Jamiat-i-Islami (Leader Burhanuddin Rabbani), Hezb-i-Islami (Leader Gulbuddin Hekmatyar), National Liberation Front (Leader Sijbatullah Mojaddedi).

DIPLOMATIC REPRESENTATION

EMBASSIES ACCREDITED TO AFGHANISTAN

(In Kabul unless otherwise stated)

(E) Embassy.

Algeria: New Delhi, India (E).

Australia: Islamabad, Pakistan (E).

Austria: Zarghouna Wat (E); *Ambassador:* Dr. CHRISTOPH CORNARO.

Bahrain: Teheran, Iran (E).

Bangladesh: Wazir Akbar Khan Mena (E); *Ambassador:* C. M. MURSHED.

Belgium: Teheran, Iran (E).

Brazil: Teheran, Iran (E).

Bulgaria: Wazir Akbar Khan Mena (E); *Ambassador:* STOYAN RADOSLAVOV.

Canada: Islamabad, Pakistan (E).

Chile: Washington, D.C., U.S.A. (E).

China, People's Republic: Shah Mahmoud Ghazi Wat (E); *Ambassador:* HUANG MING-TA.

Cuba: New Delhi, India (E).

Czechoslovakia: Taimani Wat, Kale Fatullah (E); *Ambassador:* ZDENĚK KARMELITA.

Denmark: Teheran, Iran (E).

Finland: Moscow, U.S.S.R. (E).

France: Nedjat Wat (E); *Ambassador:* GEORGE PERRUCHE.

German Democratic Republic: Wazir Akbar Khan Mena (E); *Ambassador:* Dr. HERMANN SCHWIESAU.

Germany, Federal Republic: Wazir Akbar Khan Mena (E); *Ambassador:* Dr. F. J. HOFFMAN.

Ghana: New Delhi, India (E).

Greece: Teheran, Iran (E).

Hungary: Wazir Akbar Khan Mena (E); *Ambassador:* DEZSŐ KISS.

India: Malalai Wat (E); *Ambassador:* JASKARA SINGH TEJA.

Indonesia: Wazir Akbar Khan Mena (E); *Ambassador:* ABDURRAHMAN GUNADIRDJA.

Iran: Malekyar Wat (E); *Ambassador:* (vacant).

Iraq: Malalai Wat, Shar-e-Nau (E); *Ambassador:* (vacant).

Italy: Khwaja Abdullah Ansari Wat (E); *Ambassador:* FRANCESCO LO PRINZI.

Japan: Wazir Akbar Khan Mena (E); *Ambassador:* TOSHIKAYA MAEDA.

Jordan: Teheran, Iran (E).

Korea, Democratic People's Republic: Wazir Akbar Khan Mena (E); *Ambassador:* (vacant).

Kuwait: Teheran, Iran (E).

Lebanon: Teheran, Iran (E).

Libya: Wazir Akbar Khan Mena (E); *Ambassador:* AL HADI OMAR ELHERIK.

Malaysia: Teheran, Iran (E).

Mexico: New Delhi, India (E).

Mongolia: Wazir Akbar Khan Mena (E); *Ambassador:* (vacant).

Morocco: Teheran, Iran (E).

Nepal: New Delhi, India (E).

Netherlands: Teheran, Iran (E).

Norway: Teheran, Iran (E).

Pakistan: Zarghouna Wat (E); *Ambassador:* RIAZ PIRACHA.

Philippines: New Delhi, India (E).

Poland: Guzargah Wat (E); *Ambassador:* E. BARADZIEJ.

Qatar: Teheran, Iran (E).

Romania: Teheran, Iran (E).

Saudi Arabia: Wazir Akbar Khan Mena (E); *Ambassador:* AL SHEIKH ABDULLAH SALEH HABIBI.

Senegal: Teheran, Iran (E).

Spain: Teheran, Iran (E).

Sri Lanka: New Delhi, India (E).

Sweden: Teheran, Iran (E).

Switzerland: Teheran, Iran (E).

Syria: New Delhi, India (E).

Thailand: New Delhi, India (E).

Turkey: Shah Mahmoud Ghazi Wat (E); *Ambassador:* ILHAM BAKAY.

U.S.S.R.: Dar-ul-Aman Wat (E); *Ambassador:* ALEKSANDR PUZANOV.

United Kingdom: Karte Parwan (E); *Ambassador:* K. R. CROOK, C.M.G.

U.S.A.: Khwaja Abdullah Ansari Wat (E); *Ambassador:* (vacant).

Viet-Nam: Wazir Akbar Khan Mena (E); *Ambassador:* NGUYEN SI HOACH.

Yugoslavia: Wazir Akbar Khan Mena (E); *Ambassador:* BOGDAN MALBASIC.

Afghanistan also has diplomatic relations with Argentina, Burma, Laos, Portugal, Sudan, Tunisia, the United Arab Emirates and the People's Democratic Republic of Yemen.

JUDICIAL SYSTEM

The Revolutionary Council has declared that the powers of the Supreme Court incorporated in the Law of Judicial Authority and Organization of 1966 are transferred to the Supreme Judicial Council of the Democratic Republic of Afghanistan. The Supreme Judicial Council (SJC) is accountable to the Revolutionary Council and is composed of the following: The Minister of Justice as the President, the Deputy Minister of Justice for Judicial Affairs, the President of the Cassation Court, the Deputy Minister of Justice for Administrative Affairs, the Assistant Attorney-General and one or more other persons who may be appointed on the proposal of the Minister of Justice and with the approval of the President of the Revolutionary Council.

A Military Revolutionary Court acts as a circuit court, on an itinerant basis, to try military and civilian persons who commit crimes against the revolution or in violation of the internal and foreign security of the Democratic Republic of Afghanistan. Judges of the Military Revolutionary Court are appointed by the Revolutionary Council.

RELIGION

The official religion of Afghanistan is Islam. Ninety-nine per cent of Afghans are Muslims, approximately 80 per cent of them of the Sunni and the remainder of the Shi'ite sect. There are small minority groups of Hindus, Sikhs and Jews.

THE PRESS

PRINCIPAL DAILIES

Anis (*Friendship*): Kabul; f. 1927; evening; Independent; Persian and Pashtu; news and literary articles; Chief Editor DUR MOHAMMAD WAFAKISH; circ. 24,000.

Badakshan: Faizabad; f. 1945; Persian and Pashtu; circ. 3,000.

Bedar: Mazar-i-Sharif; f. 1920; Persian and Pashtu; circ. 1,500.

Daiwan: Sheberghan.

De Sowr Enqelab: Kabul; f. 1978; Chief Editor ALIGOL PAYWAND.

Ettehadi-Baghlan: Baghlan; f. 1922; Persian and Pashtu; circ. 3,500.

Ettifaqi-Islam: Herat; f. 1919; Persian and Pashtu; circ. 2,500.

Helmand: Bost; f. 1953; twice weekly; Pashtu.

Hewad: Kabul; f. 1959; Pashtu; Editor-in-Chief AMIN AFGHANPUR; circ. 5,000.

Kabul Times: Kabul; f. 1962; English; Chief Editor MOHAMMAD KAZEM AHANG; circ. 5,000.

Khalq: Kabul; resumed publication 1979; organ of the People's Democratic Party; Editor-in-Chief A. K. NURZAI.

Nangarhar: Jalalabad; f. 1918; Persian and Pashtu; circ. 1,500.

Seistan: Farah; f. 1947; twice weekly; circ. 1,800.

Tulu-i-Afghan: Kandahar; f. 1924; Pashtu; circ. 1,500.

Wolanga: Gardiz; f. 1941; Pashtu; circ. 2,000.

PERIODICALS

Adab: Kabul; f. 1953; organ of the Faculty of Literature, Univ. of Kabul.

Afghan Journal of Public Health: Institute of Public Health, Ansari Wat, Kabul; 2 per month; Editor Dr. G. FAROUQ.

Afghan Tebbi Mojalla: Faculty of Medicine, Kabul University; monthly.

Afghanistan: Historical Society of Afghanistan, Kabul; f. 1946; quarterly; English and French; historical and cultural; Editor MALIHA FAZEL ZAFAR.

Akhbare Erfani: Ministry of Education, Kabul; f. 1952; fortnightly.

Aryana: Historical Society of Afghanistan, Kabul; f. 1943; quarterly; Pashtu and Dari; cultural and historical; Editor FAQIR MOHAMMAD KHAIRKHAN.

Badany Rauzana: Department of Physical Education, Kabul University; quarterly.

Eqtesad: Afghan Chambers of Commerce and Industry, Mohd Jan Khan Waat, Kabul; monthly; Editor MOHAMMED TAHIR PAYAM.

Herat: Ministry of Information and Culture, Kabul; monthly; Persian and Pashtu.

Irfan: Ministry of Education, Kabul; f. 1923; monthly; Persian.

Jamalmeena: Ministry of Agriculture, Kabul; f. 1955; monthly; Editor S. M. S. PEERZADA.

Kabul: Pashto Academy, Sher Alikhan St., Kabul; f. 1937; monthly; Pashtu; literature, history, social sciences; Editor ALI MOHD.

Kabul Pohantoon: Kabul University; monthly.

Kocheniano Zhaqh: Ministry of Education, Kabul; f. 1957; monthly.

Mairmun: Kabul; f. 1955; Persian and Pashtu; produced by the Women's Welfare Association.

Pamir: Kabul; f. 1951; organ of the Municipality; fortnightly.

Pashtun Zhaqh: Ansari Wat, Kabul; f. 1940; programmes of broadcasts; issued by Kabul Radio; 2 per month.

Sera Miasht: Red Crescent Society, Kabul; f. 1958.

Talim wa Tarbia: Kabul; f. 1954; monthly; published by Institute of Education.

Urdu: Kabul; f. 1922; monthly; military journal; issued by the Ministry of National Defence.

Yolduz (*Star*): Ministry of Information and Culture, Kabul; weekly; Uzbeki and Turkmani.

Zhwandoon: Kabul; Persian; illustrated; Editor NAJEEBULLAH RAHEQ; circ. 10,000.

Zery: Pashto Academy, Sher Alikhan St., Kabul; f. 1949; weekly; Editor ZALMAI HIWADMAL.

NEWS AGENCIES

Bakhtar News Agency: Ministry of Information and Culture, Kabul; f. 1939; Dir. ABDOLQODDUS TANDER.

FOREIGN BUREAUX

The following foreign agencies are represented in Kabul: APN (U.S.S.R.), TASS (U.S.S.R.), Tanjug (Yugoslavia) and Hsinhua (People's Republic of China).

PRESS ASSOCIATION

Journalists' Association: c/o Department of Press and Information, Sanaii Wat, Kabul.

PUBLISHERS

Afghan Book: P.O.B. 206, Kabul; f. 1969 by Kabir A. Ahang; books on various subjects, translations of foreign works on Afghanistan, books in English on Afghanistan and Dari language textbooks for foreigners; Man. Dir. JAMILA AHANG.

Afghanistan Publicity Department: c/o Kabul Times, Kabul; publicity materials; answers enquiries about Afghanistan.

Baihaqi Book Publishing Institute: Ministry of Information and Culture, Government Printing House, Kabul; f. 1971 by co-operation of the Government Printing House, Bakhtar News Agency and leading newspapers.

Book Publishing Institute: Herat; f. 1970 by co-operation of Government Printing House and citizens of Herat; books on literature, history and religion.

Book Publishing Institute: Kandahar; f. 1970 by citizens of Kandahar, supervised by Government Printing House; mainly books in Pashtu language.

Educational Publications: Ministry of Education, Kabul; textbooks for primary and secondary schools in the Pashtu and Dari languages; also three monthly magazines in Pashtu and in Dari.

Government Printing House: Kabul; f. 1870 under supervision of the Ministry of Information and Culture; four daily newspapers in Kabul, one in English; weekly, fortnightly and monthly magazines, one of them in English; books on Afghan history and literature, as well as textbooks for the Ministry of Education; thirteen daily newspapers in thirteen provincial centres and one journal and also magazines in three provincial centres; Dir. MOHAMMAD 'Ayan 'Ayan.

Historical Society of Afghanistan: Kabul; f. 1931; mainly historical and cultural works and two quarterly magazines: *Afghanistan* (English and French), *Aryana* (Dari and Pashtu); Pres. AHMAD ALI MOTAMEDI.

Institute of Geography: Kabul University; geographical and related works.

Kabul University Press: Kabul; publishes textbooks for Kabul and Nangarhar Universities, College Journals, etc.

Pashto Tolana (*Pashto Academy*): Sher Alikhan St., Kabul; f. 1937 by the Department of Press and Information; research works on Pashtu language and literature; Pres. POHAND RSHTEENE; publs. *Zery* (weekly), *Kabul* (monthly).

RADIO AND TELEVISION

National Radio-TV of Afghanistan: P.O.B. 544, Kabul; Dir.-Gen. of Radio and Television BASHIR ROIGAR; Dir. of Radio Broadcasting Dr. MOHAMMAD SADEQ FETRAT; the Afghan Broadcasting station is under the supervision of the Ministry of Communications; Home service in Dari, Pashtu, Nuristani, Uzbeki, Turkmani and Balochi; Foreign service in Urdu, Arabic, English, Russian, German, Dari and Pashtu.

Number of radio receivers: 1m. (approx.) in 1977.

Television broadcasting began in August 1978 with a transmission range of 50 kilometres.

Number of television sets: 20,000 in August 1978.

FINANCE

BANKING

(cap.=capital; auth.=authorized; p.u.=paid up; res.= reserves; m.=million; Afs.=Afghanis).

In June 1975 all banks were nationalized.

Da Afghanistan Bank (*Central Bank of Afghanistan*): Ibne Sina Wat, Kabul; f. 1939; main functions: banknote issue, foreign exchange regulation, credit extensions to banks and leading enterprises and companies, government and private depository, government fiscal agency; 67 local brs.; cap. Afs. 1,000m.; dep. Afs. 5,544.6m. (March 1979); Gov. MOHAMMED HAKIM.

Agricultural Development Bank of Afghanistan: P.O.B. 414, Kabul; f. 1955; makes available credits for farmers, co-operatives and agro-business; aid provided by IBRD and UNDP; auth. share cap. Afs. 1,000m.; Pres. Eng. ABDUL WAHAD ASSEFI; Gen. Man. J. HOTTER.

Banke Millie Afghan (*Afghan National Bank*): Jada Ibn Sina, Kabul; f. 1932; 12 brs.; cap. Afs. 500m.; total resources Afs. 3,154m. (March 1977); Pres. M. JAFAR MOKHTARZADA.

Export Promotion Bank of Afghanistan: Pres. Prof. Dr. ZABIOULLAH A. ELTEZAM.

Industrial Development Bank of Afghanistan: P.O.B. 14, Kabul; f. 1973; provides financing for industrial development; total financial resources including cap. Afs. 842m.; Pres. K. M. SULTANI; Gen. Man. SUNIT GUPTA.

Mortgage and Construction Bank: 2 Jade' Maiwand, Kabul; f. 1955 to provide short and long term building loans; cap. Afs. 100m.; Pres. (vacant).

Pashtany Tejaraty Bank (*Afghan Commercial Bank*): Mohammad Jan Khan Wat, Kabul; f. 1954 to provide long- and short-term credits, forwarding facilities, opening letters of credit, purchase and sale of foreign exchange, transfer of capital, issuing travellers cheques; cap. p.u. Afs. 400m.; total assets Afs. 3,099m. (March 1978); Pres. HAKIM HAMIDI; 18 brs. in Afghanistan and abroad.

There are no foreign banks operating in Afghanistan.

INSURANCE

There is one national insurance company:

Afghan Insurance Co.: P.O.B. 329, Pashtoonistan Square, Kabul; f. 1964; marine, aviation, fire, motor and accident insurance; Pres. AMON SALIMI (acting).

No foreign insurance companies are permitted to operate in the country.

TRADE AND INDUSTRY

CHAMBER OF COMMERCE

Afghan Chambers of Commerce and Industry: Mohd Jan Khan Waat, Kabul; since 1978 acts as the sole agent for the 22 Importers Associations and controls all import business; Pres. AMIR MOHAMMAD.

TRADING CORPORATIONS

Afghan Carpet Exporters Guild: Charrahi, Anssari Shah-i-nau, P.O.B. 3159, Kabul; f. 1966; exports traditional hand-knotted carpets and rugs; Pres. BASHARIAR; Vice-Pres. A. RAHIM ANDKHOY.

Office S. M. Azam Azimi: P.O.B. 498, Kabul; f. 1972; carries out import-export transactions.

Balkh Union: export and import agency handling exports of wool, hides and karakul.

Wool Company: deals with wool exports.

TRADE UNIONS

Trade Union Organization of Afghanistan: Kabul; f. 1978 to establish and develop the Trade Union movement; total membership of Trade Unions 170,000 (mid-1979); Chair. M. A. SHAFIQ.

TRANSPORT

RAILWAYS

In 1977 the Government approved plans for a railway system. The proposed railway (1,815 kilometres long) will connect Kabul to Kandahar and Herat, and will run through Islamqala and Mashed to join the Iranian railway network. Another branch will run from Kandahar to link with Pakistan Railways at Quetta. By mid-1979 work had not yet begun on the proposed railway because of political difficulties.

ROADS

Ministry of Communication and Ministry of Public Works: Kabul; in 1977 there were 2,787 kilometres of paved roads out of a total distance of 18,580 kilometres. All-weather highways now link Kabul with Kandahar and Herat in the south and west, Jalalabad in the east and Mazar-i-Sharif and the Oxus in the north. Road development continues with the aid of foreign loans.

Afghan Motor Service and Parts Co.: Zendabanon Workshops, P.O.B. 86, Kabul; passenger services in Kabul; long-distance freight and passenger services from Kabul to most parts of the country; trucking services in all towns; Pres. HAFIZULLAH RAHIMI; Vice-Pres. KHAWJA MOENODDIN.

The Millie Bus Enterprise: Kabul; government-owned and run.

INLAND WATERWAYS

River ports on the Oxus are linked by road to Kabul.

CIVIL AVIATION

Civil Aviation and Tourism Authority: Ansari Wat, P.O.B. 165, Kabul; Pres. NOOR MOHAMMAD DALILI; Dir. ABDUL WASEH HAIDARI.

There are international airports at Kabul and Kandahar.

NATIONAL AIRLINES

Ariana Afghan Airlines Co. Ltd.: P.O.B. 76, Ansari Wat, Kabul; f. 1955; services to India, Iran, Pakistan (suspended March 1979), U.S.S.R., Turkey, Europe; Pres. Col. MOHD NADIR; 1 DC-10-30, 2 727-100C.

Bakhtar Afghan Airlines: Ansari Wat, P.O.B. 165, Kabul; f. 1968; internal services between Kabul and 12 regional locations; 3 DHC-6 Twin Otter projects, 7 YAK-40 jets; Pres. NIAZ MOHAMMAD; Dir. of Operations Capt. R. NAWROZ.

The following airlines also operate services to Afghanistan: Aeroflot (U.S.S.R.), Indian Airlines, Iran Air and PIA (Pakistan).

TOURISM

Afghan Tourist Organization: Ansari Wat, Kabul; f. 1958; Pres. HASSAN KASSEEM; Vice-Pres. G. R. AMIRI; publ. *Statistical bulletin* (quarterly) and *Annual Report*.

Afghan Tour: Kabul; official travel agency supervised by A.T.O.

ATOMIC ENERGY

Atomic Energy Commission: Faculty of Science, Kabul University, Kabul; Pres. of Commission and Dean of Faculty Dr. F. M. RAOUFY.

DEFENCE

Supreme Defence Council: Kabul; founded March 1979 to improve defence, supervise the armed forces, approve the Defence Budget and safeguard internal security.

Armed Forces: (July 1978) Total strength 110,000; army 100,000; air force 10,000; reserves total 162,000 and para-military forces comprise 30,000 gendarmes; military service lasting two years is compulsory for every able-bodied man.

Equipment: The army's equipment and training are very largely provided by the Soviet Union. The air force has 144 Russian-built combat aircraft.

Defence Expenditure: Estimated defence expenditure in 1977/78 was 2,700 million afghanis (U.S. $60.7 million).

EDUCATION

The traditional system of education in Afghanistan was religious instruction in Madrasas, or Mosque schools. These centres are still active, but a modern educational system has been built up since 1904.

Since 1933 primary, middle and secondary schools have been opened all over the country. The development of education since 1961 has been rapid especially at the primary level. It is estimated that the proportion of children aged 6 to 11 years receiving primary education increased from 9 per cent in 1960 to 23 per cent in 1975. Only 7 per cent of girls in this age-group were enrolled and only 8 per cent of all children aged 12 to 16 attended secondary schools. In 1979 the Government announced the introduction of compulsory education for children over seven years of age. Competitive examinations for high-school entrance were abolished in 1978 and by 1979 the Government claimed to have opened 800 new schools since April 1978.

Under the Five-year Social and Economic Development Plan (1979–84), a massive programme to combat adult illiteracy has been launched (It has been estimated that only 10 per cent of males and 2 per cent of females are literate). The programme aims to reach over 8 million people by the end of the Plan.

Teacher training began on an organized scale in the early 1950s. The University of Kabul was founded in 1932 when the Faculty of Medicine was established. It now has 11 Faculties. In 1972 a second university was founded in Jalalabad, Nangarhar province; again the nucleus was provided by a Medical Faculty.

Progress is also being made in women's education, and girls' schools are now found in all major cities.

UNIVERSITIES

Kabul University: Kabul; 1,115 teachers, 9,865 students.

University of Nangarhar: Jalalabad; 75 teachers, 613 students.

BIBLIOGRAPHY

GENERAL

AFGHAN TRANSPORT & TRAVEL SERVICE. Afghanistan—Ancient Land with Modern Ways (London, 1961).

CAROE, OLAF. The Pathans.

GRASSMUCK, GEORGE, and ADAMEC, LUDWIG. (eds.) Afghanistan: Some new approaches (Center for Near Eastern and North African Studies, University of Michigan, 1969).

GREGORIAN, VARTAN. The Emergence of Modern Afghanistan (Stanford University Press, Stanford, 1969).

GRIFFITHS, JOHN C. Afghanistan (Pall Mall Press, London, 1967).

KESSEL, FLINKER and KLIMBURG. Afghanistan (photographs, 1959).

KING, PETER. Afghanistan, Cockpit in Asia (Bles, London, 1966, Taplinger, N.Y., 1967).

KLIMBURG, M. Afghanistan (Austrian UNESCO Commission, Vienna, 1966).

SHALISI, PRITA K. Here and There in Afghanistan.

WATKINS, MARY B. Afghanistan, an Outline (New York, 1962).

Afghanistan, Land in Transition (Van Nostrand, Princeton, N.J., 1963).

WILBER, DONALD N. Afghanistan (New Haven, Conn., 1956).

Annotated Bibliography of Afghanistan (New Haven, Conn., 1962).

GEOGRAPHY AND TRAVELS

BURNES, Sir ALEXANDER. Cabool (John Murray, London, 1842).

BYRON, ROBERT. Road to Oxiana.

ELPHINSTONE, M. An Account of the Kingdom of Caubul and its Dependencies in Persia, Tartary and India (John Murray, London, 1815).

FERRIER, J. P. Caravan Journeys.

HAHN, H. Die Stadt Kabul und ihr Umland (2 vols., Bonn, 1964–65).

HAMILTON, ANGUS. Afghanistan (Heinemann, London, 1906).

HUMLUM, J. La Géographie de l'Afghanistan (Gyldendal, Copenhagen, 1959).

MASSON, CHARLES. Narrative of various journeys in Baluchistan, Afghanistan and the Punjab (Bentley, London, 1842).

MOHUN LAL. Journal.

WOLFE, N. H. Herat (Afghan Tourist Organization, Kabul, 1966).

WOOD, JOHN. A Personal Narrative of a Journey to the Source of the River Oxus by the Route of Indus, Kabu and Badakshan (John Murray, London, 1841).

HISTORY

ADAMEC, LUDWIG W. Afghanistan 1900–1923 (University of California, Berkeley, 1967).

Afghanistan's Foreign Affairs to the Mid-Twentieth Century (University of Arizona Press, Tucson, 1974).

BOSWORTH, C. E. The Ghaznavids (Edinburgh University Press, 1963).

CAMBRIDGE HISTORY OF INDIA, Vols. I, III, IV, V, VI.

DOLLOT, RENÉ. Afghanistan (Payot, Paris, 1937).

DUPREE, LOUIS and LINNET, ALBERT (eds.). Afghanistan in the 1970s (Praeger, New York, 1974 and Pall Mall Press, London).

FLETCHER, ARNOLD. Afghanistan, Highway of Conquest (Cornell and Oxford University Presses, 1965).

FRASER-TYTLER, Sir W. KERR. Afghanistan (Oxford University Press, 1950, 3rd edn., 1967).

GOVERNMENT OF INDIA. The Third Afghan War, 1919 (Calcutta, 1926).

GREGORIAN, VARTAN. The Emergence of Modern Afghanistan—Politics of Reform and Modernization 1880–1946 (Stanford University Press, 1970).

GROUSSET. L'Empire des Steppes.

KHAN, M. M. S. M. (ed.) The Life of Abdur Rahman, Amir of Afghanistan (John Murray, London, 1900).

KOHZAD, A. A. Men and Events (Government Printing House, Kabul).

MACRORY, PATRICK. Signal Catastrophe (Hodder & Stoughton, London, 1966).

MASSON, V. M., and ROMODIN, V. A. Istoriya Afghanistana (Akad. Nauk, Moscow, 1964–65).

MOHUN LAL. Life of the Amir Dost Mohammed Khan of Kabul (Longmans, London, 1846).

NORRIS, J. A. The First Afghan War, 1838–42 (Cambridge University Press, 1967).

SYKES, Sir PERCY. A History of Afghanistan (Macmillan, London, 1940).

TATE, G. P. The Kingdom of Afghanistan (London, 1911).

ECONOMY

ASIAN CONFERENCE ON INDUSTRIALIZATION. Industrial Development: Asia and the Far East (Report of Manila Conference, 1965, published by ECAFE, Bangkok).

MALEKYAR, ABDUL WAHED. Die Verkehrsentwicklung in Afghanistan (Cologne, 1966).

RHEIN, E. and GHAUSSY, A. GHANIE. Die wirtschaftliche Entwicklung Afghanistans, 1880-1965 (C. W. Leske Verlag, Hamburg 1966).

Algeria

PHYSICAL AND SOCIAL GEOGRAPHY

Algeria is the largest of the three countries in north-west Africa that comprise the Maghreb, as the region of mountains, valleys and plateaux that lies between the sea and the Sahara desert is known. It is situated between Morocco and Tunisia with a Mediterranean coastline of nearly 1,000 km. and a total area of some 2,381,741 sq. km., over four fifths of which lies south of the Maghreb proper and within the western Sahara. Its extent, both from north to south and west to east, exceeds 2,000 km. The Arabic name for the country, *al Jazair* (the Islands), is said to derive from the rocky islands along the coastline, which have always constituted a danger to ships approaching the harbours.

Based on the 1977 census, the estimated population at January 1st, 1978, was 18,250,000 (including about 828,000 Algerian nationals living abroad). The great majority of the inhabitants live in the northern part of the country, particularly along the Mediterranean coast where both the capital, Algiers (population, with suburbs, 1.8 million in 1977), and the second largest town, Oran (about 500,000), are located. The population is almost wholly Muslim, of whom a majority speak Arabic and the remainder Berber, the language of the original inhabitants of the Maghreb. Most educated Algerians, however, speak French. Nearly all the European settlers, who numbered about 1 million in 1960, have left the country since it attained its independence from France in 1962.

PHYSICAL FEATURES

The primary contrast in the physical geography of Algeria is between the mountainous, relatively humid terrain of the north, which forms part of the Atlas mountain system, and the vast expanse of lower, flatter desert to the south, which is part of the Saharan tableland. The Atlas Mountains trend from south-west to north-east across the whole of the Maghreb. Structurally they resemble the "Alpine" mountain chains of Europe north of the Mediterranean and, like them, they came into existence during the geologically recent Tertiary era. They are still unstable and liable to severe earthquakes, such as that which partially destroyed Orléansville (now El Asnam) in 1954. They consist of rocks, now uplifted, folded and fractured, that once accumulated as submarine deposits beneath an ancestral Mediterranean sea. Limestones and sandstones are particularly extensive and they often present a barren appearance in areas where a cover of soil and vegetation is only thin or absent altogether.

In Algeria the Atlas mountain system is made up of three broad zones running parallel to the coast: the Tell Atlas, the High Plateaux and the Saharan Atlas. In the north, and separated from the Mediterranean only by a narrow and discontinuous coastal plain, is the complex series of mountains and valleys that comprise the Tell Atlas. Here individual ranges, plateaux and massifs vary in height from about 500 to 2,500 metres, and are frequently separated from one another by deep valleys and gorges which divide the country into self-contained topographic and economic units. Most distinctive of these are the massifs of the Great and Little Kabyle between Algiers and the Tunisian frontier, which have acted as mountain retreats where Berber ways of village life persist.

South of the Tell Atlas lies a zone of featureless plains known as the High Plateaux of the Shotts. To the west, near the Moroccan frontier, they form a broad, monotonous expanse of level terrain about 160 km. across and over 1,000 metres high. They gradually narrow and fall in height eastward and end in the Hodna basin, a huge enclosed depression, the bottom of which is only 420 metres above sea-level. The surface of the plateaux consists of alluvial debris derived from erosion of the mountains to north and south, and only here and there do minor ridges project through the thick mantle of alluvium to break the monotony of the level horizons. The plateaux owe their name to the presence of several vast basins of internal drainage, known as shotts, the largest of which is the Hodna basin. During rainy periods water accumulates in the shotts to form extensive shallow lakes which give way, as the water is absorbed and evaporated, to saline mud flats and swamps.

The southern margin of the High Plateaux is marked by a series of mountain chains and massifs that form the Saharan Atlas. They are more broken than the Tell Atlas and present no serious barrier to communications between the High Plateaux and the Sahara. From west to east the chief mountain chains are the Ksour, Amour, Ouled Naïl, Ziban and Aurès. The latter is the most impressive massif in the whole Algerian Atlas system and includes the highest peak: Djebel Chelia, 2,328 metres. The relief of the Aurès is very bold, with narrow gorges cut between sheer cliffs surmounted by steep bare slopes, and to the east and north of the Hodna basin its ridges merge with the southernmost folds of the Tell Atlas. North-eastern Algeria forms, therefore, a compact block of high relief in which the two Atlas mountain systems cease to be clearly separated. Within it there are a number of high plains studded with salt flats but their size is insignificant compared with the enormous shotts to the west.

CLIMATE AND VEGETATION

The climate of northernmost Algeria, including the narrow coastal plain and the Tell Atlas southward to the margin of the High Plateaux, is of "Mediterranean" type with warm wet winters and hot dry summers. Rainfall varies in amount from over 1,000 mm. annually on some coastal mountains exposed to rain-bearing winds to less than 130 mm. in sheltered, lee situations, and most of it occurs during the winter when depressions pass across the western Mediterranean most frequently. Complete drought lasts for three to four months during the summer and at this time, too, the notorious sirocco occurs. It is a scorching, dry and dusty south wind blowing from the Sahara and is known locally as the Chehili. It blows on 40 or more days a year over the High Plateaux but nearer the coast its frequency is reduced to about 20 days. When it sets in, shade temperatures often rise rapidly to over 40°C. and vegetation and crops, unable to withstand the intensity of evaporation, may wither and die within a few hours. As a result of low and uneven rainfall combined with high rates of evaporation the rivers of the Tell tend to be short and to suffer large seasonal variations in flow. Many dry out completely during the summer and are only full for brief periods following heavy winter rains. The longest perennially flowing river is the Oued Chélif which rises in the High Plateaux and crosses the Tell to reach the Mediterranean east of Oran.

Along the northern margin of the High Plateaux, which approximately coincides with the limit of 400 mm. mean annual rainfall, "Mediterranean" conditions give way to a semi-arid or steppe climate in which summer drought lasts from five to six months and winters are colder and drier. Rainfall is reduced to between 200 and 400 mm. annually and tends to occur in spring and autumn rather than in winter. It is, moreover, very variable from year to year, and under these conditions the cultivation of cereal crops without irrigation becomes quite unreliable. South of the Saharan Atlas annual rainfall decreases to below 200 mm. and any regular cultivation without irrigation becomes impossible. There are no permanent rivers south of the Tell Atlas and any surface run-off following rain is carried by temporary watercourses towards local depressions, such as the shotts.

The soils and vegetation of northern Algeria reflect the climatic contrast between the humid Tell and the semi-arid lands farther south, but they have also suffered widely from the destructive effects of over-cultivation, over-grazing and deforestation. In the higher, wetter and more isolated parts of the Tell Atlas relatively thick soils support forests of Aleppo pine, cork-oak and evergreen oak, while the lower, drier, and more accessible slopes tend to be bare or covered only with thin soils and a scrub growth of thuya, juniper and various drought-resistant shrubs. Only a few remnants survive of the once extensive forests of Atlas cedar which have been exploited for timber and fuel since classical times. They are found chiefly above 1,500 metres in the eastern Tell Atlas. South of the Tell there is very little woodland except in the higher and wetter parts of the Saharan Atlas. The surface of the High Plateaux is bare or covered only with scattered bushes and clumps of esparto and other coarse grasses.

SAHARAN ALGERIA

South of the Saharan Atlas, Algeria extends for over 1,500 km. into the heart of the desert. Structurally, this huge area consists of a resistant platform of geologically ancient rocks against which the Atlas Mountains were folded. Over most of the area relief is slight, with occasional plateaux, such as those of Eglab, Tademaït and Tassili-n-Ajjer, rising above vast spreads of gravel such as the Tanezrouft plain and huge sand accumulations such as the Great Western and Eastern Ergs. In the south-east, however, the great massif of Ahaggar rises to a height of 2,918 metres. Here erosion of volcanic and crystalline rocks has produced a lunar landscape of extreme ruggedness. Southward from the Ahaggar the massifs of Adrar des Iforas and Aïr extend across the Algerian frontier into the neighbouring countries of Mali and Niger.

The climate of Saharan Algeria is characterized by extremes of temperature, wind and aridity. Daily temperature ranges reach 32°C. and maximum shade temperatures of over 55°C. have been recorded. Sometimes very high temperatures are associated with violent dust storms. Mean average rainfall is everywhere less than 130 mm., and in some of the central parts of the desert it falls to less than 10 mm. It is, however, extremely irregular and often torrential; a fall of several cm. in one day may be followed by several years of absolute drought. These rigorous conditions are reflected in the extreme sparseness of the vegetation and in a division of the population into settled cultivators, who occupy oases dependent on permanent supplies of underground water, and nomadic pastoralists who make use of temporary pastures which become available after rain.

D.R.H.

HISTORY

Algeria as a political entity is a phenomenon of the last four hundred years: the history of its peoples, however, is of considerably greater antiquity. Little is known of the origin of the Berber people who have comprised the majority of the population of this part of Africa since the earliest times, but they had long been established there in numerous nomadic tribes when, at the time of the Punic Wars, the first ephemeral state-organizations may be distinguished in the area. The most important of these states was Numidia (208–148 B.C.), established by the chieftain Masinissa, which occupied most of present-day Algeria north of the Sahara. With the destruction of Carthage in 146 B.C., Numidia, greatly reduced in extent, was transformed into a Roman vassal-state. By the time of Augustus, Numidia was merely a senatorial province of the empire, while the rest of the area formed a loose confederacy of more or less independent tribes. Roman rule lasted until the fifth century. In the coastal centres of trade and culture a certain degree of assimilation to Roman ways took place, but in the mountains and deserts of the interior the Berber tribes maintained their independence by frequent revolt.

The adoption of Christianity as the official religion of the Roman Empire, in the early part of the fourth century, provided a convenient ideological framework for Berber separatism: in particular, their adherence to the Donatist heresy provoked violent civil war and religious strife throughout this period. Under the impact of barbarian invasions, the Roman Empire in the west slowly disintegrated in the course of the fifth century, towards the end of which its rule in North Africa was replaced by the transient dominion of the Vandals. A nomadic people of Germanic origin, they established themselves in the east of present-day Algeria, but failed, like the Romans before them, to gain any real control over the Berber tribes of the hinterland. In A.D. 531, Roman, or rather Byzantine, rule was restored in North Africa, with the conquest by the emperor Justinian of the provinces of Africa (the modern Tunisia) and Numidia, and the establishment of a tenuous hold on the coast as far west as the region of modern Algiers. Elsewhere the Berber confederacies, centred in the Aurès and the Kabyle, maintained their independence.

The rise of Islam in Arabia, and its rapid expansion after the death of the Prophet (632), leading to the Arab conquest of Syria and Egypt, was quickly followed by the penetration of North Africa. The first Arab raids into North Africa (or the Maghreb, as the region comprising the present states of Morocco, Algeria, and Tunisia now came to be called) took place about the middle of the seventh century. The foundation of Kayrawan in 670 provided a permanent base for their operations, which remained for a time little more than raids. The towns remained under Byzantine control, while the Berber tribes, uniting against the invaders, killed the Arab leader, Ukba ibn Nafi (682), and set up a Berber state centred in the eastern Maghreb. Increasing Arab immigration towards the end of the seventh century finally put an end to Berber resistance, under its heroic and legendary warrior-queen Kahina (692). At the same time the last Byzantine garrisons were dislodged from their coastal strongholds, and the whole of the area was incorporated into the Ummayad Empire. The Berbers, for their part, became converted *en masse* to Islam, and, enrolling in its armies, went on with them to the conquest of the western Maghreb and of Spain.

BERBER UNREST

This new-found Islamic unity of North Africa did not long endure. Dissatisfied with their inferior position as non-Arabs in what was in fact an Arab empire, the Berbers adopted Muslim heresies as eagerly as they had previously embraced Christian ones.

The first signs of unrest appeared early in the eighth century, part of a general movement of discontent among the non-Arab peoples of the empire, which in the course of the succeeding years was to bring about the downfall of the Ummayad dynasty (750). By this time the Berbers had become converted to Kharijism, an esoteric radical Muslim sect, and in 756 under its auspices they destroyed completely the authority of the recently-established Abbasid Caliphate throughout the Maghreb. In the east of the area imperial authority was restored in 761, ushering in a period of forty years' anarchy and civil war. In the centre and west of the Maghreb, an area comprising much of present-day Algeria, a number of small, mostly heretical states arose. Later, in the ninth century, the focal point of Berber Kharijism was transferred from Tlemcen to Tiaret. Meanwhile, in the west, the authority of the caliphs had been superseded by that of an independent dynasty, the Aghlabids, who, ruling from Kayrawan, attempted to extend their control into the central Maghreb. In opposition to their rule the Berbers of the Kabyle now embraced Shi'i doctrines—in contrast with their previous adoption of Kharijism—a move which led in 910 to the establishment of the Fatimid dynasty in the central Maghreb. Fatimid rule, however, was not undisputed. From 943 to 947 they were faced with the terrible revolt of Abu Yazid, known as "The man with a donkey", and from then on Fatimid interest in and power over the central Maghreb declined. After several attempts the capital of the dynasty was in 973 transferred to Egypt, while power in the Maghreb was again disputed between various Berber confederacies. In the centre and the east the Sinhaja tribes, the successors to the Kutama who had established the Fatimids, supported the minor dynasty of the Zirids; in the west the more nomadic Zenata established themselves under the remote suzerainty of the Spanish Ummayads. In the early eleventh century the Sinhaja Banu Hammad rose to the status of a local dynasty, ruling as neighbours of the kingdom of Kayrawan.

An event of some importance in the history of the

Maghreb occurred *c.* 1050: the invasion of the Banu Hilal, a confederation of Arab tribes dislodged from Egypt. These nomads severely damaged the economy of North Africa, and represent the only considerable Arab immigration into the Maghreb since the original Arab conquest of the area. A period of anarchy ensued, but some order was restored by the Berber dynasty of the Almoravids who, coming from Morocco, brought the area of modern Algiers and Oran under their rule. The Banu Hammad, meanwhile, had become established at Bougie. Almoravid power rapidly declined, and *c.* 1147 they were succeeded by the Almohads. This dynasty, perhaps the most important to rule in North Africa in the medieval Islamic period, unified the whole of the Maghreb together with Muslim Spain. This was a time of cultural and economic prosperity for North Africa, especially at Tlemcen, and witnessed the expansion of trade with the northern shores of the Mediterranean, but the precarious unity of the Maghreb was short-lived. By 1250 the area was again in a condition of political chaos and instability, with the Zenata Banu 'Abd al-Wad exercising such power as existed. A general decline set in, which was to last for over two centuries, during which time the general prevalence of the Berber language gradually gave way to Arabic, a further legacy of the Hilali invasions.

Throughout this period the chief seat of political power was at Tlemcen. In the interior various minor princes asserted their independence, while the coastal towns, including the minor port of Algiers, organized themselves into independent republics, the chief support of which came from piracy. This state of affairs, which lasted throughout the fourteenth century, was terminated by the sudden involvement of Algiers in matters of more than local significance.

OTTOMAN RULE

The Spanish monarchy, bringing to completion its task of driving Muslim power from the Iberian peninsula with the conquest of Granada in 1492, now carried its crusade across the Mediterranean to North Africa. The fragmented political state of that area offered little obstacle to its progress. Mers el-Kebir was captured in 1505, Oran in 1509, and Bougie in 1510, while Algiers, at that time a small port of little importance except as a centre for piracy, was reduced to submission in the same year. On the death of Ferdinand of Castile in 1516 the Algerines, in an attempt to throw off Spanish rule, sent envoys to the Turkish corsair Aruj, seeking his assistance. Aruj took possession of the town, together with other places on the littoral and Tlemcen in the interior, and caused himself to be proclaimed sultan. In 1518 Aruj was killed and was succeeded by his brother Khayr al-Din Barbarossa, who, in order to consolidate his position, placed all the territories which he controlled under the protection of the Ottoman sultan. This decisive act, which brought together under a single jurisdiction the whole of the coast of North Africa and its immediate hinterland between Constantine and Oran, may be said to mark the emergence of Algeria as a political concept. Meanwhile, the struggle for North Africa, one aspect of the conflict between Ottoman and Hapsburg which ranged from the western Mediterranean to Hungary and the Indian Ocean, continued. In 1529 Khayr al-Din drove the Spaniards from the Peñón, the fortified rock which overlooks Algiers, while throughout the next decade constant Spanish efforts were made to re-establish their position in the area. Finally, in 1541, a great expedition led by the Emperor Charles V in person, failed miserably in its objectives, and after that Algeria was left for three centuries to the Muslims. Ottoman rule in Algiers had already been further strengthened. In 1533 Khayr al-Din had been summoned to Istanbul to take charge of the Ottoman fleet. In his place a more regular administration was set up, under a succession of *beylerbeys* responsible directly to the sultan. The regime of the *beylerbeys* lasted in Algiers until 1587, when it was replaced by a government headed by a series of *pashas*, who were appointed for a term of three years. These again were succeeded in power in 1659 by the *aghas* (or commanders) of the corps of janissaries, replaced later by the *deys*, who retained their power until the French occupation in 1830. All these changes were, however, very much on the surface. From the mid-sixteenth century actual Ottoman supervision of Algerian affairs became increasingly a convenient fiction, perpetuated in the interests of both the Algerines themselves and the imperial authorities at Istanbul. The real power in Algiers gradually came into the hands of two main bodies. One, the nominal representative of Ottoman power, was the janissary corps, who were for the most part of Anatolian origin; the other, the so-called *taife-i ruesa*, was the guild of corsair captains, men of widely differing origins, who for over three centuries were the main financial support of the state.

The Regency of Algiers reached the peak of its prosperity in the course of the seventeenth century. During this period the rulers of the state entered into diplomatic relations with the leading maritime states of western Europe—England, Holland and France, while these countries maintained their consuls or agents at Algiers. The profitable trade of piracy flourished throughout the century, bringing to Algiers great wealth in the form of captured ships, cargoes and men, and great notoriety as the centre of the North African slave trade. Throughout the seventeenth and eighteenth centuries Algiers looked outwards to the sea. Despite some early Turkish attempts to control the interior, many of the Berber tribes, especially in the Aurès and the Kabyle, maintained their independence throughout the period of Turkish rule; others, more accessible to Algiers, paid to the *dey* a grudging tribute, or unwillingly recognized his suzerainty. With the eighteenth century, and the growth of European seapower in the Mediterranean, conditions became less favourable for corsair activity, and a period of decline set in. From a former figure of 100,000, the population of the city itself dropped to less than thirty thousand at the beginning of the nineteenth century, while in the interior, never firmly controlled by the Turks, the tribal chiefs extended their authority and a period of relative economic prosperity ensued.

In the period of the Napoleonic wars piracy and the economy of Algiers both underwent a certain revival, but this renewal of prosperity was shortlived. On the restoration of peace the European powers called upon the *dey* to abandon piracy, and in 1816 the British fleet bombarded Algiers. It was obvious that before long one of the European powers would take advantage of the growing anti-slavery movement in Europe, and the increasing weakness of Algiers itself, to go beyond naval demonstrations, and to land forces in the country. In the event, the conquest of Algiers was the work of France.

THE FRENCH CONQUEST

The excuse for intervention was an insult offered by the *dey* to the French consul in 1827: the real cause was the pressing need of Polignac, the chief minister under Charles X, to secure some credit for his administration in the eyes of the French public. On July 5th, 1830, Algiers fell to a French expedition, the *dey* and most of the Turkish officials being sent into exile. But the Polignac administration was unable to gather the fruits of its triumph, for before further plans for the consolidation of French rule, and its extension to other coastal towns, could be put into effect, the Bourbon dynasty and its government were overthrown by revolution. A further casualty in the revolution was Polignac's plan for handing over the rest of the country, and the decision on its future, to a European congress; instead, for four years, the problem of what to do with Algiers now that it was in French hands was left to mark time. Away from Algiers itself the absence of any central authority strengthened still further the prestige of the tribal chiefs. Finally, in 1834, following the report of a special commission, the further conquest and annexation of Algeria was decided upon, and a governor-general appointed to put the new plans into effect.

The history of Algeria for the next quarter of a century is mainly concerned with the gradual reduction of the country by France, against bitter and continuing opposition. Constantine, the last stronghold of Turkish rule, was captured in 1837, and by 1841 French rule had been consolidated in most of the ports and their immediate environs. By 1844 most of the eastern part of Algeria had been brought under French control, but in the west the conquerors were faced with the formidable power of Abd el-Kadir. This Berber leader, a skilful diplomat and a military commander of genius, had at first concluded treaties with the French, which consolidated his position as leader of the Berber confederacies in the west. But in 1839 he declared war on France, achieving widespread unity between Berbers and Arabs against the invaders. He held out until 1847, when he was finally defeated by the persistence and ruthless tactics of the French general Bugeaud, the real architect of French rule in Algeria. During the late 1840s and 1850s the tribes on the edge of the Sahara were pacified, while the virtual end of the conquest was achieved by the submission of the hitherto independent Berber confederacies of the Kabyle, in 1857. Further rebellion was to occur, however, throughout the nineteenth century, and especially after France's defeat at the hands of Prussia in the war of 1870–71.

Meanwhile, a policy of colonization, with widespread confiscation of land and its transference to settler groups, had been pushed forward. Bugeaud had at first encouraged colonization in the coastal plains; after 1848 the influx of colonists was much increased, with the approval of the governments of the Second Republic and, in its early years, the Second Empire. A further stimulus to colonization was provided by the widespread confiscation of lands resulting from the unsuccessful rebellion of 1871. By 1860 much of the best land in Algeria was in French hands, and was the scene of considerable subsequent agricultural development, while the French settlers themselves rapidly became the dominant power in the land. This was well seen some ten years later. Napoleon III had been favourably disposed towards the Algerian Muslim population, and had taken steps to protect tribal lands against settler encroachments, at the same time securing for Muslims the right to acquire French nationality. These measures had provoked strong opposition among the settlers, and in 1870, in the confusion of the Franco-Prussian War, the French colonists in Algeria expelled the imperial agents and set up a revolutionary commune.

After the confusion of the period of "commune" rule, and the subsequent Muslim revolt of 1871, the situation was regularized by the new French administration under Thiers. A civil administration with the status of a French *département* was set up for much of Algeria, while the amount of territory under military rule steadily declined. From then until the end of the nineteenth century Algeria was the scene of considerable economic progress, and increasing European immigration, especially from Italy. A feature of this period was the growth of large-scale agricultural and industrial enterprises, which concentrated still more power in the hands of the most powerful members of the settler groups. In 1900 Algeria secured administrative and financial autonomy, to be exercised through the so-called "Financial Delegations", composed of two-thirds European and one-third Muslim members, and empowered to fix the annual budget and to raise loans for further economic development.

In seventy years the Muslim people of Algeria had been reduced from relative prosperity to economic, social and cultural inferiority. Three million inhabitants had died, tribes had been broken up and the traditional economy altered during the prolonged "civilizing" campaigns. In particular, the production of wine for export had replaced the traditional production of cereals for home consumption. The settlers, however, experienced a high level of prosperity and economic progress in the years before the First World War. For the present, the French ascendancy seemed assured.

BIRTH OF NATIONALISM

The spirit of nationalism was spreading throughout the Middle East, however, and it emerged among the Algerian Muslims as a force to be reckoned with after the First World War. Nationalist aspirations began to be voiced not only by Algerian veterans of the war in Europe but also by Algerians who went to France to study or take up employment. In 1924 one of these students, Messali Hadj, founded in Paris the first Algerian nationalist newspaper, in collaboration with the French communist party; the link with the communists was severed in 1927, however. Messali Hadj and his movement were driven underground by the French Government, but reappeared in 1933 as sponsors of a congress on the future of Algeria which called for total independence, the recall of French troops, the establishment of a revolutionary government, large-scale reforms in land ownership and the nationalization of industrial enterprises.

More moderate doctrines were put forward in the post-war years by an influential body of French-educated Muslims, formalized in 1930 as the Federation of Muslim Councillors. Under the leadership of Ferhat Abbas, this group called for integration with France on a basis of complete equality. The victory of the Popular Front in the French elections of 1936 gave rise to the hope that at least some of these aspirations might be peaceably achieved. The Blum-Viollet Plan, which would have granted full rights of citizenship to an increasing number of Algerian Muslims, was, however, dropped by the French Government in the face of fierce opposition from the French settlers and the Algerian civil service.

The years immediately prior to World War II were marked by growing nationalist discontent, in which Messali Hadj, released from prison in 1936, played a significant part with the formation of the Party of the Algerian People (PPA). The outbreak of war in 1939 temporarily put an end to the nationalists' activities, but the war greatly strengthened their hand for the future. Although the Vichy administration in Algeria, strongly supported by the French settlers, was antipathetic to nationalist sentiment, the Allied landings in North Africa in 1942 provided an opportunity for the Algerian nationalists to put forward constitutional demands. A group headed by Ferhat Abbas on December 22nd, 1942, presented to the French authorities and the Allied military command a memorandum calling for the post-war establishment of an Algerian constituent assembly, to be elected by universal suffrage. No demand was made for Algerian independence outside the French framework, however.

These proposals, to which the French authorities remained unresponsive, were followed early in 1943 by the "Manifesto of the Algerian People", which called for immediate reforms, including the introduction of Arabic as an official language. Further proposals submitted in May envisaged the post-war creation of an Algerian state with a constitution to be determined by a constituent assembly, and looked forward to an eventual North African Union, comprising Tunisia, Algeria and Morocco. The newly-established Free French administration in Algiers rejected the Manifesto and the subsequent proposals out of hand.

In the face of growing Muslim discontent, and following a visit to Algiers by General de Gaulle, a new statute for Algeria was put into effect in March 1944. It was an attempt at compromise which satisfied neither the Algerian nationalists nor the European settlers. Membership of the French electoral college was opened to 60,000 Muslims, but there were still 450,000 European voters, and in the event only 32,000 Muslims accepted inscription. The Muslim share of the seats in the *communes mixtes* was restricted to 40 per cent. All further discussion of Algeria's future relationship with France was ruled out.

Ferhat Abbas shortly afterwards founded the Friends of the Manifesto of Freedom (AML), to work for the foundation of an autonomous Algerian republic linked federally with France. The new movement was based mainly on the support of middle-class Muslims, though it also gained a certain following among the masses. At the same time, Messali Hadj's PPA gained many followers among the masses during 1944 and 1945.

FRENCH INTRANSIGENCE

All possibility of an evolutionary settlement was destroyed by blunders of post-war French policy and the opposition of the French settlers to any concessions to Muslim aspirations. The ruthless suppression of the riots at Sétif in May 1945, which claimed the lives of some 15,000 Muslims, and the subsequent arrest of Ferhat Abbas and the dissolution of the AML drove many of the nationalist leaders to regard force as the only means of gaining their objective.

Nevertheless, attempts to reach a compromise solution continued for some time. In March 1946 Ferhat Abbas, released under an amnesty, launched the Democratic Union of the Algerian Manifesto (UDMA), with a programme providing for the creation of an autonomous, secular Algerian state within the French Union. Despite successes in elections to the French Assembly, the UDMA failed to achieve any of its objectives. It withdrew from the Assembly in September 1946 and refused to participate in the next elections. The breach was filled by the more radical Movement for the Triumph of Democratic Liberties (MTLD), the party formed by Messali Hadj at the end of the war, which demanded the creation of a sovereign constituent assembly and the evacuation of French troops—aims which stood no chance of adoption.

In another attempt at compromise the French Government introduced a new constitution which became law on September 20th, 1947. This gave French citizenship, and therefore the vote, to all Algerian citizens, including women, and recognized Arabic as equal in status to French. The proposed new Algerian Assembly, however, was to be divided into two colleges, each of 60 members, one to represent the 1½ million Europeans, the other the 9 million Muslims. Other provisions ruled out all possibility of anti-European legislation.

The new constitution was never brought fully into operation. Following MTLD successes in the municipal elections of October 1947, the elections to the Algerian Assembly were openly and clumsily interfered with, many candidates being arrested, election meetings forbidden and polling stations improperly operated.

As a result only a quarter of the members returned to the second college in April 1948 were MTLD or UDMA; the remainder, nominally "independent", were nonentities. Such methods continued to be employed in local and national elections during the next six years, as well as in the Algerian elections to the French National Assembly in June 1951. Some of the ameliorative provisions of the 1947 constitution were never put into effect. The aim was to destroy, or at least render harmless, opposition to French rule; the result was to drive the main forces of nationalism underground.

As early as 1947 several of the younger members of the MTLD had formed the "Secret Organization" (OS), which collected arms and money from supporters and built up a network of cells throughout Algeria in preparation for armed insurrection and the establishment of a revolutionary government. Two years later the OS felt itself strong enough to launch a terrorist attack in Oran. The movement was subsequently discovered and most of its leaders were arrested. A nucleus survived, however, in the Kabyle region, ever a stronghold for dissident groups, and the organizer of the attack, Ben Bella, escaped in 1952 to Cairo.

A decisive split was taking place in the ranks of the MTLD, and the veteran Messali Hadj, now embracing nebulous doctrines of pan-Arabism, was gradually losing control of the party organization to more activist members. The first open breach occurred in 1953, and in March the following year nine former members of the OS set up the Revolutionary Council for Unity and Action (CRUA) to prepare for an immediate revolt against French rule.

WAR OF INDEPENDENCE

Plans for the insurrection were worked out at a series of CRUA meetings in Switzerland between March and October 1954. Algeria was divided into six *wilaya* (zones) and a military commander appointed for each. When the revolt was launched on November 1st the CRUA changed its name to the National Liberation Front (FLN), its armed forces being known as the National Liberation Army (ALN). Beginning in the Aurès, the revolt had spread by early 1955 to the Constantine area, the Kabyle and the whole of the Moroccan frontiers west of Oran. By the end of 1956 the ALN was active throughout the settled areas of Algeria.

Ferhat Abbas and Ahmed Francis of the more bourgeois UDMA and the religious leaders of the Ulema joined the FLN in April 1956, making it representative of all shades of Algerian nationalist feeling apart from Messali Hadj's Algerian National Movement (MNA). In August a secret congress of the FLN, held at Soummam in the Kabyle, formed a central committee and the National Council of the Algerian Revolution; drew up a socialist programme for the future Algerian republic; and approved plans for the launching of a terrorist offensive in Algiers.

In the early stages of the war the French Government was convinced that only external support kept the FLN offensive going. The Foreign Minister was therefore despatched to Cairo in an attempt to persuade President Nasser to withdraw his support for the Algerian revolution. This mission was in vain, and Guy Mollet, the French Prime Minister, then resorted to collusion with the Israelis and the British in the abortive invasion of Egypt at the end of October 1956. The Suez operation not only did not topple Nasser, nor stop the Algerian struggle, it actually strengthened the FLN's position by increasing support from newly independent and non-aligned states.

Between September 1956 and June 1957 bomb explosions engineered by the FLN caused much loss of life. This terrorism was brought to a stop only by severe French repression of the Muslim population, including the use of torture and internment, measures which aroused condemnation of French policy both at home and abroad. Guerrilla activities continued but electrified barriers were set up along the Tunisian and Moroccan borders and ALN bands attempting to cross into Algeria met with heavy losses.

In June 1957 the Bourgès-Manoury administration in France, which had replaced that of Mollet the previous month, put forward legislation intended to link Algeria indissolubly with France, but the bill was never passed. Following the Soummam conference, a joint Moroccan-Tunisian plan had been put forward for the establishment of a North African federation linked with France. FLN leaders began negotiations in Morocco in October 1957. However, Ben Bella and his companions were kidnapped on their way from Morocco to Tunisia, when the French pilot of their plane, which the Sultan of Morocco had chartered for them, landed it at Algiers. The French authorities could hardly reject this *fait accompli*, and the hijacked leaders were arrested and interned in France. Neither the internment of FLN leaders nor the bombing by French aircraft, in February 1958, of the Tunisian border village of Sakhiet, in which 79 villagers were killed, had any effect on the FLN's capacity to continue fighting, and the failure of these desperate measures only made the possibility of French negotiations with the FLN more likely. This in turn provoked a backlash from the Algerian Europeans (only half of whom were of French origin).

In May 1958 they rebelled and set up committees of public safety in the major Algerian towns. Supported by the army and exploiting the widespread fear of civil war, the colonists caused the overthrow of the discredited Fourth French Republic and General de Gaulle's return to power, believing that he would further their aim of complete integration of Algeria into France. They were very soon to be bitterly disappointed. Although de Gaulle did step up military action against the FLN by the 500,000 French troops in Algeria, this was only at the cost of increased terrorism in Algiers and of growing tension on the Tunisian and Moroccan borders. The FLN responded in August 1958 by establishing in Tunis the Provisional Government of the Algerian Republic (GPRA), headed by Ferhat Abbas and including Ben Bella and the other leaders who had been interned in

France. De Gaulle was already beginning to recognize the strength of Algerian nationalism and was moving cautiously towards accepting FLN demands.

NEGOTIATIONS AND THE COLONISTS' LAST STAND

Initially de Gaulle's public statements on Algeria were vague. When he did make an unequivocal pronouncement, in September 1959, and upheld the right of Algerians to determine their own future, the colonists did not take long to react. In January 1960 they rebelled again, this time against de Gaulle, and erected barricades in Algiers streets. However, without the support of the army the insurrection collapsed within nine days. The first exploratory talks between French and FLN delegates took place in secret near Paris in the summer of 1960 but were abortive.

In November de Gaulle announced that a referendum was to be held on the organization of government in Algeria, pending self-determination, and in December he visited Algeria himself to prepare the way. In the referendum the electorate were asked to approve a draft law providing for self-determination and immediate reforms to give Algerians the opportunity to participate in government. There were mass abstentions from voting in Algeria, however, and in February 1961 new French approaches to the FLN were made through the President of Tunisia. Secret talks led to direct negotiations between French and FLN representatives at Evian, on the Franco-Swiss border. These began in May but were finally broken off in August over the question of the Sahara and because of the French attack on Bizerta.

Europeans in Algeria and segments of the French army had meanwhile formed the Secret Army Organization (OAS) to resist a negotiated settlement and the transfer of power from European hands. On April 22nd, 1961, four generals, Challe, Zeller, Jouhaud and Salan, organized the seizure of Algiers, but this attempt at an army *putsch* proved abortive, most regular officers remaining loyal to de Gaulle. Offensive operations against the Algerian rebels, which had been suspended when the Evian talks began, were resumed by the French Government in response to rebel pressure, and fighting continued, though on a reduced scale. At the same time the OAS began its campaign of indiscriminate terrorism against native Algerians. The Mayor of Evian had already been killed by an OAS bomb, and attacks were now also mounted in Paris.

Secret contacts between the French government and the FLN were re-established in October. Negotiations were resumed in December 1961 and January 1962 in Geneva and Rome, the five members of the GPRA interned in France taking part through a representative of the King of Morocco. Meetings at ministerial level were held in strict secrecy in Paris in February and the final stage of the negotiations was concluded at Evian on March 18th with the signing of a ceasefire agreement and a declaration of future policy. The declaration provided for the establishment of an independent Algerian state after a transitional period, and for the safeguarding of individual rights and liberties. Other declarations issued the following day dealt with the rights of French citizens in Algeria and with future Franco-Algerian cooperation. In the military sphere, France was to retain the naval base at Mers el-Kebir for 15 years and the nuclear testing site in the Sahara, together with various landing rights, for five years.

In accordance with the Evian agreements a provisional government was formed on March 28th, with Abderrahman Farès as provisional President and an executive composed of FLN members, other Muslims and Europeans. Ben Bella and the other detained Algerian leaders had been released on March 18th and flown to Morocco. The Soviet Union, the East European and many African and Asian countries quickly gave *de jure* recognition to the GPRA.

The signing of the Evian agreements was the signal for a final desperate fling by the OAS. A National Council of French Resistance in Algeria was set up, with General Salan as Commander-in-Chief, and OAS commando units attempted by attacks on the Muslim population and the destruction of public buildings to provoke a general breach of the ceasefire. After the failure of the OAS to establish an "insurrectional zone" in the Orléansville area and the capture of General Salan on April 20th, and with a renewal of FLN terrorist activity and reprisals, increasing numbers of Europeans began to leave Algeria for France. Abortive secret negotiations by OAS leaders with the FLN, aimed at securing guarantees for the European population, which began in May, disclosed a split in the OAS which heralded the virtual end of European terrorist activity. By the end of June over half the European population of Algeria had left.

The final steps towards Algerian independence were now taken. In a referendum on July 1st, 91 per cent of the electorate voted for independence, which was proclaimed by General de Gaulle on July 3rd, 1962.

THE INDEPENDENT STATE

The achievement of power by the FLN revealed serious tensions and weaknesses within the government, while the problems facing the new state after eight years of civil war were formidable.

The dominant position in the GPRA of the "centralist" group, headed by Ben Khedda and consisting of former members of the MTLD, was threatened by the release of the five GPRA members who had been detained in France—Ben Bella, Mohammed Khider, Mohammed Boudiaf, Ait Ahmed and Rabah Bitat. Boudiaf and Ait Ahmed rallied temporarily to the support of Ben Khedda, while the others formed yet another opposition faction besides that of Ferhat Abbas, who had been dropped from the GPRA leadership in 1961.

The ALN leadership was also split. The commanders of the main armed forces in Tunisia and Morocco were opposed to the politicians of the GPRA, and the commanders of the internal guerrilla groups were opposed to all external and military factions.

Serious differences had appeared when the National Council of the Algerian Revolution (CRNA) met in Tripoli in May 1962 to consider policies for the new state. A commission headed by Ben Bella produced a programme which included large-scale agrarian reform, involving expropriation and the establishment of peasant cooperatives and state farms; a state monopoly of external trade; and a foreign policy aimed towards Maghreb unity, neutralism and anti-colonialism, especially in Africa. Despite the opposition of Ben Khedda's group, the Tripoli programme became the official FLN policy.

When independence came on July 3rd the GPRA cabinet, with the exception of Ben Bella, flew to Algiers, where they installed themselves alongside the official Provisional Executive, and Ben Khedda attempted to reassert control over the ALN by dismissing the Commander-in-Chief, Col. Boumedienne. Ben Bella, however, flew to Morocco to join Boumedienne and on July 11th they crossed into Algeria and established headquarters in Tlemcen. Here Ben Bella set up the Political Bureau as the chief executive organ of the FLN and a rival to the GPRA. After negotiations he was joined by some of the GPRA leaders; this left Ben Khedda isolated in Algiers, with Boudiaf and Ait Ahmed in opposition.

Several of the *wilaya* leaders, however, felt that, having provided the internal resistance, they represented the true current of the revolution, and they were opposed to the Political Bureau and Boumedienne. While ALN forces loyal to the Bureau occupied Constantine and Bône in the east on July 25th, Algiers remained in the hands of the leadership of *wilaya* IV, who refused the Bureau entry. When Boumedienne's forces marched on Algiers from Oran at the beginning of September there were serious clashes with *wilaya* IV troops. Total civil war was averted, however, partly because of mass demonstrations against the fighting which were organized by the Algerian General Workers' Union (UGTA).

The struggle for power had gone against Ben Khedda. Before the elections were held on September 20th, 1962, a third of the 180 candidates on the single list drawn up in August were purged, including Ben Khedda himself, and their places filled with lesser-known figures. Although the elections failed to produce much public enthusiasm, some 99 per cent of the electorate were declared to have voted in favour of the proposed powers of the Constituent Assembly. The functions of the GPRA were transferred to the Assembly when it met on September 25th, and Ferhat Abbas was elected its President. The Algerian Republic was proclaimed and the following day Ben Bella was elected Prime Minister, with a cabinet drawn from his personal associates and former ALN officers.

BEN BELLA IN POWER

The new government immediately set about consolidating its position. Messali Hadj's PPA (formerly the MNA), the Algerian Communist Party, largely discredited because of its role in the war, and Boudiaf's Party of the Socialist Revolution were all banned in November; the *wilaya* system was abolished the following month, and, apart from the UGTA, all organizations affiliated to the FLN were brought firmly under control.

The economic plight of the country was severe. Some 90 per cent (one million) of the Europeans, representing virtually all the entrepreneurs, technicians, administrators, teachers, doctors and skilled workers had left the country. Factories, farms and shops had closed, leaving 70 per cent of the population unemployed. Public buildings and records had been destroyed by the OAS. At the end of the war, in which over a million had died, there had been two million in internment camps and 500,000 refugees in Tunisia and Morocco. Food, money and clothing were sent by many countries to alleviate the immediate suffering. In December 1962 an emergency austerity plan was drawn up and the government was enabled to continue functioning by large loans and technical assistance from France.

By packing the first UGTA congress with FLN militants and unemployed, the FLN managed in January 1963 to gain control of the UGTA executive, which had been opposed to the dictatorial nature of the new government. The decrees of March legalized the workers' committees which, aided by the UGTA, had taken over the operation of many of the deserted European estates in the summer and autumn of 1962. The system of workers' management known as *autogestion*, under which the workers elected their own management board to work alongside a state-appointed director, became the basis of "Algerian socialism".

In April 1963 Ben Bella increased his powers by taking over the post of general secretary of the FLN, ousting Mohammed Khider, who later went into exile. In August Ben Bella secured the adoption by the Assembly of a draft constitution providing for a presidential regime, with the FLN as the sole political party. The new constitution was approved in a referendum and on September 13th Ben Bella was elected President for a period of five years, assuming the title of commander-in-chief as well as becoming head of state and head of government.

These moves towards dictatorial government aroused opposition. Ferhat Abbas, the leading spokesman for a more liberal policy, resigned from the presidency of the Assembly and was subsequently expelled from the FLN. In the Kabyle, where discontent was accentuated by Berber regionalism, a revolt broke out during the late summer led by Ait Ahmed's Front of Socialist Forces (FFS) and former *wilaya* chief Col. Mohand Ou El Hadj. After some clashes Ben Bella reached agreement with Mohand but Ait Ahmed remained in the *maquis*. In October, partly in an attempt to regain popularity, Ben Bella nationalized the remaining European estates, placing them under *autogestion*, and suppressed the remaining French-controlled newspapers.

Long-standing disputes between Algeria and Morocco over areas on their common frontiers deteriorated into open conflict in October 1963, a fact which had made the need for agreement with Col. Mohand Ou El Hadj all the more pressing. The hostilities, near the strategic posts of Hassi-Beida and Tinjoub, were not on a large scale and were soon brought to an end through the mediation of interested African states, but they left a legacy of bitterness between the two countries.

THE FALL OF BEN BELLA

In the last year of its existence the Ben Bella regime appeared to be achieving both a certain measure of internal stability and an improvement in the country's external relations.

At the long-awaited first Congress of the FLN in April 1964, despite opposition from the right and silence from army delegates, Ben Bella secured acceptance of the "Algiers Charter", which criticized past mistakes of the FLN, defined relations between party, state and army, and attempted to formulate a theoretical basis for "Algerian socialism", centred on *autogestion*. This was the last occasion on which most of the "historic chiefs" met together. Soon afterwards Ait Ahmed's FFS again led a revolt in the Kabyle and Col. Chabaani, the army commander in the south, also rebelled against the Government. Both Chabaani and Ait Ahmed were eventually captured; the former was executed but the latter was reprieved in view of his popularity. Most of the other "historic chiefs" were eliminated from public life during 1964.

In the early months of 1965 the Algerian Government was preoccupied with preparations for an Afro-Asian conference, planned for the tenth anniversary of the Bandung Conference and due to open in Algiers on June 29th, when Ben Bella was to stand revealed both as the undisputed leader of Algeria and a force to be reckoned with in Afro-Asian affairs. The conference was not to take place. On June 19th Ben Bella was deposed and arrested in a swift and bloodless military *coup d'état*, led by the Minister of Defence, Col. Houari Boumedienne, whose army had brought Ben Bella to power in 1962.

The coup successfully pre-empted Ben Bella's own plans for a political takeover to coincide with the opening of the Afro-Asian conference. Ben Bella's takeover would have brought a shift to the left and the introduction of Marxist structures of political control. Ait Ahmed would have been freed and some right-wing ministers and Boumedienne detained. Ben Bella had been preparing for this for some time; he had announced that a popular militia was to be created, and he had dismissed Medeghri, the Minister of the Interior and one of Boumedienne's supporters. Finally, at the end of May, he had attempted to force the resignation of Bouteflika, the Foreign Minister, who was closely associated with Boumedienne. In the face of Algeria's poor economic situation and Ben Bella's dictatorial tendencies, many administrators and politicians were not averse to the coup, and his elimination of most of the traditional leaders, his repeated attacks on the UGTA and his failure to turn the FLN into a broadly-based party left him without organized support once the army had turned against him. Bereft of its leader, the FLN accepted the coup, and the UGTA, while expressing no real support for Boumedienne, did not oppose it. A number of known left-wingers, including former officials of the banned Algerian Communist Party, were arrested in September 1965 and the most militant of the opposition groups, the Organization of Popular Resistance, was broken up.

THE BOUMEDIENNE REGIME

Supreme political authority in Algeria was taken over by a Council of the Revolution, consisting mostly of military figures and presided over by Col. Boumedienne. Under the Council's authority a new Government of 20 members was announced on July 10th, with Boumedienne as Prime Minister and Minister of Defence, besides being President of the Council; Rabah Bitat as Minister of State; and Bouteflika continuing as Foreign Minister. Nine members of the Government, which included technocrats and members of the radical wing of the FLN, had held office under Ben Bella. To ensure a satisfactory relationship between the government and the FLN, a five-man party secretariat under Cherif Belkacem was set up on July 17th.

The aims of the new regime, as described by Boumedienne, were to re-establish the principles of the revolution, to remedy the abuses of personal power associated with Ben Bella, to end internal divisions, and to create an "authentic socialist society" based on a sound economy. In international relations a policy of non-alignment would be pursued and support for people struggling for freedom and independence would continue.

Although the army remained the basis of Boumedienne's power, an attempt was made in 1966 to strengthen the FLN party organization and, despite general apathy, to recruit new members. Boumedienne stated that under the one-party system contradictions between army and government should not arise, the task of the FLN being to "animate and direct". Feeling against the new regime, shown in demonstrations and student strikes in Algiers in January and February, became less apparent, particularly after a number of arrests of trade union leaders in July.

Signs that discord remained, however, were provided by the defection in August of Hadj Smain, Minister of Reconstruction and Housing before his resignation in April, and of Ahmed Mahsas and Bechir Boumaza, Ministers of Agriculture and Information respectively, in September and October. Slimane Rebba, national secretary of the UGTA, also defected in October. Ait Ahmed, in detention since 1964, had escaped from Algeria in April. Boumedienne nevertheless dismissed the opposition groups in exile as "out of circulation".

Apart from preparations for elections to the Communal Councils, the regime showed no signs of seeking a popular mandate and the Algerian National Assembly remained in abeyance. New penal and civil legal codes were promulgated in 1966, the judiciary was Algerianized and tribunals to try "economic crimes" with powers to impose the death penalty were set up in July. New conditions of service and training schemes for public employees were introduced with the aim of improving the standard of administration.

In accordance with its socialist policies, the regime increased state participation during 1966 in fields previously left to private enterprise. A state-owned construction company was set up, and it was decided in March that the distribution of the income of the oil and gas industry, both inside and outside Algeria, should be subject to government supervision. In May the nationalization was announced of eleven foreign-owned mines and of property of absentee owners, and all insurance activities were placed under state control. A National Bank of Algeria, specializing in short-term credit for the nationalized sector of the economy, was inaugurated in July.

Industrial activity continued at a low level and the country remained heavily dependent on external aid for industrial development. A new investment code, designed to attract both domestic and foreign capital and promulgated in September, contained assurances of indemnification in the event of nationalization.

CAUTION IN FOREIGN POLICY

The need to consolidate and build up national strength which influenced its domestic policies also caused Boumedienne's Government to conduct Algeria's foreign relations with caution, although it remained committed to "anti-imperialism" and a militant stand on the Palestine question.

The relationship with France, Algeria's main customer and the source of substantial assistance, remained paramount. In April 1966 an agreement was concluded which provided for French technical and educational assistance for 20 years. On December 23rd another agreement was signed which cancelled Algeria's pre-independence debts and reduced indebtedness to France to 400 million dinars. Relations were strained by conflicts of economic interests, especially when, in 1967, France revoked its undertaking to import Algerian wine, causing a crisis in Algerian agriculture which was only resolved in 1968 by the U.S.S.R.'s agreeing to take approximately half the country's wine exports. France was disturbed by the growing Soviet influence in Algeria. Soviet advisers were playing a leading role in the development of mining and industry, and the Algerian army was receiving training and equipment from the U.S.S.R. However, French fears that the Soviet navy might be allowed to use the Mers el-Kebir base, handed over by France in January 1968, proved groundless.

The French cultural influence remained: there were still many French teachers, although the teaching of Arabic was being extended in the schools; large numbers of Algerians worked in France; there was a preference for such French consumer goods as were still being imported; and France continued to give assistance, including training and equipment for Algeria's armed forces.

Algerian involvement in the six-day Palestine war in June 1967 was small. When the ceasefire came, however, there were street demonstrations against Nasser's "treason" and also against the Soviet Union for lack of support for the Arab countries. At the Khartoum conference and also at the United Nations, Algeria's voice was one of the most belligerent, calling for a people's war such as had been fought against the French, and as a token of support detachments of Algerian troops were maintained in the Suez Canal area until August 1970.

A highly critical, often openly hostile attitude to the United States was maintained, and diplomatic relations were severed in 1967. Nevertheless, American oil expertise was respected and encouraged; a substantial American investment in Algeria's oil industry remained, and a contract to sell liquefied natural gas to the United States was signed in 1969.

In Africa the Boumedienne Government took a consistently anti-colonial line, breaking relations with Britain over Rhodesia in 1965 (but restoring them in 1968), and providing training and other facilities for the liberation movements of southern Africa, as well as to the Eritrean Liberation Front and the National Liberation Front of Chad. A determined effort was made to improve relations with neighbouring countries in the Maghreb. In January 1969 President Boumedienne paid his first official visit to Morocco for talks with King Hassan, and the following June frontier posts were reopened for the first time since 1963. In May 1970 King Hassan and President Boumedienne signed an agreement at Tlemcen settling the long-standing border dispute and pledging mutual cooperation on the question of the Spanish presence in North Africa. Further agreements were signed between the two leaders in June 1972, one defining the Algerian—Moroccan border, the other providing for joint exploitation of the Gara-Djebilet mines in the border regions. Algeria ratified her border settlement with Morocco in May 1973. An agreement with Mauritania was signed in December 1969 and a friendship treaty with Tunisia agreeing on common borders in January 1970. Whilst Algeria welcomed the Libyan revolution in 1969, the subsequent orientation of the Libyan leaders towards Egypt and the Sudan rather than the Maghreb, was not conducive to close relations between the two regimes; nevertheless, an agreement to coordinate oil policies was signed.

INTERNAL OPPOSITION OVERCOME

The uneasy alliance between opponents of Ben Bella which had enabled Boumedienne to take over in 1965 broke down in 1967. Boumedienne's main support came from the "Oujda group"—Bouteflika, Medeghri, Kaid Ahmed and Cherif Belkacem; ex-members of the GPRA, such as Ben Yahia, Lamine Khane and Belaid Abdessalam; and the new professionals in the administration and the army. Opposition came from certain left-wing ministers, such as Ali Yahia and Abdelaziz Zerdani, the UGTA, the students, and some sections of the army, notably the former *wilaya* leaders. These feared the imposition of a technocratic and centralized form of socialism, different from the syndicalist concepts embodied in *autogestion*, and felt that collegial rule was being supplanted by the dictatorship of the small group round Boumedienne.

During the first half of 1967 the conflict was muted. There was student unrest in February and May, and in the communal elections in February, in which the opposition elements urged abstention, although a turn-out of 71 per cent was officially claimed there were reports of low polls in the Kabyle and Oran regions and of no more than a 50 per cent poll in the Algiers region. Unity brought about by the Palestine war was short-lived. When Abdessalem, Minister of Industry and Energy, attacked union officials and left-wing employees in the socialist sector at the end of June, the UGTA threatened to call a general strike, which was averted only by Boumedienne's mediation and the appointment of a committee of enquiry. In the autumn Ali Yahia resigned from the Ministry of Agriculture over the refusal of Kaid Ahmed, Minister of Finance to supply funds to help the *autogéré* sector of agriculture. A demand by former *wilaya* leaders for a meeting of the Council of the Revolution was refused by Boumedienne, who was uncertain of getting a majority. In December Kaid Ahmed was put in charge of the FLN, replacing the executive of Cherif Belkacem and several former *wilaya* leaders.

On December 14th, 1967, Col. Tahar Zbiri, army chief of staff and a prominent former *wilaya* leader, launched an armed rising in the Mitidja. It was put down two days later, but Zbiri was not captured and was joined in hiding by Abedlaziz Zerdani, the Minister of Labour, and other supporters. Cols. Mohand Ou El Hadj, Salah Boubnida and Katib Youcef also disappeared. The rising had failed because the key posts in the army were held by the younger professionals loyal to Boumedienne, and it was followed by a wave of arrests in the unions and the administration, and selective dismissals in the FLN and the army in order to secure his position. On March 7th Boumedienne appointed three well-known supporters to vacant ministerial offices: Cherif Belkacem (Finance), Tayebi Larbi (Agriculture) and Mohand Said Mazouni (Labour).

Opposition to Boumedienne was by no means crushed, however. FLN attempts in February 1968 to impose a new loyal student committee at Algiers University provoked a long strike by students and teachers, and in the spring there were numerous reports of guerrilla activity in the Aurès and the Kabyle. The Organization of Popular Resistance (ORP) appeared to be active both in these areas and among the students. An attempt to assassinate Boumedienne was made on April 25th in Algiers, but he escaped with only minor injuries.

In the latter part of 1968 there were signs that the Government's position had strengthened and President Boumedienne made several visits to the provinces without special security precautions. In March 1969 a number of secret trials were held and numbers of less important prisoners were subsequently released. The second stage of the reform of governmental institutions (the first being the 1967 communal elections) was put into operation in May 1969 when elections were held for the 15 administrative districts (*wilaya*) and 72 per cent of the electorate voted for candidates on a single FLN list. In June 1970, following the celebration of his first five years in power, Boumedienne undertook an extensive tour of western Algeria, and when cabinet changes were made in July, his key colleagues retained their places, a fact which served to emphasize the regime's stability. On the anniversary of the revolution in November 1970 he amnestied about 100 political prisoners. The release of these former enemies gave some indication of the weakness of the underground opposition.

Only among school and university students did discontent remain in evidence. A school strike in December led to violent clashes with the police, and in January 1971 the arrest of eight Algiers university students resulted in a strike at the university and the dissolution by the government of the National Union of Algerian Students (UNEA). The attitude of many students otherwise sympathetic to the aims and achievements of the FLN was doubtless affected by poor employment prospects.

RELATIONS WITH FRANCE

The improvement in President Boumedienne's position at home enabled him to adopt a more militant attitude towards France. He could afford to demand more for Algerian oil, and the resultant dispute over the price to be paid by the French oil companies culminated in the decision to take control of them by nationalization.

The two companies concerned, the Compagnie Française des Pétroles (CFP) and the Compagnie de Recherches et d'Activités Pétrolières (ERAP), were responsible for some two-thirds of Algeria's total production. In the first half of 1970 the Algerian government pressed them to accept an increase in the posted price of petroleum, but negotiations broke down and in July the Government unilaterally fixed a new price level. Further discussions between the French and Algerian Governments proved futile, and in February 1971 Boumedienne announced the take-over by the Algerian government of a 51 per cent holding in CFP and ERAP and the complete nationalization of the companies' gas and pipeline interests.

The French Government regarded this move as a breach of the 1965 agreement but could only ask for fair compensation. The subsequent Algerian offer was found unacceptable and in April 1971 France discontinued negotiations. Relations appeared to have reached their lowest ebb. It was announced that many French technicians and teachers were to leave Algeria, and attacks were made on some of the 700,000 Algerians in France. The French Government applied a boycott against Algerian oil and tried to get other major consumers to do the same. Talks between the two French companies and SONATRACH, the Algerian state oil concern, were resumed, however, and agreements were reached in June and September under which the role of CFP and ERAP became that of minority partners of the Algerian state in return for guaranteed oil supplies. After approval by the two governments a final agreement, which also provided for compensation and reduced back claims of taxes, was signed on December 15th.

In April 1975, Valéry Giscard d'Estaing became the first French President to visit Algeria since independence. According to Boumedienne, this event marked the definitive reconciliation of the French and Algerian peoples. However, the goodwill generated by Giscard's visit was quickly dissipated. The Algerian Government resented French economic policies which maintained an imbalance in trade between the two countries. Certain French industrial projects in Algeria were blocked, and the agreement between ERAP and SONATRACH was not renewed. Two Frenchmen were among foreigners arrested for industrial espionage in December, and French secret service agents were accused of complicity in bomb attacks on Algerian public buildings. The Algerian Government regarded French support for Morocco over the Sahara dispute as a betrayal, especially when France began supplying large quantities of arms to Algeria's potential enemy.

PALESTINE AND THE SAHARA

The Boumedienne Government's stand on the Palestine question remained uncompromisingly militant. Algeria accepted neither the 1967 UN resolution nor the ceasefire, and when, after the hostilities along the Suez Canal in 1969 and 1970, a further ceasefire was agreed in August 1970, Algerian troops were withdrawn. Radio stations of Palestine liberation movements banished from Cairo in July 1970 were allowed to broadcast from Algiers and relations with Jordan were broken off in June 1971 after the final destruction of Palestinian guerrilla bases in Jordan by King Hussein's forces. During the October War in 1973 Algeria was active on the diplomatic front, encouraging African countries to break off relations with Israel. It participated fully with other Arab oil-producing states in cut-backs in production and boycotts aimed at countries regarded as hostile to the Arab cause. Relations with Jordan were restored after the dispatch of Jordanian troops to the Syrian front, but Algeria continued to support the Palestinians against any Jordanian territorial claims. In December 1977 Algeria was one of the signatories of the Declaration of Tripoli opposing President Sadat's attempts to negotiate with Israel; diplomatic relations with Egypt were broken off.

Despite Algeria's policy towards Palestine and the welcome accorded to almost any exiled foreign opposition group, it continued to co-operate in the economic field with any state willing to do so. Fears that Algeria might fall under Soviet dominance proved groundless, although the U.S.S.R. continued to be a major source of military equipment. Despite strong disagreements with the U.S.A. over Viet-Nam and the Palestinian question, full diplomatic relations were restored at the end of 1974 and trade between the two countries increased dramatically; by the end of 1977 the U.S.A. had replaced France as Algeria's leading trade partner.

From early 1975 a major confrontation developed with Morocco over the future of the Spanish Sahara. Algeria opposed Morocco's claim to the territory, advocating the founding of an independent Saharan state after decolonization. In May 1975, at the International Court of Justice, Algeria called for genuine self-determination for the Saharans and denied any self-interest in the matter. This was, however, disingenuous, since Algeria could clearly draw considerable political and economic advantage from the existence of a weak, friendly state on its western border. When, in November 1975, Spain agreed to hand over the territory to Morocco and Mauritania, Boumedienne protested vehemently and promised full support for Polisario, the Saharan liberation movement. As Moroccan troops moved into the Western Sahara, Algeria mobilized part of its armed forces, and in January and February 1976 there were heavy clashes between units of the two armies in the Sahara several hundred miles from the Algerian border. In March Algeria recognized the Saharan Arab Democratic Republic, proclaimed by Polisario, and both Morocco and Mauritania broke off diplomatic relations. The prospect of a full-scale war in the Sahara quickly receded, especially as there was little enthusiasm for war amongst the Algerian population, but the Government continued to provide support and refuge for Polisario guerrillas. Morocco and Mauritania refused to recognize the independent existence of the guerrilla movement and interpreted all armed incursions into the Sahara as Algerian attacks against their national territory. An especially successful raid by Polisario against Zouerate, the Mauritanian mining centre, in May 1977 brought relations in the Maghreb to a new pitch of tension. Two French citizens were killed and six captured during the raid, and the French Government made clear its hostility to Algeria's position over the liberation movement. The captives were released in December after negotiations between Polisario and the UN, but almost simultaneously French aircraft began a series of three bombing raids on Polisario troops, causing protests both from the Algerian press and from the left-wing opposition in France, although the French Government declared that its intervention was solely for the protection of French citizens working in the area. In January 1978 Algeria announced a boycott of imports from France, in protest not only against events in the Sahara, but also the wide trade gap between the two countries, and especially France's decision to obtain more oil from Saudi Arabia. President Giscard d'Estaing showed a conciliatory attitude when, in a television interview in February, he suggested that the Evian agreement needed updating and proposed the setting-up of commissions to examine economic relations and the safety of Algerian workers in France. Although no immediate attempts were made to put these proposals into effect, they apparently helped to lessen tension and the anti-French press campaign became less virulent. A further French air attack on the guerrillas in May again incurred accusations of neo-colonialism from President Boumedienne. It seemed that no improvement in relations could be expected while the Sahara conflict remained in a state of stalemate in spite of the coup in Mauritania in July 1978, which at first gave rise to hopes of a solution.

HOME AFFAIRS

By 1971 Boumedienne's Government felt strong enough to initiate a more active social policy. The choice of capital-intensive export industry as the basis for economic development and of centralized bureaucratic state-control as the mode of organization had saddled Algeria with many of the same problems as countries dominated by foreign capitalism. The lives of the majority of the population, especially in the rural areas and the backward regions of the country, were untouched by the economic progress. There was mass unemployment and considerable inequality in the distribution of wealth. In 1971 a programme of agrarian reform, known as the Agrarian Revolution, was initiated. The reform was to proceed in three phases, the redistribution of state-owned and foreign land, the redistribution of private estates, and the transformation of the lives of the pastoral nomads. At the same time the government resolved to develop workers' control in industry and to reanimate the FLN as a radical force. Elected workers' councils slowly spread through nationalized industries, but the reorganization of the FLN was a failure. In 1972 Kaid Ahmed, the leader of the party, resigned because of his lack of success. The initiative in promoting the Agrarian Revolution passed to a student *volontariat*, in which the more radical students participated enthusiastically. Boumedienne's determination to build a socialist society encountered resistance from conservative sectors of the population, especially after the redistribution of private estates and the nationalization of food distribution. Conflict came into the open in May 1975 when there were clashes at Algiers University between radical students devoted to the Agrarian Revolution and conservative students wishing to give priority to Arabization. Boumedienne came out strongly in favour of the radicals.

The personal authority of Boumedienne grew in the 1970s. The death of Ahmed Medeghri and Belkacem's dismissal from the cabinet in 1974 left only Bouteflika as a figure of comparable stature in the government. Encouraged by the success of local and provincial elections since 1967 and 1969 respectively, Boumedienne announced in June 1975 that national elections for an assembly and a president were to be held and that a National Charter would be drawn up to provide the state with a new constitution.

Boumedienne's decision to consolidate the regime and his personal power provoked a resurgence of opposition, including the circulation, in March 1976, of a manifesto signed by, among others, Ferhat Abbas and Ben Youssef Ben Khedda, both former presidents of the Algerian government-in-exile during the war of liberation. The manifesto criticised Boumedienne for totalitarian rule and the personality cult. The signatories were reportedly placed under house arrest. Boumedienne rejected these criticisms of his rule as the work of bourgeois reactionaries, and declared that the revolution had reached the point of no return.

In April 1976 the Algerian press began publication of the National Charter, which, after public discussion, received approval by 98.5 per cent of the voters in a referendum in June. It was a sign of the confidence of the regime that discussion of the Charter was encouraged to be vigorous and critical. The essence of the Charter was the irreversible commitment of Algeria to socialism, though a socialism specifically adapted to Third-World conditions. The dominant role of the FLN was reasserted but, as a concession to more conservative sentiment, Islam was recognized as the state religion. The following November a new Constitution embodying the principles of the Charter was also approved by referendum, and in December Boumedienne was elected President unopposed with 99 per cent of votes cast. Finally, to complete the new formal structure of power, a national assembly of 261 members was elected in February 1977 from among 783 candidates selected by a committee of the FLN. Next, steps were taken yet again to strengthen and enlarge the FLN, in order to make it the guiding political force envisaged in the National Charter. FLN officials were installed alongside local administrative officials to form the basis of a full party apparatus at all levels, and the mass organizations affiliated to the FLN (the unions of workers, peasants, war veterans, women and youth) held a series of congresses which was to culminate in a national FLN Congress (the first since 1964) early in 1979.

THE DEATH OF BOUMEDIENNE

In November 1978, however, a more urgent problem arose when it gradually became clear that President Boumedienne was seriously ill. At the end of the month he fell into a coma which lasted almost continuously until his death on December 27th. During his illness there was anxious speculation as to who should succeed him, particularly since he had nominated neither a Vice-President nor a Prime Minister and was himself Minister of Defence (a post which had included, from 1977 onwards, direct supervision of the police and secret service) and Chief of Staff. For the time being, government was taken over by the Council of the Revolution, which by now consisted of only eight members, apart from Boumedienne (five ministers, two senior army officers and the administrative head of the FLN); although it had been given no official status in the 1976 Constitution, the Council declared that it would maintain continuity and protect existing institutions, and succeeded in bringing about a smooth transfer of power.

After Boumedienne's death Rabah Bitat, the President of the National Assembly, was automatically sworn in as Head of State for a 45-day period. At the end of January the long-planned FLN Congress was held. It now had the double task of attempting to restore the party's vitality and of choosing a presidential candidate. New statutes on party structure were adopted, whereby a Central Committee of between 120 and 160 members and between 30 and 40 advisory members, meeting at least once every 6 months, was to be elected by Congress and form the highest policy-making body not only of the party but of the country as a whole. The Committee was to select a party Secretary-General who would automatically become the FLN's (and therefore the only) presidential candidate. A Political Bureau of between 17 and 20 members, nominated by the Secretary-General, would be elected by the Central Committee and responsible to it. These structures superseded the Council of the Revolution, which was formally disbanded on January 27th.

It was expected that the chosen presidential candidate would be a member of the now-disbanded Council, and the most likely choice appeared to be either Abelaziz Bouteflika, the Minister for Foreign Affairs, regarded as a moderate, or Mohamed Salah Yahiaoui, the administrative head of the FLN, regarded as a more radical socialist and favoured by the youth and workers' organizations. The eventual choice, Col. Bendjedid Chadli, the commander of the Oran military district, was something of a compromise between the two. He was inaugurated as President on February 9th, after his candidature had been approved by 94 per cent of the electorate. He declared that he would continue to uphold the policies of Boumedienne, the "irreversible option" of socialism and "national independence" in both political and economic spheres. It soon became clear that Chadli did not intend to monopolize power to the extent that Boumedienne had. For the first time since independence, a Prime Minister was named: Col. Mohamed Ben Ahmed Abdelghani, who retained his post as Minister of the Interior. A new Minister of Defence was not named, however, and it was assumed that, like Boumedienne, Chadli had kept this post for himself. Abdelaziz Bouteflika lost the portfolio of Foreign Minister which he had held for the past 15 years, and was given the post of Adviser to the Presidency. No major changes in foreign policy were expected, however, particularly with regard to the Western Sahara: Algeria continued to condemn Moroccan policy and, while welcoming the conciliatory attitude of the Mauritanians towards Polisario, urged them to act more positively in bringing about self-determination for the people of the Western Sahara.

ECONOMIC SURVEY

Algeria covers an area of 2,381,741 sq. km., of which a large part is desert. At the census of 1966 the population (including Algerians abroad) was returned at 12,090,547. The great majority of Europeans had returned to France by the early 1960s. On the basis of a census taken in February 1977, the estimated population at January 1st, 1978, had reached 18,250,000, including about 828,000 Algerians living abroad, mainly in France. About 60 per cent of the population still live in rural areas but about 100,000 peasants migrate every year to the towns in search of work. The largest towns are Algiers, the capital (estimated population 1,800,000, including the suburbs, in 1977), Ouahran (Oran 500,000 with its suburbs), Constantine (430,000), Annaba (Bône) (340,000), Tizi-Ouzou (230,000) and Sidi-Bel-Abbès (158,000). The population is growing at an estimated rate of over 3.2 per cent a year and the current birth-rate is 46 per thousand. Forty-eight per cent of the population are under the age of 15. In an effort to reduce the flow of peasants to the towns, the Government is undertaking a far-reaching programme of land reform and redistribution. According to World Bank estimates, the population of urban centres was growing at 6.6 per cent a year in the period 1960–70 but this rate had been reduced to 5.7 per cent in 1970–75.

Algeria has varied natural resources. In the coastal region are highly fertile plains and valleys, where profitable returns are made from cereals, wine, olives and fruit. However, the rest of the country serves little agricultural purpose, though in the mountains, grazing and forestry bring a small income for the population, and dates are grown in the oases of the Sahara. Mineral resources are abundant and are now the mainstay of Algeria's foreign trade. Revenues from oil and gas are being used to finance ambitious industrialization plans, although over two-fifths of the working population are still engaged in agriculture.

GOVERNMENT STRATEGY

Since independence in 1962 Algerian governments have sought to gain control of the economy and promote economic growth as a foundation for a future socialist society. They have either taken over completely or taken a controlling interest in most foreign-owned companies. In 1966 the government nationalized foreign-owned mines, unoccupied lands deserted by Europeans at independence, and insurance companies. It took control of the whole of the hydrocarbon sector in the spring of 1971.

Heavy industries are all state-run, while consumer goods industries are still largely in private hands, although parts of the textile, leather and food industries have already been nationalized. In brief, all key sectors are run by the state, which intends eventually to control all internal transport, domestic wholesale trade and foreign trade.

The Government's strategy for development involves a high degree of austerity, with heavy restrictions placed on the importation of "luxury" goods. The first Four-Year Plan, 1970–73, emphasized the establishment of a capital-intensive sector, involving the hydrocarbon, iron and steel, chemical and engineering industries and a 9 per cent annual growth rate was achieved. About 34,000 million dinars were invested (compared with only 4,200 million dinars in the initial Three-Year Plan, 1967–69).

The second Four-Year Plan, for 1974–77, aimed at laying the foundations of a sound industrial base. The Plan also emphasized improved agricultural methods, housing, health, job-creation and training. However, there was a marked lack of effective government policy with regard to agriculture and housing. Under the Plan, industry was allocated 43.5 per cent of total investment, infrastructure 14 per cent, social services and housing 13.3 per cent and agriculture 10.9 per cent. The high level of investment (40 per cent of gross domestic product—G.D.P.) has been maintained in the second Plan and an average annual growth rate of 10 per cent was aimed at. Total expenditure, originally put at 52,000 million dinars, was later increased to 110,000 million dinars, on the basis of the large increase in income resulting from oil price rises.

The country's G.D.P. grew by an annual average rate of 6.2 per cent in real terms in the period 1970–76, according to World Bank estimates. It was estimated to have reached 70,000 million dinars in 1977 and about 90,000 million dinars in 1978. During 1979 it was expected to grow by a further 12 per cent. In 1976 agriculture accounted for only 7.6 per cent of G.D.P., against 21 per cent in 1960; industry and construction provided 56.1 per cent. Per capita income in 1970 was about 1,500 dinars, which the Government aims to increase to 2,500 dinars by 1980.

The third Four-Year Plan will cover the period 1979–83 but had still not been published by May 1979. The period between the end of the previous plan and the start of the new one was being regarded by the Government as a "transition period". The new plan will probably concentrate on performance and productivity, both in agriculture and manufacturing, and light and consumer industries will receive increasing attention, as a result of a slight change of emphasis. However, the major projects will still be in the hydrocarbons, iron and steel and exploitation of mineral deposits.

A special development fund for the south was approved in 1978. It aims at opening up the region, with total investment planned at 7,000 million dinars. In 1978 the Ain Salah-Tamanrasset stretch of the Trans-Sahara highway was inaugurated. The final stretch from In-Guezzam to the Niger border is under construction.

The total economically active population at January 1st, 1978, was estimated to be 4,002,000, of whom 42.1 per cent were in the agricultural sector.

The World Bank estimates that during the 1974–77 Plan unemployment in the non-agricultural sector was reduced from over one-third to 10 per cent. About half the rural population, however, are either unemployed or underemployed. There are signs of considerable discontent among some workers. Inflation in 1978/79 was running at over 25 per cent and there was a flourishing black market in many goods which are in short supply.

AGRICULTURE

Algeria is still mainly an agricultural country. Over nine-tenths of the land consists of arid plateaux, mountains or desert, supporting scattered herds of sheep, goats or camel. Only the northern coastal strip, 100-200 km. wide, can be used for arable purposes. There are about 6.8 million hectares of cultivable land, representing less than one hectare per rural inhabitant. Forests cover about 2.4 million hectares. Most of the Sahara is devoted to semi-desert pasturage. The most valuable crop is the grape harvest, which represents 66 per cent of total agricultural exports by value; whilst wheat, barley and oats, grown for local consumption, cover a large area. Other crops include maize, sorghum, millet, rye and rice, as well as citrus fruit, olives, figs and dates, and tobacco. Agricultural development is restricted by problems such as erosion, adverse weather conditions, especially drought and flood, primitive methods of production, and under-employment.

About half the country's workforce is employed in agriculture but this sector contributed only 7.6 per cent of G.D.P. in 1976. It has been greatly neglected by the Government, receiving only about 15 per cent of total investment in the last two development plans. Output fell by an average of 8.7 per cent annually in the period 1970–76; the average annual decline in 1960–70 was 1.6 per cent. There is an urgent need to increase food production since foodstuffs at present account for about one quarter of Algeria's total imports bill. The Government's aim is to achieve self-sufficiency in basic foodstuffs by 1980. Algeria has to import about one-fifth of its cereals, one-third of its milk and almost all of its butter and sugar. A number of large dam and irrigation projects are under construction or planned.

LAND REFORM

The first regulations, introduced in October 1962, enabled the state to take over any settler's property declared vacant. Land occupied by settlers was still legally owned by them, while the state "used" it. However, in March 1963, another Government decree declared that the state was taking over ownership of abandoned land. A number of large French landowners subsequently had their land taken away, although it was still occupied. In May 1966 all remaining unoccupied property which had been evacuated by settlers was finally taken over by the state. These expropriated lands were turned into State farms run by workers' committees (*comités de gestion*).

After the total nationalization of French land in October 1963, state farm land accounted for 2.3 million ha., roughly half the cultivable land in Algeria. The modern, "self-managed" agricultural sector represents one-third of the total agricultural area, provides work for only about 135,000 in permanent employment and about 100,000 in seasonal work, but its revenue is twice that of the "traditional" private sector, which provides a living for more than 5 million people.

In July 1971 President Boumedienne announced an agrarian reform programme which provided for the break-up of large, Algerian-owned farms and their redistribution to families of landless peasants, or *fellahs*, who would be organized in co-operatives. The first stage of its implementation, the registration of land ownership, began in March 1972. By early 1979, over 6,000 agricultural co-operatives of various kinds had been set up.

A census begun in September 1972 showed that a quarter of cultivable land was in the hands of 16,500 large landowners who represented only 3 per cent of the total number of farmers. In 1973 the Agrarian Revolution entered its second phase, that of redistributing over 650,000 hectares of private land to 60,000 families of landless peasants. Those receiving land under the scheme will be granted permanent use of it but they must belong to one of the new co-operatives being set up. Through these they will be given state loans and assistance in the form of seed, fertilizers and equipment. By early 1979, 22,000 absentee landowners had been obliged either to cultivate their own land or to hand it over to peasant farmers. As part of the land reform programme, the Government plans to resettle the rural population in 1,000 co-operative villages ,of which 52, with a total population of 78,000, were in operation by 1977 and 270 were in the course of being created. The programme has fallen well behind schedule, however. Under the *volontariat* scheme, young people are encouraged to spend their vacations working and teaching in rural areas.

The third phase of the agrarian reform programme launched in January 1975, aims at increasing livestock production in the steppe areas. About 20 million hectares of pasturage, mostly in southern Algeria, grazed by the animals of 170,000 nomadic herdsmen, are to be nationalized. At present over 50 per cent of the livestock is owned by only 5 per cent of the herdsmen. The 8 million grazing animals are to be redistributed and grouped into settled co-operative units.

CROPS

The coastal areas of the Mediterranean produce grapes. Vines have been grown in Algeria since antiquity merely for local consumption; however, after the coming of the French in 1830, vine growing received substantial encouragement and wines still represent the principal agricultural export. Nevertheless, the Government regards agricultural dependence on wine as incompatible with real political independence. Thus it is tearing up the least productive vines and converting the land to cereal and dairy farming, and to forestry. The target for 1980 is 140,000 hectares under vines, compared with the present total of 200,000 hectares. Production, which in 1960 was 18.6 million hectolitres, was down to 2.3 million hectolitres by 1976. The tendency will be for better quality wines, and dessert grapes to be produced.

Foreign ownership of wheat land was particularly resented by the Algerian peasantry. Grown principally in the Constantine, Annaba, Sétif and Tiaret areas, production of all cereals fluctuates considerably, largely as a result of drought and grains have to be imported, particularly from Canada. Wheat and barley are the most important cereals. Cereal production in recent years has averaged around 2.2 million tons. In 1976 there was a record harvest of over 2.8 million tons (wheat 2.2 million tons, barley 600,000 tons) but in 1977 the wheat harvest was only 1.3 million tons and the barley harvest 400,000 tons. Yields are very low, at 26–32 cwt. of wheat per hectare, compared with U.S. average yields of 70 cwt.

Olives are grown in the western coastal belt. Production fluctuates because of the two-year flowering cycle fo the olive. In 1977 an estimated 113,000 tons of olives and 15,000 tons of olive oil were produced.

The citrus crop, grown in the coastal districts, totals between 400,000 and 500,000 tons per year. Production of potatoes is between 400,000 and 600,000 tons. About 46,000 tons of dried vegetables are produced annually. Market gardening is being encouraged, with the aim of finding a ready export market for Algerian produce in Western Europe. Algeria is the world's fifth largest date producer, with an average of 130,000–180,000 tons per year, but 80 per cent of this is consumed locally.

Tobacco is the main industrial crop, employing about 13,000 people. About 3,000 tons per year are produced.

LIVESTOCK, FORESTRY AND FISHING

Sheep, goats and cattle are raised but great improvements will have to be made in stock-raising methods, grassland, control of disease and water supply if the increasing demand for meat is to be met. At present, a large part of Algeria's requirements in dairy products have to be imported. At the end of 1977 there were about 1.3 million head of cattle, 9.5 million sheep and 2.2 million goats.

The area covered by forests has fallen rapidly in the past two decades, and the Government plans to reafforest 335,000 hectares and to rehabilitate 30,000 hectares, partly to protect cultivable land against erosion. A vast "green wall" of pines and cypresses, 20 km. wide, is being planted along 1,500 km. on the northern edge of the Sahara from the Moroccan to the Tunisian frontier, to arrest the steady northward encroachment of the Sahara desert. Work began in 1975 and the project has involved the construction of roads, reservoirs and pilot plantations of fruit trees and vegetables. However, the scheme has encountered numerous problems, including large-scale infestation by caterpillars in 1978.

The Government feels that Algeria is not exploiting its fishing potential and hopes to raise annual production to over 40,000 tons. The total sea catch in 1976 was 35,122 metric tons. In 1975 the industrial catch was 4,500 tons.

MINERALS

Algeria has rich mineral resources and, since before the petroleum era, it had mined and exported high-grade iron ore, phosphates, lead, zinc and antimony. Mining is now controlled by the state enterprise SONAREM.

Iron ore is mined at Beni-Saf, Zaccar, Timezrit and near the eastern frontier at Ouenza and Bou Khadra. The average grade of ore is between 50 and 60 per cent. Production has fluctuated greatly since independence but reached 3.8 million metric tons (metal content) in 1974, falling to 2.7 million metric tons in 1977. The deposits at Ouenza represent 75 per cent of total production. Exploitation will begin by 1980 of deposits at Gara Djebelit and at Kenadza, in the west. The Gara Djebelit reserves, which are in territory claimed by Morocco, are estimated at 1,000 million tons of medium-grade ore. Important deposits were found in 1975 at Djebel Bouari in Batua wilaya. Italy is the biggest customer, followed by the United Kingdom. Production of bituminous coal, mined at Colomb Béhar-Kenadza and Ksiksou, dropped steadily from 153,000 tons in 1958 and in 1975 was only about 8,000 tons.

The most important zinc deposit is found on the Algerian-Moroccan frontier at El-Abed-Oued Zounder, which is an extension of the Moroccan deposits. Production fell from 14,350 metric tons (metal content) in 1973 to only 6,200 metric tons in 1976. Lead is mined at El Abed on the Moroccan border; production in 1976 was 1,600 tons (metal content). A lead and zinc mine is to be developed at Kherzet-Youssef in Sétif wilaya.

Exploitation of large phosphate deposits at Djebel-Onk, 340 km from Annaba, began in 1960 and output reached 1 million metric tons by 1977. The deposits are used to feed the Arzew fertilizer plant and the surplus is exported, mainly to France and Spain.

Other mineral resources include antimony, tungsten, manganese, mercury, copper and salt. A mercury mine and refinery are being developed at Ismail. Exploration has been concentrated in the mountainous Hoggar region in the south. There are plans to launch mining operations within the next few years for tungsten, gold and uranium. Algeria is thought to have about 50,000 metric tons of uranium oxide deposits, mostly in the Tingaouine area; mining will start in 1984–85 at the rate of 1,000 metric tons per year and all the output will be exported.

PETROLEUM AND NATURAL GAS

Production of crude oil in the Sahara on a commercial scale began in 1958. The original principal producing areas were at Hassi Massaoud in Central Algeria and round Edjeleh-Zarzaitine in the Polignac Basin near the Libyan frontier. From 1.2 million tons in 1959, Algerian production of crude oil rose to a ceiling of 26 million tons in 1964 and 1965, limited by the capacity of the two pipelines to the coast, one from the eastern fields through Tunisia to La Skhirra, and the other from Hassi Messaoud to Bejaia on the Algerian coast. The Government set up its own company, *Société Nationale pour la Recherche, la Production, le Transport, la Transformation et la Commercialisation des Hydrocarbures* (SONATRACH) to be responsible for the construction of a third pipeline from Hassi Messaoud to Arzew on the coast. This pipeline came into operation early in 1966, and its maximum capacity is 22 million tons per year. In 1966 production was boosted by substantial quantities of crude from fields at Gassi Touil, Rhourde el Baguel and Rhourde Nouss. Subsequent discoveries of oil have been made at Nezla, Hoaud Berkaoui, Ouargla, Mesdar and El Borma, and more recently at Hassi Keskessa, Guellala, Tin Fouyé and El Maharis. Algeria now has seven main oil pipeline systems, the others being Mesdar-Skikda, Ohanet-Haoud el Mahra, Mesdar-El Borma and Beni Mansour-Algiers.

Production of petroleum reached 50,750,000 metric tons in 1973 but by 1974 this had fallen to 47,170,000 tons, due to cutbacks in output imposed by Algeria in connection with the Middle East crisis. By the end of 1975 production had begun to pick up again and in 1976 totalled 50.1 million tons (crude and condensate). In 1977 output rose again to 53.5 million tons (average 1,140,000 barrels per day). Production in 1978 was 7 per cent up, at 57.2 million tons. For 1979 it was expected to be around 59 million tons, of which 54 million tons would be exported. Petroleum revenues rose by $400 million in 1978 to $6,200 million. The price of Algerian crude became increasingly competitive after 1975, in relation to other North African and to Nigerian crudes, and this helped to boost output. Algeria, which produces the lighter types of crude, with a low sulphur content, is the seventh largest Middle East oil producer but accounts for only 4 per cent of the total output of the Organization of Petroleum Exporting Countries (OPEC), which it joined in 1969. Its reported reserves totalled 8,000 million barrels by the end of 1978. The United States is the most important customer for Algerian crude oil, followed by West Germany and Italy. In line with OPEC policy, Algeria has successively raised the price of its oil, except during the period of slack world demand in late 1977 and early 1978. In March 1979 a premium added to the new OPEC price brought the cost of its highest grade crude from $14.8 per barrel to $18.50; a further increase announced in May pushed the price up to $21.

SONATRACH has complete control of the Algiers refinery (capacity 2.5 million tons a year) and of the domestic distribution network, having gradually taken over the holdings formerly owned by foreign firms. A small 100,000 tons per year refinery at Hassi Messaoud supplies the Saharan market. Refineries at Arzew (built by a Japanese consortium and completed in June 1973; annual capacity 2.5 million tons) and Skikda (being built by Snamprogetti of Italy; annual capacity 15 million tons) are both owned by SONATRACH. Algeria's fourth major refinery is to be built at Bejaia by British and Italian firms and will be linked with the Hassi R'Mel complex. It will go on stream in 1979 with a capacity of 7.5 million tons a year, bringing the country's total refining capacity up to nearly 30 million tons a year. At present, about 15 per cent of Algerian crude is refined locally and some 3.5 million tons of refined products are exported each year. A liquid petroleum gas (LPG) plant with an annual capacity of 4 million tons is to be built at Bethioua near Arzew by a Japanese firm. In 1978 about 90,000 tons of LPG were produced, and one-third of this was exported.

A thirty-year plan for Algeria's hydrocarbons sector drawn up by SONATRACH and the Bechtel Corporation of the U.S.A. predicts that by 1993 Algeria will have ceased to export crude oil but will be exporting refined products. The plan provides for government investment in the sector totalling $33,000 million over the period 1978–98. These proposals for such immense financial outlay have been criticized by some Algerian and foreign observers who believe that more funds should be injected into other sectors, particularly those which would create more jobs.

As oil production begins to decline, its place as Algeria's most valuable export will be taken by natural gas, of which Algeria is likely to be the world's leading exporter by 1980. In 1976 reserves were estimated at 3,271,000 million cubic metres. A pipeline from Hassi R'Mel, one of the world's largest gas fields, to Arzew, Algiers and Oran was opened in 1961. Shipments of natural gas in liquefied form in specially constructed tankers to the United Kingdom began in October 1964 and to France in March 1965. Natural gas is currently produced from fields at Hassi R'Mel, Hassi Messaoud, Gassi el Adem, Gassi Touil, Nord In Amenas and Rhourde el Baguel. Rhourde Nouss and several other fields are to be developed. Output reached 14,200 million cubic metres in 1978.

Contracts for sales of natural gas to Western Europe and the U.S.A. have shown a spectacular increase in size in recent years and, if all of them do come on stream, Algeria will be exporting about 80,000 million cubic metres per year by the early 1980s. By the beginning of 1979 the following contracts were operational: British Gas, Gaz de France, Distrigas of the U.S.A. (two contracts) and El Paso I (U.S.A.). Two deals with U.S. firms, one with Tenneco (to supply the U.S.A. and Canada) and a second contract with El Paso, have encountered difficulties as the U.S. Energy Department delays its final decision on whether to approve them and by April 1979 it appeared that they would eventually fall through. However, Algeria has meanwhile signed a number of large sales contracts with European firms and these, together with two deals which have been approved by the U.S.A. (with Panhandle and Trunkline), were expected to absorb all of Algeria's exporting capacity well into the 1980s and probably beyond. The countries with which deals have been concluded are Belgium, France, West Germany, the Netherlands, Italy and Tunisia, while further contracts were under negotiation early in 1979 with some of these countries and with Austria, Sweden and Yugoslavia.

To fulfil these commitments Algeria is investing heavily in pipelines, liquefaction plants and tankers, although there have been serious delays in the programme to date. The first liquefaction plant at Arzew, the Camel plant, was built in 1964 and is now owned wholly by SONATRACH. Algeria's second liquefied natural gas (LNG) plant was completed at Skikda in 1972 by Technip of France and has suffered from considerable technical difficulties. The third plant, Arzew 1, began operating in February 1978. Construction of the plant was begun by Chemico of the U.S. but the contract was cancelled by SONATRACH in 1975 because of "poor performance" and the work was completed by Bechtel. The plant will eventually have an annual capacity of 10,500 million cubic metres per year. Two LNG plants are currently under construction: Arzew 2 (capacity 10,500 million cubic metres per year; being built by Pullman Kellog, for completion in 1980) and Arzew 3 (capacity 15,750 million cubic metres per year; being built by Foster Wheeler, for completion by 1982). Two further liquefaction plants, Arzew 4 and Skikda 2, are planned and the Skikda 1 plant is currently being expanded. In May 1972 the 40-in. pipeline from Hassi R'Mel to Skikda was opened. The pipeline, 577 km. long, has a capacity of 12,700 million cubic metres per year. A second 40-in. pipeline from Hassi R'Mel to Arzew went on stream in March 1978. Two further gas pipelines are to be built by the Italian company Saipem: one of 28 in., 520 km. long, from Hassi R'Mel to Arzew and the other of 40 in., 160 km. long, from the Gassi Touil field to Hassi Messaoud. Plans for a 2,500-km. trans-Mediterranean gas pipeline to Italy, which had earlier been scrapped, were revived in 1977 when contracts were signed with Tunisia and with ENI, the Italian state oil concern. A 48-in. pipeline, with an initial capacity of 14,500 million cubic metres per year, will be built from Hassi R'Mel to the Tunisian border (550 km.) and from there across Tunisia to the coast opposite Sicily (380 km.); the submarine section will be 160 km. long. ENI will extend the pipeline across Sicily and the Straits of Messina to Minerbio, near Bologna, and will own this section. Tunisia will receive 5.25 per cent of the gas and will own the section of pipeline crossing its territory. The undersea section to Sicily will be owned by a joint company set up by SONATRACH and SNAMprogetti (an ENI subsidiary). Italy will lend $1,030 million towards financing Algeria's $1,400 million share of total construction costs ($2,500 million). The revenue from this contract is expected to total about $600 million per year once it becomes fully operationa.. Work began in 1978 on laying the submarine section across the Straits of Messina. A pipeline from Algeria to Spain will probably be started in the mid-1980s. By March 1979 the Algerian national shipping line CNAN owned three LNG carriers and was expected to take delivery of another three by 1980 ,with several more on order.

In June 1970 the local interests of Shell, Phillips, Elwerath and AMIF were nationalized, following protracted negotiations which failed to achieve agreement on tax reference prices, and SONATRACH thus became Algeria's largest producer.

In February 1971, Algeria nationalized the French oil companies operating in the country, as well as pipeline networks and natural gas deposits. In April 1971 President Boumedienne issued a decree banning concession-type agreements and laying down the conditions under which foreign oil companies could operate in Algeria. SONATRACH now directly controls 77 per cent of Algeria's oil production, compared with only 31 per cent in 1970.

Despite a law of April 1972 requiring companies wishing to explore in Algeria to form a joint company with SONATRACH, in which the latter should have a controlling interest, co-operation with foreign oil firms is increasing. The U.S. firm, Getty Oil, has operated effectively as a minority partner of SONATRACH since 1968. Under the terms of the 1972 law, agreements have been signed with Sun Oil of the U.S.A., Hispanoil of Spain, Petrobras of Brazil, Total-Algérie (a subsidiary of CFP), Copex of Poland, Elf-ERAP of France, Deminex of West Germany and Amoco of the U.S.A. In 1978 Shell signed a new type of agreement under which it will finance the exploration work, in return for a percentage of oil output in the event of a commercially viable discovery. The percentage will vary according to the profitability of the venture.

MANUFACTURING

Industrialization is the keynote of the government's economic policy and the major investment effort in the 1970–73 plan was devoted to this end. Under the second Four-Year Plan, industry received about 43.5 per cent of total allocations.

At the time of independence the Algerian industrial sector was very small, being confined mainly to food processing, building materials, textiles and minerals. The departure of the French entailed loss of demand, capital and skill, thereby slowing down the industrialization process. Foreign firms became increasingly reluctant in the 1960s to invest in Algeria because of the danger of nationalization. By 1978 about 300 state-owned manufacturing plants had been set up but productivity is very low, with some factories operating at only 15–25 per cent of design capacity.

The iron and steel industry is basic to the development of other industries and very large investments have been made in the El Hadjar complex at Annaba. The smelter and tube-mill were opened in 1969 after several delays. The steelworks, mainly Soviet-built, did not go into operation until May 1972. The complex is currently operating far below its capacity of 400,000 tons per year, but it is being expanded with additional steel-rolling mills. A steel plant at Djidjelli, in the east, is to be expanded and another is to be built at La Macta, at the western end of the coast. Algeria's domestic needs of steel are about 5 million tons per year and, of this, 2 million tons are imported. The U.S.S.R. will build an aluminium electrolysis plant at M'Sila, 200 km. south-east of Algiers. The plant, which will have an annual capacity of 140,000 tons, will begin operating in 1982 and will use bauxite imported from Jamaica and Guinea. A Canadian and French consortium is to build a foundry at Rouiba to providing castings for the vehicle industry.

A vast petrochemical complex being built at Skikda by Snamprogetti of Italy and Toyo Engineering of Japan will produce polyethylene, PVC, caustic soda and chlorine. An 800,000 tons-per-year nitrogenous fertilizer plant utilizing natural gas was opened in 1970 at Arzew, where there is also a complex for the manufacture of intermediate petrochemical products. At Annaba, a 550,000 tons-per-year plant for phosphate fertilizers was opened in 1972 but output in 1976 was only 300,000 tons. Two new fertilizer complexes are to be set up at Tebessa and Annaba, for the production of sulphuric acid, phosphoric acid and triple superphosphates, using the Djebel Onk phosphate deposits.

Algeria suffers from a severe shortage of vehicles of all types but is expanding its vehicle and farm machinery industries rapidly. At Constantine there is a factory built by the West German firm DIAG to produce tractors and diesel engines. DIAG is also building a large farm machinery plant at Sidi Bel Abbes. A heavy vehicle assembly plant built by Berliet at Rouiba has a capacity of 4,550 vehicles per year to be raised to 9,000 per year by 1980. Two-thirds of the parts used by the plant are manufactured in Algeria. Other projects planned in the vehicle and machinery sector include a truck assembly plant to be built by Toyota of Japan; a construction machinery plant to be built by a West German firm; and a factory producing electric motors, generators and transformers at Aazaga, near Algiers. Since 1970, when the Renault assembly plant at Algiers closed down, Algeria has had no automobile manufacturing industry. Renault and Fiat were still competing by April 1979 for a contract to set up a 100,000 cars-per-year plant at Senia, near Oran. However, it is thought that Algeria's planners now consider the investment needed for this project to be too high and it may have to be scaled down. At Guelma there is a plant manufacturing motorcycles, bicycles and small motors. Pumps and irrigation equipment are produced at Médéa. Pirelli and Krupp are building a tyre factory at Bouira, near Algiers.

Other growth areas are the paper industry, textiles, electrical goods (including radio and television sets), flour milling and building materials. Algeria is almost self-sufficient in cement, plastics, chemicals and fertilizers. There are five state-run cement plants and six further plants are under construction. Among new projects planned or under construction are a pharmaceuticals complex which will employ 1,000 people, a pulp factory and a desalination plant at Mostaganem. The Government intends to establish a major shipyard at Oran. A new industrial complex will be established at Bethioua in the Arzew region and will eventually provide some 100,000 new jobs.

TRADE

Algeria had a consistent foreign trade deficit, with the exception of small surpluses recorded in 1967 and 1968, until the huge increases in oil prices in 1973 began to reverse the situation, altering it dramatically by 1974. Oil and natural gas exports have transformed the pattern of Algerian exports, previously limited to agricultural products and some minerals. Main exports in the past were wine, citrus fruit and iron ore, but export markets for wine are now difficult to find. Hydrocarbons accounted for 96 per cent of total export earnings in 1977. Other exports include vegetables, tobacco, hides and skins, dates and phosphates. Imports of consumer goods are severely restricted. Capital goods made up 34.2 per cent of the total value of imports in 1977; raw materials and semi-finished goods 36.7 per cent; food and tobacco 14.9 per cent; consumer goods 12.7 per cent.

Algeria's visible trade account showed a deficit of 1,397 million dinars in 1973, which turned into a surplus of 982 million dinars in 1974, mainly as a result of soaring oil revenues. However, in 1975 there was a deficit of 5,192 million dinars, due to the sharp decline of oil exports, particularly to France, as well as to higher import costs. Government curbs on imports, together with the higher price and volume of oil exports, reversed this trend in 1976 but again in 1977 there was a deficit, of 5,444 million dinars, with oil exports falling in the second half of the year and a sharp rise in imports. The deficit for 1978 was expected to be lower, at about 4,500 million dinars.

Before independence France took 81 per cent of Algeria's exports and provided 82 per cent of its imports. This dominance declined steadily, particularly at the time of the 1971 oil nationalization crisis, and France's share of Algerian trade in 1977 had dropped to only 12.7 per cent of exports and 24 per cent of imports. Continuing poor relations between France and Algeria led to a decline in the volume of trade, although relations had improved by the end of 1978. Towards the end of 1977 France decided to take a larger share of its crude oil from Saudi Arabia rather than Algeria (having already cut its Algerian oil imports sharply in 1975) and Algeria retaliated by imposing a ban on the import of French goods early in 1978. In 1977 the main suppliers, after France, were West Germany, Italy, the United States, Japan and Spain. Main customers were West Germany, France, the United States and Italy.

Under a decree of January 1978, the State trading agencies, which operate on a commercial basis and are not backed by the automatic guarantee of the Algerian Government, now have a monopoly on all foreign trade.

In January 1976 a preferential trade agreement was signed between Algeria and the EEC, after more than two years of negotiations. Under the agreement, aid is promised to Algeria in the form of loans and grants; there is an 80 per cent reduction of the common tariff on Algerian wine; the quota of Algerian petroleum products allowed into EEC countries will be steadily raised and eventually lifted altogether; and the tariffs on imports into the EEC of Algerian agricultural products will be either lowered or abolished. A new co-operation agreement, continuing the main provisions of the trade agreement, came into force in November 1978.

FINANCE

Until independence, Algeria was mostly dependent on France for its central banking and monetary system, though some of the usual central banking functions were carried out by the Banque d'Algérie. The Banque Centrale d'Algérie started its operations on January 1st, 1963, as the sole bank of issue of the new Algerian franc, and has all the usual central banking powers. The banking system has been largely taken over by the state. A state monopoly on all foreign financial transactions was imposed in November 1967; this followed a similar monopoly imposed on insurance in June 1966. The Banque Nationale d'Algérie deals in particular with finance for agriculture. The Crédit Populaire d'Algérie and the Banque Extérieure d'Algérie are concerned with the financial interests of industry, commerce and transport. In 1974 an Algerian-Libyan bank, the Banque Internationale Arabe, was opened in Paris to finance trade and investment between France and Arab countries. Two Algerian and six French banks set up the Union Méditerranéenne de Banques in 1975 to finance international trade, especially between Algeria and France.

The 1979 budget envisages government revenue of 36,901 million dinars, an increase of 4,336 million dinars over the previous year. Total government spending was estimated at 36,881 million dinars, 13.6 per cent more than in 1978. Of this, 29,621 million dinars was for the administrative budget. Education is given high priority, with 27.6 per cent of the administrative and 21.8 per cent of the development budget, allocations of 5,696 million dinars and 2,800 million dinars respectively. The second largest allocation in the administrative budget is for defence, at 2,318 million dinars, followed by public health (1,226 million dinars) and internal affairs (1,224 million dinars). Community development and urban modernization receive the second largest share of the capital budget, with 2,520 million dinars, followed by housing with 1,520 million dinars. The size of these allocations is an indication of the shift in emphasis towards development of the social sectors. Economic infrastructure is allocated 1,350 million dinars.

Much of Algeria's investment is financed by domestic saving and not more than 25 per cent of finance for the 1974–77 Plan was expected to be borrowed abroad. However, Algeria's political stability and its oil revenues have made many countries and international financial institutions willing to lend it money.

In 1978 there was continued heavy borrowing abroad, in particular for financing gas development. Borrowing on the Euromarket during the year, mainly by SONATRACH, amounted to $2,515 million and $721 million was raised in Eurobonds. Algeria also obtained loans from a number of other sources, including $500 million from Eximbank of the U.S.A. and a $1,000 million line of credit from Canada to finance imports of Canadian goods and services. During 1979 SONATRACH was expected to be seeking international loans totalling about $3,000 million, in particular to finance the Arzew 3 LNG plant and gas pipelines. The World Bank granted a $126 million loan in March 1979 for road improvement and maintenance.

Algeria has been criticized, particularly by France, for being too much in debt. Its public external debt by the end of 1977 totalled $12,300 million, of which

$7,600 million had been disbursed, and by August 1978 the total had risen to $14,700 million. It is expected to rise to $21,040 million in 1985. Debt servicing in 1978 cost about 20 per cent of the total value of exports and this ratio is expected to reach nearly 25 per cent in 1982 but by 1985 will have fallen slightly to 23.6 per cent, thereafter falling steadily as Algeria begins to export large quantities of natural gas and as most of the development projects in the hydrocarbons sector, which have required such heavy investment, come to completion.

A balance of payments surplus of $588 million in 1974 turned into a deficit of about $336 million in 1975, as a result of the unfavourable balance of Algeria's trade and in spite of a greatly increased surplus on capital account. By the third quarter of 1976, however, there was a $468 million surplus, due partly to continued large-scale borrowing abroad. Falling oil revenues led to a deficit on current account of $2,322 million in 1977; this was largely offset by a $1,975 million surplus on capital account.

International reserves fell from U.S. $1,987 million at the end of 1976 to $1,268 million in July 1978 but by the end of the year they had risen sharply to $2,233 million (of which $1,879 million was foreign exchange).

STATISTICAL SURVEY

AREA AND POPULATION

Area	Population					
	Census	Mid-Year Estimates†				
	April 4th, 1966	1973	1974	1975	1976	1977
2,381,741 sq. km.*	11,821,679	15,772,000	16,275,000	16,776,000	17,304,000	17,910,000

* 919,595 square miles.

† Including Algerian nationals living abroad, numbering 268,868 at the 1966 census.

Note: A census began throughout the country on February 12th, 1977. Based on this census, the estimated population at January 1st, 1978, was 18,250,000 (including nationals abroad), but full census details are not yet available.

AREA AND POPULATION BY WILAYAS (DEPARTMENTS)

	Area (sq. km.)	Population* (estimates at Jan. 1st, 1978)
Adrar	422,498.0	142,046
El Asnam	8,676.7	885,200
Laghouat	112,052.0	307,977
Oum El Bouaghi	8,123.0	400,182
Batna	14,881.5	589,146
Béjaia	3,444.2	554,876
Biskra	109,728.0	544,798
Béchar	306,000.0	148,101
Blida	3,703.8	909,930
Bouira	4,517.1	385,452
Tamanrasset	556,000.0	45,622
Tébessa	16,574.5	372,479
Tlemcen	9,283.7	596,677
Tiaret	23,455.6	619,826
Tizi-Ouzou	3,756.3	875,075
Algiers	785.7	1,988,000
Djelfa	22,904.8	330,406
Jijel	3,704.5	506,488
Sétif	10,350.4	990,157
Saida	106,777.4	373,366
Skikda	4,748.3	493,929
Sidi Bel Abbès	11,648.2	531,694
Annaba	3,489.3	507,806
Guelma	8,624.4	552,455
Constantine	3,561.7	686,671
Médéa	8,704.1	482,183
Mostaganem	7,023.6	766,167
M'Sila	19,824.6	438,317
Mascara	5,845.6	435,776
Ouargla	559,234.0	199,691
Oran	1,820.0	761,507
Total	2,381,741.0	17,422,000

* Excluding Algerian nationals abroad, estimated to total 828,000 at January 1st, 1978.

PRINCIPAL TOWNS

(estimated population in 1977)

Algiers (capital)	1,800,000	Blida	162,000	Tlemcen	120,000
Ouahran (Oran)	500,000	Sétif	160,000	El Asnam	118,000
Constantine	430,000	Sidi Bel Abbès	158,000	Boufarik	112,000
Annaba (Bône)	340,000	Skikda	132,000	Béjaia	108,000
Tizi-Ouzou	230,000	Batna	120,000	Médéa	106,000

Source: Commissariat National aux Recensements et Enquêtes Statistiques, Algiers.

BIRTHS, MARRIAGES AND DEATHS

	Live Births*		Marriages		Deaths*	
	Number	Rate (per 1,000)	Number	Rate (per 1,000)	Number	Rate (per 1,000)
1966	561,528	46.2	61,981	5.1	122,999	10.1
1967	534,904	42.7	59,549	4.7	118,325	9.4
1968	529,806	39.3	n.a.	n.a.	134,160	9.9

1975: Registered live births 801,720 (birth rate 47.8 per 1,000).

* Data exclude live-born infants dying before registration of birth. Birth registration was estimated to be 90 per cent complete in 1968. Death registration was estimated to be between 40 and 60 per cent complete. According to United Nations estimates, the average annual birth rate was 49.6 per 1,000 in 1965–70 and 48.7 per 1,000 in 1970–75, while the death rate was 17.4 per 1,000 in 1965–70 and 15.4 per 1,000 in 1970–75.

EMPLOYMENT

('000 wage-earning employees)

	1973	1974	1975	1976
Industry	225	242	269	303
Construction and public works	190	207	228	261
Transport	77	85	93	100
Trade	195	217	235	256
Services	180	197	216	237
Handicrafts	40	41	42	44
Administration	300	n.a.	340	365
Others*	251	276	308	346
Total	1,458	1,580	1,731	1,812

* Including students and armed forces.

Note: The total economically active population on January 1st, 1978, was estimated at 4,002,000, of whom 42.1 per cent were employed in agriculture.

Source: Secrétariat d'Etat au Plan, Algiers.

AGRICULTURE

LAND USE, 1976

('000 hectares)

Arable Land	6,500*
Under Permanent Crops	610*
Permanent Meadows and Pastures	38,452†
Forest Land	2,424†
Other Land and Inland Water	190,188
Total Area	238,174

* FAO estimate.

† Unofficial figure.

Source: FAO, *Production Yearbook*.

PRINCIPAL CROPS

('000 metric tons)

	1975	1976	1977*
Wheat	1,848	1,630	1,200
Barley	743	589	400
Potatoes	575	493	500
Onions (dry)	106	72	108
Tomatoes	135	106	136
Grapes	601	346†	500
Olives	197	123*	113
Oranges	337	359	360
Tangerines and mandarines	149	147	148
Dates	182	137	140
Tobacco	3	2	3

* FAO estimates. † Unofficial figure.

Source: FAO, *Production Yearbook*.

LIVESTOCK

('000 head, year ending September)

	1975	1976	1977*
Sheep	9,773	9,337	9,540
Goats	2,269	2,242	2,220
Cattle	1,245*	1,270*	1,300
Horses	154	139	140
Mules	195	189	180
Asses	429	463	443
Camels	155	141	135
Chickens	16,000*	16,500*	16,900

* FAO estimate.

LIVESTOCK PRODUCTS

('000 metric tons—FAO estimates)

	1975	1976	1977
Beef and veal	28	29	29
Mutton and lamb	47	51	48
Goats' meat	8	9	9
Poultry meat	36	38	40
Cows' milk	370	380	390
Sheep's milk	130	133	135
Goats' milk	125	132	138
Hen eggs	15.5	17.0	19.0
Wool (clean)	8.2	8.7	9.2

Source: FAO, *Production Yearbook*.

FORESTRY

ROUNDWOOD REMOVALS

('000 cubic metres, excluding bark)

	Coniferous (soft wood)			Broadleaved (hard wood)			Total		
	1975*	1976*	1977*	1975	1976*	1977*	1975	1976*	1977*
Sawlogs, veneer logs and logs for sleepers	15	15	15	5	5	5	20	20	20
Pitprops (Mine timber)	—	—	—	1	1	1	1	1	1
Other industrial wood	104	107	111	52*	54	55	156*	161	166
Fuel wood	808	835	863	405*	413	415	1,213*	1,248	1,278
Total	927	957	989	463	473	476	1,390	1,430	1,465

* FAO estimate.

Source: FAO, *Yearbook of Forest Products*.

SEA FISHING

('000 metric tons)

	1969	1970	1971	1972	1973	1974	1975	1976	1977
Total catch (live weight)	23.2	25.7	23.8	28.3	31.2	35.7	37.7	35.1	43.5

Source: FAO, *Yearbook of Fishery Statistics.*

MINING

		1973	1974	1975	1976
Coal	'000 metric tons	15	13	8	n.a.
Iron ore: gross weight	,, ,, ,,	3,180	3,797	3,200	2,700
metal content	,, ,, ,,	1,700	2,064	1,728	1,490
Antimony	metric tons	60†	60†	60†	60†
Lead ore*	,, ,,	3,700	3,000	2,700	1,600
Zinc ore*	,, ,,	14,350	10,446	11,200	6,200
Copper ore*	,, ,,	300	400	400	400
Mercury	,, ,,	456	486	974	1,069†
Phosphate rock	'000 metric tons	608	802	733	818
Crude petroleum	,, ,, ,,	50,748	47,175	47,662	50,423
Natural gasolene	,, ,, ,,	1,190	1,200	2,500	n.a.
Natural gas	million cu. metres	4,745	5,621	5,947	9,933

* Metal content of concentrates. † Estimates of U.S. Bureau of Mines.

Sources: UN, *Yearbook of Industrial Statistics, Statistical Yearbook* and *Monthly Bulletin of Statistics.*

1977: Crude petroleum 53.5 million metric tons; Natural gas (estimate) 10,500 million cu. metres.

1978: Crude petroleum 57.2 million metric tons; Natural gas 14,200 million cu. metres.

INDUSTRY

SELECTED PRODUCTS

		1972	1973	1974	1975
Olive oil (crude)	'000 metric tons	23	18	18	37
Flour	,, ,, ,,	580	616	659	690
Wine	'000 hectolitres	5,753	7,600*	6,282	4,319
Cigarettes	metric tons	7,641	8,012	8,724	9,300
Paints	'000 metric tons	29.9	36.9	28.2	35.9
Washing powder and detergents	,, ,, ,,	21.5	25.2	18.5	19.3
Nitrogenous fertilizers	,, ,, ,,	39*	50*	52*	75*
Superphosphates	,, ,, ,,	16*	38*	73*	103*
Naphtha	,, ,, ,,	72	434	400	460
Motor spirit (petrol)	,, ,, ,,	507	861	717	797
Kerosene	,, ,, ,,	84	153	181	180
Jet fuel	,, ,, ,,	106	185	195	182
Distillate fuel oils	,, ,, ,,	936	1,652	1,898	1,716
Residual fuel oils	,, ,, ,,	623	1,357	1,345	1,549
Liquefied petroleum gas	,, ,, ,,	131	245	240	232
Cement	,, ,, ,,	927	1,007	941	948
Pig iron	,, ,, ,,	391	360	276	245
Crude steel	,, ,, ,,	98	186	181	190
Welded steel tubes	,, ,, ,,	83	94	105	131
Buses and coaches (assembly)	number	229	303	337	n.a.
Lorries (assembly)	,,	3,991	6,156	5,962	n.a.
Electricity	million kWh.	2,325	3,002	3,249	3,744
Manufactured gas	million cu. metres	144	72	64	48

* FAO estimate.

Source: UN, *Statistical Yearbook* and *Yearbook of Industrial Statistics*; UN Economic Commission for Africa, *African Statistical Yearbook*; FAO, *Production Yearbook.*

1976: Olive oil 17,000 metric tons; Wine 2,340,000 hectolitres; Cement 1,330,000 metric tons.

1977: Olive oil 15,000 metric tons.

FINANCE

100 centimes=1 Algerian dinar (AD).
Coins: 1, 2, 5, 10, 20 and 50 centimes; 1 and 5 dinars.
Notes: 5, 10, 100 and 500 dinars.
Exchange rates (June 1979): £1 sterling=7.92 dinars; U.S. $1=3.83 dinars.
100 Algerian dinars=£12.62=$26.12.

Note: The Algerian dinar was introduced in April 1964, replacing (at par) the new Algerian franc. From January 1960 the Algerian franc (equal to the French franc) was valued at 180 milligrammes of gold. Until August 1971 the dinar was thus valued at 20.255 U.S. cents (U.S. $1=4.937 dinars). Between December 1971 and February 1973 the dinar's value was 21.991 U.S. cents ($1=4.537 dinars); from February 1973 to January 1974 it was 24.435 U.S. cents ($1=4.093 dinars). Since January 1974 the Algerian authorities have allowed the dinar to "float" on foreign exchange markets. The average exchange rate (dinars per U.S. dollar) was: 3.959 in 1973; 4.181 in 1974; 3.949 in 1975; 4.164 in 1976; 4.147 in 1977; 3.966 in 1978. In terms of sterling, the exchange rate between November 1967 and June 1972 was £1=11.849 dinars.

BUDGET
(million AD)

REVENUE	1977	1978
Direct taxation	2,150	2,400
Profits taxes	4,000	4,700
Customs duties and indirect taxes	3,950	5,300
Oil and gas revenues	16,500	18,200
Other receipts	1,310	1,965
TOTAL	27,910	32,565

EXPENDITURE	1977	1978	1979
Current budget	15,850.0	18,165.0	20,621.0
of which:			
Defence	1,600.0	1,843.0	2,317.8
Interior	853.8	975.6	1,224.3
Agriculture and agrarian reform	444.7	474.7	539.6
Primary and secondary education	2,771.3	3,348.7	4,231.9
Higher education and scientific research	719.9	883.1	1,150.5
Public health	901.2	1,033.6	1,225.9
Public works	330.7	367.6	358.8
Labour and social affairs	220.7	237.9	313.9*
Finance	339.0	390.8	456.0
Ex-servicemen	472.8	486.1	659.8
Youth and sports	216.2	267.4	244.8
General services	5,875.9	6,590.8	n.a.
Development budget	11,900.0	14,300.0	16,260.0
TOTAL	27,750.0	32,465.0	36,881.0

* Including vocational training.

1979: Estimated revenue 36,901 million dinars.

DEVELOPMENT PLAN 1974–77
EXPENDITURE (million AD)

Industry	48,000
Agriculture	12,005
Dams and water	4,400
Tourism	1,500
Fishing	115
Economic infrastructure	15,521
Education and training	9,947
Social services	14,610
Administration	1,399
TOTAL (incl. others)	110,217

CENTRAL BANK RESERVES
(U.S. $ million at December 31st)

	1976	1977	1978
Gold	223	234	252
IMF Special Drawing Rights	50	56	60
Reserve position in IMF	39	40	41
Foreign exchange	1,676	1,588	1,879
TOTAL	1,987	1,917	2,233

Source: IMF, *International Financial Statistics.*

MONEY SUPPLY
(million AD at December 31st)

	1975	1976	1977
Currency outside banks	12,742	17,241	20,579
Demand deposits at deposit money banks	13,720	19,120	22,929
Checking deposits at Post Office	2,561	2,873	3,458
Private sector demand deposits at Treasury	1,524	353	668
TOTAL MONEY	30,547	39,587	47,634

Source: IMF, *International Financial Statistics.*

COST OF LIVING

RETAIL PRICE INDEX FOR ALGIERS
(Average of monthly figures; base: 1970=100)

	1969	1971	1972	1973	1974	1975
Food	94.7	102.7	106.7	118.7	127.1	141.5
Fuel and light	100.0	100.0	100.0	100.0	100.4	101.6
Clothing	82.1	102.9	106.5	107.1	112.6	114.3
Rent	100.0	100.0	100.0	102.8	103.1	108.8
ALL ITEMS	93.8	102.6	106.4	112.9	118.2	128.0

1976 average: Food 162.3; all items 140.1.

August 1977: Food 186.6; all items 157.8.

Source: ILO, mainly *Year Book of Labour Statistics.*

NATIONAL ACCOUNTS
(million AD at current prices)

NATIONAL INCOME AND PRODUCT

	1973	1974	1975	1976
Compensation of employees	11,989	14,822	18,313	21,986
Operating surplus	11,992	23,205	21,702	25,857
DOMESTIC FACTOR INCOMES	23,981	38,027	40,015	47,843
Consumption of fixed capital	3,169	3,506	4,647	6,057
GROSS DOMESTIC PRODUCT AT FACTOR COST	27,150	41,533	44,662	53,900
Indirect taxes, *less* subsidies	7,337	10,840	12,124	14,791
G.D.P. IN PURCHASERS' VALUES	34,487	52,373	56,786	68,692
Factor income from abroad	1,554	2,309	2,239	2,340
Less Factor income paid abroad	532	1,111	1,193	1,863
GROSS NATIONAL PRODUCT	35,509	53,572	57,831	69,169
Less Consumption of fixed capital	3,169	3,506	4,647	6,057
NATIONAL INCOME IN MARKET PRICES	32,340	50,066	53,184	63,111
Other current transfers from abroad	382	213	210	243
Less Other current transfers paid abroad	181	1,821	97	94
NATIONAL DISPOSABLE INCOME	32,540	48,458	53,298	63,260

EXPENDITURE ON THE GROSS DOMESTIC PRODUCT

	1973	1974	1975	1976
Government final consumption expenditure	4,925	6,197	8,379	9,818
Private final consumption expenditure	16,790	22,821	27,059	31,356
Increase in stocks	1,523	5,111	3,863	568
Gross fixed capital formation	14,161	17,735	24,585	31,549
TOTAL DOMESTIC EXPENDITURE	37,399	51,864	63,886	73,291
Exports of goods and services	8,010	20,089	19,357	22,925
Less Imports of goods and services	10,922	19,580	26,456	27,525
G.D.P. IN PURCHASERS' VALUES	34,487	52,373	56,786	68,692

GROSS DOMESTIC PRODUCT BY ECONOMIC ACTIVITY

	1973	1974	1975	1976
Agriculture and livestock	2,762	3,304	5,160	4,878
Forestry and logging	155	158	169	167
Fishing	87	115	133	169
Mining and quarrying*	5,273	16,774	13,767	16,954
Manufacturing	5,289	6,169	6,671	9,017
Electricity, gas and water	507	604	675	867
Construction	4,014	5,407	6,627	9,164
Wholesale and retail trade	5,292	4,838	5,383	7,231
Restaurants and hotels	390	453	550	613
Transport, storage and communications	2,628	3,566	3,936	4,546
Finance, insurance, real estate and business services	1,732	1,844	2,011	2,182
Government services	3,679	4,624	6,446	7,646
Other services	632	768	836	767
SUB-TOTAL	32,440	48,624	52,363	64,201
Import duties	2,047	3,750	4,424	4,490
TOTAL	34,487	52,373	56,786	68,692

* Including production of crude petroleum and natural gas (million AD): 5,080 in 1973; 16,402 in 1974; 13,426 in 1975; 16,625 in 1976.

BALANCE OF PAYMENTS
(U.S. $ million)

	1973	1974	1975	1976	1977
Merchandise exports f.o.b.	1,832	4,601	4,441	5,202	5,925
Merchandise imports f.o.b.	−2,141	−3,666	−5,452	−4,693	−6,197
TRADE BALANCE	−309	935	−1,011	509	−272
Exports of services	142	273	300	253	330
Imports of services	−657	−1,017	−1,376	−2,107	−2,705
BALANCE ON GOODS AND SERVICES	−824	191	−2,087	−1,345	−2,647
Private unrequited transfers (net)	416	396	437	476	343
Government unrequited transfers (net)	−36	−426	−12	−14	−18
CURRENT BALANCE	−444	161	−1,662	−883	−2,322
Direct capital investment (net)	50	358	85	184	173
Other long-term capital (net)	988	166	1,286	1,574	1,724
Short-term capital (net)	122	−250	1	−45	119
Net errors and omissions	−103	153	−45	−207	−42
TOTAL (net monetary movements)	613	588	−336	622	−347
Allocation of IMF Special Drawing Rights	—	—	—	—	—
CHANGES IN RESERVES, ETC.	613	588	−336	622	−347

Sources: IMF, *International Financial Statistics*; Secrétariat d'Etat au Plan and Ministère des Finances, Algiers.

EXTERNAL TRADE

(million AD)

	1972	1973	1974	1975	1976	1977	1978
Imports c.i.f.	6,694	9,535	17,754	23,755	22,227	29,534	n.a.
Exports f.o.b.	5,854	7,479	19,594	18,563	22,205	24,090	23,216

PRINCIPAL COMMODITIES

(million AD)

Imports	1974	1975	1976	1977
Foodstuffs and tobacco	3,707	4,518	3,593	4,398
Energy and lubricants	246	401	351	300
Primary products and raw materials	1,257	1,303	956	1,596
Semi-finished products	6,027	7,601	7,586	9,237
Capital goods	4,926	7,946	8,288	10,103
Consumer goods	1,558	1,915	1,432	3,760
Others	33	68	20	40

Exports	1974	1975	1976	1977
Foodstuffs and tobacco	664	687	628	551
Energy and lubricants	18,261	17,273	21,097	23,125
Primary products and raw materials	311	214	279	212
Semi-finished products	231	222	173	170
Capital goods	81	140	11	19
Consumer goods	46	27	17	11
Others	n.a.	n.a.	n.a.	2

Source: Ministère du Commerce, Algiers.

PRINCIPAL TRADING PARTNERS*

('000 AD)

Imports	1974	1975	1976	1977†
Belgium-Luxembourg	625,939	648,048	649,219	1,164,677
Brazil	793,206	714,970	681,876	911,530
Canada	490,018	130,469	415,385	1,100,542
France	4,951,813	8,291,571	6,014,083	7,115,033
Germany, Federal Republic	2,297,836	2,702,278	3,246,395	4,275,734
Italy	1,455,333	1,960,851	1,965,092	2,861,669
Japan	532,676	872,144	1,188,584	1,805,289
Netherlands	286,323	335,950	311,609	588,728
Poland	135,563	171,883	214,315	310,070
Romania	77,425	144,407	150,249	354,010
Spain	883,181	877,815	812,730	1,446,998
Sweden	190,868	317,575	552,517	552,563
Switzerland	285,721	394,337	358,499	586,815
U.S.S.R.	487,805	283,269	468,470	374,647
United Kingdom	631,637	805,093	1,013,349	875,901
U.S.A.	2,129,667	3,571,139	2,632,137	2,561,608

[*continued on next page*

PRINCIPAL TRADING PARTNERS—*continued*]

EXPORTS	1974	1975	1976	1977†
Belgium-Luxembourg	384,459	429,023	337,836	390,031
Brazil	463,289	261,994	n.a.	n.a.
China, People's Republic	129,683	135,243	n.a.	90,627
France	3,764,313	2,764,127	3,010,625	3,057,257
Germany, Federal Republic	4,020,100	3,561,065	4,027,414	3,533,208
Italy	1,131,032	1,928,601	1,671,265	1,309,150
Japan	121,489	150,990	14,156	76,051
Morocco	238,065	3,662	n.a.	n.a.
Netherlands	322,440	581,025	214,202	547,837
Paraguay	31,937	5,912	9,668	108,187
Romania	260,378	171,668	7,184	36,343
Senegal	958	31,521	42,295	138,324
Spain	1,218,607	876,739	653,104	584,943
Sweden	219,124	11,481	32,841	336,672
Switzerland	127,284	44,255	80,297	144,008
U.S.S.R.	334,715	381,616	352,872	230,854
United Kingdom	373,968	746,327	524,037	330,287
U.S.A.	4,581,762	5,110,129	9,784,857	2,480,586

* Imports by country of production; exports by country of consignment. † Provisional figures.

Source: Ministère du Commerce, Algiers.

TRANSPORT

RAILWAYS

	1973	1974	1975	1976
Passengers carried ('000)	6,900	8,000	n.a.	n.a.
Freight carried ('000 metric tons)	6,650	7,683	n.a.	n.a.
Passenger-km. (million)	944	1,058	1,128	1,369
Freight ton-km. (million)	1,790	1,901	1,740	1,727

Source: UN, *Statistical Yearbook.*

ROAD TRAFFIC

(motor vehicles in use at December 31st)

	1972	1973	1974	1975*
Passenger cars	165,022	176,898	204,137	286,100
Commercial vehicles	90,771	96,676	103,147	154,700

* UN estimate.

Source: IRF, *World Road Statistics,* and UN, *Statistical Yearbook.*

INTERNATIONAL SEA-BORNE SHIPPING

	GOODS LOADED ('000 metric tons)		GOODS UNLOADED ('000 metric tons)	
	1974	1975	1974	1975
Algiers	1,605	1,340	2,685	2,829
Annaba	3,532	n.a.	2,076	n.a.
Arzew	1,100	21,568	149	282
Bejaia	9,776	10,240	903	907
Oran	433	332	1,908	2,098
TOTAL (incl. others)	42,841	42,673	9,447	10,603

CIVIL AVIATION

Scheduled Services

	1972	1973	1974	1975	1976
Kilometres Flown ('000)	13,800	14,800	19,200	27,600	24,700
Passengers Carried ('000)	844	923	1,090	1,618	1,682
Passenger-km. (million)	699	760	997	1,795	1,429
Freight ton-km. ('000)	4,200	4,600	5,600	720	910
Mail ton-km. ('000)	700	700	800	1,100	1,300
Total ton-km. ('000)	68,000	74,000	95,000	171,000	147,000

Source: UN, *Statistical Yearbook.*

TOURISM

Country of Origin	1974	1975	1976	1977
France	86,192	121,190	83,391	94,701
Federal Republic of Germany	7,833	11,204	10,627	13,472
Italy	11,613	13,339	10,366	15,375
Morocco	53,639	51,774	9,740	1,462
Tunisia	24,922	26,643	18,422	41,788
United Kingdom	8,294	8,376	6,495	8,167
U.S.A.	7,351	4,917	5,154	6,558
Total (incl. others)	248,964	296,510	184,795	241,713

Hotel Capacity (1978): *c.* 20,000 beds.

Source: Office National Algérien du Tourisme, Algiers.

EDUCATION*

	Schools		Pupils		Teachers	
	1976/77	1977/78	1976/77	1977/78	1976/77	1977/78
Primary	8,182	8,380	2,782,044	2,894,084	70,498	77,009
Middle and Secondary	984	1,159	612,229	741,961	22,605	27,764
General	931	1,103	589,227	718,122	20,861	25,882
Technical	16	19	11,806	11,798	843	823
Teacher training	37	37	11,196	12,041	901	1,059
Higher	10	10	50,163	51,983	n.a.	n.a.

* State institutions only.

Source (for Education): Ministère de l'Education, Algiers.

Source (unless otherwise stated): Direction Générale du Plan des Etudes Economiques, Ministère des Finances, Algiers.

THE CONSTITUTION

(*Approved by popular referendum, November 19th,* 1976; *promulgated November 22nd,* 1976).

SUMMARY

The preamble recalls that Algeria owes its independence to a war of liberation which will go down in history as one of the epic struggles in the resurrection of the peoples of the Third World. It emphasizes that the institutions established since June 1965 are intended to transform the progressive ideas of the revolution into real achievements, affecting daily life, and to develop the content of the revolution by thought and action towards a definitive commitment to socialism.

FUNDAMENTAL PRINCIPLES OF THE ORGANIZATION OF ALGERIAN SOCIETY

The Republic: The State is socialist. Islam is the state religion and Arabic is the official national language. National sovereignty resides in the people. The National Charter is the fundamental source of national policy and law. It is to be referred to on ideological questions and for the interpretation of the Constitution. The popular assemblies are the basic institution of the state.

Socialism: The irreversible option of socialism is the only path to complete national independence. The individual ownership of property for personal or family use is guaranteed. Non-exploitative private property is an integral part of the new social system. The cultural, agrarian and industrial revolutions and socialist management of enterprises are the bases for the building of socialism.

The State: The State is exclusively at the service of the people. Those holding positions of responsibility must live solely on their salaries and may not, directly or by the agency of others, engage in any remunerative activity.

Fundamental Freedoms and the Rights of Man and the Citizen: Fundamental rights and freedoms are guaranteed. All discrimination on grounds of sex, race or occupation is forbidden. Law cannot operate retrospectively and a person is presumed innocent until proved guilty. Victims of judicial error shall receive compensation from the State.

The State guarantees the inviolability of the home, of private life and of the person. The State also guarantees the secrecy of correspondence, the freedom of conscience and opinion, freedom of intellectual, artistic and scientific creation, and freedom of expression and assembly.

The State guarantees the right to join a trade union, the right to work, to protection, to security, to health, to leisure, to education, etc. It also guarantees the right to leave the national territory, within the limits set by law. The law lays down the conditions under which the fundamental rights and freedoms may be withdrawn from anyone who uses them to attack the Constitution, the essential interests of the nation, the unity of the people and of the national territory, the internal and external security of the State, and the socialist revolution.

Duties of citizens: Every citizen must protect public property and safeguard national independence. The law sanctions the duty of parents to educate and protect their children, as well as the duty of children to help and support their parents. Women must participate fully in the building of socialism and national development.

The National Popular Army: The Army safeguards national independence and sovereignty. It participates in the development of the country and the building of socialism.

Principles of foreign policy: Algeria subscribes to the objectives of the United Nations, the Organization of African Unity and the Arab League. It supports Arab, Maghreb and African unity, on a basis of popular liberation. It is non-aligned and advocates peace and non-interference in the internal affairs of states. It fights against colonialism, imperialism and racial discrimination and supports the peoples of Africa, Asia and Latin America in their liberation struggles.

POWER AND ITS ORGANIZATION

Political power: The Algerian institutional system rests on the principle of the single-party state. The Front de Libération Nationale (FLN) is a vanguard force, guiding and organizing the people for the building of socialism. Party and state organs work in different frameworks and with different means to attain the same objectives. The decisive posts in the state organization are held by members of the party leadership.

The Executive: The President of the Republic is Head of State, Head of the Armed Forces and responsible for national defence. He must be of Algerian origin, a Muslim and more than 40 years old. He is elected by universal, secret, direct suffrage. His mandate is for six years, and is indefinitely renewable. The President embodies the unity of the political leadership of the party and the state. The presidential candidate is nominated by the party congress. The President presides over joint meetings of the party and the executive. Ministers are appointed by the President. The President presides over meetings of the Council of Ministers. He may appoint a Vice-President and a Prime Minister, to whom he may delegate some of his powers. Should the Presidency fall vacant, the President of the National Popular Assembly temporarily assumes the office and organizes presidential elections within 45 days. He may not himself be a candidate in the election. The President presides over a High Security Council which advises on all matters affecting national security.

The Legislature: The National Popular Assembly prepares and votes the law. Its members are nominated by the party leadership and elected by universal, direct, secret suffrage for a five-year term. The deputies enjoy parliamentary immunity. The Assembly sits for two ordinary sessions per year, each of not more than three months' duration. The commissions of the Assembly are in permanent session. Both the President and the Assembly may initiate legislation. The Assembly may legislate in all areas except national defence. In the periods between sessions of the Assembly the President may legislate by decree, but all such legislation must be submitted to the Assembly in the following session.

The Head of State is empowered to dissolve the Assembly or call premature elections, having consulted a joint meeting of the party leadership and the Government.

The Judiciary: Judges obey only the law. They defend the socialist revolution. The right of the accused to a defence is guaranteed. The Supreme Court regulates the activities of courts and tribunals. The Higher Court of the Magistrature is presided over by the President of the Republic; the Minister of Justice is Vice-President of the Court. All magistrates are answerable to the Higher Court for the manner in which they fulfil their functions.

Surveillance of the State: Surveillance is intended to ensure the efficient functioning of state organs and their respect for the National Charter, the Constitution and the law. Popular surveillance is exercised by the elected assemblies. An Audit Office is established to examine all expenditure by state and party bodies.

Constitutional revision: The Constitution can be revised on the initiative of the President of the Republic by a two-thirds majority of the National Assembly. The basic principles of the Constitution may not be revised.

THE GOVERNMENT

HEAD OF STATE

President: Col. Bendjedid Chadli (elected February 7th, 1979)

COUNCIL OF MINISTERS

(*June* 1979)

President and Minister of Defence: Col. Bendjedid Chadli.

Prime Minister and Minister of the Interior: Col. Mohamed Ben Ahmed Abdelghani.

Minister-Advisers to the President: Abdelaziz Bouteflika, Ahmed Taleb Ibrahimi.

Secretary-General to the Presidency: Abdelmalek Benhabyles.

Minister of Foreign Affairs: Mohamed Seddik Benyahia.

Minister of Agriculture and the Agrarian Revolution: Lt.-Col. Selim Saadi.

Minister of Water Affairs: Sid Ahmed Ghozali.

Minister of Public Works: Ahmed Ali Ghozali.

Minister of Energy and Petrochemical Industries: Belkacem Nabi.

Minister of Light Industry: Saïd Aït Messaoudène.

Minister of Heavy Industry: Mohamed Liassine.

Minister of Finance: M'Hamed Hadj Yala.

Minister of Planning and Regional Development: Abdelhamid Brahimi.

Minister of Health: Abderrazak Bouhara.

Minister of Higher Education and Scientific Research: Abdelhaq Brehri.

Minister of Primary and Secondary Education: Mohamed Kharroubi.

Minister of Labour and Vocational Training: Mouloud Oumeziane.

Minister of Commerce: Abdelhani Arbi.

Minister of Posts and Telecommunications: Mohamed Zerguini.

Minister of the Environment, Construction and Town Planning: Abdelmadjid Aouchiche.

Minister of War Veterans: Chérif Messaadia.

Minister of Religious Affairs: Baki Boualem.

Minister of Sport: Djamal Houhou.

Minister of Tourism: Abdelmadjid Allaoum.

Minister of Transport: Salah Goudgil.

Minister of Justice: Lahcene Soufi.

Minister of Information and Culture: Abdelhamid Mehri.

Secretary of State for Fishing: Ahmed Houhat.

Secretary of State for Forests and Reafforestation: Commdr. Brahim Brahmia.

Secretary-General of the Government: Smaïl Hamdani.

NATIONAL ASSEMBLY

The National Assembly (*Assemblée nationale populaire*) consists of 261 deputies elected by universal suffrage for a five-year term. In February 1977 elections were held for the first time under the new constitution. A single-party list of candidates was presented by the FLN, but the electorate was offered a choice of candidates within the list. Electoral participation was 78.5 per cent.

President of the National Assembly: Rabah Bitat.

There are two subsidiary levels of assemblies in Algeria. The communal assemblies (*assemblées populaires communales*) were created in 1967. They are headed by an elected president and are renewed by democratic vote every four years. The provincial assemblies (*assemblées populaires de wilayas*) were created in 1969 and are renewed every five years. The chief of the executive, the wali, is a government appointee. As for the national assembly, representatives are elected from a single list presented by the FLN.

POLITICAL PARTY

Government is based on a one-party system.

Front de Libération Nationale (FLN): place Emir Abdelkader, Algiers; f. 1954; socialist in outlook, the party is divided into a Secretariat, a Central Committee, a Political Bureau, Federations, Dairas and Kasmas; according to party statutes adopted at the FLN Congress in January 1979, the Central Committee, elected by Congress, chooses a party Secretary-General who automatically becomes the candidate for the Presidency of the Republic. Members of the Political Bureau are nominated by the Secretary-General and elected by the Central Committee; Sec.-Gen. Col. Bendjedid Chadli; Co-ordinator Mohamed Salah Yahiaoui.

Under the aegis of the FLN there exists a number of mass political organizations, including *Jeunesse du Front de Libération Nationale* (JFLN) and the *Union Nationale des Femmes Algériennes* (UNFA).

There are several small opposition groups; all are proscribed and in exile in France or in other Arab countries.

Frente Popular para la Liberación de Sakiet el Hamra y Rio de Oro—POLISARIO: B.P. 10, El Mouradia, Algiers; f. 1973 to gain independence for Western Sahara, first from Spain and then from Morocco and Mauritania; originally based in Mauritania but later moved to Algeria where it is supported by the Algerian Government; proclaimed the Sahrawi Arab Democratic Republic in February 1976; since recognized by 19 countries in Africa and Asia; its main organs are a nine-member executive committee, a 21-member Political Bureau and a 41-member Sahrawi National Council; Sec.-Gen. Mohamed Abdelaziz; Deputy Sec.-Gen. Bachir Mustahpa Sayed.

DIPLOMATIC REPRESENTATION

EMBASSIES ACCREDITED TO ALGERIA

(In Algiers unless otherwise stated)

Afghanistan: Cairo, Egypt.

Albania: 50 rue Oukil Mohammed, Birmandréis; *Ambassador:* SYRJA LAZE (also accred. to Mauritania).

Angola: 17 rue Desfontaine; *Ambassador:* JOÃO BATISTA MAWETE.

Argentina: 7 rue Hamani; *Ambassador:* ANDRÉS G. CEUSTERMANS (also accred. to Tunisia).

Australia: 60 blvd. Colonel Bougara, El-Biar; *Ambassador:* JOHN ANTHONY PIPER.

Austria: Immeuble Dar el Kef, rue Shakespeare, El-Mouradia; *Ambassador:* (vacant).

Bangladesh: 141 blvd. Salah Bouakouir; *Ambassador:* ABUL FATEH.

Belgium: 22 chemin Youcef Tayebi, El-Biar; *Ambassador:* ROBERT GUILLOT-PINGUE.

Benin: Villa no. 4, rue no. 3, Beaulieu, El-Harrach; *Ambassador:* ANTOINE LALEYE.

Brazil: 48 blvd. Mohamed V; *Ambassador:* RONALD L. M. SMALL.

Bulgaria: 13 blvd. Colonel Bougara; *Ambassador:* STEFAN PETROV.

Burundi: 116 blvd. des Martyrs; *Ambassador:* JULIEN NAHAYO.

Cameroon: 26 chemin Sheikh Bachir Brahimi; *Chargé d'Affaires:* FRANÇOIS N'DINE EBAKISSE.

Canada: 27 *bis* rue d'Anjou, Hydra; *Ambassador:* RAYMOND ROY.

Cape Verde: 3 rue Wiasse; *Ambassador:* ADELINO NUNES CORREIA (also representing Guinea-Bissau).

Central African Empire: 14 rue Jean Rameau, Bellevue; *Ambassador:* CHRISTOPHE MAIDOU (also accred. to Tunisia).

Chad: 6 rue Sylvain Fourastier, El-Mouradia; *Ambassador:* MBAILAOU NAIMBAYE LOSSIMIAN.

China, People's Republic: 34 blvd. des Martyrs; *Ambassador:* CHOU PO-PING.

Congo: 6 rue Cheick el Kamel, Kouba; *Ambassador:* GASTON EYABO.

Cuba: 18 rue Ibn Batran, El-Mouradia; *Ambassador:* GIRALDO MAZOLA COLLAZO.

Czechoslovakia: Villa Malika, 7 chemin Ziryab, B.P. 999; *Ambassador:* VLADIMÍR BERGER.

Denmark: 29 blvd. Zirout Youcef; *Ambassador:* OLE BERNHARD OLSEN (also accred. to Tunisia).

Finland: 2 blvd. Mohammed V; *Ambassador:* OSMO ORKOMIES.

France: rue Larbi Alik, Hydra; *Ambassador:* GUY DE COMMINES DE MARSILLY.

Gabon: 80 rue Allili, B.P. 65, Bouzareah; *Ambassador:* ETIENNE M'BOUMBA MOUDOUNGA.

Gambia: Tripoli, Libya.

German Democratic Republic: 8 ave. Mohamed Rabia; *Ambassador:* EDGAR ROEDER.

Germany, Federal Republic: 165 Chemin Sfindja; *Ambassador:* Dr. MICHAEL JOVY.

Ghana: 62 rue Parmentier, Hydra; *Ambassador:* CHARLES KWASHIE MAWUENYEGAH.

Greece: 38 rue Didouche Mourad; *Ambassador:* CONSTANTIN MIGLIARESSIS.

Guinea: 43 blvd. Central Said Hamdine, Hydra; *Ambassador:* LANCINE SYLLA (also accred. to Tunisia).

Guinea-Bissau: 3 rue Wiasse; *Ambassador:* ADELINO NUNES CORREIA (also representing Cape Verde).

Hungary: 18 ave. des Frères Oughlis; *Ambassador:* ZOLTÁN SZEPHELYI (also accred. to Tunisia).

India: 119 rue Didouche Mourad; *Ambassador:* K. K. S. RANA.

Indonesia: 6 rue Etienne Baillac, El-Mouradia; *Chargé d'affaires:* SAGIRI KARTANEGARA (also accred. to Guinea, Mali and Morocco).

Iran: 60 rue Didouche Mourad; *Ambassador:* ASSAD K. SADRY.

Iraq: 4 rue Areski Abri, Hydra; *Ambassador:* (vacant).

Ireland: Madrid, Spain.

Italy: 18 rue Finalleri, El-Biar; *Ambassador:* UBERTO BOZZINI.

Ivory Coast: Parc Paradou, Hydra; *Ambassador:* EDMOND ZEGBEHI BOUAZO.

Japan: 3 rue du Dr. Lucien Reynaud; *Ambassador:* MASAMI OTA.

Jordan: 6 rue Chenoua; *Chargé d'affaires:* FAYEZ ABDEL NABI.

Kenya: Cairo, Egypt.

Korea, Democratic People's Republic: 49 rue Salvandy; *Ambassador:* KIM HI DJOUN.

Kuwait: 1 rue Didouche Mourad; *Ambassador:* YOUSOUF AL-MONAYES.

Lebanon: 9 rue Kaid Ahmed, El-Biar; *Chargé d'affaires:* AMINE ASSI.

Libya: 15 chemin Bachir Brahimi; *Ambassador:* ABDUL-FATTAH NAAS.

Madagascar: rue Abdelkadir Aouis; *Ambassador:* M. P. ZAFERA (also accred. to Tunisia).

Mali: Villa no. 15, Cité DNC/ANP, Chemin du Kaddous; *Ambassador:* (vacant).

Malta: Tripoli, Libya.

Mexico: 103 rue Didouche Mourad; *Ambassador:* OSCAR GONZÁLES CEZAR.

Mongolia: 4 rue Belkacem Amani, Hydra; *Ambassador:* SONOMYN LOUVSAN (also accred. to Mauritania).

Nepal: Cairo, Egypt.

Netherlands: 23 chemin Cheikh Bachir Ibrahimi, El-Biar; *Ambassador:* Jonkheer EDUARD OLOF VAN SUCHTELEN.

Niger: 136 blvd. Salah Bouakouir; *Ambassador:* SOUMAILA SALIFOU (also accred. to Morocco and Tunisia).

Nigeria: 27 rue Blaise Pascal; *Ambassador:* OLA M. A. ABIOLA.

Norway: Rabat, Morocco.

Oman: 126 rue Didouche Mourad; *Ambassador:* SALEM ISMAIL SUWAID.

Pakistan: 14 ave. Souidani Boudjemâa; *Ambassador:* S. A. D. BUKHARI.

Panama: Madrid, Spain.

Peru: 127 rue Didouche Mourad; *Ambassador:* SANTIAGO ROMERO MARCENARO (also accred. to Morocco and Tunisia).

Philippines: *Ambassador:* PACIFICO CASTRO.

Poland: 37 ave. Mustafa Ali Khodja, El-Biar; *Ambassador:* BOGDAN WASILEWSKY.

Portugal: 116 blvd. des Martyrs; *Ambassador:* ANTÓNIO MANUEL DA VEIGA E MENEZES CORDEIRO.

Qatar: 155 blvd. Salah Bouakouir; *Ambassador:* ABDEL-KADER BRAIK AL-AMERI.

Romania: 24 rue Si Areski, Hydra; *Ambassador:* IOAN LAZARESCU.

Rwanda: Cairo, Egypt.

Saudi Arabia: 7 chemin des Glycines; *Ambassador:* ABDALLAH AL-MOULHAQ.

Senegal: 50 ave. Souidani Boudjemâa; *Ambassador:* IBRA DÉGUÈNE KA.

Somalia: 11 blvd. des Martyrs; *Ambassador:* ABDELHAMID ALI YOUCEF (also accred. to Spain).

Spain: 10 rue Azil Ali; *Ambassador:* GABRIEL MAÑUECO DE LECEA.

Sri Lanka: Belgrade, Yugoslavia.

Sudan: 27 rue de Carthage, Hydra; *Ambassador:* TAHER MUSTAFA ABDULLA.

Sweden: 4 blvd. Mohammed V; *Ambassador:* HARALD EDELSTAM.

Switzerland: 27 blvd. Zirout Youcef; *Ambassador:* ERNST ANDRES.

Syria: Domaine Tamzali, chemin A. Gadouche, El-Biar; *Ambassador:* AHMAD MADANIYA.

Tanzania: Paris, France.

Trinidad and Tobago: Lagos, Nigeria.

Tunisia: 11 rue du Bois de Boulogne, Hydra; *Ambassador:* AMOR FEZZANI.

Turkey: Villa dar el Ouard, blvd. Colonel Bougara; *Ambassador:* FAIK MELEK.

Uganda: Cairo, Egypt.

U.S.S.R.: chemin du Prince d'Annam, El-Biar; *Ambassador:* VASSILY NAZAROVICH RYKOV.

United Arab Emirates: 26 rue Haouis Mokrane, El-Mouradia; *Ambassador:* KHALED ABDELLAH AL KASSIMI.

United Kingdom: 7 chemin des Glycines; *Ambassador:* RICHARD STANLEY FABER.

U.S.A.: 4 chemin Bachir Brahimi; *Ambassador:* ULRIC HAYNES, Jr.

Upper Volta: Cairo, Egypt.

Vatican: 1 rue de la Basilique; *Pro-Nuncio:* Mgr. SANTE PORTALUPI (also accred. to Morocco).

Venezuela: 38 rue Jean Jaures, El-Mouradia; *Ambassador:* ALFREDO MONCH-SIEGERT (also accred. to Senegal).

Viet-Nam: 30 rue de Chenoua, Hydra; *Ambassador:* TRAN VAN HUNG.

Yemen Arab Republic: 74 rue Bouraba; *Ambassador:* HAMOD MOHAMED BAYDER (also accred. to Tunisia).

Yemen, People's Democratic Republic: 105 ave. Mustapha Ali Khodja, El Biar; *Ambassador:* SAEED HADI AWAD.

Yugoslavia: 7 rue d'Anjou, Hydra; *Ambassador:* NEDJELJKO ZORIC.

Zaire: 12 rue A, Les Crêtes, Hydra; *Ambassador:* IKOLO BOLELAMA W'OKONDOLA.

Zambia: Cairo, Egypt.

Algeria also has diplomatic relations with Bolivia, Burma, Costa Rica, Cyprus, Ecuador, Ethiopia, Guyana, Jamaica, Laos, Liberia, Luxembourg, Malaysia, Seychelles, Sierra Leone, Thailand, Togo and Uruguay.

JUDICIAL SYSTEM

Ministère de la Justice: 6 rue Delcasse, El-Biar, Algiers.

The highest court of justice is the Supreme Court in Algiers. Justice is exercised through 132 courts grouped on a regional basis. Three special Criminal Courts have been set up in Oran, Constantine and Algiers to deal with economic crimes against the state. From these there is no appeal. In April 1975 the Government decided to establish a *Cour de sûreté de l'état*, composed of magistrates and high-ranking army officers, to try all cases involving state security.

President of Supreme Court: M. GATY.

Procurator-General: M. MOSTEFAÏ.

RELIGION

Ministère des Affaires Religieuses: 4 rue de Timgad, Hydra, Algiers.

Islam is the official religion and the whole Algerian population, with a few rare exceptions, is Muslim.

President of the Superior Islamic Council: AHMED HAMANI; place Cheik Abdelhamid ibn Badis, Algiers.

The Europeans, and a few Arabs, are Christians, mostly Roman Catholics.

Archbishop of Algiers: H.E. Cardinal LÉON-ETIENNE DUVAL; 13 rue Khelifa Boukhalfa, Algiers.

Protestant Church of Algeria: Pastor Dr. HUGH G. JOHNSON; 31 rue Reda Houdou, Algeris.

THE PRESS

DAILIES

al Chaab (*The People*): 1 place Maurice Audin, Algiers; f. 1962; national information journal in Arabic.

al Joumhouria (*The Republic*): 6 rue Bencenoussi Hamida, Oran; f. 1963; Arabic language; Editor ADJINA AÏSSA; circ. 30,000.

el Moudjahid: 20 rue de la Liberté, Algiers; f. 1965; FLN journal in French; circ. 130,000.

an Nasr: 100 rue Larbi Ben M'Hidi, Constantine; f. 1963; Arabic language; Dir. ABDELALI FERRAH; Editor-in-Chief KIMOUCHE M. BERTAL; circ. 30,000.

WEEKLIES

Algérie Actualité: 20 rue de la Liberté, Algiers; f. 1965; French language weekly; Dir. R. C. YOUCEF FERHI.

el Hadef: 100 rue Larbi ben M'Hidi, Constantine; f. 1972; sports; in French; Dir. ABDELALI FERRAH; Editor-in-Chief MANCERI MUSTAPHA; circ. 80,000.

Révolution Africaine: 7 rue du Stade, Hydra, Algiers; FLN journal in French; Socialist.

Révolution et Travail: 48 rue Khelifa Boukhalfa, Algiers; journal of U.G.T.A. in Arabic and French editions; Dir. RACHID AIT ALI.

PERIODICALS

al Acala: Algiers; f. 1970; published by the Ministry of Education.

Algérie Médicale: 3 blvd. Zirout Youcef, Algiers; f. 1964; publ. of *Union médicale algérienne*; twice a year; circ. 3,000.

Alger Réalités: rue Acela Hocine, Algiers; f. 1972; organ of the Popular Assembly of the Wilaya of Algiers; monthly; French.

Alouan: 119 rue Didouche Mourad, Algiers; f. 1973; cultural review published by the Ministry of Information and Culture; monthly; Arabic.

Bibliographie de l'Algérie: Bibliothèque Nationale, 1 ave. Docteur Fanon, Algiers; f. 1964; lists books, theses, pamphlets and periodicals published in Algeria; twice a year; Arabic and French.

Bulletin Economique: 7 blvd. Ché Guévara, Algiers; summary of items issued by state news agency; monthly.

al Chaab al Thakafi: Algiers; f. 1972; cultural monthly; Arabic.

el Chabab: 2 rue Khelifa Boukhalfa; journal of the JFLN; bi-monthly; French and Arabic.

el Djazairia: Villa Joly, ave. Franklin Roosevelt, Algiers; f. 1970; organ of the UNFA; monthly; French and Arabic.

el Djeich: Office de l'Armée Nationale Populaire, 3 chemin de Gascogne, Algiers; f. 1963; monthly; Algerian army review; Arabic and French.

Journal Officiel de la République Algérienne Démocratique et Populaire: 7, 9 and 13 ave. A. Benbarek; f. 1962; French and Arabic.

al Kitab: 3 blvd. Zirout Youcef, Algiers; f. 1972; bulletin of SNED; every two months; French and Arabic.

Libyca: 3 blvd. Zirout Youcef, Algiers; f. 1953; anthropology and ethnography; irregular; French; Dir. MOULOUD MAMMERI.

Nouvelles Economiques: 6 blvd. Amilcar Cabral, Algiers; f. 1969; publ. of *Institut Algérien du Commerce Extérieur*; monthly; French.

Revue Algérienne du Travail: 28 rue Hassiba Benbouali, Algiers; f. 1964; Ministry of Labour publication; quarterly; French.

Revue d'Histoire et de Civilisation du Maghreb: 3 blvd. Zirout Youcef, Algiers; f. 1966; history and civilization; irregular; French and Arabic; circ. 4,000; Dir. M. KADDACHE.

at Thakafa: 119 rue Didouche Mourad, Algiers; f. 1971; published by the Ministry of Information and Culture; cultural review; circ. 10,000; Editor-in-Chief Dr. HANAFI BENAÏSSA.

PRESS AGENCIES

Algérie Presse Service (A.P.S.): 7 blvd. Ché Guévara, Algiers; f. 1961; Dir. MOHAMED BRAHIMI.

FOREIGN BUREAUX

Algiers

Agence France-Presse (AFP): 6 rue Abdelkrim El Khettabi; Chief Mlle V. DECOUDU.

Agencia EFE (*Spain*): 10 rue Tirman; Chief JUAN MARTOS QUESADA.

Agentstvo Pechati Novosti (APN) (*U.S.S.R.*): B.P. 24, Muradia; Chief Officer YURI S. BAGDASAROV.

Agenzia Nazionale Stampa Associata (ANSA) (*Italy*): Chief (vacant).

Allgemeiner Deutscher Nachrichtendienst (ADN) (*German Democratic Republic*): 38 rue Larbi Alik, Hydra-Alger; Chief PETER GLAUNSINGER.

Associated Press (AP) (*U.S.A.*): B.P. 769; Chief MICHAEL GOLDSMITH.

Bulgarian Telegraph Agency (BTA): Zaatcha 5, Muradia; Chief GORAN GOTEV.

Middle East News Agency (*Egypt*): 10 ave. Pasteur, B.P. 800.

Reuters: 40 rue Luciani, El Biar.

The following are also represented: Maghreb Arabe Presse (Morocco), Prensa Latina (Cuba), TASS.

PUBLISHING

All privately owned publishing firms have been replaced by a single national organization:

Société Nationale d'Edition et de Diffusion (SNED): 3 blvd. Zirout Youcef, Algiers; f. 1966; publishes books of all types, and is sole importer, exporter and distributor of all printed material, stationery, school and office supplies; also holds state monopoly for commercial advertising.

RADIO AND TELEVISION

Radiodiffusion Télévision Algérienne (R.T.A.): Imm. RTA, 21 blvd. des Martyrs. Algiers; Government controlled; Dir. ABDERRAHMANE LAGHOUATI.

RADIO

Arabic Network: stations at Aïn Beïda, Algiers, Batna, Bechar, Oran, Touggourt and Souk-Ahras.

French Network: stations at Algiers, Constantine, Oran and Tipaza.

Kabyle Network: stations at Algiers and Michelet.

There were 3,220,000 radio receivers in 1974.

Dir. M. A. BOUREGHEDA.

TELEVISION

The main stations are at Algiers, Batna, Bel Abbès, Constantine, Souk-Ahras and Tlemcen. The national network was completed during 1970. Television is taking a major part in the national education programme.

There were 440,000 television receivers in 1976.

Dir. MADANI HAOUES.

FINANCE

BANKING

(cap. = capital; dep. = deposits; m. = million; AD = Algerian dinars; Fr. = French francs; brs. = branches.)

CENTRAL BANK

Banque Centrale d'Algérie: 8 blvd. Zirout-Youcef, Algiers; f. 1963; cap. 40m. AD; central bank of issue; Gov. SEGHIR MOSTAFAÏ.

Nationalized Banks

From November 1967 only the following nationalized banks were authorized to conduct exchange transactions and to deal with banks abroad, and by May 1972 these three banks had absorbed all foreign and private banks. The Banque Extérieure and the Banque Nationale enjoy a monopoly in the financing of the agricultural sector and most of the new industries.

Banque Extérieure d'Algérie: 11 blvd. Colonel Amirouche, Algiers; f. 1967; cap. (1979) 500m. AD; chiefly concerned with foreign trade transactions and the financing of industrial development in Algeria; brs. in Algiers and 20 other principal cities in Algeria; Pres. and Gen. Man. Bouasria Belghoula.

Banque Nationale d'Algérie: blvd Ernesto Che Guevara, Algiers; f. 1966; cap. 600m. AD; dep. 9,966m. AD; 170 brs.; Pres. and Gen. Man. Habib Hakiki.

Crédit Populaire d'Algérie: 2 blvd. Colonel Amirouche, Algiers; f. 1966; cap. 320m. AD (Dec. 1977); regrouping of former credit banks; finances private and public industrial and commercial enterprise; foreign trade transactions; 68 brs.; Pres. Mohamed Nour-Eddine Kerras.

Development Banks

Banque Algérienne de Développement: Villa Jolly, ave. Franklin Roosevelt, Algiers; f. 1963; a public establishment with fiscal sovereignty, to contribute to Algerian economic development through long-term investment programmes.

Caisse Centrale de Coopération Economique (CCCE): 22 rue Larbi Alik, Hydra, Algiers; f. 1968; Dir. Jean Gambrelle.

Caisse Nationale d'Epargne et de Prévoyance: 40–42 rue Larbi Ben M'Hidi, Algiers; extends loans to housing sector.

INSURANCE

Insurance is a state monopoly.

Caisse Algérienne d'Assurance et de Réassurance: 48 rue Didouche Mourad, Algiers; f. 1963 as a public corporation; Admin.-Gen. A. Belbay.

Caisse Nationale de Mutualité Agricole: 24 blvd. Victor Hugo, Algiers; Dir. O. Larfaoui.

Société Algérienne d'Assurances: 5 blvd. de la République, Algiers; f. 1963; state sponsored company; Chair. and Man. Dir. Mohamed Bensalem.

TRADE AND INDUSTRY

EXPORT INSTITUTE

Institut National Algérien du Commerce Extérieur-COMEX: 6 blvd. Amilcar Cabral, Algiers; f. 1975; publs. *Annuaire des Exportateurs Algériens, Annuaire de l'Industrie Algérienne de l'Emballage.*

CHAMBERS OF COMMERCE

Chambre de Commerce et d'Industrie d'Annaba: Palais Consulaire, 4 rue du Cénra, Annaba; Pres. Amara Amar.

Chambre de Commerce de Béjaia: B.P. 105, Béjaia; f. 1892; 11 mems.; Pres. Bencheikh Abderrahmane; Sec.-Gen. Mahdi Younés.

Chambre de Commerce et d'Industrie de Constantine: 2 ave. Zebane, Constantine; Pres. Ben Matti Abdesselam.

Chambre de Commerce et d'Industrie d'Oran: 8 blvd. de la Soummam, Oran; f. 1844; 12 mems.; Pres. Taïeb Brahim Mokhtar; Sec.-Gen. Abdelhak Nor'Eddine; publs. *Rapport Economique Bimestriel, Statistiques Mensuelles des Produits Exportés, Rapport d'Activité Trimestriel.*

Chambre de Commerce et d'Industrie de Mostaganem: avenue Bénaïed Bendehiba, Mostaganem; f. 1901; 8 mems.; Pres. Mohamed Belhadj; Sec.-Gen. Harrag Benbernou.

Chambre Française de Commerce et d'Industrie en Algérie: 1 rue du Languedoc, Algiers; Pres. François Lerges; Dir. M. G. Faulx-Briole.

Jeune Chambre Economique d'Alger: rue de Nîmes, Algiers; Pres. M. Donneaud.

There are also Chambers of Commerce at Colomb-Béchar, Ghordaia and Tlemcen.

PRINCIPAL TRADE UNIONS

Union Générale des Travailleurs Algériens—UGTA: Maison du Peuple, place du 1er Mai, Algiers; f. 1956; 1,000,000 mems.; Sec.-Gen. Demaine Debih Abellah; publ. *Révolution et Travail* (weekly, French and Arabic).

Affiliates

Fédération du Bois, du Bâtiment, des Travaux Publics et des Activités Annexes (*Federation of Building Trades Workers*): Maison du Peuple, Algiers; f. 1964; 17,000 mems.; Gen. Sec. Belhadj Bukir.

Fédération Nationale des Cheminots (*National Federation of Railwaymen*): 3 rue Alexandre Dumas, Algiers; Sec.-Gen. Azzi Abdelmoudjid.

Fédération Nationale de la Santé (*Federation of Hospital Workers*): Maison du Peuple, Algiers; f. 1962; 15,000 mems.; Gen. Sec. Djeffal Abdelaziz.

Fédération Nationale des Travailleurs du Pétrole, du Gaz et Assimilés (*Federation of Oil and Gas Workers*): 21 blvd. Colonel Amirouche, Algiers; f. 1964; 45,000 mems.; Gen. Sec. Ali Lasfer.

Fédération Nationale des Travailleurs de la Terre—FNTT (*Federation of Farm Workers*): 4 rue Arago, Algiers; f. 1964; Gen. Sec. Benmeziane Daoud.

Fédération des Ports, Docks et Aéroports (*Federation of Dock and Airport Workers*): Maison du Peuple, Algiers; f. 1964; 2,500 mems.; Gen. Sec. Said Oukali.

Fédération des Postes et Télécommunications (*Federation of Postal and Telecommunications Workers*): Maison du Peuple, Algiers; f. 1964; 6,000 mems.; Gen. Sec. Yssaad Abdelkadar.

Fédération Sonelgaz (*National Federation of Utility Workers*): 47 rue Khélifa Boukhalfa, Algiers; f. 1963; 5,000 mems.; Gen. Sec. Chabane Labou.

Fédération des Travailleurs de l'Alimentation et du Commerce (*Federation of Food and Commerce Workers*): Maison du Peuple, Algiers; f. 1965; 14,000 mems.; Gen. Sec. Djebiene Mahmoud.

Fédération des Travailleurs de l'Education et de la Culture—FTEC (*Federation of Teachers*): Maison du Peuple, Algiers; f. 1962; 13,000 mems.; Gen. Sec. Bouamrane Chaikh.

Fédération des Travailleurs des Mines et Carrières (*Federation of Mine and Quarry Workers*): Maison du Peuple, Algiers; f. 1965; Sec.-Gen. Ouali Mahoud Kahar.

Fédération des Travailleurs Municipaux d'Algérie (*Federation of Municipal Employees*): Maison du Peuple, Algiers; 15,000 mems.; Gen. Sec. Ahmed Zitouni.

Union nationale des paysans algériens (UNPA): f. 1973; 700,000 mems.

DEVELOPMENT

Société Centrale pour l'Equipement du Territoire—S.C.E.T. International: 8 rue Sergent Addoun, Algiers; Dir. A. Gambrelle.

Société Nationale d'Etudes de Gestion, de Réalisations et d'Exploitations Industrielles (SNERI): 50 rue Khélifa Boukhalfa, Algiers; f. 1968; consultants for industrial projects.

NATIONALIZED INDUSTRIES

A large part of Algerian industry is nationalized. The following are some of the most important nationalized industries, each controlled by the appropriate Ministry.

SONATRACH (*Société nationale pour la recherche, la production, le transport, la transformation et la commercialisation des hydrocarbures*): 80 ave. Ahmed Ghermoul, Algiers; f. 1963; state-owned organization for exploration, exploitation, transport, refining and marketing of petroleum, natural gas and their products. In 1976 it accounted for 79.8 per cent of output and 78.5 per cent of exports, operating through a number of subsidiary companies formed in association with foreign oil companies; Pres. Dir.-Gen. Sid Ahmed Ghozali.

Société Nationale de Recherches et d'Exploitations Minières (SONAREM): 127 blvd. Salah Bouakouir, Algiers; mining and prospecting; Dir.-Gen. Mohamed Amirouche.

Société Nationale de la Sidérurgie (SNS): 5 rue Daguerre, Algiers; f. 1964; steel, cast iron, zinc and products.

Société Nationale de Constructions Mécaniques (SONACOME): 1 Route Nationale, Birkhadem, Algiers; f. 1967; sole manufacturer and importer of motor vehicles, agricultural equipment and allied products.

Société Nationale de Constructions Métalliques (SN METAL): 38 rue Didouche Mourad, Algiers; f. 1968; production of metal goods.

Société Nationale des Industries Textiles (SONITEX): 5 rue Abane Ramdane, Algiers; f. 1966; 16,000 employees; Dir. Gen. Benaly Cherif.

Société Nationale des Industries des Lièges et du Bois (SNLB): 1 rue Kaddour Rahim, Hussein Dey, Algiers; f. 1973; production of cork and wooden goods.

Société Nationale des Matériaux de Construction (SNMC): 17 rue Hamani, Algiers; f. 1968; building materials.

Société Nationale des Industries des Peaux et Cuirs (SONIPEC): 100 rue de Tripoli, Hussein Dey, Algiers; f. 1967; hides and skins.

Société Nationale de Semouleries, Meuneries, Fabriques de Pâtes Alimentaires et Couscous (SN SEMPAC): 6 blvd. Zirout Youcef, Algiers; f. 1965; semolina, pasta, flour and couscous.

Société Nationale des Tabacs et Alumettes (SNTA): 40 rue Hocine Nourredine, Algiers; monopoly of manufacture and trade in tobacco, cigarettes and matches.

Office Algérien des Pêches: Quai d'Aigues Mortes, Port d'Alger; f. 1969; trawling, storage, processing and distribution of fish.

Office National des Travaux Forestiers (ONTF): Immeuble des Forêts, Petit Atlas, Algiers; f. 1971; production of timber, care of forests.

STATE TRADING ORGANIZATIONS

Since 1972 all international trading has been carried out by state organizations, of which the following are the most important:

Office Algérien Interprofessionel des Céréales (OAIC): 5 rue Ferhat Bousaad, Algiers; f. 1962; monopoly of trade in wheat, rice, maize, barley and products derived from these cereals.

Office des Fruits et Légumes d'Algérie (OFLA): 12 ave. des 3 Frères Bouadou, Birmandreis, Algiers; f. 1969; division of the Ministry of Agriculture and Agrarian Reform; fruit and vegetable marketing.

Office National de Commercialisation (ONACO): 29 rue Larbi Ben M'hidi, Algiers; f. 1963; monopoly of bulk trade in basic foodstuffs except cereals; brs. in over 40 towns.

Office National de Commercialisation des Produits Viti-Vinicoles (ONCV): 112, Quai-Sud, Algiers; f. 1968; monopoly of importing and exporting products of the wine industry; Dir.-Gen. A. Kara Terki.

TRADE FAIR

Foire Internationale d'Alger: Office National des Foires et Expositions, B.P. 656, Alger-Gare, Algiers; annual; fortnight in September-October.

TRANSPORT

RAILWAYS

Société Nationale des Transports Ferroviaires (SNTF): 21–23 blvd. Mohamed V, Algiers; f. 1976 to replace Société Nationale des Chemins de Fer Algériens; 3,890 km. of track, of which 256 km. are electrified and 1,258 km. are narrow gauge; daily passenger services from Algiers to the principal provincial cities and a service to Tunis; Dir.-Gen. Saddek Benmehd Jouba.

ROADS

There are about 82,000 km. of roads and tracks, of which 18,500 km. are main roads and 19,000 km. are secondary roads. The total is made up of 55,000 km. in the north, including 24,000 km. of good roads, and 27,000 km. in the south, including 3,200 km. with asphalt surface. The French administration built a good road system, partly for military purposes, which since independence has been allowed to deteriorate in parts, and only a small percentage of roads are surfaced. New roads have been built linking the Sahara oil fields with the coast, and the trans-Saharan highway is a major project. Algeria is a member of the Trans-Sahara Road Committee, organizing the building of this road, now renamed the "Road of African Unity". The first 360-km. stretch, from Hassi Marroket to Aïn Salah, was opened in April 1973, and the next section, ending at Tamanrasset, was opened in June 1978.

Société Nationale des Transports Routiers (SNTR): 27 rue des 3 Frères Bouadou, Algiers; f. 1967; holds a monopoly of goods transport by road; Dir.-Gen. Haoussine el-Hadj.

Société Nationale pour le Transport des Voyageurs (SNTV): 19 rue Rabah Midat, Algiers; f. 1967; holds monopoly of long-distance passenger transport by road.

SHIPPING

Algiers is the main port, with 23–29 metres anchorage in the Bay of Algiers, and anchorage for the largest vessels in Agha Bay. The port has a total quayage of 8,380 metres. There are also important ports at Annaba, Arzew, Béjaia, Djidjelli, Ghazaouet, Mostaganem, Oran and Skikda. Petroleum and liquid gas are exported through Arzew, Béjaia and Skikda. Algerian crude petroleum is also exported through the Tunisian port of La Skhirra.

Compagnie Nationale Algérienne de Navigation (CNAN): 2 quai d'Ajaccio, Gare Maritime, Algiers; f. 1964; state-owned company which has the monopoly of conveyance, freight, chartering and transit facilities in all Algerian ports; operates fleet of freight and passenger ships; office in Marseilles and reps. in Paris, all French ports and the principal ports in many other countries.

Office National des Ports (ONP): 2 rue d'Angkor, B.P. 830, Algiers; f. 1971; responsible for management and growth of port facilities and sea pilotage; Dir.-Gen. M. Harrati.

Société Nationale de Manutention (SONAMA): 6 rue de Béziers, Algiers; monopoly of port handling.

CIVIL AVIATION

Algeria's main airport, Dar el Beïda at Algiers, is a class A airport of international standing. At Constantine, Annaba and Oran are smaller modern airports able to accommodate jet aircraft, and there are also 65 aerodromes of which 20 are public, and a further 135 air-strips connected with the oil industry.

Air Algérie: 1 place Maurice Audin, B.P. 858, Algiers; f. 1947; internal services and extensive services to Europe, North, Central and West Africa, the Middle East and Asia; fleet of 6 Boeing 727, 13 Boeing 737, 2 Convair 640, 4 Nord 262, 14 Grumman AG-CAT, 7 Beechcraft 80, 7 Beechcraft 70, 1 King Air; Pres. Mohamed Bouzada; Asst. Dir. Larbi Hamlaoui; Admin. Dir. Abdelmalek Boudjellal.

Foreign Lines

The following foreign airlines operate services to Algiers: Aeroflot (U.S.S.R.), Air France, Air Niger, Alitalia, Aviaco (Spain), Balkan (Bulgaria), British Caledonian, ČSA (Czechoslovakia), EgyptAir, Interflug (German Democratic Republic), Iraqi Airways, Libyan Arab Airlines, LOT (Poland), Lufthansa (Federal Republic of Germany), Sabena (Belgium), Saudia, Swissair, TAAG (Angola), TAROM (Romania).

TOURISM

Office National Algérien du Tourisme (ONAT): 25–27 rue Khélifa Boukhalfa, Algiers.

Société Nationale Algérienne de Tourisme et d'Hôtellerie (ALTOUR): 8 rue du Dr. Saadane, Algiers (general affairs); 5 blvd. Ben Boulaid, Algiers (commercial affairs).

THEATRE

Théâtre National Algérien: 10 rue Hady Oman, Algiers; performances in Arabic and French in Algiers and all main cities.

ATOMIC ENERGY

Centre des Sciences et de la Technologie Nucléaires (CSTN): B.P. 1017, Alger-Gare; f. 1958 as Institut d'Etudes Nucléaires d'Alger; research into nuclear physics, solid and electronic physics; two Van de Graaff accelerators, 3 MeV and 2 MeV; one Sames accelerator 600 KeV and one isotope separator of the Saclay type; Dir. A. Bennini.

DEFENCE

Commander-in-Chief of the Armed Forces and Minister of Defence: Col. Bendjedid Chadli.

Inspector-General of the Armed Forces: Col. Abdallah Belhouchet.

Defence Budget (1979): 2,317.8 million dinars.

Military Service: compulsory national service for both sexes since 1969.

Total Armed Forces (1978): 78,800; army 70,000; navy 3,800; air force 5,000.

Paramilitary Forces: 10,000.

EDUCATION

At present, education in Algeria continues broadly to follow the pattern laid down during the French administration, but reforms initiated in 1973 should transform the system by the mid-1980s. When completed, the reformed education system should provide nine years instruction in the national language (Arabic) for all Algerian children, and training in the varied skills required to satisfy the economic and technical needs of the country. Over a quarter of the 1979 administrative budget was allotted to education.

About 80 per cent of children of school age receive an education. In 1977/78 there were 2,894,084 pupils at primary schools, compared with about 800,000 in 1962. Facilities for middle and secondary education are still very limited, although they have greatly improved since independence, accommodating about 742,000 pupils in 1977/78 compared with 48,500 in 1962. In September 1977 the total number of primary, middle and secondary school pupils was about 3,636,000, 7.1 per cent more than the previous year. Whereas before independence most teachers were French, in 1975/76 over 95 per cent of primary teachers were Algerian, as were about 65 per cent of middle and secondary teachers. Most education at primary level is in Arabic, but at higher levels French is still widely used. The majority of foreign teachers in Algeria come from Egypt, Syria, Tunisia and other Arab countries.

In 1977/78 the number of students receiving higher education was 51,983. In addition to the main universities listed below, there are a number of other *centres universitaires* and technical colleges. Several thousand students go abroad to study. Adult illiteracy, which in 1966 averaged 81.2 per cent (males 70.1 per cent, females 92.1 per cent), is being combated by a large-scale campaign, in which instruction is sometimes given by young people who have only recently left school, and in which the broadcasting services are widely used.

UNIVERSITIES

Université d'Alger: Algiers; f. 1879; 1,530 teachers, 17,086 students.

Université d'Annaba: Annaba; f. 1975.

Université de Constantine: Constantine; f. 1969; 1,023 teachers, 8,340 students.

Université d'Oran: Oran; f. 1965; 557 teachers, 6,790 students.

Université des Sciences et de la Technologie d'Alger: Algiers; f. 1974; 480 teachers, 4,500 students.

Centre Universitaire de Tlemcen: Tlemcen; f. 1974; 11 teachers, 201 students.

Centre Universitaire de Tizi-Ouzou: Tizi-Ouzou; f. 1975.

Centre Universitaire de Sétif: Sétif; f. 1978; 40 teachers, 250 students.

Centre Universitaire de Batna: Batna.

Centre Universitaire de Tiaret: Tiaret.

BIBLIOGRAPHY

ALAZARD, J. and others. Initiation à l'Algérie (Paris, 1957).

ALLAIS, M. Les Accords d'Evian, le référendum et la résistance algérienne (Paris 1962).

AMIN, SAMIR. The Maghreb in the Modern World: Algeria, Tunisia, Morocco. (Penguin, Harmondsworth, 1970).

ARON, RAYMOND. La Tragédie Algérienne (Paris, 1957).

BALOUT, L. Algérie Préhistorique (Algiers, 1958).

BOURDIEU, PIERRE. The Algerians (Boston, 1962).
Sociologie de l'Algérie (Que Sais-je, Paris, 1958).

BRACE, R. and J. Ordeal in Algeria (New York, 1960).

CHALIAND, G. L'Algérie, est-elle Socialiste? (Maspéro, Paris, 1964).

DE GAULLE, CHARLES. Mémoires d'espoir: Le Renouveau 1958–1962 (Plon, Paris, 1970).

DE GRAMMONT, H. Histoire d'Alger sous la Domination Turque (Paris, 1887).

ENCYCLOPAEDIA OF ISLAM. Algeria (New Edition, Vol. I. London and Leiden, 1960).

FANON, FRANZ. Les Damnés de la Terre (Maspéro, Paris, 1961).

FAVROD, CH.-H. Le F.L.N. et l'Algérie (Paris, 1962).

FERAOUN, MOULOUD. Journal, 1955-1962 (Paris, 1963).

FIRST, RUTH. The Barrel of a Gun: Political Power in Africa and the Coup d'Etat (Allen Lane, The Penguin Press, London, 1970).

FISHER, G. Barbary Legend (Oxford, 1957).

FRANCOS, AVIA and SÉRÉRI, J.-P. Un Algérien nommé Boumedienne (Paris, 1976).

GILLESPIE, JOAN. Algeria (Benn, London, 1960).

GORDON, DAVID. North Africa's French Legacy, 1954-1963 (London, 1963).
The Passing of French Algeria (Oxford, 1966).

HENISSART, PAUL. Wolves in the City: The Death of French Algeria (Hart-Davis, London, 1971).

HORNE, ALISTAIR. A Savage War of Peace: Algeria 1954–1962 (Macmillan, London, 1977).

HUMBARACI, ARSLAN. Algeria—A Revolution that Failed (Pall Mall, London, 1966).

IBRAHIMI, A. TALEB. De la Décolonisation à la Révolution Culturelle (1962–72) (S.N.E.D., Algiers, 1973).

JEANSON, C. and F. L'Algérie hors la Loi (Paris, 1955).

JEANSON, F. La Révolution Algérienne; Problèmes et Perspectives (Milan, 1962).

JOESTEN, JOACHIM. The New Algeria (New York, 1964).

JULIEN, CHARLES-ANDRÉ. Histoire de l'Algérie contemporaine, conquête et colonisation, 1827-1871 (Presses Universitaires de France, Paris, 1964).

LACHERAF, MOSTEPHA. L'Algérie Nation et Société (Maspéro, Paris, 1965).

LAFFONT, PIERRE. L'Expiation: De l'Algérie de papa à l'Algérie de Ben Bella (Plon, Paris, 1968).

LAMBOTTE, R. Algérie, naissance d'une société nouvelle (Editions Sociales, Paris, 1976).

LEBJAOUI, MOHAMED. Vérités sur la Révolution Algérienne (Gallimard, Paris, 1970).

LECA, JEAN and VATIN, JEAN-CLAUDE. L'Algérie politique, institutions et régime (Fondation nationale des sciences politiques, Paris, 1974).

LESCHI, L. Algérie Antique (Algiers, 1952).

MALLARDE, ETIENNE. L'Algérie depuis (Paris, La Table Ronde, 1977).

MANDOUZE, ANDRE. La Révolution Algérienne par les Textes (Paris, 1961).

MANSELL, GERARD. Tragedy in Algeria (Oxford, 1961).

MARÇAIS, G. Algérie Médiévale (Algiers, 1957).

MARTENS, JEAN-CLAUDE. Le modèle algérien de développement (1962–1972) (S.N.E.D., Algiers, 1973).

MARTIN, CLAUDE. Histoire de l'Algérie Française 1830–1962 (Paris, 1962).

MOUILLESEAUX, LOUIZ. Histoire de l'Algérie (Paris, 1962).

M'RABET, FADELA. Les Algériennes (Maspéro, Paris, 1967).

NYSSEN, HUBERT. L'Algérie en 1970 (1970).

O'BALLANCE, EDGAR. The Algerian Insurrection 1954–62. (Archon, Hamden, Conn., and Faber, London, 1967).

OTTAWAY, DAVID and MARINA. Algeria. The Politics of a Socialist Revolution (Berkeley, University of California Press, 1970).

OUZEGANE, AMAR. Le Meilleur Combat (Julliard, Paris, 1962).

QUANDT, WILLIAM B. Revolution and Political Leadership: Algeria, 1954–1968 (M.I.T. Press, 1970).

REUDY, JOHN D. Land Policy in Colonial Algeria: The Origins of the Rural Public Domain (University of California Press, Berkeley, 1967.).

ROBSON, P. and LURY, D. The Economies of Africa (Allen & Unwin, London, 1969).

SA'DALLAH, A. Q. Studies on Modern Algerian Literature (Al Adab, Beirut, 1966).

SIVAN, EMMANUEL. Communisme et Nationalisme en Algérie (1920–1962) (Paris, 1976).

SMITH, TONY. The French Stake in Algeria 1945–1962 (Cornell University Press, 1978).

SOUSTELLE, J. Le Drame Algérien et la Décadence Française: Réponse à Raymond Aron (Paris, 1957).

SULZBERGER, C. L. The Test, de Gaulle and Algeria (London and New York, 1962).

THOMAS, BENJAMIN E. Trade Routes of Algeria and the Sahara (London, 1958).

VATIN, JEAN-CLAUDE. L'Algérie politique, histoire et société (Fondation nationale des sciences politiques, Paris, 1974).

Bahrain

GEOGRAPHY

The State of Bahrain consists of a group of islands situated midway down the Arabian Gulf about 18 miles from the east coast of Saudi Arabia.

The total area of the Bahrain group of islands is 258 square miles. Bahrain itself, the principal island, is 30 miles long and 10 miles wide. To the north-east of Bahrain, and linked to it by a causeway and motor road, lies Muharraq island, which is approximately 4 miles long. The archipelago comprising the State of Bahrain consists of thirty-three islands, including Nabih Salih, Jeddah, Hawar and Umm Suban. A causeway linking Bahrain to Saudi Arabia is scheduled for completion in 1981.

The total population of Bahrain at the census of April 1971 was 216,078. This increased to an estimated 277,582 in January 1978. The port of Manama, the capital and seat of government, had a population of 88,785 (including several hundred foreigners, mainly businessmen) in 1971. The town of Muharraq had a predominantly Arab population of 37,732. Both Sunni and Shi'ite Moslems are represented in the indigenous population, the Ruling Family belonging to the Sunnis. The indigenous population represents about 70 per cent of the total population (February 1976).

HISTORY

After several centuries of independence Bahrain passed firstly under the rule of the Portuguese (1521 to 1602) and then it occasionally came under Iranian rule (1602 to 1782). The Iranians were expelled in 1783 by the Utub tribe from Arabia whose paramount family, the Al-Khalifas, became the independent Sheikhs of Bahrain and have ruled Bahrain ever since, except for a short break before 1810. Iranian claims based on the Iranian occupation of the islands in the seventeenth and eighteenth centuries nevertheless continued to be made from time to time.

In the nineteenth century European powers began to interest themselves in the Gulf area, and Britain was principally concerned to prevent French, Russian and German penetration towards India, and to suppress the slave and arms trades. In 1861, in consequence of political claims put forward by Iran and Turkey, the Sheikh of Bahrain undertook to abstain from the prosecution of war, piracy and slavery by sea in return for British support against aggression. In 1880 and 1892 the Sheikh further undertook not to cede, mortgage or otherwise dispose of parts of his territories to anyone except the British Government, nor to enter into any relationship with a foreign government other than the British without British consent.

Bahrain was naturally affected by the general post-war ferment in the Arab world. A tentative step towards democratic institutions was taken in February 1956, when elections were held for members of an Education and Health Council, the first election in Bahrain being held in 1919 for the Municipal Council. Shortly afterwards there was a strike in the oil refinery, said to be partly a protest against the paternalistic attitude of the British adviser to the Sheikh. There were further disturbances at the time of the Suez crisis. Meanwhile, further symbols of Bahrain's growing independence were the establishment of Bahraini as opposed to British legal jurisdiction over a wide range of nationalities (1957), the issue of Bahrain's own stamps (1960), and the introduction of a separate currency (1965). A small-scale distribution of village lands was started in 1960, and among economic developments the construction of a new town, Isa Town built to Western standards of amenity, was prominent. Bahrain also pioneered free education and health services in the Gulf, and good electricity and water services are available. There was another major strike in 1965 lasting from March 19th to April 30th, the principal cause being a fear of redundancies in the oil companies. In May 1966 Britain announced that her principal base in Arabia would be transferred from Aden to Bahrain in 1968, and a more realistic rent was agreed with the Bahrain Government for the military establishment. However, in 1968 the British government announced that all forces "East of Suez"—including those in the Gulf—would be withdrawn by the end of 1971, a decision which was subsequently implemented. In October 1973, at the time of the Arab-Israeli war, the Bahrain Government gave one year's notice to quit to the U.S. Navy whose ships have docking facilities in Bahrain. The evacuation was not carried out, but negotiations continued and Bahrain finally took over the base in July 1977.

Extensive administrative and political reforms came into effect in January 1970. A twelve-member Council of State became the State's supreme executive authority, this being the first formal delegation of the sheikh's powers. Only four of the initial twelve "Directors" were members of the royal family, but all were Bahrainis, and the British advisers were officially reduced to civil servant status. Equal numbers of Sunni and Shi'ite Muslims were included (the royal family apart) to represent Bahrain's religious balance. In August 1971 the Council of State became the Cabinet of the State of Bahrain, authorized to direct the internal and external affairs of the State.

After 1968 Bahrain was officially committed to membership of the embryonic Federation of Arab Emirates, but with over half the Federation's population and high educational and social welfare standards built up over 40 years, Bahrain disagreed with the richer but more backward sheikhdoms further down the Gulf over the terms of the federal constitution (especially those relating to method of government), the allocation of common finances, etc. Bahrain's position was strengthened in May 1970 when Iran accepted the United Nations' report on Bahrain's future. The UN representatives visited the island in April and found that popular opinion overwhelmingly favoured a complete independence rather than union with Iran.

By mid-1971 Bahrain was ready for complete independence, and in August full independence was proclaimed, a new treaty of friendship signed with the U.K., and Sheikh Isa took the title of Amir. In September Bahrain became a member of the Arab League and the UN. In December 1972 elections were held for a Constituent Assembly which produced a new Constitution, enabling elections to a National Assembly to be held in December 1973. In June 1974 industrial unrest occurred, and the delay in allowing trade unions to be set up, although provided for in the constitution, was thought to be responsible, together with a large increase in the cost of living. In August 1975 the Prime Minister resigned because, it was said, the National Assembly was preventing the Government from carrying out its functions. The Amir invited the Prime Minister to form a new government and two days later the National Assembly was dissolved by Amir's decree. Further arrests of "leftists" took place in December 1975. There was evidence of continued unrest beneath the surface when in November 1976 Abdullah Madani, owner of the weekly journal *Al Mawaquf*, and also a member of the former National Assembly, was murdered. In March 1977 three alleged PFLOAG supporters were executed for the offence, and in April 1977 a terrorist was sentenced to 10 years' imprisonment for an attempted bomb attack in 1975. It is thought, however, that the majority of Bahrainis feel little concern about the lack of a National Assembly and it is generally accepted that the Government has been pursuing a policy in which the provision of homes for Bahrainis and a slow-down in the increase in the cost of living are the main aims.

Although Bahrain was hitherto regarded as a "moderate" Arab State, it joined the remainder of the Arab States in condemning the peace treaty signed between Egypt and Israel in March 1979. Bahrain subsequently broke off relations with Egypt on April 26th, 1979.

ECONOMY

Bahrain's prosperity has been built on its petroleum reserves. Petroleum in commercial quantity was found in 1932. The Bahrain Petroleum Company (BAPCO), which has been the main concessionaire, was formerly owned jointly by the Standard Oil Company of California and Texaco Inc. In November 1974 an agreement giving 60 per cent participation to the Bahrain Government was reached, and in March 1975 the Bahrain Government announced that it intended to take over full ownership of BAPCO. The take-over was accomplished in early 1978, but the Government has not taken over the BAPCO refinery.

In common with other Arab oil-producing countries, Bahrain cut back its oil production after the October 1973 war with Israel, but it is estimated that the known oil reserves can be exploited for only about another 14 years at 1977 levels. Crude oil production is declining at the rate of 4–6 per cent per year. Production in 1978 averaged 55,317 barrels per day, compared with 76,000 b/d in 1970. Production from Abu Saafa, an offshore field between Bahrain and Saudi Arabia, began in 1968, and in 1976 output was 39.2 million barrels, split 50/50 between Bahrain and Saudi Arabia. The Abu Saafa field provides about 45 per cent of Bahrain's oil revenue.

Bahrain possesses the second largest refinery in the Middle East. During 1977 its average throughput was 261,000 b/d, of which over 75 per cent originated from Saudi Arabia. The Low Sulphur Fuel Oil Project, which was brought into commission in late 1973, has meant that the refinery can manufacture 50,000 barrels of oil daily with a sulphur content of 0.5 per cent.

Gas production rose in 1978 to an average of 359 million cubic feet per day from 332 million cu. ft/day in 1977. In April 1978 the Bahrain National Oil Company and the Japan Gas Company signed an agreement under which associated gas (previously flared) will be processed under a U.S. $27 million contract to make 80,000 tons of propane per annum and 75,000 tons of butane for export. The residue will be used as feedstock for power generation.

In view of the decline in oil reserves, major adjustments are being made to the economy. Bahrain is now concentrating on oil refining and gas processing, rather than crude oil production, and is expanding trade, finance and shipping activities, being to some extent helped by the decline of Beirut.

Foreign investors have found Bahrain attractive because of its freedom from taxation, its good cable, telex and air communications, and its large surplus of low-cost natural gas. Under a new commercial law which came into effect in January 1976, all companies registered in Bahrain are now required to have a majority of shares owned by Bahraini nationals. This does not apply to banks.

In October 1975 the Bahrain Government launched a plan which is making Bahrain a major commercial centre in its own right—comparable with the position Singapore holds in the Far East. By May 1977 some 40 international banks, many of whom already operate in Bahrain, had been given approval by the Bahrain Monetary Agency to set up "Offshore Banking Units" (OBUs) in Bahrain. An offshore banking unit is not permitted to provide local banking services but is allowed to accept deposits from governments and large financial organizations in the area and make medium-term loans for local and regional capital projects. By mid-1978 offshore banking assets were about $20,000 million and more than 30 OBUs were operating.

In December 1971 the new Bahrain International Airport terminal building was opened. The first terminal designed specifically for jumbo jets, this building can handle the passengers of two Boeing 747s simultaneously and has all the equipment required for the handling of the largest aircraft planned from now until the end of the century. Further expansion is planned and Gulf Air have in hand the building of a new headquarters in Manama.

The port of Mina Sulman, which is being extended under a World Bank project, has nine berths for general cargo for ocean vessels and one for cement-carrying vessels. A container terminal opened in April 1979. The port also has storage and refrigeration facilities for the transit trade, and a free zone in which many British, American and local concerns have their headquarters. The island is a major entrepôt market for the neighbouring Gulf states, and has also become the telecommunications centre of the Gulf.

A four-lane causeway and bridge joins the two main islands of Bahrain. A causeway is also planned which will link Bahrain with Saudi Arabia and which could provide much-needed employment during the construction period.

A dry dock project, backed by the Organization of Arab Petroleum Exporting Countries, and costing U.S. $340 million, was officially opened in 1977. Known as ASRY (Arab Shipbuilding and Repair Yards), the ship repair centre and dry dock take tankers of up to 500,000 deadweight tons. Management is provided by the Portuguese company Lisnave, under a 10-year contract signed in 1974. The yard is expected to operate at a loss during its first years. The Government expects ASRY to play an important role in manpower training.

Traditional occupations such as dhow building, fishing and pearling continue but on a much smaller scale than before. In recent years, several soft drink factories and brick-making plants have been established. The Bahrain Fishing Company, 35 per cent owned by the Ross Group (U.K.) and 65 per cent by Bahrainis, has now been operating successfully for several years, exporting frozen prawns to the U.S.A. and Japan. Companies are now established producing offshore oil wellhead structures, manufactured domestic and industrial plastic products and there are several assembly plants. The construction boom, which was so pronounced in 1975–77, began to ease off in 1978.

Bahrain's most ambitious project, the aluminium smelter, which is fuelled by natural gas, started production in 1970 and in 1977 produced 120,000 tons using alumina from Australia. Ancillary industries are now being established—a factory to produce aluminium powder (Bahrain Atomisers) is now in production and an aluminium extrusion plant (BALEXCO) began operating in 1977. There is, however, considerable doubt as to whether Bahrain can find enough markets for its aluminium. About 80,000 tons a year goes to Japan and 20,000 tons to the other Gulf States.

A Swiss survey of 1977 and a World Bank report of 1978 urge the development of medium and small-scale industries such as furniture manufacture and welding. Bahrain relies heavily on expatriate labour, and therefore training programmes for Bahrainis are being given priority in industrial planning.

Agriculture and cattle breeding are practised throughout the islands, the main crops being vegetables, lucerne, fodder crops and some dates. Here, experiments in modern methods are taking place to enable Bahrain to produce more of its own food.

STATISTICAL SURVEY

AREA AND POPULATION

Area	Population (census results): May 2nd, 1959†			February 13th, 1965			April 3rd, 1971		
	Males	Females	Total	Males	Females	Total	Males	Females	Total
669.4 sq. km.*	77,622	65,513	143,135	99,384	82,819	182,203	116,314	99,764	216,078

* 258.5 sq. miles.

† Excluding alien armed forces, merchant seamen and foreign diplomatic personnel, totalling 851 in 1965.

Estimated population: 277,582 (January 1978), about 75 per cent of whom are Bahrainis.

Principal towns (1971 census): Manama (capital) 88,785; Muharraq Town 37,732.

EMPLOYMENT (1971)

Agriculture and fishing	3,990
Mining and manufacturing	4,152
Oil	4,312
Public utilities	1,705
Construction	10,404
Wholesale and retail trade, and catering	7,706
Transport, storage and communications	7,743
Finance, insurance, property and business services	1,084
Community, social and personal services	13,182
Public administration and defence	5,206
Other	817
Total	60,301

CRUDE OIL PRODUCTION ('000 metric tons)

1974*	1975	1976	1977	1978
3,363	3,040	2,916	2,909	2,765

* *Source:* Bahrain Petroleum Company.

REFINERY PRODUCTION (Output in million barrels)

1973	1974	1975	1976	1977
86.3	87.9	76.4	77.8	93.0

Note: 1 metric ton equals approx. 7.3 barrels.

Industry: Building materials, clothing, soft drinks, plastic products, industrial gases, boat building, air conditioning manufacture, flour mills and an aluminium plant. Estimated production of primary aluminium (in '000 metric tons) was: 10.2 in 1971; 62.7 in 1972; 102.6 in 1973; 118.0 in 1974; 116.3 in 1975; 122.1 in 1976.

FINANCE

1,000 fils=1 Bahrain dinar (BD).

Coins: 1, 5, 10, 25, 50, 100, 250 and 500 fils.

Notes: 100, 250 and 500 fils; 1, 5, 10 and 20 dinars.

Exchange rates (June 1979): £1 sterling=798.25 fils; U.S. $1=385.85 fils.
100 Bahrain dinars=£125.27=$259.17.

Note: The Bahrain dinar was introduced in October 1965, replacing the Persian Gulf Indian rupee at the rate of 1 dinar=10 rupees=15 shillings sterling (£1=1.333 dinars). Until August 1971 the dinar was valued at U.S. $2.10 ($1=476.19 fils). Between December 1971 and February 1973 the dinar was worth U.S. $2.28 ($1=438.60 fils). In February 1973 the dinar's official parity was fixed at $2.5333 ($1=394.74 fils) but the market rate of exchange was 1 dinar=$2.5284 ($1=395.5 fils) from January 1975 to May 1976 and 1 dinar=$2.5275 ($1=395.6 fils) from May 1976 to January 1978. From January 1978 the dinar's direct link with the U.S. dollar was broken and the currency was tied to the IMF Special Drawing Right at a mid-point of 1 dinar=2.10 SDRs. In terms of sterling, the value of the Bahrain dinar between November 1967 and June 1972 was 17s. 6d. (87½ new pence), the exchange rate being £1=1.143 dinars.

BUDGET

(million Bahrain dinars)

Revenue	1976	1977	1978	1979
Oil revenue	131	150	170	280 (total of three items)
Government fees and services	34	45	69	
Grants, loans, bonds	16	40	41	
Total	181	235.5	280	280

Expenditure	1976	1977	1978	1979
Capital	100	138.5	145	130
Recurrent	90	111.0	135	150
Total	191	249.5	280	280

MONEY SUPPLY

(million Bahrain dinars at December 31st)

	1970	1971	1972	1973	1974	1975	1976	1977
Currency outside banks	18.9	21.2	23.8	14.9	16.9	23.5	33.2	41.6
Demand deposits	19.1	27.4	31.4	44.5	44.4	53.8	93.7	108.7
Total Money	38.0	48.6	55.2	59.4	61.3	77.3	126.9	150.3

EXTERNAL TRADE*

(million Bahrain dinars)

	1971	1972	1973	1974	1975	1976	1977	1978
Imports c.i.f.	148.0	165.6	212.6	473.3	458.1	659.9	802.8	791.8
Exports f.o.b.	151.6	141.7	162.4	459.0	453.7	532.5	730.1	733.1

* Figures include stores and bunkers for ships and aircraft but exclude trade in silver bullion and dust.

PRINCIPAL COMMODITIES

('000 Bahrain dinars)

IMPORTS (excl. petroleum)	1976	1977	1978
Food and live animals	39,099.9	42,823.8	51,189.1
Beverages and tobacco	8,566.7	10,185.0	10,942.1
Inedible raw materials (not fuels)	8,701.6	9,110.8	9,044.2
Mineral fuels, lubricants etc.	7,349.9	7,442.7	6,812.6
Animal and vegetable oils and fats	658.2	626.6	1,189.4
Chemicals	21,968.9	30,879.9	38,987.2
Basic manufactured goods	96,049.0	106,304.7	101,734.6
Machinery and transport equipment	155,567.0	161,031.7	171,326.8
Miscellaneous manufactured articles	49,569.9	76,259.9	61,864.4
Unclassified groups and transactions	113.4	187.6	270.2
TOTAL	387,644.5	444,852.7	453,360.6

Imports of crude petroleum (million dinars): 272.2 in 1976; 357.8 in 1977; 338.9 in 1978.

EXPORTS (excl. petroleum)	1976	1977	1978
Cereals and cereal preparations	1,424.3	883.8	1,284.9
Coffee, tea, cocoa and spices	3,380.1	3,599.0	3,164.8
Textile yarn, fabrics, etc.	13,000.4	8,655.2	19.1
Iron and steel	1,603.1	4,608.9	2,510.7
Non-ferrous metals	44,244.4	43,178.7	67,625.3
Machinery, other than electric	16,722.6	27,381.3	17,713.6
Electric machinery, etc.	6,627.6	11,296.6	4,622.5
Transport equipment	11,787.4	5,533.0	7,873.3
Clothing	10,694.9	13,363.4	4,858.4
Footwear	4,293.1	6,516.2	2,776.2
Scientific instruments, optical and photographic goods, watches and clocks	1,062.8	2,125.3	2,262.6
TOTAL (including others)	136,633.2	157,605.7	147,546.9

Exports of refined petroleum (million dinars): 395.7 in 1976; 572.5 in 1977; 585.5 in 1978.

PRINCIPAL TRADING PARTNERS

('000 Bahrain dinars)

IMPORTS (excl. petroleum)	1975	1976	1977	1978
Australia	12,338	20,336	22,988	25,592
China, People's Republic	14,441	15,204	24,590	8,141
France	7,267	9,460	11,313	10,827
Germany, Federal Republic	11,478	24,844	26,178	36,753
Hong Kong	3,814	7,277	10,230	9,045
India	5,755	13,349	13,836	14,785
Italy	11,499	8,808	14,610	17,589
Japan	27,350	53,736	68,943	65,256
Netherlands	7,423	10,589	9,968	9,357
Pakistan	2,013	5,093	3,037	3,357
United Kingdom	42,810	68,369	87,035	90,185
U.S.A.	36,321	57,395	53,268	53,166

[*continued on next page*

PRINCIPAL TRADING PARTNERS—*continued*]

EXPORTS (excl. petroleum)	1975	1976	1977	1978
Abu Dhabi	8,399	1,323	602	12,742
China, People's Republic	5,923	7,247	6,072	4
Dubai	2,893	4,816	4,998	4,774
Iran	4,249	5,157	14,020	13,672
Japan	17,761	25,684	23,513	51,775
Kuwait	1,566	3,163	5,256	8,126
Qatar	2,160	2,884	3,559	1,572
Saudi Arabia	25,636	68,219	80,511	31,930
United Kingdom	1,930	4,241	262	113

TRANSPORT

ROAD TRAFFIC
(motor vehicles registered)

TYPE OF LICENCE	1974	1975	1976	1977
Private Cars	18,689	22,389	27,509	34,284
Taxi Cabs	945	985	1,050	1,178
Vans and Lorries	6,343	8,382	11,109	11,618
Private Buses	666	802	1,007	1,305
Public Buses	207	249	259	283
Motor Cycles	2,742	2,996	3,522	3,925
TOTAL	29,592	35,803	44,456	52,593

EDUCATION

GOVERNMENT EDUCATION, 1976/77

	CLASSES	STUDENTS
Primary	1,085	42,590
Intermediate	239	9,153
Secondary (General)	220	7,265
Technical, Commercial	68	1,760
Higher (incl. Teacher Training Colleges)	15	329
Religious	8	104
TOTAL	1,635	61,201

Source: Statistical Bureau, Ministry of Finance and National Economy, Bahrain Government.

THE CONSTITUTION

A 108-article constitution was ratified in June 1973. It states that "all citizens shall be equal before the law" and guarantees freedom of speech, of the Press, of conscience and religious beliefs. Other provisions include the outlawing of the compulsory repatriation of political refugees. The constitution also states that the country's financial comptroller should be responsible to Parliament and not to the Government, and allows for national trade unions "for legally justified causes and on peaceful lines". Compulsory free primary education and free medical care are also laid down in the constitution. The constitution provides for a National Assembly, composed of the members of the Cabinet and 30 members elected by popular vote, although this was dissolved in August 1975.

THE GOVERNMENT

HEAD OF STATE

Amir: Sheikh Isa bin Sulman al-Khalifa, k.c.m.g. (succeeded to the throne on November 2nd, 1961; took the title of Amir on August 16th, 1971).

THE CABINET

(*June* 1979)

Prime Minister: Sheikh Khalifa bin Sulman al-Khalifa.

Minister of Defence: Sheikh Hamad bin Isa al-Khalifa (Heir Apparent).

Minister of Finance: Ibrahim Abdel Karim Mohamed.

Minister of Foreign Affairs: Sheikh Mohamed bin Mubarak bin Hamad al-Khalifa.

Minister of Education: Sheikh Abdul Aziz bin Mohamed al-Khalifa.

Minister of Health: Dr. Ali Mohamed Fakhro.

Minister of Interior: Sheikh Mohamed bin Khalifa al-Khalifa.

Minister of Information: Tariq Abdal-Rahman al-Muayyad.

Minister of Justice and Islamic Affairs: Sheikh Abdullah bin Khalid al-Khalifa.

Minister of Development and Industry: Yousef Ahmed al-Shirawi.

Minister of Labour and Social Affairs: Sheikh Isa bin Mohamed bin Abdulla al-Khalifa.

Minister of Transport: Ibrahim Mohamed Homeidan.

Minister of Housing: Sheikh Khalid bin Abdullah bin Khalid al-Khalifa.

Minister of Public Works, Electricity and Water: Majid Jawad al-Jishi.

Minister of National Economy, Commerce and Agriculture: Habib Ahmed Qassem.

Minister of State for Legal Affairs: Dr. Hussain al-Baharna.

Minister of State for Cabinet Affairs: Jawid Salim al-Urrayed.

NATIONAL ASSEMBLY

In accordance with the 1973 constitution elections to a National Assembly took place in December 1973. About 30,000 electors elected 30 members for a four-year term. Since political parties are not allowed, all 114 candidates stood as independents, but in practice the National Assembly was divided about equally between conservative, moderate and more radical members. In addition to the 30 elected members, the National Assembly contained the members of the cabinet. In August 1975 the Prime Minister resigned because, it was said, the National Assembly was preventing the government from carrying out its functions. The Amir invited the Prime Minister to form a new government and two days later the National Assembly was dissolved by Amiri decree.

DIPLOMATIC REPRESENTATION

EMBASSIES ACCREDITED TO BAHRAIN

(in Manama unless otherwise stated)

Afghanistan: Baghdad, Iraq (E).

Belgium: Kuwait City, Kuwait (E).

Canada: Kuwait City, Kuwait (E).

Denmark: Abu Dhabi, United Arab Emirates (E).

France: Mahooz 1785/7, P.O.B. 1034 (E); *Ambassador:* Maurice Fougerouse.

Germany, Federal Republic: Kuwait City, Kuwait (E).

Guinea: Jeddah, Saudi Arabia (E).

India: Sh. Isa Rd. 2299/7, Ad Adlia Area (E); *Ambassador:* Hari Krishan Mahajan.

Iran: Sh. Isa Rd. 1018/7 (E); *Ambassador:* Ismail Farboud.

Iraq: Almutanabi Road 911/8, Al-Mahouz (E); *Ambassador:* Abder-Razzaq Ibrahim Said.

Ireland: London, England (E).

Italy: Kuwait City, Kuwait (E).

Japan: Kuwait City, Kuwait (E).

Jordan: Sh. Isa Rd. (E); *Ambassador:* Moussa al Kilani.

Korea, Republic: Gufool 914/6, P.O.B. 5564 (E); *Ambassador:* In Du Kim.

Kuwait: Bani Atba Road 2105/7, Qudhaibiyya, nr. the new Palace (E); *Ambassador:* Ghazi Mohammed Amin al Rayyis.

Lebanon: Kuwait City, Kuwait (E).

Libya: P.O.B. 5240 (E); *Ambassador:* Ramadan al-Ru'obi.

Morocco: Kuwait City, Kuwait (E).

Netherlands: Kuwait City, Kuwait (E).

Norway: Teheran, Iran (E).

Pakistan: Sh. Isa Rd. (E); *Ambassador:* Hakim Muhammad Ahsan.

Saudi Arabia: Delmon, P.O.B. 1100 (E); *Ambassador:* Abder-Rahman al-Qadi.

Senegal: Teheran, Iran (E).

Somalia: Jeddah, Saudi Arabia (E).

Spain: Kuwait City, Kuwait (E).

Sudan: Kuwait City, Kuwait (E).

Switzerland: Jeddah, Saudi Arabia (E).

Tunisia: Kuwait City, Kuwait (E).

Turkey: Kuwait City, Kuwait (E).

United Kingdom: Government Rd. (E); *Ambassador:* Harold Walker.

U.S.A.: Sh. Isa Rd., P.O.B. 431 (E); *Ambassador:* Robert Pelletreau.

Yemen Arab Republic: Kuwait City, Kuwait (E).

Bahrain also has diplomatic relations with Australia, Chad, the Democratic People's Republic of Korea, Malaysia, Mexico, Mongolia, Niger, Oman, Portugal, Qatar, Syria, the U.S.S.R. and the United Arab Emirates.

JUDICIAL SYSTEM

Minister of Justice: Sheikh Abdullah bin Khalid al-Khalifa.

Since the termination of British legal jurisdiction in 1971, intensive work has been undertaken on the legislative requirements of Bahrain. The Criminal Law is at present contained in various Codes, Ordinances and Regulations.

Judges, both Bahraini and Arab, are all fully qualified, as are the lawyers that appear before the courts.

All nationalities are subject to the jurisdiction of the Bahrain Courts which guarantee equality before the Law irrespective of nationality or creed.

RELIGION

The great majority of the people are Muslims of the Sunni and Shi'ite sects. The ruling family is Sunni.

Religious affiliation (1971 Census):

Muslims	206,708
Christians	6,590
Others	2,780
TOTAL	216,078

THE PRESS

DAILIES

Akhbar Al Bahrain: Ministry of Information, Manama; daily news sheet.

Akhbar Al Khalij: P.O.B. 5300, Manama; Arabic.

Awali Daily News: Published by The Bahrain Petroleum Co. Ltd.; English; circ. 1,000.

Gulf Daily News: P.O.B. 5300, Manama; f. 1978; English; Editor W. STEWART OWENS.

WEEKLIES

al Adhwaa: Arab Printing and Publishing Establishment, P.O.B. 224, Old Palace Rd., Manama; f. 1965; Arabic; Editor MAHMOUD ALMARDI; circ. 5,000.

Awali Weekend: Published by The Bahrain Petroleum Co. Ltd.; English; circ. 1,000.

Al Bahrain Al-Yom (*Bahrain Today*): P.O.B. 253, Manama; Arabic; published by the Ministry of Information; Editor SALMAN TAK; circ. 4,000.

Gulf Mirror: P.O.B. 455, Manama; f. 1971; English; also circulates in Oman, Qatar, United Arab Emirates and eastern Saudi Arabia; Man. Editor ALAN BROWN; Business Man. RICHARD FAURE-FIELD; circ. 15,000.

al Jarida al Rasmiya (*Official Gazette*): Information Department, Government of Bahrain, Manama; f. 1957; Arabic.

al Mawaquf: P.O.B. 1083, Manama; f. 1973; Arabic; world news, politics, arts, religion.

al Najma al Asbuia (*Weekly Star*): Awali; Arabic; published by The Bahrain Petroleum Co. Ltd.; circ. 8,000; Editor KHALID MEHMAS.

The New Society: P.O.B. 590, Manama.

Sada Al Usbou: P.O.B. 549, Bahrain; f. 1969; Arabic; Owner and Editor-in-Chief ALI SAYYAR; circ. 6,000 (in various Gulf States).

OTHER PERIODICALS

Bahrain Trade Directory: P.O.B. 524, Manama; annually; Publisher and Man. Dir. A. E. ASHIR.

al Hiya al Tijariya (*Commerce Review*): P.O.B. 248, Manama; monthly; Arabic; published by Bahrain Chamber of Commerce and Industry.

Al-Mujtama Al-Jadid: P.O.B. 590; Editor MUSTAFA.

al Murshid: Arabian Printing and Publishing House, P.O.B. 553, Bahrain; monthly guide, including "What's on in Bahrain"; English and Arabic; Editor M. SOLIMAN.

This is Bahrain: P.O.B. 726, Manama; English; quarterly; information; published by Gulf Public Relations; advertising rep. Falcon Publishing, P.O.B. 5028; Editor CHRIS TAYLOR.

NEWS AGENCY

Reuters (*U.K.*): P.O.B. 1930, Manama.

RADIO AND TELEVISION

Bahrain Broadcasting Station: P.O.B. 253, Manama; f. 1955; state-owned and operated enterprise; two 10kW. transmitters; programmes are in Arabic only, and include news, plays and talks; Dir. of Broadcasting IBRAHIM KANOO.

Radio Bahrain: Manama; commercial radio station in English language.

Bahrain Television: P.O.B. 1075, Manama; commenced colour TV broadcasting in 1973. The station takes advertising; covers Bahrain, eastern Saudi Arabia, Qatar and United Arab Emirates; Gen. Man. E. J. W. PAYNE.

English language programmes broadcast by the U.S. Air Force in Dhahran and by ARAMCO can be received in Bahrain, as can the television service provided by the latter.

In 1976 there were approximately 85,000 radio receiving sets and 30,000 TV receiving sets.

FINANCE

BANKING

(cap. = capital; p.u. = paid up; dep. = deposits; m. = millions; br. = branch; B.D. = Bahrain Dinars)

CENTRAL BANK

Bahrain Monetary Agency: P.O.B. 27, Manama; f. 1973 and became fully operative January 1975; controls issue of currency, organization and control of banking system and bank credit; Dir.-Gen. ABDULLAH SAIF; Adviser A. E. MOORE.

LOCALLY INCORPORATED COMMERCIAL BANKS

Al-Ahli Commercial Bank, B.S.C.: P.O.B. 5491, Manama; f. 1978; private bank; cap. p.u. B.D. 4 million.

National Bank of Bahrain: P.O.B. 106, Manama; f. 1957; commercial bank with Government of Bahrain as major shareholder; total assets (Dec. 1977) 226m. B.D.; Chair. AHMED ALI KANOO; Gen. Man. JOHN HOUSE.

Bank of Bahrain and Kuwait: P.O.B. 597, Manama; cap. p.u. 5m. B.D. subscribed by Bahraini citizens and nine financial institutions in Kuwait; Gen. Man. RICHARD E. UNGER.

Continental Bank Ltd.: P.O.B. 5237, Manama; joint venture between Continental Illinois National Bank, Chicago, and Bahraini interests; Chair. and Man. Dir. DAVID GILLESPIE.

Gulf International Bank B.S.C.: P.O.B. 1017, Manama; cap. p.u. of B.D. 28 million held by Governments of Saudi Arabia, Kuwait, U.A.E., Qatar, Oman, Bahrain and Iraq; Gen. Man. Dr. KHALED M. AL-FAYEZ.

FOREIGN COMMERCIAL BANKS

Algemene Bank Nederland: Amsterdam; P.O.B. 350, Manama; Man. Jhr M. C. VAN DE POLL.

Arab Bank Ltd.: Amman, Jordan; P.O.B. 395, Manama; Man. WA'EL A. ATO'UT.

Bank Melli Iran: Teheran; Government Rd., P.O.B. 785, Manama; 1 br.; Man. M. JAFAIRIAN.

Bank Saderat Iran: Teheran; P.O.B. 825, Manama; Man. M. AHMED.

Banque du Caïre: P.O.B. 815, Manama; Man. A. FARID.

Banque de Paris et des Pays-Bas, FCB: Paris; P.O.B. 5241, Manama; Man. H. BAUDET.

British Bank of the Middle East: London; P.O.B. 57, Manama; Man. E. C. O'Brien.

The Chartered Bank: London; P.O.B. 29, Manama; Chief Man. Gulf Branches A. Wren; Bahrain Man. P. Pickering.

Chase Manhattan Bank: New York; P.O.B. 368, Manama; Man. J. McCarthy.

Citibank N.A.: New York; P.O.B. 548, Manama; 1 br.; Vice-Pres. Blaine W. Nichols.

Grindlays Bank Ltd.: London; P.O.B. 793, Manama; Regional Dir. (Middle East) A. Anderson.

Habib Bank Ltd.: Karachi; Government Rd., P.O.B. 566, Manama; Chief Man. Mazhar Abdullah.

National Bank of Abu Dhabi: Abu Dhabi; P.O.B. 5274, Manama; Man. J. Sami.

Rafidain Bank: Baghdad; f. 1969; P.O.B. 607, Manama; Man. M. Abu Alshaeer.

United Bank Ltd.: Karachi; Government Road; P.O.B. 546, Manama; Man. M. Ajmal Sheikh.

OFFSHORE BANKING UNITS

Bahrain has been encouraging the establishment of Offshore Banking Units (OBUs) since October 1975. An OBU is not allowed to provide local banking services but is allowed to accept deposits from governments and large financial organizations in the area and make medium-term loans for local and regional capital projects.

Operational OBUs

Al Saudi Bank: P.O.B. 5820.
Algemene Bank Nederland: P.O.B. 350.
American Express International: P.O.B. 93.
Arab African International Bank.
Arab Bank: P.O.B. 813.
Arab International Bank.
Arab Latin American Bank.
Arab Malaysian Development Bank: P.O.B. 5619.
BAII-Hill Samuel.
Banco de Vizcaya: P.O.B. 5307.
Banco do Brasil: P.O.B. 5489.
Bank of America: P.O.B. 5280.
Bank of Bahrain and Kuwait: P.O.B. 597.
Bank of Nova Scotia: P.O.B. 5260.
Bank Saderat Iran: P.O.B. 825.
Bankers' Trust Co. of New York: P.O.B. 5905.
Banque Arabe et Internationale d'Investissement: P.O.B. 5333.
Banque de l'Indochine et de Suez: P.O.B. 5410.
Banque de Paris et des Pays-Bas: P.O.B. 5993.
Banque Nationale de Paris: P.O.B. 5253.
Barclays Bank International: Manama Centre.
British Bank of the Middle East.
Canadian Imperial Bank of Commerce: P.O.B. 5484.
Chartered Bank: P.O.B. 29.
Chase Manhattan Bank: P.O.B. 368.
Chemical Bank: P.O.B. 5492.
Citibank: P.O.B. 548.
European Arab Bank: P.O.B. 5888.
FRAB Holdings Ltd.: P.O.B. 5290.
Grindlays Bank: P.O.B. 5793.
Gulf International Bank B.S.C.: P.O.B. 1017.
Hong Kong & Shanghai Banking Corporation: P.O.B. 5497.
Korea Exchange Bank: P.O.B. 5767.
Kredietbank: P.O.B. 5456.
Lloyds Bank International: P.O.B. 5500.
Manufacturers Hanover Trust Co.: P.O.B. 5471.
Midland Bank Ltd.: P.O.B. 5675.
National Bank of Abu Dhabi: P.O.B. 5274.
National Bank of Pakistan.
National Westminster Bank: P.O.B. 820.
Scandinavian Bank: P.O.B. 5345.
Security Pacific National Bank: P.O.B. 5589.
Société Générale: P.O.B. 5275.
State Bank of India: P.O.B. 5466.
Swiss Bank Corporation: P.O.B. 5560.
Union de Banques Arabes et Françaises: P.O.B. 5595.
United Bank of Kuwait: P.O.B. 5494.

REPRESENTATIVE OFFICES

Al Saudi Bank, Bank of Korea, Bank of New South Wales, Bank of Tokyo, Banque de l'Union Européenne, Barclays Bank, Bayerische Vereinsbank, Canadian Imperial Bank of Commerce, Citicorp International Bank, Commercial Bank of Australia, Commerzbank, Crédit Industriel et Commercial, Crédit Suisse, Dresdner Bank, First National Bank of Dallas, First National Bank of Houston, Handelsbank N.W. Zürich, Kleinwort Benson Ltd., Lazard Bros. and Co., National Bank of Australia, National Bank of Greece, Nippon Credit Bank, Royal Bank of Canada, Scandinavian Bank Ltd., Société Générale (Paris), Sumitomo Bank, Texas Commerce Bank, Thomas Cook Bankers, Union Bank of Switzerland.

INSURANCE

Al Ahlia Insurance Co.: P.O.B. 5282, Manama; f. 1976.

Bahrain Insurance Co.: P.O.B. 843, Manama; f. 1971; general accident, fire and life insurance; cap. B.D. 300,000; $66\frac{2}{3}$ per cent Bahrain owned; $33\frac{1}{3}$ per cent Iraq owned.

National Insurance Services: Bab al Bahrain Building, P.O.B. 830, Manama; f. 1977; all classes of insurance.

About fifteen foreign insurance companies are represented.

TRADE AND INDUSTRY

Bahrain Chamber of Commerce and Industry: P.O.B. 248, Manama; f. 1939; 1,200 mems.; Pres. Muhammad Yousuf Jalal; Dir. Yusuf Muhammad Saleh.

ArabConsult: P.O.B. 551, Manama; public relations consultants to the Government of Bahrain and numerous organizations and companies operating in Bahrain, Qatar, U.A.E., Saudi Arabia and Kuwait.

There are no trade unions in Bahrain, but a law to make them legal was before the National Assembly at the time of its suspension in August 1975.

STATE ENTERPRISES

Bahrain National Oil Company (BANOCO): P.O.B. 504, Manama; responsible for exploration for petroleum and other hydrocarbons and involved in their refining, transport, storage, marketing and export; holds and is responsible for the State's 100 per cent ownership of oil and gas producing facilities; responsible for distribution of oil products to all outlets; has developed a series of modern service stations; Chair. Yousef Ahmed al-Shirawi (Minister of Development and Industry); Gen. Man. Hassan Abdulla Fakhro.

Bahrain National Gas Company (BANAGAS): f. 1979.

The Bahrain Petroleum Company Ltd. (BAPCO): Awali; the sole oil producer in Bahrain; in early 1978 the Bahrain Government secured 100 per cent interest in BAPCO; the Government did not, however, take over the BAPCO refinery; Pres. W. O. Stolz.

TRANSPORT

ROADS

Most inhabited areas of Bahrain are linked by bitumen-surfaced roads. Public transport consists of taxis and privately owned bus services. A national bus company provides public services throughout the country. A modern network of dual highways is being developed and a causeway link to Saudi Arabia is planned for the early 1980s.

SHIPPING

Assistant Under-Secretary for Customs and Ports: Sheikh Daij bin Khalifa al-Khalifa.

Port Director: Eid Abdulla Yusuf.

Harbour Master: John Alan Duck.

Numerous shipping services link Bahrain and the Gulf with Britain, Europe, the United States, Pakistan, India, the Far East and Australia.

The deep water harbour of Mina Sulman was opened in April 1962; it has ten berths capable of taking vessels of draughts up to 10 metres. In the vicinity are two slipways able to take vessels of up to 1,016 tonnes and 73 metres in length, with services available for ship repairs afloat. A container terminal opened in April 1979. Further development for Mina Sulman is planned, for completion in 1979. A trawler basin is the centre of a flourishing shrimping industry, the packaged produce being exported primarily to Europe, North America and Japan.

A dry dock project, backed by OAPEC, was ready for use in October 1977. Known as Arab Shipbuilding and Repair Yards (ASRY), the yard can take tankers of up to 500,000 deadweight tons and was opened in December 1977.

CIVIL AVIATION

Bahrain Airport has a first-class runway, capable of taking the largest aircraft in use, and it was the destination of British Airways' first Concorde service. A new jumbo jet airport terminal was opened in December 1971 and expansion is still in progress.

Gulf Air: P.O.B. 138, Bahrain; f. 1950; jointly owned by the governments of Bahrain, Qatar, United Arab Emirates and Oman; services linking Bahrain, Doha, Abu Dhabi, Dubai, Sharjah, Salalah and Muscat with London, Amsterdam, Paris, Larnaca, Beirut, Cairo, Kuwait, Dharan, Shiraz, Bandar Abbas, Karachi, Bombay and Amman; fleet consists of six TriStar L-1011 (two on lease from TWA), six Boeing 737-200 (one on lease), two Boeing 737-200 on order for delivery 1978/79, four Fokker F.27, three Short Skyvan/Skyliners, two Britten Norman Islander, two Navajo (on lease from Fairflight).

Bahrain is served by the following foreign airlines: Air India, Alia (Jordan), British Airways, Cathay Pacific (Hong Kong), Cyprus Airways, Egyptair, Ethiopian Airlines, Iran Air, Iraqi Airways, KLM (Netherlands), Korean Airlines, Kuwait Airways, MEA (Lebanon), Pan American (U.S.A.), PIA (Pakistan), Qantas (Australia), Saudia, Singapore International Airlines, Thai International Airways, TWA (U.S.A.), UTA (France).

EDUCATION

Education is free in Bahrain. From the ages of six to twelve children attend primary school. The next intermediate stage lasts two years and the secondary stage three years. There are three higher educational establishments, a Men's Teacher Training College, a Women's Teacher Training College and the Gulf Technical College. Expenditure on education was budgeted at BD 11.4 million for 1976–77. There are plans to establish a Gulf University in Bahrain.

Gulf Technical College: Isa Town, Bahrain; f. 1969; 240 full-time and 480 part-time students.

BIBLIOGRAPHY

Adamiyat, Fereydoun. Bahrain Islands: A Legal and Diplomatic Study of the British-Iranian Controversy (New York, Praeger, 1955).

Albaharna, H. M. The Legal Status of the Arabian Gulf States (Manchester University Press, 1968).

Busch, B. C. Britain and the Persian Gulf 1894–1914 (University of California Press, 1967).

Fact Sheets on Eastern Arabia (Information Center on Eastern Arabia, avenue de l'Exposition 458, Brussels, Belgium).

Faroughby, Abbas. The Bahrain Islands (New York, 1951).

Hakima, A. M. The Rise and Development of Bahrain and Kuwait (Beirut, 1965).

Hay, Sir Rupert. The Persian Gulf States (Middle East Institute, Washington, 1959).

Marlowe, John. The Persian Gulf in the 20th Century (Cresset Press, London, 1962).

Miles, S. B. The Countries and Tribes of the Persian Gulf (3rd edition, Cass, London, 1970).

Nakhleh, Emile A. Bahrain: Political Development in a Modernizing Society (Lexington Books, Mass., 1976).

Rumaihi, Mohammed al-, Bahrain: Social and Political Change since the First World War (Bowker, in association with the Centre for Middle Eastern and Islamic Studies, Durham Univ., 1977).

Wilson, Sir A. T. The Persian Gulf (Oxford University Press, 1928).

Cyprus

PHYSICAL AND SOCIAL GEOGRAPHY

W. B. Fisher

The island of Cyprus, some 3,572 sq. miles in area, is situated in the north-eastern corner of the Mediterranean Sea, closest to Turkey (which is easily visible from its northern coast), but also under 100 miles from the Syrian coast. Its greatest length, including the long, narrow peninsula of Cape Andreas, is 140 miles. The population at the census of April 1st, 1973, was 631,778. By mid-1974 the total had risen to 639,000, including 496,200 Greeks and 117,300 Turks, but considerable changes have taken place since the political upheavals of 1974 (*see* History). In 1976 another census was held, in Greek Cypriot areas only, and the mid-1978 population (based on this partial enumeration) is estimated at 616,000.

PHYSICAL FEATURES

Cyprus owes its peculiar shape to the occurrence of two ridges that were once part of two much greater arcs running from the mainland of Asia westwards towards Crete. The greater part of these arcs has disappeared, but remnants are found in Cyprus and on the eastern mainland, where they form the Amanus Range of Turkey. In Cyprus the arcs are visible as two mountain systems—the Kyrenia Range of the north, and the much larger and imposing Troödos Massif in the centre. Between the two mountain systems lies a flat lowland, open to the sea in the east and west and spoken of as the Mesaoria. Here also lies the chief town, Nicosia.

The mountain ranges are actually very different in structure and appearance. The Kyrenia Range is a single narrow fold of limestone, with occasional deposits of marble, and its maximum height is 3,000 ft. As it is mainly porous rock, rainfall soon seeps below ground; and so its appearance is rather arid, but very picturesque, with white crags and isolated pinnacles. The soil cover is thin. The Troödos, on the other hand, has been affected by folding in two separate directions, so that the whole area has been fragmented, and large quantities of molten igneous rock have forced their way to the surface from the interior of the earth, giving rise to a great dome that reaches 6,000 ft. above sea-level. As it is impervious to water, there are some surface streams, rounder outlines, a thicker soil, especially on the lower slopes, and a covering of pine forest.

CLIMATE

The climate in Cyprus is strongly "Mediterranean" in character, with the usual hot dry summers and warm, wet winters. As an island with high mountains, Cyprus receives a fair amount of moisture, and up to 40 in. of rain falls in the mountains, with the minimum of 12 to 15 inches in the Mesaoria. Frost does not occur on the coast, but may be sharp in the higher districts, and snow can fall fairly heavily in regions over 3,000 ft. in altitude. In summer, despite the nearness of the sea, temperatures are surprisingly high, and the Mesaoria in particular can experience over 100° F. A feature of minor importance is the tendency for small depressions to form over the island, giving slightly greater degree of changeability in weather than is experienced elsewhere in the Middle East.

Cyprus is noteworthy in that between 50 and 60 per cent of the total area is under cultivation—a figure higher than that for most Middle Eastern countries. This is partly to be explained by the relatively abundant rainfall; the expanses of impervious rock that retain water near the surface; and the presence of rich soils derived from volcanic rocks which occur round the Troödos Mountains. The potential of the tourist trade and the export markets in wine and early vegetables add to the incentives to development. In the southern (Greek) part of the island economic recovery after partition has been considerable: less so in the north.

HISTORY

EARLY HISTORY

Cyprus first became important in recorded history when the island fell under Egyptian control in the second millenium B.C. After a long period during which the Phoenicians and the people of Mycenae founded colonies there, Cyprus, in the eighth century B.C., became an Assyrian protectorate, at a time when the Greeks of the mainland were extending their settlements in the island. From the sixth century B.C. it was a province of the Persian empire and took part in the unsuccessful Ionian revolt against Persian rule in 502 B.C. Despite the Greek triumph over Xerxes in 480 B.C., subsequent efforts by the Greek city states of the mainland to free Cyprus from Persian control met with little success, largely because of dissension among the Greek cities of Cyprus itself. For more than two centuries after 295 B.C. the Ptolemies of Egypt ruled in Cyprus until it became part of the Roman Empire.

Under the enlightened rule of Augustus the island entered upon a long period of prosperity, for trade flourished while the Romans kept the seas clear of piracy. When Jerusalem fell to the Emperor Titus in A.D. 70, many Jews found refuge in Cyprus where they became numerous enough to undertake a serious revolt in A.D. 115. Christianity, apparently introduced into the island in the reign of Emperor Claudius (A.D. 41–54), grew steadily in the next three centuries, during which Cyprus, isolated from a continent frequently ravaged by barbarian inroads, continued to enjoy a relative degree of prosperity. From the time of Constantine the Great, Cyprus was a province governed by officials appointed from Antioch and formed part of the diocese of the East. In the reign of Theodosius I (379–395) the Greek Orthodox Church was firmly established there and in the fifth century proved strong enough to resist the attempts of the Patriarchs of Antioch to control the religious life of the island.

The Arab attack of 649 began a new period in the history of Cyprus which now became, for more than 300 years, the object of dispute between the Byzantines and the Muslims. Whenever the Byzantine fleet was weak, Cyprus remained a doubtful possession of the Empire. From the decisive Byzantine reconquest of 964–5 Cyprus enjoyed for more than two centuries a period of relative calm disturbed only by occasional revolts.

WESTERN RULE

Only with the Third Crusade did Cyprus begin a new chapter of its long story. In 1192 Richard Coeur-de-Lion, having conquered the island from the Greek usurper Comnenus, bestowed it on Guy de Lusignan, formerly King of Jerusalem. There now began almost four hundred years of Western rule, which saw the introduction of Western feudalism and of the Latin Church into a land which hitherto had been Greek in its institutions and Orthodox in its religious beliefs.

In the period from 1192 to 1267 (when the direct line of the Lusignan house became extinct) the new regime was gradually elaborated. The Lusignan monarchy was limited in character, for the royal power was effective only in the military sphere, all other important business of State being decided in a High Court which consisted of the nobles, the fief-holders, and the great officers of State. This Court applied to the island a highly developed code of feudal law derived from the Assizes of Jerusalem, the Cypriots being allowed to retain their own laws and customs in so far as these did not conflict with the feudal law. The period was also marked by the determined efforts of the Latin clergy, supported by the Papacy, to establish a complete control over the Orthodox Church, a policy carried out with much harshness which the Crown and the feudal nobility often sought to mitigate in order to keep the loyalty of the subject population. The dominance of the Latin Church was finally assured by the Bulla Cypria of Pope Alexander IV (1260).

During the second half of the thirteenth century the kingdom of Cyprus (now ruled by the house of Antioch-Lusignan) played an important role in the last struggle to maintain the Latin States in Syria against the Mamluk offensive. The influence of the monarchy was further strengthened in this period, and when in 1324 Hugues IV became king, the great age of feudal Cyprus had begun. Cyprus was now of great importance in the commerce which the Italian republics maintained with the East, and Famagusta became a flourishing port. The Papacy, however, always anxious to weaken the power of Mamluk Egypt, placed on the trade of the Italian republics with that State severe limitations and charged Cyprus and Rhodes with their enforcement. Thus began a conflict between the kings of Cyprus and the great republics of Venice and Genoa which did not endanger Cyprus so long as the Papacy could mobilize sentiment in the West to support the crusading State of the Lusignans. When, as the fourteenth century advanced, the Papacy lost its power to command such support in the West, Cyprus was left to face unaided the ambitions of Genoa and Venice, which she was powerless to withstand.

Before this decline began Cyprus enjoyed, in the mid-fourteenth century, a brief period of great brilliance under her crusading King Peter I (1359–69). In 1361 he occupied the port of Adalia on the south coast of Asia Minor, then held by the Turkish emirate of Tekke; and in the years 1362–65 toured Europe in an effort to win adequate support for a new crusade. His most memorable exploit came in 1356 when he captured Alexandria in Egypt, sacking it so completely that even as late as the sixteenth century it had not recovered its former splendour. With his assassination in 1369 the great period of the Lusignan house was ended.

The reign of King Janus I (1398–1432) was a long struggle to drive out the Genoese, who had seized Famagusta during the war with Cyprus in 1372–74, and to repel the attacks of Mamluk Egypt, which had become weary of the repeated sea-raids undertaken from the ports of Cyprus. After plundering Larnaca and Limassol in 1425 the Mamluks crushed the army of Cyprus in a battle at Khoirakoitia in 1426, King Janus himself being captured, and his capital Nicosia sacked. The King was released in 1427, when he had promised the payment of a large ransom and of an annual tribute. The last years of Lusignan power were marked by dissension in the ruling house and by the increasing domination of Venice which, with the consent of Caterina Cornaro, the Venetian widow of the last Lusignan king, annexed Cyprus in 1489.

TURKISH RULE

Venice held Cyprus until 1570 when the Ottoman Turks began a campaign of conquest which led to the fall of Nicosia in September 1570 and of Famagusta in August 1571. The Turks now restored to the Orthodox Greek Church its independence and ended the former feudal status of the peasantry. The Cypriots paid a tax for their freedom to follow their own religion and were allowed to cultivate their land as their own and to hand it to their descendants on payment of a proportion of the produce, which varied from one-fifth to one-tenth according to the locality. About thirty thousand Turkish soldiers were also given land in the island, thus forming a Turkish element in the population which was later reinforced by a certain amount of immigration from Asia Minor.

The seventeenth and eighteenth centuries were a melancholy period in the history of Cyprus. Repeated droughts and ravages of locusts preceded a famine in 1640 and an outbreak of plague in 1641. In 1660 the

Ottoman government, in order to limit the extortions of its officials and of the tax-farmers, recognized the Orthodox Archbishop and his three suffragans as guardians of the Christian peasantry, but this step did not prevent revolts in 1665 and 1690. A great famine in 1757–58 and a severe attack of plague in 1760 reduced the numbers of the peasantry very considerably, causing a widespread distress which culminated in the revolt of 1764–66. Cyprus from 1702 had been a fief of the Grand Vizier who normally sold the governorship to the highest bidder, usually for a period of one year. This practice created opportunities of financial oppression which were rarely allowed to pass unused. Perhaps the most striking development of the period was the continued rise in the power of the Orthodox bishops whose influence was so great in the late eighteenth century that the Turkish administration depended on their support for the collection of the revenues. The Turkish elements in Cyprus, who resented the dominance of the Orthodox bishops, accused them in 1821 of having a secret understanding with the Greeks of the Morea who had revolted against Turkish rule, and carried out a massacre of the Christians at Nicosia and elsewhere, which brought the supremacy of the bishops to an end.

In 1833 the Sultan granted Cyprus to Muhammad Ali, Pasha of Egypt, who was forced, however, to renounce possession of it in 1840 at the demand of the Great Powers. During the period of reforms initiated by Sultan Mahmud II (1808–39) and continued by his immediate successors, efforts were made to improve the administration of the island. The practice of farming out of the taxes was abolished (although later partially reintroduced) and the Governor now became a salaried official ruling through a divan half-Turkish and half-Christian in composition.

BRITISH RULE

In 1878 the United Kingdom made an agreement with the Sultan by which Cyprus was put under British control, to be used as a base from which to protect the Ottoman Empire against the ambitions of Russia, a defence then all the more important in that the opening of the Suez Canal (1869) had made the East Mediterranean an area of great strategic importance. Under the agreement of 1878 Cyprus remained legally a part of the Ottoman Empire, to which a tribute was paid consisting of the surplus revenues of the island, calculated at a sum rather less than £93,000 per annum.

From 1882 until 1931 the island had a Legislative Council partly nominated and partly elected. Various reforms were carried out in this first period of British rule: the introduction of an efficient judicial system and of an effective police force, and considerable improvements in agriculture, roads, education and other public services.

Cyprus was offered to Greece in 1915 provided Greece joined the Allies in the war, but the offer was refused and did not remain open. In 1925 the island became a Crown Colony, at a time when the discontent of the Greek Cypriots was beginning to assume more serious proportions.

In the period since 1931 the desire to achieve self-government within the Commonwealth grew stronger, but the *Enosis* movement remained a strong influence in the political life of the island. Cypriot troops performed valuable services in the war of 1939–45, for example in Libya under Lord Wavell and in the Greek campaign of 1941. Later Cyprus was used as a place of detention for illegal Jewish immigrants into Palestine, the last of such detention camps being closed in 1949.

CONSTITUTIONAL PROPOSALS

In July 1954 the United Kingdom made known its intention to prepare a restricted form of constitution for Cyprus, with a legislature containing official, nominated and elected members. The Greek Cypriots, insisting that their ultimate goal was *Enosis*, viewed the proposed constitution with disfavour, whereas the Turkish Cypriots declared their readiness to accept it. The Greek Government at Athens now brought the problem of Cyprus before the UN. Great Britain, however, urged that the question was one with which she alone was competent to deal. The result was that, in December 1954, the UN resolved to take no immediate action in the matter.

The more extreme advocates of *Enosis*, grouped together in the EOKA (National Organization of the Struggle for the Freedom of Cyprus) now began a campaign of terrorist activities against the British administration. A conference including representatives from the United Kingdom, Greece and the Turkish Republic met in London in August 1955. The British offer of substantial autonomy for Cyprus failed to win the approval of Greece, since it held out no clear prospect of self-determination for the island, and the conference therefore ended in frustration.

A new and more violent wave of terrorism swept Cyprus in November 1955. A state of emergency was declared on November 27th whereby the death penalty was imposed for the bearing of arms, life imprisonment for sabotage and lesser sentences for looting and the harbouring of terrorists. All public assemblies of a political nature were forbidden; the British troops in Cyprus (about 10,000 in all) assumed the status of active service in war time. The Governor now ruled the island through an executive council consisting of four officials from the administration, two Greek Cypriots and one Turkish Cypriot.

At the beginning of 1956 the Governor, Sir John Harding, discussed the situation with Archbishop Makarios, head of the Greek Orthodox Church in the island. Since the United Kingdom was now willing to accept the principle of ultimate independence for Cyprus, agreement seemed to be within reach. In March 1956, however, the discussions were broken off and Archbishop Makarios, implicated in the activities of the EOKA, was deported to the Seychelles Islands.

THE RADCLIFFE PROPOSALS

The United Kingdom, confronted w th a general strike in Cyprus, with a renewed and more intense campaign of terrorism and with the first ominous signs of strife between the Greek and Turkish communities in the island, now appointed Lord Radcliffe, in July 1956, as Commissioner for Constitutional Reform. His report, published in December of that year, proposed that defence, foreign affairs and internal security should be reserved to the Governor, other spheres of rule being under the control of a cabinet of Cypriot Ministers responsible to an elected legislature. Lord Radcliffe laid down careful safeguards for the Turks in Cyprus—no laws affecting the domestic affairs of the Turks would be valid without the consent of two-thirds of the Turkish members in the legislature.

Meanwhile, in June 1956, Greece appealed once more to the United Nations. The United Kingdom, asserting that the internal affairs of Cyprus fell solely within her own competence, complained to the UN in October about the aid forthcoming from Greece for the EOKA terrorists. There were, however, talks at Athens and Ankara in December 1956, but to no effective end, since Greece rejected the proposals of Lord Radcliffe for constitutional reform in Cyprus. The UN, in February 1957, adopted a resolution urging that a peaceful and democratic settlement be found for the Cyprus problem.

RELEASE OF MAKARIOS

In March 1957 Archbishop Makarios was released from detention in the Seychelles and, since he was not allowed to return to Cyprus, went in fact to Athens. The British authorities also relaxed some of the emergency laws—e.g. the press censorship and the mandatory death penalty for the bearing of arms. These measures facilitated the holding of further discussions, but the progress made by the end of the year was inconsiderable.

The tide of violence ran high in Cyprus during the first half of 1958. EOKA carried out an intensive campaign of sabotage, especially at Nicosia and Famagusta. At the same time strife between the Greek Cypriots and the Turkish Cypriots was becoming more frequent and severe, the outbreaks in June 1958 being particularly serious. There was increased tension, too, between the governments at Athens and at Ankara.

BRITAIN'S SEVEN-YEAR PLAN

It was in this situation that in June 1958 the United Kingdom made public a new scheme for Cyprus. The island was to remain under British control for seven years; full autonomy in communal affairs would be granted, under separate arrangements, to the Greek Cypriots and the Turkish Cypriots; internal administration was to be reserved for the Governor's Council which would include representatives of the Greek Cypriot and Turkish Cypriot communities and also of the Greek and Turkish governments at Athens and Ankara. This scheme came into force in October 1958.

THE ZURICH AND LONDON AGREEMENTS

Negotiations between Greece and the Turkish Republic soon carried the Cyprus problem towards an agreed solution. As the result of a conference held at Zürich, it was announced in February 1959, that the two states had devised a compromise settlement. A further conference at London led to a full and formal publication of the details.

Cyprus was to become an independent republic with a Greek Cypriot President and a Turkish Cypriot Vice-President. There would be a Council of Ministers (seven Greeks, three Turks) and a House of Representatives (70 per cent Greek, 30 per cent Turkish) elected by universal suffrage for a term of five years. Communal Chambers, one Greek, one Turkish, were to exercise control in matters of religion, culture and education. The Turkish inhabitants in five of the main towns would be allowed to establish separate municipalities for a period of four years.

Cyprus was not to be united with another state, nor was it to be subject to partition. The United Kingdom, Greece and the Turkish Republic guaranteed the independence, the territorial integrity and the constitution of Cyprus. Greece received the right to station a force of 950 men in the island and the Turkish Republic, a force of 650 men. The United Kingdom retained under her direct sovereignty two base areas in Cyprus—at Akrotiri and at Dhekelia.

In November 1959 agreement was attained in regard to the delimitation of the executive powers to be vested in the President and Vice-President of Cyprus. A further agreement defined the composition of the Supreme Constitutional Court. In December 1959 the state of emergency (in force since 1955) came to an end and Archbishop Makarios was elected to be the first President of Cyprus. After long negotiations concluded in July 1960, the United Kingdom and Cyprus reached agreement over the precise size and character of the two military bases to be assigned to British sovereignty.

INDEPENDENCE

Cyprus became formally an independent republic on August 16th, 1960, and, in September, a member of the United Nations. The Conference of Commonwealth Prime Ministers, meeting at London, resolved in March 1961 that Cyprus be admitted as a member of the Commonwealth.

A team of experts from the United Nations visited Cyprus in the autumn of 1960. Its official report was made public in April 1961. In August 1961 Archbishop Makarios submitted to the Cyprus House of Representatives the outline of a five year plan based on the UN report. The Archbishop laid particular emphasis on reform in land-tenure and agrarian methods, on the conservation of existing and the development of new water supplies and on the introduction of long-term loans to farmers.

CONSTITUTIONAL PROBLEMS

As Cyprus entered thus into its independence, serious problems began to arise over the interpretation and working of the constitution. There was divergence of opinion between Greek Cypriots and Turkish Cypriots over the formation of a national army, as laid down in the Zürich agreement of 1959 (2,000 men; 60 per cent Greek, 40 per cent Turkish) the main point of dispute being the degree of integration to be established between the two racial components. In October 1961 the Turkish Vice-President, Dr. Küçük, used his power of veto to ban full integration which President Makarios favoured at all levels of the armed forces.

Difficulties arose also over the implementation of the 70 per cent-30 per cent ratio of Greek Cypriot to Turkish Cypriot personnel in the public services. There was friction too in the House of Representatives, about financial affairs—e.g. customs duties and income tax laws.

The year 1962 saw the growth of a serious crisis over the system of separate Greek and Turkish municipalities in the five main towns of Cyprus—Nicosia, Famagusta, Limassol, Larnaca and Paphos. In December 1962 the Turkish Communal Chamber passed a law maintaining the Turkish municipalities in the five towns from January 1st, 1963, and also establishing a similar municipality in the predominantly Turkish town of Lefka. President Makarios now issued a decree stating that from January 1st, 1963, Government-appointed bodies would control municipal organizations throughout the island—a decree which the Turkish Cypriots denounced as an infringement of the constitution.

The Constitutional Court of Cyprus, sitting in judgement on the financial disputes, ruled in February 1963 that, in view of the veto exercised by the Turkish members of the House of Representatives since 1961, taxes could be imposed on the people of the island, but that no legal machinery existed for the collection of such taxes. In April the court declared that the Government had no power to control the municipalities through bodies of its own choosing and that the decision of the Turkish Communal Chamber to maintain the separate Turkish municipalities in defiance of the Cyprus Government was likewise invalid.

Negotiations between President Makarios and Vice-President Küçük to resolve the deadlock broke down in May. Accordingly in November Archbishop Makarios put forward proposals for a number of reforms—e.g. that the President and Vice-President of Cyprus should lose their right of veto over certain types of legislation; that separate Greek Cypriot and Turkish Cypriot majorities in the House of Representatives should not be required for financial legislation; and that single municipal councils, with both Greek and Turkish Cypriot members, should replace the separate municipalities in the five chief towns of Cyprus. These proposals proved to be unacceptable to the Turkish Cypriots.

CIVIL WAR

Meanwhile, underground organizations, prepared for violence, had come into being both among the Greek and the Turkish communities. In December 1963 serious conflict broke out. The United Kingdom suggested that a joint force composed of British, Greek and Turkish troops stationed in Cyprus should be established to restore order. The Governments at Nicosia, Athens and Ankara gave their assent to this scheme. At this same moment the forces of the Turkish Republic serving in the island occupied, north of Nicosia, a strong position which gave them control of the important road to Kyrenia on the northern coast of Cyprus—a road which was to become the scene of much conflict in the future. As a result of the December crisis co-operation between the Greek Cypriots and the Turkish Cypriots in government and in other sectors of public life came almost to an end.

The general situation was now becoming extremely tense. There was renewed violence in February 1964, especially at Limassol. Arms in considerable quantities were being brought secretly into the island for both sides and the number of armed "irregulars" was increasing rapidly. These developments also gave rise to friction between Athens and Ankara.

ESTABLISHMENT OF UN PEACE-KEEPING FORCE

Cyprus, in January 1964, had asked the UN to send a representative to the island. On January 16th U Thant, the Secretary-General of the United Nations, nominated Lieutenant-General Prem Gyani of India to act in this role. Later in the same month the Cyprus Government informed U Thant that it would be glad to see a UN force established in the island. The UN Security Council debated the Cyprus question in February finally adopting a resolution in March authorizing the creation of a United Nations peace-keeping force for Cyprus. U Thant appointed Lieutenant-General Gyani to command this force. Advance units of the Canadian contingent reached the island later in the month and by May the UN Headquarters at Nicosia controlled some 7,000 men.

In March U Thant announced the appointment of Mr. S. Tuomioja, the Finnish Ambassador to Sweden, as United Nations mediator in Cyprus. In May U Thant nominated Dr. Galo Plaza, of Ecuador, to be his special representative in the island. After the death of Mr. Tuomioja Dr. Galo Plaza was to become, in September 1964, the UN mediator in Cyprus, Senhor Carlos Bernardes, of Brazil, taking his place as U Thant's Special Representative. The exploratory consultations of the UN officials—at Nicosia, at Athens and at Ankara—failed to achieve real progress in the summer of 1964.

There was more fighting between Greek and Turkish Cypriots in March and April 1964. On June 1st the Cyprus House of Representatives passed a Bill establishing a National Guard and making all male Cypriots between the ages of 18 and 59 liable to six months of service in it. Only members of the National Guard, of the regular police and of the army forces would now have the right to bear arms. One purpose of the Bill was to suppress the irregular bands which, as extremist sentiment grew stronger, tended more and more to escape from the control of the established regime.

Under the agreements concluded for the independence of Cyprus in 1959–60 the Turkish Republic maintained a contingent of troops in the island, the personnel of this force being renewed from time to time on a system of regular rotation. A new crisis arose in August-September 1964 when the Government at Nicosia refused to allow such a rotation of personnel. After much negotiation through the UN officials in the island the Cyprus Government agreed to raise its existing blockade of the Turkish Cypriots entrenched in the Kokkina district and to allow the normal rotation of troops for the Turkish force stationed at Cyprus. The Government at Ankara now consented that this force should come under the United Nations command in Cyprus.

LEGISLATIVE MEASURES

Towards the end of 1964 the Cyprus House of Representatives passed a number of important measures—a Bill for the creation of unified municipalities in Nicosia, Larnaca, Limassol, Famagusta and Paphos; a law restoring to the Government the right to exact income tax (a right inoperative since 1961 as a result of the veto of the Turkish Cypriot members in the House); and a Bill extending compulsory service in the National Guard for Greek Cypriots from six to twelve months. In July 1965 a new law was approved for unified elections on the basis of a common electoral roll, the communal distinction between Greek Cypriots and Turkish Cypriots being thus abolished.

The UN mediator in Cyprus, Dr. Galo Plaza, resigned in December 1965. Little had been done towards mediation since Dr. Galo Plaza published a detailed report in March 1965. Moreover, no clear indication existed at this time as to where the funds would be found to continue the existence of the UN forces in the island. The United Nations was in fact to renew the mandate of these forces in June 1966 and again in December 1966. In addition the UN Secretary-General, U Thant, announced in January 1967 that he had chosen Señor Bibiano Osorio-Tafall, of Mexico, to be his personal representative in Cyprus, Senhor Carlos Bernardes, of Brazil, having resigned the appointment for personal reasons.

GENERAL GRIVAS

There was further tension in Cyprus during March 1966 over the position of General Grivas, the former head of EOKA. The General had returned to the island in June 1964 at a time when it was felt that he might be able, with his high personal prestige, to bring to order the small "private armies" and "irregular bands" which had emerged among the Greek Cypriots and which were violently defying the Cyprus Government.

In March 1966 President Makarios attempted to limit the functions of General Grivas in Cyprus and so to end a situation which saw political control vested in himself, while command of the armed forces, both the Greek Cypriot National Guard and also the "volunteer" Greek troops stationed in Cyprus, rested with the General, who took his orders from Athens. The President suggested that the National Guard should be transferred to the control of the Cyprus Minister of Defence—a proposal which found favour neither with General Grivas nor at Athens, where it provoked a sharp political crisis. The whole affair underlined the distrust separating President Makarios and General Grivas and the doubts existing at Athens as to the ultimate intentions of the President.

In November 1966 the United Kingdom announced her intention to reduce her military establishment in Cyprus. Some 2,000 servicemen would be withdrawn by the summer of 1967. At the same time there was to be a scaling down in the amount of stores held at the Dhekelia base. The Royal Air Force station at Nicosia had already been run down to care and maintenance status, leaving Akrotiri to function still as a large R.A.F. headquarters.

The shipment of small arms and machine-guns from Czechoslovakia for specialized units of the Cypriot police force during the winter of 1966–67 gave rise to another crisis. Turkey declared its concern for the safety of the Turkish community, and urged the United Nations Peace-Keeping Force (UNFICYP) to take control of the arms. The Greek government persuaded the Cypriot authorities to store the arms under the custody of the Greek troops in Cyprus.

The military *coup* in Greece in April 1967 was followed by a brief improvement in Greco-Turkish relations. The Prime Ministers and Foreign Ministers of Greece and Turkey met in Thrace in September 1967, but failed to come to an agreement on Cyprus, Greece rejecting any form of partition, which was implicit in the Turkish proposal to accept *Enosis* in return for military bases and ten per cent of the island's territory.

TURKISH CYPRIOT ADMINISTRATION

On December 29th, 1967 the Turkish Cypriot community announced the establishment of a "Transitional Administration" to administer their affairs until the provisions of the 1960 Constitution were implemented. Measures were approved to establish separate executive, legislative and judicial authorities, and Dr. Fazil Küçük, Vice-President of Cyprus, was appointed President of the Transitional Administration, with Rauf Denktaş as Vice-President. A legislative body was set up, consisting of the Turkish Cypriot members of the House of Representatives elected in 1960 and the members of the Turkish Communal Chamber. The Executive Council's nine members functioned as the administration. President Makarios described the Transitional Administration as "totally illegal", but it continued to function as the *de facto* government of the Turkish community in Cyprus.

INTER-COMMUNAL TALKS

Between January and April 1968 the Cypriot Government gradually relaxed the measures it had taken against the Turkish community. With the exception of the Turkish area in Nicosia, freedom of movement for Turkish Cypriots was restored, checkpoints were removed and unrestricted supplies to Turkish areas were allowed. In April Rauf Denktaş, the Vice-President of the Turkish Cypriot Administration, was permitted to return from exile, and in May he began talks with Glavcos Clerides, the President of the House of Representatives. These talks were intended to form the basis of a settlement of the constitutional differences between the Greek and Turkish communities, but very little progress was made. After years of intermittent discussion, there was still an impasse, the Turks demanding local autonomy, the Greeks rejecting any proposals tending towards a federal solution, fearing that it might lead to partition. In June 1972 Dr. Kurt Waldheim, the UN Secretary-General, attended the talks, stressing the need for a peaceful settlement and expressing a hope that UNFICYP might be withdrawn in the near future. By the end of 1973 the Greek Cypriot representative seemed to have accepted the principle of local autonomy, but the talks still dragged on, with no acceptable compromise having been found on the scope of local autonomy or the degree of control to be exercised by the central government over local authorities. A statement by Mr. Ecevit, Prime Minister of Turkey, calling for a federal settlement of the constitutional problem, caused the talks to break down in April 1974. The Greek and Cypriot governments claimed that the talks had been conducted on the understanding that any solution would be in terms of a unitary state, Mr. Denktaş that federation would not necessarily mean partition. Mr. Dentkaş also feared that the Greek Government was giving support to the *Enosis* movement. Each side accused the other of trying to sabotage the talks.

TERRORISM AND ELECTIONS

While the talks between the Greek and Turkish communities were drifting on, there was a marked reduction in intercommunal violence, but the Greek population of the island was split between supporters of Makarios and his aim of an independent unitary state and those who demanded union with Greece. In 1969 the National Front, an organization calling for immediate *Enosis*, embarked on a campaign of terrorism, raiding police stations to steal arms, bombing British military buildings and vehicles, shooting and wounding the chief of police and making several unsuccessful bomb attacks on Government ministers. Mr. Papadopoulos, the Greek Prime Minister, denounced terrorism in Cyprus and the National Front in particular.

On March 8th, 1970 there was an attempt to assassinate President Makarios, attributed to the National Front. The President escaped unhurt. A week later, Polycarpos Georghadjis, a former Minister of the Interior, was found shot dead. At the trial of the President's would-be assassins, Georghadjis was named as a member of the conspiracy.

Despite the activities of the National Front, the Government decided to hold a general election on July 5th, 1970. The dissolved House of Representatives had been in existence since 1960, and the elections which should have been held in 1965 according to the Constitution had been postponed from year to year due to the continuing crisis. The continued absence of the 15 Turkish members, who met as part of the Turkish Legislative Assembly, meant that the Greek Cypriot House of Representatives contained only 35 members. Fifteen of the Greek Cypriot seats were won by the Unified Party, led by Glavcos Clerides, with a policy of support for President Makarios and a united independent Cyprus. The Communist party AKEL won nine seats, to become the second largest in the House. None of the candidates of DEK, the Democratic National Party, which stands for *Enosis*, won a seat. The elections held at the same time by the Turkish Cypriots resulted in a victory for the National Solidarity Party, led by Rauf Denktaş.

RETURN OF GRIVAS AND EOKA-B

The ideal of *Enosis* was still very attractive to many Greek Cypriots, despite the lack of success for pro-*Enosis* candidates in the election. Greek Cypriot students condemned President Makarios' policy of an independent unitary state, and called for an end to the inter-communal talks. General Grivas attacked the President in an article in an Athens newspaper, calling for his resignation on the grounds that, by abandoning *Enosis*, the President had betrayed EOKA's struggle for freedom.

At the beginning of September 1971 General Grivas returned secretly to Cyprus and began to hold meetings with the leaders of the National Front and his followers in the EOKA movement of the 1950s. President Makarios threatened to arrest the General for setting up armed bands, and declared his opposition to the achievement of *Enosis* by violent means. His opponents, pro-*Enosis* Greek Cypriots, condemned the inter-communal talks and rejected the idea of a negotiated compromise with the Turkish community. The Cyprus Government imported a considerable quantity of arms from Czechoslovakia as a precautionary measure, but after protests from the Greek and Turkish Foreign Ministries that the distribution of these arms would serve only to aggravate an already tense situation, the consignment was placed under the custody of UNFICYP. In April 1972 President Makarios expressed his support for the Turkish Prime Minister's suggestion that each community should gradually disarm, but nothing came of this move.

The President had been under pressure from the Greek Government to dismiss ministers considered hostile to Athens for some time. In February 1972 it was suggested in Athens that a Cypriot government of national unity should be formed, including moderate representatives of General Grivas. For some months the President resisted this pressure, and it seemed that the Greek Government in alliance with dissident bishops and General Grivas, was intent on forcing his resignation. In May Spyros Kyprianou, the Foreign Minister who had been the main target of Greek hostility and one of the President's closest collaborators, resigned, and in June the President gave way and carried out an extensive reorganization of his cabinet.

General Grivas organized a new guerilla force, which became known as EOKA-B, and launched a series of attacks on the Makarios Government similar to those against British rule in the 1950s. While the Committee for the Co-ordination of the *Enosis*

Struggle, his political front organization, demanded a plebiscite on *Enosis* and rejected inter-communal agreement as a means of settling the future of Cyprus, EOKA-B raided police stations, quarries and warehouses, stealing arms, ammunition, dynamite and radio transmitters.

PRESIDENTIAL ELECTIONS

The demand for a plebiscite from supporters of General Grivas was put forward as an alternative to the election for the presidency, called by President Makarios as a test of strength. The President's speech of February 8th, 1973 explained his position. While believing in *Enosis*, he considered that talks with the Turkish community on the basis of an independent Cyprus were the only practical possibility. He condemned terrorism and violence as counter-productive, likely to lead to Turkish intervention and unsupported by the Greek and Cypriot authorities. The Greek Government also repudiated terrorism and expressed its support for a constitutional solution.

On February 8th, 1973 Makarios was returned unopposed for a third five year term as President, and in the Turkish quarter of Nicosia Rauf Denktaş was declared elected Vice-President following the withdrawal of Ahmet Berberoğlu.

EOKA-B continued its terrorist activities throughout 1973, concentrating on bombings and raids on police stations. In July the Minister of Justice, Christos Vakis, was kidnapped, and there were over 80 bomb explosions throughout Cyprus on the three following nights. The President refused to give in to violence or to blackmail, rejecting the terms put forward by Grivas for the release of Mr. Vakis. Numerous police and National Guard officers, suspected of being Grivas sympathizers, were dismissed, and Mr. Vakis was released in August. Action by security forces against secret EOKA bases resulted in many arrests, the seizure of quantities of munitions and the discovery of plans to assassinate the President. President Papadopoulos of Greece publicly condemned the activities of "the illegal organization of General Grivas", which undermined the Greek policy of "support for the finding of a solution to the Cyprus problem through the enlarged local talks aimed at ensuring an independent, sovereign and unitary state."

MAKARIOS AND THE BISHOPS

In March 1972 the three bishops of the Orthodox Church of Cyprus—Anthimos of Kitium, Yennadios of Paphos and Kyprianos of Kyrenia—called on Archbishop Makarios to divest himself of the temporal power of the Presidency, on the ground that his political role was incompatible with his ecclesiastical position under the rules of the Church. This provoked massive popular demonstrations and a resolution in the House of Representatives in support of the President. It appeared that the bishops had the support and protection of General Grivas. When the President rejected their demand for his resignation, they charged him with abandoning the ideal of *Enosis*, tolerating the growth of Communism and permitting the rise of anti-Greek attitudes.

The clergy of the diocese of Paphos voted Bishop Yennadios out of office in June 1972, but he and the other two bishops refused to accept this decision and continued their campaign against Archbishop Makarios. In March 1973 they held what they called a Holy Synod of the Church of Cyprus, and announced that in view of the Archbishop's refusal to resign the presidency they would strip him of his episcopal titles. Makarios disregarded this move and the bishops' declaration in April that he had been reduced to the rank of layman. While the bishops were attempting to gain control of the administration and finances of the Church, claiming that Yennadios had been appointed to the vacant archiepiscopal throne, Makarios was taking counter-measures. He called an election for the diocese of Paphos in succession to Yennadios, and in July 1973 held a synod of the Orthodox Churches in Nicosia. The synod, presided over by the Patriarch of Alexandria, gave its support to Archbishop Makarios. It ruled that the Presidency and the Archbishopric were not incompatible under canon law, that the bishops' attempt to depose the Archbishop was invalid and that the bishops were guilty of schism. The dissident bishops were replaced.

MILITARY COUP

Following the deposition of the three bishops, and the demonstrations of popular support for the President which their actions provoked, the Cypriot Government was able to take strong measures against other supporters of General Grivas. Forces loyal to the President waged guerrilla war against EOKA—B, and carried out a purge of the armed forces and police, some of whose members had collaborated with EOKA and helped their raids on police stations in search of arms. The Grivas campaign of terrorism seemed to have been checked by the beginning of 1974, and when General Grivas died of a heart attack in January 1974 the President granted an amnesty to 100 of his imprisoned supporters, hoping to restore normality in Cyprus.

In June 1974 President Makarios ordered a purge of EOKA supporters in the police, civil service, schools and National Guard, and on July 2nd wrote to President Ghizikis of Greece, accusing the Greek military regime of giving arms and subsidies to EOKA and using the Greek army officers attached to the Cyprus National Guard as a centre of subversion. The President demanded that the Greek officers who had collaborated with EOKA should be withdrawn, and began to take steps to ensure that the Guard should be loyal to Cyprus rather than to Greece and *Enosis*. The National Guard, apparently with Greek support, then staged a coup. On July 15th former EOKA gunman Nicos Sampson was appointed President. Makarios fled to Britain, the resistance of his supporters was crushed, and Greece sent more officers to reinforce the National Guard.

Rauf Denktaş, the Turkish Cypriot leader, called for military action by the United Kingdom and Turkey, as guarantors of Cypriot independence, to prevent Greece imposing *Enosis*. Having failed to induce the United Kingdom to intervene, Turkey acted unilaterally. Turkish troops landed in Cyprus on July 20th, and seized the port of Kyrenia and a corridor connecting it to the Turkish sector in Nicosia. A ceasefire on July 22nd did not prevent further Turkish advances, and the UN Peace-Keeping Force had little success in its efforts to interpose itself between the two Cypriot communities. Massacres and other atrocities were reported from many bi-communal villages, reinforcing the hostility between Greeks and Turks.

TURKEY OCCUPIES NORTHERN CYPRUS

The successful Turkish invasion had foiled Greek plans to take over Cyprus using the National Guard, and when the military government of Greece resigned on July 23rd, Nicos Sampson did likewise. Glavcos Clerides, the moderate Speaker of the House of Representatives who had led the Greek Cypriot delegation to the intercommunal talks, was appointed President, and began negotiations with Rauf Denktaş. In Geneva, Britain, Greece and Turkey also held talks, seeking a settlement, but negotiations broke down following Turkish demands for the establishment of a cantonal federation giving almost a third of the area of Cyprus to the Turkish Cypriots.

On August 14th, the day after the Geneva talks ended, the war was renewed. Turkish forces seized the whole of Cyprus north of the Attila Line, running from Morphou through Nicosia to Famagusta, and the new civilian government in Greece announced its inability to intervene. Turkey announced that, by this *fait accompli*, the boundaries of an autonomous Turkish Cypriot administration had been established, while Mr. Denktaş spoke of establishing a completely independent Turkish Cypriot state north of Attila Line and of encouraging the immigration of Turkish Cypriots from areas still under Greek Cypriot control, to produce a permanent ethnic and political partition of the island. Dr. Kurt Waldheim, the UN Secretary-General, succeeded in arranging talks between Mr. Clerides and Mr. Denktaş, but was unable to bring about any constructive results from these negotiations. Possibly the most crucial round of peace talks on the Cyprus problem began in Vienna between Mr. Clerides and Mr. Denktaş in January 1975 under the aegis of Dr. Waldheim. The success of the talks hinged on whether the two sides could reach agreement on the political future of the island: the Turkish Cypriots wanting a Greek-Turkish bi-regional federation with strong regional governments, whereas the Greeks, whilst not ruling out a bi-zonal solution, favoured a multi-regional or cantonal federation with strong central government. Both parties stressed the need for an independent, non-aligned, demilitarized Cyprus.

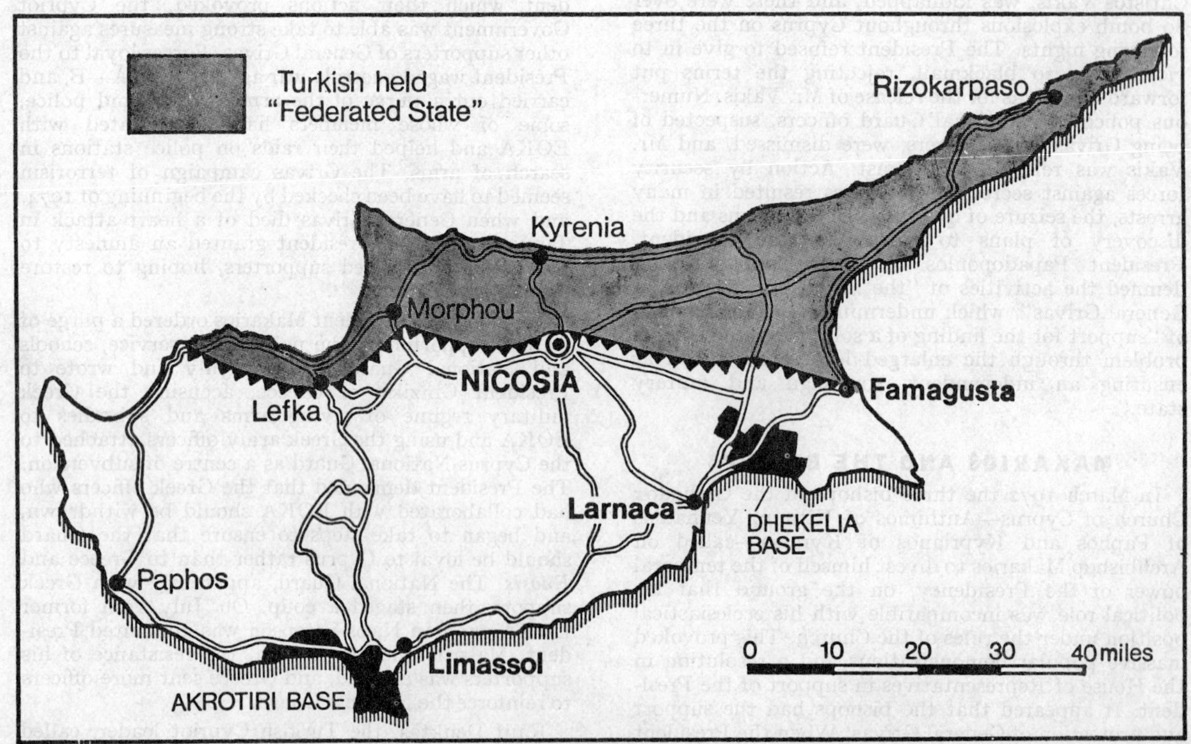

Cyprus, showing "Turkish Federated State".

On February 13th a "Turkish Federated State of Cyprus" was proclaimed in the part of the island under Turkish occupation. The new state was not proclaimed as an independent republic but as a restructuring of the Autonomous Turkish Cypriot Administration, a body established after the invasion, "on the basis of a secular and federated state until such time as the 1960 Constitution of the Republic . . . is amended in a similar manner to become the Constitution of the Federal Republic of Cyprus". Rauf Denktaş was appointed President of the new state. Greece denounced this move as a threat to peace and declared that the issue would be taken to the UN Security Council where a resolution was passed, on March 13th, regretting the unilateral decision to set up a Federated Turkish State. Talks were resumed in April and the foundation laid for intercommunal reconciliation and co-operation, when the Cypriot leaders agreed to form an expert committee, under the auspices of Dr. Luis Weckmann-Muñoz, Special Representative of the UN Secretary-General, to consider the powers and functions of a central government for Cyprus and present their findings in June to the Cypriot negotiators in Vienna.

The flight of Turkish Cypriots to British bases after the National Guard coup and the withdrawal of Greek Cypriot civilians before the advancing Turkish army had produced a major problem in Cyprus. In August 1974 the United Nations estimated that there were some 225,600 refugees in Cyprus, of whom 183,800 were Greek Cypriots. In the southern part of Cyprus, under Greek Cypriot control, were 198,800 of these refugees, of whom 35,000 were Turkish Cypriots, including prisoners of war. This problem remained unsolved in 1976, with an estimated 200,000 refugees on the island. However, 9,000 Turkish Cypriots were given the opportunity to move to the northern sector in August 1975. In return the Turkish Cypriot authorities allowed 800 relatives of Greeks who remained in the North to join them in the Turkish sector. The concern over the treatment of Greeks in the Turkish-occupied area gave rise in August 1975 to an investigation by the European Commission of Human Rights which, in a report published in January 1977, found Turkey guilty of committing atrocities in Cyprus.

In December 1974 Archbishop Makarios returned to Cyprus, and resumed the Presidency. In January 1975 Britain decided to permit the resettlement of over 9,000 Turkish Cypriot refugees from the British Sovereign Base at Akrotiri. In retaliation for the alleged ill-treatment of Turkish Cypriots still living in Greek areas and in order to force a decision on the release of the refugees and their resettlement, the Turks threatened to expel all remaining Greek Cypriots in northern Cyprus and launched a massive scheme to colonize the area, bringing thousands of farmers and peasants from mainland Turkey and settling them in Greek-owned property. Before the Turkish invasion of July 1974, Cyprus' 650,000 population was 18 per cent Turkish Cypriot and about 80 per cent Greek Cypriot.

THE SEARCH FOR A POLITICAL SETTLEMENT

In September 1975 talks between the two sides were resumed in New York. However, these failed to produce any significant results, with both sides unwilling to submit concrete proposals. It was hoped that, with the strengthening of the position of the Turkish leadership in the Senate elections in October and the relaxation of the arms embargo on Turkey by the United States, moves towards a settlement would be possible. But the negotiations were not reconvened until February 1976. These talks were as unproductive as previous meetings, with each side unwilling to compromise on the major areas of dispute: the question of Turkish withdrawal and the future constitutional character of Cyprus. The Greek Cypriot negotiator, Glavkos Clerides, appeared ready to accept the principle of a bi-zonal federation but the opposition of President Makarios to the idea of a weak central government undermined hopes of progress, together with the Turkish refusal to make proposals for territorial concessions. The divergence in the policies of Archibishop Makarios and Mr. Clerides eventually led to the resignation of the latter from his position as chief negotiator for the Government in April 1976. This led to the changing of the Turkish negotiator, with the withdrawal of Rauf Denktaş from the negotiating table, bringing about further disruption to the progress towards a settlement.

The talks were not resumed until May, with Mr. Tassos Papadopoulos representing the Greek Cypriot Government and Mr. Umit Suleyman Onan negotiating for the Turkish Cypriot authorities. The main purpose of this round of talks was the discussion of humanitarian issues but broader political problems were also discussed. Turkish proposals, laying down guidelines for the settlement of the territorial issue, were submitted at the end of May, reiterating the principle of a bi-zonal federation divided along national lines. The Turkish Cypriots insisted on retaining a militarily defensible area of territory, viable as an independent economic unit. These proposals were rejected by Archbishop Makarios.

During 1976 general elections were held on both sides of the "Attila Line". In June Rauf Denktaş was elected President of the "Turkish Federated State of Cyprus", defeating his only serious rival for power, Mr. Berberoglu, the leader of the Republican Turkish Party, by 41,059 votes to 11,869. Denktaş's election placed him constitutionally above party politics but in fact his position depends upon the support of the National Unity Party (NUP). Under the terms of the constitution promulgated by the Turkish Cypriot authorities, 40 deputies were elected to a legislative assembly, with the National Unity Party gaining a majority. Nejat Konut, the Secretary-General of the NUP, was appointed Prime Minister. In September general elections were held in the government-controlled area. A new party under Spyros Kyprianou, the Democratic Front, supporting the policies of Archbishop Makarios, won a decisive victory, gaining 21 of the 35 seats. The party of Glavcos Clerides, the Democratic Rally, did not win any seats.

In January 1977 Rauf Denktaş initiated a meeting with Archbishop Makarios to establish preliminaries for resuming inter-communal talks (suspended since February 1976); Archbishop Makarios made it clear that he was prepared to accept bi-zonal federation provided that he was prepared to accept bi-zonal federation provided that the Turkish authorities made territorial concessions, and only if there was provision for a central government with adequate powers. A sixth round of talks, which opened in Vienna in March 1977, broke down, was resumed in Nicosia in May but was suspended until after the general elections in Turkey in June 1977. The death of Archbishop Makarios on August 3rd, 1977, put an end to hopes for an immediate continuation of negotiations and gave rise to fears about the stability of the Greek Cypriot regime in his absence, especially because there was no obvious successor. Spyros Kyprianou, the President of the House of Representatives, was elected on August 31st to serve the remainder of Makarios's term of office. His style of government was very different from that of his predecessor, firm but less flamboyant. Just before the elections of January 1978 his son was kidnapped by the EOKA-B and the opposition candidate, Glavcos Clerides, withdrew in protest; Kyprianou was re-elected unopposed and formed a new Cabinet with an increased membership of 13. Following the release unharmed of the President's son and the granting of pardons to the kidnappers, the EOKA-B announced its dissolution, but in April 1978, after the discovery of a plot, 22 of its members were arrested. In the same month, following criticism in the Turkish Cypriot press about rising prices, Nejat Konut resigned as Prime Minister of the "Turkish Federated State of Cyprus" and was replaced by Osman Orek, former President of the National Assembly, who formed, a new Cabinet.

Turkish policy changed with the return to power of Bülent Ecevit as Prime Minister in January 1978. Reacting against the continued U.S. embargo on the supply of arms to Turkey under the 1976 defence agreement, Ecevit talked of a new direction in foreign policy and made moves towards a closer relationship with the U.S.S.R. In March 1978, reversing the whole of U.S. Mediterranean policy, President Carter announced that he would ask Congress to lift the embargo and approve a new defence agreement, hoping to reverse Turkish moves towards the U.S.S.R. and prompt Turkish proposals for a Cyprus settlement.

President Kyprianou reacted strongly both to the Soviet declaration of support for Turkey and to President Carter's initiative. He postponed the inter-communal talks which had been scheduled for April 11th and criticized the Soviet attitude. He also postponed indefinitely local elections which had been scheduled for June 4th, earning the disapproval of the AKEL pro-Communist party which in the Democratic Front had helped him to power.

On April 14th the Turkish government put forward new proposals for a bi-communal republic which combined specific constitutional proposals with a very small territorial concession which would return about 2 per cent of the island to the Greak Cypriots. The Greek reaction to these proposals was hostile, and on May 30th, when the Greek and Turkish premiers met at the instigation of Cyrus Vance, the U.S. Secretary of State, to reopen negotiations on defence and other matters, the Cyprus issue was not on the agenda for discussion.

During July Kyprianou's authority came under pressure from the powerful left wing and from followers of Makarios. He dismissed his chief negotiator with the Turkish Cypriots, Tassos Papadopoulos, after he had accused the President of moving away from the Makarios line on the future of Cyprus and of wanting to break off the talks. At the same time Kyprianou announced that a conspiracy to overthrow the Government had been discovered. No details of this emerged and Papadopoulos challenged Kyprianou to prove against him in court any connection with the plot. Four members of the moribund EOKA-B were arrested and the affair blew over.

A week later both sides relented on their refusal to enter into discussions. The Turkish Cypriots put forward a set of proposals on the future of Varosha, the Greek area of Famagusta, formerly the island's most important tourist area and a crucial issue in the settlement of the conflict. They demanded the repatriation of all the Greeks to the south and the establishment of an interim administration supervised by the UN, a plan dependent upon the resumption of talks. Partly as a result of these proposals, the U.S. Senate ratified President Carter's defence agreement with Turkey. The Greek Cypriot response was to demand the withdrawal of Turkish troops to allow all residents to return, while limiting the UN's role to that of a security force, a plan to precede the resumption of talks. These proposals were not discussed and in November the U.S. Government submitted a 12-point plan for settlement to the Greek and Turkish Governments and the Greek and Turkish Cypriots. The plan was to provide a framework for the resumption of the inter-communal talks under the auspices of Dr. Waldheim. It urged the Turkish Cypriots to agree to a significant geographical readjustment in favour of the Greek Cypriot side, and proposed a formula under which a *de facto* federal republic would be set up. The proposals were received favourably by Denktaş but more cautiously by Kyprianou and were the basis of further proposals by Dr. Waldheim in December which took more account of the Greek Cypriot view. This time Denktaş expressed reservations. Meanwhile, Kyprianou called on the United Nations to enforce by sanctions the resolutions often adopted calling for the withdrawal of Turkish troops. Sanctions, however, were not imposed though a time limit was recommended for Turkey to comply with the resolutions.

In December there was a crisis in the "Turkish Federated State" as a result of factional fighting in the NUP. In the midst of widespread rumours about the establishment of a multi-national company to which the Turkish Cypriot unions were opposed, all nine Cabinet Ministers resigned, followed by the Prime Minister. A new Cabinet was formed under Mustafa Çağatay, formerly Minister of Labour, Social Affairs and Health. In April 1979 a new party, the Democratic Party, was formed by the former Prime Minister, Nejat Konut, as the NUP lost support in the Legislative Assembly.

As a result of the efforts of the U.S. Government and the UN, Kyprianou and Denktaş finally resumed the inter-communal talks suspended since 1977. Though a 15-point plan was agreed beforehand, no concessions were made at the meetings held in Nicosia and talks ended abruptly after a week. The issues appeared as intractable as ever. The Greek Cypriots are committed to the Makarios-Denktaş agreement but reject the Turkish Cypriot interpretation of it as providing for a bi-zonal federation and are anxious to end the long series of talks that have served only to allow the Turkish Cypriots to entrench themselves on the north. They, on the other hand, while owing their territorial strength to the presence of the Turkish army, estimated at 26,000 in June 1979, are increasingly uneasy at their isolation and dependence on the ailing Turkish economy, especially in comparison with the economic progress made in the south.

ECONOMIC SURVEY

Geographically Cyprus may be divided into four regions distinguished by their natural and climatic features. These are the north coastal belt including the narrow Kyrenia mountain chain; the central plain, known as the Mesaoria, from Famagusta and Larnaca to Morphou Bay; the mountainous area of the south centre, dominated by the Troödos massif with its highest point of Mount Olympus (6,400 feet); and the coastal plain of the south running from a point west of Larnaca to Limassol and Paphos.

Of these areas the most significant in the island's economy are the central plain, which is the most densely populated and the centre of the island's grain production, the mountains, in which are situated the mineral deposits, the vineyards and the state forests, and the coastal plain, whose beaches form the principal tourist attraction on Cyprus.

The population of Cyprus increased rapidly in the period after the island passed under British rule, and had reached 639,000 by June 1974. The population rise was mainly the result of a fall in the death rate due to advances in public health. The emergence of a young, mostly literate population, unable to be contained by the old agricultural economy, has been at the root of most of the island's political and economic problems in the last two decades. G.D.P. per head had risen from U.S. $575 in 1963 to $1,419 in 1973.

Since the middle of 1974, however, the economy has been gravely disrupted by the political coup, the intervention of the Turkish army and the effective partition of the island. As well as the physical damage caused by the fighting, the flight of more than a third of the population as refugees and the collapse of essential services in many areas reduced economic activity to a low level. Crops were not harvested, and the citrus groves suffered from lack of irrigation. Buildings and plant were destroyed or lost their workforce. About 30 per cent of the island's factories, 80 per cent of the citrus fruit groves, all the tobacco fields, 10–15 per cent of the potato crop, 80 per cent of the carrots and 40 per cent of the carobs were north of the "Attila line" (*see* map).

The economy of the area south of the "Attila line" is recovering and finding new markets but it is still dependent on foreign aid. Greece offered U.S. $27.2 million in economic aid for 1979. The ordinary budget expenditure for 1978 was £C87 million, with the main expenditure on defence and social services. The development budget expenditure totalled £C27.7 million. The 1979 ordinary budget provided for expenditure of £C97 million and revenue of £C115 million (including £C10 million Government support from Greece), the surplus to be transferred to the development budget.

The economy of the area north of the "Attila line" has not recovered so quickly and an extensive programme of reconstruction, based on aid from Turkey, has been launched. The Five-Year Plan for 1978–82 envisages a total expenditure of TL 8,760 million, and an average annual growth of G.D.P. of 7.5 per cent. The principal areas of development are seen as the improvement of communications, irrigation and the restoration of the damaged citrus groves. In 1977 fruit production in the Turkish-controlled area recovered sufficiently for 61,000 metric tons to be exported. Total agricultural exports in 1977 were worth $10.3 million, much of it paid for in Turkish currency.

This reliance on Turkey, both as a market and as a source of aid, has led to a rise in the cost of living, not helped by devaluations of the Turkish lira. The lira's real value fell but the exchange rate remained the same. Petroleum products have to be imported from the southern part of the island and Turkey, and paid for in hard currency. The draft budget for 1979 provided for current expenditure of TL 1,243 million and capital investment of TL 457.1 million, with heavy dependence on foreign aid. Domestic revenue was expected to be TL 1,120 million. Turkey has agreed to give TL 742 million towards financing the Five-Year Plan, as well as a TL 250 million soft loan.

AGRICULTURE

Agriculture is the most important single economic activity in Cyprus. In mid-1974 it employed 33 per cent of the labour force. After the political upheaval in the middle of 1974 the Cyprus Government (controlling the area south of the "Attila line") launched an Emergency Economic Action Plan which envisaged spending £C18.5 million on agricultural and rural development over 1975 and 1976. Agriculture continued to be the major item of the development budget in 1977, at £C3.1 million, with water development second at £C2.6 million. In 1978 the Government announced a 10-year programme of agricultural and water development.

Agricultural exports in 1975 were at a low-point of £C23 million. Under the emergency Plan, loans were given to farmers and vegetable cultivation was increased. Agricultrual production responded rapidly. Agricultural exports for 1977 were worth $132 million in foreign exchange, compared with $95 million from the whole island in 1973. Exports of fruit and vegetables rose from £C18.2 million in 1975 to £C31.7 million in 1976 and £C37.9 million in 1977. While citrus fruit exports dropped from £C16.2 million in 1973 (the last "normal" year) to £C5.2 million in 1975 and remained low at £C5.1 million in 1976 and £C6.6 million in 1977, potato production increased steadily from 110,000 tons in 1975 to 200,000 tons in 1977, well above pre-1974 levels, and exports rose from £C7.7 million in 1975 to £C19.4 million in 1977, accounting for 41 per cent of food exports and 17.7 of total domestic exports. Carob production rose from 6,000 tons in 1974 to 32,000 tons in 1976 but dropped back to 19,000 tons in 1977. Cereal production in 1977, however, remained at about half of the 1974 level. In 1974 viticulture employed nearly one third of all agricultural workers but production of grapes fell from 170,000 tons in 1975 to 153,000 tons in 1977.

In 1978 the value of potato exports fell sharply, to £C10.8 million, equal to 10.4 per cent of total domestic exports. Overall, exports of fruit and vegetables decreased to £C29.3 million.

The largest irrigation scheme currently being implemented is the Paphos project, which will irrigate about 5,000 hectares along the coast at a cost of $45 million, of which the World Bank is contributing $23 million. The actual network is being built by a British firm and in 1978 the United Kingdom agreed on a loan of £7.5 million sterling for rural development.

INDUSTRY

Industry, also, was severely affected by the war of 1974. It was estimated that the Greek Cypriots lost 70 per cent of gross domestic manufacturing output, and the Emergency Economic Action Plan for 1975 and 1976 provided for expenditure of £C12.3 million on building and municipal projects, £C8.3 million on industry, trade and tourism and £C5.9 million on transport and communications. The plan has had some effect. Electricity consumption in 1975 exceeded that of 1974 and was not far short of the 1973 level. Increased demand has made it necessary to plan two more power stations. Cement production increased from 338,000 tons in 1974 to 1.1 million tons in 1977. Cement exports rose from £C500,000 in 1974 to £C10.7 million in 1977. Nevertheless, by 1978 there was a cement shortage caused by the need for homes for refugees. The boom also led to increased production of tiles, bricks and other building materials, although the loss of the Kyrenia quarries in the north meant that raw materials for tile manufacture had to be obtained from the Paphos area. Timber requirements are now met domestically and the profits and sales of Cyprus Forest Industries rose considerably in 1977. The extractive industries have not recovered from the setback of 1974 although production is rising. Exports of clothing and footwear increased from £C3.2 million in 1974 to £C23.4 million in 1978. Other industries which make a contribution to exports are transport equipment, cigarettes and foodstuffs, including wine-making. Wine production, which was 42.6 million litres in 1974, had recovered by 1977 to 38.2 million litres.

Overseas investment in Cyprus was not as high as had been hoped in 1975, although it forms a large part of total private investment. Although investment in the private sector in 1977 had risen to $287 million, only 20 per cent was from domestic sources, the remainder being derived from workers' remittances, foreign capital and borrowing abroad. Industrialists are also concerned that increased taxation on private industries will curb industrial development, already affected by rising costs of raw materials and labour. Another limiting factor in industrial growth is a chronic shortage of skilled labour. Tax concessions are being introduced to discourage the emigration of workers and to encourage those abroad to return.

The Turkish-occupied area has few industrial resources. It is estimated that 90 per cent of Cyprus's mining operations are in the Greek sector while the Turkish sector has no petroleum refinery and no power stations. The Cyprus Electrical Authority supplies to both sectors and the Turkish north's debt for unbilled consumption amounted to £C11 million between 1974 and 1978. Only 19 per cent of the manufacturing industries in the Turkish area were operational by May 1976 and there is considerable unemployment.

TRADE, TOURISM AND COMMUNICATIONS

Cyprus has experienced a trade deficit for many years, but in 1976, at £C71.4 million, it was considerably less than the 1973 figure of £C97.0 million. In 1977, however, the trade deficit widened again to £C124.3 million, 74 per cent up on the previous year, and in 1978 it grew to £C154.3 million. The United Kingdom is the main trading partner of both the Government-controlled and the Turkish-occupied areas. In recent years, however, Cyprus's trade, notably in wine and fruit and vegetables, has been threatened by EEC regulations restricting their import into the United Kingdom. Cyprus's association agreement with the EEC, which came into force in 1973, did not prove altogether satisfactory from Cyprus's point of view. The EEC fixed a 28 per cent duty and an increase in the fixed price of the Cypriot grape crop. In 1974 about 90 per cent of all wine exported went to the United Kingdom, but Cyprus is now obliged to seek new markets, for example in the U.S.S.R. and the U.S.A. The potato quota to the United Kingdom was limited to 100,000 tons in 1978 and reduced still further to 60,000 tons in 1979. Cyprus is, however, pressing for easier access to the markets in developed countries, maintaining that the amounts involved would not seriously affect EEC trade. There has also been a dispute with the EEC over recognition of the Turkish north in trade agreements. Cyprus has also concluded barter agreements with Eastern bloc states to exchange machinery and textiles for food products. A recent development is an increase in exports to Arab markets, particularly in the Gulf. Cyprus has also benefited from the large numbers of businessmen who left Beirut during the civil war in Lebanon in 1975–76. Mineral exports in 1977 were worth £C8.45 million, little more than the 1976 figure of £C8.73 million, despite increases in quantity. This was due to a fall in the prices of asbestos, copper concentrate, iron pyrites and chrome concentrate.

The Turkish sector's main exports in 1978 were citrus fruit, potatoes and tobacco, the principal markets being the United Kingdom, Lebanon, the Netherlands and Turkey. Total exports amounted to TL 705 million and imports to TL 1,984 million.

Tourism was one of the areas of the economy hardest hit by the 1974 war. Ninety per cent of the hotels fell into Turkish hands, and receipts from tourism in 1975 (to the Greek sector) amounted to only £C5 million in 1975, compared with £C24 million in 1973. Following the introduction of a government loan plan, however, the number of hotel beds increased from a low point of 3,880 in 1975 to over 6,000 in 1978. Tourist receipts rose to £C33.3 million in the same year. Closer links with the Arab states have resulted in an increase in visitors to Cyprus, particularly from the Gulf. A target for the Greek sector is 320,000 long-stay visitors in 1981 and about 20 new hotels are planned, as well as large-scale tourist development of Limassol. Since the Turkish sector already possesses good hotels it remains to exploit the tourism industry and encourage investment there.

Famagusta used to handle 83 per cent of Cyprus's cargoes but, now that it is in Turkish hands, its place has been largely taken by Larnaca and Limassol. In 1977, 26,539 containers passed through Limassol, compared with 17,084 in 1976. Port development schemes for Larnaca and Limassol will cost $45 million, and a new port is also planned for Paphos. There has been a suggestion that Cyprus should be used as an entrepôt for distributing food supplies to Saudi Arabia and the Gulf states. Cyprus has to some extent benefited from the paralysis of Beirut, although none of its ports has the capacity of Beirut.

PROSPECTS

The political situation poses great problems for the future of the Cyprus economy. The Ecevit proposals of 1978 envisaged development on bi-communal lines but by June 1979 there were few indications of a political settlement being reached. Meanwhile with both Greeks and Turks in practice tacitly accepting the *status quo* and going ahead with their own plans for development, there is no reason why crops should not continue to improve, tourism recover, and a reasonable degree of prosperity return to the island.

STATISTICAL SURVEY

Note: **The figures in this survey have been provided by the Department of Statistics and Research at the Ministry of Finance in Nicosia. Since July 1974 the northern part of Cyprus has been under Turkish control, so some of the statistics relating to subsequent periods may not cover the whole island.**

AREA AND POPULATION

Area	Population						
	Census Results		Mid-Year Estimates				
	Dec. 11th, 1960	April 1st, 1973	1974	1975†	1976†	1977†	1978†
9,251 sq. km.*	577,615	631,778	639,000	618,200	612,900	613,100	616,000

* 3,572 sq. miles. † Based on a partial census in 1976.

ETHNIC GROUPS

('000 persons at mid-year)

	1974	1977	1978
Greeks	504.2	494.8	497.2
Turks	117.3	115.0	115.5
Others	17.5	3.3	3.3
TOTAL	639.0	613.1	616.0

PRINCIPAL TOWNS

(estimated population at mid-1974)

Nicosia (capital)	117,100	Larnaca	19,800
Limassol	80,600	Paphos	9,100
Famagusta	39,400	Kyrenia	3,900

BIRTHS AND DEATHS

	BIRTH RATE (per '000)	DEATH RATE (per '000)
1974	16.5	10.8
1975	16.0	7.9
1976	18.7	8.6
1977	18.4	9.0
1978	19.2	8.5

ECONOMICALLY ACTIVE POPULATION

(Greek community only)

	1976	1977	1978
Agriculture, hunting, forestry and fishing	46,520	46,700	44,300
Mining and quarrying	2,332	2,300	2,017
Manufacturing	30,285	33,655	34,753
Electricity, gas and water	1,350	1,350	1,321
Construction	11,310	14,990	16,821
Trade, restaurants and hotels; Financing, insurance, real estate and business services	24,781	27,345	29,155
Transport, storage and communications	7,696	8,161	8,325
Community, social and personal services	36,413	36,147	36,474
Other activities (not adequately described)	46,618	32,007	38,380
TOTAL	204,305	202,655	201,552

AGRICULTURE

PRINCIPAL CROPS ('000 tons)

	1976	1977	1978
Wheat	34	23	20
Barley	55	56	67
Potatoes	180	200	145
Carrots	10	12	6
Carobs	32	19	18
Olives	10	9	10
Grapes	165	153	180
Oranges	36	39	36
Grapefruit	33	47	40
Lemons	10	13	12

LIVESTOCK ('000 head in December each year)

	1973	1976	1977	1978
Cattle	33	17	18.7	20
Sheep	430	255	280	275
Goats	340	230	240	233
Pigs	163	141	200	164
Chickens	3,085	2,100	2,000	2,000

Fishing: (metric tons, live weight): Total catch 1,216 in 1974; 950 in 1975; 1,083 in 1976; 1,190 in 1977; 1,245 in 1978.

MINING

EXPORTS (tons)

	1975	1976	1977	1978
Asbestos	27,930	33,022	34,783	28,875
Chromite	27,682	12,142	14,009	10,972
Cupreous concentrates	38,690	41,848	30,722	25,811
Cupreous pyrites	19,466	—	—	—
Iron pyrites	402,178	144,534	171,607	121,718
Gypsum, calcined	—	870	4,120	n.a.
Gypsum (stones)	20	10,161	34,370	4,928
Terra umbra	4,139	9,955	10,664	10,189
Yellow ochre	217	435	230	305
Other minerals	11,678	7,717	14,191	6,945

INDUSTRY

SELECTED PRODUCTS

		1975	1976	1977	1978
Cement	'000 metric tons	611.5	1,025.5	1,070.8	1,107.0
Bricks	million	9.7	12.5	26.2	35.7
Tiles	'000 sq. metres	207	498	895	1,155
Cigarettes	million	1,391.5	2,043.7	2,408.3	2,896.0
Shoes*	'000 pairs	2,025	3,027	4,094	4,730
Beer	million litres	11.2	11.3	13.5	15.2
Wines	,, ,,	29.0	32.6	39.4	39.4
Intoxicating liquors	,, ,,	2.6	2.5	2.6	2.9

* Excluding plastic and semi-finished shoes.

FINANCE

1,000 mils = 1 Cyprus pound.

Coins: 1, 3, 5, 25, 50, 100 and 500 mils; 1 pound.

Notes: 250 and 500 mils; 1, 5 and 10 pounds.

Exchange rates (June 1979): £1 sterling = 753.0 mils; U.S. $ = 364.0 mils.

Cyprus £100 = £132.80 sterling = $274.75.

Note: From November 1967 to August 1971 the par value of the Cyprus pound was U.S. $2.40 ($1 = 416.7 mils). Between December 1971 and February 1973 the Cyprus pound was valued at U.S. $2.6057 ($1 = 383.8 mils). From February to July 1973 the exchange rate was Cyprus £1 = U.S. $2.8952 ($1 = 345.4 mils). The Cyprus pound was at par with the pound sterling until the latter was allowed to "float" in June 1972; and it has itself been "floating" since July 1973. The average mid-point market value of the Cyprus pound was $2.861 in 1973; $2.743in 1974; $2.716 in 1975; $2.437 in 1976; $2.451 in 1977; $2.680 in 1978.

BUDGET ESTIMATES, 1979
(Cyprus £)

Revenue		Expenditure	
Direct taxes	25,358,000	Agriculture and forests	2,700,761
Indirect taxes	54,208,950	Water development	821,403
Sale of goods and services	6,415,210	Public works	1,095,287
Interest, dividends, rents and royalties	7,707,460	Cyprus army and Tripartite Agreement	1,469,150
Transfers	4,068,450	Customs and excise	3,287,147
Greek Government grants	10,300,000	Public debt charges	9,862,158
Loan proceeds	5,850,000	Pensions and grants	3,841,360
Other	1,294,800	Medical	7,658,797
		Police	9,803,565
		Subsidies, subventions and contributions	14,447,988
		Education grants	16,673,542
		Other	23,815,424
Total	115,202,870	Total	98,998,746

DEVELOPMENT BUDGET
(Cyprus £)

	1975	1976	1977	1978
Water Development	1,508,566	1,657,962	2,593,099	4,703,000
Road Network	1,739,978	1,315,657	1,648,196	1,988,163
Harbours	630,529	513,267	3,157	39,974
Agriculture	2,343,769	2,664,938	3,067,730	3,434,266
Commerce and Industry	409,190	519,841	948,034	1,384,257
Airports	429,631	1,244,098	704,508	908,836

1979 Development Budget: Total proposed expenditure £31,687,613.

INTERNATIONAL RESERVES

(U.S. $ million at December 31st)

	1972	1973	1974	1975	1976	1977	1978
Gold	16.3	18.1	18.4	17.6	17.4	18.7	20.2
IMF Special Drawing Rights	11.3	12.6	12.8	11.8	9.2	6.2	2.2
Reserve position in IMF	7.1	7.9	—	—	—	—	8.5
Foreign exchange	284.9	268.2	237.3	185.9	265.3	307.3	334.6
TOTAL	319.6	306.8	268.5	215.2	291.9	332.2	365.5

Source: IMF, *International Financial Statistics.*

MONEY SUPPLY

(Cyprus £ million at December 31st)

	1971	1972	1973	1974	1975	1976	1977
Currency outside banks	21.76	26.26	29.73	35.75	33.71	39.31	43.16
Demand deposits at deposit money banks	24.96	31.18	31.11	31.26	30.68	44.02	45.10
TOTAL MONEY	46.72	57.44	60.84	67.01	64.39	83.33	88.26

RETAIL PRICE INDEX

(1973=100)

	1975	1976	1977	1978
All Items	121.56	126.15	135.21	145.25
Food and Drinks	131.14	134.59	145.95	154.21
Rent	101.13	101.30	104.52	113.32
Fuel and Light	147.93	154.80	160.37	171.00
Household Equipment	120.16	126.04	137.65	149.75
Household Operations	149.51	155.98	162.08	165.96
Clothing and Footwear	114.10	117.27	127.56	138.49
Miscellaneous	123.84	132.78	142.80	154.61

NATIONAL ACCOUNTS
(Cyprus £ million)

	1975	1976	1977	1978*
GROSS DOMESTIC PRODUCT AT FACTOR COST	239.8	299.6	392.5	448.4
of which:				
Agriculture, etc.	40.4	53.6	56.4	51.9
Manufacturing	35.3	47.4	67.0	79.5
Construction	12.2	18.3	25.8	37.4
Wholesale and retail trade	38.8	50.3	71.9	80.9
Income from abroad	14.1	13.9	19.8	20.5
GROSS NATIONAL INCOME	266.2	333.0	445.1	511.5
Less depreciation allowances	−12.0	−15.0	−20.0	−23.0
NET NATIONAL INCOME	254.2	318.0	425.1	488.5
Indirect taxes less subsidies	12.3	19.5	32.8	42.6
NET NATIONAL PRODUCT AT FACTOR COST	241.9	298.5	392.3	445.9
Depreciation allowances	12.0	15.0	20.0	23.0
GROSS NATIONAL PRODUCT AT FACTOR COST	253.9	313.5	412.3	468.9
Balance of exports and imports of goods and services, and borrowing	54.4	41.7	84.8	126.7
AVAILABLE RESOURCES	308.3	355.2	497.1	595.6
of which:				
Private consumption expenditure	214.6	244.3	336.9	390.3
Government consumption expenditure	47.0	48.5	64.3	82.1
Gross fixed capital formation	38.3	58.0	97.6	134.4
Increase in stocks	5.2	10.0	11.3	10.9

* Provisional.

BALANCE OF PAYMENTS
(Cyprus £ million)

	1975	1976	1977	1978
Exports f.o.b.	52.4	102.7	124.2	122.0
Imports f.o.b.	−110.9	−163.4	−288.2	−255.6
TRADE BALANCE	−58.5	−60.7	−104.0	−133.6
Invisible Receipts	86.1	112.1	137.6	148.9
Invisible Payments	−41.3	−55.7	−69.6	−74.9
Invisible Balance	44.8	56.4	68.0	74.0
CURRENT ACCOUNT BALANCE	−13.7	−4.3	−36.0	−59.6
Short-term Capital	−1.6	−5.2	0.9	2.2
Long-term Loans	0.8	9.4	17.9	37.1
Other Private Long-term Capital	3.8	13.3	16.9	20.0
Other Official Long-term Capital	—	—	—	—
Net Capital Movement	3.0	17.5	34.8	59.3
Net Errors and Omissions	−3.6	4.6	3.4	4.9
OVERALL BALANCE	−14.3	17.8	2.2	4.6

EXTERNAL TRADE
(Cyprus £'000)

	1971	1972	1973	1974	1975	1976	1977	1978
Imports c.i.f.*	106,869	121,480	157,442	148,028	113,709	177,763	254,008	282,686
Exports f.o.b.	47,279	51,305	60,474	55,287	56,012	106,332	129,751	128,370

* Excluding NAAFI imports and imports of military stores but including imports of gold (Cyprus £'000): 379 in 1971; 519 in 1972; 564 in 1973; 213 in 1974; 684 in 1975; 905 in 1976; 1,200 in 1977; 1,845 in 1978.

PRINCIPAL COMMODITIES*

(Cyprus £'000)

Civil Imports c.i.f.	1975	1976	1977	1978
Food and live animals	24,346	32,077	32,705	34,777
Cereals and cereal preparations	8,354	12,867	11,563	11,845
Barley (unmilled)	6,223	5,453	5,025	3,581
Beverages and tobacco	2,339	8,220	8,746	9,745
Tobacco and tobacco manufactures	1,821	5,616	6,509	8,366
Crude materials (inedible) except fuels	1,284	2,433	5,766	6,007
Mineral fuels, lubricants, etc.	18,067	26,801	35,206	30,979
Petroleum and petroleum products	17,072	25,655	34,201	30,099
Crude and partly refined petroleum	9,675	14,565	17,508	17,785
Petroleum products	7,397	11,090	16,693	12,314
Residual fuel oils	5,531	4,723	12,395	8,524
Chemicals	10,246	15,015	19,003	19,193
Plastic materials, etc.	1,845	4,275	5,113	6,014
Basic manufactures	28,726	49,662	73,069	76,329
Paper, paperboard and manufactures	5,469	7,708	9,051	8,940
Paper and paperboard	3,323	5,175	8,452	6,631
Textile yarn, fabrics, etc.	9,679	17,191	23,976	25,091
Woven textile fabrics (excl. narrow or special fabrics)	5,094	8,482	12,416	13,608
Iron and steel	3,321	8,953	13,754	12,809
Bars, rods, angles, shapes, etc.	936	4,405	7,161	7,004
Bars and rods (excl. wire rod)	689	3,614	5,987	6,206
Machinery and transport equipment	17,499	28,669	57,187	76,608
Telecommunications equipment, etc.	2,158	2,897	4,791	4,281
Transport equipment	3,584	7,439	17,915	32,601
Road motor vehicles and parts	3,410	7,176	15,155	21,439
Passenger cars (excl. buses)	1,796	3,719	10,972	11,914
Miscellaneous manufactured articles	7,296	10,838	17,474	22,277
Total (incl. others)	113,709	177,763	254,008	282,686

Exports f.o.b.‡	1975	1976	1977	1978
Food and live animals	18,832	33,779	41,517	32,754
Fruit and vegetables	18,205	31,651	37,865	29,283
Fresh fruit and nuts (excl. oil nuts)†	7,887	8,302	10,434	11,401
Oranges, tangerines and mandarines†	1,776	2,154	2,580	2,736
Other citrus fruit†	3,436	2,960	4,051	3,965
Fresh or simply preserved vegetables	8,649	19,917	24,529	15,071
Fresh potatoes	7,725	17,707	19,435	10,772
Beverages and tobacco	5,497	10,959	12,673	13,904
Beverages	4,176	7,578	8,773	7,945
Alcoholic beverages	4,164	7,341	7,208	6,440
Wine (incl. grape must)	3,780	4,925	6,041	5,778
Wine of fresh grapes	3,750	4,556	4,673	4,982
Crude materials (inedible) except fuels	8,382	8,970	9,927	8,835
Crude fertilizers and crude minerals	4,011	4,471	6,084	4,984
Asbestos (crude, washed or ground)	2,127	3,316	4,381	3,724
Metalliferous ores and metal scrap	3,394	3,823	2,623	2,028
Copper ores and concentrates	2,630	3,339	1,864	1,462
Cupreous concentrates	2,495	3,339	1,864	1,462
Basic manufactures	9,089	13,854	17,132	15,643
Non-metallic mineral manufactures	6,015	9,358	11,202	8,807
Lime, cement, etc.	5,980	9,170	10,678	8,488
Cement	5,980	9,168	10,664	8,474
Miscellaneous manufactured articles	5,777	14,288	20,474	26,738
Clothing (excl. footwear)	3,450	8,355	11,983	16,322
Footwear	1,758	4,557	5,933	7,104
Total (incl. others)	48,813	85,165	109,501	103,575

* Beginning in 1976, the classification has been revised and figures are not all strictly comparable with those for earlier years. † Dried citrus fruit are included with "fresh fruit and nuts".

‡ Excluding re-exports (£6,514,000 in 1975; £19,584,000 in 1976; £16,964,000 in 1977; £20,071,000 in 1978) and stores for ships and aircraft (£686,000 in 1975; £1,584,000 in 1976; £3,286,000 in 1977; £4,724,000 in 1978.)

PRINCIPAL TRADING PARTNERS*

(Cyprus £'000)

Imports c.i.f.	1976	1977	1978
Algeria	3,636	4,464	2,798
Argentina	4,219	2,885	1,908
Austria	2,642	4,119	3,433
Belgium	2,603	4,918	3,626
Canada	1,337	1,135	3,836
France	9,712	13,193	13,488
Germany, Fed. Republic	12,457	19,821	20,986
Greece	17,362	21,124	17,802
Iraq	7,502	11,811	15,022
Israel	3,616	5,307	5,043
Italy	16,427	23,569	32,779
Japan	7,872	12,761	15,399
Netherlands	5,756	5,644	6,852
Spain	2,359	5,217	5,659
Sweden	2,354	3,653	3,707
U.S.S.R.	6,615	12,937	9,882
United Kingdom	35,080	48,156	62,448
U.S.A.	9,815	14,200	15,749
Total (incl. others)	177,763	254,008	282,686

Exports f.o.b.†	1976	1977	1978
Bahrain	1,240	2,066	2,319
Egypt	829	4,571	2,864
Germany, Fed. Republic	597	1,578	2,662
Greece	2,233	3,714	3,554
Jordan	538	1,359	2,337
Kuwait	2,294	3,170	5,752
Lebanon	18,025	12,012	12,953
Libya	5,836	6,970	5,727
Netherlands	1,877	1,060	2,407
Nigeria	222	1,151	3,107
Saudi Arabia	6,313	16,465	11,527
Spain	2,109	1,054	1,088
Syria	6,419	3,653	6,803
U.S.S.R.	4,844	4,180	3,401
United Arab Emirates	2,251	3,847	3,720
United Kingdom	29,466	37,505	30,040
Yemen Arab Republic	1,109	3,030	1,183
Total (incl. others)	104,749	126,206	123,391

* Imports by country of production; exports by country of consignment.

† Excluding stores for ships and aircraft (Cyprus £'000): 1,584 in 1976; 3,286 in 1977; 4,724 in 1978. Also excluded are unspecified items sent by parcel post (Cyprus £'000): 259 in 1977; 255 in 1978.

TRANSPORT

ROAD TRAFFIC

(motor vehicles in use)

	1975	1976	1977	1978
Cars	63,543	66,493	71,793	76,435
Taxis	3,655	2,634	2,669	1,297
Lorries	16,172	17,204	16,753	17,227
Motor cycles	10,987	11,715	13,378	14,208
Tractors, etc.	4,498	5,152	7,722	5,031
Total	98,855	103,198	112,315	114,198

SHIPPING

	1975	1976	1977	1978
Vessels* entered ('000 net reg. tons)	3,232	4,236	4,741	5,675
Goods loaded ('000 tons)	1,309	1,777	1,787	1,362
Goods unloaded ('000 tons)	1,133	1,632	1,750	1,778

* Steam or motor vessels and sailing vessels.

CIVIL AVIATION

Cyprus Airways

	1975	1976	1977	1978
Kilometres flown	2,424,577	4,401,000	5,590,000	7,407,000
Passenger arrivals	89,767	182,870	256,000	1,296,900
Passenger departures	89,234	208,486	255,153	294,656
Freight landed (tons)	870	3,418	3,544	4,049
Freight cleared (tons)	4,478	10,378	17,277	19,786

Communications: Over 82,000 telephones in use in December 1977.

TOURISM

FOREIGN VISITORS BY COUNTRY OF ORIGIN*

	1973	1975†	1976†	1977†	1978†
Greece	15,017	7,506	15,826	22,376	25,518
Israel	5,863	2,672	4,159	4,408	5,340
Lebanon	10,067	4,312	77,887	26,307	25,866
United Kingdom	116,026	17,474	34,501	55,565	74,593
U.S.A.	14,808	2,090	4,967	7,477	7,049
TOTAL (incl. others)	264,066	47,084	180,206	178,185	216,679

* Excluding one-day visitors. † Figures do not apply to the Turkish occupied zone.

Tourist earnings: (1975) £5.4m.; (1976) £20.7m.; (1977) £23.8m; (1978) £33.3m.

Number of hotel beds: (1975) 3,880; (1976) 4,681; (1977) 5,065; (1978) 6,032.

Number of tourist nights: (1975) 247,538; (1976) 678,878; (1977) 798,799; (1978) 1,047,070.

EDUCATION

GREEK (1978/79)

	ESTABLISHMENTS	TEACHERS	PUPILS
Elementary	439	2,260	54,309
Secondary (public)	55	1,950	37,999
Secondary (private)	26	316	4,442
Technical and vocational (public)	10	504	6,445
Teacher training	1	16	113
Other post-secondary	10	136	1,342

Source (unless otherwise stated): Department of Statistics and Research, Ministry of Finance, Nicosia.

"TURKISH FEDERATED STATE OF CYPRUS"

Note: The "Turkish Federated State of Cyprus" was established in 1975 after the Turkish invasion of northern Cyprus. The United Nations considers it to be an illegal regime in relation to the U.N. Charter, and only Turkey has granted it international recognition.

Population: 140,000 (October 1975 estimate).

Finance: Turkish currency (q.v.) is in use.

BUDGET 1979/80

(Turkish liras)

REVENUE		EXPENDITURE	
Local taxes	1,234,617,100	Housing and rehabilitation	105,187,500
Local loans	34,000,000	Water projects	153,217,000
Foreign aid	1,079,258,186	Communications	180,595,956
		Health and Social Services	223,227,027
		Other (incl. company investment, tourism, education, agriculture and industry)	1,685,647,803
TOTAL	2,347,875,286	TOTAL	2,347,875,286

EXTERNAL TRADE

Principal export: Citrus fruit (first and second grade, metric tons) 66,174 (1976/77); 87,991 (1977/78).

1977 (Cyprus £): Imports 41,722,222; Exports 12,586,410.

PRINCIPAL TRADING PARTNERS
(Turkish lira)

Imports	1977	Exports	1977
Germany, Federal Republic	80,332,992	Netherlands*	41,872,320
Turkey	562,683,580	Turkey	120,999,924
United Kingdom	378,859,536	United Kingdom	213,879,388
Total (incl. others)	1,492,123,752	Total (incl. others)	435,018,016

* Not including October and November.

Tourism (visitors from mainland Turkey): 1975, 68,000; 1976, 93,000; 1977, 96,488 by sea, 50,228 by air, total 146,716.

EDUCATION

(1976/77)

	Establishments	Teachers	Pupils
Basic education			
Nursery	6	19	585
Primary (1st stage)	177	593	18,220
Junior secondary (2nd stage)	12	114	2,157
Secondary education	10	400	8,347
Adult education	42	42	1,780
Technical schools	5	134	811
Teacher training college	1	4	68

Source: Office of the London Representative of the "Turkish Federated State of Cyprus".

THE CONSTITUTION

The Constitution entered into force on August 16th, 1960, on which date Cyprus became an independent republic. In March 1961 Cyprus was accepted as a member of the Commonwealth.

Article 1

The State of Cyprus is an independent and sovereign Republic with a presidential regime, the President being Greek and the Vice-President being Turkish, elected by the Greek and the Turkish Communities of Cyprus respectively as hereinafter in this Constitution provided.

Articles 2–5

The Greek Community comprises all citizens of the Republic who are of Greek origin and whose mother tongue is Greek or who share the Greek cultural traditions or who are members of the Greek Orthodox Church.

The Turkish Community comprises all citizens of the Republic who are of Turkish origin and whose mother tongue is Turkish or who share the Turkish cultural traditions or who are Moslems.

Citizens of the Republic who do not come within the above provisions shall, within three months of the date of the coming into operation of this Constitution, opt to belong to either the Greek or the Turkish Community as individuals, but, if they belong to a religious group, shall opt as a religious group and upon such option they shall be deemed to be members of such Community.

The official languages of the Republic are Greek and Turkish.

The Republic shall have its own flag of neutral design and colour, chosen jointly by the President and the Vice-President of the Republic.

The Greek and the Turkish Communities shall have the right to celebrate respectively the Greek and the Turkish national holidays.

Articles 6–35
Fundamental Rights and Liberties

Articles 36–53
President and Vice-President

The President of the Republic as Head of the State represents the Republic in all its official functions; signs the credentials of diplomatic envoys and receives the credentials of foreign diplomatic envoys; signs the credentials of delegates for the negotiation of international treaties, conventions or other agreements; signs the letter relating to the transmission of the instruments of ratification of any international treaties, conventions or agreements; confers the honours of the Republic.

The Vice-President of the Republic as Vice-Head of the State has the right to be present at all official functions; at the presentation of the credentials of foreign diplomatic envoys; to recommend to the President the conferment of honours on members of the Turkish Community which recommendation the President shall accept unless there are grave reasons to the contrary. The honours so conferred will be presented to the recipient by the Vice-President if he so desires.

The election of the President and the Vice-President of the Republic shall be direct, by universal suffrage and secret ballot, and shall, except in the case of a by-election, take place on the same day but separately.

The office of the President and of the Vice-President shall be incompatible with that of a Minister or of a Representative or of a member of a Communal Chamber or of a member of any municipal council including a Mayor or of a member of the armed or security forces of the Republic or with a public or municipal office.

The President and Vice-President of the Republic are invested by the House of Representatives.

The President and the Vice-President shall hold office for a period of five years.

The Executive power is ensured by the President and the Vice-President of the Republic.

The President and the Vice-President of the Republic in order to ensure the executive power shall have a Council of Ministers composed of seven Greek Ministers and three Turkish Ministers. The Ministers shall be designated respectively by the President and the Vice-President of the Republic who shall appoint them by an instrument signed by them both.

The decisions of the Council of Ministers shall be taken by an absolute majority and shall, unless the right of final veto or return is exercised by the President or the Vice-President of the Republic or both, be promulgated immediately by them.

The executive power exercised by the President and the Vice-President of the Republic conjointly consists of:

Determining the design and colour of the flag.
Creation or establishment of honours.
Appointment of the members of the Council of Ministers.
Promulgation by publication of the decisions of the Council of Ministers.
Promulgation by publication of any law or decision passed by the House of Representatives.
Appointments and termination of appointments as in Articles provided.
Institution of compulsory military service.
Reduction or increase of the security forces.
Exercise of the prerogative of mercy in capital cases.
Remission, suspension and commutation of sentences.
Right of references to the Supreme Constitutional Court and publication of Court decisions.
Address of messages to the House of Representatives.

The executive power exercised by the President consists of:

Designation and termination of appointment of Greek Ministers.
Convening and presiding of the meetings of the Council of Ministers.
Right of final veto on Council decisions and on laws or decisions of the House of Representatives concerning foreign affairs, defence or security.
Right of recourse to the Supreme Constitutional Court.
Publication of the communal laws and decisions of the Greek Communal Chamber.
Prerogative of mercy in capital cases.
Addressing messages to the House of Representatives.

The executive power exercised by the Vice-President consists of:

Designation and termination of appointment of Turkish Ministers.
Asking the President for the convening of the Council of Ministers and being present and taking part in the discussions.
Right of final veto on Council decisions and on laws or decisions of the House of Representatives concerning foreign affairs, defence or security.
Right of recourse to the Supreme Constitutional Court.
Publication of the communal laws and decisions of the Turkish Communal Chamber.
Prerogative of mercy in capital cases.
Addressing messages to the House of Representatives.

Articles 54–60

Council of Ministers

The Council of Ministers shall exercise executive power in all matters, other than those which are within the competence of a Communal Chamber, including the following:

General direction and control of the government of the Republic and the direction of general policy.
Foreign affairs, defence and security.
Co-ordination and supervision of all public services.
Supervision and disposition of property belonging to the Republic.
Consideration of Bills to be introduced to the House of Representatives by a Minister.
Making of any order or regulation for the carrying into effect of any law as provided by such law.
Consideration of the Budget of the Republic to be introduced to the House of Representatives.

Articles 61–85

House of Representatives

The legislative power of the Republic shall be exercised by the House of Representatives in all matters except those expressly reserved to the Communal Chambers.

The number of Representatives shall be fifty:

Provided that such number may be altered by a resolution of the House of Representatives carried by a majority comprising two-thirds of the Representatives elected by the Greek Community and two-thirds of the Representatives elected by the Turkish Community.

Out of the number of Representatives 70 per cent shall be elected by the Greek Community and 30 per cent by the Turkish Community separately from amongst their members respectively, and, in the case of a contested election, by universal suffrage and by direct and secret ballot held on the same day.

The term of office of the House of Representatives shall be for a period of five years.

The President of the House of Representatives shall be a Greek, and shall be elected by the Representatives elected by the Greek Community, and the Vice-President shall be a Turk and shall be elected by the Representatives elected by the Turkish Community.

Articles 86–111

Communal Chambers

The Greek and the Turkish Communities respectively shall elect from amongst their own members a Communal Chamber.

The Communal Chambers shall, in relation to their respective Community, have competence to exercise legislative power solely with regard to the following:

All religious, educational, cultural and teaching matters.

Personal status; composition and instances of courts dealing with civil disputes relating to personal status and to religious matters.

Imposition of personal taxes and fees on members of their respective Community in order to provide for their respective needs.

ARTICLES 112–121, 126–128

Officers of the Republic

ARTICLES 122–125

The Public Service

The public service shall be composed as to 70 per cent of Greeks and as to 30 per cent of Turks.

ARTICLES 129–132

The Forces of the Republic

The Republic shall have an army of two thousand men of whom 60 per cent shall be Greeks and 40 per cent shall be Turks.

The security forces of the Republic shall consist of the police and gendarmerie and shall have a contingent of two thousand men. The forces shall be composed as to 70 per cent of Greeks and as to 30 per cent of Turks.

ARTICLES 133–164

The Courts

(See section Judicial System)

ARTICLES 165–199

Financial, Miscellaneous, Final and Transitional Provisions

Note: The following measures have been passed by the House of Representatives since January 1964, when the Turkish members withdrew:

1. The amalgamation of the High Court and the Supreme Constitutional Court.
2. The abolition of the Greek Communal Chamber and the creation of a Ministry of Education.
3. The unification of the Municipalities.
4. The unification of the Police and the Gendarmerie.
5. The creation of a military force by providing that persons between the ages of eighteen and fifty can be called upon to serve in the National Guard.
6. The extension of the term of office of the President and the House of Representatives by one year intervals from July 1965 until elections in February 1968 and July 1970 respectively.
7. New electoral provisions; abolition of separate Greek and Turkish rolls; abolition of post of Vice-President, which was re-established in 1973.

THE GOVERNMENT*

HEAD OF STATE

President: Spyros Kyprianou (took office August 3rd, 1977)

COUNCIL OF MINISTERS

(*June* 1979)

Minister of Finance: Andreas Patsalides.

Minister of Foreign Affairs: Nicos A. Rolandis.

Minister-Delegate to the Presidency: Georghios X. Ioannides.

Minister of the Interior and of Defence: Christodoulos Veniamin.

Minister of Agriculture and Natural Resources: Georghios C. Tombazos.

Minister of Health: Dr. Andreas Michaelides.

Minister of Education: Dr. Chrysostomos Sofianos.

Minister of Commerce and Industry: Andreas Papageorghiou.

Minister of Communications and Works: Marios G. Eliades.

Minister of Labour and Social Insurance: Emilios Theodolou.

Minister of Justice: Petros B. Michaelides.

Deputy Minister of the Interior: Stelios Katsellis.

Deputy Minister of Education: Costas Hadjistefanou.

* Under the Constitution of 1960 the Vice-Presidency and three posts in the Council of Ministers are reserved for Turkish Cypriots. However, there has been no Turkish participation in the government since December 1963. In 1968 President Makarios announced that he considered the office of Vice-President in abeyance until Turkish participation in the government is resumed, but the Turkish community elected Rauf Denktaş Vice-President in February 1973.

HOUSE OF REPRESENTATIVES

The House of Representatives originally consisted of 50 members, 35 from the Greek community and 15 from the Turkish community, elected for a term of five years. In January 1964 the Turkish members withdrew and set up the Turkish Legislative Assembly of the Turkish Cypriot Administration.

President: Alecos Michaelides.

ELECTIONS FOR THE GREEK REPRESENTATIVES
(September 5th, 1976)

Party	Seats
Democratic Front* . . .	21
AKEL (Communist Party) .	9
EDEK (Unified Democratic Union)	4
Independents (Pro-Government) .	1
Total . . .	35

* Renamed Democratic Party.

POLITICAL PARTIES

AKEL—Progressive Party of the Working People (*Anorthotikon Komma Ergazomenou Laou*): Akamantos St., P.O.B. 1827, Nicosia; f. 1941; successor to the Communist Party of Cyprus (f. 1926); over 14,000 mems.; Sec.-Gen. EZEKIAS PAPAIOANNOU; publs. *Haravghi* (daily), *Democratia* (weekly).

Democratic Party (*Demokratiko Komma*): f. 1976; supports settlement of the Cyprus problem based on UN resolutions; Chair. SPYROS KYPRIANOU.

Democratic Rally (*Democratikos Synagermos*): f. 1976; opposition party; absorbed Democratic National Party (DEK) in 1977; calls for more active involvement of the West in the settlement of the Cyprus problem; Chair. GLAVCOS CLERIDES.

EDEK—Unified Democratic Union of Cyprus (*Eniea Democratiki Enosis Kyprou*): f. 1969; the Socialist Party of Cyprus; supports independent, non-aligned, unitary, demilitarized Cyprus; stands for a socialist structure; Chair. Dr. VASSOS LYSSARIDES; publs. *Ta Nea* (daily), *Anexartitos* (weekly).

DIPLOMATIC REPRESENTATION

EMBASSIES AND HIGH COMMISSIONS ACCREDITED TO CYPRUS

(In Nicosia, except where otherwise stated)

(E) Embassy; (HC) High Commission.

Algeria: Damascus, Syria (E).

Argentina: Rome, Italy (E).

Australia: 4 Annis Komninis St., 2nd Floor (HC); *High Commissioner:* LESLIE WILSON JOHNSON, C.B.E.

Austria: Athens, Greece (E).

Barbados: London, England (HC).

Belgium: Beirut, Lebanon (E).

Brazil: Tel-Aviv, Israel (E).

Bulgaria: 15 St. Paul St. (E); *Ambassador:* MARIN ILIEV BANGUIEV.

Canada: Tel-Aviv, Israel (HC).

China, People's Republic: 27 Clementos St., P.O.B. 4531 (E); *Ambassador:* TSAO CHIH.

Colombia: Jerusalem, Israel (E).

Cuba: Halkydonos 9, Lycavitos (E); *Ambassador:* FERMIN RODRÍGUEZ PAZ.

Czechoslovakia: 39 Agapinoros St. (E); *Ambassador:* JOSEF HEJC.

Denmark: 3 Gregori Afxentiou St.

Egypt: 3 Egypt Ave., P.O.B. 1742 (E); *Ambassador:* (vacant).

Finland: Tel-Aviv, Israel (E).

France: 6 Ploutarchou St., Engomi, P.O.B. 1671 (E); *Ambassador:* PHILIPPE OLIVIER.

German Democratic Republic: 115 Prodromos St. (E); *Ambassador:* KARL WILDAU.

Germany, Federal Republic: 10 Nikitaras St., P.O.B. 1795 (E); *Ambassador:* GERHARD SÖHNKE.

Greece: 8/10 Byron Ave., P.O.B. 1799 (E); *Ambassador:* MIHALIS C. DOUNTAS.

Hungary: Athens, Greece (E).

India: Beirut, Lebanon (HC).

Iraq: Beirut, Lebanon (E).

Israel: 44 Archbishop Makarios III Ave., P.O.B. 1049 (E); *Ambassador:* NAHUM ESHKOL.

Italy: 5 Dinokratos St., Lycavitos, P.O.B. 1452 (E); *Ambassador:* GIORGIO STEA ANTONINI.

Japan: Beirut, Lebanon (E).

Lebanon: 1 Queen Olga St., P.O.B. 1924 (E); *Ambassador.* MUNIR TAKIEDDINE.

Libya: 9A Kyranoros St., P.O.B. 3669 (E); *Chargé d'affaires a.i.:* YOUSEF O. AZZABI.

Malta: London, England (HC).

Mexico: Beirut, Lebanon (E).

Netherlands: Beirut, Lebanon (E).

Nigeria: Rome, Italy (HC).

Norway: Tel-Aviv, Israel (E).

Pakistan: Beirut, Lebanon (E).

Poland: 5 Svoronou St., P.O.B. 1952 (E); *Chargé d'affaires a.i.:* WLADYSŁAW WIECZOREK.

Portugal: Rome, Italy (E).

Romania: 10 Dramas St. (E); *Chargé d'affaires a.i.:* ION ANGHEL.

Spain: Damascus, Syria (E).

Sweden: Cairo, Egypt (E).

Switzerland: Tel-Aviv, Israel (E).

Syria: Corner Androcleous and Thoukidides Sts., P.O.B. 1891 (E); *Chargé d'affaires a.i.:* ZOUHEIR SHALABI.

Turkey: 10 Server Somuncuoğlu St. (E); *Chargé d'affaires:* CANDEMIR ÖNHON.

U.S.S.R.: 4 Gladstone St., P.O.B. 1845 (E); *Ambassador:* SERGEY T. ASTAVIN.

United Kingdom: Alexander Pallis St. (HC); *High Commissioner:* PEREGRINE ALEXANDER RHODES, C.M.G.

U.S.A.: Dositheon St. and Therissos St. (E); *Ambassador:* GALEN STONE.

Vatican: 2 Victoria Rd., P.O.B. 1964 (Apostolic Nunciature); *Apostolic Pro-Nuncio:* WILLIAM ALQUIN CAREW.

Yugoslavia: 2 Vasilissis Olgas St. (E); *Chargé d'affaires (a.i.):* DANILO BOSIC.

Cyprus also has diplomatic relations with the Bahamas, Burundi, Chile, Ethiopia, Ghana, Iceland, the Ivory Coast, Kuwait, Mongolia, New Zealand, Papua New Guinea, Seychelles, Somalia, Uganda, Uruguay, Zaire and Zambia.

JUDICIAL SYSTEM

Supreme Court: Nicosia.

President: Hon. Mr. Justice M. A. Triantafyllides.

Judges: Hon. Mr. Justice L. N. Loizou, Hon. Mr. Justice T. Hadjian-astassiou, Hon. Mr. Justice A. N. Loizou, Hon. Mr. Justice Y. Ch. Malachtos, Hon. Mr. Justice D. Gr. Demetriades, Hon Mr. Justice L. Savvides.

The Constitution of 1960 provided for a separate Supreme Constitutional Court and High Court but in 1964, in view of the resignation of their neutral Presidents, these were amalgamated to form a single Supreme Court.

The Supreme Court is the final appellate court in the Republic and the final adjudicator in matters of constitutional and administrative law, including recourses on conflict of competence between state organs on questions of the constitutionality of laws, etc. It deals with appeals from Assize Courts and District Courts as well as from the decisions of its own single judges when exercising original jurisdiction in certain matters such as prerogative orders of *habeas corpus*, *mandamus*, *certiorari*, etc., and in admiralty and certain matrimonial causes.

Assize Courts and District Courts:

As required by the Constitution a law was passed in 1960 providing for the establishment, jurisdiction and powers of courts of civil and criminal jurisdiction, i.e. of six District Courts and six Assize Courts.

Ecclesiastical Courts:

There are seven Orthodox Church tribunals having exclusive jurisdiction in matrimonial causes between members of the Greek Orthodox Church. Appeals go from these tribunals to the appellate tribunal of the Church.

Supreme Council of Judicature: Nicosia.

The Supreme Council of Judicature is composed of the Attorney-General, the President and Judges of the Supreme Court.

It is responsible for the appointment, promotion, transfer, etc., of the judges exercising civil and criminal jurisdiction in the District Courts and the Assize Courts.

"TURKISH FEDERATED STATE OF CYPRUS"

The Turkish intervention in Cyprus in July 1974 saw the establishment of a separate area in northern Cyprus under the control of the Autonomous Turkish Cypriot Administration with a Council of Ministers, and separate judicial, financial, military and educational machinery serving the Turkish community.

On February 13th, 1975, the Turkish-occupied zone of Cyprus was declared the "Turkish Federated State of Cyprus" and Rauf Denktaş elected President. At the second joint meeting held by the Executive Council and Legislative Assembly of the Autonomous Turkish Cypriot Administration it was decided to set up a Constituent Assembly which would prepare a Constitution for the "Turkish Federated State of Cyprus" within 45 days. This constitution, which was approved by the Turkish Cypriot population in a referendum held on June 8th, 1975, is regarded by the Turkish Cypriots as a first step towards a federal republic of Cyprus. The main provisions of the constitution are summarized below.

The "Turkish Federated State of Cyprus" is a democratic, secular republic based on the principles of social justice and the rule of law. It shall exercise only those functions which fall outside the powers and functions expressly given to the [proposed] Federal Republic of Cyprus. Necessary amendments shall be made to the constitution of the "Turkish Federated State of Cyprus" when the constitution of the Federal Republic comes into force. The official language is Turkish.

Legislative power is vested in a Legislative Assembly, composed of 40 deputies, elected by universal suffrage for a period of five years.

The President is Head of State and is elected by universal suffrage for a period of five years. No person may be elected President for more than two consecutive terms.

The Council of Ministers shall be composed of a Prime Minister and 10 Ministers.

Judicial power is exercised through independent courts. Other provisions cover such matters as the rehabilitation of refugees, property rights outside the "Turkish Federated State", protection of coasts, social insurance, the rights and duties of citizens, etc.

The "Turkish Federated State of Cyprus" has neither sought nor received international recognition as an independent state, and in March 1975 the UN Security Council adopted a resolution regretting its creation.

Vice-President of the Republic and President of the "Turkish Federated State of Cyprus": Rauf R. Denktaş.

CABINET

(*June* 1979)

Prime Minister: Mustafa Çağatay.

Minister of Foreign Affairs, Defence and Tourism: Dr. Kenan Atakol.

Minister of Economy and Finance: Hakki Atun.

Minister of Construction and Communications: Erdinc Gürçağ.

Minister of Education, Culture and Youth: Kubilay Çaydamli.

Minister of Agriculture, Natural Resources and Energy: Irsen Küçük.

Minister of Trade, Industry and Co-operatives: Taşkent Atasayan.

Minister of Health and Welfare Services: Dr. Ali Atun.

Minister of the Interior and Housing: Recep Gurler.

LEGISLATIVE ASSEMBLY

The forty-member Assembly replaced the former Constituent Assembly in June 1976. It is the only body empowered by the Constitution to exercise the Federated State's legislative functions. The 40 deputies are elected for a period of five years.

Speaker: Oguz Ramadan Korhan.

Deputy Speaker: Şemsi Kazim.

ELECTION JUNE 1976

PARTY	SEATS*
National Unity	29
Communal Liberation . . .	6
Republican Turkish . . .	2
Populist	2
Independent	1
TOTAL	40

* Resignations had brought the balance of seats in June 1979 to National Unity Party 21, Communal Liberation 8, Democratic People's 6, Republican Turksih 2, Populist 1, Independents 2.

POLITICAL PARTIES

Cumhuriyetçi Türk Partisi (*Republican Turkish Party*): Mirata Flats, First Floor, Osman Pasha Avenue, Nicosia; f. 1970 by members of the Turkish community in Cyprus; socialist principles with labour stand; district organizations at Famagusta, Kyrenia, Morphou and Nicosia; Leader ÖZKER ÖZGÜR.

Ulusal Birlik Partisi (*National Unity Party*): Nicosia; f. 1975; party of Government; based on Atatürk's reforms, social justice and peaceful co-existence in an independent, bi-zonal, federal state of Cyprus; Leader MUSTAFA ÇAĞATAY; Gen. Sec. IRSEN KÜÇÜK.

Halkçı Party (*The Populist Party*): Nicosia; f. 1975; party programme follows rigid social democratic principles; Leader ALPER Y. ORHON.

Toplumcu Kurtulus Partisi (*Communal Liberation Party*): Nicosia; f. 1976; based on Atatürk's reforms, social democratic principles, social justice and peaceful co-existence in an independent, bi-zonal, federal state of Cyprus free of British bases; Leader ALPAY DURDURAN.

Demokratic Halk Partisi (*Democratic People's Party*): Nicosia; f. 1979; based on social democratic principles; nationalist, revolutionist and secular; aims at bi-zonal, bi-communal Federal Republic of Cyprus; Leader NEJAT KONUK.

JUDICIAL SYSTEM

Supreme Council of Judicature:

The Supreme Council of Judicature, composed of the President and Judges of the Supreme Court, a retired member of the Supreme Court, the Attorney-General of the "Turkish Federated State of Cyprus" and the elected President of the Cyprus Turkish Bar, is responsible for the appointment, promotion, transfer, leave and discipline of all judges in accordance with the powers vested by the Constitution of the "Turkish Federated State of Cyprus". The appointment of the President and judges of the Supreme Court must be approved by the President of the "Turkish Federated State of Cyprus".

Supreme Court:

President: Hon. Mr. Justice ÜLFET EMIN.

Judges: Hon. Justices AHMED İZZET, ŞAKİR SIDKI İLKAY, SALİH DAYIOĞLU, ERGIN SALÂHI.

In the areas governed by the "Turkish Federated State of Cyprus" the Supreme Court exercises the powers vested in the Supreme Council of Judicature and the Supreme Court by the 1960 Constitution. It is the final appellate court dealing with appeals from Assize and District Courts and from the decisions of its own judges when exercising original jurisdiction. It is the final adjudicator in matters of constitutional and administrative law.

Assize Courts and District Courts:

The courts of civil and criminal jurisdiction, established by the law of 1960, amended by the Constitution of the "Turkish Federated State".

Turkish Communal Courts:

Civil disputes relating to the personal status of members of the Turkish community are dealt with by two Communal Courts. There is also a communal appellate court to which appeals may be made from the courts of first instance.

BRITISH SOVEREIGN BASE AREAS

AKROTIRI and DHEKELIA

Headquarters at Episkopi, British Forces Post Office 53.

Administrator: Maj.-Gen. W. R. TAYLOR.

Chief Officer of Administration: P. G. ADAMS, D.F.C.

Senior Judge of Senior Judge's Court: W. A. SIME, M.B.E., Q.C.

Resident Judge of Judge's Court: J. K. HAVERS, O.B.E., Q.C.

Under the Cyprus Act 1960, the United Kingdom retained sovereignty in two sovereign base areas and this was recognized in the Treaty of Establishment signed between the U.K., Greece, Turkey and the Republic of Cyprus in August 1960. The base areas cover 99 square miles. The Treaty also conferred on Britain certain rights within the Republic, including rights of movement and the use of specified training areas.

UNITED NATIONS PEACE-KEEPING FORCE IN CYPRUS

(UNFICYP)

Headquarters at Nicosia

Set up for three months in March 1964 (subsequently extended at intervals of three or six months) to keep the peace between the Greek and Turkish communities and help to solve outstanding issues between them.

Commander: Maj.-Gen. JAMES QUINN (Ireland).

Special Representative of the UN Secretary-General: REINALDO GALINDO-POHL (El Salvador).

See page 144.

RELIGION

Greeks form 80 per cent of the population and most of them belong to the Orthodox Church. Most Turks (18 per cent of the population) are Muslims.

Greek Orthodox	449,000
Muslims	104,000
Armenian Apostolic	3,500
Maronite	3,000
Anglican, Roman Catholic, Other	18,000

(1960 census)

The Orthodox Church of Cyprus: Archbishopric of Cyprus, P.O.B. 1130, Nicosia; f. 45 A.D.; the Autocephalous Orthodox Church of Cyprus is part of the Eastern Orthodox Church; the Church is independent, and the Archbishop, who is also the Ethnarch (national leader of the Greek community), is elected by universal suffrage; 500,000 members.

Archbishop of Nova Justiniana and all Cyprus: Archbishop CHRYSOSTOMOS.

Metropolitan of Paphos: Bishop CHRYSOSTOMOS.
Metropolitan of Kitium: Bishop CHRYSOSTOMOS.
Metropolitan of Kyrenia: Bishop GREGORIOS.
Metropolitan of Limassol: Bishop CHRYSANTHOS.
Metropolitan of Morphou: Bishop CHRYSANTHOS.
Suffragan Bishop of Salamis: Bishop BARNABAS.

Islam: Most of the adherents in Cyprus are Sunnis of the Hanafi Sect. The religious head of the Muslim community is the Mufti.

The Mufti of Cyprus: Dr. MUSTAFA RIFAT YÜCELTEN, P.O.B. 142, Nicosia, Mersin 10, Turkey.

Roman Catholic Church: Archbishopric of Cyprus of the Maronite rite, subject to the Sacred Congregation for the Oriental Churches; 108 parishes, 54 educational institutes, 38 resident priests, 95,000 Catholics (1977).

Archbishop of Cyprus: Mgr. ELIE FARAH, Maronite Archbishopric, Antelias, Lebanon (winter); Cornet-Chahouane, Lebanon (summer).

Other Churches: Armenian Apostolic and Church of England.

THE PRESS

DAILIES

Agon (*Struggle*): Tryfonos Bldg., Eleftherias Sq., P.O.B. 1417, Nicosia; f. 1964; morning; Greek; Independent; Owner and Editor N. KOSHIS; circ. 12,000.

Apogevmatini (*Afternoon*): Grivas Dighenis Ave., P.O.B. 1094, Nicosia; f. 1972; afternoon; Greek; pro-Government; Editor M. HADJIEFTHYMIOU; circ. 5,000.

Bozkurt (*Grey Wolf*): 142 Kyrenia St., Nicosia, Mersin 10, Turkey; f. 1951; morning; Turkish; Independent; Editor SADI CEMAL; circ. 5,000.

Cyprus Mail: P.O.B. 1144, 24 Vasiliou Voulgaroktonos St., Nicosia; f. 1945; English; Independent; Editor C. H. W. GOULT; circ. 5,740.

Demokratiko Virna: 13 Andreadis Demitriou St., Nicosia; extreme right-wing opposition.

Eleftheri Kypros (*Free Cyprus*): 6 Themistocli Thervi St., Nicosia; f. 1978; organ of Democratic Party; Dir. G. FILIS.

Halkin Sesi (*Voice of the People*): 172 Kyrenia St., Nicosia, Mersin 10, Turkey; f. 1942; morning; Independent Turkish Nationalist; Editor AKAY CEMAL; circ. 5,000.

Haravghi (*Dawn*): P.O.B. 1556, 8 Akamandos St., Nicosia; f. 1956; Greek; organ of AKEL (Communist Party); Editor GEORGE SAVVIDES; circ. 13,500.

Kurtulush: Atatürk Meydani, Nicosia, Mersin 10, Turkey; Turkish.

Makhi (*Battle*): P.O.B. 1105, Grivas Dighenis Ave., Nicosia; f. 1960; morning; Greek; circ. 12,000.

Mesimviri: 4 Costis Palamas St., Nicosia; Greek.

News Bulletin: c/o T.F.S.C. Public Information Office, Mersin 10, Turkey; f. 1963; morning; English; published by Public Information Office of "Turkish Federated State of Cyprus"; five times a week; circ. 1,500.

Phileleftheros (*Liberal*): Tryfonos Bldg., P.O.B. 1094, Nicosia; nationalist; Greek; morning; Chief Editor CHR. KATSAMBAS; circ. 20,000.

Simerini (*Today*): P.O.B. 1836, Princess Zena Bldg., Nicosia; f. 1976; morning; Greek; independent; Editorial Committee.

Ta Nea (*The News*): 23B Constantine Palaelogos Ave., P.O.B. 1064, Nicosia; f. 1970; Greek; organ of EDEK party; morning; Editor TAKIS KOUNNAFIS; circ. 4,000.

Yeni Duzen: 18 Belig Pasha St., Nicosia, Mersin 10, Turkey.

Zaman (*Time*): 43 Yediler St., Nicosia, Mersin 10, Turkey; f. 1973; supports National Unity Party; Chief Editor RAIF DENKTAŞ; circ. 3,000.

WEEKLIES

Alithia (*Truth*): P.O.B. 1965, Arsinoe St. (Manglis Bldg.), Nicosia; f. 1951; Greek; Pancyprian; Liberal; Editor ANTONIOS PHARMAKIDES; circ. 14,500.

Allaghi (*Change*): Aura Bldg., P.O.B. 1209, Nicosia; Greek.

Ammokhostos: 10 Florinis St., P.O.B. 3561, Famagusta; Greek.

Anexartitos (*Independent*): Tryphonos Bldg., Eleftherias Sq., Nicosia; f. 1974; Greek; independent socialist; Dir. RENOS PRENTZAS; circ. 7,500.

Cyprus Bulletin: Nicosia; f. 1964; Arabic, English, French, German, Greek, Russian, Spanish, Turkish; published by the Cyprus Public Information Office; circ. 40,000.

Cyprus News: 29 Ekim St. No. 1, Nicosia, Mersin 10, Turkey; f. 1975; English; Editor TREVOR TAYLOR; circ. 1,000.

Dimokratia (*Democracy*): P.O.B. 1963, Nicosia; f. 1975; pro-Government; organ of AKEL Party; Dir. K. PARTASIDES; circ. 8,000.

Dimocratiki: Grivas Dighenis Ave., Nicosia; Greek; pro-Government; Editor ANTHOS LYKAVGHIS.

Eleftherotis (*Liberator*): 26 Apollo St., Nicosia; f. 1975; independent; Dir. K. KALATHAS.

Ergatiki Phoni (*Workers' Voice*): 35 Zenon St., Limassol; f. 1946; Greek; organ of Cyprus Workers' Confederation; Editor CHRISTODOULOS MICHAELIDES; circ. 5,500.

Ergatiko Vima (*Workers' Tribune*): P.O.B. 1885, Archermos St. 31–35, Nicosia; f. 1956; Greek; organ of the Pancyprian Federation of Labour; Editor-in-Chief ZAKHARIAS PHILIPPIDES; circ. 8,300.

Kypros (*Cyprus*): P.O.B. 1491, 10 Apostolos Varnavas St., Nicosia; f. 1952; Greek; non-party; circ. 12,000; Editor J. KYRIAKIDIS.

Middle East Economic Survey: Middle East Research and Publishing Centre, P.O.B. 4940, Nicosia; f. 1957; oil topics; Editor and Publr. FUAD W. ITAYIM.

Official Gazette: Printing Office of the Republic of Cyprus, Nicosia; f. 1960; Greek; published by the Government of the Republic of Cyprus.

Phakos Tis Epikerotitos (*Mirror of Current Events*): Manglis Mansions, 1st Floor, No. 13, Nicosia; Greek; independent; Editor PHAEDON KOTSONIS.

Radio News: Maglis Bldg., 23 Bouboulius St., Strovolos, Nicosia.

Satiriki (*Satirical*): 23 Bouboulinas St., Nicosia; Greek; Dir. G. MAVROGENIS.

Tharros (*Courage*): P.O.B. 1105, Grivas Dighenis Ave., Nicosia; f. 1961; Greek; Independent; circ. 9,200.

PERIODICALS

Apostolos Barnabas: Archbishopic of Cyprus, Nicosia; monthly; organ of the Orthodox Church of Cyprus; Dir. Dr. ANDREAS N. MITSIDES; circ. 1,200.

Countryman: Nicosia; f. 1943; every two months; Greek; published by the Cyprus Public Information Office; circ. 5,000.

Cyprus Medical Journal: P.O.B. 93, Nicosia; f. 1947; monthly; English and Greek; Editor Dr. G. N. MARANGOS.

Cyprus Today: c/o Ministry of Education, Nicosia; f. 1963; every two months; cultural and information review of the Ministry of Education; published and distributed by Public Information Office; English; free of charge; Chair. Editorial Board P. SERGHIS; circ. 12,000.

Dimossios Ypallilos: 2 Andreas Demetriou St., Nicosia; fortnightly; published by the Cyprus Civil Servants' Trade Union; circ. 8,000.

Eğitim Bülteni (*Education Bulletin*): Nicosia; f. 1972; monthly; Turkish; published by Ministry of Education of the "Turkish Federated State of Cyprus"; circ. 3,000.

International Crude Oil and Product Prices: Middle East Petroleum and Economic Publications, P.O.B. 4940, Nicosia; f. 1971; twice yearly review and analysis of oil price trends in world markets; Publisher FUAD W. ITAYIM.

Kooperatif (*Co-operative*): Nicosia; f. 1970; monthly; Turkish; published by Department of Co-operative Development of the "Turkish Federated State of Cyprus"; circ. 2,000.

Kypriacos Logos: 10 Kimonos St., Engomi, Nicosia; f. 1969; every two months; Editor P. STYLIANOY; circ. 6,000.

Mathitiki Estia (*Student Hearth*): Pancyprian Gymnasium, Nicosia; f. 1950; annually; Greek; organ of the Pancyprian Gymnasium students; Editor STELLA DYMIOTOU.

Nea Epochi: 11 Stasandrou St., P.O.B. 1581, Nicosia; f. 1959; every two months; Greek; literary material; Editor ACHILLEAS PYLIOTIS; circ. 2,500.

Öğretmen (*Teacher*): Nicosia; f. 1972; monthly; Turkish; organ of Cyprus Turkish Secondary Schools Teachers Asscn.; circ. 1,200.

Paediki Hara: 18 Archbishop Makarios III Ave., Nicosia; monthly; for students; published by the Pancyprian Union of Greek Teachers; Editor ANDREAS P. POLYDOREOU; circ. 15,000.

Panta Embros: P.O.B. 1156, Nicosia; monthly; published by the Cyprus Scouts' Association; Greek; circ. 3,700.

Pnevmatiki Kypzos: Nicosia; f. 1960; monthly; Greek; literary.

Radio Programme: Cyprus Broadcasting Corpn., P.O.B. 4824, Nicosia; fortnightly; published by the CBCr radio and TV programme news; Script Superviso; TAKIS G. MAGOS; circ. 25,000.

Synergatistis (*The Co-operator*): P.O.B. 4537, Nicosia; f. 1961; monthly magazine; Greek; official organ of the Pancyprian Confederation of Co-operatives; Editor G. I. PHOTIOU; circ. 4,300.

Trapezikos: P.O.B. 1235, Nicosia; f. 1960; bank employees' magazine; Greek; monthly; Editor G. S. MICHAELIDES; circ. 17,500.

Türk Sen (*Turkish Trade Unions*): 7–7A Şehit Mehmet R. Hüseyin Sok., P.O.B. 829, Nicosia; f. 1971; weekly; Turkish; organ of Cyprus Turkish Trade Unions Federation; circ. 5,000.

NEWS AGENCIES

Cyprus News Agency: c/o Director-General, Cyprus Broadcasting Corpn., Nicosia; f. 1976; Greek; Dir. ANDREAS CHRISTOFIDES.

FOREIGN BUREAUX

Agentstvo Pechati Novosti (APN) (*U.S.S.R.*): Kreontos 6, P.O.B. 4051, Nicosia; Rep. GAREGIN SHAHOUNIAN.

Associated Press (AP) (*U.S.A.*): P.O.B. 4853, Andreas Zakos St. 4, Engomi, Nicosia; Rep. Mr. DOELLING.

Athenagence (Athens News Agency) (*Greece*): Andreas Patsalides 10, Engomi; Rep. GEORGE LEONIDAS.

Československá tisková kancelář (ČTK) (*Czechoslovakia*): 30 Evagoros Pallikarides St., Strovolos; Rep. STAVROS ANGELIDES.

Deutsche Presse Agentur (dpa) (*Federal Republic of Germany*): Daidalon 9, Nicosia; Rep. ANDREAS LYKAVGIS.

EastMed News (Cyprus) and (Overseas) (*U.K. and U.S.A.*): P.O.B. 3779, Nicosia; representing BBC Radio and TV, Reuters (U.K.), *The Guardian* (U.K.), NBC Radio and TV (U.S.A.), *Middle East Magazine* (U.K.), *Washington Post* and *Los Angeles Times* (U.S.A.); Dirs. CHRIS DRAKE, M.B.E., and JOHN BIERMAN.

Iraqi News Agency: P.O.B. 1098, Nicosia; Rep. CHRISTAKIS KATSAMBAS.

Novinska Agencija Tanjug (*Yugoslavia*): Demophon St. 10, Nicosia; Rep. MANO ALKOVIC.

Polska Agencja Prasowa (PAP) (*Poland*): Prodromos St. 24, P.O.B. 2373, Nicosia; Rep. MICHALAKIS PANTELIDES.

Prensa Latina (*Cuba*): Nicodemos Mylonas 21A, Nicosia; Rep. ANDREAS KANNAOUROS.

Telegrafnoye Agentstvo Sovietskovo Soyuza (TASS) (*U.S.S.R.*): 3 Philellinon St., Nicosia; Rep. VLADISLAV CHERTENKOV.

United Press International (UPI) (*U.S.A.*): Flat 42, 40 Nikis St., Nicosia; Rep. ANDREAS HADJIPAPAS.

PUBLISHER

MAM: P.O.B. 1722, Nicosia; specializes in publications on Cyprus and international organizations and by Cypriot authors.

RADIO AND TELEVISION

Cyprus Broadcasting Corporation: P.O.B. 4824, Nicosia; Chair. ANDREAS PHILIPPOU; Dir.-Gen. A. N. CHRISTOFIDES; Deputy Dir.-Gen. I. HADJIOSSIF; Chief Engineer P. ASTREOS; Head of Radio Programmes P. IOANNIDES (acting), Head of Television Programmes CH. PAPADOPOULOS; publ. *Radio Programme*.

Radio: f. 1952; programmes in Greek, Turkish, English, Arabic and Armenian; two medium wave transmitters of 20 kW. in Nicosia, relay stations at Paphos and Limassol, two 20 kW. VHF transmitters on Mount Olympus; international service in English and Arabic; relays Radio Monte Carlo to the Middle East from a station on Cape Greco.

Television: f. 1957; one Band III 40/8 kW transmitter on Mount Olympus with 25 transposer stations.

Radio Bayrak (B.R.T.): Atatürk Sq., Nicosia; f. 1963; Turkish Cypriot State Radio; home service in Turkish, overseas services in Turkish, Greek and English; broadcasts 18 hours a day; Dr.-Gen. HAKKI SÜHA; Dir. of Programmes MEHMET FEHMİ.

Bayrak TV: f. 1976; transmits programmes in Turkish, Greek and English on three channels; Gen. Dir. HARID FEDAİL; Programme Dir. UNER ULUTUG.

British Forces Broadcasting Service, Cyprus: British Forces Post Office 58; broadcasts continuously in English; VHF and medium wave; second channel to begin in 1979; Station Controller K.U.P. DOHERTY; Engineer-in-Charge M. E. TOWNLEY; publ. *Listen Out* (weekly).

Türkiye Radyo Televizyon (T.R.T.): Turkish television programmes are transmitted to the Turkish sector of Cyprus.

In December 1976, in the Government-controlled areas, 96,500 households possessed one or more radio receivers and 67,850 possessed television receivers.

FINANCE

(br.=branch; cap.=capital; p.u.=paid up; dep.=deposits; m.=million; amounts in Cyprus pounds)

BANKING

CENTRAL BANK

Central Bank of Cyprus: P.O.B. 1087, 36 Metochiou St.. Nicosia; f. 1963; became the Bank of Issue in 1963; cap p.u. £100,000; dep. £88.1m. (Dec. 1978); Gov. C. C. STEPHANI; publs. *Report* (annual), *Bulletin* (quarterly),

CYPRIOT BANKS

Bank of Cyprus Ltd.: P.O.B. 1472, 86-90 Phaneromeni St., Nicosia; f. 1899; cap. p.u. £6m.; dep. £133.3m. (Dec. 1977); Gov. MICHAEL COLOCASSIDES; Chair. M. S. SAVIDES; 46 branches throughout Cyprus.

Co-operative Central Bank Ltd.: P.O.B. 4537, Nicosia; f. 1938; banking and credit facilities to member societies; Sec.-Man. R. CLERIDES.

Cyprus Popular Bank Ltd.: P.O.B. 2032, Archbishop Makarios III Avenue, Nicosia; f. 1901; cap. p.u £1.5m.; dep. £34.3 (Dec. 1977); Chair. EVAGORAS C. LANITIS; Gen. Man. KIKIS N. LAZARIDES; 21 brs.

Cyprus Turkish Co-operative Central Bank, Ltd.: P.O.B. 1861, Mahmout Pasha St., Nicosia; banking and credit facilities to member societies, bodies and individuals; Gen. Man. MEHMET ESHREF.

Hellenic Bank Ltd.: 92 Dhigenis Akritas Ave., P.O.B. 4747, Nicosia; f. 1976; affiliated to Bank of America N.T. and S.A.; cap. p.u. £1.5m.; dep £15m. (Dec. 1977); Chair. P. L. PASCHALIDES; Gen. Man. P. C. GHALANOS; 9 brs.

Kıbrıs Kredi Bankası (*Cyprus Credit Bank*): Nicosia, Mersin 10, Turkey; f. 1978; cap. p.u. £1m.; Chair. MACIT FERDI.

Turkish Bank Ltd.: 92 Kyrenia St., Nicosia; f. 1901; cap. p.u. £1.01m. (1978); dep. £21.4m. (Dec. 1978); Chair. UMIT S. ONAN; Gen. Man. KIAMURAN M. JELALEDDIN; 10 brs.

DEVELOPMENT BANK

Cyprus Development Bank, Ltd.: P.O.B. 1415, Nicosia; f. 1963; cap. p.u. £1m.; provides medium and long term loans for productive investments, particularly in manufacturing and processing industries, tourism and agriculture, and technical, managerial and administrative assistance and advice; performs related economic and technical research; Chair. MIKIS TSIAKKAS; Gen. Man. JOHN G. JONANNIDES; Asst. Gen. Man. L. D. SPARSIS.

FOREIGN BANKS

Barclays Bank International Ltd.: P.O.B. 2081, Eleftheria Sq., Nicosia; Local Dir. D. G. FOGDEN; 19 brs.

The Chartered Bank: P.O.B. 1047, Corner of Makarios III and Evagoras Aves., Nicosia; Cyprus Man. J. C. HENDERSON; 10 brs.

Grindlays Bank Ltd.: 11-13 Makarios III Ave., P.O.B. 2069, Nicosia; Gen. Man. in Cyprus K. O. DANCEY; 21 brs.

Lombard Banking (Cyprus) Ltd.: P.O.B. 1661, Mitsis Bldg., Eleftheria Square, Nicosia; f. 1960; owns a subsidiary, Lombard (Cyprus) Ltd., specializing in hire purchase business; Man. Dir. H. M. KEHEYAN; 7 brs.

National Bank of Greece, S.A.: P.O.B. 1191, 36 Makarios III Ave., Nicosia; Regional Man. ARMANDOS KYRIAKIS; 11 brs.

Türkiye Cumhuriyeti Ziraat Bankası (*Agricultural Bank of Turkey*): Ankara, Turkey; Cyprus branch Kyrenia; Man. DOĞAN ERDOĞAN; acts as central bank for Turkish-occupied area of Cyprus.

Türkiye İş Bankası: 9 Kyrenia St., Nicosia; br. at Famagusta and Kyrenia.

INSURANCE

Office of the Superintendent of Insurance: 35 Dem. Severis Ave., Nicosia; f. 1969 to control insurance companies and agents in Cyprus.

Commercial Union Assurance (Cyprus) Ltd.: 42E Archbishop Makarios Ave., P.O.B. 1312, Nicosia; f. 1974; Chair. J. CHRISTOPHIDES; Gen. Man. G. GEORGALLIDES.

The General Insurance Company of Cyprus Ltd.: 24 Lycourgou St., P.O.B. 1668, Nicosia; f. 1951; Chair. M. S. SAVVIDES; Gen. Man. S. SOPHOCLEOUS.

Minerva Insurance Co. Ltd.: 1B Naxou St., P.O.B. 3554, Nicosia.

Universal Life Insurance Company Ltd.: Palace Princess Zena de Tyra, P.O.B. 1270, Nicosia; f. 1970; Gen. Man. ANDREAS GEORGHIOU; Life Man. ZENIOS DEMETRIOU.

About 35 foreign insurance companies operate in Cyprus.

TRADE AND INDUSTRY

CHAMBERS OF COMMERCE

Cyprus Chamber of Commerce and Industry: Evagoras Ave., Hadjisavva Bldg. (6th Floor), P.O.B. 1455, Nicosia; Pres. MICHEL S. SAVIDES; Vice-Pres. GEORGE ROLOGIS, CHR. MAVROUDES; Sec.-Gen. P. LOIZIDES; 2,000 members, 17 affiliated trade associations; publ. *Directory, Monthly Information Bulletin.*

Famagusta Chamber of Commerce and Industry: P.O.B. 777, Famagusta; temporary address: P.O.B. 347, Limassol; Pres. PHANOS N. EPIPHANIOU; Vice-Pres. PHOTOS LORDOS; Sec.-Gen. PAUL VANEZIS.

Larnaca Chamber of Commerce and Industry: 33 King Paul's Sq., Flat No. 22, 2nd Floor, P.O.B. 287, Larnaca; Pres. Dr. A. FRANCIS; Vice-Pres. KYPROS ECONOMIDES.

Limassol Chamber of Commerce and Industry: Spyros Araouzos St., P.O.B. 347, Limassol; Pres. KYRIACOS HAMBOULLAS; Vice-Pres. NICOS ROSSOS.

Nicosia Chamber of Commerce and Industry: Evagoras Ave., Hadjisavva Building, P.O.B. 1455, Nicosia; Pres. A. AVRAAMIDES; Vice-Pres. G. VASILIOU.

Paphos Chamber of Commerce and Industry: 14–34 Nicolaou Ellina St., P.O.B. 61, Paphos; Pres. LOIZOS M. HAVOUZARIS; Vice-Pres. POLIDEFKIS GEORGIOU.

Turkish Cypriot Chamber of Commerce: 1 Cengiz St., Köşklüciftlik, P.O.B. 718, Nicosia; Pres. R. MANYERA; Sec.-Gen. SALÂHI KARAHASAN.

EMPLOYERS' ORGANIZATIONS

Cyprus Employers' Federation: Charalambides Bldg., Grivas-Dhigenis Ave., P.O.B. 1657, Nicosia; f. 1960; 12 member Trade Associations, 310 direct and 550 indirect mems.; Dir.-Gen. ANT. PIERIDES; Chair. RENOS SOLOMIDES; publ. *Newsletter-Bulletin* (monthly).

There are also 13 independent employers' associations, among the largest of which are:

Cyprus Building Contractors' Association: 2 Voulgari St., Nicosia; 256 mems.; Sec. G. PARASKEVAIDES.

Employers' Union of Car Owners: 1 Menandrou St., Nicosia; 1,636 mems. Gen. Sec. GEORGE TOUMAZIS.

Limassol Enterprises Contractors' Association: 18 Ipiros St., Limassol; 66 mems.; Sec. E. CONSTANTINOU.

TRADE UNIONS

Cyprus Civil Servants' Trade Union: 2 Andreas Demetriou St., Nicosia; f. 1949, registered 1966; restricted to persons in the civil employment of the Govt.; 6 brs. with a total membership of 9,000; Pres. A. PAPANASTASSIOU; Gen. Sec. G. IACOVOU; publ. *Dimossios Ypallilos* (Public Servant), fortnightly.

Demokratiki Ergatiki Omospondia Kyprou (*Democratic Labour Federation of Cyprus*): 10 Kimonos St., Engomi, Nicosia; f. 1962; 4 unions with a total membership of 3,500; Hon. Pres. PETROS STYLIANOU; Gen. Sec. EVANGELOS PANAYIOTOU.

Kıbrıs Türk Işçi Sendikalari Federasyonu (*Turkish Cypriot Trade Unions Federation*): Sehit Mehmet R. Hüseyin Sok., P.O.B. 829, Nicosia, Mersin 10, Turkey; f. 1954, registered 1955; 15 unions with a total membership of 13,000; affiliated to ICFTU and the Federation of Trade Unions of Turkey; Pres. NECATI TASKIN; publ. *Türk Sen* (Turkish Trade Unions), weekly.

Pankypria Ergatiki Omospondia (*Pancyprian Federation of Labour*): P.O.B. 1885, 31-35 Archermos St., Nicosia; f. 1946, registered 1947; previously the Pancyprian Trade Union Committee f. 1941, dissolved 1946; 11 unions and 212 brs. with a total membership of 52,047; affiliated to the World Federation of Trade Unions; Gen. Sec. A. ZIARTIDES; publ. *Ergatiko Vima* (Workers' Forum), weekly.

Pankyprios Omospondia Anexartition Syntechnion (*Pancyprian Federation of Independent Trade Unions*): 1 Menadrou St., Nicosia; f. 1956, registered 1957; has no political orientations; 7 unions with a total membership of 780; Pres. COSTAS ANTONIADES; Gen. Sec. KYRIACOS NATHANAEL.

Synomospondia Ergaton Kyprou (*Cyprus Workers' Confederation*): 23 Athanasiou Diakou St., P.O.B. 5018, Engomi, Nicosia; f. 1944, registered 1950; 7 Federations, 5 Labour Centres, 47 unions, 12 branches with a total membership of 34,479; affiliated to the Greek Confederation of Labour and the ICFTU; Gen. Sec. MICHAEL IOANNOU; publ. *Ergatiki Phoni* (Workers' Voice), weekly.

In December 1975, there were 24 employers' associations with a total membership of 2,761, 111 unions with 245 branches and 7 Union Federations and 5 Confederations with 10 branches and a total membership of 98,367.

TRADE FAIRS

Cyprus International Fair: P.O.B. 3551, Nicosia; fifth scheduled for May–June 1980.

TRANSPORT

There are no railways in Cyprus.

ROADS

In 1977 there were 9,885 kilometres of roads, of which 4,644 kilometres were paved and 5,241 kilometres were earth or gravel roads. Bus and taxi services between Nicosia and the principal towns and villages were severely disrupted by the Turkish invasion. The north and south are now served by separate transport systems, and there are no services linking the two sectors.

SHIPPING

Until 1974 Famagusta was the island's most important harbour, handling about 83 per cent of the country's cargo. Famagusta is a natural port capable of receiving ships of a maximum draught of 9.2 metres. Since its capture by the Turkish army in August 1974 the port has been officially declared closed to international traffic. However, it continues to serve the Turkish-occupied region.

The ports which serve the country's maritime trade at present are Limassol and Larnaca which are both newly constructed. In 1976 Larnaca handled 32 per cent of the general cargo traffic with the remaining 68 per cent handled by Limassol. Paphos, in the west, an open roadstead, provides anchorage for small vessels drawing less than 3 metres.

Limassol, already in 1974 the main passenger port of the

island has, since the closure of Famagusta, developed into the principal port of Cyprus, handling in 1976, 1,584,000 tons of cargo, 4 per cent more than Famagusta's pre-1974 level. Larnaca is the island's main oil port, handling in addition, 96,000 tons in imports and 613,000 tons in exports in 1976.

Both Kyrenia and Karavostassi are under Turkish occupation and have been declared closed to international traffic. Karavostassi used to be the country's major mineral port dealing with 76 per cent of the total mineral exports. However, since the war minerals are being passed through Vassiliko and Limni which are open roadsteads. In 1977 a hydrofoil service was started between Kyrenia and Mersin on the Turkish mainland.

In recent years the number of merchant vessels registered in Cyprus has risen sharply from 314 (1,575,702 g.r.t.) in 1970 to 1,190 (2,765,299 g.r.t.) in 1977.

Allied Industries Ltd.: Nicosia; part of Chandris Group, London, U.K.; one cargo vessel, one tanker.

Evelpis Shipping Co. Ltd.: Nicosia; London agents Lemos Bros. Co. Ltd.; one cargo vessel.

Hellespont Shipping Co. Ltd.: c/o MM. Montanios and Montanios, Flat 2, 3rd Floor, Co-operative Bldg., Archbishop Kyprianos St., Limassol.

Kornos Shipping Co. Ltd.: Nicosia; cargo services; one cargo vessel; Gen. Man. N. M. PAPAIONNOU.

Madouri Maritime Co. Ltd.: Nicosia; managed by Kratigos Shipping Co., 145 Filonos St., Piraeus, Greece; one roll-on, roll-off.

Marifoam Shipping Co. Ltd.: Nicosia; part of Chandris Group, London, U.K.; one tanker.

CIVIL AVIATION

There is an international airport at Nicosia, which can accommodate all types of aircraft, including jets. It was closed in July 1974 following the Turkish invasion. A new airport was constructed at Larnaca from which flights operate to neighbouring countries.

In 1975 the Turkish authorities opened Ercan (formerly Tymbou) airport.

Cyprus Airways: 21 Athanasiou Diakou St., P.O.B. 1903, Nicosia; f. 1946; jointly owned by Cyprus Government, British Airways and local interests; charter subsidiary Cyprair Tours; Chair. G. ELIADES; Gen. Man. E. SAVVA; services to Amman, Athens, Bahrain, Beirut, Benghazi, Cairo, Damascus, Dubai, Frankfurt, Kuwait, London, Manchester, Paris, Salonika, Tel-Aviv and Zürich from Larnaca Airport; fleet of 3 Boeing 707, 2 BAC One-Eleven 500, 1 Canadair CL4F.

Cyprus Turkish Airlines Ltd.: Atatürk Cad., Nicosia; f. 1974; jointly owned by "the Turkish Federated State of Cyprus" and Turkish Airlines; Chair. ORHAN ÜÇOK; routes from Ercan Airport, Nicosia, to Ankara, Adana and Istanbul; fleet of one Boeing 720.

Under normal conditions Cyprus is also served by the following foreign airlines: Aeroflot (U.S.S.R.), Alia (Jordan), Alitalia, Balkan (Bulgaria), British Airways, ČSA (Czechoslovakia), EgyptAir, El Al (Israel), Gulfair (Bahrain), Interflug (German Democratic Republic), KLM (Netherlands), Kuwait Airways, MALÉV (Hungary), MEA (Lebanon), Olympic (Greece), Sabena (Belgium), Swissair, Syrian Arab Airlines, TAROM (Romania), THY (Turkey) and Zambian Airways.

TOURISM

Cyprus Tourism Organization: Zena Building, 18 Th. Theodotou St., P.O.B. 4535, Nicosia; Chair. FRIXOS PETRIDES; Dir.-Gen. A. ANDRONICOU.

CULTURAL ORGANIZATIONS

E. Ka. Te: Pancyprian Chamber of Fine Arts, P.O.B. 2179, Nicosia; f. 1964; Pres. A. SAVVIDES; Sec.-Gen. A. LADOMMATOS; publ. *Bulletin* (monthly).

TH.O.C.: Cyprus Theatrical Organization; 10A King Paul St., Nicosia; f. 1971; Dir. EVIS GABRIELIDES.

EDUCATION

Until March 31st, 1965, each community in Cyprus managed its own schooling through its respective Communal Chamber. Intercommunal education had been placed under the Minister of the Interior, assisted by a Board of Education for Intercommunal Schools of which the Minister was the Chairman. On March 31st, 1965, the Greek Communal Chamber was dissolved and a Ministry of Education was established to take its place. Intercommunal education has been placed under this Ministry

Greek-Cypriot Education

Elementary education is compulsory and is provided free in six grades to children between 6 and 14 years of age. In some towns and large villages there are separate junior schools consisting of the first two or three grades. In some large rural centres there are schools where children can take a two-year post-elementary course if they are not proceeding to a secondary school. Apart from schools for the deaf and blind, and the Lambousa School for juvenile offenders there are also 7 schools for handicapped children. The Ministry runs 18 kindergartens for children from low-income families, but most pre-primary education is privately run. There were 439 primary schools (including privately run institutions) with 54,309 pupils and 2,260 teachers in 1978/79.

Secondary education is free for the first three years and is fee-paying for the rest, although senior pupils can be wholly or partially exempt from payment. Secondary schooling lasts six years, three years at the Gymnasion followed by three years at the Lykeion. There are four types of Lykeia: classical, science, economic and agricultural. There are also five-year vocational (trade) schools and six-year technical schools. In 1978/79 there were 81 secondary schools with 2,266 teachers and 42,441 pupils.

Post-Secondary education is provided at the Pedagogical Academy, which organizes three-year courses for the training of pre-primary and primary school teachers, and at the Higher Technical Institute, which provides three-year courses for technicians in civil, electrical and mechanical engineering. Specialized training is also provided at the Forestry College, the Hotel and Catering Institute, a Nurses' and Midwives' School and a School for Health Inspectors, all of which are State institutions. Adult education is conducted through Youth Centres in rural areas and Foreign Language Institutes in the towns, and in addition a number of private institutions offer courses in business administration, secretarial work etc. There are no universities in Cyprus, and in 1976 approximately 12,400 Cypriot students were studying in universities abroad, mainly in Greece and the United Kingdom.

Turkish-Cypriot Education

Education in the Turkish occupied zone is divided into two sections, formal and adult education. Formal education covers nursery, primary and secondary education. Adult education caters for special training outside the school system.

Formal education is organized into two categories: basic and secondary. Basic education caters for children from 6 to 15 years old and is free and compulsory. There are two stages of basic education, the first stage lasting six years and the second three years. Secondary education consists of a three-year course of one of three types: preparing for higher education; preparing for higher education and vocational training; preparing for vocational training only. All pupils who have completed their basic education are entitled to proceed to a course of secondary education according to their interest and ability. Secondary education is free for those who cannot afford the fees of a maximum of £18. It is not compulsory. In 1976 there were 189 primary schools (20,377 pupils) and 10 secondary schools (8,347 pupils).

The only higher education institution in the "Turkish Federated State of Cyprus" is a teacher training college, attended by 68 pupils in 1976.

BIBLIOGRAPHY

ALASTOS, D. Cyprus in History (London, 1955).

ARNOLD, PERCY. Cyprus Challenge (London: Hogarth Press, 1956).

BARKER, DUDLEY. Grivas (London, Cresset Press, 1960).

BYFORD-JONES, W. Grivas and the Story of EOKA (London, Robert Hale, 1960).

CASSON, S. Ancient Cyprus (London, 1937).

CRAWSHAW, NANCY. The Cyprus Revolt: An Account of the Struggle for Union with Greece (London, Allen & Unwin, 1978).

EMILIANIDES, ACHILLE. Histoire de Chypre (Paris, 1963).

ESIN, EMEL. Aspects of Turkish Civilization in Cyprus (Ankara University Press, Ankara, 1965).

FOLEY, CHARLES. Island in Revolt (London, Longmans Green, 1962).
Legacy of Strife (Penguin, London, 1964).

FOOT, SYLVIA. Emergency Exit (Chatto and Windus, London, 1960).

FOOT, Sir HUGH. A Start in Freedom (London, 1964).

GRIVAS (DIGHENIS), GEORGE. Guerilla Warfare and EOKA's Struggle (London, Longmans, 1964).
Memoirs of General Grivas (London, Longmans, 1964).

HARBOTTLE, MICHAEL. The Impartial Soldier (Oxford University Press, 1970).

HILL, Sir GEORGE. A History of Cyprus (4 vols., London, 1940-1952).

JENNES, D. The Economics of Cyprus (Montreal, 1962).

KYRIAKIDES, S. Cyprus—Constitutionalism and Crisis Government (Philadelphia, University of Pennsylvania Press, 1968).

LAVENDER, D. S. The Story of Cyprus Mines Corporation (San Marino, Calif., 1962).

LUKE, Sir H. C. Cyprus under the Turks 1571-1878 (Oxford, 1921).
Cyprus: A Portrait and an Appreciation (London, Harrap, 1965).

MEYER, A. J. (with S. VASSILIOU). The Economy of Cyprus (Harvard University Press, 1962).

NEWMAN, PHILIP. A Short History of Cyprus (1940).

PAPADOPOULLOS, T. The population of Cyprus (1570–1881) (Nicosia, 1965).

PURCELL, H. D. Cyprus (London, Benn, 1969).

RICHARD, J. Chypre Sous les Lusignan (Paris, 1962).

ROYAL COMMONWEALTH SOCIETY. Notes on Conditions in Cyprus (London, 1973).

SPYRIDAKIS, Dr. C. A. Brief History of Cyprus (Nicosia, 1964).

STORRS, Sir RONALD. A Chronology of Cyprus (Nicosia, 1930).

STYLIANOU, A. and J. Byzantine Cyprus (Nicosia, 1948).

XYDIS, S. G. Cyprus—Conflict and Conciliation 1945-58 (Ohio State University Press, Columbus, Ohio, 1967).

OFFICIAL BOOKS OF REFERENCE:
Cyprus: Documents relating to Independence of Cyprus and the Establishment of British Sovereign Base Areas (Cmnd. 1093, H.M.S.O., London, July 1960).
Cyprus: Treaty of Guarantee, Nicosia, August 16th, 1960.

Egypt

PHYSICAL AND SOCIAL GEOGRAPHY

W. B. Fisher

SITUATION

The Arab Republic of Egypt occupies the north-eastern corner of the African continent, with an extension across the Gulf of Suez into the Sinai region which is usually, but not always, regarded as lying in Asia. The area of Egypt is approximately 385,200 sq. miles (997,667 sq. km.); but of this only 3.5 per cent can be said to be permanently settled, the remainder being desert or marsh. Egypt lies between Lat. 22° and 32° N.; and the greatest distance from north to south is about 674 miles (1024 km.), and from east to west 770 miles (1240 km.), giving the country a roughly square shape, with the Mediterranean and Red Seas forming respectively the northern and eastern boundaries. Egypt has political frontiers on the east with Israel, on the south with the Democratic Republic of Sudan, and on the west with the Libyan Arab Republic. The actual frontiers run in general as straight lines drawn directly between defined points and do not normally conform to geographical features. Between June 1967 and October 1973 the *de facto* frontier with Israel was the Suez Canal. Now, with the 1979 Peace Treaty, the frontier has moved much further east.

Egypt occupies an almost unique place in the world as a region where, in all probability, the earliest developments of civilization and organized government took place. Though many archaeologists would not wholly subscribe to the view of Egypt as actually the first civilized country, there can be no doubt that from very early times the lower Nile Valley has been prominent as possessing strongly marked unity, with a highly specialized and characteristic way of life. Empires with fluctuating boundaries and with varying racial composition have arisen in neighbouring lands of the Middle East, but Egypt has seemed able to stand relatively unchanged, with the facility of absorbing immigrants and outside ideas, of surviving military occupation and defeat, and of maintaining her own culture, finally shaking clear of foreign influence and rule.

PHYSICAL FEATURES

The reasons for this remarkable persistence of cultural cohesion amongst the Egyptian people may be found in the geography of the country. Egypt consists essentially of a narrow, trough-like valley, some 3 to 15 km. wide, cut by the River Nile in the plateau of north-east Africa. At an earlier geological period a gulf of the Mediterranean Sea probably extended as far south as Cairo, but deposition of silt by the Nile has entirely filled up this gulf, producing the fan-shaped Delta region (22,000 sq. km. in area), through which flow two main distributary branches of the Nile—the eastern, or Damietta branch (240 km. long), and the western, or Rosetta branch (235 km.), together with many other minor channels. As deposition of silt takes place large stretches of water are gradually impounded to form shallow lakes, which later became firm ground. At the present there are four such stretches of water in the north of the Delta: from east to west, and, in order of size, Lakes Menzaleh, Brullos, Idku and Mariut.

Upstream from Cairo the Nile Valley is at first 10 to 15 km. in width, and, as the river tends to lie close to the eastern side, much of the cultivated land, and also most of the big towns and cities, lie on the western bank. Towards the south the river valley gradually narrows until, at about 400 km. from the frontier of Sudan, it is no more than 3 km. wide. Near Aswan there is an outcrop of resistant rock, chiefly granite, which the river has not been able to erode as quickly as the rest of the valley. This gives rise to a region of cascades and rapids which is known as the First Cataract. Four other similar regions occur on the Nile, but only the First Cataract lies within Egypt. The cataracts form a barrier to human movement upstream and serve to isolate the Egyptian Nile from territories farther south. In Ancient Egypt, when river communciations were of chief importance, there was a traditional division of the Nile Valley into Lower Egypt (the Delta), Middle Egypt (the broader valley above the Delta), and Upper Egypt (the narrower valley as far as the cataracts). Nowadays it is usual to speak merely of Upper and Lower Egypt, with the division occurring at Cairo.

The fertile strip of the Nile Valley is isolated on the south by the cataracts and by the deserts and swamps of the Sudan; on the north by the Mediterranean Sea; and to east and west by desert plateaux, about which a little more must be said. The land immediately to the east of the Nile Valley, spoken of as the Eastern Highlands, is a complex region with peaks that rise 1,800 to 2,100 metres but also much broken up by deep valleys that make travel difficult. Owing to aridity the whole region is sparsely populated, with a few partly nomadic shepherds, one or two monasteries and a number of small towns associated chiefly with the exploitation of minerals—petroleum, iron, manganese and granite—that occur in this region. Difficult land-ward communications mean that contact is mostly by sea, except in the case of the ironfields. The Sinai, separated from the Eastern Highlands by the Gulf of Suez, is structurally very similar, but the general plateau level is tilted, giving the highest land (again nearly 2,100 metres in elevation) in the extreme south, where it rises in bold scarps from sea-level. Towards the north the land gradually slopes down, ultimately forming the low-lying sandy plain of the Sinai desert which fringes the Mediterranean Sea. Because of its low altitude and accessibility, the Sinai, in spite of its desert nature, has been for many centuries an important corridor linking Egypt with Asia. It is now crossed only by a motor road, the railway having been torn up in 1968 by occupying Israeli forces.

West of the Nile occur the vast expanses known as the Western Desert. Though by no means uniform in height, the land surface is much lower than that east of the Nile, and within Egypt rarely exceeds 300 metres above sea-level. Parts are covered by extensive masses of light shifting sand that often form dunes; but in addition there are a number of large depressions, some with the lowest parts actually below sea-level. These depressions seem to have been hollowed out by wind action, breaking up rock strata that were weakened by the presence of underground water, and most hollows still contain supplies of artesian water. In some instances (as for example, the Qattara depression, and the Wadi Natrun, respectively south-west and south-east of Alexandria) the subterranean water is highly saline and consequently useless for agriculture; but in others—notably the oases of the Fayyum, Siwa, Dakhla, Behariya, and Farafra—the water is sufficiently sweet to allow use for irrigation, and settlements have grown up within the desert. In the last few years, much attention has been given to irrigation development in these oases, which are sometimes spoken of as "the New Territories."

CLIMATE

The main feature of Egyptian climate is the almost uniform aridity. Alexandria, the wettest part, receives only 20 cm. of rain annually, and most of the south has 8 cm. or less. In many districts rain may fall in quantity only once in two or three years, and it is apposite to recall that throughout most of Egypt, and even in Cairo itself, the majority of the people live in houses of unbaked, sun-dried brick. During the summer temperatures are extremely high, reaching 38° to 43°C. at times and even 49°C. in the southern and western deserts. The Mediterranean coast has cooler conditions, with 32°C. as a maximum; hence the wealthier classes move to Alexandria for the three months of summer. Winters are generally warm, with very occasional rain; but cold spells occur from time to time, and light snow is not unknown. Owing to the large extent of desert, hot dry sand-winds (called *khamsin*) are fairly frequent particularly in spring, and much damage can be caused to crops; it has been known for the temperature to rise by 20°C. in two hours, and the wind to reach 150 km. per hour. Another unusual condition is the occurrence of early morning fog in Lower Egypt during spring and early summer. This, on the other hand, has a beneficial effect on plant growth in that it supplies moisture and is a partial substitute for rainfall.

IRRIGATION

With a deficient rainfall over the entire country, human existence in Egypt depends closely on irrigation from the Nile; in consequence it is now necessary to consider the regime of the river in some detail. More detailed reference to conditions outside Egypt is made in the section on the geography of Sudan (below); but it may here be stated in summary that the river rises in the highlands of East Africa, with its main stream issuing from Lakes Victoria and Albert. In the southern Sudan it wanders sluggishly across a flat open plain, where the fall in level is only 1:100,000. Here the shallow waters become a vast swamp, full of dense masses of papyrus vegetation, and this section of the Nile is called the Sudd (Arabic for "blockage"). Finally, in the north of the Sudan, the Nile flows in a well-defined channel and enters Egypt. In Upper Egypt the river is in process of cutting its bed deeper into the rock floor; but in the lower part of its course silt is deposited, and the level of the land is rising—in some places by as much as 10 cm. per century.

The salient feature of the Nile is, of course, its regular annual flood, which is caused by the onset of summer rains in East Africa and Ethiopia. The flood travels northward, reaching Egypt during August, and within Egypt the normal rise in river level was at first 6.4 metres, which had declined to 4.6 metres as irrigation works developed. This cycle of flood had been maintained for several thousand years until, in 1969, construction of the Aswan High Dam made it a feature of the past (see the section on the High Dam below) so far as Egypt is concerned.

Originally, the flood waters were simply retained in specially prepared basins with earthen banks, and the water could then be used for three to four months after the flood. Within the last century, building of large barrages held water all the year round, allowing cultivation at any season. The old (basin) system allowed one or two crops per holding per year, the newer (perennial) system, three or even four. In the past, barley and wheat were the main crops; under perennial irrigation maize and cotton, which can tolerate the great summer heat provided they are watered, take first and second place.

Changeover from basin to perennial irrigation allowed a considerable population increase in Egypt, from about 2½ million in 1800 to about 40 million in 1978, giving rural densities of over 2,300 per square km. in some areas; and as 99 per cent of all Egyptians live within the Nile valley (only 4 per cent of its area) there is considerable pressure on the land.

With most Egyptians entirely dependent upon Nile water, the point has now been reached that almost all the water entering Egypt is fully utilized. However, there are enormous losses by evaporation which at present amount to some 70 per cent of the total flow. A political problem is concerned with the effects of devoting an increased area of the Nile Valley to the growing of commodities for export: cotton, rice and vegetables. Such a change from agricultural self-sufficiency to a cash economy involves the purchase abroad of fertilizers and even foodstuffs, and is inducing considerable social changes within the country. Moreover, so long as only one or two crops were taken per year, the silt laid down by the annual floods maintained soil fertility, but now that three or four crops are taken the import of fertilizer is essential. Hence Egypt has become increasingly sensitive to world trade prices. The position of the merchant and capitalist has greatly improved, often at the expense of the peasant farmer. This was to some extent true in Nasserist times and is certainly true of the situation since 1970.

Difficulties and opportunities over use of Nile water are exemplified in the High Dam scheme at Aswan, which has created a lake 350 miles (500 km.) in length and 6 miles (10 km.) wide that has extended southwards across the Sudanese frontier and inundated the town of Wadi Halfa, whose 55,000–60,000 inhabitants were re-settled at Kashm el Girba, a district lying south east of Khartoum, whilst displaced Egyptians were settled in 33 villages around Kom Ombo: total costs of re-settlement were about £14 million. Prior to 1959 technical and political objections delayed the High Dam scheme; and as the cost of the dam (estimated at £345–400 million) could not be met by the Egyptian Government alone, application was made to the World Bank, America and Britain for a loan, This was refused (Sudanese opposition being one, but only one, factor in this refusal), whereupon Egyptian reaction was to expropriate the Suez Canal Company, in order to finance part of the Aswan scheme.

Soviet offers to assist were made and accepted; and in 1959 a first Soviet credit of £33 million allowed preliminary work to begin in December of the same year. In 1960 further agreement was reached by which the U.S.S.R. supplied credits up to £81 million (making a total of £194 million) together with technical and material assistance; and in 1964 further proposals for credit and loans were made by Nikita Khrushchev, then the Soviet head of government. Egypt must thus find at least £200 million in addition to repayments at a later stage of the Soviet credits.

In May 1964 the first phase of the High Dam was inaugurated by President Nasser and Mr. Khrushchev. The High Dam is 3,600 metres across, with a girth of 980 metres at the river bed and 40 metres at the top. It holds back the largest artificial lake in the world, and makes possible large scale storing of water from year to year, and a regular planned use of all Nile water independently of the precise amount of annual flood. Its irrigation potential is 2 million feddans for Lower Egypt alone, and the total for the Nile valley (including Upper Egypt) is adding 30 per cent to the total cultivable area of Egypt. Twelve generator units incorporated in the dam give considerable quantities of low-cost electric power (lower than costs in much of Europe and less than 50 per cent of that of electricity in London). This power is already a most important aid to industrialization, especially for the new metal industries. Started in January 1960, the Dam was completed in July 1970 and officially inaugurated in January 1971.

Some relatively minor adverse effects have been noticed: scouring of the Nile bed below the dam; increased salinity in the lower stretches; reduced sedimentation below the dam and heavy deposition within the basin; effects of blowing sand on the electric power lines; and, perhaps more seriously, the disappearance of fish (particularly sardines) off the Mediterranean coast of Egypt. It is hoped that this last can be compensated by new fishing within Lake Nasser.

Perhaps the most serious of all is a notable rise in the water-table in some areas, due to hydrostatic pressures, and all-the-year-round presence of water. Besides disturbing irrigation systems (which are adapted to pre-existing conditions), salinity and gleying of a more permanent nature are appearing; bilharzia and other parasitic diseases are spreading, and there is the appearance of the plant water hyacinth, which, if uncleared, can choke irrigation systems.

RACE

The racial origins of the Egyptian people present certain problems. In the deserts to east and west of the Nile Valley the population is of unmixed Mediterranean strains; but within the Nile Valley itself there is a special native Egyptian type that would seem to have developed partly from intermixture. The Egyptian peasant is more heavily built and muscular than the nomadic Bedouin, and his colouring is intermediate between the lighter brown of Syrian and Palestinian Arabs and the dark skins of the negroid peoples of the Sudan and Abyssinia. Facial features show some resemblance to those of other Arabs, but despite this there is often more than a hint of the features depicted in ancient monuments. It might thus be reasonable to suggest that there seems to have developed within Egypt a special racial sub-type, basically Mediterranean, with smaller elements both from the south and the north, but also greatly affected by local indigenous conditions which have given rise to a specific Egyptian racial type.

LANGUAGE

Arabic is the language of almost all Egyptians, though there are very small numbers of Berber-speaking villages in the western oases. Most educated Egyptians also speak either French or English, often with a preference for the former. This is a reflection of the traditional French interest in Egypt, which is reciprocated: governmental decrees are sometimes published in French, as well as Arabic, and newspapers in French have an important circulation in Cairo and Alexandria. Small colonies of Greeks and Armenians are also a feature of the larger Egyptian towns. It should perhaps be noted that the Arabic name for Egypt, Misr, is always used within the country itself.

HISTORY

Geography has influenced the history of Egypt from the earliest times. The narrow strip of cultivable land along the banks of the Nile between the First Cataract and the Delta is distinct from the extensive and fertile plain of the Delta itself, but the resultant tendency to separatism has been counterbalanced by the dependence of the people on the annual Nile flood: the control and exploitation of the water and silt have necessitated co-operation and obedience to routine and authority. The eastern and western deserts seal off the lower reaches of the Nile Valley from the neighbouring territories in Africa and Asia. Until recent times communication with the outside world was largely restricted to the route up the river into Nubia, the sea route across the Mediterranean to Syria and the land route to Palestine across the northern fringe of Sinai. The effect of Egypt's relative isolation has been to produce a high degree of cultural individuality.

PHARAONIC EGYPT TO 671 B.C.

Traditionally Egyptian history begins with the semi-legendary Menes, the first ruler of the united kingdom of Upper and Lower Egypt at the end of the fourth millenium B.C. But the flowering of the Old Kingdom came in the third millenium under the IVth Dynasty, which had its capital at Memphis, near the apex of the Delta. The technical and engineering progress of this period is witnessed by the pyramids. These and other works indicate a powerful monarchy commanding great resources.

This efflorescence was followed by a decline. Not until the XIth and XIIth Dynasties (*c.* 2000 B.C.) does the resurgence of a united Egypt in the Middle Kingdom become clear. The powerful provincial nobles were slowly brought under royal control. Improved conditions were reflected in reclamation works in the Fayyum and temple building at numerous sites. Egyptian armies penetrated into Nubia, a land at that time rich in gold, and the conquest of the region to a point above the Second Cataract was accomplished.

Another obscure period followed and the course of Egyptian history was interrupted by the invasion from Palestine of the Hyksos who established themselves as rulers in the Delta. Although they adopted Egyptian customs, they were never assimilated. About 1620 B.C. a revolt began under a southern prince and ultimately the Hyksos were expelled and Egypt was reunited.

Under the XVIIIth Dynasty, ancient Egypt reached her zenith. This period of the New Kingdom has left its mark up and down the land especially around the capital, Thebes, near the modern Luxor. Abroad the name of the pharaoh was feared in western Asia. The greatest of the conquerors was Thothmes III who established an Egyptian empire in Syria. Egyptian rule was restored and extended in Nubia.

The empire decayed during the reign of Akhenaten (*c.* 1380–1362), whose religious innovations antagonized the powerful priesthood of Thebes. On his death the old polytheism was restored. The outstanding figure of the XIXth Dynasty was Rameses II (*c.* 1300–1234). He fought the rising power of the Hittites in Syria for twenty years and was both a great builder and a usurper of other men's works.

After him Egypt passed into decline. The XXth Dynasty closed with a long series of insignificant pharaohs and under their successors Egypt was divided between a ruler in the Delta and a priest-king at Thebes. In the eighth century B.C. a dynasty originating from Nubia held Upper Egypt and even for a time the Delta. But Egypt was soon to pass under completely alien domination.

EGYPT UNDER FOREIGN RULERS: 671 B.C.-A.D. 640

In 671 the Assyrians conquered Egypt and drove out the Nubian pharaoh. The Assyrians, however, did not long maintain their hold and a native ruler succeeded in reuniting the country. The dynasty which he founded encouraged Greek traders and was supported by Greek mercenaries.

This last native dynasty came to an end in 525, when Persia conquered Egypt. The Persian kings patronized the religion of their subjects and were officially regarded as pharaohs. Darius I (522–485) completed the work of an Egyptian predecessor in cutting a canal linking the Nile and the Red Sea. His successors fought native pretenders to keep Egypt within their empire.

Under Alexander the Great another change of masters occurred. The Persian satrap surrendered in 332 and Alexander was recognized as pharaoh. His visit to the oracle at Siwa shows his fascinated interest in Egyptian religion, while by founding the city of Alexandria he conferred on Egypt a lasting benefit. After Alexander's death, Egypt fell to his general, Ptolemy. The Ptolemaic Dynasty was Greek in origin and outlook. Its capital was Alexandria, which was in effect a Greek rather than an Egyptian city. Egypt was the private estate of the Ptolemies, who taxed its people through a competent bureaucracy.

When Cleopatra committed suicide in 30 B.C., Egypt passed under Roman rule. Although the emperors were regarded as successors of the pharaohs the country sank into a mere province of a great Mediterranean empire. Egyptian Christianity had a distinctive doctrinal character and, by fostering monasticism, originated an important institution. In the dogmatic disputes of the Byzantine period, the adherence of the Coptic church of Egypt to monophysite beliefs in face of the official theology was a form of national self-assertion.

ARAB EGYPT: 640-969

In the early seventh century two great powers dominated the Middle East: the Byzantine empire and the Sasanian empire of the Persians. In 616 the Sasanian army invaded Egypt but Byzantine supremacy was soon restored. Meanwhile a third power was arising, the Arabs, summoned by Muhammad to belief in Islam.

The Prophet's death in 632 was followed by wars against the Byzantines and Sasanians. Egypt, the granary of the Byzantine Empire, soon attracted the Muslim warriors. In the reign of the Caliph Umar I an Arab army under 'Amr ibn al-As took the invasion route from Syria. The frontier towns fell after short sieges and in April 641 the key-fortress near the head of the Delta was captured. Alexandria, the capital, surrendered and was evacuated by the Byzantine garrison. A camp-city at Al-Fustat, again in the strategic position near the apex of the Delta, became the headquarters of the Muslim army and the new capital.

For some centuries Egypt remained an occupied rather than a Muslim country. The Copts, who disliked Byzantine rule, had not opposed the conquest. Under the Arabs they found less oppression and paid lower taxes at first than under Constantinople. In course of time, however, Egypt became an Arabic-speaking country with a Muslim majority. But to this day the Coptic Christian minority remains and uses the ancient language in its liturgy.

For over two centuries Egypt was administered as a province of the Arab Empire. By the middle of the ninth century the remoter territories were slipping from the grasp of the Abbasid caliphs of Baghdad. Egypt was obviously well-fitted to be the domain of an autonomous governor. Two short-lived Sunnite Dynasties, founded by men of central Asian origin, the Tulunids and the Ikhshidids, ruled in virtual independence of the caliph between 868 and 969. Each rapidly degenerated after the death of its founder. Ahmad ibn Tulun in 877 occupied Syria and thus once again created an empire based on Egypt.

THE FATIMIDS AND AYYUBIDS: 969-1250

Ikshidid rule was terminated in 969 by an invasion from Tunisia. Here the rival caliphate of the Fatimids had been set up by Muslims of the Shia sect, who believed that the caliphate could only pass through the direct descendants of 'Ali, the husband of Muhammad's daughter, Fatima. The fourth of these anti-caliphs, Al-Mu'izz, was made the master of Egypt by his general, Jawhar. Jawhar laid out a new capital, just outside Al-Fustat, which has developed into the modern city of Cairo, and was the founder of the mosque of Al-Azhar, the greatest centre of Islamic theological learning.

Under the early Fatimids Egypt enjoyed a golden age. The country was a well-administered absolute monarchy and it formed the central portion of an empire which at its height included North Africa, Sicily, Syria and western Arabia. Agriculture and industry were encouraged. Trade with Europe and India brought prosperity to the land and wealth to the ruler.

Soon, however, Fatimid rule began to decay. Ali Hakim (996–1021) departed from the tolerant policy towards Christians and Jews which was normal in Muslim states. The long reign of Al-Mustansir (1035–94) witnessed the break-up of the Fatimid Empire and the growing insubordination of the slave-soldiery. In 1073 the caliph was obliged to send for Badr al Jamali, the governor of Acre, to take control of the country. This he did and Egypt passed under the government of a military autocracy who kept the Fatimid caliphs under their tutelage. Thus the collapse of the Fatimid state was postponed for nearly a century but, after the death of Al-Mustansir, the six succeeding caliphs had no power.

Meanwhile a new enemy was on the threshold—the Crusaders who after 1098 established feudal, Christian states along the Syrian coast. Neither the Abbasids nor the Fatimids were capable of resisting them but in the later twelfth century the tide began to turn. The Muslim reconquest of Syria was largely due to the energy and ability of the Kurdish leader, Salah al-Din ibn Ayyub, known in European history as Saladin. In 1169 he became minister to the Fatimid caliph. In 1171 the last Fatimid was quietly deposed and Egypt restored to Sunni orthodoxy. The remainder of Saladin's life was a struggle against the crusading states but when he died in 1193 he was sultan over Egypt and practically the whole of the former Crusader territory.

Saladin's Empire was divided amongst his heirs, one branch of which, the Egyptian Ayyubids, reigned in Cairo. Dynastic struggles weakened the family and the Crusaders were able to recover some lost ground. Louis IX of France led an attack directly on Egypt. Damietta was occupied in 1249 but the advance of the Crusaders through the difficult and pestilential Delta was stopped at the battle of Al-Mansura in 1250. Louis was made prisoner but subsequently regained his liberty on paying a ransom and restoring Damietta.

THE MAMLUK SULTANATE: 1250-1517

During this Crusade the Ayyubid sultan, al-Malik al-Salih, died. This was virtually the end of the dynasty. After a short confused period the commander of the forces, a certain Aybak became the first of the Mamluk sultans who ruled Egypt from 1250 to 1517. These sultans were of slave origin. The Ayyubids had built up bodyguards of slave-troops, whose power increased as that of their masters declined. The earlier Mamluks, until 1390, were mainly of Turkish and Mongol origin, while their successors, originally the bodyguard of the former, were mostly Circassians. The Mamluk sultans did not form a dynasty in the hereditary sense but a caste from which successive rulers emerged after election or a struggle for power. The ranks of the Mamluks were replenished by fresh purchases.

The Mamluks were thus an alien element which was never fully assimilated in Egypt. They exploited the land for their own benefit and the Egyptians played a passive role under their domination. Nevertheless they protected Egypt and Syria against the Mongols and the Crusaders. The Mongol threat developed in the middle of the thirteenth century when Hulagu, the grandson of Jenghiz Khan, advanced through Persia. Baghdad was taken and the Abbasid caliphate extinguished in 1258. From Northern Syria the Mongol army advanced southwards until at Ain Jalut, near Nazareth, it was overwhelmed in 1260 by the Mamluk Sultan, Baibars. Spared from the ravages of the Mongols, Egypt became the principal centre of Arab culture. The change in the centre of gravity of Islam was symbolized when Baibars brought to Cairo an Abbasid prince, who was formally recognized as titular caliph.

This victory also ensured that the Mamluk sultans would rule over a combined empire of Egypt and Syria. The remaining pockets of Crusader territory were regained by Baibars and his successors. Baibars also intervened in the affairs of the Christian kingdom of Nubia and virtually established a protectorate.

The numerous mosques and public works of the Mamluk period indicate the wealth of Egypt. But from the middle of the fourteenth century the condition of the country declined owing to plague and civil war, while heavy taxation oppressed all classes of the native Egyptians. Another Mongol invasion under Tamerlane in 1401 devastated Syria, although Egypt itself was again spared. The valuable transit trade through Egypt was subjected to a close monopoly, which diminished its flow. Finally Vasco da Gama's voyage to India around the Cape (1496–99) sounded the doom of Egyptian prosperity. European ships henceforward by-passed Egypt and traded directly with the east, while the Portuguese destroyed the Mamluk fleets and harried Arab shipping in the Indian Ocean, Red Sea and Persian Gulf.

OTTOMAN EGYPT: 1517-1798

At the beginning of the sixteenth century a powerful state was created in Persia under the Safavid dynasty, while Anatolia and the Balkan peninsula were ruled by the Ottomans. The Mamluks were by comparison a declining power and sought by a secret understanding with the Persian Shah to hold their own against the expansionist and militant Ottomans.

In 1516 at the battle of Marj Dabiq north of Aleppo the Ottoman Sultan, Selim I, defeated the Mamluks and advanced southwards. A second battle in January 1517, outside Cairo, resulted in the overthrow of the last Mamluk sultan. The whole of his empire fell into Selim's hands and Cairo sank to a provincial status. The Turkish conquest together with the change in international trade-routes marked the beginning of a period of political and economic insignificance. The great mosque of Al-Azhar retained its primacy among the theological schools of Islam but its teaching was set in a conservative tradition that remained unbroken until the nineteenth century.

Selim recognized the individuality of Egypt and his successors usually interfered but little with the administration. The Mamluk soldiery and their leaders, the beys, were allowed to continue receiving their revenues. A garrison of Turkish janissaries was stationed in Egypt but in the course of a few generations they became useless as a military force, while constant recruiting from the slave-markets kept the Mamluks in unimpaired vigour. Ottoman governors were appointed but for the most part they were utterly dependent on the Mamluk beys.

From time to time Mamluk grandees were virtually sovereign in Egypt. The most famous of these was Ali Bey, who ruled from 1761 to 1766, was then driven into exile, but regained power from 1767 to 1772. He made an alliance with a Syrian Arab chief, and contacted a Russian squadron, which was then cruising in the eastern Mediterranean, during the course of hostilities against the Ottoman Empire. A Mamluk force attacked Damascus, and drove out the Ottoman governor, but Ali's general betrayed him, and returned to Egypt. Ali fled to his Syrian friend, but was defeated in an attempt to reconquer Egypt in 1773 and died a prisoner.

Ali Bey's career illustrated the weakness of the Mamluks. They had no roots in Egypt and the Egyptians viewed with indifference their struggles for mastery. Their power to achieve their ambitions was limited by the difficulty of financing their factions and they became unpopular by the extortions which they practised on the native Egyptians. At the end of the century a shock from Europe was to reveal the hollowness of their power.

THE FRENCH IN EGYPT: 1798-1801

During the eighteenth century, the British obtained the chief share of Eastern commerce. With the outbreak of the Revolutionary War between Britain and France, the French decided that the occupation of Egypt and the revival of the transit trade might lead to the disruption of British commerce and the overthrow of British rule in India. Bonaparte landed at Alexandria in July 1798.

His aim was to colonize Egypt, break the Mamluk hold and introduce Western ideas. Although he professed sympathy with Islam, his expedition was essentially inspired by the nationalist and secular ideology of the French Revolution. The Egyptians saw in it a new crusade and Bonaparte's attempts to win support by appeals to Muslim sentiment miscarried.

Defeated in the decisive "Battle of the Pyramids" on July 21st, the Mamluks fled and the sudden collapse of their administration was followed by disorder and pillage in Cairo until the entry of French troops. The following month, however, Bonaparte was cut off from France by the destruction of his fleet by Nelson in the "Battle of the Nile". In September the Ottoman Sultan declared war and news of this, combined with Mamluk intrigues and hostility towards the alien French, led in October to a serious revolt in Cairo, centred around Al-Azhar which was subjected to an artillery bombardment.

Early in 1799 Bonaparte invaded Syria to attack the combined forces of the Mamluks and the Ottomans under the governor of Acre. The latter was supported by a British naval squadron and after besieging Acre for two months Bonaparte withdrew to Egypt, his forces much reduced by fighting and disease. He repulsed a Turkish landing near Alexandria in July and succeeded in August in getting away to France with a few companions. His army held out until 1801 when a British force, subsequently joined by Ottoman troops, compelled them to capitulate.

The shock to Egypt of the French occupation was great. The Mamluk ruling caste was unseated, Egyptian Muslim leaders were associated with the administration and consulted on public matters, and the Copts were placed on an equal footing with the Muslims. The immediate effect was to confuse and irritate Egyptian opinion, but the way to future developments had been opened.

The French did not abandon the idea of gaining control over Egypt and their interest in Egyptian affairs was maintained. French scholars who had accompanied Bonaparte produced monographs which became the basis of modern studies of the country. In the hands of Champollion, the Rosetta Stone was to be the key to the hieroglyphs.

MUHAMMAD ALI PASHA AND HIS SUCCESSORS: 1805-63

The expulsion of the French was followed by a struggle for power in which the victor was an Albanian officer in the Ottoman forces, Muhammad Ali. In 1805 he was recognized by the Sultan as Governor of Egypt. In 1807 he defeated a British force which had occupied Alexandria. In 1811 the Mamluk chiefs were massacred in Cairo. His prestige was increased by the success of his forces in a campaign in Arabia, undertaken between 1811 and 1818 at the request of the Sultan, against the Wahhabi conquerors of the Hijaz, led by the family of Saud, who threatened the Fertile Crescent. Between 1820 and 1822 his army conquered most of the northern Sudan, the source of gold and slaves.

The gaps in his army resulting from these campaigns were made up first by slaves, who were found unsuitable because of their high mortality, and then by the conscription—unprecedented, brutal and unpopular—of native Egyptians. The new army had Turks, Albanians and Circassians for officers and was trained by European military instructors.

In 1824 Muhammad Ali sent his son Ibrahim with an Egyptian force to assist the Sultan to suppress the Greek revolt, but European intervention in 1827 led to the destruction of the Turkish and Egyptian fleets at Navarino. On the rejection by the Sultan of Muhammad Ali's demand that Syria should be given to him in recompense, Ibrahim invaded that country in 1831. War with the Ottomans followed and Ibrahim advanced into Anatolia. A convention in 1833 gave Muhammad Ali the Syrian provinces, which were ruled by Ibrahim for seven years as his viceroy. A second Ottoman war then broke out, and international intervention once again resulted in Ibrahim's defeat. Muhammad Ali's dominions were restricted to Egypt and the Sudan but his governorship was made hereditary. He died in 1849, having been predeceased by Ibrahim.

Within Egypt Muhammad Ali reformed the administration and controlled the national wealth. An ambitious educational system was organized under European teachers, and Egyptian students were sent abroad, especially to France. A press was set up, primarily for the production of textbooks and manuals. Towards the end of his reign a Western-educated class was emerging and the ferment of ideas characteristic of modern Egyptian intellectual life had begun.

Muhammad Ali was succeeded by his grandson, Abbas I (1849–54), under whom the westernizing trend was reduced, and he by Said (1854–64), Muhammad Ali's surviving son.

THE MAKING OF THE SUEZ CANAL: 1854-69

During Muhammad Ali's reign, Egypt regained importance as a link between Europe and the East. The overland route via Alexandria, Cairo and Suez, which was improved with the construction of a railway by British enterprise, reduced the passage between England and India from five months to forty days. This route was used by passengers and mail but heavy merchandise continued to go by the Cape. The scheme for a maritime canal, regarded by the British Government as a threat to India, was backed by France but Muhammad Ali refused to grant the necessary concession, seeing a canal as a threat to the independence he sought

Said proved more pliant and in 1854 granted a concession to de Lesseps which included an undertaking to supply labour but which required ratification by the Sultan. This was delayed owing to British opposition and work did not begin until 1859, in anticipation of ratification after de Lesseps had gained the support of Napoleon III.

Said was succeeded by Ismail, Ibrahim's son, who inherited something of his grandfather's imagination and his father's energy. At his insistence the concession (and particularly the clause concerning the provision of labour) was modified, but he was obliged to pay £3 million in compensation to the Suez Canal Company after the matter had been submitted to the arbitration of Napoleon III. The canal was opened with great festivities.

At first the British Government tried to ignore the canal and none of the 80,000 shares reserved for Britain (one-fifth of the total) were bought. Ismail, who had originally been allotted 64,000 shares, took up these and others which remained unsubscribed, bringing his total holding to 182,023 shares. Said and Ismail had together paid about £11½ million in connection with the canal which cost approximately £16 million to cut. Ismail was to receive 15 per cent of the net profits, in addition to the interest on his shares.

THE KHEDIVE ISMAIL AND INTERNATIONAL CONTROL: 1863-81

As part of the Ottoman Empire, Egypt was bound by the Capitulations—treaties with European powers giving European communities in Ottoman territories a considerable degree of autonomy under the jurisdiction of their consuls. Originally they had applied to small groups of merchants but with the growth of trade with Egypt in the nineteenth century consular protection came to be enjoyed by sizeable foreign communities, who were exempt from Egyptian jurisdiction and largely free of Egyptian taxation. After prolonged negotiations Mixed Courts, which reduced the scope of consular jurisdiction, were introduced in 1875; these, however, had a majority of European judges and were not insensitive to diplomatic pressures.

Ismail was to deliver Egypt into far greater international control. His ambitions made him careless of financial considerations, and high cotton prices during the American Civil War gave him a false idea of his country's wealth. In 1866 he obtained the title of Khedive. He extended his Sudanese dominions, cut canals, built railways and constructed telegraph lines. No distinction was drawn between the debts of the state and those of the ruler, whose personal expenses were high, and between 1863 and 1876 Egyptian indebtedness rose from £7 million to nearly £100 million. Much of this was in the form of loans from European financial houses at steep rates of interest.

In 1875 Ismail staved off a financial crisis by selling his Suez Canal shares to the British Government for nearly £4 million, a profitable investment by Disraeli who sought to prevent French control. The crisis came in 1876 when Ismail suspended payment of his treasury bills, a declaration of bankruptcy which led to international control. A khedival decree of May 1876 established the "Caisse de la Dette Publique", administered by four foreign members—British, French, Austrian and Italian—to provide for the service of Egyptian debts. When this arrangement proved unsuccessful the French insisted on reform of the fiscal system to provide for repayment of the debts and in 1878 Ismail was forced by France and Britain, in return for a new loan, to surrender his powers and revenues to a ministry, headed by Nubar Pasha, which included a British and a French minister. Ismail chafed under foreign control, aligned himself with Egyptian opposition to it and in May 1879 dismissed the ministry. The French and British Governments retaliated by securing his deposition by the Ottoman Sultan.

Ismail was succeeded by his son Tawfik, who, ostensibly, governed through a responsible Egyptian ministry. Strict financial control was exercised, however, by a French and a British controller, and under the law of liquidation of 1880 an international Debt Commission, consisting of two French and two British members together with one German, one Austrian and one Italian, administered 66 per cent of the country's revenue for the benefit of foreign creditors. Furthermore, a maximum was laid down for government expenditure and the Commissioners were empowered to draw on any surplus administrative revenue. Such was the burden laid upon the Egyptian people by Ismail's improvidence.

THE ARABI EPISODE: 1881-82

Meanwhile a nationalist outlook was developing among those classes who had been touched by Western influences, particularly the younger Egyptian army officers whose way to promotion was barred by Turks and Circassians. Liberal reformers led by Cherif Pasha resented Turkish overlordship and wanted a Western-style constitution. Moslem leaders were opposed to the spread of Christian influence. The great landowners, many of whom were, like the ruling house, Turkish in origin, fought to retain their privileges which were threatened by foreign control. The peasantry, who had been squeezed to pay for Ismail's schemes were being squeezed again to pay his debts. The Khedive, Tawfik, was revealed as a puppet maintained by France and Britain.

By 1881 the country seethed with unrest and a climax was reached in February when, in protest against cuts imposed on the army, a group of officers led by Arabi Pasha forced Tawfik to dismiss his Circassian War Minister. In September, after surrounding his palace, they compelled him to agree to the formation of a new ministry, and to summon the Chamber of Notables, a consultative body originally set up by Ismail. France was opposed to any concession to moderate Egyptian opinion, Britain agreed rather than risk a split with France, and a Franco-British note was sent proclaiming the resolve to maintain the Khedive and the established order.

The effect of the note was to align the Chamber of Notables with Arabi against foreign intervention. In February 1882 the Khedive was forced to dismiss the ministry led by Cherif Pasha and appoint a nationalist ministry with a supporter of Arabi as Prime Minister and Arabi himself Minister for War. The Dual Control ceased to exist and, although anxious to avoid sending an expedition to Egypt, the British and French Governments in May sent naval squadrons to Alexandria as a demonstration. On their arrival Egyptian opinion became so inflamed that in June fanaticism took control and riots broke out in Alexandria and other places in which numbers of Europeans were killed.

At a conference in Constantinople neither Germany nor Turkey would support the sending of an expeditionary force and the French Chamber of Deputies refused to sanction French intervention. On July 11th, the Egyptians having refused to cease work on the fortifications of Alexandria, the British squadron bombarded the forts. The town was evacuated by the Egyptian army, while the Khedive placed himself under British protection and subsequently proclaimed Arabi a rebel. The French ostentatiously dissociated themselves from the British action. A British expeditionary force landed at Ismailia and routed the Egyptian army at Tel el Kebir. Cairo was occupied and Tawfik's prerogatives were restored, to be subsequently exercised under British control.

THE RULE OF CROMER AND HIS SUCCESSORS: 1883-1914

The British Government hoped to set Egyptian affairs in order and then to withdraw, but the execution of this policy was frustrated. The Arabi episode had brought Egypt once again to the verge of bankruptcy. Difficulties were increased by a cholera epidemic, a poor Nile, the Mahdist revolt in the Sudan and the unremitting hostility of France. Evacuation was repeatedly deferred and the occupation gradually assumed the character of a veiled protectorate.

From 1883 to 1907 the Egyptian Government was dominated by the British Agent and Consul-General, Sir Evelyn Baring, who in 1891 became Lord Cromer. He was in title only the equal of the other consuls-general and British control was established with diplomatic care, German support being canvassed to counterbalance French obstruction. A policy of severe economy was necessary to satisfy foreign bondholders. In spite of the limitation on his freedom of action, Cromer obtained remarkable results. An international convention in 1885 eased the financial strain by permitting a further loan and modifying the rigidity with which Egyptian revenues were assigned. British financial advisers brought about increased revenues, solvency was restored and taxation reduced. Irrigation works were improved and paid labour replaced the corvée for the annual clearance of the canals. The Aswan dam was constructed. A new Egyptian army was trained by British officers.

In 1892 Tawfik died. He was succeeded by his son, Abbas II, who was barely eighteen at his accession and soon resented Cromer's authority. The possibility of a conjunction between Abbas and a new nationalist movement led by Mustafa Kamil, a young lawyer who had been trained in France, caused the British some anxiety but the Khedive's attempts to assert himself resulted in humiliation which further embittered him against Britain. A series of puppet governments preserved a façade of constitutionalism but educated youth turned increasingly to opposition.

At the turn of the century Britain gained a freer hand in Egypt. The Sudan was reconquered between 1896 and 1898. A clash between British and French at Fashoda on the Upper Nile was narrowly averted and the liquidation of this problem led ultimately to the Entente Cordiale of 1904 and the diminution of French opposition in Egypt. At the same time senior British officials, who had increased in number from about 100 in 1885 to over 1,000 in 1905, were out of touch with the growing strength of nationalist feeling.

Cromer was succeeded in 1907 by Sir Eldon Gorst, who managed to establish better relations with the Khedive and adopted an attitude of informality which contrasted with Cromer's proconsular pomp. On his death in 1911 he was followed by Lord Kitchener, who, as conqueror of the Sudan, was treated with more deference than had been grudgingly accorded to Gorst and whose arrival marked a return to more autocratic methods. Nevertheless a Legislative Assembly was created in 1913 which provided a platform from which the voice of nationalism could make itself heard with constitutional propriety, and it is to the credit of British rule throughout this period that the press was uncensored and the expression of opinion free.

THE FIRST WORLD WAR AND ITS CONSEQUENCES: 1914-22

After Turkey entered the First World War in November 1914 on the side of Germany, Egypt, still nominally a province of the Ottoman Empire, was declared a British protectorate and Britain assumed responsibility for the defence of the Suez Canal. On December 20th Abbas II was deposed and the British Government offered the title of Sultan to Husain Kamil, the brother of Tawfik. When Husain died in 1917 he was succeeded by his brother Fuad.

Under the protectorate the combination of British and Egyptian officials in the administration continued. Kitchener was succeeded by Sir Henry McMahon, the first High Commissioner, and he in turn was succeeded in 1917 by Sir Reginald Wingate, who had served in the Egyptian army under Kitchener and had since 1899 been Governor-General of the Sudan.

The Constantinople Convention of 1888 provided that the Suez Canal should be "always free and open, in time of war as in time of peace, to every vessel of commerce or war, without distinction of flag", but, by a blockade against enemy shipping outside the three-mile limit covered by the Convention, Britain was able to deny the use of the Canal to enemy shipping.

The pressure of military necessity was increasingly felt by the Egyptians. Martial law, censorship, the dearth of officials of good quality, the forcible recruitment of labour and the requisition of animals for the advance into Palestine, rising prices and profiteering all combined to intensify opposition to the protectorate. The nationalist movement, antagonistic to both the British administration and the Sultan, fed on popular discontent and at the end of the war, in November 1918, a delegation, headed by Saad Zaghlul, presented Wingate with a demand for autonomy. The British Government's refusal to deal with the nationalists and the deportation of Zaghlul and three of his associates resulted in riots and murders early in 1919 and order had to be restored by military action.

Wingate, who had given warning of the danger, was superseded by Allenby, fresh from his successful campaign against the Turks. Allenby made overtures to Egyptian opinion and Zaghlul and his friends were released, only to fail to get a hearing at the Peace Conference and to be rebuffed by the recognition of the British protectorate by the United States. Known now as the *Wafd* (i.e. Delegation), they set to work to organize support in Egypt and boycotted the British mission under Lord Milner, sent to report on the situation. Britain was prepared to negotiate a treaty in exchange for the abolition of the protectorate, and discussion between Milner and Zaghlul subsequently took place in Paris. After inciting further unrest in Egypt, Zaghlul was again deported, however.

On February 28th, 1922, the British Government issued a declaration unilaterally announcing the abolition of the protectorate and the recognition of Egypt as an independent sovereign state. Four matters were absolutely reserved to the discretion of the British Government, pending the conclusion of negotiated agreements. These were: the security of the communications of the British Empire in Egypt; the defence of Egypt; the protection of foreign interests and of minorities in Egypt; and the Sudan.

In March 1922 the Sultan, Fuad, took the title of King of Egypt and in April a committee was set up to draft a constitution.

THE TRIANGULAR STRUGGLE: 1922-39

The period after the declaration of independence saw a triangular struggle in Egypt between the King, the Wafd and the British Government. The Wafd was organized to carry out a revolution, not to direct affairs of state. The King owed his throne to the British and his presence guaranteed their interests, yet obvious subservience to them might have enabled the Wafd to rob him of his throne.

The new constitution, which made Egypt a parliamentary monarchy on the Belgian model, was promulgated in 1923. The Wafd triumphed in the elections which were then held and Saad Zaghlul became Prime Minister for a brief period in 1924. In the succeeding years political instability continued as the struggle for power between the Wafd and the throne went on. Elections usually gave the Wafd a majority but a Wafd ministry was unacceptable to King Fuad and in this he normally had the concurrence of the British Government. Hence Palace influence was predominant in the ministries appointed and at times legislation had to be enacted by decree. In 1928 the Parliament was suspended for three years, in 1930 modifications were made to the constitution which altered the electoral law, but in 1935 the original provisions were restored and in elections the following year the Wafd again obtained a majority. The month before the elections King Fuad had been succeeded by his son, Farouk, a minor. The new Prime Minister was Nahas Pasha, who had led the Wafd since Zaghlul's death in 1927.

Until 1936 negotiations for an Anglo-Egyptian treaty invariably broke down over questions of defence and the Sudan. The continued presence of British troops was regarded by Egyptians as denying the reality of independence. The Egyptians also felt that they had been ousted by Britain from dominion over the Sudan and control over their water supply. When the Governor-General of the Sudan was assassinated in Cairo in 1924, Allenby demanded the withdrawal of Egyptian troops from the Sudan, and also the unlimited extension of the irrigation of the Sudan Gezira. Although these demands were later modified, the Egyptian share in the Condominium was to remain nominal.

In 1929 the Nile Waters Agreement allotted the respective shares of Egypt and the Sudan, to Egypt's advantage. The deadlock over a treaty ended in 1936 when the rise of Italian power threatened British and Egyptian interests alike. On August 26th an Anglo-Egyptian treaty of twenty years duration was signed which formally terminated British occupation but empowered Britain to station forces in the Suez Canal zone until the Egyptian army was in a position to ensure the security of the Canal. The Sudan was to continue to be administered as in the past. The protection of foreign interests and of minorities in Egypt was recognized as the exclusive responsibility of the Egyptian Government. The abolition of the Capitulations was secured by the Convention of Montreux in May 1937. In the same month Egypt was admitted to the League of Nations.

THE SECOND WORLD WAR AND ITS CONSEQUENCES: 1939-52

In the Second World War Egypt was a vital strategic factor as the British base in the Middle East. Her treaty obligations were fulfilled but the ruling classes were by no means committed to the Allied cause and on occasions popular support for Germany became manifest. Nevertheless the presence of British forces ensured co-operation.

The young King Farouk, who had assumed full royal powers in 1937, was a popular national figure but as determined as his father to avoid domination by the Wafd. Although still the dominant political party, the Wafd was losing its revolutionary fervour and its appeal to youth was diminishing. Fascist influence appeared in the Greenshirt organization, while the Muslim Brotherhood, a puritanical religious body, developed a terrorist wing and threatened the established authorities.

The critical year was 1942. Alamein had not yet been fought, the King was disposed to appease the Axis powers and the government was under Palace influence. The Wafd, however, favoured co-operation with Britain. In February the British Ambassador, supported by an armed escort, entered the Palace and insisted on the formation of a Wafdist government. Threatened with deposition, Farouk acquiesced and Nahas Pasha became Prime Minister and Military Governor of Egypt.

Nahas held office until 1944. During this period Nuri al-Said, the Prime Minister of Iraq, and King Abdulla of Transjordan separately put forward proposals for a union of Arab states in the Fertile Crescent. These were opposed by Egypt as they seemed to favour Iraqi hegemony. Nahas took the initiative, proposing a broader league of Arab states, and a conference was held which in October 1944 produced the Alexandria Protocol. On this the Arab League was founded the following year. From the beginning Egypt held a position of leadership in the League, which was bitterly hostile to the idea of establishing a Jewish state in Palestine. Previously, preoccupied with her own national problems, Egypt had shown little interest in the Palestine problem.

By 1944 the danger to Egypt had passed. Nahas was no longer indispensable and his government fell, discredited by co-operation with the British and by the corruption which had flourished during its tenure of office. The struggle between the Wafd and the

Palace revived. Communism, made attractive, especially among students, by the Russian successes in the war, gained new adherents, and the Muslim Brotherhood continued its subversive activities. Negotiations in the immediate post-war years for a new treaty with Britain broke down over the questions of the British occupation of the Canal Zone and the future of the Sudan.

In Palestine Britain's renunciation of the Mandate on May 14th, 1948, was followed immediately by the declaration of the State of Israel and military action by Egypt, Iraq, Syria and Jordan. The Egyptian army was badly defeated. Although the fact was long concealed from the Egyptian public, it eventually recoiled on the ruling classes. The King's early popularity had vanished; military failure and the scandal of the supply of faulty arms, in which members of the Palace clique were implicated, undermined the loyalty of the army, which was his last support.

The fall of the discredited regime did not come immediately. The Communists, although widespread, lacked the means to capture the administration. A terrorist campaign by the Muslim Brotherhood was suppressed and the organization driven underground in 1949. Nahas, again in power, made a last bid for royal and popular support in 1951 by abrogating the Treaty of 1936 and the Condominium Agreement and proclaiming Farouk "King of Egypt and Sudan". New British proposals on the Sudan were rejected, as also were proposals on defence, involving the creation of an Allied Middle East Command with Egyptian participation, put forward jointly by Britain, France, Turkey and the United States. Terrorism and economic sanctions were then employed in an attempt to force the withdrawal of British forces from the Canal Zone. Clashes occurred, resulting in many deaths, and on January 26th, 1952, an anti-British demonstration in Cairo developed into rioting, looting and a conflagration, brought to an end only by army intervention.

THE REVOLUTION: 1952-56

On July 23rd, 1952, a group of young army officers, the "Free Officers", who had long been planning a *coup d'état*, seized power in Cairo. They invited the veteran politician, Ali Maher, to form a government under their control, and secured the abdication of King Farouk in favour of his infant son, Ahmed Fuad II, on July 26th. Farouk sailed to exile.

General Muhammad Neguib, an associate of the Free Officers who had incurred the enmity of King Farouk and who had earlier made himself popular by his condemnation of the British action in 1942, was made Commander-in-Chief of the armed forces and head of the military junta. A Council of Regency was formed in August. On September 7th, after an attempt by the Wafd and other parties to resume the political battle on their own terms, a new cabinet with General Neguib as Prime Minister was substituted for that of Ali Maher. Real power, however, lay with the nine officers who formed the Revolutionary Command Council.

The Revolution soon gained momentum. In September 1952 land ownership was limited to 300 acres in any one family and the power of the feudal class which had for so long dominated Egyptian political life was destroyed. Land owned by the royal family was confiscated. On December 10th the constitution was abolished and on January 16th, 1953, all political parties were dissolved. It was announced that there would be a three-year transition period before representative government was restored. On June 18th the monarchy was abolished and Egypt declared a republic, with Neguib as President and Prime Minister as well as Chairman of the Revolutionary Command Council. Colonel Gamal Abdel Nasser, who, although leader of the Free Officers, had hitherto remained in the background, became Deputy Prime Minister and Minister of the Interior, and Abdel Hakim Amer was appointed Commander-in-Chief of the armed forces.

A struggle for power soon developed between General Neguib, whose personal tendencies were Islamic and conservative, and Colonel Nasser. On February 25th, 1954, Neguib was relieved of his posts as President, Prime Minister and Chairman of the Revolutionary Command Council and accused of having attempted to concentrate power in his own hands. Nasser became Prime Minister and Chairman of the Revolutionary Command Council in his place for a few days but Neguib was restored as President and took back both the other posts, only to be ousted again as Prime Minister by Nasser in April. Neguib had suffered a defeat and his liberal measures were rescinded. When in October a member of the Muslim Brotherhood attempted to assassinate Nasser, its leaders and several thousand alleged supporters were arrested and in subsequent trials a number of death sentences were passed. On November 14th, 1954, General Neguib was relieved of the office of President and accused of being involved in a Muslim Brotherhood conspiracy against the regime. He was placed under house arrest and Colonel Nasser became acting head of state.

A settlement of the Sudan and Suez problems had been facilitated by the expulsion of King Farouk. The claim to the joint monarchy of Egypt and the Sudan was dropped and negotiations with Sudanese leaders were helped by the fact that Neguib himself was half-Sudanese and popular in the Sudan. An Anglo-Egyptian agreement, signed on February 12th, 1953, ended the Condominium and offered the Sudanese the choice of independence or union with Egypt. Egyptian expectation that they would choose the latter was disappointed; the overthrow of Neguib and the suppression of the Muslim Brotherhood fed the century-old suspicion of Egyptian motives.

An Anglo-Egyptian agreement on Suez was signed on October 19th, 1954; this provided for the withdrawal of British troops from the Canal Zone within twenty months. The agreement recognized the international importance of the Suez Canal (which was described as "an integral part of Egypt") and expressed the determination of both parties to uphold the 1888 convention.

Under Nasser Egypt began to assert her importance in world affairs. He sought influence in three circles: the Islamic, the African and the Arab, and his visit to the Bandung conference in 1955 added a fourth: the "non-aligned". Egypt led the opposition among certain Arab states to the Baghdad Pact (on which was founded the Central Treaty Organization). In October 1955 Egypt concluded defence agreements with Syria and with Saudi Arabia and in April 1956 a military pact was signed between Egypt, Saudi Arabia and the Yemen. Tension with Israel remained high, and raids and counter-raids across the border of the Gaza Strip called for unceasing vigilance on the part of the United Nations observers stationed on the frontier. In September 1955 Nasser announced an arms deal with Czechoslovakia which was to supply large quantities of military equipment, including Soviet tanks and aircraft, in return for cotton and rice.

In 1956 a constitutional basis for Colonel Nasser's authority was established. A new constitution providing for a strong presidency was proclaimed in January and on June 23rd approved in a plebiscite in which the citizens of the Egyptian Republic also elected Nasser as President.

THE SUEZ CRISIS AND ITS CONSEQUENCES: 1956-57

President Nasser's policy of non-alignment, which implied willingness to deal with both power blocs, was followed in the Egyptian attempt to obtain funds for the ambitious High Dam project at Aswan. By this project the Egyptian Government aimed to increase cultivable land and generate electricity for industrialization, which was seen as the main solution to Egypt's increasing population problem. Following offers of assistance from the United States and Britain and, separately, by the U.S.S.R., the International Bank for Reconstruction and Development offered a loan of $200 million in February 1956, on condition that the United States and Britain lent a total of $70 million and that the agreement of the riparian states to the scheme was obtained; Egypt was to provide local services and material.

The last British troops were withdrawn from Egypt in June 1956, in accordance with the 1954 agreement. Relations with the West were not helped, however, by Egyptian opposition to the Baghdad Pact and strong propaganda attacks on Britain, France and the United States. On July 20th the United States and Britain withdrew their offers of finance for the High Dam, pointing out that agreement between the riparian states had not been achieved and that Egypt's ability to devote adequate resources to the scheme was doubtful. The U.S.S.R. made no compensating move. On July 26th President Nasser announced that the Suez Canal Company had been nationalized and that revenue from the Canal would be used to finance the High Dam.

Britain, France and the United States protested strongly at this action and after an international conference had met in London in August a committee under the chairmanship of Mr. Menzies, the Prime Minister of Australia, went to Cairo to submit proposals for the operation of the Canal under an international system. These were rejected by the Egyptian Government. At a second London conference, in September, a Suez Canal Users' Association took shape and was later joined by sixteen states. On October 13th the UN Security Council voted on an Anglo-French resolution embodying basic principles for a settlement agreed earlier between the British, French and Egyptian Foreign Ministers in the presence of the UN Secretary-General. The first part of this, setting out the agreed principles, was adopted unanimously; the second, endorsing the proposals of the first London conference and inviting Egypt to make prompt proposals providing no less effective guarantees to users, was vetoed by the U.S.S.R.

Britain and France, thus frustrated in their attempts to retain some measure of control over the Suez Canal, at this stage reached a secret understanding with Israel involving military action. Following the disclosure on October 24th that a unified military command had been formed by Egypt, Jordan and Syria, Israeli forces on October 29th crossed into Sinai, ostensibly to attack Egyptian *fedayeen* bases, and advanced towards the Suez Canal. On October 30th France and Britain called on Israel and Egypt to cease warlike action and withdraw their forces from either side of the Canal; Egypt was requested to agree to an Anglo-French force moving temporarily into key positions at Port Said, Ismailia and Suez. Israel agreed but Egypt refused. The same day in the UN Security Council Britain and France vetoed United States and Soviet resolutions calling for an immediate Israeli withdrawal and calling on all UN members to refrain from the use of force or the threat of force.

Anglo-French air operations against Egypt began on October 31st but paratroops and seaborne forces landed in the Port Said area only on November 5th. Meanwhile, on November 2nd, the UN General Assembly called for a cease-fire and two days later adopted a Canadian proposal to create a United Nations Emergency Force to supervise the ending of the hostilities. On November 6th, following heavy United States pressure, the British Prime Minister, Sir Anthony Eden, announced that, subject to confirmation that Egypt and Israel had accepted an unconditional cease-fire, the armed conflict would end at midnight.

The organization of the UN force was rapidly put in hand and the first units reached Egypt on November 15th. The withdrawal of the Anglo-French forces was completed the following month. The Israelis, who had occupied the entire Sinai peninsula, withdrew from all areas except the Gaza strip, which they wished to prevent becoming a base for more raids, and Sharm el-Sheikh at the entrance to the Gulf of Aqaba, which commanded the seaway to the port of Eilat. These areas were returned to Egyptian control in March 1957 after pressure on Israel by the United States.

The Suez Canal, which had been blocked by the Egyptians, was cleared by a UN salvage fleet and reopened at the end of March 1957. The Egyptian Government rejected in February a plan proposed by

Britain, France, Norway and the United States, for the Canal to be operated by Egypt but the tolls collected by an outside agency. The Egyptian terms, announced on March 18th, which users of the Canal were subsequently obliged to accept, were full control by the Egyptian Canal Authority and respect for the Constantinople Convention of 1888. Disputes would be settled in accordance with the UN Charter or referred to the International Court of Justice.

UNION OF EGYPT AND SYRIA

Elections to the Egyptian National Assembly, provided for in the 1956 constitution, were held in July 1957. Only candidates approved by President Nasser and his colleagues were permitted to stand and it was clear that the 350 members elected (who included women) were not expected to exert much influence on the government.

Following the defence agreement in 1955, discussions had been held in the following two years on union between Egypt and Syria. Both countries were aligned against the West and looked to the U.S.S.R. and other Communist states for support, and in Syria pro-Egyptian elements were in the ascendant. On February 1st, 1958 the union of Egypt and Syria under the title of the United Arab Republic (U.A.R.) was announced. Both parliaments then formally approved the union and seventeen principles on which the constitution of the U.A.R. would be based were proclaimed. A plebiscite, held in both countries on February 21st, confirmed the union and made Nasser the first President of the United Arab Republic

The implementation of the union took time, and it was not until July 21st, 1960, that the first National Assembly of the U.A.R. was opened in Cairo by President Nasser. It consisted of 400 deputies from Egypt and 200 from Syria, appointed by him from candidates nominated by the National Union. Over half the deputies were former members of the dissolved national assemblies of Egypt and Syria.

EXTERNAL RELATIONS: 1958-61

During this period President Nasser was actively concerned with changes in the rest of the Arab world.

An invitation was extended to other Arab states to join the new Union and in March 1958 the U.A.R. and the Yemen entered into a loose association referred to as the United Arab States. This association did not prosper, however, and was terminated by the U.A.R. in December 1961.

The military revolution in Iraq in July, in which the royal family and the Prime Minister, Nuri al-Said, were murdered, destroyed the only Arab regime in the Middle East to have identified itself explicitly with the West. The immediate dispatch of American troops to the Lebanon and British forces to Jordan drew strong protests from the U.A.R. which were echoed by the U.S.S.R. The U.S.A. and Britain gave warning of the grave consequences of any conflict between their forces and those under the control of Egypt and Syria. President Nasser visited Moscow and on his return received in Damascus a delegation from the new republican regime in Baghdad. A joint communiqué on July 19th declared that the U.A.R. and Iraq would assist each other to repel any foreign aggression.

U.A.R. propaganda voiced support for a revolt which broke out at Mosul in Iraq in March 1959, and there were mass demonstrations in Cairo and Damascus in sympathy with the rebels. The Iraqi Government of General Kassem countered with the accusation that the revolt had been engineered from Syria. The political committee of the Arab League met at Beirut in April in an attempt to reduce the prevailing tension but Iraq took no part in the principal activities of the League until 1960 when relations with the U.A.R. improved.

President Nasser's hostility to the West found favour with the U.S.S.R., with which the U.A.R. established closer ties during these years. In addition to purchases of arms and industrial equipment, Soviet aid for the construction of five airfields and for industrial projects in Egypt was announced in December 1958 and the same month an agreement was concluded which ensured Soviet assistance for the building of the Aswan High Dam. Work on the first stage of the High Dam began in January 1960 and it was announced that the U.S.S.R. had agreed to participate in the second stage, due to begin in 1962. Soviet assistance was also obtained for other industrial enterprises.

Relations with the West improved during 1959 and 1960. Through the mediation of the International Bank for Reconstruction and Development an agreement with Britain was signed on March 1st, 1959, providing for the payment by the U.A.R. of £27½ million as compensation for British private property taken over at the time of the Suez crisis in 1956. Diplomatic relations with Britain were resumed at chargé d'affaires level in December 1959 and raised to ambassadorial level early in 1961. A $56.5 million loan to improve the Suez Canal was obtained from the World Bank in 1959, and other aid came from the U.S.A. in 1960.

SYRIAN WITHDRAWAL FROM U.A.R.

President Nasser replaced the two Regional Executive Councils and the Central Cabinet of the U.A.R. with a single Central Government in August 1961. By this time, however, the increasing subordination of Syria was breeding resentment and the issue of decrees in July of that year nationalizing most large-scale industrial and commercial concerns had provoked further Syrian discontent. Colonel Seraj, a Syrian Vice-President of the U.A.R., resigned on September 26th and on September 28th the Syrian army seized control in Damascus and Syria withdrew from the U.A.R. President Nasser at first called for resistance to the Syrian *coup d'état* but, when the rebels were seen to be in firm control, said on October 5th that he would not oppose recognition of Syria's independence.

The loss of Syria was a bitter blow to President Nasser and his Egyptian colleagues who now set about a re-examination of their policies which resulted in a renewal of revolutionary fervour.

The U.A.R. Government (Egypt retained the full title) was re-formed on October 18th and a National Congress of Popular Forces, consisting of 1,750 delegates, representing not geographical areas but economic and professional interests and other social groups, met in Cairo on May 21st, 1962. President Nasser presented the National Congress with a draft National Charter outlining his programme for developing the U.A.R. on Arab socialist lines. A new democratic system of government was proposed, based on the Arab Socialist Union (replacing the National Union) and including popular councils at least half the members of which would be workers or *fellahin*. The National Congress approved the Charter on June 30th and then dispersed.

MORE ATTEMPTS AT UNION

The Syrian *coup d'état* had been preceded by the overthrow in February 1963 of the regime of General Kassem in Iraq. These changes in power brought Syria and Iraq into closer alignment with Egypt and it was announced on April 17th that agreement had been reached on the formation of a federation of the three countries under the name of the United Arab Republic. Rivalries, however, arose in both Baghdad and Damascus between supporters of the Baath Party and "Nasserists" and by August President Nasser had withdrawn from the agreement, claiming that the Baathists had set up one-party dictatorships in Syria and Iraq and ignored his insistence on wider nationalist representation.

A month later President Arif of Iraq called for a Baathist union of the three countries, but after the expulsion of Baath leaders from Iraq in November 1963 and the consolidation of power in Arif's hands the unity movement between Iraq and Syria fell apart and Iraq and Egypt again moved closer together. A Unified Political Command between Iraq and Egypt began work in early 1965, but progress towards unity was slow.

During 1964 President Nasser took an important initiative in Arab League affairs by calling two Arab summits in Egypt, which determined Arab policy on the use of water from the River Jordan and also strengthened the armies of Syria, Lebanon and Jordan. A further £E1 million was set aside for the formation of the Palestine Liberation Organization.

The Arab reconciliation and presentation of a united front lasted until the spring of 1965. Iraq, Kuwait, Yemen (Republic), Algeria and the Lebanon continued to follow President Nasser's lead, only Syrian critics complaining that U.A.R. policy was not sufficiently anti-Israeli. U.A.R. relations with Jordan improved strikingly and, after a conference of heads of Arab governments in Cairo in January 1965 to discuss co-ordination of Arab policies, King Hussein, previously the object of U.A.R. attacks and derision, himself paid a visit to Cairo.

The general atmosphere of cordiality was shattered in April 1965 by President Bourguiba who criticized Arab policy on Israel as unrealistic and suggested negotiation with Israel on the basis of the 1947 UN partition plan (which would have involved Arab recognition of Israel, Israeli withdrawal to the borders proposed in the plan and the return of the Palestinian Arab refugees). This was attacked by the U.A.R. as a betrayal of the agreement at Alexandria in 1964 that the Arabs should work in concert.

At the third Arab summit conference, at Casablanca in September 1965, President Nasser found himself on the defensive, in the face of charges made by President Bourguiba (who did not attend the conference) of attempting to dominate the Arab world and interfering in the internal affairs of other Arab states.

In the Yemen, despite Egyptian support, the republican regime seemed no closer to victory over the royalists, who held the mountainous regions of the north-east and were assisted by Saudi Arabian finance and supplies of arms. This military stalemate and the financial burden of maintaining some 50,000 troops in the Yemen moved President Nasser to attempt to disengage. On August 24th, 1965, after a two-day conference at Jeddah, he and King Faisal reached agreement on a peace plan to end the civil war. A cease-fire was to be declared immediately, a national conference of Yemeni leaders was to meet to form a provisional government, Saudi Arabia was to cease supplying arms to the royalist forces, and Egyptian troops were to be withdrawn by November 1966.

The conference of republicans and royalists at Haradh in November 1965 ended in deadlock, however, owing to republican intransigence, and the Egyptian troops remained in the Yemen. On February 22nd, 1966, the day the British Government announced that British forces would leave Aden and South Arabia when that territory became independent in 1968, President Nasser stated that Egyptian troops would not be withdrawn until the revolution in the Yemen could "defend itself against the conspiracies of imperialism and reactionaries".

CHANGES OF INTERNATIONAL ALIGNMENT

The years 1964 and 1965 saw a deterioration of U.A.R. relations with the West and increasing dependence on the Soviet Union.

Relations with the United States were adversely affected by U.A.R. support for the Stanleyville rebels in the Congo during the winter of 1964–65. Diplomatic relations with Britain, already worsened by Egyptian encouragement of dissident elements in South Arabia, were severed by the U.A.R. in December 1965 over the Rhodesia issue, in common with eight other members of the Organization of African Unity.

Relations with the U.S.S.R. had been strengthened in May 1964 when the Soviet Premier, Nikita Khruschev, made a sixteen-day visit to Egypt to attend the ceremony marking the completion of the first stage of the Aswan High Dam, being built with Soviet aid. President Nasser paid his third visit to the U.S.S.R. in August 1965 and (Khruschev having been overthrown) the new Soviet Premier, Alexei Kosygin, visited the U.A.R. in May 1966, expressing support for U.A.R. policies and again demonstrating Soviet interest in the Middle East.

DOMESTIC TROUBLES

Although President Nasser obtained over 99 per cent of the votes cast in the presidential referendum in March 1965, there were subsequently more signs of discontent in the U.A.R. than at any time since he had come to power. In a speech to Arab students during his visit to Moscow in August 1965, he disclosed that a plot against his life had been discovered, in which the banned Muslim Brotherhood was thought to have been involved.

In September 1965 a new government headed by Zakaria Mohieddin replaced that of Ali Sabri, who became Secretary-General of the Arab Socialist Union. Thereafter, administrative changes were made and the security system was tightened up. Taxation was increased and measures of retrenchment were introduced because of increasing economic difficulties particularly the acute shortage of foreign exchange. United States wheat supplies were continued, credits from France, Japan and Italy and a loan from Kuwait were obtained and there were increased drawings from the International Monetary Fund. Nevertheless the level of imports, particularly food to feed the growing population, and the debt service burden resulting from the first five-year plan caused a continuing drain on foreign exchange reserves and the U.A.R. faced a balance of payments crisis. The second five-year plan was revised and extended over seven years and President Nasser gave public warnings that sacrifices were necessary in every field as Egypt lacked the foreign currency to pay for imports. He refused, however, to abandon the expensive commitment in the Yemen. Zakaria Mohieddin's replacement in September 1966 by Sidki Soliman (a technocrat who retained his post as Minister of the High Dam) was seen as the outcome of disagreement over retrenchment measures. When the U.A.R. defaulted on repayments due to the International Monetary Fund in December 1966, the country was seen to be on the verge of bankruptcy.

WIDENING RIFT WITH SAUDI ARABIA

The rift between the U.A.R. and Saudi Arabia widened. President Nasser in February 1966 expressed opposition to an Islamic grouping which King Faisal was promoting, and in the succeeding months propaganda warfare between the two countries was intensified. In the middle of the year the President gave notice that he would not attend an Arab summit conference with Saudi Arabia and Jordan, both of whom he stigmatized for obtaining British and United States military aid, and called for the indefinite postponement of the conference planned for September. A majority of Arab states agreed, but in October Tunisia broke off relations with the U.A.R. over continued differences on Arab League policies.

In the Yemen Egyptian forces had been withdrawn from northern and eastern areas and concentrated in the triangle between Sana'a, Hodeida and Taiz. Egyptian control over the republican armed forces and administration was increased and when, in September 1966, after President Sallal had returned to the Yemen from a year's absence in Cairo, the republican Prime Minister, Hassan al-Amri, and seven senior members of his cabinet visited Egypt to make a plea for greater independence, they were arrested and detained there. The following month about 100 senior Yemen officials were dismissed and arrests and executions were carried out.

WAR WITH ISRAEL

The events of May 1967 were to transform the Middle East scene. There had been an increase of Syrian guerrilla activities in Israel during the previous six months and on April 7th the tension had led to fighting in the Tiberias area in which six Syrian aircraft had been shot down. Israeli warnings to the Syrian Government, culminating on May 12th in the threat by Premier Eshkol of severe reprisals if terrorist activities were not controlled, evoked Syrian allegations that Israel was about to mount a large-scale attack on Syria. President Nasser, who had been reproached for not aiding Syria in the April fighting in accordance with the mutual defence agreement, responded immediately, moving large numbers of troops to the Israel border, He secured the dissolution of the UN Emergency Force, whose presence on the Egyptian side of the frontier depended on Egyptian permission. and re-occupied the gun emplacement at Sharm el Sheikh on the Straits of Tiran. He later justified these steps by claiming that he had received Syrian and Soviet warnings that Israeli troops were concentrated on the Syrian border (an allegation subsequently disproved by reports of UN truce observers) and an invasion of Syria was imminent.

When on May 23rd President Nasser closed the Straits of Tiran to Israeli shipping, thereby effectively blockading the Israeli port of Eilat, his prestige in the Arab world reached an unparalleled height. Britain and the United States protested that the Gulf of Aqaba was an international waterway; Israel regarded the blockade of the Straits as an unambiguous act of war. As tension increased, with frequent belligerent pronouncements from Arab leaders and the threat by President Nasser that any aggressive act by Israel would lead to an all-out battle in which the Arab aim would be Israel's destruction, King Hussein of Jordan concluded a mutual defence pact with the U.A.R. which was immediately joined by Iraq. Gestures of support were made to Nasser by all Arab leaders, including President Bourguiba and King Faisal.

On the morning of June 5th Israel launched large-scale air attacks on Egyptian, Jordanian, Syrian and Iraqi airfields and Israeli ground forces made rapid advances into the Gaza Strip, Sinai and western Jordan; there was also fighting on the Israeli-Syrian border. The outcome was decided within hours by the air strikes, which destroyed the bulk of the Arab air forces, and the Israeli ground forces were everywhere successful. By June 10th, when all participants had accepted the UN Security Council's call for a cease-fire, Israeli troops were in control of the Sinai peninsula as far as the Suez Canal (including Sharm el Sheikh), the west bank of the Jordan (including the Old City of Jerusalem), the Gaza Strip and Syrian territory extending twelve miles from the Israel border. The Suez Canal was blocked by Egypt in the course of the fighting.

On June 9th, the day after he had accepted the cease-fire, President Nasser announced his resignation in a speech in which he assumed full responsibility for the nation's plight, but the following day, in response to huge street demonstrations of popular support, he agreed to continue in office. A number of senior army officers were immediately replaced and on June 19th Nasser took over the duties of Prime Minister and Secretary-General of the Arab Socialist Union.

The implications of the catastrophe were only gradually realized. It was estimated that the loss of revenue from the Suez Canal, from oil produced in Sinai and from tourism amounted to some £12.5 million a month, or almost half Egypt's foreign currency earnings. Also, the withdrawal of a large part of the Egyptian force in the Yemen reduced Nasser's ability to influence affairs both in that country and in Aden and South Arabia (which became independent as the Republic of Southern Yemen on November 30th, 1967, after the withdrawal of British troops).

The Soviet Union, which had given the Arab cause strong verbal support throughout the crisis, continued to take a strong pro-Arab stand at the United Nations and President Podgorny paid a lengthy visit to Cairo to discuss future Egyptian policy. The U.S.S.R. replaced about half the lost Egyptian aircraft and provided other military supplies and instructors. Further economic assistance was also offered by the Soviet Union and in May 1968 an agreement was announced for the construction of a steel complex at Helwan.

Israel demanded direct negotiations with the Arab states for a peace settlement but the fourth conference of Arab heads of state, held in Khartoum at the end of August 1967, decided against recognition or negotiation with Israel. At this conference, in which Syria did not participate, it was agreed that the embargo on oil supplies to Western countries (applied the previous June) should be lifted, that the Suez Canal should remain closed until Israeli forces were withdrawn, and that Saudi Arabia, Kuwait and Libya should give special aid of £95 million a year to the U.A.R. (and also £40 million a year to Jordan) until the "effects of the aggression" were eliminated. King Faisal and President Nasser announced their agreement on a peace plan for the Yemen under which Egyptian troops were to be withdrawn within three months and Saudi Arabia was to stop supplying the royalists; the withdrawal was subsequently completed by December (President Sallal being deposed by republican leaders in November).

After repeated violations of the cease-fire by both sides, the UN Security Council on November 22nd, 1967, adopted a British resolution laying down the principles for a just and lasting peace in the Middle East and authorizing the appointment of a special UN representative to assist in bringing about a settlement. This was Resolution 242 (*see* Documents on Palestine, page 67) which later formed the basis of most attempts to restore peace to the Middle East. Dr. Gunnar Jarring was appointed special UN representative, and quickly began discussions with Arab and Israeli leaders which continued for a number of years.

U.A.R. AFTER THE JUNE WAR

Meanwhile President Nasser faced daunting economic difficulties and a disturbed political situation in Egypt. An austerity budget had been framed in July 1967. The cost of re-equipping the armed forces forced a cut in investment, in spite of Soviet aid and assistance from other Arab governments. Socialist policies were still followed, as was shown by the decision to nationalize the wholesale trade, announced in October. The continuing shortage of foreign exchange made desirable an improvement in the U.A.R.'s relations with the West and in December diplomatic relations with Britain were resumed. A bridging loan from British, West German and Italian banks, obtained in February 1968, enabled the U.A.R. to make the repayments to the International Monetary Fund which had been due since the end of 1966, and in March the IMF approved further drawings. Another hopeful development was the increased production of oil from Egyptian oilfields, which made up for the loss of Sinai.

As a result of the military débâcle the Egyptian army was subjected to major reorganization, involving the dismissal of large numbers of officers and the reorganization of the armed forces supreme command.

Widespread demonstrations of students and workers took place in Cairo, Helwan and other centres, towards the end of February 1968. Initially in protest at the leniency of sentences on air force officers, they revealed widespread discontent. A number of persons were killed in clashes with police, and the universities were closed; nevertheless President Nasser realized the need for immediate conciliatory action. Re-trials were ordered and sweeping cabinet changes announced, a number of civilian experts in various fields being brought in. Ali Sabri, who had been reinstated as Secretary-General of the Arab Socialist Union in January, was also included but Zakaria Mohieddin left the government. President Nasser continued to exercise the functions of Prime Minister.

On March 30th President Nasser announced a new plan for building a modern state in Egypt based on democracy, science and technology. The single party would remain but there would be free elections from top to bottom of the Arab Socialist Union and changes were promised among leaders in all spheres. An announcement of the distribution to the people of land taken over by the state or reclaimed was made on April 6th. In a plebiscite on May 2nd the "Declaration of March 30th" was overwhelmingly approved. The first Arab Socialist Union elections were held in June; the 75,000 persons chosen then elected a national congress in July; this in turn chose a central committee which then chose the party's higher executive. These proceedings, however, did not appear to arouse much public interest. President Nasser dissolved the U.A.R. National Assembly on November 14th and elections for a new Assembly were held on January 8th, 1969.

November 1968 saw further student riots, resulting in many injuries and some deaths, in Alexandria and Mansoura. The universities were again closed. Although these disturbances were officially attributed to the activities of an Israeli agent arrested by the police and to indignation at the continued occupation of Sinai by Israeli forces, they were seen by many observers as further evidence of frustration with the restrictions imposed by President Nasser's government and of disillusion with its performance, particularly in relation to Israel. Moreover, in uncertain health, his popularity diminished, the President appeared in 1968 to be increasingly isolated and exposed.

Deprived of foreign exchange by the continued closure of the Canal and the drop in the tourist trade, the U.A.R. remained dependent on the regular aid payments from Saudi Arabia, Kuwait and Libya and on Soviet assistance, both humiliating to a people strongly nationalist in outlook. There were signs that the civilian economic ministers favoured some relaxation of over-rigid state control in industry and more encouragement of private enterprise and foreign investment. Military expenditure in 1968 and 1969 remained high. Soviet arms deliveries continued, as also did the presence of about 3,000 Russian military advisers and instructors.

The efforts of Dr. Jarring, the representative of the UN Secretary-General, to bring Israel, the U.A.R. and Jordan closer together had, by the end of 1968, yielded little success. In April 1969, following initiatives by the U.S.S.R. and France, those two countries together with Britain and the United States, as permanent members of the Security Council, began talks at the United Nations in New York in an unsuccessful attempt to promote a settlement.

A pattern of sporadic action, involving artillery duels across the Suez Canal, commando raids and air combat developed throughout 1969 and into 1970, with growing Soviet involvement in Egypt's defence. In the summer of 1970 the U.S. Secretary of State, Mr. William Rogers, put forward a set of proposals for solving the continuing Middle East crisis. After lengthy negotiations and a visit by President Nasser to Moscow, both Egypt and Israel agreed to a 90 days ceasefire in August 1970. Talks between the U.A.R. and Jordan on the one hand and Israel on the other began later in August in New York under the guidance of the UN mediator Gunnar Jarring. They soon broke down following accusations from both sides of violations of the ceasefire agreement, but despite this the ceasefire was renewed, on its expiry, for another three months.

EGYPT AFTER NASSER

Although President Nasser had had his differences with the Palestinian guerrillas over their rejection of the U.S. peace proposals and the hijackings of the western airliners at the beginning of September, one of his last acts was to secure agreement in Cairo between King Hussein and Yassir Arafat for an end to the fighting between the Jordanian army and the guerrillas.

Nasser's death on September 28th, 1970, came as a profound shock and it was feared by many that it would materially lessen chances of achieving peace in the Middle East. A close associate of Nasser, and Vice-President at the time of his death, Col. Anwar Sadat, was immediately appointed provisional President by the Cabinet and Party, being later elected President in a national referendum, and by mid-1971 he was firmly in control of the government of Egypt.

In November 1970 President Sadat (whose mother is Sudanese) had agreed to the federation of the U.A.R. with Sudan and Libya. Sudan, however, later postponed her membership of a union and it was Syria who in April became the third member of the Federation. The federation proposals, together with Sadat's plan for the reopening of the Canal, precipitated a crisis in the leadership which led to a comprehensive purge by Sadat of opponents at all levels of the government. Ali Sabri, one of the two Vice-Presidents, and strongly pro-Moscow, was the first to go, on May 2nd, just before U.S. Secretary of State, William Rogers, arrived in Cairo. On May 13th, President Sadat, convinced of an impending coup, dismissed six other ministers and important Party and National Assembly members. In July new elections were held, not only for all levels of the Party, but also for trade unions and professional bodies. A new constitution, the first permanent one since the 1952 revolution, was voted in September. It contained important clauses governing personal freedoms and discarded at last the name of United Arab Republic, the state being known henceforward as the Arab Republic of Egypt.

The year 1971 was marked by repeated Egyptian declarations of the intention to fight Israel—but only when the time was ripe—and Egypt mounted an extensive diplomatic campaign to state her case in the West. In September 1971 came the first large-scale military operations on the canal since the August 1970 ceasefire and in December the UN passed a resolution calling for the resumption of the Jarring peace mission.

Dr. Mahmoud Fawzi, who was appointed Prime Minister in October 1970, resigned in January 1972 and was made a joint Vice-President. His successor was Dr. Aziz Sidqi, who had been First Vice-Premier since September 1971.

Egypt was becoming increasingly dependent on the U.S.S.R., both militarily and economically. In spite of Russian assurances that aid would be continued, the Egyptians were becoming very dissatisfied. This was partly because they felt the arms deliveries were not up to standard, and partly because of the frustration engendered in the country by the prolonged state of uncertainty. Student riots at the beginning of 1972 brought assurances from President Sadat that an armed confrontation with Israel was definitely intended. Against this background of increasing internal uneasiness Egypt intensified efforts to diversify sources of development aid and armaments. The Suez-Alexandria (Sumed) pipeline received promises of Western backing and in May 1972 a five-year preferential trade agreement was concluded with the EEC.

CRISIS IN EGYPTIAN-SOVIET RELATIONS

The most striking event of 1972 was the dismissal of Soviet military advisers from Egypt in July and the manning of installations by Egyptians. This did not lead to a rupture in Egyptian-Soviet relations but neither did it result in any significant rapprochement with the West, anti-American feeling remaining very strong. A new round of diplomatic visits to state Egypt's case, particularly in the West and the Far East, was embarked upon and arms supplies requested from France and Britain. With the announcement on August 2nd, 1972, of Egypt's plan to merge with Libya, France stated that supplies of Mirage fighters to Libya would continue, Libya not being in direct conflict with Israel.

Contacts with the U.S.S.R. continued and economic relations appeared unaffected by the events of July but it was clear that the U.S.S.R. was looking elsewhere to maintain its presence in the Mediterranean. It was unclear to what extent Sadat's hand had been forced in ordering the Soviet withdrawal.

INTERNAL UNREST

A law passed in August 1972 provided for penalties up to life imprisonment for offences endangering national unity, including opposing the Government by force and inciting violence between Muslims and the Coptic minority. Clashes between these two communities were growing more frequent and, along with increasing student unrest, were seen as an expression of dissatisfaction with the state of "no-peace-no-war". The Government resorted to repeated assurances of military preparations. In December 1972, Sadat in fact ordered preparations for fighting, after strong criticism in the People's Assembly of the Government's policies. Another cause of uneasiness was the proposed merger with Libya, which many people felt might give Colonel Gaddafi too much control over Egypt's destiny.

January 1973 saw violent clashes between police and students and the universities had to be closed for a short time. In February a number of left-wing elements, among them many journalists, were expelled from the ASU, student unrest continued and in March President Sadat took over from Aziz Sidqi as Prime Minister. The new administration's policies were approved by the People's Assembly but the Government was criticized for failing to follow a clear-cut economic policy, particularly with regard to the five-year plan.

RELATIONS WITH LIBYA

Egypt and Libya had agreed on a programme of full union by stages at a meeting between the two Heads of State in Benghazi in August 1972, and a merger of the two countries was planned to take place on September 1st, 1973. The Libyan leader, Colonel Gaddafi, showed more enthusiasm than President Sadat for total union, and in July 1973 Gaddafi organized a march of 40,000 Libyans on Cairo in order to bring pressure to bear on Egypt. The march was turned back about 200 miles from Cairo, however, and Sadat, although showing support for eventual union, stated that "enthusiasm and emotional impulses are not a sufficient basis for unity." An agreement in principle was nevertheless signed on August 29th, but few practical steps were taken to implement the agreement.

Relations between Egypt and Libya have since deteriorated. Gaddafi was very critical of Egypt's strategy in the early days of the October war, and when, in April 1974, a terrorist attack took place on the Military Technical Academy at Heliopolis, outside Cairo, it was suspected in Egyptian circles that the attack was the beginning of an attempted *coup* in which Libya was implicated. Throughout 1974 and early 1975 relations between the two countries deteriorated to such an extent that President Sadat asserted in a press interview in April 1975 that Gaddafi was "100 per cent sick". At the time Libya had been threatening to take action against Egyptians working in Libya. In spite of the apparent temporary success in May 1975 of attempts by a mission from the National Assembly of the Federation of Arab Republics to mediate between Sadat and Gaddafi, relations soon worsened when a large Soviet-Libyan arms deal was revealed later in the month. President Sadat hastily accused Libya and the Soviet Union of conducting an international campaign against him and his Middle East policy. Libya was among the Arab countries severely critical of the Second Interim Disengagement Agreement between Egypt and Israel in September 1975, and relations between Egypt and Libya showed little sign of improvement during 1976 and 1977. In fact, when severe riots against food prices took place in Cairo in January 1977, Gaddafi was among the people whom Sadat accused of being responsible. In July 1977 open warfare took place on the border between Egypt and Libya, and when Sadat visited Israel in November 1977 (*see* below), relations deteriorated even further, with Egypt breaking off diplomatic relations with Libya in December. Subsequent events have brought about a further deterioration in relations. Libya joined the rest of the Arab world in condemning the Egyptian-Israeli peace treaty in March 1979, and it was reported that renewed outbreaks of war on the Egyptian-Libyan border were prevented only by the intervention of the U.S.A.

THE OCTOBER WAR AND ITS AFTERMATH

Between the June 1967 war and October 1973 Egyptian leaders frequently stated that the war against Israel would be resumed, but when Egyptian forces crossed the Suez Canal on October 6th, 1973, it came as a surprise to Israel and to the rest of the world. The course of the war, and the political questions involved, are dealt with in the chapter "The Arab-Israeli Confrontation 1967–79", pages 37–54. For President Sadat the war was a considerable triumph. It appeared to end the years of stalemate with Israel, and his personal reputation was greatly enhanced. As a result of the Disengagement Agreement which Israel and Egypt signed on January 18th, 1974, Egyptian forces regained a strip of territory to the east of the Suez Canal (see map on page 72).

After the war extensive and far-reaching changes took place in Egypt. An amnesty was extended to many important political prisoners in January 1974, and in April an amnesty was extended to more than 2,000 persons who had been imprisoned for political or criminal offences. Press censorship was lifted in February, and in April about 8.5 million voters gave a 99.95 per cent endorsement to a programme of economic and social reform which concentrated on reconstruction, attracting foreign investment, limiting police interference in everyday life, and the introduction of a private enterprise sector in the economy while still maintaining the public sector (*see* Economic Survey).

One result of the October war was Egypt's improved relations with the U.S.A. Diplomatic relations between Egypt and the U.S.A. were restored in November 1973 and the U.S. Secretary of State, Dr. Henry Kissinger, had a cordial relationship with President Sadat during the disengagement talks. American initiatives in peacemaking were generally welcomed by Egypt, while the Americans became more conscious of the extent of their dependence on Arab oil. It was in this atmosphere of *rapprochement* that President Nixon visited Cairo in June 1974, and the U.S.A. and Egypt agreed to set up a Joint Co-operation Commission and to begin negotiating an agreement for co-operation in the field of nuclear energy.

RETURN TO STALEMATE

The euphoria which the crossing of the Suez Canal had produced began to disappear during 1974. Increases in the cost of living, and the slowness with which the promised economic reform was proceeding, led to riots in Cairo on January 1st, 1975, and to further disturbances among textile workers in March 1975, when the textile complex at El Mahalla el Kubra was closed for several days after violent clashes over pay demands. Inflation was estimated at the time to be running at an annual rate of about 24 per cent.

As a result of these disturbances Dr. Abdel-Aziz Higazi, who had taken over the premiership from President Sadat in September 1974, resigned as Prime Minister and was replaced in April 1975 by Gen. Mamdouh Muhammad Salem, the former Minister of the Interior and Deputy Prime Minister. On May 1st, 1975, President Sadat announced that all lower-paid public-sector employees would receive additional cost-of-living allowances equal to 30 per cent of their pay, and later in May, in a speech to the People's Assembly, the new Prime Minister promised that steps would be taken to ensure that the economic programme of 1974 would be implemented and that foreign investors, whether from Western countries or from the Eastern bloc, would be given every facility.

During the first eight months of 1975 Dr. Kissinger engaged in considerable "shuttle diplomacy" and in September Egypt and Israel signed the Second Interim Disengagement Agreement. In brief, Israel withdrew from the Giddi and Mitla passes and Egypt recovered the Abu Rudais oilfield in Sinai, while Article I of the Agreement stated that Egypt and Israel have agreed that "the conflict between them and in the Middle East shall not be resolved by military force but by peaceful means." This agreement brought upon President Sadat the strong disapproval of other Arab interests, particularly Syria, Jordan, Iraq and the PLO, as it appeared to them that Egypt was seeking to commit the whole Arab world to a policy of peace with Israel. The position had also been complicated by the fact that, at the Arab Summit at Rabat in October 1974, the PLO had achieved the status of the sole legitimate representative of the Palestinian people. At the end of May 1976 Egypt attempted to consolidate an improvement in relations with the PLO by asking the Arab League to admit the PLO as a full member. Relations with Syria, at a particularly low ebb during the Lebanese civil war, improved after the Riyadh and Cairo summits in October 1976.

The rest of the Arab world was also aware that Egypt was drawing even closer to the United States. Certainly, Sadat was becoming disillusioned with the Soviet Union. In March 1976 he abrogated the Treaty of Friendship with the U.S.S.R. which Egypt had signed in 1971. In a speech to the Egyptian People's Assembly Sadat accused the Soviet Union of exerting political, economic and military pressure on Egypt by criticising his Middle East policies, refusing to reschedule Egypt's debts, and refusing supplies of weapons and spares.

POLITICAL ADVANCE AND DOMESTIC DIFFICULTIES

During 1976 and for most of 1977, President Sadat was forced to involve himself increasingly in domestic issues. In March 1976 three political "platforms" were allowed to form within the Arab Socialist Union, and in the November 1976 elections to the People's Assembly the "platforms" entered the contest as full-scale political parties. The Arab Socialists (a party of the centre, supporting Sadat) won 280 seats, while the Liberal Socialists (supporting political and economic liberalization) won 12 seats. The left-wing National Progressive Unionist Party won 2 seats. After the elections President Sadat announced that the Arab Socialist Union would fade into the background and would become merely a watchdog for the three parties' activities.

Egypt's economy, during 1976, was experiencing great difficulties (*see* Economic Survey), and when in January 1977 Sadat announced a budget which, because of the withdrawal of subsidies, meant large increases in food and other prices, severe riots broke out in Cairo and other centres.

In the face of this opposition Sadat had to revoke the price increases and in February he introduced a law which made a wide range of new offences punishable by hard labour for life. Among these offences were forming a political group other than the three legal parties; forming a group to destroy public or private property; failing to submit an accurate account of earnings and property; tax evasion; stirring up the people or impeding the Government, or public and private sectors, or the institutions of learning; and premeditated striking. These measures were put to a referendum in which 96.9 per cent of the enfranchised population voted, and 99.4 per cent of the votes cast approved of the measures.

By June 1977 Sadat considered the internal situation in Egypt to be sufficiently under control to regularize the current position on political parties. A law was adopted by the People's Assembly stating that each party must include at least 20 members of the People's Assembly (current parties excepted). This effectively excluded the Communist Party, the Muslim Brotherhood and the New Wafd Party.

PROGRESS TOWARDS A PEACE TREATY WITH ISRAEL

In November 1977, however, domestic questions were completely overshadowed by a dramatic event which surprised the world. President Sadat visited Israel and addressed the Knesset in Jerusalem. It was by no means certain whether any tangible peace proposals would result from Sadat's talks with Menachem Begin, the newly-elected Likud Premier of Israel whose hitherto "hawkish" attitude did not seem to augur well for the cause of peace, but who might use his newly-acquired power in putting forward a daring initiative. In the event, no significant breakthrough was made immediately. The status of any future Palestine state seemed to present the main obstacle. Talks continued in 1978 at various levels at several locations, in spite of the opposition of much of the Arab world, who regarded Egypt's unilateral bid for peace with Israel as detrimental to Arab unity. In September 1978 there came a somewhat unexpected breakthrough when, after talks at Camp David in the U.S.A. under the guidance of President Carter, Sadat and Begin signed two agreements. The first was a "framework of peace in the Middle East" (*see* p. 73) and the second was a "framework for the conclusion of a peace treaty between Egypt and Israel". The first agreement provided for a five-year transitional period during which the inhabitants of the Israeli-occupied West Bank of the Jordan and the Gaza Strip would obtain full autonomy and self-government, and the second agreement provided for the signing of a peace treaty within three months. In the event the signing of the peace treaty was delayed because of the question of whether there should be any linkage between the conclusion of the peace treaty and progress towards autonomy in the Israeli-occupied areas, but on March 27th, 1979, after another intervention by President Carter, the signing took place. The treaty (*see* p. 77) provided for a phased Israeli withdrawal from Sinai over a period of three years. El Arish was, in fact, returned to Egypt on May 16th, 1979.

Proposals for Palestinian autonomy were contained in a separate letter published with the treaty, and provided for negotiations to begin within one month of ratification of the treaty and for both sides to attempt to complete negotiations within twelve months. There would then be elections of Palestinian local councils and a five-year transitional period would follow during which the final status of the West Bank and Gaza would be negotiated. The autonomy negotiations began in May 1979.

The Camp David agreements and the subsequent peace treaty resulted in Egypt's isolation in the Arab world. Syria, Algeria, Libya and the PLO had met in Damascus in September 1978 and strongly condemned the Camp David agreements, and in March 1979, after the signing of the peace treaty, the Arab League Council met in Baghdad and passed a series of resolutions (*see* p. 79) comprising the withdrawal of Arab ambassadors to Egypt, the severing of economic and political links with Egypt, the withdrawal of Arab aid and the ultimate removal of the headquarters of the Arab League from Cairo to Tunis. Egypt had already been threatened with these sanctions at an earlier Arab summit in Baghdad in November 1978. Some Arab States were reluctant to honour these decisions, but when Saudi Arabia finally broke off diplomatic relations with Egypt in late April, Egypt's isolation became a reality. As a result Egypt is having to rely even more heavily than before on financial and military aid from the U.S.A., although an arms agreement has also been signed with the People's Republic of China.

INTERNAL POLITICAL CHANGE

Since 1976 President Sadat had been trying to allow the formation of political parties while at the same time ensuring that dangerous opposition did not achieve too much influence. In a law of June 1977 political parties were legalized. Disturbed by the revival of the Wafd Party (the New Wafd Party) and the criticisms of the National Progressive Unionist Party, Sadat won approval in a referendum for a new set of regulations on political parties which resulted in the disbanding of the New Wafd Party and the suspension of the National Progressive Unionist Party. In July Sadat announced the creation of a new political party, the National Democratic Party, with himself as leader, which in practice replaced the Arab Socialist Party. In September 1978 an official opposition party, the Socialist Labour Party, was formed.

The signing of the Camp David agreements in September 1978, although causing the resignation of the Egyptian Foreign Minister, Muhammad Ibrahim Kamel, was popular in Egypt and in October Sadat appointed a new government, specially geared to peace, with Mustapha Khalil as Prime Minister. Khalil also became Foreign Minister in February 1979. The signing of the peace treaty in March was followed by a referendum in April in which 99.95 per cent of the voters approved the treaty. Another simultaneous referendum resulted in 99.9 per cent of the voters approving Sadat's plan for fresh general elections, greater freedom to form political parties and the formation of a second parliamentary-style consultative body. Elections took place for a new 392-member National Assembly (30 of whom are to be women) in June 1979, and preliminary results show an overwhelming victory for President Sadat's Social Democratic Party, who won 302 out of the 382 seats which were contested (10 are nominated).

By August 1979 talks on Palestinian autonomy had achieved very little, but were planned to continue.

ECONOMIC SURVEY

INTRODUCTION

The Egyptian economy in mid-1979 was entering a period of great uncertainty. Since 1973 there had been great efforts made to repair the material damage caused by the most recent war with Israel and to harness some of the euphoria generated by Egypt's victory in revitalizing the economy. The socialist planning which had been inherited from President Nasser gave way in 1974 to a policy of greater liberalization. Sadat's Law No. 43 of 1974 aimed at encouraging the inflow of investment from abroad, particularly from the U.S.A. Although bureaucratic obstacles and the threat of renewed war discouraged many investors, foreign banks began to operate and some projects were begun.

The wealthier Arab States, moreover, had begun to help Egypt on an ever-increasing scale. From 1967–73 Arab aid to Egypt was estimated at an annual average of US $310 million. In 1973 this increased to $720 million, and in 1974 it rose to $1,260 million, while by 1977 it had risen to between $1,700 million and $2,000 million. Much of this aid was coming from the Gulf Organization for the Development of Egypt (GODE), set up by Saudi Arabia, Kuwait, the United Arab Emirates and Qatar in 1977. Saudi sources, in fact, claimed in May 1979 that Egypt had received more than US $13,000 million from the four GODE countries in the past six years.

By signing the peace treaty with Israel in March 1979, however, Sadat undertook the risk of losing this Arab aid. The Arab League Council which met in Baghdad immediately after the signing of the peace treaty, agreed on a policy of economic and political isolation of Egypt (*see* p. 79). At first it seemed unlikely that the economic sanctions would be stringently carried out by some of the Arab countries but when in late April Saudi Arabia broke off diplomatic relations with Egypt, some of the more "moderate" Arab States gave effect to the boycott. The Arab Fund for Economic and Social Development suspended all future aid and credit relations with Egypt, although honouring transactions already in progress, and in May Saudi Arabia, Qatar and the United Arab Emirates withdrew from the Arab Organization for Industrialization, which was an Egypt-based Arab arms enterprise, causing its collapse and jeopardizing the employment of 15,000 Egyptians. Egypt, however, responded by planning to set up its own arms industry with Western capital. The Arab trade boycott never posed a serious threat, as only about seven per cent of Egypt's total trade is with Arab countries.

It is impossible to determine exactly how effective or long-lasting the withdrawal of Arab aid will be, but it has forced Sadat to rely on aid from the West, and mainly from the U.S.A. His difficulties have been compounded by the breakdown of an arrangement for a US $730 million extended facility from the IMF and difficulties in arranging a US $300 million loan on the Eurocurrency market. Sadat hopes that Egypt's economic difficulties will be alleviated by the "Carter Plan", which he sees in the same light as the "Marshall Plan", by which Egypt would receive US $12,250 million over a period of five years, mainly from the U.S.A., Western Europe and Japan.

RECONSTRUCTION

After the October 1973 war, the most pressing need was to restore and reopen the Suez Canal and by March 1975 the Suez Canal Authority pronounced the canal ready for reopening. No-one expected the step to be taken, however, before the Israelis had made a further withdrawal into Sinai, but after the failure of U.S. Secretary of State Henry Kissinger's step-by-step approach to peace-making President Sadat took the bold decision to seize the initiative and announce that the waterway would be reopened on June 5th, 1975, the eighth anniversary of the outbreak of war which led to its closure in 1967. The next stage was to restart the interrupted programme of expansion of the canal, which is scheduled to take six years to complete. Such expansion has been made even more urgent because of the vast increase in oil-tanker sizes since June 1967 which the closure of the canal then helped provoke. The existing dimensions of the canal allow the passage of ships of 70,000 dwt or 200,000 dwt in ballast. The first part of the development programme would allow 150,000 dwt tankers to pass through fully loaded, and the second part would enable tankers of up to 260,000 dwt fully laden or 300,000 dwt partly laden to pass. A Japanese company, the Penta-Ocean Construction Company, was contracted to begin the work of widening and deepening the southern end of the canal at a cost of $172 million, backed by a Japanese Government loan. A new $113 million contract was given to Penta in November 1976 for expansion work in the Great Bitter Lake sector. The present state of depression in the tanker market seems to make such a programme an investment with doubtful returns for the foreseeable future. The state of the tanker market also means that the impact of the reopening on the oil trade is marginal for the moment, though for dry cargo the advantages of the shorter Suez route over the Cape route are much clearer. The Canal Authority set the dues for ships using the canal 90–100 per cent higher than in 1967. They are calculated in the Special Drawing Rights of the International Monetary Fund, although actual payment is in dollars. Revenue in the first year of operation was $230 million; by 1978 net revenue had risen to $520 million and was expected to rise to $580 million in 1979. Tolls are to remain constant at least until 1980.

Reconstruction of the canal cities, some of them up to 80 per cent destroyed, was put in hand and by 1979 more than a million Egyptians had returned to Port Said, Ismailia and Suez. Work began in 1977 on a tunnel under the Suez Canal near Suez, which will be essential for the eventual resettlement of Sinai.

GENERAL

The total area of Egypt is about 998,000 square km., but 96 per cent of the country is desert. With no forested land, and hardly any permanent meadows or pastures, the arable land available is greatly over-crowded. Relating the population, numbering 41 million in 1979, to the inhabited area, a density of over 1,000 persons per square kilometre gives 5.5 persons per acre of arable land, representing one of the highest man/land ratios in the world. At the root of Egypt's poverty lies its birth rate, which is adding about a million people a year to the population. Lack of employment opportunities has driven people from the country into already over-crowded cities and hastened the emigration of qualified personnel the country can ill afford to lose. Many have gone to much better paid jobs in the rich Gulf states. Poor job prospects have also helped swell the bureaucracy, since the government is committed to giving a post to every Egyptian graduate who is unable to find other employment. Gross Domestic Product per head was estimated at $385 in 1977.

Despite this low level of income, certain aspects of the Egyptian economy indicate a relative state of advance, notably communications, the irrigation system, public administration and education. Although the illiteracy rate remains high (the 1960 population census showed an illiteracy rate of 69.7 per cent among people of over ten years of age), both secondary and higher education are quite developed and Egypt is a net exporter of skills, especially to other Arab countries. Remittances sent back by Egyptians working abroad amounted to nearly US $1,000 million in 1978/79. The diet of the average Egyptian is poor and contains little animal protein.

From 1918–39 when the Egyptian pound was tied to sterling and a fairly free trade policy was being pursued, manufacturing industry had little chance of developing and agricultural production, though expanding, could not keep up with the rapidly rising population. A gradual deterioration of living standards set in. This trend did not change direction until the immediate post-war period, when cotton prices improved. These reached their greatest heights during the Korean boom of 1951–52, when "soft-currency cotton", including Egyptian cotton, enjoyed high premia over dollar-cotton. But the collapse of the boom, the easing up of the world dollar scarcity and the beginning of American subsidization of cotton exports in the mid-1950s, marked a turning point in raw cotton terms of trade which, until quite recently, showed a declining trend.

The regime which assumed power in 1952 and ended the monarchy gave urgent attention to Egypt's economic problems. Its policies included measures of agrarian reform, land reclamation, the High Dam, and a programme of industrialization which was accelerated in 1960 by the formation of a comprehensive social and economic development plan.

Egypt's first five-year plan aimed at increasing real national income by 40 per cent between 1960 and 1965, this being advertised as the first lap of a ten-year programme to double real national income by 1970. The five-year growth target was virtually fulfilled, so that the second lap was initially replaced by a more ambitious plan to double real income in seven years (i.e. by 1972). Lack of finance, however, frustrated this new plan, and after two years of uncertainty, a three-year "accomplishment" plan, beginning July 1967, was proclaimed. This was to aim at a target growth rate of 5 per cent per annum (compared with 7.2. per cent under the first five-year plan) with a total investment of £E1,085 million (against £E1,513 million in 1960–65), and would concentrate on completing projects already started, rather than initiating new ones. This plan was dropped as a result of the 1967 war and was substituted by annual development appropriations (£E320 million in 1968–69 and £E350 million in 1969–70). Apart from a few select new projects, the whole emphasis of Egyptian planning was turned towards rationalizing the existing industries, and introducing incentives to improve their performance.

This plan was, however, to be superseded by a more ambitious ten-year scheme under a Programme of National Action, proclaimed by President Sadat in July 1971. The ten-year programme was to be implemented under two consecutive five-year plans, the first starting in July 1972. The target of the Programme was to double national income within ten years to £E5,000 million, but the ten-year plan was never put into operation and the Government reverted to annual development appropriations until 1974.

In mid-1974 a transitional plan was announced to prepare the ground for a new full-scale five-year plan to begin in 1976. The transitional plan envisaged total investment up to the end of 1974 of £E 454 million and in 1975 of £E 1,165.6 million, the bulk of which was to be in the public sector. The foreign component of the plan total was set at £E 467.7 million.

The 1978–82 five-year plan foresees total expenditure at some £E12,000 million ($17,000 million at the parallel rate). The main objective is to achieve annual economic growth rates of 8 per cent. The biggest allocation is for industry ($4,700 million).

AGRICULTURE

Agriculture's contribution to G.D.P. has remained fairly constant at around 30 per cent with industry accounting for 20–21 per cent. Agriculture still employs about 40 per cent. of the labour force and accounts for over 60 per cent of total export earnings. In spite of the diminishing stress on agriculture in Government plans, the volume of agricultural production has been increasing, although population growth has cancelled out most of the benefits of this increase. In recent years, production has risen at an annual rate of 2–3 per cent, disappointingly low and insufficient to cancel out the population increase. This has meant continuing dependence on substantial imports of foodstuffs.

The arable area is 6 million feddans (one feddan = 1.038 acres) but not much more than a third of this is serviced by main and secondary drains. This deficiency is significant because an unforeseen effect of the high dam (*see* below) has been to make the water table rise (because of more abundant water and more intensive cropping) and lead to widespread waterlogging and high soil salinity. At the same time, some 20,000 feddans a year is being lost through the physical expansion of towns and villages.

The extension of the cultivable area through reclamation has been slow, difficult and costly. The increasing pressure of people on the land has led to an intensification of cultivation almost without parallel anywhere. Dams, barrages, pumps and an intricate network of canals and drains bring perennial irrigation to almost the whole area. The strict pursuit of crop rotation, lavish use of commercial fertilizer and pesticides, and the patient application of manual labour not only make multiple cropping possible, but also raise land yields to exceptionally high levels.

The bulk of agricultural production is intended for the market place and not for subsistence. Nearly three-quarters of agricultural income comes from field crops, the remainder deriving from fruit, vegetables, livestock and dairy products. Long-staple cotton is the most important field crop but the area under cultivation declined from two million acres in 1968 to just over one million acres in 1978. Peasants have been finding it unprofitable to grow.

Rice is another important crop and now, after cotton, is almost as important as fruit in the agricultural sector as a foreign currency earner. Rice yields have also been improving steadily and more is being cropped in spite of lower acreage. Other important grain crops grown include wheat, maize, millet and barley. Population pressure has resulted in Egypt becoming a net importer of cereals, mostly wheat.

Another high-yielding crop is sugar-cane. It is nurtured by an expanding sugar industry, supplying the bulk of national requirements. Other crops include lucerne, a nitrogen-fixing fodder, beans, potatoes and onion and garlic.

The many kinds of fruit, vegetables and horticultural products grown are capable of great expansion and are potentially important as exports. Special efforts are being made to promote the production of these items, especially citrus fruit, and special areas are being allocated along the Mediterranean coast for their cultivation. Recent attention has been given to animal husbandry in an attempt to raise dairy and meat production. Egypt has become a net importer of meats and meatless days have been decreed to reduce consumption.

Egypt produces about a third of the world crop of long-staple cotton ($1\frac{1}{8}$ in. and longer). Many factors combine to give the high yields and excellent quality of Egyptian cotton. Among these should be mentioned climatic, soil and labour conditions, and a long experience with careful planting, watering and picking. Government assistance, which has increased of late, has always been important. The development of new varieties, seed distribution, area selection, timing of farm operations and marketing are all carried out under strict government supervision. Fertilizers and pesticides are distributed through the government-sponsored agricultural credit banks, and agricultural co-operatives which are multiplying and expanding their area of activity. All the cotton ginning industry and the cotton exporting business had been nationalized by 1963. The cotton exchanges were closed, and the Government undertook to guarantee prices to regulate internal trade. A public organization for cotton was set up to regulate all aspects of cotton growing, marketing and manufacturing, but was abolished in 1976, being replaced by a loose supervisory council. Plantings for the 1978/79 season remained low compared with earlier in the 1970s—1.2 million feddans compared with 1.48 million feddans in 1974/75 and 1.5 million feddans in 1973/74—as more land is turned over to food production. Exports in the calendar year 1977 stood at £E182 million for raw cotton, £E67 million for cotton yarn and £E24.5 million for cotton piece goods.

Demand for long-staple cotton has been shifting away towards man-made fibres, a fact which has tended to weaken Egypt's previous position of pre-eminence, and consequently the premia Egyptian cotton commanded over rival cottons. The shortage of land, however, together with the increasing requirements of the domestic textile industry (874 million metres of cotton fabrics were produced in 1976) set a limit on the quantity available for export. About half of Egypt's cotton exports has gone to Communist countries in recent years under various bilateral agreements. Egyptian preference for trading with the Western countries, with which Egypt has a balance of payments deficit, has tended to be frustrated by a number of factors, including U.S. trade restrictions (on raw cotton imports), the decline of the high-grade sections of the European cotton industries, political considerations and shortage of finance. The availability of credits (to finance imports) from the Communist countries has also tended to encourage Egyptian foreign trade with the Communist states, although since 1975 the U.S.A. and West Germany have been the two leading suppliers of Egypt's imports.

AGRARIAN REFORM

Immediately after the Egyptian Revolution of 1952 an experiment in land reform was started. This has been among the more successful of such attempts, though only the very large estates were dismembered while medium-sized estates remained untouched. Among other measures, a limit of 200 feddans was imposed on individual ownership of land. This limit was lowered to 100 feddans in 1961 and again to 50 feddans in 1969. The primary aim of this reform was the destruction of the feudal power of the old politicians, an aim which was easily realized. In 1952, 5.8 per cent of all landowners held 64.5 per cent of the total area, but only a quarter of the national acreage (some 1.5 million feddans) was in plots of over 100 acres each. By 1961, however, this area had dwindled to about 1 million feddans, nearly all of which had been appropriated by the Ministry of Agrarian Reform and redistributed to landless peasants. The 1969 land reform affected a further 1.13 million feddans owned by 16,000 land-owners. By 1975 only 12.6 per cent of the total cultivated area was held by owners with 50 feddans or more.

Other measures of agrarian reform included rent control; the regulation of land tenure; consolidation of fragmented holdings for production purposes; and the drive to build co-operatives. Under Government supervision both the number and activities of agricultural co-operatives increased. By 1963 there were 4,897 such co-operatives (compared with 1,727 in 1952) which offered more than £E46 millions in loans to 920,000 borrowers. The value of services provided by the agrarian reform co-operatives (set up to help the recipients of land under the land reform programme) increased more than fivefold between 1958 and 1965 and the activities provided covered the supply of seeds, sacks, fertilizer, insecticides and pest-control machinery. However, co-operatives were not a complete success since they readily lent themselves to corruption. Also in the process of dispossessing the large landowners and promoting co-operatives, the authorities unwittingly helped to eliminate many highly efficient medium-sized farmers. On balance, however, the redistribution of land was accompanied by improved land productivity and not the reverse.

Since land reform affected only about one-sixth of the total land, the main structure of land-ownership remained unaffected; in 1975, 5.4 per cent of the owners still held 42.9 per cent of the land while 94.6 per cent of the owners shared the remaining 57 per cent. The fundamental land tenure problem is not so much one of distribution but an overall scarcity.

Given the land shortage, special attention has naturally been paid to increasing the arable area. In view of the fact that the land to be reclaimed is often arid desert, reclamation is a costly process requiring substantial capital outlays, and the question has to be asked whether new investment should not be directed to the development of manufacturing industry instead, where returns to the scarce capital may well be higher. Between 1952 and 1976 912,000 feddans were reclaimed, 536,000 feddans being reclaimed during the 1960–65 Plan period.

THE HIGH DAM

The decision to invest more than £E400 million in the High Dam project (including initial Russian credits of £E113 million, supported subsequently by another loan of £E81 million for the later stages) was, therefore, taken with an eye also on the development of cheap hydro-electric energy for industry. The official estimate of the dam's contribution to the increase in national production was £E234 million. By 1974 revenue from the dam had exceeded the cost of its construction. The project was started in January 1960, completed in July 1970, and officially inaugurated in January 1971. The power station's generating capacity, at 10,000 million kWh. exceeds by a considerable margin the 6,012 million kWh. produced in all Egypt in 1967 mostly from thermal stations with some hydro-electric energy from the old Aswan dam. Transmission lines carry the current from the Dam site to Cairo and further north, and a major scheme aiming at the complete electrification of Egypt's villages has already started. The storage lake behind the dam, which is 500 km. long and 10 km. wide, is the centre of a developing fishing industry which is expected to replace the sardine catch in the Mediterranean, lost as a result of building the dam.

When construction of the dam was agreed in 1958, a target of 1.2 million feddans was set for desert reclamation. However, costs have far outweighed returns and it has taken on average about ten years to raise any reclaimed area up to even marginal levels of production. Reclamation has started on some 900,000 feddans, but each year over the last 15 years or so the government has had to cover a deficit of around £E10 million on operations in reclaimed areas. In 1972 the Government stopped all new desert reclamation projects. But the country's very limited options in the face of acute pressure of population on the land have brought the idea of reclamation back into the Government plans. A figure of nearly 400,000 feddans has been mentioned in ministerial pronouncements on reclamation targets in the latest development plan, and other conservative ministerial estimates have put the amount to be reclaimed by the end of the century at 2–4 million feddans.

MANUFACTURING INDUSTRY

The establishment of Bank Misr, and the group of companies it supported in the 1920s, coincided with a rising tide of Egyptian nationalism and it became patriotic to buy Egyptian industrial products. A number of manufacturing industries, mainly catering for domestic consumption and with cotton textiles at their head, came to be established and grew rapidly. On the eve of World War II local industry satisfied a substantial part of the domestic demand for textiles, cement, sugar, edible oils, soap and other consumer products. In 1937 industrial employment in establishments employing 10 persons and over totalled 155,000; two years later, however, the contribution of mining, manufacturing and public utilities to the national product was still only about 8 per cent.

The war greatly stimulated Egyptian industry which, in conditions of acute shortages, especially of equipment and raw materials, strove to meet the expanded demand. A wide variety of goods came to be produced and sometimes exported to neighbouring countries. Considerable expansion took place in the production of textiles, chemicals, building materials and processed foods, while entirely new industries sprang up, including rubber and pharmaceutical manufacturing. By 1947, and in spite of some decline in activity, industrial employment in establishments employing 10 persons and over had risen to 278,000. Industrial growth slowed down after the war owing to a period of relatively free trade, although industry was immensely encouraged by the opening up of foreign sources of machinery. Industrial production continued to expand, however, and in 1951 it reached about 140 per cent of its level in 1938. Throughout the decade of the 1950s industrial production grew steadily at an average rate of about 7 per cent per annum, helped by the chronic deficit which developed in the balance of external payments. The exchange controls that have ruled during most of the post-war period have given Egyptian industry added protection. A great drive toward self-sufficiency after the 1956 war resulted in an intensive industrialization programme which began tentatively in 1957, but was later incorporated in the first five-year economic and social development plan, 1960–65. In the six years from 1959–60 to 1965–66, gross value added by industry and mining rose, at constant prices, at an average rate of 9.5% per annum.

In recent years manufacturing industry has been held back by lack of foreign exchange, and some excess capacity has resulted from shortages of spare parts and raw materials. The total value of industrial production (including mining and electricity) has been increasing steadily and reached £E 1,883 million in 1974. Food processing and textiles still dominate the industrial sector, contributing 55–60 per cent of the total value of industrial output. Provisional data for employment in 1977 indicate a work force of 1,247,400 in manufacturing industry, 51,600 in electricity and 593,700 in construction, totalling 19 per cent of employed labour compared with 43 per cent for agriculture.

The expansion of the iron and steel complex at Helwan is going ahead. The first stage of the complex was completed in December 1973 when the third blast furnace was officially opened and production will now be able to expand up to 900,000 tons a year. Further expansion up to 2 million tons is planned by 1982, the end of the old plan period. The complex has so far cost £E150 million.

Another long-standing project is the Nag Hammadi aluminium complex which opened in 1975, with initial capacity of 40,000 tons rising to 100,000 tons, using Australian and Guinean bauxite. The establishment of a phosphorus complex awaits the start of exploitation of the Hamrawein phosphate deposits with Romanian assistance which has been postponed. Phosphate reserves at Abu Tartur have been estimated at 1,000 million tons and will eventually provide income of $240 million per year.

A major fertilizer project is taking shape at Talkha which will cost $130 million and will use $88 million in loans from the IDA, the KFAED, the AFESD, Libya, Qatar and Abu Dhabi. The plant will be fed with gas from the Abu Madi field and will have a capacity of 570,000 tons of urea fertilizer per year.

Other heavy industry plans include sponge iron plants, a steel pipe plant, expansion of cement output and a glass factory.

In manufacturing industry textiles still account for over a third of total output. The Government has embarked on a three-stage rehabilitation of the cotton-ginning industry costing $40.4 million and assisted by an $18.5 million loan from the IDA. The Arab Fund for Economic and Social Development (AFESD) is lending Egypt $40 million to finance a spinning and weaving project at Kafr al-Dawar and Bayda.

A truck and diesel engine plant is to be built by Ford of the U.S. and American Motors is examining a jeep plant. In January 1979 it was announced that Egypt is to build Volkswagen "Beetle" cars under a licensing agreement. Volkswagen is to invest US $30 million in the project. In the same month Michelin announced plans to invest $81 million in a tyre factory near Alexandria.

The needs of heavy industry, and the plan to extend electric power to all Egypt's rural communities by 1982, has underlined the need for more power generation than that supplied by the High Dam. Hence, plans to implement the Qattara Depression scheme to generate energy by flooding the depression with waters from the Mediterranean have been speeded up, and the potential for nuclear energy is being explored, notably as part of the agreement with the U.S.

OIL AND GAS

Production of crude petroleum in 1978 averaged 480,000 barrels per day (b/d), compared with 420,000 b/d in 1977. The Middle East News Agency claimed in May 1979 that Egypt had earned some £E612 million from oil operations in 1978, an increase of 15 per cent on 1977.

The main producing fields are Morgan, Ramadan and July in the Gulf of Suez. These are operated by the Gulf of Suez Petroleum Company (GUPCO), which accounted for 73.8 per cent of Egypt's total crude output in 1977. This was originally a joint venture between the Egyptian General Petroleum Corporation (EGPC) and Amoco of the U.S.A. In 1976 the relationship between the two companies was changed to a production-sharing basis, similar to nearly all the other agreements between Egypt and foreign oil companies—and the EGPC was converted into the Egyptian General Petroleum Authority (EGPA). GUPCO has already made three significant discoveries during further exploration in the Gulf of Suez in 1976. GUPCO's output in 1977 averaged 304,400 b/d against 219,200 in 1976.

WEPCO's Alamein field, discovered at the end of 1966, got off to a promising start and early in 1970 was producing 43,000 barrels per day, but its output has since declined considerably and by 1977 WEPCO's average (including production from a more recent discovery, Yidma) was only 12,200 b/d.

The Abu Gharadeq field which came on stream in 1973 has been disappointing for oil but its operator, FAPCO, has struck it rich in gas. The Razzaq field, operated by NIPCO, the other Amoco-EGPA venture in the Western Desert, has more potential than Abu Gharadeq and estimates of eventual production range up to 60,000 barrels per day. The field is already linked to the Mediterranean by pipeline.

Over 30 foreign oil groups are prospecting. The Government target is 1 million b/d by 1980, but this looks unrealistic in the light of present production.

Apart from Phillips, Amoco and Hispanoil, the Italian state concern ENI and Conoco of the U.S. are involved in Egyptian oil through the International Egyptian Oil Company, which partners EGPA in the Delta Petroleum Company (Delpco), a joint venture operating company. Braspetro, the Brazilian state monopoly, is involved in several areas, notably in the Western Desert. Deminex of West Germany has a separate agreement with the EGPA covering 2,000 square kilometres in the Gulf of Suez, as well as a joint agreement with Shell and BP and the EGPA in the same area concluded in July 1974. Elf-Aquitaine of France and the Egyptian Petroleum Development Company, a Japanese company, both signed agreements with EGPC in 1975. Conoco and British Petroleum each signed agreements in 1978 for exploration in Sinai and further agreements were signed with other oil companies in 1979. Most of the other foreign participants with the EGPA are American—Transworld (Tripco), Mobil, Exxon, Union, Pexamin Pacific (Pexpac)/LVO, Sante Fe International, Chevron, Quintana and Atlantic Richfield. Some of the companies—for instance, Amoco, Conoco and Mobil—have more than one agreement, most of which are of the production-sharing type.

The Egyptians believe that the Western Desert contains an overlap from the giant Libyan field and the interest shown by foreign companies in this area, previously unsuccessfully explored by the U.S.S.R., seems to justify their confidence. Delta and offshore Mediterranean areas are being rapidly opened up for exploration too, but it is the virgin areas of the Red Sea and Eastern Desert which are now attracting most interest as the map gradually becomes filled in with a maze of lines showing areas allotted and areas under offer. U.S., Japanese and German firms are also understood to have expressed interest in exploring in Sinai, pending an Israeli withdrawal.

There are six oil refineries: at Suez (two), Musturud near Cairo, Amiriyah and Mex both near Alexandria, and Tanta. The two refineries at Suez, of 85,000 b/d and 55,000 b/d capacity, were closed between 1969 and 1975. They are located where the bulk of the crude was produced and their closure caused great problems. Under the reconstruction plan petroleum and petrochemical industries are to be established at Suez. The Mex refinery has been enlarged to a capacity of 75,000 barrels per day and the Amiriyah refinery, opened in 1972, has a capacity of 32,000 barrels per day. The Tanta refinery, designed to meet the needs of lower Egypt and with a capacity of only 15,000 barrels per day was opened in August 1973. There is a good network of product pipelines.

A major crude pipeline has been built between Ain-Sukhna on the Gulf of Suez and Sidi-Krer, west of Alexandria. Operations started initially on a test basis in December 1976 and the line was officially opened in July 1977. This Suez-Mediterranean pipeline (Sumed) had been under discussion for several years. At the end of 1973 Egypt formed with Saudi Arabia, Kuwait, Qatar and Abu Dhabi the Arab Company for Oil Pipelines-Sumed to finance the pipeline. Egypt's share in this is 50 per cent or $200 million. Of this, $80 million was raised in the Eurodollar markets by Chase Manhattan and Orion Bank, based in London.

The pipeline's capacity is 80 million tons per year and there is the possibility of expansion up to 120 million. However, use of the line has been lower than forecast, and the Government has had to reduce the original fee of $1.60 per ton to $1.52, with a sliding scale down to $1.00 per ton for large amounts. Some major oil companies use Sumed. The Sumed Company also purchases oil on its own behalf at the Suez end, and sells it off at the Mediterranean end. Sumed is not expected to compete with the Canal for oil shipments. The Government expects the two to be complementary.

The first of Egypt's gas-fields to come on stream was Abu Madi, in the Nile Delta, in October 1974. Its capacity is 3.5 million cubic metres a day or one million tons of oil equivalent a year. Reserves are estimated at some 20 million tons. Abu Gharadeq, in the Western Desert, started production in April 1976; Abukir, offshore near Alexandria, was due to start in 1976/77 but operations were delayed. These two fields are said to have the same producing capacity and reserves as Abu Madi. Abu Madi is to be linked with the industrial centres of the Delta, in particular with the fertilizer plant to be built at Talkha, and Abu Gharadeq with the industrial centre of Helwan and notably the iron and steel complex. Abukir will eventually supply fertilizer and sponge iron plants in the Alexandria region (though these plans are a long way in the future). In February 1978 Egypt signed an agreement with the Montedison company of Italy for installation of a $350 million polyethylene plant near Alexandria.

BANKING

In late 1971 reorganizations of the banking system resulted in the merger of three of the banks into others and each of the rest being entrusted with specialized functions. The National Bank of Egypt was entrusted with foreign trade, the Bank of Port Said merged into Misr Bank which was to deal with home trade, including agricultural finance, the Industrial Bank merged into the Bank of Alexandria which was to deal with manufacturing, the Mortgage Credit Bank merged with the *Crédit Foncier Egyptian* and was to deal with construction and housing and the Bank of

Cairo left to deal with operations of the public sector. In 1975, in line with the liberalization of the banking system, these restrictions on the sectoral operations of the major banks were removed. A new bank, the Nasser Social Bank, was created to deal with pensions and other forms of social security. The Egyptian International Bank for Foreign Trade and Development was also created in 1971 to promote foreign trade and attract foreign investment but was later transformed into the Arab International Bank for Foreign Trade and Development with Egypt, Libya and other Arab investors holding shares. These banks are additional to the Central Bank of Egypt, which was created from the issue department of the National Bank of Egypt in 1960, and the Public Organization for Agricultural Credit and Co-operatives, which the *Crédit Agricole* became in 1964.

Foreign banks are welcome in Egypt since it began liberalizing its economy in earnest in 1974. American Express, Citibank, Crédit Suisse and Lloyds Bank International are among those that have set up foreign currency branches. Manufacturers Hanover Trust Company has a "free zone" foreign currency branch. A number of other international banks have representative offices. The biggest impact on the Egyptian banking system from foreign banks, however, has come from the joint ventures established with Egyptian banks. These include Chase National Bank, which pairs Chase Manhattan and the National Bank of Egypt; Misr International Bank, which partners Misr Bank with First National Bank of Chicago, Banco di Roma and UBAF Bank (London); Egyptian-American Bank, which pairs American Express and Bank of Alexandria; Cairo Barclays International Bank, a venture between Banque du Caire and Barclays Bank International; Misr-America International Bank, owned 40 per cent by Bank of America, 4.5 per cent by the Kuwait Real Estate Bank and 4.5 per cent by First Arabian Corporation on the foreign partners' side, and 26 per cent by the Development Industrial Bank (the former Industrial Bank recently hived off again from the Bank of Alexandria) and 25 per cent by Misr Insurance Company on the Egyptian side; and Banque du Caire et de Paris, a pairing of Banque Nationale de Paris and Banque du Caïre. All these, with the exception of Cairo Barclays, are 51/49 ventures in favour of the Egyptian side; this allows them to act in domestic commercial operations, as well as foreign currency operations. Cairo Barclays, being a 50/50 venture, is not permitted domestic banking activity.

BUDGET

Egypt draws up six budgets—the current services budget, the public authorities' current budget, the economic organizations' current budget, the special finance fund's current budget, the investment budget and the emergency fund—but in practice they can be grouped together. The calendar year has been the fiscal year since the end of 1972 when a July-December budget was drawn up to aid the changeover.

The 1979 budget provides for expenditure of £E12,929 million and revenue of £E10,249 million, leaving a deficit of £E2,680 million, which is above the ceiling of £E2,300 million set by the IMF in June 1978 and caused the blocking of the IMF's U.S. $730 million three-year facility. One reason for the rise in government spending was the increase in subsidies (mainly food) from £E680 million in 1978 to £E1,177 million in 1979. Prices of petrol, cigarettes and luxury goods were increased but subsidies enabled Sadat to hold down the prices of essential goods.

FOREIGN TRADE AND PAYMENTS

The external trade deficit has persisted almost without interruption since before the Second World War. According to the IMF, the visible trade deficit was $357 million in 1972, $429 million in 1973, $1,242 million in 1974, $2,374 million in 1975, $2,233 million in 1976 and $2,128 million in 1977. In most years there is also a net loss on "invisibles", so the deficit on goods and services is usually even greater. However, private and government unrequited transfers transformed a current account deficit into a surplus of $77 million in 1973, and transfers of $1,035 million in 1974 reduced the deficit to only $327 million. The current account deficit increased to $1,397 million in 1975, easing to $807 million in 1976 and $814 million in 1977. The Government keeps a constant vigil on all external payments, but the pressure of population on resources helps to keep the balance of payments in a critical state. The problem is unlikely to be solved without a breakthrough in the pattern of imports and exports which may be brought about by the development of the petroleum sector.

Exports are still largely traditional agricultural goods, with raw cotton accounting for almost one third by value in 1977. The high import figures are mainly the result of the need to buy vital food supplies, mainly wheat.

There is also a geographical imbalance in Egypt's trade: in 1976 over half of exports went to the Eastern bloc, because of supply contracts to pay off debts, but most imports come from the West (with the U.S. recording a startling rise in sales to Egypt) and only 15 per cent of imports from the Eastern bloc. In 1977, however, the proportion of exports going to the Eastern bloc had fallen to less than 50 per cent.

ECONOMIC POLICY

According to the Permanent Constitution of 1971 the economy of Egypt is one based on socialism with the people controlling all means of production. In practice this means that the Government owns or controls practically every economic unit in the economy worth controlling. Although the doctrine of socialism was invoked from the first land reform in 1952, the economy remained largely in private hands until 1961, except for the nationalization of the Suez Canal company in 1956 and that of British and French property during the Suez attack. During 1961, all cotton exporting firms were nationalized, and the Alexandria futures market was closed; 275 industrial and trading concerns were taken over by the state in whole or in part; taxation was made so progressive that individual income was virtually limited to the official maximum of £E5,000; the maximum limit on land ownership was reduced from 200 to 100 feddans (before it was reduced again in 1969); individual shareholding was limited to £E10,000; 25 per cent of the net profits of industrial companies was to be distributed to the workers, who were to be represented on the boards of directors, and to work only a 42-hour week.

Other nationalization measures followed, so that the only sectors of the economy remaining outside complete government ownership are agriculture and urban real estate, but even these are overwhelmingly regulated by laws and decrees. Concerns are grouped under boards and boards under Chairmen and Ministers, and a constant stream of directives helps to bring the activities of all the controlled units in line with Government policies.

After 1967 the Government introduced yet more restrictive measures aimed at curbing consumer demand including a variety of taxes, forced savings and compulsory contributions out of wages and salaries. Since then, however, the trend has been towards "denasserization", the sequestrations of the 1960s have been ruled illegal, new laws are being passed to allow private-sector participation in former state preserves like exporting and importing and transport, and foreign investment is seen as the key to development.

TRANSPORT

The Government is aiming to expand both the Mediterranean and Red Sea port capacities as well as reviving Port Said, Ismailia and Suez to cope with traffic passing through the reopened Suez Canal. Alexandria port is being expanded, aided by a $95 million loan from the World Bank, and a completely new port is planned, west of Alexandria, at Dakheila, with a capacity of 20 million tons per year, compared with Alexandria's present capacity of 13 million tons. Safaga on the Red Sea is also being developed but mainly to handle mineral imports and exports.

River transport is being expanded to relieve the load on roads and railways for internal distribution. Navigable waterways total about 3,100 km., of which about half is the Nile and the rest canals. Canals such as the Nubariya canal in the delta and the Bahr Youssef between Fayoum and Asyut make it possible to link Alexandria with Upper Egypt through Cairo.

Egypt was one of the first countries to have a railway—in 1851—and a good network was built up at an early stage of its development. Now with over 4,000 kilometres of track modernization is urgently needed. A project using loans from various sources of up to $165 million is being undertaken to modernize the railway system and expand its carrying capacity, as well as to draw up a comprehensive national transport survey. A French consortium won a contract for 52 electric trains for the first stage of the Cairo metro system in January 1979.

Good roads connect Cairo with Alexandria, the canal towns and Upper Egypt. There are plans to expand the output both of locally produced goods vehicles and of vehicles from joint-venture projects set up with foreign companies.

EgyptAir, the state airline, operates a network of domestic and international routes.

STATISTICAL SURVEY

AREA AND POPULATION

Area	Census Population		Estimated Mid-year Population			
	Nov. 22nd-23rd, 1976	Jan. 24th, 1979 (Preliminary)	1975	1976†	1977†	1978†
997,667 sq. km.*	38,228,180	40,500,000	37,233,000	37,866,000	38,741,000	39,636,000

* 385,201 sq. miles. Inhabited and cultivated territory accounts for 35,580 sq. km. (13,738 sq. miles).

† Including Egyptian nationals abroad.

GOVERNORATES*

(1965)

Governorate	Area (sq. km).	Capital	Governorate	Area (sq. km.)	Capital
Cairo	214.2	Cairo	Munufia	1,532.1	Shibin el-Kom
Alexandria	2,679.4	Alexandria	Behera	10,129.5	Damanhur
Port Said	72.1	Port Said	Giza	1,009.6	Giza
Ismailia	1,441.6	Ismailia	Beni Suef	1,321.7	Beni Suef
Suez	17,840.4	Suez	Fayum	1,827.2	Fayum
Damietta	589.2	Damietta	Menia	2,261.7	Menia
Dakahlia	3,470.9	Mansura	Asyut	1,530.2	Asyut
Sharkia	4,179.6	Zagazig	Suhag	1,547.2	Suhag
Kalyubia	1,001.1	Benha	Kena	1,850.7	Kena
Kafr el-Sheikh	3,437.1	Kafr el-Sheikh	Aswan	678.5	Aswan
Gharbia	1,942.2	Tanta			

* Excluding the four sparsely-populated "frontier districts".

PRINCIPAL TOWNS

(preliminary results of census of November 1976, excluding nationals abroad)

Town	Population	Town	Population
El Qahira (Cairo, the capital)	5,084,463	Asyut	213,983
El Iskandariyah (Alexandria)	2,318,655	Zagazig	202,637
El Giza	1,246,713	El Suweis (Suez)	194,001
Subra-El Khema	393,700	Damanhur	188,927
El Mahalla el Kubra	292,853	El Faiyum	167,081
Tanta	284,636	El Minya	146,423
Bur Sa'id (Port Said)	262,620	Isma'ilia	145,978
El Mansura	257,866	Aswan	144,377

Greater Cairo (November 1976): 6,818,318, (June 1979): 8,539,000.

CIVILIAN LABOUR FORCE

('000 employed)

	1974	1975	1976	1977*
Agriculture, forestry and fishing	4,214.4	4,252.8	4,223.9	4,290.9
Manufacturing and mining	1,149.5	1,186.8	1,209.5	1,247.4
Construction	312.2	423.0	434.0	593.7
Electricity	38.3	41.2	47.0	51.6
Transport, communications and storage	405.0	418.9	422.1	472.5
Finance and commerce	883.2	925.0	1,016.4	1,044.1
Housing	139.1	142.4	144.0	145.2
Public utilities	43.0	47.0	53.4	55.2
Other services	1,853.1	1,910.5	2,077.9	2,187.0
Total	9,038.8	9,297.6	9,628.2	9,987.6

* Provisional.

AGRICULTURE

AREA AND PRODUCTION OF LINT COTTON

	1975/76		1976/77		1977/78	
	'000 feddans*	'000 kantars†	'000 feddans*	'000 kantars†	'000 feddans*	'000 kantars†
Giza 70	211	1,125	257	1,688	334	1,945
Menoufi	206	958	117	624	—	—
Giza 68	107	594	117	606	156	774
Giza 69	113	791	98	696	156	1,032
Giza 67	205	1,170	208	1,421	241	1,643
Dandara	103	642	98	708	145	860
Giza 66	180	858	200	1,028	263	843
Giza 72	165	166	24	141	16	51
TOTAL (incl. others)	1,346	7,642	1,247	7,925	1,423	7,974

* 1 feddan=1.038 acres (0.42 hectare). † 1 metric kantar=50 kg.

OTHER PRINCIPAL CROPS

	AREA ('000 feddans*)				PRODUCTION ('000 metric tons)			
	1974	1975	1976	1977‡	1974	1975	1976	1977‡
Wheat	1,370	1,394	1,304	1,207	1,884	2,033	1,960	1,998
Maize	1,755	1,830	1,891	1,765	2,640	2,781	3,047	2,724
Millet	499	489	475	409	823	775	756	648
Barley	77	100	104	95	89	118	123	111
Rice	1,053	1,053	1,078	1,040	2,242	2,423	2,300	2,272
Beans†	244	246	260	292	234	234	254	270
Lentils	66	58	64	48	61	39	38	24
Onions†	39	27	31	36	730	572	652	723
Sugar Cane	208	218	242	n.a.	7,018	7,902	8,446	n.a.

* 1 feddan=1.038 acres (0.42 hectare).
† Dry crop and the production of onions includes interplanted crop.
‡ Provisional.

LIVESTOCK

('000 head, year ending September)

	1975	1976	1977*
Cattle	2,102	2,079	2,148
Buffaloes	2,204	2,236	2,294
Sheep	1,926	1,878	1,938
Goats	1,321	1,349	1,393
Pigs	15	15	15
Horses	29	21	21
Asses	1,533	1,568	1,574
Camels	105	101	101
Chickens	26,069	26,375	26,681
Ducks	3,246	3,294	3,343
Turkeys	696	705	714

*FAO estimates.

Source: FAO *Production Yearbook*.

LIVESTOCK PRODUCTS

('000 metric tons)

	1975	1976	1977*
Beef and veal	128	123	128
Buffalo meat	106	106	107
Mutton and lamb	27	26	27
Goats' meat	18	19	20
Pig meat	2	2	2
Poultry meat	78	82	88
Other meat	38	43	42
Edible offals	52*	53*	55*
Cows' milk	626	633	655
Buffaloes' milk	1,136	1,160	1,188
Sheep's milk	19	19	19
Goats' milk	7	8	8
Butter	63.9	64.5	64.9
Cow and buffalo cheese	222.4	225.5	229.2
Hen eggs	68.9	76.0*	78.8
Honey	8.4	9.3	9.0
Wool: greasy	2.9	2.8	2.8
clean	1.4	1.4	1.4
Cattle and Buffalo hides	29.8*	30.4*	31.3
Sheep skins	3.5*	3.1*	3.2
Goat skins	2.6*	2.7*	2.8

* FAO estimates.

Source: FAO, *Production Yearbook*.

FORESTRY

ROUNDWOOD REMOVALS

(FAO estimates, '000 cubic metres, all non-coniferous)

	1975	1976	1977
Industrial wood	75	77	79
Fuel wood	113	115	118
TOTAL	188	192	197

Source: FAO, *Yearbook of Forest Products*.

FISHING

('000 metric tons, live weight)

	1975	1976	1977
Marine	25.9	30.5	29.6
Fresh water	80.7	72.3	75.0
TOTAL CATCH	106.6	102.8	104.5

Source: FAO, *Yearbook of Fishery Statistics*.

MINING

		1973	1974	1975	1976
Crude petroleum	'000 metric tons	8,479	7,453	11,734	16,756
Iron ore*	,, ,, ,,	320	651	560	621
Manganese ore*	,, ,, ,,	1.1	2.1	1.5	1.8
Salt (unrefined)	,, ,, ,,	454	485	631	508
Phosphate rock	,, ,, ,,	553	507	404	486
Natural gas†	million cu. metres	87	418	1,116	1,180

Small quantities of lead and zinc are also mined.

* Figures refer to the metal content of ores. † Estimated production (*Source:* U.S. Bureau of Mines).

1977: Crude petroleum 21.0 million metric tons.

INDUSTRY

SELECTED PRODUCTS

		1973	1974	1975	1976
Wheat flour[1]	'000 metric tons	2,335	2,593	2,732	2,878
Raw sugar	,, ,, ,,	572	534	537	576
Margarine	,, ,, ,,	87.7	103.2	131.7	127
Cottonseed oil	,, ,, ,,	131	149	161	160
Wine	'000 hectolitres	60*	30*	65*	69*
Beer	,, ,,	320	293	286	300
Cigarettes	million	20,572	18,442	20,795	n.a.
Manufactured tobacco	metric tons	4,718	7,987	8,123	n.a.
Cotton yarn (pure)	'000 metric tons	182.7	179.0	181.3	193.2
Woven cotton fabrics (pure and mixed)	,, ,, ,,	118.2	120.0	121.7	n.a.
Flax yarn[2]	,, ,, ,,	3.9	3.9	n.a.	n.a.
Jute yarn	,, ,, ,,	28.1	31.6	36.0	36.5
Wool yarn (pure and mixed)	,, ,, ,,	11.2	10.9	12.2	n.a.
Woven woollen fabrics (pure and mixed)	,, ,, ,,	8.9	7.1	n.a.	n.a.
Woven rayon and acetate fabrics	,, ,, ,,	21.0	17.2	17.7	n.a.
Paper and paperboard	,, ,, ,,	127	104	106	118
Rubber tyres	'000	391	364	459	468
Ethyl alcohol	'000 hectolitres	315	294	323	n.a.
Sulphuric acid (100%)	'000 metric tons	20	31	40	31
Caustic soda (Sodium hydroxide)	,, ,, ,,	14	30	37	37
Nitrogenous fertilizers (*a*)[3]	,, ,, ,,	50.7	100.2	150.5	199.7
Phosphate fertilizers (*b*)[3]	,, ,, ,,	81.0	95.0	77.0	90.0
Motor spirit (petrol)[4]	,, ,, ,,	961	1,225	1,335	1,976
Kerosene	,, ,, ,,	982	1,155	1,142	1,320
Jet fuel	,, ,, ,,	153	180	150	117
Distillate fuel oils	,, ,, ,,	1,199	1,550	1,607	1,717
Residual fuel oil (Mazout)	,, ,, ,,	3,050	2,800	4,165	5,056
Petroleum bitumen (asphalt)	,, ,, ,,	143	65	118	135
Coke-oven coke	,, ,, ,,	344	555	695	700
Cement	,, ,, ,,	3,616	3,264	3,584	3,290
Pig-iron	,, ,, ,,	440	275	420	569
Crude steel	,, ,, ,,	290	400	348	457
Radio receivers	'000	148	157	221	117
Television receivers	,,	49	71	77	88
Passenger motor cars (assembly)	,,	5.6	9.6	11.5	9.8
Electric energy	million kWh.	8,104	8,915	10,386	11,000

1977: Residual fuel oil 5,264,000 metric tons.

* FAO estimate.

[1] *Source:* International Wheat Council, *World Wheat Statistics.*

[2] Including waste and yarn made from tow.

[3] Production in terms of (*a*) nitrogen or (*b*) phosphoric acid.

[4] Including naphtha.

FINANCE

1,000 millièmes = 100 piastres = 5 tallaris = 1 Egyptian pound (£E).
Coins: 1, 2 and 5 millièmes; 1, 2, 5 and 10 piastres.
Notes: 5, 10, 25 and 50 piastres; 1, 5, 10 and 20 pounds.
Exchange rates (June 1979): £1 sterling = £E1.4025; U.S. $1 = 678.0 millièmes.
£E100 = £71.30 sterling = $147.49.

Note: **From September 1949 to May 1962 the Egyptian pound was valued at U.S. $2.87156 ($1 = 348.24 millièmes).** Between May 1962 and February 1973 the pound's value was $2.30 ($1 = 434.783 millièmes). From February 1973 to December 1978 the official exchange rate was £E1 = $2.55556 ($1 = 391.304 millièmes) but there were other rates for tourism and since September 1975 a legal free currency market has operated in Port Said. Since May 1976 the "parallel" rate, previously fixed by the Government, has been subject to managed "floating". On January 1st, 1979, the official rate was abolished and the "parallel" rate came into use for all transactions. The unified rate was initially $1 = 700 millièmes (£E1 = $1.4286). From November 1967 to August 1971 the exchange rate was £1 sterling = £E1.0435; from December 1971 to June 1972 it was £1 sterling = £E1.1328.

BUDGET ESTIMATES
(£E million)

CURRENT BUDGETS

REVENUE	1977	1978
Sovereignty revenue	1,741.0	2,115.9
Current and transfer	3,761.7	4,400.2
TOTAL	5,502.7	6,516.1

EXPENDITURE	1977	1978
Wages	942.6	1,100.0
Current and transfer	4,560.1	5,416.1
TOTAL	5,502.7	6,516.1

CAPITAL BUDGETS

REVENUE	1977	1978
Sundry	1,027.4	1,246.3
Loans and credit facilities	618.0	1,120.6
TOTAL	1,645.4	2,366.9

EXPENDITURE	1977	1978
Investments	762.7	1,321.9
Capital transfers	882.7	1,045.0
TOTAL	1,645.4	2,366.9

Source: National Bank of Egypt, *Economic Bulletin*, Vol. XXXI, No. 1, 1978.

1979 Budget: Revenue: £E10,249 million; Expenditure £E12,929 million.

PLANNED SECTORAL OUTPUT TARGETS 1976–80
(at constant 1975 prices—£E million)

	ACTUAL		PLANNED			
	1975	1976	1977	1978	1979	1980
Agriculture	2,052	2,116	2,182	2,247	2,315	2,384
Industry and mining	3,382	3,449	3,665	4,103	4,595	5,145
Oil and products	385	581	598	747	859	989
Power	90	100	123	145	171	200
Construction	465	416	513	589	678	780
Suez	42	146	200	230	264	304
Transport and communications	300	371	456	501	551	606
Trade and other services	2,612	2,830	3,100	3,410	3,751	4,126
TOTAL GROSS OUTPUT	9,278	10,009	10,889	11,975	13,186	14,538

CENTRAL BANK RESERVES
(U.S. $ million at December 31st)

	1976	1977	1978
Gold	99	103	113
IMF Special Drawing Rights	24	29	11
Foreign exchange	216	402	481
TOTAL	339	534	605

Source: IMF, *International Financial Statistics.*

MONEY SUPPLY
(£E million at December 31st)

	1976	1977	1978
Currency outside banks	1,387.8	1,749.5	2,183.7
Demand deposits at commercial banks	848.8	1,193.5	1,344.2

Source: IMF, *International Financial Statistics.*

BALANCE OF PAYMENTS
(U.S. $ million)

	1972	1973	1974	1975	1976	1977
Merchandise exports f.o.b.	813	1,000	1,672	1,567	1,609	1,993
Merchandise imports f.o.b.	−1,170	−1,429	−2,914	−3,941	−3,842	−4,121
TRADE BALANCE	−357	−429	−1,242	−2,374	−2,233	−2,128
Exports of services	308	421	708	1,078	1,975	2,551
Imports of services	−417	−556	−829	−1,178	−1,260	−1,681
BALANCE OF GOODS AND SERVICES	−466	−564	−1,363	−2,473	−1,518	−1,258
Private unrequited transfers (net)	5	6	42	90	87	61
Government unrequited transfers (net)	290	635	993	986	623	384
CURRENT BALANCE	−170	77	−327	−1,397	−807	−814
Long-term capital (net)	117	−62	−552	1,785	748	1,923
Short-term capital (net)	75	111	375	−271	−272	−1,040
Net errors and omissions	−7	−10	334	−144	185	30
TOTAL (net monetary movements)	15	117	−170	−28	−147	99
Allocation of IMF Special Drawing Rights	22	—	—	—	—	—
CHANGES IN RESERVES, ETC.	37	117	−170	−28	−147	99

Source: IMF, *International Financial Statistics.*

EXTERNAL TRADE
(£E million)

	1971	1972	1973	1974	1975	1976	1977
Imports c.i.f.	400.0	390.8	361.1	920.1	1,539.3	1,489.9	1,884.3
Exports f.o.b.	343.2	358.8	444.2	593.3	548.6	595.4	668.5

PRINCIPAL COMMODITIES

(£E million)

Imports c.i.f.	1974	1975	1976	1977
Foodstuffs	397.7	534.9	405.0	399.6
Cereals and milling products	288.6	286.6	220.8	208.0
Animal and vegetable oils	47.3	136.6	39.2	35.1
Other consumer goods	80.4	126.8	158.3	209.5
Paper and paper products	27.8	50.2	47.8	51.1
Tobacco	11.5	20.7	26.3	41.3
Raw materials and capital goods	442.0	877.6	926.6	1,275.2
Crude petroleum	1.2	71.8	21.2	—
Mineral products	100.8	185.9	198.3	254.3
Chemical products	118.5	189.5	117.5	148.0
Wood, hides and rubber	57.5	96.5	89.1	173.1
Machinery and electrical apparatus	78.6	169.8	280.1	389.5
Transport equipment	55.5	112.4	142.9	207.8
Total	920.1	1,539.3	1,489.9	1,884.3

Exports f.o.b.	1974	1975	1976	1977
Textile fibres and products	395.0	322.0	266.5	312.1
Raw cotton	279.1	201.0	154.8	182.3
Cotton yarn	65.1	63.0	57.6	68.6
Cotton fabrics	20.1	16.2	17.4	24.5
Other agricultural crops	78.3	70.5	97.9	103.0
Potatoes	5.9	3.2	17.2	16.4
Rice	39.7	24.2	31.0	23.4
Edible fruits	11.8	20.6	22.5	26.0
Manufactured products	35.9	59.6	42.8	49.7
Sugar and sugar confectionery	11.5	15.4	11.4	11.4
Raw hides, skins, footwear, etc.	11.0	19.3	9.7	10.1
Raw materials and capital goods	78.2	96.5	188.2	203.7
Crude petroleum	23.9	23.1	109.8	119.1
Gasoline, kerosene and fuel oil	0.2	5.7	10.9	13.1
Total	587.4	548.6	595.4	668.5

PRINCIPAL TRADING PARTNERS
(£E million)

Imports c.i.f.	1975	1976	1977
Australia	67.2	58.3	54.7
Belgium/Lux'bourg	19.4	33.6	n.a.
China, People's Rep.	14.5	17.6	20.4
Czechoslovakia	23.0	27.9	29.6
France	165.0	91.2	118.9
German Dem. Rep.	39.5	25.6	32.3
Germany, Fed. Rep.	129.0	172.1	201.8
Greece	9.4	21.3	n.a.
India	25.6	38.1	32.1
Iran	24.0	5.5	3.8
Italy	91.0	118.7	168.2
Japan	50.9	74.1	97.3
Lebanon	32.9	11.7	9.1
Netherlands	42.0	37.9	50.3
Romania	56.3	20.8	31.5
Saudi Arabia	52.1	28.4	12.0
Spain	12.6	21.4	22.3
Switzerland	31.8	24.3	35.5
U.S.S.R.	91.1	74.9	106.0
United Kingdom	70.0	85.1	109.8
U.S.A.	296.2	244.2	308.4
Yugoslavia	21.1	24.1	46.2
Total (incl. others)	1,539.3	1,489.9	1,884.3

Exports f.o.b.	1975	1976	1977
Brazil	4.3	13.0	1.1
Bulgaria	13.4	13.4	5.7
China, People's Rep.	20.5	20.1	13.4
Czechoslovakia	40.4	33.1	44.5
France	8.3	21.1	23.8
German Dem. Rep.	32.2	30.5	33.4
Germany, Fed. Rep.	7.8	11.4	17.9
Greece	2.6	21.0	n.a.
Italy	24.6	50.0	70.6
Japan	4.2	20.2	24.1
Libya	11.4	7.7	8.3
Netherlands	12.1	15.6	19.3
Poland	17.8	13.6	11.5
Romania	25.3	11.2	7.9
Saudi Arabia	7.9	8.0	13.9
Syria	2.5	5.7	10.9
U.S.S.R.	237.2	145.7	154.8
United Kingdom	8.2	23.5	27.8
U.S.A.	0.8	23.0	12.7
Yugoslavia	9.1	12.9	14.7
Total (incl. others)	548.6	595.4	668.5

TRANSPORT

RAILWAYS

	1975	1976
Total Freight (million ton km.)	2,259	2,021
Total Passengers (million passenger km.)	8,831	8,748
Track Length (km.)	4,385	4,385

ROAD TRAFFIC
(motor vehicle licences at December 31st)

	1975	1976	1977
Buses	9,542	10,827	10,337
Lorries	36,776	46,575	53,713
Cars	215,533	245,629	283,240
Motor Cycles	49,565	63,463	77,887

SHIPPING
Suez Canal Traffic

		1966	1976	1977	1978
Transits	number	21,250	16,806	19,703	21,266
Net tonnage	'000	274,250	187,759	220,477	248,260
Goods traffic	'000 tons	241,913	117,653	128,693	149,280
Transiting tankers	number	n.a.	2,610	2,620	n.a.
Net tonnage of tankers	'000	n.a.	77,903	75,568	73,924

Source: Suez Canal Authority, *Yearly Report,* 1977 and monthly reports.

CIVIL AVIATION
(tons)

	1971	1972	1973	1974	1975	1976	1977
Cargo	17,433	21,608	18,760	22,036	25,572	30,409	39,781
Mail	1,201	1,299	1,437	1,276	1,236	1,238	1,461

TOURISM

TOURIST ARRIVALS BY COUNTRY

	1974	1975	1976	1977
Arabs	412,622	437,513	534,531	475,000
Europeans	152,074	214,139	283,270	343,000
Americans	55,922	75,785	89,512	97,000
Others	55,176	64,992	76,182	89,000
TOTAL	675,794	792,429	983,495	1,004,000

EDUCATION

(1976/77)

	Institutions		Teachers	Pupils
	Public	Private		
Pre-primary	—	312	1,073	47,252
Primary	9,234	819	126,397	4,151,956
Preparatory	1,562	600	34,914	1,435,529
Secondary general	309	135	17,786	392,561
Secondary technical	354	207	25,215	408,540
Teacher training	65	—	2,830	32,744
Higher	164	26	24,969	717,053

Sources (unless otherwise stated): Central Agency for Public Mobilization and Statistics, Cairo; Research Department, National Bank of Egypt, Cairo; International Monetary Fund.

THE CONSTITUTION

The Permanent Constitution of the Arab Republic of Egypt was approved by referendum on September 11th, 1971. There are six chapters with 193 articles, many of them based on the 1964 Interim Constitution, but chapters 3 and 4 show a considerable degree of liberalization of the former statutes.

CHAPTER I

The State

Egypt is an Arab Republic with a democratic, socialist system based on the alliance of the working people and derived from the country's historical heritage and the spirit of Islam.

The Egyptian people are part of the Arab nation, who work towards total Arab unity.

Islam is the religion of the State; Arabic is its official language and the Islamic code is a principal source of legislation. The State safeguards the freedom of worship and of performing rites for all religions.

Sovereignty is of the people alone which is the source of all powers.

The protection, consolidation and preservation of the socialist gains is a national duty: the sovereignty of law is the basis of the country's rule, and the independence of immunity of the judiciary are basic guarantees for the protection of rights and liberties.

The Arab Socialist Union is the political organization of the State which represents the alliance of the working forces of the people; the farmers, workers, soldiers, the intelligentsia and national capitalism.

CHAPTER 2

The Fundamental Elements of Society

Social solidarity is the basis of Egyptian society, and the family is its nucleus.

The State ensures the equality of men and women in both political and social rights in line with the provisions of Moslem legislation.

Work is a right, an honour and a duty which the State guarantees together with the services of social and health insurance, pensions for incapacity and unemployment.

The economic basis of the Republic is socialism based on sufficiency and justice. It is calculated to prevent exploitation and to level up differences between classes.

The people control all means of production and regulate the national economy according to a comprehensive development plan which determines the role of Arab and foreign capital.

Property is subject to the people's control.

Property shall be expropriated only by law and against fair compensation. Nationalization shall also be by law for public interest considerations or socialist objectives.

Agricultural holding may be limited by law.

The State follows a comprehensive central planning and compulsory planning approach based on quinquennial socio-economic and cultural development plans whereby the society's resources are mobilized and put to the best use.

The public Sector assumes the leading role in the development of the national economy. The State provides absolute protection of this Sector as well as the property of co-operative societies and trade unions against all attempts to tamper with them.

CHAPTER 3

Public Liberties, Rights and Duties

All citizens are equal before the law. Personal liberty is a natural right and no one may be arrested, searched, imprisoned or restricted in any way without a court order.

Houses have sanctity, and shall not be placed under serveillance or searched without a court order with reasons given for such action.

The law safeguards the sanctities of the private lives of all citizens; so have all postal, telegraphic telephonic and other means of communication which may not therefore be confiscated, or perused except by a court order giving the reasons, and only for a specified period.

Public rights and freedoms are also inviolate and all calls for atheism and anything that reflects adversely on divine religions is prohibited.

The freedom of opinion, the Press, printing and publications and all information media are safeguarded.

Press censorship is forbidden, so are warnings, suspensions or cance'lations through administrative channels. Under exceptional circumstances as in cases of emergency or in war time, censorship may be imposed on information media for a definite period.

Egyptians have the right to permanent or provisional emigration and no Egyptian may be deported or prevented from returning to the country.

Citizens have the right to private meetings in peace provided they bear no arms. Egyptians also have the right to form societies which have no secret activities or are hostile to the government. Public meetings are also allowed within the limits of the law.

CHAPTER 4

Sovereignty of the Law

All acts of crime should be specified together with the penalties for the acts.

Recourse to justice, it says, is a right of all citizens, and those who are financially unable, will be assured of means to defend their rights.

Arrested persons may protest against their detention and their protests should be decided upon within a prescribed period otherwise they should be released.

CHAPTER 5

System of Government

The President, who must be at least 40 years old, is nominated by at least one-third of the members of the People's Assembly, approved by at least two-thirds, and elected by popular referendum. His term is for six years and he 'may be re-elected for another subsequent term.' He may take emergency measures in the interests of the state but these measures must be approved by referendum within 60 days.

The People's Assembly, elected for five years, is the legislative body and approves general policy, the budget and the development plan. It shall have 'not less than 350' elected members, at least half of whom shall be workers or farmers, and the President may appoint up to ten additional members. In exceptional circumstances the Assembly, by a two-thirds vote, may authorize the President to rule by decree for a specified period but these decrees must be approved by the Assembly at its next meeting.

The Assembly may pass a vote of no confidence in a Deputy Prime Minister, a Minister or a Deputy Minister, provided three days' notice of the vote is given, and the minister must then resign. In the case of the Prime Minister, the Assembly may "prescribe" his responsibility and submit a report to the President: if the President disagrees with the report but the Assembly persists, then the matter is put to a referendum: if the people support the President the Assembly is dissolved; if they support the Assembly the President must accept the resignation of the Government. The President may dissolve the Assembly prematurely, but his action must be approved by a referendum and elections must be held within 60 days.

Executive Authority is vested in the President, who may appoint one or more vice-presidents and appoints all ministers. He may also dismiss the vice-presidents and ministers. The President has 'the right to refer to the people in connection with important matters related to the country's higher interests. ' The Government is described as 'the supreme executive and administrative organ of the state'. Its members, whether full ministers or deputy ministers, must be at least 35 years old. Further sections define the roles of Local Government, Specialized National Councils, the Judiciary, the Higher Constitutional Court, the Socialist Prosecutor General, the Armed Forces and National Defence Council and the Police.

CHAPTER 6

General and Transitional Provisions

No law shall normally have retroactive effect, but this may be changed, except in criminal matters, with the approval of a majority of the Assembly. Articles of the constitution may be revised, at the suggestion of the President or one-third of the Assembly, but the revision must be submitted for approval by a public referendum. The term of the present President shall date from his election as President of the United Arab Republic.

Political Parties

In June 1977 the People's Assembly adopted a new law on political parties, which, subject to certain conditions, permitted the formation of political parties for the first time since 1953. A new draft law was enacted in June 1978 by which the operation of political parties was made much more difficult but in July 1978 President Sadat announced the formation of his own political party, the National Democratic Party.

THE GOVERNMENT

THE PRESIDENCY

President: Col. MUHAMMAD ANWAR SADAT (acting President September 28th, 1970; took office October 17th, 1970; re-elected September 1976).

Vice-President: Lt.-Gen. MUHAMMAD HOSNI MUBARAK.

COUNCIL OF MINISTERS

(*August* 1979)

Prime Minister and Minister of Foreign Affairs: MUSTAPHA KHALIL.

Deputy Prime Minister for People's Assembly Affairs: FIKRI MAKRAM OBAID.

Deputy Prime Minister: HASSAN ANWAR TAHA HABIB.

Minister of Defence and War Production: KAMALEDDIN HASSAN ALI.

Minister of Petroleum: AHMAD IZZEDDIN HILAL.

Minister of Economy, Foreign Trade and Economic Co-operation: HAMED ABDUL-LATIF SAYEH.

Minister of Interior: MUHAMMAD NABAWI ISMAIL.

Minister of Tourism and Civil Aviation: MAHMOUD AMIN ABDEL-HAFEZ.

Minister of Social Welfare and Insurance: Dr. AMAL ABDUL RAHIM OTHMAN.

Minister of Land Reclamation: TAWFIQ HAMED KARARA.

Minister of Irrigation and Minister of State for Sudanese Affairs: MUHAMMAD ABDEL-HADI SAMAHA.

Minister of Transport, Communications and Shipping: ALI FAHMI DAGHASTANI.

Minister of Housing: MUSTAFA METWALLI HEFNAWI.

Minister of Industry and Mining: IBRAHIM ABDER-RAHMAN ATALLA.

Minister of Electricity and Energy: MUSTAPHA KAMAL SABRI.

Minister of Planning: ABDUL RAZZAK ABDUL MEGUID.

Minister of Health: Dr. MAMDUH KAMAL JABR.

Minister of Reconstruction and New Towns: HASBALLA MUHAMMAD KAFRAWI.

Minister of Manpower and Vocational Training: SAAD MUHAMMAD AHMED.

Minister of Justice: ANWAR ABDEL FATTAH ABU SEHLI.

Minister of Finance: ALI LUTFI.

Minister of Supply and Internal Trade: NASEF ABDEL-MAQSOUD IBRAHIM TAHOUN.

Minister of Agriculture: MAHMOUD MUHAMMAD DAWOUD.

Minister of Education and Scientific Research: Dr. MUSTAFA KAMAL HILMI

Minister of Waqfs and Minister of State for Azhar Affairs: Dr. ABDUL MUNIM AHMAD AN-NIMR.

Minister of State for Foreign Affairs: BUTROS BUTROS GHALI.

Minister of State for War Production: KAMAL TAWFIQ AHMAD NASSAR.

Minister of State for Cabinet Affairs, Local Government, Follow-up and Control: SULAIMAN METWALLI SULAIMAN.

Minister of State for People's Assembly Affairs: ABDEL-AKHER MUHAMMAD OMAR ABDEL-AKHER.

Minister of State for the Presidency: MANSUR MUHAMMAD MAHMUD HASAN.

Minister of State for Economic Co-operation: ALI GAMAL NASSER.

Minister of State for Youth and Sports: ABDEL-HAMID HASAN.

PEOPLE'S ASSEMBLY

The law governing the composition of the People's Assembly was amended on May 2nd, 1979. 176 constituencies now elect two members, at least one of which must be from among the workers and peasants, and in 30 constituencies a third member, who must be a woman, is elected in addition to the other two members. Ten members are appointed by the President.

Speaker: Dr. SUFI ABU TALIB.

Deputy Speakers: MUHAMMAD RASHWAN (workers), MUHAMMAD ABDUL HAMID RADWAN (other groups).

Leader of the Opposition: IBRAHIM SHUKRI (Socialist Labour Party).

ELECTIONS, JUNE 7th and 14th, 1979

	SEATS
National Democratic Party	302
Socialist Labour Party	29
Liberal Socialist Party	3
Independents	8
Women candidates (mostly NDP)	30
Copts (appointed)	10
TOTAL (inc. others)	392

POLITICAL PARTIES

Arab Socialist Union: Cairo; f. 1961 as the alliance of all working people's forces; was sole legal political organization until People's Assembly elections of 1976, when Arab Socialist Party, Liberal Socialist Party and National Progressive Unionist Party were formed. In February 1978 the New Wafd Party was formed, but tighter regulations forced it to disband in June 1978. In 1976 President Sadat announced that the Arab Socialist Union would merely act as a watchdog for the parties' activities, and in July 1978 he announced that the Arab Socialist Union would be only a Consultative Council and meet once a year. President Sadat announced the formation of his own party, the National Democratic Party, in July 1978.

Details of active and recently dissolved parties are given below:

Arab Socialist Party: f. 1976, but merged with National Democratic Party in October 1978; had been government party and Leader was MAMDUH MUHAMMAD SALEM.

Liberal Socialist Party: Cairo; f. 1976; advocates expansion of 'open door' economic policy and greater freedom for private enterprise; Leader MUSTAFA KAMEL MURAD.

Nasserite Party: Cairo; f. April 1979; Leaders MUHAMMAD HASSANEIN HEIKAL and Mrs. HODA NASSER.

National Democratic Party: Cairo; f. July 1978; government party founded by President Sadat; has absorbed Arab Socialist Party; Pres. MUHAMMAD ANWAR SADAT; Vice-Pres. MUHAMMAD HOSNI MUBARAK; Sec.-Gen. FIKRI MAKRAM OBAID.

National Front Party: Cairo; f. Aug. 1978; Leader MUMTAZ NASSER and MAHMOUD QADI (formerly independent Deputies).

National Progressive Unionist Party: f. 1976; left wing; Leader KHALED MOHIEDDIN; became politically inactive in June 1978.

New Wafd Party: f. February 1978; Leader FUAD SERAGEDDIN; Sec.-Gen. HELMI MURAD; while active had 24 mems. in People's Assembly; disbanded June 1978.

Socialist Labour Party: Cairo; f. September 1978; official opposition party; Leader IBRAHIM SHUKRY.

DIPLOMATIC REPRESENTATION

EMBASSIES ACCREDITED TO EGYPT

(In Cairo, unless otherwise stated)

(E) Embassy.

Albania: 29 Sh. Ismail Muhammad (Zamalek) (E); *Ambassador:* SULEJMAN TOMCINI (also accred. to Pakistan).

Argentina: 8 Sh. As-Saleh Ayoub (Zamalek) (E); *Ambassador:* MARIO A. PEPE (also accred. to Kuwait).

Australia: 1097 Corniche el Nil (Garden City) (E); *Ambassador:* PIERRE NORMAN BRUCE HUTTON.

Austria: 21 Sh. Sadd El-Aaly (Dokki) (E); *Ambassador:* Dr. HERIBERT TSCHOFEN (also accred. to the People's Democratic Republic of Yemen).

Bangladesh: 18 Souria St., Madinet El Mohamdessin (Dokki) (E); *Ambassador:* M. SULTAN.

Belgium: 20 Kamel El Shnaoui St. (Garden City) (E); *Ambassador:* RENÉ PANIS.

Bolivia: 6 Rue Nawal (Dokki) (E); *Ambassador:* (vacant).

Brazil: 1125 Corniche El Nil (Maspiro) (E); *Ambassador:* MARCUS ANTÔNIO DE SALVO COIMBRA.

Bulgaria: 36 El Messaha St. (Dokki) (E); (*diplomatic relations broken off, December 5th,* 1978).

Burma: 24 Rue Muhammad Mazhar (Zamalek) (E); *Ambassador:* (vacant) (also accred. to Turkey).

Burundi: 8 Abdel Rahman El Rafei St. (Dokki) (E); *Ambassador:* ALBERT SHIBURA.

Cameroon: 42 Babel St. (Dokki) (E); *Ambassador:* El Hadj IBRAHIM MBOMBO NJOYA (also accred. to Turkey).

Canada: 6 Sh. Muhammad Fahmy El Sayed (Garden City) (E); *Ambassador:* JEAN-MARIE DERY.

Central African Empire: 10 Sh. Sadd El-Aaly (Dokki) (E); *Ambassador:* MICHEL ADAMA TAMBOUX.

Chad: 26 El Kurum St. (Dokki) (E); *Ambassador:* MUHAMMAD HASSANE (also accred. to Morocco and Tunisia).

Chile: 5 Sh. Chagaret El-Dorr (Zamalek) (E); *Ambassador:* SERGIO NUNO BAWDEN.

China, People's Republic: 14 Sh. Bahgat Aly (Zamalek) (E); *Ambassador:* YAO KUANG.

Colombia: 15 Sh. Aboul Feda (Zamalek) (E); *Ambassador:* MIGUEL DURAN ORDOÑEZ.

Congo: 12 Midan El Nasr (Dokki) (E); *Ambassador:* Commandant ALFRED RAOUL (also accred. to Lebanon).

Cuba: 2 Al Anab St. (Dokki) (E); *Ambassador:* DOMINGO GARCÍA RODRÍGUEZ.

Cyprus: 23A Ismail Muhammad St. (Zamalek) (E); *Ambassador:* ANTIS G. SOTERIADES (also accred. to Iraq and Lebanon).

Czechoslovakia: 43 Sh. Muhammad Mazhar (Zamalek) (E); *Ambassador:* MIROSLAV SULEK (also accred. to the People's Democratic Republic of Yemen).

Denmark: 12 Sh. Hassan Sabri (Zamalek) (E); *Ambassador:* J. KORSGAARD-PEDERSEN (also accred. to Somalia and Sudan).

Ecuador: 8 Salamlek St. (Garden City) (E); *Ambassador:* AUGUSTO PÉREZ ANDA.

El Salvador: Madrid, Spain (E).

Ethiopia: 12 Midan Bahlawi (Dokki) (E); *Ambassador:* Ato BETROU KIDANE MARIAM (also accred. to Iraq and Lebanon).

Finland: 2 El-Malek El-Fadel (Zamalek) (E); *Ambassador:* JOEL PEKURI.

France: 29 Sh. Giza (E); *Ambassador:* JACQUES SÉNARD.

Gabon: 11 Sh. Moderiat El Tahrir (Garden City) (E); *Ambassador:* JULES MBAHA.

Gambia: Jeddah, Saudi Arabia (E).

German Democratic Republic: 13 Sh. Hussein Wassef (Dokki) (E); *Ambassador:* OTTO BECKER.

Germany, Federal Republic: 20 Boulos Hanna St. (Dokki) (E); *Ambassador:* WOLFGANG BEHRENDS.

Ghana: Villa 24, Sh. 22 (Dokki) (E); *Ambassador:* Commodore P. F. QUAYE.

Greece: 18 Sh. Aïcha El-Taïmouria (Garden City) (E); *Ambassador:* JEAN YANNAKAKIS.

Guatemala: 1 Sh. Amrika El Latinia (Garden City) (E); *Ambassador:* JULIO A. MERIDA.

Guinea: 46 Sh. Muhammad Mazhar (Zamalek) (E); *Ambassador:* SALIMOU SISSOKO (also accred. to Iraq, Jordan, Lebanon, Libya and Turkey).

Guinea-Bissau: 37 Rue Lebanon, Madinet el Mohandesin (E); *Ambassador:* HAIDARA CHERIF MOHAMED LAMINE.

Hungary: 29 Sh. Muhammad Mazhar (Zamalek) (E); *Ambassador:* MIKLÓS NAGY (also accred. to the People's Democratic Republic of Yemen).

India: 5 Aziz Abaza St. (Zamalek) (E); *Ambassador:* ASHOKE SEN CHIB.

Indonesia: 13 Sh. Aicha El-Taimouria (Garden City) (E); *Ambassador:* Dr. FUAD HASSAN.

Ireland: 2 Maarouf St., Apt. 17 (E); *Ambassador:* BRIAN O CEALLAIGH.

Italy: 15 Sh. Abdel Rahman Fahmi (Garden City) (E); *Ambassador:* GIAN LUIGI FERRETI.

Japan: 10 Sh. Ibrahim Naguib (Garden City) (E); *Ambassador:* MIZUO KURODA (also accred. to the People's Democratic Republic of Yemen).

Kenya: 12 Madina El Munawara (Dokki) (E); *Ambassador:* RAPHAEL MULI KIILU (also accred. to Algeria, Iraq, Kuwait, Lebanon and Saudi Arabia).

Korea, Democratic People's Republic: 6 El Saleh Ayoub St. (Zamalek) (E); *Ambassador:* CHONG TU-HWAN.

Lesotho: Nairobi, Kenya (E).

Liberia: 2 Rue El Batal Ahmed Abdel Aziz, Madinet El Awkaf (Dokki) (E); *Ambassador:* MARTINUS L. JOHNSON (also accred. to Iran, Kuwait and Saudi Arabia).

Malaysia: 7 Wadi El Nil St. (Agouza) (E); *Ambassador:* MON BEIN GAMAL ODIN (also accred. to Lebanon).

Mali: 3B Bhagat Ali St. (Zamalek) (E); *Ambassador:* HALIDOU TOURÉ (also accred. to Ethiopia, Kenya, Somalia, Sudan, Tanzania and Uganda).

Malta: Tripoli, Libya (E).

Mauritania: 31 Souria St. (Dokki) (E); *Ambassador:* ISMAIL OULD MOULOUD (also accred. to Iran and Lebanon).

Mauritius: 47 Ahmed Hechmat (Zamalek) (E); *Ambassador:* ABDOOL HACK MOHAMED OSMAN.

Mexico: 5 Dar El Chifa (E); *Ambassador:* ANTONIO DE ICAZA (also accred. to Algeria).

Mongolia: 3 Midan El Nasr (Dokki) (E); *Ambassador:* DALKHYN LUBSANRENCHIN.

Nepal: 9 Rue Tiba (Madinet El Kodah) (E); *Ambassador:* BISHWA PRADHAN (also accred. to Algeria, Jordan, Kuwait, Lebanon and Yugoslavia).

Netherlands: 18 Sh. Hassan Sabri (Zamalek) (E); *Ambassador:* (vacant).

New Zealand: Rome, Italy (E).

Niger: 28 Sh. Bahlawi (Dokki) (E); *Ambassador:* ABDOULAYE DIALLO (also accred. to Turkey).

Nigeria: 13 Sh. Gabalaya (Zamalek) (E); *Ambassador:* A. M. S. IMAM (also accred. to Iraq, Lebanon and Syria).

Norway: 8 Gezira St. (Zamalek) (E); *Ambassador:* TANCRED IBSEN (also accred. to Jordan, Lebanon, Libya, Sudan and Syria).

Oman: 30 Montaza St. (Zamalek) (E); *Ambassador:* ABDULLA GHAZALI. (also accred. to Chad).

Pakistan: 8 Sh. El Salouli (Dokki) (E); *Ambassador:* S. A. PASHA (also accred. to the Yemen Arab Republic).

Panama: 8 Salamlek St., Apt. 41 (E); *Ambassador:* LORENZO E. SÁNCHEZ GALAN.

Peru: 9 Shagaret El Dorr St. (E); *Ambassador:* ENRIQUE DE LOS HEROS RIQUELME (also accred. to Lebanon and Tunisia).

Philippines: 5 Sh. Ibn El-Walid (Dokki) (E); *Ambassador:* J. V. CRUZ.

Poland: 5 Sh. Aziz Osman (Zamalek) (E); *Ambassador:* STANISLAW TURBANSKI (also accred. to the Yemen Arab Republic and the People's Democratic Republic of Yemen).

Portugal: 15a Mansour Muhammad St. (Zamalek) (E); *Ambassador:* Dr. ROBERTO PEREIRA DE SOUSA.

Romania: 6 Sh. El Kamel Muhammad (Zamalek) (E); *Ambassador:* ION IOSEFIDE.

Rwanda: 13 Aswan St. (E); *Ambassador:* TEHAMA JUSTIN (also accred. to Algeria).

Senegal: 2 Sh. Ahmed Ragheb (Garden City) (E); *Ambassador:* MUSTAPHA CISSÉ (also accred. to Libya).

Sierra Leone: 47 Ahmad Hishmat St. (Zamalek) (E); *Ambassador:* Sheikh HAROUN OLUWOLE ZUBAIRU (also accred. to Lebanon and Yugoslavia).

Singapore: 40 Babel St. (Dokki) (E); *Ambassador:* KIRPA RAM VIJ (also accred. to Ethiopia, Lebanon, Pakistan and Yugoslavia).

Somalia: 38 Rue El Shahid Abdel Moneim Riad (Dokki) (E); *Ambassador:* ABDURRAHMAN FARAH ISMAIL.

Spain: 28 Ahmed Hechmat St. (Zamalek) (E); *Ambassador:* MANUEL ALABARTE (also accred. to the Yemen Arab Republic).

Sri Lanka: 8 Sh. Yehia Ibrahim (Zamalek) (E); *Ambassador:* (vacant) (also accred. to Algeria and Libya).

Sudan: 4 Sh. El Ibrahimi (Garden City) (E); *Ambassador:* MOHAMED MIRGHANI.

Sweden: 13 Sh. Muhammad Mazhar (Zamalek) (E); *Ambassador:* ERNST AXEL EDELSTAM (also accred. to Cyprus).

Switzerland: 10 Sh. Abdel Khalek Saroit (E); *Ambassador:* DANIEL GAGNEBIN.

Tanzania: 9 Abdel Hamid Lotfi St. (Dokki) (E); *Ambassador:* ALI H. MWINYI (also accred. to the United Arab Emirates).

Thailand: 2 Sh. El Malek El Afdal (Zamalek) (E); *Ambassador:* SUNTHORM SUWARNASARN (also accred. to Lebanon).

Turkey: Avenue El Nil (Giza) (E); *Ambassador:* (vacant).

Uganda: 9 Midan El Missaha (Dokki) (E); *Ambassador:* Lt.-Col. JACK-WILLIAM BUNYENYEZI (also accred. to Algeria, Iraq, Mauritania, Morocco, Spain, Syria, Tunisia and Turkey).

U.S.S.R.: 95 Sh. Giza (Giza) (E); *Ambassador:* VLADIMIR POLIAKOV.

United Kingdom: Kasr El Doubara (Garden City) (E); *Ambassador:* MICHAEL WEIR.

U.S.A.: 5 America El Latinia St. (Garden City) (E); *Ambassador:* ALFRED ATHERTON.

Uruguay: 6 Sh. Loutfallah (Zamalek) (E); *Ambassador:* JUAN PEDRO AMESTOY.

Vatican City: 5 Sh. Muhammad Mazhar (Zamalek) (Apostolic Nunciature); *Nuncio:* (vacant).

Venezuela: 15A Sh. Mansour Muhammad (Zamalek) (E); *Ambassador:* Col. JESÚS MANUEL PÉREZ MORÁLES.

Viet-Nam: 24 Mossadek St. (Dokki) (E); *Ambassador:* CHU DUC THANH.

Yugoslavia: 33 Sh. El Mansour Muhammad (Zamalek) (E); *Ambassador:* ALEXANDER BOZOVIC.

Zaire: 5 Mansour Mohammad St. (Zamalek) (E); *Ambassador:* MUTUALE TSHIKANKIE (also accred. to Lebanon and Turkey).

Zambia: 13 Souria St. (Madinet El Mohandessine) (E); *Ambassador:* M. JOSHUA S. SIYOLWE (also accred. to Algeria, Iran, Iraq, Kuwait, Lebanon, Morocco and the People's Democratic Republic of Yemen).

Egypt also has diplomatic relations with Cape Verde, the Comoros, Costa Rica, Fiji, Grenada, Guyana, Haiti, Honduras, Iceland, the Ivory Coast, Laos, Luxembourg, Madagascar, Monaco, Mozambique, Nicaragua, Papua New Guinea, Seychelles, Suriname, Swaziland, Togo, Upper Volta and Western Samoa.

JUDICIAL SYSTEM

The Courts of Law in Egypt are basically divided into four categories as follows:

1. *The Supreme Court* (called *The Court of Cassation*)
2. *The Courts of Appeal*
3. *The Primary Tribunals*
4. *The Summary Tribunals*

Each Court contains criminal and civil chambers.

1. The Supreme Court

The highest Court of Law in Egypt. Its sessions are held at Cairo and its jurisdiction covers the whole Egyptian territory.

Final judgements rendered in criminal and civil matters may be referred to the Supreme Court—by the accused or the Public Prosecution in criminal matters, and by any of the litigants in civil matters—in cases of misapplications or misinterpretations of the law as applied by the competent court in final judgement, as well as in cases of irregularity in the form of the judgement or the procedures having effect on that judgement.

The Supreme Court is composed of the Chief Justice, four Deputy-Chief Justices and thirty-six Justices.

2. Courts of Appeal

There are six Courts of Appeal situated in the more important Governorates of Egypt: Cairo, Alexandria, Asyut, Mansura, Tanta, and Beni Suef. Each of these courts contains a criminal chamber, *The Assize Court*, to try cases of felonies, and a civil chamber to hear appeals filed by any of the litigants in civil matters against a judgement rendered by the primary tribunal, where the law so permits.

President in Cairo: M. MAHMOUD ABD-EL-LATIF.

3. Primary Tribunals

In each Governorate, there is a Primary Tribunal, each of which contains several chambers. Each chamber is composed of three Judges. Some of these chambers try criminal cases, whilst others hear civil litigations.

Primary Tribunals sit as Courts of Appeal in certain cases, according to circumstances.

4. Summary Tribunals

Summary Tribunals are branches of the Primary Tribunals and are situated in the different districts of Egypt. Each of these tribunals is composed of a single Judge.

Summary Tribunals hear civil and criminal matters of minor importance according to certain details.

The Public Prosecution

The Public Prosecution is headed by the Attorney-General and consists of a large number of Attorneys, Chief Prosecutors and Prosecutors, who are distributed among the various districts of Egypt. The Public Prosecution is represented at all criminal Courts and also at litigation in certain civil matters. Furthermore, the enforcement of judgement rendered in criminal cases is controlled and supervised by the Public Prosecution.

Public Prosecutor: AHMED ALI MUSA.

The Supreme Judicial Council

This Council exists to guarantee the independence of the judicial system from outside interference. Under the presidency of the Chief Justice, the Supreme Judicial Council contains the following members:

the Chief Justice
two Deputy Chief Justices
the Under-Secretary of State for the Ministry of Justice
the Attorney-General
the President of the Court of Appeal in Cairo
the President of the Primary Tribunal in Cairo.

All matters concerning the promotion, discipline or otherwise of the members of the judicial system are referred to this Council.

An Arbitration Bureau was set up in 1966 to investigate cases between state and public sector organizations.

RELIGION

Over 90 per cent of Egyptians are Muslims, and almost all of these follow Sunni tenets. There are over a million Copts in Egypt forming the largest religious minority. Besides the Copts there are other Christian minorities numbering about a quarter of a million and consisting of Greek Orthodox, Roman Catholics, Armenians and Protestants. There is also a small Jewish minority.

Grand Sheikh of Al Azhar: Dr. MUHAMMAD ABDUL RAHMAN BISAR.

Grand Mufti of Egypt: ALI GAD AL-HAQ.

Coptic Orthodox Church: Anba Ruess Building, Ramses St., Abbasiya, Cairo; f. A.D. 61; Leader Pope SHENOUDA III; about 8 million followers in Egypt, Sudan, other African countries, the U.S.A., Canada, Australia; Europe and the Middle East.

Coptic Catholic Church: Patriarch Cardinal STEPHANOS I, SIDAROUSS, 34 Sh. Ibn Sandar, Koubbeh Bridge,

Cairo; 4 dioceses; 150,000 mems.; publs. *Al Salah, Sadik el Kahen, Al Risalat.*

Greek Catholic Patriarchate: P.O.B. 50076 Beirut, Lebanon; 16 rue Daher, Cairo; Patriarch of Antioch, of Alexandria and of Jerusalem His Beatitude MAXIMOS V. HAKIM; 500,000 mems. in the Middle East.

Greek Orthodox Church: Patriarch NIKOLAUS VI.

Armenian Apostolic Church: 179 Ramses Ave., Cairo, P.O.B. 48-Faggala; Archbishop MAMPRE SIROUNIAN.

Armenian Catholic Patriarchate: 36 Mohammed Sabri Abou Alam Street, Cairo; Archbishop RAPHAEL BAYAN.

Maronite Church: 15 Hamdi Street, Daher, Cairo; Archbishop JOSEPH MERHI.

Syrian Catholic Church: 46 rue Daher, Cairo; Bishop BASILE MOUSSA DAOUD.

Jewish Community: Office of the Chief Rabbi, Rabbi HAIM DOUEK; 13 Sebil-el-Khazindar St., Abbassia, Cairo.

THE PRESS

Despite a fairly high illiteracy rate, the Egyptian Press is well developed. Cairo is the biggest publishing centre in the Middle East.

Legally all newspapers and magazines come under the control of the Arab Socialist Union. All the important newspapers and magazines are owned by the Union, although the four big publishing houses of al-Ahram, Dar al-Hilal, Dar Akhbar al-Yom and Dar al-Gomhouriya, operate as separate entities and compete with each other commercially. Dar al-Hilal is concerned only with magazines and publishes *al-Mussawar, Hawa'a* and *al-Kawakeb.* Dar Akhbar al-Yom publishes the daily newspaper *al-Akhbar*, the weekly newspaper *Akhbar al-Yom* and the weekly magazine *Akher Saa.*

Dar al Gomhouriya publishes the daily *al-Gomhouriya*, the daily English language paper *Egyptian Gazette*, the daily French newspaper *Le Progrès Egyptien* and the afternoon paper *al-Misaa.*

The most authoritative daily newspaper is the very old established *al-Ahram.* Other popular large circulation magazines are *Rose al-Youssef, Sabah al-Kheir* and *al Izaw w'al Television.*

In February 1974 President Sadat ended press censorship, except on military matters, and foreign correspondents in Cairo were relieved of the duty of submitting their reports, except those on military matters, for censorship.

In May 1975 President Sadat set up the Supreme Press Council, under the Chairmanship of the First Secretary of the Arab Socialist Union, to develop the Press and find solutions to its problems. Extensive personnel changes were made in the Egyptian Press in March 1976 and subsequently an inquiry into journalists critical of the government was instigated.

In November 1978, however, President Sadat abolished the Ministry of Culture and Information, ostensibly freeing the Press from government control. Although the censors have been removed, publishing houses and newspapers remain government-owned, and Editors are personally appointed by the President.

DAILIES

ALEXANDRIA

Barid al-Charikat: P.O.B. 813; f. 1952; Arabic; evening; commerce, finance, insurance and marine affairs, etc.; Editor S. BENEDUCCI; circ. 15,000.

al-Ittihad al-Misri: 13 Sharia Sidi Abdel Razzak; f. 1871, Arabic; evening; Propr. ANWAR MAHER FARAG; Dir. HASSAN MAHER FARAG.

Le Journal d'Alexandrie: 1 Sharia Rolo; French; evening; Editor CHARLES ARCACHE.

La Réforme: 8 Passage Sherif; f. 1895; French; noon; Propr. Comte AZIZ DE SAAB; circ. 7,000.

al-Safeer: 4 El-Sahafa St.; f. 1924; Arabic; evening; Editor MOSTAFA SHARAF.

Tachydromos-Egyptos: 4 Sharia Zangarol; f. 1882; Greek; morning; liberal; Publisher PENY COUTSOUMIS; Editor DINOS COUTSOUMIS; circ. 11,000.

CAIRO

al-Ahram (*The Pyramids*): Gallaa St.; f. 1875; Arabic; morning; Editor ALI HAMDI EL-GAMAL; circ. 400,000.

al-Akhbar: Dar Akhbar al-Yom, Sharia al-Sahafa; f. 1952; Arabic; Chair. and Editor MOUSA SABRY; Man. Editor AHMED ZEIN; circ. 695,000.

Arev: 3 Sharia Soliman Halaby; f. 1915; Armenian; evening; official organ of the Armenian Liberal Democratic Party; Editor AVEDIS YAPOUDJIAN.

Egyptian Gazette: 24 Sharia Galal; f. 1880; English daily; morning; Editor Dr. AMIN MOHAMED ABOUL-ENEIN; circ. 19,000.

al-Gomhouriya (*The Republic*): 24 Sharia Zakaria Ahmed; f. 1953; Arabic; morning; Chair. and Editor-in-Chief MOHSEN MOHAMED; circ. 400,000.

Journal d'Egypte, Le: 1 Borsa Guédida St.; f. 1936; French; morning; Propr. and Gen. Man. LITA GALLAD; Editor-in-Chief MOHAMED RACHAD; circ. 63,000.

al-Misaa (*The Evening*): 24 Sharia Zakaria Ahmed; Arabic; evening; Chief Editor AHMED ADEL; circ. 70,000.

Misr: f. 1977; organ of the Arab Socialist Party.

Phos: 14 Zakaria Ahmed St.; f. 1896; Greek; morning; Editor S. PATERAS; Man. BASILE A. PATERAS; circ. 20,000.

Le Progrès Egyptien: 24 Sharia Zakaria Ahmed; f. 1890; French; morning including Sundays; Chief Editor NAGUIB HENEIN; circ. 15,000.

PERIODICALS

ALEXANDRIA

al Ahad Al Gedid: 88 al-Tatwig Street; Editor-in-Chief MAHMUD ABDEL MALAK KORITAM; Gen. Man. MUHAMMAD KORITAM.

Alexandria Medical Journal: 4 G. Carducci; f. 1922; English, French and Arabic; quarterly; publ. by Alexandria Medical Asscn.; Editor AMIN RIDA; circ. 1,500.

Amitié Internationale: 59 Avenue Hourriya; f. 1957; publ. by Assn. Egypt. d'Amitié Inter.; Arabic and French; quarterly; Editor Dr. ZAKI BADAOUI.

L'Annuaire des Sociétés Egyptiennes par Actions: 23 Midan Tahrir; f. 1930; annually in December; French; Propr ELIE I. POLITI; Editor OMAR EL-SAYED MOURSI.

L'Echo Sportif: 7 rue de l'Archevêché; French; weekly; Propr. MICHEL BITTAR.

L'Economiste Egyptien: 11 rue de la Poste, Alexandria; P.O.B. 847; f. 1901; weekly; Propr. MARGUERITE and JOFFRE HOSNY.

Egypte-Sports-Cinéma: 7 Avenue Hourriya; French; weekly; Editor EMILE ASSAAD.

Egyptian Cotton Gazette: P.O.B. 433; organ of the Alexandria Cotton Exporters Association; English; twice yearly; Chief Editor Dr. FOUAD A. TAWFIK.

Egyptian Cotton Statistics: English; weekly.

Egyptian Customs Magazine: 2 Sharia Sinan; deals with invoicing, receipts, etc.; Man. MUHAMMAD ALY EL BADAWY.

La Gazette d'Orient: 5 rue de l'Ancienne Bourse; Propr. MAURICE BETITO.

Guide des Industries: 2 Sharia Adib; French; annual; Editor SIMON A. BARANIS.

Informateur des Assurances: 1 Sharia Adib; f. 1936; French; monthly; Propr. ELIE I. POLITI; Editor SIMON A. BARANIS.

La Réforme Illustrée: 8 Passage Sherif; f. 1925; French; weekly; Propr. Comte AZIZ DE SAAB; circ. 20,000.

Répertoire Permanent de Législation Egyptienne: 27 Ave. El Guesch, Chatby-les-Bains; f. 1932; French and Arabic; Editor V. SISTO.

Revue Economique Trimestrielle: c/o Banque de Port-Said, 18 Talaat Harb St., Alexandria; French (f. 1929) and Arabic (f. 1961) editions; quarterly; Editor MAHMOUD SAMY EL ADAWAY.

Sanaet El-Nassig (*L'Industrie Textile*): 5 rue de l'Archevêché; Arabic and French; monthly; Editor PHILIPPE COLAS.

Voce d'Italia: 90 Sharia Farahde; Italian; fortnightly; Editor R. AVELLINO.

CAIRO

Akhbar al-Yom: 6 Sharia al-Sahafa; f. 1944; Arabic; weekly (Saturday); Editor-in-Chief ABDEL-HAMID ABDEL-GHANI; Editing Man. SAID SONBOL; circ. 1,099,962.

Akher Saa: Dar Akhbar al-Yom, Sharia al-Sahafa; f. 1934; Arabic; weekly (Wednesday); independent; Editor-in-Chief RUSHDY SALEH; circ. 133,817.

al-Ahd al-Goumhouri: 132 Sharia Kalaa; Editor ABDEL-KHALEK TAKIA.

al-Ahra: f. 1977; weekly; published by Liberal Socialist Party.

al Ahram Al Iqtisadi: United Arab Press, Gallaa St.; economic and political affairs; owned by *Al Ahram*; Editor AHMAD LUFTI MUHAMMAD ABDUL-AZIM; circ. 12,000.

al-Azhar: Sharia al-Azhar; Arabic; Dir MUHAMMAD FARID WABDI.

al-Doctor: 8 Hoda Shaarawy St.; f. 1947; Arabic; monthly; Editor Dr. AHMAD M. KAMAL; circ. 30,000.

al-Fussoul: 17 Sharia Sherif Pasha; Arabic; monthly; Propr. and Chief Editor MUHAMMAD ZAKI ABDEL KADER.

al-Garida al-Togaria al-Misriya: 25 Sharia Nubar Pasha; f. 1921; Arabic; weekly; circ. 7,000.

al-Hilal: Dar al-Hilal, 16 Sharia Muhammad Ezz El-Arab; f. 1895; Arabic; literary monthly; Editor SALEH GAWDAT.

al-Hurriya: Arabic; weekly; published by Arab Socialist Union; Editor-in-Chief MUHAMMAD SUBAIH.

al-Izaa wal-Television: 13 Sharia Muhammad Ezz El-Arab; f. 1935; Arabic; weekly; Editor and Chair. AHMED BAHGAT; circ. 120,000.

al-Kawakeb (*The Stars*): Dar al-Hilal, 16 Sharia Muhammad Ezz El-Arab; f. 1952; Arabic; film magazine; Editor KAMAL EL-NAGMI; circ. 38,500.

al-Magalla al-Ziraia: monthly; agriculture; circ. 30,000.

al-Mussawar: Dar al-Hilal, 16 Sharia Muhammad Ezz El-Arab; f. 1924; Arabic weekly; Editors MORSI EL SHAFEE and SABRI ABDUL MAGD; circ. 162,000.

al-Sabah: 4 Sharia Muhammad Said Pasha; f. 1922; Arabic; weekly; Editor MOSTAFA EL-KACHACHI.

al-Tahrir: 5 Sharia Naguib-Rihani; Arabic; weekly; Editor ABDEL-AZIZ SADEK.

al-Tuqaddam (*Progress*): f. 1978; organ of National Progressive Unionist Party; replaced *Al-Ahali*.

Ana Wa Inta: Sharia Central; Arabic; monthly; Editor MOHAMED HASSAN.

Arab Observer: published by the Middle East News Agency, 11 Sh. Sahafa; f. 1960; weekly international news magazine; English; Editor-in-Chief Dr. ABDEL HAMID EL-BATRIK.

Contemporary Thought: University of Cairo; quarterly; Editor Dr. Z. N. MAHMOUD.

Echos: 1;5 Sharia Mahmoud Bassiouni; f. 1947; French weekly Dir. and Propr. GEORGES QRFALI.

The Egyptian Directory: 19 Sharia Abdel Khalek Sarwat; B.P. 500; f. 1887; French and English; annual; Man. and Editor TAWHID KAMAL.

Egyptian Mail: 24 Sharia Zakaria Ahmed; f. 1910; English; weekly; Editor Dr. AMIN ABOUL-ENEIN.

Études Médicales: Collège de la Ste. Familie Faggalah, Cairo; Editor HUBERT DE LEUSSE.

Études Scientifiques: Collège de la Ste. Familie Faggalah, Cairo; scientific and technical quarterly; Editor HUBERT DE LEUSSE.

La Femme Nouvelle: 48 Sharia Kasr-el-Nil; French; twice yearly.

Hawa'a (*Eve*): Dar al-Hilal, 16 Sharia Muhammad Ezz El-Arab; women's magazine; Arabic; weekly.

Images: Dar Al-Hilal, 16 Sharia Muhammad Ezz El-Arab; French; illustrated; weekly; Editors EMILE and CHOUCRI ZEIDAN.

Industrial Egypt: P.O.B. 251, 26A Sharia Sherif Pasha, Cairo; f. 1924; Bulletin of the Federation of Egyptian Industries; English and Arabic; quarterly; Editor DARWISH M. DARWISH.

Industry and Trade Information: 13 Sharia Abdel Hamid Said; English; weekly; commercial and industrial bulletin; Dir. and Propr. NICOLAS STAVRI; Editor N. GHANEM.

Informateur Financier et Commercial: 24 Sharia Soliman Pasha; f. 1929; weekly; Dir. HENRI POLITI; circ. 15,000.

Kitab al-Hilal: 16 Sharia Muhammad Ezz El-Arab; monthly; Proprs. EMILE and CHOUKRI ZEIDAN.

Lewa al-Islam: 11 Sharia Sherif Pasha; Arabic; monthly; Propr. AHMED HAMZA; Editor MUHAMMAD ALY SHETA.

Lotus Magazine (*Afro-Asian Writings*): 104 Kasr El Eini St.; f. 1968; quarterly; English, French and Arabic.

Magalet al-Mohandeseen: 28 Avenue Ramses; f. 1945; published by The Engineers' Syndicate; Arabic and English; ten times a year; Editor and Sec. MAHMOUD SAMI ABDEL KAWI.

Medical Journal of Cairo University: Manyal University Hospital, Sharia Kasr el-Aini; f. 1933; Kasr el-Aini Clinical Society; English; quarterly.

The Middle East Observer: 8 Chawarby St.; f. 1954; weekly; English; specializing in economics of Middle East and African markets; also publishes supplements on law, foreign trade and tenders; Man. Owner AHMED FODA; Chief Editor AHMED SABRI; circ. 30,000.

October: Cairo; monthly; Editor-in-Chief ANIS MANSUR.

Progrès Dimanche: 24 Sharia Galal; French; weekly; Editor M. YACCARINI.

Riwayat al-Hilal: 16 Sharia Muhammad Ezz El-Arab Arabic; monthly; Proprs. EMILE and CHOUKRI ZEIDAN

Rose el Youssef: 89A Kasr el Ainei St.; f. 1925; Arabic; weekly; political; circulates throughout all Arab countries, includes monthly English section; Chair. ABDEL RAHMAN EL SHARKAWI; Chief Editor ABDUL AZIZ KHAMIS; Editors FATHI GHANEM and SALAH HAFEZ; Editor English section IBRAHIM EZZAT; circ. 35,000.

Sabah al-Kheir: 18 Sharia Mohamed Said; Arabic; weekly; light entertainment; Editor HASSAN FOUAD.

Tchehreh Nema: 14 Sharia Hassan El-Akbar (Abdine); f. 1904; Iranian; monthly; political, literary and general; Editor MANUCHEHR TCHEHREH NEMA MOADEB ZADEH.

Up-to-Date International Industry: 10 Sharia Galal; Arabic and English; foreign trade journal.

NEWS AGENCIES

Middle East News Agency: 4 Sharia Sherrifin, Cairo; f. 1955; regular service in Arabic, English and French; Chair. MOHAMED ABDEL GAWAD; Editors MOHAMED AL BIALI, KAMAL AMER and MUSTAFA NAGUIB.

Misr Egyptian News Agency: 43 Sharia Ramses, Cairo.

FOREIGN BUREAUX

Agence France-Presse (AFP): 33 Kasr El Nil St., Cairo; Man. GEORGES HERBOUZE.

Agencia EFE (*Spain*): 8 Sharia Dr. Handusa, Apt. 18, Garden City; Correspondent ANA MARIA DE NORIEGA.

Agenzia Nazionale Stampa Associata (ANSA) (*Italy*): 19 Sh. Abdel Khalek Sarwat, Cairo; Chief MARIO RISPOLI.

Allgemeiner Deutscher Nachrichtendienst (ADN) (*German Democratic Republic*): 17 Sharia el Brazil, Apt. 59, Cairo-Zamalek; Correspondent EBERHARD AMME.

Associated Press (AP) (*U.S.A.*): 33 Kasr El Nil, Cairo; Chief HARRY A. DUNPHY.

Bulgarian Telegraph Agency: 13 Sh. Muhammad Kamel Morsi, Aguza, Cairo; Chief DIMITER MASLAROV.

Deutsche Presse Agentur (dpa) (*Federal Republic of Germany*): 33 Kasr el Nil St., Apt. 13/4, Cairo; Correspondent PETER FISCHER.

Kyodo News Service (*Japan*): Flat 12, 33 Abdel Khalek Tharawta, Cairo; Chief HIDEO YAMASHITA.

Reuters (*United Kingdom*): Apt. 43, Immobilia Bldgs., 26 Sh. Sherif Pasha, Cairo, P.O.B. 2040.

United Press International (UPI) (*U.S.A.*): 4 Sh. Eloui, P.O.B. 872, Cairo; Chief MAURICE GUINDI.

PUBLISHERS

Egyptian General Organization for Publishing and Printing: 117 Corniche el Nil St., Cairo; affil. to Min. of Culture.

ALEXANDRIA

Alexandria University Press: Shatby.

Artec: 10 Sharia Stamboul.

Dar Nashr ath-Thagata.

Egyptian Book Centre: A. D. Christodoulou and Co., 5 Sharia Adib; f. 1950.

Egyptian Printing and Publishing House: Ahmed El Sayed Marouf, 59, Safia Zaghoul; f. 1947.

Maison Egyptienne d'Editions: Ahmed El Sayed Marouf, Sharia Adib; f. 1950.

Maktab al-Misri al-Hadith li-t-Tiba wan-Nashr: 7 Nobar St.; also at 2 Sherif St., Cairo; Man. AHMAD YEHIA.

CAIRO

Al Ahram Establishment: Gallaa St., Cairo; f. 1875; publishes newspapers, magazines and books, inc. *Al-Ahram.*

Akhbar El Yom Publishing House: 6 Sharia al-Sahafa; f. 1944; publishes *al-Akhbar* (daily), *Akhbar al-Yom* (weekly), and colour magazine *Akher Saa;* Pres. MOUSA SABRI; Dir.-Gen. Dr. HUSSEIN EL GHAMRY.

Al-Hilal Publishing House: 16 Sharia Muhammad Ezz El-Arab; f. 1895; publishes *Al-Hilal, Riwayat Al-Hilal, Kitab Al-Hilal* (monthlies); *Al Mussawar, Al Kawakeb, Hawa* (weeklies).

Argus Press: 10 Zakaria Ahmad St., Cairo; Owner HRASTAN EKMEKJIAN.

Dar al-Gomhouriya: 24 Sharia Zakaria Ahmad; publications include the dailies, *al-Gomhouriya, al-Misaa, Egyptian Gazette* and *Le Progrès Egyptien*; Pres. MOHSEN MOHAMED.

Dar al-Hilal: Al Hilal Bldg., 16 Sharia Mohammed Ezz El-Arab; f. 1892; publishes magazines only, including *al-Mussawar, Hawa'a* and *al-Kawakeb*; Chair. AMINA AS-SAID.

Dar al Kitab al Arabi: Misr Printing House, Sharia Noubar, Bab al Louk, Cairo; f. 1968; Man. Dir. Dr. SAHAIR AL KALAMAWI.

Dar al Maaref Egypt: 1119 Cornich El-Nil St.; f. 1890; Arabic books in all fields; distributor of books in English, French and German; Chair. ANIS MANSOUR; Man. Dir. Dr. MUHAMMAD FOUAD IBRAHIM.

Documentation and Research Centre for Education (Ministry of Education): 33 Falaky St.; f. 1956; Dir. Mrs.

ZEINAB M. MEHREZ; bibliographies, directories, information and education bulletins.

Editions Horus: 1 Midan Soliman Pasha.

Editions le Progrès: 6 Sharia Sherif Pasha, Propr. WADI CHOUKRI.

Editions et Publications des Pères Jésuites: 1 rue Boustan al Maksi, Faggala; religious publications in Arabic.

Les Editions Universitaires d'Egypte: 41 Sharia Sherif Pasha.

Higher University Council for Arts, Letters and Sciences: University of Cairo.

Lagnat al Taalif Wal Targama Wal Nashr (*Committee for Writing, Translating and Publishing Books*): 9 Sharia El-Kerdassi (Abdine).

Librairie La Renaissance D'Egypte (Hassan Muhammad & Sons): 9 Adly St., P.O.B. 2172; f. 1930; Man. HASSAN MUHAMMAD; religion, history, geography, medicine, architecture, economics, politics, law, philosophy, psychology, children's books, atlases, dictionaries.

Maktabet Misr: P.O.B. 16, 3 Kamel Sidki St., Cairo; f. 1932; publ. wide variety of fiction, biographies and textbooks for schools and universities; Man. AMIR SAID GOUDA EL SAHHAR.

Middle East Publishing Co.: 29 Rue Abdel Khalek Sarwat.

Mohamed Abbas Sid Ahmed: 55 Sharia Nubar.

National Library Press (*Dar al Kutub*): Midan Ahmed Maher; bibliographic works.

New Publications: J. Meshaka and Co., 5 Sharia Maspero.

The Public Organization for Books and Scientific Appliances: Cairo University, Orman, Ghiza; f. 1965; state organization publishing academic books for universities, higher institutes, etc.; also imports books, periodicals and scientific appliances; Chair. KAMIL SEDDIK; Vice-Chair. FATTHY LABIB.

Senouhy Publishers: 54 Sharia Abdel-Khalek Sarwat; f. 1956; Dirs. LEILA A. FADEL, OMAR RASHAD.

Other Cairo publishers include: *Dar al-Fikr al-Arabi, Dar al-Fikr al-Hadith Li-t-Tab wan-Nashr, Dar wa Matabi, Dar al-Nahda al-Arabiya, Dar al-Misriya Li-t-Talif wat-Tardjma, Dar al-Qalam, Dar ath-Thagapa, Majlis al-Ala Li-Riyyat al-Funun, Maktaba Ain Shams, Maktaba al-Andshilu al-Misriya, Maktabat al-Chandshi, Maktabat al-Nahira al-Hadith, Markaz Tasjil al-Athar al-Misriya, Matbaat ar-Risala, al-Qaumiya li-t-Tibaa wan-Nashr-Wizarat az-Ziraa Maslahat al-Basatin.*

RADIO AND TELEVISION

RADIO

Egyptian Radio and Television Federation (ERTV): Radio and TV Building, Corniche El Nil, P.O. Box 1186, Cairo; f. 1928; 194 hours daily; Pres. MOHAMAD MAHMOUD ARAFA ZAYEN; Head of Int. and Public Relations and Liaison Officer Mrs. SANIA MAHER. Home Service programmes in Arabic, English, French, Armenian, German, Greek, Italian and Hebrew; foreign services in Arabic, English, Swahili, Hausa, Persian, Bengali, Urdu, German, Spanish, Indonesian, Thai, Hindi, Pushtu, Turkish, Somali, Portuguese, Fulani, Russian, Italian, Sesotho, Zulu, Chishona, Sindebele, Nyanja, Lingala, Amharic, Yoruba, Wolof, Bambara, Dankali.

Middle East Radio: Société Egyptienne de Publicité, 24-26 Sharia Zakaria Ahmed, Cairo; f. 1964; commercial service with 500-kW. transmitter; U.K. Agents: Radio and Television Services (Middle East) Ltd., 21 Hertford St., London, W.1.

In 1976 there were 8 million radio receivers and 850,000 television sets.

TELEVISION

Egyptian Television Organization: Corniche el Nil, Cairo; f. 1960; 19½ hours daily (two channels); Chair. Mrs. TOMADER TAWFIK.

FINANCE

BANKING

(cap.=capital; p.u.=paid up; dep.=deposits; res.=reserves; m.=million; amounts in £ Egyptian)

The whole banking system was nationalized in 1961.

CENTRAL BANK

Central Bank of Egypt: 31 Kasr-el-Nil St., Cairo; f. 1961; cap. 5.0m.; dep. £2,097m. (Dec. 1978); Gov. MUHAMMAD ABDEL-FATTAH IBRAHIM; publs. *Economic Review* (quarterly), *Annual Report.*

COMMERCIAL AND SPECIALIZED BANKS

Arab Land Bank: 33 Abdel-Khalek Sarwat St., Cairo; Pres. AHMED AMIN ALY FAHMI.

Bank of Alexandria, S.A.E.: 6 Salah Salem St., Alexandria; and 49 Kasr El-Nil St., Cairo; f. 1864; cap. p.u. 5m.; dep. 623.7m. (Dec. 1978); 85 brs.; Chair. MOHAMED M. EL BAYOUMI.

Banque du Caire: 22 Adly St., Cairo; f. 1952; cap. and res. 93.3m. dep. 970.3m. (Dec. 1978); 82 brs.; Chair. MUHAMMAD EZZAT FAHMY; Dep. Chair. MAHMOUD F. LABAN.

Banque Misr, S.A.E.: 151 Mohamed Farid St., Cairo; f. 1920; 156 brs.; cap. 4m.; dep. 886.8m. (Dec. 1976); Chair. AHMED FOUAD MAHMOUD FOUAD; publ. *Economic Bulletin.*

Crédit Foncier Egyptien: 11 El Mashadi St., Cairo; Chair. Dr. ALI SABRI YASSIN.

Development Industrial Bank: 110 El-Gala St., Cairo; Chair. ABDEL HAMID KABOODAN.

National Bank of Egypt, S.E.A.: 24 Sherif St., Cairo; f. 1898; nationalized 1960; handles all commercial banking operations; cap. and res. 47.0m.; dep. 974.8m. (Dec. 1978); 103 brs.; Chair. MOHAMED ABDEL MONEIM ROUSHDY; publ. *Quarterly Economic Bulletin.*

The Principal Bank for Development and Agricultural Credit: 110 El-Kasr El-Eini St., Cairo; f. 1976 to succeed former Credit organizations; Chair. FATAHALLA RIFATA MOHAMED.

DEVELOPMENT BANK

Nasser Social Bank: 35 Kasr El Nil St., Cairo; f. 1971; interest-free savings and investment bank for social and economic development; Chair. I. M. LOTFY.

MULTINATIONAL BANKS

Arab African International Bank: 44 Abdel Khalek Sarwat St., Cairo; f. 1964; cap. U.S. $100m.; commercial investment bank; shareholders are Governments of Kuwait, Egypt, Iraq, Algeria, Jordan and Qatar; Chair. and Man. Dir. IBRAHIM EL IBRAHIMY; Deputy Chair. and Man. Dir. MAHMOUD BAHIR ONSY (Egypt); brs. in Beirut, Dubai, Mutrah and Abu Dhabi; Rep. Offices in Khartoum and London.

Arab International Bank: 35 Abdel Khalek Sarwat St., Cairo; f. 1971; cap. U.S. $100m.; res. U.S. $70m. (Dec. 1978); aims to promote trade and investment in shareholders' countries and other Arab countries; Chair. Dr. AHMED NAZMY ABDEL HAMID.

COMMERCIAL JOINT VENTURE BANKS

Alexandria-Kuwait International Bank: 49 Kasr El-Nil St., Cairo; Bank of Alexandria/Misr Insurance has 51 per cent interest, Kuwaiti and Egyptian private capital 39 per cent, Sharjah Group 10 per cent.

Banque du Caïre et de Paris: 14 El-Saraia El-Koubra, Garden City, P.O.B. 2441, Cairo; f. 1977; Banque du Caïre has 51 per cent interest and Banque Nationale de Paris 49 per cent; Chair. MUHAMMAD EZZAT FAHMI; Gen. Man. FATHY SOLIMAN.

Banque du Caïre-Far East: 104 Nile St., Agouza, Cairo.

Chase National Bank (Egypt): 12 El Birgas St., Garden City, P.O.B. 2430, Cairo; National Bank of Egypt has 51 per cent interest and Chase Manhattan Bank 49 per cent; cap. 10m.; Chair. ALY DABBOUS.

Egyptian-American Bank: 23 Gamal El-Din Abul Mahassen St., Garden City, P.O.B. 1825, Cairo; f. 1976; Bank of Alexandria has 51 per cent interest and American Express Banking Corporation 49 per cent; cap. 10m.; dep. 54m.; Chair. MOUSTAFA NOUR ELDIN; Man. Dir. Dr. FARID W. SAAD.

Misr International Bank: 14 Alfy St., P.O.B. 631, Cairo; Bank Misr has a 51 per cent interest and First National Bank of Chicago, Banco di Roma and UBAF hold 49 per cent.

Misr-America International Bank: 1 Behlar Passage, Kasr El Nil St., Cairo; Development Industrial Bank has 26 per cent interest, Misr Insurance Co. has 25 per cent; while Bank of America has 40 per cent, Kuwait Real Estate Bank 4.5 per cent and First Arabian Corporation 4.5 per cent.

Misr-Romanian Bank: 15 Abul-Feda St., Zamalek, Cairo; f. 1977; Misr Bank has 51 per cent interest, while Romanian Bank for Foreign Trade has 19 per cent, Romanian Bank for Agriculture and Food Industries 15 per cent, and Romanian Investments Bank 15 per cent; cap. U.S. $5m.; Dep. Chair., Man. Dir. and Gen. Man. GHORGHE IDITOIV; Man. Dir. and Gen. Man. BAHIR ABDEL KERIM FAHMI.

Nile Bank, S.A.E.: 35 Ramses St., Cairo; f. 1978; cap. U.S. $20m.

Suez Canal Bank: 11 Mohamed Sabry Abou Alam St., P.O.B. 2620, Cairo; f. 1978; Chair. ZAKARIA TAWFIK ABDEL FATAH; Gen. Man. MUHAMMAD HAMZA EL ADAWI.

JOINT VENTURE BANKS (FOREIGN CURRENCIES)

Arab Union Bank for Development and Investment: 5 Kounaish El-Nil St., Cairo.

Banque National Soçiété Général: 4 Talaat Harb St., Cairo.

Cairo Barclays International Bank: 12 El-Shekh Youssef Square, Garden City, Cairo.

Crédit International d'Egypte: 2 Talaat Harb St., Cairo.

Crédit Suisse: Cairo; Man. GIOVANNI GROPPI.

Misr Iran Development Bank: 8 Adly St., Cairo.

Soçiété Arabe International de Banque: 10 Abdel Salam Arref St., Cairo.

FOREIGN BANKS

American Express International Banking Corporation, Arab Bank Ltd., Banca Commerciale Italiana, Bank Melli Iran, Bank of America, Bank of Credit and Commerce-International, Bank of Nova Scotia, Bank Saderat Iran, Citibank, Gamal Trust Bank, Grindlays Bank Ltd., Lloyds Bank International Ltd., National Bank of Abu Dhabi, National Bank of Greece, National Bank of Pakistan, Oman Limited Bank, Rafidain Bank.

OFFSHORE BANK

Manufacturers Hanover Trust Co.

STOCK EXCHANGES

Cairo Stock Exchange: 4A Cherifein St., Cairo; f. 1883; Pres. MUHAMMAD ALY HASSAN.

Alexandria Stock Exchange: Pres. FOUAD SHAHEEN.

INSURANCE

Misr Insurance Company: 7 Sharia Talaat Harb, Cairo; Chair. FATHI MOHAMED IBRAHIM.

Arab International Insurance Co.: P.O.B. 2704, 28 Talaat Harb Str., Cairo; a joint-stock free zone company established by Egyptian and foreign insurance companies; Chair. A. G. EL BOROLLOSSY; Man. Dir. HASSAN M. HAFEZ.

Al Chark Insurance Company, S.A.E.: Cairo; 15 Sharia Kasr-el-Nil; f. 1931; Chair. AMIN EL-HIZZAWI; general and life.

Commercial Insurance Company of Egypt, S.A.E.: 7 Midan E. Tahrir, Cairo; f. 1947; life, fire, marine, accident; Man. Dir. AHMED ZAKY HELMY.

The Egyptian Reinsurance Company, S.A.E.: 7 Dar el Shifa St., Garden City, P.O.B. 950, Cairo; f. 1957; Chair. FOUAD ABDEL RAHMAN.

L'Epargne, S.A.E.: Immeuble Chemla Sharia 26 July, P.O.B. 548, Cairo; all types of insurance.

Al Iktisad el Shabee, S.A.E.; 11 Sharia Emad El Dine, P.O.B. 1635, Cairo; f. 1948; Man. Dir. and Gen. Man. W. KHAYAT.

Al Mottahida: 9 Sharia Soliman Pasha, P.O.B. 804, Cairo; f. 1957.

National Insurance Company of Egypt, S.A.E.: 33 Sharia Nabi Danial, P.O.B. 446, Alexandria; f. 1900; Chair. MOSTAFA EL-SAYED EL-ESNAWY.

Provident Association of Egypt, S.A.E.: 9 Sharia Sherif Pasha, P.O.B. 390, Alexandria; f. 1936; Man. Dir. G. C. VORLOOU.

TRADE AND INDUSTRY

CHAMBERS OF COMMERCE

Alexandria

Egyptian Chamber of Commerce, Alexandria: El-Ghorfa Eltegareia St.; Pres. Abdel Hamied Serry; Sec. Ahmed El Alfi Muhammad; Gen. Dir. Muhammed Fathy Mahmoud.

Cairo

Cairo Chamber of Commerce: 4 Midan El Falaki St.; f. 1913; Pres. Muhammad Ali Sheta; Gen. Dir. Said El-Barrad; publ. *Monthly Bulletin.*

Other Towns

Egyptian Chamber of Commerce for Aswan Governorate: Abtal El-Tahrir St., Aswan.

Egyptian Chamber of Commerce for Asyut Governorate: Asyut.

Egyptian Chamber of Commerce for Behera Governorate: Gomhouriya St., Damanhoru.

Egyptian Chamber of Commerce for Beni-Suef Governorate: Mamdouh St., Moqbel El-Guedid, Beni-Suef.

Egyptian Chamber of Commerce for Dakahlia Governorate, Mansura: El-Saleh Ayoub Square, Mansura.

Egyptian Chamber of Commerce for Damietta Governorate: Damietta.

Egyptian Chamber of Commerce for Fayum Governorate: Fayum.

Egyptian Chamber of Commerce for Gharbia Governorate: Tanta.

Egyptian Chamber of Commerce for Giza Governorate: El-Saa Square, Giza.

Egyptian Chamber of Commerce for Ismailia Governorate: Ismailia.

Egyptian Chamber of Commerce for Kafr-el-Sheika Governorate: Kafr-el-Sheikh.

Egyptian Chamber of Commerce for Kena Govornorate: El-Gamil Street, Kena.

Egyptian Chamber of Commerce for Menia Governorate: Menia.

Egyptian Chamber of Commerce for Manufia Governorate: Sidi Fayed Street, Shibín-El-Kom.

Egyptian Chamber of Commerce for Port Said Governorate: Port Said.

Egyptian Chamber of Commerce for Kalyubia Governorate: Benha.

Egyptian Chamber of Commerce for Sharkia Governorate: Zagazig.

Egyptian Chamber of Commerce for Suez Governorate: Suez.

Egyptian Chamber of Commerce for Suhag Governorate: Suhag.

FOREIGN INVESTMENT ORGANIZATION

General Authority for Investment and Free Zones: 8 Adly St., P.O.B. 1007, Cairo; Dep. Chair. Dr. Gamal Al-Nazer.

NATIONALIZED ORGANIZATIONS

It was reported in August 1975 that the General Organizations would be replaced by Higher Councils which would allow companies greater freedom, and in November 1975 a Presidential Decree ratified the establishment of Higher Councils for sectors listed below. During 1978, however, various Government Ministries took increasing control of industries.

Food industries (21 companies).

Spinning, weaving and garments (28 companies).

Chemical industries (22 companies).

Metallurgical industries and products thereof (31 companies and an aluminium complex).

Mining (5 companies and the Egyptian General Geological Survey).

Petroleum (8 companies and the Egyptian General Petroleum Corporation).

Military production (15 companies).

Electricity (4 companies and 4 authorities).

Banking (8 banks).

Foreign trade (14 companies and the General Authority for International Fairs and Exhibitions).

Cotton (12 companies).

Insurance (14 companies and 5 authorities).

Supply and domestic distribution (32 companies).

Internal transport (11 companies and 4 authorities).

Maritime transport (9 companies and 2 authorities).

Housing and public utilities (8 companies and 5 authorities).

Construction and building materials (49 companies).

Agriculture and irrigation (14 companies, 7 authorities and 2 agricultural water research centres).

Cooperation and agricultural credit (5 authorities, 2 co-operatives and one agricultural and cooperative credit bank).

Livestock production (6 companies).

Tourism and airlines (7 companies, 4 authorities and the National Civil Aviation Training Institute.

Pharmaceuticals (12 companies).

Paper, printing and publications (8 companies, 2 authorities, Central Agency for University and School Books and Educational Systems).

Culture and information (Agencies of the Ministries of Culture and Information).

Communications (Agencies of the Ministry of Communications).

PETROLEUM

Egyptian General Petroleum Authority (EGPA): P.O.B. 2130, Cairo; State supervisory authority generally concerned with the planning of policies relating to petroleum activities in Egypt with the object of securing the development of the oil industry; has entered into 50-50 partnership agreements with a number of foreign companies; Pres. Eng. Mohamed Ramzy El-Leithy; Gen. Man. Dr. Mostafa Kamal El Auoty.

Belayim Petroleum Company (PETROBEL): 155 Sharia Mohamed Farid, Cairo; has absorbed Delta Petroleum Co.; Chair. Eng. Mohamed Tawfik Shawky.

Compagnie Orientale des Pétroles d'Egypte: 155 Muhammad Farid St., Cairo; f. 1957; capital equally shared between EGPA and International Egyptian Oil Co., which is a subsidiary of ENI of Italy; exploration and production of crude petroleum.

General Petroleum Company (GPC): P.O.B. 743, Cairo; f. 1962; wholly owned subsidiary of EGPA; operates mainly in Eastern Desert.

Gulf of Suez Petroleum Company (GUPCO): 1097 Sharia Corniche El Nil, Cairo; f. 1965; partnership between EGPA and Amoco-Egypt Co., U.S.A.; developed the El Morgan oilfield in the Gulf of Suez, also holds other exploration concessions in the Gulf of Suez and the Western Desert; output averaged 304,400 b/d in 1977; Chair. Dr. Eng. Hamdi El Banbi.

Western Desert Petroleum Company (WEPCO): P.O.B. 412, Alexandria; f. 1967 as partnership between EGPC and Phillips Petroleum and later Hispanoil with 15 per cent interest; developed Alamein, Yidma and Umbarka fields in the Western Desert and later Abu Qir offshore gas field in 1978; Chair. Eng. Hassan El Dewy.

Arab Petroleum Pipelines Company (SUMED): 9 Amin Yehia St., Zizinia, P.O.B. 2056, Alexandria; owns and operates an oil pipeline (80 million tons per year) from the Gulf of Suez to the Mediterranean; Chair. and Managing Dir. Mohamed Abdulhamid Kroush.

Numerous foreign oil companies are prospecting for oil in Egypt under agreements with EGPA.

EMPLOYERS' ORGANIZATIONS

Federation of Egyptian Industries: P.O.B. 251, 26a Sharia Sherif Pasha, Cairo, and P.O.B. 1658, 65 Horia Rd., Alexandria; f. 1922; Pres. Dr. Eng. Mahmoud Aly Hassan; represents the industrial community in Egypt.

Affiliated Organizations

Chamber of Food Industries: 26a Sherif St., Cairo; Pres. Prof. Dr. Hassan Ashmawi.

Chamber of Building Materials and Construction: Pres. Eng. Hassan Muhammad Hassan.

Chamber of Cereals and Related Products Industry: Pres. Dr. Fawzi Youssef Refai.

Chamber of Chemical Industries: Pres. Dr. Hassan Ibrahim Badawi.

Chamber of Engineering Industries: 13 Sherif St., Cairo; Man. Dipl.-Ing. Adel Schoeib; 850 means.

Chamber of Leather Industry: Pres. Dr. Hassan Ibrahim El-Sissy.

Chamber of Metallurgical Industries: P.O.B. 251, 13 Sherif St., Cairo; Dir. Eng. Adel A. Shoeib.

Chamber of Petroleum and Mining: Pres. Dr. Hamed Hasanein Amer; Dir. Abdallah Abdelrahim.

Chamber of Printing, Binding and Paper Products: Pres. Eng. Youssef Moustafa Bahgat.

Chamber of Spinning and Weaving Industry: Pres. Hamed el-Maamoun Habib.

Chamber of Woodworking Industry: Pres. Eng. Zohair Nassef.

TRADE UNIONS

Egyptian Trade Union Federation (ETUF): 90 El Galaa St., Cairo; f. 1957; 21 affiliated unions; 2.5 million mems.; affiliated to the International Confederation of Arab Trade Unions and to the Organization of African Trade Union Unity; Pres. Saad M. Ahmed; Gen. Sec.Ibrahim Shalaby; publ. *El Omal* (weekly, Arabic).

General Trade Union of Agriculture: 31 Mansour St., Bab el Louk, Cairo; 150,000 mems.; Pres. Mokhtar Abdel Hamied; Gen. Sec. Mohamed Abdel Khalek Gouda.

General Trade Union of Air Transport: 5 Ahmed Sannan St., St. Fatima, Heliopolis; 11,000 mems.; Pres. Abdel Monem Farag Eisa; Gen. Sec. Shekata Abdel Hameid.

General Trade Union of Banks and Insurance: 2 El Kady El Fadel St., Cairo; 56,000 mems.; Pres. Mahmoud Mohamed Dabbour; Gen. Sec. Abdou Hassan Mohamed Ali.

General Trade Union of Building Workers: 9 Emad El Din St., Cairo; 150,000 mems.; Pres. Hamid Hassan Barakat; Gen. Sec. Salem Abdel Razek.

General Trade Union of Business and Management Services: 2 Mohamed Haggag St., Midan El Tahrir, Cairo; 100,000 mems.; Pres. Abdul Rahman Khedr; Gen. Sec. Mahmoud Mohamed.

General Trade Union of Commercial Workers: 70 El Gomhourria St., Cairo; 100,000 mems.; Pres. Abdel Razek El Sherbeeny; Gen. Sec. Yahia Fadel Megahed.

General Trade Union of Educational Services: 91 Magles El Shaab St., Cairo; 80,000 mems.; Pres. Mokhtar Yousif Mohamed; Gen. Sec. Halabi Abdel Hadi Halabi.

General Trade Union of Food Industries: 3 Housni St., Hadaek El Koba, Cairo; 111,000 mems.; Pres. Saad M. Ahmed; Gen. Sec. Adly Tanus Ibrahim.

General Trade Union of Health Services: 22 El Sheik Kamar St., El Sakakiny, Cairo; 56,000 mems.; Pres. Ibrahim Abou El Mooty Ibrahim; Gen. Sec. Ahmed Abdel Latif Salem.

General Trade Union of Maritime Transport: 36 Sharif St., Cairo; 46,000 mems.; Pres. Thabet Mohamed El Sefary; Gen. Sec. Mohamed Ramadan Abou Tor.

General Trade Union of Military Production: 90 El Galaa St., Cairo; 39,000 mems.; Pres. Moustafa Mohamed Moungy; Gen. Sec. Ibrahim Loutfy Zanaty.

General Trade Union of Mine Workers: 5 Ali Sharawi St., Hadaek El Koba, Cairo; 14,000 mems.; Pres. Abbas Mahmoud Ibrahim; Gen. Sec. Amin Hassan Amer.

General Trade Union of Petroleum and Chemical Industries: 90 El Galaa St., Cairo; 103,000 mems.; Pres. Ahmed Ahmed El Amawi; Gen. Sec. Abdel Kader Hassan Abdel Kader.

General Trade Union of Posts, Telegrams and Telephones: 90 E. Galaa St., Cairo; 60,400 mems.; Pres. Mohamed Khairy Hashem; Gen. Sec. Mohamed Abdel Raoof Dirraz.

General Trade Union of Press, Printing and Information: 90 El Galaa St., Cairo; 43,100 mems.; Pres. Mohamed Ali El Fikky; Gen. Sec. Abdel Aziz Mohamed Basuny.

General Trade Union of Public Utilities: 22 Sharif St., Cairo; 64,000 mems.; Pres. Mansour Abdel Monem Mansour; Gen. Sec. Mohamed Talaat Hassan.

General Trade Union of Railways: 15 Emad El Din St., Cairo; 89,000 mems.; Pres. Mahmoud Atito; Gen. Sec. Said Moustafa Abou El Ela.

General Trade Union of Road Transport: 90 El Galaa St., Cairo; 243,000 mems.; Pres. Mohamed Mohamed Ahmed El Okaly; Gen. Sec. Mohamed Kamal Labib.

General Trade Union of Textile Workers: 327 Shoubra St., Cairo; 244,000 mems.; Pres. Ali Mohamed Doufdaa; Gen. Sec. Hassan Toulba Marzouk.

General Trade Union of Tourism and Hotels: 90 El Galaa St., Cairo; 21,400 mems.; Pres. Amin Mawad Ali; Gen. Sec. Moustafa Ibrahim Moustafa.

General Trade Union of Workers in Engineering, Metal and Electrical Industries: 90 El Galaa St., Cairo; 130,000 mems.; Pres. Said Gomaaa Ali; Gen. Sec. Gamal Tarabishi.

TRANSPORT

RAILWAYS

Egyptian Railways: Midan Ramses, Cairo; f. 1851; length 4,872 km.; 2,420 km. auxiliary lines; 25 km. electrified; Chair. Eng. Abdel Moneim Heshmat.

Alexandria Passenger Transport Authority: 21 Saad Zaghloul Square, P.O.B. 466, Alexandria; controls City Tramways (28 km.), Ramleh Electric Railway (16 km.), suburban buses (201 km.); Chair. Eng. Aly Hosny Mahmoud; Tech. Dir. Eng. Eid Mohamed Moukhtar.

Heliopolis Company for Housing and Inhabiting: 28 Ibrahim El Lakkany St., Heliopolis, Cairo; 50 km., 148 railcars; Gen. Man. Abdel Moneim Seif.

A 6½-mile underground railway is under consideration in Cairo, and a 430 km. line to carry iron ore from the Bahariya mines to the Helwan iron and steel works was opened in August 1973.

ROADS

Egyptian General Organization of Inland Transport for Provinces Passengers: Sharia Kasr-el-Aini, Cairo; Pres. Hasan Mourad Kotb.

There are good metalled main roads as follows: Cairo-Alexandria (desert road); Cairo-Benna-Tanta-Damanhur-Alexandria; Cairo-Suez (desert road); Cairo-Ismailia-Port Said or Suez; Cairo-Fayum (desert road); in 1970 there were over 13,000 miles of good metalled roads.

SHIPPING

Alexandria Shipping and Navigation Co.: 557 El Horreya Ave., P.O.B. 812, Alexandria; services between Egypt, N. and W. Europe, U.S.A., Red Sea and Mediterranean; Chair. and Man. Dir. Eng. Mahmoud Ismail.

Egyptian Navigation Co.: 2 Elnasr St., Alexandria; f. 1930; services Alexandria/Europe, U.S.A., Black Sea, Adriatic Sea, Mediterranean Sea, Indian Ocean and Red Sea; 48 vessels; Chair. H. Z. Yacout.

Pan Arab Shipping Co.: 13 Salah Salem St., P.O.B. 39, Alexandria; Arab League Company; Chair. Ezzeldin Rifaat.

THE SUEZ CANAL

Suez Canal Authority (*Hay'at Canal Al Suess*): Irshad Building, Ismailia; Cairo Office: 6 Lazokhli St., Garden City, Cairo; Pres. Eng. Mashhour Ahmed Mashhour.

Length of Canal 173 km.; maximum permissible draught: 38 ft.: breadth of canal at water level 160-200m.; breadth between buoys defining the navigable channel 110m. The Canal was closed between June 1967 and June 1975.

CIVIL AVIATION

EgyptAir: Cairo International Airport, Heliopolis, Cairo; f. 1932 as Misr Airwork; operates internal services in Egypt and external services throughout the Middle East, Far East, Africa and Europe; Chair. Muhammad Nabil Hashad; fleet of 7 Boeing 707, 8 Boeing 737, 2 Cessna 207.

The following foreign airlines serve Egypt: Aeroflot (U.S.S.R.), Air France, Air India, Alia (Jordan), Austrian Airlines, British Airways, British Caledonian, CSA (Czechoslovakia), Cyprus Airways, Ethiopian Air Lines, Garuda (Indonesia), Ghana Airways, Interflug (German Democratic Republic), Iraqi Airways, JAL (Japan), JAT (Yugoslavia), Libyan Arab Airlines, KLM (Netherlands), Kuwait Airways, LOT (Poland), Lufthansa (Fed. Repub. of Germany), MALÉV (Hungary), MEA, Olympic Airways (Greece), Pan Am, PIA (Pakistan), Qantas (Australia), Sabena (Belgium), SAS (Sweden), Saudia, Sudan Airways, Swissair, TAROM (Romania), TWA (U.S.A.), and UTA (France).

TOURISM

Ministry of Tourism: 110 Sh. Kasr-el-Aini, Cairo; f. 1965; branches at Alexandria, Port Said, Suez, Luxor and Aswan; Minister of Tourism and Civil Aviation Dr. Eng. Mahmoud Amin Abdel-Hafez.

Egyptian General Company for Tourism and Hotels: 4 Latin America St., Garden City, Cairo; f. 1961; affiliated to the Ministry of Tourism.

Authorized foreign exchange dealers for tourists include the principal banks and the following:

American Express of Egypt Ltd.: 15 Kasr-el-Nil St., Cairo; f. 1919; 7 brs.

Thomas Cook Overseas Ltd.: 4 Sharia Champollion, Cairo.

CULTURAL ORGANIZATION

Ministry of Culture: Cairo; Minister of Information and Culture Abdel-Moneim Mahmoud Sawi.

PRINCIPAL THEATRES AND ORCHESTRA

Pocket Theatre: Cairo; f. 1961.

Egyptian General Organization of Cinema, Theatre and Music: Ministry of Culture and Information.

Departments include the following: **Opera Lyric Troupe, Opera Ballet, Opera Chorale, Cairo Symphony Orchestra.**

Members frequently take part in performances with visiting opera companies.

National Puppet Theatre: Cairo.

NATIONAL DANCE TROUPES

National Folklore Dance Troupe: Cairo; frequently performs on tours abroad.

Reda Folklore Dance Troupe: 50 Kasr-el-Nil St., Cairo; f. 1959; frequently performs on tours abroad: Dirs. Mahmoud Reda, Ali Reda; Principal Dancer Farida Fahmy; Choreographer Mahmoud Reda.

ATOMIC ENERGY

A 32-man Higher Nuclear Council, with President Sadat as Chairman, was formed in August 1975.

Atomic Energy Organization: Dokki, Cairo; f. 1955; Dir Dr. Salah Hedayet. First reactor with 2,000 kW power, opened at Inchass in 1961.

Regional Radioisotope Centre: Cairo; f. 1957; eleven laboratories for research and development in scientific medical, agricultural and industrial fields; in 1963 the Centre was transformed into a Regional Centre for the Arab countries of the Middle East, in co-operation with UN I.A.E.A.

DEFENCE

Supreme Commander of the Armed Forces: President Anwar Sadat.

Minister of Defence and Commander-in-Chief: Gen. Kamal Hasan Ali.

Chief of Staff of the Armed Forces: Lieut.-Gen. Ahmad Badawi.

Commander of the Air Force: Lieut.-Gen. Mahmoud Chaker Abdul Moneim.

Commander of Air Defence: Lieut.-Gen. Hilmi Afifi.

Commander of the Navy: Vice-Admiral Ali Muhammad.

Defence Budget, 1979: U.S. $1,500 million.

Military service: 3 years.

Total armed forces: 395,000: army 350,000; navy 20,000; air force 25,000. Reserves 515,000. Paramilitary forces: about 50,000 (National Guard, etc.).

EDUCATION

It is estimated that 72 per cent of children aged 6 to 11 years were enrolled at primary schools in 1975, while 40 per cent of those aged 12 to 17 attended secondary schools.

Administration

Responsibility for education and training lies with the Ministry of Education and Scientific Research, except for the ministries which train manpower for their own specialized needs. The universities are outside ministerial jurisdiction.

The Ministry of Education is responsible for primary, preparatory, secondary general, secondary technical (commercial, agricultural and industrial), primary teacher training and Higher Education.

The universities, however, maintain their individual independence even though the President of the Supreme Council is the Minister of Education. The Council is a planning and co-ordinating body and comprises the Rectors, Vice-Rectors and some representatives of different disciplines of university education.

Structure

Education is compulsory for the primary level with entry allowed within the 6–8 years age range. The system has a four-tiered structure:

(i) Primary—Years 1–6 (Grades 1–6).

(ii) Preparatory—Years 1–3 (Grades 7–9).

(iii) Secondary—Years 1–3 (Grades 10–12).

(iv) Higher-Technician Training—Years 1 and 2.
Higher Technical Institutes—Years 1–4 or 5.
Universities—Years 1–4 or 5 or 6.

For the present, entry from one level into the next is based on success in a final year examination. Promotion from one grade to another in each level is also by final examination, except in primary education where promotion was until recently virtually automatic except for an examination at the ends of Grades 4 and 6.

At the end of the preparatory stage, students may enter:

(*a*) General Secondary Schools which after a common first-year divide into a humanities branch and a maths-science branch;

(*b*) Technical Schools—either industrial or commercial or agricultural;

(*c*) Training institutions administered by other ministries.

Numerical details or numbers of schools, teachers and pupils for the year 1976/77 can be found in the Statistical Survey.

UNIVERSITIES

Ain Shams University: Kasr el Zaafran, Abbasiyah, Cairo; 1,262 teachers, 68,759 students.

Alexandria University: Shatby, Alexandria; 2,955 teachers, 75,007 students.

Al-Azhar University: Cairo; 1,354 teachers, 31,867 students.

American University in Cairo: 113 Sh. Kasr el Aini, Cairo; 175 teachers, 1,500 students.

Helwan University: Garden City, Cairo; 1,000 teachers, 35,000 students.

Mansoura University: Mansoura; 500 teachers, 26,000 students.

Minia University: Minia; 400 teachers, 10,000 students.

Tanta University: Tanta; 1,151 teachers, 26,833 students.

University of Assiut: Assiut (Asyut); 13,177 students.

University of Cairo: Orman, Ghiza (Giza); 3,302 teachers 61,953 students.

Zagazig University: Zagazig.

BIBLIOGRAPHY

GENERAL

ABDEL-MALEK, ANWAR. Egypte, société militaire (Paris, 1962).

Idéologie et renaissance nationale/L'Egypt moderne (Paris, 1969).

AHMED, J. M. The Intellectual Origins of Egyptian Nationalism (London, Royal Institute of International Affairs, 1960).

ALDRIDGE, JAMES. Cairo: Biography of a City (Macmillan, London, 1970).

AYROUT, H. H. The Egyptian Peasant (Boston, 1963).

BADDOUR, ABD. Sudanese-Egyptian Relations. A Chronological and Analytical Study (Nijhoff, The Hague, 1960).

BADEAU, J. S. The Emergence of Modern Egypt (New York, 1953).

BAER, GABRIEL. A History of Landownership in Modern Egypt 1800–1950 (Oxford University Press, London, 1962).

The Evolution of Landownership in Egypt and the Fertile Crescent, the Economic History of the Middle East 1800–1914 (University of Chicago Press, Chicago and London, 1966).

Studies in the Social History of Modern Egypt (University of Chicago Press, Chicago and London, 1969).

BAKER, RAYMOND WILLIAM. Egypt's Uncertain Revolution under Nasser and Sadat (Harvard University Press, 1978).

BERGER, MORROE. Bureaucracy and Society in Modern Egypt: a Study of the Higher Civil Service (Princeton University Press, 1957).

Islam in Egypt Today: Social and Political Aspects of Popular Religion (Cambridge University Press, 1970).

BERQUE, JACQUES. Egypt: Imperialism and Revolution (Faber, London, 1972).

BOKTOR, AMIN. The Development and Expansion of Education in the U.A.R. (The American University, Cairo, 1963).

COULT, LYMAN H. An Annotated Bibliography of the Egyptian Fellah (University of Miami Press, 1958).

CROMER, EARL OF. Modern Egypt (2 vols., London, 1908).

DAWISHA, A. I. Egypt in the Arab World. (Macmillan, London, 1976).

DODWELL, H. The Founder of Modern Egypt (Cambridge, 1931, reprinted 1967).

DRIAULT, E. L'Egypte et l'Europe (5 vols., Cairo, 1935).

ELISOFAN, E. The Nile (New York, 1964).

GARZOUZI, EVA. Old Ills and New Remedies in Egypt (Dar al-Maaref, Cairo, 1958).

HARRIS, C. P. Nationalism and Revolution in Egypt: the Role of the Muslim Brotherhood (Mouton and Co., The Hague, 1964).

HARRIS, J. R. (Ed) The Legacy of Egypt (2nd ed. Oxford University Press, 1972).

HOLT, P. M. Egypt and the Fertile Crescent (Longmans, London, 1966).

HOPKINS, HARRY. Egypt, The Crucible (Secker and Warburg, London, 1969).
HURST, H. E. The Nile (London, 1952).
The Major Nile Projects (Cairo, 1966).
LACOUTURE, JEAN and SIMONNE. Egypt in Transition (London, Methuen, 1958).
LANDAU, JACOB M. Parliaments and Parties in Egypt (Israel Publishing House, Tel-Aviv, 1953).
LAUTERPACHT, E. (Editor). The Suez Canal Settlement (Stevens and Sons, London, 1960, under the auspices of the British Institute of International and Comparative Law).
LENGYE, EMIL. Egypt's Role in World Affairs (Public Affairs Press, Washington, D.C., 1957).
LITTLE, TOM. Modern Egypt (Ernest Benn, London, 1967, Praeger, New York 1967).
LLOYD, LORD. Egypt since Cromer (2 vols., London, 1933-34).
MAHMOUD, ZAKI NAGIB. Modern Egyptian Thought (London, 1946).
MARLOWE, J. Anglo-Egyptian Relations (London, 1954).
MORINEAU, RAYMOND. Egypte (Lausanne, 1964).
NASSER, ABDEL GAMAL. Egypt's Liberation: The Philosophy of the Revolution (Washington, 1955).
NEGUIB, MOHAMMED. Egypt's Destiny: A Personal Statement (New York, 1955).
OWEN, ROBERT and BLUNSUM, TERENCE. Egypt, United Arab Republic, The Country and its People (Queen Anne Press, London, 1966).
RIAD, HASSAN. L'Egypte Nassérienne (Editions de Minuit Paris, 1964).
RUSSELL PASHA, Sir THOMAS. Egyptian Service, 1902-1946 (London, 1949).
STEVENS, GEORGIANA G. Egypt Yesterday and Today (New York, 1963).
STEWART, DESMOND. Cairo (Phoenix House, London, 1965).
VAUCHER, G. Gamal Abdel Nasser et son Equipe, 2 vols. (Brill, Leiden, 1950).
VIOLLET, ROGER and DORESSE, JEAN. Egypt (New York, Cromwell, 1955).
WATERFIELD, GORDON. Egypt (Thames & Hudson, London, 1966).
WATT, D. C. Britain and the Suez Canal (London, Royal Institute of International Affairs, 1956).
WAVELL, W. H. A Short Account of the Copts (London, 1945).
WILBUR, D. N. The United Arab Republic (New York, 1969).
WILSON, JOHN A. The Burden of Egypt (Chicago, 1951).
WYNN, WILTON. Nasser of Egypt: The Search for Dignity (Cambridge, Mass., 1959).
YOUSSEF BEY, AMINE. Independent Egypt (London, 1940).

ANCIENT EGYPT

ALDRED, CYRIL. Egypt to the End of the Old Kingdom (Thames and Hudson, London, 1965).
BERNARD, JEAN-LOUIS. Aux origines de l'Egypte (Laffont, Paris, 1976).
BREASTED, JAMES HENRY. A History of Egypt from the Earliest Times to the Persian Conquest (Harper and Row, New York, 1959).
DE LUBICZ, A. S. The Temples of Karnak (2 vols., London, 1961).
ERMAN, ADOLF. The Ancient Egyptians; a Sourcebook of their Writings (trans. A. M. BLACKMAN, Harper, New York, 1966).
FISCHEL, WALTER J. Ibn Khaldun in Egypt (University of California Press, 1967).
FORSTER, E. M. Alexandria: a History and a Guide (Doubleday, New York, 1961).
GARDINER, Sir ALAN HENDERSON. Egypt of the Pharaohs (Clarendon Press, Oxford, 1961).
GLANVILLE, S. R. K. (editor). The Legacy of Egypt (Oxford, 1942).
GREENER, L. The Discovery of Egypt (Cassell, London 1966, Viking Press, New York, 1967).
JOHNSON, ALLAN C. Egypt and the Roman Empire (Ann Arbor, 1951).
MEYER-RANKE, PETER. Der Rote Pharao (Christian Wegner Verlag, Hamburg, 1964).
MONTET, PIERRE. Das Leben der Pharaonen (Frankfurt/Berlin/Vienna, 1970).
PIRENNE, JACQUES. Histoire de la Civilization de l'Egypte antique (Neuchâtel, 1966).
La Religion et la Morale de l'Egypte antique (La Baconnière, Neuchâtel, 1966).
POSENER, G. (Ed.). A Dictionary of Egyptian Civilization (Methuen, London, 1962).

MODERN HISTORY

AVRAM, BENNO. The Evolution of the Suez Canal State 1869–1956. A Historico-Juridical Study (Librairie E. Droz, Libraire Minard, Geneva, Paris, 1958).
BARAWAY, RASHED EL. The Military Coup in Egypt (Cairo, Renaissance Bookshop, 1952).
BARRACLOUGH, GEOFFREY, Ed. Suez in History (London, 1962).
BLUNT, WILFRED SCAWEN. Secret History of the English Occupation of Egypt (Martin Secker, London, 1907).
CONNELL, JOHN. The Most Important Country. The Story of the Suez Crisis and the Events leading up to It (Cassell, London, 1957).
EFENDI, HUSEIN. Ottoman Egypt in the Age of the French Revolution (trans. and with introduction by Stanford J. Shaw) (Harvard Univ. Press, Cambridge, 1964).
FARNIE, D. A. East and West of Suez. The Suez Canal in history, 1854–1956 (Clarendon Press, Oxford, 1969).
HEIKAL, MUHAMMAD. The Road to Ramadan (Collins, London, 1975).
Sphinx and Commissar: The Rise and Fall of Soviet Influence in the Arab World (Collins, London, 1978).
HILL, R. Egypt in the Sudan 1820–1881 (Oxford University Press, London and New York, 1959).
HOLT, P. M. Political and Social Change in Modern Egypt (Oxford University Press, 1967).
HUSSEIN, MAHMOUD. La Lutte de Classes en Egypte de 1945 à 1968 (Maspero, Paris, 1969).
ISSAWI, CHARLES. Egypt in Revolution (Oxford, 1963).
JOESTEN, JOACHIM. Nasser: The Rise to Power (London, Odhams, 1960).
KINROSS, LORD. Between Two Seas: The Creation of the Suez Canal (John Murray, London, 1968).
LACOUTURE, JEAN. Nasser: A Biography (Secker and Warburg, London, 1973).
LANE-POOLE, S. History of Egypt in the Middle Ages (4th edn., reprinted, Frank Cass, London, 1967).
LOVE, K. Suez: the Twice-fought War (Longman, 1970).
MANSFIELD, PETER. Nasser's Egypt (Penguin Books London, 1965).
Nasser (Methuen, London, 1969).
The British in Egypt (Weidenfeld and Nicolson, London, 1971).
MARLOWE, JOHN. Cromer in Egypt (Elek Books, London, 1970).
NUTTING, ANTHONY. No End of a Lesson; the Story of Suez (Constable, London, 1967).
Nasser (London, Constable, 1972).
O'BALLANCE, E. The Sinai Campaign 1956 (Faber, London, 1959).
RICHMOND, J. C. B. Egypt, 1798-1952: Her Advance towards a Modern Identity (Methuen, London, 1977).

ROYAL INSTITUTE OF INTERNATIONAL AFFAIRS. Great Britain and Egypt, 1914–51 (London, 1952).

SADAT, ANWAR AL. Revolt on the Nile (London, Allen Wingate, 1957).

SAFRAN, NADAV. Egypt in Search of Political Community. An analysis of the intellectual and political evolution of Egypt, 1804–1952 (Harvard University Press, Cambridge, Mass., Oxford University Press, London, 1961).

SAYYID, AFAF LUTFI AL. Egypt and Cromer: A Study in Anglo-Egyptian Relations (John Murray, London, Praeger, New York, 1968).

SCHONFIELD, HUGH A. The Suez Canal in Peace and War, 1869–1969 (Vallentine, Mitchell, London, 2nd revised edn., 1969).

SHAW, STANFORD J. Ottoman Egypt in the Eighteenth Century (Harvard University Press, 1962).

STEPHENS, R. Nasser (Allen Lane The Penguin Press, London, 1971).

TIGNOR, R. L. Modernization and British Colonial Rule in Egypt 1882-1914 (Princeton, 1966).

VATIKIOTIS, P. J. A Modern History of Egypt (Praeger, New York, 1966: Weidenfeld and Nicolson, London, 1969).

The Egyptian Army in Politics (Indiana University Press, Bloomington, 1961).

ZAKI, ABDEL RAHMAN. Histoire Militaire de l'Epoque de Mohammed Ali El-Kebir (Cairo, 1950).

ECONOMY

EL GHONEMY, M. RIAD. Economic and Industrial Organization of Egyptian Agriculture since 1952, Egypt since the Revolution (Allen and Unwin, London, 1968).

EL KAMMASH, M. M. Economic Development and Planning in Egypt (London, 1967).

HANSON, BENT and MAZOUK, GIRGIS. Development and Economic Policy in the U.A.R. (Egypt) (North Holland Publishing Co., Amsterdam, 1965).

KARDOUCHE, G. S. The U.A.R. in Development (Praeger New York, 1967).

MABRO, ROBERT. The Egyptian Economy 1952-1972 (Oxford University Press, London, 1974).

MEAD, DONALD C. Growth and Structural Change in the Egyptian Economy (Irwin, Homwood, Ill., 1967).

O'BRIEN, PATRICK. The Revolution in Egypt's Economic System 1952-65 (Oxford, 1966).

RADWAN, SAMIR. Capital Formation in Egyptian Industry and Agriculture 1882-1967 (St. Antony's Middle East Monographs, published by Ithaca Press, London, 1975).

SAAB, GABRIEL S. The Egyptian Agrarian Reform 1952–1962 (Oxford University Press, London and New York, 1967).

WARRINER, DOREEN. Land Reform and Economic Development (Cairo, 1955).

Land Reform and Development in the Middle East—A Study of Egypt, Syria and Iraq (2nd ed. Oxford University Press, London, 1962).

Iran
(Persia)

PHYSICAL AND SOCIAL GEOGRAPHY

W. B. Fisher

SITUATION

The Islamic Republic of Iran is bounded on the north by the Caspian Sea and by the Transcaucasian and Turkistan territories of the U.S.S.R., on the east by Afghanistan and Pakistan, on the south by the Persian Gulf and Gulf of Oman, and on the west by Iraq and Turkey.

PHYSICAL FEATURES

Structurally, Iran is an extremely complex area; and owing partly to political difficulties and partly to the difficult nature of the country itself, complete exploration and investigation have not so far been achieved. In general, it can be stated that Iran consists of an interior plateau, 1,000 to 1,500 metres in height, that is ringed on almost all sides by mountain zones of varying height and extent. The largest mountain massif is that of the Zagros, which runs from the north-west of Iran, where the frontiers of Iran, Russia, Turkey and Iraq meet, first south-westwards to the eastern shores of the Persian Gulf, and then eastwards, fronting the Arabian Sea, and continuing into Baluchistan. Joining the Zagros in the north-west, and running along the southern edge of the Caspian Sea, is the narrower but equally high Elburz range; whilst along the eastern frontier of Iran are several scattered mountain chains, less continuous and imposing than either the Zagros or the Elburz, but sufficiently high to act as a barrier.

The Zagros range begins in north-west Iran as an alternation of high tablelands and lowland basins, the latter containing lakes, the largest of which is Lake Urmia. This lake, having no outlet, is saline. Further to the south-east the Zagros becomes much more imposing, consisting of a series of parallel hog's-back ridges, some of which reach over 4,000 metres in height. In its southern and eastern portions the Zagros becomes distinctly narrower, and its peaks much less high, though a few exceed 3,000 metres. The Elburz range is very much narrower than the Zagros, but equally, if not more abrupt, and one of its peaks, the volcanic cone of Mt. Damavand (5,601 metres), is the highest in the country. There is a sudden drop on the northern side to the flat plain occupied by the Caspian Sea, which lies about 27 metres below sea-level, and is shrinking rapidly in size. The eastern highlands of Iran consist of isolated massifs separated by lowland zones, some of which contain lakes from which there is no outlet, the largest being the Hirmand Basin, on the borders of Iran and Afghanistan.

The interior plateau of Iran is partly covered by a remarkable salt swamp (termed *kavir*) and partly by loose sand or stones (*dasht*), with stretches of better land mostly round the perimeter, near the foothills of the surrounding mountains. In these latter areas much of the cultivation of the country is carried on, but the lower-lying desert and swamp areas, towards the centre of the plateau, are largely uninhabited. The Kavir is an extremely forbidding region, consisting of a surface formed by thick plates of crystallized salt, which have sharp, upstanding edges. Below the salt lie patches of mud, with, here and there, deep drainage channels—all of which are very dangerous to travellers, and are hence unexplored. Because of this great handicap from the presence of an unusually intractable "dead heart", it has proved difficult to find a good central site for the capital of Iran—many towns, all peripheral to a greater or lesser degree, have in turn fulfilled this function, but none has proved completely satisfactory. The choice of the present capital, Teheran, dates only from the end of the eighteenth century.

Iran suffers from occasional earthquakes, which can cause severe loss of life, damage to property and disruption of communications. A particularly bad example occurred around Tabas in the north-eastern Khurasan province in September 1978; estimates placed the toll from this disaster at up to 20,000 deaths and severe damage over 2,000 square kilometres.

The climate of Iran is one of great extremes. Owing to its southerly position, adjacent to Arabia and near the Thar Desert, the summer is extremely hot, with temperatures in the interior rising possibly higher than anywhere else in the world—certainly over 55°C. has been recorded. In winter, however, the great altitude of much of the country and its continental situation result in far lower temperatures than one would expect to find for a country in such low latitudes. Minus 30°C. can be recorded in the north-west Zagros, and −20°C. is common in many places.

Another unfortunate feature is the prevalence of strong winds, which intensify the temperature contrasts. Eastern Iran in particular has a violent visitation in the so-called "Wind of 120 Days", which blows regularly throughout summer, reaching at times over 160 km. per hour and often raising sand to such an extent that the stone walls of buildings are sometimes scoured away and turn to ruins.

Most of Iran is arid; but in contrast, parts of the north-west and north receive considerable rainfall—up to 2,000 mm. along parts of the Caspian coast, producing very special climatic conditions in this small region, recalling conditions in the lower Himalayas. The Caspian shore has a hot, humid climate and this region is by far the most densely populated of the whole country. Next in order of population density comes the north-west Zagros area—the province of Azerbaizhan, with its capital, Tabriz, the fourth city of Iran. Then, reflecting the diminished rainfall, next in order come the central Zagros area, and adjacent parts of the interior plateau, round Isfahan, Hamadan, Shiraz, and Kermanshah, with an extension as far as Teheran. The extreme east and south, where rainfall is very scanty, were for long extremely lightly populated, except in the few parts where water is available, by nomadic groups. Over the past few years, however, a development programme has been initiated, and the effects are seen in the expansion of the towns, some of which have grown by 25 per cent since 1972.

ECONOMIC LIFE

Owing to the difficulties of climate and topography there are few districts, apart from the Caspian plain, that are continuously cultivated over a wide area. Settlement tends to occur in small clusters, close to water supplies, or where there are especially favourable conditions—a good soil, shelter from winds, or easy communications. Away from these cultivated areas, which stand out like oases among the barren expanses of desert or mountain, most of the population live as nomads, by the herding of animals. The nomadic tribesmen have had great influence on the life of Iran. Their principal territory is the central Zagros, where the tribal system is strongly developed; but nomads are found in all the mountain zones, though their numbers are very few in the south and east. Reza Shah (see "History") made considerable efforts to break the power of the nomadic tribes and to force them to settle as agriculturalists. Now, with the development of the economy, most nomads have moved into towns (though there are still a few remaining).

Economic activity has suffered from the handicaps of topography and climate, prolonged political and social insecurity (with constant pressure by foreign powers), and widespread devastation in the later Middle Ages by Mongol invaders, from which Iran has never fully recovered. Agricultural methods in particular are primitive, so that yields are low; but the drawbacks to efficient production mentioned in the general introduction to this volume—archaic systems of land tenure, absentee landlords, lack of education, and shortage of capital—are gradually being overcome. In the north and west, which are by far the most productive, a wide variety of cereals (including wheat, barley, and rice) and much fruit are grown, but in the south and east the date is the principal source of food. Some Iranian fruit is of remarkable quality (especially the apricots and grapes) and melons weighing more than 45 kg. are known.

Iran has a number of mineral resources, some of which are exploited on a commercial scale. The newly discovered copper deposits at Sar Cheshmeh could be among the largest in the world. Iran has the second largest natural gas deposits in the world; and during 1977 there was an announcement that large deposits of good quality coal had been discovered near Kirman. Iranians have always had a high reputation as craftsmen—particularly in metal work and in carpet making; and Reza Shah attempted to develop modern mechanized industry by placing state-owned factories in most of the big towns. Some of these have proved successful, others not, but bazaar manufactures still remain the more important. Teheran is now a major manufacturing centre, with a considerable spread of activities from processing of foodstuffs to manufacture of consumer and construction goods and an increasing range of more complex items: electronics, motor manufacturing and high-grade chemicals. Teheran is the headquarters of more than 90 per cent of all industrial firms in Iran; whilst a major industrial complex based on the steel mill at Isfahan is now taking shape. Carpet-making retains importance owing to considerable demand from the U.S.A. and Europe (West Germany especially), but major emphasis in Iran is now very much on modern manufacturing in metals, machinery, electronics and chemicals of an increasingly sophisticated kind, with the beginnings of attention to nuclear energy.

The adverse nature of geographical conditions has greatly restricted the growth of communications in Iran. The country is very large in relation to its size of population—it is 2,250 km. from north-west to south-west—and because of the interior deserts, many routes must follow a circuitous path instead of attempting a direct crossing. Then, too, the interior is shut off by ranges that are in parts as high as the Alps of Europe, but far less broken up by river valleys. Road construction is everywhere difficult, but since the mid-1960s increasing effort has gone into providing an all-weather surface set of trunk routes between major cities: special allocations are made in the Five-Year Plans. An important link is the railway constructed with great effort before the Second World War between the Caspian coast, Teheran and the Persian Gulf. Other rail links with bordering countries have already been and are still being built: from Teheran there are now direct links with the U.S.S.R., and more recently with Turkey, whilst a line is being pushed southeastwards that could one day link with Pakistan. Though there are mountain streams, many flowing in deep, inaccessible gorges, only one, the Karun river, is at all navigable. The Caspian ports are subject to silting, whilst in the south most harbours are either poorly sheltered or difficult of access from the interior. However, the last few years have seen a deliberate focusing of development on the Gulf, in response to the enhanced economic and political status of the region, now one of the wealthiest parts of the world. As well, the improvement of the frontier with Iraq, negotiated during 1975, will help Iranian development in the Shatt al-Arab. Small ports like Bushire and Lingeh, resorts such as Chah Behar and other centres are being developed as part of Iran's drive towards greater contacts in the Gulf and Indian Ocean.

RACE AND LANGUAGE

Iran has numerous ethnic groups of widely differing origin. In the central plateau there occurs a distinctive sub-race, termed by some anthropologists Iranian or Irano-Afghan. The distinguishing qualities are a moderate to rather tall stature, a moderately round head, pronounced features, but less so than among

Armenoids, and a colouring generally lighter than that of many surrounding peoples. In the mountain districts there are many other smaller groups of separate racial composition. A number of nomads, including the Bakhtiari tribes, would seem to be of Kurdish stock; whilst Turki (Mongoloid) strains are apparent in others, such as the Qashqai tribes. Smaller groups from the Caucasus (Georgians and Circassians) are represented in Azerbaizhan and the Caspian provinces, whilst Turki influence is again apparent in the racial composition of the eastern districts of Iran, especially round Meshed. The Southern Zagros near the Arabian Sea has a small population that tends to be of mixed Iranian, Afghan, and Hindu stock. Some observers have suggested that in this region there may also be representatives of a primitive negrito race, related to the hill-tribes of India and of south-east Asia.

With so many differing ethnic groups, it is not surprising to find that several languages are current in Iran. Persian, an Indo-Aryan language related to the languages of western Europe, is spoken in the north and centre of the country, and is the one official language of the State. As the north is by far the most densely peopled region of Iran, the Persian language has an importance somewhat greater than its territorial extent would suggest. Various dialects of Kurdish are current in the north and central Zagros mountains, and alongside these are found several Turki-speaking tribes. Baluchi occurs in the extreme south-east. English and French are spoken by most of the educated classes.

HISTORY

EARLY HISTORY

The Achaemenid empire, the first Persian empire, was founded by Cyrus who revolted against the Median empire in 533 B.C. After the defeat of the Median empire Babylon was taken in 539 B.C., and in 525 B.C. under Cambyses, the successor of Cyrus, Egypt was conquered. The period of conquest was rounded off by Darius who reduced the tribes of the Pontic and Armenian mountains and extended Persian dominion to the Caucasus. The main work of Darius, however, lay not in the conquest but in the organization which he gave to the empire. During his reign wars with Greece broke out and in 490 B.C. the Persian army suffered a major defeat at Marathon; an expedition under Xerxes, the successor of Darius, which set out to avenge this defeat was, after initial successes, defeated at Salamis in 480 B.C. The empire was finally overthrown by Alexander who defeated the Persian army at Arbela in 331 B.C. and then burnt Persepolis, the Achaemenid capital; the last Darius fled and was killed in 330 B.C. Alexander thereafter regarded himself as the head of the Persian empire. The death of Alexander was followed by a struggle between his generals, one of whom, Seleucus, took the whole of Persia, apart from northern Media and founded the Seleucid empire. About the year 250 B.C. a reaction against Hellenism began with the rise of the Parthian empire of the Arsacids. Although by origin nomads from the Turanian steppe, the Arsacids became the wardens of the north-east marches and were largely preoccupied in defending themselves in the east against the Scythians who, with the Tocharians and Sacae, repeatedly attacked the Parthian empire, while in the west they were engaged in fending off attacks by the Romans.

The Arsacids were succeeded by the Sasanians, who, like the Achaemenids, came from Fars and, like them, were Zoroastrians. Ardashir b. Babak, after subduing the neighbouring states (*c.* A.D. 212), made war on the Arsacid, Artabanus V, whom he eventually defeated. The empire which he founded largely continued the traditions of the Achaemenids, although it never equalled the Achaemenid empire in extent. The monarchy of the Sasanian period was a religious and civil institution. The monarch who ruled by divine right was absolute but his autocracy was limited by the powers of the Zoroastrian hierarchy and the feudal aristocracy. In the reign of Qubad (A.D. 488–531) a movement of revolt, partly social and partly religious, led by Mazdak, gained ground. Under Qubad's successor Anushiravan (531–679) orthodoxy was restored, but at the cost of the imposition of a military despotism. Like the Arsacids before them the Sasanians were occupied in the west with wars with Rome and in the east with repelling inroads of the nomads from Central Asia.

MUSLIM PERSIA

By the beginning of the seventh century A.D. Persia had been greatly weakened by these wars, and when the Muslim Arabs attacked, little effective resistance was offered. The decisive battles were fought at Qadisiyya (A.D. 637) and Nihavand (*c.* A.D. 641). Persia did not re-emerge as a political entity until the sixteenth century A.D., although with the decline of the Abbasid empire semi-independent and independent dynasties arose in different parts of Persia and at times even incorporated under their rule an area extending beyond the confines of present day Persia. As a result of the Arab conquest Persia became part of the Muslim world. Local administration remained largely in the hands of the indigenous population and many local customs continued to be observed. In due course a new civilization developed in Persia, the unifying force of which was Islam.

With the transfer of the capital of the Islamic empire from Damascus to Baghdad (*c.* A.D. 750) Persian influence began to be strongly felt in the life of the empire. Islam had already replaced Zoroastrianism and by the tenth century modern Persian, written in the Arabic script and including a large number of Arabic words in its vocabulary, had established itself. Its emergence was of immense importance; the literary tradition for which it became the vehicle has perhaps more than any other factor kept alive a national consciousness among the Persians and preserved the memory of the great Persian empires of the past, however much the details became blurred and even distorted in the course of transmission.

By the eighth century A.D. the Abbasid caliphate had begun to disintegrate and when in the eleventh century control of the north-eastern frontiers broke down, the Ghuzz Turks invaded Persia. This movement, of which the Seljuqs became the leaders, was ethnologically important since it altered the balance of population, the Turkish element from then on being second only to the Persian in numbers and influence. Secondly, it was in the Seljuq empire that the main lines of the politico-economic structure, which was to last in Persia in a modified form down to the twentieth century A.D., were worked out. The basis of this structure was the land assignment, the holder of which was often virtually a petty territorial ruler, who was required, when called upon to do so, to provide the ruler with a military contingent. This system was to some extent forced upon the Seljuqs and others after them, because they were unable to establish an effective system of direct administration or to exercise financial control over their military forces and because they could not integrate the settled and semi-settled elements of the population: the weakness of the system was that whenever the central control slackened, the empire tended to split up into independent or semi-independent units.

The Seljuq empire itself broke up in the twelfth century into a number of succession states; the thirteenth century saw the Mongol invasion and in 1258 Hulagu, the grandson of Chinghiz (Jenghiz) Khan, sacked Baghdad and destroyed the caliphate. For some years the Ilkhan dynasty, founded by Hulagu, ruled Persia as vassals of the Great Khan in Qaraqorum, but from the reign of Abaqa (1265–1281) onwards they became virtually a Persian dynasty. Their empire, like that of the Seljuqs before them—and for very much the same reason—broke up at the beginning of the fourteenth century into a number of succession states. Towards the end of the century Persia again fell under the dominion of a military conqueror, when Timur, who had started his career as the Warden of the marches in the Oxus-Jaxartes basin against the nomads of Central Asia, undertook a series of military campaigns against Persia between 1381 and 1387. The kingdom founded by him was shortlived and rapidly disintegrated on the death of his son Shahrukh, the western part falling first to the Turkomans of the Black Sheep and then to the Turkomans of the White Sheep, while Transoxania passed into the hands of the Uzbegs.

THE PERSIAN MONARCHY

The sixteenth century saw the foundation of the Safavid empire, which was accompanied by an eastward movement of the Turkomans from Asia Minor back into Persia. For the first time since the Muslim conquest Persia re-emerged as a political unit; her frontiers became more or less fixed, although there was a general movement of contraction in the eighteenth and nineteenth centuries, notably in the north-west and north-east. The foundations of the Safavid empire were laid by Isma'il Safavi (1502–24). He deliberately fostered a sense of separateness and of national unity vis-à-vis the Ottoman Turks with whom the Safavids were engaged in a struggle for supremacy in the west, and the main weapon he used to accomplish his purpose was Shi'ism. Not only the Turks but the majority of his own subjects were at the time Sunni—nevertheless he imposed Shi'ism upon them by force and created among the population of his dominions, many of whom, especially among his immediate followers, were Turks, a sense of national unity as Persians. Apart from a brief interlude under Nadir Shah, Shi'ism has since then remained the majority rite in Persia and is the official rite of the country at the present day. Under Shah Abbas (1587–1629) the Safavid empire reached its zenith and Persia enjoyed a power and prosperity which she has not since achieved.

GREAT POWER RIVALRY

During the Safavid period, intercourse with Europe increased. Various foreign embassies interested mainly in the silk trade reached the Safavid court via Russia and via the Persian Gulf. In the latter area in the early years of the sixteenth century a struggle for supremacy developed between the British and the Dutch. "Factories" were established by the East India Company in the Gulf from the early sixteenth century.

Under the later Safavids internal decline set in and from 1722–30 Persia was subject to Afghan invasion and occupation while in the west and north she was threatened by Turkey and Russia. After the death of Peter the Great there was a temporary slackening of Russian pressure, but the Turks continued to advance and took Tabriz in 1725, peace being eventually made at Hamadan in 1727. The Afghans were finally evicted by Nadir Shah Afshar whose reign (1736–47) was remarkable chiefly for his military exploits. The Afsharids were succeeded by Karim Khan Zand (1750–79) whose relatively peaceful reign was followed by the rise of the Qajars who continued to reign until 1925. Under them the capital was transferred from Isfahan to Teheran. During the Qajar period events in Persia became increasingly affected by Great Power rivalry until not only Persia's foreign policy was dominated by this question, but her internal politics also.

With the growth of British influence in India in the late eighteenth and early nineteenth centuries the main emphasis in Anglo-Persian relations, which during the sixteenth and seventeenth centuries had been on commerce, began to shift to strategy. Persia and the Persian Gulf came to be regarded as one of the main bastions to India and the existence of an independent Persia as a major British interest. In the early nineteenth century fear of a French invasion of India through Persia exercised the mind of the British in India and Whitehall. French envoys were active in Persia and Mesopotamia from 1796 to 1809, and to counter possible French activities Captain (afterwards Sir John) Malcolm was sent to Persia in 1800 by the Governor-General of India; he concluded a political and commercial treaty with Fath Ali Shah, the main purpose of which was to ensure that the Shah should not receive French agents and would do his utmost to prevent French forces entering Persia. With the defeat of Napoleon in Egypt the matter was no longer regarded as urgent and the agreement was not ratified. Subsequently the French made proposals to Persia for an alliance against Russia and in 1807 Persia concluded the Treaty of Finkenstein with France after which a military mission under General Gardanne came to Persia. In 1808 another British mission was sent under Malcolm. Its object was "first, to detach the Court of Persia from the French alliance and to prevail on that Court to refuse the passage of French troops through the territories subject to Persia, or the admission of French troops into the country. If that cannot be obtained, to admit English troops with a view of opposing the French army in its progress to India, to prevent the creation of any maritime post, and the establishment of French factories on the coast of Persia". Malcolm's task was complicated by the almost simultaneous arrival of a similar mission from Whitehall. In 1809 after the Treaty of Tilsit, which debarred the French from aiding the Shah against Russia, Gardanne was dismissed.

WARS WITH RUSSIA AND TURKEY

Meanwhile the formal annexation of Georgia by Russia in 1801 had been followed by a campaign against Russia. This proved disastrous to Persia and was temporarily brought to an end by the Treaty of Gulistan (1813) by which Persia ceded Georgia, Qara Bagh and seven other provinces. British policy continued to be exercised over the possibility of an invasion of India via Persia and in 1814 the Treaty of Teheran was concluded with Persia by which Great Britain undertook to provide troops or a subsidy in the event of unprovoked aggression on Persia. Although the treaty provided for defence against any European power it was primarily intended to provide against the designs of Russia. In fact it proved ineffective and when the Perso-Russian war recommenced in 1825 Great Britain did not interfere except as a peacemaker and discontinued the subsidy to Persia, who was technically the aggressor. The war was concluded in 1828 by the Treaty of Turkomanchai, under the terms of which Persia ceded Erivan and Nakhjivan and agreed to pay an indemnity; in addition, she was prohibited from having armed vessels on the Caspian.

During this period Persia was also engaged in hostilities with Turkey. Frontier disputes in 1821 culminated in the outbreak of war, which was concluded by the Treaty of Erzerum (1823).

By the nineteenth century the Persian Government had ceased to exercise effective control over the greater part of Khurasan. Russian policy, which became conciliatory towards Persia during the twenty-five years or so after the Treaty of Turkomanchai, encouraged the Shah to reimpose Persian rule on the eastern provinces. British policy, on the other hand, having come to regard Afghanistan as an important link in the defence of India, urged moderation upon the Persian Government. Nevertheless a Persian expedition set out, took Quchan and Sarakhs and laid siege to Herat; on the death of Abbas Mirza, the heir apparent and commander of the Persian forces in the east at the time, the siege was raised. After the accession of Muhammad Shah in 1834, a new expedition was sent against Herat. The sending of this, too, was encouraged by Russia while the Barakzai chiefs of Kandahar also offered the Persians assistance against their Saduzai rivals in Herat. The siege of Herat began in 1837 but was raised when the Shah was threatened with British intervention. Subsequently local intrigues headed by Sa'id Muhammad had enabled the Persians to enter Herat, and when Muhammad Ysuf Saduzai seized Herat some years later in 1855 and put Sa'id Muhammad to death, relatives of the latter went to Teheran to enlist the support of the Shah who thereupon ordered the governor of Meshed to march on Herat. The seizure of the city by Persia led to the outbreak of the Anglo-Persian war in 1856, which was terminated by the Treaty of Paris (1857) after a British force had occupied the island of Kharg in the Persian Gulf.

In the second half of the century the subjection of the Turkoman tribes by Russia, her capture of Marv in 1854, and the occupation of the Panjeh, meant that Russian influence became dominant in Khurasan in the same way as the advance of Russia to the Araxes after the Persian wars in the early part of the nineteenth century had made Russian influence dominant in Azerbaizhan.

INCREASED FOREIGN INTERVENTION

Internally the second half of the nineteenth century was remarkable chiefly for the beginnings of the modernist movement, which was stimulated on the one hand by internal misgovernment and on the other by increased intervention in the internal affairs of the country by Russia and Britain. Towards the end of the century numerous concessions were granted to foreigners largely in order to pay for the extravagances of the court. The most fantastic of these was the Reuter concession. In 1872 a naturalized British subject, Baron de Reuter, was given by the Shah a monopoly for seventy years of railways and tramways in Persia, all the minerals except gold, silver and precious stones, irrigation, road, factory and telegraph enterprises, and the farm of customs dues for twenty-five years. Eventually this concession was cancelled and permission instead given for the foundation of a Persian state bank with British capital, which was to have the exclusive right to issue banknotes; and accordingly in September 1889 the Imperial Bank of Persia began business. In the same year Dolgoruki obtained for Russia the first option of a railway concession for five years. In November of the following year the railway agreement with Russia was changed into one interdicting all railways whatsoever in Persia. In 1889 after negotiations for foreign loans Belgian officials were put in charge of the customs administration. By the turn of the century there had been "a pronounced sharpening of Anglo-Russian hostility as a consequence of a whole series of Russian actions, not only in northern Persia where Russian ascendancy to a large extent had to be admitted, but as well in southern and eastern Persia which had hitherto been predominantly British preserves". In 1900 a Russian loan was given, to be followed by another in 1902 secured on the customs (excluding those of Fars and the Gulf). Subsequently various short-term advances and subsidies from the Russian treasury including advances to the heir apparent, Muhammad Ali, were made so that by 1906 some £7½ million were owing to the Russians. Under the 1891 Russo-Persian tariff treaty, trade between the two countries had increased, and when under the 1901 Russo-Persian commercial treaty a new customs tariff was announced in 1903, Russian exports to Persia were considerably aided and up to 1914 Russian commerce with Persia continued to grow.

The grant of these various concessions to foreigners and the raising of foreign loans gave rise to growing anxiety on the part of the Persian public. Further, large numbers of Persians had fled the country and were living in exile. When a tobacco monopoly was granted to a British subject in 1890, various elements of the population, including the intellectuals and the religious classes, combined to oppose it. Strikes and riots threatened and the monopoly was rescinded. No effective steps, however, were taken to allay popular discontent. In 1901 protests were made against the loans and mortgages from Russia which were being contracted to pay for Muzaffar ud-Din Shah's journeys to Europe. By 1905–6 the demand for reform had grown in strength and finally on August 5th, 1906, after 12,000 persons had taken sanctuary in the British legation, a constitution was granted. A long struggle then began between the constitutionalists and the Shah. The Cossack Brigade, formed during the reign of Nasir ud-Din Shah, which was under Russian officers and was the most effective military force in the country, played a major part in this struggle and was used by Muhammad Ali Shah to supress the National Assembly in 1908. Civil war ensued and Muhammad Ali Shah's abdication was forced in 1909.

Meanwhile in 1907 the Anglo-Russian convention had been signed. The convention, which included a mutual undertaking to respect the integrity and independence of Persia, divided the country into three areas, that lying to the north of a line passing from Qasri Shirin to Kakh where the Russian, Persian and Afghan frontiers meet in the east, that lying to the south of a line running from Qazik on the Perso-Afghan frontier through Birjand and Kerman to Bandar Abbas on the Persian Gulf, and that lying outside these two areas. Great Britain gave an undertaking not to seek or support others seeking political or economic concessions in the northern area; Russia gave a similar undertaking with reference to the southern area. In the central area the freedom of action of the two parties was not limited and their existing concessions (which included the oil concession granted to D'Arcy in 1901) were maintained. The conclusion of this convention—which had taken place partly because of a change in the relative strength of the Great Powers and partly because the British Government hoped thereby to terminate Anglo-Russian rivalry in Persia and to prevent further Russian encroachments—came as a shock to Persian opinion which had hoped for much from the support which the British Government had given to the constitutional movement. It was felt that Persian interests had been bartered away by Great Britain for a promise of Russian support in the event of a European war. In fact, the convention failed in its object. Russian pressure continued to be exercised on Persia directly and indirectly. In 1909, 1911 and 1912 Russian troops occupied Tabriz and other towns in north Persia; and in 1911, as a result of Russian pressure, the National Assembly was suspended and the resignation forced of the American Administrator-General of the Finances, Shuster, who had been appointed in the hope of bringing order into the finances of Persia.

THE FIRST WORLD WAR

During the 1914–18 War Persia was nominally neutral but in fact Turkish; British and Russian forces and German agents were active in the country, and on the conclusion of the armistice between Russia and Turkey in 1917 two British expeditionary forces set out for Russia through Persia on what proved to be abortive missions. By the end of the war the internal condition of Persia was chaotic. To the British Government the restoration of order was desirable and with this end in view the Agreement of 1919 was drawn up whereby a number of men were to be lent to reorganize the Persian army and to reform the Ministry of Finance and a loan of £2 million was to be given. There was opposition to this agreement in the U.S.A. and France and in Persia, and the treaty was not ratified. A *coup d'état* took place in 1921, Reza Khan (later Reza Shah) becoming Minister of War. In February 1921 the Soviet-Persian Treaty was signed whereby the U.S.S.R. declared all treaties and conventions concluded with Persia by the Tsarist Government null and void. Under Article VI the U.S.S.R. was permitted "to advance her troops into the Persian interior for the purpose of carrying out the military operations necessary for its defence" in the event of a third party attempting "to carry out a policy of usurpation by means of armed intervention in Persia, or if such a Power should desire to use Persian territory as a base of operations against Russia. . . ." In a letter dated December 12th, 1921, from the Russian diplomatic representative at Teheran to the Persian Minister for Foreign Affairs, it was stated that this article was intended to apply "only to cases in which preparations have been made for a considerable armed attack upon Russia or the Soviet Republics allied to her, by the partisans of the régime which has been overthrown or by its supporters among those foreign Powers which are in a position to assist the enemies of the Workers' and Peasants' Republics and at the same time to possess themselves, by force or by underhand methods, of part of the Persian territory, thereby establishing a base of operations for any attacks—made either directly or through the counter-revolutionary forces—which they might meditate against Russia or the Soviet Republics allied to her".

REZA SHAH 1925-1941

In 1923 Reza Khan became Prime Minister and finally in 1925 the crown of Persia was conferred upon him. His first task was to restore the authority of the central government throughout the country, and the second to place Persia's relations with foreign countries on a basis of equality. All extra-territorial agreements were terminated from 1928. Lighterage and quarantine duties on the Persian littoral of the Persian Gulf, hitherto performed by Great Britain, were transferred to the Persian Government in 1930. The Indo-European Telegraph Company, which had been in operation since 1872, had almost entirely been withdrawn by 1931 and the British coaling stations were transferred from Basidu and Henjam to Bahrain in 1935.

In 1932 the cancellation of the Anglo-Persian Oil Company's concession was announced by Persia. The original concession obtained by D'Arcy in 1901 had been taken over by the Anglo-Persian Oil Company (later the Anglo-Iranian Oil Company) in 1909 and the British Government had acquired a controlling interest in the company in 1914. Thenceforward the main emphasis of British policy towards Persia had been on oil rather than strategy, though from 1941 onwards the strategic aspect again became important. The Persian Government's action in cancelling the concession was referred to the League of Nations. Eventually an agreement was concluded in 1933 for a new concession whereby the concession area was materially reduced and the royalty to be paid to the Persian Government increased. The concession was to run to 1993.

Internally Reza Shah's policy aimed at modernization and autarchy. In the later years of his reign the Government became increasingly totalitarian in its nature. Compulsory military service was introduced and the army much increased in size. Communications were greatly improved; the construction of a trans-Persian railway was begun. Education was remodelled on western lines. Women were no longer obliged to wear the veil after 1936. Foreign trade was made a state monopoly, currency and clearing restrictions were established. These arrangements fitted in with the economy of Germany and by the outbreak of World War II, Germany had acquired considerable commercial and political influence in Persia.

On the outbreak of war Persia declared her neutrality. In 1941 the Allies demanded a reduction in the number of Germans in the country, and when no satisfaction was obtained sent another communication demanding the expulsion of all German nationals, except such as were essential to Persian economy and harmless to the Allies. This demand was not complied with and on August 26th, 1941, Persia was invaded. Hostilities lasted some two days. On September 16th Reza Shah abdicated in favour of his son Muhammad Reza. In January 1942 a Tripartite Treaty of Alliance was concluded with Great Britain and the U.S.S.R. whereby Great Britain and the U.S.S.R. undertook jointly and severally "to respect the territorial integrity, sovereignty and political independence of Persia" and "to defend Persia by all means in their command from aggression" and the Persian Government undertook to give the Allies for certain military purposes the unrestricted right to use, maintain and guard, and in the case of military necessity, to control, all means of communications in Persia. Allied forces were to be withdrawn not later than six months after the conclusion of hostilities between the Allied Powers and Germany and her associates. In so far as the establishment of communications with the U.S.S.R. was concerned the Treaty was effective; its operation in other respects was less satisfactory. In the Russian zone of occupation the Persian authorities were denied freedom of movement and effective administration made impossible. American advisers were appointed by the Persian Government in 1942 and 1943 in the hope of reorganizing certain aspects of the administration. Their efforts were for a variety of reasons in no case attended by more than a limited measure of success and in due course their services were terminated.

In 1943 a British company applied for an oil concession in south-east Persia and in 1944 the Socony Vacuum and Sinclair Oil Companies made various proposals to the Persian Government. In September the Persian Cabinet issued a decree deferring the grant of oil concessions till after the war. The U.S.S.R. meanwhile asked for an oil concession in the north and brought heavy, though unavailing, pressure to bear on the Persian Government to accede to this demand. Persian security forces were prevented by Soviet forces from entering Azerbaizhan or the Caspian Provinces and an autonomous government was set up in Azerbaizhan with Russian support in December 1945. In January 1946 the Persian Government had recourse to the Security Council. In March the Tripartite Treaty expired and British and American forces evacuated Persia, Soviet forces remaining. The Persian Government again presented a note to the Security Council. In April an oral understanding, confirmed by an exchange of letters between the Persian Prime Minister and the Soviet Ambassador, was arrived at whereby a joint Soviet-Persian company to exploit the oil in the northern provinces was to be formed. In May Soviet forces evacuated the country. Soviet pressure, however, continued to be exerted through the Tudeh party, the Democrat movement in Azerbaizhan, and the Kurdish autonomy movement, and the Persian Government was unable to re-enter Azerbaizhan until December. In the following October, the Soviet Oil Agreement was presented to the National Assembly but was not ratified. In October 1947 an agreement was signed with America, providing for a U.S. military mission in Persia to co-operate with the Persian ministry of war in "enhancing the efficiency of the Persian army".

NATIONALIZING THE OIL INDUSTRY

Meanwhile unrest and discontent at internal misgovernment increased, culminating in the Nationalist movement of 1950/51. In July 1949 a Supplemental Oil Agreement with the Anglo-Iranian Oil Company was initialled. Opposition to this agreement (whereby Persia was offered considerable financial gains) was strong. In November 1950 the oil commission of the National Assembly recommended its rejection. Meanwhile Persia had received a loan of $25 million from the Export & Import Bank of Washington and a grant of $500,000 under the Point IV allocation. Subsequently in 1952 the Point IV aid programme was expanded. In April 1951 the National Assembly passed a Bill for the nationalization of the oil industry, and in May, Dr. Muhammad Musaddiq, who had led the campaign for nationalization of oil, became Prime Minister. The Company and the British Government severally filed petitions with the International Court, the former asking the Court to declare Persia bound by the 1933 agreement to agree to accept the Company's request for arbitration and the latter asking the Court to nominate an arbitrator. The Persian Government declined to recognize the Court's jurisdiction. Eventually the British Government referred the dispute to the Security Council, which decided on October 19th, 1951, to defer consideration of the Persian case pending a final pronouncement of the International Court. The *status quo*, however, could not be maintained in Persia and the Anglo-Iranian Oil Company evacuated the country, being unable to continue operations.

On July 22nd, 1952, the International Court found that it had no jurisdiction in the oil dispute. This decision, however, was not a decision on the merits of the case. The Company accordingly maintained its claim to be entitled to all crude oil and oil products derived from the area covered by its concession agreement, and stated its intention to take such action as was necessary to protect its interests. American policy showed an increasing interest in Persian affairs. During the period August to October 1952, considerable correspondence passed between the British, American and Persian Governments in the oil dispute, culminating in a joint offer by Sir Winston Churchill and President Truman, making proposals concerning the assessment of the compensation to be paid to the Anglo-Iranian Oil Company and the re-starting of the flow of oil to world markets. The Persian Government rejected these proposals and put forward counter proposals which were unacceptable. On October 22nd the Persian Government broke off diplomatic relations with Great Britain. Further Anglo-American proposals for an oil settlement were put forward in February 1953, which the Persian Government rejected. Meanwhile dissension between Musaddiq and some of his supporters broke out, and a rift also developed between him and the Shah. The economic situation of the country began to deteriorate rapidly, culminating in the overthrow of Mussadiq by General Zahedi in August 1953. Musaddiq was tried and sentenced to three years solitary confinement for trying to overthrow the régime and illegally dissolving the *majlis*.

The new government resumed diplomatic relations with Great Britain in December 1953, and negotiations with British and American oil interests began for the solution of the oil problem. In September 1954 an agreement was signed, and ratified by the *majlis* and senate in October, granting a concession to a consortium of eight companies (subsequently increased to seventeen) on a percentage basis.

It was also agreed that the claims of the Anglo-Iranian Oil Company and the Persian Government against each other were to be settled by the payment of a lump sum to the Company, which was also to receive compensation from the other members of the consortium. The profits arising within Persia from the oil operations were to be equally shared between the Persian Government and the consortium. The agreement was for a period of twenty-five years with provision for three five-year extensions, conditional upon a progressive reduction of the original area. The National Iranian Oil Company was to operate the Naft-i Shah oilfield and the Kermanshah refinery to meet part of Persia's own needs and to handle the distribution of oil products in Persia and to be responsible for all facilities and services not directly part of the producing, refining, and transport operations of the two operating companies set up under the agreement. The greater part of the cost of these facilities and services, which would include industrial training, public transport, road maintenance, housing, medical care, and social welfare, would be recovered by the NIOC from the operating companies.

GROWING POWER OF THE SHAH

Internally order was restored. The Tudeh party was proscribed, but continued to exist underground, and in January and August 1954, Tudeh conspiracies were uncovered. The failure of the Government to push forward actively with reform, however, led in due course to a reappearance of unrest and discontent. In April 1955 Zahedi resigned and was succeeded by Ala, the Shah henceforward taking a more active part in the administration. In October, Persia joined the Baghdad Pact. The change of government, however, did not materially lessen the mounting discontent, and in November an attempt was made on the Prime Minister's life. Meanwhile, the country had not recovered from the financial difficulties brought on by the Musaddiq régime, in spite of the considerable financial aid granted to Persia by the U.S. to enable the country to carry on until oil revenues began to come in. U.S. aid continued after oil revenues began to come in, and over 800 million U.S. dollars were poured into Iran between the end of the Second World War and September 1960. On March 5th, 1959, a bilateral defence agreement was signed in Ankara between the United States and Iran. Under the agreement the Government of the United States "will, in case of aggression, take such appropriate action, including the use of armed force, as may be mutually agreed, and as envisaged in the Joint Resolution to promote peace and security in the Middle East". (The Joint Resolution refers to the "Eisenhower Doctrine".)

Relations with the U.S.S.R. in the years following the fall of Musaddiq were not cordial, but in December

1954 an agreement providing for (1) the repayment by the U.S.S.R. of her war debts to Persia for goods supplied and services rendered, and (2) mapping of the revised frontiers was signed.

On April 3rd, 1957, Hussein Ala resigned and was succeeded as Prime Minister by Dr. Manoutchehr Egbal, who formed a new government. Immediately after taking office Dr. Egbal issued a decree ending martial law and declared his intention of forming a democratic two-party system, in accordance with the desires of the Shah. In February 1958, the formation Government-Nation-Party was announced. An Opposition-People's-Party had been formed in 1957. Elections contested by both these political parties were held for the first time in August 1960, but after accusations that electoral irregularities had enabled the government party to secure an overwhelming majority the Shah declared the elections annulled, and the Prime Minister, Dr. Egbal, resigned. A new cabinet was formed under the leadership of Jaafar Sharif-Emami, the former Minister of Mines and Industries. New elections were held in January 1961 but National Front supporters alleged that the elections had again been rigged. Dr. Emami was again elected Prime Minister, but it was generally agreed that the existing electoral law was unsatisfactory and the Shah, in his speech to the new *majlis*, stated that its first task must be the passing of a new electoral law.

In May 1961, however, Dr. Emami resigned as a result of criticism of his handling of a teachers' strike, and the Shah called upon Dr. Ali Amini, the leader of the opposition, to form a new government.

Dr. Amini quickly took stern measures to halt the political and economic chaos in Iran. A drive against corruption in the Government and civil service was coupled with policies of land reform, decentralization of administration, control of government expenditure and limitation of luxury imports. Both Houses of Parliament were dissolved pending the passing of a new electoral law which would make free and fair elections possible. Postponement of elections, in July 1962, led to disorder in Teheran, and the added difficulty of producing a reasonably balanced budget led Dr. Amini to tender his resignation.

A new government was quickly formed by Mr. Assadollah Alam, the leader of the *Mardom* (People's) Party. Mr. Alam, one of Iran's largest landowners and administrator of the Pahlevi Foundation, had previously distributed much of his land voluntarily amongst the peasants. He stated that Iran would remain closely linked to the West, and that he would continue the land reform programme and the struggle against internal political corruption. A reform programme was approved by a national referendum held in January 1963. Presenting the new budget in April, Mr. Alam announced that elections restoring the country to a parliamentary government would be held in June or July 1963.

REFORMS OF THE SHAH

In 1950 the Shah began distributing his estate amongst the peasants. By the end of 1963 he had disposed of all his Crown Properties. The Pahlavi Foundation was established in 1958 and received considerable gifts from the Shah for the purpose of improving standards of education, health and social welfare amongst the poorer classes. In October 1961 the Shah created the £40 million Pahlavi Dynasty Trust, the income of which was used for social, educational and health services for the Iranian people.

In January 1963 a referendum was held, as a result of which overwhelming approval was given to the Shah's six-point plan for the distribution of lands among the peasants, the promotion of literacy, the emancipation of women, etc. The break-up of great estates began almost immediately, and the programme was finally completed in September 1971; another important measure was the formation of the Literacy Corps (and later of the Health Corps), in which students could serve their period of national service as teachers, working in the villages. This aspect of the Shah's reforms was widely publicized, and in September 1965 an international anti-illiteracy conference was held in Teheran, attended by a number of Ministers of Education.

The elections scheduled for July 1963 eventually took place in September of that year. The result was an overwhelming victory for the National Union of Mr. Alam; his party was in fact a coalition of several political groups, all pledged to support the reform programme of the Shah. The elections, in which for the first time women were allowed to vote, were held in the face of strenuous opposition from the left-wing parties of Iran, notably the National Front and the Communist Tudeh party, which called unsuccessfully for a boycott. The new Parliament—the first since both houses were dissolved by Dr. Amini in May 1961—was opened in October; in a speech from the throne, the Shah called on Parliament to inaugurate a new 20-year programme of economic and social reform and political development and he also announced a second phase of the land reform programme, whereby it was hoped that another 20,000 villages would be added to the 10,000 already handed over to the tenants. The Alam government continued until March 1964, when without tendering any reason, Mr. Alam resigned. The new leader was Hassan Ali Mansur, a former Minister and founder of the Progressive Centre, which had played a prominent part in the coalition of Mr. Alam the previous year. In December 1963 he had formed the New Iran Party, which by now had the support of some 150 members of the *majlis*. In his policy statement, Dr. Mansur said that the major objectives of his party would be the implementation of the Shah's reform programme, the protection and expansion of home industries, and the diversification of Iran's export trade, which hitherto had consisted of little more than oil. The second stage of the land reform plan was placed before the *majlis* in May; this aimed to break down the great estates more thoroughly; the maximum permissible size was to be from 120 hectares in arid regions to 30 hectares in more fertile areas.

REGIONAL CO-OPERATION

In July 1964 the Heads of State of Iran, Turkey and Pakistan announced the formation of a new tripartite scheme of collaboration to be known as "Regional Co-operation for Development". The scheme provided for regular thrice-yearly meetings between the Foreign Ministers of the countries concerned, with the possible addition at a later date of Afghanistan; there would be close collaboration in the economic and technical spheres, and many projects could be undertaken together in the fields of communications, agriculture, industry, education, health, tourism and regional development; cultural links, based on the common Islamic heritage of the three nations, would be strengthened, especially at University level. It was emphasized that although the scheme was to exist independently of the Central Treaty Organization, it was not intended to usurp its functions; a large area existed outside the province of CENTO in which collaboration on national projects was possible.

On January 21st, 1965, Mr. Mansur was assassinated by members of the right-wing religious sect Fedayan Islam, but there was no suggestion that the murder was other than an internal affair. The accused men were tried *in camera* by a military tribunal in Teheran and on May 9th the four principal accused were sentenced to death by firing squad. The others received varying terms of imprisonment. The assassins were reportedly followers of the Ayatollah Ruhollah Khomeini, a Shi'i Muslim religious leader exiled in 1964 for his opposition to the Shah's reforms.

Amir Abbas Hoveida, the Finance Minister, was immediately appointed Acting Premier, and became Prime Minister on the day following Mr. Mansur's death, retaining his post at the Finance Ministry. He pledged himself to the continuation of his predecessor's policies, and was given the massive support of the *majlis*. More active than some of his predecessors, he made a particular point of visiting the provinces in order to study their problems at first-hand. Although elections took place in 1967, 1971 and 1975, and there were several Cabinet reshuffles, Mr. Hoveida continued as Prime Minister until August 1977, when he was succeeded by Dr. Jamshid Amouzegar.

In April 1965 an attempt was made on the Shah's life. The trial of the six people accused of organizing the attempt attracted world wide publicity; two received a death sentence, but these sentences were eventually reduced to life imprisonment. All six were apparently members of a militant Communist group.

Several more trials followed; 55 men were accused of plotting armed insurrection, and their leader was sentenced to death; thirteen former Tudeh leaders were sentenced to death *in absentia*; and in February 1966 Khalil Maleki, a former Tudeh leader who broke away to form a moderate socialist group, was sentenced to three years' imprisonment in another public trial. In April 1966 the discovery of another Tudeh network was announced.

FOREIGN RELATIONS

Iran began a period of good relations with the U.S.S.R. in 1964/65 when various mutually beneficial trading and technical agreements were signed, and a regular air service between Teheran and Moscow was inaugurated. It had been an avowed part of Mr. Mansur's policy that Iran should be as much interested in maintaining links with the Soviet Union as with the West. In June 1965 the Shah visited Moscow, and in October an agreement was signed for the construction by Soviet engineers of a steel mill. Relations with other countries were mainly commercial, including the U.S.A., Federal Germany, Japan, Romania, Hungary and Czechoslovakia.

The Shah also took seriously his role as a mediator, remaining firmly neutral in the Pakistan-India dispute of September 1965, and discussing the Viet-Nam situation with Averell Harriman in January 1966. Only with Iraq were relations strained during the winter, when the long-standing disagreement over the Shatt-al-Arab erupted into a series of border incidents, protest notes and popular demonstrations. By the spring of 1966 the situation had eased.

The magnificent coronation of the Shah in October 1967 seemed to augur forthcoming prosperity and the stability of Iran was emphasized, not only by economic development and expansion and by the organization of international gatherings ranging from the Regional Co-operation Organization for Development (in which Iran continued to be an active partner) to the International Congress of Iranian Art and Archaeology, but also by the formal ending in November of U.S. economic aid under the "Point Four" scheme. Iran, which had been the first country to accept this aid in 1951, was now the second (after the Republic of China) to find herself able to dispense with it. Military aid, however, was to continue. At the same time economic co-operation with the U.S.S.R. was developed, and an agreement was made for the purchase of £40,000,000 of munitions, the first time the Soviet Union had concluded an arms transaction with a member of the Western bloc.

In January 1968 the British Government announced its decision to withdraw all its forces from the Gulf by the end of 1971. Since these forces had apparently helped to preserve the local status quo, a revival of the ancient rivalry between Arabs and Persians over supremacy in the Gulf then seemed a likely prospect following their removal. The Iranian Government's reiteration of its claim to Bahrain in February 1968 did not help relations with the Arab world, but Iran cautiously welcomed the proposed Federation of Arab Emirates (which it was thought would incorporate Bahrain). In October the Government signed an agreement with Saudi Arabia delineating the important oil-bearing continental shelf between the two countries.

The Bahrain dispute was submitted to the United Nations early in 1970, and a special mission visited the island in the spring. As was generally expected, it found that the large Arab majority overwhelmingly preferred full independence to joining Iran or remaining a British protectorate. Iran had previously agreed to accept the mission's findings, and it did so without complaint, though expressing concern for the future of Iranians in the Gulf states. In June 1970 a dispute with other Gulf states also arose over Iran's claim to the islands of Abu Musa and the Tumbs belonging to

Sharjah and Ras al Khaimah respectively. The dispute was only settled at the beginning of December 1971. The Sheikh of Sharjah agreed to share his island of Abu Musa with Iran. The Sheikh of Ras al Khaimah was less accommodating, so Iran invaded his possessions of the Greater and Lesser Tumbs and took them by force. Seven people were killed and all the Arab inhabitants expelled to the mainland. Britain's treaty of protection with Ras al Khaimah was about to expire, as a prerequisite of the formation of the United Arab Emirates, and the British therefore took no action, causing strong reactions from Iraq and Libya in particular. Since occupying Abu Musa and the Tumbs Iran has developed them as military bases to command the straits of Hormuz which lie at the neck of the Gulf. Iran regarded maintaining freedom of passage through the Straits of Hormuz as vital to her strategic and economic interests, and it is for this reason that she strengthened military forces in the region and also sent troops to help the Sultan of Oman in his struggle against the rebels of the Popular Front for the Liberation of Oman (PFLO). It was announced in January 1977, however, that the Iranian Government was withdrawing its military forces from Oman because Dhofar province was now calm, and all remaining Iranian forces were withdrawn in early 1979, after the fall of the Shah.

Iran's relations with the more radical Arab states were less friendly under the Shah. These states had long been suspicious of Iran's close ties with the West, and especially of the generous American military aid to the powerful Iranian armed forces. Moreover, the Arab States distrusted Iran's attitude to Israel. Although no formal diplomatic links existed, trade, particularly in oil, was conducted with Israel, and one of the early acts of the Khomeini regime in early 1979 was to end any ties with Israel and to align Iran firmly behind the Arab cause, by allowing, for example, the opening of a PLO office in Teheran.

Iran's only frontier with an Arab state is with Iraq. Near the Gulf the border is delineated by the Shatt al-Arab waterway, and, by the terms of the 1937 treaty, it actually runs along the eastern, i.e. Iranian bank; thus Iraq legally has sovereignty over the whole waterway. Iran has long resented this position and in April 1969 it decided to abrogate the treaty by sending Iranian vessels flying the national flag through the waterway, whilst heavy naval forces stood by. The aim was apparently to force a re-negotiation of the treaty. In September 1969, there were further armed clashes on the border—reports differed as to the extent of the casualties. In January 1970, Iraq accused the Iranian Government of backing the abortive *coup* in Iraq, and diplomatic relations between the two countries were broken.

Relations between the two countries continued to be bad until diplomatic relations between Iran and Iraq were restored soon after the outbreak of the Arab-Israeli war in October 1973, and the Iranian Government gave assurances to Iraq that it would not exploit the absence of Iraqi forces on the Syrian front. After the October war, however, fighting again broke out on the border with Iraq. A United Nations Mediator was appointed, and in March 1974 a cease-fire was arranged which gave a temporary respite until more border incidents occurred in August. Further clashes occurred in December 1974, and secret talks in Istanbul in January 1975 between the Foreign Ministers of Iran and Iraq failed to prevent fresh clashes in February. It was therefore something of a surprise when, at the OPEC meeting in Algiers in March 1975, it was announced that the Shah and Sadam Hussein Takriti (the Vice-President of the Iraqi Revolution Command Council) had signed an agreement which "completely eliminated the conflict between the two brotherly countries". Not only did this agreement settle the outstanding border differences, but it also deprived the Kurds in Iraq of the help which they had been receiving from Iran in their struggle against the Iraqi Government, thus causing a Kurdish collapse and a virtual end to the Kurdish war.

The border agreement provided that Iran and Iraq would define their frontiers on the basis of the Protocol of Constantinople of 1913 and the verbal agreement on frontiers of 1914 and that the Shatt al-Arab frontier would be defined according to the Thalweg Line (i.e. the middle of the deepest shipping channel). The treaty giving effect to this agreement was signed on June 15th, 1975.

INTERNAL PROBLEMS

Internally, signs of opposition to the Shah's régime, never far from the surface of Iranian life, became more and more evident as the celebrations for the 2,500th anniversary of the Persian monarchy were in preparation for October 1971. The combination of the very unequal distribution of the enormous earnings from oil and the suppression of any sign of dissent was made more politically explosive as the lavishness of the celebrations (estimates of the cost range from $50 million to $300 million) and the massiveness of the security precautions (600–1,000 people were interned in the few months before October) began to make their impact. From then, until the final fall of the Shah in early 1979, there were countless stories of how opposition was stifled only by the ruthless activities of SAVAK, the Government security agency.

In March 1975 the Shah, dissatisfied with the current structure of party politics in Iran and wanting to weld together all those who supported the principles of his "White Revolution" policy (later known as the "Revolution of the Shah and People"), announced the formation of a single party system, the Iran National Resurgence Party (*Rastakhiz*), with the Prime Minister, Amir Abbas Hoveida, as Secretary-General. At elections held towards the end of June 1975 it was thought that as many as 80 per cent of those elected to the 268-seat Majlis were new members. By 1978 it became clear that the single-party *Rastakhiz* system was not solving the problem of internal opposition in Iran, but few people in early 1978 would have forecast that, within a year, a completely new political system was to be introduced.

FALL OF THE SHAH

Demonstrations, particularly at the universities, and political violence built up during 1977 and 1978. All the Shah's attempts to control the situation, first by greater liberalization and then by firmer suppression, proved of little avail. In August 1977 Dr. Jamshid Amouzegar, Secretary-General of *Rastakhiz*, replaced the long-serving Amir Abbas Hoveida as Prime Minister but he resigned a year later. In August 1978 Jaafar Sharif-Emami was appointed Prime Minister (an office he had previously held in 1960–61) and, in response to the emerging mood of the country, promised that his government would observe Islamic tenets. Unrest continued, however. Martial law was introduced in September, and in November the Shah set up a military government headed by the Army Chief of Staff, General Gholamreza Azhari. Censorship was imposed, and strikes in the oil industry and public services presented the Shah with a desperate situation, and in early January 1979 he charged Dr. Shapour Bakhtiar, a former Deputy Leader of the National Front, with forming a "last-chance" government. Dr. Bakhtiar undertook to dissolve SAVAK (the security police), stop the export of oil to South Africa and Israel and support the Palestinians. However, opposition to the Shah continued and it was evident that the Shah would have to leave Iran, and he finally left the country on January 15th, with the unspoken assumption that he would not return.

The opposition within Iran had stemmed from two main sources, theoretically opposed but in practice united in their desire to overthrow the Shah. By the time the Shah left Iran opposition from the left and the more liberal National Front had been overshadowed by the success of the opposition coming from the exiled religious leader Ayatollah Khomeini, who was conducting his campaign from France where he had arrived in early October after 14 years of exile in Iraq for opposing the Shah's "White Revolution" because it conflicted with traditional Islamic customs.

In January Khomeini formed an Islamic Revolutionary Council from near Paris and pressure in Iran grew for his return. The Bakhtiar Government tried to delay his return for as long as possible, but on February 1st Khomeini arrived in Teheran from Paris to a tumultuous welcome from the Iranian people. Bakhtiar refused to recognize Khomeini but, after several demonstrations and outbreaks of violence, the army withdrew its support from Dr. Bakhtiar and he resigned on February 12th. Dr. Mehdi Bazargan, who had been named "Provisional Prime Minister" by Khomeini on February 6th, formed a provisional government later in the month but it soon became clear that real power rested with Khomeini's 15-man Islamic Revolutionary Council.

IRAN UNDER AYATOLLAH KHOMEINI

Various tensions have been evident in Iran during the first six months of the Khomeini regime. First, there has been obvious tension between the Government, headed by Mehdi Bazargan in Teheran, and the Islamic Revolutionary Council, which Khomeini has been directing from Qom. The Islamic Revolutionary Council has been able to give effect to its policies through a network of *Komitehs* extending throughout Iranian life. Bazargan and his government have been uneasy about the power of the *Komitehs* and also about the trials by Islamic Revolutionary Courts which by June 1979 had accounted for the deaths of more than 250 officials of the Shah's regime, including the former Prime Minister, Amir Abbas Hoveida.

Secondly, tension has developed over Iran's ethnic minorities. The Kurds in the west rebelled in March, with demands for autonomy. Later, demands for various forms of autonomy came from the Baluchis in the south-east, the Arabs in the south-west, the Turkomans in the north-east and the Azerbaijanis in the north-west. Tension was increased by the fact that these minorities are Sunni Muslims, while the Khomeini regime and the majority of Iranians are Shi'ite. The Jews, also, were fearful that Iran's new alignment against Israel would result in persecution for them.

At the end of March Khomeini held a referendum on the question "Do you favour an Islamic Republic?" The result was an almost unanimous "yes" and on April 1st Khomeini declared Iran an Islamic Republic. A new constitution should have appeared within days of the referendum but, although several leaks appeared in the press, the text of the draft constitution was not released until mid-June. By then other tensions had developed. A dispute with Iraq over Kurds allegedly crossing into Iran, coupled with accusations that Iraq was smuggling arms to dissident Arabs in Khuzestan, was exacerbated by Iraqi concern about the possible persecution of Sunni Muslims in Iran. Further internal differences appeared in Iran when Ayatollah Khalkholi stated that no action would be taken against anybody who assassinated the Shah and various members of his family, and, although the Iranian Foreign Minister stated that Khalkholi had no authority to make such a statement, it was reported that Khomeini was supporting Khalkholi. In late June it was certainly Khalkholi who was responsible for sending a team of gunmen to Mexico in an attempt to kill the Shah.

The draft constitution, although undoubtedly Islamic in content, was not so extreme as to be unacceptable to some of the Islamic "moderates", such as Ayatollah Shariatmadari. It proposed that Iran be governed by a President, Prime Minister and a single-chamber parliament of 270 deputies. The official religion is the Shi'ite Muslim faith, but Christians, Jews and Zoroastrians will be free to practise, and will have deputies in parliament. Considerable authority is placed in the hands of the President who is to be elected by direct vote to a four-year term of office. He is Commander-in-Chief of the Armed Forces, chooses the Prime Minister and has the power to dissolve parliament in the event of an emergency.

Ethnic minorities are guaranteed equal rights, but there is no mention of autonomy. The constitution provides for freedom to form political parties, freedom of the press and of assembly, but it carries the proviso that no party could oppose the principles of the

Islamic Republic, or Iran's freedom, independence, unity and national sovereignty.

Although there was pressure in Iran to submit the draft constitution to a newly-elected Constituent Assembly, Khomeini resisted this, and it was finally arranged that the constitution would be discussed for a month and then submitted to a "Council of Examiners" consisting of 75 elected members. Meanwhile banks and insurance companies were nationalized in June.

The election of the "Council of Examiners" took place on August 3rd, 1979, and resulted in a definite win for candidates supporting Ayatollah Khomeini. At least five political groups, including the National Democratic Front and the Muslim People's Republican Party, boycotted the election.

ECONOMIC SURVEY

At the census of 1966 the population was returned as 25,788,722. Of this total, some 9,800,000 were urban residents. The preliminary figures from the 1976 census show a total population of 33,591,875. Since the mid-1930s there has been an accelerating migration from rural to urban areas. The population of Teheran and its suburbs reached an estimated 4,496,159 in 1976. Much of the population is concentrated in the fertile northern areas of the country and the central desert lands are sparsely populated. The rate of population growth, now nearly 3 per cent a year, has risen in recent years due to the reduction in deaths from malnutrition and famine and great advances in public health, particularly the virtual eradication of malaria over wide areas. The size of the nomadic population, now between 3 and 4 million, has declined since the 1940s, as a result of Government attempts to settle the nomads in villages. These tribes are in fact semi-nomadic, moving between traditional winter quarters in the plains, and summer pastures in the mountains.

Whereas the urban population had achieved over 65 per cent literacy by the beginning of the 1970s, the rural population had reached only 15 per cent literacy. However, the Literacy Corps programme under which high school graduates spent part of their military service teaching children in villages to read and write, helped to achieve a drop in the rural illiteracy rate from 1962 to 1979, when the programme was abandoned.

The revolutionary government that followed the Shah's downfall has been reassessing nearly all of Iran's economic and social priorities. After the massive spending spree that marked the Shah's last five years in power and contributed to his downfall, Iran's new rulers were setting more modest targets. The Shah never abandoned his dream of turning Iran into one of the world's industrial powers within his lifetime, even though it had become obvious by 1975 that this was impossible. The new regime was proving more inward-looking and was in addition saddled with the disastrous economic and social consequences of the artificial boom years and the effects of revolutionary disruption. The post-revolutionary trend was from industry to agriculture, from heavy military spending to social welfare projects—from "big" to "small".

In 1978, the last year of the Shah's reign, per capita income was calculated at about U.S. $2,500, up from about $200 in 1963. During the period of the Fourth Plan (1968–73) Iran's Gross National Product (G.N.P.) rose at an annual average of 11.2 per cent in real terms. Over the period of the 1973–78 Plan G.N.P. rose in real terms from $17,000 million to $55,300 million. The growth rate of G.N.P., which was as much as 41 per cent in 1974/75, slowed down to about 17 per cent the following year, due to declining oil revenues (which provided about 40 per cent of the total G.N.P.). In real terms the Gross Domestic Product (G.D.P.) was estimated to have grown by as little as 2.6 per cent in 1975/76. Iran's balance of payments difficulties during that year highlighted many problems connected with the rapid growth it had been experiencing, including the acute lack of skilled manpower at all levels which made ambitious development projects difficult to implement. In 1976/77 G.D.P. grew at over 14 per cent in real terms, but during 1977 the economy showed signs of further deceleration, partly as a result of very serious power shortages which hit the industrial sector. Total G.D.P. for 1977/78 was estimated at $56,500 million, representing growth in real terms of about 10 per cent over the previous year.

In the latter part of 1978 these trends continued and, combined with politically motivated industrial and business strikes, left the economy in near paralysis. The Shah felt forced to announce some cutbacks in industrial projects and military equipment purchases. By the time the Shah's last Prime Minister was ousted, announced cutbacks totalled over $15,000—mostly in U.S. and British-made military equipment.

AGRICULTURE

Out of a total surface area of 165 million hectares, 19 million (11.5 per cent) are under cultivation and over half is classified as uncultivable, non-agricultural land. About 5.3 million hectares of agricultural land are fed with perennial irrigation water supplies from modern water-storage systems or from the ancient system of qanats (underground water channels), although these have fallen into disrepair in recent years. Rain-fed agriculture is important in the western provinces of Kermanshah, Kurdestan and Azerbaizhan. Agriculture is the principal economic activity of the Iranian people. However, whilst agriculture employs over 35 per cent of the total labour force, it accounts for less than 15 per cent of G.D.P., and as a result peasants' incomes remain low. The chief factors limiting the size of agricultural production are inadequate communications, limiting access to markets; poor seeds, implements and techniques of cultivation; lack of water and under-capitalization, chiefly the result of the low income of the peasant. About four-fifths of all farms are of less than 11 hectares. Iran was self-sufficient in foodstuffs until the late 1960s but then began importing vast quantities, due to the failure of agricultural output to keep pace with increasing domestic consumption and the failure of the Government to produce a really sound agricultural policy. In 1975/76 imports of foodstuffs totalled $1,555 million, or 13 per cent of total imports. By mid-1978 foodstuff imports were estimated at around $2,000 million. Although official figures gave a 7 per cent annual growth rate for the agricultural sector in the past few years (compared with the Fifth Plan target of 8 per cent), it was generally believed that the real rate was at most 2 per cent.

The structure of agriculture has remained basically unchanged in the twentieth century, although there has been a general tendency since the 1930s away from subsistence farming to the production of cash crops. A large variety of crops are cultivated in the diverse climatic regions of Iran. Grains are the chief crops, including wheat (the major staple), barley and, in the Caspian provinces, rice. Cotton, sugar-beet, tea, almonds, pistachios and dates are of commercial importance and olives and a variety of fruits and vegetables, as well as tobacco, are also grown. Cane sugar is being grown at Haft Teppeh, in the southern province of Khuzestan and a paper plant has been established in association with the plantation. There are plans to make Iran nearly self-sufficient in carbohydrates through increased wheat, barley and rice production although some imports will still be necessary in years of poor harvests. Food requirements, as a result of improved living standards and increased population, have been growing at over 11.5 per cent a year. Per capita consumption of red meat is only 18 kg. per year (compared with more than 100 kg. in the United Kingdom) but this figure is already double that of five years ago and is expected to continue its growth. In 1976/77 wheat production was about 6 million metric tons, compared with 5.5 million metric tons the previous year. Production of barley also increased in 1976/77 to 1.5 million tons from 1.4 million tons the previous year.

Before the Land Reform Act of 1962 about 70 per cent of the fertile land was owned by a small number of large landowners. This led to a situation in which a share-cropping peasant cultivated the land on behalf of an absentee landlord. Until 1962 various half-hearted attempts at land reform failed. In 1962 a new land reform law was promulgated, limiting landholding to one village. All land above this was to be sold to the peasants. The project was accompanied by a drive to organize the peasants into co-operatives. The second phase of reform was implemented from 1965 and involved the redistribution of all land in excess of a maximum varying according to soil fertility between 30 and 150 hectares (hectare—2.5 acres approx.). The effect of the programme was somewhat cushioned by escape clauses which allowed landlords, for a transitional period, to keep up to 500 hectares of "mechanized land" and an unlimited further amount of land if it could be shown that this had been virgin land which the farmer had himself brought under mechanization. These measures had the double advantage of softening the blow for the richer landlords, and encouraging the continued use of mechanized farming with hired labour. The government would also pay to the landlord one-third of the price of any land sold to a peasant, in cash, which was to be repaid by the peasant over 14 months; and there were further financial inducements to landlords designed to speed the process of changeover. The third phase was implemented slowly from 1967 onwards and aimed at encouraging mechanization and the consolidation of fragmented holdings. In 1971, when the land reform programme was officially completed, the Government claimed that 761,931 families had benefited from phase I of the reform and 1,535,510 from phase II. By the end of 1977, 2,909 co-operatives with a membership of nearly 3 million persons had been set up. The Government was establishing groups of farm corporations, joint stock companies in which the peasants are shareholders, around a number of large dams. These corporations covered about 23,000 farmers on 400,000 hectares.

The Government encouraged the development of large-scale commercial farming with related industries under the Fifth Plan. Schemes include sugar plantations, almond plantations and meat complexes. In Khuzestan, in the south-west, four joint ventures were set up with foreign companies in 1970 and were allocated 60,800 hectares. However, only one of these ventures has been successful and three of the four foreign partners have withdrawn, since the schemes have been beset by problems, particularly to do with lack of skilled manpower and delays in irrigation projects. The schemes in Khuzestan, which involved the moving and resettlement of 6,500 peasant families, were in the process of being wound up.

The principal products of the nomad sector of Iranian agriculture are livestock products—dairy produce, wool, hair and hides. In 1976 there were about 6.7 million head of cattle, 35.3 million sheep, 14.3 million goats, 130,000 buffaloes and 60,000 camels. About 40 per cent of sheep and goats are raised by semi-nomadic tribal herdsmen. Production is limited by the prevalence of animal pests and the apparently inevitable lower productivity of pastoral as compared with domestic stock breeding, although account must be taken of the fact that most of the land grazed by the nomads' herds is land which could not be made economically viable in any other way. During the reign of Reza Shah (1923–41) the Iranian Government tried to enforce settlement on the nomads but the tribes rebelled. Since the early 1960s, government "encouragement" and economic pressures resulted in significant settlement.

About 11.5 per cent of Iran is under forest or woodland, including the Caspian area—the main source of commercial timber—and the Zagros Mountains. Forestry in an economic sense is a recent activity and it is only since the nationalization of forest land in 1963 that effective attempts have been made, under the Forestry Commission, at protection, conservation and reafforestation.

Although Iran has direct access to both the Caspian Sea and the Gulf, fishing remains poorly developed in both areas. Production in the Gulf amounts to about 14,000 tons per year and is largely consumed by the fishing community itself. The Caspian fisheries are chiefly noted for an annual production of over 200 tons of caviar. The biggest customer for Iranian caviar is the U.S.S.R. Pollution and the steadily falling water-level of the Caspian Sea are two serious problems being tackled under a Soviet-Iranian agreement signed in 1973. The Shah's Government had plans to increase the fishing fleet and build canning and fish-meal plants along the Gulf coast. One survey estimated that, when fully developed, Iran's southern fisheries could earn as much as U.S. $200 million annually, chiefly from high-grade shrimp and prawn.

PETROLEUM

The major industry of Iran is the petroleum industry, to which the large town of Abadan owes its entire existence. The history of commercial exploitation dates back to 1901, when W. K. D'Arcy was granted a sixty-year monopoly of the right to explore for and exploit oil in Iran, with the exception of the five northern provinces, which fell within the sphere of Russian influence. Oil was eventually discovered in commercial quantities at Masjid-i-Sulaiman in 1908 and in 1909 the Anglo-Persian Oil Company was formed. The Company was renamed Anglo-Iranian in 1935. A long series of disputes between the Iranian Government and Anglo-Iranian ended with the nationalization of the oil industry by Iran in 1951 and the replacement of Anglo-Iranian by what became known as the Consortium until it was dissolved in March 1979. The Consortium was an amalgam of interests (British Petroleum 40 per cent; Royal Dutch Shell 14 per cent; Gulf Oil, Socony, Mobil, Exxon, Standard Oil of California and Texaco each with 7 per cent; *Compagnie Française des Pétroles* 6 per cent; a group of independents under the umbrella of the Iricon Agency 5 per cent) formed to produce oil in the area of the old Anglo-Iranian concession as redefined in 1933. The Consortium's concession was to have lasted until 1979 with the possibility of a series of extensions under modified conditions for a further fifteen years. Ownership of oil deposits throughout Iran and the right to exploit them or to make arrangements for their exploitation was vested in the National Iranian Oil Company (NIOC), an Iranian state enterprise.

Until 1973 Iran had a leasing agreement with the Consortium, but the Iranian Government then insisted that the companies should either continue under existing arrangements until 1979 and then become ordinary arm's-length buyers, or else negotiate an entirely new "agency" agreement immediately. The Consortium opted for the latter plan, and on July 31st, 1973, a contract was signed in Teheran under which NIOC formally took over ownership and control of the oil industry in the Consortium area, while the Consortium was to set up a new operating company, Oil Service Company of Iran, which would act as production contractor for NIOC. In return the western companies were granted a 20-year supply of crude as privileged buyers, which they would take in proportion to their shareholding in the Consortium. The companies also agreed to put up 40 per cent of new development costs in the form of pre-payments for future purchases of crude. In 1978 NIOC opened talks with the former Consortium companies, with the aim of renegotiating the 1973 crude oil supply agreement on the basis of higher offtake levels.

The Shah's growing political problems resulted in a series of inconclusive negotiations which were eventually abandoned in September 1978, without a date being set for a new round. In late September oil workers supporting Ayatollah Khomeini began small-scale strikes in the Khuzestan oilfields and at the Abadan refinery. At first their demands concerned higher salaries and NIOC managed to prevent disruption of production levels with promises of more pay, but by late October the strikers were becoming organized as a political force and production began to fall dramatically. Oil exports dropped by about 80 per cent in the first week of November. Heavy government pressure and threats, combined with increased use of expatriate staff in the fields, succeeded in bringing production and exports to near normal level by the end of the month. The see-saw battle between the Shah's regime and his political opponents, trying to force him out by crippling oil exports, continued until almost the very end of the year.

The turning point came with the assassination at Christmas of an American oil executive in the south. Most expatriate staff were flown out of the country in the days after the killing and the strikers successfully stopped all exports of oil. Production, at about 270,000 barrels per day (b/d), was below even domestic requirements which in winter vary between 800,000 and 900,000 b/d. The strikers announced that exports would not resume until the Shah left the country. Iranian oil did not flow to the rest of the world until March 5th, 1979. The first shipments were sold on the "spot" market, fetching prices as high as $20 per barrel, but NIOC said that this was a temporary measure. Within a matter of weeks three dozen long-term contracts were signed with international companies for the supply of Iranian oil and production hit a 1979 peak of 4.7 million barrels per day on April 13th—about 78 per cent of the average level maintained under the Shah's regime.

NIOC has cancelled the 1973 agreement to market Iranian oil through the Consortium and has since March 5th been selling oil directly to individual companies and countries. After initial resistance the former members of the Consortium accepted the new arrangement and signed new nine-month supply agreements effective from April 1st. The provisional government said that small numbers of expatriate staff would in future be welcome to help with exploratory and secondary recovery work, but only on a contract basis.

In order to conserve the country's oil resources, NIOC intends to keep average production below the 4 million b/d level which, with 700,000 b/d held back for domestic consumption, allows for exports of 3 million b/d or more. In line with the country's new pro-Palestinian policy, supplies to Israel were stopped.

The shortage of oil in international markets allowed NIOC practically to dictate its own terms on supply levels and prices. Most OPEC producers who had raised their own production to compensate for the shortfall in Iranian supplies agreed to reduce export levels at their March 27th meeting in Geneva. By May 10th Iran had imposed a surcharge of about $2.50 per barrel above the basic OPEC rate—receiving $17.17 per barrel for its light crude and $16.64 per barrel for its heavy crude. At an export level of over 3 million barrels per day and with later OPEC price increases, Iran seemed assured of oil revenues of at least $20,000 million over the Iranian year 1979/80.

Before the revolution, NIOC participated in several joint-venture companies, usually with a 50 per cent share (*see* p. 381) but these accounted for only about 10 per cent of total Iranian production. NIOC itself was a major exporter, accounting for average exports of 1.2 million barrels per day during 1977 and somewhat higher in 1978.

At the end of 1974 Iran's output of crude petroleum from all sources was about 5.9 million barrels per day (b/d). This began falling during 1975 and average offtake for the year was 5.35 million b/d, and total output 11.2 per cent less than in the previous year. As a result of this decline, oil revenues for 1975 were estimated to be $19,900 million, or around $3,000 million less than the expected level. Production recovered during 1976 and the average for the whole year was 5.9 million b/d (of which 5.4 million from the Agreement, or former Consortium, area). Oil revenues for the year were about $22,000 million (compared with the $18,000 million forecast). OPEC's new two-tier pricing agreement increased the price of Iranian oil by 10 per cent (to $12.81 per barrel for light and $12.49 for heavy), making it less competitive than oil from Saudi Arabia and the U.A.E., whose prices were increased by only 5 per cent. Production slumped in the first half of January 1977 but picked up again during the month and average offtake during the first half of the year was 5.4 million b/d. Estimated revenue for 1977 was $23,000 million. In 1978 strikes and partial halts in exports reduced revenues by over $1,000 million. Iran's proven reserves, published in 1973, were 8,219.2 million tons, or 9.2 per cent of known world reserves. It is the second largest oil producer in the Middle East, accounting for about 26.7 per cent of the region's output; from 1975 to 1979 its share of world output was about 10 per cent, decreasing to about 7 per cent after the revolution.

Before the revolution NIOC aimed at acquiring a stake in "downstream" operations in purchaser countries, and did this mainly on a barter system. Among barter deals under negotiation or signed before 1979 were agreements with the Federal Republic of Germany (supply of manufactured goods; construction of copper refinery); the United Kingdom (goods including military equipment); the U.S.A. (supply of F-16 fighter aircraft and other military equipment); Italy (construction of steel complex; supply of helicopters; participation of NIOC in the distribution operations of ENI, the Italian state hydrocarbons concern); Japan (construction of an oil refinery); Spain (building shipyards and hospitals); the U.S.S.R. (Soviet goods and services, including assistance in building a second gas pipeline to the U.S.S.R.). After the revolution most of these agreements were cancelled or suspended.

NIOC's refinery at Shiraz was opened in November 1973 with an initial output of 40,000 b/d, or 2 million tons a year. The Abadan refinery, the largest exporting refinery in the world, reached a record output of 484,000 b/d in March 1974 and its capacity was later expanded to 600,000 b/d. A lubricants plant beside the refinery is to start operating in early 1981. There are also refineries at Teheran and Kermanshah. NIOC is building a refinery in the Neka region of Mazandaran in the north with a 130,000 b/d capacity. A new 80,000 b/d refinery at Tabriz started operations in the spring of 1978, and another at Isfahan (200,000 b/d) was nearly complete when construction was halted by the revolution. NIOC set up a joint tanker fleet in 1976 with BP, operating five tankers with an aggregate cargo capacity of 400,000 d.w.t. and with larger units on order. Iran was also participating in refinery projects in Senegal, South Korea, Greece and the U.S.A.

NATURAL GAS

Iran's natural gas reserves were, until recently, unofficially estimated at some 398 million million cubic feet, which makes them greater than those of the U.S.A. and second only to reserves in the Soviet Union. However, huge new finds both offshore and in the mountainous Kangan region have pushed Iran's reserves to about 600 million million cubic feet. Exploitation is controlled by the National Iranian Gas Company (NIGC), a subsidiary of NIOC. Pure gas is found in fields offshore from Bushehr in the Gulf and at Sarrakhs in the north-east. In the past, most of the associated gas found in the southern oilfields was flared but in the late 1960s a pipeline, known as the Iranian Gas Trunkline (IGAT) was constructed from Ahwaz in the south-west to Astara on the Soviet border. The gas was sold at the low price of 21 cents per cubic foot to the Soviet Union as part of an agreement signed in 1965, whereby Soviet contractors constructed the Isfahan steel mill, a heavy machine plant at Arak and a machine tool factory at Tabriz, as well as providing a certain amount of light military equipment. In November 1977 Iran raised its gas price to the Soviet Union by more than 30 per cent; this increased its gas earnings from $220 million to $300 million per annum. Over 10,000 million cubic metres per year were pumped to the U.S.S.R. and a further 6,000 million cubic metres were utilized by communities along the pipeline route. In 1977 about 45 per cent of all gas extracted was flared. Natural gas, which provided 17 per cent of Iran's energy needs in 1978, is expected to provide at least 35 per cent by 1983.

The revolution put several massive gas export projects in doubt. Even the IGAT line was not being fully utilized in 1979 as reduced oil production necessitated a one-third drop in IGAT's throughput. Construction of a second parallel line to the Soviet Union, IGAT II, was suspended and then cancelled in July 1979.

IGAT II, being built by Soviet, Italian, French, Polish and Iranian companies, was to have supplied the southern industrial region of the U.S.S.R. with 17,000 million cubic metres of gas per year, starting in 1981 and reaching full flow in 1983. The U.S.S.R. was, in turn, to export an equivalent amount from its northern gas fields to East and West Europe. The estimated revenue to Iran was to have been $600 million per year.

Several other projects to export liquefied natural gas (LNG) to the U.S.A. and Japan have also been suspended and seem likely to be scrapped. Late in 1978 U.S. and Norwegian companies dropped a preliminary agreement with NIGC to build a gas-gathering network for the Kangan field and a floating liquefaction terminal off the port of Bushehr, and to export the LNG in half a dozen carriers. The entire project was expected to cost about $2,000 million. Columbia Gas Company and Consolidated Natural Gas Company of the U.S. were to import $8,000 million worth of LNG over 20 years, starting in 1983.

Also in 1978, an agreement was signed with Japan to supply 52 million tons of LNG over 20 years, starting in 1982. Japan was to provide all the finance in loans and credits to the joint-venture Kangan Liquefied Natural Gas Company of Iran (Kalingas) to build two liquefaction plants near the Gulf, at a cost of more than $700 million.

The two projects, as well as several other smaller ones, are unlikely to receive the go-ahead because of political uncertainty, the drop in oil production and expected plans to make greater use of gas for domestic energy generation and heating. Another factor which reduces the chances of Iran's becoming a major exporter of gas in the near future is the probable use of gas for secondary oil recovery to extend the lives of the southern oilfields.

OTHER MINERALS

The mineral resources of Iran have not been surveyed completely. Lead-zinc is mined at Bafq near Yazd, at Khomein, west of Isfahan and at Ravanj near Qom, with a combined potential of 600 tons of concentrates daily, though current plans for development are limited to Bafq. Chrome from the Elburz mountains and near Bandar Abbas, red oxide from Hormuz in the Persian Gulf and turquoise from Nishapur are all produced for export. Sulphur and salt are produced on the coast of the Gulf, near Bandar Abbas and Iran is the leading sulphur exporter in the region. The major iron ore deposits are in the Kerman province in south-east Iran, in particular at Bafq, where proven reserves total 600 million tons, with probable reserves amounting to a further 400 million tons of ore. The ore from Bafq is carried 540 kilometres by a specially developed railway to the Isfahan steel plant. Reserves at Gol-e-Gohar are estimated at more than 200 million tons. Total coal reserves, at Kerman and in the Elburz Mountains, are estimated at more than 1,000 million tons but Iran has to import higher-grade coal for some purposes.

Deposits of copper ore have been found in Azerbaizhan, Kerman and in the Yazd and Anarak areas. A number of very important deposits have been discovered since 1967 in the Kerman area, the most important being at Sar Cheshmeh. It is predicted that Iran could soon become the world's seventh largest copper producer. The Sar Cheshmeh deposits are to be exploited with technical assistance from U.S. interests. The mine's projected output is expected to provide 145,000 tons of blister copper per year during the first ten years and its lifespan could be between 30 and 50 years. Reserves are estimated at over 400 million tons averaging 1.12 per cent copper content, with another 400 million tons of lower grade beneath. The giant project includes the construction of road and rail links to link the mine with Bandar Abbas 400 km. away on the Gulf, a training school, and a new town for the families of the 3,000 men who will work the mine. A large refinery and associated rolling mill and two continuous casting mills are to be constructed by Krupp of West Germany and Mechim of Belgium in partnership with the National Iranian Copper Industries Company (NICIC). The complex was expected to go on stream in 1980, but construction was halted during the revolution, delaying completion by at least a year.

In March 1976 it was announced that important uranium deposits had been found in Iran's northern and western regions and in 1978 agreements were signed with West German and French companies to carry out surveys.

INDUSTRY

The post-revolution regime has dropped the Shah's plans for Iran to become a major industrial power by the end of the century. In order to achieve this, the Shah had concluded a number of trade and joint venture agreements with the governments of industrialized countries, for the transfer of technology and skills to Iran on a massive scale. Major "package" deals of this type were made with the U.S.A., France, the United Kingdom, Japan, Italy and the U.S.S.R. The industry and mining sector of the Iranian economy has grown extremely rapidly since 1963, first with the help of fairly large foreign loans and then with the investment of huge oil revenues. The average annual growth of this sector was 20 per cent in the period 1963 to 1974 but since then the growth rate has fluctuated (17 per cent in 1975/76, 17.2 per cent in 1976/77) and in the first half of 1977/78 it slowed down considerably, to little more than 8 per cent for large establishments. Over two million people are employed in industry and mining, but most of them were idle for months after the revolution. Many factory owners and managers fled the country and in many cases the government and workers' committees took over operations. In a bid to get industries moving again the Government announced in May that over $500 million in easy-term loans would be available to industrialists. Nationalization measures were introduced in July 1979.

Iran's industry concentrated initially on turning local or imported raw materials into goods for the home market. These industries can be divided into three groups: textiles, food processing and construction materials. The largest cotton-producing area is Isfahan and this is the centre of cotton textile production, followed by Shahi in Mazanderan and Behshahr in Gurgan. Isfahan is also the centre of woollen production, drawing supplies from the nomad producers of the area. Tabriz, in Azerbaizhan, is also a big woollen centre. Jute and silk are produced in Mazanderan. Persian carpets are still entirely the products of a handicraft industry. They are Iran's second non-oil foreign exchange earner (after cotton). However, there is an alarming trend towards shoddy workmanship and inferior materials which the Government is anxious to check, in order to save the reputation of the Persian carpet. Food processing includes sugar refining, flour milling and canning. Finnish and Canadian firms are to set up a major forestry industry project in Mazandaran in northern Iran. With industrial development, the rapid growth of new urban centres, and the Shah's social development policy involving the building of schools and housing, the building industry was expanding fast in recent years. Cement production grew rapidly in recent years to about 9.5 million tons per year but over 2 million tons per year still had to be imported.

In the 1970s industrial centres were created in the provinces. In 1960, of 4,430 factories in Iran, nearly half were in Teheran. Main industrial growth points are now Isfahan, Tabriz and Arak, and the secondary ones are Rasht, Meshed and Shiraz. In the mid-1970's the Shah introduced a share allocation programme whereby over 320 firms in manufacturing were required to sell 49 per cent of their shares to the workers or to the public. Foreign ownership was to be limited to 25 per cent in most sectors; 15 per cent in textiles and food and 35 per cent in high technology industries.

The petrochemical industry in Iran began with the opening in 1961 of a nitrogenous fertilizer plant at Shiraz. State-run activities in the petrochemicals field are the responsibility of the National Petroleum Company (NPC), once again a subsidiary of NIOC after being made an autonomous entity in March 1977. The Government had planned an ambitious programme of development for this sector during the Fifth Plan period, mostly with foreign participation in joint-venture projects, but a number of major projects have been shelved because of financing and other difficulties. The main petrochemical complexes now in operation are all situated near the oilfields of the south: at Abadan, Bandar Shapur, Ahwaz, Kharg Island and Shiraz. These plants produce liquefied petroleum gas, ammonia products, phosphate and compound fertilizers, nitric and sulphuric acid, carbon black, detergents, polyvinylchloride (PVC), and polyester and acrylic fibres. Output of fertilizers, from Shiraz and Bandar Shapur, just covered domestic requirements of around 400,000 tons per year, and increased consumption was to be largely met by expanding the capacity of the Bandar Shapur plant, which is totally owned by the NPC. A new giant complex for olefins and aromatics being built at Bandar Shapur will be owned and run on a 50-50 basis with Japanese interests. Its completion date of 1980 has been delayed by the revolution and a shortage of funds. A new agreement was being negotiated with the Japanese partners. With the probable exception of their complex, all other petrochemical plants were scheduled to be nationalized.

Iran's first steel mill was established at Isfahan under a $286 million credit agreement concluded in 1965 with the Soviet Union. The Arya Mehr plant began operating in March 1973, after a number of teething troubles and lack of suitable coal supplies. It is run by the National Iranian Steel Corporation. Local consumption of steel has been growing at 20 per cent annually. In 1977/78 it was estimated at 6 million tons and was expected to reach 18 million tons by 1983. The Shah's Government hoped that national output would be 15 million tons by 1983, but the new Government revised estimates and was expected to scrap a number of planned steel mills. Projects in doubt included a new complex under construction near Ahwaz, involving direct reduction plants with a total annual capacity of 3 million tons. The first phase of the complex, a gas-fed steel mill, began operating on a trial basis in January 1977; it has an annual capacity of 330,000 tons. Other doubtful projects include a rolling mill at Bandar Abbas in a joint venture with Italy, a steelworks to be built at Isfahan by the British Steel Corporation, and a complex to be set up at Bushehr in collaboration with a consortium of West German firms. Also unlikely to be implemented is a December 1977 agreement signed with the Soviet Union to expand the capacity of the Isfahan plant from less than 1 million metric tons to 6 million tons.

An aluminium smelter with an annual capacity of 50,000 tons went into production at the beginning of 1973 and its capacity was to be increased to 120,000 tons by 1980/81. Partners in the projects are the Iranian and Pakistan Governments and Reynolds Metals. An agreement was signed in 1976 with the U.S.S.R. to build an aluminium plant with a capacity of 500,000 tons per year.

A well-established industry is that of motor manufacturing, which mainly comprises assembly plants. Until recently, parts were all imported but these are increasingly being manufactured in Iran. The present annual production capacity is about 160,000 vehicles, of which some 120,000 are private cars. Nevertheless, rapidly growing demand meant that over 60,000 vehicles per year were imported until a ban was imposed in 1979.

The largest of Iran's twelve motor manufacturers, Iran National, produces a version of the Hillman

Hunter under licence from Chrysler UK, called the Peykan, which is Iran's best-selling car, as well as a range of other vehicles. Iran National produces nearly 100,000 Peykans per year, and this output was to be increased to 150,000. A version of the Citroen Dyane, called the Jyane, is also manufactured as well as versions of Renault cars and Land Rovers. In November 1977 Peugeot-Citroen signed a deal with Iran National for the production of a new middle range car with a Chrysler engine, but the revolutionary government was reviewing the project. Buses and lorries are made under licence from Leyland Motors, Volvo and Daimler-Benz. Before the revolution, General Motors was planning to set up a huge lorry plant to produce 100,000 vehicles per year by 1980. Iran National had planned a $100 million project to build its own engines, aimed at producing eventually an all-Iranian car.

Diesel engines by British Leyland and Daimler-Benz are made at Tabriz. Some 45,000 tractors per year are produced in Iran. A tractor assembly plant has been set up at Tabriz as a joint venture with Massey Ferguson with an initial capacity of 5,000 units per year. Electrical goods and machine tools are also manufactured. Provisional agreement was reached in January 1977 for the creation of three new machine tool ventures with the participation of British firms. Projects for underground railway systems for Teheran and other cities, and for the electrification of Iranian railways, were included in a financial agreement signed with France in June 1974, but were suspended after the revolution.

Iran was also planning a large military industrial centre at Isfahan with the assistance of Millbank Technical Services, a British Government agency, under a £750 million arms deal signed in May 1978. This agreement was cancelled in February 1979.

The Shah's plans to generate half of Iran's estimated electric energy requirements in 1994 by nuclear power plants were scrapped in the period after the revolution. The plans, first announced in 1974, had called for 20 nuclear reactors to be installed by 1994 for a total generating capacity of 23,000 MW. Six plants were expected to be built by Kraftwerk Union of West Germany, another six by Framatome of France and eight by Westinghouse and General Electric of the U.S.A. In-principle agreements were signed with France and West Germany for 12 reactors and work was started by Framatome on two 900 MW reactors on the Karun River and by Kraftwerk on two 1,200 MW reactors at Bushehr. Construction was halted during the revolution and the indications were that it would not resume. The nuclear power generation programme was criticized on several grounds. An initial estimated cost for the 20 reactors of $30,000 million was later revised to nearly $70,000 million to take into account infrastructural and transmission requirements. Lack of water and the frequency of earthquakes meant that the plants had to be sited near the Gulf and other areas away from population centres. Thousands of workers and technicians had to be imported to build and run the plants. Gas, argued the critics, was in abundant supply and would produce the same amount of electricity at one-tenth the cost.

During the rapid industrialization years under the Shah, demand for electricity was growing at 20 per cent annually and there were frequent power cuts as a result of insufficient capacity. Generating capacity in 1978 was estimated at 6,300 MW—from gas and oil-fuelled plants and several large dams. The Reza Shah, the Great Dam on the Karun River, went into operation in 1977; and in 1978 Acres International of Canada was awarded the design contract for another $1,500 million dam on the same river. Yet another dam is under construction in the Lar Valley east of Teheran. Widespread power cuts in the summers of 1977 and 1978 led to an accelerated building programme for gas-fuelled plants. A 1,380 MW plant, just south of Teheran, was brought on stream in mid-1978 and another three plants, with a total generating capacity of over 3,300 MW, were nearing completion at the time of the revolution.

TRADE AND COMMUNICATIONS

Iran's imports of goods during 1976/77 were worth about $14,100 million, an increase of 23 per cent over 1975/76 (compared with an average of 77 per cent in the two previous years). In 1977/78 they were estimated to have increased by 14.2 per cent, to $16,000 million. Military imports account for about 27 per cent of total imports. Non-oil exports, which account for only about 3 per cent of total export earnings, declined slightly in 1976/77 and rose by 7.3 per cent in 1977/78 to about $668 million. West Germany was the leading supplier in 1976/77, with 17.7 per cent of total imports. Japan was in second place (17.4 per cent) and the United States third (15.6 per cent), followed by the United Kingdom, Italy and France. The EEC countries together account for over 40 per cent of Iran's total imports and about 40 per cent of both oil and non-oil exports.

The new government has significantly reduced imports and some officials expect the level to be about half that under the Shah's regime.

Traditional exports include cotton, carpets, fresh and dried fruit, hides and caviar. "New" industrial products include knitwear, textiles, clothes, metal ores, pharmaceuticals, chemicals, soaps, detergents and shoes. Processed foodstuffs and vehicles are also exported. Main customers for Iran's non-oil exports are the U.S.S.R., West Germany, the U.S.A., Italy and Kuwait.

Iran's principal imports, excluding military equipment, are machinery and equipment, iron and steel goods, chemical products, synthetic fibres and foodstuffs. Imports of vehicles have been declining in recent years, as Iran builds up its own industry.

Iran has been pressing for the conclusion of a preferential trading agreement with the EEC.

Under the auspices of CENTO, railway lines are planned, or have been constructed, to link the Iranian system to the European system by building a line from Sharafkhaneh in West Iran to Mus in East Turkey and to the South Asian system by building a line from Yazd to Zahedan. The rail link with Turkey was inaugurated in 1971. In addition two roads are under construction to link Iran with Pakistan, one from Kerman to Quetta and the second from Bandar Abbas to Karachi via Mekran, to be part of the Asian Highway.

FINANCE

The 1979/80 budget was still being drawn up several months after the February revolution, but indications were that spending would be cut significantly—perhaps as much as 40 per cent down on the previous year's $59,200 million target. The Government's budget for the period up to the end of June was drawn up on a monthly basis, but the Economy and Finance Ministry planned to draw up a comprehensive budget for the remaining nine months of the Iranian year. In contrast to the previous year's projected deficit of $10,700 million—$8,700 million to be covered by planned foreign and domestic borrowing—the Ministry was predicting that the Government's revenue and spending would be balanced.

Salary increases for civil servants and others, promised by the last few governments under the Shah, were likely to be a major item in the new Government's expenditures. So were payments for projects and equipment ordered by the Shah but cancelled by the new regime.

Iran said that it would no longer go abroad for the massive loans that the Shah had secured over the previous four years. At the same time the provisional Government insisted that it would repay the more than $5,000 million in foreign debts left behind by the Shah. The largest loans included $300 million raised on the Euromarket for NIGC, and $360 million for the National Petrochemical Company. U.S. banks were owed more than $2,200 million, Japanese banks $700 million, and Canada nearly $400 million. The rest of the debts were spread among west European banks.

Foreign exchange reserves are apparently healthy despite the economic and financial disruptions of the revolution. In May 1979 the Central Bank put reserves at $10,400 million, more than $2,000 million lower than the February record of 12,839 million. The reserves were expected to drop further as payments for imports—halted during the months of the revolution—resumed. The Central Bank, however, estimated that Iran had more than $5,000 million overseas in assets and investments.

Unofficial estimates in May 1979 put the current balance of payments deficit at $3,000 million. The balance of payments had started going into the red in late 1978 and a deficit of about $900 million had been predicted for mid-1979.

Foreign exchange restrictions introduced under the last few months of the Shah's reign were continued by the new regime. A ceiling of $3,000 was imposed on each person leaving the country. At the same time the Central Bank was considering a devaluation of the rial to bring it in line with the "black market" rate of over 100 rials to the U.S. dollar. A two-tier exchange rate was introduced to bring the "black market" rate down before the Government decided on its devaluation level.

Inflation in 1979 was unofficially estimated at about 30 per cent, roughly the same level as in the previous four years. There was little expectation of a fall in the inflation rate in the immediate future, as the Central Bank made it clear that this was a problem to be tackled after the economy got going and enough jobs were created to reduce significantly the level of unemployment.

FIFTH DEVELOPMENT PLAN

In March 1973 Iran embarked upon her Fifth Development Plan (1973–78). Whereas the main thrust for the Fourth Plan had been concentrated on oil and industry, the emphasis in the Fifth Plan was on improved living standards, education and training, closely followed by agriculture. Total expenditure was originally planned at U.S. $35,500 million, which was greater than the combined investment of the previous four plans put together. However, total anticipated oil revenues, originally estimated at $24,600 million for the period of the Plan, were later put at some $100,000 million. Total Plan expenditure was therefore raised to $68,600 million in August 1974. The largest single allocation went to housing, followed by industry. In the latter sector, the emphasis was on developing the hydrocarbons and steel industries, and atomic energy projects. Agriculturally-based industries also received special attention. The original target of the Plan was for an average annual growth rate of 14 per cent, but the very high growth rates achieved in 1973/74 and 1974/75 led to a revision of the Plan's target for average growth to 26 per cent. However, the deceleration experienced by the economy during 1975/76, combined with lack of adequate infrastructure, shortage of trained manpower and technical expertise, has meant that a large number of Plan projects have been slowed down or postponed. By March 1977 fulfilment ratios were: agriculture 60 per cent of target investment, industry 70 per cent and power only 40 per cent. Although the Fifth Plan was due to end in March 1978, no more than the broad outlines of the Sixth Plan (1978–83) had been published by that date. It was eventually overtaken by the revolution.

STATISTICAL SURVEY

(The Iranian year runs from March 21st to March 20th)

AREA AND POPULATION

Area	Population (census results)			
	November 1966	November 1976		
	Total	Males	Females	Total
1,648,000 sq. km.*	25,785,210	17,277,656	16,314,219	33,591,875

* 636,296 sq. miles.

Estimated population: 34,274,000 (July 1st, 1977); 35 million in 1978.

PRINCIPAL TOWNS

(November 1976 census)

Tehran (Teheran)	4,496,159*	Abadan	296,081	Ardebil	147,846
Isfahan	671,825	Kermanshah	290,861	Khorramshahr	146,709
Mashad (Meshed)	670,180	Qom	246,831	Kerman	140,309
Tabriz	598,576	Rasht	187,203	Karaj	138,774
Shiraz	416,408	Rezaiyah	163,991	Qazvin	138,527
Ahwaz	329,002	Hamedan	155,846	Yazd	135,978

* Including suburbs.

Births and Deaths: Average annual birth rate 45.3 per 1,000 in 1965-70 and 1970-75; death rate 17.4 per 1,000 in 1965-70, 15.6 per 1,000 in 1970-75 (UN estimates).

ECONOMICALLY ACTIVE POPULATION*

(1971 sample survey)

	Males	Females	Total
Agriculture, Forestry, Hunting and Fishing	3,616,537	83,850	3,700,387
Mining and Quarrying	14,290	107	14,397
Manufacturing	931,657	487,835	1,419,942
Construction	532,777	2,822	535,599
Electricity, Gas, Water Supply	45,404	1,615	47,019
Commerce	706,473	10,385	716,858
Transport, Storage and Communications	293,028	2,547	292,569
Services	720,000	165,058	885,058
Others (not adequately described)	20,363	907	21,270
Total in Employment	6,880,529	755,120	7,635,649
Unemployed	77,000	12,000	89,000
Total	6,957,529	767,120	7,724,649

* Excluding nomadic tribes and other unsettled population.

AGRICULTURE

PRINCIPAL CROPS
('000 metric tons)

	1975/76	1976/77	1977/78
Wheat	5,500	6,000	5,500
Barley	1,400	1,500	1,230
Rice (paddy)	1,430	1,600	1,400
Maize	65	75	45
Sugar beet	4,670	5,200	4,150
Sugar cane	1,100	800	1,000
Tea (green)	80	88	116
Oilseeds	100	130	105
Tobacco	15	19	15
Pulses	225	230	187
Pistachios	25	40	27

LIVESTOCK
('000 head, FAO estimates)

	1975	1976	1977
Horses	350	350	350
Mules	120	120	121
Asses	1,800	1,800	1,800
Cattle	6,500	6,650	6,650
Buffaloes	130	130	130
Camels	60	60	60
Pigs	67	68	68
Sheep	35,000	35,300	35,441
Goats	14,000	14,300	14,375
Chickens	55,000	60,000	63,382
Ducks	148	149	151

Source: FAO, *Production Yearbook.*

LIVESTOCK PRODUCTS
(FAO estimates, '000 metric tons)

	1975	1976	1977
Beef and veal	104	108	109
Buffalo meat	8	8	8
Mutton and lamb	167	171	176
Goats' meat	59	60	61
Pig meat	4	4	4
Poultry meat	106	130	139
Other meat	17	17	18
Cows' milk	1,230	1,250	1,256
Buffaloes' milk	33	34	36
Sheep's milk	593	617	640
Goats' milk	222	222	222
Cheese	85.4	86.8	87.8
Butter	54.4	55.7	56.7
Hen eggs	110	130	132
Honey	5.2	6.0	6.3
Wool: greasy	17.5	18.0	18.3
clean	9.7	9.7	9.9
Cattle and buffalo hides	21.8	22.7	22.9
Sheep skins	27.9	28.5	29.3
Goat skins	9.4	9.6	9.8

Source: FAO, *Production Yearbook.*

FORESTRY

ROUNDWOOD REMOVALS
('000 cubic metres, all broadleaved)

	1972	1973	1974*
Sawlogs, veneer logs and logs for sleepers	584	413*	318
Pitprops (Mine timber)	20*	20	4
Other industrial wood	4,528*	4,003*	4,003
Fuel wood	1,000*	1,061*	1,997
TOTAL	6,132	5,497	6,322

*FAO estimate.

Sawlogs, etc. ('000 cubic metres): 350 per year in 1975 and 1976; 369 in 1977 (FAO estimates).

SAWNWOOD PRODUCTION
('000 cubic metres, all broadleaved)

	1975	1976	1977
Sawnwood (incl. boxboards)*	90	90	90
Railway sleepers	80	54	73
TOTAL	170	144	163

*FAO estimate.

Source: FAO, *Yearbook of Forest Products.*

FISHING

('000 metric tons, live weight)

	1971	1972	1973
Inland waters	6.3	3.0	3.1
Marine fishes	13.3*	13.5*	13.5*
Marine crustaceans	4.7*	3.0*	3.4*
TOTAL CATCH	24.3	19.5	20.0

* FAO estimate.

1974–77: Annual catch as in 1973 (FAO estimates).

Source: FAO, *Yearbook of Fishery Statistics.*

MINING

CRUDE PETROLEUM

(net production, million barrels)

	1973	1974	1975	1976	1977
Oil Service Company of Iran (OSCO)	1,968.1	2,022.9	1,779.5	1,980.5	1,861.2
National Iranian Oil Company	6.1	6.6	6.2	6.8	6.4
Irano-Italian Oil Company (SIRIP)	26.2	27.7	19.3	16.7	16.5
Iran-Pan American Oil Company (IPAC)	46.8	48.3	64.5	75.9	99.5
Lavan Petroleum Company (LAPCO)	67.2	71.0	64.0	55.6	66.5
Iranian Marine International Oil Company (IMINOCO)	24.9	21.3	19.2	17.4	16.7
TOTAL	2,139.3	2,197.8	1,952.7	2,153.0	2,066.8

NATURAL GAS

(million cubic metres)

	1973	1974	1975	1976	1977
Production	48,163.8	49,993.2	45,403.1	50,378.7	57,336.1
Consumption	19,705.9	22,259.8	21,834.3	22,477.0	30,659.7
of which: Exports to U.S.S.R.	8,679.5	9,086.8	9,565.2	9,274.2	9,148.9

OTHER MINERALS

('000 metric tons)

	1970/71	1971/72	1972/73
Coal	530	600	1,000
Iron ore	10	150	980
Copper	1	1	1
Lead and zinc	200	210	220
Chromite	180	180	180
Barites	77	77	80

INDUSTRY

PETROLEUM PRODUCTS

('000 metric tons)

	1970	1971	1972	1973
Liquefied petroleum gas	112	143	161	194
Naphtha	508	311	400	346
Motor spirit (Petrol)	2,146	2,419	2,412	2,559
Aviation gasoline	667	622	643	606
Kerosene	2,301	2,503	2,618	2,641
White spirit	125*	120*	110*	99
Jet fuel	1,641	1,388	1,729	1,694
Distillate fuel oils	4,726	5,114	5,085	5,457
Residual fuel oil	12,580	13,236	12,646	13,325
Lubricating oils	80	80	106	154
Petroleum bitumen (asphalt)	357	440	416	514

* Estimated production.

1974 ('000 metric tons): Distillate fuel oils 5,493; Residual fuel oil 14,781.

OTHER PRODUCTS

(twelve months ending March 20th)

		1973/74	1974/75	1975/76	1976/77
Vegetable ghee	'000 metric tons	188	244	265	300
Sugar	" " "	697	747	770	690
Cigarettes and cigars	million	13,449	14,389	15,314	n.a.
Paints	'000 metric tons	24.6	33	36	n.a.
Cement	" " "	3,489	4,628	5,145	6,100
Refrigerators	'000	257	309	437	500
Heaters	"	216	307	336	190
Gas stoves	"	313	291	327	1,150
Radios	"	281	351	345	230
Televisions	"	242	326	356	303
Vehicles	"	77	107	140	169

FINANCE

100 dinars = 1 Iranian rial.

Coins: 50 dinars; 1, 2, 5, 10 and 20 rials.

Notes: 5, 10, 20, 50, 100, 200, 500, 1,000, 5,000 and 10,000 rials.

Exchange rates (April 1979): £1 sterling = 145.8 rials; U.S. \$1 = 70.5 rials.
1,000 Iranian rials = £6.86 = \$14.19.

Note: From December 1946 to May 1957 the official exchange rate was U.S. \$1 = 32.25 rials (1 rial = 3.1008 U.S. cents) but other rates were in operation for certain commercial transactions. From 1956 the trade rate was \$1 = 75.75 rials (1 rial = 1.3201 U.S. cents) and this was the official parity from May 1957 to February 1973, despite the devaluation of the U.S. dollar in December 1971. In terms of sterling, the exchange rate was £1 = 181.80 rials from November 1967 to August 1971; and £1 = 197.38 rials from December 1971 to June 1972. In February 1973 a new par value of \$1 = 68.175 rials was established but the Iranian authorities introduced market rates of \$1 = 67.50 rials (buying) or 67.75 rials (selling), with a mid-point of \$1 = 67.625 rials. In February 1975 the direct link with the dollar was broken and the rial has since been tied to the IMF Special Drawing Right (at a mid-point of 82.24 rials per SDR), whose value is determined by changes in a weighted "basket" of 16 national currencies. The market rate against the U.S. dollar has been frequently adjusted. It was \$1 = 66.641 rials from February to July 1975, \$1 = 69.275 rials from October 1975 to March 1976, \$1 = 70.625 rials from June 1976 to December 1977 and \$1 = 70.475 rials since December 1977. The average exchange rate (rials per U.S. dollar) was: 67.64 in 1975; 70.22 in 1976; 70.62 in 1977.

ADMINISTRATION BUDGET ESTIMATES

('000 million rials, 12 months ending March 20th)

REVENUE	1977/78	1978/79
Taxation	420.8	614.2
Oil and gas	1,372.7	1,541.8
Government monopolies	30.3	40.8
Sales of goods and services	28.0	34.0
Miscellaneous	94.4	143.9
Foreign borrowing	100.0	400.0 (Foreign and Domestic borrowing)
Domestic borrowing	150.0	
Interest on loans abroad	20.3	21.3
Other	—	—
TOTAL	2,188.6	2,796.0

EXPENDITURE	1977/78	1978/79
Public affairs	200.8	194.1
Defence	560.5	700.4
Education	220.9	689.0 (Education, Health, Welfare, Housing)
Health	77.4	
Welfare	84.7	
Housing	89.4	
Agriculture	75.7	1,205.9 (Agriculture, Electricity, Industry)
Electricity	212.4	
Industry	115.7	
TOTAL (incl. other)	2,311.2	2,935.9

Source: Iran Trade and Industry, August–September 1977, and Minister of Finance's Budget Speech.

GOVERNMENT OIL REVENUES

Total oil revenues received by Iran, in U.S. $ million: (1971) 1,870, (1972) 2,308, (1973) 5,600, (1974) 22,000, (1975) 20,500 (1976) 22,000 approx., (1977) 23,000 approx.

FIFTH DEVELOPMENT PLAN 1973–78

('000 million rials)

	ORIGINAL MARCH 73	REVISED AUGUST 74
Agriculture	121	239.6
Water	106	160.0
Industry	180	352.1
Mining	46	62.0
Oil	130	333.0
Gas	24	51.0
Power	53	240.0
Communication	177	404.0
Telecommunication	36	91.4
Rural development	36	60.0
Urban development	32	45.0
Government building	91	320.0
Housing	90	230.0
Education	127	130.0
Arts and culture	5	10.0
Tourism	7	11.0
Health	24	43.0
Welfare	5	9.0
Sports	9	15.0
Provincial development	0	10.0
Public affairs	0	32.0
TOTAL GOVERNMENT EXPENDITURE	1,299	2,848.1
Expenditure by government companies		445.0
Estimated expenditure by private sector		1,570.0
Less government loans to private sector		−229.0
TOTAL (NET)		4,364.0

Source: The Royal Road to Progress, Ministry of Information, Teheran, 1974.

CENTRAL BANK RESERVES

(U.S. $ million at December 31st)

	1976	1977	1978
Gold	152	160	175
IMF Special Drawing Rights	75	85	125
Reserve position in IMF	1,160	1,197	945
Foreign exchange	7,447	10,824	10,907
TOTAL	8,833	12,266	12,152

Source: IMF, *International Financial Statistics.*

MONEY SUPPLY

('000 million rials at March 20th)

	1976	1977	1978
Currency outside banks	182.78	251.41	326.36
Official entities' deposits at Central Bank	63.78	136.78	143.49
Demand deposits at commercial banks	257.77	385.33	487.83
TOTAL	504.33	773.52	957.68

Source: IMF, *International Financial Statistics.*

BALANCE OF PAYMENTS

(U.S. $ million)

	1972	1973	1974	1975	1976	1977
Merchandise exports f.o.b.	3,966	6,122	21,356	20,432	23,959	24,356
Merchandise imports f.o.b.	−2,591	−3,985	−7,257	−12,898	−15,973	−15,823
TRADE BALANCE	1,375	2,137	14,099	7,534	7,986	8,533
Exports of services	318	649	1,354	2,472	2,886	3,629
Imports of services	−2,086	−2,629	−3,153	−5,280	−6,139	−7,071
BALANCE ON GOODS AND SERVICES	−392	156	12,300	4,725	4,734	5,090
Unrequited transfers (net)	4	−2	−33	−18	−20	−9
CURRENT BALANCE	−388	154	12,267	4,707	4,714	5,081
Direct capital investment (net)	91	561	324	141	744	802
Other long-term capital (net)	531	628	−2,263	−3,010	−2,580	−441
Short-term capital (net)	13	−730	−3,127	−1,079	−3,238	−2,961
Net errors and omissions	219	−547	−176	−648	800	925
TOTAL (net monetary movements)	467	66	7,026	110	440	3,406
Allocation of IMF Special Drawing Rights	22	—	—	—	—	—
CHANGES IN RESERVES, ETC.	489	66	7,026	110	440	3,406

Source: IMF, *International Financial Statistics.*

EXTERNAL TRADE

('000 million rials, 12 months ending March 20th)

	1970/71	1971/72	1972/73	1973/74	1974/75	1975/76	1976/77	1977/78
Imports c.i.f.	128.2	157.7	193.7	253.2	448.2	800.8	901.7	1,029.2
Exports f.o.b.*	21.2	26.3	33.9	42.8	41.2	40.7	38.0	47.2

* Excluding crude petroleum, petroleum products and natural gas. The total value of such exports (in '000 million rials) was: 1,401.7 in 1974/75; 1,348.1 in 1975/76; 1,671.1 in 1976/77; 1,637.5 in 1977/78 (*Source:* IMF, *International Financial Statistics*).

PRINCIPAL COMMODITIES

(U.S. $ million)

IMPORTS c.i.f.	1974/75	1975/76	1976/77	1977/78
Food and live animals	852	1,555	1,232	1,486
Beverages and tobacco	13	26	77	130
Crude materials (inedible) except fuels	344	369	365	437
Mineral fuels, lubricants, etc.	13	17	23	30
Animal and vegetable oils and fats	240	291	137	164
Chemicals	649	835	858	1,003
Basic manufactures	2,198	3,342	4,202	4,316
Machinery and transport equipment	2,109	4,973	5,526	6,063
Miscellaneous manufactured articles	195	286	345	494
Other commodities and transactions	1	2	1	1
TOTAL	6,614	11,696	12,766	14,124

[*continued on next page*

PRINCIPAL COMMODITIES—*continued*]

EXPORTS (excl. petroleum and gas)	1974/75	1975/76	1976/77	1977/78
Carpets	119.1	105.6	94.5	114.5
Cotton	85.3	136.2	122.3	92.6
Fresh and dried fruits	71.8	74.7	70.3	90.4
Skins and leather	27.8	28.3	31.9	39.9
Minerals and metal ores	32.8	32.8	10.2	1.1
Detergents and soap	12.1	22.1	19.3	16.1
Glycerine and chemicals	22.0	18.5	31.6	12.1
Confectionery and biscuits	3.4	5.0	11.3	11.3
Clothing, knitwear and textiles	44.2	28.7	26.7	23.9
Road vehicles	21.2	28.3	24.2	9.9
TOTAL (incl. others)	581.5	592.2	539.9	523.2

Crude petroleum (U.S. $ million): 15,724.2 in 1974/75; 17,470.6 in 1975/76.
Petroleum products (U.S. $ million): 1,367.9 in 1974/75; 966.6 in 1975/76.
Natural gas (U.S. $ million): 124.9 in 1974/75; 137.2 in 1975/76.

PETROLEUM EXPORTS

('000 barrels per day)

	1973/74	1974/75	1975/76	1976/77	1977/78
Crude petroleum	5,317	5,244	4,617	5,278	4,817
Refined oil products	280	281	263	214	199*

* Daily average for first nine months.

Value of crude petroleum exports ('000 million rials): 1,322.8 in 1974/75; 1,268.2 in 1975/76; 1,598.9 in 1976/77; 1,569.4 in 1977/78 (*Source:* IMF, *International Financial Statistics*).

PRINCIPAL TRADING PARTNERS

(U.S. $ million)

IMPORTS c.i.f.	1975/76	1976/77	1977/78
Australia	192	172	209
Austria	77	98	142
Belgium	295	277	340
France	516	714	648
Germany, Fed. Repub.	2,024	2,273	2,747
India	435	315	185
Italy	417	735	798
Japan	1,853	2,201	2,215
Netherlands	330	443	464
Romania	167	147	190
South Africa	63	103	191
Sweden	151	143	191
Switzerland	271	473	444
U.S.S.R.	168	117	271
United Kingdom	1,033	904	971
U.S.A.	2,287	1,972	2,205
TOTAL (incl. others)	11,696	12,766	14,124

EXPORTS f.o.b.*	1975/76	1976/77	1977/78
Bahrain	6.8	6.4	8.8
China, People's Repub.	22.8	8.2	9.5
Czechoslovakia	10.5	9.7	8.9
France	17.1	14.4	13.1
Germany, Fed. Repub.	80.7	86.3	79.2
Hungary	23.2	15.1	21.8
Iraq	4.4	6.3	24.9
Italy	29.4	33.1	25.0
Kuwait	25.8	16.9	19.4
Saudi Arabia	17.0	25.0	23.1
South Africa	6.4	1.6	19.9
Taiwan	13.0	7.0	8.4
U.S.S.R.	110.4	79.3	87.8
United Arab Emirates	11.7	10.4	10.4
United Kingdom	14.3	16.2	15.3
U.S.A.	46.4	35.6	44.2
TOTAL (incl. others)	592.2	539.9	523.2

* Excluding petroleum and gas exports.

PERCENTAGE GEOGRAPHICAL DISTRIBUTION OF CRUDE OIL EXPORTS
(companies affiliated with Oil Service Co. of Iran)

	1973	1974	1975	1976	1977
Western Europe	41.2	44.5	46.6	41.6	43.3
Japan	34.9	26.9	27.1	18.9	16.4
Asia	7.2	5.0	2.3	7.8	9.3
Central and North America	11.7	16.7	15.0	14.1	20.5
Africa	3.5	5.3	6.8	13.5	7.2
Australasia	0.2	0.2	0.7	0.9	0.7
South America	0.3	0.5	0.4	2.1	2.3
Other regions	1.0	0.9	1.1	1.1	0.3

Source: National Iranian Oil Company.

TRANSPORT

RAILWAYS

	1975/76	1976/77
Passenger journeys ('000)	5,443	6,200
Freight ('000 metric tons)	8,912	9,100

Source: Iran Trade and Industry, August–September 1977.

Passenger-kilometres: 2,126 million in 1974.

ROAD TRAFFIC
('000 vehicles in use)

	1976
Cars	1,892
Buses	35
Trucks	105
Ambulances	2
Motor cycles	100

Source: Iran Almanac 1976.

CIVIL AVIATION

	1975/76	1976/77
Passenger-km. ('000)	2,402,000	2,889,000

MERCHANT SHIPPING FLEET
('000 gross registered tons at June 30th)

	1972	1973	1974	1975	1976	1977
Oil tankers	56	62	59	181	297	617
Other vessels	125	130	233	299	386	385
TOTAL	181	192	292	480	683	1,002

INTERNATIONAL SHIPPING TRAFFIC*
('000 metric tons, year ending March 20th)

	1972/73	1973/74	1974/75	1975/76	1976/77
Goods loaded	237,251	274,503	279,064	243,280	n.a.
Goods unloaded	4,144	5,516	8,529	10,964	13,642

* Including goods imported and exported other than by sea.

TOURISM

	1975/76	1976/77
Visitors	588,768	657,930
Approximate Money Spent (million U.S. $)	135	148

EDUCATION
(1975/76)

	Schools	Pupils ('000)
Elementary	22,210	3,819
Literacy Corps	14,732	655
Orientation Course	4,289	1,284
Secondary	1,601	705
Technical and Vocational	530	152
Primary Teacher Training	162	44
Universities and Colleges	207	152

Sources (except where otherwise stated): Statistical Centre of Iran, Teheran.

THE CONSTITUTION

Under the draft constitution published in mid-June 1979, it is proposed that Iran will be governed by a President, Prime Minister and a single-chamber parliament of 270 deputies. The official religion is the Shi'ite Muslim faith but religious minorities will be free to practise.

The President is to be elected by direct vote for a four-year term of office. The President chooses the Prime Minister, is Commander-in-Chief of the Armed Forces and is responsible for co-ordinating the work of the executive, legislative and judicial branches of government. The President, once in his term of office, has the power to dissolve parliament in the event of an emergency.

The draft constitution will be submitted to an elected 75-member "Council of Examiners" towards the end of July 1979.

PROVINCIAL DIVISIONS

According to the latest state division (May 1977), Iran is divided into 23 provinces (*Ostans*), 472 counties (*Shahrestan*) and 499 municipalities (*Bakhsh*).

All towns have a municipal administration, the Mayor of which is chosen by the town council. The nomination must be approved by the Ministry of the Interior.

THE GOVERNMENT

PROVISIONAL CABINET

(*July* 1979)

Prime Minister: Dr. Mehdi Bazargan.

Minister of Foreign Affairs: Dr. Ibrahim Yazdi.

Minister of Interior: Hashem Sabbaghian.

Minister of Justice: Sadr Hajj Seyyed Javadi.

Minister of Economy and Finance: Ali Ardalan.

Minister of National Defence: Gen. Taqi Riyahi.

Minister of Higher Education and Culture: Dr. Ali Shariatmadari.

Minister of Education: Gholam Hussein Shokoohi.

Minister of Posts and Telecommunications: Dr. Muhammad Islami.

Minister of Housing and Urban Development: Eng. Mostafa Katira'i.

Minister of Roads and Transport: Eng. Yusof Taheri Ghazveni.

Minister of Labour and Social Affairs: Dariush Foruhar.

Minister of Mines and Industries: Mahmud Ahmadzadeh.

Minister of State and Head of the Plan Organization: Eng. Ali Akbar Mo'infar.

Minister of State for Revolutionary Projects: Dr. Yadollah Sahabi.

Minister of Energy: Eng. Abbas Taj.

Minister of Agriculture: Dr. Ali Muhammad Izadi.

Minister of Commerce: Dr. Reza Sadre.

Minister of National Guidance: Dr. Nasser Minachi.

Deputy Prime Minister: Hashem Saghian.

Deputy Prime Minister for Public Relations: Amir Entezam.

Deputy Prime Minister for Revolutionary Affairs: (vacant).

Deputy Prime Minister for Co-operation between the Government and the People: Hossein Bani-Asadi.

Minister of Health and Welfare and Deputy Prime Minister in charge of Red Lion and Sun Society of Iran: Dr. Kazem Sami.

PARLIAMENT

Under the Shah, Parliament had consisted of a Senate of 60 members and a National Consultative Assembly (*Majlis*) of 268 members. Parliament does not exist under the Provisional Revolutionary and Islamic Government which came to power in mid-February 1979, but under the draft constitution published in mid-June 1979 a single-chamber parliament of 270 deputies is proposed.

POLITICAL PARTIES

During the last three years of the Shah's regime the only legal political party was *Rastakhiz* (the Iran National Resurgence Party), formed at the instigation of the Shah in 1975. By late 1978 mounting opposition to the Shah made it evident the *Rastakhiz* was discredited, and it was abolished. Under the Provisional Revolutionary and Islamic Government of February 1979 no political parties are constitutionally legal, but the parties and groups listed below are some of the most important operating openly. The draft constitution permits political parties, providing they do not oppose the principles of the Islamic Republic, or threaten Iran's freedom, independence, unity and national sovereignty.

Fedayeen Guerrillas: urban Marxist guerrillas.

Heib-e Komyunist-e Iran (*Communist Party of Iran*): f. 1979 on grounds that Tudeh Party was Moscow-controlled; Sec.-Gen. 'Azaryun'.

Iran Liberation Movement: Islamic; Leader Dr. Mehdi Bazargan.

Islamic Republican Party: party identified with policies of Ayatollah Khomeini.

Kurdistan Democratic Party: Leader Abdurrahman Qassemlou.

Mujaheddin Guerrillas: Islamic guerrilla group; Leader Massoud Rajavi.

National Democratic Front: f. March 1979; Leader Hedayatollah Matine-Daftari.

National Front (*Union of National Front Forces*): comprises Iran Nationalist Party, Iranian Party, and Society of Iranian Students.

Pan Iranist Party: extreme right-wing; calls for a Greater Persia; Leader Mohsen Pezeshkpour.

Sazmane Peykar da Rahe Azadieh Tabaqe Kargar (*Organization Struggling for the Freedom of the Working Class*): Marxist-Leninist.

Tudeh Party (*Communist*): f. 1941; declared illegal 1949.

DIPLOMATIC REPRESENTATION

EMBASSIES ACCREDITED TO IRAN

(In Teheran unless otherwise stated)

Afghanistan: Ave. Abbas Abad, Pompe Benzine, Angle de la 4ème Rue; *Ambassador:* Dr. Raee.

Algeria: Ave. Roosevelt (Nord), rue No. 8, No. 13; *Ambassador:* Hafid Keramane.

Argentina: Mirdamad Ave. (Tajrish), Blvd. Nahid, No. 35; *Ambassador:* Isvaldo Guillermo García Pineiro.

Australia: Ave. Soyaya, P.O.B. 3408; *Ambassador:* M. L. Johnstone.

Austria: Takhte Jamshid, Forsat Ave.; *Ambassador:* Christoph Cornaro.

Bahrain: 31 Ave. Vozara; *Ambassador:* Ibrahim Ali Ibrahim (also accred. to Afghanistan).

Bangladesh: Ave. Kakh No. 350–352; *Ambassador:* Rashid Ahmed.

Belgium: Ave. Takht-e-Tavous, 49 Ave. Daryaye Noor; *Ambassador:* Marcel van de Kerckhove (also accred. to Afghanistan).

Brazil: Mirdamad Ave., Rue Alavi No. 59; *Ambassador:* Aluysio Regis Bittencourt (also accred. to Afghanistan).

Bulgaria: Ave. Aryamehr, Place Iran Novin, rue Shabnam No. 23; *Ambassador:* Kiril Shterev.

Burma: Islamabad, Pakistan.

Cameroon: Jeddah, Saudi Arabia.

Canada: Ave. Takhte-Tavous, Ave. Darya-e-Nour No. 50 *Ambassador:* Kenneth Douglas Taylor (also accred. to Bahrain, Kuwait, Oman and Qatar).

Chad: Moscow, U.S.S.R.

Chile: Ave. Park, Ave. Passargade No. 30; *Ambassador:* Brig.-Gen. Felipe Geiger Stahr.

China, People's Republic: Ave. Saltanatabad, Ave. Golestan 1 No. 51; *Ambassador:* Chiao Jo-yu.

Colombia: Ave. Bihaghi, No. 15; *Ambassador:* (vacant).

Czechoslovakia: Sarshar No. 61; *Ambassador:* Dr. Vladimir Polacek.

Denmark: Copenhagen Ave., P.O.B. 31; *Ambassador:* Troels Munk (also accred. to Afghanistan and Pakistan).

Ecuador: *Ambassador:* Filoteo Samaniego Salazar.

Ethiopia: Ankara, Turkey.

Finland: Ave. Gandhi, corner of 25th St.; *Ambassador:* Martti Salomies.

France: France Ave.; *Ambassador:* René Saint-Légier de la Sausaye.

Gabon: Ave. Roosevelt, rue Darafeh; *Ambassador:* Pierre-Claver Eyeghet.

Gambia: Jeddah, Saudi Arabia.

German Democratic Republic: Ave. Nader Shah, rue Afshin 15; *Ambassador:* Klaus Wolf (also accred. to Afghanistan).

Germany, Federal Republic: 324 Ferdowsi Ave.; *Ambassador:* Gerhard Ritzel.

Ghana: Ave. Shah Abbas, Rue Varahram No. 12; *Ambassador:* C. C. Lokko.

Greece: Ave. Park, Rue 35 No. 20; *Ambassador:* PANAYIOTIS ECONOMOU (also accred. to Afghanistan and Pakistan).

Guinea: Rome, Italy.

Hungary: Ave. Park, rue 13, No. 18; *Ambassador:* JÓZSEF MIKO (also accred. to Afghanistan).

Iceland: Bonn, Federal Republic of Germany.

India: Ave. Saba Shomali, No. 166; *Ambassador:* V. K. AHUJA.

Indonesia: Vozara, rue 31, No. 11; *Ambassador:* NASRUN SYAHRUN.

Iraq: Ave. Mirdamad, *Ambassador:* AHMED HUSSEIN AS-SAMARAI.

Ireland: Ave. Mirdamad, Ave. Razan-e-Shomli No. 8; *Chargé d'affaires a.i.:* DONAL HURLEY.

Italy: France Ave. 81; *Ambassador:* GIULIO TAMAGNINI.

Ivory Coast: Bad Jordan Ave., Tour No. 3; *Ambassador:* EMMANUEL NOUMAMA.

Japan: Ave. Mirdamad, Ave. Nahid, No. 46; *Ambassador:* TSUTOMA WADA.

Jordan: Bukharest Ave., 16th Ave. No. 55; *Ambassador:* TAYSIR TOUKAN (also accred. to Afghanistan).

Korea, Democratic People's Republic: Ave. Tavanir No. 87; *Ambassador:* CHA PYONG-OK.

Korea, Republic: Kakh Ave., Heshmatoddowleh No. 427; *Ambassador:* KIM DONG WHIE.

Kuwait: Maikadeh Ave., 3-38 Sazman-Ab St.; *Ambassador:* AHMED ABDUL AZIZ AL-JASSIM (also accred. to Afghanistan).

Lebanon: Bukharest Ave., 16th Street, No. 43; *Ambassador:* KHALIL AL-KHALIL (also accred. to Afghanistan).

Lesotho: Bukharest Ave., 9th Street, No. 20; *Ambassador:* VITUS MOOKI MOLAPO (also accred. to Romania).

Liberia: Cairo, Egypt.

Malaysia: Bukharest Ave., No. 8; *Ambassador:* (vacant) (also accred. to Afghanistan).

Malta: London, U.K.

Mauritania: Bukharest Ave., Rue 1, No. 2/20; *Ambassador:* SIDI BOUNA OULD SIDI.

Mexico: Ave. Mirdamad, rue Dolatshahi, No. 22; *Ambassador:* ALFONSO CASTRO VALLE.

Mongolia: Prague, Czechoslovakia.

Morocco: Ave. Nader Shah, rue Afshine No. 1; *Ambassador:* ABDELHADI TAZI (also accred. to Afghanistan and Turkey).

Nepal: Ave. Pakistan; *Ambassador:* (vacant).

Netherlands: Takhte Tavous, Near Pahlavi Ave., Rue Moazami Rue Jahansouz No. 36; *Ambassador:* WILLY SILVIO JULIEN CAMPAGNE (also accred. to Afghanistan).

New Zealand: Ave. Nader Shah, Ave. Afshin, No. 29; *Ambassador:* CHRISTOPHER BEEBY.

Niger: Cairo, Egypt.

Nigeria: Ave. Vozara; *Ambassador:* Brig. GEORGE KURUBO.

Norway: Aban Ave. 3; *Ambassador:* KNUT A. S. SVERRE (also accred. to Afghanistan, Bahrain, Kuwait, Pakistan and Qatar).

Oman: Ave. Abbas-Abad, Ave. Bukharest, 17th Ave. No. 10; *Ambassador:* MALALLAH ALI HABIB (also accred. to Turkey).

Pakistan: Ave. Aryamehr. Jamshidabad Chomali, Ave. Khorshid No. 1; *Ambassador:* ALI ARSHAD.

Peru: Ave. Bihaghi No. 21; *Ambassador:* CÉSAR A. DE LA FUENTE LOCKER.

Philippines: Boulevard Elizabeth, rue Meikadeh No. 19 *Ambassador:* Gen. RAFAEL M. ILETO (also accred. to Turkey).

Poland: 140 Takhte Jamshid Ave.; *Ambassador:* (vacant).

Portugal: Rodsar Ave. No. 41; *Ambassador:* PAULO FRANICISCO MENDES DA LUZ.

Qatar: Ave. Jordan, Ave. Golazin, Parke Davar No. 4; *Ambassador:* AHMED HAMD AL-ATEYAH (also accred. to Afghanistan).

Romania: Fakhrabad Ave. 12; *Ambassador:* NICOLAE STEFAN (also accred. to Afghanistan and Oman).

Saudi Arabia: Ave. Bucharest, P.O.B. 2903; *Ambassador:* IBRAHIM S. BAKR.

Senegal: Ave. Park, 8th St. No. 4; *Ambassador:* MASSAMBA SARRE (also accred. to Afghanistan, Bahrain and Turkey).

Singapore: New Delhi, India.

Somalia: Abbassabad, Ave. Pakistan, rue 16; *Ambassador:* Dr. MOHAMED ALI SHARMANI (also accred. to Turkey).

Spain: Ave. Shah-Abbas, rue Varahram No. 14; *Ambassador:* AURELIO VALLS (also accred. to Afghanistan).

Sri Lanka: Islamabad, Pakistan.

Sudan: Ave. Park, rue 16, No. 5; *Ambassador:* ALI ABDEL RAHMAN NIMERY (also accred. to Turkey).

Sweden: Takhte Jamshid Ave., Forsat Ave.; *Ambassador:* KAY SUNDBERG (also accred. to Afghanistan).

Switzerland: Pasteur Ave.; *Ambassador:* ERIK LANG (also accred. to Afghanistan).

Syria: Ave. Muhammad Reza Shah, Ave. 34, No. 9; *Ambassador:* (vacant).

Thailand: Baharestan Ave., No. 4; *Ambassador:* LUCKIE WASIKSIRI.

Trinidad and Tobago: Beirut, Lebanon.

Tunisia: Abbas Abad, Ave. Park No. 113; *Ambassador:* ABDELAZIZ HAMZAOUI.

Turkey: Ferdowsi Ave. No. 314; *Ambassador:* TURGUT TULUMEN.

U.S.S.R.: Churchill Ave.; *Ambassador:* VLADIMIR VINOGRADOV.

United Arab Emirates: Ave. Zafar, No. 355–7; *Ambassador:* ISSA KHALPHAN AL-HUREYMIL.

United Kingdom: Ferdowsi Ave.; *Ambassador:* Sir JOHN GRAHAM, K.C.M.G.

U.S.A.: Takhte Jamshid Ave., Roosevelt Ave.; *Ambassador:* WILLIAM H. SULLIVAN.

Vatican: France Ave. 97 (Apostolic Internunciature): *Ambassador:* Mgr. ANNIBALE BUGNINI.

Venezuela: Ave. Bucharest, 9th St., No. 31; *Ambassador:* AGUSTÍN ANTONIO BERZARES MORALES.

Viet-Nam: Federal Republic of Germany.

Yemen Arab Republic: Ave. Bukharest, rue 6, No. 23; *Ambassador:* AHMED MOHAMED AL-SHEGNI.

Yugoslavia: Ave. Arak, rue Shahrivar; *Ambassador:* (vacant).

Zaire: Ave. Bucharest, 10th St., No. 37; *Ambassador:* ANGAMA KUSSU.

Zambia: Cairo, Egypt.

Iran also has diplomatic relations with Barbados, Grenada, Libya, Maldives, Mozambique, Seychelles, Sierra Leone and Uruguay.

JUDICIAL SYSTEM

SUPREME COURT

A new Supreme Court was appointed in March 1979.

Judges: Mehdi Sajjadiyan, Fatollah Banisadr, Dr. Hassan Faqih Nakhjiri, Nur Shams Shahshahani, Sheikh Hossein Tabatabai.

Prosecutor-General: Mehdi Hadavi.

ISLAMIC REVOLUTIONARY COURTS

These were in operation after the revolution and by June 1979 more than 250 persons had been tried and executed. A regular judicial system is outlined in the draft constitution (Articles 126-140) published in mid-June 1979.

RELIGION

According to the draft constitution the official religion is Islam and the Ja'fari Sect (Shi'ite), but other Islamic sects including Zeydi, Hanafi, Maleki, Shafe'i and Hanbali will be valid and respected. Zoroastrians, Jews and Christians will be recognized as official religious minorities.

MUSLIMS

The great majority of the Iranian people are Shi'i Muslims, but there is a minority of Sunni Muslims.

During 1978 there was a revival of the influence of the *Ayatollahs* (or senior Shi'ite divines). It appeared to be the general wish of the Iranian people that a return to a closer observance of the tenets of Islam was necessary. Ayatollah Ruhollah Khomeini of Qom, who had been exiled to Iraq in 1964 and moved to near Paris in October 1978, conducted a campaign of opposition to the Shah, returning to Iran in February 1979 and bringing about the downfall of the Shah's regime. Other important Ayatollahs include Ayatollah Talleganji of Teheran and the Ayatollahs Shariatmadari, Marashi-Najani and Golpayegani of Qom.

ZOROASTRIANS

There are about 20,000 Zoroastrians, a remnant of a once widespread sect. Their religious leader is Moubad.

OTHER COMMUNITIES

Communities of Armenians, and somewhat smaller numbers of Jews, Assyrians, Greek Orthodox, Uniates and Latin Christians are also found as officially recognized faiths. The Baha'i faith, which originated in Iran, has about 60,000 adherents.

Baha'i faith: Shirkat-i-Nawnahalan, Manuchehri Avenue, Teheran; 1,854 centres, 1 school.

Roman Catholic (Chaldean) Archbishop of Teheran: Ave. Forsat 91, Teheran; Most Rev. Youhannan Semaan Issayi; 28,395 Catholics (1976).

Anglican Bishop in Iran and President-Bishop, Episcopal Church in Jerusalem and the Middle East: Rt. Rev. Hassan Barnaba Dehqani-Tafti, Bishop's House, P.O.B. 12, Isfahan; Diocese founded 1912.

Synod of the Evangelical (Presbyterian) Church in Iran: Assyrian Evangelical Church, Khiaban-i Shapur, Khiaban-i Aramanch, Teheran; Moderator Rev. Adle Nakhosteen.

THE PRESS

Teheran dominates the press scene as many of the daily papers are published there and the bi-weekly, weekly and less frequent publications in the provinces generally depend on the major metropolitan dailies as a source of news. In the city are published some 10 daily and 6 weekly newspapers, and 18 weekly and 29 monthly magazines. There are at least 19 registered provincial papers.

With the exception of a small number of political organs and official publications, all newspapers are owned by private individuals, but *Kayhan* was taken over by an Islamic Committee in May 1979. A draft press law which appeared in June 1979, prescribes up to three years' imprisonment for insulting religious and revolutionary leaders, Cabinet Ministers or people's representatives.

PRINCIPAL DAILIES

Alik: Naderi Ave., Teheran; f. 1931; morning; political and literary; Armenian; Propr. Dr. R. Stepanian; circ. 20,000.

Andesha: P.O.B. 77, Kirman.

Ayandegan: 322 Shah Ave., Guiti Sq., Teheran; f. 1967; morning; political, social, economic; Man. Dir. and Editor (vacant); circ. 75,000; suspended publication May 1979.

Bahari: Khayaban Khayam, Shiraz.

Bamead: Teheran; f. 1979.

Bourse: Kh. Sevom Esfand No. 80, Teheran; f. 1961; financial; Propr. and Dir. Dr. Y. Rahmati.

Ettela'at: Khayyam Ave., Teheran; f. 1925; evening; political and literary; Editor H. Baniahmad; circ. 220,000.

Le Journal de Téhéran: Khayyam Ave., Teheran; f. 1935; morning; French; Editor Hossein Baniahmad; circ. 15,000; ceased publication March 1979.

Kayhan: Ferdowsi Ave., Teheran; f. 1941; evening; political; taken over by Islamic Committee May 1979; Chief Editor Asadollah Mobasheri; circ. 350,000.

Kayhan International: Ferdowsi Ave., Kuche Atabak, Teheran; f. 1964; morning; English; political; Editor Kazem Zarnegar; circ. 40,000; ceased publication March 1979.

Khorassan: Meshed; Head Office: Khorassan Daily Newspapers, 14 Zohre St., Roosevelt St., Teheran; f. 1948; Propr. Muhammad Sadegh Tehranian; circ. 40,000.

Peyghame Emrouz: Sevom Esfand Ave., Azizkhan Sq., Teheran; f. 1959; evening; political and social; Propr. and Dir. (vacant); circ. 25,000.

Rahnejat: Darvazeh Dowlat, Isfahan; political and social; Propr. N. Rahnejat.

Tehran Journal: Khayyam Ave., Teheran; f. 1954; morning; English; Editor Hossein Baniahmad; circ. 30,000; ceased publication March 1979.

Teheran Times: Teheran; f. 1979; pro-Islamic Revolutionary Government, English.

PRINCIPAL PERIODICALS

Akhbare Pezeshki: 86 Shahabbas Ave., Teheran; weekly; medical; Prop. Dr. T. Foruzin.

Al-Akha: Khayyam Ave., Tehran; f. 1960; Arabic; weekly; Dir. Sen. Abas Massoudi; Editor Nazir Fenza.

Armaghan: Baghe Saba, Salim Street, Teheran; literature; Prop. M. Vahid-Dastgerdi.

Around Iran: published by The Echo of Iran, Hafiz Ave., Teheran; English; tourist; Man. Editor J. Behrouz.

Ashur: Takhte-Tavous Ave., Teheran; Assyrian; Propr. Dr. V. Bitmansur.

Auditor: Q. 77, Khayaban Firdowsi North, Teheran; financial and managerial studies.

Caricature: Sevom Esfand Ave., Teheran; weekly; critical, political, humour; Propr. and Dir. Mohsen Davallo.

Cinemaha: M. Khayaban Takhte-Jamshid, Teheran.

Daneshkade Pezeshki: Faculty of Medicine, Teheran University; medical magazine; monthly; Editor Dr. Davood Kazemi.

Daneshmand: Baharestan St., Teheran 11; Scientific and Technical magazine; monthly; Editor Dr. N. Shifteh.

Die Post: Baghe Saba Ave., Danesh St. No. 1/1; German; weekly; Propr. and Dir. Mansur Nodushani.

Dokhtaran and Pesaran: Khayyam Ave., Teheran; f. 1947; weekly teenage magazine; Editor Nader Akhavan Haydari.

Donaye Varzesh: Khayaam Ave., Ettala'at Bldg., Teheran; sport; Prop. M. Farzanah.

Ettela'at Banovan: Khayyam Ave., Teheran; women's weekly magazine; Editor Mrs. Pari Abasalti; circ. 85,000.

Ettela'at Haftegi: Akhavan Ave., Teheran; weekly; Editor Rasoul Anvani Kermani; circ. approx. 200,000.

Ettela'at Javanan: Khayyam Ave., Teheran; f. 1958; youth weekly; Editor R. Ettemadi.

Farhang-e-Iran Zamin: Shiraz Ave., Ku Sepid, P.O.B. 1021, Teheran; literature; Prop. Iraqi Afshar.

Faza: Shareza Ave., Teheran; aviation; Prop. H. Kamali-Taqari.

Ferdowsi: Bahar Ave., Teheran; weekly; Editor N. Jahanbanoie; circ. 26,000.

Film-Va-Honar: Roosevelt Ave., Teheran; weekly; Editor A. Ramazani.

Honar va Memar: Shahreza Ave. No. 256, Teheran; scientific and professional monthly; Propr. A. H. Echragh.

Hoquqe Mardom: Villa Ave., 46 Damghan Street, Teheran; judicial; Prop. J. Mansurian.

Iran Economic Service: Hafiz Ave., 4 Kucheh Hurtab; P.O.B. 2008, Teheran; weekly, economic.

Iran Political Digest: Echo Bldg., Hafiz Ave., P.O.B. 2008; English; weekly; Editor J. Behrouz.

Iran Trade and Industry: Echo of Iran, P.O.B. 2008, Hafiz Ave., Teheran; f. 1965; monthly economic periodical; English; Editor J. Behrouz; circ. 16,500.

Jam: Shah Ave., Sabuhi Bldg., P.O.B. 1871, Teheran; arts; Prop. A. Vakili.

Jame'e Dandan-Pezeshkan: 85 Hafez Ave., Teheran; medical; Prop. Dr. M. Hashemi.

Javanane Rastakhiz: Vesale Shirazi Ave., Bozorgmehr Square, Teheran; youth organ of Rastakhiz party; Editor Dr. Muhammad Ali Zarnegar.

Kayhan Bacheha (*Children's World*): Kh. Ferdowsi, Teheran; weekly; Editor Djaafar Badii; circ. 150,000.

Kayhan Varzeshi (*World of Sport*): Kh. Ferdowsi, Teheran; weekly; Dir. Mahmad Monseti; circ. 125,000.

Khandaniha:: Kh. Ferdowsi, Teheran; f. 1939; weekly; Propr. and Dir. A. A. Amirani; circ. 30,000.

Khorak: 24 Esfand Square, Teheran; health and food; Prop. Dr. M. Olumi.

Maktabe Mam: Shah-Abbas-Kabir Ave., Ku Ziba No. 29, Teheran; education; Prop. Mrs. A. A. Assaf.

Massaele Jahan: Anatole France Ave. 48, Teheran; research, social scientific monthly; Propr. and Dir. Mahmoud Tolower.

Music Iran: 1029 Amiriye Ave., Teheran; f. 1951; monthly; Editor Bahman Hirbod; circ. 7,000.

Navaye-Khorasan: Meshed; political; weekly; Prop. H. Mahbodi.

Neda-e-Nationalist: W. Khayaban Hafiz (Khayaban Rish Kutcha Bostan), P.O.B. 1999, Teheran.

Negin: Mirdamad Ave., Adl St. 52, Teheran; scientific and literary monthly; Propr. and Dir. M. Enayat.

Pars: Shiraz, twice weekly; Propr. and Dir. L. Shanghi; circ. 10,000.

Pezhuhshgar: Mirdamad Ave., Teheran; scientific; Prop. Dr. R. Olumi.

Rangin-Kamin Now: W. Khayaban Shah Crossing Culistan, Teheran.

Salamate Fekr: M.22, Kharg St., Teheran.

Sepahan: Baharestan Square, Teheran; literary; weekly.

Sepid va Siyah: Kh. Ferdowsi; popular monthly; Editor Dr. A. Behzadi; circ. 30,000.

Setaraye Cinema: 91 Iranshahr Ave., Teheran; cinema; Prop. P. Galustian.

Setareye Esfahan: Isfahan; political; weekly; Prop. A. Mihankhah.

Sobhe Emroug: Ferdowsi Ave., Teheran; Editor Mrs. Amidi Nuri.

Sokhan: Hafiz Ave., Zomorrod Passage, Teheran; f. 1943; Khanlari; literary and art monthly; Propr. Parviz Nahel.

Sport: P.O.B. 342, Ebne Sina St., Park Aminodoleh, Kakhe Markazi Taj, Teheran; sports, weekly.

Taj Magazine: Sepah Ave., Teheran; sport; Chair. Parviz Khosravani.

Taj-e-Varzeshi: Park Amiliod- dowleb., Teheran; sport; weekly; Prop. Gen. P. Khusravni.

Tamasha: Ave. Takhte Tavoos, Roosevelt Square, Teheran; weekly; radio and TV.

Tarikhe Eslam: Amiriyeh 94 Ku, Ansari, Teheran; religious; Prop. A. A. Tashayyod.

Tebb-O-Daru: 545 Shahreza Ave., Teheran; medical; Prop. Dr. N. Darvish.

Tehran Economist: 99 Sevom Esfand Ave., Teheran 11; f. 1953; Persian and English; weekly; Editor Dr. Bagher Shariat; circ. 15,500 Persian, 5,600 English.

Teheran Mossavar: Lalezar Ave., Teheran; political and social weekly; Editor and Publisher Abdullah Vala; circ. 120,000.

Vahid: 55 Shah Ave., Jam St., Teheran; literature; weekly; Prop. Dr. S. VAHIDNIA.

Yaghma: 15 Khanequah Ave., Teheran; literature; Prop. H. YAHMA'I.

Zan e Ruz (*Today's Woman*): Kh. Ferdowsi, Teheran; women's weekly; Editor MAJID DAVAMI; circ. 200,000.

NEWS AGENCIES

Pars News Agency (PANA): 873 Mirdamad Ave., P.O.B. 764, Teheran; f. 1936; Man. Dir. MUHAMMAD REZA SHARIF.

FOREIGN BUREAUX

Agence France-Presse (AFP): P.O.B. 1535, Teheran; Correspondent JEAN RAFAELLI.

Agenzia Nazionale Stampa Associata (ANSA) (*Italy*): North Keradmand, 8th St., Teheran; Chief ANTONELLA TARQUINI.

Associated Press (AP) (*U.S.A.*): 5 Fifth St., Park Ave., Abbas-Abad, Teheran; Correspondent PARVIZ RAEIN.

Deutsche Presse-Agentur (dpa) (*Federal Republic of Germany*): Tadayon/Koui Dehghan 11, Darrous, Teheran; Correspondent GERD RAINER NEU.

Reuters (*U.K.*): P.O.B. 1607, Teheran; Correspondent and Man. ALI MEHRAVARI, M.B.E.

Telegrafnoye Agentstvo Sovietskovo Soyuza (TASS) (*U.S.S.R.*): Kehyaban Hamid, Kouche Masoud 73, Teheran; Correspondent VLADIMIR DIBROVA.

United Press International (UPI) (*U.S.A.*): 11 Iranyad St., Malek Ave., Old Shemiran Rd., Teheran 15.

PUBLISHERS

Ali Akbar Elmi: Shahabad Ave., Teheran; Dir. ALI AKBAR ELMI.

Amir Kabir: 28 Vessal Shirazi St., Teheran; f. 1950; historical, social, literary and children's books; Dir. ABDULRAHIM JAFARI.

Boroukhim: Avenue Ferdowsi, Teheran; dictionaries.

Bungah Tarjomeh va Nashr Ketah: Teheran; affiliated to the Pahlavi foundation.

Danesh: 357 Ave. Nasser Khosrow, Teheran; f. 1931 in India, transferred to Iran in 1937; literary and historical (Persian); imports and exports books; Man. Dir. NOOROUAH IRANPARAST.

Ebn-e-Sina: Meydane 25 Shahrivar, Teheran; f. 1957; educational publishers and booksellers; Dir. EBRAHIM RAMAZANI.

Eghbal Publishing Co.: Shahabad Ave., Teheran; Dir. DJAVAD EGHBAL.

Franklin Book Programs Inc.: 2 Alborz Ave., Shahreza Ave., Teheran; f. 1952; a non-profit organization for International Book Publishing Development; main office in New York; Dir. ALI ASGHAR MOHAJER.

Ibn-Sina: Shahabad St., Teheran.

Iran Chap Company: Ave. Khayyam, Teheran; f. 1966; newspapers, books, magazines, colour printing and engraving; Man. Dir. FARHAD MASSOUDI.

Kanoon Marefat: 6 Ave. Lalehzar, Teheran; Dir. HASSAN MAREFAT.

Khayyam: Shahabad Avenue, Teheran; Dir. MOHAMMAD ALI TARAGHI.

Majlis Press: Avenue Baharistan, Teheran.

Pirouz: Shahabad Avenue; Dir. MIRMOHAMMADI.

Safiali Shah: Baharistan Square; Dir. MANSOUR MOSHFEGH.

Taban Press: Ave. Nassir Khosrow, Teheran; f. 1939; Propr. A. MALEKI.

Teheran Economist: Sevom Esfand Ave. 99, Teheran-11.

Teheran University Press: Avenue Shah-Reza.

Towfigh: Istanbul Ave., Teheran; publishes humorous Almanac and pocket books; distributes humorous and satirical books; Dir. Dr. FARIDEH TOWFIGH.

Zawar: Shahabad Avenue; Dir. AKBAR ZAWAR.

RADIO AND TELEVISION

Network of the Islamic Revolution: P.O.B. 33-200, Teheran; semi-autonomous governmental authority; f. 1971 by merger of Radio Iran and National Iranian Television; re-named 1979; 5,000 employees.

Radio (Voice of the Revolution): covers entire area of Iran; in addition the Voice of the Revolution reaches half Europe and the whole of Asia and Africa; medium-wave and short-wave regional broadcasts in local languages and dialects; foreign broadcasts in English, French, Arabic, Russian, Armenian, Pashtu, Kurdish, Urdu, Turcoman and Baluchi; 44 transmitters; Dir.-Gen. SADEGH GHOTBZADEH.

Number of radio receivers: 5 million (1975).

Television: production centres in Teheran (2), Abadan, Bandar Abbas, Isfahan, Kerman, Kermanshah, Mahabad, Meshed, Rasht, Rezaieh, Sanandaj, Sari, Shiraz, Tabriz, Yazd, Zahedan, Latian Dam; 287 relay stations; black and white at present, with some programmes transmitted in colour.

Number of TV receivers: 2.5 million (1976).

International Radio and Television: broadcasts mainly in English; news bulletins in English, German, French, Russian.

FINANCE

BANKING

At the time of the revolution in early 1979 22 of the 37 banks in Iran were privately-owned, while 10 were under government control and five were quasi-public. In early June 1979 the government announced that the private banks were to be nationalized.

(cap. = capital; p.u. = paid up; dep. = deposits; m. = million; amounts in rials)

CENTRAL BANK

Bank Markazi Iran: Ferdowsi Ave., Teheran; f. 1960; central note-issuing bank of Iran, government banking; cap. 25,000m.; dep. 1,019,600m. (March 1978); Gov. Dr. MOHAMMED ALI MOWLAVI.

COMMERCIAL BANKS

Agricultural Development Bank of Iran: Farahzad Expressway Valiahd Street, Teheran; f. 1968; cap. 14m. (March 1977); Pres. MEHDI SAMII.

Azarbayjan Development Bank: Tabriz; formerly Bank Gosstaresh Azarbayjan; f. 1975; cap. p.u. 750m.; Chair. MORTEZA RAHIMZADIKHOYI; Pres. ABBAS ZAREH.

Bank Bazargani Iran: Maidan Sepah, P.O.B. 2258, Teheran; f. 1949; cap. p.u. 3,500m.; dep. 76,973m. (March 1978); 382 brs.; Chair. Dr. DJAVAD SADR; Man. Dir. Senator MOSTAFA TADJADOD.

Bank Bimeh Iran (*Iran Insurance Bank*): 420 N. Saadi Ave., Teheran 11; f. 1958; under auspices of government-sponsored Sherkate Sahami Bimeh Iran (Insurance Company of Iran); cap. p.u. 900m.; 22 brs. and sub-brs. in Teheran, 21 brs. in other towns; Chair. and Man. Dir. MOHAMMED REZA TEHERANI.

Bank Binolmelali Iran: Avenue Mirdamad Dameshgh St., No. 4, P.O.B. 41–1852, Teheran; f. 1957; in association with Chase Manhattan Bank N.A. New York; cap. p.u. 2,000m. (1976); Pres. ROSTAM PIRASTEH.

Bank Dariush: Karim Khan Zand Ave., Teheran; Chair. JAFAR AKHAVAN; Man. Dir. AHMAD ASKARI YAZDI.

Banque Etebarate Iran (*Iran Credit Bank*): 50 Ave. Sevom Esfand, Teheran; f. 1958; cap. p.u. 2,000m., dep. 23,020m. (March 1977); 87 brs.; Chair. MUHAMMAD ABOO NASR AZOD; Man. FEREIDUN MEIKADEH.

Bank Etebarat Sanati (*Industrial Credit Bank*): Khiaban Ateshkadeh, Teheran; f. 1956; stock owned by the Government; cap. p.u. 8,775m.; total assets 130,094m. (March 1978); Man. Dir. MUHAMMAD HOSSEIN MESHKINI.

Bank Gosstaresh Khazer: Rasht; f. 1975; cap. p.u. 1,000m.; Chair. ABOL-HASSAN BEHNIA; Exec. Man. ALI AKBAR NAJAFI.

Bank Iran-Arab: Avenue Soria No. 248, Teheran; f. 1975; cap. p.u. 1,000m.; Chair. and Pres. CYRUS SAMII.

Bank Iranshahr: 955 Pahlavi Avenue, Teheran; formerly Bank Assnaf Iran; f. 1958, change of name, capital and management 1975; cap. p.u. 3,000m. (1976); 281 brs.; Chair. A. GHASSEM KHERADJOO; Man. Dir. Dr. SOLEIMAN AGHAI.

Bank Kar: Ave. Hafez, Teheran; f. 1958; cap. 5,170m., dep. 21,201m. (March 1978); Chair. SAID HEDAYAT; Man. Dir. SHAHIN BARKHORDARIAN.

Bank Melli Iran (*The National Bank of Iran*): Ferdowsi Ave., Teheran; state-owned bank; f. 1928; cap. and res. 32,098m.; dep. 822,535m.; total assets 1,106,996m. (July 1978); over 1,760 brs. throughout Iran, 16 brs. abroad; Pres. JALIL SHORAKA.

Bank of Iran and the Middle East: Kucheh Berlin, Ave. Ferdowsi, P.O.B. 1680, Teheran; f. 1959; 19 brs.; The British Bank of the Middle East owns 35 per cent of the issued capital; 65 per cent is held by Iranian interests; cap. p.u. 2,000m., dep. 13,593m.; Chair. M. T. BARKHORDAR; Dir. and Adviser K. V. R. JEFFERIES; Gen. Man. M. H. VAKILY.

Bank of Teheran: P.O.B. 184, 211 Mirdamad Ave., Teheran; f. 1952; cap. p.u. 6,000m.; dep. 153,240m. (March 1978); Pres. MOSTAFA FATEH; Man. Dir. ALI AFGHANI.

Bank Omran: 101 Istanbul Ave., Teheran; f. 1952; cap; p.u. 3,000m.; dep. 60,000m. (March 1977); 273 brs.; Chair. and Man. Dir. HOUSHANG RAM; Vice-Chair. and Deputy Man. Dir. A. MIRMOTAHARI.

Bank Pars: Pars Building, 193 Avenue Takhte Jamshid, Teheran; f. 1953; cap. p.u. 1,750m. (March 1978); 215 brs.; Chair. E. NIKPOUR; Pres. Dr. M. R. ETMINAN.

Bank Rahni Iran (*The Mortgage Bank of Iran*): Ferdowsi St., Teheran; f. 1939; Government bank (affiliate of Ministry of Development and Housing) which grants loans for building houses; cap. p.u. 7,362m., total assets 71,269m. (Aug. 1976); Chair. and Man. Dir. M. AHARI.

Bank Refah Kargaran (*Workers' Welfare Bank*): 125 Roosevelt Ave., Teheran; f. 1960; cap. p.u. 10,000m.; 83 brs.; state-owned bank; Chair. MUHAMMAD MAJIDI.

Bank Russo-Iran: Behestij Ave., Teheran; cap. p.u. 1,250m.; branch in Isfahan.

Bank Saderat Iran (*The Export Bank of Iran*): 124 Ave. Shah, P.O.B. 2751, Teheran; f. 1952; cap. p.u. 18,000m.; dep. 420,091m. (March 1978); 3,000 brs. in Iran, brs. throughout Middle East and Europe; Chair. Eng. M. A. MOFARAH; Man. Dir. HABIB AKHAVEN.

Bank Sakhteman: 164 Blvd. Elizabeth II, Teheran; Chair. FATHOLLAH SOUTADEH; Man. Dir. A. RADPAY.

Bank Sanaye Iran: 106 Sepahbod Zahedi Ave., Teheran; cap. p.u. 7,000m., dep. 29,106m. (March 1977).

Bank Sepah (*Army Bank*): Ave. Sepah, Teheran; f. 1925; cap. p.u. 8,000m.; dep. 313,378m. (June 1978); 650 brs.; Chair. Gen. ALI ASGHAR MASUDI.

Bank Shahryar: 1/99 Sepahbod Zahedi Ave., Teheran; cap. p.u. 3,750m.; Chair. ALI REZAI; Man. Dir. Dr. AZAT ALI MOMTAZ.

Bank Taavon Keshavarzi Iran (*Agricultural Cooperative Bank of Iran*): Khiaban Park Shahr (North), Teheran; f. 1933; cap. p.u. 38,300m. (Aug. 1976); government bank; Pres. HASSAN EMAMI KHOIE.

Bank Tosee Keshavarzi Iran: 23 Takhte Jamshid Ave., Teheran; Chair. H. A. MEHRAN; Man. Dir. MEHDI SAMII.

Bank Tosee Na Sarmayehgozani Iran: 16 Naser St., Teheran; Chair. and Man. Dir. G. MOGHADAM.

Distributors' Co-operative Credit Bank: 37 Ave. Ferdowsi, Teheran; f. 1963; cap. 1,000m., dep. 13,761m. (1976); Chair. and Pres. ASSADOLLAH RASHIDIAN.

Foreign Trade Bank of Iran (*Bank Tedjarat Kharedji Iran*): Avenue Saadi, Teheran; f. 1960; jointly owned by Bank Melli Iran, Bank of America, Banca Comerciale Italiana and Deutsche Bank A.G.; cap. p.u. 1,050m., dep. 13,388m. (Aug. 1976); Chair. YOUSSEF KHOSHKISH; Man. Dir. ASHOT SAGHATELIAN.

Industrial and Mining Development Bank of Iran (IMDBI): 593 Hafez Ave., P.O.B. 1801, Teheran; f. 1959; 84.7 per cent of shares held by more than 8,400 Iranian individuals and institutions, 15.3 per cent held by France, U.K., Netherlands, Italy, Japan, U.S.A. and Federal Germany; to develop, encourage and stimulate private industrial, mining and transportation enterprises in Iran; cap. p.u. 12,000m., total assets 145,316m. (March 1977); Chair. SAEED HEDAYAT; Man. Dir. A. GASEM KHERADJOU.

International Bank of Iran and Japan: 57 Takhte Jamshid Ave., P.O.B. 1837, Teheran; f. 1959; cap. 3,000m. (Sept. 1978); 31.5 per cent Japanese owned; Chair. of Exec. Board GHASSEM LADJEVARDI; Pres. I. AZARM.

Iranians' Bank: 184 Takhte Jamshid Ave., Teheran; f. 1960, cap. 1,000m.; dep. 16,322m. (March 1978); associated with Citibank; Pres. ATA SALMANPOUR.

Irano-British Bank: Avenue Saadi, P.O.B. 1584, Teheran; f. 1959; associated with the Standard and Chartered Bank Ltd., London; 21 brs.; cap. p.u. 1,000m.; Chair. and Man. Dir. A. G. NEYSARI.

Mercantile Bank of Iran and Holland: Ave. Saadi, P.O.B. 1522, Teheran; f. 1959; affiliated with Algemene Bank Nederland N.V., Amsterdam; cap. p.u. 2,500m., dep. 25,437m.; 23 brs. in Teheran, 23 other brs.; Chair. SOLEYMAN VAHABZADEH; Man. Dir. AHMAD VAHABZADEH; Resident Dir. A. VAN DE WINT.

FOREIGN BANKS

More than 40 foreign banks have representative offices in Teheran, including: Bank of America N.T. & S.A., Bank of Tokyo, Banque de Bruxelles, Banque de Paris et des Pays-Bas, Barclays, Bayerische Vereinsbank, Berliner Bank, Chase Manhattan Overseas Corporation, Commerzbank, Deutsch Bank, Dresdner Bank, Grindlays Bank, Lloyds Bank International, Midland Bank International, Vereinsbank in Hamburg.

Association of Iranian Banks: 21 Jabarzadegan St., Takht-e-Tavous Ave., Teheran; Man. Dir. H. EMAMI; Dep. Man. Dir. Dr. A. KARIMI.

STOCK EXCHANGE

Teheran Stock Exchange: Taghinia Bldg., Saadi Ave., Teheran; f. 1968; Chair. of Council H. A. MEHRAN; publs. *Monthly Bulletin* and *Annual Report*.

INSURANCE

(The nationalization of insurance companies, was announced on June 25th, 1979).

Bimeh Iran (*Iran Insurance and Reinsurance Co.*): Avenue Saadi, Teheran; f. 1935; state-owned insurance company; all types of insurance; cap. p.u. 3,500m.; Man. Dir. MUHAMMAD BAGHER TAJBAKHSH.

Bimeh Markazi Iran (*Central Insurance Co.*): 149 Takhte Jamshid Ave., Teheran; Pres. HADI HEDAYATI.

Alborz Insurance Co. Ltd.: Alborz Bldg., 234 Sepahbod Zahedi Ave., Teheran; f. 1959; most classes of insurance; Management Habibollah Nahai and Brothers.

Dana Insurance Co. Ltd.: P.O.B. 2868, Shah Reza Avenue, Teheran; in association with Commercial Union Assurance Co. Ltd.

Hafez Insurance Co.: Takhte Tavoos Ave., 44 Daraye Noor St., Teheran; f. 1974; most classes of insurance; Man. Dir. K. HELMI.

Iran-American International Insurance Co.: Ave. Zohre, Teheran.

Pars, Société Anonyme d'Assurances: Avenue Saadi, Teheran; f. 1955; fire, marine, motor vehicle, third party liability, personal accident group life, contractor's all-risk and medical insurance; Gen. Man. MANOUCHEHR KASHANIAN; Tech. Man. PARIZ MELIK VARTANIAN.

Shirkat-i-Sahami Bimeh Dan: 315 Shah Reza, Teheran; f. 1974; cap. 500m.; joint venture between Iranian interests and Commercial Union Insurance Co., London; Man. Dir. MANSOOR AKHWAN.

Shirkat Sahami Bimeh Arya (*Arya Insurance Co. Ltd.*): 202 Soraya Ave., Teheran; f. 1952; cap. 1,000m.; Chair. ASSADOLLAH RASHIDIAN; Man. Dir. NOUREDDIN HEKMATI.

Shirkat Sahami Bimeh Asia (*Asia Insurance Co. Ltd.*): Sepahbod Zahedi-Takht Jamshid Ave., Teheran; f. 1960; Man.-Dir. ABBAS SAIRFI.

Shirkat Sahami Bimeh Iran and America: 8 Apartments Kavah, 20 Mitu Zohra Roovelt Ave.; f. 1974; cap. 1,000m.; Man. Dir. KHOSROW SHABAI.

Shirkat Sahami Bimeh Omid: Boulevard Karimkhan Zand, Ave. Kheradniand Jonoubi 99, Teheran; f. 1960.

Shirkat Sahami Bimeh Sharq: North Saadi Ave., Teheran; f. 1950; cap. 200m.; Man. Dir. ALI AUSAT SANJANI.

Shirkat Sahami Bimeh Teheran: 43 Khayaban Khushbin Villa, Teheran; f. 1974; cap. 500m.; Man. Dir. ERAJ ALI ABADI.

Shirkat Sahami Khass Bimeh Melli (*The National Insurance Co. Ltd.*): Takhte Jamshid Ave., Rasekh St., P.O.B. 1786, Teheran; f. 1956; all classes of insurance; Chair. (vacant); Man. Dir. Dr. JAHANGIR AMIR EBRAHIMI.

Shirkati Sahami Bimeh Sakhtiman Va Kar (*Construction and Labour*): Apartments Bank Kar, Khayaban-i-Hafiz; f. 1964; cap. 200m.; Man. Dir. SAMAD TAHERI.

All insurance companies are members of the Syndicate of Iranian Insurance Companies.

OIL

National Iranian Oil Company (NIOC): Takhte Jamshid Ave. (P.O.B. 1863), Teheran; A state organization controlling all petroleum, petrochemical and natural gas operations in Iran. In February 1979 it was announced that in future Iran would sell oil direct to the oil companies.

NIOC

The National Iranian Oil Company (NIOC) was incorporated April 1951 on nationalization of oil industry to engage in all phases of oil operations; auth. cap. 100,000 million rials, in 10,000 shares, 50 per cent paid up; all shares held by Iranian Government and are non-transferable; Chair. of Board and Gen. Man. Dir. Hasan Nazih; Directors: Ehsanollah Butorabi (Engineering), Abdolali Granmayeh (Refining), Ghobad Fakhimi (Distribution and Pipelines), Seyed Salah Banafti (Administration), Ezzatollah Shamida (Legal Affairs), Reza Azimi Hoseini (International Affairs), Manuchehr Parsa (Corporate Planning Affairs), Rahim Maarufion (Commercial Affairs), Jahangir Raufi (Oil Production).

Iran concluded five agreements for oil exploration and production in 1974. As a result of these agreements the following companies were formed in Iran, but their future became uncertain after the revolution in early 1979:

Deminex Iran Oil Company: Ave. North Kakh, No. 18, Teheran; Deminex of Germany holds two areas in Shiraz and Abadan respectively; Gen. Man. Dir. Dr. W. Reinecke.

Ultramar Iran Oil Company: No. 11-1, 5th Kouche, Ave. Gandy, Teheran; Ultramar (U.K.); Gen. Man. Dir. W. J. Sheptych.

AGIP Iran Petroleum Company: No. 60, Ave. North Farah, Teheran; AGIP (Italy); Gen. Man. Dir. G. C. Giuliani.

Lar Exploration Company: 5th Floor, Corner of Bozorgmehr, Ave. Kakh, Teheran; Ashland Group (Ashland, U.S.A.; Pan Canadian, Canada); Gen. Man. Dir. Mr. Ghadimi.

Other Oil Companies Active in Iran

Hormoz Petroleum Company (HOPECO): 216 Ave. Villa, IBM Building, Teheran; f. 1972; partnership—50 per cent NIOC, 25 per cent Mobil, 25 per cent Braspetro Internacional S.A.; Chair. A. B. Aghevli; Man. Dir. J. M. Roberts.

Iran Nippon Petroleum Company (INPECO): 130 Ave. Shah Abbas Kabir, Teheran; f. 1971; partnership—50 per cent NIOC, 50 per cent Japanese group; Man. Dir. Sh. Hikata.

Iran-Pan American Oil Co. (IPAC): 583 Hafez Ave., Soraya Cnr, Teheran; f. 1958; owned jointly by NIOC and Amoco Iran Oil Co.; to exploit Persian Gulf offshore deposits in their agreement area; Man. Dir. A. E. Piper.

Iranian Marine International Oil Company (IMINOCO): 128 Roodsar Ave., Teheran; f. 1965; formed with National Iranian Oil Co. on the one hand and Phillips Petroleum Co., AGIP (a subsidiary of the Italian ENI) and Hydrocarbons India Ltd. (a subsidiary of the Oil and Natural Gas Commission of India) on the other; operates off-shore fields near Lavan Island; Chair. R. Kalhor; Man. Dir. C. Trampini.

Lavan Petroleum Company (LAPCO): 3 Elizabeth II Boulevard, Teheran; f. 1965; formed with Atlantic Richfield, Murphy Oil Corporation, Sun Oil Co., and Union Oil Co. of California, who own 50 per cent interest, and the National Iranian Oil Co., who own the remaining 50 per cent; Man. Dir. N. E. Dietzel.

Phillips Petroleum Company Iran: P.O.B. 3184, Teheran; assumed operations of area previously operated by CONOCO under agreement signed with NIOC in April 1969 for exploration and development of a 5,000 sq. mile area in South Iran; owns one-sixth interest in IMINOCO; Vice-Pres. and Man. Dir. William B. Belknap.

Société Irano-Italienne des Pétroles (SIRIP): Ave. 25th Shahrivar no. 339, P.O.B. 1434, Teheran; f. 1957; owned jointly by NIOC and AGIPS.p.A.; Man. Dir. K. Mahdavi.

Sofiran: P.O.B. 3220, Teheran; NIOC General Contractor; Gen. Man. Dir. J. Alliot.

Wholly Owned Subsidiaries of NIOC

National Iranian Gas Company
National Petrochemical Company
National Iranian Tanker Company
Ahwaz Pipe Mills
Iran Oil Company
Iranian Oil Company (U.K.) Ltd.
Iranian International Oil Company (U.S.A.).
NIOC/DEN A/S (Greenland).

TRADE AND INDUSTRY

CHAMBERS OF COMMERCE

Iran Chamber of Commerce, Industries and Mines: 254 Ave. Takht-Jamshid, Teheran; f. 1970; supervises the affiliated 20 Chambers in the provinces; Pres. Sen. Dr. Taher Ziai.

R.C.D. Joint Chamber of Commerce: P.O.B. 3273, Teheran; f. 1965 with Pakistan and Turkey under auspices of Regional Co-operation for Development.

EMPLOYERS' ASSOCIATION

Association des Employeurs Industriels de l'Iran: Teheran.

LABOUR ORGANIZATIONS

All Trade Unions were dissolved in 1963, and syndicates of workers must be registered with the Government. In March 1963 there were 67 syndicates representing various trades, of which the largest included the *National Iranian Oil Company Workers' Syndicate* with 6,000 members.

Co-operatives

Central Organization for Rural Co-operatives of Iran (C.O.R.C.): Teheran; Man. Dir. Abdollah Javansheer.

Following the implementation of the Land Reform Act, the C.O.R.C. was established by the Government in 1963. The aim of the organization is to offer educational, technical and credit assistance to rural co-operative societies and their unions. The C.O.R.C. will gradually transfer its stocks to rural co-operative unions and become the national body for rural co-operatives. By the end of March 1978, after the consolidation programme, the number of rural Co-operative societies had been reduced to 2,925 with a total membership of 2,983,522 and share capital of 8,385,118,300 rials. There are 150 Co-operative Unions with capital of 366,534,500 rials. The number of member co-operative societies of the Unions is 2,907.

TRANSPORT

RAILWAYS

Iranian State Railway: Teheran; f. 1938; Pres. MUHAMMAD HUSSAIN BADI; Technical Vice-Pres. A. NAJAFIAN; Planning and Research Vice-Pres. H. CHOBINEH; Admin and Financial Vice Pres. A SHAHRESTANI.

The Iranian railway system includes the following main routes.

Trans-Iranian Railway runs 1,392 km. from Gorgan, in the north, through Teheran, and south to Bandar Shahpur on the Persian Gulf.

South Line links Teheran to Khorramshahr via Qom, Arak, Dorood, Andimeshk and Ahwaz; 937 km.

North Line links Teheran to Gorgan via Garmsar, Firooz Kooh and Sari; 499 km.

Teheran-Tabriz Line linking with the Azarbaizhan Railway; 736 km.

Garmsar-Meshed Line connects Teheran with Meshed via Semnan, Damghan, Shahrud and Nishabur; 812 km.

Qom-Zahedan Line when completed will be an intercontinental line linking Europe and Turkey, through Iran, with India. Zahedan is situated 91.7 km. west of the Baluchistan frontier, and is the end of the Pakistani broad gauge railway. The section at present links Qom to Kerman via Kashan, Sagsi, Yazd, Bafgh and Zarand; 926 km. A branch line from Sagsi was opened in 1971 via Isfahan to Aryamehr steel mill at Zarrinshahr; 112 km.

Ahwaz-Bandar Shahpur Line connects Bandar Shahpur with the Trans-Iranian railway at Ahwaz; 123 km.

Azarbaizhan Railway extends from Tabriz to Julfa (146.5 km.), meeting the Caucasian railways at the Soviet frontier. A line from Sharaf-Khaneh to the Turkish frontier at Razi was opened in 1971.

The total length of main lines is 4,604 km.

Underground Railway. An agreement was signed in March 1976 between the Municipality of Teheran and French contractors for the construction of a subway. Four lines are to be built with a total length of 143 km. Construction began during 1978, but it was announced in May 1979 that the whole project was under revision.

ROADS

Ministry of Roads: Ministry of Roads and Communications, Teheran.

In early 1979 there were 22,209 km. of paved roads, 20,819 km. of gravel roads and 6,672 km. of earth roads. There is a paved highway (A.1) from Bazargan on the Turkish border to the Afghanistan border. The A.2 highway runs from the Iraqi border to Mir Javeh on the Pakistan border. The A.2 highway is finished from Shurguz to Kerman (2,000 km.) and the remainder (300 km.) is under construction.

INLAND WATERWAYS

Principal waterways:

Lake Rezaiyeh (Lake Urmia) 50 miles west of Tabriz in North-West Iran; and River Kharun flowing south through the oilfields into the River Shatt al Arab, thence to the head of the Persian Gulf near Abadan.

Lake Rezaiyeh: From Sharafkhaneh to Golmankhaneh there is a twice-weekly service of tugs and barges for transport of passengers and goods.

River Karun: Regular cargo service is operated by the Mesopotamia-Iran Corpn. Ltd. Iranian firms also operate daily motor-boat services for passengers and goods.

SHIPPING

Persian Gulf: Principal ports are Khorramshahr, Bushire, Bandar Abbas, Bandar Shahpur. Oil exports from the Abadan refinery are handled by the Mahshahr installations and Kharg Island terminal in the Persian Gulf. Bushire is being developed to supplement the facilities at Khorramshahr, while the capacity of Bandar Abbas has recently been increased.

Caspian Sea: Principal port Bandar Pahlavi.

Arya National Shipping Lines: P.O.B. 353, Arya Building, 127 Shah Abbas Ave., Teheran; 32 vessels; liner services between the Persian Gulf and Europe; Man. Dir. F. R. MOASSER.

CIVIL AVIATION

The two main international airports are Mehrabad (Teheran) and Abadan.

Iran National Airlines Corporation (*Iran Air*): Iran Air Building Mehrabad Airport, Teheran; f. 1962; Man. Dir. GASSEM SHAKIBNIA; serves Persian Gulf area, Baghdad, Istanbul, Athens, Jeddah, Frankfurt, Geneva, London, Moscow, Paris, Rome, Vienna, Zürich, New York, Tokyo, Peking, Kabul, Karachi and Bombay; fleet of five Boeing 707, five Boeing 727-200, four Boeing 727-100, four Boeing 737, five F-27, two Boeing 747-200, three Boeing 747-SP.

Iran is also served by the following foreign lines: Aeroflot (U.S.S.R.), Air France, Air India, Alia (Jordan), Alitalia (Italy), Ariana Afghan Airlines, British Airways, ČSA (Czechoslovakia), Iraqi Airways, JAL (Japan), KLM (Netherlands), Kuwait Airways, Lufthansa (Federal Republic of Germany), MEA (Lebanon), PIA (Pakistan), Qantas (Australia), Sabena (Belgium), SAS (Sweden), Swissair, Syrian Arab Airlines.

TOURISM

Tourism has suffered considerably from the disturbances caused by the revolution.

Ministry of Higher Education and Culture: Teheran; f. 1964 to replace the Fine Arts Administration; 7 Under Secretaryships of State, including (i) Artistic Activities; (ii) Cultural Heritage; (iii) Cultural Relations with Foreign Countries; (iv) Cinematograph Activities; (v) Plans and Studies.

The following organizations come under the direction of the Ministry of Higher Education and Culture: National Library, Board of Trustees of Public Libraries, Centre for Cultural Studies and Co-ordination, Department of International Film Festivals, Rudaki Hall (Teheran Opera), Teheran Symphony Orchestra, Jeunesse Musicale of Iran, etc.

The following organizations are affiliated to the Ministry of Higher Education and Culture: Iranian Academy of Languages, Academy of Letters and Arts, High Council of Culture and Arts, National Organization for the Conservation of Ancient Monuments of Iran, National Society for Iranian Folklore, *Sahname* Foundation, Iranian Calligraphers' Association;

Schools: School of Dramatic Arts, School of Decorative Arts, Conservatory of Music, Conservatory of National Music, Ballet School, School of Local Dances, etc.

Shiraz-Persepolis Festival of Arts: Shiraz; c/o Festival of Arts, P.O.B. 33-200, Teheran; f. 1967; plays, dance, films and music, representing both Eastern and Western culture; held for a short fortnight at end of Aug. and beginning of Sept.; partly staged in the ruins at Persepolis; Pres. R. Ghotbi; publs. various books and brochures in Persian on music and drama, festival brochure annually.

ATOMIC ENERGY

Atomic Energy Organization of Iran: P.O.B. 12-1198, Teheran; f. 1973; set up to produce nuclear power to provide for the base load electricity needs of the country; to secure fuel needs of Iran's nuclear energy programme; to utilize nuclear energy in industry and medicine; to provide research and development work and training for greater national self-sufficiency in nuclear technology; Pres. Ahmed Sotudehnia.

Teheran University Nuclear Centre: Institute of Nuclear Science and Technology, P.O.B. 2989, Teheran; f. 1958; research in nuclear physics, electronics, nuclear chemistry, radiobiology and nuclear engineering; training and advice on nuclear science and the peaceful applications of atomic energy; a 5-MW pool-type research reactor on the new campus of Teheran University went critical in November 1967; a 3-MeV Van de Graaff-type accelerator became operational in 1972; Dir. Dr. J. Moghimi.

DEFENCE

Defence Budget: The revolutionary government plans to cut back considerably on defence expenditure.

Military service: 1 year.

Total armed forces: 413,000; army 285,000; navy 28,000; air force 100,000 (July 1978).

Chief of the Combined General Staff: Brig-Gen. Hossein Shaker.

Commander of Army: Brig.-Gen. Falahi.

Commander of Air Force: Brig. Asfar Ima'ian.

Commander of Navy: Admiral Madani.

Commander of Gendarmerie: Brig.-Gen. Elias Daneshvar.

EDUCATION

Primary and Secondary Education

When compulsory primary education was established by Reza Shah in the 1930s there were no more than 36,000 children attending school. In 1975/76 over six million children were attending many thousands of primary and secondary schools all over the country.

Primary education for five years is compulsory for all children and, along with a three years' guidance period, was declared free in 1974. An increasing number of children are now proceeding to secondary schools after obtaining their primary education certificate. It was reported in early 1979 that the government intended to abolish co-education.

Higher Education

Iran has 16 universities, including six in Teheran. There are several other institutes of higher education, four teachers' training colleges, a college of advanced technology in Abadan and colleges of agriculture in Karaj, Rezaiyah and Kerman. Vocational training schools also exist in Teheran, Shiraz, Tabriz, Rasht and other cities.

In recent years much emphasis has been put on improving higher education facilities as well as expanding research.

UNIVERSITIES

University of Azarabadegan: Tabriz; 566 teachers, 7,894 students.

Baluchistan University: Zahedan; 32 teachers, 206 students.

Bou Ali Sina University: Hamadan; 66 teachers, 206 students.

Farabi University: Teheran; 17 teachers, 38 students.

Farah Pahlavi University: Teheran; 173 teachers, 1,403 students.

University of Ferdowsi: Meshed; 546 teachers, 6,724 students.

Free University of Iran: Teheran; scheduled to open in 1978.

Gilan University: Rasht; 60 teachers, 450 students.

University of Isfahan: Isfahan; 472 teachers, 6,526 students.

Jundi-Shapur University: Ahwaz, Khouzestan Province; 402 teachers, 4,000 students.

University of Kerman: Kerman; 100 teachers, 1,000 students.

National University of Iran: Evin, Teheran; 654 teachers, 7,677 students.

Pahlavi University: Shiraz; 688 teachers, 4,338 students.

Reza Shah Kabir University: Mazandaran; postgraduate; 15 teachers; 12 students.

University of Teheran: Ave. Shah Reza, Teheran; 2,021 teachers, 17,958 students.

Arya Mehr University of Technology: Eisenhower Blvd., Teheran; 304 teachers, 3,080 students.

BIBLIOGRAPHY

GENERAL

ABDALIAN, S. Damavand (Iran) (Teheran, 1943).

BARTH, F. Nomads of South Persia (London, 1961).

CAMBRIDGE HISTORY OF IRAN.
Volume I: The Land of Iran.
Volume V: The Saljuq and Mongol Periods.
(Both Cambridge University Press, 1968).

CURZON, Lord. Persia and the Persian Question (2 vols., London, 1892).

DE PLANHOL, X. Recherches sur la Géographie humaine de l'Iran Septentrional (Paris, 1964).

ELWELL-SUTTON, L. P. Modern Iran (London, 1941).
A Guide to Iranian Area Study (Ann Arbor, 1952).
Persian Oil: A Study in Power Politics (London, 1955).

ENGLISH, P. W. City and Village in Iran (Wisconsin, 1967).

ESKELUND, KARL. Behind the Peacock Throne (Alvin Redman, New York, 1965).

FIELD, HENRY. Contributions to the Anthropology of Iran (Chicago, 1939).

FRYE, RICHARD N. Persia (Allen and Unwin, London, 3rd ed. 1969).

FURON, RAYMOND. L'Iran (Paris, 1952).
Géologie du Plateau iranien (Paris, 1941).
La Perse (Paris, 1938).

GAIL, MARZIEH. Persia and the Victorians (London, 1951).

GRAVES, PHILIP. The Life of Sir Percy Cox (1941).

GROSECLOSE, ELGIN. Introduction to Iran (New York, 1947).

HAAS, WILLIAM S. Iran (New York, 1946).

HUOT, JEAN LOUIS. Persia Vol. I (Muller, London, 1966).

IQBAL, MUHAMMAD. Iran (London, 1946).
Iran Almanac (Echo of Iran, Teheran, annually).
Iran: A Selected and Annotated Bibliography (Washington, 1951).

KEDDIE, NIKKI R. Historical Obstacles to Agrarian Change in Iran (Claremont, 1960).

KEMP, N. Abadan (London, 1954).

LAMBTON, A. K. S. Landlord and Peasant in Persia (New York, 1953).
Islamic Society in Persia (London, 1954).
A Persian Vocabulary (Cambridge, 1961).
The Persian Land Reform 1962-66 (Clarendon Press, Oxford, 1969).

MARLOWE, JOHN. Iran, a Short Political Guide (Pall Mall Press, London and New York, 1963).

MEHDEVI, A. S. Persian Adventure (New York, 1954).
Persia Revisited (London, 1965).

MILLSPAUGH, A. C. Americans in Persia (Washington, 1946).

MOTTER, T. H. VAIL. The Persian Corridor and Aid to Russia (Washington, 1952).

RAMAZANI, ROUHOLLAH K. The Persian Gulf: Iran's Role (Charlottesville, University Press of Virginia, 1972).

SANGHVI, RAMESH. Aryamehr: The Shah of Iran (Macmillan, London, 1968).

SHAH OF IRAN. Mission for My Country (Hutchinson, London 1961).

SHEARMAN, I. Land and People of Iran (London, 1962).

SIRDAR, IKBAL ALI SHAH. Persia of the Persians (London, 1929).

SMITH, A. Blind White Fish in Persia (New York, 1953).

STARK, FREYA. The Valleys of the Assassins (London, 1934).
East is West (London, 1945).

THARAUD, JÉRÔME. Vieille Perse et Jeune Iran (Paris, 1947).

VREELAND, H. H. Iran (Human Relations Area Files, 1957).

WARD, PHILIP. Touring Iran (Faber & Faber, London, 1971).

WICKENS, G. M. and SAVORY, R. M. Persia in Islamic Times, a practical bibliography of its history, culture and language (Institute of Islamic Studies, McGill University, Montreal, 1964).

WILBER, DONALD N. Iran: Past and Present (Princeton University Press, 1955, 8th edn. 1977).
Iran: Oasis of Stability in the Middle East (Foreign Political Association, Inc., New York, 1959).

ZABIH, SEPEHR. The Communist Movement in Iran (University of California Press 1967).

CIVILIZATION AND LITERATURE

ARBERRY, A. J. (ed.). The Legacy of Persia (London and New York, 1953).
Shiraz: The Persian City of Saints and Poets (Univ. of Oklahoma Press, 1960).
Tales from the Masnavi (London, 1961).
More Tales from the Masnavi (London, 1963).
(ed). The Cambridge History of Iran (Cambridge University Press 1969).

BAUSANI, A. Der Perser: von den Anfängen bis zur Gegenwart (Kohlhammer, Stuttgart, 1965).

BELL, GERTRUDE L. Persian Pictures (London, 1928).

BROWNE, E. G. A Literary History of Persia (4 vols., Cambridge, 1928).

COLLEDGE, M.A.R. The Parthians (Thames and Hudson, London, 1968).

CULICAN, WILLIAM. The Medes and the Persians (1965).

DUCHESNE-GUILLEMIN, JACQUES. The Hymns of Zarathustra (trans. with commentary) (Beacon, L. R., Boston, Mass., 1963).

GHIRSHMAN, R. L'Iran: des Origines à Islam (Paris, 1951).
Iran from the Earliest Times to the Islamic Conquest (London, 1954).
Arts of Ancient Persia from the Origins to Alexander the Great (London, 1963).
Iran (New York, 1964).

HERZFELD, E. Iran in the Ancient East (Oxford, 1941).

KAMSHAD, H. Modern Persian Prose Literature (Cambridge, 1966).

LEVY, REUBEN. The Persian Language (New York, 1952).
Persian Literature (1928).

LOCKHART, L. Famous Cities of Iran (London, 1939).
The Fall of the Safavi Dynasty and the Afghan Occupation of Persia (Cambridge University Press, 1958).

MONTEIL, V. Les Tribus du Fars et la sédentarisation des nomades (Mouton, Paris and The Hague, 1966).

OLMSTEAD, A. T. History of the Persian Empire, Achaemenid Period (Chicago, 1948).

POPE, ARTHUR. Survey of Persian Art from Prehistoric Times to the Present. Vols. 1–6 (Oxford University Press, 1938–58).

RICE, CYPRIAN. The Persian Sufis (Allen and Unwin, London, 1964).

ROSS, Sir DENISON. Eastern Art and Literature (London, 1928).
The Persians (London, 1931).

STOREY, C. A. Persian Literature (London, 1927).

SYKES, Sir PERCY. Persia (Oxford, 1922).
A History of Persia (2 vols.; 3rd edition, with supplementary essays) (London, 1930).

WIDENGREN. Die Religionen Irans (Kohlhammer, Stuttgart, 1965).

WULFF, H. E. The Traditional Crafts of Persia (M.I.T. Press, Cambridge, Mass., 1966).

RECENT HISTORY

BANANI, AMIN. The Modernization of Iran, 1921–1924 (Stanford, 1961).

BUNYA, ALI AKBAR. A Political and Diplomatic History of Persia (Teheran, 1955).

CHUBIN, SHARAM and ZABIH, SEPEHR. The Foreign Relations of Iran: A Developing State in the Zone of a Great-Power Conflict (University of California Press, 1975).

COTTAM, R. W. Nationalism in Iran (Pittsburgh University Press, 1964).

FATEMI, NASROLLAH S. Diplomatic History of Persia 1917–1923 (New York, 1952).

HALLIDAY, FRED. Iran: Dictatorship and Development (London, 1978).

HAMZAVI, A. H. K. Persia and the Powers: An Account of Diplomatic Relations, 1941–46 (London, 1946).

ISSAWI, CHARLES. The Economic History of Iran, 1800–1919 (University of Chicago Press, 1972).

LAING, MARGARET. The Shah (Sidgwick & Jackson, London, 1977).

LENCZOWSKI, GEORGE. Russia and the West in Iran (Cornell Univ. Press, 1949).

LENCZOWSCI, G. (Ed.). Iran under the Pahlavis (Stanford: Hoover Institution Press, 1978).

NAKHAI, M. L'Evolution Politique de l'Iran (Brussels, 1938).

RAMAZANI, ROUHOLLAH K. The Foreign Policy of Iran 1500–1941 (University Press of Virginia, Virginia, 1966).

SKRINE, Sir CLARMONT. World War in Iran (Constable, London, 1926).

STEPPAT, FRITZ. Iran zwischen den Grossmächten, 1941-48 (Oberursel, 1948).

UPTON, JOSEPH M. The History of Modern Iran: An Interpretation (Harvard University Press, 1960).

VILLIERS, GERARD DE. The Imperial Shah: An Informal Biography (Weidenfeld and Nicolson, London, 1977).

ECONOMY AND OIL

AMUZEGAR, JAHANGIR. Technical Assistance in Theory and Practice: the Case of Iran (Praeger Special Studies in International Economics, New York, 1966).

AMUZEGAR, JAHANGIR and ALI FEKRAT, M. Iran: Economic Development under Dualistic Conditions (University of Chicago Press, 1971).

BALDWIN, GEORGE B. Planning and Development in Iran (Johns Hopkins Press, Baltimore, 1967).

BHARIER, JULIAN. Economic Development in Iran 1900–1970 (Oxford University Press, London, 1971).

GHOSH, SUNIL KANTI. The Anglo-Iranian Oil Dispute (Calcutta, 1960).

GORELIKOV, SEMEN GERASIMOVICH IVAN. A study in the Geography and Economics of Persia (Russian text), (Moscow, 1961).

GUPTA, RAJ NARAIN. Iran: An Economic Study (New Delhi, 1947).

MASON, F. C. Iran: Economic and Commercial Conditions in Iran (H.M.S.O., London, 1957).

NAHAI, L. and KIBELL, C. L. The Petroleum Industry of Iran (Washington: U.S. Department of the Interior, Bureau of Mines, 1963).

NIRUMAND, BAHMAN. Persien, Modell eines Entwicklungslande, oder Die Diktatur der freien Welt (Rowohlt-Verlag, Reinbek-bei-Hamburg, 1967).

SOTOUDEH, H. L'Evolution Economique de l'Iran et ses Problèmes (Paris, 1957).

MODERN IRAN

AMIRSADEGHI, HOSSEIN. Twentieth Century Iran (Heinemann, London, 1977).

ARASTEH, REZA. Educational and Social Awakening in Iran (E. J. Brill, Leiden, 1962).
Man and Society in Iran (Leiden, 1964).

AVERY, PETER. Modern Iran (Benn, London, 1967).

BINDER, LEONARD. Iran, Political Development in a Changing Society (University of Calif. Press, 1962).

VON BLÜCHER, WIPERT. Zeitenwende in Iran: Erlebnisse und Beobachtungen (Biberach an der Riss, 1949).

BROWNE, E. S. The Press and Poetry of Modern Persia (Cambridge, 1914).
A Year Amongst the Persians (London, 1950).

GRAEFE, A. VON. Iran, Das neue Persien (Berlin, 1937).

NIRUMAND, BAHMAN. Iran: the new imperialism in action (Modern Reader Paperbacks, New York and London, 1971).

WILBER, D. N. Contemporary Iran (New York, 1963).

WOODSMALL, RUTH. Moslem Women Enter a New World (London, 1936).

Iraq

PHYSICAL AND SOCIAL GEOGRAPHY

W. B. Fisher

Iraq is bounded on the north by Turkey, on the east by Iran, on the south by Kuwait and the Persian Gulf, on the south-west by Saudi Arabia and Jordan, and on the north-west by Syria. The actual frontier lines present one or two unusual features. In the first place, there exists between Iraq, Kuwait, and Saudi Arabia a "neutral zone", rhomboidal in shape, which was devised to facilitate the migrations of pastoral nomads, who cover great distances each year in search of pasture for their animals and who move regularly between several countries. Hence the stabilization or closing of a frontier could be for them a matter of life and death. Secondly, the frontier with Iran in its extreme southern portion below Basra follows the course of the Shatt al-Arab channel, but from 1936 until March 1975 the frontier was at the left (east) bank, placing the whole of the river within Iraq. This situation had become increasingly unacceptable to Iran, and in March 1975 the border was restored to the thalweg line in the middle of the deepest shipping channel in the Shatt al-Arab estuary. Thirdly, the inclusion of the northern province of Mosul within Iraq was agreed only in 1926. Because of its oil deposits, this territory was in dispute between Turkey, Syria and Iraq. Again the presence of large numbers of migratory nomads journeying each season between Iran, Turkey, Syria and Iraq was a further complicating factor.

PHYSICAL FEATURES

The old name of Iraq (Mesopotamia=land between the rivers) indicates the main physical aspect of the country—the presence of the two river valleys of the Tigris and Euphrates, which merge in their lower courses. On the eastern side of this double valley the Zagros Mountains of Persia appear as an abrupt wall, overhanging the riverine lowlands, particularly in the south, below Baghdad. North of the latitude of Baghdad the rise to the mountains is more gradual, with several intervening hill ranges, such as the Jebel Hamrin. These ranges are fairly low and narrow at first, with separating lowlands, but towards the main Zagros topography becomes more imposing, and summits over 3,000 metres in height occur. This region, lying north and east of Baghdad, is the ancient land of Assyria; and nowadays the higher hill ranges lying in the extreme east are called Iraqi Kurdistan, since many Kurdish tribes inhabit them.

On the western side of the river valley the land rises gradually to form the plateau which continues into Syria, Jordan, and Saudi Arabia, and its maximum height in Iraq is about 1,000 metres. In places it is possible to trace a cliff formation, where a more resistant bed of rock stands out prominently, and from this the name of the country is said to be derived (Arabic *Iraq*=cliff). There is no sharp geographical break between Iraq and its western neighbours comparable with that between Iraq and Iran; the frontier lines are artificial.

THE RIVERS

It remains to describe the valley region itself and the two rivers. The Tigris, 1,150 miles in length (1,850 km.), rises in Turkey, and is joined by numerous and often large tributaries both in Turkey and Iraq. The Euphrates, 1,460 miles in length (2,350 km.), also rises in Turkey and flows first through Syria and then Iraq, joining the Tigris in its lower course at Qurna, to form the stream known as the Shatt al-Arab, which is 115 miles (185 km.) in length. Unlike the Tigris, the Euphrates receives no tributaries during its passage of Iraq. Above the region of Baghdad both rivers flow in well-defined channels, with retaining valley-walls. Below Baghdad, however, the vestiges of a retaining valley disappear, and the rivers meander over a vast open plain with only a slight drop in level—in places merely 1.5 or 2 metres in 100 km. Here the rivers are raised on great levees, or banks of silt and mud (which they themselves have laid down), and now lie several feet above the level of the surrounding plain. One remarkable feature is the change in relative level of the two river beds—water can be led from one to the other according to the actual district, and this possibility, utilised by irrigation engineers for many centuries, still remains the basic principle of present-day development. At the same time, the courses of both rivers can suddenly alter. A flood may breach the wall of the levee, and the water then pours out on to the lower-lying plain, inundating many square miles of territory. Ultimately, the river finds a new course and builds a fresh levee. Old river channels, fully or partially abandoned by the river, are thus a feature of the Mesopotamian lowland, associated with wide areas of swamp, lakes, and sandbars. The Tigris, though narrower than the Euphrates, is swifter, and carries far more water.

As the sources of both rivers lie in the mountains of Turkey, the current is very fast, and upstream navigation is difficult in the middle and upper reaches. In spring, following the melting of snows in Asia Minor, both rivers begin to rise, reaching a maximum in April (Tigris) and May (Euphrates). The spring is a very anxious time, since floods of 3.6 to 6.0 metres occur, and 10 metres is known—this in a region where the land may fall only 4 metres or less in level over 100 km. Immense areas are regularly inundated, levees often collapse, and villages and roads, where these exist, must be built on high embankments. The Tigris is particularly liable to sudden flooding, and can rise at the rate of one foot per hour. Contrasts with the Nile of Egypt will be noted. The latter river is confined in a steep-sided valley over most of its length, and floods do not spread far away from the river. In lower Iraq, on the other hand, wide expanses are inundated every year, e.g. as in early 1954 when a flood of 9 metres occurred and many thousands were rendered homeless.

CLIMATE AND ECONOMIC ACTIVITY

The summers are overwhelmingly hot, with shade temperatures of over 43°C.; and many inhabitants retire during the heat of the day to underground rooms. Winters may be surprisingly cold: frost, though very rare at Basra, can be severe in the north. Sudden hot spells during winter are another feature in the centre and south of Iraq. Rainfall is scanty over all of the country, except for the north-east (Assyria), where 40 to 60 cm. occur—enough to grow crops without irrigation. Elsewhere farming is entirely dependent upon irrigation from river water. The great extent of standing water in many parts of Iraq leads to an unduly high air humidity, which explains the notorious reputation of the Mesopotamian summer.

The unusual physical conditions outlined present a number of obstacles to human activity. The flood waters are rather less "manageable" than in Egypt, and there is less of the regular deposition of thick, rich silt that is such a feature of the Nile. The effects of this are strikingly visible in the relatively small extent of land actually cultivated—at most, only one-sixth of the potentially cultivable territory and 3 per cent of the total area of the country. The population, of over 12 million, is about 30 per cent that of Egypt. Because of the easy availability of agricultural land, wasteful, "extensive" farming methods are often followed, giving a low yield. On the whole, Iraq is underpopulated, and could support larger numbers of inhabitants.

A feature of the last few years has been the use of oil royalties (approximately U.S. $11,000 million in 1978) for development schemes, particularly in irrigation. Various Plans allocated up to £30 million annually, but this was not always used. Now, with much higher oil revenues, the figure has been revised upward, and far more extensive development is planned. A further favourable factor is the discovery in 1975 of a major new oilfield, which could make Iraq the third largest Middle Eastern oil producer.

The unusual physical conditions have greatly restricted movement and the development of communications of all kinds. In the upper reaches of the rivers boat journeys can only be made downstream, whilst nearer the sea the rivers are wider and slower but often very shallow. Roads are difficult to maintain because of the floods, and the railways have two differing gauges—standard and metre; the latter is however in process of replacement and with decreasing risk of flooding, standard gauge has been laid between Baghdad and Basra via Kut. The effect has been to leave in isolation many communities that have differing ways of life and even differing languages and religious beliefs. Numerous minority groups are hence a feature of Iraq.

THE PEOPLE

In the marshes of the extreme south there are communities of Arabs who spend most of their lives in boats and rafts. Other important minorities live in, or close to, the hill country of the north: the Kurds, who number over one million and migrate extensively into Syria, Turkey and Iran (*see* Recent History); the Yazidis of the Jebel Sinjar; the Assyrian Christians (the name refers to their geographical location, and has no historical connection); and various communities of Uniate and Orthodox Christians. As well, there were important groups of Jews—more than in most other Muslim countries—though since the establishment of the State of Israel much emigration has taken place. It should also be noted that whilst the majority of the Muslims follow Shi'a rites, the wealthier Muslims are of Sunni adherence.

Ethnically, the position is very complicated. The northern and eastern hill districts contain many racial elements—Turki, Persian, and proto-Nordic, with Armenoid strains predominating. The pastoral nomads of western Iraq are, as might be expected, of fairly unmixed Mediterranean ancestry, like the nomads of Syria, Jordan, and Saudi Arabia; but the population of the riverine districts of Iraq shows a mixture of Armenoid and Mediterranean elements. North of the Baghdad district the Armenoid strain is dominant, but to the south, it is less important, though still present.

Arabic is the official and most widely used language. Kurdish and dialects of Turkish are current in the north, whilst variants of Persian are spoken by tribesmen in the east. An estimate, probably over-generous to the Arabic speakers, puts the relative numbers at: Arabic 79 per cent, Kurdish 16 per cent, Persian 3 per cent, and Turkish 2 per cent of the total population.

HISTORY

Iraq was one of the earliest centres of civilization. Before 3000 B.C. the Sumerians, a people of problematical origin, had established a complete civilization in the marshy alluvial areas at the head of the Persian/Arabian Gulf. Here a number of city states developed, cities like Eridu, Uruk, Ur, Kish and Lagash. These states were supported by a highly developed agricultural economy, based on an intricate irrigation system.

Around 2500 B.C., Lagash gained ascendency over several other cities, until, not long afterwards, Lugalzaggisi, the governor of Umma, overran Uruk and embarked on a career of widespread conquest. Lugalzaggisi was in turn defeated by Sargon of Agade, who united the whole of Mesopotamia under Akkadian rule and conquered Elamite Susa, and whose armies penetrated as far as the Mediterranean. Akkadian dominions were extended even further under his successors, but the Sumerians of the south took every opportunity to revolt and attacks by Elamites and mountain tribesmen, the Gutians, caused the empire to collapse around 2200 B.C. After a period of chaos, a new Sumerian kingdom, centered at Ur (the Third Dynasty of Ur) established supremacy over the south, lasting through the twenty-first century B.C. It was finally sacked by invaders from Elam, and by the Amorites from the north-west, and was never again of great historical importance.

The Amorites were Semites, whose homeland was Arabia. They came into conflict with the Elamites in Sumer, and in the eighteenth century B.C. Hammurabi created an extensive empire famous for the splendour of its civilization. Pressure from the Caucasian tribes, Hurrians and Kassites, was increasing, but the empire finally crumbled before the onslaught of the Hittites, who sacked Babylon in the seventeenth century B.C.

In the north, new powers were emerging, notably the Mitanni, who occupied northern Iraq. At last their rule disintegrated under constant pressure from the Hittites of Asia Minor, whose influence, in the years following the reign of their great king Subbiluliuma (*c.* 1390–1350 B.C.), was advanced almost to the Persian/Arabian Gulf. Meanwhile, on the higher reaches of the Tigris, the warlike Assyrians, who hastened the decline of the Mitanni and the Hittite empire, embarked from time to time on a career of conquest destined to be of brief duration, as under Adad-nirari I (*c.* 1300 B.C.) and Tiglath-pileser I (*c.* 1200 B.C.). In the reign of Ashur-nasir-pal II (883–859 B.C.) Assyrian ambition burst forth once more, re-establishing control over northern Mesopotamia. Syria and Cilicia were subdued under Shalmaneser III (860–825 B.C.) and the Assyrian empire in its heyday comprised Van and other Armenian territories, Babylonia, Syria, Egypt and large areas of Persia. An army of unprecedented efficiency, mass deportations on a vast scale, relentless cruelty, a régime of rigid and despotic centralization—these features of Assyrian rule evoked the bitter enmity of the subject peoples, who, when the empire weakened as a result of incessant warfare and of Scythian invasion from the north, rose in combined revolt and sacked Nineveh in 612 B.C. Iraq now became the centre of a neo-Babylonian state which, under Nebuchadnezzar (604–562 B.C.) included much of the Fertile Crescent, but was soon to fall before the Persians, who seized Babylon in 539–538 B.C.

Thereafter, Iraq was a mere province of the vast Achaemenid empire, which extended from Asia Minor to the Punjab in north-west India and from southern Russia to Egypt. Alexander the Great brought Persian rule to an end in a series of brilliant campaigns (334–327 B.C.). After his death in 323 B.C., one of his generals, Seleucus, controlled most of the Asiatic lands which the conqueror had dominated. The Seleucids maintained their hold on Iraq for more than a hundred years and then, in the course of prolonged warfare, lost it to the Parthians, who during the third and second centuries B.C. founded a powerful state in Persia.

Under the Parthians Iraq was a frontier province over against the might of Rome. To the north and west of Mesopotamia a line of strong fortresses, e.g., Carrhae (Harran), Edessa (modern Urfa), Diyarbakir, Dara, Nisibin, marked the ground where the rival armies fought. At Carrhae, in 54 B.C., the Parthian horsemen severely defeated the Romans but from the time of Augustus until the reign of the Emperor Trajan there was no major war between the two states. Between A.D. 113 and 117, Trajan conquered much of Iraq, yet his successor, Hadrian, felt that it would be too expensive to defend the new territories and so abandoned them. Rome resumed the offensive under Marcus Aurelius (162–166), Septimius Severus (195–199) and Caracalla (216–218), her rule being now extended from the middle Euphrates to the Khabur river.

The Parthian domination came to an end in 224 owing to internal revolt in Persia; the emergence of the Sasanid régime now began. In 260 Sapor I crushed the Romans in battle near Edessa and captured the Emperor Valerian. The endless frontier hostilities flared out once more into violent war under Diocletian, Constantius and Julian (third-fourth centuries), the Romans being forced back behind the line of the Euphrates. The conflict then died down for more than a hundred years and was not resumed on a large scale until the Sasanid state recovered much of its old vigour under Kobad I (488–531) and Khusran Anushirvan (531–579). The prolonged warfare of the sixth–seventh centuries came to an end with the brilliant campaigns of the Byzantine Emperor Heraclius in Armenia and Iraq (622–628). Byzantium and Persia were by now exhausted and in the meantime a formidable danger had arisen in the far south.

THE RISE OF ISLAM

The prophet Muhammad (d. 632) had created at Mecca and Medina a religious and political organization that aroused powerful forces long latent in Arabia.

The Arab nomads of the great desert, united within the community of Islam, were forbidden to pursue their ancient tribal feuds. The restless energy thus concentrated in the Muslim state found an outlet in war outside Arabia and the Arabs overran Syria and Egypt. By 634 the Arab warriors had begun the conquest of Iraq. The battle of Qadisiya in 635 led to the fall of the Persian capital, Ctesiphon, in June of that year. A further battle at Jalula in 637 marked the end of Sasanid power in Iraq, although resistance continued in the north until the Arabs took Mosul in 641. Kufa and Basra became the two great garrison cities on which Muslim rule in Iraq was to be based for the next hundred years.

The murder of the Caliph 'Uthman in 656 brought about a civil war between his successor, 'Ali, and Mu'awiya, a kinsman of 'Uthman, who had long been governor of Syria. After an indecisive battle at Siffin in 657 the two rivals had recourse to arbitration, as a result of which, at Adhruh in January 659, both men were deposed from their respective positions, a judgment which deprived 'Ali of his real status as Caliph and Mu'awiya of a pretension to that office which as yet he had not ventured openly to avow. The outcome of the conflict remained uncertain during the next two years, until at length the murder of 'Ali at Kufa in January 661 left the way clear for Mu'awiya to become Caliph. The war revealed that effective power within the new empire was passing from Mecca and Medina to the great garrison cities where the main Arab armies were stationed. 'Ali had been obliged to go from the Hijaz to Iraq, his chief support coming from Kufa. Mu'awiya relied for his success on the strength of Syria. The real issue had been whether Iraq or Syria should be the metropolitan province of the empire. With the emergence of Mu'awiya as Caliph in 661, the question was decided, for almost a hundred years, in favour of Syria.

During the period of the Umayyad dynasty (661–750) Iraq became the centre of the movement known as Shi'atu 'Ali, i.e. "the party of Ali". Born amongst the Arabs themselves, it assumed at first the form of a "legitimist" opposition to Umayyad rule, asserting that the Caliphate should of right belong to the descendants of 'Ali, the son-in-law of the Prophet. As a purely Arab and political faction, resting to a large degree on the bitter dislike of Iraq for the hegemony of Syria, it was to meet with failure, for the armies of Kufa and Basra could not overcome the military pre-eminence of the Syrians. At Karbala, in October 680, Husain, the son of 'Ali, fell in battle against the Umayyad forces in Iraq. This event, by giving to the Shi'a an illustrious martyr, inaugurated a new and rapid growth of the party, not on the political level but as a religious sect.

UMAYYAD RULE

The Umayyad state was based on the fundamental assumption that a vast subject population, non-Muslim and non-Arab, would continue indefinitely to yield tribute to a dominant Arab and Muslim warrior aristocracy, the revenues derived from the conquered territories and from the *jizya*, i.e. the poll-tax imposed on those who did not belong to the faith of the Prophet, being shared out amongst the members of that aristocracy. Whether from a genuine acceptance of the new religion or from motives of self-interest, e.g. to escape the poll-tax and to secure the financial, economic and social privileges of the Arab Muslims, the subject peoples began to adopt Islam. The revenues of the state fell and the decline could not be made good through the acquisition of rich new lands, for the age of rapid conquest was over. Since Muhammad had declared all Muslims to be equal, the new converts, or Mawali, demanded that the Arabs concede to them a due participation in the rewards of empire. When it became clear that the Arab aristocracy meant to defend its pensions, privileges and other exclusive rights—the available resources of the state were insufficient to meet the claims of the ever-increasing numbers of Mawali—a crisis of the first magnitude threatened the Umayyad régime.

The Mawali now gave their allegiance to the Shi'a, transforming the movement into a means for the expression of their social and economic grievances against the established order and, at the same time, remoulding it as a religious sect which embraced ideas not of Muslim origin but derived from their previous Christian, Jewish and Zoroastrian traditions. This radical change in the Shi'a was already visible in the years 685–687, when a serious revolt occurred at Kufa in the name of Muhammad ibn al-Hanafiya, a son of 'Ali by a wife other than Fatima, the daughter of the Prophet.

The Umayyad Caliph 'Umar II (717–720) introduced a series of financial reforms designed to conciliate the Mawali, a policy which met only with a transient success, for the ultimate effect of his measures was to increase the expenditure and lower the revenue of the state. Disillusionment grew apace amongst the non-Arab Muslims. An efficient propaganda machine, known under the name of the Hashimiya, made its appearance in Iraq, its task being to disseminate extreme Shi'i ideas. In 716 control of this organization fell into the hands of Muhammad ibn 'Ali ibn al- 'Abbas, descended from an uncle of the Prophet. Its chief centre of activity was in the great frontier province of Khurasan, in north-east Persia, where Arab colonies from Basra and Kufa had settled in about 670. Abu Muslim, a Persian Mawla of Iraq, was sent to Khurasan as confidential agent of the Hashimiya in 743 and there raised the standard of revolt against the Umayyads. Syria, long since weakened by fierce tribal feuds amongst the Arabs, could not withstand the storm. In 750 Umayyad rule came to an end and was replaced by that of the 'Abbasid dynasty, while Iraq at last achieved her ambition of becoming the dominant province of the empire.

'ABBASID RULE

The 'Abbasid caliphs had now an immediate and urgent task to perform. It was impossible for them to govern as the representatives of the more advanced elements in the Shi'a, when most of their Muslim subjects were of the Sunni or orthodox faith. The second 'Abbasid, al-Mansur (754–775), the real founder of the new régime, therefore abandoned the extremists who had done so much to bring his house to power. He also built a new garrison city in Iraq for his main army, the hard core of which consisted largely of regiments from Khurasan. This capital of the 'Abbasid empire, Baghdad, soon developed into a great emporium of trade and a political centre of vast importance. An autocratic caliph, claiming divine authority for his power, which rested on regular armed forces and was exercised through a paid bureaucracy; a cosmopolitan ruling class of officials and landowners, of merchants and bankers; the 'Ulama, i.e. the hierarchy of religious scholars, jurists, teachers and dignitaries—these were the main characteristics of the 'Abbasid Caliphate, which for a time brought to Iraq and, indeed, to the Islamic state as a whole a splendid prosperity derived from a flourishing agriculture and industry and from the lucrative transit trade between India and the Mediterranean.

It was in regard to political unity that the 'Abbasid empire proved most vulnerable. The relative cohesion which the Muslim state had enjoyed owing to the dominance of the Arab warrior aristocracy did not survive the revolution of 750. The new dynasty sought to use the Muslim faith itself as a means of binding together the varied ethnic and social elements of the population, but the attempt was soon shown to be a failure. After the death of Harun ar-Rashid (786–809), whose reign marked the apogee of 'Abbasid power as well as fostering a great flowering of Arabic culture, civil war broke out between his sons Amin and Ma'mun, the former depending largely on the support of Iraq, the latter on the strength of Persia and, above all, on the troops of Khurasan. The conflict was, in one sense, a battle between Persia and Iraq for pre-eminence within the empire. Ma'mun conquered Baghdad in 813, but for a time considered the idea of making Marv in Khurasan his capital, a project which he abandoned only when he realized that it would lead to repeated revolt in Iraq. In August 819 he returned to Baghdad.

Persia, disappointed in its hopes, now began to break away from the caliphs of Baghdad. Local dynasties made their appearance in the east, the Tahirids in 820, the Saffarids in 867, the Samanids in *c.* 892. A similar process occurred in the west, Spain after 756, Morocco after 788, Tunisia after 800 being virtually independent of Baghdad. In 868 the dynasty of the Tulunids arose in Egypt. The more extreme elements of the Shi'a were also active, especially in Persia and the neighbouring regions, inspiring repeated insurrections against the 'Abbasid régime. Southern Iraq suffered heavily in the Zanj Rebellion (869–883), when one Ali ibn Muhammad founded a state of Negro slaves at Basra, which was sacked in 871. The Qarmatians, a religious movement of communistic and revolutionary tendencies, founded a strong régime of their own in the province of Bahrain (now called al-Hasa) and for most of the tenth century carried out frequent raids into Iraq. Meanwhile, at Baghdad, the power of the army was growing. The corps gathered for the Caliph's protection consisted of slaves (mamluks), mostly of Turkish origin, commanded by free officers. Since the reigns of al-Mu'tasim (833–842) and al-Wathiq (842–847), their officers had also been Mamluks. As power fell more and more into the hands of the army, the Mamluks were able to appoint and depose the caliphs at will. Iraq fell at length under the domination of Daylamite mountain dwellers from the region south of the Caspian Sea, Shi'i in religion and led by a family of *condottière* chieftains, the Buwaihids, who, after subduing most of western Persia, occupied Baghdad in 945. Buwaihid rule—a period of the deepest degradation for the Caliphate, since the Commander of the Faithful was now a mere puppet obedient to the orders of a Shi'i—lasted until 1055. It then collapsed before the assault of Turks from the steppe lands beyond the Oxus, who, led by the Seljuqs, a family also of *condottière* origin, overran Persia and then seized Baghdad under Tughril Beg. The Seljuq Turks were Sunni Muslims and their success was not unwelcome amongst the orthodox, who regarded it as a liberation from the yoke of the Shi'i Buwaihids. Yet the Caliph, although treated with deference, was still only in name the head of the state, all effective power being concentrated in the hands of the Seljuq Sultan.

After the death of Malik Shah in 1092, dynastic dissension and revolt amongst the Turkish tribesmen brought about a rapid decline of the new régime and the rise of succession states ruled by princes or by officers of the Seljuq house. In Iraq a series of nine Seljuq sultans ruled from 1118–94, almost all of them fated to die a violent death in conflict with rival claimants or with their Atabegs, i.e. amirs, who were the most powerful figures in the land. Some of these Atabegs established independent principalities of their own, e.g. the Zangid dynasty at Mosul, which played an important role in arousing the Muslims to defend Islam against the Christian Crusaders in Syria. The last Seljuq Sultan of Iraq, Tughril (1177–94), was defeated in battle with the Turkish ruler of Khwarizm (the region of Khiva, south of the Aral Sea). The victor, Takash (1172–1200), and his successor, 'Ala'ad-Din Muhammad (1200–20), sought to extend their rule over Iraq, but, before this ambition could be realised, the Mongols destroyed the power of the Khwarizm shahs.

THE MONGOL INVASIONS

By 1220 the great conqueror Jenghiz Khan had overrun all Transoxania and was threatening to invade Persia. His death in 1227 led to a long pause in the Mongol advance. In 1253 Hülakü, a grandson of Jenghiz Khan, moved westward in force, captured Baghdad in 1258 and thus made an end of the Abbasid caliphate. Subordinated henceforth to the Mongol Khan of Persia, Iraq became a mere frontier province, bereft of all its former wealth and splendour and much neglected by its rulers. On the death of the Mongol Khan Abu Sa'id in 1335, Iraq, after a brief period of confusion, passed into the hands of a new dynasty, the Jala'irids, who ruled over the land until the early years of the fifteenth century. During this period Iraq was again overrun by Mongols and in

1401 Timur Beg sacked Baghdad with merciless severity. The Jala'irid régime did not long outlast the death of Timur in 1405.

To the north of Iraq, around Lake Van, a powerful Turcoman confederation, known as the Black Sheep (Kara Koyunlu) was rising into prominence. The Turcomans defeated the last Jala'irid, Ahmed, and created a new state which, under Jihan Shah (1444–67), extended from Tabriz to the Shatt al-'Arab. The power of the Kara Koyunlu soon collapsed in war with a rival Turcoman confederation, that of the Ak Koyunlu (White Sheep), who, led by their famous chieftain, Uzun Hasan (1423?–78), crushed Jihan Shah and took over the territories which he had ruled. Dynastic quarrels brought about a rapid disintegration of the White Sheep ascendancy.

In the years 1499–1508 the now crumbling Ak Koyunlu régime was destroyed by the Safavid, Isma'il. (His ancestors were hereditary masters of a powerful religious order notable for its advanced Shi'i teaching and, from their main centre at Ardabil near the Caspian Sea, had fashioned their numerous adherents amongst the Turcoman tribes of Asia Minor into a formidable military movement). Isma'il made himself Shah of Persia and also conquered Iraq. To the Ottoman Sultan, the dissemination of Shi'i beliefs among the tribes of Anatolia was a menace which had to be eliminated, for it threatened to undermine his own control in that region, the Ottomans being Sunni, i.e. orthodox Muslims. Selim I made war on Shah Isma'il in 1514 and so began a protracted conflict between the Ottomans and the Safavids which was to last, with long intervals of precarious peace, until 1639. Sultan Suleyman, in the course of his first campaign against Persia, conquered Baghdad in 1534–35.

OTTOMAN IRAQ

The Ottomans were to find Iraq a most difficult and expensive province to administer. Religious animosities proved to be a constant source of trouble. Northern Iraq and Kurdistan followed largely the Sunni faith; Baghdad itself was divided in its allegiance between Sunni and Shi'i Islam; southern Iraq was a region under strong Shi'i influence. The task of restraining nomad tribes from raiding the settled lands was an endless and wearisome business. Moreover, the tribes of the delta marshlands and of the mountainous areas close to the frontier with Persia were ever liable to rise in revolt against the administration. From time to time Iraq was the scene of warfare between the Ottomans and the Safavids, e.g., in the years 1578–90, and indeed came once more under Persian control, when Shah Abbas (1587–1629) seized Baghdad in 1623 and retained it in the face of a determined Ottoman counter-offensive in 1625/26. After a second attempt at reconquest in 1629/30 had failed, the Ottomans at last recovered Baghdad in 1638 and in the next year made peace with the Safavids.

As the Ottoman state fell into decline, the Sultan at Istanbul became less able to dominate the course of events in so distant a province as Iraq. From about 1625 until 1668, Basra and the Delta marshlands were in the hands of local chieftains independent of the Ottoman administration at Baghdad, a state of affairs which recurred in the period 1694–1701. The appointment of Hasan Pasha to command at Baghdad in 1704 marked a new phase in the history of Ottoman Iraq. The pashalik was to pass from himself to his son, then to the husbands of his grand-daughters, and thereafter to a series of Mamluk governors raised and trained in the household of his immediate successors. From 1704 to 1831, therefore, the Sultan failed to enforce at Baghdad an appointment of his own choice.

Hasan Pasha died in 1723, just at the moment when the Ottomans had become involved in a new war against Persia. The last of the Safavids had been deposed in 1722 by the Afghan Mir Mahmud. Hasan Pasha's son, Ahmed Pasha, occupied Kermanshah, which Hasan himself had seized in the first stage of the conflict, and then overran Hamadan and Luristan, but these lands were lost once more to Persia when Nadir Shah, in the years after 1729, drove out the Afghans and invaded Iraq. Baghdad itself withstood a siege in 1733 and Mosul underwent the same experience in 1743. The war brought much suffering to Iraq, the province falling, as a result of frequent revolt amongst the restless tribesmen and the devastation caused by repeated campaigns, into a state of anarchy. None the less, Ahmed Pasha remained throughout this period in firm control of Baghdad and Basra and also exercised a strong influence over the affairs of Mosul and Kirkuk. He lived to see peace made with Persia in 1746 on terms which restored the general position to what it had been before the war. A few months later in 1747, he died, leaving no son to succeed him.

The palace household which his father had created and which he himself had further developed contained Mamluks recruited for the most part from Georgia, converted to Islam and trained in their youth for subsequent service in the administration of Iraq. After a brief interval of confusion, in which the Porte tried to impose its own nominee but soon had to admit failure, Suleyman Agha, one of the Mamluks whom Hasan Pasha had bought and educated, became the governor of Baghdad and Basra, an office which he held with great success for twelve years until his death in 1762. Yet another Mamluk, 'Umr Agha, ruled Iraq from 1764 to 1775. Internal strife and a frontier war which led to a Persian occupation of Basra marked the period immediately following his death.

At length, in 1780, the most famous of the Mamluk pashas, Suleyman the Great, assumed the government of Baghdad and Basra. Much of his time was spent in curbing the Kurdish chieftains in the north and the Arab tribes, above all the powerful Muntafiq confederation in the south of Iraq. From about 1790 he had to face the enmity of the formidable Wahhabi state recently founded in central Arabia. The raids of the Wahhabi tribesmen into Iraq intensified until in 1801 the great Shi'i sanctuary of Karbala was taken and sacked. The death of Suleyman in the next year threw Iraq into even greater confusion. There were further Wahhabi *razzias*, e.g. against Najaf in 1803 and Basra in 1804, and constant trouble with the tribes along the Persian border. It was only in 1817 that the last of the Mamluk pashas, Da'ud, secured control of the province and restored some semblance of order by repeated punitive campaigns against the Kurds and the nomads of the desert lands.

Meanwhile, reforms were being introduced at Istanbul which foreshadowed the end of the Mamluk régime in Iraq. Selim III (1789–1807) and Mahmud II (1808–39) sought to refashion the administration and the military forces of the empire on European lines. The moment when the Ottoman Sultan would attempt to end the Mamluk system and regain direct possession of Iraq was now at hand. Mahmud II sent 'Ali Ridha Pasha to perform this task in 1831. A severe outbreak of plague crippled the resistance of the Mamluks, Da'ud Pasha was deposed and the Mamluk regiments were at once exterminated. A new phase in the history of Iraq was about to begin.

WESTERN INFLUENCE

Although some of the European nations had long been in contact with Iraq through their commercial interests in the Persian/Arabian Gulf, western influences were slow to penetrate into the province. By 1800 there was a British Resident at Basra and two years later a British Consulate at Baghdad. France also maintained agents in these cities. French and Italian religious orders had settlements in the land. It was not, however, until after 1831 that signs of more rapid European penetration became visible, such as steam-boats on the rivers of Iraq in 1836, telegraph lines from 1861 and a number of proposals for railways, none of which was to materialise for a long time to come. The Ottoman government did much in the period between 1831 and 1850 to impose direct control over Kurdistan and the mountainous areas close to the Persian border, but the introduction of reforms was not, in fact, begun until in 1869 Midhat Pasha arrived at Baghdad. Much of his work, performed in the brief space of three years, proved to be superficial and ill-considered, yet he was able to set Iraq on a course from which there could be no retreat in the future. A newspaper, military factories, a hospital, an alms-house, schools, a tramway, conscription for the army, municipal and administrative councils, comparative security on the main routes and a reasoned policy of settling tribesmen on the land—these achievements, however imperfect, bear solid witness to the vigour of his rule. After his departure in 1872, reform and European influence continued to advance, although slowly. Postal services were much developed, a railway from Baghdad to Samarra was completed in 1914 (part of the projected *Baghdadbahn*, which betokened the rapid growth of German interest in the Ottoman Empire) and the important Hindiya Barrage on the Euphrates was rebuilt between 1910 and 1913. The measures of reform and improvement introduced between 1831 and 1914 must indeed be judged as belated and inadequate—the Iraq of 1900 differed little from that of 1500—yet a process of fundamental change had begun, which no régime, however inept, could reverse.

In November 1914 Britain and the Ottoman Empire were at war. British troops occupied the Shatt al-Arab region and, under the pressure of war needs, transformed Basra into an efficient and well-equipped port. A premature advance on Baghdad in 1915 ended in the retreat of the British forces to Kut, their prolonged defence of that town and, when all attempts to relieve it had failed, the capitulation to the Ottomans in April 1916. A new offensive launched from Basra in the autumn of that year brought about the capture of Baghdad in March 1917. Kirkuk was taken in 1918, but, before the Allies could seize Mosul, the Ottoman government sought and obtained an armistice in October. For two years, until the winter of 1920, the Commander-in-Chief of the British Forces, acting through a civil commissioner, continued to be responsible for the administration of Iraq from Basra to Mosul, all the apparatus of a modern system of rule being created at Baghdad—e.g., departments of Land, Posts and Telegraphs, Agriculture, Irrigation, Police, Customs, Finance, etc. The new régime was Christian, foreign and strange, resented by reason of its very efficiency, feared and distrusted no less by those whose loyalties were Muslim and Ottoman than by important elements who desired self-determination for Iraq.

The last phase of Ottoman domination in Iraq, especially during the years after the Young Turk Revolution in 1908, had witnessed a marked growth of Arab nationalist sentiment. Local circles in Iraq now made contact with the Ottoman Decentralization Party at Cairo, founded in 1912, and with the Young Arab Society, which moved from Paris to Beirut in 1913. Basra, in particular, became a centre of Arab aspirations and took the lead in demanding from Istanbul a measure of autonomy for Iraq. A secret organization, al-'Ahd (the Covenant) included a number of Iraqi officers serving in the Ottoman armies. The prospect of independence which the Allies held out to the Arabs in the course of the war strengthened and extended the nationalist movement. In April 1920 Britain received from the conference at San Remo a mandate for Iraq. This news was soon followed by a serious insurrection amongst the tribesmen of the south. The revolt, caused partly by instinctive dislike of foreign rule but also by vigorous nationalist propaganda, was not wholly suppressed until early in the next year. In October 1920 military rule was formally terminated in Iraq. An Arab Council of State, advised by British officials and responsible for the administration, now came into being and in March 1921 the Amir Faisal ibn Husain agreed to rule as King at Baghdad. His ceremonial accession took place on August 23rd, 1921.

The Najdi (Saudi Arabian) frontier with Iraq was defined in the Treaty of Mohammara in May 1922. Saudi concern over loss of traditional grazing rights resulted in further talks between Ibn Saud and the U.K. Civil Commissioner in Iraq, and a Neutral Zone of 7,000 sq. km. was established adjacent to the western tip of the Kuwait frontier. No military or permanent buildings were to be erected in the zone and the nomads of both countries were to have unimpeded access to its pastures and wells. A further agreement concerning the administration of this zone was signed between Iraq and Saudi Arabia in May 1938.

MODERN IRAQ

Despite the opposition of the more extreme nationalists, an Anglo-Iraqi Treaty was signed on October 10th, 1922. It embodied the provisions of the mandate, safeguarded the judicial rights of foreigners and guaranteed the special interests of Britain in Iraq. An Electoral Law prepared the way for the choice of a constituent assembly, which met in March 1924 and, in the face of strong opposition by the nationalists, ratified the treaty with Britain. It accepted, too, an Organic Law declaring Iraq to be a sovereign state with a constitutional hereditary monarchy and a representative system of government. In 1925 the League of Nations recommended that the *vilayet* of Mosul, to which the Turks had laid claim, be incorporated into the new kingdom, a decision finally implemented in the treaty of July 1926 between the interested parties, Britain, Turkey and Iraq. By this year a fully constituted Parliament was in session at Baghdad and all the ministries, as well as most of the larger departments of the administration, were in effective control. Moreover, the state now possessed a competent judicial organization, a small army of about 7,500 men and a police force well equipped to deal with the refractory desert tribesmen. In 1930 a new treaty was signed with Britain, which established between the two countries a close alliance for a period of 25 years and granted Britain the use of air bases at Shu'ayba and Habbaniya. On October 3rd, 1932, Iraq entered the League of Nations as an independent power, the mandate being now terminated.

The difficulties which confronted the Kingdom in the period after 1932 required much time and effort for their solution: e.g. the animosities between the Sunni Muslims and the powerful Shi'i tribes on the Euphrates, which tended to divide and embitter political life; the problem of relations with the Kurds, some of whom wanted a state of their own, and with other minorities like the Assyrians; the complicated task of reform in land tenure and of improvement in agriculture, irrigation, flood control, public services and communications. As yet the Government itself consisted of little more than a façade of democratic forms concealing a world of faction and intrigue. The realities of the political scene were a xenophobe press often ill-informed and irresponsible; "parties" better described as cliques gathered around prominent personalities; a small ruling class of tribal sheikhs; landowners; and the intelligentsia—lawyers, students, journalists, doctors, ex-officers—frequently torn by sharp rivalries. It is not surprising, therefore, that the first years of full independence showed a rather halting progress towards efficient rule. The dangerous nature of the tensions inside Iraq was revealed in the Assyrian massacre of 1933 carried out by troops of the Iraq army. Political intrigue from Baghdad had much to do with the outbreak of tribal revolt along the Euphrates in 1935/36. The army crushed the insurrection without much trouble and then, under the leadership of General Bakr Sidqi and in alliance with disappointed politicians and reformist elements, brought about a *coup d'état* in October 1936. The new régime failed to fulfil its assurances of reform, its policies alienated the tribal chieftains and gave rise to serious tensions even within the armed forces, tensions which led to the assassination of Bakr Sidqi in August 1937.

Of vast importance for Iraq was the rapid development of the oil industry during these years. Concessions were granted in 1925, 1932 and 1938 to the Iraq, Mosul and Basra Petroleum Companies. Oil had been discovered in the Kirkuk area in 1927 and by the end of 1934 the Iraq Petroleum Company was exporting crude oil through two 12-inch pipelines, one leading to Tripoli and the other to Haifa. Exploitation of the Mosul and Basra fields did not begin on a commercial scale until after World War II.

In 1937 Iraq joined Turkey, Persia and Afghanistan in the Sa'dabad Pact, which arranged for consultation in all disputes that might affect the common interests of the four states. A treaty signed with Persia in July 1937 and ratified in the following year provided for the specific acceptance of the boundary between the two countries as it had been defined in 1914. Relations with Britain deteriorated in the period after 1937, mainly because of the growth of anti-Zionist feeling and of resentment at British policy in Palestine. German influence increased very much at this time in Iraq, especially amongst those political and military circles associated with the army group later to be known as the Golden Square. Iraq severed her diplomatic connections with Germany at the beginning of World War II, but in 1941 the army commanders carried out a new *coup d'état*, establishing, under the nominal leadership of Rashid 'Ali al-Gaylani, a régime which announced its non-belligerent intentions. A disagreement over the passage of British troops through Iraq left no doubt of the pro-German sympathies of the Gaylani government and led to hostilities that ended with the occupation of Basra and Baghdad in May 1941. Thereafter Iraq co-operated effectively with the Allied war effort and became an important base from which aid was sent northward through Persia to Russia. In 1943 Iraq declared war on the Axis powers and in 1945 signed the Charter of the United Nations.

Iraq, during the years after World War II, was to experience much internal tension and unrest. Negotiations with Britain led to the signing at Portsmouth in January 1948 of a new Anglo-Iraqi agreement designed to replace that of 1930 and incorporating substantial concessions, amongst them the British evacuation of the airbases at Shu'ayba and Habbaniya and the creation of a joint board for the co-ordination of all matters relating to mutual defence. The animosities arising from the situation in Palestine called forth riots at Baghdad directed against the new agreement with Britain, which were sufficiently disturbing to oblige the Iraqi Government to repudiate the Portsmouth settlement.

ARAB-ISRAEL WAR 1948

With anti-Jewish and anti-Western feeling so intense, it was inevitable that troops should be sent from Iraq to the Arab-Israeli war which began on May 15th, 1948. The Iraqi troops shared in the hostilities for a period of just over two months, their participation terminating in a truce operative from July 18th. Their final withdrawal from Palestine did not commence, however, until April 1949. Subsequently, there was a considerable emigration of Jews from Iraq to Israel, especially in the years 1951–52.

The expense of the war against Israel, bad harvests, the general indigence of the people—all contributed to bring about serious tensions resulting in rioting at Baghdad in November 1952 and the imposition of martial law until October 1953. None the less, there were some favourable prospects for the future—notably a large expansion of the oil industry. New pipelines were built to Tripoli in 1949 and to Banias in Syria in 1952; the oil-fields of Mosul and Basra were producing much crude petroleum by 1951–52. A National Development Board was created in 1950 and became later, in 1953, a national ministry. An agreement of February 1952 gave to the Iraq Government 50 per cent of the oil companies' profits before deductions for foreign taxes. Abundant resources were thus available for development projects of national benefit (e.g. the flood control and irrigation works opened in April 1956 on the Tigris at Samarra and on the Euphrates at Ramadi).

THE BAGHDAD PACT

Iraq, in the field of foreign relations, was confronted during these years with a choice between the Western powers, eager to establish in the Middle East an organized pattern of defence, and the Soviet Union, entering at this time into a diplomatic propaganda and economic drive to increase her influence in the Arab lands. Baghdad, in February 1955, made with Ankara an alliance for mutual co-operation and defence. Britain acceded to this pact in the following April, agreeing also to end the Anglo-Iraqi agreement of 1930 and to surrender her air bases at Shu'ayba and Habbaniya. With the adherence of Pakistan in September and of Iran in October 1955 the so-called Baghdad Pact was completed: a defensive cordon now existed along the southern fringe of the Soviet Union.

CONSEQUENCES OF THE SUEZ CRISIS

The outbreak of hostilities between Israel and Egypt on October 29th, 1956, and the armed intervention of British and French forces against Egypt (October 31st–November 6th) led to a delicate situation in Iraq, where strong elements were still opposed to all connections with the Western Powers. Iraq, indeed, broke off diplomatic relations with France on November 9th and announced that, for the immediate future at least, it could give no assurance of taking part in further sessions of the Council of the Baghdad Pact, if delegates from Britain were present.

The attitude of the Baghdad Government during the Suez crisis had provoked unrest in Iraq. Disturbances at Najaf and Mosul resulted in some loss of life. Student demonstrations against the Anglo-French intervention in Egypt and the Israeli campaign in Sinai led the Iraqi Government to close colleges and schools. Martial law, imposed on October 31st, 1956, was not raised until May 27th, 1957.

The tension born of the Suez crisis persisted for some time to come. President Eisenhower, concerned over the flow of Soviet arms to Syria and Egypt, sought from Congress permission to use the armed forces of the United States to defend nations exposed to danger from countries under the influence of international communism. He also requested authorization to disburse 200 million dollars in economic and military aid to the Middle East states prepared to co-operate with the West. This programme received the formal approval of the Congress and Senate of the United States in March 1957. On March 16th the U.S.A. pledged some $12,500,000 of the funds available under the "Eisenhower Doctrine" to the Muslim members of the Baghdad Pact and also made it known that it would participate actively in the work of the military committee of the Pact.

RELATIONS WITH SYRIA AND JORDAN

At the time of the Suez crisis there had been sharp tension between Iraq and Syria. Pumping-stations located inside Syria and belonging to the Iraq Petroleum Company were sabotaged in November 1956 with the result that Iraq suffered a large financial loss through the interruption in the flow of oil to the Mediterranean coast. Not until March 1957 did Syria allow the Iraq Petroleum Company to begin the repair of the pipelines.

Since the Suez crisis of 1956 troops of Iraq and Syria had been stationed in Jordan as a precaution against an Israeli advance to the east. Iraq, in December 1956, announced that her troops would be withdrawn; the Syrian forces, however, still remained in Jordan. The fear that Syria might intervene in favour of the elements in Jordan opposed to King Hussein brought about further recriminations between Baghdad and Damascus. The danger of an acute crisis receded in April 1957, when the U.S.A. declared that the independence of Jordan was a matter of vital concern and underlined this statement by sending its Sixth Fleet to the eastern Mediterranean. In February 1958 King Faisal of Iraq and King Hussein of Jordan joined together in an abortive Arab Federation.

OVERTHROW OF THE MONARCHY

King Faisal II, together with the Crown Prince of Iraq and General Nuri as-Sa'id, lost their lives in the course of a *coup d'état* begun on July 14th, 1958, by units of the Iraqi Army. Iraq was now to become a Republic. Power was placed in the hands of a council of sovereignty exercising presidential authority and of a cabinet led by Brigadier 'Abd al-Karim Kassem, with the rank of Prime Minister.

A struggle for power was now to develop between the two main architects of the July *coup d'état*—Brigadier (later General) Kassem, the Prime Minister, and Colonel (later Field-Marshal) Abd al-Salam Muhammad Aref, the Deputy Prime Minister and Minister of the Interior. Colonel Aref was associated with the influential Baath Party and had shown himself to be a supporter of union between Iraq and the United Arab Republic. Now, in September 1958, he was dismissed from his offices and, in November, was tried on a charge of plotting against the interests of Iraq. As reconstituted in February 1959 the new régime might be described as hostile to the United Arab Republic and inclined to favour a form of independent nationalism with left-wing tendencies. In March 1959 a rebellion in Mosul was suppressed almost immediately.

General Kassem announced the withdrawal of Iraq from the Baghdad Pact on March 24th, 1959. Since the revolution of July 1958 Iraq's adherence to the Pact had been little more than nominal. One result of this withdrawal was the termination of the special agreement existing between Britain and Iraq since 1955 under the first article of the Baghdad Pact. On March 31st it was made known that the Royal Air Force contingent at Habbaniyah would be recalled.

PROBLEMS OF THE KASSEM RÉGIME

Earlier in 1959 the Communist elements in Iraq had been refused representation in the government. The Communists operated through a number of professional organizations and also through the so-called People's Resistance Force. Communist elements had infiltrated into the armed forces of Iraq and into the civil service. General Kassem now began to introduce measures which would limit Communist influence inside the government and administration of the country. In July 1959 fighting occurred at Kirkuk between the Kurds (supported by the People's Resistance Force) and the Turcomans, with the result that Kassem disbanded the People's Resistance Force. How strong the internal tensions had become in Iraq was underlined when, on October 7th, 1959, an attempt was made on the life of General Kassem.

REBELLION OF THE KURDS

Much more important for the government at Baghdad was the fact that, in March 1961, a considerable section of the Kurdish population in northern Iraq rose in rebellion under Mustafa Barzani, the President of the Democratic Party of Kurdistan—a party established in 1958 after the return of Barzani from an exile occasioned by an earlier unsuccessful revolt in 1946. The refusal of the central régime at Baghdad to grant the reiterated Kurdish demands for an autonomous status had contributed greatly to bring about the new insurrection. Mustafa Barzani in March 1961 proclaimed an independent Kurdish state. By September 1961 the rebels controlled some 250 miles of mountainous territory along the Iraqi-Turkish and Iraqi-Persian frontiers, from Zakho in the west to Sulaimaniya in the east. The Kurds were able to consolidate their hold over much of northern Iraq during the course of 1962. Military operations tended, in these years, to follow a regular pattern—a spring and summer offensive by the government forces, with the ground then won being lost again to the Kurds in the autumn and winter. The Kurds used guerrilla tactics with much success to isolate and deprive the government garrisons in the north of supplies. By December 1963 Kurdish forces had advanced south towards the Khanaqin area and the main road linking Iraq with Iran. The government troops found themselves in fact confined to the larger towns such as Kirkuk, Sulaimaniya and Khanaqin. Negotiations for peace began near Sulaimaniya in January 1964 and led to a cease-fire on February 10th. The national claims of the Kurds were to be recognized in a new provisional constitution for Iraq. Moreover, a general amnesty would be granted by the Iraqi Government. The Kurdish tribesmen, however, refused to lay aside their arms until their political demands had been given practical effect. Despite the negotiation of this settlement it was soon to become clear that no final solution of the Kurdish problem was as yet in sight.

FALL OF KASSEM

A military *coup* carried out in Baghdad on February 8th, 1963, overthrew the régime of General Kassem, the General himself being captured and shot. The *coup* arose out of an alliance between nationalist army officers and the Baath Party. Colonel Aref was now raised to the office of President and a new cabinet created under Brigadier Ahmed al-Bakr. The Baath Party, founded in 1941 (in Syria) and dedicated to the ideas of Arab unity, socialism and freedom, drew its main support from the military elements, the intellectuals and the middle classes. It was, however, divided in Iraq into a pro-Egyptian wing advocating union with the United Arab Republic and a more independent wing disinclined to accept authoritarian control from Egypt. The coup of February 1963 was followed by the arrest of pro-Kassem and of Communist elements, by mass trials and a number of executions, by confiscations of property and by a purge of the officer corps and of the civil service.

A number of efforts were made, during the years 1963–65, to further the cause of Arab unification, but agreements made between Syria and Iraq, and between Egypt, Syria and Iraq, had little practical effect.

MANOEUVRES OF THE BAATH PARTY

These same years saw in Iraq itself a conflict for control between the extremist and the more moderate Baath elements. At the end of September 1963 the extremists dominated the Baath Regional Council in Iraq. An international Baath Conference held at Damascus in October 1963 strengthened the position of the extremists through its support of a federal union between Syria and Iraq and its approval of more radical social and economic policies. A further Baathist conference at Baghdad in November 1963 enabled the moderates to elect a new Baath

Regional Council in Iraq with their own adherents in control. At this juncture the extremists attempted a *coup d'état*, in the course of which air force elements attacked the Presidential Palace and the Ministry of Defence.

On November 18th, 1963, President Aref assumed full powers in Iraq, with the support of the armed forces, and a new Revolutionary Command was established at Baghdad. Sporadic fighting occurred (November 18th–20th) between the government troops and the pro-Baathist National Guard. A main factor in the sudden fall of the Baathists was the attitude of the professional officer class. Officers with Communist, Kassemite or pro-Nasser sympathies, or with no strong political views, or of Kurdish origin, had all been removed from important commands and offices. The privileged position of the National Guard caused further resentment in the army. The long drawn-out operations against the Kurds, the known dissensions within the Baathist ranks in Iraq and the intervention of Baath politicians from abroad in Iraqi affairs also contributed to discredit the extreme elements amongst the Baathists. On November 20th, 1963, a new Cabinet was formed at Baghdad, consisting of officers, moderate Baathists, independents and non-party experts.

THE ARAB SOCIALIST UNION

On July 14th, 1964, President Aref announced that all political parties would be merged in a new organization known as the "Iraqi Arab Socialist Union". At the same time it was revealed that all banks and insurance companies, together with thirty-two important industrial concerns, would undergo nationalization. The firms now nationalized included steel, cement and tobacco concerns, flour mills, food industries, building material firms and tanneries.

In July 1965 a number of pro-Nasser ministers handed in their resignations. At the beginning of September 1965 a new administration came into being with Brigadier Aref Abd al-Razzaq as Prime Minister. The Brigadier, reputed to be pro-Nasser in his sympathies, attempted to seize full power in Iraq, but his attempted *coup d'état* failed and, on September 16th, he himself, together with some of his supporters, found refuge in Cairo. On April 13th, 1966, President Abd al-Salam Aref of Iraq was killed in a helicopter crash. His brother Major-General Abd al-Rahman Aref succeeded him as President with the approval of the Cabinet and of the National Defence Council. In late June 1966 Brigadier Aref Abd al-Razzaq, who had staged the unsuccessful *coup d'état* of September 1965, led a second abortive coup, which was foiled by the prompt action of President Aref.

KURDISH NATIONALISM

The war against the Kurds, halted only for a short while by the cease-fire of February 1964, dragged out its inconclusive course during 1964–66. Some of the fighting in December 1965 occurred close to the Iraq-Iran border, leading to a number of frontier violations which gave rise to sharp tension between the two states during the first half of 1966. In June of 1966 Dr. Abd al-Rahman al-Bazzaz, Prime Minister of Iraq since September 1965, formulated new proposals for a settlement of the conflict with the Kurds. Kurdish nationalism and language would receive legal recognition; the administration was to be decentralized, allowing the Kurds to run educational, health and municipal affairs in their own districts; the Kurds would have proportional representation in Parliament and in the Cabinet and the various state services; the Kurdish armed forces (some 15,000 strong) were to be dissolved. Mustafa Barzani, the Kurdish leader, declared himself to be well disposed towards these proposals.

This entente was implemented only to a limited extent. The cabinet formed in May 1967 contained Kurdish elements, and President Aref, after a visit to the north in late 1967, reaffirmed his intention to make available to the Kurds appointments of ministerial rank, to help with the rehabilitation of the war-affected areas in Kurdistan, and to work towards effective co-operation with the Kurds in the Government of Iraq. This state of quiescence was, however, broken in the first half of 1968 by reports of dissension amongst the Kurds themselves, with open violence between the adherents of Mustafa Barzani and the supporters of Jalal Talabani, who had co-operated with the Government.

OIL DISPUTES AND THE JUNE WAR

Although the winter of 1966–67 brought an improvement in relations with Iran, it also witnessed a dispute between Syria and the Iraq Petroleum Company—a dispute which was to have a serious effect on the oil revenues accruing to Iraq. The government at Damascus claimed that it had not been receiving from the IPC the full amount of revenue due to it under an agreement reached in 1955. To compensate for the alleged loss of revenue, levied on oil carried across Syria from the IPC fields in northern Iraq to ports on the Mediterranean coast, the Damascus Government demanded large back payments, increased the transit charges, and envisaged also the imposition of a surcharge. The Iraqi Government was also considering a request to the IPC that oil production in Iraq be raised 10 per cent. It was embroiled, moreover, in a long argument with the IPC over concession areas confiscated from the company five years earlier, but as yet unsettled by the national oil organization created to take them over. On December 8th, 1966, Syria impounded the property of the Iraq Petroleum Company within its territories. On December 12th–13th Iraqi oil ceased to flow across Syria to Banias and to Tripoli. Iraq was thus confronted with a potential loss of revenue amounting to about £8 million per month. Several delegations from Baghdad went to Damascus in order to urge that a settlement be found for the dispute. Not until the beginning of March 1967, however, was a new agreement signed between the IPC and the Syrian Government. It was announced early in May 1967 that the IPC had also reached agreement in principle with the Iraqi Government on the royalties payable for the first quarter of 1967, when the pipeline across Syria was out of use.

When the Arab-Israeli war broke out in June 1967, the movement of Iraqi oil was again affected. Problems connected with its production and export constituted a major preoccupation of the Baghdad Government during the period immediately following the war. Iraq had at the outset severed diplomatic relations with the U.S.A. and Britain after Arab charges that the two states had aided Israel in the war and she also banned the export of oil to them. When, at the end of June, supplies of Iraqi oil began to be moved once more from the pipeline terminals on the Mediterranean, this embargo remained. In August Iraq, Syria and the Lebanon resolved to allow the export of Iraqi oil to most of the countries of Europe, the United Kingdom being still subject, however, to the embargo.

Relations with the West improved slightly during the autumn and winter of 1967. The remaining oil embargoes were gradually removed, and in December General Sabri led a military delegation to Paris. This was followed by President Aref's official visit to France in February 1968, and in April France agreed to supply Iraq with 54 Mirage aircraft over the period 1969–73. In May diplomatic relations with the United Kingdom were resumed.

THE 1968 COUP AND ITS AFTERMATH

Throughout the first half of 1968 the régime conspicuously lacked popular support, being commonly thought to be both corrupt and inefficient, and the sudden bloodless *coup d'état* of July 17th did not surprise many observers. General Ahmed Hassan al-Bakr, a former Prime Minister, became President; the deposed President Aref went into exile and his Prime Minister, Taher Yahya, was imprisoned on corruption charges. A new government was soon dismissed by the President, who accused it of "reactionary tendencies". He then appointed himself Prime Minister and Commander-in-Chief and chose a new cabinet in which Generals Hardan Takriti and Saleh Ammash (formerly Interior Minister) were seen as the other major figures.

During the second half of 1968 the internal political situation deteriorated steadily. By November there were frequent reports of a purge directed against opponents of the new régime, and freedom of verbal political comment seemed to have disappeared. Numerous Western teachers and professional people were expelled. A former Foreign Minister, Dr. Nasser al-Hani, was found murdered, and a distinguished former Prime Minister, Dr. al-Bazzaz, and other members of former governments were arrested as "counter-revolutionary leaders"; most were later given long jail sentences. Open hostilities with the Kurds broke out in October 1968 for the first time since the June 1966 ceasefire, and continued on an extensive scale throughout the winter. Iraqi army and air force attempts to enforce the writ of the Baghdad Government had little success; the régime claimed that the rebels were receiving aid from Iran and Israel. Fighting continued unabated through 1969, the Kurds demanding autonomy within the state and asking for UN mediation.

SETTLEMENT WITH THE KURDS

The most important event of 1970 was the settlement with the Kurds when, in March, a fifteen-article peace plan was announced by the Revolutionary Command Council and the Kurdish leaders. The plan conceded that the Kurds should participate fully in the Government; that Kurdish officials should be appointed in areas inhabited by a Kurdish majority; that Kurdish should be the official language, along with Arabic, in Kurdish areas; that development of Kurdish areas should be implemented; and that the provisional constitution should be amended to incorporate the rights of the Kurds.

The agreement was generally accepted by the Kurdish community and fighting ceased immediately. The war had been very expensive for Iraq, in terms of both lives and money, and it had seriously delayed the national development programme. It had also absorbed a large part of Iraq's army, which consequently became available for service on Israel's eastern front—joining the Iraqi force already stationed in Jordan—or for defensive duties on the Iranian frontier.

The Kurdish settlement, although not entirely satisfactory, did introduce an element of stability into life in Iraq and allowed a number of reforms to be initiated. In October 1970 the state of emergency, in operation almost continuously since July 1958, was lifted. Many political detainees, including former ministers, were released. Censorship of mail was abolished at the end of the year, having lasted for over thirteen years, and a month later the censorship of foreign correspondents' cables was brought to an end after a similar period.

Kurdish unity was boosted in February 1971 by the decision of the Kurdish Revolutionary Party to merge with the Kurdish Democratic Party of Mustafa Barzani and in July 1971 a new provisional constitution was announced, which embodied many of the points contained in the 1970 settlement. The Kurds were directed by the Supreme Committee for Kurdish Affairs to give up their arms by August 1971 and the situation in the north continued to be normal.

Evidence of unrest, however, was growing both in Kurdistan and in the Government itself. In July 1971 an attempted coup by army and air force officers was put down by the Government but dissatisfaction continued to be reported. The Kurds were beginning to show discontent with the delays in implementing the 1970 agreement. Their demand for participation in the Revolutionary Command Council was refused and in September 1971 an attempt was made on Barzani's life.

THE CONTINUING KURDISH PROBLEM

During 1972, possibly because of increasing preoccupation with foreign affairs, dissension within the Government was less in evidence. Clashes with the Kurds, however, became more frequent and there was another plot to assassinate Barzani in July. The Baath Party's deteriorating relations with the Kurds brought a threat from the Kurdish Democratic Party to renew the civil war. One of the main Kurdish grievances was that the census agreed upon in 1970 had still not taken place. The two sides met to discuss their differences, the Kurdish side pointing to the unfulfilled provisions of the 1970 agreement and the Baath reiterating the various development projects carried out in Kurdish areas. In December 1972, a break appeared in the Kurdish ranks when it was reported that a breakaway party was to be set up in opposition to Barzani's party.

FOREIGN RELATIONS 1968-71

The more radical section of the Arab world had initially greeted the July 1968 coup with disfavour and the new régime was at pains to prove itself as militant an exponent of Arab nationalism as its predecessor. The régime gradually became an accepted member of the nationalist group, but there was some Arab criticism of its policies, notably the public hangings and their effect on world opinion. In March 1969, a joint Eastern Command was established comprising Jordan, Syria and Iraq.

Like Algeria, on the opposite flank of the Arab world, Iraq took a hard line on the Palestinian problem (having moved substantial forces into Jordan on the outbreak of war in 1967). All peace proposals—American, Egyptian and Jordanian—were rejected. In theory total support was given to the Palestine liberation movement but, despite a threat to the Jordanian Government at the beginning of September 1970 to intervene in Jordan on behalf of the Palestinian guerrillas, the Iraqi forces stationed there did not take part in the fighting. In January 1971, most of Iraq's 20,000 troops were withdrawn from both Jordan and Syria. In March it was reported in Cairo that Iraq's monthly contribution to the Palestine Liberation Army had ceased. Iraq's attitude to Middle East peace proposals opened up a rift with Egypt even before President Nasser's death and her contempt for the proposed Egypt-Libya-Syria federation, as well as for any negotiated settlement with Israel, kept her well isolated from Egypt and almost all the other Arab states. In July 1971 there were signs that Iraq wished to reduce her isolation, offering to co-operate again with the Arab states if they abandoned attempts to negotiate with Israel, but the renewal of hostilities between the Jordanian Government and the guerrillas caused a break in relations with Jordan. Iraq closed the border, called for Jordan's expulsion from the Arab League and banned her from participating in the Eighth International Baghdad Fair.

Meanwhile, relations with Iran continued to be poor. Iraq frequently accused the Teheran Government of assisting the Kurdish rebellion and had responded by mass expulsions of Persians resident in Iraq. In April 1969 the Shatt al-Arab waterway again caused a minor confrontation. Iraq had benefited by a 1937 treaty (engineered by the British Government which then effectively controlled Iraq, but not Iran) which gave it control of the waterway. Iran tried to force a re-negotiation of the treaty by illegally sending through vessels flying the Iranian flag. Being unwilling (or politically unable) to yield any of its sovereignty, and unable to challenge Iran militarily, Iraq was obliged to accept this situation. Iraq proposed referring the dispute to the International Court of Justice, but Iran rejected the suggestion. Minor border clashes between the two sides' forces continued to occur sporadically and both Iran and Iraq accused each other of attempting to foment coups. Not surprisingly, the two countries were also divided on policy towards the Gulf States. Iraq broke off diplomatic relations with Iran (and Britain) after Iran's seizure of the Tumb Islands in the Persian/Arabian Gulf in November 1971. The deportation of ever larger numbers of Iranians from Iraq was reported at the end of 1971 and their expulsion continued into 1972.

Relations with the Western world, and the U.S.A. in particular, remained poor, several people arrested or expelled in late 1968 being accused of spying for the Americans. The friendship with the Soviet Union remained the major factor in Iraq's foreign policy, particularly since the U.S.S.R. was supplying the bulk of Iraq's military equipment.

THE PROBLEM OF OIL

Relations between the Government and the IPC continued to be strained, the Government continually maintaining its intention of eventually exploiting its own oil resources. An agreement reached in March 1972 provided for a 20 per cent Government participation in the concessions of the Iraq, Basra and Mosul Petroleum Companies but the details of the agreement were left for further negotiation. The North Rumeila field, expropriated from the IPC in 1962, started production in April 1972, its development having been financed by a Russian loan. Nevertheless, Iraq was still dependent on Western oil interests and the Government was anxious that output should be maintained at a high level in order to safeguard revenues. Thus the cutback in production from the northern oilfields in early 1972 caused the Government to protest. In June 1972 IPC's interests were nationalized and the company immediately announced that it would take legal action to prevent the marketing of the oil.

Immediately after the break with IPC, Iran concluded an agreement with France for the sale of 23.75 per cent of oil from the nationalized Kirkuk field. This was, the Government explained, in token of France's continued friendly attitude towards the Arab World. Contacts were also made with Spain, Italy, Greece, India, Japan and Brazil. By the end of 1972 it was clear that Iraq was maintaining sales, although the situation was marred by a dispute over transit dues for use of the IPC pipeline which Syria had nationalized on June 2nd, 1972. Syria was insisting on higher rates than those originally paid by

IPC and an agreement was only reached in January 1973.

Meanwhile, contacts between IPC and the Government to determine compensation had continued, and IPC had repeatedly postponed its deadline for beginning legal proceedings. With the mediation of Nadim Pachachi of OPEC and Jean Duroc-Danner of CFP, an agreement was finally reached on February 28th, 1973. The company agreed to settle Iraqi claims for back royalties by paying £141 million, and to waive its objections to Law No. 80 under which the North Rumeila fields were seized in 1961. The Government agreed to deliver a total of 15 million tons of crude from Kirkuk, to be loaded at Eastern Mediterranean ports, to the companies as compensation. The Mosul Petroleum Company agreed to relinquish all its assets without compensation and the Basrah Petroleum Company, the only one of the group to remain operational in Iraq, undertook to increase output from 32 million tons in 1972 to 80 million tons in 1976. This agreement was regarded on the whole as a victory for the Iraqi Government, although the companies were by no means net losers by it.

With the IPC dispute out of the way, Iraq showed its unwillingness to continue indefinitely with exporting oil on a barter basis to the Eastern Bloc countries. The Government made it clear that it would press for a cash basis to future agreements.

FOREIGN RELATIONS 1972–73

The nationalization of IPC brought expressions of approval from a number of countries, including Arab States and the Soviet Union. The 15-year friendship treaty with the Soviet Union, signed in March 1972, was ratified in July and Iraq's relations with the Eastern Bloc states continued to be good. Despite this, however, the Government was well aware of the dangers of too close and exclusive a relationship with the Soviet Bloc. France was specifically singled out as the Western country most friendly towards the Arabs and the President's fourth anniversary speech in July revealed that Iraq would not be unwilling to open up friendly relations with Western countries. Although diplomatic relations with the United States were still severed, the U.S.A. established an "interests section" in Baghdad.

CONSTITUTIONAL CHANGE

In July 1973 an abortive *coup* took place, led by the Security chief, Nazim Kazzar, in which the Minister of Defence, General Hammad Shehab, was killed. It is thought that it was an attempt by a civilian faction within the Baath Party to get rid of President Bakr and the military faction. One result of the attempted *coup* was an amendment to the constitution giving more power to the President, and the formation of a National Front between the Baath Party and the Iraq Communist Party. There seemed a possibility at this time that the Kurdistan Democratic Party might be persuaded to join the National Front, but later events were to prove these hopes groundless.

CLIMAX AND END OF KURDISH WAR

According to the agreement made between the Iraq Government and the Kurds in March 1970 the deadline for implementation of the agreement was March 11th, 1974. An uneasy peace between the Kurds and the Iraqis had existed between those two dates. When March 11th, 1974, arrived Sadam Hussein Takriti, the Vice-President of the Revolution Command Council and the "strong man" of the regime, announced the granting of autonomy to the Kurds. Barzani and his Kurdish Democratic Party felt that the Iraqi offer fell short of their demands for full government representation, which included membership of the Revolution Command Council. A minority of Kurds, who belonged to Abdel Satter Sharif's Kurdish Revolutionary Party welcomed the proposals, however. Barzani and his militia, the Pesh-Merga, began armed resistance in north Iraq. In April 1974 the Iraqi Government replaced five Kurdish Ministers known to support Barzani by five other Kurds who supported the Government plan for giving the Kurds a measure of autonomy. Later in April the Iraqi Government appointed a Kurd, Taha Moheddin Marouf, as Vice-President of Iraq, but since he had long been a supporter of the Baghdad Government, it seemed unlikely that this would pacify the Kurds of the K.D.P.

By August 1974 the Kurdish war had reached a new level of intensity. The Baghdad Government was directing large military resources against the *Pesh Merga*, as Barzani's forces were called, and were deploying tanks, field guns and bombers. About 130,000 Kurds, mainly women, children and old men, took refuge in Iran. The *Pesh Merga* were able to keep up their resistance in Iraq only with the help of arms and other supplies from Iran. When, therefore, an agreement to end their border dispute was signed by Iraq and Iran at the OPEC meeting in Algiers on March 6th, 1975, both countries also agreed to end "infiltrations of a subversive character" and the Kurdish rebellion collapsed. Barzani felt that he could not continue his struggle without Iran's aid, and fled to Teheran. A ceasefire was arranged on March 13th, and Iraq announced that an amnesty would be granted to all Kurds who surrendered by April 1st. About 200,000 Kurds fled to Iran when the rebellion collapsed, but only between 50,000 and 60,000 were expected to settle permanently in Iran. The amnesty was later extended for two months, and by November 1975 a substantial part of the Kurdish population had returned to the mountain towns and villages, and many houses and buildings that were destroyed were being rebuilt. By February 1976, however, it was reported that the K.D.P. was secretly reorganizing inside Iraqi Kurdistan and preparing to resume its struggle. In March there were reports of clashes between Kurds and Iraqi security forces in the Ruwanduz area, after Iraqi attempts to clear the frontier area with Iran and resettle Kurds in less sensitive areas of Iraq. A new political organization, the National Union of Kurdistan, was also set up in Damascus quite separately from the K.D.P., which, in the opinion of the National Union of Kurdistan, had become discredited. Kurdish guerrilla units were allegedly undergoing secret training in preparation for a renewed war to begin later in 1976. Renewed skirmishing, led by Jalal Talabani, certainly began, but it was not serious enough to weaken the Iraqi claim that the Kurdish problem had been solved. Reconstruction and school-building was certainly undertaken in Kurdish areas in 1977, and in April 1977 the Iraqi authorities allowed 40,000 Kurds who had been compulsorily settled in the south in 1975 to return to their homes in the north. It was also decided in April 1977 by the Executive Council of the Kurdish Autonomous Region that Kurdish should become the official language to be used in all communications and by all government departments in the Kurdish Autonomous Region which had no connection with the central government.

FOREIGN AFFAIRS 1973–76

On the outbreak of the October 1973 war between the Arabs and Israel, Iraq sent considerable land forces to the Syrian front and took advantage of Iran's offer to resume diplomatic relations. The Iraqi Government, however, had taken offence because President Sadat had not consulted Iraq in advance, and because of this Iraqi forces were withdrawn from Syria as soon as the ceasefire went into effect, and Iraq boycotted the Arab summit meeting in Algiers in November.

Relations deteriorated with Iran in the early months of 1974, when frontier fighting broke out, and it was only after the appointment of a UN Mediator in March that "normal" relations on the frontier were restored, and they deteriorated again in August in spite of talks in Istanbul between Iraqi and Iranian diplomats. Further border clashes took place in December 1974, and secret talks in Istanbul between the Iraqi and Iranian Foreign Ministers in January 1975 failed to prevent the outbreak of fresh clashes in February. It was therefore something of a surprise when at the OPEC meeting at Algiers in March 1975 it was announced that Sadam Hussein Takriti, Vice-President of the Iraqi Revolutionary Command Council, and the Shah of Iran had signed an agreement which "completely eliminated the conflict between the two brotherly countries". This agreement also ended the Kurdish war (*see* above), and was embodied in a treaty signed between the two countries in June 1975. The frontiers were defined on the basis of the Protocol of Constantinople of 1913 and the verbal agreement on frontiers of 1914. The Shatt al-Arab frontier was defined according to the thalweg Line, which runs down the middle of the deepest shipping channel.

THE BAATH PARTY AND RELATIONS WITH SYRIA

Iraq was one of the many Arab states who were severely critical of the second interim disengagement agreement signed between Egypt and Israel in September 1975. Iraqi reaction to the agreement was similar to that of Syria, but this condemnation was perhaps the only thing upon which the two countries agreed upon between 1975 and 1978. Rivalry between the two wings of the Baath party in Baghdad and Damascus, and a dispute over the sharing of the water from the Euphrates were just two areas of contention. In February 1976 Iraq was reported to be diverting much of its oil from pipelines to the Mediterranean to terminals near Basra, thus depriving Syria of valuable pipeline revenues. Iraq was also very critical of Syria's intervention in the Lebanon. Syrian agents were also blamed for the violence which took place in the Shia holy cities of Najaf and Kerbala in February 1977. Rioting took place when Iraqi authorities banned a Shia procession. The secular wing of the Baath party are distrustful of Shia religious feelings and, on the other hand, the Shia element have always felt under-represented in Baghdad. Relations with Syria deteriorated even further in late 1977, and Iraq became somewhat isolated after President Sadat of Egypt's peace initiative in visiting Jerusalem in November 1977. At the Tripoli Conference, summoned by the States who disagreed with President Sadat's approach, Iraq wanted a specific rejection of UN Resolution 242. The stand taken by the other participants (Syria, Libya, Yemen P.D.R., Algeria and the Palestine Liberation Organization) seemed too moderate for Iraq, who walked out of the Conference. Iraq subsequently boycotted the Algiers conference of "rejectionist" States in February 1978, hoping unsuccessfully to form its own "steadfastness and liberation front" at a Baghdad conference.

NEW ALIGNMENTS

Iraq opposed the Camp David agreements made between Egypt and Israel in September 1978, but, continuing its attitude of boycott, it stayed away from the Damascus Arab summit which immediately followed the Camp David agreements. Iraq's period of isolation was almost at an end, however. In October President Assad of Syria visited Baghdad and, as a result, Iraq and Syria signed a Charter outlining plans for political and economic union between the two countries. Old rivalries and animosities were set aside in an effort to form a political and military power which would be a sizeable counterweight to Egypt in Middle Eastern affairs. In November Iraq successfully called a Pan-Arab summit which threatened sanctions against Egypt if a peace treaty with Israel should be signed, and in March 1979, when the peace treaty became a fact, Baghdad was the venue for the meeting of the Arab Foreign and Economic Ministers which resolved to put into practice the threats made to Egypt in the previous November.

The plans for complete political and economic union between Iraq and Syria have not advanced as quickly as the two Presidents had hoped. After four days of unity talks in Baghdad in June 1979 President Assad repeated that "our aim is total unity between Syria and Iraq as a strong, solid and genuine nucleus for comprehensive Arab unity." In practical terms, however, the meeting produced little more than fresh plans and fresh committees.

Relations with Iran had been quite friendly since the treaty between the two countries which was signed in June 1975. Iraq expressed support for the revolutionary regime when it first came to power in Iran in early 1979, but by June 1979 relations had deteriorated. Iraq was suspicious of the trend of Iran's Islamic policy, which stemmed from the Shia sect, whereas the leadership in Iraq belong to the Sunni sect. Iran accused Iraq of fomenting trouble and supplying arms to Iran's Arab (Sunni) minority in Kuzestan.

INTERNAL DIFFICULTIES

During 1979 the unity of the National Progressive Front, the alliance of the Baathists and the Communists, appeared to be breaking up. In the summer of 1978 21 army personnel were executed for conducting communist political activity in the army, and, although Sadam Hussein visited Moscow in December 1978 and relations with the U.S.S.R. improved temporarily, another 27 army personnel were purged in April 1979. Communist sources claim that a campaign of executions and harassment of Communists has reached a very high level, whereas Iraqi sources maintain that only law-breakers have been punished. Certainly, the Communist Party declared that they were no longer part of the National Progressive Front, the Communist daily *Tarik al Shaab* was suspended for thirty days in April and two Communist Ministers lost their posts. Further trouble seemed likely to develop with the Kurdish minority, with reports that Kurds were once again being removed from northern areas and forced to re-settle in the south.

On July 16th, 1979, Sadam Hussein replaced Bakr as President of Iraq and Chairman of the Revolutionary Command Council (RCC). A few days later an attempted coup was reported. Several members of the RCC were sentenced to death for their alleged part in the plot, and the newly-formed Syrian alliance seemed to be at risk as speculation grew that Syria was implicated.

ECONOMIC SURVEY

Iraq is traditionally an agricultural country, but its economic development has been largely attributable to its oil industry. Revenues from oil were stagnant in the early 1960s at ID 120–135 million but in the year ending March 31st, 1972, they had risen to ID 354 million as a result of increased production and revised agreements with the oil companies. The improvement in revenues was for a short time halted by the nationalization of the Iraq Petroleum Company in 1972, which led to a temporary loss of production.

As a result of price increases since 1973, the value of petroleum exports rose from ID 340 million in 1972 to ID 2,415 million in 1975, ID 2,691 million in 1976 and ID 2,807 million in 1977, and were estimated at ID 2,690 million in 1978.

Iraq is an underpopulated country which, according to both historical evidence and present estimates of possible expansion, could support a population of, perhaps, twice the size of her present 12 million.

These great advantages have certain limitations placed upon them by the nature of the country and the degree of social evolution attained by its people. Salination of the soil and the spreading of malaria as a result of big irrigation projects are dangers that have to be guarded against. The two great rivers, the Tigris and Euphrates, which must be the basis of the country's entire system of irrigation, are difficult to control. In addition, the country, with the exception of its northern area, is extremely flat and only a little above sea-level. This makes drainage and irrigation difficult and explains why most of the land at present consists of either desert or swamps. On the human side there may be a shortage of labour, and, particularly at the present moment, of the skilled labour that will be required to accomplish and operate the vast and up-to-date schemes of agricultural and industrial development that are contemplated or actually in process of execution.

The total population was estimated at 12.2 million in 1977, mostly living in the alluvial plain of the Tigris and Euphrates or the foothills of the north-east. Between 1965 and 1977 the population increased by 3.3 per cent annually. The working population was estimated at 4 million in 1975. There is little unemployment in the agricultural and public service sectors, although much labour is not fully utilized. Rural areas have some under-employment, but the labour pool is decreasing: rural migration in the decade to 1975 lowered the percentage of the population living in a rural environment from 49 per cent to 35 per cent and the movement has continued. The October 1977 census indicated that only 27 per cent of the population live outside the urban areas. Though many women work in agriculture, women are not generally employed elsewhere and at the present time cannot be regarded as making a substantial contribution to the non-agricultural labour force.

Since the Baath Socialist Party came to power in 1968, the Government has steadily expanded its control of the economy. Government organizations currently account for 78 per cent of Iraq's G.N.P. and purchase 90 per cent of imported goods. Output from the oil sector (entirely owned by the Government) now constitutes about 60 per cent of G.N.P. State companies own and operate all heavy industries and the Government, through the Industrial Bank, owns major shares of small "mixed" public sectors, which include electronics and several other light industries. The private sector, contributing about 20 per cent of G.N.P. and purchasing about 9 per cent of imports, is concentrated in food processing, textile manufacturing, tourism, services and retailing.

In the years 1973–76 Iraq's oil exports increased by 61 per cent in volume and by 312 per cent in price. As a result, Iraq's G.N.P. at current prices increased from US $5,300 million in 1973 to an estimated US $16,000 million in 1976. In 1976 per capita G.N.P. was estimated at $1,390. Financed by this new-found wealth, Iraq's imports increased fourfold in the period 1973–76. However, a decline in Iraq's oil revenues in the first half of 1976 (the result of a drop in oil production caused by distribution difficulties and the loss of international markets after the nationalization of the Basrah Petroleum Company) caused the Government temporarily to curtail imports, and also led to a slowing down of growth in domestic G.N.P. There was a sharp recovery in the volume of oil production and exports in the second half of 1976 but in 1977 demand weakness affected both output and exports which, for the year as a whole, were respectively 5.1 per cent and 8.1 per cent lower than in 1976. Oil export revenues in 1977 were 4.3 per cent higher than in 1976.

AGRICULTURE

Agriculture is the main source of employment and, next to oil, the most important sector. Although the country's latest development plan (1976–80) gives high priority to industry, agriculture remains important; the aim is to produce an agricultural surplus for export by reducing dependence on weather conditions and solving the salinity problems which affect irrigated land. The development plan has allocated funds for several vast land reclamation and integrated farming projects adding nearly one million acres to the country's arable land.

Until 1958 agricultural improvement was often inhibited by the need for adequate land reform. In October 1958 the Government announced a new and more radical land reform project. This provided for the break-up of large estates whose owners were to be compelled to forfeit their "excess" land to the Government which would redistribute the land to new peasant owners. Under the terms of the reform the largest holding permitted on flow-irrigated land is 1,000 dunums (about 600 acres), and on land watered by rainfall 2,000 dunums. The estates broken up were to be allotted to farmers in holdings of a maximum of 60 or 120 dunums, according to the type of land, and the formation of agricultural co-operatives was planned to help the new owners with capital, machinery and technical advice. Landowners losing land were to be compensated in state bonds (in 1969 all the state's liabilities to recompense land-owners were cancelled). It was hoped that the reform would take only five years to complete but the application of the law was initially mismanaged and the expropriation of land consistently ran ahead of the ability of the administration to distribute it. By the end of 1972 some 4.73 million dunums had been requisitioned from landlords and distributed to 100,646 families, but considerable areas of land remain awaiting distribution. The Government has been promoting the growth of co-operatives and collective farms since 1967.

The general system of cultivation is fallow farming and crop rotations are rare. Despite changes in recent years, the most common type of farm operation is by share tenancy, the farmer surrendering to the land-owner a share of his crop, usually 50 per cent, in return for pump irrigation, water and other facilities. Other forms of operation are: (1) plantation farming, when the landowner or tenant of a rented farm employs paid labour; and (2) individual peasant proprietorships, when the farmer owns or rents his land and works it himself with his family.

The farm worker is concerned primarily with subsistence and grows crops and keeps animals to provide for himself and his family. Cash crops are grown by plantation farmers and peasant proprietors. Types of agriculture vary considerably but the largest and most commonly grown crops are barley and wheat. Together with lentils, vetch and linseed they constitute the main winter crops. Normally Iraq produces an exportable surplus of barley, though in years of low rainfall barley exports are not possible. After several years poor harvest there was a successful cereal crop in 1972 with a total output of 3.5 million tons of cereals, of which 1.75 million tons were exported. The good crop was thought to be largely due to the new high-yielding varieties of seed used. In 1973, wheat and barley output was 1.4 million tons, it rose to 1.9 million tons in 1974, but fell back to 1.3 million tons in 1975. Wheat and barley output totalled 1.9 million tons in 1976. The wheat crop in 1977 was affected by lack of rain and was only 696,000 tons, compared with 1.3 million tons in 1976, but the 1978 wheat crop was expected to be good. The target for 1980 is 4 million tons of cereals.

The principal summer crops include rice, dates, tobacco and sesame, and these are grown much more extensively where better irrigation is available, as in the northern zone between Fallujah, Baghdad and Diyalah. Rice production has fluctuated widly from 306,000 tons in 1971 to 60,500 tons in 1975. The figure for 1977 was 199,200 tons, from 253,900 dunums under cultivation.

Dates are, after oil, one of the biggest export commodities. In 1974 Iraq made new agreements for the supply of dates to Australia and China. Cotton is grown on a small scale in central Iraq. Around the major towns a comparatively sophisticated market gardening organization has developed. The date crop has varied between 350,000 and 400,000 tons per year since 1973.

Generally, agricultural output varies according to rainfall, flooding and political disturbances. In recent years harvests have proved poor, the weather has been unfavourable and fears of massive land collectivization have caused uncertainty, while the Government's promises of greatly increased aid for agricultural development have not been fulfilled. To meet targets set for 1979/80, however, generous loans were to be provided to all areas of production. From a fund of ID 42.8 million, ID 28.3 million was earmarked for the state and collective sectors.

The cost of food imports remains at a very high level having reached a total of U.S. $600 million in 1974, or 30 per cent of all imports, but dropping to $425 million, or 13 per cent of all imports, in 1976. The 1976 budget allocated ID 150 million for food subsidies of which ID 20 million was for sugar. In the 1977 budget food subsidies amounted to ID 93 million. The main suppliers of cereals were the U.S.A. and Australia; rice was supplied by Pakistan and the U.S.A. and large amounts of meat came from New Zealand. A new meat supply agreement was signed with Australian interests early in 1979 for the supply of 5,000 tons of beef and 7,000 tons of lamb. It is expected that Australia and New Zealand will continue to provide important volumes of livestock to the growing Iraqi market. Cuba signed a contract in April 1975 to supply Iraq with 100,000 tons of sugar per year for five years and the Cubans are to assist in the development of Iraq's sugar cane production and refining. The 1976–80 development plan aimed to achieve self-sufficiency in food supplies with a 25 per cent increase in land under cultivation. A total of $11,500 million was to be spent in the agricultural sector over the five year period.

So far funds have been channelled into projects for the production of poultry, eggs, meat and sugar as well as for the necessary construction of dams and the improvement of agricultural mechanization. In April 1978 three cattle and dairy centres were opened at a total cost of ID 18.5 million. The centres were built with technical assistance supplied by Dutch companies. A further ID 42 million is to be spent on establishing poultry farms in the north of Iraq as part of the Government's development drive in the predominantly Kurdish areas.

A survey undertaken by the Central Statistical Organization of Iraq in November 1976 showed that there were 8.4 million sheep and 1.4 million cattle in the country; in 1977 holdings of 11.4 million sheep and 2.6 million cattle were reported. In 1976 there were 3 million goats, 460,000 donkeys, 146,000 buffaloes, 69,000 horses, 52,000 camels and 28,000 mules.

RIVER CONTROL AND IRRIGATION

River control policy in Iraq has three main objects: the provision of water for irrigation, the prevention of devastating floods, and the creation of hydro-electric power. It is southern and central Iraq that are affected in all three cases, since northern Iraq is rain-fed and for the most part the terrain is unsuitable for large-scale irrigation from the stored water of major dams. Minor local reservoirs and tube wells are enough to supplement the rain in the north.

At present the main systems providing flow irrigation are based on the Euphrates (serving nearly 3 million dunums), the Tigris (1.7 million dunums), the Diyalah River and the Lesser Zab River. Pumps are used extensively along both the Euphrates and the Tigris. Four dams, barrages or reservoirs (at Samarra, Dokan, Derbendi Khan and Habbaniyah) provide security against flood dangers. When the waters of the Euphrates and Tigris are fully utilized through dams and reservoirs, the area of cultivated land in Iraq will be almost doubled.

Great emphasis has been placed on the country's need for improved irrigation and an agreement has been signed with the U.S.S.R. for joint co-operation in irrigation affairs. Soviet experts are studying the Bakhma, Hindujah, Haditha, Fallujah and Kirkuk irrigation projects. The current development plan envisages outlays on a number of major water storage and control schemes of which the most important are the Euphrates dam, the Himrin dam, the Eski-Mosul dam and the Bakhma dam, while work on smaller scale canal, drainage and diversion works will also form a continuing element in the overall water control programme. The first phase, 1975–80, of the Kirkuk irrigation project has already begun, and a $10 million contract has been awarded to Italian suppliers for the provision of heavy equipment for this project. Following phases will take a further seven years with the ultimate objective of irrigating 1.5 million dunums. In all ID 250 million will be spent at the Kirkuk site before the field level irrigation and reticulation system is complete. Construction of the Tharthar-Euphrates canal, begun by a U.S.S.R. concern in 1972, was due for completion in 1976. The Lower Khalis irrigation project, financed by the World Bank, will increase the irrigated area by 625,000 dunums. In addition, the Diwaniyah-Dalmaj scheme is due for completion soon and four other schemes—the Abu Gharab, Al Ishaqi, Duja ila and Nahr Saad—will also increase irrigation facilities as well as being interlocked with general agricultural development. In August 1978 the first stage of the Himrin dam project was completed as part of a scheme which will divert the waters of the Diyalah river for hydro-electric power generation and flood-water control. The project will cost ID 60 million, but the only direct benefit to agriculture will be the irrigation of 300 sq. km. when the final stage is completed in the 1980s.

PETROLEUM

The oil industry is the country's principal source of wealth and provides the bulk of capital for all state and municipal industries. Production up to 1972 came almost exclusively from the Iraq Petroleum Company (IPC) and its associated companies, the Mosul Petroleum Company (MPC) and the Basrah Petroleum Company (BPC). The IPC group represented a consortium of British, Dutch, French and American oil companies together with the Gulbenkian interest.

The major oil field controlled by the group was at Kirkuk with subsidiary production from the Jambur, Bai Hassan, Ain Zalah and Butmah fields.

The IPC concession in Iraq dates from 1925 but relations between the oil companies and the Government were first comprehensively formalized in 1952. The companies undertook to pay the Government 50 per cent of their theoretical profit (based on posted prices) as well as certain other revenues, and guaranteed revenue and production minima. In December

1961, after prolonged negotiations for a revision of concession agreements had broken down, the Government passed Law No. 80, under which the companies' area of operations was restricted to their producing oilfields, less than 0.5 per cent of their previous area, and the remainder of their concessions withdrawn.

However, by Law No. 97 of 1967, the Government's oil policy changed direction. Under this law the Iraq National Oil Company (INOC), a state oil company formed in 1964, was given exclusive rights over all areas except those left to IPC in Law No. 80. INOC was to be allowed to operate jointly in association with foreign companies, if it wished, as long as no concession was awarded.

Despite negotiations with several foreign companies, INOC finally announced, early in 1968, that it would develop the rich North Rumeila field by itself. This field, discovered by IPC but expropriated under Law 80, was thought to be capable of producing 42 million tons per year. The Al Rafidain Bank agreed to extend a loan of ID 6 million to INOC to finance the first stage of exploitation. The U.S.S.R. has actively participated in the development of Rumeila under an agreement signed in 1969. A protocol of 1971 provided for the second stage of the Rumeila development, further exploration and a link from the Nahr Umr field to the North Rumeila-Fao pipeline. Production from North Rumeila began in the second quarter of 1972.

Meanwhile, under an agreement signed with INOC, the French firm ERAP (*l'Entreprise de Recherches et d'Activités Petrolières*) began drilling in 1968 near Basra, and discovered oil at Buzurgan, Abu Gharab and Siba. The development of these fields was delayed for some two years by disputes between ERAP and the Iraqi Government but in 1973 a contract was signed complementing the 1968 agreement and allowing for the export of 8 million tons of crude oil a year from the Abu Gharab and Buzurgan fields on completion of the Fao deepwater terminal. The Buzurgan field in fact was due to come on stream at the end of 1976, with Japan also participating in its development.

In February 1971 Iraq participated in the Teheran agreement between the Western oil companies and the six oil-producing countries of the Gulf. The agreement provided for a 35 cents per barrel increase in posted prices on oil shipped from the Gulf as well as for a higher (55 per cent) tax rate on relevant company profits.

In January 1972 the signatories of the Teheran agreement, meeting at Geneva, agreed to a further 8.57 per cent increase in posted prices at the Gulf to offset the effect of the dollar devaluation that resulted from the currency realignment of December 1971. The postings for Iraqi and Saudi Arabian crude oil at East Mediterranean terminals were similarly increased. The additional payments would be linked to an index reflecting changes in the values of nine industrialized countries' currencies and would vary with the appreciation or depreciation of the U.S. dollar as measured by this index. The producing countries later claimed payments in excess of this index which they contended did not sufficiently account for the effects on their revenue of the currency realignments of February 1973. The oil companies finally agreed to meet the full demands of the producing countries in June 1973.

In the event, the situation was totally changed by the Arab-Israeli war of October 1973. Iraq opposed the restrictive policy of the Organization of Arab Petroleum Exporting Countries (OAPEC), even increasing sales to favoured countries. The Government did, however, follow OAPEC's policy in embargoing supplies to the U.S.A. and Holland and nationalized unfriendly states' oil interests in Iraq. In spite of warnings against consumer backlash following the 70 per cent price rises in October 1973, Iraq raised its prices by a further 134 per cent in January 1974. This, combined with increased production, meant that oil revenues in 1973 reached ID 555.3 million.

The year 1973 also saw the settlement, after prolonged and acrimonious discussions, of the long-standing dispute between IPC and the Government. Cutbacks in production in 1972 (necessitated, IPC claimed, by purely commercial considerations) exacerbated the situation. Finally, however, in February 1973 the IPC group conceded the nationalization of its assets in Iraq with the exception of the BPC operation. IPC agreed to the loss of the Kirkuk oilfields in return for a total of 15 million tons of crude oil to be loaded at Eastern Mediterranean ports, free of all charges and at the rate of at least one million tons a month from March 1st, 1973. IPC also agreed to waive its objection to the seizure of the North Rumeila fields in 1961 and also agreed to pay the Government the sum of £141 million as settlement of all Government claims on the group. The MPC agreed to hand over all its assets and installations as of March 31st, 1973, without seeking any compensation.

The IPC pipeline and port facilities in Lebanon were also scheduled to be handed over to the Iraqi Government but Lebanon refused to allow this and a subsequent agreement, signed in Beirut on March 5th, 1973, provided for a Lebanese takeover of the pipeline and loading installations. The American, Dutch and Portuguese interests in BPC were taken over in October 1973 and BPC was completely nationalized in December 1975. Some outstanding claims have still to be settled.

Iraq, as a founder member of OAPEC, has consistently favoured steep oil price increases and the Government wants to increase substantially the country's oil production. With the third largest oil reserves in the Middle East, the Iraqis argue that lack of exploration during the thirteen years of talks which ended in 1975 in the nationalization of IPC has unfairly limited Iraq's above-ground crude oil capacity in comparison to that of neighbouring OPEC countries.

Total oil production in Iraq was 22 million tons in 1957 and 47.3 million tons in 1960. By 1970 output had reached 76.5 million tons, only marginally more than in the previous year, but in 1971 it increased sharply to 83.8 million tons following agreements between the Government and the oil companies on higher production targets for the southern oilfields. A sharp decline in production in 1972 to 71.1 million tons was caused by disputes between IPC and the Government. With the dispute settled, and aided by the output from the new North Rumeila field, production reached 99.4 million tons in 1973. Output fell to 96.9 million tons in 1974, but picked up again in 1975 to reach 110.4 million tons. Production in 1976 fell back to 104 million tons. However, this fall concealed a very sharp increase in the second half of the year when output was well up on that of the corresponding period of 1975. This was partly due to the Buzurgan oil field's coming on stream. This new field's output averages between 8 million and 15 million tons per year. Output in 1977 fell back to 98.7 million tons, but increased to 130 million tons in 1978. A new INOC field, the Lahis field, came on stream in April 1978. Initial capacity is 2.5 million tons. There have also been reports of a major oil strike in Basra which could be one of the biggest in the Middle East. However, initial claims of 2,000 million barrels of reserves for this field have been reduced to 1,000 million.

An oil pipeline linking the Baghdad and Basra refineries was opened in March 1977. The 545 kilometre pipeline was built with Soviet and Japanese aid, and can carry four oil products—gas oil, kerosene, benzine and super-benzine. When associated facilities are completed the project will have cost ID 16 million.

One of Iraq's weaknesses has been its dependence on the transit routes to the Eastern Mediterranean terminals at Tripoli and Banias. The payment of transit dues to Syria and Lebanon, agreed in the 1973 settlement with IPC, was seen as an unjustifiable drain on Iraq's resources. In fact, although the transit agreement was for a 15 year term the financial clauses expired in December 1975 and lengthy negotiations took place in 1976 to replace them. Accordingly, a new strategic pipeline between Haditha and Fao was planned to provide a terminal on the Gulf. This was completed in December 1975 and it was proposed in the absence of agreement with Syria on transit to switch Kirkuk exports to the Gulf terminal. A number of companies agreed to lift oil from the Gulf instead of the Mediterranean. The total capacity of the two Gulf terminals, Khor-al-Amaya and Mina al Bakr, is about 160 million tons annually. Another pipeline, this time through Turkey to the Dortyol terminal on the Mediterranean, was also proposed in 1973 but the agreement was not ratified until 1975.

In April 1976 the Iraqi Government decided to suspend Mediterranean deliveries through the Kirkuk pipeline across Syria to Tripoli because of a dispute with Syria over transit fees and other political issues. As a result of this and the loss of international markets because of the nationalization of BPC in December 1975, crude oil production dropped sharply in the first half of 1976 before recovering equally sharply in the second half of the year. The Iraqis seem to have fully regained their overseas markets and to have overcome delivery problems by using the strategic pipeline linking the Kirkuk fields in the north to Iraq's Gulf port of Fao. More recently, the opening in early 1977 of the new pipeline from the Kirkuk fields across southern Turkey to the Turkish port of Dortyol has further eased production limitations caused by pipeline capacity. Following chronic disputes regarding transit fees, an agreement was signed in August 1978 between Iraq and Turkey in which Iraq guaranteed a minimum transit fee payment to Turkey set on a nominal 15 million tons of crude per year, and the pipeline is now in moderate use. In conjunction with the pipeline to Fao, this new pipeline will allow Iraq to market crude from both its northern and southern oil fields at either Mediterranean or Gulf prices, whichever are the more advantageous. Also recently re-opened is the Kirkuk-Mediterranean pipeline through Syrian territory, closed in 1976 when talks on transit fees broke down. Iraq has continued to press OPEC for further increases in posted prices.

In common with most oil producing nations, Iraq is anxious to break into downstream operations. The construction of refineries for export production, as opposed to those serving domestic needs, and petrochemical plants and other oil based industries requires heavy investment. The Japanese Mitsubishi Heavy Industries is building a fertilizer plant at Khor al-Zubair and plans for a petrochemical complex and two refineries are also under discussion. An American-West German venture won a contract in 1976 for the construction of another petrochemical plant, near Basra. An Italian firm is building an LPG plant at Khor al-Zubair and has been awarded contracts to manage the construction of a $400 million, 150,000 b/d refinery at Baiji. Management contracts have also been awarded for two gas gathering systems in the Rumailak fields. A state-owned sulphur recovery plant has been operating at Kirkuk since 1968, producing 120,000 tons of sulphur a year. The by-product gases are sent by pipeline to Baghdad. New oil-related projects include a refinery at the Bai Hussan field in northern Iraq, with an estimated final capacity of 150,000 b/d, a hydrofiner (18,000 b/d) for light and heavy naphtha, and a reformer (10,000 b/d) for production of 95-octane petroleum to be constructed by the Italian firm Technipetrol under a $20 million award.

INOC's activities too, extend beyond the exploration for and production of crude oil. In 1972 it established an autonomous company to be responsible for the operation and management of a tanker fleet. Seven tankers were delivered from Spanish yards and several more vessels ordered from Sweden and Japan were expected to bring the Iraqi Oil Tankers Company's (IOTC) total tonnage to 1,402,000 tons in 1977.

In the aftermath of the 1973 crisis and the subsequent panic among consumers, Iraq was able to conclude several sales contracts on an oil-for-technology basis. Contracts of note included an agreement with France to supply at least 12.5 million tons a year for 10 years and with Japan for 160 million tons of crude oil and petroleum products in return for $100 million in credits to be used for building petrochemical factories and refineries. Such barter agreements for oil became an increasing feature of Iraq's international trade but sales did not always go as planned.

Despite the presently depressed market for oil tankers, the total tonnage of the Iraqi oil tanker fleet, which was estimated at 365,000 tons in early 1976, is expected to rise rapidly. Total tonnage was officially scheduled to more than double by the end of 1977.

INDUSTRY

Iraq has not the same impelling reasons for rapid and large-scale industrialization as countries with an increasing population that is too large to be supported by agriculture. Government policy aims therefore at an industrial development that will not be so accelerated as to seriously outrun the available skilled labour. It also prescribes that the industries to be encouraged should be carefully selected as based upon domestic resources and assured of a domestic market.

Accordingly, until the 1970s Iraq had few industries of any size, apart from oil. In greater Baghdad the larger enterprises were concerned with electricity and water supply and the building materials industry. In addition there was a large number of smaller-unit industries concerned with food and drink processing (date-packing, breweries, etc.), cigarette-making, textiles, chemicals, furniture, shoe-making, jewellery and various metal manufactures. The Government controls most manufacturing and mining through the General Industrial Organization, set up in 1964.

In recent years Iraq has moved into a wider range of secondary industry, directed mainly towards import substitutions. Where local manufacturing capacity is able to meet local demand, import control is normally introduced to protect it against foreign competition. The Government, while recognizing the role of the private sector in industrial development, in practice restricts the scale of private sector operations.

As a result, industry is now much more diversified, and on a larger scale. Major state factories include a bitumen plant at Qaiyarah, south of Mosul; a textile factory at Mosul, producing calico from local cotton; brick and cement factories capable of covering domestic demand; three sugar refineries at Kerbala, Sulaimaniya and Mosul, with another four planned; a tractor assembly plant which produced 2,500 tractors in 1975; the Basra fertilizer plant which uses sulphur from Kirkuk and gas from the Rumeila field; a paper board factory at Basra, now in course of expansion; a synthetic fibres complex, also being extended, at Hindiyah; and a number of flour mills. Shoe and cigarette factories serve the domestic market. Seven cement factories were due to start operation in 1977/78, raising Iraq's cement production from 2.7 million tons per year to 7 million tons per year. Shortage of cement has delayed a number of construction projects. By 1980 Iraq plans to produce some 10 million tons of cement annually. The construction industry remains very important, particularly the building of schools and training establishments. Finnish concerns have signed contracts for six agricultural colleges at a cost of $112 million, and smaller schemes using local contractors are under way to provide schools and colleges. The State Housing and Reconstruction Organization is to provide as many as 400,000 homes in 1979/80 and up to 4 million in the years 1981–2000.

The latest developments in the manufacturing sector have been in the production of pharmaceuticals, electrical goods, telephone cables and plastics. Large scale developments are under way at the Basra petrochemicals plant and a steel mill is under construction. An iron and steel plant at Khor al-Zubair was scheduled to be completed in 1978; Brazil is to supply 5.3 million tons of iron ore under a 5-year agreement. There are also plans to build an aluminium smelter in the Basra area, which would use waste oil-field gas. The food processing industries are being expanded with such projects as the vegetable oil plant planned for Baiji. Metalexport of Poland is to equip a bicycle factory at Mahmudiya which will produce 130,000 bicycles per year.

There are deposits of iron ore, chromite, copper, lead and zinc in the north, where test drilling is now being carried out, and important deposits of limestone, gypsum, salt, dolomite, phosphates and sulphur have also been located. The main sulphur deposit discovered at Mishraq in North Central Iraq, is being developed by the Iraq National Minerals Company in conjunction with the Polish state firm, Centrozap. The plant was commissioned in 1972 and a production rate of 1.5 million tons annually is the eventual target. Special port facilities for handling sulphur exports have been constructed at Um Qasr. Phosphates are being exploited at Akashat by Belgian interests. A Belgian firm has a large contract to build a phosphate fertilizer complex at Qaim and a number of firms from other countries are also involved. Poland is giving aid for phosphate development in return for fertilizer and crude oil deliveries to Poland.

The Soviet Union has assisted with the construction of eleven factories, including a steel mill and an electrical equipment factory at Baghdad, a drug factory at Samarra and a tractor plant at Musayib. A large share of industrial development is expected to take place in co-operation with Eastern bloc countries and several agreements have been signed. These include loans from Bulgaria, to pay for complete industrial plants and technical aid in mineral exploration, which will be repaid in crude oil shipments, and a loan from Hungary, some two-thirds of which is also repayable in oil. The U.S.S.R. is to receive oil to the value of ID 50 million in return for services in connection with industrial projects and, under a similar contract, Czechoslovakia is to build an oil renfiery at Basra.

Two trade agreements have been completed with China. Under the terms of the first, Iraq will supply 100,000 tons of sulphur each year over a five-year period while China will make available ID 14 million to Iraq for the purchase by China of 250,000 tons a year of chemical fertilizer from the Basra fertilizer plant. Western countries, France and Japan in particular, are making an equally large contribution to industrial development.

As far as local finance is concerned the commercial banks (which were nationalized in 1964) provide short-term credit, while longer term credit and aid for industry and agriculture is provided by several state-owned agencies—the Industrial, Agricultural,

Mortgage and Co-operative banks. The Industrial Bank, whose board is appointed by the Council of Ministers, is a shareholder in several large plants and in the private Light Industries Company which is establishing plants for the manufacture or assembly of kerosene heaters, cookers, radio sets, animal fodder, bicycles and electric wire.

Along with growth in the industrial base there is a continuing increase in the generation and consumption of electricity. In the years 1953–65 consumption of electricity rose substantially from 343 to 1,200 million kWh. Consumption in Baghdad rose from 206.4 million kWh. in 1960/61 to 1,383.5 million kWh. in 1968/69. The capacity of the power station on the Lesser Zab, near Kirkuk, will eventually be raised to 150,000 kW., when it will supply Mosul, Kirkuk, Arbil and Sulaimaniyah. Baghdad's power station is similarly raising its capacity to 200,000 kW. There are other hydro-electric stations at Basra, and based on the Samarra barrage, and more are planned at Dokan and Derbendi. A 250 MW power station at Khor al-Zubair and the Daura station extension was started in 1976. The target for electricity generating capacity is 4,000 MW by 1980. The 1976–80 plan allocates ID 76 million for a rural electrification programme to supply 9,000 villages.

Iraq is also moving into the field of nuclear power. France is building a 600 MW reactor and a co-operation agreement was signed with Italy in 1976.

It was officially claimed that the industrial sector was achieving the target growth of 17.8 per cent annually for the 1976–80 plan; however, it is clear that the state is experiencing great difficulties in implementing even a much reduced programme for the development of industries. New government restrictions will hit all major development schemes, including the Basra petrochemical complex and the Maissan papermill. The emphasis is now on the effective use of existing capacity before the creation of more.

COMMUNICATIONS

The Public Works Department is responsible for the control and maintenance of the 6,500 kilometres of main roads in Iraq, but major road and bridge construction is the responsibility of the Ministry of Planning. The main artery runs from the Jordanian frontier through Baghdad to the Iranian border but the road system is under complete reconstruction with the assistance of a World Bank loan of $23 million as part finance for a $54 million building programme. This project was nearing completion in 1979. Recently bids have been invited for road-building contracts worth ID 63 million including a new 475 km. road connecting Kirkuk with Rutba which will cost ID 35 million. The first section of the trans-Arabian highway between Baghdad and Hillah is to be constructed by the Yugoslav firm Union Engineering. The 106 km. section is expected to be completed in 33 months and to cost ID 91.8 million.

Iraq's main port is at Basra. A new port has been constructed at Um Qasr with facilities for loading sulphur, and the oil terminals are at Khor al Amaya and Fao. The dispute with Iran over the approaches to Basra on the Shatt-al-Arab river, which was settled in 1975, made it necessary to develop Um Qasr as an alternative port and military base. Iraq has been extremely anxious to secure the approaches to Um Qasr which lies at the head of a lagoon whose entrance is controlled by Kuwait. River navigation is of some importance, particularly on the Tigris between Basra and Baghdad. A scheme to build an industrial port complex at Khor al-Zubair was announced in 1976. The scheme was subsequently extended and estimates of its final cost range up to $500 million. The development of the port itself will involve the digging of a canal to allow the passage of 60,000 d.w.t. ships through the Gulf and the construction of docks and warehouses. The port will also serve for the export of phosphate fertilizers from Qaim and urea from the Khor al-Zubair plant under construction, as well as for imports of iron ore.

There are major international airports at Basra and Baghdad and civil airports at Mosul (which is being developed to take international services) and Kirkuk, as well as an IPC field at Kirkuk. A new airport is to be constructed at Baghdad, but the award of contracts has been delayed as after studying the bids of 10 international companies the Government was considering a re-tender in 1979.

The Railways Administration is a semi-autonomous body operating under a Director-General who is responsible to a government-appointed board. The principal lines run from Baghdad through Mosul to Tel Kotchek (529 km.) and from Basra to Baghdad (569 km.). Plans have been drawn up for the construction of about 1,800 kilometres of railways including a line to link Baghdad with Um Qasr via Basra, a line from Kirkuk to Haditha, a line to transport phosphates from Akashat to the Qaim complex and railways to transport sulphur from Mishraq. Total track length is expected to be about 3,000 kilometres by 1980, the last year of the development plan, and eventually the Government hopes to expand the system to provide links with Kuwait, Saudi Arabia, Lebanon and Iran. Negotiations for the establishment of rail links with Saudi Arabia and Kuwait were under way in 1979 and feasibility studies were expected to take place in the near future.

Iraq has been modernizing its telecommunication system for some years and has introduced crossbar telephone switching, a telex system, a micro-wave link between major cities and an earth satellite connection for international communications. Recently 51,000 lines have been added to the system with the completion of telephone exchanges in three cities, and, with a planned goal of 7 telephones per 100 people, further investment is expected. Investment in the country's communication network is likely to continue at a high level throughout the development plan years 1976–1980 and to include new radio and television stations. Pacific Consultants are to build and equip a $33.8 million television station in Baghdad.

FINANCE

Development spending is a potential cause of rising consumer prices and by early 1971 inflation was a cause of some concern to the Government, anxious for its political popularity. Increased imports and tighter price controls resulted in a fall in prices in the second half of 1971 and by the end of that year inflation appeared to be under control, or at least not significantly in excess of other comparable economies. Since then, however, consumer prices have risen steadily. In 1972 they rose by 5.2 per cent, in 1975 by 9.5 per cent and in 1976 by 10.3 per cent. The rate of inflation slowed during 1977, however, and by the third quarter consumer prices were running 7.6 per cent higher than in the corresponding period of the previous year. Wholesale prices have broadly matched the movement in consumer prices.

The budgeting procedure has been rationalized in recent years and a consolidated account consisting of the Ordinary Budget, the Development Budget, and the Budget for the Autonomous Agencies, is now presented. Despite the receipt of 50 per cent of all state oil revenues the budget has tended to show a deficit. In the 1972–73 budget, Government revenue was estimated at ID 331 million in the Ordinary Budget and ID 243 million in the Development Budget, together showing an increase of seven per cent over the previous year, almost all attributable to increased oil revenues. Expenditure during 1972–73 was estimated at ID 347 million in the Ordinary Budget and ID 243 million in the Development Budget. Between 1973–74 and 1974–75 total expenditure doubled from ID 1,375 million to ID 2,933 million. The 1975 Budget was for a nine month transitional period running from April to December, with expenditure estimated at ID 3,640 million. Expenditure for the calendar year 1976 was set at ID 5,045 million, while the official estimate for expenditure in 1977 was ID 6,339 million and in 1978 ID 7,457 million. The 1979 budget set total expenditure at ID 9,467 million, of which ID 2,616 million was for the ordinary budget, ID 3,282 million for the development plan and ID 3,569 million for the autonomous Government agencies. High expenditure on defence may, however, necessitate some transfer from the development budget to the ordinary budget, as has been the case in recent years.

FOREIGN TRADE AND PAYMENTS

On external account Iraq usually runs a deficit on trade (excluding oil) which is more than offset by foreign exchange earnings from the oil sector. Imports rose steadily, from a total ID 182 million in 1970 to ID 1,245 million in 1975, a large proportion of which was accounted for by iron and steel. In 1976 imports fell back to ID 1,024.7 million, increasing only slightly in 1977 to ID 1,151.3 million, as a result of the decline in oil revenues and the relative slowing down in domestic economic growth. The strengthening external position was indicated by the rise in gold and foreign exchange reserves held by the Iraq Central Bank from $781 million at the end of 1972 to $4,601 million at the end of 1976 and to $6,996 million at the end of 1977.

The Soviet Union and Eastern European countries dominated the Iraqi market during the late 1960s and early 1970s, but in 1973 the Iraqi Government opened the Iraqi market to the U.S.A. and other western countries. Excluding military sales, OECD countries accounted for 76 per cent of Iraq's imports in 1975, whilst Eastern European countries accounted for a mere 8 per cent. In 1976 Arab countries accounted for only 19 per cent of Iraqi exports and Eastern bloc countries for 24 per cent, the bulk of the rest going to Asia.

DEVELOPMENT AND PLANNING

The bulk of financing for development comes from the Government's oil revenues, supplemented by the net profits from government agencies and by external loans. In recent years Eastern Bloc countries have been an increasingly important source of external finance; the Soviet Union has been the major lender here, but other communist countries have provided sizeable loans.

The latest five-year Development Plan (1976–80) called for a total expenditure of more than ID 10,000 million at an annual rate of investment of about ID 2,130 million. The country's investment programme for 1977 provided for expenditure totalling ID 2,360 million, a massive 58 per cent increase on the 1976 figure and in 1978 the development budget allowed for ID 3,282 million, again a huge increase. Whilst major objectives remain diversification of industry and self-sufficiency in agriculture, heavy emphasis is placed on improvements in education and the social services. Spending on education was up by 84 per cent in 1977 and spending on social services, especially in rural areas, was up by 90 per cent. A further increase of 32 per cent in education spending was projected for 1978. An important aim is to narrow the gap between standards of living in urban and in rural areas.

The Government's ambitious investment plans explains why Iraq is among the "hawks" in the OPEC camp, and has been particularly concerned by the fall in the value of the dollar. Valued in dinars, Iraq's oil exports increased by 246 per cent in 1974, by 25.7 per cent in 1975, by 11.5 per cent in 1976 but by only 4.3 per cent in 1977. In 1978 oil production increased and the value of exports rose by 14.1 per cent.

STATISTICAL SURVEY

AREA AND POPULATION

Area	Population (census results)†					Density (per sq. km.)
	October 12th, 1957	October 14th, 1965	October 17th, 1977 (provisional)			
			Males	Females	Total	1977
434,924 sq. km.*	6,298,976	8,047,415	6,224,200	5,805,500	12,029,700	27.7

* 167,925 sq. miles. This figure includes 924 sq. km. (357 sq. miles) of territorial waters but excludes the Neutral Zone, of which Iraq's share is 3,522 sq. km. (1,360 sq. miles). The Zone lies between Iraq and Saudi Arabia, and is administered jointly by the two countries. Nomads move freely through it but there are no permanent inhabitants.

† Excluding Iraqis abroad, estimated at 141,720 in 1977.

GOVERNORATES
(estimated population at October 14th, 1976)

	Area* (sq. km.)	Population† ('000)	Density (per sq. km.)
Nineveh	41,320	1,158	28.0
Salah al-Deen	21,326	356	16.7
Al-Ta'meem	9,426	439	46.6
Diala	19,047	663	34.8
Baghdad	5,023	3,036	604.4
Al-Anbar	89,540	405	4.5
Babylon	5,503	565	102.7
Kerbela	52,856	243	4.6
Al-Najaf	26,834	354	13.2
A.l-Qadisiya	8,569	395	46.1
Al-Muthanna	49,206	184	3.7
Thi-Qar	13,668	617	45.1
Wasit	17,922	409	22.8
Maysan	16,774	419	25.0
Basrah	19,702	897	45.5
Autonomous Regions:			
D'hok	6,374	217	34.0
Arbil	14,428	492	34.1
Al-Sulaimaniya	16,482	656	39.8
Total	434,000	11,505	26.5

* Excluding territorial waters.

† Figures are projected from the 1965 census result and not revised in accordance with the 1977 census.

PRINCIPAL TOWNS
(population at 1965 census)

Baghdad (capital)	1,490,759	Kirkuk	175,303
Basrah (Basra)	310,850	Najaf	134,027
Mosul	264,146	Hillah	84,704

Births, Marriages and Deaths (annual average rates per 1,000 in 1973–75): Births 42.6; Marriages 14.7; Deaths 10.6 (estimates based on results of a sample survey).

EMPLOYMENT

(1973 estimate)

Agriculture	1,540,400
Mining	18,500
Manufacturing	170,000
Electricity, Gas and Water	14,300
Construction	73,000
Commerce	164,000
Transport	162,000
Services	330,000
Others	380,400
Unemployed	200,100
TOTAL LABOUR FORCE	3,052,700

AGRICULTURE

DATE CROP

(tons)

1973	1974	1975	1976*	1977*
385,000	350,000	400,000	371,980	578,310

Source: FAO, *Production Yearbook.*

* Official figure.

AREA AND PRODUCTION OF COTTON

	1974	1975	1976	1977
Area (dunums)	113,000	105,100	101,320	79,360
Production (tons)	40,000	38,600	33,890	25,730

OTHER PRINCIPAL CROPS

	1975		1976		1977	
	Area ('000 dunums)	Production ('000 tons)	Area ('000 dunums)	Production ('000 tons)	Area ('000 dunums)	Production ('000 tons)
Winter crops						
Wheat	5,630.6	845.4	6,070.4	1,312.4	3,430.0	695.7
Barley	2,269.2	437.0	2,399.3	579.3	2,143.5	457.7
Linseed	9.2	1.3	4.0	0.7	3.9	0.1
Lentils	20.6	4.8	22.8	5.1	25.5	5.9
Vetch (Hurtman)	1.7	0.4	2.7	0.3	3.2	0.4
Broad beans	45.6	80.0	72.3	97.1	69.5	93.9
Summer crops						
Rice	119.5	60.5	212.6	163.3	253.9	199.2
Sesame	46.7	7.6	53.6	7.0	36.7	4.6
Green grams	52.3	7.0	56.4	7.6	45.3	7.6
Millet	n.a.	n.a.	n.a.	n.a.	n.a.	n.a.
Giant millet	n.a.	n.a.	n.a.	n.a.	n.a.	n.a.
Maize	37.8	23.5	81.8	54.9	126.3	82.2

LIVESTOCK
('000 head)

	1975	1976	1977*
Horses	75*	69	65
Mules	22*	28	28
Donkeys	550*	459	450
Cattle	2,533	2,600	2,550
Buffaloes	221	220*	218
Camels	230*	225*	228
Sheep	11,479	11,900*	11,400
Goats	3,524	3,800*	3,600
Poultry	15,400*	15,395	15,923

* FAO estimate.

Source: FAO, *Production Yearbook.*

FISHING
('000 metric tons, live weight)

	1973	1974	1975	1976	1977
Freshwater fishes	21.4	14.1	14.6	19.0	17.5
Marine fishes	6.3	10.1	7.2	9.3	8.6
TOTAL CATCH	27.7	24.2	21.8	28.3	26.1

Source: FAO, *Yearbook of Fishery Statistics.*

MINING

PRODUCTION OF CRUDE PETROLEUM
(million barrels per day)

	1965	1974	1975	1976	1977
Total production	1.315	1.975	2.230	2.280	2.210

PRODUCTION OF NATURAL GAS
(million standard cubic feet)

	1972	1973	1974	1975	1976
Total production	262,000	308,253	328,963	368,921	468,476

Source: Ministry of Oil.

INDUSTRY

('000)

	1971	1972	1973	1974	1975
Leather tanning:					
Upper leather (sq. ft.)	n.a.	n.a.	11,001.1	11,658.2	10,169.2
Toilet Soap (tons)	15.3	19.1	35.4	43.6	28.0
Vegetable oil (tons)	84.1	72.4	89.3	92.7	90.9
Woollen textiles:					
Cloth (metres)	1,001.1	n.a.	1,112.4	1,187.9	n.a.
Blankets (number)	577.8	653.0	724.4	710.1	654.0
Cotton textiles (metres)	59,326.1	71,000.0	76,031.8	71,844.9	n.a.
Beer (litres)	8,983.8	10,238.0	12,723.1	12,321.4	19,297.0
Matches (gross)	1,629.3	1,861.0	2,101.3	2,253.1	n.a.
Cigarettes (million)	6.2	6.3	7.3	6.4	9.9
Shoes (pairs)	n.a.	n.a.	4,597.4	5,820.6	8,321.3

FINANCE

1,000 fils=20 dirhams=1 Iraqi dinar (I.D.).

Coins: 1, 5, 10, 25, 50 and 100 fils.

Notes: 250 and 500 fils; 1, 5, and 10 dinars.

Exchange rates (June 1979): £1 sterling=610.9 fils; U.S. $1=295.3 fils.
100 Iraqi dinars=£163.68=$338.62.

Note: From September 1949 to August 1971 the par value of the Iraqi dinar was U.S. $2.80 ($1=357.14 fils). Between December 1971 and February 1973 the dinar's value was $3.04 ($1=328.95 fils). In February 1973 the par value of the dinar was fixed at $3.3778 ($1=296.05 fils), with a market rate of 1 dinar=$3.3862 ($1=295.31 fils). From 1976 the latter also became the rate for calculating the value of foreign trade transactions. The Iraqi dinar was at par with the pound sterling until November 1967, after which the exchange rate was £1=857.14 fils (1 dinar=£1.167) until June 1972.

1978 Budget: Total I.D. 7,457 million (ordinary budget I.D. 1,850 million, official, semi-official and socialist sector I.D. 2,807 million, annual investment plan I.D. 2,800 million).

1979 Budget: Total I.D. 9,467.3 million.

1976-80 Five-Year Plan: Total expenditure I.D. 10,000 million.

CENTRAL BANK RESERVES

(U.S. $ million at December 31st)

	1973	1974	1975	1976	1977
Gold	173.1	175.7	168.0	166.7	176.1
IMF Special Drawing Rights	24.2	28.2	26.9	32.5	41.5
Reserve Position in IMF	32.9	33.4	31.9	31.7	33.4
Foreign Exchange	1,322.9	3,035.9	2,500.5	4,369.8	6,744.7
TOTAL	1,553.1	3,273.2	2,727.3	4,600.7	6,995.7

Source: IMF, *International Financial Statistics*.

CONSUMER PRICES INDEX (IFS)

(1963=100)

1970	1971	1972	1973	1974	1975	1976
116.8	121.0	127.3	133.5	144.6	158.2	174.6

EXTERNAL TRADE

('000 I.D.)

	1973	1974	1975	1976	1977
Imports	270,317	773,432	1,426,858	1,150,898	1,151,268
Exports*	32,523	28,129	35,565	46,530	42,670
Re-exports	272	8.5	1.7	—	—
Transit	56,095	89,724	118,141	121,947	150,075

* Excluding exports of crude petroleum (million I.D.): 555.3 in 1973; 1,921.0 in 1974; 2,414.6 in 1975; 2,691.4 in 1976; 2,807.3 in 1977; 3,204.4 in 1978.

PRINCIPAL COMMODITIES

('000 I.D.)

Imports	1973	1974	1975
Tea	4,712	9,426	8,485
Sugar	14,599	18,839	35,649
Pharmaceutical products	1,270	9,027	15,503
Clothing	191	679	1,746
Boilers and engines	47,898	84,536	202,315
Automobiles and parts	10,867	39,689	174,382
Timber	2,235	3,741	5,074

Exports	1973	1974	1975
Crude oil	621,100	2,031,300	2,457,000
Barley	n.a.	n.a.	n.a.
Dates	10,016	8,284	11,493
Straw and fodder	371	60	4
Raw wool	611	1,021	1,013
Raw cotton	84	77	20
Hides and skins	3,657	2,402	1,635
Cement	3,402	1,292	597

OIL REVENUES

(U.S. $ million)

Year		Year	
1967	361	1973	1,900*
1968	476	1974	6,000*
1969	483	1975	8,000*
1970	521	1976	8,500*
1971	340	1977	9,500*
1972	575	1978	11,600*

* Estimate.

PRINCIPAL TRADING PARTNERS

('000 I.D.)

Imports	1974	1975	1976	1977
Australia	26,139	15,230	29,006	24,085
Belgium	15,474	30,790	20,539	21,064
Brazil	n.a.	67,331	22,810	20,405
Canada	6,527	24,677	21,232	18,898
China, People's Republic	14,902	20,505	16,908	20,735
Czechoslovakia	16,789	20,027	20,329	13,782
Egypt	3,841	3,019	5,672	4,578
France	51,706	89,262	91,270	62,857
German Democratic Republic	8,312	8,219	14,337	14,462
Germany, Federal Republic	56,449	273,832	250,476	189,883
India	16,634	21,672	16,844	15,322
Italy	23,506	65,939	56,789	61,495
Japan	79,867	240,471	153,076	216,317
Lebanon	n.a.	16,293	4,863	5,922
Netherlands	11,343	20,787	22,139	48,373
Pakistan	—	4,810	14,374	13,196
Poland	10,495	14,279	12,694	13,507
Sweden	15,892	29,982	24,189	15,252
Switzerland	n.a.	15,676	11,855	22,911
U.S.S.R.	32,108	34,224	24,604	42,374
United Kingdom	37,378	83,008	80,620	82,872
U.S.A.	55,686	120,089	64,341	55,879

[*continued on next page*

PRINCIPAL TRADING PARTNERS—*continued*]

EXPORTS (excluding oil)	1974*	1975	1976	1977
China, People's Republic	2,342	2,105	3,572	4,927
Egypt	2,331	2,409	778	1,920
India	3,361	1,897	5,456	6,931
Kuwait	2,542	1,565	2,490	3,360
Lebanon	3,502	2,059	293	700
Pakistan	n.a.	2,346	3,874	3,650
Switzerland	n.a.	1,678	3,020	1,463
Syria	2,792	2,068	2,250	1,362
U.S.S.R.	929	1,905	2,164	724
U.S.A.	415	1,615	1,077	541
Viet-Nam	n.a.	—	3,912	4,209

TRANSPORT

RAILWAYS

	1974/75	1975/76	1976/77
Passenger km. ('000)	644,816	634,919	797,315
Freight ton km. ('000)	1,871,138	1,883,580	2,254,119

ROAD TRAFFIC

('000 licensed motor vehicles)

	1972	1973	1974	1975
Cars	75.5	77.3	85.7	118.3
Goods Vehicles	45.5	46.1	49.1	65.5
Buses	11.2	11.6	16.4	19.6
Motor Cycles	7.8	8.2	8.9	9.4

Source: International Road Federation.

SHIPPING

Movement of Cargo Vessels in Iraqi Ports.

	1975		1976		1977	
	Entered	Cleared	Entered	Cleared	Entered	Cleared
Number of vessels	828	827	891	892	984	977
Gross registered tonnage ('000)	8,343	8,305	8,861	9,393	11,855	11,872
Cargo ('000 tons, excl. crude oil)	3,406	1,441	3,430	1,279	3,772	964

SHIPPING OF CRUDE OIL

Export by tankers from all ports.

	1971	1972	1973	1974	1975
Crude oil ('000 tons)	19,288	21,955	26,669	35,710	37,052

CIVIL AVIATION

(Revenue traffic on Iraq airways)

	1975	1976	1977
Number of passengers . .	407,338	618,113	728,266
Cargo handled (tons) . .	3,034	7,523	10,090
Post handled (kg.) . . .	468,229	688,842	790,596

TOURISM

	1974	1975	1976	1977
Visitors .	544,800	482,090	n.a.	593,611

EDUCATION

(1976/77)

	Schools	Pupils
Primary . . .	8,156	1,947,182
Secondary (General) .	1,320	555,184
Vocational . . .	82	28,365
Teacher Training . .	43	21,186
Universities . . .	6	71,536
Colleges and Technical Institutes . . .	15	9,962

Source: Central Statistical Organization, Ministry of Planning, Baghdad, *Annual Abstract of Statistics.*

THE CONSTITUTION

The following are the principal features of the Provisional Constitution issued on September 22nd, 1968:

The Iraqi Republic is a popular democratic and sovereign state. Islam is the state religion.

The political economy of the state is founded on socialism.

The state will protect liberty of religion, freedom of speech and opinion. Public meetings are permitted under the law. All discrimination based on race, religion or language is forbidden. There shall be freedom of the Press, and the right to form societies and trade unions in conformity with the law is guaranteed.

The Iraqi people is composed of two main nationalities: Arab and Kurds. The Constitution confirms the nationalistic rights of the Kurdish people and the legitimate rights of all other minorities within the framework of Iraqi unity.

The highest authority in the country is the Council of Command of the Revolution (or Revolutionary Command Council—RCC), which will promulgate laws until the election of a National Assembly. The Council of Command of the Revolution has six members including the President and the Vice-President. The Council exercises its prerogatives and powers by a two-thirds majority.

Two amendments to the constitution were announced in November 1969. The President, already Chief of State and head of the government, also became the official Supreme Commander of the Armed Forces and President of the Command Council of the Revolution. Membership of the latter body was to increase from five to a larger number at the President's discretion. In September 1977 the members of the Iraq Regional Command of the Baath Party were appointed members of the RCC, thus raising RCC membership to 22.

Earlier, a Presidential decree replaced the 14 local government districts by 16 governorates, each headed by a governor with wide powers. In April 1976 Tekrit (Saladin) and Kerbala became separate governorates, bringing the number of governorates to 18, although three of these are designated Autonomous Regions.

The fifteen-article statement which aimed to end the Kurdish war was issued on March 11th, 1970. In accordance with this statement a form of autonomy was offered to the Kurds in March 1974, but some of the Kurds rejected the offer and fresh fighting broke out. The new Provisional Constitution was announced in July 1970. Two amendments were introduced in 1973 and 1974, the 1974 amendment stating that "the area whose majority of population is Kurdish shall enjoy autonomy in accordance with what is defined by the Law".

The President and Vice-President are elected by a two-thirds majority of the Council. The President, Vice-President and members of the Council will be responsible to the Council. Vice-Presidents and Ministers will be responsible to the President.

In July 1973, President Bakr announced a National Charter as a first step towards establishing the Progressive National Front. A National Assembly and People's Councils are features of the Charter.

THE GOVERNMENT

HEAD OF STATE

President: SADDAM HUSSAIN (assumed power July 16th, 1979).

Vice-President: TAHA MOHEDDIN MARUF.

REVOLUTIONARY COMMAND COUNCIL

Chairman: SADDAM HUSSAIN.

Vice-Chairman: IZZAT IBRAHIM.

Secretary-General: TARIQ HAMAD ABDULLA.

MEMBERS

SAADOUN GHAIDAN
TAHA YASIN RAMADAN
NAIM HADDAD
TAYEH ABDEL-KARIM
TAHER TAUFIQ
ABDEL-FATTAH MUHAMMAD AMIN
HASAN ALI AMRI
SAADOUN SHAKER
JAAFAR QASEM HAMMOUDI
ABDULLA FADL
TAREQ AZIZ
Gen. ADNAN KHAIRALLAH TALFAH
HIKMAT MIQDAM IBRAHIM
BURHANEDDIN ABDER-RAHMAN

COUNCIL OF MINISTERS

(*August* 1979)

First Deputy Prime Minister: TAHA YASIN RAMADAN.

Deputy Prime Minister: NAIM HADDAD.

Deputy Prime Minister: TARIQ AZIZ.

Deputy Prime Minister, Minister of Transport and Communications: SA'ADOUN GHAIDAN.

Deputy Prime Minister, Head of Presidency Diwan: (vacant).

Deputy Prime Minister and Minister of Defence: Lt.-Gen. ADNAN KHAIRALLA.

Minister of Foreign Affairs: Dr. SA'ADOUN HAMMADI.

Minister of Education: ABDUL JABBAR ABDUL MAJID.

Minister of Justice: Dr. MUNDHIR IBRAHIM.

Minister of Finance: THAMIR RZOUQI.

Minister of Housing and Construction: MUHAMMAD FADHEL.

Minister of Planning: Dr. TAHA IBRAHIM AL-ABDULLA.

Minister of Health: Dr. RIYADH IBRAHIM HUSSEIN.

Minister of Industry and Minerals: TAHIR TAWFIQ.

Minister of Higher Education and Scientific Research: JASIM MUHAMMAD KHALAF.

Minister of Oil: TAYEH ABDUL KARIM.

Minister of Trade: HASSAN ALI.

Minister of Youth: KARIM MAHMOUD HUSSEIN.

Minister of Agriculture and Agrarian Reform: AMIR MAHDI.

Minister of State for Foreign Affairs: HAMID ALWAN.

Minister of Culture and Information: LATIF NASEEF AL-JASIM.

Minister of Irrigation: ABDUL WAHAB MAHMOUD ABDULLA.

Minister of Labour and Social Affairs: BAKR MAHMOUD RASOUL.

Minister of Awqaf: Dr. AHMED ABDUL SATTAR.

Minister of State for Co-ordination with Autonomy Administrations: KHALID ABED OTHMAN.

Ministers of State: HASHIM HASSAN, OBAIDULLA MUSTAFA, ABDULLA ISMAIL AHMED, AZIZ RASHEED.

KURDISH AUTONOMOUS REGION

Executive Council: Chair. AHMED ABDEL QADER.

NATIONAL ASSEMBLY

No form of National Assembly has existed in Iraq since the 1958 revolution which overthrew the monarchy. The existing provisional constitution contains provisions for the election of a new assembly at a date to be determined by the Government. The members of the Assembly are to be elected from all political, social and economic sectors of the Iraqi people. A Kurdistan Legislative Council was set up at Arbil in March 1974. The Council sits for a three-year term and has 80 members.

POLITICAL PARTIES

National Progressive Front: Baghdad; f. July 1973, when Arab Baath Socialist Party and Iraqi Communist Party signed a joint manifesto agreeing to establish a comprehensive progressive national and nationalistic front. In 1975 representatives of Kurdish parties and organizations and other national and independent forces joined the Front; the Iraqi Communist Party was reported to have left the National Progressive Front in mid-March 1979; Sec.-Gen. NAIM HADDAD (Baath).

Arab Baath Socialist Party: Baghdad; revolutionary Arab socialist movement founded in Damascus in 1947; has ruled Iraq since July 1968, and since July 1973 in alliance with the Iraqi Communist Party in the National Progressive Front; in September 1977 the membership of the Regional Command of the Arab Baath Socialist Party and the Revolutionary Command Council became identical; Sec.-Gen. MICHAEL AFLAQ; Regional Sec. SADDAM HUSSEIN; Deputy Regional Sec. IZZAT IBRAHIM; Asst. Secs.-Gen. SHIBLI AYSAMI, Dr. MUNIF AL-RAZZAZ.

Iraqi Communist Party: Baghdad; f. 1934; became legally recognized in July 1973 on formation of National Progressive Front; First Sec. AZIZ MOHAMMED (said to have fled the country May 1979).

Kurdistan Democratic Party: Aqaba Ben Nafia Square, Baghdad; f. 1946; Kurdish Party; supports the National Progressive Front; Sec.-Gen. AZIZ AQRAWI; publ. *Al-Iraq* (daily).

Kurdistan Revolutionary Party: f. 1972; succeeded Democratic Kurdistan Party; admitted to National Progressive Front 1974; Sec. Gen. ABDUL-SATTAR TAHER SHAREF.

Patriotic Union of Kurdistan (PUK): f. 1977 by merger of Kurdistan National Party, Socialist Movement of Kurdistan and Association of Marxist-Leninists of Kurdistan; Leader JALAL TALBANI.

There is also a Kurdistan Democratic Party in opposition to the Iraqi Government; Leader MASOUD BARZANI.

DIPLOMATIC REPRESENTATION

EMBASSIES ACCREDITED TO IRAQ

(In Baghdad unless otherwise stated)

(E) Embassy.

Afghanistan: Maghrib St., al-Difa'ie, 27/1/12 Waziriyah (E); *Ambassador:* FAIZ MOHAMMAD (also accred. to Bahrain, Qatar and the United Arab Emirates).

Algeria: Karradat Mariam (E); *Ambassador:* ABDERRAHMAN SHARIF (also accred. to Turkey).

Argentina: Damascus, Syria (E).

Australia: Al Karada Al-Sharqiya Masbah 39B/35, P.O.B. 661 (E); *Ambassador:* H. NEIL TRUSCOTT.

Austria: 27/7/35 Al Karada Al-Sharqiya Masbah (E); *Ambassador:* Dr. HERBERT GRUBMAYR.

Bahrain: 26/2/13 Deragh Quarter (E); *Ambassador:* SALMAN ABDUL WAHHAB AL-SABBAGH.

Bangladesh: 13H/9/35 Al Karada Al-Sharqiya Masbah (E); *Ambassador:* ABDUL BARI (also accred. to the People's Democratic Republic of Yemen).

Belgium: Sa'adoun St. (E); *Ambassador:* ANDRÉ RAHIR.

Belgium (US Interest Section): Al Karada Al-Sharqiya Masbah 52/5/35; *Officer:* EDWARD L. PECK.

Brazil: 59/7/21 Karrada Sharquiya Arkheta (E); *Ambassador:* MARIO LOUREIRO DIAS COSTA.

Bulgaria: 9/12 Harthiya (E); *Ambassador:* ANGEL GEORGIEV ANGELOV.

Canada: Mansour, P.O.B. 323 (E); *Ambassador:* ROBERT GAYNER.

Central African Empire: 208/406 Al Zawra, Harthiya (E); *Ambassador:* FRANÇOIS-SYLVESTRE SANA.

Chad: 97/4/4 Karradat Mariam (E); *Chargé d'affaires:* SALIM ABDERAMAN TAHA.

China, People's Republic: 82/1/1a Jadriya, P.O.B. 223 (E); *Ambassador:* HOU YEH-FENG.

Congo: 183/406 Harthiya (E); *Ambassador:* ALBERT FOUNGUI.

Cuba: Al Karada Al-Sharqiya 24/22 (E); *Ambassador:* JUAN CARRETERO IBAÑEZ.

Cyprus: Cairo, Egypt (E).

Czechoslovakia: Dijlaschool St., No. 37, Mansoor (E); *Ambassador:* MIROSLAV JIRASKA.

Denmark: 3-G2/6/33 Alwiyah, Mazraat Hamdi al-Pachachi (E); *Ambassador:* RUDOLPH A. THORNING-PETERSEN (resident in Nicosia, Cyprus).

Finland: P.O.B. 2041, Alwiyah (E); *Ambassador:* JAN GROOP.

France: Kard el Pasha 9G/3/1 (E); *Ambassador:* JACQUES MORIZET.

German Democratic Republic: Al Karada Al-Sharqiya Masbah 34/33/32 and 52/53/54/354 (E); *Ambassador:* KARL-HEINZ LUGENHEIM.

Germany, Federal Republic: Al Karada Al-Sharqiya 224/225/377 (E); *Ambassador:* FRITZ C. MENNE.

Greece: 15/2/8 Al Karada Al-Sharqiya Masbah (E); *Ambassador:* P. SCALIERIS.

Guinea: Cairo, Egypt (E).

Hungary: Karradat Mariam 22/1/11 (E); *Ambassador:* LAJOS GONDA.

India: Taha St., Najib Pasha, Adhamiya (E); *Ambassador:* D. S. KAMTEKAR.

Indonesia: 24/6/33 Alwiya, Wathiq Street (E); *Ambassador:* ZAINUL ARIFIN SAMIL (also accred. to Kuwait).

Iran: Karradat Mariam (E); *Ambassador:* Mulla HUJATUL-ISLAM MAHMOUD DUAI.

Italy: 3/4 Nidhal St. (E); *Ambassador:* VALERIO BRIGANTE COLONNA ANGELINI.

Japan: 41/7/35 Al Karada Al-Sharqiya Masbah (E); *Ambassador:* KUNIYOSHI DATE.

Jordan: Harthiyah; *Ambassador:* FALEH ABDEL-KARIM TAWIL.

Kenya: Cairo, Egypt (E).

Korea, Democratic People's Republic: Al Fatih Square (E); *Ambassador:* RI YOK-IK.

Kuwait: 13/1/2 Al-Zuwiya, al Jadiriya, al-Karada al-Sharqiya (E); *Ambassador:* ABDUL AZIZ ABDULLAH AL-SAR'AWI.

Lebanon: 13/21/5D Husamuddin St. (E); *Ambassador:* SUHAIL SHAMMAS.

Libya: Al Mansour (E); *Chargé d'affaires:* MELOD AHMAD AHTEWISH.

Malaysia: 61/2/35 Al Karada Al-Sharqiya Masbah (E); *Ambassador:* Dato WAN ABDUL RAHIM BIN NGAH.

Mauritania: Mansour (E); *Ambassador:* MUHAMMAD ABDUL QADER WALAD DIDI.

Mongolia: Prague, Czechoslovakia (E).

Morocco: Mansour Hay Dragh No. 13/1/69 (Almoutanbe) (E); *Ambassador:* ABDELLOUAHED BELKEZIZ.

Netherlands: *Chargé d'affaires:* C. J. M. MEEUWIS (also accred. to Oman).

New Zealand: P.O.B. 2530, Alwiyah (E); *Chargé d'affaires:* JOHN PRESTON.

Niger: Cairo, Egypt (E).

Nigeria: Jadriyah (E); *Chargé d'affaires:* A. O. ADEYEMI.

Norway: Ankara, Turkey (E).

Oman: al-Zaitoon St., Harithia, House No. 25B/406, Hay al-Zawra (E); *Ambassador:* MUSLIM BIN ALI BIN SALIM.

Pakistan: 4725/7 Opposite Mashtal Al-Mansour (E); *Chargé d'affaires a.i.:* EITIZAZ HUSSAIN.

Poland: Al Karada Al-Sharqiya Masbah 2/1/27, P.O.B. 2051 (E); *Ambassador:* HENRYK ZEBROWSKI.

Portugal: P.O.B. 3014 (E); *Ambassador:* LEONARDO MATHIAS.

Qatar: 152/406 Harithia, Hay Al Kindi (E); *Ambassador:* ALI HUSAIN MUFTAH.

Romania: 303/7/19 Al Karada Al-Sharqiya Masbah (E); *Ambassador:* GHEORGE VASILE.

Saudi Arabia: Waziriyah (E); *Ambassador:* Sheikh AHMED AL-KUHAYIMI.

Senegal: Jadiriyah, 75G 31/15 (E); *Ambassador:* SALIOU KANDJI.

Somalia: 49/5/35 Al Karada Al-Sharqiya Masbah (E); *Ambassador:* ABDULLA HAJ ABUBAKAR.

Spain: 12/9/21 Al Karada Al-Sharqiya Masbah (E); *Ambassador:* JOSÉ MARÍA ULLRICH Y ROJAS.

Sri Lanka: 10 B/6/12 Alwiyah (E); *Chargé d'affaires:* V. ARULANANTHAM.

Sweden: 23A/2 Al Nidhal St. (E); *Ambassador:* FREDERIK BERGENSTRAHLE.

Switzerland: Al Karada Al-Sharqiya Masbah, House No. 41/2/35 (E); *Ambassador:* ARNOLD HUGENTOBLER.

Syria: Al Karada Al-Sharqiya Masbah (E); *Ambassador:* MUNIR AL-KHAIR.

Thailand: Islamabad, Pakistan (E).

Tunisia: Mansour 34/2/4, P.O.B. 6057 (E); *Ambassador:* MARWAN IBN AL-ARABI.

Turkey: 2/8 Waziriya (E); *Ambassador:* SENCER ASENA.

U.S.S.R.: 140 Mansour St., Karradat Mariam (E); *Ambassador:* ANATOLY BARKOVSKY.

United Arab Emirates: Al-Mansour, al Mansour Main St. (E); *Ambassador:* MUHAMMAD ALI AL-USSAIMI.

United Kingdom: Sharia Salah Ud-Din, Karkh (E); *Ambassador:* A. J. D. STIRLING.

Vatican: 20/4 Karradat Mariam (Apostolic Nunciature); *Apostolic Pro-Nuncio:* Mgr. FRANCISCO NAVARRO-RUÍZ.

Venezuela: Al-Mansour, House No. 4/4/56 (E); *Ambassador:* JOSÉ DE JESÚS OSIO.

Viet-Nam: (E); *Ambassador:* HOANG DUC PHUONG.

Yemen Arab Republic: Al Karada Al-Sharqiya Masbah 19/935 (E); *Ambassador:* GHALEB ALI JAMIL.

Yemen, People's Democratic Republic: Al Karada Al-Sharqiya Masbah No. 1/9/21 (E); *Ambassador:* ABDUL HAFIDH QAYID FARI.

Yugoslavia: 16/35/923 Babil Area, Jadriyah, P.O.B. 2061 (E); *Ambassador:* ZIVKO MUCALOV.

Zambia: Cairo, Egypt (E).

Iraq also has diplomatic relations with Cape Verde, the Comoros, Djibouti, Ecuador, Iceland, Jamaica, Laos, Malta, Mauritious, Mexico, Panama, the Philippines, Tanzania and Uruguay.

JUDICIAL SYSTEM

Courts in Iraq consist of the following: The Court of Cassation, Courts of Appeal, First Instance Courts, Peace Courts, Courts of Sessions, Shara' Courts and Penal Courts.

The Court of Cassation: This is the highest judicial bench of all the Civil Courts; it sits in Baghdad, and consists of the President and a number of Vice-Presidents and not fewer than fifteen permanent judges, delegated judges and reporters as necessity requires. There are four bodies in the Court of Cassation, these are: (*a*) The General body, (*b*) Civil and Commercial body, (*c*) Personal Status body, (*d*) The Penal body.

Courts of Appeal: The country is divided into five Districts of Appeal: Baghdad, Mosul, Basrah, Hilla, and Kirkuk, each with its Court of Appeal consisting of a President, Vice-Presidents and not fewer than three members, who consider the objections against the decisions issued by the First Instance Courts of first grade.

Courts of First Instance: These courts are of two kinds: Limited and Unlimited in jurisdiction.

Limited Courts deal with Civil and Commercial suits, the value of which is five hundred Dinars and less; and suits, the value of which cannot be defined, and which are subject to fixed fees. Limited Courts consider these suits in the final stage and they are subject to Cassation.

Unlimited Courts consider the Civil and Commercial suits irrespective of their value, and suits the value of which exceeds five hundred Dinars with first grade subject to appeal.

First Instance Courts consist of one judge in the centre of each *Liwa*, some *Qadhas* and *Nahiyas*, as the Minister of Justice judges necessary.

Revolutionary Courts: These deal with major cases that would affect the security of the state in any sphere: political, financial or economic.

Courts of Sessions: There is in every District of Appeal a Court of Sessions which consists of three judges under the presidency of the President of the Court of Appeal or one of his Vice-Presidents. It considers the penal suits prescribed by Penal Proceedings Law and other laws. More than one Court of Sessions may be established in one District of Appeal by notification issued by the Minister of Justice mentioning therein its headquarters, jurisdiction and the manner of its establishment.

Shara' Courts: A Shara' Court is established wherever there is a First Instance Court; the Muslim judge of the First Instance Court may be a *Qadhi* to the Shara' Court if a special *Qadhi* has not been appointed thereto. The Shara' Court considers matters of personal status and religious matters in accordance with the provisions of the law supplement to the Civil and Commercial Proceedings Law.

Penal Courts: A Penal Court of first grade is established in every First Instance Court. The judge of the First Instance Court is considered as penal judge unless a special judge is appointed thereto. More than one Penal Court may be established to consider the suits prescribed by the Penal Proceedings Law and other laws.

One or more Investigation Court may be established in the centre of each *Liwa* and a judge is appointed thereto. They may be established in the centres of *Qadhas* and *Nahiyas* by order of the Minister of Justice. The judge carries out the investigation in accordance with the provisions of Penal Proceedings Law and the other laws.

There is in every First Instance Court a department for the execution of judgments presided over by the Judge of First Instance if a special President is not appointed thereto. It carries out its duties in accordance with the provisions of Execution Law.

RELIGION

ISLAM

About 95 per cent of the population are Muslims. The Arabs of northern Iraq, the Bedouins, the Kurds, the Turkomans, and some of the inhabitants of Baghdad and Basra, are mainly of the Sunni sect, the remaining Arabs south of the Diyala, belong to the Shi'i sect. Leaders: Mr. ALWAIDH (Sunni), Prof. ABDUL QASSEM AL MOUSAWI AL KHOUI (Shi'i).

CHRISTIANITY

There are Christian communities in all the principal towns of Iraq, but their principal villages lie mostly in the Mosul district. The Christians of Iraq fall into three groups. (*a*) the free Churches, including the Nestorian, Gregorian, and Jacobite; (*b*) the churches known as Uniate, since they are in union with the Roman Catholic Church including the Armenian Uniates, Jacobite Uniates, and Chaldeans; (*c*) mixed bodies of Protestant converts, New Chaldeans, and Orthodox Armenians.

Catholic:

Latin Rite: Most Rev. ERNEST NYARY, Archbishop of Baghdad, Alwiyah 23/1/31, Baghdad; approx. 3,500 adherents.

Armenian Rite: Archbishop of Baghdad: P.O.B. 2344, Baghdad: Most Rev. JEAN KASPARIAN.

Chaldean Rite: Archbishop of Mosul, Most Rev. EMMANUEL DADDI; Patriarch of Bayblon of the Chaldeans: His Beatitude PAUL II CHEIKHO, with 15 Archbishops and Bishops in Iraq, Iran, Syria, Turkey and Lebanon. Approx. 475,000 adherents.

Syrian Rite: Archbishop of Mosul: Most Rev. CYRIL EMANUEL BENNI; Archbishop of Baghdad: Most Rev. ATHANASE J. D. BAKOSE; approx. 35,000 adherents.

Orthodox Syrian Community: 12,000 adherents.

Armenian Orthodox (*Gregorian*) **Community:** 25,000 adherents, mainly in Baghdad; Primate: (acting) Rev. KEGHAM PASHAYAM; Primate of the Armenian Diocese, Younis Al-Saba'awi Square, Baghdad.

JUDAISM

Unofficial estimates put the present size of the community at 2,500, almost all living in Baghdad.

OTHERS

About thirty thousand Yazidis and a smaller number of Turkomans, Sabeans, and Shebeks make up the rest of the population.

Sabean Community: 20,000 adherents; Head Sheikh DAKHIL, Nasiriyah; Mandeans, mostly in Nasiriyah.

Yazidis: 30,000 adherents; TASHIN BAIK, Ainsifni.

THE PRESS

DAILIES

Baghdad Observer: P.O.B. 257, Karantina, Baghdad; f. 1967; state-sponsored; English; Editor-in-Chief ABDUL JABBAR EL-SHATOB; circ. 7,000.

Al-Iraq: P.O.B. 5717, Baghdad; f. 1976; formerly *Al-Ta'akhi*; organ of the National Progressive Front; circ. 30,000.

al-Jumhuriya (*The Republic*): Waziriya, Baghdad; f. 1963, re-founded 1967; Editor-in-Chiet SA'AD QASSIM HAMMOUDI; circ. 25,000.

al Riyadhi (*Sportsman*): Baghdad; f. 1971; published by Ministry of Youth; circ. 30,000.

Tarik al Shaab (*People's Path*): Sadoun, Baghdad; f. 1973; organ of Iraqi Communist Party.

al Thawra (*Revolution*): Aqaba bin Nafi's Square, P.O.B. 2009, Baghdad; f. 1968; organ of Baath Party; Editor-in-Chief SAAD QASSEM HAMMOUDI; circ. 70,000.

WEEKLIES

Alif Ba (*Alphabet*): Karantina, Baghdad; Editor-in-Chief AMIR MA'ALA.

al-Fikr al-Jadid (*New Thought*): f. 1972; weekly; literary; Editor HUSAIN QASIM AL-AZIZ; circ. 30,000.

al-Mizmar: Ministry of Information, Baghdad; children's newspaper; circ. 50,000.

al-Mutafarrij: Rashid St., Hayderkhana, P.O.B. 409, Baghdad; f. 1965; Editor MOUJIB HASSOUN.

al-Rased (*The Observer*): Baghdad; general.

Sabaa Nisan: Baghdad; f. 1976; organ of the General Union of the Youth of Iraq.

Saut al Fallah (*Voice of the Peasant*): Karadat Mariam, Baghdad; f 1968; organ of the General Union of Farmers Societies; Editor-in-Chief LATIF AL-DILAIMI; circ. 40,000.

Waee Ul-Omal (*The Workers' Consciousness*): Headquarters of General Federation of Trade Unions in Iraq, Gialani St., Senak, P.O.B. 2307, Baghdad; Iraq Trades Union organ; Chief Editor MOHMMAD AYESH; circ. 25,000.

al-Idaa'h Wal-Television: Iraqi Broadcasting and Television Establishment, Karradat Maryam, Baghdad; radio and television programmes and articles; weekly; Editor-in-Chief KAMIL HAMDI AL-SHARKI; circ. 40,000.

PERIODICALS

al Adib al-Muasser (*Contemporary Writer*): Andalus Square, P.O.B. 217, Baghdad; published by Iraqi Union of Writers; f. 1970; literary; every two months; Editor FUAD AL JAKARLI.

Afaq Arabiya (*Arab Horizons*): Baghdad; literary and political; monthly.

al Aqlam (*The Pen*): Ministry of Culture and Arts, Baghdad; f. 1964; literary; monthly; circ. 20,000.

al-Funoon al-Ida'aiya: Iraqi Broadcasting and Television Establishment, Salihiya, Baghdad; supervised by Broadcasting and TV Training Institute; engineering and technical; quarterly.

L'Iraq Aujourd' hui: Ministry of Information, P.O.B. 4074, Baghdad; f. 1976; bi-monthly; political; French; Editor KHALIL EL-KHOURI; circ. 9,000.

Iraq Oil News: P.O.B. 6118, Baghdad; f. 1973; publ. by the Dept. of Information and General Relations of the Ministry of Oil; monthly; English.

Journal of the Faculty of Medicine, The: College of Medicine, University of Baghdad, Baghdad; f. 1941; quarterly; Arabic and English; medical and technical; Editor Prof. YOUSIF D. AL NAAMAN, M.D., D.SC.

Majallat-al-Majma al-Ilmi al-Iraqi (*Iraq Academy Journal*): Iraqi Academy, Waziriyah, Baghdad; f. 1947; quarterly; scholarly magazine on Arabic Islamic culture; Gen. Sec. Dr. F. AL-TA'I.

Majallat al-Thawra al-Ziraia (*Magazine of Iraq Agriculture*): Baghdad; quarterly; agricultural; published by the Ministry of Agriculture.

al-Masrah Wal-Cinema: Iraqi Broadcasting, Television and Cinema Establishment, Salihiya, Baghdad; artistic, theatrical and cinema; monthly.

al-Mawrid: Ministry of Culture and Arts, Baghdad; f. 1971; cultural quarterly.

al-Mu'allem al-Jadid: Ministry of Education, Baghdad; f. 1935; quarterly; educational, social, and general; Editor KHALIL AL-SAMARRAI; circ. 105,000.

Al Naft Wal Aalam (*Oil and the World*): publ. by the Ministry of Oil, P.O.B. 6118, Baghdad; f. 1973; Editor-in-Chief TAYEH ABDEL KARIM (Minister of Oil); monthly; Arabic.

Sawt al-Talaba (*The Voice of Students*): al-Maghreb St., Waziriya, Baghdad; f. 1968; organ of National Union of Iraqi Students; monthly; circ. 25,000.

al-Sina'a (*Industry*): P.O.B. 5665, Baghdad; publ. by Iraqi Federation of Industries; Arabic and English; every two months; Editor-in-Chief HATEM ABID AL-RASHID; circ. 16,000.

Sumer: Directorate-General of Antiquities, Jamal Abdul Nasr St., Baghdad; f. 1945; archaeological, historical journal; Chair. of Ed. Board Dr. M. SAID; annual.

al-Thaquafa (*Culture*): Place al-Tarir, Baghdad; f. 1970; Marxist; Editor-in-Chief SALAH KHALIS; monthly; circ. 5,000.

al-Thaquafa al-Jadida (*The New Culture*): Baghdad; f. 1969; pro-Communist; Editor-in-Chief SAFA AL-HAFIZ; monthly; circ. 3,000.

al-Turath al-Sha'abi (*Popular Heritage*): Dar Al-Jahidh, Ministry of Culture and Arts, Baghdad; specializes in Iraqi and Arabic folklore; Editor-in-Chief LUTFI AL-KHOURI; monthly; circ. 15,000.

al-Waqai al-Iraqiya (*Official Gazette of Republic of Iraq*); Ministry of Justice, Baghdad; f. 1922; Dir. SABAH SALMAN; Arabic and English weekly editions; circ. Arabic 9,000, English 750.

NEWS AGENCIES

Iraqi News Agency (INA): Abu Nawwas St., P.O.B. 3084, Baghdad; f. 1959; Dir.-Gen. TAHA YAEEN AL-BASRI.

FOREIGN BUREAUX

Allgemeiner Deutscher Nachrichtendienst (ADN) (*German Democratic Republic*): Zuqaq 24, Mahalla 906, Hai al-Wahda, Beit 4, Baghdad; Correspondent RAINER HOHLING.

Deutsche Presse Agentur (dpa) (*Federal Republic of Germany*): P.O.B. 5699, Baghdad; Correspondent NAJHAT KOTANI.

Middle East News Agency (MENA) (*Egypt*): Rasheed Str., al-Morabaa, Zaki Gamil Building, P.O.B. 2, Baghdad.

TASS (U.S.S.R.) also has an office in Baghdad.

PUBLISHERS

al Hurriyah Printing Establishment: Baghdad; f. 1970; largest printing and publishing establishment in Iraq; state-owned; controls al Jumhuriyah (see below).

al-Jamaheer Press House: Sarrafia, Baghdad; f. 1963; publisher of a number of newspapers and magazines, *Al-Jumhuriyah*, *Baghdad Observer*, *Alif Baa*, *Yord Weekly*; Pres. SAAD QASSIM HAMMOUDI.

al Ma'arif Ltd.: Mutanabi St., Baghdad; f. 1929; publishes periodicals and books in Arabic, Kurdish, Turkish, French and English.

al-Muthanna Library: Mutanabi St., Baghdad; f. 1936; booksellers and publishers of books in Arabic and oriental languages; Man. MOHAMED K. M. AR-RAJAB.

al Nahdah: Mutanabi St., Baghdad; politics, Arab affairs.

Kurdish Culture Publishing House: Baghdad; f. 1976; attached to the Ministry of Information.

National House for Distributing and Advertising: Ministry of Information, Al-Jumhuriyah St., Baghdad; f. 1972; importers, exporters and marketers of all kinds of books and periodicals; controls all advertising activities, inside Iraq as well as outside.

al-Thawra Printing and Publishing House: Baghdad; f. 1970; state-owned; Chair. SAAD QASSEM HAMMOUDI.

Thnayan Printing House: Baghdad.

RADIO AND TELEVISION

RADIO

Broadcasting Station of the Republic of Iraq: Iraqi Broadcasting and Television Establishment, Salihiya, Baghdad; home service broadcasts in Arabic, Kurdish, Syriac and Turkuman; foreign service in French, German, English, Russian, Persian, Swahili, Turkish and Urdu; there are 4 medium wave and 13 short wave transmitters; Dir.-Gen. SUHAIL AL-NAJM.

Idaa'h Baghdad: f. 1936; 22 hours daily.

Idaa'h Sawt Al-Jamahir: f. 1970; 21 hours daily.

Number of radio receivers (1978): 2.1 million.

TELEVISION

Baghdad Television: Ministry of Information, Iraq, Broadcasting and Television Establishment, Salihiya, Karkh, Baghdad; f. 1956; government station operating 7 hours daily; Dir.-Gen. LATEEF AL-DELAIMY.

Kirkuk Television: f. 1967; government station; commercial; 6 hours daily.

Mosul Television: f. 1968; government station; commercial; 6 hours daily.

Basrah Television: f. 1968; government station; commercial; 6 hours daily.

Missan Television: f. 1974; government station; commercial; 6 hours daily.

Kurdish Television: f. 1974; government station; commercial; 6 hours daily.

Muthanna station opened in mid-1976 and Um Qasr station is under construction.

Number of TV receivers (1978): 623,000.

FINANCE

All banks and insurance companies, including all foreign companies, were nationalized in July 1964. The assets of foreign companies were taken over by the state.

BANKING

(cap.=capital; p.u.=paid up; dep.=deposits; res=reserves; m.=million; amounts in Iraqi dinars.)

CENTRAL BANK

Central Bank of Iraq: Banks St., Baghdad; f. 1947 as National Bank of Iraq; brs. in Mosul and Basra; has the sole right of note issue; cap. p.u. 25m., dep. 860.7m. (Aug. 1977); Gov. Dr. FAKHRY KADDORI.

COMMERCIAL BANKS

Rafidain Bank: New Banks St., 11360, Massarif, Baghdad; f. 1941; Commercial Bank of Iraq was merged with Rafidain Bank, June 1974; 162 brs.; cap. p.u. 30m., res. 37.9m., dep. 1,194m. (Dec. 1977); Pres. and Chair. ADNAN AL-TAYYAR.

SPECIALIZED BANKS

Agricultural Bank of Iraq: Rashid St., Baghdad; 24 branches; cap. p.u. 6.4m.; Gen. Man. ABDUL RAZZAK AL-HILALI.

Estate Bank of Iraq: Hassan ibn Thabit St., Baghdad; f. 1949; 19 branches; gives loans to assist the building industry; cap. p.u. 34m.; acquired the Co-operative Bank in 1970; Dir.-Gen. LABEED AL-KARAGULLY.

Industrial Bank of Iraq: P.O.B. 5825, Khullari Square, Baghdad; 8 brs.; f. 1940; cap. p.u. 25m.; Gen. Man. ABDUL SALAM ALLAWI.

INSURANCE

Iraqi Life Insurance Co.: 25 S/21 Curd Al-Pasha, Karadah Al-Sharqiah, P.O.B. 989, Baghdad; Chair. and Gen. Man. MEDHAT FADHIL AL-JARRAH.

Iraq Reinsurance Company: Yousif R. Al-awi Bldg., Sa'adoon St., P.O.B. 297, Baghdad; f. 1961; to transact reinsurance business on the international market; Chair and Gen. Man. Dr. MUSTAFA RAJAB.

National Insurance Co.: Al-Aman Bldg., Al-Khulani St., P.O.B. 248, Baghdad; f. 1950; cap. p.u. 1m.; state monopoly for all direct non-life insurance; Chair. and Gen. Man. ABDULBAKI REDHA.

OIL AND GAS

Iraq National Oil Company (INOC): P.O.B. 476, Kullani Square, Baghdad; f. in 1964 to operate the oil industry at home and abroad; when Iraq nationalized its oil, structural changes took place in INOC and it has become solely responsible for exploration, production, transportation and marketing of Iraqi crude oil and oil products. The Iraq Company for Oil Operations (ICOO) has become the Northern Petroleum Organisation (NPO) and is under the control of INOC; Chair. TAYEH ABDUL-KARIM (Minister of Oil).

Northern Petroleum Organisation: formerly Iraq Company for Oil Operations (ICOO); under control of INOC (*see* above).

Entreprise des Recherches et d'Activités Petrolières (ERAP): signed a contract with INOC in 1968 under which it acts as contractor to INOC. This contract was amended in 1973 and development of the Abu Gharab and Buzurgan fields is in progress. ERAP has joined the Southern Petroleum Organisation.

State Establishment for Distribution of Oil Products and Gas: South Gate, Baghdad; is responsible for distribution and marketing of all distillates, lubricating oils, greases, natural gas and liquid gas all over Iraq. It supplies ships and tankers entering Iraqi waters and the Arabian Gulf with fuels by means of a special fleet of 4 tankers and 4 coasters. It also supplies aircraft in Iraqi airports; Chair. HAZIM TALIB.

State Establishment for Oil Refining and Gas Processing: Baghdad; operates refineries at Baghdad, Khanaqin, Kirkuk, Hadithah, Qayarah and Basra with a total capacity of 180,000 BPSD and sulphur recovery plant at Kirkuk that utilizes associated gas of Kirkuk field to produce sulphur, natural gas and liquid gas. Two gas lines were laid between Kirkuk and Baghdad where gas is processed at Taji Plant (12,000 BPSD); total capital investment ID 80m.; annual turnover ID 50m. approx.; Chair. FAROUQ ASSIM.

State Organization for Oil Projects: Baghdad; responsible for building the oil projects inside Iraq either through direct execution or contracting with foreign enterprises; supervises study of proposed projects, laying down their designs, etc.; Chair. ISSAM ABDUL RAHEEM AL-CHALEBI.

TRADE AND INDUSTRY

CHAMBERS OF COMMERCE

Federation of Iraqi Chambers of Commerce: Mustansir St., Baghdad; f. 1969; all Iraqi Chambers of Commerce are affiliated to the Federation; Chair. SA'AD ABDUL-HADI EL-RAHEEM; Sec.-Gen. KADHIM ABDUL HAMEED AL-MHAIDY; publs. *Iraq Trade Directory, Annual Trade Report, Monthly Economic News Bulletin, Wholesale Price Bulletin.*

Amarah Chamber of Commerce: Al-Amarah; f. 1950; Pres. KAMAL LEFTA HASSAN; Sec. N. J. MANSHAMI.

Arbil Chamber of Commerce: Arbil; f. 1966; Pres. ANUAR SALIH IBRAHIM; Sec. JALAL K. KARIM.

Baghdad Chamber of Commerce: Mustansir St., Baghdad; f. 1926; 13,848 mems.; Pres. SA'AD ABDUL-HADI EL-RAHEEM; Sec. FO'AD ABDUL-MAJEED; Dir.-Gen. N. H. AL-JORANI; publs. *Weekly Bulletin, Commerce* (quarterly magazine), *Trade Directory.*

Basrah Chamber of Commerce: Basrah; f. 1926; Pres. ABDUL KARIM AL-ATTAR; Sec. ABDUL RAZAK S. MAHDI; publ. *al Tajir* (monthly).

Dahok Chamber of Commerce: Dahok; Pres. K. D. MALKONIAN; Sec. T. A. AL-DAHER.

Diwaniya Chamber of Commerce: Diwaniya; f. 1961; Pres. HATEM HAMZA DHAHIR; Sec. AMIN A. MOSA.

Diyala Chamber of Commerce: Diyala; f. 1966; Pres. N. M. SALEH; Sec. TAHA H. HASSAN.

Hillah Chamber of Commerce: Hillah; f. 1949; Pres. KASSIM SAAD; Sec. A. H. SALMAN.

Karbala Chamber of Commerce: Karbala; f. 1952; 3,600 mems. Pres, JAWAD R. ABULHAB; Sec. RASHEED ABDUL WAHAB; Man. SAHIB H. HILME.

Kut Chamber of Commerce: Kut; Pres. R. S. YOUNIS; Sec. A. H. ABDUL BARI.

Mosul Chamber of Commerce: Khalid ibn Al-Waleed, P.O.B. 35, Mosul; f. 1926; 7,350 mems.; Pres. MUDHAFAR A. AL-LAWAND; Sec. F. S. AL-MOULAH; publ. *Bulletin.*

Najaf Chamber of Commerce: Najaf; f. 1950; Pres. ABDUL ILAH I. LEFTA; Sec. N. H. HASSOWA.

Nasiriya Chamber of Commerce: Nasiriya; f. 1958; Sec. ABDUL HADI M. ALI.

Ramadi Chamber of Commerce: Ramadi; Pres. R. H. HMAYIM; Sec. R. SHOKER.

Sulaimaniya Chamber of Commerce: Sulaimaniya; f. 1967; Pres. N. I. AL-JAF; Sec. A. M. MOHAMMED.

EMPLOYERS' ORGANIZATION

Iraqi Federation of Industries: Iraqi Federation of Industries Bldg., Al-Khulani Square, Baghdad; f. 1956; 6,000 mems.; Pres. HATAM ABDUL RASHID; publs. *Al-Sina'a* (bi-monthly), Directory of Iraqi Industries and monthly reports.

INDUSTRIAL ORGANIZATIONS

General Establishment for Industry: Baghdad; state organization controlling most of Iraq's industry; organized into 5 departments covering (1) Clothing, Hides and Cigarettes, (2) Construction industries, (3) Weaving and Textiles, (4) Chemicals and Foodstuffs, (5) Engineering.

Iraqi Dates Administration: Museum Square, Jamel Abdul-Nasir St., Baghdad; responsible for date exports; Acting Dir. GEORGE BATTAH.

State Establishment for Phosphate: Al-Qaim; f. 1976; state organization responsible for all aspects of phosphate mining, treatment and marketing; also responsible for production of phosphatic fertilizers, etc.; initial cap 350m. dinars.

State Organization for Minerals: P.O.B. 2330, Alwiyah Baghdad; f. 1969; 1,210 mems.; responsible for exploiting all minerals in Iraq except oil; Pres. Dr. ABDUL RAZZAK AL-HASHIMI.

TRADE UNIONS

General Federation of Trade Unions of Iraq: P.O.B. 3046 Sadoun, Aleppo Square, Baghdad; f. 1964; 14 general unions and 17 local trade union federations in the governorates of Iraq. Number of workers in industry is 489,102 and in agriculture 110,708 and in other services 400,190; GFTU is a member of the International Confederation of Arab Trade Unions and of the World Federation of Trade Unions; Pres. MOAYAD ABDULLAH HUSSEIN; Sec.-Gen. SALMAN DAWOOD NAJRIS; publ. *Wai al-Ummal*.

Union of Teachers: Baghdad; Pres. IBRAHIM MARZOUK.

Union of Palestinian Workers in Iraq: Baghdad; Sec.-Gen. SAMI AL SHAWISH.

There are also unions of doctors, pharmacologists, jurists, artists, and a General Federation of Iraqi Women.

CO-OPERATIVES

By the end of 1977 there were 1,606 co-operatives with 287,672 members.

PEASANT SOCIETIES

General Federation of Peasant Societies: Baghdad; f. 1959; has 734 affiliated Peasant Societies.

TRADE FAIR

Baghdad International Fair: Damascus St., Al Mansour, Baghdad; administered by Iraqi Fairs Administration; held annually in October; f. 1954.

TRANSPORT

RAILWAYS

Iraqi Republic Railways: Baghdad Central Station Building, Baghdad; total length of track (1975): 1,955 km., consisting of 1,130 km. of standard gauge, 825 km. of one-metre gauge; Dir.-Gen. SUHAIL M. SALEH.

The metre gauge line runs from Baghdad through Khanaqin, Kirkuk to Erbil and from Baghdad through Musayab to Kerbela. The standard gauge line covers the length of the country from Rabia on the Syrian border via Mosul to Baghdad and from Baghdad to Basra and Um-Qasr on the Arabian Gulf. A 550 km. line is planned, linking Baghdad to Hsaibah, near the Iraqi-Syrian frontier. All standard gauge trains are now hauled by diesel-electric locomotives. As well as the internal service, there is a regular international service between Baghdad and Istanbul.

ROADS

The most important roads are: Baghdad–Mosul–Tel Kotchuk (Syrian border), 521 km.; Baghdad–Kirkuk–Arbil–Zakho (border with Turkey), 544 km.; Kirkuk–Sulaimaniya, 109 km.; Baghdad–Amara–Basra–Safwan (Kuwaiti border), 595 km.; Baghdad–Rutba–Syrian border (to Damascus), 555 km.; Baghdad–Babylon–Diwaniya, 181 km.

Under the 1970–75 Development Plan $91m. were allocated to rebuilding and extending the road system. The World Bank has made a $19m. loan towards the project. In 1975 there were 6,566 km. of main roads and 5,293 km. of secondary roads.

SHIPPING

State Organization of Iraqi Ports: Basra; Acting Pres. FALEH MAHMOUD EL MOOSA.

The Ports of Basra and Um Qasr are the commercial gateway of Iraq. They are connected by various ocean routes with all parts of the world, and constitute the natural distributing centre for overseas supplies. The Iraqi Maritime Company maintains a regular service between Basra, the Gulf and north European ports. Other shipping lines operate cargo and passenger services from Basra and Um Qasr to all parts of the world. There are fast mail and passenger services from Basra to Bombay via Khorramshahr. Orient Mail Services to England, Australia, South Africa and the Far East.

At Basra there is accommodation for 12 vessels at the Maqal Wharves and accommodation for 7 vessels at the buoys. There are 1 silo berth and 2 berths for oil products at Muftia and 1 berth for fertilizer products at Abu Flus. There is room for 8 vessels at Um Qasr.

There are deep-water tanker terminals at Fao and Khor Al-Amaya for 4 and 3 vessels respectively.

For the inland waterways, which are now under the control of the State Organization of Iraqi Ports, there are 1,036 registered river craft, 48 motor vessels and 105 motor boats.

Iraq National Oil Co.: Basra; 2 supertankers.

Iraqi Maritime Transport Co.: P.O.B. 3052, Baghdad; f. 1952; 13 cargo vessels; Acting Dir.-Gen. and Chair. M. A. AL-ANI.

Iraqi Oil Tanker Co.: P.O.B. 37, Basra; 8 tankers.

CIVIL AVIATION

There are international airports near Baghdad, at Bamerni, and at Basra. Internal flights connect Baghdad to Basra and Mosul.

Iraqi Airways: Al Kharkh, Baghdad; f. 1945; Dir.-Gen. MOHAMED TAHIR YASSIN; regular services from Baghdad to Abu Dhabi, Algiers, Amman, Amsterdam, Athens, Bahrain, Bangkok, Basra, Beirut, Belgrade, Berlin, Bombay, Bucharest, Budapest, Cairo, Casablanca, Copenhagen, Damascus, Dhahran, Doha, Dubai, Frankfurt, Geneva, Istanbul, Jedda, Karachi, Khartoum, Kuala Lumpur, Kuwait, London, Madrid, Moscow, Mosul, Munich, New Delhi, Paris, Prague, Rome, Sofia, Teheran, Tripoli, Tunis, Vienna, Warsaw; fleet: 3 Tridents, 3 Boeing 707, 3 Boeing 727, 3 Boeing 737, 2 Boeing 747.

The following airlines also operate services to Iraq: Aeroflot (U.S.S.R.), Air France, Alitalia (Italy), Ariana Afghan, Balkan (Bulgaria), British Airways, ČSA (Czechoslovakia), Egyptair, Interflug (German Democratic Republic), KLM (Netherlands), Kuwait Airways, LOT (Poland), Lufthansa (Federal Republic of Germany), MALÉV (Hungary), MEA (Lebanon), PIA (Pakistan), SAS (Sweden), Saudia (Saudi Arabia), Swissair, Syrian Arab.

TOURISM

Ministry of Information, Tourism and Resorts Administration: Ukba bin Nafi Sq., Baghdad; f. 1956; Dir.-Gen. Dr. ALI GHALIB AL-ANI; publs. *Tourism in Iraq* (bimonthly), guide books, posters, tourist maps and pamphlets.

DEFENCE

Estimated defence expenditure 1977/78: 491.5 million dinars.

Military service: 2 years.

Total armed forces: 212,000; army 180,000, navy 4,000, air force 28,000. Reserves 250,000. Para-military forces 54,800.

Chief of the General Staff: General ABDEL-JABBAR SHANSHAL.

Deputy Commander of Armed Forces: Gen. ADNAM KHAIRALLA.

EDUCATION

Since the establishment of the Republic in 1958 there has been a marked expansion in education at all levels. Spending on education has increased substantially since 1958, reaching I.D. 170.4 million in the 1976 budget, representing 11.5 per cent of total regular expenditure. During 1974-75 two decisions were promulgated which constitute a landmark in the history of the Iraqi educational System. The first was a decision of the Revolutionary Command Council announcing free education in all stages from pre-primary to higher. The second decision abolished private education and transferred all existing private schools into state schools. Pre-school education is expanding although as yet it reaches only a small proportion of children in this age group. Primary education, lasting six years, is now officially compulsory, and there are plans to extend full-time education to nine years as soon as possible. At present, secondary education, which is expanding rapidly, is available for six years. An anti-illiteracy campaign is being implemented during the 1978/79 academic year.

Science, Medical and Engineering faculties of the universities have undergone considerable expansion, although technical training is less developed. Two branches of Baghdad University at Basra and Mosul became independent universities in 1967.

UNIVERSITIES

University of Baghdad: Baghdad; 1,509 teachers, 19,274 students.

University of Basra: Basra; 484 teachers, 9,395 students.

al Mustansiriya University: Baghdad; 481 teachers, 11,021 students.

Mosul University: Mosul; 576 teachers, 9,897 students.

University of Sulaimaniya: Sulaimaniya; 291 teachers, 4,167 students.

University of Technology: Baghdad; 300 teachers, 6,042 students.

BIBLIOGRAPHY

GENERAL

BELL, Lady FLORENCE (Ed.). The Letters of Gertrude Lowthian Bell (2 vols., London, 1927).

BURGOYNE, ELIZABETH (Ed.). Gertrude Bell, from her personal papers, 1914-26 (London, 1961).

HARRIS, GEORGE L. Iraq, Its People, Its Society, Its Culture (HRAF Press, New Haven, 1958).

LLOYD, SETON F. H. Iraq: Oxford Pamphlet (Bombay, 1943).
Twin Rivers: A Brief History of Iraq from the Earliest Times to the Present Day (Oxford, 1943).
Foundations in the Dust (Oxford, 1949).

LONGRIGG, S. H. and STOAKES, F. Iraq (Ernest Benn, London, 1958).

QUBAIN, FAHIM I. The Reconstruction of Iraq 1950-57 (Atlantic Books, London, 1959).

SALTER, Lord, assisted by PAYTON, S. W. The Development of Iraq: A Plan of Action (Baghdad, 1955).

STARK, FREYA. Baghdad Sketches (John Murray, London, 1937).

STEWART, DESMOND, and HAYLOCK, JOHN. New Babylon: a Portrait of Iraq (London, Collins, 1956).

VERNIER, B. L'Irak d'Aujourd'hui (Paris, 1962).

ANCIENT HISTORY

BRAIDWOOD, R. J. and HOWE, B. Prehistoric Investigation in Iraqi Kurdistan (Chicago, 1961).

CAMBRIDGE ANCIENT HISTORY (Vols. I and II, New Ed. Cambridge, 1962).

CHATERJI, S. Ancient History of Iraq (M. C. Sarkar, Ltd. Calcutta, 1961).

FIEY, J. M. L'Assyrie Chrétienne (Imprimerie Catholique, Beirut, 1965).

FRANKFORT, H. Archæology and the Sumerian Problem (Chicago, 1932).
The Birth of Civilization in the Near East (Anchor, New York, 1951).

LLOYD, SETON F. H. The Art of the Ancient Near East (London, 1961).
Ruined Cities of Iraq (Oxford, 1945).
Mesopotamia (London, 1936).
Mounds of the Near East (Edinburgh, 1964).

MALLOWAN, M. E. L. Early Mesopotamia and Iran (Thames and Hudson, London, 1965).

OATES, E. E. D. M. Studies in the Ancient History of Northern Iraq (British Academy, London, 1967).

OPPENHEIM, A. LEO. Ancient Mesopotamia (Chicago U.P., 1964).
Letters from Mesopotamia (Chicago U.P., 1967).

PARROT, A. Nineveh and Babylon (London, 1961).
Sumer (London, 1961).

PIGGOTT, S. (Ed.). The Dawn of Civilization (London, 1962).

ROUX, GEORGES. Ancient Iraq (London, 1964).

SAGGS, H. W. F. The Greatness that was Babylon (Sidgwick and Jackson, London, 1962).

STARK, FREYA. Rome on the Euphrates (John Murray, London, 1966).

WOOLLEY, Sir C. L. Abraham (London, 1936).
Mesopotamia and the Middle East (London, 1961).
The Sumerians (Oxford, 1928).
Ur of the Chaldees (London, 1950).
Ur Excavations. 8 vols. (Oxford, 1928-).

ISLAMIC PERIOD

CRESWELL, K. A. C. Early Muslim Architecture (3 vols., Oxford, 1932-50).

HITTI, P. K. A History of the Arabs (2nd ed., London, 1940).

LE STRANGE, GUY. The Lands of the Eastern Caliphate (Cambridge, 1905).

LOKKEGAARD, FREDE. Islamic Taxation in the Classical Period, with a Special Reference to Circumstances in Iraq (Copenhagen, 1950).

RECENT HISTORY

ADAMSON, DAVID. The Kurdish War (London, 1964).

AL-MARAYATI, ABID A. A Diplomatic History of Modern Iraq (Speller, New York, 1961).

DANN, URIEL. Iraq under Qassem: A Political History 1958–63 (Praeger, New York, 1969).

FOSTER, H. A. The Making of Modern Iraq (London, 1936).

GALLMAN, W. J. Iraq under General Nuri (Johns Hopkins Press, 1964).

HALDANE, Sir J. A. L. The Insurrection in Mesopotamia, 1920 (Edinburgh, 1922).

HASANI, ABDUL RAZZAQ. Ta'rikh al-'Iraq al-Siyasi al-Hadith (Political History of Modern Iraq) (Sidon, 1948).

KHADDURI, MAJID. Independent Iraq 1932-58, A Study in Iraqi Politics (2nd edition, Oxford University Press, 1960).
Republican Iraq: A study in Iraqi Politics since the Revolution of 1958 (Oxford University Press, 1970).

KENT, MARIAN. Oil and Empire: British Policy and Mesopotamian Oil, 1900–1920 (Macmillan, London, 1976).

LONGRIGG, S. H. Four Centuries of Modern Iraq (Oxford, 1925).
Iraq 1900-1950: A Political, Social and Economic History (London, 1953).

MILLAR, RONALD. Kut: The Death of an Army (London, 1969).

MOBERLY, F. J. The Campaign in Mesopotamia, 1914-1918 (4 vols., London, 1923-27).

PAIFORCE: the official story of the Persia and Iraq Command, 1941-1946 (London, 1948).

PENROSE, EDITH and E. F. Iraq: International Relations and National Development (Benn, Tonbridge, 1978).

WILSON, Sir A. T. Loyalties: Mesopotamia, 1914-17 (London, 1930).
Mesopotamia, 1917-20: a Clash of Loyalties (London, University Press, 1931).

ZAKI, SALIH. Origins of British Influence in Mesopotamia (New York, 1941).

ECONOMY

AINSRAWY, ABBAS. Finance and Economic Development in Iraq (Praeger, New York, 1966).

DLADEN, HORST. Eine sozio-ökonomische Betrachtung (Leske, Opladen, 1969).

JALAL, FERHANG. The Role of Government in the Industrialization of Iraq 1950–1965 (Frank Cass, London, 1972).

LANGLEY, KATHLEEN M. The Industrialisation of Iraq (Harvard University Press, 1961).

LONGRIGG, S. H. Oil in the Middle East (London, 1954).

MINORITIES

ARFA, HASSAN. The Kurds (Oxford University Press, Oxford, 1966).

BADGER, G. P. The Nestorians and their Rituals (2 vols., London, 1888).

BLUNT, A. T. N. Bedouin Tribes of the Euphrates (2 vols., London, 1879).

DAMLUJI, S. The Yezidis (Baghdad, 1948) (in Arabic).

DROWER, E. S. Peacock Angel (Being some account of Votaries of a Secret Cult and their Sanctuaries) (London, 1941).
The Mandeans of Iraq and Iran (Oxford, 1937).

EMPSON, R. H. W. The Cult of the Peacock Angel. (A Short Account of the Yezidi Tribes of Kurdistan) (London, 1928).

FIELD, H. Arabs of Central Iraq: Their History, Ethnology, and Physical Characters (Chicago, 1935).
The Anthropology of Iraq (4 vols., 1940, 1949, 1951, 1952, Chicago (first 2 vols.), Cambridge, Mass. (last 2 vols.).

KINNANE, DIRK. The Kurdish Problem (Oxford, 1964).
The Kurds and Kurdistan (Oxford, 1965).

LUKE, Sir H. C. Mosul and its Minorities (London, 1925).

O'BALLANCE, EDGAR. The Kurdish Revolt 1961–1970 (Faber and Faber, London, 1974).

SALIM, S. M. Marsh Dwellers of the Euphrates Delta (New York, 1961).

SHORT, MARTIN and MCDERMOTT, ANTHONY. The Kurds (Minority Rights Group, London, 1975).

THESIGER, WILFRED. The Marsh Arabs (London, 1964).

Israel

PHYSICAL AND SOCIAL GEOGRAPHY

W. B. Fisher

The pre-1967 frontiers of Israel are defined by armistice agreements signed with neighbouring Arab states, and represent the stabilization of a military front as it existed in late 1948 and early 1949. These boundaries are thus in many respects fortuitous, and have little geographical basis. It may be pertinent to recall that prior to 1918 the whole area now partitioned between Syria, Israel and the kingdom of Jordan formed part of the Ottoman Empire, and was spoken of as "Syria". Then after 1918 came the establishment of the territories of the Lebanon, Syria, Palestine, and Transjordan—the frontier between the last two lying for the most part along the Jordan river.

The present State of Israel is bounded on the north by the Lebanon, on the north-east by Syria, on the east by the Hashemite Kingdom of Jordan, and on the south and south-west by the Gulf of Aqaba and the Sinai Desert, now an occupied territory. The so-called "Gaza strip", a small piece of territory some 40 km. long, formed part of Palestine, but was, under the Armistice Agreement of February 1949, then left in Egyptian control. The territories occupied after the war of June 1967 are not recognized as forming part of the State of Israel, although it seems unlikely that she will give up her annexation of the Old City of Jerusalem. The geographical descriptions of these territories are, therefore, given in the chapters on the countries which controlled them before June 1967*.

Because of the nature of the frontiers, which partition natural geographical units, it is more convenient to discuss the geography of Israel partly in association with that of its neighbour, Jordan. The Jordan Valley itself, which is divided territorially between the two states, is dealt with in the chapter on Jordan, but the uplands of Samaria-Judaea, from Jenin to Hebron, and including Jerusalem, which form a single unit, will be discussed below, though a large part of this territory lies outside the frontiers of Israel.

PHYSICAL FEATURES

The physical geography of Israel is surprisingly complex and though the area of the state is small, a considerable number of regions are easily distinguished. In the extreme north the hills of the Lebanon range continue without break, though of lower altitude, to form the uplands of Galilee, where the maximum height is just over 1,200 metres. The Galilee hills fall away steeply on three sides: on the east to the well-defined Jordan Valley (*see* Jordan), on the west to a narrow coastal plain, and to the south at the Vale of Esdraelon or "Emek Yezreel". This latter is a rather irregular trough formed by subsidence along faults, with a flat floor and steep sides, and it runs inland from the Mediterranean south-eastwards to reach the Jordan Valley. At its western end the vale opens into the wide Bay of Acre, 25 to 30 km. in breadth, but it narrows inland to only a mile or two before opening out once again where it joins the Jordan Valley. This lowland area has a very fertile soil and an annual rainfall of 40 cm., which is sufficient, with limited irrigation, for agriculture. Formerly highly malarial and largely uncultivated, the vale is now very productive. For centuries it has been a corridor of major importance linking the Mediterranean coast and Egypt with the interior of south-west Asia, and has thus been a passage-way for ethnic, cultural, and military invasions.

South of Esdraelon there is an upland plateau extending for about 150 km. This is a broad upfold of rock, consisting mainly of limestone and reaching 900 metres in altitude. In the north, where there is a moderate rainfall, the plateau has been eroded into valleys, some of which are fertile, though less so than those of Esdraelon or Galilee. This district, centred on Jenin and Nablus, is the ancient country of Samaria, until 1967 part of Jordan. Further south rainfall is reduced and erosion is far less prominent; hence this second region, Judaea proper, stands out as a more strongly defined ridge, with far fewer streams and a barer open landscape of a more arid and dusty character. Jerusalem, Bethlehem and Hebron are the main towns. Towards the south-east rainfall becomes scanty and we reach the Wilderness of Judaea, an area of semi-desert. In the extreme south the plateau begins to fall in altitude, passing finally into a second plateau only 300 to 450 metres above sea-level, but broader, and broken by occasional ranges of hills that reach 900 metres in height. This is the Negev, a territory comprising nearly half of the total area of Israel, and bounded on the east by the lower Jordan Valley and on the west by the Sinai Desert. Agriculture, entirely dependent on irrigation, is carried on in a few places in the north, but for the most part the Negev consists of steppe or semi-desert. Irrigation schemes are now being developed in those areas where soils are potentially productive.

Between the uplands of Samaria-Judaea and the Mediterranean Sea there occurs a low-lying coastal plain that stretches southwards from Haifa as far as the Egyptian frontier at Gaza. In the north the plain is closely hemmed in by the spur of Mount Carmel (550 metres), which almost reaches the sea; but the plain soon opens out to form a fertile lowland—the

* For the state of the *de facto* boundaries after the various agreements of 1974, 1975 and 1979 with Egypt and Syria, *see* maps, pp. 72, 74 and 80.

Plain of Sharon. Further south still the plain becomes again broader, but with a more arid climate and a sandier soil—this is the ancient Philistia. Ultimately the plain becomes quite arid, with loose sand dunes, and it merges into the Sinai Desert.

One other area remains to be mentioned—the Shephelah, which is a shallow upland basin lying in the first foothills of the Judaean plateau, just east of the Plain of Sharon. This region, distinguished by a fertile soil and moister climate, is heavily cultivated, chiefly in cereals.

CLIMATE

Climatically Israel has the typical "Mediterranean" cycle of hot, dry summers, when the temperature reaches 32 to 38°C., and mild, rainy winters. Altitude has a considerable effect, in that though snow may fall on the hills, it is not frequent on the lowlands. Jerusalem can have several inches of snow in winter, and Upper Galilee several feet. The valleys, especially Esdraelon and adjacent parts of the upper Jordan, lying below sea-level, can become extremely hot (over 40°C.) and very humid.

Rainfall is very variable from one part of Israel to another. Parts of Galilee receive over 100 cm. annually, but the amount decreases rapidly southwards, until in the Negev and Plain of Gaza, it is 25 cm. or less. This is because the prevailing south-westerly winds blow off the sea to reach the north of Israel, but further south they come from Egypt, with only a short sea track, and are hence lacking in moisture.

RACE AND LANGUAGE

Discussion over the racial affinities of the Jewish people has continued over many years, but there has been no unanimity on the subject. One view is that the Jewish people, whatever their first origin, have now taken on many of the characteristics of the peoples among whom they have lived since the Dispersal—e.g., the Jews of Germany were often closely similar in anthropological character to the Germans; the Jews of Iraq resembled the Arabs; and the Jews of Abyssinia had a black skin. Upholders of such a view would largely deny the separateness of ethnic qualities amongst the Jews. On the other hand, it has been suggested that the Jews represent an intermixture of Armenoid and other Middle-Eastern racial strains, with the former predominating—and evidence for this may be found in the head-form and facial appearance of many Jews, which are often strongly Armenoid. The correctness of either viewpoint is largely a matter of personal interpretation.

Under British mandatory rule there were three official languages in Palestine—Arabic, spoken by a majority of the inhabitants (all Arabs and a few Jews); Hebrew, the ancient language of the Jews; and English. This last was considered to be standard if doubt arose as to the meaning of translation from the other two.

Since the establishment of the State of Israel the relative importance of the languages has changed. Hebrew is now dominant, Arabic has greatly declined following the flight of Arab refugees, and English is also less important, though it remains the first foreign language of most Israelis.

Hebrew, once widely current in biblical days, underwent considerable eclipse after the dispersal of Jewish people by the Romans, and until fairly recently its use was largely restricted to scholarship, serious literature and religious observance. Most Jews of Eastern and Southern Europe did not employ Hebrew as their everyday speech, but spoke either Yiddish or Ladino, the former being a Jewish-German dialect current in East and Central Europe, and the latter a form of Spanish. Immigrants into Israel since 1890 have, however, been encouraged to use Hebrew as a normal everyday speech, and Hebrew is now the living tongue of most Israeli Jews. The revival has been a potent agent in the unification of the Israeli Jewish people because, in addition to the two widely different forms of speech, Yiddish and Ladino, most Jewish immigrants usually spoke yet another language according to their country of origin, and the census of 1931 recorded over sixty such languages in habitual use within Palestine.

It is only by a revival of Hebrew that the Jewish community has found a reasonable *modus vivendi*—yet this step was not easy, for some devout Jews opposed the use of Hebrew for secular speech. Furthermore, there was controversy as to the way Hebrew should be pronounced, but the Sephardic pronunciation was finally adopted.

HISTORY

Tom Little

(with subsequent revisions by the Editor)

For most Jews the creation of the State of Israel in 1948 was the fulfilment of Biblical prophecy; to some in this more secular age it is a country justifiably won by political skill and force of arms in a world that denied them one for nearly 2,000 years; but, however regarded, it is seen as the fulfilment of Jewish history.

Although clearly a more ancient people from east of the Euphrates, the Jews trace their descent from Abraham, the first of the Patriarchs, who departed from Ur, the centre of the ancient Chaldean civilization, about 2,000 years B.C. Oral tradition as recorded in the Old Testament states that he was instructed by God to leave Chaldea with his family and proceed to Canaan (Phoenicia), or Palestine, the land of the Philistines, where he would father a great nation which would play an important part in human history. The authors of the Old Testament were primarily concerned to establish the descent of the Jewish people from Abraham under the guidance of God but in so doing they preserved the ancient history of the Jews which archaeology has tended to confirm within a debateable chronology.

Abraham's nomad family eventually reached Canaan and grazed their flocks there for a time before crossing Sinai to the richer pastures of Egypt. They remained in Egypt probably about 400 years and multiplied greatly, but their separateness in race, religion and customs at last excited the fears of the pharaohs, who enslaved them. Moses, who had escaped this slavery because he was brought up an Egyptian, fled with the Jews from the country (c. 1,200 B.C.) and gave them his law (the Torah) proclaiming the absolute oneness of God and establishing the disciplines of His worship.

They wandered for some decades in the wilderness before reaching the river Jordan. Moses' successor, Joshua, led some of the families (or tribes) across it and conquered Canaan. It was a stormy occupation of constant conflict with the indigenous peoples until the warrior Saul triumphed and became the first 'king'. His successor, David, completed the subjugation of the Israelites' enemies and briefly united all the tribes. King Solomon, his son, raised the country to its peak and built the Temple of Jerusalem which came to be recognized as the temple of all the Jews and the focal point of worship. His magnificence burdened the people, and this and his tolerance of the worship of idols provoked a successful revolt of the ten northern tribes under Jereboam who established Israel as his own kingdom. This division into two parts, Israel and Judah (which contained Jerusalem), was disastrous, for Israel was soon overcome by the Assyrians and its people were taken into captivity and lost to history. About 100 years later Judah fell victim to the Babylonians and its people were also taken captive, but their community endured to become an important element in the future of Judaism. The Babylonians destroyed Solomon's temple.

When the Persian leader Cyrus conquered Babylon he gave the Jews permission to return to Jerusalem, and some did so. There they set about rebuilding the Temple which was completed about 500 B.C. and in 200 years of relative tranquility their religion was consolidated by a series of great teachers. Palestine was in turn conquered by Alexander the Great and it and the Jews became part of his empire; but Alexander was tolerant, as were his successors in Egypt, the Ptolemies, with the result that Alexandria became the centre of a learned school of Hellenic Judaism.

The results were tragic in the successor Roman empire. The Jews rebelled against the oppressive Roman rule and Nero sent his greatest general, Vespasian, and his son, Titus, to suppress them. The conquest was completed by Titus; Jerusalem and the second temple were destroyed (c. 70 A.D.), and the Diaspora which began with the Assyrian conquest of Israel was complete. A small community of Jews remained in Jerusalem and the surrounding countryside, and devoted themselves to their religion, producing their version of the Talmud, the repository of Judaic history, learning and interpretation which, with the Torah and the Old Testament, became the essence of the faith, but it was the version of the Talmud produced by the Babylonian scholars which became the accepted document.

Scattered across the world, throughout Arabia, Asia as far as China, North Africa and Europe as far as Poland and Russia, Jewish communities continued to exist, sometimes powerful, often persecuted, but held in their exclusiveness and survival by religion and certain central themes: their belief in the oneness of God, his promise to Abraham, the promise of the 'return', and the Temple as the temple of all Jews. In terms of time their occupation of Palestine was relatively short and for even less of that time did they hold or rule it all, but the scattered communities continued to look towards Jerusalem.

THE ZIONIST MOVEMENT

In the late nineteenth century there were affluent and even powerful groups of Jews in Europe but the people as a whole were usually treated as second-class citizens in the countries where they lived. The large, pious and orthodox groups in Eastern Europe, in particular, were subject intermittently to persecution, and in 1881 there was a series of pogroms in Russia which stirred the conscience of world Jewry into forming plans for their escape. For the eastern

Jews there could be only one destination: Palestine. The pogroms lead directly to the formation in Russia of a movement called the Lovers of Zion (*Hovevei Zion*), and within that movement another was formed, called the *Bilu*, by a large community of young Jews in the Kharkov region. In 1882 a *Bilu* group in Constantinople issued a manifesto demanding a home in Palestine. They proposed that they should beg it from the Sultan of Turkey, in whose empire Palestine lay, and that if he would not give them absolute possession he should at least let them have an autonomous 'State within a larger State.'

The word Zionism was coined by a Russian about a decade later as a spiritual-humanitarian concept but Theodor Herzl, who became the leader of the movement, defined its aim specifically at the Basle Congress of 1897 (*see* Documents on Palestine, p. 57): 'Zionism', he said, 'strives to create for the Jewish people a home in Palestine secured by public law'. He wrote in his journal after the congress: 'At Basle I founded the Jewish State . . . perhaps in five years, and certainly fifty, everyone will know it'. He is recognized as the founder of political Zionism.

He was concerned essentially with the creation of a safe refuge for the suffering communities of Eastern Europe and thought that their migration and settlement could and should be financed by prosperous Jews. When he failed to get help from the Sultan he considered other possible 'homes' as far apart as Uganda and Latin America, but even safe places could never have the appeal to orthodox Jews as had Palestine, sanctioned in their scriptures and 'promised' to them by God. Some of the Jews of Russia and Poland escaped persecution to make their own way to Palestine and became the earliest immigrant communities there.

When the Turkish empire was destroyed by Allied forces in the 1914–18 war new possibilities of getting their 'home' or State in Palestine opened up before the Zionists. In the years 1915–16 Sir Mark Sykes for Britain and M. Charles Georges-Picot for France had, in fact, drafted an agreement (*see* Documents on Palestine, p. 57) in which, while undertaking 'to recognize and protect an independent Arab State or Confederation of Arab States', the two powers in effect carved the Middle East into their respective spheres of influence and authority pending the time of its liberation from Turkey. Influential Zionists, notably Dr. Chaim Weizmann, saw their opportunity to press Britain for a commitment to provide a home for the Jews in Palestine and secured the help of Judge Louis Brandeis, a leading United States Zionist and principal adviser to President Woodrow Wilson, in bringing the U.S. into the war on the side of the Allies in April 1917. The outcome was the Balfour Declaration (*see* Documents on Palestine, p. 58) which was contained in a letter from Arthur James Balfour to Lord Rothschild on behalf of the Zionist Federation, dated November 2nd, 1917. It stated:

"His Majesty's Government view with favour the establishment in Palestine of a national home for the Jewish people, and will use their best endeavours to facilitate the achievement of this object, it being clearly understood that nothing shall be done which may prejudice the existing civil and religious rights of existing non-Jewish communities in Palestine, or the rights and political status of Jews in other countries".

The San Remo Conference decided on April 24th, 1920 to give the Mandate under the newly formed League of Nations to Britain (the terms of which were approved by the United States, which was not a member of the League) before they were finally agreed by the League Council on July 24th, 1922. The terms (*see* Documents on Palestine, p. 61) included a restatement of the Balfour Declaration and provided that "an appropriate Jewish agency" should be established to advise and cooperate with the Palestine Administration in matters affecting the Jewish national home and to take part in the development of the country. This gave the Zionist Organization a special position because the Mandate stipulated that it should be recognized as such an agency if the mandatory authority thought it appropriate. Britain took over the Mandate in September 1923.

THE MANDATE

Herzl's first aim had thereby been achieved: the national home of the Jewish people had been "secured by public law"; but major obstacles were still to be overcome before the home, or State, became a reality. When the Mandate was granted, the Arabs constituted 92 per cent of the population and owned 98 per cent of the land in Palestine, and it could clearly not be a home unless the demography and land ownership were changed in favour of the Jews. It was to these ends that the Zionist movement now directed itself, but Britain and it had different views concerning what was meant by "favouring" the establishment of the home, both in the matter of boundaries and immigration, even though Britain was consistently sympathetic to the enterprise. This was important, for although she was nominally under the supervision of the Mandates Commission of the League, she was able to run Palestine very much as a Crown Colony and administered it through the Colonial Office.

The World Zionist Organization had presented a memorandum to the Paris Peace Conference in 1919 setting forth its territorial concept of the home, as follows:

The whole of Palestine, southern Lebanon, including the towns of Tyre and Sidon, the headwaters of the Jordan river on Mount Hermon and the southern portion of the Litani river; the Golan Heights in Syria, including the town of Quneitra, the Yarmuk river and Al-Himmeh hot springs; the whole of the Jordan valley, the Dead Sea, and the eastern highlands up to the outskirts of Amman, thence in a southerly direction along the Hedjaz railway to the Gulf of Aqaba; in Egypt, from El-Arish, on the Mediterranean coast, in a straight line in a southerly direction to Sharm as-Sheikh on the Gulf of Aqaba.

The League of Nations and the Peace settlement did not accept these boundaries but the mandate given to Britain included Transjordan, the territory East of the river and beyond Amman. Britain allotted Transjordan as an Emirate to Emir Abdullah in 1921 and with the grant of full independence in 1946 it became a kingdom.

The Arabs bitterly opposed the Balfour Declaration and Jewish immigration and called for the prohibition of land sales to Jews. Britain would neither accede to their demands nor to Jewish claims to a majority in Palestine. There were intermittent outbreaks of Arab violence, notably in 1922 and 1929, which brought the Arabs into conflict with the mandatory government and there were four British Commissions of Inquiry and two White Papers were issued (*see* Documents on Palestine, p. 63) on the situation before 1936, none of which envisaged a Jewish majority. In 1936 there was an effective six-months general strike of the Arab population followed by a large scale rebellion which lasted until the outbreak of the Second World War and in 1939 another Commission issued the third White Paper (*see* Documents on Palestine, p. 64) which stated that Britain would not continue to develop the Jewish national home beyond the point already reached, proposed that 75,000 more Jews should be admitted over five years and then Jewish immigration would cease. Finally, it proposed that self-governing institutions should be set-up at the end of the five years. This would have preserved the Arab majority in the country and its legislature.

THE BILTMORE PROGRAMME AND AFTER

The world emotional context at that time was conditioned by the horrifying Nazi policy of exterminating Jews—a policy which was to reach even more frightful proportions after the outbreak of war. Zionists and Jews generally regarded the White Paper as a betrayal of the terms of the Mandate and when David Ben Gurion, Chairman of the Jewish Agency Executive, was in New York in 1942 an Extraordinary Zionist Conference held at the Biltmore Hotel utterly rejected the White Paper and reformulated Zionist policy. The declaration of the conference (*see* Documents on Palestine, p. 65) issued on May 11th, 1942, concluded as follows:

> The conference urges that the gates of Palestine be opened; that the Jewish Agency be vested with control of immigration into Palestine and with the necessary authority for upbuilding the country, including the development of its unoccupied and uncultivated lands; and that Palestine be established as a Jewish Commonwealth integrated into the new structure of the democratic world.

This policy brought the Jews into head-on collision with the Palestine Government before the war was over. Those in Europe who escaped the Nazi holocaust were herded into refugee camps and some who could do so with organized Zionist help tried to reach Palestine, but the British authorities, in accordance with the 1939 policy, tried to prevent their entry.

The British failed. The Jewish population which had been 56,000 at the time of the Mandate was 608,000 in 1946 and was estimated to be 650,000 on the eve of the creation of Israel, or about two-fifths of the entire population. Further, the Jewish Agency had formed its own military organizations, the Haganah and its units of shock troops, the Palmach, which were strengthened by those Jews who had fought on the side of the British during the war, and supported by two smaller extremist groups, the Irgun Zvaei Leumi and the Stern Gang. Towards the end of the war they embarked on a policy of violence designed to impose the Biltmore programme. They successfully made the Mandate unworkable and Britain referred it to the United Nations (which had replaced the League) on April 2nd, 1947.

The UN General Assembly sent a Special Commission (UNSCOP) to Palestine to report on the situation and its report issued on August 31st, 1947 proposed two plans: a majority plan for the partition of Palestine into two States, one Jewish and one Arab, with economic union; and a minority plan for a federal State. The Assembly adopted the majority plan (*see* Documents on Palestine, p. 66) on November 29th by 33 votes for and 13 against, with ten abstentions. The plan divided Palestine into six principal parts, three of which, comprising 56 per cent of the total area were reserved for the Jewish State and three, with the enclave of Jaffa, comprising 43 per cent of the area, for the Arab State. It provided that Jerusalem would be an international zone administered by the UN as the holy city for Jews, Moslems and Christians. The Arabs refused to accept this decision and in the subsequent disorders about 1,700 people were killed. In April 1948 the Jewish forces swung into full-scale attack and by the time the Mandate was terminated on May 14th, 400,000 Arabs had evacuated their homes to become refugees in neighbouring Arab countries.

THE STATE ESTABLISHED

The Mandate was relinquished by Britain at 6 p.m. Washington time; at 6.01 the State of Israel was officially declared by the Jewish authorities in Palestine; at 6.11 the United States accorded it recognition and immediately afterwards the Soviet Union did likewise. Thus Israel came into existence only one year late on Herzl's 50-year diary prophecy. The Arab States belatedly came to the help of the Palestinian Arabs but their attempt to overthrow the new state failed and Israel was left in possession of more territory than had been allotted to her under the UN partition plan, including new (non-Arab) Jerusalem. Israel rejected the proposed internationalization of the city, for the Jews considered the return to Jerusalem to be at the heart of the divine promise to them.

A provisional government was formed in Tel-Aviv the day before the Mandate ended, with Ben Gurion as Prime Minister and other members of the Jewish Agency Executive in leading ministerial posts. The constitution and electoral laws had already been prepared and the first general elections were held in January 1949 for a single-chamber Knesset (or parliament) elected by proportional representation. This enabled several parties to gain representation, with Mapai usually in the majority but never predominant. As a result, government has since been conducted by uneasy coalitions, except during military confrontations with the Arabs.

After the war another 400,000 Arabs fled from the additional territory conquered by Israel and in the course of another year about 300,000 more left the impoverished Arab West Bank for Transjordan. (In 1950 King Abdullah held a referendum in which the West Bank Arabs agreed to be part of his kingdom which then became known as Jordan.) The Israeli Government maintained the mandatory military control, established in the earlier disorders, over those Arab populations which remained within its territory but allowed "co-operative" Arabs to be elected to the Knesset; four were elected to the first parliament.

A gigantic programme of immigration was launched immediately the Provisional Government took over and within three years the Jewish population was doubled. This result, unparalleled in history, was assisted by Iraq which expelled the larger part of its age-old Jewish communities. The 1961 census gave Israel's population as 2,260,700, of whom 230,000 were Arabs. The two-millionth Jew arrived in May 1962 and the three-millionth early in 1972. A massive plan for land development to provide for the new people was executed concomitantly with the early immigration programme; the Jewish National Fund took over 3,000,000 dunums of former Arab land and used heavy mechanical equipment to bring it rapidly back into production. This was made possible by the stupendous support from abroad which came in the form of private gifts from world Jewry, State loans and aid, and private Jewish investments. The United States was both privately and publicly the major contributor, but at the Hague in 1952 West Germany agreed to pay reparations for Nazi crimes, and these payments amounted to £216 million in Deutsche Marks before they were concluded in 1966. The effect of this influx of unearned money from all sources was to cause serious inflation which in 1962 forced devaluation of the Israel pound by 40 per cent and was still a grave problem in the 1970s (*see* Economic Survey).

Israel was admitted to the United Nations, albeit on conditions concerning Jerusalem and refugees which were contrary to her overall policy and were never fulfilled. Her relations with the Arab States were governed by a series of armistice agreements reached in Rhodes in 1949 which, in effect, established an unsteady truce without an Arab commitment to permanent peace. The Arabs continued to insist that the creation of Israel was a usurpation of Arab territory and right and a denial of UN principles. Defence policy therefore dominated Israel's political thinking and firmly established the principle that she would remain militarily superior to any combination of Arab States. In the early 1950s, however, it was the Palestinian refugees who caused intermittent frontier trouble, mainly from Syria and Jordan, but to some extent from the Gaza strip which, since the 1948 war, had been administered by Egypt.

Whenever one of the frontiers became too troublesome, Israel mounted a retaliatory raid *pour décourager les autres*. Acting on the principle that Nasser's Egypt was the only serious danger, Mr. Ben Gurion ordered a raid which on February 28th, 1955, wiped out the small Egyptian garrison at Gaza and the reinforcements travelling by road to its support. The result was contrary to Ben Gurion's intention; Nasser determined to secure adequate military strength and to that end entered in to the "Czech" arms agreement in August 1955, by which he bartered cotton and took credits from the U.S.S.R. for substantial quantities of arms and planes which began to arrive quickly. The threat to Israel was therefore increased.

SUEZ

On July 26th, 1956, Nasser nationalized the Suez Canal company of which Britain and France were the principal shareholders (*see* Egypt) and the two European powers prepared to retake control of it. Neither could expect any support from the two super-powers, or from world opinion in general, for open invasion, but in October Ben Gurion entered into a secret pact with them by which Israel would invade Sinai and thus justify Britain and France intervening to keep the combatants apart. The Israelis invaded on October 29th with powerful armoured columns and rapidly advanced towards the canal. The following day Britain and France issued their ultimatum that both sides should withdraw to 20 miles from the canal. Israel, which had by this time taken almost all of the Sinai, including the Gaza strip and Sharm as-Sheikh at the entrance to the Gulf of Aqaba, readily agreed to comply with the ultimatum, but Egypt refused on the grounds that she was being asked to withdraw from her own territory.

The Anglo-French force thereupon invaded the Port Said area and advanced some miles along the Suez Canal. There it was halted by Sir Anthony Eden, the British Prime Minister, in face of the forthright condemnation of the UN and financial sanctions threatened by the U.S.; a decision which the French Prime Minister, M. Guy Mollet, reluctantly accepted. Both countries withdrew their troops before the year was out. This was a severe blow to Mr. Ben Gurion who had counted on holding at least a security buffer zone on a line from El Arish, on the Mediterranean coast, to Sharm as-Sheikh (the Zionist 1919 frontier proposal). Therefore Israel delayed her final withdrawal from Egypt until January, and from the Gaza strip until March 1957 when a UN Emergency Force was safely established on the Sinai frontier and at Sharm as-Sheikh. Even so, Egypt kept detaining ships in the Suez Canal and confiscating cargoes bound for Israel, against which Mrs. Golda Meir, then Foreign Minister, strongly protested to the United Nations in September 1959.

A development of great consequence to Israel at this time was the increasing involvement of the Soviet Union in the Middle East, especially in Egypt. The U.S.S.R. took no less than 50 per cent of Egyptian exports in 1957, and in 1958 agreed to finance and direct the building of the mammoth High Dam at Aswan. In keeping with this policy, the Soviet Union adopted a strongly pro-Arab and anti-Israeli line and steadily rearmed Nasser's forces.

Mr. Ben Gurion resigned "for personal reasons" in June 1963 and was succeeded by Levi Eshkol, his Finance Minister, who had been a minister continuously since joining the provisional government from the Jewish Agency in 1948. He was in modern terminology a "dove", inclined to a more conciliatory policy which he hoped would in time erode Arab enmity. This was opposed by many in the ruling hierarchy, notably the veteran Ben Gurion and Gen. Moshe Dayan, who had commanded the Israeli forces in their brilliant victory in 1956.

There was a notable increase in Arab guerrilla activity across the frontiers of Egypt, Jordan and Syria in the mid-1960s. The Palestinians formed a guerrilla organization called Al-Fatah for which the Syrian Prime Minister publicly declared his support in 1966. Mutual accusations of frontier violations followed, and President Nasser warned that he would have to activate the Egypt-Syrian Joint Defence Agreement if Israel's "aggression" did not cease. In May, King Hussein brought Jordan into the agreement and in that same month Nasser received information, which proved later to be untrue, that Israeli troops were massing on the Syrian frontier. In response Nasser ordered the withdrawal of the United Nations Emergency Force from the Gaza strip, the Sinai Desert and Sharm as-Sheikh. U Thant immediately obeyed, and Nasser then imposed a total blockade on Israeli shipping in the Straits of Tiran, although Israel had always made it plain that this would be considered a *casus belli*.

U Thant flew to Cairo on May 22nd, but by that time Nasser had already strengthened his forces in the Sinai and called up his reserves. Israel, Jordan and Syria had also mobilized. Israel formed a national government by bringing to the cabinet one representative of each of the three opposition parties. General Moshe Dayan, the victor of the 1956 Sinai campaign, was brought in as Defence Minister.

THE JUNE WAR

Israel made its pre-emptive strike in the early hours of June 5th when its armoured forces moved into Sinai. At 0600 hours GMT Israeli planes attacked 25 airfields in Egypt, Jordan, Syria and Iraq, destroying large numbers of planes on the ground and putting the runways out of action, thus effectively depriving the Egyptian and Jordanian ground forces of air cover. There were some fierce armoured battles in the Sinai but Israeli forces were in position along the Suez Canal on June 8th. They took Sharm as-Sheikh without a fight. On the eastern front, they reached the Jordan river on June 7th and entered and conquered Old (Arab) Jerusalem on the same day. Their main forces destroyed, President Nasser and King Hussein accepted a cease-fire on the 8th. Israel then turned its attention to the Syrian fortifications on the Golan Heights from which Israeli settlements were being shelled. In a brilliant but costly action, armour and infantry captured the heights. Syria accepted a cease-fire on the 9th but Israel ignored it until the 10th, by which time her troops were in possession of Kuneitra, on the road to Damascus. The "six-day war", as it became known, was over; Israel had achieved a victory more sweeping even than that of 1956.

Israel had recovered Jerusalem and access to the Western Wall of the Temples of Solomon and Herod, which were the most sacred places of worship for all Jews but to which they had been denied access since the division of the city between the Arabs and Israel in 1948. Israel immediately tore down the barriers, reunited the city, put the administration of Arab Jerusalem under her existing city administration, and effectively annexed it. The UN General Assembly passed a resolution on July 4th, which Israel disregarded, calling on her to rescind all the measures taken and to desist from any further action that would change the status of the holy city. Israel made it plain from the beginning that there could be no question of returning Old Jerusalem to Arab possession in any peace settlement.

The United Nations and the world powers busied themselves with the search for peace. On August 29th the heads of the Arab States began a Summit conference in Khartoum at which they decided to seek a political settlement but not to make peace with or recognize Israel or to negotiate directly with her, and meanwhile "to adopt necessary measures to strengthen military preparation to face all eventualities". On November 22nd, after many attempts, the UN Security Council agreed to Resolution 242, which stated that the establishment of a just and lasting peace in the Middle East should include the application of the following principles:

(i) withdrawal of Israeli armed forces from territories occupied in the recent conflict; and (ii) termination of all claims or states of belligerency and respect for and acknowledgement of the sovereignty,. territorial integrity, and political independence of every State in the area, and their right to live in peace within secure and recognized boundaries free from threats or acts of force. The Council affirmed also the necessity for (*a*) guaranteeing freedom of navigation through international waterways in the area, and (*b*) achieving a just settlement of the refugee problem.

The Secretary-General designated Ambassador Gunnar Jarring of Sweden as Special Representative to assist the process of finding a peaceful settlement on this basis.

The essential ambiguity of the Council resolution was contained in the phrase "withdrawal . . . from territories occupied . . ." (which in the French translation became "les territoires"), and the Israeli

Government has contended ever since that it meant an agreed withdrawal from some occupied territories "to secure and recognized boundaries". This was, in Israel's view, precluded by the Arab States' Khartoum resolution and their insistence that Resolution 242 meant total withdrawal from the 1967 occupied territories. Further, Israel insisted that she would only negotiate withdrawal directly with Egypt and the Arab States as part of a peace settlement and that the function of Jarring was to bring this about and not to initiate proposals of his own for a settlement.

UNEASY SECURITY

Meanwhile Israel based her policy on retention of the occupied territories as warranty of her security. The 1967 defeat had severely damaged the U.S.S.R.'s prestige in the Arab world, and to repair her position she began immediately to restore the Egyptian armed forces, including the air force. Meanwhile in 1967 President de Gaulle imposed an arms embargo on Israel and refused to deliver 50 supersonic Mirage IV fighters which Israel had ordered and paid for. Israel therefore turned to the United States, arguing that the balance of military power must, for her security, be maintained in her favour. This point was conceded by the U.S. in 1968 with a contract to deliver 50 Phantom jet fighter-bombers, which brought Cairo within range and were more powerful than any MiGs in Egypt.

Using powerful artillery installed by the U.S.S.R. west of the canal, Nasser began in 1968 a "war of attrition" in order to force Israel to accept his terms. Relatively heavy casualties were caused to the Israeli troops, notably in July and October, and throughout the period Israel retaliated punitively with air and artillery attacks which forced Egypt to evacuate the canal zone towns. Suez and its oil refineries were destroyed. The zone remained disturbed until 1970, a climax being reached in February when 80 civilians were killed in an Israeli bombing raid on Soviet SAM-II missile installations.

Israel's Prime Minister, Levi Eshkol, died on February 26th, 1969, and was succeeded in the following month by Mrs. Golda Meir, who had been Minister for Foreign Affairs from 1956 to 1966.

President Nixon, who had taken office in the United States, supported an initiative by his Secretary of State, William Rogers, "to encourage the parties to stop shooting and start talking". This was announced on June 25, 1970, and was unfavourably received in the Arab world. Nasser flew to Moscow with a proposal to accept it on condition that Russia supplied SAM-III missiles capable of destroying low-flying aircraft. He returned to Cairo and stunned Egypt and the Arab world with an unconditional acceptance of the Rogers plan and its related canal zone 90 day ceasefire. King Hussein immediately associated Jordan with Nasser's acceptance. Israel accepted the Rogers plan on August 7th but immediately complained that Egypt had broken the ceasefire agreement by moving SAM-III missile sites into the 30-mile wide standstill area along the canal.

President Nasser died suddenly on September 28th, 1970, but President Sadat, who succeeded him, sustained his policy. Although he only agreed to extend the ceasefire for another 90 days, it continued indefinitely. The American effort was directed towards securing an interim agreement by which Israel would withdraw from the Suez Canal and allow it to be reopened, but Israel, again on the basic principle of her security, would only consider a limited withdrawal and would not agree that Egyptian troops should cross the canal, terms which Egypt would not accept. U.S.-Israeli relations, vital to Israel, were uneasy during most of 1971 while the State Department pressed the Tel-Aviv Government to concede unacceptable terms of withdrawal from the canal. President Sadat gave the end of the year as a deadline for "peace or war", but before the year was out Mrs. Golda Meir secured a commitment to Israeli security from President Nixon firmer than any obtained in the past; the Rogers plan thereupon died, but 1972 dawned without the threatened outbreak of war from Egypt.

An upsurge of Palestinian guerrilla activity disturbed Israel after the 1967 war. People in frontier villages and settlements were forced to sleep in underground shelters. Although security was more than adequate to secure the State, it could not prevent isolated raids and terror acts. Direct guerrilla attacks on Israel declined after 1969, as divisions developed within the Palestinian movement itself. Two left-wing guerrilla groups, the Popular Front for the Liberation of Palestine (PFLP) and its offshoot, the Popular Democratic Front (PDFLP) embarked on a series of terrorist acts against Israeli planes and passengers at European airports and challenged the authority of King Hussein within Jordan. The King proceeded to drive the guerrillas out of his country, an operation which was not finally concluded until July 1971 (*see* Jordan). Israel's troubles along the Jordan frontier thereupon ceased. There were intermittent raids from Syria and Lebanon but Israel was able to control these disturbances by retaliatory attacks. In May 1972 the PFLP returned to airport terrorist acts, and a three-man Japanese "Red Army" suicide squad sent by the PFLP landed at Lod in an Air France plane and indiscriminately shot to death 28 people in the airport and wounded 80 before two of them were killed and the third captured. A new Palestinian terrorist group calling itself Black September (*see* Jordan) seized the Israeli team at the Munich Olympics on September 5th; eleven of the team and four terrorists were killed in a battle with West German police who captured the remaining three terrorists. There were a number of letter-bomb attacks on Israelis in Europe in the last quarter of the year, but it soon became evident that Israeli security services were retaliating when fourteen PLO members were killed or wounded by similar attacks in the space of a few weeks. It developed into a silent war between the Palestinian terrorists and a terrorist wing of the Israeli secret service, and by mid-1973 five Arabs and five Israeli agents had been murdered in European capitals and Cyprus.

Punitive raids were made on the Syrian Golan Heights in January 1973 and on February 21st an

Israeli Phantom shot down a Libyan airliner which had strayed over Sinai, causing 108 deaths, including some French crew members. This caused a world outcry which was muted ten days later when eight Palestinians seized the Saudi Arabian Embassy in Khartoum and held the retiring U.S. Ambassador and his successor, the Belgian Chargé d'Affaires, the Saudi Ambassador and the Jordanian Chargé d'Affaires as hostages for the release of Palestinians in several countries. They killed the American and European diplomats before surrendering to the Sudanese authorities.

The stated objective of Israeli punitive raids on Syria and Lebanon was to compel both countries to prevent the Palestinian resistance groups from mounting raids from within their borders, whether against Israel or in other countries. This objective seemed most successfully achieved in Lebanon on April 10th by a daring commando raid into the heart of Beirut, where the raiders killed three resistance leaders, while other commando units attacked two refugee camps outside the city and destroyed the PDFLP headquarters, killing one of its leaders. The Israeli authorities were able to make a number of arrests in the occupied territories from information gained in this raid. It caused a political crisis in Lebanon and led to open conflict between Palestinian groups and the Lebanese Army, which only came to an end when the Palestinian leaders agreed to revise the Cairo agreement of 1970, by which they had had virtual autonomy within the refugee camps.

THE OCCUPIED TERRITORIES

About 380,000 Arabs fled from the West Bank to Jordan, but nearly a million remained under Israeli occupation; of these, the 70,000 in East (Arab) Jerusalem, which was annexed, were treated as Israeli citizens and the remainder brought under military administration. This was of necessity strict for the first three years because of help given to Palestinian guerrillas by the Arabs in the occupied territories and, in some instances, in Israel proper. The Gaza strip was by far the most troublesome and it was not until the end of 1971 that Israeli security operations, including the clearance of one large refugee camp which had proved particularly difficult, brought the area under control. It was announced in March 1973 that the strip would be incorporated into Israel, that Jewish settlement in the strip would continue and that Arab inhabitants could circulate freely in Israel during the day. Higher living standards enjoyed by the Arabs under the occupation, 60,000 of whom found work in Israel itself, the inevitable growth of collaboration with the Israeli authorities and, finally, the disarray in which the Palestinian movement found itself by late 1970 rendered the security problem inside the country minimal during 1971. In March of the following year the Israeli military authorities successfully held elections for the mayors and municipalities in the main Arab towns, despite guerrilla threats of reprisals against any Arabs taking part.

Government policy was officially that in a peace settlement there would be substantial territories returned to the Arabs but there was no clear consensus in the Government or the country as to what they would amount to, except to the extent that Israel should have "secure frontiers". However, statements by Ministers made it clear that in addition to East Jerusalem and the Gaza strip, which had been effectively annexed, the Golan Heights of occupied Syria and parts of the Jordanian West Bank would not be returned. There was also increasing evidence on the ground. An extensive building programme to house immigrants was rapidly being executed in and around Jerusalem; 42 settlements had been established by January 1973 although, according to Israeli figures, only 3,150 Israeli civilians had been allowed to take up permanent residence in the areas.

Israel radio announced on August 18th, 1973 that another 35 settlements would be built in the occupied territories, bringing the total to 77. The Jewish National Fund and the Israeli Lands Administration had between them acquired 15,000 acres of Arab land and the army was in occupation of another 20,000 acres. A plan advanced by Deputy Prime Minister Yigal Allon, although not publicly approved by the Government, seemed to be in process of *de facto* execution. He proposed that a chain of Israeli settlements should be established along the Jordan river, which was effectively being done, a second chain along the Samarian Hills on the West bank, and a third along the road from Jerusalem to Jericho, in order to establish Israel's security. The rest of the West Bank and the main towns, excepting Jericho, would then be returned to Jordan.

The virtue of the Allon plan for most Israelis was that it would absorb few Arabs, for the core of the dispute within Israel remained the question of demographic balance between Arabs and Jews which would be changed in the Arabs' favour by the absorption of territory in which there were many of them resident. For that reason, the Government refused the request, submitted by the newly elected mayors of the Arab towns on the West Bank, that those Arabs who had fled the area after the 1967 war should be allowed to return. To restore the population balance the Jewish Agency, which was responsible for organizing immigration, concentrated upon Jews in Soviet Russia who were the largest reservoir of would-be immigrants. Russia began to relax its stringent opposition to Jewish emigration in 1971, with the result that thousands of Soviet Jews began to arrive in Israel. Of the 57,000 immigrants in the year 1972–73, 33,000 were from the Soviet Union.

THE YOM KIPPUR WAR

The failure to strike against Israel created great difficulties for President Sadat with his own people throughout 1972 and increased the over-confidence that had existed in Israel ever since the brilliant victory of 1967. It was believed firmly that Egypt was afraid to go to war again and that the Bar-Lev defences along the eastern bank of the Suez Canal could not be overcome, but in fact Sadat was working steadily towards war, against the advice of his Soviet ally. He secured the financial support of King Faisal of Saudi Arabia to buy arms for hard currency, the agreement of Syrian President Hafez Assad to a limited war for the recovery of territories lost in 1967, made his peace with King Hussein of Jordan and finally secured the arms required from the Soviet Union.

By the late Summer of 1973 he was ready for war on two fronts, Syria and Egypt, with King Hussein standing aside to tie-up a part of Israeli forces facing Jordan. At 2 p.m. on October 6th—the most important religious festival in Israel, Yom Kippur—the Egyptians launched their attack, breaking down the assumed impregnable sand banks of the Bar-Lev line with powerful water-jets, throwing pontoon bridges across the Suez Canal and breaking into Sinai. The line was undermanned. By midnight that day, the Egyptians had 500 tanks and missiles across the canal and destroyed 100 Israeli tanks. Almost simultaneously the Syrians had broken through the Israeli lines on the Golan heights.

Israel began the rapid mobilization of its reserve forces, the highly trained and numerically most important part of its defensive system, but before they could play an effective part the Egyptians had occupied the East bank of the canal to a depth of several miles and by the third day were advancing to the strategic Mitla pass in Sinai. The Syrian forces had by that time reached five miles from the Israeli frontier in Golan.

While fierce tank battles raged in Sinai, said to be bigger than any in the second World War, Israel halted the Syrians on its vulnerable northern frontier and counter-attacked successfully, driving the Syrians in a fighting retreat back over the 1967 cease-fire lines to within 20 miles of Damascus, where its forces were halted on the Syrian second line of defence. The Egyptians held their positions in Sinai but did not reach the Mitla pass. By this time an Iraqi armoured division, Iraqi MiGs, and a crack Jordanian armoured brigade had reinforced the Syrian Eastern flank.

The Egyptian High Command blundered on the twelfth day when it allowed a small Israeli commando force to cross to the West bank of the Suez Canal near Deversoir at the northern end of the Great Bitter Lake. The Israelis were able to reinforce the bridgehead with a force strong enough to swing southwards to Suez and endanger the Egyptian Third Army on the East bank. Losses were very heavy on both sides.

After three UN Security Council resolutions, a ceasefire became precariously effective on October 25th, but even then it was honoured more in the breach than observance until the end of the year. The U.S. Secretary of State, Dr. Henry Kissinger, did much to maintain a peace-making momentum by tours of the Arab countries to secure negotiations for a permanent settlement in Geneva on December 18th and in November Israel had accepted "in principle" the terms of an agreement Dr. Kissinger had reached with President Sadat for the "scrupulous" observance of the ceasefire. Dr. Kissinger made a second tour in mid-December as a result of which Egypt, Jordan and Israel sent high-calibre representatives to Geneva for negotiations on December 21st. Syria refused to attend.

Talks were soon adjourned to an unspecified date in order to allow time for the Israeli general elections, which had been postponed from October 30th to December 31st because of the war. Dr. Henry Kissinger returned to the Middle East in January and after days of intensive diplomatic activity, shuttling back and forward between Israel and Egypt, he secured the agreement of both countries to a disengagement of their forces which was announced on January 17th (*see* Documents on Palestine, p. 70). Israel agreed to withdraw its troops in Sinai to a line approximately 20 miles from the Suez Canal and Egypt to reduce its forces on the East bank. There was to be a neutral buffer zone between the two armies manned by troops of the UN Emergency Force.

Agreement for the disengagement of forces on the northern front was not signed until May 31st (*see* Documents on Palestine, p. 70), and then only after Dr. Kissinger had flown back and forward between Jerusalem and Damascus almost daily between the 16th and 29th. Israel and Syria agreed to withdraw their troops to lines on each side of the 1967 cease-fire line, and the ruined town of Kuneitra, capital of the Golan Heights, was handed back to Syria. Both countries then handed over the prisoners they had taken in the 1973 war.

Two important factors weakened the Israeli position. In the last days of the war the Arab oil producing States banned the supply of oil to the United States and Holland and reduced supplies to Western Europe. (Britain and France were exempted but in fact were unable to get their full supplies.) This, combined with steep increases in oil prices which caused serious balance-of-payment problems for the European countries—although this had nothing to do with the war—led the EEC to issue a joint declaration in the Arab favour. Even more damaging to Israel was the confrontation which almost developed between the U.S.S.R. and the U.S.A. when they both began heavy supplies of war equipment to the Arabs and Israel respectively. Dr. Kissinger made it clear to Israel that the United States would continue to support Israel, but only within the limits imposed by détente with the U.S.S.R.. It was unquestionably a form of pressure on Israel, although this was denied. Whatever anxiety Israel felt was allayed, at least in part, when President Nixon gave his blessing to any undertakings his Secretary of State had entered into by making a tour of Egypt, Saudi Arabia, Syria, Israel and Jordan in June. Shortly afterwards Israel's Finance Minister, Shimon Peres visited Washington and the outcome was the conversion of a $500 million loan into a gift and an undertaking to supply a powerful force of warplanes to ensure Israel's security.

THE AFTERMATH

The war had a profoundly disturbing effect on Israeli public opinion. The country had never suffered such losses before: nearly 3,000 dead and missing, which was a substantial proportion of so small a population. The ease with which the Egyptians had crossed the canal and over-run the Bar-Lev line and the firmness with which the Syrians held the second line of defence 20 miles from Damascus were not off-set in Israeli eyes by the fact that Israeli troops had broken through and recrossed the canal and had made territorial gains in Syria; the Arab forces had fought with hitherto unknown determination and had used their sophisticated Soviet weaponry with great skill. The public's total confidence in the overwhelming superiority of their own army and air force was severely shaken, with the result that a sharp division of opinion occurred between those who thought the war emphasized the need to keep defensible frontiers at all costs and those, less numerous, who viewed it as an argument for a more diligent search for a permanent peace. There was widespread dissatisfaction with the Government and a public debate ensued over the failure to anticipate the outbreak of war and the breakdown of military intelligence. There were mutual recriminations among the generals and Defence Minister Moshe Dayan's popularity in the country slumped. General Ariel Sharon, whose forces had made the breakthrough and canal crossing in Egypt, resigned from the army to join the right-wing Likud Party—the "hawks" of Israeli politics.

The elections of December 1973 reflected this confusion. The Labour alignment, led by Mapai, emerged as the strongest party with 51 seats. Likud, the main opposition, made substantial gains and won 39 seats. Mrs. Golda Meir reformed her coalition but resigned in April 1974 when the report on the 1973 war was published. She was succeeded in June by General Yitzhak Rabin, whose cabinet contained neither Moshe Dayan nor Abba Eban, who had been Foreign Minister since 1966. General Rabin, and his Foreign Minister, Yigal Allon, were both willing to make territorial sacrifices to achieve a settlement with the Arabs, and a Second Disengagement Agreement was signed with Egypt in September 1975 whereby Israel withdrew from some territory in the Sinai peninsula (*see* Documents on Palestine, page 71).

Meanwhile the PLO had achieved added status in 1974 by their recognition by the Arabs as "sole representative of the Palestinian people" at the Rabat summit of November 1974, but Mr. Rabin asserted Israeli policy, which he was to continue to hold throughout his premiership, of refusing to recognize a PLO delegation at any renewed Geneva peace talks.

Mr. Rabin was never able to command the support he needed as Prime Minister. The exact demarcation of functions between his role as Prime Minister and that of Shimon Peres, his Minister of Defence, and Yigal Allon, his Minister of Foreign Affairs, was never totally clear. Moreover, it soon became clear that, while Rabin could be considered something of a "dove" in his attitude towards the Arabs, Peres was more of a "hawk". This became apparent over the question of Israeli settlements in the occupied territory on the West Bank of the Jordan. The settlement at Kaddum illustrates the problem. This was officially a "temporary" settlement, but there were considerable efforts by many groups in Israel, particularly the *Gush Emunim* movement, to make it permanent. Mr. Rabin, in 1976, announced that he would evict the rebels from Kaddum, but it was a decision that he never carried out, not least because of the opposition of Mr. Peres.

Moreover, Israel's economic difficulties (fully described in the Economic Survey) cost Mr. Rabin considerable popularity, and it seemed that the unpopular measures that he was forced to introduce to combat inflation won him few hearts, discouraged immigration, and made little visible progress towards a sounder economy.

In December 1976 the National Religious Party abstained in a confidence vote in the Knesset arising from charges that the Sabbath had been desecrated at a ceremony marking the arrival of three U.S. aircraft. Mr. Rabin subsequently dismissed two of the NRP ministers from his cabinet, and the consequent withdrawal of NRP support left the Government in a minority in the Knesset, thus precipitating Mr. Rabin's resignation.

Mr. Rabin carried on in a caretaker capacity until the election of May 1977, but in April 1977 he experienced a fresh setback. The Government had been making investigations into various allegations of corruption among politicians and in public life, and in February 1977, Asher Yadlin, the Government's nominee as the new Governor of the Bank of Israel, was convicted of bribery charges. Early in April 1977 it was revealed that Mr. Rabin had been using a bank account in Washington, in the joint names of himself and his wife, in excess of the legal limit, and he therefore resigned as Leader of the Labour Party. On April 10th the Labour Party selected Shimon Peres as its new leader. Peres had earlier been narrowly defeated by Rabin in the February poll for the leadership of the Labour Party.

ISRAEL UNDER BEGIN

When the elections for the 9th Knesset took place on May 17th, 1977, the result was a surprise victory for the Likud, under Menachem Begin, who won 43 out of the 120 seats—the largest single total. The Likud victory removed the Labour Party from the predominant position it had held in Israel since 1949. With the support of the National Religious Party, Agudat Israel and Shlomzion, Mr. Begin was able to form a government on June 19th, and his position was strengthened in October 1977 when the Democratic Movement for Change (DMC) joined the Likud coalition. In September 1978, however, the DMC split into two factions, with seven Knesset members leaving Begin's coalition because they felt that his policy of announcing plans for further Israeli settlements on the West Bank was endangering prospects for peace.

Prospects for a permanent peace settlement had received a great boost when President Sadat of Egypt visited Jerusalem in November 1977 and addressed the Knesset. Talks continued, and it soon became clear that, although Israel would consent to some form of administrative autonomy for the Palestinian Arabs in the West Bank and Gaza, Egypt and, in particular, the Palestinians were thinking in terms of an independent Palestinian State. In September 1978 there came a somewhat unexpected breakthrough when, after talks at Camp David in the U.S.A. under the guidance of President Carter, Begin and Carter signed two agreements. The first was a "framework of peace in the Middle East" (*see* p. 73) and the second was a "framework for the conclusion of a peace treaty between Egypt and Israel". The first agreement provided for a five-year transitional period during which the inhabitants of the Israeli-occupied West Bank and the Gaza Strip would obtain full autonomy and self-government, and the second agreement provided for the signing of a peace treaty within three months. The signing was delayed over the question of whether there should be any linkage between the conclusion of the peace treaty and progress towards autonomy in the West Bank and Gaza, but on March 27th, 1979, after further intervention by President Carter, the signing took place. The treaty (*see* p. 77) provided for a phased Israeli withdrawal from Sinai over a period of three years. El Arish was, in fact, returned to Egypt on May 16th, 1979.

Proposals for Palestinian autonomy were contained in a separate letter published with the treaty, and provided for negotiations to begin within one month of ratification of the treaty and for both sides to complete negotiations within twelve months. There would then be elections of Palestinian local councils and a five-year transitional period would follow during which the final status of the West Bank and Gaza would be negotiated. The autonomy negotiations began in late May 1979, but little headway had been made by the beginning of August.

It seems that Begin is being forced in two different directions by groups of opinion within Israel. The Minister of Defence, Ezer Weizmann, is against provocative Israeli settlements in the West Bank and feels that Begin's "autonomy plan" is too rigid. The *Gush Emunim* movement, on the other hand, wants to establish numerous Israeli settlements on the West Bank and tends to have the support of the Minister of Agriculture, Ariel Sharon. In mid-1979 the *Gush Emunim* element appeared to be exerting the greater influence over Begin. In early June Israel established a settlement at Eilon Noreh on Arab land near the West Bank "capital" of Nablus, and it was a move which threatened to jeopardize the recently opened autonomy talks.

ECONOMIC SURVEY

The hostility of both the natural and human environment in the eastern Mediterranean has continued to affect not only Israel's political arena but also its economy and development. The defence allocation dominates the national budget, and defence imports are a major factor in determining the deficit.

In many ways 1978 (and perhaps 1979) differed from its immediate forerunners. In fact, the year 1978 was the first complete year during which the economy functioned according to the regime introduced on October 27th, 1977, whereby exchange rates were to be determined mainly by factors of supply and demand, the Bank of Israel intervening only to prevent irregular fluctuation. Thus the selling rate of the dollar moved from I£15.32 at December 31st, 1977, to I£18.74 at December 31st, 1978: a devaluation of the Israeli pound by 18.2 per cent. During the first five months of 1979 the devaluation process was accelerated markedly, with the selling rate of the dollar moving to I£24.40, representing a depreciation of 23.2 per cent in the Israeli currency since the end of 1978. During 1978 the tide of economic growth turned. G.N.P. rose in that year from I£77,223 million to I£81,209 million (at 1975 prices). That increase of 5 per cent contrasted with the 1–2 per cent rise in the previous years. The renewed economic growth experienced in 1978 was due to domestic demand in the private sector. A particularly rapid increase was recorded in the consumption of durables—furniture, household equipment and private cars.

On the inflation front one may suppose that 1978 merely perpetuated the trends of the previous years with a rise of 48 per cent in the consumer price index following 42.5 per cent in 1977 and 38 per cent in 1976. On closer analysis it appears, however, that, unlike previous years, inflation in 1978 was engendered more by increased demand than by a rise in cost. The inflationary process was accelerated during the first four months of 1979, which witnessed a rise of 23.4 per cent in the cost of living index (an annual rate of 90 per cent). Another change—also negative—occurred in the field of balance of payments. After having declined from $4,100 million in 1975 to $2,500 million in 1977, the current deficit increased once again and by the end of 1978 reached $3,400 million. That change was mainly attributable to an increase of $528 million in direct defence imports and there was also a $300 million growth in the other components of the deficit. The unemployment rate remained almost unchanged at 3.6 per cent.

AREA AND POPULATION

The total area of the State of Israel within its 1949 armistice frontiers amounts to 20,700 sq. km. (including the Sea of Galilee and the Dead Sea); the territories occupied in 1967 (i.e. Sinai, the West Bank and the Golan Heights) multiplied fourfold the original area of Israel. This compares with the area of Palestine under British mandate which totalled 27,090 sq. km. By March 1979 the population of Israel proper was 3,748,000, including about 3,149,000 Jews.

In addition there were one million persons in the areas brought under Israeli administration as a result of the 1967 war.

The population density of Israel was 181.1 per square kilometre on February 28th, 1979. The population is heavily concentrated in the coastal strip, with about three-quarters of the Jewish and nearly two-thirds of the non-Jewish population located between Ashkelon and Naharia. The Tel-Aviv—Jaffa area, which had a population of 976,100 on December 31st, 1977, accounts for 26 per cent of the total population. A further 19.6 per cent live in the central area between Tel-Aviv and Jerusalem, 14.7 per cent around Haifa, 11.9 per cent in the southern district, 15.3 per cent in the northern area and 11.3 per cent around Jerusalem. Large desert areas are uninhabited except for nomadic Bedouin tribes numbering about 55,100 people in 1977. Approximately 85 per cent of the population was classified as urban in 1976, the urban population being made up of 2,783,100 Jews and 367,600 non-Jews.

The main reason for the growth of the Jewish population was immigration. Immigration accounted for 58 per cent of the yearly increase in the Jewish population between 1948 and 1977. In 1976, 47.8 per cent of the Jewish population had been born abroad. Twenty-six per cent was born in Europe and America, 11.3 per cent in Africa and 10.1 per cent in Asia. Of the 1,574,600 Israeli-born Jews, only 21 per cent were second generation Israelites. Immigration up to 1948 totalled 452,158 persons, of whom nearly 90 per cent came from Europe and America. The biggest wave of immigrants—over 576,000—arrived during the first six years of the new State. These were refugees from war-torn Europe, followed by Jews emigrating from the Arab States. Large numbers have come from North Africa as a result of political developments there and during 1955–64 a total of over 200,000 emigrated from Africa into Israel. Since 1956 immigration from Eastern Europe has been resumed. In the mid-1960s immigration declined, falling from 54,716 in 1964 to 14,327 in 1967, but the level of immigration picked up considerably after the 1967 war, bringing the total numbers of immigrants between 1965 and 1974 to over 300,000. Almost 70 per cent of these came from Europe and America. After the Yom Kippur war immigration dropped once more, falling from 54,886 in 1973 to 31,979 in 1974, and again to 19,754 in 1976. In 1978 immigrants totalled 26,394. With emigration running at about 18,000 per year, the decline of immigration posed a serious threat to the Israeli economy, which had always depended on an increasing supply of manpower to stimulate growth.

The Jewish birth rate was 23.3 per thousand in 1977, compared with a rate of 39.8 for non-Jews, but the infant mortality rate was much higher for the latter. The total yearly rate of increase (including immigration) of the Jewish population was only 2.0 per cent in 1975, compared with 3.1 per cent in 1973 and a peak annual rate of increase of 23.7 per cent during 1949–51.

The Israeli civilian labour force at the end of 1978 (seasonally adjusted) totalled 1,279,000, or 50.1 per cent of the population aged 14 years and over, and was made up of roughly 33 per cent women and 67 per cent men. The growth in the labour force from 735,800 in 1960 has been due chiefly to the rise in total population, since the participation rate has declined slightly.

An important characteristic is the relatively high proportion of dependents in the population, with one-third aged 14 years and under. As a result of this, the ratio of the labour force to total population—under 35 per cent—is low by European and American standards.

On December 31st, 1978, of 1,228,000 employees, some 6.3 per cent were employed in agriculture, forestry and fishing; 23.4 in industry, mining and manufacturing; 1.1 in electricity and water; 7.4 in construction; 12.5 in commerce, restaurants and hotels; 7.0 in transport, storage and communications; 7.1 were engaged in financing and business services; 27.5 in public and community service, and the rest (7.7 per cent) in personal and other services.

AGRICULTURE

The agriculture sector is relatively small, accounting for just under 6 per cent of domestic product and employing 6 per cent of the labour force. In spite of this, Israeli agriculture has attracted a great deal of international attention. Agriculture, more than any other sector of the economy, has been the focus of ideological pressure. For centuries Jews in the Diaspora were barred from owning land and the Zionist movement therefore saw land settlement as one of the chief objectives of Jewish colonization. Since the establishment of the State, government agricultural policy has centred chiefly on the attainment of self-sufficiency in foodstuffs, in view of military considerations and Israel's possible isolation from its chief foreign food supplies; on the saving of foreign exchange through import substitution and the promotion of agricultural exports; and on the absorption of the large numbers of immigrants in the agricultural sector. In line with these objectives, the promotion of mixed farming and of co-operative farming settlements has also been an important element in government policy. Although the increase in agricultural production has resulted in Israel becoming largely self-sufficient in foodstuffs—it is seriously deficient only in grains, oils and fats—and important savings have been made in foreign exchange, government intervention in the agricultural sector has been criticized as having resulted in a misallocation of resources and in impairment of the economic efficiency of agriculture.

Cultivation has undergone a profound transformation and from an extensive, primitive and mainly dry-farming structure it has developed into a modern intensive irrigated husbandry. A special feature of Israel's agriculture is its co-operative settlements which have been developed to meet the special needs and challenges encountered by a farming community new both to its surroundings and its profession. While there are a number of different forms of co-operative settlements, all are derived from two basic types: the *moshav* and the *kibbutz*. The *moshav* is a co-operative smallholders' village. Individual farms in any one village are of equal size and every farmer works his own land to the best of his ability. He is responsible for his own farm, but his economic and social security is ensured by the co-operative structure of the village, which handles the marketing of his produce, purchases his farm and household equipment, and provides him with credit and many other services.

The *kibbutz* is a collective settlement of a unique form developed in Israel. It is a collective enterprise based on common ownership of resources and on the pooling of labour, income and expenditure. Every member is expected to work to the best of his ability; he is paid no wages but is supplied by the *kibbutz* with all the goods and services he needs. The *kibbutz* is based on voluntary action and mutual liability, equal rights for all members, and assumes for them full material responsibility.

During the years following the establishment of the State a large-scale expansion of the area under cultivation took place. This was caused by the heavy influx of immigrants and the recultivation and rehabilitation of the area from which the Arabs had been forced to flee. The cultivated area increased from 1.6 million dunums in the crop of 1948–49 to over 4.31 million dunums in 1975–76, of which some 1.86 million dunums are irrigated. Total water consumption at present amounts to 1,600 million cubic metres, of which 1,200 million cubic metres is consumed by agricultural users.

Without taking into consideration the cost or availability of irrigation water, it is estimated that the land potential ultimately available for farming under irrigation is 5.3 million dunums, while 4.1 million dunums is the figure given for the area potentially available for dry farming. There are also 8.5 million dunums available for natural pasture and 0.9 million dunums for afforestation.

The main factor limiting agricultural development is not land, but the availability of water.

Since on average 800 cubic metres of water are needed per annum to irrigate one dunum of cultivated area, it is obvious that Israel must harness all water resources. For this reason, the Government established a special Water Administration headed by a Water Commissioner who has statutory powers to control and regulate both the supply and the consumption of water.

The Water Administration has been charged, among other tasks, with the implementation of the national water project. The purpose of this project is to convey a substantial part of the waters of the River Jordan and of other water sources from the north to southern Judea and to the Negev, to store excess supplies of water from winter to summer and from periods of heavy rainfall to periods of drought, and to serve as a regulator between the various regional water supply systems. The backbone of the national water project is the main conduit from Lake Tiberias to Rosh Haayin (near Tel-Aviv), known as the National Water Carrier, which has an annual capacity of 320 million cubic metres. Two other large schemes, also in operation, are the Western Galilee-Kishon and the Yarkon-Negev projects. Small desalination plants have been built at Eilat and elsewhere, and will be used more extensively if costs are eventually reduced. Desert farming in the Negev, using brackish water found underground, has achieved considerable success on an experimental basis.

Climatic conditions during 1976–77 were more favourable to Israeli agriculture than those of the preceding year, which was characterized by frost and drought. The wheat plantation area was reduced by 100,000 dunums in 1976–77 to 700,000 dunums, but due to a better harvest the total crop amounted to 230,000 tons, against 205,000 tons in 1975–76. The fall in wheat prices in the world markets stimulated the reduction of the plantations and a search for alternative crops such as spices and medicinal plants.

Cultivation of citrus fruits is one of the principal agricultural branches and produces the main export crop (U.S. $245 million in 1978/79). The total crop reached 1,465,000 tons, as in the previous years, but the composition in terms of varieties was modified: fewer "shamouti" oranges and more "late" oranges, grapefruit, lemons, tangerines, and citrons. A Citrus Marketing and Control Board supervises all aspects of the growing and marketing of the fruit, particularly exports. The area under cultivation continued to expand as a result of new plantings; the total area reached 420,000 dunums for the 1976–77 season, and with the stress laid on modern methods and techniques both in the groves and packing houses the yield increases each year.

Chief markets were West Germany, the United Kingdom and France. During the early part of 1978, exports were affected by a strike in the merchant navy, and by the panic caused after Palestinians injected mercury into some oranges in Europe.

Increasing emphasis is being laid on the growing of floral plants. During 1977–78, 480 million flowers (of which 220 million were spray carnations) were exported, earning $50 million. Today about 4,500 dunums are under glasshouse flower cultivation. The Flower Marketing Board is increasing the number of its packing houses and investing heavily in modern equipment.

After good progress had been recorded in sugar beet planting, from 49,000 dunums in 1974–75 to 60,000 dunums in 1975–76, a drop to 57,000 dunums was registered in 1976–77. Nevertheless, the sugar beet harvest reached 343,000 tons, an increase of 6 per cent. Local production satisfied 30 per cent of sugar consumption.

Cotton plantations increased in area by 25 per cent and reached 500,000 dunums in 1976–77. Fibre production rose by 20 per cent and totalled 65,000 tons, 60 per cent of which was exported. Average crops per dunum decreased due to pestilence. During

1978 Israel exported cotton to the value of $52.3 million, groundnuts to the value of $10.8 million, vegetables and potatoes estimated at $41.9 million and fruit with an estimated value of $35.4 million. This category included apples and stonefruit (mainly avocado), sub-tropical fruits and grapes.

After a shortage in milk production in 1973 (when production totalled 295 million litres against a demand of 550 million litres), in 1976–77 production reached 642 million litres (an increase of 3 per cent in comparison with a 13 per cent increase in the previous year). In the poultry sector, the increase was even less: egg production rose in 1976–77 by only 1.8 per cent and totalled 1,500 million. In the same year meat poultry totalled 119,000 tons; this sector had been affected for two years by excess production, because of the slight difference between the price of poultry meat and that of frozen imported cattle meat, causing a preference for the latter. The Ministry of Agriculture discouraged investment in the poultry sector in order to check the acceleration in development of recent years.

At the end of 1977 cattle in Israel totalled 308,000 head and there were 218,000 sheep and 142,000 goats.

CONSTRUCTION AND INDUSTRY

As a unit, construction is the leading sector in Israel since it constitutes 15 per cent of G.N.P., which totalled I£222,412 million in 1978, and 50 per cent of gross investment. Together with affiliated industries, (cement, wood, glass, ceramics), its part in the G.N.P. comes to 20 per cent. During 1978 there were 5,315,000 sq. metres of building area begun and completed, of which 1,665,000 sq. metres were public buildings and 3,650,000 sq. metres private. These data mark a sharp decline since 1976, when total building reached a peak of 7,230,000 sq. metres of building area begun and completed. At the end of 1978, there were some 80,300 persons employed in this industry.

Israel derives more of its national income—some 30 per cent—from industry than does any other Middle Eastern country. From 1968–77 industrial production rose by 85 per cent. Gross domestic capital formation rose in industry (mining and manufacturing at current prices) from I£824 million in 1970 to I£5,008 million in 1977. Industrial growth was particularly vigorous after 1967. Output in the period 1968–72 in real terms rose by 80 per cent while exports rose over five years by 124 per cent. The expansion was particularly rapid in the more sophisticated industries—electrical and electronic equipment, transport equipment, machinery, metal and polished diamonds. Value of industrial exports rose by 26 per cent during 1974, but declined the following year.

In 1977 there were 12,083 establishments which engaged employees whose number totalled 284,400. Of these establishments 301 engaged between 100 and 300 persons and 155 more than 300 persons. In the latter category 109,100 were employed. On the other hand, 5,091 establishments engaged four or less persons, and 3,175 between five and nine persons; 11,540 establishments belonged in 1977 to the private sector, 508 to the Histadrut (Trade Union Syndicat) and 35 to the public sector (mainly Government companies). The main branches of these establishments were: metal products 2,062; wood and its products 1,704; clothing and made-up textiles 1,543; food, beverage and tobacco 1,052; and diamonds and miscellaneous 1,317.

Israel's industry originally developed by supplying such basic needs as soap, oil and margarine, bread, ice, printing and electricity. It used raw materials available locally to produce citrus juices and other citrus by-products, canned fruit and vegetables, cement, glass and bricks. In order to save foreign exchange, imports of manufactured goods were curtailed, thus giving local industry the opportunity of adding local labour value to the semi-manufactures imported from abroad.

To stimulate investment and encourage the inflow of foreign capital the Law for the Encouragement of Capital Investments was enacted in 1950, broadened in 1959 and amended in 1967 and 1977. The Law sets up an Investment Centre and provides for the approval of projects contributing to the development of industrial potential, the exploitation of natural resources, the creation of new sources of employment —particularly in development areas—and to the absorption of new immigrants. Among the concessions granted to approved projects, particularly those financed in foreign currency, are remittance of profits and withdrawal of capital, and tax benefits in respect of income tax, indirect taxes and depreciation allowances.

Although most of Israel's industrial production still goes for home consumption, industrial exports constituted about 86 per cent of total exports in 1978. Here again there has been a very rapid expansion as a result of tax and investment incentives from the Government. Israeli industrial exports, worth $18 million in 1950, had risen to $780 million by 1971, and by 1978 had reached $3,466 million.

Israel's most important industrial export product is diamonds, most of the expertise for the finishing of which was supplied by immigrants from the Low Countries. In 1978 Israel exported some $1,477.4 million worth of diamonds; the country's share of international trade in polished diamonds has risen to 30 per cent and as high as 80 per cent in medium-sized stones, in which she specializes.

Apart from diamonds (which account for 37.2 per cent of industrial exports), industrial exports were constituted of 6.5 per cent food stuffs; 8.2 per cent textiles, clothing and leather; 2.8 per cent mining and quarrying products; 10 per cent chemical and oil products; 6.9 per cent metal products; 5.6 per cent machinery; 4.5 per cent electrical and electronic equipment. The figures show clearly the trend of an increase in metal and electrical products and a parallel decline in all other branches.

Israel Aircraft Industries, employing some 20,000, is Israel's largest single industrial enterprise. At its main plant adjacent to Lod Airport it produces the Kfir combat and multi-mission aircraft, the Arava, a twin-turboprop passenger/cargo transport, the Commodore Jet, a 10-place twin-jet executive aircraft, the Gabriel sea-to-sea missile, as well as other weapons.

The food, beverage and tobacco industries accounted in 1978 for about 20 per cent of manufactures and employed some 40,500 persons. About 90 per cent of output is sold on the local market; the rest, such as juices, wines, chocolate and coffee, goes abroad.

The textiles and clothing industry, which was developed chiefly because of its low capital-labour ratio, employed some 51,600 persons in 1978, when it exported goods worth some $254.7 million.

There is also a rapidly expanding electronics industry, specializing in equipment for military and communications purposes. Exports by this sector and by that of metal products have grown from $12.8 million in 1970 to $438.7 million in 1978.

In view of the heavy power needs of irrigation and the water installations, agriculture as well as industry is a large-scale consumer of electricity. Total installed generating capacity was at the end of 1977 2,385 Megawatts, and generation totalled 10,874 million kWh. Out of 9,500 million kWh total sales of electricity, industry used 34.6 per cent. Total water production reached during 1976–77 1,861 million cubic metres out of which industry used 6 per cent, while agriculture consumed 75 per cent.

MINERALS

The Petroleum Law of 1952 regulates the conditions for the granting of licences for oil prospecting, divides the country into petroleum districts and fixes a basic royalty of 12.5 per cent. Oil was discovered in 1955 at the Heletz-Bror field on the coastal plain and later at Kokhav, Brur and Negba. Signs of oil were also discovered near Ashdod. About 34 wells in Israel are now producing, and their output was 42,200,000 litres in 1976. From the time of the 1967 war to the 1975 disengagement agreement, Israel was able to exploit the oil resources of the Sinai and, from 1978 onwards, those of the Suez Gulf (Alma Fields).

Output of gas from Rosh-Zohar in the Dead Sea area, Kidod, Hakanaim and Barbur is transported through a 29 km. 6-inch pipeline to the Dead Sea potash works at Sodom and through a 49 km. 4-inch and 6-inch line to towns in the Negev and to the Oron phosphate plant. Production totalled 57 million cubic metres in 1978, exactly as in 1977.

Lacking large resources of fuel and power, Israel is very dependent on imports of petroleum and petroleum products, which rose in value from $210.6 million in 1973 to $597 million the following year, and reached $775 million in 1978; at current prices. Most imported crude oil is refined at the Haifa oil refinery, which has a capacity of over 6.0 million tons per year.

The Dead Sea, which contains potash, bromides, magnesium and other salts in high concentration, is the country's chief source of mineral wealth. The potash works on the southern shore of the Dead Sea, are owned by Dead Sea Works Ltd. The works are linked by road to Beersheba, from where a railway runs northward. Phosphates are mined at Oron in the Negev, and in the Arava. During 1978 Israel produced 107,175 tons of ammonium sulphate, 9,405 tons of potassium sulphate, 197,000 tons of sulphuric acid, 26,275 tons of chlorine, 303,200 tons of superphosphate 16 per cent; and 3,616 tons of potassium carbonate.

At Timna, in the southern Negev near Eilat, geological surveys have located proven reserves of 20 million tons of low-grade copper ore (about 1.5 per cent Cu). The building of a mill to make use of these ores and for producing copper-cement was completed in 1958. The ore was mined by open cast and underground methods until 1975 when copper production from the Timna complex totalled 8,000 tons. Due to the fall of the copper prices in the world markets, and following accumulated losses, the Government closed the mines in 1976 (copper imports during 1978 were worth $40 million).

FINANCE

The problems confronting Israel made a certain degree of inflationary financing unavoidable; in the early years of the State, when the Government financed its deficits through the printing press and banks expanded their credits, efforts were made to maintain a low level of prices by means of controls and rationing. The result was a large surplus of purchasing power in the hands of the public. The attempt of the public to expand this surplus gave rise to a black market in controlled goods and to a sharp rise in the prices of uncontrolled goods and services.

On October 28th, 1977, a basic change was initiated in the Government's exchange rate policy. Until that day, the policy in force had been one of a crawling devaluation of the Israeli pound, which had been pegged to a basket of five currencies. (U.S.$, DM, £ sterling, French franc and the Netherlands guilder). The aim of this policy was to encourage exports and to increase the cost of imports by means of frequent adjustments of the exchange rate of the Israeli pound to the rising level of domestic prices. Thus during the first nine months of 1977 the consumer price index rose by 20.6 per cent and the Israeli pound was devalued vis-à-vis the basket mentioned above by a total of 15.8 per cent. Following the change of government, and according to the economic philosophy which characterizes the political parties that compose it, a decision was taken at the end of October to reduce markedly the foreign currency controls and to let the Israeli pound find its value in the market. The immediate result was the devaluation of the pound by about 33 per cent. Thus the selling rate of the dollar when the trade in foreign exchange started on October 31st was I£15.5 compared with the official rate of I£10.4 three days earlier. In addition all exchange rates were unified by cancelling export incentives and import levies (imposed at a rate of 15 per cent). On May 27th, 1979, the selling rate of the dollar was I£24.30.

The liberalization measures in the domain of foreign currency were accompanied by a tight monetary policy and some contractionary fiscal steps. Thus bank regular credit was frozen for three months and liquidity requirements of 90 per cent and 80 per cent were imposed on new demand and time deposits respectively in foreign exchange. On November 1st, 1977, the VAT rate was raised from 8 per cent to 12 per cent, together with some reduction in purchase tax rates.

Despite appraisals at the beginning of 1978 which suggested a slowdown in price rises, the increase in the consumer price index reached 48 per cent during the year, compared with 42.5 per cent in 1977 and 38 per cent in 1976. During the first four months of 1979 prices rose even more quickly—by 23.4 per cent, equivalent to an annual rate of 90 per cent. While it is tempting to view this increase as a continuous upward inflationary spiral, analysis indicates that the factor determining the rise of prices underwent a change in 1978. In previous years, inflation developed primarily as a reaction to increased costs. During these years, the government on several occasions cut the subsidies on basic necessities, raised the rate of various other controlled commodities, imposed new taxes and devalued the currency. These measures, however, were themsleves insufficient to push prices significently upwards had not the government continued to infuse money. As opposed to previous years, the government refrained in 1978 from cutting subsidies or raising commodity rates or taxes during the seven months following an agreement with the Histadrut, but nevertheless prices continued to increase. It can be supposed that the inflationary level was determined to a large extent by demand factors, of which the following would appear to be the most important:

(i) Government infusions of money as mentioned above; this factor was also present in the previous year. It should, however, be noted that its relative influence declined in that year.

(ii) Foreign currency loans to residents presented a new factor which stimulated demand in 1978. Until October 1977 Israeli residents were limited by special government permit from obtaining loans on foreign currency. This permit regulation was lifted in 1978. Such borrowings have proved attractive in view of the high cost of marginal credit from local sources and the lengthy time lag in adjusting the rate of the dollar following domestic price increases. The foreign currency thus introduced and converted to domestic currency contributed markedly to the creation of demand factors.

(iii) It is reasonable to assume that there was a certain real conversion of financial assets into physical property. The demand factor has been assisted by the fact that 1978 was a year of increased redemption of government bonds and it can be assumed that the funds redeemed were channelled into consumption.

The slowdown which characterized the economy in 1976–77 constrasted sharply with the boom that characterized the stock market, commencing in July 1976 and lasting with occasional setbacks until it reached its apparent peak in November 1977. During that period, share prices rose almost fourfold; the turnover of securities totalled I£30,000 million in 1977, four times the 1976 figure. During 1978 turnover reached I£34,701 million. Thus while the yield rate index stood at 100 on December 23rd, 1976, it rose to 277.9 on November 23rd, 1977. On January 23rd, 1978, it attained, after the November decrease, the level of 212.0. 1978 witnessed a recovery and on March 23rd, 1979, it climbed to 305.7.

In 1978 imports of goods and services (worth U.S. $10,044 million) exceeded exports by U.S. $3,400 million (in 1977 the deficit totalled $2,563 million). About 71 per cent of the 1978 deficit ($2,249 million) was financed by transfer payments, compared with 81 per cent of the 1977 deficit. These transfer payments were composed of compensation payments from Germany ($406 million), other personal remittances ($430 million), institutional remittances $438 million) and, principally, intergovernmental transfer payments ($1,153 million). The remainder of the deficit was financed due to the increase in liabilities. Liabilities to lenders abroad rose by $2,400 million in 1978 ($1,200 million in 1977) and influenced the rise in the foreign assets of the Israeli market which in 1978 totalled $1,900 million (as against $1,100 million in 1977). On the other hand, obligations of the Israeli market abroad reached $16,500 million at the end of 1978 (compared with $13,700 million in 1977).

This increase was due, inter alia, to the growth of liabilities and loans of the monetary sector (banks), stimulated by the liberalization of foreign exchange controls in 1977. It should be noted that this growth reached its peak in the last quarter of 1978, when merchant bank liabilities grew by $1,000 million. The increase reflected not only a rise in the volume of imports but the extensive use of external credit to finance economic activity, especially after domestic credit was frozen.

Government obligations rose during 1978 by U.S. $800 million, with only a third of the rise accounted for by liabilities abroad. About 85 per cent of that increase corresponded to U.S. government loans to cover larger arms imports. Out of the total debt of $16,500 million, government obligations totalled $9,034 million at the end of 1978.

TRADE

Israel's balance of trade inevitably shows a heavy deficit, reflecting its dependence on foreign consumer and capital goods—if not foodstuffs—and raw materials.

During 1978 imports of goods and services exceeded exports by $3,400 million, compared with the 1977 deficit which totalled $2,563 million. This increase of 32.6 per cent followed the 23 per cent increase constituted by the 1977 deficit. Unilateral receipts amounted to $2,423 million in 1978, some 16 per cent more than in 1977. The rise of $827 million is mainly attributed to an increase of $528 million in direct defence imports, which, with transportation charges deducted, reached $1,612 million, the highest level since 1976.

The goods accounts, which include figures for the administered territories, show an increase of 25 per cent in exports, following a 27 per cent increase in 1977. Goods imports were augmented by only 17 per cent. Imports of consumer goods amounted to some $420.1 million in 1977 (at current prices). Production imports totalled $4,614.2 million. This includes the import of diamonds which amounted to $1,246.2 million, and fuel, totalling $774.9 million. Investment goods imports came to $818.9 million, of which ships and aircraft totalled $94.7 million. Industrial exports amounted to $3,466 million, of which diamonds accounted for $1,477.4 million. Agricultural exports came to $455.3 million. Israel's trade deficit in 1978 thus attained $2,838 million.

This deficit has been a permanent drain on foreign reserves, endurable only because of a constant inflow of grants, loans, reparations and private investment. Thus total capital movement net reached $599 million during 1978, while total goods, services and transfer payments imports exceeded exports by $971 million during that period.

The focus of Israel's foreign trade is mainly the EEC and North America, but efforts are being made to penetrate Central and South America. Israel concluded a three-year agreement with the EEC for tariff reductions in 1964, and a further five-year preferential trade agreement in 1970. On November 10th, 1976, a financial and economic protocol was settled, providing for the progressive dismantling of all tariff and quota barriers on industrial goods. On agricultural goods, the EEC agreed to make tariff cuts on some 85 per cent of Israel's exports.

BANKING, TRANSPORT AND TOURISM

Israel possesses a highly developed banking system, consisting of the central bank (Bank of Israel), 26 commercial banks and credit co-operatives, 16 mortgage banks, and other financial institutions. Nevertheless three bank-groups—namely Bank Leumi group, Bank Ha-Poalim and Bank Discount hold 92 per cent of the total assets of the banking system. Their subsidiaries are represented all over the world and enjoy a growing reputation; due to devaluation their share in the consolidated balance sheet is increasing markedly. Long-term credits are granted by mortgage banks, the Israel Agricultural Bank, the Industrial Development Bank and the Maritime Bank. In January 1979 the amount of outstanding credit allocated by the banks to the public reached the sum of I£146,862.7 million in Israeli and foreign currency.

The function of the Central Bank is to issue currency (and commemorative coins), to accept deposits from banking institutions and extend temporary advances to the Government, to act as the Government's sole fiscal and banking agent and to manage the public debt. Its Governor supervises the liquidity position of the commercial banks and regulates the volume of bank advances.

The continued severance of nearly all lines of communication with her Arab neighbours (expect the open bridges on the Jordan River) has not only intensified Israel's dependence on maritime and air communications, but has also given great impetus to the establishment of a national merchant marine and airline.

Since 1949, Israel has operated its own international air carrier—El-Al Israel National Airlines Ltd. Regular scheduled services to West Europe, U.S.A., Canada, Cyprus, Romania and parts of Africa and Asia are maintained. In 1976 a new private company—CAL, which specializes in cargo air transportation to Europe, was constituted. In addition some 14 international airlines call at Ben Gurion Airport, Lod (Lydda), near Tel-Aviv. Passenger-kilometres reached 3,234.9 million. Domestic services are provided by Arkia, a national carrier which in 1977 carried over 631,000 passengers. Israel's merchant navy has been undergoing expansion, while the passenger fleet has been practically abolished. The number of ships under the Israeli flag in 1977 totalled 105, consisting of 74 cargo ships, 7 refrigerating ships and 24 tankers. Their gross tonnage was 2,498,502. Israel Shipyards Ltd. at Haifa can build ships up to 10,000 dwt. In the north, the port of Haifa and its Kishon harbour extension provide Israel's main port facilities. The south is served by the port of Eilat—Israel's only non-Mediterranean port at the head of the Gulf of Aqaba, and mainly by the new deep water port at Ashdod, some 30 miles south of Tel-Aviv. Gaza port assures the needs of the Gaza Strip.

By 1977 Israeli railways operated some 520 km. of main lines and 395 km. of branch lines. The service extends from Nahariya, north of Haifa to Jerusalem and Tel-Aviv and then, southwards through Beer-sheba. In 1965 it reached Dimona and in 1970 the phosphate works at Oron; the construction of a huge bridge over Tsin Valley will enable the extension to Eilat. Traction is wholly by diesel locomotives. In 1977 traffic consisted of 268 million passenger-kilometres and 462 million ton-kilometres of freight.

Roads are the chief means of transport. In 1977 there were some 11,669 km. of paved roads, of which 3,200 km. were inter-urban, out of which 250 km. were four or more lane motorways. Travelling them in 1977 were 310,000 private vehicles, nearly 85.2 per thousand of the Israeli population.

The drop in the number of tourists entering Israel which began in 1973 (a slowdown had already been recorded in the second half of 1972), continued in 1975, but at a more moderate rate of 0.8 per cent; 1976 witnessed a recovery, and the number of tourists rose, reaching 1,070,813 in 1978. Income from tourism reached $620 million.

Overall administration of Israeli tourism is sponsored by the Ministry of Tourism which maintains 20 offices abroad. It is also in charge of regulating tourist services in Israel, including arrangement of "package" tours and the provision of multilingual guides. In 1976 the Ministry promoted the inauguration of charter-flights from the U.S. and Europe to Israel.

STATISTICAL SURVEY

AREA AND POPULATION

AREA	POPULATION April 1979	BIRTH RATE (per '000) 1977	MARRIAGE RATE (per '000) 1977	DEATH RATE (per '000) 1977
20,325 sq. km.*	3,760,000	26.4†	8.1†	6.9†

* 7,848 square miles.

† These figures include the population of the Old City of Jerusalem and the surrounding areas (area 70 sq. km.), which Israel annexed in 1967.

ADMINISTERED TERRITORIES*

	AREA (sq. km.)	POPULATION (Oct. 31st, 1978)
Golan	1,150	n.a.
Judea and Samaria	5,879	684,300
Gaza Strip (incl. El-Arish)	378	} 448,700
Sinai	61,181	
TOTAL	68,588	n.a.

* The area and population of the Administered Territories have changed as a result of the October 1973 war.

The area figures in this table refer to October 1st, 1973. No later figures are available.

POPULATION OF CHIEF TOWNS*

(January 1978)

Jerusalem (capital)	376,000	Ramat Gan	120,900
Tel-Aviv—Jaffa	343,300	Petach-Tikva	112,200
Haifa	227,800	Beersheba	101,000
Holon	121,200	Bene Beraq	85,900

* Provisional.

GROWTH OF POPULATION AND JEWISH IMMIGRATION, 1965–78

END OF YEAR	PERMANENT POPULATION	JEWS	OTHERS	IMMIGRATION
1965	2,598,400	2,299,100	299,300	30,736
1966	2,657,400	2,344,900	312,500	15,730
1967*	2,773,900	2,383,600	390,300	14,327
1968*	2,841,100	2,434,800	406,300	20,544
1969*	2,929,500	2,506,800	422,700	23,510
1970*	3,022,000	2,582,000	440,100	20,624
1971*	3,120,500	2,662,000	458,700	41,930
1972*	3,225,000	2,752,700	472,300	55,888
1973*	3,338,200	2,845,000	493,200	54,886
1974*	3,421,600	2,906,900	514,700	31,979
1975*	3,493,400	2,959,400	533,800	20,028
1976*	3,570,900	3,017,500	553,400	17,092
1977*	3,653,000	3,077,300	575,900	18,641
1978*	3,730,000	3,135,000	595,000	26,200

* These figures exclude the population of the areas administered by Israel since June 1967 (*see* above), but include the population of the Old City of Jerusalem and the surrounding areas.

EMPLOYMENT

('000)

	1974	1975	1976	1977
Agriculture, Forestry and Fishing	71.5	71.1	72.1	72.6
Mining, Quarrying and Manufacturing	278.4	274.4	273.8	277.6
Electricity, Gas and Water	10.4	11.1	11.5	13.5
Construction	88.5	90.2	86.3	85.0
Trade, Restaurants and Hotels	131.2	136.2	139.6	140.9
Transport, Storage and Communications	83.3	80.3	78.6	82.9
Financing, Insurance and Business Services	68.4	73.8	76.3	83.0
Community, Social and Personal Services	357.8	369.2	381.6	397.9
Others	7.1	6.2	7.1	8.2
TOTAL	1,096.7	1,112.6	1,126.9	1,159.2

AGRICULTURE

AGRICULTURAL LAND USAGE

('000 dunums or '00 hectares)

	1971/72	1972/73	1973/74	1974/75	1975/76	1976/77
Field Crops	2,650	2,672	2,739	2,624	2,595	2,662
Fruit incl. citrus	845	861	870	861	870	885
Vegetables, potatoes, etc.	396	354	376	368	339	367
Nurseries, flowers, fish ponds, etc.	274	283	285	242	244	239
TOTAL Cultivated Area	4,165	4,170	4,270	4,095	4,048	4,153

PRINCIPAL CROPS

(production in metric tons)

	1971/72	1972/73	1973/74	1974/75	1975/76	1976/77
Wheat	301,400	241,500	274,000	243,300	205,500	220,000
Barley	32,800	17,900	30,200	20,600	18,200	16,600
Sorghum	40,400	29,700	34,200	32,200	12,600	13,500
Hay	132,500	126,800	138,000	148,400	140,100	111,100
Groundnuts	19,800	14,600	18,000	18,800	23,500	22,500
Cotton lint	40,300	37,400	49,800	48,800	53,650	64,000
Cottonseed	67,400	63,400	84,000	82,000	87,000	108,000
Sugar beet	248,500	217,300	116,700	259,000	323,600	320,000
Melons and pumpkins	161,700	127,000	124,000	134,800	134,800	132,000
Vegetables	502,000	532,700	496,200	609,200	581,100	582,100
Potatoes	143,100	165,100	152,400	163,000	174,700	214,000
Citrus fruit	1,552,800	1,688,600	1,698,000	1,506,000	1,513,350	1,528,100
Grapefruit	334,300	390,800	395,500	416,800	456,450	497,200
Lemons	39,900	45,400	36,500	37,700	37,350	40,800
Oranges: Shamouti	842,200	817,000	834,400	679,800	648,100	578,500
Lates	273,500	362,600	358,500	299,700	298,250	329,000
Other varieties	62,900	72,800	73,100	72,000	73,200	82,600
Other fruit	359,800	297,000	332,600	347,950	376,950	370,600
Milk (kl.) (incl. sheep and goat milk)	519,200	565,900	590,900	627,700	704,250	720,000

LIVESTOCK
('000 head)

	1975	1976	1977
Cattle	323	345	309
Poultry*	12,500	14,000	30,500
Sheep	202	218	242
Goats	140	142	148

* Except broilers

FISHING
(tons)

1973/74	1974/75	1975/76	1976/77
22,700	22,200	24,350	24,500

MINING

		1974	1975	1976	1977
Crude petroleum . . .	million litres	45	40	41	31
Natural gas	million cu. metres	66	60	58	57
Copper ore	'000 metric tons	9.5	8.0	n.a.	n.a.
Phosphate rock . . .	,, ,, ,,	1,026	882	639	1,218

INDUSTRY
SELECTED PRODUCTS

		1974	1975	1976	1977
Wheat flour	'000 metric tons	401	452	443	460
Refined sugar . . .	,, ,, ,,	11.5	28.4	35.6	33.6
Margarine	,, ,, ,,	34.8	33.1	31.2	30.6
Wine	'000 litres	n.a.	15,869	16,775	n.a.
Beer	'000 hectolitres	340.9	355.1	350.9	353.3
Cigarettes	metric tons	5,243	5,553	5,488	4,751
Cotton yarn	,, ,,	20,241	21,533	21,244	22,370
Woven cotton fabrics* . .	,, ,,	12,098	11,100	n.a.	n.a.
Newsprint	,, ,,	7,095	7,472	12,689	16,051
Writing and printing paper .	,, ,,	45,405	45,742	39,498	50,369
Other paper	,, ,,	27,494	26,232	30,593	29,201
Rubber tyres	'000	1,650	1,466	1,680	1,720
Sulphuric acid . . .	'000 metric tons	187	194	208	198
Caustic soda	metric tons	20,458	24,156	24,009	26,836
Cement	'000 metric tons	1,796	2,189	2,042	1,852
Passenger cars . . .	number	2,936	2,382	3,934	3,896
Commercial vehicles . .	,,	5,388	3,922	3,097	3,485
Electricity	million kWh.	9,153	9,712	10,354	11,106

* After undergoing finishing processes.

FINANCE

100 agorot (singular, agora) = 1 Israeli pound (I£).
Coins: 1, 5, 10, 25 and 50 agorot; 1 pound.
Notes: 50 agorot; 1, 5, 10, 50, 100 and 500 pounds.
Exchange rates (June 1979): £1 sterling = I£50.40; U.S. $1 = I£24.36.
I£1,000 = £19.84 sterling = $41.05.

Note: The Israeli pound was introduced in August 1948, replacing (at par) the Palestine pound, equal to the pound sterling, then worth U.S. $4.03. In September 1949 the Israeli pound was devalued (in line with sterling) to $2.80 and this valuation remained in effect until February 1952. Multiple exchange rates were in operation between February 1952 and mid-1955. The official exchange rate was U.S. $1 = I£1.80 (I£1 = 55.56 U.S. cents) from July 1955 to February 1962; $1 = I£3.00 (I£1 = 33.33 U.S. cents) from February 1962 to November 1967; $1 = I£3.50 (I£1 = 28.57 U.S. cents) from November 1967 to August 1971; $1 = I£4.20 (I£1 = 23.81 U.S. cents) from August 1971 to November 1974; $1 = I£6.00 (I£1 = 16.67 U.S. cents) from November 1974 to June 1975. Since June 1975 the currency has been frequently devalued. In July 1976 the Israeli pound was linked to a "basket" of five currencies of the country's main trading partners, instead of being linked to the U.S. dollar alone, and since October 1977 the currency has been allowed to "float". The average market rate (I£ per U.S. $) was: 4.50 in 1974; 6.39 in 1975; 7.98 in 1976; 10.46 in 1977; 17.47 in 1978. The exchange rate was £1 sterling = I£8.40 from February 1962 to August 1971; and £1 sterling = I£10.944 from December 1971 to June 1972.

CENTRAL GOVERNMENT BUDGET
(I£ million, twelve months ending March 31st)

REVENUE	1975/76	1976/77	1977/78*	1978/79*
Ordinary Budget	35,364.3	50,143.7	71,826	97,520
Income Tax and Property Tax	13,164.5	18,824.0	28,805	39,900
Customs and Excise	9,056.8	10,743.1	13,780	12,280
Purchase Tax	4,721.2	5,874.1	7,550	9,250
Employers' Tax	864.0	1,274.0	1,900	3,200
Value Added Tax	—	4,899.5	9,930	17,700
Other Taxes	1,534.2	1,819.3	2,500	3,120
Interest	1,417.1	2,031.6	2,073	3,050
Loans	1,135.9	1,233.6	1,775	2,800
Other Receipts	3,470.6	3,444.3	3,513	6,220
Development Budget	27,406.0	36,609.7	52,134	84,480
Foreign Loans	14,865.2	22,971.1	28,850	44,700
Internal Loans	5,762.9	9,618.9	17,200	30,100
Other Receipts	6,777.9	4,019.7	6,084	9,680
TOTAL	62,770.3	86,753.4	123,960	182,000

EXPENDITURE	1975/76	1976/77	1977/78*	1978/79*
Ordinary Budget	49,719.1	69,400.2	96,560.0	135,000.0
Ministry of Finance	320.6	430.5	595.1	1,081.7
Ministry of Defence	25,623.3	35,288.0	40,775.0	55,300.0
Ministry of Health	1,320.1	1,528.2	1,646.7	3,470.0
Ministry of Education and Culture	3,681.4	4,689.3	6,868.0	11,535.0
Minstry of Police	753.9	1,054.6	1,348.5	2,284.3
Ministry of Labour and Social Welfare	785.7	1,121.1	1,409.6	2,935.5
Other Ministries	1,666.1	2,482.2	3,205.2	4,142.0
Interest	5,209.4	9,144.9	14,750.0	21,500.0
Pensions and Compensations	392.0	595.0	764.0	1,502.8
Transfer to National Insurance Institute	1,849.8	2,690.6	4,101.0	5,756.0
Transfers to Local Authorities	2,333.5	3,082.9	4,227.0	5,575.0
Subsidies	4,927.8	6,363.7	8,805.0	11,200.0
Other Expenditures	855.5	929.2	1,240.5	1,821.3
Reserve	—	—	6,824.4	7,196.4
Development Budget	13,009.1	17,331.7	27,400.0	46,700.0
Agriculture	277.0	210.7	936.7	1,407.3
Industry, Trade and Tourism	691.4	1,079.1	1,744.5	3,135.0
Housing	3,391.0	3,506.5	4,325.0	5,490.0
Public Buildings	1,169.3	1,411.2	1,413.8	1,768.0
Development of Energy Resources	162.5	364.6	640.0	1,650.0
Debt Repayment	5,482.1	9,158.7	15,780.0	30,000.0
Other Expenditures	1,835.8	1,600.9	2,560.0	3,249.7
TOTAL	62,728.2	86,731.9	123,960.0	182,000.0

* Estimates.

GENERAL CONSUMER PRICE INDEX

(1970=100)

1973	1974	1975	1976	1977	1978
151.6	211.9	295.1	387.6	521.7	785.4

MONEY SUPPLY

(I£ million at year end)

	1973	1974	1975	1976	1977
Currency held by the public	2,716	3,173	3,970	4,777	6,319
Current deposits	4,677	5,549	6,644	8,709	12,398
TOTAL MONEY SUPPLY	7,393	8,722	10,614	13,486	18,717

EXTERNAL TRADE

(U.S. $ million)

Excluding trade with the administered territories.

	1970	1971	1972	1973	1974	1975	1976	1977
Imports c.i.f.	1,433.5	1,811.6	1,961.4	2,968.6	4,176.5	4,108.7	4,068.6	4,760.7
Exports f.o.b.	733.6	915.1	1,099.8	1,391.8	1,737.4	1,834.6	2,306.6	2,964.2

PRINCIPAL COMMODITIES

(U.S. $'000)

IMPORTS	1974	1975	1976	1977
Diamonds, rough	442,960	469,126	670,252	1,011,723
Boilers, machinery and parts	327,955	434,502	403,501	431,542
Electrical machinery	212,141	241,252	182,722	190,043
Iron and steel	428,642	349,153	253,970	245,895
Vehicles	263,651	188,848	194,760	194,499
Chemicals	244,144	301,362	282,515	291,878
Crude oil	583,568	628,319	675,516	726,947
Cereals	226,972	267,650	235,854	218,319
Textiles and textile articles	130,911	106,958	119,690	137,397
Ships, boats, aircraft, etc.	166,462	42,658	53,250	94,674

EXPORTS	1974	1975	1976	1977
Diamonds, worked	641,131	640,744	799,726	1,098,784
Edible fruits	137,528	200,797	203,922	231,297
Textiles and textile articles	160,234	164,748	209,105	242,945
Fruit and vegetable products	88,654	77,905	99,079	101,888
Fertilizers	67,246	72,263	51,377	76,549
Organic chemicals	59,287	67,904	75,161	80,072
Inorganic chemicals	36,473	45,428	33,930	45,614
Iron and steel	51,685	98,604	169,142	259,091
Non-electric machinery	46,887	54,471	67,387	76,853
Electrical machinery	42,704	78,112	93,467	105,128

PRINCIPAL TRADING PARTNERS
(U.S. $ '000)

Imports	1975	1976	1977
Argentina	29,723	26,230	29,398
Austria	28,955	25,827	24,719
Belgium/Luxembourg	159,162	126,609	207,447
Brazil	52,576	13,471	17,042
Canada	40,479	43,156	55,269
Denmark	18,095	16,826	19,641
Finland	34,211	30,108	32,206
France	154,969	150,563	188,385
Germany, Fed. Rep.	457,538	416,632	442,759
Italy	205,877	171,498	193,984
Japan	88,768	106,870	124,951
Netherlands	182,070	241,794	413,849
Romania	34,553	39,733	35,758
South Africa	20,242	45,229	55,052
Spain	30,929	18,963	19,428
Sweden	67,305	62,219	60,897
Switzerland	124,361	158,255	421,568
United Kingdom	560,698	633,580	482,681
U.S.A.	1,001,511	888,268	955,958
Uruguay	16,717	7,280	64,316
Yugoslavia	13,844	18,136	15,207

Exports	1975	1976	1977
Australia	18,563	24,863	26,328
Austria	17,989	20,443	23,720
Belgium/Luxembourg	79,798	102,079	159,226
Canada	29,769	39,125	41,137
France	112,097	134,737	161,436
Germany, Fed. Rep.	151,492	200,587	276,362
Greece	28,466	25,415	49,597
Hong Kong	113,196	139,344	188,859
Iran	92,402	103,608	103,183
Italy	56,599	76,856	79,976
Japan	99,382	79,284	99,365
Netherlands	129,218	163,644	182,059
Romania	17,479	15,431	18,218
Singapore	23,531	25,643	31,047
South Africa	34,724	26,786	23,943
Sweden	27,859	32,561	31,086
Switzerland	80,994	93,313	116,953
Turkey	15,890	10,811	29,490
United Kingdom	171,086	185,638	225,123
U.S.A.	307,282	436,513	578,926
Yugoslavia	15,307	15,291	16,293

TRANSPORT

RAILWAYS

	1975	1976	1977
Passengers ('000)	3,579	3,498	n.a.
Freight ('000 metric tons)	3,332	3,467	4,105

ROADS 1977

Motor Vehicles ('000)

Private Cars	307.8
Trucks, Trailers	101.4
Buses	6.2
Taxis	4.9
Motorcycles, Motorscooters	26.6
Other Vehicles	3.4
Total	450.4

SHIPPING

('000 tons)

	1975	1976	1977
Cargo Loaded	3,486	3,668	4,748
Cargo Unloaded	5,359	5,121	5,035

* Estimates.

CIVIL AVIATION

(El Al revenue flights only, '000)

	1975	1976	1977
Kilometres flown	27,656	31,970	35,564
Revenue passenger-km.	3,234,900	4,339,900	4,889,900
Mail (tons)	770	917	938

TOURISM

	1973	1974	1975	1976	1977	1978
Tourist arrivals	661,651	624,727	619,554	796,598	986,534	1,070,000

COMMUNICATIONS MEDIA

	1975 (December)	1976 (December)	1977 (December)
Telephones	796,300	869,042	929,200
Daily newspapers	27	27	27

Radio receivers: 750,000 in 1978/79.

TV receivers (number of households): 465,000 in 1978/79.

EDUCATION

(1977/78: provisional figures)

	Schools	Pupils
Jewish:		
Kindergarten	4,912	150,107
Primary schools	1,243	395,683
Secondary schools	287	64,154
Vocational schools	318	67,260
Agricultural schools	28	5,601
Teachers' training	53	11,606
Others (handicapped)	227	13,949
Intermediate schools	220	65,843

	Schools	Pupils
Arab:		
Kindergarten	260	17,460
Primary schools	297	114,922
Secondary schools	81	15,800
Vocational	11	1,668
Agricultural schools	2	776
Teachers' training	2	604
Others (handicapped)	15	669
Intermediate schools	39	11,499

Source: Central Bureau of Statistics, Jerusalem.

THE CONSTITUTION

There is no written Constitution. In June 1950, the Knesset voted to adopt a State Constitution by evolution over an unspecified period. A number of laws, including the Law of Return (1950), the Nationality Law (1952), the State President (Tenure) Law (1952), the Education Law (1953) and the "Yad-va-Shem" Memorial Law (1953) are considered as incorporated into the State Constitution. Other constitutional laws are: The Law and Administration Ordinance (1948), the Knesset Election Law (1951), the Law of Equal Rights for Women (1951), the Judges Act (1953), the National Service and National Insurance Acts (1953), and the Basic Law (The Knesset) (1958).

The President

The President is elected by the Knesset for five years.

Ten or more Knesset Members may propose a candidate for the Presidency.

Voting will be by secret ballot.

The President may not leave the country without the consent of the Government.

The President may resign by submitting his resignation in writing to the Speaker.

The President may be relieved of his duties by the Knesset for misdemeanour.

The Knesset is entitled to decide by a two-thirds majority that the President is incapacitated owing to ill-health to fulfil his duties permanently.

The Speaker of the Knesset will act for the President when the President leaves the country, or when he cannot perform his duties owing to ill-health.

The Knesset

The Knesset is the parliament of the State. There are 120 members.

It is elected by general, national, direct, equal, secret and proportional elections.

Every Israeli national of 18 years or over shall have the right to vote in elections to the Knesset unless a court has deprived him of that right by virtue of any law.

Every Israeli national of 21 and over shall have the right to be elected to the Knesset unless a court has deprived him of that right by virtue of any law.

The following shall not be candidates: the President of the State; the two Chief Rabbis; a judge (*shofet*) in office; a judge (*dayan*) of a religious court; the State Comptroller; the Chief of the General Staff of the Defence Army of Israel; rabbis and ministers of other religions in office; senior State employees and senior Army officers of such ranks and in such functions as shall be determined by law.

The term of office of the Knesset shall be four years.

The elections of the Knesset shall take place on the third Tuesday of the month of Cheshven in the year in which the tenure of the outgoing Knesset ends.

Election day shall be a day of rest, but transport and other public services shall function normally.

Results of the elections shall be published within fourteen days.

The Knesset shall elect from among its members a Chairman and Vice-Chairman.

The Knesset shall elect from among its members permanent committees, and may elect committees for specific matters.

The Knesset may appoint commissions of inquiry to investigate matters designated by the Knesset.

The Knesset shall hold two sessions a year; one of them shall open within four weeks after the Feast of the Tabernacles, the other within four weeks after Independence Day; the aggregate duration of the two sessions shall not be less than eight months.

The outgoing Knesset shall continue to hold office until the convening of the incoming Knesset.

The members of the Knesset shall receive a remuneration as provided by law.

The Government

The Government shall tender its resignation to the President immediately after his election, but shall continue with its duties until the formation of a new Government.

After consultation with representatives of the parties in the Knesset, the President shall charge one of the Members with the formation of a Government.

The Government shall be composed of a Prime Minister and a number of Ministers from among the Knesset Members or from outside the Knesset.

After it has been chosen, the Government shall appear before the Knesset and shall be considered as formed after having received a vote of confidence.

Within seven days of receiving a vote of confidence, the Prime Minister and the other Ministers shall swear allegiance to the State of Israel and its Laws and undertake to carry out the decisions of the Knesset.

THE GOVERNMENT

HEAD OF STATE

President: YITZHAK NAVON (took office May 29th, 1978).

THE CABINET

(July 1979)

Prime Minister: MENACHEM BEGIN (Likud).

Deputy Prime Minister: YIGAEL YADIN (Democratic Movement).

Minister of Defence: EZER WEIZMANN (Likud).

Minister for Foreign Affairs: MOSHE DAYAN (Independent).

Minister of Finance: SIMCHA EHRLICH (Likud).

Minister of Education: ZEVULUN HAMMER (National Religious Party).

Minister of Interior: Dr. YOSEF BURG (National Religious Party).

Minister of Agriculture: ARIEL SHARON (Likud).

Minister of Health: ELIEZER SHOSTAK (Likud).

Minister of Religious Affairs: AHARON ABU-HATZEIRA (National Religious Party).

Minister of Absorption, Construction and Housing: DAVID LEVY (Likud).

Minister of Commerce, Industry and Tourism: GIDEON PATT (Likud).

Minister of Energy, Infrastructure and Communication: YITZHAK MODAI (Likud).

Minister of Justice: SHMUEL TAMIR (Democratic Movement).

Minister of Social Welfare: ISRAEL KATZ (Democratic Movement for Change).

Minister of Transport: HAIM LANDAU (Likud).

Minister without Portfolio: MOSHE NISSIM (Likud).

KNESSET

Speaker: YITZHAK SHAMIR.

The state of the parties in the 9th Knesset, following the General Election of May 1977, was as follows:

PARTY	VOTES	SEATS
Likud	583,361	43
Labour-Mapam Alignment	430,117	32
Democratic Movement for Change	202,515	15
National Religious Party	160,583	12
Communist Party (RAKAH)	78,732	5
Agudat Israel	58,379	4
Shlomzion (A. Sharon)	33,975	2
Shelli-Left-Wing Peace List	27,289	2
Poalei Agudat Israel	24,061	1
Independent Liberal Party	21,051	1
Civil Rights Party	20,264	1
United Arab List	23,063	1
Flatto-Sharon	33,240	1

POLITICAL PARTIES

Agudat Israel (f. 1912) and **Poalei Agudat Israel** (f. 1924) are Orthodox Judaist parties, the membership of the Poalei Agudat Israel being drawn largely from wage-earners. Both parties support the Likud-NRP coalition. The official organ of Agudat Israel is the daily *Hamodia*; that of the Poalei Agudat Israel is the daily *Shearim*.

Civil Rights Party: breakaway movement from Labour Party.

Communist Party of Israel (RAKAH): f. 1919; Jewish-Arab membership; favours full implementation of UN Security Council Resolutions 242 and 338, Israeli withdrawal from all Arab territories occupied since 1967, formation of a Palestinian Arab state in the West Bank and Gaza Strip, recognition of national rights of State of Israel and Palestine people, democratic rights and defence of working class interests, and demands an end of discrimination against Arab minority in Israel and against oriental Jewish communities, publishes *Zo-Haderekh* (Hebrew); *Al-Ittihad* (Arabic); *Der Weg* (Yiddish).

Democratic Movement: f. 1978 when Democratic Movement for Change split into two parties; centrist party; continues to be part of Begin's coalition; Leader YIGAEL YADIN; Sec.-Gen. RAM RON.

Flatto-Sharon: Samual Flatto-Sharon is a Polish-born businessman who successfully contested the elections to the 9th Knesset on a platform stressing the need to refurbish Israel's economy and to raise the people's standard of living.

Independent Liberal Party: P.O.B. 23076, Tel-Aviv; f. 1965 by 7 Liberal Party Knesset members after the formation of the Herut Movement and Liberal Party Bloc; 20,000 mems.; Chair. MOSHE KOL; Gen. Sec. NISSIM ELIAD; publs. *Temurot* (Hebrew, monthly), *Die*

Liberale Rundschau (German, monthly), *Igeret* (Hebrew, quarterly).

Israel Labour Party: P.O.B. 3263, Tel-Aviv; f. 1968 as a merger of the three Labour groups, Mapai, Rafi and Achdut Ha'avoda; a Zionist democratic socialist party, was in government from 1949 to 1977; together with Mapam is forming the main opposition bloc under name of Labour-Mapam Alignment; Chair. of Israel Labour Party SHIMON PERES; Gen. Sec. HAIM BAR-LEV.

Likud: Tel-Aviv; f. September 1973; is a parliamentary bloc of Herut, the Liberal Party of Israel (Chair. SIMCHA EHRLICH), Laam (Leader YIGAEL HOROWITZ) and Ahdut (Leader HILLEL SEIDEL); aims: territorial integrity (advocates retention of all the territory of post-1922 mandatory Palestine); absorption of newcomers; a social order based on freedom and justice, elimination of poverty and want; development of an economy that will ensure a decent standard of living; improvement of the environment and the quality of life. Likud became the government party in June 1977 with the support of the National Religious Party and Agudat Israel. The Democratic Movement for Change joined the coalition in October 1977, but split in September 1978 when the Movement for Change and Initiative left the coalition; Leader of Likud MENACHEM BEGIN.

Movement for Change and Initiative: f. 1978 when Democratic Movement for Change split into two parties; centrist party; left Begin's coalition in Sept. 1978 at time of split; Leaders AMNON RUBINSTEIN and MEIR AMIT.

National Religious Party: f. 1956; stands for strict adherence to Jewish religion and tradition, and strives to achieve the application of religious precepts of Judaism in everyday life; it is also endeavouring to establish the constitution of Israel on Jewish religious law; withdrew from (Labour) government coalition in December 1976 and now supports the Likud coalition, occupying 3 cabinet posts.

Sheli-Israel Peace and Equality Movement: 24 Huberman St., P.O.B. 41609, Tel-Aviv; f. 1977; an alliance of patriotic socialist and patriotic peace groups, which includes the *Ha'olam Hazeh* party, *Mokked*, Arieh Eliav's Independent Socialists, and others.

United Arab List: Arab party affiliated to Labour Party.

United Workers Party - Mapam: P.O.B. 1777, Tel-Aviv, f. 1948; left-wing Socialist-Zionist party; since January 1969 grouped in Labour-Mapam Alignment with Israel Labour Party.

DIPLOMATIC REPRESENTATION

EMBASSIES AND LEGATIONS ACCREDITED TO ISRAEL

(E) Embassy; (L) Legation.

Argentina: 112 Rehov Hayarkon, 2nd Floor, Tel-Aviv (E); *Ambassador:* JORGE E. CASAL.

Australia: 185 Rehov Hayarkon, Tel-Aviv (E); *Ambassador:* WALTER P. J. HANDMER.

Austria: 11 Hermann Cohen St., Tel-Aviv (E); *Ambassador:* Dr. INGO MUSSI.

Barbados: London, United Kingdom (E).

Belgium: 266 Rehov Hayarkon, Tel-Aviv (E); *Ambassador:* JACQUES EGGERMONT.

Bolivia: Kiryat Wolfson, Rehov Diskin, Villa 7, Jerusalem (E); *Ambassador:* Brig.-Gen. JOSÉ ANTONIO ZELAYA S.

Brazil: 14 Hei Be'Yiar, Tel-Aviv (E); *Ambassador:* Dr. VASCO MARIZ (also accred. to Cyprus).

Burma: 12 Mateh Aharon St., Ramat Gan (E); *Ambassador:* U SHWE ZAN AUNG.

Canada: 220 Hayarkon St., Tel-Aviv (E); *Ambassador:* JOSEPH STEPHEN STANFORD (also accred. to Cyprus).

Chile: 10 Brenner St., Jerusalem (E); *Ambassador:* Gen. JOSÉ BERDICHEWSKY.

Colombia: 12 Jabotinsky St., Jerusalem (E); *Chargé d'affaires a.i.:* Dr. JAIME QUIÑONES REYES.

Costa Rica: 5 Even Israel St., Jerusalem (E); *Ambassador:* RONALD FERNÁNDEZ-PINTO.

Denmark: 23 Bnei Moshe St., Tel-Aviv (E); *Ambassador:* OLE N. KOCH.

Dominican Republic: 3 Bustenai St., Jerusalem (E); *Ambassador:* JOSÉ VILLANUEVA.

Ecuador: P.O.B. 4089, 6 Hillel St., Jerusalem (E); *Ambassador:* Gen. CARLOS AGUIRRE ASANZA.

El Salvador: 7 Rehov Diskin, Bldg. 2, Apt. 12, Kiryat Wolfson, Jerusalem (E); *Ambassador:* Col. NAPOLEÓN ARMANDO GUERRA.

Finland: 224 Hayarkon St., Tel-Aviv (E); *Ambassador:* MATTI KAHILUOTO.

France: 112 Tayelet Herbert Samuel, Tel-Aviv (E); *Ambassador:* MARC BONNEFOUS.

Germany, Federal Republic: 16 Soutine St., Tel-Aviv (E); *Ambassador:* KLAUS SCHÜTZ.

Greece: 35 Sderot Shaul Hamelech, Tel-Aviv (L); *Diplomatic Representative:* E. S. SPYRIDAKIS.

Guatemala: 3 Azza St., Jerusalem (E); *Ambassador:* (vacant) (also accred. to Greece).

Haiti: 16 Kovshei Katamon St., Jerusalem (E); *Ambassador:* MUSSET PIERRE-JEROME.

Honduras: Rome, Italy (E).

Iceland: Copenhagen, Denmark (E).

Ireland: Berne, Switzerland (E).

Italy: 24 Huberman St., Tel-Aviv (E); *Ambassador:* GIROLAMO NISIO.

Jamaica: Bonn-Bad Godesberg, Federal Republic of Germany (E).

Japan: Asia House, 4 Rehov Weizman, Tel-Aviv (E); *Ambassador:* NAGAO YOSHIDA.

Malawi: London, United Kingdom (E).

Malta: London, United Kingdom (E).

Mexico: 14 Hei Beiyar St., Tel-Aviv (E); *Ambassador:* ROBERTO CASELLAS LEAL.

Nepal: Paris, France (E).

Netherlands: Beit Yoel, 33 Yaffo St., Jerusalem (E); *Ambassador:* CHRISTIAAN B. ARRIENS

Nicaragua: Rome, Italy (E).

Norway: 10 Heh Iyar St., Kikar Hamedina, Tel-Aviv (E); *Ambassador:* ODD G. JAKOBSEN.

Panama: 6 Rehov Yeshayahu Press, Jerusalem (E); *Chargé d'affaires a.i.:* MARCOS ANDRÉS VILLAREAL.

Peru: 52 Rehov Pinkos, Apt. 31, 8th Floor, Tel-Aviv (E); *Ambassador:* BERNARDO ROCA REY.

Philippines: 14 Hei Beiyar St., Kikar Hamedina, Tel-Aviv (E); *Ambassador:* Dr. RAFAELITA SORIANO.

Romania: 24 Adam Hacohen St., Tel-Aviv (E); *Ambassador:* ION COVACI.

South Africa: 2 Kaplan St., Tel-Aviv (E); *Ambassador:* DEREK STUART FRANKLIN.

Sweden: 198 Hayarkon St., Tel-Aviv (E); *Ambassador:* F. IWO DÖLLING.

Switzerland: 228 Hayarkon St., Tel-Aviv (E); *Ambassador:* ERNEST BAUERMEISTER (also accred. to Cyprus).

Thailand: Rome, Italy (E).

Turkey: 34 Rehov Amos, Tel-Aviv (L); *Chargé d'affaires a.i.:* METIN SIRMAN.

United Kingdom: 192 Hayarkon St., Tel-Aviv (E); *Ambassador:* JOHN MASON.

U.S.A.: 71 Hayarkon St., Tel-Aviv (E); *Ambassador:* SAMUEL LEWIS.

Uruguay: 20 Uziya St., Katamon, Jerusalem (E); *Ambassador:* Prof. BAUTISTA ETCHEVERRY BOGGIO.

Venezuela: 28 Rachel Imenu St., Jerusalem (E); *Ambassador:* NAPOLEÓN GIMÉNEZ.

Israel also has diplomatic relations with the Bahamas, Botswana, Cyprus, Fiji, Grenada, the Republic of Korea, Lesotho, Monaco, New Zealand, Papua New Guinea, Portugal, Singapore, Suriname, Swaziland, Tonga, Trinidad and Tobago and Western Samoa.

THE JEWISH AGENCY FOR ISRAEL

P.O.B. 92, Jerusalem.

Organization:

The governing bodies are the Assembly which determines basic policy, the Board of Governors which manages the Agency between Assembly meetings and the Executive responsible for the day to day running of the Agency.

Chairman of Executive: LEON DULZIN.

Chairman of Board of Governors: MAX M. FISHER.

Director-General: SHMUEL LAHIS.

Secretary-General: HARRY M. ROSEN.

Functions:

According to the Agreement of 1971, the Jewish Agency undertakes the immigration and absorption of immigrants in Israel, including absorption in agricultural settlement and immigrant housing, social welfare and health services in connection with immigrants, and education, youth care and training.

Budget (1978/79): U.S. $350 million.

JUDICIAL SYSTEM

The law of Israel is composed of Ottoman law, British law, Palestine law, applicable in Palestine on May 14th, 1948, when the independence of the State of Israel was declared, the substance of the common law and doctrines of equity in force in England, as modified to suit local conditions, and religious law of the various recognized religious communities as regards matters of personal status, in so far as there is nothing in any of the said laws repugnant to Israeli legislation and subject to such modifications as may have resulted from the establishment of the State of Israel and its authorities, and also of the laws enacted by the Israeli legislature. The pre-1948 law is increasingly being replaced by original local legislation.

CIVIL COURTS

The Supreme Court is the highest judicial instance in the State. It has jurisdiction as an Appellate Court from the District Courts in all matters, both civil and criminal (sitting as a Court of Civil Appeal or as a Court of Criminal Appeal), and as a Court of First Instance (sitting as a High Court of Justice) in matters in which it considers it necessary to grant relief in the interests of justice and which are not within the jurisdiction of any other court or tribunal. This includes applications for orders in the nature of *habeas corpus*, *mandamus*, prohibition and *certiorari*, and enables the court to review the legality of acts of administrative authorities of all kinds.

President of the Supreme Court: Y. SUSSMAN.

Permanent Deputy President of the Supreme Court: M. LANDAU.

Justices of the Supreme Court: A. WITKON, H. COHN, I. KAHAN, M. SHAMGAR, S. ASCHER, Mrs., M. BEN-PORAT, M. EYLON, D. BEHOR, A. BARAK.

The District Courts: Jerusalem, Tel-Aviv-Jaffa, Haifa, Beersheba, Nazareth. They have unlimited jurisdiction as Courts of First Instance in all civil and criminal matters not within the jurisdiction of a Magistrates' Court, all matters not within the exclusive jurisdiction of any other tribunal, and matters within the concurrent jurisdiction of any other tribunal so long as such tribunal does not deal with them, and as an Appellate Court in appeals from judgments and decisions of Magistrates' Courts and judgments of Municipal Courts and various administrative tribunals.

Magistrates' Courts: There are 26 Magistrates' Courts, having criminal jurisdiction to try contraventions and misdemeanours, and civil jurisdiction to try actions concerning possession or use of immovable property, or the partition thereof whatever may be the value of the subject matter of the action, and other civil actions where the amount of the claim, or the value of the subject matter, does not exceed I£150,000.

Labour Courts: Established in 1969. Regional Labour Courts in Jerusalem, Tel-Aviv, Haifa and Beersheba, composed of Judges and representatives of the Public. A National Labour Court in Jerusalem, presided over by Judge Z. Bar-Niv. The Courts have jurisdiction over all matters arising out of the relationship between employer and employee; between parties to a collective labour agreement; matters concerning the National Insurance Law and the Labour Law and Rules.

Municipal Courts: There are 5 Municipal Courts, having criminal jurisdiction over any offences against municipal regulations and by-laws and certain other offences, such as town planning offences, committed within the municipal area.

RELIGIOUS COURTS

The Religious Courts are the Courts of the recognized religious communities. They are competent in certain defined matters of personal status concerning members of their community. Where any action of personal status involves persons of different religious communities the President of the Supreme Court will decide which Court shall have jurisdiction. Whenever a question arises as to whether or not a case is one of personal status within the exclusive jurisdiction of a Religious Court, the matter must be referred to a Special Tribunal composed of two Justices of the Supreme Court and the President of the highest court of the religious community concerned in Israel.

The judgments of the Religious Courts are executed by the process and offices of the Civil Courts.

Jewish Rabbinical Courts: These Courts have exclusive jurisdiction in matters of marriage and divorce of Jews in Israel who are Israeli citizens or residents. In all other matters of personal status they have concurrent jurisdiction with the District Courts with the consent of all parties concerned.

Muslim Religious Courts: These Courts have exclusive jurisdiction in matters of marriage and divorce of Muslims who are not foreigners, or who are foreigners subject by their national law to the jurisdiction of Muslim Religious Courts in such matters. In all other matters of personal status they have concurrent jurisdiction with the District Courts with the consent of all parties concerned.

Christian Religious Courts: The Courts of the recognized Christian communities have exclusive jurisdiction in matters of marriage and divorce of members of their communities who are not foreigners. In all other matters of personal status they have concurrent jurisdiction with the District Courts with the consent of all parties concerned. But neither these Courts nor the Civil Courts have jurisdiction to dissolve the marriage of a foreign subject.

Druze Courts: These Courts, established in 1963, have exclusive jurisdiction in matters of marriage and divorce of Druze in Israel, who are Israeli citizens or residents, and concurrent jurisdiction with the District Courts in all other matters of personal status of Druze with the consent of all parties concerned.

MILITARY COURTS

Courts-Martial: A Court-Martial is competent to try a soldier within the meaning of the Military Justice Law, 1955, who has committed an act constituting a military offence, without prejudice to the power of any other Court in the State to try him for that act if it constitutes an offence under any other law. A Court-Martial is also competent to try a soldier for any offence which is not a military offence, but the Attorney General may order that he be tried by another Court if he is of the opinion that the offence was not committed within the framework of the Army or in consequence of the accused's belonging to the Army.

RELIGION

JUDAISM

Judaism, the religion evolved and followed by the Jews, is the faith of the great majority of the population. Its basis is a belief in an ethical monotheism.

There are two main Jewish communities: the Ashkenazim and the Sephardim. The former are the Jews from Eastern, Central, or Northern Europe, while the latter originate from the Balkan countries, North Africa and the Middle East. Although they have separate synagogues, and differ somewhat in their ritual and pronunciation of Hebrew, there is no doctrinal distinction. The prevailing influence is that of the Ashkenazim Jews, who are more modern and westernized, but the recent Hebrew revival has been based on the Sephardi pronunciation of the ancient Hebrew tongue.

The supreme religious authority is vested in the Chief Rabbinate, which consists of the Ashkenazi and Sephardi Chief Rabbis and the Supreme Rabbinical Council. It makes decisions on interpretation of the Jewish law, and supervises the Rabbinical Courts. There are 8 regional Rabbinical Courts, and a Rabbinical Court of Appeal presided over by the two Chief Rabbis.

According to the Rabbinical Courts Jurisdiction Law of 1953, marriage and divorce among Jews in Israel are exclusively within the jurisdiction of the Rabbinical Courts. Provided that all the parties concerned agree, other matters of personal status can also be decided by the Rabbinical Courts.

There are 195 Religious Councils, which maintain religious services and supply religious needs, and about 405 religious committees with similar functions in smaller settlements. Their expenses are borne jointly by the State and the local authorities. The Religious Councils are under the administrative control of the Ministry of Religious Affairs. In all matters of religion, the Religious Councils are subject to the authority of the Chief Rabbinate. There are 365 officially appointed rabbis. The total number of synagogues is about 7,000, most of which are organized within the framework of the Union of Israel Synagogues.

Head of the Ashkenazi Community: The Chief Rabbi Shlomo Goren.

Head of the Sephardic Community: The Chief Rabbi Ovadia Yossef.

Two Jewish sects still loyal to their distinctive customs are:

The Karaites, a sect which recognizes only the Jewish written law and not the oral law of the Mishna and Talmud. The community of about 12,000 many of whom live in or near Ramla, has been augmented by immigration from Egypt.

The Samaritans, an ancient sect mentioned in 2 Kings xvii, 24. They recognize only the Torah. The community in Israel numbers about 500; about half of them live in Holon, where a Samaritan synagogue has been built, and the remainder, including the High Priest live in Nablus, near Mt. Gerizim, which is sacred to the Samaritans.

ISLAM

The Muslims in Israel are in the main Sunnis, and are divided among the four rites of the Sunni school of Muslim thought: the Shafe'i, the Hanbali, the Hanafi, and the Maliki. Before June 1967 they numbered approximately 175,000; in 1971, approximately 343,900.

CHRISTIAN COMMUNITIES

The Greek Melkite Church: P.O.B. 279, Haifa; numbers about 41,000 and Haifa is the seat of the Archbishop of Acre, Haifa, Nazareth and all Galilee; Archbishop Maximos Salloum; publs. *Ar-Rabita* (Arabic monthly; circ. 4,000), *Message de Galilée* (3 a year in French and Flemish; circ. 2,000).

The Greek Orthodox Church in Israel has approximately 22,000 members. The Patriarch of Jerusalem is His Beatitude BENEDICTOS.

The Latin (Roman Catholic) Church has about 10,000 native members in Israel plus about 2,000 Polish and Hungarian Catholic refugees. The Latin Patriarch of Jerusalem is His Beatitude JAMES JOSEPH BELTRITTI; Representative in Israel H.E. Bishop HANNA KALDANY.

The Maronite Community, with 6,350 members, has communal centres in Isfyia, Haifa, Jaffa, Jish, Nazareth and Jerusalem. The Maronite Patriarch, Mgr. JOSEPH KHOURY, resides in the Lebanon. The Vicar-General, Mgr. AUGUSTIN HARFOUCHE, is resident in Jaffa.

Episcopal Church in Jerusalem and the Middle East, belongs to the Anglican Communion; was reorganized in 1976; has Jerusalem Diocese and also Diocese of Iran, Egypt, Cyprus and the Gulf; Presiding Bishop Rt. Rev. HASSAN DEHQANI-TAFTI, P.O.B. 12, Isfahan, Iran.

Other denominations include the *Armenian Church* (900 members), the *Coptic Church* (700 members), the *Russian Orthodox Church,* which maintains an Ecclesiastical Mission, the *Ethiopian Church,* and the *Baptist Lutheran* and *Presbyterian Churches.*

THE PRESS

Tel-Aviv is the main publishing centre, only three dailies being published in Jerusalem. Largely for economic reasons there has developed no local press away from these cities; hence all papers regard themselves as national. Friday editions, Sabbath eve, are increased to up to twice the normal size by special weekend supplements, and experience a considerable rise in circulation. No newspapers appear on Saturday.

Most of the daily papers are in Hebrew, and others appear in Arabic, English, French, Polish, Yiddish, Hungarian and German. The total daily circulation is 500,000–600,000 copies, or twenty-one papers per hundred people, although most citizens read more than one daily paper.

Most Hebrew morning dailies have strong political or religious affiliations. *Al Hamishmar* is affiliated to Mapam, *Hatzofeh* to the National Religious Front—World Mizrahi. *Davar* is the long-established organ of the Histadrut. Mapai publishes the weekly *Ot.* Although the revenue from advertisements is increasing, very few dailies are economically self-supporting; most depend on subsidies from political parties, religious organizations or public funds. The limiting effect on freedom of commentary entailed by this party press system has provoked repeated criticism.

The Jerusalem Arabic daily *Al Anba* has a small circulation (10,000) but an increasing number of Israeli Arabs are now reading Hebrew dailies. The daily, *Al Quds,* was founded in 1968 for Arabs in Jerusalem and the West Bank; the small indigenous press of occupied Jordan has largely ceased publication or transferred operations to Amman.

There are around 400 other newspapers and magazines including some 50 weekly and 150 fortnightly; over 250 of them are in Hebrew, the remainder in eleven other languages.

The most influential and respected dailies, for both quality of news coverage and commentary, are *Ha'aretz* and the trade union paper, *Davar,* which frequently has articles by government figures. These are the widest read of the morning papers, exceeded only by the popular afternoon press, *Ma'ariv* and *Yedioth Aharonoth.* The *Jerusalem Post* gives detailed and sound news coverage in English.

The Israeli Press Council, established in 1963, deals with matters of common interest to the Press such as drafting the recently published code of professional ethics which is binding on all journalists.

The Daily Newspaper Publishers' Association represents publishers in negotiations with official and public bodies, negotiates contracts with employees and purchases and distributes newsprint, of which Israel now manufactures 75 per cent of her needs.

DAILIES

Al-Anba: P.O.B. 428, 7 Harikma St., Jerusalem; f. 1968; published by Jerusalem Publications Ltd.; Arabic Editor YAACOV HAZMA; circ. 10,000.

Al Hamishmar (*The Guardian*): Al Hamishmar House, 4 Ben Avigdor St., Tel-Aviv; f. 1943; morning; organ of the United Workers' Party (Mapam); Editors MARK GEFEN, HAIM SHUR; circ. 25,000

Al Quds (*Jerusalem*): P.O.B. 19788, Jerusalem; f. 1968; Arabic; Editor ABU ZALAF.

Chadshot Hasport: Tushia St., P.O.B. 20011, Tel-Aviv 61200; f. 1954; Hebrew; sports; independent; circ. 30,000.

Davar (*The Word*): P.O.B. 199, 45 Sheinkin St., Tel-Aviv; f. 1925; morning; official organ of the General Federation of Labour (Histadrut); Editor HANNAH ZEMER; circ. 50,000.

Ha'aretz (*The Land*): 21 Salman Schocken St., Tel-Aviv; f. 1918; morning; liberal, independent; Editor GERSHOM G. SCHOCKEN; circ. 55,000 (week-days), 75,000 (week-ends).

Hamodia: Kikar Hacheruth, P.O.B. 1306, Jerusalem; organ of Agudat Israel; morning; Editor YEHUDA L. LEVIN; circ. 8,000.

Hatzofeh: 66 Hamasger St., Tel-Aviv; f. 1938; morning; organ of the National Religious Front; Editor S. DANIEL; circ. 11,000.

Israel Nachrichten: 52 Harakevet St., Tel-Aviv; f. 1974; morning; German; Editor S. HIMMELFARB; circ. 20,000.

Israelski Far Tribuna: 113 Givat Herzl St., Tel-Aviv; Bulgarian.

Jerusalem Post: P.O.B. 81, Romema, Jerusalem; f. 1932; morning; independent; English; Editor and Man. Dir. ARI RATH; Editor ERWIN FRENKEL; circ. 30,000 (weekdays), 44,000 (weekend edition); there is also a weekly international edition (*q.v.*).

Le Journal d'Israel: 26 Agra St., P.O.B. 28330, Tel-Aviv; independent; French; Dir.-Chief Editor J. RABIN; circ. 10,000; also overseas weekly selection; circ. 15,000.

Letzte Nyess (*Late News*): 52 Harakevet St., Tel-Aviv; f. 1949; Yiddish; morning; Editor S. HIMMELFARB; circ. 23,000.

Ma'ariv: Ma'ariv House, P.O.B. 20010, Tel-Aviv; f. 1948; mid-morning; independent; Editor SHALOM ROSENFELD; circ. daily 147,000, Friday 245,000.

Nowiny i Kurier: 52 Harakevet St., Tel-Aviv; f. 1952; Polish; morning; Editor S. HIMELFARB; circ. 15,000.

Omer: 45 Sheinkin St., Tel-Aviv; Histadrut popular vowelled Hebrew paper; f. 1951; Chief Editor MEIR BARELI; circ. 10,000.

Sha'ar: 52 Harakevet St., Tel-Aviv 64284; economy and finance; Hebrew and English; Editor J. KANSHAN.

Shearim: 64 Frishman St., Tel-Aviv; organ of Poalei Agudat Israel; Editor YEHUDA NAHSHONI; circ. 5,000.

Uj Kelet: 52 Harakevet St., Tel-Aviv; f. 1918; morning; Hungarian; independent; Editor S. HIMMELFARB; circ. 20,000.

Viata Noastra: 52 Harakevet St., Tel-Aviv; f. 1950; Romanian; morning; Editor MEIR ZAIT; circ. 30,000.

Yedioth Aharonoth: 138 Petah-Tikva Rd., Tel-Aviv; f. 1939; evening; independent; Editor Dr. H. ROSENBLUM; circ. 180,000, Friday 280,000.

Yom Yom: P.O.B. 1194, Tel-Aviv; f. 1964; morning; economy and finance; Editor P. MERSTEN.

WEEKLIES AND FORTNIGHTLIES

Al Ta'awun: P.O.B. 303, Tel-Aviv; f. 1961; published by the Arab Worker's Dept. of the Histadrut and the Co-operatives Dept. of the Ministry of Labour; co-operatives quarterly; Editor TUVIA SHAMOSH.

Al Harriya: 38 King George St., Tel-Aviv; Arabic weekly of the Herut Party.

Al-Ittihad: P.O.B. 104, Haifa; f. 1944; Arabic; journal of the Israeli Communist Party; Chief Editor EMILE TOUMA.

Al-Mirsad: P.O.B. 736, 4 Ben Avigdor St., Tel-Aviv; Mapam; Arabic.

Bama'alah: P.O.B. 303, Tel-Aviv; journal of the young Histadrut Movement; Editor N. ANAELY.

Bamahane: Military P.O.B. 1013, Tel-Aviv; f. 1948; military, illustrated weekly of the Israel Armed Forces; Editor-in-Chief YOSSEF ESHKOL; circ. 70,000.

Bitaon Heyl Ha'avir (*Air Force Magazine*): Doar Zwai 1560, Zahal; f. 1948; Man. Editor D. MOLAD; Technical Editor Y. BODANSKY; circ. 20,000.

Dvar Hashavua: 45 Sheinkin St., Tel-Aviv; f. 1946; popular illustrated; weekly; published by Histadrut, General Federation of Labour; Editor O. ZMORA; circ. 50,000.

Ethgar: 75 Einstein Street, Tel-Aviv; twice weekly; Editor NATHAN YALIN-MOR.

Glasul Popularui: Eilath St., P.O.B. 2675, Tel-Aviv; weekly of the Communist Party of Israel; Romanian; Editor MEÏR SEMO.

Haolam Hazeh: P.O.B. 136, 3 Gordon St., Tel-Aviv; f. 1937; independent; illustrated news magazine; weekly; Editor-in-Chief URI AVNERY.

Harefuah: 39 Shaul Hamelech Blvd., Tel-Aviv; f. 1920; with English summary; fortnightly journal of the Israeli Medical Association; Editor I. SUM, M.D.; circ. 6,000.

Hed Hahinukh: 8 Ben-Saruk Street, Tel-Aviv; f. 1926; weekly; educational; published by the Israeli Teachers' Union; Editor ORA GADELL; circ. 25,000.

Illustrirte Weltwoch: P.O.B. 2571, Tel-Aviv; f. 1956; Yiddish; weekly; Editor M. KARPINOVITZ.

The Israel Digest: P.O.B. 92, Jerusalem; f. 1957; World Zionist Organization digest of news and views; fortnightly; circ. 20,000; Editor ZVI VOLK.

Jerusalem Post Overseas Weekly: P.O.B. 81, Romema, Jerusalem; f. 1959; English; Overseas edition of the *Jerusalem Post* (*q.v.*); circ. 36,000 to 95 countries.

Kol Ha'am (*Voice of the People*): 37 Eilath St., P.O.B. 2675, Tel-Aviv; f. 1947; organ of the Communist Party of Israel; Editor B. BALTI.

Laisha: P.O.B. 28122, 7 Fin St., Tel-Aviv; f. 1946; Hebrew; women's magazine; Editor DAVID KARASSIK.

Maariv Lanoar: 2 Carlebach St., Tel-Aviv; f. 1957; weekly for youth; Editor AMNON BEI-RAV; circ. 35,000.

Magallati: Arabic Publishing House, P.O.B. 28049, Tel-Aviv; f. 1960; children's fortnightly; Editor-in-Chief IBRAHIM MUSA IBRAHIM; Editors GAMIL DAHLAN, MISHEL HADDAD, MAZIR SHIMALI; circ. 11,000.

MB (*Mitteilungsblatt*): P.O.B. 1480, Tel-Aviv; f. 1932; German weekly journal of the Irgun Olei Merkas Europa; Editor Dr. HANS CAPELL.

Min Hayesod: Tel-Aviv; fortnightly; Hebrew; news and political commentary.

Reshumot: Ministry of Justice, Jerusalem; f. 1948; Hebrew, Arabic and English; official Government gazette.

Sada-A-Tarbia (*The Echo of Education*): published by the Histadrut and Teachers' Association, P.O.B. 506, Rehovot; f. 1952; Arabic; educational; fortnightly; Editor TUVIA SHAMOSH.

OTHER PERIODICALS

Al-Bushra: P.O.B. 6088, Haifa; f. 1935; monthly; Arabic; organ of the Ahmadiyya movement; Editor JALAL-UD-DIN QAMAR.

Al Hamishmar: 20 Yehuda Halevy Street, Tel-Aviv; Bulgarian monthly of United Workers' Party.

Al Jadid: P.O.B. 104, Haifa; Arabic; literary monthly; Editor SAMEKH EL KASSEM.

Ariel: Cultural and Scientific Relations Division, Ministry for Foreign Affairs, Jerusalem; Publishers, Editorial and Distribution: The Jerusalem Publishing House, P.O.B. 7147, Jerusalem; f. 1962; quarterly review of the arts and letters in Israel; edns. in English, Spanish, French and German; Editor YAEL LOTAN.

Avoda Ubituach Leumi: P.O.B. 915, Jerusalem; f. 1949; monthly review of the Ministry of Labour and Social Affairs, and the National Insurance Institute, Jerualem; Editor Z. HEYN; circ. 3,000.

Bekalkala Uvemis'har (*Economics and Trade*): P.O.B. 852, Tel-Aviv; f. 1932; monthly; Hebrew; published by Federation of Israeli Chambers of Commerce; Editor ZVI AMIT; circ. 5,000.

Business Digest Trade Lists: 37 Harbour St., Haifa; f. 1947; weekly; English, Hebrew; shipping movements, import licences, stock exchange listings, business failures, etc.; Editor G. ALON.

Christian News from Israel: 23 Shlomo Hamelech St., Jerusalem; quarterly issued by the Ministry of Religious Affairs; in English, French, Spanish; Editor SHALOM BEN-ZAKKAI; circ. 10,000.

Di Goldene Keyt: 30 Weizmann St., Tel-Aviv; f. 1949; Yiddish; literary quarterly; published by the Histadrut; Editor A. SUTZKEVER; Co-Editor E. PINES; Man. Editor SHMUEL CHORESH.

Divrei Haknesset: c/o The Knesset, Jerusalem; f. 1949; records of the proceedings of the Knesset, published by the Government Printer, Jerusalem; Editor D. NIV; circ. 300.

The Family Physician: 148 Arlosoroff St., P.O.B. 16250; Tel-Aviv; f. 1970; three times a year; medical; Hebrew with English, French and Russian summaries; Editor Dr. M. R. POLLIACK; circ. 4,500.

Folk un Zion: P.O.B. 92, Jerusalem; f. 1950; bi-monthly; current events relating to Israel and World Jewry; circ. 3,000; Editor EPHRAIM SHEDLETSKY.

Frei Israel: P.O.B. 8512, Tel-Aviv; Yiddish, progressive monthly, publ. by Assen. for Popular Culture.

Gazit: 8 Zvi Brook St., P.O.B. 4190, Tel-Aviv; f. 1932; monthly; Hebrew and English; art, literature; Publisher G. TALPHIR.

Hameshek Hahaklai: 21 Melchett St., Tel-Aviv; f. 1929; agricultural; Editor ISRAEL INBARI.

Hamizrah Hehadash (*The New East*): The Hebrew University of Jerusalem; f. 1949; quarterly of the Israel Oriental Society; Hebrew with English summary; Middle Eastern, Asian and African Affairs; Editor AHARON LAYISH.

Hamlonai (*The Hotelier*): P.O.B. 11586, Tel-Aviv; f. 1962; monthly of the Israel Hotel Association; Hebrew and English; Editor Z. PELTZ.

Hapraklit: P.O.B. 14152 Tel-Aviv: f. 1943; quarterly; published by the Israel Bar Association; Editors A. POLONSKY, J. GROSS; circ. 6,500.

Hassadeh: 8 Shaul Hamelech Blvd., P.O.B. 40044, Tel-Aviv; f. 1920; monthly; review of agriculture; English summaries; Director MARION R. COHN; Editor J. M. MARGALIT; circ. 10,000.

Hed Hagan: 8 Ben Saruk St., Tel-Aviv; f. 1935; educational; Editor Mrs. ESTHER RABINOWITZ; circ. 3,500.

Innovation: P.O.B. 8100, Jerusalem; f. 1975; monthly; English; industrial research and development in Israel; Editor A. GREENFIELD.

Israel Annals of Psychiatry: Jerusalem Academic Press, Givat Saul, P.O.B. 3640, Jerusalem; f. 1963; quarterly; Editor-in-Chief Prof. H. Z. WINNIK.

Israel Business: P.O.B. 8100, Jerusalem; f. 1961; monthly; English; business and economic development; Editor A. GREENFIELD.

Israel Economist: P.O.B. 7052, 6 Hazanowitz St., Jerusalem; f. 1945; monthly; English; political and economic; independent; Editor J. KOLLEK, M.JUR.; also publishes *The Tel-Aviv Stock Exchange Information Card Service.*

Israel Export and Trade Journal, The: P.O.B. 11586, Tel-Aviv; f. 1949; monthly; English; commercial and economic; published by Israel Periodicals Co. Ltd.; Man. Dirs. F. A. LEWINSON and ZALMAN PELTZ.

Israel Industry and Commerce and Export News: P.O.B. 1199, Tel-Aviv; English; monthly; serves Israeli exporters; Editor SHALOM YEDIDYAH.

Israel Journal of Medical Sciences: P.O.B. 1435, Jerusalem; f. 1965; monthly; Editor-in-Chief Dr. M. PRYWES; circ. 5,500.

Israel-South Africa Trade Journal: P.O.B. 11587, Tel-Aviv; f. 1973; bi-monthly; English; commercial and economic; published by Israel Publications Corpn. Ltd.; Man. Dir. Z. PELTZ.

Israels Aussenhandel: P.O.B. 11586, Tel-Aviv; f. 1967; monthly; German; commercial; Editor Z. PELTZ.

Kalkalan: 8 Akiva St., P.O.B. 7052, Jerusalem; f. 1952; monthly; Hebrew commercial and economic; independent; Editor J. KOLLEK, M.JUR.

Kiryat Sefer: P.O.B. 503, Jerusalem; f. 1924; bibliographical quarterly of the Jewish National and University Library, Jerusalem; Editor Mrs. A. NEUBERG.

Labour in Israel: 93 Arlosoroff St., Tel-Aviv; periodic bulletin of the Histadrut; English, French, German and Spanish.

Leshonenu: Academy of the Hebrew Language, P.O.B. 3449, Jerusalem; f. 1929; quarterly; for the study of the Hebrew language and cognate subjects; Editor S. ABRAMSON.

Leshonenu La'am: Academy of the Hebrew Language, P.O.B. 3449, Jerusalem; f. 1945; popular Hebrew philology; Editors E. ETAN, M. MEDAN.

Ma'arachot: Ha'Kirya Rechov Gimmel 1, Tel-Aviv; f. 1939; military.

Mada: Weizmann Science Press of Israel, P.O.B. 801 Jerusalem; f. 1956; popular scientific bi-monthly in Hebrew; Editor-in-Chief KAPAI PINES; circ. 11,000.

Melaha Vetaassiya (*Trade and Industry*): P.O.B. 11587, Tel-Aviv; f. 1969; bi-monthly review of the Union of Artisans and Small Manufacturers of Israel; Man. Dir. Z. PELTZ.

Mibifnim: 27 Sutin St., P.O.B. 16040, Tel-Aviv; f. 1924 quarterly of the United Collective Settlements (Hakibbutz Hameuchad); Editor ZERUBAVEL GILEAD; circ. 8,000.

Molad: P.O.B. 1165, Jerusalem; f. 1948; quarterly; independent political and literary periodical; Hebrew; published by Miph'ale Molad Ltd.; Editor EPHRAIM BROIDO.

Monthly Bulletin of Statistics: Israel Central Bureau of Statistics, P.O.B. 13015, Jerusalem; f. 1949.

Administered Territories Statistics Quarterly: f. 1971; Hebrew and English.

Foreign Trade Statistics: f. 1969; Hebrew and English; appears twice a year 2 vols.; imports/exports.

Tourism and Hotel Services Statistics Quarterly: f. 1973; Hebrew and English.

Price Statistics Monthly: f. 1959; Hebrew.

Foreign Trade Statistics Monthly: f. 1950; Hebrew and English.

Immigration Statistics Quarterly: f. 1970; Hebrew.

Moznayim (*Balance*): P.O.B. 7098, Tel-Aviv; f. 1929; literature and culture; monthly; circ. 2,500; Editor B. Y. MICHALY.

Na'amat: 5 Ben-Shaprut St., P.O.B. 303, Tel-Aviv; f. 1934; monthly journal of the Council of Women Workers of the Histadrut; Hebrew; Editor ZIVIA COHEN; circ. 16,500.

Ner: Ihud, P.O.B. 451, Jerusalem; f. 1948; monthly on political and social problems; advocates Arab-Jewish reconciliation; Hebrew, English, Arabic; circ. 1,500.

New Outlook: 8 Karl Netter St., Tel-Aviv; f. 1957; Israeli and Middle Eastern Affairs; monthly; circ. 10,000; Editor SIMHA FLAPAN.

Proche-Orient Chrétien: B.P. 19079, Jerusalem; f. 1951; quarterly on churches and religion in the Middle East.

Quarterly Review of the Israel Medical Association (*Mif'al Haverut Hutz*—Non-resident Fellowship of the Israel Medical Association): 39 Shaul Hamelekh Blvd., Tel-Aviv; English; also published in French and Spanish; quarterly; Editor Dr. V. RESNEKOV.

Refuah Veterinarit: P.O.B. 18, Beit Dagan; f. 1943; quarterly review of veterinary medicine; Editor Dr. A. HADANI.

La Revue de l'A.M.I. (Non-resident Fellowship of the Israeli Medical Association): 39 Shaul Hamelekh Blvd., Tel-Aviv; French, English and Spanish; quarterly; Editor Dr. S. ZALUD.

Scopus: Hebrew University of Jerusalem; f. 1946; published by Department of Information and Public Affairs, Hebrew University of Jerusalem; yearly; English; Editor D. GETZLER.

The Sea: P.O.B. 33706, Haifa; f. 1978; shipping monthly; English and Hebrew; Man. Dir. E. GLASER; circ. 5,000.

Shituf (*Co-operation*): 24 Ha'arba St., Tel-Aviv, P.O.B. 7151; f. 1948; bi-monthly; economic, social and co-operative problems in Israel; published by the Central Union of Industrial, Transport and Service Co-operative Societies; Editor L. LOSH; circ. 12,000.

Sinai: P.O.B. 642, Jerusalem; f. 1937; Torah, science and literature; Editor Dr. YITZCHAK RAPHAEL.

Sindibad: P.O.B. 28049, Tel-Aviv; f. 1970; children's monthly; Editors WALID HUSSEIN, JAMIL DAHLAN; circ. 10,000.

Sulam: 2 Ben Yehuda St., Jerusalem; political; monthly; Editor Dr. ISRAEL ELDAD.

Terra Santa: P.O.B. 186, Jerusalem; f. 1921; monthly; published by the Custody of the Holy Land (the official custodians of the Holy Shrines); Italian, Spanish, French, English and Arabic editions published in Jerusalem, by the Franciscan Printing Press, German edition in Vienna, Maltese edition in Valletta.

Tmuroth: 48 Hamelech George St., P.O.B. 23076, Tel-Aviv; f. 1960; organ of the Liberal Labour Movement; monthly; Editor D. SHLOMI.

Urim La-Orim: 93 Arlosoroff St., P.O.B. 303, Tel-Aviv; educational problems in the family; monthly; published by the Histadrut; Editor HAYIM NAGID.

Vilner Pinkas: P.O.B. 28006, Tel-Aviv; f. 1968; periodical review of current affairs for Vilna-Jews the world over, and for the history of Yerushdayim Delito; Yiddish; Editor M. KARPINOVITZ.

WIZO Review: Women's International Zionist Organization, 38 Sderoth David Hamelekh, Tel-Aviv; English, Spanish and German editions; Editor SYLVIA SATTEN BANIN; circ. 20,000.

Yam: Israeli Maritime League, P.O.B. 706, 5 Habankim St., Haifa; f. 1937; review of marine problems; Editor Z. ESHEL; Pres. MOSHE M. POMROCK; circ. 5,500.

Zion: P.O.B. 4179, Jerusalem; f. 1935; research in Jewish history; twice yearly; Hebrew and English; Editors I. F. BAER, S. ETTINGER, M. STERN.

Zraim: 7 Dubnov St., P.O.B. 40027, Tel-Aviv; f. 1953; journal of the Bnei Akiva (Youth of Hapoel Hamizrachi) Movement; Editor AMNON SHPIRA.

Zrakor: 37 Harbour St., Haifa; f. 1947; monthly; Hebrew; news digest, trade, finance, economics, shipping; Editor G. ALON.

The following are all published by Weizmann Science Press Israel, P.O.B. 801, Jerusalem 91000; Exec. Editor L. LESTER.

Israel Journal of Botany: f. 1951; Editor Prof. MOSHE NEGBI; quarterly.

Israel Journal of Chemistry: f. 1951; Editor Prof. S. SAREL, quarterly.

Israel Journal of Earth-Sciences: f. 1951; Editor Y. WEILER; quarterly.

Israel Journal of Mathematics: f. 1951; Editors S. A. AMITSUR, H. FURSTENBERG; monthly, 3 vols. of 4 issues each per year.

Israel Journal of Technology: f. 1951; Editor Prof. D. ABIR, 6 issues per year.

Israel Journal of Zoology: f. 1951; Editor Prof. Y. L. WERNER; quarterly.

Journal d'Analyse Mathématique: f. 1955; Editor Prof. S. AGMON; 2 vols. per year.

PUBLISHERS' ASSOCIATION

Daily Newspaper Publishers' Association of Israel: P.O.B. 2251, 4 Kaplan St., Tel-Aviv; safeguards professional interests and maintains standards, supplies newsprint to dailies; negotiates with trade unions, etc.; mems. all daily papers; affiliated to International Federation of Newspaper Publishers.

NEWS AGENCIES

Jewish Telegraphic Agency (JTA): Israel Bureau, Jerusalem Post Building, Romema, Jerusalem 94467; Dir. DAVID LANDAU.

ITIM, News Agency of the Associated Israel Press: 10 Tiomkin St., Tel-Aviv; f. 1950; co-operative news agency; Dir. and Editor ALTER WELNER.

FOREIGN BUREAUX

Agence France-Presse: 7 Schderot Khen, Tel-Aviv; Chief EROL GUINEY.

Agencia EFE (*Spain*): Hasoreg 2, Binlan Gad Hajadash Bldg., Jerusalem; Correspondent ELIAS SAMUEL SCHERBACOVSKY.

Agenzia Nazionale Stampa Associata (ANSA) (*Italy*): P.O.B. 21342, Tel-Aviv; Bureau Chief FABIO CANNILLO.

Associated Press (AP) (*U.S.A.*): 49 Petah Tikva Rd., Tel-Aviv; Chief of Bureau FRANK CREPEAU.

Deutsche Presse-Agentur (dpa) (*Federal Republic of Germany*): P.O.B. 33 189, Tel-Aviv; Correspondents GEORG SPIEKER and GIDEON BERLI.

Middle East Bureau: Jerusalem Post Bldg. Jerusalem, 94 467.

Reuters (*U.K.*): 8 Bilu Street, Tel-Aviv.

United Press International (UPI) (*U.S.A.*): 138 Petah Tikva Rd., Tel-Aviv; Bureau Man. RICHARD C. GROSS.

The following are also represented: North American Newspaper Alliance, Tass.

PUBLISHERS

Achiasaf Ltd.: 13 Yosef Hanassi St., Tel-Aviv; f. 1933; general; Man. Dir. SCHACHNA ACHIASAF.

Am Hassefer Ltd.: 9 Bialik St., Tel-Aviv; f. 1955; Man. Dir. DOV LIPETZ.

"Am Oved" Ltd.: 22 Mazah St., P.O.B. 470, Tel-Aviv; f. 1942; fiction, biography, history, social science; reference books, school and university textbooks, technical and professional works, juvenile; Man. Dir. DOV GORFUNG.

Amichai Publishing House Ltd.: 5 Yosef Hanassi St., Tel-Aviv; f. 1948; Man. Dir. YEHUDA ORLINSKY.

Arabic Publishing House: 17A Hagra St., P.O.B. 28049, Tel-Aviv; f. 1960; established by the Histadrut (trade union) organization; periodicals and books; Dir. JOSEF ELIAHU; Editor-in-Chief IBRAHIM M. IBRAHIM.

Bialik Institute, The: P.O.B. 92, Jerusalem; f. 1935; classics, encyclopaedias, criticism, history, archaeology, art, reference books, Judaica; Dir. CHAIM MILKOV.

Carta, The Israel Map and Publishing Co. Ltd.: Yad Haruzim St., P.O.B. 2500, Jerusalem 91020; f. 1958; the principal cartographic publisher; Man. Dir. EMANUEL HAUSMAN.

Dvir Publishing Co. Ltd., The: 58 Mazah St., P.O.B. 149, Tel-Aviv; f. 1924; literature, science, art, education; Man. Dir. ALEXANDER BROIDO.

Eked Publishing House: 29 Bar-Kochba St., Tel-Aviv; f. 1959; poetry; Dirs. ITAMAR YAOZ-KEST, MARITZA ROSMAN.

Encyclopedia Publishing Co.: 46 Beit Lehem Rd., Jerusalem; f. 1947; Hebrew Encyclopedia and other Encyclopedias; Chair. Mrs. BRACHA PELI, ALEXANDER PELI.

Rodney Franklin Agency: 5 Karl Netter St., P.O.B. 37727, Tel-Aviv; exclusive representative of various British and U.S.A. publishers; Dir. RODNEY FRANKLIN.

Gazit: 8 Zvi Brook St., Tel-Aviv, P.O.B. 4190; art publishers; Editor GABRIEL TALPHIR.

Haifa Publishing Co. Ltd.: c/o P.O.B. 4044, Jerusalem; f. 1960; fiction and non-fiction.

Hakibbutz Hameuchad Publishing House Ltd.: P.O.B. 16040, 15 Nehardea St., Tel-Aviv; f. 1940; general; Dir. A. AVISHAI.

Hamenorah Publishing House: 24 Zangwill St., Tel-Aviv; f. 1958; books in Hebrew, Yiddish and English; Dir. MORDECHAI SONNSCHEIN.

Israeli Music Publications Ltd.: 105 Ben Yehuda St., P.O.B. 6011, Tel-Aviv; f. 1949; books on music and musical works; Dir. Dr. PETER E. GRADENWITZ.

Izre'el Publishing House Ltd.: 76 Dizengoff St., Tel-Aviv; f. 1933; Man. ALEXANDER IZREEL.

Jerusalem Academic Press: Givat Shaul, P.O.B. 3640, Jerusalem; f. 1959; scientific and technical publications; Gen. Man. LARRY LESTER.

Jerusalem Publishing House: 39 Tchernechovski St., Jerusalem, P.O.B. 7147; f. 1967; history, encyclopaedias, archaeology, art and other reference books; Dir. SHLOMO S. GAFNI.

Jewish Agency Publishing Department: P.O.B. 704; Jerusalem; f. 1945; Palestinology, Judaism, scientific, classics, and publicity brochures; Dir. M. SPITZER.

Karni Publishers Ltd.: 58 Maze St., P.O.B. 149, Tel-Aviv; f. 1951; children's and educational books; Dir. ALEXANDER BROIDO.

Keter Publishing House Jerusalem Ltd.: P.O.B. 7145, Givat Shaul B, Jerusalem; f. 1959; original and translated works in all fields of science and humanities, published in English, French, German, other European languages and Hebrew; publishing imprints: Israel Program for Scientific Translations, Israel Universities Press, Keter Books, Encyclopedia Judaica; Man. Dir. ELIAV COHEN.

Kiryath Sepher: 15 Arlosorov St., Jerusalem; f. 1933; dictionaries, textbooks, maps, scientific books; Dir. SHALOM SIVAN (STEPANSKY).

Koren Publishers Jerusalem Ltd.: P.O.B. 4044, Jerusalem; Bible, religion and Judaism.

Lewin-Epstein Ltd.: 9 Yavneh St., Tel-Aviv; f. 1930; general fiction, education, science; Man. Dir. ABRAHAM GOTTESMANN.

Magnes Press, The: The Hebrew University, Jerusalem; f. 1929; biblical studies, judaica, and all academic fields; Dir. BEN-ZION D. YEHOSHUA.

Massada Press Ltd.: 21 Jabotinsky Rd., Ramat Gan; f. 1932; encyclopedias, judaica, the arts, educational material; Chair. ALEXANDER PELI.

Ministry of Defence Publishing House: Hakiriya, Tel-Aviv; f. 1939; military literature; Dir. SHALOM SERI.

M. Mizrachi Publishers: 67 Levinsky, Tel-Aviv; f. 1960; children's books, novels; Dir. MEIR MIZRACHI.

Mosad Harav Kook: P.O.B. 642, Jerusalem; editions of classical works, Torah and Jewish studies; Dir. Rabbi M. KATZENELENBOGEN.

Otsar Hamoreh: 8 Ben Saruk, Tel-Aviv; f. 1951; educational; Dir. MENACHEM LEVANON.

I. L. Peretz: 31 Allenby Rd., Tel-Aviv; f. 1956; mainly books in Yiddish; Man. Dir. MOSHE GERSHONOWITZ.

Rubin Mass: 11 Marcus St., P.O.B. 990, Jerusalem; f. 1927; Hebraica, Judaica; Dir. RUBIN MASS.

Schocken Publishing House Ltd.: P.O.B. 2316, Tel-Aviv; f. 1938; general; Dir. Mrs. RACHELI EDELMAN.

Shikmona Publishing Co. Ltd.: P.O.B. 4044, Jerusalem; Zionism, archaeology, art, fiction and non-fiction.

Sifriat-Ma'ariv Ltd.: Dereh Petah Tikva 72A, Tel-Aviv; f. 1954; Publisher and Editor-in-Chief NAFTALI ARBEL.

Sifriat Poalim Ltd.: 73 Allenby St., P.O.B. 526, Tel-Aviv 65-171; f. 1939; textbooks; Gen. Man. YAAKOV ZVIELI.

Sinai Publishing Co.: 72 Allenby Rd., Tel-Aviv; Hebrew books and religious articles; Dir. AKNAH SCHLESINGER.

Tarbut Ve'Hinuch Publishers: 93 Arlozorov St., Tel-Aviv; f. 1956; educational; Man. IZAAK KOTUNSKY.

Tarhish Books: P.O.B. 4130, 91-040 Jerusalem; f. 1940; plays, poetry, bibliophile, classics; Man. Dir. Dr. MOSHE SPITZER.

Weizmann Science Press of Israel: 8A Horkanya St., P.O.B. 801, Jerusalem 91000; f. 1955; publishes scientific books and periodicals; Man. Dir. RAMI MICHAELI; Exec. Editor L. LESTER.

Yachdav United Publishers Co. Ltd.: 29 Carlebach St., P.O.B. 20123, Tel-Aviv; f. 1960; educational; Chair. MORDECHAI BERNSTEIN; Dir. BENJAMIN SELLA.

Yavneh Ltd.: 4 Mazeh St., Tel-Aviv; f. 1932; general; Dir. AVSHALOM ORENSTEIN.

S. Zack and Co.: 2 King George St., Jerusalem; f. *c.* 1930; reference books, textbooks, dictionaries, judaica, children's books; Dirs. DAVID and MICHAEL ZACK.

Israel Book Publishers Association: 29 Carlebach St., P.O.B. 20123, Tel-Aviv; f. 1939; mems.: 79 publishing firms; Pres. MORDECHAI BERNSTEIN; Exec. Dir. BENJAMIN SELLA.

Jerusalem International Book Fair: 22 Jaffa Rd., Jerusalem 91000; f. 1961; takes place biennially; 52 countries were represented in 1977; Exec. Dir. GERSHON POLAK; Deputy Dir. DINA SHAPIRA.

RADIO AND TELEVISION

RADIO

Israel Broadcasting Authority (I.B.A.): 21 Heleni Hamalka, P.O.B. 7139, Jerusalem; f. 1948; station, Jerusalem with additional studios in Tel-Aviv and Haifa; Dir.-Gen. Y. LIVNI. I.B.A. broadcasts five programmes for local and overseas listeners on medium, shortwave and VHF/FM in thirteen languages; Hebrew, Arabic, English, Yiddish, Ladino, Romanian, Hungarian, Moghrabit, Persian, French, Russian, Georgian and Spanish.

Number of radio receivers: 750,000 (1978/79).

Galei Zahal: A.P.O. 81005, Zakal; f. 1951; Army broadcasting station, Tel-Aviv with studios in Jerusalem; broadcasts one programme on medium wave in Hebrew.

TELEVISION

Israel Broadcasting Authority (I.B.A.): broadcasts began in 1968; station in Jerusalem with additional studios in Tel-Aviv; Dir.-Gen. Y. LIVNI; one black and white network (VHF with UHF available in some areas); broadcasts in Hebrew and Arabic.

Instructional Television Centre: Ministry of Education and Culture, 14 Klausner St., Tel-Aviv; f. 1963 by Hanadiv (Rothschild Memorial Group) as Instructional Television Trust; began transmission in 1966; now broadcasts on a national scale to 1,300 schools with 540,000 pupils, 85 per cent of the elementary school population and 60 per cent of the high school population; the programmes form an integral part of the syllabus in a wide range of subjects; also adult education; Gen. Man. YA'AKOV LORBERBAUM.

Number of TV receivers: 465,000 (1978/79).

FINANCE

BANKING

cap.=capital; p.u.=paid up; dep.=deposits; m.=million; I£=Israeli £; brs.=branches.)

CENTRAL BANK

Bank of Israel: Mizpeh Bldg., 29 Jaffa Rd., Jerusalem P.O.B. 780; f. 1954 as the Central Bank of the State of Israel; cap. I£10m., reserves I£10m., dep I£98,634m. (Dec. 1978); Gov. ARNON GAFNY; Dep. Gov. and Dir.-Gen. Dr. E. SHEFFER; Dep. Gov. Dr. Z. SUSSMAN; Mans. J. SARIG, M. MEIRAV, S. PELED, O. MESSER, A. LOZOWICK, D. WAINSHAL; 2 brs.

ISRAELI BANKS

American Israel Bank Ltd.: 9-11 Rothschild Blvd., Tel-Aviv; f. 1975 as a result of a merger between Japhet Bank Ltd. and Exchange National Bank of Chicago; cap. I£30.8m.; dep. I£2,797m. (Dec. 1977); Chair. E. REINER; Man. Dir. A. GEVA; 18 brs.

Arab Israel Bank Ltd.: 14 Hatishim Veshalosh St., Haifa; subsidiary of Bank Leumi le-Israel B.M.; f. 1959 to serve primarily the Arab sector of the economy; cap. p.u. I£3.5m., dep. I£132.2m. (Dec. 1974); Chair. J. ROSH; Gen. Man. E. ASHKENAZI

Bank Hapoalim B.M.: 50 Rothschild Blvd., Tel-Aviv; f. 1921; cap. p.u. I£2,971.4m., dep. I£105,255m. (Dec. 1977); Chair. J. LEVINSON; Man. Dirs. E. REINER, B. RABINOW, M. OLENIK.

Bank Kupat-Am Le-Israel Ltd.: 13 Ahad Ha'am St., Tel-Aviv; f. 1918; subsidiary of Bank Leumi le-Israel B.M.; cap. I£4m.; reserves I£9.6m.; Chair B. YEKUTIELI; Man. Dir. M. OSTFELD; 17 brs.

Bank Lemelacha Ltd.: 18 Shoken St., Tel-Aviv; f. 1953; cap. p.u. I£66.6m.; dep. I£518.5m. (Dec. 1977); Chair. B. WINE; Man. Dir. Y. GAL'ON.

Bank Leumi le-Israel B.M.: 24–32 Yehuda Halevy St., Tel-Aviv; f. 1902; total capital funds I£5,687m.; dep. I£142,329m. (June 1978); Chair. and Chief Exec. E. I. JAPHET; 353 brs.; publ. *Review of Economic Conditions in Israel* (quarterly).

First International Bank of Israel Ltd.: Shalom Mayer Tower, 9 Ahad Ha'am St., P.O.B. 29036, Tel-Aviv; f. 1972 as a result of a merger between The Foreign Trade Bank Ltd. and Export Bank Ltd.; cap. p.u. I£311.6m.; dep. I£9,539m. (Dec. 1977); Chair. of Board MARK MOSEVICS; Man. Dir. DAVID GOLAN; 60 brs.

Industrial Development Bank of Israel Ltd.: 2 Dafna St., Tel Aviv; cap. I£360.8m.; dep. I£9,159m. (Dec. 1977); Chair. A. FRIEDMANN.

Israel Ampal Industrial Development Bank Ltd.: 5 Druyanov St., Tel-Aviv; f. 1956; cap. p.u. I£12m.; dep. I£1,591m. (Dec. 1978); Chair. M. OLENIK; Gen. Mans. M. BACHAR, R. COHEN.

Israel Bank of Agriculture Ltd.: 83 Hashmonayim St., Tel-Aviv; f. 1951; cap. p.u. I£371m., dep. I£3,674m. (March 1978); Chair. A. BRUM; Man. Dir. D. CALDERON.

Israel Continental Bank Ltd.: 70 Ibn Gvirol St., Tel-Aviv; f. 1973; capital held jointly by Bank Hapoalim B.M. and Bank für Gemeinwirtschaft A.G.; cap. p.u. I£52.6m.; dep. I£1,582.9m. (Dec. 1977); Chair. Dr. WALTER HESSELBACH.

Israel Discount Bank Ltd.: 27–31 Yehuda Halevy St., Tel-Aviv; f. 1935 as Palestine Discount Bank Ltd.; cap. p.u. I£455m.; dep. I£101,610m. (Dec. 1978); Chair. DANIEL RECANATI; 240 brs. including sub-brs.

Israel General Bank Ltd.: 28 Ahad Ha'am St., Tel-Aviv; f. 1964; cap. p.u. I£15.7m., dep. I£1,278.4m. (Dec. 1977); Chair. Baron EDMOND DE ROTHSCHILD; Man. Dir. DAVID SHOHAM; 3 brs.

Israel Industrial Bank Ltd.: 13 Montefiore St., Tel-Aviv; f. 1933; cap. I£8.2m., total resources I£366.1m. (Dec. 1974); Chair. A. FROMCENKO; Man. Dir. A. D. KIMCHI; 9 brs.

Israel Loan and Savings Bank Ltd.: 21 Herzl St., Tel-Aviv; cap. I£10.3m.; Chair. E. AVEYNON; Man. Dir. I. GAFNI.

Mercantile Bank of Israel Ltd.: P.O.B. 512, 24 Rothschild Blvd., Tel-Aviv; f. 1924; subsidiary of Barclays Discount Bank; cap. p.u. I£6m.; dep. I£399.4m. (Dec. 1977); Chair. DANIEL RECANATI; Gen. Man. SHLOMO MAGRISO.

Union Bank of Israel Ltd.: 6–8 Ahuzat Bayit St., P.O.B. 2428, Tel-Aviv; f. 1951; subsidiary of Bank Leumi le-Israel B.M.; cap. p.u. I£519m., dep. I£21,971.2m. (Dec. 1978); Chair. E. I. JAPHET; Man. Dir. M. M. MAYER; Gen. Man. S. SOROKER; 23 brs.

United Mizrahi Bank Ltd.: 48 Lilienblum St., Tel-Aviv; f. 1923; cap. p.u. I£150m., dep. I£9,429m. (Dec. 1977); Chair. N. FEINGOLD; Man. Dir. A. MEIR; 60 brs.

MORTGAGE BANKS

General Mortgage Bank Ltd.: 13 Ahad Ha'am St., Tel-Aviv; f. 1921; subsidiary of Bank Leumi le-Israel B.M.; cap. p.u. I£152.2m., dep. I£3,008m. (Dec. 1978); Chair. S. TULCHINSKY; Man. Dir. Z. BIRNBAUM.

Housing Mortgage Bank Ltd.: 2 Kaplan St., Tel-Aviv; f. 1950; subsidiary of Bank Hapoalim B.M.; cap. p.u. I£62.9m., dep. I£1,843m. (Dec. 1977); Chair. Y. RAVIN; Dir. and Gen. Man. U. VARDY-ZER.

Israel Development and Mortgage Bank Ltd.: 16 Simtat Beit Hashoeva, Tel-Aviv; f. 1959; subsidiary of Israel Discount Bank Ltd.; Chair. M. B. GITTER; Man. Dir. K. REICH.

Tefahot, Israel Mortgage Bank Ltd.: 9 Heleni Hamalka St., Jerusalem; f. 1945; cap. and reserves I£439m.; total assets I£8,361m.; Man. Dir. MOSHE MANN. *Affiliated Bank:* **Carmel Mortgage and Investment Bank Ltd.,** 207 Hameginim Blvd., Haifa.

Unico Investment Co. Ltd.: 30 Yavneh St., Tel-Aviv; f. 1961.

FOREIGN BANKS

Barclays Discount Bank Ltd.: 103 Allenby Rd., Tel-Aviv; f. 1971 in association with Israel Discount Bank Ltd.; incorporating former brs. of Barclays Bank International Ltd.; cap. p.u. I£303m.; Chair. DANIEL RECANATI; Gen. Man. GIDEON LAHAV; 63 brs. *Affiliated Bank:* **Mercantile Bank of Israel Ltd.,** 24 Rothschild Blvd., Tel-Aviv.

STOCK EXCHANGE

Tel-Aviv Stock Exchange: 113 Allenby Rd.; Chair. Dr. M. HETH; Exec. Dir. D. OTENSOOSER; publs. *Official Quotations* (daily, monthly, annually), *Bond Guide* (quarterly) and *Stock Guide* (annually).

INSURANCE

Ararat Insurance Company Ltd.: Ararat House, 32 Yavneh St., Tel-Aviv; f. 1949; Man. Dir. PHILIP ZUCKERMAN.

Aryeh Insurance Co. Ltd.: Shalom Tower, Tel-Aviv; f. 1948; Chair. AVINOAM M. TOCATLY.

Hassneh Insurance Co. of Israel Ltd.: 115 Allenby St., P.O.B. 805, Tel-Aviv; f. 1929; Man. Dir. EITAN AVNEYON.

Israel Phoenix Assurance Company Ltd., The: 30 Levontin St., Tel-Aviv; f. 1949; Chair. of Board DAVID J. HACKMEY; Man. Dir. JOSEPH D. HACKMEY.

Israel Reinsurance Company Ltd., The: 5 Drujanov St., P.O.B. 11589, Tel-Aviv; f. 1951; Chair. Board of Dirs., Dr. J. GRUENGARD; Gen. Man. S. JANNAI.

Maoz Insurance Co. Ltd.: 26 Se'adya Gaon St., Tel-Aviv; f. 1945; formerly Binyan Insurance Co. Ltd.; Chair. B. YEKUTIELI.

Mazada Insurance Service Ltd.: 3 Ahuzat Bait St., Tel-Aviv; f. 1932; Mans. A. SPIGELMAN, M.A., M. SPIGELMAN, L.L.M.

Menorah Insurance Company Ltd.: Menorah House, 73 Rothschild Blvd., Tel-Aviv; f. 1935; Gen. Man. DAVID HIRSCHFELD.

Migdal-Binyan Insurance Co. Ltd.: 26 Se'adya Gaon St., Tel-Aviv; f. 1934; Chair. B. YEKUTIELI; Vice-Chair. Dr. Y. GRUENGARD; Gen. Man. A. ROM.

Palglass Palestine Plate Glass Insurance Co. Ltd.: 30 Achad Ha'am St., Tel-Aviv; f. 1934; Gen. Man. AKIVA ZALZMAN.

Sahar Insurance Company Ltd.: Sahar House. 23 Ben-Yehuda St., Tel-Aviv 63806, P.O.B. 26222; f. 1949; Chair. and Man. Dir. A. SACHAROV.

Samson Insurance Co. Ltd.: 27 Montefiore St., P.O.B. 29277, Tel-Aviv; f. 1933; Chair. A. AVNION.

Sela Insurance Co. Ltd.: 13 Achad Haam St., Tel-Aviv; f. 1938; Gen. Man. E. SHANI.

Shiloah Company Ltd.: 2 Pinsker St., Tel-Aviv; f. 1933; Gen. Man. Dr. S. BAMIRAH; Man. Mme BAMIRAH.

Yardenia Insurance Company Ltd.: 22 Maze St., Tel-Aviv; f. 1948; Man. Dir. H. LEBANON.

Yuval Insurance Co. Ltd.: 27 Keren Hayesod, Jerusalem; f. 1962; Man. Dir. J. KAPLAN.

Zigug Glass Insurance Co. Ltd.: 34 Sheinkin St., Tel-Aviv; f. 1952; Chair. D. HIRSCHFELD.

Zion Insurance Company Ltd.: 120 Allenby Rd., Tel-Aviv; f. 1935; Chair. HAIM TAIBER.

THE HISTADRUT

Hahistadrut Haklalit shel Haovdim Beeretz Israel, 93 Arlosoroff St., Tel-Aviv

(GENERAL FEDERATION OF LABOUR IN ISRAEL)

Secretary-General: YERUHAM MESHEL.

The General Federation of Labour in Israel, usually known as the Histadrut, is the largest voluntary organization in Israel, and the most important economic body in the State. It is open to all workers, including members of co-operatives and of the liberal professions, who join directly as individuals. The Histadrut engages in four main fields of activity: trade union organization; economic development; social insurance based on mutual aid; and educational and cultural activities. Dues—3.9 per cent of wages (up to I£6,000 per month)—cover all its trade union, health and social services activities. The Histadrut was founded in 1920.

ORGANIZATION

In 1978 the Histadrut had a membership of 1,575,000, including over 160,000 in collective, co-operative and private villages (*kibbutzim* and *moshavim*) affiliated through the Agricultural Workers' Union, and 390,000 wives (who have membership status); 125,000 of the members were Arabs. In addition some 110,000 young people under 18 years of age belong to the Organization of Working and Student Youth, a direct affiliate of the Histadrut. The main religious labour organizations, *Histadrut Hapoel Hamizrahi* and *Histadrut Poalei Agudat Israel*, belong to the trade union section and welfare services, which thus extend to 90 per cent of all workers in Israel.

All members take part in elections to the Histadrut

Convention (*Veida*), which elects the General Council (*Moetsa*) and the Executive Committee (*Vaad Hapoel*). The latter elects the 32-member Executive Bureau (*Vaada Merakezet*), which is responsible for day-to-day implementation of policy. The Executive Committee also elects the Secretary-General, who acts as its chairman as well as head of the organization as a whole and chairman of the Executive Bureau. Nearly all political parties are represented on the Histadrut Executive Committee. Throughout Israel there are 68 local Labour Councils.

The Executive Committee has the following departments: Trade Union, Arab Affairs, Mutual Security Centre, Organization, International, Finance, Legal, Employment, Vocational Training, Absorption and Development, Academic Workers, Culture and Education, Institute of Economic and Social Research, Diaspora Communities, Youth and Sport, Consumers' Authority, Industrial Democracy, Religious Affairs and Higher Education.

TRADE UNION ACTIVITIES

Collective agreements with employers fix wage scales, which are linked with the retail price index; provide for social benefits, including paid sick leave and employers' contributions to sick and pension and provident funds; and regulate dismissals. Dismissal compensation is regulated by law. The Histadrut actively promotes productivity through labour management boards and the National Productivity Institute, and supports incentive pay schemes.

There are unions for the following groups: clerical workers, building workers, teachers, engineers, agricultural workers, technicians, textile workers, printing workers, diamond workers, metal workers, food and bakery workers, wood workers, government employees, seamen, nurses, civilian employees of the armed forces, actors, musicians and variety artists, social workers, watchmen, cinema technicians, institutional and school staffs, pharmacy employees, medical laboratory workers, X-ray technicians, physiotherapists, social scientists, microbiologists, psychologists, salaried lawyers, pharmacists, physicians, occupational therapists, truck and taxi drivers, hotel and restaurant workers, workers in Histadrut-owned industry, garment, shoe and leather workers, plastic and rubber workers, editors of periodicals, painters and sculptors and industrial workers.

ECONOMIC ACTIVITIES AND SOCIAL SERVICES

These include *Hevrat Ovdim* (Economic Sector, employing 260,000 workers in 1978), *Kupat Holim* (the Sick Fund, covering almost 70 per cent of Israel's population), seven pension funds, and *NA'AMAT* (women's organization which runs nursery homes and kindergartens, organizes vocational education and promotes legislation for the protection and benefit of working women).

TRADE AND INDUSTRY

CHAMBERS OF COMMERCE

Federation of Israeli Chambers of Commerce: P.O.B. 501, Tel-Aviv; co-ordinates the Tel-Aviv, Jerusalem, Haifa and Beersheba Chambers of Commerce; Dir. ZVI AMIT.

Jerusalem Chamber of Commerce: P.O.B. 183, Jerusalem 91000; f. 1908; about 300 mems.; Pres. M. H. ELIACHAR; Vice-Pres. CH. COHEN, A. DASKAL, SH. P. DORON, Y. PEARLMAN, M. YANOWSKI; publ. *Bulletin* (Hebrew and English).

Haifa Chamber of Commerce and Industry *(Haifa and District)*: P.O.B. 33176, 53 Haatzmaut Rd., Haifa; f. 1921; 700 mems.; Pres. EMANUEL GORALI; Gen. Sec. A. MEHOULAL.

Chamber of Commerce, Tel-Aviv-Jaffa: P.O.B. 501, 84 Hachashmonaim St., Tel-Aviv; f. 1919; 1,500 mems.; Pres. AVNER BEN-YAKAR; Dir.-Gen. ZVI AMIT; Secs. J. FEINER, Z. SEGAI, J. SHOSTAK, F. B. WAHLE,; publ. *Economy and Trade.*

Federation of Bi-National Chambers of Commerce with and in Israel: 99 Ahad Haam St., Tel-Aviv, P.O.B. 1127; federates: Israel-America Chamber of Commerce and Industry; Anglo-Israel Chamber of Commerce; Australia-Israel Chamber of Commerce; Chamber of Commerce and Industry Israel-Africa; Chamber of Commerce Israel-Belgique-Luxembourg; Canada-Israel Chamber of Commerce and Industry; Israel-Danish Chamber of Commerce; Chambre de Commerce Israel-France; Chamber of Commerce and Industry Israel-Germany; Camera di Commercio Israeli-Italia; Israel-Japan Chamber of Commerce; Israel-Latin America, Spain and Portugal Chamber of Commerce; Netherlands-Israel Chamber of Commerce; Israel-Norway Chamber of Commerce; Handelskammer Israel-Schweiz; Israel-South Africa Chamber of Commerce; Israel-Sweden Chamber of Commerce; Pres. A. CHELOUCHE; Exec. Dir. H. ZUCKERMAN, O.B.E.; and also incorporates Bi-National Chamber of Commerce existing in 20 foreign countries with Israel.

Anglo-Israel Chamber of Commerce (Israel): 99 Ahad Haam St., Tel-Aviv, P.O.B. 1127; f. 1951; 420 mems.; Hon. Pres. Dr. A. S. ARNON, C.B.E., A. S. COHEN, C.B.E., E. IZAKSON, C.B.E.; Chair. A. SACHAROV.

TRADE AND INDUSTRIAL ORGANIZATIONS

The Agricultural Union: Tchlenov 20, Tel-Aviv; consists of more than 50 agricultural settlements and is connected with marketing and supplying organizations, and Bahan Ltd., controllers and auditors.

Central Union of Artisans and Small Manufacturers: P.O.B. 4041, Tel-Aviv; f. 1907; has a membership of 40,000 divided into 70 groups according to trade; the union is led by a seventeen-man Presidium; Chair. JACOB FRANK; Gen. Sec. PINHAS SCHWARTZ; publ. *Hamlakha;* 30 brs.

Citrus Control and Marketing Boards: 69 Haifa Rd., P.O.B. 2590, Tel-Aviv; the government-established institution for the control of the Israel citrus industry; Boards made up of representatives of the Government and the Growers. Functions: control of plantations, supervision of picking and packing operations, marketing of the crop overseas and on the home markets; shipping; supply of fertilizers, insecticides, equipment for orchards and packing houses and of packing materials, technical research and extension work; long-term financial assistance to growers.

Farmers' Union of Israel: P.O.B. 209, Tel-Aviv; f. 1913; membership of 7,000 independent farmers, citrus and winegrape growers; Pres. E. IZAKSON; Chair. Council IZCHAK-ZIV-AV; Dir.-Gen. SHLOMO REISMAN; publ. *The Israeli Farmer, Journal.*

General Association of Merchants in Israel: 6 Rothschild Boulevard, Tel-Aviv; the organization of retail traders; has a membership of 30,000 in 60 brs.

Israel Diamond Exchange Ltd.: P.O.B. 3222, Ramat Gan; f. 1937; production, export, import and finance facilities; estimated exports (1978) U.S. $1,500m.

Israel Journalists' Association Ltd.: 4 Kaplan St., Tel-Aviv; Sec. MOSHE RON.

Manufacturers' Association of Israel: 13 Montefiore St., P.O.B. 29116, Tel-Aviv; Pres. AVRAHAM (BUMA) SHAVIT; Gen. Man. Col. PELEG TAMIR.

TRADE UNIONS

Histadrut Haovdim Haleumit (*National Labour Federation*): 23 Sprinczak St., Tel-Aviv; f. 1934; 100,000 mems.; publ. *Lapid*.

Histadrut Hapoel Hamizrahi (*National Religious Workers' Party*): 166 Even Gavirol St., Tel-Aviv; 125,000 mems. in 81 settlements.

Histadrut Poalei Agudat Israel (*Agudat Israel Workers' Organization*): Geula Quarter, Corner Yehezkel St., Jerusalem; has 19,000 members in 12 settlements.

TRANSPORT

RAILWAYS

Israel State Railways: Central Station, P.O.B. 44, Haifa; all lines are managed and operated from Haifa. The total length of main line is 550 km.; gauge 1,435 mm.

Freight traffic consists mainly of grain, phosphates, potash, containers, oil and building materials. Rail service serves Haifa and Ashdod, ports on the Mediterranean Sea, while a combined rail-road service extends to Eilat port on the Red Sea. A rail link from Dimona to Eilat is planned. Passenger services operate between the main towns: Nahariya, Haifa, Tel-Aviv, Jerusalem, Beersheba and Dimona.

Gen. Man. ZVI TSAFRIRI; Deputy Gen. Man. I. BAR-ILAN; Deputy Gen. Man. (Admin.) L. HEYMAN.

UNDERGROUND RAILWAYS

Haifa Underground Funicular Railway: 12 Hanassi Ave., Haifa; opened 1959; 2 km. in operation; Man. D. SCHARF.

Tel-Aviv Metropolitan Area Rapid Transit: 3 Eliashberg St., Tel-Aviv; a feasibility study has been made on the possibility of building a 60 km. rapid transit line (8 km. underground).

ROADS

Ministry of Labour, Public Works Dept., Jerusalem.

There are 3,700 km. of metalled main roads not including roads in towns and settlements.

Automobile and Touring Club of Israel (MEMSI): 19 Petah Tiqva Rd., P.O.B. 36144, Tel-Aviv 61630; f. 1949; over 20,000 mems.; Sec.-Gen. B. YACOBI; publ. *Memsi* (bi-monthly).

SHIPPING

The Israel Ports Authority: Maya Building, 74 Petah Tiqva Rd., Tel-Aviv; f. 1961; to plan, build, develop, administer, maintain and operate the ports. In 1979/80 investment will amount to I£776m. for the Development Budget in Haifa, Ashdod and Eilat Ports. Cargo traffic in 1978/79 amounted to 10.7m. tons (oil excluded).

ZIM Israel Navigation Co. Ltd.: 7–9 Palyam Ave., P.O.B. 1723, Haifa; f. 1945; runs cargo services in the Mediterranean and to N. Europe, N. and S. America, Far East, Africa and Australia; operates 50 ships totalling 2m. d.w.t.; Chair. H. STOESSEL; Man. Dir. Y. ROTHEM.

Cargo Ships "El-Yam" Ltd.: 22 Shalom Aleichem St., P.O.B. 3169, Tel-Aviv; f. 1952; Chair. and Joint Man. Dir. RAPHAEL RECANATI; a world-wide cargo tramp service.

Haifa and Ashdod are the main ports in Israel. The former is a natural harbour, enclosed by two main breakwaters and dredged to 37 ft. below mean sea-level. An auxiliary harbour was opened in 1955. In 1965 the new deep water port was completed at Ashdod which has a capacity of about 4 million tons per year.

In 1977 Israel had a merchant fleet of 105 ships, with a gross tonnage of 2,498,502.

The port of Eilat is Israel's gate to the Red Sea. It is a natural harbour, operated from a wharf. A new port, to the south of the original one, started operating in 1965.

CIVIL AVIATION

El Al Israel Airlines Ltd.: P.O.B. 41, Ben Gurion Airport, Lod, Tel-Aviv; f. 1949; daily services to most capitals of Europe; over twenty flights weekly to New York; services to the U.S.A., Canada, Greece, Kenya, Mexico, Portugal, Romania, South Africa and Turkey; fleet of 3 Boeing 747-258B, 2 Boeing 747-258C, 2 Boeing 747-124SF, 3 Boeing 707-458, 3 Boeing 707-358B, 2 Boeing 707-358C, 2 Boeing 720-058B; (on order) 1 Boeing 747-258F, Chair. M. BEN-ARI; Pres. M. HOD.

Arkia, Israel Inland Airlines Ltd.: 88 Ha'hashmonaim St., Tel-Aviv; f. 1950; scheduled services from Tel-Aviv, Jerusalem and Haifa to Eilat, Ophira (Sharm-el-Sheikh), Santa Katarina (Mt. Sinai), Rosh Pina, Dead Sea, Beersheba and Mizpeh Ramon; fleet of 2 BAC 1-11, 6 Viscounts.

The following airlines also serve Israel: Air France, Alitalia (Italy), Austrian Airlines, British Airways, Canadian Pacific, Cyprus Airways, KLM (Netherlands), Lufthansa (Federal Republic of Germany), Olympic Airways (Greece), Sabena (Belgium), SAS (Sweden). Swissair, Tarom (Romania), THY (Turkey), TWA (U.S.A.),

TOURISM

Ministry of Tourism: P.O.B. 1018, Jerusalem; Minister of Tourism GIDEON PATT; Dir.-Gen. AVRAHAM ROZENMAN.

CULTURAL ORGANIZATIONS

The Israel Festival: 5th Flr., Shalom Tower, Ahad Ha'am St., Tel-Aviv, P.O.B. 29874; organizes the Israel Festival which takes place in July/August in Jerusalem, Tel-Aviv, Caesarea and Haifa; Chair. Exec. Cttee. A. BEN-NATHAN; Artistic Adviser GARY BERTINI; Dir. J. BISTRITZKY.

Israel Music Institute: P.O.B. 11253, Tel-Aviv; f. 1961; publishes and promotes Israeli music, educational music and musicological works abroad; member since 1969 of International Music Information Centres; Chair. Prof. HERZL SHMUELI; Man. Dir. and Editor-in-Chief WILLIAM ELIAS.

The National Council of Culture and Art: Hadar Daphna Bldg., Shaul Hamelech Blvd., Tel-Aviv.

PRINCIPAL THEATRES

Cameri Theatre: Tel-Aviv; f. 1944; public trusteeship; repertory theatre; tours abroad.

Habimah National Theatre of Israel: P.O.B. 222, Tel-Aviv; f. 1918 in Russia, moved to Palestine 1928; Jewish, classical and modern drama.

Israel National Opera: 1 Allenby St., Tel-Aviv; f. 1947 by Edis de-Philippe (Dir.); classical and modern opera; open 50 weeks of the year.

PRINCIPAL ORCHESTRAS

Haifa Symphony Orchestra: 50 Pevsner St., P.O.B. 5210, Haifa; Music Dir. Mrs. Ora Gill.

Israel Chamber Orchestra: Dafna Street, Tel-Aviv; f. 1965; Musical Dir. Rudolf Barshai; Gen. Man. Roni Abramson.

Israel Philharmonic Orchestra: Frederic R. Mann Auditorium, Tel-Aviv; f. 1936; Music Director Zubin Mehta; Concertmasters Chaim Taub, Uri Pianka.

The Jerusalem Symphony Orchestra: Israel Broadcasting Authority, Y.M.C.A. Building, Jerusalem; f. 1938; 90 mems.; Dir. Yehuda Fickler; Chief conductor and musical dir. Gary Bertini.

DANCE TROUPES

Bat-Dor Dance Company: 30 Ibn Gvirol St., Tel-Aviv; contemporary repertory dance company; owns theatre in Tel-Aviv; frequent tours abroad; Producer Batsheva de Rothschild; Artistic Dir. Jeannette Ordman; Gen. Man. Barry Swersky.

Batsheva Dance Company: 9 Sderot Hahaskala, Tel-Aviv.

Inbal Dance Theatre: 74 Arlosoroff St., Tel-Aviv; f. 1949; modern Israeli dance theatre specializing in their traditional folk art, with choreographic themes from the Bible; frequent tours abroad; Founder and Artistic Dir. Sara Levi-Tanai.

FESTIVALS

Israel Festival: 5th Floor, Shalom Tower, Ahad Ha'am St., P.O.B. 29874, Tel Aviv; organizes the Israel Festival held annually in July-August in Jerusalem, Tel Aviv, Haifa and Caesarea; Chair. Exec. Cttee. A. Ben-Natan; Dir. J. Bistritzky.

Ein Gev Music Festival: Kibbutz Ein Gev, Kinneret; international festival; annually for one week at Passover.

Zimriya: World Assembly of Choirs, comprising Israeli and international choirs; f. 1952; triennial.

ATOMIC ENERGY

Israel Atomic Energy Commission: 26 Rehov Ha Universita, Ramat Aviv, Tel-Aviv; and P.O.B. 17120, Tel-Aviv; f. 1952; advises the Government on long term policies and priorities in the advancement of nuclear research and development; supervises the implementation of policies approved by the government; including the licensing of nuclear power plants; represents Israel in its relations with scientific institutions abroad and international organizations engaged in nuclear research and development (Israel is a member of IAEA); Chair. The Prime Minister; Dir.-Gen. Uzi Eilam.

The Atomic Energy Commission has two research and development centres: the Soreq Nuclear Research Centre and the Negev Nuclear Research Centre near Dimona. The main fields of research are: nuclear physics and chemistry, reactor physics, reactor engineering, radiation research and applications, application of isotopes, metallurgy, electronics, radiobiology, nuclear medicine, nuclear power and desalination. The centres also provide national services: health physics including film badge service, isotope production and molecule labelling, activation analysis, irradiation, advice to industry and institutions, training of personnel, technical courses, documentation.

Soreq Nuclear Research Centre: Yavne; f. 1952; equipped with a swimming pool type research reactor IRR-1 of 5 MW thermal; Dir. Dr. Y. Ettinger.

Negev Nuclear Research Centre: Dimona; equipped with a natural uranium fuelled and heavy water moderated reactor IRR-2 of 26 MW thermal; Dir Abraham Seroussi.

Weizmann Institute of Science: Rehovot; Department of Nuclear Physics engaged in research and graduate teaching in experimental and theoretical nuclear structure and elementary particle physics, as well as in applied physics; a new *14 UD Pelletron* accelerator has been installed; Head Prof. Z. Fraenkel.

Department of Isotope Research engaged in research and teaching in a broad area, ranging from environmental research to brain chemistry, using isotope techniques; it also operates a product on-scale plant for the separation of o^{17} and o^{18} from o^{16}; Head J. R. Gat.

The Hebrew University of Jerusalem: Jerusalem; engages in atomic research and teaching in chemistry, physics biology and medicine.

Technion: Israel Institute of Technology: Haifa; the Dept. of Physics engages in undergraduate teaching in physics, as well as graduate teaching and research mainly in nuclear physics, high energy physics, foundations of quantum mechanics, atomic physics, relativity and astrophysics, solid state spectroscopy, very low temperature physics, phase transitions, semiconductor physics, magnetism and quantum optics; Chair. Dept. of Physics Prof. A. Ron; the Dept. of Nuclear Engineering undertakes teaching and graduate work in applied nuclear science and engineering; research groups work in the fields of theoretical and experimental nuclear reactor physics, neutron physics, nuclear desalination, heat transfer, nuclear radiations; Head, Nuclear Engineering Dept. Prof. N. Shafrir.

DEFENCE

The General Staff

This consists of the Chiefs of the General Staff, Manpower, Logistics and Intelligence Branches of the Defence Forces, the Commanders of the Air Force and the Navy, and the officers commanding the three Regional Commands (Northern, Central and Southern). It is headed by the Chief of Staff of the Armed Forces.

Chief of Staff of the Armed Forces: Maj.-Gen. RAFAEL EITAN.

Commander of the Air Force: Maj.-Gen. DAVID IVRI.

Commander of the Navy: Commodore ZEEV ALMOG.

Expenditure (1978/79): I£54,400 million.

Military Service (Jewish population only): Men under 29 and some unmarried women under 26 are called for regular service of up to 36 months for men and 24 months for women. Physicians may be called up to the age of 34.

Total Armed Forces: 164,000: including 123,000 conscripts; this can be raised to 400,000 by mobilizing reservists within 48–72 hours; army 18,000 regular, 120,000 conscripts (375,000 when fully mobilized); navy 5,000 regular, 1,000 conscripts (8,000 when fully mobilized); air force 21,000 regular, 2,000 conscripts (25,000 conscripts when fully mobilized).

Paramilitary Forces: 9,500.

EDUCATION

The present-day school system is based on the Compulsory Education Law (1949), the State Education Law (1953) and on some provisions of the 1933 Education Ordinance dating back to the British Mandatory Administration. The former introduced free compulsory primary education for all children between the ages of 5 and 15 (one kindergarten, eight years elementary schooling); in addition, those aged 14–18 who have not completed their elementary schooling may attend special evening classes until they reach the necessary standard.

The State Education Law abolished the old complicated Trend Education System, and vested the responsibility for Primary Education in the Government, thus providing a unified State-controlled elementary school system. The law does, however, recognise two main forms of Primary Education—(*a*) State Education; (*b*) Recognised Non-State Education. State Education may be sub-divided into two distinct categories of schools—State Schools and State Religious Schools for Jews, and State Schools for Arabs. Schools and kindergartens of the State system are in the joint ownership of the State and the Local Authorities, while the recognized non-State institutions are essentially privately-owned, although they are subsidised, and supervised by the State and the Local Authorities.

The two largest non-State school systems are the Agudat Israel Schools (of an ultra-orthodox religious character) and the boarding schools, mostly agricultural, for young immigrants, run by various voluntary bodies.

State Primary Education is financed by a partnership of the Central Government and the Local Authorities. Since 1953 the salaries of all teachers and kindergarten mistresses of State Schools have been paid by the Central Government, whilst the cost of maintenance and of maintenance services, and the provision of new buildings and equipment have been the responsibility of the Local Authorities. The State does not impose an Education Tax but local authorities may, with the Ministry's approval, levy a rate on parents for special services.

The State provides different schools for the Jewish and Arab children, because of the distribution of population and the language difference. Nevertheless many Arab children attend Jewish primary, secondary, vocational, agricultural and even teacher-training colleges. In the Jewish sector there is a distinct line of division between the secular State schools and the Religious State Schools, which are established on the demand of parents in any locality, provided that a certain minimum number of pupils have first been enrolled. In the Arab Schools all instruction is in Arabic, and there is a special department for Arabic Education in the Ministry of Education and Culture. Some 90 per cent of the Arab children attend school regularly.

Particular attention is paid to retarded children, and special classes are provided for them in the ordinary schools, besides the moderate-sized schools for backward and handicapped children which have been established by the Ministry.

Working Youth Schools are provided for boys and girls, between the ages of 14–17, who have not completed their primary education. These schools provide a four-year course, their grades corresponding to grades 5–8 in the primary schools, but there are also two preparatory classes for beginners, mostly for the children of new immigrants.

Post Primary Education is of three main types: Secondary, Vocational and Agricultural. Secondary Education is under the jurisdiction of the Ministry of Education and Culture. The other two categories were administered by the Ministries of Labour and Agriculture respectively, but passed over to the Ministry of Education in September 1960.

Secondary Schools. In 1974-75 the Ministry of Education and Culture had under its supervision 206 Hebrew and 77 Arab secondary schools, with 54,878 and 12,860 pupils respectively. No direct financial aid is given by the State to secondary schools, except building loans. On the other hand the central government and local authorities assist children who have passed a preliminary test to pay their school fees. This assistance is given on a sliding scale according to the parents' means and obligations, and may even cover the total cost. An official proposed syllabus has been published by the Ministry, for use in these schools.

Vocational Training. There are three types of training available in this section of the Education System: Vocational Schools, Apprenticeships and Vocational Training Courses for Adults.

In the school year 1977/78 there were 318 Hebrew and 11 Arab vocational schools with 67,260 and 1,668 pupils respectively. Almost all the courses extend over a period of three or four years, and the students are boys and girls between the ages of 14 and 18. The curriculum consists of some 20 hours practical training, and 24 hours instruction on industrial and general subjects, each week.

A programme of Pre-Vocational Training for pupils in the last two grades of the Government Primary Schools was launched in 1955. This programme includes training in various trades, handicrafts and agriculture, and was intended to enable pupils continuing in the Vocational Schools to begin their studies in the second year of those schools. In fact they are now absorbed in the two-year secondary schools and thus get four years of a mixed general and vocational education. The training is given in addition to the Primary School curriculum.

Vocational training for adults is divided into two sections: basic trade courses (day courses) which are intended for persons who have had no previous vocational training or have to change their occupation (mostly new immigrants), and supplementary training courses (evening classes), intended for the further education of already skilled workers. The courses are from 3–18 months.

Agricultural Schools: there are various kinds of schools offering training in agriculture, ranging from the Faculty of Agriculture of the Hebrew University, and the Rupin Institute courses for adults to the agricultural secondary schools and other training centres for youth.

In 1977/78 there were 30 agricultural schools of which two were for Arab pupils, including a fishing school, a school of horticulture, and an agricultural technical institute providing a diploma-course. Five of these (including the fishing school and the technical institute) are government schools; the others are financed by various organizations such as the Women Workers' Council, Women's International Zionist Organization, etc.

In 1977/78 there were 5,601 Hebrew and 776 Arab pupils. Most schools have well developed farms in which the pupils work for 3–4 hours a day. A 3-year course is usual and only a few have a 4-year course. Some 2-year courses are being opened in regional schools for farm-youth.

Teachers' Training. As the enrolment in schools throughout the country increases by about 20,000 pupils each year, the need for additional teachers is keenly felt. There are 53 Hebrew and two Arab teacher training colleges with 11,606 Hebrew and 604 Arab students respectively. To qualify as a teacher the student must have taken 14 years of study. Pupils normally complete the 12-year secondary school course and then go to a teachers' training college for a further two years. In these two years the student has practical teaching experience before sitting for the examination of the Ministry of Education and Culture.

Adult Education. Numerous facilities for adult education are offered both by institutions of higher learning and by various organizations. Special attention is being paid to the study of the Hebrew language and new immigrants have the opportunity to study Hebrew in intensive 5–6 month courses (*ulpanim*) some of which are conducted in agricultural settlements where students work for half the day to cover their living expenses.

The Occupied Territories. The educational system in the occupied parts of the adjacent Arab countries has been taken over with few changes. In 1973-74 the West bank had 970 schools (86 run by UNRWA) with 207,729 pupils. In the Gaza strip were 149 state and 126 UNRWA schools with 2,476 teachers and an enrolment of 123,556.

UNIVERSITIES

Bar-Ilan University: Ramat-Gan; 1,022 teachers, 7,600 students.

Ben Gurion University of the Negev: P.O.B. 653, Beersheba; 960 teachers, 4,500 students.

Everyman's University: Ramat-Aviv, Tel-Aviv; 5,600 students.

Haifa University: Mount Carmel, Haifa; 600 teachers, 7,000 students.

The Hebrew University of Jerusalem: Jerusalem; 2,200 teachers, 14,000 students.

Tel-Aviv University: Ramat-Aviv, Tel-Aviv; 1,320 teachers, 17,326 students.

Technion, Israel Institute of Technology: Haifa; 1,500 teachers, 5,800 undergraduate, 1,800 graduate students.

Weizmann Institute of Science, Feinberg Graduate School: Rehovot; 480 students.

BIBLIOGRAPHY

GENERAL

AVNERY, URI. Israel without Zionists (Collier-Macmillan, London, 1969).

GLUECK, NELSON. The River Jordan (Philadelphia, 1946.) Rivers in the Desert (London, 1959).

HILLEL, MARC. Israel en danger de paix (Fayard, Paris, 1969).

KOHN, HANS. Nationalism and Imperialism in the Hither East (London, 1932).

KOLLEK, TEDDY, and PEARLMAN, MOSHE. Jerusalem, Sacred City of Mankind (Weidenfeld and Nicholson, London, 1968).

MALLISON, W. T. (Jr.) The Zionist-Israel Juridical Claims to Constitute "The Jewish People" Nationality Entity and to Confer Membership of it. (*George Washington Law Review*, Vol. 32, No. 4-June 1964).

MARMORSTEIN, EMILE. Heaven at Bay: The Jewish Kulturkampf in the Holy Land (Oxford University Press, 1969).

ORNI, E. and EFRAT, E. The Geography of Israel (Darey, New York, 1965).

ORON, YITZHAK. Middle East Record, Vol. II (Daniel Davey and Co., New York, 1966).

PARKES, J. W. The Emergence of the Jewish Problem, 1878-1939 (Oxford, 1946).

A History of Palestine from A.D. 135 to Modern Times (Gollancz, London, 1949).

End of Exile (New York, 1954).

Whose Land? A History of the Peoples of Palestine (Pelican, Harmondsworth, 1970).

PATAI, R. Israel Between East and West (Philadelphia, 1953).

Culture and Conflict (New York, 1962).

SHAPIRO, HARRY L. The Jewish People: a biological history (UNESCO, 1960).

TOYNBEE, ARNOLD J. Survey of International Affairs, Vol. I (London, 1925).

TUCHMAN, BARBARA W. Bible and Sword (Redman, London, 1957; Minerva, New York, 1968).

WEINGROD, ALEX. Reluctant Pioneers, Village Development in Israel (Cornell University Press, New York, 1966).

ZANDER, WALTER. Israel and the Holy Places of Christendom (Weidenfeld and Nicolson, 1972).

ANCIENT HISTORY

DE VAUX, R. Ancient Israel: Its Life and Institutions (NEW York, 1961).

ORLINSKY, H. M. Ancient Israel (Cornell University Press).

SMITH, Sir G. A. Historical Geography of the Holy Land (24th ed., London, 1931).

YADIN, YIGAEL. Message of the Scrolls (Grosset and Dunlap, New York).

Masada (Weidenfeld and Nicolson, London, 1966).

YEWIN, S. A Decade of Archaeology in Israel 1948-58 (Istanbul, 1960).

RECENT HISTORY

ALLON, YIGAL. The making of Israel's Army (Vallentine, Mitchell, London, 1970).

BARBOUR, NEVILL. Nisi Dominus: a survey of the Palestine Controversy (Harrap, London, 1946, reprinted by the Institute for Palestine Studies, Beirut, 1969).

BENTWICH, NORMAN and HELEN. Mandate Memories, 1918-1948 (Hogarth Press, London, 1965).

BERMANT, CHAIM. Israel (Thames and Hudson, London, 1967).

BERGER, EARL. The Covenant and the Sword, Arab-Israel Relations 1948–56 (University of Toronto Press, Toronto, 1965).

BETHELL, NICHOLAS. The Palestine Triangle: the Struggle between the British, the Jews and the Arabs, 1935–48 (André Deutsch, London, 1979).

BURNS, E. L. M. Between Arab and Israeli (Harrap, London, 1962; Astor-Honor, New York, 1963).

CATTAN, HENRY. Palestine, the Arabs and Israel (Longmans Green, London, 1969).

CHURCHILL, RANDOLPH and WINSTON. The Six Day War (Heinemann/Penguin, London, 1967).

COHEN, MICHAEL J. Palestine, Retreat from the Mandate: The Making of British Policy (Elek, London, 1978).

CROSSMAN, R. H. S. Palestine Mission (London, 1947).

DRAPER, T. Israel and World Politics: Roots of the Third Arab-Israeli War (Secker and Warburg, London, 1968).

ESCO FOUNDATION FOR PALESTINE. Palestine: A Study of Jewish, Arab and British Policies (2 vols., New Haven, 1947).

GABBAY, RONY E. A Political Study of the Arab-Jewish Conflict, the Arab Refugee Problem (Geneva and Paris, 1959).

HOWARD, M., and HUNTER, R. Israel and the Arab World (Institute of Palestine Studies, Beirut).

JIRYIS, SABRI. The Arabs in Israel (Institute for Palestine Studies, Beirut, 1968).

KADER, RAZZAK ABDEL. The Arab-Jewish Conflict (1961).

KHALIDI, WALID. From Haven to Conquest: Readings in Zionism and the Palestine Problem until 1948 (Institute for Palestine Studies, Beirut, 1971).

KIMCHE, JON. Palestine or Israel (Secker & Warburg, London, 1973).

KIMCHE, JON and DAVID. Both Sides of the Hill: Britain and the Palestine War (Secker and Warburg, London, 1960).

KOESTLER, ARTHUR. Promise and Fulfilment: Palestine, 1917-1949 (London, 1949).

Thieves in the Night (New York and London, 1946).

LANDAU, JACOB M. The Arabs in Israel (Oxford University Press, London, 1969).

LAQUEUR, WALTER. The Road to War 1967 (Weidenfeld and Nicolson, London, 1968).

The Israel-Arab Reader (Weidenfeld and Nicolson, London, 1969).

LILIENTHAL, ALFRED M. The Other Side of the Coin: An American Perspective of the Arab-Israeli Conflict (New York, 1965).

LORCH, N. The Edge of the Sword: Israel's War of Independence 1947-49 (Putnam, New York, 1961).

LUCAS, NOAH. The Modern History of Israel (Weidenfeld and Nicolson, London, 1974/75).

MARLOWE, JOHN. The Seat of Pilate, An Account of the Palestine Mandate (Cresset, London, 1959; Dufour, Philadelphia, 1958).

O'BALLANCE, E. The Arab-Israeli War (New York, Praeger, 1957).

The Third Arab-Israeli War (Faber & Faber, London, 1972).

PERETZ, DON. Israel and the Palestine Arabs (The Middle East Institute, Washington, 1958).

PERLMUTTER, AMOS. Military and Politics in Israel, 1948–1967 (2nd edition, Frank Cass, London, 1977).

Politics and the Military in Israel, 1967–1976 (Frank Cass, London, 1977).

RIZK, EDWARD. The Palestine Question, Seminar of Arab Jurists on Palestine, Algiers, 1967 (Institute for Palestine Studies, Beirut, 1968).

RODINSON, MAXIME. Israel and the Arabs (Penguin Books, Harmondsworth, 1968; Pantheon, New York, 1969).

ROULEAU, ERIC and HELD, JEAN-FRANCIS. Israël et les Arabes (Editions du Seuil, Paris, 1967).

ROYAL INSTITUTE OF INTERNATIONAL AFFAIRS. Great Britain and Palestine 1915-45 (London, 1946).

SHARABI, HISHAM B. Palestine and Israel: The Lethal Dilemma (Van Nostrand Reinhold, New York, 1969).

SYKES, CHRISTOPHER. Crossroads to Israel (Collins, London, 1965).

TEVETH, SHABTAI. Moshe Dayan (Weidenfeld and Nicolson, London, 1972).

THE STATE

AVI-HAI, AVRAHAM. Ben Gurion, State Builder (Israel Universities Press, 1974).

BADI, JOSEPH. Fundamental Laws of the State of Israel (New York, 1961).

BAR-ZOHAR, MICHAEL. Ben-Gurion: A Biography (London, Weidenfeld & Nicolson, 1978).

BARUTH, K. H. The Physical Planning of Israel (London, 1949).

BEN GURION, D. Rebirth and Destiny of Israel (New York, 1954).

Israel: A Personal History (London, New English Library, 1972).

BENTWICH, NORMAN. Fulfilment in the Promised Land 1917-37 (London, 1938).

Judæa Lives Again (London, 1944).

Israel Resurgent (Ernest Benn, 1960).

The New-old Land of Israel (Allen and Unwin, 1960).

Israel, Two Fateful Years 1967–69 (Elek, London, 1970).

BENTWICH, J. S. Education in Israel (Routledge and Kegan Paul, London, 1965).

BERNSTEIN, MARVER H. The Politics of Israel (London, 1958).

BRECHER, MICHAEL. The Foreign Policy System of Israel (Oxford University Press, London, 1972).

COMAY, JOAN. Everyone's Guide to Israel (New York, 1962).

Introducing Israel (London, Methuen, 1963).

COMAY, JOAN and PEARLMAN, MOSHE. Israel (New York, 1965).

CROSSMAN, R. H. S. A Nation Reborn (London, Hamish Hamilton, 1960).

DAVIS, MOSHE (Ed.). Israel: its Role in Civilisation (New York, 1956).

DAYAN, SHMUEL. The Promised Land (London, 1961).

DE GAURY, GERALD. The New State of Israel (New York, 1952).

EBAN, A. The Voice of Israel (New York, Horizon Press. 1957).

The Story of Modern Israel (Weidenfeld & Nicolson, London, 1973).

ELDEMAN, MAURICE. Ben Gurion, a Political Biography (Hodder and Stoughton, London, 1964).

HALPERIN, HAIM. Changing Patterns in Israel Agriculture (London, 1957).

JANOWSKY, OSCAR I. Foundations of Israel: Emergence of a Welfare State (Anvil Nostrand Co., Princeton, 1959).

KRAINES, O. Government and Politics in Israel (Allen and Unwin, London, 1961).

LIKHOVSKI, ELIAHU S. Israel's Parliament: The Law of the Knesset (Oxford, Clarendon Press, 1971).

MEDDING, PETER. Mapai in Israel: Political Organisation and Government in a New Society (Cambridge U.P., London, 1972).

MEIR, GOLDA. This is our Strength (New York, 1963).

PATINKIN, D. The Israel Economy; the first decade (Jerusalem, 1960).

PEARLMAN, Lt.-Col. MOSHE. The Army of Israel (New York, 1959).

PREUSS, W. Co-operation in Israel and the World (Jerusalem, 1960).

SACHAR, H. M. ALIYAH. The Peoples of Israel (New York, 1962).

SAFRAN, NADAV. The United States and Israel (Harvard U.P., 1963).

SAMUEL, The Hon. EDWIN. Problems of Government in the State of Israel (Jerusalem, 1956).

SEGRE, V. D. Israel: A Society in Transition (Oxford U.P., London, 1971).

SHATIL, J. L'économie Collective du Kibboutz Israëlien (Paris, Les Editions de Minuit, 1960).

SITTON, SHLOMO. Israël: Immigration et Croissance 1948-58 (Editions Cujas, Paris, 1963).

ZIONISM

BEIN, ALEX. Theodor Herzl (East and West Library, London, 1957).

COHEN, ISRAEL. A Short History of Zionism (London, Frederick Muller, 1951).

FISCH, HAROLD. The Zionist Revolution: A New Perspective (London, Weidenfeld & Nicolson, 1978).

FRANKL, OSCAR BENJAMIN. Theodor Herzl: The Jew and Man (New York, 1949).

LAQUEUR, WALTER. A History of Zionism (Weidenfeld & Nicolson, London, 1972).

LIPSKY, L. A Gallery of Zionist Profiles (New York) Farrar, Straus and Cudahy, 1950).

LOWENTHAL, MARVIN (ed. and trans.). Diaries of Theodor Herzl (Grosset and Dunlap, New York, 1965).

PETUCHOWSKY, J. J. Zionism Reconsidered (Twayne, New York, 1966).

SCHAMA, SIMON. Two Rothschilds and the Land of Israel (London, Collins, 1978).

SCHECHTMAN, J. Rebel and Statesmen: the Jabotinsky Story (New York, Thomas Yoseloff, 1956).

SOKOLOW, NAHUM. History of Zionism (2 vols., Longmans, London, 1919; Ktav, New York, 1969).

STEIN, LEONARD and YOGEV, GEDILIA (Editors). The Letters and Papers of Chaim Weizmann; Volume I 1885-1902 (Oxford University Press, 1968).

SOKOLOW, NAHUM. History of Zionism (2 vols., London, 1919).

WEISGAL, MEYER, and CARMICHAEL, JOEL. Chaim Weizmann—a Biography by Several Hands (London, Weidenfeld and Nicolson, 1962).

WEIZMANN, Dr. CHAIM. The Jewish People and Palestine (London, 1939).

Trial and Error: the Autobiography of Chaim Weizmann (Hamish Hamilton, London, 1949; Schocken, New York, 1966).

OFFICIAL PUBLICATIONS

Report of the Palestine Royal Commission, 1937 (Cmd. 5479), London.

Report of the Palestine Partition Commission, 1938 (Cmd. 5854), London.

Statement of Policy by His Majesty's Government in the United Kingdom (Cmd. 3692), London, 1930; (Cmd. 5893), London, 1938; (Cmd. 6019), London, 1939; (Cmd. 6180), London, 1940.

Government Survey of Palestine (2 vols., 1945-46), Jerusalem. Supplement, July 1947, Jerusalem.

Report of the Anglo-American Committee of Enquiry, Lausanne, 1946.

Report to the United Nations General Assembly by the UN Special Committee on Palestine, Geneva, 1947.

Report of the UN Economic Survey Mission for the Middle East, December 1949 (United Nations, Lake Success, N.Y.; H.M. Stationery Office).

Annual Yearbook of the Government of Israel.

Israel Government. The Arabs in Israel (1952).

Jewish Agency for Palestine. Documents Submitted to General Assembly of UN, relating to the National Home (1947).

The Jewish Plan for Palestine (Jerusalem, 1947).

Statistical Survey of the Middle East (1944).

Statistical Abstract of Israel. Central Bureau of Statistics (annual).

Jordan

PHYSICAL AND SOCIAL GEOGRAPHY

W. B. Fisher

The Hashemite Kingdom of Jordan (previously Transjordan) came officially into existence under its present name in 1947 and was enlarged in 1950 to include the districts of Samaria and part of Judaea that had previously formed part of Arab Palestine. The country is bounded on the north by Syria, on the north-east by Iraq, on the east and south by Saudi Arabia, and on the west by Israel. The total area of Jordan is approximately 37,500 sq. miles. The territory west of the Jordan river—some 2,165 sq. miles—has been occupied by Israel since June 1967.

PHYSICAL FEATURES

The greater part of the State of Jordan consists of a plateau lying some 2-3,000 ft. above sea-level, which forms the north-western corner of the great plateau of Arabia (see "Saudi Arabia"). There are no natural topographical frontiers between Jordan and its neighbours Syria, Iraq, and Saudi Arabia, and the plateau continues unbroken into all three countries, with the artificial frontier boundaries drawn as straight lines between defined points. Along its western edge, facing the Jordan Valley, the plateau is uptilted to give a line of hills that rise 1-2,000 ft. above plateau-level. An old river course, the Wadi Sirhan, now almost dry with only occasional wells, breaks up the plateau surface on the south-east and continues into Saudi Arabia.

The Jordanian plateau consists of a core or table of ancient rocks, covered by layers of newer rock (chiefly limestone) lying almost horizontally. In a few places (e.g. on the southern edge of the Jordan Valley) these old rocks are exposed at the surface. On its western side the plateau has been fractured and dislocated by the development of strongly marked tear faults that run from the Red Sea via the Gulf of Aqaba northwards to the Lebanon and Syria. The narrow zone between the faults has sunk, to give the well-known Jordan rift valley, which is bordered both on the east and west by steep-sided walls, especially in the south near the Dead Sea, where the drop is often precipitous. The valley has a maximum width of 14 miles, and is now thought to have been produced by lateral shearing of two continental plates that on the east have been displaced by about 80 km. (50 miles).

The floor of the Jordan Valley varies considerably in level. At its northern end it is just above sea-level; the surface of Lake Tiberias (the Sea of Galilee) is 686 ft. below sea-level, with the deepest part of the lake 700 ft. lower still. Greatest depth of the valley is at the Dead Sea (surface 1,300 ft. below sea level, maximum depth 1,298 ft.).

Dislocation of the rock strata in the region of the Jordan Valley has had two further effects: firstly, earth tremors are still frequent along the valley (Jerusalem has minor earthquakes from time to time); and secondly, considerable quantities of lava have welled up, forming enormous sheets that cover wide expanses of territory in the State of Jordan and southern Syria, and produce a desolate, forbidding landscape. One small lava flow, by forming a natural dam across the Jordan Valley, has impounded the waters to form Lake Tiberias.

The River Jordan rises just inside the frontiers of Syria and the Lebanon—a fruitful source of dispute between the two countries and Israel. The river is 157 miles long, and after first flowing for 60 miles in Israel it lies within Jordanian territory for the remaining 95 miles. Its main tributary, the Yarmuk, is 25 miles long, and close to its junction with the Jordan forms the boundary between Jordan State, Israel and Syria. A few miles from its source, the River Jordan used to open into Lake Huleh, a shallow, marsh-fringed expanse of water which was for long a breeding ground of malaria, but which has now been drained. Lake Tiberias, also, like Huleh, in Israel, covers an area of 122 sq. miles and measures 14 miles from north to south, and 16 miles from east to west. River water outflowing from the lake is used for the generation of hydro-electricity.

The river then flows through the barren, inhospitable country of its middle and lower valley, very little of which is actually, or potentially, cultivable, and finally enters the Dead Sea. This lake is 40 miles long and 10 miles wide. Owing to the very high air temperatures at most seasons of the year evaporation from the lake is intense, and has been estimated as equivalent to 8½ million tons of water per day. At the surface the Dead Sea water contains about 250 grams of dissolved salts per litre, and at a depth of 360 feet the water is chemically saturated (i.e. holds its maximum possible content). Magnesium chloride is the most abundant mineral, with sodium chloride next in importance; but commercial interest centres in the less abundant potash and bromide salts.

Climatically, Jordan shows close affinity to its neighbours. Summers are hot, especially on the plateau and in the Jordan Valley, where temperatures up to 120° F. have been recorded. Winters are fairly cold, and on the plateau frost and some snow are usual, though not in the lower Jordan Valley. The significant element of the climate of Jordan is rainfall. In the higher parts (i.e. the uplands of Samaria and Judaea and the hills overlooking the eastern Jordan Valley) 15 to 25 inches of rainfall occur, enough for agriculture; but elsewhere as little as 8 inches or less may fall, and pastoral nomadism is the only possible way of life. Only about 25 per cent of the total area of Jordan is sufficiently humid for cultivation.

Hence the main features of economic life in Jordan are subsistence agriculture of a marginal kind, carried on in Judaea-Samaria and on the north-eastern edge of the plateau, close to Amman, with migratory herding of animals—sheep, goats, cattle and camels—over the remaining and by far the larger portion of the country. As a result, the natural wealth of Jordan is small and tribal ways of life exist in many parts. Before the June 1967 War tourism (with which must be included religious pilgrimage, mainly to the Holy Christian places of Jerusalem) had developed into a very important industry but this has been seriously jeopardized by the Israeli occupation of the West Bank territory and annexation of Jerusalem. However, civil war in the Lebanon and re-opening of the Suez Canal (which greatly affects the Jordanian port of Aqaba) have been very favourable factors, and thanks to transfer of activities from the Lebanon, a better relationship with Syria, and assistance from outside, the economy of Jordan has greatly improved over the past few years.

RACE AND LANGUAGE

A division must be drawn between the Jordanians living east of the River Jordan, who in the main are of pure Mediterranean stock, ethnically similar to the desert populations of Syria and Saudi Arabia, and the Arabs of the Jordan Valley and Samaria-Judaea. These latter are slightly taller, more heavily built, and have a broader head-form. Some authorities suggest that they are descendants of the Canaanites, who may have originated far to the north-east, in the Zagros area. An Iranian racial affinity is thus implied—but this must be of very ancient date, as the Arabs west of the Jordan Valley have been settled in their present home for many thousands of years. Besides the two groups of Arabs there are also small colonies of Circassians from the Caucasus of Russia, who settled in Jordan as refugees during the nineteenth and twentieth centuries A.D.

Arabic is spoken everywhere, except in a few Circassian villages, and, through the contacts with Britain, some English is understood in the towns.

HISTORY

Jordan, as an independent State, is a twentieth-century development. Before then it was seldom more than a rugged and backward appendage to more powerful kingdoms and empires, and indeed never had any separate existence. In Biblical times the area was covered roughly by Gilead, Ammon, Moab and Edom, and the western portions formed for a time part of the kingdom of Israel. During the sixth century B.C. the Arabian tribe of the Nabateans established their capital at Petra in the south and continued to preserve their independence when, during the fourth and third centuries, the northern half was incorporated into the Seleucid province of Syria. It was under Seleucid rule that cities like Philadelphia (the Biblical Rabbath Ammon and the modern Amman) and Gerasa (now Jerash) rose to prominence. During the first century B.C. the Nabateans extended their rule over the greater part of present-day Jordan and Syria; they then began to recede before the advance of Rome, and in A.D. 105–6 Petra was incorporated into the Roman Empire. The lands east of the Jordan shared in a brief blaze of glory under the Palmyrene sovereigns Odenathus (Udaynath) and Zenobia (al-Zabba') in the middle of the third century A.D., and during the fifth and sixth centuries formed part of the dominions of the Christian Ghassanid dynasty, vassals of the Byzantine Empire. Finally, after fifty years of anarchy in which Byzantine, Persian and local rulers intervened, Transjordania was conquered by the Arabs and absorbed into the Islamic Empire.

For centuries nothing more is heard of the country; it formed normally a part of Syria, and as such was generally governed from Egypt. From the beginning of the sixteenth century it was included in the Ottoman *vilayet* of Damascus, and remained in a condition of stagnation until the outbreak of the Great War in 1914. European travellers and explorers of the nineteenth century rediscovered the beauties of Petra and Gerasa, but otherwise the desert tribes were left undisturbed. Even the course of the war in its early stages gave little hint of the upheaval that was to take place in Jordan's fortunes. The area was included in the zone of influence allocated to Britain under the Sykes-Picot Treaty of May 1916 (*see* Documents on Palestine, p. 57), and Zionists held that it also came within the area designated as a Jewish National Home in the promise contained in the Balfour Declaration of November 1917. Apart from these somewhat remote political events the tide of war did not reach Jordanian territory until the capture of Aqaba by the Arab armies under Faisal, the third son of King Hussein of the Hijaz, in July 1917. A year later, in September 1918, they shared in the final push north by capturing Amman and Deraa.

The end of the war thus found a large area, which included almost the whole of present-day Jordan, in Arab hands under the leadership of Faisal. To begin with, the territory to the east of the River Jordan was not looked on as a separate unit. Faisal, with the assistance of British officers and Iraqi nationalists, set up an autonomous government in Damascus, a step encouraged by the Anglo-French Declaration of November 7th, 1918, favouring the establishment of indigenous governments in Syria and Iraq. Arab demands, however, as expressed by Faisal at the Paris Peace Conference in January 1919, went a good deal further in claiming independence throughout the Arab world. This brought them sharply up against both French and Zionist claims in the Near East, and when in March 1920 the General Syrian Congress in Damascus declared the independence of Syria and Iraq, with Faisal and Abdullah, Hussein's second son, as kings, the decisions were denounced by France and Britain. The following month the San Remo Conference awarded the Palestine Mandate to Britain, and thus separated it effectively from Syria proper, which fell within the French share. Faisal was forced out of Damascus by the French in July and left the country.

THE KINGDOM OF TRANSJORDAN

The position of Transjordania was not altogether clear under the new dispensation. After the withdrawal of Faisal the British High Commissioner informed a meeting of notables at Es Salt that the British Government favoured self-government for the territory with British advisers. In December 1920 the provisional frontiers of the Mandates were extended eastwards by Anglo-French agreement so as to include Transjordania within the Palestine Mandate, and therefore presumably within the provisions regarding the establishment of a Jewish National Home. Yet another twist of policy came as the result of a conference in Cairo in March 1921 attended by Winston Churchill, the new British Colonial Secretary, Abdullah, T. E. Lawrence and Sir Herbert Samuel, High Commissioner for Palestine. At this meeting it was recommended that Faisal should be proclaimed King of Iraq, while Abdullah was persuaded to stand down in his favour by the promise of an Arab administration in Transjordania. He had in fact been in effective control in Amman since his arrival the previous winter to organize a rising against the French in Syria. This project he now abandoned, and in April 1921 was officially recognized as *de facto* ruler of Transjordan. The final draft of the Palestine Mandate confirmed by the Council of the League of Nations in July 1922 contained a clause giving the Mandatory Power considerable latitude in the administration of the territory east of the Jordan (*see* Documents on Palestine, p. 61). On the basis of this clause a memorandum was approved in the following September expressly excluding Transjordan from the clauses relating to the establishment of the Jewish National Home, and although many Zionists continued to press for the reversal of this policy, the country thenceforth remained in practice separate from Palestine proper.

Like much of the post-war boundary delineation, the borders of the new state were somewhat arbitrary. Though they lay mainly in desert areas they frequently cut across tribal areas and grazing grounds with small respect for tradition. Of the three or four hundred thousand inhabitants only about a fifth were town-dwellers, and these confined to four small cities ranging in population from 30,000 to 10,000. Nevertheless Transjordan's early years were destined to be comparatively peaceful. On May 15th, 1923, Britain formally recognized Transjordan as an independent constitutional State under the rule of the Amir Abdullah with British tutelage, and with the aid of a British subsidy it was possible to make some slow progress towards development and modernization. A small but efficient armed force, the Arab Legion, was built up under the guidance of Peake Pasha and later Glubb Pasha; this force distinguished itself particularly during the Iraqi rebellion of May 1941. It also played a significant role in the fighting with Israel during 1948. Other British advisers assisted in the development of health services and schools.

The Amir Abdullah very nearly became involved in the fall of his father, King Hussein, in 1924. It was in Amman on March 5th, 1924, that the latter was proclaimed Caliph, and during the subsequent fighting with Ibn Sa'ud Wahhabi troops penetrated into Transjordanian territory. They subsequently withdrew to the south, and in June 1925, after the abdication of Hussein's eldest son Ali, Abdullah formally incorporated Ma'an and Aqaba within his dominions. The move was not disputed by the new ruler of the Hijaz and Najd, and thereafter the southern frontier of Transjordan has remained unaltered.

INDEPENDENCE

In February 1928 a treaty was signed with Great Britain granting a still larger measure of independence, though reserving for the advice of a British Resident such matters as financial policy and foreign relations. The same treaty provided for a constitution, and this was duly promulgated in April 1928, the first Legislative Council meeting a year later. In January 1934 a supplementary agreement was added permitting Transjordan to appoint consular representatives in Arab countries, and in May 1939 Britain agreed to the conversion of the Legislative Council into a regular Cabinet with ministers in charge of specified departments. The outbreak of war delayed further advances towards independence, but this was finally achieved in name at least by the Treaty of London of March 22nd, 1946. On the following May 25th Abdullah was proclaimed king and a new constitution replaced the now obsolete one of 1928.

Transjordan was not slow in taking her place in the community of nations. In 1947 King Abdullah signed treaties with Turkey and Iraq and applied for membership of the United Nations; this last, however, was thwarted by the Russian veto and by lack of American recognition of Transjordan's status as an independent nation. In March 1948 Britain agreed to the signing of a new treaty in which virtually the only restrictive clauses related to military and defence matters. Britain was to have certain peace-time military privileges, including the maintenance of airfields and communications, transit facilities and co-ordination of training methods. She was also to provide economic and social aid.

Transjordan had, however, not waited for independence before making her weight felt in Arab affairs in the Middle East. She had not been very active before the war, and, in fact her first appearance on the international scene was in May 1939, when Transjordanian delegates were invited to the Round Table Conference on Palestine in London. Transjordan took part in the preliminary discussions during 1943 and 1944 that led finally to the formation of the Arab League in March 1945, and was one of the original members of that League. During the immediately following years it seemed possible that political and dynastic differences would be forgotten in this common effort for unity. Under the stresses and strains of 1948 however, the old contradictions began to reappear. Abdullah had long favoured the project of a "Greater Syria", that is, the union of Transjordan, Syria, and Palestine, as a step towards the final unification of the Fertile Crescent by the inclusion of Iraq. This was favoured on dynastic grounds by various parties in Iraq, and also by some elements in Syria and Palestine. On the other hand it met with violent opposition from many Syrian nationalists, from the rulers of Egypt and Saudi Arabia—neither of whom were disposed to favour any strengthening of the Hashemite house—and of course from the Zionists and the French. It is in the light of these conflicts of interest that developments subsequent to the establishment of the State of Israel must be seen.

FORMATION OF ISRAEL

On May 14th–15th, 1948, British troops were withdrawn into the port of Haifa as a preliminary to the final evacuation of Palestine territory, the State of Israel was proclaimed, and Arab armies entered the former Palestinian territory from all sides. Only those from Transjordan played any significant part in the fighting, and by the time that major hostilities ceased in July they had succeeded in occupying a considerable area. The suspicion now inevitably arose that Abdullah was prepared to accept a *fait accompli* and to negotiate with the Israeli authorities for a formal recognition of the existing military boundaries. Moreover, whereas the other Arab countries refused to accept any other move that implied a tacit recognition of the *status quo*—such as the resettlement of refugees—Transjordan seemed to be following a different line. In September 1948 an Arab government was formed at Gaza under Egyptian tutelage, and this was answered from the Transjordanian side by the proclamation in December at Jericho of Abdullah as King of All-Palestine. In the following April the country's name was changed to Jordan and three Palestinians were included in the Cabinet. In the meantime armistices were being signed by all the Arab countries, including Jordan, and on January 31st, 1949, Jordan had at last been recognized by the United States.

On the three major problems confronting the Arab States in their dispute with Israel, Jordan continued to differ more or less openly with her colleagues. She refused to agree to the internationalization of Jerusalem, she initiated plans for the resettlement of the Arab refugees, and she showed a disposition to accept as permanent the armistice frontiers. In April 1950, after rumours of negotiations between Jordan and Israel, the Arab League Council in Cairo succeeded in getting Jordan's adherence to resolutions forbidding negotiations with Israel or annexation of Palestinian territory. Nevertheless in the same month elections were held in Jordan and Arab Palestine, the results of which encouraged Abdullah formally to annex the latter territory on April 24th, 1950. This step was immediately recognized by Britain.

At the meeting of the Arab League that followed, Egypt led the opposition to Jordan, who found support, however, from Iraq. The decisions reached by the Council were inconclusive; but thereafter Jordan began to drift away from Arab League policy. Jordan supported the United Nations policy over Korea, in contradistinction to the other Arab states, and signed a Point Four agreement with the United States in March 1951. Though there was at the same time constant friction between Jordan and Israel the unified opposition of the Arab States to the new Jewish State seemed to have ended, and inter-Arab differences were gaining the upper hand.

ABDULLAH ASSASSINATED

On July 20th, 1951, King Abdullah was assassinated in Jerusalem. Evidence brought out at the trial of those implicated in the plot showed that the murder was as much as anything a protest against his Greater Syria policy, and it was significant that Egypt refused to extradite some of those convicted. Nevertheless the stability of the young Jordanian State revealed itself in the calm in which the King's eldest son Talal succeeded to the throne, and the peaceful elections held shortly afterwards. In January 1952 a new constitution was promulgated. Even more significant, perhaps, was the dignity with which, only a year after his accession, King Talal, whose mental condition had long been giving cause for anxiety, abdicated in favour of his son, Hussein, still a minor. In foreign policy Talal had shown some signs of a reaction against his father's ideas in favour of a *rapprochement* with Syria and Egypt, one step being Jordan's signature of the Arab Collective Security Pact which she had failed to join in the summer of 1950.

This policy was continued during the reign of his son, King Hussein, notably by the conclusion of an economic and financial agreement with Syria in February 1953, and a joint scheme for the construction of a dam across the Yarmuk River to supply irrigation and hydro-electric power.

One problem which became pressing in 1954 was the elaborate scheme sponsored by the United States for the sharing of the Jordan waters between Jordan, Iraq, Syria and Israel, which could make no progress in the absence of political agreement. In May, amid mounting tension, the cabinet of Fawzi al-Mulqi resigned, and a new government was formed by Tawfiq Abu'l-Huda, which was reorganized on October 25th, 1954, after the elections of October 16th.

During December a financial aid agreement was signed in London with the United Kingdom, and the opportunity was taken to discuss the revision of the Anglo-Jordanian Treaty of 1946. Agreement over this was not possible owing to British insistence that any new pact should fit into a general Middle East defence system. In May 1955 Abu'l-Huda was replaced by Sa'id al-Mufti, while an exchange of state visits with King Sa'ud hinted at a *rapprochement* with Saudi Arabia. Nevertheless, in November Jordan declared its unwillingness to adhere either to the Egyptian-Syrian-Saudi Arabian bloc or to the Baghdad Pact.

DISMISSAL OF GLUBB PASHA

On December 15th, following a visit to General Sir. G. Templer, Chief of the Imperial General Staff, Sa'id al-Mufti resigned and was replaced by Hazza al-Majali, known to be in favour of the Baghdad Pact. The following day there were violent demonstrations in Amman, and on December 20th Ibrahim Hashim became Prime Minister, to be succeeded on January 9th by Samir Rifai. In February 1956 the new Prime Minister visited Syria, Lebanon, Iraq, Egypt and Saudi Arabia, and shortly after his return, on March 2nd, King Hussein announced the dismissal of Glubb Pasha, commander-in-chief of the Jordanian armed forces, and replaced him by Major-General Radi 'Annab. The Egyptian-Syrian-Saudi Arabian bloc at this juncture offered to replace the British financial subsidy to Jordan; but the latter was not in fact withdrawn, and King Hussein and the Jordanian government evidently felt that they had moved far enough in one direction, and committed themselves to a policy of strict neutrality. In April, however, the King and the Prime Minister paid a visit to the Syrian President in Damascus, and in May Major-General Annab was replaced by his deputy, Lt.-Colonel Ali Abu Nuwar, generally regarded as the leader of the movement to eliminate foreign influence from the Jordanian army and government. This coincided with the reappointment of Sa'id al-Mufti as Prime Minister. During the same period discussions culminated in agreements for military co-operation between Jordan and Syria, Lebanon and Egypt, and in July Jordan and Syria formed an economic union. At the beginning of the same month al-Mufti was replaced by Ibrahim Hashim.

RELATIONS WITH ISRAEL AND WITH THE OTHER ARAB STATES

Meanwhile relations with Israel, including the problem of the Arab refugees, the use of Jordan waters, the definition of the frontier, and the status of Jerusalem, continued to provide a standing cause for anxiety. Tension between Jordan and Israel was further increased after the Israeli, British and French military action in Egypt. A new cabinet, headed by Suleiman Nabulsi, had taken office in October, and new elections were followed by the opening of negotiations for the abrogation of the Anglo-Jordan Treaty of 1948, and the substitution of financial aid from the Arab countries, notably Saudi Arabia, Egypt and Syria. Owing to subsequent political developments, however, the shares due from Egypt and Syria were not paid. On March 13th, 1957, an Anglo-Jordanian agreement was signed abrogating the 1948 treaty, and by July 2nd the last British troops had left. In the meantime Nabulsi's evident leanings towards the Soviet connection, clashing with the recently-enunciated Eisenhower doctrine, led to his breach with King Hussein and his resignation on April 10th, to be succeeded by Ibrahim Hashim. All political parties were suppressed, and plans to establish diplomatic relations with Russia were dropped. Gen. Ali Aby Nuwar was removed from the post of Commander-in-Chief, and the United States announced its determination to preserve Jordan's independence—a policy underlined by a major air-lift of arms to Amman in September in response to Syria's alignment with the Soviet Union. In May Syrian troops serving under the joint Syro-Egypto-Jordanian command were withdrawn from Jordanian territory at Jordan's request, and in June there was a partial rupture of diplomatic relations with Egypt.

On February 14th, 1958, the merger of the Kingdoms of Iraq and Jordan in a federal union to be called the Arab Federation was proclaimed in Amman by King Faisal of Iraq and King Hussein. This new federation, made in response to the formation of the United Arab Republic a fortnight before, was dissolved by decree of King Hussein on August 2nd, following the revolution in Iraq. Samir Rifai became Prime Minister of Jordan in May, on the resignation of Ibrahim Hashim who took up the appointment of Vice-Premier in the short-lived Arab Federation.

British troops were flown to Amman from Cyprus on July 17th, in response to an appeal by King Hussein. They had all been withdrawn by the beginning of November—under UN auspices—and in the two years that followed Jordan settled down to a period of comparative peace. Hazza' al-Majali succeeded Rifai as Prime Minister on May 6th, 1959. Firm measures were taken against communism and subversive activities and collaboration with the West was, if anything, encouraged by the country's isolation between Iraq, Israel and the two halves of the United Arab Republic. American loans continued to arrive at the rate of about $50,000,000 a year, and there was also technical aid of various kinds from Britain, Western Germany and other countries. An important development was the official opening of the port of Aqaba on the Red Sea, virtually Jordan's only outlet.

Relations with Jordan's Arab neighbours continued to be uneasy, though diplomatic relations with the United Arab Republic, broken off in July, 1958, were resumed in August 1959. Incidents on the Syrian border were almost as frequent as on the Israeli, and there were no signs of a rapprochement with Iraq. In January 1960, both the King and the Prime Minister condemned the Arab leaders' approach to the Palestine problem, and in February Jordanian citizenship was offered to all Arab refugees who applied for it. On the other side of the balance sheet, King Hussein paid a flying visit to King Sa'ud in February, 1960, and in March strongly anti-Zionist statements appeared in the Jordanian press. Nevertheless there seemed to be no change in the general position that Jordan wished for formal recognition of her absorption of the Palestinian territory west of the Jordan, while the United Arab Republic and other Arab countries favoured the establishment of an independent Palestine Arab government.

On August 29th, 1960, the Jordanian Prime Minister, Hazza al-Majali, was assassinated by the explosion of a time-bomb in his office. Jordan was quick to attribute the outrage to persons in the United Arab Republic. A curfew was imposed, but after a cabinet reshuffle comparative stability was restored, with Bahjat Talhouni as Prime Minister.

INTERNAL DEVELOPMENTS

The calm and even enthusiasm with which the King's marriage to an English girl in May 1961 was received by the Jordanian population was generally seen as a sign of the strength of the Throne. In January 1962, Wasfi al-Tal had taken over the premiership, and in December after the completion of elections, the formation of political parties was once again permitted.

Mr. Al-Tal's government was short-lived. In March 1963 he was replaced by Samir Rifai, a nominee of the King. But shortly after the news of a plan to federate Egypt, Syria and Iraq, rioting broke out against Mr. Rifai who resigned on April 20th after only 23 days in office and was eventually succeeded by Sherif Hussein bin Nasser, the King's great-uncle.

In July 1964 King Hussein demonstrated his personal control over the Government when Hussein bin Nasser resigned, and Bahjat Talhouni was asked to take over once again. Talhouni, who had previously been head of the Royal Cabinet and the official representative of the King since the Arab summit conference in January 1964, stated that his government would work "in accordance with the spirit of the Arab summit conference and based on King Hussein's instruction". In August Jordan signed the Arab Common Market agreement, and in September the King attended the Arab Summit Conference in Alexandria, at which the problem of the Jordan waters was one of the main topics of discussion. Talhouni resigned in February 1965, and was replaced by Wasfi al-Tal. In April a constitutional uncertainty was resolved, with the nomination of the King's brother Hassan as Crown Prince; the infant son of the formerly British Princess Muna was thus excluded.

WAR WITH ISRAEL

During the latter part of 1966 Jordan's foreign relations were increasingly worsened by the widening breach with Syria. Charges and counter-charges were made of plots to subvert each other's governments, and while the U.A.R. and the U.S.S.R. supported Syria, Jordan looked for backing to Saudi Arabia and the U.S. This situation made it increasingly difficult for Jordan's relations with Israel to be regularized. In July 1966 Jordan suspended support for the Palestine Liberation Organization, accusing its secretary Shukairy of pro-Communist activity .In November an Israeli reprisal raid aroused bitter feeling in Jordan and elsewhere. While Jordan introduced conscription and Saudi Arabia promised military aid, Syria and the Palestine Liberation Organization called on the Jordanians to revolt against King Hussein. Negotiations to implement the resolution of the Supreme Council for Arab Defence that Iraqi and Saudi troops should be sent to Jordan to assist in her defence broke down in December. This was followed by clashes on the Jordan/Syria frontier, by PLO-sponsored bomb outrages in Jordan (resulting in the closure of the PLO headquarters in Jerusalem), and by worsening relations between Jordan and the U.A.R. and a ban by the latter on aircraft carrying British and American arms to Jordan. In retaliation Jordan withdrew recognition of the Sallal régime in Yemen, and boycotted the next meeting of the Arab Defence Council. On March 5th Wasfi al-Tal resigned and was succeeded by Hussein bin Nasser at the head of an interim government.

As the prospect of war with Israel drew nearer, King Hussein composed his differences with Egypt, and personally flew to Cairo to sign a defence agreement. Jordanian troops, together with those of the U.A.R., Iraq and Saudi Arabia, went into action immediately on the outbreak of hostilities in June. By the end of the Six Days War, however, all Jordanian territory west of the River Jordan had been occupied by Israeli troops, and a steady stream of West Bank Jordanians began to cross the River Jordan to the East Bank. Estimated at between 150,000 and 250,000 persons, they swelled Jordan's refugee population and presented the government with intractable social and economic problems.

King Hussein formed a nine-man Consultative Council in August 1967, composed of former premiers and politicians of varying sympathies, to meet weekly and to participate in the "responsibility of power". Later a Senate was formed consisting of fifteen representatives from the inhabitants of the west bank area, and fifteen from eastern Jordan. Several changes of government took place and the King took over personal command of the country's armed forces. U.S. arms shipments to Jordan were resumed on February 14th, 1968.

Meanwhile the uneasy situation along the frontier with Israel persisted, aggravated by the deteriorating economic situation in the country. Reprisal actions by Israel after numerous commando raids directed against her authority in Jerusalem and the West Bank and operating from Jordanian territory provoked Jordan to appeal for UN intervention. In June 1969 Israeli commandos blew up the diversion system of the Ghor Canal, Jordan's principal irrigation project.

THE GUERRILLA CHALLENGE

The instability in Amman after the June War was reflected in the short life of Jordanian cabinets—it became rare for one to remain unchanged for more than three months. A careful balance had to be struck between the Palestinians and the King's traditional supporters. Thus, in the new cabinet announced after the June 1970 crisis, Palestinians were given more of the key ministries, including that of the Interior. Abdul Munem Rifai, Jordan's senior diplomat, became Prime Minister for the second time.

The main factor in Jordan's internal politics between June 1967 and 1971 was the rivalry between the official government and the guerrilla organizations, principally Al Fatah. These organizations gradually assumed effective control of the refugee camps and commanded widespread support amongst the Palestinian majority of Jordan's present population. They also received arms and training assistance from other Arab countries, particularly Syria, and finance from the oil-rich Gulf states. Some camps became commando training centres, the younger occupants of these, almost all unemployed, welcoming the sense of purpose and relief from idleness and boredom that recruitment into a guerrilla group offered. The fedayeen movement virtually became a state within a state. Its leadership has stated that "We have no wish to interfere in the internal affairs of Jordan provided it does not place any obstacles in the way of our struggle to liberate Palestine". In practice, however, its popularity and influence represented a challenge to the government, whilst its actions attracted Israeli reprisals that did serious damage to the east bank, now the only fertile part of Jordan, and generally reduced the possibilities of a peace settlement on which Jordan's long-term future depended.

A major confrontation between the two forces occurred in November 1968, after massive demonstrations in Amman on the anniversary of the Balfour Declaration. Extensive street fighting broke out between guerrillas and the army, which, being mainly Bedouin, has little in common with the Palestinians anyway, and for a short period a civil war seemed possible, but both sides soon backed down. Some sources attributed the trouble to the government's attempt (subsequently abandoned) to disarm the refugee camps; others pointed out that small extremist groups had led the fighting which was discouraged by the more responsible Al Fatah leadership. Similar confrontations followed in February and June 1970, and on both occasions the Government was forced to yield to Palestinian pressures. King Hussein and Yasser Arafat, the Al Fatah leader (whose own position was threatened by the rise of small extremist groups in Jordan), jointly drew up and signed an agreement redefining their respective spheres of influence. The guerrillas appeared to have granted little or nothing, but Hussein was forced to dismiss his Commander-in-Chief and a cabinet minister, both relatives. These were regarded as the leaders of the anti-fedayeen faction, which remained strong amongst the Bedouin sheikhs. Despite the agreement, the tension between the government and the guerrillas continued, aggravated by opposition to the government's concessions from hard-line army officers.

A new and dangerous stage in the relations between the two sides in Jordan was reached in July with the acceptance by the government of the American peace proposals for the Middle East. The guerrilla groups, with few exceptions, rejected these, and, as the cease-fire between the U.A.R. and Israel came into operation on August 7th, it was clear that the Jordanian Government was preparing for a full-scale confrontation with them.

CIVIL WAR

Bitter fighting between government and guerrilla forces broke out at the end of August. In the first part of September the violence was increased by two factors: the assassination attempt on King Hussein and the hijackings by PLFP of four Western Airliners. The threat of intervention on the side of the commandos by Iraq and Syria; the transference of Libyan aid from the Jordanian government to the guerrillas; a succession of cease-fire agreements between the two sides; the release of all but 54 hostages taken from the aircraft to secure the release of Palestinian commandos held by Western governments; none of these developments were enough to prevent the escalation into full civil war in the last half of the month, and thousands of death and injuries. The continued detention of any hostages by the PFLP was a direct challenge to the government's authority. On September 16th a military cabinet was formed under Brig. Muhammad Daoud—in any case martial law had been in force since the end of the June 1967 war—and immediately Field Marshal Habis Majali replaced as Commander-in-Chief Lt.-Gen. Mashour Haditha, who had been sympathetic to the commandos and had tried to restrain their severest opponents in the army.

In the fighting that followed, the guerrillas claimed full control in the north, aided by Syrian forces and, it was later revealed, three battalions of the Palestine Liberation Army sent back by President Nasser from the Suez front. The Arab states generally appealed for an end to the fighting. Libya threatened to intervene and later broke off diplomatic relations; Kuwait stopped its aid to the government; but the Iraqi troops stationed on the Eastern front against Israel notably failed to intervene. On the government side talks were held with the U.S.A. about direct military assistance. In the event such a dangerous widening of the Palestinian confrontation was avoided by the scale of the casualties in Jordan and by the diplomacy of Arab heads of state (reinforced by President Nasser's reported threat to intervene on the guerrillas' behalf) who prevailed upon King Hussein and Yasser Arafat to sign an agreement in Cairo on September 27th ending the war. The previous day a civilian cabinet had been restored under Ahmed Toukan. Five military members were retained.

A definitive agreement, very favourable to the liberation organizations, was signed by Hussein and Arafat on October 13th in Amman, but this proved to be simply the beginning of a phase of sporadic warfare between the two parties, punctuated by new agreements, during which the commandos were gradually forced out of Amman and driven from their positions in the north back towards the Syrian frontier. At the end of October a new government, still containing three army officers, was formed under Wasfi al-Tal. By January 1971 army moves against the Palestine guerrillas had become much more blatant, and the U.A.R., Syria and Algeria all issued strong protests at the Jordanian Government's attempt to "liquidate" the liberation movements. All but two brigades of Iraqi troops were, however, withdrawn from Jordan.

By April the Jordanian Government seemed strong enough to set a deadline for the guerrillas' withdrawal of their remaining men and heavy armaments from the capital. Isolated outbreaks of fighting between government and commando forces were still being reported from the north, however. More important was the declaration issued on June 5th by seven commando organizations, including even the more moderate Fatah, calling for the overthrow of Hussein. However, it was the Jordanian authorities who in July moved first to resolve the contest for political power in Jordan. On July 13th a major Government attack began on the guerrillas entrenched in the Jerash-Aljoun area. Four days later it was all over. The Government claimed that all the bases had been destroyed and that 2,300 of 2,500 guerrillas in them had been captured. Most of the Palestinians taken prisoner by the Jordanian government were released a few days later, either to leave for other Arab states or to return to normal life in Jordan.

The "solution" (in King Hussein's word) of the guerrilla "problem" provoked strong reaction from other Arab governments. Iraq and Syria closed their borders with Jordan; Algeria suspended diplomatic relations; and Egypt, Libya, Sudan and both Yemens voiced public criticism. Relations with Syria deteriorated fastest of all, but normal trading and diplomatic relations were restored by February 1972.

In the meantime, Saudi Arabia had been attempting to bring together guerrilla leaders and Jordanian Government representatives to work out a new version of the Cairo and Amman agreements. Meetings did take place in Jeddah but were fruitless, and the Palestinians responded in their own way to the events of July. Three unsuccessful attemps were made in September to hijack Jordanian airliners. Then, on September 28th, 1971, Wasfi al-Tal, the Prime Minister and Defence Minister, was assassinated by members of a secret Palestinian guerrilla group, the Black September Organization, and other assassination attempts were made.

HUSSEIN'S ANSWER

Throughout the period since the liquidation of the guerrillas in July 1971 Hussein had been seeking to strengthen his political position. In August he announced the creation of a tribal council—a body of sheikhs or other notables, appointed by him and chaired by the Crown Prince—which was to deal with the affairs of tribal areas. A month later the formation of the Jordanian National Union was announced. This (renamed Arab National Union in March 1972) was to be Jordan's only legal political organization. It was not to be a party in the usual sense; proponents of "imported ideologies" were debarred from membership; the King became President and the Crown Prince Vice-President; and appointed the 36 members of the Supreme Executive Committee.

However, the King's boldest political move, and an obvious attempt to regain his standing in the eyes of Palestinians, was his unfolding of plans for a United Arab Kingdom in March 1972. This kingdom was to federate a Jordanian region, with Amman as its capital and also federal capital, and a Palestinian region, with Jerusalem as its capital. Each region was to be virtually autonomous, though the King would rule both and there would be a federal council of ministers.

Outside Jordan there was almost universal criticism of this plan from interested parties—Israel, the Palestinian organizations and Egypt, which in the following month broke off diplomatic relations. Jordan's isolation in the Arab world had never been more complete.

Throughout the rest of 1972 and the first half of 1973 Hussein continued to stand by his original plans for a United Arab Kingdom, but at the same time insisting that peace with Israel can only come within the framework of UN Resolution 242 (*see* Documents on Palestine, page 67) and hotly denying suggestions from other Arab states that he was considering signing a separate peace treaty with Israel.

The internal security of Jordan was threatened in November 1972 when an attempted military coup in Amman by Major Rafeh Hindawi was thwarted. It was alleged that the attempted coup had the support of Libya and the Palestinian guerrillas. In February 1973 Abu Daoud, one of the leaders of Al Fatah, and 16 other guerrillas were arrested on charges of infiltrating into Jordan for the purpose of subversive activities.

The latter affair took place while King Hussein was on a visit to the U.S.A. requesting defence and financial aid. On his return he commuted the death sentences passed on the guerrillas by a Jordanian military court and previously confirmed by himself, to life imprisonment. In May 1973 Hussein's Prime Minister, Ahmed Lauzi, resigned for health reasons and a new government under Zaid-al Rifai, who was known to be against the Palestinian guerrillas, was formed.

In September 1973 Hussein attended a "reconciliation summit" with Presidents Sadat of Egypt and Assad of Syria. This was Jordan's first official contact with the two states since they had broken diplomatic relations, and they were restored after the summit. The meeting was condemned by Al Fatah, Libya and Iraq but Jordan regained some stature in the Arab world after Hussein's general amnesty for all political prisoners; among those released was Abu Daoud.

During the Middle East War in October 1973 Jordan sent troops to support Syria on the Golan Heights but was otherwise not actively involved, and did not open a third front against the Israelis as in the 1967 War. Jordan was represented at the Geneva talks in December 1973. During February 1974 there was considerable unrest among sections of the army though this was settled by increases in pay ordered by Hussein who was out of the country when the disturbances started. In April Hussein announced that the Arab National Union, which was then the sole political organization in Jordan, was to be reorganized with an executive and council of reduced numbers.

During most of 1974 the main characteristic of Hussein's policy towards the PLO and the status of the West Bank was extreme ambiguity. He continued to try to preserve the West Bank as part of his kingdom despite strong pressure from other Arab states and the increasing influence of the PLO. In September 1974 after a meeting between Egypt, Syria and the PLO expressing support for the PLO as the "only legitimate representative of the Palestinian people", Jordan refused to participate in further Middle East peace talks. However, in October 1974 at the Arab Summit Conference at Rabat (*see* Documents on Palestine, page 71), representatives of twenty Arab heads of state unanimously recognized the PLO as the sole legitimate representative of the Palestinians, and its right to establish a national authority over any liberated Palestinian territory. Effectively ceding Jordan's claim to represent the Palestinians and re-incorporate the West Bank, when recaptured, into the Hashemite Kingdom, Hussein reluctantly assented to the resolution. He said that Jordan would continue to strive for the liberation of the West Bank and recognize the full rights of citizenship of Palestinians in Jordan. The prospect of a separate, independently ruled Palestinian state was strongly condemned by Israel.

JORDAN AFTER THE RABAT SUMMIT

Following the Rabat Conference Hussein was given more extensive powers in revisions to the Jordanian constitution approved by parliament in November. He was allowed to rule without parliament for a year and reorganize his Kingdom in order to lessen the numbers of Palestinians in the executive and legislative branches of government, his 1972 plan for a United Arab Kingdom now being wholly defunct. Parliament was dissolved and a new government formed in November, with Zaid al-Rifai remaining Prime Minister. Palestinian representation was decreased, and the question of citizenship of the estimated 800,000 Palestinians on the East Bank became contentious. Elections in Jordan were postponed in March 1975 and when Parliament was briefly reconvened in February 1976 a constitutional amendment was enacted to suspend elections indefinitely.

The success of the PLO at the Rabat Conference had, despite internal feuds (*see* Palestine Organizations, page 81), considerably strengthened its position. This was further the case when the UN acknowledged the PLO as the legitimate representative of the Palestinians by an overwhelming majority in November. The PLO was also granted observer status at the UN.

One of the most notable results of the Rabat Summit Conference and Hussein's virtual abandonment of his claim to the West Bank was an improvement in relations with the Arab world in general, and with Syria in particular. During 1975 various links with Syria were forged and strengthened. Early in the year Hussein visited Damascus and President Assad visited Jordan in June. A supreme joint committee was set up to co-ordinate military and political planning, with the two prime ministers as Chairmen. In August a Supreme Command Council, headed by the King and President Assad, was formed to direct military and political action against Israel, and in December 1976 it was announced that a form of political union would be worked out between the two countries.

This close relationship, however, was put into jeopardy by President Sadat's visit to Israel in November 1977, and subsequently overshadowed by Syria's *rapprochement* with Iraq. Jordan, unlike Syria, was anxious not to condemn Sadat's peace initiative, but did not want to destroy its growing relationship with Syria. King Hussein, therefore, "sat on the fence" and tried to act as a conciliator between Egypt on the one hand and the "rejectionist" States on the other (Algeria, Libya, Iraq, Syria and Yemen P.D.R.). Jordan, however, emphatically rejected Israel's peace proposals which were put forward by Prime Minister Begin in December 1977, and maintained its policy of demanding an Israeli withdrawal from Gaza and the West Bank, including East Jerusalem, leaving no Jewish settlements. Jordan also wanted the creation of a Palestinian homeland, the nature of whose link with Jordan should be decided by a referendum.

It was these factors which helped to determine Jordan's attitude to the Camp David agreements (see p. 73) in September 1978 and the subsequent peace treaty between Egypt and Israel (see p. 77) in March 1979. Jordan refused to be drawn into the Camp David talks by the United States, and joined the other Arab States at the Baghdad Arab summit in drawing up a list of sanctions against Egypt.

Immediately prior to the signing of the peace treaty Jordan showed its commitment to the PLO by welcoming Yasser Arafat on an official visit, and after the treaty was signed Jordan was the first Arab country still having diplomatic relations with Egypt to break them off. In July 1979, however, Dr. Henry Kissinger was forecasting that Jordan would, before long, be joining Egypt, Israel and the U.S.A. in the Palestinian autonomy talks.

King Hussein had dissolved Parliament by Royal Decree in November 1974, but in April 1978 he formed a National Consultative Council consisting of 60 members appointed by Royal Decree, three of the members being current Ministers and another 16 being former Ministers. The Council is to serve for two years, after which it can be re-formed. The King has the right to dismiss any member or dissolve the Council. It was intended that the Council would provide a forum for discussion of legislation.

ECONOMIC SURVEY

Jordan's economy has twice been completely disrupted by war between the Arabs and the Israelis, first in 1948, and then in 1967. While Jordan in 1948 acquired some 2,165 square miles of new territory—the vast salient which juts out into Israel west of the River Jordan—the country's population also increased more than threefold. In 1948, before the war broke out, the country's population was perhaps 400,000. The number of those living on the West Bank of the River Jordan in the territory acquired in 1948 was well over 800,000. This territory was occupied by the Israelis in 1967, but perhaps 350,000 of the inhabitants fled to non-occupied Jordan. The disruption caused by the October 1973 war between the Arabs and Israel was by no means as severe, since Jordanian territory was not directly involved. According to the latest statistics, the population of the East Bank in 1977 was 2,126,540, compared with 2,018,407 in 1976 when the East and West Banks had a combined population of 2,792,000. Population growth is estimated at 3.6 per cent per annum.

The absorption of the refugees of 1948 and of 1967 into Jordan's economy has presented the country with problems for which few precedents could be found in modern times. These problems were accentuated by ethnic, cultural and religious differences. Jordanians before 1948 were mainly Bedouin and mostly engaged in pastoral, and even nomadic, activities. They therefore had little in common with the Palestinians, many of whom established themselves in Jordan as traders and professional men. The vast majority of the country's original inhabitants were Sunni Muslims, but until 1967 at least there were also 180,000 Christians. Also in 1967 some 53 per cent of the population was classified as urban.

Again, the loss of the West Bank of the Jordan to Israel in the summer of 1967 created a whole series of new problems. For the result was the loss not only of some efficiently farmed agricultural land, but also of the important and growing tourist industry, and the large sums in foreign exchange received from the people who annually visited the old city of Jerusalem and Bethlehem. Some of the immediate problems brought by the war of 1967 were met by aid from Arab countries, but Jordan's economic future in the long run will obviously depend on the nature of any settlement which may be reached with Israel.

The area of the country, including the 2,165 square miles of the West Bank territory, was about 25,000 square miles. A large part of it, however, consisted of desert which spreads eastwards from a narrow, fertile strip of country running south from the Syrian frontier to Ma'an, and probably no more than about 5 per cent of the country's total area was cultivable. East of the Jordan river the country is mostly plateau, averaging about 2,000 ft. above sea level. The climate is of the Mediterranean variety, but, owing perhaps to the height above sea level, the extremes of heat and cold are greater than on the Levantine littoral. West of the Hedjaz railway there is an abundant and fairly regular rainy season, beginning in October or November and ending in April, and following the same pattern as in Israel. East of the railway line the annual rainfall tends to decrease very rapidly. From May to September there is generally no rainfall at all.

AGRICULTURE

Agriculture accounted for 10.3 per cent of the gross domestic product in 1975, and the National Planning Council estimate that the proportion will fall to 8.3 per cent by 1980. Great improvements were achieved in the years prior to the 1967 war but the war and subsequent events on the East Bank resulted in almost complete disruption. In recent years, however, the economic situation on the East Bank has stabilized and agricultural production has begun to progress, although wheat and barley production have been affected by drought and have not been able to match the record levels of 1974.

The size of the average agricultural holding varies according to its location. In the Jordan Valley, which is worked by nearly a third of the country's economically active population, the average plot is under five acres, whereas in the highland region above the valley, where yields are much lower, farms tend to be large, sometimes exceeding 500 acres. Crop cultivation peters out altogether as the semi-arid lands east of the valley give way to desert and the sparse vegetation on the desert fringes serves only as grazing for sheep and goats belonging to the Bedouin nomads. Attempts to intensify farming have centred on irrigation schemes in the Jordan Valley, based on the diversion of rivers flowing directly into the Jordan from the eastern highlands into canals along the valley floor. The valley is administered by a special authority and has its own development scheme, drawn up in 1972. Irrigation targets are being met mainly by extensions to the East Ghor canal and by the Zarqa river project. The East Ghor canal runs parallel to the Jordan carrying water diverted from the Yarmuk river. Work on the scheme began in 1958 and by 1963 it had added 300,000 acres to the country's irrigated area, but the installations were severely damaged by Israeli bombardment in 1967 and repairs were not carried out until after the 1970 civil war. Almost JD 13.5 million has been allocated in the 1976–80 Five-Year Plan to extending the East Ghor canal to the Dead Sea. The Zarqa river project hinges on the construction of the King Talal dam to divert the river water and increase the irrigated area still further. An integrated planning approach in the Jordan Valley is designed to triple sprinkler-irrigated land and increase the valley's population to 150,000 in the 1980s. Most of the JD 42 million earmarked for agricultural development in the 1976–80 Five-Year Plan was to be used for development of the valley. As well as irrigation, crop-raising has also been improved by the introduction of special strains of seed, inorganic fertilizers and mechanization. There were 2,856 tractors in use on the East Bank alone at the end of 1971, compared with 2,000 in the whole of Jordan in 1966.

Cereals, fruit and vegetables are the mainstays of Jordan's agriculture and 1974 was a record year for the cereal crop, with production of wheat, at 244,500 tons, and barley, at 40,200 tons, reaching its highest since Jordan lost one-quarter of its cereal acreage with the Israeli occupation of the West Bank. The combined wheat crop from both banks in 1964 had totalled 294,700 tons and the barley crop 97,200 tons. The success of the East Bank harvest in 1974 was particularly welcome after the serious drought of 1973 which had reduced wheat production to only 50,400 tons and barley production to 5,900 tons, levels comparable with those of 1970 when civil war had lowered output. Wheat and barley production fell considerably in 1975, with wheat totalling only 50,000 tons and barley 11,800 tons. There was a slight improvement in 1976, with wheat totalling 66,600 tons and barley 13,200 tons. Since then there has been a steady decline in wheat production, which amounted to 62,500 tons in 1977 and 53,300 tons in 1978. Barley production, on the other hand, rose from 12,000 tons in 1977 to 15,600 tons in 1978.

The loss of the West Bank had a serious effect on cereal production but its effect on fruit and vegetable cultivation was disastrous, lopping off some 80 per cent of the fruit-growing area and 45 per cent of the area under vegetables and depriving Jordan of an important and expanding source of some of its major export commodities. Production of fruit and vegetables on the East Bank has fluctuated violently, partly because of the weather and partly as a result of political instability in 1969 and 1970. However, vegetable production more than doubled from 204,400 tons to 410,000 tons between 1977 and 1978. Tomatoes showed the largest increase, rising from 85,700 tons to 208,800 tons, approaching the 1967 level of 259,700 tons. Total fruit production also rose from 103,600 tons in 1977 to 179,200 tons in 1978, with banana production showing the largest rise from 3,400 tons to 21,000 tons, again approaching the 1967 total of 22,200 tons. Current estimates give Jordan 500,000 sheep, 250,000 goats, 40,000 cattle and less than 10,000 camels.

INDUSTRY AND MINING

Industry, which is almost entirely of recent origin and accounted for approximately 18 per cent of the gross domestic product in 1976, 1977 and 1978, is concentrated around Amman and in Nablus on the West Bank. About 65 per cent of all factories produce food products or clothing but the major industrial income derives from the three heavier industries—phosphate extraction, cement manufacture and petroleum refining.

The country's mineral wealth lies predominantly in its phosphate reserves which are estimated at 2,000 million tons. There are also known to be deposits of good quality copper ore. Other minerals include gypsum, manganese ore, abundant quantities of glass sand and the clays and feldspar ore required for ceramics manufacture. Foreign investors have been found to finance the establishment of companies to produce ceramics and sheet glass and also to exploit potash deposits in the Dead Sea. The Arab Potash Company (APC), formed in 1956 as one of the earliest Arab joint ventures, is 51 per cent owned by the Jordanian Government. APC is proceeding with a $430 million scheme to produce potash from a solar evaporation plant. Production was under way in 1979 and the plant is due to come on stream in 1981, with an estimated maximum production of 1.2 million tons. Quantities of uranium and vanadium are now known to be mixed in with the phosphate reserves. A concession for oil prospection, granted to a Canadian firm in 1972, was withdrawn nine months later with no positive results having been reached, but the possibility of a big oil strike near Ramalla on the Israeli-occupied West Bank was announced by Israeli geologists in January 1975 and in April the Jordanian Government awarded a 30-year 8,400-square-kilometre concession to the American Filon Corporation. Under the agreement this company will bear all the exploration and exploitation expenses, recouping these from its share of any eventual liftings of oil. The Jordanian Government will remain sole owner of all reserves in the concessionary area. The Compagnie Française des Pétroles (CFP) has reached agreement with the Jordanian Government and is now conducting survey work under the Red Sea. In 1977 CFP and Fuyo Petroleum Company of Japan each took a 37.5 per cent stake in the Filon exploration contract.

Rich beds of phosphates exist at Rusaifa, a few miles north-east of Amman, and have been exploited since 1963 by a local company financed partly by the Government. Other deposits in the Wadi Hasa area, south of Amman, have been developed by American and Italian interests. By 1968 the country's total production of natural phosphates was 1,162,000 tons, more than five times the production in 1956. Production fell, however, to 651,000 tons in 1971, mainly as a result of the closure of the Syrian borders to Jordanian traffic, but rose again to 715,000 tons in 1972 and 1,674,800 tons in 1974, surpassing for the first time the record set in 1968. Phosphates are Jordan's biggest single export commodity. Although in 1975, production fell slightly, 1976 was a record year with production exceeding 1.76 million tons. Export earnings from phosphates, constant in 1974 and 1975 at JD 19.5 million, dropped to JD 19.2 million in 1976. This was due to a fall in the international price of phosphate rock and prompted Jordan in 1976 to join with Morocco, Tunisia and Senegal in an association of phosphate exporters. Under the 1976–80 plan phosphate production is expected to increase to 6 million tons in 1980 but is currently running behind schedule. Exports were slightly higher in 1977, at 1.8 million tons, but revenue was 8 per cent lower than in 1976. Export earnings from phosphates in the first ten months of 1978 were JD 16.8 million, while the figure for the full year of 1977 was JD 17.3 million. The Al-Hasa mine in central Jordan is being expanded to double its 3 million ton capacity and a new mine in the Shadiya region will be opened by 1980.

A phosphate fertilizer plant at Aqaba was due to start operations in 1980, having been delayed for two years by technical and financial problems, but production is not now expected to start until 1981. The project which will be managed by the Jordanian Fertiliser Industry Company, will cost $320 million. In 1977 one of the equity partners, the U.S. firm Agrico, withdrew from the project. Agrico was also technical adviser. Mitsui of Japan is now providing technical advice. The finance for the project has had to be restructured. The Jordanian Government is the principal shareholder but much of its finance is coming from suppliers' credits, international organizations and bank loans. Full production is not expected to be achieved until 1983.

Output of petroleum products from Jordan's only oil refinery at Zarqa has increased steadily from 445,800 tons in 1970 to 748,000 tons in 1974, and to 1,114,600 tons in 1976. Production capacity was scheduled to reach 3.5 million tons per year by the end of 1979. This would be more than sufficient to meet Jordan's domestic requirements. Plans to form a joint venture with Romania to build a second refinery in the south were agreed in April 1975. This project, if it proceeds, will refine petroleum for export. There are also long-term plans for a second cement plant in the south but in the meantime the existing plant at Fuheis near Amman is undergoing an expansion programme which will raise output capacity from 620,000 tons per year in 1975 to 1.2 million tons per year in 1978 and to 2.25 million tons by 1980. Cement production, badly hit by the troubles of 1970, rose to its peak in 1972 at 661,600 tons, but declined to 598,200 tons in 1975, to 533,000 tons in 1976 and again to 500,800 tons in 1977. Two sulphuric acid plants are also to be built, each with a daily production of 1,800 tons. A fertilizer plant will eventually be added to process the acid into phosphate fertilizers. This latter project is due to be commissioned in 1980, with full capacity being reached in 1983. Other goods produced in Jordan include batteries, cigarettes, detergents, pharmaceutical products, paper, spirits and alcoholic drinks and leather. There is also potential for the development of a flourishing fishing industry centred on the Gulf of Aqaba.

TRANSPORT

The development of the Jordanian economy has, in the past, been hampered by the difficulty of communication. Though there is a good road from Amman to Beirut through Syria, transport costs on this route are heavy and overland routes from Jordan northwards were cut three times between 1972 and 1973. The re-opening of the Suez Canal on June 5th, 1975, has also had important repercussions on the amount of trade passing through Aqaba, especially with the congested state of most Eastern Mediteranean ports.

A vital railway link between Aqaba and the Al-Hasa phosphate mines has been built with financial backing from the Federal Republic of Germany. Freight carried on the railway system increased from 12,300 tons to 606,300 tons between 1976 and 1977. A road between the port and the agricultural and mining installations of the southern Ghor is under construction. Cargo handled at Aqaba declined in the years immediately following 1967, falling from an average 100,000 tons a month in 1966 to 32,000 tons in 1970 but this figure rose again to 104,000 tons in 1973 although Aqaba was closed for a month during the Arab-Israeli war. It reached a monthly average of 250,000 tons in 1976 and by the end of 1977 annual unloading capacity had been increased to more than 2 million tons. Congestion had also been relieved by the use of a floating jetty while expansion of port facilities goes ahead at a cost of $54 million, with assistance of $25 million provided by Saudi Arabia. Future road schemes will include the construction of a network of roads inside Amman and a motorway from Rum, near Aqaba, through Ras al-Naq to Maan. The latter will be financed by a United States loan. What was formerly Jordan's only railway, the single-track Hedjaz line, used to run through Maan northwards to Damascus and south to Mecca and Medina in Saudi Arabia, and, though the Jordanian section of the railway is the only one still in operation, plans exist to reconstruct the section between Damascus and Al-Hasa.

The state airline is taking over a growing role in handling the country's freight and passenger transport. It made a net profit in 1973 for the first time in its 10-year existence, and increased this profit in 1974 and 1975. The airline set up an air freight company in April 1975 to operate on routes to other Middle Eastern capitals, Europe and the Far East.

The Government plans to invest JD 119.9 million on transport under the 1976–80 plan. JD 25.5 million will be spent on the construction of a new international airport at Amman and JD 37 million on road construction and improvement. JD 28.8 million will be devoted to the expansion of Aqaba port, with two new phosphate stores and four new berths. JD 14 million will be used to improve the Aqaba to Al-Hasa railway link.

EXTERNAL TRADE

The war of 1967 disrupted the country's foreign trade less, perhaps, than might have been expected. By 1970 imports had recovered to JD 65.9 million, roughly the level of 1966, and by 1975 they had almost quadrupled to JD 234 million. By 1976 imports had reached a record JD 340 million, with a trade deficit of JD 271 million. In 1977 the trade deficit had reached JD 394 million, with imports at JD 454 million. Items which have shown the largest increase since 1973 include transport equipment, chemical products, grain and textiles. Exports in 1977 amounted to JD 60.3 million, with phosphates forming the largest single item at JD 17.3 million. This represents a drop of approximately ten per cent on the 1976 figure for exports. Tomatoes, vegetables and fruit are other important exports. Jordan's principal supplier in 1977 was the U.S.A. (15 per cent of the total), followed by Federal Germany (14 per cent) and Saudi Arabia (8 per cent). Saudi Arabia was the main purchaser of Jordan's exports in 1977, taking 25 per cent of the total, followed by Syria (12 per cent).

FINANCE

Before 1967 net earnings from the tourist trade and income from private donations constituted the only important invisible export. After 1967 income from tourism and private transfers fell dramatically and the JD 6 million surplus on the travel account in 1966, when tourism earned JD 11.3 million, was already reduced to a deficit by 1968. In 1974, however, the Jordanian Government decided to allow its visitors to cross over to the West Bank and the number of tourists arriving in the country that year rose by 79 per cent on the 1973 total to reach 554,913, nearly regaining the 1966 level of 617,000, while income from tourism exceeded it, reaching JD 17.3 million. Tourism was even more successful in 1975, with 707,623 visitors bringing in revenue of about JD 23 million. The number of visitors in 1976 rose to 1,063,294 but in 1978, contrary to expectations, only 937,000 people visited Jordan, a drop of 2 per cent on 1977, generating an income of approximately $300 million. The Jordanian Government is planning to develop Aqaba as an international tourist resort. The Jordanian airline Alia has reached agreement with a Danish tour company to operate package tour flights and feasibility studies have been prepared for a major expansion of hotels in Aqaba. By the end of 1981 the number of hotel rooms should have risen from 1,869 to 4,724, on completion of 25 new hotels.

Another important source of earnings is the remittances from Jordanians working abroad. These totalled $360 million in 1976.

For many years Jordan's increasing trade deficit has been made good mainly by capital imports and subventions. Before 1967 these used to come principally from Britain and the United States but since 1967 there have been similar payments from Saudi Arabia and other Arab states (*see* below). These subventions have enabled the country's exchange reserves to be maintained and even increased. At the end of 1977 net foreign assets stood at JD 252.1 million, compared with JD 180.8 million at the end of 1976, and international reserves were $677.5 million, compared with $491.3 million at the end of 1976. At the end of March 1979 reserves were $932.2 million, 21.3 per cent higher than a year earlier.

Money supply at the end of December 1978 was JD 370.5 million. The Arab Bank, which possesses branches in most of the countries that are members of the Arab League, has its head office in Amman. Recently two new institutions operating along the lines of merchant banks have opened and a degree of financial maturity is evidenced by the establishment of secondary market bond trading and the introduction of certificates of deposit. In addition, about 125 firms have opened offices in Amman attracted by a Jordanian decree of late 1975 offering attractive benefits to any company that settles in Amman, and disillusioned with Beirut. As a result, Amman is experiencing a minor boom. There is also a Development Bank of Jordan and an Agricultural Bank and the Government has interests in both of these.

Before 1967 most of Jordan's financial support had come from the United Kingdom and the United States. After the June 1967 war Kuwait, Saudi Arabia and Libya undertook to pay Jordan quarterly sums of $112 million. These budgetary grants were suspended in the autumn of 1970 in protest against the Government's treatment of Palestinian guerrillas, and the revenue from foreign grants fell from JD 37.6 million in 1969 to JD 33 million in 1970, the only two years when subventions to the Government were exclusively from Arab sources. The United States, whose direct budgetary support ceased altogether in 1967, one year after Britain's, stepped in again in 1971 to make up the deficit. Budget support from Arab sources sank still further to JD 19.9 million in 1971, but since 1971 direct Arab budget assistance has risen to JD 75.5 million in 1976. Total external assistance in 1976 through transfer payments amounted to over JD 140 million. In 1977, budgetary support from Saudi Arabia was expected to amount to JD 11 million, while support from Kuwait was expected to be JD 9 million. The U.S.A. was expected to be the largest single source of budgetary aid, with JD 15 million. A further JD 52 million was to come from other countries while JD 83 million was expected in loans for project aid. In 1978 Jordan received $477 million in aid, $80 million of which came from the U.S.A., its major supplier. In 1979 Jordan was expected to receive $1,250 million from a fund provided by Saudi Arabia, Libya, Iraq and other Arab countries for the confrontation states, in addition to U.S. aid.

State expenditure, which was running at about JD 70 million a year immediately before the 1967 war, rose to JD 105 million in 1972 and JD 218 million in 1975. Spending under the 1976 budget was put at JD 263 million, including JD 127 million for development projects. Budget revenue in 1976 was given as JD 251 million, including JD 144 million in grants and loans. In 1977 revenue was budgeted at JD 234 million, with expenditure at JD 333 million. In 1978 these figures were JD 356.8 million and JD 371.8 million. Estimated expenditure for 1979 was JD 513 million.

The hundreds of thousands of refugees from the Israelis are the ultimate responsibility of the United Nations Relief and Works Agency (UNRWA), which pays out about JD 3.3 million per year for rations for them, and also employs probably the largest number of people in Jordan, some 2,500. Meanwhile, Jordan has still had to devote most of its own resources to the solution of pressing short-term problems. The 1966–73 Seven-Year Plan was suspended after the 1967 war and a new Three-Year Plan covering the period 1973–75 was introduced, with a total expenditure of JD 179 million. The three largest items of expenditure were transport (JD 35.8 million), housing and government buildings (JD 34.9 million) and mining and industry (JD 26.1 million). The 1976–80 plan, which has followed the 1973–75 plan, envisages a total expenditure of JD 765 million, with the public and private sectors contributing in equal proportions. The Government felt that the Jordanian economy was too heavily biased towards the services sector, and one of the chief aims of the plan is the development of the commodity producing sector and its increased contribution to G.D.P. It is for this reason that mining and manufacturing receive JD 229.1 million, or 29.9 per cent of the total—by far the largest single item). Transport receives JD 119.9 million (15.7 per cent. while agriculture and irrigation receive JD 112.1 million (14.6 per cent). The services sector of the economy (housing, municipal and rural affairs, education, health, etc.) receives JD 184.6 million, or 24.2 per cent of the total.

STATISTICAL SURVEY

AREA AND POPULATION

(East and West Banks)

Area	Estimated Population (mid-year)			
	1973	1974	1975	1976
97,740 sq. km.*	2,535,000	2,618,000	2,702,000	2,779,000

* 37,738 square miles.

Population of the East Bank (1978): 2,217,800.

Principal towns (population in 1978): Amman (capital) 775,800; Zarka 282,700; Irbid 146,070.

Births, marriages and deaths (East Bank only: Births 79,882* (1977), Marriages 14,791 (1978), Deaths 5,210* (1977).

* Preliminary.

AGRICULTURE

LAND USE

('000 hectares, East and West Banks)

	1972	1973	1974	1975	1976
Arable land	1,140*	1,140*	1,170*	1,170*	1,175*
Land under permanent crops	180*	185*	190*	190*	190*
Permanent meadows and pastures	100	100	100	100	100
Forests and woodland	125	125	125	125	125
Other land	8,173	8,168	8,133	8,133	8,128
Inland water	56	56	56	56	56
Total Area	9,774	9,774	9,774	9,774	9,774

* FAO estimate.

Source: FAO, *Production Yearbook.*

PRINCIPAL CROPS
(East Bank only)

	Area ('000 dunums)			Production ('000 metric tons)		
	1976	1977	1978	1976	1977	1978
Barley	536.4	462.8	524.3	13.2	12.0	15.6
Maize	5.1	2.3	1.0	0.6	0.3	0.1
Sesame	2.9	n.a.	n.a.	0.1	n.a.	n.a.
Wheat	1,369.5	1,264.5	1,345.7	66.6	62.5	53.3
Broad Beans	3.3	3.8	2.2	0.2	0.4	0.2
Chick Peas	16.3	13.6	12.5	0.4	0.6	0.4
Kersenneh	47.5	44.3	44.2	0.8	1.9	3.0
Lentils	229.7	134.5	144.1	9.4	6.0	8.3

FRUIT AND VEGETABLES
(East Bank only)
(production in '000 metric tons)

	1976	1977	1978		1976	1977	1978
Almonds	0.6	0.4	0.4	Tomatoes	87.9	85.7	208.8
Apples and Pears	0.7	1.2	6.0	Eggplants (Aubergines)	42.8	24.6	64.1
Apricots	0.2	0.6	0.3	Onions and Garlic	1.3	0.4	3.0
Citrus Fruits	16.5	36.5	32.9	Cauliflowers and Cabbages	7.7	6.3	27.7
Figs	0.3	0.6	0.8	Watermelons and Melons	23.1	28.1	40.3
Bananas	4.5	3.4	21.1	Potatoes	13.0	13.0	8.8
Plums and Peaches	0.4	0.8	0.4	Broadbeans (green)	4.7	6.5	5.0
				Cucumbers	12.9	13.6	30.1

LIVESTOCK
(East Bank only)
('000 head)

	1975	1976*	1977
Horses	2*	3	3*
Mules	9*	10	9*
Donkeys	38	45	50*
Cattle	41	33	24.8†
Camels	18	19	17.9†
Sheep	773	800	} 1,236†
Goats	481	500	
Poultry	4,163	4,300	4,500*

* FAO estimates.

† Figures from Department of Statistics, Amman.

Source: FAO, *Production Yearbook.*

FORESTRY

ROUNDWOOD REMOVALS
('000 cubic metres, all non-coniferous)

	1975	1976	1977
Industrial wood	4	7	4
Fuel wood	5	3	3
TOTAL	9	10	7

FISHING
(East Bank only)

	1975	1976	1977
Quantity of fish landed at Aqaba and on Jordan and Yarmuk rivers (tons)	65.1	48.6	31.0

MINING AND INDUSTRY

(East Bank only)

('000 tons)

	1975	1976	1977	1978
Phosphates	1,352.5	1,767.9	1,758.6	2,320.1
Cement	572.2	533.0	500.8	553.0
Alcohol ('000 litres)	323.8	317.7	250.4	197.0
Beer ('000 litres)	4,436.5	5,035.0	4,686.7	4,735.0
Tobacco (kg.)	6,144.0	10,691.0	7,997.0	12,497.0
Cigarettes (kg.)	1,997,888.0	2,408,023.0	2,700,164.0	2,888,556.0
Electricity (million kWh.)	407.3	501.2	594.9	n.a.

FINANCE

1,000 fils=1 Jordanian dinar (JD).

Coins: 1, 5, 10, 20, 25, 50, 100 and 250 fils.

Notes: 500 fils; 1, 5, 10 and 20 dinars.

Exchange rates (March 1979): £1 sterling=616.5 fils; U.S. $1=298.0 fils.

100 Jordanian dinars=£162.21=$335.57.

Note: The Jordanian dinar was introduced in July 1950, with a value of £1 sterling, then equal to U.S. $2.80 ($1=357.14 fils). This valuation in terms of U.S. currency remained in effect until February 1973, so that from December 1971 (when the U.S. dollar was devalued) the dinar became equivalent to 2.579 Special Drawing Rights (SDRs). In February 1973, when the dollar was again devalued, the dinar's par value was fixed at $3.111 ($1=321.43 fils), thus maintaining the exchange rate in terms of SDRs. Until the end of 1973 the market rate against the U.S. dollar was allowed to fluctuate above and below this valuation. During the first six months of 1974 the par value and market rate were unified. Since July 1974, when the fixed relationship between the SDR and the U.S. dollar was ended, the exchange rate has been maintained at a mid-point of 1 dinar=2.579 SDRs, with a market rate of 1 dinar=2.584 SDRs. The average market value of the dinar was $3.0549 in 1973; $3.1198 in 1974; $3.1305 in 1975; $3.0115 in 1976; $3.0373 in 1977; $3.2620 in 1978. The dinar was at par with the pound sterling until November 1967, after which the exchange rate was £1=857.14 fils (1 dinar=£1.167) until August 1971. The rate was £1=930.61 fils (1 dinar=£1.075) from December 1971 to June 1972.

BUDGET ESTIMATES*

(East Bank only)

(JD'000)

Revenue	1976	1977	1978
Direct taxes	17,830	24,640	27,023
Indirect taxes	31,259	58,889	68,506
Fees	12,231	25,436	30,239
Other internal receipts	45,680	28,335	33,049
	107,000	137,300	158,817
Grants and loans	144,000	97,000	198,000
Total	251,000	234,300	356,817

Expenditure	1976	1977	1978
Education	16,350	20,299	24,360
Health and social welfare	6,626	8,738	10,025
Defence and police	60,000	78,000	95,300
Other current expenditure	52,254	71,463	71,839
Development expenditure	127,770	153,700	170,289
Total	263,000	332,600	371,813

* Total expenditure comprises regular, military and development budgets.

1979: Revenue JD 401.5 million; Expenditure JD 513 million.

DEVELOPMENT EXPENDITURE ESTIMATES

Five-Year Plan, 1976-80

(JD million)

Agriculture	40.0	Education and welfare	34.6
Water	97.4	Health	9.0
Mining and industry	229.1	Social welfare	1.0
Tourism and antiquities	24.4	Work and vocational training	3.8
Electricity	42.8	Housing and government buildings	88.0
Trade	3.8	Municipal and village affairs	38.8
Transport	119.9	Miscellaneous	11.4
Communication	20.1		
Culture and information	2.9	TOTAL	765.0

Source: National Planning Council.

NATIONAL ACCOUNTS

(East Bank only)

(JD million)

	1977	1978
GROSS DOMESTIC PRODUCT (at current prices)	477.6	561.6

EXTERNAL TRADE

(JD'000)

	1974	1975	1976	1977	1978
Imports	156,507	234,013	339,458	454,518	458,943
Exports	49,752	49,143	69,445	60,289	64,136

PRINCIPAL COMMODITIES

(JD'000)

IMPORTS	1976	1977	1978
Animals and products	11,781.0	14,414.0	22,903.0
Grains and legumes	19,498.0	18,878.0	19,916.0
Vegetables	3,336.0	3,502.0	3,554.0
Fruits	10,554.0	9,924.0	9,369.0
Spices	2,677.0	4,827.0	5,621.0
Other agriculture	5,548.0	7,310.0	8,630.0
Forestry products	4,832.0	5,739.0	6,139.0
Mining and quarrying	35,470.0	37,995.0	44,747.0
Food manufactures	34,135.0	23,548.0	27,283.0
Textiles	15,290.0	18,395.0	19,349.0
Clothing	5,250.0	8,945.0	10,599.0
Wood and cork	2,429.0	3,523.0	5,213.0
Paper and products	4,479.0	7,534.0	6,025.0
Printing and publishing	714.0	1,233.0	1,697.0
Rubber and products	4,177.0	5,605.0	4,785.0
Chemical products	19,688.0	26,956.0	26,406.0
Petroleum (refined)	2,538.0	5,790.0	3,269.0
Non-metallic minerals	7,782.0	16,658.0	20,513.0
Metallic minerals	36,102.0	55,854.0	48,020.0
Non-electric machines	38,942.0	44,850.0	10,268.0
Electric machines	16,080.0	24,783.0	29,758.0
Transport equipment	45,930.0	86,925.0	53,000.0

EXPORTS	1976	1977	1978
Phosphates	19,232.8	17,304.0	19,460.0
Tomatoes	2,516.9	2,480.0	3,699.0
Lentils	243.6	1,374.0	28.0
Water Melons	69.5	7.0	6.0
Other vegetables and fruit	11,543.1	12,994.0	10,534.0
Cigarettes	808.6	997.0	1,227.0
Bananas	29.9	7.0	2.0
Raw Hides and Skins	230.6	252.0	313.0
Electric Accumulators	69.4	71.0	33.0
Olive Oil and Prepared Olives	613.1	194.0	733.0

PRINCIPAL TRADING PARTNERS
(JD'000)

IMPORTS	1976	1977	1978
China, People's Repub.	3,231.9	7,425.0	7,199.0
Egypt	9,575.1	9,589.0	8,544.0
France	10,534.9	13,424.0	16,839.0
Germany, Fed. Repub.	52,985.6	63,564.0	60,125.0
India	13,238.8	4,112.0	2,778.0
Italy	19,534.4	25,973.0	30,489.0
Japan	21,512.3	28,717.0	30,819.0
Lebanon	7,346.4	11,656.0	18,782.0
Netherlands	7,770.0	10,268.0	9,349.0
Romania	9,464.9	20,333.0	22,871.0
Saudi Arabia	34,448.0	37,144.0	43,449.0
Syria	7,449.7	11,097.0	11,930.0
U.S.S.R.	1,698.4	2,586.0	3,120.0
United Kingdom	23,720.1	33,016.0	36,549.0
U.S.A.	31,047.3	67,355.2	33,636.0

EXPORTS	1976	1977	1978
China, People's Repub.	1,998.1	—	780.0
Czechoslovakia	1,521.4	318.0	301.0
India	1,711.5	3,891.0	3,531.0
Iraq	2,327.5	4,304.0	3,446.0
Kuwait	3,281.5	2,796.0	4,211.0
Lebanon	1,660.0	2,921.0	1,824.0
Saudi Arabia	7,466.4	15,091.0	17,695.0
Syria	6,392.2	7,542.0	10,425.0
Turkey	1,365.3	1,362.0	2,293.0
Yugoslavia	189.9	142.0	1,064.0

TRANSPORT

RAILWAYS
(East Bank only)

	1976	1977	1978
Passengers carried	96,649	64,949	53,135
Freight carried (tons)	12,329	606,311	1,173,994

SHIPPING
(East Bank only)
(Aqaba port)

	1976	1977	1978
Number of vessels calling	1,064	944	1,197
Freight loaded ('000 tons)	1,636.8	1,389.4	1,551
Freight unloaded ('000 tons)	1,368.6	1,722.3	2,108

ROAD TRAFFIC
(motor vehicles registered, East Bank only)

	1976	1977	1978
Cars (private)	28,615	39,613	50,905
Taxis	7,258	9,312	10,072
Buses	862	1,024	918
Lorries and vans	12,493	16,419	20,033
TOTAL (incl. others)	60,455	79,493	97,402

CIVIL AVIATION
(East Bank only)

	1976	1977	1978
Passengers (number)	475,500	580,464	710,414
Freight ('000 tons)	9,680.0	14,436.4	19,067

TOURISM
(East Bank only)

	1976	1977	1978
Visitors to Jordan	1,063,294	1,772,894	1,184,290

COMMUNICATIONS MEDIA
(East Bank only)

Telephones (1977)	43,109
Radio sets (1974)	200,000

EDUCATION
(East Bank)

	SCHOOLS	TEACHERS	PUPILS
1975–76	2,356	19,826	577,469
1977–78	2,432	21,514	618,673
1978–79	2,522	23,930	653,630

Source: Department of Statistics, Amman.

THE CONSTITUTION

(Revised Constitution approved by King Talal I on January 1st, 1952)

THE Hashemite Kingdom of Jordan is an independent, indivisible sovereign state. Its official religion is Islam; its official language Arabic.

Rights of the Individual. There is to be no discrimination between Jordanians on account of race, religion or language. Work, education and equal opportunities shall be afforded to all as far as is possible. The freedom of the individual is guaranteed, as are his dwelling and property. No Jordanian shall be exiled. Labour shall be made compulsory only in a national emergency, or as a result of a conviction; conditions, hours worked and allowances are under the protection of the State.

The Press, and all opinions, are free, except under martial law. Societies can be formed, within the law. Schools may be established freely, but they must follow a recognized curriculum and educational policy. Elementary education is free and compulsory. All religions are tolerated. Every Jordanian is eligible to public office, and choices are to be made by merit only. Power belongs to the people.

The Legislative Power is vested in the National Assembly and the King. The National Assembly consists of two houses: the Senate and the House of Representatives.

The Senate. The number of Senators is one-half of the number of members of the House of Representatives. Senators must be unrelated to the King, over 40, and are chosen from present and past Prime Ministers and Ministers, past Ambassadors or Ministers Plenipotentiary, past Presidents of the House of Representatives, past Presidents and members of the Court of Cassation and of the Civil and Sharia Courts of Appeal, retired officers of the rank of General and above, former members of the House of Representatives who have been elected twice to that House, etc. . . . They may not hold public office. Senators are appointed for four years. They may be reappointed. The President of the Senate is appointed for two years.

The House of Representatives. The members of the House of Representatives are elected by secret ballot in a general direct election and retain their mandate for four years. General elections take place during the four months preceding the end of the term. The President of the House is elected by secret ballot each year by the Representatives. Representatives must be Jordanians of over 30, they must have a clean record, no active business interests, and are debarred from public office. Close relatives of the King are not eligible. If the House of Representatives is dissolved, the new House shall assemble in extraordinary session not more than four months after the date of dissolution. The new House cannot be dissolved for the same reason as the last. (Parliament was dissolved by Royal Decree in November 1974, and a National Consultative Council was formed in April 1978.)

General Provisions for the National Assembly. The King summons the National Assembly to its ordinary session on November 1st each year. This date can be postponed by the King for two months, or he can dissolve the Assembly before the end of its three months' session. Alternatively, he can extend the session up to a total period of six months. Each session is opened by a speech from the throne.

Decisions in the House of Representatives and the Senate are made by a majority vote. The quorum is two-thirds of the total number of members in each House. When the voting concerns the Constitution, or confidence in the Council of Ministers, "the votes shall be taken by calling the members by name in a loud voice". Sessions are public, though secret sessions can be held at the request of the Government or of five members. Complete freedom of speech, within the rules of either House, is allowed.

The Prime Minister places proposals before the House of Representatives; if accepted there, they are referred to the Senate and finally sent to the King for confirmation. If one house rejects a law while the other accepts it, a joint session of the House of Representatives and the Senate is called, and a decision made by a two-thirds majority. If the King withholds his approval from a law, he returns it to the Assembly within six months with the reasons for his dissent; a joint session of the Houses then makes a decision, and if the law is accepted by this decision it is promulgated. The Budget is submitted to the National Assembly one month before the beginning of the financial year.

The King. The throne of the Hashemite Kingdom devolves by male descent in the dynasty of King Abdullah Ibn al Hussein. The King attains his majority on his eighteenth lunar year; if the throne is inherited by a minor, the powers of the King are exercised by a Regent or a Council of Regency. If the King, through illness or absence, cannot perform his duties, his powers are given to a Deputy, or to a Council of the Throne. This Deputy, or Council, may be appointed by *Iradas* (decrees) by the King, or, if he is incapable, by the Council of Ministers.

On his accession, the King takes the oath to respect and observe the provisions of the Constitution and to be loyal to the nation. As head of the State he is immune from all liability or responsibility. He approves laws and promulgates them. He declares war, concludes peace and signs treaties; treaties, however, must be approved by the National Assembly. The King is Commander-in-Chief of the Navy, the Army and the Air Force. He orders the holding of elections; convenes, inaugurates, adjourns and prorogues the House of Representatives. The Prime Minister is appointed by him, as are the President and members of the Senate. Military and civil ranks are also granted, or withdrawn, by the King. No death sentence is carried out until he has confirmed it.

Ministers. The Council of Ministers consists of the Prime Minister, President of the Council, and of his Ministers. Ministers are forbidden to become members of any company, to receive a salary from any company, or to participate in any financial act of trade. The Council of Ministers is entrusted with the conduct of all affairs of State, internal and external.

The Council of Ministers is responsible to the House of Representatives for matters of general policy. Ministers may speak in either House, and, if they are members of one House, they may also vote in that House. Votes of confidence in the Council are cast in the House of Representatives, and decided by a two-thirds majority. If a vote of "no confidence" is returned, the Ministers are bound to resign. Every newly-formed Council of Ministers must present its programme to the House of Representatives and ask for a vote of confidence. The House of Representatives can impeach Ministers, as it impeaches its own members.

Amendments. Two amendments were passed in November 1974 giving the King the right to dissolve the Senate or to take away membership from any of its members, and to postpone general elections for a period not to exceed a year, if there are circumstances in which the Council of Ministers feels that it is impossible to hold elections. A further amendment in February 1976 enabled the King to postpone elections indefinitely.

THE GOVERNMENT

HEAD OF STATE

King HUSSEIN IBN TALAL; proclaimed King by a decree of the Jordan Parliament on August 11th, 1952; crowned on May 2nd, 1953.

Chief of Royal Court: SHAREF ABED AL-HAMID SHARAF.

Minister of Royal Court: AMER KHAMMASH.

CABINET

(*July* 1979)

Prime Minister, Minister of Defence and Foreign Affairs: MUDAR BADRAN.

Minister of Interior: SULAIMAN ARAR.

Minister of Finance: MUHAMMAD AD-DABBAS.

Minister of Information and in charge of West Bank Affairs: ADNAN ABU-AUDA.

Minister of Tourism and Antiquities: GHALEB BARAKAT.

Minister of Justice: AHMED ABDEL-KARIM TARAUNA.

Minister of Agriculture: HIKMAT SAKET.

Minister of Reconstruction and Development and Minister of State for Foreign Affairs: HASAN IBRAHIM.

Minister of Labour: ISSA AJLOUNI.

Minister of Supply: MARWAN QASSEM.

Minister of Municipal and Rural Affairs: IBRAHIM AYYOUB.

Minister of Health: ABDER-RAOOF RAWABDEH.

Minister of Communications: Dr. SAID TALL.

Minister of Education and Minister of State for Cabinet Affairs: ABDES-SALAM MAJALI.

Minister of Trade and Industry: NAJMADDIN AD-DAJANI.

Minister of Public Works: Eng. SAID BINOU.

Minister of Transport: Eng. ALI SUHAIMAT.

Minister of Waqfs, Islamic Affairs and Holy Places: KAMIL SHARAF.

Minister of Culture and Youth: SHARIF FAWWAZ SHARAF.

NATIONAL ASSEMBLY

THE SENATE

(HOUSE OF NOTABLES)

President: BAHJAT TALHOUNI.

The Senate consists of 30 members, appointed by the King. A new Senate was appointed by the King on January 20th, 1979.

HOUSE OF REPRESENTATIVES

Elections to the 60-seat House of Representatives took place in April 1967. There were no political parties. The House was dissolved by Royal Decree on November 23rd, 1974, but reconvened briefly on February 15th, 1976. Elections have been postponed indefinitely.

In April 1978 a National Consultative Council was formed by Royal Decree. It consists of 60 members appointed by the King, and serves for two years. The King has the right to dissolve the Council or dismiss members. The President is AHMAD ABDEL-KARIM LAUZI.

POLITICAL PARTIES

Political parties were banned before the elections of July 1963. In September 1971 King Hussein announced the formation of a Jordanian National Union. This was the only political organization allowed. Communists, Marxists and "other advocates of imported ideologies" were ineligible for membership. In March 1972 the organization was renamed the Arab National Union. In April 1974 King Hussein dissolved the executive committee of the Arab National Union, and accepted the resignation of the Secretary-General and in February 1976 the Cabinet approved a law abolishing the Union. Membership was estimated at about 100,000.

DIPLOMATIC REPRESENTATION

EMBASSIES AND LEGATIONS ACCREDITED TO JORDAN

(E) Embassy, (L) Legation.

Afghanistan: Jeddah, Saudi Arabia (E).
Algeria: Amman (E); *Ambassador:* MUHAMMAD ABDES-SAMI BEN AL-SHEIKH AL-HUSSEIN.
Argentina: Beirut, Lebanon (E).
Australia: Beirut, Lebanon.
Austria: Beirut, Lebanon (E).
Bahrain: Amman (E); *Ambassador:* SALEM BIN-RASHED AL-ABSI.
Bangladesh: Kuwait City, Kuwait (E).
Belgium: Amman (E); *Ambassador:* JACQUES HOLVOET.
Brazil: Beirut, Lebanon (E).
Bulgaria: Amman (E); *Ambassador:* NICOLA COLIOUVISKI.
Canada: Beirut, Lebanon (E).
Chad: Beirut, Lebanon (E).
Chile: Amman (E); *Ambassador:* FERNANDO CONTRERAS TAPIA.
China, People's Republic: Amman (E); *Ambassador:* KU HSIAO-PO.
Czechoslovakia: P.O.B. 2213, Amman (E); *Ambassador:* FRANTIŠEK MATAL.
Denmark: Nicosia, Cyprus (E).
Finland: Beirut, Lebanon (E).
France: Amman; *Ambassador:* CLAUDE HAREL.
German Democratic Republic: Damascus, Syria (E).
Germany, Federal Republic: Amman (E); *Ambassador:* Dr. HORST SCHMIDT-DORNEDDEN.
Greece: Damascus, Syria (E).
Guinea: Cairo, Egypt (E).
Hungary: Damascus, Syria (E).
India: P.O.B. 2168, Amman; *Ambassador:* ABDUL GANI GONI.
Indonesia: Jeddah, Saudi Arabia (E).
Iran: Amman; *Ambassador:* ALI REZA BAYYAT.
Iraq: Amman (E); *Ambassador:* KHALID MAKKI AL-HASHIMI.
Italy: Amman (E); *Ambassador:* FABRIZIO ROSSI LONGHI.
Japan: Amman (E); *Ambassador:* FUMIYA OKADA.
Korea, Democratic People's Republic: Amman (E); *Ambassador:* LEE SYOUK YUNG.
Korea, Republic: Jabal Amman, 3rd Circle, Abu Tammam St., P.O.B. 3060, Amman (E); *Ambassador:* SOH JIN-CHUL.
Kuwait: Amman; *Ambassador:* (vacant).
Lebanon: Amman (E); *Ambassador:* ABDEL RAHMAN SOLH.
Libya: Amman (E); *Ambassador:* SALEH AS-SENOUSSI.
Malaysia: Jeddah, Saudi Arabia (E).
Malta: Tripoli, Libya (E).
Mauritania: Jeddah, Saudi Arabia (E).
Morocco: Amman (E); *Ambassador:* MUHAMMAD AL-GHARBI.
Nepal: Cairo, Egypt (E).
Netherlands: Beirut, Lebanon (E).
Nigeria: Jeddah, Saudi Arabia (E).
Norway: Cairo, Egypt (E).
Oman: Amman (E); *Ambassador:* NAZAR MUHAMMAD ALI (also accred. to Syria).
Pakistan: Jabal Lewebdeh, Block 33, P.O.B. 1232, Amman (E); *Ambassador:* (vacant).
Poland: Amman (E); *Ambassador:* TADEUSZ CRESMENSKI.
Portugal: Beirut, Lebanon (E).
Qatar: Amman; *Ambassador:* Sheikh HAMAD BIN MOHAMMAD BIN JABER AL-THANI.
Romania: Amman (E); *Ambassador:* VASILE GANDILA.
Saudi Arabia: Um-Uthaina, Amman (E); *Ambassador:* Sheikh IBRAHIM MUHAMMAD AL-SULTAN.
Senegal: Jeddah, Saudi Arabia (E).
Somalia: Jeddah, Saudi Arabia (E).
Spain: Amman (E); *Ambassador:* JAIME AGUIRRE DE CÁRCER.
Sri Lanka: Cairo, Egypt (E).
Sudan: Amman (E); *Ambassador:* (vacant).
Sweden: Beirut, Lebanon (E).
Switzerland: Amman; *Ambassador:* GUSTAV DUBOIS (also accred. to Kuwait).
Syria: Amman (E); *Ambassador:* ABDUL KARIM SABBAGH.
Tunisia: Beirut, Lebanon (E).
Turkey: Amman (E); *Ambassador:* RECHAT ARIM.
U.S.S.R.: Amman (E); *Ambassador:* ALEXEI VORONIN.
United Arab Emirates: Amman; *Ambassador:* ABDUL AZIA NASSIR UWAYYES.
United Kingdom: 3rd Circle, Jebel Amman, P.O.B. 87, Amman (E); *Ambassador:* ALAN URWICK.
U.S.A.: Amman (E); *Ambassador:* NICHOLAS FILTOSS.
Uruguay: Beirut, Lebanon (E).
Vatican: Jerusalem, Israel (L).
Venezuela: Beirut, Lebanon (E).
Yemen Arab Republic: Amman (E); *Ambassador:* MUHAMMAD ABDUL KODDOUS AL-WAZIR.
Yugoslavia: Amman (E); *Ambassador:* DUŠAN ZAVASNIK.

Jordan also has diplomatic relations with Mexico, the Philippines and the People's Democratic Republic of Yemen.

JUDICIAL SYSTEM

With the exception of matters of purely personal nature concerning members of non-Muslim communities, the law of Jordan was based on Islamic Law for both civil and criminal matters. During the days of the Ottoman Empire, certain aspects of Continental law, especially French commercial law and civil and criminal procedure, were introduced. Due to British occupation of Palestine and Transjordan from 1917 to 1948, the Palestine territory has adopted, either by statute or case law, much of the English common law. Since the annexation of the non-occupied part of Palestine and the formation of the Hashemite Kingdom of Jordan, there has been a continuous effort to unify the law.

Court of Cassation. The Court of Cassation consists of seven judges, who sit in full panel for exceptionally important cases. In most appeals, however, only five members sit to hear the case. All cases involving amounts of more than JD 100 may be reviewed by this Court, as well as cases involving lesser amounts and cases which cannot be monetarily valued. However, for the latter types of cases, review is available only by leave of the Court of Appeal, or, upon refusal by the Court of Appeal, by leave of the President of the Court of Cassation. In addition to these functions as final and Supreme Court of Appeal, the Court of Cassation also sits as High Court of Justice to hear applications in the nature of habeas corpus, mandamus and certiorari dealing with complaints of a citizen against abuse of governmental authority.

Courts of Appeal. There are two Courts of Appeal, each of which is composed of three judges, whether for hearing of appeals or for dealing with Magistrates Courts' judgments in chambers. Jurisdiction of the two Courts is geographical, with the Court for the Western Region sitting in Jerusalem (which has not sat since June 1967) and the Court for the Eastern Region sitting in Amman. The regions are separated by the River Jordan. Appellate review of the Courts of Appeal extends to judgments rendered in the Courts of First Instance, the Magistrates Courts, and Religious Courts.

Courts of First Instance. The Courts of First Instance are courts of general jurisdiction in all matters civil and criminal except those specifically allocated to the Magistrates' Courts. Three judges sit in all felony trials, while only two judges sit for misdemeanor and civil cases. Each of the seven Courts of First Instance also exercises appellate jurisdiction in cases involving judgments of less than JD 20 and fines of less than JD 10, rendered by the Magistrates' Courts.

Magistrates' Courts. There are fourteen Magistrates' Courts, which exercise jurisdiction in civil cases involving no more than JD 250 and in criminal cases involving maximum fines of JD 100 or maximum imprisonment of one year.

Religious Courts. There are two types of Religious Court: The Sharia Courts (Muslims): and the Ecclesiastical Courts (Eastern Orthodox, Greek Melkite, Roman Catholic and Protestant). Jurisdiction extends to personal (family) matters, such as marriage, divorce, alimony, inheritance, guardianship, wills, interdiction and, for the Muslim community, the constitution of Waqfs (Religious Endowments). When a dispute involves persons of different religious communities, the Civil Courts have jurisdiction in the matter unless the parties agree to submit to the jurisdiction of one or the other of the Religious Courts involved.

Each Sharia (Muslim) Court consists of one judge (Qadi), while most of the Ecclesiastical (Christian) Courts are normally composed of three judges, who are usually clerics. Sharia Courts apply the doctrines of Islamic Law, based on the Koran and the Hadith (Precepts of Muhammad), while the Ecclesiastical Courts base their law on various aspects of Canon Law. In the event of conflict between any two Religious Courts or between a Religious Court and a Civil Court, a Special Tribunal of three judges is appointed by the President of the Court of Cassation, to decide which court shall have jurisdiction. Upon the advice of experts on the law of the various communities, this Special Tribunal decides on the venue for the case at hand.

RELIGION

Over 80 per cent of the population are Sunni Muslims, and the King can trace unbroken descent from the Prophet Muhammad. There is a Christian minority, living mainly in the towns, and smaller numbers of non-Sunni Muslims.

Prominent religious leaders in Jordan are:

Sheikh Ibrahim Qattan (Chief Justice and President of the Supreme Muslim Secular Council).

Sheikh Subhi al-Muwqqat (Director of Sharia Courts).

Sheikh Muhammad Abdo Hashem (Mufti of the Hashemite Kingdom of Jordan).

THE PRESS

DAILIES

Al-Destour (*The Constitution*): P.O.B. 591, Amman; f. 1967; Arabic; publ. by the Jordan Press and Publishing Co.; circ. 45,000.

Al-Rai (*Opinion*): P.O.B. 6710, Amman; f. 1971; independent; published by Jordan Press Foundation; Gen. Man. Juma'a Hammad; Editor-in-Chief Mahmoud Kayed; circ. 50,000.

Al-Urdun: P.O.B. 6194, Amman; f. 1909; Editor Hanna Nasr.

The Jordan Times: P.O.B. 6710, Amman; f. 1975; English; Editor-in-Chief Mohammad Amad; circ. 6,000.

PERIODICALS

Akhbar al-Usbu: Amman; f. 1954; Arabic; weekly; Chief Editor Abdul-Hafiz Muhammad.

Al Aqsa: Amman; armed forces magazine; weekly.

Huda El Islam: Amman; f. 1956; monthly; Islamic; scientific and literary; published by the Department of Islamic Affairs; Editor Abdullah Kalkeli.

Jordan: P.O.B. 224, Amman; f. 1969; published quarterly by Jordan Information Bureau, Washington; circ. 100,000.

Al-Liwa: Amman; f. 1972; Arabic; weekly; Chief Editor Hasan Attel.

Military Magazine: Army Headquarters, Amman; f. 1955; quarterly; dealing with military and literary subjects; published by Armed Forces.

Rural Education Magazine: P.O.B. 226, Amman; f. 1958; published by Khadouri Agricultural College, Teachers' Training College at Beit Haninah and Teachers' Training College at Howwarah (jointly).

Sharia: P.O.B. 585, Amman; f. 1959; fortnightly; Islamic affairs; published by Sharia College; circ. 5,000.

NEWS AGENCIES

Jordan News Agency (JNA): P.O.B. 6845, Amman; f. 1965; government-controlled; Dir.-Gen. Y. Abuleil.

Foreign News Bureaux

Agence France-Presse (AFP): P.O.B. 3340, Amman; Bureau Man. Fouad Naim.

Reuters (*U.K.*): P.O.B. 667, Amman.

dpa (Federal Republic of Germany) and TASS (U.S.S.R.) maintain bureaux in Amman.

PUBLISHERS

Jordan Press and Publishing Co. Ltd.: Amman; f. 1967 by *al-Manar* and *Falastin*; cap. JD 250,000; publishes *ad-Destour* (daily); circ. 40,000.

Other publishers in Amman include: *Dairat al-Ihsaat al-Amman, George N. Kawar, al-Matbaat al-Hashmiya* and *The National Press.*

RADIO AND TELEVISION

The Hashemite Jordan Broadcasting Service (H.B.S.): P.O.B 909, Amman; f. 1959; station at Amman broadcasts daily 20 hours in Arabic to the Arab World, 7 hours in English to Europe and 1 hour in Arabic to Europe; takes advertising; Dir.-Gen. NASHOU MAJALI.

Jordan Television Corporation: P.O.B. 1041, Amman; f. 1968; government station broadcasting for 60–65 hours weekly in Arabic and English; in colour; advertising accepted; Dir.-Gen. M. KAMAL; Dir. Engineering T. NASEREDDIN.

Number of radio receivers 200,000, number of TV receivers 180,000 (East Bank only).

FINANCE

BANKING

(cap.=capital; p.u.=paid up; dep.=deposits; m.=million; res.=reserves; JD=Jordanian dinars.)

CENTRAL BANK

Central Bank of Jordan: P.O.B. 37, Amman; f. 1964; cap. JD 2m.; total resources JD 360.7m. (Sept. 1978); Gov. Dr. SAID NABULSI; Deputy Gov. HUSAYN EL-KASIM.

NATIONAL BANKS

Agricultural Credit Corporation: P.O.B. 77, Amman; f. 1960; cap. p.u. JD 6.5m.; total assets JD 11.3 m. (Dec. 1978); government-owned credit institution; Dir.-Gen. MUHAMMAD O. QURAN.

Arab Bank Ltd.: King Faisal St., P.O.B. 68, Amman; f. 1930; cap. p.u. and reserves JD 50m.; dep. 1,000m.; total assets 1,655m. (Dec. 1978); Chair. ABDUL MAJEED SHOMAN.

Bank of Jordan Ltd.: P.O.B. 2140, Jabal Amman on 3rd Circle, Amman; f. 1960; cap. p.u. JD 1,500,000; dep. 24.5m. (Dec. 1978); Chair. HUSNI SIDO AL-KURDI; Gen. Man. ZUHAIR IZZAT DARWAZA.

Cairo Amman Bank: P.O.B. 715, Prince Hassan St., Amman; f. 1960; cap. and res. JD 1.9m.; dep. 28.3m. (Nov. 1978); 10 brs.; Chair. JAWDAT SHASHA'A; Gen. Man. HAIDAR CHUKRI; associated with Banque du Caire, Cairo, and succeeded their Amman Branch.

Jordan—Gulf Bank: P.O.B. 2804, Amman; f. 1978; cap. p.u. JD 5m.; 60 per cent Jordanian-owned and 40 per cent by Gulf businessmen; Chair. M. N. ARMOUTI; Gen. Man. Dr. KHALDOUN AL-THAHER.

Jordan Kuwait Bank: P.O.B. 9776, Amman; f. 1977; cap. p.u. JD 2.5m.; dep. JD 14.2m.; Chair. Sheikh NASSER AL-SABAH; Gen. Man. SUFIAN IBRAHIM YASSEEN.

Jordan National Bank S.A.: P.O.B. 1578, Amman; f. 1956; cap. p.u. JD 3.3m.; dep. JD 26.5m. (Nov. 1978); 13 brs. in Jordan, 3 brs. in Lebanon; Chair. and Gen. Man. H.E. SULEIMAN SUKKAR; Deputy Gen. Mans. H.E. ABDUL-KADER TASH and Dr. ABDER RAHMAN S. TOUQAN.

Petra Bank: P.O.B. 6854, Amman; f. 1978; cap. p.u. JD 3m.; dep. JD 3.2m. (Oct. 1978); 60 per cent owned by Jordanians and 40 per cent by other Arab interests; Chair. MUHAMMAD TOUQAN; Gen. Man. Dr. AHMAD CHALABI.

FOREIGN BANKS

British Bank of the Middle East: P.O.B. 444, Amman; f. 1889; Chair. P. E. HUTSON; Area Man. A. D. E. DAWSON.

Chase Manhattan Bank (*U.S.A.*): P.O.B. 20191, On the First Circle, Jabal Amman; f. 1976; Gen. Man. ANIL K. SARIN; Deputy Man. THOMAS KINCAID.

Grindlays Bank (*United Kingdom*): P.O.B. 9997, Amman; acquired the Ottoman Bank interests in Jordan in 1969; brs. in Amman (8 brs.) Aqaba, Irbid (sub-branch in Northern Shouneh), Zerak and Kerak; Gen. Man. in Jordan R. S. CORDINGLEY.

Rafidain Bank (*Iraq*): P.O.B. 11941, Amman; f. 1941; Area Man. MUHAMMAD F. AL-LOSI.

Other foreign banks include Arab Land Bank, Citibank, Bank Al Mashrek, Bank of Credit and Commerce International.

SPECIALIZED CREDIT INSTITUTIONS

Agricultural Credit Corporation: P.O.B. 77, Amman; cap. p.u. JD 6.4m.; total assets JD 12.1m. (Sept. 1978); Gen. Man. MOHAMAD O. KUR'AN.

The Arab Jordan Investment Bank: P.O.B. 8797; Amman; f. 1978; cap. p.u. JD 5m.; Chair. and Gen. Man. ABDUL QADER QADI.

Housing Bank: P.O.B. 7693, Amman; cap. p.u. JD 11.9m.; total assets JD 75m. (Sept. 1978); Chair. and Gen. Man. ZUHAIR KHOURI.

Housing Corporation: P.O.B. 2210, Amman; cap. p.u. JD 4.8m.; total assets JD 15.5m. (Sept. 1978); Chair. and Gen. Man. HAMADALLAH NABULSI.

Industrial Development Bank: P.O.B. 1982, Majles Al-Omeh St., Amman; f. 1965; cap. p.u. JD 3m., of which JD 1m. owned by the government; total assets JD 14.3m. (Sept. 1978); Chair. RAWHEE EL-KHATEEB.

Jordan Co-operative Organization: P.O.B. L343, Amman; cap. p.u. JD 1.6m.; total assets JD 5.4m. (Sept. 1978); Gen. Man. Dr. HASSAN NABULSI.

Municipal and Village Loans Fund: P.O.B. 1572, Amman; cap. p.u. JD 4.1m.; total assets JD 12.8m. (Sept. 1978); Gen. Man. Dr. HAJEM EL-TAL.

STOCK EXCHANGE

Amman Financial Market: P.O.B. 8802, Amman; Gen. Man. Dr. HASHIM SABAGH.

INSURANCE

Al-Ahlia Insurance Co. (Jordan) Ltd.: P.O.B. 2938, 2nd Circle, Jabal Amman; cap. p.u. JD 240,000.

Jordan Insurance Co. Ltd.: P.O.B. 279, King Hussein St., Amman; cap. p.u. JD 400,000; brs. in five Arab countries.

Middle East Insurance Co. Ltd.: P.O.B. 1802, King Hussein St., Amman; cap. p.u. JD 125,000.

United Insurance Co. Ltd.: P.O.B. 7521, Abujaber Bldg., King Faisal St., Amman; cap. p.u. JD 250,000; all types of insurance.

Fourteen local and 14 foreign insurance companies operate in Jordan.

TRADE AND INDUSTRY

CHAMBERS OF COMMERCE AND INDUSTRY

Amman Chamber of Commerce: P.O.B. 287, Amman; f. 1923; Pres. MOHAMAD ALI BDEIR; Dir. MAHER JA'OUNI.

Amman Chamber of Industry: P.O.B.1800, Amman; Pres. WALID ASFOUR; Exec. Dir. ALI DAJANI.

Chamber of Commerce, Irbid: P.O.B. 13; f. 1950; Pres. MUFLEH HASSAN GHARAIBEH; Dir. HASSAN M. MURAD.

PUBLIC CORPORATION

East Ghor Canal Natural Resources Authority: P.O.B. 878, Amman; the 50-mile canal is now completed, and work is in progress on the irrigation system; the U.S.A. has provided $12m. towards the cost of the canal; the project provides irrigation for some 20,000-30,000 acres. An additional 6 miles of main canal and irrigation system have been completed with an additional irrigated area of 5,000 acres, financed by Kuwait Government grants of $3m. Sprinkler irrigation in the Jordan valley was completed in December 1977.

TRADE UNIONS

The General Federation of Jordanian Trade Unions: Wadi as-Sir Rd., P.O.B. 1065, Amman; f. 1954; 33,000 mems.; member of Arab Trade Unions Confederation; Chair. SAMI HASAN MANSOUR; Gen. Sec. ABDER-RAZZAQ HAMAD.

There are also a number of independent unions, including:

Drivers' Union: P.O.B. 846, Amman; Sec.-Gen. SAMI MANSOUR.

Union of Petroleum Workers and Employees: P.O.B. 1346, Amman; Sec.-Gen. BRAHIM HADI.

PHOSPHATE

Jordan Phosphate Mines Co. Ltd.: P.O.B. 30, Amman; engaged in production and export of rock phosphates; Sec.-Gen. TAHASEEN KHREIS; production (1978) 2.25 million tons.

TRANSPORT

RAILWAYS

Hedjaz Jordan Railway: (administered by the Ministry of Transport): P.O.B. 582, Amman; f. 1902; length of track 618 km.; Gen. Man. M. R. QOSEINI.

This was formerly a section of the Hedjaz railway (Damascus to Medina) for Muslim pilgrims to Medina and Mecca. It crosses the Syrian border and enters Jordanian territory south of Dera'a, and runs for approximately 366 km. to Naqb Ishtar, passing through Zarka, Amman, Qatrana and Ma'an. Some 844 km. of the line, from Ma'an to Medina in Saudi Arabia, have been abandoned for the past fifty years. Reconstruction of the Medina line, begun in 1965, was scheduled to be completed in 1971 at a cost of £15 million, divided equally between Jordan, Saudi Arabia and Syria. However, the reconstruction work has been suspended at the request of the Arab States concerned, pending further studies on costs. The line between Ma'an and Saudi Arabia (114 km.) is now completed, as well as 15 km. in Saudi Arabia as far as Haret Ammar Station. A new 115 km. extension to Aqaba was financed by a JD 12 million loan from the Federal Republic of Germany; this line became operational in October 1975. It is used mainly for transporting phosphates and connects Aqaba to Beirut.

ROADS

Ministry of Public Works: Amman.

Amman is linked by road with all parts of the kingdom and with neighbouring countries. All cities and most towns are connected by a 2-lane paved road system. In addition, several thousand km. of tracks make all villages accessible to motor transport. At the end of 1977, the latest inventory showed the East Bank of Jordan to have 1,910 km. of main roads, 818 km. of secondary roads and 2,097 km. of village roads, all of which are asphalted.

SHIPPING

The port of Aqaba is Jordan's only outlet to the sea and has two general berths of 340 metres and 215 metres, with seven main transit sheds, covered storage area of 4,150 sq. metres, an open area of 50,600 sq. metres and a phosphate berth 210 metres long and 10 metres deep. Four new berths and storage facilities are being built, and a separate potash berth is planned.

PIPELINES

Two oil pipelines cross Jordan. The former Iraq Petroleum Company pipeline, carrying petroleum from the oilfields in Iraq to Haifa, has not operated since 1967. The 1,067-mile pipeline, known as the Trans-Arabian Pipeline (Tapline) carries petroleum from the oilfields at Dharan in Saudi Arabia to Sidon on the Mediterranean seaboard in Lebanon. It traverses Jordan for a distance of 110 miles and has frequently been cut by hostile action.

CIVIL AVIATION

There are international airports at Amman and Aqaba. Work is in progress on a new international airport, the Queen Alia International Airport, at Amman.

Alia (The Royal Jordanian Airline): Head Office: P.O.B. 302, Arab Insurance Building, First Circle, Jabel Amman, Amman; f. 1963; government-owned; services to Middle East, Europe, Far East and U.S.A.; fleet of two Boeing 747-200, four Boeing 707-320C, three Boeing 727 200, one Boeing 720 B72, one freighter Boeing 707 320C 70F; Chair. and Pres. ALI GHANDOUR.

Arab Wings Co. Ltd.: P.O.B. 3038, Amman; f. 1975; subsidiary of Alia; executive jet charter service; Chair. and Pres. ALI GHANDOUR.

Jordan World Airlines: f. 1974; subsidiary of Alia; initial Fleet: one Boeing 707; Chair. and Pres. ALI GHANDOUR.

The following airlines also serve Jordan: Air France, British Airways, EgyptAir, Gulf Air, Iran Air, Iraqi Airways, KLM (Netherlands), Kuwait Airways, Libyan Arab Airlines, MEA (Lebanon), Saudia, Syrian Arab Airlines, Tarom (Romania).

TOURISM

Ministry of Tourism and Antiquities: P.O.B. 224, Amman; f. 1952; Dir.-Gen. MICHEL HAMARNEH; publ. *Jordan* (quarterly).

DEFENCE

Commander-in-Chief of the Armed Forces: Lieutenant-General ZAID BIN SHAKAR.

Assistant Commander-in-Chief of the Armed Forces and Commander of the Royal Jordanian Air Force: Maj-Gen. (Air) SALIH AL-KURDI.

Chief of Staff of the Armed Forces: Maj.-Gen. ABDEL HADI MAJALI.

Defence Expenditure (1978): JD 95.3 million.

Military Service: 2 years.

Total Armed Forces: 67,850: army 61,000; navy 200; air force 6,650.

Paramilitary Forces: 10,000 (3,000 Mobile Police Force, 7,000 Civil Militia).

EDUCATION

Education in Jordan is both centralized and decentralized. The Ministry of Education prescribes textbooks and curricula for all schools, both public and private. On the other hand, Jordan is divided into 18 districts of education, called directorates (5 are located on the West Bank), each headed by a Director who takes many decisions without reference to the Ministry of Education.

Ministry of Education schools and institutes of higher education accommodated 68.7 per cent of total school enrolment in 1976/77. Another 0.8 per cent of school enrolment was in the schools of the Ministry of Defence, Ministry of Public Health, Ministry of Social Affairs and Labour, and the Ministry of Religious Affairs and Inalienable Properties (AWQAF). The University of Jordan and the University of Yarmouk offered education for 1.1 per cent of total student enrolment, while UNRWA provided education for 19.4 per cent of the student population. Foreign and national private schools took 10 per cent of the school enrolment. Most of the foreign private schools are run by religious bodies, while the national private schools are run by secular as well as religious bodies.

Children normally start the six years of elementary education at the age of six. The elementary cycle is followed by three years of the preparatory cycle (junior high). The nine years of the elementary and preparatory cycles are compulsory. At the end of the compulsory years of education, more than 80 per cent of students are entitled to pursue their education in the three-year secondary cycle education schools (senior high) depending upon the number of vacancies available in the tenth grade (the first secondary year) in the various districts.

Higher secondary education is provided either by secondary general schools or secondary vocational schools. Students of both types of secondary schools sit for the public secondary education examination. Those who pass are entitled to pursue their education in institutes of higher learning, both in Jordan and abroad.

For the year 1977 the Ministry of Education budget was JD 22.3 million, or 7 per cent of the total national budget. For details of number of pupils, etc., *see* Statistical Survey.

UNIVERSITIES

University of Jordan: near Jubaiha, P.O.B. 1682, Amman; 415 teachers, 7,018 students.

University of Yarmouk: P.O.B. 566, Irbid; f. 1976; 50 teachers; 1,350 students.

Bethlehem University and Birzeit University are on the West Bank.

BIBLIOGRAPHY

ABDULLAH OF TRANSJORDAN, KING. Memoirs, trans. G. Khuri, ed. P. Graves (London and New York, 1950).

ABIDI, A. H. H. Jordan, a Political Study, 1948–1957 (Asia Publishing House, Delhi, 1966).

CROSS, FRANK M. (Jr.). Ancient Library of Qumran (Anchor Books, New York).

DEARDEN, ANN. Jordan (Hale, London, 1958).

GLUBB, J. B. The Story of the Arab Legion (London, 1948).

A Soldier with the Arabs (Hodder and Stoughton, 1957).

Britain and the Arabs: A Study of Fifty Years 1908–1958 (Hodder and Stoughton, London, 1959).

War in the Desert (London, 1960).

The Middle East Crisis—A Personal Interpretation (London, 1967).

Syria, Lebanon, Jordan (London, 1967).

Peace in the Holy Land (London, 1971).

GOICHON, A. M. L'Eau: Problème Vital de la Région du Jourdain (Brussels, Centre pour l'Etude des Problèmes du Monde Musulmane Contemporain, 1964).

GRANQVIST, HILMA. Birth and Childhood among the Arabs: Studies in a Muhammadan Village in Palestine (Helsinki, 1947).

Family Life among the Arabs.

Marriage Conditions in a Palestinian Village.

HACKER, JANE M. Modern Amman: a social study (Durham, 1960).

HARRIS, G. L. Jordan, Its People, Its Society, Its Culture (Human Relations Area Files, New Haven, 1958).

HUSSEIN, HIS MAJESTY KING. Uneasy Lies the Head (London, 1962).

HUTCHISON, Cmdr. E. H. Violent Truce (New York, Devin-Adair, 1956).

INTERNATIONAL BANK FOR RECONSTRUCTION AND DEVELOPMENT. The Economic Development of Jordan (Baltimore, Johns Hopkins Press, 1957).

JARVIS, C. S. Arab Command: the Biography of Lt.-Col. F. W. Peake Pasha (London, 1942).

JOHNSTON, CHARLES. The Brink of Jordan (London, Hamish Hamilton, 1972).

KENNEDY, Sir ALEXANDER. Petra: Its History and Monuments (London, 1925).

KOHN, HANS. Die staats- und verfassungsrechtliche Entwicklung des Emirats Transjordanien (Tübingen, 1929).

KONIKOFF, A. Transjordan: An Economic Survey (2nd edn., Jerusalem, 1946).

LUKE, Sir HARRY C., and KEITH-ROACH, E. The Handbook of Palestine and Transjordan (London, 1934).

LYAUTEY, PIERRE. La Jordanie Nouvelle (Juilliard, Paris, 1966).

MINISTRY OF FOREIGN AFFAIRS, AMMAN. Jordan: Some aspects of its growing importance in the Middle East (Amman, 1951).

MORRIS, JAMES. The Hashemite Kings (Faber, London, 1959).

PALESTINE GOVERNMENT. Memorandum on the Water Resources of Palestine (Jerusalem, 1947).

PATAI, R. The Kingdom of Jordan (Princeton, 1958).

PEAKE, F. G. History of Jordan and Its Tribes (Univ. of Miami Press, 1958).

PEROWNE, STEWART. The One Remains (London, 1954).

Jerusalem and Bethlehem (A. S. Barnes Ltd., South Brunswick, New Jersey, 1966).

PHILLIPS, PAUL G. The Hashemite Kingdom of Jordan: Prolegomena to a Technical Assistance Programme (Chicago, 1954).

SANGER, RICHARD H. Where the Jordan Flows (Middle East Institute, Washington, 1965).

SHWADRAN, B. Jordan: A State of Tension (Council for Middle Eastern Affairs, New York, 1959).

SMITH, Sir G. A. Historical Geography of the Holy Land (24th ed., London, 1931).

SNOW, PETER. Hussein: A Biography (London, Barrie and Jenkins, 1972).

SPARROW, GERALD. Hussein of Jordan (the authorized biography) (Harrap, London, 1961).
Modern Jordan (Allen and Unwin, 1961).

TOUKAN, BAHA UDDIN. A Short History of Transjordan (London, 1945).

U.S. GOVERNMENT PRINTING OFFICE. Area Handbook for the Hashemite Kingdom of Jordan (Washington, D.C., 1970).

VATIKIOTIS, P. J. Politics and the Military in Jordan 1921-57 (Praeger, New York, 1967).

VERDES, JACQUES MANSOUR. Pour les Fidayine (Paris) 1969).

Kuwait

PHYSICAL AND SOCIAL GEOGRAPHY

Kuwait lies at the head of the Persian Gulf, bordering Iraq and Saudi Arabia. The area of the State of Kuwait is 17,818 sq. km., including the Kuwaiti share of the Partitioned Zone (see below).

For long it was generally held that the Gulf extended much further north, but geological evidence suggests, first, that the coastline has remained broadly at its present position and, second, that the immense masses of silt brought down by the Tigris and Euphrates cause irregular downwarping at the head of the Gulf. Local variation in the coastline is therefore likely, with possible changes since ancient times. Kuwait grew up because it has a zone of slightly higher, firmer ground that gives access from the Gulf inland to Iraq, and because it has a reasonably good and sheltered harbour in an area that elsewhere has many sandbanks and, further south, coral reefs.

The territory of Kuwait is mainly almost flat desert with a few oases. With an annual rainfall of 1 to 37 centimetres, almost entirely between November and April, there is a spring "flush" of grass. Summer shade temperature may reach 120°F., though in January, the coldest month, temperatures range between 27° and 85°, with a rare frost. There is little drinking water within the state, and supplies are largely distilled from sea water, and brought by pipeline from the Shatt al-Arab.

Kuwait's population has increased very rapidly in recent years. It is unofficially estimated to have been 152,000 in 1950 but recent census results have produced totals of 206,473 (February 1957), 321,621 (May 1961), 467,339 (April 1965), 738,662 (April 1970) and 994,837 (April 1975). By July 1978 it was estimated that the population had reached 1,198,500. Between 1963 and 1970 the average increase in Kuwait's population was 10.0 per cent, the highest growth rate recorded in any independent country. The average annual increase between 1970 and 1977 was 6.1 per cent.

Much of Kuwait's population growth has resulted from immigration, though the country also has one of the highest natural increase rates in the world. Between 1957 and 1978 the non-Kuwaiti population grew from less than 93,000 (45 per cent of the total) to nearly 625,000 (52 per cent), most of them from other Arab states. In 1976 the natural increase of the population was 4.0 per cent, with 46,039 recorded births (44.1 per 1,000 inhabitants) and only 4,661 deaths (4.5 per 1,000). The high birth rate is particularly remarkable in view of the unequal distribution of the sexes, owing to the preponderance of males among the immigrant population. In 1975 the non-Kuwaitis comprised 307,168 males and 215,581 females. Among the 472,088 Kuwaiti citizens, by contrast, there were 236,600 males and 235,488 females. The birth rate for the Kuwaiti population alone exceeded 50 per 1,000 in some recent years.

At the 1975 census Kuwait City, the capital and principal harbour, had a population of 78,116 (slightly less than in 1970), though the largest town was Hawalli, with 130,565 inhabitants. Other sizeable localities, all in Hawalli Governorate, were Salmiya (113,943), Abraq Kheetan (59,443) and Farawaniya (44,875). In all these towns, non-Kuwaitis formed a large majority. Kuwait City had only 11,777 Kuwaitis (15.1 per cent of the inhabitants), Hawalli had 9,816 Kuwaitis (7.5 per cent) and Salmiya had 16,764 (14.7 per cent).

Immediately to the south of Kuwait, along the Gulf, is a Partitioned Zone of 5,700 sq. km. which is divided between Kuwait and Saudi Arabia. Each country administers its own half, in practice as an integral part of the state. However, the oil wealth of the whole Zone remains undivided and production from the on-shore concessions in the Partitioned Zone is shared equally between the two States.

HISTORY

Although Kuwait is situated on the fringe of the Mesopotamian basin it has always belonged rather to the nomadic desert of Arabia than to the settled populations of the plains watered by the Euphrates and Tigris rivers. Thus the successive rule of the 'Abbasid Caliphate of Baghdad (750–1258), the Mongols (1258–1546) and the Ottoman Turks (1546–1918) had little direct influence on the area around Kuwait.

The origin of the present town of Kuwait is usually placed about the beginning of the 18th century, when a number of families of the famous Anaiza tribe migrated from the interior to the Arabian shore of the Gulf. These migrants included such important families as as-Sabah, al-Khalifa, az-Zayed, al-Jalahima and al-Ma'awida, from whom many of the present Kuwaitis are descended.

The foundation of the present Sabah ruling dynasty dates from about 1756, when the settlers of Kuwait decided to appoint a Sheikh to administer their affairs, provide them with security and represent them in their dealings with the Ottoman Government. The town prospered and in 1765 it was reported to contain some 10,000 inhabitants possessing 800 vessels and living by trading, fishing and pearling.

In 1776 war broke out between Persia and Turkey and the Persians captured Basra, which they held until 1779. During this time the East India Company moved the southern terminal of its overland mail route to Aleppo from Basra to Kuwait, and much of the trade of Basra was diverted to Kuwait. Sheikh Abdullah bin Sabah was reported to have been well disposed to the British, who for their part held him in high regard as being a man of his word.

About this time Kuwait was repeatedly threatened by raids from the Wahhabis, fanatical tribesmen from central Arabia, and the need for protection against these enemies led to closer contacts with the East India Company, who had a depot in the town. Ottoman dominion over the mainland was accepted in return for recognition of British trading interests over the route from the Mediterranean to India through the Gulf. The depredations of pirates and the threat from the Wahhabis caused Kuwait's prosperity to decline in the early years of the 19th century, but the British Navy restored peace to the Gulf, and by 1860 prosperity had returned.

In order to retain their autonomy the Kuwaitis had to maintain good relations with the Turks. Although not under direct Turkish administration the Sheikh of Kuwait recognized a general Ottoman suzerainty over the area by the payment of tribute and Sheikh Abdullah bin Sabah al-Jabir (1866–92) accepted the title of *Qa'immaqam* (Commandant) under the Turkish *Vali* (Governor) of Basra in 1871. His successor, Sheikh Mubarak "the Great", feared that the Turks would occupy Kuwait, and in 1899, in return for British protection, he signed an agreement with the British not to cede, mortgage or otherwise dispose of parts of his territories to anyone except the British Government, nor to enter into any relationship with a foreign government other than the British without British consent. This agreement prevented Germany from securing Kuwait as a terminal for the projected Berlin to Baghdad railway.

The reign of Sheikh Mubarak from 1896 to 1915 marked the rise of Kuwait from a Sheikhdom of undefined status to an autonomous state. In 1904 a British political agent was appointed, and in 1909 Great Britain and Turkey opened negotiations which, although never ratified because of the outbreak of the First World War, in practice secured the autonomy of Kuwait.

Sheikh Mubarak's second son, Sheikh Salim, who succeeded to the Sheikhdom in 1917, supported the Turks in the World War, thus incurring a blockade of Kuwait. Sheikh Salim was succeeded in 1921 by his nephew, Sheikh Ahmad al-Jabir. Kuwait prospered under his rule and by 1937 the population had risen to about 75,000.

Under Sheikh Ahmad the foundation of Kuwait's great oil industry was laid. After considerable prospecting, he granted a concession in 1934 jointly to the Gulf Oil Corporation of the U.S.A. and the Anglo-Persian Oil Co. of Great Britain who formed the Kuwait Oil Co. Ltd. Deep drilling started in 1936, and was just beginning to show promising results when war broke out in 1939. The oil wells were plugged in 1942 and drilling was suspended until the end of the war.

After the war the oil industry in Kuwait was resumed on an extensive scale (*see* Economic Survey) and in a few years the character of Kuwait town was changed from an old-fashioned dhow port to a thriving modern city supported by the revenues of the oil industry. In 1950 Sheikh Ahmad died and was succeeded by Sheikh Abdullah as-Salim. His policy was to use the oil revenues substantially for the welfare of his people, and in 1951 he inaugurated a programme of public works and educational and medical developments which has turned Kuwait into a planned and well-equipped country.

THE MODERN STATE

The economic aspects of post-war development are dealt with in the survey following. Here it should be noted that Kuwait has gradually built up what are probably the most comprehensive welfare services in the world, very largely without charge, at least to native Kuwaitis. Education is completely free in Kuwait, and this includes free food and clothing for students. Medical attention is also free to all and the health service is generally considered to be of a very high standard. A heavily subsidized housing programme has now provided accommodation for most residents meeting the country's generous criteria of "poverty". Even local telephone calls are free.

In June 1961 the United Kingdom and Kuwait terminated the 1899 agreement which had given the U.K. responsibility for the conduct of Kuwait's foreign policy, and Kuwait therefore became a fully independent state. The ruling Sheikh took the new title of Amir. In July Kuwait was admitted as a member of the Arab League.

Shortly after attaining independence, Kuwait was threatened by an Iraqi claim to sovereignty over the territory. British troops landed in Kuwait in response to a request from the Amir for assistance. The Arab League met in July and agreed that an Arab League Force should be provided to replace the British troops as a guarantee of Kuwait's independence. This force, composed of contingents from Saudi Arabia, Jordan, the United Arab Republic and the Sudan, arrived in Kuwait in September 1961. The United Arab Republic contingent was withdrawn in December 1961, and those of Jordan, Saudi Arabia and the Sudan before the end of February 1963. On May 14th, 1963, Kuwait became the 111th member of the United Nations.

In December 1961, for the first time in Kuwait's history, an election was held to elect 20 members of the Constituent Assembly (the other members being Ministers). This Assembly drafted a new Constitution which was published on November 11th, 1962. Under the new Constitution a National Assembly of 50 members was elected in January 1963, and the first session was held on January 29th, with Sheikh Sabah as-Salim as-Sabah, brother of the Amir and Heir Apparent, as the Prime Minister of a new Council of Ministers.

In October 1963 the new Iraqi government announced that it had decided to recognize Kuwait's complete independence; Iraq wanted to clear her relations with Kuwait and remove the atmosphere created by the Kassem regime. Kuwait is thought to have made a substantial grant to Iraq to improve relations at this juncture. In February 1964 an agreement (never implemented) was subsequently signed whereby Iraq would supply to Kuwait 120 million gallons of water daily; and in November the two countries concluded a Trade and Economic Agreement which virtually abolished customs duties between them.

In January 1965 a constitutional crisis, reflecting the tension between the paternalist ruling house and the democratically-minded National Assembly, resulted in the formation of a strengthened cabinet under the Heir Apparent, Sheikh Sabah as-Salim. In July 1965 Kuwait decided not to ratify the agreement to set up an Arab Common Market with Iraq, Jordan, Syria and the U.A.R. There was strong feeling in the National Assembly that such an association would be disadvantageous to Kuwait.

On November 24th, 1965, Sheikh Abdullah died and was succeeded by Sheikh Sabah. His post as Prime Minister was taken over by another member of the ruling family, Sheikh Jabir al-Ahmad, who became Heir Apparent in May 1966.

In the developments of 1966 and 1967 within the Arab community Kuwait continued to play a neutral role, and in particular tried to act as mediator in inter-Arab disputes such as the Yemen and South Arabian problems. Sheikh Sabah paid visits to Iraq and Lebanon, and Kuwait supported Syria in the dispute with the Iraq Petroleum Company.

Kuwait declared her support for the Arab countries in the 1967 war with Israel, and joined in the oil embargo on the U.S.A. and the United Kingdom. No Kuwaitis had, however, reached any theatre of war before the ceasefire was announced. The Government donated KD 25 million to the Arab war effort. At the Khartoum Conference in September 1967 Kuwait joined Saudi Arabia and Libya in offering financial aid to the U.A.R. and Jordan whilst their economies recovered from the June war. The Kuwaiti share of this amounted to KD 55 million annually.

On May 13th, 1968, it was announced that the agreement of June 1961—whereby Britain had undertaken to give military assistance to Kuwait if asked to do so by her ruler—would terminate on May 13th, 1971. This followed an earlier announcement that Britain would withdraw all troops from the Gulf region by the end of 1971. At this time, Kuwait continually encouraged the formation of a federation of Bahrain, Qatar and the Trucial States but her qualities as a go-between were insufficient to persuade the first two states to join what eventually became the United Arab Emirates.

Since the June 1967 war Kuwait has no longer been a frequent target of radical Arab criticism. Its financial support for the countries hit by the war and other generous economic assistance have no doubt contributed to this, while the lavish financing of the Palestinian guerrillas has been even more important. A factor behind this assistance is the large Palestinian community, said to be over 70,000 strong, in Kuwait; many of the most able and educated Palestinians have made a career in the country in recent years. Financial aid to Jordan, however, was cut off for a time in September 1970 following the war between government and guerrilla forces.

During the 1960s the Kuwaiti leadership's policies led to extensive redistribution of income, through the use of oil revenues in public expenditure and through the land compensation scheme. At the same time, however, there was popular discontent about corruption and inefficiency in public services and the manipulation of the Press and the National Assembly.

In response to public opinion, the ruling family permitted the Assembly elections of January 1971 to be held on the basis of a free vote, though women, illiterates and all non-Kuwaitis still have no voting rights. There was a lively election campaign, with 184 candidates contesting the 50 seats, despite the non-existence of political parties, which are still illegal. Several members and supporters of the Arab Nationalist Movement, founded in the 1950s by Dr. George Habash (now leader of the Popular Front for the Liberation of Palestine), were elected. This radical group, led by Dr. Ahmad al-Khatib, is generally regarded as the principal opposition to the Government.

After the 1971 elections the Crown Prince was re-appointed Prime Minister and formed a new Cabinet. The representation of the ruling family was reduced from five to three and, for the first time, the Cabinet included two Ministers drawn from the elected members of the National Assembly. After the elections in January 1975 a 16-member cabinet was appointed with the Crown Prince continuing as Prime Minister. Seven new Ministers were appointed, a new post of Deputy Prime Minister was created and the functions of the former Ministry of Oil and Finance were separated.

The main domestic problem is the difference in status between native-born Kuwaitis and immigrants, the latter comprising 52 per cent of the population in 1978. Whilst the living conditions of the immigrants are very good by Arabian standards, most senior positions are reserved for Kuwaitis, as is the suffrage and free use of some welfare services. The creation of sufficient employment opportunities to avoid the unsettling effects of idleness and boredom, a social problem even with generous unemployment benefits, is a major difficulty now confronting the Government.

In March 1973 Iraqi troops and tanks occupied a Kuwaiti outpost at Samtah, on the 100-mile border with Iraq. Iraq later withdrew its troops, but a source of potential dispute remains. Since the crisis in 1973 Kuwait has allocated large sums for the expansion of its armed forces and has announced intentions to establish its own navy. Legislation to introduce conscription was approved in 1975.

In January 1973, in common with several other Middle East countries, the Kuwait Government signed a participation agreement with the country's main oil-producing concern, the Kuwait Oil Company (KOC), owned equally by British Petroleum (BP) and Gulf Oil. KOC produced over 90 per cent of Kuwait's oil output in 1972. This agreement was not ratified by the National Assembly, however, and more far-reaching agreements were negotiated in 1974 and 1975.

During the Arab-Israeli war of October 1973 Kuwaiti forces stationed along the Suez Canal were involved in fighting. Kuwait also contributed to the Arab cause by giving considerable financial aid, totalling KD 100 million, to other Arab states. While the war was still in progress, Kuwait called for a meeting of OAPEC to draw up a common Arab policy for the use of oil as a weapon to put pressure on Western countries, particularly the U.S.A., to force an Israeli withdrawal from occupied Arab territory. This meeting took place in Kuwait, where OAPEC's ten member-states decided to reduce petroleum production by at least 5 per cent progressively each month. Kuwait was also one of the Arab countries which imposed a total embargo on oil shipments to the U.S.A. and, later, to the Netherlands.

Immediately before the OAPEC meeting, Kuwait joined other Gulf states in announcing a unilateral increase of 70 per cent in the posted price of crude petroleum (the reference price used for tax and royalty purposes) from November 1st, 1973. This followed similar moves by Algeria, Indonesia and Venezuela.

In November, at a further meeting in Kuwait, Oil Ministers from the Arab states agreed on an extra 5 per cent reduction in output for November, with the combined effect of the embargoes and production cutbacks expressed as an overall drop in supply of 25 per cent compared with September levels, to be followed by further reductions in the future. Later in November the Arab group in OPEC agreed on the next 5 per cent cut for December, but exempted EEC countries except the Netherlands.

At the next OAPEC meeting, held in Kuwait in December, an additional 5 per cent cut, without exemptions, was agreed for January 1974. A second December meeting, also in Kuwait, partly reversed earlier decisions to reduce oil production. Just before this, the Gulf states belonging to OPEC had agreed on a further sharp increase in the posted price of oil, effective from January 1st, 1974.

Kuwait played a leading part in all these moves and made considerable reductions in national oil output. Monthly production (in million metric tons) fell from 13.4 in September 1973 to 12.0 in October and 9.8 in November. There was later a reversal in this trend and monthly output was more than 10 million tons in the first half of 1974.

Following the conclusion in January of a disengagement agreement between Egypt and Israel and the consequent improvement in Arab relations with the U.S.A., seven of the Arab oil-producing states (including Kuwait) agreed in March to lift the embargo on supplies to the U.S.A. In July 1974 the Arab countries also lifted the oil embargo on the Netherlands. Kuwait's policy of conserving her oil reserves, and the fall in the world demand for oil, has meant that production fell below the considered optimum level of 2 million b/d during 1974. After this fall of 18 per cent in 1974 production fell a further 19.2 per cent in 1975 to 1.84 million b/d but rose to 1.95 million b/d in 1976, falling again to 1.79 million b/d in 1977 and recovering to 1.9 million b/d in 1978.

While the fuel crisis was developing, negotiations continued between the Government and KOC for new participation terms. Agreement was reached in January 1974 for the acquisition by the Government of a 60 per cent share, with the right to acquire the remaining 40 per cent in 1979. Although this gave Kuwait an immediate controlling interest in KOC, some members of the National Assembly, encouraged by the nationalization of foreign-owned oil companies in Iraq and Libya, demanded a third round of negotiations to achieve 100 per cent ownership. In November 1975 after long negotiations agreement was reached with the oil companies. The take-over cost the Government $50.5 million in compensation on the basis of net book value backdated to March 1975. BP and Gulf Oil agreed to lift 950,000 b/d over the next five years, using Kuwaiti tankers.

After the National Assembly elections in January 1975 the Ministry of Finance and Oil was divided and oil affairs became the sole responsibility of the Ministry of Oil. In April 1975 the Government decided to take over the Kuwait National Petroleum Company, which was already 60 per cent government-owned. The KNPC came under the authority of the Supreme Oil Council and its Co-ordinating Committee and controlled all oil operations. KOC was therefore limited to production. Nationalization of the oil industry was almost complete when, in 1977, the Government acquired Aminoil and created the Kuwait Wafra Oil Company.

Until 1973 Kuwait's financial support for the leading Palestinian organizations had protected the country from active involvement in the guerrilla struggle. However, the activities of extremist groups, lacking such links with Kuwait, have resulted in incidents which embarrassed the Kuwait Government. In September 1973 Arab gunmen occupied the Saudi Arabian Embassy in Paris and later flew to Kuwait with five hostages. The gunmen surrendered to the Kuwaiti authorities, who later handed them over to the Palestine Liberation Organization (PLO), which had condemned the incident.

Kuwait was later involved in two further terrorist incidents, in December 1973 and February 1974, and the Kuwaiti authorities fear that such incidents will encourage extremists to regard Kuwait as a safe refuge.

In August 1976 the Amir suspended the National Assembly for four years on the grounds that, amongst other things, it had been delaying legislation. A committee was ordered to be formed to review the constitution.

On December 31st, 1977, the Amir (Sheikh Sabah) died and was succeeded by his cousin, the Crown Prince, Sheikh Jaber al-Ahmad al-Sabah, who had been Prime Minister since 1966. The new heir apparent was Sheikh Saad al-Abdullah al-Sabah, who became Prime

Minister as well as Crown Prince. In a Cabinet appointed in February 1978 Sheikh Ali al-Khalifa al-Sabah was introduced as Minister of Oil, and a policy of conservation of oil and a slow-down in the pace of new development has been introduced. Both the Amir and the Prime Minister have publicly reaffirmed the Government's intention to restore the National Assembly in the near future. A committee was to be set up in 1979 to review the constitution and determine the form of a revived legislature.

In line with its policy of oil conservation the Government imposed a production ceiling of 2 million b/d in 1978. The ceiling was maintained throughout the year despite pressure to increase output after disruption to Iranian oil exports following the revolution there. In June 1979 Kuwait announced that it was considering lowering the ceiling to 1.5 million b/d from 1980. Indications by the U.S.A. that it was prepared to intervene in the Gulf to protect its oil interests if necessary are thought to have contributed to this move.

At the Baghdad summit in November 1978 Kuwait pressed for solidarity among the Arab nations in condemning the Egypt-Israeli peace agreement and supported the use of sanctions against Egypt. The Kuwaiti Ambassador has been recalled from Cairo and all aid, except for specific development projects, has been withdrawn. Anxious to preserve Arab unity, Kuwait mediated successfully in the conflict between North and South Yemen in 1979, eventually bringing about a ceasefire, and was instrumental in resolving the crisis in the United Arab Emirates.

ECONOMIC SURVEY

The State of Kuwait has an area of 17,818 square kilometres. Until petroleum was produced, the only town was the harbour of Kuwait on the Gulf. But for some 150 years this port was of some significance because it was a centre for pearl fishing and the building of dhows or "booms"; and several of the plans for building a railway across Mesopotamia envisaged Kuwait as the eastern terminus.

The rapid development of the oil industry since about 1950 has dramatically changed all this. In 1977 Kuwait had oil reserves of 67,400 million barrels, representing a further 95 years of production at 1976 levels. In 1978 Kuwait's oil output was the ninth largest in the world. The revenue from oil, estimated at U.S. $9,500 million for 1978, has brought to the area a prosperity unimaginable in 1950. Estimates suggest that in 1977 per capita income was $12,700, second only to the United Arab Emirates.

The population grew at the rate of 8.2 per cent per year between 1965 and 1973; it has been increasing at an annual rate of 6 per cent in recent years, and in mid-1978 was estimated at 1,198,500. This growth is the result of immigration from the surrounding countries, resulting from higher wages and better working conditions than anywhere else in the Middle East. Of the total population in 1978, less than half (some 574,000) were Kuwaitis. An important part of the annual revenue from oil has been spent on health, education and other social services such as the distillation of fresh water from sea water, and as a result the standard of living in Kuwait is at present among the highest in the world. Most of the social services, such as education and health, are free for Kuwaiti citizens; it has been said that, as a welfare state, Kuwait now probably has no parallel. In recent years the Government has distributed some of its wealth to other parts of the Arab world and increasingly to less developed countries in Africa and Asia, by loans and grants.

PETROLEUM

In 1933 the Anglo-Persian Oil Company, now the British Petroleum Company Limited, and Gulf Oil Corporation applied jointly to the Ruler of Kuwait for a concession to explore the territory. The two companies formed an operating unit, the Kuwait Oil Company, each holding 50 per cent of its share capital. A large oilfield was discovered at Burgan, about 25 miles south of the town of Kuwait, in 1938, but the onset of World War II delayed development until 1945. By 1948 six million tons were produced, but the main impetus to speed up development was supplied by the Abadan affair in 1951, which in effect denied Iranian production to the rest of the world for three years. By 1956 Kuwait's production had increased to 54 million tons, and was then the largest in the Middle East. Further fields were found by the company, notably at Raudhatain, north of Kuwait, and the company's production had reached over 148 million tons by 1972, although large areas of the original concession had been relinquished to the State in accordance with the Agreement. To handle this vast production, a huge tanker port has been constructed at Mina al-Ahmadi, not far from the Burgan field, which from a terminal some 10 miles offshore can now handle the largest tankers. At Ahmadi there is also a town of more than 20,000 inhabitants, of whom about 5,000 are employees of the company, and there is a refinery with an annual throughput capacity of 12 million tons.

Beginning in October 1973, Kuwait joined other Arab countries in a campaign of restricting oil production. The total 1973 oil output in Kuwait (excluding the Partitioned Zone) was 138 million metric tons, a fall of 8.3 per cent from the 1972 figure—and the first decline in the country's oil production since exploitation began in 1946. Production in 1974 was 18 per cent lower than in 1973 and dropped a further 19.2 per cent in 1975. Production increased slightly in 1976, but fell sharply in the early months of 1977 as a result of the two-tier price increase decided at the OPEC conference in Doha in December 1976. Kuwait was one of the 11 OPEC members who decided to raise their prices by 10 per cent, while Saudi Arabia and the United Arab Emirates decided on a 5 per cent price rise. Subsequently,

Kuwait offered a 10 per cent discount on contracted liftings and oil production rose strongly in the second half of 1977. Nevertheless, total output for the year was 8.5 per cent lower than in 1976 and crude exports fell by 7.5 per cent to their lowest level for more than a decade. However, revenues from oil in the year ending March 1978 were the highest on record, at more than KD2,500 million. Average production, estimated at 1.9 million b/d in 1978, is expected to remain at 2 million b/d throughout 1979. In 1974 the Kuwait Government acquired a 60 per cent interest in the Kuwait Oil Company and in November 1975 the Kuwait Government took over the remaining 40 per cent (*see* also History, page 496).

Two other companies have been permitted by Kuwait and Saudi Arabia to operate in the Partitioned Zone, and produce oil. These were Aminoil, the American Independent Oil Company, owned by the U.S. firm Reynolds, which has a joint operating agreement with Getty Oil Co. under which Aminoil and Getty bear one-half of certain expenses such as drilling; and Arabian Oil Company in which Japanese interests own 75 per cent of the share capital, the governments of Kuwait and Saudi Arabia each holding 12.5 per cent. So far the production of these companies is small compared with that of the Kuwait Oil Company. In February 1976 it was announced that the Government had begun negotiations for a 100 per cent take-over of Aminoil. This was fully completed in September 1977, when Aminoil's name was changed to the Wafra Kuwait Oil Company. The latter was dissolved in April 1978 and its operations merged with the Kuwait Oil Company and the KNPC. In addition KNPC markets, in Kuwait, oil products produced by the Kuwait Oil Company, and owns a refinery at Shuaiba.

NATURAL GAS

In November 1976 the Amir laid the foundation stone for the Kuwait Oil Company's Gas Project. The Gas Project is one of the largest development projects undertaken in Kuwait, and involves the construction of extensive facilities to utilize the gas associated with crude oil output for the production of liquefied natural gas (LNG) and such derivatives as propane and butane. By the end of 1978 all the gas associated with crude petroleum production should be utilized. During 1977 an average of 28.6 per cent of gas was flared off, compared with 54.4 per cent in 1973.

A three-train LPG plant and a gas-gathering system, which came on stream in 1979, gather the gas produced with the oil at well-heads, remove LPG components and natural gasoline, treat them to conform to international standards and distribute them to fuel users and to pressure-maintenance facilities. A major contract was awarded to the Kuwait Metal Pipe Industries for the engineering, procurement and construction of a 300-mile network of gathering and transmission pipelines.

The plant, built at a cost of over U.S. $1,000 million, has a capacity of 3.15 million metric tons of LPG per year (60 per cent propane, 40 per cent butane) at the expected crude oil production rate of 2 million b/d. It was originally designed to take crude oil production of 3 million b/d but, with the 2 million b/d ceiling in force, will be used to only two-thirds capacity.

Natural gas production from the plants in operation in 1977 averaged 927.2 million cubic feet per day, 8.8 per cent lower than in 1976. This fall was mainly due to the slowdown in oil output.

OTHER INDUSTRIES

The government has done much to foster the growth of other industries in order to diversify the economy and to provide an alternative source of employment to oil. Not surprisingly, however, oil-related activities still contribute an overwhelming proportion of Kuwait's total industrial output. A law of 1965 empowers the government to grant exemption from import duties on capital goods, subsidized rates for water and power, and preference in government purchases for locally manufactured products. An Industrial Development Committee assists the development of local industry. A Petrochemical Industries Company was formed in 1963 to manufacture fertilizers, and in 1964 a larger concern, Kuwait Chemical Fertilizer Company, was set up. An industrial area has been developed at Shuaiba, between Kuwait City and Ahmadi, close to KNPC's refinery. With a new fertilizer plant at Shuaiba, owned by KNPC, Kuwait now has a potential production capacity of 1.65 million tons per year, mainly in the form of urea and ammonia products. The profitability of these products is proving difficult to maintain because of technical problems and weak market conditions.

There are also plans by PIC to construct an aromatics complex for the production of benzene and xylenes at a cost of KD 72 million. Pre-feasibility studies are also being undertaken for a possible Olefin complex to produce ethelynes. This project might cost KD 230 million. PIC had an estimated surplus of KD 7.3 million in 1978 but has postponed these two expansionist projects. The Kuwaiti Insulating Materials Manufacturing Company, however, is to go ahead with its glass fibre insulation plant. It will take two years to build and have an initial output of 4,000 tons per year. The construction contract has gone to Technipetrol. Two sizeable contracts were also awarded early in 1979 as part of the general extension of the road system and a feasibility study for a national railway to link Kuwait with Iraq is under way.

There are several factories in Kuwait supplying consumer requirements, such as processed food and soft drinks, and there is a flour mills company. The construction industry is of some importance, owing to the vast amount of house and office building there has been in the last decade, not to mention the construction of public works such as roads, power stations, schools and hospitals, much of this work having been undertaken, however, by foreign contractors.

At the 1975 census there were more than 24,000 persons (not including construction) employed in manufacturing, compared with only 4,476 in the production of crude petroleum and natural gas. In 1975/76 manufacturing accounted for 5.0 per cent of G.D.P., while crude oil, natural gas and other mining and quarrying accounted for 70.0 per cent.

PUBLIC UTILITIES

To support the increase of population brought about by the development of oil, a vast infrastructure of public works had to be created. There are desalination plants in Kuwait City and the Shuaiba industrial area, and IHI of Japan is to build three multi-flash type desalination plants for a new power station at Doha. Important sources of fresh water have been found at Raudhatain and Al Shigaia but desalination provides 90 per cent of Kuwait's daily consumption of 60 million imperial gallons of potable water. Distillation capacity was to be increased to 70 million gallons per day during 1978. In 1975 Kuwait produced 4,653 million kWh of electric energy for public use.

The harbour of Kuwait City has been completely reconstructed; four deep-water berths have been provided. However, it is proving difficult to expand facilities as quickly as port traffic. In October 1977 South Korea was awarded a contract for $100 million to further develop the ports. An international airport has also been built. There is a national airline with an international service, Kuwait Airways Corporation, which is owned by the State. All these facilities were created at the expense of the Government, the oil ports at Mina al-Ahmadi and nearby at Mina al-Abdullah having been made by the Kuwait Oil Company. However, there are several shipowning companies owned by the private sector, including the Kuwait Oil Tanker Company, in which the Kuwait Government has taken a 51 per cent share. The company had a fleet capacity of some 2.1 million tons at the beginning of 1978 and the Oil Ministry has started including the use of Kuwaiti tankers in the terms of sale of its crude oil. The Kuwait Shipping Company has become part of the United Arab Shipping Company (UASC), formed by Kuwait and five other Gulf states. The UASC began operations in August 1976, using mainly Kuwaiti ships.

AGRICULTURE AND FISHERIES

Owing to the present lack of water, little grain is grown, and most of the food consumed in Kuwait has to be imported. In 1977 the total cultivable area was estimated at 17,000 dunums, of which vegetables and crops occupy about 6,000 dunums, with another 1,000 dunums occupied by orchards and timber. However, the Government has done much to encourage animal husbandry, the main activity (before the development of the oilfields) of the bedouin, who still rear camels, sheep and goats. There is an experimental farm of 90 acres owned by the Government, and in the private sector there is a growing poultry and dairy industry. The first phase of the Kuwait United Poultry Company project for egg farms (producing 67 million eggs per year) and a feedmill (producing 48,000 tons of feed per year) was completed in August 1978 and further poultry-related projects are expected to be completed by other companies in 1979. The growing of dates has also increased in recent years. Fishing, on the other hand, is of some importance, because the Gulf, in particular Kuwait's territorial waters, abounds in sea creatures, notably prawns (some of which are exported to the U.S.A.) and shrimps. There were four fishing companies based on the abundance of fish in Kuwait's territorial waters, until they were amalgamated into Kuwait United Fisheries in 1972.

FOREIGN TRADE AND BALANCE OF PAYMENTS

According to IMF data, total exports in 1978 were valued at KD 2,896 million, of which crude petroleum and petroleum products accounted for KD 2,625 million (just over 90 per cent). Total exports were only just above the 1974 figure of KD 2,890 million. In 1975, 26.4 per cent of Kuwait's total exports went to Japan, while 31.3 per cent went to EEC countries and 8.1 per cent went to the American continent. The value of imports was KD 972.0 million in 1976 and KD 1,387.1 million in 1977. Import growth has been explosive in recent years. Imports were KD 262.2 million in 1972 and KD 310.6 million in 1973. The most important item is machinery and transport equipment, which accounted for 46 per cent of total imports by value in 1975. Basic manufactures accounted for 17 per cent and food and live animals 15 per cent. Kuwait's principal suppliers in 1975 were the EEC, the U.S.A. and Japan, who supplied 34 per cent, 18 per cent and 16 per cent respectively of total imports by value.

According to provisional estimates, the balance of payments surplus on current account was KD 2,100 million in 1976, compared with KD 1,950 million in 1975. Official reserves grew by US $273 million during 1976 and by US $1,061 million during 1977 to reach US $2,989.9 million at the end of 1977. Reserves fell to $2,615.6 million at the end of 1978.

CURRENCY, BANKING AND FINANCE

The currency in circulation is the Kuwaiti dinar, details of which are given in the Statistical Survey.

The only foreign bank previously allowed to operate in Kuwait, the British Bank of the Middle East, was taken over by the Government in 1971 and now manages the Bank of Kuwait and the Middle East under agreement. However, there are a number of commercial banks financed by local capital, and the management of one of these, the Alahli Bank, is provided by the French Credit Lyonnais. Of the local banks, by far the largest is the National Bank of Kuwait, founded in 1953. The other banks include the Gulf Bank and the Commercial Bank of Kuwait, founded respectively in 1960 and 1961. The United Bank of Kuwait, founded in London in 1966, represents the National Bank, the Commercial Bank and the Gulf Bank, which hold part of its share capital. The net foreign assets of the commercial banks at December 31st, 1977, amounted to KD 402.6 million and by the end of 1978 this figure had risen to KD 612.9 million. In 1960 the Government founded a Savings and Credit Bank. Its paid-up capital in 1975 was KD 31 million, all provided by the State, to promote savings and to provide finance for small industries, agriculture, property and small businesses. A new commercial bank, the Burgan Bank, was established in 1976 with a capital of KD 10 million, The Government holds 51 per cent of the shares. The authorities are keen to establish Kuwait as a financial centre. To this end, a secondary market in dinar-denominated bonds has been encouraged and in 1977 several commercial banks began a market in dinar-denominated certificates of deposit. In addition, in February 1979 the Central Bank started issuing 91-day bills sold on a discount basis and a secondary market in these bills is envisaged.

There is now an active stock market in Kuwait, and for some time the State has been active in encouraging investment. The value of shares quoted on the stock exchange at the beginning of 1977 was KD 2,400 million and this rose by 35 per cent in 1978. In 1962 a Kuwait Investment Company was created, of which the State owns half the capital, to engage in portfolio investment and in property dealing in Kuwait. A similar concern, the Kuwait Foreign Trading & Investment Company, was established by the State, which owns 98 per cent of the share capital, to undertake business transactions abroad, and reference has already been made to the reserves of the State overseas. There is no official information about the amount of private portfolio investment overseas by Kuwaitis, but it is known to be substantial and about £82.5 million was revealed to be invested in leading British financial institutions when the Kuwait Investment Office disclosed its holdings of more than 5 per cent in U.K. quoted companies in April 1977.

PUBLIC FINANCE

The budgeted expenditure for the 1977/78 fiscal year (July 1st to June 30th) was set at KD 1,988 million. Of this total, KD 1,511 million was allocated for current expenditure and the remainder for development projects. The total represents a 56 per cent increase over the previous year. Revenues were projected to rise by 4.6 per cent to KD 2,272 million. However, the 1978/79 budget entails a 2.3 per cent cut in total spending and the allocation for development spending, at KD 390 million, is less than was actually spent in 1977/78.

In recent years Kuwait has become a significant financial power and the state has invested a large amount overseas. Government investment income, most of it from foreign assets, totalled KD 300 million in 1976/77. Nevertheless, Kuwait has played a leading role in aiding less prosperous countries in the region. At the end of 1961 the Government established the Kuwait Fund for Arab Economic Development (KFAED) to provide loan capital for development projects in the other Arab countries. KFAED has an authorized capital of KD 1,000 million, and it was increased to this figure from KD 200 million in 1974. Also, the fund's loan area was extended from the Arab world to all developing countries. Since 1973 the value of loans approved by the KFAED has leapt from KD 140 million in March of that year to KD 320 million in June 1976 and to KD 490 million by June 1978. Kuwait also subscribes to the Arab Fund for Economic and Social Development and to the Islamic Development Bank as well as participating in the Arab-African Oil Assistance Fund, the Arab Bank for African Industrial and Agricultural Development and the Organization of Arab Oil Exporting Countries (OAPEC). Kuwait's disbursements in aid are thought to represent about 8 per cent of G.N.P.

DEVELOPMENT

The efforts of the last few years to diversify the economy have had some success. In 1963 the G.D.P. of Kuwait was estimated to be KD 500 million. Of this KD 444 million, or 89 per cent, was provided by the oil industry. For the year 1975/76 oil, natural gas and other mining and quarrying accounted for 70.0 per cent of the G.D.P. During the last few years, it is true, there have been slight setbacks to those parts of the economy which do not depend directly on oil, and the years 1968 to 1970 are regarded as a period of relative recession. The cause of this lay mainly in the June 1967 war, after which Kuwait undertook to pay large subsidies to Egypt and Jordan. At the same time, the slowing down of the growth in oil production necessitated restraints in public spending. The greatly increased oil revenues of the 1970s have brought Kuwait out of this period of stagnation, even though oil production decreased substantially from 1973 to 1975 and in 1977 was 40.3 per cent below that of 1972. All the same, efforts to diversify the economy and maximize the increase in G.D.P. have continued.

At the end of 1976 the Government set up the "Reserves for Future Generations". This means that 50 per cent of the present General Reserves will be set aside and 10 per cent of the State Revenue added for Kuwait's coming generations. The capita land the cumulative interest are earmarked for the use of Kuwaitis when the oil eventually runs out. The initial amount is estimated to be about KD 700 million.

STATISTICAL SURVEY

AREA AND POPULATION

Area	Census Population†				Estimated Population (mid-year)		Density (per sq. km.)
	April 19th, 1970	April 21st, 1975					
		Males	Females	Total	1977	1978	1978
17,818 sq. km.*	738,662	543,768	451,069	994,837	1,129,200	1,198,500	67.3

* 6,880 square miles. † Including Kuwaiti nationals abroad: 754 in 1970; 636 (males 345, females 291) in 1975.

Principal Towns (1975 Census): Kuwait City (capital) 78,116; Hawalli 130,565; Salmiya 113,943; Abraq Kheetan 59,443; Farawaniya 44,875.

ECONOMICALLY ACTIVE POPULATION
(1975 Census)

	Kuwaitis	Non-Kuwaitis	Total
Agriculture, hunting and fishing	3,983	3,531	7,514
Mining and quarrying	1,779	3,080	4,859
Manufacturing industries	2,258	22,209	24,467
Electricity, gas and water	2,034	5,237	7,271
Construction	1,756	30,500	32,256
Trade and restaurants	6,327	33,232	39,559
Transport, storage and communications	4,567	11,118	15,685
Financial institutions, insurance	1,377	5,146	6,523
Services (including defence)	62,888	97,391	160,279
Total*	86,971	211,444	298,415

* Including two Kuwaitis of unstated activity.

AGRICULTURE

LAND USE, 1976
('000 hectares)

Arable land	1
Permanent meadows and pasture	134
Forests and woodlands	2
Other land	1,645
Total	1,782

PRINCIPAL CROPS
('000 metric tons)

	1975	1976*	1977*
Tomatoes	3	3	3
Onions (dry)	1	1	1
Watermelons	3	3	3
Dates	1	1	1

* FAO estimates.

Source: FAO, *Production Yearbook*.

LIVESTOCK
('000 head)

	1975	1976*	1977*
Cattle	8	9	9
Camels	6*	6	6
Sheep	111	111	114
Goats	86	86	89
Poultry	5,741	5,800	6,110

* FAO estimates.

Source: FAO, *Production Yearbook*.

LIVESTOCK PRODUCTS

('000 metric tons)

	1975	1976*	1977*
Beef and veal	2*	2	2
Mutton and lamb	9*	9	9
Poultry meat	7	7	7
Cows' milk	11	11	11
Sheep's milk	5	5	5
Goats' milk	5*	5	5
Hen eggs	2.0	2.0	2.1
Sheep skins	1.6*	1.6	1.6

* FAO estimates.

Source: FAO, *Production Yearbook*.

SEA FISHING

('000 metric tons, live weight)

	1972	1973	1974	1975	1976	1977
TOTAL CATCH	3.9*	5.2	4.7	5.1	4.7	4.7*

* FAO estimate.

Source: FAO, *Yearbook of Fishery Statistics*.

MINING

PETROLEUM PRODUCTION

(million barrels)

	1973	1974	1975	1976	1977
Kuwait*	1,004.8	830.6	670.9	700.0	650.8
Kuwait/Saudi Arabia Partitioned Zone:					
Onshore†	25.8	30.0	30.4	29.5	32.5
Offshore‡	71.9	68.7	59.5	55.7	34.8
TOTAL	1,102.5	929.3	760.7	785.2	718.1

* Kuwait Oil Co. † Kuwait Wafra Oil Co. (Kuwait's share). ‡ Arabian Oil Co. (Kuwait's share).

NATURAL GAS PRODUCTION

(million cu. ft.)

	GAS PRODUCED	USED BY COMPANIES	USED FOR INJECTION	USED BY STATE	TOTAL GAS USED
1974	466,939	94,324	63,186	93,940	251,450
1975	381,135	78,048	42,223	104,076	226,012
1976	395,776	89,562	46,655	107,537	243,754
1977	362,623	92,118	34,091	119,049	245,258

INDUSTRY

SELECTED PRODUCTS

		1975	1976	1977
Motor spirit (petrol)	'000 barrels	4,524	5,841	6,218
Kerosene and jet fuel	,, ,,	6,199	7,569	11,023
Distillate fuel oils	,, ,,	27,558	36,623	31,419
Residual fuel oils	,, ,,	50,471	62,406	60,179
Naphtha	,, ,,	13,383	19,154	18,891
Ammonium hydroxide	metric tons	522,743	513,776	487,913
Electricity generated	million kWh.	4,653	5,202	6,018
Potable water	million gallons	11,601	14,380	17,321
Brackish water	,, ,,	8,329	9,059	9,328
Sodium chloride	tons	18,057	15,426	16,703
Chlorine	,,	7,271	5,370	5,759
Caustic soda	,,	8,203	6,059	6,499
Hydrochloric acid	,,	197,254	219,140	333,430
Lime-sand bricks	cubic metres	170,477	213,553	215,020
Milling (Kuwait Flour Mills Co.)	tons	94,755	108,697	113,260

FINANCE

1,000 fils=10 dirhams=1 Kuwaiti dinar (KD).

Coins: 1, 5, 10, 20, 50 and 100 fils.

Notes: 250 and 500 fils; 1, 5 and 10 dinars.

Exchange rates (June 1979): £1 sterling=576.0 fils; U.S. $1=278.4 fils.

100 Kuwaiti dinars=£173.61=$359.16.

Note: The Kuwaiti dinar was introduced in April 1961, replacing the Persian Gulf Indian rupee. The dinar's initial value of U.S. $2.80 ($1=357.14 fils) remained in force until August 1971. Between December 1971 and February 1973 the dinar's par value was $3.04 ($1=328.95 fils). From February 1973 to March 1975 it was $3.3778 ($1=296.05 fils) but a fluctuating market rate was also in operation. The Kuwaiti dinar was at par with the pound sterling until November 1967, after which the exchange rate was £1=857.14 fils (1 dinar=£1.167) until June 1972. Since March 1975 the dinar's value has been determined in relation to a weighted group of currencies of the country's main trading partners. The average market value of the Kuwaiti dinar was $3.39 in 1973; $3.41 in 1974; $3.45 in 1975; $3.42 in 1976; $3.49 in 1977; $3.64 in 1978.

BUDGET

(KD million, April 1st to March 31st)

Revenue	1973/74	1974/75	1975/76*
Oil taxes and royalties	543.9	715.2	543.5
Sales of crude oil	—	1,688.4	1,143.2
Investment income	89.1	161.7	270.0
Other receipts (net)	42.3	38.7	47.8
Total	675.3	2,604.0	2,004.5

Expenditure	1973/74	1974/75	1975/76*
Current (net)	438.4	732.0	609.3
Development	73.2	106.1	249.3
Land purchase	25.1	27.1	50.0
Total	536.7	865.2	908.6

* Estimates. The 1975/76 fiscal year was subsequently extended for three months to June 30th, 1976. Budget allocations for the extra period have been set at 25 per cent of the annual figures.

1976/77 (July 1st to June 30th): Budget expenditure KD 1,035 million.

1977/78: Revenue KD 2,273 million; Expenditure KD 1,988 million.

1978/79: Revenue KD 2,301 million; Expenditure KD 1,950 million.

1976–81 DEVELOPMENT PLAN

Proposed Expenditure
(KD million)

	Private Sector	Total
Agriculture	20.7	33.2
Mining	4.9	88.7
Manufacturing	125.1	909.5
Land transport	81.6	311.7
Sea transport	93.6	334.2
Air transport	—	29.2
Communications	—	53.8
Transport contingency	3.9	50.1
Trade and finance	24.0	32.8
Electricity and water	—	538.9
Housing	695.4	1,400.8
Education	—	275.6
Health	—	133.4
Social welfare	—	68.8
Religion	—	16.4
Internal security	—	34.1
Information	—	25.7
Public buildings and utilities	—	104.1
Total	1,049.2	4,885.0

CENTRAL BANK RESERVES

(U.S. $ million at December 31st)

	1976	1977	1978
Gold	226.8	106.8	115.2
Reserve position in IMF	862.9	877.2	766.6
Foreign exchange	838.9	2,005.9	1,733.8
Total	1,928.6	2,989.9	2,615.6

Source: IMF, *International Financial Statistics.*

MONEY SUPPLY

(KD million at December 31st)

	1976	1977	1978
Currency outside banks	129.1	150.9	177.0
Demand deposits at commercial banks	264.6	339.8	459.4
Total Money	393.7	490.7	636.4

Source: IMF, *International Financial Statistics.*

EXTERNAL TRADE

(KD million)

	1970	1971	1972	1973	1974	1975	1976	1977	1978
Imports c.i.f.	223.3	232.3	262.2	310.6	455.1	693.2	972.0	1,387.1	n.a.
Exports f.o.b.	679.1	918.8	1,005.4	1,128.2	3,212.7	2,663.0	2,874.0	2,806.1	2,835.2

Source: UN, *Monthly Bulletin of Statistics.*

PRINCIPAL COMMODITIES

(KD '000)

Imports c.i.f.	1973	1974	1975	1976
Food and live animals	53,068	69,315	106,029	121,236
Cereals and cereal preparations	8,818	12,511	24,344	21,435
Fruit and vegetables	13,245	17,230	23,518	31,647
Chemicals	13,493	19,100	26,819	30,119
Basic manufactures	65,512	112,913	123,768	214,691
Textile yarn, fabrics, etc.	25,022	29,871	40,301	61,557
Non-metallic mineral manufactures	9,063	19,380	17,645	34,575
Iron and steel	11,819	32,449	28,455	56,587
Machinery and transport equipment	106,915	156,223	316,212	406,706
Non-electric machinery	19,509	31,520	62,816	103,131
Electrical machinery, apparatus, etc.	40,246	48,495	75,916	130,262
Transport equipment	47,160	76,208	177,480	173,313
Miscellaneous manufactured articles	51,153	68,633	92,011	140,120
Clothing (excl. footwear)	19,108	22,789	33,686	51,212
Scientific instruments, watches, etc.	7,902	10,365	15,326	23,070
Total (incl. others)	310,582	455,090	693,150	971,992

PRINCIPAL COMMODITIES *continued*]

EXPORTS f.o.b.	1973	1974	1975	1976
Petroleum and petroleum products	1,043,773	3,046,524	2,442,658	2,617,647
Crude petroleum	n.a.	n.a.	n.a.	2,151,600*
TOTAL (incl. others)	1,129,689	3,214,759	2,662,989	2,874,373

* *Source:* IMF, *International Financial Statistics.*

PRINCIPAL TRADING PARTNERS
(KD '000)

IMPORTS	1974	1975	1976
Arab countries (excl. Lebanon)	13,010	13,480	16,533
China, People's Republic	13,652	14,369	21,904
EEC	151,076	234,466	317,363
Eastern Europe	17,446	23,118	30,462
Western Europe (excl. EEC)	26,657	25,004	54,263
Hong Kong	6,428	9,180	16,506
India	12,916	15,400	37,959
Japan	77,691	112,356	201,423
Lebanon	16,371	14,600	7,765
Oceania	6,856	18,323	22,575
Pakistan	5,412	9,854	9,137
U.S.A.	64,161	124,923	142,408
TOTAL (incl. others)	455,090	693,150	971,992

EXPORTS (excl. petroleum and gas)	1974	1975	1976
Arabian Gulf countries (excl. Saudi Arabia)	14,073	18,163	24,101
China, People's Republic	6,376	943	2,860
EEC	5,118	5,916	3,286
Egypt	541	1,057	3,708
India	9,736	13,310	4,346
Iran	8,660	12,833	22,205
Iraq	6,635	7,429	18,686
Pakistan	2,441	2,022	2,492
Saudi Arabia	21,009	35,718	104,509
Syria	3,611	1,883	3,950
U.S.A.	1,618	3,797	1,826
TOTAL (incl. others)	117,179	170,826	215,636

PETROLEUM AND GAS EXPORTS
(KD '000)

	1973	1974	1975	1976
Africa (excl. Arab countries)	3,135	12,490	4,436	6,057
America	50,739	133,115	203,743	193,513
Arab countries	13,663	56,510	45,219	65,958
Asia (excl. Arab countries)	399,655	1,377,787	1,215,368	1,278,118
EEC	510,003	1,263,997	803,520	837,168
Eastern Europe	1,459	—	38,260	37,718
Western Europe (excl. EEC)	8,793	29,377	45,780	91,071
Oceania	41,782	129,295	81,082	79,754
Others	30,568	95,009	54,755	69,378
TOTAL	1,059,797	3,097,580	2,492,163	2,658,736

TRANSPORT

Shipping (1976): *Arrivals:* 1,804 ships; passenger arrivals 19,324; passenger departures 25,603.

Vehicles: Total (1972) 175,526; (1973) 197,777; (1974) 223,788; (1975) 272,232; (1976) 320,656; (1977) 379,101.

Civil Aviation: Kuwait Airport, total aircraft movements (1972 13,549; (1973) 14,768; (1974) 16,963; (1975) 19,042; (1976) 23,625; (1977) 28,465.

EDUCATION

(1977/78)*

	Schools	Teachers	Students
Kindergarten	56	1,196	15,412
Primary	145	6,923	113,509
Intermediate	114	6,085	78,631
Secondary	56	4,354	39,635
Commercial	2	135	1,211
Industrial college	1	92	184
Religious institutes	2	99	583
Special training institutes	12	472	2,321
Teacher training colleges	2	206	1,037

* Data for government schools only; in 1976/77 there were 2,555 teachers and 51,917 pupils at 86 private schools.

Sources: Central Statistical Office, Planning Board, Kuwait; Ministry of Finance and Oil, Kuwait; Ministry of Education, Kuwait; National Bank of Kuwait, S.A.K.; Kuwait Oil Co. Ltd., Ahmadi, Kuwait.

THE CONSTITUTION

(Promulgated November 16th, 1962)

On August 29th, 1976, the Amir suspended four articles of the Constitution dealing with Press freedom and the National Assembly, and dissolved the National Assembly. A committee will suggest constitutional amendments which must be approved by referendum within four years.

The principal provisions of the Constitution are as follows:

SOVEREIGNTY

Kuwait is an independent sovereign Arab State; her sovereignty may not be surrendered, and no part of her territory may be relinquished. Offensive war is prohibited by the Constitution.

Succession as Amir is restricted to heirs of the late MUBARAK AL-SABAH, and an Heir Apparent must be appointed within one year of the accession of a new Amir.

EXECUTIVE AUTHORITY

Executive power is vested in the Amir, who exercises it through a Council of Ministers. The Amir will appoint the Prime Minister "after the traditional consultations", and will appoint and dismiss Ministers on the recommendation of the Prime Minister. Ministers need not be members of the National Assembly, though all Ministers who are not Assembly members assume membership *ex officio* in the Assembly for the duration of office. The Amir also lays down laws, which shall not be effective unless published in the *Official Gazette.* The Amir sets up public institutions. All decrees issued in these respects shall be conveyed to the Assembly. No law is issued unless it is approved by the Assembly.

LEGISLATURE

A National Assembly of 50 members will be elected for a four-year term by all natural-born literate Kuwait males over the age of 21, except servicemen and police, who may not vote. Candidates for election must possess the franchise and be over 30 years of age. The Assembly will sit for at least eight months in any year, and new elections shall be held within two months of the last dissolution of the outgoing Assembly.

Restrictions on the commercial activities of Ministers include an injunction forbidding them to sell property to the Government.

The Amir may ask for reconsideration of a Bill passed by the Assembly and sent to him for ratification, but the Bill would automatically become law if it were subsequently passed by a two-thirds majority at the next sitting, or by a simple majority at a subsequent sitting. The Amir may declare Martial Law, but only with the approval of the Assembly.

The Assembly may pass a vote of no confidence in a Minister, in which case the Minister must resign. Such a vote is not permissible in the case of the Prime Minister, but the Assembly may approach the Amir on the matter, and the Amir shall then either dismiss the Prime Minister or dissolve the Assembly.

An annual budget shall be presented, and there shall be an independent finance control commission.

CIVIL SERVICE

Entry to the Civil Service is confined to Kuwait citizens.

PUBLIC LIBERTIES

Kuwaitis are equal before the law in prestige, rights and duties. Individual freedom is guaranteed. No one shall be seized, arrested or exiled except within the rules of law.

No punishment shall be administered except for an act or abstaining from an act considered a crime in accordance with a law applicable at the time of committing it, and no penalty shall be imposed more severe than that which could have been imposed at the time of committing the crime.

Freedom of opinion is guaranteed to everyone, and each has the right to express himself through speech, writing or other means within the limits of the law.

The Press is free within the limits of the law, and it should not be suppressed except in accordance with the dictates of law.

Freedom of performing religious rites is protected by the State according to prevailing customs, provided it does not violate the public order and morality.

Trade unions will be permitted and property must be respected. An owner is not banned from managing his property except within the boundaries of law. No property should be taken from anyone, except within the prerogatives of law, unless a just compensation be given.

Houses may not be entered, except in cases provided by law. Every Kuwaiti has freedom of movement and choice of place of residence within the state. This right shall not be controlled except in cases stipulated by law.

Every person has the right to education and freedom to choose his type of work. Freedom to form peaceful societies is guaranteed within the limits of law.

THE GOVERNMENT

HEAD OF STATE

Amir of Kuwait: His Highness Sheikh Jaber al-Ahmad al-Sabah (succeeded on the death of his cousin, December 31st, 1977).

COUNCIL OF MINISTERS

(*July* 1979)

Crown Prince and Prime Minister: Sheikh Saad al-Abdullah al-Salem al-Sabah.

Deputy Prime Minister and Minister of Information: Sheikh Jaber al-Ali al-Salem al-Sabah.

Deputy Prime Minister and Minister of Foreign Affairs: Sheikh Sabah al-Ahmad al-Jaber al-Sabah.

Minister of Education: Jasem Khalid al-Marzuq.

Minister of Housing: Humud Mubarak al-Ayyar.

Minister of Public Works: Humud Youssef al-Nisf.

Minister of Defence: Sheikh Salem al-Sabah al-Salem al-Sabah.

Minister of Communications and Transport: Sulaiman Humud al-Zaid al-Khalid.

Minister of the Interior: Nawaf al-Ahmad al-Jabir.

Minister of Finance: Abdel-Rahman Salem al-Atiqi.

Minister of Health: Dr. Abdel-Rahman Abdullah al-Awadi.

Minister of Social Affairs and Labour: Abdel-Aziz Mahmoud.

Minister of State for Amiri Diwan Affairs: Sheikh Khaled al-Ahmed al-Sabah.

Minister of State for Cabinet Affairs: Abdel-Aziz Husain.

Minister of Justice: Abdullah Ibrahim al-Muffarij.

Minister of Islamic Affairs: Youssif Jassim al-Haji.

Minister of Oil: Sheikh Ali al-Khalifa al-Sabah.

Minister of Trade and Industry: Abdel-Wahhab Youssef al-Nifisi.

Minister of Planning: Muhammad Youssif al-Adasani.

Minister of Electricity and Water: Khalaf Ahmad al-Khalaf.

Minister of State for Administrative and Legal Affairs: Sheikh Suliman Duaij al-Sabah.

PROVINCIAL GOVERNORATES

Ahmadi: Sheikh Jabir Abdullah Jabir al-Sabah.

Hawalli: Sheikh Nawaf al-Ahmad al-Jabir.

Kuwait: (vacant).

NATIONAL ASSEMBLY

In elections held for the fourth time under the new Constitution on January 27th, 1975, 260 candidates were nominated for the 50 seats (5 seats in each of 10 districts). There are no official political parties, the candidates standing as individuals. In the 1975 elections, however, several opposition leaders were re-elected. The National Assembly was suspended on August 29th, 1976 (*see* under Constitution).

DIPLOMATIC REPRESENTATION

EMBASSIES ACCREDITED TO KUWAIT

(In Kuwait City unless otherwise indicated)

(E) Embassy.

Afghanistan: Al Rawdah, Jabrieh St., Villa No. 3 (E); *Ambassador:* Khalillullha Khalili.

Algeria: Istiqlal St. (E); *Ambassador:* Boualem Bessaieh.

Argentina: Jeddah, Saudi Arabia (E).

Australia: Jeddah, Saudi Arabia (E).

Austria: Room 518, Sheraton Hotel; *Chargé d'affaires:* Dr. George Markhof.

Bahrain: Riyadh St., Al-Doha District, Birgis Humoud Bldg. 8 (E); *Ambassador:* Saif J. al-Musalam.

Bangladesh: Istiqlal St., Dasmah, Area No. 4, House No. 19 (E); *Ambassador:* Abdul Faiz Bashirul Alam.

Belgium: Mohammed Al-Ghunaiman Villa, Damascus St., P.O.B. 3280, Safat (E); *Ambassador:* Jean Davaux.

Brazil: Istiqlal St. (E); *Ambassador:* Paulo H. Parangfa.

Bulgaria: Mansuria, Parcel No. 1, Street No. 11, Naqi Bldg. (E); *Ambassador:* Asen I. Zlatanov.

Cameroon: Jeddah, Saudi Arabia (E).

Canada: (E); *Ambassador:* STUART HAY.

China, People's Republic: Sheikh Ahmed Jaber Bldgs., Dasman (E); *Ambassador:* TING HAO.

Colombia: Beirut, Lebanon (E).

Costa Rica: Beirut, Lebanon (E).

Cuba: Beirut, Lebanon (E).

Czechoslovakia: No. 14, Cairo St., P.O.B. 1151 (E); *Chargé d'affaires:* FRANTIŠEK MATEJKA.

Denmark: Abdulla Al Salem District, Block No. 1, Parcel No. 175 (E); *Chargé d'affaires:* PER S. ANDERSEN.

Ecuador: Teheran, Iran (E).

Finland: Beirut, Lebanon (E).

France: Qabazard Bldg., Istiqlal St. (E); *Ambassador:* PIERRE BLOUIN

Gambia: Jeddah, Saudi Arabia (E).

German Democratic Republic: Shuwaikh (E); *Ambassador:* Dr. GÜNTER DABERENZ.

Germany, Federal Republic: Shamiya District, Al Mamoun St., Villa Shaikh (E); *Ambassador:* FRIEDRICH LANDAU (also accred. to Bahrain).

Greece: 17 Al Mansour St., Shuwaikh "B" (E); *Ambassador:* LEONIDAS VRAILAS.

Guinea: Jeddah, Saudi Arabia (E).

Hungary: Dhahia District, Parcel No. 1 Villa 44 (E); *Ambassador:* KÁROLY SZIGETI.

India: 34 Shara, Istiqlal (E); *Ambassador:* G. RAJ.

Indonesia: Nuzha District, Block 3, Nuzha Main St. No. 32 (E); *Ambassador:* MUNAWIR SJADZALI.

Iran: Haj Abdulla Dashti Bldg., Istiqlal St. (E); *Ambassador:* Dr. ALI SHAMS ARDEKANI.

Iraq: Plot No. 26, Istiqlal St., Al-Musa Bldg. (E); *Ambassador:* THAMER R. AL-SHAIKHALI.

Ireland: Jeddah, Saudi Arabia (E).

Italy: Villa No. 6, F. Omar Ben Al-Khatab, Mulla Bldgs., Sharq (E); *Ambassador:* Dr. GERARDO ZAMPAGLIONE (also accred. to Bahrain, Oman and the United Arab Emirates).

Japan: House No. 5, Plot No. 1, Street No. 13, Rowdah Area (E); *Ambassador:* YUKIO TAKAMATSU (also accred. to Bahrain).

Jordan: Mansour Qabazard Bldg., Istiqlal St. (E); *Ambassador:* MUHYIDDIN AL-HUSEINI.

Kenya: Cairo, Egypt (E).

Lebanon: Istiqlal St. (E); *Ambassador:* FAISAL SULTAN (also accred. to Bahrain).

Liberia: Cairo, Egypt (E).

Libya: Istiqlal St. (E); *Ambassador:* HUSNI S. AL-MUDEER.

Malaysia: Block 1, Parcel 2, Mansuria (E); *Chargé d'affaires:* WAN HUSSAIN MUSTAPHA.

Mali: Cairo, Egypt (E).

Malta: Tripoli, Libya (E).

Mauritania: Villa No. 5, Sheikh Salman Duaij, Riad St. (E); *Ambassador:* MUHAMMAD ABDUL-RAHMAN OULD AMIN.

Mexico: Mubarak Al Kabeer St., Al Awadhi Bldg., 3rd Floor, Apt. 22 (E); *Ambassador:* JORGE M. RODRÍGUEZ.

Morocco: Shuwaikh Area B (E); *Ambassador:* ABDUL HADI AL-SUBAIHI. (also accred to Bahrain and Oman).

Nepal: Cairo, Egypt (E).

Netherlands: Istiqlal St., Sha'b Area, P.O.B. 21822 (E); *Ambassador:* G. W. BENDIEN (also accred. to Bahrain, Qatar and the United Arab Emirates).

Nigeria: Jeddah, Saudi Arabia (E).

Norway: Jeddah, Saudi Arabia (E).

Oman: Istiqlal St. (E); *Ambassador:* QASSIM A. AL-JAMALI.

Pakistan: Sharah-i-Istiqlal, P.O.B. 988 (E); *Ambassador:* MEHDI MASOOD.

Poland: Al Rawdah, Block 4, 3rd Ring Road (E); *Chargé d'affaires:* TADEUSZ KLEJNOCKI.

Qatar: Istiqlal St. (E); *Ambassador:* MUHAMMAD M. AL-KHELAIFI.

Romania: Sheikh Duaij Ibrahim Bldg., Istiqlal St. (E); *Ambassador:* Dr. CONSTANTIN CARUNTU.

Saudi Arabia: Istiqlal St. (E); *Ambassador:* Sheikh FAHD KHALED AS-SUDAIRI.

Senegal: P.O.B. 23892, Al Nougra, Safat (E); *Ambassador:* ALIOUNE DAT.

Somalia: Nasir St., Shuwaikh "B" (E); *Chargé d'affaires:* ADAM HASHI MOHAMMAD.

Spain: Abdullah Salem District (E); *Ambassador:* FERNANDO SCHWAITZ GIRON (also accred. to Bahrain, Oman and the United Arab Emirates).

Sudan: Al Rawdah, Abu Hayen Tawhidi St. (E); *Ambassador:* MOUSA AWAD BILAL.

Sweden: Hilali St. (E); *Ambassador:* GORAN BUNDY.

Switzerland: House No. 12, Road No. 32, Adeliyah Area (E); *Chargé d'affaires:* OTTO GRITTI.

Syria: No. 33 Diiyah District (E); *Ambassador:* ABDER-RAZZAQ SHAKER.

Thailand: Jeddah, Saudi Arabia (E).

Tunisia: Sheikh Duaij Ibrahim Bldg., Istiqlal St. (E); *Ambassador:* MUHAMMAD MHAKDEESH (also accred. to Bahrain and Oman).

Turkey: Bneid Al-Gar (E); *Chargé d'affaires a.i.:* TULUY TANC (also accred. to Bahrain).

Uganda: Jeddah, Saudi Arabia (E).

U.S.S.R.: Baghdad St., House No. 6 (E); *Ambassador:* NIKOLAI N. SIKATCHEV.

United Arab Emirates: Istiqlal St. (E); *Ambassador:* MUHAMMAD SULTAN ABDULLA.

United Kingdom: Arabian Gulf St. (E); *Ambassador:* JOHN CAMBRIDGE, C.M.G.

U.S.A.: Bneid Al-Gar (E); *Ambassador:* FRANK MAESTRONE.

Venezuela: Dahiya Abdulla Salem, Nusuf Al Nusuf St., No. 76 (E); *Ambassador:* JOSÉ A. S. GORRIN.

Yemen Arab Republic: Abdullah Al-Salem Area, Morocco St. (E); *Ambassador:* ABDULLAH RAEI (also accred. to Bahrain).

Yugoslavia: Al-Mansour St., Shuwaikh "B" (E); *Ambassador:* JOZE INGOLIC.

Zaire: Al Rawdah, Street No. 34, Villa No. 24 (E); *Ambassador:* NDEZE MATABARO.

Zambia: Cairo, Egypt (E).

Kuwait also has diplomatic relations with Albania, Djibouti, Gabon, Guinea-Bissau, Guyana, the Republic of Korea, Lesotho, Madagascar, Maldives, the Philippines, Tanzania, Trinidad and Tobago, Upper Volta and Viet-Nam.

JUDICIAL SYSTEM

There is a codified system of law based largely upon the Egyption system. In criminal matters, minor contraventions are dealt with by Magistrates Courts, felonies by Criminal Assize Courts. Appeal in the case of misdemeanours is to a Misdemeanours Court of Appeal.

Civil cases are heard by a General Court within which are separate chambers dealing with commercial cases, other civil cases and matters of personal status. Appeal is to a High Court of Appeal. Matters of personal status may go beyond the High Court of Appeal to a Court of Cassation.

In criminal cases, investigation of misdemeanours is the responsibility of the police, while responsibility for the investigation of felonies lies with the Attorney-General's Office.

RELIGION

MUSLIMS

The inhabitants are mainly Muslims of the Sunni and Shiite sects.

CHRISTIANS

Roman Catholic: Right Rev. Mgr. V. San Miguel, o.c.d., Administrator Apostolic of Kuwait, Bishop's House, P.O.B. 266, Kuwait.

National Evangelical Church in Kuwait: Rev. Yusef Abdul Noor, Box 80, Kuwait; a United Protestant Church founded by the Reformed Church in America; services in Arabic, English and Malayalam.

There are also Armenian, Greek, Coptic and Syrian Orthodox Churches in Kuwait.

THE PRESS

DAILIES

Al-Anbaa: P.O.B. 23915, Kuwait; f. 1976; Arabic; general; Editor-in-Chief Nasser Abdelaziz Al Marzooq.

Al-Qabas: P.O.B. 21800, Airport Rd., Shuwaikh, Kuwait; f. 1972; Arabic; Editor Jassim Ahmad al-Nusuf; Gen. Man. Zulficar Kobeissi; circ. 60,000.

Al-Rai al-Amm (*Public Opinion*): P.O.B. 695, International Airport Rd., Shuwaikh Industrial Area, Kuwait; f. 1961; Arabic; political, social and cultural; Editor Yousef al-Messaeed; circ. 35,000.

Al-Siyasa: P.O.B. 2270, Kuwait; f. 1965; Arabic; political; Editor Ahmed Al-Jarallah; circ. 42,000.

Al-Watan (*The Homeland*): P.O.B. 1142 Safat, Kuwait; f. 1974; Arabic; political; Editor-in-Chief and Chair. Mohamed Mussad al-Saleh; circ. 55,000.

Arab Times: P.O.B. 2,270, Kuwait; f. 1977 (formerly *Daily News*); English; Editor-in-Chief Mohammed G. Rumaihi; circ. 20,000.

Kuwait Times: P.O.B. 1301, Safat, Kuwait; f. 1961; English; political; Owner and Editor-in-Chief Yousuf Alyan; Man. Editor Dara Kadwa; circ. 24,000.

WEEKLIES AND PERIODICALS

Kuwait Al-Youm (*Kuwait Today*): P.O.B. 193, Kuwait; f. 1954; Sunday; the "Official Gazette"; Amiri Decrees, Laws, Govt. announcements, decisions, invitations for tenders, etc.; published by the Ministry of Information; circ. 5,000.

Adhwa al-Kuwait: P.O.B. 1977, Kuwait; f. 1962; Arabic; literature and arts; weekly; free advertising magazine; Editor Myrin Al Hamad; circ. 5,000.

Al-Arabi: P.O.B. 748, Kuwait; f. 1958; Arabic; science, history, arts; monthly; published by the Ministry of Information; Editor Ahmad Baha-idin; circ. 250,000.

Al-Balagh: Kuwait; weekly.

Al-Hadaf (*The Aim*): P.O.B. 1142, Safat-Kuwait; f. 1961; Arabic; political and cultural; weekly; Editor-in-Chief J. M. al-Muttawa; Chair. D. M. al-Saleh; circ. 63,000.

Al Kuwaiti: Information Dept., Ahmadi 22; f. 1961; Arabic; weekly journal of the Kuwait Oil Co. (KSC); circ. 7,000.

Al-Mujtama'a: P.O.B. 4850, Kuwait; f. 1969; Arabic weekly issued by the Social Reform Society.

Al Nahdha (*The Renaissance*): P.O.B. 695, International Airport Rd., Shuwaikh Industrial Area, Kuwait; f. 1967; Arabic; weekly; social and political; Editor Youssuf Al-Massaeed; circ. 45,000.

Arab Oil: P.O.B. 2270, Kuwait; f. 1977; international magazine for the oil industry; monthly; Editor David Lynn Price; circ. 14,000.

Ar-Raid (*The Pioneer*): P.O.B. 11259, Cairo Rd., Kuwait; f. 1969; weekly; issued by Kuwaiti Teachers' Association; circ. 4,000.

Ar Ressaleh (*The Message*): P.O.B. 2490, Shuwaikh, Kuwait; f. 1961; Arabic; political, social and cultural; weekly; Editor Jassim Mubarak.

At-Tali'a: P.O.B. 1082, Mubarak al-Kabir St., Kuwait; f. 1962; Arabic; weekly; Editor Sami Ahmed Al-Munais; circ. 10,000.

Al-Yaqza (*The Awakening*): P.O.B. 6000, Kuwait; f. 1966; political, economic, social and general; weekly; Editor-in-Chief Ahmed Yousuf Behbehani; Gen. Man. Mustafa Jundi; circ. 67,000.

Hayatuna (*Our Life*): P.O.B. 1708, Kuwait; f. 1968; Arabic; medicine and hygiene; fortnightly; published by Al-Awadi Press Corporation; Editor Dr. Abdul Rahman Al-Awadi; circ. 6,000.

Kuwaiti Digest: Information Dept., Ahmadi 22; English; quarterly; journal of Kuwait Oil Co.; circ. 6,000.

Mejallat al-Kuwait (*Kuwait Magazine*): P.O.B. 193, Kuwait; Arabic; news and literary articles; fortnightly illustrated magazine; published by Ministry of Information.

Saut al-Khaleej (*Voice of the Gulf*): P.O.B. 659, Kuwait; f. 1962; political weekly; Editor Baqer Khraibitt; circ. 20,000.

Osrati (*My Family*): P.O.B. 2995, Kuwait; Arabic; women's magazine; weekly; Editor Ghanima F. al-Marzouk; published by Fahad al-Marzouk Establishment; circ. 65,000.

NEWS AGENCIES

Kuwait News Agency (KUNA): 2nd Floor, Al-Nakib Bldg., Fahed Al-Salem St., Kuwait; f. 1976; Chair. and Dir-Gen. Barges Hamoud al-Barges.

FOREIGN BUREAUX

Hsinhua (*People's Republic of China*): P.O.B. 22168, nr. Dasman Palace, Kuwait.

Middle East News Agency (MENA) (*Egypt*): P.O.B. 1927, Fahd El-Salem St., Kuwait; Dir. REDA SOLIMAN.

Reuters (*United Kingdom*): 3rd Floor, al-Thuwaini Bldg., Ali as-Salem St., P.O.B. 5616, Safat, Kuwait.

Telegrafnoye Agentstvo Sovietskovo Soyuza (TASS) (*U.S.S.R.*): P.O.B. 1455, Kuwait.

The Jamahiriya News Agency (Libya) is also represented.

PUBLISHER

Ministry of Information: P.O.B. 193, Kuwait.

RADIO AND TELEVISION

RADIO

Kuwait Broadcasting Station: P.O.B. 397, Kuwait; f. 1951; broadcasts in Arabic, Persian, English and Urdu, some in stereo; Asst. Under-Sec. for Broadcasting Affairs ABDUL AZIZ MOHAMED JA'FFER; Asst. Under-Sec. for Engineering Affairs ABDUL-RAHMAN IBRAHIM AL-HUTY.

Number of radio receivers (1977): 700,000.

TELEVISION

Television of Kuwait, Ministry of Information: P.O.B. 621, Kuwait; f. 1961; broadcasts in Arabic; colour television started in spring 1973; a second channel was opened in 1979. Asst. Under-Sec. of TV Affairs MUHAMMAD SANOUSSI; Dir. of Programmes RISA AL-FEELI.

Number of television receivers (1978): 200,000.

FINANCE

BANKING

(cap. = capital; p.u. = paid up; dep. = deposits; res. = reserves; m. = million; amounts in Kuwaiti dinars)

CENTRAL BANK

Central Bank of Kuwait: P.O.B. 526, Kuwait; f. 1969; cap. 2m., reserves 3m.; Governor HAMZAH ABBAS HUSSAIN.

NATIONAL BANKS

Alahli Bank of Kuwait K.S.C.: Commercial Centre 5, P.O.B. 1387, Kuwait; 10 brs.; cap. p.u. 9.om.; dep. 586.7m. (Dec. 1978); Chair. SAOUD AL ABDUL RAZZAK; Gen. Man. PHILIPPE DUJARDIN.

Bank of Bahrain and Kuwait B.S.C.: Ahmad Al-Jaber St., P.O.B. 24396, Safat, Kuwait; 50 per cent government owned; cap. and res. 8.98 m; dep. 66.6 m.; total assets 160.8 m (Dec. 1978); Man. Dir. BADER ALI AL-DAWOOD; Gen. Man. FRANK R. LEHMANN.

Bank of Kuwait and the Middle East K.S.C.: P.O.B. 71, Safat, Kuwait; 49 per cent owned by the Government; began operations in Dec. 1971 when it took over former branches of the British Bank of the Middle East; cap. p.u. 8m.; Chair. FAHAD AL BAHAR; Man. Dir. FAWZI HAMAD AL-SULTAN; Gen. Man. HUE T. KEMPER;

Burgan Bank, S.A.K.: P.O.B. 5389, Safat, Kuwait; f. 1975; 51 per cent owned by the Government; cap. and res. 12.04m; dep. 231m; total assets 276.75m. (Dec. 1978); 4 brs.; Chair. and Man. Dir. ABDULRASOOL ABDUL-HASAN; Gen. Man. ABDULAZIZ AL-JASSAR.

Commercial Bank of Kuwait, S.A.K.: Mubarak Al Kabir St., P.O.B. 2861, Kuwait; cap. and res. 43m., dep. 305m. (Feb. 1978); 22 brs.; Chair. HAMAD A. A. AL HAMAD; Gen. Man. H. J. KWANT.

Gulf Bank K.S.C.: P.O.B. Safat 3200, Mubarak Al Kabir St., Kuwait; f. 1961; cap. p.u. 9.om., dep. 603m., total assets 731.5m (Dec. 1978); 19 brs.; Chair. KHALID YUSIF AL-MUTAWA; Gen. Man. S. WEBSTER.

Industrial Bank of Kuwait: P.O.B. 3146, Safat, Kuwait; 49 per cent owned by the Government; f. 1973; cap. p.u. 10m.; Chair. and Man. Dir. ANWAR A. AL-NOURI; Exec. Man. LUCIEN S. TOUTOUNJI.

Kuwait Real Estate Bank K.S.C.: P.O.B. 22822, Safat; Kuwait; Chair. and Man. Dir. SAAD ALI AL-NAHED, Gen. Man. ALI R. AL-BADER.

National Bank of Kuwait, S.A.K.: Abdullah Al-Salim St., P.O.B. 95, Kuwait; f. 1952; cap. and res. 63m., total assets 1,036.8m. (Dec. 1978); 35 brs.; Chair. YACOUB YOUSUF AL HAMAD; Chief Gen. Man. C. D. FEARS.

Savings and Credit Bank: P.O.B. 1454, Kuwait; f. 1960; nominal cap. 320m., dep. 77.5m. (June 1978); Chair. ABDUL RAHMAN ALMUJHAM; Dir.-Gen. YOUSEF M. SHAIJI.

INSURANCE

Al Ahleia Insurance Co., S.A.K.: P.O.B. 1602, Ali Al-Salim St., Kuwait; f. 1962; covers all classes of insurance; cap. 2.7m.; Chair. MUHAMMAD Y. AL-NISF; Man. Dir. ABDULLA A. AL-RIFAI; Gen. Man. Dr. RAOUF H. MAKAR.

Gulf Insurance Co. K.S.C.: P.O.B. 1040, Kuwait; f. 1962; cap. 2.6m.; Gen. Man. ELIAS N. BEDEWI.

Kuwait Insurance Co.: Abdullah As-Salim St., P.O.B. 769, Kuwait; f. 1960; cap. p.u. 5.25m.; Gen. Man. MAHMOUD S. GHUNAIM; Deputy Gen. Man. FOUAD A. AL-BAHAR.

Some 20 Arab and other foreign insurance companies are active in Kuwait.

STOCK EXCHANGE

Kuwait Stock Exchange: Kuwait City.

OIL

Kuwait National Petroleum Co., K.S.C.: P.O.B. 70—Safat, Kuwait; f. 1961; refining and marketing company; Chair. AHMAD ABDUL MUHSIN AL-MUTAIR; publ. *Al-Wataniah* (monthly).

Kuwait Oil Co., K.S.C.: Ahmadi 22, Kuwait; f. 1934; state-owned; 697 wells producing at end of December 1977; oil production in 1977 was 650,822,004 barrels; an average of 1,783,074 barrels per day; Chair. and Man. Dir. AHMAD MOHAMED JA'AFAR.

Kuwait Shell Petroleum Development Co. (*Royal Dutch Shell*): Fahad al-Salim St., Kuwait; has concession, signed January 1961, of 5,595 sq. km. offshore from Kuwait; operations suspended pending clarification of the offshore boundary disputes with Iraq, Iran and Saudi Arabia.

Kuwait Spanish Petroleum Co.: P.O.B. 20467, Kuwait; f. 1968; 51 per cent owned by Kuwait National Petroleum Co., 49 per cent by Hispanoil of Spain; holds concessions of 435,200 hectares for a period of 35 years from 1968: drilling began in 1970, was suspended in 1973, but resumed in 1975.

Kuwait Wafra Oil Co.: P.O.B. 69, Kuwait; formerly American Independent Oil Co., nationalized Sept. 1977; its operations merged with those of Kuwait Oil Co. and KNPC; shares with Getty Oil Co. (from Saudi Arabia) concessions in Kuwait/Saudi Arabia Partitioned Zone onshore; combined oil production in 1976 was 8,488,082 long tons.

Arabian Oil Co.: Head Office Tokyo; Kuwait Office P.O.B. 1641, Kuwait; Field Office Ras Al-Khafji, Divided Zone, Saudi Arabia; a Japanese company which has concessions offshore of the Partitioned Zone; there are 147 producing wells as well as four flow stations in operation; in 1978 crude oil production averaged 308,400 barrels per day.

TRADE AND INDUSTRY

CHAMBER OF COMMERCE

Kuwait Chamber of Commerce and Industry: P.O.B. 775, Chamber's Bldg., Ali Salem St., Kuwait State; f. 1959; 6,500 mems.; Pres. ABDUL AZIZ AL-SAGER; Vice-Pres. YOUSEF AL-FULEIJ and MOHAMAD A. AL-KHARAFI; Adviser and Acting Sec.-Gen. MAJED JAMAL UD-DIN; publs. *The Kuwaiti Economist* (monthly) and annual economic and administrative reports.

DEVELOPMENT

Kuwait Foreign Trading, Contracting and Investment Co.: P.O.B. 5665, Kuwait; f. 1965; overseas investment company; 80 per cent government holding; cap. and res. KD 30m., total assets KD 61.8m. (1975); Chair. and Man. Dir. ABDULWAHAB A. AL-TAMMAR.

Kuwait Fund for Arab Economic Development: Mubarak Al-Kabir, P.O.B. 2921, Kuwait; cap. KD 1,000m.; wholly government owned; provides and administers financial and technical assistance to the countries of the developing world; Chair. ABDULREHMAN SALEM AL-ATEEQY; Dir.-Gen. ABDLATIF Y. AL-HAMAD.

Kuwait Investment Co. S.A.K.: P.O.B. 1005 Safat, Kuwait; f. 1961; total resources KD 237m. (December 1978); investment banking institution owned 50 per cent by the Government and 50 per cent by Kuwaiti nationals; international banking and investment; Chair. and Man. Dir. BADER ALI AL-DAWOOD; Gen. Man. HAMAD MUHAMMAD AL-BAHAR.

Kuwait National Industries Company: P.O.B. 417, Kuwait; f. 1960; 51 per cent government-owned company with controlling interest in various construction enterprises.

Kuwait Planning Board: Kuwait City; f. 1962; supervises long-term development plans; through its Central Statistical Office publishes information on Kuwait's economic activity; Dir.-Gen. AHMED ALI AL DUAIJ.

Petrochemical Industries Co. K.S.C.: P.O.B. 1084, Kuwait; owns and operates the Fertilizer Division which produces ammonia, urea, ammonium sulphate and concentrated sulphuric acid; also owns and operates the Salt and the Chlorine Division, which produces salt, chlorine, caustic soda, hydrochloric acid, sodium hypochlorite, chlorsal and compressed hydrogen.

Shuaiba Area Authority: P.O.B. 4690, Kuwait; f. 1964; an independent governmental authority to supervise and run the industrial area and Port of Shuaiba. It has powers and duties to develop the area and its industries which include an oil refinery, cement factory, fishing plant, power stations and distillation plants, chemical fertilizer and petrochemical industries.

TRADE UNIONS

General Confederation of Kuwaiti Workers: f. 1968 central authority of which all trade unions are affiliated

KOC Workers Union: f. 1964; Chair. JASSIM ABDUL WAHAB AL TOURA.

Federation of Petroleum and Petrochemical Workers: f. 1965; Chair. JASSIM ABDUL WAHAB AL TOURA; publ. *The Worker.*

TRANSPORT

ROADS

Roads in the towns are metalled and the most important are dual carriageway. There are metalled roads to Ahmadi, Mina Al-Ahmadi and other centres of population in Kuwait, and to the Iraqi and Saudi Arabian borders. A four-lane trunk road to Damman in Saudi Arabia is under construction and a motorway system is being developed.

Kuwait Transport Co. S.A.K.: Kuwait; provides internal bus service; regular service to Iran inaugurated in December 1968.

SHIPPING

A modern port has been built at Shuwaikh, two miles west of Kuwait City, which is being expanded to bring the number of berths to 19. Ships of British and other lines make regular calls.

There is a second port at Shuaiba to the south of Kuwait containing 15 berths and a liquid products pier with 4 berths.

The oil port at Mina Al-Ahmad, 40 km. south of Kuwait City is capable of handling the largest oil tankers afloat, and oil exports of over 2 million barrels per day.

Arab Maritime Petroleum Transport Co.: Khalid al-Essa Bldg., P.O.B. 22525, Kuwait City; eight tankers; sponsored by OAPEC and financed by Algeria, Abu Dhabi, Bahrain, Iraq, Kuwait, Libya, Qatar and Saudi Arabia; Chair. Dr. A. H. TAHER; Vice-Chair. and Man. Dir. A. RAHMAN AL-SULTAN.

Kuwait Oil Tanker Co. S.A.K.: P.O.B. 810, Kuwait; f. 1957; state-owned; owns 9 tankers totalling 2,140,000 d.w.t., and 2 LPG carriers of 71,650 cu. m., with 4 further LPG carriers on order; sole tanker agents for Mina al-Ahmadi and Shuaiba and agents for other ports; LPG filling and distribution; Chair. FUAD MOHAMED THUNYYAN AL-GHANEM.

United Arab Shipping Co. S.A.G.: P.O.B. 3636, Safat, Kuwait; f. 1976; a national company of the Arabian Gulf countries, with Kuwait Shipping Co. as nucleus of the amalgamation; services to Europe, U.K., Far East, Mediterranean ports, Japan and East Coast of U.S.A.; 61 vessels totalling 1,201,780 tons; cap. p.u. KD 180m.; Chair. MUHAMMAD SAYID AL-MULLA; Gen. Man. D. H. TOD.

CIVIL AVIATION

Kuwait Airways Corporation: Al-Hilali St., P.O.B. 394, Aden, Amman, Amsterdam, Athens, Baghdad, Bahrain, Bangkok, Beirut, Belgrade, Bombay, Cairo, Casablanca, Copenhagen, Damascus, Delhi, Dhahran, Doha, Dubai, Frankfurt, Geneva, Istanbul, Jeddah, Karachi, Khartoum, London, Madrid, Muscat, Paris, Prague, Ras al-Khaimah, Rome, Sana'a, Teheran, Tripoli, Tunis; fleet of 7 Boeing 707, 3 Jumbo 747; Chair. and Man. Dir. GHASSAN AL-NISSIF; Gen. Man. AHMED AL MISHARI; publs. *Al-Boraq* (Magazine), *KAC News.*

Kuwait is also served by the following airlines: Air France, Air India, Alia (Jordan), British Airways, ČSA (Czechoslovakia), Democratic Yemen Airlines, EgyptAir, Gulf Aviation, Iranair, Iraq Airways, KLM (Netherlands), Lufthansa (Federal Republic of Germany), MAS (Malaysia), MEA (Lebanon), Olympic Airways (Greece), PIA (Pakistan), Saudia (Saudi Arabia), Syrian Arab Airlines and Yemen Airways.

DEFENCE

The armed forces number 12,000, and include 10,500 in the army and 1,000 in the air force. The navy consists of a coastguard force of 500 and there is a para-military force of 1,500. Defence expenditure amounted to KD 93 million in 1977. There is a period of Military Service lasting 9, 12 or 18 months.

Chief of Staff of Armed Forces: Lieutenant-General MUBARAK AL-ABDULLAH.

EDUCATION

Within the last few years a comprehensive system of kindergarten, primary, intermediate and secondary schools has been built up, and compulsory education between the ages of 6 and 14, was introduced in 1966–67. However, many children spend two years before this in a kindergarten, and can go on to complete their general education at the age of 18 years. In 1977/78 about 252,000 pupils attended 390 government schools staffed by about 19,500 teachers. The general policy of the Government is to provide free education to all Kuwaiti children from kindergarten stage to the University. Pupils are also provided, free of cost, with food, textbooks, clothing and medical treatment. In 1976/77 there were about 52,000 pupils at private schools.

Children may spend two preliminary years at a kindergarten, and at the age of 6 commence their compulsory education at a primary school. This lasts four years, after which the pupils move on to an intermediate school where they stay for another four years. Secondary education, which is optional and lasts four more years, is given mainly in general schools. There are also a Commercial Institute, an Institute of Technology, a health institute, a religious institute (with intermediate and secondary stages) and eleven institutes for handicapped children. Adult education centres have 21,305 students.

Two-year courses at post-secondary teacher training institutes provide teachers for kindergartens and primary schools and the University provides for intermediate and secondary schools. The number of graduates is not enough to meet all the teaching staff requirements and so the Ministry of Education meets this shortage by recruiting teachers from other Arab countries.

Scholarships are granted to students to pursue courses which are not offered by Kuwait University. In 1975–76 there were 2,787 Kuwaiti scholarship students studying mainly in Egypt, Lebanon, U.K. and the U.S.A. There were also 527 pupils from Arab, African and Asian states studying in Kuwait schools on Kuwait Government scholarships. Kuwait University also provides scholarships for a number of Arab, Asian and African students.

UNIVERSITY

Kuwait University: P.O.B. 5969, Kuwait; f. 1966; *c.* 400 teachers, *c.* 9,375 students.

BIBLIOGRAPHY

BERREBY, JEAN-JACQUES. Le Golfe Persique; mer de légende—réservoir de pétrole (Payot, Paris 1959).

CHISHOLM, A. H. T. The First Kuwait Oil Concession: A Record of the Negotiations 1911–1934 (Cass, London).

DANIELS, JOHN. Kuwait Journey (White Crescent Press, Luton, England, 1972).

DEPARTMENT OF SOCIAL AFFAIRS. Annual Report (Kuwait).

DICKSON, H. R. P. Kuwait and her Neighbours (Allen and Unwin, London, 1956).

EL MALLAKH, RAGAEI. Economic Development and Regional Co-operation: Kuwait (University of Chicago Press, 1968).

FREETH, Z. Kuwait was my Home (Allen and Unwin, London, 1956).

GOVERNMENT PRINTING PRESS. Education and Development in Kuwait (Kuwait).

Port of Kuwait Annual Report (Kuwait).

HAKIMA, A. A. The Rise and Development of Bahrein and Kuwait (Beirut, 1964).

HAY, Sir RUPERT. The Persian Gulf States (Middle East Institute, Washington, 1959).

INTERNATIONAL BANK FOR RECONSTRUCTION AND DEVELOPMENT. The Economic Development of Kuwait (Johns Hopkins Press, Baltimore, 1965).

KHOUJA, M. W., and SADLER, P. G. The Energy of Kuwait: Development and Role in International Finance (Macmillan, London, 1978).

KOCHWASSER, FRIEDRICH H. Kuwait. Geschichte, Wesen und Funktion eines modernen Arabischen Staates (Tübingen, Eldmann, 1961).

KUWAIT OIL CO. LTD. The Story of Kuwait (London).

MARLOWE, JOHN. The Persian Gulf in the 20th Century (Cresset Press, London, 1962).

MEZERIK, AVRAHAM G. The Kuwait-Iraq Dispute, 1961 (New York, 1961).

WILSON, Sir A. T. The Persian Gulf (Oxford University Press, 1928).

WINSTONE, H. V. F., and FREETH, ZAHRA. Kuwait: Prospect and Reality (Allen and Unwin, London, 1972).

Lebanon

PHYSICAL AND SOCIAL GEOGRAPHY

W. B. Fisher

The creation, after 1918, of the modern State of the Lebanon, first under French Mandatory rule and then as an independent territory, was designed to recognize the nationalist aspirations of a number of Christian groups that had lived for many centuries under Muslim rule along the coast of the eastern Mediterranean and in the hills immediately adjacent. At least as early as the sixteenth century A.D. there had been particularist Christian feeling that ultimately resulted in the grant of autonomy, though not independence, to Christians living in the territory of "Mount Lebanon", which geographically was the hill region immediately inland and extending some 20–30 miles north and south of Beirut. The territory of Mount Lebanon was later expanded, owing to French interest, into the much larger area of "Greater Lebanon" with frontiers running along the crest of the Anti-Lebanon mountains, and reaching the sea some miles north of Tripoli to form the boundary with Syria. In the south there is a frontier with Israel, running inland from the promontory of Ras an-Nakura to the head of the Jordan Valley. In drawing the frontiers so as to give a measure of geographical unity to the new State, which now occupies an area of 10,400 sq. kilometres, large non-Christian elements of Muslims and Druzes were included, so that at the present day the Christians of the Lebanon form only about half the total population.

PHYSICAL FEATURES

Structurally, the Lebanon consists of an enormous simple upfold of rocks that runs parallel to the coast. There is, first, a very narrow and broken flat coastal strip—hardly a true plain—then the land rises steeply to a series of imposing crests and ridges. The highest crest of all is Qurnet as-Sauda, just over 10,000 ft. high, lying south-east of Tripoli; Mount Sannin, north-east of Beirut, is over 9,000 ft. A few miles east of the summits there is a precipitous drop along a sharp line to a broad, troughlike valley, known as the Bekaa (Biqa), about 10 miles wide and some 70 to 80 miles long. The eastern side of the Bekaa is formed by the Anti-Lebanon mountains, which rise to 9,000 ft., and their southern continuation, the Hermon Range, of about the same height. The floor of the Bekaa Valley, though much below the level of the surrounding mountain ranges, lies in places at 3,000 ft. above sea-level, with a low divide in the region of Baalbek. Two rivers rise in the Bekaa—the Orontes, which flows northwards into Syria and the Gharb depression, ultimately reaching the Mediterranean through the Turkish territory of Antioch; and the River Litani (Leontes). This latter river flows southwards, and then, at a short distance from the Israeli frontier, makes a sudden bend westwards and plunges through the Lebanon mountains by a deep gorge.

There exists in the Lebanon an unusual feature of geological structure which is not present in either of the adjacent regions of Syria and Israel. This is the occurrence of a layer of non-porous rocks within the upfold forming the Lebanon mountains; and, because of this layer, water is forced to the surface in considerable quantities, producing large springs at the unusually high level of 4,000 to 5,000 ft. Some of the springs have a flow of several thousand cu. ft. per second and emerge as small rivers; hence the western flanks of the Lebanon mountains, unlike those nearby in Syria and Israel, are relatively well watered and cultivation is possible up to a height of 4,000 or 5,000 ft.

With its great contrasts of relief, and the configuration of the main ranges, which lie across the path of the prevailing westerly winds, there is a wide variety in climatic conditions. The coastal lowlands are moderately hot in summer, and warm in winter, with complete absence of frost. But only 5 or 10 miles away in the hills there is a heavy winter snowfall, and the higher hills are covered from December to May, giving the unusual vista for the Middle East of snow-clad peaks. From this the name Lebanon (*laban*—Aramaic for "white") is said to originate. The Bekaa has a moderately cold winter with some frost and snow, and a distinctly hot summer, as it is shut off from the tempering effect of the sea.

Rainfall is on the whole abundant, but it decreases rapidly towards the east, so that the Bekaa and Anti-Lebanon are definitely drier than the west. On the coast, between 30 and 40 inches fall annually, with up to 50 inches in the mountains, but only 15 inches in the Bekaa. As almost all this annual total falls between October and April (there are three months of complete aridity each summer) rain is extremely heavy while it lasts, and storms of surprising intensity can occur. Beirut, for example, has slightly more rain than Manchester, but on half the number of rainy days. Another remarkable feature is the extremely high humidity of the coastal region during summer, when no rain falls. The sultry heat drives as many as can afford it to spend the summer in the hills.

ECONOMIC LIFE

The occurrence of high mountains near the sea, and the relatively abundant supplies of spring water have had a marked influence on economic development within the Lebanon. Owing to the successive levels of terrain, an unusually wide range of crops can be grown, from bananas and pineapples on the hot, damp coastlands, olives, vines and figs on the lowest foothills, cereals, apricots and peaches on the middle slopes, to apples and potatoes on the highest levels. These latter are the aristocrats of the Lebanese markets, since they are rarest, and, with the growing market in the oilfield areas of Arabia and the Persian Gulf, they fetch the highest price. Export of fruit is therefore an important item. Then, too, abundant natural water has led to the growth of pinewoods and evergreen groves, which add greatly to the already considerable scenic beauty of the western hill country. There has hence grown up an important tourist trade, centred in the small hill villages, some of which have casinos, luxury hotels, and cinemas. Main activity is during the summer months, when wealthy Middle Easterners and other arrive; but there is a smaller winter sports season, when ski-ing is carried on.

In addition, the geographical situation of the Lebanon, as a "façade" to the inland territories of Syria, Jordan, and even northern Iraq and southern Turkey, enables the Lebanese ports to act as the commercial outlet for a very wide region. The importance of Beirut as a commercial centre is due in large part to the fact that the Lebanon is a free market. Over half of the volume of Lebanese trade is transit traffic, and the Lebanon normally handles most of the trade of Jordan. Her own exports are mostly agricultural products. Byblos claims to be the oldest port in the world; Tyre and Sidon were for long world-famous, and the latter is now reviving as the Mediterranean terminal of the Tapline (Trans-Arabian Pipe Line) from Saudi Arabia. Another ancient centre, Tripoli, is also a terminal of the pipeline from Iraq (now closed). Beirut is now, however, the leading town of the country, and contains one-quarter of the total population. Though local resources are not in general very great (there are no minerals or important raw materials in the Lebanon) the city in normal times lives by commercial activity on a surprising scale, developed by the ingenuity and opportunism of its merchant class. The opening in 1951 of a commercial airport designed for jet airliners, before any such aircraft were actually in use in the world, is typical of the forward-looking attitude of many Lebanese.

Beirut has of recent years come to serve as a financial and holiday centre for the less attractive but oil-rich parts of the Middle East. Transfer of financial credit from the Middle East to Zürich, Paris, London, New York and Tokyo; a trade in gold and diamonds; and some connexion with the narcotic trade of the Middle East—all these give the city a very special function. In addition, the town provides discreet distraction for all types of visitor. Whether the traditional economic basis of the country—extreme individualism and "laisser-faire" for entrepreneurs—can revive is uncertain, but strenuous efforts began in 1977 to bring about reconstruction and re-development, assisted by loans from outside.

RACE AND LANGUAGE

It is difficult to summarize the racial affinities of the Lebanese people. The western lowlands have an extremely mixed population possibly describable only as "Levantine". Basically Mediterranean, there are many other elements, including remarkably fair individuals—Arabs with blonde hair and grey eyes, who are possibly descendants of the Crusaders. The remaining parts of the country show a more decided Armenoid tendency, with darker colouring, broader head-form, and more pronounced facial features. In addition, small refugee groups, who came to the more inaccessible mountain zones in order to escape persecution, often have a different racial ancestry, so that parts of the Lebanon form a mosaic of varying racial and cultural elements. Almost all Middle Eastern countries are represented racially within the Lebanon.

Arabic is current over the whole country, but owing to the high level of education (probably the highest in any Middle Eastern country) and to the considerable volume of temporary emigration, English, French and even Spanish are widely understood. French is probably still the leading European language (though English is tending to replace it) and some of the higher schools and one university teach basically in this language. In addition, Aramaic is used by some religious sects, but only for ritual—there are no Aramaic speaking villages as in Syria.

HISTORY

ANCIENT AND MEDIEVAL HISTORY

In the Ancient World the Lebanon was important for its pine, fir, and cedarwood, which neighbouring powers, poorly supplied with timber resources, coveted so much that during the long period of Egyptian, Assyrian, Persian, and Seleucid rule, the exploitation of the forests of the Lebanon was normally a royal privilege. The area was also mined for its iron and copper in the time of the Ptolemies and the Romans. Gradually the Lebanon came to have a distinct history of its own, for the mountainous character of the region prevented any complete subjugation to outside authority. It is probable that the Arab conquest of Syria did not include the "Mountain", to which fled all those who, for one reason or another, were opposed to the Arab domination. The Caliph Mu'awiya (661–80) made some effort to assert a greater control, but the resistance of the native Aramaean Christians was reinforced by the arrival of the Mardaites from the fastnesses of the Taurus and the Amanus. These Christian nomads, led by Byzantine officers, made determined advances into the Lebanon, late in the seventh century, and seem to have united with the Maronite Christians who were later to become a Uniate Church of the Roman communion and to have a predominant role in the history of the Lebanon. The Caliph Abd al-Malik (685–705) paid tribute to Byzantium in return for a withdrawal of most of the Mardaite forces; but it is clear that the "Mountain" had begun to assume its historic function of providing a sure refuge for racial and religious minorities.

The Lebanon maintained its Christian character until the ninth century when, amongst other elements, the Arab tribe of Tanukh established a principality in the region of al-Gharb, near Beirut, and acted as a counterpoise to the Maronites of the North Lebanon, and as a bulwark against Byzantine threats from the sea. Gradually, Islam and, more slowly still, the Arabic language penetrated the "Mountain" where, however, Syriac lingered on in the Maronite districts until the seventeenth century (it is still spoken in three villages of the Anti-Lebanon). In the ninth and tenth centuries Muslim sects began to take root in the "Mountain" as, for example, the Shi'i, known in the Lebanon under the name of Mitwali and, in the eleventh century, the Druze faith, which won a firm hold in the South Lebanon.

The Crusaders established in this area the County of Tripolis and the lordships of Gibelet and Batron which enjoyed considerable support from the Christian population of the North Lebanon and were protected by a network of fortresses, the most famous of which is Hisn al-Akrad (Crac des Chevaliers). In the Mamluk period the rulers of the Lebanon continued to practise the art of political manoeuvring, thus maintaining for themselves a considerable degree of autonomy. The Tanukhid Amirs, after a long period in which they had played off the Crusaders against the Muslim amirates, had eventually taken the Mamluk side. In the North Lebanon the Maronites, under their bishop, maintained contact with the Italian Republics and also with the Roman Curia. Less fortunate were the Druzes and the Mitwali who, in the last years of the thirteenth century, took advantage of the Mamluk preoccupation with the Mongol threat from Persia and began a protracted revolt which led to widespread devastation in the Central Lebanon.

THE OTTOMAN PERIOD

In the sixteenth century the Turcoman family of Assaf and, after them, the Banu Saifa rose to prominence in the area from Beirut to the north of Tripoli; while in the south the Druze house of Ma'an supplanted the Tanukhid amirs.

After the conquest of 1516–17, the Ottoman Sultan Selim I had confirmed the amirs of the Lebanon in their privileges and had imposed only a small tribute; yet not infrequently there was open conflict with the Ottomans, as in 1584–5 when, after an attack on a convoy bearing the tribute from Egypt to Constantinople, the Sultan Murad III sent a punitive expedition to ravage the lands of the Banu Saifa and of the Druzes.

The power of the House of Ma'an now reached its zenith in the person of Fakhr ad-din II (1586–1635), who by every possible means—bribery, intrigue, foreign alliance, and open force—set out to establish an independent power over the whole of the Lebanon and parts of Palestine to the south. To this end he entered into close relations with the Grand Duke of Tuscany, negotiating in 1608 a commercial agreement which contained a secret military clause directed against the Sultan. In 1613 a naval and military expedition sent from the Porte compelled Fakhr ad-din to seek refuge with his Tuscan ally; but, returning in 1618, he rapidly restored his power and within a few years was virtual ruler from Aleppo to the borders of Egypt. The Sultan, heavily engaged in repressing revolt in Anatolia, and in waging a long struggle with Persia, could do no more than recognise the *fait accompli*. Fakhr ad-din now embarked on an ambitious programme of development for the Lebanon. He sought to equip a standing army with arms imported from Tuscany. Italian engineers and agricultural experts were employed to promote a better cultivation of the land and to increase the production of silk and olives. The Christian peasantry were encouraged to move from the North to the South Lebanon. Beirut and Sidon flourished as a result of the favour he showed to commerce; and religious missions from Europe—Capuchins, Jesuits, Carmelites—were allowed to settle throughout Syria, a development of great importance for France which strove to assert a "protectorate" over all the Catholic and other Christian elements in the Ottoman Empire. However, the ambitions of Fakhr ad-din were doomed to failure when by 1632 the Sultan Murad IV assumed effective control at Constantinople. The Pasha of Damascus, supported by a naval squadron, began a campaign to end the independent power of the Lebanon, and in 1635 Fakhr ad-din was executed at Constantinople.

In 1697, the Ma'an family became extinct, and was succeeded by the House of Shihab, which maintained its predominance until 1840. In the course of the eighteenth century, the Shihab Amirs gradually consolidated their position against the other factions of the "Mountain" and for a while recovered control of Beirut. While normally they took care to remain on good terms with the Turkish Pashas of Tripoli, Sidon and Damascus, the Pashas, for their part, strove to exercise an indirect control by fomenting the family rivalries and religious differences which always marked the course of Lebanese politics. With the advent of Bashir II (1788–1840) the House of Shihab attained the height of its influence. Not until the death of Ahmed Jazzar, Pasha of Acre (1804), was he free to develop his power, which he maintained by the traditional methods of playing off one Pasha against the other, and by bribing the officials of the Porte whenever it seemed expedient. In 1810 he helped the Ottomans to repel an invasion by the Wahhabi power of Arabia; but in 1831 he sided openly with Muhammad Ali of Egypt, when that ruler invaded Syria. Holding the Lebanon as the vassal of Egypt, he was compelled, however, to apply to the "Mountain" the unpopular policy imposed by Ibrahim Pasha, the son of Muhammad Ali, with the result that a revolt broke out, which, after the Egyptian withdrawal of 1840, led to his exile. The age of the Lebanese Amirs was now at an end, for the Ottomans assumed control of the "Mountain", appointing two Kaimakams to rule there, one Druze and the other Maronite, under the supervision of the Pashas of Sidon and Beirut.

The period of direct Ottoman rule saw the rapid growth, between the Druzes and the Maronites, of a mistrust already visible during the time of the Egyptian dominance, and now fostered by the Ottomans as the only means of maintaining their influence over the Lebanon. As a result of social and economic discontent, due to the slow disintegration of the old feudal system which had existed in the Lebanon since the Middle Ages, the Maronite peasantry revolted in 1858 and destroyed the feudal privileges of the Maronite aristocracy, thus clearing the way for the creation of a system of independent smallholdings. The Druze aristocracy, fearing the consequences of a similar discontent among their own Maronite peasantry, made a series of attacks on the Maronites of the North Lebanon, who, owing to their own dissensions, could offer no effective resistance. The dubious attitude of the Turkish Pashas, in the face of these massacres of 1860, led to French intervention, and in 1864 to the formation of an organic statute for the Lebanon, which was now to become an autonomous province under a non-Lebanese Ottoman Christian governor, appointed by the Sultan and approved by the Great Powers. He was to be aided by an elected administrative council and a locally recruited police force. The statute also abolished legal feudalism in the area, thus consolidating the position won by the Maronite peasantry in 1858. The period from 1864 to 1914 was one of increasing prosperity, especially among the Christian elements, who also played an important role in the revival of Arab literature and Arab national feeling during the last years of the nineteenth century.

THE FRENCH MANDATE

The privileged position of the Lebanon ended when the Turks entered the war of 1914–18; and by 1918 the coastal areas of the Lebanon were occupied by British and French forces. In September 1920 the French created the State of the Greater Lebanon which included not only the former autonomous province but also Tripoli, Sidon, Tyre and Beirut, some of which had in earlier times been under the control of the amirs of the Lebanon. The period from 1920–36 was for the Lebanon one of peaceful progress. A constitution was devised in 1926, which proved unworkable and was suspended in 1932, from which time the President of the Republic carried on the administration. He was, by convention, a Christian, while the Prime Minister was a Muslim, and both worked towards the achievement of a careful balance between the various religious communities of the new State. The Lebanon was not unaffected by the growth of the nationalist movement in Syria, some sections of which demanded the reduction of the Lebanon to its pre-war limits and even the abolition of its existence as a separate State. These demands found some support amongst the Sunni Muslims of the areas added to the Lebanon proper in 1920, with the result that the Syrian revolt of 1925–26 spread to parts of the southern Lebanon. The Maronite Christians, on the whole, supported the idea of a separate Lebanon, but were not united in their attitude towards France on the one hand, and the Arab States on the other. The Franco-Lebanese Treaty of 1936 differed little from that which France negotiated at the same time with Syria, the chief difference being that the military convention gave France wider military powers in the Lebanon than in Syria. A reformed constitution was promulgated in 1937; but the French refusal to ratify the treaty in 1938, and the advent of war prolonged a situation which, if outwardly calm, concealed a considerable discontent beneath the surface. In November 1941 the Free French Commander, General Catroux, formally proclaimed the Lebanon a sovereign independent State. In September

1943 a new Parliament which had a strong nationalist majority soon came into conflict with the French authorities over the transfer of the administrative services. When, in November 1943, the Lebanese Government insisted on passing legislation which removed from the constitution all provisions considered to be inconsistent with the independence of the Lebanon the French Delegate-General arrested the President and suspended the constitution. The other Arab States, together with Great Britain and America, supported the Lebanese demands and in 1944 France began to transfer to Lebanese control all important public services, save for the *Troupes Spéciales*, i.e. local levies under French command, whose transfer the French authorities at first made conditional on the signing of a Franco-Lebanese Treaty. But in 1945 the *Troupes Spéciales* were handed over to the Lebanon without such conditions, and an agreement between France and the Lebanese Government in 1946 provided for the withdrawal of French troops.

MODERN HISTORY

Since 1946 the Lebanon has continued to view with great reserve all projects for a Greater Syria, or for the union of Syria and Iraq. Like the other Arab States, the Lebanon was at war with the new State of Israel from May 1948; but negotiated an armistice in March 1949. Just as in Syria the ill-success of the Arab arms had led eventually to the *coup d'état* of March 1949, so in the Lebanon the widespread disillusionment of Arab nationalist hopes prepared the ground for a conspiracy against the Government. This conspiracy was easily suppressed in June 1949 and its leader, Antun Sa'ade, was executed.

In internal affairs, the Lebanese Government had to face considerable economic and financial difficulties soon after the end of the 1939-45 war. When, in January 1948, France devalued the franc (to which both the Lebanese and the Syrian currencies were linked) the Lebanon, economically weaker than Syria, felt obliged to sign a new agreement with France (February 1948). Syria refused to do so and began a long and complicated dispute with the Lebanon over the precise nature of the economic and financial arrangements which were to exist between the two States. In March 1950 the Lebanese Government refused a Syrian demand for full economic and financial union between Syria and the Lebanon. The severance of economic relations which now ensued did not end until the signing, in February 1952, of an agreement which arranged for the division of royalties due from oil companies, and for the status, for customs purposes, of agricultural and industrial products passing between the two states.

In September 1952 the Lebanon had to face a severe crisis in her internal affairs. Political and economic unrest brought about the fall of the Lebanese Government and the resignation of President al-Khuri, who had held office since 1943. Charges of corruption were made against the President. During his long tenure of power he had indeed used all the arts of political influence and manoeuvre in order to impose a real degree of unity on a state where the divergent interests of Maronites, Sunni and Shi'i Muslims, Druzes, and other religious communities underlined the need for firm and coherent rule.

To an even greater degree, however, the crisis was due to causes of an economic order. The Lebanon had attained its independence in the period of war-time prosperity. The end of the war meant a progressive diminution of foreign expenditure in the Lebanon, e.g., by the French and British forces stationed there, and the gradual disappearance of war shortages which had favoured Lebanese trade. The devaluation of the French franc, the unsuccessful war with Israel, and above all the economic rupture with Syria gave rise to further difficulties. The break with Syria hit the Lebanon hard, for Syria was the chief provider of agricultural goods to the Lebanon and the chief customer for Lebanese industrial products. The effect of these developments was the more serious in that the Lebanon has a permanent adverse balance of trade, her annual deficit being largely covered by the revenues accruing to her from a wide variety of financial, commercial and transit services and by royalties paid to her by the oil companies. By 1952 there was much discontent arising from the high cost of living and from considerable unemployment. It was in fact a loose coalition of all the elements of opposition, both political and economic, which brought about the fall of the al-Khuri regime.

CONSTITUTIONAL REFORM

As a result of the crisis Camille Chamoun became the new President of the Republic. The new administration, with the Amir Khalid Chehab as Prime Minister, bound itself to introduce reforms, including changes in the electoral laws, the grant of the vote to women, revision of the Press laws and the reorganization of justice. The elections held in July 1953 led to the formation of a Chamber of Deputies, 44 in number and divided as follows: 13 Maronites, 9 Sunni Muslims, 8 Shi'i Muslims, 5 Orthodox Christians, 3 Greek Catholics, 3 Druzes, 2 Orthodox Armenians and one member for other minorities.

The elections held in the Lebanon during the summer of 1953 were carried out under the provisions of the electoral law of November 1952. Since the foundation of the republic, all seats in the Chamber of Deputies had been distributed among the various religious communities in proportion to their numerical strength. Parliament was thus an institution reflecting in itself the religious and social structure of the state and capable of harmonious function, provided that the electoral system which maintained a delicate balance between the communities suffered no violent and prejudicial change. At the same time, it contained a strong "feudal" element—the tribal and religious leaders who, with their trusted retainers, formed powerful groups within the Parliament and were often criticised as being "anti-national" in their aims and methods. To end or at least weaken this "feudalization" of Lebanese political life, without, however, impairing the vital equilibrium between the Muslim and Christian communities, had long been the purpose of those who advocated a reasonable and well-considered policy of reform. The law of 1952 created 33 electoral districts (during the previous life of the republic the number had been, as a rule, five) and allotted to eleven of them two seats, and to the remainder one seat each. Of the sum-total of 44 seats the Maronites were now to receive 13, the Sunni Muslims 9, the Shi'i Muslims 8, the Greek Orthodox Christians 5, the Druzes 3, the Greek Catholics 3, the Armenian Catholics 2 and the other confessions (Protestant, Jewish, Nestorian, etc.) 1 seat.

FOREIGN RELATIONS 1953-56

In the period 1953–56 financial and economic relations with Syria remained on a provisional basis much the same as that which had prevailed in the years 1950–53, earlier short-term arrangements being renewed from time to time, as need arose. Discussions with Syria in November 1953 over problems of currency, loan policy, banks and exchange difficulties made no effective progress. The Lebanese Government was more successful, however, in its efforts to promote internal development. It was announced in August 1955 that the International Bank had granted to the Lebanon a loan of 27 million dollars for the Litani river scheme which, when completed, was expected to more than double the electric power available within the republic and also to irrigate a large acreage in the coastal region. The Lebanon signed a number of commercial treaties at this time, which bore witness to the growing penetration of the Eastern bloc into Arab lands.

At the Asian-African conference held at Bandung in April 1955 the Lebanese delegates expressed themselves in terms unfavourable to Communism. Since that time the Beirut government has not allowed its relations with Russia and her allies to pass beyond the limits of normal commercial intercourse. In regard to the Baghdad Pact, concluded between Iraq and the Turkish Republic in February 1955, the Lebanon adopted a neutral attitude. When, in March 1955, Egypt, supported by Saudi Arabia and (although with some hesitation) by Syria, attempted to form an alliance of Arab states from which Iraq was to be excluded, the Lebanese Government declined to enter into the proposed scheme, but also assured Cairo that it did not intend to join the Baghdad Pact. Its efforts were in fact directed, and not unsuccessfully, towards allaying, at least for the immediate future, the sharp tension then existing between Egypt and Iraq.

THE EISENHOWER DOCTRINE

A state of emergency was declared in the Lebanon during the Sinai-Suez crisis at the end of October 1956. The Chamber of Deputies announced its support of Egypt, but the Lebanon did not break off diplomatic relations with Great Britain and France. In November there were disturbances, however, at Tripoli and Beirut against the attitude of the Government. Reports issued at this time intimated that the Egyptian military attaché at Beirut had been implicated in the recent disorders. The "Eisenhower Doctrine", a new programme, made known in January 1957, of financial, economic and military aid by the United States to those countries of the Middle East which were prepared to accept it, evoked a favourable response in Lebanese official circles. The Foreign Minister of the Lebanon declared that the government was willing to collaborate closely with the U.S.A. in the implementation of the programme. During the visit to Beirut in March of Mr. Richards, special adviser to President Eisenhower on Middle Eastern affairs, it was announced that the Lebanon would co-operate with the United States in the task of opposing the growth of Communist influence in the area and would receive, under the new programme, assistance to the amount of some 20 million dollars. The United States was also to help in the strengthening of the Lebanese armed forces. Some of the political groups in the Lebanon protested against this pro-Western alignment, asserting that it could not fail to isolate the Lebanon from the other Arab states and thus impair Arab solidarity. None the less, in April, the government obtained from the Chamber of Deputies a vote of confidence in its policies.

The problem of electoral reform had been under consideration in the Lebanon in the course of 1956. The main proposal now to be given effect was that the number of seats in the Chamber of Deputies should be raised from 44 to 66. As election time drew near in the summer of 1957, riots occurred in Beirut, the government being compelled to call out troops for the maintenance of order. According to reports current at this time more than one hundred Communists were arrested for their share in the disturbances. The tense electoral campaign of June 1957 was fought out between two blocs, the one supporting the government, the other opposing it in the form of a United National Front. When the election results were made known, it became clear that the government had won a marked triumph. A first provisional estimate suggested that it might count on the adherence of some three-quarters of the deputies in the new Chamber. Of the total of 66 seats the Maronites now received 20, the Sunni Muslims 14, the Shi'i Muslims 12, the Greek Orthodox Christians 7, the Druzes 4, the Greek Catholics 4, the Orthodox Armenians 3, the Armenian Catholics 1 and the other religious minorities (Protestants, Jews, etc.) also 1 seat.

It was announced in July 1957 that the Lebanon would receive from the United States, under the Eisenhower Doctrine, economic and military aid to the value of approximately 15 million dollars in the course of the fiscal year 1958. Military equipment granted under the Doctrine had in fact begun to reach Beirut in June 1957. The Lebanese Government reiterated in August 1957 its firm desire to continue co-operation with the United States.

There had been sharp disturbances in the Lebanon at the time of the elections held in June 1957. It became clear that unrest, especially amongst those elements of the population which opposed the pro-Western policies of the Lebanese Government and favoured an alignment with Egypt and Syria, was in no wise dead, when further incidents (bomb outrages, assassinations) occurred in November 1957. The government, in its desire to halt these subversive activities, now imposed a close control over all Palestine refugees in the Lebanon. Indeed, after renewed outbreaks of violence in December, the northern area of the Lebanon was declared to be a military sector. It was also announced in January 1958 that a national guard would be formed for the protection of important installations.

The Lebanese Government stated in March 1958 that it would not join the United Arab Republic (Egypt and Syria), the Arab Federation (Iraq and Jordan) or indeed any association which might limit its own independence and sovereignty. Large sections of the Muslim population, both in the north (at Tripoli) and in the south (at Tyre and Sidon), were inclined to be pro-Arab rather than pro-Lebanese in sentiment—a mood greatly stimulated by the emergence of the new United Arab Republic and by the propaganda emitted from Cairo and Damascus for the return to Syria of those predominantly Muslim areas which had been joined to the old Lebanon in the time of the French Mandate. There was conflict, too, between those who, although reluctant to see the Lebanon lose its separate political existence, were none the less strongly opposed to the pro-Western attitude of the Lebanese Government and those who, fearing the possible absorption of the Lebanon into the framework of a larger Arab state, felt themselves bound to support fully the policies of the Beirut regime. The danger was real that these complex tensions might explode in the form of a "confessional" conflict between Muslims and Christians, in which, if not the continued independence, then at least the entire political orientation of the Lebanon would be at stake.

THE CRISIS OF 1958

A reorganization of the government, carried out in March 1958 and designed to remove certain members who were critical of the pro-Western policies of the Lebanon and favoured closer co-operation with the United Arab Republic, brought no relief to the grave situation then developing. Serious disturbances, originating in Tripoli and the northern areas adjacent to the Syrian border, broke out in the second week of May and spread rapidly to Beirut and also to Tyre and Sidon in the southern Lebanon. The Druze population in the south-east was involved, too, in the disorders, being sharply divided into pro- and anti-government factions. Hostile demonstrations led to the destruction of the United States Information Service centres at Tripoli and Beirut. At the request of the Lebanese Government, the United States agreed to dispatch in all haste supplies of arms and police equipment and decided at the same time to reinforce the American 6th Fleet stationed in the Mediterranean. The U.S.S.R. now accused the United States of interference in Lebanese affairs and declared that Western intervention might have grave consequences. The Lebanese Government itself charged the United Arab Republic with interference in its internal affairs and appealed for redress to the Arab League which, meeting at Benghazi in June, failed to agree on a course of action. The problem was now brought before the United Nations which resolved to send an Observer Corps to the Lebanon. The Secretary General of U.N.O., Dr. Hammarskjöld, also visited the Middle East, conferring both with leaders in the Lebanon and with President Nasser at Cairo.

The Lebanese Government was now, in fact, confronted with a widespread insurrection, in which the Muslim elements in the population were ranged against the Christian elements. The forces opposed to the existing regime controlled parts of Beirut, Tripoli and Sidon, as well as large areas in the north and the south of the Lebanon. Attempts to negotiate a settlement led to no favourable result. The Prime Minister, Sami al-Sulh, gave an assurance that President Chamoun did not intend to ask for a constitutional amendment which would enable him to seek re-election to his office in September 1958, the date when his present tenure of it was due to end. To this assurance the leaders of the insurrection replied with a firm demand for the immediate resignation of the President, who made it clear, however, that he would not relinquish his office until September.

On July 14th—the date of the *coup d'état* which led to a change of regime in Iraq—President Chamoun requested the United States to send American troops into the Lebanon with a view to the maintenance of security and the preservation of Lebanese independence. By July 20th, some 10,000 men of the United States forces were stationed in and around Beirut. Meanwhile, Mr. Robert Murphy of the American State Department had come to the Lebanon with the aim of discussing the situation with leaders of both sides in the conflict. The United States also made it known that action on the part of forces under the control of the United Arab Republic against American troops in the Lebanon might lead to most serious consequences. At this juncture, the U.S.S.R. and the Chinese People's Republic made strong protests against the American intervention and asked for the prompt withdrawal of the United States forces landed in the Lebanon. In August 1958, the General Assembly of the United Nations met to discuss the problem. On August 18th, the United States gave a written undertaking to withdraw its troops, either at the request of the Lebanese Government, or in the event that the United Nations took appropriate measures to ensure the integrity and peace of the country. The General Assembly thereupon adopted a resolution, framed by its Arab members, which provided for the evacuation of American troops under the auspices of the United Nations and of the Arab League.

PRESIDENT CHEHAB, 1958-64

Meanwhile, the Lebanese Chamber of Deputies had, on July 31st, elected as the new President of State General Fuad Chehab, the Commander-in-Chief of the Lebanese Army—a choice supported by members from both sides involved in the internal conflict. He assumed office on September 23rd, in succession to President Chamoun and at once invited Rashid Karami, the leader of the insurgents at Tripoli, to become Prime Minister. An agreement was made on September 27th to the effect that the United States forces were to leave the Lebanon by the end of October.

In October 1959 the Lebanese Cabinet was increased from four to eight members, so that greater representation might be given to the various political groups. The Chamber of Deputies approved in April 1960 an Electoral Reform Bill, which imposed for the first time the principle of the secret ballot in Lebanese elections and also enlarged the Chamber itself from 66 to 99 deputies—a total figure that maintained the existing ratio (laid down in 1943) of six Christian to every five Muslim (including Druze) deputies in the Chamber. The Chamber was dissolved by the President of the Lebanon on May 5th, 1960, the government of Mr. Rashid Karami resigning nine days later. A general election was then held in four separate stages on June 12th, 19th and 26th and July 3rd, 1960.

The election took place in an atmosphere of complete calm, strict security measures being enforced throughout the various stages of the electoral process. In the new Chamber of Deputies there were 30 Maronite Christians, 20 Sunni Muslims, 19 Shi'i Muslims, 11 Greek Orthodox Christians, 6 Greek Catholics, 6 Druzes, 4 Armenian Orthodox Christians, 1 Armenian Catholic, 1 Protestant and 1 member representing other elements. A large number of the "rebel" personalities prominent in the events of 1958 and hitherto not seated in the Chamber were now returned as members. Of the Deputies who had formed the previous Chamber 31 (out of 66) retained their seats. Some of the traditional "feudal" notabilities also recovered their places in the Chamber.

President Chehab announced on July 20th, 1960, that he intended to resign his office. He was persuaded, however, to reverse his decision. A new government, under the leadership of Mr. Saeb Salam, took the oath of office on August 2nd, 1960. The Cabinet, which included several personalities active on one side or the other in the troubles of 1958, was prompt to reaffirm the traditional policies of non-expropriation, of minimal government intervention in private enterprise, of encouragement for private investment both foreign and domestic, and of currency convertibility. Economic trends during 1960 revealed that the Lebanon had recovered almost completely from the effect of the disturbances in 1958.

CABINET REFORM

It had come to be felt, since August 1960, that the Lebanese Cabinet, 18 members strong, was too large for the maintenance of an efficient administration. Internal dissension, having weakened the Cabinet for some time past, brought about a crisis leading to the resignation of six ministers on May 9–10th, 1961. On May 22nd, the Prime Minister established a new Cabinet consisting of eight ministers only. Mr. Salam, as the result of a dispute with some members of his government, notable amongst them being Mr. Jumblatt, the Druze leader, who was Minister of Works and Planning, resigned his office on October 24th, 1961. Mr. Rashid Karami, a former Prime Minister, formed a new government on October 31st, 1961.

Military elements, acting in conjunction with civilians described as supporters of the extremist National Social Party, made an unsuccessful attempt, on December 31st, 1961, to overthrow the Lebanese government. The National Social Party was in fact the old Parti Populaire Syrien founded in the 1930s by Antoine Saadé with the aim of uniting several Arab States into a Greater Syria. Its current leader, Dr. Abdallah Saadé, was now arrested and the party itself dissolved by the Lebanese government on January 1st, 1962. The Lebanese government took firm action against all the elements suspected of implication in the revolt, and crushed it within a few days.

EXTERNAL AGREEMENTS

In February 1962 the Lebanese Government entered into an agreement with the Tunisian Government envisaging co-operation between the two states in the fields of educational, cultural and technical assistance. During the remainder of 1962 the Lebanon entered into various agreements with the Egyptian half of the United Arab Republic, Niger, Cameroon, Guinea and Senegal. These agreements were mainly on technical and cultural co-operation.

The dispute, now six years old, over payments connected with the pipelines passing oil through the Lebanon to the Mediterranean coast was at last brought to an end. At Beirut in August 1962 a settlement was made between the Lebanese Government and the Trans-Arabian Pipeline Company (Tapline), an American organization. In return for facilities relating to the transit of oil, to the loading of the oil and to the security of the pipelines the Lebanon was to receive about $4,500,000 (as against $1,250,000 under earlier agreements). The new and higher rate of payment included a sum of $500,000 in lieu of supplies of oil at reduced prices which Tapline had undertaken to make available to the national oil refineries in Syria and Jordan—the Lebanon itself does not possess such oil refineries. Tapline also promised to pay the sum of $12,500,000 in settlement of all past claims made by the Lebanese Government.

During the course of 1963 the government negotiated new economic and commercial agreements with Poland (April), the German Federal Republic (May), Sweden (October), and the U.S.S.R. (November). Syria and Lebanon agreed in September to ease restrictions in travel, employment, trade and finance between their respective territories and also reached an understanding in regard to their protracted dispute over the sharing of oil-transit dues. A brief period of sharp tension ensued, however, during the second half of October, as the result of a frontier clash between Syrian and Lebanese troops, which led to the death of several Lebanese soldiers. Syrian and Lebanese delegations met in January, 1964, to discuss questions relating to their common frontier and in particular the delimitation of certain areas hitherto not clearly demarcated.

On February 19th, 1964, the Cabinet led by Rashid Karami (which had held office for the last two years) resigned, after President Chehab had signed a decree dissolving the Chamber of Deputies (elected in 1960) and ordering elections to be held on four successive Sundays from April 5th, 1964 to May 3rd, 1964. A caretaker cabinet was appointed to supervise the elections for the new Chamber of Deputies.

PRESIDENT HÉLOU

General Chehab, whose six-year term of office as President of the Republic was due to end in September 1964, rejected all appeals that he should submit himself as a candidate for a second time. Even when the Chamber of Deputies passed a motion in favour of an amendment to the Constitution which would enable him to stand for a further term of office, General Chehab persisted (June 3rd, 1964) in his refusal. On August 18th, 1964, M. Charles Hélou, Minister of Education in the caretaker administration, succeeded General Chehab as President. M. Hélou pledged himself to follow the policies and reforms introduced under General Chehab.

On September 25th, 1964, Hussein Oweini, the Head of the caretaker Cabinet in office since February of that year, formed an administration at the request of President Hélou. The new administration aroused dissatisfaction, however, in the Chamber of Deputies, since, deriving from the Cabinet appointed originally to act as a caretaker during the period of the 1964 elections, it was in fact composed wholly of non-members of the Chamber. Having resigned on November 13th, 1964, Oweini now, on November 18th, 1964, gathered together a new Cabinet which, save for himself and the Foreign Minister, consisted of members drawn from the Chamber of Deputies and reflected in itself all the main trends of opinion within the Chamber.

FOREIGN RELATIONS

On July 20th, 1965, the Prime Minister, Mr. Hussein Oweini, resigned. There had been much debate in the Chamber of Deputies about a proposed agreement to guarantee private American investment in the Lebanon against expropriation, war or revolution—an agreement construed in some political circles as giving to the United States a possible excuse for intervention, at need in Lebanese affairs. On July 26th, Rashid Karami became the new Prime Minister, with nine Cabinet Ministers to assist him, all chosen from outside the Chamber of Deputies.

There was friction during the first months of 1965 between Federal Germany and the Arab States because of the decision by Bonn to enter into formal diplomatic relations with Israel. Anti-German demonstrations occurred at Tripoli and Beirut and on May 13th, 1965 the Lebanon broke off diplomatic relations with Federal Germany. In May 1965 Lebanon signed an agreement on trade and technical co-operation with the European Economic Community (EEC). There was some friction between Israel and the Lebanon over border incidents during the summer and autumn of 1965. Members of the Palestinian guerrilla organization, al-Fatah, raided into Israel, provoking Israeli reprisals against the Lebanese village of Noule.

FINANCIAL CRISIS

Rashid Karami modified his cabinet in December 1965 and January 1966, these changes arising from difficulties which hindered the full implementation of an administrative and judicial reform programme, one of the main advocates of which was President Hélou. Between December 1965 and March 1966 an estimated 150 officials including 100 civil servants were compelled to withdraw from public life. This sustained attempt to curb corruption and the abuse of office in government circles and to ensure efficient and honest administration inevitably caused considerable tension. There was strong pressure in the Chamber of Deputies for a return to a cabinet chosen mainly from the Chamber itself. This and other difficulties obliged Karami to offer his resignation to President Hélou who appointed Dr. Abdallah al-Yafi as the new Premier.

Dr. al-Yafi assembled a ten-man Cabinet drawn entirely from the Chamber of Deputies with the exception of himself and M. Philippe Takla, the new Foreign Minister. The constitution of the cabinet represented a balance between the various religious interests and, from the point of view of politics, between the left-wing and right-wing elements in the Chamber of Deputies.

In October 1966 the Intra Bank of the Lebanon was compelled to close its doors because of a run of withdrawals amounting to more than £11 million in the preceding month. One result of that financial crisis was that the Government resolved to discourage the creation of new commercial banks, foreign or Lebanese, for a period of five years. Hitherto there had been an almost complete freedom to establish new banks in the Lebanon and there had been a large expansion of the banking system based on the flow into the Lebanon of vast oil revenues from Saudi Arabia and from the states of the Persian Gulf.

On December 2nd the Prime Minister of the Lebanon Dr. Abdullah al-Yafi, offered the resignation of his government to President Hélou. Mr. Rashid Karami formed a new administration on December 7th, 1966. It was composed of men drawn from outside Parliament, six of whom held ministerial posts for the first time.

In June 1967 the Lebanese Government aligned itself with the Arab states then engaged in war against Israel. On June 8th the Government asked the Ambassadors of Britain and the U.S.A. to leave the Lebanon. Pro-Egyptian demonstrations at Beirut in June caused some damage to British and American properties there. Some trouble was also reported from Tripoli, where a West German cultural centre was subjected to attack. However, the months following the war witnessed a gradual easing of the tensions arising out of the conflict, and in September 1967 the Lebanese Cabinet agreed to reinstate its ambassadors in Washington and London.

POLITICAL INSTABILITY

Rashid Karami's Cabinet resigned from office in February 1968. President Hélou then asked Dr. Abdallah al-Yafi to form an interim administration, whose main task was to be the preparation and conduct of the general election in March 1968. The two most successful parties elected in the Chamber of Deputies were the Maronite-dominated Triple Alliance, of a right-wing complexion, and the Democratic Block aligned further to the left. However, Dr. al-Yafi's interim administration remained in office until October, when it was forced to resign, owing to bitter rivalry between the two main political groups, the "Chamounists" and the "Chehabists" (both named after former Presidents), disputes over sectional representation in the Cabinet, and the Government's inability to command a majority in the Chamber of Deputies. After a week of confusion, during which the President, Charles Hélou, offered his own resignation, a new four-man government was announced on October 20th, still headed by Dr. al-Yafi.

THE GUERRILLAS AND ISRAEL

May 1968 had seen the first clash between Lebanese and Israeli forces on the border for over two years. But as the activities of the Palestinian guerrillas increased, so the Lebanon became more and more the scapegoat for Israel's grievances against the Palestinians. On December 26th an Israeli airliner was machine-gunned by Arab guerrillas at Athens airport, causing two casualties (one fatal). Two days later Israeli commandos raided Beirut airport and destroyed thirteen aircraft, all belonging to Lebanese lines, without loss of life. Israel said the raid should be seen as a reprisal for the Athens attack, a warning to the Arab world not to make any repetition of it, and a further warning to the Lebanon to police the activities of the fedayeen movement in the country more effectively. The financial cost to the Lebanon was relatively small as most were insured abroad. The major after-effects of the raid were, firstly, the widespread criticism it attracted even from countries normally favourable to Israel. The Lebanon was seen as a country which had taken little active part in the campaign against Israel, while the *fedayeen* within it were only enjoying the freedom available to them in Lebanon's open, tolerant society. The UN Security Council unanimously condemned Israel for the raid. The second effect was the fall of the Government on January 7th, 1969, its alleged lack of preparedness for Israeli aggression being the final blow to bring down a weak administration. After much political manoeuvring, a new ministry was formed on January 20th headed by Mr. Rashid Karami, Prime Minister for the seventh time.

This government was immediately confronted with the basic problems underlying the Lebanese situation. Foremost amongst these is the Christian-Muslim balance; in theory both religions are equally represented in the Lebanon, but no census has been held since 1939 mainly because the authorities fear that the balance has shifted to a 60 per cent Muslim predominance, which would seriously affect the political situation. The Christian community has a disproportionate share of the wealth and important positions, and is the mainstay of the modest armed forces; it is generally conservative by Arab standards and takes a moderate position on the Israel question. The less privileged Arab majority is more in favour of both domestic reform (Lebanon has, for example, only the beginnings of a welfare state) and of a more militant position towards Israel. Early in 1969 numbers of Syrian guerrillas entered the country and apparently spent as much time in action against the Lebanese army as against Israel. Unrest also appeared amongst the 260,000 Palestinian refugees in the Sidon camp; part of the frontier with Syria was eventually closed. Numerous strikes and demonstrations continued. The Karami government felt unable to maintain the necessary coalition from the two communities and their various factions and resigned on April 25th, but it continued to function as a caretaker administration as no stronger government could be formed.

In the late summer of 1969 a number of guerrilla groups were reported to have moved to new bases better sited for attacks on Israel, which continued to raid these bases in reprisal; the combination of these factors created some friction between the guerrillas and the Lebanese army. In October the army apparently attacked some of these camps in an attempt to restrict or direct their activities. This triggered off a crisis that continued through the second half of October and threatened to develop into a full-scale civil war. The caretaker government resigned, claiming that it had not authorized the army's actions, and the President and the armed forces administered the country directly. Radical elements and guerrillas took over Tripoli, the second largest city, for several days, and most of the Palestinian refugee camps became fully converted into military training and equipment centres. Militant support for the guerrillas was voiced throughout the Arab world, and there were threats of military intervention by Syria and Iraq. Despite the tension, no extensive fighting occurred and there were few deaths.

On November 2nd the Lebanese Commander-in-Chief and Yasser Arafat, the leader of al-Fatah, signed a ceasefire agreement in Cairo. This limited the guerrilla freedom of movement to certain areas; as further defined in January 1970, it also provided that camps had to be set up some distance from towns, that military training must cease in refugee camps, and that guerrillas must enter Israel before starting to shoot. The intention was not to prevent guerrilla attacks, but to stop innocent Lebanese getting hurt, or their property being damaged, by Israeli counter-attacks.

The calmer atmosphere that followed the ceasefire enabled Mr. Karami to form another cabinet towards the end of November. There was much concern about the weakness of the country's southern defences, and in January 1970 the new ministry felt strong enough to fire the Commander-in-Chief, appointing instead Brigadier Jean Njeim. In March there was a series of street battles in the Beirut area between the Palestinian guerrillas and militant right wing Falangist groups, but the Government and the army managed to avoid becoming involved. In May, Israel launched a major air and ground attack on guerrilla positions in southern Lebanon, a substantial area being occupied for nearly two days. Syria sent air assistance for the small Lebanese air force. The result of the raid was as usual disputed.

POLITICAL CRISES

Sulaiman Franjiya was elected President in August 1970, and a new cabinet was formed by Saeb Salam. Some measures of political liberalization, such as the relaxation of press, radio and television censorship and the removal of the ban on extremist parties (the Lebanese Communist Party, Parti Populaire Syrien, pro-Iraq Baath Party, etc.), did little to curb domestic unrest. Strikes and demonstrations against unemployment and inflation, student disorders and fighting between Phalangists and the Parti Populaire Syrien continued throughout 1971. The parliamentary elections of April 1972 produced a marked swing towards left-wing political groups.

The Palestinian guerrillas remained Lebanon's major problem. Their bases in the refugee camps became more important following the expulsion of the guerrillas from Jordan in July 1971, and guerrilla operations against Israel produced violent Israeli reprisals in which both Palestinians and Lebanese suffered. The villages of southern Lebanon bore the brunt of Israeli raids, and their inhabitants secured a greater measure of Lebanese army control over guerrilla activities in March 1972. Arab terrorist actions still produced Israeli reprisals against Lebanon, even when there was little connection between the terrorists and Israel's vulnerable northern neighbour. The killing of Israeli athletes at the Olympic Games in Munich in September 1972 led to Israeli ground and air attacks on guerrilla bases, in which the Lebanese army suffered a number of casualties. The Lebanese Government was unable to persuade the guerrillas to suspend their activities against Israel, and there were several clashes between the Lebanese army and the guerrillas in December.

In February 1973 Israeli commandos attacked guerrilla training bases in refugee camps about 100 miles north of the Lebanese frontier, and escaped virtually unopposed. A further Israeli raid, in which three guerrilla leaders were shot in their homes in the centre of Beirut, and an attempt to blow up oil storage tanks at the Zahrani terminal, attributed to Palestinian extremists, resulted in the fall of the Salam Government. Mr. Salam resigned, dissatisfied with the inability of the Lebanese armed forces to prevent an Israeli military action in the capital, and Dr. Amin Hafez formed a new government. Several members of the Salam cabinet remained in office, the new government including representatives of most of the major political and religious groups.

Tension between the Lebanese army and the guerrillas culminated in May 1973 in Lebanese ground and air attacks on the refugee camps. An invasion by guerrillas based in Syria was repulsed and a ceasefire was brought about by the mediation of other Arab states. The guerrillas apparently agreed to remove heavy weapons from the refugee camps, to stop their terrorist activities within Lebanon and to cease using the camps as bases for training guerrillas.

The Hafez Government lasted only seven weeks. The Prime Minister resigned on June 14th, unable to settle the Sunni Muslim claim for a greater share in the allocation of government posts, and it was not until July 8th that Takieddin Solh was able to form a new ministry. A moderate, Mr. Solh enjoyed the support of many Sunni factions, and his cabinet included representatives of all the main religious blocs. Outside Parliament, however, violent disorders continued, with industrial disputes and the claims of tobacco growers, for instance, resulting in demonstrations and clashes with police. The Phalange party maintained training camps for its own militia, and the danger of the formation of private armies became apparent.

The potential religious hostility within Lebanon, and the political implications of the division of government and administrative posts on a confessional basis were again demonstrated in February 1974. Civil service reforms, intended to overcome the sectarian nature of certain appointments, were opposed by Maronites who feared that they would lose posts traditionally reserved to their community. The National Liberal Party threatened to withdraw its three cabinet members, and the proposed reforms were also condemned by the Phalange and the Bloc National. The Shi'i Muslims of southern Lebanon also made demands for increased representation and more investment and development in the south. The Shi'i leader, Imam Moussa as-Sadr, implied that he would organize his followers and arm them as protection against Israeli raids, which he has since done.

Although Lebanon was not directly involved in the October 1973 Arab-Israeli war, southern regions had continued to serve as a guerrilla base and to suffer Israeli reprisals. Southern villages were shelled intermittently, and small-scale raids across the border and acts of terrorism became commonplace. In the first six months of 1974 there were three notable Israeli attacks on Lebanese targets, each following guerrilla outrages in Israel, despite Lebanese denials that the terrorists involved came from Lebanon.

In July there were clashes between Palestinians and Phalangists who continued to demand more government controls on guerrilla activities. Throughout 1974 and into 1975 Israeli shelling, air raids and incursions into Lebanon continued, together with guerrilla attacks against the Israelis. Consequently the situation on the border remained tense. In September 1974, unable to curb internal sectarian violence by its ineffective ban on the possession of firearms, Takieddin Solh's cabinet resigned. In October a new government was formed under Rashid Solh though violence continued, finally erupting in a bloody clash between troops and citizens of the port of Sidon. The cabinet split amid the granting of a Muslim demand to confer citizenship to long-time residents of the country. Letter bomb and dynamite explosions and further border fighting between the Israelis and guerrilla groups were followed by further fierce conflict between the Phalangists and Palestinians, in which over 150 died and 300 were wounded. Much damage was caused in Beirut and, after an agreement by Solh to normalize relations with the Palestinians and the fact that the security forces had not intervened in the fighting, the Phalangists appeared to be on the defensive.

CIVIL WAR

Intercommunal strife had never been far from the surface in Lebanon. (*See* under The Guerrillas and Israel, p. 520). An incident in April 1975, when Palestinians made an attack on some Phalangists, led to the Phalangists killing the passengers of a bus, who were mainly Palestinians. From this incident inter-communal fighting between Christians and Muslims quickly spread, and continued, with short interruptions, until October 1976. At this point the official policy of the PLO under Yasser Arafat was to stand aloof from the conflict and Arafat himself was in fact instrumental in securing some of the many ceasefires.

In May 1975, shortly after the fighting began, Rashid Solh resigned as Prime Minister, and was replaced by Rashid Karami, who continued as Prime Minister through an exceedingly turbulent period until December 1976. In September 1975 a National Dialogue Committee was formed, consisting of 20 members from all political and confessional groups, to try to restore "normal life"—a task in which they were unsuccessful. By October 1975 there was evident dissatisfaction with President Franjiya and his inability to bring the fighting to an end, and it also became increasingly evident that in spite of the official policy of the

PLO not to interfere in the internal affairs of the Lebanon, members of extremist Palestinian groups, particularly those of the "rejectionist front", were being drawn into the fighting on the side of the Muslims. It was also, at this point, the official policy of the Lebanese army not to intervene, although later, breakaway groups became involved in the fighting.

By the middle of January 1976 the PLO was becoming increasingly drawn into the conflict, and several Syrian-based units of the Palestine Liberation Army were in Lebanon fighting on the side of the Muslims. Under these increasingly ominous conditions the term of the Chamber of Deputies was extended by a year (later increased to two years) and the general elections scheduled for April 1976 were postponed for up to 26 months. In January 1978 the Chamber's term was further extended until June 1980.

At the end of January 1976 Lebanon enjoyed a brief respite from the civil war. A Syrian mediation mission, led by the Syrian Foreign Minister, Abdel Halim Khaddam, achieved a ceasefire on January 22nd which lasted some weeks, and life began to return to normal. President Franjiya put forward a plan for constitutional reform which was rejected by his opponents. By March, however, no agreement had been reached on political reforms, fighting had flared up again, and 70 deputies signed a petition asking President Franjiya to resign. Further weight was given to this request in April when a Parliamentary Session took place and 90 deputies voted unanimously to amend Article 73 of the Constitution to allow Presidential elections to be held up to 6 months before the expiry of the present incumbent's term of office. President Franjiya signed this amendment on April 23rd but, in spite of the election of his successor, refused to resign until the completion of his term of office in September 1976, when he was succeeded by Elias Sarkis, who had been Governor of the Central Bank.

INCREASED SYRIAN INTERVENTION

By May 1976 Syria was becoming increasingly involved in Lebanese affairs. By May 20th it was estimated that about 40,000 Syrian-controlled troops were in Lebanon. Yasser Arafat had ordered pro-Damascus Palestinian units to withdraw, and it now became clear that Arafat and the PLO had become entirely sympathetic to the Lebanese left wing. In early June Syria launched a full-scale invasion of Lebanon officially to end the civil war and restore peace, but unofficially, it became clear, to crush the Palestinians. The conflict threatened to grow to world proportions and an emergency meeting of the Arab foreign ministers met in Cairo under the sponsorship of the Arab League. It was agreed to send a joint Arab peace-keeping force to Lebanon and after considerable mediation by Major Abdul Salam Jalloud, the Libyan Prime Minister, and Mahmoud Riad, Secretary-General of the Arab League, it was agreed that the introduction of the Arab peace-keeping force should be accompanied by a phased, but not complete, withdrawal of Syrian troops. The Arab peace-keeping force was to include participants from Syria, Libya, Algeria, Sudan, Saudi Arabia and the Palestine Liberation Organization, under an Egyptian Commander-in-Chief, General Muhammad Hassan Ghoneim, but by the end of June 1976 the 1,000 man force was made up of 500 Syrian troops merely under a different guise, and 500 Libyans. Meanwhile, fierce fighting broke out in the area of two Palestinian refugee camps, Tal al Zaatar and Jisr al Basha, and most of Beirut was without water or electricity. The Arab League took steps to hasten the arrival of further contingents of the peace-keeping force, and the Secretary-General, Mahmoud Riad, headed another mediation mission, but fighting continued unabated until October 1976, when Arab summit meetings in Riyadh and Cairo secured a lasting cease-fire. During the course of the fighting there had been more than 50 abortive cease-fires and it was estimated that up to 60,000 people had been killed and up to 100,000 injured.

The Riyadh and Cairo summits arranged for a 30,000-strong Arab Deterrent Force (mainly Syrians) to police the Lebanon, and a four-party disengagement committee was set up to attempt to implement the terms of the 1969 Cairo agreement between the Lebanese Government and the Palestine guerrillas, as this was considered to be one of the keys to a lasting peace. The disengagement committee consists of Col. Muhammad Khouli (Syria), Abdel-Hamid Buaijan (the Kuwaiti Ambassador in Beirut), General Ali al-Shaer (Saudi Arabian Ambassador in Beirut), and Ahmad Loutfi Moutawalli, the Egyptian Ambassador in Beirut. The committee began by scaling down the level of heavy weapons allowed to the various factions, and then tried to find agreement on the proportion of armed men allowed in the Palestinian guerrilla camps. The Shtoura Agreement of July 1977 provided an attempted settlement of this problem, by endeavouring to regulate the Palestinian base camps and introduce a reconstituted Lebanese army into the border area.

In December 1976 President Sarkis appointed Dr. Selim Hoss as Prime Minister, who formed a cabinet of eight "technocrats" charged with rebuilding and reconstruction, and the Government was granted the power to rule by decree for six months, subsequently extended. A Reconstruction and Development Council was set up under the Chairmanship of Muhammad Atalla, and this Council took over the functions of the former Ministry of Planning. In January 1977 censorship was imposed on the press, initially both on Lebanese and foreign journalists, but the restrictions on foreign despatches were lifted after three weeks.

The Druze chief and leader of the Lebanese left, Kamal Jumblatt, was assassinated by unknown gunmen on March 16th, 1977. Although his murder was followed by a wave of "revenge" killings, it did not lead to any renewed outbreak of major fighting. The southern area of Lebanon, however, between the Litani river and the Israeli border, became the scene of renewed fighting during 1977. This area was largely spared during the civil war and fighting developed when the Palestinians moved to the hills of south Lebanon after being subdued by the Syrians in the civil war. A war "by proxy" developed, with Syria allied with the Palestine guerrillas and Israel supporting the Lebanese Government. The Shtoura Agreement in July 1977, and a later ceasefire in September 1977, arranged with the intervention of the United States, proved largely ineffective and frequent violations took place.

The precarious situation flared up in March 1978 as a result of a raid by Fatah guerrillas into Israel on March 11th, when a bus was attacked near Tel-Aviv in which more than 35 people were killed. As a retaliation, and to prevent further raids, Israeli forces advanced into southern Lebanon three days later. The UN Security Council called for an Israeli withdrawal and set up a United Nations Interim Force in Lebanon (UNIFIL) of 4,000 to maintain peace in the area. Israeli forces withdrew from southern Lebanon in June 1978 but handed over to a right-wing, mainly Christian Lebanese militia who, it appeared, were maintaining links with the Israelis.

In July 1978 fighting flared up again in Beirut between the Syrian troops of the Arab Deterrent Force and right-wing Christian militias. A ceasefire was proclaimed in early October and the Foreign Ministers of the Arab Deterrent Force states (Kuwait, Lebanon, Qatar, Saudi Arabia, Sudan, Syria and the U.A.E.) met at Beiteddin, near

Beirut, aud agreed on a Declaration which they hoped would bring peace to the area. It maintained that Lebanese central authority must be imposed, armed militias must be curbed and a truly national army must be formed. By July 1979 these aims still seemed far from realization. In April Major Saad Haddad, a right-wing Lebanese army officer, proclaimed "independent free Lebanon"—700 square miles of territory next to the Israeli border. He was immediately dismissed from the army, but independent militias continued to wield influence. In late June and early July the southern border was still troubled by Israeli raids and clashes between Christian and leftist militias, although the Lebanese Government had announced that a conscripted Lebanese army, balanced between Christians and Moslems, would be formed, with the conscription of 18,000 men within 18 months of the beginning of July 1979. Meanwhile the mandate of UNIFIL was extended to December 19th, 1979, and that of the Arab Deterrent Force, now composed entirely of Syrians, to December 30th, 1979.

In the middle of May 1979. Dr. Hoss tendered his resignation to President Sarkis. He felt that the time had come for a government of parliamentarians rather than technocrats. There seemed little enthusiasm to be associated with such a Government, however, and at the beginning of July Sarkis requested Hoss to try to form a broadly-based government. On July 16th Dr. Hoss announced his new Government. It consisted of twelve members, seven of whom were deputies and five of whom were not. It was generally regarded as a compromise government, and the Phalangist leader, Pierre Gemayel, referred to it as yet another interim government".

ECONOMIC SURVEY

The Lebanon, for long the commercial and financial centre of the Middle East, was brought to a standstill in 1975–76 by nineteen months of civil war. This was not the first civil war in Lebanon's recent history; indeed the events of 1975/76 were widely seen as the inevitable, if belated, outcome of the "no victor, no vanquished" situation in which the war of 1958 came to an end. But, in terms of loss of life and its effects on an economy so heavily dependent on the confidence of international business and banking circles, on tourism, transit trade and other services, the fighting that followed April 1975 caused unprecedented damage.

Life did appear to return slowly to something near normal in the last few weeks of 1976, giving the country a chance to take stock of its losses and make a start on reconstruction during 1977, but, far from fading, the atmosphere of hopelessness left in the aftermath of the fighting was reinforced by the disruptive events of March 1978, namely the Israeli invasion of the South and the renewal of fighting in Beirut. These events added further to the already huge numbers killed, orphaned and made homeless during the hostilities of 1975–76 and left the country sliding ever nearer to partition, with different factions consolidating their hold over specific zones.

The small Cabinet of technocrats formed under Dr. Selim Hoss in December 1976 set about implementing three overlapping programmes of action, dealing first with relief, then reconstruction and finally development. Armed with statistics and considerable expertise, but without the political muscle to see its actions through, Hoss's team set up a special 12-man Council for Reconstruction and Development, headed by economist Muhammad Atalla and, like the Cabinet, formed of economists and engineers. This Council, endowed with executive powers and authorized to negotiate loans, was intended to outlive the first stages of reconstruction, its members being appointed for periods of three to five years. By mid-1977 the Cabinet and the Council had calculated that they would have to provide £L700 million in immediate assistance to relieve the plight of the homeless, orphaned and unemployed, with further sums for immediate reconstruction of the port, airport and other basic amenities. The reconstruction process was subsequently interrupted by the hostilities of 1978 but in early 1979 a revised reconstruction plan, worth some £L22,000 million, was presented in the hope that sufficient financial backing would be forthcoming from Arab oil-exporting states to give the economy the momentum necessary to keep people employed and diverted from militaristic activities.

However, the whole question of which should come first—the funds or the climate of confidence—has proved a difficult one. Funds were provided by the World Bank, the U.S.A., West Germany and various Arab aid institutions during 1977 but in some cases the facilities repaired with the help of these loans and grants were damaged yet again the following year, leaving the donors reluctant to contribute heavily a second time. Arab heads of state, meeting in Baghdad at the end of 1978, agreed that Lebanon should receive a share of a $3,500 million fund pledged for confrontation states (excluding Egypt) but that this share should be disbursed only on achievement of a solution to the Lebanese conflict.

Amid the confusion that returned to the country in the early months of 1978, the only statement that could be made with any certainty about the economy to emerge from the ruins was that it would inevitably be greatly different from that of the past, influenced by the dictates of Lebanon's unwonted dependence on outside financial and military support and subjected to tighter government control.

POPULATION

No proper census has been held in the country since 1932 for fear of upsetting the delicate political balance between the various sects or confessions. All political and administrative offices have been allocated on the basis of the 1932 census which showed Christians in the majority by six to five over non-Christians. It has been thought for some time, however, that the Muslims compose about 60 per cent of the total population, in part because of the higher ratio of Muslims in the Palestinian population in Lebanon and in part because the Muslims have tended to have a higher birth rate and to emigrate less than Christians. Changes in the population make-up have strained to the limit the delicate system of allocating offices on a sectarian basis adopted under the National Pact of 1943. As a result there have been demands in some quarters for taking a new census and for abandoning the National Pact altogether.

The effects of the civil war on the size, composition and geographical distribution of Lebanon's population have been dramatic. From an estimated 3.1 million inhabitants in 1974 (which made Lebanon one of the most densely-populated countries of the Middle East), the total is believed to have dropped to 2.6 million in 1979, or 2.26 million if non-Lebanese residents (mostly Palestinians) are excluded.

The total of those killed or disabled during 1975–76 has been put by the Lebanese Chamber of Commerce, Industry and Agriculture at 30,000 but other estimates run as high as 60,000, while thousands more were killed or wounded during the spring and autumn of 1978. Of those who escaped death or injury, many fled the country altogether. A private survey conducted during the summer of 1975 reported that 1.5 million people, nearly half the population, were non-Lebanese. This figure was said to include 350,000 Syrian residents, 315,000 visiting Syrians, 370,000 Palestinians (of whom 275,000 were living in refugee camps), 75,000 Egyptians, 78,000 other Africans, 30,000 French, 15,000 Americans and 14,000 British. Not only did most of these foreigners leave because of the war, but thousands of skilled and semi-skilled Lebanese went with them, settling in every continent. By 1979 the number of Lebanese employed in Saudi Arabia alone was estimated to have reached 100,000. This means that Lebanon will have to undertake any reconstruction effort with a sadly depleted workforce—a fact belied by the huge numbers of unemployed among those left behind. The widespread destruction of industrial and other enterprises put whole communities out of work. Unofficially, the unemployment total for early 1978 stood at 270,000.

AGRICULTURE

Of the total area of the country, about 52 per cent consists of mountain, swamp or desert, and a further 7 per cent of forest. Only 23 per cent of the area is cultivated, although a further 17 per cent is considered cultivable. The coastal strip enjoys a Mediterranean climate and is exceedingly fertile, producing mainly olives, citrus fruits and bananas. Many of the steep valleys leading up from the coastal plain are carefully terraced and very productive in olives and soft fruit. In the Zahlé and Shtaura regions there are vineyards, while cotton and onions are grown in the hinterland of Tripoli. The main cereal-growing district is the Bekaa, the fertile valley between the Lebanon and the Anti-Lebanon ranges, to the north of which lies the source of the river Orontes. The river Litani also flows southwards through the Bekaa before turning west near Marjayoun to flow into the Mediterranean just north of Tyre. This valley is particularly fertile and cotton is now grown there with some success. Throughout the country the size of the average holding is extremely small and, even so, a smallholding, particularly in the mountains, may be broken up into several fragments some distance apart. The contribution of the agricultural sector to the national income in 1974 amounted to £L685 million or 11 per cent.

Though both wheat and barley are grown, the Lebanon is far from being self-sufficient in grains. The wheat crop, which can fall in bad years to 40,000 tons, is provisionally estimated by the International Wheat Council to have reached 70,000 tons in 1975, down from 75,000 tons produced on an area of 65,000 hectares in 1974. Fruit growing, on the other hand, plays an important part in the economy and has increased substantially over the last two decades. The citrus fruit crop, which totalled an average 75,000 tons in the years from 1948 to 1952, provided 186,354 tons for export in 1974 and 189,478 tons in 1977. A rush to plant apple trees in the 1950s resulted in gluts, followed by a reduction in output in the late 1960s. Apple exports in 1977 amounted to 91,775 tons. Grapes, figs, bananas and sugar beet are also grown, and so is tobacco, although the tobacco-growing area of the south has been badly affected by Israeli attacks. It is estimated that the Israeli invasion in March 1978 may have prevented the harvesting of $30 million worth of citrus fruits and tobacco.

Important vegetable crops are potatoes, onions, tomatoes, cucumbers and melons. All these appear to have suffered in recent years, although accurate statistics for the immediate post-war period are not available. Potato production amounted to an estimated 80,000 tons in 1975, from an area of 9,000 hectares. This was down from 94,000 tons in 1974 and 117,000 tons the year before that. Tomatoes are thought to have dropped to 60,000 tons in 1975 from 70,000 tons in 1974. The 1975 onion crop is put at 35,000 tons and that of chick-peas at 2,000 tons.

The country's forests are well regulated, but have been greatly thinned by the ravages of the goat, and the number of the famous cedars of Lebanon has sadly diminished.

INDUSTRY

Until the time of the oil price explosion in 1973–74, the only minerals known to exist or exploited in Lebanon were lignite and some iron ore, smelted in Beirut. The Lebanon Petroleum Company, an affiliate of the Iraq Petroleum Company, relinquished its exploration rights in 1948, having failed to find any oil. But reports in 1974 of a big oil find in Akkar were quickly followed by the appointment of a Romanian firm to undertake a geological survey of the entire country. In April 1975 sources close to the Ministry of Industry and Oil said that commercially viable reserves had been discovered in Akkar, the Western Bekaa area and in the Mairoba area near the central coast. At the time of the announcement three Lebanese companies held concessions covering about 90 per cent of Lebanese territory and the Government immediately decided to cancel these firms' licences because of their failure to meet financial obligations and undertake drilling. Many foreign companies, from the United States, Canada, France, Italy and the Soviet Union, were expressing interest in Lebanese oil concessions and one 15-year agreement was actually signed in April 1975 with the U.S. firm Tripco Petroleum, providing for prospection off the Lebanese coast and an eventual production-sharing arrangement if oil were found. Tripco, having paid the Government $1 million before drilling, would take an initial 40 per cent of output to cover exploration costs, giving the Government 80–85 per cent of all subsequent production. But doubts about the future of the Tripco contract were soon raised when the Government invited further bids for offshore exploration on more lenient production-sharing terms and simultaneously ordered a review of all existing concessions and exploration permits. By September 1975 14 companies were said to have submitted offers and another 60 to have expressed interest. Nevertheless, the deadline for bids was postponed until later in the year and the issue became suspended pending an end to the civil war. In January 1977, within weeks of the final ceasefire, the Government set up a new Higher Oil Committee, putting it in charge of oil imports, exploration agreements and the country's two refineries. In February 1979 oil finds were again reported 2 kilometres offshore but the unsettled situation prevailing in 1978–79 precluded any intensive resumption of the oil search.

Even before hopes of an oil find were raised, the Lebanon was of considerable importance to the oil industry. Two of the world's most important oil pipelines cross the country, one from the Kirkuk oil wells in Iraq to Tripoli and the other from Saudi Arabia to Zahrani near Sidon. At each terminal there is an important oil refinery. Both the pipelines and the refineries have, however, been the subject of disputes.

Revenues from the Kirkuk-Tripoli pipeline, which was run by the Iraq Petroleum Company (IPC), were reduced after both Iraq and Syria nationalized IPC assets in their countries on June 1st, 1972. Once the Iraqi Government and IPC had reached a settlement on the nationalization in 1973 a dispute over the ownership of the IPC refinery in Lebanon followed, as a result of which the Lebanese Government took over the refinery and agreed to compensate IPC. The Government started out with one considerable advantage in that Iraqi oil supplies were temporarily maintained at little over the pre-1974 price of $2.5 a barrel. But the cheap supplies ended when the financial clauses of the transit agreement expired in December 1975 and in April 1976 Iraq actually suspended pumping, choosing to direct its Kirkuk oil to the Gulf instead. The Lebanon was thus faced with a loss of around £L30 million a year in royalties as well as the loss of cheap oil. During the early part of 1977, as the economy was getting back in motion, the Tripoli refinery was processing only 5,000 barrels a day compared with an average 36,000 barrels a day in 1975. By 1978, however, it was operating at around 75 per cent of capacity on oil reaching Tripoli by sea or from nearby Zahrani. Iraq finally resumed pumping to Syria through the former IPC pipeline in early 1979 but throughput of Kirkuk crude via Lebanon remained dependent on conclusion of a new bilateral transit and supply agreement.

The Zahrani refinery is run by the Mediterranean Refinery Company (Medreco), jointly owned by Caltex and Mobil. Mobil, Caltex's two parent firms (Texaco and Standard Oil of California) and Exxon also own the Trans-Arabian Pipeline Company (Tapline), which in turn operates the Saudi-Lebanese pipeline. Tapline suspended its pumping operations in early February 1975, on the grounds that oil tankers found it cheaper to lift oil directly from the Saudi terminal at Ras Tanura in the Gulf. This shutdown cost the Lebanon more than £L20 million in royalties. Meanwhile the company also demanded that the Lebanese Government pay for the higher cost of Saudi oil (previously supplied to the Zahrani refinery at a price of $5 a barrel), claiming that it was owed $100 million in back payments. A settlement was reached in August 1975, but when the refinery—which had been put out of action for much of 1976—started up again at the end of November 1976, the question of back payments arose again. Accumulated debts over 1975/76 were estimated at $120 million, and in August 1977 it was finally agreed that these would be settled by the Saudi Government. However, it was not until early 1979, in the wake of the Iranian revolution and the drop in Iranian oil exports, that Tapline resumed operations on its former scale.

Manufacturing industry in the Lebanon has for many years been highly developed in comparison with other states in the area, although it suffered from political disruptions and strikes even before the 1975/76 civil war. Industrial exports increased by 90 per cent between 1973 and 1974 to reach just under £L846 million and the industrial sector in 1974 provided £L1,040 million, or 16 per cent of national income. The number of workers employed in industry that year stood at over 120,000.

Coming immediately after the success of 1974, the effects of the war were all the more dramatic, leaving an estimated 200 factories damaged or destroyed. A study carried out by the Industrial Development Centre for Arab States during 1977 estimated that 15 per cent of total capital invested in industry had been lost and that war damage represented another 35-40 per cent. By mid-1977 Lebanese industry was operating at scarcely one-third of capacity, not only because of the destruction but because industrialists were having difficulty in obtaining credit. Despite this, total industrial exports for 1977 seemed encouraging, earning £L836 million with some estimates putting the equivalent figure for 1978 at over £L1,000 million. Measured against inflation and the increasing cost of imports, however, these figures are less impressive.

Industry in the Lebanon has traditionally been a small-scale operation run by individuals employing a handful of people. Before the disruption of 1975, however, the number of limited liability companies was growing and had reached 44 in 1974 from only

18 the previous year. Food processing, yarn and textile firms accounted for about 44 per cent of industrial output and furniture and woodworking factories about 29 per cent. Mechanical industries accounted for only about 7 per cent of total production and the rest was divided among cement, ceramics, pharmaceutical and plastics industries. Imports by industrial establishments were estimated at about £L800 million a year, accounting for about 40 per cent of the total import bill.

With the exception of the oil companies, the largest industrial employers in the pre-war period were probably the food-processing industries, followed by the well-developed textile industries. The inflow into real estate of funds from Lebanese abroad, mainly those whose property was sequestrated in West Africa, also helped to stimulate the building industry, bringing a sharp rise in land prices and construction activity in 1974. At the same time the production capacity of Lebanon's two cement factories was sufficient to leave a surplus for export and a third plant was planned for Siblin. In addition there were several government-sponsored efforts aimed at promoting industrial expansion. In March 1972, in a measure similar to one of 1954, all industries created between 1971 and 1976 were exempted from income tax for six years. Industries created before 1971 benefited from a partial tax holiday if they expanded their activities before the end of 1975.

As the reconstruction effort began to get under way in 1977 a series of fresh investment incentives was formulated, aimed at restoring confidence. A government-run body called the National Establishment for Investment Insurance was set up to provide investments taking the form of fixed assets with insurance cover at low premiums against hazards of civil war, revolutions, dissension and acts of violence. Legislation applying to foreign banks was amended to encourage them to contribute to the reconstruction programme by investing in the Housing Bank and the National Bank for the Development of Industry and Tourism. The Housing Bank in turn embarked on a large-scale lending programme, providing 15-year loans at an interest rate of only 2 per cent.

The lack of adequate sources of power hindered industrial development in the 1960s but Lebanon gradually achieved the position of having excess capacity. In 1972 it started supplying power through a 100 million kWh. line to southern Syria and in March 1976 the two countries agreed on the exchange of power through a similar line between Tripoli and Tartous. Work on implementing the power link-up project was given the go-ahead as part of moves to repair the country's badly damaged electricity network in 1977. A seven-year electrification scheme costing some £L1,260 million was drawn up, which was expected to be financed by the World Bank and the Arab Fund for Economic and Social Development.

EXTERNAL TRADE

Lebanon has suffered from an adverse balance of visible trade for many years. Exports in 1974, for example, covered only 62 per cent of imports. Before the war, however, this deficit was generally amply covered by invisible earnings from services and tourism, transit trade and remittances from Lebanese working abroad, particularly in the U.S.A., South America and West Africa. The war inevitably brought about a heavy drop in income from tourism and transit traffic but set against this was a parallel reduction in expenditure on imports and a sizeable increase in remittances flowing in from the ever-growing numbers of Lebanese abroad. These remittances, averaging some $100 million per month, more than compensated for the trade deficits of 1977–78 but signs of a drop in income from this source at the beginning of 1979 caused concern over the balance of payments outlook.

The most recent disruption to Lebanese trade before 1975–76 occurred during the October 1973 Arab-Israeli war. The following year, 1974, exports reached a level of £L1,740 million. By 1976 they had dropped back to only £L550 million but in 1977 they showed a remarkable recovery to £L2,364 million. Imports for 1977 were also well over their pre-war level, rising from £L4,200 million in 1974 to £L4,500 million in 1977, leaving a trade deficit for the latter year of £L2,136 million, which was actually lower than that recorded in 1974. However, provisional figures for 1978, with exports down again to about £L1,800 million and imports over £L4,800 million, showed that recovery was by no means complete. The need for capital goods to replace war-damaged installations is bound to influence the value of imports for some time to come ,but traditionally Lebanon's chief imports have been precious metals, stones, jewellery and coins, machinery and electrical apparatus, transport equipment and industrial raw materials. Imports of cars in 1977 were well down on previous levels, however, with only 28,998 new registrations during the year, compared with 41,124 in 1974. Lebanon's most important exports in 1977 were building materials (which represented just under 41 per cent of the total), followed by food and agricultural products (representing 26 per cent). Tools, machinery and electrical appliances were the third most important category (8 per cent of the total), taking equal place with chemicals and chemical products.

Five major western suppliers alone account, on average, for almost half the country's imports. Heading the list in 1978 was Italy, which provided Lebanon with goods worth £L714 million (compared with approximately £L546 million in 1977 and £L94 million in 1976). Next was France, with goods worth £L574 million (against £L530 million in 1977 and £L148 million in 1976), followed by the U.S.A. with £L379 million (compared with £L377 million and £L139 million), West Germany with £L376 million (£L352 million and £L101 million) and finally the United Kingdom which supplied goods to a value of £L347 million, compared with £L257 million in 1977 and £L52 million in 1976.

Analysis of Lebanese sales to these five trading partners in 1977 shows that they played only a minor role in the country's remarkable export performance. In fact Saudi Arabia proved the most important market in 1977 and 1978, absorbing approximately 40 per cent of total exports in both years, with Arab countries together taking as much as 85–87 per cent. Exports to the West have been badly hit by the war. The United Kingdom, one of Lebanon's biggest Western customers in 1978, bought only £L47.6 million worth of goods in that year. The U.S.A. (£L44.2 million) bought even less, followed by the Federal Republic of Germany with £L29.5 million, Italy with £L24.7 million and France with £L17.8 million. However, provision has been made for long-term expansion in Lebanon's trade with the European Economic Community with the coming into effect of a trade and aid agreement, signed in May 1977, which provides tariff concessions for a variety of Lebanese agricultural and industrial goods entering Europe, together with $33 million in grants or low-interest project loans from the European Investment Bank.

CURRENCY AND FINANCE

The importance of Beirut as the commercial and financial centre of the Middle East derived, in the 1950s and onwards, from the almost complete absence of restriction on the free movement of goods and capital and from the transference of the Middle Eastern headquarters of many foreign concerns from Cairo to Beirut after 1952. Moreover, large sums were earned in the Gulf by Arabs who were seeking investment locally, especially in property, and for them Beirut was a convenient centre. Its dominance was further strengthened later by the massive increases in surplus oil revenues earned by the producing states, much of which was channelled through Lebanon. Early in 1966 the Government introduced new regulations controlling the establishment of new banks (notably a minimum capital of £L3 million) and subjected the opening of additional branches to the consent of the central bank. The failure of the Intra Bank, the largest purely Lebanese bank, in 1966 resulted in a thorough reform of the banking system, and some smaller commercial banks of local origin were merged into larger concerns.

By June 1975 the number of representative offices opened by foreign banks in Beirut had reached 72. But by February 1976, when a lull in the fighting encouraged the banks to open again after a two-month closure, 26 of these branches had been partially or totally destroyed. The calm was short-lived but was just long enough to quell fears of massive withdrawals as, even at the most active branches, the banks' reopening was believed to have resulted in withdrawals equivalent to only 7–8 per cent of total deposits and savings accounts. Another 10-month closure was to follow, however, before the banks formally reopened again in Beirut in mid-January 1977. By this time damage and losses through looting of vaults and safety deposit boxes were believed to amount to around $500 million, though even this figure was thought to be conservative. But again fears of a flood of withdrawals proved unfounded. Instead, the liquidity accumulated outside the banking system during the war began to flow back to the extent that, by mid-1978, total bank deposits had reached more than £L12,400 million, exceeding the previous peak of £L11,500 million recorded for February 1975.

The growing competitiveness of European and Gulf financial centres had, even before the disruption of 1975/76, led the Government to seek ways of enhancing Beirut's attractions as a banking centre. The need for such incentives is now infinitely greater. A banking free-zone law which came into effect in April 1977, exempting non-residents' foreign currency accounts from taxes on interest earned, from payment of a deposit guarantee tax and from reserve requirements was a step in this direction. Moreover, in June 1977 the Government decided to lift the moratorium on new bank licences which had been imposed in the wake of the Intra Bank crash of 1966. In April 1978 two new commercial banks, the International Commerce Bank and Universal Bank, were granted licences.

Confidence in Lebanon as a banking centre may waver but confidence in the Lebanese pound has remained virtually unshaken. This confidence had led in 1972 to the first ever granting of a Lebanese currency loan by Lebanese banks to a foreign borrower. Such loans rose to £L240 million the following year, of which £L75 million went to the World Bank. Foreign loans absorbed some of the growing liquidity surplus, as did the reinvestment of Lebanese currency deposits abroad in foreign currencies. Gold and foreign exchange reserves, which stood at $861.6 million by the end of 1973, had almost doubled to $1,673.7 million by the end of 1974, largely because of deposits from Arab oil-producing states. At December 1978 they stood at $2,255.2 million.

The continuing strength of the Lebanese pound throughout and after the war can chiefly be attributed to the absence of restrictions on withdrawals or foreign exchange transactions, an increase in the supply of foreign currencies to finance the war, the pound's strong gold backing and the flow of remittances safeguarding the balance of payments. Before the onset of fighting in early 1975 the exchange rate against the U.S. dollar was £L2.25. By the third quarter of 1976 it had sunk to its lowest, £L3.31, but it quickly recovered after the ceasefire and subsequently stabilized at a level of under £L3. A spell of heavy trading of the pound in early 1979, caused by the more favourable interest rates obtainable on other currencies, prompted Central Bank intervention to bring the pound back from £L3.24 against the U.S. dollar to the preferred level of £L3.10.

Internal inflationary pressures, resulting from the relative freedom of the banks in granting loans and from the floating of the Lebanese pound, have for several years presented one of the country's most pressing problems. By early 1975 the consumer price index was averaging 130.7, (1970=100) and the civil war removed all last vestiges of price restraint, bringing with it an inflation rate of 85–90 per cent a year. The periodic closures of Beirut port, even after 1976, meant continued pressure on prices and an increase of at least 20 per cent was recorded during 1978 alone. The minimum monthly wage was increased to £L310 in 1977, then to £L415 and from that to £L525 in 1979, but this measure alone could do little to relieve the chronic post-war hardship facing much of the population.

TOURISM AND COMMUNICATIONS

Beirut's hotels, its port and airport as well as the Lebanon's largest non-government employer, Middle East Airlines (MEA), were all severely hit by the 1975–76 crisis. Tourism was just beginning to recover from the effects of the October 1973 war when the fighting broke out. The number of tourists arriving during the first quarter of 1975 exceeded the figure for the corresponding period of 1974 by 31 per cent but by the end of that year it had dropped by an overall 39 per cent.

As the war progressed the prosperous hotel district in the centre of Beirut became the scene of some of the fiercest fighting—buildings such as the Hotel St. Georges, the Phoenicia Hotel and Holiday Inn being destroyed or hopelessly damaged. According to the Lebanese Hotel Owners Association, 145 hotels were damaged, incurring losses of some £L218 million. In Beirut alone the number of hotels dwindled from 130 (with 10,486 beds) in 1975 to 44 (with 4,631 beds) by 1979. The contribution of tourism to G.N.P., which was 20 per cent in the pre-war period, shrank to 7.4 per cent in 1977 and continued falling in the face of the widespread disruption of 1978.

Rebuilding of the city centre and the seafront district, according to a master plan for a "new" Beirut drawn up by a group of French architects and planners in the early part of 1977, was hampered by the 1978 hostilities. The plan, expected to cost some £L350,000 million, envisaged the introduction of traffic-free zones, the relocation of previously obtrusive warehousing and the replacement of damaged port facilities and warehousing in central Beirut by shopping precincts, parking spaces, theatres and public gardens. The central reconstruction plan was due to start in July 1978 and to take about seven to ten years to complete.

Middle East Airlines (MEA) suffered a loss of £L14 million in 1975, which rose to £L69.1 million in 1976. The following year saw some recovery, with over 1 million passengers carried and profits of £L22 million, but 1978 was again disappointing, with staff prevented by the fighting from reporting for duty and passenger traffic some 16 per cent below expectations. Despite this setback, however, in the early months of 1979 the airline announced plans for the acquisition of as many as 19 aircraft over the next seven years, at a cost of around $150 million.

There has been an increase in airfreight, due to companies' reluctance to store goods in Lebanon, which in turn necessitates a faster turnaround which can be provided only by air. Lebanon's chief cargo-carrier, Trans-Mediterranean Airways (TMA), in operation since 1953, is also likely to profit from this transport trend. Estimates of freight movements through Beirut International Airport in 1977 appeared to indicate that these were not far off the 1974 level of 118,431 metric tons. In contrast, movement of passengers through the airport dropped to 1,417,802 in 1977, compared with 2,806,628 in 1974. This was predictable in view of the airport's vulnerability to attack and closure during the war. Because of this, Phalangist groups built their own independent airport in 1976/77, in the mountains north of Beirut.

Congestion at Beirut port was already chronic before the troubles, largely because of the volume of goods bound for Saudi Arabia, Kuwait and Iraq, where oil revenues were boosting development spending. A total of 3,972 ships called at Beirut port in 1974 and cargo handled, including cargo in transit, amounted to 5,057,545 tons. During the war, unloading was badly hindered by Muslim workers' reluctance to cross over into Christian areas and by a huge fire in April 1976 which destroyed a dozen major warehouses. During 1977, however, reconstruction of the port was given top priority, enabling 2,783 ships to call and 2,454,287 tons of cargo to be handled. However, persistent fighting in 1978 caused shipping agents to lose confidence and to rely more and more on the ports of Tripoli and Sidon instead. In the meantime Gulf and other Mediterranean ports have expanded and developed in their own right so that the transit role of Lebanon in future may be somewhat diminished.

PUBLIC FINANCE AND DEVELOPMENT

The effects of inflation are clearly seen in the evolution of Lebanon's budget expenditure. The overall state budget of 1977, the first to be adopted after the war, set spending at £L1,661.5 million and was already over 32 per cent higher than the budget for 1974. The draft budget for 1978, however, was up to £L2,083 million, with a projected budget deficit of £L700 million, while that for 1979, at £L2,806 million, envisaged a deficit of £L1,000 million. These "post-war" budgets have been characterized, on the one hand, by a removal of subsidies on basic commodities such as sugar and petrol (with the money going towards civil service salary increases instead) and, on the other, by large allocations to defence, education and public works. In keeping with the need to establish a credible army, the defence allocations of 1978 and 1979 both accounted for approximately one-quarter of total spending—the defence budget for 1979 standing at £L738 million. Along with the 1979 budget, approval was also given for the sum of £L3,000 million to be set aside for the army over the next ten years, the money coming from loans and extraordinary revenues.

The government's expanding role in directing economic activity in the country, where previously state interference had been minimal, was evident in the breakdown of the £L22,000 million five-year reconstruction and development plan announced at the beginning of 1979. This plan, involving some 17 major projects, envisaged that £L10,000 million of total expenditure would be channelled through the public sector.

With the exception of the Palestinian refugee camps, the general standard of living in Lebanon before 1975/76 was relatively high. World Bank statistics put G.N.P. per capita at $1,070 in 1974, aligning Lebanon more closely with certain of the more populous oil-producers of the Middle East than with other non-oil states. Inevitably, since 1974 this lead has been undermined, though statistics to prove it are not available.

STATISTICAL SURVEY

AREA AND POPULATION

Area	Estimated Population (November 15th, 1970)†		
	Males	Females	Total
10,400 sq. km.*	1,080,015	1,046,310	2,126,325

* 3,950 sq. miles.

† Figures are based on the results of a sample survey, excluding Palestinian refugees in camps. The total of registered Palestinian refugees was 187,529 at June 30th, 1973.

Principal towns (estimated population in 1972): Beirut (capital) 800,000; Tripoli 150,000.

Births and deaths: Average annual birth rate 39.3 per 1,000 in 1965–70, 39.8 per 1,000 in 1970–75; death rate 11.8 per 1,000 in 1965–70, 9.9 per 1,000 in 1970–75 (UN estimates).

AGRICULTURE

PRINCIPAL CROPS

	Area Harvested ('000 hectares)			Production ('000 metric tons)		
	1975	1976*	1977*	1975	1976*	1977*
Wheat	75	25	25	79	30	30
Barley	7	5	5	5	5	5
Sugar Beet	3*	1	1	145*	36	40
Potatoes	9*	9	9	80*	85	90
Onions	2*	2	2	31*	32	34
Tobacco	8	8	4	10	14	4
Citrus Fruit	n.a.	n.a.	n.a.	284*	289	294
Apples	n.a.	n.a.	n.a.	170*	173	177
Grapes	17*	17	17	100*	100	100
Olives	n.a.	n.a.	n.a.	35*	46	46
Tomatoes	5*	5	5	60*	65	70

* FAO estimates.

Source: FAO, *Production Yearbook.*

LIVESTOCK

(FAO estimates, '000 head, year ending September)

	1975	1976	1977
Goats	330	330	330
Sheep	232	234	237
Cattle	84	84	84
Donkeys	26	26	26
Pigs	22	23	24
Chickens	7,074	7,398	7,723

Source: FAO, *Production Yearbook.*

INDUSTRY

PETROLEUM PRODUCTS

('000 metric tons)

	1968	1969	1970	1971	1972	1973	1974
Petrol	347	347	374	397	446	517	814
Kerosene*	190	207	212	218	155	224	229
Gas oil	281	318	338	343	329	369.8	420.7
Fuel oil	897	884	958	947	1,082	895.1	910.7
Butane	24	23	22	24	26	48.8	63.1

* Prior to 1972, figures include jet fuel.

OTHER PRODUCTS

		1971	1972	1973	1974
Tobacco manufactures	metric tons	3,122	3,250	3,893	6,337
Timber	cu. metres	48,793	57,748	66,285	54,451
Cement	'000 metric tons	1,499	1,626	1,659	1,744
Electricity	million kWh.	1,375	1,548	1,791	1,975

FINANCE

100 piastres = 1 Lebanese pound (£L).

Coins: 1, 2½, 5, 10, 25 and 50 piastres; 1 pound.

Notes: 1, 5, 10, 25, 50, 100 and 250 pounds.

Exchange rates (June 1979): £1 sterling = £L6.70; U.S. $1 = £L3.24.

£L100 = £14.93 sterling = $30.38.

Note: A basic official exchange rate of U.S. $1 = £L3.08 was introduced in January 1956. This remained in effect until February 1973, despite the devaluation of the U.S. dollar in December 1971. The official exchange rate was £1 sterling = £L7.392 from November 1967 to August 1971; and £1 sterling = £L8.026 from December 1971 to June 1972. However, the basic rate was used only for official exchange operations and for the valuation of official assets and customs duties. All commercial transactions take place on the basis of a fluctuating free market rate, established in November 1948. From 1954 to 1972 the exchange rate in the free market fluctuated between £L2.97 and £L3.37 per U.S. dollar. In February 1973, when the U.S. dollar was again devalued, the Lebanese pound appreciated considerably on the free market. At the same time a new official rate of $1 = £L2.772 was introduced but this became inoperative in March 1973, since when official valuations have been based on an "effective" rate whose parity is adjustable from month to month. The average market rates (£L per U.S. dollar) were: 3.1568 in 1968; 3.2546 in 1969; 3.2690 in 1970; 3.2277 in 1971; 3.0507 in 1972; 2.6104 in 1973; 2.3278 in 1974; 2.3095 in 1975; 2.9037 in 1976; 3.0690 in 1977; 2.9554 in 1978.

ORDINARY BUDGET ESTIMATES

(Expenditure—million £L)

	1975	1976
President's Office	2.28	2.27
Chamber of Deputies	5.92	6.02
Prime Minister's Office	48.77	54.88
Ministry of Justice	18.76	17.97
Ministry of Foreign Affairs	39.67	4.52
Ministry of Interior	118.28	29.10
Ministry of Finance	34.75	35.39
Ministry of National Defence	314.90	326.95
Ministry of National Education	263.52	279.32
Ministry of Health	47.99	52.63
Ministry of Labour	37.82	47.28
Ministry of Information	14.58	14.37
Ministry of Public Works	233.30	217.00
Ministry of Agriculture	42.79	44.29
Ministry of National Economy	179.09	19.01
Ministry of Posts and Telecommunications	16.77	18.10
Ministry of Planning	3.77	4.18
Ministry of Hydraulic Resources	48.34	64.24
Ministry of Tourism	30.86	29.35
Ministry of Industry and Oil	1.46	1.50
Ministry of Housing and Co-operatives	3.35	3.92
Payments on debt	89.00	100.60
Reserves	40.90	32.61
TOTAL	1,636.84	1,716.56

1978 Budget: Expenditure £L2,083 million; Revenue £L1,403 million.

1979 Budget: Expenditure £L2,806 million; Revenue £L1,806 million.

EXTERNAL TRADE

(£L million)

	1970	1971	1972	1973	1974*
Imports c.i.f.	2,135	2,357	2,818	3,335	4,066
Exports f.o.b.	628	796	1,149	1,587	2,542

* Estimated.

PRINCIPAL COMMODITIES

(£L '000)

Imports	1972	1973
Precious Metals, Stones, Jewellery and Coins	252,406	640,237
Vegetable Products	240,437	292,868
Machinery and Electrical Apparatus	402,660	479,325
Textiles and Products	354,314	413,261
Non-precious Metals and Products	250,286	346,365
Transport Vehicles	248,657	322,734
Animals and Animal Products	124,135	131,140
Industrial Chemical Products	239,331	259,480
Mineral Products	169,658	187,469
Beverages and Tobacco	157,673	150,428

Exports*	1972	1973
Vegetable Products	136,720	145,354
Precious Metals, Stones, Jewellery and Coins	114,612	333,989
Animals and Animal Products	56,781	51,874
Machinery and Electrical Apparatus	123,707	168,238
Non-precious Metals and Products	95,992	114,037
Textiles and Products	122,307	172,662
Beverages and Tobacco	81,400	87,559
Transport Vehicles	126,631	150,162

* Including re-exports.

PRINCIPAL COUNTRIES

(£L '000)

Imports	1971	1972	1973
Belgium	54,773	70,149	91,941
Czechoslovakia	41,384	56,463	70,057
France	266,549	300,434	361,915
Germany, Fed. Rep.	264,295	316,107	380,839
Iraq	98,017	121,819	119,919
Italy	187,269	246,474	293,724
Japan	103,370	120,785	126,233
Jordan	13,895	16,605	21,021
Netherlands	56,897	56,598	69,055
Saudi Arabia	32,983	52,537	69,506
Switzerland	228,307	189,587	141,886
Syria	35,312	69,125	51,544
Turkey	56,574	38,664	55,225
United Kingdom	198,054	239,685	261,409
U.S.A.	250,408	322,355	377,542

Exports	1971	1972	1973
France	13,896	52,750	161,912
Germany, Fed. Rep.	13,496	12,039	19,315
Greece	2,083	1,739	6,388
Iraq	68,641	69,440	50,075
Italy	14,855	16,875	22,695
Jordan	37,843	23,513	51,020
Kuwait	88,690	110,621	105,497
Saudi Arabia	125,387	190,284	260,910
Spain	1,207	3,023	5,294
Syria	75,654	83,366	77,403
U.S.S.R.	9,404	8,192	13,833
United Kingdom	26,508	44,962	148,288
U.S.A.	23,164	71,636	72,069

TRANSPORT

RAILWAYS

	Passengers ('000)		Goods ('000)		Revenue ('000 £L)		
	Journeys	Passenger-km.	Tons	Ton-km.	Passengers	Goods	Total
1969	78	7,278	313	24,455	178	2,018	2,196
1970	76	7,430	258	20,082	187	1,916	2,103
1971	71	7,187	325	26,789	184	2,236	2,420
1972	55	5,004	417	33,116	134	2,313	2,447
1973	36	2,829	512	35,063	81	2,446	2,527

ROAD TRAFFIC
(motor vehicles in use)

	1969	1970	1971	1972	1973	1974
Passenger cars (incl. taxis)	129,674	136,016	146,270	164,790	185,935	220,204
Buses	1,763	1,794	1,905	2,067	2,258	2,397
Lorries	14,473	14,795	15,656	17,130	19,151	20,983
Motor cycles	12,004	9,800	9,731	10,734	12,036	13,179

SHIPPING (Beirut)

	Ships Entered		Merchandise (Metric Tons)	
	Number	Tonnage	Entered	Cleared
1970	2,685	4,385,247	2,289,321	728,144
1971	2,910	4,790,713	2,456,517	626,384
1972	3,265	5,958,425	2,666,821	677,378
1973	3,098	5,112,983	2,819,534	717,870
1974	2,613	5,276,000	3,411,546	667,841

CIVIL AVIATION
(International traffic through Beirut)

	Aircraft Using Airport	Passengers Using Airport	Freight Through Airport (metric tons)
1970	41,553	1,558,246	57,691
1971	39,643	1,832,514	69,742
1972	38,735	2,090,634	87,991
1973	40,037	2,258,474	109,560
1974	44,406	2,807,000	145,897

TOURISM

	1971	1972	1973	1974
Total Foreign Visitors (except Syrians)	1,015,772	1,048,159	884,997	1,510,260
of which:				
Visitors from Arab countries	619,171	577,186	535,641	892,203
Visitors from Europe	213,698	250,932	171,338	316,080
Visitors from the Americas	94,076	102,281	75,606	143,000
Syrian Visitors	1,241,633	1,233,903	1,019,498	1,498,131
TOTAL	2,257,405	2,281,062	1,904,495	3,008,391

EDUCATION
(1972–73)

	SCHOOLS	PUPILS	TEACHERS
Public:			
Primary and kindergarten	740	202,913	17,077
Upper primary	549	77,161	
Secondary	65	18,240	
Private:			
Primary and kindergarten	742	366,987	16,168
Upper primary and secondary	390		

Source (unless otherwise stated): Direction Centrale de la Statistique, Ministère du Plan, and Direction Générale des Douanes, Beirut.

THE CONSTITUTION

(Promulgated May 23rd, 1926; amended by the Constitutional Laws of 1927, 1929, 1943 and 1947.)

According to the Constitution, the Republic of the Lebanon is an independent and sovereign State, and no part of the territory may be alienated or ceded. Lebanon has no State religion. Arabic is the official language. Beirut is the capital.

All Lebanese are equal in the eyes of the law. Personal freedom and freedom of the Press are guaranteed and protected. The religious communities are entitled to maintain their own schools, provided they conform to the general requirements relating to public instruction as laid down by the State. Dwellings are inviolable; rights of ownership are protected by law. Every Lebanese citizen who has completed his twenty-first year is an elector and qualifies for the franchise.

Legislative Power

Legislative power is exercised by one house, the Chamber of Deputies, with 99 seats, 53 of which are allocated to Christians and 45 to Muslims (for full details of allocation, *see* Parliament, p. 515). Its members must be over 25 years of age, in possession of their full political and civil rights, and literate. They are considered representative of the whole nation, and are not bound to follow directives from their constituencies. They can be suspended only by a two-thirds majority of their fellow-members. Secret ballot was introduced in a new election law of April 1960.

The Chamber holds two sessions yearly, from the first Tuesday after March 15th to the end of May, and from the first Tuesday after October 15th to the end of the year. The normal term of the Chamber of Deputies is four years; general elections take place within sixty days before the end of this period. If the Chamber is dissolved before the end of its term, elections are held within three months of dissolution.

Voting in the Chamber is public—by acclamation, or by standing and sitting. A quorum of two-thirds and a majority vote is required for constitutional issues. The only exceptions to this occur when the Chamber becomes an electoral college, and chooses the President of the Republic, or Secretaries to the Chamber, or when the President is accused of treason or of violating the Constitution. In such cases voting is secret, and a two-thirds majority is needed.

Executive Power

The President of the Republic is elected for a term of six years, and is not immediately re-eligible. He and his ministers deal with the promulgation and execution of laws passed by the Chamber of Deputies. The Ministers and the Prime Minister are chosen by the President of the Republic.

They are not necessarily members of the Chamber of Deputies, although they are responsible to it and have access to its debates. The President of the Republic must be a Maronite Christian and the Prime Minister a Sunni Muslim; and the choice of the other Ministers has to reflect the division between the communities in the Chamber.

The President himself can initiate laws. Alternatively, the President may demand an additional debate on laws already passed by the Chamber. He can adjourn the Chamber for up to a month, but not more than once in each session. In exceptional circumstances he can dissolve the Chamber and force an election. Ministers can be made to resign by a vote of no confidence.

Elections to the Chamber of Deputies, due in April 1976, were postponed for up to 26 months. In January 1978 the Chamber's term was further extended to June 1980.

In December 1976 the Chamber of Deputies gave the Government power to rule by decree for six months, subsequently extended until January 1978. In March 1979 the Chamber of Deputies was renamed the National Assembly.

THE GOVERNMENT

HEAD OF STATE

President: ELIAS SARKIS (elected May 8th, 1976; took office September 23rd, 1976).

THE CABINET

(*August* 1979)

Prime Minister: Dr. SELIM HOSS (Sunni).

Deputy Prime Minister and Minister of Foreign Affairs: FUAD BUTROS (Greek Orthodox).

Minister of Interior and Tourism: BAHIJ TAQIEDDIN (Druze).

Minister of Defence and Agriculture: JOSEPH SKAF (Greek Catholic).

Minister of Posts, Telecommunications, Housing and Co-operatives: MICHEL MURR (Greek Orthodox).

Minister of Hydroelectric Resources, Oil and Industry: ANWAR SABBAH (Shi'a).

Minister of Finance: ALI KHALIL (Shi'a).

Minister of Labour and Social Affairs: NAZEM QADRI (Sunni).

Minister of Education, Public Works, and Transport: BUTROS HARB (Maronite).

Minister of Economy and Trade, and Public Health: TALAL MARIBI (Sunni).

Minister of Justice and Information: YOUSEF JUBRAN (Maronite).

Minister of State: (vacant).

NATIONAL ASSEMBLY

The electoral reform bill of April 1960 maintained the existing ratio of 6 Christians to 5 Muslims in the Chamber of Deputies. It is the custom for the President of the Chamber of Deputies to be a Shi'i Muslim. The Chamber was renamed the "National Assembly" in March 1979.

President: KAMAL ASAAD.

Deputy President: MUNIR ABU-FADEL.

There was a General Election in May 1972, but the diversity of allegiance in the Chamber makes a strict analysis by party groupings impossible. The distribution of seats among religious groups is laid down by law. The elections due in April 1976 were postponed for up to 26 months and in January 1978 the term of the Chamber of Deputies was further extended until June 1980.

RELIGIOUS GROUPS

Maronite Christians	30
Sunni Muslims	20
Shi'i Muslims	19
Greek Orthodox	11
Greek Catholics	6
Druzes	6
Armenian Orthodox	4
Armenian Catholics	1
Protestants	1
Others	1
TOTAL	99

POLITICAL PARTIES

al-Baath: f. in Syria, 1940, by MICHEL AFLAK; secular party with policy of Arab union, branches in several Middle Eastern countries; 2 mems. in Chamber of Deputies; Leader ASSEM QANSOU, Beirut.

al-Baath: pro-Iraqi wing of al-Baath party; Sec.-Gen. ABDEL-MAJID RAFEI.

Bloc National: f. 1943; policy of power-sharing and the exclusion of the military from politics; 5 mems. in the Chamber of Deputies; Leader RAYMOND EDDÉ; Vice-Pres. SAYED AQL; Sec.-Gen. ANTOINE ABU-ZAID, Chambre des Députés, Place de l'Étoile, Beirut.

ad-Dustour (*Constitutional Party*): f. 1943; led struggle against French mandate, established 1943 Constitution; party of the political and business élite; Leader MICHEL BECHARA AL-KHOURY, rue Michel Chiha, Kantari, Beirut.

al-Harakiyines al-Arab: Beirut; f. 1948 by GEORGES HABACHE; Arab nationalist party, with Marxist tendencies.

al-Hayat al-Wataniya: Beirut; f. 1964 by AMINE ARAYSSI.

al-Jabha al-Damukratiya al-Barlamaniya (*Parliamentary Democratic Front*): Beirut; mainly Muslim support; Leader RASHID ABDUL HAMID KARAMI, Chambre des Députés, Place de l'Étoile, Beirut.

al-Kata'eb (*Phalanges Libanaises, Phalangist Party*): P.O.B. 992, Place Charles Hélou, Beirut; f. 1936; nationalist, reformist, democratic social party; 70,260 mems.; 7 mems. in Chamber of Deputies; announced merger with Parti National Liberal, May 79; Leader PIERRE GEMAYEL; Gen. Sec. JOSEPH SAADE; pulbs. *al-Amal* (Arabic daily), *Action—Proche Orient* (French political and scientific monthly).

Mouvement de l'Action Nationale: f. 1965; Founder and Leader OSMAN MOSBAH AD-DANA, P.O.B. 5890, Centre Starco, Bloc Sud, Beirut.

an-Najjadé: f. 1936; unionist; 3,000 mems.; Founder and Pres. ADNANE MOUSTAPHA AL-HAKIM, Sawt al-Uruba, P.O.B. 3537, Beirut; publ. *Sawt al-Uruba* (Arabic daily).

an-Nida' al-Kawmi: f. 1945; Founder and Leader KAZEM AS-SOLH, Ramlet al-Baïda, Imm. Chammat, Beirut.

Parti Communiste Libanais (*Lebanese Communist Party*): rue al-Hout, Imm. du Parti Communiste Libanais, Beirut; f. 1924; officially dissolved 1948–71; Marxist, much support among intellectuals; 1 mem. in Chamber of Deputies; Leader and Sec.-Gen. GEORGE HAWI; publs. *an-Nida* (daily), *al-Akhbar* (weekly), *al-Tarik* (monthly), *Gantch* (Armenian weekly).

Parti Démocrate: f. 1969; supports a secuar, democratic policy, private enterprise and social justice; Sec.-Gen. JOSEPH MUGHAIZEL; co-founder ÉMILE BITAR, rue Kantari, Imm. Labban, Beirut.

Parti National Liberal (*al-Wataniyin al-Ahrar*): f. 1958; liberal reformist party; 9 mems. and assocs. in Chamber of Deputies; announced merger with Phalanges Libanaises, May 1979; Founder and Pres. CAMILLE CHAMOUN, Chambre des Députés, Place de l'Etoile, Beirut; Deputy Leader KAZEM KHALIL; Sec.-Gen. DORY CHAMOUN.

Parti Nationaliste Syrien: f. 1932, banned 1962–69; advocates a "Greater Syria", composed of Lebanon, Syria, Iraq, Jordan, Palestine and Cyprus; 1 supporter in Chamber of Deputies; leader ABDULLA SAADA.

Parti Socialiste Progressiste (*al-Takadumi al-Ishteraki*): P.O.B. 2893, Zkak el-Blat, Beirut; f. 1948; progressive party, advocates constitutional road to socialism; over 16,000 mems.; 10 mems. in Chamber of Deputies; Pres. WALID JOUMBLATT; publ. *al-Anba'* (weekly).

Parti Socialiste Révolutionnaire: Beirut; f. 1964; Leader YOUSSEF MOUBARAK.

Parti Tachnag: f. 1890; principal Armenian party; collective leadership; 5 mems. in Chamber of Deputies, including KHATCHIG BABIKIAN, Chambre des Députés, Place de l'Étoile, Beirut.

The *Lebanese Front* (Secretary EDWARD HUNAIN) is a grouping of right-wing parties (mainly Christian) and the *National Front* (Sec.-Gen. KAMAL SHATILA) is a grouping of left-wing parties (mainly Muslim). Other parties include the *Independent Nasserite Movement* (Leader IBRAHIM QULAYAT) and the *Union of Working People's Forces* (Sec.-Gen. KAMAL SHATILA).

DIPLOMATIC REPRESENTATION

EMBASSIES AND LEGATION ACCREDITED TO LEBANON

(Beirut unless otherwise indicated)

(E) Embassy; (L) Legation.

Afghanistan: Cairo, Egypt (E).

Algeria: Jnah (opposite Coral Beach) (E); *Ambassador:* MUHAMMAD YAZID.

Argentina: 149 ave. Fouad 1er (E); *Ambassador:* LUIS RAÚL DE LA FAGA (also accred. to Jordan and Saudi Arabia).

Australia: rue Bliss (E); *Chargé d'affaires:* J. M. C. WATSON (also accred. to Jordan).

Austria: Quartier Sursock, rue Négib Trad, Villa Nicolas Cattan (E); *Ambassador:* HERBERT AMRY (also accred. to Kuwait).

Bahrain: Sami Fouad Hamzeh Bldg., Bir Hassan (E); *Chargé d'affaires:* HUSSEIN RASHED SABBAGH (also accred. to Turkey).

Bangladesh: rue Tabet (Verdun), Imm. Said Jaafar (E); *Ambassador:* KHONDKER GOLAM MUSTAFA.

Belgium: 15th Floor, Centre Verdun, rue Dunant (E); *Ambassador:* HUBERT BEDUWE (also accred. to Cyprus and Jordan).

Bolivia: Sarba-Jounieh (E); *Chargé d'affaires:* NAJIB BICHARA GHOSN.

Brazil: Raabda, Imm. Amin Helou (E); *Ambassador:* PAULO DA COSTA FRANCO (also accred. to Jordan).

Bulgaria: blvd. Chiah-Hadath, Imm. Lati (E); *Ambassador:* GUEORGUI TANEV.

Cameroon: Cairo, Egypt (E).

Canada: rue Hamra, Centre Sabbagh (E); *Ambassador:* THÉODORE JEAN ARCAND (also accred. to Jordan and Syria).

Chad: blvd. Sami Solh, Forêt Kfoury, Imm. Kalot Frères (E); *Ambassador:* MUHAMMAD RAHAMA SALEH (also accred. to Jordan).

Chile: Corniche Chouran (E); *Chargé d'affaires:* THOMAS VÁSQUEZ FLORES.

China, People's Republic: rue 62, Nicolas Ibrahim Sursock, Ramlet El-Baida (E); *Ambassador:* XU WENYI.

Colombia: P.O.B. 1496, Chouran, Imm. Jaber al-Ahmad al-Sabbah (E); *Chargé d'affaires a.i.:* Dr. RAFAEL OLAYA PERDOMO.

Congo People's Republic: Cairo, Egypt (E).

Costa Rica: rue Hamra (E); *Chargé d'affaires:* RIAD ABDEL-BAKI (also accred to Kuwait).

Cuba: rue Abdel Sabbah between rue Sakiet el-Janzir and rue de Vienne, Imm. Ghazzal (E); *Ambassador:* ALBERTO VELAZCO SAN JOSÉ (also accred. to Greece).

Cyprus: Cairo, Egypt (E).

Czechoslovakia: ave. de 22 Novembre, B.P. 1529 (E); *Ambassador:* VLADIMIR ZAK.

Denmark: Imm. New Maras, rue California, P.O.B. 11-5190 (E); *Ambassador:* R. THORNING PETERSON (also accred. to Cyprus, Iraq, Jordan and Syria).

Dominican Republic: Raouché, Imm. Minkara (E).

Ethiopia: Cairo, Egypt (E).

Finland: Centre Gefinor, rue Clemenceau (E); *Ambassador:* ARTO ENSIO TANNER (also accred. to Jordan and Kuwait).

France: rue Clemenceau (E); *Ambassador:* LOUIS DE LAMAR.

Gambia: Jeddah, Saudi Arabia.

German Democratic Republic: ave. de Paris (E); *Ambassador:* ACHIM REICHARDT.

Germany, Federal Republic: rue Mansour Jourdak, Imm. Daouk (E); *Ambassador:* HORST SCHMIDT-DORDENEN.

Ghana: Cairo, Egypt (E).

Greece: rue de France (E); *Ambassador:* EUSTACHE KALAMIDAS.

Guinea: Cairo, Egypt (E).

Haiti: rue du Fleuve, Imm. Sarkis (E); *Ambassador:* PIERRE SARKIS.

Hungary: Jnah, Imm. Cheikh Salem Al-Sabah (E); *Ambassador:* JÁNOS VERES.

India: rue Kantari, Imm. Samharini (E); *Ambassador:* YUDISHTAR RAJ DHAWAN (also accred. to Cyprus).

Indonesia: Cairo, Egypt (E).

Iran: Jnah, Imm. Sakina Mattar (E); *Chargé d'affaires:* PARVIZ ATABALI.

Iraq: Jnah, Face Eden Rock (E); *Ambassador:* ABDEL HUSAIN MUSLEM (also accred. to Cyprus).

Italy: rue Makdissi, Imm. Cosmidis (E); *Ambassador:* STEFANO D'ANDREA.

Ivory Coast: ave. Sami Solh, Imm. Georges Tazbek (E); *Ambassador:* AMADOU BOCOUM.

Japan: Corniche Chouran, Imm. Olfat Nagib Salha (E); *Ambassador:* (vacant) (also accred. to Cyprus).

Jordan: rue Verdun, Imm. Belle-Vue (E); *Ambassador:* (vacant).

Kenya: Cairo, Egypt (E).

Kuwait: Bir Hassan, The Stadium Roundabout (E); *Ambassador:* ABDEL-HAMID BUAIJAN.

Liberia: Rome, Italy (E).

Libya: Jnah, Imm. Cheikh Abdallah Khalifé Al-Sabbah (E); *Ambassador:* ABDEL-WAHAB ZANTANI.

Malaysia: Cairo, Egypt (E).

Mali: Cairo, Egypt (E).

Mauritania: Cairo, Egypt (E).

Mexico: P.O.B. 4332, rue Hamra, Imm. Arida (E); *Ambassador:* Lic. JORGE E. MARTÍN RODRÍGUEZ (also accred. to Cyprus and Pakistan).

Morocco: Corniche Masraa, Imm. Chamat (E); *Ambassador:* DRISS BENNOUNA.

Nepal: Cairo, Egypt (E).

Netherlands: rue Kantari, Imm. Sahmarani (E); *Ambassador:* AUGUST HYACINTH CROIN (also accred. to Cyprus and Jordan).

Nigeria: Cairo, Egypt (E).

Norway: Cairo, Egypt (E).

Oman: Bir Hassan (E); *Ambassador:* ABDULLAH ALI AL-QUTABI.

Pakistan: 2699 Layon St. (E); *Ambassador:* Commodore KHATEEB MAQSOOD HUSSAIN (also accred. to Cyprus).

Panama: Corniche Mazraa, Imm. Saab (L).

Peru: Cairo, Egypt (E).

Poland: Furn el-Chebbak, Rue Asile des Vieillards, Imm. Haddad Frères (E); *Ambassador:* JANUSZ ZABLOCKI.

Portugal: rue Beyhum, Villa Omar Beyhum (E); *Ambassador:* (vacant) (also accred. to Jordan).

Qatar: Dibs Building, Chouran Street (E); *Ambassador:* MUHAMMAD IBN HAMAD AL-THANI.

Romania: ave. Sami el-Solh, 215 Forêt Kfouri, Imm. Boutros et Chammah (E); *Ambassador:* FLOREA CHITU.

Saudi Arabia: Rue Bliss, Manara (E); *Ambassador:* General ALI AL-SHAER.

Senegal: Corniche Mazraa, rue Ibn el-Assir, Imm. Kholy el-Kataby (E); *Ambassador:* SAMBA N'DIAYE (also accred. to Pakistan).

Singapore: Cairo, Egypt (E).

Spain: Ramlet el Baida, Imm. White Sands (E); *Ambassador:* MARIANO SANZ BRIZ.

Sri Lanka: Cairo, Egypt (E).

Sudan: rue Mme Curie, Imm. Minkara (E); *Ambassador:* JALAL HASSAN ATABANI.

Sweden: rue Clemenceau, Imm. Moukarzel et Rubeiz (E); *Ambassador:* JEAN-JAQUES VON DARDEL (also accred. to Cyprus and Jordan).

Switzerland: rue John Kennedy, Imm. Achou (E); *Ambassador:* MARCEL-RENÉ LUY.

Thailand: Jeddah, Saudi Arabia (E).

Trinidad and Tobago: 486 rue Verdun, Imm. Heliopolys, Apt. 8; *Ambassador:* (vacant) (also accred. to Iran).

Tunisia: Ramlet el-Baida, Imm. Rock and Marble (E); *Ambassador:* MUHAMMAD AMAMOU.

Turkey: Bir Hassan (E); *Ambassador:* NECMETTIN TUNCEL.

U.S.S.R.: rue Mar Elias el-Tina (E); *Ambassador:* ALEXANDER SOLDATOV.

United Arab Emirates: Jnah, Face Eden Rock, Imm. Wafic Tabbara (E); *Ambassador:* RASHED MAKKAWI.

United Kingdom: ave. de Paris, Ain el-Mreissé (E); *Ambassador:* BENJAMIN STRACHAN.

U.S.A.: ave. de Paris (Corniche), Imm. Ali Reza (E); *Ambassador:* JOHN GUNTHER DEAN.

Uruguay: rue Verdun, Fayoumé, Imm. Mohamad Hussein Ben Moutahar (E); *Ambassador:* RODOLFO COMAS AMARO (also accred. to Jordan and Syria).

Vatican: rue Badaro; *Apostolic Nuncio:* Mgr. CARLO FURNO.

Venezuela: rue Kantari, Imm. Sahmarani (E); *Ambassador:* JOSÉ NIGUEL QUINTANA GUEVARA (also accred. to Jordan and Kuwait).

Yemen Arab Republic: blvd. Khaldé-Quzai, Imm. Ingénieur Ryad Amaiche (E); *Ambassador:* ABDUL-QUDDOUS AL-WAZIR.

Yemen, People's Democratic Republic: Ramlet el Baida, Imm. Ramlet el Baida (E); *Ambassador:* MUHAMMAD ABDEL-QAWI.

Yugoslavia: Imm. Daouk, Arts et Metiers Quarter (E); *Ambassador:* NUSRET SEFEROVIC.

Zaire: Cairo, Egypt (E).

Zambia: Cairo, Egypt (E).

Lebanon also has diplomatic relations with Albania, Benin, the Central African Empire, Ecuador, El Salvador, Gabon, Guatemala, Honduras, Iceland, Ireland, Luxembourg, Madagascar, Monaco, Nicaragua, Niger, Paraguay, the Philippines, Sierra Leone, Togo and Upper Volta.

JUDICIAL SYSTEM

Law and justice in the Lebanon are administered in accordance with the following codes, which are based upon modern theories of civil and criminal legislation:

(1) Code de la Propriété (1930).
(2) Code des Obligations et des Contrats (1932).
(3) Code de Procédure Civile (1933).
(4) Code Maritime (1947).
(6) Code de Procédure Pénale (Code Ottoman Modifié).
(7) Code Pénal (1943).
(8) Code Pénal Militaire (1946).
(9) Code d'Instruction Criminelle.

The following courts are now established:

(*a*) Fifty-six "Single-Judge Courts", each consisting of a single judge, and dealing in the first instance with both civil and criminal cases; there are seventeen such courts at Beirut and seven at Tripoli.

(*b*) Eleven Courts of Appeal, each consisting of three judges, including a President and a Public Prosecutor, and dealing with civil and criminal cases; there are five such courts at Beirut.

(*c*) Four Courts of Cassation, three dealing with civil and commercial cases and the fourth with criminal cases. A Court of Cassation, to be properly constituted, must have at least three judges, one being the President and the other two Councillors. The First Court consists of the First President of the Court of Cassation, a President and two Councillors. The other two civil courts each consist of a President and three Councillors. If the Court of Cassation reverses the judgement of a lower court it does not refer the case back but retries it itself.

First President of the Court of Cassation: EMILE ABOUKHEIR.

(*d*) The Council of State, which deals with administrative cases. It consists of a President, Vice-President and four Councillors. A Commissioner represents the Government.

President of the Court of the Council of State: ANTOINE BAROUD.

(*e*) The Court of Justice, which is a special court consisting of a President and four judges, deals with matters affecting the security of the State.

In addition to the above, Islamic, Christian and Jewish religious courts deal with affairs of personal status (marriages, deaths, inheritances, etc.).

There is also a Press Tribunal.

RELIGION

PRINCIPAL COMMUNITIES

	1958	1974*
Christians	792,000	n.a.
Roman Catholics	529,500	1,141,740
Armenian Rite	14,500	24,500
Chaldean Rite	n.a.	6,459
Greek (Melkite) Rite	} 91,000	191,889
Latin Rite		20,000
Maronite Rite	424,000	878,892
Syrian Rite	n.a.	20,000
Orthodox	219,000	n.a.
Greek	150,000	n.a.
Armenian	69,000	n.a.
Protestant	14,000	n.a.
Muslims	624,000	n.a.
Sunni	286,000	n.a.
Shi'i	250,000	n.a.
Druzes	88,000	n.a.
Jews	6,600	n.a.

* The 1974 figures for members of the Roman Catholic churches are based on estimates by the curias of dioceses based in the Lebanon. National and diocesan boundaries do not necessarily correspond.

It will be seen that the largest single community in the Lebanon is the Maronite, a Uniate sect of the Roman Church. The Maronites inhabited the old territory of Mount Lebanon, i.e. immediately east of Beirut. In the south, towards the Israeli frontier, Shi'i villages are most common whilst between the Shi'i and the Maronites live the Druzes (divided between the Yazbakis and the Jumblatis). The Bekaa has many Greek Christians, whilst the Tripoli area is mainly Sunni Muslim. Altogether, of all the regions of the Middle East, the Lebanon probably presents the closest juxtaposition of sects and peoples within a small territory. As Lebanese political life is organized on a sectarian basis, the Maronites also enjoy much political influence, including a predominant voice in the nomination of the President of the Republic.

ROMAN CATHOLIC CHURCH

ARMENIAN RITE

Patriarchate of Cilicia: Patriarcat Arménien Catholique, Jeitaoui, 2400 Beirut; includes Patriarchal Diocese of Beirut; 28 priests, 24,500 Catholics; Patriarch HEMAIGH PIETRO XVII GHEDIGHIAN.

CHALDEAN RITE

Diocese of Beirut: Evêché Chaldéen-Catholique, B.P. 8566, Beirut; 8 priests, 6,459 Catholics; Bishop RAPHAEL BIDAWID.

LATIN RITE

Apostolic Vicariate of Beirut: Vicariat Apostolique, Villa Maria, B.P. 4224, Beirut; 12 parishes, 20,000 Catholics; Vicar Apostolic PAUL BASSIM.

MARONITE RITE

Patriarchate of Antioch: Patriarcat Maronite, Bkerké (winter), Dimane (summer); includes Patriarchal Diocese of Gibail and Batrun; 203 priests, 197,266 Catholics; Patriarch ANTOINE KHORAICHE. The Maronite Rite includes the Archidioceses of Beirut, Tripoli, Aleppo and Tyre, and the Dioceses of Baalbek, Saida, Jounieh, Latakia, Cairo, Australia, Brazil, U.S.A. and Sarba.

MELKITE RITE

Patriarchate of Antioch: Melkite-Greek-Catholic Patriarchate, P.O.B. 50076, Beirut; jurisdiction over one million Melkites throughout the world; publs. *Sophia* (English—in U.S.A.), *Le Lien* (French—Beirut); Patriarch of Antioch and all the East, of Alexandria and of Jerusalem MAXIMOS V HAKIM. The Melkite Rite includes the 3 Patriarchates of Damascus (Syria), Egypt, Sudan and Lybia and Jerusalem; 7 Archdioceses in Lebanon (Tyre, Beirut, Baalbek, Baniyas, Saida, Tripoli and Zahleh); 4 Archdioceses in Syria (Aleppo, Latakia, Homs and Hauran); one in Jordan (Amman); one in Israel (Acre and Nazareth).

SYRIAN RITE

Patriarchate of Antioch: Patriarcat Syrien-Catholique, rue de Damas, B.P. 116/5087, Beirut; jurisdiction over 75,000 Syrian Catholics in Palestine, Jordan, Lebanon, Syria, Iraq, Egypt and Turkey; publs.: *Revue penseé chrétienne* (monthly), *Revue La Vigne* (quarterly), *Revue Diocesonine d'Alebe* (annually); Patriarch IGNACE ANTOINE II HAYEK.

Patriarchal Vicariate of the Lebanon: Vicariat Patriarcal Syrien, rue de Syrie, Beirut; 12 priests, 18,000 Catholics; Vicar Patriarchal FLAVIEN ZACHARIE MELKI.

Note: The statistics of priests and Catholics are estimates by the diocesan curias for the situation on December 31st, 1974.

OTHER RELIGIOUS GROUPS

Armenian Orthodox: Leader His Holiness KOHREN I (PAROYAN), Catholicos of Cilicia, Armenian Catholicossate of Cilicia, Antélias.

Greek Orthodox: Leader (vacant), Patriarch of Antioch and All the East, Patriarcat Grec-Orthodoxe, P.O.B. 9, Damascus, Syria.

Syrian Orthodox: Leader Mgr. IGNATIOS III YACOUB, Patriarch of Antioch and All the East, Patriarcat Syrien Orthodoxe, Beirut.

Shi'i Muslims: Leader Imam SAYED MOUSSA AS-SADR (missing since August 1978); Pres. of the Supreme Islamic Council of the Shi'i Community of the Lebanon, Dar al-Iftaa al-Jaafari, Beirut.

Sunni Muslims: Leader S.G. Sheikh HASSAN KHALED, Grand Mufti of the Lebanon, Dar El-fatwa, Ilewi Rushed Street, Beirut.

Druzes: Leader S.G. Sheikh MUHAMMAD ABOUCHACRA, Supreme Spiritual Leader of the Druze Community, rue Abou Chacra, Beirut.

Jews: Leader CHAHOUD CHREIM, Beirut.

Protestants: Leader Rev. Dr. FARID AUDEH, Pres. of Nat. Evangelical Union of the Lebanon, P.O.B. 5224, rue Maurice Barrès, Beirut.

Union of the Armenian Evangelical Churches in the Near East: P.O.B. 377, Beirut; Moderator Prof. Hov P. AHARONIAN; the Union includes some thirty Armenian Evangelical Churches in Syria, Lebanon, Egypt, Cyprus, Greece, Iran and Turkey.

THE PRESS

The most important dailies are *al-Anwar* and *an-Nahar*, which have the highest circulations, *The Daily Star*, *al-Jarida* and *L'Orient-Le Jour*, the foremost French paper. The latter two are owned by Georges Naccache, former Lebanese ambassador to France, and tend to take a pro-government line. In a country where most of the élite speak French the other French daily, *Le Soir*, is also influential, and, for the same reason, the twice-weekly publication *Le Commerce du Levant* occupies an important place in the periodical Press.

The civil war hindered the operation of the Press, but even at the height of the civil war about two dozen newspapers and magazines appeared, reflecting every shade of political opinion. In January 1977, however, censorship was imposed on all publications. Some papers ceased publication, if only temporarily. Before this, Lebanon enjoyed the reputation of having one of the freest presses in the Middle East and was an important base for foreign correspondents. Some Lebanese papers have since introduced London and Paris editions.

DAILIES

al-Amal: P.O.B. 992, place Charles Hélou, Beirut; f. 1939; Phalangist Party; Arabic; circ. 29,000; Editor GEORGES OMEIRA.

al-Anba': P.O.B. 955, Beirut; f. 1948; Arabic.

al-Anwar: P.O.B. 1038, Beirut; f. 1959; independent; Arabic; Supplement, Sunday, cultural and social; published by Dar Assayad S.A.L.; circ. 75,200; Propr. SAID FREIHA; Editor ISSAM FREIHA.

Ararat: P.O.B. 756, Nor Hagin, Beirut; f. 1937; Communist; Armenian; circ. 5,000; Editor KRIKOR HAJENIAN.

Ayk: P.O.B. 2623, Beirut; f. 1953; Armenian.

Aztag: P.O.B. 11-587, rue Selim Boustani, Beirut; f. 1927; Armenian; circ. 6,500.

al-Bairaq: P.O.B. 1800, rue Monot, Beirut; f. 1911; Arabic; published by Soc. Libanaise de Presse; Editors ASSAD and FADEL AKL; circ. 3,000.

Bairut: P.O.B. 7944, Beirut; f. 1952; Arabic.

ach-Chaab: P.O.B. 5140, Beirut; f. 1961; Arabic; Nationalist; Propr. and Editor MUHAMMAD AMIN DUGHAN; circ. 7,000.

ach-Chams: P.O.B. 7047, Beirut; f. 1925; Arabic.

ach-Charq: P.O.B. 838, rue de la Marseillaise, Beirut; f. 1945; Arabic; Editor KHAIRY AL-KA'KI.

Daily Star: P.O.B. 11-987, rue al-Hayat, Beirut; f. 1952; independent; English; Chief Editor JIHAD KHAZEN; circ. 19,220.

ad-Dastour: P.O.B. 886, Beirut; f. 1968; Arabic; Owner and Editor ALI BALLOUT; circ. 53,400.

ad-Dunia: P.O.B. 4599, Beirut; f. 1943; Arabic; political; circ. 25,000; Chief Editor SULIMAN ABOU ZAID.

al-Hadaf: P.O.B. 212, rue Béchir, Imm. Esseilé, Beirut; f. 1969; Arabic.

al-Hayat: P.O.B. 11-987, rue al-Hayat, Beirut; f. 1946; independent; Arabic; circ. 32,538.

al-Jarida: P.O.B. 220, place Tabaris, Beirut; f. 1953; independent; Arabic; Editor ABDULLA SKAFF; circ. 22,600.

Joural al-Haddis: P.O.B. 5858, Jounieh; f. 1927; Arabic; political; Owners GEORGES ARÈG-SAADÉ, ALFRED ARÈG-SAADÉ.

al-Joumhouria: P.O.B. 7111, Beirut; f. 1924; Arabic.

al-Khatib: P.O.B. 365, rue Georges Picot; Arabic.

al-Kifah al-Arabi: P.O.B. 5158-14, Chouran, rue Andalous, Beirut; f. 1950; Arabic; political, socialist, Pan-Arab; Publisher and Chief Editor WALID HUSSEINI.

Lissan-ul-Hal: P.O.B. 4619, rue Chateaubriand, Beirut; f. 1877; Arabic; Editor GEBRAN HAYEK; circ. 33,000.

al-Liwa': P.O.B. 2402, Beirut; f. 1970; Arabic.

an-Nahar: P.O.B. 11-226, rue Banque du Liban—Hamra; Pres. Co-operative Bldg., Beirut; f. 1933; Arabic; independent; Publisher and Editor-in-Chief GHASSAN TUENI; Co-Editors MICHEL ABOU JAOUDÉ and LOUIS EL-HAJJ; circ. 75,000.

an-Nass: P.O.B. 4886, Fouad Shihab St., Beirut; f. 1959; Arabic; circ. 16,000; Editor HASSAN YAGHI.

Nida: P.O.B. 4744, Beirut; f. 1959; Arabic; published by the Lebanese Communist Party; Editor KARIM MROUÉ; circ. 10,000.

Nida' al-Watan: P.O.B. 6324, Beirut; f. 1937; Arabic.

an-Nidal: P.O.B. 1354, Beirut; f. 1939; Arabic.

L'Orient-Le Jour: P.O.B. 2488, rue Banque du Liban, Beirut; f. 1942; French independent; Dir. PIERRE EDDÉ; Editor JEAN CHOUERI; circ. 21,500.

Raqib al-Ahwad: P.O.B. 467, rue Patriarche Hoyek, Beirut; f. 1937; Arabic; Editor SIMA'N FARAH SEIF.

Rayah: P.O.B. 4101, Beirut; Arabic.

Le Reveil: Beirut; French; Editor-in-Chief JEAN SHAMI.

ar-Ruwwad: P.O.B. 2696, rue Mokhalsieh, Beirut; f. 1940; Arabic; Editor BESHARA MAROUN.

Sada Lubnan: P.O.B. 7884, Beirut; f. 1951; Arabic.

as-Safa: P.O.B. 9192, Beirut; f. 1972; French; published by Soc. Nat. de Presse et d'Edition S.A.L.; Editor RENÉ AGGIOURI; circ. 15,000.

Sawt al-Uruba: P.O.B. 3537, Beirut; f. 1959; Arabic; an-Najjadé Party; Editor ADNANE AL-HAKIM.

Le Soir: P.O.B. 1470, rue de Syrie, Beirut; f. 1947; French; political independent; Dir. DIKRAN TOSBATH; Editor ANDRÉ KECATI; circ. 16,500.

at-Tayyar: P.O.B. 1038, Beirut; Arabic; independent; issued weekly for the time being; circ. 75,000.

Telegraf—Bairut: P.O.B. 1061, rue Béehara el Khoury, Beirut; f. 1930; Arabic; political, economic and social; Editor TOUFIC ASSAD MATNI; circ. 15,500 (5,000 outside Lebanon).

al-Yawm: P.O.B. 1908, Beirut; f. 1937; Arabic; Editor WAFIC MUHAMMAD CHAKER AT-TIBY.

az-Zamane: P.O.B. 6060, rue Boutros Karameh, Beirut; f. 1947; Arabic; Editor ROBERT ABELA.

Zartonk: P.O.B. 617, rue de l'Hôpital Français, Beirut; f. 1937; Armenian; official organ of Armenian Liberal Democratic Party; Editor P. TOUMASSIAN.

WEEKLIES

Achabaka: Dar Assayad, P.O.B. 1038, Beirut; f. 1956; society and features; Arabic; Founder SAID FREIHA Editor GEORGE IBRAHIM EL-KHOURY; circ. 126,500.

al-Ahad: Quartier Chourah, rue Andalous, P.O.B. 1462, Beirut; Arabic; Editor RIAD TAHA; circ. 32,000.

al-Akhbar: Beirut; f. 1954; Arabic; published by the Lebanese Communist Party; circ. 21,000.

al-Anba': Rue Maroun Naccache, P.O.B. 2893, Beirut; Progressive Socialist Party; Arabic.

al-Anwar Supplement: P.O.B. 1038, Beirut; cultural-social; every Sunday; supplement to daily *al-Anwar*; Editor ISSAM FREIHA; circ. 90,000.

Argus: Bureau des Documentations Libanaises et Arabes, P.O.B. 11-3000, Beirut; weekly news bulletin; English; circ. 1,000.

al-Ash-Shir': 144 rue Gouraud, Beirut; f. 1948; Catholic; Arabic; Editor Father ANTOINE CORTBAWI.

Assayad: Dar Assayad, P.O.B. 1038, Beirut; f. 1943; Propr. SAID FREIHA; Editor RAFIQUE KHOURY; circ. 94,700.

al-Awassef: Homsi Bldg., P.O.B. 2492, Beirut; f. 1953; Arabic; political, independent; Dir. DAHER KHALIL ZEIDAN; circ. 10,500.

Le Commerce du Levant: P.O.B. 687, Kantari St., Commerce and Finance Bldg., Beirut; f. 1929; weekly and quarterly; commercial; French; circ. 15,000; Editor: Société de la Presse Economique; Pres. MAROUN AKL.

Dabbour: Museum Square, Beirut; f. 1922; Arabic; Editors MICHEL RICHARD and FUAD MUKARZEL; circ. 12,000.

al-Dyar: P.O.B. 959, Verdun St., Bellevue Bldg., Beirut; f. 1941; Arabic; political; Editor YASSER HAWARI; circ. 46,000.

al-Hawadess: P.O.B. 1281, Beirut; reported to be transferring to London, October 1978; f. 1911; Arabic; political; Chair., Gen. Man. and Editor-in-Chief SALIM EL-LOZI; Deputy Gen. Man. ALEX AYOUB; circ. 167,500.

al-Hurriya: P.O.B. 857, Beirut; f. 1960; voice of Arab Nationalist Movement; Arabic; Chief Editor MUHSIN IBRAHIM; circ. 12,000.

al-Iza'a: rue Selim Jazaerly, P.O.B. 462, Beirut; f. 1938; politics, art, literature and broadcasting; Arabic; circ. 11,000; Editor FAYEK KHOURY.

al-Jamhour: Mussaïtbeh, P.O.B. 1834, Beirut; f. 1936; Arabic; illustrated weekly news magazine; Editor FARID ABU SHAHLA; circ. 45,000, of which over 30,000 outside Lebanon.

Kul Shay': rue Béehara el Khoury, P.O.B. 3250, Beirut; Arabic.

al-Liwa: rue Abdel Kaim Khalil, P.O.B. 2402, Beirut; Arabic; Propr. ABDEL GHANI SALAAM.

al-Moharrer: P.O.B. 5366, Beirut; f. 1962; Arabic; circ. 87,000; Gen. Man. WALID ABOU ZAHR.

Magazine: Quartier Sursock, Achrafieh, P.O.B. 1404, Beirut; f. 1956; in French; political and social; Publ. Les Editions Orientales S.A.L.; Publisher GEORGE ABOU ADAL; Editor-in-Chief JOSEPH G. CHAMI; circ. 10,200.

Massis: place Debbas, Beirut; f. 1949; Armenian; Catholic; Editor F. VARTAN TEKEYAN; circ. 2,000.

an-Nahda: Abdul Aziz St., P.O.B. 3736, Beirut; Arabic; independent; Man. Editor NADIM ABOU-ISMIL.

Middle East Economic Survey: Middle East Research and Publishing Centre, P.O.B. 4940, Nicosia, Cyprus; f. 1957 (in Beirut); oil topics; Editor and Publr. FUAD W. ITAYIM.

al-Ousbou' al-Arabi (Arab Week): Quartier Sursock, Achrafieh, P.O.B. 1404, Beirut; f. 1959; Arabic; political and social; Publishers Les Editions Orientales, S.A.L.; Publisher GEORGE ABOU ADAL; circ. 125,000 (circulates throughout the Arab world).

al-Rassed: P.O.B. 11-2808, Beirut; Arabic; Editor GEORGE RAJJI.

Revue du Liban: rue Issa Maalouf, Beirut; f. 1928; French; Editor MELHEM KARAM; circ. 18,000.

Sada Janoub: 71 Seif Ed-dine Khatib St., Nasra, Beirut; f. 1937; Arabic; political.

Samar: P.O.B. 1038, Beirut; photorama magazine; circ. 50,000.

OTHER SELECTED PERIODICALS

Note: published monthly unless otherwise stated.

al-Adib: P.O.B. 11-878, Beirut; f. 1942; Arabic, artistic, literary, scientific and political; Editor ALBERT ADIB.

al-Afkar: rue Mère Gelas, Beirut; international; French; Editor RIAD TAHA.

Alam Attijarat (*Business World*): Strand Bldg., Hamra St., Beirut; f. 1965 in association with Johnston International Publishing Corpn., New York; monthly; commercial; Editor NADIM MAKDISI; international circ. 17,500.

Arab Economist: Gefinor Tower, Clemenceau St., P.O.B. 11-6068, Beirut; monthly; published by Centre for Economic, Financial and Social Research and Documentation S.A.L.; Chair. Dr. CHAFIC AKHRAS; Man. Dir. Dr. SABBAN AL HAJ.

L'Economie des Pays Arabes: B.P. 6068, Beirut; f. 1969; French; published by Centre d'Etudes et de Documentation Economiques Financières et Sociales S.A.L.; Pres. Dr. CHAFIC AKHRAS; Dir.-Gen. Dr. SABBAH AL HAJ; circ. 5,000.

al-Idary: P.O.B. 1038, Beirut; f. 1975; business management; Arabic; Gen. Man. BASSAM FREIHA; Chief Editor HASSAN EL-KHOURY; circ. 15,000.

International Crude Oil and Product Prices: Middle East Petroleum and Economic Publications, P.O.B. 4940, Nicosia, Cyprus; f. 1971 (in Beirut); twice yearly review and analysis of oil price trends in world markets; Publisher FUAD W. ITAYIM.

al-Intilak: c/o Michel Nehme, al-Intilak Printing and Publishing House, P.O.B. 4958, Beirut; f. 1960; literary; Arabic; Chief Editor MICHEL NEHME.

Lebanese and Arab Economy: Allenby St., P.O.B. 1801, Beirut; f. 1951; fortnightly; Arabic, English and French; Publisher Beirut Chamber of Commerce and Industry and SAMI N. ATIYEH; Editor and Dir. ABDEL-WAHAB RIFA'I.

Majallat al Izaat al Loubnaniat: Lebanese Broadcasting Corporation, Beirut; Arabic; broadcasting affairs.

Naft al Arab: Beirut; f. 1965; monthly; Arabic; oil; Publisher ABDULLAH AL TARIQI.

Nous Ouvriers dy Pays: 144 rue Gouraud, Beirut; Catholic; English-French; social welfare; Editor Father ANTOINE CORTBAWI.

Rijal al Amal (*Businessmen*): P.O.B. 220, Corniche Square, Beirut; business magazine; Arabic, with special issues in English and French; Editor G. W. SKAFF; circ. 12,000.

Sawt al-Mar'ah: Dar al-Kitab, P.O.B. 1284, Beirut; Lebanese Women's League; Arabic; Editor: Mrs. J. SHEIBOUB.

Tabibok: P.O.B. 4887, Beirut; f. 1956; medical, social, scientific; Arabic; Editor Dr. SAMI KABANI; circ. 78,000.

al-Tarik: Beirut; cultural and theoretical; published by the Lebanese Communist Party; circ. 5,000.

al-'Ulum: Dar al Ilm Lil Malayeen, rue de Syrie, P.O.B. 1085, Beirut; scientific review.

Welcome to Lebanon and the Middle East: Tourist Information and Advertising Bureau; Starco Centre, North Block 711, P.O.B. 4204, Beirut; f. 1959; on entertainment, touring and travel; English; Editor SOUHAIL TOUFIK ABOU-JAMRA; circ. 6,000.

NEWS AGENCIES

FOREIGN BUREAUX

Agence France-Presse (AFP): B.P. 11-1461, Beirut; Dir. HUBERT HAYE.

Agencia EFE (*Spain*): P.O.B. 113/5313, Beirut; Correspondent MARY ANGELES JUNQUERA.

Agenzia Nazionale Stampa Associata (ANSA) (*Italy*): rue Verdun, Immeuble Safieddine, B.P. 1525, Beirut; Correspondent GRAZIANO MOTTA.

Allgemeiner Deutscher Nachrichtendienst (ADN) (*German Democratic Republic*): P.O.B. 6105, Beirut; Correspondent FRANK KLUWE.

Associated Press (AP) (*U.S.A.*): Abu Arraj Bldg., Spears St., Beirut; Correspondent HARRY KOUNDAKJIAN.

Československá tisková kancelář (CTK) (*Czechoslovakia*): P.O.B. 5069, Beirut; Chief Middle East Correspondent VLADIMIR OTRUBA.

Deutsche Presse-Agentur (dpa) (*Federal Republic of Germany*): P.O.B. 1266, Beirut; Correspondent HANS-ARMIN REINARTZ.

Middle East News Agency (MENA) (*Egypt*): 72 Al Geish St., P.O.B. 2268, Beirut.

Agentstvo Pechati Novosti (APN) (*U.S.S.R.*): Beirut Correspondent SUREN G. SHIROYAN.

United Press International (UPI) (*U.S.A.*): Press Co-operative Bldg., rue Hamra, Beirut; Chief Middle East Correspondent DAVID D. PEARCE.

Iraq News Agency, Jamahiriya News Agency (Libya), Reuters (United Kingdom) and TASS (U.S.S.R.) also have offices in Beirut.

PRESS ASSOCIATIONS

Lebanese Press Syndicate: P.O.B. 3084, Beirut; f. 1911; 18 mems.; Pres. RIAD TAHA; Vice-Pres. FARID ABOU SHAHLA; Sec. ABDUL GANI SALAM.

Foreign Press Syndicate: rue Clemenceau, Beirut; Pres. GEORGES BITAR.

PUBLISHERS

Arab Institute for Research and Publishing: Carlton Tower Building, Saquet Janzecr, 3rd Floor, P.O.B. 5460, Beirut; works in Arabic and English.

Dar al Adab: Beirut; literary and general.

Dar El-Ilm Lilmalayin: Nassif Yazigi St., P.O.B. 1085, Beirut; f. 1945; dictionaries, textbooks, Islamic cultural books; Owners: MUNIR BA'ALBAKY and BAHIJ OSMAN; Dir. Dr. ROHI BAALBAKI.

Dar-Alkashaf: P.O.B. 112091, A. Malhamee St., Beirut; f. 1930; publishers of *Alkashaf* (Arab Youth Magazine), maps and atlases; printers and distributors; Propr. M. A. FATHALLAH.

Dar al-Makshouf: rue Amir Beshir, Beirut; scientific, cultural and school books; owner: Sheikh FUAD HOBEISH.

Dar Al-Maaref Liban S.A.L.: P.O.B. 2320, Esseily Bldg., Riad Al-Solh Square, Beirut; f. 1959; children's books and textbooks in Arabic; Gen. Man. JOSEPH NASHOU.

Dar Al-Mashreq (Imprimerie Catholique): P.O.B. 946, Beirut; f. 1853; religion, art, literature, history, languages, science, philosophy, school books, dictionaries and periodicals; Dir. PAUL BROUWERS, S.J.

Dar An-Nahar S.A.L.: B.P. 226, Beirut; f. 1967; publishes *Kadaya Moua'ssira* (quarterly); circ. 7,000; Pres. MOHAMED ALI HAMADÉ.

Dar Assayad S.A.L.: P.O.B. 1038, Beirut; f. 1943; publishes in Arabic *Al-Anwar* (daily), *Assayad* (weekly), *Al-Tayar* (weekly), *Achabaka* (weekly), *Samar* (weekly), *Dar-Assayad Yearbook*; has offices and correspondents in Arab countries and most parts of the world; Centre for Research, Studies and Archives; Chair. SAID FREIHA; Man. Dir. BASSAM FREIHA.

Dar Beirut: Immeuble Lazarieh, rue Amir Bechir, Beirut; f. 1936; Propr. M. SAFIEDDINE.

Institute for Palestine Studies, Publishing and Research Department: Nsouli-Verdun St., P.O.B. 11-7164, Beirut; f. 1963; independent non-profit Arab research organization; to promote better understanding of the Palestine problem; publishes books, reprints research papers; Chair. Prof. CONSTANTINE ZURAYK; Exec. Sec. Prof. WALID KHALIDI.

The International Documentary Center of Arab Manuscripts: Maqdissi St., Ras Beirut Hanna Bldg., P.O.B. 2668, Beirut; f. 1965; publishes and reproduces ancient and rare Arabic texts; Propr. ZOUHAIR BAALBAKI.

Khayat Book and Publishing Co. S.A.L.: 90–94 rue Bliss, Beirut; Middle East, Islam, oil, Arab publications and reprints; Man. Dir. PAUL KHAYAT.

Librairie du Liban: Riad Solh Sq., P.O.B. 945, Beirut; f. 1944; dictionaries, Middle East, travel, Islam; Proprs. KHALIL and GEORGE SAYEGH.

Middle East Publishing Co.: Beirut, rue George Picot, Imm. El Kaissi; f. 1954; publishes *Medical Index* and *Revue Immobilière* (Real Estate); Man. Editor ELIE SAWAF.

New Book Publishing House: Beirut.

Rihani Printing and Publishing House: Jibb En Nakhl St., Beirut; f. 1963; Propr. ALBERT RIHANI; Man. DAOUD STEPHAN.

Other publishing houses in Beirut include: *Dar al-Andalus, Dar Majalaat Shiir, Imprimerie Catholique, Imprimerie Universelle, Al Jamiya al Arabi, Al Kitab al Arabi, Librairie Orientale, Al Maktab al-Tijari, Middle East Stamps Inc., Mu'assasat al-Marif, Nofal and Bait at Hikmat, Saidar.*

RADIO AND TELEVISION

RADIO

Lebanese Broadcasting Station: rue Arts et Métiers, Beirut; is a part of the Ministry of Information; f. 1937; Dir.-Gen. K. HAGE ALI; Technical Dir. J. ROUHAYEM; Dir. of Programmes N. MIKATI; Head of Administration A. AOUN; Public Relations FAOUZI FEHMY.

The Home Service broadcasts in Arabic on short wave, the Foreign Service broadcasts in Portuguese, Arabic, Spanish, French and English.

Number of radio receivers: 605,000.

TELEVISION

Compagnie Libanaise de Télévision (C.L.T.): P.O.B. 4848, Beirut; f. 1959. commercial service; programmes in Arabic, French and English on four channels; Dir.-Gen. PAUL TANNOUS; Technical Manager M. S. KARIMEH.

Télé-Liban S.A.L.: P.O.B. 11-5054, Beirut; f. 1978; commercial service; programmes in Arabic, French and English on three channels, and relays on three channels; Chair. and Dir.-Gen. Dr. CHARLES RIZK.

Télé-Management: P.O.B. 113-5310, Beirut; airtime sales and programme sales contractor to Télé-Liban S.A.L.; Gen. Man. CLAUDE SAWAYA.

Number of TV receivers: 425,000.

FINANCE

BANKING

(cap. = capital; p.u. = paid up; dep. = deposits; m. = million; L£ = Lebanese £; res. = reserves)

Beirut has for long been the leading financial and commercial centre in the Middle East, as can be seen from the extensive list of banking organizations given below. However, public confidence in the banking system was strained by the closing of the Intra Bank, the largest domestic bank, late in 1966 when its liquid funds proved insufficient to cope with a run of withdrawals. The bank obtained enough guarantees to re-open in January 1968, though it is now an investment bank managed by a New York company. In 1970 the decision was taken to grant no new licences (except for medium-term lending institutions) until 1976, and foreign banks have therefore been acquiring interests in Lebanese-owned banks to establish a foothold in Beirut. The civil disturbances between April 1975 and October 1976 considerably disrupted Beirut's banking and commercial facilities. The war forced 15 of the 70 Lebanese banks and 25 foreign banks to shift their operations to Athens, Cairo and the Persian Gulf. During 1977 many of the banks which had moved returned to Beirut. By November 1977 it was estimated that banking operations had reached between 40 and 50 per cent of the pre-war level.

CENTRAL BANK

Banque du Liban: P.O.B. 5544, rue Masraf Loubnane, Beirut; f. 1964; central bank; cap. L£15m.; dep. L£5,757m. resources L£7,152m. (Dec. 1977); Gov. JOSEPH OUGHOURLIAN.

PRINCIPAL LEBANESE BANKS

Advances and Commerce Bank S.A.L.: P.O.B. 11-2431, Sehnaoui Bldg., Riad el-Solh St., Beirut; f. 1960; cap. p.u. L£6m.; dep. L£40.5m. (1977); Chair. and Gen. Man. HENRI SFEIR.

Arab Libyan Tunisian Bank S.A.L.: Riad Solh Sq., Shaker & Oueni Bldg., P.O.B. 9575, Beirut; f. 1973; subsidiary of Libyan Arab Foreign Bank and Société Tunisienne de Banque; cap. p.u. L£10m.; Pres. MOHAMED ABDEL JAWAD; Gen. Man. AHMED SHERIF.

Bank Almashrek S.A.L.: Bank Almashrek Bldg., Riad el-Solh St. 52, Beirut; Affil. with Morgan Guaranty Trust; cap. L£15m., dep. L£414m. (1977); Chair. FAHD AL-BAHAR; Man. Dir. PETER DE ROOS.

Bank of Beirut S.A.L.: P.O.B. 7354, Gefinor Centre, rue Clemenceau, Beirut; cap. p.u. L£3m.; Man. Dir. Dr. A. BARAKAT.

Bank of Beirut and the Arab Countries S.A.L.: rue Clemenceau, P.O.B. 11-1536, Beirut; f. 1957; cap. L£5m.; dep. L£293.2m. (1977); Chair. TOUFIC S. ASSAF; Vice-Chair. and Gen. Man. NASHAT SHEIKH EL-ARD; Joint Gen. Man. AMEEN M. ALAAMY.

Bank of Credit and Commerce International (Lebanon) S.A.L.: P.O.B. 1889, Piccadilly Bldg., 2nd Floor, Hamra St., Beirut; f. 1974; cap. p.u. L£3.5m.; Man. NAZIR AL-REHMAN.

Bank Handlowy for the Middle East S.A.L.: P.O.B. 11-5508, Sehnaoui Bldg., rue Banque du Liban, Beirut; cap.

p.u. L£5m.; subsidiary of Bank Handlowy w Warszawie, Warsaw; Chair. JUBRAN TAWK; Gen. Man. STANISLAW ZDZITOWIECKI.

Bank of Kuwait and the Arab World S.A.L.: P.O.B. 3846, Sehnaoui Bldg., Riad el-Solh St., Beirut; f. 1959; cap. p.u. L£12m.; dep. L£30m.; Chair. Dr. RAFIK A. NAJA; Gen. Man. ABDOU S. KARNABE.

Bank of Lebanon and Kuwait S.A.L.: P.O.B. 11-5556, Arab Bank Bldg., Riad el-Solh St., Beirut; f. 1974; cap. p.u. L£5m.

Banque al-Ahli (Banque Nationale) Foncière, Commerciale et Industrielle S.A.L.: rue Foch, P.O.B. 2868, Beirut; f. 1953; cap. L£10m.; res. L£3.16m.; Pres. and Gen. Man. BOUTROS EL KHOURY.

Banque Audi S.A.L.: ave. Fouad Chehab, St. Nicolas Area, P.O.B. 11-2560, Beirut; f. 1962; cap. p.u. L£10m.; dep. L£637.2m. (1978); Chair. and Gen. Man. GEORGES OIDIH AUDI.

Banque de la Bekaa, S.A.L.: Centre Fakhoury, Zahle; cap. p.u. L£3m.; Pres. and Gen. Man. E. W. FAKHOURY.

Banque Beyrouth pour le Commerce S.A.L.: P.O.B. 10-216, Arab Bank Bldg., Riad el-Solh St., Beirut; f. 1961; Chair. and Gen. Man. RIFAAT S. AL-NIMER.

Banque de Crédit Agricole, Industriel et Foncier: Oueini Bldg., Riad el-Solh St., Beirut; f. 1954; Dir.-Gen. Sheikh BOUTROS EL KHOURY; took over several banks in 1967–68, including Banque de l'Economie Arabe, Banque d'Epargne and Union National Bank.

Banque de Credit National S.A.L.: Beirut Riyad Bank Bldg., Riad el-Solh St., P.O.B. 11-0204, Beirut; f. 1959; cap. and reserves L£4.8m.; dep. L£18.7m. (1977); Pres. and Gen. Man. EDMOND J. SAFRA; Deputy Gen. Man. HENRI KRAYEM.

Banque du Crédit Populaire, S.A.L.: P.O.B. 5292, Riad el-Solh St., Beirut; f. 1963; cap. p.u. L£5m.; dep. L£266m. (Dec. 1978); Chair. JOE I. KAIROUZ.

Banque de l'Essor Economique Libanaise S.A.L.: Manassa Bldg., nr. Municipal Playground, Jounieh; cap. p.u. L£3m.

Banque de Financement S.A.L.: P.O.B. 5044, Intra Investment Company Bldg., Hamra, Beirut; Chair. and Gen. Man. ISSAM ASHOUR.

Banque de l'Industrie et du Travail, S.A.L.: B.P. 11-3948, rue Riad Solh, Beirut; f. 1961; cap. L£10m.; dep. L£195m. (1977); Chair. LAURA EMILE BUSTANI; Gen. Man. Dr. ASSAAD F. SAWAYA; Dep. Gen. Man. REDA G. ABUJAWDEH.

Banque Joseph Lati et Fils S.A.L.: P.O.B. 1983, Bradawil Bldg., Adib Ishaq St., Beirut; f. 1925; Chair. and Man. ISSAC LATI.

Banque du Liban et d'Outre-Mer (S.A.): P.O.B. 11-1912, Spears Street, Beirut; f. 1951; cap. p.u. L£16m.; dep. L£845m. (1977); Chair. and Gen. Man. Dr. NAAMAN AZHARI.

Banque Libanaise des Emigrés S.A.L.: Raouche, Beirut; cap. p.u. L£3m.; dep. L£4.3m.

Banque Libanaise pour le Commerce S.A.L.: P.O.B. 1126, rue Riad el-Solh, Beirut; f. 1950; cap. L£5m.; res. L£15m. (Dec. 1973); Pres. Dir.-Gen. ELIA ABOU JAOUDÉ.

Banque Libano-Française: 1 rue Riad el-Solh, Beirut; f. 1968; cap. p.u. L£15m.; dep. L£820m. (Dec. 1977); Pres. and Chair. JEAN GIBERT; Gen. Man. M. VALENTIN-SMITH.

Banque Libano-Bresilienne S.A.L.: P.O.B. 3310, Maarad St., Beirut; f. 1962; cap. L£5m.; res. L£1.3m. (Dec. 1973); Pres. N. A. GHOSN; Gen. Man. J. A. GHOSN.

Banque de la Méditerranée S.A.L.: P.O.B. 348, Beirut; f. 1944; cap. L£5m.; dep. L£167m. (1974); Pres. and Gen. Man. JOSEPH A. EL-KHOURY.

Banque Misr Liban, S.A.L.: Head Office: P.O.B. 7, Beirut.

Banque Nasr Libano-Africaine, S.A.L.: P.O.B. 798, Beydoun Bldg., Riad el-Solh St., Beirut; f. 1963; Pres. DIAB ISKANDAR NASR.

Banque Sabbag et Française pour le Moyen-Orient S.A.L.: P.O.B. 11-0393, Imm Centre Sabbag, rue Hamra, Beirut; f. 1921; formerly known as Banque Française pour le Moyen-Orient S.A.L.; affiliated to Banque de l'Indochine et de Suez; cap. L£14m.; dep. L£254m. (1977); Chair. R. BRAVARD; Gen. Man. HABIB NAUPHAL.

Banque Saradar S.A.L.: Trad Bldg., Sursock St., P.O.B. 11-1121, Beirut; f. 1948; cap. L£5m.; dep. L£318m. (1977); Pres.-Gen. Man. JOE MARIUS SARADAR; Asst. Gen. Man. ABDO I. JEFFI.

Banque Tohme S.A.L.: P.O.B. 837, Gabriel Bachour Bldg., St. Nicholas St., Ashrafieh, Beirut; f. 1919; cap. p.u. L£3m.; dep. L£22m.; Pres. and Gen. Man. ROGER TOHME.

Banque G. Trad (Crédit Lyonnais) S.A.L.: P.O.B. 113, Trad Palace, Tabariz, Ashrafieh, Beirut; f. 1951; cap. L£3m.; dep. L£329m. (Dec. 1973); Pres. G. A. TRAD.

Beirut-Riyad Bank S.A.L.: Beirut-Riyad Bank Bldg., Riad Solh St., P.O.B. 11-4668, Beirut; f. 1959; cap. p.u. L£12.5m.; dep. L£184m. (1977); Pres. and Gen. Man. HUSSEIN MANSOUR.

British Bank of the Lebanon S.A.L.: rue Trablos, P.O.B. 11-7048, Beirut; f. 1971; dep. L£60.8m. (1977); subsidiary of British Bank of the Middle East; Chair. E. C. O'BRIAN; Man. Z. N. AUDEH.

Byblos Bank: P.O.B. 11-5605, Verdun St., Beirut; f. 1962; cap. L£11m.; res. L£2m.; dep. L£427m. (1977); Pres. SEMAAN M. BASSIL; Gen. Man. FRANÇOIS S. BASSIL.

Chemical Bank (Middle East) S.A.L.: Rabiya Metn, Beirut; subsidiary of Chemical Bank, New York.

Continental Development Bank, S.A.L.: Beydoun Bldg., Arz St., P.O.B. 11-3270, Beirut; f. 1961; subsidiary of Continental Bank, Chicago; cap. L£8m.; total resources L£140.6m. (Dec. 1977); Chair. and Gen. Man. JOHN BURN.

Crédit Libanais S.A.L.: P.O.B. 11-1458, Riad el-Solh Square, Esseily Bldg., Beirut; f. 1961; cap. L£12m.; dep. L£504m. (1978); Chair. and Gen. Man. B. Y. OBÉGI; Gen. Man. H. Y. OBÉGI.

Federal Bank of Lebanon S.A.L.: Parliament Square, P.O.B. 2209, Beirut; f. 1952; cap. L£10m.; Pres. and Gen. Man. MICHEL A. SAAB.

First National Bank of Chicago (Lebanon) S.A.L.: P.O.B. 11-1629, Riad el-Solh St., Beirut; f. 1958; wholly-owned subsidiary of First National Bank of Chicago, U.S.A.; cap. L£5m.; total resources L£165m. (Dec. 1978); Chair. ZIAD H. IDILBY; Gen. Man. RICHARD J. GILGAN.

Jammal Trust Bank, S.A.L.: Jallad Bldg., Riad el-Solh St., Beirut; f. 1963 as Investment Bank, S.A.L.; cap. p.u. L£20m.; dep. L£70m. (1974); Chair. A. A. JAMMAL; Gen. Man. MUHAMMAD A. SALLAB.

MEBCO BANK—Middle East Banking Co. S.A.L.: B.P. 3540, Beydoun Bldg., Beirut; f. 1959; cap. p.u. L£6.25m.; dep. L£277.8m. (1978); Chair. and Gen. Man. JAWAD CHALABI.

Prosperity Bank of Lebanon S.A.L.: P.O.B. 5625, Acra Bldg., Place des Martyres, Ashrafieh, Beirut; cap. p.u. L£3m.; Gen. Man. S. S. WEHBE.

Rifbank S.A.L.: Head Office: P.O.B. 5727, rue Kantari, Beirut; f. 1965; in association with Commerzbank A.G., The National Bank of Kuwait S.A.K., The Commercial Bank of Kuwait S.A.K.; cap. p.u. L£4m.; dep. L£118m. (1973); Chair. and Gen. Man. A. A. BASSAM.

Royal Bank of Canada (Middle East) S.A.L.: Hanna Ghantous Bldg., Dora, P.O.B. 11-250, Beirut; f. 1969; cap. L£5m.; dep. L£86m. (1973); Pres. BRUCE LAMONT; Gen. Man. EDWARD BROKES; Man. KHALIL KIKANO.

Société Bancaire du Liban S.A.L.: Beirut Riyad Bank Bldg., Riad el-Solh St., Beirut; P.O.B. 11-435; f. 1899; cap. p.u. and reserves L£5m.; dep. L£68.6m. (Dec. 1973); Chair. S. S. LEVY.

Société Générale Libano-Européenne de Banque S.A.L.: Riad el-Solh St., P.O.B. 11-2955, Beirut; f. 1953; cap. p.u. L£5m.; dep. L£422m. (1977); Chair. A. M. SEHNAOUI; Gen. Man. JEAN DUBOIS.

Société Nouvelle de la Banque de Syrie et du Liban S.A.L.: P.O.B. 957, Beirut; f. 1963; cap. p.u. L£15m.; dep. L£433m. (1977); Pres. GUY TRANCART; Gen. Man. JEAN PIERRE DE CALBIAC.

Toronto Dominion Bank (Middle East) S.A.L.: P.O.B. 5580, Rue Banque du Liban, Beirut; f. 1964; cap. L£3m.; Chair. IBRAHIM AL-AHDAB; Man. Dir. E. ACHKAR.

Transorient Bank: P.O.B. 11-6260, Beirut; f. 1966; cap. p.u. L£5m.; dep. L£122m. (1978); joint venture with the International Bank of Washington and Lebanese private investors; Chair. HAMED BAKI; Gen. Man. GABRIEL ATALLAH.

United Bank of Lebanon & Pakistan, S.A.L.: P.O.B. 5600; Beydoun Bldg., Arz St., Beirut; f. 1963; cap. L£3m.; Chair. MAK YOUSUFI.

DEVELOPMENT BANKS

National Bank for Industrial and Touristic Development: Tabriz Sq., ave. Fouad Chehab, S.N.A. Bldg., 5th Floor, B.P. 8412, Beirut; f. 1973; cap. L£60m.; Chair. and Gen. Man. Dr. SALIM HOSS; Dir. of Loans Dr. ROY KARAOGLAN; Dir. of Research Dr. JOSEPH FULEIHAN.

Investment and Finance Bank S.A.L. (INFI): P.O.B. 16-5110, ave. Fouad Chehab, St. Nicolas Area, Beirut; f. 1974; medium- and long-term loans, 60 per cent from Lebanese sources; associated with Banque Audi (Lebanon), NCB Bank AG (Zürich), Investbank (U.A.E.).

PRINCIPAL FOREIGN BANKS

Algemene Bank Nederland N.V. (*General Bank of the Netherlands*): P.O.B. 11-3012, Beirut.

Arab African Bank (*Egypt*): Riad el-Solh St., P.O.B. 11-6066, Beirut.

Arab Bank Ltd. (*Jordan*): Beirut Main Branch: Riad Solh St., Beirut.

Banco Atlántico S.A. (*Spain*): P.O.B. 7376, Beirut; Rep. ENRIQUE DE CEANOVIVAS.

Banco di Roma S.p.A. (*Italy*): Beirut, Saida and Tripoli; Dir.-Gen. MARCELLO CONTENTO.

Bank of America N.T. and S.A. (*U.S.A.*): P.O.B. 3965, Beirut; Man. C. HOLLANDER.

Bank of Nova Scotia (*Canada*): Riad el-Solh St., P.O.B. 4446, Beirut; Man. P. KLUGE.

Bank Saderat Iran (*Iran*): Beirut Branch, P.O.B. 5126, Beirut.

Banque Nationale de Paris Intercontinentale S.A. (*France*): P.O.B. 1608, Beirut; Beirut Dir. HENRI TYAN.

British Bank of the Middle East: Bab Edriss, Beirut; brs. at Ras Beirut, St. George's Bay, Mazra'a and Tripoli; Lebanon Area Man. E. C. O'BRIAN.

Československá Obchodni Banka A.S. (*Commercial Bank of Czechoslovakia Ltd.*): Prague, Czechoslovakia; Middle East office: P.O.B. 5928, Beirut.

The Chartered Bank (*United Kingdom*): P.O.B. 11-3996, Riad el-Solh St., Beirut; Man. in Beirut D. R. HOBBY.

Chase Manhattan Bank, N.A. (*U.S.A.*): P.O.B. 11-3684, Beirut; Man. GUNTER NEUBERT.

Chemical Bank (*U.S.A.*): P.O.B. 9506, Rabbiya, Matn, nr. Beirut; Rep. MICHAEL DAVIES.

Citibank N.A. (*U.S.A.*): P.O.B. 11-3648, Arab Bank Bldg., Riad el-Solh St., Beirut; Resident Vice-Pres. JOHN H. BERNSON.

Crédit Commercial de France S.A.: P.O.B. 11-6873, Port St., Beirut; Rep. M. HEMAYA.

Crédit Suisse: P.O.B. 11-35155, Mme Curie St., Beirut; cap. p.u. L£10m.; dep. L£77.3m.; Rep. MAJED DAJANI.

Deutsche Bank A.G. (*Federal Republic of Germany*): P.O.B. 11-710, Beirut; Rep. SIEGFRIED BRUNNENMILLER.

Habib Bank (Overseas) Ltd. (*Pakistan*): P.O.B. 5616, Beirut; Man. A. RASHID KHAN.

Jordan National Bank, S.A.: P.O.B. 5786, Beirut; Tripoli and Saida.

Manufacturers Hanover Trust Co. (*U.S.A.*): B.I.T. Bldg., Riad el-Solh St., Beirut; Man. VAHEK T. TAHMAZIAN.

Morgan Guaranty Trust Co. (*U.S.A.*): P.O.B. 5752, Beirut Riyad Bank Bldg., rue Riad Solh, Beirut; Rep. SELWA B. LORENZ (acting).

Moscow Narodny Bank Ltd. (*United Kingdom*): P.O.B. 5481, Beirut; Man. in Beirut V. BARISHEV.

Rafidain Bank (*Iraq*): Beirut Branch: Beydoun Bldg., place de l'Etoile, Beirut, P.O.B. 1891; f. 1941.

Saudi National Commercial Bank: P.O.B. 2355, Beirut; f. 1938.

State Bank of India: P.O.B. 7275, 5th Floor, Arab Bank Bldg., Riad el-Solh St., Beirut.

Union Bank of Switzerland: P.O.B. 11-5734, Starco South 1001-4, Beirut; Rep. G. E. SALAWI.

Numerous foreign banks have Representative Offices in Beirut.

BANKING ASSOCIATION

Association of Banks in Lebanon: P.O.B. 976, Riad el Solh Square, Beirut; f. 1959; serves and promotes the interests of the banking community in the Lebanon; mems.: over 100 banks and banking rep. offices. Pres. Dr. ASSAAD SAWAYA; Gen. Sec. Dr. PIERRE NASRALLAH.

INSURANCE

NATIONAL COMPANIES

"La Phenicienne" (S.A.L.) (formerly *al Ahli*): Centre Géfinor, rue Clemenceau, P.O.B. 5652, Beirut; f. 1964; Chair., Gen. Man. ANTOINE K. FEGALY; Dep. Gen. Man. NICOLAS MAASSAB.

al-Ittihad al-Watani: Immeuble Fattal, P.O.B. 1270, Beirut; Chair. JOE I. KAIROUZ.

Arabia Insurance Co. Ltd. S.A.L.: Arabia House, Phoenicia St., P.O.B. 11-2172, Beirut; Vice-Chair. and Gen. Man. BADR S. FAHOUM.

Commercial Insurance Co. S.A.L.: Starco Centre, P.O.B. 4351, Beirut; f. 1962; Chair. MAX R. ZACCAR; Gen. Man. MYRIAM R. ZACCAR.

Compagnie Libanaise d'Assurances (S.A.L.): Riad el-Solh St., P.O.B. 3685, Beirut; f. 1951; Man. Dir. ELIA F. S. ABOUJAOUDÉ; Man. BAHJAT DAGHER.

Libano-Suisse Insurance Co. (S.A.L.): Commerce and Finance Bldg., Rond-Point Kantari, Beirut; Pres. and Gen. Man. PIERRE J. SEHNAOUI; Man., Lebanon Branch, ANTOINE MAILA.

Some twenty of the major European companies are also represented in Beirut.

TRADE AND INDUSTRY

DEVELOPMENT ORGANIZATION

Council of Development and Reconstruction: Beirut; f. 1976; aims to achieve reconstruction after civil war; Chair. Dr. MUHAMMAD ATALLAH.

CHAMBERS OF COMMERCE AND INDUSTRY

Beirut Chamber of Commerce and Industry: Sanayeh, Spears St., Chamber of Commerce & Industry Bldg., P.O.B. 111801, Beirut; f. 1898; 10,000 mems.; Pres. ADNAN KASSAR; Gen. Dir. WALID NAJA; publ. *The Lebanese and Arab Economy* (13 issues per annum).

Tripoli Chamber of Commerce and Industry: Tripoli.

Sidon Chamber of Commerce and Industry: Sidon.

Zahlé Chamber of Commerce and Industry: Zahlé; f. 1939; 497 mems.; Pres. ALFRED SKAFF.

EMPLOYERS' ASSOCIATIONS

Association of Lebanese Industrialists: Chamber of Commerce and Industry Bldg., Justinian St., P.O.B. 1520, Beirut; Chair. FUAD ABI SALAH.

Conseil National du Patronat: Beirut; f. 1965.

TRADE UNION FEDERATIONS

Confédération Générale des Travailleurs du Liban (C.G.T.L.): Beirut; confederation of the following four federations; Pres. GABRIEL KHOURY.

Federation of Independent Trade Unions: Central Bldg., rue Mère Galace, Beirut; f. 1954; estimated 6,000 mems. in 7 trade unions; affiliated to Confed. of Arab T.U.'s; Pres. MOHAMED EL-ASSIR; Sec.-Gen. ALI HOURANI; publ. *Sawt al 'Amel.*

Federation of Unions of Workers and Employees of North Lebanon: Al-Ahram Building, Abu-Wadi Square, Tripoli; f. 1954; affiliated to Confed. of Arab T.U.'s; 3,700 mems. in 14 trade unions; Pres. MOUSTAFA HAMZI; Sec.-Gen. KHALED BARADI; publ. *Al A'mel.*

Ligue des Syndicats des Employés et des Ouvriers dans la République Libanaise (*League of Trade Unions of Employees and Workers in the Lebanese Republic*): Immeuble Rivoli, Place des Canons, Beirut; f. 1946; estimated 6,000 mems. in 21 trade unions; affiliated to ICFTU; Pres. HUSSEIN ALI HUSSEIN; Vice-Pres. HALIM MATTAR; Sec.-Gen. FOUAD KHARANOUH; Foreign Sec. ANTOINE CHIHA; Del. to ICFTU and mem. of Exec. Cttee. ANTOINE CHIHA; publ. *Al-Awassef.*

United Unions for Employees and Workers: Imm. Waqf Bzoummar, rue Béchara el Khoury, Beirut, B.P. 3636; f. 1952; affiliated to ICFTU; 16,000 mems. in 21 trade unions; Pres. GABRIEL KHOURY; Sec.-Gen. ANTOINE AOUN; publ. *La Gazette.*

TRANSPORT

RAILWAYS

Office des Chemins de Fer de l'Etat Libanais et du Transport en Commun de Beyrouth et de sa Banlieue: P.O.B. 109, Souk el-Arwam, Beirut; since 1959 all railways in Lebanon have been state-owned. There are 335 km. of standard-gauge railway and 90 km. of narrow-gauge local lines; the coastal line between Israeli and Syrian frontiers is open only from Zahrani to Tripoli, due to political disturbances; Chair. ADEL HAMIÉ; Dir.-Gen. ANTOINE BAROUKI.

ROADS

Lebanon has 7,100 km. of roads, of which 1,990 km. are main roads. Most are generally good by Middle Eastern standards. The two international motorways are the north-south coastal road and the road connecting Beirut with Damascus in Syria. Among the major roads are that crossing the Bekaa and continuing South to Bent-Jbail and the Chtaura-Baalbek road. Hard-surfaced roads connect Jezzine with Moukhtara, Bzebdine with Metn, Meyroub with Afka and Tannourine.

SHIPPING

Beirut is the principal port of call for the main shipping and forwarding business of the Levant; the port was closed during the civil war, but reopened in December 1976. It was closed again for five months during 1978. Tripoli, the northern Mediterranean terminus of the oil pipeline from Iraq (the other is Haifa), is also a busy port, with good equipment and facilities. Saida is still relatively unimportant as a port. Shipping was disrupted by the civil war.

There are many shipping companies and agents in Beirut. The following are some of the largest:

"Adriatica" S.p.A.N.: Rue du Port, Immbilière du Port de Beyrouth, P.O.B. 1472; Gen. Man. J. WEHBE.

American Eastern Tanker Agencies S.A.L.: P.O.B. 215, Aboucharache Bldg., Rue Verdun, Beirut; f. 1956; Pres. M. S. SPITERI, Man. N. BALTAGI.

American Lebanese Shipping Co. S.A.L.: P.O.B. 215, Aboucharache Bldg., Rue Verdun, Beirut; f. 1951; Pres. P. PARATORE; Man. N. BALTAGI.

American Levant Shipping & Distributing Co.: P.O.B. 1429, Rue Patriarch Hoyek, Immeuble Anwar Dassouki & Co.; agents for: Holland America Line, Lykes Bros. Steamship Co.; correspondents throughout Middle East; Pres. EDWIN B. HOUSE; Man. Dir. SAMIR ISHAK.

Arab Shipping and Chartering Co.: P.O.B. 1084; agents for China National Chartering Corpn., China Ocean Shipping Co., Kiu Lee Shipping Co. Ltd., Chinese-Tanzanian Joint Shipping Co.

Barrad Shipping Co. S.A.L.: P.O.B. 181, Beirut; refrigerated tramp services; 3 cargo reefer vessels; Chair. P. H. Helou.

British Maritime Agencies (Levant) Ltd.: rue du Port, agents for: Ellerman and Papayanni Line Ltd., Ellerman's Wilson Line Ltd., Prince Line Ltd., etc.

Catoni & Co. S.A.L.: P.O.B. 800, rue du Port; f. 1960; Chair. H. J. Beard; agents for: British Maritime Agencies (Levant) Ltd., Royal Netherlands Steamship Co., Lloyd's.

Ets. Derviche Y. Haddad: rue Derviche Haddad, P.O.B. 42; agents for: Armement Deppe, Antwerp and Compagnie Maritime Belge, Antwerp.

Daher & Cie. S.A.L.: Byblos Bldg., Place des Martyrs, P.O.B. 254; importer and distributor of cars and building materials. Agence Maritime Daher are agents for: Cie. de Navigation Daher, Concordia Line, Navale et Commerciale Havraise Peninsulaire, Société Maritime des Petroles B.P., Cie Navale des Petroles, Cie. Générale Transatlantique, Nouvelle Cie. de Paquebots, Sudcargos, Medcar, Stolt Nielsen Inc.

O. D. Debbas & Sons: Head Office: Sahmarani Bldg., Kantary St., P.O.B. 11-003, Beirut; Man. Dir. Elie O. Debbas.

Fauzi Jemil Ghandour: P.O.B. 1084; agents for: Denizçilik Bankası T.A.O. (Denizyollari), D.B. Deniz Nakliyati T.A.Ş. (Dbcargo), Iraqi Maritime Transport Co., Kuwait Shipping Co. (S.A.K.)

T. Gargour & Fils: rue Foch, P.O.B. 371; f. 1928; agents for: Assoc. Levant Lines S.A.L.; Dirs. Nicolas T. Gargour, Habib T. Gargour.

Globe Shipping, Chartering and Tourist Co.: P.O.B. 6986, Beirut; agents for Hellenic Mediterranean Lines Piraeus Uiterwyk Shipping Co., Tampa Linea C, Genoa, Sintra S.p.a., Palermo, Lykiardopulo & Co., Livanos Shipbrokers, General Steam Navigation, etc.

Henry Heald & Co. S.A.L.: Imm. Fatal, rue du Port, P.O.B. 64; f. 1837; agents for: Canadian Pacific Lines, Nippon Yusen Kaisha, P. & O. Group, Royal Mail Lines, Scandinavian Near East Agency, Vanderzee Shipping Agency, Worms and Co.; Chair. J. L. Joly; Dir. G. Hani.

Hitti Frères: Rue de Phenicie, P.O.B. 511; airlines and shipping agents.

Khedivial Mail Line: Rue du Port.

Raymond A. Makzoumé: rue de la Marseillaise, P.O.B. 1357; agents for: Jugoslav Lines, Italian Lines, Hellenic Lines Ltd. (N.Y.), Fenton Steamship Co. Ltd. (U.K.).

Mediterranean Maritime Co. S.A.L.: P.O.B. 1914, Bourse Bldg., Hoyek St., Beirut; managers for National Maritime Agencies Co. W.LL., Kuwait.

Mena Shipping and Tourist Agency: P.O.B. 11-884, Modern Bldg., El Arz St., Beirut; 5 cargo vessels; Man. Dir. W. Leheta.

Messageries Maritimes: rue Allenby, P.O.B. 880.

Rudolphe Saadé & Co. S.A.L.: Freight Office: P.O.B. 2279, rue de la Marseillaise; Travel Office: ave. des Français; agents for American Export Lines, Rosade Lines and Syrian Arab Airlines; f. 1964; Pres. Jacques R. Saade.

Union Shipping & Chartering Agency S.A.L.: P.O.B. 2856; agents for Yugoslav vessels.

CIVIL AVIATION

MEA (*Middle East Airlines, Air Liban*): MEA Bldgs., Airport Blvd., Beirut, P.O.B. 206; f. 1945; regular services throughout Europe, the Middle East and Africa; fleet of 3 Boeing 747, 3 Boeing 707/320C, 16 Boeing 707/720B; Chair. of Board and Pres. Asad Nasr; Gen. Man. Salim Bey Salaam.

Trans-Mediterranean Airways (TMA): Beirut International Airport, P.O.B. 11-3018, Beirut; f. 1953; world-wide cargo services between Europe, Middle East, S.-E. Asia, the Far East and U.S.A.; fleet of 11 Boeing 707/320C; Pres. and Chair. Munir Abu-Haidar.

The following foreign companies also operate services to Lebanon: Aeroflot (U.S.S.R.), Air Algérie, Air France, Air India, Air Maroc (Morocco), Alia (Jordan), Alitalia (Italy), Ariana Afghan Airlines, Austrian Airlines, British Airways, CSA (Czechoslovakia), EgyptAir, Ethiopian, Garuda (Indonesia), Ghana Airways, Iberia (Spain), Interflug (German Democratic Republic), Iranair, Iraqi Airways, JAL (Japan), JAT (Yugoslavia), KLM (Netherlands), Kuwait Airways, Libyan Arab Airlines, LOT (Poland), Lufthansa (Federal Republic of Germany), Malev (Hungary), Olympic Airways (Greece), PIA (Pakistan), Sabena (Belgium), SAS (Sweden), Saudia, Sudan Airways, Swissair, Syrian Arab Airlines, Tarom (Romania), THY (Turkey), TWA (U.S.A.), UTA (France), Varig (Brazil), Viasa (Venezuela) and Yemen Republic Airlines.

TOURISM

Ministry of Tourism: Beirut; f. 1966; official organization; Head of International Relations and Conventions Dept. Antoine Accaoui; Head Speleological Service Sami Karkabi.

National Council of Tourism: P.O.B. 5344, rue de la Banque du Liban, Beirut; government-sponsored autonomous organization; overseas offices in New York, Paris, Frankfurt, Stockholm, Brussels, Cairo, Jeddah and Baghdad; Pres. Cheikh Habib Kayrouz; Vice-Pres. Selim Salam.

Baalbeck International Festival: Beirut; Dir. Wagih Ghossoub.

Theatres

Baalbeck Festival Modern Theatre Group: Baalbeck; Dir. Mounir Abu-Debs.

National Theatre: Beirut; Dir. Nizar Mikati.

DEFENCE

Commander of the Arab Deterrent Force: Col. Sami Khatib.

Commander-in-Chief of the Armed Forces: Bashir al-Jumayyil.

Defence Budget (1978): L£491 million.

The 18,000 Lebanese army virtually disintegrated during the civil war, when it split up into factions, but a new army is being formed.

In March 1978 a 4,000-strong UN Interim Force in Lebanon (UNIFIL) took up positions to try to keep the peace near the border with Israel.

EDUCATION

Free primary education was introduced in 1960, but private institutions still provide the main facilities for secondary and university education. Private schools enjoy almost complete autonomy except for a certain number which receive government financial aid and are supervised by the Ministry's inspectors.

The primary course lasts for five years. It is followed either by the four-year intermediate course or the three-year secondary course. The baccalaureate examination is taken in two parts at the end of the second and third years of secondary education, and a public examination is taken at the end of the intermediate course. Technical education is provided mainly at the National School of Arts and Crafts, which offers four-year courses in electronics, mechanics, architectural and industrial drawing, and other subjects. There are also public Vocational schools providing courses for lower levels.

Higher education is provided by twelve institutions, including five universities. In 1972–73 50,803 students attended these centres, of whom 45.7 per cent were Lebanese citizens. Teacher training is given at various levels. A three-year course which follows the intermediate course trains primary school teachers and another three-year course which follows the second part of the baccalaureate trains teachers for the intermediate school. Secondary school teachers are trained at the Higher Teachers' College at the Lebanese University. Two Agricultural Schools provide a three-year course for pupils holding the intermediate school degree.

For the year 1973 the budget of the Ministry of National Education amounted to L£201.5 million or 18.64 per cent of state expenditure. By 1972–73 there were altogether 1,354 public schools and 1,927 private schools, containing some 800,500 pupils and 39,000 teachers.

UNIVERSITIES

American University of Beirut: Beirut; 500 teachers, 3,800 students.

Beirut Arab University: Tarik El-Jadidé, P.O.B. 5020, Beirut; 180 teachers, 27,000 students.

Université Libanaise (*Lebanese University*): Bir Hassan, Beirut; 733 teachers, 14,826 students.

Université Saint Joseph: B.P. 293, Beirut; 479 teachers, 5,663 students.

Université Saint-Esprit De Kaslik: Jounieh; 230 teachers, 1,510 students.

BIBLIOGRAPHY

Abouchdid, E. E. Thirty Years of Lebanon and Syria (1917–47) (Beirut, 1948).

Agwani, M. S. (Ed.). The Lebanese Crisis, 1958: a documentary study (Asia Publishing House, 1965).

Atiyah, E. An Arab tells his Story (London, 1946).

Besoins et Possibilités de Développement du Liban, Étude Préliminaire, 2 Vols. (Lebanese Ministry of Planning, Beirut, 1964).

Binder, Leonard (Ed.). Politics in Lebanon (Wiley, New York, 1966).

Bulloch, John. Death of a Country: The Civil War in Lebanon (Weidenfeld and Nicolson, London, 1977).

Burckhard, C. Le Mandat Français en Syrie et au Liban (Paris, 1925).

Cardon, L. Le Régime de la propriété foncière en Syrie et au Liban (Paris, 1932).

Catroux, G. Dans la Bataille de Méditerranée (Julliard, Paris, 1949).

Chamoun, C. Les Mémoires de Camille Chamoun (Beirut, 1949).

Corm, G. C. Politique Economique et Planification au Liban 1953–63 (Beirut, 1964).

Eddé, Jacques. Géographie Liban-Syrie (Beirut, 1941).

Fedden, R. Syria (London, 1946) (also covers the Lebanon).

France, Ministère des Affaires Etrangères. Rapport sur la Situation de la Syrie et du Liban (Paris, annually, 1924–39).

Ghattas, Emile. The monetary system in the Lebanon (New York, 1961).

Gulick, John. Social Structure and Culture Change in a Lebanese Village (New York, 1955).

Hachem, Nabil. Liban: Sozio-ökenomische Groundlagen (Opladen, 1969).

Haddad, J. Fifty Years of Modern Syria and Lebanon (Beirut, 1950).

Harding, G. Lankester. Baalbek, a New Guide (Beirut, 1964).

Harik, Iliya F. Politics and Change in a Traditional Society—Lebanon 1711–1845 (Princeton University Press, 1968).

Hepburn, A. H. Lebanon (New York, 1966).

Himadeh, Raja S. The Fiscal System of Lebanon (Khayat, Beirut, 1961).

Hitti, Philip K. Lebanon in History (3rd ed., Macmillan, London 1967).

Hourani, Albert K. Syria and Lebanon (London, 1946).

Hudson, Michael C. The Precarious Republic: Political Modernization in the Lebanon (Random House, New York, 1968).

Jidejian, Nina. Byblos Through the Ages (Dar El-Mashreq, Beirut, 1968).

Longrigg, S. H. Syria and Lebanon under French Mandate (Oxford University Press, 1958).

Mills, Arthur E. Private Enterprise in Lebanon (American University of Beirut, 1959).

Penrose, S. B. L. That They Have Life: the story of the American University of Beirut 1866–1941 (Princeton, New Jersey, U.P., 1941).

PUAUX, G. Deux Années au Levant; souvenirs de Syrie et du Liban (Hachette, Paris, 1952).

QUBAIN, FAHIM I. Crisis in Lebanon (Middle East Institute, Washington, D.C., 1961).

RONDOT, PIERRE. Les Institutions Politiques du Liban (Paris, 1947).

SABA, ELIAS S. The Foreign Exchange Systems of Lebanon and Syria (American University of Beirut, 1961).

SAFA, ELIE. L'Emigration Libanaise (Beirut, 1960).

SALIBI, K. S. The Modern History of Lebanon (Praeger, New York, and Weidenfeld & Nicolson, London, 1964); Cross Roads to Civil War: Lebanon 1958–76 (Caravan Books, New York, 1976).

SAYIGH, Y. A. Entrepreneurs of Lebanon (Cambridge, Mass., 1962).

STEWART, DESMOND. Trouble in Beirut (Wingate, London, 1959).

SULEIMAN, M. W. Political Parties in Lebanon (Cornell University Press, Ithaca, N.Y., 1967).

SYKES, JOHN. The Mountain Arabs (Hutchinson, London, 1968).

TIBAWI, A. L. A Modern History of Greater Syria, including Lebanon and Palestine (Macmillan, London, 1969).

VALLAUD, PIERRE. Le Liban au Bout du Fusil (Librairie Hachette, Paris, 1976).

WARD, PHILIP. Touring Lebanon (Faber and Faber, London, 1971).

ZIADEH, NICOLA. Syria and Lebanon (Praeger, New York, 1957).

Libya

(The Socialist People's Libyan Arab Jamahiriya)

PHYSICAL AND SOCIAL GEOGRAPHY

W. B. Fisher

The Socialist People's Libyan Arab Jamahiriya (Libya) is bounded on the north by the Mediterranean Sea, on the east by Egypt and the Sudan, on the south and south-west by Chad and Niger, on the west by Algeria, and on the north-west by Tunisia. The three component areas of Libya are: Tripolitania, in the west, with an area of 285,000 sq. km.; Cyrenaica, in the east, area 905,000 sq. km.; and the Fezzan, in the south, area 570,000 sq. km.—total for Libya, 1,760,000 sq. km. The independence of Libya was proclaimed in December 1951; before that date, following conquest from the Italians, Tripolitania and Cyrenaica had been ruled by a British administration, at first military, then civil; and the Fezzan had been administered by France. The revolutionary government which came to power in September 1969 has formally re-named the three regions: Tripolitania became known as the Western provinces, Cyrenaica the Eastern provinces, and the Fezzan the Southern provinces.

PHYSICAL FEATURES

The whole of Libya may be said to form part of the vast plateau of North Africa, which extends from the Atlantic Ocean to the Red Sea; but there are certain minor geographical features which give individuality to the three component areas of Libya. Tripolitania consists of a series of regions of different level, rising in the main towards the south, and thus broadly comparable with a flight of steps. In the extreme north, along the Mediterranean coast, there is a low-lying coastal plain called the Jefara. This is succeeded inland by a line of hills, or rather a scarp edge, that has several distinguishing local names, but is usually alluded to merely as the Jebel. Here and there in the Jebel occur evidences of former volcanic activity—old craters, and sheets of lava. The Jefara and adjacent parts of the Jebel are by far the most important parts of Tripolitania, since they are better watered and contain most of the population, together with the capital town, Tripoli.

South of the Jebel there is an upland plateau—a dreary desert landscape of sand, scrub, and scattered irregular masses of stone. After several hundred miles the plateau gives place to a series of east-west running depressions, where artesian water, and hence oases, are found. These depressions make up the region of the Fezzan, which is merely a collection of oases on a fairly large scale, interspersed with areas of desert. In the extreme south the land rises considerably to form the mountains of the central Sahara, where some peaks reach 3,500 metres in height.

Cyrenaica has a slightly different physical pattern. In the north, along the Mediterranean, there is an upland plateau that rises to 600 metres in two very narrow steps, each only a few miles wide. This gives a bold prominent coastline to much of Cyrenaica, and so there is a marked contrast with Tripolitania where the coast is low-lying, and in parts fringed by lagoons. The northern uplands of Cyrenaica are called the Jebel Akhdar (Green Mountain), and here, once again, are found the bulk of the population and the two main towns Benghazi and Derna. On its western side the Jebel Akhdar drops fairly steeply to the shores of the Gulf of Sirte; but on the east it falls more gradually, and is traceable as a series of ridges, only a few hundred feet in altitude, that extend as far as the Egyptian frontier. This eastern district, consisting of low ridges aligned parallel to the coast, is known as Marmarica, and its chief town is Tobruk.

South of the Jebel Akhdar the land falls in elevation, producing an extensive lowland, which except for its northern fringe, is mainly desert. Here and there occur a few oases—Aujila (or Ojila) Jalo, and Jaghbub in the north; and Jawf, Zighen, and Kufra (the largest of all) in the south. These oases support only a few thousand inhabitants and are of much less importance than those of the Fezzan. In the same region, and becoming more widespread towards the east, is the Sand Sea—an expanse of fine, mobile sand, easily lifted by the wind into dunes that can sometimes reach several hundred feet in height and over 100 miles in length. Finally, in the far south of Cyrenaica, lie the central Saharan mountains—the Tibesti Ranges, continuous with those to the south of the Fezzan.

The climate of Libya is characterised chiefly by its aridity and by its wide alternation of temperatures. Lacking mountain barriers, the country is open to influences both from the Sahara and from the Mediterranean Sea, and as a result there can be abrupt transitions from one kind of weather to another. In winter it can be fairly raw and cold in the north, with sleet and even light snow on the hills. In summer it is extremely hot in the Jefara of Tripolitania, reaching temperatures of 40°–45°C. In the southern deserts conditions are hotter still. Garian once (incorrectly) claimed the world record in temperature, but figures of over 49°C are known. Several feet of snow can also occur here in winter. Northern Cyrenaica has a markedly cooler summer of 27°–32°C, but with high air humidity near the coast. A special feature is the *ghibi*—a hot, very dry wind from the south that can raise temperatures in the north by 15°C or even 20°C in a few hours, sometimes giving figures of 20°C or 25°C in January. This sand-laden, dry wind may blow at any season of the year, but spring and autumn are the most usual seasons. Considerable damage is done to growing crops, and the effect even on human beings is often marked.

The hills of Tripolitania and Cyrenaica receive annually as much as 40 to 50 cm. of rainfall, but in the remainder of the country the amount is 20 cm. or less. A special difficulty is that once in every five or six years there is a pronounced drought, sometimes lasting for two successive seasons. Actual falls of rain can also be unreliable and erratic.

ECONOMIC LIFE

Such conditions impose severe restriction on all forms of economic activity. Although oil has been found in considerable quantities in Libya, physical and climatic conditions make exploitation difficult, and until the closing of the Suez Canal in 1967 the remote situation of the country, away from the currents of international trade, was a further handicap. But production of crude oil has increased rapidly and proximity to southern and central Europe presents a considerable advantage (no Suez dues) that can be reflected in the price charged for Libyan oil. The availability of oil revenues is transforming the economic situation of Libya. Plans for extensive development are being drawn up by foreign consultants, with the aim of improving housing, and the fostering of consumer goods industry. Roads, electricity, better water supplies and re-organized town planning are in process of being achieved.

In the better-watered areas of the Jafara, and to a smaller extent in northern Cyrenaica, there is cultivation of barley, wheat, olives, and Mediterranean fruit.

The Fezzan and the smaller oases in Cyrenaica are almost rainless, and cultivation depends entirely upon irrigation from wells. Millet is the chief crop, and there are several million date palms, which provide the bulk of the food. Small quantities of vegetables and fruit—figs, pomegranates, squashes, artichokes, and tubers—are produced from gardens. Along the northern coast, and especially on the lower slopes both of the Tripolitanian Jebel and the Jebel Akhdar, vines are widely grown, chiefly for wine-making. An edict imposing complete prohibition upon Libyan Muslims has, however, led to a restriction of production.

Over much of Libya pastoral nomadism, based on the rearing of sheep and goats, and some cattle and camels, is the only possible activity. In Cyrenaica nomads for long outnumbered the rest of the population, but in Tripolitania the main emphasis is on agriculture, though herding is still carried on. Within the last few years a number of industries have developed or are in prospect—refining, of course, plus some petrochemical activity—but overall the scale of industrial activity is still very small and, with notable exceptions, still on a local scale.

The original population of Libya seems to have been Berber in origin, i.e. connected with many of the present-day inhabitants of Morocco, Algeria, and Tunis. The establishment of Greek colonies from about 650 B.C. onwards seems to have had little ethnic effect on the population; but in the ninth and tenth centuries A.D. there were large-scale immigrations by Arabic-speaking tribes from the Najd of Arabia. This latter group, of relatively unmixed Mediterranean racial type, is now entirely dominant, ethnically speaking, especially in Cyrenaica, of which it has been said that no other part of the world (central Arabia alone excepted) is more thoroughly "Arab".

A few Berber elements do, however, survive, mainly in the south and west of Libya; whilst the long-continued traffic in Negro slaves (which came to an end in the 1940s) has left a visible influence on peoples more especially in the south but also to some extent in the north.

Arabic, brought in by the tenth century invaders, is now current as the one official language of Libya, but a few Berber-speaking villages remain.

HISTORY

Until very modern times, the history of Libya consisted basically of a series of local histories of small cities, and it is difficult to obtain a clear conspectus of the history of the country as a whole.

Where harbours and roadsteads existed in Libya, which had more or less fertile immediate hinterlands, and which were conveniently sited with respect to the northern ends of caravan routes trading from the interior of Africa, those peoples of the Mediterranean who from time to time were active as seamen and traders, established, or maintained, "emporia"—small city colonies. These conditions existed in Libya only at the west and the east ends of the bleak and forbidding Gulf of Sirte where the desert reaches to the sea and separates the modern provinces of Tripolitania and Cyrenaica by a vacuum 250 miles across.

Where there was desert, there was nothing; where the semi-desert lay, and around the distant oases of the interior, there were the nomads and the semi-nomads, whose way of life changed little throughout the centuries and in whose history the main event was their conversion to Islam. Intolerant of all external controls, they seem perpetually to have resented the civilizing influences from without which clung to the two extremities of the Mediterranean coastline around Sabratha, Tripoli, Leptis at the west end, and ancient Cyrene, Barca, Berenice (now Benghazi) and Derna at the east. When the coastal cities were in strong hands, their civilizing influence was pushed inland to the limits of cultivable land. When they were in weak hands, their influence stopped at their city gates, and the very sands of the desert invaded what under stronger rulers of the cities bore crops of corn, olives and grapes.

From the evidence of Herodotus, and also from that of modern archaeological research, it appears that in the earliest historical times two races inhabited Libya—the "Libyans" and the "Ethiopians"—the former, of Mediterranean stock, inhabited the coastal areas; the latter, of negroid and African stock, inhabited the interior. They used neolithic stone instruments. They knew how to cultivate. The Garamantes of the Fezzan raised cattle over a thousand years before Christ, when Phoenician sailors from the cities of Tyre and Sidon in Syria began to visit Libya to trade for gold and silver, ivory, apes, and peacocks. The perils of their voyages in little ships and the advantages of having emporia at or near the northern ends of the caravan routes led the Phoenicians eventually to establish permanent colonies on the coast, at Leptis, Uai'at (Tripoli) and Sabratha, where more or less safe roadsteads existed. Their most famous colony, Carthage, lay to the west of the boundary of what is now called Libya. But this city, in its maritime and commercial struggle with the ancient Greeks, extended its influence eastward and by 517 B.C. had incorporated the three cities into its Empire.

By this time the Greeks had colonized Cyrene (about 600 B.C.) and raised it to be a powerful city. The Carthaginians, sensitive to competition in Libya, not only drove off an attempt by the son of a Spartan King to found a colony near Leptis, but advanced to contact with Cyrene, where, some time about the beginning of the fourth century B.C., a firm frontier was established against the Cyrenaicans at the Mounds of Philainos, where Mussolini's "Marble Arch" now stands. Cyrene herself fell under the domination of Alexander the Great, and although he was never able to carry out his threat of marching against Carthage, Ptolemy I Soter, heir to Alexander's Egyptian conquests, conquered Cyrenaica for Egypt and extended his empire westwards as far as Sirte.

By about 250 B.C. Carthage was at the height of her power. Her monopolistic policy in commercial and foreign relations reduced the three "emporia" to political non-entity, although their agriculture flourished.

By this time the Romans had substituted themselves for the Greeks as the most powerful Europeans in the Mediterranean. During the struggle between Rome and Carthage which followed, the Tripolitanian half of Libya fell into the power of the Numidians under Massinissa, who allied himself with Rome. After the destruction of Carthage, the three emporia remained under nominal Numidian suzerainty, but in ever closer trading relationship with Italy, until Caesar's war against Pompey, when, after his victory at Thapsus over the Pompeians and their Numidian allies, Caesar created the Roman province of Africa Nova. Augustus set this province under a proconsul responsible to the Senate who also commanded the Legio III Augusta. Meanwhile Cyrenaica had passed under Roman sovereignty by the testament of the last of her Ptolemaic Kings—Ptolemy Apion—and was eventually created a province about 75 B.C.

The Pax Romana extended itself during the first century after Christ from the Mediterranean to the Fezzan. The second century was for Libya a period of prosperity, peace and civilization, the like of which she has never seen again. In particular under Septimius Severus, himself born in Leptis, and the successors of his family, the cities, and especially Leptis, attained the height of their splendour.

This condition did not last. Decline had set in by the middle of the fourth century. The general economic disease which was affecting Roman civilization affected also Africa. Christianity had challenged the spiritual values of the classical world but was itself too full of schisms to provide unity and strength. Libya itself was the scene of fierce internecine struggles caused by the Donatist heresy. Barbarians broke into the province, devastating the countryside, destroying its agricultural system, and spreading insecurity which caused depopulation through flight to the towns. In A.D. 431, Genseric and his Vandals appeared, overran the country, beat down the city walls, and brought ruin in their train. They were the first to introduce that piracy for which its harbours in a later age became notorious. A hundred years later the Emperor Justinian's general Belisarius found little difficulty in reconquering the country for the Byzantine Empire. There was a temporary revival of prosperity but continual rebellions by the Berber tribes soon reduced the country to anarchy.

THE MUSLIM PERIOD

In this condition the first Arab invaders found it. In the Caliphate of Omar, Amr ibn al-As, the conqueror of Egypt, overran the country as far as the Fezzan and Tripoli, the walls of which city he razed. This was in A.D. 643. There followed successive expeditions, mostly for booty, fiercely resisted by the Berbers, in the course of which Oqba ibn Nafi founded Qairawan (A.D. 670) and actually reached the Atlantic. The majority of the Berbers rapidly embraced Islam, but for the most part in its schismatic forms as Kharijites, Ibadites, and Shi'ites. An outlet for their turbulence was found in joining them with the Arabs in the invasion of Spain (A.D. 711).

Schism and continual rebellion induced the Caliph of Baghdad, Harun ar-Rashid, to appoint, in A.D. 800, Ibrahim ibn al-Aghlab as Governor with capital at Qairawan. He founded the Aghlabid dynasty, which became virtually independent of the Abbasid Caliph of Baghdad, but which brought little peace to Libya. A hundred years later a Shi'ite rising overthrew the Aghlabids and founded the Shi'ite Fatimid Dynasty, which from Tunisia conquered Egypt, transferred the seat of their Government to Cairo in A.D. 972, and made Bulukkin ibn Ziri Governor of Ifriqiya. He in turn set up a dynasty under which the land enjoyed considerable prosperity. But, at the beginning of the eleventh century, the Zirid Amir returned to orthodox Sunnism and acknowledged the sovereignty of the Caliph of Baghdad.

The Fatimid Caliph of Egypt, Al-Mustansir, reacted by sending against Libya two nomad Arab tribes which had been kept in Upper Egypt—the Banu Hilal and the Banu Suleim (A.D. 1049). This invasion was a final catastrophe for medieval Libya. The country was devastated, agriculture abandoned. The fortified cities, and in particular Tripoli, alone retained some vestiges of civilization. The next two centuries tell of little but intertribal wars, and the gradual fusion of the Arab and Berber races. Nor do the fourteenth and fifteenth centuries offer much more to record in "Ifriqiya". Murabit dynasts from Morocco contended with Muwahhid dynasts from the Balearic Islands. From these struggles emerged a dynasty in Tunisia called the Hafsids, whose power declined into a weak and anarchic state that attracted the attention of the new, crusading and imperialistic power of Christian Spain which could not overlook the fact that the cities of the northern coast of Africa had become dens of pirates.

Ferdinand the Catholic sent an expedition under Cardinal Ximenes and Don Pietro of Navarre which took Oran, Bugia, Algiers, and Tunis, and then, in 1510, Tripoli. These conquests produced a profound impression on the Muslim world, which at that time had become more united under the Ottoman Turks than it had been since the Abbasid Caliphs were at their zenith six hundred years earlier. The people outside the cities resisted the Spanish with Ottoman encouragement. Within the cities the Spanish were exposed to the dangers of conspiracy. Moreover they could make little effort to extend their power inland since, after the accession of the Emperor Charles V, Spain became heavily involved in European politics. The citizens of Tripoli intrigued unsuccessfully with the corsair Khair ad-Din, known as Barbarossa, who had made himself Lord of Algeria and had later become the Admiral of the Ottoman Sultan.

In these circumstances, the Emperor Charles V confided (A.D. 1530) the Lordship and the defence of Tripoli to the Knights Hospitallers of St. John (later to be known as the Knights of Malta) who had in A.D. 1522 lost Rhodes to the Ottoman Sultan, Suleyman the Magnificent. The Knights were able to maintain themselves there for only 21 years and then Sinan Pasha, who had been sent to reduce Malta but had failed in the attempt, invaded the town and forced the Knights to capitulate.

The Ottoman rulers of Constantinople now proceeded to organise their North African possessions into three Regencies—Algeria, Tunisia, and Tripoli, the last including also Cyrenaica and the Fezzan—each under a Pasha. But their organization contained from the first the germs of the disease to which it ultimately succumbed. The population of the interior was left almost unadministered. Tribute was levied and collected by a few regular troops, and by the "Maghzen" tribes from the remaining tribes, in return for the privilege of exemption from tithe and capitation tax. The system gave obvious opportunities for oppression and rebellion, and the division of the people into feudal lords and serfs. Worse still was the hardening of the professional soldiery of the garrisons, the Janissaries, of slave origin, into a military caste in which promotion was by seniority alone, and the retired officers of which had the right to a seat in the Pasha's Divan, or Council. The Janissaries became a power within the state. No less dangerous was the influence of the pirate captains—the corsairs. The Pashas subsidized them with arms and equipment and took their recognized share of their prizes. The Captains' Guild, called at-Ta'ifa, also became a power within the State. As early as A.D. 1595 the Divan was conceded by the Sultan the right of deciding foreign affairs and taxation. At the beginning of the seventeenth century the Janissaries introduced the custom of electing a "Dey" who sometimes reduced the Ottoman Pasha to a nonentity, sometimes shared with him the power, and sometimes was himself both Dey and Pasha. The history of the seventeenth and eighteenth centuries is one of intrigue, rebellion, sudden death, occasional outbreaks of pestilence, and of a country supported mainly by the depredations of the corsairs upon the merchant-fleets of Christian powers and the enslavement of their crews. In A.D. 1654 Admiral Blake was the first to bombard Tripoli in reprisal for such piracies. The great de Ruyter of Holland followed in 1669 and again in 1672.

In 1711 a local notable, Ahmed Karamanli, of Ottoman origin, and an officer of Janissaries, was proclaimed Dey. He succeeded not only in killing the former Dey and in defeating and killing the new Pasha sent from Constantinople, but also in persuading the Sultan Ahmed III to recognise him as Pasha. For the first time Libya had some sort of autonomous existence. The Karamanli dynasty lasted until 1835. Several of these rulers, and in particular the first and the last (Yusuf ibn Ali Karamanli, who was in power during the period of the Napoleonic wars) were men of strong personality, and capable statesmen who controlled the whole of Libya and improved the political and economic condition of the country. Like the former Pashas, they relied for much of their revenue on piracy. But the Karamanlis learned to make treaties with the maritime powers, bargaining with them to refrain from attacking their ships for a consideration, and for the most part restraining their Captains from breaking such treaties. When they failed to do so the powers would take strong action, as did the United States of America in 1805. The lesser powers naturally suffered most from the corsairs.

Such vast profits had the rulers of the Barbary coast made from piracy during the Napoleonic wars that the smaller powers made the abolition of piracy and of the enslavement of Christians points for discussion at the Congress of Vienna. England was entrusted with the suppression of these evils. It took ten years of naval and diplomatic action on the part of England and the Kingdom of the Two Sicilies to effect this. The suppression of piracy spelt the ruin of the Karamanlis. Yusuf Pasha fell into dire financial straits from which his expedients of adulterating the currency, of state trading, and of pledging in advance the already exorbitant taxes, so far from rescuing him served only to ruin both him and Libya. In 1830 French pressure compelled him to give up even the payments formerly exacted from Christian States for the right to maintain Consuls in Tripoli and for the right to unmolested navigation. In desperation, Yusuf demanded a special "aid" from both Jews and Muslims and this was the signal for revolt.

Probably through fear of the extension of French power in Algiers and Tunis, the Sultan decided to reoccupy Libya and to bring it once more under the direct rule of the Porte. This was in 1835. The rest of Libya's story in the nineteenth century is similar to that of most of the possessions of "The Sick Man of Europe"—corruption, oppression, revolts and their suppression—the towns alone being held by the Turks, with an occasional more energetic or more honest Governor. The period was, however, marked by the diffusion of Sanusi influence. The Sanusi were a religious brotherhood, founded by one Muhammad ibn Ali al Sanusi who settled in Cyrenaica on Jebel al Akhdar in 1834. From there the order spread, founding fraternities (*zawia*) throughout Libya and North Africa. In 1855 the Sanusi headquarters were transferred to Jaghbub to avoid opposition to the order of the Turks and, to some extent, Europeans. Al Sanusi was succeeded on his death in 1859 by his son Muhammad al Mahdi, who led the brotherhood until 1901.

ITALO-TURKISH CONFLICTS

On September 29th, 1911, Italy declared war on Turkey for causes more trivial than those which twenty-four years later led to her war with Ethiopia and her denunciation as an aggressor. After a short bombardment Italian troops landed at Tripoli on October 3rd. Italy knew the Turks to be involved in the Balkans, and knew, through her commercial infiltration of Libya, their weakness in Africa. But her attack on Libya was not the easy exercise she expected. The Turks withdrew inland. But the Libyans organized themselves and joined the Turks, to whom the Porte sent assistance in the form of arms and of two senior officers, Ali Fethi Bey and Enver Pasha. The presence in the Italian army of Eritrean troops was a spur to the pride of the Libyans. In October and November a number of actions were fought around Tripoli in which the Italians had little success. A seaborne Italian force then descended on Misurata and seized it, but could make no progress inland. At Ar-Rumeila they suffered a considerable reverse. Turkey, however, defeated in the Balkan War, was anxious for a peace, which was signed on October 18th, 1912. One of the conditions of this peace was that the Libyans should be allowed "administrative autonomy". This was never realized.

Peace with Turkey did not, however, mean peace in Libya for the Italians. Although most of the Tripolitanians submitted and were disarmed within two years, the Sanusiya of Cyrenaica under Sayyid Ahmad ash-Sharif, and their adherents in the Fezzan and Tripolitania, refused to yield. The Sanusiya maintained a forward post at Sirte under Sayyid Ahmad's brother, Sayyid Safi ad-Din as-Sanusi. What contact there was between this Sayyid and one Ramadan as-Sueihli of Misurata is obscure. Ramadan had been in the resistance to the Italians and two years later had appeared to be submissive. At all events, he found himself commanding Libyans in an action started by the Italians at Al-Qaradabia in 1914, to push back Sayyid Safi ad-Din. Ramadan and his Misuratis changed sides in this action to the discomfiture of the Italians. By the time that the First World War had started, the Italians held only the coast towns of Tripoli, Benghazi, Derna and Tobruk, and a few coast villages near Tripoli.

The First World War gave Turkey and her German allies the opportunity of fermenting trouble against Italy in Libya. Arms and munitions were sent by submarine. Nuri Pasha from Turkey and Abdurrahman Azzam (late Secretary-General of the Arab League) from Egypt joined Sayyid Ahmad ash-Sharif in Cyrenaica. Ramadan as-Sueihli became head of a government at Misurata. The Sultan, to prevent quarrels, sent as Amir Osman Fu'ad, grandson of Sultan Murad; and Ishaq Pasha as commander in chief in Tripolitania. The strategical objective of these efforts was to tie up Italian forces in Libya and British forces in the Western Desert. The climax of Nuri Pasha's efforts with the Sanusi was their disastrous action in the Western Desert against the British, as a result of which Sayyid Ahmad ash-Sharif handed over the leadership to Sayyid Muhammad Idris. He was compelled to make the treaty of az-Zawiatna with the British and the Italians who recognised him as Amir of the interior of Cyrenaica, provided he desisted from attacks on the coastal towns and on Egypt.

The end of the war in 1918 left Italy weak and the Libyans, deserted by the Turks, weary. The Tripolitanians attempted to form a republic with headquarters at Gharian and with Abdurrahman Azzam as adviser. The Italians made a truce with them at Suani ibn Adam, permitting a delegation to go to Rome and entertaining the idea of "administrative independence". Ramadan as-Sueihli visited Tripoli. In Cyrenaica, Sayyid Muhammad Idris as-Sanusi likewise attempted to come to terms. In 1921 at Sirte the Tripolitanian leaders agreed with him to join forces to obtain Libya's rights and to do homage to him as Amir of all Libya. Meanwhile the delegation to Rome had returned empty-handed and Ramadan as-Sueihli had been slain in a tribal fight.

ITALIAN COLONIZATION

The advent of the Fascists to power in Italy (1922) coincided with the appointment in Tripoli of a vigorous Governor, Count Volpi. Thereafter, it took them until 1925 to occupy and pacify the province of Tripolitania and disarm the population. In Cyrenaica, however, the famous Sayyid Omar al-Mukhtar, representing the Amir Muhammad Idris, whose health had broken down, kept up the struggle. The Italians realized that the only effective policy was to deprive the Sanusiya of their bases, the oases of the South. Jaghbub was occupied in 1925, Zella, Ojila and Jalo in 1927. In 1928 Marshal Badoglio was appointed Governor General and in 1929 he occupied Mizda in the Fezzan. Omar Mukhtar still resisted. The Italians removed into concentration camps at al-Aqeila the tribes of the Jebel Akhdar. In 1930 Graziani was appointed to Cyrenaica, and the famous barbed-wire fence was erected along the frontier of Egypt. Finally, in 1931, cut off from all support, Omar Mukhtar, now an aged man, was surrounded, wounded, captured, and hanged.

Starting in the early 1920s, the Italians proceeded to colonize, in the sense of that word which is now in disrepute, those parts of Libya which they had occupied, and which geographical and ecological conditions rendered profitable for development. They enlarged and embellished the coastal towns. They extended throughout the cultivable areas a most excellent network of roads. They bored wells. They planted trees, and stabilized sand-dunes. But their civilizing policy was weighted heavily in favour of their own race. The object was clearly the settlement in Africa of as much as possible of Italy's surplus peasant population. These were encouraged to come in large numbers. Skilled cultivators of olives, vines, tobacco, barley, they needed the best lands and were provided with them. The priority given to the progress of the Libyans was a low one. Primary education for the Libyans was encouraged and schools provided for them. But the main medium of instruction was Italian. Very few Libyans were accepted into Italian secondary schools.

INDEPENDENCE

There followed the Second World War, and the occupation in 1942 of Cyrenaica and Tripolitania by a British Military Administration and of the Fezzan by French Forces. Thereafter until 1950 the country was administered with the greatest economy on a care and maintenance basis. Its final fate was long in doubt, until the United Nations decreed its independence by 1952. On December 24th, 1951, Libya was declared an independent United Kingdom with a federal constitution under King Idris, the former Amir Muhammad Idris, hero of the resistance.

According to the Constitution promulgated in October 1951, the state of Libya was a federal monarchy ruled by King Muhammad Idris al-Mahdi al-Sanusi and his heirs, and divided into the three provinces of Tripolitania, Cyrenaica and the Fezzan. The Federal Government consisted of a bicameral legislature, i.e., a Chamber of Deputies, to which was responsible a Council of Ministers appointed by the King, and a Senate of 24 members, 8 for each province. The King had the right to nominate half the total number of Senators, to introduce and to veto legislation, and to dissolve the Lower House at his discretion. The Constitution also provided that Provincial Legislatures should be created for the subordinate provinces of the new realm.

On the attainment of full independence serious political financial and economic problems confronted Libya. Not the least of these was the task of fostering amongst the population a sense of national identity and unity. The loyalties of the people were still given to the village and the tribe, rather than to the new federal state. Poor communications and the great spaces of desert land, together with the lack of trained personnel and lingering provincial rivalries, were great obstacles to the establishment of a stable and efficient modern administration.

These rivalries revealed themselves in the next two years. The Party of Independence, which supported the constitution, won control in the February 1952 elections for the Federal Chamber of Deputies. The National Congress Party of Tripolitania, however, was opposed to the federal principle and advocated a unitary state with proportional representation (which would have given Tripolitania the main voice). Disorders arising from this disagreement led to the outlawing of the Tripolitania party and the deportation of its leader al-Sa'adawi. A Legislative Council for Tripolitania was formed in 1952 but had to be dissolved in 1954 because of continued friction with the Federal Government and the King.

About 80 per cent of the population of Libya was engaged in agriculture; but owing to the low rainfall, the hot desert winds and primitive farming methods, the average yield was small. There were no important mineral resources and only a few industries, most of them in Italian hands. Since 1945 exports had sufficed to meet only about 50 per cent of the cost of imports, most of which had been in the form of consumer goods needed to maintain the already low standards of life, and not of capital equipment and machinery. Income from foreign military establishments had been estimated as being 50 per cent above the total value of exports.

Efforts were undertaken, with Western technical aid, to increase the economic resources of Libya, e.g., to improve irrigation and initiate schemes for water catchments, to extend reafforestation, to teach better methods of farming, and to explore the possibilities of extending industries which could process local products and raw materials such as edible oils, fruits, vegetables, fish, etc.

FOREIGN RELATIONS IN THE 1950s

The first important development in the sphere of foreign relations was the admission of Libya to the Arab League in March 1953. The second development reflected the economic difficulties of the new state and its close links with Western Europe. In July 1953 Libya concluded a twenty-year treaty with Britain. In return for permission to maintain military bases in Libya, Britain undertook to grant the new state £1 million annually for economic development and a further annual sum of £2,750,000 to meet budgetary deficits. The financial obligations of the treaty were subject to review after five years.

In September 1954 a similar agreement was signed with the United States. A number of air bases were granted to the U.S. in return for economic aid amounting to $40 million over twenty years, which amount was later substantially increased. Libya also consolidated relations with France and Italy, signing a friendship pact with France in 1955 and a trade and financial agreement with Italy in 1956. In addition Libya was attempting to cement relations with her Arab neighbours. In May 1956 Libya concluded a trade and payments pact with Egypt, arranging the exchange of Libyan cattle for Egyptian foodstuffs.

The critical problem for Libya was to ensure that enough funds from abroad should be available to meet the normal expenses of the Government and to pay for much-needed improvements. At this time, her strategic position was all Libya had to sell, hence her involvement with the Western military alliance and in particular with Britain, France, Italy, Turkey and the United States. The

Libyan attitude to the Communist world was much more reserved.

Reliance on income from foreign military bases continued, therefore, to dominate foreign policy. In April 1958 the Prime Minister, Abd al Majid Kubar, who had taken office in May 1957 on the resignation of his predecessor, Mustafa ibn Halim, went to London to discuss the financial assistance that would be given to Libya during the five years 1958–63 under the terms of the Anglo-Libyan agreement signed in 1953. He announced to the Libyan Parliament in May 1958 that in the five-year period ending on April 1st, 1963, Great Britain would provide subsidies to the amount of £3,250,000 per annum, would make available light arms and equipment for 5,000 Libyan troops and would also continue the programme of free military training. He also stated that the British Government would no longer give £1 million per annum to the Libyan Development Agency, as it had done since 1953, and that the United States intended to contribute to the Agency $5.5 million during the next five years.

In September 1958 Libya became a member of the International Monetary Fund and of the International Bank for Reconstruction and Development. Official sources stated in May 1959 that Libya would henceforward receive financial aid from the United States, not through the various aid organizations of the United States, but directly from the United States Government. In June 1959 the U.S. Development Loan Fund made available to Libya $5 million for electric power generation and transmission facilities designed to serve Tripoli and the surrounding region.

In August 1960 the Libyan Government announced that the U.S.A. had agreed to pay $10 million per annum for the use of military bases in Libya. Aid was also obtained from Federal Germany at this time.

OIL DISCOVERIES

After 1955–56, when Libya granted concessions for oil exploration to several American companies, the search for oil resources became one of the main interests of the Libyan Government. By the end of 1959 some fifteen companies held oil concessions in Libya. An oilfield at Zelten in Cyrenaica was discovered in June 1959. Before the year was out, six productive wells had been found in Tripolitania, four in Cyrenaica and one in the Fezzan. By the beginning of July 1960 there were thirty-five oil wells in production, yielding altogether a little less than 93,000 barrels of oil per day. The development of the oil fields is dealt with in greater detail in the *Economic Survey* which follows this history.

In the month of August 1964 British Petroleum discovered large oil reserves in eastern Libya, not far from the Egyptian frontier, and stated that a pipeline would be built to Tobruk for the exploitation of this field. The Esso Libya corporation confirmed in November that it intended to construct a gas liquefaction plant at Mersa Brega. December 1964 witnessed the opening of a pipeline from the Hofra oilfield to a new loading terminal at Ras Lanuf on the Gulf of Sirte. Oil production showed a tremendous increase in the 1962–66 period, with exports rising from 8 million tons in 1962 to over 70 million in 1966.

A UNITARY REALM

A general election was held in Libya on January 17th, 1960. Most of the 55 seats were contested, but there was no party system in operation. The election was fought mainly on a personal basis. Secret ballotting, limited in earlier elections to the urban areas, was now extended to the rural districts. The Prime Minister, Abd al Majid Kubar, and the other members of his Cabinet retained their seats.

Libya's increasing wealth was making the business of government more complex and several changes of administration ensued between 1960 and 1963. Finally, in March 1963, a new cabinet under the premiership of Dr. Mohieddin Fekini was appointed.

Dr. Fekini stated in April 1963 that his government intended to introduce legislation designed to transform Libya from a federal into a unitary state—a change which would mean increased efficiency and considerable economies in administration. On April 15th the Prime Minister presented to the Chamber of Deputies a Bill which contained a number of important reforms: (1) the franchise was to be granted to women; (2) Libya would have (as before) a bicameral parliamentary system, but henceforward the King was to nominate all the 24 members of the Senate (heretofore half nominated and half elected); (3) the Kingdom of Libya would cease to be a federal state comprising three provinces (Tripolitania, Cyrenaica and Fezzan), becoming instead a unitary realm divided into ten administrative areas; (4) the administrative councils established in each of the three provinces were to be abolished, the exercise of executive power residing now in the Council of Ministers. Libya became a unitary state by royal proclamation on April 27th, 1963.

THE REALITY OF INDEPENDENCE

In the field of foreign relations, Libya was by now helped by the prospect of financial independence and was making her voice heard in international affairs, particularly in Africa. As a result of decisions taken at the Addis Ababa conference of African Heads of State in May 1963 Libya closed her air and sea ports to Portuguese and South African ships. The signing of pacts with Morocco (1962) and Algeria (1963) meant that Libya now had closer links with all the Maghreb countries. Libya was also showing signs of throwing off her dependence on the West. The 1955 agreement with France had allowed France to retain in Libya certain military facilities—notably in the field of communications—for the defence of her African territories. The future of this agreement was raised by Dr. Fekini in November 1963. He expressed the view that the recently acquired independence (1960) of Libya's southern neighbours, Niger and Chad, rendered the agreement obsolete and he thought that the whole matter should be considered anew.

The question of foreign military bases in Libya now came to the fore. On January 22nd, 1964, Dr. Fekini resigned his office of Prime Minister after student demonstrations at Benghazi and Tripoli. The new Prime Minister was Mahmud Muntasser, hitherto Minister of Justice. The Government issued a statement on February 23rd to the effect that it did not propose to renew or extend its military agreements with Great Britain and the United States and that it supported the other governments of the Arab world in the resistance to imperialism. Mr. Muntasser defined the aim of his government as the termination of the existing agreements with Great Britain and the United States and the fixing of a date for the evacuation of the bases in Libya. The Chamber of Deputies now passed a resolution calling for the achievement of this aim and providing that, if negotiations were unsuccessful, the Chamber would pass legislation to abrogate the treaties and close the bases.

The Anglo-Libyan treaty of 1953 was due to expire in 1973. Under the treaty Great Britain maintained a Royal

Air Force staging post near Tobruk, an Air Force detachment at Idris airport in Tripoli and Army District Headquarters at Tripoli and Benghazi. The American-Libyan agreement of 1954 was to expire in 1971. Near Tripoli was situated the largest American air-base outside the United States. Under the treaties Libya had received large amounts of financial, economic and military aid from the United States and from Great Britain. Libyan dependence on such aid had diminished, however, as a result of the swift development of the oil fields, which provided the state with increasing revenues. Great Britain withdrew the bulk of her forces in February and March 1966.

At elections for the Libyan Parliament held in October 1964 moderate candidates won most of the 103 seats. Women received the right to vote in this election. King Idris dissolved the Parliament, however, on February 13th, 1965, as the result of complaints about irregularities in the election procedure of October 1964.

The Prime Minister resigned, to be succeeded by Husayn Maziq, Minister for Foreign Affairs. A new election for Parliament was held on May 8th, 1965, over two hundred candidates contesting the 91 seats, 16 members being returned unopposed.

The outbreak of the six-day Arab-Israeli war in June 1967 was followed by serious disturbances in Tripoli and Benghazi, in which port and oil workers and students, inflamed by Egyptian propaganda, played a prominent part. The British and United States embassies were attacked and the Jewish minorities were subjected to violence and persecution which resulted in the greater part of them emigrating to Italy, Malta and elsewhere. The Prime Minister, Husayn Maziq, proved unable to control the situation and was dismissed by the King on June 28th. Firm measures by his successor, Abdul Qadir Badri, brought a return to order but the antagonisms he aroused forced him to resign in turn in October. He was succeeded as Prime Minister on October 28th by the Minister of Justice, Abdul Hamid Bakkush, a Tripoli lawyer.

An immediate result of the June war was a fall in the Libyan output of crude oil of about 80 per cent because of the boycott of oil supplies from Arab countries to Britain, the United States and Federal Germany. There was a gradual return to full production in the months following the conflict, however, and the ban on the export of oil was lifted in September. The closure of the Suez Canal brought about a considerable increase in Libya's oil exports and general prosperity, although the Libyan Government agreed to make annual aid payments totalling £30 million to the U.A.R. and Jordan to alleviate the consequences of the war. Libya's oil output increased by about 50 per cent in 1968 and the country became after only 7½ years the second largest producer in the Arab world with the great advantage, as a supplier to Europe, of being on the right side of the Suez Canal.

The new Prime Minister, Abdul Hamid Bakkush, was a progressive. His relatively young and well-educated administration immediately embarked on a programme of rapid change, seeking to modernize Libya's administration, reform the civil service and improve the educational system. He also sought to provide the armed forces with up-to-date equipment, and under a contract announced in April 1968 the purchase from a British firm of a surface-to-air missile defence system costing £100 million was arranged. An agreement to buy British heavy arms, notably the advanced Chieftain tanks, followed in spring 1969. In September 1968, however, Mr. Bakkush was replaced as premier by Wanis el Qaddafi, the pace of his reforms having apparently alienated some conservative elements. Both ministries enjoyed close relationships with the Western countries but played little part in Arab politics.

THE 1969 COUP

On September 1st, 1969, a military coup was staged in Tripoli whilst the King was in Turkey for medical treatment. Within a few days the new régime gained complete control of the entire country. The coup was remarkable for the absence of any opposition, relatively few arrests, virtually no fighting and no deaths at all being reported. A "Revolution Command Council" (RCC) took power and proclaimed the Libyan Arab Republic. The RCC initially remained anonymous but was soon revealed as a group of young army officers, the leader, Muammar Gaddafi, being only 27. The aged King refused to abdicate but accepted exile in Egypt when it became obvious that the revolution had been completely accepted by his people.

The provisional constitution announced in November stated that supreme power would remain in the hands of the RCC which appointed the cabinet; there was no mention of any future general election or of a National Assembly, and the royal ban on political parties continued. A largely civilian cabinet was appointed under close military supervision. The Ministers of Defence and of the Interior were accused of organizing an abortive counter-revolution in December, and were tried and sentenced in 1970. In January Col. Gaddafi himself became Prime Minister and several of his colleagues also joined the cabinet.

The principal force underlying the régime's policies was undoubtedly the professed one of Arab nationalism. Internally this led to the strict enforcement of the royal law requiring businesses operating in Libya to be controlled by Libyans—banks being particularly affected. The remaining British military establishment in Libya, requested to leave as soon as possible, was finally removed in March 1970, and the much larger U.S. presence at Wheelus Field followed suit in June. Most of the European and American managers, teachers, technicians and doctors were replaced by Arabs, mainly from Egypt. English translations disappeared from street signs, official stationery and publications, and most hoardings, the use of Arabic alone being permitted; similarly, the Islamic prohibitions on alcoholic drinks and certain Western clothes were officially revived. In July 1970 the property of all Jews and Italians still living in Libya—some 25,000 people—was sequestrated by the Government, and both communities were encouraged to leave without delay; some Jews were, however, offered compensation in government bonds. In the same month the three main oil marketing companies—Shell, Esso and an ENI subsidiary—had their distribution facilities nationalized.

Another anti-government plot was reported crushed in July 1970. In the autumn two ministers resigned and there were signs of a power struggle developing in the Revolutionary Command Council. The internal dissension apparently increased in the first part of 1970 over the proposed federation with the U.A.R., Syria and Sudan, and over President Gaddafi's promises of a constitution, and political institutions, including an elected president. A step towards introducing these was the announcement in June 1971 that an Arab Socialist Union was to be created as the state's sole party.

FOREIGN POLICY AFTER THE COUP

The new régime almost immediately received recognition—indeed acclaim—from the radical Arab countries and the U.S.S.R., and the rest of the world also granted recognition within a few days. As would be expected from the Arab nationalist inspiration behind the revolution, the monarchy's close ties with the Western powers were abandoned in favour of close relations with the Arab world and Egypt in particular; this friendship became the basis of an important triple alliance announced late in 1969, the Sudan being the third member. The alliance was intended to develop both politically—as a strong bulwark against Israel and the West—and economically, in that the economies of the three countries complemented each other to a considerable extent. However, when a federation agreement was signed in April 1971, it was Syria which became the third member. Libya also adopted a militant position on the Palestine question, and this created some diplomatic problems regarding arms contracts, particularly with Britain.

Although in July 1970 the Libyan Government followed Egypt in accepting the American proposals for a cease-fire with Israel, it continued its militant statements on the Middle East problem. President Gaddafi stated that a peaceful solution was impossible and rejected the UN Security Council resolution on which the Rogers initiative was based. During the fighting between Palestine guerrillas and the Jordanian army in September 1970, Libya redirected its financial aid from the Government to the guerrillas and broke off diplomatic relations with Hussein's government.

Nearer home, the coup appeared to have reorientated Libya away from the Maghreb; in the summer of 1970 Libya withdrew from the Maghreb Permanent Consultative Committee. Relations with Tunisia improved in the last half of 1970, after initial concern in Tunis in 1969 at the radical leanings of the new régime, and President Gaddafi headed a delegation which visited Tunisia in February 1971. Relations with Morocco were severed in July 1971 after the Libyan Government prematurely gave its support to an attempt to overthrow King Hassan, which failed within twenty-four hours.

There was little evidence of any closer relationship with the communist powers, although China was recognized in June 1971 and the U.S.S.R. was given due credit for its Middle East policies. But communism was regarded in Libya as a "foreign" ideology, antipathetic to more "progressive" Arab socialism (as in Sudan). Hence, in July 1971, Gaddafi was ready to help President Nimeri of Sudan to regain power after a coup led by communists had ousted him. A regular BOAC flight from London to Khartoum was forced down over Libya and two leaders of the coup, one of whom, Major al-Nur, was travelling back to become head of state, were taken from the plane and handed over to Sudan. They were almost immediately executed by the restored regime.

OIL POWER

In April 1971 the negotiations with the oil companies operating in Libya, which had begun soon after the 1969 coup, finally ended in a new five-year agreement raising the total posted price for Libyan crude to $3.447 per barrel. In the last stage of the negotiations, conducted in Tripoli, the Libyan Government also represented the interests of the Algerian, Iraqi and Saudi Arabian Governments. Threats of an embargo on the export of crude oil were used as a lever in the negotiations.

In ten years Libya's position had changed from one of penury and dependence to one of power based entirely on her ability to cut off oil supplies. The pronouncements of President Gaddafi were, therefore, by now of great moment to the West. In July 1971, the Deputy Prime Minister, Major Abd al Salam Jalloud, visited West Germany, France and Britain. Germany, which buys a particularly large proportion of its crude oil from Libya, needed to maintain good relations. France was anxious over the use to which Libya would put the Mirage jet fighters being supplied under the 1970 agreement. The same anxiety was revealed in Britain over the supply of armaments, but none of these countries could afford to alienate Libya.

In December 1971, avowedly in retaliation for Britain's failure to prevent the Iranian occupation of the Tumb islands in the Gulf, Libya nationalized the assets of British Petroleum. This began the process of nationalizing the foreign oil companies which is described in more detail in the Economic Survey.

Relations with Egypt and Syria were somewhat strained at the end of 1971, the cause of the friction being largely Gaddafi's uncompromising hard line on the Arab/Israel conflict. In October, President Sadat and Gaddafi met for talks on the problem and Gaddafi continued to press for all-out war.

Relations with Britain were also very much strained in the winter of 1971/72, not only because of the nationalization of BP but also because of Libyan intervention in the dispute with Malta over the British bases there. Libya had for some time been actively fostering relations with Malta, talks on possible Libyan aid being held in August 1971. In January 1972 the British naval training mission was ordered to leave Libya. And in February the 1954 agreement with the United States was abrogated.

Libya's attitude towards the Soviet Union had remained cool, and the Government was violently opposed to the Iraqi/Soviet treaty, signed in April 1972. Nevertheless, in February 1972, Major Jalloud visited Moscow and in March an agreement on oil co-operation was signed. It was also reported that the U.S.S.R. might supply arms to Libya.

At home, President Gaddafi continued to attempt to run the legislature and the Government entirely in accordance with Islamic principles. At the end of March 1972 the Arab Socialist Union held its first national congress. At subsequent sessions of the ASU resolutions were passed, clarifying its position and policies, and abolishing censorship of the Press, while at the same time maintaining financial control of newspapers.

In July 1972 disagreement within the RCC led to Maj. Jalloud taking over as Prime Minister from Gaddafi, a new cabinet being formed in which all but two of the ministers were civilians.

ARAB UNITY

A recurrent feature of President Gaddafi's foreign policy was the announcement of proposals for the union of Libya with neighbouring states, and their later collapse. The Tripoli Charter of December 1969 establishing a revolutionary alliance of Libya, Egypt (then the United Arab Republic) and Sudan was followed by gradual moves towards federation and the adhesion of Syria. Sudan withdrew, but in September 1971 referenda in Libya, Egypt and Syria approved the constitution of the Federation of Arab Republics, which officially came into existence on January 1st, 1972, but has had few practical consequences.

The Federation was not Gaddafi's only attempt to export his ideals by means of merger. At the time of Malta's dispute with Britain over the use of bases, in 1971, he proposed a union of Malta with Libya, but was rebuffed. In December 1972, in a speech in Tunis, he proposed the union of Libya and Tunisia, much to the surprise of his audience, not least President Bourguiba, who immediately rejected the idea, making some pointed remarks about Gaddafi's inexperience.

A merger of Libya and Egypt was agreed in principle in August 1972, but as the date when it should come into force approached, certain difficulties became apparent. Gaddafi, who had recently launched his Cultural Revolution of April 1973, was seen as a reactionary Islamic puritan in Egypt, and he was openly critical of Egyptian moral laxity. Some 40,000 Libyans attempted to stage a "march on Cairo" in July 1973, to bring pressure to bear on the Egyptian Government. The marchers destroyed an Egyptian border post, but were halted some 200 miles from Cairo. This incident served only to increase Egyptian suspicion of Libyan revolutionary enthusiasm, which was seen as unsuitable for Egypt's more advanced and cosmopolitan society. The union nevertheless came into effect on September 1st, 1973, with the establishment, on paper, of unified political leadership and economic policy and a constituent assembly. The union soon fell apart, wrecked by Gaddafi's opposition to Egypt's conduct of the October 1973 Arab-Israeli war.

President Gaddafi's attitude towards the Palestine problem had long been a source of discord between Libya and other Arab states. He gave financial support to the Palestinian guerrillas, and a number of Libyan volunteers were sent to assist them, Gaddafi's objective being the complete destruction of Israel. He was extremely critical of what he saw as the lack of total commitment to the Palestinian cause on the part of Egypt and Syria, and frequently expressed the opinion that the Arab states could not, and did not deserve to defeat Israel. He accused Egypt and Syria of being more interested in the recovery of territory lost in the 1967 war than in aiding the Palestinian resistance movement, which was being "destroyed by the Arabs in co-operation with Israel". Gaddafi was not informed of the Egyptian and Syrian plan to attack Israel in October 1973, was strongly critical of their battle plan, and refused to attend the Algiers meeting of Arab heads of state after the war, declaring that it would only ratify Arab capitulation. Libya was nevertheless an enthusiastic proponent of the use of the Arab oil embargo against countries considered to be pro-Israel. During the war, Libya's participation had been limited to the supply of arms and equipment, and its conclusion seemed only to complete Gaddafi's disillusionment with the union with Egypt.

Presidents Gaddafi and Bourguiba announced the union of Libya and Tunisia on January 12th, 1974, following two days of talks. A referendum to approve the decision was to be held on January 18th, but was almost immediately postponed. The decision had been taken in the absence of the Tunisian Prime Minister, Hedi Nouira. When he returned to Tunisia, the pro-merger foreign minister was dismissed, and Tunisia's attitude changed to one of indefinite deferment of the union. Gaddafi's impetuous action seemed to have produced a unified state, but Tunisia now treated the agreement as merely a declaration of principle, without any practical effect.

Gaddafi's enthusiasm for Arab unity continued unabated, but the failure of political mergers led him to propound a new course. His speeches attacked the Arab leaders who blocked unity and failed to "liberate" Palestine, and he spoke of Libyan aid for revolution and the achievement of Arab union by popular pressure on the governments of Tunisia, Egypt, Algeria and Morocco. Libya had for some time been providing money, arms and training for subversive or "liberation" organizations operating in Ireland, Eritrea, the Philippines, Rhodesia, Portuguese Guinea, Morocco and Chad, as well as providing aid for sympathetic countries such as Pakistan, Uganda, Zambia, Togo and, after May 1973, Chad. Now it appeared that Libya was supporting subversion in Egypt and Sudan. Attempted coups in Egypt in April and Sudan in May 1974 were believed to have had Libyan support, and relations between Libya and other Arab states became increasingly hostile. Gaddafi's failed mergers and his interference in the internal affairs of other countries were believed to have been major factors in his withdrawal from an active political role in April 1974, when it was seen that he had failed in his policy of exporting the ideals of the Libyan Cultural Revolution.

THE CULTURAL REVOLUTION

President Gaddafi's somewhat idiosyncratic political and social philosophy first obtained full expression in a speech in April 1973, when he called for the immediate launching of a "cultural revolution to destroy imported ideologies, whether they are eastern or western" and for the construction of a society based on the tenets of the Koran. The form which this revolution was to take was laid down in a five-point programme: "people's committees" would be set up to carry out the revolution, the "politically sick" would be purged, the revolutionary masses would be armed, a campaign would begin against bureaucracy and administrative abuses, and imported books which propagated Communism, atheism or capitalism would be burned. The people's committees set about their task of supervision of all aspects of social and economic life, criticizing and dismissing officials and business executives who failed to show the required revolutionary fervour, and offensive books and magazines were seized and destroyed.

In May 1973 Gaddafi presented his Third International Theory, "an alternative to capitalist materialism and communist atheism". In effect, it appeared to be a call for a return to Muslim fundamentalism, together with a rather confused combination of socialism and respect for private property, and much talk of tolerance and the rights of oppressed nationalities. Whilst the Cultural Revolution proceeded apace in Libya, Gaddafi seemed more concerned with foreign policy and his new-found role as revolutionary philosopher, who had put forward a universally applicable theory which would replace existing ideologies. Gaddafi concentrated on the formulation and propagation of his theory, and his erratic and unsuccessful attempts to export the Libyan revolution by merger or by subversion, while the mundane details of administration were increasingly left to Major Jalloud, the Prime Minister.

The return to the Koran and the rejection of external influences took several forms, some petty, such as the insistence upon the use of Arabic in foreigners' passports, some macabre, as in the revival of such features of Koranic law as the amputation of thieves' hands. The theory was also invoked in the disputes with foreign oil companies in 1973 (dealt with in detail in the Economic Survey), presented as an expression of Libyan independence. The revolution seemed to peter out as Gaddafi became more involved with foreign affairs, and it was rumoured that there was some discord within the RCC, some of whose members were dissatisfied with Gaddafi's eccentricities and the failure of his schemes for Arab union.

On April 5th, 1974 it was announced that Gaddafi, while remaining head of state and commander-in-chief, had been relieved of political, administrative and ceremonial duties, and was to devote himself to ideological and mass organization work. It appeared that, willingly or otherwise, Gaddafi had effectively been replaced by Prime Minister Jalloud. After a five-month withdrawal from active direction of the Government, Gaddafi re-emerged in the autumn of 1974 and it soon became apparent that he was more than ever in command. Relations with Egypt deteriorated after Gaddafi boycotted the Rabat summit of Arab Heads of State in October. Gaddafi was unhappy about the decision to recognize the PLO, under Yasser Arafat, as the sole legitimate representative of the Palestinians, and Gaddafi has subsequently shown his support for the "rejectionist front"—the wing of the Palestine guerrilla movement which rejects the idea of a possible settlement of the Arab-Israeli conflict under terms acceptable to Arafat and President Sadat.

The war of words with Egypt continued in 1975, with articles in the Libyan press containing bitter personal attacks on President Sadat and with the Egyptian press accusing Gaddafi of preparing to mount an invasion of Egypt. A delegation from the National Assembly of the Federation of Arab Republics, which visited Tripoli and Cairo in May, was able to bring about a temporary reconciliation, but at the end of May relations deteriorated again after reports that Libya was to allow the establishment of Soviet military bases on its territory in return for huge supplies of Soviet weapons. It later appeared that the arms deal did not include the establishment of Soviet military bases in Libya, and was in fact smaller than at first reported. Relations with Egypt, however, have remained strained, and Libya was very critical of Egypt's part in the signing of the second interim disengagement between Egypt and Israel in September 1975. Relations with Egypt did not improve in 1976 or 1977, and in July 1977 relations were so bad that, for a while, frontier clashes had all the appearances of open war.

Relations with Egypt were not improved when in November 1977 President Sadat of Egypt launched his peace initiative by visiting Israel. Gaddafi condemned Sadat's move and was a leading instigator of the Tripoli summit of "rejectionist" States who formed a "front of steadfastness and confrontation" against Israel in December 1977. Gaddafi remained strongly opposed to Sadat's peace initiative throughout 1978 and, following the signing of the Egyptian-Israeli treaty in March 1979, there were reports of Libyan troop movements along the Egyptian border. Gaddafi subsequently walked out of the Baghdad summit meeting of Arab States on the grounds that the sanctions contemplated against Egypt were insufficiently far-reaching. Relations with the U.S.A. came under recurrent strain during the first half of 1979, following threats by Gaddafi to cut off oil exports unless President Carter lifted a ban on sales to Libya of agricultural and electronic equipment and transport aircraft. At mid-1979 Libyan oil accounted for an estimated 600,000 of the 8 million barrels per day imported by the U.S.A.

For many years Libya had been supporting the FROLINAT rebels in Chad in their struggle against the Chad Government. In 1973 Libya occupied the mineral-rich Aozou strip, a region of 114,000 sq. km. in the north of Chad, basing its action on a territorial agreement made between Italy and Vichy France during the Second World War. Chad raised this grievance at the OAU conference in Gabon in July 1977, and a committee of reconciliation was set up but without results. In March 1978 the FROLINAT rebels were achieving such success against the Chad army that General Malloum (the President of Chad) was forced to appeal to Libya to arrest the progress of the rebels. A cease-fire was arranged at the end of March at reconciliation meetings held in Sebha and Benghazi in Libya. Sporadic fighting continued, however, amid allegations that certain factions of FROLINAT were still receiving substantial Libyan support. A series of military reverses brought down the Malloum government in March 1979 and, following an initiative by Nigeria, a ceasefire was signed at Kano by the four opposing Chadian factions. A coalition government dominated by former FROLINAT insurgents was formed, but by mid-April Gaddafi, although a signatory of the Kano agreement, had reportedly launched a new offensive from bases in the Aozou strip.

Gaddafi's cordial relations with Idi Amin led to Libyan military involvement in Uganda during March and April 1979. An estimated 1,500 troops, with air support, were sent to the aid of the Amin regime; heavy casualties were suffered and at the end of April, when the last of the Libyan forces were withdrawn, Gaddafi agreed to pay the new Ugandan government a ransom of $40 million for the release of Libyan army prisoners.

The termination of the British military presence in Malta in April 1979 was marked by the presence of Gaddafi at celebrations on the island. Promises of financial assistance were made to the Maltese, including the sale of oil at preferential rates, to make up for revenue lost from the closure of the British bases. Disagreements, however, later developed between the two governments over seabed oil rights. The direction of Gaddafi's foreign policy towards the establishment of a Libyan sphere of influence in Africa has created increasing unease among Libya's neighbours.

THE CREATION OF THE SOCIALIST PEOPLE'S LIBYAN ARAB JAMAHIRIYA

President Gaddafi's theories had, since 1973 when he presented his Third International Theory, shown a strong desire to foster people's assemblies at all levels of Libyan life. Under a decree promulgated by the ruling RCC in November 1975, provision was made for the creation of a 618-member General National Congress of the Arab Socialist Union (ASU), the country's only permitted political party. The Congress, which held its first session in January 1976, comprised members of the RCC, leaders of existing "people's congresses" and "popular committees", and trade unions and professional organizations. Subsquently the General National Congress of the ASU became the General People's Congress (GPC), which first met in November 1976. Gaddafi announced plans for radical constitutional changes and these were endorsed by the GPC in March 1977. The official name of the country was changed to The Socialist People's Libyan Arab Jamahiriya, and power was vested in the people through the GPC and the groups represented in it. The RCC disappeared and a General Secretariat of the GPC with Gaddafi as Secretary General, was established. The Council of Ministers was replaced by the General People's Committee, with 26 members, each a Secretary of a Department. In early March 1979 Gaddafi resigned from his post of Secretary General of the General Secretariat of the GPC to devote more time to "revolutionary work". The General Secretariat was reorganized, as was the General People's Committee, which was reduced to 21 members.

ECONOMIC SURVEY

Oil has transformed the Libyan economy. Before its discovery in commercial quantities in the 1950s, agriculture was the basis of the economy and domestic revenue covered only about half of the Government's ordinary and development expenditure. But between 1962 and 1968, national income increased from LD 131 million to LD 798 million and gross national product (G.N.P.) increased from LD 163 million to LD 909 million. Oil exports during the period increased by 835 per cent, accounting for 51 per cent of gross domestic product (G.D.P.) in 1968. Since then, the country's G.N.P., according to official estimates, rose to LD 3,534 million in 1974 before falling slightly to LD 3,497 million in 1975, when oil exports accounted for 46.3 per cent of G.D.P., and subsequently rising strongly with a recovery in the price and volume of oil exports.

In foreign trade over 99 per cent of recorded exports for every year since 1965 have consisted of crude petroleum, and a healthy trade surplus is being maintained. The merchandise trade surplus in 1977 was $5,170 million; the current account surplus in that year was $2,905 million.

Since the 1969 revolution, state intervention in the economy has increased, in line with Colonel Gaddafi's ideas of "Islamic socialism". The Government has at least a 51 per cent share in a number of sectors including banking and insurance, public transport, some sections of the construction industry and some manufacturing concerns. Apart, however, from the nationalization of distribution and marketing of oil in Libya in 1970, the Government refrained from directly taking over oil company assets until the dispute with BP in 1971.

Until the country's oil resources began to be exploited not more than 25 per cent of the population lived in the towns. This is no longer true, and the drift to the towns has caused a serious problem. Something like half of the non-urban population is settled in rural communities, and the other half are semi-nomads, who follow a pastoral mode of life. The majority of the population of Libya is Arab or Berber by race, with Negroid races predominating in the Fezzan (Southern Province). The estimated population in mid-1978 was 3,014,100, compared with 2,444,000 in mid-1975.

AGRICULTURE

Agriculture dominated the economy until the discovery of oil. Even now the oil industry gives direct employment to no more than a small fraction of the population and the present Government regards the agricultural sector as of the first importance. At present only a very small proportion of the total area of the country is cultivable and of this a high percentage is used for grazing in some regions. In mid-1970 all Italian-owned land and property in Libya, including 37,000 hectares of cultivated land, was confiscated and plans were made to distribute the expropriated lands to Libyan farmers, with government credits for seed, fertilizers and machinery. The area under irrigation is increasing and, according to 1976 figures, had reached 300,000 hectares. A number of very large contracts has been awarded for reclamation and irrigation work in various scheduled areas. The best-known schemes are the Kufra Oasis project to irrigate 10,000 hectares; the Tawurgha project to reclaim 3,000 hectares; the Sarir reclamation project; the Jebel el-Akhdar project; the Jefara plain project; and the Wadi Qattera reclamation project. The Wadi Jaref dam, one of the biggest in Libya, went into operation in 1976. In 1974 an allocation of LD 3.4 million was announced for six more agricultural projects, covering over 10,000 hectares. All projects are meant to be fully integrated, providing for the establishment of farms, the building of rural roads, irrigation and drainage facilities and, in some cases, the introduction of agro-industries. New ideas are: a scheme to turn unused oil tankers into water carriers to meet agricultural needs; and the construction of two refuse composting plants at Tripoli and Benghazi to produce fertilizer for desert areas.

After a successful year in 1972–73, as far as the implementation of investment projects was concerned, the Government decided to make a great effort in agriculture, allocating to it a sum of LD 700 million over the 10-year period 1973–83 and it is now the major sector in Libya's development plan. The Three-Year Plan, as revised in February 1975, provided LD 566.9 million for agricultural development and agrarian reform. The revised 1976–80 Development Plan provides LD 498 million plus LD 977 million for integral developments. Indeed, an important feature of Libya's economic planning is the relatively high priority which is being given to agriculture—an activity in which more than 50 per cent of the population is engaged. In 1975, agricultural development absorbed 21 per cent of total budget expenditure whilst in 1976 it had shot up to a corresponding 30 per cent. In the 1978 financial year, the agricultural sector was allocated 18.9 per cent of budgeted development expenditure and 14.6 per cent of overall budget spending. In most other oil-rich countries, agriculture hardly receives more than 10 per cent of development funds.

In spite of the money poured into the sector, however, results in terms of production were largely unsatisfactory, certainly up to 1973. Climatic and soil factors will, it is hoped, cease to play such a large part in fluctuations of output, once irrigation projects are under way and the distribution and use of fertilizers is well established. There have been signs in the production figures since 1973 that this is indeed happening; total foodstuffs production increased in each year from 1973 to 1976 when output, in aggregate, surpassed the previous record of 1970, and the Planning Secretariat announced that there had been considerable increases in the production of all major crops in 1978. The other problems, those of lack of trained technicians and administrators and poor education among the farming communities, are not so easily solved. Libya is obliged for the present to rely on foreign expertise.

Animal husbandry is the basis of farming in Libya and is likely to remain so until irrigation and reclamation measures really start to take effect. Sheep and goats are used for meat, milk and wool. Cattle, like the donkeys and camels, were used mainly for draught and transport but in recent years breeding for dairy produce has been expanded and milk production reached 61,000 tons in 1977. Livestock is being imported on an increasing scale from a number of sources. Breeding cattle have been supplied by the United Kingdom, and stock-raising co-operation agreements signed with Argentina, Romania and Australia. In 1974 contracts were awarded for fodder factories at Sebha, Zleiten and Zawia. Estimates of livestock numbers in 1977 showed a rise in the sheep, goat and cattle population as compared with 1970, but a drop in numbers of camels, reflecting the current emphasis on meat and dairy production.

Of the cereal crops, barley, which is the staple diet of most of the population, is by far the most important. Production of barley in 1977, at 200,000 metric tons, almost reached the 1973 record level of 204,000 metric tons, but wheat production (70,000 metric tons in 1977) was approximately half that of 1976, although the Planning Secretariat reported production of 98,000 tons in 1978.

Olives and citrus fruit are grown mainly in the west of the country, and other important food crops are tomatoes, almonds, castor beans, groundnuts and potatoes, also grown mainly in the west. Dates are produced in oases in the south and on the coastal belt. Esparto grass, which grows wild in the Jebel, is used for the manufacture of high quality paper and banknotes and was formerly Libya's most important article of export. The agricultural sector accounted for only 2.1 per cent of G.D.P. in 1976 and Libya still has to import over 80 per cent of its food requirements. The 1976–80 development plan envisages an annual growth of 15.8 per cent in domestic production so that Libya will be self-sufficient in vegetables and dairy products by 1980 and should also be able to produce 92 per cent of its fruit requirements and 75 per cent of its meat and wheat consumption.

The Government is continuing to further land development and reform. Polish assistance is being used to open up new farms in eastern Libya and in March 1978 the Government transferred the ownership of 1,011 farms formerly owned by politicians to farmers at a subsidized price.

An interesting new development, only possible in an oil-rich economy, is the development of hydroponic farming. A contract was signed with a U.S. firm in 1974 to develop a number of hydroponic farms. Similar experiments are being carried out in the Arabian Gulf states but it is doubtful whether such methods will be employed on a large scale in Libya, in view of the scope for reclamation.

Some attempts have been made by the Government at reafforestation, including a successful small-scale experiment in 1971 to stabilize the soil with a synthetic rubber spray and then plant eucalyptus saplings. Since then, a number of co-operation agreements signed with other countries have included schemes for dune stabilization.

The offshore waters abound in fish, especially tunny and sardines, but most of the fishing is done by Italians, Greeks or Maltese. The total catch amounted to an estimated 4,800 metric tons in 1975, an increase on the catch in each of the three preceding years, but well below the annual catch in the late 1960s. Of special importance are the sponge-beds along the wide continental shelf. These are exploited by foreign fishermen and divers, mainly Greeks from the Dodecanese.

OIL

That oil was present in both Tripolitania and Cyrenaica had long been suspected, and for several years after Libya became independent, a large number of the bigger oil companies carried out geological surveys of the country. In 1955 a petroleum law came into force setting up a petroleum commission, which was empowered to grant concessions on a fifty-fifty profit sharing basis, with parts of each concession being handed back to the Government after a given period. Under this law, concessions were granted to many American companies and to British, French and other foreign groups. By 1972 eleven groups, involving 21 companies, held concession rights.

Important oil strikes first began to be made in 1958, and ten years later Libya was already the fourth largest exporter in the world. The growth of the oil industry was particularly rapid after the closing of the Suez Canal in 1967, but it still employs only a relatively small proportion of the population.

Exports take place from five different ocean terminals connected to the various fields by pipelines built by the five groups which have made the major finds. The pipeline system and the terminals are, however, available to other groups. The first of the five terminals to be opened was that at Mersa Brega on the Gulf of Sirte, in 1961. The pipeline was built to Bir Zelten, some 200 miles south of Benghazi, where Esso Standard (Libya) had found oil in 1959. This group also operates a refinery at Mersa Brega and a gas liquefaction plant to prepare gas for shipment to Italy and Spain. The terminal for the Oasis group's Hofra field is at Ras el Sidr, to the west of Mersa Brega. The Mobil/Gelsenberg group also found oil near Hofra, but built another pipeline to Ras Lanuf, just east of Ras el Sidr. From a fourth terminal at Mersa el-Hariga, near Tobruk, a pipeline some 320 miles long runs to Sarir, then the BP/Bunker Hunt concession. The most recent terminal is at Zuetina, and was opened in 1968 to serve the Augila and Idris fields. Here an American company, Occidental, which did not even obtain its concession until early in 1966, had found oil in large quantities. The Amoseas group, which produces oil from the Nafoora field, not far from Augila, has a pipeline connected to the Ras Lanuf terminal.

In 1965 a law was passed bringing the arrangements under which the producing companies pay tax and royalties to the Libyan Government into line with those in force in the other Middle Eastern members of OPEC, which Libya joined in 1962. Hitherto the price used by the companies to calculate the profits on which tax was assessed had been the price they actually realized on world markets. The new law stipulated amongst other things that the price used should be the so-called posted price instead, which for many years had been much higher; this the operating companies eventually accepted. Negotiations began in the autumn of 1969 between the Government and the companies with the object of increasing the posted price, and came to fruition in April 1971 with the signing of the Tripoli agreements which raised the base posted price per barrel of 40° API crude to $3.07 with temporary adjustments bringing the total posted price per barrel to $3.447.

The agreement also included annual incremental price rises until 1975; settlement of company income tax rates at 55 per cent (except for Occidental Oil); an assured reinvestment in exploration, secondary recovery or gas projects; and a guaranteed supply of crude to the Libyan National Petroleum Corporation (LINOCO) sufficient for local consumption.

Further adjustments were made in May 1972, when agreement was reached in principle on an 8.49 per cent increase in posted prices to offset the realignment of world currencies in December 1971. Detailed agreements on this issue had been concluded by early June 1972 with all the oil companies in Libya except Mobil/Gelsenberg and Esso. Libya's disagreement with the latter stemmed from the Government's argument, not accepted by Esso, that the 8.49 per cent price increase should apply also to liquefied natural gas produced from the Brega plant. Esso is believed to have lost as much as $200 million on the Brega project due to building and technical difficulties and price quarrels with the Government. The plant cost $350 million and was completed in June 1970, but deliveries to Spain, the first customer, did not begin until March 1971, and to Italy until the summer of 1971.

A further agreement on a new formula for adjusting oil prices was signed between Libya and the oil companies in Geneva in June 1973.

The October 1973 war with Israel caused further upheavals in the price situation and Libya doubled the posted price of 40°API crude to $18.768 a barrel, effective from January 1st, 1974. In March 1974 a three-tier price system was proposed, giving preference to Islamic countries, followed by developing countries, with the industrial powers paying the highest prices. In April and May 1974 cuts in prices to contract customers, and in the buy-back prices to companies with participation agreements, were announced. Reductions were reported in September 1974 and again in January 1975, when Libya also announced 5 per cent royalty increases on equity crude lifted by companies, bringing the rate to 65 per cent, in line with OPEC policy. Further cuts were made in February and June 1975. Reports varied as to the exact amounts by which prices were reduced, but it was generally agreed that competition from the cheaper Gulf crudes, combined with a fall in demand, had occasioned the cuts. Demand is, however, partly seasonal and, moreover, Libya supports the general principle of higher world oil prices to meet inflation. Libya's policy of conserving its oil has also led to disputes with the companies. In October 1975 Occidental was ordered to reduce output to 210,000 b/d and a vigorous dispute ensued. It was finally settled in December 1975. Occidental was allowed an output of 300,000 b/d over three years with subsequent reductions.

Libya was a leader of those oil producers which demanded participation in oil company activities. In September 1972 it negotiated an agreement with ENI under which Libya received an immediate 50 per cent share in ENI's Libyan activities. ENI was induced to make this agreement by Libya's refusal to allow exports from Concession 100, the Italian company's first source of Libyan oil, and by the awarding of the Zawia refinery contract to an ENI subsidiary. Libya, for its part, reduced its initial demand, which was for a 51 per cent share.

Talks on participation began in earnest in January 1973. Agreements for 51 per cent participation were concluded with Occidental, Marathon, Continental and Amerada Hess, but the major oil companies, with interests elsewhere in the Arab world, proved recalcitrant, since any agreement concluded with Libya would inevitably affect those already made with, for example, the Arabian Gulf states. The result of a long round of negotiations was that the Government came to a 51 per cent share in the Libyan operations of Agip, Continental/Marathon/Amerada Hess, Exxon, Mobil and Occidental, while it has completely nationalized the holdings of Amoseas, BP/Bunker Hunt, Shell, Texaco, California Asiatic and Atlantic Richfield. Most outstanding claims by the companies were settled in 1977 following arbitration.

In fact, for some time the Government refrained from any general nationalization measures, apart from the takeover of distribution in 1970. But in December 1971 it took over BP's Libyan interests in retaliation for the British Government's failure to prevent the Iranian occupation of the Arabian Gulf islands of Abu Musa and the Tumbs. British Petroleum had operated the 400,000 barrels-a-day (b/d) Sarir field with Bunker Hunt and Libya set up the Arabian Gulf Exploration Company to operate BP's half of the field. Production dropped to a little over 200,000 b/d and BP warned that it would take legal action against any buyer of crude from AGEC. Meanwhile, talks with the other partner in the Sarir field, Bunker Hunt, dragged on until in June 1973 Libya nationalized the company's assets. Both BP and Bunker Hunt brought a number of actions against companies who bought Sarir crude after nationalization and the dispute lasted for many months. In 1974, however, following a compensation agreement between Shell and the Libyan Government, agreement was finally reached with BP and subsequently Bunker Hunt.

Following all the above upheavals production fell from 159.7 million metric tons in 1970 to 71.5 million metric tons in 1975. In 1976, however, output rose to 93.5 million tons under the influence of more reasonable prices and generally rising demand. This recovery in output countinued in 1977, when production rose to 100 million metric tons but output fell by 5 per cent in 1978 in response to competition from North Sea oil and generally depressed market conditions. In mid-1979 it seemed that Libya was ready to limit its oil production as a weapon to persuade the U.S.A. to allow delivery of transport aircraft.

At present the Oasis group (comprising Continental, Marathon and Amerada) is responsible for over one-third of total crude oil output, while the NOC—including the production from the fully nationalized fields at Sarir (formerly BP/Hunt) and Nafoora (formerly Amoseas)—accounts for only about 21 per cent of overall production. The NOC is looking to the Sarir field in particular for increased production, since it has rarely produced at more than half its rate since being nationalized. The Government would like to raise the field's output by 50 per cent to reach 50,000–60,000 b/d by 1980, but will need foreign help to do so.

The fact is that, although Libya is still committed to its stated goal of "gaining full control of the sources of oil wealth", it is agreeable for the time being to foreign oil companies continuing to explore for and market crude oil and to provide specialized services. Indeed, in present circumstances, Libya's interests on the oil front appear to be best served by co-operation with foreign companies. This is why the Libyan Government has not in general, followed a policy of complete nationalization.

Colonel Gaddafi is recently on record as saying that Libya would not hesitate to take full control of the oil industry "whenever we can manage our fields". In the meantime, however, Dr. Muntasser—Chairman of the NOC—considers present arrangements with foreign oil companies satisfactory and rules out the possibility of nationalization and the award of service contracts to the companies on the Venezuelan model.

A new phase in exploration involving much greater Government participation is now under way in Libya. In particular, the Government is keen to maintain an active exploration campaign to evaluate the oil potential of parts of the country outside the Sirtica Basin in north-central Libya, where the currently commercial fields are grouped. There are two main areas of interest—western Libya (formerly Tripolitania) and the offshore, with particular stress on the Tripolitanian offshore. Indeed, exploration interest in areas off the Tripolitanian coast has been stimulated in recent years by the discovery of a series of commercial oil and gas fields—Ashtart, Miskar and Isis—in the Gulf of Gabes in the neighbouring Tunisian offshore. In 1976, the NOC announced the discovery of potentially the largest oilfield in Libya, about 100 kilometres north of the port of Zuara. The find was made by a consortium comprising Aquitaine, Elf, Austria's OMV and Wintershall. According to Elf-Aquitaine anhydrous oil has been tested at the bottom of a productive formation nearly 2,300 metres below the seabed.

Exploration also continues in other parts of the country, with some work being undertaken in the largely unexplored south. New finds continue to be made in the Sirtica Basin, despite the intensive exploration of previous years. In 1976, Occidental brought the new Almas field into production and the Libyan Umm-al-Jawaby company also has two commercial finds, one on the eastern side of the Sirtica Basin and one on the west, which it hopes to bring into production.

On the marketing side, Libya has up to now tended to conclude agreements involving the exchange of crude oil for specific goods or services. Poland agreed to exchange oil for ships and machinery; a similar agreement was made with Yugoslavia to supply tankers; France signed a long-term agreement to barter technical assistance for oil; Italy is supplying industrial goods in return for oil; and, perhaps most controversial, co-operation agreements were signed in 1974 with the U.S.S.R. which provided for arms supplies and development assistance.

Libya, however, in common with other large oil producers, would much prefer to refine and process its own oil, rather than export it in its crude state. In this respect, the country is rather behind the older-established producers, having one refinery at Zawia, opened in September 1974 and now being expanded, with a present capacity of 120,000 b/d, and two other small privately-owned plants. Three more refineries are planned: for Zuetina (400,000 b/d); Misurata (220,000 b/d) and Tobruk (220,000 b/d). Contracts were awarded in 1975 for the Tobruk plant. Libya planned to have enough refining capacity to refine all its crude production by 1978, but the Government announced that these projects would be put back in 1976. Latest information is that the Tobruk refinery is not expected to come on stream before 1980 and the others not until 1985. However, the work involved in doubling (to 120,000 b/d) the throughput capacity of the NOC's existing refinery at Zawia (commissioned in September 1974) was completed in June 1977. Hitherto supplied by tanker with crude oil shipped from Marsa Brega, the refinery will eventually draw all of its materials from fields near the Algerian frontier through a new 400-km. pipeline (diameter 20 inches or 50 cm.) to be constructed by the Dutch company Protech International.

In the petro-chemical sphere, the NOC—together with an American company and a West German firm—has won contracts for the construction at Marsa Brega of a 1,000 tons per day ammonia plant, which opened in October 1977, a 1,000 tons per day methanol plant, which was due to open in 1978, and a 350 tons per day urea plant for completion in 1979. Sited near Exxon's liquefied natural gas (L.N.G.) plant, the new units will process natural gas and are expected to make Marsa Brega the country's foremost petrochemical centre. The programme for the improvement of port facilities at Marsa Brega is also approaching completion.

Significantly, the Libyans have shown no desire to take a share in Exxon's gas liquefaction and export projects which are now operating smoothly after years of financial and technical troubles. The technical difficulties at Marsa Brega's L.N.G. plant and at similar plants in neighbouring Algeria seem to have made a strong impression on the Libyan Government and Exxon is—for the time being at least—fully in charge of this highly skilled operation. The U.S.S.R. is to build a gas pipeline joining coastal centres to Brega and Misurata.

Libya is also investing in refining ventures abroad, notably the refinery at Koper in Yugoslavia and the Adriatic pipeline from Libya to Eastern Europe. Clauses covering refining and petrochemicals development are now being included in new exploration agreements.

Despite the fact that most of Libya's oil is carried in foreign tankers, and there are vessels lying idle, the tanker fleet has been enlarged in recent years with three tankers ordered from Japan, two from Yugoslavia and four from Sweden. In fact, Libya's Grand National Maritime Transport Company (GNMTC) has refused to take delivery of three of the Swedish vessels, which are 154,000 d.w.t. tankers, and has demanded repayment of almost $100 million in contract payments. The GNMTC argues that Sweden has violated Libya's regulations on boycotting Israel and that the tankers do not meet technical specifications. Libya rejected an international arbitration decision in April 1978 that it accept delivery of the tankers, which have been ready since late 1976 according to the Swedish builders, Gotaverken.

INDUSTRY

Manufacturing in Libya has been largely confined to the processing of local agricultural products and such traditional crafts as carpet weaving, tanning and leather working and shoe making. Plans were made several years ago for a whole range of factories to make such diverse articles as prefabricated construction materials, cables, glass, pharmaceuticals, woollen and synthetic textiles, among others. Most of these factories did not get past the tendering stage, but the Government is now settling down to getting Libyan development going again.

Contracts for industrial plant have in the past been awarded mainly to Western European and U.S. companies, but Japanese firms are becoming more active in Libya and links with Eastern Europe, particularly Yugoslavia are much closer. At the beginning of 1975 a joint venture agreement to manufacture carbon paper was signed with a Japanese firm and an aluminium plant is planned with Yugoslavian participation. Libya's first ready-made clothing factory at Derna, and a new tannery at Tajura, were opened in 1974. Other manufacturing projects planned are: a canning factory for Zawia; a tyre factory at Tajura; a hypodermic syringe plant; a soap factory, and a glass factory for Tripoli. President Gaddafi also said in January 1975 that Libya had plans for the establishment of a heavy industry sector involving vehicle and tractor assembly plants, shipbuilding and iron and steel works. A French firm won a contract in 1976 for the construction of two organic fertilizer plants at Tripoli and Benghazi. An Italian firm in 1977 won a contract for setting up a steel frame factory in Libya which will have an annual capacity of 35,000 tons. Also in 1977, a German company was awarded a $35 million contract to build a blanket factory, plans were announced for a joint venture with the United Kingdom to establish an electrical equipment plant, and an Italian company was awarded a contract to build refrigeration plants in Libya. Modest plans are under way to improve tourist facilities.

Notwithstanding its support for these smaller projects, the Government is giving more attention, and resources, to a few major ventures in heavy industry and in infrastructure development.

Iron ore reserves estimated at over 700 million tons were discovered in 1974 at Wadi Shatti, in southern Libya and plans for their exploitation are under way. A steelworks is to be constructed at Misurata for completion in 1985 at a cost of some $1,000 million. There are plans for Yugoslav agencies to build an aluminium plant at Zawara, at a cost of $900 million, with technical assistance from Japan; a chemical complex is being built by the West German company Salzgitter at Abu Kammesh and a Belgian company, Tractionel, has prepared feasibility studies for a $300 million industrial complex at Murada.

The construction work now being carried out under the development programme has given rise to a rapidly increasing demand for cement, which is imported in large quantities. The existing cement plant at Homs is being expanded and two more are being built at Souk el-Khemis and Derna, with others planned. A new Benghazi cement factory was opened in August 1978. A completely new $150 million plant is being built at Homs by a French firm, and was due to go into operation in 1979. It is hoped that production will reach 4 million tons per year once all the plants are fully operational.

Infrastructure expenditure has put great emphasis on power generation. Since 1974 the Government has awarded several large contracts for power stations, some in association with desalination plants, and it is planned that national generating capacity will be raised to 4,000 MW by 1980, with some use of nuclear power.

As might be expected, the large and increasing volume of imports has led to severe congestion at the main ports of Tripoli and Benghazi, and Libya has an agreement with Tunisia to use facilities at Gabes and Sfax to relieve the situation. In addition, Derna and Misurata ports are being reconstructed. Both Tripoli and Benghazi are undergoing large-scale expansion, the Tripoli project being, in fact, one of the larger projects in the 1976–80 Plan, involving an investment of LD 125 million. Port expansion is necessarily a long-term process and the development of rail, road and to some extent air freight is very important. There is an extensive road-building programme, and a number of large road-building contracts, such as the Sebha-Waddan road and the Mirzuk link, have gone to Egyptian companies. A Turkish company is to build a road between Kusbat and Tarunah at a cost of $14.5 million. The road—a 12 metre wide, asphalt-surfaced dual carriageway—will take two years to construct, with work starting in 1977.

The telecommunications network is constantly being expanded; a new company was set up in 1976 to oversee all telecommunications contracts and imports of equipment. The first major contract awarded to a Japanese firm in Libya went to Nippon Electric for the installation of a microwave network. A number of contracts were awarded for telecommunications development in 1977; they included contracts with Nippon Electric, the United Kingdom Post Office Consultancy Services and Marconi U.K. In March 1978 Plessey Telecommunications of the United

Kingdom was awarded a $9 million contract to supply electronic automatic branch exchanges for Libya's National Telecommunications Company.

The estimated cost of the new international airport at Benghazi, on which construction work began in 1977, has risen to roughly $200 million; the airport is scheduled for completion in 1980. The contract for a new airport at Ghat went to an Indian company in 1976. The new Tripoli International Airport was opened in August 1978.

EXTERNAL TRADE

Until production of oil began, Libya's exports consisted almost entirely of agricultural products, and its imports of manufactured goods. In 1960, for instance, imports were valued at LD 60.4 million and exports at LD 4.0 million, leaving an adverse balance of LD 56.4 million (although LD 21 million of the total value of imports in 1960 was accounted for by goods imported for the account of the oil companies). Oil was first exported in the autumn of 1961, and by 1969, according to IMF data, imports totalled LD 241.3 million and exports LD 937.9 million, of which LD 936.5 million (or almost 100 per cent) was officially accounted for by crude petroleum. Oil exports in 1974 were worth LD 2,109.5 million (74 million tons), compared with LD 1,031.7 million (105 million tons) in 1973. In 1975 the value of oil exports fell to LD 1,786.8 million but there was a significant rise to LD 2,456.7 million in 1976 and to LD 2,886.1 million in 1977, when total recorded exports were worth LD 2,889.7 million. Oil exports in 1978 fell to LD 2,809.6 million, while total recorded exports were worth LD 2,813.3 million. The minute proportion of remaining exports were mainly hides and skins, groundnuts, almonds, metal scrap and re-exports.

Imports now consist of a wide variety of manufactured goods, such as textiles, motor vehicles and luxury consumer goods. In the last few years imports of timber, chemicals and raw materials and, in particular, cement and building materials, have been stepped up. In addition, many foodstuffs have to be imported, for example tea, sugar, coffee and, in years of drought, wheat and flour. The value of imports almost quadrupled between 1972 and 1977, rising from LD 343.2 million to LD 1,119.7 million.

Since oil has been exported, Libya has experienced a considerable trade surplus. In 1971, exports f.o.b. were valued at LD 1,010.1 million and imports c.i.f. at LD 250.4 million, leaving a trade surplus of LD 759.7 million. In 1977, the trade surplus, measured on the same basis, was LD 1,770.0 million.

In 1976 Libya's principal supplier was Italy, with 25 per cent of total imports. West Germany supplied 16.8 per cent, France 9.9 per cent, Japan 6.7 per cent and the United Kingdom 5 per cent of total imports. Eastern Bloc countries are likely to take a larger share of the market as more trade and co-operation agreements are signed. In 1976, for example, Libya signed a trade and co-operation agreement with Yugoslavia. Yugoslav firms have won a number of large contracts in Libya and exports to Libya rose by over 60 per cent between 1973 and 1974. A similar agreement has been signed with India, whose exports to Libya have risen by much the same percentage. Libya also has an agreement with the Soviet Union, which has agreed to supply arms.

Libya's best oil customers in 1975 were the United Kingdom, France, West Germany, Italy and the U.S.A. Sales to Italy were stimulated by the ENI settlement and to the U.S.A. by the much-publicized American fuel crisis. The events of 1973, and the embargo on sales to America (since lifted) and the Netherlands, altered the pattern somewhat, with sales to the U.S.A. later increasing rapidly. In 1977 the U.S.A. took 25 per cent of Libya's oil exports. The U.S.A. and Western Europe together accounted for almost 90 per cent of total oil exports from Libya.

FINANCE

Before the 1969 coup most Libyan banks were subsidiaries of foreign banks. However, amongst the first decrees issued by the Revolutionary Council was one which required 51 per cent of the capital of all banks operating in Libya to be owned by Libyans; the majority of directors, including the chairman, of each bank had to be Libyan citizens. The royal Government had followed a similar policy without compulsion, and a number of foreign banks had accordingly already "Libyanized" themselves. In December 1970, all commercial banks were nationalized, with government participation set at 51 per cent. There are now only six commercial banks in the country including one formed at the same time by the amalgamation of the former commercial section of the central bank with two small Libyan banks.

The development of the oil industry has enabled Libya to maintain a high degree of stability in the external value of its currency. Indeed, the Libyan currency has maintained its dollar parity of $3.378 (or LD 0.296 per U.S. dollar) since it was established after the February 1973 U.S. dollar devaluation. The fact is that the Libyan authorities do not consider the country's exchange rate as an instrument of domestic economic policy which can be employed to counteract inflationary pressures. The dollar's weakness during 1974 and again in early 1977 undoubtedly has raised the cost of imported goods when converted into dinars at the official rate of exchange; but in respect of important items, such as food, the Government has tended to prefer introducing subsidies in order to dampen the impact of increased costs on local consumers. Since subsidies can be applied to specific goods, whereas a change in the exchange rate necessarily affects all commodities, the authorities have felt that relying on subsidies would be more equitable as well as simple. Further, the authorities have felt that pursuance of a neutral exchange rate policy made economic sense in endeavouring to diversify the country's export industries away from almost total reliance on foreign sales of crude petroleum to include exports of refined products, plastics, fertilizers and many other goods. Clearly, had the Libyan currency been allowed to appreciate against the dollar and other major currencies, this would have adversely affected prospects for domestic industries in international markets.

Until December 1971 Libya was a member of the Sterling Area, but the nationalization of BP and the withdrawal of deposits of £200 million from British banks resulted in her expulsion.

The massive growth in oil revenue has also allowed the Government to devote about half its income to development expenditure. It has even been able to give generous aid abroad, in particular to the Yemen P.D.R., Egypt, Syria and Jordan, although the Government is somewhat capricious in implementing aid agreements. Aid was cut off from the Jordanian Government in September 1970 when it attacked the Palestinian guerrillas. Egypt was criticized over its conduct of the war with Israel and in 1974 Libya demanded the return of a loan to the Sudan. Future aid to Egypt is suspended as a result of Egypt's signing the peace treaty with Israel in March 1979. There is no comparable organization in Libya to the Kuwait Fund for Arab Economic Development, but in 1974 Libya made a contribution to the Islamic Development Bank.

Recent developments in the Libyan banking sector include the establishment of joint development banks with Algeria and Turkey and an agreement to establish a joint Libyan-Mali bank. In March 1977 the Libyan Arab Foreign Bank (LAFB) took up a 9.6 per cent stake in the equity of Fiat, the Italian motor car company. The deal is backed by a loan to Fiat from the LAFB of $105 million repayable over ten years (with two years grace). Until this purchase the LAFB had pursued a cautious and selective policy of putting Libyan capital into banking, hotel and tourism in many countries, as well as joint-stock ventures in agriculture, fishing and forestry projects in some African countries. Whilst Libya does not envisage any immediate new purchases into Western manufacturing, it seems clear that the Libyans regard the Fiat purchase as the vanguard of Libyan investment into industrial countries' manufacturing base.

Although Libya enjoys a substantial trade surplus, it also experiences a substantial deficit on "invisibles" (services and transfer payments). This "invisible" deficit increased from $1,450 million in 1973 to $2,265 million in 1977. In most years it partly offsets the trade surplus, leaving a fluctuating surplus on current account, but in 1975 (when the trade surplus was reduced) the current account was pushed into deficit. Aid payments and arms purchases tend to bring about a substantial outflow on capital account—so that Libya's basic balance of payments often yields a deficit. International reserves totalled $4,216 million at December 31st, 1978, compared with $2,127 million at the end of 1973.

At the end of April 1972 the Government published a one-year development budget to cover the period ending March 31st, 1973, and a three-year development budget to end on March 31st, 1975. The one-year budget involved total spending of LD 367 million, a record figure (the 1970–71 budget totalled LD 300 million), and the three-year programme called for expenditure of LD 1,165 million. Despite the fact that many of the allocations in the 1972–73 budget were not spent (in some sectors probably less than half the funds available were utilized), the Government was sufficiently encouraged by its experience to revise the three-year plan dramatically. In the spring of 1973 the three-year budget was amended to provide for a LD 800 million increase in spending to bring the three-year total to LD 1,965 million, with increased emphasis placed on agriculture. A further increase in total spending, to LD 2,115 million, was approved in 1974. In February 1975 the allocations were revised yet again to give total expenditure of LD 2,571 million, with even more emphasis on agriculture. Power, transport, housing and education all received increased allocations, reflecting mainly the continued upsurge in construction activity and prestige projects such as the universities of Benghazi and Tripoli. Actual average growth during the Three-Year Plan is estimated at 23.5 per cent overall but varies between sectors.

The latest Development Plan, drawn up for the period 1976–80, involves a total investment of LD 9,250 million, with priority again given to agriculture, although industrial and communications sectors also receive large allocations. The Plan aims at an annual increase of 10.5 per cent in G.N.P. and a 26 per cent rise in industrial production. Industry received an allocation of LD 1,205 million, transport and communications LD 930 million and oil and gas exploitation LD 670 million. Housing allocations were LD 1,131 million.

STATISTICAL SURVEY

AREA AND POPULATION

AREA (sq. km.)	POPULATION	
	1964 Census	1973 Census
1,759,540	1,564,369	2,290,734

Estimated Population: 3,014,100 (June 30th, 1978)

POPULATION BY DISTRICT
(1973 Census)

District	Population	District	Population
Tripoli	735,083	Gharian	155,958
Benghazi	337,423	Jebel Akhdar	131,940
Zawia (Zavia)	247,628	Derna	122,984
Misurata	177,939	Sebha	113,006
Khoms	162,126	Kalig	106,647

PRINCIPAL TOWNS
(1973 census)

Town	Population	Town	Population
Tripoli (capital)	551,477	Zawia	72,207
Benghazi	140,000	Gharian	65,439
Misurata	103,302	Tubruq (Tobruk)	58,869
Homs-Cussabat	88,695		

AGRICULTURE

LAND USE, 1976
(FAO estimates, '000 hectares)

Arable land	2,400
Land under permanent crops	144
Permanent meadows and pastures	6,780
Forests and woodlands	534
Other land	166,096
Total	175,954

PRINCIPAL CROPS
(FAO estimates, '000 metric tons)

	1975	1976	1977
Barley	192	196	200
Wheat	75	133	70
Olives	95	95	100
Citrus fruits	27	28	28
Groundnuts	14	14	15
Almonds	5.2	5.4	5.6
Tomatoes	180	192	204
Dates	65	67	70
Potatoes	80	80	80
Grapes	12	12	12

LIVESTOCK
(FAO estimates, '000 head)

	1975	1976	1977
Horses	15	15	15
Asses	73	73	73
Cattle	151	152	152
Camels	60	60	60
Sheep	2,900	2,950	3,000
Goats	1,170	1,200	1,250
Poultry	5,000	5,100	5,200

Source: FAO, *Production Yearbook.*

LIVESTOCK PRODUCTS
(FAO estimates, '000 metric tons)

	1975	1976	1977
Beef and veal	9	9	10
Mutton and lamb	35	36	37
Goats' meat	7	7	7
Poultry meat	6	6	6
Other meat	5	6	7
Cows' milk	15	15	16
Sheep's milk	29	30	31
Goats' milk	14	14	14
Hen eggs	3.1	3.2	3.3
Wool: greasy	4.8	5.1	5.2
clean	1.3	1.4	1.4
Sheep skins	7.7	7.8	8.0
Goat skins	1.7	1.8	1.8

Source: FAO, *Production Yearbook.*

FORESTRY

ROUNDWOOD REMOVALS

('000 cubic metres, all non-coniferous)

	1970	1971	1972	1973	1974	1975	1976	1977*
Industrial wood	36	44	34	70	62	39	43	44
Fuel wood*	400	416	434	452	470	488	504	520
TOTAL	436	460	468	522	532	527	547	564

* FAO estimate.

1976: Production as in 1975 (FAO estimates).

Source: FAO, *Yearbook of Forest Products.*

SEA FISHING

('000 metric tons)

	1968	1969	1970	1971	1972	1973	1974	1975
Total catch	5.5	11.3	5.5	5.7	2.4	2.9	3.8	4.8*

* FAO estimate.

1976–77: Annual catch as in 1975 (FAO estimates).

Source: FAO, *Yearbook of Fishery Statistics.*

MINING

		1972	1973	1974	1975	1976	1977
Crude petroleum	'000 metric tons	107,478	104,882	73,364	71,533	93,460	100,040
Natural gas*	million cu. metres	2,536	3,071	2,710	3,368	3,808	n.a.

* Estimated production.

INDUSTRY

(Value of Output in LD'000—Large establishments only)

	1972	1973	1974
Food manufacturing	11,072	12,823	20,806
Beverage industries	3,218	4,265	5,301
Tobacco manufactures	13,585	17,077	21,146
Chemicals and products	5,086	7,294	10,535
Textiles	1,795	2,004	2,400
Cement and products	4,718	5,701	11,752
Fabricated metal products	2,363	3,487	4,096
TOTAL (incl. others)	45,837	58,799	84,978

FINANCE

1,000 dirhams=1 Libyan dinar (LD).
Coins: 1, 5, 10, 20, 50 and 100 dirhams.
Notes: 250 and 500 dirhams; 1, 5 and 10 dinars.
Exchange rates (June 1979): £1 sterling=612.47 dirhams; U.S. $1=296.05 dirhams;
100 Libyan dinars=£163.27=$337.78.

Note: The dinar is equivalent to the former Libyan pound (of 1,000 millièmes), which it replaced in September 1971. The Libyan pound had been introduced in March 1952, with a value of U.S. $2.80 ($1=357.14 millièmes). This valuation remained in effect until August 1971. Between December 1971 and February 1973 the new Libyan dinar (replacing the pound was worth $3.04 ($1=328.95 dirhams). The present dollar valuation became effective in February 1973. The Libyan pound was at par with the pound sterling until November 1967, after which the exchange rate was £1 sterling=857.14 millièmes or dirhams (Lib£1 or 1 dinar=£1.167 sterling) until June 1972.

ADMINISTRATIVE BUDGET EXPENDITURE 1976
(LD million)

Interior and police	42.0	Industry and mineral wealth	3.0
Foreign affairs	11.5	Oil	0.9
Education	151.1	Support of state corporations	31.3
Health	62.0	Miscellaneous	22.8
Communications authorities	16.3	Local administration	23.5
Social affairs and social insurance	7.5	Armed forces	72.0
Housing	7.0		
Agriculture and agrarian reform	14.5	TOTAL (incl. others)	500.0

1978: LD 695 million budgeted, LD 741 million actual.

1976–80 DEVELOPMENT PLAN AND EXPENDITURE FOR 1978
(LD '000)

	Original Allocations 1976–80	Revised Allocations 1976–80	Revised Allocations 1978
Agriculture and agrarian reform	412,269	498,000	109,000
Integral agricultural development	857,760	977,660	227,600
Dams and water resources	80,040	139,115	26,000
Nutrition and marine wealth	49,161	63,673	157,500
Industry and mineral wealth	1,149,418	1,204,980	221,500
Oil and gas exploitation	670,000	670,000	90,000
Electricity	683,195	896,825	170,000
Education	491,655	521,820	122,000
Information and culture	99,168	121,925	24,500
Manpower	56,002	62,712	13,000
Public health	197,655	273,640	62,700
Social affairs and social insurance	13,157	33,757	62,500
Youth and sports	52,020	62,000	16,000
Housing	794,236	1,131,040	211,000
Security services	35,000	60,000	13,500
Municipalities	565,108	755,729	170,000
Transport and communications	659,854	929,798	144,200
Marine transport	353,500	373,500	60,000
Trade and marketing	36,730	44,740	65,000
Planning and scientific research	13,045	16,800	35,000
Reserve for projects	230,027	409,586	72,000
TOTAL (incl. others)	7,525,000	9,250,000	1,785,000

Source: The Guardian, September 1st, 1978

CENTRAL BANK RESERVES
(U.S. $ million at December 31st)

	1976	1977	1978
Gold	99	104	112
Reserve position in IMF	7	7	8
Foreign exchange	3,099	4,779	4,097
TOTAL	3,206	4,891	4,216

Source: IMF, *International Financial Statistics.*

MONEY SUPPLY
(LD million at December 31st)

	1975	1976	1977
Currency outside banks	346.0	436.0	585.0
Private sector deposits at Central Bank	185.8	210.5	265.9
Demand deposits at commercial banks	335.7	492.9	425.1
TOTAL MONEY	867.5	1,139.4	1,276.0

Source: Central Bank of Libya.

BALANCE OF PAYMENTS
(U.S. $ million)

	1971	1972	1973	1974	1975	1976	1977
Merchandise exports f.o.b.	2,714	2,470	3,528	7,213	6,418	8,748	10,384
Merchandise imports f.o.b.	−930	−1,291	−2,011	−3,746	−4,424	−4,277	−5,214
TRADE BALANCE	1,784	1,179	1,516	3,467	1,994	4,471	5,170
Exports of services	172	225	216	434	375	349	416
Imports of services	−1,034	−1,012	−1,466	−1,864	−2,241	−2,203	−2,489
BALANCE ON GOODS AND SERVICES	922	392	266	2,037	128	2,617	3,097
Private unrequited transfers (net)	−48	−52	−44	−137	−32	−37	−40
Government unrequited transfers (net)	−90	−102	−156	−69	−164	−144	−152
CURRENT BALANCE	784	238	66	1,832	−68	2,435	2,905
Direct capital investment (net)	140	−4	−148	−241	−616	−521	−425
Other long-term capital (net)	−10	−39	−362	−182	−908	−987	−878
Short-term capital (net)	10	244	410	373	307	286	125
Net errors and omissions	−52	−25	−1,023	−59	−262	−163	−235
TOTAL (net monetary movements)	872	414	−1,057	1,723	−1,547	1,051	1,492

Source: IMF, *International Financial Statistics.*

EXTERNAL TRADE
(LD million)

	1969	1970	1971	1972	1973	1974	1975	1976	1977
Imports c.i.f.	241.3	198.0	250.4	343.2	539.9	817.8	1,052.1	950.8	1,119.7
Exports f.o.b.	773.9	844.9	962.5	966.3	1,197.1	2,445.7	2,024.1	2,830.7	2,993.9

SELECTED COMMODITIES
(LD'000)

IMPORTS	1973	1974	1975
Food and live animals	85,055	129,758	162,058
Beverages and Tobacco	1,779	3,037	3,471
Mineral fuel	10,627	13,265	28,195
Animal and vegetable oils and fats	9,515	9,035	20,394
Inedible crude materials excl. fuel	24,535	32,311	14,239
Chemicals	21,244	29,862	39,017
Manufactures	137,244	230,650	306,097
Machinery	183,572	273,929	359,217
Miscellaneous	66,367	95,996	116,013

EXPORTS	1973	1974	1975
Crude petroleum	1,161,666	2,388,347	1,925,314
Groundnuts	—	—	n.a.
Hides and skins	1,366	388	77
Castor oil seed	10	8	n.a.
Wool and other animal hair	972	118	n.a.

Exports (LD million): 2,459.0 (crude petroleum 2,456.7) in 1976; 2,889.7 (crude petroleum 2,886.1) in 1977; 2,813.3 (crude petroleum 2,809.6) in 1978 (*Source:* IMF, *International Financial Statistics*).

PRINCIPAL TRADING PARTNERS
(U.S. $ million)

	IMPORTS c.i.f.			EXPORTS f.o.b.		
	1975	1976	1977	1975	1976	1977
Argentina	100	48	n.a.	113	10	n.a.
Bahamas	n.a.	n.a.	n.a.	302	367	n.a.
Belgium	493	115	253	27	28	17
Brazil	n.a.	3	n.a.	188	117	n.a.
China, People's Republic	72	27	24	n.a.	n.a.	n.a.
France	314	354	438	252	348	281
Germany, Federal Republic	431	615	716	1,332	1,809	1,966
Hong Kong	31	53	38	n.a.	n.a.	n.a.
India	6	14	n.a.	8	n.a.	n.a.
Italy	921	1,069	n.a.	1,496	1,610	n.a.
Japan	294	342	307	232	223	102
Netherlands	73	94	101	141	130	134
Romania	98	125	n.a.	69	142	n.a.
Spain	89	153	176	351	512	456
Turkey	28	10	15	113	243	215
United Kingdom	195	234	334	272	224	277
U.S.A.	142	277	345	1,499	2,188	3,656
Yugoslavia	52	59	n.a.	45	36	n.a.
TOTAL (incl. others)	3,554	3,203	5,148	6,837	8,442	10,113

TRANSPORT

ROAD TRAFFIC
(motor vehicles in use)

	1973	1974	1975
Private Cars	188,985	222,904	250,697
Taxis	9,630	11,396	12,360
Lorries	88,850	105,451	129,730
Buses	1,176	1,296	1,556

INTERNATIONAL SEA-BORNE SHIPPING

	Ships ('000 N.R.T.)		Cargo ('000 metric tons)	
	Entered	Cleared	Loaded	Unloaded
1972	5,450	5,433	109,958	5,649
1973	5,146	5,023	107,300	5,051
1974	5,166	5,012	75,045	6,413
1975	6,400	5,947	72,994	9,619

CIVIL AVIATION

	1973	1974	1975
Number of Passengers			
Entering	282,070	315,046	363,239
Leaving	276,911	339,206	345,991
Cargo Unloaded (tons)	15,090	23,059	30,182
Cargo Loaded (tons)	1,929	1,881	2,294

EDUCATION
(1975/76)

State Schools	Schools	Students	Teachers
Primary	2,042	556,172	24,331
Preparatory	510	122,419	7,739
Secondary	74	18,069	1,725
Teacher Training	91	20,748	1,832
Technical	12	3,285	340

Source (unless otherwise stated): Census and Statistical Dept., Ministry of Planning, Tripoli.

THE CONSTITUTION

The Libyan Arab People, meeting in the General People's Congress in Sebha from March 2nd to March 28th, 1977, proclaimed its adherence to freedom and its readiness to defend it on its own land and anywhere else in the world. It also announced its adherence to socialism and its commitment to achieving total Arab Unity; its adherence to the moral human values, and confirmed the march of the revolution led by Col. Muammar al-Gaddafi, the revolutionary leader, towards complete People's Authority.

The Libyan Arab People announced the following:

(i) The official name of Libya is henceforth *The Socialist People's Libyan Arab Jamahiriya*.

(ii) The Holy Koran is the social code in The Socialist People's Libyan Arab Jamahiriya.

(iii) The Direct People's Authority is the basis for the political order in The Socialist People's Libyan Arab Jamahiriya. The People shall practise its authority through People's Congresses, Popular Committees, Trade Unions, Vocational Syndicates, and The General People's Congress, in the presence of the law.

(iv) The defence of our homeland is the responsibility of every citizen. The whole people shall be trained militarily and armed by general military training, the preparation of which shall be specified by the law.

The General People's Congress in its extraordinary session held in Sebha issued four decrees:

The first decree announced the establishment of The People's Authority in compliance with the resolutions and recommendations of the People's Congresses and Trade Unions.

The second decree stipulated the choice of Col. Muammar al-Gaddafi, the Revolutionary Leader, as Secretary-General of the General People's Congress.

The third decree stipulated the formation of the General Secretariat of the General People's Congress (*see* The Government, below).

The fourth decree stipulated the formation of the General People's Committee which comprises 26 Secretaries (reduced to 21 in March 1979) to carry out the tasks of the various former ministries (*see* The Government, below).

In February 1979 it was announced that the Secretariats were to be reorganized and their functions delimited. In March 1979, when Col. Gaddafi resigned from the post of Secretary General of the General People's Congress, the number of Secretaries of the General People's Committee was reduced to 21.

THE GOVERNMENT

HEAD OF STATE

President: Col. MUAMMAR AL-GADDAFI (took office as Chairman of the Revolution Command Council September 8th, 1969 elected Head of State by the General People's Congress March 1977).

GENERAL SECRETARIAT OF THE GENERAL PEOPLE'S CONGRESS

Secretary General: ABDUL ATI AL-OBEIDI.

Assistant Secretary General: MOHAMMED ABDUL-QASSIM AL-ZUWAI.

Secretary for Affairs of the Congress: ALI ABU AL-KHAYIR.

Secretary for Affairs of the People's Committees: ABDULLAH ZAHMUL.

Secretary for Trade Unions, Federations and Vocational Affairs: MUKHTAR QURBU.

GENERAL PEOPLE'S COMMITTEE

(*June* 1979)

Secretary of the General People's Committee: Eng. JADALLAH AZZUZ AT-TALHI.

Secretary for Liaison: Eng. ABDUL-MAJID AL-MABRUK AL-QU'UD.

Secretary of the General People's Committee (GPC) for Justice: MUHAMMAD ALI JADI.

Secretary of the GPC for Health: Dr. MUFTAH AL-USTA UMAR.

Secretary for Petroleum: IZZADIN AL-MABRUK.

Secretary of the GPC for Housing: Eng. MUHAMMAD AL-MANQUSH.

Secretary of the GPC for Economy: ABU BAKR AS-SHARIF.

Secretary of the GPC for the Treasury: MUHAMMAD ZARRUQ RAJAB.

Secretary of the GPC for Education: Dr. MUHAMMAD AHMAD AS-SHARIF.

Secretary of the GPC for Light Industries: Dr. UMAR AHMAD AL-MAQSI.

Secretary of the GPC for Electricity: Eng. JUMAH AL-ARBASH.

Secretary of the GPC for Communications and Maritime Transport: Eng. NURI AL-FITURI AL-MADANI.

Secretary of the GPC for Municipalities: ABU ZAYID UMAR DURDA.

Secretary of the GPC for Jamahiriya Sports: MUFTAH KUAYBAH.

Foreign Secretary: Dr. ALI ABDESSALEM AL-TREIKI.

Secretary of the GPC for Planning: MUSA ABU FURAYWAH.

Secretary of the GPC for Land Reclamation and Land Reform: BASHIR JUDAH.

Secretary for Heavy Industries: UMAR MUSTAFA AL-MUNTASIR.

Secretary of the GPC for Information: MUHAMMAD SUWAIDI.

Secretary of the GPC for the Civil Service: MUHAMMAD ABDULLAH AL-MABRUK.

Secretary of the GPC for Social Security: IBRAHIM HASAN.

GENERAL PEOPLE'S CONGRESS

The Senate and House of Representatives were dissolved after the *coup d'état* of September 1969, and the provisional constitution issued in December 1969 made no mention of elections or a return to Parliamentary procedure. However, in January 1971 Col. Gaddafi announced that a new Parliament would be appointed, not elected; no date was mentioned. All political parties other than the Arab Socialist Union were banned. In November 1975 provision was made for the creation of the General National Congress of the Arab Socialist Union, which met officially in January 1976. This later became the General People's Congress, which met for the first time in November 1976 and in March 1977 began introducing the wide-ranging changes outlined in "The Constitution" (above).

Secretary General: ABDUL ATI AL-OBEIDI.

DIPLOMATIC REPRESENTATION

EMBASSIES ACCREDITED TO LIBYA

(Tripoli unless otherwise stated)

(E) Embassy.

Afghanistan: Sharia Moher Aftas (E); *Ambassador:* PACHA GUL WAFADAR.

Algeria: Sharia Qayrouan 12 (E); *Ambassador:* Col. BIN MUSTAFA BIN AUDA.

Argentina: Sharia Moher Aftas (E); *Ambassador:* VICENTE CAYETTI.

Australia: Shalti Andalus (E); *Chargé d'affaires:* BRUCE CONDUIT.

Austria: Sharia Khalid Ben Walid/corner (former) Sharia Arismondi, Dahra Area, Garden City (E); *Ambassador:* Dr. HELMUT SCHURZ.

Bangladesh: Hadaba Al Khadra (E); *Ambassador:* ZAMIRUDDIN AHMED (also accred. to Tunisia).

Belgium: Abu Ubaida Ibn Al Jarah (E); *Ambassador:* JEAN-PAUL DESCAMPS (also accred. to Malta).

Benin: (E); *Ambassador:* HASAN ABOUDO.

Brazil: Sharia Bin Ashur (E); *Ambassador:* CARLOS F. LECKIE LOBO (also accred. to Malta).

Bulgaria: Sharia Murad Agha (E); *Ambassador:* VLADIMIR MEDAROV.

Burundi: Sharia Ras Hassan (E); *Ambassador:* MANGONA IBRAHIM.

Cambodia (Kampuchea): Algiers, Algeria (E).

Canada: Cairo, Egypt (E).

Central African Empire: (E); *Ambassador:* MUKHTAR ADOPIAT.

Chad: Sharia Muhammad Mussadeq (E); *Ambassador:* (vacant).

Chile: Cairo, Egypt (E).

China, People's Republic: (E); *Chargé d'affaires* LU DEFANG.

China (Taiwan): Sharia al-Hadi Ka'bar (E); (relations suspended September 1978).

Cuba: Sharia Al Zubier Ibn al Awwam (E); *Ambassador:* LUIS MARISY FIGUEREDO.

Czechoslovakia: Ahmed Lutfi Street, Ben Ashour Area (E); *Ambassador:* JOSEF VARHOLIK.

Denmark: Gamhouria St. and Khadisia Sq., Garden City (E); *Chargé d'affaires:* BJØRN SUHR.

Ethiopia: Libya Palace Hotel (E); *Ambassador:* MOHAMMED ABDUL RAHMAN.

Finland: Garden City (E); *Ambassador:* JYRKI AIMONEN.

France: Sharia Ahmad Lutfi Said (E); *Ambassador:* (vacant).

Gabon: (E); *Ambassador:* MIMON AKOMI.

Gambia: Maidan At-Tahrir, P.O.B. 10972 (E); *Ambassador:* Alhaji MUSA DERBOE (also accred. to Algeria and Malta).

German Democratic Republic: Sharia Jumhuriya (E); *Ambassador:* FREIMUT SEIDEL.

Germany, Federal Republic: Sharia Hassan al-Masha (E); *Ambassador:* OSKAR MARIA NEUBERT.

Greece: Sharia Jalal Bayar, 18 (E); *Ambassador:* EMMANUEL E. MEGALOKONOMOS.

Guinea: Sharia Bin 'Ashur (E); *Ambassador:* DIAWO KONTEH.

Hungary: Sharia Talha Bin Abdullah (E); *Ambassador:* PÁL SZÜTS.

India: Sharia Mahmud Shaltut (E); *Ambassador:* NARENDRA SINGH.

Iran: Tunis, Tunisia (E).

Iraq: Sharia Nasser (E); *Ambassador:* SABAH AL-HURANI.

Italy: Sharia 'Oran 1 (E); *Ambassador:* ALDO CONTE MAROTTA.

Japan: 37 Sharia Ubei Ben Ka'ab (E); *Ambassador:* KENICHIRO NISHIZAWA.

Jordan: Sharia Ali ibn Uloff (E); *Ambassador:* HISHAM SHAWA.

Korea, Democratic People's Republic: Sharia Al Thul (E); *Ambassador:* KYE CHANG-HWAN.

Kuwait: Sharia Bin Yassir (E); *Ambassador:* ABDUL HAJJI AL-MAHMID.

Lebanon: Sharia Bin Yassir (E); *Ambassador:* JOSEPH FORACE.

Malaysia: (E); *Chargé d'affaires:* SYED ARIFF FADZILLAH.

Mali: Cairo, Egypt (E).

Malta: Sharia Ubei Ben Ka'ab (E); *Ambassador:* (vacant). (also accred. to Algeria, Bahrain, Egypt, Iraq, Jordan, Kuwait, Lebanon, Morocco, Saudi Arabia, Sudan, Syria, Tunisia and United Arab Emirates).

Mauritania: Sharia Aissa Wokwak (E); *Ambassador:* MUHAMMAD MAHMUD OULD WADDADI (also accred. to Chad and Niger).

Morocco: Sharia Bashir al-Ibrahim (E); *Ambassador:* IDRIS AL-FALLAH (also accred. to Chad and Malta).

Netherlands: Sharia Jelal Bayar 20 (E); *Chargé d'affaires:* H. J. VAN PESCH.

Niger: Sharia Bin 'Ubaydallah (E); *Ambassador:* Al Hadji ABU-BAKR BELLO.

Nigeria: Sharia Ammar Ben Yaser (E); *Ambassador:* D. A. WAZIRI.

Norway: Cairo, Egypt (E).

Pakistan: Sharia al-Khitabi (E); *Ambassador:* Lt.-Gen. AFTAB AHMAD KHAN.

Philippines: (E); *Ambassador:* RODOLFO G. TUPAS.

Poland: Sharia Ben Ashur (E); *Ambassador:* SYKSTUS OLESIK.

Qatar: Garden City (E); *Ambassador:* (vacant).

Romania: Sharia Ben Ashur (E); *Ambassador:* NICOLAE VERES.

Rwanda: Hay al Andalus (E); *Ambassador:* KABANDA CELESTIN.

Saudi Arabia: Sharia al-Qayrounan 2 (E); *Ambassador:* Sheikh ABDULLAH BIN SALAH AL-FADL (also accred. to Malta).

Senegal: Brach Hotel (E); *Ambassador:* ABOUBALAH SY.

Somalia: Sharia Khalid Ben Elwalid (E); *Ambassador:* TAHER YOUSEF MAHMOUD.

Spain: Sharia al-Jazayri (E); *Ambassador:* FRANCESCO JAVIR.

Sri Lanka: Cairo, Egypt (E).

Sudan: (E); *Ambassador:* ABDUL MAGID BASHIR EL-AHMADI (also accred. to Malta).

Sweden: Sharia Mugaryef (E); *Ambassador:* B. H. HOLMQUIST.

Switzerland: Sharia Jeraba (E); *Chargé d'affaires:* HERMANN RIEDER.

Syria: Sharia Muhammed Rashid Rida 4 (Relations Office); *Acting Head:* 'ALY HASAN.

Togo: Fashloum (E); *Ambassador:* Al Hadji KASSIM MENSAH.

Tunisia: Sharia Bashir al-Ibrahimi (E); *Commissioner-General:* MUSTAFA ILMI (also accred. to Malta).

Turkey: Sharia Gamal Abdel Nasser 36 (E); *Ambassador:* MUSTAFA ASHULA.

Uganda: Sharia Jekaba (E); *Chargé d'affaires:* AMIN MUTYABA.

U.S.S.R.: Sharia Solaroli (E); *Ambassador:* ANATOLY ANISSIMOV.

United Arab Emirates: Sharia Ben Ashur (E); *Ambassador:* HAMAD SALIM AL-MAKAMI (also accred. to Malta).

United Kingdom: Sharia Gamal Abdul Nasser (E); *Ambassador:* A. J. WILLIAMS.

U.S.A.: Sharia al-Nasr (E); *Chargé d'affaires:* ROBERT J. CARLE.

Venezuela: Sharia Abdulrahman Kwakby (E); *Ambassador:* JOSÉ GREGORIO GONZÁLES RODRÍGUES (also accred. to Morocco).

Viet-Nam: Sharia Ben Abdullah (E); *Ambassador:* NGUYEN VAN SAO.

Yemen Arab Republic: Sharia Ubei Ben Ka'ab 36 (E); *Ambassador:* AHMAD MUHAMMAD AL-ROUKHI (also accred. to Malta).

Yemen, People's Democratic Republic: Sharia Bin 'Ashur (E); *Ambassador:* (vacant).

Yugoslavia: Sharia Bashir al-Ibrahimi (E); *Ambassador:* SAFET SERIFOVIC.

Zaire: Aziz al Masri (E); *Ambassador:* (vacant).

Libya also has diplomatic relations with Costa Rica, Cyprus, Djibouti, Guinea-Bissau, Ireland, Jamaica, the Republic of Korea, Laos, Madagascar, Mauritius, Mexico, Panama, São Tomé and Príncipe, Seychelles, Suriname, Thailand and Tonga.

JUDICIAL SYSTEM

President of the Supreme Court: MUHAMMAD ABDULKAREEM AZZUZ.

The law of the Judicial System of 1954 established the following courts: the Federal Supreme Court, the Courts of Appeal, the Courts of First Instance and the Summary Courts. Sittings are in public, unless the court decides to hold them *in camera* in the interests of decency or public order. Judgment is in all cases given in public. The language of the courts is Arabic, but there is a translation office attached to each Court to help non-Arabic speaking parties or lawyers.

In October 1971 the Revolution Command Council decreed that all legislation should conform with the basic principles of Islamic Law and set up committees to carry this out. In April 1973 Colonel Gaddafi declared that any legislation likely to impede the progress of the revolution or to defeat public interest must be repealed.

The **Supreme Court** consists at present of a Chief Justice and ten justices.

Courts of Appeal exist in Tripoli, Benghazi and Misurata, consisting of a President, Vice-President and three judges; judgments must be given by three judges. Each Court of Appeal includes a Court of Assize consisting of three judges.

Courts of First Instance are set up in the provinces, consisting of a President, Vice-President and a number of judges; judgment in these courts is given by one judge.

Summary Courts, composed of one judge, exist within the territorial jurisdiction of every Court of First Instance.

The People's Court is a special court set up by decree in October 1969 and is particularly concerned with cases of political or administrative corruption.

RELIGION

Muslims: The Libyan Arabs practically without exception follow Sunni Muslim rites.

Chief Mufti of Libya: Sheikh TAHER AHMED AL ZAWI.

Roman Catholic Church: Apostolic Vicariates of Benghazi, Derna and Tripoli, Apostolic Prefecture of Misurata; 17,000 Catholics (1976).

THE PRESS

In October 1973 the Revolution Command Council decreed the nationalization of all private newspapers, which were to be handed over to the Public Press Organization.

DAILIES

TRIPOLI

Al-Fajr al-Jadid: Sharia Tariq; f. 1969; official journal; Editor ABD AR-RAHMAN SHALGAM; circ. 35,000.

Al Jihad: Sharia Jamia Siala; f. 1974; official journal; Editor SALIM WALIY.

PERIODICALS

TRIPOLI

Al Shura: monthly.

Socialist People's Libyan Arab Jamahiriya Official Gazette: published by the Secretariat of Justice; legal; weekly.

Al Thaqafa al Arabiya: P.O.B. 4587; f. 1973; cultural; circ. 25,000.

Al Usbu Al Thaqafiy: P.O.B. 4845; weekly; cultural; Editor MUSTAFA AL-MISULLATI.

NEWS AGENCIES

Jamahiriya News Agency (JANA): P.O.B. 2303, Tripoli; branches and correspondents throughout Libya; main foreign bureaux: London, Paris, Beirut, Cairo and Kuwait; serves Libyan and foreign subscribers; Dir.-Gen. SULAIMAN AL-AZZABI.

FOREIGN BUREAU

Tass (U.S.S.R.) has an office in Tripoli.

PUBLISHER

Dar Libya Publishing House: P.O.B. 2487, Benghazi.

RADIO AND TELEVISION

Socialist People's Libyan Arab Jamahiriya Broadcasting Corporation: P.O.B. 333, Tripoli; P.O.B. 274, Benghazi; f. 1957 (TV 1968); broadcasts in Arabic and English from Tripoli and Benghazi; from September 1971 special daily broadcasts to Gaza and other Israeli-occupied territory were begun; under the direction of the Information Secretary; Dir.-Gen. N. DHAW EL-HOMIDE.

Number of radio receivers: 130,000 (1978).

A national television service was inaugurated in December 1968. Number of TV receivers: 155,000 (1978).

FINANCE

BANKING

(br.=branch; cap.=capital; p.u.=paid up; dep.=deposits; LD=Libyan Dinar; m.=million; res.=reserves)

CENTRAL BANK

Central Bank of Libya: Sharia al Malik Seoud, P.O.B. 1103, Tripoli; f. 1955; bank of issue and central bank carrying government accounts and operating exchange control; commercial operations transferred to National Commercial Bank 1970; publs. *Economic Bulletin, Annual Report*; cap. LD 1m.; res. LD 7m.; dep. LD 155.5m. (Dec. 1975); Governor K. M. SHERLALA.

OTHER BANKS

Jamahiriya Bank: P.O.B. 3224, Sharia Emhamed El Megarief, Tripoli; f. 1969 as successor to Barclays Bank International in Libya; known as Masraf al Gumhouria until March 1977; government-owned; 27 brs. throughout Libya; cap. LD 750,000; res LD 14.4m.; dep. LD 209.2m. (Dec. 1977); Chair. SHTEWI K. ETTIR.

Libyan Arab Foreign Bank: 1st September St., P.O.B. 2542, Tripoli; government bank wholly owned by Central Bank of Libya; cap. p.u. and res. LD 34m. (Nov. 1977); Chair. and Gen. Man. ABDALLA A. SAUDI.

National Commercial Bank: Shuhada Square, P.O.B. 4647, Tripoli; f. 1970 to take over commercial banking division of Central Bank and brs. of Aruba Bank and Istiklal Bank; 22 brs.; cap. LD 2.5m.; dep. LD 262.2m.; res. LD 17.5m. (Dec. 1976); Chair. and Gen. Man. MUHAMMAD MUSTAFA GHADBAN.

Sahara Bank: Sharia 1 September, P.O.B. 270, Tripoli; f. 1964 to take over br. of Banco di Sicilia; 12 brs.; Chair. and Gen. Man. FARAG A. GAMRA.

Umma Bank S.A.L.: 1 Sharia Omar Mukhtar, P.O.B. 685; Tripoli; f. 1969 to take over brs. of Banco di Roma, 17 brs.; cap. LD 500,000; res. LD 32m.; dep. LD 160.0m. (December 1976); Chair. and Gen. Man. YOUSEF I. AGHIL.

Wahda Bank: Jamal Abdul Naser St., P.O.B. 452, Benghazi; f. 1970 to take over Bank of North Africa, Commercial Bank, S.A.L., Nahda Arabia Bank, Société Africaine de Banque, Kafila Ahly Bank of Libya; 24 brs.; cap. and res. LD 13.7m.; dep. LD 176.9m. (Dec. 1977); Chair. and Gen. Man. MOHAMED SALEH KHLEIF.

INSURANCE

Libya Insurance Co.: P.O.B. 2438, Tripoli; P.O.B. 643, Benghazi; all classes of insurance.

Al Mukhtar Insurance Co.: 230 Muhammad Lemgarief St., P.O.B. 2548, Tripoli; all classes of insurance; Chair. and Gen. Man. IBRAHIM FELFEL.

OIL

Petroleum affairs in Libya are dealt with primarily by the Secretariat of Petroleum. Since 1973 Libya has been entering into participation agreements with some of the foreign oil companies (concession holders), and nationalizing others. It has concluded 85–15 per cent production sharing agreements with various oil companies.

Secretariat of Petroleum: P.O.B. 256, Tripoli.

NATIONAL COMPANIES

National Oil Corporation (NOC): P.O.B. 2655, Tripoli; f. 1970 as successor to the Libyan General Petroleum Corporation, to undertake joint ventures with foreign companies; to build and operate refineries, storage tanks, petrochemical facilities, pipelines and tankers; to take part in arranging specifications for local and imported petroleum products; to participate in general planning of oil installations in Libya; to market crude oil and to establish and operate oil terminals; Chair. OMAR MUNTASSER.

Agip Oil, Co. (North Africa and Middle East, Libyan Branch Ltd.): P.O.B. 346, Tripoli; Gen. Man. NOURI ESSANOUSSI.

Arabian Gulf Exploration Co.: P.O.B. 263, Benghazi; Chair. Operations Man. H. A. LAYASS.

Brega Oil Marketing Co.: P.O.B. 402, Tripoli; Chair. and Gen. Man. ALI EL-FITURI.

Esso Standard Libya Inc.: P.O.B. 385, Tripoli; Chair. Management Cttee. ABUSSALAM M. ZAGGAR.

Mobil Oil Libya: P.O.B. 690, Tripoli; Chair. DOKALI B. MEGHARIEF.

Oasis Oil Co.: P.O.B. 395, Tripoli; Chair. and Dir.-Gen. Dr. MUKHTAR A. EL-AGELI.

Occidental of Libya: P.O.B. 2134, Tripoli; Chair. and Gen. Man. MASSAOUD JARNAZ.

National Drilling Co.: P.O.B. 1454, Tripoli; Chair. and Gen. Man. MUHAMMAD AHMED ATTIGA.

Umm Al-Jawaby Petroleum Co.: P.O.B. 693, Tripoli; Chair. and Gen. Man. MUHAMMAD TENTTOUSH.

Zawiya Oil Refining Co.: affiliated with NOC, P.O.B. 6451, Tripoli, and P.O.B. 15715, Azzawiya; Chair. and Gen. Man. ALI HABBOUNI.

FOREIGN COMPANIES

Aquitaine Libya: P.O.B. 282, Tripoli; Man. JEAN LE BRETON.

Wintershall-Libya and Elwerath Oil Co. Libya: P.O.B. 469 and 905, Tripoli; Man. HORST BOERNECKE.

TRADE AND INDUSTRY

CHAMBERS OF COMMERCE

Chamber of Commerce and Industry for the Western Province: Al-Jomhourieh St., P.O.B. 2321, Tripoli; f. 1952; Pres. SALEM EL-SAGHIR GADDAH; Sec.-Gen. BASHIR K. EL-GENAYYEN; 40,000 mems.; publs. *Quarterly Bulletin, Trade Acquaintance* (bi-weekly) and *Commercial Directory* (annual, English and Arabic).

Chamber of Commerce, Trade, Industry and Agriculture for the Eastern Province: P.O.B. 208–1286, Benghazi; f. 1953; Pres. HASAN H. MATAR; Sec.-Gen. YOUSEF EL GIAMI; 5,400 mems.

DEVELOPMENT

General National Organization for Industrialization: P.O.B. 4388, Tripoli; f. March 1970; a public organization controlling various heavy and light industries; Chair. is Sec. of Industry and Minerals.

Kufrah and Serir Authority: Council of Agricultural Development, Benghazi; f. 1972 to develop the Kufrah Oasis and Serir area in south-east Libya.

NATIONALIZED INDUSTRIES

General Tobacco Company: P.O.B. 696, Tripoli; develops the production and curing of tobacco; leaf production 1,000,000 kilos, manufactured tobacco production 2,800,000 kilos (1973).

TRADE UNIONS

National Trade Unions' Federation: (affiliated to ICFTU); P.O.B. 734, 2 Sharia Istanbul, Tripoli; f. 1952; Sec.-Gen. HAMIED ABUBAKER JALLUD; 18 trade unions with 275,000 members; Publ. *Attalia* (weekly).

Union of Petroleum Workers of Libya: Tripoli; also branch in Benghazi.

TRADE FAIR

Tripoli International Fair: P.O.B. 891, Tripoli; under control of General Board of Tourism and Fairs; annual fair March 1st–20th; Chair. and Dir.-Gen. SALEH F. AZZABI.

TRANSPORT

ROADS

The most important road is the 1,822 km. national coast road from the Tunisian to the Egyptian border, passing through Tripoli and Benghazi. It has a second link between Barce and Lamluda, 141 km. long. The other national road runs from a point on the coastal road 120 km. south of Misurata through Sebha to Ghat near the Algerian border (total length 1,250 km.). There is a branch 260 km. long running from Vaddan to Sirte. There is a road crossing the desert from Sebha to the frontiers of Chad and Niger.

In addition to the national highways, the west of Libya has about 1,200 km. of black-top and macadamized roads and the east about 500 km. Practically all the towns and villages of Libya, including the desert oases, are accessible by motor vehicle.

SHIPPING

Principal ports are Tripoli, Benghazi, Port Brega and the Oasis Marine Terminal at Es-Sider. Port Brega was opened to oil tankers in 1961. A 30-inch crude oil pipeline connects the Zelten oilfields with Marsa El Brega. Another pipeline joins the Sarir oilfield with Marsa Hariga, the port of Tobruk, and a pipeline from the Sarir field to Zuetina was opened in 1968. There is another oil port at Ras Lunuf. Libya also has the use of Tunisian port facilities at Sfax and Gabes, to alleviate congestion at Tripoli.

Libyan General Maritime Transport Organization: 10 Garnaia St., P.O.B. 4673, Tripoli; f. 1970 to handle all projects dealing with maritime trade.

CIVIL AVIATION

There are four civil airports: the International Airport, situated at Ben Gashir, 21 miles from Tripoli; Benina Airport, 12 miles from Benghazi; Sebha Airport; Misurata Airport (domestic flights only).

Libyan Arab Airlines: P.O.B. 2555, Tripoli; f. 1965; passenger and cargo services from Tripoli and Benghazi to London, Paris, Zürich, Frankfurt, Warsaw, Rome, Belgrade, Istanbul, Amman, Athens, Madrid, Malta, Beirut, Damascus, Jeddah, Tunis, Algiers, Casablanca and Niamey; domestic services throughout Libya; fleet of 10 Boeing 727-2000, 8 F-27; Chair. of People's Committee BADRI HASAN; Commercial Man. MUHAMMAD GHEBALI.

Libya is also served by the following foreign airlines: Aeroflot (U.S.S.R.), Air Algérie, Alitalia (Italy), British Caledonian, ČSA (Czechoslovakia), EgyptAir, JAT (Yugoslavia), KLM (Netherlands), Lufthansa (Federal Republic of Germany), Malta Airlines, Saudia (Saudi Arabia), Sudan Airways, Swissair, Syrian Arab, Tunis Air, UTA (France).

TOURISM

General Board of Tourism and Fairs: Tripoli; f. 1964.

DEFENCE

Commander-in-Chief of Armed Forces: Brig. ABU-BAKR YOUNES.

Defence Budget (1978): LD 130 million.

Military Service: 3 years for ground forces, 4 years for air and naval forces (since May 1978).

Total Armed Forces: 37,000: army 30,000; navy 3,000; air force 4,000; Libya possesses over 2,000 tanks.

EDUCATION

By 1939 there were in Tripolitania 70 Italo-Arab primary schools with 6,884 Arab and 170 Italian pupils, 13 girls' trades schools with 944 pupils, a secondary school, and an arts and crafts school with 85 students. In addition, evening classes were started for adult Arab illiterates, and in 1928 Arabs were permitted to join Italian secondary schools. Small numbers of Arabs also gained admittance to Italian and Egyptian universities. Koranic schools also increased in numbers from 52 with 1,792 pupils in 1921 to 496 schools with 10,165 pupils in 1939. For Jews there were 19 primary schools (2,645 students), 2 trade secondary schools with 101 pupils, and 15 private schools catering for 1,939 pupils.

Up to the year 1939 the educational system for Arabs in Cyrenaica was similarly under-developed. At that time not more than 37 elementary schools were in existence with a total of 2,600 Arab pupils, and for Jews there were 5 elementary schools with 621 students.

Due to the destruction of towns and communications and to the evacuation of many people to the interior during the Second World War, education was badly disrupted, and at the end of the war there was a great demand for educational facilities. Secondary education was no longer limited to the few places permitted in Italian schools and Libyan schools of all grades rapidly increased in number. A steady expansion of all educational services occurred between 1943 and 1949, followed by a considerable acceleration after the United Nations' decision of November 21st, 1949.

The numbers attending kindergarten, primary and secondary schools increased from a total of 6,808 in 1943/44 to 696,660 in 1975/76. The number of teachers rose similarly, from 219 in 1943/44 to 31,795 in 1975/76. Elementary education is compulsory for children of both sexes. The above statistics do not include "Kuttabs"—self-efforts at small groups of children being educated collectively in villages.

In 1958 the University of Libya opened in Benghazi with Faculties of Arts and Commerce, followed the next year by the Faculty of Science near Tripoli. Faculties of Law, Agriculture, Engineering, Teacher Training, and Arabic Language and Islamic Studies have since been added to the University. In 1973 the University was divided into two parts, to form the Universities of Tripoli and Benghazi, later renamed Alfateh and Ghar Yunis Universities.

In the 1976–80 Development Plan LD 122 million was allocated to education.

UNIVERSITIES

Alfateh University: P.O.B. 398, Tripoli; f. 1973; 340 teachers, 4,125 students.

Ghar Yunis University: P.O.B. 1308, Benghazi; f. 1955; 354 teachers, 8,765 students.

BIBLIOGRAPHY

ANSELL, MEREDITH O. and AL-ARIF, IBRAHIM M. The Libyan Revolution (The Oleander Press, London, 1972).

DI AGOSTINI, Col. ENRICO. La popolazione della Tripolitania (2 vols.; Tripoli, 1917).

La popolazione della Cirenaica (Benghazi, 1922-23).

Amministrazione Fiduciaria all'Italia in Africa (Florence, 1948).

Archivio bibliografico Coloniale (Libia) (Florence, 1915-21).

BARUNI, OMAR. Spaniards and Knights of St. John of Jerusalem in Tripoli (Arabic) (Tripoli, 1952).

BERLARDINELLI, ARSENIO. La Ghibla (Tripoli, 1935).

BLUNSUM, T. Libya: the Country and its People (Queen Anne Press, London, 1968).

CACHIA, ANTHONY J. Libya under the Second Ottoman Occupation, 1835-1911 (Tripoli, 1945).

CECCHERINI, UGO. Bibliografia della Libia in continuazione .... de F. Minutilli (Rome, 1915).

COLUCCI, MASSIMO. Il Regime della Proprieta Fondiaria nell'Africa Italiana: Vol. I. Libia (Bologna, 1942).

CORÒ, FRANCESCO. Settantasei Anni di Dominazione Turca in Libia (Tripoli, 1937).

CUROTTI, TORQUATO. Gente di Libia (Tripoli, 1928).

DESPOIS, JEAN. Géographie Humaine (Paris, 1946).
Le Djebel Nefousa (Paris, 1935).
La Colonisation italienne en Libye; Problèmes et Méthodes (Larose-Editeurs, Paris, 1935).

EPTON, NINA. Oasis Kingdom: The Libyan Story (New York, 1953).

EVANS-PRITCHARD, E. E. The Sanusi of Cyrenaica (London, 1949).

FARLEY, RAWLE. Planning for Development in Libya (Pall Mall, London, 1971).

FIRST, RUTH. Libya—the Elusive Revolution (Penguin, London, 1974).

FISHER, W. B. Problems of Modern Libya (*Geographical Journal*, June 1953).

FORBES, ROSITA. The Secret of the Sahara: Kufara (London, 1921).

FRANCA, PIETRO, and others. L'Italia in Africa: Incivilimento e Sviluppo dell'Eritrea, della Somalia, e della Libia (Rome, 1947).

GADDAFI, Col. MUAMMAR AL-. The Green Book (3 vols., Tripoli, 1976–79).

HAJJAJI, S. A. The New Libya (Tripoli, 1967).

HERRMANN, GERHARD. Italiens Weg zum Imperium (Goldman, Leipzig, 1938).

HESELTINE, NIGEL. From Libyan Sands to Chad (Museum Press, London, 1960).

HILL, R. W. A Bibliography of Libya (University of Durham, 1959).

JONGMANS, D. G. Libie-land van de dorst (Boom, Meppel, 1964).

JUIN, A-P. Le Maghreb en Feu (French) (Paris, Librairie Plon, 1957).

KHADDURI, MAJID. Modern Libya, a Study in Political Development (Johns Hopkins Press, 1963).

KHALIDI, I. R. Constitutional Developments in Libya (Beirut, Khayat's Book Co-operative, 1956).

KUBBAH, ABDUL AMIR Q. Libya, Its Oil Industry and Economic System (The Arab Petro-Economic Research Centre, Baghdad, 1964).

LEBLANC, M. E. Anthropologie et Ethnologie (du Fezzan) (1944-45).

LEGG, H. J. Libya: Economic and General Conditions in Libya (London, 1952).

LETHIELLEUX, J. Le Fezzan, ses Jardins, ses Palmiers: Notes d'Ethnographie et d'Histoire (Tunis, 1948).

LINDBERG, J. A General Economic Appraisal of Libya (New York, 1952).

MICACCHI, RODOLFO. La Tripolitania sotto il dominio dei Caramanli (Intra, 1936).

MINUTILLI, FEDERICO. Bibliografia della Libia (Turin, 1903).

MURABET, MOHAMMED. Tripolitania: the Country and its People (Tripoli, 1952).

NORMAN, JOHN. Labour and Politics in Libya and Arab Africa (Bookman, New York, 1965).

OWEN, R. Libya: a Brief Political and Economic Survey (London, 1961).

PELT, ADRIAN. Libyan Independence and the United Nations (Yale U.P., 1970).

PICHOU, JEAN. La Question de Libye dans le règlement de la paix (Paris, 1945).

Lord RENNELL. British Military Administration of Occupied Territories in Africa during the years 1941-47 (London, H.M.S.O., 1948).

RIVLIN, BENJAMIN. The United Nations and the Italian Colonies (New York, 1950).

ROYAL INSTITUTE OF INTERNATIONAL AFFAIRS. The Italian Colonial Empire (London, 1940).

ROSSI, P. Libya (Lausanne, 1965).

RUSHDI, MUHAMMAD RASIM. Trablus al Gharb (Arabic) (Tripoli, 1953).

SCARIN, Prof. La Giofra e Zella (Florence, 1938).
L'Insediamento Umano nella Libia Occidentale (Rome, 1940).
Le Oasi Cirenaiche del 29° Parallelo (Florence, 1937).
Le Oasi del Fezzan (2 vols.; Florence, 1934).

SCHLUETER, HANS. Index Libycus (G. K. Hall, Boston, 1972).

SCHMEIDER, OSKAR and WILHELMY, HERBERT. Die faschistische Kolonisation in Nordafrika (Quelle and Meyer, Leipzig, 1939).

STEELE-GREIG, A. J. History of Education in Tripolitania from the Time of the Ottoman Occupation to the Fifth Year under British Military Occupation (Tripoli, 1948).

VILLARD, HENRY S. Libya: The New Arab Kingdom of North Africa (Ithaca, 1956).

WARD, PHILIP. Touring Libya. 3 vols. (1967–69).
Tripoli: Portrait of a City (1970).

WILLIAMS, G. Green Mountain, an Informal Guide to Cyrenaica and its Jebel Akhdar (London, 1963).

WILLIMOTT, S. G. and CLARKE, J. I. Field Studies in Libya (Durham, 1960).

WRIGHT, JOHN. Libya (Ernest Benn, London, and Praeger, New York, 1969).

Morocco

PHYSICAL AND SOCIAL GEOGRAPHY

The Kingdom of Morocco is the westernmost of the three North African countries known to the Arabs as Jeziret al Maghreb or "Island of the West". Intermediate in size between Algeria and Tunisia, it occupies an area of 458,730 sq. km. (excluding the portion of the former Spanish Sahara annexed in 1976, covering some 200,000 sq. km.), and has an extensive coastline facing both the Atlantic and the Mediterranean. However, as a result of both its position and the existence of massive mountain ranges within its borders, Morocco has remained relatively isolated from the rest of the Maghreb and has served as a refuge for descendants of the original Berber-speaking occupants of north-west Africa.

The population at mid-1977 was estimated to be 18,245,000. About 35 per cent of the total are Berber-speaking peoples, living mainly in mountain villages, while the Arabic-speaking majority is concentrated in towns in the lowlands, particularly in Casablanca, which is the largest city in the Maghreb, in Marrakesh, the old southern capital, and in Rabat (population 435,510, including Salé, in 1971), the modern administrative capital. There were some 450,000 Europeans living in Morocco before the country attained its independence from the French in 1956 but since then their number has greatly diminished.

PHYSICAL FEATURES

The physical geography of Morocco is dominated by the highest and most rugged ranges in the Atlas Mountain system of north-west Africa. They are the result of a phase of mountain-building that took place in the geologically recent Tertiary era when sediments deposited beneath an ancestral Mediterranean Sea were uplifted, folded and fractured. The mountains remain geologically unstable and Morocco is liable to severe earthquakes, such as the appallingly destructive one that took place at the port of Agadir in 1960.

In Morocco the Atlas Mountains form four distinct massifs which are surrounded and partially separated by lowland plains and plateaux. In the north, in the zone of the former Spanish Protectorate, the Rif Atlas comprise a rugged arc of mountains that rise steeply from the Mediterranean coast to heights of over 2,200 metres. There limestone and sandstone ranges are difficult to penetrate and have functioned as an effective barrier to east-west communications. They are inhabited by Berber farmers who live in isolated mountain villages and have little contact with the Arabs of Tétouan (population 137,080 in 1971) and Tangier (185,850) at the north-western end of the Rif chain.

The Middle Atlas lie immediately south of the Rif from which they are separated by the Col of Taza, a narrow gap which affords the only easy route between western Algeria and Atlantic Morocco. They rise to about 3,000 metres and form a broad barrier between the two countries. They also function as a major drainage divide and are flanked by the basins of Morocco's two principal rivers, the Oum er Rbia which flows west to the Atlantic and the Moulouya which flows north-east to the Mediterranean. Much of the Middle Atlas consists of a limestone plateau dissected by river gorges and capped here and there by volcanic craters and lava flows. Semi-nomadic Berber tribesmen spend the winter in valley villages and move to the higher slopes in summer to pasture their flocks.

Southward the Middle Atlas chain merges into the High Atlas, the most formidable of the mountain massifs, which rises to about 4,000 metres and is heavily snow-clad in winter. The mountains are aligned in a chain from south-west to north-east, and they rise precipitously from both the Atlantic lowland to the north and the desert plain of Saharan Morocco to the south. The contrast between the two sides is very striking; the northern slopes are covered by forest and scrub while the southern slopes consist of bare, sunbaked rock. Eastward the chain loses height and continues into Algeria as the Saharan Atlas. The central part of the massif is made up of resistant crystalline rocks which have been eroded by former glaciers and present streams into a wilderness of sharp peaks and steep-sided valleys, but elsewhere limestones and sandstones give rise to more subdued topography. There are no easily accessible routes across the High Atlas, but numerous mountain tracks make possible the exchange of goods by pack animal between Atlantic and Saharan Morocco. A considerable Berber population lives in the mountain valleys in compact, fortified villages.

The Anti Atlas is the lowest and most southerly of the mountain massifs. Structurally it forms an elevated edge of the Saharan platform which was uplifted when the High Atlas were formed. It consists largely of crystalline rocks and is joined to the southern margin of the High Atlas by a mass of volcanic lavas which separates the valley from the river Sous, draining west to the Atlantic at Agadir, from that of the upper Draa, draining south-east towards the Sahara. On the southern side of the chain barren slopes are trenched by gorges from which cultivated palm groves extend like green tongues out into the desert.

Stretching inland from the Atlantic coast is an extensive area of lowland, enclosed on the north, east and south by the Rif, Middle and High Atlas. It consists of the Gharb plain and the wide valley of the River Sebou in the north and of the plateaux and plains of the Meseta, the Tadla, the Rehamna, the Djebilet and the Haouz farther south. Most of the Arabic-speaking people of Morocco live in this region.

CLIMATE AND VEGETATION

Northern and central Morocco experiences a "Mediterranean" type of climate, with warm wet winters and hot dry summers, but this gives way southward to semi-arid and eventually to desert conditions. In the Rif and the northern parts of the Middle Atlas mean annual rainfall exceeds 75 cm. and the summer drought lasts only 3 months, but in the rest of the Middle Atlas, in the High Atlas and over the northern half of the Atlantic lowland rainfall is reduced to between 40 and 75 cm. and the summer drought lasts for 4 months or more. During the summer intensely hot winds from the Sahara, known as the Sirocco or Chergui, occasionally cross the mountains and sweep across the lowland desiccating all that lies in their path. Summer heat on the Atlantic coastal plain is tempered however by breezes that blow inland after they have been cooled over the cold waters of the Canaries current offshore.

Over the southern half of the Atlantic lowland and the Anti Atlas semi-arid conditions prevail and rainfall decreases to between 20 and 40 cm. per year. It also becomes very variable and is generally insufficient for the regular cultivation of cereal crops without irrigation. East and south of the Atlas Mountains, which act as a barrier to rain-bearing winds from the Atlantic, rainfall is reduced still further and regular cultivation becomes entirely dependent on irrigation.

The chief contrast in the vegetation of Morocco is between the mountain massifs, which support forest or open woodland, and the surrounding lowlands which, when uncultivated, tend to be covered only by scrub growth of low, drought-resistant bushes. The natural vegetation has however been widely altered, and in many places actually destroyed, by excessive cutting, burning and grazing. This is particularly evident in the lowlands and on the lower mountain slopes where such scrub species as juniper, thuya, dwarf palm and gorse are common. There is little doubt that cork oak covered a large part of the Atlantic lowland but today only the "forest" of Mamora remains to suggest the former abundance of this valuable tree. The middle and upper slopes of the mountains are often quite well wooded, with evergreen oak dominant at the lower and cedar at the higher elevations. The lowlands to the east and south of the Atlas Mountains support distinctive types of steppe and desert vegetation, in which esparto grass and the argan tree (which is unique to south-western Morocco) are conspicuous.

NEWLY-ANNEXED TERRITORY

After independence the Moroccan Government claimed a right to control a large area of the western Sahara, including territory in Algeria and Mauritania and the whole of the Spanish Sahara. The claim was based on the extent of Moroccan rule in medieval times. The existence of considerable deposits of phosphates in the Spanish Sahara and of iron ore in the Algeria-Morocco border region further excited Moroccan interest in expansion. After Spanish withdrawal from the Sahara in 1976 Morocco and Mauritania divided the former Spanish Sahara between them, Morocco annexing the northern part of the territory, including the phosphate mines of Bu Craa. The new border between the two countries runs in a straight line from the intersection of the 24th parallel with the coast to the intersection of the 23rd parallel with Mauritania's western frontier.

The territory annexed by Morocco has an area of some 200,000 sq. km., extending from the former southern border of Morocco along the Atlantic coast for some 500 km. and reaching between 200 and 450 km. inland to the western border of Mauritania. The population of the territory are mostly nomadic pastoralists, of Moorish or mixed Arab-Berber descent with some negro admixture, who depend for their existence on herds of sheep, camels and goats which they move seasonally from one pasture to another. The main tribes are the R'gibat, Uld Delim, Izargien and Arosien. In July 1975 the population of the Spanish Sahara was estimated at 117,000, but since annexation a considerable number of the former inhabitants have fled to refugee camps in Algeria. The principal towns in the area annexed by Morocco are Laayoune (formerly El Aaiún) and Essmara (Smara).

The relief of most of the area is gentle. The coast is backed by a wide alluvial plain overlain in the south by extensive sand dunes aligned from south-west to north-east and extending inland over 250 km. Behind the coastal plain the land rises gradually to a plateau surface diversified by sandstone ridges that reach 300 m. in height. In the north-east, close to the Mauritanian frontier, isolated mountain ranges, such as the Massif de la Guelta, rise to over 600 m. There are no permanent streams and the only considerable valley is that of the Sekia el Hamra which crosses the northernmost part of the area to reach the coast at El Aaiún north of Cape Bojador. The whole of the region experiences an extreme desert climate. Nowhere does mean annual rainfall exceed 10 cm. and over most of the territory it is less than 5 cm. Vegetation is restricted to scattered desert shrubs and occasional patches of coarse grass in most depressions. Along the coast summer heat is tempered by air moving inland after it has been cooled over the waters of the cold Canaries current which flows off shore from north to south.

HISTORY

The Phoenicians and after them the Carthaginians established staging posts and trading factories on the coasts of Morocco. Still later, the Romans established in what is now northern Morocco the province of Mauritania Tingitana, the frontier or *limes* passing a little to the south of Rabat, Meknès and Fez. Muslim warriors raided into Morocco under Uqba b. Nafi in A.D. 684–85. It was not, however, until the first years of the eighth century that the Muslims began to bring Morocco under durable control, their forces, under Musa b. Nusair, reaching the Tafilalet and the Wadi Draa. The Berber tribesmen of Morocco rallied to the cause of Islam and had a large share in the Muslim conquest of Spain after A.D. 711. Religious ideas of a heterodox character—i.e., the ideas of the Khawarij, who constituted the first of the great schismatic movements inside Islam—won much support among the Berbers of Morocco. The spread of Kharijite beliefs, the fierce particularism of the Berbers and their refractoriness towards all forms of political control, led to a great rebellion in 739–40, which had as its chief consequence the fragmentation of Morocco into a number of small Muslim principalities.

It was Idris, a descendant of al-Hasan, the son of the Caliph 'Ali and of Fatima, the daughter of the Prophet Muhammad, who, fleeing westward after an unsuccessful revolt against the Abbasid Caliph in Iraq, founded the first of the great Muslim dynasties ruling in Morocco. The Idrisid regime lasted from 788–89 to 985–86. Idris, the founder of the new state, died in 792–93, after reducing most of Morocco and also Tlemcen to obedience with the aid of the Berber tribesmen who had rallied to his cause on his arrival in the western Maghreb. His son, Idris II, founded Fez, the capital of the Idrisids and a notable centre of Muslim life and civilization in the Maghreb. After the death of Idris II (d. 828–29) the regime fell into decline. Morocco now endured for some two hundred years a long period of internecine conflict, of tribal revolt and of warring principalities. At the same time it had to face external danger in the form of pressures from the Umayad Caliphate of Cordoba in Spain (at the apogee of its power and splendour in the reigns of Abd al-Rahman III (912–61) and al-Hakam II (961–76)) and also from the Fatimid Caliphate established and consolidated in Ifriqiya (i.e. modern Tunisia and eastern Algeria) during the years 908–69.

It was after this long period of turmoil and fragmentation that Morocco entered into the most splendid phase of its medieval history. There now arose, amongst Berbers of Sanhaja descent who followed a nomadic mode of life in the regions near the Senegal, the religious movement of the Almoravids (al-Murabitun—"people of the ribat", i.e., of a fortified abode devoted to spiritual retreat and also to jihad or war against the infidel). The chieftain of these Berbers, Yahya b. Ibrahim, brought back from Mecca Abd Allah b. Yasin to spread the true doctrine of Islam among his people. The Almoravids soon passed over from the pursuit of the ascetic life to war on behalf of the true faith. The tide of conquest in Morocco gathered momentum under the amir Abu Bakr and led, after his death, to the establishment of a vast Almoravid state in the time of Yusef b. Tashufin (d. 1106), who in 1062 founded Marrakesh and extended the domination of the Almoravids over all Morocco and much of Algeria. In 1086 he halted the southward advance of the Christian *reconquista* in Spain and then annexed the Muslim lands there to the Almoravid territories in North Africa. His successor Ali b. Yusuf (d. 1142) consolidated and maintained the empire, but thereafter the power of the Almoravids fell into a rapid decline. The Saharan nomads who had been the dynamic force behind the movement became absorbed, as it were, into the rich milieu of Andalusian Muslim civilization. Dynastic discord and incompetence among the Almoravid amirs hastened the collapse of the regime. The Christians in Spain took Saragossa in 1118 and began a new phase of their *reconquista*. And in the Atlas mountains of Morocco a new religious force was preparing to burst out over the Moroccan scene. Seven years later, in Morocco, the Almohads rose in revolt against the Almoravids and after 22 years of stubborn conflict took Marrakesh in 1147.

A religious leader, Muhammad b. Tumart (d. 1130), who had studied at Cordoba, Mecca and Baghdad, taught amongst the Masmuda Berbers of the High Atlas doctrines of a strict unitarian character and assumed for himself the designation of al-Mahdi, "the rightly guided one". Amongst the Masmuda he gathered around himself a nucleus of Berber adherents—the "Unitarians", i.e., al-Muwahhidun or Almohads. After the death of Ibn Tumart in 1130 one of his ardent disciples, a Berber of the Kumiya tribe named Abd al-Mumin, became the Khalifa of the Mahdi. Under the guidance of Abd al-Mumin (d. 1163) the Almohads took Marrakesh in 1147 and then in the years 1151–59 overran the rest of Morocco and the North African lands as far east as Tripolitania and Cyrenaica. The Almohads reached the summit of their splendour in the reign of al-Mansur (1184–98), who brought Muslim Spain under Almohad control and checked the menacing advance of the Christians at the battle of Alarcos (1196). Under his successor Muhammad al-Nasir (1199–1214) the Almohads suffered a serious defeat in battle against the Christians of Spain at Las Navas de Tolosa (1212). Thereafter the Almohad empire began to decline. The Hafsids made themselves independent in Ifriqiya (1235–56). Much of the Central Maghreb came under the control of the Abd al-Wadid amirs ruling at Tlemcen. At the same time a new Berber house—the Merinids, of Zenata Berber origin—rose into prominence, conquering Fez in 1248 and Marrakesh in 1269 and thus bringing to an end the last remnants of Almohad rule.

THE MERINIDS

The Merinids, whose effective power lasted for about one hundred years, came from eastern Morocco, overran first the northern regions of Morocco and then the lands in the South. Their attempts to reconstitute the empire of the Almohads met with no durable success. Revolt against their domination was not infrequent in the southern regions of Morocco. Several campaigns undertaken to regain control of the eastern Maghreb brought no more than transient gains, both Ifriqiya and Tlemcen escaping from their domination. Nor could the Merinids establish themselves in Spain, although their interventions there did hinder the Christian *reconquista* and gave the Muslim state of Grenada enough time to consolidate its resources and thus gain the strength to resist the Christians until 1492. The decline of the Merinid regime saw the culmination of a process long since in train. Nomadic tribes of Arab origin—the Hilal and the Sulaym—penetrated into the Maghreb during the course of the 11th and 12th centuries. Other Badawi elements infiltrated through the northern reaches of the Sahara during the later phases of Almohad rule. With the gradual disintegration of the Merinid state the Badawi tribes thrust westward through the Atlas mountains and penetrated into the heart-lands of Morocco. These Badawi invasions, although causing widespread disruption and confusion, contributed much to the Arabization of Morocco and the neighbouring lands. During the years of Merinid decline, dynastic quarrels led to political disintegration, with the result that rival states came into being at Fez and Marrakesh. Morocco, until 1465, was a prey to prolonged internal discords, which ended, at least in part, only with the emergence of another regime of Zenata Berber origin—the Wattasid regime (1465–1549). The Wattasids had no long pre-eminence, their failure to halt the progress of the Portuguese and the Spaniards, who had begun to establish themselves along the Atlantic and the Mediterranean shores of Morocco, being one of the main reasons for their rapid decline.

THE LINE OF SHARIFS

A new movement of resistance to the intrusions of the Spaniards, and, above all, of the Portuguese (by 1500 the masters of Ceuta, Tangier, Arcila, Agadir, Mazagan and Safi on the western coast of Morocco) was born amongst the religious confraternities, amongst the *marabouts* and the "shorfa" (descendants of the Prophet) in Morocco, who now led the Jihad, or war on behalf of the Muslim faith, against the Christians. Out of this situation arose the Saadian regime, originating in a line of Sharifs from the region of the Wadi Draa on the Saharan side of the Atlas mountains. The Saadians took Fez in 1520 and Marrakesh in 1548. Their prestige was due to their status as descendants of the Prophet and to their success in driving the Portuguese from most of their possessions on the Atlantic littoral of Morocco—a success which culminated in their defeat of the Portuguese at the battle of Alcazarquivir in 1578. The most famous of the Sharifs, Ahmad al-Mansur (1578–1603) resisted the pressure of the Ottoman Turks on his eastern frontier with Algeria and in 1591 sent out a large expedition which seized Timbuktu and Goa on the Western Sudan, returning with rich plunder in the form of slaves and gold. Al-Mansur, realising that his house had no strong tribal support, such as earlier dynasties had owned, organised the Saadian regime on a new foundation (the Makhzan)—a system under which various Arab tribes enjoyed exemption from taxes in return for armed service to the state. Much depended, in such a system, on the character of the Sultan. If he were strong and able, all might be well, but in practice the political influence of the sultans tended to fluctuate in accordance with their skill or incompetence. The tribal rivalries would break out anew, the endless tensions between the nomadic and the settled elements in the population became intensified whenever the central government was weak or ill-directed. At such times the "Bled as-Siba" (the areas of dissidence—in particular the Atlas Mountains) set their tribal autonomies against the forces of the "Bled al-Makhzan" (the controlled areas). The period of Saadian rule, which ended in 1668, was, however, one of considerable prosperity for Morocco. Sugar cane culture was encouraged; gold brought by caravan from the Sudan added to the resources of the regime; close commercial contact was made with the lands of southern and western Europe, amongst them England.

Yet another wave of popular religious sentiment brought to power a new house—known under the designations Alawi, Hasani or Filali—which still reigns in Morocco. The Alawi Sharifs had their origin amongst the Berbers located in the oases of Tafilalet, i.e., Saharan Morocco. Under the guidance of the Alawi house Berber forces took

Fez in 1644 and Marrakesh in 1668. The reigns of Rashid II (1664–72) and, above all, of Mulai Ismail (1672–1727) established the Alawi regime on a firm basis and saw Morocco more thoroughly pacified and more solidly united than it was ever to be again until the time of the French occupation. Ismail used as one of his main instruments of rule a powerful corps of negro troops, some stationed close to his capital, Meknès, others established in a network of Qasbahs (fortresses) which covered most of the land. He also had at his command a strong force of European renegades. Among the main achievements of Mulai Ismail must be numbered the occupation, in 1684, of Tangier (English since 1662) and the capture, in 1689, of Larache (Spanish since 1610). Mulai Ismail concluded with France in 1682 a commercial agreement, which was confirmed later in 1787, precedence being then accorded to the consuls of France over the consuls of all other nations.

Mulai Ismail had managed to thrust back the pressure of the Sanhaja Berbers, who were beginning to move down from the Middle Atlas into the lowland areas of Morocco. His successors did not win the same degree of success, with the result that, after the death of Ismail in 1727, a period of confusion ensued in Morocco until the rise of yet another able prince, the Sharif Muhammad b. Abdallah (1757–1790). Muhammad founded Mogador in 1765 and drove the Portuguese from Mazagan in 1769. He entered into a pact of friendship and commerce with Spain in 1767. A brief period of conflict with Spain followed in 1774, but a new agreement was negotiated between Morocco and Spain in 1780.

Muhammad b. Abdallah and his immediate successors, Mulai Sulaiman (1792–1822) and Mulai Abd al-Rahman (1822–59) made strenuous efforts to maintain the control of the central regime in the face of tribal dissidence, and to ward off the possibilities of foreign intervention in the affairs of Morocco. The French conquest of Algiers in 1830 was bound, however, to have repercussions in Morocco. Mulai Abd al-Rahman gave assistance to Abd al-Qadir, the amir who led the Muslim resistance to France in Algeria during the years 1832–47. During the course of their campaigns against Abd al-Qadir the French met and defeated a Moroccan force at Wadi Isly in 1844.

A dispute over the limits of the Ceuta enclave, which was under Spanish rule, led in 1860 to a brief war between Morocco and Spain. Spanish troops under General O'Donnell defeated the Moroccans at Los Castillejos and seized Tetuan. A further engagement at Wadi Ras in March 1860 brought the war to a close. A peace settlement followed, under the terms of which the Ceuta enclave was enlarged and Spain was given indemnities amounting to 100 million pesetas. Morocco also granted to Spain a territorial enclave on the Atlantic coast opposite the Canaries (Santa Cruz de Mar Pequeña, now Ifni). In 1884 Spain claimed a protectorate over the coastal zone to the south of Morocco, from Cape Bojador to Cape Blanco, the future Spanish Sahara. The borders between this territory, known as the Río de Oro, and the French possessions to the south and east were agreed between France and Spain in June 1900.

FRENCH RULE

France, with her hold on Algeria secure, had begun to turn her eyes towards the Western Maghreb, but the rivalries among the great Powers long hindered the establishment of a French protectorate over Morocco. In April 1904, however, Great Britain agreed to recognize the pre-eminence of French interests in Morocco in return for a similar recognition of English interests in Egypt. A convention between France and Spain in October 1904 assigned to Spain two zones of influence, one in northern and the other in southern Morocco. The southern border of Morocco was set at 27° 40″N., beyond which latitude Spain's Saharan territories were deemed to begin. The Germans now sought to intervene in Moroccan affairs and at the conference of Algeciras in 1906 secured the adherence of the Great Powers to the economic "internationalization" of Morocco. A sharp crisis in 1911, when the German gunboat *Panther* appeared at Agadir, ended in a Franco-German settlement, the Germans now recognizing Morocco as a French sphere of influence in return for territorial concessions in the Congo. In March 1912 Morocco became a Protectorate of France, with a French Resident-General empowered to direct foreign affairs, to control defence and also to introduce internal reforms. A new convention of 1912 between France and Spain revised the earlier agreement of 1904: Spain now received her zones of influence in Morocco (though somewhat diminished in extent)—but from France as the protecting power and *not* from the Sultan.

The first French Resident-General in Morocco was General Lyautey (1912–25). He established effective control, before 1914, over the plains and lower plateaux of Morocco from Fez to the Atlas mountains south of Marrakesh; then, before 1918, over the western Atlas, the Taza corridor connecting with Algeria and some areas of the northern highlands. French troops helped Spain to subdue the formidable rebellion (1921–26) of the Rif tribesmen under Abd al-Krim. This success meant the subjugation of the northern mountains and allowed the French to turn with unimpeded vigour to the reduction of the Middle Atlas and the Tafilalet—a task accomplished by 1934, when the pacification of the whole of Morocco could be regarded as complete.

It was at this time that nationalist sentiment began to make itself felt in Morocco. A "Comité d'Action Marocaine" now asked for a limitation of the protectorate. This "Comité" was dissolved in 1937, but nationalist propaganda continued against the French regime. Morocco rallied to the cause of France in 1939 and to the Free French movement in 1942. A Party of Independence (Istiqlal), formed in 1943, demanded full freedom for Morocco, with a constitutional form of government under Sultan Muhammad b. Yusuf, who supported the nationalist movement. The Istiqlal, strong in the towns, did not find great favour at this time among the conservative tribesmen of Morocco, who tended to concentrate their resistance to reform on western lines around Thami al-Glawi, the Pasha of Marrakesh. The tensions between the new and the old ideas in Morocco became much sharper in 1953. Sultan Muhammad b. Yusuf had long adhered to the aims of the Istiqlal movement. He had fallen into disagreement with the French administration, refusing to issue *dahirs* (decrees) authorising various measures that the French desired to see in force. In May 1953 a number of Pashas and Caids, with al-Glawi, the Pasha of Marrakesh, at their head, asked for the removal of the Sultan. Berber tribesmen began to converge in force towards the main urban centres in Morocco such as Rabat, Casablanca and Fez. On August 20th, 1953, the Sultan agreed to go into exile in Europe, but not to abdicate. Muhammad b. Arafa, a prince of the Alawi house, was now recognised as Sultan. Attempts to assassinate him occurred in September 1953 at Rabat and again in March 1954 at Marrakesh. The situation continued to be tense, with outbreaks of violence occurring here and there throughout Morocco in 1954–55 and nationalist fervour running high.

INDEPENDENCE—1956

Sultan Muhammad b. Arafa renounced the throne and withdrew to Tangier in 1955. Muhammad b. Yusuf, on November 5th in that year, was recognised once more as the legitimate Sultan. A joint Franco-Moroccan declaration of March 2nd, 1956, stated that the Protectorate agreement of 1912 was obsolete and that the French government now recognised the independence of Morocco. A Protocol of the same date covered the transitional phase before new agreements between France and Morocco, still to be negotiated, could come into effect. The Sultan would now have full legislative powers in Morocco. Henceforward a High Commissioner was to represent France in the new state. France undertook also to aid Morocco with the organization of its armed forces and to assist in the re-assertion of Moroccan control over the zones of Spanish influence, the sole legal basis for which was the Franco-Spanish convention of 1912. On November 12th, 1956, Morocco became a member of the United Nations.

In August 1956 the Istiqlal proclaimed the need to abrogate the Convention of Algeciras (1906), which had "internationalized" the economic life of Morocco, and also to secure the withdrawal of all foreign troops from the land. Following an international conference in October 1956 Tangier was restored to Morocco. A Royal Charter of August 1957 maintained in general the former economic and financial system in force at Tangier, including a free money market, quota-free trade with foreign countries and a low level of taxation. In 1959 Tangier lost its special status and was integrated financially and economically with Morocco, but a Royal decree of January 1962 made it once more a free port. The Istiqlal, in 1956, had envisaged the creation of a "Great Morocco" which, according to a map published in July of that year, would include certain areas in South-West Algeria, the Spanish territories in North-West Africa and also Mauritania, together with the French Sudan (i.e., the Republic of Mali). The Sultan of Morocco and his government reiterated these claims in the years which followed the achievement of Moroccan independence, beginning in 1960 an intensive propaganda and diplomatic campaign against Mauritania.

The problem of the Spanish territories in North-West Africa also came to the fore at this time. Spain had recognised the independence of Morocco, renouncing also the northern zone of the protectorate assigned to her in Morocco under the terms of the Franco-Spanish convention of 1912. No agreement was reached, however, on the enclaves of Ceuta and Melilla in the north, the enclave of Ifni in the south, or the Spanish territories to the south of Morocco. These territories had since 1934 been divided in two parts, the northern Seghia el Hamra and the southern Río de Oro, both administered jointly with Ifni, and separately from the contiguous southern zone of Spain's protectorate in Morocco. Raids on Ifni and the western Sahara by Moroccan irregular forces (the "Armée de Libération du Grand Sahara"), reputed to have some connection with the Istiqlal, caused serious truble between 1956 and 1958, although the Moroccan Government declared that it was not responsible for these incursions. Negotiations between Morocco and Spain, held at Cintra in Portugal, led in April 1958 to an agreement under which Spain, in accordance with the settlement reached in April 1956, relinquished to Morocco the southern zone of her former protectorate. Spain retained possession of the enclaves and of Seghia el Hamra and Río de Oro, which were renamed the Spanish Sahara and separated from Ifni.

KING HASSAN II AND ROYAL DOMINANCE OF GOVERNMENT

The dominant political force after independence remained the Istiqlal, which obtained a majority in the Government. At the same time Sultan Muhammad strengthened the position of the monarchy. In July 1957 Prince Moulai Hassan was proclaimed heir to the throne and in August the Sultan assumed the title of king. Istiqlal's efforts to reduce the power of the monarch were hampered by divisions within the party itself. Tension between the conservative and radical wings reached breaking-point in December 1958 when a Government was formed by Abdullah Ibrahim, a leader of the radical tendency. In the following months Ben Barka led a movement to establish a radical party organization independent of the conservative Istiqlal leadership of Allal El Fassi. In September 1959 this new organization became an independent party, the National Union of Popular Forces (UNFP). Although the UNFP supported Ibrahim's government, it became the object of repressive measures by the police and the army who were under the control of the king or of "king's men" in the cabinet. In May 1960 a new government was formed with the King himself as Prime Minister and Prince Hassan as his deputy, and the UNFP went into opposition. On the death of King Muhammad in February 1961 the prince ascended the throne as King Hassan II, and also became Prime Minister. In December 1962 a new constitution was approved by referendum, establishing a constitutional monarchy with guaranteed personal and political freedoms. In January 1963 a cabinet reshuffle deprived the Istiqlal leaders of their posts in the government, and when elections for the House of Representatives were held in May both Istiqlal and the UNFP appeared as opposition parties. The King was represented by the newly-formed Front for the Defence of Constitutional Institutions (FDIC). The election, by universal direct suffrage, failed to produce the expected clear majority for the government party, the results being: FDIC 69 seats; Istiqlal 41 seats; UNFP 28 seats; Independents 6 seats. In the following months repressive action was taken against both opposition parties. Several Istiqlal deputies were arrested for protesting against corruption and mismanagement of the election, leading the party to boycott further elections later in the year. Almost all the leaders of the UNFP were arrested in July 1963 in connection with an alleged coup attempt. Many of them were held in solitary confinement, tortured and eventually sentenced to death. In November the King gave up the post of Prime Minister, installing a Government of FDIC men devoted to his interests.

RELATIONS IN THE MAGHREB

In July 1962 Moroccan troops entered the region south of Colomb-Béchar in Algeria—a region never officially demarcated. The Moroccan press also launched a strong campaign in support of the view that the Tindouf area in the extreme south-west of Algeria should belong to Morocco—a claim of some importance, since the area contains large deposits of high-grade (57 per cent) iron ore and also considerable resources of oil and natural gas.

An arbitration commission was established by the OAU, and Algeria and Morocco submitted evidence in support of their respective territorial claims. On February 20th, 1964, an agreement was reached on the establishment of a demilitarized zone. A swift improvement in relations between the two countries followed.

A more amicable relationship also became evident between Morocco and Mauritania. The Ministers of Information of these two states met at Cairo in July 1964 during the course of an African Summit Conference. An understanding was reached to bring an end to the "war" of radio propaganda and criticism hitherto active between Morocco and Mauritania.

INTERNAL UNREST

In August 1964 the Moroccan Government was reorganized, although it remained composed largely of FDIC members. The reshuffle was the preparation for an attempt to attract the opposition parties back into a coalition government, since the FDIC had an inadequate majority in the House of Representatives and was itself split into two factions, the Democratic Socialist Party (PSD) and the People's Movement. The weakness of the government contributed to the tense political situation which developed in the first half of 1965 as unemployment and rising prices generated discontent among the urban working class. In March an unpopular Ministry of Education circular led to student protests. On March 23rd student demonstrations in Casablanca developed into rioting with the participation of workers, and over a hundred people are estimated to have been killed when police and troops fired on the demonstrators. Meanwhile negotiations were going on between the King and political leaders of all parties in an attempt to form a government of National Union. As a conciliatory gesture the King declared an amnesty for all political prisoners on April 14th. He proposed a programme of industrial development and agrarian reform, plus a campaign against corruption in the administration. Both Istiqlal and the UNFP refused coalition, however, demanding democratic elections to be followed by the formation of a government by the majority party. Faced with continuing political deadlock, on June 7th King Hassan proclaimed a state of emergency, under which he himself assumed full legislative and executive power. New elections, it was stated, would be held after the constitution had been revised and submitted to a referendum. In October 1965 the UNFP leader Ben Barka disappeared in France never to be seen again. Gen. Oufkir, one of the King's sturdiest supporters, was found guilty in France in his absence of complicity in Ben Barka's disappearance. Relations between Morocco and France became very strained and there were anti-government protest strikes in Morocco.

In July 1967, King Hassan relinquished the post of Prime Minister to Dr. Mohammed Benhima, and in 1967 and 1968 there were eight major cabinet reshuffles. Considerable student and trade union unrest continued during this period, but the King won some popularity by extensive nationalization measures and a degree of land redistribution.

There was a gradual return to full political activity in 1969, though still under royal direction. Municipal and rural communal elections were held in October, although these were boycotted by opposition parties and the successful candidates mostly stood as independents. Following this Dr. Mohammed Benhima was replaced as Prime Minister by Dr. Ahmed Laraki, formerly Foreign Minister. A national referendum on a new constitution was at last held in July 1970; official figures claimed that over 98 per cent of the votes were affirmative, despite general opposition from the main political parties, trade unions and student organizations. Elections for a new single chamber legislature were held in August. Of the 240 members, 90 were elected by direct suffrage, 90 by local councils and 60 by an electoral college. The results were that 158 elected members were Independents, 60 were of the government party *Mouvement Populaire* and 22 from opposition parties.

In July 1971 there was an unsuccessful attempt to overthrow the King and establish a republic, apparently engineered by right-wing army officers, angered by the level of corruption in the royal administration and by the King's too lenient treatment of dissent on the left. During the months following the attempted coup, a series of conciliatory talks was held between the Government and members of Istiqlal and the UNFP who had united to form a National Front in July 1970, but they refused to compromise with government policies.

In February 1972 King Hassan announced a new Constitution, under which executive power would be vested in the Government and the Assembly, and two-thirds of the Assembly's members were to be elected by universal suffrage compared to half under the previous constitution. The National Front urged a boycott of the constitution referendum and accused the Government of rigging the results, according to which 93 per cent of voters took part and approved the constitution in 98.75 per cent of valid votes cast. The constitution was promulgated in March, and in April a new cabinet, substantially the same as its predecessor, was appointed to organize elections. On April 30th, however, King Hassan announced that Parliament, which was due to be reopened, would remain dissolved, and that elections for the new assembly were being postponed until new electoral lists had been drawn up. In July a split occurred in the UNFP which separated the Rabat section from the rest of the party. As a consequence the National Front became a dead letter.

In August 1972 King Hassan survived another attempt on his life, which had apparently been planned by General Oufkir, the Minister of Defence and Army Chief of Staff, whose death occurred immediately afterwards. The King himself took over the command of the armed forces and defence matters and did not appoint a new Defence Minister until March 1973. He approached the opposition parties again, asking for their co-operation in supervising general elections and collaboration with the Government. However, both Istiqlal and the UNFP demanded that a number of far-reaching reforms be introduced, which were unacceptable to the King, as they included curtailing the King's powers and guaranteeing political freedom. The elections, which had been postponed until October, were further postponed indefinitely, and a new cabinet was formed in November without opposition participation.

FOREIGN RELATIONS 1967-72

In the Arab-Israeli war in June 1967, the Moroccan government gave voice to its support of the Arabs' anti-Zionist cause, but did not commit its troops to the fighting.

Morocco continued to press her claim to Spanish-held territories in north-west Africa. In December 1967 the United Nations passed a resolution urging Spain to hold a referendum in the Spanish Sahara to allow the population to determine its future; the referendum should be held in consultation with Morocco and Mauritania, which had also asserted a claim to the territory. Spain accepted the principle of self-determination, but positions hardened in June 1970 after riots in the major Sahara town, El Aaiún, were quelled with loss of life. Further UN resolutions were passed in support of decolonization, and Morocco, Mauritania and Algeria each gave some backing to three rival Saharan liberation movements. In contrast, the question of Ifni was settled amicably in June 1969, when Spain handed over the small coastal enclave to Morocco.

Morocco's claim to Mauritania was dropped in 1969. Full diplomatic recognition and an exchange of ambassadors followed in January 1970; in June 1970, a treaty of solidarity, good neighbourliness and co-operation was signed between the two countries. Relations with France improved following the general pattern in the Arab world, and the diplomatic missions in Paris and Rabat were returned to full ambassadorial status for the first time since the Ben Barka affair in 1966.

In May 1970 final agreement was reached in the frontier dispute with Algeria, and a joint commission mapped out a delineation maintaining the boundaries of the colonial period. The disputed region of Gara-Djebilet, rich in iron ore deposits, thus became the property of Algeria, but Morocco was to have a share in a joint company to be established to exploit these deposits. The Algerian-Moroccan border was agreed by both heads of state, and the agreement was ratified on May 17th, 1973.

HASSAN IN CONTROL

At the end of 1972 King Hassan's position appeared precarious. He was politically isolated since the main political parties continued in opposition and the armed forces could no longer be relied upon to support him. Many observers doubted his ability to survive. However, the King took strong measures against dissidents and won support by adopting nationalist policies.

In March 1973 the King announced plans for the Moroccanization of parts of the economy in the course of the next two years. At the same time he reinforced his traditional support in the rural areas by ordering the confiscation of foreign-owned lands and their distribution among the peasantry. Since most of the landowners were French, relations between France and Morocco cooled and French aid was suspended pending an agreement on compensation. In the same month relations with Spain became strained when Morocco announced the extension of its territorial waters from 12 to 70 miles. Intrusions of Spanish trawlers into the new limits led to frequent confrontations until an agreement was reached between the two governments in January 1974 allowing a limited number of Spanish vessels to fish in Moroccan waters. The new nationalist policy also led Morocco to take a more active part than previously in the Arab-Israeli conflict. In February troops were despatched to the Syrian front and during the October War further detachments were sent to Egypt. The common cause produced a degree of rapprochement between Morocco and the more revolutionary Arab states.

In the early months of 1974 political trials continued. Another round of arrests followed the announcement in February of the discovery of a plot to free prisoners in Kenitra jail. The King, however, made some conciliatory gestures. In March he announced plans for university and judicial reforms, and in April several imprisoned UNFP leaders were released. Relations with France improved and French aid was resumed in February, but despite the settlement of the fishing dispute relations with Spain remained bad, since Morocco continued to press her claim to the Spanish Sahara. The growth of phosphate mining in the territory posed a threat to the Moroccan economy which was itself dependent on revenue from phosphate exports. The opposition parties, motivated by a mixture of anti-colonialism and nationalism, urged the government to take action. In July 1974 the King held consultations with military leaders, ministers and leaders of all the political parties to prepare an international campaign for the annexation of the Sahara. An extraordinary degree of national unity was achieved, opposition leaders agreeing to act as government envoys to foreign capitals. Discussions with Spain in August produced no result. The Spanish pursued their own plan for the decolonization of the Sahara, involving the establishment of an independent state closely linked with Spain. This project was contested not only by Morocco but also by Mauritania which reasserted its old claim to the area. Both countries rejected Spain's plan to hold a referendum in the Sahara under UN supervision. In October the issue was debated in the UN General Assembly at the initiative of Morocco. Two months later the Assembly formally approved Morocco's suggestion that the matter be brought before the International Court of Justice at the Hague, and the UN Special Committee on Colonialism was instructed to send a mission to the territory. The referendum proposed by Spain was to be postponed for the time being.

In the atmosphere of national unity produced by the Sahara issue in the second half of 1974 there was an effervescence of political activity. New parties were formed and existing parties reorganized. Most notably the split in the UNFP was confirmed, as the Rabat section of the party became the USFP. King Hassan once more promised elections for the following year, and once more postponed them indefinitely, but even the opposition were not enthusiastic about elections before the settlement of the Sahara dispute. Harassment of opposition parties did not cease and no opposition figures were invited into the Government, but some political prisoners were released. Social and political conflicts were temporarily obscured by a mist of nationalist sentiment.

SAHARAN TAKEOVER

The situation in the Western Sahara developed rapidly Since Spain reiterated its readiness to withdraw from the Sahara, it became clear that the chief conflict was between the rival North African countries and liberation movements. After Morocco and Mauritania reached some agreement on the future division of the territory Algeria became the main butt of Moroccan invective, because of its support for *Frente Popular para la Liberación de Sakiet el Hamra y Río de Oro* (*Polisario*), a Saharan liberation movement hostile to Moroccan claims and close to the Algerian Government in ideology.

On October 15th, 1975, a UN investigative mission reported that the majority of Saharans favoured independence, and the following day the World Court ruled in favour of self-determination. King Hassan responded immediately by ordering a march of 350,000 unarmed civilians to take possession of the Spanish Sahara. The Green March, as it was called, began on November 6th. The Spanish authorities allowed the marchers to progress a few miles across the border before halting their advance. On November 9th Hassan called off the march, declaring that it had achieved its objective, and on November 14th a tripartite agreement was signed in Madrid, by which Spain agreed to withdraw from the Sahara in 1976 and hand over to a joint Morocco-Mauritanian administration. Algeria reacted angrily to this agreement, stepping up its support for Polisario and making veiled threats of direct military intervention. Moroccan armed forces quickly moved into the territory, entering the capital, El Aaiún, on December 11th. They met sharp resistance from Polisario guerrillas, and many Saharans fled towards the Algerian border to avoid the Moroccan advance. The last Spanish troops left in January 1976, a month before they were due to go under the terms of the tripartite agreement.

The Moroccan Prime Minister, Ahmed Osman, visited France in January and French arms supplies to Morocco were stepped up. On January 27th Algerian and Moroccan forces clashed at Amgalla, inside the Western Sahara, and there was further fighting in February. On March 4th a Saharan government-in-exile was formed in Algeria and on March 7th Morocco broke off diplomatic relations with Algeria. The prospect of general war between the two countries faded, however, as Algeria contented itself with arming and training Polisario guerrillas for raids into the Sahara and providing camps for civilian refugees from the area, believed to number some 60,000.

Despite the fighting, there is no doubt that King Hassan benefited greatly in prestige and popularity at home from the Saharan takeover. The staging of the Green March had particularly appealed to the Moroccan imagination. The King at last felt secure enough to hold the long-awaited elections. With the exception of the UNFP, the opposition parties agreed to participate, despite the continuation of political trials connected with the March 1973 uprising which resulted in heavy prison sentences for many of the accused in early 1977. Municipal elections were held in November 1976, and these were followed by provincial elections in January 1977 and elections for professional and vocational chambers the following March.

At each stage "independents", mostly pro-government and conservative, won over 60 per cent of the seats. Istiqlal and the USFP protested against electoral irregularities and administrative interference. On March 1st four party leaders, including M'Hamed Boucetta of Istiqlal and Abderrahim Bouabid of the USFP, agreed to join the Government as Ministers of State without Portfolio, in the hope of ensuring that the national elections to be held on June 3rd would be fairly conducted. Press censorship was also abolished. In the elections, Independents won a total of 141 of the 264 seats in the new Chamber of Representatives, while Istiqlal and the Mouvement Populaire won 49 and 44 respectively, the USFP won 16 and other opposition parties 14. The new Government, announced in October, included former opposition members, notably M'Hamed Boucetta as Foreign Minister, with seven other members of Istiqlal, four members of the Mouvement Populaire and Maati Bouabid of the UNFP, whose party, however, subsequently disowned him. Thus the King won over the major part of the opposition, and appeared to have succeeded in his plan to combine the forms of democracy with strong royal authority.

In April 1976 Morocco and Mauritania reached agreement on the division of the Saharan territory, of which the greater part, containing most of the known mineral wealth, was allotted to Morocco, which then set about absorbing the new territory as three new provinces of the Kingdom. By placing strong army garrisons in the territory's few scattered urban settlements the Moroccans were able to secure them against guerrilla attacks, but Polisario incursions into the surrounding desert areas could not be checked. The conveyor belt from the important Bu Craa phosphate mines to the sea was sabotaged, and clashes between the Moroccan army and guerrillas caused heavy casualties on both sides. Polisario proved too strong for Mauritania's very limited armed forces in the south and Morocco took increasing responsibility for the defence of the region. The two countries formed a joint defence committee in May 1977 after a successful Polisario raid on the Mauritanian mining town of Zouérate, in which two French nationals were killed and six captured. In November King Hassan warned Algeria that Moroccan troops would pursue Polisario forces into Algerian territory if necessary; the Algerian Government retorted that any such incursion would mean war. Tension was increased by the direct intervention of France, following the release of the French captives in December, with three air attacks on the Polisario; although the French Government maintained that its action was for the protection of the French nationals working at the Saharan mines, and had been undertaken at the request of Mauritania, it was also clear that France favoured the expansion of Moroccan interests in the area rather than those of Algeria, for both economic and strategic reasons. During the first half of 1978 the situation of stalemate continued, with intermittent fighting and a further French air-raid in April. Proposed meetings of the OAU to discuss the issue were postponed on three occasions, revealing an apparent unwillingness on the part of many African leaders to commit themselves. The intransigence of both Morocco and Algeria was at least partly due to the fact that their governments relied to a great extent on their respective Saharan policies for popular support at home; in Morocco, the various opposition parties were still united in support of the King in this respect, despite the enormous expense of the war, which accounted for at least a quarter of the 1979 budget, and the cost of confirming Morocco's hold on the Saharan provinces by installing facilities such as schools, hospitals and housing for those inhabitants remaining in the area. In January 1978 a $292 million Sahara Development Programme had been announced, providing for the settlement of the nomads and the creation of a sedentary economy.

The war was having a still worse effect on the economy of Mauritania, and this was the chief reason for the coup which took place there in July 1978. Polisario at once announced a ceasefire in its hostilities against Mauritania, whose new President, Col. Moustapha Ould Salek, announced that the country was eager for peace; it was soon clear that he would be willing to renounce the Saharan province altogether, were it not for the 10,000 Moroccan troops still stationed in Mauritania who might be used against the new regime if it antagonized Morocco. The coup was followed by renewed diplomatic activity, in which France played an important role. President Houphouët-Boigny of the Ivory Coast also offered to act as mediator, proposing the creation of a Saharan Republic in the Mauritanian sector of Western Sahara alone, a suggestion which was as unlikely to satisfy Polisario as it was unacceptable to King Hassan, who declared in August that Morocco would not tolerate the presence of any state other than Mauritania on its southern frontier. In September he accepted the proposal by the President of the OAU, President Nimeri of Sudan, that the Heads of State of six African countries (Guinea, the Ivory Coast, Mali, Nigeria, Tanzania and Sudan) should form a committee of "wise men" to mediate in the dispute, although by the following June this appeared to have achieved very little. Spain, too, became increasingly involved, evidently uneasy about its role in the partition of the area which had been one of the final acts of General Franco; it was anxious, too, to maintain good relations with Algeria and avoid provoking it into increasing its support for the independence movement in the Canary Islands; on the other hand, Spain also needed to avoid offending Morocco if it was to safeguard its fishing rights in Moroccan waters and, still more, its claim to the enclaves of Ceuta and Melilla, long coveted by Morocco. Nevertheless, the Spanish Prime Minister, Adolfo Suárez, visited Algeria in May 1979, held talks with the Secretary-General of Polisario, and declared his support for self-determination by the Saharan people.

Meanwhile, the death of President Boumedienne in December 1978 had not led to a softening of Algeria's attitude: the new Government under President Chadli was equally uncompromising in its support for Polisario. Fighting continued, and in January 1979 Polisario made an attack on the town of Tan-Tan, well within Morocco's pre-1975 borders. In March King Hassan declared that the situation had "reached the verge of the intolerable": he proposed, and the Chamber of Representatives approved, the formation of a National Defence Council to formulate defence policy. This Council comprised members of all the main political groups (independents, Istiqlal, Mouvement Popularie, USFP, Mouvement Populaire Constitutionnel et Démocratique, and Parti du Progrès et du Socialisme), a composition which suggested that the King was seeking to strengthen support for the war by enlarging the number and the political range of those responsible for its direction. At the same time the Chamber of Representatives showed that its attitude was still belligerent by reaffirming Morocco's right to its Saharan territory and recommended that the right of pursuit into foreign (i.e. Algerian) territory should be exercised. Among the Moroccan people as a whole, support for the war still appeared to be almost universal, but there were signs of discontent which could be at least partly attributed to the heavy cost of the fighting. During the first few months of 1979 there were strikes by many different sections of the work-force demanding higher wages, while the visit of the deposed Shah of Iran in March provided an excuse for the expression of discontent, particularly among students and the unemployed. On March 21st the Prime Minister, Ahmed Osman, resigned, ostensibly to devote himself to the organization of the newly formed Independents' party (RNI). He was replaced by Maati Bouabid, the Minister of Justice and a former trade union leader, who had been a member of the left-wing UNFP before it expelled him for joining the Government in 1977. The new Prime Minister held talks with union leaders, after which wage rises were announced, including an increase of 40 per cent in the minimum wage. Although this provided a short-term answer to social unrest, it could only add to the burden on the economy, and the need to find a solution to the Sahara problem became more pressing than ever.

Relations with the U.S.A. cooled slightly when President Carter insisted on remaining neutral with regard to the Saharan problem, and when Congress refused to allow the sale of military aircraft to Morocco for possible use against the Polisario, causing King Hassan to postpone for a year the state visit to Washington which he was due to make in December 1977. Nevertheless, Morocco continued to hold a strongly anti-communist and pro-Western stance, even while maintaining important commercial links with the U.S.S.R., particularly after the 1978 agreements on phosphates and fisheries. Evidence of growing links with France and pro-Western African states was provided in April 1977 and again in June 1978, when Moroccan troops were ferried to Zaire in French and American military aircraft to defend President Mobutu's regime against invasion by Katangan rebels.

Morocco continued to take a moderate view of the conflict in the Middle East, giving a cautious welcome to President Sadat's peace initiative in December 1977 and encouraging emigrants to return to its own Jewish community. However, Morocco joined the other Arab nations in condemning the Egyptian-Israeli peace treaty, and broke off diplomatic relations with Egypt in April 1979.

ECONOMIC SURVEY

Morocco has a congenial climate, varied soils with good agricultural potential and important mineral resources. There is an emerging industrial sector, a small, but growing managerial class and the beginnings of an industrial force. The economic infrastructure (transport, communications, electric energy) is at an advanced stage. The beauty of the country and its climate offer opportunities for the growth of tourism. However, the movement out of the country of capital and trained personnel in the period immediately before and after independence was a severe setback to economic growth. A series of poor harvests also limited growth but favourable capital movements resulted in an average annual growth of 3.9 per cent in the Gross National Product between 1963 and 1969 to 16,110 million dirhams in 1969. The fastest growth was recorded in mining and industry (4.3 per cent). Agricultural production rose by less than 1 per cent annually over this period, as did the activity in the various service sectors while construction and public works showed a decline. The five-year development plan introduced in 1968 aimed at an annual rate of growth of 4.3 per cent, and a slightly bigger increase was achieved, despite a fall off in investment because of political instability and severe floods in early 1970. The G.N.P. in 1972, the final year of the plan, reached 20,600 million dirhams. Agriculture remained the most important sector of production and output increased by four per cent, but this was scarcely sufficient to offset population growth. Industry has a small but growing place in the economy. In 1972 industrial production reached 1,840 million dirhams compared with 1,420 million dirhams at the beginning of the plan period. The mining and power sectors also registered favourable increases in production but growth in the building and public works sector was slower than in the first five-year plan.

The problems that Morocco has to face are familiar among developing countries. The fast-rising population, increasing by 3 per cent per annum, is supported for the most part by an out-of-date agricultural system, and any substantial increase in the country's productive capacity is dependent on foreign finance. The population in 1977 was estimated at 17.6 million (by the World Bank) and is expected to reach 28 million by 1990. Per capita G.N.P. stood at $570 in 1977, but most of the wealth is distributed among landowners and a small number of urban industrialists and merchants. The rural masses and small but growing urban proletariat are much poorer than per capita income figures indicate.

The share of G.N.P. devoted to investments has generally been low by world standards, although the 1973–77 development plan attempted to reverse this trend. Unemployment is a serious problem: it is estimated that about 40 per cent of the population between the ages of 20 and 30 are unemployed. The economy has also been damaged by inflation: the annual rise in consumer prices jumped from 4.2 per cent in 1973 to 17.7 per cent in 1974. It fell slightly to 12.5 per cent in 1977 and again to 9.8 per cent in 1978, as a result of the Government's austerity policy introduced in 1978 and of measures to check speculation.

Morocco has considerable potential for economic growth but defence spending has, since 1976, put severe constraints on development. The sudden rise in phosphate prices in 1974–75 boosted government revenue and allowed the expansion of development plans. Since then, however, income from this source has dropped as a result of decreased world demand. At the same time, outlay on defence and capital equipment has risen. Long-term prospects are good, however, since world demand for phosphate rock—a raw material essential for the manufacture of fertilizers—is bound to pick up and Morocco has other valuable mineral deposits which have not yet been fully exploited. Capital investment continues to be actively encouraged but the government has been forced by shortage of funds to reduce its own share of investment. The three-year plan for 1978–80, announced at the end of 1978, puts total proposed investment at 36,900 million dirhams, of which only 9,700 million dirhams will be provided by the state, the remainder being from the private sector. Priorities are roughly the same as in the 1973–77 five-year plan, which put emphasis on industry, agriculture and irrigation, tourism and vocational training. However, some industries, particularly import-substitution or export-oriented industries, like those of sugar refining and cement, are being given special attention. Labour-intensive light industry is also encouraged. Remittances from expatriate workers, which make an important contribution to the balance of payments, declined from 1973 because of recession and higher unemployment in Europe, but they rose in 1978 after the Government—in June of that year—introduced a preferential exchange rate for remittances in an attempt to stimulate repatriation of earnings. Tourism is also an important source of income. The number of tourists entering Morocco increased rapidly to 1.4 million in 1973, fell to 1.2 million in 1975 but rose to about 1.5 million in 1977 and 1978, as a result of increased hotel capacity and intensive marketing. Receipts from tourism in 1978 were estimated at 1,650 million dirhams, 10 per cent more than in 1977. The country also has the natural advantages of a convenient geographical position, considerable natural resources and an excellent communications system.

AGRICULTURE AND FISHERIES

Agriculture is the key to the economy of Morocco. Three-quarters of Morocco's population live in the countryside, and 55 per cent of the active labour force is engaged in agriculture, livestock-raising and fishing. Thus agriculture provides the means of livelihood of the majority of the population, supplies 80–90 per cent of the country's domestic food requirements and in the region of 30 per cent of the country's total merchandise exports. In 1978 agriculture contributed about 14 per cent of total domestic production.

Changing climatic conditions cause substantial year-to-year variations in agricultural output. In years with bumper harvests the contribution of agriculture to the gross domestic product rises to over 20 per cent (at 1969 prices), whereas in years with particularly poor crops the corresponding contribution is in the region of 14 per cent. Grain production in 1976/77 dropped from 5.5 million tons the previous season to 3 million because of severe drought. It improved to about 4.6 million tons in 1977/78 but about 1.6 million had to be imported to build up depleted stocks.

The prinicipal crops are cereals (especially wheat, barley and maize), citrus fruit, potatoes, tomatoes, beans, chick peas and olives. Canary seed, cumin, coriander, linseed and almonds are also grown, and tea cultivation has recently started in the Loukkos. Esparto grass is put to several uses including the manufacture of vegetable horsehair and is exported for paper making. Vast areas of esparto grass have been brought into economic use by the establishment of a pulp industry based on this grass and on the eucalyptus tree. Forest resources, almost entirely under state control, include cork (covering approximately 370,000 hectares), cedar, argon, oak and various conifers. Tizra wood is exported for tanning.

Livestock numbers have been declining and the quality of herds is generally poor. Milk production, estimated at 620 million litres in 1977, falls far short of domestic demand, and some 36,000 metric tons of dairy products had to be imported in that year, at a cost of about 150 million dirhams. The Government has introduced subsidies to encourage production, and plans to develop five million hectares of pasture land.

In the past Morocco has been largely self-sufficient in foodstuffs, but population growth is fast outpacing increases in agricultural production. Food imports, particularly cereals, sugar and dairy products, have become substantial and the purchase of cereals costs $100–200 million per year.

Until 1973 agricultural produce accounted for by far the largest proportion of total exports, but their importance has declined since the sharp rise in phosphate prices in 1974. In 1978 sales of foodstuffs accounted for about 32 per cent of total exports. Main agricultural exports are citrus fruits (mostly oranges), tomatoes, processed fish and vegetables. Morocco is the world's second largest exporter of citrus fruits: citrus exports in 1976/77 were worth 987 million dirhams and amounted to 590,000 metric tons. In 1977/78 exports rose to 669,000 tons, worth 1,161 million dirhams. A fruit processing industry is being developed, and preserved fruit, jam and fruit juice exports now contribute substantially to earnings.

Under its co-operation treaty with the EEC, Moroccan citrus fruits can enter the Community subject to a small duty. However, stiff competition is provided by Spanish and Israeli fruit. Efforts to obtain further concessions from the EEC for exports of citrus fruits and vegetables met with resistance from Italy, but the revised trade agreement with the EEC in 1976 apparently satisfied Moroccan demands.

The agricultural sector is one of contrasts: on the one side, a system of holdings inherited from European farmers, with an emphasis on cash and export crops; and, on the other, the Muslim farmers, who are much less prosperous, and who raise crops mainly for their own consumption. The traditional arable farming comprises 800,000 to 1,000,000 holdings covering approximately 4 million hectares and is characterized by the small size of the holdings, the legal complexity of rights governing their tenure, low productivity, and the predominance of cereals and stock-raising. Irrigation plans have not made great headway due to the conservatism of the farmers and the complexity of the legal situation. Much of farming and grazing land is owned by the state, tribes and religious communities. Individual ownership formalized by title deeds is still relatively unusual but is spreading. The last colonial lands were nationalized in March 1973 when King Hassan decreed that 250,000 hectares of land belonging to foreign farmers, mainly French, should be taken over by the State. Nearly 2,000 foreign settlers are believed to have been affected by the decree. The demands of French farmers for compensation from the Moroccan Government were not immediately dealt with. This resulted in some tension in Franco-Moroccan relations and French aid to Morocco was suspended. However, France agreed to give Morocco aid totalling 200 million French francs for 1974 when Morocco consented to transfer proceeds from the sale of the 1972–73 season crops of the expropriated farms to the former owners.

Cereals are grown on more than 80 per cent of cultivated land and this is being increased as part of attempts to offset falling production, while the Government has also called for a major effort to increase yield. The Government has pressed strongly for increases in sugar beet and cane production, and by 1976 sugar beet was being grown on over 67,000 hectares. In 1975/76 the sugar beet crop came to 2,362,000 tons, producing 310,000 tons of refined sugar, 60 per cent of total domestic demand. The beet crop fell in 1976/77 to 1,473,700 tons because of bad weather and only 213,400 tons of sugar were refined, but state investment in the sugar industry, which aims to meet all domestic demand by 1985, should ensure that production increases. Market gardening, especially in irrigated areas yields more income per unit of land than most other crops. Output of tomatoes and miscellaneous green vegetaales is fairly constant, but potato output fluctuates widely from one year to another. A year of weak prices can be diastrous for small market gardeners, who are nevertheless unwilling to submit to output controls. Output of pulses, especially broad beans and chick peas, has expanded fairly steadily but in 1976/77 it declined sharply, again because of bad weather, falling to 158,400 tons after a total of 496,200 tons in 1975/76. Production of olives and olive oil has fluctuated considerably, but the Government plans to stabilize production through an intensive tree-planting programme. By 1980 output should reach 400,000 tons of olives.

A total sum of $140 million was allocated to dams and irrigation networks under the five-year plan (1968–72) with a view to increasing the irrigated area by 158,000 hectares. The first of a series of six dams to be built during the plan period was completed in November 1970. The dam, located at Ait Aidel on the River Tersaout, has increased the irrigated area in the Haouz plain from 3,000 to 30,000 hectares. In May 1972 the Mansour Eddahbi dam in southern Morocco was inaugurated and in April 1971 the Hassan Eddakhil Dam was finished, which should irrigate a total area of 40,000 hectares. By the end of the 1973–77 plan Morocco had an estimated 450,000 hectares of land under irrigated cultivation and the ultimate aim is to raise this figure to one million hectares. A total of 23 dams have been, or are being, built for this purpose. Irrigation projects benefiting from World Bank assistance include the $53.7 million expansion of the Gharb Sebou region and the Souss Valley project.

Fishing is an important industry and the total catch varies from 200,000 to 400,000 metric tons per year. The principal species caught is the European pilchard (sardine). Agadir has taken over from Safi as the main fishing port although Casablanca and Eassaouira are also important. Most fish is processed before being consumed or exported. Exports of canned fish were worth 249 million dirhams in 1977/78 and the volume sold was 39,700 tons, most of which went to the EEC. Moroccan sardines are renowned on the world market for their flavour and high quality. There are also substantial exports of fish meal and other products for use as fertilizers and animal foodstuffs.

Fish catches had been declining up to 1972 and Moroccan fishermen blamed European boats, especially those from Spain, for catching too many fish and depleting stocks. In March 1973 King Hassan announced that Morocco was extending its jurisdiction over territorial waters from 12 to 70 miles. Foreign fishing vessels are no longer allowed into the 70-mile area unless their government has a fishing agreement with Morocco. Spain refused to accept this measure, and several incidents involving the Spanish and Moroccan navies occurred. In January 1974 an agreement was reached which did not include Spanish recognition of the new limit, but allowed 200 Spanish vessels to fish near the Moroccan coast as part of a joint Moroccan-Spanish fishing company, *Maropêche*. This company has a capital of 4.4 million dirhams and intends to operate a fleet which will include ocean-going tuna-fishing vessels. The success of such joint ventures could do much to ease a difficult situation. The extension of territorial waters and increasing world prices of fish products should mean that fishing will make an increasingly important contribution to the national economy. In early 1978 a fishing agreement was signed by Morocco and the Soviet Union, providing for co-operation in research and training.

MINING

The most important mineral deposits are phosphates. Morocco accounts for 66 per cent of world reserves and is the third most important producer and the largest exporter in the world. Phosphates represent about 90 per cent of the value of total exports of minerals from Morocco. In addition, Morocco is estimated to be the fourth largest producer of cobalt and also possesses important deposits of lead, manganese and zinc and lesser resources of several other metals, including copper and tin. The exploitation of uranium, associated with phosphate, is being considered.

The chief phosphate deposits are at Khouribga, Youssoufia and Bu Craa, in the former Spanish Sahara, and are controlled by the state *Office Chérifien des Phosphates* (OCP). National consumption of phosphates is very small, about 1.8 million metric tons in 1978 out of total production of 19.1 million tons. Exports account for the bulk of production but, because of a decline in prices from 1974/75 onwards, earnings fell to 2,034 million dirhams in 1978, compared with 4,233 million dirhams in 1974. Prices were increased from $14 per ton in 1973 to a peak of $68 per ton in March 1975, but the world recession reduced demand and prices slipped back to an average of $30 per ton in 1978. From a peak of 19.7 million tons in 1974 production fell back to 14.1 million tons in 1975. It then rose to 19.1 million tons in 1978, of which 17.3 million tons were exported. The biggest purchasers of Moroccan phosphates in 1978 were Spain, France, Belgium, Mexico and Poland.

Morocco's plan is to produce 50 million tons of phosphates per year by the year 2000 by phasing in new mines, at Ben Guerir, Sidi Hajjaj and Meskala. The latter is to be developed by the U.S.S.R. under the terms of a major agreement initialled in January 1978. The deal could be worth $9,000 million over 30 years. It involves the exchange of phosphate rock for crude petroleum, chemical products, timber and technical and financial help at Meskala. Exports of phosphate rock to the U.S.S.R. will initially run at 5 million tons per year, but will rise to 10 million tons per year by 1990. The phosphate industry's prospects were also improved by Morocco's acquisition in February 1976 of territory in the former Spanish Sahara, including the rich Bu Craa deposits, under an agreement concluded with Spain and Mauritania in the previous year. So far, however, production from these deposits has been interrupted because of the activity of Polisario guerrillas.

Morocco has put considerable investment into the phosphate-processing industry, with the aim of increasing the value of its phosphate exports. There are three phosphate-processing plants in operation at Safi, and a $225 million contract to build a fourth was awarded to Heurtey Industries of France in mid-1977. One of the three now operating—Maroc Phosphore I—is being extended by Polimex-Cekop of Poland. The World Bank and Poland are providing loans to cover the cost of the extension. Other expansion plans include the construction of a fifth phosphate processing plant, Maroc Phosphore III, at Jorf Lasfar, where a phosphates port is now under construction. Investment in the phosphates industry is a heavy burden and Morocco has resorted increasingly to foreign borrowing to help to pay for it. The OCP borrowed about $500 million on the international financial market in 1977 and 1978.

Most of the other mineral products have not fared as well as phosphates since independence. Iron ore production fell to only 63,000 metric tons (55 to 60 per cent iron) in 1978, from 407,000 tons in 1977 and 343,000 tons in 1976. It is almost all exported. The lack of a steel industry in the country has not encouraged high activity in the sector. Production of manganese ore was 126,000 tons (gross weight) in 1978, compared with 114,000 tons in 1977. Lead and zinc are often found together in deposits, e.g. at Boukber, Touissit, Aouli and Mikbladen. Production of zinc concentrates dropped to 9,000 tons (gross weight) in 1978 from 22,000 tons in 1977. In contrast, the output of lead concentrates rose in 1978 to a peak of 166,000 tons (gross), because of the opening of a new mine at Touissit. The Oued al-Heimer lead smelter, which now smelts 30,000 tons of lead per year, is to be extended and a new smelter, to produce 80,000 tons of refined lead annually, is planned at Meknès. Cobalt is produced at Bou Azzer. Production fell to 7,000 tons (gross weight) in 1976 from 14,000 tons in 1975 but has since remained steady at the 1976 level. Copper is mined at Blida. A Moroccan-Japanese venture is to invest 70 million dirhams in exploiting the Blida copper deposits and production is expected to reach 225,000 tons of ore per year. The value of mining exports (excluding phosphates) was 425.2 million dirhams in 1977.

Mining has been placed on the list of industries which benefit under the Investment Code introduced in July 1973 to promote private investments, and replacing the first decree published in December 1969. Another decree virtually abolished the export tax on minerals by lowering it from 5 per cent *ad valorem* to 0.5 per cent on iron, antimony, cobalt, manganese, barytine and fluorine ores, fuller's earth, lead, zinc and silver metals. For lead, zinc and copper ores the tax is reduced on a variable scale related to world prices of these minerals.

Morocco also has coal and small quantities of petroleum. The coal deposits are at Djerada south of Oujda and are controlled by the Government Bureau of Mining Research and Participation (BRPM). Production rose sharply from 565,000 tons in 1973 to 720,000 tons in 1978. Big increases in oil prices in 1973 mean that Morocco relies more on domestic supplies of coal in preference to high-priced oil imports, which meet about 80 per cent of domestic energy requirements. In the past the coal industry has been affected by the concentration on hydro-electricity at the expense of thermal generation. Until the mid-1960s hydraulic power was the major source of electricity generation, accounting for 90 per cent of the total in 1965. Thermal power has since expanded rapidly and now accounts for two-thirds of electricity production, the remaining third being hydraulic based. Total electricity production grew by an average 10 per cent annually between 1965 and 1978, reaching 4,061 million kWh in 1978. Production and distribution are state-controlled through the *Office National de l'Electricité*; the frequency is 50 cycles per second.

Oil price rises in 1973 and 1974 added new impetus to the Government's attempts to develop a domestic oil industry. Production in 1973 amounted to an almost negligible 42,000 tons which fell to 20,000 tons in 1975. Apart from small oil deposits in the Doukkala, Dara and Tafaya regions the only significant find since 1962 has been the oil shale deposits found in 1974 at Tamahdid, where reserves are estimated at 2,000 million tons. Occidental Petroleum of the U.S.A. signed a contract with BRPM in 1978 to study extracting oil from the deposits. The company, which is to use a method it has tested in Colorado, estimates that Tamahdid could yield 3 million tons of oil per year by 1985. All Morocco's production is refined in the country at a topping unit built at Mohammedia by the Italian firm ENI. The refinery is now run by the Société Anonyme Marocaine du Raffinage (SAMIR), formerly a Moroccan-Italian company, of which the Moroccan Government took full control in August 1974. A great part of the refinery's need for crude oil is satisfied by imports from Iraq and the U.S.S.R. and oil continues to be an expensive import item. An extension to the refinery, increasing its annual capacity from 2.5 million to 5 million tons, is now under construction.

BRPM is undertaking large-scale prospecting for hydro-carbons and other minerals, both alone and in association with private partners. Phillips Petroleum of the U.S.A. started drilling in October 1978 in the off-shore Cap Sim concession in the Atlantic. Phillips is the operator for the concession, which is held jointly with Agip of Italy, Getty Oil of the U.S.A. and British Petroleum (BP). The same consortium has other off-shore concessions, one at Simmou in the same area, and another off the Saharan coast. Phillips is sole operator for an onshore concession, near Tafrata and Ksabi about 200 miles east of Rabat. In 1978 Elf Aquitaine of France signed a letter of intent to explore for petroleum onshore. However, despite the efforts of these companies and of others before them, no petroleum had been found in commercially exploitable quantities by mid-1979.

INDUSTRY

Industry has shown a fairly rapid rate of growth in the last few years, as a result of Government efforts to develop industry and reduce dependence on agriculture. The 1973–77 plan's final capital investment target was 50,000 million dirhams, 34 per cent of which was allocated to industry, compared with 15 per cent for agriculture. In 1977 industry and mining contributed 34.9 per cent of Gross Domestic Product (at 1969 prices), or 8,875 million dirhams. The sector suffered in 1978, however, from the reduction in capital equipment imports imposed as part of the package of austerity measures, and from a credit squeeze. Lending by the state development bank, the Banque Nationale pour le Développement Economique, dropped by nearly 60 per cent and the growth of industrial production slowed to 3 per cent from 8 per cent in 1977. Some branches, like the metal, paper and construction industries, were hit more than others. The industrial development effort is nevertheless to be sustained and nearly a third of the 36,000 million dirhams scheduled for investment in the 1978–80 plan is for industry and mining.

The growth of manufacturing in Morocco has been directed largely towards the light industries. Although the majority of the population has very little purchasing power, there is nevertheless a fairly large market for many consumer goods among the two to three million people who are better off. Encouraged by government promotion, many new enterprises have been established to produce goods that formerly had to be imported. An export-orientated industry has also emerged during the past few years, particularly in the field of food-processing. This consists mainly of fruit juice plants and canneries (fish and vegetables) as well as the edible oil industry. Of special importance for the domestic market are the flour-milling, sugar refining and tobacco processing industries. Next to the food industries in importance are the textile and leather industries. A metal products industry is also well established, while in the chemical sector the most significant plants are a crude oil refinery and the Safi phosphate complex. Bids are being assessed for contracts for construction of a 950,000 tons per year steel works at Nador, but the Government is having difficulties in raising funds for the plant, whose cost is estimated to have risen from $600 million in 1976, when the project was given the go-ahead, to $1,300 million.

Several foreign companies contribute to the country's manufacturing capacity. A $17 million tyre plant has been completed by Goodyear near Casablanca. The Safi chemical complex helps to supply the country's great need for agricultural fertilizers. A 14 million dirham chemical plant built by the West German Hoechst concern was opened in Casablanca in May 1972 to produce plastics, medicines and other chemical goods. Morocco has its own car assembly company, which increased its output of cars by 17 per cent in 1973 to 20,769. Renault-Saviem-Berliet is to invest 200 million dirhams in an assembly plant and other production units over the next five years.

Morocco is at present heavily dependent on imported textiles but considerable investment (some of it from the World Bank) has been made in increasing the capacity of the local industry, especially in cotton cloth. Industrialization plans for the future include projects for the manufacture of vegetable oil, PVC, iron and steel and artificial fibres. Particularly worthy of note is Morocco's long-term sugar plan which is designed to promote national sugar production in such a way as to bring about a steady reduction in imports. According to the plan, an integrated sugar industry will be formed, through the addition of sugar work to the existing refineries and through the development of sugar crops, notably beet, which is already being grown successfully in some parts of the country. There are at present eight sugar mills with twelve more planned, and Morocco hopes eventually to become self-sufficient in sugar.

About half of the industrial labour force is concentrated in Casablanca. There is substantial unemployment and after the last shipments of agricultural exports this is swelled by the seasonal laying off of workers (packers, etc.). Official estimates put unemployment at 11 per cent of the labour force of 5 million in 1977, but the actual figure could be higher. Many workers emigrate because of the lack of employment opportunities, although the rate of emigration has slowed down as a result of the recession in Europe. The remittance of these workers' wages, amounting to 2,652 million dirhams in 1977, helps to strengthen the balance of payments.

The conditions under which Morocco's industrial development has surged forward since 1945 explain to some extent the present structure of industry. Some sections such as fish canning and edible oils and fats are over-equipped, while others are under-equipped. The textile industry, for instance, meets only about 35 per cent of local demand. Often the equipment is not fully integrated or balanced; for example, textiles have had an imbalance between spinning and weaving capacity. Recent trends indicate that many of these problems are being faced. The latest modern equipment is being installed to improve quality and increase profits.

"Moroccanization" of the country's business is taking place gradually. In April 1971 King Hassan II outlined that several hundred enterprises owned by foreigners in Morocco would gradually be transferred to Moroccan control. The King has taken particular care to point out that Moroccanization does not mean nationalization. Instead he sees it as the negotiated transfer of private enterprises from foreign to Moroccan hands with adequate indemnities paid. In March 1973 King Hassan indicated that the pace of Moroccanization was to be accelerated. In April the details were published of the requirements for a "Moroccan" company: the chairman, the managing director, a majority of the board and at least half of the shareholders must be Moroccan. Under a timetable published in May 1973 wholesale and retail businesses, import agencies and industrial concerns had to be Moroccanized by April 30th, 1974, and the banking and insurance sectors would be taken over within the following year. Ten of the foreign banks in Morocco anticipated the move by taking in Moroccan shareholders, two of them majority holdings. The deadlines for completion of the programme proved flexible as Morocco is anxious not to alienate foreign investors.

TRADE AND PAYMENTS

Morocco runs a deficit in her trade with other countries. Chief exports are agricultural goods and minerals. Agricultural production is extremely sensitive to changes in the weather, and a bad year has considerable adverse effect on the balance of trade. Mineral exports too are subject to fluctuation with changes in world demand. The sharp rises in mineral prices in 1973–74 helped boost the value of Morocco's mineral exports, particularly phosphates, and the balance of trade showed considerable improvement over previous years. In 1975, however, exports of phosphates fell back, while capital equipment, food and oil imports continued to rise, boosted by world inflation. The trade gap widened to 4,156 million dirhams from 852 million dirhams in 1974. World demand for phosphates failed to pick up and by 1977 the deficit had doubled again to 8,541 million dirhams. The Government then stepped in to arrest the deterioration and in June 1978 announced a 25 per cent import cut as part of a package of austerity measures. Almost all luxury goods and some items of capital equipment were banned as a result of the cut. By the end of the year the measures appeared to have had a significant effect and the balance of trade improved. The value of imports fell by 14.2 per cent over the whole year to 12,361 million dirhams and the value of exports increased by 7 per cent to 6,261 million dirhams, giving a deficit of 6,100 million dirhams. The export improvement was attributable entirely to higher exports of citrus fruit, vegetable and industrial goods. The value of phosphate rock exports actually declined by 3.6 per cent.

In 1969 Morocco concluded a treaty of association with the European Economic Community which provided for duty-free entry into the EEC of Moroccan goods. Restrictions were lowered on Moroccan exports of certain food products including citrus fruits, olive oil and fish. In return Morocco reduced duties on manufactured goods from the EEC. Tomatoes, wine and some preserved foods were excluded from the agreement. In February 1973 Morocco conducted an agreement amending its treaty with the EEC to take into account the entry into the Community of Britain, Denmark and Ireland. The enlarged EEC accounts for over half Morocco's imports and exports. Morocco's treaty with the EEC expired in March 1974 but negotiation of a new agreement was delayed by internal problems in the EEC and delays in formulating a new approach by the enlarged EEC on links with associated countries. When negotiations began, it was in the context of a global Mediterranean policy decided by the EEC and involving initially six Mediterranean countries, including Morocco's Maghreb neighbours. Morocco's own negotiations became deadlocked towards the end of 1974, but after prolonged discussions in 1975 over concessions for Morocco's citrus fruit, a trade and aid agreement with the EEC was initialled in March 1976. Under the agreement Morocco was to receive $160 million in aid from the EEC. The agreement has smoothed Morocco's trade relations with the EEC but it was not sufficient to prevent the EEC from imposing, in 1977, import quotas on textile imports from outside countries, including Morocco, which was badly affected. Morocco has since reached a three-year (1979–81) agreement on textiles with the EEC which should save Morocco's textile industry from the quotas' worst effects.

More and more state control has been introduced into the export trade. The export of phosphates is controlled by the *Office Chérifien des Phosphates*, and the export of citrus fruit, other agricultural products, fish products and handicraft goods by the *Office de Commercialisation et d'Exportation* (OCE).

TRANSPORT AND COMMUNICATIONS

The road network of Morocco is well developed, incorporating 29,301 kilometres of roads (84 per cent paved) at the end of 1978. Most of Morocco's roads are built to design standards well in advance of the traffic which they are currently carrying. Many of these were built by the French army, primarily for strategic purposes. In 1973, there were over 370,000 vehicles in Morocco. The tonnage transported on Moroccan roads in 1975 was 6.8 million tons.

The country's railway network is good, there being 1,856 km. of track, much of which is electrified. Traction is by electric or diesel locomotives. Casablanca is connected by a track that continues through Alegria to Tunis. A second railway track between Rabat and Casablanca is under construction and should be completed by 1980. The feasibility of building an 850 km. railway to link Marrakesh with Laayoune (El Aaiún) and the phosphate mines of the former Spanish Sahara is being studied by Parsons Brinckerhoff and Centrex, both of the U.S.A., the

Société Française de Réalisations Ferroviaires (SOFRERAIL) and Laboratories Publics d'Essais et d'Etudes (LPEE) of Casablanca.

Morocco currently has thirty commercial airfields, of which eight are open to international traffic, the most important being Tanger-Boakhalf, Casablanca-Nouaceur and Rabat-Salé. Substantial runway and terminal improvements are being carried out at major airfields to encourage the tourist industry. Moroccan air transport is now mainly provided by Royal Air Maroc, which is an autonomous corporation in which the Moroccan State has an 81.7 per cent share, the remainder being held by Air France, by private transportation companies or by individuals. The number of passengers carried has shown a steady upward trend, numbering 1.2 million in 1978 compared with 849,018 in 1976. A second air company, Royal Air-Inter, which serves Morocco's internal lines, hitherto largely covered by Air France, came into operation in April 1970. Royal Air Maroc has an 80 per cent holding in the company.

On its 2,000 km. of coastline, Morocco has seven major ports: Agadir, Casablanca, Laayoune (El Aaiún), Kénitra, Mohammedia, Safi and Tangier. The coast is generally not very favourable for port installations since it is particularly rocky and the Atlantic swell is one of the strongest in the world. In 1977, the ports handled 45.4 million tons of cargo, most of which went through Casablanca and Safi. The volume of cargo shipped has increased steadily in recent years (although with considerable variations between the different ports). Casablanca handled 16.7 million tons of cargo in 1976, of which 67 per cent was phosphates. Mohammedia is the principal petroleum port at present, but Safi is being developed to take large tankers. Maritime passenger traffic is concentrated at Tangier and Casablanca, with most at the former being based on the ferry service across the Straits of Gibraltar, and most at the latter on cruise visitors making relatively short visits.

FINANCE AND FOREIGN AID

The serious external payments position, caused by high expenditure on industrial development combined with a decline in the value of the main export (phosphate rock), led the Government to adopt a cautious budgetary policy in 1978. State budget allocations dropped to 24,963 million dirhams from 26,104 million dirhams in 1977. All ministries, with the notable exceptions of defence and education, were allotted less. However, defence, which is considered essential because of the Saharan conflict, received no less than a third of the total budget. Import tax was raised from 8 to 12 per cent; the car tax was also raised; and new taxes were put on real estate profits and undeveloped land.

The same austere policy was maintained in 1979. Budget spending increased slightly, to 26,480 million dirhams, but the rise was less than Morocco's rate of inflation so that in real terms there was little change. Most of the increase was in the administrative budget, which rose by 12 per cent to 10,622 million dirhams. The investment, or development, budget rose by only 7 per cent to 8,735 million dirhams. (The difference between the total budget figure and the sum of the administrative and investment budgets is accounted for by spending on the public debt service and on annexed budgets, like that of Casablanca port). Defence spending again accounted for a considerable share of the total but there was a marked attempt to divert more funds into social sectors such as housing, education and transport. Taxes on higher income groups were also increased in an effort to boost Government revenue.

The Government had hoped that increased revenue and cutbacks in spending would help the state to balance its books. However, an unexpected wage increase of 40 per cent, which the government found itself obliged to introduce in May 1979 to end a wave of strikes in many key sectors of the economy, seemed certain to lead to a wide budget deficit. The increase, to be introduced in two stages (on May 1st, 1979, and January 1st, 1980), was to bring the basic wage to 1.40 dirhams per hour.

Revenues from tourism and workers' remittances have to some extent compensated for the trade deficits but, since 1975, Morocco has turned increasingly to foreign borrowing to help to cover the gap. The payments deficit amounted to only 17 million dirhams in 1977, compared with 51 million dirhams in 1976, but this was because foreign loans and export credits had substantially increased and were being counted as receipts. The external public debt more than doubled from 9,556 million dirhams ($2,133 million) in 1976 to 21,150 million dirhams ($5,437 million) in 1978. Almost all the debt is long term. About 7,000 million dirhams ($1,799 million) is in Eurocredits and a further 4,000 million dirhams ($1,028 million) is debt contracted with Middle East states. Debt service in 1976 was equivalent to only 7 per cent of exports and net transfer payments but by 1978 the ratio had risen to about 17 per cent.

Despite the deterioration in the payments position, Morocco has had little difficulty in obtaining foreign funds. It borrowed $605 million on the Euromarket in 1978, compared with $797 million in 1977 and $641 million in 1976. Several major Euroloans raised in 1978 were at favourable rates and "soft" loans were provided by the World Bank, the Islamic Development Bank, the OPEC Special Fund, the Kuwait Fund for Arab Economic Development and the International Monetary Fund.

DEVELOPMENT

The growth in income resulting from the 1974 rise in phosphate rock prices led to substantial increases in investment allocations under the 1973–77 development plan. The investment target was more than doubled during the course of the plan to 50,037 million dirhams. An overall growth rate of 7.5 per cent a year was officially planned, with agriculture rising by 3 per cent a year, industry by 11 per cent a year and services by 6.9 per cent a year. King Hassan announced in January 1975 that the increases would be concentrated mainly on irrigation, mineral prospecting, industry and vocational training. Under the plan some 26.8 per cent of investment was allocated for industry, 15.9 per cent for agriculture, 16.9 per cent for social and cultural affairs and 12.1 per cent for infrastructure. Gross fixed capital formation was to rise from 18.6 per cent of G.N.P. to 23 per cent over the plan period. Import growth was to be held to 8 per cent a year, while exports were planned to rise by 10 per cent a year. However, many of these targets were not fully achieved. The state industrial development office (ODI) attained only 45 per cent of planned investments during the 1973–77 plan period—1,388 million dirhams instead of the projected 3,075 million. Public sector investments reached about 80 per cent of what was projected, but the private sector could manage only 23 per cent. The growth in gross domestic product suffered too. G.D.P. grew by only about 5 per cent per year in the period 1973–77, instead of the planned 7.5 per cent. In 1977 growth of only 1 per cent was realized, against 10 per cent in 1976. G.D.P. (computed at 1969 prices) stood at 26,500 million dirhams in 1978, against 25,400 million in 1977 and 19,000 million in 1973. G.N.P., at current prices, was 42,740 million dirhams in 1977.

The five-year plan which was to have followed the 1973–77 plan was shortened to three years (1978–80) because of financial constraints resulting mainly from defence expenditure. The hope was that by 1980 the world price of phosphate rock might have improved and a solution to the Saharan dispute—the cause of the high defence costs—been found. The plan's investment target of 36,000 million dirhams was announced only at the end of 1978. It relies much more on private investment than the last plan did. The state maintains responsibility for rural development, hydraulics and education, but private investment is encouraged in industry and housing.

STATISTICAL SURVEY

Statistics for Morocco exclude the portion of the former Spanish Sahara annexed in February 1976 unless otherwise stated

AREA AND POPULATION

Area (sq. km.)	Population (Census of July 20th, 1971)		
	Total	Moroccans	Aliens
458,730	15,379,259	15,267,000	112,000

Estimated population: 17,305,000 (July 1st, 1975), 17,828,000 (July 1st, 1976), 18,245,000 (July 1st, 1977).

ADMINISTRATIVE DISTRICTS*
(1976 estimates)

	Area (sq. km.)	Population	Density (per sq. km.)
Provinces:			
Agadir	18,855	876,300	46.5
Al-Hocima	3,550	282,500	79.6
Azizal	10,050	368,300	36.7
Beni Mellal	7,075	519,700	73.5
Boujdour	100,120	n.a.	n.a.
Boulemane	14,790	130,600	8.8
Chaouen	4,350	279,500	64.3
El Jadida	6,000	659,400	109.9
El Kellaa Srarhna	10,070	520,400	51.7
Essaouira	6,335	510,500	64.8
Essmara	61,760	n.a.	n.a.
Fès	10,145	1,155,000	113.8
Figuig	55,990	100,100	1.8
Kemisset	8,305	396,200	123.6
Kénitra	8,805	1,088,700	47.7
Khenifra	11,115	278,100	25.0
Khouribga	4,250	385,800	90.8
Laayoune	39,360	n.a.	n.a.
Marrakech	14,755	1,129,800	76.6
Meknès	8,510	705,700	82.9
Nador	6,130	557,700	91.0
Ouarzazate	56,990	286,900	10.3
Oujda	20,700	695,300	33.6
Rachidia	59,585	376,500	6.3
Safi	7,285	614,200	84.3
Settat	11,445	754,100	65.9
Tanger	1,195	340,200	284.7
Tan-Tan	43,420	77,900	1.8
Taza	15,465	605,900	39.2
Tétouan	6,025	625,500	301.8
Tiznit	23,585	395,200	16.8
Prefectures:			
Casablanca	1,855	2,116,300	1,140.9
Rabat-Salé	2,100	793,400	337.8
Total	659,920*	17,825,700	38.9

* Area figures include 205,270 sq. km. annexed from Western Sahara but population figures exclude the three new Saharan provinces. The estimated population of Western Sahara (including the Mauritanian-held portion) was 128,000 at July 1st, 1976.

PRINCIPAL TOWNS

(1971 census)

Rabat (capital)*	435,510	Tanger (Tangier)	185,850
Casablanca	1,371,330	Oujda	155,800
Marrakech (Marrakesh)	330,400	Tétouan	137,080
Fès (Fez)	321,460	Kénitra	135,960
Meknès	244,520	Safi	129,100

* Including Salé.

Births and Deaths: Average annual birth rate 48.2 per 1,000 in 1965–70, 46.2 per 1,000 in 1970–75; death rate 17.4 per 1,000 in 1965–70, 15.7 per 1,000 in 1970–75 (UN estimates).

ECONOMICALLY ACTIVE POPULATION*

(1971 census)

Agriculture, hunting, forestry and fishing	1,988,060
Mining and quarrying	44,540
Manufacturing	369,264
Electricity, gas and water	10,810
Construction	171,695
Trade, restaurants and hotels	289,082
Transport, storage and communications	100,425
Financing, insurance, real estate and business services	5,602
Community, social and personal services	501,728
Activities not adequately described	155,412
TOTAL IN EMPLOYMENT	3,636,618
Unemployed	343,900
TOTAL LABOUR FORCE	3,980,518
of which:	
Males	3,375,363
Females	605,155

* Figures are based on a 10 per cent sample tabulation of census returns. The figure for females excludes unreported family helpers in agriculture.

AGRICULTURE

LAND USE

('000 hectares)

	1971	1976
Arable land	7,075	7,400*
Land under permanent crops	429	430*
Permanent meadows and pastures	12,500	12,500
Forests and woodland	5,164	5,190*
Other land	19,466	19,110
Inland water	21	25
TOTAL AREA	44,655	44,655

*FAO estimate.

Source: FAO, *Production Yearbook*.

PRINCIPAL CROPS
('000 metric tons)

	1975	1976	1977
Wheat	1,575	2,135	1,288
Barley	1,587	2,862	1,347
Maize	371	493	184
Olives	312	306†	252†
Dates	50†	70*	70*
Pulses	453	470	162
Tomatoes	542	450	470*
Oranges	477	566	610*
Tangerines	106	118	130*
Potatoes	195	170	180*
Sugar Beet	1,792	2,362	1,474
Seed Cotton	15	22	22†
Grapes	220†	210*	215*

* FAO estimate.
† Unofficial figure.

Source: FAO, *Production Yearbook.*

LIVESTOCK
('000 head, year ending September)

	1974	1976	1977
Cattle	3,620	3,620†	3,650†
Sheep	14,800	14,270†	14,300†
Goats	6,800	5,740†	4,940†
Camels	200	210*	210*
Horses	320†	315†	312†
Asses	1,200*	1,200*	1,200*
Chickens	19,000*	20,000*	21,000*

* FAO estimate
† Unofficial figure.

Source: FAO, *Production Yearbook.*

LIVESTOCK PRODUCTS
('000 metric tons)

	1975	1976	1977
Beef and veal	81†	79†	74†
Mutton and lamb	43*	41†	37†
Goats' meat	23†	13†	10†
Poultry meat	40*	45†	50†
Cows' milk	457	480*	473*
Sheep's milk	20*	20*	20*
Goats' milk	23*	24*	25*
Hen eggs	52.5*	56.7*	59.8*
Wool (greasy)	20†	21†	21*

* FAO estimate.
† Unofficial figure.

Source: FAO, *Production Yearbook.*

FORESTRY

ROUNDWOOD REMOVALS
('000 cubic metres)

	Coniferous (soft wood)			Broadleaved (hard wood)			Total		
	1975	1976	1977	1975	1976	1977	1975	1976	1977
Sawlogs and veneer logs	105*	73	85	—	—	—	105*	73	85
Pitprops (Mine timber)	—	—	—	25	17	20	25	17	20
Pulpwood	—	—	—	184	223	200	184	223	200
Other industrial wood	18*	19*	20*	80	80	138	98*	99*	158*
Fuel wood	525*	541*	558*	2,100*	2,165*	2,231*	2,625*	2,706*	2,789*
Total	648*	633*	663*	2,389*	2,485*	2,589*	3,037*	3,118*	3,252*

* FAO estimate.

Source: FAO, *Yearbook of Forest Products.*

FISHING

('000 metric tons, live weight)

	1972	1973	1974	1975	1976	1977
Total catch	247.8	400.0	288.4	229.0	286.6	260.6
of which:						
European pilchard (sardine)	185.0	349.3	224.2	167.4	225.1	129.6

Source: FAO, *Yearbook of Fishery Statistics.*

MINING

('000 metric tons)

	1974	1975	1976	1977
Phosphate rock	19,750	14,119	15,656	17,572
Iron ore*	534	554	343	407
Coal	574	652	702	707
Manganese ore*	175	131	117	114
Lead concentrates*	142	104	99	158
Petroleum	24	20	8	22
Zinc concentrates*	27	36	30	22
Cobalt ore*	13	14	7	8
Copper concentrates (metal content)	5.3	4.8	4.6	n.a.

* Figures refer to the gross weight of ores and concentrates. The metal content (in '000 metric tons) was: Iron 324 in 1974; 336 in 1975; 202 in 1976; Manganese 89.4 in 1974, 67.0 in 1975, 60.1 in 1976; Lead 83.7 in 1974, 67.8 in 1975, 68.1 in 1976; Zinc 13.8 in 1974, 16.9 in 1975, 15.4 in 1976; Cobalt 2.0 in 1974, 1.9 in 1975; 0.8 in 1976.

Natural gas (million cubic metres): 63 in 1974; 76 in 1975; 86 in 1976.

INDUSTRY

SELECTED PRODUCTS*

		1973	1974	1975	1976
Cement	'000 metric tons	1,619	1,914	2,028	2,140
Refined sugar	,, ,, ,,	473	446	466	445
Textiles	metric tons	48,947	45,044	45,644	50,393
Electricity	million kWh.	2,599	2,609	2,816	3,079
Cars†	number	20,769	23,510	24,969	25,154
Tyres	,,	533,000	n.a.	n.a.	n.a.
Shoes	'000 pairs	n.a.	18,974	17,173	15,209
Flour	metric tons	781,000	n.a.	14,605	18,760
Phosphatic fertilizers‡	'000 metric tons	171.0	147.5	420	449
Carpets	number	249,000	25,489	311,192	393,967
Wine	'000 hl.	1,200	1,273	690	n.a.
Olive oil	metric tons	38,000§	22,000	44,000	41,000
Beer	'000 hl.	281	246	254	316
Cigarettes	million	6,423	7,732	9,339	9,043
Sulphuric acid	'000 metric tons	43	389	284	357
Motor spirit (petrol)	,, ,, ,,	372	352	368	n.a.
Kerosene	,, ,, ,,	85	86	93	94
Distillate fuel oils	,, ,, ,,	688	686	785	872
Residual fuel oils	,, ,, ,,	755	968	1,064	1,194
Jet fuels	,, ,, ,,	70	70	67	62

* Major industrial establishments only. † Assembly only.
‡ In terms of phosphoric acid. § FAO estimate.

FINANCE

100 Moroccan francs (centimes) = 1 Moroccan dirham.
Coins: 1, 2, 5, 10, 20 and 50 francs; 1 and 5 dirhams.
Notes: 5, 10, 50 and 100 dirhams.

Exchange rates (April 1979): £1 sterling = 8.166 dirhams; U.S. $1 = 3.968 dirhams.
100 Moroccan dirhams = £12.25 = $25.20.

Note: The dirham was introduced in October 1959, replacing the Moroccan franc (at par with the old French franc until December 1958) at the rate of 1 dirham = 100 francs. At the same time the currency was devalued by 17.0 per cent, with the former exchange rate (U.S. $1 = 420 Moroccan francs) being replaced by a new rate based on a relationship with French currency, initially fixed at 1 French franc = 1.025 Moroccan francs (1 French franc = 1.025 dirhams after the introduction of the new French franc in January 1960). In terms of U.S. currency, the rate was $1 = 5.0605 dirhams (1 dirham = 19.761 U.S. cents), which remained in operation until August 1971, while the relationship to French currency became 1 French franc = 91.111 Moroccan francs after August 1969. From December 1971 to February 1973 the official exchange rate was $1 = 4.661 dirhams (1 dirham = 21.455 U.S. cents). A new par value of $1 = 4.195 dirhams (1 dirham = 23.84 U.S. cents) was established in February 1973 but in March 1973 the French authorities ceased to maintain the franc-dollar rate within previously agreed margins. Morocco maintained a link with the French franc, although the fixed relationship was ended in May 1973. As a result of these changes, the market exchange rate since March 1973 has fluctuated widely above and below the par value, although the latter continued to be the basis for calculating the value of foreign trade transactions until the end of 1974. In June 1978 it was announced that the dirham would be treated as being at par with the French franc for remittances from Moroccan workers in France. The average market rates (dirhams per U.S. dollar) were: 4.5959 in 1972; 4.1069 in 1973; 4.3698 in 1974; 4.0525 in 1975; 4.4193 in 1976; 4.5034 in 1977; 4.1667 in 1978. In terms of sterling, the exchange rate between November 1967 and June 1972 was £1 = 12.145 dirhams.

BUDGET

(million dirhams)

Revenue	1977	1978
Taxation:		
Direct taxation	2,482	3,229
Customs duties	2,001	2,903
Other indirect taxes	3,160	4,043
Stamp duties	660	1,000
	8,303	11,175
Contributions from state corporations and other ordinary receipts	1,987	1,633
Extraordinary receipts and borrowing	7,115	6,270
Total	17,405	19,078

Expenditure	1977	1978
Current expenditure	9,936	11,349
of which:		
Education	2,202	2,672
Defence	1,560	1,925
Interior	871	1,203
Health	407	498
Agriculture	409	469
Debt servicing	1,050	1,880
Other	3,437	2,702
Capital expenditure	11,744	8,128
Total	21,680	19,477

CENTRAL BANK RESERVES

(U.S. $ million at December 31st)

	1976	1977	1978
Gold	24	27	31
IMF Special Drawing Rights	12	10	16
Foreign exchange	455	495	602
Total	491	532	649

MONEY SUPPLY

(million dirhams at December 31st)

	1976	1977	1978
Currency outside banks	5,732	6,650	7,676
Private sector deposits at Bank of Morocco	207	219	265
Demand deposits at deposit money banks	7,837	9,445	10,873
Demand deposits at Post Office	687	853	912
Private sector demand deposits at Treasury	705	918	1,182
Total Money	15,168	18,085	20,908

Source: IMF, *International Financial Statistics.*

BALANCE OF PAYMENTS
(U.S.$ millon)

	1972	1973	1974	1975	1976	1976
Merchandise exports f.o.b.	642	913	1,704	1,530	1,277	1,284
Merchandise imports f.o.b.	−709	−1,037	−1,690	−2,264	−2,308	−2,822
TRADE BALANCE	−67	−124	14	−734	−1,031	−1,538
Exports of services	304	389	427	497	472	587
Imports of services	−327	−412	542	803	−1,315	−1,466
BALANCE ON GOODS AND SERVICES	−90	−148	−101	−1,040	−1,874	−2,417
Private unrequited transfers (net)	138	237	324	512	528	574
Government unrequited transfers (net)	0	7	6	−5	−23	−29
CURRENT BALANCE	48	97	229	533	−1,369	−1,872
Direct capital investment (net)	13	−1	−20	−1	38	54
Other long-term capital (net)	34	10	64	391	1,260	1,693
Short-term capital (net)	−47	−105	−142	158	82	89
Net errors and omissions		2	1	−45	−28	22
TOTAL (net monetary movements)	48	−2	131	−30	−17	−14
Allocation of IMF Special Drawing Rights	13	—	—	—	—	—
CHANGES IN RESERVES, ETC.	61	−2	131	−30	−17	−14

Source: IMF, *International Financial Statistics.*

EXTERNAL TRADE
(million dirhams)

	1972	1973	1974	1975	1976	1977	1978
Imports c.i.f.	3,577	4,684	8,292	10,394	11,555	14,401	12,361
Exports f.o.b.	2,953	3,746	7,440	6,238	5,579	5,860	6,261

PRINCIPAL COMMODITIES
(million dirhams)

IMPORTS	1975	1976	1977
Food, drink and tobacco	2,594	1,976	1,944
Wheat	960	725	587
Sugar	971	610	510
Tea	104	88	103
Dairy products	124	140	149
Energy and lubricants	1,121	1,303	1,669
Crude petroleum	897	1,050	1,241
Animal and vegetable products	891	865	1,161
Crude vegetable oils	409	n.a.	345
Timber	175	246	336
Minerals	105	169	231
Semi-finished products	2,005	2,366	2,964
Iron and steel goods	522	n.a.	n.a.
Chemical products	268	264	331
Fertilizers	144	92	81
Plastics	158	n.a.	239
Paper and cardboard	99	129	157
Agricultural equipment	139	} 3,444 {	174
Industrial equipment	2,375		4,797
Machinery (non-electric)	1,437	n.a.	n.a.
Electrical machinery	393	n.a.	n.a.
Consumer goods	1,120	1,326	1,351
Passenger cars and spares	412	286	n.a.
TOTAL	10,394	11,555	14,401

EXPORTS	1975	1976	1977
Food, drink and tobacco	1,456	1,801	1,705
Citrus fruit	406	593	673
Fresh tomatoes	173	127	115
Potatoes	74	81	38
Fresh vegetables	43	81	50
Pulses	118	n.a.	n.a.
Preserved vegetables	109	105	197
Preserved fruits and jam	39	n.a.	57
Wines, etc.	36	41	47
Preserved fish	171	235	229
Energy and lubricants	57	78	92
Animal and vegetable products	242	279	227
Olive oil	94	66	64
Pulp for paper	48	n.a.	46
Minerals	3,686	2,484	2,520
Phosphates	3,430	2,190	2,111
Lead ore	65	63	155
Semi-finished products	252	297	564
Fertilizers	106	n.a.	109
Agricultural equipment	2	} 21	30
Industrial equipment	44		
Consumer goods	497	619	723
Carpets	114	154	209
Clothes	99	n.a.	188
TOTAL	6,238	5,579	5,860

PRINCIPAL TRADING PARTNERS
(million dirhams)

IMPORTS	1975	1976	1977
Algeria	10	—	—
Belgium/Luxembourg	225	273	360
Brazil	116	165	189
Cuba	131	37	141
France	3,140	3,368	3,935
Germany, Fed. Republic	826	936	958
Iraq	561	587	709
Italy	405	644	1,003
Netherlands	390	244	472
Poland	170	262	217
Saudi Arabia	41	184	178
Spain	457	732	1,245
Sweden	194	222	284
U.S.S.R.	298	297	377
United Kingdom	340	470	509
U.S.A.	795	990	908

EXPORTS	1975	1976	1977
Algeria	113	30	—
Belgium/Luxembourg	420	309	297
Brazil	83	128	125
France	1,356	1,324	1,449
Germany, Fed. Republic	406	536	613
Italy	465	406	357
Japan	143	118	103
Mexico	52	115	114
Netherlands	224	242	246
Poland	438	265	118
Romania	130	110	126
Spain	332	300	437
U.S.S.R.	186	238	226
United Kingdom	418	322	252
Yugoslavia	213	133	97

1977 (million dirhams): *Imports:* Argentina 331, Canada 238, China 119, Norway 369; *Exports:* U.S.A. 115.

Source: Ministry of Finance, Rabat.

TRANSPORT

RAILWAYS

	1974*	1975*	1976
Passenger-kilometres (million)	776	835	830
Freight ton-kilometres (million)	3,603	2,890	3,143

* Provisional.

ROAD TRAFFIC
(motor vehicles in use)

	1975	1976
Cars	320,064	347,444
Buses and coaches	5,441	5,790
Lorries and vans	106,742	121,637
Motor cycles	16,045	16,609

SHIPPING

		1975	1976
Passenger arrivals	number	995,179	392,845
Passenger departures	,,	24,829	451,997
Freight loaded	'000 tons	15,447	17,340
Freight unloaded	,, ,,	7,282	7,902

CIVIL AVIATION

	1974	1975	1976*
Passenger arrivals	738,390	862,599	2,436,455 (arrivals and departures)
Passenger departures	773,804	880,489	
Freight loaded and unloaded (metric tons)	19,157	17,762	205,651

* Provisional.

TOURISM

Country of Origin	1974	1975	1976
Algeria	147,956	84,353	1,234
Belgium	24,149	25,572	25,142
Canada	26,539	26,695	18,421
France	216,422	280,726	225,693
Federal Germany	82,157	94,343	95,117
Italy	26,954	27,370	25,751
Netherlands	33,360	29,830	23,702
Scandinavia	29,392	45,267	n.a.
Spain	70,184	48,098	115,736
Switzerland	21,256	20,995	18,581
United Kingdom	107,839	115,683	96,438
U.S.A.	173,217	128,436	97,113
Total (incl. others)*	1,338,028	1,334,454	1,218,473

* Total includes arrivals of Moroccan nationals returning from abroad, numbering 152,646 in 1974, 218,214 in 1975. It also includes cruise visitors (not classified by country), numbering 133,364 in 1974, 89,638 in 1975, 110,757 in 1976.

The total number of arrivals in 1977 was 1,501,890, including 74,423 cruise visitors.

Hotel Capacity (1977): 51,761 beds. (*Source:* Crédit Immobilier et Hôtelier).

EDUCATION

	1974/75	1975/76	1976/77	1977/78
Primary school pupils	1,413,993	1,547,647	1,667,331	1,793,772
Secondary school pupils	399,551	471,575	524,555	582,197
Students engaged in higher education	33,772	45,081	57,085	77,400

Source: Ministère de l'Education.

Source (unless otherwise stated): Direction de la Statistique, Rabat.

THE CONSTITUTION

(Promulgated March 10th, 1972, after having been approved by national referendum.)*

Preamble: The Kingdom of Morocco, a sovereign Moslem State, shall be a part of the Great Maghreb. As an African State one of its aims shall be the realization of African unity. It will adhere to the principles, rights and obligations of those international organizations of which it is a member and will work for the preservation of peace and security in the world.

General Principles: Morocco shall be a constitutional, democratic and social monarchy. Sovereignty shall pertain to the nation and be exercised directly by means of the referendum and indirectly by the constitutional institutions. All Moroccans shall be equal before the law, and all adults shall enjoy equal political rights including the franchise. Freedoms of movement, opinion and speech and the right of assembly shall be guaranteed. Islam shall be the state religion.

The Monarchy: The Crown of Morocco and its attendant constitutional rights shall be hereditary in the line of H.M. King Hassan II, and shall be transmitted to the oldest son, unless during his lifetime the King has appointed as his successor another of his sons. The King is the symbol of unity, guarantees the continuity of the state, and safeguards respect for Islam and the Constitution. The King shall have the power to appoint and dismiss the Prime Minister and Cabinet Ministers and shall preside over the Cabinet. He shall promulgate legislation passed by the Chamber of Representatives and have the power to dissolve the Chamber; is empowered to declare a state of emergency and to initiate revisions to the Constitution. The Sovereign is the Commander-in-Chief of the Armed Forces; makes appointments to civil and military posts; appoints Ambassadors; signs and ratifies treaties; presides over the Council for National Development Planning and the Supreme Judiciary Council; and exercises the right of pardon.

Legislature: This shall consist of a single assembly, the Chamber of Representatives, which shall comprise 264 members elected for a four-year term. Two-thirds of the members shall be elected by direct universal suffrage, and one-third by an electoral college composed of councillors in local government and employers' and employees' representatives. The Chamber shall pass legislation, which may be initiated by its members or by the Prime Minister; authorize any declaration of war; and approve any extension beyond thirty days of a state of emergency.

Government: The Government shall be responsible to the King and the Chamber of Representatives and shall ensure the execution of laws. The Prime Minister shall be empowered to initiate legislation and to exercise statutory powers except where these are reserved to the King. He shall put before the Chamber the Government's intended programme and shall be responsible for co-ordinating ministerial work.

Relations between the Authorities: The King may request further consideration of legislation by the Chamber of Representatives before giving his assent; submit proposed legislation to a referendum by decree; and dissolve the Chamber if a Bill rejected by it is approved by referendum. He may also dissolve the Chamber by decree, but the succeeding Chamber may not be dissolved within a year of its election. The Chamber of Representatives may defeat the Government either by refusing a vote of confidence moved by the Prime Minister or by passing a censure motion; either eventuality shall involve the Government's collective resignation.

Judiciary: The Judiciary shall be independent. Judges shall be appointed on the recommendation of the Supreme Council of the Judiciary presided over by the King.

* For the most part the Constitution is unchanged from the one drawn up by King Hassan II and promulgated in 1962. This provided for two houses of parliament, one elected by universal suffrage and one by electoral colleges, and was superseded by that of July 1970, which introduced a unicameral Chamber of Representatives, of which two-thirds of the members were to be elected by universal suffrage, and increased the powers of the monarch.

THE GOVERNMENT

HEAD OF STATE

H.M. King HASSAN II (acceded March 3rd, 1961).

CABINET

(*June* 1979)

Prime Minister and Minister of Justice: MAATI BOUABID.

Minister of State for Foreign Affairs and Co-operation: M'HAMED BOUCETTA.

Minister of State for Posts and Telecommunications: MAHJOUBI AHERDANI.

Minister of State for Culture: MOHAMED BAHNINI.

Minister of State for the Interior: IDRIS BASRI.

Minister of Equipment and National Revival: MOHAMED DOUIRI.

Minister of Finance: ABDELKAMEL REGHAY.

Minister of Agriculture and Agrarian Reform: ABDELLATIF GHISSASSI.

Minister of Information: ABDELOUAHED BELKZIZ.

Minister of Religious Endowments (Habous) and Islamic Affairs: Dr. AHMED RAMZI.

Minister of Labour and Vocational Training: MOHAMMED ARSALAN JEDIDI.

Minister of Administrative Affairs: MANSOURI BEN ALI.

Minister of Relations with Parliament: MOHAMED HADDOU ECHIGUER.

Minister of Education and Cadre Training: Dr. AZZEDINE LARAKI.

Minister of Youth and Sports: ABDELHAFID KADIRI.

Minister of Housing and National Territory: ABBES EL FASSI.

Minister of Social Affairs: ABDALLAH GHARNIT.

Minister of Transport: MOHAMED NASSER.

Minister of Trade and Industry: AZZEDINE JASSOUS.

Minister of Health: Dr. RAHAL RAHHALI.

Minister of Energy and Mining Research: MOUSSAS SAADI.

Minister of Tourism: ABDESSALEM ZNINED.

Secretary of State for Saharan Affairs: KHALI HANNA OULD RASHID.

CHAMBER OF REPRESENTATIVES

Elections for the Chamber of Representatives (*Majlis al Nuwab*) provided for under the 1972 Constitution took place for the first time in June 1977. Two-thirds of the Chamber's members are elected by universal suffrage and one-third by an electoral college comprising representatives of commune and municipal councils, professional bodies and employees.

President: DEY OULD SIDI BABA.

(General Election, June 3rd, 1977)

	Votes in Direct Election	Seats by Direct Election	Seats by Indirect Election	Total Seats
Independents*	2,254,297	81	60	141
Istiqlal	1,090,960	45	4	49
Mouvement Populaire	625,786	29	15	44
USFP	738,541	16	—	16
MPCD	102,358	2	1	3
Parti de l'Action	90,840	2	—	2
PPS	116,470	1	—	1
Others	26,111	—	8†	8†
Total	5,045,363	176	88	264

* Candidates of a pro-Government, monarchist tendency.

† Includes six members of the Union marocaine du travail (UMT), one member of the Union générale des travailleurs marocains (UGMT) and one non-party member.

POLITICAL PARTIES

Istiqlal: f. 1944; aims to raise living standards, to confer equal rights on all, stresses the Moroccan claim to Mauritania and the Western Sahara; Sec.-Gen. M'Hamed Boucetta; publs. *Al Alam* (daily), and *L'Opinion* (daily).

Mouvement Populaire: f. 1957; conservative; Leader Mahjoubi Aherdan.

Mouvement Populaire Constitutionnel et Démocratique—MPCD: breakaway party from *Mouvement Populaire*; Leader Abdelkrim Khatib.

Parti de l'Action: Rabat; f. 1974; advocates democracy and progress; Sec.-Gen. Abderrahim Mounadi.

Parti Démocratique Constitutionnel.

Parti Libéral Progressiste—PLP: Casablanca; f. 1974; advocates individual freedom and free enterprise; Leader Aknoush Ahmadou Belhaj.

Parti du Progrès et du Socialisme—PPS: B.P. 152, Casablanca; f. 1974; successor to the Parti Communiste Marocain banned in 1952, and the Parti de la Libération et du Socialisme banned in 1969; left-wing; advocates nationalization and democracy; Sec.-Gen. Ali Yata; publ. *Al Bayane* (Arabic and French daily).

Rassemblement National des Indépendants—RNI: Rabat; f. 1978 from the pro-Government group forming the majority in the Chamber of Representatives; Pres. Ahmed Osman.

Union National des Forces Populaires—UNFP: B.P. 747, Casablanca; f. 1959 by Mehdi Ben Barka from a group within Istiqlal; left wing; opposition party; in July 1972 a split occurred between the Casablanca and Rabat sections of the party; Leader Abdullah Ibrahim.

Union Socialiste des Forces Populaires—USFP: 10 rue Fatima El Fihrya, Rabat; f. 1959 as UNFP, Rabat section of UNFP became USFP in 1974; left-wing opposition party, 100,000 mems.; First Sec. Abderrahim Bouabid; publ. *Al Mouharir* (Arabic daily), *Libération* (French weekly).

DIPLOMATIC REPRESENTATION

EMBASSIES ACCREDITED TO MOROCCO

(In Rabat unless otherwise stated)

Afghanistan: Cairo, Egypt.

Argentina: 4 blvd. Moulay Hassan; *Chargé d'affaires:* Jorge Ernesto Blanco (also accred. to Mali).

Australia: Paris, France.

Austria: 2 rue de Tedders; *Ambassador:* Hariad Vavrik.

Bangladesh: Algiers, Algeria.

Belgium: 6 ave. de Marrakech; *Ambassador:* Luc Putman.

Brazil: 34 Zankat Al-Hatimi; *Ambassador:* Everaldo Deyrell Delima.

Bulgaria: 32 rue Jaafar As-Sadiq, Agdal; *Ambassador:* Stoyan Vladimirov Zaimov.

Cameroon: Paris, France.

Canada: B.P. 543, 2 rue Assafi; *Ambassador:* Michel Gauvin.

Central African Empire: 2 rue Ouedal Makhazine; *Ambassador:* Bernard Beloum.

Chad: Cairo, Egypt.

Chile: Madrid, Spain.

China, People's Republic: 6 Zankat Ibn Al Abbar; *Ambassador:* (vacant).

Costa Rica: Madrid, Spain.

Cuba: 18 blvd. du Front d'Oued; *Ambassador:* Jorge Manfugas Lavigne (also accred. to Mauritania).

Czechoslovakia: 4 rue Abou Faris Al Marini; *Ambassador:* Jan Juda.

Denmark: 4 rue de Khemisset; *Ambassador:* Svend Aage Sandagar Jeppesen (also accred. to Mauritania).

Finland: Madrid, Spain.

France: 6 ave. Mohamed V; *Ambassador:* Jean Herly.

Gabon: 19 ave. de Meknès; *Ambassador:* RENÉ KOMBILA.

Gambia: Dakar, Senegal.

German Democratic Republic: 4 ave. de Meknès; *Ambassador:* HANS SCHARF.

Germany, Federal Republic: Zankat Madina, B.P. 235; *Ambassador:* HANS SCHWARZMANN.

Greece: 9 rue de Kairouan; *Ambassador:* PANYOTIS RELLAS.

Guatemala: Madrid, Spain.

Guinea: 2 Zankat ibn Mokla, Orangers; *Ambassador:* MOULOUKOU SOULEYMAN TOURE.

Hungary: 12 rue d'Agadir; *Ambassador:* FRIGYES LEDERER.

India: 18 ave de Champagne, Agdal; *Ambassador:* UDAY CHAND SONI (also accred. to Tunisia).

Indonesia: Algiers, Algeria.

Iran: 7 rue El Qassar; *Ambassador:* (vacant).

Iraq: 6 ave. de la Victoire; *Ambassador:* ADNAN SHARIF SHIHAB.

Ireland: Paris, France.

Italy: 2 rue de Sebou; *Ambassador:* FRANSISCO MEZZALAMA.

Ivory Coast: 21 rue de Tedders; *Ambassador:* SULEIMAN SAKO.

Japan: 19 ave. Tarik Ibn Ziad; *Ambassador:* OSAMU KATAOKA.

Jordan: route des Zaers, Souissi; *Ambassador:* HANI TABARAH.

Kenya: Cairo, Egypt.

Korea, Republic: 23 ave. de France, Agdal; *Ambassador:* TEAK KEUN LEE.

Kuwait: 48 ave. Al Mouwahidine; *Ambassador:* ABDALLAH AHMED HOSSEIN.

Lebanon: 5 rue de Tedders; *Ambassador:* Dr. ADEL ISMAIL.

Libya: 1 rue Lavoisier; *Ambassador:* ABDALLAH ESSAOUISSI.

Malaysia: Angle Zankat Achafii et Zankat Hamzah, Agdal; *Ambassador:* Raja Tan Sri AZMAN BIN RAJA haji AHMAD.

Mali: Algiers, Algeria.

Malta: Tripoli, Libya.

Mauritania: 64 Zankat Oum Errabia; *Ambassador:* SAAD BOUH.

Mexico: Accra, Ghana.

Nepal: Cairo, Egypt.

Netherlands: 38 rue de Tunis; *Ambassador:* (vacant).

Niger: Algiers, Algeria.

Nigeria: 2 rue Al Bousiri; *Ambassador:* AL-AJI ADO SANUSI.

Norway: 20 Charia As-Saouira; *Ambassador:* IVER MALHUUS (also accred. to Algeria, Libya and Tunisia)

Oman: 27 rue Hamza; *Ambassador:* CHABIB BEN TAIMUR AL SAID.

Pakistan: 20 ave. d'Alger; *Ambassador:* AHMED GHIATEDDIN.

Paraguay: Madrid, Spain.

Peru: Cairo, Egypt.

Poland: 25 Zankat Oqbah, Agdal; *Ambassador:* ZDZISŁAW PACHOWSKI.

Portugal: 45 rue Maurice Pascouet; *Ambassador:* JOSÉ JOAQUIM DE MINA E MENDONÇA.

Qatar: 4 Chariaâ Tarik Ibn Ziad; *Ambassador:* ABDALLAH YOUSSEF AL JIDA.

Romania: 10 rue d'Ouezzane; *Ambassador:* Dr. OVIDIU CORNELIU POPESCU.

Saudi Arabia: 43 place de l'Unité Africaine; *Ambassador:* FAKRI SHEIKH EL ARD.

Senegal: 3 rue Descartes, B.P. 365; *Ambassador:* ALY DIOUM.

Spain: 3 rue Mohamed al Fatih; *Ambassador:* MANUEL ALBABART MIRANDA.

Sudan: 9 rue de Tedders; *Ambassador:* ABBES MOUSA MUSTAPHA.

Sweden: 6 Zankat Jabal Al Ayachi; *Ambassador:* KNUT JOHN RICHARD BERNSTRON (also accred. to The Gambia and Mauritania).

Switzerland: Square Condo de Satriano; *Ambassador:* JEAN-PIERRE WEBER.

Syria: 27 rue d'Oqbah, Agdal; *Ambassador:* MOHAMMED ADNAN AL-ZUBAIR.

Tunisia: 6 ave. de Fès; *Ambassador:* SALADDIN ABDULLAH.

Turkey: 19 ave. de Meknès; *Ambassador:* NECDEK ILCI.

Uganda: Cairo, Egypt.

U.S.S.R.: 18 ave. Aneggai; *Ambassador:* YEVGENIY NERSESOV.

United Arab Emirates: 8 Zankat Ifrane, B.P. 478; *Ambassador:* AHMED ALI ATTAJIR.

United Kingdom: 28 bis ave. Allal-Ben-Abdallah; *Ambassador:* S. Y. DAWBARN.

U.S.A.: 2 ave de Marrakech; *Ambassador:* RICHARD PARKER.

Vatican City: Algiers, Algeria.

Venezuela: Tunis, Tunisia.

Yugoslavia: 39 ave. Omar Ibn Khattab; *Ambassador:* BRANICA GVIDO.

Zaire: 34 ave. de la Victoire; *Ambassador:* LOMBO LO MANGAMANGA.

Zambia: Cairo, Egypt.

Morocco also has diplomatic relations with Albania, the Bahamas, Burma, Guinea-Bissau, Jamaica, Mauritius, Monaco, Mongolia, the Philippines and Sierra Leone.

JUDICIAL SYSTEM

The **Supreme Court** (*Majlis el Aala*) is responsible for the interpretation of the law and regulates the jurisprudence of the courts and tribunals of the Kingdom. The Supreme Court sits at Rabat and is divided into five Chambers.

First President and Attorney-General: BRAHIM KEDDARA.

The nine **Courts of Appeal** hear appeals from lower courts and also comprise a criminal division.

The **Sadad Tribunals** pass judgment, without possibility of appeal, in personal, civil and commercial cases involving up to 300 dirhams. These tribunals also pass judgment, subject to appeal before the Regional Tribunals, in the same cases up to 900 dirhams, in disputes related to the personal and successional statutes of Moroccan Muslims and Jews, and in penal cases involving misdemeanours or infringements of the law.

The **Regional Tribunals** deal with appeals against judgments made by the Sadad Tribunals; and pass judgment in the first and last resort in cases of personal property of 900 to 1,200 dirhams or property producing a yield of up to 80 dirhams. The Regional Tribunals also pass judgment, subject to appeal before the Court of Appeal, in actions brought against public administrations in administrative affairs, and in cases of minor offences in penal matters.

Labour Tribunals settle, by means of conciliation, disputes arising from rental contracts or services between employers and employees engaged in private industry. There are 14 labour tribunals in the Kingdom.

A special court was created in 1965 in Rabat to deal with corruption among public officials.

RELIGION

ISLAM

Most Moroccans are Muslims and Islam is the state religion.

CHRISTIANITY

There are about 70,000 Christians, mostly Roman Catholics.

Archbishop of Rabat: Jean Marcel Chabbert, 1 rue Abou Inane, B.P. 258, Rabat.

Archbishop of Tangier: Carlos Amigo Vallejo; 55 Sidi Bouabid, B.P. 2116, Tangier.

Evangelical Church: 33 rue d'Azilal, Casablanca; f. 1920; established in 9 towns; Pastor Gilbert Schmid; publ. *Vie Nouvelle* (monthly).

JUDAISM

There are about 30,000 Jews.

Grand Rabbi of Casablanca: 167 blvd. Ziraoui, Casablanca; Chalom Messas, President of the Rabbinical Court of Casablanca, Palais de Justice, Place des Nations Unies.

THE PRESS

DAILIES

Casablanca

Al Bayane: 32 rue Ledru-Rollin, B.P. 152, Casablanca; Arabic and French; Dir. Ali Yata.

Maroc Soir: 34 rue Mohammed Smiha; f. Nov. 1971 to replace *La Vigie Marocaine*, closed down by the Government; French; Pres. Dir.-Gen. Moulay Ahmed Alaoui; circ. 35,000.

Le Matin du Sahara: rue Mohammed Smiha; f. Nov. 1971 to replace *Le Petit Marocain*, closed down by the Government; French; Pres. Dir.-Gen. Moulay Ahmed Alaoui; circ. 50,000.

Al Mouharir: 11 rue Soldat Roch; Arabic; organ of USFP; Dir. Mohamed Lyazghi.

Rabat

Al Alam (*The Flag*): 11 ave. Allal Ben Abdullah; organ of the Istiqlal Party; f. 1946, Arabic; Dir. Abdelkrim Ghallab; circ. 44,000; also *Al Alam Book*.

Al Anba'a (*Information*): Zankat Al Medina, B.P. 65; Arabic; Dir. Ahmed Al Yaakoubi; circ. 15,000.

Al Maghreb: French; Dir. Abdallah Stouky.

Al Maghreb al Arabi: 16 rue Al Abral, Agdal; Arabic; Dir. Amr Aloiquouti; circ. 10,000.

L'Opinion: 11 ave Allal Ben Abdullah; f. 1965; Istiqlal party newspaper; French; Dir. Mohamed Idrissi Kaitouni; circ. 35,000.

PERIODICALS

Casablanca

Annidal: 10 rue Cols Bleus, Sidi Bousmara, Médina Kédima; f. 1973; weekly; Dir. Ibrahimi Ahmed.

CAF Omnisports: ave. Jean Mermoz; f. 1955; monthly; French; Dir. Léon Verrax.

Cedies Informations: 23 blvd. Mohamed Abdouh; weekly; French; Admin. Fayçal Chraibi.

Construire: 25 rue d'Azilal, Immeuble Ortiba; f. 1946; weekly; French; Dir. Bouchaib Tallal.

Le Courrier Economique: 28 ave. de l'Armée Royale; weekly; French; Dir. Betoul Tahiri.

Les Echos Africains: B.P. 140, 27 ave. des F.A.R.; f. 1972; monthly; news, economics; French; Dir. Mohamed Choufani Elfassi.

L'Espoir: 167 ave. Hassan; twice monthly; French; Dir. Idris Charaf.

Al-Ittihad ul Watani: 46 rue de la Garon; organ of UNFP; weekly; Arabic; Dir. Ahmed Shakur.

Lamalif: 27 rue d'Epinal; f. 1966; French; monthly; economic, social and cultural magazine; Dir. Mohamed Loghlam.

Al Mabadie: rue Caporal Paul; monthly; Arabic; Dir. Abdeslam Bourkia.

La Marche Verte: 34 rue Mohammed Smiha; weekly; Pres. Dir.-Gen. Moulay Ahmed Alaoui.

Maroc Fruits: 44 rue Mohamed Smiha; f. 1958; fortnightly; French; organ of ASPAM; Dir. Ahmed Ben Mansour Nejjai; circ. 6,000.

Al Mouharir: 11 rue Soldat Roch; weekly; Arabic; organ of USFP; Dir. Mohamed Elyazghi.

Nous les Bêtes: 42 ave. des F.A.R.; twice monthly; French; Dir. Raoul Fayaux.

Al-Oummal: 9 rue Rif; weekly; French and Arabic; organ of the U.G.T.M.; Dir. Abderrazak Afilal.

La Quinzaine du Maroc: 8 rue Voltaire; twice monthly; French; Dir. Gabriel Gauthey.

Revue Automobile Africaine: 38 blvd. de la Gironde; monthly; French; Dir. Robert Perrier.

Revue Fiduciaire Marocaine: 81 rue Colbert; twice monthly; French; Dir. Maurice Bernard.

Réalités Maghrebines: f. 1965; monthly; French; general economic review; Dir. MOHAMED ELMERGAOUI.

Revue Marocaine de Droit: monthly; Arabic; Dir. MEYLAN BENCHALEL.

Revue Mensuelle de la Chambre de Commerce et d'Industrie de Casablanca: B.P. 423; monthly; French; Dir. ABDELLAH SOUIRI.

Télé Sport: 8 rue Voltaire; weekly; French; Dir. GABRIEL GAUTHEY.

La Tribune Economique: f. 1977; weekly; Editor ABDELHAFID ROUISSI.

La Vie Economique: 5 boulevard Ben Yacine; f. 1921; French; weekly; Dir. MARCEL HERZOG.

La Vie Industrielle et Agricole: 142 blvd. Mohamed V; twice monthly; French; Dir. AHMED ZGHARI.

La Vie Touristique: 142 blvd. Mohamed V; weekly; French; Dir. AHMED ZGHARI.

Vie Nouvelle: 33 rue d'Azilal; f. 1930; monthly; French; journal of the Protestant churches of the Maghreb; Dir. ROGER CHATAIGNE.

Fez

Fès: rue Etats-Unis; monthly; Arabic; Dir. MOHAMED SLAOUI.

Rabat

Al Aamak: 291 ave. Mohamed V; monthly; Arabic; Dir. EL WAKILI THAMI.

Achaab (*The People*): 2 rue Parmentier, B.P. 364; independent; twice weekly; Arabic; Founder and Editor M. MEKKI NACIRI; Dir. MUSTAPHA BELHAJ; circ. 25,000.

Achorta: B.P. 437; monthly; Arabic; Dir. Directeur de la Sûreté Nationale.

Al Aklam: B.P. 2229; monthly; Arabic; Dir. ABDERRAHMANE BEN AMAR.

Asdae: 10 rue Port Said; weekly; Arabic; Dir. HASSAN ARABI.

Attadamoun: 23 ave. Allal ben Abdellah; monthly; Arabic; Dir. ABDELMAJID SEMLALI EL HASANI.

Barid el Maghreb: 281 ave. Mohamed V; monthly; Arabic; Dir. MUSTAPHA ALAOUI.

Daouat Elhak: Ministry of Waqfs; monthly; Arabic; Dir. MOHAMED BEN ABDELLAH.

Al Iman: B.P. 356, rue Akenssous; f. 1963; monthly; Arabic; Dir. ELKADIRI BOUBKER.

Al Irchad: Ministry of Waqfs; monthly; Arabic.

Al Khansa: 154 ave. Souss Mohamedia; monthly; Arabic; Dir. ABOUZAL AICHA.

Tangier

Actualités Touristiques: 80 rue de la Liberté; monthly; French; Dir. TAYEB ALAMI.

Le Journal de Tanger: 11 ave. de Rabat, B.P. 2002; f. 1905; French, English, Spanish and Arabic; weekly; Dir. AHMED BENCHEKROUNE; circ. 6,500.

Tanjah: 8 place de France, B.P. 1055; f. 1956; French and Arabic; weekly; Dir. MOHAMMED MEHDI ZAHDI.

NEWS AGENCIES

Maghreb Arabe Presse: 10 rue Al-Yamama, B.P. 1049, Rabat; f. 1959; Arabic, French and English; government-owned; Man. Dir. ABDULJALIL FENJIRO.

FOREIGN BUREAUX

Agence France-Presse (AFP): place Mohammed V; B.P. 118, Rabat; f. 1920; French; Dir. ANDRÉ DAVY; Sec. and Editor MANOUBI MEKNASSY.

Reuters (*United Kingdom*): 17 rue de Baghdad, Rabat; *Representative:* STEPHEN HUGHES.

Hsinhua (People's Republic of China) and TASS (U.S.S.R.) also have bureaux in Rabat.

PUBLISHERS

Dar El Kitab: place de la Mosquée, B.P. 4018, Casablanca; f. 1948; philosophy, law, novels, educational books; Arabic and French; Dir. BOUTALEB ABDOU ABDELHAY.

Editions La Porte: 281 ave. Mohammed V; Rabat; law, guides, educational books; Man. Dir. PAUL SOUCHON.

Editions Maghrébines: 5–13 rue Soldat Roch, Casablanca; f. 1962; general non-fiction.

Imprimerie Artistique: 31 ave. Es-Sellaoui, Fez.

RADIO AND TELEVISION

Radiodiffusion Télévision Marocaine: 1 Zenkat Al Brihi, Rabat; government station; *Radio:* Network 1 in Arabic, Network 2 in French, Network 3 in Berber, Spanish and English; Foreign Service in Arabic, French and English; *Television:* began 1962; 60½ hours weekly; French and Arabic; carries commercial advertising; Dir.-Gen. BENNACER DRISSI QEYTONI; Deputy Dir. Progs. ABDELLATIF BEKKALI; Dir. Foreign Service ABDALLAH CHAKROUN; publ. *Al ladaa wa Talvaza al Maghribia.*

Voice of America Radio Station in Tangier: c/o U.S. Consulate General, Chemin des Amoureux, Tangier.

Number of radios (1978): 2,400,000.

Number of televisions (1978): 605,000.

FINANCE

BANKING

(cap. = capital; p.u. = paid up; dep. = deposits; m. = million; brs. = branches; amounts in dirhams unless otherwise indicated)

CENTRAL BANK

Banque du Maroc: P.O.B. 445, 277 ave. Mohammed V, Rabat; f. 1959; cap. 30m.; dep. 624m. (Dec. 1975); Gov. Prince MOULAY HASSAN BEN MEHDI; Vice-Gov. AHMED BENNANI.

Algemene Bank Marokko S.A.: place du 16 Novembre, Casablanca; branches in Tangier, Rabat and Agadir; f. 1948; 50 per cent participation of Algemene Bank Nederland N.V., Amsterdam, Netherlands; cap. 10m.; Pres. M. KASSIDI; Gen. Man. B. HANSEN.

Arab Bank Maroc: 174 blvd. Mohammed V, B.P. 810, Casablanca; f. 1975; cap. 10m.; Pres. Hadj OMAR ABDELJALIL; Gen. Man. FAROUK ABDELMAJEED.

Banque Commerciale du Maroc S.A.: 81 ave. de l'Armée Royale, Casablanca; f. 1911; affiliated to Crédit Industriel et Commercial, Paris, France; cap. 24m., dep. 1,509m. (Dec. 1976); Pres. ABDELAZIZ ALAMI; Vice-Pres. R. BELIN; 43 brs.

Banque Marocaine du Commerce Exterieur: 241 boulevard Mohammed V, Casablanca; f. 1959; took over Société de Banque du Maghreb, 1971, Banco Español en Marruecos, 1975; partly state-owned; cap. 54m., res. 53m. (Dec. 1975); Chair. and Chief Exec. Hadj ABDEL MAJID BENGELLOUN; Man. Dir. MOHAMMED BENNIS; 75 brs.

Banque Marocaine pour l'Afrique et l'Orient: 80 ave. Lalla Yacout, B.P. 880, Casablanca; formerly British Bank of the Middle East (Morocco).

Banque Marocaine pour le Commerce et l'Industrie: 26 place Mohammed V, Casablanca, P.O.B. 573; f. 1964; cap. 29m., res. 32m. (Nov. 1977); Pres. Hadj Ahmed Bargach; Gen. Man. Mohamed Benkirane; 47 brs.

Banque Nationale pour le Développement Economique: B.P. 407, place des Alaouites, Rabat; f. 1959; cap. 70m.; Pres. and Gen. Man. Mustapha Faris.

Compagnie Marocaine de Crédit et de Banques S.A.: 1 ave. Hassan II, Casablanca; f. 1964; affiliated to Banque de l'Indochine et de Suez, Paris, France; cap. 20m., res. 8.1m.; Pres. Ali Kettani; 50 brs.

Crédit du Maroc S.A.: B.P. 579, 48–58 blvd. Mohammed V, Casablanca; f. 1963; cap. 33m., res. 27m. (Dec. 1977); Pres. M. Karim-Lamrani; Dir.-Gen. Jawad Ben Brahim.

Société de Banque et de Crédit: 26 ave. de l'Armée Royale, B.P. 972, Casablanca; f. 1951; affil. to Swiss Bank Corporation, Crédit Commercial de France and Continental Illinois National Bank & Trust Co. of Chicago; cap. 4.5m., res. 2.9m.; Mans. Louis Fourat, E. F. Veldhuyzen.

Société Générale Marocaine de Banques: 84 blvd. Mohammed V, B.P. 90, Casablanca; f. 1962; cap. 35.4m., res. 17.2m. (Dec. 1977); Chair. Hamed Bargach; Man. Dir. Abdelaziz Tazi; 40 brs.

Société Marocaine de Dépôt et Crédit: 79 ave. Hassan II, Casablanca; Pres. Abdelkader Bensalah; Gen. Man. Omar Akalay.

Unión Bancaria Hispano Marroquí: 69 rue du Prince Moulay Abdullah, Casablanca; f. 1958; cap. 16m., dep. 339m. (Dec. 1977); Pres. Mohamed ben Ahmed Benabud; Gen. Man. Pedro Landra Velon; 15 brs.

Bank Organizations

Groupement Professionnel des Banques du Maroc: 71 ave. de l'Armée Royale, Casablanca; f. 1967; groups all commercial banks for organization, studies, inquiries of general interest, and contacts with official authorities; Pres. Hadj Abdelmajid Bengelloun.

Association Professionelle des Intermédiaires de Bourse: 71 ave. de l'Armée Royale, Casablanca; f. 1970; groups all banks and brokers in the stock exchange of Casablanca, for organization, studies, inquiries of general interest and connection with official authorities; Pres. Hadj Abdelmajid Bengelloun.

STOCK EXCHANGE

Bourse des Valeurs de Cassablanca: Chamber of Commerce Building, 98 boulevard Mohammed V, Casablanca; f. 1929; Dir. Abderrazak Laraqui; publ. *Bulletin de la Cote*.

INSURANCE

Atlanta: 243 blvd. Mohammed V, Casablanca; f. 1947; Dir. M. Poirrier.

Cie. Africaine d'Assurances: 123 blvd. Rahal el Meskini, Casablanca; Dir.-Gen. M. Sekkat.

Cie. d'Assurances SANAD: 28 place Mohammed V, Casablanca; Dir.-Gen. Pierre Croze.

Cie. Nordafricaine et Intercontinentale d'Assurances (C.N.I.A.): 157 ave. Hassan II, Casablanca; cap. 1.8m.; Pres. Abdelkamel Rerhrhaye.

Cia. Marroqui de Seguros: 62 rue de la Liberté, Tangier; Dir. M. Buisan.

COMAR Paternelle-Prévoyance: 42 avenue de l'Armée Royale, Casablanca; cap. 3.1m.; Gen. Man. Bernard Pagezy.

L'Entente: 2 rue Mohammed Smiha, Casablanca; f. 1960; Pres. Abdelkader ben Salah; Dir.-Gen. Mohamed Cherkaoui.

Mutuelle Agricole Marocaine d'Assurances: B.P. 27, 16 rue Abou Inane, Rabat; Dir.-Gen. Yacoubi Soussane.

La Providence Marocaine: 1 rond-point St. Exupéry, Casablanca; Dir. M. de Roquefeuil.

La Royale Marocaine d'Assurance: 67 ave. de l'Armée Royale, Casablanca; cap. 1.1m.; Dir.-Gen. Mahomed Ben Jilali Bennani.

Es Saada, Cie. Générale d'Assurances et de Réassurances: 123 ave. Hassan II, Casablanca; f. 1961; cap. 5m.; Chair. Izarab Ouazzani; Man. Dir. Mehdi Ouazzani.

Société Central de Réassurance: B.P. 183, Tour Atlas, Place Zallaqa, Casablanca; f. 1960; Dir.Gen. M. Aimarah.

Société Marocaine d'Assurances: 1 rond-point Saint Exupéry, Casablanca; Dir. M. Giustiniani.

Société Nouvelle d'Assurances: 10 rue Mohamed Diouri, Casablanca; f. 1972; Chair. A. Kettani; Gen. Man. J. Kettani.

Fédération Marocaine des Sociétés d'Assurances et de Réassurances: 300 rue Mustafa el Maani, Casablanca; f. 1958; Pres. M'Hamed Ben Jilali Bennani; Dir. Bekkaye-Driss.

TRADE AND INDUSTRY

CHAMBERS OF COMMERCE

La Fédération des Chambres de Commerce et d'Industrie du Maroc: B.P. 218, 11 ave. Allal Ben Abdullah, Rabat; f. 1962; groups the 15 Chambers of Commerce and Industry; Pres. Abdellah Souira; publ. *Revue Trimestrielle*.

British Chamber of Commerce for Morocco: 291 blvd. Mohammed V, Casablanca; Pres. Evan Llewellyn.

Chambre de Commerce et d'Industrie de Casablanca: 98 blvd. Mohammed V, B.P. 423, Casablanca; Pres. Mohamed Drissi.

Chambre Française de Commerce et d'Industrie du Maroc (CFI): 15 avenue Mers Sultan, B.P. 73, Casablanca; Pres. Bernard Larmigny; Dir. Pierre Rousselot.

DEVELOPMENT ORGANIZATIONS

Bureau de Recherches et de Participations Minières (BPRM): 5–7 Charii Moulay Hassan, B.P. 99, Rabat; f. 1928; a state agency to develop geological, mining and oil research; Dir.-Gen. Abderrafih Guessous.

Caisse Marocaine des Marchés (*Marketing Fund*): 52 ave. Hassan II, Casablanca; f. 1950; cap. 10m.; dep. 5m.; Pres. Dir.-Gen. Abdelkader Benslimane; Man. Hassan Kissi.

Caisse Nationale de Crédit Agricole (*Agricultural Credit Fund*): B.P. 49, Rabat.

Crédit Immobilier et Hôtelier: 68 rue de Reims, Casablanca; f. 1920; cap. 80m.; Pres. Dir.-Gen. El Fihri El Habib.

Office National Interprofessionel des Céréales et des Légumineuses: 25 ave. Moulay Hassan, B.P. 154, Rabat; f. 1937; Dir. Mohamed Brick.

Office de Commercialisation et d'Exportation (OCE): 45 ave. des F.A.R., Casablanca; f. 1932 (nationalized 1965); turnover (1977/78) c. 2,400m. dirhams; takes part in productivity planning, industrialization, local marketing and overseas trade; Dir. ABDALLAH LAHLOU; Sec.-Gen. MOHAMMED GUESSOUS.

Office du Développement Industriel (ODI): 8 rue Gandhi, Rabat; f. 1958; a state agency to develop industry; Dir.-Gen. ABDELAZIZ BENJELLOUN.

Société de Développement Agricole (SODEA): 12 Zankat Tanja, Rabat; state agricultural development organization.

Société de Gestion des Terres Agricoles (SOGETA): 11 rue de Salé, Rabat; oversees use of agricultural land.

PRINCIPAL STATE ENTERPRISES

Complexe Textile de Fès (COTEF): B.P. 267, Fez; f. 1967; 99 per cent state participation; started full activity in Jan. 1972; Dir.-Gen. MAHROUCH ABDESLAM.

Office Chérifien des Phosphates (OCP): 305 ave. Mohammed V, Rabat; f. 1921; a state company to produce and market rock phosphates and derivatives; Dir.-Gen. MOHAMMED KARIM LAMRANI.

Office National de l'Eau Potable (ONEP): 6 *bis* rue Patrice Lumumba, Rabat; responsible for drinking-water supply.

Office National de l'Electricité: B.P. 498, Casablanca; state electricity authority.

Office National des Pêches: 13/15 rue Chevalier Bayard, Casablanca; state fishing organization.

Société d'Exploitation du Fer du Rif (SEFERIF): B.P. 14, Nador; mines began production 1914, nationalized 1967; open and underground mines produce iron ore for export and for the projected Nador iron and steel complex.

Société Nationale de Sidérurgie (SONASID): 63 ave. Moulay Youssef, Rabat; f. 1974; to build and operate an iron and steel complex at Nador.

EMPLOYERS' ORGANIZATIONS

Association Marocaine des Industries Textiles: 58 rue Lughérini, Casablanca; f. 1958; mems. 550 textile and ready-made factories; Pres. MOHAMED DRISSI; Sec.-Gen. A. MIKOU.

Association des Producteurs d'Agrumes du Maroc (ASPAM): 44 rue Mohamed Smiha, Casablanca; links Moroccan citrus growers; has its own processing plants.

Confédération Générale Economique Marocaine (C.G.E.M.): 23 blvd. Mohammed Abdouh, Casablanca; Pres. MOHAMED AMOR; Sec.-Gen. M. FAYÇAL CHRAÏBI.

Union Marocaine de l'Agriculture (U.M.A.): rue Gandhi, Rabat; Pres. M. NEJJAI.

TRADE UNIONS

Confédération Démocratique du Travail (C.D.T.): Rabat; f. 1978; associated with Union socialiste des forces populaires; Sec.-Gen. MOHAMED AMAWI.

Union Générale des Travailleurs du Maroc (U.G.T.M.): 9 rue du Rif, angle Route de Médiouna, Casablanca; f. 1960; associated with Istiqlal; supported by unions not affiliated to U.M.T.; 673,000 mems.; Sec.-Gen. ABDERRAZZAQ AFILAL; publ. *Al Oummal* (weekly).

Union Marocaine du Travail (U.M.T.): Bourse du Travail, 222 avenue de l'Armée Royale, Casablanca; left wing and associated with UNFP; most unions are affiliated; 700,000 mems.; Sec. MAHJOUB BEN SEDDIQ; publs. *Maghreb Informations* (daily, suspended March 1975).

Union Syndicale Agricole (U.S.A.): agricultural section of U.M.T.

Union Marocaine du Travail Autonome: Rabat; breakaway union from U.M.T.

Union Nationale des Travailleurs du Maroc (UNTM): Casablanca; associated with the MPCD.

Syndicat National Libre: blvd. Hansali (prolongé), Casablanca; f. 1958; 69,000 mems.; Sec.-Gen. MEEKI IBRAHIMY.

TRADE FAIR

Foire Internationale de Casablanca: 11 rue Jules Mauran, Casablanca; f. 1950; international trade fair; every two years for 18 days in April-May.

TRANSPORT

Office National de Transport: 10 rue Annaba (Chellah), Rabat.

RAILWAYS

Railways cover over 1,800 km. of which 161 km. are double track; 730 km. of lines are electrified and diesel locomotives are used on the rest. All services are nationalized.

Office National des Chemins de Fer du Maroc (ONCFM): 19 ave. Allal Ben Abdallah, Rabat; f. 1963; runs all Morocco's railways; Pres. MOHAND NACEUR; Dir. MOUSSA MOUSSAOUI.

ROADS

There are over 29,300 km. of roads, of which 84 per cent are surfaced. In 1973 there were 14 km. of modern motorway (70 km. in 1977, between Casablanca and Rabat) and 7,141 km. of main roads. In 1978 a new 980 km. road between Bou Craa and Ajoujt in Mauritania was planned.

Compagnie de Transports au Maroc "Lignes Nationales" (CTM-LN): 303 blvd. Brahim Roudani, Casablanca; Agencies in Tangier, Rabat, Meknès, Oujda, Marrakesh, Agadir, El Jadida, Safi, Essouira, Ksar-Es-Souk, Fez and Ouarzazate.

SHIPPING

The chief ports of Morocco are Casablanca, Tangier, Safi, Mohammedia, Kenitra and Agadir. In January 1962 the port of Tangier became an International Free Zone. Tangier is the principal port for passenger services. Casablanca is the principal freight port, handling 70 per cent of Morocco's trade. New ports are being built at Nador and Jorf Lasfar.

Agence Gibmar S.A.: 3 rue Henri Regnault, Tangier; also at Casablanca; regular sea services from Tangier to Gibraltar.

Compagnie Chérifienne d'Armement: 5 ave. de l'Armée Royale, Casablanca; f. 1929; Pres. BENNANI SMIRES; regular lines to North France and Europe.

Compagnie Marocaine d'Agences Maritimes (COMARINE): 65 ave. de l'Armée Royale, B.P. 60, Casablanca; f. 1969; Dir.-Gen. MICHEL BOUKHTIAROFF.

Compagnie Marocaine de Navigation (COMANAV): 28 rue de Lille, Casablanca; f. 1946; Pres. Dir.-Gen. A. BOUAYAD; regular lines to Mediterranean, North-west European and West African ports; tramping.

Limadet-ferry: 3 rue Henri Regnault, Tangier; f. 1966; operates between Malaga and Algeciras and Tangier; Dir.-Gen. AZIZ BOUZOUBAA.

Société Marocaine de Navigation Fruitière: 27 ave. de l'Armée Royale, Casablanca; Pres. M. SEGUENI.

Société de Navigation Maghribine: B.P. 746, 15 rue de Foucauld, Casablanca; oil and chemicals.

Transmediterranea S.A. (Intercona): 31 rue Quevedo, Tangier; daily services Algeciras to Tangier; two services weekly Malaga to Tangier.

Voyages Paquet: 65 ave. de l'Armée Royale, Casablanca; f. 1970; Dir.-Gen. MICHEL BOUKHTIAROFF.

CIVIL AVIATION

There are international airports at Casablanca, Rabat, Tangier, Marrakesh, Agadir and Fez.

NATIONAL AIRLINES

Royal Air Maroc: Aéroport International Casablanca-Nouasseur; f. 1953; 81.7 per cent owned by the Government; domestic flights and services to Western Europe, North America, Brazil, North Africa, Senegal, the Ivory Coast, the Canary Islands, Saudi Arabia and Kuwait; fleet of 3 Boeing 737, Boeing 727, 3 Boeing 707, 1 Boeing 747; Chair. Gen. DRISS BEN AOMAR EL ALAMI; Man. Dir. SAID BEN ALI YAALA.

Royal Air Inter: Aéroport Casablanca-Anfa; f. 1970; operates domestic services from Casablanca and foreign services to the Canary Islands, Gibraltar, Mauritania and Spain; fleet of 2 F-27, 1 Boeing 737; Dir.-Gen. HASSAN YACOUBI SOUSSANE.

Casablanca is served by the following foreign airlines; Aeroflot (U.S.S.R.), Air Afrique (Ivory Coast), Air Algérie, Air France, Air Mali, Balkan (Bulgaria), British Caledonian, Iberia (Spain), KLM (Netherlands), Lufthansa (Federal Republic of Germany), TWA (U.S.A.), Sabena (Belgium), Saudia (Saudi Arabia), Swissair and Tunis Air. In addition, ČSA (Czechoslovakia) fly to Rabat, British Airways to Marrakesh and Agadir, and Gibair (Gibraltar) to Tangier.

TOURISM

Office National Marocain de Tourisme: B.P. 19, 22 ave. d'Alger, Rabat; f. 1946; Dir. ABDELLATIF AMOR; publ. *Maroc-Tourisme* (quarterly).

CULTURAL ORGANIZATIONS

Ministry of Cultural Affairs: rue Gandhi, Rabat; consists of departments of Cultural Activities and Art Education, Museums and Historic Monuments, together with administrative and legal divisions; publs. *Bulletin d'Archéologie Marocaine, Etudes et Travaux d'Archéologie*, etc.

Associations des Amateurs de la Musique Andalouse: 26 rue de Strasbourg, Casablanca; f. 1957; centres in 13 Moroccan towns; Dir. Hadj DRISS BENJELLOUN.

PRINCIPAL THEATRES

Théâtre National Mohammed V: Rabat; f. 1961; Morocco's national theatre with its own troupe, subsidized by the state; Dir. M. A. SEGHROUCHNI.

Théâtre Municipal de Casablanca: blvd. de Paris, Casablanca; f. 1922, reorganized 1934 and 1949; presents a large number of foreign and national productions; maintained by the Casablanca Municipality; Dir. TAIB SASSIKI; Gen. Administrator ALI KADIRI.

PRINCIPAL ORCHESTRAS

Orchestre Symphonique du Conservatoire National de Musique: Rabat; European classical music and Andalusian (Arabic) music; chamber orchestra.

Orchestre du Conservatoire de Tétouan: Tetuan; specializes in Andalusian (Arabic) music; Dir. M. TEMSEMANI.

Orchestre du Conservatoire Dar Adyel: Fez; specialising in traditional music; Dir. Hadj ABDELKRIM RAIS.

DEFENCE

Defence Budget (1978): 1,925 million dirhams.

Military Service: 18 months.

Total Armed Forces (1978): 89,000; army 81,000; navy 2,000; air force 6,000. Paramilitary forces: 30,000.

EDUCATION

Since independence in 1956 Morocco has had to tackle a number of educational problems: a youthful and fast-growing population, an urgent need for skilled workers and executives, a great diversity of teaching methods between French, Spanish, Muslim and Moroccan Government schools, and, above all, a high degree of adult illiteracy. Morocco spends about 15 per cent of her national budget on education, of which a considerable proportion is devoted to constructing buildings for higher studies and technical education. In many small towns and villages, local craftsmen have co-operated together in the building of elementary schools.

In 1977/78 there were 1,793,772 pupils in primary schools. At this level nearly 97 per cent of instruction is given in government schools, where syllabuses have been standardized since 1967. Great progress was made in providing new schools between 1957 and 1964, but since then the increase in the number of places has slowed down. A decree of November 1963 made education compulsory for children between the ages of seven and thirteen, and this has now been applied in most urban areas, but throughout the country only 51 per cent of the age-group attended school in 1970–71. That year there were 5,034 government primary schools with 32,050 teachers, all Moroccan, trained in the 18 regional teacher training colleges. Instruction is given in Arabic for the first two years and in Arabic and French for the next three years, with English as the first additional language.

Secondary education lasts for three or four years, depending on the type of course, and in 1977/78 provided for 582,197 pupils. Approximately a quarter of these pupils attended technical schools, where reforms have taken place since 1970 to attract more pupils and to provide relevant training to meet the country's need for technical manpower. In 1971 there were 12,364 qualified teachers in secondary schools, of whom just under half were Moroccan and most of the rest French. Instruction is given mainly in French, but about a third of teachers use Arabic, and this trend is increasing.

Higher education has a long history in Morocco. The Islamic University of Al Quarawiyin at Fez celebrated its eleventh centenary in 1959-60. The Mohammed V University opened in Rabat in 1957 and now has over 16,000 students in four faculties. In addition there are institutes of higher education in business studies, agriculture, mining, law, and statistics and advanced economics.

Adult education is being tackled through the means of radio, simplified type, a special newspaper for the newly literate, and the co-operation of every teacher in the country. Another notable development in recent years has been the increasing attention given to education for girls. In 1976/77 about 64 per cent of primary school pupils were boys and 36 per cent girls. There are now a number of mixed and girls' schools, and the proportion is growing every year, especially in urban areas.

UNIVERSITIES

Al Quarawiyin University: Cité Cherarda, Fez; f. in the 9th century A.D.; 90 teachers, 1,647 students (1977/78).

Université Hassan II: Casablanca; 256 teachers, 11,582 students (1977/78).

Université Mohammed V: ave. Moulay Chérif, Rabat; f. 1957; 1,188 teachers, 30,294 students (1977/78).

Université Mohamed Ben Abdallah: Dhar Mehraz, Fez; 309 teachers, 9,877 students (1977/78).

BIBLIOGRAPHY

AMIN, SAMIR. The Maghreb in the Modern World (Penguin, Harmondsworth, 1971).

ASHFORD, D. E. Political Change in Morocco (Princeton U.P., 1961).
Perspectives of a Moroccan Nationalist (New York, 1964).

AYACHE, A. Le Maroc (Editions Sociales, Paris, 1956).

BARBOUR, NEVILL. Morocco (Thames and Hudson, London, 1964).

BELAL, ABDEL AZIZ. L'investissement au Maroc (1912–1964) et ses enseignements en matière de développement économique (Mouton, Paris, 1968).

BEN BARKA, MEHDI. Problèmes de l'édification du Maroc et du Maghreb (Plon, Paris, 1959).
Option Révolutionnaire en Maroc (Maspéro, Paris, 1966).

BENNETT, NORMAN ROBERT. A study guide for Morocco (Boston, 1970).

BERNARD, STÉPHANE. Le Conflit Franco-Marocain 1943–1956, 3 vols. (Brussels, 1963; English translation, Yale University Press, 1968).

BERQUE, JAQUES. Le Maghreb entre deux guerres (Eds. du Seuil, Paris, 1962).

BIDWELL, ROBIN. Morocco under Colonial Rule: French Administration of Tribal Areas 1912–56 (Frank Cass, London, 1973).

BOVILL, E. W. The Golden Trade of the Moors (London, 1958).

CLASEN, DIRK. Stauffacher-Reiseführer Marokko (Stauffacher Verlag, Zürich, 1964).

COHEN, M. I., and HAHN, LORNA. Morocco: Old Land, New Nation (Praeger, New York, 1964).

COULAU, JULIEN. La paysannerie marocaine (Paris, 1968).

HALL, L. J. The United States and Morocco, 1776–1956 (Scarecrow Press, Metuchen, N.J., 1971).

HALSTEAD, JOHN P. Rebirth of a Nation: the Origins and Rise of Moroccan Nationalism (Harvard University Press, 1967).

HASSAN II, King of Morocco. Le Défi (Albin Michel, Paris, 1976).

JULIEN, CHARLES-ANDRÉ. Le Maroc face aux Impérialismes (1415–1956) (Editions Jeune Afrique, Paris, 1978).

KININMONTH, C. The Travellers' Guide to Morocco (Jonathan Cape, London, 1972).

LACOUTURE, J. and S. Le Maroc à l'épreuve (du Seuil, Paris, 1958)

LANDAU, ROM. The Moroccan Drama 1900–1955 (Hale, London, 1956).
Morocco Independent under Mohammed V (Allen and Unwin, London, 1961).
Hassan II, King of Morocco (Allen and Unwin, London, 1962).
The Moroccans—Yesterday and Today (London, 1963).
Morocco (Allen & Unwin, London, 1967).

LANDAU, ROM and SWANN, WIM. Marokko (Cologne, 1970).

LE TOURNEAU, ROGER. Evolution politique de l'Afrique du Nord musulmane (Armand Colin, Paris, 1962).

MAXWELL, GAVIN. Lords of the Atlas (Longmans, London, 1966).

METCALF, JOHN. Morocco—an Economic Study (First National City Bank, New York, 1966).

PERROUX, F. and BARRE, R. Développement, croissance, progrès—Maroc-Tunisie (Paris, 1961).

ROBERT, J. La monarchie marocaine (Librairie générale de droit et de jurisprudence, Paris, 1963).

STEWART, CHARLES F. The Economy of Morocco 1912-1962 (Oxford Univ. Press, 1965).

TERRASSE, H. Histoire du Maroc des origines à l'établissement du protectorat français, 2 vols. (Casablanca, 1949–50) (English trans. by H. Tee, London, 1952).

TIANO, ANDRÉ. La politique économique et financière du Maroc indépendant (Presses universitaires de France, Paris, 1963).

TROUT, FRANK E. Morocco's Saharan Frontiers (Geneva, 1969).

WATERSON, ALBERT. Planning in Morocco (Johns Hopkins, Baltimore, 1963).

WATERBURY, JOHN. The commander of the Faithful. The Moroccan political élite (London, 1970).

WORLD BANK. The Economic Development of Morocco (Johns Hopkins Press, Baltimore, 1966).

ZARTMAN, I. W. Morocco: Problems of New Power (Atherton Press, New York, 1964).

Oman

GEOGRAPHY

The Sultanate of Oman lies on the east of the Arabian Peninsula and is flanked by the United Arab Emirates on the north and west, by Saudi Arabia on the west and by Southern Yemen on the south-west. Its sea coast extends for over 1,600 km. and its total area, including Dhofar, is about 120,000 square miles (300,000 sq. km.). The country's frontiers with its neighbours have never been clearly demarcated on the ground but agreement exists on their general lines.

No census has ever been held in Oman and estimates of the country's population are based on conjecture. Official estimates placed the mid-year total at 550,000 for each year between 1949 and 1958; at 565,000 between 1959 and 1966; and at 600,000 in 1972. Based on a mid-1965 estimate of 565,000, the UN Population Division has projected a total of 657,000 for mid-1970 and 766,000 for mid-1975. Preliminary surveys for a census were taken in 1975.

At Muscat the mean rainfall is 10 cm. and the average mean temperature varies between 69°F. and 110°F. Rainfall on the hills of the interior is somewhat heavier and the south-western province of Dhofar is the only part of Arabia to benefit from the summer monsoon. Although most of the country is arid, there is cultivation on the coastal plain of the Batinah and in a number of valleys in the interior irrigation has been developed. The *Rub Al Khali* (or empty quarter) on Oman's western border is a rainless unrelieved wilderness of shifting sand almost entirely without human habitation.

HISTORY

Oman was probably the land of Magan mentioned in Sumerian tablets with which cities like Ur of the Chaldees traded in the third millenium B.C. The province of Dhofar also produced frankincense in vast quantities which was shipped to markets in Iraq, Syria, Egypt and the West. Roman geographers mention the city of Omana, although its precise location has not been identified, and Portus Moschus, conceivably Muscat. Masirah was also known to Pliny as the Island of Turtles. Oman at various times came under the influence of the Himyaritic kingdoms of South Arabia and of Iran, to which the introduction of the falaj irrigation systems is probably attributable, though legend attributes it to Sulaiman bin Daoud (Solomon).

The people of Oman come from two main stocks, the Qahtan who immigrated from South Arabia, and the Nizar who came in from the North. Tradition attributes the first important invasion from South Arabia to the leadership of Malik ibn Faham after the final collapse of the Marib dam in the Yemen in the first or second century A.D. Oman was one of the first countries to be converted to Islam by Amr ibn al As, who later converted Egypt to Islam. Omanis of the tribe of al Azd played an important part in the early days of Islam in Iraq. They subsequently embraced the Ibadhi doctrine which holds that the caliphate in Islam should not be hereditary or confined to any one family and established their own independent Imamate in Oman in the eighth century A.D. Subsequently, though subject to various invasions from time to time by the Caliphate, Iranians, Moguls and others, Oman has largely maintained its independence.

During the 10th century Sohar became probably the largest and most important city in the Arab world and Omani mariners, together with those from Basrah and other Gulf ports, went as far afield as China. Sohar, though subject to decline and recovery, remained an important port until, and indeed after, the Portuguese conquests. When the Portuguese under Albuquerque arrived in 1507 on their way to India, they found the Omani seaport under the suzerainty of the King of Hormus, himself of Omani stock. The towns of Qalhat, Quryat, Muscat and Sohar were all then thriving and prosperous.

The arrival of the Portuguese in the Indian Ocean changed the balance of power in the area radically. Previously the Omanis had been ubiquitous on the seas and it was an Omani pilot who guided Vasco da Gama across from Malindi to Calicut in India. The Portuguese established themselves in the Omani ports, concentrating principally on Sohar and Muscat, where they built the two great forts, Merani (1587) and Jalali (1588). British and Dutch traders followed in the wake of the Portuguese, though they did not establish themselves by force of arms in Oman in the same way. In 1650 the Imam Nasir bin Murshid of the Yaariba dynasty, who also inaugurated a period of Omani renaissance during which learning flourished, effectively turned the Portuguese out of Muscat and the rest of Oman. The country's external power grew and by 1730 the Omanis had conquered the Portuguese settlements on the coast of East Africa, including Mogadishu, Mombasa and Zanzibar.

The country was, however, ravaged by civil war in the first half of the eighteenth century when the strength and authority of the Imam diminished. During this period the Iranians were called in to assist one of the contenders for the Imamate, but they were finally expelled by Ahmad bin Said who was elected Imam in 1749 and was the founder of the Al Bu Said dynasty, which still rules Oman. The Al Bu Said is thus one of the oldest dynasties in the Middle East. The country prospered under the new dynasty and its maritime importance again grew. In about 1786 the capital of the country was moved from Rostaq to Muscat, a move which led to a dichotomy between the coast and the interior, creating political problems between the two regions at various times.

The Imam Said bin Sultan ruled Oman from 1804 until 1856. He was a strong and much beloved ruler, who also gained the respect and friendship of European nations, in particular the British. Treaties providing for the exchange of consular relations were negotiated with the British in 1839 (there had been earlier treaties of friendship in 1798 and 1800), the United States in 1833, France in 1844 and the Netherlands in 1877. British relations with Oman were maintained for the greater part of the period from the early eighteenth century until the present day, whilst the relations of the other states concerned were somewhat spasmodic.

Said bin Sultan revived Omani interest in Zanzibar and during the latter part of his reign spent an increasing amount of his time there. He started the clove plantations which were later to bring the territory great wealth and was the founder of the dynasty which ruled in Zanzibar until the revolution in 1964. When he died, his dominions were split between two of his sons, one of whom became Sultan of Oman and the other of Zanzibar. Following British mediation Zanzibar, which was the richer part of the heritage, agreed to pay Oman an annual subsidy of $6,400. During Said's time, Omani dominions reached their greatest extent in modern times. Dhofar became one of the constituent parts of the Sultanate in 1829, which it has remained ever since.

The next half of the century was one of some difficulty for the Sultanate on account of the erosion of the basis of its former prosperity. Not only had it lost its East African possessions but the series of treaties with Britain by which the slave trade was curbed also assisted the decline as Muscat had been an important port for this lucrative traffic.

Britain's only formal links with the Sultanate have been a series of Treaties of Friendship, Commerce and Navigation signed in 1891, 1939 and 1951. Britain has, however, given military assistance to Oman on a number of occasions in the past and is continuing to do so, though this is not based on any treaty obligation.

Several insurrections took place towards the end of the nineteenth century and in 1913 a new Imam was elected in the Interior, the Sultan who ruled from Muscat not having been elected. This led to the expulsion of the Sultan's garrisons from Nizwa, Izki and Sumail. In the same year Sultan Faisal bin Turki, who had ruled since 1888, died and he was succeeded by his son Taimur. Efforts to come to terms with the rebels failed but in 1920 an agreement between the Sultan and the principal dissidents, led by Isa bin Salih, was reached providing for peace, free movement of persons between the interior and the coast, limitation of customs duty and non-interference by the Government of the Sultan in the internal affairs of the signatory tribes. Relations between the Imam, Mohammad bin Abdullah al Khalili, and the Sultan remained good until the Imam died in 1954 when rebellion again broke out under the Imam's successor Ghalib bin Ali, who sought foreign help to establish a separate principality. In December 1955, forces under the Sultan's control entered the main inhabited centres of Oman without resistance. The former Imam was allowed by the Sultan to retire to his village but his brother, Talib, escaped to Saudi Arabia and thence to Cairo. An "Oman Imamate" office was set up there and the cause of the Imam was supported by Egyptian propaganda. In the summer of 1957 Talib returned and established himself with followers in the mountain areas north-west of Niswa. The Sultan appealed for British help and fighting continued until early 1959 when the Sultan's authority was fully re-established. In October 1960 ten Arab countries secured the placing of the "question of Oman" on the agenda of the General Assembly of the United Nations, despite British objections. In 1961 a resolution calling for the independence of Oman failed to get the necessary majority, and in 1963 a UN Commission of Inquiry refuted the Imamate charges of oppressive government and strong public feeling against the Sultan. Nevertheless, a Committee was set up to study the "question of Oman" and after its report had been submitted to the General Assembly in 1965 a resolution was adopted which among other things demanded the elimination of British domination in any form. The question was raised again in the United Nations on several occasions until more than a year after Sultan Qaboos's accession, Oman became a member of the UN in October 1971.

THE SULTANATE SINCE 1970

By 1970 Sultan Said's government had come to be regarded as the most reactionary and isolationist in the area, if not the world—slavery was still common, and many mediaeval prohibitions were in force. The Sultan's refusal to use the oil revenues for any purpose other than the building up of his armed forces had particularly embarrassed Britain, the oil companies and most neighbouring states, and this attitude had provided ideal conditions for the rebellion which broke out in Dhofar province in 1964. On July 24th, 1970, the Sultan was deposed by a coup led by his son, Qaboos bin Said, at the royal palace in Salalah. Qaboos, aged 29 and trained at Sandhurst, thus became Sultan to general acclaim both within the Sultanate and abroad, including support from the army; reports of British complicity in the coup were strongly denied by London. The new Sultan announced his intention to transform the country by using the oil revenues for development, following the example of the Gulf sheikhdoms to the north. He asked the rebels for their co-operation in developing the country, but only the Dhofar Liberation Front reacted favourably. The Popular Front for the Liberation of the Occupied Arabian Gulf (reported to control much of Dhofar, and to be receiving Chinese aid through the Yemen P.D.R.) and its ally the National Democratic Front for the Liberation of the Occupied Arab Gulf appeared to think that the palace coup changed little.

In August 1970 "Muscat" was dropped from the title of the country, which became simply the "Sultanate of Oman". Sultan Qaboos appointed his uncle, Tariq bin Taimur, as Prime Minister, but he resigned his office in December 1971, since when the Sultan has himself presided over cabinet meetings and acted as his own Prime Minister, Minister of Defence and Minister of Foreign Affairs. Government policy is aimed at providing the basic social and economic infrastructure which the former Sultan was rigidly opposed to—housing, education, communications, health services, etc. (Before the coup there were only three primary schools and one hospital). In addition, restrictions on travel have been lifted, many prisoners released, and many Omanis have returned from abroad. However, a substantial proportion of the annual budget has been devoted to defence and to quelling the Dhofar insurgency.

Oman's admission to the UN was achieved in face of opposition from the Yemen P.D.R., which supported the Popular Front for the Liberation of Oman and the Arab Gulf (PFLOAG), formed in 1972 by the unification of the two nationalist liberation fronts. The name of this organization was changed in July 1974 to People's Front for the Liberation of Oman. Oman's relationship with Britain also compromised Oman's candidature for UN membership. Britain still supplies arms and ammunition to the Oman Government and officers on secondment or contract. The progress achieved since the palace coup of 1970 has had some impact on the insurgents' following, with a number of defections to the Sultan's forces, but fighting continued until December 1975. Omani forces attacked the border area of the Yemen P.D.R. for the first time in May 1972, the guerrillas having increasingly operated from beyond the border as the Sultan's forces advanced into Dhofar. In 1973 Iranian troops entered the conflict on the side of the Sultan, who also received assistance from Jordan, Saudi Arabia, the U.A.E., Pakistan and India. The Sultan's forces have gradually been gaining the upper hand and development in the Jebel area of Dhofar has been considerable. The war has turned out to be prolonged, however, and during October 1975 the rebels were using sophisticated weapons such as SAM-7 missiles. By December 1975, after an offensive, the Sultan was claiming a complete victory over the insurgents. On March 11th, 1976, a ceasefire between Oman and the Yemen P.D.R. was negotiated by Saudi Arabia, and Sultan Qaboos granted an amnesty to Omanis who had been fighting for the PFLO. Since then only desultory conflicts have taken place and many rebels have returned to their homes in Oman. In January 1977 Iran decided to withdraw the bulk of her forces who had been engaged in Dhofar, but a token force remained until the revolution in Iran in early 1979. A renewal of the insurrection against Sultan Qaboos occurred in June 1978, when a party of British engineers were attacked in the Salalah region of Dhofar. Reports from South Yemeni exiles would seem to indicate that there has been an increase in support for the PFLO from the Cubans. The PFLO has become largely an external force, however, and has achieved little success in attracting adherents within Oman, although the Governor of Dhofar was assassinated at the beginning of June 1979 and renewed insurgency from the PFLO was reported.

The United Kingdom withdrew its forces from Masirah Island in the spring of 1977. There were rumours that the Sultan was intending to allow the U.S.A. to make use of Masirah Island as a base, but this was later denied by Qaboos. Oman's relations with her Arab neighbours have improved rapidly over the last few years. During the reign of Sultan Said the Omani dependence on British military forces was viewed with disfavour by her neighbours and this suspicion served only to deepen the isolation of Oman from the rest of the Arab world. However since the accession of Sultan Qaboos, and more especially since the defeat of the Dhofar insurgents, relations have improved considerably. Both Kuwait and the U.A.E. have supplied much-needed financial support to Oman, while Iraq, formerly a supporter of the PFLO, has established diplomatic relations. As an outward sign of this developing co-operation between the Gulf States, a number of Arab Heads of State visited Oman during 1977 and 1978. The establishment of close economic and diplomatic links with Saudi Arabia was an important step in the full emergence of Oman from her former isolated position in the Arab world. Oman's support of the Israeli-Egyptian peace treaty, however, could result in the distancing of relations with some of the "hard-line" members of the Arab League, and in closer ties with the U.S.A. and with Egypt, which has promised to respond to any request from Oman for military aid.

ECONOMIC SURVEY

AGRICULTURE AND FISHERIES

About 70 per cent of the working population is engaged in agriculture and the Sultanate's long-term plans for development foresee a considerable increase in agricultural production. At present subsistence farming dominates Oman's agriculture: because of the very wide variations in rainfall from one year to another farming is heavily dependent on irrigation. The oases of the interior rely on a system of underground water channels, known as *falaj* (plural *aflaj*), to tap water tables. On the Batinah coast irrigation is by pump from wells. About half of the estimated 36,000 hectares under cultivation are planted with dates. Other crops include lucerne, limes, mangoes, melons, bananas and onions. Local tomatoes and cucumbers are also coming on to the town markets. Some wheat is grown in the interior around Nizwa. The estimated value of agricultural production in 1975 was OR 31 million, of which OR 18 million was accounted for by fruit, OR 6.6 million by crops and the remainder by vegetables. The 1976–80 development plan aims to increase the cultivable area to 50,000 hectares by 1980.

In encouraging agricultural development the Department of Agriculture (which is a part of the Ministry of Development) hopes to increase production of traditional export crops and to reduce the level of food imports by producing more for the home market. The Department has five experimental and production farms and 22 extension centres throughout the country. A series of 5 surveys of water resources in Northern Oman by international consultants will provide the basis for future agricultural planning. A contract worth $6 million was given to the American Farm Machinery Corporation for the establishment of demonstration and experimental farms.

Agriculture in Dhofar is the responsibility of the Dhofar Development Department. Because the province enjoys monsoon rains from June to September, the agricultural scene differs markedly from that in Northern Oman. Cattle are raised on the hills north of Salalah and coconut palms and a wide variety of vegetables are grown on the coastal plain. Although the insurgency delayed development on the hills, the Government is now establishing administrative centres and drilling for water.

Livestock farming in Dhofar is also under study. Among existing projects is the Garziaz cattle station, originally managed by a British company. A Swiss firm then took it over as a joint venture known as Sun Farms of Oman. Sun Farms will control livestock projects in Dhofar, Sahnut, Sohar and Saham, and will take over a vegetable farm and nusery in Salalah. The constraints on agricultural development in Dhofar are the shortage of labour and the distance from markets, rather than any lack of water.

Fishing is a traditional industry in Oman and employs about 10 per cent of the working population. The inshore waters are rich in fish which is the main source of protein in the diet of many Omanis. Most fishing is done from canoes equipped with outboard motors, but the Government has signed two agreements with the U.S. firm Mardela to develop commercial fishing in the Gulf of Oman. A new South Korean company, the Korea Overseas Fishing Company, is now catching around 20 tons of fish per day in a concession formerly held by a Japanese company. The agreement, which runs until 1980, provides for a fishmeal factory, 60 per cent of whose production is to be given to Oman. Similarly 30 per cent of the total catch belongs to Oman. Other fisheries projects are being planned in co-operation with Kuwait.

PETROLEUM AND NATURAL GAS

The economy of Oman is dominated by the oil industry which provides almost all Government revenue. In 1937 Petroleum Concessions (Oman) Ltd., a subsidiary of the Iraq Petroleum Co., was granted a 75-year oil concession extending over the whole area except the district of Dhofar. A concession covering Dhofar was granted in 1953 to Dhofar Cities Service Petroleum Corporation; it expires in 25 years from the date of commercial production, with option to renew for another 25 years.

In 1964 Petroleum Development (Oman) Ltd., re-formed in 1967 as a subsidiary of Royal Dutch/ Shell (with an 85 per cent interest), Compagnie Française des Pétroles (with 10 per cent) and Gulbenkian interests (with 5 per cent), announced that drilling had proved sufficient reserves for the company to go into commercial production. Production began in 1967 at a rate of 200,000 barrels per day and expanded to 360,000 barrels per day by the end of 1969. However, during late 1970 and early 1971 technical difficulties affected production and the 1971 production of 105.56 million barrels was 15 million down on 1970. Total oil exports in 1972 were 103.2 million barrels and by 1977 they had risen to 122 million barrels. Total oil production in 1977 was 124 million barrels. Oman's oil reserves were estimated at about 2,500 million barrels in January 1979, representing 22 more years of production at 1978 levels.

In 1973 the four connected oil fields at Fahud, Natih, Yibal and Al-Huwaisah together produced at an average rate of 293,000 barrels per day. The average rose to about 340,000 barrels per day in 1975, but increased to 385,900 b/d in December 1975, when the three Ghaba fields started production. The 1976 average rate of 368,000 b/d is expected to fall to 244,000 b/d by 1980. Natural gas reserves in Oman are estimated at 4,000,000 million cubic feet. The Yibal gas fields are expected to be capable of a daily yield of 140 million cubic feet although the 1977 production rate was only about 50 million cubic feet. A pipeline to the power/desalination plant at Ghubra was completed in 1978 and a liquefaction plant is also being built at Yibal.

Petroleum Development (Oman) Limited is currently exploiting the Marmul and Amal fields in southern Dhofar. Development will prove to be costly because the oil is very heavy. The extra production should amount to some 30,000 barrels per day by 1981. Plans to build a pipeline linking the fields with a new terminal at Raysut have been abandoned in favour of pumping the oil north to blend with that from the northern fields. Lighter oil found at Qaharit may have been a factor in making this decision.

Sun Oil Company heads a group exploring in offshore areas south of Masirah Island, and in 1975 a concession was granted to Elf/Sumitomo to explore in the Butabul region. This was later changed to a production-sharing agreement and in 1978 20 per cent of the area was assigned to the West German Wintershall company. Drilling was due to start in mid-1978. The offshore Musandam concession is held by Elf-Aquitaine, Gulf Oil and a U.K. independent company, Cluff Oil.

In December 1973 the Oman Government purchased a 25 per cent share in Petroleum Development (Oman), and increased this to 60 per cent in July 1974. The present distribution of the remaining shares is Royal Dutch/ Shell 34 per cent, Compagnie Française des Pétroles 4 per cent and Gulbenkian 2 per cent. Oman is not a member of the Organization of Petroleum Exporting Companies (OPEC), nor of the Organization of Arab Petroleum Exporting Countries (OAPEC), but under the terms of the concessions the Government of the Sultanate is assured of treatment equal to that received by members of OPEC.

INDUSTRY AND MINERALS

Before 1964 industry in Oman was confined to small traditional handicrafts. The development of oil generated activity in the construction sector, but it was not until the change of regime in 1970 that Government investment in infrastructure projects and private spending on housing started a boom in construction. Some of the new projects were not well conceived, resulting in the drain of resources abroad to foreign contractors. With oil revenues declining and a chronic shortage of manpower, Oman is not well placed to develop heavy industry or manufacturing on a large scale. The Government is, accordingly, turning more towards the development of agriculture and fisheries, and encouraging building in the rural areas with the emphasis on social projects and roads. Some industrial projects have been completed. A paint factory was opened in 1977 under Danish supervision. A large proportion of the workforce is Indian and Pakistani, illustrating Oman's dependence on foreign labour. A cement works in Muscat, built as a joint venture with Kuwait, will have a capacity of 350,000 tons per year.

Geological surveys are being carried out to locate mineral deposits. So far, sizeable reserves of copper and chromite have been found. Chromite reserves, estimated at 2 million tons of medium grade ore, exist on the coastal side of the Jebel Akhdar. The concession is held by a Canadian-based company. The Oman Mining Company, owned 75 per cent by the Government and 25 per cent by Canadian and U.S. interests, is developing three copper mines at Sohar, north-west of Muscat. Production will be an estimated 20,000 tons per year. The Japanese have also shown an interest in the copper mining project.

FINANCE AND DEVELOPMENT

With the expected decline in revenue from oil, the Government has had to tailor its development programme accordingly, although the oil exploration programme is to continue. Expenditure on defence, however, continues to be a heavy burden. In 1979 the budget allocation was RO 238 million, compared with RO 265 million in 1978, and $15 million in defence aid was requested from the U.S.A. Infrastructural and communications projects are gradually being completed. Radar was installed at Salalah airport in 1978; previously Thumrait airport had to be used in bad weather and the monsoon season. The opening of twelve new berths at Mina Qaboos has improved port facilities and a West German firm is engaged on harbour expansion at Mina Raysut. A road network for the mountainous region inland from Salalah is planned at a cost of $72 million.

The targets of the 1976–80 development plan were relatively modest, concentrating on establishing a workable basis for light industry and agriculture. The Omani Development Bank was established in December 1977 to encourage private sector investment. Nevertheless, expenditure still lags behind allocations. Budget expenditure for 1977 was set at RO 684 million, but only some RO 500 million was spent. Similarly, in 1978, development allocations of RO 136 million remained unspent. In 1979, RO 760 million in expenditure was budgeted, with an expected income of RO 652 million. Development expenditure for 1979 was put at RO 217 million. Oil revenues account for over 80 per cent of total income.

Missions from the World Bank and the International Monetary Fund, which visited Oman in 1977 and 1978, recommended that Oman should make more use of local capital, rather than relying on grants from abroad and should exercise tighter controls over budgeting and project planning and monitoring.

STATISTICAL SURVEY

Area: 300,000 sq. km. (120,000 sq. miles).

Population: 750,000 (estimate for mid-1974); Capital area (Muscat to Seeb) estimated 50,000. Estimated number of gainfully employed 150,000; agriculture 109,000; fisheries 15,000; government 10,000; construction 6,000; oil, banking, services 5,000; others 5,000 (1972.)

Agriculture: Land utilization 1971 (hectares): Batinah 13,800; Interior 19,920; capital area 1,080; Musandam 400; Dhofar 800. Crops include dates, lucerne, limes, onions, wheat, bananas, mangoes, tobacco, sorghum, sweet potatoes, chickpeas and coconuts.

Livestock (1976 estimates, '000 head): goats 164.6, sheep 57.2, cattle 133.8, camels 13.5.

MINING

		1974	1975	1976	1977	1978
Crude petroleum . .	'000 metric tons	14,466	17,016	18,290	17,031	15,750

ELECTRICITY

		1972	1973	1974	1975	1976	1977
Electric energy .	million kWh.	130.0	172.5	229.9	306.3	412.9	537.8

FINANCE

1,000 baiza = 1 rial Omani (RO).
Coins: 2, 5, 10, 25, 50 and 100 baiza.
Notes: 100, 250 and 500 baiza; 1, 5, 10 and 20 rials.
Exchange rates (June 1979): £1 sterling = 714.6 baiza; U.S. $1 = 345.4 baiza.
100 rials Omani = £139.95 = $289.52.

Note: The rial Saidi (renamed the rial Omani in 1972) was introduced in May 1970, replacing the Persian Gulf Indian rupee at the rate of 1 rial = 21 rupees = £1 sterling. The initial value of the rial was U.S. $2.40 ($1 = 416.7 baiza), which remained in operation until August 1971. From December 1971 to February 1973 the rial's value was $2.6057 ($1 = 383.8 baiza). The present dollar valuation has been effective since February 1973. The rial was at par with the pound sterling until the latter was allowed to "float" in June 1972.

BUDGET ESTIMATES*
(RO million)

Revenue	1977	1978	1979	Expenditure	1977	1978	1979
Oil revenues . .	482.0	415.0	482.0	Defence . . .	142.0	265.0	238.0
Other receipts . .	39.0	280.0	170.0	Other current expenditure . . .	144.0	178.0	162.0
				Capital expenditure .	211.3	302.0	360.0
Total .	521.3	695.0	652.0	Total .	497.3	745.0	760.0

*Provisional figures. The revised estimate of 1977 oil revenues was RO 546.0 million.

EXTERNAL TRADE

(RO million)

	1971	1972	1973	1974	1975	1976	1977
Imports							
Recorded	13.8	18.7	40.7	135.6	264.3	250.5	302.1
Unrecorded estimate .	26.4	42.9	45.1	78.5	120.0	155.0	104.0
Total . . .	40.2	61.6	85.8	214.1	371.3	405.5	406.2
Exports							
Government oil receipts .	47.9	49.6	114.3	418.7	488.1	543.8	546.0
Other	0.4	0.4	0.6	0.4	1.1	1.4	1.5
Total . . .	48.3	50.0	114.9	419.1	489.2	545.2	547.5

Source: Central Bank of Oman.

RECORDED IMPORTS
(RO '000)

PRINCIPAL COMMODITIES

	1977	1978
Food and live animals	38,116	42,363
Beverages and tobacco	6,322	11,548
Crude materials (inedible) except fuels	6,414	4,833
Mineral fuels and lubricants	21,461	27,542
Animal and vegetable oils and fats	1,973	3,134
Chemicals	11,139	13,618
Basic manufactures	53,782	58,649
Machinery and transport equipment	123,563	125,933
Miscellaneous manufactured articles	39,295	39,601
TOTAL	302,065	327,221

PRINCIPAL TRADING PARTNERS

	1977	1978
Australia	7,612	6,249
Bahrain	7,981	9,043
Belgium	1,635	2,129
France	6,318	9,214
Germany, Fed. Repub.	19,612	20,810
India	14,710	14,534
Iran	1,796	1,643
Italy	6,229	6,637
Japan	41,056	50,749
Kuwait	1,117	732
Netherlands	14,249	8,045
Singapore	6,713	8,121
United Arab Emirates	44,330	51,405
United Kingdom	69,755	67,696
U.S.A.	21,579	20,660
TOTAL (incl. others)	302,064	327,221

EXPORTS

Non-oil exports consist mainly of limes, dates, fish and tobacco: 1972 RO 394,100; 1973 RO 609,049; 1974 RO 430,300; 1975 RO 1,078,231; 1976 RO 1,409,500; 1977 RO 1,527,900; 1978 RO 3,322,900.

TRANSPORT

ROAD TRAFFIC
(vehicles in use)

	1977
Private cars	18,984
Taxis	2,308
Public service	928
Commercial	23,657
Government	5,935
Motor-cycles	4,063
Private hire	21
Diplomatic	146
TOTAL	50,042

CIVIL AVIATION
(Seeb International Airport)

	1975	1976	1977
Passengers ('000)	263.8	323.7	373.8
Cargo handled ('000 tons)	10.8	12.6	13.3

EDUCATION

	PRIMARY		PREPARATORY		SECONDARY	
	Boys	Girls	Boys	Girls	Boys	Girls
1973/74	27,430	7,795	239	79	22	—
1974/75	36,351	12,225	437	134	63	19
1975/76	39,640	14,817	925	170	143	57
1976/77	44,668	17,962	1,609	406	233	97
1977/78	49,294	21,377	3,819	861	397	139

THE GOVERNMENT

Head of State, Premier and Minister of Foreign Affairs, Defence and Finance:
Sultan QABOOS BIN SAID (assumed power July 24th, 1970).

CABINET

(*June* 1979)

Deputy Premier for Security and Defence: Sayyid FAHAR BIN TAIMOUR AL-SAID.

Deputy Premier for Legal Affairs: Sayyid FAHAD BIN MAHMOUD AL-SAID.

Personal Adviser to the Sultan and Governor of Muscat: Sayyid THUWAINI BIN SHIHAB.

Minister of Diwan Affairs: Sayyid HAMAD BIN HAMUD SAID.

Minister of Justice: Sayyid HILAL BIN HAMAD AL-SAMMAR.

Minister of State for Foreign Affairs: QAIS ABDUL MUNIM AL-ZAWAWI.

Minister of Information, Youth Affairs and Tourism: ABDULAZIZ AL-ROWASS.

Minister of Electricity and Water: HAMOUD ABDULLA AL-HARTHY.

Minister of Posts, Telegraphs and Telephones: KARIM AHMED AL-HAREMY.

Minister of Civil Aviation, Ports and Roads: SALIM BIN NASSIR AL-BUSAIDY.

Minister of Education: YAHYA MAHFOUZ AL-MUNZIRI.

Minister of Land Affairs and Muncipalities: AHMAD AL-GHAZALI.

Minister of Social Affairs and Labour: KHALFAN BIN NASSIR AL-WAHAIBI.

Minister of Awkaf and Islamic Affairs: Sheikh WALID BIN ZAHIR AL-HINAWI.

Minister of National Heritage and Culture: Sayyid FAISAL BIN ALI AL-SAID.

Minister of the Interior: BADR BIN SAYD BIN-HAREB.

Minister of Commerce and Industry: MUHAMMAD ZUBAIR.

Minister of Petroleum and Minerals: SAID AHMED AL-SHANFARI.

Minister of Agriculture and Fisheries: ABDEL HAFIZ SALEM RAJAB.

Minister of Health: Dr. MUBAREK AL-KHADDURI.

Governor of Dhofar and Minister of State: (vacant).

Minister of the Environment: ASSEM AL-JAMALI.

DIPLOMATIC REPRESENTATION

EMBASSIES ACCREDITED TO OMAN

(In Muscat unless otherwise stated)

Austria: Jeddah, Saudi Arabia.

Bangladesh: Jeddah, Saudi Arabia.

Belgium: Jeddah, Saudi Arabia.

Brazil: Jeddah, Saudi Arabia.

Canada: Teheran, Iran.

Chile: Amman, Jordan.

China, People's Republic: *Ambassador:* YUAN LOUNIN.

Denmark: Jeddah, Saudi Arabia.

Egypt: P.O.B. 5252; *Ambassador:* YAHYA REFAT.

Finland: Jeddah, Saudi Arabia.

France: P.O.B. 591; *Ambassador:* ROBERT ODDOS.

Germany, Federal Republic: P.O.B. 3128; *Ambassador:* THEODOR MEZ.

Guinea: Jeddah, Saudi Arabia.

India: P.O.B. 4727; *Ambassador:* AHMAD HAMMOUD AL-AMRI.

Iran: P.O.B. 702; *Ambassador:* (vacant).

Iraq: P.O.B. 4848; *Ambassador:* TAHA RAJAB AREEM.

Japan: Jeddah, Saudi Arabia.

Jordan: P.O.B. 900; *Ambassador:* SAHAIL AL-TAL.

Korea, Republic: P.O.B. 5220; *Ambassador:* CHUNG KOO WOOK.

Kuwait: P.O.B. 4798; *Ambassador:* MOHAMED AHMED AL-SAAD.

Mali: Jeddah, Saudi Arabia.

Mauritania: Jeddah, Saudi Arabia.

Niger: Jeddah, Saudi Arabia.

Pakistan: P.O.B. 1005; *Ambassador:* ANWAR SAID.

Qatar: P.O.B. 802; *Ambassador:* ALI ABDUL REHMAN AL-MIFTAH.

Romania: Teheran, Iran.

Saudi Arabia: P.O.B. 873; *Ambassador:* MUHAMMAD AL-MUTLAQ.

Somalia: P.O.B. 4767, Ruwi; *Ambassador:* (vacant).

Spain: Jeddah, Saudi Arabia.

Sudan: P.O.B. 5205; *Ambassador:* MUBARAK A. AL-HADI.

Sweden: Jeddah, Saudi Arabia.

Switzerland: Jeddah, Saudi Arabia.

Turkey: Jeddah, Saudi Arabia.

United Arab Emirates: P.O.B. 335; *Ambassador:* (vacant).

United Kingdom: P.O.B. 300; *Ambassador:* Hon. IVOR LUCAS.

U.S.A.: P.O.B. 966; *Ambassador:* MARSHALL WILEY.

Yemen Arab Republic: P.O.B. 3701; *Ambassador:* ABDUL JABBER A. MAJAHID.

Oman also has diplomatic relations with Algeria, Djibouti, Italy, Lebanon, Kenya, Morocco, the Netherlands, Tunisia and Yugoslavia.

JUDICIAL SYSTEM

Jurisdiction is exercised by the Sharia Courts, applying Islamic Law. Local courts are officered by *Qadhis* appointed by the Minister of Justice. The Chief Court is at Muscat. Appeals from local courts, including the court in the capital, go to the Court of Appeal at Muscat.

RELIGION

The majority of the population are Ibadhi Muslims; about a quarter are Sunni Muslims.

THE PRESS

NEWSPAPERS

Al Watan (*The Nation*): P.O.B. 463, Muscat; daily.

Oman: P.O.B. 600, Muscat; produced by Ministry of Information; twice weekly; Editor MUHAMMAD AMIN ABDULLAH.

ENGLISH LANGUAGE

Akhbar Oman: P.O.B. 3959, Muscat; weekly; Chief Editor SAID SALIM SHANFARI.

Gulf Mirror: P.O.B. 455, Manama, Bahrain; f. 1971, weekly; Man. Editor ALAN G. BROWN; circ. 16,000 in Bahrain, Oman, Qatar, U.A.E., Kuwait and eastern Saudi Arabia.

Times of Oman: P.O.B. 3770, Ruwi, Muscat; weekly; Editor-in-Chief G. REID ANDERSON.

PERIODICALS

Al-Akidah (*The Faith*): P.O.B. 4001, Ruwi; weekly illustrated magazine; Editor SAID AL-SAMHAN AL-KATHIRI; circ. 18,000.

Al Mawared Al Tabeiah: Ministry of Agriculture, Fisheries, Petroleum and Minerals, P.O.B. 551, Muscat; English and Arabic; Editor KHALID AL-ZUBAIDI.

Al Nahda (*The Renaissance*): P.O.B. 1178, Mutrah; fortnightly illustrated magazine; Editor TALEB SAID AL-MEAWALY.

Al Usra (*The Family*): P.O.B. 3959, Ruwi; socio-economic; fortnightly illustrated magazine; Chief Editor SADEK ABDOWANI.

Jund Oman (*Soldiers of Oman*): P.O.B. 113, Muscat; monthly illustrated magazine of the Department of Defence; Supervisor: Deputy Minister for Defence.

RADIO AND TELEVISION

Radio Oman: Muscat; f. 1970; transmits in Arabic 13 hours daily, English 2 hours daily; Dir. of Arabic DIYAB AL-AMRI; Dir. of English Service LYUTHA SULTAN AL-MUGHERY.

Radio Salalah: f. 1970; transmits daily programmes in Arabic and the Dhofari languages; Director: HAMMAD AL-GHAFRY.

A colour television station built at Qurm outside Muscat by the German Company Siemens A.G. was opened in November 1974. A colour television system for Dhofar has been constructed by Pye of Great Britain and Phillips of the Netherlands. It opened in late 1975.

The British Broadcasting Corporation has built a powerful new medium-wave relay station on the island of Masirah, off the Oman coast. It is used to expand and improve the reception of the B.B.C.'s Arabic, Farsi and Urdu services.

There were an estimated 25,000 TV receivers in use in 1978.

FINANCE

BANKING

(cap.=capital; p.u.=paid up; dep.=deposits; m=million; br.=branch; RO=rials Omani)

CENTRAL BANK

Central Bank of Oman: P.O.B. 4161 Ruwi, Muscat; f. 1975; cap. RO 10m.; dep. RO 28m.; Chair. SAYYID TARIQ BIN TAIMUR; Deputy Chair. and Pres. Dr. ABDUL WAHAB KHAYATA.

COMMERCIAL BANKS

Arab Bank Ltd.: P.O.B. 991, Muscat; Man. ABDUL QADER ASKALAN.

Al Bank al-Ahli al-Omani S.A.O.: P.O.B. 3134, Ruwi, Muscat; f. 1978; cap. p.u. RO 2m.; 20 per cent French, 80 per cent Omani; Chair. Sheikh ZAHER AL-HARTHY; Gen. Man. DEREK J. FLETCHER.

Bank of Baroda: P.O.B. 3142, Mutrah; Man. S. N. AMIN; P.O.B. 4610, Ruwi.

Bank of Credit and Commerce Int. S.A.: P.O.B. 840, Muscat; Man. S. ABRAR H. ZAIDI.

Bank Melli Iran: P.O.B. 410, Muscat; Man. MOHSEN PIRZADEH.

Bank of Oman, Bahrain and Kuwait S.A.O.: P.O.B. 4708, Ruwi; f. 1974; cap. p.u. RO 1.4m.; dep. RO 6.7m. (Dec. 1977); 6 brs.; Chair MOHSIN HAIDER DARWISH; Gen. Man. CHARLES LLEWELLYN.

Bank Saderat Iran: Muscat; Man. MUHAMMAD HASSAN PASHMI.

Banque de Paris et des Pays-Bas: P.O.B. 425, Muscat; Man. MUHAMMAD BECHIR BEN OTHMAN.

British Bank of the Middle East: London; f. 1889; P.O.B. 234, Muscat; 15 brs.; Area Man. J. R. H. JAMES.

The Chartered Bank: P.O.B. 210, Muscat; Man. K. F. WAINFORTH; brs. in Mutrah, Ruwi, Salalah, Birka and Sur.

Citibank: P.O.B. 918, Muscat.

Commercial Bank of Oman: P.O.B. 4696, Ruwi, Muscat; Gen. Man. SHAHID HUSSAIN ABIDI.

Grindlays Bank Ltd.: London; P.O.B. 3550, Ruwi; Gen. Man. I. G. MCINTOSH; 6 brs. in Muscat, Muttrah, Seeb and Salalah.

Habib Bank AG-Zürich: P.O.B. 1338, Muttrah.

Habib Bank (Overseas) Ltd.: P.O.B. 1326, Mutrah; br. in Greater Mutrah; Man. R. ALVI.

National Bank of Abu Dhabi: P.O.B. 5293, Ruwi, Muttrah; Man. ALI ABDEL SADEQ.

National Bank of Oman S.A.O.: P.O.B. 3751, Ruwi, Muscat; f. 1973; cap. p.u. RO 2m.; dep. RO 68.1m. (March 1979); Dir. and Gen. Man. S. M. SHAFI.

Oman Arab African Bank: P.O.B. 1117, Mutrah; Man. BASEM R. NAJJAR.

Union Bank of Oman: P.O.B. 4565, Ruwi, Muscat; f. 1976; Man. Dir. ABDUL KARIM HIJAZI.

In 1977 the Government gave permission for the opening of The Bank of Oman and the Gulf.

DEVELOPMENT BANKS

Oman Development Bank; P.O. 309, Muscat; f. 1976; cap. RO 10m.; 40 per cent Oman Government, 40 per cent foreign, 20 per cent Omani private.

Oman Housing Bank: Muscat; f. 1977; cap. RO 10m.; 51 per cent Oman Government, 39 per cent Government of Kuwait, 10 per cent British Bank of the Middle East; Gen. Man. R. K. M. SCOULER.

INSURANCE

Oman National Insurance Co.: Muscat.

Oman United Agencies Ltd: Muscat; representatives of several British insurance companies; subsidiary of Gray, MacKenzie and Co. Ltd.

OIL

Petroleum Development (Oman) Ltd.: P.O.B. 81, Muscat; f. 1937; since July 1974 60 per cent owned by Oman Government, 34 per cent by Shell, 4 per cent by Compagnie Française des Pétroles and 2 per cent by Gulbenkian interests; exports oil from 5 fields in the Fahud area and 4 fields centred on the Qarn Alam area of Central Oman via a pipeline to a terminal at Mina al Fahal near Muscat; there are plans to develop the oil fields in the Dhofar region; production in 1978 averaged 314,000 b.p.d.

Amoco: holds concession area of 13,000 square km. south of Masirah Island; consortium composed of Amoco, Sun Oil, Home Oil of Canada, Canadian Superior, Deutsche Schachtbau and three others; exploration is in progress.

Elf/Sumitomo: concession granted in 1975 for exploration in the onshore region of Butabul; area of 7,000 square km.; converted to a production sharing agreement in October 1976; 48 per cent owned by Elf, 32 per cent by Sumitomo and 20 per cent by Wintershall.

The Government is hoping that more oil will be found in Dhofar and recently granted exploration rights over a large area of western and south-western Dhofar to a consortium consisting of BP, Deminex, AGIP, Hispanoil, Elf/Aquitane I, Quintana/Gulf and Cluff Oil.

TRADE AND INDUSTRY

Oman Chamber of Commerce and Industry: P.O.B. 4400 Ruwi-Muscat; Pres. ALI SULTAN; Dir.-Gen. MOHAMMED ABDEL RAHMAN FAKIR.

TRANSPORT

ROADS

A network of adequate graded roads links all the main centres of population and only a few mountain villages are not accessible by Land Rover. A rapid road construction programme began in 1970 and by 1977 there were 1,447 km. of asphalt road and 10,500 km. of graded roads. The final link in the 362 km. Dubai-Oman highway was finished in November 1977. A new coastal highway between Muscat and Mutrah was opened in November 1978. In Dhofar tarmac roads have been completed from Raysut through Salalah to Taqa. Roads between Seeb and Nizwa and Salalah and Thumrait have been completed and a rural bus service started operations in 1975.

SHIPPING

Port Services Corporation Ltd.: P.O.B. 133, Muscat.

The new port at Mina Qaboos, which was completed in 1974 at a cost of RO 18.2 million, provides 13 berths. Nine of these can take vessels with draughts of up to 36 feet. The port also provides warehousing facilities and a harbour for dhows and coastal vessels. In 1977 over 1,000 ships visited the port and 850,000 metric tons of general cargo was handled.

The oil terminal at Mina-al-Fahal can also accommodate the largest super-tankers on off-shore loading buoys. Similiar facilities for the import of refined petroleum products exist at Mina-al-Fahal and Riyam (near Muscat). In 1977 the Government created the Port Services Corporation to operate Mina Qaboos. The Corporation is 60 per cent Government financed, with the remainder being supplied by the private sector.

The major shipping lines using the port are: Hansa, Nedlloyd, P & O, Scindia, United Arab Shipping Co., Yugolinja, NYK, K Line Philippine President Lines, Concordia, Far East Express Line, NOSAC, Compagnie Maritime Belge, Central Gulf, Showa, Wilhelmson, Scanmel, NCHP. There are 13 major shipping agencies represented.

Loading facilities for smaller craft exist at Sohar, Khaboura, Sur, Marbat and Salalah.

CIVIL AVIATION

Domestic and international flights operate from Seeb International Airport. Its runway is being extended from the present 10,000 feet to 12,000 feet. Oman's second international airport at Salalah was completed in 1978. Most towns of any size have small air strips.

Gulf Aviation Ltd (Gulf Air): P.O.B. 138, Bahrain; f. 1950, jointly owned by the Governments of Bahrain, Qatar; the United Arab Emirates and Oman; services linking Bahrain, Doha, Abu Dhabi, Dubai, Sharjah, Salalah and Muscat with London, Amsterdam, Paris, Larnaca, Beirut, Cairo, Kuwait, Dharan, Shiraz, Bandar Abbas, Karachi, Bombay, Basra, Baghdad, Amman and Athens; fleet consists of four TriStars, five VC-10, four BAC 1-11, three F27, four Skyvans, two Islanders, two Beechcraft B80 and five Boeing 737.

Other airlines using Seeb for passenger flights include Alia (Jordan), Air India, British Airways, EgyptAir, Kuwait Airlines, MEA (Lebanon), PIA (Pakistan), Saudia, Somali Airlines and UTA (France). Cargo flights are operated by TMA (Lebanon) and Tradewinds Airways (United Kingdom).

DEFENCE

Defence Expenditure, 1978: 265 million Omani rials.

Military service: voluntary.

Total armed forces: 19,200: army 16,200; navy 900; air force 2,100.

Paramilitary forces: 3,000: tribal Home Guard.

EDUCATION

Until 1970 there were only three primary schools, offering a six-year course of basic education for boys only. There were no schools for girls. In the years since the accession of Sultan Qaboos emphasis has been placed on the expansion of education horizontally as well as vertically all over the Sultanate. From three primary schools before 1970 there were in 1977 a total of 261 schools, of which 213 were primary, 45 were preparatory and 3 were secondary. Out of these there are 58 schools for girls and there is co-education in the lower classes of 77 primary schools. Altogether the number of pupils attending school in 1977 was 75,887, of whom 22,377 were girls. The large majority of teachers are seconded from other Arab countries such as Egypt, Jordan and the Sudan, but preparations are well ahead for the opening of a Teacher Training Institute in 1978. There are plans in hand also for the starting of agricultural technical education in the same year. Adult literacy and adult education classes have met with great success in most regions.

BIBLIOGRAPHY

ADMIRALTY. A Handbook of Arabia (London, 1916).

AITCHISON, C. V. (Ed.). Government of India Foreign Department—Collection of Treaties Relating to India and Neighbouring Countries. Volume XII (Calcutta 1932).

BADGER, G. P. The History of the Imams and Sayyids of Oman, by Salilbin-Razik, from AD 661 to 1856 (Hakluyt Society 1871).

BUSCH, B. C. Great Britain and the Persian Gulf 1894–1914 (University of California Press, 1967).

DEPARTMENT OF INFORMATION, MUSCAT. Oman (London, 1972).

FACT SHEETS ON EASTERN ARABIA (Information Center on Eastern Arabia, Brussels, Belgium).

GIBB, H. A. R. Ibn Battuta—Travels in Asia and Africa 1325–1354 (London, 1929).

HAWLEY, DONALD. Oman and its Renaissance (Stacey International, London, 1977).

HOLDEN, D. Farewell to Arabia (London, 1966).

HOPWOOD, D. (Ed.). The Arabian Peninsula: Society and Politics (London, 1972).

KELLY, J. B. Great Britain and the Persian Gulf, 1793–1880 (London).

KELLY, J. B. Eastern Arabia Frontier (Faber and Faber, London).

LANDEN, R. G. Oman Since 1856 (Princeton University Press, 1967).

LORIMER, J. C. Gazeteer of the Persian Gulf, Oman and Central Arabia, 2 vols. (Calcutta 1908 and 1915).

MILES, S. B. The Countries and Tribes of the Persian Gulf (3rd edition, Frank Cass, London, 1966).

MORRIS, JAMES. Sultan in Oman (Faber, London, 1957).

PETERSON, J. E. Oman in the Twentieth Century (Croom Helm, London, 1978).

PHILLIPS, WENDELL. Unknown Oman (Longmans, London, 1966).

Oman. A History (Longmans, London, 1967).

ROYAL INSTITUTE OF INTERNATIONAL AFFAIRS. Sultanate and Imamate in Oman (Oxford University Press, 1959).

RUBINACCI, R. Religion in the Middle East (Ed. Arberry, A. J.) Vol. 2, Chapter 16 (Cambridge).

SKEET, IAN, Muscat and Oman: The End of an Era (Faber and Faber, 1974).

THESIGER, WILFRED. Arabian Sands (Longmans, London, 1959).

TOWNSEND, JOHN. Oman: The Making of the Modern State (Croom Helm, London, 1977).

WILSON, Sir A. T. The Persian Gulf (London, 1928).

Qatar

GEOGRAPHY

The Emirate of Qatar is a peninsula roughly 100 miles in length, with a breadth varying between 35 and 50 miles, on the west coast of the Persian Gulf. The total area is 11,000 sq. km. and in 1978 the estimated population was 200,000, two-thirds of whom are concentrated in the town of Doha, on the east coast. Two other ports, Zakrit on the west coast and Umm Said on the east, owe their existence to the discovery of petroleum. Zakrit is a convenient, if shallow, harbour for the import of goods from Bahrain, while Umm Said affords anchorage to deep-sea tankers and freighters.

Qatar is stony, sandy and barren; limited supplies of underground water are unsuitable for drinking or agriculture because of high mineral content. Over half the water supply is now provided by sea water distillation processes. The inhabitants have traditionally lived from pearl-diving, fishing and nomadic herding.

HISTORY

Owing to the aridity of the peninsula the early history of Qatar is of little interest, though archaeological expeditions have found evidence of inhabitation in the Stone and Iron ages and as early as 4,000 B.C. In 1916 Great Britain, in order to exclude other powers from the area, made an agreement with the Sheikh of Qatar, who undertook not to cede, mortgage or otherwise dispose of parts of his territories to anyone except the British Government, nor to enter into any relationship with a foreign government other than the British without British consent. Similar agreements had been concluded with Bahrain in 1880 and 1892, with the Trucial States in 1892 and with Kuwait in 1899. In return Britain undertook to protect Qatar from all aggression by sea, and to lend her good offices in case of an overland attack.

The discovery of oil in the 1930s promised greater prosperity for Qatar, but because of the Second World War production did not begin on a commercial scale until 1949 (*see* below). An ambitious development programme has now been put into operation with the revenues from the production and export of oil. The Sheikhdom took a leading part in moves towards the formation of a Gulf Federation; it also enjoys close relations with Saudi Arabia. In January 1961 Qatar joined the Organization of Petroleum Exporting Countries, and in May 1970 it also became a member of OAPEC (the Organization of Arab Petroleum Exporting Countries).

In April 1970 a provisional constitution was announced which, it was said, would assist Qatar's entry into the Federation of Arab Emirates. The first cabinet was formed in May; the Ruler became Prime Minister with responsibility for oil, and six of the other nine members were also members of the Royal Family. However, Qatar decided to remain outside a Gulf Federation and became independent on September 1st, 1971, joining the UN and the Arab League. Qatar, however, still feels enthusiastic about the idea of some form of enlarged Gulf Federation in the future. Qatar and the United Kingdom immediately signed a new treaty of friendship. Sheikh Ahmad bin Ali al-Thani became Amir on September 4th, but apparently took little interest in affairs of the State. He was deposed on February 22nd, 1972, in a bloodless coup staged by his cousin Sheikh Khalifa bin Hamad al-Thani. Sheikh Khalifa seized power with the support of the ruling al-Thani family, although his avowed purpose included the curtailment of some of the family's long-held privileges. The coup also thwarted the ambitions of the deposed Amir's son, Sheikh Abdul Aziz, who went into exile. Qatar is closely allied with Saudi Arabia and is usually considered as one of the more moderate Arab states. It opposed the Camp David agreements between Egypt, Israel and the U.S.A. and the subsequent Egyptian-Israeli treaty signed in March 1979.

Since his accession in 1972 the Amir has introduced discreet changes, but has preserved the Islamic pattern of life. In accordance with the 1970 constitution, Sheikh Khalifa decreed the first Advisory Council, to complement the ministerial government. Its 20 members, selected from representatives elected by limited suffrage, were increased to 30 in December 1975. In May 1978 the term of the Consultative Assembly was extended for a further three years, to expire at the end of May 1981. The Advisory Council's constitutional entitlements include power to debate legislation drafted by the Council of Ministers before ratification and promulgation. It also has power to request ministerial statements on matters of general and specific policy inclusive of the draft budget.

ECONOMIC SURVEY

Agriculture is still developing but outside the capital most of the population is employed in the oil industry, which is the state's principal source of wealth. Fishing, apart from shrimp fishing and processing, is carried on to supply local demands. Unlike many of the other Sheikhdoms, Qatar has no entrepôt trade.

Interest in the petroleum possibilities of Qatar was first stimulated by the entry of Standard Oil of California into Bahrain in 1930. Shortly afterwords the Anglo-Iranian Company received permission from the ruler to make a surface survey of his territories, and in 1935 they were granted a concession. This gave exclusive petroleum rights in the Sheikhdom and its territorial waters for 75 years. The concession was later transferred to Petroleum Concessions Ltd., which formed an operating company, Petroleum Development (Qatar) Ltd.

Petroleum Development started exploration in 1937 and oil was discovered in 1939. Field activities were interrupted during the war, but resumed in 1947.

By 1949 the company had completed a drilling programme, the laying of a pipeline system from the field of Dukhan, on the west coast, to Umm Said, and the construction of terminal facilities. At the end of that year the first shipment was made from the Umm Said offshore berths. In 1953 the name of the company was changed to Qatar Petroleum Company (QPC). From 1963 to 1970 production remained steady at about 9 million tons per year but expanded rapidly during 1971 to reach 10.3 million tons. The increase was maintained when production reached 11.4 million tons in 1972 and 11.7 million tons in 1973. As demand fell in 1974, production was reduced to 10.3 million tons and fell yet further to 8.0 million tons in 1975. It recovered in 1976 to 11.9 million tons.

An offshore grant was awarded to the Shell Overseas Exploration Company in 1952. This covered an area of approximately 10,000 square miles and was due to expire in 2027. Exploration started in 1953. Test production from the offshore field at Idd el Shargi through temporary facilities began in January 1964. Construction of permanent facilities on Halul Island, some 60 miles off the cost of Qatar, were completed early in 1966. This also enabled production to be commenced from Shell's second field in Maydam Mazam. Shell Qatar began commercial production of oil in 1966 at an annual rate of more than 5 million long tons, increasing to 15.4 million tons by 1973 but falling to 13.9 million tons in 1974 and 12.1 million tons in 1976. Production from a third field, Bul Hanine, began in 1972. In 1963 the Continental Oil Company of Qatar was granted a concession over land and offshore areas relinquished by the Qatar Petroleum Company and the Shell Company of Qatar, and over a strip of territory in the south of the peninsula not previously included in any concession. In 1969 a Japanese consortium was granted an exploration concession in the south-eastern offshore area, but discontinued its search and returned the concessionary rights to the Government in 1974. Also in 1969 Qatar and Abu Dhabi agreed on the joint exploration of the al-Bunduq field, which is shared by the two countries. This is being developed by the al-Bunduq Co. Ltd., which is owned by British Petroleum, Compagnie Française des Pétroles and Qatar Oil Japan. Production began in 1976.

By the 1970s the relationships between state and oil companies in the oil-producing countries were radically different from those existing 20 years earlier. In April 1972 the Amir signed a law to create the Qatar National Petroleum Co., with power to carry out a comprehensive range of production, refining and marketing functions. In January 1973 the Qatar Government signed participation agreements with both local crude-producing companies—Qatar Petroleum Co. Ltd. and Shell Company of Qatar Ltd.—whereby it acquired a 25 per cent share in the operations of each company, this to rise to a controlling interest by 1982. Following the Arab-Israeli war of October 1973, however, a movement developed in all the Arab oil-producing states towards increased participation in the operations of the western-owned oil companies (*see* chapter *Oil in the Middle East and North Africa*). Accordingly, the Qatar Government held negotations with QPC and Shell Company of Qatar in February 1974 and reached agreement on the immediate acquisition by the Government of a 60 per cent interest in each of the companies. Two months later it was further agreed that the companies should buy back at least 60 per cent of the Government's 60 per cent share of production at an average price of 93 per cent of posted prices. After the first six months the price was to be subject to quarterly review. The Government retained its option to sell its remaining 40 per cent of production on world markets or to sell it to the two companies at the price agreed. In September 1976 an agreement was signed for the take-over of the remaining 40 per cent in QPC, and in February 1977 the process was completed when Qatar General Petroleum Corporation (QGPC) signed an agreement for the take-over of the concession originally held by Shell Qatar.

Equally significant results of the Arab-Israeli conflict were severe but temporary cut-backs in oil production among Arab states and sharp but sustained increases in oil prices. Between October 1973 and January 1974 the "take" of the governments of the Gulf producer states (which include Qatar) rose from $3 per barrel to $7. Qatari revenue, which was $197.8 million in 1971 and $254.8 million in 1972 had risen to $2,000 million in 1976. In 1977 revenue dropped slightly, along with production, to $1,887 million. Total oil production in 1976 was 182 million barrels, falling to 162.3 million in 1977. It rose again to 171 million barrels in 1978 but 1979 production was expected to fall short.

In order to avoid complete dependence on oil the Government has encouraged the growth of other industries, and the proportion of the revenue from oil used to finance development projects has been rising steadily. In 1975 it became clear that Qatar intended to use its oil wealth in developing heavy industry, with plans for an iron and steel complex, petrochemicals projects, a cement plant and an aluminium smelter. The steel works at Umm Said, built by Japanese firms at a cost of $250 million, opened in April 1978. The complex processes iron ore imported from Australia and the United States and local scrap iron to produce mainly round bars for export to the neighbouring Gulf States. Feasibility studies indicated that prices would be lower than those for European or Japanese products because of lower transport costs but a temporary tariff was introduced on imported steel bars to protect the new industry. The plant, which is expected to employ 1,000 people, will use natural gas for smelting. The Qatar Fertiliser Company, whose Umm Said plant annually produces 244,000 metric tons of ammonia and 330,000 tons of urea, was expected to double its capacity by mid-1979. The company received a $30 million Euro-credit in 1978. Two French companies are constructing a polyethylene plant at Umm Said as the first part of a petrochemical complex for QPC which will go into production in 1980. An export refinery is planned by the QGPC, with a capacity of 150,000 barrels per day.

The natural gas industry received a setback in 1977 when the liquefaction plant NGL-1 at Umm Said was destroyed by fire. An extension to NGL-2 is now under consideration. Studies in the NW Dome gasfield, where reserves of over 31 million cubic feet exist, are under way.

Other developments have been in diverse fields. The Qatar Flour Mills Co., which, though privately owned, was set up at the prompting of the Government, operates a mill which can process 100 tons of flour per day. The Qatar National Fishing Co., originally formed in 1966 as an extension of the local shrimp-fishing industry, now has refrigeration and processing plant near Doha harbour capable of handling seven tons of shrimps daily. The Qater National Cement Manufacturing Co. at Umm Bab began production at a rate of 100,000 tons per year early in 1969; its capacity has since been expanded. A ready-mixed concrete factory, a joint venture with a British firm, started production in 1978. There is a sand-processing plant at Hofuf, and a plastics factory, making pipes, hoses and plastic bags.

One of Qatar's problems in developing its industrial sector is shortage of electrical power. The new steelworks may even experience difficulty in achieving its target production in the first year because of this. New power plants are under construction, fed by natural gas, and a nuclear power/desalination plant was at one time considered.

The Department of Agriculture has already succeeded in making the country self-sufficient in vegetables, production of which was negligible as recently as 1960; fruit production and the planting of trees are making rapid progress. Some vegetables, mainly tomatoes, marrows and cucumbers, are now exported to other Gulf states.

Despite the fact that the bias has rather been towards heavy industry in recent years, in the 1978 budget the allocation for industrial development was cut to QR 1,174 million, against QR 2,780 million in 1977. Cuts were also made in other sectors in an effort to deal with inflationary pressures. The trend is now very definitely away from prestige projects, reflecting the Government's reaction to the country's dependence on oil revenues. Natural gas exports in 1977/78 were also badly affected by the destruction of the Umm Said plant. The budget surplus has been decreasing in recent years, and a deficit was recorded in 1977/78, with the drop in oil revenues. An International Monetary Fund mission, which visited Qatar in 1978, warned against drastic cutbacks in expenditure which could slow the economy down too much. The 1978 budget projected an increase in expenditure.

Considerable sums have, of course, been invested in large projects. There is an international airport at Doha, the Doha earth satellite station is to be expanded and Doha port has been much improved with a consequent reduction in delays. Hospitals and schools have, in the past, received large allocations in the development budget, but their share was cut in 1978. Allocations for housing projects, however, were increased from QR 643 million in 1977 to QR 920 million in 1978. Part of Qatar's oil income has been used to provide foreign aid through various agencies such as the United Nations and the OPEC Special Fund.

The volume of trade has been increasing, particularly with Japan, now Qatar's major trading partner. Imports in 1978 amounted to QR 4,590 million, compared with QR 4,850 million in 1977, the decline being due to the completion of some industrial projects and a resultant decrease in imports of machinery and equipment. Qatar's non-oil export and re-export trade is conducted mainly with the neighbouring Arab states and Iran.

STATISTICAL SURVEY

AREA AND POPULATION

Area	Estimated Population†			
	March 1976			1978
	Males	Females	Total	
11,000 sq. km.*	129,518	54,082	183,600	200,000

* 4,247 sq. miles.

† Inclusive of immigrant communities. Native Qataris were estimated to number about 40,000 in 1978.

Capital: Doha (estimated population 140,000 in 1975).

Labour force (March 1976): 86,727 (males 84,834; females 1,893).

AGRICULTURE

VEGETABLES

	1973	1974	1975	1976	1977
Area (dunums*)	9,413	9,703	9,812	n.a.	13,167
Production (tons)	17,781	18,342	18,644	20,284	24,369

* 1 dunum=4,201 sq. metres (1.038 acres).

LIVESTOCK
('000 head)

	1975	1976	1977
Cattle	5.6	9.5	9.8
Camels	8.1	8.5	10.5
Sheep	35.1	38.0	38.6
Goats	49.3	42.0	35.0
Horses	0.3	1.0	1.2

Livestock products (FAO estimates, '000 metric tons, 1977): Meat 3; Cows' milk 5; Sheep's milk 2; Goats' milk 9.

Source: FAO, *Production Yearbook*.

Sea fishing: Total catch 1,000 metric tons per year (FAO estimate).

MINING

		1973	1974	1975	1976	1977	1978
Crude petroleum	'000 metric tons	27,502	24,698	21,102	24,018	21,000	23,200
Natural gas*	million cu. metres	1,580	1,300	2,209	1,476	n.a.	n.a.

* Gas utilized only.

Source: OPEC, *Annual Statistical Bulletin*.

CRUDE OIL PRODUCTION
(b.p.d.)

	1977	1978
Offshore	232,000	249,000
Onshore	200,000	234,000
Bunduq	10,000	2,500
TOTAL	442,000	485,000

Source: Financial Times, February 22nd, 1979.

INDUSTRY

SELECTED PRODUCTS

		1973	1974	1975	1976
Nitrogenous fertilizers*	'000 metric tons	—	14.0	55.5	87.0
Motor spirit (petrol)	,, ,, ,,	8	6	65	78
Jet fuel	,, ,, ,,	—	—	29	52
Distillate fuel oils	,, ,, ,,	10	6	72	116
Natural gasolene†	,, ,, ,,	—	2	96	110
Liquefied petroleum gas†	,, ,, ,,	—	—	138	150
Electric energy	million kWh.	425	465	640	816

Nitrogenous fertilizers: 86,600 metric tons in 1976/77.

* Estimated production in terms of nitrogen; figures refer to the 12 months ending June 30th of the year stated.

† Produced at natural gas processing plants.

Source: UN, *Statistical Yearbook* and *Yearbook of Industrial Statistics.*

FINANCE

100 dirhams=1 Qatar riyal (QR).

Coins: 1, 5, 10, 25 and 50 dirhams.

Notes: 1, 5, 10, 50, 100 and 500 riyals.

Exchange rates (June 1979) £1 sterling=7.79 riyals; U.S. $1=3.76 riyals.

100 Qatar riyals=£12.84=$26.57.

Note: Before June 1966 Qatar's currency was the Persian Gulf Indian rupee, valued at 1s. 6d. sterling (£1=13.33 rupees). When the Indian rupee was devalued in June 1966 Qatar adopted Saudi Arabian currency prior to the introduction of the Qatar/Dubai riyal (at par with the old rupee) in September 1966. This new currency was also used in the states of Trucial Oman (now the United Arab Emirates) except Abu Dhabi. The Q/D riyal was valued at 21 U.S. cents ($1=4.762 riyals) until August 1971. The riyal's value was 22.8 U.S. cents ($1=4.386 riyals) from December 1971 to February 1973; and 25.333 U.S. cents ($1=3.947 riyals) from February 1973 to March 1975. In terms of sterling, the value of the Q/D riyal between November 1967 and June 1972 was 1s. 9d. (8.75 new pence), the exchange rate being £1=11.429 riyals. When the United Arab Emirates adopted a national currency in May 1973 the Q/D riyal was superseded by the Qatar riyal, with the same value as the old currency. Since March 1975 the Qatar riyal has been linked to the IMF Special Drawing Right (at a mid-point of 1 riyal=0.21 SDR), whose value is determined by changes in a weighted "basket" of 16 national currencies. The average exchange rate (riyals per U.S. dollar) was: 3.931 in 1975; 3.962 in 1976; 3.956 in 1977; 3,877 in 1978.

GOVERNMENT FINANCE
(million Qatar riyals—Fiscal year)

	1976	1977	1978*
Revenue	8,811.3	8,754.4	8,700.0
Oil and gas	7,944.4	7,450.8	8,000.0
Other	568.9	703.6	700.0
Expenditure	5,392.7	7,312.9	6,500.0
Foreign grants	309.7	582.1	110.0
Other	5,083.0	6,735.8	6,390.0

* Provisional

Source: International Monetary Fund Survey.

OIL REVENUES
(million U.S. dollars)

1974	1975	1976	1977	1978
1,650	1,700	2,000	1,900	2,200

EXTERNAL TRADE
(million Qatar riyals)

	1972	1973	1974	1975	1976	1977	1978
Imports c.i.f.	616.4	778.3	1,070.0	1,621.6	3,290.4	4,850.1	4,589.7
Exports f.o.b.	1,739.8	2,466.4	7,956.0	7,107.0	8,754.1	7,863.8	8,982.2

Exports of crude petroleum (million Qatar riyals): 2,399.2 in 1973; 7,813.8 in 1974; 6,906.0 in 1975; 8,466.7 in 1976; 7,793.5 in 1977; 8,887.7 in 1978.

Source: IMF, *International Financial Statistics.*

PRINCIPAL TRADING PARTNERS
('000 Qatar riyals)

Imports	1975	1976	1977	1978
Australia	33,800	36,169	39,660	54,372
China	24,000	35,043	55,880	57,846
France	56,600	143,900	277,462	333,831
Germany, Federal Republic	150,700	252,100	344,138	851,364
India	44,700	54,803	106,709	98,980
Italy	47,700	127,583	135,490	213,326
Japan	242,200	933,697	1,293,864	906,473
Kuwait	36,000	110,108	102,760	44,369
Lebanon	64,700	21,224	42,124	41,905
Netherlands	52,600	96,148	167,223	188,392
Saudi Arabia	23,700	32,281	20,055	10,897
Switzerland	42,000	97,350	156,264	48,204
United Arab Emirates	50,000	157,183	224,551	59,471
United Kingdom	342,300	547,596	915,338	721,270
U.S.A.	201,600	257,807	463,816	460,879

EXPORTS OF UREA AND AMMONIA

Urea: Total exports in 1976: QR 101.6 million, of which India received QR 41.5 million and China QR 30.3 million; total exports in 1977: QR 60.3 million, of which India received QR 19.0 million and Viet-Nam QR 12.3 million; total exports in 1978: QR 166.8 million, of which Pakistan received QR 72.6 million and India QR 66.7 million.

Ammonia: Total exports in 1976: QR 20.6 million, of which Brazil received QR 9.6 million and Turkey QR 8.0 million; total exports in 1977: QR 10.3 million, of which India received QR 8.1 million and Kuwait QR 2.2 million; total exports in 1978: QR 20.5 million, of which India received QR 15.6 million and Italy QR 3.2 million.

EDUCATION

(1975/76)

	Pupils		Schools	Teachers
	Boys	Girls		
Primary	11,658	10,543	87	1,912
Preparatory	3,014	2,631	11	
Secondary	1,959	1,311	10	
Total	16,631	14,535	108	1,912

THE CONSTITUTION

A provisional constitution came into effect in July 1970. Executive power is put in the hands of the Council of Ministers, appointed by the Head of State, and assisted by an Advisory Council of 20 members (increased to 30 in December 1975), whose term was extended for three years in May 1975 and for a further three years in May 1978. All fundamental democratic rights are guaranteed. In December 1975 the Advisory Council was granted power to summon individual ministers to answer questions on legislation before promulgation. Previously the Advisory Council was restricted to debating draft bills and regulations before framing recommendations to the Council of Ministers.

THE GOVERNMENT

HEAD OF STATE

Amir: Sheikh KHALIFA BIN HAMAD AL-THANI (assumed power February 22nd, 1972).

COUNCIL OF MINISTERS

(*June* 1979)

Prime Minister: Sheikh KHALIFA BIN HAMAD AL-THANI.

Heir Apparent and Minister of Defence: Maj.-Gen. Sheikh HAMAD BIN KHALIFA AL-THANI.

Minister of Finance and Petroleum: Sheikh ABDUL-AZIZ BIN KHALIFA AL-THANI.

Minister of Foreign Affairs: Sheikh SUHAIM BIN HAMAD AL-THANI.

Minister of Education, Culture and Youth Care: Sheikh MUHAMMAD BIN HAMAD AL-THANI.

Minister of Public Health: KHALED MUHAMMAD AL-MANI.

Minister of the Economy and Commerce: Sheikh NASSIR BIN KHALID AL-THANI.

Minister of Electricty and Water: Sheikh JASSIM BIN MUHAMMAD AL-THANI.

Minister of Justice: (vacant).

Minister of the Interior: Sheikh KHALID BIN HAMAD AL-THANI.

Minister of Industry and Agriculture: Sheikh FAISAL BIN THANI AL-THANI.

Minister of Public Works: KHALID BIN ABDULLAH AL-ATIYYAH.

Minister of Information: ISSA GHANIM AL-KAWARI.

Minister of Municipal Affairs: Sheikh MUHAMMAD BIN JABR AL-THANI.

Minister of Labour and Social Affairs: ALI BIN AHMAD AL-ANSARI.

Minister of Communications and Transport: ABDULLAH BIN NASSIR AL-SUWAIDI.

Minister of State for Foreign Affairs: Sheikh AHMED BIN SAIF AL-THANI.

Adviser to the Emir: Dr. HASAN KAMEL.

DIPLOMATIC REPRESENTATION

EMBASSIES ACCREDITED TO QATAR

(In Doha, unless otherwise indicated)

Afghanistan: Baghdad, Iraq.
Austria: Jeddah, Saudi Arabia.
Bangladesh: P.O.B. 2080; *Ambassador:* (vacant).
Belgium: Kuwait City, Kuwait.
Brazil: Jeddah, Saudi Arabia.
Cameroon: Jeddah, Saudi Arabia.
Canada: Teheran, Iran.
Czechoslovakia: Kuwait City, Kuwait.
Denmark: Jeddah, Saudi Arabia.
Finland: Jeddah, Saudi Arabia.
France: P.O.B. 2699; *Ambassador:* JEAN BELLIVIER.
Gabon: P.O.B. 3566; *Ambassador:* JAN BATIST M'BATSHI.
Gambia: Jeddah, Saudi Arabia.
Germany, Federal Republic: P.O.B. 3064; *Ambassador:* Dr. JUERGEN HELLNER.
Greece: Kuwait City, Kuwait.
Guinea: Jeddah, Saudi Arabia.
India: P.O.B. 2788; *Ambassador:* KRISHNAN MOHAN LAL.
Indonesia: Kuwait City, Kuwait.
Iran: P.O.B. 1633; *Ambassador:* HAMZEH AKHAVAN.
Iraq: P.O.B. 1526; *Ambassador:* MOHAMED GHANEM AL-ENNAZ.
Ireland: Jeddah, Saudi Arabia.
Italy: Kuwait City, Kuwait.
Japan: P.O.B. 2208; *Ambassador:* TOSHIO TADA.
Jordan: P.O.B. 2366; *Ambassador:* AZIZ AL-KABARITY.
Korea, Republic: P.O.B. 3727; *Ambassador:* KYUNG SUK SUH.
Kuwait: P.O.B. 1177; *Ambassador:* ABDUL RAHMAN AHMED AL-BAKR.
Lebanon: P.O.B. 2411; *Ambassador:* MUHAMMAD TAUFIQ SHATILA.
Libya: P.O.B. 3361; *Ambassador:* MOHIDIN AL-SADEQ AL-MASAUDI.
Malaysia: Kuwait City, Kuwait.
Malta: Tripoli, Libya.
Mauritania: P.O.B. 3132; *Ambassador:* BA ALI HAMADI.
Morocco: P.O.B. 3242; *Ambassador:* MUHAMMAD EL-TAHER BANNANI.
Netherlands: Kuwait City, Kuwait.
Norway: Jeddah, Saudi Arabia.
Oman: P.O.B. 1525; *Ambassador:* ABDULLAH ALI AL-NAJJAR.
Pakistan: P.O.B. 334; *Ambassador:* SELIMUZ ZAMAN.
Saudi Arabia: P.O.B. 1255; *Ambassador:* MOHAMED AL-FAHD AL-ISSA.
Senegal: Cairo, Egypt.
Somalia: P.O.B. 1948; *Ambassador:* ABDULLAH HAJI ABDEL-RAHMAN.
Spain: Abu Dhabi, United Arab Emirates.
Sudan: P.O.B. 2999; *Ambassador:* SHARIF AHMAD.
Sweden: Kuwait City, Kuwait.
Switzerland: Amman, Jordan.
Syria: P.O.B. 1257; *Ambassador:* ABDUL AZIZ AL-RIFAI.
Tunisia: P.O.B. 2707; *Ambassador:* ABDEL RAZEK SHATA.
Turkey: Jeddah, Saudi Arabia.
Uganda: Jeddah, Saudi Arabia.
United Kingdom: P.O.B. 3; *Ambassador:* COLIN BRANT.
U.S.A.: P.O.B. 2399; *Ambassador:* ANDREW KILLGORE.
Yemen Arab Republic: P.O.B. 3318; *Ambassador:* (vacant).
Zaire: Jeddah, Saudi Arabia.

Qatar also has diplomatic relations with Algeria, Bahrain, the United Arab Emirates and Yugoslavia.

JUDICIAL SYSTEM

Justice is administered by five courts (Higher Criminal, Lower Criminal, Civil, Appeal and Labour) on the basis of codified laws. In addition traditional Sharia courts apply the Holy Law in certain cases. Non-Muslims are invariably tried by a court operating codified law. Independence of the judiciary is guaranteed by the provisional Constitution.

RELIGION

The indigenous population are Muslims of the Sunni sect, most being of the strict Wahhabi persuasion.

THE PRESS

Al-Ahad: P.O.B. 2531, Doha; weekly magazine; Arabic; published by ABDULLA AL-HUSSINI.

Al-Doha Magazine: Ministry of Information, P.O.B. 1836, Doha; f. 1969; monthly; Arabic; circ. 40,000.

Al-Fajr: Qatar National Printing Press and Publicity Establishment, P.O.B. 2908, Doha; weekly; political; Arabic.

Al-Jawhara: P.O.B. 2531, Doha; monthly; women's magazine; Arabic.

Al-Khalij al-Jadeed: Doha; monthly magazine; Arabic.

Al Mash'al: Qatar Petroleum Producing Authority, P.O.B. 70; Doha; monthly; English and Arabic:

Daily News Bulletin: P.O.B. 3299, Doha; daily; English and Arabic editions; Dir.-Gen. OSMAN ABU ZEID.

Dar Al-Ouroba: P.O.B. 633, Doha; Newspaper Printing and Publishing, Doha; f. 1957; publ. daily Arabic newspaper *Al-Arab*, circ. 8,000; weekly Arabic magazine *Al-Ouroba*, circ. 15,000; and weekly English magazine *Gulf News*, Proprietor and Editor-in-Chief ABDULLA HUSSAIN NAAMA.

Diaruna Wal Alam: Ministry of Finance and Petroleum, P.O.B. 3594, Doha; monthly; English and Arabic.

Gulf Times: P.O.B. 2888, Doha; weekly; English; f. 1978; circ. 9,500; Editor BRIAN NICHOLLS.

NEWS AGENCY

Qatar News Agency: P.O.B. 3299, Doha; Dir.-Gen. OSMAN ABU ZEID.

RADIO AND TELEVISION

Radio Qatar (Q.B.S.): P.O.B. 1414, Doha; f. 1968; government service transmitting for 18 hours in Arabic daily, and in English for 18 hours daily; Dir. M. MADHADI.

Qatar Television: P.O.B. 1944, Doha; f. 1970; two 5 kW transmitters began transmissions throughout the Gulf in 1972. Colour transmissions began in 1974. Channel 11, with two 54W transmitters, was due to operate from May 1978. Dir. of TV YOUSUF MUZAFFAR. There were an estimated 52,000 TV receivers in use in 1978.

FINANCE

BANKING

Qatar Monetary Agency: P.O.B. 1234, Doha; f. 1966 as Qatar and Dubai Currency Board; became Qatar Monetary Agency 1973 when Qatar issued its own currency, the Qatar riyal; currency in circulation (Dec. 1977) QR 561m.; Dir. MAJED AL-MAJED.

Qatar National Bank, S.A.Q.: P.O.B. 1000, Doha; f. 1965; cap. and res. QR 231m.; dep. QR 3,151m. (1978); Chair. Sheikh ABDUL AZIZ BIN KHALIFA AL-THANI; Gen. Man. H. A. ALAMI.

Arab Bank Ltd.: Amman, Jordan; P.O.B. 172, Doha; Man. Dr. MUHAMMAD M. ABDUL HADI.

Bank Al-Mashrek, S.A.L.: P.O.B. 388, Doha.

Bank of Cairo: P.O.B. 553, Doha.

Bank of Oman: P.O.B. 173, Doha.

Bank Saderat Iran: P.O.B. 2256, Doha.

Banque de Paris et des Pays-Bas: Paris; P.O.B. 2636, Doha; Man. R. LAMBERT.

British Bank of the Middle East, The: P.O.B. 57, Doha; Man. A. A. TRACHY.

Chartered Bank, The: London; P.O.B. 29, Doha.

Citibank N.A.: P.O.B. 2309, Doha.

Commercial Bank of Qatar Ltd.: P.O.B. 3232, Doha; f. 1975; cap. QR 15m., dep. QR 290.8m. (Dec. 1978); Gen. Man. D. J. HAYEK.

Doha Bank: P.O.B. 3818, Doha.

Grindlays Bank Ltd.: London; P.O.B. 2001, Doha; Gen. Man. L. B. CANT.

United Bank of Pakistan: P.O.B. 242, Doha.

INSURANCE

Qatar Insurance Co.: P.O.B. 666, Doha; f. 1964; assets and reserves QR 17m. (1977); branches in Dubai and Riyadh; Man. FATHI I. GABR.

COMMERCE

Qatar Chamber of Commerce: P.O.B. 402, Doha; f. 1963; 13 mems. appointed by decree; Pres. AHMED MUHAMMAD AL-SOWAIDI; Dir.-Gen. KAMAL ALI SALEH.

TRADE AND INDUSTRY

STATE ENTERPRISES

Qatar General Petroleum Corporation: P.O.B. 3212, Doha; capital QR 3,000 million; the State of Qatar's interest in companies active in petroleum and related industries has passed to the Corporation. In line with OPEC policy, the Government agreed a participation agreement with the Qatar Petroleum Company and Shell Company of Qatar in 1974 to secure Qatar's interest and obtained a 60 per cent interest in both. In late 1976, under two separate agreements, the Government secured a 100 per cent interest in both companies. Qatar Petroleum Producing Authority (QPPA) was established in 1976 as a subsidiary wholly owned by the Corporation to carry out all operations previously carried out by the two companies.

Qatar General Petroleum Corporation wholly or partly owns: Qatar Petroleum Producing Authority (QPPA), National Oil Distribution Co. (NODCO), Qatar Fertilizer Co. Ltd. (QAFCO), Qatar Petrochemical Co. Ltd. (QAPCO), Qatar Gas Co. (QGC), Compagnie Petrochemique du Nord (COPENOR), Arab Maritime Petroleum Transport Co. Ltd., Arab Pipelines Co. (SUMED), Arab Shipbuilding and Repair Yard Co., Arab Petroleum Services Co. and Arab Petroleum Investments Corp. (APICORP); Chair. Sheikh ABDUL AZIZ BIN KHALIFA AL-THANI (Minister of Finance and Petroleum); Dir.-Gen. ALI MUHAMMAD AL-JAIDA.

Qatar Petroleum Producing Authority (Onshore Operations): Doha; produces and exports crude oil and natural gas liquids from the Dukhan oilfield (onshore). The operation is now run by personnel seconded by the Dukhan Service Co. and by hire personnel; production in 1978 was 237,371 b/d.

Qatar Petroleum Producing Authority (Offshore Operations): P.O.B. 47, Doha; state-owned organization for offshore oil/gas exploration and production; Chair. ABDULLA SALATT; Gen. Man. MENNO SCHEPERS; production in 1978 averaged 246,000 b/d.

Qatar Gas Company: Doha; f. 1974; natural gas; Qatar Government owns 70 per cent and Shell the remaining 30 per cent; capital QR 400 million.

Wintershall: leads a consortium of five companies carrying out exploration.

TRANSPORT

ROADS

There are some 600 miles of surfaced road linking Doha and the oil centres of Dukhan and Umm Said with the northern end of the peninsula. A 65-mile long road from Doha to Salwa was completed in 1970, and joins one leading from Al Hufuf in Saudi Arabia, giving Qatar land access to the Mediterranean. A 260-mile highway, built in conjunction with Abu Dhabi, links both states with the Gulf network. Road construction is a continual process.

PIPELINES

Oil is transported by pipeline from the oilfields at Dukhan to the loading terminal at Umm Said. Natural gas is brought by pipeline from Dukhan to Doha where it is used as fuel for a power station and water distillation plant.

SHIPPING

Qatar National Navigation and Transport Co. Ltd.: P.O.B. 153, Doha; shipping agents, lighterage contractors, ship chandlers, clearing and forwarding agents at the ports of Qatar.

Director of Ports: ABDULREHMAN JABER MUFTAH, P.O.B. 313, Doha.

Doha Port: At the end of 1977 there were 5 berths of 9.1m. depth and 4–5 berths of 7.5m. depth. Total length of berths is 1,853m.

Umm Said Harbour: Although accommodating smaller tankers (up to 60,000 d.w.t.) Umm Said still has the country's main oil terminal. A 220,000 ton capacity tank farm is connected by a series of pipelines with QPC's three main gathering stations. A jetty 210 metres long is linked to a grain mill and a newly constructed fertilizer plant. In addition, the new Umm Said Port, opened in 1977, has a total length of 4.5 km., of which 2.5 km. has been developed to provide deep-water berths. There are three berths of 15.5 metres depth, five berths of 13 metres depth and two berths of 10 metres depth.

CIVIL AVIATION

Doha international airport is equipped to receive jumbo jets; its runway was extended to 15,000 ft. in 1970. Plans for a new civil airport, which will have one of the longest runways in the world (14,993 ft.), are under preparation.

Gulf Air Co. Ltd.: jointly owned by Bahrain, Qatar, the U.A.E. and Oman (*see* Oman—Civil Aviation).

Gulf Helicopters: P.O.B. 811, Doha; owned by Gulf Aviation Co. Ltd.; fleet of six Bell 212 and two Bell 205s.

Doha is also served by the following airlines: Air France, Alia (Jordan), British Airways, Cathay Pacific Airlines (Hong Kong), EgyptAir, Iranian Airways, Iraqi Airways, KLM (Netherlands), Korean Airlines (Republic of Korea), Kuwait Airways, MEA (Lebanon), PIA (Pakistan), Sabena (Belgium), Saudia, SIA (Singapore), Sudan Airways, Syrian Arab Airlines, TMA (Lebanon), Yemen Airlines.

DEFENCE

Defence Expenditure, 1978: 238 million Qatar rials.

Total armed forces: 4,000: army 3,500; navy 200; air force 300.

EDUCATION

All education within Qatar is free and numerous scholarships are awarded for study overseas. The state education system was inaugurated in 1956, when 1,388 boys attended 17 primary schools; by 1974–75 some 20,152 children (10,528 boys and 9,624 girls) attended primary school. The six-year primary stage is followed by a three-year preparatory stage (2,683 boys and 2,241 girls in 1974–75) and a further three-year secondary stage. General secondary education facilities are complemented by a teacher-training institute, a technical school, a school of commerce and an institute of religious studies. 1,399 boys and 816 girls received general secondary education in 1974–75, while there were 307 trainee teachers enrolled. In 1976/77 902 Qataris were sent on scholarships to higher education institutions abroad, almost all in other Arab countries, Britain, or the U.S.A. The number of schools (97 in 1975) and of teachers (1,695), together with expenditure under the 1973–74 budget of about £380 per pupil indicates the importance given to education in Qatar. In October 1973 the first two Higher Teacher Training Colleges were opened providing education to university level. The Ministry of Education has made substantial efforts to mitigate the effects of social deprivation on equal educational opportunity.

UNIVERSITY

University of Qatar: Doha; 925 students.

BIBLIOGRAPHY

See Bibliography on Bahrain, p. 257, and United Arab Emirates, p. 822.

Saudi Arabia

PHYSICAL AND SOCIAL GEOGRAPHY OF THE ARABIAN PENINSULA

The Arabian peninsula is a strongly marked geographical unit, being delimited on three sides by sea—on the east by the Persian Gulf and Gulf of Oman, on the south by the Indian Ocean, and on the west by the Red Sea—and its remaining (northern) side is occupied by the deserts of Jordan and Iraq. This isolated territory, extending over more than one million square miles, is, however, divided politically into several states. The largest of these is Saudi Arabia, which occupies over 2,000,000 sq. km.; to the east and south lie much smaller territories where suzerainty and even actual frontiers are in some instances a matter of doubt. Along the shores of the Persian Gulf and Gulf of Oman there are first the State of Kuwait, with two adjacent patches of "neutral" territory; then, after a stretch of Saudi coast, the island of Bahrain and the Qatar peninsula, followed by the United Arab Emirates and the much larger state of Oman. The People's Democratic Republic of Yemen, composed of the former British colony of Aden and former (British) Protectorate of South Arabia, occupies most of the southern coastline of the peninsula. To the north of it, facing the Red Sea, lies the Yemen Arab Republic. The precise location of frontiers between these states and Saudi Arabia, which adjoins them all, is still in some doubt, and atlases show varying positions. The granting of oil concessions and continued discoveries of oil may ultimately lead to a more accurate delimitation.

PHYSICAL FEATURES

Structurally, the whole of Arabia is a vast platform of ancient rocks, once continuous with north-east Africa. In relatively recent geological time a series of great fissures opened, as the result of which a large trough, or rift valley, was formed and later occupied by the sea, to produce the Red Sea and Gulf of Aden. The Arabian platform is tilted, having its highest part in the extreme west, along the Red Sea; and it slopes gradually down from west to east. Thus the Red Sea coast is often bold and mountainous, whereas the Persian Gulf coast is flat and low-lying, being fringed with extensive coral reefs that make it difficult to approach the shore in many places.

Dislocation of the rock strata in the west of Arabia has led to the upwelling of much lava, which has solidified into vast barren expanses known as *harras*. Volcanic cones and flows are also prominent along the whole length of the western coast as far as Aden, giving peaks that rise well above 3,000 metres. The maximum height of the mountains is attained in the south, in the Yemen Arab Republic, where summits reach 4,000 metres; and the lowest part of this mountain wall occurs roughly half-way along its course, in the region of Jeddah, Mecca, and Medina. One main reason for the presence of these three towns is the geographical fact that they offer the easiest route inland from the coast, and one of the shortest routes across Arabia.

Further to the east the ancient platform is covered by relatively thin layers of younger rocks. Some of the strata have weathered away to form shallow depressions; others have proved more resistant, and now stand out as ridges. This central area, diversified by shallow vales and upstanding ridges and covered in many places by desert sand, is called the Najd, and is spoken of as the homeland of the Wahhabi sect, which now rules the whole of Saudi Arabia. Farther east still, practically all the land lies well below 300 metres in altitude, and both to north and south lie desert areas. The Nefud in the north has some wells, and even a slight rainfall, so life is possible for a few oasis cultivators and pastoral nomads. But south of the Najd lies the Rub' al-Khali, or Empty Quarter, a rainless, unrelieved wilderness of shifting sand, too difficult for occupation even by nomads.

Though most of the east coast of Arabia (termed al-Hasa) is low-lying, there is an exception in the imposing ridge of the Jebel Akhdar of Oman, which also produces a fjord-like coastline along the Gulf of Oman. One other feature of importance is the presence of several large river valleys, or *wadis*, cut by river action at an earlier geological period, but now almost, or entirely, dry and partly covered in sand. The largest is the Wadi Hadhramaut, which runs parallel to the southern coast for several hundred miles; another is the Wadi Sirhan, which stretches from the Nefud north-westwards into Jordan.

CLIMATE

Because of its land-locked nature, the winds reaching Arabia are generally dry, and almost all the area is arid. In the north there is a rainfall of 10 to 20 cm. annually; further south, except near the coast, even this fails. The higher parts of the west and south do, however, experience appreciable falls—rather sporadic in some parts, but copious and reliable in the Yemen Arab Republic. There are even small, regularly flowing streams in the higher parts of the Yemeni mountains, but none manages to reach the sea. The Jebel Akhdar (Green Mountain) of Oman, as its name indicates, also has more rainfall than the surrounding districts.

Because of aridity, and hence relatively cloudless skies, there are great extremes of temperature. The summer is overwhelmingly hot, with maxima of over 50°C., which are intensified by the dark rocks, whilst in winter there can be general severe frost and even weeks of snow in the mountains—sheepskins are worn in the Yemen Arab Republic. Another feature, due to wide alternations of temperature, is the prevalence of violent local winds. Also, near the coast, atmospheric humidity is very high, and this makes living conditions extremely unpleasant. The coasts of both the Red Sea and Persian Gulf are notorious for their humidity.

Owing to the tilt of the strata eastwards, and their great elevation in the west, rainfall occurring in the hills near the Red Sea apparently percolates gradually eastwards, to emerge as springs along the Persian Gulf coast. This phenomenon, borne out by the fact that the flow of water in the springs greatly exceeds the total rainfall in the same district, would appear to indicate that water may be present underground over much of the interior. Hence irrigation schemes to tap these supplies have been developed, notably in Najd at al-Kharj. Results are, however, fairly limited.

ECONOMIC LIFE

Over much of Arabia life is dependent on the occurrence of oases. Many wells are used solely by nomads for watering their animals, but in some parts, more especially the south, there is some regular cultivation. The Yemen Arab Republic, in particular, has a well-developed agriculture, showing a gradation of crops according to altitude, with cereals, fruit, coffee and *qat* (a narcotic) as the chief products. Other agricultural districts occur in Aden and the Hadhramaut (in Yemen P.D.R.), in Oman, and in the large oases of the Hijaz (including Medina and Mecca). Despite this, however, it must be emphasized that in the main, conditions in Arabia are harsh, and human life depends for existence partly on resources brought in from outside—the revenues from pilgrimage, trading by dhow in the Indian Ocean, or trading in the East Indies. A major change in the economy of Saudi Arabia and the Gulf states has taken place following the exploitation of oil, the revenues from which are transforming these states, and *inter alia* allowing the import of food for Arab oil workers.

RACE

The inhabitants of the centre, north, and west are of almost unmixed Mediterranean stock—lightly built, long-headed, and dark. In coastal districts of the east, south, and south-west intermixture of broader-headed and slightly heavier peoples of Armenoid descent is a prominent feature; and there has been some exchange of racial type with the populations on the Persian shores of the Persian Gulf and Gulf of Oman. Owing to the long-continued slave trade, negroid influences from Africa are also widespread. On this basis it is possible to delimit two ethnic zones within Arabia: a northern, central and western area, geographically arid and in isolation, with a relatively unmixed racial composition; and the coastlands of the south, south-west, and east, showing a mixed population.

LANGUAGE

Arabic is the only language of Arabia. Unlike many other parts of the Middle East, European languages are not current.

HISTORY

ANCIENT AND MEDIEVAL HISTORY

Although there is some support for the belief that Arabia was at one time a land of great fertility, there is little evidence of this in historical times. For the most part Arabian history has been the account of small pockets of settled civilization, subsisting mainly on trade, in the midst of an ocean of nomadic tribes whose livelihood was derived mainly from camel-breeding and raiding. The earliest urban settlements developed in the south-west, where the flourishing Minaean kingdom is believed to have been established as early as the twelfth century B.C. This was followed by the Sabaean and Himyarite kingdoms, which lasted with varying degrees of power until the sixth century A.D. The term "kingdom" in this connection implies rather a loose federation of city states than a centralized monarchy. As an important trading station between east and west, southern Arabia was brought into early contact with the Persian and Roman empires, whence spread the influence of Judaism, Zoroastrianism, and later Christianity. Politically, however, the south Arabian principalities remained independent, though there was an abortive Roman expedition in A.D. 24, and two brief periods of Abyssinian rule in the fourth and sixth centuries A.D.

By the end of the sixth century the centre of gravity had shifted to the west coast, to the Hijaz cities of at-Ta'if, Mecca and Medina. While the southern regions fell under the somewhat spasmodic control of the Sasanid rulers of Persia, the Hijaz grew in independence and importance as a trade route between the Byzantine Empire, Egypt, and the East. From the fifth century onwards Mecca was dominated by the tribe of Quraish, through whose extensive commercial activities influences from Byzantine, Persian, Aramaic and Judaic sources began to make themselves felt. Meanwhile the central deserts remained obstinately nomadic, and the inhospitable east coast formed for the most part a corner of the Persian sphere of influence.

It is not necessary here to relate in detail the events that led to the spectacular outbreak of the Arabs from the Arabian peninsula and their political and social domination within a century of an area extending from Spain to northern India. Ostensibly the driving force behind this great movement was the Islamic religion preached by Muhammad, a humble member of the Quraish tribe; and so powerful was its appeal that not only was the faith itself widely adopted, but even the language of its holy book, the Koran, has left an indelible impression on the speech of all the peoples it reached.

But this flowering and development of Arabism was to proceed for the most part outside the confines of the Arabian peninsula itself. The Islamic unification of the Near and Middle East reduced the importance of the Hijaz as a trade route. Mecca retained a unique status as a centre of pilgrimage for the whole Muslim world, but Arabia as a whole, temporarily united under Muhammad and his successors, soon drifted back into disunity. The Yemen was the first to break away from the weakening Abbasid Caliphate in Baghdad, and from the ninth century onwards a variety of small dynasties established themselves in Sana'a, Zabid, and other towns. Mecca also had its semi-independent governors, though their proximity to Egypt made them more cautious in their attitude towards the Caliphs and the later rulers of that country, particularly the Fatimids of the tenth to twelfth centuries. In Oman in the south-east a line of spiritual Imams arose who before long were exercising temporal power; to the north the Arabian shores of the Persian Gulf provided a home for the fanatical Carmathian sect whose influence at times extended as far as Iraq, Syria, Mecca, and the Yemen.

THE OTTOMAN PERIOD

Arabia continued to be restless and unsettled until the beginning of the sixteenth century, when the whole peninsula came nominally under the suzerainty of the Ottoman Sultans at Istanbul. It was a hold that was never very strong, even in the Hijaz, while in Oman and the Yemen native lines of Imams were once again exercising unfettered authority before the end of the century. More important for the future of the peninsula was the appearance of European merchant adventurers in the Indian Ocean and the Persian/Arabian Gulf. The Portuguese were the first to arrive in the sixteenth century, and they were succeeded in the seventeenth and eighteenth centuries by the English, Dutch and French. By the beginning of the nineteenth century Britain had eliminated her European rivals and had established her influence firmly in the Gulf and to a lesser extent along the southern coast.

The political structure of Arabia was now beginning to take the shape it has today. The Yemen was already a virtually independent Imamate; Lahej broke away in the middle of the eighteenth century, only to lose Aden to Britain in 1839 and to become the nucleus of the Aden Protectorate. To the north of the Yemen was the principality of the Asir, generally independent, though both countries were occupied by the Turks from 1850 to the outbreak of the Great War. The Hijaz continued to be a province of the Ottoman Empire. In 1793 the Sultanate of Oman was established with its capital at Muscat, and during the nineteenth century all the rulers and chieftains along the Persian Gulf coast, including Oman, the sheikhdoms of the Trucial Coast, Bahrain and Kuwait, entered into close and "exclusive" treaty relations with the British Government. Britain was principally concerned to prevent French, Russian and German penetration towards India and to suppress the slave and arms trades.

Meanwhile the Najd in the centre of Arabia was the scene of another upheaval with religious inspirations. The puritanical and reforming Wahhabi movement, launched in the middle of the eighteenth century, had by 1800 reached such strength that its followers were able to capture Kerbela and Najaf in Iraq, Damascus in Syria, and Mecca and Medina in the Hijaz. They were defeated by Muhammad Ali of Egypt, acting in the name of the Ottoman Sultan, in 1811–1818 and again in 1838; but the Wahhabi ruling house of Sa'ud continued to rule in the interior. Towards the end of the century they were in danger of being eclipsed by the Shammar line of Rashid to the north, who had Turkish support; but in 1902 Abd al-Aziz ibn Sa'ud, the late ruler of Saudi Arabia, succeeded in recapturing the Wahhabi capital of Riyadh, and by the outbreak of the Great War was master of the whole of central Arabia, including the Hasa coast of the Persian Gulf. In 1910, with the aim of reviving the ideals of the Wahhabi movement, he established the *Ikhwan* or Brethren and proceeded to settle them in colonies throughout the Najd, thus forming the basis of a centralized organization that was to prove a powerful instrument in later years.

MODERN HISTORY

When Turkey entered the war on the side of Germany in October 1914 Arabia inevitably became a centre of intrigue, if not necessarily of military action. British influence was paramount along the eastern and southern coasts, where the various sheikhs and tribal chiefs from Kuwait to the Hadhramaut lost no time in severing their last slender connections with the Ottoman Empire. On the other hand, the Turks had faithful allies in Ibn Rashid of the Shammar to the north of the Najd, and in Imam Yahya of the Yemen; they also retained their garrisons along the west coast, both in the Asir, whose Idrisi ruler was impelled by his long-standing enmity with the Imam of the Yemen to intrigue against them, and in the Hijaz, where Sharif Hussein of Mecca still acknowledged Ottoman suzerainty. In the centre Ibn Sa'ud, who had accepted Turkish recognition in 1913 of his occupation of the Hasa coast, was in close and friendly relations with the Government of India.

British military strategy developed as the war dragged on into a two-pronged thrust against the Turks from both Egypt and the Persian Gulf. In the implementation of this plan opinions were divided on the extent to which use could be made of the Arab population. The Indian Government on the eastern wing, while favouring the pretensions of Ibn Sa'ud, preferred to see the problem in purely military terms, and opposed any suggestion of an Arab revolt. This, however, was the scheme favoured by the Arab Bureau in Cairo, whose views eventually prevailed in London. They were alarmed at the Ottoman declaration of a *Jihad* (Holy War) and possible repercussions in Egypt and North Africa. Negotiations were started at a very early stage with Arab nationalist movements in Syria and Egypt, but these met with comparatively little success. More progress was made when the British negotiators turned their attentions to the Sharif of Mecca, Hussein, member of the Hashimi family that had ruled in Mecca since the eleventh century A.D. The support of such a religious dignitary would be an effective counter to Turkish claims. Hussein was inclined to favour the Allied cause, but was reluctant to act independently, and it was only after he had elicited from the British (in the MacMahon correspondence—*see* DOCUMENTS ON PALESTINE, p. 52) promises which he believed would meet Arab nationalist aspirations that he decided to move. On June 5th, 1916, he proclaimed Arab independence and declared war on the Turks. By November things had gone so well that he felt able to claim the title of King of the Hijaz. Military operations continued throughout the winter, and in July 1917 the port of Aqaba was captured and the Hijaz cleared of Turkish troops except for a beleaguered and helpless garrison in Medina.

Arabia thereafter remained comparatively peaceful, and was not even greatly disturbed by the complicated post-war political manoeuvres in the Middle East. Hussein played a somewhat ineffectual role in maintaining the Arab point of view at the peace conferences and over the allocation of mandates, and as a result forfeited the favour of the British Government. When, therefore, he was unwise enough to challenge the growing power of his old enemy Ibn Sa'ud, he found himself entirely without support. Ibn Sa'ud's stature had been steadily growing since the end of the war In November 1921 he had succeeded in eliminating the house of Ibn Rashid and annexing the Shammar, and a year later he was recognized by the Government of India as overlord of Ha'il, Shammar and Jawf. On March 5th, 1924, King Hussein laid claim to the title of Caliph, vacant by the deposition of the Ottoman Sultan. His claims were nowhere recognized, and Ibn Sa'ud, declaring him a traitor, overran the Hijaz in a campaign of a few months, captured Mecca and forced Hussein's abdication. Hussein's eldest son, Ali, continued to hold Jeddah for another year, but was then driven out, and on January 8th, 1926, Ibn Sa'ud proclaimed himself King of the Hijaz, so formally marking the establishment of the Saudi Arabian kingdom.

THE KINGDOM OF SAUDI ARABIA*

Ibn Sa'ud's new status was recognized by Britain in the Treaty of Jeddah of 1927, while Ibn Sa'ud in his turn acknowledged his rival Hussein's sons, Abdallah and Faisal, as rulers of Transjordan and Iraq, and also the special status of the British-protected sheikhdoms along the Gulf coast. The northern frontier of his domains had previously been established by the Hadda and Bahra agreements of November 1925, which set the Mandate boundaries as the limit of his expansion; while the border war with Yemen was, after protracted negotiations and a brief war, settled in 1934. (For a fuller account of this, *see* the Yemen Arab Republic chapter, History.)

During the years that followed, the new king continued to be absorbed in his primary task of unifying and developing his country. The colonization policy begun in 1910 was pursued vigorously; land settlements were established and Bedouin unruliness was suppressed. A start was made at the modernization of communications, and the need for economic development along modern lines was emphasized by the falling-off in the pilgrimage during the early 1930s. The serious crisis that this produced might indeed never have been averted had it not been for the discovery of oil in Bahrain in 1932 and the subsequent extension of prospecting to the mainland.

Saudi Arabia's chief sufferings during the war were economic, though there was an Italian air raid on Dhahran (and also on Bahrain) in October 1940. The pilgrimage traffic dropped away almost to extinction, and in April 1943 it was found necessary to include Saudi Arabia in the benefits of Lease-Lend. Up to September 1946 $17,500,000 had been received, and in August of that year there was a further £10,000,000 from the Export-Import Bank. Two years later, however, as a protest against American policy over Palestine, an American loan of $15,000,000 was turned down. But by this time the oil industry alone was enough to establish the Saudi Arabian economy firmly on its feet.

In January 1944 the California Arabian Standard Oil Company, owned jointly by the Standard Oil Company of California and the Texas Company, was re-formed as the Arabian American Oil Company. This was reconstructed once more in December 1948 to include the Standard Oil Company of New Jersey and Socony Vacuum—a move that brought protests from the French Government. Under an agreement of 1928 shareholders in the Iraq Petroleum Company, who included the latter two American companies as well as French and British interests, had agreed not to secure rival concessions within an area including the Arabian peninsula. A settlement was finally reached at the end of 1948, by which this so-called "Red Line" clause was abandoned. Meanwhile production had been mounting steadily as new fields were developed; a refinery was opened at Ras Tanura in October 1945, and two years later work was started on a pipeline to connect the Arabian fields with the Mediterranean. In spite of a year's suspension owing to events in Palestine, the task was completed before the end of 1950, and oil first reached the Lebanese port of Sidon on December 2nd of that year. In the same month a new "fifty-fifty" agreement was signed with the Arabian American Oil Company which was to set an interesting example to other foreign oil interests in December 1951. In 1956 a government-owned National Oil Company was formed to exploit areas not covered by the Aramco concession.

Saudi Arabia was an original member of the Arab League formed in 1945, and to begin with played a loyal and comparatively inconspicuous part. Ibn Sa'ud sent a small force to join the fighting against

* For subsequent developments in the rest of the Arabian Peninsula, *see* separate chapters on Bahrain, Kuwait, Oman, Qatar, United Arab Emirates, Yemen Arab Republic and Yemen People's Democratic Republic.

Israel in the summer of 1948. When the solidarity of the League began to show signs of cracking, it was natural that he should side with Egypt and Syria rather than with his old dynastic enemies, the rulers of Iraq and Jordan. In course of time, however, he began to turn once more to internal development, and to forget his political quarrel with the United States in his need for economic advice and aid. The $15,000,000 Export-Import Bank loan was finally taken up in August 1950; in January 1951 a Point Four Agreement was signed, and in June a Mutual Assistance Pact. But the real basis of development was the revenue from the ever-expanding oil industry. This was sufficient to justify the announcement in July 1949 of a $270,000,000 Four Year Plan, in which an ambitious programme of railway development was the main item. A railway now links the oilfields in the east with Riyadh in the centre, and extends to the port of Dammam. For the rest the King's policy was one of cautious modernization at home, and the enhancement of Saudi Arabian prestige and influence in the Middle East and in world affairs generally.

AFTER IBN SA'UD

On November 9th, 1953, King Ibn Sa'ud died at the age of 71, and was succeeded peacefully by the Crown Prince, Sa'ud. It was assumed that there would be no major changes, but the policy already adopted of strengthening the governmental machine and of relying less on one-man rule was continued by the formation of new ministries and of a regular cabinet. In March 1958 King Sa'ud conferred upon his brother, the Amir Faisal, full powers over the foreign, internal and economic affairs of Saudi Arabia, with the professed aim of strengthening the machinery of government and centralizing responsibilities. In December 1960, however, the Amir Faisal resigned, and the King took over the office of Prime Minister himself. In the following month a High Planning Council, with a team of international experts, was set up to survey the country's resources, and thereafter there has been slow but steady progress in the modernization of the country.

Throughout his reign the King regarded his role as that of a mediator between the conflicting national and foreign interests in the Arab Middle East. He refused to join either the United Arab Republic or the rival Arab Federation. Relations with Egypt ranged from the mutual defence pacts between Egypt, Syria and Saudi Arabia in October 1955 (to which Yemen and Jordan adhered the following year) to the open quarrel in March 1958 over an alleged plot to assassinate President Nasser. Subsequently, relations improved, and the King visited Cairo in September 1959. Contacts with the United States have always been close, owing to the extensive American oil interests. The Saudi Arabian Government also played a leading role in bringing the Arab governments together after Egypt's nationalization of the Suez Canal in July 1956 and the Israeli, British and French military action in the Sinai peninsula in November. In 1961 Saudi Arabia supported the Syrians in their break with the United Arab Republic, and in general relations with the U.A.R. deteriorated. By 1964, however, in spite of the tensions over the Yemen revolution, there were signs of improved relations. King Sa'ud attended the Cairo conference on the Jordan waters dispute in January, and in March, after a meeting in Riyadh, diplomatic relations with the U.A.R. were resumed. In September Prince Faisal attended the Arab Summit Conference in Alexandria, and afterwards had talks with President Nasser on the Yemen situation.

THE REIGN OF KING FAISAL

Meanwhile, in March 1964 King Sa'ud had relinquished all real power over the affairs of the country to his brother, Crown Prince Faisal, who had again acted as Prime Minister intermittently during 1962, and continuously since the middle of 1963. The rule of Prince Faisal was expected to result in many concessions to "Westernization" such as more cinemas and television, with more profound social and economic reforms to follow. The division of the country into provinces, each with a thirty-man council, was under study early in 1964. The change of power, by which King Sa'ud retired as active monarch, was supported in a statement by the *ulema* council of religious leaders "in the light of developments, the King's condition of health, and his inability to attend to state affairs". In November 1964 Sa'ud was formally deposed, and Faisal became King, as well as head of the Council of Ministers with the exclusive power of appointing and dismissing Ministers. His younger brother Khalid was appointed Crown Prince. On August 24th, 1965, King Faisal confirmed his stature as an important Arab leader, when he concluded an agreement at Jeddah with President Nasser of the U.A.R. on a peace plan for the Yemen.

Although the Yemen problem remained unsolved, there was evidence of Saudi Arabia's genuine anxiety that a solution should be found, even though in April 1966 the construction of a military airfield near the frontier brought protests from the Yemeni Republican Government and the U.A.R. Representatives of Saudi Arabia and the U.A.R. met in Kuwait in August 1966 in an attempt to implement the Jeddah agreement. But relations with both the U.A.R. and the Arab League continued to be tense, and no progress was evident. Matters were not improved by the appearance in Cairo of ex-King Sa'ud, with a public declaration of his support for U.A.R. policy in Yemen.

During 1966 and 1967 King Faisal made extensive visits abroad. In the June 1967 Arab-Israeli war, Saudi forces collaborated with Jordanian and Iraqi forces in action against Israel. At a summit conference of Arab leaders held in Khartoum at the end of August 1967 Saudi Arabia agreed to put up £50 million of a total £135 million fund to assist Jordan and the U.A.R. in restoring their economic strength after the hostilities with Israel. At the same time an agreement was concluded with President Nasser on the withdrawal of U.A.R. and Saudi military support for the warring parties in the Yemen. By way of recompense for these concessions the Saudi Arabian Government persuaded the other Arab states that it was in their best interests to resume production of oil, shipments of which to western countries had been suspended for political reasons after the war with Israel.

EVENTS SINCE THE 1967 WAR

Though outwardly calm, the internal political situation was apparently disturbed by abortive coups in June and September 1969. Plans for both are presumed to have been discovered in advance, the only visible evidence of the attempts being the arrests of numbers of army and air force officers. A flight of private capital abroad was also reported. Some observers drew parallels with developments in Libya. In the Yemen the Royalist cause which the Saudi Government had strongly supported appeared to be within sight of victory early in 1968, but by mid-1969 its remaining adherents had largely been driven into exile and the civil war seemed to have come to an end, although further hostilities were reported during the 1969-70 winter. Dissension amongst the Royalists, which led to the withdrawal of Saudi assistance, was a principal factor in this decline. Discussions between Sana'a representatives and Saudi officials took place at Jeddah in March 1970, and the Yemen Republic was officially recognized in July. Relations with Southern Yemen deteriorated, however, and an extensive battle on the disputed frontier took place in December 1969, with Saudi Arabia apparently winning easily owing mainly to its superior air power.

The important relationship with Iran, under some strain at the beginning of 1968 over the Bahrain question, improved greatly later in the year. In October the two countries signed a treaty which at last delineated their offshore boundaries. In November the Shah paid a state visit to Saudi Arabia; the occasion, which included a pilgrimage, was acclaimed as symbolic of Muslim unity. The Saudi Government took a favourable view of the proposed Gulf federation, and gave financial assistance for the road linking the Trucial sheikhdoms. Together with Kuwait the government was closely involved in 1971 in the diplomatic efforts to secure Bahrain's and Qatar's membership of a nine-member Gulf federation, but the two sheikhdoms eventually decided to remain apart from the Trucial States, which formed the United Arab Emirates.

Relations with Sudan have become closer since the communist-inspired coup attempt there in July 1971, and President Nimeri visited Saudi Arabia in November 1971 and April 1972. Saudi Arabia also played an important role in attempting to bring about agreement between the Palestinian guerrillas and the Jordanian Government after the final confrontation between them in north Jordan in July 1971.

In 1972 and 1973 Faisal visited a large number of countries, including Morocco, Italy, Algeria, Tunisia, Egypt, France, Uganda, Chad, Senegal, Mauritania and Niger. The growing tension in the Gulf area generally was illustrated by an agreement with the U.S.A. in May 1973 for the supply of Phantom jets to Saudi Arabia, and the signing of a £250 million contract in June 1973 for British Aircraft Corporation to supply Saudi Arabia with air defence support systems. Saudi Arabia, however, warned the United States that she might be prepared to withhold oil supplies unless the U.S.A. changed her attitude in the Arab-Israeli dispute.

The warning was prophetic but went unheeded. When the Arab-Israeli war of October 1973 broke out, therefore, and when United States aid to Israel continued, Saudi Arabia, despite her traditionally good relationship with the West, led a movement by all the Arab oil-producing countries to exert political pressure by cuts in oil production. Since there was no immediate response from the U.S.A., OPEC members placed an embargo on oil supplies to that country and to several other developed western countries as well. Supplies to the western world were not cut off entirely, but it was announced that production would be progressively reduced until attitudes towards support for Israel changed. The Arab states having thus made clear the strength of their determination to achieve a Middle East settlement more favourable to the Palestinian cause, there then began, in the closing months of 1973 and the first months of 1974, a period of extremely active negotiating for a settlement that would mean more than simply an end to Arab-Israeli hostilities. On the one hand the western nations attempted to repair their links with the oil-producing countries; on the other hand these latter debated among themselves how far they should wield the "oil weapon" to achieve their ends.

As the possessor of 40 per cent of Middle East oil reserves, and one quarter of world reserves, Saudi Arabia, together with Egypt, was in the very forefront of these negotiations. It soon became apparent, however, that the Saudis held views that differed from those of other producer nations (notably Libya, Algeria and Iran) on the extent to which oil could be safely used to put pressure on the West. It was feared in Riyadh that too much of this pressure would have economic repercussions that nobody wanted. The more radical OPEC members wanted to retain the oil embargo until a satisfactory outcome to the October hostilities was reached. At a meeting in March 1974, though, Saudi Arabia pressed for a resumption of supplies to the U.S.A. and, when this was agreed, resisted any moves to increase oil prices, which, by January 1974, had risen to nearly four times the pre-hostilities level. It was reported that, in order to achieve their aim, the Saudis threatened to leave OPEC and lower prices unilaterally. Reluctantly, therefore, the radical OPEC members agreed to a freeze on oil prices.

Meanwhile, in negotiations with consumer countries, the Saudis made it clear that the continued supply of oil was dependent not only on a change in attitudes towards supporting Israel but on assistance to Saudi Arabia itself in industrializing and diversifying its economy against the day when oil reserves become depleted. The U.S.A. in particular showed itself eager to satisfy these conditions and an important economic and military co-operation agreement was signed in May 1974.

On March 25th, 1975, King Faisal was assassinated by one of his nephews, Prince Faisal ibn Masaed ibn Abdul Aziz. Although at first it was feared that the assassination was a deep-seated plot it soon became clear that the assassin, although not mentally deranged, had acted on his own. King Faisal was succeeded by his half-brother, Khalid, the Crown Prince, and Khalid's brother Prince Fahd became Crown Prince, retaining his post as Minister of the Interior. Prince Fahd also became First Deputy Prime Minister.

No major change of policy resulted from Khalid's succession. He quickly announced that Saudi Arabia would follow the late King Faisal's policies involving Islamic solidarity and the strengthening of Arab unity, and that the objectives remained "the recovery of occupied Arab territories" and the "liberation of the City of Jerusalem from the claws of Zionism". At a press interview in May 1975 King Khalid said that Saudi Arabia would concede Israel's right to exist in its pre-1967 borders in return for total Israeli withdrawal from Arab lands occupied in 1967 and the establishment of a Palestinian state between Israel and Jordan.

In March 1976 Saudi Arabia established diplomatic relations with the Yemen People's Democratic Republic. Although both countries have been ideological enemies since Aden achieved independence from Britain in 1967, both also were concerned about the presence of Iranian forces in Oman. A Saudi loan was made to the needy Yemen P.D.R. and it was expected that in return the Yemenis would abandon their support for the PFLO. The border conflict between the two Yemeni States has remained a source of concern to Saudi Arabia.

An indication of the growth in stature of Saudi Arabia in Arab affairs in recent years was the key role she played in October 1976 in bringing about the Riyadh summit—a meeting which was instrumental in ending the civil war in the Lebanon and also brought about reconciliation between Egypt and Syria. Saudi Arabia also asserted herself at the OPEC summit in Doha in December 1976 when she, along with the United Arab Emirates, showed herself firmly committed to only a 5 per cent increase in oil prices while the other OPEC countries insisted on a 10 per cent rise (*see* Economic Survey for further details).

Saudi Arabia has traditionally supported President Sadat of Egypt, fearing that his fall from power would result in Egypt's moving to the left. When Sadat visited Israel in November 1977 Saudi Arabia gave him discreet support in his peace initiative. This position, however, was abandoned following the signing of the Egyptian–Israeli treaty in the following spring. At the Arab Summit meeting held in April 1979 Saudi Arabia aligned itself with the "moderate" states in supporting the sanctions against Egypt which had been outlined at the Arab League meeting the previous November. In July 1979 the Saudi Government withdrew from its arms manufacturing consortium with Egypt.

In the spring of 1978 relations with the United States came under strain when there was some doubt whether the U.S. Senate would allow the purchase of 60 F-15 fighters (the U.S.'s most advanced military aircraft), by Saudi Arabia. In May, however, the deal eventually received the approval of the U.S. Senate. While relations with the United States have remained generally cordial, attempts are being made to broaden international contacts.

In domestic affairs the Saudi Government continues to allow social change to unfold organically and at a moderate pace, without using its huge wealth to force the pace, although the 1975–80 Five-Year Plan is certainly bringing about economic change. Because of the official belief in organic change, despite the great improvement in communications, welfare services and the standard of living in general over recent years, Saudi Arabia remains the most traditional and conservative of the Arab countries; the ancient restrictions on smoking, alcohol, dress, etc., have been continuously observed, as have the Muslim calendar and religious festivals.

ECONOMIC SURVEY

AREA AND POPULATION

The area of Saudi Arabia has been estimated at 830,000 square miles but the borders have not all been defined and therefore no precise figure can be arrived at. Estimates of the kingdom's population have been a subject of dispute for some years. An official estimate for January 1st, 1956, put the figure at 6,036,400. A census was held in 1962–63 but the results were officially repudiated. The UN Population Division estimated the mid-1965 population at 6,750,000 and projected figures of 7,740,000 for mid-1970 and 8,966,000 for mid-1975. Meanwhile, Saudi officials were still quoting figures of 5–6 million in 1975. A census was held in September 1974, a necessary preliminary to the ambitious second five-year development plan (1975–80), but even then the facts were not made clear. First reports put the census total for Saudis at 4.3 million. Later a figure of 7,012,642 was announced, though many observers still believe the lower figure to be more realistic. Half the population is thought to be urban by now, with the other half about equally divided between farmers clustered around oases and the Bedouin.

Foreigners working in Saudi Arabia number between 1.5 and 2 million, though the last official estimate put them at only 400,000. Most of them are Arabs from poorer states, such as Yemenis and Egyptians.

The population of Riyadh, the royal capital, was estimated at 667,000 in 1976 and that of Jeddah, the leading port and commercial centre, at 561,000. The other main towns are the holy cities of Mecca (367,000) and Medina (198,000), the east coast commercial centres, Al-Khobar and Dammam (combined population 176,000), two agricultural centres, Hofuf (150,000) and Haradh (100,000), the summer capital, Ta'if (100,000), Yanbu, Abha, Jizan, Dhahran and Ras Tanura.

AGRICULTURE

Agriculture contributed 0.9 per cent of G.D.P. in 1976/77 although it employs about half the population. Cultivation is confined to oases and to irrigated regions, comprising a mere 0.2 per cent of the total land area: the remaining agricultural land is used for low-grade grazing. The chief crops cultivated on irrigated or cultivated soil are wheat, lucerne, millet and maize, while fruits of many varieties, particularly dates, grow in abundance in oases. Production of wheat, which is, after dates, the second largest crop, provided only 25 per cent of requirements in 1972–73. Experiments with new wheat varieties, undertaken in collaboration with the FAO, have, however, shown that yield can be doubled. Sheep and goats are bred extensively, both for meat and for wool; camels are also bred.

The Government has recognized the importance of developing agriculture as a means of reducing the dependence on imported food, and as a means of diversifying the economy and of raising rural living standards. Since scarcity of water constitutes the chief factor limiting the development of agriculture, the Government has launched an ambitious programme to overcome this obstacle. Execution of this programme—which includes surveys for underground water resources, construction of dams, irrigation and drainage networks, combined with distribution of fallow land, settlement of Bedouin and the introduction of mechanization—is aimed at eventually raising agricultural production to the level of near self-sufficiency in food. Consequently, budgetary allocations for the agricultural sector have increased considerably in recent years and the second five-year plan (1975–80) projects spending on agriculture at 4,000 million riyals and on water (mainly desalination plants) at no less than 34,000 million. During the second plan, irrigated farm land is to be expanded by 50,000 hectares over its present area of 121,000 hectares, though success in reaching this target will largely depend on studies on the development of water resources.

During the 1960s, surveys were carried out over 393,800 square miles—45 per cent of the total area of the country—on behalf of the Government by foreign consulting firms. The reports indicated a large potential for considerably increasing agricultural production in nearly all areas under cultivation by improving water distribution and drainage systems. Four other important projects which have been undertaken by the Government include the al-Hasa irrigation scheme, the Faisal Model Settlement scheme, the Wadi Jizan dam project and the Abha dam.

The al-Hasa irrigation and drainage scheme, inaugurated in December 1971, was completed over five years at a cost of 260 million riyals and will result in the reclamation of 12,000 hectares. It is the country's biggest agricultural scheme and about 50,000 persons will benefit from it. The Faisal Model Settlement scheme, which cost 100 million riyals, has involved extensive land reclamation and irrigation and has provided permanent farmland and housing for 1,000 Bedouin families. The Wadi Jizan dam, which was inaugurated in March 1971, has a reservoir with a capacity of 71 million cubic metres of water and was built at a cost of 42 million riyals. It constitutes the first stage in a plan for development of Wadi Jizan which will increase the irrigated area by 8,000 hectares and will contribute about 8.8 million riyals annually to agricultural and livestock production. A second dam, due for completion in 1980, will add a further 68 million cubic metres to water storage capacity in the Jizan-Najran area. The Abha dam in the Asir region was opened in April 1974 with a reservoir capacity of 2.4 million cubic metres.

During the 1975–80 plan, seawater desalination capacity will be increased from 13 million gallons per day to 145 million gallons per day. Eight desalination plants will be built, seven will be expanded for a second time and five for a third time. By 1980 there should be 27 plants in the kingdom.

Government encouragement to farmers is substantial. Interest-free loans are available through the Agricultural Bank, set up in 1963, and chemical fertilizer, domestic or imported, is distributed at half-price. There are also large subsidies or incentives for irrigation pumps, farm machinery or imported rearing stock.

PETROLEUM

The most important industry in Saudi Arabia is the production of crude petroleum and petroleum products. Saudi Arabia is the biggest oil producer within OPEC, with almost 30 per cent of the organization's output, and is the second or third biggest producer in the world (its rank varies with fluctuations in production), with about 15 per cent of world output. Saudi proven reserves were given as 165,700 million barrels at January 1st, 1979, allowing 55 more years of production at 1978 levels.

In 1933 a Saudi concession was granted to Standard Oil Company of California to explore for oil. The operating company, the Arabian American Oil Company (Aramco), began explorations for oil in 1933 and was soon drilling. It discovered oil in commercial quantities in 1938. By the end of the Second World War it had discovered four oil fields and had established the necessary facilities, including a large refinery, to meet post-war demands for crude oil and refined products.

At the end of 1977, Aramco's proven reserves of crude oil were estimated to be 110,443 million barrels. Probable reserves are estimated at 177,500 million barrels. Production comes from fourteen major oilfields: Ghawar, Abqaiq, Safaniya, Berri, Abu

Hadriya, Abu Sa'fah, Qatif, Fadhili, Manifa, Khursaniyah, Dammam, Marjan, Zuluf and Khurais. Of these the four first-named are by far the most important. Ghawar is generally accepted as the world's largest oilfield and Safaniya is the world's largest offshore field. Production mounted steadily each year from 1956 to reach 2,996 million barrels in 1974 but fell steadily from the average 8.2 million barrels per day in 1974 to an average of 6.8 million b/d in 1975. The recovery of 1976 continued into 1977 when the 10 million b/d mark was passed early in the year as the kingdom endeavoured to raise production sufficiently to force down prices charged by the majority of OPEC, but Aramco's final production rate in 1977 was 9.1 million b/d (3,291 million barrels)—still a record nevertheless. Eleven OPEC members decided at the December 1976 OPEC conference in Qatar to raise their prices by 10 per cent from January 1st, 1977, and a further 5 per cent from July 1st. Saudi Arabia and the U.A.E. decided to put up their prices by only 5 per cent for the whole of 1977, and Saudi Arabia announced that it would step up its production to try to enforce its will. However, a compromise had been reached by the time the OPEC conference convened in Stockholm in July 1977, and Saudi Arabia and the U.A.E. raised their prices 5 per cent, while the rest of OPEC forwent their proposed extra 5 per cent increase. From 1975 onwards, Saudi Arabia has consistently pursued a moderate line on price increases and has opposed moves within OPEC to co-ordinate members' production programmes. In the plentiful world supply conditions of the first three quarters of 1978, Saudi Arabia limited its production, but again increased its output between December 1978 and April 1979 to help offset the Iranian export shortfall. This was again reduced when Iranian shipments were resumed. At the OPEC conference in June 1979, Saudi Arabia was joined by Qatar and the U.A.E. in imposing a lower scale of price increases than other OPEC members. In July 1979 Saudi Arabia announced that production would again be temporarily increased, although the amount involved was not initially specified. It was understood that the additional revenue was needed to fund the final stages of the second five-year development plan (1975–80). (*See* also Oil in the Middle East and North Africa.) The Ras Tanura refinery on the Gulf, which was completed in 1945, had an average throughput of 376,934 b/d in 1975.

A 30/31-inch pipeline system, 1,068 miles long, runs from Aramco's oil fields to the Mediterranean port of Sidon, Lebanon. It was brought into operation in 1950 and by 1958 its capacity was 470,000 barrels per day. It is operated by the affiliated Trans-Arabian Pipe Line Company (Tapline).

The area of Aramco's original concession was about 673,000 square miles. The company has, however, agreed to relinquish progressively parts of its concession areas. Following relinquishments in 1960, 1963, 1968 and 1973, its concession has been reduced to 85,000 square miles.

In 1949 the Saudi Arabian government granted the Getty Oil Corporation a 60-year exclusive concession covering its undivided half interest in the Saudi Arabian-Kuwait Neutral Zone, now called the Partitioned Zone. Getty's production in 1977 amounted to 32 million barrels. In 1969 Japanese interests, which had obtained concessions from Saudi Arabia and Kuwait in 1957 and 1958 covering an offshore area of the neutral zone of the Gulf, found oil which is now being exploited by the Arabian Oil Co. Production in 1977 was 34.8 million barrels, compared with 55.7 million barrels in 1976.

In 1965 the French state company Auxerap concluded an agreement for offshore exploration in the Red Sea. The agreement provided for the Saudi Arabian state organization Petromin (General Petroleum and Mineral Organization) to participate in exploitation of any commercial discoveries. In December 1967 two further agreements were signed. One was between Petromin and the Italian state oil corporation, Agip, and Phillips Petroleum of the U.S., by which the latter two firms were permitted to explore for oil during a period of six years in some 77,000 square km. of the Rub'al-Khali and 9,600 square km. in the Eastern Province. This concession was relinquished in 1973. The other was between Petromin and a group led by two American corporations, Sun Oil Co. and Natomas, under which the group was granted similar rights in the Red Sea area. In both cases the prospecting concerns were to act as contractors for Petromin which retained the legal title to the concessions.

Revenues from oil rose steadily throughout the 1960s, from $334 million in 1960 to $949 million in 1969. This process accelerated at the beginning of the next decade, however, and the Saudi Government received $1,885 million in 1971 and $2,734 million in 1972. By far the largest proportion of this sum derived from one company, Aramco, which contributed $2,633 million in 1972. As a result of a participation agreement, effective from January 1973, the Government acquired a 25 per cent share in Aramco, which was scheduled to rise to a controlling interest by 1982. But following the Arab-Israeli war oil prices were pushed up drastically, and the Arab oil-producing countries in general made moves to acquire controlling shares in the oil companies. The Saudi Government waited until June 1974 before following the example of other governments and acquiring a 60 per cent interest in Aramco, backdated to January of that year. Negotiations on a full Saudi takeover of Aramco were being finalized in 1979. As a result of these developments revenues from oil have risen dramatically. Total oil revenue in 1977 reached U.S. $38,000 million, but fell to $36,700 million in 1978.

RELATED AND MANUFACTURING INDUSTRIES

The development of modern industry is at an early stage, and most of the kingdom's manufacturing is geared to the local market—building materials, some consumer products and some oil-related activities. The big local enterprises are the Ras Tanura oil refinery, three private-sector cement plants, and several Petromin projects (*see* below). The smaller industries include cement and plastic pipes; brick, marble and tile; furniture; cotton textile and carpet mills; a shoe factory; detergent, paint and chemical plants; and food processing and soft drink industries.

In terms of output, construction has been the most important industry after oil in recent years, contributing around 12.6 per cent to G.D.P. at current prices in 1976/77.

The chief instrument of industrial development has been Petromin, set up in 1962 to implement the long-run objective of diversifying the economy through the establishment of industries based on hydrocarbons and other minerals. But the Ministry of Industry and Electricity was set up in October 1975 to take overall control of industrial development, and responsibility for all Petromin's interests outside oil in the narrowest sense is being transferred to the new ministry. The ministry has set up a 10,000 million riyal Saudi Arabian Basic Industries Corporation (SABIC) to run all the heavy industrial projects. Existing industrial projects include a steel rolling mill in Jeddah which produces reinforcing bars. This started production in 1968 with an annual capacity of 45,000 tons, which will eventually be expanded to 300,000 tons. Petromin set up an oil refinery in Jeddah, which came on stream in 1968 with a capacity of 12,000 barrels per day, since raised to 45,000 barrels a day, and a lubricating oil plant. Petromin also had a 51 per cent holding in the Saudi Arabian Fertilizer Company (SAFCO), whose plant at Dammam started producing fertilizer and sulphuric acid in 1969.

The big oil price increase of late 1973 made much more ambitious industrialization programmes possible, and in the second five-year plan investment in industrial projects in the Eastern Region will amount to SR 37,800 million ($10,900 million) and in the Western Region SR 10,800 million ($3,100 million). The nucleus of the plans for the Eastern Region is the gas gathering, treatment and distribution plant, announced in March 1974 and contracted to Aramco in March 1975. Originally costs were put at $4,500 million. By 1976 they had risen to $16,000 million. The plant will be designed to handle around 6,000 million cubic feet of gas a day, corresponding to an oil production level of 12 million b/d, and will produce around 12 million tons a year of natural gas liquids (NGL), of which Saudi Arabia expects to become the world's biggest exporter. At the end of 1977, gas reserves were estimated at 85,000,0000 million cubic feet. The gas plant will feed petrochemical and industrial ventures, power an electricity network and supply Aramco's operations.

Pipeline projects within the framework of the second five-year plan are a crude line from the eastern fields to Yanbo on the Red Sea, a gas liquids line along the same route to allow the export of NGL from Yanbo, and a 500,000-b/d spur line from Tapline to the Red Sea port of Duba.

SABIC plans three export refineries, with an initial capacity of 750,000 b/d, rising to 1.5 million b/d. Two of these will be in the east and one in the west. Shell is to build one at Jubail on the east coast, and Mobil is at an advanced stage of negotiation to build one at Yanbo. The third is likely to be built by either Mitsubishi or Gulf. The first large industrial project to be completed within the framework of the five-year plan—a lubricating oil refinery with an initial capacity of 1 million barrels per year—was officially opened in Jeddah in March 1978.

There are to be three petrochemical complexes in the east and one in the west, as well as two or three fertilizer plants. A West German firm is to build a direct-reduction steel plant at Jubail, but final agreement on the project is awaited.

The only minerals, apart from hydrocarbons, being produced at present are limestone (for cement production), gypsum, marble, clay and salt. Substantial iron ore deposits are known to exist, as well as copper, gold, lead, zinc, silver and some uranium. The British Steel Corporation is evaluating a 350 million tonne iron ore deposit in a remote part of the kingdom and other British and foreign firms are studying or prospecting for phosphorite and other minerals.

Industrial projects which are joint ventures between foreign companies and Saudi interests include an assembly plant for Mercedes trucks, which began operating in April 1978, and a steel-pipe plant.

TRANSPORT

Until 1964 the only surfaced roads, besides those in the oil network, were in the Jeddah-Mecca-Medina area. Since then roads have been given priority with 20 per cent of the development budget. There are now over 7,000 miles of asphalted roads, and over 8,000 miles of new surfaced roads are planned for the period 1975–80.

There are three chief ports: Jeddah and Yanbu on the Red Sea and Dammam on the Gulf. These ports have been undergoing expansion and improvement in recent years. Jeddah, for example, has been modernized with the construction of nine new piers at a cost of about 273 million riyals. Projects are in hand for the development of Jizan and Jubail ports and for a completely new and separate $1,100 million industrial port at Jubail. Major projects include the expansion of the annual capacities of Jeddah and Dammam ports to about two million tons each.

The chief international airports are Jeddah, Dhahran and Riyadh. Although both Jeddah and Riyadh have been considerably improved in recent years, schemes are under way for the expansion of Riyadh and the building of a new airport to the north of Jeddah at a total cost of SR 750 million and SR 1,045 million respectively. Medina and Bisha airports are being improved and new airports have been built at Abha, Hayil and Badanah and other new airports are planned at Tayif, Turayf, Al Khafji and Al Qurayat. The Government operates the airline, Saudia, which links important Saudi cities, with regular flights to many foreign countries. The airline carried 3.4 million passengers in 1977.

The Government operates a single track railway connecting the port of Dammam on the Gulf with Riyadh, the capital, some 370 miles inland. A Saudi-Syrian-Jordanian technical committee is studying the feasibility of reconstructing the historic Hijaz railway from Damascus to Medina.

A causeway linking Bahrain with the Saudi mainland is to be built at a cost of almost $1,000 million. The Saudi Government is to foot the entire bill. Design work is well advanced and construction is scheduled to start in mid-1980.

FOREIGN TRADE

According to data compiled by the International Monetary Fund, the total value of the country's exports, which consist almost entirely of oil, amounted to $27,996 million in 1975, $36,437 million in 1976 and $41,210 million in 1977. The value of exports fell in 1978 to $37,935 million. Western Europe is the major market for Saudi oil and accounted for 39.5 per cent of total exports in 1977, with 33.0 per cent going to EEC countries, mainly France (9.6 per cent) and Italy (7.3 per cent). Exports to Asia were 34.5 per cent of the total, with 19.0 per cent going to Japan. In 1977 there was a sharp increase in exports to the U.S.A., which took 9.5 per cent of the total. Other important sources of foreign exchange derive from the local expenditure of Aramco and from the Pilgrimage traffic.

The value of Saudi Arabia's imports has increased steadily in recent years, rising from $4,214 million in 1975 to $8,695 million in 1976, $14,656 million in 1977 and $24,148 million in 1978. Imports cover a wide range of manufactured goods, particularly machinery and transport equipment (accounting for 40 per cent of total imports in 1977). Other significant imports are base metals, foodstuffs and textiles. The pattern of imports reflects the Saudi development effort and the country's poor agricultural resources. The U.S.A. has been the leading exporter to Saudi Arabia in recent years, accounting for 18.6 per cent of Saudi imports in 1977, followed by Japan (11.6 per cent), the Federal Republic of Germany (8.4 per cent), the United Kingdom (6.2 per cent) and Italy (6.1 per cent).

Saudi Arabia had a deficit on current account in 1968 and 1969 but there has since been a surplus each year, reaching a peak of $23,007 million in 1974, compared with $2,203 million in 1973. The current account surplus for 1977 was $12,793 million but this could fall to about $5,000 million by 1980, according to Morgan Guaranty Trust Company estimates, even allowing for net investment income flows which will reach about $4,000 million per year by then.

FINANCE

The currency is described in the Statistical Survey. Since mid-1977, and particularly since July 1978, the Saudi Arabian Monetary Agency (SAMA) has made a series of frequent small adjustments in the exchange rate against the U.S. dollar. By June 1979 the rate was $1 = 3.395 riyals, an overall revaluation of 4 per cent since mid-1977. From June 1st, 1978, the Saudi riyal was included in the "basket" of 16 currencies which determine the value of the International Monetary Fund's Special Drawing Right (SDR). SAMA, established in 1952, is the central bank, its total holdings of gold, foreign currencies and other international reserve assets standing at $30,034 million at the end of 1977. This compared with $23,319 million at the end of 1975, $14,285 million at the end of 1974 and only $3,877 million at the end of 1973. At the end of 1977 Saudi reserves were surpassed only by those of West Germany. From April 1978 Saudi Arabia's reserves were redefined to exclude foreign exchange cover against the note issue, then about $5,300 million. Under the new definition, reserves at December 1978 were $19,407 million.

There are 12 commercial banks in Saudi Arabia—two wholly Saudi, eight wholly foreign and two joint-ventures. The biggest Saudi commercial bank is the National Commercial Bank and the fastest-growing the Riyad Bank, both with headquarters in Jeddah. The foreign banks are the British Bank of the Middle East, Citibank, Banque du Liban et d'Outre Mer, Arab Bank, Banque du Caire, Banque de l'Indochine et de Suez, United Bank and Bank Melli Iran. The Bank al-Jazira was the National Bank of Pakistan until it underwent "Saudization" in 1975, taking in 65 per cent Saudi participation. Algemene Bank Nederland was "Saudi-ized" in 1977, becoming Al-Bank al-Saudi al-Hollandi, with the Dutch retaining a 40 per cent shareholding. The Government gave the other foreign banks a deadline of June 1978 to complete the same process and by September the change-over had been virtually completed.

The major Saudi source of project finance is the Saudi Industrial Development Fund, set up by the Government in 1974 and in full operation by early 1975. It grants loans carrying only 2 per cent for up to 50 per cent of the total cost of a project (up to 80 per cent in the case of electricity projects). The SIDF is managed by Chase Manhattan Bank.

The other main state financial institution to aid development (and another recent creation) is the Real Estate Development Fund, whose capital has been raised successively from 250 million riyals to 23,800 million riyals. The REDF lends interest-free for up to 70 per cent of the total cost of building homes or other types of accommodation. By contrast, the Agricultural Bank, set up as long ago as 1964, still only benefits a very small proportion of farmers. The Saudi Credit Bank was set up in 1973 to advance interest-free loans to low-income Saudis for purposes such as getting married or carrying out home repairs.

The Saudi Investment Banking Corporation, in which Chase Manhattan Bank has a 20 per cent stake, opened in 1977.

Saudi banks have recently become slightly more outward-looking. The most obvious example of this is the 55 per cent Saudi-owned Saudi International Bank which opened as a fully-fledged merchant bank in London in March 1976. SAMA holds 50 per cent and National Commercial Bank and Riyad Bank 2.5 per cent each. The biggest non-Saudi partner is Morgan Guaranty Trust Company, which also provides management. The other shares are held by leading Western and Japanese banks. The first wholly private Saudi bank abroad—Al Saudi Banque—opened in Paris in the autumn of 1976. Riyad Bank has a share in the Paris-based Union de Banques Arabes et Françaises, and in the Gulf Riyad Bank in Bahrain. The NCB has small stakes in the European-Arab Holding and the Compagnie Arabe et Internationale d'Investissement, both based in Luxembourg, and in the Amman-based Arab-Jordanian Investment Bank, which opened in the spring of 1978.

INVESTMENT

SAMA is also the kingdom's investment authority, responsible for looking after the vast foreign assets of some $61,500 million at the end of November 1977. Of the total of $52,000 million assets at the end of 1976, $27,000 million was reserves and $25,000 million "SAMA Investments", according to the IMF's *International Financial Statistics*. Most of this money is held in the U.S.A. and Europe. Though SAMA has been of late investing more long-term, the vast bulk of its assets are still thought to be liquid. One estimate in mid-1977 was that $17,500 million of the SAMA Investments were probably highly liquid, about $4,000 million were bonds and about $3,500 million were private placements with country or "triple-A" company borrowers. Very little official Saudi money goes into equities and almost nothing into property Big Western banks seem to be the main beneficiaries of the vast funds at SAMA's disposal, and SAMA's investment department is advised by a small team seconded from London merchant bankers Barings and the U.S. investment bank White Weld.

AID

In 1976 Saudi Arabia committed $2,803 million in concessional aid and disbursed $2,316 million, equivalent to 5.77 per cent of its gross national product, according to the OECD. The commitment for 1976 compares with $2,790 million in 1975, $1,288 million in 1974 and $568 million in 1973; the disbursement in 1976 contrasts with $1,997 million in 1975, $1,029 million in 1974 and $305 million in 1973. Most Saudi aid goes to Arab states, especially the frontline ones, and other Muslim states, notably Pakistan. Saudi Arabia pledged $1,000 million in aid to Africa at the 1977 Afro-Arab summit. Saudi contributions to the frontline states after 1967 amounted to $188 million per year; from the 1974 Rabat Arab summit $1,000 million per year. The country has generally been the biggest contributor to the various Arab funds set up to help poor Arab and poor African states, as well as to the IMF oil facilities (1,000 million SDRs in 1974 and 1,250 million SDRs in 1975). It has also lent the World Bank at commercial rates a total of $890.8 million, $750 million in the biggest ever borrowing by the Bank. The Saudi Fund for Development, set up in 1974, makes "soft" loans to Africa, Asia and Latin America, as well as to the Arab world.

BUDGET AND ECONOMIC DEVELOPMENT PLAN

Oil revenues traditionally provide over 90 per cent of the state's budget revenue. In the 1975/76 Saudi financial year expenditure notionally exceeded revenue for the first time in years. In fact, SAMA has admitted, its actual revenues that year were 101,170 million riyals, compared with the 95,840 million budgeted, and its actual expenditure 77,480 million riyals, compared with the budgeted 110,935 million. However, the amount actually spent was a long way ahead of the previous fiscal year, when expenditure totalled only 35,000 million riyals, even though revenue was still about the same at 100,100 million. For 1976/77, expenditure has been fixed at exactly the same as the previous year, 110,935 million riyals, with revenue projected at the same amount. Project expenditure at 74,430 million is also nearly the same as for 1975/76, despite some cutbacks and delays in development schemes. Expenditure was maintained at the same level in 1977/78, but in 1978/79 expenditure rose to 147,400 million riyals, exceeding revenue by 14,530 million riyals. For 1979/80 revenue and expenditure were projected to balance at 160,000 million riyals. The biggest items of expenditure are defence and internal security, which accounted for 35 per cent of the 1979/80 allocations.

Saudi Arabia ran a budget deficit in 1969/70, but bigger and bigger budget surpluses at the end of each financial year led the Government to budget in 1974/75 for a surplus for the first time—a massive 52,504 million riyals. There was a return to deficit financing in the 1977/78 and 1978/79 budgets, however, and the 1979/80 budget, which was the last of the second five-year development plan, reflected government intentions of cutting public expenditure.

The second five-year development plan (1975–80) provides for expenditure of no less than 498,000 million riyals (about $142,000 million). Described by the Saudi Minister of Planning, Hisham Nazer, as an "experiment in social transformation", the plan aims at raising G.D.P. by 114 per cent from 148,000 million riyals to 318,000 million riyals, and to reduce the proportion of G.D.P. accounted for by oil from about 86 per cent to 82 per cent.

Sixty-three per cent of the plan total (314,000 million riyals) has been allocated to economic and social development, 18 per cent (89,600 million riyals) to defence, 8 per cent (39,800 million riyals) to administration and 11 per cent (54,700 million riyals) to other items, including foreign aid. Within the economic and social sector, education has been given 23 per cent (114,500 million riyals) of the total plan expenditure.

The plan aims to create two industrial "poles" around Jubail on the Gulf coast and Yanbo on the Red Sea coast. Several oil refineries, petrochemical complexes and fertilizer plants are planned at both places, and an iron and steel complex at Jubail. Cross-country oil and gas lines will link Yanbo with the Eastern oilfields and make its development possible. Desalination plants, 100,000 houses, schools, thousands of miles of roads, etc., are also projected.

Three years after the plan started in July 1975, the problems that the Planning Ministry and its advisers from the Stanford Research Institute foresaw have perhaps proved greater than was expected. Port congestion, manpower shortages, lack of supplies of basic materials and equipment and inflation have introduced some nightmarish qualities into the Saudi boom. But the Government is determined to press on and try to meet its ambitious targets, rescheduling some of the bigger projects to give an even bigger boost to the main hindrance to rapid development—physical infrastructure. This has involved extending the plan period to seven years, in practice, and admitting that investments will probably reach $200,000 million.

A third development plan has been in preparation since 1978. It is expected to continue to emphasize primary industry, and the expansion of import substitution, particularly in the agricultural sphere. It is also likely that the plan will promote the development of the private sector and the lessening of domestic economic dependence on government spending.

STATISTICAL SURVEY

AREA AND POPULATION

Area (estimated)	Population (September 1974)
830,000 sq. miles*	7,012,642

* 2,149,690 square kilometres.

PRINCIPAL TOWNS
(estimated population in 1976)

Riyadh (royal capital)	667,000
Jeddah (administrative capital)	561,000
Mecca	367,000
Medina	198,000
Dammam }	176,000
Al-Khobar }	

SAUDI ARABIA-IRAQ NEUTRAL ZONE

The Najdi (Saudi Arabian) frontier with Iraq was defined in the Treaty of Mohammara in May 1922. Later a Neutral Zone of 7,044 sq. km. was established adjacent to the western tip of the Kuwait frontier. No military or permanent buildings were to be erected in the zone and the nomads of both countries were to have unimpeded access to its pastures and wells. A further agreement concerning the administration of this zone was signed between Iraq and Saudi Arabia in May 1938. In July 1975 Iraq and Saudi Arabia signed an agreement providing for an equal division of the diamond-shaped zone between the two countries, with the border following a straight line through the zone.

SAUDI ARABIA-KUWAIT PARTITIONED ZONE

A Convention signed at Uqair in December 1922 fixed the Najdi (Saudi Arabian) boundary with Kuwait. The Convention also established a Neutral Zone of 5,770 sq. km. immediately to the south of Kuwait in which Saudi Arabia and Kuwait held equal rights. The final agreement on this matter was signed in 1963. Since 1966 the Zone has been divided between the two countries and each administers its own half, in practice as an integral part of the state. However, the oil wealth of the whole Zone remains undivided and production from the on-shore oil concessions in the Partitioned Zone is shared equally between the two states' concessionaires (Aminoil and Getty).

Births and Deaths: Average annual birth rate 50.0 per 1,000 in 1965–70, 49.5 per 1,000 in 1970–75; death rate 22.7 per 1,000 in 1965–70, 20.2 per 1,000 in 1970–75 (UN estimates).

AGRICULTURE

PRINCIPAL CROPS

('000 metric tons)

	1975	1976	1977
Wheat	132	93	135*
Barley	17	12	15*
Millet	11	7	10
Sorghum	128	67	86
Sesame seed	n.a.	1*	1*
Tomatoes	301	305*	310*
Onions (dry)	50	50*	50*
Grapes	61	68	70*
Dates	262*	262*	265*
Oranges	20	20*	20*

* FAO estimate.

Source: FAO, *Production Yearbook.*

LIVESTOCK

(FAO estimates, '000 head, year ending September)

	1975	1976	1977
Cattle	180	170	170
Sheep	1,350	1,380	1,410
Goats	765	770	775
Asses	102	103	103
Camels	602	610	620
Chickens	9,200	9,300	9,800

Source: FAO, *Production Yearbook.*

LIVESTOCK PRODUCTS

(FAO estimates, '000 metric tons)

	1975	1976	1977
Beef and veal	11	11	12
Mutton and lamb	19	20	21
Goats' meat	13	13	13
Poultry meat	13	14	14
Other meat	20	20	21
Cows' milk	33	34	34
Sheep's milk	56	57	59
Goats' milk	39	39	40
Hen eggs	11.6	14.9	19.3

Source: FAO, *Production Yearbook.*

SEA FISHING

('000 metric tons, live weight)

	1972	1973	1974	1975*	1976	1977
Marine fishes	18.7	20.3	20.3*	20.0	18.5	16.8
Shrimps and prawns	5.1	6.1	3.3	3.0	4.8	1.6
TOTAL CATCH	23.8	26.4	23.6	23.0	23.3	18.4

*FAO estimate.

Source: FAO, *Yearbook of Fishery Statistics.*

MINING*

	1972	1973	1974	1975	1976	1977
Crude petroleum ('000 metric tons)	300,198	377,788	422,705	352,394	425,804	457,100
Natural gas (million cubic metres)†	2,806	4,531	6,201	6,330	8,261	9,442

1979: Crude petroleum: 410.3 million metric tons.

* Including half the total output of the Partitioned Zone, shared with Kuwait.

† *Source:* OPEC, *Annual Statistical Bulletin.* Figures from 1973 onwards are estimates.

CRUDE OIL PRODUCTION BY COMPANY
(million barrels)

	Total	Aramco	Getty Oil	Arabian Oil
1938	0.5	0.5	—	—
1946	59.9	59.9	—	—
1955	356.6	352.2	4.4	—
1970	1,386.3	1,295.3	28.3	62.7
1971	1,740.8	1,641.6	33.7	65.5
1972	2,201.7	2,098.4	28.3	75.0
1973	2,772.7	2,677.4	23.4	71.9
1974	3,095.1	2,996.5	29.8	68.7
1975	2,582.5	2,491.8	31.2	59.5
1976	3,139.3	3,053.9	29.7	55.7
1977	3,358.0	3,291.2	32.0	34.8

Source: SAMA, *Statistical Summary.*

OIL REVENUES BY SOURCE
(U.S. $ million)

	Total	Aramco	Getty Oil	Arabian Oil	Other Companies
1939	3.2	3.2	—	—	—
1946	10.4	10.4	—	—	—
1955	340.8	338.2	2.6	—	—
1970	1,214.0	1,148.4	17.2	40.3	3.8
1971	1,884.9	1,806.4	20.6	44.2	13.7
1972	2,744.6	2,643.2	28.0	68.7	4.7
1973	4,340.0	4,195.0	22.0	91.4	31.7
1974	22,573.5	2,375.0	53.3	113.6	31.6
1975	25,676.2	24,838.6	191.1	642.7	3.8
1976	30,747.5	29,937.3	247.6	559.2	3.3
1977	36,538.2	35,701.9	263.4	571.6	1.2

Source: SAMA, *Statistical Summary.*

INDUSTRY

SELECTED PRODUCTS

		1973	1974	1975	1976
Nitrogenous fertilizers	'000 metric tons	69	61	81	87
Liquefied petroleum gas*	" " "	2,200	3,255	3,410	4,030
Motor spirit (petrol)†	" " "	5,644	5,555	5,202	6,548
Kerosene	" " "	715	957	1,137	1,098
Jet fuel	" " "	1,696	1,008	462	559
Distillate fuel oils	" " "	3,769	3,847	3,448	3,723
Residual fuel oil	" " "	17,217	16,048	13,137	15,790
Petroleum bitumen (asphalt)	" " "	259	322	408	840
Quicklime	" " "	12	12	11	n.a.
Cement	" " "	964	1,056	1,140	1,104
Electric energy‡	million kWh	1,164	1,220	2,000	2,250

* Estimated production from natural gas processing plants. † Including naphtha.

‡ Public sector only, excluding industrial establishments generating electricity primarily for their own use.

1977 ('000 metric tons): Motor spirit and naphtha 6,630; Kerosene and jet fuel 1,346; Distillate fuel oils 3,707; Residual fuel oil 14,087.

Source: UN, mainly *Statistical Yearbook*.

FINANCE

100 halalah = 20 qursh = 1 Saudi riyal (SR).

Coins: 1, 5, 10, 25 and 50 halalah; 1, 2 and 4 qursh.*

Notes: 1, 5, 10, 50 and 100 riyals.

Exchange rates (June 1979): £1 sterling = 7.024 Saudi riyals; U.S. $1 = 3.395 Saudi riyals.

100 Saudi riyals = £14.24 = $29.46.

* The coins of 1, 2 and 4 qursh are being gradually withdrawn from circulation.

Note: Prior to January 1960 the prevailing exchange rate was U.S. $1 = 3.75 Saudi riyals (1 riyal = 26.67 U.S. cents). From January 1960 to August 1971 the exchange rate was $1 = 4.50 riyals (1 riyal = 22.22 U.S. cents). Between December 1971 and February 1973 the rate was $1 = 4.145 riyals (1 riyal = 24.13 U.S. cents). It was $1 = 3.730 riyals (1 riyal = 26.81 U.S. cents) from February to August 1973; and $1 = 3.55 riyals (1 riyal = 28.17 U.S. cents) from August 1973 to March 1975, when the riyal's direct link with the dollar was ended and the currency was valued in terms of the IMF Special Drawing Right (based on a weighted "basket" of 16 national currencies since July 1974), with a mid-point of 1 SDR = 4.28255 riyals. Wide fluctuations around this are allowed in order to permit a fixed rate against the U.S. dollar for extended periods of time. From August 1975 to July 1977 the rate was $1 = 3.53 riyals. The average exchange rate (riyals per U.S. dollar) was: 3.518 in 1975; 3.525 in 1977. Since July 1978 there have been frequent small adjustments in the riyal-dollar rate. The average rate in 1978 was $1 = 3.400 riyals. In terms of sterling, the exchange rate between November 1967 and June 1972 was £1 = 10.80 riyals.

BUDGET ESTIMATES

(million riyals, July 1st to June 30th)

Revenue	1977/78	1978/79	Expenditure	1977/78	1978/79
Oil royalties	31,817	27,042	Council of Ministers	6,508*	9,147*
Income tax (incl. tax on oil receipts)	99,337	89,492	Municipal and rural affairs	1,703	2,300
Customs	1,000	1,400	Defence and aviation	5,135	6,088
Other items	14,339	12,066	Interior	4,692	5,699
			Labour and social affairs	2,185	1,838
			Health	1,626	2,185
			Education	7,212	10,099
			Communications	719	969
			Agriculture and water resources	676	1,086
			Subsidies	3,829	3,982
			Projects expenditure (*see* below)	74,866	83,048
Total	146,493	130,000	Total (incl. others)	111,400	130,000

* Includes foreign aid.

PROJECTS BUDGET
(planned expenditure in million riyals)

	1975/76	1976/77	1977/78	1978/79
Council of Ministers	4,761.8	4,756.9	4,924.5	4,399.4
Municipal and rural affairs	13,221.6	14,758.0	11,681.3	7,966.8
Public works and housing	185.7	9,061.4	7,856.8	5,649.4
Information	636.7	959.8	1,064.0	723.5
Civil aviation	4,469.9	4,469.9	4,370.0	3,912.8
Interior	2,301.3	3,078.9	3,293.4	3,330.5
Labour and social affairs	1,408.5	2,040.8	2,237.0	1,452.3
Health	2,061.6	1,737.0	1,758.3	1,855.0
Education	6,355.1	6,367.6	7,955.3	5,123.1
Communications	10,994.2	15,380.7	7,822.5	7,377.0
Finance and national economy	7,030.1	3,984.8	3,754.3	3,309.5
Industry, electricity and commerce	586.7	1,081.0	488.0	337.3
Agriculture and water resources	1,718.0	1,721.4	1,511.4	1,854.4
Public investment fund	1,600.0	—	—	4,000.0
Other	17,047.8	25,396.3	39,022.7	50,433.0
Less: Earmarked expenditure	—	−20,361.1	−22,853.5	−18,676.3
TOTAL	74,379.0	74,433.4	74,866.0	83,047.7

FIVE YEAR PLAN—1975–80
(proposed expenditure in million riyals)

Water and desalination	34,065
Agriculture	4,685
Electricity	6,240
Manufacturing and minerals	45,058
Education	74,161
Health	17,302
Social Programmes and youth welfare	14,649
Road, ports and railroads	21,283
Civil Aviation	14,845
Telecommunications and post	4,225
Municipalities	53,328
Housing	14,263
Holy Cities and the Hajj	5,000
Other Development	9,312
TOTAL DEVELOPMENT	318,416
Defence	78,157
General Administration	38,179
Funds	63,478
SUB-TOTAL OTHER	179,814
TOTAL PLAN	498,230

INTERNATIONAL RESERVES*
(U.S. $ million in December each year)

	1972	1973	1974	1975	1976	1977	1978
Gold	117	130	132	126	125	131	207
Reserve position in IMF	36	40	729	1,838	2,563	2,691	2,470
Foreign exchange	2,347	3,707	13,424	21,355	24,337	27,212	16,730
TOTAL	2,500	3,877	14,285	23,319	27,025	30,034	19,407

*From April 1978 reserves were redefined to exclude the foreign exchange cover against the note issue (then about $5,300 million).

Source: IMF, *International Financial Statistics.*

NATIONAL ACCOUNTS

(million riyals at current prices, twelve months ending June 30th)

Gross Domestic Product by Economic Activity

	1972/73	1973/74	1974/75	1975/76
Agriculture, Forestry, Fishing	1,139	1,242	1,392	1,586
Mining and Quarrying:				
Crude petroleum and natural gas	26,284	78,345	104,696	109,560
Other	90	146	248	576
Manufacturing:				
Petroleum refining	1,811	4,347	5,766	5,962
Other	617	730	931	1,191
Electricity, Gas and Water	319	328	318	342
Construction	1,809	2,720	4,949	11,522
Wholesale and Retail Trade, Restaurants and Hotels	1,554	2,355	3,045	4,642
Transport, Storage and Communication	2,121	2,718	3,946	5,776
Finance, Insurance, Real Estate, Business Services:				
Ownership of dwellings	1,000	1,333	2,000	3,000
Other	523	746	1,107	1,655
Community, Social and Personal Services	339	403	523	712
Sub-Total	37,606	95,413	128,921	146,524
Less Imputed Bank Service charge	−51	−64	−77	−96
Domestic Product of Industries	37,555	95,349	128,844	146,428
Public Administration and Defence	1,363	1,858	2,689	3,742
Other Government Services	1,170	1,632	2,301	4,413
G.D.P. in Producers' Values	40,088	98,839	133,834	154,583
Import Duties	463	475	376	470
G.D.P. in Purchasers' Values	40,551	99,513	134,211	155,053

BALANCE OF PAYMENTS

(U.S. $ million)

	1971	1972	1973	1974	1975	1976	1977
Merchandise exports f.o.b.	3,505	4,328	7,531	30,091	27,150	35,467	40,084
Merchandise imports f.o.b.	−866	−1,275	−2,103	−3,713	−5,998	−10,396	−14,355
Trade Balance	2,640	3,053	5,428	26,379	21,152	25,071	25,729
Exports of services	341	464	764	2,556	3,296	4,647	6,127
Imports of services	−1,795	−1,619	−3,098	−4,394	−6,537	−11,118	−13,674
Balance on Goods and Services	1,186	1,898	3,094	24,540	17,911	18,600	18,183
Private unrequited transfers (net)	−208	−267	−392	−518	−852	−1,473	−1,504
Government unrequited transfers (net)	−68	−157	−498	−1,015	−3,128	−3,328	−3,887
Current Balance	910	1,473	2,203	23,007	13,931	13,798	12,793
Direct capital investment (net)	−111	35	−696	−4,470	1,876	−368	822
Other long-term capital (net)	−11	19	−4	−39	−7,136	−8,810	−9,786
Short-term capital (net)	23	−341	130	−616	56	−738	−3,036
Net errors and omissions	−14	—	—	—	—	—	1
Total (net monetary movements)	796	1,187	1,633	17,882	8,727	3,881	794

Source: IMF, *International Financial Statistics.*

EXTERNAL TRADE

(million riyals)

	1971	1972	1973	1974	1975	1976	1977	1978
Imports c.i.f.	3,625	4,665	7,270	10,149	14,823	30,691	51,639	n.a.
Exports f.o.b.	17,304	22,758	33,296	126,223	104,394	135,153	153,209	128,390

Source: UN, *Monthly Bulletin of Statistics.*

PRINCIPAL COMMODITIES

(million riyals)

Imports	1975	1976	1977
Foodstuffs	2,301	3,536	5,365
Non-metallic minerals	324	919	1,827
Chemical products, etc.	668	900	1,739
Wood and wooden articles	372	1,535	2,138
Textiles and clothing	1,291	2,170	3,496
Precious stones and jewellery	429	1,374	1,906
Base metals and metal products	1,383	3,586	7,650
Machinery (incl. electric)	2,883	7,454	13,961
Transport equipment	3,063	5,632	6,607
Optical and surgical instruments, etc.	516	1,139	1,714
Total (inc. others)	14,823	30,691	51,662

Exports*	1976	1977	1978
Crude petroleum	118,990	135,950	120,010
Refined petroleum	9,190	8,990	8,400
Others	430	330	330
Total	128,620	145,260	128,730

*Source: IMF, *International Financial Statistics.*

PRINCIPAL TRADING PARTNERS

(million riyals)

Imports	1975	1976	1977
Bahrain	201	640	762
Belgium	243	512	832
France	332	821	1,728
Germany, Fed. Repub.	1,017	2,538	4,320
Greece	43	341	638
India	153	329	601
Italy	578	1,504	3,168
Japan	2,267	3,731	5,981
Jordan	135	620	429
Korea, Republic	81	218	665
Kuwait	722	2,690	2,300
Lebanon	1,537	739	1,165
Netherlands	430	1,135	2,278
Singapore	169	269	550
Switzerland	419	1,094	1,510
Syria	681	2,019	1,816
Taiwan	188	320	783
United Kingdom	1,147	1,815	3,182
U.S.A.	2,538	5,739	9,621
Total (inc. others)	14,823	30,691	51,662

Exports*	1975	1976	1977
Bahamas	3,436	6,008	4,361
Bahrain	2,249	2,548	3,370
Belgium	3,090	3,480	5,237
Brazil	3,462	4,341	4,586
Canada	1,353	1,331	2,217
France	11,290	15,582	14,704
Germany, Fed. Repub.	3,659	4,238	4,435
Italy	7,894	8,587	11,182
Japan	20,483	27,097	29,080
Korea, Republic	2,219	2,559	3,804
Netherlands	5,291	6,951	8,123
Singapore	2,579	4,658	5,738
Spain	5,205	5,704	5,579
Taiwan	903	1,573	1,741
Thailand	1,033	1,092	1,780
Trinidad and Tobago	2,244	3,087	2,345
United Kingdom	6,271	6,618	6,491
U.S.A.	4,031	6,377	14,575
Total (inc. others)	104,412	135,154	153,209

***Figures for individual countries exclude bunker fuel.**

TOURISM

Pilgrims to Mecca: 1974/75 918,777; 1975/76 894,573; 1976/77 719,040; 1977/78 739,319; 1978/79 830,236.

TRANSPORT

RAILWAYS

	1971	1972	1973	1974
Passenger-kilometres (million) . . .	42	48	61	72
Freight tonne-kilometres (million) . .	39	69	62	66

Source: United Nations, *Statistical Yearbook.*

ROAD TRAFFIC
(motor vehicles in use)

	1968	1969	1970	1974
Passenger cars	52,700	61,100	64,900	59,400
Commercial vehicles . . .	35,300	43,200	50,400	52,600

* Figures for 1971–73 are unavailable.

Source: United Nations, *Statistical Yearbook.*

INTERNATIONAL SEA-BORNE SHIPPING*
('000 metric tons)

	1972	1973	1974	1975
Goods loaded	246,560	321,210	390,510	377,710
of which: Ras Tanura . . .	246,540	321,190	n.a.	n.a.
Goods unloaded	3,000	3,500	4,000	5,000

* Provisional figures.

Source: United Nations, *Monthly Bulletin of Statistics.*

CIVIL AVIATION
(total scheduled services)

	1973	1974	1975	1976
Kilometres flown ('000)	17,500	21,800	27,500	38,900
Passengers carried ('000) . . .	968	1,282	1,836	3,268
Passenger-kilometres (million) . .	939	1,268	1,827	3,122
Freight tonne-km. ('000) . . .	26,500	35,800	50,100	82,600
Mail tonne-km. ('000) . . .	1,400	1,600	2,000	2,600
Total tonne-km. ('000) . . .	112,000	151,000	217,000	366,000

Source: UN, *Statistical Yearbook.*

EDUCATION

(Academic year 1976/77)

	SCHOOLS	TEACHERS	PUPILS
Kindergarten . .	3	51	822
Elementary . .	2,987	25,188	466,836
Intermediate . .	669	7,926	123,548
Secondary . .	190	2,263	44,036
Teacher training .	39	815	10,363
Technical . .	27	785	5,169
Special . . .	52	711	1,690
TOTAL (incl. others)	3,967	37,739	3,967

THE CONSTITUTION

After Ibn Saud had finally brought the whole of present-day Saudi Arabia under his control in 1925, the territory was made into a dual kingdom.

Six years later, in 1932, the realm was unified by decree and became the Kingdom of Saudi Arabia. Saudi Arabia as a whole has in practice been developing, in recent years particularly, from monarchical towards ministerial rule. The power of the Cabinet was increased in May 1958, when several ministries were delegated to the Crown Prince. In December 1960, however, the Crown Prince resigned and King Saud assumed the Prime Ministership. In 1962, Prince Faisal resumed the Prime Ministership. In 1964 King Saud was relieved of his duties and his brother Prince Faisal was proclaimed King. King Faisal was assassinated in 1975 and succeeded by his brother Khalid.

The organs of local government are the General Municipal Councils, the District Council and the tribal and village councils A General Municipal Council is established in the towns of Mecca, Medina and Jeddah. Its members are proposed by the inhabitants and must be approved by the King. Functioning concurrently with each General Municipal Council is a General Administration Committee, which investigates ways and means of executing resolutions passed by the Council. There are also elected district councils under the presidency of local chiefs, consisting of his assistant, the principal local officials and other important persons of the district. Every village and tribe has a council composed of the sheikh, who presides, his legal advisers and two other prominent personages. These councils have power to enforce regulations.

The principal administrative divisions are as follows:

Najd: capital Riyadh. Najd is sub-divided as follows:

1. The principality of Riyadh, to which are associated Wadi al-Dawasir, al-Aflaj, al-Hariq, al-Kharj, al-'Aridh, al-Washm and Sudair.
2. The principality of al-Qasim, comprising 'Unaizah, Buraidah, al-Ras and their villages, and al-Mudhanban and its dependencies.
3. The Northern principality (capital Hayil). This includes the tribes of Shammar, 'Anzah, al-Dhafir and Mutair, the Town of Taima in the south and some northerly towns.

Hijaz: capital Mecca. Includes the principalities of Tabuk, al-'Ula, Dhaba, al-Wajh, Amlaj, Yanbu', Medina, Jeddah, al-Lith, al-Qunfundhah, Baljarshi and Tayif.

Asir: capital Abha. Includes Abha, Qahtan, Shahran, Rijal Alma', Rijal al-Hajr, Banu Shahr, Mahayil, Bariq, Bisha, Najran and its villages.

Eastern Province (*Al Hasa*): capital Dammam. Includes Hofuf, Al-Mubarraz, Qatif, Dhahran, Al-Khobar and Qaryat al-Jubail.

THE GOVERNMENT

HEAD OF STATE

H.M. King KHALID IBN ABDUL AZIZ

(Acceded to the throne March 25th, 1975)

Crown Prince: FAHD IBN ABDUL AZIZ.

COUNCIL OF MINISTERS

(*July* 1979)

Prime Minister: H.M. King KHALID IBN ABDUL AZIZ.

First Deputy Prime Minister: H.R.H. Prince FAHD IBN ABDUL AZIZ.

Second Deputy Prime Minister and Commander of the National Guard: H.R.H. Prince ABDULLAH IBN ABDUL AZIZ.

Minister of Defence and Aviation: H.R.H. Prince SULTAN IBN ABDUL AZIZ.

Minister of Public Works and Housing: H.R.H. Prince MUTAIB IBN ABDUL AZIZ.

Minister of Municipal and Rural Affairs: H.R.H. Prince MAJED IBN ABDUL AZIZ.

Minister of the Interior: H.R.H. Prince NAYEF IBN ABDUL AZIZ.

Minister of Foreign Affairs: H.R.H. Prince SAUD AL-FAISAL.

Minister of Oil and Mineral Wealth: Sheikh Ahmed Zaki Yamani.

Minister of Labour and Social Affairs: Sheikh Ibrahim ibn Abdullah al-Angari.

Minister of Higher Education: Sheikh Hassan ibn Abdullah As-Sheikh.

Minister of Communications: Sheikh Hussein Ibrahim al-Mansouri.

Minister of Finance and National Economy: Muhammad Ali Abdul-Khail.

Minister of Information: Dr. Muhammad Abdou Yamani.

Minister of Industry and Power: Dr. Ghazi Abder-Rahman Algosaibi.

Minister of Commerce: Dr. Sulaiman Abdul Aziz al-Sulaim.

Minister of Justice: Sheikh Ibrahim ibn Muhammad ibn Ibrahim As-Sheikh.

Minister of Education: Dr. Abdul Aziz al-Abdullah al-Khuwaiter.

Minister of Planning: Sheikh Hisham Nazer.

Minister of Pilgrimage Affairs and Waqfs: Sheikh Abdul Wahhab Ahmad Abdul Wasi.

Minister of Agriculture and Water: Dr. Abder-Rahman ibn Abdul Aziz ibn Hasan As-Sheikh.

Minister of Health: Dr. Hussein Abdul Razzak Jazairi.

Minister of Posts, Telegraphs and Telecommunications: Dr. Alawi Darwish Kayyal.

Ministers of State: Sheikh Muhammad Ibrahim Masoud, Dr. Abdullah Muhammad Omran, Dr. Muhammad Abdel Latif Milham.

DIPLOMATIC REPRESENTATION

EMBASSIES ACCREDITED TO SAUDI ARABIA

(In Jeddah, unless otherwise indicated)

Afghanistan: *Ambassador:* Muhammad Akbar Parwani. (also accred. to Jordan).

Algeria: *Ambassador:* Mohammad Kadri.

Argentina: *Ambassador:* Juan Manuel Figuerero.

Australia: Villa Ruwais Quarter, P.O.B. 4876; *Ambassador:* D. J. Kingsmill (also accred. to Kuwait).

Austria: P.O.B. 767; *Ambassador:* Dr. Franz Schmid (also accred. to Bahrain, Oman, Qatar, the United Arab Emirates and the Yemen Arab Republic).

Bahrain: *Chargé d'affaires:* Yusuf Abdullah Khalifah.

Bangladesh: *Ambassador:* Humayun Rasheed Choudhury.

Belgium: *Ambassador:* André de Schutter (also accred. to Oman and the Yemen Arab Republic).

Brazil: *Ambassador:* Murillo Gurgel Valente (also accred. to Oman and Qatar).

Cameroon: *Ambassador:* Alhaji Hammadou Alim (also accred. to Iran and Kuwait).

Canada: P.O.B. 5050; *Ambassador:* Edward L. Bobinski (also accred. to the Yemen Arab Republic and the People's Democratic Republic of Yemen).

Chad: *Ambassador:* Mahamat Rahma Saleh.

China (Taiwan): *Ambassador:* Hsueh Yu-chi.

Denmark: P.O.B. 5333; *Ambassador:* Paul Bent Sønder-gaard (also accred. to Bahrain, Kuwait, Oman, Qatar, the Yemen Arab Republic and the People's Democratic Republic of Yemen).

Ethiopia: *Chargé d'affaires a.i.:* Tilahun Teguado.

Finland: *Ambassador:* Kai Helenius (also accred. to Bahrain, Oman, Qatar and the United Arab Emirates).

France: *Ambassador:* Michel Drumetz.

Gabon: *Ambassador:* Lieut.-Col. Diop Mamadou.

Gambia: *Ambassador:* Mustahpa Sossesh (also accred. to Ethiopia and Iran).

Germany, Federal Republic: *Ambassador:* Reinhard Schlagintweit.

Ghana: *Ambassador:* Abdul Raouf Alando.

Greece: *Ambassador:* Pantelis Menglidis (also accred. to the Yemen Arab Republic).

Guinea: *Ambassador:* Thierno Nabiko Diallo (also accred. to Bahrain, Kuwait, Oman and Qatar).

India: *Ambassador:* Abdul Kadir Hafizka.

Indonesia: *Ambassador:* Dhanamar Adjam (also accred. to Jordan).

Iran: 116 Madina Rd.; *Ambassador:* (vacant).

Iraq: *Ambassador:* Taha Ahmed al-Dawood.

Ireland: *Ambassador:* Eamon O'Tuathail.

Italy: *Ambassador:* Alberto Solera.

Japan: P.O.B. 1260; *Ambassador:* Nobuo Okuchi (also accred. to Oman and the Yemen Arab Republic).

Jordan: *Ambassador:* Tharwat Talhouni.

Kenya: *Ambassador:* Mwabili Kisaka.

Korea, Republic: Villa North, Hamra Palace; *Ambassador:* Yu Yang-su (also accred. to Oman).

Kuwait: *Ambassador:* Saud al-Asaymi.

Lebanon: *Ambassador:* Zafer al-Hasan.

Libya: El Sharifia; *Ambassador:* Ahmed Fouzi Hilal ben Faid.

Malaysia: *Ambassador:* Dato Sri Haji Kamarubbim bin Mohamed Isa (also accred. to Jordan).

Mali: Cairo, Egypt.

Malta: *Chargé d'affaires:* Maurice Lubrano.

Mauritania: *Ambassador:* Ahmed Wald Taliah (also accred. to Jordan, Kuwait and Oman).

Mexico: *Ambassador:* Jorge A. Martín.

Morocco: *Ambassador:* Mohammed Naciri.

Nepal: *Chargé d'affaires:* Sayed Anwar Shah.

Netherlands: *Ambassador:* Jonkheer Hubert Van Nispen (also accred. to the Yemen Arab Republic).

Niger: P.O.B. 1394, *Ambassador:* Oumarou Amadou.

Nigeria: *Ambassador:* Alhaji Muhammadu Bello (also accred. to Jordan and Kuwait).

Norway: P.O.B. 6251; *Ambassador:* Bjarne Grindem (also accred. to Bahrain, Kuwait, Qatar, the United Arab Emirates and the Yemen Arab Republic).

Oman: P.O.B. 2271; *Ambassador:* Sheikh Ibrahim Hammad al-Harthi.

Pakistan: *Ambassador:* Maj.-Gen. Fazal Muqeem Khan.

Philippines: P.O.B. 4794; *Ambassador:* Lininding P. Pangadaman.

Qatar: *Ambassador:* ABDUL-AZIZ BIN SA'AD AL-SA'AD (also accred. to the Yemen Arab Republic).

Senegal: P.O.B. 1394; *Ambassador:* SHEMSADDIN NADAWI (also accred. to Jordan).

Sierra Leone: *Ambassador:* SULIMAN BABA TENBU.

Somalia: *Ambassador:* ABDULLAH MOHAMOUD (also accred. to Bahrain and Jordan).

Spain: P.O.B. 453; *Ambassador:* JOSÉ ANTONIO ACEBAL.

Sudan: *Ambassador:* Lieut.-Gen. EL FATIH M. B. BUSHARA.

Sweden: *Ambassador:* CARL GUSTAF GAZRIEL BIELKE (also accred. to Oman, Qatar and the Yemen Arab Republic).

Switzerland: *Ambassador:* ANDRÉ MAILLARD (also accred. to Oman and the Yemen Arab Republic).

Syria: *Ambassador:* ABDUL HAMID DARKAL.

Thailand: P.O.B. 2224; *Ambassador:* PRASONG SUWANPRADHES (also accred. to Lebanon).

Tunisia: *Ambassador:* KACEM BOUSNINA (also accred. to the Yemen Arab Republic).

Turkey: *Ambassador:* FIKRAT BARAKAT (also accred. to Oman, Qatar and the Yemen Arab Republic).

Uganda: *Ambassador:* Lieut.-Col. MUSA ASUMEN EYEGA (also accred. to Qatar and the People's Democratic Republic of Yemen).

United Arab Emirates: *Ambassador:* AHMED MOHAMMAD BU-REHAIMA.

United Kingdom: P.O.B. 393; *Ambassador:* Sir ARTHUR WILTON, K.C.M.G.

U.S.A.: *Ambassador:* JOHN C. WEST.

Venezuela: *Ambassador:* JOSÉ RAMÓN DOVALE.

Yemen Arab Republic: *Ambassador:* HOMOOD BIN HOMOOD AL-JAIFI.

Yemen, People's Democratic Republic: *Ambassador:* MUHAMMAD M. BANAFA.

Zaire: *Ambassador:* KIMASI MATWIKU BASAULA.

Zambia: Cairo, Egypt.

Saudi Arabia also has diplomatic relations with Burundi, Djibouti, Jamaica, Luxembourg, Singapore and Sri Lanka.

JUDICIAL SYSTEM

Judges are independent and governed by the rules of Islamic *Sharia*. The following courts operate:

Supreme Council of Justice: consists of eleven members and supervises work of the courts; reviews legal questions referred to it by the Minister of Justice and expresses opinions on judicial questions; reviews sentences of death, cutting and stoning.

Court of Cassation: consists of Chief Justice and an adequate number of judges; includes department for penal suits, department for personal status and department for other suits.

General (Public) Courts: consist of one or more Judges; sentences of public courts are issued by a single judge, with the exception of death, stoning and cutting, which require the decision of three judges.

Summary Courts: consist of a single judge or more; sentences are issued by a single judge.

Specialized Courts: Article 26 of the judicial system stipulates that the setting up of specialized courts is permissible by Royal Decree on a proposal from the Supreme Council of Justice.

RELIGION

Arabia is the centre of the Islamic faith and includes the holy cities of Mecca and Medina. Except in the Eastern Province, where a large number of people follow Shi'a rites, the majority of the population are of the Sunni faith. The last seventy years have seen the rise of the Wahhabi sect, who originated in the eighteenth century, but first became unified and influential under their late leader King Ibn Saud. They are now the keepers of the holy places and control the pilgrimage to Mecca.

Mecca: Birthplace of the Prophet Muhammad, seat of the Great Mosque and Shrine of Ka'ba visited by a million Muslims annually.

Medina: Burial place of Muhammad, second sacred city of Islam.

THE PRESS

Since 1964 most newspapers and periodicals have been published by press organizations administered by boards of directors with full autonomous powers, in accordance with the provisions of the Press Law. These organizations, which took over from small private firms, are privately owned by groups of individuals widely experienced in newspaper publishing and administration (*see* Publishers).

There are also a number of popular periodicals published by the Government and by the Arabian American Oil Co. and distributed free of charge. The press is subject to no legal restriction affecting freedom of expression or the coverage of news.

DAILIES

Arab News: P.O.B. 4556, Jeddah; f. 1976; English; published by Al-Madina Press Establishment; Editor MUHAMMAD A. HAFIZ.

al-Bilad: King Abdul Aziz St., Jeddah; f. 1934; Arabic; published by al-Bilad Publishing Corporation; Editor ABDULMAJID AL-SHUBUKSHI; circ. 25,000.

al-Jazirah: P.O.B. 354, Apt. 88, Municipality Bldg., Safat, Riyadh; Arabic; Editor KHALID HAMDUL MALIK, circ. 5,000.

al-Madina al-Munawara: Jeddah, P.O.B. 807; f. 1937; Arabic; published by al-Madina Press Establishment; Editor AHMED M. MAHMOUD; circ. 45,000.

al-Nadwah: Mecca; f. 1958; Arabic; published by Mecca Press and Information Organization; Editor HAMED MUTAWI'E; circ. 10,000.

Okaz Newspaper: P.O.B. 1508, Jeddah; f. 1960; Arabic; Editor ALI HUSAIN SHOBOKSHI; circ. 20,000.

al-Riyadh: P.O.B. 851, Riyadh; Arabic; published by Yamamah Press Organization; Editor TURKI A. AL-SUDARI; circ. 10,000.

Saudi Gazette: Mina Rd., P.O.B. 5576, Jeddah; f. 1975; English; published by Okaz Organization; Dir.-Gen. ALI H. SHOBOKSHI; Editor AYAD A. MADANI; Man. Editor TERENCE L. RYLE.

Saudi Review: P.O.B. 4288, Jeddah; f. 1966; English; daily newsletter from Saudi newspapers and broadcasting service; Publisher and Chief Editor MUHAMMAD SALAHUDDIN; Man. Dir. SHAKER AL-SANTAWI; circ. 5,000.

al-Yaum (*Today*): P.O.B. 565, Dammam; f. 1964; Dir. HAMAD AL-MUBARAK; circ. 42,000.

WEEKLIES

Akhbar al-Dhahran (*Dhahran News*): Dammam; f. 1958; Editor 'ABD AL-AZIZ AL-ISA; circ. 1,500.

Arabian Sun: Aramco, Dhahran; English; published by the Arabian American Oil Co., Dhahran.

Child: P.O.B. 1508, Jeddah; f. 1976; circ. 5,000.

al-Dawa: Islamic University, Shahrah Ibn Khaldun, Riyadh; Arabic.

Hasan: Jeddah; f. 1977; children's magazine; Editor-in-Chief JACOB MUHAMMAD ISSAC; circ. 10,000.

Iqra'a: King Abdul Aziz St., P.O.B. 6360, Jeddah; f. 1974; Arabic; published by al-Bilad Publishing Corporation; Editor Dr. HASAN ABU RUKKAH.

Rabita al Alam Islami (*Journal of Muslim World League*): P.O.B. 537 and 538, Mecca: weekly and monthly in both Arabic and English; Editors MUHAMMAD MAHMOUD HAFIZ (Arabic), SAYYID HASAN MUTAHAR (English).

Saudi Business: Arab News Bldg., off Sharafia, P.O.B. 4556, Jeddah; Editor MUHAMMAD A. HAFIZ.

Saudi Economic Survey: P.O.B. 1989, Jeddah; Editor ABDUL HAKIM GHAITH.

Al-Yamana: Shahrah Al Khalyli Arabii, P.O.B. 4058, Riyadh; Editor ABDULLAH AL-QARAWI.

MONTHLIES

Al-Arab: King Faisal St., Riyadh; Editor HAMDUL JANIR.

Ahlan wa Sahlan (*Welcome*): P.O.B. 620, Jeddah; flight journal by Saudi Arabian Airlines.

Al-Lequ'a: P.O.B. 812, Riyadh; Editor IBRAHIM AL ULAI AL MAIMAN.

Al-Manhal: 44 Shahrah Arafet, P.O.B. 2925, Riyadh; literary and cultural; Arabic; Editor ABDUL QUDOOS ANSARI.

Mujalla al-Iqtisad wa Edara (*Economics and Administrative Review*): Centre of Research and Development, King Abdul Aziz Univ., P.O.B. 1540, Jeddah; Editor HASAN ABDULLAH ALI.

Oafla-e-Zaid (*Oil Caravan*): P.O.B. 1389, Dhahran; published by Arabian American Oil Company.

Al-Saqor (*Falcon*): P.O.B. 2973, King Faisal Air Academy, Riyadh; air-force journal; Editor ABDUL RAHIM AL KASIR.

Al-Sharkiah-Elle (*Arab Women's Magazine*): Al-Jabbul Ahalie Bldg., P.O.B. 6, Riyadh; Editor SAMIRA M. KHASHAGGI.

Al-Tadhamon Al-Islami (*Islamic Solidarity*): Hajj Ministry, Mecca; Editor Dr. MUSTAAF ABDUL WAHID.

al-Tijarah: P.O.B. 1264, Jeddah; f. 1960; for businessmen; published by Jeddah Chamber of Commerce and Industry; Chair. Sheihk ISMAIL ABUDAWOOD; Gen. Man. WAHAB ABUZINADA; circ. 1,800.

NEWS AGENCIES

Saudi Press Agency: Nasiriya St., Riyadh; f. 1970; Dir.-Gen. ABDULLA HILAIL.

PUBLISHERS

al-Bilad Publishing Organization: King Abdul Aziz St., Jeddah; publishes *al-Bilad* and *Iqra'a*; Dir.-Gen. ABDULLAH DABBAGH.

Dar al-Yaum Press and Publishing Establishment: P.O.B. 565, Dammam; f. 1964; publishes *al-Yaum*; Dir.-Gen. HAMAD AL-MUBARAK.

al-Jazirah for Press Printing and Publishing: P.O.B. 354, Riyadh; f. 1964; 29 mems.; publishes *al-Jazirah* (daily); Dir.-Gen. SALEH AL-AJROUSH; Editor-in-Chief KHALID EL MALEK.

al-Madina Press Establishment: P.O.B. 807, Jeddah; f. 1937; publishes *al-Madina al-Munawara*; Dir.-Gen. AHMED SALAH JAMJOON.

Okaz Organization for Press and Publication: Al-Mina St., P.O.B. 1508, Jeddah; publishes *Okaz, Saudi Gazette* and *Child*; Gen. Man. ALI H. SHOBOKSHI.

Saudi Publishing and Distributing House: Al-Jauhara Bldg., Flats 7 and 12, Baghdadia, P.O.B. 2043, Jeddah; books in Arabic and English; Chair. MUHAMMAD SALAHUDDIN; Gen. Man. MUHAMMAD ALI AL-WAZIR.

al-Yamamah Press Establishment: Riyadh; publishes *al-Riyadh, al-Yamamah* and *She*; Dir.-Gen. ABDULLAH QAR'AWI.

RADIO AND TELEVISION

RADIO

Saudi Arabian Broadcasting Service: Ministry of Information, Airport Rd., Jeddah; stations at Jeddah, Riyadh, Dammam and Abha, broadcast programmes in Arabic and English; overseas service in Urdu, Indonesian, Persian, French, Somali and Swahili; Dir.-Gen. KHALID H. GHOUTH.

ARAMCO Radio: P.O.B. 96, Dhahran; broadcasts music and programmes in English for the entertainment of employees of Arabian American Oil Company.

There are about 290,000 radio receivers (1978).

TELEVISION

Saudi Arabian Government Television Service: Information Ministry, P.O.B. 570, Riyadh; stations at Riyadh, Jeddah, Medina, Dammam, Qassim, Abha, Hail, Albaha, Sakaka, Al-Qurayat, Wadiadda-Wasir and Tabuk operate 8 hours daily; major stations and relay points are under construction to serve all principal towns; Dir.-Gen. MOHAMMAD AL-FHAID.

Dhahran-HZ-22-TV. Aramco TV: Arabian American Oil Co., Room 300, Administration Bldg., Dhahran; non-commercial; started 1957, since 1970 English language film-chain operation only; Man. (Residential and Recreation Services) WALTER L. JOHNSTON; Man. (Communications) J. C. WEBB.

There are about 305,000 television sets (1978).

FINANCE

BANKING

The Saudi Arabian banking system consists of: the Saudi Arabian Monetary Agency, as central note-issuing and regulatory body; twelve commercial banks (two national and ten foreign banks); and three specialist banks. There is a policy of 'Saudization' of the foreign banks.

The rising volume of oil revenues imposed a need for a central monetary authority and in 1952 the Saudi Arabian Monetary Agency (SAMA) was established in Jeddah. SAMA's functions include: bankers to the Government; stabilization of the value of the currency; administration of monetary reserves; issue of coin and notes; and regulation of banking.

In June 1966, a Banking Control Law formalized SAMA's control of the commercial banking system. Commercial banks are obliged to maintain a certain proportion of their deposit liabilities (currently, 10 per cent of demand deposits, and 5 per cent of time and savings deposits) as statutory deposits with SAMA. They must also maintain liquid reserves equivalent to a certain proportion (currently 20 per cent) of their total deposit liabilities and are required to be Saudi Joint Stock Companies, and may not trade for purposes other than banking. Their paid-up capital must be not less than 2.5 million Saudi riyals; banks' total deposit liabilities may not exceed 15 times their paid-up capital and reserves; and banks must plough back 25 per cent of their undistributed profits in the form of reserves, until such reserves equal, as a minimum, their paid-up capital.

(cap. = capital; p.u. = paid up; dep. = deposits; m. = million amounts in Saudi Riyals)

Central Bank

Saudi Arabian Monetary Agency: P.O.B. 2992, Airport Rd., Riyadh; f. 1952; gold, foreign exchange and investments 134,240m. (Dec. 1977); Pres. and Gov. Abdul Aziz Al Quraishi; Vice-Gov. Sheikh Khalid Mohammad Algosaibi; Controller-Gen. Abdul Wahab M. S. Sheikh; publs. *Statement of Affairs* (fortnightly); *Annual Report; Statistical Summary* (twice a year); 10 brs.

National Banks

National Commercial Bank: P.O.B. 3555, King Abdul Aziz St., Jeddah; f. 1938; cap. and reserves 140m.; dep. and current account 13,976m. (Dec. 1977); Partners Sheikh Saleh Abdullah Mosa Alkaaki, Sheikh Abdulaziz Muhammad Alkaaki, Sheikh Salim bin Mahfooz (Gen. Man.); 45 brs.

Riyad Bank Ltd.: P.O.B. 1047, King Abdul Aziz St., Jeddah; f. 1957; cap. p.u. and res. 624m.; dep. 6,946m.; total assets 13,298m. (June 1978); Chair. H. E. Sheikh Abdullah bin Adwan; Man. Dir. H.E. Sheikh Abdul Rahman al-Sheikh; Gen. Man. P. D. Brewer; 37 brs.

Specialist Banks

Agricultural Credit Bank: Jeddah; f. 1964; cap. 31.5m.; Dir.-Gen. Izzat Husni al-Ali.

Arab Investment Co. S.A.A.: P.O.B. 4009, Riyadh; f. 1974 by 15 Arab countries for industrial investment.

Saudi Credit Bank: Jeddah; f. 1973; provides interest-free loans for specific purposes to Saudi citizens of moderate means.

Saudi Investment Banking Corporation: P.O.B. 3533, Riyadh; f. 1977; provides medium- and long-term finance to business and individuals; foreign sponsors, particularly Chase Manhattan Bank, have provided 20 per cent of capital; Dir. and Gen. Man. Jamal M. Radwan.

Banks with Foreign Interests

Al-Bank al-Saudi al Britani (*Saudi British Bank*): P.O.B. 109, Jeddah; formerly British Bank of the Middle East, but Saudi Arabia acquired 60 per cent interest in 1978; cap. 100m; Chair. Sheikh Suliman Saleh Olayan; Man. Dir. J. C. Kelly, c.b.e.; 6 brs.

Al-Bank al-Saudi al-Fransi (*Saudi French Bank*): P.O.B. 1, King Abdul Aziz St., Jeddah; cap. 100m.; brs. at Al-Khobar, Riyadh, Jubail, Hofuf and Dammam; 40 per cent interest held by Banque de l'Indochine et de Suez.

Al-Bank al-Saudi al-Hollandi (*Saudi Netherlands Bank*): P.O.B. 67, Jeddah; formerly Algemene Bank Nederland, N.V., but Saudi Arabia acquired 60 per cent participation in 1977; 4 brs.

Arab Bank Ltd.: Amman, Jordan; P.O.B. 344, Jeddah; 6 brs.

Bank al-Jazira: P.O.B. 6277, Jeddah; formerly National Bank of Pakistan, Jeddah, but Saudi Arabia acquired 65 per cent participation in 1976; cap. p.u. 50m., dep. 414m. (March 1978); Chair. Sheikh Abdul Aziz Abdullah Al-Sulaiman; Gen. Man. M. S. Ansari.

Bank Melli Iran: Ferdowsi Ave., Teheran; Jeddah.

Banque du Caire: Cairo; P.O.B. 472, Jeddah; 3 brs.

Banque du Liban et d'Outre-Mer S.A.: Beirut, Lebanon; P.O.B. 482, Jeddah.

Citibank: New York; Riyadh, P.O.B. 833, Al Batha St.; Vice-Pres. Michael A. Callen; Jeddah, P.O.B. 490; Vice-Pres. Robert Wilcox.

United Bank Ltd.: Karachi; P.O.B. 619, Dammam.

INSURANCE COMPANIES

Al-Alamiya Insurance Co. Ltd.: P.O.B. 209, Jeddah; managed by Sun Alliance, London.

Credit and Commerce Insurance Co. (Saudi) Ltd.: 1001 Queens Bldg., King Abdul Aziz St., Jeddah.

Independent Insurance Co. of Saudi Arabia Ltd.: Jeddah Towers Bldg., Sharafia, Jeddah; all classes of insurance; Gen. Man. N. J. N. Rowton.

National Insurance Co. S.A.: P.O.B. 5832, Jeddah; all classes.

Pan Arabian Insurance Co.: El-Khereiji Bldg., Dammam; f. 1978; majority shareholder Sheikh Abdul Karim El-Khereiji.

Red Sea Insurance Co. Ltd.: Attar Bldg., King Abdel Aziz St., Jeddah.

Saudi United Insurance Co. Ltd.: P.O.B. 464, Al-Khobar; f. 1976; fire, accident and marine; majority shareholding held by Ahmed Hamad Algosaibi & Bros.; Gen. Man. Ahmed Muhammad Sabbagh.

TRADE AND INDUSTRY

CHAMBERS OF COMMERCE

Chamber of Commerce and Industries: Jeddah, P.O.B. 1264; f. 1950; Pres. Sheikh Ismail Abudawood; Man. Wahab Abuzinada; publ. *Al-Tijara*.

Dammam Chamber of Commerce: P.O.B. 719, Dammam.

Mecca Chamber of Commerce and Industry: P.O.B. 1086, Al-Ghazza St., Mecca; f. 1945; Pres. Saleh Mohamed Jamal; Sec.-Gen. Fouad A. Himdy; publ. *Al Tijarah Wassina'Ah* (monthly).

Medina Chamber of Commerce: P.O.B. 443, Medina.

Riyadh Chamber of Commerce and Industry: P.O.B. 596, Riyadh; f. 1961; acts as arbitrator in business disputes, information centre; Pres. Sheikh Mohamed A. Al Fraih; Sec.-Gen. Saleh Toaimi; 4,000 mems.; publs. monthly magazine, trade directory, twice-weekly bulletin.

OIL

General Petroleum and Mineral Organization (PETROMIN): P.O.B. 757, Riyadh; f. 1962 to establish oil and mineral industries and collateral activities in Saudi Arabia; Gov. Dr. Abdul Hadi Taher.

The following projects have been set up by Petromin but, as a result of a government decision announced in November 1975, Petromin is to give up responsibility for industrial projects, including petrochemicals, and will concentrate on the distribution, refining and marketing of oil abroad. The Saudi Basic Industries Corporation (SABIC) was set up in December 1976 to oversee the petrochemical industry and also the State's share in other hydrocarbon-based organizations:

Arabian Drilling Co.: P.O.B. 932, Riyadh; f. 1964; shareholding 51 per cent, remainder French private capital; undertakes contract drilling for oil, minerals and water both inside and outside Saudi Arabia.

Arabian Geophysical and Surveying Co. (ARGAS): P.O.B. 2109, Jeddah; f. 1966; shareholding 51 per cent owned by General Petroleum and Mineral Organization (PETROMIN); remainder provided by Cie. Générale de Géophysique; geophysical exploration for oil, minerals and ground water, as well as all types of land, airborne and marine surveys; Man. Dir. Fadlullah Farouq; Tech. Dir. Paul Clary.

Arabian Marine Petroleum Co. (MARINCO): P.O.B. 50, Dhahran Airport; f. 1968; shareholding 51 per cent, remainder held by McDermott Co. of New Orleans, U.S.A.; undertakes marine construction work (pipelines, rigs, sea terminals, etc.).

Jeddah Oil Refinery: P.O.B. 1604, Jeddah; f. 1968; shareholding 75 per cent, remainder held by Saudi Arabian Refining Co. (SARCO); the refinery at Jeddah, Japanese-built and American-staffed, has a capacity of 69,000 b/d.; distribution in the Western Province is undertaken by Petromin's **Department for Distribution of Oil Products.**

Petromin Lubricating Oil Co. (PETROLUBE): P.O.B. 1432, Jeddah; f. 1968; for the refining, processing and manufacture of lubricating oils and other related products; also distribution.

Petromin Lubricating Refinery (LUBREF): P.O.B. 1604, Jeddah; f. 1975; has initial production capacity of one million barrels of lubricating oil per year.

Petromin Marketing (PETMARK): P.O.B. 50, Dhahran Airport; f. 1967; wholly-owned by Petromin; operates the installations and facilities for the distribution of petroleum products in the Eastern, Central and Northern provinces of Saudi Arabia; Gen. Man. S. S. Abu Al-Jadayil.

Petromin Services Department (PETROSERV): f. 1975; operates medical and social centres; meets health and recreational needs of personnel of Petromin and its contractors.

Petromin Steel Project (PETROMAR): Jubail; f. 1975; steel processing plant with capacity of 3.3 million tons per year.

Petromin Sulphuric Acid Plant (PETROCID): P.O.B. 757, Riyadh; plant began production mid-1971; wholly-owned by Petromin; produces sulphuric acid at Dammam.

Petromin Tankers and Mineral Shipping Co. (PETROSHIP): P.O.B. 1600, Jeddah; f. 1968; wholly owned by Petromin; operates tanker fleet.

Riyadh Refinery: P.O.B. 3946, Riyadh; f. 1974.

Saudi Arabian Fertilizers Co. (SAFCO): P.O.B. 553, Dammam; f. 1965; 51 per cent shareholding, remainder open to public subscription; the plant at Dammam has a capacity of about 1,100 tons of urea and 35 tons of sulphur a day; construction and management have been undertaken by Occidental Petroleum Co. of U.S.A.

Sulb: P.O.B. 1826, Jeddah; wholly-owned by Petromin; steel rolling mill at Jeddah.

Foreign Concessionaires

Arabian-American Oil Co. (Aramco): Dhahran; f. 1933; holds the principal working concessions in Saudi Arabia, covering approx. 85,000 square miles; production (1977) 3,291.2 million barrels; Saudi Government acquired 60 per cent participation in 1974 and negotiations are still in progress by which the Saudi Government would increase its interest to 100 per cent; Pres. and Vice-Chair. R. W. Powers; Chair. and Chief Exec. Officer John J. Kelberger.

Arabian Oil Co. Ltd.: P.O.B. 335, Riyadh; f. 1958; holds concession for offshore exploitation of Saudi Arabia's half-interest in the Kuwait-Saudi Arabia Partitioned Zone; total oil production (1977) 69.6m. barrels; natural gas production (1974) 56.7m. cubic feet; Chair. Sohei Mizuno; Pres. Yoshihisa Ojimi; Dir. in Saudi Arabia Takashi Hayashi.

Getty Oil Co.: P.O.B. 363, Riyadh; also office in Kuwait; f. 1928; holds concession for exploitation of Saudi Arabia's half-interest in the Saudi Arabia-Kuwait Partitioned Zone, both on-shore and in territorial waters; total Zone production (1977) 64.0 million barrels.

TRANSPORT

RAILWAYS

Saudi Government Railroad Organization: P.O.B. 92, Dammam; Pres. Faysal M. al-Shehail.

The Saudi Government Railroad is a single track, standard gauge line 580 km. long. In addition, the total length of spur lines and sidings is 160 km. The main line connects Dammam Port at the Arabian Gulf with Riyadh, and passes Dhahran, Abqaiq, Hofuf, Harad, Khurais and al-Kharj. Plans to construct lines linking Dammam with Jeddah and Dammam with Jubail were under study in 1979.

The Organization is an independent entity with a Board of Directors headed by the Minister of Communications.

ROADS

Asphalted roads link Jeddah to Mecca, Jeddah to Medina, Medina to Yanbo, Taif to Mecca, Riyadh to al-Kharj, and Dammam to Hofuf as well as the principal communities and certain outlying points in Aramco's area of operations. Work is proceeding on various other roads, including one which will link Medina and Riyadh. A road from Taif to Jizan in the south, near the Yemeni border, was officially opened in 1976. The trans-Arabian highway, linking Dammam, Riyadh, Taif, Mecca and Jeddah, was completed in 1967. Under the 1975–80 Plan some 13,000 km. of paved roads will be added to the existing network, bringing the total to over 24,000 km. by 1980.

National Transport Company of Saudi Arabia: P.O.B. 1312, Jeddah; specialises in all aspects of containers, general and heavy road haulage operations; Gen. Man. IAN FITZGERALD.

SHIPPING

Saudi Arabian Ports Authority: P.O.B. 5162, Riyadh; Pres. and Chair. Dr. FAYEZ BADR; Dir. Gen. MUHAMMAD A. BAKR.

The ports of Jeddah, Dammam, Yanbu, Gizan and Jubail, as well as a number of minor ports, are under the exclusive management of the Ports Authority.

Jeddah is the principal port and the main point of entry for pilgrims bound for Mecca. It had 30 berths in April 1979 and there are 15 more under construction, which are due for completion in 1981. These berths have draughts ranging from 10 to 14 metres. A tanker terminal was due to begin operation in July 1979.

Dammam is the second largest port and had 28 berths in December 1978, with a further 10 under construction. Draughts at this port range from 9 to 14 metres.

Yanbu is a busy cargo port as well as being the main port used by pilgrims bound for Medina. It is currently being extended and modernized with new docks, storage space and a special Pilgrims' Hall. The port has two berths with an additional seven under construction. The draughts range from 10 to 12 metres.

Gizan, which is the main port for the southern part of the country, is also undergoing improvement with the construction of two berths of 10 metres draught.

At *Jubail* a new deep-water port is being built which will include 25 berths with draughts ranging from 12 to 14 metres plus an Open Sea Tanker Terminal with four 28-metre draught berths. Two berths were in operation by April 1978 and the others will be completed by the end of 1979.

The Ports Authority has strongly encouraged the growth of container traffic in its ports, and at the start of 1979 three container berths were operational at Jeddah and two at Dammam. Two more will be provided later in the year at Jubail.

In addition to the ports mentioned, there are a number of minor ports including Haql, Wejh, Umludj, Rabigh, Al Lith, Qunsudah, Farasan, Qudayma and Muwaih on the Red Sea coast and Al-Khobar, Qatif, Uqair, Ras Al-Ghar and Darin on the Arabian Gulf coast. Most of these are suitable only for small craft. Ras Mishab on the Arabian Gulf coast is operated by the Ministry of Defence and Aviation.

Nashar Saudi Lines: P.O.B. 6697, Jeddah; owners of livestock carriers trading in Arabian Gulf, Red Sea, Mediterranean and Black Sea.

Saudi Lines: P.O.B. 66, Jeddah; regular cargo and passenger services between Red Sea and Indian Ocean ports.

Saudi National Lines: P.O.B. 4181, Jeddah; regular container, Ro/Ro and general cargo service from U.S.A. to Saudi Arabia, Gulf and Red Sea ports.

CIVIL AVIATION

Saudia—Saudi Arabian Airlines: Saudia Bldg., P.O.B. 620, Jeddah; f. 1945; regular internal services to all major cities of Saudi Arabia; regular international services to London, Paris, Geneva, Frankfurt, Athens, Rome, New York, Beirut, Casablanca, Algiers, Tunis, Tripoli, Dubai, Doha, Bahrain, Muscat, Port Sudan, Khartoum, Cairo, Kuwait, Baghdad, Damascus, Amman, Asmara, Karachi, Bombay, Istanbul, Shiraz, Abu Dhabi, Sana'a, Aden and Teheran; fleet of 54 aircraft, principally Lockheed TriStar L-1011, Boeing 747, 707, 720-B-737, Douglas DC-8, Fokker F-27, DC-3 and Convair 340; Dir.-Gen. Sheikh KAMIL SINDI; Exec. Vice-Pres. and Deputy Dir.-Gen. T. BURDETTE.

Saudi Arabia is also served by the following foreign airlines: Air Algérie, Air France, Air India, Alia (Jordan), Alitalia (Italy), British Airways, China Airlines (Taiwan), Cyprus Airways, EgyptAir, Ethiopian Airlines, Gulf Air, Iranair, Iraq Airways, KLM (Netherlands), Korean Airlines (Republic of Korea), Kuwait Airways, Libyan Arab Airlines, Lufthansa (Federal Republic of Germany), MEA (Lebanon), Olympic Airways (Greece), PIA (Pakistan), Royal Air Maroc, Somali Airlines, Sudan Airways, Swissair, Syrian Arab Airlines, TMA (Lebanon), Tunis Air, Turkish Airlines, Yemen Airways (Yemen Arab Republic).

TOURISM

Saudi Hotels and Resort Areas Company: P.O.B. 5500, Riyadh; Saudi Government has 22 per cent interest.

ATOMIC ENERGY

Saudi Arabia joined the International Atomic Energy Agency in January 1963. Radio isotopes are used in the oil industry and are being introduced into state-controlled agricultural schemes.

DEFENCE

Defence Budget (1978/79): 33,300m. riyals.

Military Service: voluntary.

Total Armed Forces: 58,500; army 45,000; navy 1,500; air force 12,000.

Paramilitary Forces: 35,000 National Guard and 6,500 Frontier Force and Coastguard.

EDUCATION

The educational system in Saudi Arabia resembles that of other Arab countries. Educational institutions are run mainly by the government. The private sector plays a significant role at the first and second levels, but its total contribution is quite small compared with that of the public sector.

Pre-elementary education is provided on a small scale, mainly in urban areas. Elementary education is of six years' duration and the normal entrance age is 6+. The total number of pupils in 1976/77 was 72,602, with 38,185 teachers. Intermediate education begins at 12+ and lasts for three years. The total number of pupils in this stage for 1976/77 was 77,952, with teachers numbering 10,543. Secondary education begins at 15+ and extends for three years. After the first year, successful pupils branch into science or arts groups. Total number of pupils in this stage for 1976/77 was 59,933, with 3,230 teachers.

Industrial and commercial schools can be entered after the completion of the intermediate stage. There are two higher technical and three higher commercial colleges offering two-year courses. Vocational craft training institutes are maintained in six centres, providing courses in electrical, mechanical and allied trades. Facilities exist for the training of teachers. A college of art was due to open in Jeddah in 1979.

There are six universities (*see* below) and also the Colleges of Education for Girls at Riyadh, Jeddah and Dammam, and the Higher Islamic Judicial Institute. Adult education is divided into two categories: (a) to combat illiteracy; (b) follow-up. The duration of study in each is 16 months.

Budgetary allocations for education in the fiscal year 1976/77 were SR 13,977 million out of total budget allocations of SR 110,935 million.

UNIVERSITIES

Imam Mohammed bin Saud Islamic University: Riyadh; 267 teachers, 4,604 students.

Islamic University: Medina; 85 teachers, 1,055 students.

King Abdulaziz University: P.O.B. 1540, Jeddah; 546 teachers, 9,986 students.

King Faisal University: Dammam; 28 teachers, 170 students.

University of Petroleum and Minerals: Dhahran; 288 teachers, 2,369 students.

Riyadh University: Riyadh; 1,107 teachers, 10,274 students.

BIBLIOGRAPHY

ARMSTRONG, H. C. Lord of Arabia (Beirut, 1962).

ASSAH, AHMED. Miracle of the Desert Kingdom (Johnson, London, 1969).

ATLAS OF SAUDI ARABIA (Edward Stanford, London, 1978).

BENOIT-MÉCHIN, S. Ibn Séoud ou la naissance d'un royaume (Albin Michel, Paris, 1955).

BROWN, E. HOAGLAND. The Saudi-Arabia-Kuwait Neutral Zone (Beirut, 1964).

BUTLER, GRANT C. Kings and Camels: An American in Saudi Arabia (The Devin-Adair Co., New York, 1960).

DE GAURY, GERALD. Faisal (Arthur Barker, London, 1969).

DEQUIN, HORST. Saudi Arabia's Agriculture and its Development Possibilities (Frankfurt, 1963).

GHARAYBEH, A. Saudi Arabia (London, 1962).

HOWARTH, DAVID. The Desert King: Ibn Sa'ud (McGraw Hill, New York, 1964).

LEBKICHER, ROY, RENTZ, GEORGE, and STEINCKE, MAX. Saudi Arabia (New York, 1952)

LIPSKY, GEORGE A., and others. Saudi Arabia: Its People, Its Society, Its Culture (New Haven, 1959).

PHILBY, H. ST. J. B. Arabia and the Wahhabis (London, 1928).

Arabia (London, Benn, 1930).
Arabian Jubilee (London, 1951).
The Empty Quarter (London, 1933).
The Land of Midian (London, 1957).
A Pilgrim in Arabia (London, 1946).
Saudi Arabia (London, 1955).

SARHAN, SAMIR (Ed.). Who's Who in Saudi Arabia (Tihama, Jeddah, and Europa, London, 2nd edn., 1978).

SOULIÉ, G. J. L., Le Royaume d'Arabie Séoudite face à l'Islam révolutionnaire 1953–64 (Armand Colin, Paris, 1966).

TROELLER, GARY. The Birth of Saudi Arabia: Britain and the Rise of the House of Sa'ud (London, Frank Cass, 1976).

TWITCHELL, KARL S., with the co-operation of JURJI, EDWARD J. Saudi Arabia (Princeton, 1953).

VAN DER MEULEN, D. The Wells of Ib'n Saud (John Murray, 1957).

WILLIAMS, K. Ibn Sa'ud: the Puritan King of Arabia (London, Cape, 1933).

WINDER, R. BAYLY. Saudi Arabia in the Nineteenth Century (Macmillan, London, 1965).

Spanish North Africa

GEOGRAPHY

CEUTA

The ancient port and walled city of Ceuta is situated on a rocky promontory on the North African coast overlooking the Strait of Gibraltar. It was retained by Spain as a *plaza de soberania* when Morocco became independent in 1956 and is administered as part of Cádiz Province. The Portuguese first established a fort at Ceuta in 1415 and it was ceded to Spain by Portugal in 1668. It developed as a military and administrative centre for the former Spanish Protectorate in Morocco and now functions as a bunkering and fishing port. In 1977 its population was 67,187.

MELILLA

Melilla is situated on a small peninsula jutting out into the Mediterranean on the North African coast. It was retained by Spain as a *plaza de soberania* when Morocco became independent in 1956 and is administered from Málaga. It was annexed by Spain in 1471 and served as a military stronghold up to the present. In 1977 it had a population of 64,942 and it is an active port which exports over 1 million tons of iron ore annually from mines inland at Kelata, Morocco.

PEÑÓN DE VÉLEZ, PEÑÓN DE ALHUCEMAS AND CHAFARINAS

These three rocky islets, situated respectively just west and east of Alhucemas and east of Melilla off the north coast of Morocco, are administered with Melilla. In 1977 their populations were 71, 63 and 195.

HISTORY

Ceuta, Melilla and the island dependencies are known as the Plazas de Soberanía—i.e. *presidios*, or fortified enclaves, over which Spain has full sovereign rights. Children born in these dependencies, whether Christian or Muslim, are Spanish citizens and subjects. Both Ceuta and Melilla have municipal councils (*ayuntamientos*). They are administered as an integral part of Spain by an official responsible to the Ministry of the Interior. In respect of ecclesiastical and judicial affairs Ceuta is integrated with the province of Cádiz, and Melilla with the province of Málaga in Spain.

CEUTA

Ceuta is situated on the African shore opposite Gibraltar, the Straits being here about 25 km. wide. The Portuguese took Ceuta in 1415. On the union of the crowns of Spain and Portugal in 1580 Ceuta passed under Spanish rule and in 1694, when Portugal was formally separated from Spain, asked to remain under Spanish control. During the sixteenth, seventeenth and eighteenth centuries Ceuta had to endure a number of sieges at the hands of the Muslims. Ahmad Gailan, a chieftain in northern Morocco, blockaded the town in 1648–55. The Sultan of Morocco, Mulai Ismail (1672–1727), attacked Ceuta in 1674, 1680 and 1694, after which he maintained a blockade against the town until 1720. Ahmad Ali al-Rifi, a chieftain from northern Morocco, made yet another unsuccessful assault in 1732. A pact of friendship and commerce was negotiated between Spain and Morocco at Aranjuez in 1780, a peaceful agreement following in the next year over the boundaries of the Ceuta enclave. There was in 1844–45 a sharp dispute once more about the precise limits of Ceuta. Further disagreement in 1859 led to the war of 1860. Spanish forces, after an engagement at Los Castillejos, seized Tetuán from Morocco. After another battle at Wadi Ras in March 1860 the conflict came to an end. A settlement was now made which enlarged the enclave of Ceuta and obliged Morocco to hand over to Spain 100 million pesetas as war indemnities. In 1874 the town became the seat of the Capitanía General de Africa.

MELILLA

Spain secured control of Melilla in 1496, the town being infeudated thereafter to the ducal house of Medina Sidonia, which was empowered to appoint the governor and seneschal with the approval of the Spanish Crown. The Rif tribesmen attacked Melilla in 1562–64. Later still, the Sultan of Morocco, Mulai Ismail (1672–1727) assaulted the town in 1687, 1696 and 1697. Sultan Muhammad b. Abdallah (1757–90) besieged Melilla in 1771 and 1774. An agreement concluded between Spain and Morocco in 1780 at Aranjuez led, however, in the following year, to a peaceful delimitation of the Melilla enclave. There was a brief period of tension in 1844 and then, in 1861, under the terms of an agreement signed at Madrid, after the Spanish-Moroccan campaign of 1860, Melilla received an extension of its boundaries. Trouble with the Rif tribesmen gave rise in 1893–94 to the so-called "War of Melilla", which ended with a settlement negotiated at Marrakesh. It was not until 1909 that Spanish forces, after a hard campaign, occupied the mountainous hinterland of Melilla between the Wadi Kert and the Wadi Muluya—a region in which, some ten miles behind Melilla, are situated the rich iron mines of Beni Bu Ifrur. In July 1921 the Rif tribes, under the command of Abd al-Krim, defeated a Spanish force near Anual and threatened Melilla itself. Only in 1926, with the final defeat of the Rif rebellion, was Spanish control restored over the Melilla region. Melilla was the first Spanish town to rise against the Government of the Popular Front on July 17th, 1936, at the beginning of the Spanish Civil War. Since 1939 both towns have been ruled as integral parts of Spain.

OTHER POSSESSIONS

The Chafarinas Islands, lying about 2½ miles off the Cabo de Agua, came under Spanish control in 1847. Peñón de Alhucemas is situated some three-quarters of a mile from the coast opposite Ajdir. It was occupied in 1673. Peñón de Vélez de la Gomera, about 50 miles farther west, came under Spanish rule in 1508, was then lost not long afterwards and reoccupied in 1564.

ECONOMIC SURVEY

CEUTA AND MELILLA

Ceuta and Melilla, both free ports, are in fact of little economic importance, while the other possessions, with a population of 530, mostly fishermen, are of negligible significance. The basic reason for Spanish retention of these areas is their overwhelmingly Spanish population. For instance, in the Melilla census of 1960 (the latest complete figures available), of a total population of 79,056 only 6,300 Muslims and 3,100 Jews were recorded. The 80,000 population of Ceuta was similarly composed. Ceuta's population had fallen to 64,576 by 1973, owing to the lack of economic opportunities in the town, but rose slightly to 67,187 in 1977. The hinterland of the two cities is small: the total extent of Ceuta is 19 square kilometres, and of Melilla 12 square kilometres. Accordingly most of the population's food needs have to be imported, with the exception of fish which is obtained locally. Sardines and anchovies are the most important items, in an annual catch of about 16,000 tons. A large proportion of the tinned fish is sold outside Spain. More important to the economies of the cities is the port activity; most of their exports take the form of fuel supplied—at very competitive rates—to ships. Most of the petroleum fuels come from the Spanish refinery in Tenerife. Ceuta's port is the busier but, apart from the ferries from Málaga in Spain, Melilla's port is not so frequented and its exports are correspondingly low. But i. figures importantly as an export point for the iron ore mined in the Uixan mines of the Moroccan Rif. Ceuta exports wood, cork, foodstuffs and beverages. Industry is limited to meeting some of the everyday needs of the citiest In both cities less than two per cent of the working population are employed in agriculture. Most of the industry is located in the port area. The total labour force in Ceuta in 1962 numbered 13,080 (construction 2,083, textiles 1,276, fishing 1,384 and commerce 1,768). Unemployment in both towns is about 600–700. Business and port activity are sufficiently high to permit the municipalities budgets which, by Spanish standards, are high in relation to the numbers of population. More than a million tourists visit the enclaves each year, mainly attracted by the duty-free goods on sale.

In 1975 Spain granted 14 million pesetas for the development of facilities in the enclaves.

STATISTICAL SURVEY

CEUTA

Area: 19 square km.

Population (1977): 67,187.

Finance: Spanish currency: 100 céntimos = 1 peseta. Exchange rates (June 1979): £1 sterling = 136.80 pesetas; U.S. $1 = 66.14 pesetas; 1,000 pesetas = £7.31 = $15.12.

External Trade: Ceuta is a duty-free port. Trade is chiefly with Spain, the Balearic and Canary Islands and Melilla.

Transport: Much of the traffic between Spain and Morocco passes through Ceuta; there are ferry services to Algeciras, Spain.

Education: (1975/76): Primary: 263 schools, 10,101 pupils; Secondary: 1,654 pupils.

Government: In both Ceuta and Melilla civil authority is vested in an official directly responsible to the Ministry of the Interior and military authority is vested in a Commandant-General. At present both these positions are held by one official. A Mayor administers the town. Deputy elected to The Congress in Madrid Francisco Olivencia Ruiz.

Religion: Most Africans are Muslims; Europeans are nearly all Catholics; there are a few Jews.

Press: *El Faro de Ceuta*, Solís 4, Ceuta; morning; Dir. Antonio de la Cruz Agustí; Editor Antonio Ferrer Peña.

Radio: *Radio Ceuta*, Virgilio Oñate 1, Ceuta; commercial; owned by Sociedad Española de Radiodifusión; Dir. J. Solera.

MELILLA

Area: 12.3 square km.

Population (1977): 65,271 (Melilla 64,942, Alhucemas 63; Chafarinas 195, Peñón de Vélez de la Gomera 71).

Finance: Spanish currency (*see* Ceuta).

External Trade: Melilla is a duty-free port. Most imports are from Spain but over 90 per cent of exports go to non-Spanish territories. Chief exports: fish and iron ore from Moroccan mines.

Transport: There is a daily ferry service to Málaga and a weekly service to Almería. Melilla airport is served by a daily service to Málaga, operated by Iberia.

Education (1975/76): Primary 251 schools, 8,338 pupils; Secondary: 1,431 pupils.

Government: A mayor administers the town. Deputy elected to the Congress in Madrid José Manuel García-Margallo.

Press: *El Telegrama de Melilla*, Ejército Español 16, Melilla; morning; Dir. Tomás Galbán Noguera.

Radio: *Radio Melilla*, O'Donell 26, Melilla; commercial; owned by Sociedad Española de Radiodifusión; Dir. G. Palau.

BIBLIOGRAPHY

Areilza, J. Ma. De, and Castiella, F. Ma. Revindicaciones de España (Madrid, 1941).

Boucher, M. Spain in Africa (3 articles, *Africa Institute Bulletin*, May–July 1966).

Habsbourg, Otto D. E. Européens et Africains: L'Entente Nécessaire (Hachette, Paris, 1963).

Pélissier, René. Los Territorios Españoles de Africa (Madrid, 1964).

Sudan

PHYSICAL AND SOCIAL GEOGRAPHY

L. Berry

THE NILE

The Democratic Republic of Sudan is the largest state in Africa (2,500,000 sq. km.), stretching across nearly 18° of latitude and from sub-equatorial forest to some of the driest desert in the world. These vast spaces of contrasting terrain are, however, linked by the unifying Nile. Any account of Sudan should perhaps start with the river, so vital is it to the republic. The Nile enters Sudan from Uganda in the south and the "Bahr el Jebel" is fed by a number of streams draining the south-west of the country. Some miles north of Mongalla, the river enters the Sudd region where seasonal swamps cover a large part of the area. The White Nile drains the Sudd region northward, though half of the flow is lost by irrigation in the Sudd. The Blue Nile drains a large part of the Ethiopian Highlands and joins the White Nile at Khartoum. The two rivers are very different. In August the Blue Nile is in flood and, rising seven metres above its low level, makes up nearly 90 per cent of the total discharge at Khartoum (7,000 cu. m. per sec.). At low water the more regularly flowing White Nile provides 83 per cent of the discharge and the Blue Nile is reduced to a mere 80 cu. m. per second. North of Khartoum the Nile is the focus of most agricultural activity and pump irrigation along its banks provides a green strip through the desert to Wadi Halfa and Lake Nasser. The Atbara, which is the only tributary north of Khartoum, flows for about six months of the year and then dries up into a series of pools.

PHYSICAL FEATURES

Away from the Nile Sudan is mainly a plainland and plateau country, although there are a number of important mountain ranges such as the Imatong and the Nuba Mountains (rising to over 1,500 m.) in the south; Jebel Marra, a largely extinct volcano (over 3,500 m.) in the west; and the Red Sea Hill ranges (over 2,000 m.) in the north-east. Elsewhere the plainlands, diversified in places by smaller hill ranges, slope gently to the north and towards the Nile.

CLIMATE

Sudan has a range of tropical continental climates, with a marked climatic gradient from south to north and from the Ethiopian plateau north-westwards. In the south the rainy season lasts up to eight months, producing over 1,000 mm. of precipitation, while at Atbara, north of Khartoum, there is a one-month rainy season in August and only 50 mm. of rainfall. In the north high summer temperatures are common, mean daily maxima reaching about 104°F. in Khartoum in May and June, though there is usually a marked diurnal range (about 68°F.). In the south temperatures are lower (average daily maxima 86°F.), the hottest months being February and March.

VEGETATION AND SOILS

Vegetation types are related to the climatic gradient. Tropical rain forest is found only in the uplands of the extreme south; and the south-east is dominated by a wooded-grassland complex, which merges northwards in Kordofan, Darfur and Blue Nile Provinces to a "low woodland savannah", dominated by acacia and with large areas of short grassland. Northward is a gradation through semi-desert to desert. The pattern is broken in the south by the large swamp grasslands of the Sudd area.

In the south-east areas from east of Khartoum to Juba alkaline clay soils dominate, and the south-western part of the country has red latosols, but elsewhere soils are predominantly sandy with pockets and strips of finer materials along the water courses.

POPULATION

The population of Sudan at the census of April 1973 was 14,819,271, compared with 10,262,536 at the time of the previous population survey in January 1956. The total population is small in relation to the size of the country, but there is a very uneven distribution, with over 50 per cent of the people concentrated in 15 per cent of the total national area. High densities occur along the Nile and around Khartoum, but parts of Kordofan near the railway line, the Nuba mountains and parts of Bahr el Ghazal and Darfur have average densities of 15 per sq. km. with much higher local concentrations. The people of northern Sudan are of mixed Arabic and African origin and traditionally are nomadic or semi-nomadic; in the south Nilotic peoples predominate, the Nuer, the Dinka and the Shilluk being the most important.

The major towns are the provincial centres, with the three towns of Khartoum, Omdurman and Khartoum North forming by far the largest urban centre. The Khartoum urban complex, with a population of about 800,000, is the main industrial, commercial, communication and administrative centre, and handles 90 per cent of the external trade. Of the other towns Atbara, the centre of the railway industry, Wad Medani, first town of the Gezira, El Obeid and Juba are the most important. Sudan has a well-developed railway system which now provides good links with the most populated parts of the country. The road system is poorly developed, and outside the main towns well maintained roads are rare. Communications suffered considerable damage in the civil war.

HISTORY

Muddathir Abdel-Rahim

The geographic position of the Sudan, between the Mediterranean-Middle Eastern world on the one hand and Central Africa on the other, has played an important part in determining the character and politics of the country since Biblical times at least. In almost all the contacts between the Sudan and the outside world Egypt has been the most important link, and, especially since the rise of Islam, the dominant one. Thus the Pharaohs, the Persians, the Greeks, the Romans, the Arabs, the Turks and the British, all those who governed or conquered Egypt in the past, have in turn found it either necessary or desirable to extend their influence, if not their power, beyond the traditional boundaries of Egypt (between the first and second cataracts) into the lands which now constitute the Republic of Sudan. Conversely, the inhabitants of those lands, or at any rate those of them who lived in the northern parts of the country, have always had to choose between three alternative policies: domination by Egypt; independence from their neighbours; or conquest of Egypt; at one time or another each of these possibilities was actually realized. At no time, however, could either of the two countries ignore the other—a fact which, with modern Egyptian nationalists, became the justification for making the Unity of the Nile Valley for many years the *raison d'être* of Egyptian foreign policy.

ANCIENT AND MEDIEVAL

From the time of Tuthmosis I (1530–1520 B.C.) until the eighth century B.C. northern Cush (as the area as far as the Gezira was called in ancient times) was, for the most part, under the effective control of the Pharaohs. And even after the political supremacy of the Pharaohs had been completely shaken off the Cushites continued to be so thoroughly Egyptianized that, at times, they regarded themselves as the champions of true Egyptian culture.

The political mastery of the Pharaohs in Cush gradually diminished from the tenth century onwards, and by 725 B.C. the balance of power was finally turned by a series of competent Cushite leaders who established themselves as the twenty-fifth Pharaonic dynasty. The most renowned Pharaoh of this Cushite dynasty was Tirhaka (688–663 B.C.) under whose leadership the empire extended from Cush to Syria and whose wars in Syria and Judea are recorded in the Bible. Tirhaka's empire, however, did not last long; a number of setbacks led to his final defeat by the Assyrians in 666 B.C. The kingdom of Cush survived for a thousand years, during which it expanded to the south, the capital being transferred from Napata, near the fourth cataract, to Meroe, near Kaboshiya, about 100 miles north of Khartoum. But under the pressure of Nubian migrants from the south-west and the new power of Axum in the east, the Meroitic kingdom declined and there was little of its former glory left when the first Christian king of Axum raided the Nile valley in A.D. 350.

From this cataclysm emerged three Nuba kingdoms into which Christianity was introduced from Egypt under the patronage of the Empress Theodora early in the sixth century A.D.

By A.D. 639, when the Arab Muslims invaded Egypt, two Christian Nuba kingdoms occupied approximately the territory formerly covered by the Meroitic realm. With the more northerly of these the Arab invaders made a treaty which subsisted for six hundred years. Under the terms of this agreement Islam began to spread into Nubia and Arab immigration—especially after the rise in Egypt of the Bahri Mamluks around A.D. 1250—gathered momentum. As a result of the twin processes—greatly facilitated by the fact that Muslim Arab immigrants readily intermarried with the indigenous population—Nubia was gradually transferred into a largely Islamized and Arabized society. The process culminated in the collapse of the last of the Nubian Christian kingdom in 1504 and the establishment thereafter of the Islamic Sultanate of the Funj.

The Islamic Sultanate of The Funj, otherwise known as "the Black Sultanate", was, in effect, a confederation of smaller Sultanates or tribal chieftainships, each ruled from Sinnar, the new capital city on the Blue Nile, about 170 miles south of Khartoum. The authority of the Sultan at Sinnar was recognized throughout the former lands of Cush and Nubia, including the Gezira, but was contested in Kordofan by the dynasty of Sultan Suleiman Solong, which established itself in Darfur in 1596. Largely as a result of internecine warfare and wars with the Furs in the west and the Abyssinians in the east the energies of the Funj were sapped and, by the nineteenth century, when Muhammad Ali Pasha of Egypt challenged them, their Sultanate was already in decline.

THE NINETEENTH CENTURY

Muhammad Ali had two main objectives in the Sudan: gold and slaves, both of which he needed in order to build an Egyptian-Arab empire independent of that of the Sultan in Istanbul. His ambitions in this respect were frustrated by the European powers and his dreams about gold were proved to be false. But Muhammad Ali did succeed in establishing an empire in the Nile Valley which lasted from 1821, when the last of the kings of Sinnar surrendered, until 1885 when Khartoum fell to the Mahdi. Kordofan and Darfur were subsequently added to Sinnar and, under his successors, principally Khedive Ismail, the boundaries of the empire were extended to the Great Lakes, and by 1877 the Somali coast as far as Ras Hofun was also recognized as Egyptian territory under the suzerainty of the Sultan.

Within this vast but loosely organized empire the Sudan was, at first, viewed as a province of Egypt but its administration, centred on the new capital of Khartoum, was afterwards decentralized and put under a Hakimdar (or Governor General) to whom provincial governors were responsible. And the provinces were likewise divided into smaller units which tended to follow the traditional tribal and territorial boundaries of the Funj period. The personnel of the new regime was a mixture of Circassian, Turkish, European and Armenian officers of the Ottoman-Egyptian army who were assisted, especially at the lower levels, by Sudanese sheikhs and tribal leaders.

Like its counterparts in other parts of the later Ottoman empire the Sudan administration was corrupt and far from efficient. Its difficulties, arising from the general malaise of the declining empire, were further accentuated, on the one hand by frequent and arbitrary interference from Cairo and, on the other, by the policy of rapid but poorly organized expansion which was followed by Muhammad Ali's successors, especially Khedive Ismail. Ismail furthermore was determined to abolish slavery in his own lifetime. Slavery had been part of the social system throughout the Nile Valley including the southern Sudan. But trading rights in the newly opened south had been sold to armed adventurers, and searching for slaves was carried to extremes which were in many cases reminiscent of the barbarities of the triangular slave trade. Ismail hoped to mitigate these evils by administrative means and through the agency of European expatriates such as Sir Samuel Baker and General Charles Gordon. But the violent methods used by these men in order to abolish the slave trade alienated large sections of the population, caused considerable social and economic dislocation and to that extent weakened the government's control over the country and played into the hands of the Sudanese religious rebel Muhammad Ahmed Abdulla. In March 1881, Abdulla declared that he was the Mahdi and called upon the people to rally with him against the Turks and for the reformation of Islam. This was not, at first, taken seriously by the government. The Mahdi on the other hand showed remarkable skill in manoeuvre and organization, and under his able leadership the apparently minor rebellion was rapidly transferred into a nation-wide "jihad" which by January 1885 resulted in the fall of Khartoum. Thus began a new chapter in the history of the country during which the Sudan was governed by Sudanese; first under the Mahdi and after his death in June 1885, by the Khalifa Abdullahi whose rule lasted for more than thirteen years.

In the meantime Britain had occupied Egypt and assumed effective, but indirect, control of its government. Thus, in 1883, the Government of the Khedive, acting on what was officially described as the advice of the British Government, concluded that it could not hold the Sudan against the Mahdists and therefore decided to evacuate the country and concentrate, instead, on the development of Egypt's own resources. It was in order to execute this policy that Gordon was sent to Khartoum where he was killed when the town fell to the Mahdi. The Egyptian nationalists greatly resented this policy of evacuation which they felt was dictated by British, not Egyptian, interests.

Ten years later Britain, in order to safeguard its own position in Egypt and to ward off the Italians, the Belgians and, most importantly, the French—all engaged in the general scramble for Africa, including the Upper Nile—decided that the Sudan also should be brought under its effective control. But since conquest would have brought Britain in direct conflict with the French and the other European powers in Central Africa, the British Government decided that the conquest should be done in the name of the Khedive and Egypt who, it was contended, were now in a position to reaffirm their control over what was described as Egyptian territory which had been temporarily disrupted by the Mahdist rebellion. The reconquest, as it was called, was as unpopular with the Egyptian nationalists as the policy of evacuation had been ten years previously—and for the same reasons. Opposition notwithstanding, the reconquest was executed by combined Egyptian and British forces under the general command of General Herbert Kitchener. It took three years: from 1896 to 1898, when, on September 2nd, the last of the Mahdist forces were destroyed at the battle of Omdurman.

THE CONDOMINIUM

The scramble for Africa which dominated the closing decades of the nineteenth century convinced the British government that, in order to safeguard Britain's interests in Egypt and to ward off the Italians, the Belgians and, above all, the French from the upper reaches of the Nile, it was necessary that the Sudan be brought under British control. Since this would have brought Britain in direct conflict with the French and other European powers in central Africa, however, the British government decided that the conquest should be done in the name of the Khedive and Egypt who, it was contended, were now in a position to reaffirm their control over what was described as Egyptian territory which had been temporarily disrupted by the Mahdist rebellion. The reconquest, as it was called, was as unpopular with the Egyptian nationalists as the policy of evacuation which had been imposed on Egypt after the fall of Khartoum to the Mahdi in 1885. In spite of opposition, the reconquest was executed by combined Egyptian and British forces under the general command of Gen. Herbert Kitchener. It took three years: from 1896 to 1898 when, on September 2nd, the last of the Mahdist forces were destroyed in the battle of Omdurman.

The Anglo-Egyptian Agreement of 1899 laid the foundations of the new régime in the Sudan. The important, but thorny question of sovereignty over the country was, however, deliberately left out of the Agreement. For, from Britain's point of view, the acceptance, as binding law, of the theory that the new régime was a restoration of the Ottoman-Egyptian régime overthrown by the Mahdi was undesirable because it would have left Britain without legal basis for its presence in the Sudan, while the alternative—the theory that Britain was sovereign or had a share in sovereignty over the Sudan—would have aroused the hostility, not only of the Egyptians and the Sultan, but also of the French and the other European powers, and was therefore similarly undesirable. While emphasizing the claims which accrued to Britain by virtue of her participation in the reconquest, therefore, the Agreement was silent as to the juridical positions of the two conquering powers in the Sudan. This allowed Britain considerable scope for political and diplomatic manoeuvre. Thus, when the French questioned Britain's presence in the Sudan the British Government insisted that it was acting on behalf of the Khedive; when the Egyptian nationalists raised the same question they were reminded of Britain's role in the reconquest; and when they protested their inferior position in the administration of the country, though they had contributed the larger share of men and money during the reconquest and almost all the expenses of the administration, Britain maintained that this was only fair as the country was reconquered in the name of Egypt which, however, was unable to govern itself let alone the Sudan. This was perhaps illogical but from a practical point of view, it made little difference so long as Britain was in effective control of Egypt as well as the Sudan. After Egypt's independence in 1922 however, and especially after the abolition of the Caliphate, in whom sovereignty over the Sudan had theoretically resided during the Ottoman-Egyptian régime, the silence of the Agreement as to the subject of sovereignty became a source of increasing embarrassment to Britain.

The juridical dispute aside, the Agreement established in the Sudan an administration which was nominally Anglo-Egyptian but was actually a British colonial administration. Like the Ottoman-Egyptian administration it was headed by a Governor-General in whom all civil and military authority was vested. He was appointed by Khedivial decree but on the recommendation of the British Government, without whose consent he could not be dismissed. Nothing was mentioned in the Agreement about his nationality but it is not surprising that all the Governors-General of the Sudan—like the Province Governors and District Commissioners who assisted them—were British. The British character of the régime became more obvious after 1924, when the Egyptian troops, officers and civilians who had hitherto acted as intermediaries between the British and the Sudanese were evacuated from the Sudan following the murder in Cairo of Sir Lee Stack, the then Governor-General of the Sudan and Sirdar (i.e. C.-in-C.) of the Egyptian Army. The administration of the country was until then based on the principle of Direct Rule and was, especially before the First World War, carried out along military lines. This was necessitated by the fact that resistance to the new régime did not cease after the battle of Omdurman and risings against it occurred annually. By the end of the war, however, the process of pacification, except in the south, was completed, and the last stronghold of Mahdism was taken when, in 1916, Sultan Ali Dinar of Darfur was killed and his Sultanate made a province of the Sudan.

INDIRECT RULE

The evacuation of the Egyptians from the Sudan in 1924 was generally unpopular with the Sudanese, especially the non-Mahdists and the small but influential educated class, who sympathized with the Egyptians on grounds of common language and religion, and saw in Egypt a natural ally against the British. Demonstrations were therefore organized in order to show solidarity with the Egyptians, and a Sudanese battalion mutinied and clashed with British troops. The rising was, however, ruthlessly crushed. Relations between the Sudan Government and educated Sudanese deteriorated rapidly and a period of intense bitterness began which lasted well into the 1930s and was much aggravated by the depression and the subsequent retrenchment of salaries.

It was against this background that Indirect Rule, through the agency of tribal sheikhs and chiefs, was introduced, which soon replaced Direct Rule as the guiding principle in administration. Tribalism, which had been greatly weakened during the Mahdiyya, was revived and encouraged not only for purposes of administrative decentralization but also, and more importantly, as an alternative to bureaucratic government which necessitated the creation and employment of more and more educated Sudanese. These, because of their education, however limited, were politically more conscious than tribal leaders and therefore more difficult to control. Simultaneously with the stimulation of tribalism and tribal institutions therefore, training centres such as the military college were closed down; courses for training Sudanese administrators were discontinued; and harsh discipline which "savoured strongly of the barracks" was introduced in the Gordon College—an elementary institution which had been opened in 1902 for the training of artisans and junior officials. In general, the period from 1924 to the mid-thirties may be described as the golden age of Indirect Rule, or Native Administration; but from the point of view of education—always, under the British, closely connected with policy and administration—it was, in the words of a distinguished British scholar, "a period of utter stagnation". Economically, however, it was notable for the development of the Gezira scheme, whose cotton crops were largely responsible for the growth of the government's revenue from £1,654,149 in 1913, when the budget was balanced for the first time since the reconquest, to over £S4 million in 1936 and nearly £S46 million in 1956. Today the scheme covers nearly 2,000,000 acres and is the basis for the country's prosperity.

The introduction of Native Administration in the Northern Sudan after 1924 was paralleled in the south, by the launching of the government's new "Southern Policy". Until then official policy in the south was, apart from the maintenance of law and order, largely limited to the provision of various forms of assistance to Christian missionary societies which, in the words of an official Annual Report, worked for the proselytization of the population and "teaching these savages the elements of common sense, good behaviour, and obedience to government authority". After the rising of 1924 which, incidentally, was led by an officer of southern (Dinka) origin, the "Southern Policy" was introduced. It had two main objectives: the prevention of the spirit of nationalism, which had already taken root in Egypt, from spreading across the Northern Sudan to the south and to other East African "possessions"; and the separation of the three southern provinces from the rest of the country with a view to their eventual assimilation by the government of neighbouring British territories which, it was hoped, would then emerge as a great East African Federation under British control. Accordingly, Muslim and Arabic speaking people in the south, whether they were of Egyptian, northern Sudanese or west African origins, were evicted from the region while stringent systems of permits and "Closed Districts" were introduced to prevent others from entering. Southerners, on the other hand, were discouraged from visiting or seeking employment in the north, and those among them who had adopted the Muslim religion or used Arabic names, clothes or language were persuaded, by administrative means (which sometimes involved the burning of Arab clothes) to drop them and use, instead, Christian, English or native equivalents. Whereas education was then stagnating in the north and had so far been neglected in the south it was now enthusiastically supported by the government—but along lines calculated to eradicate all traces of Islamic and Arabic culture, and thus gradually sever relations between the northern and southern provinces.

TOWARDS SELF-GOVERNMENT

As may be expected the Southern Policy, like Native Administration, was most unpopular with the nationalists who, by the mid-1930s, had recovered from the shocks they had suffered after the failure of 1924. Encouraged by the challenge which the Axis powers were then presenting to Britain and by the restoration of Egypt's position in the Sudan in 1936, itself largely the result of the changing international scene, they began to mobilize themselves and prepared to resume their offensive. The Graduates' Congress, representing the *literati* of the country, was established early in 1938. Stimulated by the war, the Atlantic Charter and the open competition of the Egyptian and Sudan Governments for their sympathy and support, the graduates, in 1942, submitted to the government a famous Memorandum in which they demanded, *inter alia*, the abolition of the Closed Districts Ordinance; the cancellation of subventions to missionary schools and the unification of syllabuses in the north and the south; an increase in the share of the Sudanese in the administration of their country and the issue of a declaration granting the Sudan the right of self-government directly after the war. The government rebuffed the graduates by refusing to receive their Memorandum but nevertheless proceeded to react, on the local level, by the gradual transformation of Native Administration into a modern system of local government and, in central government administration, by launching, in 1943, an Advisory Council for the Northern Sudan which was replaced, in 1948, by a Legislative Assembly for the Sudan as a whole. The development of local government, however, was a very slow process (the first comprehensive local government Ordinance being promulgated as late as 1951); and it was in any case peripheral to the main wishes of the nationalists. The Advisory Council and the Legislative Assembly on the other hand failed to satisfy them because, among other things, they had very little power to exercise (in the case of the Council no power at all), while their composition, largely based on the principle of appointment rather than free elections, only partially reflected political opinion in the country.

The limitations of the Council and the Assembly notwithstanding, the promulgation of these institutions had the effect of accentuating differences within Congress and eventually splitting it into two rival groups. Some worried about Egypt's continued claims over the Sudan and, feeling that independence could best be achieved by co-operating with the government, thought that Congress should participate in the Council and the Assembly however defective they were. This group, led by the Umma Party, was supported by the Mahdists, and their motto was "The Sudan for the Sudanese". Others being more distrustful of the British, felt that independence could best be achieved through co-operation with Egypt which was an Arabic-speaking and Muslim neighbouring country and, like the Sudan, despite its formal independence, a victim of British imperialism. They therefore stood for "The Unity of the Nile Valley" and, supported by the Khatmiyya, the chief rival of the Mahdists among the religious fraternities, boycotted both the Council and the Assembly.

In the meantime successive negotiations between the British and Egyptian governments led from one deadlock to another and the unhappy schism between "the Unionists" and "the Independence Front" continued until the outbreak of the Egyptian Revolution in July 1952. The new régime promptly disowned the king and the Pasha class with whom "The Unity of the Nile Valley under the Egyptian Crown" was a basic article of political faith, and thus cleared the way for a separate settlement of the Sudan question. Neguib, Nasser and Salah Salem, all of whom had served in the Sudan and knew the Sudanese well, then staged a diplomatic *coup* which put the initiative in their hands.

The British had consistently justified their continued presence in the Sudan in terms of their desire to secure self-determination for the Sudanese as opposed to imposing on them a unity with Egypt which many Sudanese were prepared to resist by force of arms if necessary. Having got rid of the king the new Egyptian régime now declared that it was equally willing to grant the Sudanese the right of self-determination. On the basis of this declaration an Anglo-Egyptian Agreement was signed in 1953. This Agreement provided, among other things, for the Sudanization of the police and the civil service and the evacuation of all British and Egyptian troops in preparation for self-determination within a period of three years. Elections, held under the supervision of an international commission, resulted in the victory of the National Unionist Party, whose leader Ismail El Azhari became the first Sudanese Prime Minister in January 1954 and proceeded to put the terms of the Agreement into effect. The Egyptians had supported the NUP during the elections and it was naturally expected that Azhari would try to lead the country in the direction of union with Egypt. However, by the time the Sudanization programme was completed and the Egyptian and British troops had left the country, it was clear that he stood for independence. Several reasons led to this apparent reversal of attitude. Among these was the fact that the overwhelming majority of the NUP had looked upon solidarity with the Egyptians as a means for achieving the independence of the Sudan. Besides, the official opening of Parliament on March 1st, 1954, witnessed a violent demonstration by the Mahdists of their determination to split the country if the government wanted to lead the Sudan along the path of unity with Egypt rather than independence. Several people were killed and the ceremony to which guests from many countries, including Gen. Neguib, had been invited, was postponed. It then became obvious that independence would not only satisfy the aspirations of the Sudanese but would also save the country from civil war. One thing, however, could still frustrate the country's progress to independence: namely the mutiny of southern troops at Juba in August 1955. This was the prelude to an attempted revolt in the south in which nearly three hundred northern Sudanese officials, merchants and their families were massacred. The disorders, except for some sporadic outbursts, did not spread to the two provinces of Upper Nile and Bahr El Ghazal but were centred in Equatoria. Order was restored in due course but the political problem of the south which, springing from the geographic and social differences between the northern and southern provinces, had been greatly accentuated by the "Southern Policy" of the British administration, continued to present a serious challenge to the Sudanese and the unity of the Sudan. Before they could vote for independence southern members of Parliament insisted that their request for a federal form of government be given full consideration. This they were duly promised.

The agreement had prescribed a plebiscite and other protracted procedures for self-determination. Azhari, supported by all Sudanese parties, decided to sidestep these arrangements, and on December 19th, 1955, Parliament unanimously declared the Sudan an independent republic and, at the same time, resolved that a committee of five elected by Parliament exercise the powers of the Head of State in place of the Governor-General. Faced with this *fait accompli* Britain and Egypt had no choice but to recognize the Sudan's independence, which was formally celebrated on January 1st, 1956.

THE INDEPENDENT SUDAN

Since achieving independence the Sudan (renamed Sudan in 1975) has had four regimes: a civilian parliamentary regime, which lasted until November 1958; a military régime, which, under Gen. Ibrahim Abboud, continued in office until it was overthrown by a "civilian *coup*" in October 1964; a second civilian régime, which was then ushered in and lasted until May 1969 when the existing régime of Gen. Gaafar Nimeri came to office. Successive governments under all four régimes have been faced, above all, by three major problems: that arising from the country's dependence on one cash crop, i.e. cotton; the problem of the southern Sudan which was inherited from the British colonial régime; and the search for a permanent constitution for the country.

Throughout the greater part of the first régime the Sudan was governed by an improbable Mahdist-Khatmiyya coalition which, led by Abdalla Khalil, replaced Azhari and the non-sectarian rump of his NUP shortly after independence. During this period the Sudan established itself in the international field, joining the UN, the Arab League and, later on, the OAU. Internally, social services were expanded; the University College of Khartoum was raised to full university status, railway extensions in the Blue Nile south of Sinnar and in Darfur were completed; and the first stages of the Managil extension began operating, in July 1958, with a gross irrigable area of 200,000 acres. But serious economic and financial problems arising from rapid expansion on the one hand and difficulty in selling cotton crops on the other began to face the country. Politically the unnatural coalition was strained by serious differences between the Mahdist Umma Party and the People's Democratic Party, the political organ of the Khatmiyya. Thus, during the Suez crisis, the PDP felt that Egypt should have been given greater support than the Prime Minister was prepared to give, while some Umma spokesman accused the PDP of softness towards, if not actual complicity with, Egypt when a minor border dispute arose between the two countries in February 1958. And whereas the Umma Party favoured a presidential form of government, with Sayyid Abdel Rahman al-Mahdi as first president, the PDP and the Khatmiyya could not agree. A third difficulty arose from the deteriorating financial and economic situation which, having initially resulted from failure to dispose of the cotton crop of 1957, was compounded by exceptionally poor crops in 1958. With the country's reserves falling rapidly, severe and unpopular restrictions had to be imposed and, the Prime Minister felt, foreign aid had to be sought. But the PDP, already worried by what it considered was the unduly pro-western policy of Abdalla Khalil, opposed acceptance of American aid. Elections, held in February 1958, resulted in no change and the already strained coalition was returned to power. The president of the Umma Party, Sayyid Siddiq al-Mahdi, then sought an alliance with Azhari's NUP. But this was unacceptable to the Prime Minister who was the secretary of the Umma Party. Khalil—who was the Minister of Defence as well as Prime Minister and who had been an army officer—then started consultations with senior army officers about the possibility of a military *coup*.

ABBOUD'S MILITARY GOVERNMENT

The *coup* was launched on November 17th, 1958. To the people in general it came as a relief after the wrangling and differences of the parties. The two Sayyids, al-Mahdi and al-Mirghani, gave their blessing to the régime on the understanding that the army would not stay in power longer than was necessary for the restoration of stability. Gen. Abboud assured the country that his aim was the restoration of stability and sound administration at home and the fostering of cordial relations with the outside world, particularly Egypt.

In the economic field a good start was made by following a realistic cotton sales policy which ensured the sale of both the carry-over from past seasons and the new crop. Loans from various international institutions and aid from the U.S.A., the U.S.S.R. and elsewhere were successfully negotiated. The money was used to finance such projects as the completion of the Managil extension and the construction of the Roseires Dam on the Blue Nile, and the Khashm al-Girba Dam on the Atbara. The latter was used for the purpose of irrigating an area for the resettlement of the people of Halfa whose ancient town had been submerged by waters of the High Dam at Aswan.

But discontent soon began to grow. Prompting this was the feeling that too many officers—encouraged by the absence of democratic procedures of control and accountability—had become corrupt and used public funds for private gain. The result was that when the country was again gripped by financial and economic difficulties in 1964 the public was convinced that this could not be accounted for in terms of the poor cotton crop of that year, nor in terms of over-ambitious economic development schemes; they no longer trusted the government. In the field of administration other than financial a system of provincial administrations not unlike Pakistan's "Basic Democracies" was introduced in 1961 and this was crowned in 1962 by the creation of a Central Council which met for the first time in November 1963. While these arrangements, aimed at the training of the people in self-government, were in principle acceptable to most Sudanese, the actual working of the system—very much under the control of military personnel—not only failed to win the politically sophisticated but also alienated the civil service and professional administrators, many of whom were involved in friction with army officers. Thus when the civil service was called to join the judiciary, university staff, workers and others in the general strike which followed the outbreak of the revolution in October 1964, the response was both complete and enthusiastic.

THE CIVILIAN COUP

The immediate cause of the revolution was the government's heavy-handed administration in the south. This was based on the mistaken idea that the problem of the southern Sudan was a military, not a political, problem and that it was mainly the result of the activities of the missionaries who had participated in the implementation of the "Southern Policy" of the British administration. But the expulsion of missionaries in February 1964 dramatized the problem for the outside world rather than helped to solve it, while military action against both the *Anya Nya* rebels and the civilian villagers who were sometimes obliged to give them food and shelter had the effect of forcing thousands of southerners to live as refugees in neighbouring countries and convinced many that the only solution of the problem was for them to have a separate and independent state in the south. Concerned for the unity of the country, politicians, university students and others started campaigning for the view that the country could not be saved except by the removal of the military from authority and the restoration of democratic government. Orders forbidding public discussion of the southern problem and other political matters were issued but were defiantly disregarded by students. On October 21st the police, determined to break up such a discussion, opened fire on the students within the precincts of the University. One student died and the revolution was thereby set in motion. A general strike brought the country to a standstill and Gen. Abboud was forced to start negotiations with a Committee of Public Safety, to which he subsequently agreed to surrender political power. His decision was partly dictated by the fact that the army was known to be divided and that the younger officers especially were reluctant to open fire on unarmed civilian demonstrators with whom they generally sympathized.

A transitional government in which all parties including, for the first time, the Communist Party and the Muslim Brotherhood, were represented, was sworn in under Sirr al-Khatim al-Khalifa, an educationalist with a good record of service in the south, as Prime Minister. As a result of the inclusion as ministers of representatives of the communist-dominated Workers' and Tenants' Trades Unions and certain front organizations, the cabinet as a whole was dominated by the Communist Party.

After restoring the freedom of the press, raising the ban on political parties and starting a purge of the administration (which was subsequently abandoned on account of its being carried along personal and partisan lines) the new government turned to the most important problem facing it: the problem of the southern Sudan.

One of the first acts of the government had been a declaration of a general amnesty in the south. On March 16th, 1965, a round table conference in which northern and southern parties participated was opened in Khartoum. It was also attended by observers from seven African countries. The northern parties proposed to set up a regional government in the south which would, among other things, have its own parliament, executive and public service commission. The southern parties which attended the conference were divided. Some wanted federation; others a separate state; while the unionists (who were not represented in the conference because the two other groups would boycott the conference if they were allowed to participate) favoured the *status quo*. The conference failed to reach a general agreement on the constitutional future of the country and the subject was then referred to a Twelve Man Committee on which all parties—except the unionists—were represented. But agreement was reached on a constructive programme of immediate action which included the repatriation of refugees and the restoration of order, freedom of religion and unrestricted missionary activity by Sudanese nationals and the training of southerners for army, police and civil service.

Externally, the transitional government supported national liberation movements in Southern Arabia, Congo (K.) and among the Eritreans in Ethiopia. But this, like the purging of the administration, was controversial and was especially disliked by the Umma Party and the NUP who, together with the Islamic Charter Front (at the core of which was the Muslim Brotherhood), formed a front against the more left-wing PDP and the Communist Party. As a result of mounting pressure on the part of the former elections were held in June 1965. They were boycotted by the PDP but were heavily contested by all other parties. The Umma Party won 76 seats, the NUP 53, the Communists 11 (out of the 15 seats in the graduates' constituency) and the Islamic Charter Front 7. For the first time tribal groups fought elections, winning 21 seats: 10 for the Beja and 11 for the Nuba of Kordofan.

COALITION GOVERNMENT AGAIN

The new government had to be a coalition. This was formed by the Umma and the NUP with Muhammad Ahmad Mahgoub (Umma) as Prime Minister and Azhari the permanent President of the Committee of Five which collectively acted as Head of State.

To pacify the Ethiopian and Chad governments, both of which had been provoked by the policy of the transitional government with regard to liberation movements in their territories, Mahgoub hastened to affirm his government's adherence to the Accra pledges of non-interference and signed a border pact with Ethiopia in June 1966. This was followed by a number of visits to neighbouring countries with a view to confirming the new government's position in this respect and, at the same time, making arrangements whereby the return of Sudanese refugees from these countries would be facilitated.

Internally, the government ran into a number of difficulties. In July 1965 there was serious rebel activity at Juba and Wau, and large numbers of southerners were killed in the course of reprisals by government troops. Subsequently there were severe difficulties in retaining southern representatives in the government. Personal animosity between Azhari and Mahgoub led to a crisis within the coalition in October which was only solved by the mediation of the young Umma Party President, Sadiq al-Mahdi. Government policies meanwhile became increasingly right-wing, and in November 1965 the Communist Party was banned and its members unseated from the Assembly. This was contested in the courts which, in December 1966, ruled that it was illegal. But the Constituent Assembly, acting in its capacity as constitution-maker, overruled the courts' judgement. A crisis in which the judiciary and the Assembly confronted one another was thereby precipitated, but this was finally resolved in favour of the Assembly.

In the meantime a serious split was developing between the right wing of the Umma Party, led by Imam al-Hadi (Sadiq's uncle) which supported Premier Mahgoub, and the younger and more moderate elements who looked to Sadiq for more effective leadership. Sadiq, however, was reluctant to accept the Premiership not only on account of his young age (30), but also because failure (which was likely, in view especially of the mounting financial and security problems of the country) would prejudice his political future. But events and the pressure of his supporters finally obliged him to change his mind. After a heavy defeat in a vote of censure, on July 25th, 1966, Mahgoub resigned and Sadiq was then elected Prime Minister.

Sadiq's government was also a coalition of Umma and NUP but included, as Minister of Finance, an able expert of Khatmiyya background, Hamza Mirghani, who had been Principal Under-Secretary of the Ministry of Finance and a senior official at the IBRD. There were also two southern Ministers.

With the help of stringent controls and loans from the IBRD and IMF the economy gradually began to recover and the country's reserves of foreign currency, which had dropped to £S13 million, began to improve. Meantime the Twelve Man Committee had made considerable progress towards the settlement of the southern problem on the basis of regional government. A "Parties Conference" continued the Committee's work and, in April 1967, submitted a report in which it also recommended a regional solution. By this time the long-awaited supplementary elections in the south had been held, bringing 36 members to the Constituent Assembly of whom 10, led by William Deng, represented SANU, the leading southern party. It was now possible to speed up the process of drafting the permanent constitution and the settlement, *inter alia*, of the southern problem.

The relative success of Sadiq's government, however, coupled with the announcement that he would stand for the Presidency under the proposed constitution, resulted in the break-up of the coalition between his wing of the Umma Party and the NUP whose leader, Azhari, like the leader of the Ansar, Imam al-Hadiq, also aspired to the Presidency. Thus, on May 1967, Sadiq was defeated in the Assembly and Mahgoub was once again elected Premier.

Under his leadership the new coalition of NUP and al-Hadi's branch of the Umma Party pursued a vigorous foreign policy, particularly in the Middle East after the Six Days War. As a result the first Arab Summit Conference after the war was convened in Khartoum (August 1967) and Mahgoub, together with Iraqi and Moroccan colleagues, was subsequently entrusted with the task of finding a formula for the settlement of the Yemeni dispute. Deterioration of relations with Western Powers, culminating in severence of diplomatic relations with the U.K. and the U.S.A. after the June War, was accompanied by the development of closer relations with the eastern bloc, and the conclusion of an arms deal with the U.S.S.R. resulted in the lifting, without formal announcement, of the ban which had previously been imposed on the Sudanese Communist Party. The internal affairs of the country, particularly the already precarious financial situation, had in the meantime been somewhat neglected. The result was that when the Constituent Assembly was reconvened after the prolonged recess which followed the outbreak of hostilities in the Middle East, the opposition, under the vigorous leadership of Sadiq al-Mahdi and William Deng (who, together with the ICF, now formed the New Forces Congress), was able to defeat the government on several occasions. This, together with the growing PDP and Communist opposition to the Draft Permanent Constitution based on Islam, regionalism and a strong executive on the presidential model, induced the government to dissolve the Constituent Assembly on January 7th, 1968, following a mass resignation of the government members in the Assembly. Sadiq and his allies contested the constitutionality of this act in the courts. Before any judgment was pronounced, however, new elections were held in April, which were contested for the first time since 1958 by the PDP, now merged with the NUP in the new Democratic Unionist Party. This won the largest number of seats, 101, followed by Sadiq's Umma, which won 38, and al-Hadi's Umma, with 30 seats. As the DUP did not command a majority on its own, a new coalition, also with Imam al-Hadi's faction of the Umma Party, and under the leadership of Mahgoub, was formed when the Assembly was convened on May 27th.

Mahgoub's third government, however, was unable to improve the economic and financial situation while the situation in the southern provinces continued to deteriorate. Mahgoub, moreover, fell ill and the situation was aggravated by the cabinet crisis of April-May over the reallocation of ministerial responsibilities between the Umma and Democratic Unionist Parties. The result was the bloodless *coup* of May 25th, 1969, when the government was overthrown by a group of officers and civilians led by Col. (later Gen.) Gaafar Mohammed Nimeri.

SUDAN UNDER NIMERI

Already the longest surviving in Sudanese history since the achievement of independence 22 years ago, Nimeri's regime can be said to have passed through two principal phases.

During the first phase, from May 1969 until July 1971, the regime followed distinctly radical policies. This tendency—inherent in Nimeri's declared commitment to a programme of "Sudanese Socialism", which was regarded as an expression of the essential spirit of the October Revolution of 1964—was accentuated by the fact that the Communist Party and its supporters then enjoyed a uniquely dominant position in governmental and policy-making processes. The close alliance which was then forged between the officially dissolved Communist Party and the new military rulers of the country was a function of the fact that the leaders of the more effectively banned traditional political parties and of the Tariqas (i.e. the Ansar and the Khatmiyya) were regarded as having betrayed the October Revolution of which Nimeri and his friends saw themselves as the true heirs and perpetrators. Accordingly, and in order to effectively exclude the traditional parties from the political arena, Nimeri decided to work in close co-operation with like-minded civilians—not on a personal and purely administrative basis as had been the case with Abboud—but with a view to building a permanent base of popular support on the model of the Arab Socialist Union, Egypt's one-party organization. Thus were laid the foundations of the Sudanese Socialist Union.

In the meantime Nimeri announced the formation of a predominantly civilian cabinet some of whose members—including a number of communists who had chosen to follow his lead rather than that of their officially dissolved party—had played prominent parts in the October Revolution. At first Sayyid Babiker Awadalla, a former Chief Justice, was appointed Prime Minister and thus became the only civilian member of the Revolutionary Council. But he was subsequently replaced as Prime Minister by General Nimeri who had been President of the Revolutionary Council and was subsequently elected first President of the Sudan.

Under this leadership the country was given the new name of "The Democratic Republic of the Sudan". Banks, together with a wide variety of firms and companies, were nationalized. The property of certain persons, including members of the Mahdi family, was confiscated. Several former ministers and members of traditional parties were put on trial on charges of bribery and corruption. Following an attempt on the life of General Nimeri, the chief source of opposition to the regime—namely Imam al-Hadi al-Mahdi, who had for some time been gathering weapons and supporters at Aba Island on the White Nile—was crushed in March 1970.

With regard to the southern provinces in particular, the regime declared its commitment to a policy of regional administrative autonomy supported by a programme of economic development and reconstruction on socialist lines. A special Ministry for Southern Affairs was created which, under the guidance as Minister of Joseph Garang—a Southern Sudanese lawyer who was a member of the Communist Party—was charged with the responsibility of spelling out the details of that policy and the supervision of their implementation.

In the field of foreign affairs, one of the first decisions taken by the regime was to recognize the German Democratic Republic. This was followed by the forging of closer diplomatic and trade relations with China, the U.S.S.R. and Eastern Europe. In the Middle East the regime's policy was, above all, characterized by its militant support for the Arab cause over the Palestine question and, for some time after the Libyan coup of September 1969, with Gaddafi of Libya as well as with Nasser and the U.A.R. Subsequently, General Nimeri personally participated in the resolution of the Jordanian crisis and, in November 1970, it was declared that Presidents Nimeri, Sadat and Gaddafi had decided to unite the Sudan, Libya and the U.A.R. into one federal state.

This was unacceptable to the Communists who, having already suffered serious internal strains resulting from differences over the question of how best to handle the new regime, now feared that they would be subjected to the same fate as their Egyptian counterparts. The growing mistrust and hostility culminated in an open bid for power by the Communists. This took the form of a coup which, led by Major Hashim al-Ata, resulted in the overthrow of General Nimeri on July 19th, 1971, and the subsequent liquidation of some thirty officers who were known to favour him and his policies.

The communist coup, however, proved abortive. Its proclaimed head of state, Colonel Babiker al-Nur and his lieutenant, Major Faruq Hamadalla had been in London and while on their way back home the BOAC plane carrying them was forced down in Libya. The Libyan authorities then handed them over to Nimeri who had in the meantime regained power as a result of a popular rising which brought the newly-born communist regime to an end only three days after the *putsch* of July 19th. A massive purge of communists followed and fourteen people were executed. Apart from Major Hashim al-Ata, who had set the coup in motion in Khartoum, and the two leaders back from London, the Communist Party's Secretary General, Abd al-Khaliq Mahjoub and two prominent members of the party, al-Shafia Ahmed al-Shaikh, the Secretary General of the Federation of Sudanese Workers' Union, and Joseph Garang, who had been Minister for Southern Affairs, were eliminated after summary trials before a military tribunal.

The events of July 1971 ushered in the second phase of Nimeri's regime.

In so far as foreign relations were concerned, this phase was characterized by a cooling-off of relations with the Soviet Union and its East European allies, which was matched by a gradual improvement of relations with the U.S.A. and Western European countries. This reversal of attitudes was prompted by the open encouragement which had been given by Bulgaria and the German Democratic Republic to the abortive coup of July 1971 and also by the unusually strong condemnation, by Soviet and East European governments, of the executions which followed Nimeri's return to power. Diplomatic relations, however, remained intact. In the meantime Nimeri received strong support from President Sadat of Egypt.

Commonly regarded as the nation's saviour from militant atheism, Nimeri's personal popularity rapidly soared in the wake of the abortive coup. When the first Presidential elections in Sudanese history were held in October 1971 he received almost four million votes with only 56,000 opposed. A new government was formed, the Revolutionary Command Council was dissolved and the Sudanese Socialist Union was recognized as the only legal political party in the Sudan.

The vitally important Addis Ababa Agreement between the Sudanese Government and the *Anya Nya* southern Sudanese rebels was signed in March 1972. As a result the long standing dispute was settled on the basis of regional autonomy for the three southern provinces. A Regional People's Assembly for the south was established at Juba with representatives in the National People's Assembly and a High Executive Council of its own. The Head of the Executive Council would also be a Vice-President of the Republic—a post which was held until 1978 by the former judge and politician Abel Alier. The Agreement also provided for the return and rehabilitation of southern Sudanese refugees abroad and for the integration of the former *Anya Nya* rebels into the Sudan armed forces. The ceasefire came into effect on March 12th, 1972, and the process of rehabilitation and reconstruction of the region has since been gathering momentum with continued support from Khartoum and President Nimeri personally.

At the national level these developments have been matched by a gradual disengagement from the ideologically inspired postures of earlier days and the adoption, instead, of measures for the economic and social development of the country on the basis of a more pragmatic approach. Thus in January 1973, a presidential decree repealed the previous orders of expropriation and a policy of "denationalization" affecting some of the firms and companies which had previously been taken over by the state has been inaugurated. Laws intended to encourage foreign investments have also been promulgated and a strategy aimed at the marriage of Western technology and Arabian petrodollars to the vast agricultural potential of the Sudan at a time of pressing shortage of international and regional food supplies has been launched. Thus the political and economic strategies of the country—whether internally or in regard to its relations with the outside world—have been greatly transformed since 1971.

Throughout its two phases, however, the regime showed a consistent determination to exclude the leaders of the traditional parties and their generally right-wing supporters from the political arena. These accordingly organized themselves into a "National Front" which, supported (since 1971) by the Communist Party and its sympathizers, operated as a largely external opposition to the regime. Reportedly harboured and sustained by Libya's Gaddafi (since the deterioration of relations between Libya and the Sudan which had followed Sudan's interception of Libyan planes carrying weapons intended for Uganda's General Amin in 1972) as well as by Ethiopia since its more recent revolution, the National Front on several occasions attempted to topple Nimeri by force.

The latest in this series of abortive attempts took place in September 1975 and July 1976. The first of these—a standard coup attempt which was led by an army officer named Hassan Husain—was rapidly put down and its leaders executed. The July 1976 attempted coup—officially decribed as an invasion based and financed from Libya—was a more sophisticated affair which, however, also came to grief and over one hundred of its leaders and others accused of complicity in it were executed.

Since the prolonged stalemate—though it seriously strained the resources of the National Front, the Government and the country as a whole—did not bring about the results desired by either side, alternative courses of action began to be considered: not only on account of what has just been said, but also because the ideological cleavage which had separated the Government and the National Front between 1969 and 1971 had since been rapidly shrinking. In addition such powers as Saudi Arabia and the U.S.A., with both of which the two parties to the conflict had close relations, also favoured a peaceful resolution of the conflict, for both strategic and economic reasons. As a result, protracted and partly secret negotiations were initiated, an important stage being reached in July 1977 when Sayid Sadiq al-Mahdi, who had been under sentence of death, met President Nimeri in Port Sudan. "National Reconciliation", as it was designated, gathered momentum in the course of the following months and, in consequence, the State Security Act of 1974 was abolished, large numbers of political detainees were released and many members of the National Front who had been living in exile, including Sadiq al-Mahdi himself, now returned home, some being appointed to High Office, either as Ministers, or in the SSU, the country's only party organization.

Certain supporters both of the Government and of the National Front, however, have shown a considerable degree of ambivalence towards reconciliation. This may be explained partly in terms of the bitterness generated in the course of the prolonged conflict between the Government forces and the National Front, especially since the events of March 1970, and partly in terms of the controversy within the National Front, including Sadiq al-Hajdi's Ansar itself, over the nature and the terms of the agreement reached between Sadiq and Nimeri.

In an effort to meet some of the objections and reservations made by al-Sharif Husain al-Hindi and his Democratic Unionist faction of the National Front, a supplementary agreement, which more explicitly stressed the need for the restoration of the rule of law and respect for the independence of the judiciary, was reached and formally announced in London in April 1978. But al-Hindi, reportedly supported by Libya, still refuses to return to the Sudan, his argument being that the terms of the agreement with him have not yet been fully implemented.

In the meantime, Sadiq al-Mahdi, who had returned to the Sudan and some of whose supporters now hold senior posts in the administration, has shown his dissatisfaction—especially over President Nimeri's support for the Camp David accord—by leaving the Sudan to live in exile once again. Nimeri, however, is still keeping the door open for him to return.

The February 1978 elections, following which some of Sadiq's supporters as well as supporters of the Islamic Charter Front were integrated into the administration, resulted, in the Southern region, in the defeat of Vice-President Abel Alier and his team of regional ministers, some of whom were considered ineffective as well as corrupt. Instead a new regional government, under General Joseph Lagu, the former *Anya Nya* guerrilla leader, was returned to office with a number of the old guard, such as Clement Mboro and Joseph Uduhu, holding ministerial posts.

But the country as a whole has been suffering the rigours of a deteriorating economy which has resulted in a number of strikes as well as the acceleration of an already serious "brain drain" and exodus of skilled workers, particularly to the oil-rich neighbouring countries. In the field of foreign relations there has been controversy over the Camp David accord as well as over the proposed integration with Egypt which, as may be expected, is particularly resented by Southern Sudanese. Some of the Southern representatives in the National Assembly submitted a strongly-worded statement of protest in January 1979 when the second joint session of the Egyptian and Sudanese Assemblies was convened in Khartoum.

There was more of a consensus, however, over the handling of issues affecting Africa. Here the Sudan continued its traditional policy of reconciliation between, for example, the Eritreans and the Government of Ethiopia and, in the Chad conflict, between the forces led by Prime Minister Habré and those backing President Malloum. Progress here, however—as in the consolidation of the reconciliation exercise at home—has been slow. But, having successfully brought about a peaceful settlement to the 17-year-old North-South conflict within the Sudan in 1972, President Nimeri, who in the year of his tenth anniversary as ruler of the Sudan symbolically combined the Chairmanship of the OAU and the Presidency of the Arab League's Solidarity Committee, continued to pursue reconciliation and co-operation as the principal features of his policy at home, within neighbouring countries to the east and to the west of the Sudan, and also between African and Arab countries in general.

ECONOMIC SURVEY

Ali Ahmed Suliman

THE MAIN CHARACTERISTICS OF THE ECONOMY

Sudan is primarily an agricultural and pastoral country. Agriculture, including forestry, livestock and fishing, contributed 38.7 per cent of G.D.P. in 1974/75 (the most recent year for which national accounts are published). Livestock, though very undeveloped, contributed 18.4 per cent of G.D.P. in 1974/75. The significance of agriculture in the Sudanese economy is also reflected in the distribution of manpower among the different economic sectors. About 85 per cent of those economically active (according to 1955/56 figures) are engaged in primary production. Manufacturing industries contributed only about 2 per cent of the G.D.P. up to 1962/63, increasing to 9.2 per cent of G.D.P. in 1974/75, while the share of minerals is less than 1 per cent. No important minerals have yet been found in Sudan in significant enough quantities to be exploited economically. Sudan not only depends on agriculture, but on one main crop for its exports. In fact the share of extra-long staple cotton in the exports of Sudan reaches more than 70 per cent in some years. Such dependence on one major export crop, with wide fluctuations in price and quantity exported, has caused political, as well as economic, instability.

With such a traditional agricultural sector it is not surprising that Sudan has a low per capita income, which was only U.S. $97 in 1963/64, rising a little to $109 in 1970/71 and reaching $242 in 1974/75 at current prices, which reflected merely an inflationary rise in prices, estimated to be not less than 15 per cent per annum. From 1961–71 G.D.P. in Sudan grew at an annual rate of 4 per cent in current prices but overall, economic growth has been negligible. The population was believed to have been growing annually at a rate of about 2.8 per cent but the results of the 1973 census suggested a much lower rate of increase. The 1973 census figures were subsequently revised upwards, but they have not as yet been officially released.

The average density of population in Sudan is low and there is no population pressure on the available resources at present. Open unemployment is very insignificant. In fact, Sudan suffers from a shortage of labour, particularlv during the cotton-picking season. Sometimes this problem is soived by immigrant labour from neighbouring countries. Sudan is a large country with large unproductive areas. Unfortunately it is these vast unproductive parts which are close to the Red Sea, whereas the more productive regions are separated from the sea and from Port Sudan by distances ranging between 500 and 1,500 miles. Their remoteness was a major factor in retarding economic development in the past. For the present, inadequacy of transport is one of the important bottle-necks in the economy, and this has been worsened by the 17 years of civil war up to 1972, when there were only 8 miles of tarred road in the southern region.

Perhaps one of the most striking features of the Sudanese economy is the dominant role which is played by the public sector in all important economic activities. The government owns the majority of modern capital establishments in the economy. In the current Six-Year Plan (1977/78–1982/83), the share of the government in the total proposed investment of £S2,670 million is 59 per cent, while the share of the private sector is 41 per cent. In the period 1955/56–1974/75 the share of the government in gross fixed capital formation ranged between a half and two-thirds. However, it seems that the role of the public sector as a whole in gross fixed capital formation declined in the 1970s. In 1970/71, out of a total of £S73.2 million of gross fixed capital formation, the share of the public sector was only £S20.6 million. The Government is not only the chief investor in public utilities, but is the main promoter of industries such as sugar, cotton-ginning, food processing, tanning and printing. Governmental efforts to develop the country have expanded to such an extent that all large hotels in the various parts of Sudan are owned and managed by the Government. With the nationalization of all commercial banks and several leading commercial firms in May and June 1970 the economic significance of the public sector has become even greater. However, after 1976, the Government policy seems to be changing and it has begun to denationalize some of the nationalized firms (e.g. Bata Shoe Factory) and if such a policy continues, it may lead to a further decline in the size of the public sector.

AGRICULTURE

The availability of water is the governing factor for agriculture in Sudan. In most parts of the rainlands of Sudan drinking water for humans and animals is a crucial factor, especially before the rainy season, when land is prepared for cultivation, and after it during harvest time. However, land does not impose any constraint on the agricultural development of the country. The cultivable land is estimated to be about 200 million feddans (one feddan=1.038 acres). Only about 8 per cent of this cultivable land is being utilized in agriculture, and less than four million feddans are under irrigation. Half of this area is in the Gezira scheme (with its Managil extension), and the rest is irrigated by the flood waters of two small rivers in eastern Sudan, Gash and Baraka, by the flood waters of the Nile and by pumps.

Prior to the Nile Waters agreement of 1959 the distribution of water between Sudan and the U.A.R.

was governed by the Nile Waters agreement of 1929, which allocated 4,000 million cubic metres to Sudan. However, with the 1959 agreement and the construction of the Roseires and Khashm el Girba dams, the water problem has been solved. Sudan is now entitled to draw 18,500 million cubic metres at Aswan High Dam or the equivalent of about 20,500 million cubic metres in Sudan, and the way has been opened for considerable expansion of irrigated agriculture. At present Sudan is drawing about half of its entitlement—about 10,000 million cubic metres annually—but with the development of new areas along the White and Blue Nile, Atbara River and the Main Nile, as well as the intensification of the Gezira scheme by reducing fallow, and its diversification by such crops as wheat, groundnuts and *philipesara* vegetables, Sudan is expected to utilize all its entitlement within the coming five years or so. The proposed first phase of Jonglei Project, which is estimated to take about five years, aims at conserving more of the Nile water and thus providing an extra yield of 3,800 million cubic metres at Aswan which is equivalent to 4,700 million cubic metres at Malakal. This extra yield will be divided equally between the Sudan and Egypt, while the total cost, which is estimated to be about £S70 million, will also be divided equally between them. This joint Sudanese-Egyptian project would increase Egypt's share of the Nile water by 1,900 million cubic metres per year and cultivate an extra 300,000 feddans in each of them. One of the main development projects in Sudan is the Rahad project, which will need about four milliard cubic metres of water for an area of about half a million feddans. The Roseires Dam, built at a cost of £S60 million will serve this project. Of the area available, half will be given to cotton, and the remainder to wheat, groundnuts and vegetables. A pump station at Meira on the Blue Nile will feed a supply canal 50 miles long across the Rahad. The project's main canal will be 100 miles long. Railway construction, clearance of land and building of nearby villages are to be undertaken and finance is to be provided by the World Bank, the U.S.A. and Kuwait. About 200,000 feddans are expected to be brought under cultivation by early 1977 and 500,000 acres by 1980. The Sukki project, which has also started, may reach an area of 170,000 feddans, while the pump-irrigated areas of the Northern Province may increase by about 165,000 feddans within a few years to come.

In spite of the significant role played by irrigation (particularly gravity irrigation) in the economic development of Sudan, the rainlands are more important. Total cropped area in Sudan—in spite of its increase in the long run—tends to fluctuate from year to year because of variations in the rainfall. The total cropped area increased from 10.3 million feddans in 1970/71 to 16.7 million feddans in 1977. The total area under irrigation continued to increase and reach approximately 4 million feddans in 1978. With the exception of cotton, pulses and a proportion of groundnuts, Sudan's foodstuffs and most exported agricultural products come from the rainlands. In fact Sudan is self-sufficient in the essential foods: millet, meat, edible oils and salt.

The agricultural sector of the Sudan does not face any serious land tenure problems. The rainlands, in particular, are very free from such problems, and also enjoy the advantage of relatively low production costs. The present Government has already started an anti-thirst campaign and has promised the economic and social development of those areas. The current Six-Year Plan, like all the previous development plans, is more concerned with the modern sector and the irrigated areas, where the rate of return is assumed to be greater in the near future.

Sudan has an animal wealth which contributes on average about 10 per cent of G.D.P. annually. It was estimated in 1977 as 15.9 million cattle, 15.2 million sheep, 11.6 million goats and 2.8 million camels. In 1976 the estimated production of milk was 1,350,000 metric tons and meat 340,000 metric tons. The share of livestock (live animals, hides and skins) in total exports was over 5 per cent between 1971 and 1977. However, this percentage is not expected to increase very much in the future because domestic consumption of meat and hides is increasing at a faster rate than that of production. The Government has occasionally restricted the export of animal products in order to satisfy the local market.

In the year 1962/63 forest reserve estates, which are completely owned by the government, increased by 7,000 feddans to a total of 2,574,000 feddans. Beside gum arabic, the other important forest products are the various types of timber which are processed by the forest department of the ministry of agriculture. In 1972/73 the forest department produced 74,729 railway sleepers, 31,612 poles and 635,000 cubic metres of sawn timber. The main consumer of these products is the government itself.

Sudan is rich in fish and other aquatic resources. The inland fisheries cover more than 20,000 sq. km., while marine fisheries extend for a distance of about 700 km. along the Red Sea. It is estimated that the annual total value of the output of fish and aquatic resources in Sudan is about £S10 million. Potential output of fish from the Nile is 60,000 tons annually (1977) but only a small percentage of this wealth is utilized at present. Since the actual output of fish from inland fisheries is estimated at around 20,000 tons annually, therefore about 40,000 tons are not utilized.

Cotton is the most important crop in Sudan from the economic point of view. It is the major export crop, the chief exchange earner and the main generator of income in the Sudan. A proportion of it is consumed locally by the textile industry. Its average share of exports over the five years 1965–69 was 53 per cent, not including its by-products, and 63 per cent including them. The cotton is of two types: long-staple varieties, Skallarides and its derivatives (commonly known as *Sakel*), and short-staple varieties, which are mainly American types and are consumed locally. The *Sakel* varieties are exclusively for export and are grown in the large schemes of the Gezira and the Gash and Tokar deltas, while the American types are grown in the rainlands of Equatoria, the Nuba mountains, Gedaref and also in some of the pump schemes in the

Northern Province. The volume of output of the American types fluctuates more than the *Sakel*, but is generally increasing at a faster rate. In 1974/75 the total production of *Sakel* was 521,945 tons, while the total production of American types was 121,863 tons.

Owing to competition from synthetic fibres and a policy of self-sufficiency in wheat, the Government is to reduce the area under cultivation for long-staple cotton in the Gezira by a third. This should slightly lessen the Sudan's dangerously high reliance on cotton which was highlighted by the poor export figures in 1974 due to low production and bad marketing arrangements for cotton. In 1973, 1.2 million bales were exported with a value of £S85 million and in 1974 this fell to half a million bales worth £S53.2 million. The share of cotton in the Sudan's exports declined to under 50 per cent in the mid-1970s.

The Sudan's main cereal crop is sorghum (durra). It is the most important staple food in Sudan and is mainly grown in the rainlands. Sudan produces annually about 1.5 million tons of durra, which is usually sufficient for domestic consumption.

With urbanization and social development the consumption of bread made out of wheat flour is increasing by about 10 per cent annually. There seems to be a shift in consumption from *kisra* made out of durra to bread made out of wheat. Wheat is grown mainly as a cash crop. A small proportion of rural people use wheat flour in their diet. To meet the rapidly expanding demand of the urban population the government is growing wheat in the Gezira scheme and other suitable areas. It is also paying a subsidy to encourage its production and at the same time keep the price of bread reasonably low. In March 1975 it was announced that the area for growing wheat in the Gezira was to be increased from 400,000 feddans to 600,000 feddans in 1976, and that for groundnuts was to rise from 370,000 to 600,000 feddans in the Gezira. The value of groundnut exports rose by 40 per cent to £S18.2 million in 1974 and increased to £S34.4 million in 1975.

Reductions in the government's sugar subsidy led to riots in Khartoum in 1974, and radical moves to increase sugar production. The government has a 50 per cent share in the Kenana Sugar Company, set up to create a huge sugar estate 180 miles south of Khartoum, producing 350,000 tons of white sugar annually by 1979 on 100,000 feddans of land. This is the world's largest single sugar project, destined to provide 20,000 jobs, but estimated costs rose from $180 million in 1974 to $600 million in 1977. Plans for sugar refineries at Hassaheisa, Sinnar, Melut (with Belgian aid) and Mongalla (with Czechoslovak aid) are part of a scheme to produce 815,000 tons of sugar annually by 1980.

Sudan gums have been known in trade for at least two thousand years. Gum arabic, which constituted about 10 per cent of Sudan's exports in 1969 and 5 per cent in 1973 was for many years the second export crop, until overtaken by groundnuts in 1971. In 1974, however, its share of exports rose to 12 per cent, valued at £S14.2 million. It is the most important forest product and, though collected in the traditional sector, it is a purely cash crop. It is almost entirely exported, as the confectionery industry manufactures only a very small percentage of it. In the 1960s Sudan was the largest producer of gum arabic, accounting for about 92 per cent of world production in 1962–66. Its monopolistic position has declined in the 1970s. In 1973/74 world production amounted to 62,100 tons but Sudan produced only 29,722 tons.

INDUSTRY

The ginning of cotton encouraged the beginning of industry in Sudan early in this century. With the expansion of cotton production the number of ginning factories have increased until the Gezira Board alone has the largest ginning enterprise under single management in the world. The processing of cotton has not gone beyond ginning. Cotton seeds are partly decorticated, while the exports of cotton-seed oil and oil cakes are increasing. Groundnuts are also shelled for export. Minerals (copper, iron, mica and chromite), which constitute less than 1 per cent of exports, are exported in the crudest form.

With the exception of the soap, soft drinks and oil-pressing industries, large industries manufacturing import substitutes started only after 1960. The government was not involved in any industry until 1959 but from 1960 the involvement in industry began to increase and in 1962 the Government formed the Industrial Development Corporation to look after the large factories of the public sector. By 1968 the Industrial Development Corporation was managing nine manufacturing factories. There are also factories in the public sector managed by the ministries, such as the Government printing press and the mint.

The first factory to be established was the Guneid sugar factory, which, in response to the great increase in the consumption of sugar in the 1950s, came into production in November 1961 with a capacity of 60,000 tons of refined sugar annually. A second factory was needed to meet the local demand and in 1963 Khashm el Girba sugar factory was started, with a capacity similar to that of Guneid. In addition to a tannery, opened in November 1961, the government also has five food processing plants: one cannery and one date factory in Kareima, another cannery in Wau, an onion dehydrating plant in Kassala and a milk factory in Babanousa. What is very striking about these food processing industries is that the supply of raw materials is not high enough to match the productive capacity, and therefore, the weakness in these factories is not technical but agricultural.

The private sector has also played an important role in the industrial development of this country. In the period 1960–69 the private sector invested £S35.9 million in industries of which £S16.1 million was Sudanese and £S19.8 foreign capital. The foreign capital is mainly savings of foreign residents accumulated from the profits of the import and export trade. The bulk of the investment has gone into the textile, soap, oil-pressing, footwear, soft drinks, printing, packing, flour, and knitwear industries. In the 1970s, the role of the private sector increased. In 1970/71, the private sector invested £S52.6 million in fixed capital formation, of which £S22 million is transport and £S14.8 million is machinery and equipment. The private sector is increasingly tending to invest in transport because of the serious inadequacy of the present system of transport available in the Sudan.

The government has encouraged industrialization in Sudan by various means. The Approved Enterprises (Concessions) Act, 1959, gave generous concessions to infant industries. The Organization and Promotion of Industrial Investment Act, 1967, has been even more generous to industry. It gives exemption from the business profits tax for a number of years, depending on the size of the invested capital, allows very high rates of depreciation, gives very fair treatment to losses, reduces import duties on imported machinery and materials, protects domestic production by high tariffs and import restrictions and allocates building lands at reduced prices. In addition to this, the Industrial Bank, which was established in 1961, assists in the financing of private industrial enterprises with up to two-thirds of the capital required. In 1974 a new act was introduced for the development and encouragement of industrial investment which gave generous terms like the previous acts. The 1974 Development and Encouragement of Industrial Investment Act is not very different from the 1972 Act which it has superceded. The major changes made by the 1974 Act have eliminated only one of the seven conditions of the 1972 Act regarding the eligibility for concessions, namely that enterprises must be established in rural areas. Under the 1972 Act a total exemption from Business Profits Tax was allowed for a period of five years; a further total exemption for five years was also allowed if profits did not exceed 10 per cent of the capital employed by the enterprise and a 50 per cent exemption from the tax was given if the profits were between 10 and 20 per cent of the capital employed. Under the 1974 Act any profits over 10 per cent of capital are subject to Business Profits Tax. The provisions relating to depreciation in 1972 Act are taken over by the 1974 Act but with the addition of the further incentive of allowing an enterprise to keep a reserve to cover increases in the prices of fixed assets. However, the provisions contained in the 1974 Act on transfers of capital abroad are more restrictive than those of the 1972 Act.

The industrial scene in Sudan is changing because of the dramatic expansion in textile and sugar industries which resulted from the Government's policy of self-sufficiency and the rise in the prices of sugar in 1974/75. While the South West Sennar Sugar Factory was completed in October 1976, the Hagar Asalaya, Melut and Mongala sugar factories are under construction. The Kenana Sugar Factory (a joint venture between the Government and the private sector) is in its final stages of construction. Seven textile factories, which are expected to meet all the local demand for popular textiles and to export yarn (by the end of the Six-Year Plan in 1982), are planned. Five of these factories are completed, while the Friendship Weaving and Textile Factory, built by the Chinese, completed its first stage in 1976. The construction of a cement factory at Dordaib, which is a joint venture between the Government and the private sector, has started. Most probably, production will start in 1982 and then the acute problem of cement shortage may be eased. The construction of a fertilizers factory should have started by the second quarter of 1978. Sudan has been importing all the fertilizers it needs, and it seems that it will continue to do so until the early 1980s.

In 1973 several international companies showed interest in exploring for oil in Sudan. An exploration concession covering 3,360,000 acres on the Red Sea coast and offshore, north and south of Port Sudan, had been granted to several international companies, mainly American, by mid-1975. The government has the right to a 50 per cent interest in the project and intends to build a further refinery at Port Sudan. The oil pipeline between Port Sudan and Khartoum was completed in 1977. It is designed for the transport of motor gasoline, gas-oil and kerosene, including aviation turbine fuel. It has a capacity of 600,000 metric tons, a length of about 850 km. and a diameter of 8 inches. At present, because of technical problems, the pipeline is carrying gas-oil of about 420,000 metric tons per annum. It seems that the under-utilization of the pipeline is partly caused by the shortage of crude oil. Because of the Sudan's balance of payments difficulties, the Bank of Sudan has not been able to meet Iraqi payments at the due date. Sudan has been importing crude oil from Iraq since mid-1975. Some time ago, Iraq imposed a policy of "no money, no oil", and vessels carrying Basra light crude oil for Sudan were ordered not to unload until payments were made, thus causing cut-offs in supply to the refinery and ultimately hardship to industry and the country as a whole.

FOREIGN TRADE

The value of Sudan's exports rose from £S63.4 million in 1960 to £S193.0 million in 1976, while the value of imports rose from £S63.7 million to £S341.4 million. The balance of payments would have become a more serious problem if it had not been for the government's policy of clamping down on imports and encouraging exports. There are import restrictions and high import duties on a large number of goods, though in 1975 further categories were exempted, but export taxes are light and no licence is required for export, with the exception of goods consumed locally and in short supply.

Imports rose considerably in 1973 to £S166.9 million compared with exports of £S143.5 million, thus putting renewed strain on the balance of payments.

Owing to the poor cotton crop and low market prices for what was produced, the trade deficit widened enormously to £S77.6 million in 1974 and £S183.1 million in 1975, the Sudan's heavy debts adding further to the serious economic situation.

Sudan's main exports are primary agricultural products, and since the establishment of the Gezira Scheme in 1925, cotton has dominated Sudan's exports. Between 1960 and 1971 the share of lint cotton alone ranged between 46 and 65 per cent. In 1971 the U.S.S.R. was the largest buyer of Sudan's cotton, followed closely by India, the People's Republic of China, whose share had doubled since the previous year, and the EEC. However, after the attempted *coup* in 1971 the U.S.S.R.'s purchases dropped to nil in 1973 when the People's Republic of China took the largest share, 51,903 tons, followed by Japan, Italy and India. A trade agreement with China in 1975 envisaged that imports and exports should be £S36 million for that year, and guaranteed a market for a large share of the Sudan's cotton crop, which had been hit by lower world market prices during 1974 and 1975. In the last ten years, due to the expansion of production in the traditional sector, the relative importance of oil seeds as exports has increased and in 1973 groundnuts formed the second most important export crop with a share of about 9 per cent of exports, rising to 14.9 per cent in 1974. The EEC is the largest buyer of Sudan's groundnuts (60 per cent). The east European countries buy about 20 per cent of the groundnuts and the rest go to various west European countries. Gum arabic has been overtaken in importance in the 1970's. In 1975 and 1976, while gum arabic formed about 5 per cent of exports, groundnuts formed 22.6 and 20.2 per cent of exports in the same years. As a result of the Lomé Convention which the Sudan signed in April 1976, trade relations between the Sudan and the EEC have been further strengthened. However, the technical and financial co-operation achieved so far does not appear to be significant.

The major imports are vehicles, transport equipment, machinery, appliances and textiles, and in 1973 sugar imports greatly increased. In 1963 Sudan produced only 61 per cent of its domestic sugar needs. There are new plans to expand the sugar industry, so as to produce a surplus for export in the late 1970s. The growth of industries which are manufacturing import substitutes has affected the pattern of imports since the mid-1960s. The imports of footwear and cigarettes are declining in relative and absolute terms.

Perhaps a more striking change has taken place in the pattern of suppliers and buyers, if the late 1960s are compared with the early 1950s. The U.K. used to be the largest seller and buyer from Sudan (30–40 per cent before independence). In 1976 only 3.5 per cent of Sudan's exports went to the U.K., and only 5.5 per cent of imports were brought from the U.K. Trade with socialist countries increased since independence until 1971 as a result of several bilateral agreements. Their share in Sudan's trade has, with the exception of the People's Republic of China, drastically declined since the attempted coup in 1971. Exports to the U.S.S.R. fell from £S18,351,000 in 1971 to £S3,000 in 1973. Since 1973 the U.S.S.R. has almost ceased cotton purchases from the Sudan. Trade with the Arab countries has been expanding in recent years and exports to them have reached about 10 per cent, but imports from these countries form a smaller percentage.

Exports of animals and other foodstuffs to Arab countries are not expected to increase because the surplus of such materials is diminishing in the Sudan. Unless large Arab investment flows into such fields, the percentage of such exports to Arab countries is not expected to increase and may even decline.

Trade with the EEC continued to grow in importance. In 1977 about half of Sudan's exports and imports were traded with EEC countries. Within this group, the U.K. is still the largest supplier. However, trade with the U.S.S.R., India, China and Egypt declined in late the 1970s compared with the early 1970s. After 1973 the U.S.S.R. almost ceased to buy any Sudanese cotton—for political reasons. Trade with Egypt declined in the mid-1970s, in spite of bilateral trade agreements. However, as a result of the protocol ratified in January 1977, Egypt's share of Sudan's exports has remained about the same, but Sudan's imports from Egypt declined from about 5 per cent in the early 1970s to about 2 per cent in 1978. Trade with India is expected to be insignificant, as the trade agreement with India was terminated in March 1977.

The government tried to redress the chronic balance of payments deficit, which has persisted since 1956, by introducing in March 1972 an exchange tax on all transfers abroad and a subsidy paid on all receipts from abroad of about 15 per cent. This was also meant to discourage black market dealings in foreign currencies. However, despite a three-year refusal to concede to the demands of the IMF—which included devaluation—the increasingly precarious foreign exchange position made the government agree to devalue the Sudanese pound in June 1978 from $2.87 to $2.50, in addition to raising the exchange tax from 15 per cent to 25 per cent. This effectively increased the devaluation to about 25 per cent. In March 1979 the government increased the incentive paid to non-residents to encourage them to transfer their savings to the Sudan. The balance of payments deficit seems to be a growing problem without a foreseeable solution.

FOREIGN AID

The Ten-Year Plan of Economic and Social Development, 1961/62–1970/71, was the country's first experience in planning, although there had been three previous attempts to develop Sudan in a systematic manner: 1946–51, 1951–56 and the Managil extension programme. In contrast to the Ten-Year Plan, the development programmes were not comprehensive, being concerned only with some projects in the public sector and depending on finance from savings of the public sector.

The total gross investment of the plan was estimated to be £S565 million, of which 40 per cent (£S228 million) was to be sponsored by the private sector and 60 per cent (£S337 million) by the public sector. Out of the total investment £S415.9 million was to be financed by domestic savings and £S219.7 million from foreign financial assistance. The £S415.9 would consist of £S219.7 million public savings and £S196.2 million private savings.

The amount of foreign aid which was actually received in the period 1960–69 did not fall very much short of the target of the plan. While £S150 million of foreign aid was forecast for the period 1961/62–1970/71, £S141 million of aid in the form of grants, long-term and medium-term loans and in kind was received in the period 1960–69. However, in spite of the small difference between projected and realized foreign aid, the plan could not be properly implemented, mainly because of a shortage of domestic and foreign finance.

The Khashm el Girba and Roseires dams could not be utilized fully because the lack of finance prevented the associated works being completed. Additional reasons, such as wastage and corruption, also contributed to hampering the completion of projects of the public sector.

From the Eastern Bloc, aid to Sudan from Yugoslavia has included a tannery, a cardboard factory and 3 ships, which form part of the Sudan Shipping Line. By 1973 a second tannery at Khartoum had been completed and a third was to be built at Malakal. Romania was assisting the development of river transport and in prospecting for petroleum in 1973. The U.S.S.R. has provided Sudan with two grain elevators, factories for processing agricultural and dairy products, a hospital and veterinary laboratories. The change in Sudanese foreign policy, however, has since 1971 led to more aid from Western countries and from the People's Republic of China. China has built a foundry, completed the construction of a textile mill at Hassaheisa in 1976 and a conference hall in Khartoum, as well as a section of the Khartoum-Port Sudan highway. This will run from Wad Medani to Gedaref, with two bridges across the Blue Nile and Rahad rivers, which were completed in 1977.

By early 1976 Sudan appeared to be in a favourable position to benefit from Arab aid, with close relations with most Arab states. In 1975 the Arab Fund for Economic and Social Development (AFESD) announced a ten-year plan to double G.D.P. in Sudan, and in 1975 plans were being prepared for a massive investment of $6,000 million of Arab funds in Sudan for a scheme which would produce a substantial amount of the food requirements of Arab countries by 1985. This would involve a projected annual growth rate in Sudan of 5.8 per cent between 1975 and 1980 and 8 per cent between 1980 and 1985, with greatly increased production of cereals, meat and sugar. In 1960-69 Arab aid totalled about 30 per cent of the total received. In 1972 relations with Egypt and Libya deteriorated, and Sudan received aid mainly from Kuwait and Saudi Arabia. In 1974 Saudi Arabia agreed to co-operate with Sudan in developing the resources of the Red Sea as part of a reported Saudi Arabian investment aid programme in Sudan of an estimated $2,000 million. Saudi Arabia also guaranteed a large loan on the Euro-dollar market over 10 years for Sudan in February 1974, and Sudan negotiated a further Euro-dollar loan of $20 million in June 1974. Saudi budgetary aid of $5 million was announced in April 1974. In 1973 Kuwait granted assistance for financing the construction of a sugar refinery at Sinnar. Kuwait also agreed to finance excess cotton unsold in the 1974–75 season. In 1975 Kuwait increased its promised contribution to the important Rahad Project to $62 million, and the IDA promised an increase to $50 million with the AFESD contributing $9 million, the U.S. Government $11 million, and Saudi Arabia a loan of $39 million in June 1975. Relations with Egypt improved in 1974 and the Higher Ministerial Committee for Co-ordination and Integration between Egypt and the Sudan have set up three joint companies, for Agriculture and Irrigation, for River Transport and for Construction.

Aid from the United Kingdom and U.S. also has often been dependent on political circumstances. In 1973 the U.S.A. donated wheat worth £S3.6 million and made a loan of £S9.6 million to enable Sudan Airways to purchase two Boeings. The U.S.A. also made a contribution of £S3.9 million to the Rahad Project and assisted in the construction of a dry batteries factory completed in September 1975. The United Kingdom had contributed to the development of the electricity system in Juba and guaranteed £S10 million to help build the Sinnar sugar refinery. Norway is to provide $4 million in general aid and the Norwegian Church Research Agency is to provide aid for the South. Belgium is assisting with the construction of a sugar refinery at Melut. The Netherlands and UNHCR collaborated in a project to build a bridge across the Nile which was completed in 1973. The Federal Republic of Germany has played an important role in financing the economic development of the country by contributing to the financing of the Roseires Dam, and credit from German firms helped to finance the Guneid and Khashm el Girba sugar factories. In 1973 funds were loaned to the Sudan for railways, telecommunications aid and improvements in the television and veterinary services.

The benefits for Sudan in aid from international organizations are considerable. For 1972-76 the UN promised $88 million in aid. A $40 million grant for food research from the FAO, announced in April 1975, will include the expansion of research facilities at Khartoum University. In May 1975 the World Bank offered a loan of $10 million for educational expansion, especially in the South, and the IDA also offered $10 million for a similar scheme particularly to benefit the South, as well as $23 million for the development of power resources. The World Bank has played a vital role in Sudan's aid projects, contributing loans of $245 million under generous terms since 1958. The Bank has financed vital projects such as the Roseires Dam, mechanized farming, Sudan Railways extension and dieselization, and the Managil Extension.

In 1973 Sudan was also granted loans of £S25.7 million from the World Bank for the Rahad scheme, railway improvements and electricity generation. IMF special drawing rights up to £S9 million were granted to support balance of payments stabilization. The vast relief operation to rehabilitate and resettle southern refugees was covered by aid from the UN which contributed over $20 million, aid organizations and foreign governments.

Total external resources received in 1978 amounted

to £S68 million, which was more than twice the amount received in 1977. This capital inflow included £S10 million representing drawings on a $200 million loan granted by Saudi Arabia and £S39.5 million as short-term credit from the IMF. However, the inflow of gross external resources to be used for development, amounted to only £S2.5 million, compared with £S9.5 million in 1977. Debt servicing during 1978 amounted to £S46.8 million against £S38.3 million in 1977. The ratio of debt servicing to export proceeds marginally increased from 13.3 per cent in 1977 to 14.3 per cent in 1978.

Three EEC members, the Federal Republic of Germany, the U.K. and the Netherlands, decided to write off their governments' outstanding debts on the Sudan in 1978 and consider them as grants. The outstanding debts amounted $218 million, £S10.1 million and $19 million in respect of loans from the Federal Republic of Germany, the U.K. and the Netherlands. Such a generous move reduced the foreign liability of the Sudan government by about 16 per cent in 1978.

PUBLIC FINANCE

The Sudan government, like governments in many other underdeveloped countries, depends heavily on indirect taxes as a major source of revenue. In the fiscal year 1972/73 indirect taxes contributed 43 per cent of the central government's revenue, while in 1975/76 they yielded about 47.8 per cent. In recent years the relative share of indirect taxes declined because of increased import restrictions, and also because of the increased revenue from direct taxes and proceeds from government agricultural enterprises. The main source of revenue from indirect taxation is import duties. Because of balance of payments deficits in recent years the Government has been trying to restrict imports of consumer goods, particularly luxuries, and those which bear the highest rates. Excise duties are growing in importance because of the growth of industries producing import substitutes. Thus, the share of excise duties in revenue from indirect taxation, 5 per cent in 1964/65, rose to 36.9 per cent in 1975/76. This change is also reducing the rate of increase of revenue from indirect taxation.

The revenue from direct taxes was about 9 per cent of the total revenue of the central government in 1975/76, having been 2.7 per cent in 1963/64. The present direct taxes of Sudan (1977/78) are income taxes, and a stamp duty. The revenue for the fiscal year 1968/69 for all the units in the public sector was estimated at £S171,878,116, and the maximum limit of borrowing by the Government from the Central Bank was fixed at £S24.5 million, while the actual borrowing of the Government during that fiscal year was £S24.3 million. The ceiling for central government borrowing from the Bank of Sudan during the fiscal year 1976/77 was fixed at £S44.8 million. However, actual temporary borrowing by the Government amounted to £S73.88 million by end of June 1976. By the end of December 1976 temporary borrowings dropped to £S44.8 million because £S33.7 million was transferred from temporary borrowings to the long-term loan account which stood at £S217.7 million at the end of that year. Revenue for all units in 1974/75 was £S277.5 million, and in 1975/76 it was estimated to be £S337.3 million.

Since the mid-1960s the Sudan government has been finding it more and more difficult to make all its local cash payments, whether wages and salaries or payment to contractors, on time. This seems to be the result of two main factors: underestimation of expenditure and ineffective financial control of government accounts. This problem of the illiquidity of the public sector has forced the government to seek various ways to increase revenue and reduce expenditure, but it has not yet been solved. Deficit finance from the Bank of Sudan has been increasingly used to finance the government's expenditure, but this is reaching a critical limit and adding to existing inflationary pressure.

The expenditure of the central government has been rising very fast since independence in 1956. In 1949 the total current expenditure of the central government was £S10 million; by 1975/76 it was an estimated £S304.5 million. Besides the rise in prices and the normal expansion in government services, increased expenditure on education, national defence and the rise in wages and salaries of the employees of the public sector have accentuated the rate of increase of the total current expenditure in recent years. The expenditure of the Ministry of Defence increased from £S14.1 million in 1965/66 to £S37.7 million in 1975/76, while the expenditure of the Ministry of Education increased from £S5.8 million in 1965/66 to £S15.9 million in 1975/76. In February 1979, President Nimeri took the country by surprise and announced a decentralization programme which gave power to the provinces. Seven ministries were abolished and four ministries had their powers reduced. If this policy is maintained in the long term, political authority will be developed in the provinces and, with it, public finance in the Sudan will witness important changes. Provincial and local councils will spend more, and local taxes will have to be developed to support them, and taxes collected by the central government will have to be divided among them in an equitable and acceptable manner.

LABOUR AND WAGES

The number of persons five years of age and over reported in the 1955/56 census as mainly engaged in economic activity was 3,800,000 out of a population of 10.2 million. In addition it was estimated, on the basis of detailed tabulations of the census returns, that 1,116,000 persons, whose main activity was not economic, took part in subsidiary economic activity. So the total number engaged to any degree in economic activity was approximately 4,916,000 or 48 per cent of the population. Sudan's labour force is overwhelmingly male. Men made up 56 per cent of the total economically active population, women 24.7 per cent, boys 14.4 per cent and girls 4.9 per cent.

Of all the males and females in the labour force 86.7 per cent were primary producers, 3.3 per cent secondary producers and 10 per cent tertiary pro-

ducers. All these percentages of sex and industrial distribution of the Sudan's labour force have not, it is thought, changed very much since 1955/56.

As the figures of the 1973 census have not been released officially, it is still difficult to get any reasonably accurate data beyond 1956 in order to assess the labour situation in the Sudan. However, according to an ILO Employment Mission (1975), the labour force of the country, broadly defined, is estimated at 7 million persons, of whom about one million move around Sudan during any year in response to geographical disparities in employment opportunity. These are mainly migrants from Western Sudan to the Gezira Scheme and to the mechanized rain-fed farming schemes in the Gadaref area, the Nuba Mountains and Kordofan. They include rural-urban as well as rural-rural migrants, but the figure excludes the movements of nomadic cattle-herding tribes in response to variations in rainfall, which amount perhaps to another million. Rural-urban labour migration in Sudan, though not yet very dramatic, is beginning to cause some concern because of its social effects as well as increasing urban unemployment.

Until about 1965 one of the country's major problems was considered to be the shortage of skilled workers. There was heavy dependence on expatriates of Greek and Armenian descent, who filled a high proportion of skilled jobs and managerial and executive posts.

However, by 1965 the major development projects were finished. The most important factories in both private and public sectors, as well as Khashm el Girba and Roseires dams, were finished by that year. In the early 1960s institutes of technical education and training centres were established and by 1965 their graduates could meet the demand for skilled labour.

In fact, after 1965, unemployment began to appear among skilled workers in the towns, and some economists and businessmen began to believe that the shortage of skilled workers was no longer a serious problem to the industrialization of Sudan. Sudan has already started to export skilled workers, clerical staff and teachers to the Arab countries. However, the increasing "brain-drain" of high-level manpower (e.g. doctors, engineers, university lecturers, etc.) to the Arab oil-producing countries is causing concern in Sudan.

The only available figures on unemployment come from the registrations at employment exchanges in major towns. In 1967/68 31,919 were registered as unemployed. In 1974/75 registered unemployment totalled 73,881. However, it is obvious that this **figure does not represent total open unemployment in Sudan. Not all the workers register themselves when they are unemployed, particularly unskilled workers.** On the other hand, some workers may register more than once, while, when other workers find a job, neither they nor their employers report to the employment exchanges. Therefore, the present figures of unemployment in Sudan should be viewed with great caution.

In 1974 a new minimum wage was introduced in the private sector in stages, to become £S16.5 per month by October 1977, for enterprises which employ ten workers or more in Khartoum and Gezira Provinces as well as in large towns in the other provinces. However, in 1979 the minimum wage was raised to £S28 per month, while the minimum pay for unskilled workers rose to 150 piastres per day. With the increase in inflation, especially after the devaluation of the Sudanese pound in June 1978, wages and salaries rose considerably during the second half of 1978 and continued to rise in 1979. In addition, the government introduced a job evaluation and classification scheme which was partly implemented as from January 1979. This scheme has resulted in a large increase in the cost of wages and salaries paid by the public sector and added further to inflation in the Sudan. Some economists—in the absence of reliable price indices—have estimated that the general price level approximately doubled between June 1978 and April 1979, because of devaluation and the job evaluation scheme. Although the main objective of the scheme is to make wages and salaries in the public sector as a whole more rational, it has increased the wage bill of the public sector by about £S100 million and created a series of strikes and discontent among employees of the public sector who are seeking to retain their acquired rights.

PLANNING AND DEVELOPMENT

The first development plan was a ten-year plan, 1961/62 to 1970/71. Then a five-year plan 1970/71 to 1974/75 was published in 1970 and later in the year **it was revised. Because of nationalization, the share of the public sector in investment increased from £S200 million to £S215 million. The private sector's share in capital investment has been fixed at £S170 million. The major targets of the plan are: to increase G.D.P. at an average rate of 7.6 per cent annually; to increase the revenue of the Government to £S953 million compared to £S516.5 million for the previous five years; to increase the share of commodity production to 65 per cent in 1974/75 as against 61.1 per cent in 1969/70; to increase industrial production by 57.4 per cent, and to increase the volume of agricultural production by 60.8 per cent. In June 1974 it was announced that the Plan would be extended to June 1977 and named the Amended Five-Year Plan.** The allocations to the 1974/75 development budget totalled £S194 million though actual expenditure did not exceed £S65 million, of which £S43.8 million was provided by external sources. The estimated 1975-76 development budget was £S281.8 million, of which £S69.3 million was allocated to industry, £S58.9 million to agriculture and £S58.9 million to transport and communications.

The general aim of the plan is to promote welfare through an increase in productivity, realization of full employment and an expansion of public services. The number of projects in the plan for the public sector was 276, of which 239 projects have actually been started. In 1970/71 40 projects (17 per cent of the total planned) were completed.

To accelerate the implementation of development projects earmarked in the Five-Year Plan, many of which were behind schedule, the Interim Action Programme was formulated in December 1973. This was an extension of the period of the plan to 1976/77. The programme emphasized self-sufficiency in the daily necessities of the population, but it failed to achieve its objectives. The current Six-Year Plan (1977/78–1982/83) envisages a total investment of £S2,670 million, of which £S1,570 million (59 per cent) is to be invested by the public sector and £S1,100 million (41 per cent) by the private sector. Foreign sources will provide 53 per cent of the finance for the plan, while deficit finance provides 18 per cent and current budget surpluses represent only 6 per cent. The additional fiscal effort of the Government is expected to provide 23 per cent of the resources needed to finance the plan. It is obvious that there is too much reliance on foreign sources and deficit finance, especially in the face of inflationary pressures from which the economy has been suffering.

The sectoral shares in the allocations of the Six-Year Plan are very similar to those in previous plans: agriculture and irrigation 32 per cent; industry, mining, power and tourism 25 per cent; transport and communications 24 per cent; and social services and public administration 19 per cent. One of the important features of the latest plan is that it has a very limited degree of flexibility in these proposed allocations because of on-going projects. In the case of the public sector, such projects account for £S370 million, or 23.6 per cent of the total planned investment of £S1,570 million. These on-going projects could not be completed during the amended Five-Year Plan and therefore they were carried over to the Six-Year Plan. However, the rate of financial implementation of the Six-Year Plan in 1977/78 was 60 per cent of the planned expenditure.

The main current problems facing the implementation of the Six-Year Plan are the shortage of local and foreign finance and the inadequacy of the transport system (especially railways), as well as the shortage of power and cement.

POWER AND TRANSPORT

The installed generating capacity of Sudan in 1977 was 112,900 kW. thermal and 19,600 kW. hydro. The total power generated in 1976 was 641,842,742 kWh. The number of consumers is 68,529 residential and commercial, 558 agricultural and 844 industrial. All the main towns of Sudan are supplied with electricity and some of the small towns which lie near to the transmission lines, such as Kamlin, also enjoy this facility. Seventeen towns altogether are provided with electricity. In June 1975 it was announced that the World Bank was to provide $23 million out of a total of $40 million for a project to spread electricity in the Sudan. The African Development Bank has loaned $5 million.

The volume of electricity used by industry is 118,353,000 kWh. (1972), while the volume of electricity used by agriculture for pumps is 26,200,000 kWh. The electricity consumption of industry does not include that of ginning factories, the large oil mills and Guneid and Khashm el Girba sugar factories. All these generate their own electricity from by-products. The grain silos at Gedaref and Port Sudan have their own generating sets.

Sudan depends mainly on railways for transport. Steamers and motor transport play only a secondary role. All-weather roads are very limited. The total length of asphalt main roads is 821 km. The length of cleared tracks covered with gravel is 4,936 km. The length of just cleared tracks is 12,496 km. and these make up the main network of roads in Sudan. However, they are usually impassable immediately after the rains. Road bridges cross the Blue and White Niles at four points, and four dams on the river also carry traffic. The Civil War caused considerable damage to communications in the South where 1,600 km. of road and 70 bridges were destroyed. A major reconstruction programme is under way. Construction of the Khartoum-Port Sudan road is progressing and 789 km. had been completed by the end of March 1978. This has roughly trebled the length of asphalt roads the Sudan. The total number of trucks in Sudan in 1977 amounted to 29,795, operating mainly between Khartoum and Port Sudan. The government is believed to intend to introduce a system of tolls on this road. The completed section of the Khartoum-Port Sudan road has already helped to ease the transport problem on that route. However, it is not expected that the road alone can solve the problem of transport between these two important centres because about two-thirds of Sudan's traffic is of the bulk type which is very expensive to transport by road for such long distances.

Rail facilities, though improved, are far from adequate. The length of the railway network is 4,781 km. and the average density of railways for the whole country is only 1.9 km. per 1,000 sq. km. The river fleet comprises 386 low-speed old steamers of various types. River transport is mainly used between Kosti and Juba (1,435 km.) and between Dongola and Kareima (187 km.); these routes are navigable all year round. The total length of the river navigation routes is about 4,068 km., of which 1,723 km. are open all the year and the rest are seasonal. River transport between Wadi Halfa and Shellal, which lies partly on Lake Nasser, is under development at present. As far as sea transport is concerned, the government company, the Sudan Shipping Line, one of the successful public enterprises, owns seven dry cargo ships of total deadweight of 52,338 tons, which carried about nine per cent of Sudan's imports and exports in 1976. After the reopening of the Suez Canal in June 1975 work began on installing new equipment at Port Sudan, and enlarging its capacity. Congestion is still a problem. The communications facilities have been expanded to provide a wider geographical coverage. The telex exchange, the microwave television network and telephone automation were some of the key projects which were implemented during the last development plan. However, the telephone service in the Sudan is far from satisfactory.

The government-owned Sudan Airways, formed in 1947, operates internal and international services. It connects Khartoum with twenty important Sudanese towns as well as with Europe, the Middle East and Africa. In 1976 it carried 265,000 passengers and approximately one million kg. of freight.

STATISTICAL SURVEY

AREA AND POPULATION

Area	Population				
	Census (April 3rd, 1973)	Mid-year Estimates			
		1973	1974	1975	1976
967,500 sq. miles*	14,819,271†	15,000,000	15,340,000	15,730,000	16,126,000

* 2,505,813 sq. kilometres.

† Including an estimate for nomadic tribes and an adjustment for underenumeration in the Blue Nile province.

PROVINCES
(April 3rd, 1973)

	Area (sq. miles)	Population		Area (sq. miles)	Population
Bahr el Ghazal	82,530	1,387,842	Kordofan . .	146,930	2,202,977
Blue Nile .	54,880	3,804,399	Northern . .	184,200	963,609
Darfur . .	191,650	2,180,570	Red Sea . .	82,092	459,365
Equatoria .	76,495	758,412	Upper Nile .	91,190	798,813
Kassala .	49,436	1,112,886			
Khartoum .	8,097	1,150,398	Total .	967,500	14,819,271

PRINCIPAL TOWNS

	POPULATION (April 3rd, 1973)
Khartoum (capital)	333,906
Omdurman	299,399
Khartoum North	150,989
Port Sudan	132,632
Wadi Medani	106,715
El Obeid	90,073
Atbara	66,116

Because of the flooding of the Wadi Halfa and adjacent areas by the Aswan High Dam, over 50,000 inhabitants have been resettled in Khashm el Girba, on the Atbara River.

Births and Deaths (1966): Registered births 143,052 (birth rate 10.1 per 1,000); registered deaths 13,416 (death rate 1.0 per 1,000). Birth registration is believed to be about 20 per cent complete and death registration 5 per cent complete. UN estimates for 1965–70 put the average annual birth rate at 48.5 per 1,000 and the death rate at 19.0 per 1,000. These figures indicate that the natural increase rate is nearly 3.0 per cent per year, but the results of the 1973 census suggest a much lower increase rate.

ECONOMICALLY ACTIVE POPULATION

(1973 census, provisional)

Agriculture, hunting, forestry and fishing	2,950,000
Mining and quarrying	4,000
Manufacturing	179,000
Electricity, gas and water	45,000
Construction	87,000
Trade, restaurants and hotels	244,000
Transport, storage and communications	154,000
Financing, insurance, real estate and business services	6,000
Community, social and personal services	456,000
Activities not adequately described	315,000
TOTAL	4,442,921*

* Males 3,518,680; Females 924,241.

AGRICULTURE

LAND USE, 1976

('000 hectares)

Arable land	7,450*
Land under permanent crops	45*
Permanent meadows and pastures	24,000
Forests and woodlands	91,500
Other land	114,605
TOTAL LAND	237,600
Inland water	12,981
TOTAL AREA	250,581

* FAO estimate.

Source: FAO, *Production Yearbook.*

PRINCIPAL CROPS
('000 metric tons)

	1975	1976	1977
Wheat	276	264	336
Maize	55	50*	45*
Millet	432	430	410*
Sorghum (Durra)	2,026	1,762	1,600*
Rice	7	12	8*
Sugar cane	1,289	1,174	1,640
Potatoes	27	25*	22*
Sweet potatoes	39	41	42
Cassava (Manioc)	130	131*	131*
Other roots and tubers	115	115*	111*
Onions	20*	20*	20*
Water melons	80*	82*	85*
Dry beans	4	3	3*
Dry broad beans	18	19	20*
Chick-peas	1	3	3*
Other pulses	51	52	54*
Oranges and tangerines	42*	43*	44*
Lemons and limes	35*	36*	36*
Grapefruit	52*	53*	53*
Mangoes	60*	61*	61*
Dates	102*	105*	106*
Bananas	80*	83*	83*
Groundnuts (in shell)	931	827	850
Seed cotton	656	357	599
Cottonseed	418	233	350
Sesame seed	238	235	220*
Castor beans	16	15	19
Cotton lint	229	124	208
Tomatoes	140*	142*	143*
Pumpkins, etc.	55*	56*	57*
Aubergines	75*	76*	76*
Melons	10*	10*	10*

* FAO estimate.

Source: FAO, *Production Yearbook*.

LIVESTOCK
('000 head, year ending September)

	1975	1976*	1977
Cattle	14,720	15,300	15,892
Sheep	14,840	15,300	15,248
Goats	9,855	10,600	11,592
Pigs*	7	7	8
Horses*	20	20	20
Asses*	668	670	675
Camels	2,736	2,800	2,813
Chickens	22,000	23,000	24,000*

* FAO estimate.

Source: FAO, *Production Yearbook*.

LIVESTOCK PRODUCTS
(FAO estimates, '000 metric tons)

	1975	1976	1977
Beef and veal	151	158	163
Mutton and lamb	92	95	97
Goats' meat	21	22	23
Poultry meat	12	13	13
Other meat	61	62	64
Cows' milk	844	850	885
Sheep's milk	115*	118	121
Goats' milk	353	360	370
Butter	9.7	9.9	10.1
Cheese	48.6	49.8	50.5
Hen eggs	19.8	20.8	21.8
Wool: greasy	14.5	14.8	15.0
clean	5.8	6.0	6.2
Cattle hides	19.2	20.2	20.8
Sheep skins	11.5	11.8	12.2
Goat skins	4.1	4.3	4.4

* Official estimate.

Source: FAO, *Production Yearbook*.

FORESTRY

ROUNDWOOD REMOVALS
('000 cubic metres, all non-coniferous)

	1970	1971	1972	1973	1974	1975	1976
Sawlogs, veneer logs and logs for sleepers	40	80	88	90	60	93	127
Other industrial wood	1,130	1,160	1,190	1,254	1,295	1,319	1,319*
Fuel wood	19,800	19,800	19,800	18,700	20,250	20,925	20,925
TOTAL	20,970	21,040	21,078	20,044	21,605	22,337	22,371

* FAO estimate.

Source: FAO, *Yearbook of Forest Products*.

GUM ARABIC PRODUCTION
(tons)

	1972/73	1973/74	1974/75	1975/76
Gum kashab	32,418	32,410	19,697	43,030
Gum talh	2,649	3,804	1,107	888
TOTAL	35,067	36,214	20,804	43,918

Fishing (metric tons): Total catch 24,700 (inland waters 23,900, sea 800) in 1976.

MINING

PRODUCTION

		1972	1973	1974	1975
Salt (unrefined)	'000 metric tons	60	75	50	75
Chromium Ore*	metric tons	12,783	16,666	10,400	7,800
Magnesite (crude)	,, ,,	100	100	100	100
Manganese Ore*	,, ,,	500	n.a.	n.a.	n.a.
Gold	kilogrammes	2	2	10	n.a.

* Figures refer to the metal content of ores.

Chromium ore (1976): 11,500 metric tons.

Source: UN, *Statistical Yearbook.*

INDUSTRY

SELECTED PRODUCTS

		1973	1974	1975	1976
Cement	'000 tons	193.6	233.8	171.2	163.3
Wheat flour	,, ,,	195.8	201	225.9	251
Sugar	'000 metric tons	100	130	139	140
Soap	'000 tons	30.7	34.7	39.4	47.1
Wine	'000 litres	3,637.7	4,369.7	4,809.4	4,709.7
Beer	,, ,,	7,459	9,321	9,987.4	8,401.6
Cigarettes	million	685	571	680	690
Canned fruit and vegetables*	million tins	21.2	19	14.2	n.a.
Shoes	million pairs	12.6	13.4	13.2	12
Woven cotton fabrics	million sq. metres	96	97	103	n.a.
Electric energy†	million kWh	500	580	640	720

* Year beginning July 1st. † Estimates.

Source: partly UN, *Statistical Yearbook.*

PETROLEUM PRODUCTS
('000 metric tons)

	1973	1974	1975	1976
Motor Spirit	106	113	114	120
Naphtha	54	40	40	11
Jet Fuels	94	44	47	50
Kerosene	18	32	36	37
Distillate Fuel Oils	356	365	447	325
Residual Fuel Oils	564	507	463	577
Liquefied Petroleum Gas	2	3	3	4

Source: UN, *Statistical Yearbook.*

FINANCE

1,000 millièmes = 100 piastres = 1 Sudanese pound (£S).
Coins: 1, 2, 5 and 10 millièmes; 2, 5 and 10 piastres.
Notes: 25 and 50 piastres; £S1, £S5 and £S10.

Exchange rates (June 1979): £1 sterling = 827.5 millièmes; U.S. $1 = 400.0 millièmes.
£S100 = £120.84 sterling = $250.00.

Note: The Sudanese pound was introduced in April 1957, replacing (at par) the Egyptian pound, valued at U.S. $2.87156 since September 1949. This valuation was maintained in Sudan until June 1978, despite two devaluations of the U.S. dollar (in December 1971 and February 1973). In June 1978 the Sudanese pound was devalued to U.S. $2.50 ($1 = 400 millièmes). The exchange rate was £1 sterling = 835.78 millièmes (£S1 = £1.1965 sterling) from November 1967 to August 1971; and £1 sterling = 907.42 millièmes (£S1 = £1.102 sterling) from December 1971 to June 1972.

BUDGET*

(£S million, twelve months ending June 30th)

Revenue	1974/75	1975/76
Income tax	30.9	29.1
Taxes on production and consumption; Stamp duty and other excise duties	63.0	72.6
Import duties	88.9	77.0
Export duties	10.8	19.1
Transfer fees	27.5	17.6
Development tax	10.9	10.2
Gezira Board	1.8	12.6
Reimbursements and interdepartmental services	9.9	8.6
Sugar monopoly	—	12.1
TOTAL (incl. others)	287.8	337.3

Expenditure	1974/75	1975/76
Education	8.6	10.3
Public health	5.2	7.2
Other social services	4.9	6.2
Agriculture and forestry	6.5	8.1
Public works	1.3	2.3
Other economic services	20.6	23.2
Defence	39.9	43.0
Settlement of loans	27.6	40.0
General administration	147.4	160.7
Internal security	2.0	3.0
TOTAL	264.0	304.4

* Figures represent consolidated cash transactions covered in the Central Budget and the Development Budget.

BALANCE OF PAYMENTS

(U.S. $ million)

	1972	1973	1974	1975	1976	1977
Merchandise exports f.o.b.	324.7	441.1	384.4	411.8	588.8	658.1
Merchandise imports f.o.b.	−316.7	−334.4	−541.7	−743.2	−625.7	−643.9
TRADE BALANCE	8.0	106.7	−157.3	−331.3	−36.9	14.2
Exports of services	46.4	41.8	61.7	98.6	119.8	166.0
Imports of services	−113.2	−125.5	−200.7	−243.0	−268.3	−273.9
BALANCE ON GOODS AND SERVICES	−58.8	23.0	−296.3	−475.7	−185.4	−93.7
Private unrequited transfers (net)	0.7	3.9	2.5	−0.4	−0.1	0.0
Government unrequited transfers (net)	6.3	−1.7	18.4	45.9	20.4	20.7
CURRENT BALANCE	−51.9	25.3	−275.4	−430.2	−165.0	−73.0
Long-term capital (net)	14.7	4.9	253.6	33.0	44.4	32.3
Short-term capital (net)	26.2	−2.5	1.4	271.7	100.8	69.6
Net errors and omissions	2.2	−2.6	14.8	2.4	2.4	−1.5
TOTAL (net monetary movements)	−8.9	25.0	−5.5	−123.0	−17.4	27.3
Allocation of IMF Special Drawing Rights	8.3	—	—	—	—	—
CHANGES IN RESERVES, ETC.	−0.7	25.0	−5.5	−123.0	−17.4	27.3

Source: IMF, *International Financial Statistics.*

EXTERNAL TRADE

(£S million)

	1969	1970	1971	1972	1973	1974	1975	1976	1977
Imports c.i.f.*	92.5	108.3	123.7	123.1	151.8	228.4	332.9	341.4	369.0
Exports f.o.b.†	86.2	103.9	115.2	125.5	152.2	165.8	152.5	193.0	230.2

* Excluding imports of crude petroleum (£S31,120,000 in 1976).

† Excluding exports of camels (£S2,420,000 in 1971).

PRINCIPAL COMMODITIES

(£S '000)

Imports	1973	1974	1975
Sugar	14,810	33,392	39,706
Tea	4,966	6,247	4,231
Coffee	1,993	2,680	2,197
Wheat	7,067	8,158	8,323
Textiles	16,135	24,149	43,000
Footwear	181	59	10
Sacks and jute	4,255	6,064	7,663
Fertilizers	2,771	6,689	9,681
Machinery	20,001	30,087	59,135
Tyres	2,035	3,852	5,193
Petroleum products	744	33,056	27,228
Pharmaceuticals	5,096	5,200	9,764
Iron and steel	8,269	9,539	13,381
Transport equipment	25,291	33,675	63,665
Metal manufactures	5,368	6,401	11,731

Exports	1973	1974	1975
Animals	7,680	7,798	1,237
Cotton, ginned	82,578	53,706	68,367
Cotton seed	530	253	n.a.
Cotton seed oil	3,017	n.a.	3,590
Durra	2,922	4,401	2,233
Groundnuts	12,993	18,163	34,382
Gum arabic	7,403	14,270	7,548
Oilseed cake	7,904	2,243	4,152
Sesame	10,706	16,511	11,939
Hides and skins	6,072	3,777	3,187

PRINCIPAL TRADING PARTNERS

(£S '000)

	Imports				Exports			
	1972	1973	1974	1975	1972	1973	1974	1975
Belgium	1,148	3,372	3,917	7,883	4,036	2,449	2,747	1,173
China, People's Republic	8,792	10,233	22,577	16,195	12,459	22,746	11,797	13,046
Egypt	5,188	3,622	5,632	6,082	7,046	5,767	3,734	10,642
France	4,174	6,358	9,664	8,455	4,527	9,247	12,652	19,258
Germany, Federal Republic	7,832	9,934	16,147	30,586	11,569	13,874	8,147	9,386
India	18,862	11,331	28,575	26,343	22,903	8,878	4,551	2,257
Iraq	—	—	117	17,588	—	—	592	291
Italy	2,660	5,315	11,354	23,433	11,594	16,866	15,502	20,059
Japan	4,749	9,098	13,073	36,487	10,087	16,887	4,307	6,520
Netherlands	2,256	3,834	3,832	7,397	4,315	7,313	4,895	6,890
Poland	1,360	1,555	759	5,633	1,818	1,742	1,047	1,396
U.S.S.R.	5,329	9,057	2,399	1,615	470	3	1,621	3,656
United Kingdom	21,493	27,366	28,523	55,056	4,687	5,453	4,188	5,520
U.S.A.	4,806	11,568	22,133	30,729	3,691	2,921	6,883	3,340
Yugoslavia	2,141	1,878	964	1,001	2,422	945	891	7,025
Total (incl. others)	117,905	151,841	247,500	359,873	124,351	152,172	122,010	152,468

TOURISM

	1974	1975
Foreign tourist arrivals	24,886	30,675

TRANSPORT

RAILWAY TRAFFIC

(July 1st to June 30th)

	1971/72	1972/73	1973/74
Freight ton-kilometres (million)	2,752	2,520	2,324

ROAD TRAFFIC

(motor vehicles in use)

	1970	1971	1972
Passenger Cars	27,400	30,000	29,200
Commercial Vehicles	16,500	18,000	21,200

Source: UN, *Statistical Yearbook.*

INTERNATIONAL SEA-BORNE SHIPPING

(Port Sudan)

	1970	1971	1972	1973
Vessels entered ('000 net registered tons)	2,522	2,563	3,199	n.a.
Goods loaded ('000 metric tons)*	989	1,053	1,167	1,168
Goods unloaded ('000 metric tons)*	1,845	1,829	2,006	1,913

* Excluding livestock.

Source: UN, *Statistical Yearbook.*

CIVIL AVIATION

(scheduled services)

	1973	1974	1975	1976
Kilometres flown (million)	6.3	6.5	7.5	7.7
Passengers carried ('000)	141	235	250	265
Passenger-km. (million)	168	244	320	345
Freight ton-km. (million)	1.8	4.4	7.2	7.3

Source: UN, *Statistical Yearbook.*

EDUCATION

(1973-74)

	Teachers	Students		
		Male	Female	Total
Pre-Primary*	334	8,880	7,999	16,879
Primary	27,185	786,628	375,619	1,162,247
Secondary: General	6,127	103,495	34,819	138,314
Higher	2,121	33,973	10,416	44,389
Vocational	365	4,347	267	4,614
Teacher Training	406	2,528	1,538	4,066
Tertiary	1,046	16,371	1,391	17,762

* 1971 figures.

Source (unless otherwise stated): Department of Statistics, H.Q. Council of Ministers, Khartoum.

THE CONSTITUTION

A Provisional Constitution was introduced by the Revolutionary Command Council in August 1971. A People's Council, including various categories of the people's working forces, was called to draft and ratify a permanent constitution. It was endorsed by the People's Assembly in April 1973 as the Permanent Constitution of Sudan.

The President

The President must be a Sudanese of at least 35 years of age. He is nominated by the Sudanese Socialist Union, is Head of State, and is responsible for maintaining the Constitution. He may appoint Vice-Presidents, a Prime Minister and Ministers who are responsible to him. He is the Supreme Commander of the People's Armed Forces and Security Forces, and the Supreme Head of the Public Service.

If satisfied that a national crisis exists, the President may declare a State of Emergency, which may entail the suspension of any or all freedoms and rights under the Permanent Constitution other than that of resort to the courts. In the event of the President's death, the First Vice-President will temporarily assume office for a period not exceeding 60 days. Following the abortive coup of September 1975, a constitutional amendment was introduced which empowers the President to take any measures and decisions he sees as "suitable".

The People's Assembly

The President may appoint up to a tenth of the members of the Assembly. The duration of a sitting is four years and sittings are held in public. A quorum consists of half the number of members. Amendments to the Constitution may be proposed by the President or one third of the membership of the People's Assembly. An amendment to the Constitution must have a two-thirds majority of the People's Assembly and the assent of the President.

Judiciary

The State is subject to the rule of law which is the basis of government. The judiciary is an independent body directly responsible to the President and judges are appointed by the President.

Religion

Unrestricted freedom of religion is allowed and mention is specifically made of the Islamic and Christian religions.

Southern Region

Under the Regional Constitution for the Southern Sudan, the southern provinces form a single region, with its own regional executive in Juba headed by a president who is also a Vice-President of the whole Republic. The regional executive is responsible for all matters except national defence, external affairs, economic and social development, education, currency and coinage, air and inter-regional river transport, communications and telecommunications, nationality and immigration, public audit, customs and foreign trade regulations except for border trade. The regional President is appointed by and responsible to a Regional People's Assembly. The Assembly may postpone legislation of the central Government which it considers adverse to the interests of the South, though the President is not compelled to accede to its request. The Regional Constitution can be amended only by a four-fifths majority of the central People's Assembly, where southerners are represented.

The National People's Assembly had 304 seats after the February 1978 elections, which include 274 members elected for four years by universal adult suffrage and 30 members nominated by workers and other groups and by the President. The Regional People's Assembly consists of 60 members of whom 30 represent the geographical areas, 21 the people's working forces alliance and 9 the administrative units. They are elected by direct secret ballot.

THE GOVERNMENT

President and Prime Minister

Gen. Gaafar Mohammed Nimeri (assumed power as Chairman of the Revolutionary Command Council May 25th, 1969; inaugurated as President October 12th, 1971; re-elected April 1977).

First Vice-President: (vacant).

Vice-President: Abel Alier.

Vice-President and President of the High Executive Council for the Southern Region: Joseph Lagu.

Vice-President and Minister of Foreign Affairs: El Rashid el Tahir Bakr.

CABINET

(*August* 1979)

Minister of Defence and Commander-in-Chief of the Armed Forces: Gen. Abd Al-Majid Khalil.

Minister of Finance and National Economy: Dr. Osman Hashim Abdel-Salam.

Minister of Health: Maj.-Gen. (retd.) Khalid Hassan Abbass.

Minister of Culture and Information: Ali Shummo.

Minister of Education and Orientation: Dafalla el Hag Yousif.

Minister of Agriculture, Food and Natural Resources: Dr. Abdalla Ahmed Abdalla.

Minister of Construction and Public Works: Mohammed Sid Ahmed Abdalla.

Minister of Industry: Beshire Abbadi.

Minister of Public Services and Administrative Reform: Karamalla el Awad.

Minister of Communications: Ahmed Abdel Karim Badri.

Minister of National Security: Maj.-Gen. (retd.) Omer Mohammed el Tayeb.

Minister of Irrigation and Hydroelectric Power: YAHIA ABDEL MAGID.

Minister of Co-operation, Trade and Supply: FAROUK EL MAGBOUL.

Minister of National Planning: Maj.-Gen. (retd.) NASR EDDIN MUSTAFA.

Minister of Cabinet Affairs: ABU BAKR OSMAN MOHAMMED SALIH.

Minister of Energy and Mining: SHARIF AL TUHAMI.

Minister of Transport: MUSTAFA OSMAN HASSAN.

Minister for the Presidency: BAHA ELDIN MOHAMED IDRIS.

Attorney-General: MAHDI EL FAHAL.

MINISTERS OF STATE

Minister of State for Presidential Affairs: KHALID EL KHEIR OMER.

Minister of State for Foreign Affairs: Dr. FRANCIS DENG.

Minister of State for Culture and Information: Dr. ISMAIL HAG MOUSA.

Minister of State for Agriculture, Food and Natural Resources: Dr. MOHAMMED SHAZALY OSMAN.

Minister of State for Finance and National Economy: UTHMAN ABDULLAH AN-NADHIR.

Minister of State for Cabinet Affairs: IZZELDIN HAMID.

Minister of State, Legal Adviser in the Ministry of the Presidency: Dr. YOUSIF MICHAEL.

Minister of State, Press Adviser to the President: MOHAMED MAHGOUB SULIMAN.

Minister of State, Adviser to the President for People's Local Government Affairs: EL SHEIKH BESHIR EL SHEIKH.

Minister of State for Co-operation, Commerce and Supply: AHMAD SALIM.

HIGH EXECUTIVE COUNCIL FOR THE SOUTHERN REGION

President: Maj.-Gen. JOSEPH LAGU.

Vice-President and Regional Minister of Finance, Industry and Economic Planning: PETER GATKOUTH GUAL.

Regional Minister of Public Service and Human Resources: JOSEPH UDUHU.

Regional Minister of Administration, Legal Affairs and Co-ordination: NATALE OLWAK AKOLAWIN.

Regional Minister of Public Works, Housing and Transport and Communications: JOSEPH JAMES TOMBURA.

Regional Minister of Health: Dr. PACIFICO LOLIK.

Regional Minister of Agriculture and Natural Resources: JUSTIN YAK ARUB.

Regional Minister of Education and Guidance: BARNABA DUMO.

Regional Minister of Co-operation, Commerce and Supply: MARTIN MAJIR.

Regional Minister of Cabinet Affairs: LAWRENCE WOL WOL.

Regional Minister of Culture and Information: AMBROSE RING THIIK.

PROVINCE COMMISSIONERS

Bahr El Ghazal: SAMUEL LUPAI.

Blue Nile: MOHAMMED EL HASSAN AWAD EL KARIM.

East Equatoria: ALEXANDER NAGIB.

Gezira: ABDEL RAHIM MAHMOUD.

Jongali: VENINSIO LORO.

Kassala: HAYDAR HUSSEIN.

Khartoum: Maj. (retd.) ABDUL GASIM MOHAMMED IBRAHIM.

Lakes: JAMES AGETH.

Nile: SA'AD AWAD.

Northern: MALIK AMIN NABREI.

Northern Darfur: EL TAYEB EL MARDI.

Northern Kordofan: ABDALLA OMER ABDEL RAHMAN.

Red Sea: ABDEL RAHMAN SALMAN.

Southern Darfur: MOHAMMED ABDEL GADIR.

Southern Kordofan: MAHMOUD HASEEB.

Upper Nile: PHILIP OBENG.

West Equatoria: BARNABA KISINGA.

White Nile: MOHAMMED EL SAYED EL SHAAR.

PEOPLE'S ASSEMBLIES

NATIONAL PEOPLE'S ASSEMBLY

The National People's Assembly has 304 members: 274 elected for four years by universal adult suffrage, and the remainder nominated by the President. The Assembly was opened in May 1974. In the elections of February 1978 only the names of successful candidates to the Assembly were published and not their political affiliations. However, it is believed that 120–140 seats were gained by members of the SSU, about 20 by members of the Uanma party, led by SADIQ AL-MAHDI, about 30 by members of the National-Unionist party, led by SHARAF AL-HINDI, about 20 by Muslim Brotherhood supporters, 40–60 by independent local dignataries and the remainder by adherents of left-wing parties.

Speaker: Maj. (retd.) ABDUL GASIM HASHIM.

Leader: BADREDDIN SULAIMAN.

REGIONAL PEOPLE'S ASSEMBLY

The Assembly was opened in 1973. The latest elections were in February 1978. Represents the Southern Region; sits in Juba.

Speaker: ISAIAH KULANG.

Controller: MICHAEL WOL.

POLITICAL ORGANIZATION

Sudanese Socialist Union (SSU): P.O.B. 1850, Khartoum; f. 1972; only recognized political organization; consists of National Conference, Central Committee, Political Bureau, Executive Bureau and Secretariat-General; Pres. GAAFAR MOHAMMED NIMERI; Sec.-Gen. Maj. ABDUL GASIM MOHAMMED IBRAHIM.

There are nine Assistant Secretaries-General.

Executive Bureau of the SSU:

Chair. Gen. GAAFAR MOHAMMED NIMERI
Maj.-Gen. MOHAMED EL BAGHIR AHMED
ABEL ALIER
PETER GATKUOTH
Dr. LAWRENCE WOL WOL
Lt.-Gen. BASHIR MOHAMMED ALI
MAHDI MUSTAFA EL HADI
BONA MALWAL
Dr. BESHIR ABBADI
HILLARY PAULO LOGALI
KHALAFALLAH RASHID
EL RASHID EL TAHIR BAKR
AHMED ABDEL HALIM
Maj. (retd.) ZEIN EL ABDIN MOHAMMED AHMED ABDEL GADIR
Maj.-Gen. (retd.) KHALID HASSAN ABBAS
Maj. (retd.) MAMOUN AWAD ABU ZEID
Maj. (retd.) ABUL GASIM HASHIM
Dr. MANSOUR KHALID
Maj.-Gen. JOSEPH LAGU
MUSA AL MUBARAK
Dr. AWN AL SHARIF GASIM
Lt.-Col. (retd.) SALAH ABDEL 'AAL MABROUK
SADIQ AL-MAHDI*
Dr. HASAN TURABI
AHMED AL-MIRGANI
SAMUEL ARU
BADREDDIN SULAIMAN
JOSEPH UDUHU
NATALE OLWAK AKOLAWIN
ABD AL-MAJID KHALIL

* From 1978 known as Sadiq Abdul Rahman.

DIPLOMATIC REPRESENTATION

EMBASSIES ACCREDITED TO SUDAN
(In Khartoum unless otherwise stated)

Afghanistan: Cairo, Egypt.

Algeria: Junction El Mek Nimr St. and 67th St., P.O.B. 80; *Ambassador:* (vacant).

Australia: Cairo, Egypt.

Austria: Slavos Bldg. 29, 3rd Floor, P.O.B. 1860 (also accred. to Chad).

Bahrain: Cairo, Egypt.

Belgium: Sharia Al Mek Nimr, House No. 4, P.O.B. 969; *Ambassador:* J. M. MELSENS.

Bulgaria: El Mek Nimr St. South 7, P.O.B. 1690; *Ambassador:* IVAN MARINOV GUNINSKI.

Central African Empire: Africa Rd., P.O.B. 1723; *Ambassador:* GILBERT MARIUS BANDIO.

Chad: St. 17, New Extension, P.O.B. 1514; *Ambassador:* MOULI SAID.

China, People's Republic: 69 31st St., P.O.B. 1425; *Ambassador:* SONG HAN-YI.

Czechoslovakia: Plot 5 Ge, House no. 39, P.O.B. 1047; *Ambassador:* JINDŘICH TISLER.

Denmark: Cairo, Egypt.

Egypt: Mogram St.; *Ambassador:* SA'AD MUHAMMAD BADAWI AL-FATATRY.

Ethiopia: 6, 11A St. 3, New Extension, P.O.B. 844; *Ambassador:* YILMA TADESSE.

Finland: Cairo, Egypt.

France: 6H East Plot 2, 19th St., P.O.B. 377; *Ambassador:* HENRI DUMONT.

German Democratic Republic: P4 (3) B2, Khartoum West, P.O.B. 1089; *Ambassador:* LOTHAR EICHELKRAUT.

Germany, Federal Republic: 53 Baladiya St., Block No. 8 D.E., P.O.B. 970; *Ambassador:* HANS KAHLE.

Greece: Block 74, 31st St., P.O.B. 1182; *Ambassador:* (vacant).

Hungary: Block 11, Plot 12, 13th St., New Extension, P.O.B. 1033; *Chargé d'affaires a.i.:* ISTVÁN FODOR.

India: El Mek Nimr St., P.O.B. 707; *Ambassador:* MUBARAK SHAH (also accred. to Chad).

Iran: Baladiya St.; *Ambassador:* Dr. MUSTAFA ELM NUTLAG.

Iraq: St. 5, New Extension; *Ambassador:* (vacant).

Italy: 39th St., P.O.B. 793; *Ambassador:* GIULIO BILANCIONI.

Japan: House no. 24, Block 10AE, St. 3, P.O.B. 1649; *Ambassador:* TOMIZO ARIMOTO.

Jordan: 25 7th St., New Extension; *Ambassador:* NAJI ABDA AL-AZIZ.

Korea, Democratic People's Republic: 2-10 BE, 7th St., New Extension, P.O.B. 332; *Ambassador:* CHO MYONG-HWANG.

Korea, Republic: House 2, St. 1, New Extension, P.O.B. 2414; *Ambassador:* DONG KUN KIM.

Kuwait: 9th St., New Extension; *Ambassador:* MOHAMMED SALEM EL BALHEN.

Lebanon: 60, St. 49; *Ambassador:* Dr. MADHAT FATFAT.

Libya: Africa Rd. 50, P.O.B. 2091; *Ambassador:* ABDUL WAHAB RANTANI.

Morocco: 32, 19th St.; *Ambassador:* ABDEL LATIF LAKHMIRI.

Netherlands: P.O.B. 391; *Chargé d'affaires a.i.:* F. B. A.M. VAN HAREN (also accred. to Somalia).

Niger: St. 1, New Extension, P.O.B. 1283; *Ambassador:* El Haj OMAROU AMADOU.

Nigeria: P.O.B. 1538; *Ambassador:* (vacant).

Pakistan: House no. 6, Block 12AE, St. 3, New Extension, P.O.B. 1178; *Ambassador:* A. A. CHOWDURY (also accred. to the Central African Empire and Chad).

Poland: 73 Africa Rd., P.O.B. 902; *Chargé d'affaires a.i.:* JAN TYBURA.

Qatar: St. 15, New Extension; *Ambassador:* (vacant).

Romania: St. 47, Plot 67, P.O.B. 1652; *Ambassador:* FLORIAN STOICA (also accred. to the Yemen Arab Republic).

Saudi Arabia: Central St., New Extension, P.O.B. 852; *Ambassador:* ARAB SAEED HASHIM.

Somalia: Central St., New Extension; *Ambassador:* JAALLE MOHAMED HAGI NUIR.

Spain: Street 3, New Extension, P.O.B. 2621; *Ambassador:* JOSÉ MANUEL DEL MORAL Y GRACIA SAEZ.

Switzerland: New Aboulela Bldg, P.O.B. 1707; *Chargé d'affaires:* WERNER HAENI.

Syria: 3rd St., New Extension; *Chargé d'affaires a.i.:* ABDEL KARIM (also accred. to Chad).

Tanzania: P.O.B. 6080; *Ambassador:* ABBAS K. SYKES.

Tunisia: Cairo, Egypt.

Turkey: 71 Africa Rd., P.O.B. 771; *Chargé d'affaires:* DARJAL BATIBAY.

Uganda: Excelsior Hotel, Room 408/410; *Ambassador:* OMAR MATARE.

U.S.S.R.: B1, A10 St., New Extension, P.O.B. 1161; *Ambassador:* VLADISLAV ZHUKOV.

United Arab Emirates: St. 3, New Extension; *Ambassador:* MOHAMED MUSBAH KHALAFAN.

United Kingdom: New Aboulela Bldg., P.O.B. 801; *Ambassador:* DERRICK CHARLES CARDEN.

U.S.A.: Gumhouria Ave.; *Ambassador:* DONALD BERGUS.

Vatican: El Safeh City, Shambat, P.O.B. 623; *Apostolic Pro-Nuncio:* UBALDO CALABRESI.

Yemen Arab Republic: St. 35, New Extension; *Ambassador:* YAHYA ABDEL RAHMAN AL-ARYAN.

Yemen, People's Democratic Republic: St. 51, New Extension; *Chargé d'affaires a.i.:* ABDEL MALIK ISMAIL.

Yugoslavia: St. 31, 79-A, Khartoum 1, P.O.B. 1180; *Ambassador:* ISNET REDZIĆ (also accred. to Chad).

Zaire: Gumhouria Ave.; *Ambassador:* MUKAMBA KADIATA-NZEMBA.

Sudan also has diplomatic relations with Afghanistan, Argentina, Bangladesh, Brazil, Burundi, Cameroon, Canada, Chile, Cyprus, Djibouti, Gabon, Ghana, Guinea, Indonesia, the Ivory Coast, Kenya, Malaysia, Mali, Malta, Mauritania, Mauritius, Mozambique, Norway, Oman, Portugal, Senegal, Sri Lanka, Sweden, Viet-Nam and Zambia.

JUDICIAL SYSTEM

The administration of justice is the function of the judiciary, as a separate and independent department of state. The judiciary is formed of two divisions, the Civil Division, headed by the Chief Justice, and the Sharia (Islamic Law) Division, headed by the Grand Kadi. The general administrative supervision and control of the judiciary is vested in the Higher Judiciary Council headed by the President of the Republic. The members are the Chief Justice, who is also the President of the Supreme Court, the Grand Kadi, the Minister of Public Service and Administrative Reform, the Minister of Finance and Economics, the Attorney General, the two deputies of the Chief Justice, the deputy Grand Kadi and the Dean of the Faculty of Law of the University of Khartoum. If the President does not preside, nor deputes one of the Vice-Presidents to preside, then the Chief Justice does so, as is often the case.

Civil Justice: is administered by the courts constituted under the 1976 Judiciary Act, namely the Supreme Court, Courts of Appeal and Other Courts. The Supreme Court consists of a president (the Chief Justice), his two deputies, the Grand Kadi and his deputy and sufficient judges of the Supreme Court. It is the custodian of the constitution under the Permanent Constitution of Sudan of 1973. The powers and jurisdiction of the courts are defined by the Code of Civil Procedure of 1974.

Criminal Justice: is administered by the courts constituted under the 1976 Judiciary Act, namely Major Courts and Magistrates' Courts, and their powers and jurisdiction are defined by the Criminal Procedure Code of 1974. Serious crimes are tried by Major Courts which are composed of a president and two members and have power to pass the death sentence. Major Courts are as a rule presided over by a magistrate of the First Class. There is a right of appeal against any decision or order of a Major Court and findings of guilty of murder and sentences of death or life imprisonment are subject to confirmation by the Supreme Court.

Lesser crimes are tried by Magistrates' Courts consisting of a single magistrate, or a bench of magistrates.

Local People's Courts: constituted under the 1976 Local People's Court Act to try a substantial portion of criminal and civil cases and work to some extent with the State Courts.

Chief Justice and President of the Supreme Court: KHALAFALLA EL RASHID.

SHARIA (ISLAMIC LAW) COURTS

Justice in personal matters for the Muslim population is administered by the courts constituted under the 1976 Judiciary Act. These courts consist of panels of judges in personal matters. The religious Law of Islam is administered by these courts in matters of inheritance, marriage, divorce, family relationships and charitable trusts.

Grand Kadi: Sheikh MOHAMED EL GIZOULI.

Mufti: AWADALLA SALIH.

RELIGION

The majority of the northern Sudanese population are followers of Islam while in the South the population is usually either Animist or Christian. It is estimated that there are more than 9 million Muslims and over 500,000 Catholics. The Government plans to create a Sudanese National Church.

CHRISTIAN COMMUNITIES

Sudan Council of Churches: P.O.B. 469, Khartoum; f. 1972; Gen. Sec. Rev. EZEKIEL KUTJOK; 11 churches.

Sudan Interior Mission: P.O.B. 220, Khartoum; f. 1937; 39 mems.

Catholic Church:

Roman Rite:

Archbishop of Khartoum: P.O.B. 49, Khartoum; Most Rev. AUGUSTINE BARONI.

Archbishop of Juba: P.O.B. 32, Juba; Most Rev. IRENEUS WIEN DUD.

Maronite Church: P.O.B. 244, Khartoum; Rev. Fr. YOUSEPH NEAMA.

Greek Catholic Church: P.O.B. 766, Khartoum; Bishop PAUL ANTAKI (Egypt); Vicar Rev. JOSEPH SUCKARIEH (Sudan).

Coptic Orthodox Church: Bishop of Nubia, Atbara and Omdurman: Rt. Rev. BAKHOMIOS.
Bishop of Khartoum, Southern Sudan and Uganda: Rt. Rev. ANBA YOUANNIS.

Episcopal Church of the Sudan: Clergy House, P.O.B. 110, Juba; Archbishop in Sudan: The Rt. Rev. ELINANA JABI NGALAMU.

Evangelical Church: P.O.B. 57, Khartoum; Chair. Rev. RADI ELIAS; about 1,500 mems.; runs schools, literature centre and training centre; publ. *El Marifa.*

Greek Orthodox Church: Metropolitan of Nubia: Archbishop SINESSIOS.

Greek Evangelical Church.

Presbyterian Church: Malakal.

THE PRESS

The Press was nationalized in August 1970. A General Corporation for Press, Printing and Publications was set up. The two main publishing houses are El-Ayam and El-Sahafa. These two houses publish most of the following newspapers and magazines.

DAILIES

El-Ayam: P.O.B. 363, Khartoum; f. 1953; Arabic; Chair. AHMED ABDEL HALIM; Editor-in-Chief ISMAIL EL HAG MUSA; circ. 50–60,000.

El-Sahafa: P.O.B. 1228, Khartoum; f. 1961; Arabic; Chair. Dr. AWN EL SHARIF QASIM; Editor-in-Chief Dr. HASSAN ABDIEN; circ. 50–60,000.

PERIODICALS

El-Eza'a: f. 1942; broadcasting, television and theatre magazine; Arabic; weekly; Sudan Broadcasting Service Magazine; publ. by Ministry of Culture and Information.

El Kibar: Arabic; monthly; publ. by Ministry of Education.

El Guwat El Musallaha: f. 1969; armed forces publications; comprising a weekly newspaper and monthly magazine, Editor-in-Chief Maj. MAHMOUD GALANDER; circ. 25–30,000.

Khartoum: Arabic; monthly; publ. by Ministry of Culture and Information.

Kordofan: weekly; local events in Kordofan Province; Editor-in-Chief MUSA EL MUBARAK.

Nile Mirror: Juba; English; weekly; publ. by Ministry of Culture and Information for the Southern Region.

Sudanow: P.O.B. 2651, Khartoum; f. 1976; English; monthly; publ. by Ministry of Culture and Information; Editor-in-Chief EL FATIH EL TIGANI; circ. 15,000.

Sudan Standard: English; two a week; publ. by Ministry of Culture and Information; Editor-in-Chief MEKKI AWAD EL NUR.

Youth and Sports: P.O.B. 2361, Khartoum; Arabic; publ. by the Ministry of Youth and Sports.

NEWS AGENCIES

Sudan News Agency (SUNA): P.O.B. 1506, Gamaa Ave., Khartoum; Editor-in-Chief MUSTAFA AMIN ISMAIL.

FOREIGN BUREAUX

Middle East News Agency (MENA) (*Egypt*): Dalala Bldg., P.O.B. 740, Khartoum.

TASS (U.S.S.R.) Hsinhua (People's Republic of China), the Iraqi News Agency and the Syrian News Agency also have bureaux in Khartoum.

PUBLISHERS

Ahmed Abdel Rahman El Tikeine: P.O.B. 299, Port Sudan.

El-Ayam Publishing and Printing House: Aboul Ela Bldg., United Nations Square, P.O.B. 363, Khartoum; f. 1953; Man. Dir. BESHIR MUHAMMAD SAID; newspapers, pamphlets and books.

El-Sahafa Publishing and Printing House: P.O.B. 1228, Khartoum; f. 1961; newspapers, pamphlets, government publications and short stories.

El-Salam Co. Ltd.: P.O.B. 944, Khartoum.

Claudios S. Fellas: P.O.B. 641, Khartoum.

Government Printing Press: government publishing office; publications include the *Sudan Almanac.*

Khartoum University Press: P.O.B. 321, Khartoum; f. 1967; academic, general and educational publishing; Dir. EL-FATIH MAHGOUB; Gen. Editor ALI EL-MUK.

RADIO AND TELEVISION

Sudan Broadcasting Service: P.O.B. 572, Omdurman; a government-controlled radio station which broadcasts daily in Amharic, Arabic, English, Somali and Tigringa; Dir. M. AWAD ALLAM.

There were an estimated 1,135,000 radio receivers in 1978.

In November 1974 an earth satellite station operated on 36 channels, was opened at Umm Haraz and this has given Sudan much improved telecommunication links. A nationwide satellite network is being established with 14 earth stations in the provinces.

Sudan Television Service: P.O.B. 1094, Omdurman; f. 1962; 35 hours of programmes per week; Dir. M. A. EL NUR.

There were 95,000 television receivers in 1978.

A microwave network to extend television transmission was begun in 1975. There is a second station at Gezira and further stations are planned at Atbarah and Port Sudan.

FINANCE

BANKING

(cap.=capital; p.u.=paid up; res.=reserves; dep.=deposits; m.=million; br.=branch; £S=Sudanese pound).

Under the Nationalization of Banks Act 1970, all banks have been nationalized and converted into limited companies controlled by the Bank of Sudan. Foreign banks were permitted to operate again in Sudan in 1976.

CENTRAL BANK

Bank of Sudan: Sharia Gamaa P.O.B. 313, Khartoum; f. 1960; acts as banker and financial adviser to the Government and has sole right of issue of Sudanese banknotes; cap. £S1.5m.; res. £S5.1m. (Dec. 1976); Gov. IBRAHIM MOHAMMED NIMIR; Deputy Gov. HASSAN BESHIR; 8 brs.

COMMERCIAL BANKS

Bank of Khartoum: 8 Sharia Gamhouria P.O.B. 1008, Khartoum; f. 1913; formerly Barclays Bank; former State Bank of Foreign Trade; cap. p.u. £S2m.; dep. £S95.9m. (Dec. 1977); Chair. of Board ALI HASSAN ABDALLA; Deputy Chair. and Gen Man. SALIH MOHAMED ALI SAKRAN; 22 brs.

El Nilein Bank: Sharia Barlaman, Sharia Khalifa, P.O.B. 466, Khartoum; f. 1965; formerly Crédit Lyonnais; authorized cap. £S5.0m.; cap. p.u. £S4.5m.; dep. £S89.1m.; Chair. (vacant); Deputy Chair. and Man. Dir. MAHMOUD MUSTAFA RIAD OLEIM; 8 brs.

People's Co-operative Bank: P.O.B. 922, Khartoum; f. 1970; formerly the Misr Bank; deals with all operations and facilities of the Sudan co-operative movement; cap. p.u. £S2.3m.; dep. £S26.5m.; Chair. SAAD ABOULELA; Gen. Man. ABDEL RAHMAN SID AHMED; 10 brs. and sub-brs.

Sudan Commercial Bank: Gamhouria Ave., P.O.B. 1116, Khartoum; f. 1960; cap. p.u. £S2.0m.; dep. £S33.2m.; Chair. MOHAMED IDRIS ABDALLA; Deputy Chair. and Gen. Man. FARID RUFAIL ELIAS; 7 brs. and sub-brs.

Unity Bank: P.O.B. 408, Khartoum; f. 1973; formerly Juba-Omdurman Commercial Bank; cap. £S1.5m.; dep. £S43.9m.; Chair. MAKI EL MANA; Deputy Chair. and Gen. Man. MOHAMED SALIH YAHYA.

FOREIGN BANKS

Bank of Credit and Commerce International SA: (*Luxembourg*): P.O.B. 5, Khartoum; dep. £S5.0m. (July 1977); Gen. Man. ASHRAF KHAN.

Chase Manhattan Bank (*U.S.A.*): P.O.B. 2679, Khartoum.

Citibank (*U.S.A.*): P.O.B. 2743, Khartoum.

Faisal Islamic Bank (*Saudi Arabia*): P.O.B. 2415, Khartoum; 40 per cent of local cap. provided by Sudan Government, 40 per cent by Saudi Arabia and 20 per cent by private investors.

National Bank of Abu Dhabi (*United Arab Emirates*): P.O.B. 2465, Khartoum; dep. £S3.5m.; Gen. Man. ELFAKI MUSTAFA.

DEVELOPMENT BANKS

Agricultural Bank of Sudan: Gamhouria Ave., Mogren. P.O.B. 1363, Khartoum; f. 1957; cap. £S9m.; provides facilities for approved agricultural projects; 14 brs.

Arab-Africa Bank: P.O.B. 2721, Khartoum; Man. (vacant),

Arab Bank for Economic Development in Africa: P.O.B. 2640, Khartoum; f. 1973; cap. U.S. $738.3m.; membership comprises 18 Arab states; Pres. and Dir.-Gen. Dr. CHEDLY AYARI; Gen. Man. AHMED OSMAN; Vice-Pres. Dr. OMAR MOHAMED OSMAN.

Industrial Bank of Sudan: UN Square, P.O.B. 1722, Khartoum; f. 1961; cap. p.u. £S3.5m.; to provide technical and financial assistance for the establishment, expansion and modernization of industrial projects in the private sector and to acquire shares in industrial enterprises; Chair .and Gen. Man. HASSAN AHMED MEKKI.

Sudanese Estates Bank: Sharia Baladia, P.O.B. 309, Khartoum; cap. £S10m.: mortgage bank to finance urban housing development in the private sector; Chair. and Man. Dir. MOHAMED MEKKI KANANI.

INSURANCE COMPANIES

Blue Nile Insurance Co. (Sudan) Ltd.: P.O.B. 2215, Khartoum; Gen. Man. MOHAMMED EL AMIN MIRGHANI.

General Insurance Co. (Sudan) Ltd.: P.O.B. 1555, Khartoum; Gen. Man. MOHAMMED TAWFIQ AHMED.

Sudanese Insurance and Re-insurance Co. Ltd.: P.O.B. 2332, Khartoum; Gen. Man. IZZEL-DIN EL SAYED MOHAMMED.

Khartoum Insurance Co. Ltd.: P.O.B. 737, Khartoum; Gen. Man. H. MYRIALLIS.

United Insurance Co. (Sudan) Ltd.: P.O.B. 318, Khartoum; Gen. Man. HASIM EL BIREIR.

TRADE AND INDUSTRY

Animal Production Corporation: P.O.B. 624, Khartoum; Dir.-Gen. Dr. Ali Hassan Mahmoud.

Agricultural Research Corporation: P.O.B. 126, Wad Medani; Dir. Mohamed Osman Mohamed Salih.

Cotton Public Corporation: P.O.B. 1672, Khartoum; f. 1970; Chair. and Gen. Man. Beshir Ibrahim Ishaq; supervises all cotton marketing operations; publs. *Sudan Cotton Bulletin* (monthly), *Sudan Cotton Review* (annual).

Alaktan Trading Co.: P.O.B. 2067, Khartoum; Gen. Man. Abdel Rahman Abdel Moneim.

National Cotton and Trade Co. Ltd.: P.O.B. 1552, Khartoum; Gen. Man. Mohamed Taha Mohamed Ali.

Port Sudan Cotton Trade Co. Ltd.: P.O.B. 590, Khartoum and P.O.B. 261, Port Sudan; Gen. Man. Sayed Mohd Adam.

Sudan Cotton Co. Ltd.: P.O.B. 2284, Khartoum; Gen. Man. Gaafar Sirel Khatim Osman.

Gum Arabic Company: P.O.B. 857, Khartoum; Gen. Man. Osman Mohammed el Hassan.

Industrial Production Corporation: P.O.B. 1034, Khartoum; Dir.-Gen. Osman Tammam; Deputy Chair. Abdel Latif Widatalla; incorporates:

Building Materials and Refractories Corporation: P.O.B. 2241, Khartoum; Dir. Magzoub el Shoush.

Food Industries Corporation: P.O.B. 2341, Khartoum; Dir. Mohamed el Ghali Suliman.

Leather Industries Corporation: P.O.B. 1639, Khartoum; Man. Bukhari Ahmed Bukhari.

Oil Corporation: P.O.B. 64, Khartoum North; Dir. Mohied Din Yassin.

Spinning and Weaving Corporation: P.O.B. 765, Khartoum; Dir. Mohammed Saieed Ali.

Sudanese Mining Corporation: P.O.B. 1034, Khartoum; Dir. Ibrahim Mudawi.

Sugar and Distilling Industry Corporation: P.O.B. 511, Khartoum; Man. Mirghani Ahmed Babiker.

Mechanised Farming Corporation: P.O.B. 2482, Khartoum; Acting Man. Dir. Awad el Kariem el Yass.

Petroleum Public Corporation: Khartoum; f. 1976; Chair. Dr. Amin Abu Sineina; Gen. Man. Dr. Omer el-Sheikh Omer.

Public Agricultural Production Corporation: P.O.B. 538, Khartoum; Chair. and Man. Dir. Abdalla Bayoumo; Sec. Saad el Din Mohammed Ali.

Public Corporation for Building and Construction: P.O.B. 2110, Khartoum; Dir. Naeim Eldin.

Public Corporation for Irrigation and Excavations: P.O.B. 123, Wad Medani; Gen. Sec. Osman En Nur.

Public Corporation for Oil Products and Pipelines: P.O.B. 1704, Khartoum; Chair. Ahmed Babiker Eisa; Exec. Dir. Abdel Rahman Suliman.

Public Electricity and Water Corporation: P.O.B. 1380, Khartoum; Gen. Man. Mohamed el Mahdi Mirghani.

Rahad Corporation: P.O.B. 2523, Khartoum; financed by the World Bank, Kuwait and the U.S.A.; designed to irrigate 820,000 acres and settle 70,000 people in 15,000 tenancies; Man. Dir. Ibrahim Mohammed Ibrahim.

The State Trading Corporation: P.O.B. 211, Khartoum; Chair. and Man. Dir. Mubarak Mahgoub Logman (acting).

Automobile Corporation: P.O.B. 221, Khartoum; importer of vehicles and spare parts; Gen. Man. Mohammed Osman Abdel Halim.

Engineering Equipment Corporation: P.O.B. 97, Khartoum; importers and distributors of agricultural, engineering and electronic equipment; Gen. Man. Amir Yousif.

Silos and Storage Corporation: P.O.B. 62, Khartoum; stores and handles agricultural products; Gen. Man. Abdel Rahman Medani.

Trade and Services Corporation: P.O.B. 215, Khartoum; largest importer of general merchandise and services in storage, shipping and insurance; Gen. Man. Bukhari Abdalla.

Sudan Gezira Board: H.Q. Barakat Wad Medani; Sales Office, P.O.B. 884, Khartoum; responsible for Sudan's main cotton producing area; the Gezira Scheme is a partnership between the Government, the tenants and the Board. The Government, which provides the land and is responsible for irrigation, receives 36 per cent of the net proceeds; the tenants, about 100,000 in 1976, receive 49 per cent. The Board receives 10 per cent, the local Government Councils in the Scheme area 2 per cent and the Social Development Fund, set up to provide social services for the inhabitants, 3 per cent. The total possible cultivable area of the Gezira Scheme is over 5 million acres and the total area under systematic irrigation is now 2.3 million acres. In addition to cotton, groundnuts, sorghum, wheat, rice, pulses and vegetables are grown for the benefit of tenant farmers; Chair. and Man. Dir. Hassan Abdalla Hashim.

Sudanese Industries Association: P.O.B. 2565, Khartoum.

Sudan Oilseeds Co.: P.O.B. 167, Khartoum; Gen. Man. Mohammed Kailani.

Sugar Trading Corporation: P.O.B. 1209, Omdurman; f. 1974; Gen. Man. Saad el Izzeirig.

CHAMBER OF COMMERCE

Sudan Chamber of Commerce: P.O.B. 81, Khartoum; f. 1908; Pres. Saad Aboul Ela; Sec.-Gen. Mohamed Hassan Abdalla.

DEVELOPMENT CORPORATION

Sudan Development Corporation: P.O.B. 710, Khartoum; f. 1974 to promote and co-finance development projects with special emphasis on projects in the agricultural, agri-business, and industrial sectors, within the framework of the Government's overall development planning; cap. p.u. U.S. $200m.; Chair. and Man. Dir. Mohamed Abdel Magid Ahmed; Deputy Chair. and Deputy Man. Dir. Mamoun Mohamed el Sayed.

TRADE UNIONS

In 1971 all existing trade unions were dissolved and reconstituted according to the 1971 Trade Unions Act.

Secretary-General of Trade Unions: Abdel Moniem Hassan Medani.

Federations

Sudan Workers Trade Unions Federation (SWTUF): P.O.B. 2258, Khartoum; includes 38 Trade Unions of public service workers and workers of the private sector with a total membership of roughly 480,000 members; affiliated to the International Confederation of Arab Trade Unions and the Organization of African Trade Union Unity; Pres. ABDALLA NASR GINAWI; Exec. Sec. MUHIE-DIEN BAKHIET.

Agricultural Sector Workers' Trade Union: Workers' Club, Khartoum North; Pres. AWAD WIDATALLA; Sec. MOHAMMED OSMAN SALIM; 30,000 mems.

Gezira Scheme Workers' Trade Union: Barakat; Pres. IBRAHIM MOHAMMED AHMED EL SHEIKH; Sec. EL SIR ABDOON; 11,500 mems.

Health Workers' Trade Union: Khartoum Civil Hospital, Khartoum; Pres. EL YAYES EL AWAD; GAAFAR MOHAMMED SID AHMED; 25,000 mems.

Local Government Workers' Trade Union: Workers' Union, Khartoum; 25,000 mems.; Pres. ISMAIL MOHAMMED FADL; Sec. SALEM BEDRI HUMAM.

Post, Telegraph and Telephone Workers' Trade Union: Workers' Club, Khartoum; 8,463 mems.; Pres. MANSOUL EL MANNA; Sec. YASSIN ABDEL GALIL.

Public Service Workers' Trade Union: Baladia St., Khartoum; 19,800 mems.; Pres. MOHIE EDDIN BAKHEIT; Sec. ALI IDRIS EL HUSSEIN.

Railway Workers' Trade Union: Railway Workers' Club, Atbara; 32,000 mems.; Pres. MOHAMMED EL HASSAN ABDALLA; Sec. OSMAN ALI FADL.

Sudan Irrigation Workers' Trade Union: Ministry of Education, Wad Medani; 19,150 mems.; Pres. MOHAMMED HABIB; Sec. MOHAMMED AHMED.

Taxi Workers' Trade Union: Workers' Union, Khartoum; 15,000 mems.; Pres. EL RAYAN YOUSIF; Sec. EL TAYEB KHALAFALLA.

Sudanese Federation of Employees and Professionals Trade Unions: P.O.B. 2398, Khartoum; f. 1975; includes 54 Trade Unions representing 250,000 mems.; Pres. ABDALLA ALI ABDALLA; Sec.-Gen. KAMAL EL DIN MOHAMED ABDALLA.

Bank Officials' Union: Bank of Sudan, Khartoum; Pres. AHMED ABDULLAHI MOHAMED KEHIR; Sec. HASSAN MOHAMED MOHAMED ALI.

Gezira Board Officials' Union: Barakat; Pres. GALAL HAMID; Sec. OSMAN ABDEL RAHIM KHEIRAWY.

Local Government Officials' Union: Ministry of Local Government, Khartoum; Pres. SALAH IBRAHIM KHALIL; Sec. MOHAMED AWAD GABIR.

Post, Telegraph and Telephone Officials: Post Office, Khartoum; Pres. ABDEL RAHMAN EL KHIDER ALI; Sec. AWAD EL KARIM OSMAN.

Railway Officials' Union: Sudan Railways Corporation, Atbara; Pres. HASSAN HAG MUSA; Sec. EL HASSAN SIR EL KATIM.

Teachers' Union: Teachers House, Khartoum; Pres. ABDALLA ALI ABDALLA; Sec. HASSAN IBRAHIM MARZOUG.

CO-OPERATIVE SOCIETIES

There are about 600 co-operative societies in Sudan, of which 570 are formally registered.

Central Co-operative Union: P.O.B. 2492, Khartoum; largest co-operative union operating in 15 provinces.

MAJOR INDUSTRIAL COMPANIES

The following are a few of the larger companies either in terms of capital investment or employment.

Aboulela Cotton Ginning Co. Ltd.: P.O.B. 121, Khartoum; cotton mills.

AGIP (Sudan) Ltd.: P.O.B. 1155, Khartoum; f. 1959; cap. £S1m.

Distribution of petroleum products.

Pres. ROSARIO DISTEFANO; Gen. Man. V. L. BELLETTI; 140 employees.

Bata (Sudan) Ltd.: P.O.B. 88, Khartoum; f. 1950; cap. £S1m.

Manufacturers and distributors of footwear.

Man. Dir. AWAD ABDUL-RAHMAN SOGHAIR; 1,600 employees.

The Blue Nile Brewery: P.O.B. 1408, Khartoum; f. 1954, cap. £S734,150.

Brewing, bottling and distribution of beer.

Man. Dirs. IBRAHIM ELYAS, HUSSEIN MOHAMED KEMAL, OMER EL ZEIN SAGAYROUN; 336 employees.

The Central Desert Mining Co. Ltd.: P.O.B. 20, Port Sudan; f. 1946; cap. £S150,000.

Prospecting for and mining of gold, manganese and iron ore.

Dirs. ABDELHADI AHMED BAASHER, ABU-BAKR SAID BAASHER; 274 employees.

Sudan Tobacco Co. Ltd.: P.O.B. 87, Khartoum; production of tobacco products.

TRANSPORT

Ministry of Transport and Communications: P.O.B. 300, Khartoum.

RAILWAYS

Sudan Railways Corporation: P.O.B. 1812, Khartoum; P.O.B. 65, Atbara; Gen. Man. MOHAMMED ABDEL RAHMAN WASFI.

The total length of railway in operation in 1979 was 4,734 route-kilometres. The main line runs from Wadi Halfa, on the Egyptian border, to El Obeid, via Khartoum. Lines from Atbara and Sinnar connect with Port Sudan on the coast. There are lines from Sinnar to Damazine on the Blue Nile (227 km.) and from Aradeiba to Nyala in the south-western province of Darfus (689 km.), with a 445 km. branch line from Babanousa to Wau in the Bahr el Ghazal Province. A six-year plan to modernize the system, with French assistance, was scheduled to begin in 1977.

ROADS

National Transport Corporation: P.O.B. 723, Khartoum; Gen. Man. MOHI EL DIN HASSAN MOHAMED NUR.

Public Corporation for Roads and Bridges: P.O.B. 756, Khartoum; f. 1976; Chair. ABDEL RAHMAN HABOUD; Dir.-Gen. ABDU MOHAMMED ABDU.

Roads in northern Sudan, other than town roads, are only cleared tracks and often impassable immediately after rain. Motor traffic on roads in the Upper Nile Province is limited to the drier months of January–May. There are several good gravelled roads in the Equatoria and Bahr el Ghazal Provinces which are passable all the year round, but in these districts some of the minor roads become impassable after rain. Rehabilitation of communications in southern Sudan is a major priority as the civil war completely destroyed 1,600 km. of roads and 70 bridges.

In 1977 construction of a 960-km. road linking Juba and Wau was begun with assistance from the Federal Republic of Germany. The Wad-Medani to Gedaref highway, financed by a loan from the People's Republic of China, was completed in March 1977. Over 48,000 km. of tracks are classed as "motorable", but only 557 km. are asphalt. A 1,190 km. tarmac road linking the capital with Port Sudan is expected to be completed during 1979.

INLAND WATERWAYS

River Transport Corporation: P.O.B. 284, North Khartoum; operates 2,500 km. of steamers on the Nile; Chair. ALI AMIR TAHA.

River Navigation Corporation: Khartoum; f. 1970; jointly owned by the Egyptian and Sudanese Governments; operates services between Aswan and Wadi Halfa.

The total length of navigable waterways served by passenger and freight services is 4,068 km. From the Egyptian border to Wadi Halfa and Khartoum navigation is limited by cataracts to short stretches but the White Nile from Khartoum to Juba is navigable at almost all seasons.

SHIPPING

Port Sudan, on the Red Sea, 784 km. from Khartoum, is the only seaport. There are plans to build a port at Suakin by 1985.

Red Sea Shipping Corporation: P.O.B. 116, Khartoum; Gen. Man. OSMAN AMIN.

Sea Port Corporation: P.O.B. 2534, Khartoum; Administrator (vacant).

Sudan Shipping Line: P.O.B. 426, Port Sudan and P.O.B. 1731, Khartoum; f. 1960; seven vessels totalling 53,000 d.w.t. operating between the Red Sea, North Europe and the United Kingdom; Chair. ISMAIL BAKHEIT; Gen. Man. SALAH EDDIN OMER AL AZIZ; Financial Man. OSMAN MAHGOUB.

United African Shipping Co.: P.O.B. 339, Khartoum; Gen. Man. MOHAMED TAHA EL GINDI.

CIVIL AVIATION

The airports at Juba and Malakal in Southern Sudan are to be repaired and new airports built at Wau and Port Sudan.

Civil Aviation Department: Dir.-Gen. SIR HASSAN BESHIR.

Sudan Airways Corporation: Gamhouria Ave., P.O.B. 253, Khartoum; f. 1947; government-owned; internal services and international services to Bahrain, Chad, Egypt, Ethiopia, Federal Republic of Germany, Greece, Kenya, Italy, Nigeria, Saudi Arabia, the U.K. and the Yemen Arab Republic; fleet of 2 Boeing 737, 2 Boeing 707, and 5 Fokker F-27; Chair. Dr. ABDEL EL MUBARAK; Gen. Man. SALAH ZUMRAWI.

Sudan is also served by the following foreign airlines: Aeroflot (U.S.S.R.), Air France, Alitalia, British Airways, EgyptAir, Ethiopian Airlines, Interflug (German Democratic Republic), Libyan Arab Airlines, Lufthansa (Federal Republic of Germany), MEA (Lebanon), SAS (Sweden), Saudi Arabian Airlines, Swissair, TWA (U.S.A.) and Yemen Airways (Yemen Arab Republic).

TOURISM

Tourism and Hotels Corporation: P.O.B. 2424, Khartoum; Chair. OMER BABIKER EL SHAFIE; Dir.-Gen. MAHGOUB MOHAMED ALI.

DEFENCE

Total Armed Forces: In 1978 the armed forces totalled 52,100: army 50,000, navy 600, air force 1,500. There are 3,500 paramilitary forces. Military service is compulsory. Sudan has defence agreements with the Arab League Unified Military Command and with Egypt.

Defence Budget: (1977/78) £S82.6 million.

Commander-in-Chief of the People's Armed Forces: Gen. ABD AL-MAJID KHALIL.

Chief of Staff of the People's Armed Forces: Maj.-Gen. Gen. IZZELDIN ALI MALIK.

Commander of the Southern Region: Maj.-Gen. JOSEPH LAGU (former *Anya Nya* leader).

EDUCATION

The administrative machinery of supervision and control is conducted through the Ministry of Education. General policy is executed through different technical and administrative bodies under the control of the Ministry. In the past education was mainly administered centrally with the delegation of certain powers to the regional directorates. The new policy has widened the authority of the regional directorates, and only matters of a technical, political, planning and financial nature remain the responsibility of the central machinery.

The Government provides free elementary education from the ages 7 to 12, intermediate from 13 to 15 and secondary from 16 to 18. In 1975/76 £S10.3 million was allocated for education from the national budget. Under the Six-Year Plan 1977–83, £S100 million has been allocated to education.

The Plan places great emphasis on reducing the level of illiteracy from 80 per cent in 1975 to 50 per cent by 1980. The Plan involves special concentration on those involved in the industrial and agricultural sectors, the government service and housewives. It is to be linked with the development projects and resettlement schemes and the target is to reach a million people per year.

Primary Education. Several important developments have taken place in primary education. The most important are those in connection with the implementation of the Five-Year Plan 1970/71–1974/75 as readjusted, including the extension of this level from four to six years and the expansion of classes which by September 1973 had been largely achieved. As regards the curricula, notable features included the introduction of "Environmental Studies", "Citizenship Education" and "National Subjects" comprising civics, history and geography. There has recently been a notable increase in the number of pupils in primary education rising from 610,798 in 1969 to 1,217,510 in 1976/77. The number of teachers rose from 12,370 in 1969 to 33,718 in 1976/77. In the south, primary school enrolment in state schools increased from 53,169 in 1971/72 to 109,552 in 1976/77.

Academic Secondary and Vocational Education. The secondary level is divided into two stages: junior secondary (intermediate) of three years' duration which is completely academic, and senior secondary (secondary) of three years which is of three types: academic, technical and teacher training. English, the first foreign language, is taught from the beginning of the junior secondary stage, while French, the second foreign language, is taught from the beginning of the senior secondary stage. In the south, senior secondary school enrolment increased from 909 in 1972 to 2,480 in 1976.

Higher and Technical Education. Under the Six-Year Plan, £S35 million has been allocated to higher education. Administration was decentralized in November 1975 with the establishment of the National Council for Higher Education. The University of Khartoum was brought under government control. The University of Cairo has a branch in Khartoum. The University of Juba concentrates on rural development, as will the University of Gezira, which opened in 1978.

The Khartoum Institute of Technical Colleges, an amalgamation of formerly independent bodies, is given priority under the 1977–83 Six-Year Plan. There are plans to triple the present number of students (1,000) by the end of that period.

Teacher Training. A number of crash programmes fo training new teachers have been implemented following the introduction of the New Plan. The raising of the status of sub-grade schools to primary schools status has created the need for at least 2,000 primary teachers who would be in charge of teaching the additional fifth class in the new primary schools. Student teachers are hence selected from the Secondary School Certificate holders. There are plans to increase the number of teachers to 40,000 by 1980.

Adult and Non-Vocational Education. Projects for increasing literacy among adults have been in progress for several years. Experiments in the improvement of syllabuses have begun supervised by the National Council of Literacy and Adult Functional Education, and new Adult Education curricula will be introduced and taught in the teacher training institutes.

UNIVERSITIES

University of Gezira: P.O.B. 20, Wad Medani.

University of Juba: P.O.B. 82, Juba; 41 teachers, 116 students.

University of Khartoum: P.O.B. 321, Khartoum; 788 teachers, 7,833 students.

Cairo University Khartoum Branch: P.O.B. 1055, Khartoum; *c.* 80 teachers, *c.* 5,000 students.

Omdurman Islamic University: P.O.B. 382, Omdurman; 65 teachers, 1,141 students.

BIBLIOGRAPHY

GENERAL

ABDEL RAHIM, MUDDATHIR. Imperialism and Nationalism in the Sudan: A Study in Constitutional and Political Developments 1899–1956 (Oxford University Press, 1969).

ALBINO, OLIVER. The Sudan, a southern viewpoint (Oxford, 1969).

AMMAR, ABBAS, and others. The Unity of the Nile Valley, its Geographical Basis and its Manifestations in History (Cairo, 1947).

BARBOUR, K. M. The Republic of the Sudan: A Regional Geography (University of London Press, London, 1961).

BESHIR, M. O. The Southern Sudan: Background to Conflict (C. Hurst, London, 1968, Praeger, New York, 1968).

BOUSFIELD, L. Sudan Doctor (London, 1954).

BUDGE, Sir E. A. T. W. The Egyptian Sudan: Its History and Monuments (2 vols., London, 1907).
By Nile and Tigris (London, 1920).

EGYPTIAN SOCIETY OF INTERNATIONAL LAW. Documents of the Sudan 1899–1953 (Cairo, 1953).

FADL, EL S. H. Their Finest Days (Rex Collings, London, 1969).

FAWZI, S. ED DIN. The Labour Movement in the Sudan, 1946–55 (Oxford University Press, London, 1957).

GAITSKELL, ARTHUR. Gezira: A Story of Development in the Sudan (Faber, London, 1959).

HENDERSON, K. D. D. The Sudan Republic (Benn, London, 1965).

HILL, R. A Bibliography of the Anglo-Egyptian Sudan from the earliest times to 1937 (Oxford, 1939).
A Bibliographical Dictionary of the Anglo-Egyptian Sudan (new edition, Frank Cass, London, 1967).
Egypt in the Sudan 1820–1881 (Oxford University Press, London and New York, 1959).
Slatin Pasha (Oxford University Press, London, 1964, New York, 1965).
Sudan Transport: a History (London, 1965).

HODGKIN, R. A. Sudan Geography (London, 1951).

HURST, H. E. and PHILIPS, P. The Nile Basin, 7 vols (London, 1932–38).

JACKSON, H. C. The Fighting Sudanese (London, 1954).
Sudan Days and Ways (London, 1954).

KNIGHT, R. L., and BOYNS, B. M. Agricultural Science in the Sudan (1950).

LANGLEY, M. No Woman's Country: Travels in the Anglo-Egyptian Sudan (New York, 1951).

LEBON, J. H. C. Land Use in Sudan (Geographical Publications Ltd., Bude, U.K., 1965).

NASRI, A. R. EL-. A Bibliography of the Sudan 1938–1958 (Oxford University Press, 1962).

NEWBOLD, Sir D. The Making of the Modern Sudan; the Life and Letters of Sir Douglas Newbold (London, Faber and Faber, 1953).

ODUHO, JOSEPH, and DENG, WILLIAM. The Problem of the Southern Sudan (Oxford University Press, 1963).

SUDANESE GOVERNMENT. Ten Year Plan of Economic and Social Development 1961-62—1971-72 (Khartoum, Ministry of Finance and Economics, 1962).

TRIMINGHAM, J. S. Islam in the Sudan (London, 1949).

ANTHROPOLOGY

CUNNISON, IAN. Baggara Arabs (Oxford University Press, New York, 1966).

EVANS-PRITCHARD, E. E. Kinship and Marriage among the Nuer (London, 1951).
The Nuer (London, 1940).
Witchcraft, Oracles and Magic among the Azande (London, 1937).

Griffiths, V. L., and **Taha, Abdel Rahman Ali.** Sudan Courtesy Customs (Sudan Government, 1936).

Haber, Hugo. Das Fortleben nach dem Tode im Glauben westsudanischer Völker (Mödling, 1951).

Nadel, S. F. The Nuba: an Anthropological Study of the Hill Tribes of Kordofan (London, 1947).

Paul, A. A History of the Beja tribes of the Sudan (Cambridge, 1954).

Seligman, C. G. Pagan Tribes of the Nilotic Sudan (London, 1932).

ECONOMICS

Ali, Mohamed Abdel Rahman. *Fluctuations and Impact of Government Expenditure in the Sudan 1955–1967.* Khartoum University Press, 1974.

Beshai, Adel Amin. *Export Performance and Economic Development in Sudan 1900–1967.* London, Ithaca Press, 1976.

International Labour Office. *Growth, Employment and Equity: A Comprehensive Strategy for the Sudan.* Geneva, 1976.

Ministry of National Planning. *The Six-Year Plan of Economic and Social Development.* Khartoum, 1977.

Nimeiri, Sayed. *Taxation and Economic Development: A Case Study of the Sudan.* Khartoum University Press, 1974.

Suliman, Ali Ahmed. *Issues in the Economic Development of the Sudan.* Khartoum University Press, 1975.

HISTORY

Abbas, Mekki. The Sudan Question: the Dispute about the Anglo-Egyptian Condominium, 1884-1951 (London, 1952).

Arkell, A. J. Outline History of the Sudan (London, 1938); History of the Sudan to 1821 (2nd. ed., London, 1961).

Boahen, A. Adu. Britain, the Sahara and the Western Sudan 1788-1816 (Oxford University Press, New York and London, 1964).

Collins, Robert O. The Southern Sudan 1883-1898 (Yale University Press, 1962).

Collins, Robert O and **Tignor, R. L.** Egypt and the Sudan (Prentice, New York, 1967).

Corbyn, E. N. Survey of the Anglo-Egyptian Sudan, 1898-1944 (London, 1946).

Eprile, Cecil, War and Peace in the Sudan 1955-1972 (David and Charles, Devon, England, 1974).

Fabunmi, L. A. The Sudan in Anglo-Egyptian Relations (Longmans, London, 1965).

Gray, Richard. History of the Southern Sudan 1839–89 (Oxford, 1961).

Hassan, Yusuf Fadl. The Arabs and the Sudan (Edinburgh University Press, Edinburgh, 1967).

Henderson, K. D. D. Survey of the Anglo-Egyptian Sudan, 1898-1944 (London, 1946).

Holt, P. M. The Mahdist State in the Sudan: 1881–98 (Oxford University Press, 2nd edn., 1970).

A Modern History of the Sudan (Weidenfeld and Nicolson, London, 1962, Praeger, New York, 1963).

MacMichael, Sir H. A. A History of the Arabs in the Sudan (2 vols., Cambridge, 1922; reprinted Frank Cass, London and Barnes & Noble, New York, 1967).

The Anglo-Egyptian Sudan (London, 1935).

The Sudan (London, 1954).

Sabry, M. Le Soudan Egyptien, 1821-98 (Cairo, 1947).

Sanderson, G. N. England, Europe and the Upper Nile (Edinburgh University Press, Edinburgh, 1965).

Shibeika, Mekki. The Sudan in the Century 1819-1919 (Cairo, 1947).

British Policy in the Sudan: 1882–1902 (London, 1952).

The Independent Sudan: The History of a Nation (New York, 1960).

Shinnie, Margaret. A Short History of the Sudan up to A.D. 1500 (Khartoum, 1954).

Shinnie, P. L. Meroe (Thames and Hudson, London, 1967).

Sylvester, Antony. Sudan under Nimeiri. (Bodley Head, London, 1977).

Theobald, A. B. The Mahdiya: A History of the Anglo-Egyptian Sudan 1881-1899 (New York, 1951).

Syria

PHYSICAL AND SOCIAL GEOGRAPHY

W. B. Fisher

Before 1918 the term "Syria" was rather loosely applied to the whole of the territory now forming the modern States of Syria, the Lebanon, Israel and Jordan. To the Ottomans, as to the Romans, Syria stretched from the Euphrates to the Mediterranean, and from the Sinai to the hills of southern Turkey, with Palestine as a smaller province of this wider unit. Though the present Syrian Arab Republic has a much more limited extension, an echo of the past remains to colour the political thinking of a few present-day Syrians and from time to time there are references to a "Greater Syria" as a desirable but possibly remote aspiration.

The frontiers of the present-day State are largely artificial, and reflect to a considerable extent the interests and prestige of outside Powers—Britain, France, and the United States—as these existed in 1918-20. The northern frontier with Turkey is defined by a single-track railway line running along the southern edge of the foothills—probably the only case of its kind in the world; whilst eastwards and southwards boundaries are highly arbitrary, being straight lines drawn for convenience between salient points. Westwards, the frontiers are again artificial, though less crudely drawn, leaving the headwaters of the Jordan river outside Syria and following the crest of the Anti-Lebanon hills, to reach the sea north of Tripoli.

PHYSICAL FEATURES

Geographically, Syria consists of two main zones: a fairly narrow western part, made up of a complex of mountain ranges and intervening valleys; and a much larger eastern zone that is essentially a broad and open platform dropping gently towards the east and crossed diagonally by the wide Euphrates Valley.

The western zone, which contains over 80 per cent of the population of Syria, can be further subdivided as follows. In the extreme west, fronting the Mediterranean Sea, there lies an imposing ridge rising to 5,000 feet, and known as the Jebel Ansariyeh. Its western flank drops fairly gradually to the sea, giving a narrow coastal plain; but on the east it falls very sharply, almost as a wall, to a flat-bottomed valley occupied by the Orontes river, which meanders sluggishly over the flat floor, often flooding in winter, and leaving a formerly malarial marsh in summer. Farther east lie more hill ranges, opening out like a fan from the south-west, where the Anti-Lebanon range, with Mount Hermon (9,000 ft.), is the highest in Syria. Along the eastern flanks of the various ridges lie a number of shallow basins occupied by small streams that eventually dry up or form closed salt lakes. In one basin lies the city of Aleppo, once the second town of the Ottoman Empire and still close to being the largest city of Syria. In another is situated Damascus, irrigated from five streams, and famous for its clear fountains and gardens—now the capital of the country. One remaining sub-region of western Syria is the Jebel Druse, which lies in the extreme south-west, and consists of a vast out-pouring of lava, in the form of sheets and cones. Towards the west this region is fertile, and produces good cereal crops, but eastwards the soil cover disappears, leaving a barren countryside of twisted lava and caverns, for long the refuge of outlaws, bandits, and minority groups. Because of its difficulty and isolation the Jebel Druse has tended socially and politically to go its own way, remaining aloof from the rest of the country.

The entire eastern zone is mainly steppe or open desert, except close to the banks of the river Euphrates, Tigris, and their larger tributaries, where recent irrigation projects have allowed considerable cultivation on an increasing scale. The triangularly-shaped region between the Euphrates and Tigris rivers is spoken of as the Jezireh (Arabic *Jazira*= island), but is in no way different from the remaining parts of the east.

The presence of ranks of relatively high hills aligned parallel to the coast has important climatic effects. Tempering and humid effects from the Mediterranean are restricted to a narrow western belt, and central and eastern Syria show marked continental tendencies: that is, a very hot summer with temperatures often above 100° or even 110° F., and a moderately cold winter, with frost on many nights. Very close to the Mediterranean, frost is unknown at any season, but on the hills altitude greatly reduces the average temperature, so that snow may lie on the heights from late December to April, or even May. Rainfall is fairly abundant in the west, where the height of the land tends to determine the amount received; but east of the Anti-Lebanon mountains the amount decreases considerably, producing a steppe region that quickly passes into true desert. On the extreme east, as the Zagros ranges of Persia are approached, there is once again a slight increase, but most of Syria has an annual rainfall of under ten inches.

ECONOMIC LIFE

There is a close relationship between climate and economic activities. In the west, where up to 30 or even 40 inches of rainfall occur, settled farming is possible, and the main limitation is difficult terrain; but from the Orontes Valley eastwards natural rainfall is increasingly inadequate, and irrigation becomes necessary. The narrow band of territory where annual rainfall lies between 8 and 15 inches is sometimes spoken of as the "Fertile Crescent", since it runs in an arc along the inner side of the hills from Jordan through western and northern Syria as far east as Iraq. In its normal state a steppeland covered with seasonal grass, the Fertile Crescent can often be converted by irrigation and efficient organization into a rich and productive territory. Such it was in the golden days of the Arab Caliphate; now, after centuries of decline, it is once again reviving. From the 1940s to the 1950s a marked change was seen and, thanks first to small-scale irrigation schemes and the installation of motor pumps to raise water from underground artesian sources, large areas of the former steppe are producing crops of cotton, cereals and fruit. Syria has now a surplus of agricultural production, especially cereals, and this allows her to export to Jordan and the Lebanon, neither of which are self-sufficient in foodstuffs. It is expected that production will increase with the eventual doubling of Syria's irrigated area (by 640,000 hectares) as the Euphrates Dam at Tabqa develops fully. However, there have been doubts cast on the possibility of this target's being achieved; difficulties have been experienced in irrigating part of the designated area and some experts believe that perhaps 300,000 hectares may be impossible to develop according to the original plans, though the first part of the plan is now being achieved.

Because of its relative openness and accessibility and its geographical situation as a "waist" between the Mediterranean and the Persian Gulf, Syria has been a land of passage, and for centuries its role was that of an intermediary, both commercial and cultural, between the Mediterranean world and the Far East. From early times until the end of the Middle Ages there was a flow of traffic east and west that raised a number of Syrian cities and ports to the rank of international markets. Since the 1930s, following a long period of decline and eclipse resulting from the diversion of this trade to the sea, there has been a revival of activity due to the new elements of air transport and the construction of oil pipelines from Iraq.

In addition, Syria has been able to develop her own deposits of petroleum and phosphate; and her greatly improved political standing (as almost the successor of Egypt as the leading Arab state) has had an economic spin-off. The Syrian economy is much stronger than it was, and the country is able to "balance" between the Soviet and Western political groups.

RACE AND LANGUAGE

Racially, we can distinguish many elements in the Syrian people. The nomads of the interior deserts are unusually pure specimens of the Mediterranean type, isolation having preserved them from intermixture. To the west and north there is a widely varying mosaic of other groups: Armenoids, such as the Kurds and Turkish-speaking communities of the north, and the Armenians themselves, who form communities in the cities; groups such as the Druzes, who show some affinity to the tribes of the Persian Zagros, and many others.

As a result, there is a surprising variety of language and religion. Arabic is spoken over most of the country, but Kurdish is widely used along the northern frontier and Armenian in the cities. Aramaic, the language of Christ, survives in three villages.

HISTORY

ANCIENT HISTORY

From the earliest times, Syria has experienced successive waves of Semitic immigration—the Canaanites and Phoenicians in the third millennium B.C., the Hebrews and Aramaeans in the second, and, unceasingly, the nomad tribes infiltrating from the Arabian peninsula. This process has enabled Syria to assimilate or reject, without losing its essentially Semitic character, the alien invaders who, time and again, in the course of a long history, have established their domination over the land. Before Rome assumed control of Syria in the first century B.C., the Egyptians, the Assyrians and the Hittites, and, later, the Persians and the Macedonian Greeks had all left their mark in greater or lesser degree. Damascus is claimed to be the oldest capital city in the world, having been continuously inhabited since about 2000 B.C., and Aleppo may be even older. Under Roman rule the infiltration and settlement of nomad elements continued, almost unnoticed by historians, save when along the desert trade routes a Semitic vassal state attained a brief importance as, for example, the kingdom of Palmyra in the Syrian desert, which the Emperor Aurelian destroyed in A.D. 272 or, later still, when the Byzantines ruled in Syria, the Arab State of Ghassan, prominent throughout the sixth century A.D. as a bulwark of the Byzantine Empire against the desert tribes in the service of Sasanid Persia.

ARAB AND TURKISH RULE

When, after the death of the Prophet Muhammad in A.D. 632, the newly-created power of Islam began a career of conquest, the populations of Syria, Semitic in their language and culture and, as adherents of the Monophysite faith, ill-disposed towards the Greek-speaking Orthodox Byzantines, did little to oppose the Muslims, from whom they hoped to obtain a greater measure of freedom. The Muslims defeated the Byzantine forces at Ajnadain in July 634, seized Damascus in September 635, and, by their decisive victory on the River Yarmuk (August 636), virtually secured possession of all Syria. From 661–750 the Umayyad dynasty ruled in Syria, which, after the conquest, had been divided into four military districts or junds (Damascus, Homs, Urdun, i.e. Jordan, and Palestine). To these the Caliph Yazid I (680–83) added a fifth, Kinnasrin, for the defence of northern Syria, where in the late seventh century, the Mardaites, Christians from the Taurus, were making serious inroads under Byzantine leadership. Under Abd al-Malik (685–705) Arabic became the official language of the State, in whose administration, hitherto largely carried out by the old Byzantine bureaucracy, Syrians, Muslim as well as Christian, now had an increasing share. For Syria was now the heart of a great Empire, and the Arab Army of Syria, well trained in the ceaseless frontier warfare with Byzantium, bore the main burden of imperial rule, taking a major part in the two great Arab assaults on Byzantium in 674–8 and in 717–18.

The new regime in Syria was pre-eminently military and fiscal in character, representing the domination of a military caste of Muslim Arab warriors, who governed on the basic assumption that a large subject population, non-Muslim and non-Arab in character, would continue indefinitely to pay tribute. But this assumption was falsified by the gradual spread of Islam, a process which meant the progressive diminution of the amount of tribute paid to the State, and the consequent undermining of the fiscal system as a whole. In theory, conversion meant for the non-Arab convert (*Mawla*; in the plural, *Mawali*) full social and economic equality with the ruling caste, but in practice it was not enough to be a Muslim, one had to be an Arab as well. The discontent of the *Mawali* with their enforced inferiority expressed itself in an appeal to the universal character of Islam, an appeal which often took the form of religious heresies, and which, as it became more widespread, undermined the strength of the Arab regime.

To the ever present fiscal problems of the Arab State and the growing discontent of the *Mawali* was added a third and fatal weakness: the hostility between those Arab tribes which had arrived in Syria with or since the conquest, and those which had infiltrated there at an earlier date. The Umayyad house strove to maintain a neutral position over and above the tribal feuds; but from the moment when, under the pressure of events, the Umayyads were compelled to side with one faction to oppose the other (battle of Marj Rahit 684), their position was irretrievably compromised.

When in A.D. 750 with the accession of the Abbasid dynasty the centre of the Empire was transferred to Iraq, Syria, jealously watched because of its association with the former ruling house, became a mere province, where in the course of the next hundred years, several abortive revolts, inspired in part by the traditional loyalty to the Umayyads, failed to shake off Abbasid control. During the ninth century Syria was the object of dispute between Egypt and Baghdad. In 878 Ahmad ibn Tulun, Governor of Egypt, occupied it and, subsequently, every independent ruler of Egypt sought to maintain a hold, partial or complete, over Syria. Local dynasties, however, achieved from time to time a transitory importance, as did the Hamdanids (a Bedouin family from Northern Iraq) who, under Saif ad-Daula, ruler of Aleppo from 946–967, attained a brief ascendancy, marked internally by financial and administrative ineptitude, and externally by military campaigns against the Byzantines which did much to provoke the great Byzantine reconquest of the late tenth century. By the treaty of 997, northern Syria became Byzantine, while the rest of the country remained in the hands of the Fatimid dynasty which ruled in Egypt from 969. Fatimid control remained insecure and from about 1027 a new Arab house ruled at Aleppo—the Mirdasids, who were soon to disappear before the formidable power of the Seljuq Turks. The Seljuqs, having conquered Persia, rapidly overran Syria (Damascus fell to them in 1075) but failed to establish there a united State. As a result of dynastic quarrels, the Seljuq domination disintegrated into a number of amirates: Seljuq princes ruled at Aleppo and Damascus, a local dynasty held Tripoli and, in the south, Egypt controlled most of the littoral.

This political fragmentation greatly favoured the success of the First Crusade which, taking Antioch in 1098 and Jerusalem in 1099, proceeded to organize four feudal States at Edessa, Antioch, Tripoli and Jerusalem, but did not succeed in conquering Aleppo, Homs, Hama, and Damascus. From the death of Baldwin II of Jerusalem in 1131, the essential weakness of the crusading States began to appear. Byzantium, the Christian State of Lesser Armenia, and the Latin principalities in Syria never united in a successful resistance to the Muslim counter-offensive which, initiated by the energetic Turkish general Zangi Atabeg of Mosul, developed rapidly in the third and fourth decades of the century. Zangi, who seized Aleppo in 1128, and the Latin State of Edessa in 1144, was succeeded in 1146 by his able son Nur ad-Din, who by his capture of Damascus in 1154 recreated in Syria a united Muslim Power. On Nur ad-Din's death in 1174, the Kurd Saladin, already master of Egypt, assumed control at Damascus and, in 1183, seized Aleppo. His victory over the Crusaders at Hattin (July 1187) destroyed the kingdom of Jerusalem. Only the partial success of the Third Crusade (1189–92) and, after his death in 1193, the disintegration of Saladin's Empire into a number of separate principalities, made it possible for the Crusaders to maintain an ever more precarious hold on the coastal areas of Syria. The emergence in Egypt of the powerful Mamluk Sultanate (1250) meant that the end was near. A series of military campaigns, led by the Sultan Baibars (1260–77) and his immediate successors, brought about the fall of Antioch (1268) and Tripoli (1289), and, with the fall of Acre in 1291, the disappearance of the crusading States in Syria.

Before the last crusading States had been reduced, the Mamluks had to encounter a determined assault by the Mongols, in the course of which Aleppo and Hama were sacked, and Damascus besieged; until, in 1260, the Mongol army of invasion was crushed at the battle of Ain-Jalut, near Nazareth. The Mongol Il-Khans of Persia made further efforts to conquer Syria in the late thirteenth century, negotiating for this purpose with the Papacy, the remaining crusader States, and Lesser Armenia. In 1280 the Mamluks defeated a Mongol army at Homs; but in 1299 were themselves beaten near the same town, a defeat which enabled the Mongols to ravage northern Syria and to take Damascus in 1300. Only in 1303, at the battle of Marj as-Suffar, south of Damascus, was this last Mongol offensive finally repelled.

The period of Mamluk rule in Syria, which endured until 1517, was on the whole one of slow decline. Warfare, periodical famine, and not least, the plague (there were four great outbreaks in the fourteenth century, and in the fifteenth century fourteen more recorded attacks of some severity) produced a state of affairs which the financial rapacity and misrule of the Mamluk governors and the devastation of Aleppo and Damascus by Timur (1400–01) served only to aggravate.

The ill-defined protectorate which the Mamluks asserted over Cilicia and considerable areas of southern Anatolia occasioned, in the late fifteenth century, a growing tension with the power of the Ottoman Turks, which broke out into inconclusive warfare in the years 1485–91. When to this tension was added the possibility of an alliance between the Mamluks and the rising power of the Safavids in Persia, the Ottoman Sultan Selim I (1512–20) was compelled to seek a decisive solution to the problem. In August 1516 the battle of Marj Dabik, north of Aleppo, gave Syria to the Ottomans, who proceeded to ensure their continued hold on the land by conquering Egypt (1517). Turkish rule, during the next three centuries, although unjustly accused of complete responsibility for a decay and stagnation which appear to have been well advanced before 1517, brought only a temporary improvement in the unhappy condition of Syria, now divided into the three provinces of Damascus, Tripoli, and Aleppo. In parts of Syria the Turkish pashas in reality administered directly only the important towns and their immediate neighbourhood; elsewhere, the older elements—Bedouin emirs, Turcoman chiefs, etc.—were left to act much as they pleased, provided the due tribute was paid. The pashas normally bought their appointment to high office and sought in their brief tenure of power to recover the money and bribes they had expended in securing it, knowing that they might, at any moment, be replaced by someone who could pay more for the post. Damascus alone had 133 pashas in 180 years. As the control of the Sultan at Constantinople became weaker, the pashas obtained greater freedom of action, until Ahmed Jazzar, Pasha of Acre, virtually ruled Syria as an independent prince (1785–1804).

The nineteenth century saw important changes. The Ottoman Sultan Mahmud II (1808–39) had promised Syria to the Pasha of Egypt, Muhammad Ali, in return for the latter's services during the Greek War of Independence. When the Sulṭan declined to fulfil his promise, Egyptian troops overran Syria (1831–33). Ibrahim Pasha, son of Muhammad Ali, now gave to Syria, for the first time in centuries, a centralized government strong enough to hold separatist tendencies in check and to impose a system of taxation which, if burdensome, was at least regular in its functioning. But Ibrahim's rule was not popular, for the landowners resented his efforts to limit their social and political dominance, while the peasantry disliked the conscription, the forced labour, and the heavy taxation which he found indispensable for the maintenance of his regime. In 1840 a revolt broke out in Syria, and when the Great Powers intervened on behalf of the Sultan (at war with Egypt since 1839), Muhammad Ali was compelled to renounce his claim to rule there.

Western influence, working through trade, through the protection of religious minorities, and through the cultural and educational efforts of missions and schools, had received encouragement from Ibrahim Pasha. The French Jesuits, returning to Syria in 1831, opened schools, and in 1875 founded their University at Beirut. The American Presbyterian Mission (established at Beirut in 1820) introduced a printing press in 1834, and in 1866 founded the Syrian Protestant College, later renamed the American University of Beirut. Syria also received some benefit from the reform movement within the Ottoman Empire, which, begun by Mahmud II, and continued under his successors, took the form of a determined attempt to modernize the structure of the Empire. The semi-independent pashas of old disappeared, the administration being now entrusted to salaried officials of the central government; some effort was made to create schools and colleges on Western lines, and much was done to deprive the landowning classes of their feudal privileges, although their social and economic predominance was left unchallenged. As a result of these improvements, there was, in the late nineteenth century, a revival of Arabic literature which did much to prepare the way for the growth of Arab nationalism in the twentieth century.

MODERN HISTORY

By 1914 Arab nationalist sentiment had made some headway among the educated and professional classes, and especially among army officers. Nationalist societies like *Al-Fatat* soon made contact with Arab nationalists outside Syria—with the army officers of Iraq, with influential Syrian colonies in Egypt and America, and with the Sharif Husein of Mecca. The Husein-McMahon Correspondence (July 1915–January 1916) encouraged the Arab nationalists to hope that the end of the Great War would mean the creation of a greater Arab kingdom. This expectation was disappointed, for as a result of the Sykes-Picot Agreement, negotiated in secret between England, France, and Russia in 1916 (*see* Documents on Palestine, page 54), Syria was to become a French sphere of influence. At the end of the war, and in accordance with this agreement, a provisional French administration was established in the coastal districts of Syria, while in the interior an Arab government came into being under Amir Faisal, son of the Sharif Husein of Mecca. In March 1920 the Syrian nationalists proclaimed an independent kingdom of Greater Syria (including the Lebanon and Palestine); but in April of the same year the San Remo Conference gave France a mandate for the whole of Syria, and in July, French troops occupied Damascus.

By 1925 the French, aware that the majority of the Muslim population resented their rule, and that only amongst the Christian Maronites of the Lebanon could they hope to find support, had carried into effect a policy based upon the religious divisions so strong in Syria. The area under mandate had been divided into four distinct units; a much enlarged Lebanon (including Beirut and Tripoli), a Syrian Republic, and the two districts of Latakia and Jebel Druse. Despite the fact that the French rule gave Syria a degree of law and order which might render possible the transition from a medieval to a more modern form of society, nationalist sentiment opposed the mandate on principle, and deplored the failure to introduce full representative institutions and the tendency to encourage separatism amongst the religious minorities. This discontent, especially strong in the Syrian Republic, became open revolt in 1925-26, during the course of which the French twice bombarded Damascus (October 1925 and May 1926).

The next ten years were marked by a hesitant and often interrupted progress towards self-government in Syria, and by French efforts to conclude a Franco-Syrian treaty. In April 1928 elections were held for a Constituent Assembly, and in August a draft Constitution was completed; but the French High Commissioner refused to accept certain articles, especially Article 2, which, declaring the Syrian territories detached from the old Ottoman Empire to be an indivisible unity, constituted a denial of the separate existence of the Jebel Druse, Latakia, and the Lebanese Republic. After repeated attempts to reach a compromise, the High Commissioner dissolved the Assembly in May 1930 and, on his own authority, issued a new Constitution for the State of Syria, much the same as that formerly proposed by the Assembly, but with those modifications which were considered indispensable to the maintenance of French control. After new elections (January 1932) negotiations were begun for a Franco-Syrian treaty, to be modelled on that concluded between England and Iraq in 1930, but no compromise could be found between the French demands and those of the nationalists who, although in a minority, wielded a dominant influence in the Chamber and whose aim was to limit both in time and in place the French military occupation, and to include in Syria the separate areas of Jebel Druse and Latakia. In 1934 the High Commissioner suspended the Chamber indefinitely. Disorders occurred early in 1936 which induced the French to send a Syrian delegation to Paris, where the new Popular Front Government showed itself more sympathetic towards Syrian aspirations than former French governments had been. In September 1936 a Franco-Syrian treaty was signed which recognised the principle of Syrian independence and stipulated that, after ratification, there should be a period of three years during which the apparatus of a fully independent State should be created. The districts of Jebel Druse and Latakia would be annexed to Syria, but would retain special administrations. Other subsidiary agreements reserved to France important military and economic rights in Syria. It seemed that Syria might now enter a period of rapid political development; but the unrest caused by the situation in Palestine, the crisis with Turkey, and the failure of France to ratify the 1936 treaty were responsible, within two years, for the breakdown of these hopes.

In 1921 Turkey had consented to the inclusion of the Sanjak of Alexandretta in the French mandated territories, on condition that it should be governed under a special regime. The Turks, alarmed by the treaty of 1936, which envisaged the emergence of a unitary Syrian State including, to all appearance, Alexandretta, now pressed for a separate agreement concerning the status of the Sanjak. After long discussion the League of Nations decided in 1937 that the Sanjak should be fully autonomous, save for its foreign and financial policies which were to be under the control of the Syrian Government. A treaty between France and Turkey guaranteed the integrity of the Sanjak, and also the Turco-Syrian frontier. Throughout 1937 there were conflicts between Turks and Arabs in the Sanjak, and in Syria a widespread and growing resentment, for it was clear that sooner or later Turkey would ask for the cession of Alexandretta. The problem came to be regarded in Syria as a test of Franco-Syrian co-operation, and when in June 1939, under the pressure of international tension, Alexandretta was finally ceded to Turkey, the cession assumed in the eyes of Syrian nationalists the character of a betrayal by France. Meanwhile, in France itself, opposition to the treaty of 1936 had grown steadily; and in December 1938 the French Government, anxious not to weaken its military position in the Near East, declared that no ratification of the treaty was to be expected.

Unrest in Syria led to open riots in 1941, as a result of which the Vichy High Commissioner, General Dentz, promised the restoration of partial self-government; while in June of the same year, when in order to combat Axis intrigues the Allies invaded Syria, General Catroux, on behalf of the Free French Government, promised independence for Syria and the end of mandatory rule. Syrian independence was formally recognized in September 1941, but the reality of power was still withheld, with the effect that nationalist agitation, inflamed by French reluctance to restore constitutional rule, and by economic difficulties due to the war, became even more pronounced. When at last elections were held once more, a nationalist government was formed, with Shukri al-Kuwatly as President of the Syrian Republic (August 1943).

Gradually all important powers and public services were transferred from French to Syrian hands; but conflict again developed over the *Troupes Spéciales*, the local Syrian and Lebanese levies which had existed throughout the mandatory period as an integral part of the French military forces in the Levant, and which, transferred to the Syrian and Lebanese Governments, would enable them to form their own armies. Other points of dispute were the so-called "Common Interests" (i.e. departments dealing with matters of concern to both Syria and the Lebanon), and the control of internal security, hitherto in French hands. Strongly supported by the newly-created Arab League, Syria refused the French demand for a Franco-Syrian Treaty as the condition for the final transfer of these administrative and military services which had always been the main instruments of French policy. In May 1945 disturbances broke out which ended only with British armed intervention and the evacuation of French troops and administrative personnel. The *Troupes Spéciales* were now handed over to the Syrian Government, and with the departure of British forces in April 1946 the full independence of Syria was at last achieved.

UNSTABLE INDEPENDENCE

After the attainment of independence Syria passed through a long period of instability. She was involved in a complicated economic and financial dispute with the Lebanon (1948–50) and also in various schemes for union with Iraq—schemes which tended to divide political opinion inside Syria itself and, in addition, to disrupt the unity of the Arab League. Syria, in fact, found herself aligned at this time with Egypt and Saudi Arabia against the ambitions of the Hashemite rulers of Iraq and Jordan. These rivalries, together with the profound disappointment felt at Damascus over the Arab failures in the war of 1948–49 against Israel, were the prelude to three *coups d'état* in 1949. Dislike of continued financial dependence on France, aspirations towards a greater Syria, the resentments arising out of the unsuccessful war against the Israelis—all help to explain the unrest inside Syria.

The intervention of the army in politics was itself a cause of further tension. Opposition to the dominance of the army grew in the Syrian Chamber of Deputies to such an extent that yet another *coup d'état* was carried out in December 1951. Syria now came under the control of a military autocracy with Colonel Shishakli as head of the state. The Chamber of Deputies was dissolved in December 1951; a decree of April 1952 abolished all political parties in Syria. After the approval of a new constitution in July 1953 General Shishakli became President of Syria in August of that year. The formation of political parties was now allowed once more. Members of the parties dissolved under the decree of April 1952 proceeded, however, to boycott the elections held in October 1953, at which President Shishakli's Movement of Arab Liberation obtained a large majority in the Chamber of Deputies. Politicians hostile to the regime of President Shishakli established in November 1953 a Front of National Opposition, refusing to accept as legal the results of the October elections and declaring as their avowed aim the end of military autocracy and the restoration of democratic rule. Demonstrations at Damascus and Aleppo in December 1953 led soon to the flight of Shishakli to France. The collapse of his regime early in 1954 meant for Syria a return to the Constitution of 1950. New elections held in September 1954 brought into being a Chamber of Deputies notable for the large number of its members (81 out of 142) who might be regarded as independents grouped around leading political figures.

INFLUENCE FROM ABROAD

There was still, however, much friction in Syria between those who favoured union or at least close co-operation with Iraq and those inclined towards an effective *entente* with Egypt. In August 1955 Shukri al-Kuwatli became President of the Republic. His appointment was interpreted as an indication that pro-Egyptian influence had won the ascendancy in Syria. On October 20th, 1955, Syria made with Egypt an agreement for the creation of a joint military command with its headquarters at Damascus.

The U.S.S.R., meanwhile, in answer to the developments in the Middle East associated with the Baghdad Pact, had begun an intensive diplomatic, propaganda and economic campaign of penetration into the Arab lands. In the years 1954–56 Syria, the only Arab state where the Communist Party was legal, made a number of barter agreements with the Soviet Union and its associates in eastern Europe. A report from Cairo intimated, in February 1956, that Syria had joined Egypt in accepting arms from U.S.S.R.

At the end of October 1956 there occurred the Israeli campaign in the Sinai peninsula, an event followed, in the first days of November, by the armed intervention of Great Britain and France in the Suez Canal region. On October 30th the President of the Syrian Republic left Damascus on a visit to the Soviet Union. A state of emergency was declared in Syria. Reports from Beirut revealed on November 3rd that Syrian forces had put out of action the pipelines which carried Iraqi oil to the Mediterranean. The damage that Syrian elements had done to the pipelines earned the sharp disapproval of such Arab states as Iraq and Saudi Arabia, both of whom were now faced with a severe loss of oil revenues. The Syrian Government declared that it would not allow the repair of the pipelines until Israel had withdrawn her troops from Gaza and the Gulf of Aqaba. Not until March 1957 was it possible to restore the pipelines, Israel having in the meantime agreed to evacuate her forces from the areas in dispute.

In April 1957 a crisis took place in Jordan where the Palestinian elements in political circles, with some support from the army, sought to draw Jordan into alignment with Egypt and Syria. At the time of the Sinai-Suez crisis in November 1956 contingents of Syrian troops had been stationed in Jordan. These troops were still on Jordanian soil. There were also reports that reinforcements might be sent to the Syrian forces in Jordan. It seemed that a major intervention in the affairs of Jordan was imminent. On April 24th the U.S.A. announced that it regarded the independence and integrity of Jordan as a matter of vital concern. The United States Sixth Fleet was now ordered to the eastern Mediterranean with instructions to assist Jordan, if aid were requested. At the same time the U.S. Government deplored the flow of Soviet arms and equipment to Egypt and Syria. In May 1957 Syria stated that, in compliance with a request from Amman, she would withdraw her forces from Jordan.

UNION WITH EGYPT

The Syrian National Assembly, in November 1957, passed a resolution in favour of union with Egypt. Earlier in the year there had been discussions concerning proposals for a customs union between the two countries and for the co-ordination of their currencies and of their economic policies. The formal union of Egypt and Syria to constitute one state under the title of the United Arab Republic received the final approval of the Syrian National Assembly on February 5th, 1958. President Nasser of Egypt, on February 21st, became the first head of the combined state. A central cabinet for the U.A.R. was established in October 1958, also two regional executive councils, one for Syria and one for Egypt. A further move towards integration came in March 1960, when President Nasser announced the formation of a single National Assembly for the whole of the U.A.R. The Assembly, consisting of 400 deputies from Egypt and 200 from Syria, held its first meeting at Cairo on July 21st, 1960.

The more extreme elements of the right and of the left—e.g. the conservative class of landowners and also the Communist following in Syria—had viewed with distrust the union of Syria and Egypt. Amongst the Baath Socialists, who had played an important role in bringing about the merger with Egypt in 1958, dissatisfaction grew as a result of the small progress made with schemes for the socialization of the Syrian economy. There was disillusionment, too, in the Syrian armed forces over the more and more frequent transfer of Syrian officers to Egypt and of Egyptian officers to Syria. Administrators and officials of Egyptian origin had come, moreover, to hold a large number of the most influential positions in the Syrian Region of the U.A.R. Syria still retained, however, at the end of 1960 and in the first months of 1961, a considerable measure of autonomy in most economic matters.

August 1961 saw the abolition of the regional executive councils for Syria and Egypt created in 1958. This attempt to hasten the integration of the two countries was the prelude to a new crisis at Damascus. On September 28th, 1961, there occurred in Syria a military *coup d'état* which aimed—successfully—at the separation of Syria from Egypt and at the dissolution of the United Arab Republic. Political figures representing most of the parties which existed in Syria before the establishment of the U.A.R. in 1958 met at Damascus and Aleppo on October 3rd, 1961, issuing a declaration of support for the new regime and calling for free elections to a new legislature. Syrian members of the National Assembly of the U.A.R. gathered at Damascus on October 4th to denounce the arbitrary and dictatorial character of the control previously exercised from Cairo over Syrian affairs. President Nasser now, on October 5th, recognized the *fait accompli*. Most foreign states made haste to grant formal recognition to the government at Damascus. On October 13th 1961, Syria became once more a member of the United Nations. A provisional constitution was promulgated in November and elections for a Constituent Assembly took place on December 1st, 1961.

The regime thus established in Syria rested on no sure foundation. At the end of March 1962 the Syrian Army intervened once more, bringing about the resignation of Dr. Nazim Kudsi, the President of the Republic, and also of the ministers who had taken office in December 1961. After demonstrations at Aleppo, Homs and Hama in April 1962, Dr. Kudsi was reinstated as President, but further ministerial resignations in May of that year pointed to the existence of continuing tensions within the government.

THE REVOLUTION OF 1963

A military junta, styled the National Council of the Revolutionary Command, seized control in Damascus on March 8th, 1963. In May the Baathists took measures to purge the armed forces and the administration of personnel known to favour a close alignment with Egypt. A new government, formed on May 13th and strongly Baathist in character, carried out a further purge in June and at the same time created a National Guard recruited from members of the Baath movement. These measures led the pro-Egyptian elements to attempt a *coup d'état* at Damascus on July 18th, 1963. The attempt failed, however, with a considerable loss of life. On July 27th Maj-Gen. Amin al-Hafiz, Deputy Prime Minister and Minister of the Interior, became President of the National Council of the Revolutionary Command, a position equivalent to Head of State.

BAATH SOCIALISM

The nationalization of all Arab-owned banks in 1963, and of various industrial enterprises, also the transfer of land to the peasants—all had contributed to bring about much dissatisfaction in the business world and amongst the influential landed elements. The Baath regime depended for its main support on the armed forces which, however, had been recruited in no small degree from the religious minorities in Syria, including adherents of the Shi'i (Alawi) faith—most Syrians being, in fact, of Sunni or orthodox Muslim allegiance. In general, conservative Muslims tended to oppose the Baath government under guidance of the *'ulama* and of the Muslim Brotherhood. The mass of the peasant population was thought to have some pro-Nasser sympathies; the working class (small in number) was divided between pro-Nasser and Baathist adherents; the middle and upper classes opposed the domination of al-Baath. The unease arising out of these frictions and antipathies took the form of disturbances and finally of open revolt—soon suppressed—at Hama (April 1964).

On April 25th, 1964, a provisional constitution had been promulgated, describing Syria as a democratic socialist republic forming an integral part of the Arab nation. A Presidential Council was established on May 14th, 1964, with General Hafiz as head of the state.

The as yet undeveloped petroleum and other mineral resources of Syria were nationalized in 1964, together with other industrial concerns. On January 7th, 1965, a special military court was created with sweeping powers to deal with all offences, of word or deed, against the nationalization decrees and the socialist revolution. General Hafiz denounced the *'ulama* and the Muslim Brotherhood as being involved in the resulting demonstrations. Further nationalization followed.

The autumn of 1965 saw a number of important changes inside Syria. A National Council, almost one hundred strong, was established in August with the task of preparing a new constitution which would be submitted to a public referendum. Meeting for the first time on September 1st, 1965, it created a Presidency Council, of five members, which was to exercise the powers of a head of state.

RADICAL REACTION

The tensions hitherto visible in al-Baath were, however, still active. Two groups stood ranged one against the other—on the one hand the older more experienced politicians in al-Baath, less inclined than in former years to insist on the unrestrained pursuit of the main Baathist objectives, socialism and pan-Arab union, and on the other hand the extreme left-wing elements, doctrinaire in their attitude and enjoying considerable support amongst the younger radical officers in the armed forces.

The tensions thus engendered found expression in a new *coup d'état* on February 23rd, 1966. A military junta representing the extreme radical elements in al-Baath seized power in Damascus and placed under arrest a number of personalities long identified with al-Baath and belonging to the international leadership controlling the organization throughout the Arab world—amongst them Mr. Michael Aflaq, the founder of al-Baath; General Hafiz, the chairman of the recently established Presidency Council; and Mr. Salah al-Din Bitar, the Prime Minister of the displaced administration.

On November 4th the United Arab Republic and Syria entered into a defence agreement for military co-ordination between the two countries. The agreement stipulated that aggression against either state would be considered as an assault on the other, to be repelled by the armed forces of the U.A.R. and of Syria acting together. A defence council and a joint military command were to be established under the terms of the agreement.

ARAB-ISRAELI WAR OF 1967

The friction ever present along the frontier between Syria and Israel had flared out from time to time during recent years into violent conflict, particularly in the region of Lake Tiberias. Now, in the winter of 1966–67, the tension along the border began to assume more serious proportions. Israel, in October 1966, complained to the Security Council of the United Nations about guerilla activities from Syria across the frontier into Israeli territory. In April 1967, mortars, cannon and air force units from Syria and Israel were involved in fighting south-east of Lake Tiberias.

The continuing tension on the Syrian-Israeli frontier was now to become a major influence leading to the war which broke out on June 5th, 1967, between Israel and her Arab neighbours Egypt, Syria and Jordan. During the course of hostilities which lasted six days Israel defeated Egypt and Jordan and then, after some stubborn fighting, outflanked and overran the Syrian positions on the hills above Lake Tiberias. With the breakthrough accomplished, Israeli forces made a rapid advance and occupied the town of Quneitra about forty miles from Damascus. On June 10th Israel and Syria announced their formal acceptance of the United Nations proposal for a cease-fire, but Syria effectively boycotted the Arab summit conference held at Khartoum in August 1967 and in September the Baath party of Syria rejected all idea of a compromise with Israel. The resolution adopted by the UN Security Council in November, urging the withdrawal of the Israelis from the lands occupied by them during the June war and the ending of the belligerency which the Arab governments had up till then maintained against Israel, was rejected by Syria, which alone maintained its commitment to a reunified Palestine.

STRUGGLE FOR POWER 1968-71

The ruling Baath Party had for some years been divided into two main factions. Until October 1968 the dominant faction had been the "progressive" group led by Dr. Atassi and Dr. Makhous, the Premier and Foreign Minister respectively. This group was distinguished by its doctrinaire and Marxist-orientated public pronouncements (not always put into effect despite its control of the government) and by the strong support it received from the U.S.S.R. It held that the creation of a strong one-party state and economy along neo-Marxist lines was of paramount importance, overriding even the need for a militant stand towards Israel and for Arab unity.

By October 1968 the government felt particularly insecure, partly owing to a feud with the new Baath régime in Iraq, and at the end of the month a new cabinet was formed including several members of the opposing "nationalist" faction. This group took less interest in ideological questions and favoured a pragmatic attitude to the economy, improved relations with Syria's Arab neighbours and full participation in the campaign against Israel, including support for the fedayeen movement. Its leader was Lt.-Gen. Hafiz al-Assad, who assumed the all-important Ministry of Defence. His critical attitude to the powerful Soviet influence on the government, seen by some "nationalists" as tantamount to colonialism in restricting Syria's freedom of action, led to a prolonged struggle with the "progressive" leadership. Cabinet reshuffles took place in March and again in May, but both Dr. Atassi and General Assad retained their positions. During the spring of 1969 a number of Communists were arrested or sent into exile, and the leader of the Syrian Communist Party, still technically an illegal organization, flew to Moscow.

General Assad attempted to take over the government in February 1969 but was forestalled by Soviet threats that if he did so all military supplies (including spares), economic and technical aid, and trade agreements would end. This would have brought about a major disruption in the national economy and the armed forces, and the "nationalists" were obliged to yield. In May General Mustafa Tlas, the Army Chief of Staff and General Assad's right-hand man, led a military delegation to Peking to buy arms. Some Chinese weapons were reported to be delivered in July. The incident indicated a new independence of Moscow. Some observers also saw this independence in the creation of a joint military command with Iraq (with whom relations improved during the spring) and Jordan. Relations with the Lebanon worsened, owing to Syria's support of the Lebanese fedayeen movement, containing many Syrian members. In the 1968–70 period this appeared to direct much of its activity towards bringing down the precarious Lebanese Government, presumably in the hope that a more militantly anti-Israel ministry would take power. Syria did, however, grant diplomatic recognition to the German Democratic Republic (East Germany) in June, and refused to resume diplomatic relations with Britain and the U.S.A.

During the year 1969–70 there was some revival of activity on the front with Israel. Several air battles took place, and there was an extensive surface conflict involving tanks in June 1970; as usual, both sides claimed sweeping victories. Syria consistently supported the guerrilla forces in their struggle with the Jordan Government.

In November 1970, following a reported *coup* attempt backed by Iraq in August, the struggle between the two factions of the Baath Party came to a head when General Assad seized power. Dr. Atassi, who was in hospital at the time, was placed under guard and a retired General, Salah Jadid, Assistant Secretary-General of the Baath Party and leader of the civilian faction, was arrested. Other members of the civilian wing were arrested or fled to the Lebanon. The coup was precipitated by attempts of Jadid and his supporters (culminating at the emergency session of the Tenth National Pan-Arab Congress of the Party) to oust

Assad and Tlas from their posts. This power struggle had become acute as a result of differences over support for the Palestine guerrillas during the fighting with the Jordanian army in September. Jadid and Yusuf Zeayen, a former Prime Minister, controlled the Syrian guerrilla organization, Saiqa, and supported the movement of tanks from Syria into Jordan to support the Palestinian guerrillas' efforts against the Jordanian army. This, Assad and the military faction opposed. Their approach to the Palestinian problem was more akin to Nasser's and they wanted to avoid giving any provocation to Israel, because they considered the Syrian armed forces to be unready to offer adequate resistance.

ASSAD IN POWER

There was no obvious opposition to the army takeover. Ahmed Khatib became acting President and General Assad Prime Minister and Party Secretary-General. A new Regional Command of the Baath Party was formed. The old leaders were removed from their posts in a purge which stretched into the new year. Following amendments to the 1969 provisional constitution in February 1971, General Assad was elected President for a seven-year term in March. In the following month Maj.-Gen. Abdel Rahman Khlefawi became Premier and Mahmoud al-Ayoubi was appointed Vice-President. In February the first legislative body in Syria since 1966, the People's Council, was formed. Of its 173 members, 87 represented the Baath Party.

The Nasserite leanings of the new regime in foreign policy soon became apparent (and presumably helped Assad establish some kind of *modus vivendi* with the U.S.S.R.). Although Syria continued to reject the November 1967 UN Security Council resolution, relations with the U.A.R. and Jordan improved, and Syria's isolation in the Arab world was soon reduced. Syria's willingness to join a union with the U.A.R., Sudan and Libya almost immediately became apparent and agreement on federation with Libya and the U.A.R. was reached in April 1971. In September the Federation of Arab Republics was established, following a referendum covering all three countries. The Federation, however, has had little practical effect.

After coming to power, the Assad regime increased the Syrian army's control over Saiqa. In April 1971 guerrilla operations against Israeli positions from the Syrian front were banned by the Government. Then, at the beginning of July, some guerrilla units were forced out of Syria into south Lebanon and arms destined for them and arriving from Algeria were seized by the Syrian authorities. Yet after the Jordanian Government's final onslaught on the Palestinian guerrillas in north Jordan in July Syria closed her border and in August broke off diplomatic relations when the tension had become so great that tank and artillery clashes developed between the two armies. Egyptian mediation reduced the chances of any more serious conflict developing but diplomatic links remained severed with Jordan until October 1973. Relations with the U.S.S.R. improved during the last half of 1971 and in 1972, and in May Marshal Grechko, the Soviet Defence Minister, visited Damascus. Syria was not prepared, however, to sign a friendship treaty with the U.S.S.R. like Egypt and Iraq. On the other hand, the Syrian Government, which had been broadened in March 1972 to include representatives of parties other than the Baath like the communists, did not follow Egypt's example in July and expel its Soviet advisers.

In December 1972 Maj.-Gen. Khlefawi resigned from the post of Prime Minister for health reasons and a new Government was formed by Mahmoud al-Ayoubi, the Vice-President, with 16 out of 31 government portfolios going to the Baath Party. At the end of January 1973 a draft Constitution was approved by the People's Council and confirmed by a referendum in March. The Sunni Muslims were dissatisfied that the Constitution did not recognize Islam as the State religion, and as a result of their pressure an amendment was passed declaring that the President must be a Muslim. Under the Constitution freedom of belief is guaranteed, with the State respecting all religions, although the Constitution recognizes that Islamic jurisprudence was "a principal source of legislation". In 1972 a National Charter, creating a National Progressive Front, a grouping of the Baath party and its allies, came into being. In May 1973 elections were organized for the new People's Council under the aegis of the Front and 140 out of the 186 seats were won by the Progressive Front while 42 seats were won by Independents and 4 by the Opposition.

THE FOURTH ARAB-ISRAELI WAR AND ITS AFTERMATH

On the afternoon of October 6th, 1973, Egyptian and Syrian forces launched war against Israel in an effort to regain territories lost in 1967. On both the Egyptian and Syrian fronts complete surprise was achieved, giving the Arabs a strong initial advantage, much of which they subsequently lost. The course of the war is described in "The Arab-Israeli Confrontation 1969–79", pages 37–54. Although Egypt signed a disengagement agreement with Israel on January 18th, 1974, fighting continued on the Syrian front in the Golan Heights area until a disengagement agreement was signed on May 31st, after much diplomacy and travel by the U.S. Secretary of State, Dr. Henry Kissinger (*see* "Documents on Palestine" pages 70–71).

Syria has continued to maintain a "hard line" policy in the Middle East, especially regarding the Palestinian question, and since the 1973 war it has received vast amounts of Soviet military aid which has fully re-equipped its forces. Contact with Moscow and Eastern European states has, for most of the time, been extremely close. Syria's strong support for the PLO was vindicated in October 1974 at the Arab Summit in Rabat, Morocco, where the PLO's claim to the West Bank was recognized.

By June 1976, however, Syria was in the position of invading Lebanon to crush the Palestinians, and finding most of the remainder of the Arab world agreeing to send a peace-keeping force to Lebanon to quell the conflict.

FOREIGN AFFAIRS 1975–78

This reversal for Syria arose out of a lengthy chain of events. An improvement in relations with Jordan took place in 1975, with King Hussein visiting Damascus in April and President Assad visiting Amman in June. A joint military and political command was set up between the two countries and by the spring of 1977 their customs, electricity networks and education systems were unified. Plans were made for the eventual union of the two countries. Relations between Syria and Jordan cooled, however, after Jordan appeared to give guarded support to Sadat's peace initiative in November 1977.

The second Egyptian-Israeli disengagement agreement in Sinai, signed in September 1975, met with Syria's strong condemnation. Syria accused Egypt of going it alone, and, by agreeing to three years of peace with Israel, weakening the general Arab position and betraying the Palestinians.

Syria had shown considerable interest in the Lebanese civil war since it began in April 1975. Initially, Syria wanted to protect the position of the Palestinians in Lebanon and perhaps also further plans for a "greater

Syria", sending in about 2,000 Saiqa troops in January 1976. After having secured a ceasefire Assad pledged that he would control the Palestinians in Lebanon, and the core of the PLO under Yasser Arafat began to be apprehensive that they would be dominated by Syria.

In May 1976 there were attempts by Saudi Arabia and Kuwait to effect a reconciliation between Syria and Egypt. A meeting was arranged to take place at Riyadh between Syria, Egypt, Kuwait and Saudi Arabia, but before the meeting could take place in June the Lebanese situation had intervened and the meeting was postponed. By early June the fighting in Lebanon was so fierce that Syria felt obliged to intervene militarily and overtly. This time, Syria's intervention was welcomed by the Christian Right and condemned by the Palestinians and the Muslim left.

Egypt's reaction was to close the Syrian Relations Bureau in Cairo, and to expel its staff. This followed an attack on the Egyptian Relations Office in Damascus by what the Egyptians alleged were "Syrian intelligence". A meeting of the Arab League Foreign Ministers towards the middle of June agreed that an Arab peace-keeping force should be sent to Lebanon to effect a ceasefire. After some delay, a peace-keeping force consisting of Syrian and Libyan troops in equal proportions did arrive in Lebanon, but the fighting continued unabated until October 1976 when Arab summits at Riyadh and Cairo secured a more lasting ceasefire. A 30,000-strong Arab Deterrent Force, consisting largely of Syrian troops, was given authority by the Arab summits to maintain the peace. President Assad's prestige in Syria and the Arab world was considerably strengthened by this success. Relations with Egypt improved after a tacit understanding that Syria would end its criticism of the September 1975 Egyptian-Israeli Sinai agreement in return for Egypt's acceptance of Syria's intervention in Lebanon.

In August 1976 the Prime Minister, Mahmoud al-Ayoubi, was replaced by his predecessor, Gen. Khlefawi. He held office until March 1978, when he was succeeded by Muhammad Ali al-Halabi, previously Speaker of the Peolpe's Council.

Relations with the U.S.S.R., which had been extremely bad during most of 1976, improved after the October 1976 summits and were consolidated when Assad visited Moscow in April 1977. With Iraq, however, relations continued to be bad. Iraq shut off the flow of oil from Kirkuk to the Syrian port of Banias as a protest against Syrian intervention in Lebanon. Another Iraqi grievance was Syria's use of Euphrates water. When an attempt to assassinate the Syrian Vice-Premier and Minister of Foreign Affairs, Abdel Halim Khaddam, was made in December 1976, voices in Syria were swift to blame terrorists trained in Iraq. Relations between Syria and Egypt deteriorated again as a result of President Sadat's peace initiative in November 1977. Syria's President Assad strongly criticized the move and diplomatic relations between the two countries were broken off in December.

Syria's rift with Egypt grew even wider after Sadat and Prime Minister Begin of Israel signed the Camp David agreements (see p. 73) in the U.S.A. in September 1978. The third summit of the "Steadfastness and Confrontation Front", comprising Arab countries strongly opposed to Egypt's attempt to make a separate peace with Israel, met in Damascus in late September 1978. When the Egyptian-Israeli peace treaty was finally signed in March 1979 Syria joined most of the other Arab League member countries at a meeting in Baghdad which endorsed political and economic sanctions against Egypt.

Egypt's *rapprochement* with Israel, however, has led Syria to improve its relations with Iraq. A united Syria and Iraq would provide a strong counterweight to Egypt in Middle Eastern affairs, and this consideration had some influence on the signing of the National Charter for Joint Action by Syria and Iraq in October 1978. Complete political and economic unity of the two countries is intended, but after the third meeting of the "Higher Political Committee" of the two countries, held in mid-June 1979 in Baghdad, it appeared that practical steps towards complete unity were proving elusive. A "Unified Political Leadership" was set up, but after the meeting the Presidents of both countries showed disappointment that more had not been achieved. Internal changes in Iraq in July and August 1979 have also threatened the union.

INTERNAL DIFFICULTIES

Although President Assad was comfortably returned for a second seven-year term of office in February 1978 (he received 99.6 per cent of the votes cast and 97 per cent of the electorate voted), there has been growing evidence of internal dissatisfaction in Syria. Important government posts are largely in the hands of Alawites, a minority Muslim sect to which Assad belongs, and over the past two years several Alawites have been assassinated. The majority of the top army commanders are also Alawites, and it was at the Aleppo military academy where the latest and most noteworthy massacre took place. In June 1979 more than 60 army cadets, most of them thought to be Alawites, were gunned down, and the slaughter was later officially attributed to the right-wing Muslim Brotherhood. Whoever was responsible, there is clearly tension between the Alawite (Shi'ite) community (15 per cent of the population) and the remaining Sunnis.

ECONOMIC SURVEY

Despite its proven resilience to the immense strains of war and periods of political instability, the Syrian economy today has still to be seen against a backdrop of geopolitics. As a confrontation state, a portion of whose land has now been under Israeli occupation for over a decade, Syria bears a heavy burden of defence expenditure which regularly consumes a quarter of its annual budget. At the same time its position at the frontline has encouraged Syria to assume responsibility for events elsewhere in the area, resulting in 1976 in its military intervention in the Lebanon, which created a further drain on financial resources and appeared for a while to put Syria out of favour with some of its principal financial supporters among the Arab oil-exporting states. Moreover, the traditional political rivalry between the Syrian and Iraqi Baath parties can have serious economic repercussions, as happened in 1976/77 when Iraq decided to stop pumping oil through Syria to Banias, thus depriving the Syrian Government of valuable transit revenues and the benefits of easily accessible oil supplies at a favourable price. In 1978, however, in the wake of Egypt's decision to sign a peace treaty with Israel, Syria and Iraq were recociled and all the Arab countries east of Suez closed ranks—a move much to Syria's advantage in purely financial terms.

Even so, the major, long-term constraints on Syria's economic progress will be removed only by a comprehensive peace settlement in the Middle East, since all attempts at sustained development since independence have so far been disrupted by political instability. In the 1950s and 1960s frequent changes of government and alternate periods of boom and slump led to a mass exodus of capital and skills and a state of lethargy among those who stayed behind. Three years of relative calm under President Assad had just started to bring about an improvement in this state of affairs when the Arab-Israeli war of October 1973 broke out, causing damage to Syria estimated at $1,800 million. Latakia port, the Banias and Tartous oil terminals and the huge Homs complex in central Syria which then housed the country's only oil refinery and generated more than 40 per cent of its power needs were virtually destroyed. The reconstruction effort needed was immense but the Government acted swiftly, bringing in economic liberalization measures to encourage investment in early 1974 and gradually, business confidence began to return, to the extent that the Third Development Plan (1971–75) ended with a flourish of unprecedented growth. This, in turn, prompted the government to reinforce investment incentives in certain sectors and to launch an ambitious Fourth Development Plan for the period 1976–80, only to find itself confronted once again with the economic repercussions of regional political problems.

Syrian leaders now look to the 1980s to bring fulfilment of the country's undoubted economic potential. If agreements reached during 1978/79 are implemented, Syria and Iraq should be co-ordinating their development plans starting in 1980. Jordan may also feature to some extent in this regional co-operation, since Syria and Jordan have been co-operating on development projects with varying degrees of enthusiasm since 1975. Other factors in Syria's favour include its ability to attract development funds from various sources, Arab, European and international, including the World Bank. These lenders recognize the diversity of the Syrian economy, based as it is not only on petroleum or cotton but on large-scale food production and an expanding services sector, particularly with regard to tourism and transit trade. It is this diversity which will help to cushion the country against further blows from outside its borders or setbacks within.

AREA AND POPULATION

Syria covers an area of about 7,1500 square miles (185,180 sq. km.), about 45 per cent of which is considered arable land. The remainder consists of bare mountain, desert and pastures suitable only for nomads. Of the total cultivable area of 8.7 million hectares little more than about 70 per cent is under cultivation. According to official statistics for mid-1978, the population (including Palestinian refugees) totalled 8,088,000. The average annual increase between 1970 and 1977 was 3.3 per cent. Census totals in September 1960 and September 1970 stood at 4,565,121 and 6,304,685 respectively. Of the total population in 1973, 35.9 per cent were aged under 10 and roughly half were under the age of 15.4 years.

There has been a continuing movement from village to town, reflected in a 60 per cent increase in the urban population between 1959, when 35 per cent of the population were classified as urban, and 1969, when 40 per cent came in this category. This movement has been amply illustrated by the growth of shanty towns along the edges of the large urban centres such as Damascus and Aleppo. The population of Damascus and its surrounding province approximately doubled between 1959 and 1973, from over half a million to an estimated 1,456,000. By early 1979 it had grown to 2.25 million. The population of Aleppo, put at 466,026 in 1959, rose to 646,000 in 1973, the total figure for the city and its province standing at 1,522,000.

The total labour force rose from 1,524,552 in 1970 to 1,994,759 in 1977. The composition of the labour force in 1977 reflected the exodus from rural to urban areas. Of the total, agriculture, forestry, hunting and fishing employed 37.8 per cent (against 49 per cent in 1970), manufacturing and mining employed 13.7 per cent (against 12.5 per cent), trade, catering and hotels 10.2 per cent (against 9.1 per cent) and transport and communications employed 6 per cent (compared with 4 per cent in 1970).

AGRICULTURE

Agriculture has for long been a mainstay of the Syrian economy in spite of the existence of a traditionally strong trading sector and relatively successful attempts at industrialization. It accounts for roughly one-fifth of the G.D.P. and employs about half the labour force. The main areas of cultivation are a narrow strip of land along the coast from the Lebanese to the Turkish frontiers which enjoys a Mediterranean climate, is exceedingly fertile and produces fruit, olives, tobacco and cotton. East of this strip lies the northward continuation of the Lebanon range of mountains, which falls sharply on the east to the Orontes River valley whose marshes were recently reclaimed to form one of Syria's most fertile areas. In central Syria this valley joins the 100-mile wide steppe-plain which runs from the Jordanian borders northeastward towards the Euphrates valley. The plain is traditionally Syria's major agricultural area, mainly grains-producing, in which are located the main cities, Damascus, Homs, Hama and Aleppo. The importance of this plain is now being rivalled by a fourth area, the Jezira, which lies between the Euphrates in Syria and the Tigris in Iraq. Although fertile lands along the banks of the Euphrates and its tributaries had previously been cultivated, the Jezira only came into its own in the early 1950s when large-scale cotton cultivation was introduced in former pasture lands. It is now vastly increasing its output with the development of the Euphrates Dam.

One of the chief characteristics of Syria's agricultural performance, in the absence of any established large-scale irrigation system, is the violent annual fluctuation in output resulting from wide variations in rainfall. Dependence on rainfall for good harvests is nowhere more clearly shown than in the Central Bank's general indices for agricultural production, which show a swing from 156 in 1972 to 103 the following year and up again to an estimated 181 in 1977 (1970=100).

Agriculture's share in the G.D.P. has fallen substantially since the early 1960s. In 1962 it had contributed 32.2 per cent of G.D.P. and in 1972 25.6 per cent. In 1977 it accounted for only 19.6 per cent (£S5,126 million out of G.D.P. totalling £S26,132 million at current prices). Initially the decline was attributable to under-use of potential caused by the discouraging effects of the 1958 agrarian reform law on investment and the removal of the large rural landowners and urban money-lenders who had formerly provided the traditional channels of credit. The area of unused cultivable land (excluding fallow) increased from 1,892,000 hectares in 1963 to 2,825,000 hectares by 1970. Suspicion of Government intentions was gradually tempered, however, by the relaxation of the reform law and, under the post-1970 Assad administration, by a number of significant amendments. The apparent continued decline in more recent years has simply resulted from the growing comparative importance of the mining and manufacturing sector. Judged in terms of gross output at producers' values and constant 1963 prices, the agricultural sector is actually showing steady improvements, with total output standing at £S2,170 million in 1977, against £S1,764 million during the highly successful season of 1972.

Extensive irrigation programmes now under way should eventually have the effect of steadying agricultural output as well as increasing it. It was with this in mind that, out of agricultural investments accounting for a sizeable 35 per cent of total investment under the Third Five-Year Plan (1971–75), the Government devoted the lion's share to the Euphrates Dam project (*see* below under Economic Development). The main task for the Fourth Development Plan ,which runs from 1976 to 1980, is to put the dam's stored waters to work and to irrigate an additional 240,000 hectares of land in the Euphrates basin by the end of the decade. This area will then be expanded to 640,000 hectares in later years. Other irrigation schemes on the Yarmouk river and in the Ghab, implemented with French, and possibly later American, assistance will reclaim still more land, increasing the acreage available for such crops as cereals, sugar beet, rice and cotton.

Cotton, for long Syria's most valuable source of export earnings, ceded this distinction to petroleum in 1974. However, it is nonetheless one of the most important crops, generating revenue of £S849 million in 1977. This compares with a figure of only £S619 million the previous year.

Although medium-staple cotton had been grown in Syria for many years, it was the high prices prevalent after the Second World War and during the Korean War that provided the greatest impetus to cotton production. The early 1950s saw the previously neglected Jezira area opened up for large-scale agriculture on a new capital intensive basis, relatively free from the traditional agricultural relations, still semi-feudal in the rest of the country. Cotton production grew from 38,000 tons in 1949 to 100,000 tons in 1950 and 220,800 tons in 1954. The area under cotton grew from 25,300 hectares in 1949 to 78,000 hectares in 1950 and 250,000 hectares in 1971/72. The increase in area planted has now peaked, however, and the current tendency is towards a reduction in the area under cotton cultivation in favour of new strains of wheat and, since the 1974 climb in the price of sugar imports, sugar beet. For the 1979/80 season cotton was sown on only 160,000 hectares, compared with 164,000 hectares in 1978/79 and 176,000 hectares in 1977/78. The 1977 crop totalled 394,500 tons of raw cotton, with a better than average yield of 2.1 tons per hectare. In 1971 the yield was only 1.6 tons per hectare.

Syria's own cotton mills take an average 44,000 tons of the annual lint out-turn but, with the installation of additional spinning capacity supplied by British, East German, Chinese and Czechoslovak firms, the proportion of ginned cotton available for export is expected to fall. Syrian planners aim to use 75 per cent of raw cotton in manufacturing by 1980.

Syria's grain crop is also of prime importance. Wheat and barley together took up some 2,549,000 hectares in 1977, or roughly two-thirds of the total cultivated area. The combined area devoted to these crops in the period 1961–65 averaged 2,136,000 hectares. Output in 1976 was above average, at 1,790,000 metric tons for wheat and 1,059,000 tons for barley, but in 1977 it dropped back again to about 1.2 million tons for wheat and only about 337,000 tons for barley because of drought in the eastern part of the country. These figures compare with the very poor harvest of 1973, when only 593,000 tons of wheat and 102,000 tons of barley were produced. In the past Syria has exported surplus grain. Wheat sales abroad in 1972 totalled 278,400 tons, worth £S84.2 million. Recently, in contrast, Syria has had to import wheat, receiving shipments of up to 100,000 tons under the U.S. food aid programme.

Syria does have a number of other actual and potential agricultural exports, however. Sugar beet is proving particularly successful, with 273,300 tons harvested in 1977. Tobacco, which declined to a minimum annual figure of 6,000 tons in 1967, was back up to 11,600 tons in 1972 and has remained at about this level since. There is considerable room for expansion in the marketing of fruit and vegetables. The fruit crop in 1977 produced 353,000 tons of grapes, 32,000 tons of apricots and 61,200 tons of apples. Tomatoes and onions are also grown and, in 1977, 453,629 tons of tomatoes and 161,493 tons of onions were produced, the size of the tomato crop comparing very favourably with previous years, although less than in 1976. A breakdown of the 1977 trade figures indicates earnings of £S119.6 million from exports of fruit and vegetables, representing nearly 3 per cent of that year's export income.

Stockraising is another important branch of agriculture which is being developed on a large scale with finance from the World Bank and other sources. Hungary has helped to set up half a dozen poultry farms throughout the country and egg production has averaged 650–700 million since 1975, more than double the output of the early 1970s.

PETROLEUM

Syria was at one time thought to have no oil. The Iraq Petroleum Company group had rights throughout Syria which it abandoned in 1951 after failing to find oil in commercial quantities. Concessions granted to an independent American operator in 1955 and to a West-German led consortium in 1956 led to the discovery first of the Karachuk field in the north-eastern corner of the country, then of the Suweidiya field and finally of the field at nearby Rumelan. But the oil at all three places was of low quality; that found by the Americans at Karachuk having a density of 19° API and a sulphur content of 4.5 per cent and that found by the German group at Suweidiya having a density of 25° API and 3.5 per cent sulphur content. By 1964, years before any of the three fields had begun production on a commercial basis, Syria became one of the first Arab states to discard the notion of oil concessions and nationalize its oil operations. Even at that early stage Syria's industrial planners were anxious to use the country's oil not only for export in its crude state but also as a raw material for domestic industry. For the next 10 years all exploration and exploitation was conducted solely by the state-owned General Petroleum Authority and its off-shoot, the Syrian Petroleum Company, with Soviet assistance.

Output from Suweidiya started in July 1968 and totalled one million tons the first year, of which 833,000 tons were exported. Output in 1969, when the Karachuk field went into operation, failed to reach expectations, totalling only 3.2 million tons, of which 2.3 million tons were exported. The October war in 1973 reduced production from a level of 6.3 million tons the previous year to just 5.4 million tons, recovering in 1974 to 6.2 million tons. Finally in 1976, the ten million ton production figure was attained, with output reaching 10,039,000 tons but it dropped back to an estimated 9,117,000 tons in 1977. During the present phase of development the aim is to keep production at around the 1977 level so as to prolong the life of the oil reserves.

The Syrian oil industry today presents a thoroughly different picture from the one that faced observers at the time of the first state takeovers. The knowledge that Syria has 75,000 square kilometres of land offering good prospects for oil exploration has led to a reversal of the no-concessions policy. In May 1975 the first Syrian concession won by any Western company for over 15 years was awarded to a U.S. group, on production-sharing terms heavily tilted in the Government's favour and stipulating that $20 million be invested in exploration offshore. In June 1975 the Government took its new policy one stage further by offering a dozen onshore oil concessions for international bidding. Altogether 50,000 square kilometres were to be made available. The oil companies' response to the invitation was initially slow and, when the first U.S. group, Tripco, relinquished its concession in March 1976, no other company had come forward to join the search. In July 1977, however, a U.S.-Syrian consortium called Samoco took up a concession in the Deir-al-Zor area and in December another concession in Raqqa province was taken by Shell subsidiaries, Syria Shell Petroleum Development and Pecten Syria Company. Both Shell and Samoco insisted on a larger share of eventual oil production than was agreed between the Government and Tripco. This softening of terms brought other firms onto the scene to negotiate concessions, including Challenger Oil of Canada and Marathon and Mobil of the U.S.A.

The outlook is further enhanced by the evidence that not all Syria's oil is of the poor quality found in the three original fields. The Jbeisseh field, between Hassakeh and the Iraqi border (an area in which the Iraq Petroleum Company had formerly found only gas), was officially opened in May 1975, producing high quality oil with a gravity of 40.5° API and a 0.62 per cent sulphur content. Rompetrol of Romania has since discovered 38° API crude in its concession in the north, but not in commercial quantities. It is clear, however, that further exploration will alter the size of Syria's proven oil reserves, which were estimated in 1979 to total some 1,300 million tons, of which about 300 million tons is recoverable.

Though Suweidiya crude is suitable for blending with lighter Algerian or Libyan crudes to produce fuel oils and the high sulphur content of the Karachuk crude makes it suitable for the production of good quality asphalt, the generally poor quality of Syrian oil, together with opposition on the part of some of the major oil companies to Syria's nationalization experiment, combined at the outset of the country's oil history to cause considerable marketing difficulties. But with the growth of sales, particularly to Greece, France, Italy and the Soviet Union, oil has become Syria's most important export. The value of oil exports, which in 1973 had amounted to £S291.2 million, soared to £S1,607.5 million in 1974 and £S2,544 million in 1977.

January 1975 saw the capacity of the Homs refinery restored to its former level of 2.5 million tons per year (following its virtual destruction by Israeli bombardment in October 1973) and in March 1976, with the addition of two extra distillation units installed by Czechoslovakia and Italy, this capacity doubled to 5 million tons. Work on a second refinery, at Banias on the Mediterranean, with a capacity of six million tons per year, was due for completion in the summer of 1979. The project, undertaken by Romania at a cost of some £S1,000 million, was delayed for over a year, partly because of a decision to alter the specifications of the facility to allow it to process different grades of crude. Once this was under way, Syria dropped plans to build a third refinery, at least for the duration of the 1980–85 development plan.

Royalties for the transit of foreign crude through Syrian territory were for many years more valuable than indigenous oil production. Two pipelines carry oil from Kirkuk through Syria. One, built in 1934, leads on to a terminal at Tripoli in Lebanon. The second, completed in 1952, branches off at Homs to the Syrian terminal at Banias. A third pipeline, belonging to the Trans-Arabian Pipeline Company (Tapline) and carrying 24 million tons of Saudi Arabian crude a year to a terminal near Sidon in Lebanon, crosses about 100 miles of Syrian territory, much of which was occupied by Israel in 1967. After nationalizing the Iraq Petroleum Company in June 1972, Iraq took over payment of royalties to Syria and, after lengthy negotiations, a transit agreement was signed in January 1973 providing both for transit dues and oil supplies for Syria's own domestic use. But, by the time the financial clauses of the agreement expired in December 1975, oil had more than quadrupled in price and Iraq was demanding that the transit agreement be radically revised. In return Syria sought a proportionate increase in transit fees, hitherto equivalent to 41 cents per barrel. Iraq's answer—the diversion of all its northern oil away from the Mediterranean and southwards to the Gulf—deprived Syria both of revenue, which has in the past amounted to £S500 million per year, and of the benefits of cheap oil. Iraq has since gained access to the Mediterranean through an alternative pipeline crossing Turkey and is no longer reliant on the Syrian route to the same extent. Nevertheless, with the improvement in Iraq-Syrian political relations in late 1978 and with the world oil shortages arising from the Iranian revolution shortly afterwards, Iraq resumed pumping through Syria in early 1979, on the basis of a commitment to put through 10 million tons per year for export in addition to providing half the throughput needed for the Homs refinery and around half of that required for Banias. Under this agreement, Syria is to receive transit royalties roughly equivalent to 35 U.S. cents per barrel and will pay market prices for its own offtake of Iraqi crude.

INDUSTRY

A remarkable industrial boom, mainly based on textiles, occurred in Syria shortly after independence and was the main cause of the dissolution of the customs union with Lebanon in 1959, since the protectionist policies adopted by the Syrian Government to safeguard this growth came into direct conflict with Lebanon's free-trade tradition. Since then the manufacturing and mining sector has grown steadily until in 1971, for the first time, it replaced agriculture as the main generator of wealth—accounting for 19.5 per cent of the G.D.P., compared with 19.1 per cent for agriculture. The value of industrial production has risen steadily since then—the general index of industrial production (based on 1970=100) reaching 191 in 1977. The contribution of mining and manufacturing to the 1977 G.D.P. (measured at current prices) stood at £S5,626 million or 21.5 per cent of the total.

The importance attached by the Government to industrial growth is clear from the allocation of 22.3 per cent of the 1979 investment budget to industry and mining and 15.7 per cent to energy and fuel. Priorities for investment, apart from oil, are electricity generation, fertilizers, iron and steel, sugar refining, textiles and cement.

Production of phosphates started from the mines in the Palmyra area in 1972, reaching 857,000 tons in 1975 but dropping to only 425,000 tons in 1977 because of insufficient demand. Disappointments in the phosphate sector have arisen not so much through a lack of capacity, which now stands at about 2 million tons per year, but from the high chlorine content of Syrian rock, which has reduced the price from $53 to $30 per ton since 1974.

New cement plant at Tartous, Aleppo, Hama and Adra are expected to raise overall cement production capcity to a level of some 6 million tons per year by 1980, compared with the level of 1,395,000 tons achieved in 1977. An integrated iron and steel complex is under construction at Hama and one aim in this development is to make maximum use of Syria's own deposits of about 530 million tons of iron ore. Chemical fertilizer manufacture in Syria, based partly on the country's phosphate reserves and partly on nitrogenous fertilizers, centres on Homs, Hama and Deir al-Zor, with factories built primarily by Romania and France. In the field of sugar refining, four new refineries are being launched with Belgian and Italian help, to process the beet produced from the Euphrates basin. Established industries include rubber, glass and paper manufacture and the assembly of tractors and electrical appliances such as refrigerators and television receivers. Plans for a car assembly plant were postponed following the financial difficulties of 1976, but Japan is involved in setting up a plant to assemble motor-cycles. Further industrial development will probably be planned in co-ordination with Jordan and Iraq. Syria decided in 1979, for example, to drop plans for a petrochemicals plant of its own so as not to overlap with Iraq's facilities. Iraq, on the other hand, is seen as a good potential market for Syrian textiles and processed foods.

The key to much of the country's future industrial development lies in the power-generating facilities linked with the Euphrates Dam, which was inaugurated in 1978. At full capacity the power station's eight turbines can produce 1,100 MW, although the normal flow of the Euphrates river is not sufficient to activate the turbines all at once. Another important power plant is situated at Mehardeh on the Orontes. Syria also has tentative plans for setting up a nuclear power station. There are believed to be substantial amounts of uranium associated with local phosphate deposits, in quantities of 200–300 grammes per ton.

Syria's principal industries centre around the major towns, Damascus, Aleppo and Homs and the port of Latakia, and these centres, with the exception of Homs and the addition of Tartous, are also the site of Syria's free zones, set up to encourage foreign investment in the establishment of light industries, assembly plants and warehouses. A further industrial free zone is to be set up jointly with Jordan on a 4,000 square metre area south of Deraa. The ports of Latakia and Tartous are being expanded to handle 3.5 million tons and 5 million tons a year respectively by 1980. Tartous will also have a drydock.

EXTERNAL TRADE

Commerce has traditionally been a major occupation of Syria's towns, especially Damascus and Aleppo as they lie on the main east-west trade route. But there have been some radical changes both in the direction and the composition of Syria's trade over the years. During the mid-1960s, Syria's main suppliers were among the Eastern European bloc. In 1968 the Soviet Union and Czechoslovakia alone provided over 20 per cent of all imported goods. In 1974, though the value of their supplies had increased, these countries accounted for just under 7.2 per cent of the total. Meanwhile the value of Syria's imports over the six-year period had risen nearly fourfold, reaching £S4,571 million in 1974, and the bulk of the increase had resulted from flourishing trade ties not with the East but with Western Europe. In 1977, out of imports worth a total of £S10,497 million, the nine countries of the European Economic Community (EEC) together provided some 38 per cent. Of these, West Germany led with 14 per cent, followed by Italy with 6.7 per cent and the United Kingdom with 4 per cent. The U.S.A. and Japan have also achieved significant increases in the past few years. American exports to Syria rose from $39.6 million in 1974 (the year diplomatic relations were resumed) to $272 million in 1976, mainly due to the delivery of aircraft, locomotives and parts. The U.S.A. accounted for 4.3 per cent of Syrian imports in 1977 and Japan for 6 per cent. Main imports are usually machinery and transport equipment. In 1977 imports in this category were worth £S3,571 million, followed by basic manufactures to a value of £S2,422 million.

Syria's exports have increased dramatically, mainly due to oil sales. But they have nowhere near succeeded in keeping pace with imports. Exports rose by 50 per cent between 1971 and 1972, but this did not prevent the trade deficit from hitting the £S1,000 million mark one year later. It has continued to widen ever since. In 1977 export earnings, at £S4,199 million, were equal to much less than half the cost of imports. A geographical analysis of Syrian trade in 1977 shows that the countries of the EEC predominated not only as suppliers but also as customers, taking 46.7 per cent of exports. Of these, Italy was the biggest customer, taking 13.2 per cent of the overall total. Centrally planned economies have generally played a less important role in the mid-1970s but there was a slight revival in 1977, mainly due to Syrian trade with Romania, with these markets taking 25.5 per cent of Syrian exports and providing 20 per cent of imports. The trend towards closer ties with the EEC is likely to continue, with the coming into effect of a trade and aid agreement signed by the EEC and Syria in early 1977 within the framework of the EEC's Mediterranean policy. Under the agreement Syria enjoys a 100 per cent tariff cut on exports of petroleum and cotton products to the EEC and will receive some $67 million in grants and low-interest loans. The first of these loans, worth $26 million, was announced in May 1979 and will help to pay for a road from Aleppo to the Iraqi border.

FINANCE

The sudden increase in Syrian exports from 1972 onwards was one of the major results of a reform in the foreign exchange regulations. All exports other than cotton and crude oil were shifted to the parallel (free) market which meant a *de facto* devaluation of Syrian currency in relation to most transactions. (For details of changes in the exchange rate, *see* the Statistical Survey, following). Another major factor influencing Syrian finances has been the level of financial support forthcoming from the wealthy Arab oil-exporting states. Figures published by the International Monetary Fund show that the country's current account deficit of $58 million in 1971 had been transformed into a $339 million surplus in 1973. In 1976, however, with the interruption in the flow of aid, there was a return to a deficit, this time equal to $772 million. Arab subsidies, paid to Syria since the Khartoum summit meeting of 1967, were reinforced when the Rabat summit in 1974 resulted in the promise of an annual $1,000 million to Syria in its capacity as a confrontation state. Some $500 million was received on this basis in 1974, $690 million in 1975 but only $355 million in 1976. Donations are thought to have risen again to $570 million in 1977.

State expenditure since the October 1973 war has also clearly reflected the inflow of foreign funds. The general budget soared from a total of £S6,976 million in 1974 to £S16,564 million in 1976. However, with the drop in aid and other income in 1976 and the rather unsettled internal situation, budget allocations have since dropped in real terms and actual spending has fallen far short of target. The overall budgets for 1977 and 1978 increased by only about 5 per cent each time, the 1978 budget of £S18,202 million including £S10,645 million for investment. In 1979, following the Baghdad summit, a big increase in defence spending brought the overall budget up again to £S22,600 million, including some £S11,000 million for development. Defence and national security, traditionally exempt from the cuts applied to the investment budget, have generally absorbed around 60 per cent of current expenditure. In 1979 this figure is believed to have risen to 69 per cent.

ECONOMIC DEVELOPMENT

The most ambitious of the projects contained in the Third Five-Year Plan (1971–75) was the Euphrates Dam project, under construction since 1968. Most of the country's future industrial and agricultural development depends on this scheme, and nearly one-quarter of public investment over the plan period was earmarked for its implementation, with £S950 million allocated for the dam itself and £S643 million for land reclamation and development in the Euphrates basin. The project involved the construction of a dam 4.6 kilometres long and 60 metres high with a width of

500 metres at the bottom. The reservoir thus created, Lake Assad, has been designed to hold 12,000 million cubic metres of water, operating eight turbines and enabling the long-term irrigation of 640,000 hectares of land, some 550,000 of these by 1990. The scheme was undertaken with the help of 1,200 Soviet technicians and about £S600 million in Soviet financial assistance, under an agreement reached with the Soviet Union in April 1966. By 1977, however, only 100 Soviet experts remained on the site. In spring 1978 the entire project was formally opened, although the dam's first turbines had started to operate, some months ahead of schedule, in early 1974. It is estimated that the cost of developing each hectare of land in the Euphrates basin will work out at £S20,000, making a total of up to £S14,000 million for the development of all 640,000 hectares. Despite its advantages, the dam has exacerbated friction between Syria and Iraq, which also relies on Euphrates water. Problems came to a head in 1974–75 when Turkey started to fill the reservoir behind its Keban dam on the river at the same time as Syria started to fill Lake Assad, leaving Iraq with much less water than usual. Tension on this score subsided in 1977–78, however, and no more problems are expected for another 10 to 15 years.

The Fourth Five-Year Plan started in 1976 but was interrupted by the events of that year and was reissued in 1977. It envisages expenditure of nearly £S53,000 million, comprising £S27,000 million for projects already under way, £S17,600 million for new projects and £S8,000 million to be held in reserve. Mining and manufacturing will take 22 per cent of the £S44,600 million earmarked for specific projects, followed by energy and fuel development (17.8 per cent) and Euphrates projects (16.6 per cent). The average annual growth rate target under the plan is 12 per cent, compared with 8.2 per cent under the previous plan. One important aspect of the plan in its original form was its emphasis on tourism, which was expected to become the country's third main source of foreign currency, after oil and cotton, by 1980. This aim has been undermined by political factors, however, and although a record total of nearly 1.4 million foreign visitors arrived in Syria in 1976 with 1.29 million arriving in 1977, this was mainly a result of people fleeing the civil war in Lebanon and not an indication of future trends.

The Fifth Five-Year Plan, to be announced in June 1980, will aim to achieve 11 per cent annual growth of G.D.P.

STATISTICAL SURVEY

AREA AND POPULATION

Area	Population†						
	Census results				Estimates (mid-year)		
	Sept. 20th, 1960	September 23rd, 1970					
		Total	Males	Females	1976	1977	1978
185,180 sq. km.*	4,565,121	6,304,685	3,233,110	3,071,575	7,596,000	7,845,000	8,088,000

* 71,498 sq. miles. † Including Palestinian refugees, numbering 193,000 at mid-1977.

REGISTERED BIRTHS, MARRIAGES AND DEATHS

	Births	Marriages	Deaths
1975	263,597	79,595	34,202
1976	272,310	79,692	35,281
1977	322,357	72,530	35,860

PRINCIPAL TOWNS
(population at 1970 census)

Damascus (capital)	836,668*	Latakia	125,716
Aleppo	639,428	Deir-ez-Zor	66,146
Homs	215,423	Hasakeh	32,746
Hama	137,421		

* Including suburbs, population was 923,253.

AGRICULTURE

LAND USE
('ooo hectares)

	1970	1976
Arable land	5,651	5,260
Land under permanent crops	258	412
Permanent meadows and pastures	7,550*	8,541
Forests and woodland	468	457
Other land	4,530	3,748
Inland water	61	100
TOTAL AREA	18,518	18,518

* Unofficial estimate.

Source: FAO, *Production Yearbook.*

AREA AND PRODUCTION OF PRINCIPAL CROPS

	1976		1977		1978	
	Hectares	Metric tons	Hectares	Metric tons	Hectares	Metric tons
Wheat	1,590,259	1,790,109	1,527,718	1,217,214	1,555,376	1,650,696
Barley	1,171,922	1,058,711	1,021,495	336,898	1,032,565	728,695
Maize	23,386	48,687	26,169	58,651	26,597	56,191
Millet	19,551	15,582	24,876	23,677	18,573	17,288
Lentils	146,479	136,227	178,346	117,308	136,116	92,375
Cotton	181,760	408,854	186,500	394,800	n.a.	n.a.
Tobacco	17,622	12,031	15,300	11,500	n.a.	n.a.
Sesame	42,641	19,028	39,318	18,283	35,723	19,018
Grapes	94,888	319,417	94,000	353,000	93,835	345,775
Olives	219,422	233,403	228,000	175,000	234,424	303,677
Figs	22,220	41,288	21,000	45,000	20,647	35,018
Apricots	11,339	46,290	12,000	32,000	12,318	47,434
Apples	18,092	70,534	19,000	61,200	21,015	67,302
Sugar beet	8,510	242,315	12,200	273,300	13,682	271,853
Pomegranates	4,437	19,944	4,900	24,000	5,227	28,560
Onions	6,953	100,302	9,433	161,493	8,429	159,561
Tomatoes	31,619	516,562	32,791	453,629	30,755	501,967
Potatoes	9,886	132,284	12,830	164,000	14,587	198,517

LIVESTOCK
('ooo head)

	1975	1976	1977
Cattle	557	574	639
Horses	55	53	55
Camels	6	7	8
Asses	233.6	233.8	235
Sheep	5,809	6,489	7,070
Goats	814	956	1,010
Chickens	8,572	9,300	8,700

DAIRY PRODUCE

		1975	1976	1977
Milk	'ooo tons	567	665	647
Cheese	tons	29,862	34,550	30,160
Butter	,,	1,283	1,083	839
Honey	,,	279	380	350
Ghee	,,	8,911	9,180	7,586
Eggs	'ooo	656,000	699,877	672,000

Fishing ('ooo metric tons): 1.5 in 1972; 1.3 in 1973; 1.6 in 1974; 2.0 in 1975.

MINING

		1974	1975	1976†	1977	1978
Crude petroleum	'000 metric tons	6,426	9,572	10,004	9,117	9,924
Phosphate rock	,, ,, ,,	650	857	512	425	747
Salt (unrefined)	,, ,, ,,	40.0	34	58	48	62
Natural gas*	million cu. metres	180	287	454	474	n.a.

* *Source:* OPEC, *Annual Statistical Bulletin.* † Estimate.

INDUSTRY

SELECTED PRODUCTS

		1974	1975	1976*	1977
Cotton Yarn	'000 tons	30.4	31.7	31.8	27.8
Silk and Cotton Textiles	,, ,,	35.1	36.7	36.4	42.4
Woollen Fabrics	tons	134.7	1,536.0	1,441.0	1,609.0
Cement	'000 tons	865.0	994.0	1,110.0	1,395.0
Natural Asphalt	,, ,,	34.9	31.0	32.0	98.8
Glass	,, ,,	24.7	25.4	26.2	26.5
Soap	,, ,,	28.3	28.9	31.2	34.6
Sugar	,, ,,	148.0	117.1	126.1	103.7
Margarine	,, ,,	8.3	6.7	6.0	24.1
Edible Oils	,, ,,	25.3	22.2	24.8	24.0
Manufactured Tobacco	,, ,,	5.8	6.7	8.5	7.8
Electricity	million kWh.	1,366.0	1,673.0	1,776.0	2,152.0
Beer	'000 litres	5,799.0	6,984.0	6,759.0	6,544.0
Wine	,, ,,	370.4	420.2	460.1	460.5
Arak	,, ,,	573.6	654.3	730.5	735.5

* Estimates.

FINANCE

100 piastres=1 Syrian pound (£S).
Coins: 2½, 5, 10, 25 and 50 piastres; 1 pound.
Notes: 1, 5, 10, 25, 50, 100 and 500 pounds.
Exchange rates (June 1979): £1 sterling=£S8,120; U.S. $1=£S3.925.
£S100=£12.32 sterling=$25.48.

Note: The official basic exchange rate of U.S. $1=£S2.19, established in 1949, is inoperative for all practical purposes. Prior to July 1962 the official selling rate, used for calculating the value of foreign trade, was U.S. $1=£S3.58 (£S1=27.97 U.S. cents). From July 1962 to February 1973 the buying rate was $1=£S3.80 and the selling rate was $1=£S3.82 (£S1=26.18 U.S. cents). Exchange rates were adjusted frequently between February and July 1973. From July 1973 to February 1974 the buying rate was $1=£S3.75 and the selling rate $1=£S3.80. From February 1974 to March 1976 the buying rate was $1=£S3.65 and the selling rate $1=£S3.70. In April 1976 new rates of $1=£S3.90 (buying) or £S3.95 (selling) were established. From January 1964 to July 1973 a "parallel" free market was also in operation. From early 1970 to February 1973 the free rates were $1=£S4.30 (buying) or £S4.32 (selling). The official exchange rates were £1 sterling=£S9.12 (buying) or £S9.168 (selling) from November 1967 to August 1971; and £1 sterling=£S9.902 (buying) or £S9.954 (selling) from December 1971 to June 1972.

ORDINARY BUDGET

(£S million)

	1975	1976	1977	1978	1979
National defence	2,613.2	3,661.4	4,136.6	4,544.9	8,246.3
Cultural and social affairs	627.1	787.7	990.4	649.8	768.0
Communications and public works	56.6	67.6	74.1	82.9	88.3
Economic affairs and planning	474.5	581.6	494.5	1,281.4	1,442.2
Administrative affairs	823.4	797.3	948.9	997.7	1,016.2
TOTAL	4,594.8	5,895.6	6,644.5	7,556.7	11,561.0

CONSOLIDATED BUDGET

(£S million)

A new consolidated budget has been issued incorporating both ordinary and development budgets

	1975	1976	1977	1978	1979
Justice and Public Authorities	768.4	1,302.9	1,351.2	1,510.9	1,879.6
National Security	3,344.8	3,690.4	4,159.6	4,573.1	8,281.5
Culture and Information	1,056.5	1,640.8	1,578.1	1,293.2	1,506.5
Social Welfare	97.9	144.7	133.6	150.3	165.8
Economy and Finance	842.6	1,110.1	1,144.4	1,769.4	2,077.8
Agriculture and Land Reclamation	1,270.1	1,416.5	1,422.1	1,470.8	1,709.2
Industry and Mining	3,188.4	4,646.6	4,794.3	4,518.6	3,857.4
Public Works, Utilities and Communications	1,253.5	2,005.7	1,675.5	1,996.4	2,145.9
Other Expenditure and Revenue	605.1	606.3	789.6	919.3	1,017.3
TOTAL	12,427.3	16,564.0	17,048.4	18,202.0	22,641.0

FOURTH FIVE-YEAR PLAN

(1976–80—£S million)

	INVESTMENT (Public Sector)
Euphrates Dam project	7,439
Irrigation and land reclamation	1,095
Agriculture	1,904
Industry	9,889
Energy and fuels	7,986
Transport and communications	5,136
Trade and commerce	944
Housing and public utilities	3,997
Services	5,194
Administration	1,034
Popular work	160
TOTAL	44,777

EXTERNAL TRADE

(£S million)

	1971	1972	1973	1974	1975	1976	1977	1978
Imports c.i.f.	1,703.5	2,081.9	2,342.0	4,571.0	6,236.2	9,203.3	10,496.7	9,658.7
Exports f.o.b.	788.9	1,140.7	1,341.3	2,914.0	3,440.9	4,141.3	4,199.0	4,159.8

COMMODITIES (£S million)

Imports	1975	1976	1977	1978
Cotton textiles, other textile goods and silk	359.8	441.8	562.6	502.6
Mineral fuels and oils	396.8	752.5	1,757.2	1,268.4
Lime, cement and salt	138.9	185.1	192.6	147.4
Cereals	203.6	107.8	191.8	275.1
Vegetables and fruit	124.4	196.8	220.8	277.2
Machinery, apparatus and electrical materials	247.6	538.1	809.3	689.9
Precious metals and coins	69.9	1,525.0	18.9	25.3
Base metals and manufactures	888.8	1,256.4	1,409.1	1,283.3
Vehicles	759.9	901.5	714.2	514.4
Chemical and pharmaceutical products	267.0	206.0	245.0	332.4
Preserved foods, beverages and tobacco	661.4	586.1	309.2	471.0
Other products	2,118.1	2,506.2	4,066.0	3,837.0

Exports	1975	1976	1977	1978
Cotton (raw, yarn, textiles)	502.5	686.3	836.1*	720.7
Other textile goods	169.4	246.7	232.6	179.4
Cereals	0.1	32.9	57.9	12.2
Vegetables and fruit	40.9	59.0	90.2	155.4
Preserved foods, beverages and tobacco	106.7	139.5	66.7	75.5
Phosphates	55.8	42.5	59.1	n.a.
Crude petroleum	2,376.6	2,585.7	2,435.7	2,988.7 (Crude petroleum and Other products)
Other products	188.9	348.7	420.7	

* Raw cotton only (£S637.7 million in 1976).

PRINCIPAL TRADING PARTNERS
(£S million)

Imports	1975	1976	1977	1978
Austria	132.0	138.0	204.7	150.2
Belgium	125.6	176.4	342.9	225.0
China, People's Republic	173.8	139.6	197.4	215.1
Czechoslovakia	199.6	174.6	128.8	179.1
France	465.8	563.0	815.4	728.7
Germany, Federal Republic	795.7	1,069.4	1,478.6	1,037.5
Greece	60.4	108.2	230.2	n.a.
Iraq	196.9	95.8	12.0	676.7
Italy	568.2	690.5	706.9	799.3
Japan	323.3	565.2	632.9	481.1
Lebanon	256.0	177.2	242.4	282.3
Netherlands	175.5	181.9	188.0	210.9
Romania	255.5	162.4	930.7	673.0
Saudi Arabia	10.2	602.0	1,087.9	218.2
Switzerland	236.5	1,634.1	176.6	141.9
U.S.S.R.	201.4	172.2	362.1	166.5
United Kingdom	261.7	357.8	423.5	336.5
U.S.A.	404.5	528.4	455.0	166.5

Exports	1975	1976	1977	1978
Belgium	364.0	288.9	265.9	128.4
China, People's Republic	84.1	144.2	218.1	131.0
France	15.2	96.2	301.4	n.a.
Germany, Federal Republic	348.2	410.3	232.2	435.0
Greece	198.4	201.9	165.4	284.3
Italy	621.7	634.9	555.5	348.3
Lebanon	29.7	25.6	86.7	36.0
Netherlands	5.9	278.8	294.2	377.9
Saudi Arabia	86.4	201.2	229.7	194.1
U.S.S.R.	238.5	360.1	421.3	387.3
United Kingdom	276.8	301.6	211.3	161.6
Yugoslavia	215.2	323.4	148.3	144.5

TRANSPORT

RAILWAYS

	1975	1976
Passenger-km.	135,598	165,761
Freight, '000 tons	1,046	1,337

ROADS

	1976	1977
Passenger cars	62,760	69,084
Buses	5,631	6,829
Lorries, trucks, etc.	52,375	70,613
Motor-cycles	11,931	24,320

SHIPPING

PORT OF LATAKIA

	1972	1973	1974	1975	1976	1977
Number of steam vessels entering harbour	1,856	1,701	1,959	2,062	2,667	2,023
Number of sailing vessels entering harbour	92	117	61	47	46	44
Cargo unloaded ('000 tons)	1,645	1,529	2,403	2,022	2,795	2,040
Cargo loaded ('000 tons)	518	312	189	150	268	367

CIVIL AVIATION

(Damascus Airport)

	1974		1975		1976		1977	
	ARRIVE	DEPART	ARRIVE	DEPART	ARRIVE	DEPART	ARRIVE	DEPART
Aircraft	7,061	7,071	7,841	7,835	9,557	9,549	10,417	10,416
Passengers	242,133	272,996	346,552	359,711	468,307	511,339	435,637	453,082

TOURISM

	JORDANIANS AND LEBANESE	TOTAL VISITORS
1972	719,601	1,038,543
1973	413,982	709,626
1974	477,037	921,854
1975	516,152	1,171,722
1976	910,249	1,389,979
1977	683,967	1,291,308

Tourist Accommodation: 20,085 tourist hotel beds (1974).

EDUCATION

(1976/77)

	PUPILS		TEACHERS	
	Public Sector	Private Sector*	Public Sector	Private Sector*
Pre-School	—	36,679	—	n.a.
Primary	1,284,766	41,648	40,091	1,459
Preparatory	352,670	10,215	—	—
Secondary	123,485	21,446	—	—
Vocational	23,854	—	—	—
Teacher Training	1,018	—	927	—
Universities	n.a.	n.a.	n.a.	n.a.

* Excluding UNRWA schools.

Source (unless otherwise stated): Central Bureau of Statistics, Office of the Prime Minister, Damascus.

THE CONSTITUTION

A new and permanent constitution was endorsed by 97.6 per cent of the voters in a national referendum on March 12th, 1973. The 157-article constitution defines Syria as a "Socialist popular democracy" with a "pre-planned Socialist economy". Under the new constitution, Lt.-Gen. al-Assad remained President, with the power to appoint and dismiss his Vice-President, Premier and Government Ministers, and also became Commander-in-Chief of the armed forces, secretary-general of the Baath Socialist Party and President of the National Progressive Front. Legislative power is vested in the People's Council, with 195 members elected by universal adult suffrage.

THE GOVERNMENT

HEAD OF STATE

President: Lt.-Gen. HAFIZ AL-ASSAD (elected March 12th, 1971, for a seven-year term; re-elected February 8th, 1978.)

CABINET

(*July* 1979)

(B) Baath, US (Unionist Socialist), AS (Arab Socialist), C (Communist), (ASU) Arab Socialist Union.

Prime Minister: MUHAMMAD ALI AL-HALABI (B).

Deputy Prime Minister and Minister for Foreign Affairs: ABDUL HALIM KHADDAM (B).

Deputy Prime Minister for Economic Affairs: JAMIL SHAYYA (B).

Deputy Prime Minister for Services (non-military): FAHMI YUSUFI (B).

Minister of Defence: Maj.-Gen. MUSTAPHA TLASS (B).

Minister for Local Administration: TAHA KHAIRAT (B).

Minister of Supply and Internal Trade: MUHAMMAD GHABASH (B).

Minister of State for Foreign Affairs: ABDUL KARIM 'ADI (B).

Minister of State for Presidency Affairs: ADIB MULHEM (B).

Minister for the Euphrates Dam: SUBHI KAHHALAH (Independent).

Minister of Education: ZUHAIR MASHARIOAH (B).

Minister of Justice: ADIB AL-NAHAWI (US).

Minister of Communications: OMAR SIBAI (C).

Minister of Agriculture and Agrarian Reform: AHMAD QABLAN (B).

Minister of Wakfs: ABDUL SAITAR SAID (Independent).

Minister of the Economy and Foreign Trade: Dr. MUHAMMAD AL-IMADI (Independent).

Minister of State at the Prime Minister's Office: ANWAR HAMADA (US).

Minister of Health: MADANI AL-KHIAMI (Independent).

Minister of Higher Education: Dr. SHAKIR FAHHAM (B).

Minister of State: DAHIR ABDUL SAMAD (C).

Minister for Social Affairs and Labour: YUSUF JU'AIDANI (ASU).

Minister of Industry: SHTEIWI SEIFO (B).

Minister of Transport: Dr. SALIM YASINE (B).

Minister of Information: AHMAD ISKANDAR AHMAD (B).

Minister of the Interior: ADNAN DABBAGH (B).

Minister of Finance: SADIQ AL-AYYUBI (Independent).

Minister of Electricity: AHMAD OMAR YUSUF (Independent).

Minister of Culture and National Guidance: NAJAH ATTAR (Independent).

Minister of Petroleum and Mineral Wealth: 'ISA DARWISH (B).

Minister for Tourism: GHASSAN CHALHOUB (Independent).

Minister of State: DIA MALUHI (US).

Minister of Housing and Utilities: MUHARRAM TAYYARA (AS).

Minister of Public Works and Water Wealth: NAZEM QADDUR (AS).

Minister of State for Planning: GEORGE HAURANIYA (Independent).

Minister of State: SAFWAN QUDSI, SHARIF KUSH (ASU).

PEOPLE'S COUNCIL

A new People's Council was elected in May 1973 under the terms of the new Constitution. 140 seats were won by the Progressive Front. In elections in August 1977 125 out of a total of 195 seats were won by the Baath Party and a further 34 seats by the other parties of the Progressive Front (Communist 6, Socialist Union 12, Syrian Arab Socialist Union 8, Arab Socialist Party 8).

Speaker: MAHMOUD HADID.

POLITICAL PARTIES

The National Progressive Front, headed by President Assad, was formed in March 1972 by the grouping of the five parties listed below:

Arab Socialist Renaissance (Baath) Party: Arab socialist party; in power since 1963; supports militant Arab unity; Sec.-Gen. Pres. HAFIZ AL-ASSAD; Asst. Sec.-Gen. ABDULLA AL-AHMAR.

Syrian Arab Socialist Union: Nasserite; Leader Dr. JAMAL ATASI; Sec.-Gen. FAUZI KAYYALI.

Unionist Socialist: Leader SAMI SOUFAN.

Arab Socialist Party: a breakaway socialist party; Leader ABDEL GHANI KANNOUT.

Communist Party of Syria: Sec.-Gen. KHALID BAGDASH.

DIPLOMATIC REPRESENTATION

EMBASSIES ACCREDITED TO SYRIA

(In Damascus unless otherwise stated)

Afghanistan: Baghdad, Iraq.

Algeria: Raouda, Imm. Noss; *Ambassador:* ABDEL-QADER BEN-KASI (also accred. to Cyprus).

Argentina: Raouda, Rue Ziad ben Abi Soufian; *Ambassador:* OTTO JACINTO SASSE (also accred. to Iraq and Jordan).

Australia: 49 Rue Hawakir Mouhajirine, West Malki; *Ambassador:* H. N. TRUSCOTT (also accred. to Iraq, Jordan and Lebanon).

Austria: West Malki-Abdel Moneim Riad St., Imm. Dr. Sawah, P.O.B. 5634; *Ambassador:* Dr. FRANZ PARAK.

Bangladesh: Cairo, Egypt.

Belgium: Rue Ata Ayoubi, Imm. Hachem; *Ambassador:* GUY BRIGODE.

Brazil: 76 Rue Ata Ayoubi; *Ambassador:* VICTOR JOSÉ SILVEIRA.

Bulgaria: 4 Rue Chahbandar; *Ambassador:* STEFEN MITEV.

Canada: Beirut, Lebanon.

Chad: Beirut, Lebanon.

Chile: 43 Rue Al-Rachid; *Ambassador:* ALIRO MUÑOZ DE LA SUATPE.

China, People's Republic: 83 Rue Ata Ayoubi; *Ambassador:* TSAO KE-CHIANG.

Colombia: Cairo, Egypt.

Cuba: 40 Rue Al-Rachid, Imm. Oustwani and Charabati; *Ambassador:* ARTURO BARBER OROZCO.

Cyprus: Cairo, Egypt.

Czechoslovakia: Place Aboul-Alaa Al-Maari; *Ambassador:* JIŘÍ KRALIK.

Denmark: Rue Chekib Arslan, Abu Rumaneh; *Ambassador:* RUDOLPH THORNING-PETERSON (also accred. to Cyprus).

Finland: Cairo, Egypt.

France: Rue Ata Ayoubi; *Ambassador:* F. ROUILLON.

German Democratic Republic: 60 Avenue Adnan el Malki; *Ambassador:* Dr. HEINZ-DIETER WINTER (also accred. to Jordan).

Germany, Federal Republic: 53 Rue Ibrahim Hanano (Imm. Kotob); *Ambassador:* JOACHIM PECKERT.

Greece: 57 Rue Ata Ayoubi; *Ambassador:* ATHANASIOS PETROPOULOS (also accred. to Iraq and Jordan).

Guinea: Cairo, Egypt.

Hungary: 13 Rue Ibrahim Hanano (Imm. Roujoulé); *Ambassador:* LÁSZLO SZIKRA (also accred. to Jordan).

India: 40/46 Ave. Al Malki, Imm. Noueilati; *Ambassador:* A. P. VENKATESWARAN.

Indonesia: 19 Rue Al-Amir Ezzeddine; *Ambassador:* MARTONO KADRI.

Iran: Rue Kawakbi, Imm. Oustwani; *Ambassador:* (vacant).

Iraq: Ave. Al Mansour 3756, Charkasieh; *Ambassador:* WALID KHASHALI.

Italy: 82 Avenue Al Mansour; *Ambassador:* GIORGIO GIACOMELLI.

Japan: 15 Ave. Al-Jalaa; *Ambassador:* MASANAO ODAKA.

Jordan: Abou Roumaneh; *Ambassador:* HUSAIN HAMAMI.

Korea, Democratic People's Republic: Rue Fares El-Khouri-Jisr Tora; *Ambassador:* KIM RYONG HA.

Kuwait: Rue Ibrahim Hanano; *Ambassador:* KHALID ABDULLATIF AL-MUSALLAM.

Libya: Place Al Malki, 10 Avenue Mansour; *Head of Office:* AHMAD ABDULSALAM BEN KHAYAL.

Mauritania: Ave. Al-Jala'a, Rue Karameh; *Ambassador:* TELMIDI OULD MOHAMED AMAR.

Mexico: Cairo, Egypt.

Mongolia: Bucharest, Romania.

Morocco: Abou Roumaneh-Abdel Malek ben Marwan St.; *Ambassador:* DRISS BANNOUNA.

Netherlands: Place Abou Ala'a Al-Maarri, Imm. Bodr Diab; *Ambassador:* HENRI C. E. VAN EDE VAN DER PALS.

Nigeria: Cairo, Egypt.

Norway: Cairo, Egypt.

Oman: Amman, Jordan.

Pakistan: Avenue Al Jala'a; *Ambassador:* SARFARAZ KHAN.

Panama: Malki, Al-Bizm St., Al-Zein Bldg., Apt. 7; *Ambassador:* MARÍA LAKAS BAHAS (also accred. to Greece).

Poland: Rue Georges Haddad, Imm. Chahine; *Ambassador:* STANISŁAW MATOZEK.

Qatar: Abou Roumaneh, Place Madfa, Imm. Allawi No. 20; *Ambassador:* HAMAD ABDUL AZIZ AL-KAWARI.

Romania: Rue Ibrahim Hanano No. 8; *Ambassador:* EMILIAN MANCIUR.

Saudi Arabia: Avenue Al Jala'a; *Ambassador:* Sheikh ABDUL MOUHSEN AL-ZEID.

Senegal: 18 Ave. Adnan Malki; *Ambassador:* AMADOU LAÏTY NDIAYE.

Somalia: Avenue Ata Ayoubi; *Ambassador:* YOUSSEF JAMA BOURALLE.

Spain: 81 Ave. Al Jala'a, Imm. Swaaf; *Ambassador:* FELIX GUILLERMO FERNÁNDEZ-SHAW (also accred. to Cyprus).

Sudan: 76 Rue Ata Ayoubi; *Ambassador:* HASAN EL-EMIR AL-BASHIR.

Sweden: Abdul M. Ben Marwan St., Abou Roumaneh; *Ambassador:* JEAN JACQUES DE DARDEL.

Switzerland: Malki, 31 Rue M. Kurd Ali; *Ambassador:* ROBERT BEAUJON.

Tanzania: Cairo, Egypt.

Trinidad and Tobago: Beirut, Lebanon.

Tunisia: Abu Rumaneh, Rue Rashid, Imm. Jabi; *Ambassador:* FARID SOUDANI.

Turkey: 58 Avenue Ziad Bin Abou Soufian; *Ambassador:* LYDEN ALACAKAPTAN.

U.S.S.R.: Boustan El-Kouzbari, Rue d'Alep; *Ambassador:* VLADIMIR YUKHIN.

United Arab Emirates: Rue Raouda No. 62, Imm. Housami; *Ambassador:* KHALIFEH AHMAD A. EL-MOUBARAK.

United Kingdom: Malki; Rue Muhammad Kurd Ali; *Ambassador:* ALBERT JAMES MCQUEEN CRAIG, C.M.G.

U.S.A.: Rue Al Mansour 2; *Ambassador:* TALCOTT SEELYE.

Uruguay: Beirut, Lebanon.

Vatican City: 82 Rue Misr, B.P. 2271 (Apostolic Nunciature): *Apostolic Pro-Nuncio:* Mgr. ANGELO PEDRONI.

Venezuela: Abou Roumaneh, Rue Nouri Pacha, Imm. Tabbah; *Chargé d'affaires a.i.:* Dr. EUGENIO OMANA MURILLO.

Viet-Nam: 9 Avenue Malki; *Ambassador:* LONG THUAN PHUOC (also accred. to Iraq).

Yemen Arab Republic: 43 Rue Al Jala'a; *Ambassador:* Lt.-Col. ALI ABU LUHUM.

Yemen, People's Democratic Republic: Beirut, Lebanon.

Yugoslavia: Ave. A. Jala'a; *Ambassador:* DIMITAR JANEVSKI (also accred. to Jordan).

Zambia: Cairo, Egypt.

Syria also has diplomatic relations with Albania, Bahrain, Burma, Djibouti, Guyana, Luxembourg, Malta, Mozambique, Portugal and Suriname.

JUDICIAL SYSTEM

High Constitutional Court: Damascus; f. 1974 in accordance with the Constitution of 1973. It is the highest court in the judicial system.

Court of Cassation: Damascus; Court of appeal.

Courts of Appeal: 13 Courts of Appeal in the 13 Prefectures try all criminal cases subject to appeal, as well as all other cases within their competence by virtue of the law in force; some of them are composed of several chambers; decisions are given by three judges, one of them being the President.

Summary Courts: 110 Summary Courts try civil, commercial and penal cases within their competence; a Summary Court is constituted by one judge known as a "Judge of the Peace".

First Instance Courts: 41 First Instance Courts, constituted by one judge, deal with all cases other than those within the competence of special tribunals. In some Prefectures are several Chambers.

Chief Justice of Syria: JAMAL NAAMANI (President of the High Constitutional Court).

PERSONAL STATUS COURTS

For Muslims: each court consists of one judge, the "Qadi Shari'i", who deals with marriage, divorce, etc.

For Druzes: one court consisting of one judge, the "Qadi Mazhabi".

For non-Muslim Communities: for Catholics, Orthodox-Protestants, Jews.

OTHER COURTS

Courts for Minors: their constitution, officers, sessions, jurisdiction and competence are determined by a special law.

Military Court: Damascus.

RELIGION

In religion the majority of Syrians follow a form of Sunni orthodoxy. There is also a considerable number of religious minorities: Muslim Shi'ites; the Ismaili of the Salamiya district, whose spiritual head is the Aga Khan; a large number of Druzes, the Nusairis or Alawites of the Jebel Ansariyeh and the Yezidis of the Jebel Sinjar.

MUSLIMS

Grand Mufti: AHMAD KUFTARO.

Most Syrians are Muslims. Nearly all are Sunnites with a small number of Ismailis and Shi'ites.

CHRISTIANS

Greek Orthodox Patriarch: His Beatitude IGNATIUS HAZIM, Patriarch of Antioch and all the Orient; P.O.B. 9, Damascus.

Greek Catholic Patriarch: H.B. MAXIMOS V HAKIM; Bab-Sharki, Damascus; P.O.B. 50076, Beirut, Lebanon; one million mems.; publ. *Le Lien* (monthly, in French).

Syrian Orthodox Patriarch: His Holiness IGNATIUS YACOB III.

THE PRESS

Since the coming to power of the Baath Arab Socialist Party the structure of the press has been modified according to socialist patterns. Most publications are published by organizations such as political, religious, or professional associations, trade unions, etc. and several are published by government ministries. Anyone wishing to establish a new paper or periodical must apply for a licence.

The major dailies are *al-Baath* (the organ of the party) and *al-Thawrah* in Damascus, *al-Jamahir al-Arabia* in Aleppo, and *al-Fida* in Hama.

PRINCIPAL DAILIES

Aravelk: Aleppo; Armenian; morning; Editor Dr. A. ANGYKIAN; circ. 3,500.

al-Baath (*Renaissance*): rue el Barazil, Damascus; Arabic; morning; organ of the Baath Arab Socialist Party; circ. 20,000.

Barq al-Shimal: rue Aziziyah, Aleppo; Arabic; morning; Editor MAURICE DJANDJI; circ. 6,400.

al-Fida: rue Kuwatly, Hama; political; Arabic; morning; Publishing concession holder OSMAN ALOUINI; Editor A. AULWANI; circ. 4,000.

al-Jamahir al-Arabia: El Ouedha Printing and Publishing Organization, Aleppo; political; Arabic; Chief Editor MORTADA BAKACH; circ. 10,000.

al-Shabab: rue al Tawil, Aleppo; Arabic; morning; Editor MUHAMMAD TALAS; circ. 9,000.

al-Thawrah: El Ouedha Printing and Publishing Organization, Damascus; political; Arabic; morning; circ. 20,000.

WEEKLIES AND FORTNIGHTLIES

al-Ajoua: Compagnie de l'Aviation Arabe Syrienne, Damascus; aviation; Arabic; fortnightly; Editor AHMAD ALLOUCHE.

Arab Press Digest: Syrian Documentation Papers, P.O.B. 2712, Damascus.

al-Esbou al-Riadi: ave. Firdoisse, Tibi Bldg., Damascus; sports; Arabic; weekly; Publisher MOUNIR BAKIR; Dir. and Editor KAMEL EL BOUNNI.

al-Fursan: Damascus; political magazine; Editor Major FIFAAT ASSAD.

Hadarat al-Islam: B.P. 808, Jadet Halbouni, Jadet El Raby, Damascus; religious; Arabic; fortnightly; Publisher MOUSTAPHA ESSIBAI; Dir. AHMAD FARHAT; Editor MUHAMMAD ADIB SALEH.

Homs: Homs; literary; Arabic; weekly; Publisher and Dir. ADIB KABA; Editor PHILIPPE KABA.

Jaysh al-Shaab: P.O.B. 3320, blvd. Palestine, Damascus; f. 1946; army magazine, Arabic; weekly; published by the Political Department.

Kifah al-Oummal al-Ishtiraki: Fédération Générale des Syndicats des Ouvriers, Damascus; labour; Arabic; weekly; Published by General Federation of Trade Unions; Editor SAID EL HAMAMI.

al-Majalla al-Batriarquia: B.P. 914, Syrian Orthodox Patriarchate, Damascus; f. 1962; religious; Arabic; monthly; Dir. and Editor SAMIR ABDOH; circ. 7,000.

al-Masira: Damascus; political; weekly; published by Federation of Youth Organizations.

al-Maukef al-Riadi: El Ouehda Organization, Damascus; sports; Arabic; weekly; Published by El Ouehda Printing and Publishing Organization; circ. 5,000.

al-Nass: B.P. 926, Aleppo; f. 1953; Arabic; weekly; Publisher VICTOR KALOUS.

Nidal al-Fellahin: Fédération Générale des Laboureurs, Damascus; peasant workers; Arabic; weekly; Published by General Federation of Workers; Editor MANSOUR ABU EL HOSN.

Revue de la Presse Arabe: 67 Place Chahbandar, Damascus; f. 1948; French; twice weekly.

al-Riada: B.P. 292, near Electricity Institute, Damascus; sports; Arabic; weekly; Dir. NOUREDDINE RIAL; Publisher and Editor OURFANE UBARI.

al-Sakafe al-Isboui; B.P. 2570, Soukak El Sakr, Damascus; cultural; Arabic; weekly; Publisher, Dir. and Editor MADHAT AKKACHE.

al-Talia (*Vanguard*): B.P. 3031, the National Guard, Damascus; Arabic; fortnightly; Editor SOHDI KHALIL.

al-Thawrah al-Ziraia (*Agricultural Revolution Review*): Ministry of Agrarian Reform, Damascus; f. 1965; agriculture; Arabic; monthly; circ. 7,000.

al-Yanbu al-Jadid: al-Awkaf Bldg., Homs; literary; Arabic; weekly; Publisher, Dir. and Editor MAMDOU EL KOUSSEIR.

MONTHLIES

al-Dad: rue El Tital, Wakf El Moiriné Bldg., Aleppo; literary; Arabic; Dir. RIAD HALLAK; Publisher and Editor ABDALLAH YARKI HALLAK.

Ecos: P.O.B. 3320, Damascus; monthly review; Spanish.

Flash: P.O.B. 3320, Damascus; monthly review; English and French.

al-Irshad al-Zirai: Ministry of Agriculture, Damascus; agriculture; every two months.

al-Kalima: Al-Kalima Association, Aleppo; religious; Arabic; Publisher and Editor FATHALLA SAKAL.

al-Kanoun: Ministry of Justice, Damascus; juridical; Arabic.

al-Maarifa: Ministry of Culture and National Guidance, Damascus; f. 1962; literary; Arabic; Edited by SAFWAN KUDSI and KHALDOUN SHAMAA.

al-Majalla al-Askaria: P.O.B. 3320, blvd. Palestine, Damascus; f. 1950; official military magazine; Editor NAKHLI KALLAS.

al-Majalla al-Toubilla al-Arabilla: Al-Jalla's St., Damascus; Published by Arab Medical Commission; Dir. Dr. SHAMSEDDIN EL JUNDI; Editor Dr. ADNAN TAKRITI.

Monthly Survey of Arab Economics: B.P. 2306, Damascus and B.P. 6068, Beirut; f. 1958; English and French editions; published Centre d'Etudes et de Documentation Economiques, Financières et Sociales; Dir. Dr. CHAFIC AKHRAS.

al-Mouallem al-Arabi (*The Arab Teacher*): Ministry of Education; Damascus; f. 1948; educational and cultural; Arabic.

al-Mouhandis al-Arabi: Al-Jala St., Damascus; published by Syrian Engineering Syndicate; scientific and cultural; Dir. HICHAM SATI; Editor Dr. MAHMOUD ABRACHE; bi-monthly.

al-Moujtama al-Arabi al-Ishtiraki: Ministry of Social Affairs, Damascus; social security; Arabic; Editor SAMI ATFE.

al-Oumran: Ministry of Municipal and Rural Affairs, Damascus; fine arts; Arabic.

Rissalat al-Kimia: B.P. 669, El Abid Bldg., Damascus; scientific; Arabic; Publisher, Dir. and Editor HASSAN EL SAKA.

Saut al-Forat: Deir-Ezzor; literary; Arabic; Publisher, Dir and Editor ABDEL KADER AYACH.

al-Shourta: Directorate of Public Affairs and Moral Guidance, Damascus; juridical; Arabic.

Souriya al-Arabilla: Ministry of Information, Damascus; publicity; in four languages.

Syrie et Monde Arabe: P.O.B. 3550, Place Chahbandar, Damascus; f. 1952; economic, statistical and political survey; French and English.

al-Tamaddon al-Islami: Darwichiya, Damascus; religious; Arabic; monthly; Published by Tamaddon al-Islami Association; Dir. MUHAMMAD EL KHATIB; Editor AHMAD MAZAR EL AZMAH.

al-Yakza: Sisi St., Al Yazka Association, Aleppo; f. 1935; Dir. and Editor PAUL GENADRI.

QUARTERLY

Les Archives Littéraires du Moyen Orient: Syrian Documentation Papers, P.O.B. 2712, Damascus.

Majallat Majma al-Lughah al-Arabiyyah-bi Dimashq: Arab Academy of Damascus; P.O.B. 327, Damascus; f. 1921; Islamic culture and Arabic literature, Arabic scientific and cultural terminology; circ. 2,000.

ANNUALS

Bibliography of the Middle East: Syrian Documentation Papers, P.O.B. 2712, Damascus.

General Directory of the Press and Periodicals in the Arab World: Syrian Documentation Papers, P.O.B. 2712, Damascus.

PRESS AGENCIES

Agence Arabe Syrienne d'Information: Damascus; f. 1966; supplies bulletins on Syrian news to foreign news agencies.

FOREIGN BUREAUX

Agencia EFE (*Spain*): Mazras El Malek El Adel Building, Al Mahdi Sabbagh, Damascus; Correspondent ZACHARIAS SARME.

Agenzia Nazionale Stampa Associata (ANSA) (*Italy*): P.O.B. 827, rue Salhié, Immeuble Tibi-Selo; f. 1962; Chief KHALIL NABKI.

Allgemeiner Deutscher Nachrichtendienst (ADN) (*German Democratic Republic*): P.O.B. 844, Damascus; Correspondent WILFRIED HOFFMANN.

Deutsche Presse-Agentur (dpa) (*Federal Republic of Germany*): P.O.B. 2712, Damascus; Correspondent LOUIS FARES.

Reuters: P.O.B. 3525, Ijl, Omary and Kassas Bldg., Damascus.

TASS (U.S.S.R.) also has a bureau in Damascus.

PUBLISHERS

Arab Advertising Organization: 28 Moutanabbi St., P.O.B. 2842 and 3034, Damascus; f. 1963; publishes Directory of Commerce and Industry, Damascus International Fair Guide, Daily Bulletin of Official Tenders, The Industrial Guide and The Professional Guide; Dir.-Gen. GEORGE KHOURY.

Damascus University Press: Damascus; art, geography, education, history, engineering, medicine, law, sociology, school books.

Office Arabe de Presse et de Documentation (OFA): P.O.B. 3550, Damascus; f. 1964; numerous periodicals, monographs and surveys on political and economic affairs; Dir.-Gen. SAMIR A. DARWICH. Has two affiliated branches, *OFA-Business Consulting Centre* (market surveys and services) and *OFA-Renseignements Commerciaux* (Commercial enquiries on firms and persons in Syria and Lebanon).

al-Ouehda Printing and Publishing Organization (*Institut al-Ouedha pour l'impression, édition et distribution*): Damascus and Aleppo; publishes *al-Jamahir al-Arabia* and *al-Thawrah* (dailies) and *al-Maukef al-Raidi* (weekly).

Syrian Documentation Papers: P.O.B. 2712, Damascus; f. 1968; publishers of *Bibliography of the Middle East* (annual), *General Directory of the Press and Periodicals in the Arab World* (annual), *Les Archives Littéraires du Moyen Orient* (quarterly), *Arab Press Digest* (weekly), and numerous publications on political, economic and social affairs and literature and legislative texts concerning Syria and the Arab world; Dir.-Gen. LOUIS FARÉS.

al-Tawjih Press: P.O.B. 3320, Palestine St., Damascus.

Other publishers include: *Dar El-Yakaza El-Arabia, Dar El-Hahda El-Arabia, Dar El-Filez, Dar El-Fatah, Dubed, El-Mouassassa El-Sakafieh.*

RADIO AND TELEVISION

Directorate-General of Broadcasting and Television: Omayyad Square, Damascus; f. 1945; Dir.-Gen. FOUAD BALLAT; Eng. Dir. ANTOINE KARKOUCHE; Broadcasts Dir. KHODR OMRANE; publ. *Here is Damascus* (fortnightly).

RADIO

Director of Radio: KHODR AMRAN.

Broadcasts in Arabic, French, English, Russian, German, Spanish, Polish, Turkish, Bulgarian.

There were 1,232,500 receivers in use in mid-1976.

TELEVISION

Director of Television: FUAD BALLAT.

Services started in 1960.

There were 302,760 receivers in use in mid-1976.

FINANCE

BANKING

(cap.=capital; res.=reserves; p.u.=paid up; dep.=deposits; m.=millions; amounts in £S)

CENTRAL BANK

Central Bank of Syria: 29 Ayar Square, Damascus; f. 1956; cap. and res. 100m.; total assets 9,912m. (Dec. 1976) Gov. RIFAT AKKAD; 10 brs.

OTHER BANKS

Agricultural Bank: P.O.B. 4325, Damascus; f. 1924; Dir.-Gen. MAAN RISLAN.

Commercial Bank of Syria: P.O.B. 933, Moawia St., Harika, Damacsus; f. 1967; 30 brs.; cap. 182m.; total resources 8,263m. (Dec. 1977); Pres. and Gen. Man. Dr. DIB ABU ASSALI.

Industrial Bank: Damascus; f. 1959; nationalized bank providing finance for industry; cap. 12.5m., dep. 304m., total investments 326m. (March 1977); 7 brs.; Chair. and Gen. Man. Dr. A. S. KANAAN.

Popular Credit Bank: Darwishieh, Harika, P.O.B. 2841, Damascus; f. 1967; governmental bank; cap. 3m., dep. 265m. (March 1977).

Real Estate Bank: P.O.B. 2337, Al Furar St., Damascus; f. 1966; cap. 115m.; 10 brs.; Dir.-Gen. FARROUK AYYASH.

INSURANCE

Syrian General Organization for Insurance: Tajheez St., P.O.B. 2279, Damascus; f. 1953; authorized cap. 10m.; a nationalized company; operates throughout Syria, with branches in Jordan and Lebanon; Chair. and Gen. Man. SALIM YAZIJI.

TRADE AND INDUSTRY

CHAMBERS OF COMMERCE

Damascus Chamber of Commerce: B.P. 1040, Mou'awiah St., Damascus; f. 1914; 9,000 mems.; Pres. BADREDDINE SHALLAH; Gen. Dir. MUHAMMAD THABET Gh. MAHAYNI; publ. *Economic Bulletin* (quarterly).

Aleppo Chamber of Commerce: Al-Moutanabbi Str., Aleppo; f. 1885; Pres. MUHAMMAD MAHROUSEH; Sec. MOUNIR EL-ZAKRI; Dir. ZEKI DAROUZI.

Hama Chamber of Commerce and Industry: Sh. Bachoura, Hama; f. 1934; Pres. ABDUL-HAMID KAMBAZ.

Homs Chamber of Commerce and Industry: Aboul-of St., Homs; f. 1938; Pres. YUSUF AL-IKHOUAN; Dir. SELIM AL-MUSANNEF.

Latakia Chamber of Commerce: Sh. Al-Hurriyah, Latakia; Pres. JULE NASRI.

CHAMBERS OF INDUSTRY

Aleppo Chamber of Industry: Moutanabbi St., Aleppo; f. 1935; Pres. ABDEL AZIZ FANSA; 4,000 mems.

Damascus Chamber of Industry: P.O.B. 1305, Harika-Mouawiya St., Damascus; Pres. SHAFIC SOUCCAR; Gen. Man. ABDUL HAMID MALAKANI; publ. *Al Siniye* (Industry) (irregularly).

EMPLOYERS' ORGANIZATIONS

FEDERATIONS

Fédération Générale à Damas: Damascus; f. 1951; Dir TALAT TAGLUBI.

Fédération de Damas: Damascus; f. 1949.

Fédération des Patrons et Industriels à Lattaquié: Latakia; f. 1953.

TRADE UNIONS

Ittihad Naqabat al-'Ummal al-'Am fi Suriya (*General Federation of Labour Unions*): Qanawat St., Damascus; f. 1948; Chair. (vacant); Sec. MAHMUD FAHURI.

STATE ENTERPRISE

Syrian Petroleum Company: P.O.B. 2849, Al-Mutanabi St., Damascus; f. 1974; state agency; holds the oil concession for all Syria; exploits the Suwadiyah, Karachuk, Rumailan and Jbeisseh oilfields; production in 1977 174,352 barrels a day; also organizes exploring, production and marketing of oil nationally; Dir. Eng. ISSA IBRAHIM YOUSSEF.

TRANSPORT

RAILWAYS

Syrian Railways: B.P. 182, Aleppo; Pres. of the Board of Administration and Gen. Man. Ing. ABDULKADER MOULAYES.

The present railway system is composed of the following network:

Meydan Ekbez (Turkish frontier)–Aleppo; Cobanbey (Turkish frontier)–Aleppo; Qamishliya (Turkish frontier)–Jaroubieh (Iraq frontier); Aleppo–Homs; Koussair (Lebanese frontier)–Aleppo; Homs–Akkari (Lebanese frontier); Latakia–Aleppo; there are 555 km. of normal gauge and 313 km. of narrow gauge track. Lines from Latakia to Djezira and from Homs to Damascus (204 km.) are under construction.

Syrian Railways: Northern Lines: 248 km, Southern Lines: 295 km.

Hejaz Railways (narrow gauge): 301 km. in Syria; the historic railway to Medina is the subject of a reconstruction project jointly with Jordan and Saudi Arabia, but little progress has been made since the June 1967 war. Trains run from Damascus to Amman.

ROADS

Arterial roads run across the country linking the north to the south and the Mediterranean to the eastern frontier. The main arterial networks are as follows: Sidon (Lebanon)-Quneitra-Sweida-Salkhad-Jordan border: Beirut (Lebanon)-Damascus - Khan Abu Chamat - Iraq border - Baghdad; Tartous - Tell Kalakh - Homs - Palmyra; Banias - Hama - Salemie; Latakia-Aleppo-Rakka-Deirezzor-Abou Kemal-Iraq border; Tripoli (Lebanon)-Tartous-Banias-Latakia; Turkish border - Antakya; Amman (Jordan) - Dera'a - Damascus-Homs-Hama-Aleppo-Azaz (Turkish border); Haifa (Israel) - Kuneitra - Damascus - Palmyra - Deirezzor-Hassetche-Kamechlie.

Asphalted roads: 6,000 km, macadam roads: 1,300 km. earth roads: 6,000 km.

Touring Club de Syrie: P.O.B. 28, Aleppo; f. 1950; the principal Syrian motoring organization; Pres. ALFRED GIRARDI.

PIPELINES

The oil pipelines which cross Syrian territory are of great importance to the national economy, representing a considerable source of foreign exchange. Iraq halted the flow of oil through the pipeline between Kirkuk and Banias in April 1976, but it was resumed in February 1979.

Following the Iraq Government's nationalization of the Iraq Petroleum Company, the Syrian Government nationalized the IPC's pipelines, pumping stations and other installations in Syria, setting up a new company to administer them:

Syrian Company for Oil Transport (SCOT): Dir.-Gen. HANNA HADDAD.

SHIPPING

The port of Latakia has been developed and the construction of a deep water harbour was completed in 1959. A new port at Tartous is under construction.

Syrian Navigation Company: Latakia.

CIVIL AVIATION

There is an international airport at Damascus.

Syrian Arab Airlines: P.O.B. 417, Red Crescent Bldg., Yousef-Al-Azmeh Square, Damascus; f. 1946, refounded 1961 after revocation of merger with Misrair forming U.A.A.; domestic services and routes to Abu Dhabi, Algiers, Athens, Baghdad, Benghazi, Budapest, Cairo, Casablanca, Copenhagen, Delhi, Dhahran, Doha, Dubai, East Berlin, Jeddah, Karachi, Kuwait, London, Moscow, Munich, Paris, Prague, Sana'a, Sofia, Teheran, Tripoli and Tunis; fleet of four Caravelles and two Boeing 707 on lease; three Boeing 727 and two Boeing 747 are on order; Chair. Major-Gen. ASSAD MOUKAYED; Man. Dir. Air. Brig.-Gen. AHMAD ANTAR.

FOREIGN AIRLINES

The following foreign airlines serve Syria: Aeroflot (U.S.S.R.), Air France, Alitalia (Italy), Ariana Afghan Airlines, Balkan (Bulgaria), British Airways, ČSA (Czechoslovakia), EgyptAir, Interflug (German Democratic Republic), Iraqi Airways, KLM (Netherlands), Kuwait Airways, Lufthansa (Federal Republic of Germany), Malév (Hungary), Pan Am (U.S.A.), PIA (Pakistan), Qantas (Australia), SAS (Sweden), Saudia and Swissair.

TOURISM

Ministry of Tourism: Abou Firas El-Hamadani St., Damascus; f. 1972; Minister of Tourism GHASSAN CHALHOUB; Dir. of Tourist Relations IHSAN CHICHAKLI; Ministerial Adviser NADIM KANAFANI.

Middle East Tourism: P.O.B. 201, Fardoss St., Damascus; f. 1966; Pres. MOHAMED DAADOUCHE; 7 brs.

DEFENCE

Minister of Defence and C.-in-C. of the Armed Forces: Maj.-Gen. MUSTAFA TLASS.

Chief of Staff of the Armed Forces: Maj.-Gen. HIKMAT SHEHABI.

Air Force Commander: Maj.-Gen. SUBHI HADDAD.

Defence Budget (1978): £S4,400 million.

Military Service: 30 months (Jewish population exempted).

Total Armed Forces: 227,500: army 200,000; navy 2,500; air force 25,000.

Paramilitary Forces: 9,500 (8,000 Gendarmerie, 1,500 Desert Guard (Frontier Force).

The Arab Deterrent Force of approximately 30,000 in Lebanon is composed entirely of Syrian troops.

EDUCATION

Compulsory schooling lasts six years up to the age of 14, and text books are issued free in the primary sector. Both primary and secondary education are expanding rapidly.

Agricultural schools prepare students mainly for work in agriculture and are open to the sons of peasants. Technical schools prepare students for work in all types of factories. Higher education is provided by the Universities of Damascus, Aleppo and Latakia, and the Homs Institute of Petroleum.

The main language of instruction in schools is Arabic, but English and French are widely taught as second languages.

UNIVERSITIES

Tichreen University: Baghdad St., Lazikiah; 50 teachers; 4,695 students.

University of Aleppo: 417 teachers; 19,122 students.

University of Damascus: 745 teachers; 39,214 students.

BIBLIOGRAPHY

ABU JABER, KAMAL S. The Arab Baath Socialist Party (Syracuse University Press, New York, 1966).

ASFOUR, EDMUND Y. Syrian Development and Monetary Policy (Harvard, 1959).

DIRECTORY OF COMMERCE AND INDUSTRY FOR THE SYRIAN ARAB REPUBLIC (Arab Advertising Organization, Damascus, 1969).

FEDDEN, ROBIN. Syria: an Historical Appreciation (London, 1946).

Syria and Lebanon (John Murray, London, 1966).

GLUBB, J. B. Syria, Lebanon, Jordan (Thames and Hudson, London, 1967).

HADDAD, J. Fifty Years of Modern Syria and Lebanon (Beirut, 1950).

HELBAOUI, YOUSSEF. La Syrie (Paris, 1956).

HITTI, PHILIP K. History of Syria; including Lebanon and Palestine (New York, 1951).

HOMET, M. L'Histoire secrète du traité franco-syrien (New Ed., Paris, 1951).

HOPWOOD, DEREK. The Russian presence in Syria and Palestine 1843–1914 (Oxford, 1969).

HOURANI, ALBERT H. Syria and Lebanon: A Political Essay (New York, 1946).

INTERNATIONAL BANK FOR RECONSTRUCTION AND DEVELOPMENT, THE. The Economic Development of Syria (Baltimore, 1955).

LLOYD-GEORGE, D. The Truth about the Peace Treaties-Vol. II (London, 1938).

LONGRIGG, S. H. Syria and Lebanon Under French Mandate (Oxford University Press, 1958).

PETRAN, TABITHA. Syria (Benn, London, 1972).

RABBATH, E. Unité Syrienne et Devenir Arabe (Paris, 1937).

RUNCIMAN, STEVEN. A History of the Crusades (London, Vol. I 1951, Vol. II 1952).

SAUVAGET, J. Les monuments historiques de Damas (Beirut, 1932).

SEALE, PATRICK. The Struggle for Syria (London, 1965).

SHARIF, A. A. Sources of Statistics in Syria (B.D.S.A., Damascus, 1964).

SPRINGETT, B. H. Secret Sects of Syria and the Lebanon (London, 1922).

STARK, FREYA. Letters from Syria (London, 1942).

SULTANOV, A. F. Souremennaya Siriya (Izdatel'stvo Vostochnoi Literaturni, Moscow, 1958).

THUBRON, C. A. Mirror to Damascus (Heinemann, London, 1967).

TIBAWI, A. L. Syria (London, 1962).

American Interests in Syria 1800–1901 (Oxford University Press, New York, 1966).

A Modern History of Syria (Macmillan, London, 1969).

TORREY, GORDON H. Syrian Politics and the Military (State University, Ohio, 1964).

TRITTON, A. S. The Caliphs and their Non-Muslim Subjects (London, 1930).

WEULERSSE, J. Paysans de Syrie et du Proche Orient (Paris, 1946).

YAMAK, L. Z. The Syrian Social Nationalist Party (Harvard University Press, Cambridge, Mass., 1966).

ZIADEH N. Syria and Lebanon (New York, Praeger, 1957).

Tunisia

PHYSICAL AND SOCIAL GEOGRAPHY

D. R. Harris

Tunisia is the smallest of the three countries that comprise the "Maghreb" of north Africa, but it is more cosmopolitan than either Algeria or Morocco. It forms a wedge of territory, 163,610 square kilometres in extent, between Algeria and Libya. It includes the easternmost ridges of the Atlas Mountains but most of it is low-lying and bordered by a long and sinuous Mediterranean coastline that faces both north and east. Ease of access by sea and by land from the east has favoured the penetration of foreign influences and Tunisia owes its distinct national identity and its varied cultural traditions to a succession of invading peoples: Phoenicians, Romans, Arabs, Turks and French. It was more completely Arabized than either Algeria or Morocco and remnants of the original Berber-speaking population of the Maghreb are confined, in Tunisia, to a few isolated localities in the south.

At mid-1977 the population was estimated to be 5,930,300 and the overall density was 36.2 per square kilometre. Most of the people live in the more humid, northern part of the country and at the May 1975 census about 10 per cent lived in Tunis (550,404). Situated strategically where the Sicilian Channel links the western with the central Mediterranean and close to the site of ancient Carthage, Tunis combines the functions of capital and chief port. No other town approaches Tunis in importance but on the east coast both Sousse (population 69,530 in 1975) and Sfax (population 171,297) provide modern port facilities, as does Bizerta (population 62,856) on the north coast, while some distance inland the old Arab capital and holy-city of Kairouan (population 54,546) serves as a regional centre. The only other sizeable town is Djerba (population 70,217).

The principal contrasts in the physical geography of Tunisia are between a humid and relatively mountainous northern region, a semi-arid central region of low plateaux and plains and a dry Saharan region in the south. The northern region is dominated by the easternmost folds of the Atlas mountain system which form two separate chains, the Northern and High Tell, separated by the valley of the River Medjerda, the only perennially flowing river in the country. The Northern Tell, which is a continuation of the Algerian Tell Atlas, consists mainly of sandstone and extends along the north coast at heights of between 300 and 600 metres. South of the Medjerda valley the much broader Tell Atlas, which is a continuation of the Saharan Atlas of Algeria, is made up of a succession of rugged sandstone and limestone ridges. Near the Algerian frontier they reach a maximum height of 1,544 metres in Djebel Chambi, the highest point in Tunisia, but the folds die away eastward towards the Cape Bon peninsula which extends north-east to within 145 kilometres of Sicily.

South of the High Tell or Dorsale ("backbone") central Tunisia consists of an extensive platform sloping gently towards the east coast. Its western half, known as the High Steppe, is made up of alluvial basins rimmed by low, barren mountains, but eastward the mountains give way first to the Low Steppe, which is a monotonous gravel-covered plateau and ultimately to the flat coastal plain of the Sahel. Occasional watercourses cross the Steppes but they only flow after heavy rain and usually fan out and evaporate in salt flats, or sebkhas, before reaching the sea.

The central Steppes give way southward to a broad depression occupied by two great seasonal salt lakes or shotts. The largest of these, the Shott Djerid, lies at 16 metres below sea-level and is normally covered by a salt crust. It extends from close to the Mediterranean coast near Gabès almost to the Algerian frontier and is adjoined on the north-west by the Shott el Rharsa which lies at 21 metres below sea-level. South of the shotts Tunisia extends for over 320 kilometres into the Sahara. Rocky, flat-topped mountains, the Monts des Ksour, separate a flat plain known as the Djeffara, which borders the coast south of Gabès, from a sandy lowland which is partly covered by the dunes of the Great Eastern Erg.

The climate of northern Tunisia is "Mediterranean" in type with hot, dry summers followed by warm, wet winters. Average rainfall reaches 150 cm. in the Kroumirie Mountains, which is the wettest area in north Africa, but over most of the northern region it varies from 40 to 100 cm. The wetter and least accessible mountains are covered with forests in which cork oak and evergreen oak predominate, but elsewhere lower rainfall and overgrazing combine to replace forest with meagre scrub growth. South of the High Tell rainfall is reduced to between 20 and 40 cm. annually, which is insufficient for the regular cultivation of cereal crops without irrigation, and there is no continuous cover of vegetation. Large areas of the Steppes support only clumps of wiry esparto grass, which is collected and exported for paper manufacture. Southern Tunisia experiences full desert conditions. Rainfall is reduced to below 20 cm. annually and occurs only at rare intervals. Extremes of temperature and wind are characteristic and vegetation is completely absent over extensive tracts. The country supports only a sparse nomadic population except where supplies of underground water make cultivation possible, as in the famous date-producing oasis of Tozeur on the northern edge of the Shott Djerid.

HISTORY

Although the creation of the present-day independent Republic of Tunisia has been a phenomenon of the post-war period, the history of this small but important part of North Africa has displayed a certain continuity since the earliest times. From the early days of Phoenician settlement in the course of the ninth century B.C., the region has alternated between being itself a focus of political control (the Carthaginian Empire, or the period of medieval Islam, for example) reaching out to colonize or dominate the adjacent shores of the Mediterranean; and being the object of imperial aggrandizement (Rome, the Ottoman Empire, France) on the part of the dominant Mediterranean power of the time. On top of this pattern must be superimposed the conquest of North Africa by the Arabs in the course of the seventh century A.D., which has determined the basic characteristics of Tunisia ever since.

The history of Tunisia may be said to begin with the establishment there of colonies of Phoenician settlers, and the rise of the Carthaginian Empire. Emerging, in the course of the sixth century B.C., from the mists of its legendary foundation by the semi-mythical Queen Dido, by *c.* 550 B.C. Carthage had reached a position of commercial and naval supremacy in the Mediterranean, controlling part of Sicily, and with trading colonies established as far as what is now southern Portugal. The empire reached its height in the course of the fourth century, but shortly afterwards became involved with the rising power of the Roman Republic in a bitter struggle for the hegemony of the Mediterranean. The Punic Wars (264–241; 218–201; 149–146), of which the second is memorable for Hannibal's invasion of Italy, ended in the utter destruction of Carthage as a political entity, and the incorporation of its domains within the growing empire of Rome.

After one and a half centuries of abandonment, the ancient site of Carthage was rebuilt by Augustus at the dawn of the Christian era: intensive colonization from this time onward brought to what had become the Province of Africa a new prosperity, and the blessings of Roman civilization. During the first two centuries A.D. Carthage was generally accounted the second city of the Empire after Rome, but with the decline of the Empire in the west in the course of the fourth century, the great days of Roman Carthage were over. In A.D. 439 the city was lost to the Vandals, a nomadic people of Germanic origin, and became the capital of their ephemeral state, to be recovered for the Byzantine Empire in 533–34.

For the next two hundred and fifty years the history of Tunisia cannot be separated from the larger account of North Africa. Although Byzantine rule was better established in Tunisia than in the rest of the area, it was by no means secure. The tendency of the local governors to free themselves of the control of Constantinople was echoed by religious dissensions among the native population, who, largely Berber in origin, adopted various Christian heresies as tokens of their opposition to Imperial rule.

It was from another quarter, however, that the final challenge to Byzantine rule was to come. The foundation in Arabia of the power of Islam, and its rapid expansion after the death of the Prophet (632), led quickly to the Arab conquest of Egypt and Syria, and to the shattering of the precarious unity of the Byzantine Empire. The first Arab raids into North Africa soon followed (647). After a confused period, in which the Arabs, the Berbers, and the forces of Byzantium all contested for the control of North Africa, Arab control over the area was finally established (698) with the conquest of Carthage, and the foundation of the town of Tunis. Islam now spread rapidly amongst the Berbers, but did not prevent them from making further attempts to regain their independence, merely providing them with new and more convenient pretexts for revolt in the shape of new Islamic religious heresies. The greater part of the eighth century is taken up with Berber-supported Kharijite risings, manifestations of extreme left-wing Islam against the central government, and with constant revolts among the occupying Arab forces. In the last years of the Umayyad dynasty (overthrown 748–50) Tunisia escaped completely from Imperial control: the new dynasty of the Abbasids, ruling from Iraq, made strong efforts to recapture the province. Kayrawan, founded in 670 as the centre of Arab rule in the Maghreb, was retaken, but lost in 767, when a period of complete anarchy ensued. After a period of rule by petty chieftains, Tunisia was restored to Abbasid control in the year 800, in the person of Ibrahim ibn Aghlab. As a reward for his services, and as a means of maintaining the form if not the actuality of imperial control over the area, the caliph Harun al-Rashid thereupon appointed him as tributary ruler of al-Ifrikiya—corresponding more or less to the Roman Province of Africa, and to the present-day state of Tunisia.

The period of Aghlabid rule is one of great importance for the history of Tunisia. For the major part of the ninth century the country enjoyed a relatively stable and prosperous existence, while the importance of the dynasty was early recognized by the arrival of an embassy from the Emperor Charlemagne. Some years later, returning in a different way the interest of Europe, Aghlabid forces began the conquest of Sicily (827–39). The middle of the ninth century was the zenith of Aghlabid rule, and was signalized by the emir Ahmed with the construction of great mosques in the major cities, and the building of an elaborate system of dams and reservoirs to supply the capital of Kayrawan. From 874 the power of the Aghlabid state began to decline; despite the virtual completion of the conquest of Sicily (878) the dynasty was finally overthrown in the course of a religious revolution from the west. Between 905 and 909 Tunisia was brought under the control of the Fatimids, adherents and fanatical propagators of the heretical doctrines of Shi'ism. Established in their new capital of Mahdiya, on the Tunisian coast, the Fatimids pursued a vigorous policy of expansion and conquest. Expeditions were sent against Egypt, and Sicily was once more ruled from North Africa, while by 933 Fatimid rule was established throughout the Maghreb. A serious threat to the regime, posed in 943–47 by the terrible Berber revolt led by "the man with the donkey", was overcome, and for the next twenty-five years Tunisia enjoyed a certain degree of prosperity. Fatimid power meanwhile was expanding in the east. In 969–70 the dynasty gained control of Egypt and Syria: three years later the caliph al-Muizz abandoned Mahdiya for his new capital of Cairo, and handed over the government of Tunisia to the Zirids, a family of Berber princes who had long supported the Fatimid regime. Under Zirid rule Tunisia enjoyed great prosperity, in which the arts and sciences, commerce and industry, all flourished, but this golden age was suddenly brought to an end in 1050 by the Zirids transferring their allegiance from Cairo to the orthodox caliph at Baghdad. Fatimid revenge was terrible. In 1051 hundreds of thousands of Hilali Arab nomads were sent against Ifrikiya from Egypt. Under the devastating impact of these marauding nomads the economy crumbled, along with the political power of the Berbers, and the country as a whole lapsed into political fragmentation. Further troubles now came from another quarter. In 1087 forces from the rising Italian city-states of Pisa and Genoa took Mahdiya, allowing the Zirids, who had held out there against the Hilali invasion, to continue as its rulers. Early in the twelfth century the Zirids renewed their loyalty to Cairo, and attempted to restore the shattered fragments of their state, but were interrupted by the Normans, who, having previously conquered Sicily and Malta, in 1148 drove the last Zirid from Mahdiya.

Norman rule in Tunisia was short-lived. By 1160 they had been ejected from their last coastal stronghold, and for the next fifty years Tunisia formed part of the empire of the caliphs of Marrakesh (the Almohads). With the thirteenth century the authority of Baghdad was briefly restored over Tunisia. In 1207 the Abbasid caliph al-Nasir set up a strong provincial government under a member of the Berber family of the Hafsids, who, having held the governorship of Tunis since 1184, were to continue as the main political force in the area until the Ottoman conquest late in the sixteenth century.

For most of the thirteenth century the Hafsids ruled over North Africa from Tripoli to central Algeria, and maintained close diplomatic and commercial relations with the trading ports and city-states of the northern shores of the Mediterranean. European interest in Tunisia had never disappeared since the temporary Norman conquest of the twelfth century: with the weakening of Hafsid rule in face of tribal and Arab unrest, Jerba came once more into Christian hands (1284–1337). In the reign of Abu'l-Abbas (1370–94) the fortunes of the dynasty once more improved, and further Christian attempts to seize coastal places were repelled. His son held off repeated Sicilian and Catalan attempts to capture Jerba, and in 1428 went on the offensive, becoming involved in operations against Malta. The last Hafsid ruler of note was Abu Amr Uthman (1435–88). Shortly after his death the Hafsid Empire began to disintegrate, and at the same time Tunisia became involved in the wider struggle between the resurgent forces of the newly-unified Spanish monarchy and the Ottoman Empire for control of the Mediterranean, the outcome of which conflict was to determine the future of Tunisia for the next four centuries, and to mark its emergence as a definite political entity.

OTTOMAN RULE

With the completion of the *reconquista* in 1492 by the incorporation of the Muslim kingdom of Granada, Spain turned her attentions to the conquest of Muslim North Africa. The first place in the crumbling Hafsid territories to fall under her control was Bougie, in 1510, and then Tripoli, in the same year. Ten years later the strategic place of Jerba also fell. But these events had already produced a reaction. In 1516 Algiers had come into the possession of the Turkish corsair Aruj. His brother, Khayr ed-Din Barbarossa, who had succeeded him in 1518, had in 1533 been summoned to Istanbul to act as high admiral of the Ottoman fleet. In this new capacity he drove the compliant Emir al-Hasan from Tunis (1534), and placed the town under Ottoman control. In the following year a great Spanish naval expedition retook the town, and al-Hasan returned as the Emperor's vassal, handing over la Goleta to Spain as the price of his restoration. Further coastal strongholds subsequently passed into Spanish hands, while in 1542 al-Hassan was deposed by his son Ahmed, who, with the not disinterested help of the Turkish corsair chiefs, made a final attempt to reunite Tunisia against Spain. After a long drawn-out struggle Ahmed fell at the siege of Malta, 1565, which, together with the Spanish naval victory of Lepanto six years later, marks the climax and virtual end of their struggle with the Ottomans for control of the sea. As far as Tunisia was concerned, the sole beneficiaries of the struggle were the Ottomans. Already well established at Algiers, in 1569 the Pasha of Algiers, Uluj Ali, placed a garrison in Tunis, only to be driven out briefly (1572) in the aftermath of the Spanish victory at Lepanto. The unfortunate Hafsid was restored for the last time as nominal ruler, but in 1574 an Ottoman expedition put an end to Spanish power in Tunis, and to the Hafsid dynasty itself.

Direct Ottoman rule in Algiers lasted only seventeen years. The provincial administration set up in 1574 took its orders at first from Algiers, and later from the Porte itself, but a military revolt in 1591 reduced the power of the Pasha, the actual representative of the sultan, to a cypher, and the affairs of the state were taken over by one of the forty *deys* or high officers of the Ottoman army of occupation. By *c.* 1600 a situation had arisen analogous to that in Algiers, the *diwan*, or governing council, coming to share a pre-eminent place with the *taifa*, or guild of the corsair chiefs. By 1606 the *de facto* independence of Tunisia had been recognized by the dispatch of a French embassy, under orders to negotiate commercial privileges with Tunis without reference to the Porte. Nevertheless, for the next two and a half centuries and more, Tunisia was regarded as part of the Ottoman Empire, a convenient fiction both flattering to the government at Istanbul, and useful to the *deys* in safeguarding their rule and bolstering their reputation with outside powers.

In the first half of the seventeenth century the situation of Tunis was fairly flourishing. Trade and commerce, especially with Marseilles and Livorno, prospered, while commercial relations were entered into with states as far distant as England and the Netherlands. From *c.* 1650 the power of the *deys* declined, and authority in the state gradually passed to the *beys*, originally subordinate in rank. Hammuda, *bey* from 1659 to 1663, became master of the entire country, and assured the maintenance of power in his family—the Muradids—until 1702. This was a period of decline, with tribal unrest away from Tunis, and incursions from the direction of Algiers. With the accession of Huseyn Ali Turki in 1705 a new line of *beys* brought some semblance of order to the country. The remainder of the eighteenth century passed fairly uneventfully for Tunisia, with a certain amount of quiet prosperity, despite the uncertainty of relations with Algeria, and the growing naval power of Europe in the Mediterranean.

With the aftermath of the Napoleonic Wars came the first real impact of Europe on Tunisia. The European powers, in congress at Vienna and Aachen (1815–17) forced upon the *bey* Mahmud (1814–24) the suppression of the corsairs and their piratical activities, which had provided a considerable part of the revenues of the state. The French occupied Algiers in 1830, and subsequently reduced the whole of Algeria to colonial status. The next fifty years witnessed desperate but unavailing efforts by Tunisia to avoid the same fate. Increasingly the influence of France and Britain, and later Italy, came to be manifest through the activities of their consuls. The *bey* Ahmed (1837–55) attempted to reform the army on western lines, and to liberalize the institutions of society: his efforts merely increased the financial dependence of Tunisia on France. Under Muhammad (1855–59) a proclamation of reform and equality based on the Ottoman Hatti-Sherif of 1839 was promulgated under European pressure: his successor Muhammad al-Sadik (1859–82) promulgated a Constitution (suspended 1864) which attempted to separate executive from legislative power, to codify the laws, and to guarantee the independence of the judiciary.

Nevertheless, Tunisia's position deteriorated. Increased taxes, imposed from the mid-fifties, provoked tribal rebellion, and the growing dependence on foreign loans led to foreign intervention. Annual debt charges eventually exceeded revenue and in 1869 the *bey* was obliged to accept international financial control by France, Britain and Italy. By 1881 the imminence of financial collapse decided France to intervene, especially as at the Congress of Berlin three years earlier Britain, confronted by French hostility to the Cyprus Convention between Britain and Turkey, had indicated that it would not contest French influence in Tunisia, which Germany actually encouraged. French forces invaded Tunisia in April 1881, the immediate occasion being incidents on the frontier with Algeria. They encountered no serious resistance and the *bey* was forced to accept the terms of the Treaty of Kassar Said (also known as the Treaty of Bardo) under which he remained the nominal ruler of his country while French officials took over the direction of military, financial and foreign affairs.

FRENCH PROTECTORATE

The French presence once established, French control was soon extended. In 1883 Ali IV, the successor to Muhammad al-Sadik, was forced to sign the Treaty of Mersa, which formally established a French protectorate over Tunisia and brought the actual government of the country under French control. Although the office of *bey* was preserved, the real power passed to the French Resident-General. The international control commission was abolished in 1884, the currency was reformed on French lines in 1891, and the extra-territorial privileges of other Europeans were abrogated. Encouraged by large-scale grants of land, there was a considerable influx of settlers from France, and also from Italy, especially after 1900. Besides being confronted with the task of sustaining the economy by something better than the proceeds of piracy, which they tackled by investment in the development of the country's resources, the French were faced with rivalry from Italy, whose ambitions in North Africa were not extinguished until the collapse of the Fascist regime in the Second World War, and with the rise of Tunisian nationalism.

Tunisian cultural and political life absorbed many French ideas but was also influenced by movements in other parts of the Islamic world. An attempt to emulate the Young Turk reformers in the Ottoman Empire was seen in the Young Tunisian movement (1908) which called for the restoration of the authority of the *bey* together with reforms on democratic lines. The achievement of independence in eastern Arab countries after the First World War, and the example of the nationalist movement in Egypt, inspired Tunisians with a greater national consciousness and in 1920 the Destour (Constitution) movement was formed under the leadership of Shaikh al-Tha'libi, one of the founders of the pre-war Young Tunisians.

The Destour called for a self-governing constitutional regime with a legislative assembly. French attempts to conciliate opinion by administrative reforms, beginning in 1920 with economic councils on which Tunisians were represented, did not satisfy the more radical elements, however, and in the face of further nationalist activity repressive measures were resorted to. Shaikh al-Tha'libi was exiled in 1923 and in 1925 the Destour movement was broken up. It revived in the years after the Depression but soon split, the old Destour leaders being accused of collaboration with France by younger members eager for political action on a broad front. In 1934, led by Habib Bourguiba, a Tunisian lawyer, these created the Néo-Destour (New Constitution) Party. The new party employed methods of widespread political agitation as a result of which Bourguiba was exiled. With the victory of the Popular Front in France in 1936 he returned to Tunisia but little was achieved in direct negotiations with the new French government, from which much had been expected in the way of reforms. The Néo-Destour was built up into a powerful organization, its influence extending into all parts of the country, and its strength was proved in a successful general strike in 1938. Widespread clashes with the police followed, martial law was proclaimed, some 200 nationalists were arrested and both the Destour and Néo-Destour parties were dissolved.

When the Second World War broke out in the following year Tunisian opinion rallied in favour of France and when Italy entered the war some 23,000 Italians in Tunisia were interned. With the fall of France Tunisia came under Vichy rule and Bizerta, Tunis and other ports were used by Germany and Italy to supply their armies in Libya. The country became a theatre of war until the defeat of the Axis forces by the Allies in 1943 brought about the eventual restoration of French authority. The *bey*, Muhammad al-Monsif, was accused of collaboration with the Axis powers and deposed; he was replaced by his cousin, Muhammad al-Amin, who reigned until Tunisia became a republic in 1957.

GROWING AUTONOMY

The virtual restoration of peace-time conditions in 1944 brought a relaxation of political restrictions and the years immediately following saw renewed agitation for political changes. French action to repress this obliged Habib Bourguiba to remove himself to Cairo in 1945 but his chief lieutenant, Salah ben Youssef, was able to remain in Tunisia. The French authorities turned their attention to political reforms and by Beylical decrees in 1945 the Council of Ministers and the Grand Council (an elected body with equal French and Tunisian representation) were reorganized, the authority of the latter being extended. These moves did not satisfy the nationalists, however, who in August 1946 at a national congress unequivocally demanded complete independence. Later in the year a ministry was formed under Muhammad Kaak which included an increased number of Tunisians (moderate leaders being appointed, the Destour and Néo-Destour having refused to participate); the French retained overriding control.

Bourguiba returned to Tunisia in 1949. In April 1950 Néo-Destour proposals were put forward for the transfer of sovereignty and executive control to Tunisian hands, under a responsible government with a Prime Minister appointed by the *bey* and an elected National Assembly which would draw up a democratic constitution. Local French interests would be protected by representation on municipal councils, and Tunisia would co-operate with France on terms of equality. These proposals were met with a reasonable response in France and a new Tunisian government was formed in August 1950, composed of an equal number of Tunisian and French ministers, with Muhammad Chenik as Chief Minister and Salah ben Youssef Minister of Justice. The object of the new Government was stated to be the restoration of Tunisian sovereignty in stages, in co-operation with France. Despite strong opposition to these developments from the European settlers (some 10 per cent of the population), who opposed all concessions to nationalist demands, further reforms were effected in September 1950 and February 1951, when French advisers to the Tunisian ministers were removed and the Resident-General's control over the Council of Ministers was diminished.

Peaceful progress towards autonomy came to a halt, however, with growing settler opposition, procrastination on the part of the French government and consequent alienation of the nationalists. Franco-Tunisian negotiations in 1951 came to nothing and Tunisian resentment erupted in strikes and demonstrations early in 1952. In February 1952 Bourguiba and other Néo-Destour leaders were arrested on the order of a new Resident-General, Jean de Hauteclocque, and a wave of violence spread throughout the country, culminating in the arrest and removal from office of the Chief Minister and the imposition of French military control.

A new Government was formed under Salaheddine Baccouche, a French-inspired scheme of reforms designed to lead to eventual internal autonomy was announced in April, and a temporary easing of tension followed, although the now-proscribed Néo-Destour took their case to Cairo and the UN General Assembly. Against a background of increasing terrorism, countered by French repressive action, and in face of opposition from both the Néo-Destour and the settlers, little in the way of reform could be achieved. The *bey* at first refused to sign French reform decrees and when he yielded in December 1952 under the threat of deposition the proposals were promptly repudiated by the Néo-Destour.

Terrorist activities continued and a secret settler counter-terrorist organization, the "Red Hand", came into prominence. The situation, which approached civil war in 1953, with bands of *fellagha* active in the western highlands and around Bizerta, and terrorism and counter-terrorism in the towns, did not improve until July 1954, when the newly-formed Mendès-France government in France offered internal autonomy for Tunisia with responsibility only for defence and foreign affairs being retained by France. The French proposals were accepted and in August a new Tunisian government headed by Tahar ben Ammar, which contained moderate nationalists but also three Néo-Destour members, was formed. Negotiations with the French government began at Carthage in September 1954 and although they had reached deadlock when the Mèndes-France government fell in February 1955 they were resumed in March and a final agreement was signed in Paris on June 2nd.

The agreement gave internal autonomy to Tunisia while at the same time protecting French interests and preserving the close links with France. France retained responsibility for foreign affairs, defence (including the control of frontiers) and internal security.

Although it was supported by a majority of the Néo-Destour, the extremist wing, headed by the exiled Salah ben Youssef, and the old Destour and Communist elements, opposed it, as also did the settlers' organizations. An all-Tunisian cabinet was formed in September 1955 by Tahar ben Ammar, with Néo-Destour members holding six of the twelve posts.

Habib Bourguiba had returned from three years' exile in June 1955, to be followed by Salah ben Youssef in September. In October, however, ben Youssef was expelled from the party for opposition to the recent agreement and for "splitting activities". A Néo-Destour party congress at Sfax in November 1955 confirmed the expulsion and re-elected Bourguiba as party president. The congress accepted the agreement but at the same time reaffirmed that it would be satisfied only with independence and demanded the election of a constituent assembly. Clashes between "Bourguibist" and "Youssefist" factions followed and in December a conspiracy to set up a terrorist organization to prevent the implementation of the agreement was discovered. Salah ben Youssef fled to Tripoli in January 1956 and many suspected "Youssefists" were placed in detention. At the same time *fellagha* activity revived, rebel bands becoming active in the remoter parts of the country and acts of terrorism being committed against both Frenchmen and members of the Néo-Destour.

INDEPENDENCE

Against the background of these events a Tunisian delegation led by Bourguiba began independence negotiations with the French Government in Paris on February 27th, 1956. In a protocol signed on March 20th France formally recognized the independence of Tunisia and its right to exercise responsibility over foreign affairs, security and defence, and to set up a national army. A transitional period was envisaged during which French forces would gradually be withdrawn from Tunisia, including Bizerta.

Elections for a Constituent Assembly, immediately held on March 25th, resulted in all 98 seats being won by candidates of the National Front, all of whom acknowledged allegiance to the Néo-Destour. The elections were boycotted by the "Youssefist" opposition. The ministry of Tahar ben Ammar resigned and Habib Bourguiba became Prime Minister on April 11th, leading a government in which 16 of the 17 ministers belonged to the Néo-Destour.

In the early years of independence Tunisia's relations with France were bedevilled by the question of the evacuation of French forces. A Tunisian demand for their withdrawal was rejected in July 1956 by a French government preoccupied with a deteriorating situation in Algeria. Bourguiba visited Paris in September in an attempt to promote a mediated settlement in Algeria based on French recognition of Algeria's right to independence but hopes of progress in this direction were shattered by the French kidnapping in October of five leading Algerian nationalists on their way from Morocco to Algeria. Tunisia immediately severed diplomatic relations with France, anti-French riots broke out and there were clashes between French troops and Tunisian demonstrators resulting in deaths on both sides.

Moves were made early in 1957 to strengthen Tunisia's relations with her neighbours. In January a treaty of good-neighbourliness was signed with Libya and proclaimed to be a step towards establishing a "Greater Arab Maghreb", and in March, at the end of a visit by Bourguiba, a twenty-year treaty of friendship was concluded with Morocco.

The *bey*, Muhammed al-Amin, had for long been the object of criticism from Tunisian nationalist leaders who saw him as having been unwilling to participate actively in the struggle for independence and apt to rely on French support. After independence his remaining powers were whittled away and on July 25th, 1957, the Constituent Assembly decided to abolish the monarchy, proclaim Tunisia a republic and invest Bourguiba with the powers of Head of State.

RELATIONS WITH FRANCE

Although diplomatic relations with France had been resumed in January 1957, differences between the two governments in connection with the Algerian revolt soon worsened. The most serious Franco-Tunisian incident of the Algerian war occurred in February 1958 when French aircraft from Algeria attacked the Tunisian border village of Sakhiet Sidi Youssef, the scene of several clashes the previous month, killing 79 people, injuring 130 and destroying many buildings. The Tunisian government's reaction was to break off diplomatic relations with France, to forbid all French troop movements in Tunisia, to demand the immediate evacuation of all French bases, including Bizerta, and to take the matter before the UN Security Council. French troops were blockaded in their barracks and the extra-territorial status of Bizerta, from which French warships were banned, was abolished. In addition some 600 French civilians were expelled from the frontier area and five of the seven French consulates closed.

British and United States mediation was accepted and on April 15th it was agreed that all French troops would be evacuated in accordance with a jointly-agreed timetable and Tunisian sovereignty over Bizerta recognized; at the same time the French consulates would be reopened and the cases of the expelled French civilians examined. When further clashes between Tunisian and French forces occurred in May, a state of emergency covering the whole country was proclaimed and Tunisia again took the matter to the Security Council and also requested further arms supplies from the United States and Britain.

A new phase in Franco-Tunisian relations began with the accession to power of General de Gaulle in June 1958. An agreement was concluded on June 17th under which French troops stationed outside Bizerta were to be withdrawn during the next four months, while negotiations for a provisional agreement on Bizerta were to follow. Restrictions on French troops were removed and diplomatic relations resumed. By October the only French troops remaining in Tunisia were in Bizerta.

Further elimination of French interests had meanwhile commenced. In June the French-owned transport services and in August the electricity services of Tunis were nationalized. On November 29th President Bourguiba announced proposals for purchasing by 1960 all agricultural land in Tunisia owned by French citizens, for distribution to landless Tunisians.

POLITICAL CONSOLIDATION

With the improvement of relations with France the Tunisian government felt free to consolidate its internal position, by reforming the party structure of the Néo-Destour and by taking court proceedings against members of the former regime and "Youssefist" opponents. Prince Chadly, the eldest son of the ex-*bey*, and the former Prime Ministers, Tahar ben Ammar and Salaheddine Baccouche, were among those tried in the latter part of 1958 on charges which included the misuse of public funds and collaboration with the French authorities; sentences imposed ranged from heavy fines to imprisonment and loss of civic rights. Salah ben Youssef (*in absentia*) and 54 of his supporters were charged with plotting the death of President Bourguiba, smuggling arms from Libya, and aiming to overthrow the government; ben Youssef and several others were sentenced to death and most of the remainder received long prison sentences.

This trial reflected a widening breach between Tunisia and the United Arab Republic, from where ben Youssef had been conducting his activities. In October 1958 Tunisia had joined the Arab League, only to withdraw from a meeting of its Council ten days later after accusing the U.A.R. of attempts at domination. Diplomatic relations with the U.A.R. were severed the same month on the grounds of Egyptian complicity in the "Youssefist" attempt to assassinate President Bourguiba, and on the eve of ben Youssef's trial the President announced the capture of Egyptian officers who had secretly entered Tunisia to assist subversive elements to overthrow his government.

A further step in the establishment of a presidential system of government was taken with the promulgation on June 1st, 1959, of a new constitution for Tunisia, which provided for the election of the President for five years and permitted his re-election for three consecutive terms. The President was empowered to lay down the general policy of the state, choose the members of the government, hold supreme command of the armed forces and make all appointments to civil and military posts. The constitution also provided for the election of a National Assembly for five years and required the approval of the Assembly for the declaration of war, the conclusion of peace and the ratification of treaties. In elections which followed on November 8th President Bourguiba was unopposed and all 90 seats in the Assembly went to the Néo-Destour, their only opponents being the Communists.

THE BIZERTA CRISIS

During 1959 and 1960 Tunisian relations with France gradually improved. A trade and tariff agreement was signed on September 5th, 1959, and further agreements on technical co-operation and the transfer of French state property in Tunisia to the Tunisian government were concluded. In October 1959 President Bourguiba announced his support for President de Gaulle's offer of self-determination for Algeria, and Tunisia was subsequently able to act as intermediary between France and the Algerian rebels in moves towards a negotiated settlement. A meeting in Paris in February 1961 between Presidents Bourguiba and de Gaulle, at the latter's invitation, was regarded as a significant step forward in relations between the two countries.

At the same time the Tunisian claim for the handing-back of the Bizerta base was maintained and the issue came to a head on July 5th, 1961, when President Bourguiba made a formal demand for its return and repeated the claim, first put forward in 1959, to Saharan territory in Algeria adjacent to the south-western part of Tunisia. Demonstrations then took place against the continued French occupation of Bizerta and on July 17th President Bourguiba referred in the National Assembly to plans to "express our will to restore the Tunisian soil in both north and south".

Fighting between Tunisian and French troops began around the Bizerta base and in the disputed area of the Sahara; on July 19th, 1961, diplomatic relations were again severed, and Tunisia called for a meeting of the UN Security Council. The fighting ended on July 22nd with the French in firm control of the base and town of Bizerta, over 800 Tunisians having been killed. In the south a Tunisian attempt to seize the fort of Garat el-Hamel also failed. A subsequent visit to Bizerta by the UN Secretary-General, Mr. Hammarskjöld, in an attempt to promote a settlement, was unsuccessful. A French statement on July 28th said that France wished to continue to use the base whilst a state of international tension persisted but was prepared to negotiate with Tunisia about its use during this period.

The immediate results of the Bizerta crisis were a rapprochement between Tunisia and other Arab states, a cooling of relations with the West and an improvement of relations with the Communist bloc.

The final settlement of the Bizerta dispute occupied the remainder of 1961 and much of 1962, talks being held in both Rome and Paris. The Algerian cease-fire in March 1962 had an immediately beneficial effect on Franco-Tunisian relations and the French base installations at Menzel Bourguiba, near Bizerta, were handed over to Tunisia on June 30th. In March 1963 agreement was reached on the transfer of some 370,000 acres of French-owned agricultural land to the Tunisian government. Other agreements, on trade and finance, were designed to reduce Tunisia's balance of payments deficit with France.

Although Algerian independence had been warmly welcomed by Tunisia the extremist doctrines of the new state conflicted with Tunisian moderation and relations quickly deteriorated. In January 1963 the Tunisian ambassador was recalled from Algiers on the grounds of alleged Algerian complicity in an unsuccessful attempt the previous month on the life of President Bourguiba in which "Youssefists" in Algeria, as well as supporters of the old Destour and army elements, were implicated. Moroccan mediation led to a conference of the Maghreb states in Rabat in February 1963 at which the Tunisians demanded the cessation of "Youssefist" activities in Algeria, and after further negotiations a frontier agreement between Tunisia and Algeria was signed in July. Algerian, and also Egyptian, leaders attended celebrations in December of the final French evacuation of Bizerta which had taken place two months earlier.

EXPROPRIATION

Despite agreement with France in February 1964 on the provision of loans and credits, it was claimed that the March 1963 agreement on the transfer of French-owned land had placed too great a strain on Tunisian financial resources and had also resulted in over-exploitation of the land held by settlers, who had been given up to five years before relinquishing it. On May 11th the Tunisian National Assembly enacted legislation authorizing the expropriation of all foreign-owned lands; this affected the proprietors of some 750,000 acres. The French immediately suspended, then cancelled, all financial aid.

This nationalization of foreign-owned land was also seen as a step towards the development of socialism in the agrarian sector of the economy. The Néo-Destour's commitment to "Tunisian socialism" was emphasized in the change of the party's name to the Parti Socialiste Destourien (PSD) at the time of the presidential and general elections in November 1964, in which President Bourguiba was again elected unopposed and the PSD, the only party to present candidates, filled all 90 seats in the National Assembly. Subsequent cabinet changes included the appointment of the President's son, Habib Bourguiba, Jr., as Foreign Minister.

From 1964 onwards internal political conditions became more settled and the attention of the government was turned to the tasks of economic development. The hold of the PSD on the country was strengthened and President Bourguiba's dominating position was unchallenged. In 1966 the setting-up was announced of a Council of the Republic, consisting of members of the government and of the political bureau of the PSD, to ensure continuing stability, one of its functions being to nominate an interim President in the event of the President's death.

FOREIGN POLICIES

Tunisia's relations with the world beyond the Arab states and Africa after 1964 tended to be influenced by the need for foreign aid, most of which was received from Western countries (particularly from the United States but also from Federal Germany) where the moderation of Tunisian policies inspired confidence. Towards the Communist world Tunisian gestures were cautious. Some economic assistance was obtained from the Soviet Union without Tunisia having shifted her non-aligned stance and, although a visit by Chou En-lai in January 1964 was followed by the establishment of diplomatic relations between Tunisia and the People's Republic of China, President Bourguiba publicly criticized Chinese policies, including the encouragement of revolution in Africa. On African issues Tunisia took a moderate line and inside the Organization of African Unity exercised a responsible influence.

Relations with the rest of the Arab world continued to be President Bourguiba's main foreign preoccupation and here his initiatives resulted in bitter controversy. In April 1965 he openly criticized Arab League policy on Palestine and advocated a more flexible approach, with direct negotiations with Israel on the UN partition plan of 1948. This provoked severe attacks from the U.A.R. and other Arab states (excepting Morocco, Libya and Saudi Arabia), and after violent demonstrations in Cairo and Tunis both countries withdrew their ambassadors. Tunisia's refusal at the end of April to follow the example of other Arab League states in breaking off relations with Federal Germany, which had exchanged ambassadors with Israel, increased the rift. A conference of Arab heads of state at Casablanca in May at which Tunisia was not represented, categorically rejected President Bourguiba's proposal that Israel should be asked to cede territory to the Palestine refugees in return for recognition by the Arab states, and reaffirmed their determination to bring about the complete overthrow of Israel. In an open letter to those attending, President Bourguiba accused President Nasser of attempting to use the Arab League as an instrument of U.A.R. national policy and of interfering in the affairs of every Arab state; Tunisia was not prepared to take part in the debates of the Arab League in the light of this situation. In October 1966, after accusations by President Bourguiba that the U.A.R. was waging a campaign of insults against Tunisia, the severance of diplomatic relations with the U.A.R. was announced.

The six-day war between Israel and the Arab states in June 1967 brought immediate reconciliation in the Arab world despite long-standing differences. Tunisian troops were dispatched to the front but the Israeli success was so swift and the cease-fire came so soon that they were recalled before they had reached the scene of the fighting. Diplomatic relations between Tunisia and the U.A.R. were resumed and Tunisia was represented at the Arab summit meeting in Khartoum in September, which agreed not to recognize nor to negotiate with Israel.

The reconciliation between Tunisia and other Arab countries was short-lived. In May 1968, following an attack on President Bourguiba by the Syrian Prime Minister, who charged him with having betrayed the Arab struggle in Palestine, the Syrian chargé d'affaires and his staff in Tunis were accused of inciting Tunisian citizens to undertake subversive activities and ordered to leave the country. The Arab League, at a meeting in Cairo on 1st September refused to hear a statement from the Tunisian delegate criticising the Arab attitude over Israel, and particularly that of the U.A.R. On 26th September the Tunisian Government announced its intention of boycotting future meetings of the League. The statement reproached the U.A.R. with having sought to dictate to the Arab states and with having followed policies which had led to successive defeats at the hands of the Israelis and excessive dependence on communist countries. Nevertheless, Tunisian support for the Palestinian guerrilla movement was reaffirmed.

An exchange of visits by the Foreign Ministers of Tunisia and Algeria in the spring of 1969 brought about an improved climate for negotiation on the demarcation of their common frontier and on economic matters, especially those arising from the nationalization by each country of property owned by nationals of the other. On January 6th, 1970, a treaty of Co-operation and Friendship was signed, settling all outstanding issues between the two countries. It provided notably for collaboration in the exploitation of the El Borma oil-field which straddles the Tunisia-Algeria border.

THE FALL OF AHMED BEN SALAH

Between 1964 and 1969 the chief issue in internal affairs was the drive to collectivize agriculture, carried out under the leadership of Ahmed Ben Salah, Minister of Finance and Planning. The programme was carried out in the face of massive opposition in affected areas and disagreement within the ruling party itself. At the beginning of 1969 it was announced that collectivization would be completed by the end of that year, but in September in a sudden *volte-face* Ben Salah was transferred to the Ministry of Education and his agricultural policy abandoned. Ben Salah's subsequent fall was spectacular. Once generally regarded as the most brilliant member of the cabinet and a possible successor to the ageing President, he was stripped of all office, arrested and tried on a variety of charges. Found guilty in May 1970, he was sentenced to ten years' hard labour. However, he escaped from prison in February 1973 and has taken refuge in Europe, from where he has issued statements condemning President Bourguiba for acting against the people in the interests of a privileged class, and acted as the leader of the radical Popular Unity Movement (MUP), which was declared illegal in Tunisia itself.

Ben Salah was the first of several ministers to experience a sharp reversal of fortune. After his re-election in November 1969, President Bourguiba spent much of his time receiving medical treatment abroad. There was speculation that the Prime Minister, Bahi Ladgham, would be his successor, especially as he ran Tunisia for six months in the President's absence. Ladgham was chairman of the committee set up to supervise the implementation of the Cairo agreement between King Hussein of Jordan and the Palestine Liberation Organization, and as such received wide publicity throughout the Arab world. However, on the pretext that Ladgham's duties in Jordan kept him too long out of the country, President Bourguiba replaced him as Premier by Hedi Nouira in October 1970. A year later the President declared that Nouira would be his successor when the time came. In March 1973 Ladgham resigned from all his political posts. Mahmoud Mestiri was the next Minister to fall into disgrace. As Minister of the Interior in 1970 and 1971, he demanded the liberalization of government. Consequently he was dismissed from the cabinet in September 1971, expelled from the party in 1972 and from the National Assembly in May 1973. When a revision of the constitution was finally proposed in March 1973 it included almost none of the measures suggested by Mestiri to modify the presidential nature of the regime. Indeed, during the next two years President Bourguiba and Prime Minister Nouira strengthened their grip on the country. In September 1974 the ninth party congress of the PSD elected Bourguiba as President-for-Life of the party and confirmed Nouira in the post of Secretary-General. Bourguiba appointed a new political bureau of 20 members, including 14 ministers, confirming a tendency to draw party and government closer together. In November Bourguiba was re-elected President of Tunisia unopposed and National Assembly elections saw all 112 PSD candidates returned, also without opposition. The new Assembly voted amendments to the constitution designating the Prime Minister as the President's successor and allowing for the appointment of a President-for-Life, a post to which the Assembly elected Bourguiba in March 1975. Further constitutional reforms in December 1975 increased presidential powers still more. The country's motto was changed from "Liberty, Order, Justice" to "Order, Liberty, Justice".

If these formal assertions of presidential authority and popularity had little substance, there could still be no doubt of Bourguiba's hold on Tunisia. Opponents of the regime received short shrift, and between 1974 and 1976 prison sentences were passed on hundreds, mostly Marxist students, for belonging to unauthorized organizations and plotting against the state.

LIBYAN MERGER

In June 1970 the President's son, Habib Bourguiba, Jr., was replaced as Foreign Minister by Mohamed Masmoudi. From that date relations with the more radical Arab states and with radical powers outside the area improved. Normal relations were resumed with the U.A.R. and Syria, and Tunisia again took up membership of the Arab League.

On January 12th, 1974, after a meeting between President Bourguiba and Colonel Gaddafi, the Libyan leader, it was announced that Tunisia and Libya were to form a union. The announcement was greeted with general surprise for, despite an improvement in relations between the two countries in previous years, President Bourguiba had always shown himself to be hostile to union. Bourguiba was to be president of the new state, with Gaddafi as his deputy. It would seem that the union agreement was managed by Mohamed Masmoudi, who was present at the meeting, without the consent of the Prime Minister, Hedi Nouira, who was out of the country at the time. Nouira returned swiftly to Tunisia and Masmoudi was dismissed from his post in the Government and the party.

In the aftermath of this confused affair, relations with Libya were tense and uncomfortable. The Libyans continued to urge fulfilment of the union agreement, and in 1975 Bourguiba expressed concern at the increase of Libyan armed strength. Another bone of contention between the two countries was the delimitation of their respective sectors of the continental shelf, in which important deposits of petroleum were to be found. In June 1977, however, both sides agreed to submit to arbitration by the International Court of Justice, and in October a joint statement was issued, saying that Tunisia and Libya had agreed to "reactivate mutual co-operation" and set up a scheme to link the electricity networks of the two countries, while experts were to discuss the possibility of other joint ventures. Relations with Algeria also improved in 1977, after Tunisia dropped its attempts at conciliation in the Sahara dispute (in which it sided with Morocco): a co-operation agreement was signed in July by the Interior Ministers of the two countries.

DOMESTIC UNREST

By 1977, with President Bourguiba in his seventies and in poor health, there was growing uncertainty over the future of the system of government which he had dominated for so long. Hedi Nouira, his designated successor, appeared to lack the powerful personality which had kept Bourguiba in command of the country, and there were signs of a succession struggle in the increasing demands for the free development of a multi-party democracy from, among others, former ministers Ahmed Ben Salah, in exile, and Mahmoud Mestiri, leader of the unofficial liberal group of Social Democrats. The arrest and trial (from June to August 1977) of 33 members of the MUP, on charges of threatening state security and defaming the President, indicated the continuing hostility of the Government to any form of organized opposition. In June Mestiri and other liberals formed a national council for the defence of public liberties (CNDLP) calling for greater political freedom; in October Mestiri, in his first meeting with President Bourguiba since his dismissal from the Government in 1971, proposed a "national pact" which would involve full acceptance by the Government of fundamental liberties such as freedom of assembly, the formation of political parties, and the publication of opposition newspapers, as stated in the Constitution. He was told that the proposed pact would not be considered in detail until the next PSD Congress in September 1979.

Meanwhile, however, a more effective political force was beginning to make itself felt. After a number of strikes by workers in 1976, a "social contract" had been drawn up early in 1977 between the Government and the General Union of Tunisian Workers (UGTT) under the leadership of Habib Achour, involving inflation-linked pay rises for the duration of the 1977–81 plan. In spite of this agreement there were further strikes in various sectors of industry towards the end of the year, demanding better pay and conditions and backed by the UGTT, which was becoming (particularly through its weekly newspaper *Ach-Chaab*) an increasingly vocal critic of government policy and an outlet for action by political dissenters in the absence of official opposition parties. As the presence of students and unemployed young people at the accompanying demonstrations suggested, the strikes reflected a sense of dissatisfaction and frustration which went beyond industrial grievances. In December Mohamed Masmoudi, the former Foreign Minister, returned from exile in Libya and declared his support for the UGTT, thereby underlining its importance as a potential political force.

Within the Government there was disagreement as to the best way of dealing with the situation. Nouira declared that extremist infiltrators were using industrial grievances as an excuse to disrupt the country, and insisted that a forceful policy was needed to restore order. Tahar Belkhodja, the Minister of the Interior, was dismissed on December 23rd, after having suggested that the unrest should be attributed not to any one sinister cause but to social and economic problems such as a fast-increasing population and serious unemployment; only by attempting to deal with these could the crisis be averted, and rule by force would not prove to be a solution. Six other moderate members of the Cabinet resigned in sympathy, but President Bourguiba reaffirmed his support for Nouira by forming a new government in which the dissidents were replaced mainly by civil servants and technical experts, all of whom could be expected to accept Nouira's tough policy; in addition, Bourguiba brought in his son as Special Adviser.

On January 10th, 1978, Achour resigned from the political bureau and central committee of the PSD after pressure from members of the UGTT who felt that his dual role had become unacceptable. The UGTT national council called for urgent changes in the method of government and an end to the use of "intimidation" in suppressing strikes and demonstrations. On January 26th the Union finally took the drastic step of calling a general strike as a warning to the Government and in retaliation for attacks on union offices. There was rioting in Tunis and several other cities, the army was called in and at least 51 people were killed, while hundreds more were injured; a state of emergency was declared and a curfew imposed. Hundreds of demonstrators were arrested tried and imprisoned, and Achour and other members of the UGTT executive were also taken into custody, charged with subversion. The Government accused the UGTT of a long-standing conspiracy against the state and hinted at foreign backing, presumably from Libya.

The trial of Achour and 30 other union leaders did not begin until August. The criminal court at Sousse ruled itself incompetent to try the case, which was then transferred to the State Security Court, thereby becoming overtly political. Lawyers engaged by the International Confederation of Free Trade Unions, of which Achour was Vice-President, had been expelled from the country, and there was widespread international criticism of the conduct of the trial, particularly in view of the fact that the defence lawyers were given only two weeks in which to study the enormous prosecution dossier. The trade unionists refused to answer the questions put by the prosecution, alleging that they were not being properly defended, since most of the defence lawyers had been dismissed after walking out in protest at the conduct of the trial: the defendants' silence was, however, interpreted as an admission of guilt by the PSD newspaper, *al-Amal*. Eventually Achour was sentenced to 10 years' hard labour, and prison sentences were also passed on all but six of the other defendants. Although Achour and some of his colleagues were given a conditional discharge in May 1979, while 263 others serving prison terms for their involvement in the riots were pardoned by the President, it was nevertheless clear that the power of the UGTT as a source of opposition had, for the moment, been crushed. A new Secretary-General, Tijani Abid, was elected in March 1978, and the Union expressed regret at the recent events and declared its willingness to co-operate with the Government.

There was no sign of greater liberalization following the disturbances. A scheme of civilian national service was begun whereby unemployed youths and students who failed to attend classes were to be drafted to work on various development projects. This plan was given a hostile reception, being seen by critics as yet another weapon to be used against opponents of the Government. In June 1978 the Social Democrats, led by Mestiri, announced that they had applied to the authorities to form an official opposition party, but permission was not granted. In a speech made to the central committee of the PSD in March 1979, Hedi Nouira acknowledged the need for an "opening-up" of politics to involve young people and other groups, but reaffirmed that this must occur within the one-party system.

ECONOMIC SURVEY

Tunisia covers an area of 163,610 square kilometres. At the 1975 census the population was 5,588,209, with over half under 25 years old. The mid-1977 estimate was 5,930,300. The annual rate of increase in the population from 1975 to 1977 averaged 2.65 per cent. Most of the towns, and also the greater part of the rural population, are concentrated in the coastal areas. In the centre and the south, the land is infertile semi-desert, the population scattered, the standard of living very low, and the rate of growth of the population even higher than in the north.

The capital and main commercial centre is Tunis (population 550,404 in 1975) which, together with the adjacent La Goulette, is also the chief port. There are about 50,000 Europeans in Tunis, mainly French and Italians, their numbers having decreased rapidly since independence. Other towns of importance are Sfax (171,297 in 1975), which is the principal town in the south, the second port and the centre for exports of phosphates and olive oil, Djerba (70,217), Sousse (69,530), Bizerta (62,856) and Kairouan (54,546). Some 316,000 Tunisians were employed abroad in 1977, thus relieving the domestic employment situation and providing a source of foreign exchange earnings through workers' remittances from overseas.

Tunisia's development record in recent years has been fairly impressive, with per capita income reaching U.S. $850 by 1979. Total Gross Domestic Product (G.D.P.) at 1972 factor cost was TD 1,236.7 million in 1976. Agriculture, forestry and fishing accounted for over 20 per cent of G.D.P., manufacturing 11 per cent and mining and energy 6 per cent. During the Fourth Plan period (1973–76) G.D.P. grew at an average annual rate of 7.2 per cent at 1972 prices (about 6.2 per cent in real terms) and per capita G.D.P. grew in real terms at 4.6 per cent a year. This rate of growth was made possible by high prices for phosphates, petroleum and olive oil, up to 1975. However, the sharp decline in world demand for these export commodities, in addition to a downturn in the tourism sector and poor agricultural output, resulted in an overall slowdown in the country's economy during 1976. In 1977 it grew by 4.1 per cent. Rapidly rising prices and growing unemployment led to social unrest and a series of strikes in the autumn of 1977. In January 1978 a general strike and violent riots took place, indicating a rift between the Government and the unions. In October 1977 the number of unemployed was officially 250,000 but this figure did not include seasonal unemployment (particularly in the agricultural sector), temporary emigration or underemployment.

AGRICULTURE

About two-thirds of the total area of Tunisia is suitable for farming. Agriculture accounts for 40 per cent of export earnings and over 17 per cent of G.D.P., and provides a livelihood for 60 per cent of the active population. For agricultural purposes the country is composed of five different districts—the north with its mountains, having large fertile valleys; the north-east including the Cap Bon, where the soil is especially suitable for the cultivation of oranges and other citrus fruit; the Sahel where the olives grow; the centre with its high tablelands and pastures; and the south with oases and gardens where dates are prolific. Harvests vary considerably in size, depending on the uncertain rainfall, since cultivation is largely by dry farming and irrigation is as yet limited. The main cereal crops are wheat, barley, maize, oats and sorghum; fruit is also important—grapes, olives, dates, oranges and figs are grown for export as well as for the local market.

In good years there is a surplus of cereal for export but imports are frequently necessary and in both 1977 and 1978 cost TD40 million. During the 1960s the agricultural sector grew at only about 1.5 per cent a year but exceptional weather conditions and improved irrigation in 1971 and 1972 resulted in excellent agricultural yields, and during the Fourth Plan period (1973–76) good weather, except in 1974, led to an average annual growth rate of 3 per cent. However, drought in the early months of 1977 caused a 7.6 per cent fall in output. Under the 1977–81 plan the agricultural sector was expected to grow by 3.5 per cent a year.

It is hoped that the country will become self-sufficient in foodstuffs and that expansion in agriculture will be sufficient for the sector not to act as a drag on the rest of the economy. The means by which this should be achieved has been the cause of political conflict in the past decade. From 1960 until 1969, under the Minister of Planning, Ahmed Ben Salah, the basis of the Government's agrarian reform programme lay in the formation of collective "agricultural units". These units, consisting of 500 hectares at least, were to be operated as collectives in order to consolidate small peasant holdings and, later, to exploit land expropriated from French farmers or to be acquired eventually from owners of large or medium-sized farms. The system was controlled through credits provided by the Agricultural Bank. By 1968 some 220 state co-operatives were in existence and several hundred more were being put together. However, opposition to the scheme was widespread. There were revelations of unsatisfactory performance, heavy debts and misappropriation of state funds. These discoveries were instrumental in the downfall and disgrace of Ben Salah, whose position was weakened by the displeasure of foreign aid donors with his agricultural policies (especially the World Bank which had previously given some support, including an $18 million loan in 1967).

Following Ben Salah's downfall farmers were given a chance to opt out of the state system which was soon dismantled. Nonetheless a law was passed providing for the eventual break-up of large private estates, to be split among individual farmers or private co-operatives. The Government has also taken a number of measures to stimulate output, including providing funds for mechanization, reducing taxes, and subsidizing fertilizers and seed purchases. In 1975 approximately half the total cultivated area of 9 million hectares was in private hands, a further 2.1 million hectares were worked by co-operative farm groups and the remainder was farmed by state or religious institutions. In April 1974 a "supervised credits scheme" was announced, whereby small and medium-sized farms could be given supervised credits on a short-term basis to improve farming methods. It is hoped that the plan will encourage the use of modern diversified crops rather than the traditional staple crops.

Grown in a belt across the northern part of the country, wheat is the most important cereal crop. The Government guarantees the price to the grower and, amongst other incentives, pays the transport costs of merchants. In 1977 Tunisia produced only 570,000 metric tons of wheat, compared with 810,000 tons in 1976. The Government has encouraged the spread of the Mexican dwarf wheat and this variety now accounts for over one-tenth of output. Production of barley fluctuates according to the rainfall, and was 100,000 metric tons in 1977, compared with 240,000 tons in 1976.

Grapes are grown around Tunis and Bizerta. Wine production reached a peak of 1,986,000 hectolitres in 1963. By 1978 it had fallen to 424,000 hectolitres. Wine used to represent Tunisia's second most important export, but in 1978 it contributed less than one per cent of total exports.

The size of olive harvests varies considerably, partly due to the two-year flowering cycle of the tree. Tunisia is usually the world's fourth largest producer of olive oil. Production reached a record 180,000 metric tons in 1975/76, fell to only 85,000 tons in 1976/77 but rose again to 136,000 tons in 1977/78. World prices fell sharply in 1976 and 1977 but in 1978 the value of olive oil exports rose from TD 25.9 million to TD 36.5 million.

Citrus fruit is grown on the north-eastern coast. Citrus fruit production in 1977 was an estimated 160,000 metric tons, against 163,000 tons in 1976. Date production fluctuates between 40,000 and 60,000 metric tons per year, with exports steady at about 7,000 tons per year. Sugar beet production is expanding (83,000 metric tons in 1976; 118,000 metric tons in 1977) and the crop is used by the sugar refinery near Béja, which has a capacity of 1,850 tons per day. A second refinery, with a daily capacity of 4,000 tons, is being considered. In 1977 the volume of sugar exports totalled 28,474 tons. Other crops include tomatoes, chillis and peppers, melons, water melons and almonds.

In 1977 Tunisia's livestock included an estimated 3.6 million sheep, 950,000 goats, 890,000 cattle, 108,000 horses, 198,000 asses and 190,000 camels. The Government is anxious to improve cattle-stock and milk production.

Some progress has been made in the last decade towards the diversification of crops, mechanization, irrigation and increased use of fertilizers. The World Bank is supervising the overall plan for a massive water development programme which includes the construction of a number of dams for irrigation and flood prevention. Among these are the Bou Heurtma dam in Jendouba, which will irrigate 20,000 hectares and which is being financed by West Germany. the Sidi Salem dam, being financed by loans from West Germany, Kuwait and Iran; and the Sidi Saad dam near Kairouan, which will irrigate more than 4,000 hectares and will be financed by a Saudi Arabian loan. At present some 80,000 hectares of land are irrigated. It is believed that the maximum area for potential irrigation is more than 200,000 hectares, most of it in the north. A study is being undertaken of underground water resources in the Sahara.

The fishing industry employs about 22,550 people. Sfax is the main centre of the industry, which is being expanded with Government encouragement and some foreign aid. The total catch has been rising steadily in recent years and in 1977 was 53,700 metric tons. Tunisia exports fresh fish, crustaceans, molluscs and sponges.

MINERALS

Some 24,000 persons are employed in the mining and quarrying sector. The Office National des Mines is responsible for exploration for fresh mineral deposits, for the reactivation of deposits which have ceased production, for the carrying out of an elaborate modernization programme in mining methods and in the improvement of productivity. A further task is to promote exploration for oil. Minerals are the most important foreign exchange earner.

Tunisia is the fourth largest producer in the world of calcium phosphates, which are mined mainly from six large deposits in central Tunisia. Phosphates and phosphatic fertilizers taken together are Tunisia's second most important export. Production of phosphate rock reached a peak of 3.9 million metric tons in 1974, when there was a huge increase in world prices, but the market collapsed during 1975 and by 1976 output was down to 3.3 million tons. Output recovered to 3.6 million tons in 1977 and to about 3.75 million tons (against a target of 4.1 million tons) in 1978. Some 60 per cent of Tunisian phosphate exports are for Western markets, particularly France, while the balance goes to Eastern European countries and China. Government policy is to develop new resources and to concentrate efforts on the local manufacture of highly profitable fertilizer and phosphoric acid. About three-quarters of phosphate output is still exported as phosphate rock but phosphoric acid exports have increased dramatically in the past few years. Output in 1978 was 226,700 metric tons. Phosphate is used by the fertilizer industry to produce hyper-phosphate, superphosphate and triple superphosphate. A vast investment programme for the processing of phosphates is now under way and when completed will enable Tunisia's annual production of fertilizers to reach 7.5 million metric tons. Phosphate mining is now concentrated in the hands of a single concern, the Compagnie des Phosphates de Gafsa, which operates under the overall financial control of the Government.

Intensive exploration for petroleum has been carried out since the discovery of oil in neighbouring Algeria. In May 1964 a subsidiary of the Italian State hydrocarbons agency ENI found oil at El Borma in the south near the Algerian border. Recoverable reserves were estimated to be 53 million tons in 1971. The Tunisian Government took a 50 per cent share in the El Borma operating company when oil was found.

Crude oil is taken from El Borma via a spur pipeline which links with the pipeline from the oil fields at Zarzaitine and Edjeleh in Algeria to the terminal at La Skhirra on the Gulf of Gabès. Thence the crude is taken to the refinery at Bizerta.

In 1968 a second field came into operation at Douleb, 125 miles north of El Borma. This field is operated by a joint French–Tunisian company, the Société de Recherches et d'Exploitations des Pétroles en Tunisie (SEREPT), together with Aquitaine-Tunisie (a wholly owned subsidiary of the French company SNPA). A six-inch pipeline has been built to the port of La Skhirra. Other fields include Tamesmida, on the Algerian border south-west of Douleb, which was joined to the Douleb-La Skhirra pipeline in 1969; and Bihrat and Sidi al-Itayem, both of which began producing in 1972. Important new finds offshore at Ashtart, east of Sfax in the Gulf of Gabès, now account for half of Tunisia's total output. The field is operated jointly with Elf/Erap and Aquitaine-Tunisie. In February 1977 an agreement was signed by CFP, ENI and Amoco to develop another offshore discovery, the Isis field, about 100 miles from Sfax, but development of the field has been postponed. Tunisia and Libya are disputing the demarcation of the Gulf of Gabès where promising new finds have been made. CFP-Total won a 6,920 sq. km. exploration concession in central Tunisia in May 1979.

Tunisia's refinery at Bizerta has a capacity of 1.2 million tons a year. It was built with Italian assistance, and was wholly nationalized in August 1975. Plans for a second refinery have been postponed indefinitely, but the Bizerta refinery is to be expanded to a capacity of 4 million tons a year. Tunisia has to import heavier grades of crude and in 1977 imported 635,000 tons of refined products.

Tunisia produces only about 0.3 per cent of the total output of members of the Organization of Petroleum Exporting Countries (OPEC). However, petroleum is the country's main export, although imports of heavier grades are necessary. Output, which fell sharply from 5 million tons in 1975 to 3.7 million tons in 1976, rose again to 4.3 million tons in 1977 and an estimated 4.8 million tons in 1978. Target production for 1979 was 5.2 million tons.

Tunisia's reserves of natural gas are thought to be sufficient to meet local needs for the next 20 years. Production in 1977, mainly from fields in the Cap Bon area and from El Borma, totalled 256 million cubic metres in 1978. The Miskar field in the Gulf of Gabès was to have been developed but this project is now being reconsidered since it is capital-intensive and would provide relatively few new jobs, and its cost and yield are uncertain. Moreover, Tunisia is to receive about 5 per cent of the gas which will be pumped through a pipeline being built from Algeria to Italy via Tunisia. The 380 km. section crossing Tunisia will cost $500 million and is being built and financed by Italy, although it will be owned by Tunisia. A gas compression plant is to be built at Cap Bon, from where the pipeline will continue under the sea to Sicily.

In 1972 the National Assembly passed a bill to set up a state company for petroleum activities, and the Government now has a 50 per cent participation in all the operating fields except for Douleb. Apart from the State oil company and SONATRACH (the Algerian state oil company which has agreed to help in efforts to inject pressure into the El Borma field), a number of foreign companies are prospecting both on- and offshore in Tunisia, including CFP, Continental Oil,

Marathon, Gulf, Santa Fe, Mobil, Shell, Agip and Gigol.

Tunisia has numerous deposits of rich non-phosphorous iron ore; the two main deposits are at Djerissa and Douaria. Production has been falling steadily in recent years, as the reserves at Djerissa are nearing exhaustion, and in 1977 totalled 179,000 metric tons (metal content), compared with 255,000 metric tons in 1976. Exports of iron ore go mostly to markets in Italy, the United Kingdom and Greece. When current studies have been concluded, other deposits may be exploited.

Lead ore is extracted in the northern coastal region. Production in terms of contained lead was 10,200 metric tons in 1977. Zinc ore is mined in the north-western corner of Tunisia and production has been declining, from 8,800 metric tons (metal content) in 1975 to 7,300 tons in 1976 and 7,100 tons in 1977. A new zinc mine, Fej Hassine, is being developed. About 90 per cent of the salt produced by COTUSAL (300–320,000 tons a year) is exported, chiefly to Japan.

INDUSTRY

During the period of the 1973–76 plan, the industrial sector grew by 7.4 per cent instead of the 10.2 per cent planned (manufacturing by 6.9 per cent instead of 9.6 per cent planned). Under the plan, industry was allocated 32 per cent of total investment. In 1976 the sector grew by only 2.5 per cent but in 1977 it grew by about 10 per cent and this level of expansion was maintained in the first nine months of 1978. This improvement was due mainly to growth in mining and electricity.

Over half of Tunisia's industry is located in Tunis. Other industrial centres are Sousse, Sfax, Gabès, Bizerta, Gafsa, Béja and Kasserine. In the past, manufacturing tended to concentrate on the processing of raw materials, particularly foodstuffs, and was aimed at meeting domestic demand. However, government policy is now to encourage export-orientated industries. After food processing, the next most important manufacturing industry is textiles and clothing, which is an important foreign exchange earner and until 1976 was growing at about 20 per cent a year, although this rate has since slackened. It has been severely affected by EEC import restrictions, which have been partly responsible for the closure of 19 textile firms. Tunisia also manufactures glass, furniture, batteries, paint and varnish, leather goods and shoes, and rubber goods; ceramics are made at Nabeul, sugar is refined at Béja and carpets are handwoven at Kairouan. A cellulose factory and paper pulp plant at Kasserine uses locally grown esparto grass. The metallurgical, mechanical and electrical industries are expanding steadily. The El Fouladh steel complex at Menzel-Bourguiba near Bizerta is supplied with iron ore from Tamera and Djerissa. It has an annual capacity of 175,000 tons of iron bars, wire and small sections. A new steel mill, with a capacity of 100,000 tons per year, is being built at Bizerta. The state-owned STIA vehicle assembly plant at Sousse produces about 6,000 Peugeot cars and 14,000 lorries and buses per year. Nearly one-third of the components are now manufactured locally.

In 1978 Tunisia produced some 881,500 metric tons of cement, compared with 610,100 tons in 1977. With several new plants planned or under construction and some existing plants being expanded, Tunisia expects to be self-sufficient in cement by 1980.

The chemicals industry is receiving special attention from the Government. The major industry within this sector is the transformation of phosphate rock into phosphatic fertilizers and phosphoric acid, by the state-owned Industries Chimiques Maghrébines at Gabès and by mixed companies at Sfax. In 1976 the Government bought out the foreign interests in the Sfax plant, when production had been halted because of declining demand. Paint, glue and detergents are also manufactured. Tunisia plans to set up factories for the production of ammonia and compound fertilizers and hopes to establish a petrochemicals complex at Gabès producing synthetic fibres and plastics.

Production of electricity in 1978 was 1,786 million kWh., most of which was produced by thermal means; hydro-electric power is of lesser importance. Altogether there are eighteen power stations and several more are planned. Plans have been drawn up for building a nuclear reactor costing 15 million dinars at Gabes. It is expected to have a capacity of 50 MW and to produce 20,000 cubic metres of desalinized water per day.

Tunisia inherited a relatively modern system of road and rail communications from the period of colonial rule. As part of an overall transport and communications agreement announced in June 1974, Libya and Tunisia are to co-operate in the building of a railway line between Gabès and Tripoli. There are four International airports at Tunis (two), Djerba and Monastir, while a new international airport is being constructed near Tozeur. The Tunisian Navigation Company began operating in 1971 and has a total fleet of 31 vessels with an aggregate capacity of 463,000 deadweight tons. In 1975 it carried only 4 per cent of the country's imports and exports but by the end of the Fifth Plan period this proportion should rise to 30 per cent.

FINANCE

The Banque Centrale de Tunisie is the sole bank of issue of the dinar; it performs all the normal central banking functions. Apart from the commercial banks, there are financial institutions such as the Société Nationale d'Investissement which specialize in providing finance for investment purposes. SNI, established as a development finance company by the Government in 1959 with assistance from the IFC, was reorganized in 1965 into a privately controlled company. Its objectives are to invest capital, both loan and equity, in private and public enterprise in manufacturing and tourism.

Gross National Savings are more than 17 per cent of G.N.P. while capital formation is consistently over

20 per cent of G.N.P. Investments in 1976 amounted to 29 per cent of Gross Domestic Product (G.D.P.), compared with 20 per cent in 1972. The availability of local savings for investment has meant firstly that the need for foreign borrowings to finance development projects has been greatly reduced and secondly that the local financial markets have expanded and become more sophisticated to meet the demand for loans. To encourage domestic savings, interest rates on deposits and loans were raised in September 1977 and the official discount rate increased from 5 per cent to 5.75 per cent. Income tax on higher incomes and other taxes was also raised in 1977, and a new capital gains tax introduced, as part of the Government's measures to ensure sufficient domestic resources for financing the new Plan.

The current budget usually shows a surplus which is directed to capital expenditure. Direct taxation normally accounts for 20 per cent of total revenue and indirect taxes for over 50 per cent. Other sources of Government revenue are profits from state monopolies and receipts from state property and forests; oil is a growing source of Government income. The Government's administrative budget for 1979 envisages revenue of TD 625.1 million, 15 per cent more than in the previous year. Administrative spending will total TD 481.6 million (14 per cent up on 1978) while TD 143.5 million will be transferred to the capital budget. The social sectors are given priority, with 52 per cent of total recurrent spending allocations. Defence receives TD 40.3 million, compared with TD 35.14 million in 1978. The capital budget for 1979 envisages total spending at TD 383.5 million (11 per cent more than in the previous year), of which 71.3 per cent is to be financed from internal sources.

Tunisia has a recurrent deficit on its balance of trade, which is normally offset by earnings from tourism and remittances of Tunisians working abroad, so that the overall position on current payments has been roughly in balance in recent years. However, in 1975 the fall in oil prices and slump in demand for phosphates widened the visible trade gap so seriously, despite continuing good harvests, that the current balance showed a deficit of $183 million, compared with a surplus of $29 million in 1974. There was a current deficit of 388 million in 1976 and this rose to 534 million in 1977. The deficit fell to $208 million in 1978. Tunisia's rising deficits on current account have been offset by net inflows of capital. The country's foreign reserves rose from $357.5 million at the end of 1977 to $450.3 million at the end of 1978 but by April 30th, 1979, they had declined again to $369.3 million.

Following a series of strikes during 1976, a "social contract" was agreed between Government, union leaders and industrialists, which will run for the duration of the new plan, 1977–81, and will involve wage rises in all sectors, including agriculture, and a 33 per cent rise in across-the-board minimum wages. A further basic wage rise of 11 per cent was agreed in 1978 and another of 8 per cent in May 1979.

PLANNING

It was not until 1961, when the Ten-Year Perspective Plan was formulated, that the Government laid down comprehensive plans for development. The broad lines of policy put forward in the Perspective Plan were embodied in the first three-year plan (1962–64), and then in successive four-year plans (1965–68, 1969–72 and 1973–76).

Two of the major difficulties facing the planners are rapid population growth, and the consistent, heavy trade deficit which, until the early 1970s, meant that 40 per cent of development expenditure had to be financed by foreign aid. However, domestic savings financed 84 per cent of the 1973–76 plan, whereas only 75.7 per cent had been envisaged. Total investment under this plan was TD 1,605 million, or nearly TD 400 million more than the amount planned. The average annual growth of the economy during the plan period was 6 per cent (the rate aimed at had been 6.6 per cent) but 164,000 new jobs were created (against 119,000 planned).

Unemployment, generally believed to cover 15–20 per cent of the active population, is a major problem. The plan for 1977–81 seeks to create 60,000 new jobs per year but only about 45,000 per year have been created since the start of the plan. A real annual growth rate of 7.5 per cent is planned and per capita income is to rise to TD 390 by the end of the plan period. Growth of consumption, which was 8.1 per cent a year during the last plan, is to be restricted to 7.1 per cent. Total planned investment is TD 4,200 million at current prices, representing a 52 per cent increase, in real terms, on the average annual investment during the previous Plan. Domestic resources will finance 72 per cent of expenditure and the Government plans to borrow up to $500 million in medium-term loans on the international financial market. Tunisia tapped the Eurocurrency market for the first time in 1977 and obtained a $125 million loan to help finance the Miskar gas field development, a new cement plant and a new phosphate fertilizer plant. Early in 1979 a $100 million loan was being arranged through a consortium of international banks to finance the Tunisian section of the Algeria-Italy gas pipeline. The Fifth Plan emphasizes mining and energy, which are allocated 25 per cent of total investment, and manufacturing (23 per cent). The hydrocarbons sector is planned to grow at 14.1 per cent annually. Other priority areas will be transport, housing and agriculture. A greater degree of self-sufficiency in food will be aimed at, and the agricultural sector is planned to grow by 3.5 per cent per year.

There has been a notable change in Tunisian policy regarding foreign private investment since the fall of Ben Salah and Ladgham, who were widely reputed to favour economic policies tending towards socialism. The law of April 1972 provided a package of incentives to attract foreign and also domestic capital to set up manufacturing industries producing solely for export. By 1976 a total of 280 export-orientated projects had been set up under the 1972 decree, involving investment of TD 114 million. West German, Italian and wholly-owned Tunisian firms predominate. Legislation was introduced in 1974 to promote investment in domestic-orientated manufacturing. The Industrial and Decentralization Fund (FOPRODI) helps Tunisians to set up in industry and gives assistance to small and medium-sized firms.

EXTERNAL TRADE

Tunisia has a persistent trade deficit which rose steadily during the 1960s and early 1970s. There was a deficit of TD 428.3 million in 1978, compared with a deficit of TD 384.2 million in 1977. Exports are heavily dependent on sales of agricultural and mineral products, and thus on the success of the harvest and the condition of world mineral markets. Total exports rose by 13.8 per cent in 1978 to TD 453.4 million and imports grew by 12.7 per cent to reach a record TD 881.7 million. Exports covered 51.5 per cent of imports, compared with 50.9 per cent in 1977.

Crude petroleum accounted for about 43 per cent of the value of all exports in 1977, phosphates and phosphoric acid 23 per cent, textiles and other manufactured goods 19 per cent and olive oil 14 per cent. During 1975 and 1976 there was a fall in exports of olive oil, petroleum and phosphates, in terms of both value and volume, due mainly to slackening world demand. Exports of textiles and clothing, however, improved considerably in 1976. Other major exports include iron ore, lead, almonds, fresh fruit, wine and light electronics.

Tunisia's main imports are machinery, crude petroleum (grades not produced locally) and petroleum products, iron and steel, sugar (raw and refined), wheat, vegetable oils and fats, electrical machinery, vehicles, timber, raw cotton and cotton yarn. Capital goods account for about one-third of the import bill and food represented 12.5 per cent of the total in 1977.

France is Tunisia's largest single trading partner. It supplies about 34 per cent of Tunisian imports and is followed by West Germany, Italy, Greece and the U.S.A. France is the most important customer for exports, followed by Italy, West Germany, the U.S.A. and Greece. Tunisia has a persistent trade deficit with France but surpluses in its trade with the U.S.A., Greece, Algeria and Libya. EEC member countries account for around 60 per cent of Tunisia's imports and 60 per cent of its exports.

Under an agreement reached with the EEC in January 1976, the import levy on Tunisian olive oil has been abolished and tariffs on all other Tunisian agricultural products imported into EEC countries are being lowered. The agreement also covers aid to Tunisia totalling $117 million over five years, in the form of loans and grants. Nevertheless, Tunisia has been disappointed with the way in which the agreement has been implemented, and particularly with the delays in lifting the olive import restrictions. In June 1977 the EEC quota of textiles and clothing imports was reduced. This measure severely affected the Tunisian textile and clothing industries although Tunisia did not in fact fulfil its EEC quotas in 1978, as a result of a two-month strike in the industry early in 1978. Nevertheless, negotiations on this issue continued into 1979 and in March Tunisia signed an agreement, under pressure from the EEC, voluntarily to limit its textile exports to EEC countries in 1979 and 1980. In return, Tunisia wants a five-year "freeze" on its obligations to eliminate tariff barriers relating to goods imported from the EEC. Tunisia has also registered its anxiety about the possible consequences of eventual accession to EEC membership of Spain, Portugal and Greece.

TOURISM

Between 1961 and 1972 total tourist arrivals grew at a rate of 30 per cent annually. Tourism was the nation's largest foreign currency earner from 1968 to 1976 (when it was overtaken by petroleum). The number of tourists each year has fluctuated but in 1978 totalled 1,141,942 (compared with 721,000 in 1973). Tourist receipts rose from TD 139 million in 1977 to TD 158 million in 1978 and they were expected to reach TD 200 million in 1979. France is the main country of origin of tourists, followed by West Germany and the United Kingdom. There are four main centres for tourists: Hammamet, Sousse, Djerba and Tunis. A major scheme under way is the Sousse-Nord tourism project which is being financed by the Tunisian Government, the IFC and the Government of Abu Dhabi, and which will provide a total of 15,000 tourist beds in a development along two miles of coast. Another major complex is being built at Mahdia (Tunis-Nord). The *Compagnie Financière et Touristique* (COFITOUR), set up in 1970, promotes and finances three types of ventures: new hotel construction; modernization of existing hotels; and other activities related to tourism such as transport, housing and real estate. The 1977–81 Plan aims to increase the number of tourists to 1.5 million per year by 1981 and the number of beds to 85,000 (from 64,000).

FOREIGN AID

The principal sources of economic aid for Tunisia continue to be Western countries and international institutions. In recent years the U.S.A., West Germany and Saudi Arabia have been among the most important bilateral aid donors.

The World Bank Group (IBRD, IDA and IFC) has been the most important multilateral donor, providing loans and credits for investment in a variety of projects—including participation in the *Société Nationale d'Investissement* (SNI) and in COFITOUR. In 1977/78 World Bank loans to Tunisia totalled $47.5 million, for water supply development, electricity generation and agricultural credit facilities, and the Bank agreed to lend a further $35 million to assist industrial enterprises. Tunisia drew $28 million in SDRs (Special Drawing Rights) on the IMF compensatory financing facility in 1976/77, to offset its shortfall in export earnings.

Tunisia's total foreign debt outstanding at the end of 1976 totalled $1,400 million, compared with $1,200 million at the end of 1975. The debt service ratio rose from 7.5 per cent of current receipts in 1974 to 10.8 per cent in 1977. It is expected to reach 17.4 per cent by the end of the 1977–81 Plan period.

STATISTICAL SURVEY

AREA AND POPULATION

Area	Census Population				Estimated Population (mid-year)		Density (per sq. km.)
	May 3rd, 1966	May 8th, 1975					
		Males	Females	Total	1976	1977	1977
163,610 sq. km.*	4,533,351†	2,840,913	2,747,296	5,588,209	5,744,900	5,930,300	36.2

* 63,170 square miles.

† Excluding adjustment for underenumeration, estimated to have been 4.0 per cent.

PRINCIPAL COMMUNES

(1975 Census)

Tunis (capital)	550,404	Sousse	69,530	Gafsa	42,225
Sfax (Safaqis)	171,297	Bizerte (Bizerta)	62,856	Gabès	40,585
Djerba	70,217	Kairouan	54,546	Béja	39,226

BIRTHS, MARRIAGES AND DEATHS*

	Registered Live Births		Registered Marriages		Registered Deaths	
	Number	Rate (per '000)	Number	Rate (per '000)	Number	Rate (per '000)
1971	198,477	37.6	37,750	14.7	49,460	13.6
1972	199,121	38.1	45,649	17.4	56,410	11.0
1973	194,764	36.5	43,817	16.4	63,450	11.9
1974	194,600	35.6	46,672	17.1	57,555	10.5
1975†	205,400	36.6	47,900	17.0	55,500	9.9
1976†	208,800	36.6	48,000	16.6	49,200	8.5
1977†	213,300	36.4	48,000	16.4	46,000	7.9

* Birth registration is reported to be at least 90 per cent complete. Death registration is estimated to be about 65 per cent complete. UN estimates for the average annual rates are: Births 42.9 per 1,000 in 1965–70, 40.0 per 1,000 in 1970-75; Deaths 15.8 per 1,000 in 1965-70, 13.8 per 1,000 in 1970-75.

† Provisional figures.

Sources: Banque Centrale de Tunisie, and Institut National de la Statistique, Tunis.

ECONOMICALLY ACTIVE POPULATION*

(1975 census, sample tabulation)

	MALES	FEMALES	TOTAL
Agriculture, hunting, forestry and fishing	456,700	69,410	526,110
Mining and quarrying	26,780	430	27,210
Manufacturing	115,820	124,820	240,640
Electricity, gas and water	11,160	520	11,680
Construction	139,560	1,180	140,740
Trade, restaurants and hotels	112,410	7,220	119,630
Transport, storage and communications	54,530	2,850	57,380
Financing, insurance, real estate and business services	5,800	1,910	7,710
Community, social and personal services	170,530	47,860	218,390
Activities not adequately described	133,260	19,950	153,210
TOTAL	1,226,550	276,150	1,502,700

* Figures refer to persons aged 15 years and over, excluding those seeking work for the first time, numbering 119,120 (males 91,760, females 27,360). In addition, the economically active population included 107,240 persons (males 65,210, females 42,030) aged 10 to 15 years. The total labour force was thus 1,729,060 (males 1,383,520, females 345,540).

Source: International Labour Office, *Year Book of Labour Statistics*.

AGRICULTURE

PRINCIPAL CROPS

('000 metric tons)

	1974	1975	1976	1977
Wheat	857	943	810	570
Barley	228	272	240	100
Potatoes	100	110	105	85
Olives	650	468	870	425
Tomatoes	238	256	250	320
Chillis and peppers	103	100	120	125
Onions	74	69	70	83
Water melons and melons	200	195	250	210
Grapes	180	169	139	185
Dates	52	43	50	50
Sugar beet	45	52	83	118
Apricots	22	25	29	28
Citrus fruit	107	131	163	160
Almonds	23	25	24	26
Tobacco	2.2	3.3	3.8	4.4

Source: Ministère du Plan, Tunis.

LIVESTOCK

(FAO estimates—'000 head)

	1975	1976	1977
Horses	104	106	108
Asses	193	195	198
Cattle	870	880	890
Camels	180	195	190
Sheep	3,400	3,526	3,600
Goats	850	900	950
Chickens	14,500	14,839	15,100

Source: FAO, *Production Yearbook*.

LIVESTOCK PRODUCTS

('000 metric tons)

	1975	1976*	1977*
Beef and veal	26†	26	27
Mutton and lamb	34†	35	36
Poultry meat	24†	25	25
Cows' milk	186	191	195
Hen eggs	16.8	17.8	18.1
Wool (greasy)	6.1	6.4	6.5
Cattle hides	6.0*	6.3	7.2
Sheepskins	5.7*	5.9	6.1

* FAO estimates. † Unofficial figure.

Source: FAO, *Production Yearbook*.

FORESTRY

ROUNDWOOD REMOVALS
('000 cubic metres, excluding bark)

	Coniferous (soft wood)			Broadleaved (hard wood)			Total		
	1975	1976	1977	1975	1976	1977	1975	1976	1977
Sawlogs, veneer logs and logs for sleepers	8	4	10	—	—	—	8	4	10
Pitprops (mine timber)	—	—	—	—	2	2	—	2	2
Pulpwood	12	12	12*	—	—	—	12	12	12*
Other industrial wood	8	7	7	57*	59*	60*	65	66	67
Fuel wood	175	175*	175*	1,550*	1,593*	1,640*	1,725	1,768*	1,815*
Total	203	198	204	1,607	1,593	1,702	1,810	1,852	1,906

* FAO estimate.

Source: FAO, *Yearbook of Forest Products.*

FISHING

('000 metric tons, live weight)

	1974	1975	1976	1977
Total catch	42.0	45.0	49.0	53.7

Source. Ministère de l'Agriculture (Direction de la Pêche), Tunis.

MINING

('000 metric tons)

	1973	1974	1975	1976	1977
Iron Ore*	433	422	326	255	179
Lead Ore*	15.6	12.5	10.8	10.5	10.2
Calcium Phosphate	3,474	3,827	3,540	3,305	3,615
Zinc Ore*	8.8	6.2	6.0	7.3	7.1
Crude Petroleum	3,878	4,139	4,609	3,710	4,265
Natural Gas (million cu. metres)	113.8	207.6	210.5	214.0	229.8

* Metal content of ore.

Source: Institut National de la Statistique.

INDUSTRY

SELECTED PRODUCTS

		1975	1976	1977	1978
Superphosphates	'000 metric tons	305	343.7	489.1	508.1
Phosphoric acid	,, ,, ,,	102	236.7	221.4	226.7
Cement	,, ,, ,,	615	478.3	610.1	881.5
Lead	,, ,, ,,	23.3	23.4	19.2	16.3
Electric power	million kWh.	1,346	1,524	1,518.0	1,786.3
Town gas	'000 cubic metres	20.2	21.7	22.1	23.6
Beer	'000 hectolitres	308	278.5	302.2	329.3
Cigarettes	millions	4,863	n.a.	n.a.	n.a.
Wine	'000 hl.	990	604	650	424
Olive oil	'000 metric tons	117	180	85	136
Semolina	,, ,, ,,	221.7	237.4	287.8	324.4
Flour	,, ,, ,,	267	284.5	299.6	321.0
Esparto pulp	,, ,, ,,	21	19.4	20.7	21.5
Refined sugar	,, ,, ,,	58	n.a.	n.a.	n.a.
Cast iron and bar iron	,, ,, ,,	377.1	331	—	443.1
Lime	,, ,, ,,	283	318.5	337.7	426.5
Petrol	,, ,, ,,	140	137.5	150	159.3
Kerosene	,, ,, ,,	84	107.6	101	n.a.
Diesel oil	,, ,, ,,	350	323.7	339.6	317.1
Fuel oil	,, ,, ,,	483	468.5	509	501.6

Source: Banque Centrale de Tunisie.

FINANCE

1,000 millimes = 1 Tunisian dinar.

Coins: 1, 2, 5, 10, 20, 50, 100 and 500 millimes; 1 and 5 dinars.

Notes: 500 millimes; 1, 5 and 10 dinars.

Exchange rates (April 1979): £1 sterling = 846.4 millimes; U.S. $1 = 411.3 millimes.

100 Tunisian dinars = £118.15 = $243.13.

Note: The Tunisian dinar was introduced in November 1958, replacing the Tunisian franc (then at par with the old French franc) at the rate of 1 dinar = 1,000 francs. In August 1957 the exchange rate was fixed at $1 = 420 Tunisian francs, so the initial rate for the new currency was $1 = 420 millimes (1 dinar = $2.381). From December 1958 the relationship to French currency was 1 dinar = 1,175 old francs (11.75 new francs from January 1960). These rates remained in force until September 1964, when the dinar was devalued by 20 per cent. Between September 1964 and August 1971 the official exchange rate was $1 = 525 millimes (1 dinar = $1.905), with the dinar valued at 9.40 French francs until August 1969 and at 10.575 French francs thereafter. From December 1971 to February 1973 the par value was $1 = 483.55 millimes (1 dinar = $2.068). In terms of sterling, the exchange rate between November 1967 and June 1972 was £1 = 1.26 dinars. In February 1973 a new par value of $1 = 435.2 millimes (1 dinar = $2.298) was established but in March 1973 the French authorities ceased to maintain the franc-dollar rate within previously agreed margins. Tunisia retained its currency link with France, thus allowing its exchange rate against the dollar to vary widely from the par value. In January 1974 the Tunisian authorities announced that the franc-dinar rate would henceforth take into account the daily quotations of the Deutsche Mark in terms of francs on the Paris exchange market. The average market rates were: $1 = 477.2 millimes in 1972; $1 = 420.0 millimes in 1973; $1 = 436.5 millimes in 1974; $1 = 402.3 millimes in 1975; £1 = 428.8 millimes in 1976; $1 = 429.0 millimes in 1977; $1 = 416.2 millimes in 1978.

CURRENT BUDGET
('000 dinars)

Ministry	1976	1977	1978
Prime Minister's Office	4,547	4,990	11,335
Finance	121,257	147,222	195,237
Education	87,235	112,733	118,300
Defence	27,008	32,199	35,143
Public health	31,925	32,626	44,130
Interior	28,425	34,102	35,483
Agriculture	23,130	28,578	31,815
Public works	10,084	11,847	13,200
Social affairs	8,334	9,639	10,543
Youth and sports	6,390	7,823	8,583
Communications and transport	5,298	6,860	6,172
Information	4,837	5,483	9,598
Cultural affairs	3,392	4,069	4,262
Justice	3,623	4,012	4,571
Planning	1,286	1,412	1,532
Total (incl. others)	381,711	467,390	541,200

Capital Budget ('000 dinars): 248,918 in 1976; 318,216 in 1977; 368,000 in 1978.

1979: Total current expenditure 625.1 million dinars.

Sources: Ministère des Finances, Tunis; (1978 figures) Banque Centrale de Tunisie.

NATIONAL ACCOUNTS
(million dinars at current prices)

Economic Activity	1974	1975	1976	1977
Agriculture and Forestry	279.2	292.3	318.0	298.0
Fishing	10.1	13.4	15.0	18.2
Crude Petroleum and Petroleum Products	117.8	116.2	102.2	122.5
Other Mining and Quarrying	57.6	55.9	26.2	27.0
Manufacturing*	151.4	155.9	177.0	200.3
Electricity, Gas and Water Supply	19.7	23.9	27.8	32.3
Construction	98.1	136.3	163.7	196.7
Transport and Communications	73.8	81.0	102.8	118.8
Tourism	44.2	65.7	68.7	68.7
Owner-occupied Dwellings	66.4	73.8	522.8	606.2
Public Administration and Defence	160.6	201.7		
Wholesale and Retail Trade	266.1	315.4		
Other Producers and Services†				
Gross Domestic Product at Factor Cost	1,345.0	1,531.5	1,653.9	1,818.5
Indirect Taxes‡	205.1	215.6	255.0	308.0
Less Subsidies	23.1			
Gross Domestic Product in Purchasers' Values	1,527.0	1,747.1	1,908.9	2,126.5
Imports of Goods and Services	542.0	629.7	715.2	813.0
Less Exports of Goods and Services	547.4	545.6	551.1	612.0
Available Resources	1,521.6	1,831.2	2,073.0	2,327.5
Government Final Consumption	202.9	245.3	288.0	351.0
Private Final Consumption	964.7	1,050.9	1,175.0	1,306.5
Increase in Stocks	36.0	85.0	40.0	670.0
Gross Fixed Capital Formation	318.0	450.0	570.0	

* Excluding petroleum products.

† Including financial institutions, business services and community, social and personal services.

‡ Including import duties.

EXTERNAL TRADE

('000 dinars)

	1972	1973	1974	1975	1976	1977	1978
Imports	222,219	286,087	488,658	572,815	656,718	782,466	881,707
Exports	150,327	178,835	397,695	345,580	338,262	398,246	453,375

PRINCIPAL COMMODITIES

('000 dinars)

Imports	1975	1976	1977	1978
Wheat and meslin (unmilled)	14,454	16,456	24,405	12,100
Sugar (raw and refined)	25,038	25,741	17,808	16,077
Soybean oil	16,334	545	2,274	9,118
Crude petroleum	34,469	45,650	43,975	35,712
Petroleum products	16,996	23,621	31,171	40,863
Pharmaceutical products	11,324	11,709	15,964	14,960
Wood	9,280	16,569	18,682	19,122
Raw cotton, cotton yarn and fabrics	10,577	15,488	20,690	19,175
Plastics and products	9,445	11,018	15,164	17,883
Iron and steel	39,213	41,869	52,422	63,344
Machinery (non-electric)	87,674	104,599	130,517	158,661
Electric machinery	29,398	48,231	52,268	57,765
Tractors	9,104	7,309	7,400	9,891
Road motor vehicles	17,134	19,690	12,151	16,168
Aircraft and air equipment	5,549	10,060	15,350	876
Optical and scientific equipment	8,995	10,928	11,948	13,847
Total (incl. others)	572,815	656,718	782,466	881,707

Exports	1975	1976	1977	1978
Fresh fruit	5,794	5,477	7,455	10,034
Olive oil	31,031	36,275	25,893	36,493
Wine	6,940	4,631	2,186	4,102
Natural phosphates	46,885	26,108	22,032	17,323
Crude petroleum	144,557	138,516	161,016	169,242
Phosphoric acid	14,988	19,811	20,699	22,544
Superphosphates	16,659	12,068	19,339	23,087
Cotton fabrics	3,089	5,781	7,648	4,874
Clothing and accessories	11,812	22,038	48,047	58,118
Iron and steel	1,138	655	846	4,235
Refined lead	3,695	3,971	4,111	3,192
Total (incl. others)	345,580	338,262	398,246	453,375

Source: Banque Centrale de Tunisie.

PRINCIPAL TRADING PARTNERS
('000 dinars)

IMPORTS	1975	1976	1977	1978
Belgium/Luxembourg	16,318	20,627	18,836	27,936
Brazil	11,337	7,629	11,977	5,047
Canada	7,079	9,296	8,475	13,571
France	196,604	210,858	219,437	301,628
Germany, Federal Republic	48,396	65,968	87,895	108,290
Greece	14,923	15,911	19,539	35,393
Iraq	23,263	23,402	17,904	11,572
Italy	53,402	58,855	77,680	88,053
Netherlands	13,716	20,473	25,521	26,609
Poland	6,478	4,412	7,067	6,178
Saudi Arabia	11,488	23,703	26,471	19,623
Spain	14,343	17,281	28,603	27,019
Sweden	7,550	15,236	7,740	6,856
U.S.S.R.	2,186	6,791	5,312	6,138
United Kingdom	29,763	19,940	22,356	18,236
U.S.A.	38,468	40,811	54,331	39,134
Yugoslavia	4,599	8,876	8,302	8,377
TOTAL (incl. others)	572,815	656,718	782,466	881,706

EXPORTS	1975	1976	1977	1978
Algeria	14,470	9,359	9,371	5,974
Belgium/Luxembourg	3,240	6,550	14,284	14,039
Brazil	993	2,733	2,136	2,456
Bulgaria	3,493	59	1,075	689
Czechoslovakia	5,105	1,689	2,452	1,688
France	65,883	57,733	71,125	75,978
Germany, Federal Republic	26,323	23,367	65,093	73,336
Greece	48,723	52,004	54,246	42,570
Italy	58,999	72,615	55,266	73,755
Libya	18,769	4,582	9,949	27,288
Netherlands	8,636	11,633	17,253	17,648
Spain	4,853	1,247	1,523	1,287
Switzerland	791	1,194	1,749	1,478
Turkey	11,682	9,451	5,221	6,120
U.S.S.R.	3,642	3,177	1,791	1,661
United Kingdom	1,976	2,131	3,303	3,692
U.S.A.	35,559	46,516	42,310	39,525
TOTAL (incl. others)	345,580	338,262	398,246	453,375

Source: Banque Centrale de Tunisie.

TRANSPORT

RAILWAYS

	1975	1976	1977
Passenger-km. (million)	588	641	713
Freight ton-km. (million)	1,283	1,277	1,339

Source: Institut National de la Statistique.

ROAD TRAFFIC
(motor vehicles in use)

	1974	1975	1976
Private cars	94,161	99,362	105,379
Buses	2,698	3,068	3,443
Commercial vehicles	53,122	59,900	68,197
Motor cycles	10,370	10,581	10,691

SEA-BORNE SHIPPING

	1973	1974	1975	1976
Vessels ('000 net registered tons):				
Total entered and cleared*	25,933	28,256	n.a.	n.a.
Passenger journeys	246,625	223,618	n.a.	n.a.
Total goods loaded ('000 metric tons)†	17,241	16,749	16,234	17,139
La Skhirra†	12,187	10,754	9,961	11,030
Other ports	5,055	5,995	6,273	6,109
International goods loaded ('000 metric tons)†	16,425	15,667	15,362	16,286
La Skhirra†	12,113	10,539	9,886	10,947
Other ports	4,312	5,128	5,476	5,339
Coastwise goods loaded ('000 metric tons)	816	1,082	872	853
Total goods unloaded ('000 metric tons)	4,184	5,059	4,778	5,566
International shipping	3,212	3,977	3,906	4,713
Coastwise shipping	972	1,082	872	853

* Excluding the petroleum port of La Skhirra.

† Including Algerian crude petroleum loaded at La Skhirra.

1977: International freight traffic ('000 metric tons, excl. La Skhirra): Goods loaded 4,394; Goods unloaded 6,558.

CIVIL AVIATION

('000)

	1976	1977
Kilometres flown	16,944	16,163
Passengers carried	1,128	1,127
Passenger-km.	1,499,858	1,496,135
Freight ton-km.	7,023	8,437
Mail ton-km.	791	825

Source: Tunis Air.

TOURISM

FOREIGN TOURIST ARRIVALS BY NATIONALITY

('000)

	1973	1974	1975	1976	1977
Algeria	18.6	25.3	34.4	23.5	60.4
Austria	13.5	20.6	32.3	28.9	27.9
Belgium	37.6	34.9	45.2	43.3	36.6
France	171.7	207.9	322.6	371.5	386.5
Germany, Federal Republic	104.8	90.5	139.9	139.4	151.0
Italy	39.7	57.2	71.1	50.8	53.5
Libya	63.1	63.4	55.6	10.1	39.6
Netherlands	21.6	28.1	42.1	38.8	29.5
Scandinavia	36.1	38.7	75.9	78.0	53.7
Switzerland	30.6	28.2	41.6	39.4	37.6
United Kingdom	124.1	64.2	72.6	79.4	58.9
U.S.A.	13.1	11.3	12.4	13.1	12.2
TOTAL (incl. others)	721.9	716.0	1,013.8	977.8	1,016.0

Tourist Accommodation: (1977) 64,097 tourist beds.

Tourist Nights: (1977) 8,117,577.

Tourist Spending: (1975) 65.7m. dinars, (1976) 127m. dinars, (1977) 139.4m. dinars.

Source: Office National du Tourisme, Tunis.

EDUCATION

	Institutions		Teachers		Pupils	
	1976/77	1977/78	1976/77	1977/78	1976/77	1977/78
Primary	2,374	2,423	23,983	24,871	957,107	981,255
Secondary	186	193	9,843	10,177	195,788	215,044
of which:						
Secondary Technical	n.a.	n.a.	n.a.	n.a.	40,688	50,887
Teacher Training	4	6	86	125	1,079	1,987
University of Tunis	1	1	1,349	2,008	17,908	20,909

Source: Institut National de la Statistique.

THE CONSTITUTION

Tunisia, which had been a French Protectorate since 1883, achieved full internal autonomy in September 1955, and was finally recognized as a fully independent sovereign State by the Protocol of Paris of March 20th, 1956, by which France abrogated the former treaties and conventions.

NATIONAL ASSEMBLY

The Constitution was proclaimed by the Constituent Assembly on June 1st, 1959. Tunisia is a free, independent and sovereign republic. Legislative power is exercised by the National Assembly which is elected (at the same time as the President) every five years by direct universal suffrage. Every citizen who has had Tunisian nationality for at least five years and who has attained twenty years of age has the vote. The National Assembly shall hold two sessions every year, each session lasting not more than three months. Additional meetings may be held at the demand of the President or of a majority of the deputies.

HEAD OF STATE

The President of the Republic is both Head of State and Head of the Executive. He must be not less than 40 years of age. There is no limit to the number of terms a President may serve. The President is also the Commander-in-Chief of the army and makes both civil and military appointments. The Government may be censured by the National Assembly, in which case the President may dismiss the Assembly and hold fresh elections. If censured by the new Assembly thus elected, the Government must resign. Should the Presidency fall vacant for any reason before the end of a President's term of office, the Prime Minister shall assume the Presidency until the end of the term.

COUNCIL OF STATE

Comprises two judicial bodies: (1) an administrative body dealing with legal disputes between individuals and State or public bodies; (2) an audit office to verify the accounts of the State and submit reports.

ECONOMIC AND SOCIAL COUNCIL

Deals with economic and social planning and studies projects submitted by the National Assembly. Members are grouped in seven categories representing various sections of the community.

THE GOVERNMENT

HEAD OF STATE

President-for-Life: Habib Bourguiba (took office as President July 25th, 1957; proclaimed Life President March 18th, 1975).

THE CABINET

(*June* 1979)

Prime Minister: Hedi Nouira.

Special Adviser to the President: Habib Bourguiba, Jr.

Minister responsible to the Prime Minister: Mohamed Sayah.

Minister responsible to the Prime Minister in charge of Planning: Mustapha Zannouni.

Minister for Foreign Affairs: Mohamed Fitouri.

Minister of National Defence: Abdallah Farhat.

Minister of Industry, Mines and Energy: Rachid Sfar.

Minister of Commerce: Slaheddine Mberek.

Minister of Health: Fouad Mbazaa.

Minister of Cultural Affairs: Mohammed Yaalaoui.

Minister of Finance: Abdelaziz Mathari.

Minister of Justice: Slaheddine Baly.

Minister of the Interior: Dhaoui Hannablia.

Minister of Agriculture: Hassan Belkhodja.

Minister of Education: Mohamed Mzali.

Minister of Higher Education and Scientific Research: Abdelaziz Ben Dhia.

Minister of Transport and Communications: Abdelhamid Sassi.

Minister of Equipment: Lassaad Ben Osman.

Minister of Social Affairs: Mohamed Jomaa.

Minister of Youth and Sport: Hedi Zghal.

Minister for Relations with the National Assembly: Othman Kecherid.

Minister of Information: (vacant).

Secretary of State for Equipment: LARBI MELLAKH.

Secretary of State for Foreign Affairs: IBRAHIM TURKI.

Secretary of State responsible to the Minister of Social Affairs, in charge of Professional Training: NOUREDDINE KTARI.

NATIONAL ASSEMBLY

Speaker: SADEK MOQADDEM.

ELECTION, NOVEMBER 1974

All 112 seats were won by the Destour Socialist Party. There were no opposition candidates.

POLITICAL ORGANIZATIONS

The Parti Socialiste Destourien (Destour Socialist Party) is the only legal party in Tunisia.

Parti Socialiste Destourien—PSD: blvd. 9 Avril 1938, Tunis; f. 1934 by Habib Bourguiba, as a splinter par tyfrom the old *Destour* (Constitution) Party; moderate left-wing republican party, which achieved Tunisian independence; 9th Congress held Sept. 1974; there is a political bureau of 20 members, including 14 ministers, and a central committee of 60 elected by the party congress; 765,310 mems. (1978); Sec.-Gen. HEDI NOUIRA; Chairman-for-Life HABIB BOURGUIBA.

The following organizations operate clandestinely:

Front National Progressiste Tunisien (FNPT): comprises the Union Socialiste Arabe de Tunisie (Nasserites), Mouvement Socialiste Arabe de Tunisie (Baathists) and the Yousefistes; Sec.-Gen. MAHREZ SAADAWI.

Mouvement de l'Unité Populaire (MUP): supports radical reform; Sec.-Gen. AHMED BEN SALAH.

Social Democrats: in favour of a pluralist political system; Sec.-Gen. MAHMOUD MESTIRI.

DIPLOMATIC REPRESENTATION

EMBASSIES ACCREDITED TO TUNISIA

(In Tunis unless otherwise indicated)

Algeria: 18 rue de Niger; *Ambassador:* ALI KEFFI.

Argentina: Algiers, Algeria.

Australia: Algiers, Algeria.

Austria: 17 ave. de France; *Ambassador:* ERICH BINDER.

Bangladesh: Tripoli, Libya.

Belgium: 47 rue du 1er Juin; *Ambassador:* J. BASSOMPIERRE.

Brazil: 15 rue Es-Sayouti, El Menzah; *Ambassador:* DONATELLO GRIECO.

Bulgaria: 16 rue Moutanabbi, El Menzah; *Ambassador:* IVAN ABADJIEV.

Cameroon: Paris, France.

Canada: 2 place Virgile, Notre Dame, Cité El Mahdi, Mutuelleville; *Ambassador:* JEAN TOUCHETTE.

Central African Empire: Algiers, Algeria.

Chad: Cairo, Egypt.

China, People's Republic: 41 ave. de Lesseps; *Ambassador:* TSUI TSIEN.

Costa Rica: Madrid, Spain.

Czechoslovakia: 98 rue de la Palestine, B.P. 680; *Ambassador:* CESPMIR JANOUT.

Denmark: Algiers, Algeria.

Finland: Algiers, Algeria.

France: place de l'Indépendance; *Ambassador:* PHILIPPE REBEYROL.

Gabon: Paris, France.

The Gambia: Tripoli, Libya.

German Democratic Republic: ave. d'Afrique, El Menzah; *Ambassador:* Dr. ALFRED PEUKERT.

Germany, Federal Republic: 18 rue Félicien Challaye *Ambassador:* KLAUS TERFLOTH.

Ghana: *Ambassador:* ANTHONY W. EPHSON.

Greece: 4 rue El Jahedh, El Menzah; *Ambassador:* DIONYSIOS XENOS.

Guinea: Algiers, Algiera.

Hungary: Algiers, Algeria.

India: Rabat, Morocco.

Indonesia: Algiers, Algeria.

Iran: 10 rue Dr. Burnet, Belvédère; *Ambassador:* IRAJ AMINI (also accred. to Libya).

Iraq: 125 ave. de la Liberté; *Ambassador:* MOHAMED SABRI AL-HADITHI.

Ireland: Madrid, Spain.

Italy: 37 rue Gamal Abdel Nasser; *Ambassador:* ELIO GIUFFRIDA.

Ivory Coast: 1 place Pasteur; *Ambassador:* CHARLES AILLOT ABOUT.

Japan: 16 rue Djebel-Aurès, Notre Dame; *Ambassador:* YUTAKA TAMURA.

Jordan: 27 ave. Lacépède, Notre Dame; *Ambassador:* SAMI CHAMAYLIH.

Kenya: Cairo, Egypt.

Korea, Democratic People's Republic: *Ambassador:* PAK CHANG-SUK.

Korea, Republic: 7 rue Teymour, El Menzah; *Ambassador:* HONG IEL.

Kuwait: 22 rue Jacques Cartier; *Ambassador:* MEJREN AHMED EL HAMAD.

Lebanon: 4 impasse Ibn Chabbat; *Ambassador:* JOSEPH SALAMA.

Libya: 48 *bis* rue du 1er Juin; *Ambassador:* ABDEL-HAMID AS-SIDI AZ-ZINTANI.

Madagascar: Algiers, Algeria.

Mali: Paris, France.

Malta: Tripoli, Libya.

Mauritania: 4 rue Apollo XI; *Ambassador:* JIDDOU OULD SALEK (also accred. to Greece and Yugoslavia).

Mexico: Rome, Italy.

Mongolia: Algiers, Algeria.

Morocco: 5 rue Didon, Notre Dame; *Ambassador:* MOHAMED TAZI.

Netherlands: 24–26 place d'Afrique; *Ambassador:* M. C. T. R. VAN BAARDA.

Niger: Algiers, Algeria.

Nigeria: Paris, France.

Norway: Rabat, Morocco.

Oman: 129, ave. de Lesseps; *Ambassador:* GHALEB ABDULLAH GIBRAN (also accred. to Algeria).

Pakistan: 29 rue Iman Mislim; *Ambassador:* BAKHTIAR ALI.

Peru: Cairo, Egypt.

Philippines: Algiers, Algeria.

Poland: 12 rue Didon, Notre Dame; *Ambassador:* HANRIK SOKOLAK.

Portugal: 2 rue Chakib Arsalane, Belvédère; *Ambassador:* HENRIQUE GUILHERME AUGUSTE DE FIGAREDO SILVA MARTINS.

Qatar: 1 rue Enée, Notre Dame; *Ambassador:* ALI OMEIR ENNOAIMI.

Romania: 6 rue Magon, Notre Dame; *Ambassador:* (vacant).

Rwanda: Cairo, Egypt.

Saudi Arabia: 16 rue d'Autriche, Belvédère; *Ambassador:* ABDELRAHMAN EL OMRAN.

Senegal: 122 ave. de la Liberté; *Ambassador:* IBRAHIM DIENG.

Spain: 75 ave. Taïeb Mehiri; *Ambassador:* EMILIO MARTIN.

Sudan: 117 ave. de Lesseps; *Ambassador:* JAAFAR ABOU HADJ.

Sweden: 17 ave. de France; *Ambassador:* OLOV TERNSTRÖM.

Switzerland: 17 ave. de France; *Ambassador:* HEINZ LANGENBACHER.

Syria: 128 ave. de Lesseps; *Ambassador:* MOHAMED ISSAM AL-NAIEB.

Tanzania: Rome, Italy.

Thailand: Madrid, Spain.

Turkey: 47 ave. Mohamed V; *Ambassador:* MUAMMER AKGER.

Uganda: Cairo, Egypt.

U.S.S.R.: 31 rue du 1er Juin; *Ambassador:* BORIS L. KOLOKOLOV.

United Arab Emirates: 84 ave. Hedi Chaker; *Ambassador:* HAMAD SALEM AL-MAQAMI.

United Kingdom: 5 place de la Victoire; *Ambassador:* J. H. LAMBERT.

U.S.A.: 144 ave. de la Liberté; *Ambassador:* EDWARD W MULCAHY.

Vatican City: Algiers, Algeria.

Venezuela: Tripoli, Libya.

Viet-Nam: 23 rue Jacques Cartier; *Ambassador:* TRAN VAN HUNG.

Yemen Arab Republic: Algiers, Algeria.

Yugoslavia: 4 rue du Libéria; *Ambassador:* MIODRAG KROZIG.

Zaire: 5 rue de Niger; *Ambassador:* AMISI TANGOLA.

Zambia: Paris, France.

Tunisia also has diplomatic relations with Afghanistan, Albania, Bahrain, Benin, the Congo, Iceland, Liberia, Luxembourg, Mauritius, Monaco, Panama, Sierra Leone, Somalia, Togo and Upper Volta.

JUDICIAL SYSTEM

Cour de Cassation: Tunis; has three civil and one criminal sections.

There are three Courts of Appeal, at Tunis, Sousse and Sfax, and thirteen courts of First Instance, each having three chambers except the Court of First Instance of Tunis which has eight chambers.

Cantonal Justices have been set up in 51 areas.

RELIGION

The Constitution of 1956 recognizes Islam as the State religion, with the introduction of certain reforms, such as the abolition of polygamy. Minority religions are Jews (20,000), Roman Catholics (20,000), Greek Orthodox and a number of French and English Protestants.

Grand Mufti of Tunisia: Sheikh MOHAMMED HABIB BELKHODJA.

Reformed Church of Tunisia: 36 rue Charles de Gaulle, Tunis; *Pastor:* MARSTON SPEIGHT.

Roman Catholic Prelature: 4 rue d'Alger, Tunis; *Titular Archbishop of Tunis:* Mgr. MICHEL CALLENS.

THE PRESS

DAILIES

TUNIS

L'Action: rue 2 Mars 1934; f. 1932; organ of the Destour Socialist Party (PSD); French; Chief Editor ABDELHAY SEGHAÏER; circ. 50,000.

al-Amal (*Action*): 15 rue 2 Mars 1934; f. 1934; organ of the PSD; Arabic; Dir. MOHAMED LARBI ABDERRAZAK; circ. 50,000.

Assabah (*The Echo*): 4 rue Ali Bach-Hamba; f. 1951; Arabic; Dir. HABIB CHEIKH-ROUHOU; circ. 50,000.

La Presse de Tunisie: 6 rue Ali Bach-Hamba; f. 1936; French; Dir. ABDELHAKIM BELKHIRIA; circ. 40,000.

Le Temps: 4 rue Ali Bach-Hamba; f. 1975; general news; French; Dir. HABIB CHEIKH-ROUHOU.

PERIODICALS

TUNIS

Ach-Chaab: 21 place M'Hamed Ali; f. 1959; organ of Union Générale Tunisienne du Travail; Arabic; weekly.

ach-Chabab: Maison du PSD, blvd. 9 Avril 1938; publ. of the Union of Tunisian youth; Arabic language; monthly.

Ar-Rai: opposition newspaper; f. 1977 by Social Democrat group; weekly (suspended for three months from January 1979); Dir. HASIB BIN-AMMAR; circ. 25,000.

Assada: 4 rue Ali Bach-Hamba; political and general; weekly; Arabic; Dir. HABIB CHEIKH-ROUHOU.

Biladi: rue 2 Mars 1934; f. 1974; political and general weekly for Tunisian workers abroad; Arabic; Dir. HOUCINE EL MAGHERBI; circ. 90,000.

Bulletin Mensuel de Statistique: Institut National de Statistique, B.P. 65, 27 rue de Liban; monthly.

Conjoncture: Banque Centrale de Tunisie, 7 place de la Monnaie; economic and financial surveys; quarterly.

Il Corriere di Tunisi: 4 rue de Russie; Italian; weekly; Dir. M. FINZI.

Démocratie: f. 1978; organ of the opposition Social Democratic Party; weekly; French.

Dialogue: Maison du PSD, blvd. 9 Avril 1938; cultural and political organ of the PSD; weekly; French; Dir. OMAR HABOU.

Etudiant Tunisien: B.P. 286, 11 rue d'Espagne; f. 1953; French and Arabic; Chief Editor FAOUZI AOUAM.

al-Fikr (*Thought*): B.P. 556; f. 1955; cultural review; Arabic; monthly; Dir. MOHAMED MZALI.

Gazette Touristique: Zone Industriel, La Changuia 2; f. 1971; tourism; fortnightly; French; Dir. TIJANI HADDAD; circ. 5,000.

IBLA: Institut des Belles Lettres Arabes, 12 rue Jamâa el Haoua; f. 1937; social and cultural review on Maghreb and Muslim-Arab affairs; French; twice yearly; Dir. A. DEMEERSEMAN.

al-Idhaa wa Talvaza (*Radio and Television*): 71 ave. de la Liberté; f. 1956; broadcasting magazine; Arabic language; fortnightly; Editor ABDELMAJID ENNAIFAR; circ. 15,000.

al-Jaich: National Defence publication; Arabic language.

Journal Officiel de la République Tunisienne: Km. 2, route de Radès, Radès; the official gazette; f. 1860; French and Arabic editions published twice weekly by the Imprimerie Officielle (The State Press); Pres./Gen. Man. ZAOUFIK NAAMOURI.

Loisirs et Tourisme: 10 rue de Suède; tourism and cultural review; French, English and German; circ. 5,000.

al-Maraa (*The Woman*): 56 blvd. Bab Benat; f. 1961; issued by the National Union of Tunisian Women; Arabic and Arabic and French; political, economic and social affairs; every 2 months; Dir. FATHIA MZALI; circ. 10,000.

Pro-mode: 10 rue du Yémen; French; Dir. MOHAMED ARBI LOUSSAIEF.

Le Sport: 6 rue Kamel Ataturk; f. 1958; French; weekly; Pres. MAHMOUD ELLAFI; circ. 30,000.

Statistiques Financières: Banque Centrale de Tunisie, 7 place de la Monnaie; statistical tables; monthly.

Tunis Hebdo: 1 passage Saint Joseph; general and sport; weekly; French; Dir. M'HAMED BEN YOUSSEF.

Tunisian Highlights: 15 rue Kamel Ataturk; every two months; English.

Tunisie Actualités: 9 rue Hooker Doolittle, Belvédère; f. 1966; quarterly; French; official journal; Dir. ABDELBAKI DALY; circ. 1,300.

NEWS AGENCIES

Tunis Afrique Presse (TAP): 25 ave. Habib Bourguiba, Tunis; f. 1961; Arab, French and English; offices in Bonn, Brussels, Cairo, Paris and New York; weekly and monthly bulletins; Chair. and Gen. Man. MAHMOUD TRIKI.

FOREIGN BUREAUX

Agence France-Presse (AFP): 45 ave. Habib Bourguiba, Tunis; Chief HENRI DE BONNIÈRES.

Agentstvo Pechati Novosti (APN) (*U.S.S.R.*): 108 ave. de la Liberté, Tunis; Chief VALERITY BOLSHOKOV.

Agenzia Nazionale Stampa Associata (ANSA) (*Italy*): 24 rue Gamal Abdel Nasser, Tunis; Representative BRUNO CAMPANINI.

Associated Press (AP) (*U.S.A.*): 35 rue Garibaldi, Tunis; Chief F. VENTURA.

Hsinhua (*People's Republic of China*): ave. de Lesseps, Tunis; Dir. HSIEH PIN YU.

Reuters (*U.K.*): 45 ave. Habib Bourguiba, Tunis; Chief GUSTAVE DEJEANNE.

Tanjug (*Yugoslavia*): 4 rue du Libéria, Tunis; Representative VUCKOVIC SIME.

TASS (*U.S.S.R.*): 2 rue de Damas, Tunis; Chief IGOR MIAKISHEV.

United Press International (UPI) (*U.S.A.*): 28 rue Gamal Abdel Nasser, Tunis; Chief MICHEL DEURE.

PUBLISHERS

Ceres Productions: 6 ave. Montplaisir, Tunis; f. 1964; Dir MOHAMMED BEN SMAIL.

Coopérative Ouvrière Publication Impression "C.O.O.P.I.": rue du Marché and ave. Taieb M'hiri, Sfax.

Dar Al Kitab: 5 ave. Habib Bourguiba, Sousse; f. 1950; Dir. TAIEB KACEM.

Dar Assabah: 4 rue Ali Bach-Hamba, Tunis; f. 1951; 200 mems.; publishes daily and weekly papers which circulate throughout Tunisia, North Africa, France, Belgium, Luxembourg and West Germany.

En Najah—Editions Hedi ben Abdelgheni: 11 ave. de France, Tunis; Arab and French books, oriental reviews.

Imprimerie Al Manar: B.P. 121, Tunis; history, religion; Man. Dir. T. EL M'HAMDI.

Imprimerie Officielle: route de Radès, Radès, Tunis; government press; Dir. HAMED ZGHAL.

Institut National de la Statistique: 27 rue de Liban, B.P. 65, Tunis; publishes a variety of annuals, periodicals and papers concerned with the economic policy and development of Tunisia.

Maison Tunisienne de l'Edition: 54 ave. de la Liberté, Tunis; f. 1966; all kinds of books, revues, etc.; Dir. AZOUZ REBAI.

S.L.I.M. (Société Librairie Imprimerie Messagerie): blvd. Président Bourguiba, El Kef.

Société Anonyme de Papeterie et Imprimerie: 12 rue de Vesoul, Tunis.

Société d'Arts Graphiques, d'Edition et de Presse: 15 rue 2 mars 1934, la Kasbah, Tunis; f. 1966; prints and publishes daily papers, magazines, books, etc.; Pres. Dir.-Gen. MOKHTAR MADJ ALI.

Société Nationale d'Edition et de Diffusion: 5 ave. de Carthage, B.P. 440, Tunis; Dir. NACEUR BEN AMOR.

RADIO AND TELEVISION

RADIO

Radiodiffusion Télévision Tunisienne: 71 ave. de la Liberté, Tunis; government service; broadcasts in Arabic, French and Italian; stations at Tunis, Gafsa, Sfax and Monastir; Dir.-Gen. SALEM BOUMIZA.

TELEVISION

Television was introduced in northern and central Tunisia in January 1966, and by 1972 transmission reached all the country. A relay station to link up with European transmissions was built at El Haouaria in 1967.

Number of television receivers (1978): 229,918.

FINANCE

(cap. = capital, p.u. = paid up, dep. = deposits, m. = million, br. = branch)

BANKING

CENTRAL BANK

Banque Centrale de Tunisie: 7 place de la Monnaie, Tunis; f. 1958; cap. 3.0m. dinars, assets 446.5m. dinars (Dec. 1977); Gov. MOHAMED GHENIMA; Dir.-Gen. MOHAMED BOUSBIA; publs. *Conjoncture* (quarterly), *Statistiques Financières* (monthly), *Rapport Annuel*.

Banque de Développement Economique de Tunisie: 68 ave. Habib Bourguiba, Tunis; f. 1959; development bank, now the main source of long term and equity finance for industrial and tourist enterprises; Pres. H. BOURGUIBA, Jr.; cap. 6.5m. dinars.

Banque Franco-Tunisienne: 13 rue d'Alger, Tunis; Pres. BEL HASSAN RIAHI; Gen. Man. BRAHIM ANANE.

Banque Internationale Arabe de Tunisie: 12 ave. de France, Tunis; f. 1976 by consortium of banks and Tunisian Government; cap. 3m. dinars (Dec. 1977); Pres. and Dir.-Gen. MANSOUR MOALLA; 10 brs.

Banque Nationale de Tunisie: 19 ave. de Paris, Tunis; f. 1959; cap. 6m. dinars (April 1978), dep. (1977) 92,929m. dinars; Pres. MOHAMED EL BEJI HAMDA; Dir. Gen. ABDELLATIF JERIJENI; 58 brs.

Banque du Sud: 14 ave. de Paris, Tunis; f. 1968; cap. 4.0m. dinars, dep. 85m. dinars (Dec. 1978); Pres., Dir.-Gen. SAID CHENIK; Asst. Dir.-Gen. MONGI BEN OTHMAN.

Banque de Tunisie: 3 avenue de France, Tunis; f. 1884; cap. 3m. dinars; dep. 52.4m dinars (Dec. 1978); Pres. BOUBAKER MABROUK; Vice-Pres. and Gen. Man. ABDERRAZAK RASSAA; 5 brs.

Crédit Foncier et Commercial de Tunisie: 13 ave. de France, Tunis; f. 1967; cap. 2.1m. dinars; Chair. and Pres. RACHID BEN YEDDER; Gen. Man MAHMOUD BABBOU.

Société Tunisienne de Banque: 1 ave. Habib Thameur, Tunis; f. 1958; cap. p.u. 4m. dinars, res. 10.5m. dinars (Dec. 1977); Chair. HABIB GHENIM; 46 brs.

Union Bancaire pour le Commerce et l'Industrie: 7–9 rue Gamal Abdel Nasser, Tunis; f. 1961; cap. p.u. 2.75m. dinars, dep. 67.5m. dinars (Dec. 1976); affiliated to Banque Nationale de Paris; Pres. and Dir.-Gen. ABDESSELAM BEN AYED; 9 brs.

Union Internationale de Banques: 65 ave. Habib Bourguiba, Tunis; f. 1963 as a merging of Tunisian interests by the Société Tunisienne de Banque with the Crédit Lyonnais and other foreign banks including Bank of America, Commerzbank, and Banca Commerciale Italiana; cap 4m. dinars, dep. 59m. dinars (1977); Man. TAWFIK TORGEMAN; Deputy Gen. Man. SLAHEDDINE MOUELHI and CLAUDE TOURNAIRE; 25 brs.

FOREIGN BANKS

Arab Bank Ltd. (*Jordan*): 21 rue Al-Djazira, Tunis.

Branches of Citibank and Chase Manhattan Bank were established in 1977.

A national Stock Exchange was opened in 1967.

INSURANCE

Astrée, Compagnie d'Assurances et de Réassurances, S.A.: 56 ave. Farhat Hached, Tunis; f. 1950; Pres., Dir.-Gen. ABDERRAZAK RASSAA; Vice-Pres., Dir.-Gen. MOHAMED HACHICHA.

Caisse Tunisienne d'Assurances Mutuelles Agricoles et Mutuelle Générale d'Assurances: 6 ave. Habib Thameur, Tunis; f. 1912; Pres. MOKTAR BELLAGHA; Dir.-Gen. SLAHEDDINE FERCHIOU.

Lloyd Tunisien: 7 ave. de Carthage, Tunis; f. 1945; Pres., Dir.-Gen. FAKHREDDINE ELKATEB; fire, accident, liability, marine, life; cap. 500,000 dinars.

Société Tunisienne d'Assurances et de Réassurances: ave. de Paris, Tunis; f. 1958; Pres./Dir.-Gen. HEDI ENNIFER; all kinds of insurance and reinsurance.

FOREIGN COMPANIES

About thirty of the major French, Swiss and British insurance companies are represented in Tunisia.

TRADE AND INDUSTRY

CHAMBERS OF COMMERCE

Chambre de Commerce de Tunis: 1 ave. Habib Thameur, Tunis; f. 1925; 25 mems.; Pres. MAHMOUD ZERZERI; publ. *Bulletin* (monthly).

Chambre de Commerce du Centre: rue Chadly Khaznadar, Sousse; Pres. HÉDI BOUSLAMA; Sec.-Gen. TOUHAMI EL HEDDA; publ. *Bulletin Economique* (every two months in French and Arabic).

Chambre de Commerce du Nord: 12 rue Ibn Khaldoun, Bizerte; f. 1903; 8 mems.; Pres. MOHAMED TERRAS; Sec.-Gen. Mme SFAXI RACHIDA; publ. *Bulletin Economique*.

Chambre de Commerce du Sud: 21–23 rue Habib Thameur, Sfax; f. 1895; 8 mems.; publ. *Bulletin Economique* (monthly).

Chambre Tuniso-Française de Commerce et d'Industrie: 14 rue de Vesoul, Tunis; f. 1974; Pres. MAHMOUD BELHASSINE.

ECONOMIC ORGANIZATIONS

Union Nationale des Agriculteurs Tunisiens (U.N.A.T.:) 6 ave. Habib Thameur, Tunis.

Union Tunisienne de l'Industrie, du Commerce et de l'Artisanat (U.T.I.C.A.): 32 rue Charles-de-Gaulle, Tunis; f. 1946; mems.: 14 national federations and 75 syndical chambers at national levels; Pres. and founder FERDJANI BEN HADJ AMMAR; First Vice-Pres. HABIB MAJOUL; Sec.-Gen. LAROUSSI GUIGA; publs. *La Tunisie Economique* (every month), *l'Annuaire Economique*, *Kompass Tunisie* (every year), *El Bayane* (weekly).

TRADE UNIONS

Union Générale des Etudiants de Tunisie (U.G.E.T.): 11 rue d'Espagne, Tunis; f. 1953; 600 mems.; Pres. MEKKI FITOURI; publ. *L'Etudiant Tunisien.*

Union Générale Tunisienne du Travail (U.G.T.T.): 29 place M'Hamed Ali, Tunis; f. 1946 by FARHAT HACHED; affiliated to ICFTU; mems. 175,000 in 23 affiliated unions; Sec.-Gen. TIJANI ABID.

Union Nationale des Femmes de Tunisie (U.N.F.T.): 56 blvd. Bab-Benat, Tunis; f. 1956; 45,000 mems.; Pres. Mme. FATHIA MZALI; Sec.-Gen. Mme. FAIZA SLAMA; Sec. for Youth and Sport Mme. DORDANA MASMOUDI.

TRADE FAIR

International Fair in Tunis: Mohammed V St., Tunis.

TRANSPORT

RAILWAYS

In 1977 the total length of railways was 2,257 km. In 1978 it was announced that the coastal railway would be converted to provide a continuous standard gauge line from Morocco to Libya.

Société Nationale des Chemins de Fer Tunisiens (S.N.C.F.T.): 67 ave. Farhat Hached, Tunis; f. 1957; State organization controlling all Tunisian railways; Pres. Dir.-Gen. SADOK BORGI.

Société Nationale des Transports: 1 ave. Habib Bourguiba, Tunis; f. 1963; controls the electrified line from Tunis to La Marsa (19.5 km.); operates 112 local and 178 long-distance domestic and international bus routes.

ROADS

In 1975 there were 21,309 km. of roads. Of these, 10,554 km. were main roads and 5,906 km. secondary roads.

Each region has a *Société Régionale des Transports* responsible for road transport.

SHIPPING

Tunisia has 4 major ports: Tunis–La Goulette, Bizerta, Sousse and Sfax. There is a special petroleum port at La Skhirra. A complex of three ports, with separate facilities for general merchandise, minerals and oil, is under construction at Gabès.

Compagnie Tunisienne de Navigation: P.O.B. 40, 5 avenue Dag Hammarskjoeld, Tunis; brs. at Bizerta, Gabès, La Skhirra, La Goulette, Sfax and Sousse; Pres. ABDERRAHMAN BEN MESSEOUD.

CIVIL AVIATION

There are international airports at Tunis-Carthage, Tunis-El Aouina, Djerba and Monastir. A new international airport is being constructed near Tozeur.

Tunis Air (*Société Tunisienne de l'Air*): 113 ave. de la Liberté, Tunis; f. 1948; 85 per cent Government-owned; flights to Abu Dhabi, Algeria, Belgium, Egypt, France, Fed. Rep. of Germany, Kuwait, Libya, Luxembourg, Morocco, Netherlands, Switzerland, Syria, U.K. and internal flights; fleet of 10 Boeing 727; Pres. SADOK BOURAOUI.

Société Tunisienne de Réparations Aéronautiques et de Constructions: Aérodrome de Tunis-Carthage, Tunis; f. 1952; internal charter flights for oil companies.

FOREIGN AIRLINES

Aeroflot (U.S.S.R.), Air Afrique (Ivory Coast), Air Algérie, Air France, Air India, Alitalia, Austrian Airlines, Balkan, (Bulgaria), British Caledonian, ČSA (Czechoslovakia), EgyptAir, Interflug (German Democratic Republic), JAT (Yugoslavia), KLM (Netherlands), Libyan Arab Airlines, LOT (Poland), Lufthansa (Federal Republic of Germany), MALÉV (Hungary), Royal Air Maroc, Sabena (Belgium), SAS (Sweden), Swissair, TWA (U.S.A.), and UTA (France) also serve Tunis.

TOURISM

Office National du Tourisme Tunisien: 1 ave. Mohammed V, Tunis; f. 1958; Dir.-Gen. B. BEN ZINEB.

Voyages 2000: 2 ave. de France, Tunis; f. 1964; Dir. MONCEF TRIKI; Man. ORMANE AMOURI; publ. *Voyages 2000.*

CULTURAL ORGANIZATIONS

Ministry of Cultural Affairs: Tunis; departments organize all national cultural events; Minister MOHAMED YALAOUI.

Institute des Belles Lettres Arabes: 12 rue Jamâa el Haoua, Tunis; f. 1930; cultural centre; Dir. A. DEMEERSEMAN; publ. *IBLA* (twice yearly) and special studies.

International Cultural Centre: Hammamet; f. 1962; organizes national and international scientific and cultural conferences, and the Hammamet International Festival; provides individual study facilities for writers, musicians and painters; Dir. TAHAR GUIGA.

PRINCIPAL THEATRES

Théâtre Municipal de Tunis: Tunis; subsidized by the state.

Hammamet Theatre: Hammamet; open air theatre built 1963; organized by International Cultural Centre of Hammamet.

CULTURAL FESTIVALS

Carthage Festival: 22 rue Amin Raihani, El Omrane, Tunis; f. 1974; international festival of arts; held every year at the site of the ancient city and in Tunis.

Hammamet International Festival: Hammamet; annual festival, July–August; theatre, music, ballet, cinema, art; based on the open-air theatre.

International Theatre Festival: c/o Comité Culturel Régional, Monastir; f. 1964; open to theatrical groups from Algeria, Libya, Morocco and Tunisia.

DEFENCE

Estimated Defence Expenditure (1978/79): 77m. dinars.

Military Service: 1 year (selective).

Total Armed Forces (1978/79): 22,200; army 18,000; navy 2,500; air force 1,700.

Paramilitary Forces (1978/79): 2,500 (1,500 Gendarmerie, 1,000 National Guard).

EDUCATION

Tunisia has better educational facilities than most developing countries. Approximately 80 per cent of children of school age receive an education. In 1977/78 there were 981,255 pupils in 2,423 primary schools and 215,044 pupils in 193 secondary schools.

Arabic only is used in the first three years of primary school, but in the higher grades French becomes progressively more important and is used almost exclusively in higher education. The University of Tunis was opened in 1959/60. It has 54 faculties and institutes.

UNIVERSITY

Université de Tunis: Tunis; f. 1959; 2,008 teachers, 20,909 students (1977/78).

BIBLIOGRAPHY

ANTHONY, JOHN. About Tunisia (London, 1961).

ARDANT, GAVRIEL. La Tunisie d'Aujourd'hui et Demain (Paris, 1961).

ASHFORD, DOUGLAS E. Morocco-Tunisia: Politics and Planning (Syracuse University Press, 1965).

BASSET, ANDRÉ. Initiation à la Tunisie (Paris, 1950).

BOURGUIBA, HABIB. La Tunisie et la France (Paris, 1954). Hadith al-Jamaa (*Collected Broadcasts*) (Tunis, 1957).

BRUNSCHVIG, ROBERT. La Tunisie au haut Moyen Age (Cairo, 1948).

CAMBON, HENRI. Histoire de la régence de Tunisie (Paris, 1948).

DE MONTETY, HENRI. Femmes de Tunisie (Paris, 1958).

DESPOIS, JEAN. La Tunisie, ses Régions (Paris, 1959).

DUVIGNAUD, JEAN. Tunisie (Editions Rencontre, Lausanne, 1965).

DUWAJI, GHAZI. Economic Development in Tunisia (Praeger, New York, 1967).

GARAS, FELIX. Bourguiba et la Naissance d'une Nation (Paris, 1956).

GERMANN, RAIMUND E. Verwaltung und Einheitspartei in Tunisien (Europa Verlag, Zürich, 1968).

GUEN, MONCEF. La Tunisie indépendante face à son économie (Paris, 1961).

KNAPP, W. Tunisia (Thames and Hudson, London, 1972).

LAITMAN, LEON. Tunisia Today: Crisis in North Africa (New York, 1954).

LING, DWIGHT D. Tunisia, from Protectorate to Republic (Indiana University Press, 1967).

MENSCHING, HORST. Tunesien: eine geographische Landeskunde (Darmstadt, 1968).

MICAUD, C. A. Tunisia, the Politics of Moderation (New York, 1964).

MOORE, C. H. Tunisia since Independence (University of California Press, Berkeley, 1965).

NERFIN, M. Entretiens avec Ahmed Ben Salah (F. Maspero, Paris, 1974).

PERROUX, F. and BARRE, R., Editors. Développement, croissance, progrès: Maroc-Tunisie (Paris, 1961).

RAYMOND, ANDRÉ. La Tunisie (Series *Que sais-je*, No. 318) (Paris, 1961).

ROMERIL, PAUL E. A. Tunisian nationalism: a bibliographical outline (*Middle East Journal* 1960, pages 206-215).

RUDEBECK, LARS. Party and People: A Study of Political Change in Tunisia (C. Hurst, London, 1969).

RUF, WERNER KLAUS, Der Burgismus und die Aussenpolitik der unabhängigen Tunesien (Freiburg, 1969).

SYLVESTER, ANTHONY. Tunisia (Bodley Head, London, 1969).

TLATLI, SALAH-EDDINE. Tunisie nouvelle (Tunis, 1957).

ZIADEH, NICOLA A. The Origins of Tunisian Nationalism (Beirut, 1962.)

Turkey

PHYSICAL AND SOCIAL GEOGRAPHY

W. B. Fisher

Turkey is, in a remarkable sense, passage land between Europe and Asia. Nearly one-half of its 2,620 km. of land frontier is with European States—Greece, Bulgaria, and Soviet Russia; and the remainder with Iran, Iraq, and Syria. The richest and most densely populated west of Turkey looks towards the Aegean and Mediterranean Seas and is very conscious of its links with Europe; whilst in culture, racial origins, and ways of life there are frequent reminders of Turkey's geographical situation primarily as a part of Asia.

Turkey consists essentially of the large peninsula of Asia Minor, which has strongly defined natural limits: sea on three sides (the Black Sea in the north, the Aegean in the west, and the Mediterranean on the south), and high mountain ranges on the fourth (eastern) side. The small region of European Turkey, containing the cities of Istanbul (Constantinople) and Edirne (Adrianople) is on the other hand defined by a purely artificial frontier, the exact position of which has varied considerably over the last century, according to the fluctuating fortunes and prestige of Turkey herself. Another small territory, the Hatay, centred on Iskenderun (Alexandretta) and lying as an enclave in Syrian territory, was acquired as a diplomatic bargain in 1939.

PHYSICAL FEATURES

The geological structure of Turkey is extremely compli cated, and rocks of almost all ages occur, from the most ancient to most recent. Broadly speaking, we may say that Turkey consists of a number of old plateau blocks, against which masses of younger rock series have been squeezed to form fold mountain ranges of varying size. As there were several of these plateau blocks, and not just one, the fold mountains run in many different directions, with considerable irregularity, and hence no simple pattern can be discerned—instead, one mountain range gives place to another abruptly, and we can pass suddenly from highland to plain or plateau.

In general outline Turkey consists of a ring of mountains enclosing a series of inland plateaus, with the highest mountains on the east, close to the U.S.S.R. and Iran. Mount Ararat, overlooking the Soviet frontier, is the highest peak in Turkey, reaching 5,165 metres, and there are neighbouring peaks almost as large. In the west the average altitude of the hills is distinctly lower, though the highest peak (Mount Erciyas or Argaeus) is over 3,900 metres. The irregular topography of Turkey has given rise to many lakes, some salt, and some fresh, and generally more numerous than elsewhere in the Middle East. The largest, Lake Van, covers nearly 4,000 sq. km. (1,100 sq. miles).

Two other features may be mentioned. Large areas of the east, and some parts of the centre of Asia Minor have been covered in sheets of lava which are often of such recent occurrence that soil has not yet been formed—consequently wide expanses are sterile and uninhabited. Secondly, in the north and west cracking and disturbance of the rocks has taken place on an enormous scale. The long, indented coast of the Aegean Sea, with its numerous oddly shaped islands and estuaries, is due to cracking in two directions, which has split the land into detached blocks of roughly rectangular shape. Often the lower parts have sunk and been drowned by the sea. The Bosphorus and Dardanelles owe their origin to this faulting action, and the whole of the Black Sea coast is due to subsidence along a great series of fissures. Movement and adjustment along these cracks has by no means ceased, so that at the present day earthquakes are frequent in the north and west of Turkey.

Because of the presence of mountain ranges close to the coast, and the great height of the interior plateaus (varying from 800 to 2,000 metres). Turkey has special climatic conditions, characterized by great extremes of temperature and rainfall, with wide variation from one district to another. In winter conditions are severe in most areas, except for those lying close to sea-level. Temperatures of minus 30° to minus 40°C. can occur in the east, and snow lies there for as many as 120 days each year. The west has frost on most nights of December and January, and (again apart from the coastal zone) has an average winter temperature below 1°C. In summer, however, temperatures over most of Turkey exceed 30°C, with 43°C. in the south-east. There can hence be enormous seasonal variations of temperature—sometimes over 50°C., among the widest in the world.

Rainfall too is remarkably variable. Along the eastern Black Sea coast, towards the Soviet frontier, over 250 cm. fall annually; but elsewhere, amounts are very much smaller. Parts of the central plateau, being shut off by mountains from the influence of sea winds, are arid, with annual totals of under 25 cm., and expanses of salt steppe and desert are frequent. Like Iran, Turkey also has a "dead heart", and the main towns of Anatolia, including Ankara, the capital, are placed away from the centre and close to the hills, where rainfall tends to be greater.

It is necessary to emphasize the contrast that exists between the Aegean coastlands, which climatically are by far the most favoured regions of Turkey, and the rest of the country. Round the Aegean, winters are mild and fairly rainy, and the summers hot, but tempered by a persistent northerly wind, the Meltemi, or Etesian wind, which is of great value in ripening fruit, especially figs and sultana grapes.

ECONOMIC LIFE

The variety of geographical conditions within Turkey has led to uneven development, and this unevenness has been intensified by poor communications, due to the broken nature of the topography. Roads are relatively few, railways slow and often roundabout, and whole districts—sometimes even considerable towns—are accessible only by bridle track. Many rivers flow in deep gorges near their sources and either meander or are broken by cascades in their lower reaches, so that none are navigable.

Thus we find that the west of Turkey, situated close to the Aegean Sea, is by far the most densely peopled and the most intensively developed. Since 1923, however, attempts have been made to develop the Anatolian plateau and the districts in the extreme east, which, following the expulsion and massacre of the Armenians in 1914-18, for a time supported only a very scanty population. Development in the central plateau has been aided by the exploitation of several small but on the whole valuable mineral deposits, and by irrigation schemes to improve agriculture. A certain degree of industrialisation (mainly undertaken by state-sponsored and owned organisations) has also grown up, based on Turkish-produced raw materials—cotton, wool, mohair, beet-sugar, olive-oil, and tobacco. The eastern districts present a more intractable problem, and development so far has been slower.

Of recent years, the considerable annual increase of population, about 2.7 per cent, has led to intensification of settlement and the bringing in of all available land for cultivation. Henceforth a principal problem for Turkey must be to improve yields from agriculture and industry. Because of the strategic importance of the country, there has been a considerable programme of road-building, largely financed by the U.S.A. In recent years absorption of Turkish labour in western Europe (chiefly the Federal Republic of Germany) provided most useful extra revenue from remittances; but with the repatriation of many of these *gastarbeiter* during the recession of the last few years, there have been problems of reabsorption (the returning workers have higher expectations) together with the need to find other sources of revenue.

RACE AND LANGUAGE

Racially, the bulk of the Turkish people show an intermixture of Mediterranean and Armenoid strains. In the western half of the country Mediterraneans and Armenoids are more or less equally represented; but further east the proportion of Armenoids steadily increases, until towards the Soviet and Iranian borders, they become almost universal. Much of south-eastern Turkey is inhabited by Kurds, a people of Indo-European descent; estimates of their number range widely, from three to over eight million. We can in addition note less important racial elements: there would seem to be small numbers of proto-Nordics in the north and west, and some authorities suggest a racial relationship between Galatia (the modern district of Ankara) and ancient Gaul. The Ottoman Turks were in the main of Turki (western Mongoloid) ancestry, but in the view of some authorities their contribution to the ethnic stocks of Turkey would seem to have been small, since they were really an invading tribal group that became an aristocracy and soon intermarried with other peoples. There are also numbers of Caucasians—particularly Circassians and Georgians—who have contributed to the racial structure of Turkey; and during 1951 a further element was added by the arrival of many thousands of Bulgarian Muslims who had been deported from their own country.

The Turkish language, which is of central Asiatic origin, is spoken over most, but by no means all of the country. This was introduced into Turkey in Seljuq times, and was written in Arabic characters, but as these are not really well adapted to the sound of Turkish, Roman (i.e. European) script has been compulsory since 1928. As well, there are a number of non-Turkish languages. Kurdish has a wide extension in the south-east, along the Syrian and Iraqi frontiers; and Caucasian dialects, quite different from either Turkish or Kurdish, occur in the north-east. Greek and Armenian were once widespread, but following the deportations of the last forty years both forms of speech are now current only in the city of Istanbul, where considerable numbers of Greeks and Armenians still live.

HISTORY

ANCIENT HISTORY

The most ancient written records so far found in Asia Minor date from the beginning of the second millennium B.C. They are in Assyrian, and reveal the existence of Assyrian trading colonies in Cappadocia. These documents, together with a growing amount of archaeological evidence, show an important Copper Age culture in Central Anatolia in the third and early second millennia. Later in the second millennium the greater part of Asia Minor fell under the rule of the Hittites. This people has long been known from references in the Old Testament and other ancient texts, but its full importance was first revealed by the excavations at Boğazköy, the site of the ancient Hittite capital of Hattushash. The Hittite Empire flourished from about 1600 to about 1200 B.C., and reached its apogee in the fourteenth and thirteenth centuries, when it became one of the dominant States of the Middle East. One of the sources of Hittite strength was iron, which was first worked in Anatolia. The production of iron was for long a monopoly of the Hittite kings, but the use of iron implements eventually spread to other parts, and revolutionised agriculture, industry and war.

After the break-up of the Hittite Empire, Asia Minor was split up among a number of dynasties and peoples—Phrygians, Cimmerians, Lydians and others—about whom not very much is known. Towards the end of the Hittite period the Greeks began to invade the Aegean coast, and entered on a long struggle with the native states that is reflected in the story of the Trojan war. Greek culture spread in western Anatolia, which was gradually incorporated into the Hellenic world. A series of political changes, of which the most important are the Persian conquest in 546, the conquest of Alexander in 334, and the constitution of the Roman province of Asia in 133 B.C., did not impede the steady spread of Greek language and culture in the cities.

In A.D. 330, the Emperor Constantine inaugurated the new city of Constantinople, on the site of the old Greek trading settlement of Byzantium. This city at once became the capital of the East Roman and then of the Christian Byzantine Empire. Asia Minor was now the metropolitan province of a great Empire, and grew in wealth, prosperity and importance. Under Byzantine rule Greek Christianity, already firmly established in Roman times, spread over most of the peninsula.

SELJUQS AND OTTOMANS

At the beginning of the eleventh century a new conquest of Anatolia began—that of the Turks. The early history of the Turkish peoples is still obscure. Some references in the ancient biography of Alexander show them to have been established in Central Asia at the time of his conquests, and Turkish tribal confederacies played an important part in the invasions of Europe from late Roman times onwards. The name "Turk" first appears in historical records in the sixth century A.D., when Chinese annals speak of a powerful empire in Central Asia, founded by a steppe people called Tu-Kiu. It is from this state that the oldest surviving Turkish inscriptions have come. From the seventh century onwards the Central Asian Turks came into ever closer contact with the Islamic peoples of the Near East, from whom they adopted the Islamic faith and the Arabic script, and with them much of the complex civilisation of Islam. From the ninth century Turks entered the service of the Caliphate in increasing numbers, and soon came to provide the bulk of its armies, its generals, and eventually its rulers.

From the tenth century whole tribes of Turks began to migrate into Persia and Iraq, and in the eleventh, under the leadership of the family of Seljuq, the Turks were able to set up a great empire comprising most of the eastern lands of the Caliphate. The Muslim armies on the Byzantine frontier had long been predominantly Turkish, and in the course of the eleventh century they began a great movement into Anatolia which resulted in the termination of Byzantine rule in most of the country and its incorporation in the Muslim Seljuq Sultanate. A Seljuq prince, Suleyman ibn Kutlumush, was sent to organize the new province, and by the end of the twelfth century his successors had built up a strong Turkish monarchy in Anatolia, with its capital in Konya (the ancient Iconium). Under the rule of the Anatolian Seljuqs, which in various forms lasted until the fourteenth century, Anatolia gradually became a Turkish land. Masses of Turkish immigrants from further east entered the country, and a Turkish, Muslim civilisation replaced Greek Christianity.

In the late thirteenth century the Sultanate of Konya fell into decay, and gradually gave way to a number of smaller principalities. One of these, in north-western Anatolia, was ruled by a certain Osman, or Othman, from whom the name Ottoman is derived. The Ottoman State soon embarked on a great movement of expansion, on the one hand in Anatolia, at the expense of its Turkish neighbours, on the other in the Balkans. Ottoman armies first crossed to Europe in the mid-fourteenth century, and by 1400 they were masters of much of the Balkan peninsula as well as of almost all Anatolia. The capital was moved first from Bursa to Edirne and then, in 1453, to Constantinople, the final conquest of which from the last Byzantine Emperor completed the process that had transformed a principality of frontier-warriors into a new great empire. Constantinople, called Istanbul by the Turks, remained the capital of the Ottoman Empire until 1922. The wave of conquest was by no means spent. For more than a century Ottoman arms continued to advance into Central Europe, while in 1516–17 Sultan Selim I destroyed the Mamluk Sultanate and incorporated Syria and Egypt into the Empire. During the reign of Sultan Suleyman I (1520–66), called the Magnificent in Europe, the Ottoman Empire was at the height of its power. In three continents the Sultan held unchallenged sway over vast territories. A skilled and highly-organised bureaucracy secured for the peoples of the Empire peace, justice and prosperity; literature, scholarship and the arts flourished; and the Ottoman armies and fleets seemed to threaten the very existence of Western Christendom.

The decay of the Empire is usually dated from after the death of Suleyman. In the West great changes were taking place. The Renaissance and the Reformation, the rapid development of science and technology, the emergence of strong, centralised nation states with constantly improving military techniques, the deflection of the main routes of international trade from the Mediterranean to the open seas, all combined to strengthen Turkey's Western adversaries while leaving her own resources unchanged or even diminished, and helped to relegate her into a backwater of cultural and economic stagnation. An imposing military façade for a while masked the internal decay that was rotting the once all-powerful Empire, but by the end of the seventeenth century the weakness of the Ottoman State was manifest. Then began the struggle of the Powers for pickings of Turkish territory and for positions of influence in the Empire. During the eighteenth century it was Austria and Russia that made the main territorial advances in the Balkans and in the Black Sea area, while England and France were content with commercial and diplomatic privileges. In a succession of wars one province after another was lost, while internal conditions went from bad to worse. During the nineteenth century England and France began to play a more active role. British policy was generally to support the Turks against their impatient heirs. In 1854 Britain and France went to war at the side of Turkey in order to check Russian aggression, and in 1877–78 British diplomatic intervention was effective to the same end. Meanwhile the ferment of nationalist ideas had spread from the West to the subject peoples of the Empire, and one by one the Serbs, Greeks, Romanians and Bulgarians succeeded in throwing off Ottoman rule and attaining independent statehood.

More significant for Turkish history were the first stirrings of a new spirit among the Turks themselves. The first serious attempts at reform were made during the reign of Selim III (1789–1807), and during the nineteenth century a series of reforming sultans and ministers worked on a programme of reform and modernisation which, though it fell short of its avowed objectives, nevertheless transformed the face of the Ottoman Empire and began a process of change, the effects of which are still visible. In 1878 the reforming movement came to an abrupt end, and from that year until 1908 the Empire was subjected to the iron despotism of Abdul-Hamid II, who ruthlessly repressed every attempt at liberal thought and reform. In 1908 the secret opposition group known as the Young Turks seized power, and in a wave of revolutionary enthusiasm inaugurated a constitution, parliamentary government, and a whole series of liberal reforms. Unfortunately the Young Turks had little opportunity to follow up their promising start. First internal dissension, then foreign wars, combined to turn the Young Turk regime into a military dictatorship. In 1911 the Italians suddenly started a war against Turkey which ended with their gaining Libya and the Dodecanese Islands; in 1912–13 a Balkan alliance succeeded in wresting from the dying Empire most of its remaining possessions on the continent of Europe. Finally, in October 1914, Turkey entered the war on the side of the Central Powers. During the reign of Abdul-Hamid German influence had been steadily increasing in Turkey, and the process continued under the Young Turks. It was certainly helped by the growing friendship between the Western Powers and Russia, which threw the Turks into the arms of the only power that seemed ready to support them against Russian designs. German officers reorganised the Turkish Army. German business-men and technicians extended their hold on the economic resources of the country, and German engineers and financiers began the construction of the famous Baghdad railway which was to provide direct rail communication between Germany and the Middle East.

The Turkish alliance was of immense military value to the Central Powers. The Turkish armies, still established in Syria and Palestine, were able to offer an immediate and serious threat to the Suez Canal and to the British position in Egypt. By their dogged and successful defence of the Dardanelles they prevented effective co-operation between Russia and the Western Powers. Their Balkan position assured the supremacy of the Central Powers in that important area. Their position as the greatest independent Muslim State and their prestige among Muslims elsewhere created a series of problems in the British and French Empires.

Despite their weakness and exhaustion after two previous wars, the Turks were able to wage a bitter defensive war against the Allies. At last, after two unsuccessful attempts, one on the Dardanelles and the other in Mesopotamia, a new British attack from Egypt and from India succeeded in expelling the Turks from Palestine, Syria, and most of Iraq. Defeated on all sides, cut off from their allies by the Salonica Expedition, the Turks decided to abandon the struggle, and signed an armistice at Mudros on October 30th, 1918. The outlook for Turkey seemed black. Allied forces controlled Istanbul and the Straits— British forces were in control of the Arab countries, and in 1919 French, Italian and British forces occupied strategic positions in parts of Anatolia itself. In the capital the Young Turk leaders had fled, and a new Government was formed, subservient to the will of the occupying Powers.

For some time the victorious Powers were too busy elsewhere to attend to the affairs of Turkey, and it was not until the San Remo Conference of April 1920 that the first serious attempt was made to settle the Turkish question. Meanwhile the victors were busy quarrelling among themselves. Partly, no doubt, with the idea of forestalling Italian ambitions, the British, French, and American Governments agreed to a Greek proposal for a Greek occupation of Izmir and the surrounding country, and on May 15th, 1919, a Greek Army, under cover of allied warships, landed at Izmir. Second thoughts on the wisdom of this step appeared in the allied camp, and in October 1919 the Inter-Allied Commission in Istanbul condemned it as "unjustifiable" and as "a violation of the terms of the Armistice". The consequences of the invasion for Turkey were momentous. Now it was no longer the non-Turkish subject provinces and the Ottoman superstructure of the Turkish nation that were threatened, but the Turkish homeland itself. Moreover, the Greeks, unlike the Western Allies, showed that they intended to stay, and that they were aiming at nothing less than the incorporation of the territories they occupied into the Greek kingdom. The Turkish reaction to this danger was vigorous and immediate. The Nationalist movement, hitherto limited to a small class of intellectuals, became the mass instrument of Turkish determination to preserve the integrity and independence of the homeland. A new leader appeared to organise their victory.

THE RISE OF ATATÜRK

Mustafa Kemal, later surnamed Atatürk, was born in Salonica, then an Ottoman city, in 1880. After a promising career as a regular army officer, he achieved his first active command in Libya in 1911, and thereafter fought with distinction in the successive wars in which his country was involved. After his brilliant conduct of the defence of Gallipoli, he fought on various fronts against the Allies, and at the time of the Armistice held a command on the Syrian front. A month later he returned to Istanbul, and at once began to seek ways and means of getting to Anatolia to organise national resistance. At length he was successful, and on May 19th, 1919—four days after the Greek landing in Izmir—he arrived at Samsun, on the Black Sea coast, ostensibly in order to supervise the disbanding of the remaining Turkish forces. Instead he set to work at once on the double task of organising a national movement and raising a national army.

Meanwhile the Allied Powers were at last completing their arrangements for the obsequies of the Sick Man of Europe. After a series of conferences, a treaty was drawn up and signed by the Allied representatives and those of the Sultan's Government at Sèvres, on August 10th, 1920. The Treaty of Sèvres was very harsh—far harsher than that imposed on Germany. The Arab provinces were to be placed under British and French Mandates, to prepare them for eventual independence. In Anatolia, Armenian and Kurdish States were to be set up in the east, the south was to be divided between France and Italy, and a truncated Turkish Sultanate confined to the interior. The Straits were to be demilitarised and placed under Allied administration, with a Turkish Istanbul surrounded by Allied forces. The rest of European Turkey was to be ceded to Greece, while the Izmir district was to be under "Ottoman sovereignty and Greek administration".

This treaty was, however, never implemented. While the Allies were imposing their terms on the Sultan and his Government in Istanbul, a new Turkish State was rising in the interior of Anatolia, based on the rejection of the treaty and the principles on which it was founded. On July 23rd, 1919, Mustafa Kemal and his associates convened the first Nationalist Congress in Erzurum, and drew up a national programme. A second Congress was held in September in the same year, and attended by delegates from all over the country. An executive committee, presided over by Mustafa Kemal, was formed, and chose Ankara, then a minor provincial town, as its headquarters. Frequent meetings were held in Ankara, which soon became the effective capital of the Nationalist movement and forces. It was there that they issued the famous National Pact, the declaration that laid down the basic programme of the Kemalist movement, renouncing the Empire and the domination of the non-Turkish provinces, but demanding the total and unconditional independence of all areas inhabited by Turks. This declaration won immediate support, and on January 28th, 1920, was approved even by the legal Ottoman Parliament sitting in Istanbul. The growth of the Nationalist movement in Istanbul alarmed the Allies, and on March 16th British forces entered the Turkish part of the city and arrested and deported many Nationalist leaders. Despite this setback, followed by a new anti-Nationalist campaign on the part of the Sultan and his political and religious advisers, the Kemalists continued to advance. On March 19th, 1920, Mustafa Kemal ordered general elections, and at the end of April a National Assembly of 350 deputies met in Ankara and voted the National Pact. The Sultan and his government were declared deposed, a provisional Constitution promulgated, and a government set up with Mustafa Kemal as President.

There remained the military task of expelling the invaders. The Greco-Turkish war falls into three stages, covering roughly the campaigns of 1920, 1921 and 1922. In the first the Nationalists, hopelessly outmatched in numbers and material, were badly defeated, and the Greeks advanced far into Anatolia. Turkish resistance was, however, strong enough to impress the Allies, who, for the first time, accorded a certain limited recognition to the Nationalist Government and proclaimed their neutrality in the Greco-Turkish war. The second campaign began with Greek successes, but the Turks rallied and defeated the invaders first at İnönü—from which İsmet Pasha, who commanded the Turkish forces there, later took his surname—and then, on August 24th, 1921, in a major battle on the Sakarya River, where the Turkish forces were under the personal command of Mustafa Kemal. This victory considerably strengthened the Nationalists, who were now generally realised to be the effective Government of Turkey. The French and Italians withdrew from the areas of Anatolia assigned to them, and made terms with the new Government. The Soviets, now established on Turkey's eastern frontier, had already done so at the beginning of the year.

A period of waiting and reorganization followed, during which the morale of the Greek armies was adversely affected by political changes in Greece. In August 1922 the third and final phase of the war of independence began. The Turkish Army drove the Greeks back to the Aegean, and on September 9th reoccupied İzmir. Mustafa Kemal now prepared to cross to Thrace. To do so he had to cross the Straits, still under Allied occupation. The French and Italian contingents withdrew, and, after a menacing pause, the British followed. On October 11th an armistice was signed at Mudanya, whereby the Allied Governments agreed to the restoration of Turkish sovereignty in Eastern Thrace. In November the Sultan's Cabinet resigned, and the Sultan himself went into exile. Turkey once more had only one government, and Istanbul, the ancient seat of Empire, became a provincial city, ruled by a governor appointed from Ankara.

The peace conference opened in November 1922. After many months of argument the treaty was finally signed on July 24th, 1923. It recognised complete and undivided Turkish sovereignty and the abolition of the last vestiges of foreign privilege. The only reservation related to the demilitarisation of the Straits, which were not to be fortified without the consent of the Powers. This consent was given at the Montreux Conference in 1936.

THE TURKISH REPUBLIC

The military task was completed, and the demands formulated in the National Pact had been embodied in an international treaty. There remained the greater task of rebuilding the ruins of long years of war and revolution—and of remedying those elements of weakness in the Turkish State and society that had brought Turkey to the verge of extinction. Mustafa Kemal saw the solution of Turkey's problems in a process of Westernisation—in the integration of Turkey, on a basis of equality, in the modern Western world. To do this it was not sufficient to borrow, as other reformers had done, the outward forms and trappings of Western civilisation. It was necessary to change the very basis of society in Turkey, and to suppress, ruthlessly if need be, the opposition that was bound to come from the entrenched forces of the old order. Between 1922 and 1938, the year of his death, Kemal carried through a series of far-reaching reforms in Turkey. These may be considered under various headings.

The first changes were political. After the deposition of Sultan Vahdeddin in November 1922, a brief experiment was made with a purely religious sovereignty, and Abdul-Mejid was proclaimed as Caliph but not Sultan. The experiment was not successful. Abdul-Mejid followed his predecessor into exile, and on October 29th, 1923, Turkey was declared a Republic, with Kemal as President. The regime of Kemal Atatürk was effectively a dictatorship—though without the violence and oppression normally associated with that word in Europe. A single party—the Republican People's Party—formed the main instrument for the enforcement of Government policy. The Constitution of April 20th, 1924, provided for an elected Parliament which was the repository of sovereign power. Executive power was to be exercised by the President and a Cabinet chosen by him.

The next object of attack was the religious hierarchy, already weakened by the removal of the Sultan-Caliph. In a series of edicts the Ministry of Religious Affairs was abolished, the religious orders disbanded, religious property sequestrated, religious instruction forbidden. With the religious leaders in retreat, the attack on the old social order began. Certainly the most striking reforms were the abolition of the fez and the Arabic alphabet, and their replacement by the hat and the Latin alphabet. But these were probably less important in the long run than the abrogation of the old legal system and the introduction of new civil and criminal codes of law adapted from Europe. In 1928 Islam itself was disestablished, and the Constitution amended to make Turkey a secular State.

Not the least of the problems that faced Mustafa Kemal was the economic one. Turkey is naturally a very rich country, but her resources were for the most part undeveloped, and what development there was had been in foreign hands. To restore the devastation of war, replace the departed foreign investors, and raise the low standard of living of the country, much capital was needed. Rather than risk the independence of Turkey by inviting foreign capital in a time of weakness, Kemal adopted the principle of *Étatisme*, and made it one of the cardinal doctrines of his regime. From 1923 to 1933 the State made its main effort in railway construction, nearly doubling the length of line in that period. At the same time a start was made in establishing other industries. The major effort of industrialization began in 1934, with the adoption of the first five-year plan—completed in 1939. While often wasteful and inefficient, State-sponsored industry was probably the only form of development possible at the time without recourse to foreign aid. The progress achieved stood Turkey in good stead in the critical years that were to follow.

The foreign policy of the Republic was for long one of strict non-involvement in foreign disputes, and the maintenance of friendly relations with as many Powers as possible. In 1935-36, however, Turkey co-operated loyally in sanctions against Italy, and thereafter the growing threat of German, and more especially Italian, aggression led to closer links with the West. In 1938 steps were taken to strengthen economic links between Turkey and the United Kingdom. A British credit of £16 million was granted to Turkey, and a number of contracts given to British firms by Turkey.

The establishment of the Republic also put an end to the prospect of Kurdish independence offered by the Treaty of Sèvres. The Kurds were opposed to Atatürk's secularist and nationalist policies and in 1925 rose up in revolt after the abolition of the Caliphate. They were ruthlessly crushed. A more nationalist uprising in 1930 and a further revolt against the repressive actions taken by the Government were also suppressed. The Kurdish provinces remained rigorously policed, garrisons were established in larger towns and Kurdish leaders were exiled. The Kurdish language was made illegal and the Government refused to recognize any aspect of the Kurds' separate ethnic identity, calling them "mountain Turks".

The death of Kemal Atatürk in November 1938 was a great shock to Turkey. Perhaps the best testimony to the solidity of his achievement is that his regime was able to survive that shock, and the stresses and strains of the war that followed shortly after.

He was succeeded as President by İsmet İnönü, who announced his intention of maintaining and carrying on the work of his predecessor. The new President was soon called upon to guide his country through a very difficult time. As early as May 12th, 1939, a joint Anglo-Turkish declaration was issued, stating that "the British and Turkish Governments, in the event of an act of aggression leading to war in the Mediterranean area, would co-operate effectively and lend each other all the aid and assistance in their power". This prepared the way for the formal Anglo-French-Turkish Treaty of Alliance signed October 19th, 1939. It had been hoped that this Treaty would be complemented by a parallel treaty with the U.S.S.R., but the equivocal attitude of the Soviet Government, followed by the Stalin-Hitler Agreement of August 1939, made this impossible, and the Turks proceeded with the Western alliance in the face of clearly expressed Soviet disapproval. They protected themselves, however, by Protocol II of the Treaty, stipulating that nothing in the Treaty should bind them to any action likely to involve them in war with the U.S.S.R.

TURKEY DURING THE SECOND WORLD WAR

The fall of France, the hostile attitude of the Soviet Government, and the extension of German power over most of Europe, led the Turkish Government to the conclusion that nothing would be gained by provoking an almost certain German conquest. While continuing to recognize the Alliance, therefore, they invoked Protocol II as a reason for remaining neutral, and in June 1941, when German expansion in the Balkans had brought the German armies within 100 miles of Istanbul, the Turks further protected themselves by signing a friendship and trade agreement with Germany, in which, however, they stipulated that Turkey would maintain her treaty obligations to Britain.

The German attack on the U.S.S.R., and the consequent entry of that country into the Grand Alliance, brought an important change to the situation, and the Western Powers increased their pressure on Turkey to enter the war. The main consideration holding Turkey back from active participation in the war was mistrust of the U.S.S.R., and the widespread feeling that Nazi conquest and Soviet "liberation" were equally to be feared. While stopping short of actual belligerency, however, the Turks, especially after 1942, entered into closer economic and military relations with the West and aided the Allied cause in a number of ways. In August 1944 they broke off diplomatic relations with Germany, and on February 23rd, 1945, declared war on Germany in order to comply with the formalities of entry to the United Nations Conference in San Francisco.

The war years subjected Turkey to severe economic strains. These, and the dangers of armed neutrality in a world at war, resulted in the imposition of martial law, of closer police surveillance, and of a generally more authoritarian form of government. And then, between 1945 and 1950, came a further series of changes, no less remarkable than the great reforms of Atatürk. When the Charter of the United Nations came up for ratification in the Turkish Parliament in 1945, a group of members, led by Celâl Bayar, Adnan Menderes, Fuad Köprülü and Refik Koraltan, tabled a motion suggesting a series of reforms in the law and the Constitution which would effectively ensure inside Turkey those liberties to which the Turkish Government was giving its theoretical approval in the Charter. The motion was rejected by the Government, and its sponsors forced to leave the party. In November 1945, however, under pressure of a by now active and informed public opinion, President İnönü announced the end of the single-party system, and in January 1946 the opposition leaders registered the new Democratic Party. Numerous other parties followed, including the National Party (formed July 1948 and reconstituted as the Republic National Party in 1954).

TURKEY UNDER THE DEMOCRATIC PARTY

In July 1946 new elections gave the Democrat opposition 70 out of 416 seats, and there can be little doubt that completely free elections would have given them many more. During the years that followed, the breach in the dictatorship grew ever wider, and a series of changes in both law and practice ensured the growth of democratic liberties. Freedom of the Press and of association were extended, martial law ended, and, on February 15th, 1950, a new electoral law was approved, guaranteeing free and fair elections. In May 1950 a new general election was held, in which the Democrats won an overwhelming victory. Celâl Bayar became President, and a new Cabinet was formed, with Adnan Menderes as Prime Minister and Fuad Köprülü as Foreign Minister. The new regime adopted a more liberal economic policy, involving the partial abandonment of *Étatisme* and the encouragement of private enterprise, both Turkish and foreign. For a while, the stability and progress of the republic seemed to be threatened by the growing activities of groups of religious fanatics, whose programme appeared to require little less than the abrogation of all the reforms achieved by the Turkish revolution. After the attempt on the life of the liberal journalist Ahmet Emin Yalman in November 1952, the government took more vigorous action against what were called the "forces of clericalism and reaction". Many arrests were made, and in the summer of 1953 the National Party, accused of complicity in reactionary plots, was for a time outlawed and legislation was passed prohibiting the exploitation of religion for political purposes. The relations between the two main parties, after a temporary improvement in the face of the common danger of reaction, deteriorated again in the course of 1953-54, though not to such an extent as to imperil national unity. On May 2nd, 1954, in Turkey's third general election since the war, the Democrats won a resounding victory.

Encouraged by this overwhelming reaffirmation of popular support, the Government proceeded to adopt a number of measures which were criticised by the opposition as undemocratic. These included new civil service laws giving the Government greatly increased powers of dismissal and compulsory retirement, and an electoral reform restricted coalition candidatures. These laws, following on the new Press law of March 7th, 1954, embittered relations between Government and opposition. Both opposition parties decided to boycott the provincial council and municipal elections (September and November 1955 respectively), in which therefore the Democrats were opposed only by the very small Peasant Party and by Independents. These were able to score some successes.

In view of the smallness and weakness of the opposition parties, and the immense parliamentary majority of the Democratic Party, it was inevitable that sooner or later splits would appear within it. In October 1955 a serious crisis culminated in the dismissal or resignation from the party of nineteen deputies. These were later joined by some others and formed a new party, the Freedom Party.

Meanwhile, in September 1955, severe anti-Greek outbreaks led to the imposition of martial law in Istanbul, Izmir and Ankara, the dismissal of several senior officers and several cabinet changes. A new Cabinet, the fourth since the Democrat victory in 1950, was presented to the assembly on December 9th.

Conflict between the Government and Opposition was sharpened by the decision taken to advance the date of the general elections by more than eight months, to October 27th, 1957. The three Opposition parties—Republicans, Freedom and National Parties—first intended to present a united front, but the electoral law was changed to make this impossible. They were therefore obliged to present separate lists in each constituency, and so, although the combined votes won by Opposition candidates were slightly more than 50 per cent of the total, the Democrats again emerged triumphant, though with a diminished majority.

In the new Assembly the themes of debate continued to centre on the economic condition of the country and what the Opposition considered inroads on liberty. A Bill was passed in December 1957 amending the rules of the Assembly, and laying down a new scale of penalties for their infraction. At the same time a proposal to channel all newspaper advertisements through a single organisation was interpreted as another device for ensuring Government control over the Press. There is no doubt that its running fight with the Press contributed much to the downfall of the Menderes regime. The new regime, while not immediately sweeping away the old bans, encouraged newspaper owners and editors to draw up a "code of self-control" which was worked out with the assistance of the International Press Institute.

FOREIGN AFFAIRS 1945-60

In foreign affairs, both the People's Party and the Democrat Governments followed a firm policy of unreserved identification with the West in the cold war. Since May 1947 the United States has extended economic and military aid to Turkey on an increasing scale, and in 1950 a first indication of both the seriousness and the effectiveness of Turkish policy was given with the despatch of Turkish troops to Korea, where they fought with distinction. In August 1949 Turkey became a member of the Council of Europe, and early in 1952 acceded to full membership of the North Atlantic Treaty Organisation, in which she began to play an increasingly important part. Thereafter other arrangements were made by which Turkey accepted a role in both Balkan and Middle Eastern defence. On

February 28th, 1953 a treaty of friendship and collaboration was signed in Ankara with Greece and Yugoslavia, which prepared the way for a subsequent alliance, and on April 2nd, 1954 a mutual aid pact was signed in Karachi between Turkey and Pakistan, with the blessing of the United States.

Despite her economic problems and her failure to secure the 300 million U.S. dollar loan which she had requested from the United States, Turkey resisted the temptation to follow the example of some other states and play the great powers off against one another. In spite of efforts from both north and south to detach her, Turkey remained faithful to the northern tier alliance, and on November 21st–22nd, 1955, the Turkish Prime Minister attended the inaugural meeting of the council of the Baghdad Pact, in which Turkey thereafter played a major role.

In January 1957 the President of the United States announced a new programme of economic and military assistance for those countries of the area which were willing to accept it. At a further meeting held in Ankara the Muslim states belonging to the Baghdad Pact expressed their approval of this "Eisenhower Doctrine". The United States, in March 1957, made known its decision to join the military committee of the Baghdad Pact, and later in March Turkey promised to co-operate with the United States against all subversive activities in the Middle East. It was announced that financial aid would be forthcoming from Washington for the economic projects previously discussed between the members of the Baghdad Pact.

From 1958 Turkey was actively involved in settling terms for the constitution of an independent Cyprus. These were eventually agreed between Turkey, Greece, the United Kingdom and the Greek and Turkish Cypriots. Cyprus achieved independence in August 1960.

Fidelity to NATO and CENTO remained the basis of Turkey's foreign policy during the late 1950s. By the beginning of 1960, Turkey, following the examples of some of her allies, decided that such a policy need not be incompatible with less frigid relations towards Russia, and in April a visit to Moscow by Mr. Menderes was announced for July. Before it could take place the Menderes regime was overthrown, but his successors continued a more flexible policy. Soon after the revolution a cordial letter from Mr. Khrushchev to Gen. Gürsel received a cordial reply, in which, however, Turkey's need for active allies was once more emphasised.

THE 1960 REVOLUTION

Economic difficulties continued to be one of the main preoccupations of the Turkish Government. The development plans envisaged since 1950 had been carried forward with financial aid from the United States and from such bodies as the World Bank .These policies had been accompanied by inflationary pressures, an unfavourable trade balance, decreased imports, a shortage of foreign exchange and, since the agricultural population was in receipt of subsidies from the Government, a higher demand for consumer goods which aggravated the prevalent inflation. Social and economic unease tended to reveal itself in a drift of people from the villages to the towns, the population of centres like Ankara, Istanbul, Izmir, Bursa and Adana being considerably increased during recent years.

The influences which led to the revolution had been long at work. Hostility between the Democrats in power and the People's Party in opposition grew steadily more marked, and was sharpened towards the end of 1959 by suspicions that the Democrats were planning to hold fresh elections in the near future ahead of time. It was feared that these would, if necessary, be rigged to keep the Democrats in power indefinitely.

In May, 1959, political tension between the two main parties had already broken into violence during a political tour of Anatolia conducted by the opposition leader İsmet İnönü. The Government banned all political meetings. Blows were struck in the Grand National Assembly, and the Opposition walked out.

Much the same pattern of events ushered in the final breakdown a year later. At the beginning of April, 1960, İsmet İnönü undertook another political tour of Anatolia. At one point troops were called on to block his progress. Three of the officers involved in this incident took the strong step of resigning. The Opposition tried, but failed, to force a debate in the Assembly. On their side the Democrats set up a commission of enquiry, composed entirely of their own supporters, to investigate "the destructive and illegal activities of the P.R.P." Again the Grand National Assembly was the scene of violence, and all political activity was suspended for three months.

At this point the students took a hand. The universities had for some time been a focus of anti-government feeling, and in consequence had, like the newspapers, found their liberties attacked. On April 28th students in Istanbul demonstrated against the Menderes Government. Troops were called on to fire, and martial law was declared in Ankara and Istanbul.

As administrator of martial law, the Turkish Army found itself, contrary to its traditions, involved in politics. A group of officers decided that their intervention must be complete if Turkey was to return to Kemalist principles. In the early hours of May 27th they struck. President Bayar, Mr. Menderes, most Democratic Deputies and a number of officials and senior officers were arrested. The Government was replaced by a Committee of National Union headed by General Gürsel, a much respected senior officer who had fought with Atatürk at Gallipoli.

The *coup* was immediately successful and almost bloodless, though Dr. Gedik, former Minister of the Interior, committed suicide after his arrest. The accusation against the Menderes regime was that it had broken the constitution and was moving towards dictatorship. The officers insisted that they were temporary custodians of authority and would hand over to the duly constituted civilians. A temporary constitution was quickly agreed, pending the drafting of a final new one. During this interval legislative power was vested in the Committee of National Unity, and executive power in a Council of Ministers, composed of civilians as well as soldiers. On August 25th, however, ten of the eighteen Ministers were dismissed, leaving only three civilians in the Government. General Gürsel was President of Republic, Prime Minister and Minister of Defence. The courts were declared independent. Commissions were set up to inquire into the alleged misdeeds of the Menderes regime.

Although the new regime did not fail to meet political opposition, particularly among the peasants and around Izmir, a stronghold of Mr. Menderes, the main problems facing it were economic. The former regime was shown to be heavily in debt in every field. Austerity measures, including restrictions on credit, had to be put into operation and an economic planning board was set up to work out a long-term investment plan with the aid of foreign experts.

THE COMMITTEE OF NATIONAL UNITY

The Committee of National Unity, which originally consisted of 37 members, was reduced to 23 on November 13th, 1960. The 14 officers dismissed represented a group led by Colonel Turkeş, who had been pressing for the army to retain its post-revolutionary powers and to introduce radical social reforms.

This purge completed, preparations for a return to political democracy continued. A new Assembly, to act as a temporary parliament, was convened at the beginning of January 1961. It consisted of the National Unity Committee of 23, acting jointly with a House of Representatives of 271 members, both elected and nominated. In this the People's Party predominated. At the same time party politics were again legalised and a number of new parties emerged. Some of them proved short-lived, but one, the Justice Party founded by General Ragip Gümüşpala, who had been Commander of the Third Army at the time of the *coup d'état*, was destined to become formidable by attracting the support of many former adherents of the Democratic Party, which had been declared illegal.

A special committee of the Assembly framed a new constitution which had some significant changes from the 1924 version. It provided for a court to determine the constitutionality of laws, for a two-chambered legislature, and it included a reference to "social justice" as one of the aims of the State.

THE YASSIADA TRIALS

These constitutional developments took place against the background of the trial of the accused members of the Menderes regime. The trial was held on the little island of Yassiada in the Bosphorus, where the accused had been confined after arrest, and lasted from October 1960 to August 1961. The sentence of the court was pronounced on September 15th. There were fifteen death sentences, twelve of which, including that on Mr. Bayar, were commuted to life imprisonment. Adnan Menderes, Fatin Zorlu, the former Foreign Minister, and Hasan Polatkan, the former Minister of Finance, were duly hanged.

The trial inevitably absorbed the attention of the country, and there were many reminders that sympathy for the former regime and its leaders was far from dead. The most serious setback for the authorities, however, appeared in the results of the referendum on the new constitution. This was approved by 6,348,191 votes against 3,934,370, and the large minority was taken as an indication of continuing loyalty to the Democrats.

It was to electioneering that the country, still stirred by the execution of Mr. Menderes and his colleagues, turned in the autumn. The campaign, perhaps because Yassiada was ruled out as a subject for discussion, proved unexpectedly quiet. On October 15th, 1961, the elections gave the People's Party 173 seats and the Justice Party 158 seats in the National Assembly, and 36 and 70 respectively in the Senate.

These figures were a blow to the hopes of the People's Party that they would achieve an overall working majority. A coalition became necessary. The election results were also further evidence of latent support for the Democrats.

THE NEW GOVERNMENT

On October 25th, 1961, Parliament opened and the transfer of power from military to civilians was made. The revolutionaries had kept their word and a new epoch began. The next day General Gürsel, the only candidate, was elected President. But forming a government proved a much harder process. On November 10th Mr. İsmet İnönü, leader of the People's Party, was asked to form a government, and after much hesitation and strong pressure from the Army, the Justice Party agreed to join forces with its rival. A Cabinet was formed with Mr. İnönü as Prime Minister, Mr. Akıf İyidoğan, of the Justice Party, as Deputy Prime Minister, and ten more Ministers from each of the two coalition parties.

The Government remained, as Mr. İnönü said, exposed to a double fire—from those who thought the Army did too much (i.e. that civil liberties were still circumscribed) and those who thought it did too little (i.e. that it did not crush all signs of counter-revolution). The resignation of Mr. İnönü at the end of May weakened the extremists in the Justice Party, who had wanted to grant an amnesty to former supporters of Mr. Menderes. They were now face to face with the Army, the original movers of the 1960 revolution, and many of them felt it wise to moderate their demands.

By the end of June Mr. İnönü had formed a new coalition government composed of twelve Ministers from the Republican People's Party, six from the New Turkey Party, four from the Republican Peasants' Nation Party, and one Independent Minister.

The new government's programme expressed attachment to the principles of Western democracy and to the NATO alliance. It covered almost every sphere of the national life, including education, taxation, employment, and the problems of a rapidly rising birth-rate and an adverse balance of trade.

The Republican People's Party, like the country as a whole, found itself divided on the pace of reforms. There were also some signs of a growing but largely unformed interest in socialism. A Socialist Cultural Association, composed of politicians, intellectuals and journalists, was formed in December. But an article on socialism in *Cumhuriyet* brought its author under arrest—a sign that the identification of socialism with communism was still prevalent.

1962 saw the publication of Turkey's long-awaited first Five-Year Plan (*see* below, *Economic Survey*). Before the Plan was published there had been considerable controversy over how the amount should be raised (about £2,400 million sterling). Four leading members of the planning organization, who favoured more drastic taxation of landowners and agriculturalists, including the director, Mr. Osman Torun, resigned in September. In January 1963 Mr. Attila Sönmez, director of economic planning, likewise resigned, on the grounds that serious inflation would result if the Plan were carried out as the Government intended. A working group set up in July by OECD in Paris was one answer to the problem of outside contributions to the Plan. This reached agreement in June 1963 and formal signature followed on September 12th. The agreement provided for the association of Turkey with the Common Market in two phases.

POLITICAL UNREST

The political climate during 1963 remained unsettled. In February the leading radical of the original Committee of National Unity, Colonel Turkeş, who had been in unofficial exile abroad, returned with plans to set up a new political organization. More immediately threatening to the regime were the disturbances which marked the temporary release of the former President, Celal Bayar, from the prison in Kayseri where he had been since his sentence. A convoy of hundreds of cars escorted the 80-year-old politician to Ankara, where he was welcomed on March 24th by large and enthusiastic crowds. The reception appeared as a direct challenge to the revolution and was countered by violent protests, in which students and members of the armed forces participated, denouncing Mr. Bayar and his supposed supporters in the Justice Party.

In the early hours of May 21st, 1963, Ankara was the scene of yet another abortive *coup d'état*. The instigator was Colonel Aydemir, who had been responsible for the attempted revolt in February 1962. On this occasion his resort to arms, in which some of the cadets at the Military

Academy were involved, was quickly suppressed. Colonel Aydemir was executed in July, 1964. One result of the attempted *coup* was the imposition of martial law in Ankara, Istanbul and Izmir. Originally proclaimed for one month, martial law was repeatedly prolonged.

Although the Bayar incident and Aydemir *coup* produced divisions inside the ranks of the Justice Party, it showed considerable successes at the local elections in November, the first to be held since 1954. These successes were mainly at the expense of the New Turkey Party and the Republican Peasants' Nation Party, Mr. İnönü's two junior partners in the coalition. They resigned from the government, and after General Gümüşpala, the leader of the Justice Party, had tried and failed to form a Ministry, the President called again on Mr. İnönü, who on December 23rd formed a minority government drawn from members of his own Republican Party and some independents. It received a vote of confidence in the Assembly.

The first months of 1964 were overshadowed by an attempt on the life of Mr. İnönü in February, and by the situation in Cyprus, where the fate of the Turkish minority created strong feeling in the mainland. Mr. İnönü's critics claimed that he had "missed the bus" by failing to intervene on the island with force when the trouble started.

RAPPROCHEMENT WITH U.S.S.R.

This, and other diplomatic efforts towards a solution, failed, and public opinion grew more irritated, not only with Greece, but also with Turkey's western allies, in particular the U.S.A. and the United Kingdom, who were accused of being lukewarm in their support for Turkey's case. In August this irritation caused a violent explosion in Izmir, when rioters wrecked the U.S. and British pavilions at the trade fair. Mr. İnönü, though moving with characteristic caution, gave a warning that the alliance with the west, the basis of Turkey's foreign policy since the war, was in danger. To reinforce his warning came several steps designed to improve relations with the U.S.S.R. When the Cyprus problem first flared up again it had appeared that the Soviet Government took the side of Greece, and the Soviet trade pavilion had also been a target for the Izmir hooligans. But feelers were out in both Moscow and Ankara, and at the end of October 1964 Mr. Erkin visited the U.S.S.R.—the first Turkish Foreign Minister to make this journey for twenty-five years. Before leaving he invoked the memory of the early days of friendship between Atatürk and Lenin, and the same precedent was made much of by his hosts, who tactfully did not try to press Turkey into premature neutralism, as they had done in the past. On Cyprus, the U.S.S.R. appeared to have moved closer to the Turkish point of view, the communiqué which ended Mr. Erkin's talks speaking favourably of a solution "by peaceful means on the basis of respect for the territorial integrity of Cyprus, and for the legal rights of the two national communities".

Mr. Erkin's journey was followed up in January 1965 by the visit to Ankara of a Soviet parliamentary delegation. A trade pact between the two countries followed in March. In May, Mr. Gromyko, the Soviet Foreign Minister, paid a five-day visit to Turkey, and in August, Mr. Ürgüplü, the Prime Minister, paid a return visit to the U.S.S.R.

FALL OF MR. İNÖNÜ

For all this, Cyprus continued to give the Opposition ammunition with which to harass the İnönü government. At the Senate elections in June, 1964, the Justice Party won 31 out of the 51 seats contested, thus increasing its already large majority in this House. Its success was clouded by the death of the Party's leader, General Gümüşpala. In November Mr. Süleyman Demirel, a trained engineer and a former Director General of the state water organization, was elected leader in his place, though he was without a seat in Parliament. Mr. İnönü survived more than one narrow vote of confidence, but was finally brought down on February 13th, 1965, by an adverse vote (225 to 197) in the Assembly on the Budget—the first time that the life of a Turkish government had been ended in this way. There was some speculation whether the Army would allow the Opposition to form a government: the previous November General Sunay, Chief of Staff of the Armed Forces, had warned Justice Party Deputies against criticizing the army. After a short delay, however, a coalition government was formed, made up from the four parties which had been in Opposition—the Justice Party, the New Turkish Party, the Republican Peasant's Party, and the National Party. An independent senator, Mr. Suat Ürgüplü, who had spent much of his previous career in diplomacy, headed the team as Prime Minister.

Turkey suffered a bitter blow when, in December, the General Assembly of the United Nations passed a resolution urging all states to refrain from intervention in Cyprus. This was seen as directly aimed at Turkey's aid for the Turkish minority there. The Government in Ankara denounced the resolution as being "against right, law, and international agreements". However, in the early months of 1966 the position improved somewhat. Direct contacts between Ankara and Athens led to renewed hopes of a negotiated settlement. Unfortunately nothing had been achieved by the early summer of 1967, when the military *coup* in Athens led to Turkish fears that Greece was entering a new phase of instability and nationalism.

1965 was election year. The general election of October 11th confirmed the growing popularity of the Justice Party. Winning 240 seats in an Assembly of 450, it achieved a majority over all its rivals. The People's Party was reduced to 134 seats, followed by the extreme right-wing National Party with 31, the New Turkish Party with 19, the Turkish Workers' Party with 15, and the Republican National Peasants' Party with 11 seats. The emergence of an organized party of the left was perhaps even more remarkable than the triumph of the Justice Party, heirs of the Menderes tradition.

DEMİREL CABINET

Mr. Süleyman Demirel formed his cabinet from members of his own party. Introducing his government to the Assembly, Mr. Demirel declared that its most important task would be to withstand communism "by the realization of social justice and measures of social security". Emphasis was to be put on industrialization.

In spite of its working majority the Demirel Government proved hardly more successful than its predecessors in getting things done. The Justice Party blamed its poor record of legislation on the obstructionist tactics of the Opposition. There had been filibusters, and several ugly scenes of violence on the floor of the Assembly. However, elections in June 1966 for a third of the seats in the Senate showed that the Justice Party was not losing popularity.

To some extent this success was attributable to the innate conservatism of the Turkish peasantry, who may have been alarmed by Mr. İnönü's statement that the People's Party was left of centre. This position was not approved by all the party—some thought it went too far, others not far enough. A convention of the party in October showed a victory for the left-wingers. Mr. Bülent Ecevit, Minister of Labour in 1961–65, was elected general secretary of the party, with the declared intention of turning it into a party of democratic socialism. Six months later 48 senators and congressmen, led by Mr. Turhan Feyzioğlu, a former Minister, resigned from the party on the grounds that it was falling into a "dangerous leftist adventure". This was denied by Mr. Ecevit and Mr. İnönü, who supported him. They claimed that, on the contrary, their progressive policies took the wind out of other left-wing parties' sails, and so was the best barrier against communism.

In May 1967 a majority of dissidents came together to form the new Reliance Party, which proclaimed its opposition to socialism and its belief in the "spiritual values of the Turkish nation." In June Mr. Ecevit forced a fresh election of the People's Party executive, and by securing the elimination of two left-wing representatives on it he was able to emphasise that his party remained left of centre rather than left wing.

The National Party also found itself in trouble when 8 of its 31 deputies resigned. But the real threat to all parties other than the governing Justice Party was the new electoral law. This, which was finally passed in March 1968 against the protests of a united opposition, did away with the so-called "national remainder system"—a change which threatened the electoral chances of all the smaller parties but was thought to be particularly aimed at the Turkish Workers' Party, which was accused by the Government of using communist tactics. Earlier a battle had been fought over the party's stormy petrel, Çetin Altan. In July 1967 a vote was taken to lift his parliamentary immunity so that he could stand trial on a charge of distributing communist propaganda. This decision was quashed by the constitutional court in August.

In March 1966 President Gursel, whose health had deteriorated (he died in September), was succeeded by Senator Cevdet Sunay.

FOREIGN POLICY 1966-1969

Turkey's relations with her allies in 1966 deteriorated. There were various demonstrations against the U.S.A., culminating in March 1966 in a riot in Adana, during which American buildings were attacked and American cars overturned. This was touched off by rumours that U.S. servicemen, of whom there were large numbers near the town, had made improper advances to Turkish women. But in effect it was the consequence of a long campaign in the press against the U.S.A.'s military presence, which reflected a general increase in xenophobia.

Parallel with these manifestations against Turkey's formerly most stalwart ally went an effort by the Demirel Government to make its whole foreign policy more flexible. This flexibility was symbolized by many official visits, given and received, between Turkey on the one hand, and the U.K., Romania, Bulgaria, Egypt, Yugoslavia and Morocco. One outcome of the exchanges with Arab leaders was that at the time of the June war with Israel the Turkish Government expressed its sympathy with the Arab cause.

As usual the touchstone of Turkey's foreign relations continued to be Cyprus. In 1967 this perennial problem oscillated between near settlement and near war. The military regime brought to power in Athens by the *coup* of April 1967 seemed ready to negotiate, but no agreement was reached.

Later in the year the situation suddenly deteriorated as a result of attacks by Greek Cypriots on the Turkish enclaves on the island on November 15th. Two days later the National Assembly voted by 432 votes to 1 to authorize the Government to send troops to foreign countries—in other words, to fight in Cyprus. There were daily Turkish flights over the island and the prospects of war seemed real. As a result of strong intervention by U.S. and UN go-betweens the worst was avoided. On December 3rd the Greeks undertook to withdraw their troops from the island and the Turks to take the necessary measures to ease tension. By February 1968 the situation had been so far restored that direct efforts to agree on a negotiated settlement for Cyprus were once again under way.

MILITARY INTERVENTION

Süleyman Demirel's Justice Party Government was faced with the growing problem of political violence from early 1968 onward. Disorders in the universities, springing from non-political educational grievances and from clashes between political extremists of the right and the left, took an increasingly violent form. Students staged anti-American riots, and in June 1969 troops had to be called in to prevent extremists disrupting examinations. The fighting between right and left factions became more serious in 1970, firearms and petrol bombs being used, and a number of political murders taking place.

Parliamentary politics also became rather confused. Elections in October 1969 produced an enlarged majority for the Justice Party, but the party soon split, a number of Mr. Demirel's right-wing opponents forming the Democratic Party. Party strengths became almost impossible to calculate, as factions and alliances formed and dissolved, and on crucial votes the support of Government and the combined Opposition parties was almost equally balanced. A new party, the National Order Party, with right-wing policies and theocratic tendencies, was formed in January 1970 by Professor Necmettin Erbakan.

The Turkish armed forces began to take an unusually close interest in political questions as internal disorders became more serious and it became apparent that factional bickering was preventing the Government from taking effective action. In May 1969 it was feared that the army would intervene to prevent the restoration of civil rights to members of the Menderes regime, and in 1970 the air force commander, General Muhsin Batur, was reported to be pressing for political and economic reforms and a return to the ideals of Atatürk. The student violence of 1970 and clashes between rival trade union organizations prompted General Tagmaç, Chief of the General Staff, to warn that the armed forces would consider it their duty to suppress disorders threatening Turkish national integrity and Atatürk's reforms. The year 1971 opened with intensified terrorism, and a wave of strikes and protests by public employees. There was a wave of bomb attacks on American-owned property, bank robberies and kidnappings of Americans, carried out by left-wing extremists, to which were added separatist agitation among the Kurds and reported Syrian encouragement for a separatist movement among the Arabs of Hatay province. It was at this stage that the armed forces intervened.

On March 12th, 1971, the Chief of the General Staff and the Army, Navy and Air Force Commanders delivered a memorandum to the President. Alleging that "Parliament and the Government, through their sustained policies, views and actions, have driven our country into anarchy, fratricidal strife and social and economic unrest; made the public lose all hope of reaching a level of contemporary civilization, a goal set by Atatürk; failed to realize the reforms stipulated by the Constitution; and placed the future of the Turkish republic in grave danger", they felt that it was "essential that, within the context of democratic principles, a strong and credible government should be formed which would neutralize the current anarchical situation". If this were not done quickly, they threatened, "the armed forces are determined to take over the administration of the State in accordance with the powers vested in them by the laws to protect and preserve the Turkish Republic". Later that day the Demirel Cabinet resigned.

MILITARY DOMINATION OF POLITICS

A new Government was formed by Dr. Nihat Erim, with the support of both the Justice Party and the Republican People's Party (RPP). Bülent Ecevit, the RPP secretary-general, resigned from office and refused to collaborate. Dr. Erim's programme promised sweeping reforms in taxation, land ownership, education, power and industry, but the Government's attention was first directed to the suppression of political violence. The military ultimatum was followed by further bombings, kidnappings and clashes between right and left-wing students and between students and police. On April 28th, 1971, martial law was proclaimed, initially for one month, in eleven provinces, including Ankara and Istanbul.

Newspapers were suppressed, strikes were banned and large numbers of left-wingers were arrested. The National Order Party was dissolved in May 1971, the Turkish Labour Party in July. The murder of the Israeli consul-general in Istanbul by the so-called Turkish People's Liberation Army provided the military authorities with an opportunity to round up nearly one thousand suspects in Istanbul alone, including many journalists, writers and intellectuals. In September 1971, Dr. Erim introduced a number of amendments to the Constitution, limiting individual civil rights and the autonomy of universities, radio and television, placing restrictions on the press and trade unions and giving the Government powers to legislate by decree. Dr. Erim's proposal to use the new powers to introduce sweeping social and economic reforms, supported by the armed forces, was opposed by the Justice Party. A Cabinet crisis in October and December 1971 led to the formation of a new coalition Cabinet, again headed by Dr. Erim, but his proposals for taking further executive powers were opposed by the four major parliamentary parties, and in April 1972 he resigned. A Cabinet formed by Suat Ürgüplü was rejected by President Sunay, and in May a Government drawn from the Justice Party, National Reliance Party and RPP, headed by Ferit Melen, was approved. There was a swing to the left within the RPP in May; the veteran party leader İsmet İnönü resigned after 34 years as chairman, and was replaced by Bülent Ecevit. Meanwhile, the terrorist activities of the Turkish People's Liberation Army continued, and martial law was prolonged at two-month intervals.

In July 1972, dissident RPP members, opposing the dominance of the left wing led by Mr. Ecevit, formed the Republican Party. In November the RPP withdrew its support from the Melen coalition Government, but its five ministers preferred to leave the party, and stay in the Cabinet. This caused further resignations from the RPP, including that of İsmet İnönü and 25 other deputies and senators. A number of these dissidents, together with the National Reliance Party and the Republican Party joined to form the Republican Reliance Party in February 1973. The RPP, without its right wing, began actively to oppose the Melen Government, which it considered to be dominated by the armed forces, and martial law, under which, it was alleged with increasing frequency, arbitrary arrest and torture were practised. In March 1973, for the first time, the RPP voted against the prolongation of martial law, following a heated debate in which the Minister of the Interior disclosed that in the two years of martial law 1,383 persons had been sentenced by military courts, 553 acquitted, and that 179 trials were then taking place and 2,991 were in preparation.

President Sunay's term of office expired in March 1973, and the Grand National Assembly began the process of electing a new president. General Gürler resigned his post as Chief of Staff in order to stand for election, his candidature receiving the strong support of the armed forces. He was opposed by members of the Justice and Democratic Parties, while the RPP decided to abstain from voting, as a protest against the military interference in the election and the censorship of electoral news in Ankara. Despite obvious military support for General Gürler, 14 ballots failed to produce a result, and eventually the Justice Party, RPP and Republican Reliance Party agreed on a compromise candidate, Senator Fahri Korotürk, former Commander-in-Chief of the Navy, who had not belonged to any political party. He was elected President on April 6th, 1973. The following day Mr. Melen resigned, and was succeeded as Prime Minister by Naim Talû, an independent senator, who formed a Cabinet with Justice Party and Republican Reliance Party participation.

The Talû Government, although considered to be merely a caretaker administration to last until the general election, due in October 1973, brought about a number of reforms, and during its term of office the armed forces gradually withdrew from political affairs. A land reform law, distributing some 8 million acres to 500,000 peasants, was passed in June 1973, and measures were taken to prevent foreign domination of the mining and petroleum industries. A strong element within the armed forces felt that the time had come to return to a strictly military role, and that martial law had achieved its objective of crushing extremism. General Sancar, who became Chief of Staff when General Gürler resigned to make his unsuccessful attempt to become President, was opposed to military intervention in politics, and retired 196 senior officers. Many close associates of General Gürler were transferred to politically insignificant posts, and the retirement of General Batur, the Air Force Commander, removed the last of the officers who had signed the armed forces' memorandum of March 1971. Martial law was gradually lifted from the affected provinces, and came to an end in September 1973.

RECENT FOREIGN POLICY

The traditional hostility between Turkey and Greece revived following the Greek announcement in February 1974 that oil had been found in Greek territorial waters in the Aegean. This led to a dispute over the extent of national jurisdiction over the continental shelf and territorial waters, with both sides making warlike moves in Thrace and the Aegean area. Turkey began a hydrographical survey of the continental shelf in this area, claiming oil exploration rights in the eastern Aegean. The Aegean issue contributed to making a preoccupation with the possibility of a confrontation with Greece rather than the U.S.S.R. the dominating issue of Turkish foreign policy during the late 1970s. The potentially tense situation in the Aegean was overshadowed by the coup in Cyprus in July (*see* page 265).

This *coup* was carried out by the Cypriot National Guard, led by officers from Greece, apparently with the support of the Greek military regime. Declaring its intention of protecting the Turkish community in Cyprus and preventing the union of Cyprus with mainland Greece, the Turkish Government proclaimed a right to intervene as a guarantor state under the Zürich agreement of 1959. On July 20th Turkish troops landed in Cyprus, and rapidly won control of the area around Kyrenia on the northern coast. The Turkish intervention in Cyprus was followed by negotiations in Geneva between Turkey, Greece and the United Kingdom. Turkey pressed for the creation of an independent federal Cypriot state, with population movements to give the Turkish community their own sector in the north. The intransigence of both Greeks and Turks, and Greece's rejection of a possible cantonal solution put forward by Turkey, led to a further successful advance by the Turkish forces in Cyprus. When a second ceasefire was called on August 16th, Turkey controlled about one-third of the total area of Cyprus.

The sector under Turkish control, all of Cyprus north of a line running from Morphou through Nicosia to Famagusta, contained more than half the livestock, citrus plantations and mineral reserves of Cyprus, with access to two major seaports. The flight of Greek Cypriot refugees from the north left the Turks a free hand to take over the administration and economy, and establish an effective partition of the island. Mr. Ecevit claimed that the Turkish military success had laid the foundation of a federal state with two autonomous administrations, allowing the Turkish Cypriot community to concentrate in the conquered area and establish their own government. On February 13th, 1975, the Turkish Cypriots unilaterally declared a "Turkish Federated State" in northern Cyprus and continued pressing for the establishment of a bi-regional federal state system in Cyprus. The State was described by the Turkish Cypriot leader, Rauf Denktaş, as the federal wing of the Republic of Cyprus, although no such Federal Republic yet existed. Greek and Turkish Foreign Ministers held talks in Rome in May 1975 on outstanding disputes between the two countries, with the future of Cyprus among the main topics. The Greek-Turkish Aegean dispute was also discussed, including the issue of who held the rights over oil exploration in the area, the equitable division of the Aegean continental shelf and the question of air space control in the area. The dispute was submitted to the International Court of Justice. In April 1978 Turkey refused to recognize the jurisdiction of the Court on this question, preferring to try to negotiate a political settlement, and in October the Court ruled that it was not competent to try the issue.

The U.S. imposed an embargo on military aid and the supply of arms to Turkey in February 1975 on the grounds that American military equipment had been used in the Turkish invasion of Cyprus in July 1974 and that Turkey had failed to make substantial progress towards resolving the Cyprus crisis. Relations between Turkey and the U.S. became further strained when, in July 1975, Turkey implemented counter-measures against the announced continuation of the U.S. arms ban, including the take-over of U.S. bases in Turkey by the Turkish Armed Forces and the abrogation of all Turkey's defence agreements with the U.S.A., although the NATO base was not affected. Nevertheless, the undermining of Turkey's confidence in the U.S. Government's support caused by the embargo cast doubts upon the value of its membership of NATO. The embargo caused considerable difficulties in the armed forces, which received most of their equipment from the U.S.A., and came at a time when economic difficulties made it impossible for them to buy elsewhere.

This embargo was slightly relaxed in October 1975 and, after lengthy negotiations, a new bilateral defence agreement was reached between the U.S. and Turkey in March 1976. However, thanks to the strength of the Greek lobby in the U.S. Congress, the agreement was not ratified during 1976 or 1977, in spite of pressure from the new U.S. President, Jimmy Carter, and widespread expectation of progress in the settlement of the Cyprus question. In January 1978, at the beginning of his term of office, Bülent Ecevit stated that his foreign policy would be aimed at relaxation rather than tension and the exploration at the highest level of possible compromises between Greece and Turkey. A summit meeting took place at Montreux, in Switzerland, on March 9th and the progress made in personal relations between Ecevit and the Greek Prime Minister, Constantine Karamanlis, contributed to a general lessening of tension in the Aegean. On March 11th, however, there was a severe dent in U.S.-Turkish relations when the U.S. Secretary of State, Cyrus Vance, made a statement about the linkage of the arms embargo relaxation and U.S. arms aid. Ecevit warned that the U.S.A. was endangering the process of negotiations and that Turkey was "not without alternatives as far as her national defence is concerned". He pressed home this point by agreeing a trade pact with the U.S.S.R. on April 7th. On May 2nd the U.S.S.R. announced that it could in principle supply arms to Turkey, and on June 23rd Turkey and the U.S.S.R. signed a friendship document which, however, was claimed by Ecevit to be not in conflict with Turkey's responsibilities as a NATO member. Nevertheless, the agreement with the U.S.S.R. marked a turning point in Turkish foreign policy. After the arms embargo, the confrontation with Greece over the Aegean and the failure of the western powers to help Turkey overcome its severe economic crisis, NATO could no longer be seen as its sole source of support abroad. The *rapprochement* with the U.S.S.R. was part of the determination to establish a ring of friendship around Turkey which also included, in 1978–79, a number of diplomatic missions with economic aims to eastern bloc and Arab countries. Turkey's more independent foreign policy was demonstrated in 1979 when Ecevit refused the U.S. Government overflying rights in Turkey to monitor Soviet military developments.

Progress on the solution of the Cyprus issue was less than had been hoped in the light of the amicability of the Montreux summit. During 1979 the inter-communal talks suspended since 1977 were the focus of attention and in June were resumed as a result of efforts by the U.S. Government and the UN. No progress was made, however, and the issues appeared as intractable as ever. Turkey continued to keep an estimated 26,000 troops in Cyprus but the economic crisis made this occupation seem not only unnecessarily expensive but also embarrassing since it makes it politically more difficult for the west to grant aid.

ECEVİT GOVERNMENT

General elections for the National Assembly and for 52 Senate seats were held on October 14th, 1973. In the National Assembly the RPP, with 185 seats, replaced the Justice Party as the largest party, but failed to win an overall majority. The RPP was believed to have won many votes from former supporters of the banned Turkish Labour Party, while the Justice Party lost support to the Democratic Party and a new organization, the National Salvation Party (NSP). The latter, led by Professor Necmettin Erbakan, was founded in 1972 to replace his banned National Order Party, and shared its traditionalist, Islamic policies, and became the third largest party in the new National Assembly. Prime Minister Talû resigned, but then continued in office for a further three months while negotiations on the formation of a coalition government dragged on. Despite this parliamentary crisis, the armed forces remained aloof from politics. Eventually, on January 25th, 1974, a Government was formed by the RPP and NSP, with Bülent Ecevit as Prime Minister and Necmettin Erbakan as his Deputy. The Cabinet had 18 RPP members and seven from the NSP.

The new Government, an apparently unlikely coalition of the left-of-centre RPP and the reactionary NSP, proclaimed its reforming intentions, but made concessions to the demands of its Muslim supporters which tended to deviate from Atatürk's strictly secular principles. In March 1974, Turkey was for the first time represented at an Islamic Summit Conference. The appointment of an NSP deputy as Minister of the Interior brought about a number of petty manifestations of Islamic puritanism, but the main lines of the Ecevit Government's policy seemed to be of a reforming, liberal nature, intended to remove the more excessive manifestations of the police state created during the period of military intervention. In May 1972, to mark the fiftieth anniversary of the founding of the republic, the Government amnestied 50,000 prisoners.

The land reform passed by the Talû administration came into operation in a pilot project in Urfa province, and in July the ban on opium production introduced under American pressure in 1972 was rescinded, a move which, together with the successful handling of the Cyprus question, increased Mr. Ecevit's popularity. The differences between the NSP and the RPP had been submerged during the Cyprus crisis, but once more became apparent in September. On September 16th, 1974, Mr. Ecevit announced that he had decided to resign, as the coalition was no longer viable, and to seek a stronger mandate in new elections. New elections, however, were not held immediately and President Korutürk sought to find a coalition government.

Following the resignation of the Cabinet of Bülent Ecevit on September 18th, 1974, Turkey remained for over six m nths without a government having parliamentary approval. Professor Sadi Irmak attempted unsuccessfully to form an interim coalition in November to prepare for new elections in 1975, but remained in office in a caretaker capacity whilst efforts were made to form a new government. Internal unrest increased during the lengthy government crisis, with serious clashes between opposing political factions and between students.

DEMİREL RETURNS TO POWER

In March 1975 Mr. Süleyman Demirel returned to power, leading a right-wing coalition, the Nationalist Front, consisting of four parties: Mr. Demirel's Justice Party (the biggest), the National Salvation Party (NSP), the Republican Reliance Party (CGP) and the neo-fascist National Action Party (NAP) founded by a retired Colonel, Alparslan Türkeş, who became a Deputy Prime Minister. Of the cabinet of 30 the Justice Party occupied 16 of the seats, the NSP eight, the CGP four, and the NAP two. The coalition did not have an overall majority in the National Assembly, but support from other parties was virtually assured. However, the precarious nature of this coalition meant that the Government had to avoid taking radical measures which would upset the co-operation between the four parties. This prevented Mr. Demirel's cabinet from tackling the pressing problems of a deteriorating economy and increasing political violence, for Erbakan refused to countenance the austerity measures demanded by the IMF while Türkeş stood in the way of a crackdown on political violence, most of which the "Grey Wolves" of the NAP were thought to have instigated. The weakness of the coalition also hampered progress towards a settlement of the Cyprus question, with Mr. Demirel having to make concessions to the militant views of the extreme right wing represented by Necmettin Erbakan's National Salvation Party. Even though Mr. Demirel's position in relation to his coalition partners was strengthened by the results of the elections to the Senate held in October 1976, when the Justice Party gained 27 of the 54 seats contested, the opposition leader, Bülent Ecevit, also increased his representation in the Upper House and the smaller parties of the coalition continued to exert pressure disproportionate to their actual strength. Between 1974 and 1977 the fortunes of the NSP fell drastically and their representation in the National Assembly was reduced from 48 to 24. Erbakan became increasingly discredited, although his deputy and chief rival, Korbut Ozal, grew in influence. At the same time the star of the NAP rose rapidly. It combines anti-Communism, Islamic values and a desire for centrally-directed free enterprise with a nationalism that would dispense with democracy. During Demirel's administration, the NAP was able to build up a system of militant cadres by placing its supporters in the police and civil service.

In spite of its difficulties, the Demirel Government continued in power in 1976 and 1977 by suspending all action over controversial issues, such as the economy, Cyprus and Greece and relations with the EEC and NATO, pending the general election scheduled for October 1977. Increasing political violence throughout Turkey and especially in the universities, between left- and right-wing groups, persuaded the authorities to bring forward the general elections to June. The political inactivity was matched by economic paralysis as it became clear that the economy was overloaded with short-term debt and banks struggled to pay foreign currency bills of payment.

Amid this financial uncertainty the election of June 1977 failed to produce the hoped-for decisive majority. While the Republican People's Party (RPP) increased its National Assembly seats to 213 out of 450, the Justice Party also increased its share from 149 to 189 seats. Bülent Ecevit, the leader of the RPP, formed a Council of Ministers but failed to agree a coalition with the smaller parties, and a week later was defeated in a vote of confidence in the Grand National Assembly. Süleyman Demirel, the leader of the Justice Party, was then invited to form a government and on August 1st a coalition came to power which gave key ministerial posts to members of Necmettin Erbakan's right-wing National Salvation Party and the National Action Party. As a result there was penetration of the university and college administrations by extreme right-wing factions and a consequent flare-up of violence on campuses. By mid-December a third of the universities were shut and 250 people had died in political violence.

The National Salvation Party contributed to the financial crisis by blocking attempts to follow IMF prescriptions for the economy, insisting on the maintenance of a 5.5 per cent growth rate and refusing to implement monetarist curbs to reduce inflation. Failure to agree on economic remedies led to the withdrawal of an IMF team on December 19th, 1977, without agreeing the necessary restructuring for the foreign debt position.

Frustration at the coalition's powerlessness led to the progressive diminution of the Justice Party's support in the Assembly between October and December 1977 as members resigned. By December 27th the coalition could muster only 214 votes and Bülent Ecevit was preparing a new coalition. Following a vote of "no confidence" in the Grand National Assembly, the Demirel government resigned on December 31st and formed a caretaker administration. On January 2nd, 1978, Bülent Ecevit formed a new government.

After the chaos of Demirel's administration, the appointment of Ecevit as Prime Minister was greeted with great popular enthusiasm and high hopes were entertained of his promise to deal with the economic crisis and the political violence. In the economic field there was an urgent need to restore confidence by rescheduling Turkish debts, devaluing the lira and obtaining foreign finance for desperately needed arms modernization for NATO commitments. By appointing a former general, Irfan Özaydinli, to the Interior Ministry and a former police chief and Interior Minister, Necdet Uğur, to the Education Ministry, Ecevit hoped to curb the political violence that had racked the universities. Ecevit's popular support, however, was not reflected in the National Assembly. His majority rested on the defectors from the Justice Party, to 10 of whom he gave places in his Cabinet, while the number of deputies who had "crossed the floor" had resulted in a pool of about 20 independents with fickle allegiances. Radical reforms were urged on Ecevit (particularly in retrospect) but the insecure parliamentary majority, the country's economic weakness and the unwanted reputation of the RPP in the conservative rural areas as a radical party enjoined on him the necessity for caution. He began a painstaking, relentless purge of right-wing elements in the public administration (including in September the Governor of the Central Bank) in response to the cramming of their ministries by Demirel, Erbakan and Türkeş in 1975–77. He adopted an economic stabilization programme, signed a stand-by arrangement with the IMF (providing for a total of U.S. $450 million over two years) and began work on restructuring the severe short-term debt burden. He was, however, unable to secure the huge amounts of international financial assistance necessary to make the stabilization programme work and few of the targets aimed at were reached. Inflation continued at about 60–70 per cent, unemployment reached 20 per cent and, for lack of raw materials, industry was working half time. Nevertheless, Ecevit was unwilling to take further austerity measures demanded by the IMF as a condition for further aid. More seriously still, the extent of political violence went from bad to worse. Although the universities returned to normal, elsewhere more and more people were killed in acts of terrorism. Both the police force and the internal security forces (MIT) were riven by factions of left and right which made them unable to intervene. Here, too, the process of purging extremists was begun and in September Ecevit replaced the chief of security but, while the civilian tools of authority remained weak and unreformed, the maintenance of law and order depended on the armed forces and Ecevit was forced to ask the *gendarmerie* to undertake policing duties in urban areas. By December 1978 over 800 people had been killed, particularly in the eastern provinces. These new areas of violence reflected a change of tactics by the NAP, which during 1978 campaigned in Central and Eastern Anatolia, where the traditional elements of society have been least affected by modernization and which are most threatened by its arrival. Türkeş' appeal to nationalism gained him supporters, particularly in areas where Turks lived with other ethnic groups, notably the Kurds. The violence culminated in December at the south-eastern town of Karamanmaraş in the most serious outbreak of ethnic fighting since the 1920s. There the historic enmity between the orthodox Sunni majority and the Alevi (Shi'a) minority had been exacerbated by the activities of right- and left-wing agitators. On December 21st the funeral of two members of the left-wing teachers' association, murdered the day before, was turned into a large-scale demonstration by the Alevis. The mourners were fired on by Sunni supporters of Turkeş and indiscriminate rioting erupted. After three days, over 100 people had been killed, over 1,000 injured and large parts of the Alevi quarters reduced to ruins. The MIT had failed to alert the Government to the incidents leading up to the massacre and order was not restored until the intervention of the army on the 24th.

The violence led to the imposition of martial law on December 26th. Although he had long been urged to take this step by Demirel, Ecevit had refused both in view of Turkey's previous experiences of martial law and to ensure the continuation of parliamentary democracy. It was imposed for two months (and renewed in February, April and June) in 13 provinces, all, excepting Istanbul and Ankara, in the east, although the mainly Kurdish areas of the south-east were excluded to prevent friction. Ecevit announced it was to be "martial law with a human face" and instituted a co-ordination committee to implement it comprising himself, Gen. Kenan Evren, the Chief of the General Staff, and Lt.-Gen. Sahap Yardimoğlu, the chief martial law administrator. Special military courts were established to hear cases of those arrested for martial law violations.

Following the riots at Karamanmaraş, Özaydinli, the Minister of the Interior, resigned in response to criticisms of his handling of the affair. The resignations of two more ministers (including Hasan Isik, the Minister of Defence) revealed the strains being placed on Ecevit's cabinet. The fact that Isik's resignation followed a visit to Turkey by the U.S. Under-Secretary of State suggested that he had disagreed with the Prime Minister over foreign policy, in particular over the new defence agreement being negotiated between the two countries and over the negotiations on the multilateral aid programme.

The first two months of martial law failed to halt the now endemic violence. A number of extreme organizations and journals, including two Kurdish periodicals, were closed down. In February 1979 the violence claimed its most distinguished victim, Abdi Ipekçi, the editor of the Istanbul newspaper *Milliyet*, a close associate of Ecevit and outspoken opponent of terrorism. The murder made it clear that martial law was powerless to prevent individual acts of terror and that extremists were killing off respected citizens of moderate views in their attempt to overthrow first the Government, then democracy. When martial law was renewed at the end of February, the Justice Party voted against the proposal on the grounds that it was being enforced with insufficient rigour and that the army's powers were too circumscribed.

In March the beleaguered Government gained two victories on the economic front, in getting an austere budget through the National Assembly and agreeing on a new stabilization package, but the victories proved hollow as the measures failed to boost the economy while at the same time a crisis blew up on the political front. On April 17th six ministers, all members of the group of defectors from the Justice Party, issued a public memorandum criticizing Ecevit for taking insufficient account of their views and demanding tougher measures to combat political violence, particularly of the left-wing variety, and Kurdish separatism. They also demanded a redirection of economic policies to allow more western investment and greater freedom for private enterprise. The gulf between these views and those of Ecevit's left-wing supporters in the RPP, the unions and the country appeared absolute but, after a 17-hour cabinet meeting, a compromise was reached under which Ecevit placated the group by acceding, to some extent, to their demands. The grounds for this agreement were minimal and a week later the impossibility of reconciling the irreconcilable elements in the coalition became evident. In response to the growth of Kurdish separatism, and alarmed by Kurdish violence in Iran, Ecevit agreed to extend martial law into six more provinces, all in the Kurdish south-east. Three RPP deputies promptly resigned, reducing the party's minority representation in the National Assembly to 211 out of 450. The revolt of the six ministers seemed to have unleashed forces that posed the threat of permanent instability to the coalition and to the Government's survival.

As violence continued throughout the country, the authorities were forced to take the drastic measure of imposing an all-day curfew in Istanbul and Ankara on May Day to prevent riots at the traditional parades. A march planned by the more radical of the union confederations, DISK, was banned and the army ordered the arrest of its whole leadership, a severe blow to Ecevit's reputation as a champion of workers' rights and an indication of the army's increasing involvement in politics. The cabinet defections continued with the resignation of another Minister of State. Talks with the IMF resumed, however, and finally, in June, agreement was reached in principle and the Minister of Finance, Ziya Müezzinoglu, signed a letter of intent outlining new austerity measures which effectively granted most of the IMF's demands. Meanwhile, at the General Convention of the RPP, Ecevit's position in the party was shown to be both unassailable (he was re-elected Chairman unopposed) and subject to fierce criticism (from the left for not adopting more radical policies and from the right for his highly personal style of leadership).

In June the crisis in the National Assembly, which had been imminent since April, broke (during intense activity before the July recess) over Ecevit's failure to stop the economic decline and the terrorist violence. There was a wave of resignations. Another Minister and four deputies resigned from the RPP and, most seriously, Ali Rıza Septiloğlu, a Minister of State, recrossed the floor to the Justice Party. At the same time the Minister of Customs and Monopolies was accused of corruption and could be saved only by a Government boycott of the Assembly. Ecevit weathered the crisis and the recess came with Demirel still unable to muster the 226 votes needed to bring down the Government, although the prospect of its survival beyond October appeared very distant for in that month five by-elections, all of which the Justice Party seemed likely to win, could give Demirel the extra votes he needs.

In January 1978, on taking office, Ecevit had been hailed as the worthy successor to Atatürk; by June 1979, as the murders and high prices continued, his popular support had vanished, he was in a minority in the National Assembly, his right-wing supporters had gone into opposition and his left wing was fiercely critical of his policies. If the attempt to steer a middle course between these two had made radical solutions to the problems impossible, cautious reforms seemed to have been swept away by the increasing chaos. The imposition of martial law could be said to have marked the failure of Ecevit's approach to the violence as the acceptance of most of the IMF's demands did to his handling of economic policy; indeed, the continuation of these two crises cast doubt upon the effectiveness of democracy itself. The democratic alternative, Demirel, had little to offer and a newspaper characterized the parties' policies as "fishing for votes in a sea of blood". The downfall of the Shah had suggested to many the possibility that Turkey would follow Iran into turmoil. In both countries the transition from an agricultural to an industrial society threatens the established patterns of a Muslim peasant society but in fact the differences make the analogy unconvincing. What principally distinguishes the two countries is the establishment of democracy: Turkey is committed to industrialization not through political coercion but parliamentary democracy. This system had so far survived the challenge of the chaos; whether it can continue to do so, as the Prime Minister's position becomes increasingly untenable, is open to doubt.

ECONOMIC SURVEY

Turkey is about 1,449 km. long and some 483 km. wide, covering an area of 779,452 sq. kilometres. The 1975 census recorded a population of 40,347,719, and the population has been growing at over 2.5 per cent annually in recent years. The estimated total by mid-1978 was 43,144,000. Two-thirds of the population live in rural areas. Turkey's largest cities are the former capital of Istanbul (2.5 million), the port of Izmir (637,000) on the Aegean Sea, and the capital Ankara (1.7 million, 1976 estimates). In 1977 845,000 Turks were working aboard, 654,000 of them in the Federal Republic of Germany.

The country possesses great natural advantages: the land yields good grain and a wide variety of fruit and other products; it is rich in minerals; and it has a number of natural ports. The climate is varied and, on the whole, favourable, but communications are hindered by the mountain ranges that ring the Anatolian plateau to the north, east and south.

Gross National Product (G.N.P.) grew by an average of 6.9 per cent a year in real terms between 1963 and 1976. In 1977 it grew by 4 per cent and in 1978 by an estimated 2.7 per cent, to about TL 1,132,506 million.

AGRICULTURE

Turkey is still predominantly an agricultural country. The agricultural sector employs nearly two-thirds of the labour force, provides about 60 per cent of export earnings and contributes about 25 per cent of G.D.P. Nearly 25 million hectares, or about a third of total land area, are under cultivation. Most of the farms are small and the average size of a family farm is only 19 acres (7.7 hectares). In good years the country is basically self-sufficient in foodstuffs. Principal agricultural exports are cotton, tobacco, fruit and nuts.

During the period 1963–70, the agricultural growth rate was only 2.5 per cent per annum compared with a target rate of 4.2 per cent under the First Five-Year Plan (1962–67). This failure is attributed to the insufficient emphasis placed on agriculture in both the First and Second Plans. There were indications by 1971 that this relative neglect would cease, with land reforms and the improved utilization of land, machinery and farmer education resources. In fact agricultural production in 1971 increased by some 30 per cent. In 1975 real growth in agriculture was 10.9 per cent, due mainly to a good wheat harvest, but the rate dropped to 3.8 per cent in 1976 and to little more than 1 per cent in 1977, recovering to an estimated 4 per cent in 1978. If the potential for agricultural development is to be exploited, then along with land reform a larger share of government expenditure must be allocated to agriculture than it has received hitherto.

A Land and Agrarian Reform Bill was passed in 1973, which should ultimately redistribute some 8 million acres to 500,000 peasants, over 15 years: 3.5 million acres of arable State property, 2.5 million acres of uncultivated State land which will be made arable and 2 million acres of private land which will be nationalized for free distribution make up the area covered by the Bill. This area, 37,670 sq. kilometres, is significantly large compared with the total 250,730 sq. kilometres under cultivation in 1972. Many Turkish peasants own very little land, and about one-tenth of all farming families have no land at all. The reform came into operation in 1974 in a pilot project in Urfa province. The maximum holding for each family was set at 80 acres of irrigated or 250 acres of unirrigated land, the excess to be expropriated and paid for by the State. The expropriated land, together with parcels of State land, will be distributed to about 25,000 families of landless tenant-farmers, who will be organized into co-operatives with State grants and loans to provide capital. The other 12,000 landless families will be diverted from agriculture, mainly to the textile and food industries.

About half the cultivated area is devoted to cereals, the most important of which is wheat. The principal wheat-growing area is the central Anatolian plateau, but the uncertain climate causes wide fluctuations in production. Barley, rye and oats are other important crops grown on the central plateau. Maize is grown along the Black Sea coastal regions, and leguminous crops in the Izmir hinterland. Rice, normally sufficient for domestic needs, is grown in various parts of the country. In 1977 the wheat harvest rose to a record 16.7 million metric tons, due to good weather and improved cultivation methods, but this fell to an estimated 14.7 million tons in 1978.

Cotton has only recently been taken seriously by Turkey, but its cultivation, mainly in the Izmir region and in the district round Adana, in southern Turkey, has been successful and great hopes are placed in it. Production of cotton lint rose from under 200,000 metric tons in 1960 to a peak of 598,387 tons in 1974. Output fell in 1975 and 1976 but rose again to about 475,000 tons in 1977 and to an estimated 515,000 tons in 1978. Since 1975 cotton prices have been steadily climbing and cotton earned more than 12 per cent of total exports in 1977, although it was overtaken that year for the first time by hazel-nuts as the single most profitable agricultural export.

Turkey produces a particularly fine type of tobacco. The three principal producing regions are the Aegean district, the Black Sea coast, and the Marmara-Thrace region. The bulk of the crop is produced in the Aegean region, where the tobacco is notable for its light golden colour and mild taste. The finest tobacco is grown on the Black Sea coast, around Samsun. Although a traditional Turkish export, its relative position as an export has been declining in recent years. Most of the tobacco exports go to buyers in the U.S.A. and East European countries. The size of the crop fluctuates considerably: in 1976 it reached a record level of 315,000 metric tons; the estimate for 1978 was 230,000 tons.

The coastal area of the Aegean, with mild winters and hot, dry summers produces the grape, fig and the olive. The outstanding product, however, is the sultana type of raisin, which is grown also in California and elsewhere. Turkey normally ranks second in the world as a sultana producer, but in good years becomes the largest producer in the world. The 1976 sultana harvest was only 85,000 metric tons, but improved in 1977 to an estimated 121,000 tons.

The Black Sea area, notably around the Giresun and Trabzon, produces the greatest quantity of hazel-nuts (filberts) of any region in the world; in 1977 an estimated 250,000 metric tons were harvested, compared with a record 317,000 tons in 1975. The forecast for 1978 was 260,000 tons. Substantial amounts of walnuts and almonds are also grown.

Tea is grown at the eastern end of the Black Sea, around Rize, and in other areas. Production from State tea plantations is around 300,000–400,000 metric tons of fresh leaves per annum.

Turkey is also an important producer of oilseeds, the principal varieties grown being sunflower, cotton, sesame and linseed. It also produces olive oil, some of which is exported. Production fluctuates, partly because of the two-year flowering cycle of the trees; in 1977/78 it was estimated at only 75,000 metric tons, compared with 178,000 tons in 1976/77. Figs are also a fairly important export crop (exported as dried figs).

Turkey was until 1972 one of the seven countries with the right to export opium under the UN Commission on Narcotic Drugs. Much opium was, however, exported illegally, particularly to the U.S.A. and Iran; partly as a result of pressure from the U.S. Government, the Turkish Government made opium cultivation illegal in 1972, but the ban was lifted in July 1974. The opium is now made into pharmaceutical opiates in a local factory.

Sheep and cattle are raised on the grazing lands of the Anatolian plateau. Stock-raising forms an important branch of the economy. The sheep population of about 42.7 million (1977) is mainly of the Karaman type and is used primarily as a source of meat and milk. The bulk of the clip comprises coarse wool suitable only for carpets, blankets and poorer grades of clothing fabric, but efforts have been made in recent years to encourage breeding for wool and there are some 200,000 Merino sheep in the Bursa region.

The Angora goat produces the fine, soft wool known as mohair. Turkey is the second largest producer of mohair in the world; production averages 9,000 tons per annum.

MINERALS

Turkey has a diversity of rich mineral resources, including large quantities of bauxite, borax, chrome, copper, iron ore, manganese and sulphur. Mining and quarrying employed 115,000 workers in 1977. Minerals account for about 8 per cent of total export earnings. In spite of the importance of mining—particularly as a foreign exchange earner—investment in mining under the Second Five-Year Plan was set at only 3.7 per cent of total planned allocations. However, under the Third Plan, the proposed investment was more than doubled to TL 1,113 million. About 60 per cent of all mineral output and all coal production is carried out by State enterprises. The most important state enterprise in the mining sector is Etibank, which works through its subsidiaries, Eregli Coal Mines, East Chromium Mines, Turkish Copper, Keban Lead

Mines and Keçiborlu Sulphur Mines. The state enterprises increased their predominance over the private sector during the early 1960s with an investment programme backed by the Mining Investment Bank, which was set up in 1962. The policy of encouraging the private sector to play a greater part in the mining industry through the establishment of the Turkish Mining Bank Corporation (TMBC) in 1968 has failed to overcome the general reluctance on the part of private investors to view mining as a worthwhile area for long-term investment, with the result that the private sector is undercapitalized. An additional factor militating against the development of mining has been the long-held suspicion of foreign investment in mining. A Bill passed by Parliament in 1973 restricts foreign participation in mining development projects.

Bituminous coal is found at and around Zonguldak on the Black Sea coast. The seams are steeply inclined, much folded, and strongly faulted. The coal is generally mined by the longwall system or a variation of it. These mines constitute the Etibank's largest operation, and the coalfield is the largest in this part of the world, including the Balkans. Most of the seams are of good coking quality, the coke being used in the steel mills at nearby Karabük. Production of coal in the public sector rose from 3,772,000 tons in 1961 to 4,973,000 tons in 1974, but fell to 4,405,000 tons by 1977; lignite production rose from 1,594,000 metric tons in 1961 to 9,022,000 tons in 1977. It is thought that coal reserves may become exhausted by the mid-1980s when Turkey will become dependent on its lignite reserves. Lignite is found in many parts of central and western Anatolia and total reserves are estimated at 5,000 million tons. Seams located in western Turkey are operated by the West Lignite Mines. The other main mines are at Soma, Degirmisaz and Tuncbilçk.

Practically all of Turkish iron ore comes from the Divrigi mine situated between Sivas and Erzurum in the north-east of the country and run by the Turkish Iron and Steel Corporation. The average grade of ore is from 60 to 66 per cent: reserves have been put at 28 million tons. Output varies with the needs of the Turkish iron and steel industry. Output of iron ore in 1977 amounted to 3,208,000 metric tons and is expected to register a significant increase when reserves in southern Turkey begin to be worked to serve the Iskenderun steelworks which is being expanded.

Turkey is one of the world's largest producers of chrome. The richest deposits are in Guleman, south-eastern Turkey, in the vicinity of Iskenderun; in the area around Eskisehir, north-west Anatolia; and between Fethiye and Antalya on the Mediterranean coast. The Güleman mines, producing 25 per cent of the country's total, are operated by East Chromium Mines under Etibank. Other mines are owned and worked by private enterprise. Little chromium is used domestically and the mineral is the greatest foreign-exchange earner among mining exports. Chrome ore production in 1977 was 918,000 metric tons.

Copper has been mined in Turkey since ancient times. Present-day production, conducted entirely by Etibank, comes from the Ergani Mines situated at Maden in Elâziğ, and the Morgul Copper Mine at Borçka in Çoruh province. Production of blister copper, most of which is exported to West Germany, the United Kingdom and the U.S.A., declined from 30,634 metric tons in 1977 to 26,928 tons in 1978. Known reserves of copper ore are put at 90 million tons. Studies carried out by MTA have revealed the presence of a promising copper belt along the Black Sea coast, with possible reserves of 300 million tons of medium quality ore.

Eskişehir in north-west Anatolia is the world's centre of meerschaum mining. Meerschaum, a soft, white mineral which hardens on exposure to the sun and looks like ivory, has long been used by Turkish craftsmen for pipes and cigarette-holders, to which may now be added various items of costume jewellery.

Manganese, magnesite, lead, sulphur, salt, asbestos, antimony, zinc and mercury are important mineral resources. Of these, manganese ranks first in importance. Deposits, worked by private enterprise, are found in many parts of the country, but principally near Eskişehir and in the Eregli district. Production of manganese has been around 34,000 metric tons annually in the past few years. Lead is mined at Keban, west of Elazig. Development of a new lead/zinc mine and electrolytic smelter in the Zantanti/Kayseri district is being undertaken by CINKUR, a private company 35 per cent owned by Etibank. Production of sulphur from the Keciborlu mine in Isparta province was 20,000 tons in 1977. Antimony is mined in small quantities near Balikesir and Nigde. An important new find of mercury deposits, which may amount to 440,000 tons, has been made at Sizma in Konya province. Large uranium deposits have been discovered in the Black Sea, between 1 and 2 km. below sea-level.

The Uludag (Bursa) wolfram deposits have been calculated at 10,000 tons of tungsten ore, carrying an average grade of 0.43 per cent WO_3. These reserves are among the richest in the world. Etibank and the German firm of Krupp have entered into an agreement on the development of the deposits.

Turkey's bauxite deposits are now supplying the aluminium complex built at Seydisehir with Soviet aid. The plant's initial annual capacity was 60,000 tons of aluminium but this is to be expanded to 120,000 tons. The plant will also produce alumina for export, and semi-finished products. The reserves at Seydisehir are estimated at more than 30 million tons.

Petroleum was first struck in Turkey in 1950 and all subsequent strikes have been in the same area in the south-east of the country. It is mostly heavy-grade oil with a fairly high sulphur content. Production of crude petroleum rose from 2.4 million tons in 1966 to a peak of 3.5 million tons in 1973. Output dropped back again to 2.6 million tons in 1977 and 2.7 million tons in 1978. The country's import needs in 1978 were forecast at 13 million tons of crude petroleum and 2 million tons of refined products. Five companies produce oil: the Turkish Petroleum Corporation (TPAO), a 99 per cent state-owned Turkish company, at Garzan and Ramandag, with recently discovered deposits at Magrip, Batiraman and Kurtalan and the smaller fields at Kurtalan and Çelikli; Mobil and Dorchester at Bulgurdag, Silivanka and Selmo; Shell at Kayaköy, Kurkan, Beykan and Sahaban; and Ersan, a small private Turkish company, at Kahta. In 1977 the largest producer was Shell, accounting for 45 per cent of output, followed by TPAO, with 39 per cent, and Mobil (which also purchases all the output of Dorchester). Ersan accounted for only around 3,700 tons. TPAO has been exploring offshore in the Aegean Sea and claims to have drilled 96 wells in 1977 but the finds appear to have been very small.

Turkey has four oil refineries. The 4.4 million ton refinery at Mersin came on stream in 1962. It is operated by the Anatolian Refinery Company (ATAS), a Turkish-registered company owned by Mobil, Shell, B.P. and Marmara Petrol. In March 1979 the Government announced it was going to buy out Mobil's 51 per cent share in the refinery. Since February 1978 the Mersin refinery has been running at less than 50 per cent capacity because ATAS refused to import more crude until it had received payment outstanding on previous imports. The Izmit refinery, which came on stream in 1961, is wholly TPAO-owned, following the sale of Caltex's 49 per cent share to TAPO in 1972. The capacity of this refinery is to be raised from 3.2 million to 10 million tons per year with Soviet aid. TPAO operates a 660,000 tons per annum refinery at Batman, near Diyarbakir, connected by pipeline to both Garzan and Ramandag. Its capacity is being expanded to 800,000 tons per annum. A 5 million tons per annum refinery built at Aliaga with Soviet aid has been experiencing teething troubles but its capacity is to be increased to 10 million tons per year. At present, two further refineries are planned at Thrace, and at a site on the Black Sea.

TPAO operates a 310-mile, 18-inch diameter pipeline running from the oilfields around Batman to Dörtyol on the Gulf of Iskenderun. Daily throughput capacity is around 10,000 tons, bnt this may be increased to 16,000 tons. Other companies use the pipeline on a tariff basis. In May 1977 a 980 km. oil pipeline from Iraq to Turkey went on stream. Its initial annual capacity is 25 million tons and this will be increased to 35 million tons. Between January and September 1978 Iraq suspended oil exports to Turkey because of non-payment. There is a severe shortage of petroleum products, particularly following the Iranian cutback. Libya is to supply Turkey with 4 million tons of oil during 1979, compared with 3 million tons in 1978, and the U.S.S.R. has promised to supply about 1.5 million tons.

INDUSTRY

The leading role in the process of inaugurating industrialization has been played by the state economic enterprises. Since 1950, however, private enterprise has been encouraged; by the beginning of the 1970s the private sector accounted for nearly half of industrial output and its rate of capital investment had become almost equal to public sector investment. The share of industry in the economy is increasing: whereas in 1952 industry accounted for 12 per cent of domestic product this had increased to 25.8 per cent by 1976. Manufacturing accounted for 17.5 per cent of G.D.P. in 1978. Whereas in 1962 consumer goods industries accounted for over two-thirds of industrial production, by 1972 its share had fallen to 46.5 per cent. In the same period the share of the intermediate goods industries increased from 17 to 39.4 per cent and that of capital goods from 12.9 to 14.1 per cent. Turkish industrial development has been protected from overseas competition by tariff and quota restrictions, with the result that Turkish industry is geared principally to the needs of the home market and manufactured goods account for only around 4 per cent of total exports. In 1977 the number of workers in manufacturing industries was 1,652,000. Manufacturing grew at about 10 per cent in 1976 (compared with the Plan target of 11.7 per cent) but this growth shrank to 8 per cent in 1977 and to 3.8 per cent in 1978, as a result of a serious electricity shortage and dire lack of foreign exchange, which led to totally inadequate supplies of imported raw materials, semi-finished goods and components.

The textile and clothing industry is Turkey's largest, accounting for one-third of manufacturing employment and contributing about 20 per cent of manufacturing output. Cotton yarn is the most important export in this sector but exports of clothing are increasing steadily. Cotton spinning and weaving, artificial fibres and knitwear have been major areas of expansion.

The iron and steel works at Karabük, north-west Anatolia, are run by the state-controlled Turkish Iron and Steel Corporation. Capacity is 570,000 tons. A second iron and steel complex, at Eregli in west Anatolia, produces hot and cold rolled sheets, steel strip and tinplate. The plant's annual capacity is 1,250,000 tons. A new steel mill with a capacity of 1.1 million tons was opened at Iskenderun in December 1975. The plant was built with the assistance of the Soviet Union, which in 1979 agreed to lend $400 million to double the capacity of the complex. Phase I of the expansion programme brought production up to 2.2 million tons by 1977, and by 1982 this will be increased to 6 million tons a year. Turkey's total output of iron and steel products in 1978 was 3.7 million metric tons.

Production of cement has been increasing steadily over recent years and in 1978 amounted to 15 million metric tons. Some is exported to Syria and Iraq.

Among food industries, the state-controlled sugar beet industry is the most important. Sugar production in 1978 totalled 1,126,062 metric tons. Production costs are very high and exports have to be heavily subsidized by the domestic market, except when the international price is very high.

The paper and board industry is dominated by the government-owned SEKA corporation which has one old-established mill at Izmir, with an annual capacity of 126,000 metric tons of paper and board, plus six mills which have been opened since 1971. Total output of paper and board in 1977 was 252,000 metric tons but fell to 227,000 tons in 1978. A very large paper factory is being built at Tasucu, on the south coast and another is to be built on the Black Sea coast with Libyan aid.

The motor vehicle industry was established after 1956 as an import substitute industry and by 1971 had become the largest industrial employer after the textile industry. However, it accounted for only around 5 per cent of total industrial output. The total output of more than 25,000 trucks, pick-ups and buses and 58,000 saloon cars (local versions of Fiats and Renaults) is fragmented between 15 enterprises with resulting loss of economies of scale. The process of merging of firms (there were 22 in 1967) is expected to continue under the impact of heavier taxation. The capacity of Oyak-Renault (44 per cent owned by Renault) is at present 40,000–50,000 units per year but this is to be doubled. An agreement has been signed with Fiat to build 80,000 tractors and an additional 60,000 engines. The two plants, to be built at Konya, will create 10,000 new jobs.

Turkey's first petrochemicals complex, situated at Izmit, began production in 1970 in ethylene, polythene, PVC, chlorine and caustic soda. Commercial fertilizer production has increased rapidly in recent years, reaching 2,900,000 tons in 1976. The state-owned Turkish Nitrates Corporation (TNC) has a nitrates plant at Kutahya, a triple superphosphates plant at Samsun and a superphosphates plant at Elazig. The Mediterranean Fertilizer Corporation's phosphates-nitrates complex at Mersin, based on by-products of the refinery there, began trial production in 1972. The Istanbul Fertilizer Corporation (IGSAS) plans to build an ammonia and urea plant at Kirikkale, 90 km. from Ankara. There are privately-owned triple superphosphates plants at Iskenderun and Yarimca. Turkey produces 75 per cent of its requirements of fertilizers and when new plants are completed it will be self-sufficient. An ammonia plant is to be set up at Gemlik under a joint investment agreement signed with Libya in 1975.

Other manufacturing industries include tobacco, chemicals, pharmaceuticals, construction, metal working, engineering, leather goods, glassware and ferrochrome.

There has been an extensive development of electrical energy; production in 1978 totalled 21,596 million kWh. More than half is supplied by thermal sources and the remainder by hydro-electric plants. However, installed capacity is at present 8 per cent below actual demand and the severe shortages of electricity affect both domestic and industrial users. Turkey has to import electricity from Bulgaria and, from spring 1979, from the U.S.S.R.

Turkey's most ambitious power project, the Euphrates dam at Keban, began production in 1973. The 670 ft. high dam will hold back a lake 70 miles long at the confluence of the two main branches of the Euphrates. The plant will have an initial capacity of 620 MW, rising to 1,240 MW. A 1,200-MW hydro-electric project is to be constructed on the Tigris at Ilisu; it is being designed by a British firm and will be completed by about 1985. Another hydro-electric dam is being built at Karakaya on the Euphrates, in the south-east, and the Soviet Union is to build two new thermal plants. At the end of 1978 it was announced that Sweden would build a nuclear plant in Turkey and in June 1979 agreement was reached with the U.S.S.R. for the supply of another nuclear power station as one of the projects in an $8,000 million package.

FINANCE

The Central Bank (Merkez Bankası), the sole bank of issue, started its operations on October 3rd, 1931. It controls exchange operations and ensures the monetary requirements of certain state enterprises by the discounting of bonds issued by these establishments and guaranteed by the Treasury. Other banks are described in the Finance section on page 796.

The monetary unit is the kuruş (piastre) by the law of April 1916. The Turkish lira (pound), which is, in practice, employed as the monetary unit, is made up of 100 kuruş.

The principal sources of budgetary revenue are income tax, import taxes and duties, production taxes, taxes and fees on services and revenues from State monopolies. From the beginning of 1962 agricultural incomes were taxed for the first time in recent history.

The 1978/79 budget estimated consolidated revenue at TL 247,253 million and recurrent expenditure at TL 262,753 million, giving a deficit of TL 15,500 million, compared with a deficit of nearly TL 20,000 million in 1977/78. However, revenue in 1978/79 actually totalled TL 315,000 million. By far the largest expenditure allocations in the recurrent budget were for defence (TL 50,617 million) and education (TL 25,905 million). The 1979/80 budget envisages recurrent expenditure of TL 397,300 million. Defence is allocated TL 64,000 million, education TL 46,000 million and village affairs and rural development TL 16,700 million.

Taxes have been increased by unprecedented amounts over recent years, partially to counteract the traditional budget deficit, and to reduce the volume of deficit financing. Inflation, which in 1976 had been running at about 20 per cent a year, had reached an annual rate of 65 per cent by April 1978 and was still between 60 and 70 per cent in the first quarter of 1979. Unemployment was more than 20 per cent.

A serious political and economic crisis came to a head in 1977, rendering Turkey virtually bankrupt. Foreign exchange transfers for all goods except strategic materials had ceased in February and many governments imposed a block on exports to Turkey, while foreign banks refused to advance any more loans. The Turkish Government asked for assistance from the IMF and in the meantime introduced an austerity package in September, which included an 8 per cent overall devaluation of the lira, drastic price increases and various foreign exchange measures. However, this was not sufficient to satisfy the IMF, which sent a team of experts to Ankara in October to discuss further measures for rescuing the country's economy. The lira was devalued by a further 3.4 per cent in December.

Finally, in March 1978, agreement was reached on a programme which included further devaluation of the lira by about 23 per cent overall; a limit to annual growth of 6.1 per cent; increases in deposit rates; and severe cuts in public spending. The IMF agreed to grant a $450 million credit over two years and its seal of approval on Turkey's proposed measures led foreign banks and governments to relax restrictions which they had imposed during 1977. In April six international banks set up a consortium to facilitate the re-scheduling of about $2,500 million of Turkey's foreign debts and in the same month the World Bank agreed to lend $650 million. Turkey was able to resume payment for imports in May 1978. However, the crisis continued, with Turkey still unable to service most of its debts in either 1977 or 1978. The economic targets agreed under the IMF stand-by arrangement were virtually unattainable, despite successive devaluations of the lira during 1978. The IMF refused to release the third tranche of the stand-by credit which had been due in November and talks between the two sides were suspended the following month. In March 1979 the Government announced a new austerity package which included a doubling of petrol prices (which had already been increased by 60–70 per cent in September 1978) plus price rises for iron and steel, cement, sugar and some consumer durables. The lira was effectively devalued by 40 per cent and a premium introduced for foreign currencies exchanged in Turkey by tourists and for the remittances of emigrant workers, to encourage them to send more of their earnings home. The measures did not produce the hoped-for signs of recovery, partly bacause of the lack of long-term structural reforms, and partly because, although imports were drastically pared, the cost of imported fuel continued to absorb nearly all export earnings.

The Government was resisting IMF demands for a further substantial devaluation of the lira, of at least 30 per cent, but did devalue by 5.7 per cent against the dollar in April. It also announced further measures which included more price rises on staple products, especially petrol, and a sharp increase in bank interest rates. In May the IMF agreed to resume talks (although the April 1978 stand-by funds were still frozen). Meanwhile western countries and the World Bank agreed on an aid package which would involve the immediate release of about $1,450 million in extra loans and export credits, but the package was conditional on Turkey's concluding a new stand-by agreement with the IMF.

Finally, in June 1979, an agreement in principle was reached with the IMF during talks in Paris. It covers a new stand-by credit, reported to total $315 million for one year. The agreement followed a 44 per cent devaluation of the lira announced on June 11th and new austerity measures, including further increases in the price of petrol and several other goods. The new exchange rate does not apply to imports of essentials such as petroleum and fertilizers.

Turkey also signed an agreement with Saudi Arabia in April 1979 for a loan of $250 million and smaller loans from other Arab states were under discussion during the first half of the year. The Libyan Arab Foreign Bank was the main participant in a $100 million loan arranged by a consortium of international banks in August 1978, and in June 1979 Libya also promised to provide a further $600 million in loans. An international bank loan of $125 million, agreed in January 1979, was subsequently halted by the Ministry of Commerce, which objected to the use of export stocks of cotton and hazel-nuts as collateral for the credit and asked for the arrangement to be reviewed.

Turkey's short-term debts in May 1979 totalled about $6,000 million. Its total foreign debt was estimated at $12,500 million.

Turkey's persistent trade deficit is partly offset by a net surplus on "invisible" items. Turkish workers abroad sent back remittances worth $1,312 million in 1975. This sum decreased to $981.8 million in 1977 but was expected to rise to $1,300 million in 1978, as a result of a government scheme to encourage emigrant workers to deposit money in Turkey. In 1977 the trade deficit (f.o.b.) was $3,406 million and the overall current account deficit at $3,325 million; this was expected to be reduced to $2,600 million by the end of 1978. International reserves, which at the end of 1977 had stood at only $774 million, rose to $1,318 million by September 30th, 1978, but declined again to $917 million (of which $752 million was in foreign exchange) at February 28th, 1979.

In 1974 the U.S. Congress had imposed an arms embargo on Turkey, which contributed greatly to soaring import costs, since Turkey was obliged to finance its defence expenditure from its own resources. A new defence pact signed in 1976, providing for military aid from the U.S.A. in the form of arms and grants worth $1,336 million, was not approved by Congress until July 1978 after the embargo was repealed. For 1979 the U.S. House of Representatives approved aid to Turkey totalling $300 million (compared with $225 million in 1978), of which $202 million was to be in the form of military aid (compared with $175 million in 1978), but the Bill still had to be passed by Congress. In June 1979 the House of Representatives refused to approve the granting of an extra $50 million in military aid. The Federal Republic of Germany also provides military assistance to Turkey.

EXTERNAL TRADE

Before and during World War II, Turkish foreign trade figures showed a surplus of exports over imports. Since 1947 this position has been reversed, and the demands of Turkey's economic development, especially since 1950, have inflated the imports bill without making equivalent short-term additions to the country's exporting strength. Exports in 1978 rose by more than 30 per cent to $2,288 million, while imports fell by nearly 21 per cent to $4,599 million, leaving a deficit of $2,310 million, compared with a deficit of $4,043 million in 1977 and $3,168.4 million in 1976. In 1977, exports had declined by 10 per cent and imports had risen by 13 per cent. Agricultural and livestock exports, which represented 67 per cent of the total, improved by 48 per cent in value. Metal ores accounted for 5.4 per cent and industrial and processed goods about 27 per cent. In 1977, raw materials accounted for 57.5 per cent of imports, investment goods 39.5 per cent and consumer goods only 3 per cent. In the first quarter of 1979 the trade gap was $532.7 million, 10 per cent more than in the same period of 1978, although exports, particularly of industrial goods, had improved considerably.

The main exports are cotton, textiles and clothing, fruit and nuts, tobacco, livestock, cattlecake and foodstuff residues, cereals and iron, chrome, manganese and other ores. The principal imports are crude petroleum, machinery, mineral products, base metals, transport vehicles, pharmaceuticals, chemicals, vegetable products, plastic and rubber, fertilizers and textiles. In 1977, 43.8 per cent of Turkey's exports went to the EEC, which supplied nearly 50 per cent of imports. By far the most important single trading partner was the Federal Republic of Germany, which supplied 16 per cent of imports and took nearly 22 per cent of exports. Iraq, the U.S.A., the United Kingdom and Italy are also important suppliers, while other major customers are the U.S.A., Switzerland, Italy and the United Kingdom.

An association agreement with the European Economic Community (EEC) was signed in 1963, under which Turkey was granted financial aid and preferential tariff quotas. A package of minor improvements, including better access for Turkish goods into the EEC and free movement of Turkish workers within EEC countries, was introduced at the end of 1976 but Turkey has been discontented with the slow progress in implementing these decisions, the way in which its preferential treatment has been eroded by agreements signed with other Mediterranean countries and with the restrictions placed on imports of its textiles and clothing. Full membership of the EEC is not a realistic goal in the foreseeable future but at the same time Turkey is worried about the harm it will suffer when Greece is admitted as a member. Talks were held in 1979 on the possibility of a five-year "freeze" on Turkey's obligation to dismantle tariff barriers against EEC goods while the EEC continues to dismantle its own, in accordance with the association agreement. The talks also dealt with EEC assistance to Turkey which may amount to as much as $1,200 million, including "soft" loans and other aid.

PLANNING

During the years of the First Plan (1962–67) a real growth rate of 6.6 per cent per annum was achieved. The Second Five-Year Plan, covering the years 1968 to 1972, envisaged an annual growth rate of 7 per cent, which was almost exactly achieved. Total investment was set at TL 111,500 million from both the public and the private sectors. The emphasis was on industrial development and the reduction of agriculture's dependence on weather conditions. Of total investment, 22.4 per cent was allocated to manufacturing industry. The long-term target of self-sustained economic growth, i.e. independent of foreign loans, was a prominent aim of the Third Five-Plan (1973–77), which allocated almost 45 per cent of the total investment to mining and manufacturing. Priority was given to providing a modern heavy industry base to promote export opportunities and import substitution. Total investment was planned at TL 281,000 million, of which manufacturing was to receive TL 187,000 million. An annual growth rate of 7.9 per cent in G.N.P. was aimed at. However, many targets were only 60 per cent achieved and in real terms the overall growth rate was below target. The start of the Fourth Plan (1978–82) has been delayed by the economic crisis until 1979. It envisages total investment of TL 1,500,000 million and an average annual growth rate of 8.2 per cent, with total G.D.P. at 1978 prices rising from TL 1,140,200 million to TL 1,699,500 million by 1983. Energy and manufacturing receive the largest investment allocations, followed by agriculture, transport and communications, and tourism.

STATISTICAL SURVEY

AREA AND POPULATION

Total Area	Thrace	Anatolia	Estimated Population (July 1st, 1978)	Workers Abroad* (1977)
779,452 sq. km.	23,764 sq. km.	755,688 sq. km.	43,144,000	844,599

* Including workers who returned to Turkey in the same year.

Population: 40,347,719 (October 1975 census).

CHIEF TOWNS

ESTIMATED POPULATION (July 1978)

Ankara (capital)	2,018,000	Diyarbakir	181,300
İstanbul*	2,801,000	Erzurum	181,250
İzmir (Smyrna)*	742,500	Mersin (İçei)	178,600
Adana	562,200	İzmit (Kocaeli)	172,000
Bursa	390,600	Sivas	170,500
Gaziantep	349,300	Malatya	170,350
Eskişehir	286,700	Antalya	154,500
Konya	275,700	Urfa	154,250
Kayseri	236,800	Kahramanmaraş	151,300
Samsun	190,300	Elâziğ	146,500

* Excluding suburbs.

ECONOMICALLY ACTIVE POPULATION

('000 persons employed in 1977)

Agriculture, hunting, forestry and fishing	9,100
Mining and quarrying	115
Manufacturing	1,652
Electricity, gas and water	90
Construction	547
Wholesale and retail trade	639
Transport, storage and communications	497
Finance, insurance and real estate	188
Public and personal services (including restaurants and hotels)	1,686
Other activities (not adequately described)	270
Total	14,784

Workers Abroad (1977)*
('000)

Australia	14
Austria	27
Belgium	16
France	42
Germany, Federal Republic	514
Libya	13
Netherlands	41
Switzerland	16
Total (incl. others)	713

* Provisional.

WORKERS' REMITTANCES FROM ABROAD
(U.S. $ million)

1972	1973	1974	1975	1976	1977
740.1	1,183.3	1,426.3	1,312.3	982.7	981.8

AGRICULTURE

LAND USE

	AREA ('000 hectares)				
	1973	1974	1975	1976	1977
Area under cultivation	25,014	24,660	24,407	24,239	24,515
Market gardens and truck farms, orchards, olive groves, vineyards, etc.	3,274	3,268	3,244	3,460	3,457
Forests	19,136	20,170	20,170	20,170	20,170

Meadows and grazing lands: 26,135,000 hectares in 1967.

PRINCIPAL CROPS

	AREA ('000 hectares)			PRODUCTION ('000 metric tons)		
	1975	1976	1977	1975	1976	1977
Wheat	9,250	9,250	9,325	14,750	16,500	16,650
Spelt	59	58	50	80	78	70
Rye	565	530	520	750	740	690
Barley	2,600	2,635	2,620	4,500	4,916	4,750
Oats	260	243	230	390	400	370
Maize	600	600	580	1,200	1,310	1,265
Millet	25	24	20	40	34	29
Rice (milled)	55	54	58	150	158	165
Mixed grain	194	186	180	250	233	220
Dry beans	94	102	104	155	159	160
Chick peas	140	138	138	172	170	180
Lentils	125	186	240	135	210	260
Vetch	163	159	119	145	114	100
Broad beans	31	30	30	50	48	50
Potatoes	179	187	180	2,490	2,850	2,850
Onions (dry)	60	63	70	670	760	845
Garlic (dry)	11	12	12	59	60	60
Tomatoes	82†	84†	n.a.	2,300	2,750	2,900
Cabbages (incl. black)	26†	28†	n.a.	610	600	540
Melons and water-melons	220	245	220	4,000	4,500	3,810
Aubergines (eggplants)	34†	35†	n.a.	485	525	550
Cotton (lint)	670	581	777	480	470	575
Cottonseed				768	767	920
Tobacco	231	293	270	193	315	238
Sugar beet	215	248	250	6,949	7,900	8,995
Sesame seed	54	43	32	33	25	24
Sunflower seed	418	445	374	488	550	455
Olives	80.1*	81.1*	81.6*	561	1,097	400
Olive oil				94	178	75
Tea (fresh leaves)	50	52	52	262	301	396

* Number of trees (million). † FAO estimate.

FRUIT AND NUTS

('000 metric tons)

	1974	1975	1976	1977
Apples	950	900	1,000	900
Grapes	3,347	3,247	3,080	3,180
Pears	230	240	255	260
Hazelnuts (filberts)	244	317	245	290
Figs (dried)	43	52	60	48
Walnuts	110	117	135	150
Pistachios	23	31	5	40
Almonds	33	37	30	24
Chestnuts	48	47	48	48
Oranges	500	540	545	650
Lemons	265	290	278	325
Mandarins	112	105	126	135
Peaches	160	200	192	185
Plums	136	130	137	153
Apricots (incl. wild)	124	165	176	151
Cherries	67	73	85	91

LIVESTOCK

('000 head at December)

	1975	1976	1977
Cattle	13,751	14,102	14,540
Buffaloes	1,051	1,056	1,012
Sheep	41,366	41,504	42,706
Angora goats	3,547	3,535	3,524
Other goats	15,216	14,973	14,752
Horses	871	853	843
Asses	1,476	1,465	1,407
Pigs	16	15	14
Mules	300	324	311
Camels	17	17	15
Chickens*	39,327	45,711	48,427
Turkeys*	2,409	2,492	2,537

* At October.

LIVESTOCK PRODUCTS

('000 metric tons)

	1975	1976	1977
Beef and veal	223†	191†	214†
Buffalo meat	20†	21†	21†
Mutton and lamb	270†	274†	275†
Goats' meat	107†	106†	105†
Pig meat*	1	1	1
Horse meat*	8	8	8
Poultry meat*	162	165	192
Edible offals*	84	82	84
Tallow*	12	n.a.	n.a.
Cows' milk	2,910	3,100	2,950*
Buffalo milk	283	278	291*
Sheep milk	993	1,004	1,065*
Goats' milk	631	624	637*
Butter*	118.4	120.3	123.2
Cow and buffalo cheese*	74.8	114.0 (cow, buffalo and sheep cheese combined)	117.8 (cow, buffalo and sheep cheese combined)
Sheep cheese*	35.0		
Hen eggs	129.8	154.7	132.0*
Honey	21.3	24.1	23.0*
Wool: greasy	52.4	53.9	54.5*
Wool: clean	28.8	30.0	30.0*
Cattle hides*	41.9	38.6	41.2
Sheep skins*	51.1	52.1	52.3
Goat skins*	13.2	13.1	13.0

* FAO estimates.

† Unofficial figures.

Source: FAO, mainly *Production Yearbook.*

FORESTRY

ROUNDWOOD REMOVALS

('000 cubic metres, excluding bark)

	Coniferous (soft wood)			Broadleaved (hard wood)			Total		
	1974	1975	1976	1974	1975	1976	1974	1975	1976
Sawlogs, veneer logs and logs for sleepers	3,768	3,908	3,612	1,220	767	907	4,988	4,675	4,519
Pitprops (mine timber)	475	520	473	88	69	78	563	589	551
Pulpwood	1,213	823	951	150	46	15	1,363	869	966
Other industrial wood	359	397	264	47	47	44	406	444	308
Fuel wood	6,285	6,556	5,170	5,071	5,385	5,330	11,356	11,941	10,500
Total	12,100	12,204	10,470	6,576	6,314	6,374	18,676	18,518	16,844

Source: FAO, *Yearbook of Forest Products.*

SAWNWOOD PRODUCTION

('000 cubic metres)

	1972	1973	1974	1975	1976
Coniferous sawnwood	1,816	1,897	1,878	1,908	2,178
Broadleaved sawnwood	526	550	545	552	446
	2,342	2,447	2,423	2,460	2,624
Railway sleepers	24	36*	48	52	59
Total	2,366	2,483	2,471	2,512	2,683

* FAO estimate.

Source: FAO, *Yearbook of Forest Products.*

FISHING

('000 metric tons, live weight)

	1973	1974	1975	1976
Inland waters	15.1	16.2	16.7*	17.2
Mediterranean and Black Sea:				
European anchovy	90.1	188.3	130.0	79.9
Others	62.8*	55.2*	54.8*	58.3*
Total Catch	168.0*	259.7*	201.5*	155.3*

* FAO estimate.

1977: Catch as in 1976 (FAO estimates).

Source: FAO, *Yearbook of Fishery Statistics.*

MINING

PRODUCTION

('000 metric tons)

	1975	1976	1977*
Crude petroleum	3,095	2,595	2,713
Iron ore (gross weight)	2,359	3,602	3,208
Chrome ore	952	945	918
Lignite	6,939	8,252	9,022
Coal	4,813	4,632	4,405
Manganese*	35	34	34
Copper (blister)†	27	28	32
Sulphur (pure)†	19	21	20

* Provisional.
† Public sector only.

INDUSTRY

SELECTED PRODUCTS

		1975	1976	1977
Paper*	'000 tons	307	335	375
Cotton Yarn*	,, ,,	42	46	38
Woollen Yarn*	,, ,,	4.5	4.4	3.7
Cotton Fabrics*	million metres	212.4	206.2	178.9
Woollen Fabrics*	,, ,,	7.1	7.6	5.9
Raki*	'000 litres	16,651	18,239	45,204
Beer	,, ,,	48,329*	172,944	192,312
Tobacco*	'000 tons	57	57	62.1
Pig Iron	,, ,,	1,197	1,518	1,360
Steel Ingots	,, ,,	1,457	1,457	1,397
Cement	,, ,,	10,850	12,392	13,848
Sugar	,, ,,	806	982	1,080
Commercial Fertilizers	,, ,,	2,685	2,930	2,736
Sulphuric Acid (100%)*	,, ,,	36	32	32
Electrolytic Copper†	,, ,,	11.4	11.1	10.1
Aluminium Sheets	,, ,,	3†	2.9	2.6
Polyethylene	,, ,,	25.4	23.1	26.1
Coke*	,, ,,	1,402	1,821	1,740
Motor Spirit	,, ,,	2,038	1,931	2,382
Kerosene	,, ,,	414	521	596
Distillate Fuel Oils	,, ,,	3,177	3,285	3,382
Residual Fuel Oils	,, ,,	5,168	5,813	5,281
Hydro-electricity	million kWh.	5,886	8,373	8,570
Thermal Electricity	,, ,,	9,683	9,897	11,942

* Public sector only. † Private sector only.

FINANCE

100 kuruş = 1 Turkish lira (TL) or pound.
Coins: 1, 5, 10, 25 and 50 kuruş; 1, 2½, 5 and 10 liras.
Notes: 5, 10, 20, 50, 100, 500 and 1,000 liras.
Exchange rates (June 1979): £1 sterling = 97.12 liras; U.S. $1 = 47.10 liras (export rates).
1,000 Turkish liras = £10.30 = $21.23.

Note: Between June 1947 and August 1960 the exchange rate was U.S. $1 = 2.80 liras (1 lira = 35.71 U.S. cents). From August 1960 to August 1970 the rate was $1 = 9.00 liras (1 lira = 11.11 U.S. cents). Between August 1970 and December 1971 the mid-point rate was $1 = 15.00 liras (1 lira = 6.67 U.S. cents), with an export (buying) rate of $1 = 14.85 liras and an import (selling) rate of $1 = 15.15 liras. From December 1971 to May 1974 the export rate was $1 = 14.00 liras (1 lira = 7.14 U.S. cents) and the import rate was $1 = 14.30 liras. Since May 1974 the rates have been adjusted frequently. The average mid-point rate (liras per U.S. $) was 13.927 in 1974; 14.442 in 1975; 16.053 in 1976; 18.002 in 1977; 24.282 in 1978. In terms of sterling, the exchange rate between November 1967 and August 1970 was £1 = 21.60 liras; from August 1970 to December 1971 the mid-point rate was £1 = 36.00 liras; from December 1971 to June 1972 the export rate was £1 = 36.48 liras and the import rate £1 = 37.26 liras. Since January 1972, when sterling was allowed to "float", the exchange rates have been adjusted frequently.

GENERAL BUDGET

(TL million, fiscal year beginning March 1st)

Revenue	1977	1978
Tax revenues	171,700	229,716
Taxes on income	80,105	117,200
Income tax	63,265	93,250
Corporation tax	8,080	11,500
Financial balance tax	8,060	11,150
Taxes on wealth	2,700	2,600
Taxes on goods	39,115	42,160
Taxes on services	17,530	23,850
Tax on banking and insurance transactions	8,200	11,000
Taxes on foreign trade	32,250	43,906
Other normal revenues	19,560	15,528
Special revenues and funds	12,189	2,009
Total Revenue	203,449	247,253

Expenditure	1977	1978
Finance	89,370	123,697
Defence	42,500	50,617
Education	24,089	25,905
Health and social welfare	5,897	7,500
Food, agriculture and livestock	4,242	4,694
Rural affairs	10,807	8,770
Public works	3,634	4,274
Security	4,939	5,861
Gendarmerie	3,918	4,082
Energy and national resources	2,193	3,802
Justice	2,781	3,006
Housing	2,545	2,500
Industry and technology	13,871	3,249
Others	12,163	14,796
Total Expenditure	222,949	262,753

INTERNATIONAL RESERVES

(U.S. $ million, at year end)

	1973	1974	1975	1976	1977
Central Bank:					
Gold holding	146.4	146.4	146.4	146.4	149.1
Foreign exchange	1,877.6	1,462.4	879.1	842.6	397.6
Reserve Position of the Central Bank	2,024.0	1,608.8	1,025.5	989.0	546.7
Reserve Holdings of Other Banks	—	—	166.3	91.0	83.0
Total Reserves (Net)	2,024.0	1,608.8	1,191.8	1,080.0	629.7

CURRENCY IN CIRCULATION

(TL million, at year end)

	1973	1974	1975	1976	1977
Currency in public circulation*	20,700	26,151	32,905	42,466	61,988
Bank-notes	20,328	25,744	32,396	41,781	61,188
Coins	372	407	509	685	800
Total outstanding of bank-notes and coins	25,782	33,357	41,532	52,831	78,764

* Outside banks.

NATIONAL ACCOUNTS
(TL million, at current prices)

	1974*	1975*	1976*	1977*	1978†
Agriculture and livestock	102,628.2	132,411.6	172,221.6	212,654.6	263,968.0
Forestry and logging	2,136.4	2,755.6	2,851.4	4,400.7	5,394.9
Fishing	747.0	947.1	1,197.5	1,718.6	2,458.8
Mining and quarrying	5,208.7	5,936.8	7,475.1	14,199.3	19,044.3
Manufacturing	66,069.7	79,845.5	97,924.8	119,879.8	183,422.5
Electricity, gas and water	5,431.8	7,748.3	9,577.6	13,934.4	21,495.2
Construction	18,828.8	24,620.6	31,027.1	41,998.3	64,787.7
Wholesale and retail trade	52,265.0	64,752.0	81,123.0	102,357.9	138,301.4
Transport, storage and communications	35,538.5	43,281.0	54,499.9	69,558.6	91,868.7
Financial institutions	10,092.0	12,602.2	16,825.3	20,466.6	25,601.4
Ownership of dwellings	13,279.4	17,887.2	21,906.2	31,185.4	51,241.2
Other private services	19,343.7	25,047.9	31,583.6	40,593.6	54,941.5
Government services	38,203.2	50,546.6	66,477.5	101,478.0	122,757.8
GROSS DOMESTIC PRODUCT AT FACTOR COST	369,772.4	468,382.4	594,690.6	774,425.9	1,045,283.0
Indirect taxes	42,145.8	53,291.7	69,340.9	92,292.6	97,570.6
Less: Subsidies	2,172.0	2,500.8	5,042.5	12,611.0	17,511.0
G.D.P. IN PURCHASERS' VALUES	409,746.2	519,173.3	658,989.0	854,107.5	1,125,342.6
Net factor income from abroad	17,351.3	16,597.7	11,048.8	9,926.0	7,163.7
GROSS NATIONAL PRODUCT	427,097.5	535,771.0	670,037.8	864,033.5	1,132,506.3

* Provisional. † Preliminary estimate.

CONSUMER PRICE INDEX
(Ankara—1968=100)

	1973	1974	1975	1976	1977
Food	179.4	213.7	277.9	327.6	427.9
Clothing	209.3	262.5	288.0	327.6	430.4
Household Expenditures	182.4	225.7	266.2	325.7	434.6
Medical and Personal Care	146.2	156.0	177.1	192.5	264.4
Transportation	159.5	194.8	208.5	245.4	303.2
Cultural and Recreational Expenditures	178.6	216.5	255.2	290.0	410.0
Dwelling expenditures*	149.2	160.7	172.5	178.3	191.8
ALL ITEMS	176.3	209.2	251.3	289.7	372.1

* Rent is accepted as fixed.

BALANCE OF PAYMENTS
(U.S. $ million)

	1974	1975	1976	1977
Exports f.o.b.	1,532	1,401	1,960	1,752
Imports f.o.b.	−3,363	−4,235	−4,565	−5,158
MERCHANDISE TRADE BALANCE	−1,830	−2,834	−2,605	−3,406
Services (net)	−302	−438	−465	−1,022
Transfers (net)	1,498	1,424	1,106	1,104
CURRENT BALANCE	−634	−1,848	−1,964	−3,325
Long-term capital (net)	404	1,315	2,334	1,988
Short-term capital (net)	−189	−294	−585	842
CAPITAL BALANCE	215	1,021	1,749	2,830
Net errors and omissions	11	−61	14	−66
TOTAL (net monetary movements)	−408	−888	−201	−561

Source: IMF, *International Financial Statistics.*

EXTERNAL TRADE

(U.S. $ million)

	1972	1973	1974	1975	1976	1977
Imports c.i.f.	1,562.6	2,086.2	3,777.5	4,738.6	5,128.6	5,769.3
Exports f.o.b.	885.1	1,317.1	1,532.2	1,401.1	1,960.2	1,753.0

PRINCIPAL COMMODITIES

(U.S. $ million)

Imports	1972*	1973*	1974*	1975*	1976*	1977*
Machinery	499	634	811	1,256.9	1,344.0	1,351.3
Iron and steel	146	247	531	679.1	545.7	689.7
Liquid fuels	155	221	763	811.3	1,125.7	1,469.9
Medicines and dyes	150	179	280	423.7	459.0	443.1
Transport vehicles	165	213	246	332.1	517.8	572.8
Textiles and yarns	54	53	105	117.9	107.3	108.9
Synthetic plastic materials, natural and synthetic rubber	56	71	135	152.4	182.9	266.3
Fats and oils	18	3	17	123.4	103.8	20.6
Commercial fertilizers	62	132	101	48.4	98.2	214.5
Others	203	283	731	695.2	508.7	556.8
Total	1,508	2,036	3,720	4,640.4	4,993.1	5,693.9

* Provisional. Revised totals (in U.S. $ million) are: 1,563 in 1972; 2,086 in 1973; 3,778 in 1974; 4,739 in 1975; 5,129 in 1976; 5,796 in 1977.

Exports	1972	1973	1974	1975	1976	1977
Agricultural products	607.3	831.5	851.8	792.5	1,254.4	1,041.4
Cereals, leguminous seeds	36.2	64.0	25.3	33.2	76.2	128.4
Fruits and vegetables	197.3	259.1	297.0	282.4	384.8	449.3
Hazelnuts	116.5	121.7	173.2	154.2	203.1	251.0
Sultanas	30.4	56.8	53.1	45.7	52.6	75.0
Citrus fruits	17.5	25.7	26.3	25.7	47.8	42.2
Others	32.9	54.9	44.4	56.8	81.3	81.1
Industrial crops	337.5	456.3	458.5	423.0	718.4	414.9
Tobacco	130.8	132.2	197.6	183.3	251.3	175.8
Cotton	191.3	305.9	250.7	230.0	438.2	213.6
Others	15.4	18.2	10.2	9.7	28.9	25.5
Livestock and animal products	36.3	52.1	71.0	53.9	75.0	48.8
Cattle, sheep, goats	15.7	23.0	43.3	24.6	30.5	18.9
Mohair, wool	5.2	10.5	4.6	11.3	26.3	13.5
Others	15.4	18.6	23.1	18.0	18.2	16.4
Minerals	50.3	56.5	84.7	105.7	110.0	125.8
Chrome ore	11.7	13.1	23.3	46.4	54.9	47.1
Others	38.6	43.4	61.4	59.3	55.1	78.7
Industrial products	222.1	416.2	595.7	502.9	595.8	585.8
Others	5.4	12.9	—	—	—	—
Total	885.1	1,317.1	1,532.2	1,401.1	1,960.2	1,753.0

PRINCIPAL TRADING PARTNERS
(U.S. $ million)

IMPORTS	1975	1976	1977
Belgium/Luxembourg	129	103	160
France	279	309	328
Germany, Federal Republic	1,058	946	945
Iran	26	109	165
Iraq	504	644	692
Italy	358	386	454
Japan	211	228	311
Libya	78	234	276
Netherlands	139	168	154
Romania	60	90	114
Switzerland	281	280	335
United Kingdom	344	410	403
U.S.A.	426	438	503
TOTAL (incl. others)	4,739	5,129	5,769

EXPORTS	1975	1976	1977
Belgium/Luxembourg	30	86	56
France	62	108	94
Germany, Federal Republic	305	377	389
Iran	37	34	49
Iraq	45	41	49
Italy	82	171	163
Netherlands	51	64	57
Switzerland	96	179	09
U.S.S.R.	74	81	180
United Kingdom	70	138	94
U.S.A.	147	191	122
TOTAL (incl. others)	1,401	1,960	1,753

TOURISM

	1973	1974	1975	1976	1977
Number of foreign arrivals ('000)	1,342	1,110	1,541	1,676	1,661
Receipts from foreign travel (million U.S. $)	171.5	193.7	200.9	180.5	204.9

TOURISTS BY COUNTRY OF ORIGIN
('000)

COUNTRY	1973	1974	1975	1976	1977
France	93	65	113	124	150
Germany, Federal Republic	172	139	206	197	203
Greece	42	31	30	38	44
Iran	29	47	189	50	94
Italy	83	45	85	74	85
Syria	18	29	42	35	41
United Kingdom	100	66	99	90	108
U.S.A.	183	92	79	115	165
Yugoslavia	76	69	92	85	n.a.
TOTAL (incl. others)	1,342	1,110	1,541	1,676	1,661

Tourist Accommodation (1977): 466 registered hotels, motels, boarding houses and holiday villages, with 26,496 rooms and 50,379 beds.

TRANSPORT

RAILWAYS
(millions)

	1975	1976	1977
Passenger kilometres	4,731	4,656	5,088
Net ton-kilometres	7,312	7,289	6,369

ROAD TRAFFIC
('000 motor vehicles at December 31st)

	1975	1976	1977
Passenger Cars	393.8	471.5	536.2
Trucks	205.6	236.5	270.9
Buses	64.9	71.2	78.9
Motor Cycles	n.a.	94.9	110.3

SHIPPING

	1973	1974	1975	1976
Vessels Entered* . ('000 gross reg. tons)	18,376	15,942	18,990	23,015
Vessels Cleared* . (,, ,, ,, ,,)	18,169	15,942	18,546	23,098
Goods Loaded . ('000 metric tons)	4,798	4,305	3,776	3,978
Goods Unloaded . (,, ,, ,,)	16,074	17,634	17,749	22,368

* Includes vessels entered and cleared in ballast and loaded, but excludes coastal shipping.

CIVIL AVIATION

Turkish Airlines

('000)

	1974	1975	1976
Kilometres flown	23,355	25,250	28,297
Number of flights	32,888	30,650	35,516
Number of passengers	2,096	2,274	2,862
Freight (metric tons)	177	193	238
Passenger-kilometres	2,030,000	2,415,000	2,840,000
Freight ton-kilometres	181	216	252

1977: Number of passengers 3,196,000; freight carried 262,000 metric tons.

COMMUNICATIONS MEDIA

	1975	1976	1977
Telephones	680,050	769,907	851,353
Radio Licences	4,154,000	4,228,000	4,260,563
TV Licences	999,021	1,769,317	2,271,781

EDUCATION

(1975/76)

	Schools	Teachers	Pupils
Primary	42,009	172,488	5,512,700
Secondary:			
General	3,328	37,899	1,363,188
Technical and vocational	1,209	12,240	312,522
Higher (incl. academies, teacher training and other technical and vocational schools)	108	14,120	123,938
Universities	18	10,696	85,114

Source: Ministry of Education, Ankara.

Sources (unless otherwise stated): State Institute of Statistics, Prime Minister's Office, Ankara, and Türkiye İş Bankasi A.Ş., Economic Research Dept., Ankara.

THE CONSTITUTION

The main provisions of the Constitution promulgated on October 25th, 1961 are summarized below.

GENERAL PROVISIONS

The Turkish Republic is a nationalistic, democratic, secular and social State governed by the rule of law, based on human rights. The State is an indivisible whole comprising the territory and people. Its official language is Turkish. Its capital is the city of Ankara.

Sovereignty is vested in the nation without reservation and condition. Legislative power is vested in the Turkish Grand National Assembly. The right to exercise such sovereignty is not delegated to any one person, group or class.

The executive function is exercised by the President of the Republic and the Council of Ministers within the framework of law.

Judicial power is exercised by independent courts on behalf of the Turkish Nation. Laws may not be in conflict with the Constitution.

The provision of the Constitution establishing the form of the State as a republic shall not be amended.

RIGHTS OF INDIVIDUALS

Every individual is entitled, in virtue of his existence as a human being, to fundamental rights and freedoms, which cannot be usurped, transferred or relinquished. All individuals are equal before the law irrespective of language, race, sex, political opinion, philosophical views, or religion or religious sect. There are provisions regulating the status of aliens, personal immunities, freedom of communication, travel, residence, thought, belief, press and publications. All citizens have the right to controvert and rebut, to congregate, demonstrate and form associations.

GRAND NATIONAL ASSEMBLY

The Grand National Assembly of Turkey is composed of the National Assembly and the Senate of the Republic. The two bodies meet in joint session in such instances as are provided in the Constitution. The Grand National Assembly is empowered to enact, amend and repeal laws, to debate and adopt the bills on the State budget and final accounts, to pass resolutions in regard to minting currency, proclaiming pardons and amnesties, and to the carrying out of definitive death sentences passed by courts.

National Assembly

The National Assembly is composed of 450 deputies elected by direct general ballot. Elections are held every four years. The Assembly may hold new elections before the end of the four-year period.

The Senate

The Senate is composed of 150 members elected by general ballot and 15 members appointed by the President of the Republic. There are also a number of Life Senators. The term of office is six years. One-third of members are re-elected every two years.

THE PRESIDENT OF THE REPUBLIC

The President of the Republic is the Head of the State. In this capacity he represents the Turkish Republic and the integrity of the Turkish Nation.

The President is elected for a term of seven years from among those members of the Grand National Assembly who have completed their fortieth year and received higher education; election is by secret ballot, and by a two-thirds majority of the plenary session. In case this majority is not obtained in the first two ballots, an absolute majority is sufficient. The President is not eligible for re-election.

The President elect must dissociate himself from his party, and his status as a regular member of the Grand National Assembly is terminated.

The President presides over the Council of Ministers whenever he deems it necessary, dispatches the representatives of the Turkish State to foreign states, receives the representatives of foreign states, ratifies and promulgates international conventions and treaties and may commute or pardon on grounds of chronic illness, infirmity or old age the sentences of convicted individuals. The President of the Republic is not accountable for his actions connected with his duties.

All decrees emanating from the President must be signed by the Prime Minister and the relevant Ministers. The Prime Minister and the Ministers concerned are responsible for the enforcement of these decrees.

The President may be impeached for high treason upon the proposal of one-third of the plenary session of the Turkish Grand National Assembly, and conviction of high treason requires the vote of at least a two-thirds majority of the joint plenary session of both legislative bodies.

COUNCIL OF MINISTERS

The Council of Ministers consists of the Prime Minister and the Ministers. The Prime Minister is designated by the President from among the members of the Grand National Assembly. The ministers are nominated by the Prime Minister and appointed by the President from among the members of the Grand National Assembly, or from among those qualified for election as deputies.

As head of the Council of Ministers, the Prime Minister promotes co-operation among the Ministries, and supervises the implementation of the Government's general policy. The members of the Council of Ministers are jointly and equally responsible for the manner in which this policy is implemented. Each Minister is responsible for the operations in his field of authority and for the acts and activities of his subordinates. The Ministers are subject to the same immunities and liabilities as the members of the Turkish Grand National Assembly.

NATIONAL DEFENCE

The office of the Commander-in-Chief is integrated in spirit in the Turkish Grand National Assembly and is represented by the President of the Republic.

The Council of Ministers is responsible to the Grand National Assembly for ensuring national security and preparing the armed forces for war. The Chief of the General Staff is the Commander of the armed forces. The Chief of the General Staff is appointed by the President of the Republic upon his nomination by the Council of Ministers, and his duties and powers are regulated by law. The Chief of the General Staff is responsible to the Prime Minister in the exercise of his duties and powers.

The National Security Council consists of the Ministers as provided by law, the Chief of the General Staff, and representatives of the armed forces. It is presided over by the President of the Republic and, in his absence, by the Prime Minister.

THE JUDICIARY

Judges are independent in the discharge of their duties and pass judgment in accordance with the Constitution, law, justice and their personal convictions. No organ, office, agency or individual may give orders or instructions to courts or judges in connection with the discharge of their judicial duty, send them circulars or make recommendations or suggestions. No questions may be raised, debates held, or statements issued in legislative bodies in connection with the discharge of judicial power concerning a case on trial. Legislative and executive organs, and the administration are under obligation to comply with ruling of the courts. Such organs and the administration may in no manner whatsoever alter court rulings or delay their execution.

THE GOVERNMENT

HEAD OF STATE

President: Admiral Fahri Korutürk (elected April 1973).

COUNCIL OF MINISTERS

(*July* 1979)

Republican People's Party (RPP), Democratic Party (DP), Independent (Ind.)

Prime Minister: Bülent Ecevit (RPP).

Deputy Prime Ministers: Orhan Eyüboğlu (RPP), Faruk Sukan (DP), Hikmet Çetin (RPP).

Ministers of State: Lütfü Doğan (RPP), Mustafa Kiliç (Ind.), Ahmet Şener (RPP), Hasan Korkut.

Minister of Justice: Mehmet Can (RPP).

Minister of National Defence: Neset Akmandor (RPP).

Minister of the Interior: Hasan Fehmi Güneş (RPP).

Minister of Foreign Affairs: Gündüz Ökçün (RPP).

Minister of Finance: Ziya Müezzinoğlu (RPP).

Minister of Education: Necdet Uğur (RPP).

Minister of Public Works: Şerafettin Elçi (Ind.).

Minister of Trade: Teoman Köprülüler (RPP).

Minister of Public Health: Mete Tan (Ind.).

Minister of Customs and Monopolies: Tuncay Mataraci (Ind.).

Minister of Transport and Communications: Güneş Ongüt (Ind.).

Minister of Agriculture and Livestock: Mehmet Yüceler (RPP).

Minister of Labour: Bahir Ersoy (RPP).

Minister of Industry and Technology: Orhan Alp (Ind.).

Minister of Management: Kenan Bulutoğlu (RPP).

Minister of Energy and Natural Resources: Deniz Baykal (RPP).

Minister of Tourism and Information: Alev Çoşkun (RPP).

Minister of Housing and Reconstruction: Ahmet Kararslan (Ind.).

Minister of Rural Affairs and Co-operatives: Ali Topuz (RPP).

Minister of Forestry: Vecdi İlhan (RPP).

Minister of Youth and Sports: Yücsel Çakmur (RPP).

Minister of Social Security: Salih Yildiz (Ind.).

Minister of Culture: Ahmet Taner Kişali (RPP).

Minister of Regional Administration: Mahmut Özdemir (RPP).

GRAND NATIONAL ASSEMBLY

SENATE OF THE REPUBLIC

President: Sirri Atalay.

(Seats as at November 1977)

Party	Seats
Republican People's Party	78
Justice Party	64
National Salvation Party	6
Republican Reliance Party . .	4
National Action Party . .	1
Independents	11
Presidential Appointees	11
Life Senators . . .	19
Total	184

NATIONAL ASSEMBLY

President: Cahit Karakaş.

	Seats at General Election, June 1977	Seats at June 1979
Republican People's Party	214*	210
Justice Party . . .	190	177
National Salvation Party	24	23
National Action Party	16	17
Republican Reliance Party	2	1
Democratic Party	1	1
National Order Party	—	1
Independent . .	3	15
Vacant		5
Total . .	450	450

POLITICAL PARTIES

Democratic Party (*Demokratik Parti*): Ankara; f. 1970 by deputies and senators expelled from the Justice Party; nationalist and traditionalist; Leader Dr. FARUK SÜKAN.

Justice Party (*Adalet Partisi*): Ankara; f. 1961; supports private enterprise within a mixed economy; Leader SÜLEYMAN DEMİREL; Sec.-Gen. NAHIT MENTESE.

Nation Party (NP): Ankara; f. 1962; traditional and religious in character; Leader (vacant).

National Action Party (NAP): 3 Cadde 47, Bahçelievler, Ankara; f. 1969; right-wing, favours secularism, nationalism, communal progress, increased scientific activities and development; supports close co-operation between the public and private sectors; Leader ALPARSLAN TÜRKEŞ; Sec.-Gen. NECATİ GÜLTEKIN.

National Order Party (NOP): Ankara; f. 1969; dissolved in 1971 by the Constitutional Court for violating the Constitution; in 1979 ABDÜLKER DOĞRU, NSP deputy to National Assembly, resigned from NSP and joined National Order Party.

National Salvation Party (NSP): Ankara; f. 1972; traditionalist, Islamic; took place of National Order Party which was closed down by order of the Constitutional Court; traditionalist right-wing party; Leader NECMETTIN ERBAKAN.

Republican People's Party (RPP) (*Cumhuriyet Halk Partisi*): Ankara; f. 1923 by Kemal Atatürk; favours a considerable degree of State enterprise along with continuing private enterprise. In recent years the party has moved to the left of centre; Leader BÜLENT ECEVİT; Sec.-Gen. MUSTAFA ÜSTÜNDAĞ.

Republican Reliance Party (RRP): Ankara; f. 1967 as the National Reliance Party by 45 members of Parliament from the Republican People's Party, who broke away as a result of this party's "left of centre policies"; merged with Republican Party 1973; Leader Prof. TURHAN FEYZIOĞLU.

Turkish Socialist Workers' Party (*Turkiye Sosyalist Işçi Partisi*): Ankara; f. 1974; supports nationalization of major sectors of the economy, withdrawal from NATO; Chair. AHMET KACMAZ; Sec.-Gen. YALCIN YUSUFOĞLU.

Turkish Unity Party (TBP): Ankara; f. 1966; Social democratic; Leader MUSTAFA TİMISI; publ. *Birlik* (monthly).

Workers' Party of Turkey (*Türkiye İşçi Partisi*): Çemberlitaş, Piyerloti Cad. 21/5, Istanbul; f. 1975; Pres. Mrs. BEHICE BORAN; Sec.-Gen. Dr. NIHAT SARGIN; publs. *Yürüyüs* (weekly), *Görev* (biweekly), *Genç Öncü* (monthly), *Çarkbaşak* (monthly), *Yurt ve Dünya* (bimonthly).

DIPLOMATIC REPRESENTATION

EMBASSIES AND LEGATIONS ACCREDITED TO TURKEY

(In Ankara unless otherwise stated)

Afghanistan: Cemal Nadir Sok. 25, Çankaya; *Ambassador:* ABDUL MANAF QUDUS.

Albania: Nenehatun Cad. 89, Gaziosmanpaşa; *Ambassador:* GUYLANI SHEHU.

Algeria: Karyağdi Sok. 18; *Chargé d'affaires:* DJILALI KERMAD.

Argentina: Riza Şah Pehlevi Caddesi 57/1, Çankaya; *Chargé d'affaires a.i.:* (vacant).

Australia: Gaziosmanpaşa, Nenehatun Cad. 83; *Ambassador:* R. A. PEACHEY.

Austria: Atatürk Bulvarı 189; *Ambassador:* FRANZ WANDERBALDINGER.

Bahrain: Beirut, Lebanon.

Bangladesh: Cinnah Cad. 102/2; *Ambassador:* Gen. ABDUL JABBAR.

Barbados: London, England.

Belgium: Nenehatun Cad. 109; *Ambassador:* PIERRE MARCHAL.

Brazil: Çankaya, Alaçam Sokak, 10/2-4-5; *Ambassador:* Dr. WAGNER PIMENTA-BUENO.

Bulgaria: Atatürk Bulvarı 124; *Ambassador:* VLADIMIR GRANTCHAROV.

Burma: Cairo, Egypt.

Cameroon: Cairo, Egypt.

Canada: Nenehatun Cad. No. 75, Gaziosmanpaşa; *Ambassador:* C. J. MARSHALL.

Chad: Beirut, Lebanon.

Chile: Çankaya, Abdullah Cevdet Sokak 20/2; *Ambassador:* ARTURO YONANE ZUNIGA.

China, People's Republic: Yukarı Ayrancı 8, Durak Hoşdere Cad. 147; *Ambassador:* WANG YUEYI.

Cuba: Sofia, Bulgaria.

Czechoslovakia: Atatürk Bulvarı 245; *Ambassador:* JAN MALKOVIC.

Denmark: Kırlangıç Sokak 42, Gaziosmanpaşa; *Ambassador:* LORENZ PETERSEN (also accred. to Iraq).

Dominican Republic: London, England.

Egypt: Atatürk Bulvarı 126; *Ambassador:* AHMED KAMAL OLAMA.

El Salvador: Bonn, Federal Republic of Germany.

Ethiopia: Alabaş Sokak 2/10, Çankaya; *Ambassador:* ZEMENE KASSEGN.

Finland: Galip Dede Sokak 1/20, Farabi; *Ambassador:* ULF-ERIK SLOTTE.

France: Paris Cad. 70, Kavaklıdere; *Ambassador:* EMILE CAZIMAJOU.

Gabon: Rome, Italy.

German Democratic Republic: Turan Emeksiz Sok. 1, Gaziosmanpaşa; *Ambassador:* HEINZ SCHULZ.

Germany, Federal Republic: Atatürk Bulvarı 114; *Ambassador:* ULRICH SAHM.

Ghana: Rome, Italy.

Greece: Fatma Aliye Sokak 1, Kavaklıdere; *Ambassador:* GEORGES PAPOULIAS.

Guinea: Cairo, Egypt.

Hungary: Gazi Mustafa Kemal Bulvarı 10; *Ambassador:* Dr. LASZLÓ ROSTA.

Iceland: Copenhagen, Denmark.

India: Kıbrıs Sokak 24, Çankaya; *Ambassador:* Nagendra Nath Jha.

Indonesia: Abdullah Cevdet Sokak 10, Çankaya; *Ambassador:* Noermanli Aman.

Iran: Tahran Cad. 10; *Chargé d'affaires a.i.:* (vacant).

Iraq: Turan Emeksiz Sokak 11, Gaziosmanpaşa; *Ambassador:* Samir Abdul Aziz al-Najim.

Ireland: Rome, Italy.

Israel: Farabi Sokak 43, Çankaya; *Chargé d'affaires:* Shimeon Amir.

Italy: Atatürk Bulvarı 118; *Ambassador:* Eric da Rin.

Japan: Gasiosmanpaşa, Resit Galip Cad. 81; *Ambassador:* Shigeto Nikai.

Jordan: Dede Korkut Sokak 18, Çankaya; *Ambassador:* Zuhayr el Mufti.

Korea, Republic: Cinnah Caddesi Alaçam Sokak 9; *Ambassador:* Chul Soon Moon.

Kuwait: Cinnah Caddesi 88/3-4, Çankaya; *Ambassador:* Saud Abdul-Aziz al-Humaidi (also accred. to Bulgaria).

Lebanon: Cinnah Caddesi 11/3, Çankaya; *Ambassador:* Issam Beyhum.

Libya: Ebuziya Tevfik Sokak 5, Çankaya; *Ambassador:* Saadeddin M. Abushwereb.

Malaysia: Nenehatun Cad. 115 Gaziosmanpaşa, Çankaya; *Chargé d'affaires a.i.:* Hassan Mohammad Noor.

Mauritania: Cairo, Egypt.

Mexico: Abdullah Cevdet Sokak 20/1, Çankaya; *Chargé d'affaires a.i.:* (vacant).

Mongolia: Sofia, Bulgaria.

Morocco: Atatürk Bulvarı No. 219/9; *Ambassador:* Dr. Ahmed Benabud.

Nepal: Islamabad, Pakistan.

Netherlands: Şehit Ersan Cad. 4, Çankaya; *Ambassador:* J. J. Derksen.

Niger: Cairo, Egypt.

Nigeria: Farabi Sok. 8, Çankaya; *Chargé d'affaires:* Abba Abdulkadiri.

Norway: Arjantin Cad. 14, Gaziosmanpaşa; *Ambassador:* Per Thee Naevdal.

Oman: Teheran, Iran.

Pakistan: Riza Şah Pehlevi Caddesi 37; *Ambassador:* Mufti Mohammad Abbas.

Peru: Vienna, Austria.

Philippines: Teheran, Iran.

Poland: Atatürk Bulvarı 241; *Ambassador:* Kazimierz Sidor.

Portugal: Cinnah Caddesi 28/3; *Ambassador:* Armando de Paula Coelho (also accred. to Iraq).

Qatar: Beirut, Lebanon.

Romania: Bükreş Sok. 4, Çankaya; *Ambassador:* Vasile Alexandrescu.

Saudi Arabia: Abdullah Cevdet Sok. 18, Çankaya; *Ambassador:* Mohammad Ali el-Awadi.

Senegal: Teheran, Iran.

Somalia: Ankara; *Ambassador:* Hashi Abdulla Farah.

Spain: Abdullah Cevdet Sokak 8, Çankaya; *Ambassador:* Santiago Martínez-Caro.

Sudan: Teheran, Iran.

Sweden: Kâtip Çelebi Sok. 7; *Ambassador:* Rune Nyström.

Switzerland: Atatürk Bulvarı 247; *Ambassador:* Georges Bonnant.

Syria: Çankaya, Abdullah Cevdet Sok. 7; *Ambassador:* Bachir el-Kotb.

Thailand: Cinnah Caddesi 7/9, Kavaklıdere; *Ambassador:* Uthai Thongphagdi.

Tunisia: Cinnah Cad. 63/6-7; *Ambassador:* Salah Ladgham.

Uganda: Cairo, Egypt.

U.S.S.R.: Karyağdı Sokak 5, Çankaya; *Ambassador:* Alexei Rodionov.

United Kingdom: Çankaya, Şehit Ersan Cad. 46/A; *Ambassador:* Peter H. Laurence, C.M.G.

U.S.A.: Atatürk Bulvarı 110; *Ambassador:* Ronald I. Spiers.

Vatican City: Köroğlu Sok. 6, Gaziosmanpaşa; *Apostolic Pronuncio:* Mgr. Salvatore Asta.

Venezuela: Abdullah Cevdet Sok. 26/1, Çankaya; *Chargé d'affaires:* Publio Salvaverria Pérez.

Yemen Arab Republic: Amman, Jordan.

Yugoslavia: Paris Cad. 47, Kavaklıdere; *Ambassador:* Ramadan Vranici.

Zaire: Cairo, Egypt.

Zambia: Rome, Italy.

Turkey also has diplomatic relations with Djibouti, Grenada, Guinea-Bissau, Laos, Malawi, Mauritius, Sierra Leone, Solomon Islands, Suriname, the United Arab Emirates, Upper Volta, Uruguay and Viet-Nam.

JUDICIAL SYSTEM

Until the foundation of the new Turkish Republic, a large part of the Turkish civil law—the laws affecting the family, inheritance, property, obligations, etc.—was based on the Koran, and this holy law was administered by special religious (Sharia) courts. The legal reform of 1926 was not only a process of secularization, but also a radical change of the legal system. The Swiss Civil Code and the Code of Obligation, the Italian Penal Code, and the Neuchâtel (Cantonal) Code of Civil Procedure were adopted and modified to fit Turkish customs and traditions.

Constitutional Court: Consists of fifteen regular and five alternate members. Reviews the constitutionality of laws passed by the Turkish Grand National Assembly. Sits as a High Council empowered to try senior members of state. The rulings of the Constitutional Court are final. Decisions of the Court are published immediately in the Official Gazette, and shall be binding on the legislative, executive, and judicial organs of the State.

Court of Cassation: The court of the last instance for reviewing the decisions and verdicts rendered by courts of law. It has original and final jurisdiction in specific cases defined by law. Members are elected by the Supreme Council of Judges.

Council of State: An administrative court of the first instance in matters not referred by law to other administrative courts, and an administrative court of the last instance in general. Hears and settles administrative disputes and expresses opinions on draft laws submitted by the Council of Ministers.

High Military Administrative Court: A military court for the judicial control of administrative acts concerning military personnel.

Military Court of Cassation: A court of the last instance to review decisions and verdicts rendered by military courts.

Court of Jurisdictional Disputes: Settles disputes among civil, administrative and military courts arising from disagreements on jurisdictional matters and verdicts.

Supreme Council of Judges: Consists of eighteen regular and five alternate members. Decides all personnel matters relating to judges.

Public Prosecutor: The law shall make provision for the tenure of public prosecutors and attorneys of the Council of State and their functions.

The Chief Prosecutor of the Republic, the Chief Attorney of the Council of State and the Chief Prosecutor of the Military Court of Cassation are subject to the provisions applicable to judges of higher courts.

Military Trial: Military trials are conducted by military and disciplinary courts. These courts are entitled to try the military offences of military personnel and those offences committed against military personnel or in military areas, or offences connected with military service and duties. Military courts may try non-military persons only for military offences prescribed by special laws.

RELIGION

ISLAM

Diyanet İsleri Reisi (*Head of the Muslim Faith in Turkey*): TAYYAR ALTIKULAC.

Over 98 per cent of the Turkish people are Muslims, mainly Sunnis. Under the Republic, from 1923 onwards, action was taken to reduce the influence of religion on state affairs: e.g., its association with the schools was curtailed, mosques and churches were sometimes closed and facilities denied to their adherents, both Muslim and Christian. The Muslim faith was also disestablished. After 1950 there was a change, and religious life was to a certain extent revived. The revolution of 1960 brought about a return to the more secular republic of Atatürk but recent Governments have once again established links between church and state.

GREEK ORTHODOX

Archbishop of Constantinople and Ecumenical Patriarch: DIMITRIOUS I, Rum Ortodox Patrikhanesi, Fener, Istanbul.

ROMAN CATHOLIC CHURCH

ARMENIAN RITE

Patriarchate of Cilicia: Patriarchat Arménien Catholique, Beirut, Lebanon; Patriarch HEMAIAGH PIERRE XVII GHEDIGHIAN.

Archbishopric of Istanbul: Sakızağacı Cad. N. 31, P.K. 183, Beyoğlu, Istanbul; f. 1830; 3 secular priests, 6 religious priests, 1 Diacre permanent, 5,000 Catholics (1979); Archbishop JEAN TCHOLAKIAN.

BYZANTINE RITE

Apostolic Exarchate of Istanbul: Beyoğlu, Hamalbaşi Cad. 44, Istanbul; f. 1860; 1 secular priest, 70 Catholics (1978); Exarch: (vacant).

CHALDEAN RITE

Archbishopric of Diarbekir: Archevechè Chaldşen, Beyoğlu, B.P. 280, Istanbul; 6 secular priests, 11,000 Catholics (1978); Archbishop PAUL KARATAS.

LATIN RITE

Metropolitan See of Izmir: Atatürk Cad. 210/6, P.K. 267, Izmir; 10 priests, 2,700 Catholics; Metropolitan JOHN HENRY BOCCELLA, T.O.R.

Apostolic Vicariate of Asia Minor (attached to Archbishopric of Izmir): Apostolic Administrator Mgr. JOHN HENRY BOCCELLA.

Apostolic Vicariate of Istanbul: Olçek Sok. 83, Harbiye, Istanbul; 6 secular priests, 43 religious priests, 5,000 Catholics (1978); GAUTHIER PIERRE DUBOIS.

Mission of Trabzon: Katolik Kilisesi, P.K. 5, Samsun; 2 priests, 90 Catholics (1978); Superior Rev. P. GIUSEPPE GERMANO BERNARDINI.

THE PRESS

Under the Constitution of 1961, "the press is free within the limits of the law". Provision is made for recourse to a constitutional court in issues involving laws affecting the Press.

It is almost impossible to produce a correct list of the numerous provincial newspapers, which tend to be small in circulation and rather short-lived. In all, there are about 370 daily papers, 260 weeklies and magazines, over 200 fortnightly and monthly and about 25 quarterly, six-monthly and annually published magazines. The estimated total circulation of all the daily papers is 1,353,000.

Almost all Istanbul papers are also printed in Ankara and İzmir on the same day, and some in Adana. Among the most serious and influential papers are the dailies *Milliyet* and *Cumhuriyet*. *Akbaba* is noted for its political satire. The most popular dailies are the Istanbul papers *Hürriyet, Milliyet, Tercüman, Son Havadis, Günaydın* and *Cumhuriyet*; *Yeni Asir*, published in İzmir, is the best selling quality daily of the Aegean region. A major popular weekly is the illustrated magazine *Hayat*.

PRINCIPAL DAILIES

ADANA

Cukurova: Kızılay Cad.; f. 1961; political; Proprietor ADİL İKIZ; Editor REFİK SÖLEN; circ. 1,500.

Vatandaş: Dörtyolağzı 117 Sok. 11; f. 1951; political; Editor MİTHAT GÜLYAŞAR; circ. 1,700.

Yeni Adana: Kızılay Cad. 29; f. 1918; political; Proprietor ÇETİN REMZİ YÜREĞIR; Editor KUDDUSİ ÜSTÜN GÜVELEOĞLU; circ. 1,200.

ANKARA

Adalet: Agâh Efendi Sok.; f. 1962; morning; political, independent; Editor TURHAN DİLLİGİL; circ. 10,000.

Ankara Ticaret Gazetesi: Rüzgârlı Sok., O.W. Han 2/6; f. 1954; commercial; Proprietor MEHMET SÜKRÜ SENBOL; Editor CAHİT BAYDAR; circ. 4,500.

Baris: Sinasi Cad. 10; f. 1971; morning; political, supports the Republican People's Party; Editor LEVENT YALÇIN; circ. 13,500.

Hür Anadolu: Rüzgarlı Sok. 21; f. 1967; political; Publisher MUSTAFA ÖZKAN; circ. 3,400.

Resmi Gazete: Başbakanlık Neşriyat, ve Müdevvenat Genel Müdürlüğü; f. 1920; official gazette.

Turizm Ticaret: Sumer Sok. 6/10, Kızılay; f. 1970; commercial; Editor ILHAN TUNALI.

Turkish Daily News: Tunus Cad. 49/7 Kavaklıdere; f. 1961; English language; Publisher-Editor İLHAN ÇEVİK; circ. 3,000.

Turkiye Iktisat Gazetesi: Karanfil Sok. 56, Bakanlıkar; f. 1953; commercial; Editor SABAHATTİN ALPAT.

Vatan: Babiali Cad. 28; f. 1940; evening; Publisher NUMAN ESIN; Editor BÜLENT ÖZÜKAN; circ. 5,500.

Yenigün: Rüzgârlı Sok. Âgah Efendi, Ucar Han 8/5, Ulus; f. 1968; political; Editor KEMAL YAZGAN; circ. 3,200.

Yeni Halkçi: Atatürk Bulvarı 88/16; f. 1974; political; Editor IRFAN AYDIN.

Yeni Tanin: Agâh Efendi Sok, 8/3 Ulus; f. 1964; political; Proprietor BURHANETTIR GÖGÖN; Editor KEMAL ARARAT; circ. 3,500.

Zafer: Çankırı Cad. 14; f. 1963; morning; political; Proprietor MUAMMER KIRANER; circ. 5,000.

BURSA

Bursa Hakimiyet: Ünlü Cad. Çamlıbel Işhanı 34/36; f. 1959; political; Proprietor ARMAĞAN GERÇEKÇİ; Editor SARUHUAN AYBER; circ. 5,867.

Haber: Kümbet Sok. 7; f. 1964; political; Editor TURHAN TAYAN; circ. 800.

ESKİŞEHİR

Istiklal: Sakarya Cad. Kanatli Işhani; f. 1950; political; Proprietor SENGÜL MÜCAHİT; Editor SONER SARIBAYIR.

Milli Irade: 27 Mayis Cad., Eskişehir Pasaji 31; f. 1968; political; Proprietor ETHEM KARACA; Editor SADETTİN KÜSMEZ.

Sakarya: Hacet Sok. 3; f. 1947; political; Proprietor ABDURRAHMAN ÜNGÜR; Editor GÖNÜL ÖKTEM.

İSTANBUL

Akşam: Nuruosmanıye Cad. 3/4, Çağaloğlu; f. 1918; independent; Editor AYDIN UNSAL; circ. 5,200.

Apoyevmatini: Suriye Çarşısı 10-12, Beyoğlu; f. 1925; Greek language; Publisher Dr. Y. A. ADASOĞLU; Editor İSTEFAN PAPADOPOULOS; circ. 1,724.

Aydınlık: Nurosmaniye Cad. 3, 3 Çağaloğlu; f. 1977; political; Editor MEHMET ATABERK.

Bayrak: Yerebatan Cad., Salkim Söğüt Sok. 14 Çağaloğlu; political; Editor YILMAZ KARAOĞLU.

Bizim Anadolu: Ticarethane Sok. 46/5, Çağaloğlu; f. 1969; political; Editor KEMAL YAMAN.

Cumhuriyet: Turkocağı Cad. 39, Çağaloğlu; f. 1924; morning; independent political; Editor BÜLENT DİKMENER; circ. 240,675.

Dünya: Narlidere Sok. 15, Çağaloğlu; f. 1952; morning; political; Editor GÜL SÖKMEN; circ. 29,500.

Ekonomi: Ankara Cad., Cemal Nadir Sok. 22, Çağaloğlu; f. 1944; commercial; Editor SAFA ÇELİKER; circ. 1,500.

Ekspres: Çatalçesme Sok. 29/1, Çağaloğlu; f. 1962; evening; Editor COŞKUM ÖZER.

Günaydin: Eryilmaz Sok. Alemdar Mah. 3 Çağaloğlu; f. 1968; political; Proprietor HALDUN SIMAVİ; Editor NECATİ ZİNCİRKIRAN; circ. 502,200.

Günlük Ticaret: Çemberlitas Palas, Çemberlitas; f. 1947; political; Editor NESRİN TUNÇBİLEK; circ. 1,700.

Haber: Şeref Efendi Sok. 44, Çağaloğlu; f. 1934; Editor HASAN KARAYAVUZ; Publisher DÜNDAS ENGIN; circ. 3,300.

Hergün: Mimar Mehmet Aga Cad. 36; f. 1947; evening; supports National Action Party; Editor ENVER ALTAYLI; circ. 17,420.

Hürriyet: Babıalı Cad. 15-17, Çağaloğlu; f. 1948; morning; independent political; Publisher EROL SİMAVİ; Editor SALİM BAYER; circ. 850,000.

Istanbul Postası: Çatalçeşme Sok. 17, Çağaloğlu; f. 1946; commercial; Editor SEVKI CELIKSER; circ. 2,250.

Jamanak: İstiklâl Cad., Narmanlı Yurdu, Beyoğlu; f. 1908; Armenian; Editor ARAM BOĞOSYAN; circ. 1,888.

Kelebek: Babıali Cad. 15-17, Çağaloğlu; f. 1972; morning; daily home magazine; Publisher EROL SİMAVİ; Editor SADAN GALIPAGIU; circ. 100,500.

Marmara: İstiklâl Cad. 360/12, Tünel; f. 1941; Armenian language; Editor R. HADDECIYAN; circ. 1,700.

Milli Gazete: Çatalçeşme Sok. 29, Üretmen tran Kat 2, Çağaloğlu; political; Editor DURMUŞ ALI AYDIN.

Milliyet: Nuruosmaniye Caddesi 65; f. 1950; morning; political; Editor (vacant); circ. 329,000 (weekdays), 324,300 (Sunday).

Son Havadis: Şeref Efendi Sok. 44, Çağaloğlu; f. 1951; supports the Justice Party; Owner MUSTAFA ÖZKAN; Editors M. LUTFI BALLISOY, YÜKSEL BASTUNC; circ. 20,800.

Tercüman: Topkapi, Londra asfalti Tercüman Tesisleri ist; f. 1961; political; Editor-in-Chief GÜNERİ CIVALOĞLU; Editor ÜNAL SAKMAN; circ. 436,700.

Yeni Asya: Kazim Gürkan Cad. 6, Çağaloğlu; f. 1970; political; Editor SABAHATTIN AKSAKAL; circ. 9,090.

Yeni İstanbul: Dr. Emin Paşa Sok. 20, Çağaloğlu; f. 1950; independent political; Editor DOĞAN KOLOĞLU; circ. 29,200.

İZMİR

Ege Ekonomi: 2 Beyler Sok. 49; f. 1968; commercial; Editor ABDULLAH BOZKURT; circ. 1,932.

Ege Telgraf: Atatürk Cad. 150; f. 1960; evening; political; Editor NEDİM ÇAPMAN; circ. 3,600.

Ekspres: Halit Ziya Bul. 74/A; f. 1952; political; Editor ERKİN USMAN; circ. 32,000.

Ticaret: Gazi Bulvarı 18; f. 1942; commercial and political news; Editor SÜHA S. TÜKEL; circ. 10,005.

Yeni Asir: Gazi Osman Paşa Bulvarı 13/A; f. 1895; political; Proprietor DINÇ BİLGİN; Editor YUSUF RIZA DÜVENCİ; circ. 3,264.

KONYA

Yeni Konya: İş Bankası bitişiği 4; f. 1949; political; Editor ÜNAL GÜCÜYENER; circ. 2,283.

Yeni Meram: Mevlâna Cad. Sağlık Pasajı; f. 1949; political; Editor A. RIDVAN BÜLBÜL; circ. 1,660.

WEEKLIES

ANKARA

Ekonomi ve Politika: Atatürk Bulvarı, 199/A-45, Kavaklıdere; f. 1966; economic and political; Publisher ZİYA TANSU.

Hiz: Necatibey Cad., Sezenler Sok.; f. 1965; labour news; Publisher ŞERAFETTİN AKOVA; Editor NECMI ERTEZ; circ. 10,000.

Outlook: Konur Sokak 27/7, Kizilay P.K. 210; f. 1967; English language; Editor M. A. KIŞLALI.

Türkiye Ticaret Sicili: Karanfil Sok. 56, Bakanlıklar; f. 1957; commercial; Editor ISMAIL ASLAN.

Turkiye Yazıları: Selanik Cad., 7 Kizilay; literary; Proprietor-Editor AHMET SAY.

Yarın: İnkılap Sok. 25/2, Yenişehir; f. 1963; political; Publisher-Editor MÜFİT DURU.

Yanki: Konur Sokak 27/7, P.K. 210, Kizilay; f. 1970; Editor MEHMET ALİ KIŞLALI.

İSTANBUL

Akbaba: Klodfarer Cad. 8-10, Divanyolu; f. 1923; satirical; Editor ERGIM ORLÂÇ.

Doğan Kardeş: Türbedar Sok. 22, Çağaloğlu; f. 1945; illustrated children's magazine; Editor ŞEVKET RADO; circ. 40,000.

Geçit: Nuruosmaniye Cad., Atasaray Han 406; f. 1966; political; Publisher FÜRÜZAN TEKİL.

Hayat: Türbedar Sok. 22, Çağaloğlu; f. 1956; general interest illustrated magazine; Publisher ŞEVKET RADO; circ. 125,000.

Hayat Spor: Türbedar Sok. 22, Çağaloğlu; f. 1974; illustrated sport magazine; weekly; Editor MEHMET RADO; circ. 90,000.

İstanbul Ticaret: Istanbul Chamber of Commerce, Eminönü-Unkapanı Cad.; f. 1957; commercial news; Publishers Dr. YILDIRIM KILKIŞ, YÜKSEL METİN.

Pazar: Alayköskü Cad., Eryilmaz Sok., Çağaloğlu; f. 1956; illustrated; Publisher HALDUN SİMAVİ.

Resimli Roman: Türbedar Sok. 22, Çağaloğlu; f. 1965; weekly; illustrated; Editor OĞUZ ÖZDEŞ; circ. 90,000.

Şalom: Bereket Han 24/5, Karaköy; f. 1948; Jewish; Publisher AVRAM LEYON.

Ses: Türbedar Sok. 22, Çağaloğlu; f. 1962; illustrated film, TV, music magazine; Editor ŞEVKET RADO; circ. 90,000.

Tutum: Nuruosmaniye Cad. 54; f. 1967; political; Editor ERDOĞAN AKKURT.

PERIODICALS

ANKARA

Adalet Dergisi: Adalet Bakanlığı; f. 1909; legal journal published by the Ministry of Justice; Editor HÜSEYİN ERGÜL; circ. 3,500.

Azerbaycan Türk Kültür Dergisi: Vakif İş Hani 324 Anafartalar; f. 1949; literary and cultural periodical of Azerbaizhanian Turks; Editor Dr. AHMET YAŞAT.

Bayrak Dergisi: Necatibev Cad., Karakimseli Han 56; f. 1964; Publisher and Editor HAMI KARTAY.

Çiftlik Dergisi: P.K. 43, Bakanlıklar-Ankara; f. 1960; agricultural; monthly; Publisher VASFİ HAKMAN; circ. 10,000.

Devlet Opera ve Balesi Genel Müdürlügü: f. 1949; State opera and ballet; Gen. Dir. LÜTFÜ AY.

Devlet Tiyatrosu: Devlet Tiyatrosu Um. Md.; f. 1952; art, theatre.

Dost: Menekşe Sok. 16/13, Yenişehir; f. 1947; literary; Editor SALİM SENGİL.

Eğitim ve Bilim: Ziya Gökalp Cad. 48, Yenişehir; education and science; Editor TEVFİK DALGIC.

Elektrik Mühendisligi Mecmuası: Ihlamur Sokak 10/1, Yenişehir; f. 1954; published by the Chamber of Turkish Electrical Engineers.

Halk Eğitimi: Millî Eğitim Bakanlığı, Halk Eğitimi Genel Müdürlüğü, Ankara; f. 1966; published by a department of the Ministry of Education; educational.

Halkevleri Dergisi: Menekşe Sok. 11/A; f. 1966; art, literary; Publisher KADRİ KAPLAN.

Hisar: Sağlik Sok. 17/A Sıhhiye, Ankara; f. 1950; literary; monthly; Editor-in-Chief MEHMET ÇINARLI; Editor İLHAN GEÇER.

İdare Dergisi: İcişleri Bakanliği; administrative.

Ilk Oğretim: Millî Eğitim Bakanliği; educational.

İller ve Belediyeler Dergisi: Mithat Paşa Cad. 45/2; f. 1945; monthly journal of the Turkish Municipal Assen.; Pres. İSMET SEZGİN.

Karinca: Mithat Paşa Cad. 38/A, Yenişehir; f. 1934; monthly review published by the Turkish Co-operative Society; Editor NUSRET UZGÖREN; circ. 6,000.

Maden Tetkik ve Arama Enstitüsü Dergisi: İnönü Bulvarı; f. 1935; bi-annual; publ. by Mineral Research and Exploration Institute of Turkey; English Edition *Bulletin of the Mineral Research and Exploration Institute* (bi-annual).

Mühendis ve Makina: Sümer Sk. 36/1; f. 1957; engineering; monthly; Publisher Chamber of Mechanical Engineers; Dir. and Editor ISMET RİZA GEBİ.

Onasya Dergisi: P.K. 605; f. 1965; monthly; cultural; Publisher SADİ BAYRAM; circ. 5,000.

Resmi Kararlar Dergisi: Ministry of Justice, Adalet Bakanlığı; f. 1966; legal; Editor AVNİ ÖZENÇ; circ. 3,500.

Türk Arkeoloji Dergisi: General Directorate of Antiquities and Museums, Eski Eserler ve Müzeler Genel Müdürlüğü; archaeological.

Turk Dili: Türk Dil Kurumu, Atatürk Bulvarı 217, Kavaklıdere; f. 1951; monthly; literary.

Türk, Kültürü: P.K. 14, Çankaya; f. 1962; cultural studies; Editor TALİP YÜCEL.

Turkey—Economic News Digest: Karanfil Sok. 56; f. 1960; Editor-in-Chief BEHZAT TANİR; Man. Editor SADİK BALKAN.

Türkiye Bankacılık: P.K. 121; f. 1955; commercial; Publisher MUSTAFA ATALAY.

Türkiye Bibliyografyası: Millî Kütüphane Genel Müdürlüğü, Yenişehir; f. 1934; quarterly; Turkish national bibliography; published by the Bibliographical Institute of the Turkish National Library; Dir. IŞIN DURUÖZ.

Türkiye Makaleler Bibliyografyası: Millî Kütüphane Genel Müdürlüğü, Yenişehir; f. 1952; quarterly; Turkish articles bibliography; published by the Bibliographical Institute of the Turkish National Library; Dir. IŞIN DURUÖZ.

Yen Yayinlar, Aylık Bibliyografya Dergisi (*New Publications, Monthly Bibliographic Journal*): P.K. 440, Kızılay, Ankara; f. 1956; Published by Assen. of Univ. Library School Graduates; Dir. O. ÜSTÜN YILDIRIM.

İSTANBUL

Arkitekt: Anadolu Han 32, Eminönü; f. 1931; quarterly; architecture, city planning and tourism; Chair. Dr. Arch. ZEKİ SAYÂR; Sec. KETİ ÇAPANOĞLU.

Bakis: Çağaloğlu Yokuşu; f. 1945; Editor AVNİ ALTINER.

Banka ve Ekonomik Yorumlar: Çağaloğlu, Çatalçeşme Sok. 17, Kat. 4, Istanbul; f. 1964; banking, economic, social and management subjects; Dir. BÜLEND ÇORAPÇI; circ. 5,000.

Deniz: İstanbul; f. 1955; monthly; maritime news; Publisher EMEL KAZANLIOĞLU.

Filim: P.K. 307, Beyoğlu; f. 1970; cinema; Editor ONAT KUTLAR.

Iktisadi Yükseliş: P.K. 317; f. 1949; economic; Publisher ŞEMŞETTİN CURA.

Istanbul, A Handbook for Tourists: Sişli Meydanı, 364; f. 1968; quarterly; published by Türk Turing, official travel agency of the Touring and Automobile Club of Turkey; Publisher Prof. KEMAL KUTLU; Editor ÇELIK GÜLERSOY.

İstanbul Ticaret Odası Mecmuası: İstanbul Ticaret Odası, Gümüşpala Cad., Eminönü; f. 1884; every three months; journal of the Istanbul Chamber of Commerce; Turkish and English; Editor AHMET TOYDEMIR.

Kadın: Nuruosmaniye Cad., Benice Han 54, Çağaloğlu; f. 1947; serious, political, women's magazine; Publisher İFFET HALİM ORUZ.

Kemalizm: Bankalar Cad., Ankara H. 4; f. 1962; Publisher HÜSEYİN SAĞIROĞLU.

Kulis: Çağaloğlu Yokuşu 10/A; f. 1947; fortnightly arts magazine; Armenian; Publisher HAGOP AYVAZ.

Musiki Mecmuası: P.K. 666, Istanbul; f. 1948 monthly; music and musicology; Editor ETEM RUHİ ÜNGÖR.

Pirelli Mecmuası: Büyükdere Cad. 117, Gayrettepe; f. 1964; monthly; Publisher Türk Pirelli Lâstiklerí A.S.; Editor NAMI ELAGÖZ; circ. 10,000.

Ruh ve Madde Dergisi: P.K. 1157; f. 1959; organ of the Metapsychic and Scientific Research Society of Turkey; Publisher ERGÜN ARIKDAL.

Sağlık Âlemi: Divanyolu Cad. Ersoy Pasajı 1, Çağaloğlu; f. 1964; health; Editor SAMIM AKAY.

Sevgi Dünyası (*World of Love*): Larmartin Cad. 26/3, Taksim; f. 1963; Publisher and Editor Dr. R. KAYSERİLİOĞLU; circ. 5,000.

Söz: Piyerloti Cad. 7, Divanyolu; f. 1966; political; Editor GENÇAY GÜN.

Tip Dünyasi: Ankara Cad. 43/303, Konak Han, Çağaloğlu; f. 1927; monthly; organ of the Turkish Mental Health and Social Psychiatry Society; Editor Ord. Prof. Dr. FAHREDDIN KERIM GÖKAY.

Türk Anglo-Amerikan ve Almaya Postasi: P.K. 192, Beyoğlu; f. 1947; commercial; Publisher KEMAL ERKAN.

Türk Folklor Araştirmalari: P.K. 46, Aksaray; f. 1949; arts and folklore; publ. by Turkish Folklore Association; Gen. Man. and Editor İHSAN HINÇER.

Türk Ticaret Almanaği: Molla Fenari Sok. 25/4, Çağaloğlu; f. 1955; monthly; commercial; Editor AYSEL TOPALOĞLU.

Turkish Trade Directory and Telex Index: Peykhane Caddesi 14, Daire 1, Çemberlitas; f. 1962; annual; Publisher CIRO COSTANTE, COSTANTE BASIN AJANSI.

Türkiye Turing ve Otomobil Kurumu Belleteni: Halaskargazi Cad. 364, Şişli Meydanı; f. 1930; quarterly; published by the Touring and Automobile Club of Turkey; Publisher Prof. KEMAL KUTLU; Editor ÇELIK GÜLERSOY.

Türkiyede ve Dünyada Tarim: Baş Muharip Sok. 17 Seyhan İşhani Kat. 3 14 Çağaloğlu; f. 1964; agricultural news; Publisher KEMAL BAYKAL.

Ülkücü Öğretman: Divanyolu Cad. 64, Çağaloğlu; f. 1965; education; Publisher SIRET İSTEMİ; Editor-in-Chief TEVFİK MARAL.

Varlik: Çağaloğlu Yokuşu 40; f. 1933; monthly; literary; Editor YAŞAR NABİ NAYIR.

Yeditepe: P.K. 77, Çağaloğlu, Mengene Sok., Yeni Han 21; f. 1950; literary and cultural; monthly; Editor HÜSAMETTIN BOZOK.

Yelken: P.K. 639, Karaköy; f. 1955; arts; Editor RÜKNETTİN RESULOĞLU.

Yeni Sanayi Dünyası: P.K. 515, Beyoğlu; f. 1963; Editor NURETTİN ÖZŞIMŞEK.

İZMİR

İzmir Ticaret Odasi Dergisi: Atatürk Cad. 126; f. 1925; every two months; commercial; Editor and Publisher EDIP KAÇAR.

KONYA

Çağrı Dergisi: P.K. 99; f. 1957; literary; monthly; Editor FEYZİ HALICI.

NEWS AGENCIES

Akajans: Tunus Cad. 28, Kat. 4, Bakanliklar, Ankara; Gen. Dir. UĞUR REYHAN.

Anatolian News Agency: Hanimeli Sok. 7, Ankara; also in Istanbul; f. 1920; Gen. Man. AYTEKIN YILDIZ; publ. *Weekly Economical Bulletin*.

ANKA Ajansı: Portakal Çiçeği Sok. 632, Ankara; Dir.-Gen. MÜSSERREF HEKIMOĞLU.

EBA: Olgunlar Sok 2/1, Bakanliklar, Ankara; commercial; Publisher YAVUZ TOLUN.

Hurriyet Haber Ajansı: Babıali Cad. 15-17 Kat 3, Çağaloğlu, Istanbul; f. 1963; Dir.-Gen. OKTAY EKŞİ.

İKA (Economic and Commercial News Agency): Atatürk Bulvarı 199/A-45, Kavaklıdere, Ankara; f. 1954; Dir. ZİYA TANSU.

Türk Haberler Ajansı (*Turkish News Agency*): Türkocağı Cad. 1/4, Çağaloğlu, Istanbul; f. 1950; 11 brs. in Turkey; Dir.-Gen. KADRİ KAYABAL; Editor NİYAZİ DALYANCI.

Yurt Haberler Ajansı: Karanfil Sok. 18/4, Ankara; Dir. YAŞAR GEVREKÇI.

FOREIGN BUREAUX

Agence France-Presse (AFP): P.K. 30, Cankaya-Ankara, Günes Sok. 14; Correspondent GUSTAVE FUMELLI.

Agencia EFE (*Spain*): Günes Sok. 12/3, Güven Evleri Kavaklidere, Ankara; Correspondent ERCOLE MICHELINI.

Associated Press (AP) (*U.S.A.*): Tunus Cad. 49-7, Kavaklidere, Ankara; Correspondent Mrs. EMEL ANIL.

Deutsche Presse-Agentur (dpa) (*Federal Republic of Germany*): c/o ANKA Ajansi, Portakal Ciceği Sok. 63/2, Cankaya, Ankara; Correspondent RASIT GÜRDILEK.

Hsinhua (*People's Republic of China*): Ahmed Mithat Efendi Sok. 52/9, Ankara.

Reuters (*United Kingdom*): P.K. 239, Kizilay, Ankara; Correspondent JEREMY TOWN.

United Press International (UPI) (*U.S.A.*): Kurucesme Cad. 18-20, Arnavutkoy, İstanbul; Bureau Chief OGUZ SEREN.

AFP also has representatives in Istanbul and İzmir. AP is also represented in Istanbul. TASS (*U.S.S.R.*) is also represented in Turkey.

PRESS ASSOCIATION

Gazeteciler Cemiyeti: Çağaloğlu, İstanbul; Pres. BURHAN FELEK; Sec. MUSTAFA YÜCEL.

PUBLISHERS

Ağaoğlu Yayınevi: Selvilimesçit Sokak 2, Kurt İş Hanı, Çağaloğlu, Istanbul; translations and literary books; MUSTAFA KEMAL AĞAOĞLU.

Altin Kitaplar: Çağaloğlu, Istanbul; f. 1959; fiction, non-fiction, biography, memoirs, poetry, children's books, classics, history and crime; Publisher FETHİ UL; Editor-in-Chief TURHAN BOZKURT.

Ark Ticaret Ltd. ŞTI: P.K. 577, Ankara; f. 1962; import-export representation; imports technical books and exports all kinds of Turkish books, periodicals and newspapers; Gen. Man. ATILAN TÜMER; European Branch: 62 Wiesbaden, Postfach 1228, Pagenstrecher St. 1, Federal Republic of Germany.

Arkin Kitabevi: Ankara Cad. 60, P.K. 11, Istanbul; f. 1949; encyclopedias, atlases, children's books, reference; Pres. and Man. RAMAZAN GÖKALP ARKIN.

Atlas Yayınevi: Nuruosmaniye Caddesi, Mengene Sokak 7-9, Istanbul; literary; Publisher RAKIM ÇALAPALA.

Başkent Yayınevi: İzmir Cad. 55/22, Ankara; literary.

Bedir Yayınevi: P.O.B. 1060, Istanbul; Islamic and Turkish books.

Bilgi Yayinlari: Bayindir Sok. 57, Ankara; translations and literary books; Man. AHMET KÜFLÜ.

Cem Yayınevi: Çağaloğlu, Istanbul; f. 1964; novels, poetry, modern classics, cultural and historical books, children's books; Man. ÖGUZ AKKAN.

De Yayınevi: Vilâyet Han, Kat. 3, Çağaloğlu, Istanbul; literary.

Elif Kitabevi: Sahaflar Çarşısı 4, Beyazit, Istanbul; f. 1956; all types of publications, especially historical, literary; political, drama and reference; Publisher ARSLAN KAYNARDAĞ; publ. *Elif Yayınları Kitap Bütteni* (twice monthly).

Gelişim Yayinları A.Ş.: Şafak Sok. 2, Nışantaşı, Istanbul; encyclopaedias, reference and non-fiction; Man. ERCAN ARIKLI.

Hürriyet Yayınları: Cemal Nadir Sok. 7, Çağaloğlu, İstanbul; fiction, history, classics, poetry, general reference books; Dir. AYDIN EMEÇ.

Inkilâp Kitabevi: Ankara Caddesi 95, Istanbul; Dir. NAZAR FİKRİ.

Inkilâp ve Aka Kitabevleri Kollektif Şirketi: Ankara Caddesi 95, Istanbul; general publications, reference books, children's books; Dir. KARABET FİKRİ.

Kanaat Kitabevi: Ilyas Bayar Halefi, Yakup Bayar, Ankara Caddesi 133, Istanbul; f. 1896; textbooks, novels, dictionaries, posters, maps and atlases.

Kanaat Yayınları Ltd. Şti: Ankara Cad. 133/1, Istanbul; f. 1951; maps, school books; Dir. YAKUP BAYAR.

Kervan Yayinlari: Tercüman Tesisleri Londra Asfalti Topkapi, Istanbul; literary.

Koza Yayınevi: Çağaloğlu, Ozaydin Han 6, İstanbul; non-fiction, children's books; Man. TARIK DURSUN.

Kültür Kitabevi: Ankara Cad. 62, Sirkeci, Istanbul; f. 1945; technical books, school books, language books, etc.; Dirs. İZİDOR and RENE KANT.

Milliyet Yayinlari: Basin Sarayi, Çağaloğlu, Istanbul; literary; Man. ÜLKÜ TAMER.

Neşriyat A.Ş.: Mollafenari S.1, Çağaloğlu, Istanbul; classics, children's books, novels.

Oğretim Yayınevi: Ankara Cad. 62/2, Sirkeci, Istanbul; f. 1959; English, French, German, Italian, Spanish and Dutch language courses, guides and dictionaries, phrase books for tourists; Dir. İZİDOR KANT.

Remzi Kitabevi: Ankara Caddesi 93, Istanbul; f. 1930; school textbooks, fiction, children's, science and reference books; Dir. EROL ERDURAN.

Sander Yayınevi: Kiragı Sok. 78, Osmanbey, Istanbul; Man. Dir. NECDET SANDER.

Türk Dil Kurumu: Atatürk Bulvarı 217, Kavaklıdere, Ankara; f. 1932; non-fiction.

Varlık Yayınevi: Çağaloğlu Yokuşu 40, Istanbul; f. 1946; fiction and non-fiction books; Dir. YAŞAR NABİ NAYİR.

Yeditepe Yayınları: P.K. 77, Çağaloğlu, Mengene Sok., Yeni Han 21, Istanbul; publishes literature, poetry, translations, etc. and also *Yeditepe* (monthly).

PUBLISHERS' ASSOCIATION

Editörler Derneği (*Publishers' Association*): Ankara Cad. 60, Istanbul; f. 1950; Pres. RAMAZAN GÖKALP ARKIN; Sec. RAKIM ÇALAPALA.

RADIO AND TELEVISION

RADIO

Türkiye Radyo Televizyon Kurumu (T.R.T.): Nevzat Tandoğan Cad. No. 2, Kavaklıdere, Ankara; f. 1964; controls Turkish radio and television services; Dir.-Gen. Dr. İ CENGIZ TAŞER.

Home Services:

There are local radio stations in Adana, Ankara (3), Antalya, Bursa, Çukurova, Diyarbakir, Edirne, Erzurum, Eskişehir, Gaziantep, Hakkari, Istanbul (3), Izmir (2), Kars, Trabzon and Van.

Foreign Service (Voice of Turkey):

Ankara: SW 100 kW, SW 250 kW (3). Eleven daily short-wave transmissions in the following languages: Arabic, Bulgarian, English, French, German, Greek, Persian, Romanian, Serbo-Croat, Turkish, Urdu; Dir. ESİN TALU ÇELİKKAN.

There is also an educational radio service for schools and a station run by the Turkish State Meteorological Service. The American Forces have their own radio and television service.

In 1977, about 4,260,600 licensed radio receivers were in use.

TELEVISION

Türkiye Radyo Televizyon Kurumu (Ankara TV): Nevzat Tandoğan Cad. 2, Kavaklıdere, Ankara. A limited television service was set up in 1965, and regular broadcasts for Ankara began in 1968, now transmitting programmes seven days a week, averaging 50 hours a week. Head of Television Dept. YILMAZ DAĞDEVIREN; Technical Dir. ERDOĞAN GÖNÖLLÜ.

In 1977 approx. 2,271,800 licensed television receivers were in use.

FINANCE

The Central Bank of the Republic of Turkey was originally founded in 1931, and constituted in its present form in 1970. The Central Bank is the bank of issue and is also responsible for the execution of monetary and credit policies, the regulation of the foreign and domestic value of the Turkish lira jointly with the Government, and the supervision of the credit system.

There are some 41 other banks functioning in Turkey. Thirteen were created by special laws to fulfil specialized services for particular industries. The Sümerbank directs the operation of a number of state-owned factories; Etibank operates primarily in the extractive industries and electric power industries; the Agricultural Bank makes loans for agriculture; the Maritime Bank operates government-owned port facilities, the merchant marine and its own fleet of ships; the Real Estate Credit Bank participates in industrial undertakings and the construction of all types of building. Other specialized banks deal with tourism, municipalities and mortgages, etc.

The largest of the private sector Turkish banks is the Türkiye İş Bankası which operates over 700 branches. The private banks borrow at medium- and long-term mainly from the State Investment Bank.

There are several other credit institutions in Turkey, including the Industrial Development Bank of Turkey, which encourages private investment in industry by acting as underwriter in the issue of share capital. The Turkiye Sınaı Kalkînma Bankası founded in 1950 with the assistance of the World Bank to stimulate industrial growth in the private sector.

There are numerous co-operative organizations, and in the rural areas there are Agricultural Sale Co-operatives and Agricultural Co-operatives. There are also a number of savings institutions.

BANKING

(cap.=capital; p.u.=paid up; auth.=authorized; dep.=deposits; res.=reserves; m.=million; brs.=branches).

(Amounts in Turkish liras, except where otherwise stated. Figures given for capital and deposits are for the end of the calendar year, except where otherwise stated.)

State Banks

Türkiye Cumhuriyet Merkez Bankası (*Central Bank of the Republic of Turkey*): Bankalar Caddesi 48, Ankara; f. 1931; bank of issue; part of the share capital is owned by the State; cap. p.u. 1,500m.; dep. 49,416m. (1977); Gov. Ismail Hakkî Aydinoğlu; 20 brs.

Denizçilik Bankası T.A.O. (*Turkish Maritime Bank*): Rihtim Caddesi, Posta K. 1387, Istanbul; f. 1952; semi-public corporation; nominal cap. 2,000m., of which 51 per cent is subscribed by the Government, the rest by private investors and organizations; dep. 1,328.6m. (1977); operates a shipping line (*see* Shipping); Gen. Man. Recai Hanioğlu.

Devlet Sanayi ve İşçi Yatırım Bankası A.Ş. (*State Industrial and Labour Investment Bank*): Atatürk Bulvarı 44, Ulus, Ankara; f. 1976; cap. p.u. 468.7m.; Gen. Man, Faruk Molu.

Devlet Yatırım Bankası (*State Investment Bank*): Milli Müdafaa Cad., Yenişehir, Ankara; f. 1964; loans and guarantees to State enterprises; cap. 2,000m.; Gen. Man. Sükrü Akgüngör.

Etibank: (Banking Dept.), Atatürk Bulvarı 61, Sıhhiye, Ankara; f. 1935; State economic enterprise active in mining, metallurgy, the chemical industry and banking; cap. 3,250m.; dep. 4,164m. (1978); Gen. Man. Atİlla Aybay; 87 brs.

İller Bankası (*Municipal Bank*): Atatürk Bulvarı, Ankara; f. 1933; government municipalities bank; cap. p.u. 2,000m.; dep. 165.2m. (1977); Chair. of Board and Gen. Dir. Mazhar Haznedar.

Sınai Yatırım ve Kredi Bankasi A.Ş. (*Industrial Investment and Credit Bank*): Istiklal Cad., Beyoğlu, Istanbul; f. 1963; cap. 40m.; Chair. Cahit Kocaömer; Gen. Man. Vecdi Ünay.

Sümerbank: Ulus Meydanı 2, Ankara; f. 1933; holdings bank for governmental industrial undertakings; cap. p.u. 2,250m.; dep. 1,288m. (1977); Gen. Man. Celâlettin Özgen; 36 brs.

Türkiye Cumhuriyeti Turizm Bankası A.Ş.: Atatürk Bulvarı 151/9, Bakanliklar, Ankara; f. 1962; state bank to develop tourism; auth. cap. 1,000m., cap. p.u. 671.1m. (1976); Gen. Man. İlhan Evlİyaoğlu.

Türkiye Cumhuriyeti Ziraat Bankası (*Agricultural Bank of the Republic of Turkey*): Bankalar Caddesi, Ankara; f. 1863; state agricultural bank; 1,000 branches; cap. p.u. 1,500m.; dep. 57,455m. (1978); Gen. Man. Türgüt Erdem.

Türkiye Emlâk Kredi Bankası A.O.: Atatürk Bulvarı 15, Ankara; f. 1927; cap. p.u. 838.7m.; dep. 10,291m. (1978); 216 brs.; Pres. and Gen. Man. Miraç Aktuğ.

Türkiye Sınaî Kalkınma Bankası A.Ş. (*Industrial Development Bank of Turkey*): Meclisi Mebusan Cad. 137, P.O.B. 59, Fındıkhı, Istanbul; f. 1950; cap. 425.4m. (1978); 4 brs.; Chair. Cahit Kocaömer; Gen. Man. Özhan Eroğuz.

Türkiye Vakıflar Bankası T.A.O. (*Foundation Bank of Turkey*): Atatürk Bulvarı 207, Kavaklıdere, Ankara; f. 1954; cap. p.u. 200m.; dep. 9,182m. (1977); 196 brs.; Chair. Osman Nurİ Çatakli; Gen. Man. Halİl Harmanci.

Principal Commercial Banks

Akbank T.A.Ş.: Meclisi Mebusan Cad. 65-69, Fındıklı, Istanbul; f. 1948; cap. p.u. 1,000m.; dep. 44,860m. (Dec. 1978); 566 brs.; Chair. Naİm Talû; Gen. Man. Medenİ Berk.

Anadolu Bankası A.Ş.: İstiklâl Caddesi 108, Beyoğlu, Istanbul; f. 1962; cap. p.u. 150m.; dep. 3,010m. (1977); successor to Türk Ekspres Bank and Buğday Bankası; Gen. Man. Sulhi Alson.

Demirbank T.A.Ş.: 44-46 Bankalar Caddesi, Karaköy, Istanbul; f. 1953; cap. p.u. 20m.; dep. 227m. (1977); Chair. Kamİl Gündeş; Gen. Man. Nuri Cingillioğlu.

Denizli İktisat Bankası T.A.Ş.: Enverpaşa Cad., Denizli; f. 1927; cap. p.u. 25m.; dep. 68.9m. (1977); Chair. A. Fuat Dağdeviren; Gen. Man. Ismail Sarialp.

Egebank A.S.: Gazi Bulvarı 3, P.O.B. 251, İzmir; f. 1928; cap. p.u. 100m.; dep. 466.3m. (1978); Chair. Melih Özakat; Gen. Man. Tekin Değirmenci.

Eskişehir Bankası T.A.Ş.: Demirtaş Cad., Eskişehir; f. 1927; cap. p.u. 50m.; dep. 320.3m. (1977); Chair. Mesut Zeytinoğlu.

İstanbul Bankası T.A.Ş.: İstiklâl Caddesi 398-396, Müeyyet Sok. 1 Tünel, P.O.B. 350, Beyoğlu, İstanbul; f. 1953; auth. cap. 250m.; dep. 2,843m. (1978); Chair. Nevzat Alptürk; Gen. Man. Kemal Onar.

İstanbul Emniyet Sandığı: Pr. Kâzim İsmail Gürkân Cad. 40, Çağaloğu, İstanbul; f. 1968; res. 15.74m.; dep. 1,455m. (1978); Dir. M. Ali Aydaş.

Pamukbank T.A.Ş.: İstiklâl Caddesi 261, Galatasaray, Istanbul; f. 1955; cap. p.u. 400m.; dep. 2,829m. (1977); 89 brs.; Chair., Pres. Mehmet E. Karamehmet; Gen. Man. Hüseyin M. Özyeğin.

Şekerbank T.A.Ş.: Atatürk Bulvarı 55, Ankara; f. 1953; cap. p.u. 100m.; dep. 3,982m. (1978); 136 brs.; Chair. Behçet Oğur; Gen. Man. Cavit Ay.

Türk Diş Ticaret Bankası A.Ş. (*Turkish Foreign Trade Bank*): Cumhuriyet Caddesi 199-201, Harbiye, P.K. 11, Şişli, Istanbul; f. 1964; cap. p.u. 10m.; dep. 986m. (1978); jointly owned by Bank of America, Türkiye İş Bankası and Banca d'America e d'Italia; 5 brs.; Chair. and Man. Dir. A. Üsküdarli.

Türk Ticaret Bankası A.S.: Iskele Caddesi, Hayri Efendi Sokak 36, Bahçekapı, Istanbul; f. 1913; cap. p.u. 125m.; dep. 12,411m. (1977); 350 brs.; Chair. Metin Kizilkaya; Gen. Man. Turgut Sizmazoğlu.

Türkiye Garantı Bankası A.S.: İstiklâl Caddesi, Mıhçıoğlu Han, Istanbul; f. 1946; cap. p.u. 450m.; dep. 10,304m. (1978); 245 brs.; Chair. Ziya Bengü; Gen. Man. Erol Aksoy.

Türkiye Halk Bankası A.Ş.: P.O.B. 150, Anafartalar Caddesi 41, Ankara; f. 1938; cap. p.u. 695.7m.; dep. 12,343.1m. (1978); 467 brs.; Gen. Man. İsmet Alver.

Türkiye İmar Bankası T.A.Ş.: Karakoy, Istanbul; f. 1928; cap. p.u. 50m.; dep. 604.5m. (1977); Gen. Man. Hicri Haznedaroğlu.

Türkiye İs Bankası A.Ş.: P.O.B. 191, Küçükesat, Ankara; Foreign Dept.; P.O.B. 241, Karaköy, Istanbul; f. 1924; cap. p.u. 40m.; dep. 55,395m. (1977); 834 brs.; Chair. İsmail Hakkı Birler; Gen. Man. Cahit Kocaömer; publs. annual review, economic report, economic review (every 2 months).

Türkiye Öğretmenler Bankası T.A.Ş. (TÖBANK): P.O.B. 152, Ulus Atatürk Bulvarı 163, Ankara; f. 1959; cap. and res. 175m.; dep. 3,784m. (1978); Chair. Prof. Dr. Sait Kemal Mimaroğlu; Gen. Man. Bülüt Hüsrev Göle; 106 brs.

Türkiye Tütüncüler Bankası A.Ş.: Halit Ziya Bulvarı No. 45, İzmir, P.K. 239; f. 1924; 22 brs.; cap. p.u. 10m.; dep. 221.6m. (1977); Chair. Kamil Ekini.

Uluslararası Endüstrı ve Ticaret Bankasi A.Ş. (*International Industry and Commerce Bank*): Bankalar Cad. 69, P.O.B. 1326, Karaköy, Istanbul; f. 1888; cap. p.u. 2.7m.; dep. 1,230m. (1977); 9 brs.; Chair. Tacettin Baykal; Gen. Man. İlhan Köseoğlu.

Yapi ve Kredi Bankası A.Ş.: Istiklâl Caddesi, Korsan Çıkmazı 1, P.O.B. 250, Beyoğlu, Istanbul; f. 1944; cap. p.u. 600m.; dep. 30,935m. (1977); 574 brs.; Chair. Ekrem Alican.

Foreign Banks

The Arab Turkish Bank: Istanbul; f. 1977; cap. 300m.; owned 40 per cent by The Libyan Arab Foreign Bank, 20 per cent each by the Kuwait Investment Co., Türkiye İs Bankası and Anadolu Bankası.

Banco di Roma: Hayri Efendi Caddesi, Bahçekapi, P.O.B. 464, Istanbul; cap. 1.5m.; dep. 302.8m. (1977); Gen. Man. Manlio di Mase.

Holantse Bank-Uni N.V.: P.K. 624, Beyoğlu, Istanbul; cap. p.u. 1m.; dep. 230m. (1978); Gen. Man. Willem Cozijnsen.

Ottoman Bank (*Osmanli Bankası*): P.O.B. 297, Karaköy, Istanbul; f. 1863; cap. p.u. 8m.; dep. 5,587m. (1978); Gen. Man. J. Jeulin; Deputy Gen. Man. A. A. Collings-Wells; 97 brs. in Turkey.

STOCK EXCHANGE

Borsa-Komiserliği: Menkul Kıymetler ve Kambiyo Borsası, 4 Vakıf Han, Bahçekapı, Istanbul; f. 1873; 323 mems.; Pres. Refik T. Selimoğlu; Vice-Pres. Kadriye Şişman; publ. *Borsa.*

INSURANCE

Milli Reasürans T.A.Ş.: P.K. 359, Istanbul; f. 1929; state-owned with monopoly of re-insurance; supervises private insurance companies; Chair. Yalçin Ahiska; Gen. Man. Faruk Seven.

Sosyal Sigortalar Kurumu: Mithatpaşa Caddesi, Ankara; f. 1945; Social Insurance Organization; 2,300,000 mems.; cap. and dep. 55,531.7m.; Gen. Dir. Hikmet Ering; publ. *Social Security Bulletin* (monthly).

Private Insurance

Anadolu Anonim Türk Sigorta Şirketi (*Anatolia Turkish Insurance Society*): Rıhtım Caddesi 57, P.O.B. 1845, Karaköy, Istanbul.

Ankara Sigorta Şirketi (*Ankara Insurance Society*): Bankalar Cad. 80, Ankara Sigorta Hanı, Istanbul; f. 1936; Dir. Mahmut Çalişal.

Atlantik Sigorta A.Ş.: Karaköy Meydanı Aksu İş Hanı Kat. 4, Karaköy, Istanbul; f. 1964; fire, marine, accident; Chair. Ali Gomeç; Gen. Man. Okan Balci.

Destek Reasurans T.A.Ş.: Cumhuriyet Caddesi 6a/2, Harbive, İstanbul; f. 1945; Pres. Hikmet Küney; Vice-Pres. Tacettin Aliefendioğlu.

Doğan Sigorta A.Ş.: Doğan Sigorta Binası, Karaköy, Istanbul; f. 1942; fire, marine, accident and life; Chair. Erol Sabanci; Man. Dir. Bedi Yazici; Gen. Man. Engin Asal.

Güven Türk Anonim Sigorta Şirketi: Karaköy, Istanbul; f. 1924; Chair. and Gen. Man. A. Fethi Soysal.

Halk Sigorta T.A.Ş.: Kocataş iş hani, Nişantaş, Istanbul; f. 1944; Pres. Saffet Demir.

İmtaş İttihadı Milli Türk Anonim Sigorta Şirketi (*Imtaş Insurance Company*): Karaköy, Ünyon Han, Istanbul; P.K. 107; f. 1918; Man. Ali Talayman.

Istanbul Umum Sigorta, Anonim Şirketi (*General Insurance Society of Istanbul*): Bankalar Cad. 31/33, Karaköy, Istanbul; f. 1893; Pres. Selim Dirvana; Man. Haşim Ekener.

Şark Sigorta Türk Anonim Şirketi: P.O.B. 111, Karaköy, Bankalar Cad., Şark Han, Istanbul; f. 1923; Chair. Hulki Alisbah.

Şeker Sigorta Anonim Şirketi: Meclisi Mebusan Cad. 325, Şeker Sigorta Hanı, P.O.B. 187, Fındıklı, Istanbul; all types of insurance and reinsurance.

Tam Hayat Sigorta A.Ş.: Büyükdere Cad., Tamhan, Şişli, Istanbul; general life assurance.

Tam Sigorta A.Ş.: Büyükdere Cad. 15, Tamhan, Şişli, Istanbul; all types of insurance except life.

Türkiye Genel Sigorta Anonim Şirketi: Yeni Postahane Karşışı, Istanbul; f. 1948; Pres. Mehmet E. Karamehmet; Gen. Man. Ömer Erül.

TRADE AND INDUSTRY

CHAMBERS OF COMMERCE AND INDUSTRY

Union of Chambers of Commerce, Industry and Commodity Exchanges of Turkey: 149 Atatürk Bulvarı, Bakanlıklar, Ankara; Pres. SEZAİ DIBLAN; publs. *Economic Report* (annually), various specialized brochures and directories.

There are Chambers of Commerce and Industry in all towns of the Republic. Among the most important are the following:

Adana Chamber of Commerce: Adana; f. 1893; Pres. ABDULLAH ÖNGEN; Sec.-Gen. Â. İRFAN TUĞBERK; 7,019 mems.; publ. *Adana Ticaret Odası Gazetesi.*

Adana Chamber of Industry: Adana; f. 1966; Pres. SAKIP SABANCI; 230 mems.

Ankara Chamber of Commerce: Şehit Teğmen Kalmaz Caddesi 20; Pres. NECDET ESEN; Gen. Sec. Dr. AGAH OKTAY GÜNER; publ. *Bulletin* (monthly).

Ankara Chamber of Industry: İzmir Caddesi 22/2; Pres. HAMİ KARTAY; Sec.-Gen. MEHMET AYDIN.

Bursa Chamber of Commerce and Industry: Bursa; f. 1926; 4,582 mems.; Pres. ALİ OSMAN SÖNMEZ; Sec.-Gen. ERGUN KAĞITCIBAŞİ; publ. *Bursa Ticaret Haberleri* (weekly).

Chamber of Industry for the Aegean Region: Cumhuriyet Blv. 136, İzmir; f. 1954, succeeded to the İzmir Chamber of Industry; Pres. YILMAZ ADIGÜZEL; Sec.-Gen. SAMIM TURGAY; publs. *News Bulletin* (weekly), *Quarterly Review.*

Istanbul Chamber of Commerce: Ragıp Gümüspala Cad., Eminönü, Istanbul; f. 1882; 56,693 mems.; Pres. EMIN SANCER; Sec.-Gen. Prof. Dr. İSMAİL ÖZASLAN; publs. *Istanbul Ticaret Odası Mecmuasi* (bi-monthly), *Istanbul Ticaret* (weekly), *Statistical Abstract* (in English), *Exporters Directory* (tri-lingual).

İstanbul Chamber of Industry: Eminönü, Istanbul; Pres. NURULLAH GEZGİN.

İzmir Chamber of Commerce: Atatürk Caddesi 126, İzmir; f. 1885; 8,760 mems.; Pres. DÜNDAR SOYER; Sec.-Gen. ÜMRAN ÖLCÜOĞLU (acting); publ. *Izmir Ticaret Odası Dergisi* (every two months).

Mersin Chamber of Commerce and Industry: P.O.B. 212, Mersin; f. 1886; 1,711 mems.; Pres. MUSTAFA NİHAT SÖZMEN; Sec.-Gen. SUPHİ GÜZELOĞLU.

Samsun Chamber of Commerce and Industry: Samsun; f. 1923; 9 mems.; Pres. YÜCEL TÜRE; Gen. Sec. NECAT GÖKTÜRK.

EMPLOYERS' ASSOCIATION

Turkish Industrialists' and Businessmen's Association (Tusiad): Ankara; Chair. FEYYAZ BERKER.

TRADE UNIONS

CONFEDERATIONS

DİSK (*Confederation of Progressive Trade Unions of Turkey*): Merter Sitesi, Ahmet Kutsi Tecer Cad. 10, K.5 Bayrampasa, Istanbul; *c.* 600,000 mems.; Pres. ABDULLAH BAŞTÜRK; Sec.-Gen. FEHMİ IŞIKLAR; publs. *DİSK Dergisi, DİSK Ajansi.*

Türk-İş (Türkiye İşçi Sendikaları Konfederasyonu Genel Başkanlığı) (*Confederation of Turkish Trade Unions*): Baıyndır Sok. 10, Yenişehir, Ankara; f. 1952; affiliated to I.C.F.T.U.; national unions and federations with 1,570,000 mems.; Pres. İBRAHIM DENİZCİER; Sec.-Gen. SADIK ŞIDE; publs. *Türk-İş* (monthly), *English News* (monthly).

PRINCIPAL UNIONS

Unions affiliated to Türk İş with a membership of over 5,000.

Ağaç-İş (Türkiye Ağaç Sanayii İşçileri Sendikası) (*Wood and Lumber*): Necatibey Cad. No. 20/22-23, Yenişehir, Ankara; f. 1949; 20,882 mems.; also affiliated to IFBWW; Pres. KEMAL SARISOY; Gen. Sec. GÜRAL ERÇAKIR.

Basın-İş (Türkiye Gazeteciler ve Basin Sanayii İşçileri Sendikası) (*Journalists and Press Technicians*): Necatibey Cad. 20/7, Yenişehir, Ankara; f. 1964; 15,000 mems.; Pres. HÜSEYİN DÜZGÜN; Gen. Sec. EYÜP UÇAR; publ. *Gündem* (daily).

B.İ.F. (Türkiye Belediye Hizmetelri İşçi Sendikalari Federasyonu) (*Municipal and Public Employees*): Mesihi paşa Cad., Şair Haşmet Sok. 56, Lâleli, Istanbul; f. 1975; 180,000 mems.; Pres. HÜSEYİN PALA; Gen. Sec. FUAT ALAN.

Cimse-İş (Türkiye Çimento, Seramik ve Toprak Sanayiı İşçileri Sendikası) (*Cement, Ceramic and Soil*): Necatibey Cad. 20/11-12, Yenişehir, Ankara; f. 1963; 38,816 mems.; 39 local unions; Pres. AKİF KESKİN; Gen. Sec. VELİ EKER; publ. *Çimse-Iş News* (monthly).

Deri-İş (Türkiye Deri, Debbağ, Kundura ve Saraciye Sanayii İşçilerı Sendikası) (*Leather and Shoe*): Gençtürk Cad. 17, Birlik İşhanı Aksaray, Istanbul; f. 1948; 17,000 mems.; Pres. YENER KAYA; Gen. Sec. ZEYNEL SEL.

Dok Gemi-İş (Türkiye Liman Dok ve Gemi Sanayii İşçileri Sendikası) (*Port, Dock and Ship Building*): Ordu Cad., 285, Kat-6, Aksaray, Istanbul; f. 1947; 8,000 mems.; also affiliated to IUF; Pres. ASLAN SİVRİ; Gen. Sec. GÜNGÖR TARI.

Dyf-İş (Türkiye Demiryolları İşçi Sendikaları Federasyonu) (*Railways*): Necatibey Cad., Sezenler Sok. 5/4, Yenişehir, Ankara; f. 1952; 56,000 mems.; also affiliated to ITF; Pres. ŞERAFETTİN AKOVA; Gen. Sec. ÖMER SÖNMEZ; publ. *Hiz* (fortnightly).

Haber-İş (Türkiye, Posta, Telegraf, Telefon Radyo ve Television İşcileri Sendikası) (*Postal, Telegraph, Telephone, Radio and Television Workers*): İzmir Cad., Elgün Sok., Pınar Apt. 13/6, Yenişehir, Ankara; 35,000 mems.; Pres. SABRİ IŞIK; Gen. Sec. YUSUF UZUNCAN.

Harb-İş (Türkiye Harb Sanayii ve Yardımcı İşkolları İşçileri Sendikası) (*Defence Industry and Allied Workers*): Inkılap Sok. 20, Kızılay, Ankara; f. 1956; 32,000 mems.; also affiliated to PSI; Pres. KENAN DURUKAN; Gen. Sec. YILMAZ ÖRNEK; publ. *Turk harb-iş* (monthly).

Hava-İş (Türkiye Sivil Havacılık Sendikası) (*Civil Aviation*): Incirli Cad., Volkan Apt. 66/1, Bakırköy, Istanbul; 6,600 mems.; Pres. İBRAHİM ÖZTÜRK; Gen. Sec. ORHAN TARINÇ.

Kauçuk-Iş (Türkiye Kauçuk, Lastik ve Plastik Işçileri Sendikası) (*Plastic and Tyre Workers*): Atatürk Bulvarı, Yayla Palas Apt. 114/6, Aksaray, Istanbul; 5,700 mems.; Pres. FEVZİ BAŞTÜRK; Gen. Sec. YALÇIN CANBOLAT.

Koop-İş (**Türkiye Kooperatif ve Büro İşçileri Sendikası**) (*Cooperative and Office Workers*): İzmir Cad. Fevzi Çadmak Sok. 15/11-12, Yenişehir, Ankara; f. 1964; 12,000 mems.; Pres. İBRAHIM ÇAPAN; Gen. Sec. YETKİN ARÖZ.

Kristal-İş (**Türkiye Şişe, Cam ve Kristal Sanayii İşçileri Sendkası**) (*Glass and Crystal Industry*): Sahipmolla Cad. 24, Paşabahçe, Istanbul; f. 1965; 7,000 mems.; Pres. HASAN BASRI BABALI; Gen. Sec. AHMET KAYA.

Likat-İş (**Türkiye Liman ve Kara Tahmil-Tahliye İşçileri Sendikasi**) (*Longshoremen*): Necatibey Cad. Sezenler Sok. 4, Kat. 5, Yenişehir, Ankara; f. 1963; 6,000 mems.; also affiliated to ITF; Pres. AHMET KURT; Gen. Sec. YAŞAR ATICI.

Maden-İş (**Türkiye Maden, Madenî Eşya ve Makina Sanayii İşçileri Sendikasi**) (*Metal, Metal Goods and Machine Industry Workers' Union of Turkey*): Barbaros Bulvarı 58, Kat 2-3-4-5, Beşiktaş, Istanbul; f. 1947; 80,000 mems.; Pres. KEMAL TÜRKLER; Gen. Sec. MEHMET ERTÜRK; publ. *Maden-Iş* (fortnightly).

Maden Federasyonu (**Türkiye Maden İşçileri Sendikaları Federasyonu**) (*Mine Workers*): Strazburg Cad. 7, Kat. 3-5, Sıhhıye, Ankara; f. 1958; 105,000 mems.; Pres. KEMÂL ÖZER; Gen. Sec. MUSTAFA ORHAN.

Petrol-İş (**Türkiye Petrol, Kimya, Azot ve Atom İşçileri Sendikası**) (*Oil, Chemical and Atomic*): Yıldız Posta Cad., Evren Sitesi, D-Blok, Gayrettepe, Istanbul; f. 1950; 49,000 mems.; also affiliated to IFPCW; Pres. CEVDET SELVİ; Gen. Sec. ADEM YILMAZ; publ. *Petrol-Iş* (weekly).

Sağlık-İş (**Türkiye Sağlık İşçileri Sendikası**) (*Health Employees*): Necatibey Cad. 23/9-10, Yenişehir, Ankara; f. 1961; 40,000 mems.; also affiliated to PSI; Pres. MUSTAFA BAŞOĞLU; Gen. Sec. YILMAZ UÇAR.

Şeker-İş (**Türkiye Şeker Sanayii İşçileri Sendikası**) (*Sugar Industry*): Mithatpaşa Cad. 13/3, Yenişehir, Ankara; f. 1952; 26,000 mems.; Pres. A. YAŞAR DOĞUALP; Gen. Sec. HİKMET ALCAN; publ. *Şeker-Iş* (fortnightly).

Selüloz-İş (**Türkiye Selüloz ve Mamülleri İşçileri Sendikası**) (*Celluloid Industry*): Hürriyet Cad., Isılay Apt. Kat-1, Kocaeli; f. 1952; 12,000 mems.; Pres. NECATİ CANSEVER; Gen. Sec. SALİH GÜNGÖRMEZ.

Su-İş (**Türkiye Baraj, Enerji, Su ve Sulama İşçileri Sendikası**) (*Dam, Energy, Water and Irrigation Workers*): Büyükdere Cad. 56/1-2, Mecidiyeköy, Istanbul; f. 1950; 5,000 mems.; Pres. NIHAT KAYA; Gen. Sec. NEVZAT ÖZBAY.

Tarim-İş (**Türkiye Orman, Topraksu, Tarım ve Tarım Sanayii Işçileri Sendikasi**) (*Forestry and Agricultural Workers*): Necatibey Cad., Ankara Apt. 22/9-10-12, Yenişehir, Ankara; f. 1961; 120,000 mems.; affiliated to IFPAAW; Pres. ZEYNEL IRMAK; Gen. Sec. MAHMUT TELLİ; publ. *Agricultural News* (monthly).

Tekgida-İş (**Türkiye Tütün, Müskirat Gıda ve Yardımcı İşçileri Sendikası**) (*Tobacco, Drink, Food and Allied Workers' Union of Turkey*): 4 Levent Konaklar Sokak, P.K. 98, Istanbul; f. 1952; 152,000 mems.; also affiliated to IUF; Pres. İBRAHİM DENİZCİER; Gen. Sec. NAZMİ CEYLANDAĞ.

Teksif (**Türkiye Tekstil, Örme ve Giyim Sanayii İşçileri Sendikası**) (*Textile, Knitting and Clothing*): Aydoğmuş Sok. 1, Kurtuluş, Ankara; f. 1951; 120,000 mems.; also affiliated to ITGWF; Pres. ŞEVKET YILPAZ; Gen. Sec. ZEKI POLAT.

Tes-İş (**Türkiye Enerji, Su ve Gaz İşçi Sendikaları**) (*Energy, Water and Gas*): Meşrutiyet Cad. Karanfil Sokak 34/6, Yenişehir, Ankara; f. 1963; 65,000 mems.; Pres. ORHAN ERÇELİK; Gen. Sec. FARUK BARUT.

T.G.S. (**Türkiye Gazetecilar Sendikası**) (*Journalists*): Basin Sarayı, Kat. 2, Çağaloğlu, İstanbul; 6,000 mems.; Pres. OKTAY KURTBATUR; Gen. Sec. ACAR ŞÖLEN.

Tez-Büro-İş (**Türkiye, Ticaret, Banka, Sigorta, Kooperatif, Eğitim, Tezgahtarlar ve Büro İşçileri Sendikası**) (*Commercial and Clerical Employees*): Necatibey Cad. Sezenler Sok. 2/16, Sıhhiye, Ankara; f. 1962; 25,000 mems.; Pres. UĞUR BATMAZ; Gen. Sec. TURAN BARUT.

TOREYİS (**Türkiye Otel Restaurant Eğlence Yerleri İşçileri Sendikası**) (*Hotel, Restaurant and Places of Entertainment*): Kuloğu Sok., Tercioğlu Apt. 7/1, Beyoğlu, Istanbul; f. 1947; 23,000 mems.; also affiliated to IUF; Pres. SERVET SOFUOĞLU; Gen. Sec. CEMIL GİDER.

Tümtis (**Türkiye Motorlu Taşıt İşçileri Sendikası**) (*Motor Transport*): Selimpaşa Sok. 62, P.K. 292, Aksaray, Istanbul; f. 1949; 15,000 mems.; also affiliated to ITF; Pres. HÜSEYIN PALA; Gen. Sec. ABID ŞİMŞEK.

Türk Deniz Ulaş-İş (**Türkiye Deniz Taşıtmacılığı İşçi Sendikalari Federasyonu**) (*Seamen*): Rıhtım Cad., Çıraci Sok. 7, Tophane, Istanbul; f. 1959; 25,000 mems.; also affiliated to ITF; Pres. EMIN KUL; Gen. Sec. MUSTAFA YÖNDEY.

Türk-Metal (**Türkiye Metal, Çelik, Mühimmat, Makina Metalden Mamul, Eşya ve Oto, Montaj ve Yardimoi Işçileri Sendikası**) (*Auto, Metal and Allied Workers*): Gazi Mustafa Kemal Bulvarı, 40/1-2, Maltepe, Ankara; f. 1963; 55,000 mems.; Pres. MUSTAFA ÖZBEK; Gen. Sec. MUAMMER GÜR.

Yol-İş (**Türkiye Yol Yapı ve İnşaat İşçileri Sendikaları Federasyonu**) (*Federation of Turkish Road Construction and Building Workers' Unions*): İzmir Cad. 22, Kat 2, Yenişehir, Ankara; f. 1963; 70,000 mems.; also affiliated to IFBWW; Pres. HALİT MISIRLIOĞLU; Gen. Sec. MUZAFFER SARAÇ; publ. *Yol-İş* (monthly).

TRADE FAIR

İzmir Enternasyonal Fuarı (*İzmir International Fair*): Kültürpark, İzmir; f. 1929; August 20th–September 20th annually; Pres. İHSAN ALYANAK; Dir. HAMDI ASENA.

TRANSPORT

RAILWAYS

Türkiye Cumhuriyeti Devlet Demiryollari İşletmesi—TCDD (*Turkish Republic State Railways*): İşletmeşi Genel Müdürlüğü, Ankara; f. 1924; operates all railways and connecting ports; the Railway Administration acquired the status of a public corporation in 1953; Gen. Dir. ZÜHTÜ ORAL; Dir. Administration and External Relations HÜSNÜ KAYAOĞLU; publ. *Demiryol* (monthly).

The total length of the railways operated within the national frontiers is 10,125 km. (1976), of which 352 km. are electrified. Five-Year Plans for modernizing the railway system were introduced in 1963, with dieselization and electrification projects having since been carried out. A ten year Master Plan (1978–87) aims to extend electrification further. A new direct rail link between Ankara and Istanbul, cutting the distance from 577 km. to 414 km., is expected to be completed by 1983. There are direct rail links with Bulgaria and Iran.

ROADS

Bayındırlık Bakanlığı Karayolları Genel Müdürlüğü (*General Directorate of Highways*): Ankara; Dir.-Gen. SERAFETTIN UZUNER.

At the beginning of 1977 24 km. of freeway, and 67 km. of expressways were open to traffic and 189 km. of freeways were under construction. The total length of all-weather roads was 57,969 km., comprising 32,544 km. of national and 25,425 km. of provincial roads. The total length of village roads was 136,367 km.

SHIPPING

Denizcilik Bankasi T.A.O. (*Turkish Maritime Bank*): Genel Müdürlük, Karaköy, İstanbul; f. 1952; capital of TL 2,000m.; four maritime establishments operate passenger, cargo and ferry-boat lines on inter-city, coastal, Adriatic, Aegean and Mediterranean Sea routes; four Port Administrations offer loading, unloading, transfer and warehousing facilities; five shipyards and dry docks have repair and construction facilities for ships up to 20,000 tons; international concerns such as ship salvage and coastal security; other assets include: six hotels; 73,562 gross tons of shipping, 17 ships and 44,493 gross tons of inter-city communication, 68 ferries.

D.B. Deniz Nakliyati T.A.Ş. (*D.B. Turkish Cargo Lines*): Findıklı, Meclisi Mebusan Cad. 93-97, İstanbul; f. 1955; regular liner services between Turkey and Mediterranean, Europe, Black Sea, and U.S. Atlantic and Gulf ports; Chair. Retd. Admiral C. BIREN; 37 dry cargo ships, 14 bulk/ore carriers, 11 tankers.

PRIVATE COMPANIES

Denizcilik Anonim Şirketi: Meclisi Mebusan Caddesi, Fındıklı Han Kat 4, Fındıklı, Istanbul; f. 1952; tanker owners and shipbuilders up to 8,000 t.d.w., repair and dry-docking at company's shipyard in Istanbul; Chair. Board of Dirs. HAYRETTIN BARAN; Man. Dir. SABAHATTIN ÜLKÜ; 2 tankers.

Koçtuğ Denizcilik İşletmesi D.İ.: Bankalar Caddesi, Bozkurt-General Han Kat 5, Karaköy, P.K. 884, Istanbul; cargo services to and from Europe, North Africa and the U.S.A.; Owners S. KOÇMAN, S. GÖKTUĞ; 7 cargo vessels.

Marmara Transport A.S.: Yeniçarşi Sok. Vakıf Han No. 20, Kat. 3 Galatasaray, Istanbul; ship-building; 2 slipways, capacity 12,000 d.w.t.; output 20,000 d.w.t.; tanker services; Chair. M. A. MARDIN; Gen. Man. O. GIRAY; 2 tankers.

CIVIL AVIATION

There are airports for scheduled international and internal flights at Yeşilkoy (Istanbul), Esenboğa (Ankara) and Adana, while international charter flights are handled by Antalya and Cigli (Izmir). Seventeen other airports handle internal flights only.

Türk Hava Yollari A.O. (THY) (*Turkish Airlines Inc.*): Cumhuriyet Caddesi 199-201, Harbiye, Istanbul; f. 1933; 97.35 per cent state-owned; Pres. SELAHATTIN BABÜROĞLU; Chair. NIHAT KURSAT; extensive internal network and flights from Ankara and Istanbul to Beirut, Brussels, Copenhagen, Frankfurt, Geneva, London, Milan, Munich, Nicosia, Paris, Rome, Tel-Aviv, Tripoli, Vienna and Zürich; fleet of four Boeing 707, four Boeing 727, nine DC-9, two DC-10 and three F-28.

Turkey is also served by the following foreign airlines: Aeroflot (U.S.S.R.), Air France, Alia (Jordan), Alitalia, Ariana (Afghanistan), Austrian Airlines, Balkan (Bulgaria), British Airways, ČSA (Czechoslovakia), Cyprus Airways, El-Al (Israel), Iran National, Iraqi Airways, JAT (Yugoslavia), KLM (Netherlands), Kuwait Airways, LOT (Poland), Lufthansa (Federal Republic of Germany), MALÉV (Hungary), MEA (Lebanon), Olympic (Greece), Pan Am (U.S.A.), PIA (Pakistan), Sabena (Belgium), Saudia, SAS (Sweden), Swissair and TAROM (Romania).

TOURISM

Ministry of Tourism and Information: Gazi Mustafa Kemal Bulvarı 33, Ankara; Dir.-Gen. of Tourism AYDIN KEZER; Dir.-Gen. of Information NEVİN MENEMENCIOĞLU.

CULTURAL ORGANIZATIONS

Fine Arts General Directorate (*Güzel Sanatlar Akademisi Genel Müdürlüğü*): Education Ministry, Bakanlıklar, Ankara; Dir.-Gen. Prof. SADUN ERSIN.

PRINCIPAL THEATRES

State Theatre General Directorate (*Devlet Tiyatrosu Genel Müdürlüğü*): part of the above; runs eight playhouses; Dir.-Gen. ERGİN ORBEY.

Büyük Tiyatro (*Great Theatre*): Ankara.

Küçük Tiyatro (*Small Theatre*): Ankara.

Devlet Opera ve Balesi: Ankara; state opera and ballet; permanent classical and modern ballet company of 65 dancers; Gen. Dir. AYDIN GÜN.

There are three other state theatres in Ankara, and five private companies. Istanbul has thirteen private companies.

Istanbul City Opera: Taksim, Istanbul; Dir. AYDIN GÜN.

ORCHESTRAS

Istanbul State Symphony Orchestra: Taksim, Istanbul; f. 1972; Gen. Dir. MUKERREM BERK; Music Dir. MIRCEA BASARAB; 120 mems.

Presidential Symphony Orchestra: Ankara.

ATOMIC ENERGY

Turkish Atomic Energy Commission: Prime Minister's Office, Bestekar Sokak 29, Ankara; f. 1956; controls the development of peaceful uses of atomic energy; 12 mems.; Chair. Hon. MUSTAFA KEMAL ERKOVAN; Sec.-Gen. İBRAHIM DERİNER; publs. *Activity Reports, Research Reports*, etc.

There are nuclear research centres at Çekmece, near Istanbul, and at Ankara. Turkey is a member of the International Atomic Energy Agency (IAEA) and the OECD Nuclear Energy Agency (NEA).

DEFENCE

Chief of General Staff: Gen. KENAN EVREN.

Army Commander: Gen. NURETTIN ERSIN.

Navy Commander: Admiral BULEND ULUSU.

Air Force Commander: Gen. TAHSIN SAHINKAYA.

Defence Budget (1978): TL 50,617 million.

Military Service: 20 months.

Total Armed Forces: 465,000: army 375,000 men, with 2,800 medium tanks; navy 43,000 men, includes 14 submarines; air force 47,000 men, 319 combat aircraft.

Paramilitary Forces: 75,000 gendarmerie.

EDUCATION

One of the greatest problems confronting the new Republic was that of modernizing and extending the educational system, for at that time only 11 per cent of the population were literate. New schools had to be built and equipped in towns and villages; teachers and inspectors trained, and suitable schemes of training devised for them; technical courses provided to equip skilled workers for industry and agriculture; and, above all, training in reading and writing had to be provided for the millions of peasants who had received no schooling.

Under the Ottoman Empire there had been a dual system of education—religious schools existing side by side with others in which ordinary educational subjects were taught, although religious instruction played a large part. Unity of education was recognised as the first requisite; the theological schools were converted into theological seminaries for the training of clergy, or abolished; the others were secularised. The Ministry of Education was declared the sole authority in all educational matters.

One of the main obstacles to literacy was the Arabic script, which required years of study before proficiency could be attained. In 1928, therefore, a Turkish alphabet was introduced, using Latin characters. At the same time the literary language was simplified, and purged of some of its foreign elements. By 1978 the education budget amounted to TL 25,905 million, nearly 10 per cent of the state budget.

People's Schools

This change of script created a need for schools in which reading and writing in the new alphabet could be taught to adults. Temporary institutions known as "people's schools" or "national schools" were set up everywhere. During the winter months these schools gave instruction in reading and writing and other basic subjects to men and women beyond the normal school age. Between 1928 and 1935 some 2 million people received certificates of proficiency. Since then education in Turkey has made big advances, but although literacy is estimated at 65 per cent in towns, it is still much lower in the villages (30.3 per cent in 1960).

Primary Education

A compulsory school attendance law had been passed in 1913, but only under the Republic were measures taken to enforce this. Primary education is now entirely free, and co-education is the accepted basis for universal education. The number of schools has risen from 12,511 in 1950 to 42,009 in 1975, and the number of teachers from 27,144 to 172,488. In 1975–76, over 5.5 million children were attending primary schools.

Secondary Education

The reorganization of the system of secondary education began in the early 1920s. Before the reorganization there were two types of secondary schools: state schools, providing one or two educational stages, and local schools corresponding approximately to the modern middle schools. In 1926 the system of co-education was adopted in day schools of the middle-school group.

Present Organization. This period of education lasts six years, and is free.

The secondary schools are divided into two stages: middle schools and *lycées*, and students who intend to proceed to higher educational institutions must pass through both stages, spending three years in the middle school and three in the *lycée*.

The middle school, although complementary to the *lycée*, is a separate unit, designed to give a definite and complete education to those students who at the end of the course will proceed directly to work. The state examination is taken by all students at the end of the third year. Graduates of a middle school are qualified either to take up an unskilled occupation or to enter upon a vocational course at a school of a higher grade.

The *lycée* takes the student up to the age of 17 or 18 years, and those who wish to proceed to an institute of higher education must pass the state matriculation examination. The study of a modern language (English, French or German) is compulsory in middle schools and *lycées*. In addition, Latin and Greek have been taught in some *lycées* since 1940. The number of secondary schools (not including technical and vocational schools) in 1975 was 3,328 with a total of 1,363,188 students.

Adult Education. Since 1932, reading-rooms have been established in every town and many villages. They are centres of social and cultural life and provide evening classes. Their libraries, meeting-halls and recreational facilities are open to all. In the towns there are also evening trade schools which provide technical training for adults, and travelling courses are sent out to the villages.

Higher Education. Higher educational institutions in Turkey were founded, and are administered, by the State. These institutions include the universities and the higher professional schools. There are now 18 universities and 102 institutes of higher education (including teacher training colleges). Three of the universities specialize in scientific and technical subjects. The number of students at universities and other institutes of higher education was nearly 210,000 in the academic year 1975–76.

Technical Education. The problem of technical education began to be seriously considered first in 1926; specialists were invited from Europe and America, and a plan was drawn up for perfecting the existing vocational schools and for founding new ones to meet the economic needs of each region. In 1975 there were 1,209 technical and vocational *lycées*, giving training to 312,522 students. In addition, plans were made for evening schools to train craftsmen and for the founding of teachers' technical training colleges. There are two such colleges in Ankara, one for men and one for women.

Teachers' Training. In Turkey teachers' training colleges are divided into three basic categories: two-year teacher training institutes which train teachers for primary schools, three-year teacher training institutes which train teachers for middle schools and higher teacher training schools offering a four-year course qualifying teachers for the *lycées*. Students of the higher teacher training schools take specialist subject courses in the relevant university faculty and their pedagogy courses in the higher teacher training schools. In the academic year 1974–75 there were 30,749 students enrolled in 42 teacher training colleges.

UNIVERSITIES

Anadolu Üniversitesi (*University of Anatolia*): Eskişehir; 33 teachers, 203 students.

Ankara Üniversitesi (*University of Ankara*): Tandogan Meydani, Ankara; *c.* 2,000 teachers, *c.* 23,000 students.

Atatürk Üniversitesi (*Atatürk University*): Erzurum; 587 teachers, 7,985 students.

Boğaziçi Üniversitesi (*Bosporus University*): Istanbul; formerly Robert College; 370 teachers, 3,062 students.

Bursa Üniversitesi (*Bursa Universtiy*): Bursa; 107 teachers, 1,245 students.

Çukurova Üniversitesi (*University of Çukurova*): Adana; 281 teachers, 948 students.

Cumhuriyet Üniversitesi (*Republic University*): Sivas; 54 teachers, 109 students.

Diyarkabir Üniversitesi (*Diyarbakir University*): Diyarbakir; 309 teachers, 1,327 students.

Ege Üniversitesi (*Aegean University*): Bornova, İzmir; 1,369 teachers, 20,000 students.

Firat Üniversitesi (*Euphrates University*): Elâzig; 60 teachers, 580 students.

Hacettepe Üniversitesi (*University of Haceteppe*): Ankara; 1,758 teachers, 13,629 students.

Inönü Üniversitesi (*Inönü University*): Malatya; *c.* 30 teachers, 100 students.

İstanbul Üniversitesi (*Istanbul University*): Beyazit, Istanbul; 804 teachers, *c.* 33,000 students.

İstanbul Teknik Üniversitesi (*Istanbul Technical University*): Beyoğlu, Istanbul; 789 teachers, 8,053 students.

Karadeniz Teknik Üniversitesi (*Karadeniz Technical University*): Trabzon; 250 teachers, 2,810 students.

19 Mayis Üniversitesi (19 *May University*): Sarnsua; 46 teachers, 306 students.

Orta Doğu Teknik Üniversitesi (*Middle East Technical University*): Ankara; 1,011 teachers, 10,112 students.

Selçuk Üniversitesi (*Seljuk University*): Konya; 425 students.

BIBLIOGRAPHY

GENERAL

ALLEN, H. E. The Turkish Transformation (Chicago, 1935).

ARMSTRONG, H. C. Grey Wolf: Mustafa Kemal: an Intimate Study of a Dictator (London, 1937).

AUBOYNEAU & FEVRET. Essai de bibliographie pour l'Empire Ottomane (Paris, 1911).

BAHRAMPOUR, FIROUZ. Turkey, Political and Social Transformation (Gaus, New York, 1967).

BEAN, G. E. Aegean Turkey (Benn, London, 1966).

Turkey's Southern Shore (Benn, London, 1968).

BERKES, NIYAZI. The Development of Secularism in Turkey (McGill University Press, Montreal, 1964).

BIRGE, J. K. A Guide to Turkish Area Study (Washington, 1949).

BISBEE, ELEANOR. The New Turks (Philadelphia, 1951).

The People of Turkey (New York, 1946).

BRIDGE, ANN. The Dark Moment (New York, 1952).

The Falcon in Flight (New York, 1951).

COHN, EDWIN J. Turkish Economic, Social and Political Change (New York, Praeger, 1970).

COOKE, HEDLEY V. Challenge and Response in the Middle East: The Quest for Prosperity, 1919-1951 (New York, 1952).

DODD, C. H. Politics and Government in Turkey (Manchester University Press, 1969).

EDGECUMBE, Sir, C. N. E. Turkey in Europe (Barnes and Noble, N.Y., 1965).

EKREM, SELMA. Turkey: Old and New (New York, 1947).

EREN, NURI. Turkey Today and Tomorrow (New York, 1964).

FREY, F. W. The Turkish Political Elite (M.I.T. Press, Cambridge, Mass., 1965).

GÖKALP, ZIYA. Turkish Nationalism and Western Civilisation (London, 1960).

GÜNTEKİN, REŞAT NURİ (trans. Sir WYNDHAM DEEDES). Afternoon Sun (London, 1950).

The Autobiography of a Turkish Girl (London, 1949).

HALE, WILLIAM. Aspects of Modern Turkey (Bowker Publishing, Epping, 1977).

HARRIS, GEORGE S. The Origins of Communism in Turkey (Hoover Institution, Stanford, Calif., 1967).

HAYIT, B. Turkestan im XX Jahrhundert (Darmstadt, C. W. Leske Verlag, 1956) (in German).

HEYD, URIEL. Foundations of Turkish Nationalism: the Life and Teachings of Ziya Gökalp (Luzac and Harvill Press, London, 1950).

Language Reform in Modern Turkey (Jerusalem, 1954).

HOTHAM, DAVID. The Turks (John Murray, London, 1972).

JACKH, ERNEST. The Rising Crescent (New York, 1950).

JÄSCHKE, GOTTHARD. Der Islam in der Neuen Türkei: eine Rechtsgeschichtliche Untersuchung Die Welt des Islams (N.S., Vol. I, Nos. 1-2).
Die Türkei in den Jahren 1942-51 (Wiesbaden, 1954)

KARPAT, KEMAL. Turkey's Politics, The Transition to a Multi-Party System (Princeton, 1959).

KAZAMIAS, A. M. Education and the Quest for Modernity in Turkey (Allen and Unwin, London, 1967).

KELLY, MARIE NOËLE. Turkish Delights: Travels and Impressions of the Turkish Scene, 1946-1949 (London, 1951).

KINNANE, DIRK. The Kurds and Kurdistan (Oxford, 1965).

KINROSS, Lord. Within the Taurus (London, 1954).
Europa Minor: Journeys in Coastal Turkey (London, 1956).
Turkey (303 photogravure illustrations, London, 1960).
Atatürk (Weidenfeld, London, 1964).

KIŞLALI, AHMET TANER. Forces politiques dans la Turquie moderne (Ankara, 1967).

KORAY, ENVER. Türkiye Tarih Yayınları Bibliografyası 1729-1950; A Bibliography of Historical Works on Turkey (Ankara 1952).

KÜRGER, K. Die Türkei (Berlin, 1951).

LAMB, HAROLD. Suleiman the Magnificent: Sultan of the East (New York, 1951).

LEWIS, BERNARD. Turkey Today (London, 1940).
The Emergence of Modern Turkey (Oxford University Press, London and New York (rev. edition 1970)).

LEWIS, G. L. Turkey ("Nations of the Modern World" series) (London, 1955) (3rd edn., Praeger, N.Y., 1965).

LINKE, L. Allah Dethroned (London, 1937).

LUKACH (LUKE), Sir HARRY CHARLES. The Old Turkey and the New (Geoffrey Bles, London, 1955).

MANGO, ANDREW. Turkey (Thames and Hudson, London, 1967).

MARFORI, TERENZIO. La Constituzione della Repubblica Turca (Florence, 1947).

MAYNE, PETER. Istanbul (Dent, London, 1967).

MELLAART, JAMES. Earliest Civilizations of the Near East (Thames and Hudson, London, 1965).
Çatal Hüyük (Thames and Hudson, London, 1967).

MOOREHEAD, A. Gallipoli (New York, Harper, 1956).

MUNTZ, T. G. A. Turkey (New York, 1951).

NEWMAN, BERNARD. Turkish Crossroads (London, 1951)
Turkey and the Turks (Herbert Jenkins, London, 1968).

ORGA, IRFAN and MARGARETE. Atatürk (London, 1962).

PARKER, J., and SMITH, C. Modern Turkey (London, 1940).

PLATE, HERBERT. Das Land der Türken (Verlag Styria, Graz, Wien, Köln, 1957).

ROBINSON, RICHARD D. The First Turkish Republic (Harvard University Press, 1963).

SALTER, CEDRIC. Introducing Turkey (Methuen, London, 1961).

STARK, FREYA. Ionia (London, 1954).
Lycian Shore (London, 1951).
Riding to the Tigris (London, 1956).

STEINHAUS, KURT. Soziologie der turkischen Revolution (Frankfurt, 1969).

STEWART, DESMOND. Turkey (Life World Library Series, Time Inc., N.Y., 1965).

SZYLIOWICZ, JOSEPH S. Political Change in Rural Turkey: Erdemli (Mouton, The Hague, 1966).

TOYNBEE, A. J. The Western Question in Greece and Turkey (Constable, London, 1923).

TOYNBEE, A. J., and KIRKWOOD, D. P. Turkey (London, 1926).
Lycian Shore (London, 1956).

TUNAYA, T. Z. Atatürk, the Revolutionary Movement and Atatürkism (Baha, Istanbul, 1964).

UNESCO. Emancipation of the Turkish Woman (Columbia University Press, New York).

VALI, FERENC A. Bridge across the Bosphorus: the Foreign Policy of Turkey (Johns Hopkins Press, 1970).

WARD, BARBARA. Turkey (Oxford, 1942).

WARD, ROBERT E., and RUSTOW, OANKWART A. (eds.). Political Modernizations in Japan and Turkey (Princeton University Press, 1964).

WEBSTER, D. E. The Turkey of Atatürk: Social Progress in the Turkish Reformation (Philadelphia, 1939).

WILLIAMS, GWYN. Turkey: A Travellers Guide and History (Faber and Faber, London, 1967).

YALMAN, A. E. Turkey in my time (University of Oklahoma Press, 1956).

HISTORY

AHMAD, FEROZ. The Young Turks (Oxford University Press, 1969).

ALDERSON, A. D. The Structure of the Ottoman Dynasty (Oxford, 1956).

ALLEN, W. E. D., and MURATOFF, P. Caucasian Battlefields: A History of the Wars on the Turco-Caucasian Border, 1828-1921 (Cambridge, 1953).

CAHEN, CLAUDE. Pre-Ottoman Turkey (Sidgwick and Jackson, London, 1968).

CASSELS, LAVENDER. The Struggle for the Ottoman Empire, 1717-1740 (John Murray, London, 1967).

COLES, PAUL. The Ottoman Impact on Europe (Thames and Hudson, London, 1968; Brace and World, New York, 1968).

DAVIDSON, RODERIC H. Turkey (Prentice-Hall, New York, 1968).

DUDA, HERBERT W. Vom Kalifat zur Republik (Vienna, 1948).

GURNEY, O. R. The Hittites (London, 1952).

JASCHKE, G. Die Türkei in den Jahren 1952-61 (Otto Harrassowitz, Wiesbaden, 1965).

KEDOURIE, ELIE. England and the Middle East: The Destruction of the Ottoman Empire, 1914-1921 (Cambridge, 1956).

LEWIS, BERNARD. Istanbul and the Civilization of the Ottoman Empire (University of Oklahoma Press, 1963).

LEWIS, GEOFFREY. La Turquie, le déclin de l'Empire, les réformes d'Ataturk, la République moderne (Verviers/Belgique, 1968).

LIDDELL, ROBERT. Byzantium and Istanbul (London, 1956).

LLOYD, SETON. Early Anatolia (London, 1956).

MANTRAN, ROBERT. Histoire de la Turquie (Paris, 1952).

MILLER, WILLIAM. The Ottoman Empire and its Successors, 1801-1927 (Cambridge, 1934).

OSTROGORSKY, G. History of the Byzantine State (Oxford, 1956).

PALLIS, A. A. In the Days of the Janissaries (London, 1951).

PFEFFERMANN, HANS. Die Zusammenarbeit der Renaissance Päpste mit den Türken (Winterthur, 1946).

PRICE, M. PHILIPS. A History of Turkey: From Empire to Republic (London, 1956).

RAMSAUR, E. E. The Young Turks and the Revolution of 1908 (Princeton University Press, 1957).

RICE, DAVID TALBOT. Art of the Byzantine Era (Frederick A. Praeger, New York, 1963).

Byzantine Art (Penguin, London, 1962).

RICE, TAMARA TALBOT. The Seljuks (London, 1962).

RUNCIMAN, Sir STEVEN. The Fall of Constantinople, 1453 (Cambridge University Press, 1965).

SUMNER, B. H. Peter the Great and the Ottoman Empire (Oxford, 1949).

THOMAS, L. V., and FRYE, R. N. The U.S.A. and Turkey and Iran (Oxford University Press, 1952).

VAUGHAN, DOROTHY. Europe and the Turk: A Pattern of Alliances, 1350-1700 (Liverpool, 1954).

VERE-HODGE, EDWARD REGINALD. Turkish Foreign Policy, 1918-1948 (2nd (revised) edition, London, 1950).

WALDER, DAVID. The Chanak Affair (Hutchinson, London. 1968).

ECONOMY

The Economy of Turkey: an Analysis and Recommendations for Development Program: Report of the Mission sponsored by the International Bank for Reconstruction and Development; in collaboration with the Government of Turkey (Baltimore, 1951).

HERSHLAG, Z. Y. Turkey: the Challenge of Growth (Leiden, 1968).

SHORTER, FREDERIC C. (ed.). Four Studies on the Economic Development of Turkey (Cass, London, 1967; Kelley, New York, 1968).

THORNBURG, MAX, SPRY, GRAHAM, and SOULE, GEORGE Turkey: an Economic Appraisal (New York, 1949).

United Arab Emirates

ABU DHABI DUBAI SHARJAH RAS AL-KHAIMAH UMM AL-QUWAIN AJMAN FUJAIRAH

GEOGRAPHY

The coastline of the seven United Arab Emirates extends for nearly 400 miles from the frontier of the Sultanate of Oman to Khor al-Odaid on the Qatar Peninsula in the Persian Gulf. The area is one of extremely shallow seas, with offshore islands and coral reefs, and often an intricate pattern of sandbanks and small gulfs as a coastline. In contrast to the Mediterranean, there is a large tide. The waters of the Gulf contain relatively abundant quantities of fish, large and small, hence fishing plays some part in local life. The climate is arid, with very high summer temperatures; and except for a few weeks in winter, air humidity is also very high. The total area of the U.A.E. has been estimated at approximately 32,000 square miles and it has a rapidly growing population estimated at 877,000 (1978), concentrated in the oil boom areas of Abu Dhabi, the capital of the U.A.E., and Dubai. Many inhabitants are nomadic or settled Arabs. In the coastal towns live also many Persians, Indians, Pakistanis, Baluchis and Negros, the latter being descended from slaves carried from Africa during the course of several centuries of slave trading. The most important port is Dubai, capital of the U.A.E.'s second largest state. Its significance derives from its position on one of the rare deep creeks of the area, and it now has a very large transit trade.

HISTORY

In the early 16th century the Portuguese commercial monopoly of the Gulf area began to be challenged by other European traders eager for a share in the profits from the Eastern trade, first by the Dutch, later by the British. By the end of the century the Portuguese ascendency in the East had declined and in 1650 the Portuguese evacuated Oman losing their entire hold on the Arabian shore. Then followed a period of commercial and political rivalry between the Dutch and the British during which the initial Dutch predominance weakened and in 1766 came practically to an end, while the British were consolidating their supremacy in India.

Both European and Arab pirates were very active in the Gulf during the 17th, 18th and early 19th centuries. Lawlessness reached its height at the beginning of the 19th century when the seafaring Arab tribes were welded together and incited to pillage by Wahhabi emissaries who had established their supremacy over the whole Arabian coast of the Gulf. Attacks on British-flag vessels led to British expeditions against the pirates in 1806 and 1809 and, finally, in 1818 against the pirate headquarters at Ras al-Khaimah and other harbours along the 150 miles of "Pirate Coast". In 1820 a General Treaty of Peace for suppressing piracy and slave traffic was concluded between Great Britain and the Arab Tribes of the Gulf. Among the signatories were the principal Sheikhs of the Pirate Coast and the Sheikhs of Bahrain. A strong British squadron was stationed for some time at Ras al-Khaimah to enforce the treaty.

Many piratical acts continued to be committed and accordingly, in 1835, the Sheikhs were induced to bind themselves by a "Maritime Truce" not to engage, in any circumstances, in hostilities by sea for a period of six months (i.e. during the pearl-diving season). The advantages of this were so marked that they were easily persuaded to renew the truce and continually did so for increasing periods until, in May 1853 a Treaty of Maritime Peace in Perpetuity was concluded between all the Sheikhs of the "Trucial Coast"—as it was henceforth called—establishing a "perpetual maritime truce". It was to be watched over and enforced by the British Government, to whom the signatories were to refer any breach. The British, however, did not interfere in wars between the Sheikhs on land.

The British concern in stopping the slave trade had also led to contacts with the Trucial Coast, where the Sheikhs had been engaged in carrying slaves from Africa to India and Arabia. By agreements signed with the British in 1838–39 and 1847 the Sheikhs undertook to prohibit the carriage of slaves on board vessels belonging to them or their subjects, and consented to the detention and search of such vessels and to their confiscation in case of guilt.

Towards the end of the 19th century France, Germany and Russia showed increasing interest in the Gulf area and in 1892 Britain entered into separate but identical "exclusive" treaties with the Trucial rulers concluded on different dates, whereby the Sheikhs undertook not to cede, mortgage nor otherwise dispose of parts of their territories to anyone except the British Government, nor to enter into any relationship with a foreign government other than the British without British consent. Britain had already undertaken to protect the states from outside attack in the Perpetual Maritime Treaty of 1853.

In 1820 when the General Treaty was signed, there were only five Trucial States. In 1866, on the death of the Chief Sheikh of Sharjah, his domains were divided amongst his four sons, the separate branches of the family being established at Sharjah, Ras al-Khaimah Dibah and Kalba.

In 1952, Kalba was incorporated into Sharjah when its ruler undertook to accept all the treaties and agreements in force between the United Kingdom and the other Trucial States. These undertakings included recognition of the right of the U.K. Government to fix state boundaries, to settle disputes between the Trucial Sheikhdoms and to render assistance to the Trucial Oman Scouts, a British-officered Arab force set up in 1952. The Ruler of Fujairah also accepted these undertakings when his state was recognized as independent in 1952.

In 1952 on British advice a Trucial Council was established at which all seven rulers met at least twice a year under the chairmanship of the Political Agent in Dubai. It was formed with the object of inducing the rulers to adopt a common policy in administrative matters and in the hope that an eventual federation of the states would ensue.

The advent of commercial production of oil in mid-1962 gave Abu Dhabi a great opportunity for development. The deposition of the Ruler, Sheikh Shakhbut, in 1966 removed a major obstacle to implementing this opportunity, and the history of this sheikhdom since then is a classic example of a society being transformed almost overnight by the acquisition of immense wealth. Dubai has also benefited greatly from the oil boom.

In June 1965 Sheikh Saqr of Sharjah was deposed. In spite of an appeal to the UN Secretary-General, supported by Iraq and the United Arab Republic, the accession of his cousin, Sheikh Khalid, passed off without incident. There was an unsuccessful attempt on the Sheikh's life in July 1970.

After June 1966 Britain gradually built a substantial military base at Sharjah, with the object of replacing Aden as the major base in the Middle East; by July 1968 the force of 3,000 men was also larger than Bahrain's and Sharjah had become the principal base in the Gulf. Early in 1968 the British Government announced that all its forces would be withdrawn from the area by the end of 1971. The Trucial Oman Scouts, a force of some 1,600 men officered and paid for by Britain and based in Sharjah, was proposed as the nucleus of a federal security force after British withdrawal in 1971, but some states, notably Abu Dhabi, were already creating their own defence forces.

It was feared that friction might be aroused by disputes over the ill-defined state borders; those between Qatar, Abu Dhabi and Dubai were settled early in 1970, the settlement being disputed by Saudi Arabia, whose claimed territory overlapped that of Abu Dhabi to a considerable extent. In July 1970 King Faisal requested that a plebiscite be held in the Buraimi district now ruled by Abu Dhabi. In the autumn of 1974 a border agreement was signed with Saudi Arabia on the Liwa oases, whereupon Saudi Arabia recognized the U.A.E. and Ambassadors were exchanged. Further down the Gulf, offshore rights also caused trouble. Rival claims over the island of Abu Musa were made by both Sharjah and Iran when petroleum exploration began in 1970, but in 1971 an agreement was reached to split the profits from any oil production on the island.

The original proposals for the formation of a federation on the departure of British influence included Bahrain and Qatar, as well as the seven Trucial States, but negotiations on the participation of the larger and more developed states eventually broke down in 1971, and they opted for separate independence. On December 1st, 1971, Britain terminated all existing treaties with the Trucial States. The following day Abu Dhabi, Dubai, Sharjah, Umm al-Quwain, Ajman and Fujairah formed the United Arab Emirates and a treaty of friendship was made with Britain.

Ras al-Khaimah refused to join the Union until February 1972, when it had become clear that neither Britain nor any Arab government was prepared to take action on Iran's seizure of the two Tumb islands in the Gulf belonging to the sheikhdom. In December 1971 the U.A.E. became a member of both the Arab League and the United Nations.

In January 1972 the Ruler of Sharjah, Sheikh Khalid, was killed by rebels led by his cousin, Sheikh Saqr, who had been deposed as Ruler in 1965. The rebels were captured, and Sheikh Sultan succeeded his brother as Ruler. Sheikh Sultan soon confirmed that he would rule according to the relatively liberal principles of his brother and retain Sharjah's membership of the U.A.E.

Although the U.A.E. remained one of the most conservative Arab states, it gave considerable support to the Arab cause in the October War of 1973 and participated in the oil cut-backs and boycotts associated with it. It was the first state to operate a total ban on oil exports to the U.S.A. Loans and contributions by the U.A.E. to developing countries in 1974 totalled U.S. $554 million. The allocation for 1978 was $1,300 million.

In December 1973 the separate Abu Dhabi Government was disbanded and, in a cabinet reshuffle, some of its members became federal ministers. Most notably the Abu Dhabi oil minister, Mani Said al-Otaiba, became the first federal oil minister. The government reorganization involved a considerable extension of central authority and was a further step towards integration of the seven sheikhdoms. Abu Dhabi was using its economic power to encourage its partners to accept a greater degree of unity, although some seemed reluctant to abandon more of their personal authority. In May 1975, at a session of the Supreme Council, the seven Emirs gave their consent in principle to further steps for centralization. In November 1975 Sharjah merged the Sharjah National Guard with the Union Defence Force, and also handed control of its broadcasting station to the Federal Ministry of Communications, its police to the Ministry of the Interior and its courts to the Ministry of Justice. The Sharjah flag was abolished in favour of the federal tricolour. Fujairah immediately did the same, and Abu Dhabi gave up its flag.

The merger of the main defence forces (the Union Defence Force, the Abu Dhabi Defence Force and the Dubai Defence Force) was finally agreed upon in early May 1976, when General Sheikh Khalifa bin Zayed al-Nahayan, the Crown Prince of Abu Dhabi, was made Deputy Supreme Commander (Sheikh Zayed became Supreme Commander). In November 1976 Article 142 of the provisional constitution was amended so that the right to levy armed forces and acquire weapons was placed exclusively in the hands of the Federal Government.

During 1976 Sheikh Zayed had shown impatience and misgiving about the speed at which the Emirates were achieving centralization. In fact, so disillusioned was he that he threatened not to stand for a second term as President of the U.A.E., beginning in November 1976. In the event, he was re-elected unanimously after the Supreme Council had granted the Federal Government greater control over defence, intelligence services, immigration, public security and border control. A cabinet re-shuffle followed in January 1977 in which the Ministers were said to be chosen on the principle of individual merit rather than representation of the seven Emirates. The new 40-member Federal National Council, which was inaugurated on March 1st, 1977, showed the same spirit of re-invigoration, as only seven members of the first five-year session (1971–76) were included.

During 1978, however, it seemed that the unity of the Federal Defence Force was under strain. A dispute arose in February 1978, when Sheikh Zayed appointed his second son, Sheikh Sultan, as Commander-in-Chief of the Armed Forces. Sheikh Rashid of Dubai claimed that he was not consulted. Thereafter the forces of Dubai and Ras al Khaimah refused to accept orders from the Federal Commander, and Dubai independently ordered a number of British tanks.

The United Arab Emirates attempted to play a mediatory role in the divisions in the Arab world which followed President Sadat of Egypt's peace initiative in visiting Israel in November 1977. The U.A.E. supported the decision to ostracize Egypt, taken at the Baghdad summit in November 1978, and has broken off diplomatic relations and stopped all aid.

Mounting pressure from within the Emirates for a more united federation in 1978 led to the setting up of a joint Cabinet-Federal National Council committee to discuss methods of achieving this. Events in Iran in 1979 and the resultant security threat prompted a full meeting of the Council of Ministers and the Federal National Council in February. The outcome of this was a 10-point memorandum advocating the abolition of all internal borders, the unification of defence forces and the merging of revenues in a federal budget, which was subsequently submitted to the Supreme Council.

There were large-scale demonstrations throughout the Emirates in support of these demands. However, the proposals aggravated the long-standing rivalry between Abu Dhabi, the financial mainstay of the federation, and Dubai, increasingly critical of the centralized federal government in recent years. Dubai announced that it rejected the memorandum completely and, together with Ras al-Khaimah, boycotted a Supreme Council meeting in March. There was widespread agitation in Ras al-Khaimah at this and Sheikh Saqr was urged to be more co-operative with the federal government and accept more federal aid. The remaining members of the Council criticized Dubai for allegedly failing to contribute to the federal budget, maintaining a separate defence force and keeping control of its oil revenues.

It was thought that the deadlock had been broken for the time being when Sheikh Rashid, ruler of Dubai, was offered the premiership of the federal government in late April, in place of his son, and accepted it. By this time he had agreed to merge the Dubai defence force with the federal army and all the Emirates had agreed to contribute 50 per cent of their oil revenue to the federal budget. The new cabinet, announced in July, preserved a similar balance of power between the Emirates to that of the previous one.

ECONOMIC SURVEY

The seven sheikhdoms which form the United Arab Emirates cover some 32,300 square miles (83,600 sq. km.), stretching nearly 400 miles (650 km.) along the southern coast of the Gulf and part of the Gulf of Oman. The low barren coastal plain merges southward into the sandy desert of the Empty Quarter of Saudi Arabia, and eastwards along the border with Oman rise mountains of 7,000–8,000 feet (2,100–2,400 metres). The official census of 1975 put the population at 655,937, of which the two largest emirates, Abu Dhabi and Dubai, accounted for 235,662 and 206,861 respectively. The population has grown rapidly in recent years, swollen largely by foreign workers attracted by the area's vast oil wealth. The officially estimated population in 1978 was 877,340, of whom less than a quarter were citizens of the United Arab Emirates. Before the discovery of petroleum in 1959, economic activity was limited to oasis agriculture, fishing and trade. Rising oil production and recent oil price increases have boosted income to give the United Arab Emirates the highest per capita G.N.P. in the world: U.S. $14.420 in 1977, according to World Bank estimates.

The economy of the U.A.E. is dominated by petroleum. Production of crude petroleum rose steadily until 1977, when it totalled 729.5 million barrels, compared with 708.9 million barrels in 1976. Exports of crude petroleum reached 720.9 million barrels in 1977, compared with 706.7 million barrels in 1976. In 1978, however, oil output declined for the first time, falling to about 670 million barrels. Abu Dhabi is by far the biggest producer within the U.A.E., with 602.3 million barrels in 1977 (of which 596.3 million were exported). In 1977 Dubai produced 116.4 million barrels and exported 114.5 million. The only other Emirate producing oil is Sharjah, with a 1977 output of 10.3 million barrels and exports of 10.1 million. The United Arab Emirates is a member of the Organization of Petroleum Exporting Countries and Abu Dhabi has played a prominent role in helping to form OPEC policy. Abu Dhabi has taken 60 per cent participation in foreign oil company operations, but appears reluctant to effect a full 100 per cent takeover. Dubai took over foreign oil company operations completely in 1975, a move which seemed in sharp contrast to its *laissez-faire* economic policies, but it is thought that the move was actively supported by the oil companies.

Earnings from petroleum exports, which account for about 90 per cent of the U.A.E.'s income, rose steadily to Dh 6,953 million in 1973 before leaping, with the quadrupling of oil prices in that year, to Dh 24,967 million in 1974. Slackened world demand in 1975 partly offset still higher prices and the U.A.E.'s oil export revenues that year rose only slightly to Dh 26,646 million. In 1976, however, exports increased considerably and Dh 32,566 million was earned. In 1977 there was a further rise to Dh 35,607 million but in 1978, when output fell, export earnings declined to Dh 33,450 million.

The immense oil wealth has enabled the Emirates to undertake an ambitious programme of economic and social development. In the early 1960s the area was without paved roads, water and electricity services, telephones or hotels. Today roads link all the main centres of settlement, hotels and high-rise buildings have sprung up, communications are being continually expanded and health and welfare services and education are freely available to all citizens. Development has chiefly been concerned with infrastructure, but more attention is now being turned to diversifying the economy through industrialization and the development of agricultural and fishery potential. However, with its small population and paucity of natural resources other than oil, the United Arab Emirates faces immense problems in realizing development ambitions. The local workforce long ago proved too small to meet the rapidly growing demands for skilled workers, administrators and technicians by the construction industry, the civil service and the oil industry, with the result that workers from western industrialized nations, other Arab countries and the Indian sub-continent are increasingly filling the gap. The Government is keen to use local citizens wherever possible and has begun an intensive campaign to develop education and technical training facilities, although these schemes are not expected to show significant results for at east 10 years.

The lack of raw materials and the small size of the local market has led the Emirates to concentrate on developing indigenous resources to the full. Abu Dhabi is concentrating on hydrocarbon-based projects, while Dubai is building on its well-established trading pre-eminence in the Gulf, as well as promoting ambitious industrial projects. There are plans to develop tourism throughout the United Arab Emirates.

Despite the progress in the U.A.E. towards political integration, there is little co-ordination in economic policies. Abu Dhabi's wealth tends to overshadow the other Emirates but at the same time is the main factor that holds the seven Emirates together. Apart from the difference between Abu Dhabi and Dubai over participation in the oil industry, the two main Emirates do not appear to co-operate on building up their hydrocarbon-based or other industries. Indeed, there seems to be outright rivalry. When Dubai announced its plans in 1976 for a major industrial complex and special port at Jebel Ali, a few weeks later Abu Dhabi announced plans for a similar complex and port at Ruwais. The smaller Emirates also do not want to be left behind, and as a result there is already a surfeit of international airports and is likely to be an excess of cement plants. Abu Dhabi, Dubai, Sharjah and Ras al-Khaimah all boast international airports, the latter two greatly under-used. Dubai has abandoned plans for a new airport but intends to carry out expansion of the existing one by 1981, at a cost of $65 million.

The main instrument of development policy is the federal budget, which is mainly concerned with the implementation of federal infrastructure policy. Individual Emirates also draw up separate budgets for municipal expenditure and local, mainly industrial projects. The constitution provides for all services such as health and education to come under federal control but in practice the Emirates have tended to go their own way. Abu Dhabi is the moving force behind the federal budget, contributing more than 90 per cent of federal budget revenue, although both Abu Dhabi and Dubai have pledged 50 per cent of their oil revenues to the federal budget in the future.

The federal budget in 1977 was Dh 13,150 million, compared with Dh 3,114.0 million in 1976. Current expenditure in 1977 was set at Dh 9,833 million (Dh 1,451.0 million in 1976) and development expenditure at Dh 1,403.0 million (Dh 748 million in 1976). The big increase in the 1977 budget reflected the transfer of some major items from the Abu Dhabi to the U.A.E budget, notably foreign aid, education, health and information, as well as the merger of Abu Dhabi's defence force into the U.A.E.'s. However, Abu Dhabi is still likely to end up providing well over 90 per cent of the revenue to support the Union budget, though, as in previous years, full disbursement of expenditure will probably not be achieved. The federal budget for 1978 was Dh 10,500 million, and for 1979 was provisionally set at Dh 12,000 million.

Though a central monetary institution—the U.A.E. Currency Board—was established in May 1973, inter-Emirate rivalry has prevented its being given full central banking powers. This has had some unfortunate consequences in what has been described as the most over-banked country in the world. The U.A.E. has 53 retail commercial banks, five restricted license banks and several merchant banks and money brokers. Thirty-six foreign banks have branches. The Currency Board, managed mainly by expatriates, has been able to bring some order into the banking free-for-all. A moratorium on new banks opening was imposed in 1975 but was lifted temporarily in May 1976 (as a result of what appeared to be political pressure) to allow five more banks (four Arab and one British) to operate. The moratorium was then reimposed, but with the let-out for international banks of restricted licences, which allow all operations except domestic retail banking. Twelve such restricted licences were issued in 1976, but only five such banks have opened.

Early in 1977, the circumscription of the powers of the Currency Board by political factors within the U.A.E. became more apparent. First of all, there was a run on the dirham, sparked off by the failure of the Abu Dhabi and Dubai Governments to supply the Board with enough foreign exchange to support the currency. When the Board did obtain enough dollars to redress the situation, and also introduced severe controls to end the speculation, several banks found themselves in difficulties, highlighting the unhealthy policies some of them had been encouraged to follow by the severe competition for business in the U.A.E.

Later, the Ruler of Dubai gave permission for two new local banks in which influential local merchants were involved to open in defiance of the Currency Board's moratorium. A few weeks later, two banks—the Ajman Arab Bank and the Janata Bank—closed their doors because of liquidity problems and others were reported to be facing cash problems. The Currency Board announced tough new measures to ease the situation, but these were countermanded by the Government.

Missions from the IMF and the Bank of England were sent to advise on the situation and the Janata Bank re-opened. After the "Janata affair" the controversy over the Central Bank bill continued amid much dissension among the Rulers. It was proposed to introduce a rule requiring banks to have a minimum paid up capital of Dh 20 million. There is no doubt that a Central Bank would maintain tighter controls than the Currency Board has been able to; but some, notably the Ruler of Ras al-Khaimah, claim that tighter controls would alienate capital.

The Currency Board moves to squeeze liquidity dealt a final blow to the already faltering construction boom which had lasted since 1973/74 in the U.A.E.

In 1978 the Board eased liquidity restrictions a little, calculating that some Dh 500 million would be injected into the economy. 1977 and 1978 have been described as years of recession, but this is only true in comparison with the tremendous growth experienced in 1976.

The money supply has risen rapidly in line with the expansion of government revenue since 1973. Currency in circulation rose by 387 per cent in the three years to December 1976 and overall domestic liquidity by 728 per cent. Money supply expanded only 10 per cent in 1978, however. Most bank lending is for construction activities and trade. Inflation in 1978 was reckoned to be of the order of 15 per cent, compared with 40–50 per cent in 1975–76.

Official estimates of the balance of payments were published for the first time at the beginning of 1978. There has been a gradual decline in the surplus on the current account, as imports of goods and services rose more rapidly than oil exports. In 1977 the trade balance was Dh 22,200 million, compared with Dh 22,000 million in 1976, and declined even further to Dh 17,500 million in 1978. The current account surplus fell from Dh 13,500 million in 1976 to Dh 9,700 million in 1977. The biggest import items are machinery and transport equipment, basic manufactures and food and live animals. In 1977 the leading purchasers of crude oil from Abu Dhabi and Dubai were Japan (27.1 per cent), the U.S.A. (15.7 per cent), France (13.2 per cent) and the Netherlands (7.1 per cent). All of Sharjah's oil exports went to the U.S.A. The leading suppliers of imports into Abu Dhabi and Dubai were Japan (20.1 per cent), the United Kingdom (16.0 per cent), the U.S.A. (10.9 per cent) and the Federal Republic of Germany (9.2 per cent). The healthy trade balance is reflected in the growth of the U.A.E.'s international reserves, even though only part of the individual Emirates' foreign exchange reserves is deposited with the Currency Board and it was reported at the end of 1978 that the Board held no government dollar reserves.

The dirham was created in 1973 to replace the Bahraini dinar and the Qatar/Dubai riyal, formerly used in the Emirates. A timetable for achievement of a common Gulf currency has been agreed with Bahrain, Kuwait and Qatar, but the target date of 1978 proved to be unrealistically early. For travellers there is interchangeability between the U.A.E., Bahrain and Qatar currencies up to amounts of Dh 5,000, one dirham being taken as equivalent to one Qatari riyal or one-tenth of a Bahraini dinar.

ABU DHABI

Abu Dhabi's hydrocarbon wealth is substantial. Oil, first discovered in 1959 and exported in 1963, is found on and off shore and these reserves have been developed mainly by two companies, Abu Dhabi Petroleum Company (a consortium of BP, Shell, CFP, Exxon, Mobil and Partex) and Abu Dhabi Marine Areas (a consortium of BP, CFP and Japan Oil Development Co.). In September 1974 the Government took a 60 per cent share in the operations of these companies, to be handled by the state oil company, Abu Dhabi National Oil Company, which also has the local monopoly of oil distribution and is responsible for oil installations and oil-based industries. The value of natural gas reserves has only recently been realized. Gas associated with petroleum is usually flared but Abu Dhabi is now taking steps to harness these resources for local energy and industry and for export. Gas reserves are officially estimated at 20,000,000 million cubic feet and could be among the largest in the world. In 1977 the LNG plant on Das Island was finished and the first shipment to Japan began. Income from the hydrocarbon sector, mainly crude petroleum exports, rose steadily as production increased, to reach about $750 million in 1973. After the fourfold increase in prices, revenue leapt to about $4,500 million in 1974. Early in 1975 oil production dropped suddenly as world demand slackened, and the Abu Dhabi Government had to exercise tighter control on its spending for a time. The Emirate's oil appeared to be overpriced for current market conditions and premiums were therefore cut, helping production to regain its former level by the end of the year. However, revenue for the year overall suffered and was Dh 15,015 million, compared with Dh 14,131 million in 1974. By 1976 it had reached Dh 19,663 million, and it was projected to reach Dh 18,401 million in 1977.

Explosive population growth in recent years, as a result of the flood of immigration (as few as 20 per cent of Abu Dhabi's 1975 population of 235,000 were thought to be Abu Dhabi citizens), has put a severe strain on the economy, particularly services and accommodation. In 1968 Abu Dhabi initiated its first National Plan, which envisaged a total expenditure of BD 316.97 million ($662 million), of which over 90 per cent was to be spent on social services and industrial and agricultural projects during the period 1968–73. The pace and pressure of development led to a minor crisis in late 1969, when expenditure began to exceed revenues, partly because the Government had authorized more projects than it could immediately pay for, especially as inflation had driven up the cost of all construction. A policy of consolidation was introduced at the end of 1969, with a resultant slowdown in the rate of development. In the 1970 budget, development expenditure was reduced by 35 per cent from the level envisaged under the five-year plan. After the 1969–70 "freeze" the Government continued a more cautious policy of "controlled expansion" until 1972. But growth in oil production and the fourfold increase in world oil prices in 1973/74 radically altered Abu Dhabi's fortunes, boosting oil revenue more than five fold and enabling the Emirate to expand its development plans.

In 1976/77 revenue was budgeted at Dh 18,401.2 million, expenditure at Dh 18,205.2 million, leaving a small surplus, which, through underspending on development projects, is likely to have turned out much larger. Development expenditure was set at Dh 4,463.2 million. In 1977/78 and 1978/79 this part of the budget went up to about Dh 5,500 million. The total for 1978/79 was set at over Dh 8,000 million. A development plan for 1977–79 is being loosely followed which envisages expenditure of some $8,700 million and the creation of some 183,000 new jobs. Almost 80 per cent of total spending under the plan will go on services (housing, transport, telecommunications, etc.) and industry. The latter is concentrated on hydrocarbons, and will be centred on Ruwais, near the crude oil loading facility at Jebel Dhanna, some 200 km. west of Abu Dhabi town. At Ruwais will be the Emirate's second refinery, a petrochemical plant, an LNG plant, a plastic pipe factory and four desalination plants. Other industries such as iron and steel are also under consideration.

With the growth of its oil income, Abu Dhabi has evolved a generous aid programme to poorer developing countries. External assistance in the form of grants, soft loans and participations totalled Dh 2,401.6 million in 1974. Despite his straitened financial position, Sheikh Zayed stepped up his aid in 1975 to Dh 4,376.5 million. By 1976, it had reached Dh 5,309 million, equivalent to no less than 29.5 per cent of Abu Dhabi's total oil receipts that year. Some 75 per cent of the Emirate's aid was estimated to go to Egypt (its share is now channelled into the Baghdad Fund for the "confrontation states"), Syria, Jordan and the Palestine Liberation Organization. Spearheading the project-financing side of the aid programme is the Abu Dhabi Fund for Arab Economic Development (ADFAED), set up in 1971 with a capital of $120 million. In 1974, its capital was raised to $500 million and its scope of operation broadened to non-Arab Asia and Africa, though 1976 was the first year loan agreements were concluded with such countries. By the end of 1977 the ADFAED had committed 47 loans worth Dh 1,640 million, of which 79 per cent had gone to Arab countries, 13 per cent to Asian countries and 8 per cent to African countries. Electricity projects accounted for 33 per cent, industry for 27 per cent and agriculture 11 per cent.

Despite its generous foreign aid programme, Abu Dhabi has a considerable financial surplus—estimated at around $5–6,000 million at the beginning of 1978. This surplus is the responsibility of the Abu Dhabi Investment Authority, set up in early 1976 to replace the London-based Abu Dhabi Investment Board which had previously handled these funds. After the massive increase in revenue as a result of the 1973/74 oil price rises most of the surplus was kept in liquid assets but, under the guidance of the Investment Board and then the Investment Authority, a growing proportion is being transferred to a portfolio of equities, bonds and property.

DUBAI

Dubai, the second largest of the Emirates, has a long trading tradition and, in the wake of the Gulf oil boom, has developed its talents to become one of the most important financial and commercial centres in the Gulf. The discovery of oil in 1966, albeit in small quantities compared with those of Abu Dhabi, has substantially increased Dubai's wealth and enabled it to undertake a number of ambitious projects to consolidate its position.

The port of Dubai has prospered for centuries from the *entrepôt* trade practised up and down the Gulf by its merchant families. The decision taken by the Ruler, Sheikh Rashid, in the late 1960s to dredge the creek and establish a new deep-water port was critical for Dubai, enabling it to take full advantage of the growing oil wealth of the area. The four-berth deep-water harbour at Port Rashid was completed in 1972. It has since been expanded to 19 berths and another 18 are under construction. It is now one of the largest artificial deep-water harbours in the Middle East and handles much of the trade of the U.A.E. as well as considerable *entrepôt* trade with neighbouring states. The volume of goods handled by the port has expanded rapidly. In 1974 Dubai handled 2.7 million tons of imports, in 1975 3.2 million and in 1976 5.3 million. The value of Dubai's imports for the same years was Dh 4,817 million, Dh 7,115 million and Dh 9,498 million. In 1977 imports amounted to Dh 12,659 million. In 1978 the value of imports rose to Dh 12,708 million but the actual volume of goods fell by 22 per cent. This was due partly to the decline in machinery imports with the slow-down in the construction sector. Currency changes also meant that Japanese goods became dearer during the year, Japan being Dubai's leading supplier. Re-exports form the bulk of Dubai's non-oil trade. Since statistics are incomplete, their value can only be estimated but it is thought that between 40 and 50 per cent of Dubai's total imports are re-exported. Official figures for 1977 and 1978 put re-exports at Dh 1,156.8 million and Dh 1,379.4 million respectively. The main destinations were Iran and Saudi Arabia.

Oil was discovered in Dubai in 1966 by a consortium known as the Dubai Petroleum Company: production began in 1969 and has risen steadily to 319,000 b/d in 1977. Output comes from two offshore fields, Fateh and South-west Fateh. The Fallah field could start producing in 1979 at 10,000 b/d; the Rashid field could come on stream at a similar rate in 1980. Reserves are fairly small, in the order of 185 million tons, and could be exhausted by about 1985 or 1990. In July 1975 the Dubai Government took 100 per cent control of oil company operations, but the oil companies continue to produce and market oil on behalf of the Government. Net oil revenues are estimated at $1,500 million for 1979, with a further $1,500 million of income expected, deriving from customs duties and port charges.

In the late 1960s and early 1970s development was concentrated on the expansion of commerce and finance, for example, the expansion of Port Rashid bnd the encouragement of banking. Further projects aeing implemented to consolidate Dubai's financial and commercial position include a dry dock, a trade and exhibition centre, port and airport expansion and more hotels. The dry dock is by far the most ambitious project and, when completed, will be one of the largest ship repair facilities in the world with three docks, one capable of taking ships up to one million d.w.t. In view of the limited life of oil resources, industrialization is also being encouraged and the projects are equally ambitious: a $500 million aluminium smelter, natural gas liquefaction and oil refining facilities and a cement plant. In 1979 Dubai Aluminium obtained a $230 million loan for the smelter but its feasibility in the Gulf area at present, bearing in mind Bahrain's experience, is doubtful. Light industries are also being developed in the Port Rashid free zone.

Because of the close personal involvement of the Ruler, Sheikh Rashid, in the economy of Dubai, it is often difficult to differentiate between Dubai's finances and those of the Ruler. Capital projects are financed by the Ruler and foreign loans raised on his personal guarantee. Since the end of 1973 Dubai has raised $1,400 million in the Eurodollar markets. In the past no official budget figures have been published and only those close to the Ruler know the true picture, but in May 1976 a municipal budget of 635 million dirhams for 1976 to cover local infrastructure expenditure, was announced. It was also officially stated that Dubai would be spending 11,200 million dirhams on major development projects. In 1977 the Municipal budget rose 85 per cent to Dh 1.174 million. In 1978 Dubai was to spend about Dh 4,100 million on development and Dh 700 million on recurrent items.

THE NORTHERN EMIRATES

Sharjah is the most developed of the five northern Emirates. Since oil production began in 1974 the pace of economic development has accelerated, with emphasis on finance and commerce. Oil revenues are small, an estimated Dh 307 million in 1975, Dh 321 million in 1976 and about Dh 140 million in 1977 (after 30 per cent of revenue had been given to Umm al Quwain and 5 per cent to Ajman under a 1971 agreement), and Sharjah has had to seek loans from foreign bankers and aid from Abu Dhabi to finance its ambitious plans. Amoco Sharjah, which was granted a 35-year concession in 1978, considered that there were good prospects of finding oil in Wadia, west of the Hajar mountains. Sharjah has adopted an open liberal policy towards foreign banks and businesses in a determined effort to attract some of the business that might otherwise go to Dubai. There are no taxes on banks and 79 have now been licensed, of which 38 were operating in 1977. No local participation is required in foreign enterprises, in contrast to Abu Dhabi and Dubai. Port Khaled in Sharjah town has been developed to operate container services, and Khor Fakkan on the Omani coast is to become a major container cargo port. Other major enterprises include a plastic pipe factory, paint factories and a 700 tons a day cement plant. The end of the construction boom in the U.A.E. has hit Sharjah particularly hard. Sharjah town in mid-1978 was almost a ghost town with a hundred or more buildings standing incomplete or untenanted, and hotels languishing without guests, but by mid-1979, with many grandiose schemes abandoned, there was cause for more optimism.

Ras al-Khaimah has discovered oil offshore but its significance has yet to be determined. The Emirate has the most advanced agricultural sector in the U.A.E., helped by having a slightly wetter climate than its neighbours, and an increasing proportion of its food requirements is being met from domestic resources. There is a cement plant producing 700 tons a day, with expansion to an eventual 4,500 tons a day planned; the international airport; and, under construction, a 250-room hotel and a seven-berth port.

Fishing and agriculture predominate in Umm al-Quwain and Fujairah, though the former also gets a modest income from oil through its 30 per cent share of revenue received by Sharjah from the Abu Musa field. It has announced the discovery of oil offshore, but how much has yet to be revealed. Fujairah, the poorest Emirate, is also hoping for oil, exploratory drilling having begun, but the main emphasis at present seems to be on tourism, with a 110-room Hilton hotel and a garden city complex under construction.

Ajman, the smallest Emirate, also plans a garden city for 30,000 residents aimed at attracting people who work in nearby Dubai and Sharjah. Its main project so far, however, has been a small dry dock which began operating in December 1976 and which has proved very successful. Ajman's credibility was set back by the closure of the Ajman Arab Bank in May 1977. The bank—owned 40 per cent by the ruling family and 60 per cent by a bank set up by a Cuban exile in Florida—was financing a number of projects. The bank has now reopened as the First Bank of the Gulf.

STATISTICAL SURVEY

AREA AND POPULATION

Area (sq. miles)		Population* (1975 Census)							
Total	Abu Dhabi (estimate)	Total	Abu Dhabi	Dubai	Sharjah	Ras al-Khaimah	Fujairah	Ajman	Umm al-Quwain
32,000	25,000	655,937	235,662	206,861	88,188	57,282	26,498	21,566	16,879

* Provisional figures.

The population of the United Arab Emirates in 1978 was estimated at 877,340.

Capital: Abu Dhabi (estimated population 250,000 in 1978).

SEA FISHING

('000 metric tons)

	1972	1973	1974	1975	1976
Total catch (live weight) . .	43.0	43.0	68.0	68.0	64.4

1977: Catch as in 1976.

Source: FAO, *Yearbook of Fishery Statistics.*

MINING

		1973	1974	1975	1976	1977	1978
Crude petroleum . .	'000 metric tons	74,194	81,441	82,058	95,265	98,700	90,000
Natural gas . . .	million cu. metres	849	934	793	878	n.a.	n.a.

PRODUCTION OF CRUDE PETROLEUM
(million barrels)

	1973	1974	1975	1976	1977
Abu Dhabi . . .	475.6	515.1	513.3	580.5	602.8
Dubai	80.2	88.1	92.8	114.8	116.4
Sharjah	—	8.5	13.9	13.5	10.3
TOTAL . .	555.8	611.7	620.1	708.9	729.5

INDUSTRY

PETROLEUM PRODUCTS
('000 metric tons)

	1976
Motor spirit (petrol)	65
Kerosene	3
Distillate fuel oils (gas oil, etc.) . . .	129
Residual fuel oil	105

Liquefied natural gas: 609,468 metric tons in 1977.

ELECTRICITY
(million kWh., Abu Dhabi)

	1969	1970	1971	1972	1973	1974	1975	1976
Estimated production .	100	140	210	255	382	454*	500*	600*

* Provisional.

Source: UN, *Statistical Yearbook.*

FINANCE

100 fils=1 U.A.E. dirham.
Coins: 1, 5, 10, 25 and 50 fils; 1 dirham.
Notes: 1, 5, 10, 50 and 100 dirhams.
Exchange rates (June 1979): £1=sterling=7.94 dirhams; U.S. $1=3.84 dirhams.
100 U.A.E. dirhams=£12.59=$26.06.

Note: Before June 1966 the currency used by the states of Trucial Oman (now the United Arab Emirates) was the Persian Gulf Indian rupee, valued at 1s. 6d. sterling (£1=13.33 rupees). When the Indian rupee was devalued in June 1966, Abu Dhabi adopted the Bahrain dinar (of 1,000 fils) while the other states used Saudi Arabian currency prior to the introduction of the Qatar/Dubai riyal (at par with the old rupee) in September 1966. The Bahrain dinar, equal to 10 old rupees, was valued at U.S. $2.10 ($1=476.19 fils) until August 1971; at $2.28 ($1=438.60 fils) from December 1971 to February 1973; and at $2.533 ($1=394.74 fils) from February 1973. The Q/D riyal, also used in Qatar, was valued at 21 U.S. cents ($1=4.762 riyals) until August 1971; at 22.8 U.S. cents ($1=4.386 riyals) from December 1971 to February 1973; and at 25.33 U.S. cents ($1=3.947 riyals) from February 1973. Between November 1967 and June 1972 the Bahrain dinar was valued at 17s. 6d. sterling (87½ new pence) and the Q/D riyal at 1s. 9d. (8.75 new pence), the exchange rates being £1=1.143 dinars=11.43 riyals. In May 1973 the U.A.E. adopted a common currency, the dirham, which was at par with the Q/D riyal (renamed the Qatar riyal) and thus valued at 25.33 U.S. cents. The market exchange rate has been frequently adjusted. It corresponded to the original par value ($1=3.947 dirhams) from January to November 1976 and was $1=3.898 dirhams from February 1977 to January 1978. The rate was $1=3.978 dirhams from January to September 1978; and $1=3.838 dirhams from October 1978 to June 1979. The average rates (dirhams per dollar) were: 3.996 in 1973; 3.959 in 1974; 3.961 in 1975; 3.953 in 1976; 3.903 in 1977; 3.871 in 1978.

FEDERAL BUDGET EXPENDITURE
(1977/78—'000 U.A.E. dirhams)

Cabinet secretariat	10,921
State Ministry for cabinet affairs	14,547
Finance and industry	1,959,666
Interior	620,240
Public works and housing	292,414
Justice, Islamic affairs and endowments	136,632
Electricity and water	288,618
Communications	396,927
Health	903,366
Agriculture and fisheries	121,058
Information and culture	249,060
Labour and social affairs	169,267
Planning	24,050
Education and youth	1,241,418
State Ministry	1,004
Ministry for Supreme Council affairs	1,489
Federal National Council	11,808
Foreign affairs	117,201
Economy and trade	10,034
Petroleum and mineral resources	34,837
Audit Chamber	19,230
Defence	2,565,000
TOTAL	9,188,788
Investments	2,011,000
Allocation for projects in hand (approx.)	2,000,000
GRAND TOTAL	13,200,148

1978/79: Expenditure 10,500 million dirhams, of which 3,000 million for defence.
1979/80 (Provisional): Expenditure 12,000 million dirhams.

ABU DHABI BUDGET
(1976/77—'000 U.A.E. dirhams)

Current Expenditure	4,296,000
Development Budget	5,000,000
Support of Federal Budget	4,000,000
International Aid	4,500,000
Capital Payments	409,000
TOTAL (incl. others)	18,205,000

EXTERNAL TRADE
United Arab Emirates
(million U.A.E. dirhams)

	1972	1973	1974	1975	1976	1977	1978
Imports c.i.f.	2,113	3,279	6,750	10,571	13,150	18,060	20,500
Exports f.o.b.	4,745	7,198	25,305	27,250	33,770	37,082	35,158

Export of crude petroleum (million dirhams): 24,996 in 1974; 26,647 in 1975; 32,566 in 1976; 35,607 in 1977; 33,450 in 1978.

Source: mainly IMF, *International Financial Statistics*.

Dubai

(million U.A.E. dirhams)

	1972	1973	1974	1975	1976	1977	1978
Imports	1,474.7	2,341.0	4,816.6	7,115.1	9,497.8	12,659.4	12,707.9
Exports*	168.2	215.5	295.6	566.6	980.2	1,156.8	1,387.7

* Excluding petroleum.

COMMODITY GROUPS

('000 U.A.E. dirhams)

IMPORTS	1976*	1977	1978
Food and live animals	948,100	1,021,546	1,226,128
Beverages and tobacco	147,900	164,520	178,313
Crude materials (inedible) except fuels	198,800	251,159	215,949
Mineral fuels, lubricants, etc.	732,800	1,004,073	510,297
Animal and vegetable oils and fats	20,200	18,572	31,993
Chemicals	356,400	478,145	580,027
Basic manufactures	2,454,600	3,185,768	3,267,146
Machinery and transport equipment	3,614,800	4,972,761	4,796,572
Miscellaneous manufactured articles	902,100	1,434,155	1,715,172
Other commodities and transactions	122,000	128,761	186,308
TOTAL	9,497,800	12,659,460	12,707,905

There is a large and officially authorized trade in gold which is not, however, included in the official trade statistics for Dubai.

* Figures rounded.

PRINCIPAL TRADING PARTNERS

('000 U.A.E. dirhams)

IMPORTS	1975	1976	1977	1978
Australia	133,358	160,705	102,598	149,525
China, People's Republic	211,282	182,533	292,347	278,557
France	261,738	258,023	316,639	391,031
Germany, Federal Republic	304,061	483,405	855,801	969,116
Hong Kong	199,007	187,786	245,932	282,627
India	285,664	514,181	657,576	510,181
Iran	341,007	230,020	218,877	96,797
Japan	1,355,440	1,805,484	2,536,726	2,614,709
Kuwait	93,018	111,356	30,865	9,521
Netherlands	177,866	279,594	439,928	414,967
Pakistan	121,719	102,975	124,893	95,872
Saudi Arabia	65,803	370,208	472,707	272,876
Switzerland	99,681	136,533	160,435	145,392
United Kingdom	1,073,326	1,539,948	2,109,686	2,385,650
U.S.A.	973,085	1,256,718	1,336,948	1,403,517

Abu Dhabi

(million U.A.E. dirhams)

	1972	1973	1974	1975	1976	1977	1978
Imports	757.6	1,018.9	2,266.1	3,795.0	4,103.0	5,430.2	6,307

Figures for total exports are not available. Re-exports (in million dirhams) were: 29.0 in 1973; 43.0 in 1974; 36.1 in 1975; 223.9 in 1976; 318.5 in 1977.

COMMODITY GROUPS
(million U.A.E. dirhams)

IMPORTS	1976	1977
Food and live animals	302.2	418.6
Beverages and tobacco	50.9	53.7
Crude materials (inedible) except fuels	107.1	88.5
Mineral fuels, lubricants, etc.	197.9	211.9
Animal and vegetable oil and fats	8.6	13.1
Chemicals	118.2	163.8
Basic manufactures	896.4	1,231.2
Machinery and transport equipment	2,118.8	2,776.5
Miscellaneous manufactured articles	302.7	470.6
TOTAL (incl. others)	4,103.0	5,430.2

PRINCIPAL TRADING PARTNERS
(million U.A.E. dirhams)

IMPORTS	1976	1977
France	272.0	200.7
Germany, Fed. Rep.	532.7	817.4
India	100.2	142.4
Italy	160.6	238.8
Japan	563.8	1,110.0
Kuwait	118.1	157.1
Lebanon	86.1	155.2
Netherlands	108.1	106.2
Romania	83.1	81.8
United Kingdom	753.0	785.1
U.S.A.	568.7	692.5

TRANSPORT

INTERNATIONAL SEA-BORNE SHIPPING
(estimated freight traffic in '000 metric tons)

	1970	1971	1972	1973	1974	1975
Goods loaded	37,977	51,770	58,900	74,833	82,891	81,626
Crude petroleum	37,940	51,730	58,297	73,668	81,691	80,376
Other cargo	37	40	603	1,165	1,200	1,250
Goods unloaded	800	830	840	900	1,020	1,250

Source: United Nations, *Statistical Yearbook.*

COMMUNICATIONS

(Abu Dhabi)

	1971	1972	1973	1974	1975	1976
Telephone exchange capacity	5,050	5,250	5,950	7,850	12,648	14,373
Telephone subscribers	n.a.	3,870	5,201	6,871	9,153	12,290

The number of telephone lines in the United Arab Emirates as a whole was 52,000 (April 1978).

EDUCATION

United Arab Emirates

	1974–75	1975–76	1976–77	1977–78
Schools	167	185	204	350
Students	52,321	61,803	71,314	94,425
Teachers	3,828	4,856	5,966	7,849

Source: Ministry of Education, *Annual Report.*

THE CONSTITUTION

A provisional constitution for the U.A.E. was set up in December 1971. This laid the foundation for the federal structure of the Union of the seven sheikhdoms, previously known as the Trucial States.

The highest federal authority is the Supreme Council which comprises the rulers of the seven Emirates. It elects a president and vice-president from among its members. The president appoints a prime minister and a cabinet. The legislature is the Federal National Council, a consultative assembly comprising 40 members appointed by the emirates for a two-year term.

In July 1975 a committee was appointed to draft a permanent federal constitution, but the National Council decided in 1976 to extend the provisional constitution for five years. In November 1976, however, the Supreme Council amended Article 142 of the provisional constitution so that the right to levy armed forces was placed exclusively in the hands of the federal government.

THE GOVERNMENT

HEAD OF STATE

President: Sheikh ZAYED BIN SULTAN AL-NAHAYAN (Ruler of Abu Dhabi).

Vice-President: Sheikh RASHID BIN SAID AL-MAKTUM (Ruler of Dubai).

SUPREME COUNCIL OF THE UNION

(with each ruler's date of accession)

Ruler of Sharjah: Sheikh SULTAN BIN MUHAMMAD AL-QASIMI (1972).

Ruler of Ras al-Khaimah: Sheikh SAQR BIN MUHAMMAD AL-QASIMI (1948).

Ruler of Umm al-Quwain: Sheikh AHMAD BIN RASHID AL-MU'ALLA, M.B.E. (1929).

Ruler of Ajman: Sheikh RASHID BIN HUMAID AL-NU'AIMI (1928).

Ruler of Dubai: Sheikh RASHID BIN SAID AL-MAKTUM (1958).

Ruler of Abu Dhabi: Sheikh ZAYED BIN SULTAN AL-NAHAYAN (1966).

Ruler of Fujairah: Sheikh HAMAD BIN MUHAMMAD AL-SHARQI (1974).

UNION COUNCIL OF MINISTERS

(*July* 1979)

Prime Minister: Sheikh RASHID BIN SAID AL-MAKTUM.

Deputy Prime Minister: Sheikh MAKTUM BIN RASHID AL-MAKTUM.

Deputy Prime Minister: Sheikh HAMDAN BIN MUHAMMAD AL-NAHAYAN.

Minister of the Interior: Sheikh MUBARAK BIN MUHAMMAD AL-NAHAYAN.

Minister of Finance and Industry: Sheikh HAMDAN BIN RASHID AL-MAKTUM.

Minister of Defence: Sheikh MUHAMMAD BIN RASHID AL-MAKTUM.

Minister of Foreign Affairs: AHMED KHALIFA AS-SUWEIDI.

Minister of Economy and Trade: Sheikh SULTAN BIN AHMED AL-MUALLA.

Minister of Information and Culture: Sheikh AHMED BIN HAMED.

Minister of Communications: AHMED SAID AL MULLA.

Minister of Public Works and Housing: MUHAMMAD KHALIFA AL-KINDI.

Minister of Education and Youth Affairs: SAID SALMAN.

Minister of Petroleum and Natural Resources: MANI SAID AL OTEIBA.

Minister of Electricity and Water: HAMAD BIN NASIR AL-UWAIS.

Minister of Justice, Islamic Affairs and Endowments: MUHAMMAD ABDEL AR-RAHMAN AL-BAKR.

Minister of Health: HAMAD ABD AR-RAHMAN AL-MIDFA.

Minister of Labour and Social Affairs: SAIF AL-JARWAN.

Minister of Planning: SAEED GHOBASH.

Minister of Agriculture and Fisheries: SAID AR-RUQBANI.

Minister of State for the Interior: HAMOUDA BIN ALI AL-DHAHIRI.

Minister of State for Foreign Affairs: ABDULLAH RASHID.

Minister of State for Cabinet Affairs: SAID AL-GHAITH.

Minister of State for Supreme Council Affairs: Sheikh ABDEL-AZIZ BIN HUMAID AL-QASIMI.

Minister of State without Portfolio: Sheikh AHMED BIN SULTAN AL-QASIMI.

FEDERAL NATIONAL COUNCIL

Formed under the provisions of the temporary constitution, it is composed of 40 members from the various Emirates (8 each from Abu Dhabi and Dubai, 6 each from Sharjah and Ras al-Khaimah, and 4 each from Ajman, Fujairah and Umm al-Quwain). Each Emirate appoints its own representatives separately. The Council studies laws proposed by the Council of Ministers and can reject them or suggest amendments. The second five-year session of the Federal National Council was inaugurated in Abu Dhabi on March 1st, 1977.

Speaker: TARYAM OMRAN TARYAM (Sharjah).

DIPLOMATIC REPRESENTATION

EMBASSIES ACCREDITED TO THE UNITED ARAB EMIRATES

(In Abu Dhabi unless otherwise stated)

Afghanistan: Baghdad, Iraq.

Algeria: P.O.B. 3070; *Chargé d'affaires:* MOHAMED AISSA MESSOUDI.

Australia: Jeddah, Saudi Arabia.

Austria: P.O.B. 3095; *Chargé d'affaires:* Dr. PETER SINGER.

Bangladesh: P.O.B. 2504; *Ambassador:* FARUQ AHMAD CHOUDHURY.

Belgium: P.O.B. 3686; *Ambassador:* MICHEL GEUENS (also accred. to Bahrain).

Brazil: P.O.B. 3027; *Chargé d'affaires:* CYRO GABRIEL DO ESPIRITO SANTO CARDOSO.

Canada: Kuwait City, Kuwait.

Denmark: P.O.B. 6666; *Chargé d'affaires:* KURT EBERT.

Finland: Jeddah, Saudi Arabia.

France: P.O.B. 4014; *Ambassador:* JEAN-CLAUDE GUISSET.

Gabon: P.O.B. 2653; *Ambassador:* (vacant).

Germany, Federal Republic: P.O.B. 2591; *Ambassador:* HANS JOACHIM NEUMANN.

Greece: Kuwait City, Kuwait.

India: P.O.B. 4090; *Ambassador:* MOHAMMED HAMID ANSARI.

Indonesia: Kuwait City, Kuwait.

Iran: P.O.B. 4080; *Ambassador:* EBRAHIM TEYMOURI.

Iraq: P.O.B. 4030; *Ambassador:* MOHAMED JASSIM AL-AMIN.

Ireland: Jeddah, Saudi Arabia.

Italy: Kuwait City, Kuwait.

Japan: P.O.B. 2430; *Ambassador:* RYOKEI MURATA.

Jordan: P.O.B. 4024; *Ambassador:* ALI AINAD KHRAIS.

Kuwait: P.O.B. 926; *Ambassador:* QASIM OMER AL-YAGOUT.

Lebanon: P.O.B. 4023; *Ambassador:* MAHMOUD HAMMOUD.

Libya: P.O.B. 2091; *Ambassador:* ABDUL QADIR QOGHA.

Malaysia: Kuwait City, Kuwait.

Mauritania: P.O.B. 2714; *Ambassador:* AHMAD OULD SEYDI OULD HASSAN.

Mexico: Beirut, Lebanon.

Morocco: P.O.B. 4066; *Ambassador:* HASSAN AL FASSI AL FIHRI.

Netherlands: P.O.B. 6560; *Chargé d'affaires:* DIGNUS H. VISSCHER.

Niger: Khartoum, Sudan.

Norway: Jeddah, Saudi Arabia.

Pakistan: P.O.B. 846; *Ambassador:* ANWAR UL HAQ.

Qatar: P.O.B. 3503; *Chargé d'affaires:* IBRAHIM A. H. NIMAH.

Saudi Arabia: P.O.B. 4057; *Ambassador:* Shaikh MUHAMMAD MANSUR AL-RUMAIH.

Senegal: Cairo, Egypt.

Somalia: P.O.B. 4155; *Ambassador:* ABDI NUR ALI YUSSUF.

Spain: P.O.B. 6474; *Ambassador:* CAMILO BARCIA.

Sudan: P.O.B. 4027; *Ambassador:* SULEIMAN BABIKER SULEIMAN.

Sweden: Kuwait City, Kuwait.

Switzerland: P.O.B. 6116; *Commercial Counsellor:* WILLY FRIES.

Syria: P.O.B. 4011; *Ambassador:* ADNAN SAFI.

Tanzania: Cairo, Egypt.

Tunisia: P.O.B. 4166; *Ambassador:* ABDELAZIZ GASSAB.

Turkey: Kuwait City, Kuwait.

United Kingdom: P.O.B. 248; *Ambassador:* DAVID ARTHUR ROBERTS, C.M.G.

U.S.A.: P.O.B. 4009; *Ambassador:* FRANCOIS M. DICKMAN.

Venezuela: Kuwait City, Kuwait.

Yemen Arab Republic: P.O.B. 2095; *Ambassador:* MUHAMMAD SAID QUBATI.

Zaire: P.O.B. 2592; *Ambassador:* DEDE KABIKA MWENE-NGABWE.

The U.A.E. also has diplomatic relations with Chile, Ecuador, Honduras, Maldives, Mauritius, Oman and Thailand.

JUDICIAL SYSTEM

The 95th article of the provisional constitution of 1971 provided for the setting up of a Union Supreme Court and Union Primary Tribunals.

The Union has exclusive legislative and executive jurisdiction over all matters that are concerned with the strengthening of the federation such as foreign affairs, defence and Union armed forces, security, finance, communications, traffic control, education, currency, measures, standards and weights, matters relating to nationality and emigration, Union information, etc.

President Sheikh Zayed signed the law establishing the new federal courts on June 9th, 1978. The new law effectively transferred local judicial authorities into the jurisdiction of the federal system.

Primary tribunals in Abu Dhabi, Sharjah, Ajman and Fujairah are now primary federal tribunals and primary tribunals in other towns in those Emirates have become circuits of the primary federal tribunals.

The primary federal tribunal may sit in any of the capitals of the four Emirates and have jurisdiction on all administrative disputes between the Union and individuals, whether the Union is plaintiff or defendant. Civil disputes between Union and individuals will be heard by primary federal tribunals in the defendant's place of normal residence.

The new law requires that all judges will now take a constitutional oath before the Minister of Justice and Islamic Affairs and that the courts apply the rules of Sharia (Islamic religious laws) and that no judgment contradicts Sharia. All employees of the old judiciaries will be transferred to the federal authority without loss of salary or seniority.

Chief Sharia Justice: AHMED ABDUL AZIZ AL-MUBARAK.

RELIGION

Most of the inhabitants are Muslims of the Sunni and Shi'ite sects.

THE PRESS

Abu Dhabi Chamber of Commerce Review: P.O.B. 662, Abu Dhabi; monthly; Arabic, some articles in English.

al-Dhafra: P.O.B. 4288, Abu Dhabi; independent; published by Dar al-Wahdah; Arabic; weekly.

Emirates News: P.O.B. 791, Abu Dhabi; published by Al Ittihad Press and Publishing Corporation; daily; English.

Gulf News: P.O.B. 1112, Abu Dhabi; daily; English.

Hie Ladies Magazine: P.O.B. 2488, Abu Dhabi; published by Dar al-Wahdah.

al-Ittihad (*Unity*): P.O.B. 17, Abu Dhabi; f. 1972; daily; Editor-in-Chief KHALED MUHAMMAD AHMAD.

Recorder: P.O.B. 2310, Abu Dhabi; daily news bulletin; English.

U.A.E. and Abu Dhabi Official Gazette: P.O.B. 899, Abu Dhabi; Arabic.

U.A.E. Press Service Daily News: P.O.B. 2035, Abu Dhabi; daily; English; Editor RASHID AL MAZROUI.

al-Wahdah: P.O.B. 2488, Abu Dhabi; f. 1973; independent; daily; Man. Editor RASHID AWEIDHA; Gen. Man. KHALIFA AL MASHWI.

Akhbar Dubai: Department of Information, Dubai Municipality, P.O.B. 1420, Dubai; f. 1965; weekly; Arabic.

Al Khaleej Times: P.O.B. 11253, Dubai; English; daily.

Dubai External Trade Statistics: P.O.B. 516, Dubai; monthly; English.

Dubai Official Gazette: P.O.B. 516, Dubai; Arabic; quarterly or as necessary.

Dubai Trade and Industry Magazine: P.O.B. 1457; f. 1975; published by Dubai Chamber of Commerce and Industry; Arabic and English; monthly; circ. 5,000.

Gulf Mirror: P.O.B. 874, Dubai; branch office of the Gulf weekly newspaper; English; circ. 16,000.

Recorder: P.O.B. 1579, Dubai; daily news bulletin; English.

Ras al-Khaimah: P.O.B. 87, Ras al-Khaimah; Chamber of Commerce magazine; quarterly; Arabic and English.

Ras al-Khaimah Magazine: P.O.B. 200, Ras al-Khaimah; monthly; Arabic, Chief Editor AHMED AL TADMORI.

---

al Tijarah: Sharjah; monthly; Arabic; published by Sharjah Chamber of Commerce and Industry.

NEWS AGENCY

Emirates News Agency (WAM): Abu Dhabi; f. 1977.

FOREIGN BUREAU

Reuters (*U.K.*): P.O.B. 5010, Deira, Dubai.

RADIO AND TELEVISION

United Arab Emirates Radio: f. 1969; stations in Abu Dhabi, Dubai, Umm al-Quwain and Ras al-Khaimah all broadcasting in Arabic over wide area; Abu Dhabi also broadcasts in English, French and Urdu, Dubai in English and Ras al-Khaimah in Urdu. There is colour TV in Abu Dhabi, Dubai and Ras al-Khaimah. TV takes advertisements but only Dubai of the four radio stations does; estimated radio receivers 150,000 and TV sets 80,000 in U.A.E.

Abu Dhabi Television: P.O.B. 637, Abu Dhabi.

Dubai Radio and Dubai Colour Television: P.O.B. 1695, Dubai.

FINANCE

BANKING

The United Arab Emirates are served by 56 banks with 302 branches. A further 130 have been approved, and it is considered to be the most over-banked area in the world. Early in 1977 several banks found themselves in difficulties and stricter regulations had to be introduced, which were later eased in February 1978. In addition to the banks listed below, 12 banks have offshore licenses, although are not yet operating, and 12 banks have representative offices.

United Arab Emirates Currency Board: P.O.B. 854, Abu Dhabi; f. 1973; functions as a central bank and acts as issuing authority for local currency; Man. Dir. ABDUL MALIK AL-HAMR.

United Arab Emirates Bankers' Association: P.O.B. 2734, Abu Dhabi; Chair. for 1979 K. G. STIRZAKER (Barclays Bank International).

PRINCIPAL BANKS

Al Ahli Bank: P.O.B. 1719, Dubai; Man. K. RAFLA.

Algemene Bank Nederland N.V.: Amsterdam, Netherlands; P.O.B. 2720, Abu Dhabi; P.O.B. 2567, Deira, Dubai br. at Sharjah; Gen. Man. T. W. S. DEFABRE.

Al Khalij First Bank: P.O.B. 414, Ajman; formerly Ajman Arab Bank.

Al-Nilein Bank: P.O.B. 6013, Abu Dhabi.

Arab Bank: Amman, Jordan; P.O.B. 875, Abu Dhabi; P.O.B. 1650, Dubai; P.O.B. 130, Sharjah; P.O.B. 20, Ras al-Khaimah; Ajman; Man. G. BAKRI.

Arab-African International Bank: P.O.B. 1049, Dubai; P.O.B. 928, Abu Dhabi; and Sharjah; Chair. and Man. Dir. A. H. HASSAN; Dep. Chair. and Man. Dir. MAHMOUD BAHIR ONSY.

Arab Bank for Investment and Foreign Trade: P.O.B. 2484, Abu Dhabi; cap. p.u. Dh. 60m.; Man. B. E. NOUIOUA.

Bank of the Arab Coast: P.O.B. 342, Ras al-Khaimah.

Bank of Baroda: P.O.B. 2303, Abu Dhabi; P.O.B. 3162, Dubai; Man. S. V. SHOSHI; also branches in Sharjah.

Bank of Credit and Commerce International and Overseas: Middle East Regional Office: P.O.B. 4021, Abu Dhabi; 11 brs. in Abu Dhabi, 9 brs. in Dubai, 4 in Sharjah and one each in Ajman, Umm al-Quwain, Ras al-Khaimah and Fujairah; Gen. Man. SALEEM SIDDIQI.

Bank Melli Iran: P.O.B. 2656, Abu Dhabi; P.O.B. 1894, Dubai; P.O.B. 459, Sharjah; P.O.B. 248, Fujairah; P.O.B. 1888, Al-Ain; P.O.B. 448, Ajman; Man. S. A. TAMERI.

Bank of Oman Ltd.: P.O.B. 2111, Dubai; f. 1967; cap. p.u. 27m. dirhams (May 1977); 13 brs. in U.A.E.; Gen. Man. ABDULLAH AL-GHURAIR.

Bank Saderat Iran: P.O.B. 700, Abu Dhabi; P.O.B. 4182, Dubai; also Sharjah, Ajman, Ras al-Khaimah and Fujairah; Man. M. SHARAZI.

Bank of Sharjah: P.O.B. 1394, Sharjah.

Banque de l'Indochine et de Suez: P.O.B. 4005, Dubai.

Banque de Paris et des Pays-Bas: Paris, France; P.O.B. 2742, Abu Dhabi; P.O.B. 1944, Dubai; Gen. Man. G. Tabet.

Banque du Caire: P.O.B. 533, Abu Dhabi; P.O.B. 1502, Dubai; P.O.B. 254, Sharjah; Ras al-Khaimah; Gen. Man. M. al Faham.

Banque du Liban et d'outre mer: P.O.B. 4370, Dubai; f. 1951; Chair. and Pres. Dr. Naaman Azhari.

Banque Libanaise pour le Commerce: P.O.B. 4207, Dubai; P.O.B. 854, Sharjah; also in Abu Dhabi and Ras al-Khaimah; Man. E. B. al Zeenny.

Banque Omran: P.O.B. 19, Dubai; Man. H. Zavich.

Barclays Bank International: P.O.B. 2734, Abu Dhabi; P.O.B. 1891, Dubai; P.O.B. 1953, Sharjah; Man. R. T. Woolston.

British Bank of the Middle East, The: London; brs. in Dubai, Sharjah, Khorfakan, Ras al-Khaimah, Abu Dhabi, Fujairah, Kalba, Diba, Ajman and Umm al-Quwain; Man. J. C. Duncan.

Chartered Bank: London; P.O.B. 240, Abu Dhabi; P.O.B. 999 and 1125, Dubai; P.O.B. 5, Sharjah; P.O.B. 1240, Al Ain; Man. R. E. Cannings.

Citibank: New York; P.O.B. 749, Dubai; P.O.B. 346, Sharjah; P.O.B. 999, Abu Dhabi; P.O.B. 294, Ras Al Khaimah; Man. K. al-Hassan.

Commercial Bank of Dubai: P.O.B. 1709, Dubai; f. 1969; owned by Chase Manhattan Bank, Commerzbank A.G. and the Commercial Bank of Kuwait; brs. in Dubai (4), Abu Dhabi (1), Sharjah (1), Ras al Khaimah (1); Gen. Man. R. W. Robertson.

Commercial Development Bank of Sharjah: Sharjah.

Distributors Co-operative Credit Bank of Iran: P.O.B. 888, Abu Dhabi; Man. N. C. Chauan.

Dubai Bank: P.O.B. 2545, Deira, Dubai; f. 1970; control is held by local interests, but Swiss, British, French and American banks are also participating; p.u. cap. 50m. dirhams; Chair. Abdul Rahim bin Ibrahim Galadari; Gen. Man. P. J. Reynolds.

Dubai Islamic Bank: P.O.B. 1080, Dubai; Gen. Man. S. A. Lootah.

Emirates Commercial Bank: P.O.B. 939, Abu Dhabi; Man. D. Twell.

Emirates National Bank: P.O.B. 26, Dubai; f. 1977; cap. p.u. Dh. 150m.; Chair. Muhammad Majed al-Ghurair; Gen. Man. A. Davies.

Federal Commercial Bank Ltd.: P.O.B. 2934, Abu Dhabi; Man. P. R. Maqsood.

First National Bank of Chicago, The: P.O.B. 1655, Dubai; P.O.B. 2747, Abu Dhabi; P.O.B. 1278, Sharjah; Man. I. B. Irving.

Grindlays Bank Ltd.: London; P.O.B. 241, Abu Dhabi; P.O.B. 225, Ras al Khaimah; P.O.B. 357, Sharjah; P.O.B. 4166, Dubai; P.O.B. 1100, Al Ain; P.O.B. 452, Ajman; P.O.B. 92, Fujairah; P.O.B. 490, Umm al-Quwain and 4 other brs. in United Arab Emirates; Man. A. Anderson.

Habib Bank AG Zürich: P.O.B. 2681, Abu Dhabi; P.O.B. 1166, Sharjah; P.O.B. 3306, Dubai; Man. R. A. Chowdhry.

Habib Bank Ltd.: Karachi; P.O.B. 888, Dubai; P.O.B. 897, Abu Dhabi; f. 1941; 17 other brs. in United Arab Emirates; Man. W. Raza.

Investment Bank for Trade and Finance: P.O.B. 2875, Abu Dhabi; P.O.B. 1885, Sharjah; Man. A. H. Kanaan.

Janata Bank: P.O.B. 2630, Abu Dhabi; P.O.B. 3342, Dubai; Man. Ali Kabir.

Khalij Commercial Bank: P.O.B. 2832, Abu Dhabi; f. 1975; Gen. Man. D. H. Alexander.

Lloyds Bank International: P.O.B. 3766, Dubai.

National Bank of Abu Dhabi: P.O.B. 4, Abu Dhabi; f. 1968; cap. p.u. Dh. 100m.; res. Dh. 92.3m.; dep. 12,660m. (Dec. 1977); Chief Exec. Abdullah M. Mazrui.

National Bank of Dubai: P.O.B. 777, Dubai; f. 1963; brs. in Abu Dhabi and Umm al-Quwain; cap. p.u. Dh. 45.1m.; Gen. Man. D. W. Mack, M.B.E.

National Bank of Ras al-Khaimah: P.O.B. 5300, Ras al-Khaimah; f. 1977; cap. p.u. Dh. 11.25m.; Gen. Man. D. R. E. Murray.

National Bank of Sharjah: P.O.B. 4, Sharjah; Gen. Man. I. W. McNab.

Rafidain Bank (Iraq): P.O.B. 2727, Abu Dhabi; Man. H. A. Hafidh.

Royal Bank of Canada: P.O.B. 3614, Dubai.

Toronto Dominion Bank: P.O.B. 898; Abu Dhabi; P.O.B. 2294, Dubai; Gen. Man. W. H. Eagle.

Union Bank of the Middle East: P.O.B. 2923, Dubai; f. 1977; cap. Dh. 500m. (Dec. 1978); Man. H. Pano.

United Arab Bank: P.O.B. 881, Sharjah; brs. in Abu Dhabi, Dubai and Ras al-Khaimah; Man. Yasin al-Khatib.

United Bank: P.O.B. 1000, Dubai; P.O.B. 237, Abu Dhabi; 17 other brs. in U.A.E.; Man. Ahmed Raza.

There are also 5 banks operating on restricted licences and 12 banks which have representative offices.

INSURANCE

Abu Dhabi National Insurance Co.: Shaikha Mariam Bldg., Leewa St. off Sh. Khalifa St., P.O.B. 839, Abu Dhabi; f. 1973; cap. 10m. dirhams subscribed 25 per cent by the Government of Abu Dhabi and 75 per cent by United Arab Emirates nationals; Gen. Man. Wasef Salim Jabsheh.

Al Ahlia Insurance Co.: P.O.B. 128, Ras al-Khaimah; f. 1977; cap. 2.9m.; Gen. Man. Desmond Reynolds.

Al Ain Ahlia Insurance Co.: P.O.B. 3077, Abu Dhabi; f. 1975; cap. 5m. dirhams; Chair. Hamil al-Gaith; Gen. Man. Jamil Hajjar.

Arabian Security Insurance Co.: P.O.B. 1737, Dubai.

Dubai Insurance Co.: P.O.B. 3027, Dubai; Chair. Majid al Futtaim; Gen. Man. Farouk Huwaidi.

Sharjah Insurance Co.: P.O.B. 792, Sharjah; f. 1970; cap. 4m. dirhams.

Union Insurance Co.: Head Office: P.O.B. 460, Umm al-Quwain; P.O.B. 4623, Dubai; P.O.B. 3196, Abu Dhabi.

CHAMBERS OF COMMERCE

Abu Dhabi Chamber of Commerce and Industries: P.O.B. 662, Abu Dhabi; f. 1969; 5,000 mems.; Pres. Saeed bin Ahmed al-Otaiba; publ. monthly magazine in Arabic.

Ajman Chamber of Commerce and Industry: P.O.B. 662, Ajman; Chair. Salim Saeed al-Suweidi.

Dubai Chamber of Commerce and Industry: Ben Yass St., P.O.B. 1457, Dubai; f. 1965; 5,500 mems.; Pres. Saif Ahmed al-Ghurair; Dir.-Gen. Nizar Sardast; publ. *Dubai Trade & Industry Magazine.*

Ras al-Khaimah Chamber of Commerce, Industry and Agriculture: P.O.B. 87, Ras al-Khaimah; f. 1967; 2600 mems.; Chair. Sheikh Abdul Malik al-Qassimi; Dir. Zaki Saqr; publ. quarterly magazine in Arabic.

Sharjah Chamber of Commerce and Industry: P.O.B. 580, Sharjah; f. 1970; Pres. Abdul Rehman Bu Khatr; publ. *Al-Tijara.*

Umm al-Quwain Chamber of Commerce and Industry: P.O.B. 436, Umm al-Quwain; Dir.-Gen. A. AQUEEL ABU BAQR.

DEVELOPMENT

Capital projects include inter-state roads, urban water and electricity schemes, housing and other urban development, rural water supplies, agricultural extension schemes and harbour works. Investigations into water resources, mineral prospects, soil, agricultural marketing and fisheries have been conducted.

Federal Ministry of Planning: P.O.B. 2847, Abu Dhabi; Under-Sec. AHMED MANSOUR.

United Arab Emirates Development Bank: P.O.B. 2449, Abu Dhabi; f. 1974; participates in development of real estate, agriculture, fishery, livestock and light industries; cap. p.u. Dh. 500m.; Gen. Man. MOHAMED SALEM AL-MELEHY.

Abu Dhabi Fund for Arab Economic Development (ADFAED): P.O.B. 814; f. 1971; purpose is to offer economic aid to other Arab States and other developing countries in support of their development; capital limited at inception to U.S. $120 million paid by Abu Dhabi Government; in June 1974 capital was raised to U.S. $500 million; Man. Dir. NASSER M. AL-NOWAIS.

Abu Dhabi Planning Department: P.O.B. 12, Abu Dhabi; supervises Abu Dhabi's Development Programme; Chair. Sheikh SAIF BIN MOHD AL-NAHYAN; Under-Sec. H. E. HASSAN MOUSA AL-QAMZI.

Abu Dhabi Development Finance Corpn.: P.O.B. 30, Abu Dhabi; purpose is to provide finance to the private sector.

Abu Dhabi Investment Authority (ADIA): P.O.B. 3609, Abu Dhabi.

TRADE AND INDUSTRY

PRINCIPAL PETROLEUM CONCESSIONS

In September 1974 the Government of Abu Dhabi acquired a 60 per cent interest in ADPC and ADMA, and early in 1975 an increase of this interest to 100 per cent was under consideration. In the Spring of 1975 Abu Dhabi withdrew from pressing for 100 per cent interest, but in July 1975 it was announced that Dubai had successfully concluded a 100 per cent participation with the companies represented offshore and onshore in Dubai.

Ministry of Petroleum and Mineral Resources: P.O.B. 59, Abu Dhabi; Minister Dr. MANA SAEED AL-OTAIBA.

ABU DHABI

Abu Dhabi Company for Onshore Oil Operations (ADCO): P.O.B. 270, Abu Dhabi; shareholders are ADNOC (60 per cent), British Petroleum, Shell and Compagnie Française des Pétroles (9.5 per cent each), Exxon and Mobil (4.75 per cent each) and Partex (2 per cent); Chair. Sheikh TAHNOON BIN MOHAMED AL-NAHAYAN; Gen. Man. G. K. TAYLOR.

Abu Dhabi Marine Operating Company (ADMA-OPCO): P.O.B. 303, Abu Dhabi; operates a concession 60 per cent owned by the Abu Dhabi National Oil Co. and 40 per cent by Abu Dhabi Marine Areas Ltd., Britannic House, Moor Lane, London, EC2 9BU, England (BP-Japan Oil Development Co. Ltd. 26⅔ per cent; Compagnie Française des Pétroles 13⅓ per cent). The concession lies in the Abu Dhabi offshore area and currently produces oil from Zakum and Umm Shaif fields. ADMA-OPCO was created in 1977 as an operator for the concession which between September 1974 and October 1977 was operated by ADMA Ltd. in its role as an interim operator. The new company is owned by the shareholders of the concession in the same proportion of ownership. ADMA-OPCO also operates the Bunduq field on behalf of the Bunduq Company; production (1978) 180,868,216 barrels (23,900,971 metric tons); Gen. Man. Dr. A. J. HORAN.

Abu Dhabi Gas Liquefaction Company (ADGLC): P.O.B. 3500, Abu Dhabi; owned by Abu Dhabi National Oil Co., 51 per cent; the British Petroleum Co., 16⅓ per cent; Compagnie Française des Pétroles, 8⅙ per cent; Mitsui and Co., 22$\frac{1}{20}$ per cent; Bridgestone Liquefied Gas Co., 2$\frac{9}{20}$ per cent. The LNG plant on Das Island which cost about $500m. was commissioned in 1977. The plant uses natural gas produced in association with oil from offshore fields and has a design capacity of approx. 2.2 m.t.a. LNG and 0.8 m.t.a. LPG. The liquefied gas is sold to the Tokyo Electric Power Co., Japan. Gen. Man. Dr. D. G. B. HORNE.

Abu Dhabi National Oil Company (ADNOC): P.O.B. 898, Abu Dhabi; f. 1971; state company; deals in all phases of oil industry; inaugurated its own refinery on Umm Al-Nar island, May 1976; holds 60 per cent participation in operations of ADMA-OPCO and ADCO; has 100 per cent control of Abu Dhabi National Oil Company for Distribution and interests in numerous other companies; Chair. Sheikh TAHNOUN BIN MOHAMED AL-NAYHAN; Gen. Man. MAHMOUD HAMRA KROUHA.

Abu Dhabi Oil Company (Japan) (ADOCO): Abu Dhabi; consortium of Japanese oil companies including Maruzen, Daikyo and Nihon Kogyo; holds offshore concession, extended by 1,582.5 sq. km. in 1979; oil strikes reported in September 1969 and January 1970; export of oil from Mubarraz Island terminal began in June 1973; production 21,000 b.p.d. (1977).

Abu Dhabi Petroleum Company Ltd. (ADPC): P.O.B. 270, Abu Dhabi; engaged in exploration, production and export of crude oil from onshore areas of Abu Dhabi. Export started from Bab field in December 1963. In 1965 the Bu Hasa field was brought on stream, to be followed in 1973 by the Asab field and in 1975 by the Sahil field. Crude oil from Asab, Bu Hasa, Bab and Sahil is exported from Jebel Dhanna Terminal. Production (1977) 373,984,196 barrels; total exports (1977) 367.6 million barrels. Operations are now conducted by ADCO.

Bunduq Oil Co.: revenues are shared equally between Abu Dhabi and Qatar; owners: BP 33.3 per cent, CFP 16.7 per cent, Japanese interests 50 per cent.

Total Abu al Bukhoosh: P.O.B. 4058, Abu Dhabi; owned by Compagnie Française des Pétroles, Amerada Hess, Korr McGee Oils and Nepco Eastern; began production from the Abu al-Bukhoosh offshore field in July 1974; average production of 75,000 b/d in 1977.

Another concession is held by the Amerada-Hess Group.

DUBAI

Department of the Ruler's Affairs and Petroleum Affairs: P.O.B. 207, Dubai; government supervisory body: Dir. MAHDI AL TAJIR.

Dubai Petroleum Company: Dubai; holds offshore concession which began production in 1969; average production rate (1977) 319,028 b/d, (1978) 362.3466/d.

Sedco-Houston Oil Group: Dubai; holds onshore concession of over 1 million acres as well as the offshore concession formerly held by Texas Pacific Oil.

SHARJAH

Concessions are owned by the Buttes Group, the Crescent Group (25.7 per cent owned by Buttes) and Amoco and Forman Explorations.

TRANSPORT

ROADS

Roads are rapidly being developed in the United Arab Emirates, and Abu Dhabi and Dubai are linked by a good road which is dual carriageway for most of its length. This road forms part of a west coast route from Shaam, at the U.A.E. border with the northern enclave of Oman, through Dubai and Abu Dhabi to Tarif. An east coast route links Dibba with Muscat. Other roads include the Abu Dhabi-Al Ain highway and roads linking the northern Emirates. An underwater tunnel links Dubai Town and Deira by dual carriageway and pedestrian subway.

SHIPPING

Dubai has been the main commercial centre in the Gulf for many years. In 1968 work was begun on a new artificial deep-water port to supplement the traditional harbour. Port Rashid has been expanded to 19 deep-water berths. Further expansion to 37 berths is scheduled for completion in 1980. Abu Dhabi has also become an important port since the opening of the first section of its artificial harbour, Port Zayed. Eventually it is planned to create 17 deep-water berths and extensive storage facilities. There are smaller ports in Sharjah and Ras al-Khaimah. Work on a dry-dock scheme for Dubai began in 1973 and was completed in 1979. It will have two docks capable of handling 500,000-ton tankers, seven repair berths and a third dock able to accommodate 1,000,000-ton tankers. This will make Dubai the biggest supertanker complex in the Gulf. Part of a 66-berth port under construction at Jebel Ali, Dubai became operational to break bulk and container cargo in May 1979. Five deep-water berths are due for completion at Port Saqr, Ras al-Khaimah in 1979. Current modernisation of Port Khalid in Sharjah will double its berth capacity.

United Arab Shipping Co.: Kuwait; f. 1977; shareholders are Kuwait, U.A.E., Saudi Arabia, Qatar and Iraq; Chair. MOHAMED SAID AL-MUALLA (United Arab Emirates).

CIVIL AVIATION

There are international airports at Dubai, Abu Dhabi and Ras al-Khaimah, and a smaller one at Sharjah. New airports for Abu Dhabi and Al Ain are scheduled to be completed by 1980 and 1982 respectively.

Gulf Air Dubai: Dubai National Air Travel Agency, P.O.B. 1515, Dubai; daily service to Abu Dhabi, Bahrain, Beirut, Doha, Karachi, London, Muscat and Salalah; six times weekly to Bombay; five times weekly to Amman; four times weekly to Cairo, Kuwait; three times weekly to Larnaca; and twice weekly to Amsterdam, Paris and Shiraz.

Gulf Air Sharjah: Sharjah Aircraft Handling Agency, P.O.B. 8; Oman Travel Agency, P.O.B. 15; Kanoo Travel Agency; weekly flight Shiraz–Muscat, weekly flight Abu Dhabi–Doha–Bahrain–Sharjah.

Aeroflot (U.S.S.R.), Alia(Jordan), Air France, Air India, British Airways, ČSA (Czechoslovakia), EgyptAir, Ethiopian Airlines, Iran Air, Kuwait Airways, Middle East Airlines (Lebanon), PIA (Pakistan), KLM (Netherlands), Gulf Air (Bahrain), Iraqi Airways, Sabena (Belgium), Saudi, Syrian Arab Airlines, Tunis Air and TMA (Lebanon) all serve Dubai and Abu Dhabi, while Gulf Air, Air Ceylon and Syrian Arab Airways serve Sharjah. Ras al-Khaimah is served only by Kuwait Airways.

TOURISM

Ministry of Information and Culture: P.O.B. 17, Abu Dhabi.

Ministry of Information and Culture: P.O.B. 67, Dubai.

Ministry of Information and Culture: P.O.B. 55, Sharjah.

Dubai Information Department: P.O.B. 1420, Dubai (local government); Dir. OMAR DEESI.

Ras al-Khaimah Information and Tourism Department: P.O.B. 200, Ras al-Khaimah (local government); Dir. AHMED TADMORI.

DEFENCE

Commander-in-Chief of Federal Armed Forces: Sheikh SULTAN BIN ZAYED AL-NAHAYAN.

The Union Defence Force and the armed forces of the various Emirates were formally merged in May 1976, although difficulties have since been experienced (*see* History). An 18-month period of conscription was introduced in October 1978.

Total armed forces: 25,900; army 23,500; navy 600; air force 1,800.

EDUCATION

The U.A.E. is engaged in an expansion of education which is seen as a unifying force for the future of the federation. In 1971 there were about 28,000 pupils in the U.A.E., and by 1977 the number had increased to an estimated 90,000. There are primary and secondary schools in all the states and further education in technical fields is available in the more advanced areas. Teachers from other Arab countries, most notably Kuwait, Egypt and Jordan, supplement the U.A.E.'s inadequate native teaching staff. Many students receive higher education abroad. A university opened at Al Ain in Abu Dhabi in the autumn of 1977. The first intake was 300 students, but the university is expected to handle 3,000 students by 1980.

UNIVERSITY

United Arab Emirates University: Al. Ain; 105 teachers, 320 students.

BIBLIOGRAPHY

ABDULLAH, M. MORSY. The Modern History of the United Arab Emirates (Croom Helm, London, 1978).

ALBAHARNA, H. M. The Legal Status of the Arabian Gulf States (Manchester University Press, May 1969).

BUSCH, B. C. Britain and the Persian Gulf 1894–1914 (University of California Press, 1967).

DANIELS, JOHN. Abu Dhabi: A Portrait (Longman, London, 1974).

FACT SHEETS ON EASTERN ARABIA (Information Center on Eastern Arabia, Brussels, Belgium).

FENELON, K. G. The United Arab Emirates: an Economic and Social Survey (Longman, London, 1973).

HAWLEY, DONALD FREDERICK. Courtesies in the Trucial States (1965).

The Trucial States (George Allen and Unwin, London, 1971).

HAY, Sir RUPERT. The Persian Gulf States (Middle East Institute, Washington, 1959).

MANN, CLARENCE. Abu Dhabi: birth of an Oil Sheikhdom (Khayats, Beirut, 1964).

MARLOWE, JOHN. The Persian Gulf in the 20th Century (Cresset Press, London, 1962).

MILES, S. B. The Countries and Tribes of the Persian Gulf (3rd edition, Cass, London, 1966).

OTAIBA, AL-, MANI SAEED. Petroleum and the Economy of the United Arab Emirates (Croom Helm, London, 1977).

SADIQ, MUHAMMAD T., and SNAVELY, WILLIAM P. Bahrain, Qatar and the United Arab Emirates: Colonial Past, Present Problems, and Future Prospects (Heath, Lexington, Mass., 1972).

ZAHLAN, ROSEMARIE SAID. The Origins of the United Arab Emirates (Macmillan, London, 1978).

Yemen Arab Republic

GEOGRAPHY

The Yemen Arab Republic lies at the south-west corner of the Arabian peninsula and comprises two well-defined areas—the highlands inland, and the coastal strip along the Red Sea. The climate of the highlands is considered the best in all Arabia since it experiences a régime rather like that of East Africa, with a warm temperate and rainy summer, and a cool, moderately dry winter with occasional frost and some snow. As stated below (*see* Yemen P.D.R.) these conditions are thought to be produced by an upper air current that brings very moist air from the Atlantic, giving rise to a minor monsoonal effect of heavy summer rainfall. As much as 35 inches of rain may fall annually on the higher parts of the interior, with 15–20 inches over much of the plateau; but the coast receives under 5 inches generally, and in the form often of irregular downpours. There is therefore the phenomenon of streams and even rivers flowing perennially in the highlands, but failing to reach the coast.

Because of this climatic gradation, from desert to temperate conditions, the Yemen has a similar gradation of crops and vegetation. The highest parts appear as "African", with scattered trees and grassland. Crops of coffee, qat, cereals and vegetables are grown, whilst lower down, "Mediterranean" fruits appear, with millet and, where irrigation water is available, bananas. Finally, near the coast, the date palm becomes the only tree.

The area of the Yemen is approximately 75,000 square miles and its population was estimated at 6.5 million in 1975. The capital is Sana'a (on the d'El Jehal plateau, altitude 7,260 ft.).

HISTORY

In classical times the Yemen formed part of the south-eastern area of Arabia Felix. One of the best-known kingdoms in that region was that of Sheba, which lasted from 950 to 115 B.C. From then until the sixth century A.D. Arabia Felix was ruled by the Himyarite dynasty, from whom the modern Imams claim descent. In A.D. 525 the Ethiopians conquered the Himyarite Kingdom, and they in turn were overthrown by a Persian invasion in 575. During the seventh century the country nominally accepted Islam and the Sunnis of the Shafi'i rite established their power in the Tihama (the coastal region), and the Zaidis, a moderate branch of the Shia, held the highlands.

During the ninth century the Zaidi Imam Yahya al-Hadi ila'l-Haqq founded the Rassid dynasty of the Yemen, which has survived, with some interruptions, to the present time.

In 1517 the Yemen was conquered by the Ottoman Turks, but their power was continually contested by other European powers, and their authority was not great. Fierce tribal and religious warfare led the Turks to establish in 1872 a full occupation of the country under a Turkish *Vali*. This occupation lasted until the Mudros armistice of 1918, but in 1911 the Imam Yahya had led a full-scale revolt which secured a treaty confirming Turkish suzerainty, but dividing administrative control between the Imam in the highlands and the Turks in the Tihama and on the coast.

During the First World War the Imam had supported the Turks, and the British had therefore supported Idrisi invaders from the small state of the Asir to the north of the Yemen. A succession dispute broke out in the Asir in 1923 in the course of which Imam Yahya of the Yemen had occupied the port of Hodeida and the coastal areas. By the Treaty of Mecca in October 1926 the Sheikh of the Asir was placed formally under the protection of Ibn Sa'ud; this position, however, was never enthusiastically accepted by the Imam, who continued to bait the new king of Arabia and also to encroach on the British-protected territory of the Aden Protectorate. In these activities he seemed to have had the support of Italy, with whom he signed a treaty of friendship in 1926; and a Soviet trade delegation made a brief appearance in the country at this time. In 1930 following on a dispute over his Hijaz borders he encouraged the Sheikh of the Asir to revolt against Ibn Sa'ud; the latter attempted to settle the dispute by peaceful means, and negotiations dragged on until 1934. In April of that year, however, Ibn Sa'ud decided on more drastic action; marching on the Yemen, he drove the Yemeni troops out of Hodeida, and in a bloodless campaign of a month forced them back into Sana'a. The peace treaty of Ta'if allotted Tihama and Najran to Ibn Sa'ud but otherwise left the boundaries of the Yemen undisturbed —a policy of moderation that won him considerable prestige. At the same time Britain formally recognized the independence of the Yemen by treaty, and ended for a time a long series of frontier disputes.

The despotic and conservative Imam Yahya continued to rule until February 1948, when an attempted *coup d'état* by Sayyid Abdullah al-Wazzir resulted in his murder; his eldest son, Saif al-Islam Ahmad, however, succeeded to the throne and drove out the insurgent. Since then the Yemen has been co-operating in international affairs; in January 1951 a start was made on the development of the country with British, American and French technical aid, and at the same time full diplomatic relations were established for the first time with foreign powers, including Britain, the U.S.A. and Egypt.

In the winter of 1953 Yemen, with Arab support, began pressing before the United Nations her claims to Aden and the territories of the Aden Protectorate, and throughout the summer of 1954, and again in 1955, there was a series of frontier incidents.

In April 1955 an attempted *coup d'état* against the Imam Ahmad was defeated, and the royal conspirators executed; but one consequence may have been the Imam's decision in August of that year to set up a formal cabinet. During 1956 relations were established with the Soviet Union and a military pact was concluded with Egypt, Saudi Arabia and Syria.

The frontier dispute between Britain and the Yemen was continued late in December 1956 and in 1957, when Yemeni tribesmen were reported to have attacked villages in the Aden Protectorate. The Crown Prince visited London for talks in November 1957, but hostilities flared up again in the spring of 1958 and the political committee of the Arab League denounced the actions of Great Britain in the Aden territories. Two bomb incidents in Aden itself led to the enforcement in May 1958 of a temporary state of emergency. Unsuccessful talks to settle the dispute were held in July 1958 and May 1959. (For a fuller account of the border dispute see the chapter on Yemen P.D.R.)

A Yemeni delegation, headed by the Crown Prince, visited Cairo in February 1958 for negotiations which led to a federal union between the United Arab Republic and the Yemen, established by an agreement signed in Damascus on March 8th. The new union was named the United Arab States, and was to have a unified defence and foreign policy, and later a Customs union and common currency. Few practical steps were taken to that end and although, in November 1961, the Yemen renewed the agreement for a further three years, the Federation was formally dissolved by the United Arab Republic in December 1961.

In May 1959 disorders followed the departure of the Imam Ahmad to Europe and the Crown Prince Muhammad al-Badr introduced various reforms, including the innovation of a Representative Council. This policy was reversed on the return of the Imam in August.

CIVIL WAR 1962—1969

In March 1961 there was an unsuccessful attempt to assassinate the Imam, who was wounded in the shoulder. The Imam died in September 1962, and was briefly succeeded by his son Muhammad Badr. But a week later a revolt broke out, led by Colonel Abdullah Sallal, supported by troops from the U.A.R. The new Imam fled into the hills after a series of attempts to regain the capital, and Republican forces gained control of most of the country. The Republic was soon recognized by the U.S.S.R. and the United States, and early in 1963 was admitted to the United Nations. Britain, however, continued to give recognition to the Royalist régime, and stated on a number of occasions that she would only recognize the Republic when U.A.R. forces were withdrawn. Fighting continued throughout the year and did not cease until the summer of 1969, having been particularly severe during the winter of 1963–64 and much of 1968. An Observer Mission dispatched by the United Nations found that an agreement for simultaneous withdrawal of U.A.R. troops and Saudi Arabian military supplies had not been implemented by either side. The Mission operated from July 1963 to September 1964.

The rapprochement between U.A.R. and Saudi Arabia in February 1964 suggested that a solution would not be long delayed, and recognition by Jordan of the Republican régime was a further important step towards complete acceptance of the Revolution and its consequences. Britain, nevertheless, maintained her stand in support of the Royalists; the interest of the U.A.R. in driving British influence out of South Arabia (the Yemen Republican leaders were less vehement in this aim than their Egyptian colleagues) only strengthened the determination of the United Kingdom Government.

In May 1964 a new Republican Government was announced under the terms of a new Constitution published in April. The Prime Minister, Hamud Al Jaifi, soon displayed his command of the situation, which was emphasised by the frequent absences of the President for medical treatment in Cairo and Europe. In a policy statement in June a programme of school, hospital and road building was announced, and in July an agreement was signed in Cairo to establish a U.A.R./Yemen co-ordinating council and a joint military command; 90 per cent of the expenses of these ventures would be provided by Egypt, which had already sent an estimated 40,000 troops into the country in support of the Republicans.

In September the UN military observers left the country, while at the same time Sallal was attending the Arab Summit Conference in Alexandria. Following this meeting President Nasser and King Faisal discussed the Yemen situation, and this led in November to a meeting at Erkwit in the Sudan, at which republican and royalist delegations agreed to a cease-fire and the convening of a national congress. Differences over procedure forced the postponement of this, and in December the royalists resumed the offensive. During January the Imam al-Badr proclaimed a constitutional charter. This military and political offensive led to dissensions in the republican cabinet, culminating in the fall of Hamud Al Jaifi in January 1965, and his replacement by Lieut.-Gen. Hassan Al-Amri with a mandate to stiffen the war effort. In April, however, Lieut.-Gen. Amri resigned, and was replaced by the moderate Muhammad Ahmad Noman, who embarked on a policy of conciliation. The long postponed National Congress met in May in the village of Khamer, though without the participation of the royalists, and on May 9 the text was published of an interim constitution, setting up a supreme Consultative Assembly with power to make laws, remove members of the Republican Council, and nominate the President. Despite the energetic efforts of Mr. Noman to achieve a peace settlement, it was not long before his sympathy for the Baathist cause ran him into opposition from the Egyptian authorities, who retained a measure of financial control over the Yemen. In July Noman resigned and after a few days of uncertainty President Sallal announced a new cabinet headed by Lieut.-Gen. Amri. The return to prominence of the military, pro-Egyptian element coincided with a number of important Royalist advances, and relations between the U.A.R. and Saudi Arabia worsened dangerously as each accused the other once again of complicity in the civil war.

THE SEARCH FOR A SETTLEMENT

In late summer events took a more hopeful turn when President Nasser agreed to discuss the Yemen situation with King Faisal at Jeddah. On August 24th, after their two-day conference, the two leaders concluded an agreement on a plan to bring the war to an end and to establish, within fifteen months, a Yemeni government free from outside interference. The agreement stipulated that a cease-fire was to be declared immediately; Saudi Arabia was to stop supplying arms to the Royalist forces; an interim government of moderate politicians, excluding both the Imam al-Badr and President Sallal, was to be set up within three months; after which the Egyptian forces, numbering about 50,000, were to be withdrawn during the ten-month period ending September 23rd, 1966. By November 23rd, 1966, a plebiscite would be held to enable the Yemenis to choose the political form they wished their state to assume.

Although the immediate effects of the Jeddah agreement were hopeful, including the establishment of a more representative Presidency Council for the Republic, and of a U.A.R./Saudi Arabian Peace Committee, the good intentions of the participants to the agreement were soon eroded. In November 1965 a conference of Republican and Royalist envoys meeting at Haradh reached deadlock over the next steps to be taken, and through 1966 the implementation of the agreement seemed less and less likely as relations between Egypt and Saudi Arabia deteriorated. Egyptian troop numbers in the Yemen, far from being reduced, were built up; despite a further U.A.R./Saudi meeting in August in Beirut, chaired by Kuwait, a solution seemed no nearer. Worse still, in September 1966 friction between Lt.-Gen. Amri and President Sallal came into the open when the latter returned to Sana'a. A large delegation, led personally by the Premier, then flew to Cairo to demand complete independence from U.A.R. for the Yemen régime, and the permanent removal of the President. The U.A.R. response to this was to arrest the members of the delegation, and Sallal himself assumed the duties of the premiership. This was followed by a drastic purge of the republican armed forces and administration, and a wave of riots, trials and executions. The dissident republican elements took refuge in the mountains to the north of Sana'a.

During the latter months of 1966 republican and royalist operations began to escalate. Egyptian aircraft were in action, and on several occasions air raids were made on the Saudi Arabian towns of Jizan and Najran. In January allegations were made of the use of poison gas, a charge denied by the U.A.R.

Meanwhile there was considerable diplomatic activity. In January Sallal formed the Popular Revolutionary Union at a meeting attended by Makkawi (*see* Yemen P.D.R.). Outside Yemen, a Union of Popular Forces was formed, led by Ibrahim al-Wazir, who visited Riyad and Geneva calling for an Islamic State of Yemen, the withdrawal of Egyptian troops, and the ending of Saudi Arabian aid. On February 11th, 1967, Tunisia and Jordan withdrew their recognition of the Sallal régime. However, Jordanian recognition was subsequently restored, in consequence of the diplomatic rapprochement with Egypt at the time of the Arab-Israel war of June 1967.

In July, following a major government reorganization, the Royalists took advantage of the run-down in Egyptian troops to stage one of the fiercest land offensives for two years. Republican forces were driven from Haradh and the port of Maydi, and refugees from the coastal town of al-Luhayya had to be evacuated to the British-administered island of Kamaran. Later in July the Egyptian military build-up was resumed, and these localities were retaken.

THE EGYPTIAN WITHDRAWAL

Early in August 1967, on the occasion of the meeting of Foreign Ministers at Khartoum to prepare an agenda for an Arab summit conference, the U.A.R. delegate announced that the Egyptian Government was once again prepared to put into effect the agreement drawn up with King Faisal of Saudi Arabia at Jeddah in August 1965. The supervision of the withdrawal of troops would be entrusted to a committee of three Arab states. According to Radio Sana'a, a principal factor influencing this change of heart by the Egyptians was the British decision on a definite date for the withdrawal of troops from Aden, in January 1968. The implication appeared to be that Egypt saw no further need for the presence of her forces in Yemen after the British withdrawal from South Arabia had taken place. The fact that the U.A.R. was now partially dependent on financial aid from more conservative Arab countries, notably Saudi Arabia, was not mentioned.

On August 31st an agreement on these terms was finally reached by King Faisal and President Nasser at the Arab leaders' conference at Khartoum. Egyptian troops were to be withdrawn within three months; a plebiscite to determine the political future of the Yemen was to be held within a further six months; President Sallal was to lead a transitional government; the whole agreement to be carried out under the supervision of representatives of three independent Arab states, Iraq, Morocco and Sudan. Although President Sallal immediately protested against the peace plan, his opposition did not prove an obstacle.

The Egyptian army, with an estimated strength of up to 80,000 men, had effectively colonized the Republican-held sector of the Yemen, and was in general neither popular nor well regarded for its military prowess. Thus its withdrawal, which was completed by January 1968, was not altogether unwelcome although it naturally encouraged the Royalist forces to become bolder. It also led to the deposition of President Sallal in November, carried out while he was on an official visit to Iraq, and the institution of a three-man Presidency Council headed initially by Abdul Rahman al-Iriani. In December 1967 General Hassan Al-Amri, a militant republican, replaced the moderate Muhammad Noman on the Council; shortly afterwards he also became Prime Minister, again replacing a more moderate man. The National Liberation Front, the left-wing force that had come to power in the newly independent territory of Southern Yemen, also came to possess considerable influence in the Yemen at this time.

The Royalist army continued to make progress early in 1968, and for some time the Republican capital of Sana'a was virtually besieged. Its defendants claimed that the Imam was still receiving generous aid from Saudi Arabia, while much of their own equipment had been taken by the Egyptians. In January the Iraqi, Sudanese and Moroccan foreign ministers arranged a peace meeting in Beirut, but it proved abortive as the rival factions could not even agree to meet. By April the pressure on Sana'a had relaxed somewhat; a left-wing plot to overthrow the Al-Amri government was unsuccessful. In June the Royalist leader, Imam Muhammad al-Badr, was deposed by his followers in favour of his son (his cousin according to some accounts), Muhammad bin Hussein. A ministerial delegation from Southern Yemen met the leaders of the Republican government in July, apparently for talks regarding the rebels in the hinterland of both countries.

THE END OF THE CIVIL WAR

During the 1968–69 period it became evident that the Royalist military effort was in decline after its major offensive following the Egyptian withdrawal; some accounts claimed that the Royalists ceased to exist as a regular fighting force after a defeat at Hajja in December 1968. By the summer of 1969 the leading members of the Royalist camp were all in exile, and their followers had apparently accepted the Sana'a government. The principal cause of this swift collapse appeared to be a feud within the royal family following the deposition of the Imam. The Saudi Arabian Government's confidence in the Royalists, already weakened by their failure to capture Sana'a, thus diminished further; eventually the Saudis ceased their financial and military assistance on which the Royalists had depended. Since the Republicans were apparently in receipt of substantial arms supplies from other Arab countries and the U.S.S.R. their success was assured.

Nevertheless, there was a short-lived revival of military activity in the north-east during the winter of 1969–70. Rebel tribesmen, said to be opposed to rule from Sana'a rather than positive supporters of the Imam, surrounded the town of Saada for some weeks. This development, plus the massive economic problems faced by the government, led to the resignation of the Prime Minister, Abdallah Kurshoumi, in February 1970, only six months after he had succeeded General Al-Amri. Muhsin Al-Aini, the Ambassador in Moscow, was then appointed Prime Minister.

In March 1970 the Premier and the Foreign Minister met Saudi Arabian officials privately during the Islamic Foreign Ministers Conference at Jeddah. Although no formal announcement of the outcome was made, it appeared that an informal peace settlement was agreed upon. As a result, the leading Royalists, apart from the Imam and the royal family itself, returned to Sana'a in May 1970 and were offered a number of posts in the administration. Ahmed Al Shami, the former Royalist foreign minister, joined the Presidential Council, four Royalists joined the cabinet, and others were given high diplomatic or civil service posts or became members of the National Assembly.

The government was said to be anxious to open relations with the Western countries which had recognized the Royalist régime; in July 1969 diplomatic relations with Federal Germany were restored at a time when several Arab states followed an opposite policy in recognizing the G.D.R. (East Germany). One result was a generous offer of economic and financial aid from Bonn. In July 1970 Saudi Arabia formally opened diplomatic relations with the republic, followed, within a few days, by Britain and France.

In December 1970, a new constitution was promulgated, providing for a Consultative Council to replace the National Assembly. Elections were held in February and March 1971.

In July 1971 there were rumours of an attempt by senior army officers to overthrow the Government, and several officers were dismissed. In September the Prime Minister, Lt.-Gen. Hassan al-Amri, went into exile (until 1975) after reportedly murdering a man in his office. Tension between Sana'a and Aden increased in the first half of 1972 as supporters of FLOSY and the South Arabian League, opponents of the Aden Government, gathered on the borders between the two states.

Serious fighting broke out on the border in September, but an Arab League mission was able to mediate and a ceasefire became effective in October. A peace agreement and an agreement on eventual unification of the two Yemens were signed in Cairo on October 28th. Further details were discussed in Tripoli (Libya) in November by the Presidents of the two Yemens, and it was agreed that the people of Yemen would establish a single state, to be known as the Yemen Republic, with Sana'a as its capital, Islam as the State religion and Arabic as the official language. Committees were set up to discuss details of the unification. In January 1973 it appeared that certain obstacles had arisen in the progress towards union, but in February a new political organization, the Yemeni Union, was formed in Sana'a in anticipation of the forthcoming union. At the end of May fighting again broke out on the border between the two Yemens, and on May 30th, Sheikh Muhammad al-Othman, a member of the three-man Presidential Council, was assassinated by unknown gunmen. Although this incident temporarily soured relations between the two Yemens, it was announced in June that talks on unity would continue.

In December 1972 Mohsin al-Aini resigned as Prime Minister and a new government was later formed under Abdullah al-Hajari. The Government of Abdullah al-Hajari had to contend with a great deal of violence, particularly in the south of the country, and in September 1973 President Iriani and President Salem Rubayi Ali of South Yemen met in Sana'a and decided to extend the one year period originally decided upon for the unification of their two countries, and to concentrate on suppressing terrorism and sabotage.

A new Government under Hassan Makki took office in March 1974, pledged to continue the policies of the former Prime Minister, Abdullah al-Hajari, and in particular to work for unification with South Yemen. On June 13th, however, a bloodless *coup* took place in which a seven-man military junta, under the leadership of pro-Saudi Colonel Ibrahim al-Hamadi, suspended the Constitution and Consultative Council and dissolved the armed forces high command and the Yemeni National Union. Colonel Hamadi later stated that the *coup* had been necessary to remedy economic and administrative chaos. The former President, Qadi Abdul Rahman al-Iriani, later left for Damascus. A provisional constitution was issued on June 19th and on June 21st a new Government was formed under Mohsin al-Aini. The policy of the new Government was stated to include openness to all Arab States, support for non-alignment and adherence to the Arab League Charter and the UN Charter. The goal of ultimate unity with South Yemen was to be preserved.

In January 1975 Mohsin al-Aini was relieved of his post of Prime Minister and replaced by the former Chairman of the central bank, Abdel-Aziz Abdel-Ghani. Although it was hoped that a return to constitutional government would be made in June 1975 (after one year of military rule), Col. Hamadi merely announced in May 1975 that he would nominate a commission to supervise the election of a Popular Assembly which would in turn amend the constitution. In October 1975 Col. Hamadi issued a decree proroguing the Constituent Assembly and calling for new elections to be held under the supervision of the supreme electoral committee, but no date was fixed for the elections.

During 1975 there were signs that the Yemen Arab Republic was drawing closer to Saudi Arabia and the U.S.A. In August, King Khaled of Saudi Arabia gave 810 million Saudi riyals to the Yemen as budget and development project support, and in April 1976 a plan was announced whereby Saudi Arabia would bear the expense of re-equipping sections of the Yemeni army with U.S. weapons. In contrast to this, President Hamadi had declared, in August 1975, that his relations with the Soviet Union were "frozen" and that the Yemen Arab Republic had turned down offers of help with arms from the Soviet Union.

Eventual union of the two Yemens appeared to have been brought slightly nearer in February 1977 when the two Heads of State met at Qaataba, near the border with South Yemen, and established a joint council consisting of their respective Ministers of Foreign Affairs, Economy, Trade and Planning. The Council decided to meet for discussion every six months, alternately in Sana'a and Aden. A joint economic, trade and planning sub-committee was also set up.

In April 1977 Qadi Abdullah al-Hajari, Prime Minister between December 1972 and February 1974, was assassinated in London. He had been a minister under the Imam and had been slow to transfer his allegiance to the republican government. As Prime Minister he had also forged close links with Saudi Arabia, and had never been enthusiastic about effecting the union of the two Yemens.

In July 1977 Hamadi had to face a rebellion of the northern tribes, mainly supporters of the former Imamate. In October Hamadi was assassinated in Sana'a, and there has since been much speculation about who was responsible. Another member of the Military Command Council, Lt.-Col. Ahmed ibn Hussein al-Ghashmi, took over as Chairman. Although he survived an assassination attempt within two weeks of taking over as Chairman, he placated some of the dissident elements in the Yemen for a while by doubling the pay of the army and giving every soldier a daily ration of the narcotic qat. At the same time he became increasingly dependent on Saudi Arabia for aid, and was apparently unwilling to promote the long-awaited unification with South Yemen, although regular discussions continued.

Towards the end of May 1978 there were reports of a rebellion against President al-Ghashmi, led by Major Abdulla Abdel Alem, in the south of the country. Major Alem had been one of the members of al-Ghashmi's Presidential Council, and after the rebellion fled to South Yemen. At the end of June President al-Ghashmi was assassinated. The Yemen Arab Republic claimed that the assassination was engineered by South Yemen, and suspected that Major Alem had been instrumental. A suitcase carried by a South Yemen envoy contained a bomb which exploded and killed both President al-Ghashmi and the envoy. Whatever was the truth of the matter, the affair had repercussions in South Yemen, where President Salem Rubayi Ali was ousted and executed, and fighting broke out on the frontier between the two countries in July 1978 (*see* Yemen P.D.R., History).

In spite of the insecurity and assassinations, the Yemen Arab Republic has made some advance towards a more democratic form of government. In February 1978 the Command Council appointed a Constituent People's Assembly of 99 members for a term of between two and three years, whose task was to propose the form of the Presidency (it later elected al-Ghashmi President), to review the Constitution and prepare the way for eventual elections. The Constituent People's Assembly appears to have survived al-Ghashmi's assassination in June 1978, since, together with the Council of Ministers, it set up a four-man Presidential Council, with Qadi Abdul Karim al-Arshi (also Speaker of the Constituent Assembly) as its Chairman. The main task of the Presidential Council was to maintain power until the election of a new President. Lt.-Col. Ali Abdullah Saleh was elected President on July 17th, 1978.

President Saleh survived an assassination attempt in September 1978 and an attempted coup by senior military officers in October, thought to have external backing. Suspicion of South Yemeni involvement in both these events put increased strain on the relations between North and South Yemen. Between October 1978 and January 1979 the North Yemen Government repeatedly accused South Yemen of territorial violations and sabotage. Sporadic border clashes during these months escalated into open warfare during February and March 1979. The North Yemen opposition group, the National Democratic Front, carried out disruptive action in cities of the North and claimed to have captured several towns which it refused to relinquish. A mediation team from Syria, Jordan and Iraq arranged a ceasefire on March 2nd but, when this failed to hold and the fighting worsened, the Arab League intervened to enforce its implementation and supervise withdrawals from occupied territory in the second half of March.

At a meeting arranged by the Arab League in Kuwait on March 29th the Heads of State of North and South Yemen agreed that the only permanent way of settling the countries' differences was by unification, and they pledged their commitment to this in a peace treaty. A constitutional committee, containing representatives from North and South Yemen, would be formed and charged with drawing up a "proposal for a united state" within four months which would then be submitted to the Yemeni peoples for approval in a referendum. Free direct elections to the Government of the new state were also promised and committees were subsequently formed to reconcile, amongst other things, the differing economic, judicial, legal and education systems.

President Saleh has thought it wise to continue the gradual democratization of the North Yemen Government. On May 8th he appointed a 15-member advisory council and expanded the membership of the Constituent Assembly to 159. On May 16th he opened the second session of the Constituent Assembly which will continue the work of preparation for a general election.

In July 1979 it was reported that Saleh had crushed yet another military coup.

ECONOMIC SURVEY

AGRICULTURE

Despite considerable progress in recent years, the Yemen Arab Republic remains one of the poorest countries in the world. Per capita income was estimated at $250 in 1977. The economy is dominated by the agricultural sector, which provides about 50 per cent of G.D.P., employs 73 per cent of the labour force and provides over 80 per cent of visible exports.

Yemen contains some of the most fertile land in the Arabian Peninsula, both in the highlands, where agriculture has always been extensively practised, and in the dry coastal plain of the Tihama. Total cultivated area, according to estimates made in 1977 by the U.N. Economic Commission for Western Asia, amounts to 1,500,000 hectares, equivalent to 8 per cent of Yemen's area. Of this cultivated land, 85 per cent is irrigated solely by rainwater. Yemen's best-known crop is coffee, grown mainly in the hills behind the Tihama, although it is cultivated in various degrees all over the country. It used to be Yemen's largest foreign exchange earner, but the amount of land devoted to it has decreased, partly because of fluctuation in demand on the world market, partly because the farmers found the narcotic, qat, to be a more profitable crop. In 1972, however, the Government announced measures to limit the growing of qat, whereby its cultivation was banned on state-owned land or on *Waqf* (religious endowment) land. In any case, cotton has now replaced coffee as the main cash crop.

Yemen's major cereal crop is sorghum (durra), grown at any altitude up to 9,000 feet. The annual harvest of sorghum and millet is usually about one million tons, but in 1974/75 it rose appreciably to 1.57 million tons. Other cereals are wheat, barley and maize. Although a comparatively large area is allocated to cereals, the yield is poor and Yemen relies on imports of staple foods. A prolonged drought in the years 1968 to 1970 caused the failure of many crops and the resultant famine obliged the Government to import even larger quantities of wheat and cereals. The 1971 season saw increased yields, and production in 1975, estimated at over 2 million tons, was enough for Yemen's needs. The maintenance of increased yields depends, however, on weather conditions; floods as well as drought can cause loss of output. The 1976 crop fell sharply to 859,000 tons. The Government is planning a grain distribution system involving the building of silos at Hodeida and setting up flour mills and bakeries. Other cereal crops are as yet of lesser importance but the Government hopes that their growth will be more rapid than that of sorghum. Maize production in 1976 was 72,000 tons, barley 75,000 tons and wheat 52,000 tons. Under the first Five-Year Plan (1976/77 to 1980/81) wheat output is projected to increase by 146 per cent above that of

1975/76, while sorghum and millet output are projected to be only 21 per cent greater than in 1975/76.

The highland areas also produce many fruits and vegetables, citrus fruits, apricots, peaches, grapes, tomatoes and potatoes being the main crops; but others, such as cauliflowers, lettuces, peas, cucumbers and water melons are being introduced at the instigation of the Ministry of Agriculture. The Government is seeking finance from the United Arab Emirates and the World Bank to develop agriculture further in the central highlands.

The hot Tihama plain produces dates, and tobacco and cotton plantations are being established there to form the basis for local industries. Cotton in particular is assuming some importance as a cash crop; in 1971/72, the first year in which cotton and cotton seeds were exported, their value was 9.9 million riyals and in 1972/73 it amounted to 10.8 million riyals. In 1973/74 total cotton and cottonseed exports more than trebled to total 35.2 million riyals. This was followed by a small drop in cotton exports to 28.2 million riyals in 1974/75.

Since 1974/75 cotton production has fallen sharply, from 27,238 tons to 9,200 tons in 1976/77, while the area planted with cotton fell from 39,493 hectares to 13,233 hectares. This decline appears to have been due to the low prices maintained by the Government in 1975 and 1976 and partly due to a shortage of agricultural credit facilities and lack of improved seeds. Nevertheless, cotton and cottonseeds remain by far the principal visible export, providing, in 1975/76, 32.3 million riyals out of total exports of 55.1 million riyals. By 1980/81 cotton output is projected to increase to 32,000 tons.

The Government plans to introduce Friesian cattle to the upland regions to improve the local stock, and breeding stations are being built in Sana'a, Taiz and Hodeida. In 1975 an agreement was made with U.S. interests to establish a poultry farm project.

Because droughts are so frequent, Yemen's major concern is to achieve efficient irrigation systems and water storage schemes and to utilize the ground water which exists in the Tihama.

The largest project now in hand is the $17.5 million agricultural scheme for the Tihama region, assisted by the United Nations, the International Development Association (IDA) and the Kuwait Fund for Arab Economic Development (KFAED). The scheme involves irrigation works in the Wadi Zebid area, the development of 60,000 hectares at Wadi Mawr, the establishment of a Tihama Development Authority and provision of credit schemes and various other services. Output of cotton and vegetables in the area should almost double when the project is completed and substantially increased yields of cereals and oilseeds are expected. Other UN schemes are a pilot project for the development of a sugar cane industry and the expansion of the government-run model farm near Taiz into an agricultural advisory centre. An Agricultural Credit Bank has been set up with a $3.4 million grant from the Government. The International Fund for Agricultural Development, based in Rome, has agreed to lend $12 million for land development on the Red Sea coast. In 1979 the IDA approved a $10 million credit for secondary education aimed mainly at agricultural training, and a training school at Surdud is planned.

Yemen is also receiving agricultural aid from the Netherlands, China and other Arab states. In 1976 a Livestock Development Corporation (LDC) was set up with total credit facilities of $32 million—of which $17 million emanated from foreign sources. The LDC will establish eight 50-cow dairy farms, a livestock fattening farm, a poultry unit and a feedmill, construct three urban slaughterhouses and about 154 municipal retail market stalls, improve production of hides and skins, aid animal health services and ensure supervised credit to some 900 traditional sector landowners, smallholder livestock and poultry owners and irrigated fodder crop producers. At the same time, a livestock and range improvement centre will be established with a village range development programme under which 1,250 hectares of suitable land will be improved for grazing. A group of Dutch and West German firms plan to set up a chicken farm to provide 37 million eggs and 1,550 tons of broiler meat per year. In the same area of agricultural development it was announced in 1976 that the Swiss firm Electrowatt had been commissioned to prepare studies for the rehabilitation of the ancient dam at Marib which would irrigate 1,000 hectares. Efforts are also to be made to exploit the country's fish resources. The annual catch, in the region of 10,000 tons, could be increased to 28,500 tons, it is estimated, with proper investment.

INDUSTRY

It is calculated that industry accounts for only 5 per cent of Yemen's Gross Domestic Product and employs less than 4 per cent of the labour force. With a few exceptions, the existing and projected new industries are mainly based on the traditional occupations such as textiles, leather work, basketry, jewellery and glass-making, and, where possible, local raw materials. The Government's aim is to become self-sufficient in food processing, clothing and construction industries, that is, those sectors which could be made independent of imported raw materials. There is a state-owned spinning and weaving factory at Sana'a, established under an agreement of 1958 between Yemen and China, and completed in 1967. The plant, the Sana'a Textile Factory, employs 1,500 workers, many of them women. China is continuing to make aid available for the textile industry, with plans to set up a mill in Hodeida. The Bajil textile factory, set up by French and Syrian interests in the 1950s, encountered financial difficulties and never went into production. A United Nations report of 1968 recommended its urgent rehabilitation and repair, and a Dutch firm conducted a study. Modernization was proposed under the Three-Year Plan (1973/74 to 1975/76). In addition, there are two cotton-cleaning plants in Hodeida, and one in Zebid, and a cotton seed oil and cake plant in Hodeida; these are privately owned. The textile industry is clearly the most promising line of industrial development in Yemen. The Yemen Cotton Company, owned 51 per cent by the Government, 30 per cent by the Yemeni Bank for Reconstruction and Development and 19 per cent by private interests, provides the plants with raw cotton, over which it has monopoly rights. In 1974 a new factory making school, police and military uniforms was opened and a similar plant for medical clothing is under consideration.

The rock salt factory at Salif, managed by the Ministry of Economy, utilizes local salt deposits, estimated to contain at least 25 million tons. Until 1975, the salt, which is of high quality, was nearly all exported to Japan. The Salt Company had invested about $400,000 to raise production to 500,000 tons per year and the KFAED provided loans to extend bulk-loading facilities at Salif port. A further KFAED loan of KD 1.2 million was given to exploit the deposits further and to raise production to 1 million tons per year by 1974. In 1975, however, Japanese customers ceased imports of salt, claiming that it contained impurities. The Government was understandably concerned in view of the large investments in the industry and the amount of goods imported from Japan. In 1976 the U.S.S.R. agreed to buy salt from Yemen.

During 1977 the planned expansion of salt mining facilities begun under the Three-Year Plan was completed. Design capacity is 1 million tons per year and Salif is likely to be profitable in the long term due to fairly high salt purity, proximity to deep water and low-cost open pit mining. The Yemen Salt Mining Corporation is now seeking new market outlets. In 1977 shipments were made to North Korea and Bangladesh, both new markets, but full capacity working at Salif may have to await the completion of new chloralkali plants in other Middle East countries.

The salt at Salif is the only mineral at present exploited in Yemen on any scale. There are also salt deposits at Maarib in the east and at Qumah, near Salif. A mineral resources survey has been started by the U.S. Agency for International Development (AID). Other minerals known to exist in Yemen are: coal, copper (at Hamoura, near Taiz), iron, sulphur, lead, zinc, silver, gold and uranium. The exploitation of copper deposits at Hamoura, near Taiz, is being studied by KFAED experts. Talks are being held with South Yemen on the working of copper deposits in the Beida area. The Government has plans to exploit marble deposits in the Mawzah region. It was reported in the second half of 1977 that large copper reserves had been found in the Al-Baidah and Al-Hamoura regions.

The Yemen Petroleum Company, a joint venture between the Government and the YBRD, has the monopoly of imports, storage and distribution of oil products.

In 1970 a joint company, the Yemen Oil and Mineral Industrial Company, was formed by the Yemeni Government with the Algerian state-owned oil concern, SONATRACH. It was announced in 1972 that oil had been found in the Tihama but in the same year the company had to be dissolved because of lack of capital. The Government made it known that it would welcome foreign firms who wished to prospect for oil. In January 1974 an agreement was signed with Shell (Hamburg) to prospect for oil in the northern territorial waters, the company also having the right to refine any oil found. The agreement was extended in 1976 to cover part of the southern offshore area. Yemen Shell Explorations (YSE), formed in 1976 and registered in West Germany, is exploring the coast north of Hodeida. In early 1977 YSE indicated that its first well had proved negative, but stressed that a second well would be started shortly. American and Japanese companies also have offshore concessions and the Government is optimistic about the prospects of finding oil. Toyo Menka Kaisha of Japan has a 2,500 sq. km. concession off the southern coast. Exploration costs have been shared with Santa Fe International of the U.S.A. A refinery is now being built at Hodeida and another is proposed for Salif. Yemen Shell Exploration's exploration agreement was renewed in June 1977.

Other industries include soft drinks factories, a cigarette plant at Hodeida, built with Italian aid, an oxygen plant, originally set up by the U.S.S.R. and now state-operated, and a plant making aluminium products. A plastics plant outside Taiz, built in 1973, produces mattresses, plastic tubes and plasticized paper. The IFC granted a $3 million loan in 1978 for a dairy and fruit juice plant in Hodeida. An IDA credit of $2.3 million to set up a pilot industrial project in Sana'a was announced in 1974. Through this scheme, the establishment of an iron foundry and plants manufacturing building fixtures and fitting, tools, clothing, and water pumps, among other things, will be attempted. Technical aid is being provided by the United Nations. The Yemeni Company for Industrial Development was formed to develop light industry, particularly in Sana'a, Taiz and Hodeida but industrialization is progressing very slowly, even with the increased aid which has been made available. New industries are, where possible, based on the traditional ones; for example, a textile plant has been set up at Sana'a with Chinese aid and another is planned at Hodeida.

The Soviet-built cement factory at Bajil, which uses local limestone deposits, is one of the more successful ventures. Its current output is only 62,000 tons per year, however. Although it should eventually achieve an output of 250,000 tons per year, this has to be seen against Yemen's rapidly growing needs. Estimates of cement imports in 1977 range from 500,000 tons to 800,000 tons. The Five-Year Development Plan (1976/77 to 1980/81) envisages the construction of two new plants, the first at Omran and the second at Taiz, each capable of an annual output of 500,000 tons, and a ready-mix concrete plant is to be sited near Sana'a. Denmark lent the Yemen 37 million riyals in 1978 to set up light industries.

COMMUNICATIONS

It is only since the revolution in 1962 that Yemen has established regular links with the outside world, and that good roads have been built connecting the main towns. Road construction now has high priority in development plans. The Sana'a–Hodeida road, completed in 1962, was built by Chinese engineers and is a spectacular achievement. The Sana'a-Saada road of 242 kilometres, also built with Chinese aid, was completed during the Three-Year Plan. The Sana'a-Taiz, the Mocha–Taiz and the Sana'a–Ibb–Taiz roads were built with American aid. The World Bank and KFAED are financing the Taiz–Turbah road and Dutch and Saudi aid is being provided for the Dhamar–Rada road. The U.A.E. provided finance for a road from Sana'a to Marib, through the remote eastern region, which was also completed during the Three-Year Plan. This road is to be extended to Baida on the border with Yemen P.D.R., across difficult mountainous terrain, and is planned for completion in 1979. The repair and maintenance of these roads is proving a problem, since neither the equipment nor the personnel are available locally. Altogether there were estimated in 1977 to be about 4,000 km. of roads, of which only 976 km. were asphalted. In addition there are a number of gravel feeder roads under construction. These are of great importance for the transport of agricultural produce which otherwise cannot reach centres of distribution. More asphalting is being done, especially around Sana'a, and a number of hard-surfaced roads are planned, notably the Amran–Hajja road. World Bank aid has been requested for the surfacing of the Taiz–Mocha and Dhamar–Rada roads, and Saudi Arabia is giving extensive aid for roads, mainly in the north-east and connecting with Saudi Arabia. Saudi-financed roads are: Hodeida–Jizan (204 km); Saada–Zahran al Janoub (79 km.); Yerim–Qatabati (96 km.); and Beit Marwan-Al Hazm (112 km.). West Germany is adding to its already sizeable aid to Yemen, by providing assistance equivalent to $13 million for a number of projects in the Five-Year Development Plan (1976/77 to 1980/81), notably further road development between Sana'a and Taiz. The Kuwait Fund for Arab Economic Development has agreed to build a hard-surfaced road from Taiz to link up with the Soviet-built road which runs from the port of Hodeida to a point some 64 km. from Taiz.

Improvement in the roads system is reflected in the increasing imports of motor vehicles, both commercial and private.

There are three ports in Yemen: Hodeida, Mocha and Salif, of which the most important is Hodeida. A new harbour, completed in 1962 by the U.S.S.R., has since been deepened and is now being expanded still further with Iraqi aid. Mocha cannot be used by ships of any size at present, but in 1973 the Government allocated 2.5 million riyals for its improvement with Italian assistance. With the expansion of salt mining at Salif, the harbour is being rebuilt to enable it to take ships of up to 5,000 tons and a bulk petrol plant is also planned. Since Hodeida suffers badly from silting, there are tentative plans to develop Salif into the country's main port, but these are very much in the future. In the meantime, the Yemen Port Corporation obtained finance totalling $6 million in May 1977 from the International Development Association to develop the port of Hodeida. The envisaged project involves construction of a deep-sea berth, restoration of existing berth facilities, dredging and the installation of new equipment. The project also involves the improvement of existing port facilities at Mocha. Hodeida is one of the world's most congested ports, with waiting times of up to six months for unloading.

There are airports at Sana'a, Hodeida and Taiz and smaller airstrips in other towns. Sana'a airport, built by the U.S.S.R. and equipped by West Germany, is capable of taking large aircraft, and both Hodeida and Taiz can take international flights. Facilities for air travel are poor by international standards. Work began in late 1976 on the expansion of Sana'a airport to proper international standards. This work is being primarily Saudi Arabian financed. The Iraq Development Fund is to provide a $15 million loan to be used mainly for the constructicn of an international airport at Hodeida. A contract for the work has been awarded to Costain International and Amay Roadstone Construction of the U.K. In May 1977 a Yemeni-Saudi Arabian airline company was established to take over the national airline, Yemen Airways. The joint company has a capital of $30 million, of which 51 per cent has been subscribed by the Yemeni Government and the remaining 49 per cent is subscribed by Saudi Arabia. The company will also be involved in developing airport facilities in the Yemen. In March 1977 it was reported that Yemen Airways had made a profit of $11 million in 1976.

Much work is now being done on providing Yemen with a telecommunications system, one of the Development Plan priorities. The three main towns, Sana'a, Taiz and Hodeida are linked by a 600 km. telephone line, built by East German experts, and are also connected to a number of other towns where telephone exchanges are in operation: Bajil, Ibb, Dhamar, Yerim, Manakha, Zebid, Beit-el-Faqih and Hais. East Germany also helped to found a Communications College at Sana'a. A six-channel microwave scatter system linking Sana'a and Taiz is being implemented by the United Nations and Sana'a is linked via Aden with the rest of the world. There are radio transmitters at Sana'a and Taiz and various small wireless communications posts scattered throughout the country. Work has started on a television network to operate from Sana'a. There were some 14,000 telephone lines at the end of 1976 and work has begun on an automatic system. An earth satellite station was completed in October 1976 by Cable and Wireless (U.K.) and Nippon Electric of Japan. Sited at Ghuraff, near Sana'a, and costing close to $1 million, it is linked to the INTELSAT (International Telecommunications Satellite Organization) system and can provide over 100 channels. As a further development, Cable and Wireless has proposed an internal microwave system.

FOREIGN TRADE

Yemen's trade is characterized by an ever-growing deficit which had reached 1,292 million riyals in 1975 and 1,666 million riyals in 1976, compared with 539.1 million riyals in 1973. The deficit rose still further to 2,980 million riyals in 1977 as development projects got under way. The payments problem was aggravated in 1973 when oil prices rose and the Government was obliged to subsidize oil products. Kuwait agreed in 1976 to supply products over a three-year period.

Yemen's exports consist almost entirely of agricultural produce: cotton, coffee, salt, skins and products of the artisan industries. The principal import is food and this has contributed most to the large trade gap in recent years. Food imports rose from 30 million riyals in 1966 to over 100 million riyals in 1970 because of the drought and famine experienced during that period. Although in 1971 food imports fell to 66 million riyals, the trend is for them to increase, partly because of rises in the world price of wheat. In 1974 food imports were worth 310 million riyals and in 1976 they were worth 775.9 million riyals, accounting for 45.1 per cent of total visible imports. A substantial proportion of the remainder of Yemen's imports is made up of finished goods, vehicles, electrical machinery and fuel.

Yemen used to import most from Australia, which supplies foodstuffs, and the Soviet Union, but in 1972–73 a change in the pattern of trade took place because of the growing importance of imports of machinery and motor vehicles. As a result, Japan has forged ahead as the country's main supplier. In 1975/76 Japan accounted for 14 per cent of total imports, while India, China, Australia and Saudi Arabia were other important suppliers. Figures for trade with Yemen P.D.R. are inflated due to the volume of transit trade *via* Aden but, with the development of Hodeida as a port capable of handling all Yemen's trade, the importance of Aden is declining.

The amount of trade with the Eastern Bloc is increasing, with China and the Soviet Union taking deliveries of Yemen cotton and coffee in return for aid with industrial projects and the supply of machinery. This has tended to stimulate the production of coffee but coffee exports in 1975/76 were only 1.7 million riyals.

FINANCE AND FOREIGN AID

During the civil war there was a considerable inflow of foreign exchange from Saudi Arabia and Egypt. This, coupled with continued remittances from Yemenis living abroad, tended to soften the effects of the decline in agriculture which took place after 1966. These flows resulted, however, in a rise in liquidity which, with increasing government expenditure, led in turn to inflation, a sharp rise in imports and the depreciation of the Yemeni riyal.

Yemen has a very large budgetary deficit, which in 1968–69 amounted to 70 million riyals and reached 83 million riyals in 1971–72 quite apart from foreign loan commitments. The instability of the Government in 1971 meant that no firm measures were taken to deal with the situation. In July 1971 the Government of Muhammad Ahmed Noman resigned because of its inability to deal with the state's financial difficulties. The administration under Mohsin al-Aini announced that it would make a sharp reduction in government spending, would do all it could to attract foreign investment and would try to establish light industry in Yemen. Subsequent administrations have pursued much the same policies, but the budget deficit continues to grow, not least because the defence allocation is so large. In the 1978/79 budget, expenditure was set at 3,177.1 million riyals and revenue at 2,193.4 million riyals. Saudi Arabia has consistently made available budgetary aid to Yemen, including a payment of 120 million Saudi riyals in 1974 and SR 345 million in 1979. The Saudi Fund for Development has also agreed to provide some $570 million for Plan projects and has already completed schemes worth $63 million in Yemen. These include a large number of school and hospital buildings, as well as larger schemes such as the Taiz water supply and drainage project.

After the civil war the country had to rely more and more on foreign assistance for development. Extensive aid was offered by China, the Soviet Union and the United Nations and smaller amounts by Hungary, Yugoslavia, Bulgaria and Romania. Western aid came mainly from the United States and West Germany. The richer Arab countries, notably Algeria and Kuwait, also started to take an interest in Yemen; Algeria in oil and mineral exploitation, and Kuwait in the agricultural sector through loans from the Kuwait Fund for Arab Economic Development. Between 1962 and 1969 a total of $141 million was offered by China, the Soviet Union and the United Nations alone and Yemen had since 1956 accumulated a total debt of about $190 million. Even so, aid offered has been in excess of aid drawn and many development projects have been held up.

With the relative stabilization of the Government in 1971–72 foreign interests showed themselves more ready to invest in and aid Yemen, but political events in 1972 and 1973 had an unfortunate effect on the economy, the fighting with the South being most unlikely to inspire confidence in foreign investors. The unity agreement signed at the end of 1972 between North and South Yemen achieved only a pause in hostilities but at the end of 1973 the two countries were discussing economic integration and the outlook was more hopeful. The Government continued to reiterate its intention to pursue unification plans, although political developments tend to make unification something that is striven for rather than anything that is attained.

Much practical aid in the fields of health, education and social welfare has flowed into Yemen, particularly from China, the Soviet Union, the World Health Organization and UNICEF. The Arab states appear to be increasingly ready to co-operate with Yemen in providing both financial and practical assistance. Kuwait and Saudi Arabia and, more recently, the United Arab Emirates, have provided schools, hospitals and clinics and many other Arab countries have sent teachers to Yemen. At the end of 1972 the U.A.E. provided a loan of $19 million and further aid was expected in 1974. Qatar has provided aid for schools, hospitals and roads, and radio and television staff training. In 1974 Iraq announced aid for education, health and transport projects and is helping with the Hodeida port improvements. In 1977 Kuwait announced that it aimed to invest about 2,000 million riyals ($441 million) in joint-venture development projects in the private and public sectors, to be carried out under the Yemen's Five-Year Development Plan (1976/77 to 1980/81). The projects include an oil pipeline linking the cities of Sana'a, Hodeida and Taiz, a Kuwaiti-Yemeni bank, a cement plant with a capacity of 500,000 tons per year, a textile plant in Damaar, the Sana'a Hilton hotel, two hotels in Hodeida and Taiz and a number of building projects.

Yemen relies heavily on teachers recruited from Egypt to staff its schools. In 1979 Yemen requested another 1,340 teachers, in addition to about 2,700 already working there. Other Arab countries also make their contribution.

Before 1975 the Government of Yemen had relied rather more on aid from the Eastern bloc countries and had secured arms supplies mainly from the Soviet Union. Since then, however, arms have been purchased increasingly from the U.S.A., with finance provided by Saudi Arabia.

Increased aid is an important factor in the country's economic planning and has played a part in the Yemen's dramatically improved financial position. However, the main factor here has been the flow of remittances from Yemenis working abroad. According to some estimates, there are 1.5 million Yemenis working in Saudi Arabia and the Gulf countries alone and they remitted around $1,000 million in 1977, although the figure has been put as high as $1,500 million. In 1975/76, the most recent year for which payments figures are available, Yemen's trade deficit was 1,666 million riyals and its deficit on goods and services together was 1,470.1 million riyals. However, this was more than offset by net private transfers of 2,057.3 million riyals and net official transfers, including aid, of 513.2 million riyals, so that the current account was actually in surplus by 1,100.4 million riyals. In addition, there was a net capital inflow of 352.3 million riyals. During the period of the Three-Year Plan the cumulative current account surplus was 1,323.4 million riyals and there was also a net capital inflow of 625.2 million riyals.

As a result, the country's international reserves rose from $126.9 million at the end of 1973 to $1,240.4 million at the end of 1977 and were $1,613.1 million at the end of March 1979.

Other relevant indicators are the latest figures for currency in circulation outside the banking system and money supply. Currency in circulation (outside banks) totalled 465.5 million riyals at the end of 1973 and had more than doubled to 1,080.5 million riyals at the end of 1975. By the end of 1976, the relevant figure had doubled yet again in the space of one year to total 2,329 million riyals. By the end of 1978 currency in circulation outside the banks had increased to 4,963 million riyals. Similar growth marked the money supply (currency in circulation plus demand deposits at commercial banks), which rose from 540.9 million riyals at the end of 1973 to 2,787 million riyals at the end of 1976, with a very strong expansion in demand deposits from 91.5 million riyals at the beginning of 1975 to 457.8 million riyals at the end of 1976. By the end of 1978 demand deposits stood at 654.8 million riyals. The total of demand, time and saving deposits increased more than fivefold in the two years to December 1976. The money supply rose by a further 61 per cent to 4,492.3 million riyals in 1977, and to 5,617.8 million riyals in 1978. This monetary expansion has been accompanied by strong inflationary pressures. Consumer prices, on official estimates, rose by 45 per cent in 1973, 25 per cent in 1974, 25 per cent in 1975 and 15 per cent in 1976. Unofficial estimates put the annual rate of inflation as high as 40 per cent.

THE FIVE-YEAR PLAN

Yemen's first development plan was drawn up in 1973 to cover the years 1973/74 to 1975/76, and revised in 1974. Some of the successes of this plan, which laid emphasis on the improvement of basic infrastructure, agriculture and communications, have already been mentioned. During the Plan period G.D.P. grew by 7 per cent per annum. Total allocations amounted to 936 million riyals, of which transport alone received 292 million riyals. Education allocations amounted to 195 million riyals, spending on industry to 91 million riyals and on agriculture to 138 million riyals. Health spending was cut to 48 million riyals in the revised plan. The plan was, of course, financed mainly by foreign investment, the largest source being the World Bank. Considerable support is also expected from the United Nations and the oil-rich Arab states, with some aid from the Eastern block, but on nothing like the scale received by the PDRY. Much work still needs to be done in the social sphere to combat the effects of malnutrition, disease and ignorance and here the United Nations is helping by mounting programmes to teach the ordinary people the principles of nutrition and hygiene. Particular attention was paid in the plan to the development of water resources, both for agriculture and in the towns. Water supply schemes are under way in Sana'a, Hodeida, Taiz and Hajja. There is, however, some indication that injudiciously planned water supply schemes may dangerously lower the water table. An electricity scheme for the Taiz, Sana'a and Hodeida areas is being partly financed by the Arab Fund for Economic and Social Development.

In mid-1977 a new Five-Year Plan was put forward which will involve investment expenditure of 16,600 million riyals ($3,640 million) in the period to 1980/81. Transport and communications will receive the largest share of investment, followed by industry (including electricity and water supplies) and agriculture. Growth in G.D.P., which was around 7 per cent in 1976/77 is expected to accelerate through the Plan period to average at least 8.2 per cent per annum. Specific plan targets include an increase in installed electricity generating capacity from 13.4 MW to 55.2 MW; an increase in potable water capacity in Sana'a, Taiz and Hodeida to four times the present 13,500 cubic metres; the construction of 2,604 kilometres of main roads, of which 685 km. will be asphalt; an increase in installed telephone lines to 42,115 in 1980/81; construction and completion of the Omran cement project, a liquid paper plant in Zubeida and a steel pouring, smelting and rolling plant in Hodeida. In addition, of course, a variety of smaller industrial projects is envisaged in the Plan. Internal finance is expected to provide only 58.6 per cent of total investment requirements. The remainder will, it is hoped, be financed by aid, loans and direct investment.

Saudi Arabia, Kuwait and the ADFAED have already agreed to provide more than half the required aid and loan finance, and discussions are under way with other potential sources of finance, including the World Bank and the UN. A continued flow of aid and, especially, remittances will be vital to maintain external equilibrium as well as to finance investment. The trade deficit, if the Plan is achieved, is projected to increase to 5,878 million riyals in 1980/81, even measured in 1975/76 prices. The new Plan will also face the same non-financial constraints as its predecessor, including lack of basic infrastructure and shortage of skilled labour. The latter problem creates something of a policy dilemma. On the one hand the Government encourages workers to emigrate, partly for training but largely in order to earn foreign currency; on the other hand it attempts to entice skilled labour back again, but this is not easily done without adequate financial incentives.

STATISTICAL SURVEY

AREA AND POPULATION

Area	Total* (1975)	Sana'a (capital) (1975)	Taiz (1975)	Hodeida (1975)
200,000 sq. km.	6,471,893	447,898	320,323	147,982

* Provisional census result.

AGRICULTURE

PRINCIPAL CROPS
(July 1st to June 30th)

	1973/74		1974/75		1975/76	
	Area ('000 hectares)	Production ('000 metric tons)	Area ('000 hectares)	Production ('000 metric tons)	Area ('000 hectares)	Production ('000 metric tons)
Sorghum and millet	952	639	1,215	1,008	1,145	859
Wheat	70	71	50	56	50	52
Barley	77	85	73	80	68	80
Maize	52	80	50	79	50	72
Pulses	65	64	71	71	76	76
Potatoes	5.9	64	6.5	71	6.8	76
Vegetables	16	150	8	168	20	183
Grapes	8.5	31	8.5	40	8.8	42.4
Coffee	4.5	3.5	4	3	4	3
Cotton	20	20	28.3	27.2	15	13.9
Tobacco	4.2	5	4.2	5	4.6	5.6

LIVESTOCK

(FAO estimates, 'ooo head, year ending September)

	1975	1976	1977
Horses . . .	4	4	4
Asses . . .	650	640	650
Cattle . . .	923	1,000	1,050
Camels . . .	83	120	121
Sheep . . .	2,940	3,200	3,300
Goats . . .	6,860	7,400	7,600
Poultry . . .	2,850	3,170	3,230

Source: FAO, *Production Yearbook.*

LIVESTOCK PRODUCTS

(FAO estimates, 'ooo metric tons)

	1975	1976	1977
Beef and veal . .	14	14	14
Mutton and lamb .	12	13	13
Goats' meat . .	37	37	38
Poultry meat . .	2	2	2
Cows' milk . .	60	60	64
Sheep's milk . .	49	49	50
Goats' milk . .	128	128	128
Cheese . . .	16.2	16.2	16.5
Butter . . .	3.7	3.7	3.8
Hen eggs . .	2.7	2.8	2.9
Cattle hides . .	2.2	2.2	2.2
Sheep skins . .	2.1	2.1	2.2
Goat skins . .	6.1	6.1	6.2

Source: FAO, *Production Yearbook.*

SEA FISHING

('ooo metric tons, live weight)

	1972*	1973*	1974	1975	1976	1977
Indian mackerel	3.8	4.2	3.3	3.9	4.5	4.7
Other fishes .	5.5	5.8	9.1	10.7	12.0	12.8
TOTAL CATCH .	9.3	10.0	12.4	14.6	16.5	17.5

* FAO estimate.

Source: FAO, *Yearbook of Fishery Statistics.*

INDUSTRY

SELECTED PRODUCTS

		1973/74	1974/75	1975/76
Cotton textiles . .	million yards	11.1	10.1	8.4
Electricity . . .	million kWh.	25.8	31.6	34.3
Aluminium products . .	tons	200.0	200.0	200.0
Paints	'ooo gallons	48.0	54.0	60.0
Mineral drinks . . .	million bottles	27.2	27.5	27.8
Cement	hundred tons	50.0	55.0	63.0

Source: Central Bank of Yemen.

FINANCE

100 fils = 1 Yemeni riyal.
Coins: 1, 5, 10, 25 and 50 fils.
Notes: 1, 5, 10, 20, 50 and 100 riyals.
Exchange rates (June 1979): £1 sterling = 9.44 Yemeni riyals; U.S. $1 = 4.56 Yemeni riyals.
100 Yemeni riyals = £10.59 = $ 21.92.

Note: The Yemeni riyal was introduced in 1964, with an initial value of 6s. 8d. sterling (£1 = 3.00 riyals) or 93.33 U.S. cents (U.S. $1 = 1.071 riyals). Thereafter, the authorities allowed the currency to depreciate on the free market while applying a system of multiple official exchange rates. By 1970 the free rate was $1 = 5.50 riyals (£1 = 13.20 riyals). In June 1971 multiple practices were eliminated, leaving a single rate which held fairly stable at $1 = 5.00 riyals until February 1973, since when the Central Bank has set a selling rate of $1 = 4.50 riyals. The mid-point rate was $1 = 4.575 riyals until April 1975, since when it has been $1 = 4.5625 riyals. Before 1975 the riyal was divided into 40 buqsha, rather than 100 fils. Notes of 10 and 20 buqsha have been withdrawn from circulation but coins of ½, 1 and 2 buqsha are still in use.

BUDGET

('000 riyals, year ending June 30th)

	Revenue	Expenditure
1977/78	1,550,000	2,053,000
1978/79	2,193,375	3,177,090
1979/80	3,013,000	4,384,000

Source: Ministry of Treasury and Central Bank of Yemen.

DEVELOPMENT PLAN, 1976/77 to 1980/81

(proposed expenditure in million riyals)

Transport and communications	4,600
Industry and mining	4,300
Electricity and water	2,000
Housing	2,000
Agriculture	2,600
Other	3,000
Total	16,500

EXTERNAL TRADE

('000 riyals, year ending June 30th)

	1972/73	1973/74	1974/75	1975/76	1976/77	1977/78
Imports	410,666	744,980	981,004	1,706,894	3,035,329	6,194,926
Exports	25,269	55,382	52,966	50,063	50,534	33,416

PRINCIPAL COMMODITIES
('000 riyals)

IMPORTS	1974/75	1975/76	1976/77	1977/78
Food and live animals	418,631	741,569	868,352	1,543,388
Beverages and tobacco	29,113	44,375	48,985	134,645
Crude materials (inedible) except fuels	3,100	6,599	12,689	31,155
Mineral fuels, lubricants, etc.	35,964	81,118	58,897	169,870
Animal and vegetable oils and fats	3,565	7,852	11,200	44,588
Chemicals	66,154	82,834	155,335	350,738
Basic manufactures	193,114	310,679	668,207	1,533,400
Machinery and transport equipment	149,585	289,561	965,678	1,816,690
Miscellaneous manufactured articles	79,642	140,413	243,043	534,043
Unspecified items	2,136	1,894	2,943	36,410
TOTAL	981,004	1,706,894	3,035,329	6,194,926

EXPORTS	1973/74	1974/75	1975/76	1976/77
Cotton	35,180	28,188	24,221	24,953
Coffee	6,461	4,972	7,588	10,223
Hides and skins	6,241	4,404	8,040	6,129
Cotton seed	1,873	2,766	362	—
Biscuits	1,315	1,131	2,093	3,156
Dried fish	781	736	325	56
Live animals	643	443	6	—
Potatoes	195	141	135	17
Rock salt	26	1	1	—
Qat	—	—	395	796
Cotton fabrics	—	1,193	775	165
Cotton sheets	325	257	609	472
TOTAL (incl. others)	55,382	52,966	50,063	50,534

PRINCIPAL TRADING PARTNERS
('000 riyals)

IMPORTS	1974/75	1975/76	1976/77	1977/78
Australia	44,172	133,298	160,050	249,581
China, People's Republic	114,095	139,358	134,474	209,146
Djibouti	28,216	77,126	129,273	177,606
France	29,583	56,064	117,009	353,116
Germany, Federal Republic	59,417	80,254	177,348	352,272
Hong Kong	24,799	43,327	53,843	138,848
India	27,062	146,950	178,223	290,153
Italy	24,964	40,859	121,876	322,845
Japan	170,712	239,590	409,971	785,143
Netherlands	37,424	105,801	109,450	239,024
Saudi Arabia	56,750	118,650	374,277	987,517
Singapore	26,064	57,773	143,617	264,870
United Kingdom	49,673	89,961	169,565	306,172
Yemen, People's Democratic Republic	47,243	84,229	138,660	349,372

EXPORTS	1974/75	1975/76	1976/77	1977/78
China, People's Republic	22,092	24,625	24,939	40
Djibouti	434	534	846	2,898
France	316	688	60	279
Italy	4,340	8,693	5,988	2,866
Japan	7,258	150	200	91
Saudi Arabia	2,542	4,592	4,510	4,998
U.S.S.R.	1,012	—	—	485
Yemen, People's Democratic Republic	6,349	8,423	12,592	20,067

Source: Central Bank of Yemen.

TRANSPORT

ROAD TRAFFIC 1973

Private cars 2,288, motor cycles 6,063, taxis 3,329, trucks 6,957.

SHIPPING

	Vessels Entering Hodeida Port	Tonnage Unloaded
1972	506	506,991
1973	520	530,943

CIVIL AVIATION
(Yemen Airways)

	Passengers Carried	Freight (tons)
1972	48,600	567
1973	43,400	431

EDUCATION

(1976/77)

	Pupils		
	Male	Female	Total
Primary	191,258	30,224	221,482
Intermediate	15,249	2,427	17,676
Higher Secondary (General)	6,485	712	7,197
Higher Secondary (Commercial)	212	—	212
Higher Secondary (Trades)	291	—	291
Primary Teacher Training	626	486	1,112
Secondary Teacher Training	363	175	538

Source (except where otherwise stated): Yemen Arab Republic Central Planning Organization.

PROVISIONAL CONSTITUTION

(*Published June 19th*, 1974)

In the name of the people, the Chairman of the Command Council, having taken cognizance of Command Council Proclamation No. 1 for 1974, Command Council Proclamation No. 4 for 1974 suspending the Constitution, and Command Council Proclamation No. 5 for 1974 increasing the membership of the Command Council, and desiring to consolidate the bases of authority during the transitional period and to regulate the rights and duties of all employees in a manner conducive to fruitful production to raise the country to the level which we all hope it will attain, we announce in the name of the people that during the transitional period the country will be governed in accordance with the following rules:

Chapter One: General Principles: the State:

Article 1: Yemen is an Arab, Islamic, and independent state enjoying full sovereignty. Its system is republican. The Yemeni people are a part of the Arab nation.

Article 2: The people are the source of all authority.

Article 3: Islam is the state religion and Arabic the official state language.

Article 4: The Islamic Sharia is the source of all laws.

Article 5: Yemen is an indivisible whole and its defence is the sacred duty of all citizens.

Chapter Two: Rights and Duties:

Article 6: Yemenis have equal rights and general duties.

Article 7: Personal freedom is guaranteed in accordance with the provisions of the law.

Article 8: There shall be no crime and no penalty except as laid down by law and there shall be no penalty for acts except those committed after the promulgation of the law (applying to them).

Article 9: Homes are inviolate: it is therefore inadmissible to enter them except in such instances as prescribed by the law.

Article 10: The confiscation of funds is prohibited, except within the confines of the law.

Article 11: No person's property shall be expropriated except in the public interest, in the instances prescribed by the law, and with just compensation to the person.

Article 12: The citizens have the right to express their thoughts by means of speech, writing, or voting within the confines of the law.

Article 13: Places of worship and learning have immunity which cannot be violated except in instances required by security needs and as prescribed by the law.

Chapter Three: The System of Government:

Article 14: The Chairman of the Command Council shall assume the function of general sovereignty, particularly in taking the measures he deems necessary to protect the revolution and the republican régime.

Article 15: The Command Council shall assume the functions of the legislative and executive authorities of the state. It shall also have the power to lay down general policy and define its general framework.

Article 16: The Government is the executive and administrative body responsible for carrying out the state's general policy as laid down by the Command Council.

Article 17: The judiciary is independent, and there shall be no authority over it except for the law. Its verdicts shall be handed down and executed in accordance with the principles of the Sharia.

Chapter Four: Concluding Rules:

Article 18: All the rules determined by the laws, bylaws and decisions prior to the issuance of this constitutional declaration shall remain in force unless they conflict with the rules of this declaration or unless they are amended or revoked.

Article 19: During the transitional period action shall be taken to restore constitutional and democratic life on sound bases in view of the need to provide the Yemeni people with a dignified life and a bright future.

Article 20: This constitutional declaration shall come into force from the date of its issuance and it shall be published in the Official Gazette.

In February 1978 a Constituent People's Assembly was appointed by the Command Council to (i) propose the form of the presidency; (ii) amend the constitution, (iii) carry out various functions related to the eventual holding of parliamentary elections; (iv) review and give recommendations on the budget, domestic and foreign affairs, draft laws, etc.

THE GOVERNMENT

HEAD OF STATE

President: Lt.-Col. Ali Abdullah Saleh (took office July 17th, 1978).

Vice-President: Qadi Abdul Karim al-Arashi.

CABINET

(*July* 1979)

Prime Minister: Abdel-Aziz Abdel-Ghani.

Minister of the Interior: Lt.-Col. Muhammad Hamud Khamis.

Deputy Premier for Economic Affairs and Minister of Finance: Muhammad Ahmed Junaid.

Deputy Premier for Domestic Affairs: Lt.-Col. Mujahid Abu Shawrib.

Deputy Premier for Foreign Affairs and Foreign Minister: Hasan Muhammad Makki.

Minister of Transport and Communications: Ahmed Muhammad Ansi.

Minister of Development and Chairman of Central Planning Organization: Ali Lutfi Thor.

Minister of Economy: Muhammad Hezam Shohaji.

Minister of Information and Culture: Yahya Hussein al-Arashi.

Minister of Justice: Ismail Ahmad Wazir.

Minister of Education: Muhammad Khadim Wajih.

Minister of Waqfs: Ali bin Ali Samman.

Minister of Supply and Trade: Saleh Jamali.

Minister of Health: Muhammad Ahmad Asbahi.

Minister of Social, Labour and Youth Affairs: Ahmed Saleh Ruaini.

Minister of Agriculture: Abd al-Wahab Mahmud Abd al-Hamid.

Minister of Works: Abdulla al-Kurshumi.

Minister of Municipalities: Ahmad al-Mihanni.

Minister of State and Chairman of the Oil and Mineral Resources Organization: Ahmad Sayed Barakat.

Minister of State and Adviser to the Prime Minister for Information Affairs: Lt.-Col. Lutfi al-Kilabi.

Minister of State and Adviser to the Presidency and Cabinet: Hussein Ali al-Hubayshi.

CONSTITUENT PEOPLE'S ASSEMBLY

Speaker: Qadi Abdul Karim al-Arashi.

Composed of 99 members appointed by the Command Council in February 1978 for a term of between three and five years. In May 1979 it was announced that the Assembly would be iucreased to 159 members.

DIPLOMATIC REPRESENTATION

EMBASSIES ACCREDITED TO THE YEMEN ARAB REPUBLIC

(In Sana'a unless otherwise stated)

Algeria: Ali Abdul Moghni St.; *Ambassador:* Mohammed Sabbagh (also accred. to the People's Democratic Republic of Yemen).

Austria: Jeddah, Saudi Arabia.

Belgium: Jeddah, Saudi Arabia.

Bulgaria: Cairo, Egypt.

China, People's Republic: Zubairy St.; *Ambassador:* Shao Chin.

Czechoslovakia: Gamal Abdul Naser St.; *Chargé d'Affaires:* František Kropacek.

Denmark: Jeddah, Saudi Arabia.

Ethiopia: Zubairy St.; *Ambassador:* (vacant).

France: Gamal Abdul Naser St.; *Ambassador:* Luc Baldit.

German Democratic Republic: 26 September St.; *Ambassador:* Walter Issleib.

Germany, Federal Republic: Republican Palace St.; *Ambassador:* Klaus Max.

Greece: Jeddah, Saudi Arabia.

Hungary: Cairo, Egypt.

India: Haddah St.; *Ambassador:* B. D. Goswami.

Iran: *Ambassador:* Amireddin Eftekhar.

Iraq: Ali Zubiri St.; *Ambassador:* Taha'a Yasin Ali.

Italy: Gamal Abdul Naser St.; *Ambassador:* Lorenzo Baracchi Tua.

Japan: Tareeq Al-Darie, Safaye Al-Garbiya; *Ambassador:* (vacant).

Jordan: Hadda Rd.; *Ambassador:* SALEH AL-SHERE (also accred. to the People's Democratic Republic of Yemen).

Korea, Democratic People's Republic: Zubairy St.; *Chargé d'affaires:* CHOI IN SAB.

Kuwait: Hadda Rd.; *Ambassador:* TALA'AT AL-GHOSSAIN (also accred. to the People's Democratic Republic of Yemen).

Lebanon: Hadda Rd.; *Chargé d'affaires:* HIKMAT NASIR (also accred. to the People's Democratic Republic of Yemen).

Libya: Zubairy St.; *Ambassador:* FARAJ ALI BIN GALIL.

Netherlands: House of Abdullah Safaar, nr. Old Radio Station; *Ambassador:* D. T. SCHUURMAN VOKLER.

Norway: Jeddah, Saudi Arabia.

Oman: Hadda Rd.; *Ambassador:* MOHAMED SAEED AL-MANHOUR.

Pakistan: Cairo, Egypt.

Poland: Cairo, Egypt.

Qatar: Jeddah, Saudi Arabia.

Romania: Khartoum, Sudan.

Saudi Arabia: Arman Bldg.; *Ambassador:* TARRAD AL-HARES.

Somalia: Wadi Dahr St.; *Ambassador:* ABDUL NOOR AHMED MAHMOUD.

Spain: Cairo, Egypt.

Sudan: Al Rasda St.; *Ambassador:* MAJIID BASHIR AL-AHMADI.

Sweden: Jeddah, Saudi Arabia.

Switzerland: Jeddah, Saudi Arabia.

Syria: Zubairy St.; *Ambassador:* ASSAF HASSOUN (also accred. to the People's Democratic Republic of Yemen).

Tunisia: Jeddah, Saudi Arabia.

Turkey: Jeddah, Saudi Arabia.

U.S.S.R.: 26 September St.; *Ambassador:* VASILI KORNEV.

United Arab Emirates: Hadda Rd.; *Ambassador:* SAIF SA'IID SAA'ID.

United Kingdom: 11/13 Qasr Al Jumhuri St., P.O.B. 1287; *Ambassador:* JULIAN WALKER, M.B.E. (also accred to Djibouti).

U.S.A.: Beit Al-Halali; *Ambassador:* GEORGE M. LANE.

Viet-Nam: Cairo, Egypt.

Yugoslavia: Kuwait City, Kuwait.

The Yemen Arab Republic also has diplomatic relations with Albania, Djibouti, Mali, Malta, Mexico, Nigeria, Portugal and Uganda.

JUDICIAL SYSTEM

President of the State Security Court: Qadhi GHALIB ABDULLA RAJEH (political cases).

Public Prosecutor: Lt.-Col. MUHAMMAD KHAMIS.

Attorney General: Lt.-Col. MUHSIN MUHAMMAD AL-ULUFI.

Sharia Court: Sana'a; deals with cases related to Islamic law.

Disciplinary Court: prosecution office for maladministration and misappropriation of public funds; Chair. MUHAMMAD ABDO NUMAN.

THE PRESS

DAILIES

Al Gumhuryyah (*The Republic*): Information Office, Taiz; Arabic; government-owned.

Al Thawra (*The Revolution*): Ministry of Information, Sana'a; Arabic; government-owned.

WEEKLY AND OTHER

Al Bilad: P.O.B. 1438, Sana'a; Arabic; weekly; inclined to right.

Mareb: Dar Al-Qalam, Taiz; Arabic; weekly; supports Nasserite ideas.

Al Risalah: 26 September St., Sana'a; Arabic; weekly.

As-Sabah: P.O.B. 599, Hodeida; Arabic; weekly; reformist.

As-Salam: P.O.B. 181, Sana'a; f. 1948; Arabic; weekly; political, economic and general essays; circ. 7,000; Editor ABDULLA ASSAKAL.

Sana'a: P.O.B. 193, Sana'a; Arabic; fortnightly; inclined to left.

Al Shab: Al-Andalus Bookshop, Sana'a; Arabic; weekly; slightly left-inclined.

Al-Ta'wn: Al Ta'wn Building, Jubairi St., Sana'a; Arabic; weekly; supports co-operative societies.

Al-Yemen: Sana'a; Arabic; fortnightly; inclined to right.

NEWS AGENCY

Saba News Agency: Sana'a; f. 1970; Dir. HASSAN AL-ULUFI.

RADIO AND TELEVISION

Radio Hodeida: Hodeida; government-controlled local radio; broadcasts in Arabic, 4 hours daily.

Radio Sana'a: Sana'a; government-controlled station, broadcasts in Arabic, 15 hours daily; Dir.-Gen. ABDUL RAHMAN AL-MUTARIB.

Radio Taiz: Taiz; government-controlled station; broadcasts in Arabic, 4 hours daily.

There are 250,000 receiving sets.

A television station opened in September 1975 and a new TV station opened in Taiz in December 1978.

FINANCE

BANKING

(cap.=capital; p.u.=paid up; m.=million; br.=branch; amounts in riyals)

Central Bank of Yemen: P.O.B. 59, Sana'a; f. 1971; cap. p.u. 10m.; Gov. and Chair. (vacant); Deputy Gov. and Deputy Chair. ABDULLA SANABANI; Gen. Man. ABDULLAH A. AL-BARAKANI.

Yemen Bank for Reconstruction and Development: P.O.B. 541, Sana'a; f. 1962; cap. 10m.; consolidated bank; 8 brs.; Chair. MOHSIN SIRRY.

Bank of Credit and Commerce International S.A.: P.O.B. 160, Sana'a.

Arab Bank Ltd.: P.O.B. 68, Amman, Jordan; Tahrir (Liberation) Square, Sana'a; br. in Hodeida.

British Bank of the Middle East: P.O.B. 3932, Hodeida:. Man. I. M. REVOLTA; P.O.B. 4886, Taiz; Man. M. W. MALCOLM.

Citibank: P.O.B. 2133, Sana'a.

Habib Bank Ltd.: Karachi, Pakistan; P.O.B. 3927, Al-Akhwa, Hodeida.

United Bank of Pakistan: Ali Abdul Mugni St., Sana'a.

INSURANCE

Yemen General Insurance Co. S.A.Y.: Asia Hotel Bldg., Sana'a St., P.O.B. 3952, Hodeida; all classes of insurance.

TRADE AND INDUSTRY

CHAMBERS OF COMMERCE

Hodeida Chamber of Commerce: Azzoubairi St., P.O.B. 3370, Hodeida.

Sana'a Chamber of Commerce: Bab El-Yemen, P.O.B. 195, Sana'a.

Taiz Chamber of Commerce: 26th September St., P.O.B. 1029, Taiz.

Ibb also has a Chamber of Commerce.

NATIONALIZED ORGANIZATIONS

General Cotton Organization: Sana'a.

Hodeida Electricity and Water Company: P.O.B. 3363, Hodeida; affiliate of Yemen Bank for Reconstruction and Development.

National Tobacco and Matches Co.: P.O.B. 3571, Hodeida; f. 1964; monopoly importing and sales organization for tobacco and matches; cigarette manufacture and tobacco growing; Chair. A. A. NAGI.

Yemen Company for Foreign Trade: Hodeida.

Yemen Petroleum Co.: YPC Bldg., P.O.B. 3360, Hodeida; sole petroleum supplier; Chair. HUSSAIN ABDULLAH AL MAKDANI; Gen. Man. YEHIA ABDULLAH AL-DAILAMI.

Yemen Printing and Publishing Co.: P.O.B. 1081, Sana'a; f. 1970; publishes ten newspapers (including two government newspapers); Chair. AHMAD MUHAMMAD HADI.

TRANSPORT

ROADS

There are about 1,650 km. of main roads, of which about 600 km. are asphalted and the rest gravelled. Highways run from Hodeida to Sana'a, and from Moka to Taiz, Ibb and Sana'a. A highway from Sana'a to Saada was opened in May 1977.

SHIPPING

Hodeida is a Red Sea port of some importance, and the Yemen Navigation Company runs passenger and cargo services to many parts of the Middle East and Africa.

Adafar Yemenite Line: Hodeida.

Hodeida Shipping and Transport Co.: P.O.B. 3337, Hodeida.

Middle East Shipping Co.: P.O.B. 3700, Hodeida; brs. in Mocha and Saleef.

CIVIL AVIATION

There are three international airports—Al Rahaba at Sana'a, Al Ganad at Taiz and Hodeida Airport.

Yemen Airways: Zubery St., Sana'a; internal services and external services to Abu Dhabi, Aden, Cairo, Damascus, Dharan, Djibouti, Doha, Jeddah, Khartoum, Kuwait and Sharjah; supervised by a ministerial committee headed by the Minister of Communications; Chair. and Pres. SHAIF MOHAMMED SAEED; fleet of 2 DC-6, 1 Boeing 737-15, 3 DC-3.

The following airlines also serve the Yemen: Aeroflot (U.S.S.R.), Air Djibouti, Al Yamda (Yemen P.D.R.), Ethiopian Airlines, Kuwait Airways, Somali Airlines, Sudan Airways, Syrian Arab Airlines and Saudi Arabian Airlines in addition to charter flights by various carriers.

DEFENCE

Commander-in-Chief of the Armed Forces: Lt.-Col. ABDEL-AZIZ BARTI.

Defence Budget: 360 million riyals (1977/78).

Military Service: 3 years.

Total Armed Forces: 38,000: army 36,000, navy 500, air force 1,500; paramilitary forces: 20,000 tribal levies.

EDUCATION

The development of a modern educational system in the Yemen Arab Republic gained impetus after the 1962 revolution. However, the implementation of extensive educational reform was delayed by the civil war which extended until 1967. The latest statistics on the number of pupils can be found in the Statistical Survey. The University of Sana'a had 2,760 pupils in the 1976/77 academic year.

In addition to military colleges, more specific institutions are being established under the Educational Development Project, especially in the field of vocational training.

UNIVERSITY

University of Sana'a: P.O.B. 1247, Sana'a; f. 1974; 89 teachers, 3,139 students.

BIBLIOGRAPHY

ANSALDI, C. Il Yemen nella storia e nella leggenda (Rome, 1933).

ATTAR, MOHAMED SAID EL-. Le sous-développement Economique et Social du Yémen (Editions Tiers-Monde, Algiers, 1966).

BALSAN, FRANÇOIS. Inquiétant Yémen (Paris, 1961).

BETHMANN, E. W. Yemen on the Threshold (American Friends of the Middle East, Washington, 1960).

COLONIAL OFFICE. Aden and the Yemen (H.M.S.O., London, 1960).

DEUTSCH, ROBERT. Der Yemen (Vienna, 1914).

DOE, BRIAN. Southern Arabia (Thames and Hudson, London, 1972).

FAROUGHY, A. Introducing Yemen (New York, 1947).

FAYEIN, CLAUDE. A French Doctor in the Yemen (Robert Hale, London, 1957).

HELFRITZ, H. The Yemen: A Secret Journey (Allen and Unwin, London, 1958).

HEYWORTH-DUNNE, G. E. Al-Yemen: Social, Political and Economic Survey (Cairo, 1952).

INGRAMS, HAROLD. The Yemen; Imams, Rulers and Revolutions (London, 1963).

MACRO, ERIC. Bibliography of the Yemen, with Notes on Mocha (University of Miami Press, 1959).

Yemen and the Western World since 1571 (C. Hurst, London, and Praeger, New York, 1968).

O'BALLANCE, EDGAR. The War in the Yemen (Faber, London, 1971).

PAWELKE, GUNTHER. Der Yemen: Das Verbotene Land (Econ. Verlag., Düsseldorf, 1959).

SCHMIDT, DANA ADAMS. Yemen, the Unknown War (Bodley Head, London, 1968).

SCOTT, H. In the High Yemen (Murray, London, 1942).

U.S.G.P.O. Geology of the Arabian Peninsula: Yemen (Washington, 1967).

WENNER, MANFRED W. Yemen: a selected Bibliography of Literature since 1960 (Library of Congress Legislative Reference Service, Washington, D.C., 1965).

Modern Yemen, 1918-1966 (Johns Hopkins Press, Baltimore, U.S.A., 1967).

People's Democratic Republic of Yemen

(Southern Yemen)

PHYSICAL AND SOCIAL GEOGRAPHY

W. B. Fisher

On November 30th, 1967, the People's Republic of Southern Yemen came into existence, formed from the former British Colony and Protectorate of Aden (75 sq. miles and 111,000 sq. miles respectively), together with the islands of Perim (5 sq. miles) and Kamaran (22 sq. miles). Socotra (1,400 sq. miles) elected to join the new state. The Kuria Muria group of islands were returned to Muscat by Britain but the new Republican government revoked this decision. In November 1970 the name of the Republic was changed to the "People's Democratic Republic of Yemen". The capital is Aden. The state is divided into eight governorates which replace Aden and the 20 states of the old South Arabian Protectorate. The Republic lies at the southern end of the Arabian peninsula, approximately between longitude 43° and 56°E., with Perim Island a few miles due west, in the strait marking the southern extremity of the Red Sea; Kamaran Island some 200 miles north of Perim; Socotra and the Kuria Muria groups in the extreme east, the former at the entrance to the Gulf of Aden, the latter near the coast of Oman. The Republic has frontiers with the Yemen Arab Republic, Saudi Arabia, and Oman, but none of these frontiers is fully delimited, and in some instances they are disputed. Atlases still show considerable variation in the precise boundaries of all four territories, or sometimes do not indicate them at all.

Physically, the Republic comprises the broken and dislocated southern edge of the great plateau of Arabia. This is an immense mass of ancient granites, once forming part of Africa, and covered in many places by shallow, generally horizontal layers of younger sedimentary rocks. The whole plateau has undergone downwarping in the east and elevation in the west, so that the highest land (over 10,000 ft.) occurs in the extreme west, near the Red Sea, with a gradual decline to the lowest parts (under 1,000 ft.) in the extreme east. The whole of the southern and western coasts of the Republic were formed by a series of enormous fractures, which produced a flat but very narrow coastal plain, rising steeply to the hill country a short distance inland. Percolation of molten magma along the fracture-lines has given rise to a number of volcanic craters, now extinct, and one of these, partly eroded and occupied by the sea, forms the site of Aden port.

An important topographic feature is the Wadi Hadhramaut, an imposing valley running parallel to the coast at 100–150 miles distance inland. In its upper and middle parts, this valley is broad, and occupied by a seasonal torrent; in its lower (eastern) part it narrows considerably, making a sudden turn south-eastwards and reaching the sea. This lower part is largely uninhabited, but the upper parts, where alluvial soil and intermittent flood water are available, are occupied by a farming population.

The details of climate in the Republic are simple to state, but extremely difficult to explain. Rainfall is everywhere scanty, but relatively more abundant on the highlands and in the west. Thus Aden itself has 5 in. of rain annually, entirely in winter (December-March), whilst in the lowlands of the extreme east, it may rain only once in five or ten years. In the highlands a few miles north of Aden, falls of up to 30 in. occur, for the most part during summer, and this rainfall also gradually declines eastwards, giving 15–20 in. in the highlands of Dhofar. Ultimately, to the north and east, rainfall diminishes to almost nil, as the edges of the Arabian Desert are reached. This unusual situation of a reversal in climatic conditions over a few miles is thought to be the result of two streams of air; an upper one, damp and unstable in summer, and originating in the equatorial regions of East Africa; and a lower current, generally drier and related to conditions prevailing over the rest of the Middle East. In this way the low lying coastal areas have a maximum of rainfall in winter, and the hills of both the Yemens a maximum in summer. Temperatures are everywhere high, particularly on the coastal plain, which has a southern aspect: mean figures of 76°F. (Jan.) to 89° (June) occur at Aden town, but maxima of over 100° are common.

Except on the higher parts, which have a light covering of thorn scrub (including dwarf trees which exude a sap from which incense and myrrh are derived), and the restricted patches of cultivated land, the territory of the Republic is devoid of vegetation. Cultivation is limited to small level patches of good soil on flat terraces alongside the river beds, on the floor and sides of the Wadi Hadhramaut, or where irrigation from wells and cisterns can be practised. The most productive areas are: Lahej, close to Aden town; two districts near Mukalla (about 300 miles east of Aden), and parts of the middle Hadhramaut. Irrigation from cisterns hollowed out of the rock has long been practised, and Aden town has a famous system of this kind, dating back many centuries.

HISTORY

ADEN COLONY

When the Portuguese first rounded the Cape of Good Hope (1497–98), Aden was a port of some commercial importance, acting as a rendezvous for ships bound from India to the Red Sea and at the same time enjoying an active local trade with the Persian Gulf and the coast of East Africa. In 1513 the Portuguese, under Albuquerque, tried to capture the town, though without success. The Ottoman Turks, in their endeavour to deny the Portuguese access to the Red Sea, seized Aden in 1538, but their hold on the Yemen proved to be precarious. There was a serious revolt against the Ottoman régime in 1547–51 and a still more dangerous rebellion in 1566–70. When in the course of the seventeenth century the Ottoman state fell into decline, the authority of the Sultan over this distant region became little more than nominal, effective power in the Yemen passing now into the hands of local chieftains, the most notable of whom, after 1735, was the Sultan of Lahej. The discovery of the Cape route to India had greatly diminished the prosperity of Aden as a commercial entrepôt, but with the Napoleonic campaign in Egypt in 1798, Aden assumed strategic importance in Britain's plan of containment. In 1799 Britain occupied the island of Perim. Shortage of water compelled a withdrawal to the mainland where friendly relations were established with the Sultan of Lahej with whom later in 1902 a commercial treaty was concluded. However, the need to possess a base in these waters under the British flag doubled with the coming of the steamship. Negotiations began for the purchase of the island of Socotra, which in 1834 was temporarily occupied by the East India Company; they might have succeeded had not the relations with the Sultan suddenly deteriorated in 1837 following the plunder near Aden of a wrecked Indian vessel flying the British flag. The incident was followed by the despatch by the East India Company of a British force from Bombay, under the command of Captain Haines of the Indian navy, which, on January 16th, 1839, captured Aden. By the peace treaty, the Sultan was guaranteed an annual sum of 6,000 dollars and Aden became part of the British Empire, administered by the government of Bombay. The Sultan did not finally abandon his efforts to regain Aden until 1857 when permanent peace was established with Britain. Perim Island was ceded in the same year. The Kuria Muria Islands had already been acquired in 1854 from the Sultan of Oman. With the opening of the Suez Canal and the revival of the Red Sea route, Aden, which had been a free port since 1853, increased in importance. In the twentieth century, with the gradual replacement of coal by oil, Aden, closely linked to the Persian Gulf area, enhanced its historic position as a fuelling station. Aden's strategic value is also based on plentiful supplies of fresh drinking water from the artesian wells at Shaikh Othman.

In 1932, the administration of Aden passed to the Governor-General of India in Council; in April 1937, it was vested in a separately appointed governor, who was also commander-in-chief, and who was assisted by an Executive Council. Crown Colony status had in fact been granted two years previously by the Government of India Act 1935. A Legislative Council for Aden, granted in 1944, was inaugurated in 1947. In 1955 the Aden Colony (Amendment) Order came into force, providing for an elected element in the Council; the first elections were held in December of the same year. Further constitutional changes were made in 1959. On January 4th, 1959, voting took place for the choice of 12 elected members of the Legislative Council. Nine Arabs, 2 Somalis and 1 Indian were elected to the Council. Large numbers of the Arab population boycotted the election.

On January 16th, 1961, Sir Charles Johnston, the Governor of Aden, announced to the Legislative Council of Aden that the (then) Colonial Secretary, Mr. Macleod, had approved a ministerial system of government for Aden and that members of the Executive Council in charge of administrative departments would soon assume ministerial status. The Governor also spoke of a possible closer association with the West Aden Protectorate and in particular with the Federation of Arab Amirates of the South. The Federation was renamed the Federation of South Arabia in April 1962. On November 30th, 1967, Aden and the Protectorate of South Arabia achieved independence under the name of the People's Republic of Southern Yemen.

SOUTH ARABIAN PROTECTORATE

Behind Aden and stretching some 600 miles along the coast is the territory of 20 former states whose rulers, between 1882 and 1914, entered into protective treaty relations with the British Government and acknowledged the authority of the Governor of Aden as Governor of the Protectorate. Many of the States later entered into closer treaty relations, and, while retaining independent control in the internal affairs of their respective territories, the rulers accepted the advice on administration offered by British Agents and Political Officers appointed by the Governor. Britain guaranteed protection to the States and they agreed not to cede territory to foreign powers.

EASTERN PROTECTORATE STATES

Formerly named the Eastern Aden Protectorate, the region covered by the States comprised the Hadhramaut (consisting of the Qu'aiti State of Shihr and Mukalla, and the Kathiri State of Sai'un), the Mahra Sultanate of Qishn and Socotra, the Wahidi Sultanates of Balhaf and Bir'ali, and the Sheikhdoms of Irqa and Haura. At July 1st, 1966, the total population of the area was estimated at 326,000. The Qu'aiti Sultan first concluded a protectorate treaty with Britain in 1888. In 1918 following an agreement between the Qu'aiti and the Kathiri Sultans, the latter accepted the protectorate treaty as extending to his State. Both Sultans agreed by further treaties, signed in 1937 and 1939, to accept the advice of a British Agent in all matters except those concerning the religion and custom of Islam. The British Agent for the Eastern Protectorate States was stationed at Mukalla in the territory of the premier chief, the Qu'aiti Sultan of Shihr and Mukalla. Both he and the Kathiri Sultan were constitutional rulers and were assisted by State Councils. Close co-operation existed between the two states in constitutional and in economic matters.

In 1949 an advisory treaty was concluded with the Wahidi Sultan of Balhaf. The Mahra Sultan of Qishn and Socotra signed a treaty of protection with Britain in 1866 and by it the Island of Socotra and the Abd Alkuri and Brothers Islands came within the protectorate.

WESTERN PROTECTORATE STATES

The former Western Protectorate comprised 17 states. Population at July 1st, 1966, was estimated at 570,000. Five of the States, in 1944 and 1945, agreed by advisory treaties with Britain to accept the advice of the Governor of Aden on administrative affairs—the Fadhli, the Lower 'Aulaqi and the Lower Yafa'i Sultans, the Sherif of Beihan and the Amir of Dhala. In 1952 similar treaties were signed by the Upper 'Aulaqi Sheikh and the 'Audhali Sultan; and a joint advisory and protectorate treaty was accepted by the newly elected Sultan of Lahej. The British Political Officers and the Arab Assistant Political Officers for the Western Protectorate States were under the supervision of the Assistant High Commissioner whose headquarters were in Al Ittihad, the Federal capital.

The British authorities, in 1954 and again in 1956, had discussed a plan of federation with local rulers in the West Aden Protectorate. On February 11th, 1959, the rulers of six (out of 17) states in the Western Protectorate signed a Federal Constitution and also a Treaty of Friendship and Protection with Great Britain. The British Government promised financial and military aid which would assist the Federation (embracing 'Audhali, Lower Yafa'i, Fadhli, Dhala, Beihan and Upper 'Aulaqi) to become eventually an independent state. The members of the Federation bound themselves not to enter into foreign relations of whatsoever kind without the approval of Great Britain. Lahej joined the Federation in October 1959, and Lower 'Aulaqi, 'Aqrabi and Dathina in February 1960. The Wahidi States of Balhaf and Bir Ali in the Eastern Aden Protectorate joined in 1962. Aden Colony became a member in January 1963, and Haushabi and Shaib joined in April. In 1965 there were three further accessions: the 'Alawi and Muflahi Sheikhdoms, and the Upper 'Aulaqi Sultanate. The new Federal capital was Al Ittihad near Bir Ahmed.

The U.K. met the cost of defence, including the R.A.F. and Protectorate levy establishments. Beside the security forces maintained by the U.K. Government there were tribal guards in the Western States partially supported by the States, and the Mukalla Regular Army maintained by the Qu'aiti State.

At the end of November 1961 the British Government handed over control of the Aden Protectorate Levies to the Federation of Arab Amirates of the South. The Levies—which would be henceforth the Army of the Federation—had been formed in 1928 to protect Aden on the landward side and to provide garrisons for the Red Sea islands of Perim and Kamaran. An Arab force trained and commanded by British officers, the Levies consisted in 1961 of five infantry battalions, an armoured car squadron, and various signals and administrative units. The Levies came under the control of the Sultan of Lahej, who was Minister of Defence to the Federation, but command of the force still rested in the hands of a British officer as hitherto; for operational purposes the Levies were at the disposal of the G.O.C. Land Forces, Middle East.

ADEN AND THE YEMEN

Relations between the Protectorate and the neighbouring State of the Yemen were at all times delicate. Frequent encroachments led to the demarcation of frontiers which were accepted in a convention signed with the Ottoman government in March 1914. During the first World War, the Turkish troops from Yemen occupied the greater part of the Protectorate, and though in 1919 most of the chiefs resumed their treaty relations with Britain, the Imam of Sana'a, who exercised the principal religious authority in Yemen, being the most powerful of the Chieftains, maintained his claim to the entire territories. He sought to enforce it by occupying the Amiri district including the Radhfan tribes and parts of Haushabi, Sha'ibi and Upper Yafa'i territory, and the Audhali plateau. He also occupied territory not then within the Protectorate, the district of the Beidha Sultan. Britain continually repelled the Imam's advance and in 1928 he was compelled to withdraw from most of the Amiri territory. The Anglo-Yemenite treaty of peace and friendship was signed in February 1934, and was to be valid for 40 years; the two powers agreed to respect the *status quo*, and to negotiate for the classification of frontiers; Britain recognized the independence of the Yemen and the Imam agreed to evacuate the remainder of the Amiri district. In 1950 they agreed further to set up a frontier commission and to exchange diplomatic missions. In 1953 Yemen pressed her claims to the territories of the Aden Protectorate before the United Nations, and in subsequent years there was a series of border incidents. In December 1956 both tribesmen and Yemeni forces were reported to have raided villages in the Protectorate and made invasions into Western Aden. Similar incidents of varying degrees of importance continued until 1959. During this period there was a substantial flow of arms and technicians into the Yemen from the U.S.S.R. and its allies, and in March 1958 a formal union with the U.A.R. was announced. Britain sent troop reinforcements and R.A.F. units to repel these attacks, and in 1958 it established a separate military command in Aden. On two occasions the Yemen brought the dispute before the United Nations on the grounds that the U.K. was committing acts of aggression against her territory.

Incidents along the ill-defined frontier between Aden and the Yemen became less numerous in 1959.

The Governor of Aden paid a visit to Taiz in November 1959 which led to the conclusion of two informal agreements with the Yemen, the first covering civil aircraft flights between Aden and the Yemen, the second establishing local frontier commissions to settle border incidents. The first frontier commission met in February 1960.

In August 1962 the Yemen denounced the agreements reached at the London conference (discussed below), and reiterated its claim to the Aden territories. The revolution which broke out in the Yemen on September 27th, 1962, led to the establishment of a Republic of the Yemen. Colonel Sallal, the leader of the revolution, stated at this time that the new régime did not intend to press a claim to the Aden territories and hoped indeed for friendship with Britain. The U.S.S.R. and the U.A.R. recognized the republican régime almost immediately, and the United States followed suit in December, but Britain refused recognition. The new Yemen government frequently accused Britain of giving assistance to the Royalist resistance during the winter of 1962–63; the British legation at Taiz was closed, there were several minor conflicts in the border area, and another Yemen protest was made at the UN.

British and Federal forces carried out extensive military operations against dissident border tribesmen in 1964 and 1965; officials claimed these measures were necessary mainly because of unrest created by Yemeni agents. Direct clashes with Yemeni forces also occurred; the situation remained complex owing to the continuing presence of Royalist forces in the area. In 1964 Britain proposed that UN observers should patrol the border areas; the republican government, however, would not accept this, claiming that no frontier was necessary as Aden and the Federation all belonged by right to the Yemen. This attitude did not help relations during the independence negotiations or with the new Southern Yemen government.

CONSTITUTIONAL DEVELOPMENTS

In August 1960 Sir Charles Johnston became Governor of Aden in succession to Sir William Luce. The new Governor announced to the Legislative Council of the Aden Colony in January 1961 that a ministerial system was to be introduced into Aden—members of the Executive Council in charge of administrative departments (twelve in all) would soon assume ministerial status. Sir Charles Johnston also noted that efforts were in progress to promote constitutional development within Aden and in particular to bring about a closer association between the West Aden Protectorate and the Federation of Arab Emirates of the South.

A constitutional conference, which included five Ministers from Aden and five from the Federation, met in London (July–August 1962) under the chairmanship of Mr. Duncan Sandys, the Colonial Secretary. The Aden Trade Union Congress and its political wing, the People's Socialist Party (both counted much on the support of Yemenis who worked in Aden and aimed at the ultimate union of the Yemen, Aden, the Federation and the other territories of the West Aden Protectorate) denounced the conference held in London. On July 23rd, 1962, they called a strike to protest against the composition of the existing Legislative Council of Aden and to demand a general election and the establishment of an autonomous government in Aden before further progress should be made towards union with the Federation of Arab Emirates.

The discussions undertaken in August 1962 led to a White Paper recommending the incorporation of Aden into the Federation as a constituent state. It specified that Britain would retain sovereignty over Aden and responsibility for its defence and internal security. These proposals were the principal features of a draft treaty between Britain and the Federation (re-named the Federation of South Arabia); Perim and the Kuria Muria islands, although administered by the governor of Aden, were to be excluded.

There was considerable opposition in Aden to incorporation into the Federation. Several political parties opposed the move, and strikes and demonstrations directed against it occurred throughout 1962. Serious riots coincided with the Aden Legislative Council's passing of the draft treaty in September. Nevertheless, Britain and the Federation duly signed the agreement in January 1963 and Aden formally became a member of the Federation later that month.

ADEN'S INCORPORATION IN THE FEDERATION

Aden's new government consisted of a nine-member Council of Ministers, all Adenis except for the British Attorney-General. Since its principal economic support remained British forces expenditure—£20 million was spent on capital projects alone in the 1962–65 period—it could hardly expect to escape the suspicions of the radical Arab nationalist movements. In May 1963 representatives of the United Nations Committee on decolonization visited Yemen but were not allowed into Aden or the Federation. In July they issued a report—later adopted by the full committee and eventually the General Assembly—which claimed that most of the population disliked "the repressive laws and police methods" of the government; it accused Britain of attempting to prolong its control whilst most South Arabians wanted union with the Yemen. Britain, of course, rejected the report. In the meantime two more states—the Haushabi Sultanate and the Shaibi Sheikdom—had joined the Federation, now 14 strong; on April 1st all customs barriers were abolished within the Federation, Aden remaining a free port.

In December 1963 an attempt to assassinate the High Commissioner in Aden killed two people and injured over fifty; a state of emergency was declared and large numbers of political activists were detained. Although no charges were made, several weeks elapsed before many activists were released, and much opinion in Aden and beyond clearly thought this police treatment was too harsh.

MOVES TOWARDS INDEPENDENCE

In June 1964 a constitutional conference was held in London and an agreement was signed whereby the Federation of South Arabia, inclusive of Aden, would become independent not later than 1968. Further discussions took place in London in August 1965, but the talks failed, and violence in Aden increased. It was estimated that between December 1963 and May 1966 60 people had been killed and 350 injured in Aden alone as a result of terrorism, one-third of the casualties being British. Meanwhile, in March 1965, Mr. Abd al-Qawi Makkawi became Chief Minister of Aden. However, in September 1965 the Aden Council of Ministers was dismissed, and the Colony's constitution suspended, because of mounting terrorism and the Council's failure either to condemn the terrorists or take any action against them.

POLITICAL REALIGNMENTS

The political scene in South Arabia, as viewed from the side of the nationalist elements, presented at this time an appearance of increasing confusion. The People's Socialist Party, led by Mr. Abdallah al-Asnag, had merged, in May 1965, with the Committee for the Liberation of Occupied South Yemen and with the South Arabian League to form the Organization for the Liberation of the Occupied South. A further development took place in January 1966, when the Organization for the Liberation of the Occupied South united with the National Front for the Liberation of the Occupied South, an extremist group operating from the Yemen with Egyptian support and responsible for the campaign of terrorism in Aden. Out of this new fusion of interests came the Front for the Liberation of Occupied South Yemen (FLOSY), in which political figures like Mr. Makkawi and Mr. al-Asnag now began to assume positions of prominence. The South Arabian League, however, declined to accept the prospect of complete absorption in a united nationalist movement and resumed its former independence. As an organization it held moderate nationalist views, rejecting the territorial claims of the Yemen, disapproving of terrorism and of influence emanating from Egypt, and aiming in general at a united state of South Arabia which should embrace Aden, the federal states and also the principalities of the East Aden Protectorate. Over against these various nationalist forces stood the "traditionalist" elements, embodied in the sheikhdoms and sultanates of the South Arabia Federation (and also of the East Aden Protectorate).

Of great importance too, as a factor influencing the affairs of South Arabia was the situation in the Yemen, itself divided between tribesmen loyal to the old Imamate and supported by Saudi Arabia, and the republican régime maintained and controlled by Egypt—a situation, in short, which reflected in itself the confrontation of Egypt and Saudi Arabia for a dominant voice in the affairs of Arabia as a whole.

NEW PROPOSALS FOR ADEN, 1966

The Federation of South Arabia made known in February 1966 proposals which, it was hoped, might serve as a basis for a constitution when South Arabia gained independence in 1968. At the request of the Federal Government in September 1965, two British experts, Sir Ralph Hone and Sir Gawain Bell, had undertaken the task of framing new proposals. Their recommendations now envisaged the creation of a United Republic of South Arabia (including the Hadhramaut area). The republic would be organized on federal lines. Aden, however, together with the federal capital al-Ittihad and the islands of Perim, Kamaran and Kuria Muria, would form within the republic a distinctive "capital territory".

THE DEFENCE QUESTION

In February 1966 the British Government issued a White Paper on Defence, which envisaged large reductions in the use of the armed forces of Great Britain overseas and in the general expenditure on them. The White Paper declared that, when Aden became independent in 1968, all British forces would be withdrawn and concentrated at Bahrain in the Persian Gulf; it also made known that the British Government did not propose to enter into defence agreements with the newly independent state of South Arabia.

This announcement gave grounds for alarm to the sheikhdoms and sultanates embraced within the Federation that the National Guard of the Federation might be confronted in the future with a Yemen able to call on large numbers of Egyptian troops. The federal authorities sent a delegation to London, hoping to persuade the British Government to at least assist with the rapid strengthening of the federal forces and with the provision of equipment. In June the British Government offered to contribute as much as £5,500,000 towards the capital cost of expanding and re-equipping the armed forces of the Federation. It also declared its readiness to continue its contribution (about £5,000,000) to the federal budget each year and to increase, to the extent of some £2,500,000, its share (hitherto about £4,600,000) in the maintenance of the federal troops. This aid was to continue for three years after independence, provided that no radical change occurred in the political situation of an independent South Arabia. The British Government still declined, however, to undertake the defence of South Arabia after it had won independence.

The extreme nationalist organizations had long advocated the acceptance in full of the UN resolutions passed in December 1963. Now, in May 1966, the Federal Government of South Arabia made known its readiness at last to take the resolutions as a basis for future action.

THE UN MISSION

In June 1966 the UN Committee on Colonialism urged that a United Nations Mission be sent to South Arabia to advise on the best means of giving effect to the UN resolutions of 1963 and 1965: resolutions which envisaged the granting of independence to South

Arabia, the withdrawal of British forces, the return of political leaders in exile or in detention and the holding of elections under international supervision. In August 1966 the British Government declared that it welcomed the appointment of such a mission, but it insisted that it could not abandon its responsibilities for the maintenance of good order in South Arabia and that it was bound to observe the agreements which it had made with the local states existing in the area.

PREPARATIONS FOR INDEPENDENCE

In April 1967 Lord Shackleton, Minister without Portfolio, was sent to South Arabia to assist the High Commissioner in examining the possibilities for the establishment of a "caretaker" régime representing all the interested elements in South Arabia. The nationalist organizations continued, however, to reject all appeals for co-operation with the British and the federal authorities.

On June 20th, 1967, the British Government made known the measures that it intended to bring into effect. The date of independence was to be January 9th, 1968. To check the growing violence in South Arabia it was proposed to suspend trial by jury in respect of terrorist activities. On the other hand, the ban on the NLF was to be removed and consideration given to the possible release of some detainees. The British Government also declared that it would be willing to accept a draft constitution which the federal régime was now circulating to its member states. This constitution would prepare the ground for eventual elections on a basis of universal adult suffrage and for the establishment, as soon as circumstances allowed, of an administration representative of all the political elements in South Arabia. Regarding the problem of the uncommitted states in the East Aden Protectorate, Great Britain favoured their union with the Federation of South Arabia. It seemed improbable, however, that such a merger, if it did indeed come about, would occur before South Arabia attained its independence.

During July 1967 Britain continued her efforts to establish in Aden and the associated territories a broad-based provisional administration which should hold office until the moment of independence in January 1968. To facilitate the achievement of this aim the Federal Government consented to invite one of its own members, Mr. Bayumi, to form an interim administration with the aid, if possible, of FLOSY and the NLF. These nationalist organizations remained adamant, however, in their refusal to recognize the federal régime, which, in their view, reflected in its structure pre-eminently the interests of the local sultans. Mr. Bayumi's endeavour to gain the co-operation of the nationalist groups ended in failure and on July 27th the federal authorities relieved him of his appointment as Prime Minister designate.

Meanwhile, in South Arabia itself, during August to October 1967 the authority of the sultans crumbled rapidly before the advancing tide of nationalism. The NLF extended its control over the sheikhdom of Maflahi and over most of the other tribal states. On August 28th Sheikh Ali Musaid al-Babakri, speaking as chairman of the Supreme Council of the South Arabian Federation, admitted that the Federal Government and the Sultans had lost control of events and appealed to the armed forces of South Arabia to take command of the situation. This appeal—which marked in fact the virtual disintegration of the federal regime—was unsuccessful, the South Arabian Army refusing to accept the role thus offered to it. The swift advance of the NLF was due, not least of all, to the alignment on its side of a large measure of support amongst the local tribes against their traditional rulers, and also to the determination of the federal armed forces to maintain a neutral attitude. During September and October the NLF also moved into the territories of the Eastern Aden Protectorate, the sultanates of Qaiti, Kathiri and Mahra now passing under its influence. The High Commissioner announced on September 5th that Britain was now prepared to recognize the nationalist forces in general as representative of the local populations and would be willing to enter into negotiations with them.

THE CLASH BETWEEN NATIONALISTS

The collapse of the federal regime left the main nationalist organizations face to face. There had been discussions between them, under Egyptian auspices, at Cairo and in the Yemen, but without much sign of ultimate agreement. Now, the notable success of the NLF had done much to diminish the prospect before the Front for the Liberation of the Occupied South Yemen. This latter organization was under the disadvantage that it operated largely under Egyptian guidance and not in South Arabia itself, but from the Yemen. Its chief support in Aden had come from the numerous Yemeni elements formerly working there. Of adverse effect, too, was the fact that its leaders, Abdallah al-Asnag and Abd al-Qawi Makkawi, had been working from the Yemen as exiles during the past two years. The imminence of an Egyptian withdrawal from the Yemen also contributed to a decline in its influence.

With the federal structure now in ruins, the immediate question was whether or not the two main nationalist groups could be brought into mutual co-operation. Conflict soon broke out, however, between them, and fierce fighting developed in the northern suburbs of Aden during September. The South Arabian Army was able to enforce a brief ceasefire, and the rival organizations met in Cairo in October, but without any agreement. Fresh fighting then began, FLOSY being finally defeated when the Army high command joined forces with the NLF.

The latter then insisted that Britain should regard it as the sole valid representative of the people of South Arabia—a course of action which the authorities in London agreed to take on November 11th, 1967. On November 14th it was announced at Aden that Qahtan al-Shaabi, one of the founders of the NLF, would lead a delegation to Geneva to hold discussions with the representatives of Britain.

The evacuation of British troops from Aden had begun earlier on August 25th, 1967. As the situation unfolded itself in Aden, the British Government resolved to hasten the withdrawal of its forces and to advance the independence of South Arabia from January 9th, 1968, to a date if possible in the second half of November 1967. On November 27th, after the British troops had made over large areas of Aden to the armed forces of South Arabia, the NLF proclaimed the creation of the People's Republic of Southern Yemen. At Geneva, Qahtan al-Shaabi announced on November 28th that agreement had been reached with Great Britain over the cession of Aden and its associated territories. The last British troops in Aden were withdrawn on November 29th, 1967. Qahtan al-Shaabi, with the approval of the NLF, was appointed the first President of the Republic on November 30th. Unlike most former British dependencies, Southern Yemen did not join the Commonwealth.

[*Note:* Since Southern Yemen's independence the neighbouring Yemen Arab Republic has been sometimes referred to as "North Yemen".]

INDEPENDENCE

The prospect before the new Republic in December 1967 was still a most uncertain one. On the economic side there were great difficulties to be overcome. The withdrawal of the British troops meant a serious loss of revenue. To maintain the armed forces inherited from the era of British control would impose on the Republic a large expenditure. Moreover, the closure of the Suez Canal had brought about a great falling off in the entrepôt trade of Aden and in the bunkering of ships. The continuance, in the immediate future, of financial aid from Britain was therefore of prime importance to the new regime in Aden. During the negotiations in Geneva between Britain and the NLF in November 1967 the British representatives agreed to make available financial aid to South Arabia for a period of six months (December 1st, 1967, to May 31st, 1968) at a rate amounting to about £2 million per month. Talks held in Aden in April 1968 between a British delegation and the government led only to the rejection of a new, though reduced, offer of further financial assistance from Britain.

There was disagreement also between Southern Yemen and Britain over the Kuria Muria Islands. These islands, about 40 miles from the south coast of Arabia and 200 miles east of the border between Southern Yemen and the Sultanate of Muscat and Oman, had been handed over to Britain in 1954 and, though administered subsequently from Aden, had not been included formally within the Aden Protectorate. On November 30th, 1967, Britain had made known to the United Nations her intention to restore the Kuria Muria Islands to the Sultan of Muscat—a decision which gave rise to much bitterness amongst the members of the new government in Aden, which continued to claim these islands and also Perim and Kamaran.

INTERNAL DISSENSION

The administration of President al-Shaabi had to meet other serious difficulties also. In the first months of 1968 it had carried out a series of "purges" in the armed forces and the police of Southern Yemen. Discontent amongst the armed forces increased after the annual conference of the NLF convened at Zinjibar, east of Aden, in March 1968. The more extreme elements in the NLF were reported to have put forward at the conference resolutions designed to force the Government of Southern Yemen further to the left—amongst them resolutions calling for the appointment of political commissars to all army units, for the strengthening of the NLF militia and for the creation of "popular guards". A demand was also made, it would seem, at this conference, for the establishment of popular councils in all six of the governorates of Southern Yemen—these provincial councils having the right to elect a supreme council which would control the affairs of the new Republic. There was in March 1968 a real danger of conflict between the moderate and the extreme elements in the NLF. On March 20th the army intervened to bring about the dismissal of several ministers identified with the more radical section of the Front. The extremists indeed had been taking matters into their own hands in the eastern areas of the Republic—above all in the fifth and sixth governorates which embrace the former sultanates of Qaiti, Kathiri and Mahra (i.e. the erstwhile Eastern Aden Protectorate). Here the radical elements had established popular councils of their own choice, ignoring the governors appointed from the central regime, ousting members of the armed forces and the police, and seizing the oil installations at Mukalla. The tensions thus generated showed no sign of a rapid abatement, and on May 15th, 1968, there was a short-lived rebellion in the region of Jaar, Abyan and Shuqra—i.e. in the third governorate to the north-east of Aden.

Another more serious uprising occurred at the end of July 1968, when two groups of armed rebels cut roads in the Radfan and Aulaqi districts north and east of Aden. The leaders of this rebellion were named as Colonel Abdullah Saleh al Aulaqi ("Colonel Sabaa"), formerly the NLF commander of security forces, and Brig. Nasser Buraik al Aulaqi, who until independence had been commander of the South Arabian Army. These risings were quickly crushed by NLF forces. Both FLOSY and the rival exiled political organization, the South Arabian League, claimed credit for this threat to the Government of President al-Shaabi. Although several members of the FLOSY High Command were captured during the campaign, the economic difficulties of the country continued to act as a serious threat to the stability of the new régime. These difficulties enforced drastic cuts in government expenditure during the summer of 1968.

NEIGHBOURING HOSTILITY

Relations with neighbouring states continued to be poor, and the government blamed all unrest within the country on elements operating from these states. FLOSY, operating from Yemen and now without its Egyptian support, the deposed sheikhs and sultans from the Federation (now mostly in Saudi Arabia), and the Sultan of Muscat and Oman with his British advisers were claimed to be the most important of these. There were reports of large supplies of Soviet military equipment reaching Aden, some of which were displayed in military parades; units of the Soviet fleet visited Aden more and more frequently, while there were fewer visits by British or other Western naval vessels.

In June 1969 President al-Shaabi resigned following a reported power struggle; Salem Rubayi Ali, a former commando leader who had gone into semi-exile in the provinces after a dispute with the leadership, came to power as Chairman of a new five-man Presidential committee, and a new cabinet was formed which included several other exiles. The new regime was seen as even more left-wing and pro-Soviet than its predecessor.

In November 1969 the government announced the nationalization of 36 foreign firms, including shipping, insurance and commercial companies, but excluding the BP oil refinery at Little Aden.

In November 1970 a new Constitution was promulgated, changing the name of the country to the People's Democratic Republic of Yemen, with a view to possible Yemeni unity. However, relations with the other Yemen and with other neighbouring states failed to improve, and during 1972 the People's Democratic Republic seemed threatened on all sides. Omani forces attacked frontier posts of the Aden Government in its drive against the rebels in its Dhofar province. These are grouped under the Popular Front for the Liberation of Oman (PFLO) and have been supported by the Aden Government. Forces of FLOSY and the South Arabian League were also reported to be gathering on the Yemeni borders. Saudi Arabia, as well as the Yemen Arab Republic, gives refuge to dissidents from the People's Democratic Republic, mainly because of the Aden Government's ideology.

In March 1974 the Arab League Foreign Ministers, meeting in Tunis, set up a conciliation commission in an attempt to end the long-standing conflict between the People's Democratic Republic and Oman over the support given by the Yemen P.D.R. Government to PFLO rebels in Oman.

POSSIBLE YEMENI UNITY

Serious fighting broke out on the border with the Yemen Arab Republic in September 1972, but an Arab League mission was able to mediate and a ceasefire became effective in October. A peace agreement on eventual unification of the two Yemens was signed in Cairo on October 28th. Further details were discussed in Tripoli (Libya) in November by the Presidents of the two Yemens, and it was agreed that the people of the Yemen would establish a single state, to be known as the Yemeni Republic, with Sana'a as its capital, Islam as the state religion and Arabic as the official language. Committees were set up to discuss details of the unification. In January 1973 it appeared that obstacles had arisen in the progress towards union, but in June 1973 the People's Democratic Republic Foreign Minister received the heads of mission of all socialist, Asian and African countries represented in Aden and reiterated his government's determination to implement the Cairo and Tripoli agreements on union. By September 1973 the prospects for the union had become more remote, and President Rubayi Ali and President Iriani of the Yemen Arab Republic met in Sana'a and agreed to extend the one-year period originally decided upon for unification. The subsequent *coup* in the Yemen Arab Republic in June 1974, when a pro-Saudi military junta gained control, made the union seem even more unrealistic. Subsequent events seemed to confirm this opinion, although the inter-Yemeni joint economic and financial committee continued to hold meetings. In the spring of 1975, however, the North Yemen Government accused Southern Yemen of "acts of sabotage" over the frontier.

The possibility of a fresh direction in foreign affairs opened up in March 1976, when the Yemen P.D.R. and Saudi Arabia established diplomatic relations. Saudi Arabia hitherto had not recognized Southern Yemen since its achievement of independence in 1967. The two sides declared that they wanted to normalize their relations in order "to guarantee the security and stability of the Arab peninsula and to serve the interests of the Arab nations while excluding foreign intervention". On the next day a ceasefire was announced between the Yemen P.D.R. and Oman, and although the fighting has virtually ceased, political events in Aden in June 1978 made it seem unlikely that this question had been finally resolved.

INTERNAL TENSIONS

President Rubayi Ali had been inclining towards Peking in policy since his visit to China in 1970. He was at the same time, however, prepared to accept aid from Saudi Arabia and the West (hence the establishment of diplomatic relations with Saudi Arabia in March 1976). In contrast, Abdul Fattah Ismail, who had become Secretary-General of the NLF in 1971, favoured a much more pro-Soviet policy, and a rift grew up between them. In June 1975 the Vanguard (ex-Baathist) and the People's Democratic Union (Communist) parties were absorbed by the NLF to form the United Political Organization – National Front (UPONF), of which Abdul Fattah Ismail became Secretary-General. It was no secret that Abdul Fattah Ismail wanted to transform the National Front into a far more radical Vanguard Party during the first half of 1978, a move about which President Rubayi Ali was unenthusiastic.

The assassination of President al-Ghashmi of North Yemen on June 24th, 1978, provided the impetus which toppled President Rubayi Ali two days later. It was reported that al-Ghashmi was killed by a bomb in a suitcase carried by an envoy from South Yemen. Whether this was instigated by President Rubayi Ali, or, as seems more likely, was arranged by other forces in South Yemen to discredit President Rubayi Ali, the fact remains that Rubayi Ali was ousted and later executed. Heavy fighting ensued between troops loyal to Ali and the ruling party militias which continued even after the new President took power. The Prime Minister, Ali Nasser Muhammad, became Head of State, but there was no doubt that the power of Abdul Fattah Ismail had been made more secure, and that South Yemen had moved further into the Soviet camp. At an emergency session of the Arab League, held on July 2nd, 1978, the 16 Arab countries present voted unanimously for an economic and political boycott of South Yemen. The "steadfastness" States, i.e. those (of which South Yemen is one) who disagreed most strongly with President Sadat's peace initiative in visiting Israel, stayed away from the meeting. Quite apart from the question of whether South Yemen was responsible for al-Ghashmi's death, the more conservative Arab countries were concerned about South Yemen's growing links with the U.S.S.R., and the threat this posed to the situation in the Horn of Africa, where South Yemen had already been backing Ethiopia against Eritrean rebels and Somalia.

In July 1978 relations with the Yemen Arab Republic again reached crisis point, with South Yemen accusing its neighbour of invading its northern territory. Each subsequently accused the other of military build-ups along the border but the menace of outright war eventually subsided.

Abdul Fattah Ismail managed to hold on to his powerful position when the three parties within the National Front reorganized themselves into the Yemen Socialist Party in October. At the first session of the elected 111-member People's Supreme Assembly in December, Ismail was elected Chairman of the Presidium which was to replace the Presidential Council, and thus became Head of State. Extensive Cabinet changes took place in August 1979.

At the beginning of 1979 fierce fighting broke out between government forces and troops of the opposition movement, the United Front for South Yemen. At the same time there were reports of armed clashes between the followers of Prime Minister Muhammad and President Ismail and, simultaneously, between Ismail's supporters and supporters of the Defence Minister and, in another instance, those of the Minister of the Interior. In early February the airport at Beihan was reportedly under siege from rebels who had mutinied and joined the United Front Forces.

The continuing border skirmishes with the Yemen Arab Republic escalated into full-scale warfare in February and March. After one unsuccessful ceasefire, truce talks arranged by the Arab League ended, surprisingly, in a firm Unity agreement (see Yemen Arab Republic History). According to a newspaper report in late May, a plot had been uncovered to assassinate the heads of state of the two Yemens as they met for unity talks at Rahda. The former ruling family of North Yemen was said to be implicated.

ECONOMIC SURVEY

The People's Democratic Republic of Yemen (PDRY) consists of the former British colony of Aden and the former Eastern and Western Aden Protectorates. The country covers about 130,000 sq. miles and the population was estimated at 1,853,000 in mid-1978. The population has been growing at an average annual rate of almost 3 per cent since 1970. Per capita income is among the lowest in the Arab world; G.D.P. per capita in 1976 is estimated to have been equivalent to $280 and had shown little or no growth since 1970. The most important town is Aden, with a population of 264,326 in 1973, followed by Mukalla in the east, with a population of about 50,000. The country is now divided into eight governorates, or provinces, whose finances and administration are centrally controlled, although the provincial councils are responsible for planning and finance on a local level. The Governorates vary greatly in size, the smallest being the First Governorate in the west, consisting of Aden district and the offshore islands, and the largest being the Sixth Governorate, the former Mahra Sultanate, situated in the extreme east of the country. A new province, Revolution Province, was formed within the Fifth Governorate in 1973 and another, the Abr, was established in 1976.

Most of the population is concentrated in the west and one of the Government's hardest tasks since independence has been to unite the various regions politically, administratively and economically. Whether political and economic union with the Yemen Arab Republic will be possible or successful is open to question. The Government, however, continued (in spite of the outbreak of hostilities) in 1973 and 1974 to reiterate its commitment to the principle of unity. At the end of 1973 it was agreed to set up an organization to co-ordinate both countries' agricultural, industrial and fisheries policies. Following the signing of a formal unity agreement in March 1979, talks were held to discuss the realities of economic unity in May (*see* History).

Under British rule, the country was sustained by the position of Aden on the main shipping route to Europe from the Far East, India and East Africa via Suez. The British Petroleum refinery, completed in 1954, was the focus of industry and trade. In addition, the British troops stationed in Aden and the many foreign visitors who came ashore from ships calling at the port provided a market for services and luxury goods which encouraged local merchants and entrepreneurs and brought plenty of foreign exchange into Aden. This prosperity was, in the main, confined to the then Aden Colony where there was a boom in construction work between 1955 and 1965. The British Government was more concerned with maintaining the Aden base and the port installations than with developing the hinterland although certain agricultural areas were developed during this period. The Abyan district, where development started in 1947, became one of the major cotton-producing areas and a similar scheme was carried out in Lahej in the 1960s. In the Hadhramaut, where there are fertile valleys in an otherwise barren area, the Governments of the states of Quaiti and Kathiri financed irrigation schemes and agricultural developments.

The closure of the Suez Canal in 1967 and the withdrawal of British troops in the same year, put an end to the Republic's commercial prosperity. Furthermore, British aid and military expenditure, which amounted to about £11 million in 1960, increasing to £36 million by 1967, and had more than covered the visible trade deficit, was discontinued after withdrawal, making it impossible for the Government to cover the budget deficit. In such a situation the Republic had no choice but to turn to other countries for sources of finance and technical aid to assist it in the transition from a service economy to one based on agriculture and manufacturing. The favourable terms offered by the Communist countries, coupled with a seeming lack of interest on the part of the West, made it inevitable that the Aden Government should turn to the Eastern bloc.

In November 1969 a decree was issued nationalizing all important foreign assets in the Republic, with the exception of the BP refinery, which was not taken over until 1977. This development, although a logical one in view of the regime's socialist leanings, nevertheless tended to frighten off firms which might otherwise have risked some investment, and made the Republic more than ever dependent on the Soviet Union, China and East Germany.

The Three-Year Development Plan (1971–74), although limited by shortage of funds, aimed at the creation, firstly of a communications network, secondly the expansion of agricultural production and, thirdly, the establishment of small-scale light industries, based on locally produced raw materials. Some progress was made, notably in telecommunications, and it was estimated that about 80 per cent of the total allocation was invested.

A new Five-Year Plan (1974–79) began in Apri 1974. Total capital investment in the plan was set at 92 million dinars, preliminary allocations of 144 million dinars having been rejected as too ambitious, but this figure was later reduced to 75 million dinars. In the event, however, investment spending appears to have reached 73 million dinars by the beginning of 1978. Special attention is being given to the development of fisheries and the oil industry. The Plan was drawn up with assistance from Soviet experts, and both the U.S.S.R. and China have promised extensive aid with projects. Czechoslovakia agreed to lend $6.3 million for Plan projects and discussions were held in 1974 with Cuba, Bulgaria and North Korea. The second Five-Year Plan (1978–83) has been allocated a total of $1,200 million.

Improved relations with Saudi Arabia led to talks in 1976 on aid for development projects and the PDRY has established closer ties with other Arab states. During the first half of 1977, agreement was reached with Saudi Arabia and other Gulf States by which several investment projects in the PDRY would receive concessional finance. The principal scheme involved the Aden refinery. However, relations between Saudi Arabia and the PDRY deteriorated in the course of the year because of the PDRY's support for Ethiopia. In November Aden and Riyadh recalled their ambassadors and Saudi Arabia withdrew its aid offers, as did some other Arab states. However, talks are continuing with Saudi Arabia and, meanwhile, the Eastern bloc countries appear to have increased their support.

AGRICULTURE

Only about a quarter of the country's cultivable land is used at present, and the most intensively cultivated areas are Abyan, east of Aden, and Lahej, north of Aden. The river valleys of the Hadhramaut area in the Fifth Governorate are also fertile and relatively well-developed. The Kuwait Fund for Arab Economic Development (KFAED) financed a pre-investment study of the Abyan delta and in May 1974 agreed to lend 4.2 million Kuwaiti dinars to help finance land reclamation and irrigation in the area. Bulgaria is also aiding the project. The Abyan Dam project began in 1974 and is now completed. The IDA has provided loans worth $7 million to develop agriculture in the Hadhramaut. The Government is giving priority to several agricultural projects and an Agricultural Fund provides economic assistance to farmers. Considerable foreign assistance (mainly from the Eastern bloc, Arab and UN sources and the Kuwait Fund) continues to be given in the form of finance and technical aid projects, such as irrigation development and the introduction of new farming methods and equipment.

Cotton is produced mainly in Lahej and Abyan. The government-controlled Abyan Board supervises the whole process of growing and marketing and has its own ginnery at El Kad. Cotton is also produced in other areas and the Cotton Producers' Associations were the most flourishing co-operatives in the country. The area under cotton has been declining, in spite of cash incentives offered to growers, and it is hoped to raise the cotton acreage by two-thirds with an output of 25,000 tons per year by 1980. Two more ginneries are planned, as well as a cottonseed oil factory at Maalla.

The Republic is able, on the whole, to meet local demand for most vegetables but imports onions, potatoes and fruit. The main fruits and vegetables grown are tomatoes, carrots, salad vegetables, bananas and melons. Bananas in particular are produced in quantity and the Food and Agriculture Organization has recommended an expansion of banana-growing, provided export markets can be found. In 1972 the only foreign customer was China.

Wheat is grown mainly in the Hadhramaut and Beihan but is not enough for the country's needs. The balance is imported mainly from Australia. Other cereals produced include barley, millet and sorghum. Cereal production is expected to rise to about 130,000 tons per year by 1980. Tobacco is grown in the coastal areas, mainly in the Ghail Ba Wazir area. Livestock production has remained fairly static for the last ten years and considerable numbers of sheep and goats have to be imported to satisfy local meat demand.

The resources available at present are not sufficient to finance agricultural development schemes over the whole country and efforts are being concentrated in the Lahej, Abyan, Beihan and Hadhramaut areas. In the east, the developments most likely to take place are the expansion of tobacco growing and the development of the fishing industry, with Mukalla as its centre. In recent years agricultural production has been severely disrupted by weather conditions. Because of drought in 1976 and 1977, recourse to food aid was necessary. In 1977 the UN World Food Programme gave $5 million in aid for drought victims and $4.5 million for a school meals programme while Japan provided rice aid of over $800,000 equivalent.

FISHERIES

The Arabian Sea fishing grounds are the Republic's greatest potential source of wealth. Most of the 10,000 fishermen fish only in territorial waters, their equipment is often poor and efficient marketing of the catch is impossible with the present state of communications. The main species caught are the Indian oil-sardine (sardinella), Indian mackerels and anchovies. At the beginning of 1973 exports of fish took a very encouraging turn and several foreign countries were involved in developing the industry. The total catch in 1977 was 161,700 metric tons, compared with 117,500 metric tons in 1970.

The Soviet Union and Cuba provided modern fishing vessels as well as equipment and technical aid. A Japanese firm obtained a contract in 1969 to fish in the coastal waters, and a joint Polish/Yemeni company with a capital of $5 million was planned. Denmark lent $2 million to finance development of Nakhtun port and construct refrigeration and storage facilities. In 1974 the Arab Fund for Economic and Social Development granted a loan of KD 3.2 million to build a fish meal plant and to improve facilities at Mukalla port. In 1976 the Abu Dhabi Fund for Arab Economic Development (ADFAED) granted $7.3 million for the purchase of fishing vessels. The FAO is sponsoring a special fund for fisheries research. The fish canning factory at Mukalla, partly financed by the U.S.S.R., is due for completion at the end of 1979, and will produce 15 million tons of fish per year. There is already a freezing plant for fish at Mukalla. According to UN and Soviet sources, fishing provides the main hope for developing an export-based industry in the country.

In January 1975 a joint company was set up with Iraq to operate a deep-sea fishing fleet. A canning project for fish and turtles at Lahej is also planned, as a joint venture with Libya. In 1977 bids were invited for the supply of fishing vessels to be financed by the ADFAED. In addition, a joint fishing company was set up with Iraq and the Islamic Development Bank of Saudi Arabia.

INDUSTRY

The BP refinery, which accounted for over 80 per cent of the country's total industrial output, was taken over in Spring 1977 by the Aden Refinery Company, a partnership between the Yemeni National Petroleum Company and the Saudi Arabian state oil company, Petromin. The refinery, which was built by BP in 1954 with a capacity of some 6 million tons per year, was badly affected by the closure of the Suez Canal in June 1967. In recent years it had been running at only one-third of its capacity. BP is believed to have been glad to dispose of it, because it was not an economic proposition. Compensation will be paid at book value, with BP's 40 expatriate employees at the refinery being retained under a management, technical and marketing services contract. In April 1979 BP turned bunkering facilities over to the Government. The bunkering operation had a turnover of only 100,000 tons, compared with 2.5 million tons in 1967. The refinery, of which some units are believed to be obsolete, was to have been expanded and modernized with financial assistance from Saudi Arabia, Kuwait, Iraq and Libya. Saudi Arabia agreed to provide 1 million tons of crude petroleum per year for processing in Aden. The status of these plans is now uncertain since the cooling in relations between Saudi Arabia and the PDRY. Saudi Arabia is believed to be withholding both financial support and oil for processing. Iraqi crude was delivered in 1977 and Kuwait is holding to its agreement, reached in February 1977, to supply 300,000 tons of crude per year. In November 1977 it was reported that the U.S.S.R. had signed an agreement to process additional crude oil at Aden.

The future of the Aden oil refinery, the PDRY's only large industrial complex, is of paramount importance to the country's economic development. Its relative decline is highlighted by recent trade figures. Between 1970 and 1973 the export of petroleum products in value terms fell from 45 million dinars to 28.4 million dinars, the latter representing 72 per cent of a much reduced total export bill of 39.4 million dinars, compared with 63 per cent of exports totalling 49.7 million dinars in 1967. Imports of crude petroleum for the refinery fell from 33.3 million dinars (44.6 per cent of total imports valued f.o.b.) to 23.7 million dinars in 1973, representing 44.3 per cent of an almost equally reduced import total. With the large increase in petroleum prices, product exports appeared to soar—but only in value terms—in 1974, standing at 78.7 million dinars or 94 per cent of total exports, while imports of crude petroleum, costing 73.3 million dinars, represented 58.6 per cent of the total import bill in the same year. There was an obvious fall in any terms in 1975, when exports of petroleum products stood at only 59.9 million dinars (93 per cent of total exports) and the necessary crude imports at only 44.2 million dinars (45.9 per cent of total imports). In 1976 exports of petroleum products fell still further to 50.9 million dinars, or 83 per cent of total exports. Crude imports were 76.1 million dinars, or 74 per cent of total imports.

The Government intends to give priority to oil

prospecting and, to this end, has offered very favourable terms to oil companies. Exploration agreements have been signed with East German and Soviet firms, and Western participation is also welcomed; a Canadian firm was awarded a concession in 1975. A joint Yemeni/Algerian company did some prospecting in the Hadhramaut but went into liquidation in 1976. In 1977 Agip, the refining and distribution subsidiary of the Italian state agency ENI, signed an offshore oil exploration agreement, and Siebens Oil and Gas began drilling in the Samaha offshore concession. In June 1979 ENI signed a long-term agreement for the exploration and production of petroleum and natural gas in two more zones, one on-shore and one offshore, covering 15,000 sq. km.

Saudi Arabia has agreed to finance the construction of an oil terminal on the Hadhramaut coast, connected by pipeline to the Saudi Arabian oilfields.

Industrial developments are planned to take the form of agro-industries. The Three-Year Development Plan envisaged the establishment of a textile industry based on local cotton; fruit and vegetable processing and canning plants; a cigarette factory; fish-canning plants and a tanning industry. This last would be particularly suitable since skins are at present exported in the raw state and there is much wastage. Some progress has been made, with China building a textile factory and a cigarette factory going into operation in 1973. Although in the initial stages the tobacco for the factory will be imported from Britain, supplies will eventually come from the Hadhramaut.

Existing industries (in Aden) are: the manufacture of cement blocks, tiles and bricks; salt production; soft drinks bottling and dairy plants. In the western Governorates there are also cotton ginneries, flour mills and seed-crushing plants. The fishing industry (see above) centres on Mukalla. Consultants are working at the possibility of a $75 million cement plant, to be located in the Third Governorate, possibly using the extensive limestone deposits reported to exist to the east of Aden. The German Democratic Republic is helping with the establishment of factories making flour, biscuits, vegetable oil and animal fodder. A tomato purée factory, capable of producing 1,500 tons per year, started operating in 1976.

Known mineral resources are few but the country has not yet been fully explored. Prospecting for copper and other minerals started at the end of 1975. Experts from several countries have conducted surveys. A British firm—Hunting Surveys—won a $1.5 million contract in 1976 to carry out a mineral survey in a 1,300 sq. km. area to the south-west of Mukalla. Copper deposits have already been reported, and beach sands have been investigated. The first phase of this work was completed in late 1977 and a second phase contract has been awarded, worth $1.8 million, with finance from the ADFAED. Prospects for a commercially viable mineral deposit still seem very doubtful although surveys in Wadi Ghabar and the Eastern Governorates indicate the presence of a number of minerals, including copper, lead, zinc and molybdenum.

All mineral and raw material sources in the country were declared publicly-owned in August 1973.

TRANSPORT AND COMMUNICATIONS

Several international airlines visit Khormaksar airport (formerly an RAF base), which has been extended and improved with Soviet assistance. Another airport is being considered, possibly to be financed by the KFAED. The Democratic Yemen Airlines Company provides an air link with Yemen and other neighbouring countries. The company has had significant commercial success. Steps were being taken in 1976/77 to improve Aden port, which has not yet recovered its former greatness despite the re-opening of the Suez Canal. A small floating dock (with a capacity of ships of only up to 5,000 d.w.t.) was commissioned from a Japanese firm in March 1977, while the Yemen Ports and Shipping Corporation has invited tenders for the supply of tugs and other craft, equipment and communications facilities as part of the rehabilitation project to be financed by the World Bank. Indeed, Aden is an important cable communications centre. The Russians have built a radio station in Aden, and the Greeks another station in Mukalla. In March 1978 the U.K. firm Cable and Wireless was nationalized by the Yemen Telecommunications Corporation (YTC), which plans to replace existing equipment with a satellite system. There are good roads round Aden and motorable tracks throughout the western area. A new road has been built, with massive Chinese aid, between Aden and Mukalla. Some 22,400 vehicles were in use in the country in 1976, including over 11,900 private cars and 10,500 commercial vehicles.

FOREIGN TRADE

Aden port handles nearly all the Republic's trade, as well as some of that of the Yemen Arab Republic. Transit trade to Yemen however, is declining owing to the development of the port of Hodeida. The free port of Aden attracted a large volume of traffic and all the commercial activities associated with a large port flourished, providing comfortable livings for the Adeni merchants but contributing little to the development of the other sectors of the economy. The disadvantages of a free port in the changed situation after 1967, not least the hindrance to industrial development caused by the lack of protective tariffs, led the Government, after much deliberation, to remove Aden's free port status, although there is still a free zone for transit trade.

In view of the disastrous effect of Aden's stagnation on a precarious economy, the Government viewed the re-opening of the Suez Canal in June 1975 with a satisfaction verging on jubilation. Plans for the port include dredging, improvement of mooring and repair facilities; expansion of the duty-free shopping zone and the construction of tourist facilities. The scheme is being financed by the World Bank and the Arab Fund for Economic and Social Development. As it turned out, the increase in traffic fell short of expectations. It was reported in early 1976 that only

150 ships per month were now calling at the port compared with 100 per month before the canal was re-opened. There had been optimistic forecasts that up to 500 ships per month would use the port once the Suez Canal link was re-opened. There was some further recovery in activity during 1977, and in October a 15 per cent surcharge was introduced.

The trade deficit continued to grow up to 1969. Government austerity measures and the lack of foreign exchange, reduced imports in 1970 by over £7 million but exports continued at much the same level. In 1971 and 1972 both imports and exports declined but the value of imports, particularly of oil products, rose steeply after 1973 as a result of increased oil prices and general inflation. The Government was forced to call on the International Monetary Fund's oil facility. The trade balance deteriorated further in 1974 and in 1975 despite record exports in value terms. In 1976 exports were worth 61.2 million dinars and imports had risen to 103.3 million dinars. The main commodities exported (excluding petroleum products) are cotton, hides and skins, dried fish, rice and coffee. The chief imports (excluding petroleum) are clothing, foodstuffs and livestock. The drop in petroleum trade was particularly significant, as it made reduction of activity at the refinery inevitable, with consequent repercussions on the whole fragile economy. In 1966, bunkering made up a third of total exports, but by 1970 this proportion had fallen to less than 7 per cent and petroleum exports were moving to markets in Africa and Asia rather than Europe.

FINANCE AND FOREIGN AID

The Republic has had difficulty in maintaining financial stability since independence. In December 1966 international reserves amounted to $62.4 million. By the end of 1970 they were $59.3 million. In the same period, the budget deficit grew from 100,000 dinars to over 4 million dinars. This deficit was substantially cut in 1971, largely because more foreign grants were obtained, but expenditure still had to be held down with adverse effects on development. The situation was considered to be so serious in 1972 that the salaries of many government employees were cut by anything from 15 to 50 per cent and restrictions were placed on foreign travel. By the end of 1973 the situation was a little better and international reserves were $76.0 million. In 1975 the International Monetary Fund agreed to the purchase of SDR 7.25 million to help with balance of payments problems and general inflation. The overall payments deficit in 1974 was $24 million but the Government's measures, combined with the IMF aid, were having their effect by 1976 and the economy was being brought under control. At the end of 1975 reserves had fallen to $54.7 million, including drawings of $32.1 million on IMF facilities. At the end of 1976 reserves amounted to $82.22 million with IMF drawings having increased to $47.15 million. The situation continued to improve during 1977 and 1978. At the end of 1978 reserves were $189.24 million with IMF drawings at $46.5 million.

In the absence of recent trade figures, it must be assumed that the increase in net reserves reflects foreign aid flows resulting in part from the general *détente* with neighbouring Middle Eastern countries. The IMF, to which the country is now heavily committed, is continuing to watch over the economy. The government financial deficit remains at a high level, having increased from 7.39 million dinars in 1973/74 to 11.69 million in 1975/76.

The abrupt cessation of British aid to the Republic after the withdrawal of troops in November 1967 caused a crisis which enabled the communist bloc to step into the breach. The Soviet Union, under an agreement of February 1969, which included aid specifically for fisheries, undertook to provide technical aid and experts for a number of development projects. A separate agreement, signed in August 1969, covered aid for agriculture and irrigation. The first agreement was extended in February 1970 to include aid in kind worth 5.5 million roubles and, most important of all, a low-interest loan of 7 million roubles repayable over 12 years. This loan was significant in that actual financial aid was offered rather than aid in the form of goods or technical assistance. The U.S.S.R. was reported to have offered a further loan of 18 million roubles in 1976. Five hospitals, including a children's hospital and a maternity home, are being built with Soviet aid. The U.S.S.R. is also considering the finance of several projects included in the second Five-Year Plan, notably a power station for Aden and further modernization of the port. In 1979 a loan of 24 million roubles was made for development projects, which included mineral surveys and agricultural development. The German Democratic Republic agreed to a loan of $22 million in October 1969 and China granted a $18 million loan in 1970, both part of large aid and trade "package deals". Both covered a wide range of projects, including, in the case of the German Democratic Republic, the construction of telephone facilities and the establishment of light industries; and, in the case of China, help with the road-building programme. Most of the communist bloc countries have offered aid to the Republic, particularly for communications projects such as the Aden television station built with Czech aid. Large development loans were obtained in 1979 from Bulgaria and Czechoslovakia, while China lent a further $12.5 million for the purchase of industrial goods.

The richer Arab countries, too, are providing aid in certain sectors. The Kuwait Fund for Arab Economic Development is financing the Abyan Delta project and an economic survey of the whole country. Algeria, as well as participating in oil exploration, agreed to give $4 million worth of development aid. Libya in 1972 granted a loan of 5.8 million dinars and in 1974 approved a first payment of LD1.5 million under this agreement. Libyan aid in 1974 totalled LD3 million. The Aden Government approached the Arab League on the subject of compensation for losses incurred as a direct result of the June War of 1967 but no actual financial compensation has so far been awarded. Iraq gave a $5 million interest-free loan in 1974, of which $3 million was repayable in goods and services. In January 1975 a further $10 million loan was announced. Also in 1975, the Government launched a diplomatic offensive to improve relations with the rich Gulf states. A grant of $5 million was forthcoming from Kuwait, the United Arab Emirates agreed to finance a minerals survey, and the Abu Dhabi Fund for Arab Economic Development granted aid for the fishing industry. In 1977 the country was admitted as a member of the Islamic Development Bank. The bank, established with capital of $900 million in 1974, aims to help finance economic and social development projects in Muslim countries in Asia and Africa. In 1977, in addition to aid mentioned in previous sections, Kuwait agreed to provide $13.5 million for hospital building, the Saudi Fund for Development offered $20 million equivalent for electricity projects and also agreed on assistance for a housing scheme in Al Mansoura. The $28 million Wadi Hadhramaut electricity scheme, for which bids were invited in 1978/79, is being financed by Kuwait, Saudi Arabia and the World Bank.

The Republic's relations with the West have deteriorated not only because of the British refusal to continue aid, but as a result of the rapprochement with the Eastern bloc countries. The main source of aid, other than the socialist countries and the Arab states, has been the United Nations. However, in 1974/75 loans were obtained from the World Bank for the Saiwun–Mukhalla road project. During 1977 it was announced that an organic fertilizer plant would be built with UN Development Programme assistance and the IDA has provided over $10 million for education and training schemes. One of the country's main difficulties is lack of trained manpower, manifested in the shortage of staff to run statistical departments and to collect information on the economy. A number of countries have offered training schemes for Yemenis to study abroad.

STATISTICAL SURVEY

AREA AND POPULATION

(Census of May 14th, 1973)

	Governorates							Total
	First	Second	Third	Fourth	Fifth	Sixth	Thamoud	
Population ('000) .	291	273	311	162	451	61	41	1,590
Area (sq. miles) .	2,695	4,929	8,297	28,536	32,991	25,618	27,000	130,066

Estimated Population ('000 at mid-year): 1,749 in 1976; 1,797 in 1977; 1,853 in 1978.

Capital: Aden (population 264,326 in 1973).

The Abr Province was established by Presidential decree in July 1976.

EMPLOYMENT

(1976)

Total	Agriculture and Fishing	Mining and Quarrying	Manufacturing	Construction	Electricity, Gas and Water	Commerce	Transport	Services	Miscellaneous
370,655	182,065	2,232	15,824	16,797	3,145	27,955	14,575	87,220	20,842

AGRICULTURE

PRINCIPAL CROPS

	Area ('000 hectares)			Production ('000 tons)		
	1975	1976	1977	1975	1976	1977
Millet	47	48	40*	74	61	65*
Wheat	12	13	14	21	24	27
Barley	1	1	1	2	2	2
Sesame	4	4	4*	4	4	4*
Cotton Lint }	12*	12*	12*	5*	3*	4*
Cotton Seed }				11*	11*	11*

* Estimates.

Source: FAO, *Production Yearbook*.

LIVESTOCK

(FAO estimates, year ending September)

	1973/74	1974/75	1975/76	1976/77
Cattle	99,000	101,000	102,000	104,000
Sheep	880,000	900,000	930,000	940,000
Goats	1,150,000	1,200,000	1,230,000	1,260,000
Asses	30,000	31,000	32,000	32,000
Camels	40,000	40,000	40,000	40,000

Source: FAO, *Production Yearbook*.

LIVESTOCK PRODUCTS

(FAO estimates, metric tons)

	1974	1975	1976	1977
Mutton and lamb	6,000	6,000	6,000	6,000
Goats' meat	5,000	5,000	5,000	5,000
Cows' milk	6,000	7,000	7,000	7,000
Sheep's milk	11,000	11,000	11,000	11,000
Goats' milk	24,000	24,000	24,000	24,000
Hen eggs	1,418	1,400	1,450	1,500

Source: FAO, *Production Yearbook*.

FISHING

('000 metric tons, live weight)

	1973	1974	1975	1976	1977
Indian oil-sardine (sardinella)	91.0	96.4	91.1	97.3	98.6
Other marine fishes	35.8	41.5	40.5	41.1	46.5
Other sea creatures	6.7	7.6	11.2	14.2	16.6
Total Catch	133.5	145.5	142.8	152.6	161.7

Source: FAO, *Yearbook of Fishery Statistics*.

MINING

('000 metric tons)

	1971	1972	1973	1974	1975	1976*
Salt (unrefined)	67	75	75	75	75	76

* Estimate.

INDUSTRY

SELECTED PRODUCTS

		1973	1974†	1975†	1976†
Salted, dried or smoked fish	metric tons	2,300	2,600	1,800	n.a.
Motor spirit (Petrol)	'000 metric tons	505	400	160	98
Kerosene	" " "	104	105	100	100
Jet fuel	" " "	341	320	150	150
Distillate fuel oils	" " "	446	430	200	388
Residual fuel oil	" " "	1,520	1,400	540	1,026
Electric energy*	million kWh.	174	174	180	180

* Figures refer to Aden only. † Estimates.

Sources: United Nations, *Statistical Yearbook* and *Yearbook of Industrial Statistics.*

FINANCE

1,000 fils = 1 Yemeni dinar (YD).

Coins: 1, 2½, 5, 25 and 50 fils.

Notes: 250 and 500 fils; 1, 5 and 10 dinars.

Exchange rates (June 1979): £1 sterling = 714.6 fils; U.S. $1 = 345.4 fils.
100 Yemeni dinars = £139.95 = $289.52.

Note: Before independence (November 30th, 1967) the currency unit was the South Arabian dinar (SA dinar), introduced in April 1965 with a value of £1 sterling, then worth U.S. $2.80. On November 18th, 1967, the pound and dinar were both devalued to $2.40 ($1 = 416.67 fils). Following independence the SA dinar was replaced by the Southern Yemen dinar, with the same value. The exchange rate (1 dinar = $2.40) remained in force until August 1971. Between December 1971 and February 1973 the rate was 1 dinar = $2.6057 ($1 = 383.77 fils). The present dollar valuation has been effective since February 1973. The dinar was at par with the pound sterling until the latter was allowed to "float" in June 1972.

BUDGET

('000 dinars, April 1st to March 31st)

Revenue	1971/72	1972/73	1973/74*	Expenditure	1971/72	1972/73	1973/74*
Taxes on personal income	1,050	1,078	1,221	General administration	1,152	1,886	2,693
Taxes on corporate income	2,712	1,388	1,952	Defence and security†	9,184	9,798	10,444
Other taxes	195	132	134	Public works and communications	1,146	1,041	1,076
Import duties	5,869	4,406	5,143	Economic services	1,886	1,154	1,550
Excise duties	872	1,269	2,170	Education	2,615	2,711	3,836
Stamp duties	405	378	432	Health	1,013	996	1,152
Other indirect taxes	423	387	526	Agriculture	417	417	491
Non-tax revenue	3,550	2,100	3,763	Pensions	287	376	276
Other receipts	910	908	—	Local authorities	389	365	458
				Other services	2,646	2,937	756
Total	15,986	12,046	15,341	**Total**	20,735	21,681	22,732

* Estimates. † Including expenditure of the Ministry of the Interior.

Source: United Nations, *Statistical Yearbook*.

1974/75 ('000 dinars): Revenue 18,130; Expenditure 27,450.

1975/76 ('000 dinars): Revenue 13,860; Expenditure 25,550.

Five-Year Plan 1974/75–1978/79: Total expenditure 75 million dinars.

COST OF LIVING

(Consumer Price Index. Base: 1970 = 100)

	1971	1972	1973	1974
Food	105.4	116.7	120.5	144.5
Fuel and light	103.1	110.7	115.1	155.6
Clothing	109.8	135.1	143.3	n.a.
Rent	100.0	89.6	75.0	75.0

Source: International Labour Office, *Year Book of Labour Statistics*.

BALANCE OF PAYMENTS

(U.S. $ million)

	1971	1972	1973	1974
Merchandise exports f.o.b.	99.9	106.5	106.9	234.3
Merchandise imports f.o.b.	−147.7	−146.1	−174.1	−362.5
TRADE BALANCE	−47.8	−39.6	−67.2	−128.2
Exports of services	21.7	24.4	27.2	52.1
Imports of services	−29.3	−40.3	−44.6	−65.9
BALANCE ON GOODS AND SERVICES	−55.5	−55.5	−84.5	−142.0
Unrequited transfers (net)	44.8	27.1	33.4	41.7
BALANCE ON CURRENT ACCOUNT	−10.6	−28.3	−51.1	−100.3
Long-term capital (net)	2.4	12.6	25.6	52.6
Short-term capital (net)	—	6.7	26.3	25.1
Net errors and omissions	4.9	8.7	0.7	−1.8
TOTAL (net monetary movements)	−3.3	−0.3	1.5	−24.4

Source: IMF, *International Financial Statistics.*

EXTERNAL TRADE

(million dinars)

	1971	1972	1973	1974	1975	1976
Imports c.i.f.	64.9	57.2	59.9	140.1	108.0	115.7
Exports f.o.b.	43.4	41.2	39.4	83.6	59.0	61.2

PRINCIPAL COMMODITIES

(dinars)

	IMPORTS			EXPORTS		
	1973	1974*	1975*	1973	1974*	1975*
Live Animals	790,326	551,899	820,401	—	—	125
Dairy Produce, Eggs	1,980,192	1,364,375	1,730,645	2,719	46	—
Cereals	6,561,567	14,092,587	8,460,649	1,622	1,350	9,267
Fruit and Vegetables	1,309,034	1,120,965	1,525,484	13,403	69,343	117,518
Sugar, etc.	3,175,245	4,444,419	5,027,418	276,935	45,931	38,658
Coffee, Tea, Cocoa, Spices	2,382,734	1,619,560	2,199,512	519,187	381,402	669,184
Beverages and Tobacco	1,117,526	1,098,294	954,553	56,638	38,784	65,082
Oilseeds, Oil Nuts, etc.	863,451	1,351,333	715,909	2,038	1	—
Petroleum and Petroleum Products	26,921,482	10,440,627	8,928,498	28,713,439	52,092	24,294
Chemicals	1,616,103	2,447,851	2,785,311	56,885	40,229	24,364
Textile Yarn, Fabrics, etc.	3,454,515	3,988,973	2,597,253	473,341	187,626	18,430
Non-electric Machinery	1,288,501	2,984,236	4,215,082	23,254	8,556	8,191
Electrical Machinery	636,688	1,311,295	1,994,234	17,491	10,978	1,750
Transport Equipment	1,032,900	3,966,596	4,106,304	36,576	19,681	11,125

* Excluding imports and exports of foreign-owned companies. Total imports of crude petroleum (in million dinars) were: 23.7 in 1973; 73.3 in 1974; 44.2 in 1975; 76.1 in 1976; 58.6 in 1977. Total exports of petroleum products (in million dinars) were: 28.4 in 1973; 78.7 in 1974; 58.6 in 1975; 50.9 in 1976; 46.5 in 1977.

PRINCIPAL TRADING PARTNERS
(dinars)

Imports	1973	1974*	1975*
Hong Kong	807,467	560,546	368,309
India	1,353,561	5,038,126	2,931,431
Iran	10,774,799	1,013,005	1,010,837
Japan	3,318,810	3,818,015	4,706,804
Kuwait	4,575,315	4,613,339	2,518,259
United Arab Emirates	1,427,276	24,000	62,737
United Kingdom	4,531,992	7,655,331	12,525,940

* Excluding imports by foreign-owned companies.

Exports	1973	1974*	1975*
Australia	4,082,819	—	—
Canary Islands	1,566,200	—	—
Japan	2,935,676	1,404,233	1,297,896
Thailand	1,426,316		
United Kingdom	3,921,234	74,082	150,616
Yemen Arab Rep.	2,098,587	124,970	131,813

* Excluding exports by foreign-owned companies.

TRANSPORT

ROAD TRAFFIC
(motor vehicles registered)

	1973	1974	1975	1976
Passenger cars	10,600	10,700	11,600	11,900
Commercial vehicles	7,900	8,100	9,900	10,500

INTERNATIONAL SEA-BORNE SHIPPING
Port of Aden

	1973	1974	1975
Vessels Entered ('000 net reg. tons)	5,542	5,107	6,016
Dry Cargo Imported ('000 long tons)	310	364	327
Dry Cargo Exported ('000 long tons)	65	54	31
Oil Cargo Imported ('000 long tons)	3,343	2,885	1,655
Oil Cargo Exported ('000 long tons)	2,724	2,185	1,478

CIVIL AVIATION
(1975)

Aircraft Movements	Passengers			Freight (kilos)	
	Arrivals	Departures	Transit	Inward	Outward
6,376	91,051	85,432	22,829	1,019,044	863,258

EDUCATION

NUMBER OF SCHOOLS

(1974/75)

Primary schools	1,036
Intermediate schools	105
Secondary schools	19
Teachers' colleges for males	2
Teachers' colleges for females	1
Technical institutes	1

Source (except where otherwise stated): Central Statistical Office, Central Planning Commission, Aden.

THE CONSTITUTION

Before the 1970 constitution was drawn up existing ordinances and regulations remained in force, with Presidential authority replacing the powers of the British and Federal Governments. The National Liberation Front general command, which had 41 members, formed the interim legislative authority. The country is divided into eight administrative Governorates. The two-year term of office granted to the National Liberation Front expired on November 30th, 1969, and was formally renewed for another year. Following the adoption of the new constitution on November 30th, 1970, a Provisional Supreme People's Council of 101 selected members took over legislative powers. General elections took place in December 1978 for a 111-member Council which subsequently elected the Head of State and the Presidential Council. In March 1979 a constitutional commission from both the Yemen P.D.R. and the Yemen Arab Republic was appointed to draw up a Constitution for a unified state. Amendments to the Constitution allowing for the formation of the Yemen Socialist Party were approved by the Supreme People's Council in October 1978.

THE GOVERNMENT

HEAD OF STATE

President: ABDUL FATTAH ISMAIL (elected December 27th, 1978).

PRESIDENTIAL COUNCIL

(elected December 27th, 1978)

Chairman: ABDUL FATTAH ISMAIL.

Vice-Chairman: ALI NASSER MUHAMMAD.

Secretary-General: FADL MUHSEN ABDULLA.

Members: SAID SALEH SALEM, SULTAN MUHAMMAD AD-DOSH, AIDA ALI SAID, MUHAMMAD SAID MAHDI, ABDULLA AHMAD GHANEM, ALI AHMAD NASSER AS-SALAMI, FARES SALEM AHMAD.

CABINET

(*August* 1979)

Prime Minister and Minister of Finance: ALI NASSER MUHAMMAD.

Minister of Foreign Affairs: SALIM SALIH MUHAMMAD.

Minister of Defence: ALI AHMAD NASSER ANTAR.

Minister of the Interior: ALI SHAYI HADI.

Minister of Justice and Waqfs: KHALID FADL MANSUR.

Minister of Health: DR. ABDULLAH AHMAD BUKIR.

Ministry of Industry: ABDUL GHANI ABDUL QADIR.

Minister of Education: SAID ABDEL-KHAIR AN-NOBAN.

Minister of Communications: MAHMOUD ABDULLA OSHEISH.

Minister of Labour and Civil Service: NASR NASSER ALI.

Minister of Agriculture and Agrarian Reform: FADL MUHSIN ABDULLAH.

Minister of Culture and Tourism: MAHMUD NAJASHI.

Minister of Information: RASHID MUHAMMAD THABIT.

Minister of Construction: HAIDAR ABU BAKR AL-ATTAS.

Minister of Fishery Resources: ANIS HASAN YAHYA.

Minister of Trade and Supply: AHMAD UBAYD AL-FADLI.

Minister of Planning: DR. FARAJ Bin GHANIM.

Minister of Finance: MAHMUD SAID MAHDI.

Minister of State for Cabinet Affairs: ALI ASSAD MUTANNA.

Consists of 111 members, elected December 1978.

SUPREME PEOPLE'S COUNCIL

Chairman of Presidium: ABDUL FATTAH ISMAIL.

Deputy Chairman of Presidium: ALI NASSER MUHAMMAD.

Secretary: (vacant)

POLITICAL PARTY

Yemen Socialist Party: Aden; f. October 1978 as successor to United Political Organization—National Front (UPONF); based on "scientific socialism"; has Political Bureau (9 mems., *see* below), Executive Cttee. (13 mems.), Secretariat (7 mems.), Appeals Cttee. (6 mems.), Information Cttee. (10 mems.) and Central Cttee. (51 mems.).

POLITICAL BUREAU

Secretary-General: ABDUL FATTAH ISMAIL.
ALI NASSER MUHAMMAD.
MUHAMMAD SALEH MUTI.
ALI ABDER-RAZZAQ BADIB.
ABDEL-AZIZ ABDEL WALI.
SALEH MUSLIH QASIM.
MUHAMMAD SAID ABDULLA.
ALI SALEM AL-BID.
AHMAD HASAN YAHYA.

DIPLOMATIC REPRESENTATION

EMBASSIES ACCREDITED TO THE PEOPLE'S DEMOCRATIC REPUBLIC OF YEMEN

(In Aden unless otherwise stated)

Algeria: Sana'a, Yemen Arab Republic.

Austria: Cairo, Egypt.

Bangladesh: Baghdad, Iraq.

Belgium: Cairo, Egypt.

Bulgaria: Khormaksar; *Ambassador:* ATANAS SAMSAROV.

Canada: Jeddah, Saudi Arabia.

China, People's Republic: 145 Andalus Gardens, Khormaksar; *Ambassador:* HUANG SHIH-HSIEH.

Cuba: 36 Socotra Rd., Khormaksar; *Ambassador:* JUSTINO BARO ISASI.

Czechoslovakia: Imran St., Khormaksar; *Chargé d'affaires:* A. KUSY.

Denmark: Jeddah, Saudi Arabia.

Ethiopia: Abdulla Assaidi St., Ma'alla; *Ambassador:* SAMUEL TEFERA.

France: Sayhut St., Khormaksar; *Ambassador:* M. COURAGE.

German Democratic Republic: Khormaksar; *Ambassador:* ERNST-PETER RABENHORST.

Germany, Federal Republic: P.O.B. 6100, Aden; *Chargé d'affaires:* Dr. W. DAUM.

Guinea: Addis Ababa, Ethiopia.

Hungary: Cairo, Egypt.

India: Bremjee Chambers, Tawahi; *Chargé d'affaires:* J. P. GUBTA.

Iraq: Miswat St., Khormaksar; *Ambassador:* (*withdrawn June* 1979).

Italy: Tawahi; *Ambassador:* C. PANSERA.

Japan: Crescent Hotel, Steamer Point; *Chargé d'affaires a.i.:* HIROSHI SHIOJIRI.

Jordan: Sana'a, Yemen Arab Republic.

Korea, Democratic People's Republic: Khormaksar; *Ambassador:* YANG CHAE-TOK.

Kuwait: Sana'a, Yemen Arab Republic.

Lebanon: Sana'a, Yemen Arab Republic.

Libya: Airport Rd., Khormaksar; *Ambassador:* M. S. JIBRIL.

Mongolia: Cairo, Egypt.

Netherlands: Cairo, Egypt.

Pakistan: 34 Kassim Hilal, Khormaksar; *Chargé d'affaires:* M. SIDIQI.

Poland: Cairo, Egypt.

Romania: Abyan Beach Rd., Plot No. 106, Khormaksar; *Chargé d'affaires:* N. MEZEI.

Saudi Arabia: *Ambassador:* Sheikh MUHAMMAD ALAKI.

Somalia: Britannic Court, Dolphin Square, Ma'alla; *Ambassador:* MUHAMMAD JAMA ELMI.

Spain: Addis Ababa, Ethiopia.

Sudan: Tawahi; *Chargé d'affaires:* A. M. HASSAN.

Sweden: Addis Ababa, Ethiopia.

Switzerland: Addis Ababa, Ethiopia.

Syria: Sana'a, Yemen Arab Republic.

Uganda: Jeddah, Saudi Arabia.

U.S.S.R.: Abyan Beach Rd., Khormaksar; *Ambassador:* FELIX FEDOTOV.

United Kingdom: 28 Shara Ho Chi Minh, Khormaksar; *Chargé d'affaires a.i.:* M. T. MCKERNAN.

Viet-Nam: 110 Awadh Al-Saaidy St., Khormaksar; *Ambassador:* LEE QUANG KHAI.

Yugoslavia: Mogadishu, Somalia.

Zambia: Cairo, Egypt.

The People's Democratic Republic of Yemen also has diplomatic relations with Afghanistan, Albania, Angola, Djibouti, Iran, Kenya, Mexico, the Philippines, Senegal and Tanzania.

JUDICIAL SYSTEM

The administration of justice is entrusted to the Supreme Court and Magistrates' Courts. In the former Protectorate States Muslim law and local common law (Urfi) are also applied.

President of the Supreme Court: ABD-AL-MAJID ABD-AL-RAHMAN.

RELIGION

The majority of the population are Muslim but there are small Christian and Hindu communities.

THE PRESS

DAILIES

14 October: P.O.B. 4227, Aden; not published on Saturdays; f. 1968; Editor-in-Chief ADBULLA SHARAF SAEED; cir. 15,000.

WEEKLIES

Al-Thawri: P.O.B. 4227, Aden; published on Saturday; mouthpiece of Central Committee of National Front.

MONTHLIES

al-Thaqafa Al-Jadida: P.O.B. 1187, Aden; f. Aug. 1970; a cultural monthly review issued by the Ministry of Culture and Tourism; Arabic; circ. 3,000.

NEWS AGENCIES

Aden News Agency: P.O.B. 1207, Tawahi, Aden; f. 1970; government-owned; Dir.-Gen. UMAR AL-JAWI.

FOREIGN BUREAU

Agentstvo Pechati Novosti (APN) (*U.S.S.R.*): Aden; Correspondent NIKOLAI Y. LEVCHENKO.

RADIO AND TELEVISION

RADIO

Democratic Yemen Broadcasting Service: P.O.B. 1264, Aden; transmits 100 hours a week in Arabic; Dir.-Gen. for Broadcasting and TV: JAMAL AL-KHATIB; there are about 150,000 receivers in the country.

TELEVISION

Democratic Yemen Broadcasting Service: P.O.B. 1264, Aden; programmes for four hours daily, mainly in Arabic; other series in English and French. There are about 25,000 receivers.

FINANCE

CENTRAL BANK

Bank of Yemen: P.O.B. 452, Aden; replaced Yemeni Currency Authority 1972; cap. p.u. 500,000 YD; Governor AHMAD UBAID FADHLY; publ. *Annual Report.*

COMMERCIAL BANK

National Bank of Yemen: P.O.B. 5, Crater, Aden; f. 1969 by nationalizing and amalgamating the local branches of the seven foreign banks in Aden; cap. p.u. 1.25 million YD; total resources 57.3 million YD (December 1976); Gen. Man. AYOOB NAZIR A. WAHED; 20 brs.

INSURANCE

All foreign insurance interests were nationalized in November 1969.

National Insurance and Re-insurance Co.: P.O.B. 456, Aden; Lloyd's Agents.

TRADE AND INDUSTRY

National Chamber of Commerce and Industry: P.O.B. 473, Crater; Pres. ABDULREHMAN AL-SAILANI; Sec. MONASAR BAZARA; Gen. Man. ABDULLA SALEM KHADER.

National Company for Foreign Trade: Crater, Aden; f. 1969; incorporates main foreign trading businesses, and arranges their supply to the National Company for Home Trade; Gen. Man. HUSSEIN AHMED FADAQ.

National Company for Home Trade: Crater, Aden; f. 1969; marketing of cars, electrical goods, agricultural machinery, building materials and general consumer goods; incorporates the main foreign trading businesses which were nationalized in 1970; Gen. Man. ABDUL RAHMAN AL SAILAWI.

TRADE UNION

General Confederation of Workers of the People's Democratic Republic of Yemen: P.O.B. 1162, Ma'alla, Aden; f. 1956; affiliated to WFTU and ICFTU; 35,000 mems.; Pres. SULTAN MUHAMMAD AD-DOSH; Gen. Sec. ABDUL RAZAK SHAIF; publ. *Sout A Omal* weekly, circ. approx. 4,500.

CO-OPERATIVES AND MARKETING

There are 65 co-operative societies, mostly for agricultural products; the movement was founded in 1965 and is now the responsibility of the Ministry for Agiculture and Agrarian Reform.

STATE ENTERPRISE

Yemeni National Petroleum Co.: P.O.B. 5050, Aden; sole oil concessionaire importer and distributor of oil products in Yemen P.D.R.; Chair. and Gen. Man. ABDUL KARIM THABET.

TRANSPORT

ROADS

Yemen Bus Co. Ltd.: Adbusco Bldg., Ma'alla, P.O.B. 905, Aden; f. 1960; operates services within the Crater, Ma'alla, Steamer Point, Sheikh Othman, Al-Mansoura, Lahej and Abyan areas; affiliated to Ministry of Transport.

A new state transport monopoly, the Yemen Land Transport Company, is being formed to incorporate the Aden Bus Company and all other local public transport.

Aden has 140 miles of roads, of which 127 have bituminous surfacings. There are 6,382 miles of rough tracks passable for motor traffic in the hinterland, of which 716 have bituminous surfacing.

SHIPPING

National Shipping Company: P.O.B. 1228, Steamer Point, Aden; founded 1970 following nationalization and amalgamation of foreign shipping companies; freight and passenger services; branch in Mukalla, agents at Berbera (Somalia) and Mocha and Hodeida (Yemen Arab Republic); Aden Coasters, an affiliate, provides services for transshipment via Aden Free Zone to the Red Sea ports, East Africa and Bombay.

Port of Aden Authority: Aden; f. 1888; state administrative body. Aden Main Harbour has twenty first-class berths. In addition there is ample room to accommodate vessels of light draught at anchor in the 18-foot dredged area. There is also 800 feet of cargo wharf accommodating vessels of 300 feet length and 18 feet draught. Aden Oil Harbour accommodates four tankers of 57,000 tons and up to 40 feet draught.

During 1978 great progress was made with the Port of Aden Rehabilitation Project.

CIVIL AVIATION

Democratic Yemen Airlines Company (*Al Yamda*): Aden: Aden; f. 1971 as wholly owned Corporation by the Government.

Other companies operating services include the following: Aeroflot (U.S.S.R.), Air Djibouti, Air India, EgyptAir, Ethiopian Airways, Kuwait Airways, MEA (Lebanon), Pakistan International Airlines, Somali Airlines, Sudan Airways, Yemen Airlines.

Aden Civil Airport is at Khormaksar, 7 miles from the Port. It was established in 1952, and is operated by the Civil Aviation Department.

DEFENCE

Defence Expenditure: 19 million dinars (1978).

Total Armed Forces: 20,900: army 19,000, navy 600, air force 1,300.

EDUCATION

The educational system consists of four years of Primary, three years of Intermediate and four to six years of Secondary schooling. There are 225 Government Primary Schools, 29 Intermediate Schools and 6 Secondary Schools, and a Technical Institute at Ma'alla, Aden, with a branch at Little Aden. Other higher education is received abroad.

In addition there are 12 Government-Aided and 5 Private Primary Schools, and 10 Grant-Aided and 4 Private Intermediate Schools. Teacher-Training Centres provide over 200 places for men and women trainees while adult education is provided by evening classes.

UNIVERSITY

University of Aden: Aden; f. 1975.

BIBLIOGRAPHY

BRINTON, J. Y. Aden and the Federation of South Arabia (American Soc. of Int. Law, Washington, 1964).

CENTRAL OFFICE OF INFORMATION. Aden and South Arabia (London, H.M.S.O., 1965).

COLONIAL OFFICE. Accession of Aden to the Federation of South Arabia (London, H.M.S.O., 1962).

COLONIAL OFFICE. Treaty of Friendship and Protection between the United Kingdom and the Federation of South Arabia (London, H.M.S.O., 1964).

FEDERATION OF SOUTH ARABIA. Conference on Constitutional Problems of South Arabia (H.M.S.O., 1964).

GAVIN, R. J. Aden 1839–1967 (Hurst, London, 1973).

GEHRKE, Dr. ULRICH. Südarabien, Südarabische Föderation oder Süd-Jemen? (*Orient* Magazine, German Near and Middle East Association, Hamburg, 1967).

GOVERNMENT OF ADEN. Memorandum on the Five-Year Development Plan, 1952–53 to 1956–57 (Aden, 1958).

GOVERNMENT OF ADEN. Report of the Adenisation Committee, 1959 (London, 1959).

HARDING, H. LANKESTER. Archaeology in the Aden Protectorate (London, H.M.S.O., 1964).

HICKINBOTHAM, Sir TOM. Aden (London, Constable, 1959).

INGRAMS, DOREEN. A Survey of the Social and Economic Conditions of the Aden Protectorate (London).

INGRAMS, W. H. A Report on the Social, Economic and Political Conditions of the Hadhramaut, Aden Protectorate (London, 1936).

JOHNSTON, CHARLES. The View from Steamer Point (London, Collins, 1964).

KING, GILLIAN. Imperial Outpost–Aden (New York, Oxford University Press, 1964).

LITTLE, TOM. South Arabia (London, Pall Mall Press, 1968).

MAWER, JUNE KNOX. The Sultans Came to Tea (Murray, London, 1961).

PAGET, JULIAN. Last Post: Aden 1964–67 (Faber and Faber, London, 1969).

QAT COMMISSION OF INQUIRY. Report (Aden, 1958).

TREVASKIS, Sir KENNEDY. Shades of Amber, A South Arabian Episode (London, Hutchinson, 1967).

VAN DER MEULEN, DANIEL. Hadramaut: Some of Its Mysteries Unveiled (Leiden, 1932, reprinted 1964).

WATERFIELD, GORDON. Sultans of Aden (Murray, London 1968).

PART FOUR

Other Reference Material

WHO'S WHO IN THE MIDDLE EAST AND NORTH AFRICA

A

Abalkhail, Mohamed Ali, B.A.; Saudi Arabian government official and financial executive; b. 1935, Buraida; ed. Cairo Univ.
Began career as Asst. Dir. of Office of Minister of Communications 56, later Dir.; Dir.-Gen. of Inst. of Public Admin. 61-64; Deputy Minister of Finance and Nat. Econ. 64-70, Vice-Minister 70-71, Minister of State for Finance and Nat. Econ. 71-75, Minister 75-; Chair. of Board, Saudi Int. Bank, London, Public Investments Fund, Inst. of Public Admin., Saudi Industrial Devt. Fund, Saudi Fund for Devt.; Chair. Board of Govs. Islamic Devt. Bank; mem. Supreme Consultative Council of Petroleum and Minerals, Supreme Cttee. for Admin. Reform, Royal Comm. on Jubail and Yanbu Industrial Estates; mem. Board, Saudia-Saudi Airlines Corpn., Petroleum and Minerals Corpn. (PETROMIN), Council of Civil Service; decorations from Belgium, Egypt, France, Niger, Pakistan, Saudi Arabia, Sudan, Luxembourg, Indonesia, Spain, Zaire.
Ministry of Finance and National Economy, Riyadh, Saudi Arabia.

Abaza, Tharwat, LL.B.; Egyptian lawyer, editor and writer; b. 28 June 1927; ed. Monira Primary School, Farouk Secondary School and Cairo Univ.
Lawyer 50-54; Editor *Elmasri* daily newspaper 52-54, *Alkahira* 54-55; Publishing Consultant 56-57, 61-; mem. Cttee. on Fiction, Supreme Council for Arts, Literature and Social Sciences, and of its State Prizes Cttee.; State Prize for Fiction 59; State Decoration Grade I for Literature.
Publs. *Ibn Ammar* (Historical Fiction) 54, *Al Hayat Lana* (Life for Us—play) 55, *Hareb men Alayam* (An Escape from Fate—novel) 56, *Kasr Ala Elnil* (A Palace over the Nile—novel) 57, *Alayam Alkhadra* (Green Days—short stories) 58, *Thoma Toshrelk Alshams* (Then the Sun Rises—novel) 60, *Zhekriat Baida* (Far Echoes—short stories) 61, *Leka Honak* (An Appointment There—novel) 62, *Aldabab* (The Fog—novel) 64, *Shaion men Alkhawf* (A Little Fear—novel) 65, *Hayat El Hayah* (Life of Life—play), *Hathihi Elloba* (This Toy—short stories), *Hina Yamil Al Mizan* (When the Scales are Unbalanced—short stories).
5 Nadi Street, Maadi, Egypt.

Abbadi, Beshire Ahmed, PH.D.; Sudanese politician; b. 1936, Omdurman; ed. Univ. of Khartoum and Northwestern Univ., U.S.A.
Lecturer, Faculty of Eng., Univ. of Khartoum, Head, Dept. of Mechanical Eng. 70-71; mem. Board of Dirs. Sudan Railways 68-69, Chair. Board of Dirs. Sudan Airways 69-70; Minister of Communications Oct. 71-73, of Transport and Communications 73-77, of Industry 77-; mem. Political Bureau, Sudanese Socialist Union April 76-.
Ministry of Industry, P.O. Box 2184, Khartoum, Sudan.

Abbas, Ferhat; Algerian politician; b. 24 Aug. 1899, Taker, Constantine; ed. Algiers Univ.
Formerly a chemist at Sétif; Leader of *Association des Etudiants musulmans* 26-31; took part in org. of the Algeria People's Union 38; published "Manifesto of the Algerian People" 43; founded Amis du Manifeste et de la Liberté (A.M.L.) 44; under detention May 45-March 46; took part in the formation of the Union Démocratique du Manifeste Algérien (U.D.M.A.) 46; elected rep. to French Constitutional Assembly 46, later mem. of French Union Assembly; elected to Algerian Assembly 48 and 54; Leader of U.D.M.A. 46-56; joined Nat. Liberation Front (FLN) 55; mem. FLN del. to Eleventh Gen. Assembly of UN 57; Prime Minister of Provisional Government of the Algerian Republic (GPRA) in Tunisia 58-61; Pres. of the Chamber of Algeria 62-63; detained July 64-June 65.
Publs. *Le jeune algérien* 31, *La nuit coloniale* 62.
Konba, Algiers, Algeria.

Abboud, Gen. Ibrahim; Sudanese officer and politician; b. 1900; ed. Gordon Memorial Coll., Khartoum and Military Coll., Khartoum.
Entered Sudan Defence Force; served 39-45 war with Sudanese contingent, British Army in Eritrea, Ethiopia and Libya; Dep. C.-in-C. Sudanese Army 54, C.-in-C. 56-64; Pres. Supreme Military Council, Prime Minister and Minister of Defence 58-64.
Suakin, Sudan.

Abdalla, Abdel Rahman; Sudanese politician; b. 1933; ed. Khartoum Univ. Coll. and New York Univ.
Joined Ministry of Interior, Sub-Mamour 56; Inspector, Tokar district, later of Kassala Province; joined Halfa People's Settlement Comm. 59; Dir. Inst. of Public Admin. 63-65; Dir. African Admin. Training and Research Inst., Morocco 65; Dir. Nat. Inst. of Public Admin., Libya; Deputy Minister of Local Govt. Aug. 71; Minister of Public Service and Admin. Reform 71-77, of Industry and Mining 77, of Communications 77-78; mem. Exec. Bureau, Sudanese Socialist Union.
Sudanese Socialist Union, P.O. Box 1850, Khartoum, Sudan.

Abdalla, Ismail-Sabri, PH.D.; Egyptian economist; b. 25 Dec. 1924, Malawi; ed. Abdin and Khedive Ismail schools, Cairo and Paris Univs.
Lecturer, Alexandria Univ. 51-54, Cairo Univ. 54-56; Econ. Adviser, Econ. Devt. Org. 57-59; Chief Editor *Dar Al-Maarif* Publishing House 65-69; Dir.-Gen. Inst. of Nat. Planning 69-71, Chair. of Board 72-, Dir.-Gen. May 75-; Deputy Minister of Planning 71, Minister of State for Planning 72-74, Minister 74-75; Deputy Chair. of Board, Soc. Egyptienne d'Econ. politique, de statistique et de législation 72-; Sec.-Gen. Scientific Conf. of Egyptian Economists; mem. Acad. Advisory Board, UN African Inst. of Devt. and Planning, Dakar 71-76; mem. Gov. Council, Soc. for Int. Devt. 76-; mem. Acad. Cttee., UN Arab Inst. of Planning, Kuwait; founding mem. and now Chair. Third World Forum; mem. Board, Council for the Devt. of Econ. and Social Research in Africa.
Publs. *Economie et Structure Economique* 52, *Lectures in Economics* (Arabic) 54, *The Organization of the Public Sector* (Arabic) 69, *Confrontation with Israel* (Arabic) 69, *Political Papers* (Arabic) 72; *Towards a New Economic World Order* (in Arabic) 76; various articles in Arabic, English and French.
Institute of National Planning, Nasr City, Cairo; Home: 6 Ibn Malek Street, Guizeh, Egypt.

Abdel-Ghani, Abdul-Aziz, M.A.(ECON.); Yemeni economist and politician; b. 4 July 1939, Haifan, Yemen Arab Repub.; ed. Colorado Coll. and Colorado Univ.
Minister of Health 67-68, of Economy 68-69, 70-71; Chair. Technical Office, Board of Planning 69-70; Gov. Central Bank of Yemen 71-75; Prime Minister Jan. 75-; mem. Presidential Council.
P.O. Box 38, Sana'a, Yemen Arab Republic.

Abdelghani, Col. Mohamed Ben Ahmed; Algerian army officer and politician; b. 18 March 1927, Ghazouet, Oran region; primary and secondary educ. in Algiers.
Joined nationalist movement, Parti du Peuple Algérien 43; arrested and imprisoned 45-46; joined Nat. Liberation Front (FLN) at start of war for nat. independence 54; Commdr. of First Mil. Region (Algiers) 62-65, Fourth Mil. Region (Ouargla) 65-67, Mil. Region of Constantine 67-74;

promoted Col. 69; mem. Revolutionary Council 65-79, Political Cttee. of FLN Feb. 79-; Minister of the Interior Dec. 74-, also Prime Minister March 79-.
Office du Premier Ministre, Palais du Gouvernement, Algiers, Algeria.

Abdel Kader, H Yehia; Egyptian diplomatist; b. 1920, Alexandria; ed. Univ. of Cairo.
Secretary, Counsellor Egyptian Embassies in Belgrade, Khartoum, Milan; Amb. to Saudi Arabia 64-68, to Yugoslavia 68-71; Chair. Egyptian Radio and Television 71; Amb. to U.S.S.R. 71-74, to Greece 74-; Order of the Repub. (Egypt) 61, Order of Yugoslav Flag with Cordon 68, Order of Merit, First Class (Egypt) 70, Great Cross, Order of Phoenix (Greece) 76.
Embassy of Egypt, 3 Leoforos Vassilissis Sofias, Athens, Greece; Home: 1095, Cornish El Nil Street, Garden City, Cairo, Egypt.

Abdel Meguid, Ahmed Esmat, PH.D.; Egyptian diplomatist; b. 22 March 1923, Alexandria; ed. Faculty of Law, Alexandria Univ. and Univ. of Paris.
Attaché and Sec. Egyptian Embassy, London 50-54; Ministry of Foreign Affairs, Head of British Desk 54-56, Asst. Dir. Legal Dept. 61-63, Head, Cultural and Technical Assistance Dept. 67-68; Counsellor, Perm. Mission to European Office of UN, Geneva 57-61; Minister Counsellor, Egyptian Embassy, Paris 63-67; Official Spokesman of Govt. and Head Information Dept. 68-69; Amb. to France 69-70; Minister of State for Cabinet Affairs 70-72; Perm. Rep. to UN 72-; Chair. Cairo Preparatory Conf. for Geneva Peace Conf. 77; mem. Int. Law Asscn., took part in UN confs. on the Law of the Sea 59, on Consular Relations 63 and on the Law of Treaties 69; Ordre National de Mérite, France 67; Grand Croix 71; 1st Class Decoration, Egypt 70.
Publs. *Comparative Study of Prize Courts* 51, articles in *Revue Egyptienne de Droit International.*
Permanent Mission of Egypt to the United Nations, 36 East 67th Street, New York, N.Y. 10021, U.S.A.
Telephone: 879-6300.

Abdel-Rahman, Ibrahim Helmi, PH.D.; Egyptian international official and politician; b. 5 Jan. 1919; ed. Univs. of Cairo, London, Edinburgh, Cambridge and Leiden.
Lecturer in Astronomy and Astrophysics, later Asst. Prof. Cairo Univ. 42-54; Sec.-Gen. Council of Ministers 54-58; Dir. Egyptian Atomic Energy Comm. 54-59; mem. and Sec.-Gen. Nat. Science Council 56-58; mem. Nat. Planning Comm. 57-60; Dir. Inst. of Nat. Planning 60-63; UN Commr. for Industrial Devt. 63-66; Exec. Dir. UN Industrial Devt. Org. (UNIDO) 67-74; Senior Adviser to the Prime Minister 75; Minister of Nat. Planning and Admin. Reform 75-76; Adviser to the Prime Minister for Planning and Econ. Affairs March 76-; mem. Egyptian Acad. of Science and Institut d'Egypte.
Council of Ministers, Cairo, Egypt.

Abdessalam, Belaid; Algerian politician; b. July 1928, Dehemcha.
Former Hon. Pres. Union Générale des Etudiants Musulmans Algériens; Instructor Front de Libération Nat. (FLN) school, Oujda; in Cabinet of M. Abdelhamid Mehri, Tunisia 60; Political Adviser in Cabinet of M. Ben Khedda 61; in charge of Economic Affairs, FLN Provisional Exec. 62; Pres., Dir.-Gen. SONATRACH 64-65; Minister of Industry and Energy 65-77, of Light Industry 77-79; Chair. FLN Cttee. on Economic Affairs March 79-; Chair. Council Org. of Arab Petroleum Exporting Countries (OAPEC) 74.
Front de Libération Nationale, place Emir Abdelkader, Algiers, Algeria.

Abdoh, Djalal, LL.D.; Iranian diplomatist; b. 1909; ed. Teheran and Paris Univs.
Assistant Dir. Ministry of Justice 37-39; Public Prosecutor, Court of Govt. Employees, Teheran 41-43; Dir.-Gen. Ministry of Justice 43-44; mem. Parl. 44-49; Deputy Perm. Rep. to UN 49-53; Dir.-Gen. of Political Affairs, Ministry of Foreign Affairs 54-55; Acting Head Del. to Bandung Conf. 55; Amb. and Perm. Rep. to UN 56; Act. Rep. Security Council 56; Chair. Iranian Del. Gen. Assembly 58-59; Minister of Foreign Affairs 59; UN Plebiscite Commr., British N. Cameroons 59-60; Amb. at Large 61; Administrator, UN Temporary Exec. Authority (UNTEA), West New Guinea (West Irian) 62-63; Prof., Teheran Univ. 64-65; Amb. to India 65-68, to Italy 68-72; Man. Dir. Iranian Bankers' Asscn. 72; mem. Currency and Credit Council 72-78, Perm. Court of Arbitration 46; Pres. Iranian Asscn. for the UN 72, Iranian branch of Int. Law Asscn. 73; currently attorney-at-law.
Publs. *Civil Procedure of Iran, Comparative Law, International Private Law, Eléments psychologiques dans les Contrats, Le Ministère Public, Le régime Pénitentiaire en Iran, The Political Situation in Africa* (Persian), *The Political Situation in The Middle East* (Persian); series of articles on UN in *World Affairs.*
J. Abdoh and Associates, 49 Daryay-e-Noor Street, Takht-e-Tavous Avenue, Teheran, Iran.

Abdul-Khail, Muhammad Ali (*see* Abalkhail, Mohammed Ali).

Abdullah as Sheikh, Sheikh Hassan; Saudi Arabian politician; b. 1932; ed. Shariah Coll., Mecca and Al Azhar Univ., Cairo.
Former mem. Judicial Supervisory Cttee.; Vice-Pres. Judicial Supervisory Cttee.; Minister of Educ. and Health 62, later of Educ., of Higher Educ. 75-; Chief Dir. Council of Arts, Sciences and Literature 62-; Chancellor Univ. of King Abdelaziz, Univ. of Riyadh, Islamic Univ. of Imam Muhammad ibn Saud, Islamic Univ. at Medina; Chair. Board of Trustees, Univ. of Petroleum and Minerals; Dir. Muhammad ibn Saud, Islamic Univ. at Medina; Dir. Archaeological Dept.
Publs. *Duwarna Fi Al-Kufah* (Our Turn in the Struggle), *Brave Ideas, Dignity of The Individual in Islam.*
Ministry of Higher Education, Riyadh, Saudi Arabia.

Abdullah ibn Abdulaziz ibn Abdelrahman el Faisal el Saud, H.R.H. Prince; Saudi Arabian Prince and army officer; b. Aug. 1921; brother of H.M. King Khalid (*q.v.*).
Commander of Saudi Arabian Nat. Guard 62-; Second Deputy Prime Minister March 75-.
c/o National Guard, Riyadh, Saudi Arabia.

Abushadi, Mohamed Mahmoud, PH.D., B.COM., A.C.I.P.; Egyptian banker; b. 15 Aug. 1913, Fayoum; ed. Cairo Univ., Chartered Inst. of Patent Agents, and American Univ., Washington, D.C., U.S.A.
Controller-Gen. Insurance Dept., Ministry of Finance 49-52; Dir.-Gen. Govt. Insurance and Provident Funds 53; Chair. and Man. Dir. Development and Popular Housing Co. 54-55; Sub.-Gov. Nat. Bank of Egypt 55-60, Man. Dir. 61-67, Chair. 67-70; Chair. Social Insurance Org. 56-57; Chair. and Man. Dir. Cairo Insurance Co. 56-57; Man. Dir. Cairo Bank 56-57; Chair. Union de Banques Arabes et Françaises, Paris 70-, UBAF Bank Ltd., London 72-; Pres. Int. Bankers' Asscn. 76-; Order of the Repub., Second Class, Order of Merit, First Class.
Publs. *The Art of Central Banking and its Application in Egypt* 52, *Central Banking in Egypt* 52, *Will New York attract Arab Capital?* 74, *The Experience of Arab-French Banks* 74, *Oil Funds: the search for supplementary recycling mechanisms* 75.
Union de Banques Arabes et Françaises, 4 rue Ancelle, 92521 Neuilly sur Seine; Home: 52 avenue Foch, 75016 Paris, France.

Abuzeid, Hamdi; Egyptian diplomatist; b. 20 March 1919, Sudan; ed. Mil. Colls. in U.K., U.S.A., U.S.S.R.
Military pilot, Egyptian Air Force 40; Amb. to Yugoslavia

62, to Mexico 68, to Syria 75, to U.S.S.R. 76-; Head, European Dept., Ministry of Foreign Affairs 73; Minister of Civil Aviation 75.
Embassy of Egypt, Ul. Gertsena 56, Moscow, U.S.S.R.; Home: 31 Mazhar Street, Zamalek, Cairo, Egypt.

Abuzeid, Salah; Jordanian diplomatist and former politician; b. 21 April 1925, Irbid; ed. Law Coll. of Syrian Univ., Damascus and Syracuse Univ., U.S.A.
Government Official 50-58; Dir. Amman Radio Station 58-59; Asst. Dir.-Gen. Hashemite Broadcasting Service 59-62, Dir.-Gen. of Hashemite Broadcasting Service and Chief of Nat. Guidance 62-64; Minister of Information 64-65, 67, of Culture and Information 67-68; Amb. to U.K. 69; Minister of Culture and Information 69-70; Special Adviser to H.M. The King 70-72; Minister of Foreign Affairs 72-73; mem. Senate, Head of Foreign Relations Cttee. 74-76; Adviser to H.M. The King 76; Amb. to United Kingdom 76-78; sentenced to three years' imprisonment for misuse of funds 79; sentence later reduced to six months; numerous decorations.
Publ. *Al Hussein bin Talal* 58.
c/o Ministry of Foreign Affairs, Amman, Jordan.

Adams, Michael Evelyn, M.A.; British writer; b. 31 May 1920; ed. Sedbergh School and Christ Church, Oxford.
Commonwealth Fund Fellowship in U.S.A. 54-55; Middle East Corresp. *The Guardian* 56-62; Asst. to Dir. Voluntary Service Overseas 64-67; Dir. of Information, Council for the Advancement of Arab-British Understanding (CAABUI 68-78; Editor *Middle East International.*
Publs. *Suez and After* 58, *Umbria* 64, *Voluntary Service Overseas* 68, *Chaos or Rebirth* 68, *Handbook to the Middle East* (Editor) 71, *Publish it Not . . .* (with Christopher Mayhew) 75.
Middle East International, 21 Collingham Road, London, SW5 0NU, England.

Adams, Robert McCormick, A.M., PH.D.; American anthropologist and archaeologist; b. 23 July 1926; ed. Univ. of Chicago.
Archaeological field work at Jarmo, Iraq 50-51; joined staff of Univ. of Chicago 54, Dir. Oriental Inst. 62-68, Prof. of Anthropology 63-, Harold H. Swift Distinguished Service Prof. 75-, Dean, Div. of Social Science 70-74; Field studies of irrigation and settlement patterns in central and southern Iraq 56-58, 60, 67, 68-69, 73-75, Iran 60-61; excavations in Iran 63, Syria 70, Saudi Arabia 76; Chair. Assembly of Behavioral and Social Sciences, Nat. Research Council 73-76, American Oriental Soc.; Vice-Chair. Cttee. on Science and Public Policy, Nat. Acad. of Sciences 77-; Fellow, American Acad. of Arts and Sciences, American Anthropological Asscn., American Asscn. for the Advancement of Science; mem. German Archaeological Inst., Nat. Acad. of Science, Middle East Studies Asscn., American Philosophical Soc.; Trustee, Nat. Opinion Research Center 70-, Nat. Humanities Center 76-, Russell Sage Foundation 78-.
Publs. *City Invincible: a Symposium of Urbanization and Cultural Development in the Ancient Near East* (co-editor with C. H. Kraeling) 60, *Land Behind Baghdad: a History of Settlement on the Diyala Plains* 65, *The Evolution of Urban Society: Early Mesopotamia and Pre-hispanic Mexico* 66, *The Uruk Countryside* (with H. J. Nissen) 72, *Heartland of Cities: Surveys of Ancient Settlement and Land Use on the Central Floodplain of the Euphrates.*
The Oriental Institute, 1155 East 58th Street, Chicago, Illinois 60637; and 5805 South Dorchester Avenue, Chicago, Illinois 60637, U.S.A.

Adasani, Mahmoud, B.SC.; Kuwaiti engineer; b. 31 Jan. 1934; ed. Kuwait, American Univ., Beirut and Univ. of Southern California.
Assistant petroleum engineer, Kuwait Oil Co (KOC) 58-60, petroleum engineer 60, Dir. KOC 60-; Technical Asst., Gen. Oil Affairs Dept., Ministry of Finance and Oil 60-63, Dir. of Technical Affairs 63-66, Asst. Under-Sec. for Oil Affairs 66-75; Under-Sec., Ministry of Oil June 75-; Man. Dir. Salwa Construction Co.; Dir. Kuwait Metal Pipeline Co. 70-79; Kuwait Rep., Bureau of the Org. of Arab Petroleum Exporting Countries (OAPEC) Jan. 75- (Chair. 78); Chair. Petroleum Resources Conservation Board 76-; OPEC Gov. for Kuwait; mem. American Inst. Mechanical Engineers, Kuwait Soc. Engineers.
Publs. *Oil of Kuwait, The Greater Burgan Field, North Kuwait Oil Fields.*
Ministry of Oil, P.O. Box 5077, Kuwait.

Adib, Albert; Lebanese editor; b. 1 July 1908, Mexico.
Editor many magazines, Cairo 27-30, Beirut 30-38; Pres. Acad. of Oriental Music, Beirut 33-38; Gen. Dir. Radio-Levant Broadcasting Station, Beirut 38-43; Editor and proprietor *Al-Adib* review, Beirut 42-; mem. various acads. and foreign cultural insts.; Chevalier of the Order of the Cedar.
Publ. *Liman* (poems) 52.
P.O. Box 11-878, Beirut, Lebanon.

Adni, Daniel; Israeli concert pianist; b. 6 Dec. 1951, Haifa; ed. High Schools in Haifa and Tel-Aviv, Conservatoire of Music in Paris.
First Recital in Haifa 63; professional debut, London 70; New York debut 76; has played at most musical centres of the world incl. U.K., Fed. Repub. of Germany, Israel, U.S.A., Japan, South Africa, Switzerland, Norway, Netherlands, Romania; made over 12 records for EMI-His Master's Voice; First Prize, Paris Conservatoire; First Prize, Young Concert Artists' Auditions, New York.
c/o Dr. G. de Koos and Co. Ltd., 416 King's Road, London, SW10 0LJ, England.

Afshar, Dr. Amir Aslan; Iranian government official; b. 21 Nov. 1922; ed. Berlin and Hindenburg Schools, and Univs. of Berlin, Greifswald, Vienna and Geneva.
Joined Ministry of Foreign Affairs 47, Sec., The Hague 50-54; Del. to Bandung Conf., Indonesia 55; Eisenhower Exchange Fellowship 55-56; mem. Parl. 56-61; Del. to UN Gen. Assembly 57, 58 and 60; Adjutant to the Shah 59-79; Plenipotentiary Minister 63; mem. High Political Council 63-66; Pres. Iranian Shipping Lines 60-; Amb. to Austria 67-69, to U.S.A. and Mexico 69-73, to Fed. Repub. of Germany 73; Grand Master of Ceremonies of H.I.M. The Shahanshah Aryamehr 77-79; Chair. Board of Governors of the Int. Atomic Energy Agency, Vienna 68-69; head of del. to 10 int. confs.; numerous decorations.
Publs. in German: *The Constitution of the Third Reich* 42, *The Administration of the Third Reich* 42, *Possibilities for the Economic Development of Iran* 43; in Persian: *The End of the Third Reich* 48, *God Created the Universe and the Dutch made Holland* 55; in English: *Report on America* 56.
210 Hafez Avenue, Teheran, Iran.

Aga Khan, Prince Sadruddin; Iranian UN official; b. 1933, Paris, France; ed. Harvard Univ. and Harvard Univ. Graduate School for Arts and Sciences.
UNESCO Consultant for Afro-Asian Projects 58; Head of Mission and Adviser to UN High Commr. for Refugees 59-60; UNESCO Special Consultant to Dir.-Gen. 61; Exec. Sec. Int. Action Cttee. for Preservation of Nubian Monuments 61; UN Dep. High Commr. for Refugees 62-65, High Commr. 66-77; Consultant to Sec.-Gen. of OAU 78; Publr. *The Paris Review*; Founder and Sec. Harvard Islamic Asscn.; Pres. Council on Islamic Affairs, New York City; mem. Inst. of Differing Civilizations, Brussels, World Wildlife Fund; Founding mem. and Pres. Groupe de Bellerive; Commander's Cross with Star of the Order of Merit of the Polish People's Repub. 77; Order of St. Sylvester the Pope; Order of Star of the Nile (Sudan);

Order of Homayoun, First Class; UN Human Rights Award 78.
Château de Bellerive, Collonge, Geneva, Switzerland.

Agam, Yaacoy; Israeli artist; b. 1928, Rishon Letzon; ed. Bezalel School of Art, Jerusalem, Atelier d'art abstrait, Paris.
One-man exhbns. in Galerie Craven, Paris 53, Galerie Denise René, Paris 56, 58, Palais des Beaux-Arts, Brussels 58, Tel-Aviv Museum 58, Suzanne Bollag Gallery, Zurich 59, 62, Drian Gallery, London 59, Marlborough Gerson Gallery, New York 66, Galerie Denise René, New York 71; travelling retrospective exhbn. Paris, Amsterdam, Düsseldorf, Tel-Aviv 72-73; numerous group exhbns. 54-.
Works include: *Transformes Musicales* 61, *Double Metamorphosis*, Shalom Liner 64, *Sculptures in the City*, Reims 70, sculpture and mural, President's mansion, Israel 71, *Water Fire* fountain, St. Louis 71, environment, Elysée Palace, Paris 72, mobile wall, School of Science, Montpellier 72, design and realization of a square in defence quarter, Paris, incl. water fountain and monumental sculpture 73; films produced incl. *Recherches et Inventions* 56, *Le Désert chante*, *Micro-salon* (with I. Mambush) 57.
26 rue Boulard, Paris, France.

Ahmad, Maj.-Gen. Mohammed al-Baqir; Sudanese army officer and politician; b. 1927, El Sofi; ed Commercial Secondary School, Khartoum, Military Coll. and Cairo Univ.
Commissioned 50; Chief of Staff, Southern Command 58; Mil. Gov. Upper Nile Province 59; Mil. Attaché, London 66-67; Dir. of Training and Chief of Staff, Southern Command 68; Commdr. Mil. Coll. 68-69; Under-Sec. Ministry of Defence 69; First Deputy Chief of Staff of Armed Forces 69-70, Chief of Staff 70-71; Minister of Interior 71-73, Jan.-Aug. 75; First Vice-Pres. of Sudan 72-77; mem. Exec. Bureau, Sudanese Socialist Union, Council, Univ. of Khartoum 70-71; del. to several int. confs.; several decorations.
Executive Bureau, Sudanese Socialist Union, P.O. Box 1850, Khartoum, Sudan.

Aini, Mohsin A. al; Yemeni diplomatist and politician; b. 1932; ed. Cairo Univ. and Univ. of Paris.
Schoolteacher, Aden 58-60; Int. Confederation of Arab Trade Unions 60-62; Minister of Foreign Affairs, Yemeni Republic Sept.-Dec. 62; Perm. Rep. to UN Dec. 62-65, 65-66, 67-69; Amb. to U.S.A. 63-65, 65-66; Foreign Minister May-July 65; Prime Minister Nov. 67; Personal Rep. of Chair. Republican Council 67; Amb. to U.S.S.R. 68-70; Prime Minister and Foreign Minister Feb. 70-Feb. 71; Amb. to France July-Sept. 71; Prime Minister, Minister of Foreign Affairs 71-72, June 74-June 75; Amb. to U.K. 73-74, to France 75-76.
c/o Ministry of Foreign Affairs, Sana'a, Yemen Arab Republic.

Aktuğ, Savlet K.; Turkish diplomatist; b. 14 March 1926, Afyon; ed. Galatasaray Lycée, Istanbul, Faculty of Law, Univ. of Ankara.
Editor, Anatolian News Agency 45-49; Commentator, Ankara Radio; Dir. of Information Dept., Office of the Dir.-Gen. of the Press, Ankara; Deputy Dir.-Gen. Anatolian News Agency; served in the Ministry of Foreign Affairs 52-, in Amman, in Berne (First Sec.); Chargé d'Affaires and Counsellor, Turkish Embassy, Rio de Janeiro 63-69; Deputy Dir.-Gen. of Dept. of Information; Chef de Cabinet to the Minister of Foreign Affairs; Turkish Consul-Gen. (Ministerial rank), London 71-76; Amb. to Tunisia 76-79; several foreign decorations.
c/o Ministry of Foreign Affairs, Dişişleri Bakanliği, Müdafaa Cad. Bakanliklar, Ankara, Turkey.

Akurgal, Ekrem, PH.D.; Turkish archaeologist; b. 1911, Istanbul; ed. Germany.
Lecturer, Univ. of Ankara 41-49, Prof. of Archaeology 49-; has conducted excavations at Smyrna, Sinope, Phokaia, Daskyleion, Pitane and Erythrai 53-, at Izmir 67-; Visiting Prof., Princeton Univ. 61-62; mem. Turkish Historical Soc., Turkish High Comm. for Ancient Monuments; mem. Austrian and German Archaeol. Insts., British, Austrian and Swedish Acads.; Hon. mem. Soc. for Promotion of Hellenic Studies, London, American Inst. of Archaeol.; Dr. h.c. (Bordeaux) 61.
Publs. *Griechische Reliefs aus Lykien* 42, *Remarques Stylistiques sur les reliefs de Malatya* 46, *Späthethitische Bildkunst* 49, *Phrygische Kunst* 55, *Die Kunst Anatoliens von Homer bis Alexander* 61, *Die Kunst der Hethiter* 61, *Orient und Okzident* 66, *Treasures of Turkey* (with Mango and Ettinghausen) 66, *Urartäische und Altiranische Kunstzentren* 68, *Ancient Civilizations and Ruins of Turkey* (3rd edn.) 73.
University of Ankara, Dil ve Tarih-Coğrafya Fakültesi, Ankara; Home: Vali Dr. Reşit cad. 90/5 Çankaya, Ankara, Turkey.

Akwaa', Brig. Mohammed Ali al-; Yemeni army officer, b. 1933, Sana'a; ed. secondary scho ol, Mil.Coll., Sana'a.
Participated in the movts. against last three Imams of Yemen, Free Yemenis Revolution 48, attempted coup 55; Revolution of 26 September 1962; leading figure in movt. which ousted Pres. al-Sallal 67; has held several posts in mil. and civil service including Asst. Mil. Commdr. Taiz District, Head Criminal Investigation Dept., Head Nat. Security (Intelligence) Dept.; Chief of Staff, Army Operations, Head S. Yemen Relief Office attached to Presidency; Minister of the Interior 73-74.
Bir Al-Azab, Sana'a, Yemen Arab Republic.

Alamuddin, Sheikh Najib Salim, B.A.; Lebanese airline executive; b. 9 March 1909; ed. American Univ. of Beirut and Univ. Coll. of South West, Exeter, England.
Teacher of Engineering and Mathematics, American Univ. of Beirut 30-33; Insp. of Mathematics, Educ. Dept., Govt. of Trans-Jordan 33-36; Insp.-Gen. of Customs, Trade and Industry, Trans-Jordan 39-40; Chief Sec. Govt. of Trans-Jordan 40-42; founded Near East Resources Co. 42; Gen. Man. Middle East Airlines 52-56, Chair. and Pres. 56-77, Hon. Chair. 77-; Minister of Information and Tourism 65, of Public Works and Transport 66, 73; fmr. mem. Exec. Cttee. of Int. Air Transport Asscn.; Trustee Emeritus, American Univ. of Beirut; Dir. several Lebanese companies; numerous decorations; Hon. C.B.E. (U.K.) Nov. 76.
Middle East Airlines, Beirut International Airport, P.O. Box 206, Beirut, Lebanon.

Al-Azzawi, Hikmet: (*see* Azzawi, Hikmat al-).

Al-Hinai, Sheikh Farid Mbarek Ali: (*see* Hinai).

Ali, Ahmad Mohamed, PH.D.; Saudi Arabian administrator; b. 13 April 1934, Medina Munawwara; ed. Medina Munawwara, Cairo Univ., Univ. of Michigan, State Univ. of New York at Albany.
Vice-Chancellor, King Abdul Aziz Univ., Jeddah 67-72; Deputy Minister for Technical Affairs, Ministry of Educ. 72-75, Pres. Islamic Devt. Bank Sept. 75-.
Islamic Development Bank, P.O. Box 5925, Jeddah, Saudi Arabia.

Ali, Lieut-Gen. Kamal Hassan; Egyptian army officer and politician; b. 18 Sept. 1921, Abdin, Cairo; ed. secondary school, Mil. Acad., British Armoured School, Staff Coll., Festrel Acad., U.S.S.R., Nasser Higher Mil. Acad.
Career in Army from graduation at Mil. Acad. 42; promoted Lieut. 42, First Lieut. 46, Capt. 48; Senior Instructor, Armour School 53; Major 54; Staff Officer, 2nd Armoured Operational Group 56; Lieut.-Col. 57; Commdr. 70th Brigade 60; Instructor, Staff Coll. 61; Brigadier 65, Commdr. 2nd Armoured Brigade 66; Chief of Staff, 21st Armoured Div. 68, Commdr. 69; Chief of Operational Branch, Operations Dept. 70; Major-Gen. and Chief of Staff of Armoured Corps 71, Dir. 72; Asst. Minister of War 75; Chief of Gen. Intelligence 75; Minister of Defence and

Mil. Production, C.-in-C. of Armed Forces, Lieut.-Gen. Oct. 78-; Liberation Order 52, Memorial Order 58; many ribbons and medals.
Ministry of Defence, P.O. Box 78, Heliopolis, Cairo, Egypt.

Ali, Salah Omar al-; Iraqi diplomatist; b. 1 July 1937; ed. Al-Mustansiriyah Univ., Baghdad.
Member of Revolutionary Command Council 68-70; Editor-in-Chief of *Al-Thawra* newspaper 69; Minister for Information March-July 70; Amb. to Sweden 72-76, to Spain 76-78; Perm. Rep. to the UN July 78-; fmr. mem. leadership of Arab Baath Socialist Party.
Permanent Mission of Iraq to the United Nations, 14 East 79th Street, New York, N.Y. 10021, U.S.A.

Alier, Abel, LL.B., LL.M.; Sudanese politician; b. 1933, Bor District, Upper Nile Province; ed. Univs. of Khartoum, London, Yale.
Former advocate; District Judge in El Obeid, Wad Medani and Khartoum until 65; participant in Round Table Conf. and mem. Twelve Man Cttee. to study the Southern problem 65-66; mem. Constitution Comms. 66-67, 68; fmr. mem. Law Reform Comm.; mem. Board of Dirs., Industrial Planning Corpn. 68-69; mem. Nat. Scholarship Board 68-69; Minister of Supply and Internal Trade Oct. 69-June 70; Minister of Works June 70-July 71; Minister for Southern Affairs Aug. 71-April 72; Vice-Pres. Oct. 71-; Pres. High Exec. Council for the Southern Region 72-78; Chair. Nat. Council for Devt. of Jonglei Canal Area 77-, Tech. Cttee. to establish Regional System of Govt. in Sudan; mem. Political Bureau, Sudanese Socialist Union; Hon. LL.D. (Khartoum) 78; Most Honoured Son of the Sudan Medal.
People's Palace, Khartoum, Sudan.

Alireza, Sheikh Mohamed Ibn Abdullah; Saudi Arabian merchant and industrialist; b. 1911; ed. Saudi Arabia and India.
Former Pres. Chamber of Commerce and Industries, Jeddah; mem. Admin. Council, Jeddah 46; Ex-Pres. Jeddah Benevolent Water Supply Cttee.; mem. Board of Trustees of the Benevolent Falah School 34; Leader Saudi Arabian del. to the Int. Islamic Econ. Conf., Pakistan 49; Chair. of Jeddah Port Trust Project 50; Minister of Commerce and Industries 54-58; Ambassador to U.A.R. March-June 64; Pres. Haji Abdullah Alireza & Co. Ltd., Haji Abdullah Alireza Libyan Trading Co., Arabian Italian Engineering Contractors S.p.A., Rome, Arabian Petroleum Supply Co. S.A.; fmr. Amb. to France.
Haji Abdullah Alireza & Co. Ltd., Jeddah, Saudi Arabia.

Al-Jamali, Asim; (*see* Jamali, Asim al-).

Allegro, John Marco; British philologist and archaeologist; b. 17 Feb. 1923; ed. Wallington County Grammar School and Univ. of Manchester.
Royal Navy 41-46; Manchester Univ. 47-52; research in Hebrew dialects, Magdalen Coll., Oxford 52-53; British rep. on Int. Editing Team for Dead Sea Scrolls, Jerusalem 53-; Lecturer in Comparative Semitic Philology and Hebrew, Univ. of Manchester 54-62, in Old Testament and Intertestamental Studies 62-70; Adviser to Jordanian Govt. on Dead Sea Scrolls 61-; Trustee and Hon. Sec. Dead Sea Scrolls Fund 62-70.
Publs. *The Dead Sea Scrolls* 56, 64, *The People of the Dead Sea Scrolls* 59, *The Treasure of the Copper Scroll* 60, 64, *Search in the Desert* 64, *The Shapira Affair* 65, *Discoveries in the Judaean Desert* (Vol. 5) 68, *The Sacred Mushroom and the Cross* 70, *The End of a Road* 70, *The Chosen People* 71, *Lost Gods* 77, *The Dead Sea Scrolls and the Christian Myth* 79.
Craigmore, Ballasalla, Isle of Man.

Allon, Maj.-Gen. Yigal; Israeli soldier and politician; b. 10 Oct. 1918, Kfar Tabor, Lower Galilee; ed. Kadourie Agricultural Coll., St. Antony's Coll., Oxford, Hebrew Univ., Jerusalem.
Joined Hagana 31, Commdr. of Palmach Company 41, in Syria and Lebanon with Allies, Dep. Commdr. Palmach 43, C.-in-C. Palmach 45-48; charged with Hagana operations in Palestine 45-47; in command, Upper Galilee, Central Israel, Jerusalem Corridor, the Negev and N. Sinai 47-48; Maj.-Gen. (Reserves) Zahal (Israel Defence Forces); mem. and Co-Founder Kibbutz Genossar 37-; Minister of Labour 61-67; Minister for Absorption 67-69; Deputy Prime Minister 67-June 77; Minister of Educ. and Culture 69-74, of Foreign Affairs 74-June 77; mem. Exec. Cttee. Hakibbutz Hameuchad; fmr. Sec.-Gen. Achduth Ha-avodah Socialist Party; Chair. World Labour Zionist Movement Feb. 78-; mem. Knesset's Foreign Affairs and Defence Cttee., Labour Party and Labour-Mapam Alignment, Knesset 54-.
Publs. *The Story of Palmach* 51 (Book of Palmach), *Curtain of Sand* 60, *The Making of Israel's Army* (in English and German) 70, *Shield of David* (in English) 70, *Three Wars and one Peace* (trans. in Arabic), *My Father's House* (in Hebrew and English) 76, *Israël: la Lutte pour l'Espoir* 77, and many essays and articles on political, military, education and cultural subjects in Hebrew, Yiddish, Arabic and English.
Kibbutz Genossar, Israel.

Allouache, Merzak; Algerian film director.
Worked in Nat. Inst. of Cinema, Algiers, later in Inst. of Film, Paris; after return to Algeria worked as Adviser, Ministry of Culture; Tanit D'Or Prize, Carthage 79.
Films include: *Our Agrarian Revolution* (documentary) 73, *Omar Gatlato, Adventures of a Hero.*
c/o Ministry of Information and Culture, 119 rue Didouche Mourad, Algiers, Algeria.

Almogi, Major Yosef; Israeli politician; b. 5 May 1910; ed. secondary school.
Came to Palestine 30; mem. Haganah Command 33-39; Prisoner of War, Germany 41-45; Gen. Sec. Labour Council, Haifa 45-49; Gen. Sec. Mapai Party 59-62; Minister of State 61-62; Minister of Housing and Development 62-65; joined Israel Labour List (Rafi Party) 65; Minister of Labour 68-74; Mayor of Haifa 74-76; Chair. Jewish Agency for Israel 76-77.
120 Arlozorov Street, Haifa, Israel.

Aloni, Shulamit, LL.M.; Israeli lawyer and politician; b. 1928, Tel Aviv; ed. Teachers' Seminary, Hebrew Univ; Editor radio programmes on legal matters and civil rightst Columnist *Ydiot Achoronot* (daily); mem. 6th Knesse; (Parl.) for Mapai 65-69; Chair. Consumers' Council 66-70. founder and Pres. Citizens Rights Movement 73-; mem. 8th Knesset 73-77, 9th Knesset June 77-; Minister without Portfolio 74-75.
Publs. *The Citizen and His State* 58, (7th edn. 74), *The Rights of Children in Israel* 61, *The Arrangement—From a Halachi State to a State of Law* 70.
The Knesset, Jerusalem; Home: Kfar Shmariahu, Israel.

Alpert, Carl; Israeli journalist and university official; b. 12 May 1913; ed. Boston Univ., U.S.A.
Editor *The New Palestine* 40-47; Nat. Pres. American Young Judaea 40-41; Nat. Dir. Educ. Dept. Zionist Org. of America 47-52; emigrated to Israel 52; Dir. Public Relations Dept., Technion Israel Inst. of Technology 52-68; Exec. Vice-Chair. Technion Board of Govs. 62-; Nat. Pres. Assn. of Americans and Canadians in Israel 57-59; author int. syndicated weekly column in 42 newspapers.
Technion Israel Institute of Technology, Technion City, Haifa, Israel.

Al-Saffar, Salman Mohamed: (*see* Saffar, Salman Mohamed al-).

Alwan, Hamia; Iraqi politician and former journalist; b. 1930, Babylon Governorate; ed. American Univ. in Beirut.
Served Ministry of Finance for several years; arrested several times for political activity; Editor-in-Chief and Publisher *Al-Shaab* newspaper; served in State Org. of Commerce; Dir.-Gen. of Information 68; Minister of State for Presidential Affairs 68; Minister of Culture and Information 69, of Youth 70; Head of Iraqi-German Friendship Assen. 72; Minister of Information 72; Head of Exec. Bureau, Gen. Fed. of Iraqi Youth 74; Minister of State 74-76; Head of Bureau of Vice-Chair. of Revolutionary Command Council with rank of Minister 76-77; Minister of State for Foreign Affairs Jan. 77-.
Ministry of Foreign Affairs, Karradat Mariam, Baghdad, Iraq.

Amer, Subhi Amin, M.D.; Jordanian politician; b. 1912; ed. American Univ. of Beirut.
Physician, Transjordan 38-46, Palestine Govt. 47-48; Dir. Govt. Hosp., Nablus 48-53; Chief Physician, Nablus District 53-57; Asst. Under-Sec. to Minister of Health 57-62; Minister of Health five times 62-67; Minister of Health, Reconstruction and Devt. Oct.-Dec. 62, 68-70, of Health June-Sept. 70, of Reconstruction and Devt. Sept. 70-July 76.
Amman, Jordan.

Amin, Hafizullah, B.S., M.A.; Afghani politician; b. 1 Aug. 1929, Paghman, Kabul; ed. Teachers' Training High School, Kabul, Kabal Univ., Columbia Univ., New York, U.S.A.
Vice-Principal, Teachers' Coll., Kabul; Principal, Ibne-Sina School; Lecturer, Faculty of Educ., Kabul Univ., mem. of Teachers' Training Dept.; teacher at Rabea-Balkhi Lycée, Kabul; mem. Primary Educ. Dept., Ministry of Educ.; mem. of Parl.; Minister of Foreign Affairs April 78-; Deputy Prime Minister April 78-March 79, Prime Minister March 79-; Sec. People's Democratic Party July 78-.
Office of the Prime Minister, Kabul, Afghanistan.

Amin, Mahmoud, M.SC., PH.D.; Egyptian petroleum geologist; b. 30 April 1920, Cairo; ed. Cairo Univ., London Univ.
Deputy Gen. Man. of Exploration and Production, Egyptian Petroleum Corpn. 58-68; Chair. Western Desert Petroleum Corpn. 68-75; Asst. Sec.-Gen. OAPEC 75-79; Petroleum consultant 79-.
Publs. *Economics of Petroleum Resources*, about 25 scientific papers in geology and petroleum, about 100 articles on petroleum.
20 Mohamed Hassan Street, Heliopolis, Cairo; Home: 391 Horyia Street, Apartment 802, Alexandria, Egypt.

Amin, Mohamed el Amir; Sudanese airways official; b. 1 June 1919; ed. Gordon Memorial Coll., Khartoum.
Attached to Office of Civil Sec. (now Ministry of Interior) 38-48; Chief of Booking and Freight Office, Sudan Airways 48-54, Sales Supt. Sudan Airways 54-66; Gen. Man. Sudan Airways 66-68, 72-79; Adviser-Gen. 68-72.
c/o Sudan Airways, P.O. Box 253, Khartoum North, Sudan.

Amin, Mostafa, M.A.; Egyptian journalist; b. 21 Feb. 1914, Cairo; ed. American Univ. of Cairo and Georgetown Univ., U.S.A.
Began his career publishing or writing for magazines, incl. *El Raghaeb, Rose el Youssef* 28; Deputy Chief Editor *Akher Saa* weekly magazine 34, Editor-in-Chief 38; City Editor *Al Ahram* daily 39-44, Diplomatic Editor 40; Editor-in-Chief *Al Isnain* weekly 41-44; founder *Akhbar el Yom* weekly newspaper and publishing house, jointly with his brother Ali Amin 44; mem. House of Reps. 44; purchased *Akher Saa* weekly magazine 46; founded *Akher Lahza, El Guil* 51, weekly magazines; arrested 26 times for editorial policies during 51; co-founded *Al-Akhbar* daily 52; published *Al Mokhtar* for Reader's Digest 56-67; Vice-Chair. Press Board 60, dismissed by Pres. Gamal Abdul Nasser 60; Chair. of Board, Dar al Hilal Publishers 61; Chair. of Board, Akhbar el Yom Publishers 62-64, Editorial Man. 64-65; arrested 65, sentenced to life imprisonment 66, reprieved by Pres. Anwar Sadat 74; Editor-in-Chief *Akhbar el Yom* 74-76; staff writer 76-.
Publs. *Laughing America* 43, *First Year in Prison.*
Dar Akhbar el Yom, 6 Sharia al-Safaha, Cairo, Egypt.

Amin, Samir, D.ECON.; Egyptian economist; b. 4 Sept. 1931, Cairo; ed. Univ. of Paris.
Senior Economist, Econ. Devt. Org., Cairo 57-60; Technical Adviser for Planning to Govt. of Mali 60-63; Prof. of Econs., Univs. of Poitiers, Paris and Dakar; Dir. UN African Inst. for Econ. Devt. and Planning 70-.
Publs. *Trois expériences africaines de développement, Mali, Guinée, Ghana* 65, *L'Economie du Maghreb* (2 vols.) 67, *Le développement du capitalisme en Côte d'Ivoire* 68, *Le monde des affaires sénégalaises* 68, *Maghreb in the Modern World* 70, *L'Accumulation à l'échelle mondiale* 70, *L'Afrique de l'Ouest bloquée* 71, *Le développement inégal* 73, *The Arab Nation* 78.
African Institute for Economic Development and Planning, rue 18 Juin, B.P. 3186, Dakar, Senegal.

Amini, Ali, D.ECON. ET IUR.; Iranian politician; b. 1 July 1907; ed. Ecole de Droit, Grenoble, and Faculté de Droit, Paris, France.
Alternative Judge, Court of First Instance, and Penal Branch, Court of Appeal, Teheran 31; Asst. Dir. Opium Admin. Monopoly 33; Asst. Dir.-Gen. Customs Admin. 34, Dir. 36; Economic Dir.-Gen. Ministry of Finance 38, Under-Sec. 40; mem. Chamber of Deputies Teheran and Deputy Prime Minister 40; Iranian rep. Int. Narcotic and Opium Confs. 49 and 50; Minister of Finance 52; led Iranian del. in negotiations with Int. Oil Consortium 54; Minister of Justice 55; Amb. to U.S.A. 56-58; Prime Minister 61-62.
Publ. *L'institution du monopole de commerce extérieur en Perse.*
Chemiran Elahieh, ave. Yassaman 4, Teheran, Iran.

Ammash, Major-General Saleh Mahdi; Iraqi soldier and politician; ed. Military Coll.
Minister of Defence Feb.-Nov. 63; C.-in-C. Supreme Defence Council of Iraq and Syria Oct.-Nov. 63; Deputy Prime Minister and Minister of the Interior July 68-70; Vice-Pres. 70-71; Amb. to U.S.S.R. 71-74, to France 74.
c/o Ministry of Foreign Affairs, Karradat Mariam, Baghdad, Iraq.

Amouzegar, Jamshid, B.C.E., M.S., PH.D., Iranian politician; b. 25 June 1923; ed. Univs. of Teheran, Cornell, Washington.
United Nations Expert, Mission to Iran 51; Chief, Engineering Dept. 52-55; Deputy Minister of Health 55-58; Minister of Labour 58-59, of Agriculture 59-60; Consulting Engineer 60-64; Minister of Health 64-65, of Finance 65-74, of Employment 74, of Interior 74-76; Minister of State 76-77; Prime Minister 77-78; Sec.-Gen. Nat. Resurgence Party 76-77, Jan.-Aug. 78; Chair. Int. Civil Service Advisory Board of UN; Pres. Org. of Petroleum Exporting Countries (OPEC) 74.
Kakh Avenue, Teheran, Iran.

Amri, Gen. Hassan al-; Yemeni politician.
Took part in the Revolution against the Imamate 62; Minister of Transport Sept.-Oct. 62, of Communications Oct. 62-April 63; mem. Council of the Revolutionary Command 62-63; Vice-President of Yemen 63-66; mem. Political Bureau 63-66; Prime Minister Jan.-April 65, July 65-Sept. 66; C.-in-C. Yemen Armed Forces 67-71; mem.

Presidential Council and Prime Minister April-July 69, Aug.-Sept. 71; in exile in Lebanon until Jan. 75; returned to Yemen A.R. Jan. 75.

Amuzegar, Jahangir, PH.D.; Iranian economist and politician; b. 13 Jan. 1920; ed. Univs. of Teheran, Washington and California.
Teaching Asst., Univ. of California, Los Angeles 51-53; Lecturer, Whittier Coll. 53, Univ. of Michigan 53-55; Asst. Prof. Pomona Coll., Claremont, California 55-56; Asst. Prof. Michigan State Univ., E. Lansing, Mich. 56-58; Assoc. Prof. Occidental Coll. and Univ. of Calif., Los Angeles 58-60; Brookings Research Prof. 60-61; Lecturer, Univ. of Maryland 63-73; Adjunct Prof. American Univ. 75-; Econ. Adviser, Plan Org., Govt. of Iran 56-57; Minister of Commerce, Iran 61-62; mem. Council of Money and Credit 61-62, High Econ. Council 61-62; mem. Board of Dirs. Bank Melli Iran 61-62; Chair, Board, Foreign Trade Co. (Iranian Govt. Org.) 61-62; Minister of Finance 62; Chair. High Council of Nat. Iranian Oil Co. 62; Chief of Iranian Econ. Mission, Washington, D.C. 63-73; Amb.-at-Large 63-78; Exec. Dir. Int. Monetary Fund, Washington, D.C. 73-78.
Publs. *Technical Assistance in Theory and Practice: The Case of Iran* 66, *Iran: Economic Development under Dualistic Conditions* 71, *Energy Policies of the World: Iran* 75.
c/o International Monetary Fund, 700 19th Street, N.W., Washington, D.C. 20431, U.S.A.

Anderson, Sir (James) Norman (Dalrymple), O.B.E., Q.C., M.A., LL.D., D.D., F.B.A.; British educationalist; b. 29 Sept. 1908; ed. St. Lawrence Coll., Trinity Coll., Cambridge.
Missionary, Egypt Gen. Mission 32-40; Capt. Libyan Arab Force 40-41; Major (Political Officer for Sanusi Affairs) 41; Lieut.-Col. (Sec. for Arab Affairs, Civil Affairs Branch, G.H.Q., M.E. 43, Political Sec. 43); Col. (Chief Sec., Civil Affairs Branch) 44-45; lectured on Islamic Law in Cambridge 47-50; Lecturer in Islamic Law, School of Oriental and African Studies, Univ. of London 47; Reader in Oriental Laws, Univ. of London 51; Prof. of Oriental Laws Univ. of London 53-75; Head of Dept. of Law, School of Oriental and African Studies 53-71; Lecturer in Mohammedan Law, Council of Legal Educ. 53-71; Visiting Prof., Princeton Univ. and New York Univ. Law School 58, Harvard Law School 66; Chair. U.K. National Comm. of Comparative Law 58-60; Dir. Inst. of Advanced Legal Studies, Univ. of London 59-76; Dean, Faculty of Law, Univ. of London 64-68; Pres. Soc. of Public Teachers of Law 69-70; Chair. House of Laity, Gen. Synod of Church of England 70-; mem. Panel of Advisory Jurists to Northern Nigerian Govt. 58-62; Vice-Pres. Int. African Law Assen.; mem. Int. Cttee. of Comparative Law 63-67; Libyan Order of Independence, Class II.
Publs. *The World's Religions* (Gen. Editor) 50, *Islamic Law in Africa* 54, *Islamic Law in the Modern World* 59, *Changing Law in Developing Countries* (Editor) 63, *Family Law in Asia and Africa* (Editor) 68, *Into the World: The need and limits of Christian involvement* 68, *Christianity: the Witness of History* 69, *Christianity and Comparative Religion* 70, *Morality, Law and Grace* 72, *A Lawyer among the Theologians* 73, *Law Reform in the Muslim World* 76, *Issues of Life and Death* 76, *Liberty, Law and Justice* 78, *The Mystery of the Incarnation* 78; contributions on Islamic Law, etc., to various learned journals.
9 Larchfield, Gough Way, Cambridge, England.

Ansari, Homayoun J., M.S.; Iranian civil servant; b. 20 Dec. 1929, Isfahan; ed. in Iran and U.S.A.
Senior Exploration Geologist, Nat. Iranian Oil Co. 56-59, Head of Studies and Co-ordination, Exploration and Production Dept. 59-62; Dir.-Gen. Petroleum Affairs, Ministry of Finance 62-64; Chair. and Man. Dir. Telephone Co. of Iran 64-71; Chair. and Man. Dir. Telecommunication Co. of Iran 71-74; Minister of Housing and Urban Devt. April 74-77; Chair. Board Iran Pan American Oil Co., Teheran 77-79.
Publs. several scientific papers on petroleum exploration.
122 Sheibani Street, Darrus, Teheran, Iran.

Ansari, Dr. Hooshang, M.A.; Iranian politician; b. 1928; ed. England, U.S.A. and Japan.
Successively Special Reporter of Int. News Service and Int. News Photos; Press Attaché of Publication and Propaganda Dept. in Japan; Commercial Attaché in Japan, Econ. Attaché, Tokyo; Chief, Supervisory Comm. of Public Supplies, mem. High Council on Iranian Aviation; Technical Under-Sec., Ministry of Commerce; Special Ambassador in African countries; Amb. to Pakistan and Ceylon 65-66; Minister of Information 66-67; Amb. to U.S.A. 67-69; Minister of Economy 69-Nov. 77, concurrently of Finance 74-Nov. 77; Chair. of Board and Gen. Man. Dir. Nat. Iranian Oil Co. (N.I.O.C.) 77-79.
c/o National Iranian Oil Company, Takhte Jamshid Avenue, P.O. Box 1863, Teheran, Iran.

Anwar, Mohamed Samih; Egyptian diplomatist; b. 10 Dec. 1924, Cairo; ed. Univ. of Cairo.
Ministry of Justice 46-54; First Sec. Ministry of Foreign Affairs 54; served Embassies in U.S.S.R. 57-62, U.K. 63-65; Amb. to Kuwait 66-68; Under-Sec. Ministry of Foreign Affairs 68-70; Amb. to Iran 71-74; Minister of State for Foreign Affairs 74-75; Amb. to U.K. Oct. 75-; Order of the Repub. 2nd Class 58, Order of Merit 1st Class 68, Order of Homayoun First Class (Iran) 74, Order of the Flag (Yugoslavia) 70.
Egyptian Embassy, 26 South Street, London, W1Y 8EL, England.

Arafat, Yasser (*pseudonym* of Mohammed Abed Ar'ouf Arafat); Palestinian resistance leader; b. 1929, Jerusalem; ed. Cairo Univ.
Joined League of Palestinian Students 44, mem. Exec. Cttee. 50, Pres. 52-56; formed, with others, Al Fatah movt. 56; engineer in Egypt 56, Kuwait 57-65; Pres. Exec. Cttee. of Palestine Nat. Liberation Movement (Al Fatah) June 68-; Chair. Exec. Cttee. Palestine Liberation Org. 68-, Pres. Cen. Cttee., Head Political Dept. 73-; Gen. Commdr. Palestinian Revolutionary Forces; addressed UN Gen. Assembly Nov. 74; Joliot-Curie Gold Medal, World Peace Council Sept. 75.
Palestine Liberation Organization, Colombani Street, Off Sadat Street, Dr. Raji Nasr Building, Ras Beirut, Lebanon.

Arashi, Qadi Abdul Karim al-; Yemeni politician.
Former Minister for Local Govt. and the Treasury; Speaker of the Constituent People's Assembly Feb. 78-; Chair. Provisional Presidential Council June-July 78; Vice-Pres. Yemen Arab Republic July 78-.
Constituent People's Assembly, Sana'a, Yemen Arab Republic.

Araslan, Uajid: (*see* Arslane, Amir Majuid Toufik).

Aram, Abbas; Iranian diplomatist; b. 1906; ed. Teheran and Europe.
Entered diplomatic service 31; Asst. Chief, Third Political Div., Foreign Ministry 43; First Sec. Berne 45; First Sec., Counsellor, and Chargé d'Affaires, Washington, D.C. 46, 49, 50; Dir. Fourth Political Div., Foreign Ministry 51; Counsellor, Baghdad 53; Chargé d'Affaires and Minister, Washington, D.C. 53, 54-56; Dir.-Gen. Political Affairs, Foreign Ministry 58; Amb. to Japan 58, concurrently to Republic of China; Minister of Foreign Affairs 59-60; Amb. to Iraq 60-62; Minister of Foreign Affairs 62-67; Amb. to U.K. 67-69, to People's Repub. of China 72-75, also accred. to Dem. Repub. of Viet-Nam and Dem. People's Repub. of Korea; Senator 77-79.
Teheran, Iran.

Aref, Lt.-Gen. Abdul-Rahman Mohammed (brother of late Pres. Abdul Salam Aref); Iraqi army officer and politician; b. 1916; ed. Baghdad Military Acad.
Joined Army 36; took part in July 58 Revolution, Chief of Gen. Staff Armoured Corps Dept. 58-61; Commdr. 5th Div. 63; assisted in overthrow of Gen. Kassem 63; mem. Regency Council 65; Asst. Chief of Staff Iraqi Armed Forces 63-64; Acting Chief of Staff 64, Chief of Staff 64-68; Pres. of Iraq 66-68; also Prime Minister May-July 67.

Ariburun, Gen. Tekin; Turkish politician; b. 1905, Istip, Yugoslavia; ed. Kulei and Konya Mil. Schools, Harbiye (Mil.) Coll. and War Acad.
Staff Officer in Turkish Air Force; served as first Turkish Air Attaché in Germany, U.S.A. and first Turkish Commanding Gen. NATO Defence Coll., Paris; promoted to rank of Brig.-Gen. 50, Gen. 59; Commdr. Turkish Air Force 59-60, retd.; Senator for Istanbul 64-; Speaker of Senate 70-77; Candidate for Presidency 73; Justice Party.
The Senate, Ankara, Turkey.

Arkell, Rev. Anthony John, M.B.E., M.C., D.LITT., F.S.A.; British archaeologist; b. 29 July 1898; ed. Bradfield and Queen's Coll., Oxford.
2nd-Lieut. Royal Flying Corps 16; Flying Off. Royal Air Force 18; Sudan Political Service 20-38; Chief Transport Officer Sudan Govt. 40-44; Commr. for Archæology and Anthropology, Sudan Govt. 38-48; Chair. and Editorial Sec. *Sudan Notes and Records* 46-48; Lecturer in Egyptology, Univ. Coll. London 48-53; Reader in Egyptian Archaeology, Univ. of London 53-63; Deacon, Cuddesdon Coll. 60, Priest 61; Vicar of Cuddington with Dinton 63-71; Archaeological Adviser to Sudan Govt. 48-54; mem. German Archaeological Inst. 53-; British Ennedi Expedition 57.
Publs. *Early Khartoum* 49, *The Old Stone Age in the Anglo-Egyptian Sudan* 49, *Shaheinab* 53, *History of the Sudan* 55, (2nd edn.) 61, *Wan yanga* 64.
Cuddington, Colam Lane, Little Baddow, Chelmsford, Essex, England.

Asaad, Kamal el, L. EN D.; Lebanese politician; b. 1929; ed. Law Faculty, Beirut and Univ. de Paris.
Practising lawyer; Deputy 53-; Mayor of Marjéyoun; Minister of Education 61-64; Pres. Chamber of Deputies 64-65, 72-; Minister of Water Resources and Health 66; mem. Nat. Dialogue Cttee. Sept. 75.
Hazmieh, Imm. Haddad, Beirut, Lebanon.

Asfia, Safi; Iranian mining engineer and politician; b. 1916; ed. Polytechnic Inst., Ecole des Mines, Paris.
Professor of Economic Geology, Teheran Univ. 39-62; Deputy Dir. Plan Org. 54-61, Man. Dir. 61-68; Deputy Prime Minister 68-74; Minister of State for Econ. and Devt. 68-70; Minister of State 74-75, without Portfolio 75-77, for Econ. Affairs 77-78.
Department of Economic Geology, University of Teheran, Teheran, Iran.

Ashiotis, Costas, M.B.E.; Cypriot diplomatist; b. 1908; ed. Pancyprian Gymnasium, Nicosia, and London School of Economics.
Former journalist and editor; Govt. Service 42-; Asst. Commr. of Labour 48; Dir.-Gen. Ministry of Foreign Affairs 60; mem. Cypriot Dels. to UN and Int. Confs.; High Commr. in U.K. 66-78; Hon. M.B.E.
Publ. *Labour Conditions in Cyprus During the War Years 1939-45.*
c/o Ministry of Foreign Affairs, Nicosia, Cyprus.

Ashraf Ahmadi, Ali, LL.B.; Iranian judge and politician; b. 1910, Behbahan; ed. High School, Shiraz and Univ. of Teheran.
Chief Magistrate Province of Teheran 47-49; Chief Justice Province of Khuzistan 50; Chief Criminal Court, Teheran 51; Chief Justice, Province of Isfahan 53; Gov. Isfahan 53-55; Judge, Supreme Court 55; Deputy Prime Minister 56-60; Sec. Royal Council 56-61; Minister of State 60-61; Deputy Dir. Pahlavi Foundation 62; Chief 12th Branch Supreme Court 63; Senator 64-79; Scientific Order, 1st Class, Taj, 2nd Class, Homayoun, 1st Class.
Publs. *Laws and Justice in Ancient Imperial Iran* 60, *Five Years in the Service of His Majesty the Shahanshah* (2 vols.), *Ten Years' Work and Endeavour, 12 Years of Efforts for Reconstruction of New Iran, Iran in the Past and Present.*
176 Television Avenue, Abbas Abad, Teheran, Iran.

Ashtal, Abdalla Saleh, M.A.; Yemeni diplomatist; b. 5 Oct. 1940; ed. Menelik II Secondary School, Addis Ababa, Ethiopia, American Univ. of Beirut, Lebanon, New York Univ.
Assistant Dir. of Sana'a Branch, Yemeni Bank for Reconstruction and Devt. 66-67; mem. Supreme People's Council, 5th Province 67-68; Editor *Ash-arara* (weekly) 67-68; mem. Exec. Cttee. of Gen. Command, Nat. Liberation Front 68-72; Political Adviser, Perm. Mission to UN 70, Senior Counsellor 72-73, Perm. Rep. 73-; concurrently non-resident Amb. to Canada Oct. 74- and to Mexico Nov. 75-.
Permanent Mission of People's Democratic Republic of Yemen to the United Nations, 413 East 51st Street, New York, N.Y. 10022, U.S.A.

Asiltürk, Oğuzhan; Turkish politician; b. 1935, Malatya; ed. Tech. Univ. of Istanbul.
Served Dept. of Highways and State Irrigation Admin.; later set up own engineering firm; Provincial Chair. Nat. Order Party, Ankara; mem. for Ankara, Nat. Assembly; Sec.-Gen. Nat. Salvation Party (NSP); Minister of Interior 74-June 77, of Industry and Technology July-Dec. 77.
National Salvation Party, Ankara, Turkey.

Âşiroğlu, Vahap, L. EN D.; Turkish diplomatist; b. 14 Aug. 1916, Karamursel; ed. Galatasaray Lycée, Istanbul and Faculty of Law, Univ. of Istanbul.
Entered diplomatic service 43; served in Czechoslovakia, Turkish Ministry of Foreign Affairs and Perm. Mission of Turkey at UN 46; Head of Chancery of Turkish Mission to UN 53-59; Minister and Deputy Perm. Rep. to UN 62-65; Amb. to Denmark 65-68, to Indonesia 68-71, to U.K. 78-; Sec.-Gen. Regional Co-operation for Devt. (RCD) 71-74; mem. UN Comm. on Human Rights 53-56; Leader, Turkish del. to ICAO Assembly 56; Chair. del., GATT Ministerial meeting, Tokyo 59; Chair. UN Conciliation Comm. for Palestine 62-65.
Embassy of Turkey, 43 Belgrave Square, London, SW1X 8PA, England.

Asnag, Abdallah Al-Majid al-; Yemeni trade union official and politician; b. 1933.
Leader, People's Socialist Party, Gen. Sec. Aden Trade Union Congress until Dec. 62, 63-65; imprisoned Dec. 62-Dec. 63; Head of Political Bureau, Front for Liberation of Occupied South Yemen (FLOSY); in Yemen Arab Repub. since 65; Minister of Foreign Affairs Aug.-Sept. 71, of the Economy 71-74, of Foreign Affairs March-June 74, 75-79; Deputy Premier for Communications June 74-Jan. 75; Political Adviser to Pres., mem. People's Assembly April 79-; Orders of Al-Kawkab (Jordan) 74, Repub. of Egypt 75, Sultanate of Oman 78.
Office of the President, Sana'a, Yemen Arab Republic.

Assad, Lt.-Gen. Hafiz al-; Syrian army officer and politician; b. 1928.
Minister of Defence and Commdr. of Air Force Feb. 66-Nov. 70; Prime Minister Nov. 70-April 71; Sec. Baath Party Nov. 70-; Pres. of Syria March 71-; mem. Pres. Council, Fed. of Arab Repubs. 71-; Pres. Syrian Nat. Progressive Front 72-; Commdr. in Chief of Armed Forces 73-; Dr. h.c. (Damascus) 72.
Office of the President, Damascus, Syria.

Assar, Nassir; Iranian diplomatist; b. 1926; ed. Univ. of Teheran.
Ministry of Foreign Affairs 45-; Vice-Consul, Stuttgart 49, Hamburg 53; Deputy Dir. Dept. of Int. Org., Ministry of Foreign Affairs 53-55; First Sec. Iranian Embassy to Turkey 56, Counsellor 61; First Sec. Iranian Mission to UN 58, Counsellor 59; Deputy Dir. Dept. of Econ. Affairs, Ministry of Foreign Affairs 60; Deputy Prime Minister, Head of Iranian Public Trust and Endowments 64; Sec.-Gen. Central Treaty Org. (CENTO) 72-74; Under-Sec. Political and Parl. Affairs 75-77; Adviser to Minister of Foreign Affairs 77-79.
c/o Ministry of Foreign Affairs, Teheran, Iran.

Atassi, Nureddin, M.D.; Syrian politician; b. 1929; ed. Damascus Univ.
Minister of the Interior Aug. 63; Deputy Prime Minister Oct. 64; mem. Syrian Presidential Council May 64-Dec. 65; Pres. of Syria 66-70, also Prime Minister 68-70; Sec.-Gen. Syrian Baath Party 66-Oct. 70; in exile in Libya.

Atherton, Alfred Leroy, B.SC., M.A.; American diplomatist; b. 22 Nov. 1921, Pittsburgh; ed. Harvard Univ.
Joined Foreign Service 47; Second Sec., U.S. Embassy, Syria 53-56; Consul, Aleppo, Syria 57-58, Calcutta, India 62-65; Int. Relations Officer, Bureau of Near Eastern and S. Asian Affairs, State Dept. 59-61, Deputy Dir. 65-66, Country Dir. (Iraq, Jordan, Lebanon, Syria) 66-67, (Israel and Arab-Israeli Affairs) 67-70, Deputy Asst. Sec. of State 70-74, Asst. Sec. of State 74-79; Amb. at Large with Special Responsibility for Middle East Peace Negotiations 78-79; Amb. to Egypt May 79-.
American Embassy, 5 America El Latinia Street, Cairo, Egypt; Home: 1435 4th Street, S.W., Washington, D.C. 20024, U.S.A.

Atiqi, Abdel-Rahman Salem al-; Kuwaiti diplomatist and politician; b. 5 April 1928; ed. High School, Kuwait.
Secretary-General, Police Dept., Kuwait 49-59; Dir.-Gen. Health Dept. 59-61; Del. to UN 60-61, to WHO, Geneva 61, to UN Gen. Assembly 61; Amb. to U.S.A. 62-63; Under-Sec. Ministry of Foreign Affairs 63-67; Minister of Finance and Oil Affairs 67-75, of Finance 75-; Chair. Kuwait Fund for Arab Econ. Devt., The Public Inst. for Social Security 77-; Gov. for Kuwait, Islamic Devt. Bank.
Ministry of Finance, P.O. Box Safat 9, Kuwait.

Atiya, Aziz Suryal, M.A., PH.D., LITT.D., F.R.HIST.S.; Egyptian historian and writer; b. 7 July 1898; ed. Univs. of Liverpool and London.
Charles Beard Fellow and Univ. Fellow, Univ. of Liverpool 30-32; History Tutor, School of Oriental Studies, Univ. of London 33-34; Prof. of Medieval and Oriental History, Univ. of Bonn 35-38; Prof. of Medieval History, Cairo 38-42, Alexandria 42-54; Pres. Higher Institute of Coptic Studies, Cairo; consultant to Library of Congress, Washington, D.C. 50-51; visiting lecturer U.S. Univs., Univ. of Zurich and Swiss Inst. of Int. Affairs 50-51; Medieval Acad. Visiting Prof. of Islamic Studies, Univ. of Michigan, Ann Arbor 55-56; Luce Prof. of World Christianity, Union Theological Seminary, and Visiting Prof. of History, Columbia Univ., New York 56-57; Visiting Prof. of Arabic and Islamic History, Princeton Univ. 57-58; mem. Inst. for Advanced Study, Princeton 58-59; Dir. Middle East Center, Utah Univ. 59-67; Distinguished Prof. of History, Utah 67-; corresp. mem. UNESCO Int. Comm. for the Scientific and Cultural History of Mankind; corresp. mem. Coptic Archaeological Soc.; mem. Medieval Acad. of America, Mediterranean Acad., Rome; Hon. D.H.L.
Publs. *The Crusade of Nicopolis* 34, *The Crusade in the Later Middle Ages* 38, *Egypt and Aragon—Embassies and Diplomatic Correspondence between 1300 and 1330* 38, *Kitab Qawanin al-Dawawin by Saladin's Wazir ibn Mammati* 43, *History of the Patriarchs of the Holy Church of Alexandria* (2 vols.) 48-49, *Monastery of St. Catherine in Mt. Sinai* 49, *The Mt. Sinai Arabic Microfilms* 54, *Coptic Music* 60, *Crusade, Commerce and Culture* 62, *The Crusades—Historiography and Bibliography* 62, *History of Eastern Christianity* 68, etc. (all books in either English or Arabic).
1335 Perry Avenue, Salt Lake City, Utah, U.S.A.

Atrash, Muhammad al-, M.A., PH.D.; Syrian international official; b. 13 Nov. 1934, Tartous; ed. American Univ., Beirut, Lebanon, American Univ., Washington, D.C., U.S.A., London School of Econs.
Joined Cen. Bank of Syria 63, Research Dept. 63, Head of Credit Dept. 66-70; Alt. Exec. Dir. IMF 70-73; Deputy Gov. Cen. Bank of Syria 74; Exec. Dir. IBRD 74-76, IMF 76-78; del. to Second Cttee. of UN Gen. Assembly, to UNCTAD and other int. econ. confs. 63-70; part-time Lecturer, Univ. of Damascus 63-70; mem. Deputies of IMF Interim Cttee. of the Board of Governors on Reform of Int. Monetary System 72-74; Assoc. mem. IMF Interim Cttee. 74-76, *ex officio* mem. 76-78.
Publs. articles in *Al-Abhath* (Quarterly of the American Univ. of Beirut) 63, 64, 66.
c/o Ministry of Foreign Affairs, Damascus, Syria.

Attar, Mohammed Said al-; Yemeni diplomatist; b. 26 Nov. 1927; ed. Ecole Pratique des Hautes Etudes à la Sorbonne, Inst. d'Etudes du Développement Econ. et Social (I.E.D.E.S.), Univ. de Paris.
Research I.E.D.E.S. 60-62; Dir.-Gen. Yemen Bank for Reconstruction and Devt. 62-65, Pres. 68-71; Minister of Econ. 65, 67-68; Pres. Econ. Comm. 65-66; Pres. Board, Yemen Bank and Econ. High Comm. 66-68; Minister of Foreign Affairs 67-69; Vice-Pres. High Cttee. for Planning; mem. Int. Asscn. of Sociology; Perm. Rep. to UN 69-71, 73-74; Deputy Premier for Financial Affairs, Minister of Econ. 71; Exec. Sec. UN Econ. Comm. for Western Asia (ECWA) 74-.
Publs. *L'Industrie du gant en France* 61, *L'épicerie à Paris* 61, *Etude sur la croissance économique de l'Afrique Occidentale* 62, *Le marché industriel et les projets de l'Arabie Séoudite* 62, *Le sous-développement économique et social du Yemen* (*Perspectives de la Révolution Yemenite*) 64, Arabic edn. 65.
Economic Commission for Western Asia (ECWA), B.P. 4656, Beirut, Lebanon.

Attiga, Ali Ahmed, B.SC., M.SC., PH.D.; Libyan economist; b. Oct. 1931, Misurata; ed. Univ. of Wisconsin and Univ. of California, U.S.A.
Assistant Econ. Adviser, Nat. Bank of Libya 59-60, Dir. of Research 60-64; Under-Sec. Ministry of Planning and Devt. 64-66, Dir. Econ. Research Div. 66-68; Minister of Planning and Devt. 68-69, concurrently of the Economy 69; Gen. Man. Libya Insurance Co. 70-73, Chair. 73; Chair. Nat. Investment Co. 71-73, Libya Hotel and Tourism Co. 71-73; Sec.-Gen. Org. of Arab Petroleum Exporting Countries (OAPEC) 73-(82); mem. Board of Dirs., Arab Reinsurance Co., Beirut.
Organization of Arab Petroleum Exporting Countries (OAPEC), P.O. Box 20501, Safat, Kuwait City, Kuwait.

Attiyia, Mahmoud Ibrahim, B.SC.; Egyptian geologist; b. 1900; ed. Cairo and Imperial Coll. of Science and Technology, London.
Assistant Lecturer, School of Engineering, Giza 23-25; Geologist, Geological Survey of Egypt 29, Asst. Dir. 39, Dir. 49; Dir.-Gen. Mines and Quarries Dept. 54-56; Tech. Dir. Mineral Wealth Co. and Sinai Manganese Co., Cairo 56-62; delegated Prof. of Geology, Cairo Univ.; A.R.C.S. London 29; F.G.S. London 30; mem. Inst. d'Egypte 46-; mem. of the Board, Desert Inst. of Egypt 50; mem. Egyptian Acad. of Sciences 50, Pres. 68-; mem. Conseil d'Administration de la Société de Géographie d'Egypte 51;

State Prize in Geological and Chemical Sciences; Order of the Republic (Egypt).
Publs. *Notes on the Underground Water in Egypt* 42, *The Barramiya Mining District* 48, *New Mode of Occurrence of Iron-Ore Deposits* 49, *Iron-Ore Deposits of Egypt* 50, *Ground-Water in Egypt* 53, *Deposits in the Nile Valley and the Delta* 54, *Iron-Ore Deposits of the District East of Aswan* 55, *Manganese Deposits of Egypt* 56.
10 Diwan Street, Garden City, Cairo, Egypt.

Avidom (Mahler-Kalkstein), Menahem, B.A.; Israeli composer; b. 6 Jan. 1908; ed. American Univ. Beirut, and in Paris.
Lecturer on theory of music, Hebrew Conservatoire of Music, Tel-Aviv 36-, and Music Teachers' Training Coll. Tel-Aviv 45-; Sec.-Gen. Israel Philharmonic Orchestra 46-; Vice-Pres. Board of Dirs. Acum Ltd. (Composers and Authors Asscn.), Dir.-Gen. 56-; Dir. Arts Dept. Jerusalem Convention Centre 52; Art Adviser, Govt. Tourist Centre, Ministry of Commerce and Industry 54-; Pres. League of Composers 58; mem. Nat. Arts Council 62; Israel State Prize 61, Tel-Aviv Municipality Prize 48, 56; Israel Philharmonic Prize 53; Authors' and Composers' Asscn. Prize 62.
Compositions include: *A Folk Symphony* 47, *Symphony No. 2 David* 48, *Mediterranean Sinfonietta* 51, 2 Piano Sonatinas 49, *Concertino* for violinist Jascha Heifetz, *Concertino* for cellist Gregor Piatigorsky 51, *Alexandra Hashmonaith* (opera in 3 acts) 52, *Jubilee Suite, Triptyque Symphonique, In Every Generation* (opera) 55, *The Crook* (opera in 2 acts) 65, *B-A-C-H* Suite for chamber orchestra, *Sinfonietta* 66, *Twelve Changing Preludes* for piano 68, *Symphonie Variée* for chamber orchestra 69, *The Farewell* (opera in 1 act) 70, concerto for strings and flute, music for strings, symphonies 3, 4, 5, 6 and 7, psalms and cantatas, septet for woodwind, piano and percussion, string quartet No. 2, quartet for brass instruments, *The Pearl and The Coral* (ballet) 72, *Spring* overture for symphony orchestra 73, *Six Inventions for Piano in Homage and on the name of Arthur Rubinstein* 73, *Passacaglia for Piano* 73, *Yemenite Wedding Suite* 74, *Piece on the name of SCHoEnBerG for Piano* 74, *The Emperor's New Clothes* (one-act comic opera) 75; *Twelve Hills* cantata 76, *Five Psalms* 76, *Leachar* cantata 76, *Jodephat's cave* dramatic scene 77, *Once Upon a Time* (5 short tales for piano) 78, *The End of King Og* (children's opera) 78, *Movements for Strings* 79, *The First Sin* (opera in four scenes) 79.
30 Semadar Street, Ramat-Gan, Israel.

Avineri, Shlomo; Israeli professor of political science and diplomatist; b. 20 Aug. 1933, Bielsko, Poland; ed. Shalva Secondary School, Tel-Aviv, Hebrew Univ. Jerusalem and London School of Econs.
Professor of Political Science, Hebrew Univ. Jerusalem 71-, Dir. Eshkol Research Inst. 71-74, Dean of Faculty of Social Sciences 74-76; Dir.-Gen. Ministry of Foreign Affairs 76-77; visiting appointments at Yale Univ. 66-67, Wesleyan Univ. Middletown Conn. 71-72, Research School of Social Sciences, Australian Nat. Univ. 72, Cornell Univ. 73, Univ. of Calif., San Diego 79; mem. Presidium of Exec. Council, World Zionist Org. 78-; British Council Scholarship 61; Rubin Prize in the Social Sciences 68, Peretz Naphtali Prize in Econ. and Social Sciences 77.
Publs. *The Social and Political Thought of Karl Marx* 68, *Karl Marx on Colonialism and Modernization* 68, *Israel and the Palestinians* 71, *Marx' Socialism* 72, *Hegel's Theory of the Modern State* 73, *Varieties of Marxism* 77.
Department of Political Science, The Hebrew University, Jerusalem; Home: 50 Harlap Street, Jerusalem, Israel.

Avni, Tzvi; Israeli composer; b. 2 Sept. 1927, Germany. Arrived in Israel as a child; studied with Abel Ehrlich, Paul Ben-Haim and Mordecai Seter, Tel-Aviv Acad. of Music, with Aaron Copland and Lukas Foss at Tanglewood, Mass., and electronic music at Columbia Univ.
Compositions include: *Songs for Soprano and Orchestra* 57, *Woodwind Quintet* 59, *Prayer* for string orchestra 61, *Summer Strings* for string quartet 62, *Chaconne for Harp* 62, *Capriccio* for orchestra 63, *Vocalise* (electronic music) 64, *Two Pieces for Four Clarinets* 65, *Meditations on a Drama* for chamber orchestra 66 (ACUM Prize), *Collage* for Mezzo Soprano, Fl., Perc. and electronic tape 67, *Yerushalayim Shel Ma'ala* for mixed choir and orchestra 68, *Churban Habayit* for mixed choir and orchestra 68, *Five Pantomimes* for eight players 68, *Akeda* for chamber groups and narrator 69, *String Quartet No. 2* (Liberson Prize 69), *Requiem for Sounds* (ballet music), *Ein Dor* (ballet music) 70, *Holiday Metaphors* for symphony orchestra 70 (Engel Prize 73), *All the King's Women* (ballet music) 71, *By the Waters of Babylon* (prelude for small orchestra) 71, *Michtam* for David's harp and string quartet 75, *Two Psalms* for oboe and string quartet 75, *Al Harachamim* for choir 73, *Frames* (ballet music) 74, *On this Cape of Death* for orchestra 74, *Retrospection* for cello, percussion and tape 75, *Four Songs* for voice and piano 75, *He and She* (ballet music) 76, *Leda and the Swan* for soprano and clarinet 76, *Three Madrigals* for mixed choir 77, *Genesis Reconsidered* (ballet music) 78.
Office: Rubin Academy of Music, 7 Smolenskin Street, Jerusalem; Home: 7 Zangwill Street, Tel-Aviv, Israel.

Avriel, Ehud; Israeli diplomatist; b. 19 Oct. 1917; ed. High School, Vienna.
Israeli Minister to Czechoslovakia 48, concurrently to Hungary 49; Minister to Romania 50; Dir.-Gen. Prime Minister's Office, Jerusalem 51-57; Amb. to Ghana and to Liberia 57-60, to Congo 60-61; Dep. Dir.-Gen. Ministry of Foreign Affairs 61-65; Amb. to Italy 66-68, concurrently accred. to Malta 66-68; Chair. World Zionist Action Cttee., Jerusalem 69-72; Diplomatic Adviser and Amb. Extraordinary, Ministry of Foreign Affairs 72; Consul Gen. to Chicago and Midwest, U.S.A. 75-; Amb.-at-Large, Jerusalem; mem. Knesset 75.
Ministry of Foreign Affairs, Hakirya, Romema, Jerusalem; and Neoth Mordechai, Hagalil Hoelyon, Israel.

Awad, Muhammad Hadi; Yemeni diplomatist; b. 5 May 1934; ed. Murray House Coll. of Educ.
Teacher 53-59; Educ. Officer 60-62; Chief Insp. of Schools 63-65; Vice-Principal As-Shaab Coll. 65-67; Perm. Rep. to Arab League 68-70, concurrently Amb. to U.A.R., also accred. to Sudan, Lebanon, Libya and Iraq; Perm. Sec. Ministry of Foreign Affairs 70-73; Amb. to U.K. 73-, concurrently non-resident Amb. to Spain and Sweden 74-, to Portugal, Denmark and Netherlands 75-.
Embassy of the People's Democratic Republic of Yemen, 57 Cromwell Road, London, S.W.7, England.

Ayari, Chedly, L. EN D.; Tunisian economist and politician; b. 24 Aug. 1933.
Head of Admin., Tunisian Banking Soc. 58-59; Asst., Faculty of Law and Political and Econ. Sciences, Univ. of Tunis 59-60, Dean 65-67; Econ. Adviser, Perm. Mission to UN 60-64; Exec. Dir. Int. Bank for Reconstruction and Devt. (IBRD), Int. Devt. Asscn. (IDA), Int. Finance Corpn. (IFC) 64-65; Dir. CERES (Centre d'Etudes et de Recherches Economiques et Sociales) 67-69; Sec. of State in charge of the Nat. Plan 69-70; Minister of Educ., Youth and Sport 70-71; Amb. to Belgium and Luxembourg Feb.-March 72; Minister of the Nat. Economy March 72-74, of Planning 74-75; Chair. of Board, Pres. and Gen. Man. Arab Bank for Econ. Devt. in Africa March 75-; Pres. UN Industrial Cttee. 62; del. to UN Confs. on Commerce and Devt. 62, 64; Grand Cordon, Order of the Repub.
Publs. Numerous articles in economic journals.
Arab Bank for Economic Development in Africa, Baladia Road, P.O. Box 2640, Khartoum, Sudan; and Gammarth, La Mousa, Tunis, Tunisia.

Ayyoubi, Mahmoud; Syrian politician; b. 1932.
Former Dir.-Gen. for Admin. Affairs, Euphrates Dept.; Minister of Educ. 69-71, and Deputy Prime Minister 70-71; Vice-Pres. of Syria 71-75; Prime Minister 72-76.
c/o Office of the Prime Minister, Damascus, Syria.

Azimi, Gen. Reza; Iranian army officer and politician; b. 1913; ed. Mil. Acad., Teheran.
Joined Imperial Army 29; Commdr. Armoured Corps, Chief of Army Staff Dept., Commdr. Central Army No. 1, Deputy Commdr. Ground Forces, Commdr. Western Army, Officer Commdg. Ground Forces 60-66, Adjutant-Gen. to Shahanshah; Minister of War 71-78; various army decorations.
c/o Ministry of War, Teheran, Iran.

Azkoul, Karim, PH.D.; Lebanese former diplomatist; b. 15 July 1915; ed. Jesuit Univ. of St. Joseph, Beirut, and Univs. of Paris, Berlin, Bonn and Munich.
Professor of History, Arab and French literature, and Philosophy in various colls. in Lebanon 39-46; Dir. of an Arabic publishing house and of a monthly Arabic review, *The Arab World*, in Beirut 43-45; mem. of the Lebanese del. to UN 47-50; Acting Perm. Del. to UN 50-53; Head of UN Affairs Dept., Ministry for Foreign Affairs 53-57; Head of Perm. Del. to UN 57-59; Consul-General in Australia and N.Z. 59-61; Amb. to Ghana, Guinea and Mali 61-64, to Iran and Afghanistan 64-66; Prof. of Philosophy, Beirut Coll. for Women 68-72, Lebanese Univ. 70-72; mem. Emergency World Council, Hague 71-, PEN; mem. Board of Trustees, Board of Man., Theological School of Balamand, Lebanon; Order of Cedar (Lebanon), Order of Holy Sepulchre (Jerusalem), Order of St. Marc (Alexandria), Order of the Brilliant Star (Republic of China), Order of Southern Star (Brazil), Order of St. Peter and Paul (Damascus).
Publs. *Reason and Faith in Islam* (in German) 38, and a similar work in Arabic 46, *A Study on Freedom of Association* (French, English, Russian, Spanish) 68; transl. *Consciencism* (Nkrumah) 64; *Arabic Thought in the Liberal Age* (Albert Hourani) 69.
Union Building, Spears Street, Al-Sanayeh, Beirut, Lebanon.

Azzawi, Hikmat al-, B.A.COMM.; Iraqi politician; b. 1934, Diyalah; ed. Coll. of Commerce and Econs., Baghdad Univ.
Reserve Lieutenant 57-58; Supt. Cen. Bank of Iraq 58-63, First Supt. 63; Auditor, Dir. of Stores and Warehouses, Dir. of Marketing, State Co. for Electrical Instruments and Equipment 66-68; Dir.-Gen., Chair. Govt. Purchasing Board 68; Chair. General Trade Establishment 69; Under-Sec. Ministry of Econ. 69; mem. Board of Dirs. Cen. Bank of Iraq 69; Minister of Econ. 72-76, of Foreign Trade 75-77; Minister of State without Portfolio 77; mem. Baath Arab Socialist Party 53-, mem. of Leadership of Baghdad Branch 65, Deputy Sec. Baghdad Branch 71, mem. Regional (Iraqi) Command Jan. 77-; Chief Ed. *Al-Iktisad* (Economist) magazine, Baghdad.
Baghdad, Iraq.

B

Badawi, Major-Gen. Ahmed, B.A.; Egyptian army officer; b. 3 April 1927, Alexandria; ed. Mil. Acad., Staff Coll., U.S.S.R., Nasser Higher Mil. Acad., Ain Shams Univ., Cairo.
Career in Army from 48; Chief of Operations, 4th Infantry Brigade 61, 7th Infantry Div. 62; Commdr. 4th Infantry Bn. 63; Chief of Staff 5th Infantry Div. 65, 1st Mechanized Infantry Brigade 65; Chief of Operations, 6th Infantry Div. 66; Asst. Chief of Staff, 2nd Field Army 71; Commdr. 3rd Field Army 71; Chief of Armed Forces Training Dept. 78; Chief of Staff of Armed Forces Oct. 78-; Asst. Sec.-Gen. for Mil. Affairs, Arab League Oct. 78-; Liberation Order 52, Memorial Order 58, Star of Honour 74, Order of King Abdel Aziz (Saudi Arabia) 74, Order of Courage (Libya) 75; many medals and ribbons.
c/o Ministry of Defence, P.O. Box 78, Heliopolis, Cairo, Egypt.

Badran, Mudar, B.A.; Jordanian politician and civil servant; b. 1934, Jerash; ed. Univ. of Damascus, Syria.
Lieutenant and Legal Consultant, Jordanian armed forces 57, Capt. and Legal Adviser to the Armed Forces Treasury 62; Asst. Chief, Jordanian Foreign Intelligence 65; Deputy Chief of Gen. Intelligence 66, Chief 68; Retd. Maj.-Gen. 70; Chief Chamberlain of the Royal Court 70, Sec.-Gen.; Nat. Security Adviser to King Hussein 71; Minister in the Royal Court 72; Deputy Head, Exec. Office of Occupied Territories Affairs 72-73; Minister of Educ. 73-74; Chief of the Royal Court 74-76; Prime Minister, Minister of Defence and of Foreign Affairs July 76-; fmr. mem. Exec. Council of the Arab Nat. Union.
Office of the Prime Minister, Amman, Jordan.

Bahar, Abdul Aziz Ahmed al-, B.A.ECONS.; Kuwaiti businessman; b. 1929; ed. American Univ. Beirut.
Director-General of Housing Dept., Ministry of Finance 56-61, of Kuwait Fund for Arab Econ. Devt. 61-62; Chair. Kuwait Nat. Industries 63-65, Kuwait Insurance Co. 65-67, Kuwait Foreign Trading Contracting and Investment Co. 65-73; Dir. Rifbank 67-74; Chair. Commercial Bank of Kuwait 65-78, Arab European Financial Management Co., Kuwait; Dir. United Bank of Kuwait Ltd., London 75-78; Deputy Chair. Commercial Bank of Dubai 70-78; Dir. Arab Trust Co. 75-78; Hon. Consul Repub. of Costa Rica; mem. Int. Banking Asscn., Advisory Cttee. to American Coll. in Switzerland.
P.O. Box Safat 460, Kuwait.

Bahnini, Hadj M'Hammed, L. EN D., L. ÈS L.; Moroccan politician; b. 1914, Fez; ed. Lycée Gouraud (now "Lycée Hassan II"), Rabat.
Sec. Royal Palace; Magistrate, Haut Tribunal Chérifien; Instructor, College Impérial and Private Tutor to H.R.H. Crown Prince Moulay El Hassan, Prince Moulay Abdallah, Princess Lalla Aïcha and Princess Lalla Malika; Dir. of the Imperial Cabinet 50-61; Del. Judge, Meknés 51; Exiled Dec. 52-July 54; Sec.-Gen. of the Cabinet 55-72; Minister of Justice 58-60; Minister of Admin. Affairs 65-70; Minister of Nat. Defence 70-71; Minister of Justice 71; Vice-Premier and Minister of Justice April-Nov. 72; Minister of State for Culture April 74-.
Office of the Minister of State, Ministry of Culture, Rabat, Morocco.

Bahrain, Ruler of; (*see* Khalifa, Sheikh Isa bin Sulman al-).

Bakdash, Khalid; Syrian politician; b. 1912; ed. Damascus Inst. of Law.
Member of Parl. 54-58; Sec.-Gen. Syrian Communist Party; self-imposed exile in East Europe 58-66; returned to Syria April 66; mem. Cen. Cttee., Syrian Nat. Progressive Front 72-.
Ave. Akrad, Damascus, Syria.

Bakhtiar, Shapour; Iranian lawyer and politician; b. 1916; ed. in Paris and Beirut.
Supporter of Nat. Front opposition to Govt. of Shah Mohammad Reza Pahlavi (*q.v.*); Deputy Minister during Nat. Front Govt. of Dr. Musaddiq 51-53; imprisoned several times during reign of Shah; Deputy Leader of Nat. Front -79; Chair. Regency Council and Prime Minister Jan.-Feb. 79; resigned after return of Ayatollah Khomeini (*q.v.*) Feb. 79.
Paris, France

Bakir, Anwar, D. en D.; Egyptian postal executive; b. 24 Nov. 1914; ed. Univs. of Cairo and Paris.
Former Dir. of Int. Services, Egyptian Postal Service; fmr.

Dir. of Posts of Egypt, now mem. Admin. Council; mem. Board of Dirs., Egyptian Postal Org.; Sec.-Gen. Arab Postal Union; del. to numerous confs. of APU and int. postal confs.
General Secretariat, Arab Postal Union, 28 rue Adly, Cairo, Egypt.

Bakr, Field Marshal Ahmed Hassan al-; Iraqi army officer and politician; b. 1914; ed. Military Academy.
Army career 36-58; Commdr. First Infantry Brigade 57; forced to retire from Iraq Army 58; Prime Minister of Iraq Feb. 63 and Nov. 63; Vice-Pres. of Iraq Nov. 63-Jan. 64; Amb. Jan.-Sept. 64; President of Iraq, Prime Minister and C.-in-C. of Armed Forces July 68-July 79; Chair. Revolutionary Command Council July 68-July 79; Minister of Defence 73-77; promoted to rank of Field Marshal 69.
Baghdad, Iraq.

Bakr, El Rashid el Tahir; Sudanese politician; b. 1930, Karkoj; ed. Univ. of Khartoum.
Former advocate; imprisoned for opposition to the regime of Gen. Ibrahim Abboud (*q.v.*) 58-64; Minister of Animal Resources and Justice 65; Amb. to Libya 72-74; apptd. mem. Political Bureau, Sudanese Socialist Union (SSU) and Sec. Farmers' Union in the SSU 72; Asst. Sec.-Gen. Sectoral Orgs., SSU 74; Speaker, People's Nat. Assembly 74-76; Second Vice-Pres. of Sudan Aug. 76-; Prime Minister 76-77, Minister of Foreign Affairs Sept. 77-.
Ministry of Foreign Affairs, P.O. Box 873, Khartoum, Sudan.

Bakri-Wahab, Laman, B.A.; Iraqi cultural official; b. 8 Jan. 1929; ed. Fine Arts Inst., Baghdad and Baghdad Univ.
Law practice 54-55; Social Asst. for girl students, Baghdad Univ. 55-59; Editor-in-Chief *New Iraq Magazine* 60-61; Supt. Press Dept., Ministry of Culture and Guidance 63-64; Man. Iraqi Nat. Symphony Orchestra 64-66; Dir. Nat. Museum of Modern Art 67; Dir. of Arts 69-73; Dir. Cultural Affairs, Foundation for Technical Institutes, Ministry of Higher Educ. 73-.
44/2/55 Sulikh, Ahdamia, Baghdad, Iraq.

Balafrej, Ahmed; Moroccan politician; b. 1908; ed. Univs. of Paris and Cairo.
Secretary-General of Istiqlal (Independence) Party 44; later exiled by French, returned to Morocco 55; Minister of Foreign Affairs 55-58; Prime Minister May-Dec. 58; Ambassador-at-Large 60-61; Dep. Prime Minister June 61; Minister of Foreign Affairs 61-Nov. 63; Personal Rep. of King with rank of Minister 63-June 72.
c/o The Royal Palace, Rabat, Morocco.

Barakat, Lt.-Col. Abdullah Hosain; Yemeni politician; b. 26 Jan. 1934, Sana'a; ed. Mil. Coll., Sana'a, Police Coll., Cairo, Ain Shams Univ. and Cairo Univ.
Director of Police, Security and Passports, Taiz 61, of Public Security 62-64; Deputy, Ministry of Interior 64; Minister of Agriculture 65, of Interior 67-71; Amb. to Sudan 71, to Algeria and Tunisia 72-74; Minister of Social Affairs, Labour and Youth 74; Deputy Prime Minister for Interior Affairs 75.
Alkharabah Airport Road, Sana'a, Yemen Arab Republic.

Barakat, Gamal Eddin, LL.B., B.LITT.; Egyptian diplomatist; b. 18 Feb. 1921, Cairo; ed. Helwan Secondary School, Cairo Univ., Hague Acad. of Int. Law, Oriel Coll. Oxford.
Third Sec., Egyptian Embassy, London 50-52; with Political Dept., Ministry of Foreign Affairs 53-55; Secretariat, Anglo-Egyptian Treaty negotiations 54; Consul-Gen., Aleppo, Syria 55-58; Counsellor, Washington, D.C. 58-60; Head of In-Service Training Dept., Ministry of Foreign Affairs 61-63; mem. OAU Experts Cttee., Addis Ababa 63-64; Amb. to Uganda 64-68, also to Burundi 68, to Finland 68-73; Asst. to the President's Adviser on Nat. Security 73-74; Head of Cultural Relations and Tech. Co-operation Dept., Ministry of Foreign Affairs 75; Amb. to Iraq Jan. 76- (diplomatic relations broken off Dec. 77); Dir. Diplomatic Inst., Ministry of Foreign Affairs 79-; Order of the Repub. 54, 64, Order of Merit (Egypt) 58, 73, Order of Merit (Syria) 58, Order of the Lion (Finland) 73.
Publs. *Status of Aliens in Egypt* 49, *Diplomatic Terminology* (in English and Arabic) 61.
55 Hegaz Street, Heliopolis, Cairo, Egypt.

Barakat, Ghaleb, B.B.A.; Jordanian civil servant; b. 1927; ed. American Univ. Beirut.
Teacher, Nat. Coll., Tripoli 49-50, Teachers' Coll., Tripoli 50-52, Asst. Dir. 51-52; Chief Clerk, Jordan Tourist Dept. 52-53, Press Attaché 53-54; Tourist and Press Attaché, Royal Jordan Embassy, Rome 54-60; Dir. of Tourism 60-; Dir. Jordan Pavilion, Brussels Exhbn. 58; Commr.-Gen. Jordan Pavilion, New York World's Fair 64; Pres. Arab Int. Tourist Union 64, 70; Dir.-Gen. Tourism Authority 66, now Chair.; Dir.-Gen. Ministry of Tourism and Antiquities 68; Minister of Tourism and Antiquities 72-, concurrently of Transport 72; Chair. Board of Dirs., Hotels and Resthouses Corpn. 67-; now also Lecturer, Faculty of Econ. and Commerce, Univ. of Jordan; Jordanian, Belgian, Mexican, Romanian and Vatican decorations.
Ministry of Tourism and Antiquities, P.O.B. 224, Amman; Home: P.O. Box 9064, Amman, Jordan.

Baram, Moshe: Israeli politician, b. 1911, Zdolvinov, Ukraine.
Member of Youth and Hechalutz movts. and Hachshara group in Ukraine; emigrated to Israel 31; worked as a bldg. labourer, active in Hagana, mem. Socialist Youth movt.; Sec. Israel Workers' Party, Jerusalem 42; mem. Yishuv (Reps. Assembly of Jewish Community) 44; del. to World Zionist Congresses 46-; mem. Israel Labour Party 46-, Cen. Exec. Bodies 46-; Sec.-Gen. Histadrut (Jerusalem Workers' Council) 48; mem. Hagana HQ in Jerusalem, Emergency Comm. 48, Jerusalem Municipal Council, Chair. Coalition Exec. 55-59; mem. Fourth and subsequent Knessets 59-, Chair. Labour Comm., mem. Finance Comm.; Coalition Whip in Sixth Knesset 65; Chair. Unemployment Insurance Comm., mem. Cen. Body of Histadrut Council's Fed. of Labour; Minister of Labour 74-June 77.
Labour Party of Israel, Jerusalem, Israel.

Baramki, Dimitri Constantine, B.A., PH.D.; Jordanian archaeologist; b. 1909; ed. St. George's School, American Univ. of Beirut, Univ. of London.
Teacher, Jerusalem 25-26; Student Inspector of Antiquities, Palestine 27-28, Inspector 29; Senior Archaeological Officer 45; Archaeological Adviser and Librarian, American School of Oriental Research, Jerusalem 49-51; Curator of Museums 51-; Asst. Prof. of Ancient History, American Univ. of Beirut 51-53, Assoc. Prof. 53, Prof. 58-75; Prof. Lebanese Univ. 75-; UNESCO Expert in Prehistoric Archaeology, accred. to Libya 64-65; excavated numerous sites in Palestine.
Publs. Numerous articles in the Quarterly of the Dept. of Antiquities, Palestine and in other publications.
Lebanese University, Bir Hassan, Beirut, Lebanon.

Barenboim, Daniel; Israeli concert pianist and conductor; b. 15 Nov. 1942, Buenos Aires, Argentina; studied piano with his father and other musical subjects with Nadia Boulanger, Edwin Fischer and Igor Markevitch.
Debut in Buenos Aires at age of seven; played Bach D Minor Concerto with orchestra at Salzburg Mozarteum at age of nine; has played in Europe regularly 54-; yearly tours of U.S.A. 57-; has toured Japan, Australia and S. America; has played with or conducted New Philharmonia Orchestra, London Symphony Orchestra, New York Philharmonic, Philadelphia Orchestra, Israel Philharmonic, Vienna Philharmonic, Berlin Philharmonic, etc.; frequently tours with English Chamber Orchestra and with them records for E.M.I. (projects include complete Mozart

Piano Concertos and late Symphonies); other recording projects include complete Beethoven Sonatas and Beethoven Concertos (with New Philharmonia Orchestra conducted by Klemperer); has appeared in series of Master-classes on B.B.C. television; presented Festival of Summer Music on South Bank, London, 68, 69; leading role in Brighton Festival 67-; appears regularly at Edinburgh Festival; conductor, Edinburgh Festival Opera 73; Musical Dir. Orchestre de Paris 75-.
c/o Harold Holt Ltd., 134 Wigmore Street, London, W.1, England.

Bar-Ilan, Tuvia, PH.D., B.CH.E.; Israeli chemist and university administrator; b. 28 Dec. 1912; ed. Polytechnic Inst. of Brooklyn and Hebrew Univ., Jerusalem.
Emigrated to Palestine from U.S.A. 23; research worker, Weizmann Inst. of Science, Rehovot 36-43; War Dept. analyst and British army officer 43-46; Commdr. Scientific Corps, Jerusalem area, Israeli Defence Forces 47-48; manufacturer of plastic products 49-66; Dir. Bar-Ilan Univ., Ramat-Gan 58-63; Dir. Bar-Ilan Univ., Extension Div. (Ashkelon, Safed and Jordan Valley) 65-; Pres. B'nei-B'rith, Holon 59-62, 63-65; Chair. Exec. Cttee. Nat. Religious Party, Holon 63-66; mem. Board of Higher Studies 61-65; Town Councillor, Holon 69-74; mem. Cen. Cttee. for Colleges 72-74; AACI Henrietta Szold Award for Advancing Higher Educ. in Israel 62.
Publs. Articles and patents on organic chemistry and plastics.
3 Azar Street, Holon, Israel.

Barkovsky, Anatoly; Soviet diplomatist; b. 1921, Moscow; ed. Diplomatic Acad.
Attaché, Third Sec., Second Sec., First Sec., U.S.S.R. Embassy, Egypt 52-57, Counsellor 59-61; Consul-Gen., Syria 1961; Amb. to Syria 61-68, to Cyprus 71-73, to Iraq 74-.
Embassy of the U.S.S.R., Mansour Street 140, Karradat Mariam, Baghdad, Iraq.

Bar-Lev, Lieut.-Gen. Haim; Israeli officer and politician; b. 1924, Austria; ed. Mikhev Israel Agricultural School, Columbia Univ. School of Econs. and Admin., U.S.A.
Joined Palmach Units 42; Platoon Commdr., Beith-Ha'Arava 44; Commdr. D Co., Yesreel 45-46; Commdr. Palmach N.C.P.'s course and C.O. Eight Regt., Negev Brigade 47, Operations Officer 48; Commdr. Armoured Units 48; Instructor and later Commdr., Bn. Commdrs. course 49-52; Chief of Staff, Northern Command 52-53; C.O. Givati Brigade 54-55; Dir. G.H.Q. Training Div. 56; Commdr. Armoured Brigade during Sinai campaign; Commdr. Armoured Corps 65-71; made study tour of armoured corps of Western European countries and U.S.A. 61; visited U.S. army installations and the armies of the Philippines, Japan, Thailand and S. Viet-Nam; Dir. Gen. Staff, Operations Branch 64-66; Deputy Chief of Staff, Israel Defence Forces 67, Chief of Staff 68-72; Minister of Commerce and Industry 72-June 77; elected to Knesset June 77; Sec.-Gen. Israel Labour Party Aug. 78-.
Neve Magen, Israel.

Bayani, Mehdi, PH.D.; Iranian librarian; b. 1906; ed. Univ. of Teheran.
Librarian, Nat. Teachers' Coll., and Lecturer, Faculty of Literature, Teheran Univ. 33; Head of Educ. Dept., Ispahan Province 40; Special Inspector and Asst. Dir. of Educ. Dept., Ministry of Art and Industry 41; Dir. Nat. Library of Teheran 42; Dir. of Imperial Library 57-72; Dir.-Gen. The Nat. Library 57; Prof. Nat. Teachers' Coll. 61-; Prof. Faculty of Art 63-.
Editor: *Nimuneh-Sukhan-i-Fars-i* 38, *Rahnemaye Ganjineh Koran* 48, *Specimens of Fine Writing from the National Library, Teheran* 48, *Specimens of Fine Writing from the Imperial Library of Iran* 51, *Ahval va Athare mir Emad* 52, *Khochnevissan* (vol. 1) 66.
Publs. *Three Essays of Sheikh Shahabod-din Suhrawardi* 38-40; *Essay Sawanih-fel-Eshq Ahmad Ghazzali* 43; *Badaya ol-Azman* (Tarikhe Afzal) 47.
c/o National Library, Ghavamossaltané Street, Teheran, Iran.

Bayar, Celal; Turkish politician; b. 1883.
Minister of Nat. Economy 21; Minister of Reconstruction and Settlement (when Turkish and Greek populations were exchanged in accordance with Treaty of Lausanne) 23; founded İş Bank 24; Minister of Nat. Economy 32; Prime Minister 37-39; Vice-Pres. Republican Peoples' Party during Presidency of Kemal Atatürk; undertook leadership of new Democratic Party founded 46; Pres. of the Republic May 50-60; arrested and detained May 60; death sentence passed and changed to life imprisonment 61; released Nov. 64; pardoned 66.
Ankara, Turkey.

Bayramoğlu, Fuat; Turkish diplomatist; b. 23 March 1912, Ankara; ed. School of Political Sciences (Mülkiye), Istanbul and Univ. of Liège.
Entered Diplomatic Service 39; mem. Gen. Directorate of Press and Publication Cttee. 43; Head of Secretariat Prime Minister's Office 44-46; Chair. Press Dept. Cttee. 46; Dir. in Foreign Ministry 48; Consul, Cyprus 49; Consul-Gen., Jerusalem 51-53; Dir.-Gen. Consular and Claims Dept., Ministry of Foreign Affairs, Ankara 53-57; Amb. to Norway 57-59, to Iraq 59-60, to Iran 60-62, to Italy 62-63; Sec.-Gen. Ministry of Foreign Affairs 63-64; Amb. to Belgium 64-67, to Italy 67-69, to U.S.S.R. 69-71; Chair. Inspection Corps, Ministry of Foreign Affairs 71-72; Sec.-Gen. to the Pres. of Turkey 72-77; Homayoun Order of Iran 62, Grand Croix de Mérite Civil (Spain) 63, Gran Croce all' Ordine al merito della Repubblica (Italy) 69, Presidential and Ministry of Foreign Affairs Distinguished Service awards 73; Silver and Gold Medals from seven int. philatelic exhbns.
Publ. *Rubaiat* book of poems; several legal and sociological articles; *Rubailer* (book of quatrains) 74, revised and enlarged edn. 76; *Turk Cam Sanati ve Beykoz İşleri* (Turkish Glass Art) 74, *Turkish Glass Art and Beykoz Ware* 76, some firmans with illuminations and with the Sultan's signatures (in English) 76, (in French) 79.
Kandilli, Istanbul, Turkey.

Bayülken, Ümit Halûk; Turkish diplomatist; b. July 1921; ed. Ankara Univ.
Joined Ministry of Foreign Affairs 44, served Frankfurt, Bonn, Dir. Middle East Section 51-53; Political Adviser to UN Del. 53-59; mem. Turkish Del. to Cyprus Joint Cttee., London 59-60; Dir.-Gen. Policy Planning Group, Ministry of Foreign Affairs 60-63, appointed Minister Plenipotentiary; Asst. Sec.-Gen. for Political Affairs 63-64; Sec.-Gen. Ministry of Foreign Affairs 64-66; Amb. to U.K. 66-69; Perm. Rep. to UN 69-71; Minister of Foreign Affairs 71-74; Sec.-Gen. CENTO 75-77; Sec.-Gen. of the Presidency Aug. 77-; Head of several overseas dels. since 52, Order Isabel la Catolica (Spain), German Grand Cross of Merit, Hon. G.C.V.O. (U.K.) 67, Star, First Order (Jordan) 72, Sitara-i-Pakistan 70, Sirdar-i- Ali (Afghanistan) 72.
Publs. several papers on minorities, Cyprus and foreign policy.
Presidential Palace, Cumhurbaskanlig, Çankaya, Ankara, Turkey.

Bazargan, Mehdi; Iranian politician, businessman and university professor; b. 1905; ed. Univ. of the Sorbonne.
Assistant Prof., Teheran Univ., then Prof., then Dean; fmr. Man. Dir. Nat. Oil Co. of Iran; Founder mem. and Leader Nehzat Azardi (Freedom of Iran Movement) 61; arrested for anti-Govt. activities 62; Man. Dir. Yad Construction Co.; Founder mem. Iranian Cttee. for the

Defence of Liberty and Human Rights Dec. 77; appointed Prime Minister by Ayatollah Khomeini (*q.v.*) Feb. 79-.
Publs. Booklets on Islam and modern civilization.
Office of the Prime Minister, Qajar Palace, Teheran, Iran.

Bedjaoui, Mohammed; Algerian politician; b. 21 Sept. 1929; ed. Univ. of Grenoble and Institut d'Etudes Politiques, Grenoble.
Lawyer, Court of Appeal, Grenoble 51; research worker at Centre National de la Recherche Scientifique (C.N.R.S.), Paris 55; Legal Counsellor of the Arab League in Geneva 59-62; Legal Counsellor Provisional Republican Govt. of Algeria in Exile 58-61; Dir. Office of the Pres. of Nat. Constituent Assembly 62; mem. Del. to UN 57, 62, 77, 78; Sec.-Gen. Council of Ministers, Algiers 62-63; Pres. Soc. Nat. des chemins de fer algériens (S.N.C.F.A.) 64; Dean of the Faculty of Law, Algiers Univ. 64; Minister of Justice and Keeper of the Seals 64-70; mem., special reporter, Comm. on Int. Law, UN 65-; Amb. to France 70-; Perm. Rep. to UNESCO 71-; mem. Int. Law Comm. 76-(81); Carnegie Endowment for Int. Peace 56; Ordre du Mérite Alaouite, Morocco; Order of the Repub., Egypt.
Publs. *International Civil Service* 56, *Fonction publique internationale et influences nationales* 58, *La révolution algérienne et le droit* 61, *Succession d'états* 70, *Terra nullius, droits historiques et autodétermination* 78, *Non-alignement et droit international* 76, *Pour un nouvel ordre économique international* 78.
Embassy of Algeria, rue Hamelin 18, Paris 16e, France; and 39 rue des Pins, Hydra, Algiers, Algeria.

Begin, Menachem, M.JUR.; Israeli politician; b. 16 Aug. 1913, Brest-Litovsk, Russia; ed. Warsaw Univ.
Active in Jewish Youth Movement "Betar"; Chair. "Betar" in Czechoslovakia 36, in Poland 39; confined in Siberian labour camp by Moscow Comm. of N.K.V.D. 40-41; came with Polish army to Palestine 42; C.-in-C. Irgun Zvi Leumi 43, leading revolt against British rule in Palestine; mem. Knesset (Israel Parl.); Leader of the Opposition in Knesset 48-67, 69-77; Minister without Portfolio 67-69; Founder and Chair. Herut (Freedom Movement); joint Chair. of Likud Bloc 73-; Prime Minister June 77-; Hon. D.Litt. (Yeshiva Univ., N.Y.) 78; Nobel Prize for Peace (shared with Pres. Sadat, *q.v.*) 78.
Publs. *The Revolt, personal memoirs of the Commander of Irgun Zvi Leumi* 49, *The White Nights*, *Behmatret* 78.
Office of the Prime Minister, Jerusalem; and 1 Rosenbaum Street, Tel-Aviv, Israel.

Beheiry, Mamoun Ahmed, B.A.; Sudanese civil servant and politician; b. 3 Oct. 1925; ed. Victoria Coll., Alexandria, and Brasenose Coll., Oxford.
Deputy Perm. Under-Sec. Ministry of Finance and Economics 54-56; Chair. Sudan Currency Board 56-58; fmr. Chair. Nat. Tech. Planning Cttee. 62; First Gov. Central Bank of Sudan 58-63; Gov. IMF and IBRD for Sudan; Chair. Cttee. of Nine preparing for African Devt. Bank 63; Minister of Finance and Econ. 63-64, of Finance and Nat. Econ. 75-76, of Finance, Planning and Nat. Econ. Feb.-Oct. 76; Pres. of African Devt. Bank 64-70; Pres. Board of Trustees, Special Fund for Southern Region 72-74; Chair. Parl. Devt. and Econ. Affairs Cttee., Jan. 75-; Chair. Board of Govs., Arab Bank for Econ. Devt. in Africa 75; Gov. for Sudan, Islamic Devt. Bank.
c/o National People's Assembly, Khartoum, Sudan.

Belkhodja, Tahar; Tunisian politician and former agricultural engineer; b. 3 June 1931, Mahdia.
Active mem. Néo-Destour (now called Parti Socialiste Destour) 47-, now mem. Central Cttee.; Agricultural Eng. 56; Sec.-Gen. Union Gén. des Etudiants Tunisiens 57-59; Officer of Néo-Destour Political Bureau for Students 59; Pres. Confed. of North African Students 59; Pres. Int. Asscn. of Students of Agriculture 58; Chef de Cabinet to Sec. of State for Foreign Affairs 60; Minister Plenipotentiary, Chargé d'Affaires in Paris 61; Amb. to Guinea, Ivory Coast, Mali, Mauritania, Senegal 61-66; Chef de Cabinet to Sec. of State for Plan and Nat. Econ. 66; Head of Nat. Security 67; Amb. to Senegal 69, to Spain 70; Sec. of State, Ministry of Agriculture 70; Minister of Youth and Sports 70; Amb. to Vatican City 71, also Perm. Rep. to Geneva 71; Minister of the Interior 73-77; Grand Cordon, Order of Independence; Grand Cordon, Order of the Repub. of Tunisia; several foreign decorations.
c/o Ministry of the Interior, ave. Habib Bourguiba, Tunis, Tunisia.

Ben Abbes, Youssef, M.D.; Moroccan diplomatist and former politician; b. 15 Aug. 1921, Rabat; ed. Marrakesh, Medical Coll. of Algiers and Paris.
Joined Public Health Service 49, Dir. several hospitals, then Insp. of Health; Minister of Health 58-61, of Health and Educ. 61-62, of Educ., Youth and Sport 62-65; Mayor of Marrakesh and Pres. Provincial Council; Senator for Marrakesh; Amb. to U.A.R. 65-66, to Italy 67-69, to Algeria 69-70; Minister of Foreign Affairs Oct. 70-71; Amb. to Spain 71-72, to France and UNESCO Sept. 72- (also accred. to the Vatican 76-); Commdr., Ordre nat. du Trone, Ordre nat. du Mérite; other orders and decorations.
Embassy of Morocco, rue Le Tasse 3, Paris 16e, France.

Benabdallah, Abdel-Aziz; Moroccan professor; b. 28 Nov. 1923; ed. Univ. of Algiers.
General Dir. for the Conservation and Registry of Land Properties 57; Dir. of Higher Educ. for Scientific Research 58-61; Dir. of Nat. Arabization Centre 61-68; Dir.-Gen. Perm. Office for the Co-ordination of Arabization in the Arab World, Arab League, Rabat 69-; Prof., Faculty of Arts, Mohamed V Univ., Rabat and also Dar-el-Hadith Inst., al-Qarawiyine Univ., Fez.
Publs. in Arabic: *Philosophy and Morality in Ibn El Khatib* 49, *Aspects of Maghreb Civilization* (2 edns., third entitled *Gifts of Maghreb Cilivization*), *History of Medicine* 59, *History of Morocco* (2 vols.), *Geography of Morocco* (3 edns.), about 30 specialized dictionaries, *Dictionary of Native Arabic and Foreign Words used in Moroccan Dialects, with a Comparative Study of Dialects of the Arab World, Evolution of Thought and Language, Classical Arabic and Moroccan Dialects, Catalogue of Moroccan Commentators and Readers of the Koran, Arabization and the Future of the Arabic Language;* in French: *Les Grands Courants de la Civilisation du Maghreb* 58, *l'Art Maghrebin* 62, *Clarté sur l'Islam ou l'Islam dans ses sources* (2 edns.), *Vérité sur le Sahara*.
Bureau Permanent d'Arabization, 8 rue Angola, Rabat, Morocco.

Ben-Aharon, Yitzhak; Israeli administrator; b. 1906, Bukovina, Austria; ed. Berlin High School for Political Science and Econs.
Went to Palestine 28; founder of Kibbutz Givat Hayim; Sec. Tel-Aviv Labour Council 38-39; Lieut., British Army, Second World War, prisoner-of-war 41-45; mem. Knesset 49-62; Minister of Transport 59-62; mem. Knesset 69-; Sec.-Gen. Histadrut 69-73.
Publs. *Listen Gentile*, *Michtavim Leuni*, *Bepheta Temura*.
Kibbutz Givat Hayim (Meyuhad), Doar Hedera, Israel.

Ben Ammar, Hassib; Tunisian professor and politician; b. 11 April 1924; ed. Coll. Sadiki, Tunis and Faculty of Sciences, Paris.
Active mem. of Destour groups abroad 42-52; mem. Destour Fed., Tunis 54; Sec.-Gen. of the Econ. and Social Board 59; Sec.-Gen. of Destour Youth Movt. 60; Mayor of Tunis 63-65, Gov. 65-69; Amb. to Italy 69; Minister of Defence 70-71; mem. Cen. Cttee., Destour Socialist Party (DSP) 64; mem. Political Bureau DSP, Chair. 69-70, Supreme Cttee. DSP 70-, Council of Nat. Defence 71-;

Grand Cordon, Order of Independence, Grand Cordon, Order of the Repub.
Parti Socialiste Destourien, 10 rue de Rome, Tunis, Tunisia.

Ben-Ari, Mordechai, M.A.; Israeli business executive; b. 10 Sept. 1920, Transylvania; ed. Hebrew Univ., Jerusalem.
Arrived in Palestine 40, joined Kibbutz Maagan; active in Israel's War of Independence; joined El Al Israel Airlines 50, Man. Air Freight Dept. 50-58, Head Sales Dept. 58-60, Pres. 67-77, Exec. Chair. 77-.
Publs. *Twenty Years of El Al* 68, *Role of an International Airline in the Service of a Small Community* 69.
El Al, Ben-Gurion Airport; Home: 7 Shneur Street, Ramat Gan, Israel.

Ben Bella, Mohammed; Algerian politician; b. 1916.
Warrant Officer in Moroccan regiment during Second World War (decorated); Chief O.S. rebel military group in Algeria 47; imprisoned 49-52 (escaped); directed Algerian nat. movement from exile in Libya 52-56; arrested Oct. 56; held in France 59-62; Vice-Premier, Algerian Nationalist Provisional Govt., Tunis 62; Leader, Algerian Political Bureau, Algeria 62; Premier of Algeria Sept. 62-June 65, President of Algeria Sept. 63-June 65, concurrently Minister of Interior Dec. 64-June 65; overthrown by mil. coup and imprisoned 65; under house arrest 65-79; Lenin Peace Prize 64.
Msila, Algeria.

Bendor, Shmuel; Israeli educator and former diplomatist; b. 21 June 1909, Belfast; ed. Liverpool Univ.
Emigrated to Palestine 32; became English teacher, later Vice-Principal, Haifa Reali School 32-48; Military Service 48-49; with Ministry of Education 49; Dir. of U.S. Dept. Foreign Ministry 50-54; Counsellor, Paris 54-57; Minister to Czechoslovakia 57-59, to Rumania 59-61; Dir. Western European Dept., Foreign Ministry 61-63; Deputy Dir.-Gen. Prime Minister's Office 63-66; Dir. Foreign Relations Atomic Energy Comm. 66-69; Dir. Foreign Relations and Sec. Council for Higher Educ., Ministry of Educ. and Culture 69-72; Dir. Israel Acad. of Sciences and Humanities 72-74; Consultant, Planning and Grants Cttee., Council for Higher Education 75-.
58 Harlap Street, Jerusalem 92.342, Israel.

Benedictos (Vassilios Papadopoulos); Greek orthodox ecclesiastic; b. 1892; ed. Greek Orthodox Hieratic School, Jerusalem, and Athens Univ.
Clerk, Patriarchal Offices, Jerusalem 14; ordained deacon 14; accompanied the then Patriarch to Damascus during World War I; studies in Law and Theological Schools, Athens Univ. 21-25; rep. of Patriarch of Jerusalem at World Christian Conf. of Faith and Order, Geneva 27; Exarch of the Holy Sepulchre in Athens 29-46; ordained priest and Archimandrite 46; mem. Holy Synod, Jerusalem Patriarchate 46-; Legal Adviser and Chair. Pending Property Cttee. 47; Chair. Financial Cttee. 50; rep. of Patriarch, Internationalisation of Jerusalem Trusteeship Conf. 50; Archbishop of Tiberias 51; Greek Orthodox Patriarch of Jerusalem 57-; Grand Cross of King George of Greece, Grand Cross and Cordon of Patriarchate of Antioch, Jordanian and Lebanese orders.
Publs. Numerous historical and legal works.
Greek Orthodox Patriarchate, P.O. Box 4074, Jerusalem, Israel.

Bengelloun, Ahmed Majid, L. EN D.; Moroccan lawyer and politician; b. 27 Dec. 1927, Fez; ed. Inst. of Political Science, Paris.
Public Prosecutor, Marrakesh 56, later Public Prosecutor of Mil. Tribunal, Meknès, Gen. Counsel, Supreme Court; Public Prosecutor Court of Appeal 60-64; Minister of Information 65-67; Sec.-Gen. Ministry of Justice 67; Minister at the Royal Cabinet 67-71, of Civil Service 71-72 of Information 72-74; Prosecutor-Gen. May 74-; fmr. Prof. Inst. des Hautes Etudes Juridiques; Prof. Law Faculty, Univ. of Rabat, Ecole Marocaine d'Admin.; mem. Comm. for the Drafting of the Penal Code and Penal Procedure Code; has attended numerous int. judicial confs.; Order of the Throne, and several foreign decorations.
Bureau du Procureur Général, Rabat, Morocco.

Ben-Haim, Paul; Israeli composer; b. 5 July 1897; ed. State Acad. of Music and Univ. of Munich.
Composer, pianist and conductor in various cities in Germany 20-33; moved to Palestine 33 and settled in Tel-Aviv teaching composition and piano; guest conductor, Jerusalem Radio Orchestra and Israel Philharmonic Orchestra; Dir. New Jerusalem Acad. of Music 49-54; Hon. Pres. Israeli Composers' Asscn.; awarded Engel Prize of Tel-Aviv Municipality for *1st Symphony* 45, and for *2nd Symphony* 53; awarded Israel State Prize 57 for symphonic work *The Sweet Psalmist of Israel*; Cross of Merit (1st Class) of the Fed. Repub. of Germany 68.
Works include two symphonies, *Evocation* for violin and orchestra, *Pastorale* for clarinet and strings, Concerto for piano and orchestra, Concerto for strings, *Liturgical Cantata*, *The Sweet Psalmist of Israel*, other symphonic works include a violin and a 'cello concerto, cantatas, chamber music, songs, etc.
Aharonovitz Street 11, Tel Aviv, Israel.

Benhima, Ahmed Tahibi (brother of Mohamed Benhima, *q.v.*); Moroccan diplomatist and politician; b. 13 Nov. 1927; ed. Univs. of Nancy and Paris.
Chargé d'Affaires, Paris 56-57, Ambassador to Italy 57-59; Sec.-Gen. of Ministry of Foreign Affairs 59-61; Perm. Rep. to UN 61-64; Minister of Foreign Affairs 64-66; Dir. Cabinet of the King 66-67; Perm. Rep. to UN 67-71; Minister of Foreign Affairs 72-74; Minister of State for Information 74-77.
Rabat, Morocco.

Benhima, Mohamed, M.D. (brother of Ahmed Benhima, *q.v.*); Moroccan physician and politician; b. 25 June 1924; ed. Faculté de Médecine de Nancy, France.
Chief Medical Officer, Had Court District 54-56; Chief of Central Service for Urban and Rural Hygiene 56-57; Head of Personal Office of Minister of Public Health 57-60; Sec.-Gen., Ministry of Public Health Jan.-June 60; Gov. of Provinces of Agadir and Tarfaya 60-61; Minister of Public Works 61-62, 63-65, of Commerce, Industry, Mines, Handicrafts and Merchant Marine 62-63, of Nat. Educ. 65-67; Prime Minister July 67-69; Minister of Agriculture and Agrarian Reform 69, of Public Health 69-72, of the Interior 72-73; Minister of State for Co-operation and Training 73-77, for the Interior Feb. 77-; decorations from Govts. of Belgium, France, Morocco, Sweden, Ethiopia, Tunisia, Liberia and Egypt.
Km. 5,500, Route des Zaërs, Rabat, Morocco.

Benjenk, Munir P., B.SC. (ECON.); Turkish public servant: b. 1924; ed. English Lycée and Robert Coll., Istanbul and London School of Economics.
Worked with B.B.C., Reading, U.K. 49-51; served with Turkish Army in Korea 51-52; with OEEC (now OECD), Paris 53-63; mem. Perm. Mission to Washington, D.C. of OEEC 55-57; Dir. Sardinian Village Devt. Project 59-60; Asst. Dir. Devt. Dept., OECD 62-63; with Int. Bank for Reconstruction and Devt. 63-; Head of Econ. Advisory Mission, Algeria 64, Head of N. Africa Div. 65-67, Deputy Dir. Middle East and N. Africa Dept. 67-68, Europe, Middle East and N. Africa Dept. 68-69, Dir. 70-72, Vice-Pres. Europe, Middle East and N. Africa 72-75, 76-; Visiting Fellow, St. Antony's Coll., Oxford 75-76; Ordine al Merito della Repubblica Italiana, Order of the Cedars of Lebanon 73.

1308 28th Street, N.W., Washington, D.C. 20007; and International Bank for Reconstruction and Development, 1818 H Street, N.W., Washington, D.C. 20433, U.S.A.

Ben Khedda, Ben Yousef; Algerian politician; b. 1920.
Minister of Cultural and Social Affairs, Algerian Provisional Govt. 58-Jan 60; Missions, Moscow and Peking 60-61; Prime Minister Algerian Provisional Govt., Tunis 61-62, Algiers 62; under arrest July 64.

Ben Salah, Ahmed; Tunisian politician; b. 13 Jan. 1926; ed. Collège Sadiki, Tunis and Univ. of Paris.
Teacher, Lycée de Sousse 48-51; Del. Tunisian Trade Union Movement at Int. Confederation of Trade Unions, Brussels 51-54; Sec.-Gen. Union Générale Tunisienne du Travail 54-56; Sec. of State for Public Health and Social Affairs 57-60, for the Plan and Finance 61-64, for the Plan and Nat. Economy 64-69, for Educ. Sept. 69-70; Asst. Sec.-Gen. Destour Socialist Party 64-70; imprisoned 70, escaped Feb. 73; Sec.-Gen. Mouvement de l'Unité Populaire (M.U.P.).

Ben Seddik, Mahjoub; Moroccan trade union leader; b. 1925.
Secretary-General Union Marocaine du Travail 55-; Pres. All-African Trade Union Fed. 61, 64, 66, 71; mem. Secretariat-Gen. Union Nat. des Forces Populaires; imprisoned 52-53, July 67; mem. Admin. Council, ILO.
Bourse du Travail, 222 avenue de l'Armée, Casablanca, Morocco.

Benslimane, Abdelkader, B.A.; Moroccan politician; b. 22 Feb. 1932, Rommani; ed. Toulouse Univ., France.
Joined Ministry of Finance 57, Head of Admin. Div. 57-59, Head of Budget Dept. and Censor at Central Bank 61-63; Minister, Embassy to France 61-63; Dir.-Gen. Bureau d'Etudes et de Participations Industrielles 63-66; Del. to Maghreb Perm. Consultative Cttee. 66-72, Vice-Pres. 65-72; Amb. to Benelux and EEC Feb.-Nov. 72; Minister of Trade, Industry, Mines and Merchant Marine 72-74, of Finance 74-77; Chair. and Gen. Man. Banque Nat. pour le Développement Economique Jan. 78-; Gov. Arab Fund for Econ. and Social Devt., Arab Bank for Econ. Devt. in Africa, Islamic Devt. Bank, African Devt. Bank, African Devt. Fund.
B.P. 407, Place des Alaouites, Rabat, Morocco.

Ben Yahya, Prince Abdul Rahman; Yemeni politician.
Deputy Prime Minister until 67; Prime Minister 67-68; mem. Imamate Council 67-68; in exile 68-; royalist.

Ben Yahya, Mohammed Sedik, L. EN D.; Algerian diplomatist; b. 30 Jan. 1932, Djidjelli.
Closely associated with Ferhat Abbas in Tunisia and Yazd 59-62; Amb. to U.S.S.R. 62-65; undertook several missions for Pres. Ben Bella 63-65; Amb. to U.K. 65; mem. Algerian Del. to UN 65-66; Minister of Information 66-70, of Higher Educ. and Scientific Research 70-77, of Finance 77-79, of Foreign Affairs March 79-.
Ministry of Foreign Affairs, 6 rue Claude Bernard, El Mouradia, Algiers, Algeria.

Berenblum, Isaac, M.D., M.SC.; Israeli pathologist and experimental biologist; b. 26 Aug. 1903; ed. Bristol Grammar School and Leeds Univ.
Riley-Smith Research Fellow, Dept. Experimental Pathology and Cancer Research, Leeds Univ. Medical School 29-36; Beit Memorial Research Fellow, Dunn School of Pathology, Oxford Univ. 36-40; Departmental and Univ. Demonstrator in Pathology, Oxford Univ. 40-48; in charge of Oxford Univ. Research Centre of British Empire Cancer Campaign 40-48; Special Research Fellow, Nat. Cancer Inst., Bethesda, Md., U.S.A. 48-50; Head of Dept. of Experimental Biology, The Weizmann Inst. of Science, Rehovot, Israel 50-71; Visiting Prof. of Oncology, Hebrew Univ., Jerusalem 50-56; mem. Israel Research Council 52-57; Jack Cotton Prof. of Cancer Research, The Weizmann Inst. of Science, Rehovot, Israel 62-71, Emer. Prof. 71-; Hon. Life Mem. New York Acad. of Sciences, World Acad. of Sciences, American Asscn. of Cancer Research, Israel Acad. of Sciences and Humanities; Weizmann Prize of Municipality of Tel-Aviv-Yaffo 59; Rothschild Prize for Biology 66; Israel Prize 74, Bertner Award for Cancer Research, Texas 78.
Publs. *Science versus Cancer* 46, *Man Against Cancer* 52, *Cancer Research Today* 67, *Carcinogenesis as a Biological Problem* 74.
33 Ruppin Street, Rehovot, Israel.

Berger, Morroe, PH.D.; American educator and writer; b. 25 June 1917; ed. Columbia Univ., New York.
Assistant Prof., Princeton Univ. 52-58, Assoc. Prof. 58-61, Prof. of Sociology 62-; Dir. Program in Near Eastern Studies, Princeton Univ. 62-68, 73-77; mem., Chair. Joint Cttee. of Near and Middle East, of American Council of Learned Socs. and Social Science Research Council 62-69; Consultant to U.S. Office of Educ. 65-68; mem. Governing Boards, American Research Center, Egypt (Pres. 74-78), American Research Inst., Turkey 64-; Pres. Middle East Studies Asscn. 67; Chair. Council on Int. and Regional Studies, Princeton Univ. 68-77, Chair. Dept. of Sociology 71-74.
Publs. *Equality by Statute* 52, 67, *Bureaucracy and Society in Modern Egypt* 57, *The Arab World To-day* 62, *Madame de Staël on Politics, Literature and National Character* 64, *Islam in Egypt Today* 70, *Real and Imagined Worlds: The Novel and Social Science* 77; Editor *New Metropolis in the Arab World* 63; Translator and Adapter (with others) *The Recited Koran, A History of the First Recorded Version* 75; numerous articles in learned journals and contributions to encyclopaedias.
Jones Hall, Princeton University, Princeton, New Jersey 08540, U.S.A.

Berk, Medenî; Turkish politician.
Fmr. Dir.-Gen. Emlâk Kredi Bankası; Minister of Reconstruction and Town Planning 57-59; Deputy Prime Minister 59-60; arrested May 60; sentenced to life imprisonment, released 65; Dir.-Gen. Akbank T.A.Ş. 66-; Pres. Union of Chambers of Commerce, Chambers of Industry and Commodity Exchanges of Turkey 70-71.
Akbank T.A.Ş., Meclisi Mebusan Caddesi 65-69, Fındıklı, Istanbul; and Etiler, Camlık Sokak 6, Istanbul, Turkey.

Berk, Mükerrem; Turkish musician; b. 1917; ed. Istanbul Conservatoire.
Joined Presidential Symphony Orchestra 37, Principal Flute and Woodwind leader 41-68, Admin. Dir. 60-68; Gen. Dir. State Opera and Ballet 69-74; Dir. Istanbul State Symphony Orchestra and Izmir State Symphony Orchestra 74-; many tours in U.S.A., United Kingdom, W. Europe, Scandinavia, Middle East, India, Pakistan and U.S.S.R.
Istanbul Devlet Senfoni Orkestrasi Atatürk Kültüı Merkezi, Taksim, Istanbul; Home: Molla Bayiri Sok. no. 32/4, Fındıklı-Istanbul, Turkey.

Berk, Nurullah; Turkish artist; b. 1906; ed. Acad. of Fine Arts, Istanbul, Paris Acad. and Léger and Lhote studios, Paris.
Teacher and fmr. Dir., Acad. of Fine Arts, Istanbul; exhibited UNESCO Int. Art Exhbn., Paris 47, Exhbn. of Turkish Art, Musée Cernuschi, Paris 47, Exhbn. of Turkish Art, Amsterdam 48, Turin Art Club Exhbn. 50, Contemporary Turkish Painting, Univ. Art Gallery, New York 71, Peinture Turque Contemporaine, UNESCO, Paris 74; mem. Int. Comm. of Govt. Experts on Art, Council of Europe, Strasbourg 69-72.
Publs. *Turkish Sculpture, Leonardo da Vinci, Art in Modern Turkey, La Peinture Turque, Bellinis, Sandro Botticelli—Le Musée des Beaux-Arts d'Istanbul* 73, *Cinquante ans de*

Peinture en Turquie 74, *Istanbul chez les peintres turcs et étrangers* 77.
Abacı Latif Sokak 10, Besiktas, Istanbul, Turkey.

Berkol, Faruk N., LL.D.; Turkish diplomatist; b. 9 Sept. 1917, Istanbul; ed. Univs. of Istanbul and Paris and School of Political Science, Paris.
Joined Ministry of Foreign Affairs 41; First Sec., Washington, D.C. 45-50; Counsellor, later Chargé d'Affaires, London 52-56; Chef de Cabinet to Pres. of Turkey 56-60; Amb. to Tunisia 62-67, to Belgium 67-72; UN Under-Sec. Gen., UN Disaster Relief Co-ordinator 72-; mem. Mexican Acad. of Int. Law; decorations from Afghanistan, Belgium, Fed. Repub. of Germany, France, Italy, Liberia, Libya, Luxembourg, Spain and Tunisia.
Publs. *Le Statut juridique actuel des portes maritimes orientales de la Méditerranée* 40, and books and articles in Turkish and French on the Balkan *entente* and Turkish economic expansion.
Office of the United Nations Disaster Relief Co-ordinator, Palais des Nations, 1211 Geneva 10, Switzerland.

Berque, Jacques, D. ès L.; French oriental sociologist; b. 4 June 1910; ed. Univ. of Algiers and Univ. de Paris à la Sorbonne.
Early career as Admin. Officer in Morocco; UNESCO specialist in Egypt 53-55; Dir. of Studies, Ecole des Hautes Etudes, Sorbonne 55-; Prof. of Social History of Contemporary Islam, Coll. de France 56-; Commdr. du Ouissam Alaouite (Morocco), Chevalier Légion d'Honneur and Commdr. Palmes académiques (France); Commdr. of Merit (Syria, Tunisia).
Publs. *Structures sociales du Haut-Atlas* 55, *Les Arabes* 57, *Les Arabes d'hier à demain* 60, *Le Maghreb entre deux guerres* 62, *Dépossession du monde* 64, *L'Egypte, impérialisme et révolution* 67, *L'Orient Second* 70, *Langages arabes du Présent* 74, *L'Intérieur du Maghreb* 78.
Collège de France, 11 place Marcelin-Berthelot, Paris 5e, France.

Berrada, Abdeslam, DIP.SC.AGRI.; Moroccan agronomist; b. 3 Oct. 1931, Fez; ed. secondary schools, Fez, Ecole Nat. d'Agriculture de Grignon, Ecole Nat. des Eaux et Forêts, Nancy, France.
Several posts in Waters and Forests Admin., subsequently Dir. 65; Sec.-Gen. Ministry of Agriculture and Agrarian Reform 71-72, Minister 72-74; Pres. Soc. Cellulose du Maroc 72-; rep. to numerous regional and int. confs.
c/o Cellulose du Maroc, B.P. 429, Rabat, Morocco.

Bertini, Gary; Israeli conductor; b. 1 May 1927, Bessarabia; U.S.S.R.; ed. Israel, Univ. of Paris, Conservatorio Verdi, Milan, Conservatoire Nat. Paris and studies under Arthur Honegger.
Founder RINAT Chamber Choir 55; Founder Jeunesses Musicales d'Israel; teacher of conducting at Rubin Acad. of Music; Artistic Dir. and Conductor Israel Chamber Orchestra; Principal Guest Conductor Scottish Nat. Orchestra; Regular Guest Conductor Hamburg State Opera, Paris Opera, Scottish Opera, BBC, Israel Philharmonic Orchestra and Jerusalem Philharmonic Orchestra; Prof. Tel-Aviv Univ.; Founder, Israel Chamber Orchestra; Artistic Adviser Israel Festival; has conducted many orchestras in Israel and abroad, often performing contemporary Israeli music; composer of symphonic and chamber music, ballets, incidental music to more than 40 plays, and music for films and radio.
5 Basel Street, Tel-Aviv, Israel.

Besse, Antonin Bernard; French company director; b. 22 Feb. 1927.
Chairman Besse group of companies (import, export, finance, maritime affairs) 51-65; Chair. Besse Int. S.A. (finance); mem. Int. Council of United World Colls.; Chevalier de l'Ordre de la Couronne.
P.O. Box 8203, Beirut, Lebanon; 14 avenue de Verzy, Paris 17e, France.

Bilge, Ali Suat, LL.T.; Turkish professor of international law and politician; b. 1921, Istanbul; ed. Univs. of Ankara and Geneva.
Assistant, Faculty of Political Science, Univ. of Ankara 50, Assoc. Prof. 52, Prof. 60; Hon. Legal Adviser, Ministry of Foreign Affairs 60, First Hon. Legal Adviser 65; Judge, European Court of Human Rights 66; mem. Perm. Court of Arbitration, The Hague 66; mem. UN Cttee. of Human Rights 70; mem. Int. Law Comm. 71-76; Minister of Justice Dec. 71-72; Amb. to Switzerland Oct. 72-.
Publs. *Diplomatic Protection of Compatriots* 53, *International Politics* 66.
Embassy of Turkey, Lombachweg 33, Berne, Switzerland.

Bilgehan, Orhan Zihni; Cypriot judge and politician; b. 1929, Famagusta; ed. Turkish Lycée, Cyprus and Middle Temple, London.
District Judge, Cyprus 60; Pres. District Court of Larnaca and Famagusta 68; Minister of Education 73-75; High Court Judge Jan.-June 76; mem. Turkish Cypriot Legislative Assembly 76-; Minister of State 76, Minister of the Interior, "Turkish Federated State of Cyprus" 76-78, also of Defence 78, and Acting Minister of Educ. 77; in practice as barrister Dec. 78-.
3 Altay Street, Famagusta, Cyprus.

Binder, Leonard; American university professor; b. 20 Aug. 1927; ed. Boston Latin School, Harvard Coll., Harvard Univ., Princeton Univ. amd Oxford Univ.
Assistant Prof. Univ. Calif., Los Angeles 56-61; Assoc. Prof. and Prof. Univ. of Chicago 61-77, Chair. Dept. of Political Science 64-67, Chair. Cttee. on Near Eastern Studies 63-65; mem. New Nations Cttee. 61-; Fellow Center for Advanced Studies in the Behavioral Sciences 67-68; Field Research in Pakistan 54-55, in Iran 58-59, in Egypt 60-61, in Lebanon 64, in Tunisia 64, 65, 66, 69; Chair. Research and Training Cttee., Middle East Studies Asscn.; Pres. Middle East Studies Asscn. 73-74; Dir. Middle East Center, Univ. of Chicago 73-76; Co-Dir. Islam and Social Change Project 76-77.
Publs. *Religion and Politics in Pakistan* 60, *Iran: Political Development in a Changing Society* 61, *The Ideological Revolution in the Middle East* 64, Editor, *Politics in the Lebanon* 65, Co-author, *Crises and Sequences in Political Development* 72, Editor, *The Study of the Middle East* 76, *In a Moment of Enthusiasm; Political Power and the Second Stratum in Egypt* 78 also numerous articles in periodicals.
5512 South Harper Avenue, Chicago, Illinois 60637, U.S.A.

Bisar, Muhammad Abdul Rahman, PH.D.; Egyptian religious leader; b. *c.* 1910; ed. Univ. of London, England.
Former Sec.-Gen. of Acad. of Islamic Research, Cairo, and Dir. Islamic Cultural Centre, Washington, D.C.; Minister of Waqfs and Minister of State charged with Al-Azhar Affairs Oct. 78-Jan. 79; Grand Sheikh of Al-Azhar Jan. 79-.
Office of the Grand Sheikh, Al-Azhar Administration, Cairo, Egypt.

Bishara, Abdulla Yacoub; Kuwaiti diplomatist; b. 1936; ed. Cairo Univ., Balliol Coll., Oxford, St. John's Univ. New York.
Second Sec., Kuwait Embassy, Tunisia 63-64; Dir. Office of Minister of Foreign Affairs, Kuwait 64-71; Perm. Rep. to UN Sept. 71-; currently Amb. to Argentina; del. to numerous int. confs.
Permanent Mission of Kuwait to United Nations, 801 Second Ave., Fifth Floor, New York, N.Y. 10017, U.S.A.

Bitar, Salah Eddine el-; Syrian politician; b. 1912; ed. Damascus and Univ. of Paris.
Secondary school teacher in Damascus 34-42; entered

politics 42; co-founder, with Michel Aflak, of Arab Resurrection Party and Editor of party organ; left Syria after Shishekly *coup* 52; later returned and took part in merging of Renaissance and Socialist parties to form Baath Party; elected to Parliament after overthrow of Shishekly 54; Minister of Foreign Affairs 56; head of Syrian Del. to UN Gen. Assembly 57; Minister of Culture and Nat. Guidance, U.A.R. 58-59; Prime Minister of Syrian Arab Republic March-May 11, 63, May 13, 63-Nov. 63; concurrently Minister of Foreign Affairs May 63-Nov. 63; Vice-Pres. Council of Revolutionary Commd. Nov. 63-May 64; Prime Minister and Vice-Pres. Council of Presidency May-Oct. 64; Prime Minister and Foreign Minister Jan.-Feb. 66, expelled from Baath Party Oct. 66; returned to Syria Dec. 77.
Pacific Hotel, Beirut, Lebanon.

Bitat, Rabah; Algerian politician; b. 19 Dec. 1925, Constantine Region.
Joined Parti du Peuple Algérien 40, Mouvement pour le Triomphe des Libertés démocratiques 47; participated in formation of Organisation spéciale 48; detained, sentenced to 10 years; participated in foundation of Comité révolutionnaire d'Unité et d'Action 54, later of Front de Libération National; arrested March 55, held in France till 62; hunger strike, granted political status after being appointed Minister of State in Provisional Revolutionary Govt. of Algerian Repub. 58; mem. Political Bureau, in charge of Party Org. 62-63; Deputy Premier 62-63, Third Deputy Premier 63; in exile in France 63-65; Minister of State 65-66; Minister of State in charge of Transport 66-77; Pres. Nat. People's Assembly March 77-; acting Pres. of Algeria Dec. 78-Feb. 79.
Assemblée nationale populaire, Algiers, Algeria.

Blum, Yehuda Z., M.JUR., PH.D.; Israeli professor and diplomatist; b. 2 Oct. 1931, Bratislava, Czechoslovakia; ed. elementary schools in Bratislava and Budapest, Secondary school in Jerusalem, Hebrew Univ. Jerusalem, Univ. of London, England.
Worked as Law Clerk 55-56; Asst. to Judge Advocate Gen., Israel Defence Forces 56-59; Asst. Legal Adviser, Ministry of Foreign Affairs 62-65; Lecturer, Faculty of Law, Hebrew Univ. of Jerusalem 65-68, Senior Lecturer 68-72, Prof. 72-; Perm. Rep. to the UN 78-; Arlozoroff Prize 62, Nordau Prize 78.
Publs. *Historic Titles in International Law* 65, *Secure Boundaries and Middle East Peace* 71, *The Juridical Status of Jerusalem* 74.
Permanent Mission of Israel to the United Nations, 800 Second Avenue, New York, N.Y. 10017, U.S.A.

Bouabid, Abderrahim, LIC. EN DROIT; Moroccan lawyer, b. 23 March 1920; ed. Rabat and Univ. of Paris.
Student and Istiqlal Rep., Paris 45-50; mem. Exec. Comm. of Istiqlal, Dir. *Al Istiqlal* 50-52; Political Officer, Moroccan Trade Union Movt. 50-52; in prison 52-54; Istiqlal Rep. to France 54-55, to Aix-les-Bains Conf. 55; Minister of State, First Moroccan Govt. Nov. 55; mem. Moroccan del. to Independence Conf., Paris 56, Amb. to France April-Nov. 56; Minister of Finance 56-58; Vice-Pres. Council of Ministers 59-60; mem. left wing section of Istiqlal Party, co-founder of Union Nat. des Forces Populaires (UNFP) 59; resigned from Govt. 60; elected to Gen. Secretariat, UNFP 62; mem. Parl. for Kénitra 63; lawyer for UNFP in trial for plot against King Hassan II 63-64; mem. Central Cttee. of Nat. Front (Koutla Watania) 70; mem. Rabat (left wing) section of UNFP 72-74; co-founder of new party Union Socialiste des Forces Populaires (USFP) 74, now First Sec. of USFP; Minister of State without Portfolio March-June 77; mem. Nat. Defence Council March 79-.
Plateau de Bettana, Salé, Morocco.

Bouabid, Maati,; L. EN D.; Moroccan lawyer and politician; b. 11 Nov. 1927, Casablanca; ed. Lycée Lyautey, Casablanca, Univ. of Bordeaux, France.
In practice as Barrister, Casablanca 53-56; Public Prosecutor, Tangier 56-57; Attorney-Gen. Court of Appeal 57-58; Minister of Labour and Social Affairs 58-60, of Justice Oct. 77-; Prime Minister March 79-; fmr. Pres. of Municipal Council of Casablanca; fmr. mem. Union Nat. des Forces Populaires; Medal of the Green March.
Présidence du Conseil de Gouvernement, Rabat, Morocco.

Boucetta, M'Hamed, L. EN D.; Moroccan politician; b. 1925, Marrakesh; ed. Ecole Sidi Mohamed, Lycée Moulay Idriss, Fez, Univ. of Paris, France, Inst. des Etudes Supérieures, Paris.
Worked as lawyer in Casablanca; joined Istiqlal Party, Dir. *Al-Istiqlal* (party newspaper) 55, mem. Political Bureau 56, Exec. Cttee. 63-, Sec.-Gen. 74-; Sec. of State for Foreign Affairs 56; Minister of Justice 61-63; Minister of State without Portfolio March-Oct. 77, for Foreign Affairs and Co-operation Oct. 77-.
Ministère des Affaires Etrangères et de la Coopération, Rabat, Morocco.

Bourguiba, Habib Ben Ali; Tunisian politician; b. 3 Aug. 1902; ed. Collège Sadiki, Lycée Carnot, Univ. of Paris, Ecole Libre des Sciences Politiques.
Active in politics and journalism since 28; mem. Destour Party 21, broke away and formed Néo-Destour Party (outlawed by the French) 34; imprisoned by the French 34-36 and 38-43; escaped to Middle East 45, travelled to promote Tunisian independence 45-49, world tour 51 during Tunisian negotiations with French Govt.; arrested 52, placed under surveillance at Tabarka (Jan.), imprisoned at Remada (March), in solitary confinement, Ile de la Galite (May) until 54; released 54, under surveillance in France 54-55, during negotiations; returned to Tunisia following Franco-Tunisian Agreements 55; Pres. Tunisian Nat. Assembly, Prime Minister, Pres. of the Council, 56-59, 59-, concurrently Minister of Foreign Affairs and Defence 56-59; Pres. of Repub. July 57-, Life Pres. March 75-; Pres. Destour Socialist Party, Life Pres. 74-; Ordre du Sang, Ordre de la confiance en diamants.
Publs. *Le Destour et la France* 37, *La Tunisie et la France* 54.
Présidence de la République, Tunis, Tunisia.

Bourguiba, Habib, Jr., L. ès D.; Tunisian diplomatist and politician; b. 9 April 1927; ed. College Sadiki, Lycée Carnot de Dijon, Faculté de Droit, Paris and Grenoble Univs.
Collaborated in nat. liberation movement, especially 51-54; lawyer in training, Tunis 54-56; Counsellor, Tunisian Embassy, Washington 56-57; Ambassador to Italy 57-58, to France 58-61, to U.S.A. 61-63, concurrently to Canada and Mexico; Sec.-Gen. to Presidency of the Repub. 64; Asst. Sec.-Gen. Destour Socialist Party 64-69; mem. Nat. Assembly 64-; Sec. of State for Foreign Affairs 64-69, Minister of Foreign Affairs 69-70, of Justice June-Nov. 70; Special Adviser to the Pres. Dec. 77-; Pres. and Dir.-Gen. Banque de Développement Economique de Tunisie 71; Grand Cordon de l'Ordre de l'Indépendance de la République Tunisienne, Grand Officer, Légion d'Honneur (France), many foreign decorations.
Villa Dar Es Salaam, La Marsa, Tunisia.

Boustany, Elie J., LIC. EN DROIT; Lebanese lawyer and diplomatist; b. 20 Aug. 1918; ed. Univ. of Saint-Joseph, Beirut.
Chef de Bureau, Office of Pres. of the Repub. 42, Head of Youth Dept. 43; Sec. Lebanese Embassy, Paris 44-45; Head of Legis., Ministry of Justice 47; Counsellor, Lebanese Embassy, Rome 56-58, 62-64, Madrid 58-60, London 60-62; Head Litigation Dept., Ministry of Foreign Affairs 64-66; Amb. to Senegal 66-71, concurrently accred. to

Mali, Guinea, The Gambia; Dir. Int. Relations, Ministry of Foreign Affairs 71; Amb. to People's Repub. of China May 72-; Officer Order of Merit of the Repub. (Italy) 58, Commdr. Order of Civil Merit (Spain) 60, Grand Officer Nat. Order (Senegal) 71.
Publs. *Les codes libanais annotés et traduits* (7 vols.), *Recueil des traités* (2 vols.), *Législation libanaise* 1954-56; contribs. to Lebanese magazines and periodicals.
Lebanese Embassy, 51 Tung Liu Chieh, San Li Tun, Peking, People's Republic of China; and Ministry of Foreign Affairs, Beirut, Lebanon.

Boustany, Fouad Ephrem, DR.-ès-LETTRES; Lebanese scholar; b. 15 Aug. 1906; ed. Deir-el-Kamar Coll. and Univ. St. Joseph, Beirut.
Teacher in Arab Literature, Islamic Insts. and History of Arab Civilization, Institut des Lettres Orientales 33-; Dir. Ecole Normale 42-53; Prof. of Near Eastern History and Civilizations, Inst. des Sciences Politiques 45-55; Prof. of Arab Literature, Islamic Philosophy and Arab History, Acad. Libanaise des Beaux-Arts 47-53; Rector Univ. Libanaise 53-70; Sec.-Gen. Lebanese Nat. Comm. for UNESCO 48-55, Int. Comm. for Translation of Classic Works 49-, Acad. Libanaise; Dr. h.c. Univs. of Lyon 57, Austin, Texas 58, Georgetown, Washington, D.C. 58; decorations from: Lebanon, France, Vatican, Spain, Italy, Iran, Tunisia, Morocco and Senegal.
Publs. *Au temps de l'Emir* 26, *Ar-Rawae* (critical studies) 27, *Pourquoi* 30, *Histoire du Liban sous les Chéhab* of Amir Haïdar Chéhab (with Dr. A. Rustem) 33-35, *Bagdad, capitale des lettres abbassides* 34, *Le rôle des chrétiens dans l'établissement de la dynastie Omayyade* 38, *Le style orale chez les Arabes préislamiques* 41, *Al-Magani al Haditah* (5 vols.) 46-50 ,*Cinq jours à travers la Syrie* 50, *Les dits desmois* 73, *Le Problème du Liban* 78, *Encyclopedia Arabica* (12 vols.) 56-78.
Université Libanaise, Beirut, Lebanon.

Boutaleb, Abdelhadi; Moroccan politician; b. 23 Dec. 1923, Fez; ed. Al Qarawiyin Univ., Fez.
Professor of Arabic History and Literature, and Tutor to Prince Moulay Hassan and Prince Moulay Abdallah; Founder-mem. Democratic Party of Independence 44-51; campaigned, through the Party, for Moroccan independence, and for this purpose attended UN Session, Paris 51, and Negotiating Conf. at Aix-les-Bains 54-56; Minister of Labour and Social Questions in Bekkai Govt. 56; Chief Editor of journal *Al Rayal Am* 56-61; Amb. to Syria Feb. 62; Sec. of State, Ministry of Information Nov. 62, Ministry of Information, Youth and Sports Jan. 63; Minister of Information, Youth and Sports June 63; Interim Minister in Charge of Mauritania and Sahara Nov. 63; Minister of Justice 64-67, of Nat. Educ. and Fine Arts 67; Minister of State 68; Minister of Foreign Affairs 69-70; Pres. of Parl. 70-71; Amb. to U.S.A. Jan. 75-77; Prof. of Constitutional Law and Political Insts., Mohamed V Univ., Rabat; Adviser to King Hassan II (*q.v.*) 77-78; Minister of State in charge of Information Oct. 78-; decorations from Morocco, France, Spain, Italy, Tunisia and Egypt include Commdr. of the Throne of Morocco, Grand Cordon of the Repub. of Egypt and Commdr. du Mérite Sportif, France.
Publs. Many cultural and literary works.
Ministry of Information, Rabat, Morocco.

Bouteflika, Abdelaziz; Algerian politician; b. 2 March 1937, Oujda; ed. Morocco.
Major, Nat. Liberation Army (ALN) and Sec. of Gen. Staff; Minister of Sports and Tourism 62-63, of Foreign Affairs 63-79; Adviser to the Pres. March 79-; Head of del. to UN 63-79; mem. FLN Political Bureau 64-79, of Revolutionary Council 65-79; led negotiations with France 63-66, for nationalization of hydrocarbons 71; leader of dels. to many confs. of Arab League, OAU 68, Group of 77 67, Non-aligned countries 73, 29th Session of UN Gen. Assembly 74, Preparatory Conf. to Summit Meeting of OPEC 75, 7th Special Session of UN Gen. Assembly 75; Leader of del. to Conf. on Int. Econ. Co-operation, Paris 75-76.
c/o Office du Président, Palais du Gouvernement, Algiers, Algeria.

Bouziri, Najib; Tunisian diplomatist; b. 1925; ed. Paris Univ. and Inst. d'Etudes politiques.
Joined Néo-Destour Party (now Destour Socialist Party) 41, mem. Central Cttee. 64-; practised law in France; mem. Tunisian del., autonomy negotiations 54-55; served with Home and Foreign Ministries 55-56; Chargé d'Affaires, Paris 56; Chef de Cabinet, Foreign Ministry 57-58; Ambassador to Italy 58-61, to Fed. Repub. of Germany 61-64; Sec. of State for P.T.T. Feb.-Nov. 64; 2nd Vice-Pres. Nat. Assembly 64-65; Amb. to U.S.S.R. March 65-70, concurrently to Poland Feb. 67; Amb. to Belgium and Luxembourg 70-72, to Morocco 72-73, to Algeria 73-75, to Spain Feb. 75-; Leader, Tunisian del. to confs. on Maritime Law, Geneva 60, Diplomatic Relations, Vienna 61, Consular Relations, Vienna 63; Chair. Admin. and Budgetary Cttee. of UN Gen. Ass. 65, Grand Cordon Ordre de la République; Commdr. Ordre de l'Indépendance.
Embassy of Tunisia, Plaza Alonso Martínez 3, Madrid 4, Spain.

Bozbeyli, Ferruh; Turkish lawyer and politician; b. 21 Jan. 1927, Pazarcik, Maras Prov.; ed. Univ. of Istanbul.
Practised law until 65; mem. Parl. (Justice Party—JP) 61-70; fmr. Vice Pres. JP Parl. Group; Deputy Speaker Nat. Assembly, Speaker 65-70; founded Democratic Party (DP) 70, Leader Dec. 70-; Candidate for Presidency 73.
Democratic Party, Ankara, Turkey.

Bozer, Prof. Dr. Ali Husrev; Turkish jurist; b. 28 July 1925, Ankara; ed. Ankara Univ. and Neuchâtel Univ. Switzerland and Harvard Law School.
Assistant judge, Ankara 51; Asst., Faculty of Law, Ankara Univ. 52-60, Agrégé 55-60, Head of Dept. 61-, Prof. of Commercial Law 65-; lawyer at bar, Ankara 52-; Dir. Inst. de Recherche sur le Droit commercial et bancaire 60-; Judge, European Court of Human Rights 74-; mem. Admin. Council, Radio-TV de Turquie 68-71, Vice-Pres. 71-73.
Publs. *Les Droits d'Administration et de Jouissance des Père et Mère sur les Biens de l'Enfant, Nantissement Commercial, Aperçu général sur le Droit des Assurances Sociales en Droit turc, Droit commercial pour les Employés de Banques, Papiers valeurs pour les Employés de Banques;* monographs and articles in several reviews in Turkish and French.
Ahmet Rasim sok. 35/5, Çankaya, Ankara, Turkey.
Telephone: 271845, 191322.

Brahimi, Lakhdar; Algerian diplomatist; b. 1934; ed. Medersa Algiers, Institut des Sciences Politiques, Algiers, and Ecole des Sciences Politiques, Paris.
Perm. Rep. of F.L.N. and later of Provisional Govt. of Algeria in South East Asia 56-61; Gen. Secretariat Ministry of External Affairs 61-63; Amb. to U.A.R. and Sudan 63-70; Perm. Rep. to Arab League 63-70; Amb. to U.K. July 71-.
Algerian Embassy, 6 Hyde Park Gate, London, S.W.7; and 54 Holland Park, London W11 3RS, England.

Burg, Yosef, DR. PHIL.; Israeli politician; b. 31 Jan. 1909; ed. Univs. of Berlin and Leipzig, Pedagogical Inst., Leipzig, Rabbinical Seminary Berlin, and Hebrew Univ. of Jerusalem.
Directorate, Palestine Office, Berlin 36; Nat. Exec. Mizrachi; Zionist Gen. Council 38-51; mem. Exec. Hapoel Hamizrachi 44-; Deputy Speaker First Knesset (Israeli

Parl.) 49-51; Minister of Health, Govt. of Israel 51-52; Minister of Posts and Telegraphs 52-58; Minister of Social Welfare 59-70, of Interior 70-, of Welfare July-Nov. 75; Nat. Religious Party.
6 Ben Maimon Street, Jerusalem, Israel.

Burgan, Salih Khalil, M.D.; Jordanian politician; b. 1918; ed. American Univ. of Beirut.
Physician, Transjordan Frontier Forces 43-46, Dir. of Arab Physicians, T.F.F. 46-48; Private Physician, Zerka 48-63; M.P. 61-63; Minister of Health April 63-July 64, of Social Affairs and Labour Feb. 66, Sept. 66, 67-69, of Public Health Sept. 66-Aug. 67, of Social Labour, Home, Municipal and Rural Affairs April 67-69; mem. of Senate 63-69; Regional Dir. ILO Beirut 69-75, Asst. Dir.-Gen. ILO June 75-; Al Kawkab Medal (1st Grade); Grand Knight of the Holy Sepulchre.
Case Postale 500, CH-1211 Geneva 22, Switzerland.

Burns, Norman, M.A.; American economist and educationalist; b. 14 Nov. 1905; ed. Wittenberg Univ., Ohio, Yale Univ. and Univ. of Montpellier, France.
Assistant Prof. of Econs. American Univ. of Beirut 29-32; U.S. Govt. Service as Foreign trade economist, U.S. Tariff Comm., Dir. Foreign Service Inst. of State Dept., Dep. Dir. for Near East and South Asia, Int. Co-operation admin., Econ. Adviser, UN Relief and Works Agency, Beirut, Dir. United States operations missions, Amman 34-61; Pres. American Univ. of Beirut 61-65; Vice-Pres. Musa Alami Foundation of Jericho, Washington D.C.; mem. Board of Govs. Middle East Inst., Washington; Hon. LL.D. (Wittenberg Univ.); Commdr. Order of Cedar of Lebanon 65.
Publs. *The Tariff of Syria* 33, *Government Budgets of Middle East Countries* (Editor) 56, *Planning Economic Development in the Arab World* 59, *The Challenge of Education in the Developing Countries* 73.
3813 North 37th Street, Arlington, Va. 22207, U.S.A.

Butros, Fouad; Lebanese lawyer and politician; b. 1918; ed. Coll. des Frères, Beirut and Univ. of Lyon.
Judge, Civil and Mixed Commercial Court, Beirut 43-46; Judge Mil. Tribunal 45-46; Court Lawyer 47-; Govt. Lawyer 51-57; Minister of Nat. Educ. and of the Plan 59-60; mem. Chamber of Deputies 60-, Deputy Speaker 60-61; Minister of Justice 61-64; Vice-Pres. of the Council, Minister of Educ. and Defence 66, Minister of Foreign Affairs and of Tourism Feb.-Oct. 68; Deputy Prime Minister, Minister of Foreign Affairs Dec. 76-, of Defence 76-78; numerous decorations and honours.
Office of the Deputy Prime Minister, Beirut; Home: Sursock Street, Fouad Butros Building, Beirut, Lebanon.

C

Cagatay, Mustafa; Cypriot politician; b. 1937, Limassol; ed. Nicosia Turkish Lycée.
Started law practice in Limassol 63; elected Deputy for Limassol, Turkish Communal Chamber 70, mem. for Cyrenia, Legislative Assembly, Turkish Federated State of Cyprus 76; Minister of Finance 76, of Labour, Social Security and Health May-Dec. 78; Prime Minister Dec. 78-; mem. Turkish Cypriot Cttee., Turkish and Greek Cypriot Talks on Humanitarian issues 74; mem. Nat. Unity Party.
Office of the Prime Minister, Turkish Federated State of Cyprus, Lefkoşa, Mersin 10, Turkey.

Çağlayangil, Ihsan Sabri; Turkish politician; b. 1908; ed. Faculty of Law, Univ. of Istanbul.
Formerly with Ministry of Interior; Gov. of Yozgat, then of Antalya 48-53, of Çannakale 53-54, of Sivas 54, of Bursa 54-60; Senator for Bursa 61-; Minister of Labour Feb.-Oct. 65, of Foreign Affairs 65-71; Pres. Senate Foreign Affairs Cttee. 72-75; Minister of Foreign Affairs 75-June 77, July-Dec. 77; Justice Party.
Şehit Ersan Caddesi 30/15, Çankaya, Ankara, Turkey.

Cahen, Claude Louis Alfred, D. ès L.; French university professor; b. 1909; ed. Sorbonne, Ecole des Langues Orientales and Ecole Normale Supérieure, Paris.
Professor, Faculty of Letters, Univ. of Strasbourg 45-59, Sorbonne, Paris 59-; Lecturer, Ecole des Langues Orientales, Paris 37-54; Pres. Société Asiatique; Dir. *Journal of the Economic and Social History of the Orient*, Centre d'Etudes de l'Orient Contemporain, Inst. d'Etudes Arabes et Islamiques; mem. Acad. des Inscriptions et de Belles-Lettres, Inst. de France 73; Schlumberger Prize 45.
Publs. *La Syrie du Nord au temps des Croisades* 40, *Le régime féodal de l'Italie normande* 40, *Pre-Ottoman Turkey* 68, *Der Islam* (Fischer Weltgeschichte) 68, French edn *L'Islam* 70, *Makhzumiyyat* 77, *Les Peuples Musulmans dans l'histoire médiévale* 77, various studies in Turkish history, Islamic economic and social history, and history of the Crusaders.
62 avenue Carnot, Savigny s. Orge (S.et O.), France.

Cappelletti, Luciano, J.D., PH.D.; Italian international official; b. 22 Nov. 1930; ed. Univs. of Padua, Ferrara, Bologna and California (Berkeley).
Associate Prof., Univ. of Bologna 60-63; joined UN Devt. Programme (UNDP) 63, served in India, Burma, Uganda, Pakistan, Sudan; now Chief of Div. for Arab States, UNDP Headquarters, New York.
Publs. *Burocrazia e Società* 68, and several articles on public admin. in professional journals.
United Nations Development Programme, 1 United Nations Plaza, New York, N.Y. 10017, U.S.A.

Cayer, Rt. Rev. John Aimé, D.D.; Canadian ecclesiastic; b. 1900; ed. Quebec and Montreal Colls. and Innsbruck Univ., Austria.
Ordained priest 26; missionary in Edmonton, Alberta 27-36; apptd. Rector of St. Anthony's Coll., Edmonton 30; Prof. of Theology, R.C. Seminary Regina, Sask. 40-45; elected Commissary Provincial for the Franciscan Fathers 45, Minister Provincial for the Order in Canada 48; consecrated Bishop of Alexandria and Vicar Apostolic of Egypt, Sept. 49-; and Admin. of the Apostolic Vicariate of Port Said 57-.
Publ. *Mère Marie de Bethanie Beghian* 60.
Archbishop's Residence, 10 Sidi Metwalli, Alexandria, Egypt.

Çelik, Vedat; Cypriot politician; b. 6 May 1935, Tera; ed. English School, Cyprus and Univ. of Wales, Cardiff.
Civil Service 53-69, Under-Sec. to the Vice-Pres. 69-72; Minister of Commerce, Industry and Tourism 72-75, of Energy and Natural Resources 74, of Foreign Affairs 75; Turkish Cypriot Rep. to UN 75; mem. for Kyrenia, Legislative Assembly of "Turkish Federated State of Cyprus (TFSC)" 76-; Deputy Prime Minister, Minister of Defence and Foreign Affairs, "TFSC" 76-78, Minister of Tourism and Information 78-.
Publs. various papers on constitutional and political aspects of the Cyprus problem.
Ministry of Tourism and Information, Lefkoşa, Mersin 10, Turkey; Home: Kumsal, Lefkoşa, Mersin 10, Turkey.

Chadli, Col. Bendjedid; Algerian army officer and politician; b. 14 April 1929.
Served in French Army before start of Algerian war for nat. independence 54; joined Maquisards guerrilla forces 55; Commdr. 13th Battalion, Army of Nat. Liberation 60, mem. Gen. Staff 61; Commdr. of Constantine Mil. Region, East Algeria 63, of Second Mil. Region (Oran) 64-79; mem. Revolutionary Council 65; Acting Minister of Defence and Chief of Staff Nov. 78-Jan. 79; Sec.-Gen. Nat. Liberation

Front Jan. 79-; Pres. of Algeria and Minister of Defence Feb. 79-.
Office du Président, Palais du Gouvernement, Algiers, Algeria.

Chaker, Abdelmajid; Tunisian politician and diplomatist.
Secretary of State for Agriculture 62-64, for Information 64-66; Amb. to Algeria 66-70, to Yugoslavia 70-73, to Sweden 73-; mem. Néo Destour, later Socialist Destour Party, Dir. until Nov. 64, mem. Bureau Politique Nov. 64-71, mem. Cen. Cttee. 71-.
Tunisian Embassy, 73c Drottninggatan, Stockholm, Sweden.

Chamoun, Camille, LL.D.; Lebanese lawyer; b. 3 April 1900; ed. Coll. des Frères and Law School, Beirut.
Qualified as lawyer 24; mem. Parl. 34-; Minister of Finance 38; Minister of Interior 43-44; Minister to Allied Governments in London 44; Head of Del. to Int. Civil Aviation Conf., Chicago 44, UNESCO Conf. and UN Preparatory Comm. 45; Del. to UN Gen. Assembly, London and N.Y. 46; Lebanese rep. Interim Comm., UN 48; Pres. Lebanese Republic 52-58; leader Liberal Nationalist Party 58-; Minister of Interior, of Post Office and Telecommunications, of Hydraulic and Electrical Resources May 75-Dec. 76, of Foreign Affairs June-Dec. 76, of Defence Sept.-Dec. 76; mem. Nat. Dialogue Cttee. Sept. 75.
Home: Saadyat, Lebanon.

Chatti, Habib; Tunisian diplomatist and politician; b. 1916; ed. Sadik Coll., Tunis.
Journalist 37-52, Editor *Ez-Zohra* 43-50, *Es-Sabah* 50-52; imprisoned 52, 53; Head, Press Cabinet of Pres. of Council 54-55, Head, Information Service 55; mem. Nat. Council, Néo-Destour Party 55; Dir. *Al Amal* 56; Vice-Pres. Constituent Nat. Assembly 56; Ambassador to Lebanon and Iraq 57-59, to Turkey and Iran 59-62, to U.K. 62-64, to Morocco 64-70, to Algeria 70-72; Dir. of the Presidential Cabinet 72-74; Minister of Foreign Affairs 74-77; mem. Cen. Cttee. Destour Socialist Party 74-; Deputy to Nat. Assembly 74-; Grand Cordon Ordre de la Répub. Tunisienne, several foreign decorations.
Tunis, Tunisia.

Chaudhuri, Kamal Reheem, F.R.S.A.; Bangladesh administrator; b. 1 March 1923; ed. Calcutta Univ., Presidency Coll., Aligarh Muslim Univ., Imperial Agricultural Research Inst. and Edinburgh Univ., Scotland.
Governor Imperial Coll. of Science and Technology 57-65; Chair. British Commonwealth Scientific Offices, London 58; Assessor British Cttee. for Int. Nature Conservation 58-65; Chair. Commonwealth Agricultural Bureaux 61; Alt. Gov. IAEA 63; Head UNESCO Regional Science Office for the Arab States 70-; del. to numerous int. scientific and agricultural confs.; Egyptian Order of Merit 72.
Publs. include *Science and Ourselves* 60.
UNESCO Regional Science Office for the Arab States, 8 Abdel Rahman Fahmy Street, Garden City, Cairo, Egypt.

Chéhab, Amir Khalid; Lebanese diplomatist and politician; b. 1890; ed. Patriarchal Coll. Damascus.
Mem. comm. for drawing up Lebanese Constitution 26; Minister of Finance 27; elected Deputy 28-55, 60-; Pres. Chamber of Deputies 35; Prime Minister 38; Minister of State 43; Minister to Jordan 47; Prime Minister and Minister of Interior 52-53; Leader Dar el Fatwa.
Rue de Damas, Beirut, Lebanon.

Chéhab, Amir Maurice; Lebanese archaeologist and historian; b. 1904; ed. Univ. St. Joseph, Beirut, Ecole du Louvre, and Ecole des Hautes Etudes Historiques, Paris.
Conservator, Lebanese Nat. Museum 28, Chief of Antiquities Service 37, Dir. 44; Prof. of the History of Architecture, Lebanese Acad. of Fine Arts 42, of Lebanese History, Ecole Normale 42, of Diplomatic and Gen. History, Ecole des Sciences Politiques 45; Prof. of Oriental Archaeology, Inst. of Oriental Literature 46; Dir. Tyre and Anjar Excavations 50; Prof. of History and Archaeology, Univ. of the Lebanon 53-59; Curator of Lebanese Gen. Antiquities 53-59, Dir.-Gen. of Antiquities 59-.
Direction des Antiquités, rue de Damas, Beirut, Lebanon.

Chelli, Tijani; Tunisian politician; b. 23 March 1931, Nabeul; ed. Collège Sadiki, Tunis, Ecole Polytechnique, Paris and Ecole Nat. des Ponts et Chaussées, Paris.
Engineer, Ministry of Public Works, Kef 59-60; Deputy Chief Engineer of Roads and Bridges 60; Dir. of Transport 61; Dir. of Sea and Air Transport 62; Pres. Dir.-Gen. Société Nationale des Chemins de Fer Tunisiens 65-67; Dir. of Industry, Dept. of Planning and Nat. Economy 67-69; Pres. Dir.-Gen. Industries Chimiques Maghrébines (ICM) Jan.-Nov. 69; Minister of Public Works 69-70, of the Economy 70-72; Pres., Dir.-Gen. Investment Promotion and Industrial Land Agency 73-75, Investment Promotion Agency 76-79; Chair. Econ. and Social Council 76-79.
Agence de Promotion des Investissements, 17 rue du Royaume d'Arabie Saoudite, Tunis, Tunisia.

Choufi, Hammoud el-, B.A.; Syrian diplomatist; b. 1935, Salkhad; ed. Damascus Univ.
Secretary-General of Baath Party in Syria 63; Amb. to Indonesia 65-70, to India 70-72; Dir. American Dept., Ministry of Foreign Affairs 72-78; Perm. Rep. to the UN June 78-.
Publ. *History of the Sweida Region* 61.
Permanent Mission of the Syrian Arab Republic to the United Nations, 150 East 58th Street, Room 1500, New York, N.Y. 10022; Home: 1155 Park Avenue, Apartment 11 N.W., New York, N.Y. 10028, U.S.A.

Christofides, Andreas N., M.A.; Cypriot broadcasting official; b. 20 Aug. 1937; ed. Pancyprian Gymnasium, Nicosia, Athens Univ. and Columbia Univ., New York.
Teacher at Pancyprian Gymnasium 58-63; Dir. of Radio Programmes of Cyprus Broadcasting Corpn. 64-67; Dir.-Gen. of Cyprus Broadcasting Corpn. 67-; Chair. Cyprus State Theatre Org.; fmr. mem. Admin. Council European Broadcasting Union; first Nat. Award Prize for *Points of View I and II*.
Publs. include: Essays: *Letters from New York* 65, *Points of View I* 66, *Points of View II* 69 (First Nat. Award Prize), *Introduction to Propaganda* 66, *Love Songs from Cyprus* 64, *An Anthology of Poetry from Cyprus* (with K. Montis) 69, *An Anthology of Short Stories* (with P. Ioannides) 71, *Points of View III;* Poems: *A Strange Illustration* 69, *Analytical Propositions* 70.
Cyprus Broadcasting Corporation, P.O. Box 4824, Nicosia, Cyprus.

Christophides, Ioannis; Cypriot politician; b. 21 Jan. 1924, Nicosia; ed. Pancyprian Gymnasium, Nicosia, Gray's Inn Law School, London.
Barrister-at-Law; joined family banking and insurance firms 48, Chief Exec. 54-72; Chair. of several private cos. 54-72; Chair. Cyprus Telecommunications Authority 66-72; Vice-Chair. Commonwealth Telecommunications Board 70-72; Minister of Foreign Affairs 72-74, 75-78; Pres. Nicosia Branch, Cyprus Red Cross 64-72.
25 El. Venizelos Street, Nicosia, Cyprus.

Clerides, Glavkos John, B.A., LL.B.; Cypriot lawyer and politician; b. 1919; ed. Pancyprian Gymnasium, Nicosia, Univ. Tutorial Coll., London, King's Coll., London Univ., Gray's Inn, London.
Served with R.A.F. 39-45; shot down and taken prisoner 42-45 (mentioned in despatches); practised law in Cyprus 51-60; Head of Greek Cypriot Del., Constitutional Comm. 59-60; first Minister of Justice of the Republic 59-60; mem. House of Representatives 60-, Pres. of the House 60-76;

Acting Pres. of Repub. 60-76, Temporary Pres. July-Dec. 74; Head of Greek Cypriot Del. to London Conf. 64; Rep. to Consultative Assembly of the Council of Europe; mem. Political Cttee. and Standing Cttee.; Rep. Greek Cypriots in UN sponsored talks 68-76; Chair. Democratic Rally 76-; Gold Medal Order of the Holy Sepulchre.
56 Metochio Street, Nicosia, Cyprus.

Cluverius, Wat Tyler, IV, B.S., M.A.; American diplomatist; b. 4 Dec. 1934; Arlington, Mass.; ed. Northwestern Univ., Indiana Univ.
Officer, U.S. Navy 57-62; Third Sec. and Vice-Consul, Embassy in Jeddah 67-69; Second Sec., Tel Aviv 69-72; Deputy Dir., Office of Israeli and Arab-Israeli Affairs, U.S. Dept. of State 73-76; Amb. to Bahrain 76-78; Dir. Office of Lebanon, Jordan, Syria and Iraq, Bureau of Near Eastern Affairs, Dept. of State; U.S. Dept. of State Meritorious Honor Award 69.
Bureau of Near Eastern and South Asian Studies, Department of State, 2201 C Street, N.W., Washington, D.C. 20520, U.S.A.

Cohn, Haim H.; Israeli lawyer; b. 11 March 1911; ed. Univs. of Munich, Hamburg and Frankfurt-am-Main, Germany, Hebrew Univ. of Jerusalem, and Govt. Law School, Jerusalem.
Admitted to Bar of Palestine 37; Sec. Legal Council, Jewish Agency for Palestine, Jerusalem 47; State Attorney, Ministry of Justice, Hakirya 48, Dir.-Gen. 49; Attorney-Gen., Govt. of Israel 50; Minister of Justice and Acting Attorney-Gen. 52; Attorney-Gen. 52-60; Justice, Supreme Court of Israel 60-; mem. Perm. Court of Arbitration, The Hague 62-, UN Comm. on Human Rights 65-67; Deputy Chair. Council of Higher Educ., Israel 58-71; mem. Board of Govs., Int. Inst. of Human Rights, Strasbourg; mem. Exec. Council Asscn. Internationale de Droit Pénal, Paris; Deputy Pres. Board of Govs. Hebrew Univ. of Jerusalem; Visiting Prof. of Law, Univ. of Tel-Aviv; mem. Int. Comm. of Jurists, Geneva 73-; Pres. Israel Sec. of Criminology 75-; Pres. Int. Asscn. of Jewish Lawyers and Jurists 75-.
Publs. *The Foreign Laws of Marriage and Divorce* (English) 37, *Glaube und Glaubensfreiheit* (German) 67, *The Trial and Death of Jesus* (Hebrew) 68, English edn. 71, *Jewish Law in Ancient and Modern Israel* 72.
Supreme Court of Israel, Jerusalem; and 36 Tchernihovsky Street, Jerusalem, Israel.

Colocassides, Michael G., B.SC.(ECON); Cypriot banker; b. 9 Sept. 1933, Nicosia; ed. Pancyprian Gymnasium, London School of Econs., London Univ.
Engaged in business, mainly as an Exec. Dir. of S. & G. Colocassides Ltd. 55-70; Part-time teacher of Econs. in Commercial Section of Pancyprian Gymnasium 56-68; mem. Board of Dirs., Cyprus Devt. Corpn. Ltd. 63-72, Vice-Chair. 66-68, Chair. 68-70; Chair. Cyprus Tourism Org. 70-72; Minister of Commerce and Industry 72-76; Gov. Bank of Cyprus Ltd. Oct. 76-.
Bank of Cyprus Ltd., P.O. Box 1472, 86-90 Phaneromeni Street, Nicosia, Cyprus.

Comay, Michael, B.A., LL.B.; Israeli diplomatist; b. 17 Oct. 1908; ed. Cape Town Univ., South Africa.
Major South African Army 40-45; Special Rep. South African Zionist Fed., attached to Political Dept. Jewish Agency, Jerusalem 46-48; mem. Israel del. to UN 48, Chair. 60-67; has represented Israel at a number of int. confs.; Dir. British Commonwealth Div., Israel Foreign Ministry 48-51, Asst. Dir.-Gen. 51-53; Amb. to Canada 53-57; Asst. Dir.-Gen. Ministry for Foreign Affairs 57-59; Perm. Rep. to UN 60-67; Political Adviser to Foreign Minister and Amb.-at-Large 67-70; Amb. to U.K. 70-73; Special Adviser to Minister of Foreign Affairs Oct. 73-76; Research Fellow, Leonard Davis Inst. Int. Affairs 76-.
Leonard Davis Institute for International Affairs, Hebrew University of Jerusalem; 47 Harav Berlin Street, Jerusalem, Israel.

Coobar, Abdulmegid; Libyan politician; b. 1909; ed. Arabic and Italian schools in Tripoli, and privately.
With Birth Registration Section, Tripoli Municipal Council and later its Section Head, Adviser on Arab Affairs for the Council 43-44; resigned from Govt. Service 44; mem. Nat. Constitutional Assembly 50, and mem. its Cttee. to draft the Libyan Constitution; mem. of Parl. for Eastern Gharian 52-55, Pres. of Parl. Assembly 52-55; Dep. Prime Minister and Minister of Communications 55-56; again elected for Eastern Gharian to the new Chamber of Deputies 55, Pres. 56; mem. of Council of Viceroy 56; Dep. Prime Minister and Minister of Foreign Affairs 57; Prime Minister 57–60, concurrently Minister for Foreign Affairs 58-60; Independence Award (First Class).
Asadu el-Furat Street 29, Garden City, Tripoli, Libya.

Craig, Albert James Macqueen, C.M.G., M.A.; British diplomatist; b. 13 July 1924, Liverpool; ed. Liverpool Inst. High School, Queen's Coll., Oxford, Magdalen Coll., Oxford.
Lecturer in Arabic, Durham Univ. 48; Principal Instructor, Middle East Centre for Arab Studies 55; Foreign Office 58; H.M. Political Agent in Dubai, Trucial States 61; First Sec., Embassy in Beirut 64; Counsellor, Jeddah 67; Fellow, St. Antony's Coll., Oxford 70; Head, Near East and North Africa Dept., Foreign and Commonwealth Office 71; Deputy High Commr. in Malaysia 75; Amb. to Syria 76-.
British Embassy, Damascus, Syria; c/o Outward Bag Room (Damascus), Foreign and Commonwealth Office, London, S.W.1, England.

Crawford, David Gordon; British diplomatist; b. 10 June 1928, London; ed. Ashford Grammar School, Kent, London Univ.
H.M. Forces 47-55; Foreign Office 56; Middle East Centre for Arab Studies, Shemlan, Lebanon 57; Taiz 59; Bahrain 59; Foreign Office 62; First Sec. Perm. Mission to UN, New York 64; First Sec. and Head of Chancery, Amman 67; Consul-Gen., Muscat 69; Head of Accommodation and Services Dept., Foreign and Commonwealth Office 71; Amb. to Qatar 74-77; Consul-Gen., Atlanta, U.S.A. 78-.
British Consulate-General, Atlanta, Georgia, U.S.A.; Foreign and Commonwealth Office, London, S.W.1, England.

Crawford, William R., Jr., M.A.; American diplomatist; b. 22 April 1928; ed. Harvard Coll. and Univ. of Pennsylvania.
Political Officer, Jeddah, Saudi Arabia 51; Consul, Venice, Italy 53; Chargé d'Affaires, Taiz, Yemen 57, Principal Officer, Aden; Officer-in-Charge Lebanon-Israel Affairs, Washington, D.C. 62; Counsellor, Political Officer, Rabat, Morocco 64; Deputy Head of Mission to Cyprus 68; Amb. to Yemen Arab Repub. 72-74, to Cyprus 74-78; Deputy Asst. Sec. of State for Near East, North African and South Asian Affairs; Meritorious Service Award (U.S. Dept. of State) 59, William A. Jump Award 63.
c/o Department of State, NEA, Washington, D.C. 20520, U.S.A.

Cunbur, Fatma Müjgân, DR. PHIL.; Turkish librarian; b. 1926; ed. Lycée and Univ. of Ankara.
Librarian of Faculty of Letters, Univ. of Ankara 52-55, Lecturer in Library Science 60-; Librarian Nat. Library 55-59, Acting Dir. 59, Chief of rare books and manuscripts section 60-65, Gen. Dir. 65-; mem. Turkish Librarians' Asscn., Turkish Language Asscn., Asscn. for Studying Social Life of Women, Turkish Nat. Comm. for UNESCO, Inst. for the study of Turkish Culture; Chair. Asscn. for the Nat. Library.
Publs. *Türk Kadın Yazarları Bibliyografyasi* (Bibliography

of Turkish Women Authors) 55, *Fuzuli hakkında bir bibliyografya denemesi* (A Preliminary Bibliography of the Turkish Poet Fuzuli) 56, *Fuzuli divan* (Collected Poems of Fuzuli) 58, *Yunus Emre'nin gönlü* (The Heart of Yunus Emre) 59, *Yusuf Ağa Kütüphanesi Vakfiyesi* (The Endowment of Yusuf Ağa Library) 63, *I. Abdülhamid vakfiyesi ve Hamidiye Kütüphanesi* (The Endowment of Abdülhamid I and the Hamidiye Library) 65, *Başaklarin sesi, Türkhalk sairleri, hayatlari ve eserleri* (The Sounds of Corn Ears, Turkish folk poets, their lives and works), *Karacaoğlan, hayatı ve şiirleri* (Karacaoğlan, his life and poems) 1972, *Atatürk ve millî kültür* (Atatürk and national culture) 73, *Fârâbî bibliyografyası* (Bibliography of Farâbî) 73, *Ali Kuşçu bibliyografyası* (Bibliography of Ali Kusî) 74.
Turkish National Library, Yenişehir, Ankara, Turkey.

D

Daccak, Nassouh, L. EN D.; Syrian financial administrator; b. 1916, Damascus; ed. Damascus Univ.
Head Dept. of Foreign Trade, Ministry of Econ. 47-50; Dir. of Trade, Ministry of Econ. 50-51, Dir. of Econ. Affairs 51-59; Chair. Board of Dirs., Gen. Man. Industrial Bank 59-62; Gen. Sec. Ministry of Labour and Social Affairs 62-63; Chair. Board of Credit and Money 71-78; Gov. Cen. Bank of Syria 71-78; Alt. Gov. IMF, Arab Fund for Social and Econ. Devt.; mem. Board of Dirs., European Arab Bank.
c/o Central Bank of Syria, 29 Ayar Square, Damascus, Syria.

Dagher, Abdallah, S.J.; Lebanese ecclesiastic and university rector; b. 1 June 1914; ed. Secondary School of Univ. St. Joseph, Oriental Seminary of Beirut and Univ. de Paris à la Sorbonne.
Entered Jesuit Noviciate 32; ordained priest 45; Prefect Arabic Studies, Secondary School of Univ. St. Joseph; Dir. Oriental Seminary (Maronite) of Beirut; Rector Maronite Seminary of Ghazir, Lebanon 51-57; Jesuit Provincial for the Near East 57-65; Rector Univ. St. Joseph 65-72, Coll. Notre-Dame de Jamhour 72-; Consultant of Roman Congregation for the Non-Christian Religious (Islam); Officier de la Légion d'Honneur, du Mérite Libanais.
Collège Notre-Dame de Jamhour, P.O. Box 11-2904, Beirut, Lebanon.

Daouk, Ahmed bey; Lebanese engineer, diplomatist and politician; b. 1893; ed. Univ. of Aix-en-Provence, France.
Engineer with Sucreries et Raffineries d'Egypte 15-19; technical mission for King Hussein of Hedjaz 19-20; consultant 20-27; held various directorships 27-40; Prime Minister 41, 42, May-Aug. 60; Pres. Nat. Congress 43; Ambassador to France 44-58, to Spain; Head of Missions to U.S.A., South America and Africa; Rep. to Arab League; mem. Dels. to UN and UNESCO 44-58; Pres. Admin. Council of Banks and Socs. 60-; Leader of official dels. overseas 60-; Prime Minister 60; Pres. Ogero Radio-Orient 73-; holder of several Lebanese and foreign decorations.
Rue Omar Daouk, Beirut, Lebanon.

Dawalibi, Marouf; Syrian professor and lawyer; b. 1907; ed. Aleppo, Damascus, and Univ. of Paris, France.
Lawyer Court of Appeal Aleppo 35-39; Prof. Law Faculty, Damascus 47; Minister of Nat. Economy 49-50; Pres. Chamber of Deputies 51; Prime Minister and Minister of Defence 51; Minister of Nat. Defence 54; Prime Minister 61-62; mem. Exec. Council Motamav al Alam al Islami (World Muslim Congress) 65; living in Saudi Arabia 66.
Publs. *La Jurisprudence dans le Droit Islamique* 41, *Introduction au Droit Romain* 47, *Introduction à la science des sources du Droit Musulman* 49, *Précis du Droit Romain* 2 vols. 61, *Histoire Générale du Droit* 61.

Dayan, Gen. Moshe, LL.B.; Israeli soldier and politician; b. 20 May 1915, Degania; ed. agricultural high school, Nahalal, School of Law and Econs., Tel Aviv, Hebrew Univ. and Staff Coll., Camberley, England.
Trained in Haganah (Jewish militia) 29; second in command to Capt. Orde Wingate 37; imprisoned by British when Haganah declared illegal 39; released for training as intelligence scout in Syria 41; Colonel after 45; took leading part in war with Arabs 48-49; promoted to Gen. and Commdr. Southern Region Command 50; Commdr. Northern Region Command 51; Chief of Staff 53-58; Minister of Agriculture 59-64; Minister of Defence 67-74, of Foreign Affairs June 77-; fmr. mem. Mapai Party; elected to Knesset 59, 65, 69, 73, 77; mem. Mapai Party until 64, Rafi Party until 68, Labour Party until 77; Independent June 77-.
Publs. *Diary of the Sinai Campaign* 66, *Mapa Hadasha, Yahassim Aherim* 69, *Story of My Life* 76, *Living with the Bible* 78.
Ministry of Foreign Affairs, Hakiriya, Romema, Jerusalem; Yoav Street 11, Zahala, Tel-Aviv, Israel.

Dean, John Gunther, PH.D.; American diplomatist; b. 24 Feb. 1926, Germany; ed. Harvard Coll., Harvard Univ., Univ. of Paris.
Member of U.S. Del. to UN 63; Deputy to Commdr. 24th Army Corps, Viet-Nam 70-72; Chargé d'affaires, Laos 72-73; Amb. to Cambodia 74-75, to Denmark 75-78, to Lebanon Sept. 78-; numerous American and foreign decorations and awards.
Embassy of the U.S.A., Avenue de Paris, Imm. Ali Reza, Beirut, Lebanon; c/o Department of State, Washington, D.C. 20520, U.S.A.

de Garang, (Enok) Mading; Sudanese politican; b. 1 Jan. 1934, Kongor; ed. Malek, Atar Intermediate School, Rumbek Secondary School, Manchester Coll. of Science and Technology, England, London Univ. Inst. of Educ.
Member of Southern Nationalist Movement 56-; co-founder Sudan African Nat. Union, Manchester, U.K. 63; Ed. *Voice of Southern Sudan*, Manchester, U.K. 63; Man. Spearhead Press, Malakal 63; Ed. *Light* 63-65; Asst. Production Man., Haile Selassie Printing Press, Ethiopia 65-67; studied then taught at Africa Lit. Centre, Kitwe, Zambia 67-69; co-founder Southern Sudan Asscn., London, Later Dir.; Ed. *Grass Curtain*, London 70-72; External Spokesman, South Sudan Liberation Movement 70-March 72; mem. High Exec. Council for Southern Region, Minister for Information, Culture, Youth and Sports, Tourism and Wildlife, Social Services April 72-73, for Rural Devt. and Co-operatives 73-75, for Information and Culture 75-77, Youth and Sports July 75-76; mem. People's Regional Assembly for Bor; mem. Cen. Cttee. Sudanese Socialist Union; First Class Medal (Two Niles) for Peace.
Home: Kongor District, Jonglei Province, Sudan.

Deif, Nazih Ahmed, B.COM., M.A., PH.D.; Egyptian economist; b. 4 March 1923; ed. Cairo Univ. and Univ. of Chicago, Ill., U.S.A.
Member Expert Group collaborating with Arthur D. Little Group on Industrialization of Egypt 53; Dir. Econ. Statistics, Ministry of Finance 54; Senior Research Officer, Nat. Planning Comm. 57, Dir.-Gen. 58; Under-Sec. Ministry of Planning, U.A.R. 61-64; Gov. Int. Monetary Fund, U.A.R. 64-66; Ministry of Treasury, Egypt 64-68; Prof. Inst of Statistical Studies and Research, Cairo Univ. 69-70; Exec. Dir. for Middle East IMF 70-76.
Publs. numerous papers on national planning issues, particularly national accounting, and various UN publs.
2 Rollins Court, Rockville, Md. 20852, U.S.A.

Demirel, Süleyman; Turkish hydraulic engineer and politician; b. 1924, Islâmköy, Isparta Prov.; ed. High School, Afyon and Istanbul Technical Univ.
Qualified engineer; worked in U.S.A. 49-51, 54-55; with

Dir.-Gen. Electrical Studies, Ankara 50-52; in charge of building various hydro-electric schemes 52-54; Head of Dept. of Dams 54; Dir.-Gen. of Water Control 54-55; first Eisenhower Fellow for Study in U.S.A. 54; Dir. State Hydraulics Admin. 55-60; private practice including Consultant to Morrison-Knudsen, and lecturer Middle East Technical Univ. 61-65; Pres. Justice Party 64-; Deputy Prime Minister Feb.-Oct. 65; Prime Minister 65-71, 75-June 77, July-Dec. 77.
Adalet Partisi Genel Baskanligi, Ankara, Turkey.

Denktaş, Rauf; Cypriot lawyer; b. 27 Jan. 1924; ed. English School, Nicosia, and Lincoln's Inn, London.
Interpreter, Court Clerk, Teacher until 43; called to Bar, Lincoln's Inn 47; mem. Consultative Assembly under Colonial Govt. of Cyprus 48, also mem. Turkish Affairs Cttee. 48-49; Junior Crown Counsel, Attorney-Gen.'s Office 49-53, Crown Counsel 53-56; Solicitor-Gen. 56-57; Chair. Fed. of Turkish Cypriot Asscns. 57-60; mem. Turkish Cypriot del. to Conf. on Independence of Cyprus, London 59; rep. to Conf. on Mil. aspects of Treaty of Establishment 59; Head of Turkish Cypriot del. to Constitutional Cttee. 59-60; Pres. Turkish Communal Chamber 60-63, 68-73; Head of del. to Conf. on Cyprus, London 63; also attended UN Security Council 64; prohibited from returning by Greek Cypriot authorities 64; in exile in Turkey 64-67; detained after secretly returning to Cyprus 67; in exile in Turkey 67-68; Vice-Pres. Turkish Cypriot Admin. 68-73, Pres. 73-75; Turkish Cypriot Spokesman in intercommunal talks 68-76; Vice-Pres. of Cyprus 73-; Pres. "Turkish Federated State of Cyprus" 75-.
Publs. *Secrets of Happiness* (1st edn. 43, 2nd edn. 73), *Hell Without Fire* 44, *A Handbook of Criminal Cases* 55, *Five Minutes to Twelve* 66, *The AKRITAS Plan* 72, *A Short Discourse on Cyprus* 72, *The Cyprus Problem* 73.
Office of the President of the Turkish Federated State of Cyprus, Lefkoşa (Nicosia), via Mersin 10, Turkey.

Dimechkié, Nadim, G.C.V.O., M.A.; Lebanese diplomatist; b. 5 Dec. 1919; ed. American Univ. of Beirut.
Director-General Ministry of Nat. Economy 43-44; Lebanese del. Joint Supply Board for Syria and Lebanon 42-44; Counsellor, Lebanese Embassy, London 44-49; Consul-Gen., Ottawa 50; Dir. Econ. and Social Dept., Ministry of Foreign Affairs 51-52; Chargé d'Affaires, Cairo 52, Minister 53-55; Minister to Switzerland 55-57; Amb. to U.S.A. 58-62; Dir. Econ. Affairs, Ministry of Foreign Affairs 62-66; Amb. to U.K. 66-78; Doyen of the Diplomatic Corps 77-78; Special Adviser on Foreign Affairs to Minister of Foreign Affairs and Prime Minister 79; Lebanese Order of Cedars, Syrian Order of Merit, Tunisian Order of Merit, Greek Order of Phoenix, Egyptian Order of Ismail, etc.
Ministry of Foreign Affairs, Beirut, Lebanon.

Dimitrios I (Dimitrios Papadopoulos); Archbishop of Constantinople and Ecumenical Patriarch; b. 8 Sept. 1914, Istanbul; ed. Theological School of Halki, Heybeliada-Istanbul.
Ordained Deacon 37; Ordained Priest 42; Preacher in Edessa, Greece 37-38; Preacher, Parish of Feriköy-Istanbul 39-45; Priest of Orthodox Community, Teheran 45-50; Head Priest, Feriköy 50-64; Bishop of Elaia, Auxiliary Bishop of the Patriarch Athenagoras in Istanbul 64-72; Metropolitan of Imvros and Tenedos 72; Archbishop of Constantinople and Ecumenical Patriarch 72-.
Rum Ortodoks Patrikhanesi, Fener, Istanbul, Turkey.

Dimitriou, Nicos George, F.C.I.S.; Cypriot merchant banker, industrialist and diplomatist; b. 16 July 1920; ed. Larnaca Commercial Lyceum, Greek Gymnasium, Athens. and Maiden Erlegh Private School, Reading, England.
Manager and Sec. N. J. Dimitriou Ltd., Merchant Bankers 52-62, Man. Dir. 62-; Man. Dir. Larnaca Oil Works Ltd. 63-; dir. several Cyprus companies; Dir. Bank of Cyprus Ltd. 60-62; Chair. Cyprus Chamber of Commerce 60-63; Pres. Chamber of Commerce and Industry, Larnaca 63-68, Pezoporicos Club, Larnaca 57-68; Pres. Cyprus Soc. of Inc. Secretaries 68; Consul-Gen. of Denmark 61-; mem. Council Cyprus Chamber of Commerce and Industry 63-68; Chair. Cyprus Devt. Corpn. Ltd. 66-68; Minister of Commerce and Industry 68-70; Chair. Electricity Authority of Cyprus 70-73, Advisory Board Nat. and Grindlays Bank Ltd. 70-73; Amb. to U.S.A. 73-, High Commr. to Canada 74-; Commdr. Order of Cedar of Lebanon; Commdr. Order of Dannebrog.
Publ. *Chambers of Commerce—their Objects and Aims.*
Embassy of Cyprus, 2211 R Street, N.W., Washington, D.C., U.S.A.; and Artemis Avenue 39, Larnaca, Cyprus.

Dinitz, Simcha, M.S.; Israeli diplomatist; b. 23 June 1929; ed. Univ. of Cincinnati and School of Foreign Service and Graduate School, Georgetown Univ.
Director, Office of the Dir.-Gen., Ministry of Foreign Affairs 61-63; Political Sec. to Minister of Foreign Affairs 63-66; Minister, Embassy of Israel, Rome 66-68, Washington 68-69; Political Adviser to the Prime Minister 69, later Dir.-Gen. Office of the Prime Minister; Amb. to U.S.A. 73-78; mem. Israeli del. to the UN 63, 64, 65.
Publ. *The Legal Aspect of the Egyptian Blockade of the Suez Canal* (Georgetown Law Journal) 56.
40 Nayot, Jerusalem, Israel.

Dodson, Sir Derek Sherborne Lindsell, K.C.M.G., M.C.; British diplomatist; b. 20 Jan. 1920, Cambridge, ed. Stowe School, Royal Mil. Coll., Sandhurst.
Commissioned in Royal Scots Fusiliers 39; Mil. Asst. to British Commr., Allied Control Comm. for Bulgaria 45-46; Second Sec., Foreign Office 47-48; Vice-Consul, Salonika, Greece 48-60; in British Embassy to Spain 50-53; at Foreign Office 53-58; Head of Chancery, Ebasmsy to Czechoslovakia 53-62; Consul, Elisabethville (now Lubumbashi), Zaire 62-63; Head of Central Dept., FCO 63-66; Counsellor, Embassy to Greece 66-69; Amb. to Hungary 70-73, to Brazil 73-77, to Turkey 77-; Grand Cross of Cruzeiro do Sul (Brazil).
British Embassy, Çankaya, Şehit Ersan Cad. 46/A, Ankara, Turkey; 47 Ovington Street, London S.W.3; Gable House, Leadenham, Lincoln, England.

Doğramaci Ihsan, M.D.; Turkish pediatrician and educator; b. 3 April 1915; ed. Istanbul, Harvard, Washington Univs.
Associate Prof. of Pediatrics, Ankara Univ. 49-54, Prof. of Child Health and Head of Dept. 55-63, Dir. Inst. of Child Health, Ankara 58-63; Prof. of Pediatrics and Head of Dept. Hacettepe Faculty of Medicine 63-, Dean of Faculty June 63-Nov. 63; Pres. Ankara Univ. 63-65; Pres. Hacettepe Science Centre, Ankara 65-67; Pres. Hacettepe Children's Medical Centre 75-; mem. UNICEF Exec. Board 60-75, Chair. 68-70: Chair. Board of Trustees, Middle East Technical Univ. 65-67; Pres. Hacettepe Univ. 67-75, now Hon. Rector; Pres. Int. Pediatric Asscn. 68-77, Exec. Dir. 77-; mem. Standing Cttee. Standing Conf. of Rectors and Vice-Chancellors of the European Univs. 69-; Pres. Council of Rectors of Turkish Univs. 75-; mem. Board Int. Children's Centre (Paris) 70-; Fellow, Royal Coll. of Physicians (London) 71; Corresp. mem. Acad. Nat. de Médecine, France 73-, Deutsche Akad. der Naturforscher, Leopoldina 76; hon. mem. several foreign pediatrics socs.; Hon. LL.D. (Nebraska and Glasgow Univs.), Dr. h.c. (Nice Univ.), Hon. D.Sc. (Baghdad and Anatolian Univs.); Nat. Award for Distinguished Service (Scientific and Technical Research) 78; Chevalier Légion d'Honneur 73, Officer, Order of Duarte, Sanchez y Mella (Dominican Repub.); Editor *The Turkish Journal of Pediatrics, Bulletin of the International Pediatric Association*, Consulting Editor *Clinical Pediatrics.*

Publs. *Annenin Kitabi* (Mother's Handbook on Child Care) 8 edns. 52-74, *Premature Baby Care* 54, *Porphysis in Childhood* 64, *Care of Mother and Child* 67, various monographs and articles on child health and pediatric topics.
c/o Children's Medical Centre, Hacettepe University, Ankara, Turkey.

Dostrovsky, Israel, PH.D.; Israeli scientist; b. 1918, Odessa, U.S.S.R.; ed. Univ. Coll., London.
Engaged in research work, Univ. Coll., London 40-43; Lecturer in Chem., Univ. Coll. of N. Wales 43-48; joined staff of Weizmann Inst. of Science 48; Head of Isotope Research Dept., Weizmann Inst. 48-65; mem. Israel Atomic Energy Comm. and first Dir. of Research 53-57; Chair. Nat. Council of Research and Devt. 59-61; Senior scientist, Brookhaven Nat. Laboratory, U.S.A. 61-64; Dir.-Gen. Israel Atomic Energy Comm. 65-71; Vice-Pres. Weizmann Inst. 71-73, Pres. 73-75; Ramsay Medal, U.K. 44; Weizmann Prize, Israel 52; Dr. h.c. (Tel-Aviv Univ.) 73.
Neve Weizmann, Rehovot, Israel.

Dountas, Mihalis; Greek diplomatist; b. 1932, Athens; ed. Univ. of Athens.
Entered Greek Diplomatic Service 58; Cyprus and Turkish Desk in Ministry of Foreign Affairs 58-60; Consul in Toronto, Canada 60-63; First Sec. Embassy in Nicosia 63-66; First Sec., Washington, D.C. 66-69; Counsellor, Nicosia 69-71; Counsellor, Perm. Greek del to NATO 71-73; Head of Greek del. to talks on Mutual and Balanced Force Reductions (MBFR), Vienna 73-74; Diplomatic Adviser to Constantine Karamanlis, Prime Minister Aug. 74; Amb. to Cyprus Aug. 74-; took part in bilateral Greek-Turkish negotiations 59; mem. del. to UN Gen. Assembly 60-66; Officer, Order of Phoenix; Commdr., Order of the Holy Sepulchre; Officer, Order of Merit (Egypt).
Greek Embassy, 8-10 Byron Avenue, Nicosia, Cyprus; Home: Stratiotikou Syndesmou Athens, Greece.

Driss, Rachid; Tunisian journalist and diplomatist; b. 27 Jan. 1917; ed. Sadiki Coll., Tunis.
Joined Néo-Destour Party 34; journalist exiled in Cairo, and with President Bourguiba founder mem. Bureau du Maghreb Arabe 46-52; returned to Tunisia 55; Editor *El Amal;* Deputy, Constitutional Assembly 56; Sec. of State Post Office and Communications 57-64, mem. Nat. Assembly 59-, Political Bureau Destour Socialist Party 58-; Amb. to the U.S.A. and Mexico 64-70; Perm. Rep. to UN 70-76; Pres. Econ. and Social Council 71; Grand Cordon de l'Ordre de l'Indépendance de la République Tunisienne and foreign decorations.
P.O. Box 5, Carthage, Tunisia.

Duaij, Ahmad Ali al-, B.A.; Kuwaiti company director; b. 25 Dec. 1937; ed. Shuwaikh Secondary School, Kuwait, Reading Technical Coll., Keele Univ. and St. Antony's Coll., Oxford, England.
Joined Ministry of Foreign Affairs 62; joined Planning Board as Sec. 62, Sec.-Gen. 63, Dir.-Gen. with rank of Perm. Under-Sec. 64-75; Chair. and Man. Dir. Kuwait Real Estate Investment Consortium 75-.
Publs. Regular articles in Kuwait, Lebanese and British Press.
Kuwait Real Estate Investment Consortium (K.S.C.), P.O. Box 23411, Kuwait.

Dultzin, Leib (Leon Aryeh); Israeli business executive; b. 31 March 1913, Minsk, Russia.
Lived in Mexico 28-56, Israel 65-; mem. of the executive, Jewish Agency. Treas, 68-78, Chair. 78-; Minister without Portfolio, Govt. of Israel 70-73; Gov. Pal Land Devt. Co. Ltd., Bank Leumi le-Israel; Dir. Rassco Ltd., Yakhim Hakal Co. Ltd., Otzar Hataasiya; mem. World Directorate, Keren Hayesod; mem. of numerous Zionist orgs.
Publs. *The Economic Role of the Middle Class, The Middle Classes and their Role in the Productive Absorption of New Immigrants.*
The Jewish Agency, P.O. Box 92, Jerusalem; Home: 11 Mapu Street, Tel-Aviv, Israel.

Dupont-Sommer, André Louis; French Semiticist; b. 23 Dec. 1900; ed. Univ. of Paris.
Secretary, Collège de France 34-40; Dir. of Studies, School of Higher Studies 38-; Prof., Univ. of Paris 45-63; Pres. of Inst. of Semitic Studies, Univ. of Paris 52-; Prof. Collège de France 63-71, Hon. Prof. 72; mem. Institut de France 61-; Secrétaire Perpétuel de l'Académie des Inscriptions et Belles-Lettres 68-; Foreign mem. Accad. dei Lincei (Rome); Corresp. mem. Austrian Acad. of Sciences; Officier de la Légion d'Honneur; Commandeur des Palmes académiques.
Publs. *La Doctrine gnostique de la lettre wâw d'après une lamelle araméenne inédite* 46, *Les Araméens* 49, *Les inscriptions araméennes de Sfiré* 48, *Aperçus préliminaires sur les manuscrits de la mer Morte* 50, *Nouveaux aperçus sur les manuscrits de la mer Morte* 53, *Les Ecrits esséniens découverts près de la mer Morte* 59, 60, 64, and others.
Palais Mazarin, 25 quai de Conti, Paris 6e, France.

Duval, H.E. Cardinal Léon-Etienne; Algerian (b. French) ecclesiastic; b. 9 Nov. 1903; ed. Petit Séminaire, Roche-sur-Foron, Grand Séminaire Annecy, Séminaire français Rome, and Pontifica Universitas Gregoriana.
Ordained priest 26; Prof. Grand Séminaire Annecy 30-42; Vicar-Gen. and Dir. of works, Diocese of Annecy 42-46; consecrated Bishop of Constantine and Hippo 46; Archbishop of Algiers 54-; created Cardinal 65; took Algerian nationality 65; Officier Légion d'Honneur.
Publs. *Paroles de Paix* 55, *Messages de Paix 1955-1962* 62, *Laïcs, prêtres, religieux dans l'Eglise selon Vatican II* 67.
Archbishop's House, 13 rue Khelifa-Boukhalfa, Algiers, Algeria.

E

Eban, Abba, M.A.; Israeli politician; b. (as Aubrey Solomon) 2 Feb. 1915, South Africa; ed. Queens' Coll., Cambridge.
Liaison Officer of Allied H.Q. with the Jewish population in Jerusalem 40; Chief Instructor at the Middle East Arab Centre in Jerusalem; entered service of Jewish Agency 46; Liaison Officer with UN Special Comm. on Palestine 47; Rep. of Provisional Govt. to UN 48, Perm. Rep. with rank of Minister 49; Amb. to U.S.A. 50-59; Minister without Portfolio 59-60; Minister of Educ. and Culture 60-63; Deputy Prime Minister June 63-66; Minister of Foreign Affairs 66-74; mem. of Knesset 74-; Guest Prof. Columbia Univ. 74, Haifa Univ. 75, Inst. for Advanced Study, Princeton Univ. 78; Pres. Weizmann Inst. of Science 58-66; Hon. L.H.D., Hon. Ph.D., Hon. Dr. New York, Maryland, Boston, Chicago, Cincinnati Univs.; foreign mem. American Acad. of Arts and Sciences 60.
Publs. *Maze of Justice* 46, *Social and Cultural Problems in the Middle East* 47, *The Toynbee Heresy* 55, *Voice of Israel* 57, *Tide of Nationalism* 59, *Chaim Weizmann: A Collective Biography* 62, *Israel in the World* 66, *My People* 68, *My Country* 73, *An Autobiography* 77.
The Knesset, Jerusalem, Israel.

Ebtehaj, Abol Hassan; Iranian banker and administrator; b. 1899; ed. Lycée Montaigne, Paris, and Syrian Protestant Coll., Beirut.
Joined Imperial Bank of Iran 20; Govt. Inspector Agricultural Bank and Controller of State-owned companies 36; Vice-Gov. Bank Melli Iran 38; Chair. and Man. Dir. Mortgage Bank 40; Gov. and Chair. Bank Melli Iran (National Bank of Iran) 42-50; Chair. Iranian Del. Middle East Financial and Monetary Conf., Cairo 44; Chair. Iranian Del. Bretton Woods Conf. 44; Amb. to France

50-52; Adviser to Man. Dir., IMF 52-53, Dir. Middle East Dept. 53; Man. Dir. Plan Org. (Development Board), Teheran 54-59; Chair. and Pres. Iranians' Bank (Private Bank) 59-72, Chair. 72-77; Chair. Iran America Int. Insurance Co. 74-79.
68 Park Avenue, Teheran, Iran.

Ecevit, Bülent, B.A.; Turkish journalist and politician; b. 28 May 1925, Istanbul; ed. Robert Coll., Ankara, London and Harvard Univ.
Government official 44-50; Turkish Press Attaché's Office, London 46-50; Foreign News Editor, Man. Editor later Political Dir. *Ulus* (Ankara) 50-61, Political Columnist, *Ulus* 56-61; M.P. (Republican People's Party) 57-60, Oct. 61-; mem. Constituent Assembly 61; Minister of Labour 61-65; Political Columnist *Milliyet* 65; Sec.-Gen. Republican People's Party 66-71, Chair. 72-; Prime Minister Jan.-Nov. 74, June-July 77, Jan. 78-.
Publs. *Ortanin Solu* (Left of Centre) 66, *Bu Düzen Değismelidir* (The System Must Change) 68, *Atatürk ve Devrimcilik* (Atatürk and Revolution) 70, *Sohbet* (conversations), *Demokratik Sol* (Democratic Left) 74, *Diş Politika* (Foreign Policy) 75, *Işçi-Köylü Elele* (Workers and Peasants Together) 76, *Siirler* (Poems) 76; Translations into Turkish: *Gitinjali* (R. Tagore) 41, *Straybirds* (R. Tagore) 43, *Cocktail Party* (T. S. Eliot) 63.
Or-an Şehri, Ankara, Turkey.

Echiguer, Mohammed Haddou; (*see* Shiguer, Mohamed Haddou).

Eddé, Raymond, L. en D.; Lebanese lawyer and politician b. 1913; ed. Univ. Saint Joseph, Beirut.
Member of Parl. 53-57-60-65-68-72; Leader, Nat. Bloc Party 49-; Minister of Interior, of Public Works, of Social Affairs, and of Posts, Telegraphs and Telephones 58-59; Candidate for Presidency 58, May 76; Minister of Public Works, Agriculture, Planning, Water and Power 68-72; mem. Nat. Dialogue Cttee. Sept. 75.
Publs. *Loi sur les Immeubles de Luxe, Loi sur le Secret Bancaire, Loi sur le compte joint.*
Rue Emile Eddé, Quartier Arts et Métiers, Beirut, Lebanon.

Ehrlich, Simha; Israeli industrialist and politician; b. 15 Dec. 1915, Poland; ed. high school and econ. studies.
Industrialist; mem. Tel-Aviv Municipality Council 55-69; mem. Knesset 69-; fmr. Deputy Mayor and Head of Lighting and Water Dept. of Sanitation Dept. of Bureau of Municipal Corpn.; Nat. Sec. of Liberal Party; mem. Exec. Cttee., Gattal; mem. of Knesset Finance Cttee. and Sub-cttee. for Defence Budget; Minister of Finance June 77-; Chair. Habimah Co.; mem. Publicity Cttee. for Israel Opera; Likud.
Ministry of Finance, Hakinya, Ruppin Street, Jerusalem, Israel.

Eilts, Hermann Frederick, M.A., LL.D.; American diplomatist; b. 23 March 1922, Germany; ed. Ursinus Coll., Johns Hopkins Univ. School of Advanced Int. Studies, Univ. of Pennsylvania Nat. War Coll.
Counsellor and Deputy Chief of Mission, American Embassy, Libya 64-65; Amb. to Saudi Arabia 65-70; Diplomatic Adviser, U.S. Army War Coll. 70-73; Amb. to Egypt 73-79; retd. from foreign service June 79; Prof. of Middle Eastern Affairs, Boston Univ. 79-; Arthur S. Flemming Distinguished Govt. Service Award 58; U.S. Army Decoration for Distinguished Civilian Service 73.
Boston University, 147 Bay State Road, Boston, Massachusetts 02215, U.S.A.

Eisenstadt, Shmuel N., M.A., PH.D.; Israeli professor of sociology; b. 10 Sept. 1923, Warsaw, Poland; ed. Hebrew Univ., Jerusalem and London School of Economics.
Chairman, Dept. of Sociology, Hebrew Univ., Jerusalem 51-68, Prof. of Sociology 59-, Dean, Faculty of Social Sciences 66-68; Fellow Center for Advanced Studies in the Behavioral Sciences, Stanford Univ. 55-56; Visiting Prof., Univ. of Oslo 58, Univ. of Chicago 60, Harvard Univ. 66, 68-69; Carnegie Visiting Prof., Mass. Inst. of Technology 62-63; Chair. Council on Community Devt., Israel 62-66, Israeli Sociological Soc. 69-72; Visiting Prof., Univ. of Michigan 70, Univ. of Chicago 70, Univ. of Zurich 75, Harvard Univ. 75, 76, 77; Simon Visiting Prof., Univ. of Manchester 77; Hon. Research Fellow, Australian Nat. Univ. 77; mem. Advisory Board *International Encyclopedia of the Social Sciences*; Fellow, Netherlands Inst. of Advanced Studies 73; mem. Israel Acad. of Sciences and Humanities, Int. Sociological Soc., American Sociological Asscn.; Foreign Hon. mem. American Acad. of Arts and Sciences, American Philosophical Soc.; Hon. Fellow, London School of Econs.; McIver Award, American Sociological Asscn.
Publs. *The Absorption of Immigrants* 54, *Political Sociology* (editor) 55, *From Generation to Generation* 56, *Essays on Sociological Aspects of Economical and Political Development* 61, *The Political Systems of Empires* 63, *Essays on Comparative Institutions* 65, *Modernization, Protest and Change* 66, *Israeli Society* 68, *The Protestant Ethic and Modernization* 68, *Political Sociology of Modernization* (in Japanese) 68, *Comparative Perceptives on Social Change* (editor) 68, *Charisma and Institution Building: Selections from Max Weber* (editor) 68, *Ensayos sobre el Cambio social y la Modernización* (Spanish) 69, *Modernização e Mudança Social* (Portuguese) 69, *Political Sociology* (editor) 71, *Social Stratification and Differentiation* 71, *Tradition, Change and Modernity* 73, *The Form of Sociology: Paradigms and Crisis* (with M. Curelaru) 76, *Revolution and the Transformation of Societies* 78.
The Hebrew University, Jerusalem; Home: Rechov Radak 30, Jerusalem, Israel.

Elath, Eliahu, PH.D.; Israeli diplomatist; b. 30 July 1903; ed. Hebrew Univ. of Jerusalem and American Univ. of Beirut.
Jewish Agency 34; Jewish Agency observer to San Francisco Conf. 45; Head of Jewish Agency's Political Office in Washington, D.C.; Israeli Amb. to U.S.A. 48-50; Minister to U.K. 59-52, Amb. 52-59; Adviser, Ministry of Foreign Affairs 59-60; Pres. Hebrew Univ., Jerusalem 61-67; Vice-Pres. Jewish Colonization Asscn.; Pres. Israel Oriental Soc.; Chair. Afro-Asian Inst., Tel-Aviv; Hon. Ph.D.
Publs. *Bedouin, their Life and Manners* 34, *Trans-Jordan* 35, *Israel and Her Neighbours* 57, *The Political Struggle for the inclusion of Elath in the Jewish State* 67, *San Francisco Diary* 71, *British Routes to India* 71, *Zionism and the Arabs* 74.
17 Bialik Street, Beth Hakerem, Jerusalem, Israel.

El Bualy, Nassir Seif, B.A.ECON.; Omani diplomatist; b. 9 Jan. 1925, Dar es Salaam, Tanzania.
Assistant Dir. of Information, Zanzibar 56-60, Asst. Principal Sec. 60-65; Asst. Dir. Mwananchi Group of Cos., Dar es Salaam 65-68; Senior Admin., Dept. of Finance, United Arab Emirates 69-70; Dir. of Social Affairs and Acting Dir. of Information, Oman 71, Dir.-Gen. of Information and Tourism 72-73; Chargé d'Affaires, Omani Embassy in London Feb.-June 73, Amb. June 73-.
Embassy of the Sultanate of Oman, 64 Ennismore Gardens, London, SW7 5DN; Residence: 33 Hyde Park Gate, London, S.W.7, England.

Elias, Ibrahim; Sudanese economist and politican; b. 29 Aug. 1923, Omdurman; ed. Gordon Memorial Coll., Khartoum, Queen's Univ., Belfast and Manchester Univ.
Schoolmaster 49-56; trade officer, Ministry of Commerce, Industry and Supply 56-62; Asst. Man. Dir. Sudan Industrial Bank 62-65; Asst. Under Sec. Ministry of Econ. 65-69; Gen. Man. Gulf Fisheries, Kuwait 69-70; Man. Dir. Blue Nile Brewery, Khartoum and Chair. Leather and Plastic Industries Corpn. 70-72; Minister of the Treasury

Oct. 72-; Chair., Man. Dir. Sudan Investment Co. Ltd. 74-; Chair. El Nilein Bank 74-76.
Publ. *Studies in Sudan Economy* 69.
P.O. Box 1017, Omdurman, Sudan.

Eliraz, Israel, M.A.; Israeli writer, playwright and teacher; b. 24 March 1936, Jerusalem; ed. Hebrew Univ., Jerusalem, Tel-Aviv Univ., Sorbonne, Paris.
Plays produced in Israel, Paris, London, New York, Belgium and Germany; libretti commissioned and performed by Hamburgische Staatsoper 71, Israeli Festival 73, Bayerische Staatsoper 76; Teacher in Jerusalem; Lecturer, Hebrew Univ.; awarded two first prizes by Nat. Council for Culture and Art, Israel.
Publs. novels: *Tin Swings, Last Birds, Golden Summer, A Voyage;* plays: *Far from the Sea—Far from the Summer, The Bear, The Banana, Round Trip, Three Women in Yellow, The Persian Protocoles;* libretti: *Ashmedai, Massada 967, The Temptation, Elsa-Homage, The Fire and the Mountains, The Journey*; choreographies: *M.A.S.A.D.A. 77, Little Savage Square* 77.
6 Jabotinsky Street, Jerusalem, Israel.

Elmandjra, Mahdi, PH.D.; Moroccan international official; b. 13 March 1933; ed. Lycée Lyautey, Casablanca, Putney School, Vermont, U.S.A., Cornell Univ., London School of Economics and Univ. de Paris.
Head of Confs., Law Faculty, Univ. of Rabat 57-58; Adviser Ministry of Foreign Affairs, and to Moroccan Del. to UN 58-59; Dir.-Gen. Radiodiffusion Télévision Marocaine 59-60; Chief of African Div., Office of Relations with mem. States, UNESCO 61-63; Dir. Exec. Office of Dir.-Gen. of UNESCO 63-66; Asst. Dir.-Gen. of UNESCO for Social Sciences, Human Sciences and Culture July 66-Dec. 69; Visiting Fellow, Centre for Int. Studies, London School of Econs. and Political Sciences 70; Asst. Dir.-Gen. of UNESCO for Pre-Programming 71-75, Special Adviser to the Dir.-Gen. 75-76; Prof. Univ. Mohamed V, Rabat 77-; Pres. World Future Studies Fed.; Vice-Pres. Morocco-Japan Assn.; mem. Soc. for Int. Devt., World Acad. of Art and Science, Pugwash Movement; Chevalier, Ordre des Arts et Lettres (France).
Publ. *The United Nations System: An Analysis* 73; co-author of Club of Rome report on learning 79.
B.P. 53, Rabat, Morocco.

El-Yafi, Mohamed Selim, LL.B.; Syrian international official; b. 21 Dec. 1920; ed. Maristes Frères school, Damascus and Damascus Univ.
Ministry of Supply 43-45, of Foreign Affairs 45; Attaché, Cairo 45, Ankara 46; Consul in Mersina, Turkey 49; Chargé d'Affaires, Jeddah 52; Ministry of Foreign Affairs 54; Dir.-Gen. Arab Palestinian Org. 54; del. to Consultative Comm., UNRWA 54; Chargé d'Affaires, Berne 56; Asst. Sec.-Gen. Ministry of Social and Labour Affairs 58-62; Dir.-Gen. Palestinian Refugees Org. 58-62; mem. U.A.R. Higher Council of Radio and Television 59-62; Counsellor for Palestinian Affairs, Ministry of Foreign Affairs 62, later Dir. of Arab Affairs; Dir. of Admin. and Cultural Affairs 62; Lecturer, Faculty of Commerce, Univ. of Damascus 62-63, 63-64; Minister, Paris 64-65; Minister, Brussels, then Chargé d'Affaires, then Amb. to Belgium 66-68; Dir. of European Affairs, Ministry of Foreign Affairs 68, Asst. Sec.-Gen. Political Affairs 69, Asst. Minister 70; Asst. Sec.-Gen. Arab League 70-; Pres. Conciliation Comms. of Jordan 70, Oman 71, Yemen 72-73.
Publ. a book on the Palestinian question and its evolution 61.
League of Arab States, Khairaldin Basha Street, Tunis, Tunisia.

Eralp, Orhan, B.A., LL.B., PH.D.; Turkish diplomatist; b. 28 Jan. 1915; ed. Robert Coll. Istanbul, Univ. Coll., London, and London School of Economics.
Ministry of Foreign Affairs 39-; Sec. Washington 42-48; Adviser to Turkish Del., UN Conciliation Comm. for Palestine 49-51; Perm. Rep. to European Office of UN, Geneva 51; Counsellor, London 52; Dir.-Gen. Second Dept., Ministry of Foreign Affairs 52-56; Ambassador to Sweden 57-59, to Yugoslavia 59-64; Perm. Rep. of Turkey to UN, New York 64-69, 78-; Sec.-Gen. Foreign Ministry 69-72; Perm. Rep. of Turkey to NATO 72-76; Amb. to France 76-78.
Permanent Mission of Turkey to the United Nations, 821 UN Plaza, New York, N.Y. 10017, U.S.A.

Erbakan, Necmettin; Turkish politician; b. 1926, Sinop; ed. Inst. of Mechanics, Technical Univ. of Istanbul and Technische Universität, Aachen, Federal Republic of Germany.
Assistant Lecturer Inst. of Mechanics, Technical Univ. of Istanbul 48-51; Engineer, Firma Deutz 51-54; Prof. Technical Univ. of Istanbul 54-66; Chair. Industrial Dept., Turkish Assn. of Chambers of Commerce 66-68, Chair. of Assn. 68; mem. Nat. Assembly 69-; f. Nat. Order Party 70 (disbanded 71); Chair. Nat. Salvation Party Oct. 73-; Deputy Prime Minister Jan.-Sept. 74, April 75-June 77, July-Dec. 77; Minister of State Jan.-Sept. 74.
National Salvation Party, Ankara, Turkey.

Erim, Nihat, PH.D.; Turkish politician; b. 1912, Kandira, Kocael Province; ed. Lycée of Galatasaray, Istanbul, and Univ. of Istanbul Law School and Univ. of Paris.
Professor of Constitutional and Int. Law, Univ. of Ankara and Legal Adviser, Ministry of Foreign Affairs 42; mem. Parl. 45-50; Minister of Public Works, concurrently Deputy Prime Minister 48-50; Publr. and Editor *Ulus* (organ of the Republican People's Party) 50, subsequently Publr. and Editor of *Halkçi*; mem. for Turkey, European Human Rights Comm.; mem. Nat. Assembly 61-72; Deputy Chair. Republican People's Party Nat. Assembly Group 61-71; mem. Turkish Parl. Group, Council of Europe 61-70; Prime Minister March 71-March 72; Senator 72-.
Publs. several books on law.
Cumhuriyet Senatosu, Ankara, Turkey.

Erkmen, Nizamettin; Turkish politician; b. 1919, Giresun.
Director of Legal Affairs, Samsun; mem. Nat. Assembly for Giresun 61-; Sec.-Gen. Justice Party until 74; Minister of State, Deputy Prime Minister 73-74; Justice Party.
Dr. Mediha Eldem Sok. 73/14,
Ankara, Turkey.

Ertekun, Mehmet Necati Munir, O.B.E., Q.C., M.A.; Cypriot judge; b. 7 Dec. 1923, Nicosia; ed. Froebel School, Kyrenia, Brentwood School, Essex, St. John's Coll., Cambridge, Gray's Inn, London.
McMahon Law Studentship, St. John's Coll., Cambridge 46; Crown Counsel, Tanganyika (now Tanzania) 48-53; Solicitor-Gen., Cyprus 53-60; Turkish Judge, Supreme Constitutional Court of Cyprus 60; Pres. Supreme Court of Turkish Cypriot Admin. 67-75, of "Turkish Federated State of Cyprus (TFSC)" 75-78; Constitutional and Legal Adviser to Pres. of TFSC 79-; Legal Adviser to Turkish Cypriot del. to Mixed Constitutional Comm. on Cyprus 56-60; mem. Turkish Cypriot del. to Second Geneva Conf. on Cyprus Aug. 74; Pres. Supreme Council of Judicature of "TFSC" 75-78, of Supreme Electoral Comm. 76-78; mem. Supreme Council of Public Prosecutors 76-78.
Publs. *Inter-Communal Talks and the Cyprus Problem* 77, various papers relating to constitutional aspects of the Cyprus problem.
3 Mufit Guleroglu Street, Lefkoşa, Mersin 10, Turkey.

Esenbel, Melih; Turkish diplomatist; b. 15 March 1915, Istanbul; ed. Galatasaray Lycée, Faculty of Law, Istanbul.

Ministry of Foreign Affairs 36, Third Sec., Private Cabinet of Sec.-Gen., Later in Second Political Dept.; Second Sec., Paris and First Sec. of Protocol Dept. of Ministry of Foreign Affairs 44; First Sec., later Counsellor, Washington, D.C. 45-52; Dir.-Gen. Dept. of Int. Econ. Affairs 52; del. to UN Gen. Assembly 52, 53; Asst. Sec.-Gen. for Econ. Affairs and Sec.-Gen. of Int. Co-operation Admin. 54-56; participated in negotiations for Baghdad Pact 55; Sec.-Gen. Ministry of Foreign Affairs 57-59, participated in Zürich and London Confs. on independence of Cyprus 59; Amb. to U.S.A. 60; Senior Adviser, Ministry of Foreign Affairs 60-63; Amb. to Japan 63-66, to U.S.A. 67-74; Minister of Foreign Affairs 74-75; Amb. to U.S.A. April 75-; Chevalier, Légion d'Honneur (France) 41, Cross of Order of Isabel la Católica (Spain) 56, Gran Cruz del Mérito Civil (Spain) 59, Cavaliere di Gran Croce (Italy) 57, Order of the Sacred Treasure (Japan) 58, Grand Cordon, Order of the Brilliant Star (Repub. of China) 58, Knight, Grand Cross, Royal Order of the Phoenix (Greece) 59, Sardar Ali (Afghanistan) 58, Grand Cross (Fed. Repub. of Germany) 54.
Embassy of Turkey, 1606 23rd Street, N.W., Washington, D.C. 20008, U.S.A.

Essaafi, M'hamed; Tunisian diplomatist; b. 26 May 1930; ed. Collège Sadiki and Univ. of Paris.
Secretariat of Foreign Affairs, Tunis 56; Tunisian Embassy, London 56-57; First Sec., Washington 57-60; Dir. of American Dept., Secr. of Foreign Affairs, Tunis 60-62, American Dept. and Int. Conf. Dept. 62-64; Amb. to U.K. 64-69; Sec.-Gen. Foreign Affairs, Tunis 69-70; Amb. to U.S.S.R. 70-74, to Federal Repub. of Germany 74-76; Sec.-Gen. Ministry of Foreign Affairs 76-78; Amb. to Belgium, Luxembourg and the EEC 78-; Grand Officier de l'Ordre de la République Tunisienne.
Embassy of Tunisia, 278 avenue de Tervueren, 1150 Brussels, Belgium.

Etemadi, Noor Ahmad; Afghan diplomatist; b. 22 Feb. 1921, Kandahar; ed. Istiqlal Lycée, Kabul, and Kabul Univ.
Joined Ministry of Foreign Affairs 46, Asst. Chief of Protocol, Dir. for Econ. Relations, Dir.-Gen. for Political Affairs 57; diplomatic posts in London and Washington; Deputy Minister of Foreign Affairs 63; Amb. to Pakistan 64; Minister of Foreign Affairs 65-71, Prime Minister 67-71; Amb. to Italy 72-73, to U.S.S.R. 73-74, 75-76, to Pakistan 76-78; arrested June 78.
Kabul, Afghanistan.

Ettinghausen, Richard, PH.D.; American educationist and art curator; b. 5 Feb. 1906; ed. Univs. of Munich, Cambridge and Frankfurt a.M.
Asst. Islamic Dept., State Museum, Berlin 31-33; Asst. to Editor *A Survey of Persian Art* 33-34; Research Assoc., American Inst. for Persian Art and Archaeology, N.Y. 34-37; Lecturer on Islamic Art, Inst. of Fine Arts, N.Y. Univ. 36-38; mem. Inst. of Advanced Study, Princeton, N.J. 37-38; Assoc. Prof. of Islamic Art, Univ. of Mich., Ann Arbor 38-44; Assoc. in Near-Eastern Art, Freer Gallery of Art, Smithsonian Inst., Washington, D.C. 44-58, Curator of Near Eastern Art 58-61, Head Curator 61-66; Research Prof. of Islamic Art, Univ. of Mich. 48-67; Editor *Ars Islamica* 38-51; Near-Eastern Editor *Ars Orientalis* 51-58; Editorial Board *The Art Bulletin* 40-, *Kairos* 59-; Adjunct Prof. of Fine Arts, New York Univ. 60-67, Prof. of Fine Arts 67-; Consultant, Near Eastern Art, Los Angeles County Museum of Art 67-; Consultative Chair. Islamic Dept., Metropolitan Museum of Art, N.Y. 69-.
Publs. *The Unicorn* (*Studies in Muslim Iconography I*) 50, *The Paintings of Emperors and Sultans of India in American Collections* 61, *Persian Miniatures in the Bernard Berenson Collection* 63, *Arab Painting* 62; Editor and contributor: *A Selected and Annotated Bibliography of Books and Periodicals in Western Languages dealing with the Near and Middle East, with special emphasis on Medieval and Modern Times* 52, *Aus der Welt der Islamischen Kunst* (editor) 59, *Turkish Miniatures from the 13th to the 14th Century* (editor) 65, *Treasures of Turkey* (co-author) 66, *From Byzantium to Sasanian Iran and the Islamic World* 72.
Office: Institute of Fine Arts, New York University, 1 East 78th Street, New York, N.Y. 10021; Home: 24 Armour Road, Princeton, N.J. 08540, U.S.A.

Evenari, Michael; Israeli botanist; b. 9 Oct. 1904; ed. Univ. of Frankfurt, Germany.
Staff of Botany Dept., Univ. of Frankfurt 27-28, German Univ., Prague 28-31; Staff of Technische Hochschule, Darmstadt 31-33, Lecturer 33; External Teacher, Hebrew Univ., Jerusalem 34-37, Instructor 37-44, Lecturer 44, Chair. Dept. of Botany 45-, Prof. 51-; Vice-Pres. Hebrew Univ., Jerusalem 53-59; Fellow Linnean Soc.; Hon. Fellow American Botanical Soc.; mem. German Acad. of Science; Major Research on ancient desert agriculture and its modern application and studies in germination, physiology and ecology of desert plants; Hon. Ph.D. (Technical Univ., Darmstadt).
Publ. *The Negev—The Challenge of a Desert* 71.
Department of Botany, Hebrew University of Jerusalem, Jerusalem, Israel.

Evron, Ephraim; Israeli diplomatist; b. 1920, Haifa; ed. Reali Secondary School, Haifa, Hebrew Univ. of Jerusalem.
Served in British Army 41-46; in Israeli Foreign Service 49-56, 61-; Political Sec. to Minister of Foreign Affairs 49-51; Chief of Bureau, Office of the Prime Minister 51-52, Ministry of Defence 54-55; worked in the Histadrut (Gen. Fed. of Labour) 56-61; Counsellor, Embassy of Israel to the U.K. 61-63, Minister 63-65; Minister at Embassy to U.S.A. 65-68; Amb. to Sweden 68-69, to Canada 69-71; Asst. Dir.-Gen. of Ministry of Foreign Affairs 72-73, Deputy Dir.-Gen. 73-77, Dir.-Gen. 77-78; Amb. to U.S.A. Jan. 79-.
Embassy of Israel, 1621 22nd Avenue, N.W., Washington, D.C. 20008, U.S.A.

Eytan, Walter, M.A.; Israeli public official; b. 24 July 1910; ed. St. Paul's School, London and Queen's Coll. Oxford.
Lecturer in German, Queen's Coll., Oxford 34-46; Principal, Public Service Coll., Jerusalem 46-48; Dir.-Gen., Ministry for Foreign Affairs, Israel 48-59; Ambassador to France 60-70; Political Adviser to Minister of Foreign Affairs 70-72; Chair. Israel Broadcasting Authority 72-78; Commdr. Légion d'Honneur 76.
Publ. *The First Ten Years* 58.
18 Balfour Street, 92 102 Jerusalem, Israel.

F

Fahd ibn Abdul Aziz, H.R.H. Prince; Saudi Arabian politician; b.1922; brother of H.M. King Khalid (*q.v.*).
Minister of Educ. 53, of the Interior 62-Oct. 75; Second Deputy Prime Minister 68-75, First Deputy Prime Minister March 75-; became Crown Prince 75.
Council of Ministers, Jeddah, Saudi Arabia.

Fahmi, Ismail; Egyptian diplomatist and politician; b. 1922; ed. Cairo Univ.
Entered diplomatic service 45; mem. Perm. Mission to UN 49-57, Counsellor 57; Perm Rep. of Egypt (later United Arab Repub.) to IAEA 57-60; Dir. Dept. of Int. Orgs. and Confs., Ministry of Foreign Affairs 64-68; Amb. to Austria 68-71; Under-Sec. of State for Foreign Affairs 71-73; Minister of Tourism April-Oct. 73, of Foreign Affairs 73-77; Vice-Pres. Council of Ministers 75-77; mem. Higher Council for Nuclear Energy April 75-77.
c/o Ministry of Foreign Affairs, Cairo, Egypt.

Fahmy, Lieut.-Gen. Mohamed Ali; Egyptian armed forces officer; b. 11 Oct. 1920, Cairo; ed. Engineering Faculty of Cairo Univ., Mil. Acad., Staff Coll., Air Defence Acad. in Kalinin, U.S.S.R.
Served in Second World War 39, Palestine War 48; Instructor, Senior Officers' Studies Inst. 52-53; Army Operations Dept. 52-58; served in Suez War 56; Commdr. 2nd Light A/A Regt. 58, 14th A/A Regt. 58-59, 64th A/A Regt. 59-61, 6th Artillery Group 61-63; Chief of Staff, 5th Artillery Div. 63-66, Commdr. 66-68; took part in mil. operations 67; Air Defence Chief of Staff 68-69; C.-in-C. Air Defence Forces 69-75; served in October War 73; C.-in-C. Armed Forces 75-78; Mil. Adviser to the Pres. Oct. 78-; rank of Maj-Gen. 65, Lt.-Gen. 73; Order of Liberation 52, Memorial Order of Founding of U.A.R. 58; Mil. Star 71; Star of Honour (PLO) 74; Yugoslav Star with Gold Belt, First Class 74; Order of King Abdul-Aziz, First Class (Saudi Arabia) 74; numerous ribbons and medals.
Publs. Two books on the Palestinian Campaign, *Germany, a Threat to Peace, Germany between East and West* (in two parts), book on African unity, book on African nationalism, *The Fourth Service: The History of the Egyptian Air Defence Force.*
c/o Ministry of War, Cairo, Egypt.

Farah Diba Pahlavi; (*see* Pahlavi, Farah Diba).

Farhan, Ishaq Ahmad, M.SC., M.A., ED.D.; Jordanian educationist; b. 1934, Ein Karem; ed. American Univ. Beirut, and Columbia Univ., New York.
Science teacher 58-64; with Ministry of Educ., Amman 64, Dir. of Pedagogical Services and Head, Syllabi Section 69, Dir. of Syllabi 69-70; Minister of Educ. 70-73, of Endowments and Islamic Shrines 73; Science Consultant Royal Scientific Soc. 74, Dir. Gen. 75-; Pres. Univ. of Jordan 76-78.
Publs. several school textbooks and articles in scientific and pedagogical journals.
Royal Scientific Society, P.O. Box 6945, Amman, Jordan.

Farhat, Abdallah; Tunisian politician; b. 28 Aug. 1914, Ouerdenine; ed. Ecole Supérieure de langue Arabe, Tunis.
Member Parti Néo-Destour 34-; Dir. Féd. Nat. des P.T.T.; Dir. Féd. Gén. des Fonctionnaires, Treas.-Gen. Union Gén. des Travailleurs Tunisiens 48-56; mem. 2nd Political Bureau 52, 55; Vice-Pres. Constituent Assembly 56-59; Deputy Nat. Assembly 59-; Dir. Cabinet of the Pres. 56-63, 70-71, 71-72; Pres. and Dir.-Gen. Soc. Nat. d'Investissement 63-64; Sec. of State for Post and Telecommunications (P.T.T.) 64-69; Sec. of State for Agriculture Sept.-Nov. 69, Minister for Agriculture 69-71, for Nat. Defence 72-74, for Public Works Jan.-Sept. 74, for Transport and Communications Sept. 74-June 76, of Nat. Defence June 76-; Grand Cordon Ordre de l'Indépendence, Ordre de la République; many foreign decorations.
Ministère de la Défence, Tunis, Tunisia.

Faris, Mustapha, DIPL.ING.; Moroccan engineer, politician and banker; b. 17 Dec. 1933; ed. Ecole Nat. des Ponts et Chaussées, Paris.
Government Civil Engineer, Dept. of Public Works 56-61; Dir. of Supply, Nat. Irrigation Office 61-65; Dir.-Gen. of Hydraulic Engineering 65-69; Sec. of State for Planning attached to Prime Minister's Office 69-71; Minister of Finance 71-72; Pres., Dir.-Gen. Banque Nationale pour le Développement Economique 72-77; fmr. Vice-Pres. Int. Comm. on Large Dams; Gov. IBRD (World Bank), African Devt. Bank; Ordre du Trône.
c/o Baque Nationale pour le Développement Economique, B.P. 407, place des Alaouites, Rabat, Morocco.

Farmanfarmaian, Khodadad, M.A., PH.D.; Iranian economist and banker; b. 8 May 1928, Teheran; ed. American Univ. of Beirut, Lebanon and Stanford and Colorado Univs., U.S.A.
Instructor and Research Asst., Dept. of Econs., Colorado Univ. 52-53; Instructor, Dept. of Econs., Brown Univ. 53-55; Research Fellow, Center for Middle Eastern Studies, Harvard Univ. 55-57; Research Assoc., Dept. of Econs. and Oriental Studies, Princeton Univ. 57-58; Dir. Econ. Bureau, Plan Org. 58-61; mem. Tax Comm., Ministry of Finance 58-60; mem. High Econ. Council 59-62, 64-73; Deputy Man. Dir. Plan Org. 61-62, Man. Dir. 70-73; Deputy Gov., Bank Markazi Iran (Central Bank of Iran) 64-69, Gov. 69-70; Chair. Board of Dirs., Bank Sanaye Iran 73-79; medals from govts. of Iran and Belgium.
Publs. *Social Change and Economic Behaviour in Iran, Exploration in Entrepreneurial History* 56, *How can the World Afford OPEC Oil?* 75; has contributed to *Middle Eastern Journal.*
c/o Bank Sanaye Iran, Avenue Sepahbod Zahedi, No. 106, Teheran, Iran.

Fasi, Mohammed el; Moroccan educationist; b. 2 Sept. 1908; ed. Al Qarawiyin Univ., Fez, Univ. de Paris à la Sorbonne and Ecole des langues orientales, Paris.
Teacher, Inst. des Hautes Etudes Marocaines 35-40; Head Arab manuscript section, Bibliothèque Gén., Rabat 40; Tutor to Prince Moulay Hassan 41-44, 47-52; Rector Al Qarawiyin Univ. 42-44, 47-52; Vice-Pres. Conseil des Uléma 42-; Founder-mem. Istiqlal Party 44; under restriction 44-47, 52-54; Minister of Nat. Educ. 55-58; Rector of the Univ. of Morocco 58; Pres. Moroccan Del. to Gen. Conf. of UNESCO 56, 58, 60, 64, Vice-Pres. 62; Pres. Co-ordination Centre for Nat. Comms. of UNESCO in Arab countries; leader of numerous UNESCO Confs. in the Arab World, Pres. Exec. Board of UNESCO 64; Pres. Conseil d'Admin. Asscn. des Univs. Partiellement ou Entièrement de Langue Francaise (AUPELF) 66; Pres. Conseil Exec., Asscn. des Univs. Africains 67; Minister for Cultural Affairs and Original Educ. 68; Pres. Conseil Exec., Asscn. des Univs. Islamiques 69; mem. Exec. Council and Special Cttee., UNESCO Nov. 78-; mem. Acad. of Arabic Language, Cairo 58, Acad. of Iraq; Dr. h.c. Univ. of Bridgeport 65, Lagos 68, Jakarta 68; Tutor to H.R.H. Crown Prince Sidi Mohammed.
Publs. Numerous works including *L'évolution politique et culturelle au Maroc* 58, *La Formation des Cadres au Maroc* 60, *Chants anciens des femmes de Fès* 67.
18 rue des Saadiens, Rabat, Morocco.

Fatemi, Nasrollah, M.A., PH.D.; American (b. Iranian), professor of international affairs; b. 15 June 1910, Nain, Iran.
Formerly Ed. Bakhtar newspaper, Gov. of Fars, mem. of Majlis, Mayor of Shiraz, and del. to UN (adviser to perm. Iranian del.); Visiting Prof. Asia Inst. and Princeton Univ. 50-55; Prof. of Social Sciences, Fairleigh Dickinson Univ. 55-61, Chair. Social Sciences Dept. 61-65, Dean of the Graduate School 65-71, Distinguished Prof. of Int. Affairs and Dir. of Graduate Inst. of Int. Studies 71-; Chair. Exec. Cttee. Inter-University Centre for Post-Graduate Studies, Dubrovnik, Yugoslavia 71-; mem. Int. Asscn. of Univ. Pres., North American Council; Fellow, Royal Acad. Arts and Sciences; LL.D. (Kyung Hee Univ., South Korea) 74.
Publs. *Biography of Hafiz* 36, *Persian Literature in the 16th and 17th centuries* 37, *Modern Persian Literature* 39, *Diplomatic History of Persia* 51, *Oil Diplomacy* 54, *The Dollar Crisis* 64, *The Roots of Arab Nationalism* 65, *Humanities in the Age of Science* 67; *Problems of Balance of Payments and Trade* (editor) 74, *Multinational Corporations* 75, *Sufism, Message of Brotherhood, Harmony and Hope* 76, *Love, Beauty and Harmony in Sufism* 78.
1000 River Road, Teaneck, N.J. 07666 (Office); 47 Chestnut Ridge Road, Saddle River, N.J. 07458, U.S.A. (Home).

Fawzi, Ahmad; Jordanian engineer and politician; b. 1927; ed. U.S.A. and Baghdad Univ.
District Engineer, Public Works 50-53, Asst. Under-Sec. 53-57, Under-Sec. 57-64; Mayor of Amman 64-; Minister of Interior for Municipal and Rural Affairs 67-68, and Minister without Portfolio 67-68; Minister of Public Works April 68-Aug. 69; Sec. Civil Eng. Union; mem. Devt. Board; Chair. Housing Corpn. Board; Chair. Municipal and Rural Loan Fund; Chair. Hidjaz Railway Reconstruction Cttee.; mem. Arab Cities Org. Exec. Office; Orders of Al-Kawkab, first class, Al-Istiklal, first class, Al-Nahda, second class, Al-Jalalah Asharefah, first class (Morocco), Tunisian Repub., first class, Mallizia, Ethiopian Emperor, first class.
c/o Municipality of Amman, Amman, Jordan.

Fawzi, Mahmoud; Egyptian diplomatist and politician; b. 1900, Cairo; ed. Univs. of Cairo, Rome, Italy, Liverpool, England and Columbia Univ., U.S.A.
Vice-Consul, N.Y. and New Orleans 26-29; Consul, Kobe, Japan 29-36; Dir. Dept. of Nationalities, Ministry of Foreign Affairs 39-41; Consul-Gen., Jerusalem 41-44; rep. to UN Security Council 46, Alt. rep. to Gen. Assembly 47, Perm. Rep. to UN 49-51; Amb. to U.K. 52; Minister of Foreign Affairs Dec. 52-58; U.A.R. Minister of Foreign Affairs 58-64; mem. Presidency Council 62-64; Dep. Prime Minister of Foreign Affairs 64-67, Vice-Pres. and Presidential Asst. for Foreign Affairs 67-68; Prime Minister 70-72; Vice-Pres. 72-74.
Cairo, Egypt.

Feinberg, Nathan, DR.IUR.UTR.; Israeli emeritus professor of international law; b. 6 June 1895; ed. Univ. of Zürich and Graduate Inst. of Int. Studies, Geneva.
Head of Dept., Ministry of Jewish Affairs, Lithuania 19-21; Sec. Cttee. of Jewish Dels., Paris 22-24; law practice in Palestine 24-27 and 34-45; Lecturer, Univ. of Geneva 31-33; Lecturer, Hebrew Univ., Jerusalem 45-49, Assoc. Prof. 49-52, Prof. of Int. Law and Relations 52-66, Dean of Faculty of Law 49-51, Prof. Emer. 65-; Lectured at Acad. of Int. Law, The Hague 32, 37, 52; mem. Perm. Court of Arbitration; mem. Inst. of Int. Law; Fellow of the Int. Inst. of Arts and Letters; Dr. h.c. and mem. Board of Governors, Hebrew Univ.
Publs. *La Question des Minorités à la Conférence de la paix de 1919-1920 et l'action juive en faveur de la Protection Internationale des Minorités* 29, *La Juridiction de la Cour Permanente de Justice Internationale dans le Système des Mandats* 30, *La Juridiction de la Cour Permanente de Justice dans le Système de la Protection Internationale des Minorités* 31, *La Pétition en Droit International* 33, *Some Problems of the Palestine Mandate* 36, *L'Admission de Nouveaux Membres à la Société des Nations et à l'Organisation des Nations Unies* 52, *The Jewish Struggle Against Hitler in the League of Nations (Bernheim Petition)* (Hebrew) 57, *The Legality of a "State of War" after the Cessation of Hostilities* 61, *Palestine under the Mandate and the State of Israel: Problems of International Law* (Hebrew) 63, *The Jewish League of Nations Societies* (Hebrew) 67, *The Arab-Israel Conflict in International Law* 70, *On an Arab Jurist's Approach to Zionism and the State of Israel* 71, *Studies in International Law, with special Reference to the Arab-Israel Conflict* 79, etc.; co-editor: *The Jewish Year Book of International Law* 49; Editor *Studies in Public International Law in Memory of Sir Hersch Lauterpacht* (in Hebrew) 62.
6 Ben Labrat Street, Jerusalem, Israel.

Fernea, Robert Alan, PH.D.; American anthropologist; b. 25 Jan. 1932; ed. Reed Coll., Portland, Oregon, and Univ. of Chicago.
Assistant, Assoc. Prof. of Anthropology, American Univ. in Cairo 59-65, Social Research Center, American Univ. in Cairo 61-65; Dir. Nubian Ethnological Survey 61-65; Visiting Lecturer, Univ. of Alexandria 63, 64; Consultant, Ford Foundation in U.A.R. 63-65; Post-doctoral Fellow, Harvard Univ. 65-66; Prof. of Anthropology, Univ. of Texas at Austin 66-, Dir. Middle East Center 66-73; mem. Board of Governors, American Research Center in Egypt Inc. 78-; Fellow, American Anthropological Asscn., Founding Fellow, Middle East Studies Asscn. of N. America; Univ. of Chicago Fellow 54, Nat. Science Foundation Fellowship 56, 57, Danforth Fellow 54-59, Faculty Fulbright-Hays Fellow (Afghanistan) 67, (Morocco) 71-72.
Publs. *Symposium on Contemporary Egyptian Nubia* 67, *Shaykh and Effendi* 70, *Nubians in Egypt: Peaceful People* 73, and numerous anthropological articles.
University of Texas at Austin, Department of Anthropology, Burdine Hall, Room 370, Austin, Texas 78712, U.S.A.

Feyzioğlu, Turhan, LL.D.; Turkish lawyer, political scientist and politician; b. 19 Jan. 1922; ed. Galatasaray Lycée, Istanbul Univ. and Ecole Nat. d'Administration, Paris.
Assistant Prof. Ankara Political Science School 45-47, Assoc. Prof. 47-54; Research, Nuffield Coll., Oxford 54; Co-editor *Forum* 54-58; Prof. Ankara Univ. 55; Dean, Political Science School, Ankara 56; M.P. 57, 61, 65-; mem. Nat. Exec. Cttee. Republican People's Party 57-61; Pres. Middle East Technical Univ. 60; mem. Constituent Assembly 60; Minister of Education 60; Minister of State 61; Deputy Prime Minister 62-63; mem. Turkish High Planning Council 61-63, Asst. Sec.-Gen. Republican People's Party 64, Vice-Pres. Parl. Group 65-66; founded Nat. Reliance Party (now Republican Reliance Party) 67, Pres. 67-; mem. Consultative Assembly (now Parliamentary Assembly), Council of Europe 64-66, 72-75, Vice-Pres. 74-75; Deputy Prime Minister 75-June 77, Deputy Prime Minister and Minister of State Jan.-Sept. 78.
Publs. *Administration Law* 47, *Judicial Review of Unconstitutional Laws* 51, *Les Parties Politiques en Turquie* 53, *The Reforms of the French Higher Civil Service* 55, *Democracy and Dictatorship* 57, *The Communist Danger* 69, *In the Service of the Nation* 75.
Republican Reliance Party, Ankara, Turkey.

Field, Henry, B.A., M.A., D.SC.; American anthropologist; b. 15 Dec. 1902; ed. Eton Coll. and New Coll., Oxford.
Asst. Curator of Physical Anthropology, Field Museum of Natural History (Chicago) 26-34, Curator 34-41; Field Museum Expeditions, Near East 25-26, 27-28, 34; govt. research 41-45; research on S.W. Asia 46-47; Univ. of Calif. African Expedition 47-48; Peabody Museum-Harvard Expedition to Near East 50, and to West Pakistan 55; Honorary Associate in Physical Anthropology, Peabody Museum, Harvard 50-; Research in India 69, in Mongolia 73; Annandale Medal, Asiatic Soc. of Bengal 66.
Publs. *Arabs of Central Iraq: their History, Ethnology and Physical Characters* 35; *Contributions to the Anthropology of Iran* 39; *The Anthropology of Iraq, Part I, No.* 1 40, Nos. 2-3 49; *Part II*, No. 1 51, Nos. 2, 3 52; *Contributions to the Anthropology of the Faiyum, Sinai, Sudan and Kenya* 52; *Contributions to the Anthropology of the Caucasus* 53; *The Track of Man* 53; *Ancient and Modern Man in Southwestern Asia* I 56, II 61; *Bibliographies on S.W. Asia*, I-VII 53-63; *An Anthropological Reconnaissance in West Pakistan* 59; *North Arabian Desert Archaeological Survey 25-50*, 60; *"M" Project for F.D.R.: Studies on Migration and Settlement* 62; Editor *Peabody Museum Russian Translation Series*, Vols. I-V 59-70, *Contributions to the Anthropology of Saudi Arabia* 72, *Mongolia Diary* 78, *Mongolia Today* 78.
3551 Main Highway, Coconut Grove, Miami, Fla. 33133; Office: Peabody Museum, Harvard University, Cambridge, Mass., U.S.A.

Filali, Abdel Aziz, LL.D.; Moroccan judge and administrator; b. 10 June 1924; ed. Lycée Gouraud, Rabat, Lycée Lyautey, Casablanca, Ecole Nat. d'Org. Economique et Sociale, Paris and Grenoble Univ., France and Inst. des Hautes Etudes, Rabat.
Practised at the Bar, Casablanca 51-55; First Pres. Int. Tribunal of Tangier, Court of Appeal Tangier and Court of Appeal Rabat 55-; Lecturer Inst. des Hautes Etudes Marocaines, Ecole Marocaine d'Administration, then Asst. Dir. Ecole Marocaine; Pres. Centre Africain de Formation et de Recherche Administratives pour le Développement (C.A.F.R.A.D.), Tangier 64-; mem. Comm. for Arabization of Code of Civil Procedure 63, Comm. for Arabization of Code of Obligations and Contracts 64; Pres. Comm. for Arabization of Code of Commercial Law 65; designated Conciliator and Arbitrator, Int. Centre for Settlement of Investment Disputes, Washington, D.C., U.S.A.; Arbitrator Franco-Arab Chamber of Commerce 76-; Dr. h.c. Univ. of Grenoble.
Publs. *Marriage in Moroccan Law* (in Arabic), *Notes Judiciaires* (in French).
Chambre Commerciale Franco-Arabe, Paris, France.

Filali, Abdellatif; Moroccan diplomatist; b. 26 Jan. 1928, Fez; ed. Univ. of Paris.
Joined Ministry of Foreign Affairs, rank of Amb. 57; Perm. Rep. to the UN 58-59; Chief of Royal Cabinet 59-61; Chargé d'affaires, Embassy to France 61-62; Amb. to Belgium, the Netherlands and Luxembourg 62-63, to People's Repub. of China 65-67, to Algeria 67-68, to Spain 70-71 and 72-78; Minister of Higher Educ. 68-70, of Foreign Affairs 71-72; Perm. Rep. to the UN May 78-.
Permanent Mission of Morocco to the United Nations, 1 Dag Hammarskjöld Plaza, 245 East 47th Street, 28th Floor, New York, N.Y. 10017, U.S.A.

Fisher, Sydney Nettleton, M.A., PH.D.; American emeritus professor of Middle East history; b. 1906; ed. Oberlin Coll., Univ. of Illinois, Princeton Univ. and Univ. of Brussels.
Tutor in Mathematics and English, Robert Coll., Istanbul 28-31, 36-37; Instructor in History, Denison Univ., Granville, Ohio 35-36; Instructor in History, The Ohio State Univ. 37-42, Asst. Prof. 42-47, Assoc. Prof. 47-55, Prof. 55-72, Prof. Emer. 72-; Co-ordinator, Graduate Inst. for World Affairs 62-65; Dir. Near and Middle East Program 67-71; Assoc. Chief, Econ. Analysis Section, Middle East Div., Foreign Econ. Admin., Washington, D.C. 43-44, Country Specialist, Commercial Policy Div., Dept. of State 44-46; Lecturer on World Affairs, Chautauqua Inst., Chautauqua, N.Y. 40, 41 and 42; Visiting Prof. of History and Govt., Stetson Univ., DeLand, Fla. 49; Dir. of Publs. of The Middle East Inst. and Editor *The Middle East Journal*, Washington, D.C. 52-53; Visiting Prof. of History, Univ. of S. Calif., Los Angeles 54, 61; mem. American Historical Asscn., The Middle East Inst., Royal Historical Soc., London, Accademia del Mediterraneo, Asscn. for North American Middle East Studies, etc.
Publs. *The Foreign Relations of Turkey, 1481-1512* 48, *Evolution in the Middle East* 53, *Social Forces in the Middle East* 55, 76, *The Middle East: A History* 59, 69, 79, *The Military in the Middle East* 63, *France and the European Community* 65, *New Horizons for the United States in World Affairs* 66.
P.O. Box 162, Worthington, Ohio 43085, U.S.A.

Fisher, William Bayne, B.A., DR. DE L'UNIV. (Paris); British geographer; b. 24 Sept. 1916; ed. Univ. of Manchester and Univs. of Louvain, Caen and Paris.
Research Fellow 37-40; served in Royal Air Force 40-46, commissioned 41, O.C. R.A.F. Liaison Unit, Syria and Lebanon 44-45; Lecturer, Univ. of Manchester 46; Senior Lecturer, Dept. of Geography, Aberdeen Univ. 47-53; Reader and Head of Dept. of Geography, Univ. of Durham 54-56, Prof. 56-, Dir. Inst. of Middle Eastern and Islamic Studies 62-65, Principal Graduate Coll. 65-; Consultant H.M. Govt., Govt. of Libya and Harvard Univ., U.S.A.; Leader Univ. Expedition to Libya 51; Visiting Prof. Univ. of Louvain, Belgium 78.
Publs. *The Middle East—a Physical, Social and Regional Geography* 50, 78, *Spain* (with H. Bowen-Jones) 57, *Malta* (with H. Bowen-Jones and J. C. Dewdney), Editor Vol. I *The Cambridge History of Iran* (Land and People) 68, *Populations of the Middle East and North Africa* (with J. I. Clarke) 72.
Department of Geography, Science Laboratories, South Road, Durham DH1 3LE; and 38 Old Elvet, Durham, DH1 3JD, England.

Fitouri, Mohamed, L. EN D.; Tunisian politician; b. 4 April 1925, Kairouan; ed. Lycée Carnot, Tunis, Inst. des Hautes Etudes, Tunis and Faculté de Droit, Paris.
Called to the Bar 52; mem. Council, Nat. Asscn. of Lawyers 60; Advocate, Court of Cassation 62; mem. Econ. and Social Council 63; City Counsellor, Tunis 69; Deputy to Nat. Assembly Nov. 69-; Minister of Justice 70-71, of Finance 71-77, of Foreign Affairs Dec. 77-; mem. Political Bureau of Parti Socialiste Destourien 74; Grand Cordon, Ordre de la République, Ordre de l'Indépendance.
Ministère des Affaires Etrangères, Tunis; and 17 rue Slaheddine El Ayoubi, Tunis, Tunisia.

Franjiya, Sulaiman; Lebanese politician; b. 14 June 1910, Zgharta; ed. coll. at Zgharta, near Beirut.
Elected to Parl. as Independent mem. 60 and 64; Minister of Posts, Telegraphs and Telephones and Minister of Agriculture 60-61; Minister of the Interior 68; Minister of Justice, Minister of Econ., Minister of Public Works, Minister of Nat. Econ. 69-70; head, trade del. to negotiate Soviet-Lebanese trade and payments agreement; Pres. of Lebanon 70-76.
Beirut, Lebanon.

Frei, Ephraim Heinrich, D.PHIL.; Israeli physicist; b. 2 March 1912, Vienna, Austria; ed. Vienna Univ. and Hebrew Univ. of Jerusalem.
Broadcasting Engineer, British Army and attached to British Embassy, Athens 42-46; Head Electronics Section Scientific Dept., Ministry of Defence, Israel 48-50; with Weizmann Inst. of Science 53-, Prof. and Head Dept. of Electronics 61-77, Prof. Emer. 77-; mem. Inst. for Advanced Study, Princeton, N.J. 50; Int. Research Fellow, Stanford Research Inst., Calif. 60; Scientific Dir. and Chair. of Board Yeda Research and Devt. Co.; mem. Board, Miles-Yeda Ltd.; Chair. Combined Conf. of 12th Int. Conf. on Medical and Biological Engineering and 5th Conf. on Medical Physics; mem. Advisory Board, Jerusalem School of Applied Science, editorial board, *Medical Progress through Technology*; Chair. I.E.E.E. Comm. on Magnetics in Life Sciences, Fellow, I.E.E.E. 67; Weizmann Prize 57.
Publs. scientific papers on electronics and physics.
Weizmann Institute, Rehovot, Israel.

Freiha, Said; Lebanese newspaper proprietor; b. 1903.
Chairman Board Dar Assayad S.A.L. which publishes *Assayad* (weekly) 43-, *Achabaka* (weekly) 56-, *Al-Anwar* (daily) 59-.
Dar Assayad, Hamzieh, P.O.B. 1038, Beirut, Lebanon.

Freund, Miriam Kottler, M.A., PH.D.; American Zionist leader; b. 17 Feb. 1906; ed. Hunter Coll., New York Univ.
Teacher high schools, N.Y.C. to 44; Vice-Pres. Women's Comm., Brandeis Univ. 50-52; Nat. Board Hadassah, Women's Zionist Organization 40-, Vice-Pres. 53-56, Pres. 56-60; Chair. Nat. Youth Aliyah 53-56; mem. Actions Cttee., World Zionist Organization 56-; Chair. Exec. Cttee. American Zionist Council 60-; mem. Nat. Board Jewish Nat. Fund and Keren Hayesod 47-48; del. 21st Orientalist Congress, Moscow 60; Editor *Hadassah* magazine 66-71, Nat. Ed. Chair. 71-; mem. American Asscn. of Univ.

Women, Jewish History Soc., Nat. Council of Nat. Planning Asscn. 70; Vice-Pres. American Zionist Fed. 70-72; Nat. Vice-Pres. Mercaz 78; mem. Board of Trustees, American Friends of the Hebrew Univ. 78, Touro Coll. 79; mem. Exec. World Council of Synagogues; Nat. Assoc. Chair. Israel Bonds Women's Div.
Publs. *Jewish Merchants in Colonial America* 36, *Jewels for a Crown: The Chagall Windows* 63.
575 Park Avenue, New York, N.Y. 10021, U.S.A.

Frye, Richard Nelson, PH.D.; American orientalist; b. 10 Jan. 1920; ed. Univ. of Ill., Harvard Univ., and School of Oriental and African Studies, London.
Junior Fellow, Harvard 46-49; visiting scholar, Univ. of Teheran 51-52; Aga Khan Prof. of Iranian, Harvard 57-; Visiting Prof., Oriental Seminary, Frankfurt Univ. 58-59; Hamburg Univ. 68-69; assoc. Editor *Bulletin Asia Institute* and *Indo-Iranica;* Dir. Asia Inst. of Pahlavi Univ., Shiraz 69-74; co-founder Nat. Asscn. of Armenian Studies 60; Hon. mem. German Archaeological Inst.
Publs. *Notes on the early coinage of Transoxiana* 49, *History of the Nation of the Archers* 52, *Narshakhi, The History of Bukhara* 54, *Iran* 56, *The Heritage of Persia* 62, *The Histories of Nishapur* 65, *Bukhara, the Medieval Achievement* 65, *Corpus Iranian Inscriptions* 68, 71, *Qasr-i Abu Nasr Excavations* 73, *The Golden Age of Persia* 75; Editor: *Bulletin Asia Institute* (monographs), *Cambridge History of Iran Vol. IV*.
546 Widener Library, Cambridge 38, Mass., U.S.A.

G

Gaddafi, Col. Muammar al-; Libyan army officer and politician; b. 1942, Serte; ed. Univ. of Libya, Benghazi.
Served with Libyan Army 65-; took leading part in coup to depose King Idris Sept. 69; Chair. Revolutionary Council and C.-in-C. of Armed Forces of Libya 69-77; Prime Minister 70-72; Minister of Defence 70-77; mem. Pres. Council, Fed. Arab Repubs. 71-; rank of Maj.-Gen. Jan. 76, still keeping the title of Col.; Pres. Socialist People's Libyan Arab Jamahiriya March 77-; Sec.-Gen. of Gen. Secretariat of Gen. People's Congress 77-79.
Publ. *The Green Book* (3 vols.).
General People's Congress, Tripoli, Libya.

Gaddafi, Wanis; Libyan politician and diplomatist.
Head of Exec. Council in Cyrenaican Provincial Govt. 52-62; Minister of Foreign Affairs Jan. 62-63, of Interior 63-64, of Labour 64; Amb. to Fed. Repub. of Germany 64-65; Minister of Planning and Devt. 66-68; Minister of Foreign Affairs 68; Prime Minister Sept. 68-69; imprisoned for two years Nov. 71.
Tripoli, Libya.

Gafny, Arnon, M.A.; Israeli economist and central banker; b. 1932, Tel-Aviv; ed. Bard Coll., N.Y., U.S.A. and Hebrew Univ., Jerusalem.
Falk Inst. for Econ. Research 54-56; Asst. to Financial Adviser to Chief of Staff, Israel Defence Forces 57-59; Chief Asst., Budgets Dept., Ministry of Finance 59-61; Head, Econ. and Commercial Dept. of Ports Authority 61; Dir. Ashdod Port 61-70; Dir. of Budgets, Ministry of Finance 70-75, Dir.-Gen. Ministry of Finance 75-76; Gov. Bank of Israel Nov. 76-.
Bank of Israel, Mizpeh Building, 29 Jaffa Road, Jerusalem, P.O. Box 780, Israel.

Galili, Israel; Israeli politician; b. May 1911, Brailov, Ukraine; ed. Ahad Ha'am Primary School.
Went to Palestine 15; later worked on buildings and in printing; f. Asscn. of Working Youth 24; helped establish Kibbutz Na'an 30; Haganah activities 35-48; Deputy Minister of Defence, Israe Govt. 48; mem. Knesset; Minister without Portfolio (in charge of Information Services) 66-69; Minister without Portfolio 69-June 77; Achdut Ha'Avoda, Labour.
The Knesset, Jerusalem; Kibbutz "Na'an", Israel.

Galindo Pohl, Reinaldo, LL.D.; Salvadorian diplomatist; b. 1919.
President, Nat. Constitutional Assembly May-Sept. 50; Minister of Educ. 50-56; Prof. of Philosophy of Law, Gen. Theory of the State, Constitutional Law, and History of Ancient Thought, El Salvador Univ. 59-67; Perm. Rep. to UN Dec. 67-June 77; Dir. Legal Affairs Dept., Organization of American States; UN Special Rep. in Cyprus May 78-.
UNFICYP, Nicosia, Cyprus.

Gamassi, Gen. Muhammad Abdul Ghani al-; Egyptian army officer and government official; b. 9 Sept. 1921, al-Batanoun, Menoufia Governorate; ed. Mil. Acad., Staff Coll., Nasser Higher Mil. Acad.
Assistant Dir. of Mobilization Dept. 54-55; Commdr. 5th Reconnaissance Regt. 55-57; Staff Officer, Armoured Corps 57-59; Commdr. 2nd Armoured Brigade 59-61; Commdr. Armour School 61-66; Chief, Army Operational Branch 66-67; Chief of Staff, Eastern Mil. Zone Sept. 67-68; Deputy Dir. Reconnaissance and Intelligence Dept. 68-70; Commdr. Operational Group, Syrian Front 70-71; Chief, Armed Forces Training Dept. 71-72; Chief of Operations Dept. and Deputy Chief of Staff of Armed Forces 72-73; Chief of Staff of Armed Forces 73-74; Minister of War and War Production, and C.-in-C. of Armed Forces 74-78, also a Deputy Prime Minister 75-78; Mil. Adviser to the Pres. 78-; Order of Liberation 52, Memorial Order of Founding of U.A.R. 58, Star of Honour 73, Star of Honour (PLO) 74, Knight, Order of Mil. Honour (Syria) 74, Order of Courage (Libya) 74, Order of the Two Niles, First Class (Sudan) 74, Order of King Abdel Aziz, First Class (Saudi Arabia) 74, Order of Homayoun, First Class (Iran) 75; numerous ribbons and medals.
Office of the President, Abdeen, Cairo, Egypt.

Gammal, Ali Hamdi El, B.A.; Egyptian journalist; b. 19 Sept. 1925, Cairo; ed. Faculty of Agriculture, Cairo Univ.
Began career on *Al Zaman* evening newspaper 47; joined Akhbar el Yom publishing house 49, Asst. Chief Editor until 56; Editor-in-Chief, Middle East News Agency 56-57; Man. Editor *Al Ahram* 57-75, Editor-in-Chief March 75-.
Publs. *The Yellow Giant* 56, *The Sino-Indian Conflict* 63.
Al Ahram, Gallaa Street, Cairo; Home: 4 Sad el Aali Street, Dokki-Girza, Egypt.

Gat, Dr. Joel R., M.SC., PH.D.; Israeli geochemist; b. 17 Feb. 1926, Munich, Germany; ed. Hebrew Univ., Jerusalem.
Department of Physical Chem., Hebrew Univ. 49-50; Ministry of Defence Laboratories, Jerusalem 50-52; Israel Atomic Energy Comm., Rehovot 52-59; Fellow ISNSE, Argonne Nat. Laboratories and Enrico Fermi Inst., Univ. of Chicago, Ill. 55-56; Fellow, Scripps Inst. of Oceanography, Univ. of Calif. San Diego at La Jolla 64-65; Acting Head of Isotope Dept., Weizmann Inst. of Science 66-70, Prof. Isotope Research 71-, Head of Isotope Dept. 73-; Walther P. Reuther Chair in the Peaceful Uses of Atomic Energy 68.
Faculty of Chemistry, The Weizmann Institute of Science, P.O. Box 26, Rehovot; Home. 3 Hagrast, Rehovot, Israel.

Gaye, Amadou Karim, D.M.V.; Senegalese politician and international official; b. 8 Dec. 1913, Saint-Louis; ed. Lycée Saint-Louis, Univ. de Paris, Ecole Nat. Vétérinaire, Alfort, France, Ecole de Cavalerie, Saumur, France.
Served in Senegalese veterinary service 49-57; Gen. Counsellor of Senegal 49-52; Deputy of Union Progressiste Sénégalaise (UPS) 59-75, Asst. Sec. for Propaganda 60-70; Minister of Educ. and Culture Jan.-April 59, of Planning,

Devt. and Econ. 59-60; Minister Del. to Presidency charged with Planning and Tech. Co-operation 61-62; Minister of Labour and Civil Service Nov.-Dec. 62, of Agriculture 62-65, of Armed Forces 65-68, of Foreign Affairs 68-72; Pres. Econ. and Social Council 72-75; Sec.-Gen. of the Islamic Conf. Nov. 76-; Nat. Order of the Lion.
Islamic Conference, Secretariat-General, Kilo 6, Mecca Road, P.O. Box 179, Jeddah, Saudi Arabia.

Gazit, Mordechai, M.A.; Israeli diplomatist; b. 5 Sept. 1922; ed. Hebrew Univ., Jerusalem.
Minister, Embassy of Israel to U.S.A. 60-65; Asst. Dir.-Gen. Ministry of Foreign Affairs 65-67; Deputy Dir.-Gen. Ministry of Immigrant Absorption 69-70; Asst. Dir.-Gen. Ministry of Foreign Affairs 70-72, Dir.-Gen. 72-73; Dir.-Gen., Political Adviser Prime Minister's Office 73-75; Head of Israeli del. at Geneva talks with Egyptians 75; Amb. to France Dec. 75-.
Israeli Embassy, 3 rue Rabelais, Paris 8e, France.

Gazit, Maj.-Gen. Shlomo; Israeli army officer; b. 1926, Turkey; ed. Tel-Aviv Coll., Tel-Aviv Univ.
Joined Palmach 44, successively served in 8th Co., Sixth Regt., and as Co. Commdr. Harel Brigade; Editor *Maarachot* (Army monthly) 49-51; Regimental Commdrs.' course 51; Dir. Office of the Deputy Chief of Staff until 53; Dir. Chief of Staff's Office 53-54; Deputy Battalion Commdr. G'Vati Brigade 55; Liaison Officer with French Army Del., Sinai Campaign 56; Asst. to Mil. Attaché, France 57; Instructor Israeli Defence Forces Staff and Command Coll. 58-59; with Gen. Staff 60-61; Deputy Commdr. Golani Brigade 62; co-founder and Instructor, Nat. Defence Coll., Jerusalem 63; served in senior posts, Intelligence Branch, Gen. Staff 64-67; Dir. Dept. of Mil. Govt. 67; Co-ordinator of Administered Areas, Ministry of Defence 67-74; Rank of Maj.-Gen. 73; Dir. of Mil. Intelligence, Israeli Defence Forces 74-79; on academic vacation Feb. 79-.
Israeli Defence Forces, General Staff, 9 Itamar Ben-Avi Street, Tel-Aviv, Israel.

Geghman, Yahya Hamoud; Yemeni diplomatist; b. 24 Sept. 1934; ed. Law Schools, Cairo, Paris, Damascus and Boston and Columbia Univs.
Teacher of Arabic Language and Literature, Kuwait 57-59; Dir.-Gen. Yemen Broadcasting System, Special Adviser, Ministry of Foreign Affairs 62-63; Deputy Perm. Rep. to UN 63-66, 67-68; Minister, Yemen Arab Repub. (Y.A.R.) Embassy in U.S.A. 63-67; Minister of Foreign Affairs 68-69; Minister of State, Personal Rep. of the Pres. 69; Deputy Prime Minister 69-71; Amb. to UN 71-73, to U.S.A. 73-74; Deputy Prime Minister for Foreign and Econ. Affairs Jan. 75; Pres. Supreme Council for Youth Welfare and Sport 70; Gov. for Y.A.R., IBRD, IMF 70-71; mem. of del. to Conf. of Arab Heads of Govts. 65, 69, to U.S.S.R. 68, to UN Gen. Assembly 62-; has represented Y.A.R. at many int. functions.
Publs. articles on politics, economics and literature in various Arabic journals.
Sana'a, Yemen Arab Republic.

Gemayel, Sheikh Pierre; Lebanese politician; b. 1905; ed. Univ. St. Joseph, Beirut and Cochin Hospital, Paris.
Trained as a pharmacist; founded Parti Démocrate Social Libanais—Les Phalanges (Kataeb Party) 36, leader 37-; imprisoned 37, 43; organized general strike 43; established the first Labour Code 44; Minister of Public Works 60, of Finance 60-61, of Communications 60, of Public Health 60, 61; Minister of Public Works May 61-Feb. 64; Minister of the Interior 66-67; Deputy for Beirut 60-; mem. Nat. Dialogue Cttee. Sept. 75; Lebanese, Polish and Egyptian decorations.
Rue de l'Université St. Joseph, Beirut, Lebanon.

Ghaffari, Abolghassem, DR. SC. MATH., PH.D.; Iranian mathematician; b. 1909; ed. Darolfonoun School and Univs. of Nancy, Paris, London and Oxford, England.
Associate Prof., Teheran Univ. 37-42, Prof. of Mathematics 42-; Mathematics Research Asst. King's Coll., London 47-48; Research Fellow, Harvard 50-51, Research Assoc., Princeton 51-52; mem. Inst. for Advanced Study, Princeton 51-52; Senior Mathematician, Nat. Bureau of Standards, Washington, D.C. 56-57; aeronautical research scientist 57-64; Professorial Lecturer, American Univ., Washington, D.C. 58-62; aerospace scientist, Goddard Space Flight Center, Greenbelt, Md. 64-; Visiting Prof. of Mathematics, Arya-Mehr Univ. of Technology, Teheran 74-75; has lectured at Univs. of Harvard, Maryland, Princeton and Columbia and at Massachusetts Inst. of Technology; mem. American, French and British Mathematical Societies; Fellow Washington Acad. of Sciences, New York Acad. of Sciences, American Asscn. for the Advancement of Science; mem. Iranian Higher Council of Education 54-58; Iranian Del. to 5th Pakistan Science Conf. Lahore 53, to Int. Congresses of Mathematicians, Cambridge, Mass. 50, Amsterdam 54, Edinburgh 58, Stockholm 62, NASA del. to Int. Congress of Mathematics, Moscow 66, Nice, France 70, Vancouver, Canada 74; mem. Iranian Comm. for UNESCO 54; mem. American Astronomical Soc.; Orders of Homayoun and of Danesh (first class) and of Sepass (first class); U.S. Special Apollo Achievement Award.
Publs. *Sur l'Equation Fonctionelle de Chapman-Kolmogoroff* 36, *The Hodograph Method in Gas Dynamics* 50, over fifty research articles on mathematics, mathematical physics and astrodynamics in American, British and French scientific journals.
5420 Goldsboro Road, Bethesda, Md. 20034, U.S.A.

Ghaidan, Gen. Saadoun; Iraqi army officer and politician; b. 1930; ed. secondary educ. in Aana and Military Coll., Baghdad.
Commissioned 2nd Lieut. 53; Commdr. of Khalid bin Al-Waleed Tank Bn., Republican Palace Tank Bn., taking part in overthrow of Govt. in July 68; became Gen. Commdr. of Repub. Bodyguard Forces and mem. Revolutionary Command Council 68; Gen. Commdr. of Forces in Baghdad 69; Minister of the Interior April 70-74, of Communications 74-, Deputy Prime Minister July 79-; nemerous medals.
Ministry of Communications, Baghdad, Iraq.

Ghaleb, Mohamed Murad; Egyptian diplomatist and politician; b. 1 April 1922, Cairo.
Under-Sec. for Foreign Affairs 59-60; Amb. to Congo Republic (Léopoldville) 60, to U.S.S.R. 61-71; Minister of Foreign Affairs 71-72, of Information 73-74; Amb. to Yugoslavia June 74-Dec. 77 (resigned over Sadat's visit to Israel).
78 El Nil Street, Gueza, Cairo, Egypt.

Ghanem, Ismail, D. EN D.; Egyptian lawyer; b. 24 May 1924, Alexandria; ed. Alexandria Univ., Faculté de Droit, Paris and Inst. of Comparative Law, New York Univ.
Member Staff, Faculty of Law, Alexandria Univ. and Ain-Shams Univ. 51-; Dean Faculty of Law, Arab Univ. of Beirut, Lebanon 62-63; Dean, Faculty of Law, Ain-Shams Univ. 66-68, Vice-Rector 68-70, Rector 71-74; Amb. and Perm. Del. to UNESCO, Paris 70-71; Minister of Culture May-Sept. 71, of Higher Educ. and Scientific Research 74-75; mem. Exec. Board, Cairo Governorate; mem. Board, Acad. for Scientific Research; Chair. Council for the Social Sciences 71.
Publs. *Le Droit du Travail* 62, *La Vente* 63, *Le Droit Subjectif* 63, all in Arabic; *Les Droits réels principaux*, 2 vols., 62, *La Théorie générale des Obligations* 66-67.
c/o Ministry of Higher Education, Cairo, Egypt.

Ghanem, Mohamed Hafez, PH.D.; Egyptian lawyer and government official; b. 28 Sept. 1925; ed. Cairo Univ. and Univ. de Paris.
Lecturer, Faculty of Law, Alexandria Univ. 49; Prof. of Public Int. Law and Vice-Dean, Faculty of Law, Ain Shams Univ. 60-68; Minister of Tourism 68-69, of Educ. 69-71; Sec.-Gen. Arab Socialist Union 73; Deputy Premier and Minister of Higher Educ. April 75-76, Deputy Premier and Minister responsible for Social Devt. and Services 76-77; Head of Ministerial Cttee. for Local Govt. 76-; Deputy Prime Minister, Minister for Sudan and for Council Affairs 77-78; Attorney, Legal and Econ. Consultant 78-; Prof. of Public Int. Law, Ain Shams Univ. 78-; Pres. Egyptian Soc. of Int. Law; mem. Arbitration, Conciliation and Mediation Comm. of Org. of African Unity (OAU) 66-71; mem. Legal Consultative Comm. for Afro-Asian Countries 58-65; State Prize for best publ. in field of Int. Law and Political Science 60.
Publs. *Public International Law* (Arabic) 64, *International Organization* 67, *International Responsibility* 72.
26 Mahmoud Bassiouny, Cairo (Office); 3 Sharia El Bergass, Garden City, Cairo, Egypt.

Gherab, Mohamed Habib; Tunisian UN official.
Former Amb. to Spain; Special Adviser to Tunisian Sec. of State for Foreign Affairs 67-69; mem. del. to XXIII session of UN Gen. Assembly; Asst. Sec.-Gen. of UN and Dir. of Personnel 69-79; Sec.-Gen., UN Conf. on New and Renewable Sources of Energy March 79-.
UN Secretariat, New York, N.Y., U.S.A.

Ghirshman, Roman, D. ÈS L.; French professor and archaeologist; b. 3 Oct. 1895; ed. Sorbonne, Ecole des Hautes-Etudes, Ecole du Louvre.
Director, French archaeological mission in Iran 31-67, in Afghanistan 41-43; mem. Acad. des Inscriptions et Belles-Lettres; Pres. Asscn. pour l'avancement des études iraniennes; Dir. *Iranica Antiqua* review; Fellow British Acad; Dr. h.c. (Teheran); Cmmdr. Légion d'Honneur; Grand Croix Ordre Homayoun (Iran); Grand Officer Tadj (Iran); Croix de St. Georges; Medal of Freer Gallery of Art.
Publs. *Fouilles de Tépé Giyan* 31-32, *Fouilles de Sialk* (2 vols.) 33-37; *Bégram, Histoire des Kouchans* 46, *Les Chionites-Hephtalites* 48, *Iran, des Origines à l'Islam* 51, (second edn.) 76, *Village perse-achéménide* 54, *Bîchâpour II, mosaïques sassanides* 56, *Bîchâpour I* 70, *Iran, Parthes et Sassanides* 62, *Perse, Proto-Iraniens, Mèdes, Achéménides* 64, *Tchoga Zanbil, La Ziggourat*, vol. I 66, *Tchoga Zanbil, Temenos, Temples, Palais, Tombes* vol. II 68, *Iran Immortal Kingdom* 70, *Les Terrasses sacrées de Bard-è Néchandeh et Masjid-i Solaiman, depuis le VIIIe siècle avant notre ère au Ve siècle de notre ère* 76, *L'Iran et la migration des Indo-Aryens et des Iraniens* 77; 300 articles in reviews.
96 rue La Fontaine, 75016, Paris, France.

Ghissassi, Abdellatif; Moroccan politician; b. 19 Nov. 1937, Taza; ed. Lycée Moulay Idriss, Fez, Lycée Lyautey, Casablanca, Ecole Nat. des Ponts et Chausées, Paris, Ecole Nat. de l'Aviation Civile, Paris.
Teacher, Ecole Mohammedia d'Ingénieurs 62-72; Dir. Ministry of Public Works 62-68, Gen. Sec. 68-72, Minister 72-74; Dir. Soc. Marocaine des Industries de Raffinage 73-74; Minister of Commerce, Mines, Industry and Merchant Marine 74-77, of Finance 77-79, of Agriculture and Agrarian Reform March 79-; Officier, Ordre du Mérite 72; Commdr. Ordre Nat. du Mérite (France) 75, Ordre du Mérite (Mauritania) 77.
Ministère de l'Agriculture et de la Réforme Agraire, Rabat; 4 rue Abou Iblane, Rabat, Morocco (Home).

Ghorbal, Ashraf, PH.D.; Egyptian diplomatist; ed. Cairo Univ. and Harvard, Mass., U.S.A.
Joined Egyptian Del. to UN 49; Head Egyptian Interests Section, Indian Embassy, Washington 68-73; Press Adviser to the Pres. Feb.-Nov. 73; Amb. to U.S.A. Nov. 73-.
Embassy of Egypt, 2310 Decatur Place, N.W., Washington, D.C. 20008, U.S.A.

Ghoussein, Talat al-; Kuwaiti diplomatist; b. 1924; ed. American Univ. of Cairo.
Foreign News Editor *As-Shaab* (Jaffa, Palestine) 46-47; Controller, Arab Bank Ltd., Jaffa, Palestine 47-48; Editor Foreign News and Dir. of English Section, Broadcasting Station of Jordan 48-49; Dir. Press and Public Information Ministry of Foreign Affairs, Yemen 49-53; Sec.-Gen., Development Board, Kuwait 53-60; Dep. Private Sec. to Amir of Kuwait 60-61; Minister-Counsellor, Kuwait Embassy, Washington 62-63, Amb. to U.S.A. 63-70, concurrently to Canada 65-70; Amb. to Morocco 70-71, to Japan 71-78, also accred. to Australia, Indonesia and Malaysia.
c/o Ministry of Foreign Affairs, Kuwait City, Kuwait.

Ghozali, Sid Ahmed; Algerian petroleum executive; b. 31 March 1937, Marnia; ed. Ecole des Ponts et Chaussées, Paris.
Formerly Dir. of Energy, Ministry of Industry and Energy; Adviser, Ministry of the Economy 64; Under-Sec., Ministry of Public Works 64-65; Pres., Dir.-Gen. Société nationale de transports et de commercialisation des hydrocarbures (SONATRACH) 66-; mem. Org. technique de mise en valeur des richesses du sous-sol saharien 62-.
SONATRACH, 80 Avenue Ahmed Ghermoul, Algiers, Algeria.

Glubb, Lieut.-Gen. Sir John Bagot, K.C.B., C.M.G., D.S.O., O.B.E., M.C.; British officer; b. 16 April 1897; ed. Cheltenham and Royal Military Acad. Woolwich.
2nd Lieut. Royal Engineers 15, served France; served Iraq 20; Admin. Inspector Iraq Govt. 26; Officer Commdg. Desert Area (Transjordan) 30; Officer Commdg. Arab Legion, Transjordan (now Jordan) 38-56.
Publs. *Story of the Arab Legion* 48, *A Soldier with the Arabs* 57, *Britain and the Arabs* 59, *War in the Desert* 60, *The Great Arab Conquests* 63, *The Empire of the Arabs* 63, *The Course of Empire* 65, *The Lost Centuries* 67, *Syria, Lebanon, Jordan* 67, *A Short History of the Arab Peoples* 69, *The Life and Times of Muhammad* 70, *Peace in the Holy Land* 71, *Soldiers of Fortune* 73, *The Way of Love* 74, *Haroon al Raschid and the Great Abbasids* 76, *Into Battle: a Soldier's Diary of the Great War* 77, *Arabian Adventures* 78.
West Wood St. Dunstan, Mayfield, Sussex, England.

Goldmann, Nahum; Lithuanian-born Zionist leader; b. 10 July 1895; ed. Heidelberg, Berlin and Marburg Univs.
Editor and Publisher German Hebrew Encylopedia Judaica 22-34; mem. Zionist Political Comm. 27; Act. Chair. Zionist Action Cttee. 33; escaped from Germany 34; Rep. of Jewish Agency to L. of N.; in U.S. 41; Rep. Jewish Agency for Palestine in U.S.A. during Second World War; Pres. World Jewish Congress 51-77, World Zionist Org. 56-68, Conf. on Jewish Claims against Germany, Memorial Foundation for Jewish Culture; Chair. Cttee. on Jewish Claims against Austria 50-.
Ahad Haam 18, Jerusalem, Israel; 12 avenue Montaigne, Paris, France.

Goldstein, Rabbi Israel, M.A., D.D., D.H.L., LITT.H.D., LL.D., PH.D.; American Rabbi; b. 18 June 1896; ed. Univ. of Pennsylvania, Jewish Theological Seminary of America and Columbia Univ.
Rabbi Congregation B'nai Jeshurun N.Y.C. 18-60, Rabbi Emeritus 61-; Pres. Jewish Conciliation Board of America 29-68 (now Hon. Pres.), Jewish Nat. Fund of America 33-43 (now Hon. Pres.); Pres. Synagogue Council of America 42-44, Zionist Organization of America 44-46; Chair. World Confed. of Gen. Zionists 46-72 (now Hon. Pres.); United Palestine Appeal 47-49; Co-Chair. United

Jewish Appeal 47-49; Treas. Jewish Agency 47-49; Pres. Amidar Israel Nat. Housing Co. for Immigrants 48-49; mem. World Jewish Congress Exec. 48-, and Chair. of its Western Hemisphere Exec. 50-60, Hon. Vice-Pres. 59-; Pres. American Jewish Congress 51-58; now Hon. Pres.; Pres. World Hebrew Union; mem. Jewish Agency for Palestine Exec. 48-72; World Chair. Keren Hayesod-United Israel Appeal 61-71; mem. Board of Govs. Hebrew Univ. of Jerusalem, Weizmann Inst. of Science, Univ. of Haifa; Founder Brandeis Univ. 46; Chair. Jerusalem Artists' House 67-70; Chair in Zionism at Hebrew Univ. of Jerusalem, Synagogue of Hebrew Univ. of Jerusalem; Chair in Practical Theology, Jewish Theological Seminary of America; Hon. Pres. Asscn. of Americans and Canadians in Israel; Hon. doctorates from Brandeis Univ., New York Univ., Univ. of Pennsylvania, Hebrew Univ. of Jerusalem.
Publs. *A Century of Judaism in New York* 30, *Towards a Solution* 40, *Mourner's Devotions* 41, *Brandeis University* 51, *American Jewry Comes of Age* 55, *Transition Years* 62, *Israel at Home and Abroad* 73.
12 Pinsker Street, Jerusalem, Israel.

Golkulcu, Ahmet Feyyaz; Turkish judge and adacemic; b. 4 Oct. 1926, Mugla; ed. Univ. of Istanbul and Univ. of Neuchâtel, France.
Assistant Professor, Faculty of Political Sciences, Univ. of Ankara, Assoc. Prof. 58, Prof. 65-, Dir. School of Journalism and Broadcasting 69 and 72, Dean Faculty of Political Sciences 73-76; Judge, European Court of Human Rights 77-.
Publs. *Examination of the Accused Person in Penal Matters* 52, *Personal Liberty of the Accused in Criminal Procedure* 58, *A Research on Juvenile Delinquency in Turkey* 63, *Turkish Penal System* 65, *Mass Communication Law* 73.
Pilot Sokak 8/4, Cankaya, Ankara, Turkey.

Goodarzi, Dr. Manouchehr; Iranian administrator; b. 1925; ed. Princeton Univ. and Univ. of S. Calif., U.S.A.
Lecturer, Princeton Univ.; Lecturer in Public Admin., Teheran Univ.; Founding Dir. Org. and Management Bureau 56-57, Dir. Dept. of Social and Municipal Devt. 57-60, Deputy Man. Dir. 60-62, Plan Org.; Deputy Prime Minister, Sec.-Gen. State Org. for Admin and Employment Affairs 62-69; Minister of Agricultural Products and Consumer Goods 69-70; Minister in charge of Nat. Transport Co-ordination 70-71; Special Adviser to the Prime Minister 71-73; Pres., mem. of Board, Arj Mfg. Corpn. 73-; decorations from Iran, Repub. of Korea and Philippines.
Arj Corporation, P.O. Box 3427, Teheran, Iran.

Goren, Maj.-Gen. Shlomo; Israeli Rabbi; b. 1917, Poland; ed. Hebrew Univ., High Theological Seminar, Jerusalem.
In Israel 25-; co-founder Kfar Hassidim; Chief Chaplain, Israel Defence Forces 48-71; Chief Rabbi of Tel-Aviv (elected June 68); Ashkenazi Chief Rabbi of Israel Oct. 72-; Rabbi Kook Prize, State of Israel Prize.
Publs. *Nezer Hakodesh* (on Maimonides), *Shaarei Tahara, Talmud Yerushalmi Meforash, Torath Ha Moadim, Piskei Hilchoth Tzavah Hagrah Vehavushalmi, Responsa: Mashiv Milchama;* works on religion in military life, prayers for soldiers, etc.
Chief Rabbinate, Hechal Shlomo, Jerusalem; Private Office: 35 Shaul Hamelech Boulevard, Tel-Aviv, Israel.

Goulli, Slaheddine el, LL.D.; Tunisian diplomatist; b. 22 June 1919, Sousse; ed. Collège de Sousse and Université de Paris.
Tunisian Bar 47; in private industry 49-56; active in Tunisian Nat. Liberation Movement, Europe 47-56; Gen. Consul, Marseilles 56-57; Counsellor, Washington 58, Minister, Washington 59-61; Alt. Exec. Dir. World Bank 61; Amb. to Belgium, also accred. to Netherlands and Luxembourg 62, concurrently Perm. Rep. to EEC; Perm. Rep. to UN 69; Amb. to U.S.A. 69-73, concurrently to Mexico 70-73, to Venezuela 72-73; Special Diplomatic Adviser to Foreign Minister 74-76; Amb. to Netherlands 76-78; Grand Cordon de l'Ordre de la République Tunisienne 66, also decorations from Belgium, Netherlands and Luxembourg.
c/o Ministry of Foreign Affairs, Tunis, Tunisia.

Graham, Sir John Alexander Noble, K.C.M.G.; British diplomatist; b. 15 July 1926, Calcutta; ed. Eton Coll., Trinity Coll. Cambridge.
Served in the Army 44-47; joined Diplomatic Service 50; Principal private Sec. to Foreign Sec. 69-72; Minister, Head of Chancery, British Embassy to U.S.A. 72-74; Amb. to Iraq 74-77, to Iran 79-; Deputy Under-Sec., FCO 77-78.
c/o Foreign and Commonwealth Office, Downing Street, London, S.W.1, England.

Guiga, Driss, L. EN D.; Tunisian politician and diplomatist; b. 21 Oct. 1924, Testour; ed. Sadiki Coll., Tunis, and Paris.
Tunisian Bar; Chef de Cabinet, Ministry of Public Health 52; Dir. Nat. Security until 63; Dir.-Gen. of Tourism and Thermal Affairs 63; Sec. of State for Public Health Sept.-Nov. 69; Minister of Public Health 69-73, of Nat. Educ. 73-76; mem. Destour Socialist Party 43-, has held several party posts, currently mem. Cen. Cttee.; Amb. to Fed. Repub. of Germany.
Embassy of Tunisia, Godesberger Allee 103, 53 Bonn 2, Federal Republic of Germany.

Gümrükçüoğlu, Rahmi Kamil, B.SC., M.A.; Turkish diplomatist; b. 18 May 1927, Balçic, Roumania; ed. Haydar Pasha Coll. Istanbul, Ankara Univ. and Graduate School, Harvard Univ.
Joined Ministry of Foreign Affairs 49; Second Sec., London 52, First Sec. 58; Head of Foreign Int. Econ. Relations Dept., Ministry of Foreign Affairs 58-60; Counsellor, Cairo 60-63; Deputy Dir.-Gen. Dept. of Int. Econ. Affairs, Ministry of Foreign Affairs 63-65, Head of Special Bureau for Econ. Co-operation with U.S.S.R. 65-67, Dir.-Gen. Dept. of Int. Econ. Affairs 67-71; Amb. to Council of Europe 71-75, mem. Governing Board, European Resettlement Fund 71-75; Amb. to Iran 75-78; rep. in many bilateral and multilateral talks; negotiated over 100 int. agreements on financial, econ., tech. and industrial matters.
Publs. articles and studies on foreign investment in Turkey, econ. integration among developing countries, econ. devt. in U.S.S.R. 58, 64, 65, 66.
c/o Ministry of Foreign Affairs, Dişişleri Bakanliği, Müdafaa Cad., Bakanliklar, Ankara, Turkey.

Gur, Lieut.-Gen. Mordechai; Israeli army officer; b. 5 May 1930; ed. Hebrew Univ.
Served in Haganah; Co. Commdr. during Independence War; Deputy Commdr. Paratroop Corps 57; Instructor, Command and Staff Coll. 58; C.O. Golani Brigade 61-63; Chief of Operations 64-65; in charge of Command and Staff Coll. 65-66; Staff and Command 66-67; C.O. Paratroop Brigade during Six-Day War 67; mem. Israeli Del. to UN Emergency Session 67; C.O. Israeli Forces in Gaza and N. Sinai, Northern Command 67-72; Mil. Attaché, Washington 72-73; C.O. Northern Command during Yom Kippur War Oct. 73; Chief Mil. Negotiator at Geneva Peace Conf. Dec. 73; Chief of Staff 74-78.
Publs. several children's books.
c/o Ministry of Defence, Tel-Aviv, Israel.

Gurney, Oliver Robert, M.A., D.PHIL.; British assyriologist; b. 28 Jan. 1911; ed. Eton Coll. and New Coll. Oxford.
Army Service 39-45; Shillito Reader in Assyriology,

Oxford Univ. 45-, Prof. 65-, Emeritus Prof. 78; Fellow of British Acad. 59-, Magdalen Coll. Oxford 63-; Editor *Anatolian Studies* 59-.
Publs. *The Geography of the Hittite Empire* (with J. Garstang) 59, *The Hittites* 52, 75, *The Sultantepe Tablets I* and *II* (with J. J. Finkelstein and P. Hulin) 57, 64, *Ur Excavations—Texts VII* 74, I, *Sumerian Literary Texts* (with S. N. Kramer) 76, *Some Aspects of Hittite Religion* (The Schweich Lectures 76) 77.
Bayworth Corner, Boars Hill, Oxford, England.

Gürün, Kâmuran; Turkish diplomatist; b. 1924, Çengelköy (Istanbul); ed. studied political science.
Entered diplomatic service 48; posted to Turkish Embassy, Bonn 51; subsequently held various posts at Ministry of Foreign Affairs and diplomatic missions abroad; Dir.-Gen. Dept. for Admin. Affairs 61, subsequently Perm. Sec. to the Inter-Ministerial Cttee. on External Econ. Relations, Dir.-Gen. Dept. for Econ. and Commercial Affairs, Deputy Sec.-Gen. for Econ. Affairs and Sec.-Gen. Inter-Ministerial Econ. Council; Amb. to Romania 67-70; Perm. Rep. of Turkey at OECD 70-72; Amb. to Greece 74-76; Sec.-Gen. CENTO 78-79.
c/o Ministry of Foreign Affairs, Dişişleri Bakanliği, Müdafaa Cad., Bakanliklar, Ankara, Turkey.

H

Habash, George, M.D.; Palestinian nationalist leader; b. 1925, Lydda, Palestine; ed. American University of Beirut.
Member Youth of Avengeance 48 and Arab Nationalists' Movement early 50s; practised as doctor 50s; leader of Popular Front for the Liberation of Palestine Nov. 67-.
c/o Palestine Liberation Organization, Colombani Street, Off Sadat Street, Dr. Raji Nasr Building, Ras Beirut, Lebanon.

Habashi, Wadie; Sudanese agricultural economist and politician; b. 14 Aug. 1917, Merwi; ed. Univ. of Khartoum and Oxford Univ.
Worked on the Al Aalyab, Burgaeg and White Nile devt. schemes; Agricultural Insp. for Khartoum Province and later for Merwi, Dongla and Halfa; Technical Adviser to the Minister of Agriculture; Asst. Dir. for Planning and Devt., Dept. of Agriculture, Dir. 55-66; Rep. of Sudan to FAO Conf. 56, to Int. Tobacco Conf., Rhodesia 63; Chair. Admin. Council of El Gash Scheme Comm.; Dir. Production Section, Equatoria Schemes Comm.; Head, Advisory Comm. for Agricultural Research; mem. Gezira Scheme Admin. Council; mem. Studies Comm., Faculty of Agriculture, Univ. of Khartoum; with FAO 66-71, Dir. FAO-ECA Joint Agricultural Div., Addis Ababa; with IBRD and Kuwait Fund for Arab Econ. Devt. 71; Minister of Agriculture 71-73, of Agriculture, Food and Natural Resources 73-74; Pres. Nat. Council for Research July 74-, OAU Scientific Council for Africa May 75-.
c/o OAU Scientific, Technical and Research Commission, Nigerian Ports Authority Building, P.M.B. 2359, Marina, Lagos, Nigeria.

Haddad, Ahmed Ali al-, B.A.; Yemeni diplomatist; b. 2 Oct. 1939, Sana'a, Yemen Arab Republic; ed. Univ. of Vermont, Boston Univ., New School of Social Research, New York, U.S.A.
Director of Int. Orgs. Dept., Ministry of Foreign Affairs, Sana'a 64-65, Dir.-Gen. 65-66, Under-Sec. 66-67, Head of Branch at Taiz 68, Head of Dept. for Econ. and Tech. Affairs 69-70, Head of Political Dept. 75-76; Chargé d'affaires, Embassy to Fed. Repub. of Germany 70; mem. Del. to UN 70, Deputy Perm. Rep. 71-74, Amb. to UN Office in Geneva 77, Perm. Rep. to the UN Dec. 66-.
Permanent Mission of the Yemen Arab Republic to the United Nations, 747 Third Avenue, 8th Floor, New York, N.Y. 10017, U.S.A.

Haddad, Prof. Ghassan, D.ECON.SC.; Syrian educationist and politician; b. 26 Jan. 1926, Latakia; ed. secondary schools, Latakia and Damascus, Mil. Acad., and U.S.S.R.
Served in various mil. posts 48-61; promoted to rank of Gen. 63; mem. Higher Nat. Council of the Revolution, mem. of Gen. Leadership of the Army and Armed Forces 63; Minister of Planning 63-65, later Pres. Parl. Planning Cttee.; carried out scientific research 66-68; Conf. Prof. Univ. of Damascus, Planning Inst. for Social and Econ. Devt. 69-75; Econ. Adviser, Ministry of Planning, Iraq and Conf. Prof. Univ. of Baghdad 75-; participated in several int. seminars on problems of planning; Founder and Pres. Board of Dirs., Arab Progress Publishers; mem. Union of Arab Writers, Union of the Arab Economists; several decorations including Médaille de Mérite de Hors Classe, Médaille de la Loyauté de Premier Classe.
Publs. many articles and works.
Ministry of Planning, Baghdad, Karradat Mariam, Jamhouriya Bridge, Iraq.

Haddad, Sulaiman Ahmed el; Kuwaiti banker and politician; b. 1930; ed. Kuwait Aazamieh Secondary School, and Cairo Univ.
Secretary of Educ. Council of Kuwait; fmr. Financial Asst., Ministry of Educ. and mem. Constituent Assembly for formation of Kuwaiti Constitution; mem. National Assembly 63-; fmr. Chair. and Man. Dir. Arab African Bank; Chair. ARTOC Bank Ltd., Int. Resources and Finance Bank, Arab Investment Co. in Asia and Kuwait; mem. Board, Arab African Bank, Cairo; Deputy Chair. and Man. Dir. ARTOC (S.A.K.).
Arab African Bank, 44 Abdel Khalek Sarwat Street, Cairo, Egypt; ARTOC, El Sour Street, Arab Gulf Building, P.O. Box 23074, Safat, Kuwait.

Hadithi, Murtada al-; Iraqi politician; b. 1939, Ramadi; ed. Higher Teachers' Training Inst. and Univ. of Baghdad.
School Teacher, Fallouja 66-67; mem. Revolutionary Command Council 67; Chair. Kurdish Affairs Bureau and Peace Cttee. 67; mem. World Peace Cttee.; Minister of Labour March 70-Oct. 71; Minister of Foreign Affairs 71-74; Amb. to U.S.S.R. 74-75.
Ministry of Foreign Affairs, Baghdad, Karradat Mariam, Iraq.

Hadjioannou, Kyriacos, F.R.A.I., PH.D.; Cypriot teacher and diplomatist; b. 1909; ed. Famagusta Gymnasium, Athens Univ. and Oxford Univ.
Greek Master, Kyrenia Gymnasium 32-35, Famagusta 36-45; Principal, Famagusta Gymnasium 46-48, 57-60, 63-69; Amb. to U.A.R. 60-63; Lecturer, Teachers' Training Coll., Morphou 48-53; Principal, Morphou Gymnasium 53-57; Pres. United Nat. Solid Front 57-59; Founder and Pres. Philological and Scientific Soc. of Famagusta 60-61, 64-; Fellow, Royal Anthropological Inst. of Great Britain and Ireland 46-; Grand Cordon of the Repub. (Egypt); prizes: D. Marangos (EFSA) 73, Athens Acad. 76, Hellenic Cultural Soc. 77.
Publs. *The Loan-words of Medieval and Modern Greek Cypriot Dialect* 36, *Cypriot Fables* 48, *Literary Texts of the Medieval and Modern Greek Cypriot Dialect with Introductions and Commentaries* 61, *Ta en Diaspora* 69, *Diplomacy and machinations in the Courts of the Lusignan Kings of Cyprus* 70, *Ancient Cyprus in Greek Sources:* Vol. I, *Legendary Traditions, History and Ethnology from Prehistoric Times to the Year 395 A.D.* 71, Vol. II, *Mythology and Religion, Geography and Geology* 73, Vol. III, Part I, *Letters, Sciences, Arts and Crafts from Homeric Times to the Year 395 A.D.* 75, Vol. III, Part II, *Cyprian Glosses* 77

and articles in Greek, German, English, French and Belgian journals.
Ay. Spyridon 8, Famagusta 58; Cyprus.

Hafez, Maj.-Gen. Amin el; Syrian army officer and politician; b. 1911.
Former Military Attaché in Argentina; took part in the revolution of March 1963; Dep. Prime Minister, Mil. Gov. of Syria and Minister of Interior March-Aug. 63; Minister of Defence and Army Chief of Staff July-Aug. 63; C.-in-C. of Armed Forces July 63-64; Pres. of Revolutionary Council July 63-May 64; Pres. Presidency Council May 64-Feb. 66; Prime Minister Nov. 63-May 64, Oct. 64-Sept. 65; sentenced to death *in absentia* Aug. 71; living in exile.

Hagras, Dr. Kamal M.; Omani diplomatist; b. 15 Jan. 1927; ed. Cairo, Paris and New York Univs.
Joined diplomatic service 51, served in France, then Colombia, New York, London; also in various depts. of Foreign Office; Chief of Cabinet of Under-Sec.; Amb. to France and Switzerland, Perm. Rep. to UNESCO until 75; Amb. and Perm. Rep. to UN 75-77; Rockefeller Foundation Fellowship 63-65; fmr. Chair. London Diplomatic Asscn.; Oman Wissam First Class; Commdr. Légion d'Honneur (France).
Ministry of Foreign Affairs, Muscat, Oman.

Haidar, Mohamed Haider, LL.B.; Syrian politician; b. 1931; ed. secondary schools, Latakia, Univ. of Damascus.
Teacher, Latakia, Hama, Damascus 51-60; with Ministry of Agrarian Reform 60-63; Dir. Agrarian Reform Inst., Hama 63; Dir. Agrarian Reform, Damascus, Daraa, Al-Suaida 64; Dir. Legal and Admin. Affairs, Ministry of Agriculture and Agrarian Reform 65; Gov. Al-Hasakeh 66; mem. Command, Damascus Branch of Arab Socialist Baath Party 67, Temporal Regional Command 70, now Regional and Nat. Commands, mem. Cen. Command Progressive Nat. Front of Syria; Deputy Prime Minister, Minister of Agric. and Agrarian Reform until 73, of Econ. Affairs Sept. 73-76.
c/o Ministry of Economic Affairs, Damascus, Syria.

Haithem, Muhammad Ali; Yemeni politician; b. 1940, Dathina, Southern Arabia.
Formerly school teacher; Minister of Interior 67; mem. Presidential Council of S. Yemen 69-71; Chair. Council of Ministers 69-70; mem. Nat. Front Gen. Command.
Now living in Cairo, Egypt.

Hakim, George; (*see* Maximos V Hakim).

Hakim, George, M.A., L.en D.; Lebanese diplomatist; b. 1913; ed. American Univ., Beirut, and Univ. St. Joseph.
Adjunct Prof. of Econs., American Univ., Beirut 43; mem. of several advisory govt. cttees. on econ. and financial questions 42-46; alt. del. to UN ECOSOC 46, chief del. 49; Counsellor, Legation in Washington, D.C. 64-52, Chargé d'Affaires 48 and 51; Minister of Finance, Nat. Economy and Agriculture 52-53; del. to numerous int. confs. including Int. Health Conf. N.Y. 46, UN Conf. on Trade and Employment, London 46, Geneva 47, Havana 47-48, etc.; Gov. IBRD, IMF 47-50; Vice-Chair. UN Econ. and Financial Cttee. 49; Chair. UN Group of Experts on econ. devt. 51; Minister of Foreign Affairs and of Econ. 53; Deputy Sec.-Gen. Ministry of Foreign Affairs 55; Minister to Fed. Repub. of Germany 55-57, Amb. 57-58; Minister of Nat. Economy 56; Perm. Rep. to UN 59-65, 66; Chair. UN Comm. on Human Rights 62; Deputy Prime Minister and Minister of Foreign Affairs 65-66, 66-67; Vice-Pres. American Univ. of Beirut 68-76.
Henry Abiad Building, Rabiya, Lebanon.

Hakim, Tawfiq al-, B.A.; Egyptian novelist and playwright; b. 9 Oct. 1898, Alexandria; ed. Muhammad 'Ali Secondary School, Cairo, Law School, The Egyptian Univ., Cairo, Collège des Lois, Sorbonne, Paris.
Director-General Nat. Library 51-56; Under-Sec. Higher Council of Arts, Letters and Social Sciences 56-59, 60-; Perm. Rep. of U.A.R. at UNESCO 59-60; Dir. *Al Ahram* newspaper; mem. Cairo Arabic Language Acad. 54-; State Prize for Literature; State Prize for Merit; Republican Chain; Hon. Dr. (Egyptian Acad. of Arts).
Publs. novels: *The Soul's Return* 33, *A Rural Deputy's Diary* 37; plays: *The Cavemen* 33, *Shahrazad* 34, *Pigmalyun* 42, *Solomon the Wise* 43, *Rejuvenation* 50, *Journey into the Future* 57, *Praksa* 60, *The Sultan's Dilemma* 60, *The Tree Climber* 62, *Food for Every Mouth* 63, *Fate of a Cockroach* 66.
c/o Al Ahram, Shalia Lal-Galaa, Cairo, Egypt.

Halabi, Mohammed Ali el-; Syrian politician; b. 1937, Damascus; ed. Teachers Training School and Damascus Univ.
Teacher 54-62; mem. Regional Command of Baath Party, Damascus; Mayor of Damascus; mem. Arab Fed. Assembly; Speaker of People's Council 73-78; Prime Minister March 78-; Pres. Arab Parl. Union 74-76.
Office of the Prime Minister, Damascus, Syria.

Halefoğlu, Vahit M., K.C.V.O., M.A.; Turkish diplomatist; b. 1919; ed. Antakya Coll. and Univ. of Ankara.
Turkish Foreign Service 43-, served Vienna, Moscow, Ministry of Foreign Affairs, London 46-59; Dir.-Gen. First Political Dept., Ministry of Foreign Affairs 59-62; Amb. to Lebanon 62-65, concurrently accred. to Kuwait 64-65; Amb. to U.S.S.R. 65-66; to the Netherlands 66-70; Deputy Sec.-Gen. for Political Affairs, Ministry of Foreign Affairs 70-72; Amb. to Fed. Repub. of Germany 72-; Lebanese, Finnish, British, Greek, Italian, German and Spanish decorations.
Embassy of Turkey, Utestrasse 47, Bonn-Bad Godesberg, Federal Republic of Germany.

Halkin, Shimon, B.A., M.A., D.H.L.; American Hebrew scholar and author; b. 30 Oct. 1899, Dovsk, Russia; ed. N.Y. City Coll., Chicago, New York and Columbia Univs.
Instructor in Hebrew and Hebrew Literature, Hebrew Union School for Teachers, N.Y. 24-32; Teacher, Geulah High School, Tel-Aviv 32-39; Lecturer in Bible, Jewish, Sociology and Modern Hebrew Literature, Chicago Coll. of Jewish Studies 40-43; Prof. of Hebrew and Hebrew Literature, Jewish Inst. of Religion, New York City 43-49; Assoc. Prof. of Hebrew Literature, Hebrew Univ. of Jerusalem 49-56, Prof. and Head of Dept. 56-68; Visiting Prof., Univ. of Calif. 54-55, Jewish Theological Seminary, N.Y. 65-66; Emer., Hebrew Univ. of Jerusalem 69; mem. Acad. of Hebrew Language; Pres. Israel PEN Club; Tchernichovsky Prize for translation of Whitman 53, of Seferis 77; Bialik Prize for Literature 68, State of Isràel Prize for Literature 75.
Publs. *Yehiel Ha-Hagri* (novel) 28, *An Ethical Philosophy of Life* 28, *Hebrew Literature in Palestine* 42, *Arai va-Keva* 43, *Ad Mashber* 45, *Al Haiy* (collected poems) 46, *Modern Hebrew Literature: Trends and Values* 51, *La Littérature Hebraïque Moderne* 57, *Ma'avar Yabok* (collected poems) 65, *Literatura Hebrea Moderna* 68, *Collected Literary Essays and Studies* (3 vols., Hebrew) 70, *Adrift, Collected Short Stories* 73, *Collected Poems* 76, and numerous others; translations of Shakespeare, Maeterlinck, Whitman, Shelley, Jack London, Seferis, etc.
5 Redak Street, Jerusalem, Israel.

Hamad, Abdlatif Yousef al-; Kuwaiti economist and banker.
Director-General Kuwait Fund for Arab Econ. Devt. 63-; Dir. Kuwait Investment Co.; Chair. Prefabricated Buildings Co. of Kuwait, United Bank of Kuwait Ltd., London, Middle East Int. Fund; Dir. American Express Int. Fund; Exec. Dir. Arab Fund for Econ and Social Devt.; Chair.

Cie. Arabe et Int. Investissements; Dir. Scandinavian Securities Corpn. May 77-; Trustee Kuwait Inst. of Econ. and Social Planning in the Middle East; mem. Perm. Cttee. for Aid to the Arabian Gulf and Yemen.
Kuwait Fund for Arab Economic Development, P.O.B. 2921, Kuwait City, Kuwait.

Hammadi, Sadoon; Iraqi economist and politician; b. 22 June 1930, Karbala; ed. in Beirut, Lebanon and U.S.A.
Professor of Econs., Univ. of Baghdad 57; Deputy Head of Econ. Research, Nat. Bank of Libya, Tripoli 61-62; Minister of Agrarian Reform 63; Econ. Adviser to Presidential Council, Govt. of Syria 64; Econ. Expert, UN Planning Inst., Syria 65-68; Pres. Iraq Nat. Oil Co. (INOC) 68; Minister of Oil and Minerals 68-74, of Foreign Affairs 74-.
Publs. *Towards a Socialist Agrarian Reform in Iraq* 64, *Views About Arab Revolution* 69.
Ministry of Foreign Affairs, Baghdad, Karradat Mariam, Iraq.

Hare, Raymond Arthur, A.B.; American diplomatist; b. 3 April 1901; ed. Grinnell Coll.
Instructor, Robert Coll., Constantinople 24-27; Exec. Sec. American Chamber of Commerce for Levant 26-27; Clerk, later Vice-Consul, U.S. Consulate-Gen., Constantinople 27-28; Language Officer, Paris 29, also Vice-Consul 31; Sec. in Diplomatic Service and Vice-Consul, Cairo 31; Beirut 32; Third Sec. and Vice-Consul, Teheran 33, Consul 35; Second Sec. Cairo 39, also at Jeddah 40-44, also Consul, Cairo 40; Second Sec., later First Sec. and Consul, London 44; Dept. of State 46; Nat. War Coll. 46-47; Chief, Div. of S. Asian Affairs 47; Deputy Dir. Office of Near East and African Affairs 48; Deputy Asst. Sec. State for Near East, S. Asian and African Affairs Oct. 49; Amb. to Saudi Arabia and Minister to Yemen 50-53; Amb. to Lebanon 53-54; Dir.-Gen. U.S. Foreign Service 54-56; Amb. to Egypt 56-58, to United Arab Republic 58-59, also Minister to Yemen 59; Dep. Under-Sec. of State for Political Affairs 60-61; Amb. to Turkey 61-65; Asst. Sec. of State for Near Eastern and South Asian Affairs 65-66; Pres. Middle East Inst. 66-69, Nat. Chair. 69-.
Middle East Institute, 1761 N. Street, N.W., Washington, D.C. 20036; 3214 39th Street, N.W., Washington, D.C. 20016, U.S.A.

Harkavy, Rabbi Zvi (Hirsh Gershon), B.A., M.A., TH.D.; Israeli (b. Russian) author and bibliographer; b. 1 Feb. 1908; ed. Inst. in U.S.S.R., Jerusalem Teachers' Seminary, Haifa Technion, Hebrew Univ. of Jerusalem, Petach Tikva Yeshiva, C.S.R.A.
Leader in Zionist underground in U.S.S.R.; repatriated to Palestine 26; Commdr. in Hagana 26-47; schoolmaster and lecturer Jerusalem Teachers' Seminaries 30-; Dir. Eretz Yisrael Publishing House 35-; Chaplain in Israeli Army 48-49; Dir. Dept. of Refugees in Ministry of War Casualties and later Editor of Ministry of Religious Affairs *Monthly* 49-53; Dir. Central Rabbinical Library of Israel 53-68; Editor *Hasefer* 54-; participated in world congresses; Visiting Prof. Yeshiva Univ., N.Y. 59; lectured at U.S.S.R. Acad. of Sciences, Leningrad 62; initiator of Religious Univ. (Bar-Ian) in Israel; one of the founders of the Religious Academics and Authors Orgs. and fmr. Chair.; Leader, Hapoel Hamizrachi, "Great Israel" Movement; an Editor of the *General Encyclopaedia* and of many periodicals and books; Komemiut, Hamishmar, Haganah, Ale, Hagana-Yerushalayim and Etziony Medals.
Publs. Biographies (Ed.): *Rambam, Rabbi Shmuel Strashun, Rabbi Mates Strashun, Rabbi I. M. Pines, Professor Simcha Assaf, A. E. Harkavy, Rabbi Reuven Katz—Chief Rabbi of Petach Tikva, The Family Maskil L'eytan, The Family Harkavy*; Essays: *Jews of Salonica, The Jewish Community of Ekaterinoslav; Scepticism of Pascal; The Man, The Plant, The Animal, Inorganic Nature; The Secret of Happy Marriage, Sexual Hygiene from the Religious and Scientific Viewpoint; Shomrei Hagachelet—Responsa of Soviet Rabbis* 66, *My Father's Home* 68, *Autobibliography* 71, *Ein Roe* 72; *Book of Ekaterinoslav-Dnepropetrovsk* 73, *The Works of A. E. Harkavy* (20 vols.), *A Fragment of Anan's Sefer Hamiswot, from the Yevpatoria manuscript* 75; also 1,400 articles and papers on Rabbinics, bibliography, theology, philosophy, archaeology, philology, history and Dead Sea Scrolls.
P.O. Box 7031, 7 Haran Street, Jerusalem 91070, Israel.

Harman, Avraham, B.A.; Israeli diplomatist; b. 1914; ed. Oxford Univ.
Moved to Palestine 38; held posts in Jewish Agency 38-48; Deputy Dir. Govt. Information Bureau 48-49; Consul-Gen. Montreal 49-50; Dir. Israel Information Office, N.Y. 50-53; Consul-Gen. Washington, D.C. 53-55; Ministry of Foreign Affairs 55-56; Exec. Jewish Agency 56-59; Amb. to the U.S.A. 59-68; Pres. Hebrew Univ. 68-.
The Hebrew University, Givat-Ram, Jerusalem, Israel.

Hart, Parker T.; American business consultant; b. 28 Sept. 1910; ed. Dartmouth Coll., Harvard and Georgetown Univs., Institut Universitaire de Hautes Etudes Internationales, Geneva, and School of Foreign Service.
Translator, Dept. of State 37-38; Foreign Service Officer 38-69, served Vienna, Pará (Brazil), Cairo, Jeddah, Dhahran 38-47; Dept. of State 47-49; Consul-Gen. Dhahran 49-51; Nat. War Coll. 51-52; Dir. Office of Near Eastern Affairs, Dept. of State 52-55; Dep. Chief of Mission and Councellor Cairo 55-58; Consul-Gen. and Minister, Damascus 58; Dep. Asst. Sec. of State, Near East and South Asia Affairs 58-61; Amb. to Saudi Arabia 61-65, concurrently Minister to Kingdom of Yemen 61-62 and Amb. to Kuwait 62-63; Amb. to Turkey 65-68; Asst. Sec. of State for Near Eastern and South Asian Affairs 68-69; Dir. Foreign Service Inst. 69; Pres. Middle East Inst., Washington, D.C. 69-73; Consultant, Bechtel Corpn., RCA Corpn.; mem. Board of Govs., Middle East Inst., Washington, D.C.; Emer. mem. Board of Trustees, American Univ. Beirut; mem. Advisory Council on Near Eastern Studies, Princeton Univ.; mem. of Board, Center for Applied Linguistics; mem. of Visiting Cttee. in Near Eastern Languages and Literature, Harvard Univ.; mem. Int. Advisory Cttee., American Security Bank; Co-Pres. American-Turkish Soc.; mem. Board of Visitors, Nat. Defense Univ.; mem. Royal Soc. for Asian Affairs.
4705 Berkeley Terrace, N.W., Washington, D.C. 20007, U.S.A.

Hasani, Ali Nasir Muhammad; (*see* Muhammad, Ali Nasir).

Hasani, Baqir Husain, B.SC., LL.B.; Iraqi diplomatist; b. 1915; ed. Columbia Univ., New York and Baghdad Law Coll.
Dir. of Commerce and Registrar of Companies, Iraq Ministry of Econs. 47-51; Dir.-Gen. of Contracts and Econ. Affairs, Development Board 51-54; Dir.-Gen. of Income Tax, Ministry of Finance 56-57; Dir.-Gen. and Chair. of Board of Dirs., Tobacco Monopoly Admin. 57-59; Minister to Austria 59-62, Ambassador 62-63; Chair. Board of Govs. Int. Atomic Energy Agency (IAEA) 61-62, Special Adviser to Dir.-Gen. 63-67, 70-76; Special Adviser to Perm. Mission and Gov. of Saudi Arabia at IAEA; mem. Iraqi and later IAEA dels. to UN; Rafidain Decoration (Iraq); Grand Golden Cross with Ribbon (Austria).
43 Maidenhead Court Park, Maidenhead, Berkshire, SL6 8HN, England; and Masbah, Karradah, Baghdad, Iraq.

Haseeb, Khair El-Din, PH.D.; Iraqi economist and statistician; b. 1 Aug. 1929, Mosul; ed. Baghdad Univ. and London School of Econs., Cambridge Univ., England.
Civil service 47-54; Head of Research and Statistics Dept.,

Iraq Petroleum Co. 59-60; Lecturer, Baghdad Univ. 60-61, Assoc. Prof. 65-71, Prof. of Econs. 71-74; Dir.-Gen. Iraqi Fed. of Industries 60-63; Gov. Cen. Bank of Iraq 63-65; Pres. Gen. Org. for Banks 64-65; Acting Pres. Econ. Org. 64-65; Gov. for Iraq, IMF 63-65; Alt. Gov. for Iraq, IBRD 63-65; Chief of Natural Resources and Science and Technology Div., UN ECWA 74-.
Publs. *The National Income of Iraq, 1953-1961* 64, *Sources of Arab Economic Thought in Iraq 1900-1971* 73, *Workers' Participation in Management in Arab Countries* 71, and several articles in English and Arabic.
P.O. Box 111612, Beirut, Lebanon.

Hashim, Jawad M., PH.D.; Iraqi politician; b. 10 Feb. 1938; ed. London School of Econs. and Political Science, Univ. of London.
Professor of Statistics, Univ. of Baghdad 67; Dir.-Gen. Cen. Statistical Org. 68; Minister of Planning 68-71, 72-74; mem. Planning Board and Econ. Office, Revolutionary Command Council 74; Man. Dir. Arab Monetary Fund (AMF) April 77-; Chair. ECWA May 75.
Publs. *Capital Formation in Iraq 1957-1970, National Income—Its Methods of Estimation, The Evaluation of Economic Growth in Iraq 1950-1970,* and eighteen articles
Arab Monetary Fund, Abu Dhabi, United Arab Emirates.

Hassan II, King of Morocco; 17th Sovereign of the Alouite dynasty; b. 9 July 1929; ed. Bordeaux Univ.
Son of Mohammed V; invested as Crown Prince Moulay Hassan 57; C.-in-C. and Chief of Staff of Royal Moroccan Army 57; personally directed rescue operations at Agadir earthquake disaster 60; Minister of Defence May 60-June 61; Vice-Premier May 60-Feb. 61; Prime Minister Feb. 61-Nov. 63, June 65-67; succeeded to throne on death of his father, 26 Feb. 1961; Minister of Defence, Commdr.-in-Chief of the Army Aug. 71-; Chair. Org. of African Unity 72-73.
Publ. *The Challenge* (memoirs) 79.
Royal Palace, Rabat, Morocco.

Hassan ibn Talal, B.A.; Crown Prince of Jordan; b. 20 March 1947, Amman; ed. Harrow School, England, Christ Church, Oxford Univ.
Brother of H.R.H. Hussein ibn Talal, King of Jordan (*q.v.*), and heir to the throne; Acting Regent during absence of King Hussein; Ombudsman for Nat. Devt. 71-; Founder of Royal Scientific Soc. of Jordan 70; Hon. Gen. of Jordanian Army.
Office of the Crown Prince, The Royal Palace, Amman, Jordan.

Hassan, Abdullah el-, DIP.ARTS; Sudanese diplomatist and politician; b. 1925; ed. Gordon Secondary School, Khartoum Univ. Coll.
District Officer and Commissioner 49-56; Consul Gen. to Uganda 56-58; Head Political Section, Ministry of Foreign Affairs 58-60; Amb. to Ghana 60-64; Dir. Gen. Ministry of Information 65; Amb. to France 65-67, to Ethiopia 67-69; Under-Sec. Ministry of Foreign Affairs 69-70; Amb. to U.S.S.R. 71, to U.K. 72; Minister of Rural Devt. 72-73, of Interior 73-75; Sec. Gen. to the Presidency 75-; mem. Political Bureau, Sudanese Socialist Union 72-; Sec.-Gen. Sudanese Nat. Council for Friendship, Solidarity and Peace; mem. numerous dels.; Order of the Republic, First Class, numerous foreign decorations.
Office of the Cabinet, Khartoum, Sudan.

Hassan, Ahmad Y. al-, D.I.C., PH.D.; Syrian engineer and professor; b. 25 June 1925, Palestine; ed. Govt. Arab Coll., Jerusalem, Univ. of Cairo, Imperial Coll., London, Univ. Coll., London.
Professor of Mechanical Engineering; Dean, Faculty of Eng., Aleppo Univ. 64-67; Minister of Petroleum, Electricity and Industrial Projects 67-70; Pres. Aleppo Univ. 73-.
Publs. *Theory of Machines* 64, *Machine Design* 65, *Power Stations* 66, *Taq-al-Din and Arab Mechanical Engineering* 67; co-author, paper in *Proceedings of Royal Soc. of London* 64.
University of Aleppo, Aleppo, Syria.

Hassan, Cleto; (*see* Rial, Cleto Hassan).

Hassan, Mahmoud Ali, DR.ENG.; Egyptian engineer; b. 17 July 1915; ed. Cairo and Zürich Univs.
Director-General Industrial Control Dept. 56-59; Under-Sec. of State for Industry 59-61; Chair. Org. for Engineering Industries 61-66; Pres. Fed. of Egyptian Industries 67-74; Chair. Org. for Metallurgical Industries 71-74, Org. for Industrialization 74; Minister of Industry and Mining 74-75; now Consulting Eng.; Gen. Dir. Swissal Eng. Co.; Chair. Industrial Research Council of Acad. of Science and Tech.; Order of Trade and Industry, First Class.
Publs. *Druckverlüste in Abzweigen von quadratischen Kanälen, Anwendungen der elektrolytischen Methode auf die Betzsche Theorie der Spaltverlüste an Schaufelgittern.*
45 Road 15 Maadi, Cairo, Egypt.

Hassan Rial, Cleto; (*see* Rial, Cleto Hassan).

Hassouna, Mohammed Abdel-Khalek; Egyptian diplomatist (retd.); b. 28 Oct. 1898; ed. Cairo Univ. and Cambridge Univ.
Law practice 21; then joined Diplomatic Corps, served in Berlin 26, Prague 28, Brussels 28, Rome 30, Ministry for Foreign Affairs Cairo 32-39; Under-Sec. of State, Ministry of Social Affairs 39; served in Diplomatic Service in Belgium, Italy, Germany, Czechoslovakia; Gov. of Alexandria 42; Under-Sec. of State for Foreign Affairs 48; Minister of Social Affairs 49-50, of Education 52, of Foreign Affairs 52; Sec.-Gen. League of Arab States 52-72; Grand Cordon Order of the Nile (Egypt); Nile Collar (Egypt) 72; Legion of Honour (France); decorations conferred by Albania, Belgium, China, Ethiopia, Fed. Repub. of Germany, Greece, Italy and Yugoslavia.
3 Sharia Rifaa, Manchiet El-Bakry, Cairo, Egypt.

Hatem, Mohammed Abdel Kader, M.SC., PH.D.; Egyptian politician; b. 1918, Alexandria; ed. Military Acad., Univs. of London and Cairo.
Member, Nat. Assembly 57; Adviser to the Presidency, subsequently Deputy Minister for Presidential Affairs 57; Minister of State responsible for broadcasting and television 59; Minister for Culture, Nat. Guidance and Tourism 62; Deputy Prime Minister for Cultural Affairs and Nat. Guidance 65; Deputy Prime Minister and Minister for Culture and Information 71-74; Chair. of Board *Al-Ahram* 74; Asst. to Pres. of the Repub. and Supervisor-Gen. of Specialized Nat. Councils 74-; mem. Gen. Secr. Arab Socialist Union; hon. doctorates from two French Univs. and from Democratic People's Repub. of Korea.
Specialized National Councils, Arab Socialist Union Building, Corniche el-Nil, Cairo, Egypt.

Hawari Ahmed, Mahmoud el-; Egyptian journalist; b. 12 April 1921; ed. Polytechnic School, Cairo.
Director, Arab Information Center Press Office, New York 55-58; Man. Editor Middle East News Agency, Cairo 58-65, Chair. of Board 65-74; Dir. Magazine Dept., Nat. Publishing House 65-67; Chair. Nat. Distributing Co. 67; Publishing Man. Al-Katib Al-Arabi Publishing House 67-69; Adviser, Editing and Publishing Org. 69-71; Dir.-Gen. Egyptian Book Org. 71-72; Gold Cross, Order of King George I of Greece 60.
Isis Building, Garden City, Cairo, Egypt.

Hayek, His Beatitude Ignace Antoine, D.PHIL., D. ÈS SC., Syrian ecclesiastic; b. 14 Sept. 1910: ed. Séminaire Patriarcal, Charfé, Lebanon, Pontifical Coll. of Propaganda Fide, Rome, and Oriental Pontifical Inst., Rome.
Ordained priest 33; successively or concurrently Dir. of School, Curate and Vicar-Gen., Aleppo; Archbishop of Aleppo 59-68; Syrian Patriarch Antioch 68-.
Patriarcat Syrien Catholique d'Antioche, rue de Damas, B.P. 116/5087, Beirut, Lebanon.

Hedayati, Hadi; Iranian educationalist and politician; b. 1923; ed. Teheran Univ., Faculté de Droit, Paris Univ., and Sorbonne, Paris.
Assistant Prof. Teheran Univ. 52-62, Prof. 62-; Legal Counsellor, Iran Insurance Co. 52-57; Counsellor High Council of Econs. 57-60; High Counsellor, Ministry of Commerce 60; Exec. Man. Bimeh (Insurance) Bank 60-62; Deputy to Majlis 63-79; Advisory Minister 63; Minister of Educ. 64-68; Advisory Minister 68-73; Minister of State 73-74, Exec. Asst. to Prime Minister 74-75; Minister of State, Exec. Deputy to Prime Minister in Admin. Affairs 75-77; Homayoun Medal, Palme Académique (France); Imperial Award for best book of the year 58, 59.
Publs. *History of the Zand Dynasty in Iran, A Study of Iranian Handwritten Works in the 13th Hegyra Century, Cyrus the Great*; translations into Persian: *History of Herodotus, The Principles of Administrative Management.*
University of Teheran, Teheran, Iran.

Hedda, Ali; Tunisian diplomatist; b. 30 Oct. 1930, Sousse; ed. Inst. des Sciences Politiques, Paris.
Attaché, Washington, D.C. 56; Sec. Ministry of Foreign Affairs 57; with Secr. of State for Planning and Nat. Econ. 58-66; Minister, Rome 66; Amb. to Senegal 70-72, also accred. to Mali, Mauritania, Guinea, Liberia, Sierra Leone and The Gambia; Dir. Int. Co-operation, Ministry of Foreign Affairs 72; Dir. Cabinet of the Prime Minister 73; Amb. to U.S.A. Nov. 73-, concurrently to Mexico and Venezuela 74-; Grand Officer, Ordre de la République Tunisienne, Order of the Republic, Italy.
Tunisian Embassy, 2408 Massachusetts Avenue, N.W., Washington, D.C. 20008, U.S.A.

Hegazy, Abdel Aziz, D.PHIL.; Egyptian economist and politician; b. 3 Jan. 1923; ed. Fuad Univ., Cairo, Birmingham Univ., England.
Dean, Faculty of Commerce, Ain Shams Univ. 66-68; mem. Nat. Assembly 69-75; Minister of the Treasury 68-73; Deputy Prime Minister, Minister of Finance, Econ. and Foreign Trade 73-74; First Deputy Prime Minister April-Sept. 74, Prime Minister 74-75; now teaching and working as a management consultant and Certified Accountant in Cairo, Jeddah and Beirut.
Cairo, Egypt.

Hegelan, Sheikh Faisal Abdul Aziz al-; Saudi Arabian diplomatist; b. 7 Oct. 1929, Riyadh; ed. Faculty of Law, Fouad Univ., Cairo.
Ministry of Foreign Affairs 52-54; served Embassy in Washington, D.C. 54-58; Chief of Protocol in Ministry 58-60; Political Adviser to H.M. King Sa'ud 60-61; Amb. to Spain 61-68, to Venezuela and Argentina 68-75, to Denmark 75-76, to U.K. 76-79, to U.S.A. May 79-; Order of King Abdulaziz; Gran Cruz, Order of Isabela la Católica (Spain), Gran Cordon, Orden del Libertador (Venezuela); Grande Oficial, Orden Riobranco (Brazil).
Embassy of Saudi Arabia, 1520 18th Street, N.W., Washington, D.C. 20036, U.S.A.

Heikal, Mohammed Hasanein; Egyptian journalist; b. 1923.
Reporter Akher Saa Magazine 44; Editor *Al-Akhbar* 56-57; Editor-in-Chief *Al-Ahram* daily newspaper 57-74; ordered to resign Oct. 75; Editor and Chair. Establishment Board 60-74; mem. Central Cttee. Arab Socialist Union 68; Minister of Nat. Guidance 70.
Publs. *Nahnou wa America* 67, *Nasser: The Cairo Documents* 72, *The Road to Ramadan* 75, *Sphinx and Commissar* 79.
Cairo, Egypt.

Helaissi, Sheikh Abdulrahman al-; Saudi Arabian diplomatist; b. 24 July 1922; ed. Cairo Univ. and Univ. of London.
Official at Ministry of Foreign Affairs; Secretary Embassy London 47-54; Under-Sec. Ministry of Agriculture 54-57; Rep. to UN 47, and at conferences on Health, Agriculture, Wheat, Sugar and Locusts; Head of Del. to FAO 55-61; Amb. to Sudan 57-60; Del. to Conference of Non-Aligned Nations, Belgrade 61; Amb. to Italy 61-66, concurrently to Austria; Amb. to U.K. 66-76, also to Denmark 66-69.
Publ. *The Rehabilitation of the Bedouins* 59.
Ministry of Foreign Affairs, Jeddah, Saudi Arabia.

Hélou, Charles; Lebanese lawyer, journalist and politician; b. 1911; ed. St. Joseph (Jesuit) Univ. and Ecole Française de Droit, Beirut.
Barrister at Court of Appeal and Cassation Beirut 36; founded newspaper *L'Eclair du Nord* at Aleppo Syria 32; founded *Le Jour* Beirut 34; was Political Dir. of the latter until apptd. Lebanese Minister to the Vatican 47; fmr. Pres. Cercle de la Jeunesse Catholique Beirut; fmr. Sec.-Gen. Catholic Action of Lebanon; Minister of Justice and Health Sept. 54-May 55: Minister of Education Feb.-Sept. 64; President of Lebanon 64-70; Minister of State July-Aug. 79; Pres. Asscn. des Parlementaires de Langue Française 73-. Kaslik, Jounieh, Lebanon.

Herzog, Gen. Chaim, LL.B.; Israeli lawyer, military expert and diplomatist; b. 17 Sept. 1918, Belfast, N. Ireland; ed. Wesley Coll., Dublin, London and Cambridge Univs., Lincoln's Inn, London, Israeli Bar, Jerusalem.
Went to Palestine 35; served in British Army, World War II; rank of Maj.; Dir. Intelligence, Israeli Defence Forces 48-50; Defence Attaché, Washington, D.C., and Ottawa 50-54; Field Commands 54-59; Dir. Mil. Intelligence 59-62; Gen. 61; Man. G.U.S. Industries 62-72; Gov. West Bank of the Jordan 67; Senior Partner, Herzog, Fox and Neeman 72-; Perm. Rep. to UN 75-78; mem. Leadership Bureau, Israel Labour Party; prominent broadcaster; Hon. Doctorate (Yeshiva Univ., N.Y., Jewish Theological Seminay, N.Y., Bar Ilan Univ., Israel); Hon. K.B.E. 70.
Publs. *Israel's Finest Hour* (Hebrew and English) 67, *Days of Awe* (Hebrew) 73, *Judaism, Law and Ethics* 74, *The War of Atonement* 75, *Who Stands Accused?* 78, *Battles of the Bible* 78 and numerous articles in foreign journals.
25 Ibn Guirol Street, Tel-Aviv, Israel.

Hewedy, Amin; Egyptian diplomatist; b. 21 Sept. 1921; ed. Military and Staff Colls., Egypt, and General Staff Coll., Fort Leavenworth, U.S.A., and Press Coll., Egypt.
Former Army Officer; fmr. Political Counsellor to Pres. Abdel Gamal Nasser; fmr. Amb. to Morocco 62; Amb. to Iraq 63-65; Minister of State, then of Nat. Guidance, of War 65-70; Dir. of Gen. Intelligence 67-69.
Publs. *Speeches in Strategy* 55, *Sun-Tso* 57, *How do the Zionist Leaders Think?* 74, *Arab Security* 75, *The Israeli-Arab War 1967* 76.
Cairo, Egypt.

Hillel, Shlomo; Israeli politician; b. 23 April 1923, Baghdad, Iraq; ed. Herzliah School, Tel-Aviv, Hebrew Univ., Jerusalem.
Settled in Palestine 30s; mem. 2nd, 3rd Knessets (Parl.) 53-59; Amb. to Guinea 59-61, to Ivory Coast 61-63, concurrently to Dahomey (now Benin), Upper Volta and Niger; mem. Perm. Mission to UN 64-67; Asst. Dir.-Gen. Ministry of Foreign Affairs in charge of Middle East Affairs 67-69; Minister of Police 69-June 77; Co-ordinator of Political Contracts with the Arab leadership in the Administered Territories 70; mem. 9th Knesset; Minister for the Interior June-Oct. 74; Chair. Ministerial Cttee. for Social Welfare 74-77; Chair. Sephardi Fed. 76-; Commdr. Nat. Order of the Repubs. of the Ivory Coast, Upper Volta, Dahomey.
The Knesset, Jerusalem, Israel.

Hinai, Sheikh Farid Mbarak Ali al-; Omani diplomatist; b. 29 Aug. 1930, Ghaffat; ed. Victoria Coll., Egypt, Gray's Inn, London, Christ Church, Oxford, Kenya Inst. of Admin., Nairobi.

In Kenyan Admin. and Diplomatic Service 60-75; District Officer, Provincial Admin., Kenya 60-63; Chief of Protocol, Foreign Ministry 63-65; Counsellor at Kenyan Embassy in France 65-67, to Fed. Repub. of Germany 67-68; Amb. to Zaire 68-70, to Egypt 70-74; Dir. of Africa and Middle East Desk, Ministry of Foreign Affairs 74-75; retd. from Kenyan service 75; Minister Plenipotentiary, Ministry of Foreign Affairs of Sultanate of Oman 75-76; Amb. of Oman to Fed. Repub. of Germany 76-77, to the U.S.A. 77-; Order of Repub. of Egypt (1st class), Commdr. of Order of the Star of Honour (Ethiopia), Commdr. of Ordre Nat. du Léopard (Zaire), Officer of Nat. Order of Zaire.
Embassy of Oman, 2342 Massachusetts Avenue, N.W., Washington, D.C., U.S.A.

Hindawi, Thaugan el-, ED.M.; Jordanian politician; b. 18 Feb. 1927; ed. Arab Coll., Jerusalem, Univ. of Cairo, Univ. of Maryland, U.S.A.
Principal, Teachers' Training Coll., Bet Hannina, Jerusalem 56-60; Supervisor of Educ. 60-63; Cultural Attaché, Cairo 64; Under-Sec. Ministry of Information 64-65; Minister of Information 65, of Educ. 65-70; Amb. to Kuwait 71-73; Minister of State for Prime Minister's Affairs 73; Minister of Finance 73-74, of Educ. 74-76; Amb. to Egypt 77-79; many decorations from Jordan, Tunisia, France, Fed. Repub. of Germany and Malaysia.
Publ. *Palestinian Issue* (textbook).
c/o Ministry of Foreign Affairs, Amman, Jordan.

Horowitz, David; Israeli banker; b. Feb. 1899; ed. Vienna and Lwów.
Member Exec. Cttee. Gen. Fed. of Jewish Labour 23; journalist and writer; Econ. Adviser and Sec. American Econ. Cttee. for Palestine 32-35; Dir. Econ. Dept. of Jewish Agency for Palestine; mem. various Govt. Cttees. under Mandatory Regime, and dir. various enterprises 35-48; Lecturer, High School for Law and Econs., Tel-Aviv 46-50; Liaison Officer to UN Special Cttee. on Palestine 46; mem. Jewish Del. to Lake Success 47; Head of Israel Del. to Econ. Survey Comm. of UN 48; Head of Israel Del. Financial Talks on Sterling Releases between Israel and U.K., London 49, and in negotiations between Israel and U.K. on econ. and financial affairs in connection with termination of the Mandate; Dir.-Gen. Ministry of Finance 48-52; Gov. Designate, Bank of Israel 52-54, Gov. 54-71, Chair. Advisory Cttee. and Council 71-; Gov. for Israel, IBRD; Chair. Board of Dirs., the Eliezer Kaplan School of Econs. and Social Sciences, Hebrew Univ.; mem. State Council for Higher Educ., Board of Govs. Hebrew Univ., Exec. Council Weizmann Inst. of Science Board of Trustees of the Truman Center for the Advancement of Peace; Head, Israel Del. to UN Conf. on Trade and Devt., Geneva 64; Hon. Pres. Istituto per le Relazioni Internazionali (Rome); Dr. h.c. (Hebrew Univ. and Tel-Aviv Univ.); Israel Prize for Social Sciences 68.
Publs. *Aspects of Economic Policy in Palestine* 36, *Jewish Colonisation in Palestine* 37, *Economic Survey of Palestine* 38, *Jewry's Economic War Effort* 42, *Postwar Reconstruction* 42, *Palestine and the Middle East, An Essay in Regional Economy* 43, *Prediction and Reality in Palestine* 45, *State in the Making* 53, *Anatomie unserer Zeit* 64, *Hemispheres North and South* 66, *The Economics of Israel* 67, *The Abolition of Poverty* 69, *Anatomia de Nuestro Tiempo* 69, *The Enigma of Economic Growth—The Case Study of Israel* 72, and several publs. in Hebrew.
(*Died* 12 *August* 1979).

Hoss, Dr. Selim al-; Lebanese politician and professor of economics; b. 1930.
With Bank of Lebanon 66; Chair. Banking Control Comm. 67-73; Chair. Nat. Bank for Industrial and Tourist Devt. 73-76; Prime Minister Dec. 76-, also Minister of the Economy and Trade, and Minister of Information Dec. 76-July 79.
Office du président du Conseil des Ministres, Place de l'Etoile, Beirut, Lebanon.

Hoveyda, Fereydoun, LL.D.; Iranian diplomatist; b. 21 Sept. 1924, Damascus; ed. Univ. of Paris.
Various positions, Imperial Iranian Embassy, Paris 46-51; Programme Specialist, Mass Communications Dept., UNESCO 52-64; Under-Sec. of State for Int. and Econ. Affairs, Ministry of Foreign Affairs 65-71; Perm. Rep. to UN 71-79; del. to various int. confs. including UN Gen. Assembly 48, 51, 65, UNESCO Confs. 66, 68, 70 and ECOSOC sessions 66-69; Léopold Senghor Prize, French Language Cultural and Technical Soc. for novel *Les Neiges du Sinai* 73.
c/o Permanent Mission of Iran at United Nations, 622 Third Avenue, 34th Floor, New York, N.Y. 10016, U.S.A.

Howard, Harry Nicholas, A.B., M.A., PH.D.; American consultant on international affairs; b. 19 Feb. 1902; ed. Univs. of Missouri and California.
Gregory Fellow in History Univ. of Missouri 26-27; Research Asst. in Modern European History Univ. of California 28-29; Asst. Prof. History Univ. of Oklahoma 29-30; Associate Prof. History, Miami Univ. 30-37, Prof. 40-42; Lecturer Contemporary Problems, Univ. of Cincinnati 37-42; served Dept. of State as Head, East European Unit 42-44, mem. U.S. Del. UN Conf. on Int. Orgs. 45, Chief, Near East Branch Research Div. 45-47, Adviser Div. of Greek, Turkish and Iranian Affairs 47-49, UN Adviser, Dept. of State, Bureau of Near East, S. Asian and African Affairs 49-56; Acting U.S. Rep. Advisory Comm. UNRWA, Beirut 56-61; Special Asst. to Dir. of UNRWA 62-63; Adviser U.S. Del. UN Balkan Comm. 47-50; Prof. of Middle East Studies, School of Int. Service, American Univ., Washington, D.C. 63-68, Adjunct Prof. 68-; Chair. Middle East Program, Foreign Service Inst., Dept. of State 66, 71-72; Faculty Adviser FSI 66-67; Reserve Consultant, Dept. of State 67-; Assoc. Editor *Middle East Journal* 63-; mem. Board of Govs. Middle East Inst. 63-; Consultant, Middle East, Cincinatti Council on World Affairs 68-69; mem. Board of Dirs. ANERA 68-; Lecturer, Middle East, U.S. Army War Coll., Pa. 70-72; Visiting Prof. Missouri, Indiana, Calif. (Berkeley), Columbia and Colorado Univs.; Order of the Phoenix (Greece).
Publs. *The Partition of Turkey, A Diplomatic History 1913–1923* 31, *Military Government in the Panama Canal Zone* 31 (with Prof. R. Kerner), *The Balkan Conferences and the Balkan Entente* 30-35, *A Study in the Recent History of the Balkan and Near Eastern People* 36, *The Problem of the Turkish Straits* 47, *The United Nations and the Problem of Greece* 47, *The General Assembly and the Problem of Greece* 48, *Yugoslavia* (co-author) 49, *Soviet Power and Policy* (co-author) 55, *The King-Crane Commission* 63.
6508 Greentree Road, Bradley Hills Grove, Bethesda, Md. 20034, U.S.A.

Humaidan, Dr. Ali; United Arab Emirates diplomatist; b. 20 Sept. 1931, Bahrain; ed. Univs. of Baghdad and Paris.
Deputy Rep. of Kuwait to UNESCO 67-69; Prof. of Political Science, Univ. of Kuwait 69-70; Legal Adviser to the Abu Dhabi Govt. 71-72; Perm. Rep. of the United Arab Emirates to UN 72-.
Permanent Mission of the United Arab Emirates to the United Nations, 744 Third Avenue, 36 Floor, New York, N.Y. 10017, U.S.A.

Husain, Gen. Saddam, LL.B.; Iraqi politician; b. 1937, Tikrit; ed. Al-Karkh (Baghdad) and Al-Qasr al-Aini (Cairo) secondary schools, Cairo Univ. and al-Mustanseriya Univ. Baghdad.
Joined Arab Baath Socialist Party 57; sentenced to death for attempted execution of Gen. Kassem 59; in Egypt 62,

joined Baath Party, Cairo; returned to Iraq 63; mem. 4th Regional Congress and 6th Nat. Congress, Baath Party 63, mem. Regional Leadership 63, mem. 7th Nat. Congress, Syria 64; arrested for plotting overthrow of Pres. Aref Oct. 64; mem. Nat. Leadership, Baath Party 65, 66-, Deputy Sec. Regional Leadership 65-79, Sec. July 79-; played prominent role in Revolution of July 68; Vice-Pres. Revolutionary Command Council Nov. 69-July 79, Pres. July 79-; rank of Gen. Jan. 76; Order of Rafidain, 1st Class, Jan. 76.
Publ. *One Trench or Two.*
Revolutionary Command Council, Baghdad, Iraq.

Hussain, Abdul Aziz; Kuwaiti politician; b. 1921; ed. Teachers' Higher Inst., Cairo and Univ. of London.
Head, Kuwait Cultural Bureau, Cairo 45-50; Gen. Dir. of Education, Kuwait 52-61; Ambassador to Egypt 61-62; Minister of State for Cabinet Affairs 63-65, 71-.
Publ. *Arab Community in Kuwait* 60.
Ministry of State for Cabinet Affairs, Kuwait.

Hussein, Hamzah Abbas, B.A.(ECONS.); Kuwaiti central banker; b. 1 Oct. 1934, Kuwait; ed. American Univ. of Beirut.
Government official 59; Admin. Asst., Civil Service Comm. 59-60; attended several postgraduate courses on money and banking 60-62; Sec. and Currency Officer, Kuwait Currency Board 63-68; Deputy Gov. Cen. Bank of Kuwait 68-73, Gov. 73-; Chair. of Board, Banking Studies Centre of Kuwait 70-.
Central Bank of Kuwait, P.O. Box 526, Kuwait.

Hussein ibn Talal, King of Jordan; b. 14 Nov. 1935; ed. Victoria Coll., Alexandria, Egypt and Harrow School and Royal Mil. Acad. Sandhurst, England.
Succeeded his father August 11th, 1952; came to power May 2nd, 1953; married 55, Princess Dina, daughter of Abdel-Hamid Aoun of Saudi Arabia; daughter Princess Alia, b. 56 (marriage dissolved); married 61, Antoinette Gardiner (assumed name of Muna el Hussein); sons, Prince Abdullah, b. 62, Prince Feisal, b. 63; twin daughters, Princess Zein, Princess Aisha, b. 68 (marriage dissolved); married 72, Alia Toukan (died Feb. 77), daughter of Baha'uddin Toukan; daughter Princess Haya, b. 74; son Prince Ali, b. 75; married 78, Elizabeth Halaby; Order of Al-Nahda, of Al-Kawkab, of Al-Istiqlal; Istiqlal Medal, and many other decorations.
Publs. *Uneasy Lies the Head* 62, *My War with Israel* 67.
Royal Palace, Amman, Jordan.

I

Ibrahim, Abdel Aziz el Sayed, PH.D.; Egyptian educationist; b. 30 April 1907; ed. Teachers' Coll. and Higher Inst. of Educ., Cairo and Ohio State Univ., U.S.A.
Formerly Lecturer in Mathematics, Mil. Coll., Cairo; Prof. of Educ., Head of Dept., Ain Shams Univ.; Vice-Rector Cairo Univ., Rector Khartoum Branch, Cairo Univ.; Rector Alexandria Univ.; Minister of Higher Educ., later of Educ.; Visiting Prof. Columbia Univ., U.S.A.; Dir.-Gen. Arab Educational, Cultural and Scientific Org., Arab League until 75; mem. Arabic Language Acad. (Egypt), Scientific Acad. (Iraq); decorations from Egypt, Lebanon, Morocco, Tunisia, Jordan, German Democratic Repub.
Publs. *The Slide Rule for Military Cadets* 39, *The Preparation of Teachers in Arab States* 54, *The University and Culture* 60.
52 Merghani Street, Heliopolis, Cairo, Egypt.

Ibrahim, Major Abul Gasim Mohammed; Sudanese army officer and politician; b. 1937, Omdurman; ed. Khartoum Secondary School and Military Coll.
Commissioned 61; mem. Revolutionary Council 69; Minister of Local Govt. 69; Asst. Prime Minister for Services July 70; Minister of Interior Nov. 70; Minister of Health 71-74, and of Social Welfare 73-74, of Agriculture, Food and Natural Resources 74-76; Deputy Sec.-Gen. Sudanese Socialist Union (SSU), Sec.-Gen. Aug. 76-79; Commr. for Khartoum Province Aug. 76-79; First Vice-Pres. of Sudan Aug. 77-79.
Khartoum, Sudan.

Ibrahim, Wing Commdr. Hassan; Egyptian businessman and fmr. politician; b. 1971; ed. Egyptian Mil. Coll. and Egyptian Air Force Coll.
Served Egyptian Air Force 39-52; mem. Revolutionary Council 52-56; Minister for Presidency and for Production 54-56; Chair. Economic Development Organization 57-59; Pres. El Nasr Company (pencil and graphite production) 58-61, Paints and Chemicals Industries 59-61; mem. Presidential Council 62-64; Vice-Pres. of U.A.R. 64-65; business exec. 66-; Pres. Middle East Financing and Consultation Co., Egyptian Catering and Contracting Co., Egyptian Granite Co.; Nile Collar of Egypt; various orders and decorations from Syria, Yugoslavia, Cameroon, Niger, Yemen, Bulgaria, Poland, Lebanon, G.D.R., Morocco, Malaysia, Libya.
10 Abdel-Rahman Fahmy Street, Garden City, Cairo; Home: 6 Khartoum Street, Heliopolis, Cairo, Egypt.

Ibrahim, Izzat; Iraqi politician; b. 1942, al-Dour; ed. secondary schools.
Editor *Voice of the Peasant* 68, Head, Supreme Cttee. for People's Work 68-70; Minister of Agrarian Reform 70-74; Vice-Chair. Supreme Agric. Council 70-71, Chair. 71; Minister of Agriculture 73-74; Minister of Interior 74-79; mem. Revolution Command Council, Deputy Chair. July 79-; Asst. Sec. Regional Command of Arab Baath Socialist Party July 79-.
Revolution Command Council, Baghdad, Iraq.

Ibrahim, Sid Moulay Abdullah; Moroccan politician; b. 1918; ed. Ben Youssef Univ., Marrakesh and the Sorbonne, Paris.
Mem. Istiqlal (Independence) Party 44-59; mem. Editorial Cttee. *Al Alam* (Istiqlal organ) 50-52; imprisoned for political reasons 52-54; Sec. of State for Information and Tourism, First Moroccan Nat. Govt. 55-56; Minister of Labour and Social Affairs 56-57; Prime Minister and Minister of Foreign Affairs Dec. 58-May 60; leader Union National des Forces Populaires 59-72, suspended from party 72.
c/o Union National des Forces Populaires, B.P. 747, Casablanca, Morocco.

Idris I (Sayyid Muhammad Idris as-Sanusi); former King of Libya; b. 13 March 1890.
Son of Sayyid Muhammad al-Mahdi; succeeded his uncle, Sayyid Ahmed Sherif as-Sanusi, in charge of affairs of the Senusiya Order 16; became Amir of Cyrenaica; proclaimed King of Libya Dec. 2nd 50; ascended the throne 24 December 51; deposed by military coup Sept. 69; sentenced to death *in absentia* 71; granted Egyptian nationality April 74.

Imady, Dr. Mohammed; Syrian economist and planner; b. 1 Dec. 1930, Damascus; ed. Damascus Secondary School, Damascus Univ. and New York Univ.
Deputy Minister of Planning 68-72, Minister 72; Minister of Economy and Foreign Trade 72-79; Pres. Arab Econ. Soc. 74-75, Syrian Econ. Soc. 76, Arab Fund for Econ. and Social Devt. June 79-; chair. Board of Govs. IMF, IBRD 75-76; Gov. for Syria, IMF, Islamic Devt. Bank; Founders Day Award (New York Univ.).
Publ. *Economic Development and Planning* (textbook in Arabic for Damascus Univ.) 68, revised 69, 71.

Ministry of Economy and Foreign Trade, Damascus; Home: Tijara, Korneish Bazeih, The New Way, Damascus, Syria.

Inbal, Eliahu; British/Israeli conductor; b. 16 Feb. 1936, Jerusalem; ed. Acad. of Music, Jerusalem, Conservatoire Nat. Supérieur, Paris.
From 1963 guest conductor with numerous orchestras including Milan, Rome, Berlin, Munich, Hamburg, Stockholm, Copenhagen, Vienna, Budapest, Amsterdam, London, Paris, Tel-Aviv, New York, Chicago, Toronto and Tokyo; Chief Conductor, Radio Symphony Orchestra, Frankfurt 74-.
Hessischer Rundfunk, Bertramstrasse 8, 6000 Frankfurt, Federal Republic of Germany.

Ioannides, Georghios X.; Cypriot lawyer and politician; b. 1924, Ktima, Paphos; ed. Greek Gymnasium, Paphos.
Clerk, Civil Service 41-45; studied law, Middle Temple, London, and called to Bar 47; lawyer, Paphos 48-70; mem. House of Reps. (Patriotic Front Group) 60-70; Minister of Justice 70-72, of the Interior and Defence 72-74, of Justice and Health 76-78; Minister to the Presidency March 78-.
c/o The Presidency, Nicosia, Cyprus.

Irmak, Sadi; Turkish professor and politician; b. 15 May 1904, Seydişehir, Konya; ed. Konya, Univs. of Istanbul and Berlin.
Teacher, Gazi Educ. Inst.; Chief Medical Officer, Ankara; Lecturer in Physiology, Istanbul Univ. 32, Prof. 40; mem. Parl. for Konya 43-50; Minister of Labour 45-47; Faculty of Medicine, Munich Univ. 50-52; Senator 74-; Prime Minister Nov. 74-March 75; Pres. Istanbul Univ. Inst. of Research on Atatürk's Reforms; Republican People's Party.
Kazim Orbayc 14, Istanbul-Chichli, Turkey.

Iryani, Sheikh Qadi Abd al Rahman al-; Yemeni religious and political leader; b. 18 July 1917.
Member of Revolutionary Council 62-74; Minister of Justice 62-63; Vice-Pres. Exec. Council Oct. 63-Feb. 64; mem. Political Bureau 64-74; mem. Presidency Council 65-74, Chair. 69-74 (deposed by mil. coup); Chair. Peace Cttee. set up after Khamer Peace Talks May 65; leader of Zaidi (Shi'a) sect.
Sana'a, Yemen Arab Republic.

Isa bin Sulman al-Khalifa (*see* Khalifa, Sheikh Isa bin Sulman al-).

Işik, Hasan Esat; Turkish diplomatist and politician; b. 1916, Istanbul; ed. Lycée of Galatasaray, Faculty of Law, Univ. of Ankara.
Ministry of Foreign Affairs 40-; Consulate-Gen., Paris 45-49; Head of Section, Dept. of Commerce and Econ. Affairs, and Dept. of Int. Econ. Relations 49-52; mem. del. to UN Office, Geneva 52-54; Dir.-Gen. of Dept. of Commerce and Commercial Agreements, Ministry of Foreign Affairs 54-57; Asst. for Econ. Affairs to Sec.-Gen. of Ministry of Foreign Affairs, Sec.-Gen. Econ. Co-operation Int. Org. 57-62; Amb. to Belgium, led negotiations for Asscn. with EEC 62-64, to U.S.S.R. 64-65, 66-68; Minister of Foreign Affairs 65; Amb. to France 68-73; mem. Nat. Assembly 73; Minister of Defence 74, June-July 77, 78-79; Republican People's Party (RPP).
c/o Ministry of National Defence, Milli Savunma Bakanliği, Bakanlıklar, Ankara, Turkey.

Ismail, Abdul Fattah; Yemeni politician; b. 28 July 1939; ed. Tawani Nat. School, Aden Tech. School in Little Aden.
Engaged on technical staff of British Petroleum Co. 57; joined Nat. Liberation Front (NLF) 59; in charge of NLF mil. and political activities in Aden 64; mem. NLF Exec. Cttee. 65; Minister of Culture and Nat. Guidance and of Yemen Unity Affairs 67; Sec.-Gen. Nat. Front 69-75, United Political Org.-the Nat. Front (UPONF) 75-78; mem. Presidential Council 69-; Chair. (provisional) Supreme People's Council 71; Pres., Chair. Revolutionary Council Dec. 78-; Chair. Presidium, Supreme People's Council Dec. 78-; Sec.-Gen. Yemen Socialist Party Oct. 78-; Chair. Yemeni Council for Peace and Solidarity in the People's Democratic Repub. of Yemen; mem. Presidium of Afro-Asian People's Solidarity Org. (AAPSO) and of World Peace Council; Dr. h.c. (Moscow Univ.) Aug. 76.
Presidential Council, Aden, People's Democratic Republic of Yemen.

Ismail, Abdul Malek; Yemeni diplomatist; b. 26 Nov. 1937, Aden; ed. Tawahi and Crater, Aden, Tech. School, Maalla, Khediwi High School, Cairo and Cairo Univ. Faculty of Commerce.
Member, United Nat. Front; Editor *A-Nour* and *Hakikah* (newspapers) 61-63; Vice-Chair. Gen. Union of Petroleum Workers 61-62, Chair. Petroleum Workers Union 62-64; Vice-Pres. Arab Fed. of Petroleum Workers 62-65; leading mem. Arab Nationalist Movement 56-63; leading mem. Nat. Liberation Front for Southern Yemen (NLF) 63-65; Dir. Nat. Front Office, Cairo 65-66; mem. Gen. Command of Nat. Liberation Front 66-68; Minister of Labour and Social Affairs 67-68; Minister of Econs., Commerce and Planning 68-70; Perm. Rep. to UN 70-73.
Aden, People's Democratic Republic of Yemen.

Ismail, Ahmed Sultan, B.SC.; Egyptian engineer and politician; b. 14 April 1923, Port Said; ed. Cairo Univ.
Worked as shift engineer, maintenance engineer at various power stations 45-64; mem. Exec. Board Electrical Projects Corpn. 64-; Nat. Defence Coll. 67; Gov. Menufia Prov. 68-71; Minister of Power 71-76; Deputy Premier for Production and Minister for Electric Power and Energy 76-78; Order of Repub., First Class.
43 Ahmed Abdel Aziz Street, Dokki, Cairo, Egypt.

Issawi, Charles Philip, M.A.; American economist; b. 1916; ed. Victoria Coll. Alexandria and Magdalen Coll. Oxford.
Sec. to Under-Sec. of State, Ministry of Finance, Cairo 37-38; Head of Research Section, Nat. Bank of Egypt, Cairo 38-43; Adjunct Prof. American Univ. of Beirut 43-47; UN Secretariat Economic Affairs Officer 48-55; Visiting Lecturer, Harvard Univ. 50, Johns Hopkins 67, Princeton Univ. 74; Prof. Columbia Univ. 51-75, Princeton Univ. 75-; Pres. Middle East Studies Asscn. of N. America 73-.
Publs. *Egypt: an Economic and Social Analysis* 47, *An Arab Philosophy of History* 50, *Egypt at Mid-Century* 54, *Mushkilat Qaumia* 59, *The Economics of Middle East Oil* (co-author) 62, *Egypt in Revolution* 63, *The Economic History of the Middle East 1800–1914* 66, *The Economic History of Iran 1800-1914* 71, *Oil, the Middle East and the World* 72, *Issawi's Laws of Social Motion* 73.
Princeton University, Princeton, N.J. 08540, U.S.A.

Izzidin, Ibrahim, B.A.; Jordanian diplomatist; b. 3 Dec. 1934; Beirut, Lebanon; ed. American Univ. of Beirut.
Served in Ministry of Communications, Prime Minister's Office, and Press Section of Ministry of Foreign Affairs 55-58; Deputy Dir. Book Publishers, Beirut 58-65; Dir. of Foreign Press, Ministry of Information 65-68, Under-Sec. 71-75; Private Sec. to H.R.H. King Hussein (*q.v.*) 68-70; Dir. Public Relations for Alia (Royal Jordanian Airlines) 70-71; Amb. to Switzerland 75-77, to Fed. Repub. of Germany 77-78, to U.K. 78-; Order of Istiqlal, Second Class, Cedar of Lebanon.
Embassy of the Hashemite Kingdom of Jordan, 6 Upper Phillimore Gardens, London, W8 7HB, England.

J

Jaber al-Ahmed al-Jaber al-Sabah (*see* Sabah, Jaber al-Ahmed al-Jaber al-).

Jaber al-Ali al-Salem al-Sabah (*see* Sabah, Jaber al-Ali al-Salem al-).

Jabre, Jamil Louis; Lebanese writer; b. 1924; ed. Univ. Saint-Joseph, Beirut.
Director of *Al-Hikmal* Revue; Cultural Counsellor for dailies *Al Jaryda* and *L'Orient* and United Unions for Employees and Workers; Founder-mem. Lebanese P.E.N. Club, Amis du Livre, Club du Roman, Club de la Jeunesse Vivante.
Publs. include: *Fever, After the Storm, Agony* (3 vols.), *May Ziadé, Amine Rihani, Gébrane Khalil Gébrane, Tagore, May: Authoress, Jahiz and the Society of His Times, Views on Contemporary American Literature* (essays), *Dream of Nemrod.*
Secteur Chalhoub, Immeuble Nassim Audi, Zalka, Beirut, Lebanon.

Jaffar, Khalid Mohammed; Kuwaiti diplomatist; b. 12 June 1922; ed. Mubarakia School, Kuwait.
Teacher, Kuwait 40-42; Chief Cashier, Kuwait Municipality 43-45; Kuwait Oil Co., rose to Supt. of Public Relations 45-61; Lord Chamberlain to His Highness The Amir of Kuwait 61-62; Ambassador, Foreign Affairs, Kuwait May-Dec. 62, concurrently Head of Press and Culture Div., Ministry of Foreign Affairs; mem. Delegation to UN before admission of Kuwait as a mem. 62; deputized for Under-Sec. of State at the Ministry of Foreign Affairs 62-63; Amb. to U.K. 63-65, to France 65-67, concurrently to Lebanon 65-70, to Turkey 68-73, concurrently to Bulgaria, Greece 71-73; Amb. to U.S.A. July 75-.
Kuwaiti Embassy, 2940 Tilden Street, Washington, D.C. 20008, U.S.A.

Jaghman, Yahya Hamoud; (*see* Geghman, Yahya Hamoud).

Jahanshahi, Abdol Ali, PH.D.; Iranian economist; b. 1924; ed. Univ. de Paris.
Ministry of Justice 46-57; Univ. of Teheran 57; Bank Melli Iran 57-60; Vice-Gov. Bank Markazi Iran 62-63; Minister of Educ. 64; Minister of State 64-65; Chancellor, Nat. Univ. of Iran 65-66; Alt. Exec. Dir. IBRD 66-71; Gov. Bank Markazi Iran (Central Bank of Iran) 71-73; Amb. Extraordinary, Head of Mission to European Communities 74-79.
Avenue Louise 166, 1050 Brussels, Belgium.

Jaidah, Ali Mohammed, M.SC.; Qatari international official; b. 1941, Doha; ed. London Univ.
Head of Econs. Div. in Dept. of Petroleum Affairs, Ministry of Finance and Petroleum 66-71, Dir. of Petroleum Affairs in Dept. of Petroleum Affairs 71-76; mem. Exec. Office of OAPEC; Gov. for OPEC of Qatar until Dec. 76; Sec.-Gen. OPEC 77-79; mem. Board of Dirs., Qatar Gen. Petroleum Corpn.; Head of dels. to OPEC, OAPEC and other petroleum confs.
c/o Ministry of Finance and Petroleum, P.O. Box 36, Doha, Qatar.

Jalal, Mahsoun, PH.D.ECON.; Saudi Arabian international official; b. 26 June 1936; ed. Cairo Univ., Rutgers Univ., U.S.A., Univ. of California, U.S.A.
Professor, Chair. Dept. of Econs., Riyadh Univ. 67-75; Consultant to various Govt. agencies 67-75; formed the Consulting Centre (Man. Consultancy firm); Vice-Chair., Man. Dir. Saudi Fund for Devt. 75-; mem. Civil Service Council 75-; Dir. Saudi Int. Bank 75-; Dir. Saudi Basic Industries Corpn.; Chair. Saudi Investment Banking Corpn.; Gov. OPEC Special Fund; Trustee Arab League Org. for Educ., Culture and Science; Exec. Dir. IMF 78-; Golden Star (First Class) (Taiwan) 78, Tanda Mahputera (Indonesia) 78.
Publs. *Principles of Economics,* other books and articles on econ. devt. and econ. theory.
International Monetary Fund, 700 19th Street, N.W., Washington, D.C. 20431; 1432 Lady Bird Drive, McLean, Va. 22101, U.S.A. (Home).

Jalloud, Major Abdul Salam Ahmed; Libyan politician; b. 15 Dec. 1944; ed. Secondary School, Sebha, Mil. Acad., Benghazi.
Member Revolutionary Command Council 69-77; Minister of Industry and the Econ., Acting Minister of the Treasury until 72; Prime Minister 72-77; mem. Gen. Secretariat of Gen. People's Congress 77-79.
c/o General Secretariat of the General People's Congress, Tripoli, Libya.

Jamal, Jasim Yousif; Qatar diplomatist; b. 17 Sept. 1940; ed. Northeast Mo. State Univ., Kirksville, Mo., U.S.A. and Univ. of New York.
Ministry of Educ., Dir. Admin. Affairs 58-63, Cultural Adviser, U.S.A. 63-68; Dir. of Cultural Affairs 68-72; Perm. Rep. to UN 72-; non-resident Amb. to Canada, Brazil and Argentina.
Permanent Mission of Qatar to the United Nations, 747 Third Avenue, 22nd Floor, New York, N.Y. 10017, U.S.A.

Jamali, Asim al-; Omani politician; b. 15 Jan. 1935, Muscat; ed. Univ. of Karachi Medical Coll., Univ. of London.
Medical Officer of Health, Dubai 60-63; at London School of Hygiene and Tropical Medicine 64-65; Health Adviser to Trucial States Council, Dubai 65-70; Minister of Health, Oman 70-74, Minister without Portfolio and Special Rep. of the Sultan 74-76; Minister of Land Affairs and Municipalities 76-79, of Environment May 79-; Renaissance Medal 74, Medal of the First Order.
Ministy of the Environment, Muscat, Oman.

Jamjoom, Ahmed Salah, B.COM.; Saudi Arabian businessman and politician; b. 1925, Jeddah; ed. Fouad Univ. Cairo and Harvard Law School.
Joined Arab Bank, Jeddah 50; Minister of State and mem. Council of Ministers 58-59; Supervisor of Economic Dept. 59-60; Minister of Commerce 60; Minister of Trade and Industry 61-62; Dir. and Partner, Mohd. Nour Salah Jamjoom & Bros. 62-; Dir. Jamjoom Vehicles and Equipment and Jamjoom Construction; Gen. Man. Madina Press. Org.
Publs. *An Approach to an Integrated Economic Development* 60, *Economics of Mecca* 67.
Mohamed Nour Salah Jamjoom and Brothers, Riyadh, and P.O. Box 1247, Jeddah, Saudi Arabia.

Jaroudi, Saeb, M.A.; Lebanese international official; b. 25 Nov. 1929, Beirut; ed. Int. Coll. Beirut, Univ. of California at Berkeley, Columbia Univ.
Instructor in Econs. and Research Economist, American Univ. of Beirut 53-56; Econ. Officer, UN Secretariat, New York 56-65, detailed from UN as Econ. Adviser to Govt. of Kuwait 62-64; Chief Economist, Kuwait Fund for Econ. and Social Devt. 66-69; Minister for Nat. Econ., Lebanon 70-72; Pres. Arab Fund for Econ. and Social Devt. 72-79.
c/o Arab Fund for Economic and Social Development, P.O. Box 21923, Kuwait.

Jarring, Gunnar, PH.D.; Swedish diplomatist; b. 12 Oct. 1907; ed. Lund Univ.
Associate Prof. Turkic Languages Lund Univ. 33-40; Attaché Ankara 40-41; Chief Section B Teheran 41; Chargé d'Affaires a.i. Teheran and Baghdad 45, Addis Ababa 46-48; Minister to India 48-51, concurrently to Ceylon 50-51, to Persia, Iraq and Pakistan 51-52; Dir. Political Div. Ministry of Foreign Affairs 53-56; Perm. Rep. to UN 56-58; rep. on Security Council 57-58; Amb. to U.S.A. 58-64, to U.S.S.R. 64-73, and to Mongolia 65-73; Special Rep. of Sec.-Gen. of UN on Middle East situation Nov. 67-; Grand Cross, Order of the North Star.

Publs. *Studien zu einer osttürkischen Lautlehre* 33, *The Contest of the Fruits—An Eastern Turki Allegory* 36, *The Uzbek Dialect of Qilich, Russian Turkestan* 37, *Uzbek Texts from Afghan Turkestan* 38, *The Distribution of Turk Tribes in Afghanistan* 39, *Materials for the Knowledge of Eastern Turkestan* (Vols. I-IV) 47-51, *An Eastern Turki-English Dialect Dictionary* 64.
Karlavägen 85, S-114 59 Stockholm, Sweden.

Jezrawi, Taha al-; Iraqi politician; b. 1938, Mosul; ed. schools in Mosul and Military Coll.
Former army officer; mem. Regional Leadership, Arab Baath Socialist Party; Head, Arab Affairs Office 68; mem. Revolutionary Command Council Nov. 69; Minister of Industry and Minerals March 70-76; Acting Minister of Planning 75-76; Minister of Public Works and Housing 76-77; Head of Trade Council 72; C.-in-C. People's Army 74.
Publs. *Industrialization in Developing Countries, Industrial Administration and Requirements of Economic Growth.*
c/o Ministry of Public Works and Housing, Baghdad Karkh, Salhiya, Iraq.

Jordan, King of (*see* Hussein ibn Talal).

Joukhdar, Mohammed Saleh, B.A., M.A.; Saudi Arabian economist and politician; b. 1932; ed. Univs. of California and Southern California.
Economic Consultant to Directorate-Gen. of Petroleum and Minerals, Saudi Arabia 58; Govt. Rep. Supervisory Cttee. for Expenditure and Purchasing, Arabian Oil Co. 61, Dir. 61-66; Sec.-Gen. Org. of Petroleum Exporting Countries (OPEC) 67-68; Deputy Minister of Petroleum and Mineral Resources 69; Deputy Gov. for Oil Affairs, PETROMIN 70-73; Amb. in Charge of Petroleum and Econ. Desk, Ministry of Foreign Affairs 73-74; on leave of absence as petroleum consultant 74-; mem. American Soc. of Economists.
Ministry of Petroleum and Mineral Resources, P.O. Box 247, Riyadh, Saudi Arabia.

Juffali, Ahmed; Saudi Arabian businessman; b. 15 Oct. 1924; ed. Saudi Arabia and United Kingdom.
Managing Dir., E. A. Juffali & Bros. 45-; mem. Board of Dirs. Saudi Electric Co. 52-; Man. Dir. Saudi Cement Co. 58, Medina Electric Co. 58-; Hon. Danish Consul-Gen. 59-; Chair. Nat. Insurance Co. of Saudi Arabia 74, Petroserv 75, Nat. Automobile Industry Co. Ltd. 75, Arabian Metal Industries Ltd. 75, Flour Arabia Ltd. 76, Juffali-Sulzer Saudi Arabia Ltd. 76, Arabia Electric Ltd. 76, Marco 76, Saudi Building Systems Ltd. 76, Pool Arabia Ltd. 76, Beck Arabia 76.
E. A. Juffali & Bros., King Abdul Aziz Street, P.O. Box 1049, Jeddah, Saudi Arabia.

Juma, Midhet (brother of Saad Juma, *q.v.*); Jordanian diplomatist; b. 19 Aug. 1920; ed. Cairo Univ.
Attaché to Arab League, Cairo 45-47; First Sec. and Counsellor, Cairo 47-52; Counsellor and Chargé d'Affaires, London 52-53; Minister to Pakistan 53-55; Chief of Protocol, Royal Palace Amman 56; Under-Sec. for Press and Broadcasting 56-58; Ambassador to the U.S.A. 58-59, to Morocco 59-62, to Federal Repub. of Germany 62-65, to Lebanon 65-67, to U.K. 67-69, to Tunisia 69-70, to Spain 71-74; numerous decorations.
c/o Ministry of Foreign Affairs, Amman, Jordan.

Juma, Saad (brother of Midhet Juma, *q.v.*); Jordanian diplomatist and politician; b. 1916; ed. Syrian Univ., Damascus.
Civil Service for twenty-six years; Dir. Press and Publicity; Chief Censor; Sec. to Prime Minister; Perm. Under-Sec., Gov. of Amman; Under-Sec. for Foreign Affairs; Ambassador to Syrian Arab Republic 62, to U.S.A. 62-65; Minister of the Royal Court 65-67; Prime Minister and Minister of Nat. Defence April-Oct. 67; mem. Consultative Council 67; Amb. to U.K. 69-70; fmr. Personal Rep. to H.M. King Hussein; mem. Senate; honours from Jordan, Iran, Syria, Italy and China (Taiwan).
Publs. *Conspiracy and the Battle of Destiny, Hostile Society.*
(Died August 1979).

K

Kaddafi, Col. Muammar al- (*see* Gaddafi).

Kaddori, Fakhri Yasin, DR.RER.POL.; Iraqi economist; b. 28 Aug. 1932; ed. Adhamiya Intermediate School and Central Secondary School, Baghdad, Coll. of Commerce and Econs. (Univ. of Baghdad), State Univ. of Iowa, Cologne Univ., Int. Marketing Inst. (Harvard Univ.).
Director of Internal Trade, Ministry of the Economy 64-68; Minister of the Economy 68-71, mem. Planning Board 68-; mem. Bureau of Econ. Affairs, Revolutionary Command Council 71-73, Chair. 73-76, Acting Chair. 76-; Gov. Central Bank of Iraq 76-78; Sec.-Gen. Arab Econ. Unity Council, Cairo May 78-; Pres. Exec. Cttee. for Professional and Popular Orgs. in Iraq 75-77; Chair. Iraqi Economist Asscn. 72-74, 77-.
Arab Economic Unity Council, Cairo; Home: 20 Aisha El-Taymouria Street, Garden City, Cairo, Egypt.

Kahale, Noureddin, B.S., M.S.; Syrian engineer; b. 1911, ed. Robert Coll., Istanbul, and Purdue and Illinois Univs., U.S.A.
With Ministry of Public Works and Communications 41-51, Head Irrigation Section 41-43, Acting Dir. of Irrigation 43-46, Dir.-Gen. 47, Sec.-Gen. 48-51; Chair. Board and Dir. Latakia Port Co. 51-58; Minister of Public Works, Syrian Region, United Arab Republic 58-60, concurrently Pres. Syrian Exec. Council, Acting Minister of Planning, and Minister of State, Central Govt.; Vice-President U.A.R. and Minister of Planning, Central Govt. 60-61; Vice-President U.A.R. in charge of Production Sector 61; Chair. and Dir.-Gen. Euphrates Project Authority 61-; Sec. Asscn. of Syrian Engineers 43-49; Pres. Damascus Asscn. of Chartered Engineers 61-62; Pres. Supreme Council of Engineering Asscns. of U.A.R. 61; Syrian Rep. to various Int. Confs.; decorations from Govts. of Syria, Khmer Repub., Denmark, Ethiopia, Greece, Morocco, Spain, Sudan and Yugoslavia.
Principal works: design and execution, Hama Irrigation Scheme 45-46; planning and execution, Latakia Harbour 51-58; planning Tartousse Harbour 58-60, Euphrates Dam, Power Plant and Irrigation Project, Habur Dam and Irrigation Project 62-.
Publs. *The Solution of the Water Supply Shortage in Aleppo* 47, *The Latakia Harbour Project* 55 (Papers presented to Pan-Arab Engineers Confs.).
West Adnan Malki, Mohammed Kurd-Ali Street, Damascus, Syria.

Kaissi, Fawzi al-, PH.D.; Iraqi financial and government official; b. 1929, Baghdad; ed. Univ. of Baghdad and Univ. of Southern Calif., U.S.A.
Professor, Univ. of Baghdad; Man. of Nationalized Banks 64, then a Man. of Rafidain Bank until 70; Man. Union de Banques Arabes et Françaises (UBAF), Paris 70-73; Gov. Central Bank of Iraq 73; mem. Cttee. of Twenty Interim Cttee. on Int. Monetary Reform 73-; Gen. Sec. of Arab Economists' Fed. 74; Minister of Finance Dec. 75-July 79.
c/o Ministry of Finance, Baghdad, Jamhouriay Street, Al-Amin Square, Iraq.

Kaissouni, Abdel Moneim, B.COM., B.SC., PH.D.; Egyptian financial administrator and politician; b. 1916; ed. Univ. of Cairo and London School of Economics.
With Barclays Bank, England 42-43; Lecturer and Asst. Prof. of Econs., Univ. of Cairo 44-46; Dir. Middle East Dept. Int. Monetary Fund, Washington, and later Chief

Technical Rep. in Middle East 46-50; with Nat. Bank of Egypt 50-54; Minister of Finance, Econ. and Dep. Prime Minister 54-66, 68; Chair. Arab Int. Bank 71-76, 78-; Deputy Prime Minister for Econ. and Financial Affairs Nov. 76-May 78, also Minister of Planning Oct. 77-May 78; Chair. European Arab Holding, Luxembourg 72; mem. Higher Econ. Council, Egypt 74; Chair. IMF and IBRD annual meetings 55; Pres. Cairo Conf. on Devt. 62; Pres. UN Conf. on Trade and Devt. 64; Grand Cordon of the Repub. (Egypt).
35 Abdel Khalek Sarwat Street, Cairo, Egypt.

Kalali, Manouchehr, D.ECON.; Iranian politician; b. 1925; ed. Teheran Univ. and Paris, France.
Joined Ministry of Labour and Social Services, later Perm. Under-Sec.; mem. Parl. for Mashad 65-79; founder mem. "Kanoon Motara Ghi" (later Iran Novin Party), Sec.; mem. Exec. Board, Iran Novin Party; Asst. to Sec.-Gen. Iran Novin Party, Deputy Sec.-Gen., Sec.-Gen. 69-74; Minister of State 71; Minister without Portfolio 74-75.
Teheran, Iran.

Kamel, Hassan, LL.D.; Egyptian diplomatist and administrator; b. 6 Sept. 1907; ed. Univs. of Montpellier, Cairo and Paris.
Member Mixed Bar 30-36; Lecturer, Admin. Law, High Coll. of Police and Admin. 36-37; Ministry of Foreign Affairs 37, served in several countries including France, Italy, Iran, Syria, Portugal, Switzerland, Libya, Argentina, Turkey and Hungary until 59; Legal Adviser, Govt. of Qatar 60, Dir.-Gen. 61-67, Adviser to the Govt. 67-71; Perm. Rep. of Qatar to UN 71-72; Adviser to H.H. the Amir 73-; Adviser of several dels. to UN and Rep. on numerous Int. Confs.; mem. several Law Asscns.; mem. Board of Dirs. Shell (Qatar) Ltd., Qatar Petroleum Co. Ltd.; Grand Officer, Order of the Repub. (Egypt); Grand Officier, Légion d'Honneur (France); similar decorations from Iran, Jordan, Morocco, Saudi Arabia, Syria, Tunisia.
Publs. numerous legal articles.
P.O. Box 636, Doha, Qatar.

Kamel, Muhammad Ibrahim; Egyptian diplomatist and politician; b. 1923; graduated in law.
Second Sec., London 50, served successively in Mexico, Kinshasa, Bonn and Montreal; Amb. to Fed. Rep. of Germany 73-77; Minister of Foreign Affairs 77-78; Amb. Extraordinary, Ministry of Foreign Affairs Nov. 78-.
c/o Ministry of Foreign Affairs, Cairo, Egypt.

Karageorghis, Vassos, PH.D., F.S.A., F.R.S.A.; Cypriot archaeologist; b. 29 April 1929, Trikomo; ed. Pancyprian Gymnasium, Nicosia, Univ. Coll., and Inst. of Archaeology, London Univ.
Assistant Curator, Cyprus Museum 52-60, Curator 60-63, Acting Dir., Dept. of Antiquities, Cyprus 63-64, Dir. 64-; mem. Gov. Body, Cyprus Research Centre; Fellow, Soc. of Antiquaries, London, Univ. Coll. London; Corresp. Fellow, British Acad.; Corresp. mem. Archaeological Soc., Athens, Acad. of Athens, Austrian Acad. of Sciences; mem. German Archaeological Inst., Berlin, Royal Soc. for Humanistic Studies, Lund, Royal Swedish Acad.; Dr. h.c. (Univs. of Lyon, Göteborg, Athens, Birmingham); Commonwealth Prize 78; Chevalier de l'Ordre de la Légion d'Honneur.
Publs. *Treasures in the Cyprus Museum* 62, *Nouveaux Documents pour l'Etude du Bronze Récent à Chypre* 64, *Corpus Vasorum Antiquorum I* 63, and *II* 65, *Sculptures from Salamis I* 64, *II* 66, *Excavations in the Necropolis of Salamis I* 67, *II* 70, *III* 73, *IV* 78, *Cyprus* (Archaelogia Mundi) 68, *Salamis-New Aspects of Antiquity* 69, *Altagais und Altkypros* (with H.-G. Buchholz) 71, and *Cypriot Antiquities in the Pierides Collection, Larnaca* 73, *Excavations at Kiton I: The Tombs* 74, *The Civilization of Prehistoric Cyprus* 75, *Alaas, a Protogeometric Necropolis in Cyprus* 75, *La Céramique Chypriote de Style figuré* (with J. des Gagniers) 76, *Vases et Figurines de l'Age du Bronze à Chypre* (with J. des Gagniers) 76, *Kition, Mycenaean and Phoenician discoveries in Cyprus* 76, *Hala Sultan Tekké I, Excavations 1897-1971* (with P. Åström and D. M. Bailey) 76, *Fouilles de Kition II, Objets Egyptiens et Egyptisants* (with G. Clerc, E. Lagarce and J. Leclant) 76, *Fouilles de Kition III, Inscriptions Phéniciennes* (with M.-G. Guzzo Amadasi), *Cypriot Antiquities in the Medelhausmuseet*, Stockholm (with C.-G. Styrenius and M.-G. Winbladh) 77, *Memoirs* vol. II 77, *Two Cypriot Sanctuaries of the end of the Cypro-Archaic period* 77, *The goddess with uplifted arms in Cyprus* 77 and articles in German, American, English and French journals.
Cyprus Museum, P.O. Box 2024, Nicosia; Home: 12 Kastorias Street, Nicosia, Cyprus.

Karami, Rashid Abdul Hamid; Lebanese politician; b. 1921; ed. Fuad I Univ., Cairo.
Minister of Nat. Economy and Social Affairs 54-55; Prime Minister and Minister of the Interior Sept. 55-March 56; Prime Minister Sept. 58-May 60; Minister of Finance, Economy, Defence and Information Oct. 58-Oct. 59, of Finance and Defence Oct. 59-May 60; Prime Minister and Minister of Finance Oct. 61-April 64; Prime Minister 65-66, 66-67, 67-68, 69-70, May 75-Dec. 76; Minister of Defence May 75-Sept. 76, of Finance and Information May 75-Dec. 76; mem. Nat. Dialogue Cttee. Sept. 75; Leader Parliamentary Democratic Front.
Rue Karm Ellé, Beirut, Lebanon.

Karim-Lamrani, Mohammed; Moroccan businessman and politician; b. 1 May 1919, Fez.
Economic adviser to H.M. the King of Morocco; Gen. Dir. Office Chérifien des Phosphates 67-; Chair. Crédit du Maroc; Minister of Finance April-Aug. 71; Prime Minister 71-72.
Office Chérifien des Phosphates, Route d'El Jadida, Casablanca, Morocco.

Kassab, Adnan Ali; Iraqi civil servant; b. 1934; ed. Higher Inst. of Industrial Engineering.
Resident Engineer to Army Canal Project 61-63; Dir. of Admin. in Industrial Govt. Projects 63-64; later arrested and imprisoned; Dir.-Gen. of Iraqi Ports Admin. 68-71; Pres. Nat. Oil Co. 71-72; Pres. State Construction Contracting Co. Sept. 72-.
State Construction Contracting Co., Insurance Building, Rashid Street, Baghdad, Iraq.

Katzir, Ephraim, M.SC., PH.D.; Israeli scientist, teacher and administrator; b. (as Ephraim Katchalski) 16 May 1916, Kiev, Russia; ed. Hebrew Univ., Jerusalem.
Head of Dept. of Biophysics, Weizmann Inst. of Science 51-73, Prof. 78-; Chief Scientist, Ministry of Defence 66-68; Pres. of Israel 73-78; Prof. Tel-Aviv Univ. 78-; Ephraim Katzir Chair of Biophysics, Bar Ilan Univ. 76; Visiting Prof., Hebrew Univ. 53-61; Guest Scientist, Harvard Univ. 57-59; Senior Foreign Scientist Fellowship, Univ. of California, Los Angeles 64; Chair. Weizmann Inst. Cttee. for Katzir Centre; mem. Board of Govs., Hebrew Univ.; mem. Israel Acad. of Sciences and Humanities, Biochemical Soc. of Israel, Israel Chemical Soc., Nat. Acad. of Sciences, U.S.A., American Acad. of Arts and Sciences (Foreign Hon. mem.), Leopoldina Acad. of Science, German Democratic Repub., American Soc. of Biological Chemists (Hon.), Ciba Foundation, Int. Union of Biochemistry and many other orgs.; Foreign mem. Royal Society, London; mem. Editorial Board, *Biopolymers, Progress in Surface and Membrane Science, T.I.T. Journal of Life Sciences*, series on *Applied Biochemistry and Bioengineering* and *Advances in Experimental Medicine and Biology;* Hon. Ph.D. (Brandeis, Michigan, Hebrew, Harvard and Northwestern Univs., Polytechnic Inst. of New York, Hebrew Union Coll., Jerusalem, Weizmann Inst. of Sciences); Tchernikhovsky Prize 48, Weizmann

Prize 50, Israel Prize Natural Sciences 59, Rothschild Prize Natural Sciences 61; Linderstram-Lang Gold Medal 69, Hans Krebs Medal 72.
Publs. numerous papers and articles on polyamino acids as protein models, polymers as chemical reagents, immobilized enzymes and the structure and function of living cells.
Weizmann Institute of Science, P.O.B. 26, Rehovot, Israel.

Kayla, Ziya; Turkish economist; b. 28 Dec. 1912; ed. School of Political Sciences, Istanbul.
Ministry of Finance 34-63, Asst. Inspector, Inspector and Chief Inspector of Finance 34-60; Deputy Minister of Finance 60-63; Chair. Board of Dirs. and Dir.-Gen. Central Bank of Turkey 63-66; Alternate Gov. IBRD 61-66; Pres. Banks' Asscn. of Turkey 63-66; Sec.-Gen. Comm. of Regulation of Bank Credits 63-66, Head of Foreign Investment Encouragement Cttee. 63-66; mem. Board of Controllers of the Prime Ministry 66-70; Chair. Türkiye Vakıflar Bankası 71-76, Central Bank of Turkey 78-.
Publs. *Emission Movements in Turkey* 67, *Treasury and Central Banks Relations* 70, *Knowledge of the Economic Situation* 78.
Mesnevi sokak 8/8, Ankara, Turkey.

Kayra, Cahit; Turkish civil servant and diplomatist; b. 13 March 1917; ed. Univ. of Ankara.
Inspector of Finance 42-50; Counsellor, Gen. Dir. of Finance 50-55; private financial adviser 55-59; Head of Foreign Trade Dept., Ministry of Trade 59-60; Head of Turkish Perm. Del. to Gen. Agreement on Tariffs and Trade (GATT) 60-63; Deputy Under-Sec. of State to Min. of Finance 63-64; Head of Turkish Del. to OECD 64-67; Head of Research Dept., Ministry of Finance 67-73; Minister of Energy and Natural Resources 74; mem. Gen. Admin. Board of the Republican People's Party 77, Nat. Assembly for Ankara.
Publs. *Middle Eastern Oil* 53, *A Guide to the Turkish System of Taxation* 57, *Import Policy in Turkey* 63, *A Rational Customs Policy* 69, *Foreign Financing Techniques* 70, *Free Trade of Gold in Turkey* 71, *Balance of Payments of Turkey* 72.
Cumhuriyet Halk Partisi (Republican People's Party), Ankara, Turkey.

Kedourie, Elie, B.SC.(ECON.); British professor of politics and editor.
Assistant Lecturer, then Lecturer in Politics and Public Admin., London School of Economics 53-60; Reader in Political Studies with special reference to the Middle East, London Univ. 61-65; Prof. of Politics, London Univ. 65-; Editor *Middle Eastern Studies* 64-; Fellow, British Acad. 75-.
Publs. *England and the Middle East: the Destruction of the Ottoman Empire* 56, *Nationalism* 60, *Afghani and Abduh* 66, *The Chatham House Version* 70, *Nationalism in Asia and Africa* 71, *Arabic Political Memoirs and Other Studies* 74, *In the Anglo-Arab Labyrinth* 76, *The Middle Eastern Economy* (Ed.) 78.
London School of Economics, Houghton Street, Aldwych, London, W.C.1, England.

Kelani, Haissam; Syrian diplomatist; b. 6 Aug. 1926, Hamah; ed. Mil. Coll., Air Gen. Staff Coll., Paris and High Mil. Air Acad., Paris.
General Pilot 61-62; Amb. to Algeria 62-63, to Morocco 65-67; Sec.-Gen. Ministry of Foreign Affairs 67-69; Amb. to the German Democratic Repub. 69-72; Perm. Rep. to UN 72-76; Dir. Dept. of Int. Organizations, Ministry of Foreign Affairs; mem. Expert, Human Rights Cttee. 77-80; Hon. Dr. Contemporary History; twelve medals.
Publs. ten books, many articles in Arab reviews.
c/o Ministry of Foreign Affairs, Damascus, Syria.

Kellou, Mohamed; Algerian lawyer and diplomatist; b. 27 March 1931; ed. Univs. of Algiers and Montpellier.
Lawyer, Algiers; fmr. Vice-Pres. Union Générale des Etudiants Musulmans Algériens (U.G.E.M.A.) (in charge of Foreign Affairs); Front de Libération Nationale (F.L.N.) Rep. in U.K. 57-61; Chief of Provisional Govt. of Algeria Diplomatic Mission to Pakistan 61-62; Chief of Africa-Asia-Latin America Div., Ministry of Foreign Affairs, Republic of Algeria 62-63; Amb. to U.K. 63-64, to Czechoslovakia 64-70, concurrently to Hungary 65-70, to Poland 66-70, to Argentina, Chile, Uruguay, Bolivia and Peru. 70-75, to People's Repub. of China 75-77; mem. People's Nat. Assembly Feb. 77-, Chair. Foreign Affairs Cttee. March 77-.
People's National Assembly, Algiers, Algeria.

Kemal, Yaşar; Turkish writer and journalist; b. 1923; self-educated.
Novels transl. into English: *Memed, My Hawk* 61, *The Wind from the Plain* 63, *Anatolian Tales* 68, *They Burn the Thistles* 73, *Iron Earth Copper Sky* 74, *The Legend of Ararat* 75, *The Legend of the Thousand Bulls* 76, *The Undying Grass* 77, *The Lords of Akchasez* (Part I), *Murder in the Ironsmiths Market* 79; novels, short stories, plays and essays in Turkish; books translated into several languages.
P.K. 14, Basinköy, Istanbul, Turkey.

Khaddam, Abdel Halim; Syrian politician.
Minister of the Economy and Foreign Trade 69-70; Deputy Prime Minister and Minister of Foreign Affairs Nov. 70-; mem. Regional Command, Baath Party May 71-.
Ministry of Foreign Affairs, Damascus, Syria.

Khadduri, Majid, B.A., PH.D.; Iraqi educationist and writer; b. 27 Sept. 1909; ed. American Univ. of Beirut and Univ. of Chicago.
Sec.-Treas. Baghdad P.E.N. Club; mem. American Society of Int. Law; Iraqi Del. to the 14th Conf. of the P.E.N. Clubs in Buenos Aires 36; adviser to the Iraq Delegation at the San Francisco Conf. 45; Visiting Lecturer in Near Eastern History at Indiana Univ. 47-48; fmr. Prof. Modern Middle Eastern History at the Higher Teachers' Coll., Baghdad, Iraq 48-49; taught Middle East politics at Chicago and Harvard Univs. 49-50; Prof. Middle East Studies, Johns Hopkins Univ. 50-, Distinguished Research Prof. 70-; Dir. of Research and Education, Middle East Inst. 50-; Visiting Middle East Prof., Columbia Univ.; mem. American Pol. Science Asscn.; Pres. Shaybani Soc. of Int. Law Washington D.C.
Publs. *The Liberation of Iraq from the Mandate* (in Arabic) 35, *The Law of War and Peace in Islam* 41, *The Government of Iraq* 44, *The System of Government in Iraq* (in Arabic) 46, *Independent Iraq* 51, *War and Peace in the Law of Islam* 55, *Islamic Jurisprudence* 61, *Modern Libya* 63, *The Islamic Law of Nations* 66, *Republican Iraq* 69, *Political Trends in the Arab World* 70, *Arab Contemporaries* 73.
Office: 4454 Tindall Street, N.W., Washington, D.C. 20016, U.S.A.

Khal, Yusuf A. al-, B.A.; Lebanese writer and publisher; b. 25 Dec. 1917; ed. American Univ. of Beirut.
Teacher of Arabic Literature, American Univ. of Beirut 45-47, 55-58; Editor *Sawt al Mar'at* women's monthly 46-48; Editor-Writer, Dept. of Public Information, UN Secretariat 48-50; Information Officer Libyan Mission to UN 50-52; Editor *Al Hoda* daily, New York 52-55; Founder and Editor *Shir* poetry magazine, *Adab* literary quarterly 57-; owner Gallery One, Beirut; Editorial Dir. Dar An-Nahar Publishing Co., Beirut 67-70, Soc. Co-operative Libanaise pour l'édition et diffusion, Beirut; Pro Mundi Beneficio Medal, Brazilian Acad. of Humanities 75.
Publs. *Al Hurriyat* (poetry) 44, *Herodiat* (poetical play) 54, *Al Bi'r al Mahjourat* (poetry) 58, *Quasa'id fil Arba'yn* (poetry) 60, *Collected Poems* 73; translations of works by T. S. Eliot, Auden, Pound, Sandberg, Frost and others; numerous essays and articles of literary criticism.
Rue Patriarcat, Beirut, Lebanon.

Khalid ibn Abdul Aziz; King of Saudi Arabia; b. 1913, Riyadh; ed. religious schools.
Appointed Asst. to his brother, Prince Faisal 34; Rep. of Saudi Arabia to various Int. Confs.; Vice-Pres. Council of Ministers 62-75; nominated Crown Prince 65; acceded to throne on the death of his brother March 75; Pres. Council of Ministers March 75-, Minister of Foreign Affairs March-Oct. 75; UN Gold Medal for Peaçe 77.
Royal Palace, Riyadh, Saudi Arabia.

Khalid, Mansour, LL.D.; Sudanese diplomatist and lawyer; b. 17 Jan. 1931, Sudan; ed. Univs. of Khartoum, Pennsylvania and Paris.
Began his career as an attorney, Khartoum 57-59; Legal officer, UN, N.Y. 62-63; Deputy UN resident rep., Algeria 64-65; Bureau of Relations with Member States, UNESCO. Paris 65-69; Visiting Prof. of Int. Law, Univ. of Colorado 68; Minister of Youth and Social Affairs, Sudan 69-71; Chair. of Del. of Sudan to UN Gen. Assembly, Special Consultant and Personal Rep. of UNESCO Dir.-Gen. for UNWRA fund-raising mission 70; Perm. Rep. to UN for Sudan 71, Pres. Security Council 72; Minister of Foreign Affairs 71-75, Feb.-Sept. 77, of Educ. 75-July 76; Asst. to the Pres. for Co-ordination and Foreign Affairs 76, for Co-ordination 77; mem. Exec. Bureau of Sudanese Socialist Union; dismissed from political posts July 78; Chair. OAU Ministerial Cttee. on Impact of Petroleum Price Increase in Africa 73-75.
Publs. *Private Law in Sudan* 70, *The Nile Basin, Present and Future* 71, *Solution of the Southern Problem and its African Implications* 72, *The Decision-Making Process in Foreign Policy* 73, *The Sudan Experiment with Unity* 73, *A Dialogue with the Sudanese Intellectuals.*
People's Palace, P.O. Box 281, Khartoum, Sudan.

Khalifa, Sheikh Hamed bin Isa al-; Heir Apparent to H.H. Emir of Bahrain; b. 28 Jan. 1950; ed. Secondary School, Manama, Applegarth Coll., Godalming, Mons Officer Cadet School, Aldershot, England, and U.S. Army Command and Gen. Staff Coll., Fort Leavenworth, Kansas, U.S.A.
Founder, Commdr. Bahrain Defence Force, Head Defence Dept., Govt. of Bahrain 68-; mem. State Admin. Council 70-71; Minister of Defence 71-; awarded several foreign decorations.
Private Office of the Heir Apparent, Court of the Emir, Rifa'a Palace, Manama, Bahrain.

Khalifa, H.H. Sheikh Isa bin Sulman al-; Ruler of the State of Bahrain; b. 3 July 1933.
Appointed heir-apparent by his father, H.H. Sheikh Sulman bin Hamad al-Khalifah 58; succeeded as Ruler on the death of his father Nov. 61; took title of Amir Aug. 71; Hon. K.C.M.G.
Rifa'a Palace, Manama, Bahrain.

Khalifa, Sheikh Khalifa bin Sulman al-; Bahrain politician; b. 1935.
Son of the late Sheikh Sulman and brother of the ruler, Sheikh Isa; Dir. of Finance and Pres. of Electricity Board 61; Pres. Council of Admin. 66-70; Pres. State Council 70-73, Prime Minister 73-.
Council of Ministers, Manama, Bahrain.

Khalifa, Sirr el Khatim, G.C.M.G.; Sudanese educationalist and politician; b. 1 Jan. 1919; ed. Gordon Coll., Khartoum.
Former teacher, Gordon Coll., Khartoum, and Bakht-er-Ruda Inst.; Head, Khartoum Technical Inst. 60-64; Deputy Under-Sec. Ministry of Educ. 64; Prime Minister 64-65; Amb. to Italy 65-68, to United Kingdom 68-69; Minister of Higher Educ. and Scientific Research 72-Jan. 75.
c/o Ministry of Higher Education and Scientific Research, P.O. Box 2081, Khartoum, Sudan.

Khalifa bin Hamad al-Thani, Sheikh (*see* Thani, Sheikh Khalifa bin Hamad al-).

Khalil, Mohamed Kamal El-Din; Egyptian diplomatist.
Lecturer in Int. and Public Law 41-56; Dir. of Research Dept., U.A.R. Ministry of Foreign Affairs 56-60; Minister Plenipotentiary, London 60-61; Dir. North American Dept. U.A.R. Ministry of Foreign Affairs 61-64; Amb. to Jordan 64-66, to Sudan 66-71; Under-Sec. of State for Foreign Affairs Sept. 71-74; Amb. to Belgium 74-, also to EEC.
Publ. *The Arab States and the Arab League* (2 vols.) 62.
Embassy of the Arab Republic of Egypt, 2 Avenue Victoria, 1050 Brussels, Belgium.

Khalil, Mustafa, M.SC., D.PHIL.; Egyptian engineer and politician; b. 1920; ed. Univ. of Cairo, Illinois Univ., U.S.A.
Served in Egyptian State Railways 41-47, 51-52; Training with Chicago-Milwaukee Railways (U.S.A.) 47; Lecturer in Railways and Highway Engineering, Ain Shams Univ., Cairo 52; Tech. Consultant to Transport Cttee., Perm. Council for Nat. Production 55; Minister of Communication and Transport 56-64, of Industry, Mineral Resources and Electricity 65-66; Deputy Prime Minister 64-65; resigned from Cabinet 66; Head of Broadcasting Corpn. 70; Sec.-Gen. Central Cttee., Arab Socialist Un on 70-76; Prime Minister Oct. 78-, also Minister of Foreign Affairs Feb. 79-.
Office of the Prime Minister, Cairo, Egypt.

Khane, Abd-El Rahman, M.D.; Algerian politician, administrator and physician; b. 6 March 1931, Collo; ed. Univ. of Algiers.
Served as officer in Nat. Liberation Army until Algerian independence 62; Sec. of State provisional govt. (GPRA) 58-60; Gen. Controller Nat. Liberation Front 60-61; Head of Finance Dept. GPRA 61-62; Pres. Algerian-French tech. org. for exploiting wealth of Sahara sub-soil 62-65; Pres. Electricité et Gaz d'Algérie July-Oct. 64; mem. Board Dirs. Nat. Petroleum Research and Exploitation Co. 65-66; Minister of Public Works and Pres. Algerian-French Industrial Co-operation Org. 66-70; Physician, Cardiology Dept., Univ. Hospital of Algiers 70-73; Sec.-Gen. OPEC 73-74; Exec. Dir. UNIDO Jan. 75-.
4 Bockkellergasse, 1190 Vienna, Austria; 42 Chemin B. Brahimi, El Biar, Algiers, Algeria.

Khanlari, Parviz, PH.D.; Iranian historian and politician; b. 1913; ed. Teheran Univ. and Univ. of Paris.
Professor of Iranian Linguistics, Teheran Univ. 48-; Ed. *Sokhan* (literary monthly) 44-64, and of its *Scientific Supplement* 61-64; Dep. Minister of Interior 55; Senator 57; Minister of Education 62-64; Co-Founder *Mardom* Party 57; Gen. Sec. Imperial Foundation for Iranian Cultural Studies; Pres. Imperial Acad. of Letters and Arts 65.
Hafez Avenue, Zomorrod Passage, P.O. Box 984, Teheran, Iran.

Khatib, Ahmed al-; Syrian politician; b. 1931, Salkhad, Jabal al-Arab region.
Formerly Head, Syrian Teachers Asscn.; mem. Presidential Council Sept. 65-Feb. 66; Pres. of Syria Nov. 70-Feb. 71; Chair. People's Council Feb.-Dec. 71; Prime Minister and Chair. of Federal Ministerial Council, Fed. of Arab Repubs. Dec. 71-; mem. Baath Party, elected to Leadership Cttee. May 71.
People's Council, Damascus, Syria.

Khayyal, Abdullah al; Saudi Arabian diplomatist and politician; b. 1913; ed. Fuad I Univ., Cairo.
Private Sec. to Minister of Foreign Affairs, H.R.H. Prince Faisal 32; Dir.-Gen. of Schools, Eastern Saudi Arabia and Dir. A.H.S.A. Central School 41; Second Sec. Saudi Arabian Legation, Baghdad 43 First Sec. and Chargé d'Affaires 45; Minister to Iraq 47-55; Perm. Del. to UN

55-57; Ambassador to U.S.A. 55-63, concurrently Minister to Mexico 56-60, Ambassador 60-63: Pres. Islamic Center, Washington, D.C. 56-68; Dir. of Public Works 64; later Amb. to United Arab Emirates.
c/o Ministry of Foreign Affairs, Riyadh, Saudi Arabia.

Khene Abderrahman (*see* Khane Abd-El Rahman).

Khiary, Mahmoud; Tunisian politician and trades union official; b. 1911; ed. Ecole Normale, Tunis.
Teacher 31-55; Sec.-Gen. Tunisian Union of Teachers 41-52; Pres. Gen. Fed. of Tunisian Officials 47-58; fmr. Sec.-Gen., Gen. Union of Tunisian Workers; fmr. Minister of Posts and Telegraphs; fmr. Minister of Agriculture; mem. Nat. Constituent Ass.; Chief, UN Civil Operations in the Congo 61-62; Pres. Dir.-Gen. Soc. Nat. Tunisienne de Cellulose, Soc. Nat. Tunisienne de Papier Alfa 63-72; Pres. Dir.-Gen. Société Nationale de Mise en Valeur du Sud (SONMIVAS) 72-74; Dir.-Gen. Entreprises Gén. des Travaux Publics et de Promotion de l'Habitat 74-.
20 rue du Koweit, Tunis, Tunisia.

Khlefawi, Gen. Abdel Rahman; Syrian army officer and politician; b. 1927, Damascus; ed. schools in Damascus, Military School, Homs.
Representative of Syria, Joint Arab Command, Cairo 64-67; Head, Armoured Forces Admin., Damascus 67-68; Head, Officers' Board, Ministry of Defence 68-70; Minister of the Interior Nov. 70-April 71; Prime Minister 71-72, 76-78; mem. Regional Command, Baath Party.
Damascus, Syria.

Kholi, Hassan Sabri el-; Egyptian diplomatist: b. 25 Feb. 1922, Tanta; ed. Univ. of Cairo, Mil. and Staff Colls.
Fought in Palestine War 48; Prof., Senior Officer Studies Inst.; opened Infantry School, Syria 57; Dir. Office for Palestine at the Presidency, Office for Public Affairs; Personal Rep. of the Pres. 64-75; has represented Egypt at UN, Arab League and Arab Summit Confs.; UNICEF Rep. in Arab Countries 75-76; Chief Mediator of Arab League in Lebanon crisis 76-77; Pres. Egyptian Soc. for the Mentally Handicapped, Asscn. for Welfare of the Disabled and Handicapped; numerous foreign decorations.
Publs. *The Palestine Case, Sinai, The Policy of the Imperialism and Zionism towards Palestine during the First Half of the Twentieth Century*, and several research papers on Palestine.
c/o The Presidency, Cairo; 50 Khalifa Mamoun Street, Cairo, Egypt.

Khomeini, Ayatollah Ruhollah; Iranian religious leader; b. in town of Khomein; ed. in Khomein and at theological school, Qom.
Religious teacher in theological school, Qom; arrested in Qom after riots over Shah's land reforms June-Aug. 63; in exile, Najaf, Iraq 63-78, Neauphle-le-Château, France Oct. 78-Feb. 79; from France acted as leader in revolution which toppled Shah Mohammad Reza Pahlavi (*q.v.*) with aim of creating Islamic Repub.; returned to Iran Feb. 79; appointed Mehdi Bazargan (*q.v.*) as Prime Minister; returned to the theological seminary, Qom, but continued as leader. March 79-.
Publs. *The Government of Theologians* (lectures while in exile), numerous religious and political books and tracts.
Faizeyeh Theological Seminary, Qom, Iran.

Khoshkish, Youssof; Iranian banker; b. 1906, Teheran; ed. Teheran Secondary School and Sorbonne, Paris.
Bank Melli Iran 34-39, Asst. Man., Org. Dept. 36-38, Man. Supply Dept. 38-39; Iranian del. Ministry of Finance, Europe 39-40, India 40-44; Vice-Pres. Bank Sepah 45-61; Pres. Bank Melli Iran 61-77; Governor Bank Markazi Iran 77-79.
Bank Markazi Iran, Ferdowsi Avenue, Teheran, Iran.

Khosravani, Attaollah; Iranian politician; b. 21 March 1919, Teheran; ed. Univ. of Teheran, Univ. of Paris.
Former Labour Attaché, France; fmr. Govt. Supervisor to Workers Social Insurance Org., later Head; Founder and Dir. newspaper *Afkare Iran*; fmr. Under-Sec. (Admin.) Ministry of Labour and Under-Sec. (Parl.), Ministry of Labour; Sec.-Gen. Iran Novin Party 65; Minister of Labour and Social Affairs 61-68, of the Interior 68; Chair. Board of Inspectorate, Nat. Iranian Oil Co. 69-79; Chair. Board of Iranian Bank 77-79; Order of Homayoun (twice).
Ferechteh-Kamran Avenue No. 17, Teheran 19, Iran.

Khoury, Sheikh Maître Michel, LL.B.; Lebanese businessman and politician; b. 24 Nov. 1926; ed. Univ. St. Joseph, Beirut, Paris Univ. Faculté de Droit, Inst. d'Etudes Politiques and Coll. de France.
Political section, Ministry of Foreign Affairs 46-49; Contributor to *Le Jour* daily 44-; Dir.-Gen. Ets. Derwiche Youssef Haddad 53-; mem. Board Nat. Council of Tourism 62-66, Pres. 64-66; Minister of Defence and of Guidance, Information and Tourism Dec. 65-April 66; Minister of Planning and Tourism 66-68; Middle East Regional Editor *Columbia Journal of World Business*.
rue Michel Chiha, Kantari, Beirut, Lebanon.

Kidron, Abraham, B.A.; Israeli diplomatist; b. 19 Nov. 1919; ed. Hebrew Univ. of Jerusalem.
Joined Ministry of Foreign Affairs, Jerusalem 49-50; Attaché, Rome Embassy 50-52; Ministry of Foreign Affairs, Jerusalem 53-54; Consul, Cyprus 54-56; First Sec. (Press) London Embassy 57-59; Head of Research Dept. and Spokesman, Ministry of Foreign Affairs 59-63; Minister, Israel Legation, Yugoslavia 63-65; Amb. to Philippines 65-67; Asst. Dir.-Gen. Ministry of Foreign Affairs, Jerusalem 69-71, Deputy Dir.-Gen. 72-73, Dir.-Gen. 73-76; Amb. to Netherlands 76-77, to U.K. June 77-.
c/o Embassy of Israel, 2 Palace Green, London, W8 4QB, England.

Kikhia, Mansur Rashid; Libyan diplomatist; b. 1 Dec. 1931, Benghazi; ed. Faculty of Law, Univ. of Cairo and Paris.
Joined Diplomatic Service 57; Asst. in Nationality and Consular Affairs Section, Ministry of Foreign Affairs 57, Head, Treaties and Int. Confs. Section 58-60, 62-65; Second Sec. for Consular and Cultural Affairs, Libyan Embassy to France 60-62; Chargé d'Affaires, France Jan.-Aug. 62, Algeria Feb.-Aug. 63; Consul-Gen., Geneva 65-67; mem. Del. of Libya to UN 61, 66-70, Chair. 70, 72, 75, 76, Vice-Chair. 77-78, Rep. on Security Council 76-77; Under-Sec. Ministry of Unity and Foreign Affairs 69-72; Perm. Rep. to UN Feb.-July 72; Minister of Foreign Affairs July 72-73; private law practice, Tripoli 73-75; Amb. to UN Aug. 75-; Chair. Libyan Del. to 3rd UN Conf. on Law of the Sea 76-78, Preparatory Comm. for special session on disarmament 77-78, *ad hoc* Comm. on drafting of Int. Convention against taking of hostages 77; Chair. UN Security Council Sanctions Comm. 77.
Permanent Mission of Libya to the United Nations, 866 UN Plaza, New York, N.Y. 10017, U.S.A.

Kirk, George Eden, M.A.; American (b. British) author; b. 1911; ed. Cambridge, and Schools of Archaeology Athens and Jerusalem.
Epigraphist with Colt expedition, Palestine 35-38; Staff Officer (Int.) at G.H.Q Middle East Forces 40-45; Instructor Middle East Centre for Arab studies 45-47; M.E. specialist Royal Inst. of International Affairs 47-52; Assoc. Prof. Int. Relations, American Univ. of Beirut 53-57; Lecturer, Harvard Univ. Center for Middle Eastern Studies 57-66; Prof. of History, Univ. of Mass. 66-79, Dir. of Graduate Studies in History 70-73.
Publs. *A Short History of the Middle East* 48 (definitive edn. 64), *The Middle East in the War* 52, *The Middle East, 1945-50* 55, *Contemporary Arab Politics* 61; contributed to:

The Military in the Middle East (ed. Sydney N. Fisher) 63, *Forces of Change in the Middle East* (ed. Maurice M. Roumani) 71.
32 Cosby Ave., Amherst, Mass. 01002, U.S.A.

Kittani, Ismat T.; Iraqi United Nations official; b. 5 April 1929, Amadiya; ed. Knox Coll, Galesburg, Ill.
High School teacher, Iraq; joined Foreign Ministry 52; Attaché, Cairo 54-57; mem. Iraqi mission to UN 57, Acting Perm. Rep. 58-59; Perm. Rep. to European Office of UN 61-64; Chief, Specialized Agencies and Admin. Cttee. of Co-ordination Affairs, Dept. of Econ. and Social Affairs, UN Secr. 64; Sec. Econ. and Social Council 65-67; Principal Officer, later Dir. Exec. Office of Sec.-Gen. of UN 67-69; Deputy to Asst. Sec.-Gen. for Inter-Agency Affairs 69-70; Asst. Sec.-Gen. for Inter-Agency Affairs 71-73; Exec. Asst. to UN Sec.-Gen. 73-75; Dir.-Gen. Dept. of Int. Orgs. and Confs., Ministry of Foreign Affairs 75-; fmr. del. of Iraq to various int. comms. and confs.; mem. Gov. Board ILO 59; alt. mem. Exec. Board WHO 61.
Ministry of Foreign Affairs, Karradat Mariam, Baghdad, Iraq.

Klibi, Chédli, D.LITT.; Tunisian politician; b. 6 Sept. 1925, Tunis; ed. Sadiki Coll., Univ. of Tunis, Sorbonne, Paris.
Journalist 51-57, working successively for *Es Sabah, An Nadwa, Sawt el Amal, Al Amal*; Prof. of Arabic, Lycée Carnot 57-58; Gen. Man. Tunisian Radio and Television 58-61; Sec. of State for Information and Cultural Affairs 61-64, for Cultural Affairs Nov. 64, for Guidance and Cultural Affairs 66-69; mem. Political Bureau, Parti Socialiste Destourien Jan. 68-; Mayor of Carthage 64-79; Minister of Cultural Affairs and Information 69-73; Amb. to Egypt 73-74; Minister of Cultural Affairs 76-79; Sec.-Gen. of League of Arab States June 79-; mem. Arab Language Acad., Cairo.; Grand Cordon Order of the Repub.; Grand Cordon, Order of Independence.
Publs. *The Arabs facing the Palestinian Problem*; poetry and numerous articles.
Secretariat, League of Arab States, Tunis, Tunisia.

Koç, Vehbi; Turkish businessman; b. 1901.
Opened first grocery shop in Ankara 17; formed Koç Trading Corpn. 37, General Elektrik Türk 49, and many other companies; assoc. with numerous major firms in U.S.A. and Europe; Chair. Koç Holding Corpn. 64-; manufactured Turkey's first passenger car (Anadol) 66, second (Murat, under licence from Fiat) 71; Founded Vehbi Koç Foundation 69, Turkish Educ. Foundation 69; Order of Merit (Fed. Repub. of Germany) 74.
Publ. *My Life Story* (in Turkish) 73.
Koç Holding Corporation, Fındıklı, Ankara, Turkey.

Kol, Moshe; Israeli educator and politician; b. 1911, Russia; ed. Hebrew Secondary School, Pinsk and Hebrew Univ. Jerusalem.
Co-Founder Hanoar Hazioni (Zionist Youth) movement in Poland and its Rep. on Cen. Cttee. of Zionist Org. in Poland; came to Israel and joined Hamefales pioneer group in Kfar Saba 32; Del. to all Zionist Congresses 33-; mem. Histadrut Exec. 41-46; mem. Jewish Agency Exec. and Head of its Youth Aliya Dept. 46-66; mem. Provisional State Council 48, and Chair. of its Foreign Affairs Cttee.; Signatory to Declaration of Independence 48; mem. Knesset (Parl.) 49-66; Minister of Devt. and of Tourism 66-69, of Tourism 69-June 77; Chair. Independent Liberal Party; Vice-Pres. Liberal Int. 69-; Chair. Int. Cultural Centre for Youth, Jerusalem, Friends of Hebrew Writers Asscn., Masua, Dr. Forder Liberal Inst., Inst. of Archives and Museum of Jewish Theatre, Yesodot (Zionist Youth Villages); Co-Founder (in Israel), Oved Hazioni (Zionist Workers) Movement, World Confed. of Gen. Zionists; many Jewish Agency and govt. missions abroad; Hon. Treas. Israel Exploration Soc.
Publs. in Hebrew. *Arichim, Misholim Bezionout, Netivot Bechinouch Uveshikum, Morim Vechaverim, Youth Aliya* (also in English and French).
10 Jabotinsky Street, Jerusalem, Israel.

Kollek, Theodore (Teddy); Israeli politician; b. 1911; ed. Vienna.
Went to Palestine 34; mem. Kibbutz Ein-Gev. 37; with Zionist Youth groups in Europe and U.K. 38-40; Political Dept., Jewish Agency 42-47; Liaison with Jewish Underground in Europe 42-45; mem. Haganah mission to U.S.A. 47-48; Minister Plenipotentiary, Washington 51-52; Dir.-Gen. Prime Minister's Office, including Dept. for Applied Civilian Scientific Research, Bureau of Statistics, Govt. Press and Information Office, the devt. of broadcasting services, est. Israel Govt. Tourist Office, 52-64; Chair. Govt. Tourist Corpn. 56-65; Chair. Israel 10th Anniversary Celebrations; Mayor of Jerusalem 65-; Head of Nuclear Desalination of Water Project 64-66; Chair. Board of Governors, Israel Museum 65-; Hon. doctorate (Hebrew Univ., Jerusalem) 77; Rothschild Medal and Bublick Prize 75.
Publs. (with Moshe Pearlman) *Jerusalem: Sacred City of Mankind* 68, *Pilgrims to the Holy Land* 70, and numerous articles.
Municipality of Jerusalem, Jerusalem; Home: 6 Rashba Street, Jerusalem, Israel.

Konuk, Nejat; Cypriot lawyer, politician and writer; b. 1928, Nicosia; ed. Turkish Lycée, Cyprus and Law Faculty of Ankara Univ.
Began career as Legal Adviser in Turkish Civil Service; Sec.-Gen. and Acting Dir.-Gen. of Turkish Communal Chamber; Under-Sec. to Rauf Denktash (*q.v.*, Deputy Pres. of Turkish Cypriot Admin.) 68-69; Minister of Justice and Internal Affairs, Turkish Cypriot Admin. 69-75; mem. for Nicosia, Turkish Cypriot Legislative Assembly 70-; Minister of Interior, Turkish Cypriot Admin. 73-74; founder mem. Nat. Unity Party 75, Party Leader 76-78; Prime Minister "Turkish Federated State of Cyprus" July 76-Feb. 78.
Publs. essays on literature, various papers on Cyprus, political articles 53-77.
Kumsal, Lefkoşa, Mersin 10, Turkey.

Koper, Daniş; Turkish politician and businessman; b. 19 Dec. 1908, Diyadin; ed. Ankara Lisesi and Munich Coll. of Technology.
Engineer Water Works Dept. 36-48; Dir. Provincial Bank 51; Gen. Man. Highways Admin. 51-56; Under-Sec. Ministry of Public Works 56-57; Minister of Public Works 60; Chair. Asscn. of Chamber of Engineering and Architecture 58-60; Chair. Turkish Airlines 59-60; Trustee Middle East Technical Univ., Ankara 59-60; mem. Constitutional Assembly 61; Partner Kuyaş Construction Co., and Bormak Ltd. 60-; Chair. Board and Exec. Cttee. Ereğli Iron and Steel Co. 61-68; Chair. Board of Trustees, Middle East Technical Univ. 63-66; Chair. Board of Trustees, Ankara Koleji (High School) 63-68; Trustee, Hacettepe Univ. 70-71; Gen. Sec. Turkish Atomic Energy Comm. 70-71; Technical Counsellor Yapi ve Kredi Bank 72-, Man. 78-; Chair. Board of Dirs. Bayurdirlek Isleri Corpn. 72-; mem. Board of Dirs. Black Sea Copper Works 72-; mem. Board, Yatirimlar Holding 72-; Trustee, Pension Fund, Yapi ve Kredi Bank 72-; mem. Board, Canakka Cimenta Works 73-, Eregli Steel Works 75, Turyag Corpn. 76-; Deputy Chair. Peteter Chemical Industries 77-; Chevalier, Légion d'Honneur.
Istiklal cad. Oda Kule, Kat. 6, Istanbul; Home: 378, Bagdat Cad. 8, Swadiye, Istanbul, Turkey.

Korutürk, Admiral Fahri S.; Turkish naval officer and Head of State; b. 12 Aug. 1903, Instanbul; ed. Naval Acad. and Naval War Coll.
Joined Navy 20; Naval Attaché, Berlin 35, Rome 36,

Berlin and Stockholm 42-43; Naval Adviser to Turkish del., Montreux Conf.; Commdr. Naval War Acad. 45-46; Commdr. Submarine Fleet 53; Chief of Intelligence, General Staff, Armed Forces 54; Commdr. of Sea-going Fleet 55-56; C.-in-C. Straits Area 56-57, Admiral 57; C.-in-C. of Navy and Commdr. of Allied Forces, Black Sea 57-60; Amb. to U.S.S.R. 60-64; mem. Defence Cttee. of the Senate 68; Head Presidential Senate Group 71-73; Pres. of Turkey April 73-.
The Presidency, Ankara, Turkey.

Kotaite, Assad, LL.D.; Lebanese lawyer and aviation official; b 6 Nov. 1924; ed. French Univ. of Beirut, Univ. of Paris, Inst. des Hautes Etudes Internationales, Paris and Acad. of Int. Law, The Hague.
Practising barrister 48-49; Head, Legal Services, Int. Agreements and External Relations, Dir. of Civil Aviation, Ministry of Public Works and Transport 53-56; Rep. to Int. Civil Aviation Org. (ICAO) 56-70, Sec.-Gen. 70-76, Pres. ICAO Council Aug. 76-; mem. UN Transport and Communications Comm. 57-79; Chair. 59; Chair. Air Transport Cttee., ICAO 59-62, 65-68; Golden Medal of Merit (Lebanon), Award of Air Law Soc. (Brazil), Gran Cruz del Merito Aeronautico (Spain).
International Civil Aviation Organization, 1000 Sherbrooke Street West, Montreal, P.Q. H3A 2R2, Canada.

Kranidiotis, Nicos; Greek-Cypriot scholar and diplomatist; b. 25 Nov. 1911; ed. Pan Cyprian Gymnasium, Cyprus, Athens Univ., and Harvard Univ. Center for Int. Affairs.
Worked as schoolmaster in Cyprus; Dir. of *Hellenic Cyprus* (official political organ of Cyprus Ethnarchy) 49; Gen. Sec. Cyprus Ethnarchy 53-57, Councillor 57-60; Ambassador to Greece 60-, to Yugoslavia 63-, to Italy 64-, to Bulgaria and Romania 70-; Sec. of 2nd and 3rd Cyprus Nat. Assemblies 54, 55; Founder, Dir. and Editor (with others) of *Kypriaka Grammata* (Cyprus Literature), a literary magazine.
Publs. *Chronicles* (short stories) 45, *The Neohellenic Theatre* (essay) 50, *Studies* (poems) 51, *Forms of Myth* (short stories) 54, *The Poet G. Seferis* (essay) 55, *The National Character of the Cyprus Literature* 58, *Cyprus in her Struggle for Freedom* (history) 58, *An Introduction to the Poetry of George Seferis* 64, *Cyprus-Greece* 66, *Cyprus Poetry* 69, *Poesie* 74, *Epistrophi* 74, *The Cyprus Problem* 75.
Embassy of Cyprus, 16 Herodotos Street, Athens, Greece; Home: 16 Prometheus Street, Nicosia, Cyprus.

Kubar, Abd al-Majid (*see* Coobar, Abdulmegid).

Kudsi, Nazem el, PH.D.; Syrian former Head of State; b. 1906; ed. American Coll., Beirut, Damascus Univ. and Univ. of Geneva.
Barrister in Aleppo 30; Dep. for Aleppo 36, 47, 55; Minister Plenipotentiary, Washington 44-45; Prime Minister and Minister for Foreign Affairs 50; Pres. Council of Ministers 54-57; Leader, Populist Party; held no political office during United Arab Republic régime 58-61; Pres. of the Syrian Arab Republic 61-63, retired 63.
Aleppo, Syria.

Kuwait, H. H. The Ruler of (*see* Sabah, Amir Jaber al-Ahmed al-Jaber al-).

Kyprianou, Spyros; Cypriot politician; b. 28 Oct. 1932, Limassol; ed. City of London Coll. and Gray's Inn.
Founded Nat. Union of Cypriot Students in U.K. (EFEKA), Pres. 52-54; Sec. in London to Archbishop Makarios 52-54, London Sec. of Ethnarchy of Cyprus 54-56, 57-59; also journalist 52-56; rep. of Ethnarchy of Cyprus, New York 56-57; mem. Cttee. Nat. Democratic Front for Reconstruction (EDMA, later Patriotic Front) 59; Minister of Justice Aug. 60, of Foreign Affairs 60-72; leader of del. to UN Gen. Assembly 64-71, 74; law practice 72-76; Pres. House of Reps. 76-77; President of Cyprus Aug. 77-; Grand Cross, Order of George I (Greece) 62, Grand Cross (Fed. Repub. of Germany) 62, Grand Star of the Repub. (United Arab Repub., now Egypt) 61, Grand Cross, Order of Boyaca (Colombia) 66, Grand Cross, Order of Merit (Chile) 66, Grand Silver Cross (Austria) 73, Ecclesiastical decoration, Order of St. Aikaterini of Sinai 66.
Presidential Palace, Nicosia, Cyprus.

L

Labidi, Abdelwahab; Tunisian financier; b. 22 April 1929, Kef; ed. Coll. Sidiki, Tunis, Inst. des Hautes Etudes, Tunis, Faculty of Law, Univ. of Paris.
Former Gen. Man. Banque de Tunisie; Insp.-Gen. Banque Nat. Agricole de Tunisie; Man. Soc. Tunisienne de Banque; Man. Dir. Nat. Devt. Bank of Niger 64-69; Vice-Pres. African Devt. Bank June 69-70, Pres. 70-76; Pres. African Devt. Fund 73-76; Chair. Sifida (Geneva) 73-77; Adviser to Scandinavian Bank Ltd. (London) 77-; mem. Exec. Cttee. Club de Dakar, Governing Council of Soc. for Int. Devt.
62 bis rue de Latour, 75016 Paris, France.

Ladgham, Bahi; Tunisian politician; b. 10 Jan. 1913, Tunis.
Joined Dept. of Interior 33, subsequently moved to Finance Dept.; Sec. of State for the Presidency and Sec. of State for Defence 56-69; Prime Minister of Tunisia 69-70; Chair. Arab Cttee. supervising the ceasefire between Jordanian Govt. and the Palestinian guerrillas in Jordan 70-71; fmr. personal rep. of Pres. Bourguiba; fmr. Sec.-Gen. Destour Socialist Party (fmrly. Néo-Destour Party).
c/o Destour Socialist Party, 10 rue de Rome, Tunis, Tunisia.

Lalla Aicha, H.R.H. Princess; Moroccan diplomatist; b. 1930.
Eldest daughter of late King Mohammed V; Ambassador to United Kingdom 65-69, to Italy 69-71; Pres. Moroccan Red Crescent; Grand Cordon of Order of the Throne.
c/o Ministry of Foreign Affairs, Rabat, Morocco.

Lamrani, Mohammed Karim (*see* Karim-Lamrani, Mohammed).

Landau, Moshe, LL.B.; Israeli judge; b. 1912, Danzig, Germany (now Gdańsk, Poland); ed. London Univ.
Arrived in Palestine 33; called to Palestine Bar 37, Magistrate of Haifa 40, District Court Judge, Haifa 48, Justice Supreme Court, Jerusalem 53-, Deputy Pres. 76-.
The Supreme Court, Jerusalem, Israel.

Laraki, Moulay Ahmed, M.D.; Moroccan physician and diplomatist; b. 15 Oct. 1931, Casablanca; ed. Univ. of Paris.
With Ministry of Foreign Affairs 56-57; Perm. Rep. to UN 57-58; Head of Hospital Services, Casablanca 56-61; Ambassador to Spain 61-65, to U.S.A., concurrently accred. to Mexico, Canada and Venezuela 65-67; Minister of Foreign Affairs 67-69; Prime Minister 69-71; Minister of State for Foreign Affairs 74-77.
Ministry of Foreign Affairs, Rabat, Morocco.

Léger, Jacques; Haitian international official; b. Port-au-Prince; ed. Faculty of Law, Univ. of Haiti.
Attached to Protocol Sec., Dept. of State 34-35; Sec. to Sec. of State for Foreign Affairs 35-36; service with legation in Venezuela; Dir. Haiti Service of Inter-American Affairs; Chargé d'Affaires, Venezuela 44-47; Amb. to Cuba 47-48, to Argentina and Brazil 48-50; Sec.

of State for Foreign Affairs 50-51; Amb. to U.S.A. and Canada 52-56; Perm. Rep. to UN 56-57; research activities, N.Y. Public Library and Library of Congress 57-59; translator 59-63; UNDP Regional Rep., Ivory Coast 64-67, Democratic Repub. of Congo (now Zaire) 67-69, N.W. Africa 69-72, Kuwait 72-; Grand Officer, Légion d'Honneur, and other decorations.
United Nations Development Programme, P.O. Box 2193, Kuwait City, Kuwait.

Levinson, Jacob; Israeli banker; b. 1932; ed. Hebrew Hniv., Jerusalem.
Dember Kibbutz Rosh Hanikra 49-61; fmr. Sec. Hatnu'ah Uame'uhedet (United Youth Movement); fmr. Head Econ. Mept., Hevrat Ovdim (Gen. Co-operative Asscn. of Labour); now Chair. Board of Dirs., Bank Hapoalim B.M.; mem. Board of Man., Hevrat Ovdim; mem. Advisory Board, Bank of Israel.
Publs. numerous articles in econ. and general books and periodicals.
Bank Hapoalim B.M., 50 Rothschild Boulevard, Tel-Aviv, Israel.

Lewis, Bernard, B.A., PH.D., F.B.A., F.R.HIST.S.; British university professor; b. 31 May 1916; ed. Univs. of London and Paris.
Lecturer in Islamic History, School of Oriental Studies, Univ. of London 38; served R.A.C. and Intelligence Corps 40-41; attached to Foreign Office 41-45, Prof. of History of the Near and Middle East, Univ. of London 49-74; Cleveland E. Dodge Prof. of Near Eastern Studies, Princeton Univ. 74-, Long-term mem. School of Social Science, Inst. for Advanced Study 74-; Visiting Prof. of History, Univ. of California at Los Angeles 55-56, Columbia Univ. 60, Indiana Univ. 63, Princeton Univ. 64, Inst. for Advanced Study 69; Foreign mem. American Philosophical Soc.; Corresp. Fellow Inst. d'Egypte, Cairo; hon. mem. Turkish Historical Soc.
Publs. *The Origins of Isma'ilism* 40, *Turkey Today* 40, *British Contributions to Arabic Studies* 41, *Handbook of Diplomatic and Political Arabic* 47, *Land of Enchanters* (Editor) 48, *The Arabs in History* 50 (revised edns. 58, 64, 66, 70), *Notes and Documents from the Turkish Archives* 52, *The Kingly Crown* 61, *The Emergence of Modern Turkey* 61 (revised edn. 68), *Historians of the Middle East* (ed. with P. M. Holt) 62, 64, *Istanbul and the Civilization of the Ottoman Empire* 63, 68, *The Middle East and the West* 64, 68, *The Assassins* 67, *Race and Colour in Islam* 71, Co-editor *Encyclopaedia of Islam* 56-, *Cambridge History of Islam* 70, *Islam in History: Ideas, Men and Events in the Middle East* 73; *Islam from the Prophet Muhammad to the Capture of Constantinople* (2 vols.) 74, *History Remembered, Recovered, Invented* 75, *The World of Islam* (U.K. title, published in U.S.A. as *Islam and the Arab World*) (Editor) 76, *Population and Revenue in the Towns of Palestine in the Sixteenth Century* (with A. Cohen) 78.
110 Jones Hall, Princeton University, Princeton, N.J. 08540, U.S.A.

Lifson, Shneior, PH.D.; Israeli scientist; b. 18 March 1914, Tel-Aviv; ed. Hebrew Univ.
Member of kibbutz 32-43; served in Science Unit, Israel Defence Forces 48-49; Weizmann Inst. of Science, attached to Polymer Dept. 49, Chair. Scientific Council 61-63, Head Chemical Physics Dept. 63-, Science Dir. 63-67; Rector Everyman's Univ., Israel 74; mem. Israel Science Teaching Center, Comm. of Molecular Biophysics of Int. Union of Pure and Applied Biophysics, European Molecular Biology Org., Advisory Board *Biopolymers* and Editorial Board *Journal of Statistical Physics* (U.S.A.); Weizmann Prize 58, Israel Prize 69.
Publs. numerous scientific papers.
15 Neve Weizmann, Rehovot, Israel.

Lloyd, Seton, C.B.E., M.A., F.B.A., F.S.A., A.R.I.B.A.; British archaeologist; b. 30 May 1902; ed. Uppingham and Architectural Asscn.
Asst. to Sir Edwin Lutyens, P.R.A. 27-28; excavated for Egypt Exploration Society, Egypt 29-30, for Oriental Inst., Univ. of Chicago in Iraq 30-37, for Univ. of Liverpool in Turkey 37-39; Technical Adviser, Govt. of Iraq, Directorate-Gen. of Antiquities 39-49; Dir. British Inst. of Archaeology in Ankara 49-61, Hon. Sec. 64-74, Pres. 74-; Prof. of Western Asiatic Archaeology, Univ. of London 62-69, Emer. Prof. 69-; Pres. British School of Archaeology in Iraq 78; Hon. M.A. (Edinburgh); Lawrence of Arabia Medal (Royal Soc. for Asian Affairs) 71, Gertrude Bell Memorial Medal (British School of Archaeology in Iraq) 78; Certificate of Merit, Turkey 73.
Publs. *Mesopotamia* 34, *Sennacherib's Aqueduct at Jerwan* 35, *The Gimilsin Temple* 40, *Presargonid Temples* 42, *Ruined Cities of Iraq* 42, *Twin Rivers* 43, *Foundations in the Dust* 48, *Early Anatolia* 56, *Alanya-Ala'iyya* 58, *Art of the Ancient Near East*, *Beycesultan* 62, *Mounds of the Near East* 63, *Highland Peoples of Early Anatolia* 67, *The Archaeology of Mesopotamia* 78.
Woolstone Lodge, Faringdon, Oxon., England.

Logali, Hilary Nyigilo Paul; Sudanese politician; b. 1931, Juba, Equatoria Province; ed. Khartoum Univ., Yale Univ.
Official with Ministry of Finance and Econs. 57-64; Minister of Works and Natural Resources 65, of Communications 65; Sec.-Gen. Southern Front Party 65-67, Vice-Pres. of Party 67-69; Minister of Labour and Co-operation 67-69; political detention without trial 69-70; Man. Dir. Bata Nationalized Corpn. 70-71, Watania Distillery Corpn. 71; Commr. for Equatoria Province with Ministerial rank 71-72; Minister of Finance and Econ. Planning in Southern Regional Govt., Juba 72-75; Speaker, Regional People's Assembly 75-78; mem. Cen. Cttee. and Political Bureau of Sudanese Socialist Union (SSU) 72-77; mem. for Juba Territorial Constituency in People's Regional Assembly 73-78; Asst. Sec.-Gen. SSU and Head of Southern Regional Secretariat 76-, mem. Exec. Bureau, SSU Cen. Cttee. Jan. 77-; Chair. Univ. of Juba; Order of the Two Niles, First Class; Order of the Constitution; Order of the Repub., First Class.
Executive Bureau of the Sudanese Socialist Union, P.O. Box 1850, Khartoum, Sudan.

Lozi, Ahmad Abdel Kareem Al-; Jordanian politician; b. 1925, Jubeiha, nr. Amman; ed. Teachers' Training Coll., Baghdad, Iraq.
Teacher, 50-53; Asst. to Chief of Royal Protocol 53-56; Head of Ceremonies, Ministry of Foreign Affairs 57; mem. Parl. 61-62, 62-63; Asst. to Chief of Royal Court 63-64; Minister of State, Prime Minister's Office 64-65; mem. Senate 65; Minister of the Interior for Municipal and Rural Affairs 67; mem. Senate 67; Minister of Finance 70-71; Prime Minister 71-73; Pres. Nat. Consultative Council April 78-; various Jordanian and foreign decorations.
National Consultative Council, Amman, Jordan.

M

Maarouf, Taha Muhyiddin (*see* Maruf, Taha Muhyiddin).

Ma'ayani, Ami, M.SC., M.A.; Israeli composer; b. 13 Jan. 1936, Tel-Aviv; ed. Tel-Aviv Univ., Haifa Technion and Columbia Univ., New York.
Studied music with Paul Ben-Haim and Prof. Vladimir Ussachevsky; Chair. League of Composers of Israel 70-73; Asst. Dir. Rubin Acad. of Music 76; Musical Dir. and Conductor of Nat. Youth Orchestra 70-73; Engel Prize (Tel-Aviv) 63; Prix Divvone (France) 67.

Works include: *Toccata for Harp* 59-60, *Concerto for Harp and Orchestra No. 1* 60, *Maquamat for Harp* 60, *Music for Strings* 62, *Teamin* 64, *Electronic Music* 64-65, *Concerto for Percussion and Eight Wind Instruments* 66, *Symphonic Concerto for Harp and Orchestra* 66, *Regalim* 66, *Concerto for Violin and Orchestra* 67, *Concerto for Violoncello and Orchestra* 67, *Concerto for Two Pianos and Orchestra* 69, *Qumran-Symphonic Metaphor* 70, *The War of the Sons of Light* (opera-oratorio in one act for solos, chorus, dancers and orchestra), chamber music, song cycles, *Symphony No. 2* 75, *Concerto for Viola and Orchestra* 75, *for Guitar and Orchestra* 76.
8 Nahum Street, Tel-Aviv, Israel.

Mabrouk, Ezzidin Al-, LL.B., LL.M.; Libyan politician; b. 28 May 1932; ed. Cairo Univ. and Univ. Coll., London.
Public Prosecutor, Tripoli 56; subsequently Judge, Summary Court, Tripoli, Pres. Tripoli Court and Counsellor of Supreme Appeal Court; Senior Legal Adviser, Org. of Petroleum Exporting Countries (OPEC); Minister of Petroleum, Libya 70-77; Sec. for Petroleum, Gen. People's Cttee. March 77-.
Office of the Secretary for Petroleum, P.O. Box 256, Tripoli, Libya.

Macki, Ahmed al-Nabi; Omani diplomatist; b. 17 Dec. 1939, Muscat; ed. Cairo and Paris.
Member, Oman Del. to UNESCO 69-70; Dir. of Offices of Prime Minister and Minister of Foreign Affairs 70-71; First Perm. Rep. of Oman to UN 71-72; Under-Sec. Ministry of Foreign Affairs 72-73; Perm. Rep. to UN 73-75, Amb. to U.S.A. 73-77, Non-Resident Amb. to Canada 74-77, to Argentina 75-77.
c/o Ministry of Foreign Affairs, Muscat, Oman.

Maghribi, Mahmoud Suleiman: Libyan politician; b. 1935; ed. George Washington Univ., U.S.A.
Helped to organize strikes of port workers June 67, for which he was sentenced to four years imprisonment and deprived of Libyan nationality; released Aug. 69; following the coup of Sept. 69 became Prime Minister, Minister of Finance and Agriculture, and of Agricultural Reform; resigned from the Govt. 70; Perm. Rep. to UN 71-72; Amb. to U.K. 73-77.
Secretariat for Foreign Affairs, Tripoli, Libya.

Maguid, Yahya Abdel, C.ENG., A.M.I.C.E.; Sudanese politician; b. 7 Oct. 1925, Omdurman; ed. Gordon Memorial Coll. and Imperial Coll., London.
Received practical training in construction of irrigation projects with British companies specializing in this field; held various posts in Ministry of Irrigation, rising to Under-Sec. Sept. 69; part-time lecturer, Univ. of Khartoum; Minister of Irrigation and Hydro-electric Power 71; Minister of State for Irrigation, Agriculture, Food and Natural Resources 71-74; Minister of Irrigation and Hydro-electric Power 75-; Sec.-Gen. UN Water Conf. June 76-March 77; mem. Int. Comm. for Hydraulic Law.
Ministry of Irrigation and Hydro-electric Power, P.O. Box 878, Khartoum, Sudan.

Mahdi, Dr. Sadiq al- (since 1978 known as **Sadiq Abdul Rahman**); Sudanese politician (great-grandson of Imam Abdul Rahman al-Mahdi); b. 1936; ed. Comboni Coll., Khartoum, and St. John's Coll., Oxford.
Leader, Umma Mahdist Party 61; Prime Minister 66-67; arrested on a charge of high treason 69; exiled April 70; returned to Sudan and arrested Feb. 72; released May 73, left Sudan 73, returned Sept. 77; mem. Cen. Cttee. Sudanese Socialist Union March 78-.
Publ. *Problems of the South Sudan*.
Sudanese Socialist Union, Khartoum, Sudan.

Mahdi al Tajir, Mohamed; United Arab Emirates administrator; b. 26 Dec. 1931, Bahrain; ed. Bahrain Govt. School and Preston Grammar School, Lancs., England.
Department of Port and Customs, Govt. of Bahrain, Dir. 55-63; Dir. Dept. of His Highness the Ruler's Affairs and Petroleum Affairs March 63-; Dir. Nat. Bank of Dubai Ltd. 63-; Dir. Dubai Petroleum Co. April 63-; Dir. Dubai Nat. Air Travel Agency Jan. 66-; Dir. Qatar-Dubai Currency Board Oct. 65-73, United Arab Emirates Currency Board 73; Chair. South Eastern Dubai Drilling Co. April 68-; Amb. of the United Arab Emirates to U.K. 72-, also accred. to France 72-77; Dir. Dubai Dry Dock Co. 73-; Hon. Citizen of State of Texas, U.S.A. 63.
Department of H.H. The Ruler's Affairs and Petroleum Affairs, P.O. Box 207, Dubai; and Embassy of the United Arab Emirates, 30 Prince's Gate, London, S.W.7, England.

Mahfuz, Nagib; Egyptian author; b. 11 Dec. 1911; ed. Univ. of Cairo.
Civil servant 34-; successively with Univ. of Cairo, Ministry of Waqfs, Dept. of Arts and Censorship Board; fmr. Dir.-Gen., now Adviser, Cinema Org. of Egypt; State Prize for 1st vol. *Bain al-Kasrain* 57.
Publs. novels: *Khan al Khalili* 46, *Midaq Alley* 47, *The Castle of Desire* (Vol. I) 56, *Between the Two Castles* (Vol. II) 57, *The Sugar Bowl* (Vol. III) 57 (trilogy *Bain al-Kasrain*), *The Thief and the Dogs* 61, *Quails in Autumn* 62, *The Road* 64, *The Beggar* 65, *Gossip by the Nile* 66, *Miramar* 67; short story collections: *The Whisper of Madness* 38, *God's World* 63, *At the Sign of the Black Cat* 69, *Under the Umbrella* 69, *A Story Without Beginning or End* 71; *Mirrors* (contemporary history) 72.
c/o Cinema Organization, TV Building, Maspero Street, Cairo, Egypt.

Mahgoub, Mohammed Ahmed; Sudanese lawyer and politician; b. 1908; ed. Gordon Coll. and Khartoum School of Law.
Qualified as an architect and lawyer; practising lawyer; mem. Legislative Assembly 48-54; accompanied Umma Party Del. to Lake Success 47; mem. Constitution Amendment Comm.; non-party candidate in Gen. Election 54; Leader of the Opposition 54-56; Minister of Foreign Affairs 56-58; practising solicitor 58-64; Minister of Foreign Affairs 64-Feb. 65; Prime Minister 65-66; Prime Minister and Minister of Foreign Affairs 67-68; Prime Minister and Minister of Defence 68-69.
Publs. *Democracy on Trial*, and several vols. of poetry (in Arabic).
60c Prince's Gate, Exhibition Road, London, S.W.7, England.

Mahroug, Smail; Algerian economist; b. 21 Oct. 1926, Bougaa; ed. Univ. of Paris.
In Morocco 53-62, active in Front de Libération Nationale (FLN), also Dir. of Planning, Moroccan Govt.; returned to Algeria, Chef de Cabinet of Head of Econ. Affairs, Provisional Govt. 62; Econ. Counsellor to Pres. 63-70; Dir.-Gen. Caisse Algérienne de Développement 63-65; Dir.-Gen. Ministry of Finance 65-66; Minister of Finance 70-Feb. 76; Chair. Union Méditeranéenne de Banques 76-; Chair. Group of 24, IMF 74.
Union Méditeranéenne de Banques, 50 rue de Lisbonne, Paris 8, France.

Majidi, Abdol-Majid, PH.D.; Iranian politician and lawyer; b. 11 Jan. 1929; ed. Teheran, Paris, Harvard and Illinois Univs.
Held posts in Export Devt. Bank and in Plan Org.; Head of Budget Bureau of Plan Org. 59-60; Financial and Admin. Asst. Man. Dir. of Plan Org. 62-64; Head of Budget Bureau formed in 1964; Deputy Prime Minister, Head of Cen. Budget Bureau, Plan Org. 66; Minister of Agricultural Products and Consumer Goods 67-68, of Labour and Social Affairs 68-73, of State in charge of Plan and Budget 73-74; Sec.-Gen. The Shahbanu Farah Foundation 77-79; mem. Arts and Culture High Council 68; Sec.-Gen. Red Lion and Sun Soc.

Makhous, Dr. Ibrahim; Syrian politician.
Member of Baath Party's Supreme Command 65; Deputy Prime Minister and Minister of Foreign Affairs 65, 66-68.
Damascus, Syria.

Makki, Mohammed Hassan, D.ECON.; Yemeni politician and diplomatist; b. 22 Dec. 1933; ed. Univs. of Bologna and Rome.
Adviser, Ministry of Econ. 60-62, Deputy Minister 62, Minister 63-64; Chair. Yemen Bank for Reconstruction and Devt. 62-63; Minister of Foreign Affairs 64, 66, 67-68, of Communications 65; Adviser to the Prime Minister 65-66; Amb. to Italy 68-70, to Fed. Repub. of Germany 70-72; Deputy Prime Minister 72-74, Prime Minister March-June 74; Deputy Prime Minister for Econ. Affairs June-Dec. 74; Perm. Rep. to UN 74-76, Amb. to U.S.A. and Canada 75-76.
Ministry of Foreign Affairs, Sana'a, Yemen Arab Republic.

Maktum, H. H. Sheikh Rashid bin Said al-; Ruler of Dubai; b. 1914; ed. privately.
Succeeded his father, Said bin Maktum, as 4th Sheikh 58; Vice-Pres. United Arab Emirates (UAE) Dec. 71-; Prime Minister May 79-.
Royal Palace, Dubai, United Arab Emirates.

Malek, Reda; Algerian diplomatist; b. 1931; ed. Univs. of Algiers and Paris.
Director of weekly *El Moudjahid*, Tunis 57-61; mem. F.L.N. Del. to Evian talks 61; Amb. to Yugoslavia 63-65, to France 65-70, to U.S.S.R. 70-77; Minister of Information and Culture 77-79.
c/o Ministry of Information and Culture, 119 rue Didouche Mourad, Algiers, Algeria.

Malik, Charles Habib, M.A., PH.D.; Lebanese philosopher, educationist and diplomatist; b. 1906, Btirram, Al-Koura; ed. American Univ. of Beirut, and Harvard and Freiburg Univs.
Instructor Maths. and Physics American Univ. Beirut 27-29; with *Al Hilal* Publ. House, Cairo 29-30; with Rockefeller Found. Exped., Cairo 30-32; Asst. in Philosophy Harvard 36-37; Instructor in Philosophy American Univ. Beirut 37-39; Adjunct-Prof. 39-43, Assoc. Prof. 43-45 Head of Dept. 39-45, on leave 45-55, Dean of Graduate Studies and Prof. of Philosophy 55-60, Distinguished Prof. of Philosophy 62-; E. K. Hall Visiting Prof., Dartmouth Coll. 60; Visiting Prof. Harvard Summer School 60; Minister of Lebanon to U.S.A. 45-53, to Cuba 46-55; Minister designate to Venezuela 47-48; Amb. to U.S.A. 53-55; Lebanese del. UN Conf. and Signatory UN Charter 45; mem. and Chair. Lebanese del. to UN 45-54; Pres. 13th Gen. Assembly UN 58-59; del. to Bandung Conf. 55; Minister for Foreign Affairs 56-58, for Nat. Education and Fine Arts 56-57; mem. of Parl. 57-60; Pres. Security Council 53, 54; Pres. Economic and Social Council 48; Chair. Human Rights Comm. 51, 52; Chair. Lebanese del. for Peace Treaty with Japan 51; Grand First Magistrate of the Holy Orthodox Church; Pres. World Council of Christian Educ. 67-71; Vice-Pres. United Bible Societies 66-72; Fellow Inst. for Advanced Religious Studies at the Univ. of Notre Dame, Indiana 69; Hon. life mem. American Bible Soc. mem.; Société européenne de Culture; Fellow American Asscn. for Advancement of Science, American Geog. Soc.; mem. American Philos. Assocn., American Philos. Soc., American Acad. of Arts and Sciences, Acad. of Human Rights, etc.; founding mem. Lebanese Acad.; numerous awards and decorations.
Publs. *War and Peace* 50, *Problems of Asia* 51, *Problem of Coexistence* 55, *Christ and Crisis* 62, *Man in the Struggle for Peace* 63, *God and Man in Contemporary Christian Thought* 70, *God and Man in Contemporary Islamic Thought* 72; numerous other published works and articles.
American University, Beirut, Lebanon; and Harvard Club, 27 West 44th Street, New York, U.S.A.

Malikyar, Abdullah; Afghan diplomatist; b. 1909; ed. Isteklal Coll., Kabul, and Franco-Persian Coll., Teheran.
Secretary and Gen. Dir. Prime Minister's Office 31-35; Head, Govt. Purchasing Office, Europe 36-40; Vice-Pres. Central Bank and Deputy Minister of Commerce 41-42; Gov. of Herat 42-47, 51-52; Minister of Communications 48-50; Pres. Hillmand Valley Authority Projects 53-62; Minister of Commerce 55-57, of Finance 57-64, Deputy Prime Minister 63-64; Amb. to U.K. 64-67, to U.S.A. 67-77, concurrently to Argentina, Brazil, Canada, Chile and Mexico, to Iran 77-78; Sardar Ali Reshteen Decoration.
c/o Ministry of Foreign Affairs, Kabul, Afghanistan.

Mammeri, Mouloud; Algerian writer; b. 28 Dec. 1917; ed. Rabat, Algiers and Paris.
Director of Anthropological, Prehistoric and Ethnological Research Centre, Algiers; Prix des quatre jurys for *La colline oubliée* 53.
Publs. Novels: in French *La colline oubliée* 52, *Le Sommeil du juste* 55, *L'opium et le bâton* 65; Play: *Le Foehn* 67, *Le Banquet* 74; *Les isefra de Si Mohand* (collection of oral poems in Berber).
82 rue Laperlier, El-Biar, Algiers, Algeria.

Marei, Sayed Ahmed; Egyptian agriculturist and politician; b. 26 Aug. 1913; ed. Faculty of Agriculture, Cairo Univ.
Worked on his father's farm after graduation; subsequently with import-export, pharmaceutical, seed, and fertilizer companies; mem. Egyptian House of Commons 44; Del. mem. Higher Cttee. for Agrarian Reform 52-; Chair. of Board, Agricultural Co-operative Credit Bank 55-56; initiated "Supervised Credit System"; Minister of State for Agrarian Reform 56-57; Minister of Agriculture and Agrarian Reform 57-58; Central Minister for Agricultural and Agrarian Reform in the U.A.R. 58-61; Dep. Speaker, Nat. Assembly and Man. Dir. Bank Misr, Cairo 62-67; Minister of Agriculture and Agrarian Reform 67-70; Deputy Premier for Agriculture and Irrigation 72-73; First Sec. Arab Socialist Union (ASU) 72-73; Personal Asst. to Pres. Sadat 73; Sec.-Gen. UN World Food Conf. Rome 74; Pres. UN World Food Council 75-77; Speaker, People's Assembly 75-78; Asst. to Pres. Oct. 78-.
Publs. *Agrarian Reform in Egypt* 57, *U.A.R. Agriculture Enters a New Age* 60, *Food Production in Developing Countries* 68.
Office of the President, Cairo; and 9 Sh. Shagaret El Dorr, Zamalek, Cairo, Egypt.

Martin, Jean-Pierre, PH.D.; French United Nations official; b. 2 Jan. 1926; ed. Univs. of Montpellier and Paris.
Economist, UN Dept. of Econ. and Social Affairs 49-60; Special Asst. to the Special Rep. of Sec.-Gen. of UN in Congo 60-61; Chief, Financial Policies and Institutions Section, UN Dept. of Econ. and Social Affairs 61-62; Chef de Cabinet of Under-Sec.-Gen. of UN for Econ. and Social Affairs 62-66; Dir. UN Econ. and Social Office, Beirut 66-74, Econ. Comm. for Western Asia (ECWA), Beirut 74-.
Publs. *Les Finances de Guerre du Canada* 51, *Les Finances publiques britanniques 1939-1955* 56; articles on financial and econ. subjects.
United Nations, B.P. 4656, Beirut, Lebanon.

Maruf, Taha Muhyiddin, LL.B.; Iraqi politician and diplomatist; b. 1924, Sulaimaniyah; ed. Coll. of Law, Univ. of Baghdad.
Worked as lawyer; joined Diplomatic Service 49; Minister of State 68-70; Minister of Works and Housing 68; Amb. to Italy, concurrently non-resident Amb. to Malta and Albania 70-74; Vice-Pres. of Iraq April 74-; mem. Higher Cttee. of Nat. Progressive Front 75-; Chair. African Affairs Bureau of Revolutionary Command Council 76-.
Office of the Vice-President of the Republic, National Assembly Building, Baghdad, Iraq.

Mashhour, Mashhour Ahmed; Egyptian engineer and company executive; b. April 1918; ed. Faculty of Eng., Cairo Univ., Staff Officers' Coll.
Ministry of Transport 41; Army Eng. 42; eng. studies in Corps of Engs., British Army 43-44; tech. studies in Corps of Engs., U.S. Army; Officer, Corps of Engs., Egyptian Army; Lecturer, U.A.R. Acad. of War 48-52; Dir. of Transit, Suez Canal Authority 56; Del. Chair. of Canaltex Co. and mem. Board of Dirs. of Timsah Ship Building Co., Ismailia; Chair. and Man. Dir. Suez Canal Authority 65-; Sec. for Governorate of Ismailia, Arab Socialist Union 65-71, mem. People's Assembly 76-; mem. Nat. Council of Production; Repub. Medal (3rd Class); Mil. Service Medal (1st Class); Liberation Medal; Palestine Medal; Order of Merit (1st Class); Commdr. Légion d'honneur (France); Order of Polonia Restituta; Mono-Grand Officier (Togo).
Suez Canal Authority, Ismailia, Egypt.

Masmoudi, Mohamed, LL.B.; Tunisian politician; b. 29 May 1925; ed. Tunis and Univ. of Paris.
Member of Tunisian Nationalist Movement 34-; Minister of State in Govt. negotiating Tunisian independence 53-55; Minister of the Economy 55-56; Amb. to France 56-58, 61-70; Minister of Information 58-61; Sec.-Gen. Destour Socialist Party 69-74; Minister of Foreign Affairs 70-74; assoc. with *Action*, later renamed *Afrique Action*; in exile 74-77; returned to Tunisia 77; under house arrest Dec. 77-.
La Manouba, Tunis, Tunisia.

Mavrommatis, Andreas; Cypriot lawyer; b. 1932, Larnaca; ed. Greek Gymnasium, Limassol, and Lincoln's Inn, London.
Called to Bar 54; practised law, Cyprus 54-58; Magistrate, Paphos 58-60; District Judge 60; District Judge, Nicosia 64-70; Minister of Labour and Social Insurance 70-72; Special Legal Adviser to Ministry of Foreign Affairs 72-; Head Cyprus Del. to European Conf. on Security and Co-operation; Perm. Rep. to UN Office in Geneva 75-79, in New York Jan. 79-; Vice-Pres. ECOSOC; Head Cyprus Del., Belgrade 77; Chair. Human Rights Cttee.
Publ. *A List of Treaties of the Republic of Cyprus in Force on 1.1.1973* 74.
Permanent Mission of Cyprus at the United Nations, 820 Second Avenue, New York, N.Y. 10017, U.S.A.; 10 Plato Street, Nicosia 116, Cyprus.

Maximos V Hakim, (fmrly. **Archbishop George S. Hakim**), D.D.; Lebanese ecclesiastic; b. 18 May 1908, Tanta, Egypt; ed. St. Louis School, Tanta, Holy Family Jesuit School, Cairo and St. Anne Seminary, Jerusalem.
Teacher Patriarchal School, Beirut 30-31; Rector and Principal Patriarchal School, Cairo 31-43; Archbishop of Acre, Haifa, Nazareth and all Galilee 43-67; elected Patriarch of Antioch and all the East, Alexandria and Jerusalem Nov. 67; founded *Le Lien*, (French) Cairo 36, *Ar-Rabita* (Arabic) Haifa 43; Commdr. Légion d'Honneur; Dr. h.c. (Laval Univ. Canada, Algiers Univ. and many U.S. univs.).
Publ. *Pages d'Evangile lues en Galilée* (transl. into English Dutch and Spanish) 54.
Greek Catholic Patriarchate, P.O. Box 50076, Beirut, Lebanon; P.O. Box 22249, Damascus, Syria; Daher 16, Cairo, Egypt.

Mazar, Benjamin, D.PHIL.; Russian-born Israeli archaeologist; b. 28 June 1906; ed. Berlin and Giessen Univs.
Settled in Palestine 29; joined staff of Hebrew Univ. Jerusalem 43, Prof. of Biblical History and Historical Geography of Palestine 51-, Rector 52-61, Pres. 53-61, Pro-Rector 61-; Chair. Israel Exploration Soc.; Dir. excavations Ramat Rahel 32, Beth Shearim 36-40, Beth Yerah 42-43, Tell Qasile 48-50, 59, Ein Gedi 60, 62, 64, 65, Old City of Jerusalem 68-75; mem. Israel Acad. of Science; Hon. mem. British Soc. for Old Testament Study, American Soc. of Biblical Literature and Exegesis; Hon. D.H.L. (Hebrew Union Coll., Jewish Inst. of Religion, U.S.A., Jewish Theological Seminary of America); Hon. Ph.D. (Hebrew Univ., Jerusalem).
Publs. *Untersuchungen zur alten Geschichte Syriens und Palästinas* 30, *History of Archaeological Research in Palestine* 36, *History of Palestine from the early days to the Israelite Kingdom* 38, *Beth Shearim Excavations 1936-40* 40 (2nd edn. 58), *Historical Atlas of Palestine: Israel in Biblical Times* 41, *Excavations at Tell Qasile* 51; Chair. Editorial Board *Encyclopaedia Biblica* 50-78; *Ein Gedi* 64, *The World History of the Jewish People Vol. II* (editor) 67, *The Excavations in the Old City of Jerusalem* 69, 71, *The Mountain of the Lord* 76.
Hebrew University of Jerusalem, Jerusalem; and 9 Abarbanel Street, Jerusalem, Israel.

Mazidi, Feisal, B.ECON.; Kuwaiti economist; b. 2 May 1933; ed. Kuwait and Univ. Coll. of N. Staffordshire, Keele, England.
Appointed to Dept. of Finance and Economy 59; Dir. State Chlorine and Salt Board; Dir. Kuwait Oil Co. Ltd. 60; Econ. Asst. to Minister of Finance and Economy 60; Chair. Econ. and Industrial Cttee. 61; Dir. Kuwait Fund for Econ. Development of Arab Countries 62; mem. Kuwait Univ. Higher Council 62-64; Chair. and Man. Dir. Kuwait Chemical Fertilizer Co. 64-71; Chair. Govt. Oil Concession Cttee. 63-65, Govt. Refinery Cttee. 64-66, Kuwait Maritime Mercantile Co. 65-70; Dir. Petrochemical Industries Co. 63-71, Kuwait United Fisheries Co. 71-76; Pres. Kuwait Associated Consultants 71-; Chair. Kuwait Resources Engineering and Management International (KUREMI) 76-; mem. Kuwait Econs. Soc.; Arab League Prize for paper on Natural Gas 63.
Publs. *Natural Gas in Kuwait and its Utilization* 63, *Kuwait as a Base for Petrochemicals* 65, *International Investments* 79.
Kuwait Associated Consultants, P.O. Box 5443, Kuwait.

Meguid, Ahmet Esmat Abdel (*see* Abdel Meguid, Ahmet Esmat).

Mehr, Farhang, LL.M., PH.D., Iranian lawyer, economist and financial executive; b. 1924; ed. Univs. of Teheran, Southampton and London.
Professor of Law and Public Finance; Legal Adviser, Head of Industrial Relations Dept., Nat. Iranian Oil Co. 57; Adviser to High Council of Econs. and to Minister of Commerce 58; Dir.-Gen. Petroleum and Int. Affairs 59; Gov. for Iran, Org. of Petroleum Exporting Countries 63-68; Dir.-Gen. of Econ. Affairs 63-78; Chair. of several socs. including Ancient Iranian Cultural Soc. 63, Zoroastrian Anjuman 65; Deputy Minister of Finance 64-78; Asst. to Prime Minister 66-78; Chair. of Board, Man. Dir. Iran Insurance Co. 67; Trustee, Teheran Coll. of Insurance, Kerman Univ., Computer Coll., Inst. of Int. Political and Econ. Studies; Chancellor Pahlavi Univ. 72-79; Hon. LL.D. (Univ. of Pennsylvania) 76; Homayoun 2nd and 3rd Class, Taj 2nd Class, Sepah 1st Class, Kah 1st Class, Abadani va Pishraft 1st Class.
Publs. *Labour Law and Social Insurance* 60, *Government Corporation* 64, *Public Finance* 67.
c/o Chancellor's Office, Pahlavi University, Shiraz, Iran.

Mehran, Hassan Ali; Iranian central banker; b. 24 Dec. 1937, Teheran; ed. Univ. of Nottingham, England.
Assistant Lecturer and Research Asst., Univ. of Bristol, U.K. 65-68; worked at IMF 68-69; Dir.-Gen. of Projects and Research and Deputy Man. Dir. of Research Centre, Ministry of Econ. 69-71; Under-Sec. of Econ. 71-74; Deputy Minister of Econ. Affairs and Finance 74-75; Gov. Cen. Bank of Iran 75-78; Chair. Bank Tosee Keshavarzi Iran 78-79.
36 Pirasteh Avenue, Teheran, Iran.

Melen, Ferit; Turkish politician; b. 1906, Van; ed. School of Political Science, Univ. of Ankara.
District Officer, Local Admin. 31-33; Auditor, Ministry of Finance 33-43, Dir.-Gen. of Incomes 43-50; Deputy for Van (Repub. People's Party) 50-64; Minister of Finance 62-65; Senator for Van 64-67; mem. Council of Europe 66-67; participated in formation of Nat. Reliance Party (now part of Republican Reliance Party) 67, later Deputy Leader; Minister of Nat. Defence 71-72, 75-77; Prime Minister 72-73.
Republican Reliance Party, Ankara, Turkey.

Mellink, Machteld Johanna, PH.D.; Netherlands archaeologist; b. 26 Oct. 1917; ed. Amsterdam and Utrecht Univs.
Field Asst. Tarsus excavations 47-49; Asst. Prof. of Classical Archæology Bryn Mawr Coll. 49-53, Assoc. Prof., Chair. Dept. of Classical and Near Eastern Archæology 53-62, Prof. 62-; staff mem. Gordion excavations organized by Pennsylvania Univ. Museum 50-, during which the putative tomb of King Midas was discovered 57; field dir. excavations at Karataş-Semayük in Lycia 63-, excavations of painted tombs in Elmali district 70-.
Publs. *Hyakinthos* 43, *A Hittite Cemetery at Gordion* 56; *Archaeology in Asia Minor* (reports in *American Journal of Archaeology*) 55-, editor *Dark Ages and Nomads c. 1000 B.C., Frühe Stufen der Kunst* (with J. Filip) 74.
Department of Classical and Near Eastern Archaeology, Bryn Mawr College, Bryn Mawr, Pa. 19010, U.S.A.

Memmi, Albert; Tunisian writer; b. 15 Dec. 1920; ed. Lycée Carnot, Tunis, Univ. of Algiers and Univ. de Paris.
Teacher of Philosophy in Tunis 55; Dir. Psychological Centre, Tunis 56; Researcher, Centre national de la recherche scientifique, Paris 59-; Asst. Prof. Ecole pratique des hautes études 59-66, Prof. 66-70; Prof. Univ. of Paris 70-, Dir. Dept. of Social Sciences 73; Pres. PEN Club 76; Prix Fénéon 54, Prix de Carthage, Prix Simba 78; Commdr. Ordre de Nichan Iftikhar; Palmes Académiques; mem. Acad. des Sciences d'Outremer 75.
Publs. include: *The Pillar of Salt* 53, *Strangers* 55, *Anthologie des écrivains nord-africains* 55, *Colonizer, Colonized* 57, *Portrait of a Jew* 62, *Le français et le racisme* 65, *The Liberation of the Jew* 66, *The Dominated Man* 68, *Le Scorpion* 69, *Jews and Arabs* 74, *Entretien* 75, *La Terre Intérieure* 76, *Le désert* 77.
5 rue Saint Merri, Paris 4e, France.

Menemencioğlu, Turgut; Turkish diplomatist; b. 1914; ed. Robert Coll., Istanbul, and Geneva Univ.
Turkish Ministry of Foreign Affairs 39-; Perm. Del., European Office UN, Geneva 50-52; Counsellor, Turkish Embassy, Washington 52; Dir. Gen. Econ. Affairs, Ministry of Foreign Affairs 52-54; Dep. Perm. Rep. to UN 54-60; Ambassador to Canada 60; Perm. Rep. to UN 60-62; Amb. to U.S.A. 62-66; High Political Adviser Ministry of Foreign Affairs 67; Sec.-Gen. Central Treaty Org. 68-71; Adviser, Ministry of Foreign Affairs 71-72; Amb. to U.K. 72-78.
c/o Ministry of Foreign Affairs, Dışişleri Bakanlığı, Müdafaa Cad, Bakanlıklar, Ankara, Turkey.

Meridor, Yaacov; Israeli business executive; b. 1 Sept. 1913.
Joined Irgun Zevayi Leumi (IZL) 33, Commdr. in Chief 41-43, second in command 44-48; Co-founder of the Herut movement; mem. Knesset (Parl.) 50-52; founder, Chair. of Board, Maritime Fruit Carriers Ltd., Haifa 56-69.
Publ. *Long is the Road to Freedom.*
Maritime Fruit Carriers Ltd., 53 Shderot Hameginim, P.O. Box 1501, Haifa, Israel.

Merlin, Samuel; Israeli author and director of political studies; b. 17 Jan. 1910; ed. Lycée, Kishineff, Univ. of Paris.
Secretary-General World Exec., Zionist Revisionist and New Zionist Org. 34-38; Editor-in-Chief Yiddish daily *Di Tat*, Warsaw, Poland 38-39; Sec.-Gen. Hebrew Cttee. for Nat. Liberation 40-48; mem. First Knesset 48-51; Pres. Israel Press Ltd. 50-57; Dir. of Political Studies, Inst. for Mediterranean Affairs, N.Y. 57-; Lecturer, Middle East Studies, Fairleigh Dickinson Univ., N.J. 71-; Hon. mem. of Abu Gosh village near Jerusalem.
Publs. *The Palestine Refugee Problem* 58, *United States Policy in the Middle East* 60, *The Ascent of Man* (Co-Author) 63, *The Cyprus Dilemma* (Editor) 67, *The Big Powers and the Present Crisis in the Middle East* 68, *The Search for Peace in the Middle East* 69, *Guerre et Paix au Moyen Orient* 70.
Institute for Mediterranean Affairs, 1078 Madison Avenue, New York, N.Y. 10028, U.S.A.

Merzban, Mohammed Abdullah, M.A.; Egyptian politician; b. 20 Jan. 1918, Fayoum; ed. Fuad Univ. and Harvard Univ.
Lecturer, Faculty of Commerce, Cairo Univ. until 56; Sec.-Gen. Ministry of Industry 56-58; Gen. Man. Industrialization Authority 58-60; Chair. Al-Nasr Org. 60-61; Chair. Spinning & Weaving Org. 61-66; Chair. Bank of Cairo 66-68; Minister of Supply and Home Trade 68-70; Minister of Economy and Foreign Trade 70-73, also acting Minister of Supply and Home Trade 71-73; Deputy Prime Minister 72-73.
Publs. *Financial Management, Sales Management, Mathematics of Marketing.*
c/o INVESTRADE, 5 Talat Harb Street, Cairo, Egypt.

Meshel, Yeruham; Israeli trade unionist; b. 24 Nov. 1912, Pinsk, Russia.
Immigrated to Palestine 33; Sec. Metal Workers' Union, Tel-Aviv, mem. Tel-Aviv Labour Council Exec. 45; mem. Trade Union Centre of Histadrut Exec. Cttee., Chair. Industrial Workers' Div. 50-60, mem. Central Exec. Bureau 60-, Chair. Trade Union Centre 61, Deputy Sec.-Gen. Histadrut 64-74, Head of Histadrut Social Security Centre and Arab Workers' Dept., Acting Sec.-Gen. Histadrut 73, Sec.-Gen. 74-; Vice-Pres. ICFTU and Asian Regional Org. (ARO) of ICFTU 75-; mem. Central Cttee. and Bureau, Israel Labour Party; rep. to numerous int. labour confs.
Histadrut, 93 Arlosorof Street, Tel-Aviv, Israel.

Mesnil du Buisson, Robert du, Count, D. ès L., D. en D.; French archaeologist; b. 19 April 1895.
Dir. French Archaeological Missions in Syria, Egypt and France; Lecturer Ecole des Hautes Etudes 38-; Head Archaeological Mission, Centre Nat. de la Recherche Scientifique, Palmyra 65-; Pres. Société Nat. des Antiquaires de France 46-47; Pres. Société Historique et Archéologique de l'Orne 47-55, Hon. Pres. 56-; Pres. Soc. du Manoir d'Argentelles 57-; Dir. Centre Culturel et Touristique de l'Orne 67-; Dir. of the Review *L'Ethnographie* 69-, of *Au Pays d'Argentelles* 76-; Vice-Pres. Fédération des Sociétés normandes 47-55, Pres. Soc. d'Ethnographie de Paris 69-; Commdr. of Legion of Honour 46; Lauréat Institut de France, Acad. des Inscriptions et Belles-Lettres 40, 63, Acad. des Beaux-Arts 58; Gold Medal Soc. d'Encouragement au Progrès 74.
Publs. *Les ruines d'El-Mishrifé au Nord-Est de Homs* 27, *La technique des fouilles archéologiques* 33, *Le site archéologique de Mishrifé-Qatna* 35, *Les noms et signes égyptiens désignant des vases* 35, *Souran et Tell Masin* 35, *Le site de Qadesh* 36, *Inscriptions juives de Doura-Europos* 37, *Inventaire des inscriptions palmyréniennes de Doura-Europos* 39, *Les peintures de la Synagogue de Doura 245-256 ap. J-C.* 39, *Tessères et monnaies de Palmyre* 44, *Les ouvrages du siège a Doura-Europos* 45, *Le site archéologique d'Exmes (Uxoma)* 46, *Le sautoir d'Atargatis et la chaîne d'amulettes* 47, *Baghouz, l'ancienne Corsôté* 48, *Une voie commerciale de haute antiquité dans l'Orne* 51, *Les*

dieux et les déesses en forme de vase dans L'Antiquité Orientale, La palissade gauloise d'Alençon 52, *L'alcôve royale dite "Lit de Justice d'Argentelles"* 53, *Un constructeur du Château de la Celle-Saint-Cloud, Jacques Jérémie Roussel* 54, *Les barques de la Grande Pyramide et le voyage au Paradis* 56, *Les enceintes gauloises d'Alençon* 58, *Inscriptions sur jarres de Doura-Europos* 59, *Une famille de Chevaliers de Malte, Les Costart* 60, *Le vrai nom de Bôl, prédécesseur de Bêl, à Palmyre* 61, *Les tessères et les monnaies de Palmyre de la Bibliothèque Nationale* 62, *Origine et évolution du Panthéon de Tyr, Les Chaussons de la Salle* 63, *Les origines du Panthéon Palmyrénien* 64, *Le dieu-Griffon à Palmyre et chez les Hittites* 65, *Le dieu Ousô sur des monnaies de Tyr* 65, *Le drame des deux étoiles du matin et du soir dans l'antiquité orientale* 67, *Les origines du mythe animalier de la planète Vénus, Une ancienne famille de Normandie, les du Mesnil du Buisson* 68, *Etudes sur les dieux phéniciens* 70, *Nouvelles études sur les dieux et les mythes de Canaan* 73, *Les voyages de Gilgamesh* 74, *Le mythe de la Tour de Babel* 76.
63 rue de Varenne, Paris 7e; and Château de Champobert, par Exmes (Orne), France.

Messadi, Prof. Mahmoud; Tunisian educationist and politician; b. 28 Jan. 1911, Tazarka; ed. Coll. Sadiki and Lycée Carnot, Tunis, Univ. of Paris.
Professor Lycée Carnot 36-38, Coll. Sadiki 38-48; Asst. Prof. Centre d'Etudes Islamiques, Univ. of Paris 48-52, Inst. des Hautes Etudes de Paris 48-55; Head Dept. of Secondary Educ., Tunis 55-58; Insp.-Gen. of Public Educ 58-; Sec. of State for Nat. Educ. Youth and Sports 58-68; Minister of State 69-70; Minister of Cultural Affairs 73-Dec. 76; Deputy, Nat. Assembly; mem. Cen. Cttee. Destour Socialist Party; Grand Cordon Ordre de l'Indépendance, Ordre de la République.
Publs. *Essoud* (The Dam), *Haddatha Abou Houraira, Maouled en-Nassian* (Birth of Oblivion).
c/o Ministère des Affaires Culturelles, Place du Gouvernement, Tunis, Tunisia.

Mestiri, Mahmoud; Tunisian diplomatist; b. 25 Dec. 1929; ed. Inst. d'Etudes Politiques, Univ. de Lyons.
Served in several Tunisian Dels. to UN; Alt. Rep. to UN 58, 59; Head of Tunisian special Diplomatic Mission to Congo (Léopoldville) 60; Asst. to Personal Rep. of UN Sec.-Gen. to Govt. of Belgium 61; Deputy Perm. Rep. of Tunisia to UN 62-65; Sec.-Gen. for Foreign Affairs, Tunis 65-67; Perm. Rep. to UN 67-69; Chair. UN Special Cttee. on the Situation with Regard to Implementation of Declaration on the Granting of Independence to Colonial Countries and Peoples 68; Amb. to Belgium Sept. 69, to Luxembourg Oct. 69, to EEC Nov. 69, to Fed. Repub. of Germany 71-73, to U.S.S.R. 73-74, and to Poland 74-76, to UN 76-.
Permanent Mission of Tunisia to the United Nations, 40 East 71st Street, New York, N.Y. 10021, U.S.A.

Meulen, Daniel van der (*see* van der Meulen, Daniel).

Mhedhebi, Béchir; Tunisian politician; b. 1912.
Ambassador to Lebanon, Kuwait, Libya 65-70; Sec.-Gen. Ministry of Foreign Affairs 70-71; Minister of Defence 71-72; Amb. to U.K. 72-74, to Morocco 74-76; mem. Political Bureau, Destour Socialist Party Oct. 71-.
c/o Ministry of Foreign Affairs, Tunis, Tunisia.

Michałowski, Kazimierz; Polish archaeologist; b. 14 Dec. 1901.
Emeritus Professor of Mediterranean Archaeology, Warsaw Univ.; mem. Presidium, Polish Acad. of Sciences, Head Inst. of Mediterranean Archaeology; mem. numerous foreign acads. and scientific socs.; Vice-Dir. Warsaw Nat. Museum; in charge of Franco-Polish excavations, Egypt 37-39, Polish excavations, Crimea 56-58, Egypt 57-, Syria 59-, Sudan 60-, Cyprus 65-, Iraq 73-; Chair. Int. Working Group of Archaeologists and Landscape Architects, Abu Simbel; Pres. Soc. for Nubian Studies; Vice-Pres. Int. Asscn. of Egyptologists; Dir. of Polish Centre of Archaeology, Cairo; Prix de l'Acad. des Inscriptions et Belles Lettres 33; State Prize 55, 66; Dr. h.c. (Strasbourg, Cambridge and Uppsala); Silver Cross Virtuti Militari, Cmmdr. Cross with Star of Order Polonia Restituta, Order of Banner of Labour, Commdr. Corona d'Italia, Officier Légion d'Honneur, numerous other Polish and foreign decorations.
Publs. *Les portraits hellénistiques et romains* 32, *Fouilles Franco-Polonaises à Tell Edfou* 37-50, *Mirmeki* 56, *Fouilles Polonaises à Palmyre* 60-64, *Fouilles Polonaises à Faras* 62-65, *Die Kathedrale aus dem Wüstensand* 67, *L'Art de l'Egypte Ancienne* 68 (English edn. 69), *Faras, Wall Paintings in the Collection of the National Museum in Warsaw* 74 (German and Polish edns. 74), *Storia della Scultura nel Mondo, Egitto* 78.
Sewerynów 6, Warsaw, Poland.

Mili, Mohamed Ezzedine; Tunisian civil servant; b. 4 Dec. 1917; ed. Ecole Normale Supérieure de Saint-Cloud and Ecole Nationale Supérieure des Télécommunications, Paris.
Telecommunications Engineer, Ministry of Posts 47-56; Dir.-Gen. of Telecommunications 57-65; Vice-Pres. Plan for Africa, Int. Telecommunication Union (ITU) 60-64; Pres. Admin. Council 64, Pres. Plan for Africa ITU 64-65, Vice-Sec.-Gen. ITU 65-66, Sec.-Gen. 66-; Commdr. Ordre de la République (Tunisia), Commdr. Order of Vasa (Sweden), Officier Ordre de l'Indépendance (Tunisia), Gran Cruz de la Orden de Duarte, Sánchez y Mella con Placa de Plata (Dominican Repub.), Honor al Mérito Medal (Paraguay), Grand Star of the Order of Merit of Telecommunications (Spain), Commdr. of the Order of Leopold (Belgium); Philip Reis Medal (Fed. Repub. of Germany); Diploma of Honour (Int. Council of Archives) 78.
International Telecommunication Union, Place des Nations, 1211 Geneva 20, Switzerland.

Minai, Ahmad, M.A., PH.D.; Iranian economist and diplomatist; b. 10 Sept. 1921; ed. Teheran Univ., Univs. of Glasgow and Oxford, American Univ., Washington, D.C.
Lecturer, London Univ. 49-50; joined Foreign Service 50; Third Sec., Washington, D.C. 53; First Sec., Ankara 60; Special Aide to Prime Minister with rank of Dir.-Gen., mem. High Econ. Council 61-62; Econ. Counsellor, Washington, D.C. 63; Vice-Gov. Agricultural Bank of Iran 65-66; Dir. Dept. of Econ. Affairs, Ministry of Foreign Affairs 66-67; Minister-Counsellor, Islamabad 67; Consul-Gen., Karachi 69; Minister-Counsellor, London 70; Dir. Fourth Political Dept., Ministry of Foreign Affairs 73; Amb. 74; Sec.-Gen. Regional Co-operation for Devt. May 74-.
Publs. several articles on econ. topics.
Office of the Secretary-General, Regional Co-operation for Development, 5 Los Angeles Avenue, Teheran, Iran.

Moalla, Mansour, L. EN D., L. ÈS L., LL.D.; Tunisian economist; b. 1 May 1930, Sfax; ed. Inst. des Etudes Politiques, Ecole Nat. d'Administration, Paris.
Inspecteur des Finances 56; Technical Adviser, Ministry of Finance 57-58; Dir.-Gen. Banque Centrale de Tunisie 58-61; Dir. of Admin., Office of the Pres. 61-63, 68-69; Dir. Ecole Nat. d'Administration (ENA) 63-67; Under-Sec. of State, Ministry of Commerce and Industry 67-68; Sec. of State (then Minister) for Posts, Telegraphs and Telecommunications (PTT) 69-70; Deputy Minister in charge of the Nat. Plan 70-71, Minister 71-74; mem. Cen. Cttee., Political Bureau, Destour Socialist Party 71-; Grand Cordon, Order of the Repub., Order of Independence.
32 avenue de la République, Carthage, Tunisia.

Moberly, John Campbell, C.M.G.; British diplomatist; b. 27 May 1925, Exmouth, Devon; ed. Winchester Coll. and Magdalen Coll., Oxford.
War service in Royal Navy 43-47; entered Foreign (later Diplomatic) Service 50; service at Foreign Office and in Bahrain and Kuwait 50-59; British Political Agent in Doha, Qatar 59-62; First Sec., Athens 62-66; with FCO 66-68; Canadian Nat. Defence Coll., Kingston, Ont. 68-69; Counsellor, Washington, D.C. 69-73; Dir. Middle East Centre for Arab Studies, Shemlan, Lebanon 73-75; Amb. to Jordan 75-79; Asst. Under-Sec. of State, FCO 79-.
55 Cardigan Street, London S.E.11; and The Cedars, Temple Sowerby, Penrith, Cumbria, England.

Mohammed Reza Pahlavi (*see* Pahlavi, Mohammed Reza).

Mohammed Zahir Shah; fmr. King of Afghanistan; b. 15 Oct. 1914; ed. Habibia High School, Istiqlal Coll. (both in Kabul), Lycée Janson-de-Sailly and Univ. of Montpellier, France.
Graduated with highest honours; attended Infantry Officers' School, Kabul 32; married Lady Homira, Nov. 4th 1931; children, Princess Bilqis, Prince Ahmad Shah Khan, Princess Maryam, Prince Mohammed Nadir Khan, Prince Shah Mahmoud Khan, Prince Mohammed Daoud Jan, Prince Mirvis Jan; Asst. Min. in Ministry of Nat. Defence 32-33; acting Minister of Educ. 33; crowned King Nov. 8th, 33, deposed July 73; abdicated Aug. 73.

Mohieddin, Zakaria; Egyptian army officer and politician; b. May 1918; ed. Mil. Coll. and Staff Officers' Coll., Cairo.
Former lecturer Mil. Coll. and Staff Officers' Coll. and Dir.-Gen. Intelligence; Minister of the Interior 53-58; Minister of the Interior U.A.R. 58-62, Vice-Pres. U.A.R. and Chair. Aswan Dam Cttee. 61-62; mem. Nat. Defence Cttee. 62-69, Presidency Council 62-64; mem. Exec. Cttee. Arab Socialist Union 64-69; Deputy Prime Minister 64-65, June 67-68; Prime Minister and Minister of the Interior 65-66.
68 Khalifa al-Mamoun Street, Manchiet al-Bakri, Cairo, Egypt.

Moini, Amir-Ghassem; Iranian mechanical engineer and politician; b. June 1925; ed. Teheran Univ.
Ministry of Labour and Social Affairs 47-; Teheran Labour Dept.; Deputy Head Inspection Office; Acting Head of Fars Prov. Labour Dept., later Head; Deputy Head Teheran Branch of Workers' Social Insurance Org.; Deputy Dir.-Gen. Employment Services, later Dir.-Gen.; Sec.-Gen. Graduate Guidance Org.; Technical Under-Sec., Ministry of Labour and Social Affairs; mem. Board of Dirs. Social Insurance Org.; Acting Sec.-Gen. Iran Novin Party 71; Minister of Labour and Social Services 73-76 of the Interior 76-77; Homayoun Order, First Class.
c/o Ministry of the Interior, Teheran, Iran.

Moqaddem, Sadok; Tunisian diplomatist and parliamentarian; b. 1914; ed. Lycée Carnot, Tunis, Faculty of Sciences, Montpellier and Faculty of Medicine, Paris.
Physician, Tunis; mem. Néo-Destour 34-, mem. Political Bureau 52-; Sec. of State for Justice 54-55, for Public Health 55-56; mem. to Constituent Ass. 56-59, mem. Nat. Assembly 59-; Ambassador to Egypt 56-57; Sec. of State for Foreign Affairs 57-62; Ambassador to France 62-64; Pres. Nat. Assembly 64-69, 69-; Chair. Destour Socialist Party 70; Grand Cordon of Nat. Order of Independence, Grand Cordon, Nat. Order of the Repub.; several foreign decorations.
National Assembly, Palais du Bardo, Tunis, Tunisia.

Morocco, King of (*see* Hassan II).

Mosevics, Mark; Israeli industrialist; b. 22 Aug. 1920; ed. Dulwich Coll., London, Jesus Coll., Cambridge, England, Hebrew Univ. Jerusalem.
Chairman Board of Dirs., Israel Export Inst. 66-68; Chair. Board of Dirs., Israel Industrial Bank 68-72, mem. Board of Dirs. 72-; Chair. Board of Dirs., Elite Israel Chocolate and Sweets Mfg. Co. Ltd., Co-ordinating Bureau of Econ. Orgs. 68-; Pres. Mfrs. Asscn. of Israel 69-75; mem. Board of Dirs. Israel Corpn. Ltd. 70-; Chair. Board, First Int. Bank of Israel 73-; mem. Presidium, Prime Minister's 3rd Econ. Conf.
Elite Israel Chocolate and Sweets Manufacturing Co. Ltd., P.O. Box 19, Ramat-Gan; and 4 Wisotsky Street, Tel-Aviv, Israel.

Mostofi, Khosrow, M.A., PH.D.; Iranian professor; b. 8 July 1921; ed. Univs. of Teheran and Utah.
Assistant Prof. Political Science, Portland State Univ. 58-60, Univ. of Utah 60-65; Acting Dir. Inst. of Int. Studies, Univ. of Utah 62-63; Assoc. Prof., Univ. of Utah 65-70, Prof. 70-; Acting Chair. Dept. of Political Science 67; Dir. Middle East Center, Univ. of Utah 67-; Fulbright-Hays Fellow, Turkey and Iran 65-66; Board mem. American Inst. of Iranian Studies 68, CASA 73-; Co-Dir. American Center for Iranian Studies in Teheran 70; mem. N.D.F.L. Panel of Consultants, U.S.O.E. 68-70, 76, American Asscn. of Univ. Profs., American Acad. of Political Sciences, Western Political Science Asscn., American Acad. for Advancement of Science, American Oriental Soc.
Publs. *Suez Dispute: A Case Study of a Treaty* 57, *Aspects of Nationalism: The Sociology of Colonial Revolt* 64, *Parsee Nameh: A Persian Reader in* 8 *Vols.* Vol. I, II 63, 4th edn. Vol. I 69, *Iran* in *Encyclopaedia Britannica* 74, *Idries Shah* in *Studies in Art and Literature of the Near East* 74.
Room 19, Middle East Center, University of Utah, Salt Lake City, Utah 84112; Home: 2481 East 13th South Street, Salt Lake City, Utah 84108, U.S.A.

Moti, Mohammed Saleh (*see* Muti, Muhammad Salih).

Moulay Hassan Ben El Mehdi, H.R.H. Prince (Cousin of King Hassan II); Moroccan diplomatist; b. 14 Aug. 1912.
Caliph Northern Zone of Morocco 25; Amb. to Great Britain 57-64, to Italy 64-67; Pres. of Admin. Council, Nat. Bank for Econ. Devt. 65-67; Gov. Banque du Maroc 69-; decorations include, Ouissam Alaoui, Charles I Medal, Great Military Ouissam, Great Medal of Portugal, Great Dominican Medal, Great Naval Medal, Great Mahdaoui Medal, Great Houssni Medal.
Banque du Maroc, 277 avenue Mohammed V, Rabat, Morocco.

Mounayer, H.E. Eustache Joseph, D. en. L.; Syrian ecclesiastic; b. 6 June 1925; ed. Seminary of Benedictine Fathers, Jerusalem, Patriarchal Seminary, Charfé, Lebanon and Pontifical Univ. of Latran, Rome.
Ordained priest 49; Sec. of Archbishop of Damascus 54-59, concurrently Sec. of Apostolic Nunzio, Pres. ecclesiastic court: Sec. of Cardinal Tappouni 59-71; consecrated bishop 71; Patriarchal Auxiliary Bishop 71-; Dir. *Al-Karma* (review in Arabic).
Publs. *Les Synodes Syriens Jacobites* (in French), *Le Schihim* (in Arabic).
Patriarcat Syrien Catholique d'Antioche, P.O. Box 125087, Beirut, Lebanon.

Moussalli, Paul Michel Négib, LIC. en D.; Lebanese lawyer and United Nations official; b. 9 April 1932; ed. Lycée français de garçons, Beirut, Faculty of Law, Beirut, Univ. of Lyons, France, Max Planck Inst. für Ausländisches Öffentliches Recht und Völkerrecht, Heidelberg, Germany, and Graduate Inst. of Int. Studies, Geneva, Switzerland.
Legal Adviser, Office of UN High Commr. for Refugees (UNHCR), Geneva 61-62; UNHCR Rep. for Tunisia 62; UNHCR Rep. at Tripartite Repatriation Comm. (Algerian refugees) 62; UNHCR Rep. for Algeria 62-63; UNHCR Legal Adviser, Geneva (questions relating to refugees in Africa and Asia) 63-66; UNHCR Regional Rep. for Africa

66-70; Acting Dir. of Admin. and Management, UNHCR, Geneva 71-74, Dir. 75-.
Office of United Nations High Commissioner for Refugees, Palais des Nations, Geneva, Switzerland.

Mubarak, Lt.-Gen. Muhammad Hosni; Egyptian air force officer and politician; b. 1929.
Commander, Air Force 72-75; Vice-Pres. of Repub. April 75-; Dir.-Gen. Egyptian Arms Procurement Agency April 75-; mem. Higher Council for Nuclear Energy 75-; Vice-Pres. Nat. Democratic Party July 78-.
Office of the Vice-President, Cairo, Egypt.

Müezzinoğlu, Ziya; Turkish civil servant and diplomatist; b. 5 May 1919; ed. Ankara Univ.
Inspector of Finance, Turkish Ministry of Finance 42-53; Adviser to Treasury, Ministry of Finance 53-59; Dir.-Gen. of Treasury 59-60; Dir.-Gen. of Treasury and Sec.-Gen. Org. for Int. Econ. Co-operation in Turkey 60; mem. Constituent Assembly 60; Chair. Interministerial Cttee. for Foreign Econ. Relations 62; Sec. of State of State Planning Org. 62-64; Amb. to Fed. Repub. of Germany 64-67; Amb., Perm. Del. to EEC 67; Minister of Finance 72-73, Jan. 78-, of Trade June-July 77; mem. Nat. Security Council; mem. Senate and Foreign Relations Cttee. 75; Republican People's Party.
Ministry of Finance, Maliye Bakanlığı, Ulus, Ankara, Turkey.

Mufti, Said el-; Jordanian politician; b. 1898; ed. Turkish School, Damascus.
Governor of Amman 25, 39; Mayor of Amman 27, 38; mem. First Legislative Council 29, 31; Head of Treasury 39; Minister of Communications 44; Minister of Interior 44, 48; Minister of Finance and Communications 45; Deputy 47, 51 and 54; Minister of Commerce and Agriculture 47; Prime Minister and Minister of Foreign Affairs 55; Prime Minister 56; Deputy Prime Minister and Minister of Interior and Agriculture 57; Pres. of Senate 58; Deputy Prime Minister 63; Pres. of Senate 63-74; mem. Consultative Council 67; Jordan Medal of Independence First Class, Jordan Star First Class, and many others.
The Senate, Amman, Jordan.

Müftüoğlu, Ismail; Turkish jurist and politician; b. 1 Jan. 1939, Adapazarı; ed. High School, Adapazarı and Istanbul Univ. Law School.
Primary school teacher 60-65; legal apprenticeship 68-69, practice 69-73; mem. Nat. Assembly for Adapazarı 73-; Minister of Justice 75-77; Nat. Salvation Party.
Güvenlik Cad. Esenlik Sok 13/4, Ankara, Turkey.

Muhammad, Ali Nasser; Yemeni politician; b. 1939, Dathina Rural District.
Active mem. of Nat. Liberation Front (NLF) 63-67; Gov. of the Islands 67, of Second Province 68; mem. Nat. Front Gen. Command 68; Minister of Local Govt. 69, later of Defence; mem. Front Exec. Cttee. 70; mem. Presidential Council of People's Democratic Repub. of Yemen 71-78, Chair. June-Dec. 78, Vice-Chair. Dec. 78-; Chair. Council of Ministers (Prime Minister) 71-; mem. Supreme People's Council 71-; mem. Political Bureau of Nat. Front 72-75, of United Political Org.-Nat. Front 75-78, of Yemen Socialist Party Oct. 78-; Minister of Educ. 74-75, of Finance Dec. 78-.
Office of the Vice-Chairman, Presidential Council, Steamer Point, Aden, People's Democratic Republic of Yemen.

Mumcuoğlu, Hayri; Turkish lawyer; b. 1914, Istanbul; ed. secondary schools, Istanbul.
Assistant Judge, Bartın 37; Judge for Penal Affairs, Akçaabat, Saframbolu; Asst. Prosecutor, Ankara; Judge, Chief Prosecutor of the Repub.; Chief Prosecutor, Ministry of Justice; mem. Court of Cassation; mem. Parl. for Tekirdağ (New Turkey Party) 61; Minister of Housing and Reconstruction 63; joined Repub. People's Party 67, resigned 72; Minister of Justice 73, 74-75; Independent.
National Assembly, Ankara, Turkey.

Murphy, Richard William, B.A., A.B.; American diplomatist; b. 29 July 1929, Boston, Mass.; ed. Harvard Univ. and Emmanuel Coll., Cambridge.
United States Consul, Aleppo, Syria 60-63; Political Officer, U.S. Embassy, Jeddah 63-66, Amman 66-68; Country Dir. for Arabian Peninsula Affairs, U.S. Dept. of State 70-71; Amb. to Mauritania 71-74, to Syria 74-78; Dept. of State Superior Service Award 69.
c/o State Department, 2201 C Street, N.W., Washington, D.C. 20520, U.S.A.

Muti, Muhammad Salih; Yemeni officer and politician; b. 16 June 1944, Aden; ed. Higher Technical Inst., Cairo.
Military Commdr. NLF Commandos in Aden 67; mem. High Command, Nat. Front 68-75, Exec. Cttee. 70-75, Politbureau 72-75; mem. Political Bureau United Political Org.-Nat. Front 75-78, Yemen Socialist Party Oct. 78-; Minister of the Interior 69-73, of Foreign Affairs May 73-.
Ministry of Foreign Affairs, Medint-Al-Shaab, Aden, People's Democratic Republic of Yemen.

N

Nabulsi, M. Said, M.A., PH.D.; Jordanian banker; b. 1928, Palestine; ed. Univ. of Damascus, Syria, Univ. of California at Berkeley, Georgetown Univ., Washington, D.C.
Secretary-General, Central Bank of Syria 64-67; Head of Research, Central Bank of Jordan 68-72, Gov. and Chair. of Board. 73-; Minister of Nat. Econ. 72-73; Gov. Int. Monetary Fund, Arab Monetary Fund; mem. Board of Trustees, Univ. of Jordan, Yarmouk Univ.
Publs. numerous articles, research papers in economic journals.
Central Bank of Jordan, P.O. Box 37, Amman; Home: Shmeisani, Amman, Jordan.

Nabulsi, Omar, L. en D., M.A.; Jordanian lawyer and politician; b. 1 April 1936, Nablus; ed. Cairo, Ain Shams and London Univs.
Legal Adviser, Sasco Petroleum Co., Libya 59-61; Legal and Political Attaché, Arab League 61-69; Asst. Dir., Royal Court of Jordan 69-70; Minister of Nat. Economy 70-72; Amb., Ministry of Foreign Affairs 72; Amb. to U.K. 72-73; Minister of Agriculture and Nat. Econ. 73-Jan, 75; Legal and Econ. Adviser to Arab Fund for Econ. and Social Devt. 75-77; Lawyer and Consultant in Corporate and Business Legal Affairs Aug. 77-; Order of Al-Kawkab (First Class).
Publs. several articles in legal journals.
P.O. Box 35116, Amman, Jordan.

Naggar, Abd el Moneim el; Egyptian army officer and diplomatist; b. 1920; ed. Cairo Military Academy, Cairo Staff Academy, Cairo Univ. and Inst. de Hautes Etudes, Univ. of Paris.
Egyptian Army 39-57; Military Attaché, Paris 53-54, Madrid 55-57; Head of East European Dept., Ministry of Foreign Affairs, Cairo 58; U.A.R. Consul-General, Bombay 59-62, Hong Kong 62-63; Ambassador to Greece 63-64, to France 64-68; Minister of Foreign Affairs 69-71; Amb. to Iraq 72-76; numerous decorations.
c/o Ministry of Foreign Affairs, Cairo, Egypt.

Naguib, Ibrahim; Egyptian architect and politician; b. 24 June 1911; ed. Royal School of Engineering, Giza.
Chartered Structural Engineer, London 35; Architect State Bldg. Dept., Ministry of Public Works 31, Head Technical Dept. 44-52, Insp. N. Cairo Zone 52-55; Del. Lecturer, Alexandria Univ. 46-50, Ain Shams Univ. 54-62; Controller of Municipal and Village Affairs, Cairo Governorate

55-57; Dir.-Gen. of Technical Research and Inspection, Ministry of Municipal and Village Affairs 57-60; Deputy Minister of Housing and Public Utilities 62-67; mem. Cen. Cttee. Arab Socialist Union 68-72, Gen. Secr. 72-74; mem. People's Assembly, Vice-Chair. Services Cttee. 69-71; Minister of Tourism 71-72, of Tourism and Civil Aviation 74-77; Chair. Cttee. of Int. Experts in charge of project for salvaging Temples on Philae Island, Aswan, Cttee. for Urban Reconstruction; Pres. Afro-Asian Housing Org. 63-67; mem. Board, Egyptian Soc. of Engineers; mem. Inst. of Structural Engineers, London; Hon. Pres. Soc. of Architects; has participated in numerous int. scientific confs.
Publs. *Architectural Drawing* 40, *Buildings of Nubia* 45, *Code of Practice for Structural Engineering* 46, *Foundations of Buildings in Egypt and the Sudan* 51, *Village Buildings and the Farmer's House* 53, *The Nature of Soil, and Foundations in the City of Cairo* 59, *Housing in Developing Countries* 68, *Trends in Architecture in the Arab Countries* 69.
Cairo, Egypt.

Naguib, Gen. Mohammed (*see* Neguib, Gen. Mohamed).

Nahavandi, Houshang, L. EN D., DR. ECON. SC.; Iranian economist, educationist and politician; b. 1930; ed. Univ. of Paris.
Adviser to High Council of the Econ. 58-61, to Minister of Labour 59-61; Econ. Counsellor, Embassy in Brussels 61-63; Deputy Head of del. to EEC 62-63; Man. Dir. Foreign Trade Co. 63-64; Minister of Housing and Devt. 64-68, of Science and Higher Educ. Aug.-Oct. 78; Chancellor, Pahlavi Univ. 68-71, Teheran Univ. 71-78; Civil A.D.C. to H.I.M. Shahanshah Aryamehr 68-74; mem. High Council of Centre for Int. Studies 72, Boards of Trustees of Mashad Univ., Farabi Univ. 73, Guilan Univ. 74, also of Charity Foundation of H.I.H. Princess Shams; mem. High Council of Nat. Soc. for the Protection of Animals, High Council for Nat. Educ.; mem. Temporary Exec. Council, Rastakhiz Party 74, now of Political Bureau; Perm. mem. Int. Council for Interuniversity Co-operation at California Univ. 75-; mem. Int. Asscn. of Univs.; Homayoun Decoration 1st and 4th class, Sepasse Decoration, Chevalier Légion d'Honneur (France), Commdr. Ordre de la Couronne (Belgium), Grand Cross of Order of Merit (Italy); Dr. h.c.(Haceteppe Univ., Ankara) 73, (Pahlavi Univ., Shiraz) 74 and other awards.
Publs. numerous books and articles.
University of Teheran, Teheran, Iran.

Nahayan, H.H. Sheikh Zayed bin Sultan al-; President of the United Arab Emirates and Ruler of Abu Dhabi; b. 1918.
Governor of Eastern Province of Abu Dhabi 46-66; deposed his brother Sheikh Shakhbut and succeeded to Sheikhdom 66; Pres. Fed. of Arabian Emirates 69-71; Pres. United Arab Emirates (U.A.E.) 71-.
Amiri Palace, Abu Dhabi, United Arab Emirates.

Najmabadi, Farrokh; Iranian civil servant; b. 1922; ed. U.K.
Consultant Engineer, Central Exploration and Extraction Dept., Nat. Iranian Oil Co., Head of Dept. of Statistics, Deputy to Head of Exploration and Production; Head of Production Dept., Org. of Petroleum Exporting Countries; Deputy and Alt. Man. Dir. NIOC, Head of Oil Affairs Office NIOC Exploration and Production Dept.; Dir.-Gen. for Oil, Ministry of Finance; Pres. of Board, Man. Dir. Iran Telephone Joint Stock Co.; Industry and Mines Under-Sec., Ministry of Econ.; Minister of Mines and Industries April 74-Aug. 77.
c/o Ministry of Mines and Industries, Teheran, Iran.

Nakib, Ahmed Abdul Wahab Al-; Kuwaiti diplomatist; b. 30 July 1933, Kuwait; ed. Adam State Coll., Colorado, U.S.A.
First Sec., Kuwait Embassy, London 62-63; Counsellor, first Perm. Mission of Kuwait to UN 63-66; Consul-Gen., Nairobi, Kenya 66-67; Amb. to Pakistan 67-70, to U.K. 71-75, also accred. to Denmark, Norway and Sweden 71-75; Chair. and Man. Dir. Kuwait Projects Co. 75-.
Kuwait Projects Co., P.O. Box 23982, Safat, Kuwait.

Nashashibi, Nasser Eddin; Jordanian (b. Palestine) editor and diplomatist; b. 1924; ed. Arab Coll., Jerusalem and American Univ. Beirut.
Arab Office, Jerusalem 45-47; Chief Chamberlain, Amman 51; Dir.-Gen. Hashemite Broadcasting 52; Roving Editor *Akhbar El Yom*, Cairo; Chief Editor *Al Gomhouria*, Cairo 59-65; Roving Rep. of the Arab League June 65-67; Roving Dip. Editor *Al-Ahram*, Cairo; now freelance writer and journalist in Europe and Middle East; Jordanian Independence Star, 1st degree.
Publs. *Steps in Britain* (Arabic) 48, *What Happened in the Middle East* 58, *Short Political Stories* 59, *Return Ticket to Palestine* 60, *Some Sand* (Arabic) 62, *An Arab in China* (Arabic and English) 64, *Roving Ambassador* (Arabic) 70, *The Ink is Black* 71, *No Camel No Sand* 76, *I Am the Middle East* 77.
38 Rue Athénée, Geneva, Switzerland; and 26 Lowndes Street, London, England.

Nasir, Mohammed, B.SC., M.A., ED.D.; Iraqi educator and diplomatist; b. 1911; ed. Teacher Training Coll., Baghdad, American Univ., Beirut and Columbia Univ., New York.
Schoolteacher 31-32; Prof. of Educ. and Dean of Coll. of Educ., Baghdad Univ. 41-45, 55-63; Cultural Attaché and Perm. Rep. of Iraq to Arab League Cultural Comm. 45-48; Cultural Attaché, Washington 48-54; Alternate Del. to UN 5th Gen. Assembly; Pres. Teachers Union of Iraq 63-64; mem. Council, Univ. of Baghdad 63-64; Minister of Educ. 64; Ambassador to U.S.S.R. Nov. 64-66; Minister of Culture and Nat. Orientation 66; Prof. of Educational Admin., and Chair. Dept. of Educ. Kuwait Univ. 67-.
Publs. include many school books in Arabic, *Arabic Readings* (2 vols., joint author) 40, *Civic Education* (joint author) 40, *Guide to Higher Education in the U.S.A.* 57, *Readings in Educational Thought*, Vol. I 73, *Arabic-Islamic Educational Thought* 77.
Department of Education, Kuwait University, P.O. Box 23558, Kuwait.

Nasr, Asad Yusuf, M.A.; Lebanese airline executive; b. 11 Sept. 1927, Haifa; ed. Cambridge Univ.
Instructor in Mathematics and Statistics, American Univ. of Beirut 50-55; Expert at Ministry of Nat. Econ. 50-52; Manager for Gen. Planning and Economics, Middle East Airlines (MEA) 55-63, Exec. Vice-Pres. 63-65, Gen. Man. 65-76, Man. Dir. 76-77, Man. Dir. and Deputy Chair. 77, Chair. of the Board and Pres. Dec. 77-; Airline Tech. Man. Award, Air Transport World 75; Gold Labour Medal (Lebanon) 75; Gold Medal, Asscn. of Engineers Graduates of Esib 78; Commdr. Nat. Order of Chad 73, Officer Nat. Order of Lebanon 74, Order of Repub. of Egypt 74, Légion d'honneur 75.
Publ. *The Asna Formula: A New Concept* 78.
c/o Middle East Airlines, 80 Piccadilly, London, W1V ODR, England; MEA Headquarters, Beirut International Airport, Beirut; Home: 87 Mexico Street, Beirut, Lebanon.

Natra, Sergiu; Israeli composer; b. 1924, Romania; ed. National Conservatoire, Bucharest.
Settled in Israel 61; teaches composition at the Rubin Acad. of Music, Tel-Aviv; G. Enesco Prize 45, State Prize 51, Engel Prize 69.
Works include: *March and Chorale* 44, *Suite for Orchestra* 48, *Sinfonia* 60, *Music for Violin and Harp* 60, *Toccata for Orchestra* 63, *Music for Harpsichord and Six Instruments* 64, *Sonatina for Harp* 65, *Voices of Fire* (ballet music), *Music for Oboe and Strings* 65, *Prelude for Narrator and Orchestra*, *Commentary on Nehemia*, *Song of Deborah for*

Mezzo-Soprano and Chamber Orchestra 67, *Prayer for Harp* 70, *Trio in One Movement for Violin, Violoncello and Piano* 71, *Dedication: Two Poems for Mezzo-Soprano and Orchestra* 72, *A Book of Hebrew Songs for the Harp* 74, *Sacred Service* 75.
10 Barth Street, Ramat Aviv, Tel-Aviv, Israel.

Navon, Yitzhak; Israeli politician; b. 19 April 1921, Jerusalem; ed. Hebrew Univ. of Jerusalem.
Director, Hagana Arabic Dept., Jerusalem 46-49; Second Sec., Israel Legation in Uruguay and Argentina 49-51; Political Sec. to Foreign Minister 51-52; Head of Bureau of Prime Minister 52-63; Head Dept. of Culture, Ministry of Educ. and Culture 63-65; mem. Knesset 65-78, fmr. Deputy Speaker; fmr. Chair. Knesset Defence and Foreign Affairs Cttee.; Chair. World Zionist Council 73-78; Pres. of Israel May 78-; mem. Mapai Party 51-65, Rafi 65-68; Yediot Ahronot's Kinor David prize.
Publs. *Hollekh Birkida* 44, *Six Days and Seven Gates, Romancero Sephardi* (collection of songs) 68, *Bustan Sephardi* (play).
Office of the President, Jerusalem, Israel.

Nayeri, Abbas, PH.D.; Iranian diplomatist; b. 1925, Neishabour; ed. Iran and France.
Ministry of Foreign Affairs 48; Minister-Counsellor, Iranian Embassy, London 66; Dir.-Gen. Admin. of Econ. and Int. Affairs 66-72; Amb. to Morocco 72-76; Dir.-Gen. Admin. of Political Affairs 77-78; Amb. to Egypt 78-79; holder of First Order of Homayoun and Second Order of Taj.
c/o Ministry of Foreign Affairs, Teheran, Iran.

Nazih, Hassan, B.A.; Iranian lawyer and petroleum executive; b. 1921; ed. Univ. of Teheran.
In legal practice 45-; mem. Teheran Bar Asscn.; Chair. Iranian Bar Asscn.; Chair. and Man. Dir. Nat. Iranian Oil Co. 79-.
National Iranian Oil Company, Takhte Jamshid Avenue, P.O. Box 1863, Teheran, Iran.

Nebenzahl, Itzhak Ernst, DR.IUR.; Israeli public official; b. 24 Oct. 1907; ed. Univs. of Frankfurt and Freiburg.
Settled in Palestine 33; Dir. Jerusalem Econ. Corpn. 47-61, Jerusalem Devt. Dept., Jewish Agency 48-50, Bank Leumi le-Israel Ltd. 56-61; Hon. Consul-Gen. of Sweden 52-62; Chair. Post Office Bank 54-61, of Advisory Cttee. and Council, Bank of Israel 57-62; State Comptroller of Israel 61, re-elected 66, 71, 76-; Pres. Fifth Int. Congress of Int. Org. of Supreme Audit Insts. (INTOSAI) 65, Chair. 65-68, now mem. Gov. Board; Public Complaints Commr. (Ombudsman) 71-; Vice-Chair. Int. Ombudsman Steering Cttee. 77-; designated host of 2nd Int. Ombudsman Conf.; fmr. mem. Petroleum Board, Anti-Trust Council, and several govt. inquiry cttees, including inquiry into Yom Kippur war; Partner, Hollander Concern (Stockholm, New York, London, Buenos Aires, Paris, Tokyo, etc.), Chair. Board of Dirs. 47-61; Chevalier (First Class), Royal Swedish Order of Vasa 57.
Office of the State Comptroller, P.O. Box 1081, Jerusalem; Home: 9 Batei Mahse Street, Old City, Jerusalem, Israel.

Ne'eman, Yuval, B.SC., DIP. ING., D.E.M., D.I.C., PH.D.; Israeli soldier and scientist; b. 14 May 1925; ed. Herzlia High School, Tel-Aviv, Israel Inst. of Technology, Haifa, Ecole Supérieure de Guerre, Paris, and London Univ.
Hydrodynamics Design Engineer 45; in Hagana 46; Captain, Israeli Defence Forces (Infantry) 48, Major 49, Lieut.-Col. 50, Col. 55; Defence Attaché, London 58-60; joined Israel Atomic Energy Establishments 60, Scientific Dir., Soreq Research Establishment 61-63; Head, Physics Dept., Tel-Aviv Univ. 62-, Prof. of Physics 64-; Research Fellow, Calif. Inst. of Technology 63, Visiting Prof. of Physics 64-65; Vice-Rector and Vice-Pres., Tel-Aviv Univ. 65-66, Pres. 71-75; Senior Adviser and Chief Scientist, Ministry of Defence 75-76; mem. Israel Atomic Energy Comm. 66-, Israel Nat. Acad. of Sciences 66-; known mainly for his co-discovery of Unitary Symmetry (The Eightfold Way) 61; Foreign Hon. mem., American Acad. of Arts and Sciences 70; Foreign Assoc. Nat. Acad. of Sciences, U.S.A. 72; Hon. Life mem. New York Acad. of Sciences 73; Hon. D.Sc.; Weizmann Prize for the Sciences 66, Rothschild Prize 68, Israel Prize for Exact Sciences 69; Albert Einstein Medal and Prize (U.S.A.) 70.
Publs. *The Eightfold Way* (with M. Gell-Mann) 64, *Algebraic Theory of Particle Physics* 67, *The Past Decade in Particle Theory* (with E. C. G. Sudarshan) 73; about 150 articles on physics, astrophysics and philosophy of science.
Department of Physics and Astronomy, Tel-Aviv University, Tel-Aviv, Israel.

Neguib, Gen. Mohamed; Egyptian army officer; b. Khartoum 1901; ed. Sudan Schools, Gordon Coll., Khartoum, Royal Mil. Acad. and Egyptian Univ., Cairo.
Commissioned in infantry 17; served in Gen. Staff, Adjutant-Gen. and Q.M.-Gens'. departments during Second World War; Sub-Governor of Sinai and Governor of Red Sea Provinces in Frontier Corps; Col. Commdg. 2nd Machine Gun Bn.; Brig., 2nd in commd. of Egyptian troops in Palestine and commdg. successively 1st, 2nd, 3rd, 4th and 10th Inf. Bdes. during hostilities with Israel 48; Dir.-Gen. Frontier Corps 50, Dir.-Gen. Infantry 51, C.-in-C. Egyptian Army July 52; Prime Minister, Minister for War and Marine, C.-in-C. of the Army and Military Gov. of Egypt 52-53; Pres. of the Repub. of Egypt 53-54.
Cairo, Egypt.

Nemery, Maj.-Gen. Gaafar (*see* Nimeri).

Nimeri, Maj.-Gen. Gaafar Mohammed al-; Sudanese army officer and political leader; b. 1 Jan. 1930, Omdurman; ed. Hantaib Secondary School, Medani, Sudan Military Coll.
Former Commdr. Khartoum garrison; campaigns against rebels in Southern Sudan; placed under arrest on suspicion of plotting to overthrow the Government; led successful mil. coup May 69; promoted from Col. to Maj.-Gen. May 69; Chair. Revolutionary Command Council (R.C.C.) 69-71; C.-in-C. of Armed Forces 69-73; Minister of Defence May-June 69, 72-73, 74-76, July 78-; Prime Minister Oct. 69-Aug. 76, Sept. 77-; Minister of Foreign Affairs 70-71, of Planning 71-72, of Finance Sept. 77-March 78; Pres. of Sudan Oct. 71-; Supreme Commdr. of Armed Forces 76-; Pres. Political Bureau, Sec.-Gen. Sudanese Socialist Union 71-76; Pres. of OAU 78-79.
Office of the President, Khartoum, Sudan.

Nimir, Ibrahim Mohamed Aly, B.A., F.I.B.; Sudanese banker; b. 1922; ed. Gordon Memorial Coll. and Univ. of Wales.
Governor and Chair. Bank of Sudan 72-; Chair. Savings and Investment Council 73; mem. Ministerial Council for Nat. Econ. 73-74, Khartoum Univ. Council 74-, Islamic Univ. Council 74-, Board of Dirs. Sudanese Devt. Corpn. 74-; Alt. Gov. for Sudan, Int. Monetary Fund 72-.
Bank of Sudan, Sharia Gamaa, Khartoum, P.O. Box 313, Sudan.

Nofal, Sayed, DR. ARTS; Egyptian international civil servant; b. 1910; ed. Cairo Univ.
Head of Literary Dept. *Al Sivassa* 35-38; Teacher, Cairo Univ. 38; later Dir. of Technical Secr., Ministry of Educ. and Ministry of Social Affairs; later Dir. of Legislative Dept., Upper House of Egyptian Parl.; later Dir. Political Dept., League of Arab States, Asst. Sec.-Gen. 60-.
Publs. include *Poetry of Nature in Arabic and Western Literature* 44, *Egypt in the United Nations* 47, *The Egyptian Parliament in a Quarter of a Century* 51, *The Political Status of the Emirates of the Arab Gulf and Southern Arabia* 59, *A Comparative Study of the Arab League's, United*

Nations and American States Organisation's Systems 60, *Ben-Gurion's Version of History* 62, *The Arab-Israeli Conflict* 62, *Arab Unity* 64, *Arab Nationalism* 65, *Arab Socialism* 66, *The Record of Israel* 66, *Joint Arab Action Book I* 68, *Book II* 71, *The Arab Gulf or The Eastern Borders of the Arab Homeland* 69, *An Introduction to Israeli Foreign Policy* 72, *The Relationship between the United Nations and the Arab League* 75, *The International Function of the Arab League* 75, *The Future of Joint Arab Action* 77.
9 Khan Younis Street, Madinet al Mohandesseen, Dokki, Cairo, Egypt.

Nouira, Hedi; Tunisian politician; b. 6 April 1911, Monastir; ed. High School, Sousse, and Paris.
Secretary of Gen. Confed. of Tunisian Workers 38; in detention 38-43; Sec.-Gen. of Néo-Destour Party 42-54, 69-; Minister of Commerce 54-55; Minister of Finance 55-58; Founder and Dir. of Central Bank of Tunisia 58-70; Minister of the Economy 70; Prime Minister Nov. 70-.
Office of the Secretary-General, Parti Socialiste Destourien, boulevard 9 Avril 1938, Tunis, Tunisia.

Nowar, Ma'an Abu; Jordanian diplomatist; b. 26 July 1928, Salt; ed. London Univ.
Joined Jordanian Arab Army 43, Commdr. Infantry Brigade 57-63; Counsellor, Jordanian Embassy, London 63; Dir. Jordan Civil Defence 64-67, Jordan Public Security 67-69; Asst. Chief of Staff for Gen. Affairs 69-72; Minister of Culture and Information 72; Amb. to U.K. 73-76; Jordanian Star (1st Class).
c/o Ministry of Foreign Affairs, Amman, Jordan.

Numairy, Maj.-Gen. Gaafar (*see* Nimeri).

Nuseibeh, Hazem, M.A., PH.D.; Jordanian politician; ed. Rawda Coll., Jerusalem, Victoria Coll., Alexandria, American Univ. of Beirut, Law School, Jerusalem, Woodrow Wilson School of Public and Int. Affairs and Princeton Univ.
Under-Secretary, Ministry of Nat. Econ. 57-59; Pres. Jordan Devt. Board 59-61; Minister of Foreign Affairs 62-63, 65-66; Minister of Royal Court 63-65; Prof. of Int. Affairs, Jordan Univ. 66-67; Minister of Reconstruction and Devt. 67-69; Amb. to Egypt 69-71, to Turkey 71-73, to Italy 73-75, also accred. to Austria and Switzerland; Perm. Rep. to UN 76-.
Publ. *Ideas of Arab Nationalism* 56.
Jordanian Mission to the United Nations, 866 United Nations Plaza, Room 550-552, New York, N.Y. 10017, U.S.A.

Nutting, Rt. Hon. Sir (Harold) Anthony, Bt., P.C.; British politician and writer; b. 11 Jan. 1920; ed. Eton and Trinity Coll., Cambridge.
In British Foreign Service 40-45; mem. Parl. 45-56; Chair. Young Conservative and Unionist Movement 46, Nat. Union of Conservative and Unionist Asscns. 50, Conservative Nat. Exec. Cttee. 51; Parl. Under-Sec. of State for Foreign Affairs 51-54; Minister of State for Foreign Affairs 54-56 (resigned over British Suez policy); Leader, U.K. Del. to UN Gen. Assembly and UN Disarmament Comm. 54-56.
Publs. *I Saw for Myself* 58, *Disarmament* 59, *Europe Will Not Wait* 60, *Lawrence of Arabia* 61, *The Arabs* 64, *Gordon, Martyr and Misfit* 66, *No End of a Lesson* 67, *Scramble for Africa* 70, *Nasser* 72.
c/o Council for Arab-British Understanding, 21 Collingham Road, London, S.W.5, England.

O

Obeidi, Abdul Ati El-, M.SC.; Libyan politician; b. 10 Oct. 1939; ed. Libyan Univ., Manchester Univ., England.
Lecturer, Libyan Univ. 67-70; Acting Minister of Foreign Affairs 70; Minister of Labour 70-77, of Civil Service 74-77; Chair. Gen. Popular Cttee. 77-79; Sec.-Gen. Gen. People's Congress March 79-; decorations from Tunisia, The Philippines and Malaysia.
General People's Congress, Tripoli; Home: P.O. Box 2256, Benghazi, Libya.

Okasha, Sarwat Mahmoud Fahmy, D. ÈS L.; Egyptian diplomatist, politician and banker; b. 1921; ed. Military Coll. and Cairo Univ.
Cavalry officer 39; took part in Palestine war 48-49; Mil. Attaché, Berne 53-54, Paris and Madrid 54-56; Attaché in Presidency of Republic 56-67; U.A.R. Ambassador to Italy 57-58; Minister of Culture and Nat. Guidance and Pres. of Supreme Council for Literature, Art and Social Sciences 58-62; Chair. Board of Dirs. of Nat. Bank of Egypt 62; mem. UNESCO Exec. Board 62; mem. Nat. Assembly and Pres. Foreign Affairs Comm. 64-66; Deputy Prime Minister, Minister of Culture 66-68; Minister of Culture 68-71; Asst. to the Pres. 71-June 72; Pres. of Supreme Council for Literature, Art and Social Sciences; Pres. Egypt-France Asscn. 65-; numerous awards.
Publs. Nineteen works (incl. translations) since 42.
Villa 34, St. 14, Maadi, Cairo, Egypt.

Ökçün, Gündüz; Turkish university professor and politician; b. 1936.
Former Dean, Faculty of Political Sciences, Univ. of Ankara; Minister for Foreign Affairs June-July 77, Jan. 78-; Republican People's Party.
Ministry of Foreign Affairs, Dişişleri Bakanlığı, Müdafaa Cad., Bakanlıklar, Ankara. Turkey.

Olcay, Osman; Turkish diplomatist; b. 17 Jan. 1924; ed. St. Joseph French Coll., Istanbul, and Faculty of Political Science, Univ. of Ankara.
Joined Ministry of Foreign Affairs, Turkey 45; Lieut., Turkish Army 46; Foreign Ministry 47; Vice-Consul, London 48-50, Second Sec., London 50-52; Chief of Section, Dept. of Econ. Affairs, Ministry of Foreign Affairs 52-54; First Sec. NATO, Paris 54, Counsellor and Deputy Perm. Rep. 58-59; Asst. Dir.-Gen. NATO Dept., Min. of Foreign Affairs, Ankara 59-60, Dir.-Gen. 60-63, Asst. Sec.-Gen. 63-64; Amb. to Finland 64-66, to India and Ceylon 66-68; Deputy Sec.-Gen. of NATO, Brussels 69-71; Minister of Foreign Affairs March-Dec. 71; Perm. Rep, to UN 72-75, to NATO Aug. 78-.
Turkish Delegation to NATO, Boulevard Léopold III, 1110 Brussels, Belgium.

Oman, Sultan of (*see* Qaboos bin Said).

Omran, Adnan; Syrian diplomatist; b. 9 Aug. 1934, Syria; ed. Univ. of Damascus, Moscow, U.S.S.R. and Columbia Univ., U.S.A.
Ministry of Foreign Affairs 62-63; mem. Perm. Mission to UN 63-66; First Sec., Moscow 66-68; Consul-Gen., Embassy in Berlin, German Dem. Repub. 68-70; Dir. Int. Org. and Conf. Dept., Ministry of Foreign Affairs 70-71, Palestine Dept. 71-72, Special Bureau Dept. 72-74, concurrently mem. Del. to UN 70-73; Amb. to U.K. and Sweden 74-.
Embassy of the Syrian Arab Republic, 8 Belgrave Square, London, SW1X 8PH, England.

Onan, Umit Suleyman; Cypriot barrister and politician, b. 1928, Nicosia; ed. Turkish Lycee, Cyprus, Lincoln's Inn; London.
Member of Nicosia Municipal Council 53-58, of Cyprus House of Reps. 60; Cyprus Rep. at Consultative Assembly of Council of Europe 61; Turkish Cypriot Rep. to Tripartite Liaison Cttee. 63; mem. Turkish Cypriot Legislative Assembly 73, Deputy Leader 73-75; Turkish Cypriot Chief Negotiator at Intercommunal Talks 76-.
Office of the Chief Negotiator, Lefkoşa, Mersin 10, Turkey.

Örek, Osman Nuri; Cypriot lawyer and politician; b. 1925; ed. Turkish Lycée, Nicosia, Univ. of Istanbul and Middle Temple, London.

Founder-mem. Cyprus Turkish Asscn., London; Sec.-Gen. Cyprus Turkish Nat. Union Party 55-60; Deputy Chair. High Council of Ecvaf 56-60; rep. Turkish Cypriot Community at London Conf. 59 and subsequent Joint Cttee.; Minister of Defence 59; mem. Exec. Council of Turkish Cypriot Provisional Admin. for Defence 67-74, concurrently for Internal Affairs 67-70, and External Affairs 67-72; mem. Exec. Council of Autonomous Turkish Cypriot Admin. for Vice-Presidency and Defence 74-75; Vice-Pres. "Turkish Federated State of Cyprus" (TFSC) 75-76; Minister of Defence 75-76; Pres. TFSC Legislative Assembly 76-78; Prime Minister April-Dec. 78; Leader, Nat. Unity Party 78; Founder-mem. Democratic People's Party 79.
Law Office of Osman N. Örek and Associates, Müftü Raci Street, Ontaş Building Nos. 1 and 2, Lefkoşa, Mersin 10, Turkey; Home: 10 Ismail Beyoglu Street, Lefkosa, Mersin 10, Turkey.

Orgad, Ben Zion; Israeli composer; b. 1926, Germany; ed. Acad. of Music in Jerusalem and Brandeis Univ., U.S.A.
Studied violin with Kinory and Bergman and composition with Paul Ben-Haim and Josef Tal; studied in U.S.A. under Aaron Copland and Irving Fine; now Superviser of Musical Educ., Israel Ministry of Educ. and Culture; Chair. Israel Composers' League; recipient of several awards for compositions.
Compositions include: cantatas: *The Story of the Spies* (UNESCO Koussevitsky Prize 52), *Isaiah's Vision*; works for orchestra, *Building a King's Stage, Choreographic Sketches, Movements on "A", Kaleidoscope, Music for Horn and Orchestra, Ballad for Orchestra, Dialogues on the First Scroll* (for 21 players); for orchestra and voices: *Hatsvi Israel* (Symphony for baritone and orchestra), *Suffering for Redemption* (for mezzo-soprano, 12-women choir and orchestra); solo and chamber works: *Out of the Dust* (for solo and instruments); *Ballada* (for violin), *Taksim* (for harp) *Monologue* (for viola), *The Old Decrees, Mizmorim*; works for soloists and orchestra, songs, piano pieces, etc.
Ministry of Education and Culture, 32 Ben-Yehuda Street, Tel-Aviv; Home: 14 Bloch Street, Tel-Aviv, Israel.

Osman, Ahmed, LL.D.; Moroccan diplomatist and politician; b. 3 Jan. 1930, Oujda; *m.* Princess Lallah Nezha (sister of King Hassan II, q.v.); ed. Royal High School, Rabat, Univ. of Rabat and Univ. of Bordeaux, France.
Member of Royal Cabinet (judicial matters) 56; joined Ministry of Foreign Affairs 57; Sec.-Gen. Ministry of Nat. Defence 59-61; Amb. to Fed. Repub. of Germany 61-62; Under Sec.-of-State for Industry and Mines 63-64; Pres. and Gen. Man. Moroccan Navigation Co. 64-67; Ambassador to U.S.A., Canada and Mexico 67-70; Minister of Admin. Affairs 70-71; Dir. of Royal Cabinet 71-72; Prime Minister 72-79; Head Nat. Defence Council March 79-; Parliamentary Rep. for Oujda 77-; Leader of Nat. Independent Group in Chamber of Reps.; participated in UN sessions 57, 58, 60, 61, Conf. on Maritime Law 58, Conf. of the League of Arab States 61; Leader of Moroccan Dels. to various Int. Confs.
National Defence Council, Rabat, Morocco.

Osman, Osman Ahmed, B.SC.; Egyptian civil engineer; b. 6 April 1917; ed. Cairo Univ.
Chairman The Arab Contractors (Osman Ahmed Osman & Co.) 49-73, and of its assoc. companies, Saudi Enterprises, Kuwaiti Engineering Co., The Libyan Co. for Contracting and Devt.; Minister of Reconstruction 73-74, of Housing and Reconstruction 74-76; mem. for Ismailia, People's Assembly Oct. 76-; Chair. Syndicate of Engineers March 79-; Chair. Ismaili Football Club; Head Agricultural Projects Complex for Food Security; Hon. LL.D. (Ricker Coll. of the North East) 76; Repub. Medal (1st Class), Russian Hero of Labour Medal.
Chief works undertaken include: (in Egypt) Aswan High Dam, Suez Canal deepening and widening, Port Said Shipyard, Cairo Int. Airport, High Dam Electric Power Transmission Lines, Guiza Bridge and Ramses Bridge over the Nile, Suez Canal restoration, Suez Canal area devt. programme, western coast devt. programme; (in Saudi Arabia) Dhahran Airport, Riyadh Mil. Coll., Dammam Mil. Barracks; (in Kuwait) Municipality Centre, Kuwait drainage system; (in Libya) Benghazi drainage system, Benghazi Stadium; (in Iraq) Kirkuk area Feeder Canal; (in Jordan) Khaled Ibn El-Walid Dam and Tunnels (Yarmouk River); (in Sudan) 200 bedroom First Class Hotel.
Publ. *The High Dam* (lecture) 66.
People's Assembly, Cairo, Egypt.

Osseyran, Adel; Lebanese politician; b. 1905, Saida; ed. American Univ. of Beirut.
Deputy for Southern Lebanon 43; Minister of Supplies in first Cabinet after Independence 43; mem. of Lebanese Del. to UN 47, 48; Deputy for Zahrani 53-; Pres. Chamber of Deputies 53, 57, 58; Minister of the Interior 68-69, of Justice, of Public Works, of Economy May 75-Dec. 76; Grand Cordon of the Order of the Cedar; several foreign decorations.
Chambre des Députés, Place de l'Etoile, Beirut, Lebanon.

Otaiba, Mana Saeed al; Abu Dhabi economist; b. 15 May 1946; ed. Univ. of Baghdad.
Chairman of Board, Abu Dhabi Nat. Oil Co.; mem. Abu Dhabi Planning Board; Pres. Dept. of Petroleum, Minerals and Industry; Chair. of Board, Abu Dhabi Gas Liquifaction Co.; Minister of Petroleum and Industry (Abu Dhabi) 72-73, of Petroleum and Mineral Resources (U.A.E. Fed. Govt.) 73-79, of Petroleum and Natural Resources June 79-; Pres. OPEC 79; mem. Board of six oil cos. in Abu Dhabi; has travelled on State visits, etc. throughout Arab countries, W. Europe, U.S., Canada.
Publs. *The Abu Dhabi Planning Board, The Economy of Abu Dhabi, Organization of the Petroleum Exporting Countries, Petroleum and the Economy of the United Arab Emirates.*
Ministry of Petroleum, P.O. Box 59, Abu Dhabi, United Arab Emirates.

Othman as-Said, Muhammad; Libyan politician; b. Oct. 1922; ed. Sanusi religious institutions, Fezzan.
Head of Religious Court for Admin. Region of Brak 45; organized Libyan Nationalist Activity in Fezzan 47; imprisoned by French 48-50; Leader Fezzan Del. to Libyan Independence Comm. 50; mem. Constituent Assembly 50; mem. Advisory Comm. to UN in Libya 50; Minister of Health, Libya 51, later Minister of Public Health until 58; Deputy to Constituent Assembly 58; Minister for Econ. Affairs 60; Prime Minister 60-March 63; Deputy 64; private business 64-; numerous decorations.
Geraba Street 6, Tripoli, Libya.

Ötüken, Adnan; Turkish librarian; b. 1911, Mamastin; ed. Lycée and Univ. of Istanbul, and Staatsbibliothek, Berlin.
Asst. Turkish Language and Literature Dept., Univ. of Istanbul 40; Dir. of Publications, Acting Asst. Dir.-Gen. of Higher Education, and Asst. Dir.-Gen. of Fine Arts, Ministry of Education 52-54; Lecturer in Library Science, Univ. of Ankara; mem. Executive Cttee. Turkish Nat. Comm. of UNESCO, and Executive Board Turkish Librarians Asscn.; Dir. Turkish Nat. Library 60-65; Under-Sec. for Cultural Affairs, Ministry of Educ. 65-67; Lecturer of Turkish Language and Lit., Lycée Teachers' Training Coll., Ankara, 67-; Gen. Sec. Turkish-Iraqi Standing Cttee. of Cultural Agreement; fmr. Turkish Cultural Attaché in Germany.
Publs. *Bibliyotek bilgisi ve bibliyografi* (Library Science and Bibliography) 40, *Istanbul Universities Yayimlari Bibliyografyasi* (Bibliography of the Publications of the University of Istanbul) 41, *Seçme eserler bibliyografyasi.* I.

cilt (Selected Bibliography, Vol. 1) 46, *Millî Kütüphane kurulurken* (Establishing the National Library) 46, *Istanbul Universities Yayimlari Bibliyografyasi, 1933-45* (Bibliography of the Publications of the University of Istanbul 1933-45, with Acaroğlu) 47, *Dünya edebiyatindan tercümeler. Klasikler Bibliyografyasi, 1940-48* (Bibliography of classical and modern works translated and published by Turkish Ministry of Education, *1940-48*) 47, 2nd edn. *1940-50* 52, *Millî Kütüphane Nasil Kuruldu* (How the Turkish National Library was founded) 55, *Türk Dilimim Basina Gelenler* 68, *Trt gin Türkge Dersleri* 68, *Iki Yilda 600 den Fazla Yazi* 68, *Yeniden 645 Yazi* 69.
Lycée Teachers' Training College, Ankara; (Home) Memeviş sok 80/A, Kavaklidere, Ankara, Turkey.

Özbek, Dr. Sabahattin; Turkish agronomist and politician; b. 1915, Erzincan; ed. Secondary School, Istanbul, Faculty of Agriculture, Univ. of Ankara.
Lecturer, Faculty of Agriculture, Univ. of Ankara 38, Asst. Prof. 41, Prof. 53, Dean 55-57, 65-68; Visiting Prof. Univs. of Michigan and Calif. 50-51, 57-58; Minister of Nat. Educ. 72-73, of Communications 73-74; founded Atatürk Univ., Erzurum, later Co-Founder Faculty of Agriculture, Adana; Chair. Agricultural Cttee. for the preparation of First Five-Year Devt. Plan; mem. Turkish Atomic Energy Comm.; Prize of Professional Honour, Union of Agricultural Engineers; Independent.
Publs. 35 books in Turkish and foreign languages.
c/o Ministry of Communications, Ulaştirma Bakanlığı, Hipodrom Caddesi, Ankara, Turkey.

Özdaş, Mehmet Nimet, DR.ING.; Turkish professor of mechanical engineering; b. 26 March 1921, Istanbul; ed. Technical Univ. of Istanbul, Imperial Coll., London and London Univ.
Dozent, Technical Univ. of Istanbul 52, Prof. 61-73, Dir. Computation Centre 62-64; Visiting Prof. Case Inst. of Technology 58-59; Sec.-Gen. Scientific and Technical Research Council 64-67, mem. Science Board 68-71; Rep. to CENTO Science Council 65, to NATO Science Cttee. 66-73; Dir. Marmara Scientific and Industrial Research Inst. 69-73; Asst. Sec.-Gen. for Scientific and Environmental Affairs, NATO Sept. 73-.
Publs. about 20 articles in English in scientific periodicals, many articles in Turkish and five books.
Scientific Affairs Division, North Atlantic Treaty Organization, 1110 Brussels, Belgium.

P

Pachachi, Adnan al, PH.D.; Iraqi diplomatist; b. 14 May 1923; ed. American Univ. of Beirut and Georgetown Univ., Washington, D.C.
Joined Foreign Service 44, served Washington, Alexandria; Dir.-Gen. of Political Affairs, Council of Ministers 57-58; Dir.-Gen. Ministry of Foreign Affairs 58-59; Perm. Rep. of Iraq to UN 59-65; Minister of State Dec. 65-66; Minister of Foreign Affairs 66-67; Perm. Rep. to UN 67-69; Minister of State, Govt. of Abu Dhabi, United Arab Emirates (UAE) 71-74; Personal Rep. of Pres. of the UAE and mem. Abu Dhabi Exec. Council 74-.
c/o Manhal Palace, Abu Dhabi, United Arab Emirates.

Pahlavi, Farah Diba; former Empress of Iran; b. 14 Oct. 1938; ed. Italian School, Jeanne d'Arc School and Razi School, Teheran and Ecole Spéciale d'Architecture, Paris.
Married H.I.M. the Shah 21 Dec. 59; son Reza b. 31 Oct. 60, daughter Farahnaz b 12. March 63, son Ali Reza b. 28 April 66, daughter Leila b. 27 March 1970; fmr. Patron of 37 educ., health and cultural orgs. including Farah Pahlavi Assn. (administration of orphanages in Iran), Iran Cultural Foundation; Foreign Assoc. Fine Arts Acad. of French Inst.
Cuernavaca, Mexico.

Pahlavi, Mohammad Reza; former Shah of Iran; b. 26 Oct. 1919.
Succeeded to throne on the abdication of his father, Reza Shah Pahlavi, 16 Sept. 1941; personally led the Imperial Iranian Army in the liberation of the Province of Azerbaijan 46; went into exile Jan. 79; married (1) Princess Fawzia, sister of King Farouk of Egypt 39, divorced Nov. 48; daughter, Princess Shahnaz Pahlavi; (2) Soraya Esfandiari, 12 Feb. 51; divorced March 58; (3) Farah Diba, 21 Dec. 59; sons: Prince Reza Pahlavi and Prince Ali Reza Pahlavi; daughters: Princess Farahnaz and Princess Leila; Dr. h.c. Columbia, Michigan, Pennsylvania, California (U.C.L.A.), Harvard, Chicago, New York, Washington Univs., U.S.A. and Univs. of Teheran, Punjab, Agra, Aligarh, Istanbul, Beirut, Rio de Janeiro, Bucharest, Sofia, Malaya, Bangkok, Madras, Budapest, Nat. Univ. of Iran; 31 foreign decorations.
Publs. *Mission for My Country* 61, *The White Revolution* 67, *Towards the Great Civilization* 78.
Cuernavaca, Mexico.

Pahlbod, Mehrdad, B.SC.; Iranian politician; b. Teheran; ed. Univ. of Teheran and in France.
Former Deputy Prime Minister and Sec. of State for Fine Arts; Minister of Culture and Arts 64-79; mem. Political Bureau, Rastakhiz Party.
c/o Ministry of Culture and Art, Teheran, Iran.

Panayides, Tasos Christou, M.A.; Cypriot diplomatist; b. 9 April 1934, Ktima, Paphos; ed. Paphos Gymnasium, Teachers' Training Coll., Univ. of London, Univ. of Indiana (U.S.A.).
Instructor 54-59; First Sec. to the Pres. 60-68; Dir. of Office of the Pres. 69; Amb. to Fed. Repub. of Germany, also accred. to Switzerland, Austria and IAEA; High Commr. in the U.K. Feb. 79-; Grand Order of the Fed. Repub. of Germany.
Cyprus High Commission, 93 Park Street, London, W1Y 4ET; 5 Cheyne Walk, London, S.W.3, England.

Paoli, José; French diplomatist; b. 16 Dec. 1924, Epinal; ed. Ecole Nat. des Langues Orientales Vivantes, Paris, Faculté des Lettres, Sorbonne.
Secretary of Embassy, Cairo 51-54, Damascus 54-56, Moscow 58-61, Washington 61-64; Counsellor, Rabat 64-67, Tripoli, Libya 67-70; Asst. Dir. for Algerian Affairs, Ministry of Foreign Affairs 70-75; Amb. to Kuwait 75-79; Chevalier, Légion d'Honneur; Officier, Ordre Nat. du Mérite; Officier du Mérite egyptien; Wissam al Kuwait, First Class.
Ministère des Affaires Etrangères, 37 quai d'Orsay, 75700 Paris, France.

Papadopoulos, Tassos; Cypriot lawyer and politician; b. 1934; ed. Pancyprian Gymnasium, Nicosia, King's Coll., London, and Gray's Inn, London.
Law practice, Nicosia 55-59; fmr. mem. EOKA; mem. Constitutional Comm. drafting Cyprus Constitution 59-60; Minister of Interior *a.i.* 59-60; Minister of Labour and Social Insurance 60-70; Acting Minister of Agriculture 64-66, Minister of Health 60-70; M.P., Deputy Pres. House of Reps. July 70-; practising lawyer; Rep. of Greek Cypriot Community at Intercommunal Talks June 76-July 78.
Chanteclair Building, Apt. 105-205, Nicosia, Cyprus.

Papaioannou, Ezekias; Cypriot journalist; b. 8 Oct. 1908; ed. American Acad., Larnaca, Cyprus.
Secretary-General, Progressive Party of the Working People (Anorthotikon Komma Ergazomenou Laou—AKEL) 49-; Deputy of AKEL, House of Reps. 60-; mem.

Foreign Affairs Cttee., House of Reps. 60-, Chair. Communications and Works Cttee. 70-.
Akamantos Street, P.O. Box 1827, Nicosia; and 8 Doiranis Street, Nicosia, Cyprus.

Parker, Richard B., M.S.; American diplomatist; b. 3 July 1923, Philippines; ed. Kansas State Univ. and Princeton Univ.
Woodrow Wilson Fellow, Princeton Univ.; Second Sec., Amman 55-56; Dept. of State 57-61; First Sec., Beirut 61-64; Political Counsellor, Cairo 65-67; Country Dir. for U.A.R., Dept. of State 67-70; Minister Counsellor, Rabat 70-74; Amb. to Algeria 74-77, to Lebanon 77-78.
Publ. *Practical Guide to Islamic Monuments of Cairo* 74.
c/o Department of State, 2201 C Street, N.W., Washington, D.C. 20520, U.S.A.

Parrot, André; French archaeologist; b. 15 Feb. 1901; ed. Univ. de Paris à la Sorbonne, Faculté de Théologie Protestante, Ecole du Louvre and Ecole Archéologique Française de Jerusalem.
Professor, Faculty of Protestant Theology, Univ. of Paris 37-55, Ecole du Louvre 37-; Head Keeper of Nat. Museums 46-65, Insp.-Gen. 65-; Dir. of Louvre Museum 68-72; Dir. of French archaeological expeditions to Mari (Syrian Arab Republic) and Larsa (Iraq); mem. Institut Français (Académie des Inscriptions et Belles-Lettres); mem. British Acad., Belgian Acad.; Commandeur Légion d'Honneur; Commandeur des Arts et des Lettres; Croix de Guerre 39-45; Grand Croix, Ordre Nat. du Mérite, Grand Cordon du Mérite Syrien.
Publs. *Mari, une ville perdue* 36, *Archéologie mésopotamienne* 46-53, *Tello-vingt campagnes de fouilles* 48, *Ziggurats et Tour de Babel* 48, *Découverte des Mondes ensevelis* 52, *Mari—le temple d'Ishtar* 56, *Mari—le Palais* (3 vols.) 58-59, *Les temples d'Ishtarat et Ninni-zaza* 67, *Le trésor d'Ur* 68, *Sumer* 60, *Assur* 61, *Abraham et son temps* 62, *Terre du Christ* 65, *Clés pour l'archéologie* 67, *Mari—capitale fabuleuse* 74.
11 rue du Val de Grâce, Paris 75005, France.

Parsons, Sir Anthony Derrick, K.C.M.G., M.V.O., M.C., M.A. (OXON.); British diplomatist; b. 9 Sept. 1922, London; ed. King's School Canterbury, Balliol Coll., Oxford.
Army service 40-54; Asst. Mil. Attaché, Baghdad 52-54; Foreign Office 54-55; at British Embassy, Ankara 55-59, Amman 59-60, Cairo 60-61; Foreign Office 61-64; British Embassy, Khartoum 64-65; British Political Agent, Bahrain 65-69; with U.K. Mission to UN 69-71; Foreign and Commonwealth Office 71-74; Amb. to Iran 74-78; c/o Foreign and Commonwealth Office, London, S.W.1, England.

Patinkin, Don, PH.D.; Israeli economist; b. 8 Jan. 1922; ed. Univ. of Chicago.
Asst. Prof. of Economics, Univ. of Chicago 47-48; Research Assoc., Cowles Comm. for Economic Research 47-48; Assoc. Prof. of Economics, Univ. of Ill. 48-49; Lecturer, The Eliezer Kaplan School of Economics and Social Sciences, Hebrew Univ. 49, later Prof. of Economics; Dir. of Research, Maurice Falk Inst. for Economic Research in Israel 56-72; Pres. Econometric Soc. 74; mem. Israel Acad. of Sciences and Humanities; Foreign Hon. mem. American Acad. of Arts and Sciences; Hon. mem. American Econ. Asscn.
Publs. *Money, Interest and Prices: An Integration of Monetary and Value Theory* 56 (2nd edn. 65), *The Israel Economy: The First Decade* 59, *Studies in Monetary Economics* 72, *Keynes' Monetary Thought: a Study of its Development* 76.
Chovevei Zion 5, Talbieh, Jerusalem, Israel.

Patsalides, Andreas, B.SC.ECONS.; Cypriot politician; b. 1922; ed. Greek Gymnasium, Limassol, School of Econs. and Political Science, London, and Harvard Univ., Mass.
Various posts in Public Service; Gen. Dir., Planning Bureau 59-68; Minister of Finance 68-74, Aug. 74-.
Ministry of Finance, Nicosia, Cyprus.

Pattichis, Nicos Kyriakou, LL.B., BAR.-AT-LAW; Cypriot politician; b. 20 Feb. 1916, Kato-Dhrys, Larnaca; ed. Pancyprian Gymnasium, Nicosia, Liverpool Univ. and Middle Temple, London.
District Judge 51-57; Vice-Pres. Cyprus Fed. of Chambers of Commerce and Industry 59-62; Mayor of Limassol 64-71; Pres. Chamber of Commerce and Industry, Limassol April-Aug. 74; Minister of Communications and Works Aug. 74-Jan. 75.
Despina N. Pattichis Str. 1, Limassol, Cyprus.

Pazhwak, Abdurrahman; Afghan diplomatist; b. 7 March 1919.
Has been successively mem. Historical Section of Afghan Acad.; Dir. Foreign Publications Section of Afghan Press Dept.; Editor daily *Islah* and acting Dir.-Gen. of Bakhtar News Agency; Pres. Pashto-Tolana; Dir.-Gen. Publs. Section, Afghan Press Dept.; Press and Cultural Attaché, Afghan Embassy, London; mem. of Section of Information Dept. of ILO; Press and Cultural Attaché, Afghan Embassy, Washington; Dir. Section for East Asia and Dir. a.i., Section for UN, and Int. Confs., Afghan Ministry for Foreign Affairs; Dir.-Gen. Political Affairs in Ministry of Foreign Affairs 56; Perm. Rep. to UN 58-73; Amb. to Fed. Repub. of Germany 73, to India 73-77, to U.K. 77-78; Pres. UN Human Rights Comm. 63, 21st Session of UN Gen. Assembly 66, 5th Special Session 66 and of Emergency Session of Gen. Assembly on Middle East 66; Special Envoy to Fourth Summit of Non-Aligned Countries, Algiers 73, to Summit of Islamic Conf., Lahore 74; Special Envoy to Pres. of Bangladesh.
Publs. *Aryana or Ancient Afghanistan, Pakhtunistan* (both in English), *Tales of the People* 58 (in Persian), and many other works.
c/o Ministry of Foreign Affairs, Kabul, Afghanistan.

Peres, Shimon; Israeli politician; b. 1923, Poland; ed. New York Univ., Harvard Univ.
Immigrated to Palestine 34; fmr. Sec. Hano'ar Ha'oved Movt.; mem. Haganah Movt. 47; Head of Israel Naval Service, Ministry of Defence 48; Head of Defence Mission in U.S.A.; Deputy Dir.-Gen. of Ministry of Defence 52-53, Dir.-Gen. 53-59, Deputy Minister of Defence 59-65; mem. Knesset -59; mem. Mapai Party 59-65, founder mem. and Sec.-Gen. Rafi Party 65, mem. Labour Party after merger 68; Minister for Econ. Devt. in the Administered Areas and for Immigrant Absorption 69-70, of Transport and Communications 70-74, of Information March-June 74, of Defence 74-77; Acting Prime Minister April-May 77; elected Leader of Labour Party June 77.
Publs. *The Next Phase* 65, *David's Sling* 70, *Tomorrow is Now* 78, *With These Men* 78 and numerous political articles in Israeli and foreign publications.
Israel Labour Party, P.O. Box 3263, Tel-Aviv, Israel.

Perlman, Itzhak; Israeli violinist; b. 31 Aug. 1945, Tel-Aviv; ed. Tel-Aviv Acad. of Music, Juilliard School, U.S.A.
Gave recitals on radio at the age of 10; went to U.S.A. 58; studied with Ivan Galamian and Dorothy De Lay; first recital at Carnegie Hall 63; has played with major American orchestras 64-; has toured Europe regularly and played with major European orchestras 66-; debut in U.K. with London Symphony Orchestra 68; appearances at Israel Festival, South Bank Summer Concerts, London 68, 69.
c/o Harold Holt Ltd., 134 Wigmore Street, London, W1H 0DJ, England.

Perowne, Stewart Henry, O.B.E., K.ST.J., M.A., F.S.A.; British orientalist and historian; b. 17 June 1901; ed. Haileybury Coll., Corpus Christi Coll. Cambridge, and Harvard Univ.

English Lecturer, Govt. Arab Coll. Jerusalem 27-30; Asst. Sec. Palestine Govt. 30-32, Asst. District Commr. 32-34; Asst. Sec. Malta 34-37; Political Officer, Aden 37; Arabic Programme Organizer, B.B.C. 38; Information Officer, Aden 39-41; Public Relations Attaché, British Embassy, Baghdad 41-44, Oriental Counsellor 44-47; Colonial Sec. Barbados 47-50; Acting Gov. March-Oct. 49; Adviser, Ministry of Interior, Cyrenaica 50-51; Adviser on Arab Affairs, U.K. Del. UN Gen. Assembly 51; discovered ancient Aziris 51; Hon. Asst. Jerusalem Diocesan Refugee Organization 52; designed and supervised seven Arab refugee villages 52-56; Faculty mem. "College Year in Athens" 65-66.
Publs. *The One Remains* 54, *Herod the Great* 56, *The Later Herods* 58, *Hadrian* 60, *Caesars and Saints* 62, *The Pilgrim's Companion in Jerusalem and Bethlehem* 63, *The Pilgrim's Companion in Roman Rome* 63, *The Pilgrim's Companion in Athens* 65, *Jerusalem* 65, *The End of the Roman World* 66, *Death of the Roman Republic* 68, *Roman Mythology* 69, *The Siege within the Walls* 70, *Rome* 71, *The Journeys of Saint Paul* 73, *The Caesars' Wives: above Suspicion?* 74, *The Archaeology of Greece and the Aegean* 74, *Holy Places of Christendom* 76.
44 Arminger Road, London, W12 7BB, England.

Petrides, Frixos L.; Cypriot teacher and politician; b. 1915, Nicosia; ed. Pancyprian Gymnasium and Univ. of Athens.
In Athens during Second World War; teacher, Pancyprian Gymnasium after Second World War; Chair. Pancyprian Assсn. 47-60; Headmaster, Pancyprian Gymnasium 60; Chair. of Board, Cyprus Broadcasting Corpn. 60-70; Minister of Educ. 70-72; Chair. Cyprus Tourism Org. 72-.
Cyprus Tourism Organization, P.O. Box 4535, Nicosia, Cyprus.

Phanos, Titos; Cypriot politician; b. 23 Jan. 1929, Nicosia; ed. Pancyprian Gymnasium, Nicosia, Middle Temple, London.
Called to Bar 51; law practice 52-66; mem. EOKA fighters' union during campaign for freedom 55-59; mem. of Cttee. of Human Rights of the Nicosia Bar Assсn.; arrested by British administration and served 16 months as political detainee 56-58; mem. Consultative Body to Archbishop Makarios 59-60; mem. House of Representatives for Nicosia 60-66; Parl. Spokesman (Floor Leader) of pro-government Patriotic Front 63-66; mem. Consultative Assembly of Council of Europe 63-65; Minister of Communications and Works 66-70; Amb. to Belgium, Head of Mission to EEC 71-, concurrently Amb. to Luxembourg and Netherlands 73-.
Embassy of Cyprus, 83-85 rue de la Loi, 1040 Brussels, Belgium.

Pickering, Thomas Reeve, M.A.; American diplomatist; b. 5 Nov. 1931, Orange, N.J.; ed. Bowdoin Coll., Brunswick, Me., Fletcher School of Law and Diplomacy, Medford, Mass., Univ. of Melbourne, Australia.
Lieutenant U.S. Navy 56-59; joined Dept. of State 59-, Intelligence Research Specialist 60, Foreign Affairs Officer 61, Arms Control and Disarmament Agency 61-62; mem. U.S. Del. to Disarmament Conf., Geneva 62-64; Principal Officer, Zanzibar 65-67; Deputy Chief of Mission, Dar es Salaam 67-69; Deputy Dir. Bureau of Politico-Mil. Affairs 69-73; Exec. Sec. Dept. of State, Special Asst. to Sec. of State 73-74; Amb. to Jordan 74-78; Asst. Sec. of State, Bureau of Oceans and Int. Environmental and Scientific Affairs 78-.
OES, Room 7831, Department of State, Washington, D.C. 20520, U.S.A.

Polyakov, Vladimir Porfiriyevich, PH.D.; Soviet diplomatist; b. 1931; ed. Inst. of Oriental Studies, Moscow.
Diplomatic Service 56-; Counsellor, Syria 61-65; various posts in Ministry of Foreign Affairs 65-67; Counsellor-Minister, Egypt 68-71; Amb. to People's Democratic Repub. of Yemen 72-74, to Egypt May 74-.
Embassy of the U.S.S.R., 95 Sh. El Giza (Giza), Cairo, Egypt.

Pritchard, James Bennett, A.B., B.D., PH.D., S.T.D., D.D., L.H.D.; American orientalist; b. 4 Oct. 1909; ed. Asbury Coll., Drew Univ., Univ. of Pa.
Professor of Old Testament Literature, Crozer Theological Seminary 42-54; Annual Prof. American School of Oriental Research, Jerusalem 50-51, Visiting Prof. 56-57, 61-62; Prof. Old Testament Literature Church Divinity School of the Pacific 54-62; Prof. Religious Thought, Univ. of Pa. and Curator of Biblical Archaeology Univ. Museum 62-78, Assoc. Dir. 67-76, Dir. 76-77; Visiting Prof. of Archaeology, American Univ. of Beirut 67, Trustee 70-; mem. American Oriental Soc., Archaeological Inst. of America (Pres. 73-74), Soc. for Biblical Literature; Editor *Journal of the American Oriental Soc.* 52-54.
Publs. *Palestinian Figures* 43, *Ancient Near Eastern Texts* 50, *The Ancient Near East in Pictures* 54, *Archaeology and the Old Testament* 58, *Gibeon, Where the Sun Stood Still* 62, *The Ancient Near East: Supplementary Texts and Pictures* 69, *The Ancient Near East Vol. II* 75, *Recovering Sarepta* 78.
University Museum, 33rd and Spruce Streets, Philadelphia 4, Pa., U.S.A.

Pharaon, Ghaith Rashad, PH.D., M.B.A.; Saudi Arabian business executive; b. 7 Sept. 1940, Riyadh; ed. Stanford Univ., Harvard Univ.
Founder Saudi Arabia Research and Devt. Corpn. (Redec) 65, now Chair. of Board and Dir.-Gen.; Chair. Board Saudi Arabian Parsons Ltd., Saudi Automotive Industries Ltd., Redec Daelim Ltd., Interstal, Saudi Chemical Processors Ltd., Arabian Maritime Co., Saudi Inland Transport, etc.; Vice-Chair. Jezirah Bank Ltd., Saudi Light Industries Ltd., Arabian Chemical Industries Ltd.; mem. Board Okaz Publications, Tihama; Commendatore (Italy); King Abdul Aziz Award.
P.O. Box 1935, Jeddah; Home: Ghaith Pharaon Residence, Ruwais, Jeddah, Saudi Arabia.

Q

Qaboos bin Said; Sultan of Oman; b. 18 Nov. 1940; ed. by British tutors and at Royal Military Coll., Sandhurst.
In Britain 58-66; served in British Army and studied local government; returned to Salalah 66; deposed his father Said bin Taimur 70; Sultan July 70-, also Minister of Foreign Affairs, Defence and Finance.
The Palace, Muscat, Sultanate of Oman.

Qaddafi, Col. Muammar al- (*see* Gaddafi, Muammar al-).

Qaissi, Fawzi al- (*see* Kaissi, Fawzi al-).

Qatar, Amir of (*see* Thani, Sheikh Khalifa bin Hamad al-).

Quandt, William B., PH.D.; American educationist and administrator; b. 1942; ed. Stanford Univ., Massachusetts Inst. of Tech.
Served with RAND Corpn., California 68-72; in Bureau of Near Eastern and South Asian Affairs, State Dept. 72-79; also Assoc. Prof. of Political Science, Univ. of Pennsylvania.
Publs. *Revolution and Political Leadership: Algeria* 54-68, 69, *The Politics of Palestinan Nationalism* (Co-author), *Decade of Decisions: American Policy towards the Arab-Israeli Conflict* 67-76.
University of Pennsylvania, Philadelphia, Pa. 19104, U.S.A.

Quddus, Ihsan Abdal (son of the late Rose al-Yussuf, famous actress and writer); Egyptian writer; b. 1 Jan. 1919; ed. Univ. of Cairo.
Practised law 42; joined magazine *Rose al-Yussuf* 42, imprisoned for attack on govt. 45, released and became Chief Editor, again imprisoned 50, 51; first novel publ. 54; Editor *Akhbar al-Yom* until 74; writer for *Al-Ahram* May 74-.
Publs. include *I am Free* 54, *Do not Turn out the Sun* (two vols.) 60, *Nothing Matters* 63.
c/o Al-Ahram, Galaa Street, Cairo, Egypt.

Quraishi, Abdul Aziz al-, M.B.A., F.I.B.A.; Saudi Arabian government official; b. 1930, Hail; ed. Univ. of Southern California, U.S.A.
General Man. State Railways 61-68; Pres. Gen. Personnel Bureau 68-74; Minister of State 71-74; Gov. Saudi Arabian Monetary Agency 74-; Gov. Int. Monetary Fund, Arab Monetary Fund; Alt. Gov. for Saudi Arabia, Islamic Devt. Bank; mem. Board of Dirs., Supreme Council for Petroleum and Mineral Affairs, Gen. Petroleum and Mineral Org., Public Investment Fund, Pension Fund.
Saudi Arabian Monetary Agency, P.O. Box 2992, Jeddah; Home: Saudi Arabian Monetary Agency Staff Compound, Malaz, Riyadh, Saudi Arabia.

R

Rabin, Maj.-Gen. Yitzhak; Israeli army officer and politician; b. 1 March 1922, Jerusalem; ed. Kadoorie Agricultural School, Kfar Tabor, and Staff Coll., England.
Palmach commands 43-48, including War of Independence; represented Israel Defence Forces (I.D.F.) at Rhodes armistice negotiations; fmr. Head of Training Dept., I.D.F.; C.-in-C. Northern Command 56-59; Head, Manpower Branch 59-60; Deputy Chief of Staff and Head, Gen. Staff Branch 60-64, Chief of Staff I.D.F. 64-68; Amb. to U.S.A. 68-73; mem. Knesset Jan. 74-; Minister of Labour March-April 74; Prime Minister 74-June 77, also Minister of Communications 74-75; Leader Labour Party 74-April 77; Hon. Doctorates, Jerusalem Univ. 67, Dropsie Coll. 68, Brandeis Univ. 68, Yeshiva Univ. 68, Coll. of Jewish Studies, Chicago 69, Univ. of Miami 70, Hebrew Union Coll., Boston 71.
c/o The Knesset, Jerusalem, Israel.

Rabinowitz, Yehoshua; Israeli politician; b. 13 Nov. 1911; ed. Poland and Tel-Aviv School of Law and Econs.
Management posts in Israeli Co-operative Movement 48-56; mem. Tel-Aviv Municipal Council 56-59, Deputy Mayor 59-61, Chair. Financial, Townbuilding and Planning Cttees. 61-69, Mayor of Tel-Aviv 69-74; Minister of Housing March-May 74, of Finance 74-June 77; mem. Knesset; Labour Party.
(*Died* 14 *August* 1979)

Radji, Parviz Camran, M.A.(ECON.); Iranian diplomatist; b. 1936, Teheran; ed. Alborz Coll., Teheran, Hill School, Pa., U.S.A., Trinity Hall, Cambridge Univ., U.K.
National Iranian Oil Co. 59-62; Ministry of Foreign Affairs 63-65; Private Sec. Office of the Prime Minister 65; later Personal Asst. to the Prime Minister; Special Adviser to the Prime Minister 72-76; Amb. to U.K. 76-79.
c/o Iranian Embassy, 16 Princes Gate, London, S.W.7, England.

Rafael, Gideon; Israeli diplomatist; b. Germany 5 March 1913; ed. Univ. of Berlin.
Emigrated 34; mem. Kibbutz 34-43; active in Haganah and war services 39-42; Jewish Agency, Political Dept. 43; in charge of preparation of Jewish case for Jewish Agency, Political Dept., Nuremberg War Crimes Trial 45-46; mem. of Jewish Agency Comm. to Anglo-American Comm. of Enquiry 46, and of Jewish Agency mission to UN Special Comm. for Palestine 47; mem. Israel Permanent Del. to UN 51-52; alternate rep. to UN 53; rep. at UN Gen. Assemblies 47-66; Counsellor in charge of Middle East and UN Affairs, Ministry for Foreign Affairs 53-57; Amb. to Belgium and Luxembourg 57-60, to the European Econ. Community 59; Deputy Dir.-Gen. Ministry of Foreign Affairs 60; Head of Israel Del. Int. Conf. Law of the Sea, Geneva 60; Deputy Dir.-Gen. Ministry for Foreign Affairs 60-65; Perm. Rep. to UN, Geneva 65-66; Special Amb. and Adviser to Foreign Minister May 66-67; Perm. Rep. of Israel to UN 67; Dir.-Gen. Ministry of Foreign Affairs 67-71; Senior Political Adviser to Minister of Foreign Affairs 72-73; Amb. to U.K. 73-77, concurrently non-Resident Amb. to Ireland 75-77; Head of Del. to UNCTAD III 72.
Kiryath Yovel, Jerusalem, Israel.

Rahal, Abdellatif; Algerian diplomatist; b. 1922.
Professor of mathematics; Govt. service 62; Dir.-Gen. Presidential Cabinet 63; first Algerian Amb. to France 64; then posts in Ministry of Foreign Affairs; Sec.-Gen. Ministry of Foreign Affairs until 70; Perm. Rep. to UN 70-77; Minister of Higher Educ. and Scientific Research 77-79.
c/o Ministry of Higher Education and Scientific Research, Algiers, Algeria.

Rais Abin, Maj.-Gen.; Indonesian army officer; b. 15 Aug. 1926; ed. Army Staff Coll., Queenscliff, Australia, Nat. Defence Coll., Indonesia, Defence Management Inst., Indonesia.
Senior Asst. for Planning, Army Logistics, Indonesian Army 69-72; Deputy Commdr. of Army Staff and Command Coll., Indonesia 73-75; Chief of Staff, UNEF Jan.-Nov. 76, Acting Force Commdr. Dec. 76, Force Commdr. Jan. 77-.
United Nations Emergency Force, P.O. Box 138, Ismailia, Egypt; 50 Cik Dikiro, Jakarta, Indonesia.

Raphael, Farid; Lebanese banker and government official; b. 27 Oct. 1933, Dlebta, Kesrouan; ed. Univ. of St. Joseph, Beirut, Univ. of Lyons, France.
Fondé de Pouvoirs, Compagnie Algérienne de Crédit et de Banque, Beirut 60, Sub-Man. 62, Joint Man. 65, Gen. Man. 67, mem. Board 67-; Vice-Pres. and Gen. Man. Banque Libano Française (France) S.A., Paris 76-78; Minister of Justice, Finance, Posts, Telephones and Telecommunications Dec. 76-.
Ministry of Finance, Beirut; Home: Baroudy Building, Hazmieh, Lebanon.

Raphael, Yitzchak, M.A., PH.D.; Israeli politician; b. 5 July 1914; ed. Hebrew Univ.
Settled in Palestine 35; mem. Exec. Jewish Agency and Head, Emigration Dept. 48-54; mem. of 2nd, 3rd, 4th, 5th, 6th, 7th and 8th Knesset; Chair. Exec. Hapoel Hamizrachi (Nat. Religious Party); mem. World Exec. Nat. Religious Party Mizrachi; Chair. Legislative Cttee. Knesset; Chair. Mossad Harav Kook (Publishers); Deputy Minister of Health 62-64; Minister of Religious Affairs 74-Dec. 76; Chair. (Mosad) Yad Harav Maimon Judaic Studies Centre.
Publs. *Sefer Hachasiduth, Rishonim v'achronim, Hachasidut v'Eretz Israel, Sefer Hamanhig*; Ed. *Encyclopaedia of Religious Zionism* 59, 60.
P.O.B. 642, Jerusalem, Israel.

Rasheed, Khalafalla el-, LL.M.; Sudanese judge; b. 15 Feb. 1930, Merowe District; ed. Hantub Secondary School, Univ. Coll. of Khartoum, Cambridge and London Univs.
Joined Sudan Judiciary 55; District Judge (Second Grade) 56, First Grade 60; in practice as advocate 56-57; recalled to Judiciary 57; transferred to Attorney-Gen.'s Dept. 62; Advocate Gen. 67-72; Pres. Supreme Court (Chief Justice) 72-; mem. Exec. Bureau, Sudanese Socialist

Union; Order of King Abdul Aziz, Third Class, Order of El Nilein, First Class.
Publs. *The Law and the Citizen* (pamphlet) 67, various newspaper articles on legal topics.
The Sudan Judiciary, Law Courts, P.O. Box 763, Khartoum, Sudan.

Rashid bin Said al-Maktum (*see* Maktum, Rashid bin Said al-).

Rateb, Aisha, PH.D.; Egyptian politician; ed. Faculty of Law, Cairo Univ.
Junior Lecturer, Faculty of Law, Cairo Univ., Prof. of Int. Law; Minister of Social Affairs 71-76, of Social Affairs and Insurance 76-77; Amb. Extraordinary, Ministry of Foreign Affairs Nov. 78-; Chair. Legislative Affairs Cttee. 73-.
c/o Ministry of Foreign Affairs, Cairo, Egypt.

Razzaz, Ahmed Munif, M.B., B.CH.; Jordanian physician and politician; b. 1919; ed. Amman Secondary School, American Univ. of Beirut and Cairo.
Teacher 39-41; mem. Baath Party 49-, Jordan Regional Leadership 56-66, Sec. 60-66, Sec.-Gen. Baath Party 65-66; exiled to Syria 52-53; imprisoned 57-59, 61, 63-64; arrested Feb. 66; Arab League Prize 63.
Publs. *Features of New Arab Life* (in Arabic) 53, *Evolution of the Meaning of Nationalism* (in Arabic) 60, (English trans.) 63, *Freedom and its Problems in Underdeveloped Countries* 65.
Baath Party, rue Abdul Aziz 66, Damascus, Syria.

Razzek, Brig. Aref Abdel; Iraqi politician; b. 1914; ed. Military Acad.
Entered Air Force 36; became Commdr. Habbaniya base; Minister of Agriculture Nov. 63-Dec. 63; Commdr. of Air Forces Dec. 63-July 65; Prime Minister and Acting Minister of Defence Sept. 65; Abortive *coup d'état* Sept. 65, June 66; imprisoned June 66.
Baghdad, Iraq.

Rebeyrol, Philippe; French diplomatist; b. 14 June 1917, Paris; ed. Lycée Louis-le-Grand, Paris, Ecole Normale Supérieure, Univ. de la Sorbonne.
Professor, Inst. Français, Barcelona 42-45; Head of Inst. de Hautes Etudes, Bucharest 46-49; Counsellor for Cultural Affairs, French Embassy to Egypt 51-55; Chargé d'affaires, Algeria 62-68; Amb. to Cameroon 68-71; Dir. for African Affairs, Ministry of Foreign Affairs 72-75; Amb. to Tunisia July 74-; Officier, Légion d'Honneur; Commdr., Ordre Nat. de Mérite.
Publs. Articles on the history of Art.
Ambassade de France, Place de l'Indépendance, Tunis, Tunisia; 34 rue de Grenelle, Paris 7e, France (Home).

Recanati, Daniel; Israeli banker; b. 26 Oct. 1921, Greece.
Chairman and Man. Dir. IDB Bankholding Corpn. Ltd.; Chair. and Man. Dir. Israel Discount Bank Ltd.; Chair. Board of Dirs. Barclays Discount Bank Ltd., Discount Bank Investment Corpn. Ltd.; dir. of several cos.
Israel Discount Bank, 27-31 Yehuda Halevy Street, Tel-Aviv, Israel.

Remez, Brig.-Gen. Aharon; Israeli air force officer and diplomatist; b. 8 May 1919; ed. Herzliah Grammar School, Tel-Aviv, Harvard School of Business Administration, U.S.A., and Woodrow Wilson School of Public and International Affairs, Princeton, U.S.A.
Agricultural training in Kibbutz, Givat Haim 37-39; Emissary to Zionist Youth Movement, U.S.A. 39-41; Royal Air Force 42-47; mem. Kibbutz Kfar Blum 47-; Dir. of Planning and Operations, later Chief of Staff, Israel Air Force 48; Commdr.-in-Chief Israel Air Force 48-51; Head, Ministry of Defence Purchasing Mission, U.S.A. 51-53; Aviation Adviser to Minister of Defence 53-54; mem. Board of Dirs. Solel Boneh Ltd., Exec. Dir. Koor Industries Ltd. 54-59; mem. Knesset 56-57; Admin. Dir. Weizmann Inst. of Science, Rehovot 59-60; Dir. Int. Co-operation Dept., Ministry for Foreign Affairs 60-64, Adviser on Int. Co-operation to Minister for Foreign Affairs 64-65; Consultant to OECD 64-65; Chair. Nat. Aviation Council 63-65; Amb. to U.K. 65-70; Dir.-Gen. Israel Ports Authority 70-.
Israel Ports Authority, Maya Building, 74 Patah Tiqva Road, P.O. Box 20121, Tel-Aviv; Home: 8 San Martin Street, Jerusalem, Israel.

Riad, Mahmoud; Egyptian diplomatist; b. 8 Jan. 1917; ed. Military Acad. and General Staff Coll.
Egyptian Rep. to Mixed Armistice Comm. 49-52; Dir. Dept. of Arab Affairs, Ministry of Foreign Affairs 54-55; Ambassador to Syria 55-58; President's Counsellor on Foreign Affairs 58-62; Chair. Del. to UN Econ. Comm. for Africa 61; Ambassador and Perm. Rep. to UN 62-64; Minister of Foreign Affairs 64-72, Deputy Premier 71-72; Pres. Adviser Jan.-June 72; Sec.-Gen. League of Arab States 72-79.
c/o Ministry of Foreign Affairs, Cairo, Egypt.

Riad, Mahmoud Mohammed, PH.D.; Egyptian electrical and electronic engineer; b. 4 June 1918, Cairo; ed. Cairo Univ., Imperial Coll., London Univ.
Assistant Prof. of Telecommunications, Alexandria Univ. 43-56; Head Eng. Dept., Atomic Energy Org. 56-57; Dir.-Gen. Telecommunications Org. 57-64; Sec.-Gen. Arab Telecommunications Union 58-; Minister of Communications 64-65; Chair. Electricity Corpn. 65-66, Electrical and Electronic Industries Corpn. 66-68; Prof. of Electronics, Kuwait Univ. 68-71; Minister of Transport and Communications 71-April 75; Fellow, American Inst. of Electrical and Electronic Engineers, Inst. of Electrical Engineers, England.
Publs. various papers on science and engineering in technical journals.
Secretary-General, Arab Telecommunications Union, 83 Ramses Street, Cairo; and Ministry of Transport and Communications, Cairo, Egypt.

Rial, Cleto Hassan, B.SC., M.A.; Sudanese administrator; b. 1 Sept. 1935, Wau, Bahr El Ghazal; ed. Comboni Coll., Khartoum, Xavier Univ., Ohio, Univ. of Notre Dame, Indiana, Inst. of Social Studies, The Hague, Royal Inst. of Public Admin., London.
Executive Officer, Ministry of Local Govt. 58-59; Schoolmaster, Comboni Coll., Khartoum 59-60; Finance Insp. Ministry of Finance and Econs. 62-63; Lecturer Inst. of Public Admin. 63-72; Sec.-Gen. High Exec. Council for the Southern Region 72-; Sudanese Rep. at Conf. on African Devt. held by Massachusetts Inst. of Tech. at Athens 63; participated in Seminar on Nat. Govt. Admin., Tokyo 76; toured African countries consulting Southern Sudanese leaders in exile 69-71; mem. Second Order of the Nile.
Publ. *Methods and Techniques of Community Development Programmes* 66.
Secretariat General, P.O. Box 17, Juba, Sudan.

Rifa'i, Abdul Munem; Jordanian diplomatist and politician; b. 1917; ed. American Univ. of Beirut.
In service of King Abdullah 38; Chief Sec. of Govt. 40; Asst. Chief of Royal Court 41-42; Consul-Gen. in Cairo, Lebanon and Syria 43-44; Del. to Treaty Conf. with Great Britain 46; Under-Sec. of Foreign Affairs 47; Minister to Iran and Pakistan 49; Amb. to United States and Perm. Rep. to UN 53-57, to Lebanon 57, to Great Britain 58; Chief of Nat. Guidance 59; Perm. Rep. to UN 59-66; Amb. to U.A.R. 66, 67-68; Minister of Foreign Affairs 68-69; Prime Minister March-Aug. 69; Deputy Prime Minister, Minister of Foreign Affairs and Senator 69-70; Prime Minister June 70-71; Personal Rep. to H.M. King Hussein 72-73; Perm. Rep. to Arab League 73; Amb. to Egypt Sept.-Dec. 73; Special Adviser to H.M. King Hussein on

Int. Affairs Dec. 73-74, mem. Senate 74-; numerous decorations.
The Senate, Amman, Jordan.

Rifai, Rashid M. S. al-, M.S.ENG., PH.D., M.I.E.E.; Iraqi electrical engineer; b. 1 May 1929; ed. American Univ. of Beirut, Lebanon, Univ. of Bristol, England, Purdue and Rice Univs., U.S.A.
Engineer in Posts, Telephones and Telecommunications 54-62; Chief Engineer, Gen. Co. for Electrical Industries 68; Minister for Presidential Affairs July-Aug. 68, of Oil and Minerals 68-70; Minister of State 70; Minister of Planning 71, of Communications 72-75, of Public Works and Housing 75; Acting Minister of Defence 73-74; Amb. in Ministry of Foreign Affairs May 76; Amb. to Belgium Dec. 76-, to Luxembourg May 77-; Perm. Rep. to EEC Sept. 77-.
Embassy of Iraq, Avenue de la Floride 131, 1180 Brussels, Belgium.

Rifa'i, Zaid al-, M.A.; Jordanian diplomatist; b. 27 Nov. 1936, Amman (son of fmr. Prime Minister Samir Rifa'i and nephew of Abdul Munem Rifa'i, *q.v.*); ed. Victoria Coll., Cairo, and Harvard and Columbia Univs.
Joined diplomatic service 57; served at embassies in Cairo, Beirut and London and at the Perm. Mission of Jordan at UN; Chief of Royal Protocol 65; Sec.-Gen. of Royal Court and Private Sec. to H.M. King Hussein 67; Chief of Royal Court 69-70; Amb. to U.K. 70-72; Political Adviser to H.M. King Hussein 72-73; Prime Minister May 73-July 76: Minister of Foreign Affairs and Defence 73-76.
Amman, Jordan.

Rishtya, Kassim; Afghan writer and diplomatist (retd.); b. 1913; ed. Istiklal High School, Kabul, Banking Inst., Kabul.
Clerk in Press Section, Ministry of Foreign Affairs 31; Chief Clerk Foreign Relations Section, Ministry of Communications 32; mem. Kabul Literary Circle 33; Dir. Publs. Div. 36, Vice-Pres. 38; Editor *Kabul Almanach* and *Kabul Magazine* 36-38; Dir.-Gen. of Publs. Press Dept. 40-44, Vice-Pres. 44-47, Pres. 47-48; Pres. Govt. Econ. Planning Board 49, Govt. Co-operative Org. 49-52, Bakhtar News Agency 52-55; Minister of Information 56-59; Amb. to Czechoslovakia, Poland and Hungary 60-62, to Egypt, Greece, Sudan, Ghana 62-63; Minister of Information 63; Vice-Chair. Cttee. for Revision of Constitution 63; Minister of Finance 64-65; Rep. for Afghanistan at Second Conf. for the Support of the Arab People 69; Del. to UN Gen. Assembly 69; Amb. to Japan 70-73, also accred. to the Philippines.
Publs. *Afghanistan in the 19th Century, Jawani Afghan, Jamaluddin Afghani, Afghanistan* 77, short stories, translations and several novels.
Zarghoona Watt 26, Kolola Pushta, Kabul, Afghanistan.

Rivlin, Moshe; Israeli administrator; b. 1925, Jerusalem; ed. Teacher's Seminary, Graduate Aluma Inst. for Jewish Studies, Mizrachi Teachers' Coll. and Hebrew Univ., Jerusalem.
Joined Haganah 40; Head, Council of Youth Movts., Jerusalem 44-46; served as Maj.-Gen. in Israeli Army 48; Consul, New York 52-58; Dir. Information Dept., The Jewish Agency 58-60, Sec.-Gen. 60-66, Dir.-Gen. and Head of Admin. and Public Relations Dept. 66-71; Dir.-Gen. of reconstituted Jewish Agency 71-; Chair. Board of Dirs. of Keren Kayemeth Le Israel 77-; Assoc. mem. Exec., World Zionist Org. 71, Chair. Haganah veterans in Israel; mem. Boards of Govs. of Ben-Gurion Univ., Coll. for Public Admin., Jewish Telegraphic Agency; mem. Exec. Cttee. of Yad Ben-Zvi, Council of Yad Ben-Gurion, Boards of Dirs. of *Jerusalem Post*, El Al and the Hebrew Univ.
Keren Kayemeth Le Israel, P.O. Box 283, Jerusalem; 1 Keren Kayemeth Street, Jerusalem, Israel.

Robert, Louis; French archaeologist; b. 15 Feb. 1904; ed. Paris Univ., Ecole Normale Supérieure.
Member French School, Athens 27-32; Dir. of Studies Ecole des Hautes Etudes 32-; Prof. of Greek Epigraphy and Antiquities Coll. de France 39-74; dir. excavations at Amyzon 49 and Claros (Temple of Apollo) 50-61; Officier Légion d'Honneur.
Publs. *Villes d'Asie Mineure, Etudes Anatoliennes, Les Gladiateurs dans l'Orient Grec, Etudes de Numismatique Grecque, Hellenica* (13 vols.), *Noms Indigènes dans l'Asie Mineure, La Carie* (with his wife, Jeanne Robert), *Monnaies antiques en Troade, Documents de l'Asie Mineure méridionale, La déesse de Hiérapolis Castabala, Monnaies Grecques, Opera Minora Selecta* (4 vols.), *Bulletin Epigraphique* (with his wife) 38- (annually).
31 avenue René Coty, Paris 14e, France.

Rolandis, Nicos, BAR.-AT-LAW; Cypriot lawyer and politician; b. 10 Dec. 1934, Limassol; ed. Pancyprian Gymnasium, Nicosia, and Middle Temple, London.
Practised Law; Partner then Chair. and Man. Dir. of several industrial and commercial companies; joint founder of the Democratic Camp, (now the Democratic Party); Minister of Foreign Affairs March 78-.
Ministry of Foreign Affairs, Nicosia, Cyprus.

Rosen, Shlomo; Israeli politician; b. 21 June 1905.
Active in Histadrut, missions abroad; mem. Exec. Cttee., Jewish Agency; mem. Exec. Comm., Mapam (United Workers' Party); mem. Knesset (Parl.), Deputy Speaker 65-; Sec. Kibbutz Movement; Minister for Immigration and Absorption 74-June 77.
The Knesset, Jerusalem, Israel.

Rosenne, Shabtai, LL.B., PH.D.; Israeli lawyer and diplomatist; b. 24 Nov. 1917; ed. London Univ. and Hebrew Univ. of Jerusalem.
Advocate (Israel), Political Dept., Jewish Agency for Palestine 46-48; Legal Adviser, Ministry of Foreign Affairs 48-66; Deputy Perm. Rep. to UN 67-71; Perm. Rep. to UN (Geneva) 71-74; Ministry of Foreign Affairs 74-; mem. Del. to UN Gen. Assemblies 48-74, Vice-Chair. Legal Cttee. 60; mem. Del. to Armistice Negotiations with Egypt, Jordan, Lebanon and Syria 49; mem. Del. to UN Conf. on Law of the Sea, Chair. 73, 78-; Chair. Del. to UN Conf. on Law of Treaties 68, 69, mem. other UN conf.; Govt. Rep. before Int. Court of Justice in several cases; mem. Int. Law Comm. 62-71, UN Comm. on Human Rights 68-70; Assoc. and mem. Inst. of Int. Law 63, 75; Rapporteur, Termination and Modification of Treaties 65; Visiting Prof. Bar-Ilan Univ. 76-; Hon. mem. American Soc. of Int. Law 76; Israel Prize 60, Certificate of Merit, American Soc. of Int. Law 68.
Publs. *International Court of Justice* 57, *The Time Factor in Jurisdiction of the International Court of Justice* 60, *The Law and Practice of the International Court* (2 vols.) 65, *The Law of Treaties: Guide to the Vienna Convention* 70, *The World Court: What it is and how it works* 73; and numerous articles, mainly on law.
Ministry of Foreign Affairs, Hakiriya, Romema, Jerusalem, Israel.

Rossides, Zenon George; Cypriot diplomatist; b. 8 Feb. 1895; ed. Limassol Coll. and Middle Temple, London.
Called to Bar 23; law practice in Cyprus 25-54; mem. Nat. Del. to London 29-31; mem. Ethnarchy Council 46-48 and 58-59; mem. Exec. 50-59; Greek Cypriot Rep. on Joint Cttee. in London, leading to Independence of Cyprus 59-60; Ambassador to U.S.A. 60-73; Perm. Rep. of Cyprus to UN 60-; Vice-Pres. UN Gen. Assembly 61-62, 63-64; Chair. UN Cttee. on Portuguese Colonies 62; mem. UN Admin. Tribunal 66-, UN Cttee. on Elimination of Racial Discrimination 69-71, Int. Law Comm. 71-, Preparatory Cttee. on Conf. on Human Environment.
Publs. *The Island of Cyprus and Union with Greece* 51, *The Problem of Cyprus* 58.
Permanent Mission of Cyprus to the United Nations, 820 Second Ave., 12th Floor, New York, N.Y. 10017, U.S.A.

Rouhani, Fuad, LL.M.; Iranian lawyer and executive; b. 23 Oct. 1907; ed. Teheran and London Univ.
Anglo-Iranian Oil Co., Legal and Administrative Branches 26-51; Chief Legal Adviser, Nat. Iranian Oil Co. 51-54, Dir. 54-79, Deputy Chair. 56-79; Sec.-Gen. and Chair. Board of Govs., Organization of Petroleum Exporting Countries (OPEC) 61-64; Adviser to the Prime Minister 64; Sec.-Gen. Regional Co-operation for Devt. 64-68; Adviser to Prime Minister; now in private practice as expert on Iranian and int. law; D. en D. (Paris) 68.
16 Kh. Rasht (Behjatabad), Teheran, Iran.

Rouillon, Fernand; French diplomatist; b. 11 Dec. 1920, Condrieu (Rhône); ed. Tivoli Coll., School of Political Sciences, Bordeaux Univ.
With Ministry of Foreign Affairs 44-; Dept. of Econ. Affairs 44-47; Tunis, London (NATO) and Ottawa 47-56; Dept. of Eastern Europe 56-58, of Cultural Affairs 58-60; Rabat, New York (UN), and Athens 60-70; Asst. Dir. Dept. of Middle East 70-75; Amb. to Syria June 75-; Chevalier, Légion d'Honneur; Officier, Ordre National du Mérite.
French Embassy, rue Ata Ayoubi, Damascus, Syria.

Roussos, Nicolaos S.; Cypriot civil engineer and politician; b. 1906, Lania Village, Limassol District, ed. Greek Gymnasium, Limassol, and Athens Technical Univ.
Practised civil engineering in Greece, mainly road construction work 29-33; Municipal Engineer, Limassol 33-47; Senior Partner, N. S. Roussos & J. Pericleous (civil engineers and architects) 38-70; Minister of Communications and Works 70-72; mem. of Board, Cyprus Telecommunications Authority 60-68, Vice-Chair. 68-70, Chair. June 72-; Pres. Cyprus Civil Engineers and Architects Asscn. 46-62; Pres. UN Asscn. of Cyprus 70, Limassol Rotary 61-62, Limassol Wine Festival 64, 65.
Cyprus Telecommunications Authority, Nicosia; and P.O. Box 270, Limassol, Cyprus.

Runciman, The Hon. Sir Steven (James Cochran Stevenson), Kt., M.A., F.B.A.; British historian; b. 7 July 1903; ed. Eton Coll. and Trinity Coll., Cambridge.
Fellow Trinity Coll., Cambridge 27-38; Lecturer Cambridge Univ. 31-38; Press Attaché, British Legation, Sofia 40-41; Prof. of Byzantine Studies, Istanbul Univ. 42-45; Rep. of British Council, Greece 45-47; Chair. Anglo-Hellenic League 51-67; Trustee, British Museum 60-67; Pres. British Inst. of Archaeology at Ankara 61-75; Fellow, British Acad. 57; Hon. Fellow, Trinity Coll., Cambridge 65; Hon. Litt.D. (Cambridge, London, Chicago, Durham, St. Andrews, Oxford, Birmingham), Hon. LL.D. (Glasgow), Hon. D.Phil. (Thessalonika), Hon. D.D. (Wabash, U.S.A.).
Publs. *The Emperor Romanus Lecapenus* 29, *The First Bulgarian Empire* 30, *Byzantine Civilization* 33, *The Medieval Manichee* 47, *History of the Crusades* (3 vols.) 51-54, *The Eastern Schism* 55, *The Sicilian Vespers* 58, *The White Rajahs* 60, *The Fall of Constantinople 1453* 65, *The Great Church in Captivity* 68, *The Last Byzantine Renaissance* 70, *The Orthodox Churches and the Secular State* 71, *Byzantine Style and Civilization* 75, *The Byzantine Theocracy* 77.
Elshieshields, Lockerbie, Dumfriesshire, Scotland.

S

Saad al-Abdullah al-Salem al-Sabah, Sheikh (*see* Sabah, Sheikh Saad al-Abdullah al Salem al-).

Saba, Elias, B.LITT.; Lebanese economist and politician; b. 1932, Lebanon; ed. American Univ. of Beirut and Univ. of Oxford.
Economic Adviser to Ministry of Finance and Petroleum, Kuwait and Kuwait Fund for Arab Econ. Devt. 61-62; Chair. Dept. of Econs., American Univ. of Beirut 63-67; Assoc. Prof. of Econs., American Univ. of Beirut 67-69; Deputy Prime Minister of the Lebanon, Minister of Finance and Minister of Defence 70-72; Econ. and Financial Adviser to Pres. 72-73; Chair. and Gen. Man. St. Charles City Centre, S.A.R.L. 74-; Chair. and Chief Exec. Arab Int. Finance Co., Switzerland 74-; mem. Nat. Dialogue Cttee. Sept. 75.
Publ. *Postwar Developments in the Foreign Exchange Systems of Lebanon and Syria* 62.
Biarritz Building, P.O. Box 9500, Beirut, Lebanon.

Saba, Hanna, D. en D.; Egyptian jurist and diplomatist; b. 23 July 1909; ed. Coll. of Jesuit Fathers, Cairo, Faculté de Droit, Paris, and Ecole Libre des Sciences Politiques, Paris.
Ministry of Foreign Affairs, Cairo 42, Counsellor 46, Minister 52; Dir. of Treaties Div., UN Secr. 46-50; Juridical Adviser, UNESCO 50-67; Asst. Dir.-Gen. of UNESCO 67-71; Alt. Chair. UNESCO Appeal Board 73; Vice-Chair. Asscn. of French and Arab Jurists, Arbitration Council of Franco-Arab Chamber of Commerce, Paris; Grand Officer of Merit, Egypt; Officer of the Nile; Ordre de Malte.
Publs. *L'Islam et la nationalité* 32, *L'évolution dans la technique des traités, Les droits économiques et sociaux dans le projet de pacte des droits de l'homme, Les ententes et accords régionaux dans la Charte des Nations Unies* (Course at Acad. of Int. Law, The Hague 52), *L'Activité quasi-législative des institutions spécialisées des Nations Unies* (Course at Acad. of Int. Law, The Hague 64).
3 boulevard de la Saussaye, Neuilly (Hauts de Seine) 92.200, France.

Sabah, Hussni Yahia, M.D.; Syrian physician; b. 3 March 1900, Damascus; ed. Faculty of Medicine, Damascus Univ., Univ. of Lausanne, Switzerland, Univ. of Paris.
Assistant, Faculty of Medicine, Damascus Univ. 20-24, Instructor 24-28, Asst. Prof. 28-32, Prof. and Head of Internal Medicine Dept. 32-67; Dean of Faculty 38-42; Rector of Damascus Univ. 42-49; retd. from Univ. 67; Co-founder and fmr. Chair. Syrian Al-Muassat Asscn. 43-75; co-founder and mem. Board of Dirs. Al-Muassat Gen. Hosp. 53-; Pres. Syrian Asscn. of Diabetes and Endocrinology 72-; mem. Arab Acad. of Damascus 46-, Pres. 68-; mem. Arab Acad. of Cairo 56-; Medal of Syrian Merit, Distinguished Order; Medal of al-Jumhouria (Egypt); Al-Kawkab Medal (Jordan); Medal of Educ. (Iran).
Publs. *Principles of Internal Medicine, Elements of Pathology, Medical Semiology, General Pathology, Elements of Internal Medicine* (2 vols.), *Textbook of Internal Medicine* (7 vols.), *Elements of Neurology, Textbook of Endocrinology, Diseases of Metabolism and Intoxications, French-Arabic Glossaries of Terms in Neurology, Infectious and Parasitic Diseases, Diseases of Respiratory System and Diseases of Digestive System, French-Arabic and Arabic-French Medical Dictionary, English-Arabic Medical Dictionary* (co-author).
22 Baghdad Boulevard, P.O. Box 450, Damascus; Home: 59 al-Jalaa Street, Damascus, Syria.

Sabah, H.H. Sheikh Jaber al-Ahmed al-Jaber al-; Amir of Kuwait; b. 1928; ed. Almubarakiyyah School and privately.
Governor, Ahmedi and Oil Areas 49-59; Pres. Dept. of Finance and Econ. 59; Minister of Finance and Econ. 62, of Finance and Industry 63; Minister of Finance and Industry and Minister of Commerce 65; Prime Minister 65-77; Nominated Heir-Apparent 66; Amir of Kuwait Jan. 78-.
Office of H.H. the Amir, Amiri Diwan, Seif Palace, Kuwait.

Sabah, Sheikh Jaber al-Ali al-Salem al-; Kuwaiti politician; b. 1928.
President of Dept. of Electricity, Water and Gas 52-63; mem. High Exec. Cttee. to organize establishments and depts. 54; mem. Defence High Council; Minister of Information 64-71, 75-; Deputy Prime Minister 75-.
c/o Council of Ministers, Kuwait City, Kuwait.

Sabah, Sheikh Saad al-Abdullah al-Salem al-; Kuwaiti politician.
Deputy Pres., Police and Public Security Dept. until 61, Minister of the Interior 61-65; Minister of the Interior and Defence 65-78; Head of Ministerial Cttee. on Labour Problems 75-78; Crown Prince Jan. 78-; Prime Minister Feb. 78-.
Office of the Prime Minister, Kuwait City, Kuwait.

Sabah, Sheikh Sabah al-Ahmed al-Jabir al-; Kuwaiti politician; b. 1929; ed. Mubarakiyyah National School, Kuwait and privately.
Member Supreme Cttee. 56-61; Head of Dept. of Social Affairs and Dept. of Printing, Press and Publications 61; Minister of Guidance of News 63; Minister of Foreign Affairs 63-, acting Minister of Oil 65-67; Minister of Oil Affairs 67; Acting Minister of the Interior 78; Deputy Prime Minister Feb. 78-.
Ministry of Foreign Affairs, Kuwait.

Sabah, H.H. Sheikh Salem al-Sabah al- (son of late Sheikh Sabah al-Salem al-Sabah, Amir of Kuwait); Kuwaiti diplomatist; b. 18 June 1937; ed. Secondary School, Kuwait, Gray's Inn, London, and Christ Church, Oxford.
Joined Foreign Service 62; Head of Legal (later Political) Dept. Ministry of Foreign Affairs; Amb. to the U.K. 65-70, to U.S.A. 70-75, also accred. to Canada; Minister of Social Affairs and Labour 75-78, of Defence 78-.
Ministry of Defence, Kuwait.

Sabah, Sheikh Saud Nasir al-; Kuwaiti diplomatist; b. 3 Oct. 1944, Kuwait.
Barrister-at-Law, Gray's Inn; Legal Dept., Ministry of Foreign Affairs; Rep. to Sixth Cttee., UN Gen. Assembly 69-74, to Seabed Cttee. 69-73; Vice-Chair. del. to Conf. on Law of the Sea 74-75; rep. of del. to Conf. on Law of Treaties 69; Amb. to U.K., also accred. to Denmark, Norway and Sweden 75-.
Embassy of Kuwait, 46 Queen's Gate, London, S.W.7, England.

Saber, Mohieddin, PH.D.; Sudanese international official and former politician; b. 1919, Dalgo, Sudan; ed. Cairo Univ., Bordeaux Univ., France, Sorbonne, Paris.
Director, Ministry of Social Affairs 54; Lecturer in Anthropology, Cairo Univ. in Khartoum 56-59; Editor-in-Chief *El Esteglal* and *Sout El Sudan*, daily papers 55; Man. *El Zaman* daily paper 57-59; UNESCO Expert and Head of Social Sciences Dept., Arab States Training Centre for Community Devt., Sirs el Layyan, Menoufia, Egypt 59-68; mem. Constituent Assembly of Sudan 68-69; Minister of Educ. 69-72; Dir. Arab Literacy and Adult Educ. Org. (ARLO) 73-75; Dir.-Gen. Arab League Educational, Cultural and Scientific Org. (ALECSO) 75-; Perm. mem. Afro-Asian Writers' Asscn.; Loyal Son of the Sudan Order 71, Order of the Repub. (Egypt) 70, Nat. Order (Chad) 72.
Publs. *Cultural Change and Community Development* 62, *Researches in Community Development Programmes* 63, *Local Government and Community Development in Developing Countries* 63, *Nomad and Nomadism—Concepts and Approaches* (with Dr. Lewis Meleka) 66, *Adult Education in the Sudan* 69, *The New Educational System in the Sudan* 70, *Studies on Issues Related to Development and Adult Education* 75, *Adult Education as Science* (co-author) 75; numerous studies and papers.
Arab League Educational, Cultural and Scientific Organization, 109 Tahrir Street, Dokki, Cairo, Egypt.

Sabri, Wing Cdr. Ali; Egyptian air force officer and politician; b. 30 Aug. 1920; ed. Military Acad. and Air Force Acad.
Fought in Palestine War 48; Minister for Presidential Affairs, Egypt 57-58, U.A.R. 58-62; Pres. Exec. Council 62-64, Prime Minister 64-65; Vice-Pres. of Repub. Oct. 65-67; Sec.-Gen. Arab Socialist Union Oct. 65-67, 68-Sept. 69; Deputy Prime Minister 67 and Minister of Local Govt. 67-Oct. 67; Resident Minister for Suez Canal Zone Oct. 67-68; Vice-Pres. of Repub. 70-71; on trial for treason Aug. 71, sentenced to life imprisonment Dec. 71.
Cairo, Egypt.

Sa'd, Farid Ali, B.SC.; Jordanian economist; b. 1908; ed. American Univ. of Beirut, Lebanon.
Science Teacher, Principal, Insp. of Educ. in Transjordan and Palestine 28-35; District Officer, Palestine Govt. 35-43; Man. Arab Bank Ltd., Haifa 43-48; mem. War Econ. Advisory Council of Palestine Govt. 43-46; Senator 51-55; mem. Municipality Council, Royal Fiscal Comm., Cttee. of Educ. Moslem Coll.; Minister of Finance 72-73; Chair., Man. Dir. Jordan Tobacco and Cigarette Co. Ltd., Jordan Bata Co.; Dir. Jordan Petroleum Refinery Co. Ltd.; Chair. Advisory Board, Grindlays Bank Ltd.; mem. Arab Orphans Cttee.; Trustee, Jordan Univ., American Univ. of Beirut.
P.O. Box 59, Amman, Jordan.

Sadat, Col. Muhammad Anwar es-; Egyptian officer and politician; b. 25 Dec. 1918; ed. primary and secondary schools in Cairo, also Mil. Coll.
Signals officer 38; dismissed from Army for underground work against British occupation 42; imprisoned several times for political activity; mem. Free Officers underground org. 51; Editor-in-Chief *Al Gamhouria* newspaper 53; Sec. Islamic Congress and Nat. Union 57; Head of Afro-Asian Solidarity Council 60; Vice-Pres. of Egypt 64-66, 69-70, Pres. Oct. 70-, also Prime Minister 73-74; Chair. Arab Socialist Union; Pres. Nat. Dem. Party July 78-; Joint Nobel Peace Prize 78 (with Menachem Begin, *q.v.*); Methodist Peace Prize 78; decorations from Yugoslavia 56, Greece 58, German Democratic Repub. 65, Romania 66, Finland 67, Iran 71, Saudi Arabia 74 and others.
Publs. *Unknown Pages* 55, *The Secrets of the Egyptian Revolution* 57, *The Story of Arab Unity* 57, *My Son, this is your Uncle Gamal* 58, *The Complete Story of the Revolution* 61, *For a New Resurrection* 63, *In Search of Identity* 78.
The Presidential Palace, Abdeen, Cairo, Egypt.

Sadawi, A. M. Suhail; Libyan oil executive; b. 1928, Beirut; ed. American Univ. of Beirut.
With Gulf Oil Corpn., Libya 58-61; Int. Labour Office, Geneva 62-63; Head, Gen. Econ. Section, Org. of Petroleum Exporting Countries (OPEC) 63; participated in negotiations for amendment of Libyan Petroleum Law 65; mem. Pricing Comm., Libya 67, Chair. 68; Asst. Under Sec., Libyan Ministry of Petroleum 68; Deputy Dir. Gen. Libyan Nat. Petroleum Corpn. 68; Sec.-Gen. Org. of Arab Petroleum Exporting Countries 70-73.
Arab Economists Petroleum Affairs (Consultants), P.O. Box 8840, Beirut, Lebanon.

Sadiq Abdul Rahman (*see* Mahdi, Sadiq al-).

Sadiq, Issa, PH.D.; Iranian educationist; b. 1894, Teheran; ed. Univs. of Paris, Cambridge (England), and Columbia (New York).
Directed various depts. Ministry of Educ. 19-30; mem. Nat. Constituent Assembly 25, 49, 67; Pres. and Prof. Nat. Teachers' Coll.; Dean of Faculties of Arts and Science, Teheran Univ. 32-41, Prof. 32-72, Prof. Emer. 72-; Chancellor of Univ. 41; Minister of Educ. 41, 43-45, 47, 60-61; Vice-Pres. Persian Acad. 37-70; mem. Board of Governors, Nat. Bank of Persia 37-52; Senator for Teheran 49-52, 54-60, 63-67, 67-71, 75-79; Pres. Persia-America Relations Soc. 49-53; founding mem. Nat. Soc. for Physical Educ. 33-54, Soc. for Preservation of Nat. Heritage 44-, Nat. Soc. for Protection of Children 53-; mem. High Educ. Council 34-41, 51-58, 72-, Royal Cultural Council 62-, Higher Council Nat. Org. for the Protection of Historical Monuments 65-, mem. Acad. of Iran language 70-, mem.

Higher Council of Culture and Art 72-76, 77-79, of Educ. 78.
Publs. *Principles of Education, New Methods in Education, History of Education, Modern Persia and her Educational System* (in English), *A Year in America, The March of Education in Persia and the West, A Brief Course in the History of Education in Iran, A History of Education in Europe, History of Education in Persia from the Earliest Time till Today, Forty Lectures, Memoirs* (autobiography, 3 vols.); trans. *Past and Future of Persian Art* (by A. V. Pope); eleven essays, etc.
316 Avenue Hedayat, Valiabad, Teheran, Iran.

Saffar, Salman Mohamed al-, PH.D.; Bahrain diplomatist; b. 1931, Bahrain; ed. Baghdad Univ., Iraq and Sorbonne, Paris.
Primary school teacher, Bahrain 49-54, Secondary school teacher 59-60; with Ministry of Foreign Affairs, Bahrain; Perm. Rep. to UN Sept. 71-.
Permanent Mission of Bahrain to United Nations, 747 Third Avenue, 19th Floor, New York, N.Y. 10017, U.S.A.

Sagar, Abdul Aziz al-Hamad al; Kuwaiti businessman and politician; b. 1913; ed. Secondary School, Bombay.
Member Municipality Board 52-55, Devt. Board 52-55; Chair. Kuwait Chamber of Commerce 59-, Nat. Bank of Kuwait 59-65; Jt. Council 61-62; Chair. Kuwait Oil Tanker Co. 61-64, 65-; mem. Constituent Assembly 63-, Speaker 63-65; Minister of Health 63; Chair. Red Crescent Soc. 66-.
Kuwait Chamber of Commerce, P.O. Box 775, Ali Salem Street, Kuwait City, Kuwait.

Sahnoun, Hadj Mohamed, M.A.; Algerian diplomatist; b. 8 April 1931; ed. Lycée of Constantine, Univ. de Paris à la Sorbonne and New York Univ.
Director of African, Asian and Latin American Affairs, Ministry of Foreign Affairs 62-63, of Political Affairs 64; Del. to UN Gen. Assembly 62-63, 64-65; Asst. Sec.-Gen. Org. of African Unity (OAU) 64-73, Arab League 74; Amb. to Fed. Repub. of Germany Jan. 75-.
Publ. *Economic and Social Aspects of the Algerian Revolution* 62.
c/o Algerian Embassy, Bonn-Bad Godesberg, Rheinallee 32, Federal Republic of Germany; and Ministry of Foreign Affairs, 6 rue Claude Bernard, El Mouradia, Algiers, Algeria.

Said, Faisal bin Ali al-; Omani politician; b. 1927, Muscat.
Attached to Ministry of Foreign Affairs, Muscat 53-57; lived abroad 57-70; Perm. Under-Sec. Ministry of Educ. 70-72; Minister of Econ. Affairs 72; Perm. Rep. to UN 72-73; Minister of Educ. 73-76, of Nat. Heritage 76-, of Culture 79-.
Ministry of National Heritage and Culture, Muscat, Oman.

Said, Tarik bin Taimur al-; Omani diplomatist; b. 2 July 1923; ed. English High for Boys, Istanbul, Robert Coll., Istanbul, and Germany.
Commissioned in Muscat Army 41-44; Chair., Administrator, Muscat Mutrah Municipality 45-57; in charge of Operational Area in Jabal War 58-59; self-exile 62-70; Prime Minister 70-71; Personal Adviser for Diplomatic Affairs to Sultan of Oman, Senior Amb. Extraordinary and Plenipotentiary 72-; Chair. Cen. Bank of Oman June 75-; Order of Oman 1st Class.
P.O. Box 202, Muscat, Oman; and Leuchtturmweg 21, 2000 Hamburg 56, Federal Republic of Germany.

Saif al-Islam, Abdullah ben Hassan; Yemeni politician.
Minister of the Interior April 67-69; mem. Mil. Council 67; Prime Minister *ad interim* June 68; in exile 68-.

Saif al-Islam, al-Hassan ben Yahya, H.H.; Yemeni politician.
Crown Prince of the Yemen 62-; Prime Minister 62-67; Head of Mil. Council 67; in exile 68-.

Saif al-Islam, Mohamed al-Badr, H.R.H.; Prince of the Yemen; b. 1927; ed. Coll. for Higher Education, Sana'a.
Son of King of the Yemen; Minister for Foreign Affairs 55-61, and Minister of Defence and C.-in-C. 55-62; succeeded to Imamate on the death of his father, Imam Ahmed Sept. 62; left Taiz following Republican *coup d'état* Sept. 62, leading Royalist resistance 62-68; replaced by Imamate Council May 68; in exile 68-.

Saif al-Islam, Mohammed ben Hussein; Yemeni politician; b. 1938.
Former diplomatic rep. to Fed. Germany; Vice-Pres. Imamate Council 67-May 68, Pres. of Council May 68; Commdr. of Royalist Armed Forces 67-68; in exile 68-.

Salah, Abdullah A.; Jordanian diplomatist; b. 31 Dec. 1922; ed. Bishop Gobat's School, Jerusalem, and American Univ. of Beirut.
Field Educ. Officer, United Nations Relief and Works Agency (UNRWA), Jordan 52-62; Ambassador to Kuwait 62-63, to India 63-64, to France 64-66, 67-70; Minister of Foreign Affairs 66-67, 70-72; Amb. to U.S.A. 73-, also accred. to Mexico; several decorations.
Jordanian Embassy, 2319 Wyoming Avenue, N.W., Washington, D.C., U.S.A.

Salam, Saeb; Lebanese politician; b. 1905; ed. American Univ. of Beirut.
Elected Provisional Head Lebanese Govt. 43; deputy 43-47, 51; Minister of Interior 46, 60-61; Minister Foreign Affairs 46; Prime Minister 52, 53, 60-61, concurrently Minister of Defence 61; pioneer Lebanese civil aviation 45; Pres. Middle East Airlines Co., Beirut 45-56; Pres. Nat. Fats & Oil Co. Ltd., Beirut; Prime Minister 70-73; Pres. Makassed Philanthropic Islamic Asscn. 58-; mem. Nat. Dialogue Cttee. Sept. 75.
Rue Moussaitbé, B.P. 206, Beirut, Lebanon.

Saleh, Lt.-Col. Ali Abdullah; Yemeni army officer and politician; b. *c.* 1942.
Participated in coup 74 which brought Lt.-Col. al Hamdi to power; Security Chief, Taiz Province 77-78; mem. Provisional Presidential Council, Deputy C.-in-C. of Armed Forces June-July 78; Pres. of Yemen Arab Repub. and C.-in-C. of Armed Forces July 78-.
Office of the President, Sana'a, Yemen Arab Republic.

Salem, Gen. Mamdouh Muhammad; Egyptian police officer, administrator and politician; b. 1918, Alexandria; ed. Police Acad.
Police Commdr., Alexandria 64-68; Gov. of Assiyut 68-70, of Alexandria 70-71; Deputy Prime Minister, Minister of the Interior 71-75, Prime Minister 75-78, also Minister of Interior Feb.-Oct. 77; Asst. to the Pres. Oct. 78-; Leader Arab Socialist Party 75-78; mem. Higher Council for Nuclear Energy 75.
Office of the President, Cairo, Egypt.

Salim, Dr. Khalil, ED.D.; Jordanian diplomatist; b. 1921, Husn; ed. American Univ. Beirut, Univ. of London, Columbia Univ., U.S.A.
Teacher in secondary schools 41-49; Insp. of Educ. 50-56; Dir. of Cultural Affairs 56-59; Asst. Under-Sec. of Educ. 60-62; Minister of Social Welfare and Minister of State, Prime Minister's Office 62-63; Gov. Central Bank of Jordan 63-73; Pres. Nat. Planning Council 73-74; Amb. to France, non-resident Amb. to Belgium 75-78, also to EEC 77-78; mem. Nat. Consultative Council 78-; Pres. Authority for Tourism and Antiquities 62-63; Chair. Co-operative Union 65-68, Public Insurance Corpn. 71-73, Inst. of Banking Studies 71-73, Nat. Cttee. for Population 73-74, Cttee. for Environment 73-74; Deputy Chair. Royal Scientific Soc. 70-73, Alia Airline 71-74; mem. Exec. Board UNESCO 76-; Gov. IMF, IBRD 63-74; Al-Istiqlal Medal, Second Class 59, Al-Kawkab Medal, First Class 62, Al-Nahdah Medal, First Class 74.

Publs. books on mathematics, teaching, educ. admin. in Jordan, articles, lectures and broadcasts.
National Consultative Council, Amman, Jordan.

Sallal, Marshal Abdullah; Yemeni army officer and politician; b. 1917; ed. in Iraq.
Returned to Yemen from Iraq 39; imprisoned 39; army service 40-48, 55-; imprisoned 48-55; Gov. of Hodeida 59-62; Chief of Staff to Imam Mohammed Sept. 62; led coup against the Imam and proclaimed a Repub. Sept. 62; Pres. of the Revolutionary Council and C.-in-C. of Republican forces during civil war 62-67; Prime Minister 62-64, 66-67, concurrently Minister of Foreign Affairs 63-64.
Cairo, Egypt.

Sallam, Mohamed Abdulaziz, B.A.; Yemeni diplomatist; b. 15 Dec. 1933, Taiz; ed. secondary school in Helwan, Egypt, Stockbridge School, Mass. and Temple Univ., Philadelphia, Pa., U.S.A.
Engaged in private sector 60-61; Instructor, Belguis Coll. 61-62; Dir.-Gen. Ministry of Public Health 62-63; Minister and Chargé d'Affaires, Embassy in Baghdad 63-64; Deputy Minister of Foreign Affairs 64-65; Chair. Board, Yemen Drug Co. 65-66; Minister of Foreign Affairs 66-67; Dir.-Gen. Office of the Prime Minister 70-71; Amb. in Ministry of Foreign Affairs 71-73; Minister with rank of Amb., Embassy in London 73-74; Amb., Deputy Perm. Rep. to UN 74-76, Perm. Rep. 76-78; leader of dels. to various int. confs. incl. UN Gen. Assembly 65, Fifth Emergency Special Session, Fourth Summit Conf. of Arab League 67.
c/o Ministry of Foreign Affairs, Sana'a, Yemen Arab Republic.

Salman, Salah, M.D., F.A.C.S.; Lebanese physician and government official; b. 24 Jan. 1936, Beirut; ed. American Univ. Beirut School of Medicine, Johns Hopkins Univ. School of Medicine, U.S.A.
Minister of Public Health March-June 72; Assoc. Prof. and Chair. of Dept. of Otolaryngology, American Univ. of Beirut 74-; Minister of Interior, Housing and Co-operatives Dec. 76-; Penrose Award, Faculties of Medical Sciences 61.
Publs. 19 papers in int. and local medical journals in otolaryngology and allied subjects.
Ministry of the Interior, Beirut; American University of Beirut; Home: Lyon Street, Najjar Building, Beirut, Lebanon.

Salzman, Pnina; Israeli pianist; b. 1923; ed. Ecole Normale de Musique and Conservatoire National de Musique, Paris.
Gave first concert in Paris at age of twelve; since then has given concerts in five continents; travels all over the world every year, playing with most of the major orchestras; over 300 concerts with Israeli orchestras.
20 Dubnov St., Tel-Aviv, Israel.

Samii, Mohammad Mehdi; Iranian banker; b. 1918; ed. Inst. of Chartered Accountants in England and Wales.
Bank Melli Iran 45-51; National Iranian Oil Co. 51-53; Bank Melli Iran 53-59; Industrial and Mining Devt. Bank of Iran 59-63; Gov. Bank Markazi Iran (Central Bank of Iran) 63-68, 70-71; Man. Dir. Plan Org. 68-70; Adviser to the Prime Minister 71-73; Pres. Agricultural Devt. Bank of Iran 74-79.
c/o Agricultural Development Bank of Iran, Farahzad Express Way, Valiahd Street, Teheran, Iran.

Samiy, Abdol Hossein, M.D.; Iranian physician and minister; b. 20 June 1930, Iran; ed. Stanford Univ., Univ. of Calif., Los Angeles and Cornell Univ.
Assistant in Medicine, Cornell Univ. 56-57, Fellow in Physiology 57-58; Asst. in Medicine and later Research Fellow, Harvard Medical School 58-60; Deputy Minister of Health, Iran 62-64: Dir. Firowzgar Medical Centre 64, Pars Hosp. 69-73; Minister of Science and Higher Educ. 74-77; Chancellor, Reza Shah Kabir Univ. 75-78; fmr. Pres. Imperial Medical Center of Iran; Prof. of Medicine, Cornell Univ. Medical Coll.; fmr. Vice-Chair. Imperial Iranian Acad. of Sciences; Borden Award for Medical Research, Larken Award for Medical Research.
Publs. 16 medical papers; Co-editor: *International Textbook of Medicine* 76.
Avenue Jaleh-Avenue Iran No. 5, Teheran, Iran.

Sanbar, Moshe, M.A.(ECON.); Israeli banker and economist; b. 29 March 1926, Kecskemét, Hungary; ed. Univ. of Budapest and Hebrew Univ., Jerusalem.
Emigrated to Israel 48; Project Dir., Israel Inst. of Applied Social Research and later Deputy Dir. 51-58; Lecturer in Statistics, Hebrew Univ., Jerusalem 57-61; Dir. Research Dept., Deputy Dir. Internal State Revenue Div., Ministry of Finance 58-63, Dir. of Budgets 63-68; Econ. Adviser to Ministry of Finance 63-68; Deputy Chair., and later Chair., Industrial Devt. Bank of Israel 68-71; Chief Econ. Adviser to Minister of Finance 69-71; Acting Deputy Minister of Commerce and Industry 70-71; Gov. Bank of Israel 71-76; Chair. of Board, Electrochemical Industries (Frutarom) Ltd. 76-; Chair. Econ. Devt. and Refugee Rehabilitation Trust, Board of Dirs. Habimah Nat. Theatre; Pres. Israel Asscn. of Graduates in the Social Sciences and Humanities; Chair. Board of Trustees of Coll. of Admin.; Hon. Pres. World Fed. of Hungarian Jews.
Publs. *My Longest Year* (Yad Vashem Prize) 66; many articles and research studies on economic subjects.
44 Pincas Street, Tel-Aviv, Israel.

Sancar, Gen. Semih; Turkish army officer; b. 1911, Erzurum; ed. Artillery School, War Acad.
Served in Turkish Army as Commdr. of Artillery Battery and Battalion, Asst. Commdr. Army Corps Artillery, Dept. Chief, Branch Section Dir. in Land Forces and Gen. Staff H.Q.; then Instructor War Acad.; Dir. of Personnel, Dir. of Operations Turkish Gen. Staff; promoted to rank of Gen. 69; Commdr. of Gendarmerie 69; Commdr. 2nd Army; Commdr. Turkish Land Forces 72-73; Chief of Gen. Staff 73-78.
c/o General Staff Headquarters, Ankara, Turkey.

Sanjabi, Karim, L. EN D.; Iranian lawyer and politician; b. 1904; ed. Political Science School, Teheran, Univ. of Teheran, Univ. of the Sorbonne, Paris.
Entered Ministry of Education 34, Ministry of Finance 39; Prof. of Law; arrested by British during Second World War, banned from Kermanshah during War; founding mem. Mihan movement, then Iran Party, 43-44; supporter of Musaddiq during Nat. Front Govt., Minister of Educ. May-Dec. 51; arrested after fall of Musaddiq Govt. 53; resumed political activities 60, mem. Cen. Cttee. of Nat. Front; founder mem. Iranian Cttee. for Defence of Liberty and Human Rights Dec. 77; Minister of Foreign Affairs Feb.-April 79.
c/o Ministry of Foreign Affairs, Teheran, Iran.

Sanusi, H.R.H. Prince Hassan Rida; Former Crown Prince of Libya; b. 1934.
Son of H.M. King Idris I; became Crown Prince on death of his Great Uncle, Ahmed Sherif as-Sanusi, Dec. 50; in exile 69-.

Saouma, Edouard; Lebanese agricultural engineer and international official; b. 6 Nov. 1926, Beirut; ed. St. Joseph's Univ. School of Eng., Beirut, Ecole Nat. Supérieure d'Agronomie, Montpellier, France.
Director, Tel Amara Agricultural School 52-53, Nat. Centre for Farm Mechanization 54-55; Sec.-Gen. Nat. Fed. of Lebanese Agronomists 55; Dir.-Gen. Nat. Inst. for Agricultural Research 55-62; mem. Governing Board, Nat. Grains Office 60-62; Deputy Regional Rep. for Asia and Far East, FAO 62-65, Dir. Land and Water Devt. Div. 65-75, Dir.-Gen. of FAO 76-; Minister of Agric., Fisheries and Forestry Oct.-Nov. 70; Corresp. mem. Accademia Nazionale di Agricultura (Italy); Dr. h.c. (Universidad

Nacional Agraria, Peru, Agriculture Univ. La Molina, Peru, Univ. of Seoul, Repub. of Korea, Univs. of Uruguay and Indonesia); Order of the Cedar (Lebanon), Said Akl Prize (Lebanon); Chevalier du Mérite Agricole (France), Grand Croix Ordre National (Chad, Ghana and Upper Volta).
Publs. technical publs. in agriculture.
Food and Agriculture Organization of the United Nations, Via delle Terme di Caracalla, 00100 Rome, Italy.

Sarkis, Elias, L. EN D.; Lebanese banker and politician; b. 20 July 1924; ed. Université Saint Joseph, Beirut.
Former Magistrate, Cour des Comptes; Pres. Management Cttee. of Intra Bank 67; fmr. Dir.-Gen. Cabinet of Presidency; Gov. Bank of Lebanon 68-76; Pres. of Lebanon Sept. 76-; Pres. Comm. Supérieure des Banques; Medal of Independence, First Class, Jordan.
Présidence de la République, Palais de Baabda, Beirut, Lebanon; Home: Mar Takla, Lebanon.

Sarrûf, Fûad, B.A., LL.D.; Lebanese author and university official; b. 1900; ed. Shwaifat Nat. Coll., and American Univ. of Beirut.
Teacher and Headmaster, Lebanon 19-22; Asst. Editor *Al-Muqtataf* (monthly), Cairo 22-27, Editor 27-44; Editor *Al-Mukhtar* (Arabic edition of *Reader's Digest*), Cairo 43-47; Columnist, *Al-Ahram* (daily), Cairo 48-51; Vice-Pres. in charge of Univ. Relations, American Univ., Beirut 52-68; started Dept. of Journalism, American Univ., Cairo 35-43; Pres. Lebanese Nat. Comm. for UNESCO; mem. Exec. Board of UNESCO 66-70, Vice-Pres. 70-72, Pres. 72-74; fmr. mem., later Sec., Vice-Pres. Egyptian Asscn. for Advancement of Science 30-52; mem. Lebanese Nat. Research Council, Baalbek Int. Festival Cttee.; Hon. LL.D. (Univ. of the Pacific, Calif.) 58; several decorations.
Publs. *Pillars of Modern Science* 35, *Horizons of Modern Science* 39, *The Conquest Goes On* 44, *Horizons Without End* 58, *Man and the Universe* 61, *Modern Science in Modern Society* 66, *Scientific Papers* 72, *The Eternal Fire*, numerous other books.
55 rue du Caire, Hamra, Beirut, Lebanon.

Satir, Kemal; Turkish physician and politician; b. 1911, Adana; ed. Adana.
Practised as X-ray specialist; mem. Parl. for Adana (Republican People's Party) 43-60, 69-, for Elazig 61-69; Minister of Communications 48-50; private practice, Adana 50-57; Deputy Sec.-Gen. RPP, Sec.-Gen. 61-66; mem. Constituent Assembly; Deputy Prime Minister 63-65; resigned RPP 72; formed Republican Party which joined Nat. Reliance Party to become Republican Reliance Party, Pres. Council of RRP; Minister of State and Deputy Prime Minister 73-74.
Republican Reliance Party (C.G.P.), Ankara, Turkey.

Saud al-Faisal, H.R.H. Prince, B.A.(ECONS.); Saudi Arabian diplomatist; b. Riyadh; *s.* of late King Faisal; ed. Princeton Univ., U.S.A.
Former Deputy Minister of Petroleum and Mineral Resources; Minister of State for Foreign Affairs March-Oct. 75, Minister of Foreign Affairs Oct. 75-; leader del. to UN Gen. Assembly 76; Special Envoy of H.M. King Khaled in diplomatic efforts to resolve Algerian-Moroccan conflict over Western Sahara, and the civil war in Lebanon; mem. Saudi Arabian del. to Arab restricted Summit, Riyadh, Oct. 76, and to full Summit Conf. of Arab League, Oct. 76; Founding mem. King Faisal's Int. Charity Soc.
Ministry of Foreign Affairs, Jeddah, Saudi Arabia.

Saudi Arabia, Royal Family of (*see* under first names, as Khalid, King).

Sayah, Mohamed; Tunisian politician; b. 31 Dec. 1933; ed. Sadikia; Sfax, and Training School for Higher Education, Tunis.
Joined Néo-Destour Party 49; mem. Gen. Union of Tunisian Students 52-62, mem. Exec. Bureau 57-62, Sec.-Gen. 60-62; Asst. Dir. Néo-Destour Party and Chief Editor *L'Action* 62-64, Gen. Sec. of Destourian Youth, Gen. Sec. of Tunisian Youth 63-64; mem. High Comm. DSP 70-; Deputy Nat. Assembly 64-; Minister of Information 69-70; Perm. Rep. to UN, Geneva 70; Minister Public Works and Housing 71-73, of Youth and Sports 73; Minister at the Prime Minister's Office Nov. 73-; mem. Central Cttee., then mem. Political Bureau and Dir. Destour Socialist Party 64.
Publs. Several books on the history of the National Tunisian Movement.
c/o Office of the Prime Minister, Tunis, Tunisia.

Sayigh, Yusif A., M.A., PH.D.; Palestinian economist; b. 26 March 1916; ed. American Univ. of Beirut and Johns Hopkins Univ.
At American Univ. of Beirut, Asst. Prof. of Econ. 53-54, 56-57, Assoc. Prof. 57-58, 62-63, Prof. 63-74; Dir. Econ. Research Inst. 57-59, 62-64; Econ. Adviser, Planning Board of Kuwait 64-65; Econ. Consultant, Jordan East Ghor Study 66-67; Adviser, Org. of Arab Petroleum Exporting Countries 74-77; Chair. Planning Board, Nat. Fund of Palestine Liberation Org. (PLO) 68-74; Adviser, Arab Fund for Econ. and Social Devt. 76-; Grand Prix twice from Lebanese "Friends of the Book" Soc.
Publs. *Bread with Dignity: Socio-economic Content of Arab Nationalism* (Arabic) 61, *Enterpreneurs of Lebanon* 62, *Economics and Economists in the Arab World* 64, *Second Look at Lebanese Economy* (Co-Author) (Arabic) 66, *The Israeli Economy* (Arabic) 66, *The Strategy of Action for the Liberation of Palestine* (Arabic) 68, *Jordan: Country Study* (Mediterranean Development Project) (Co-Author), *The Economies of the Arab World: Development since 1945* 77, *The Determinants of Arab Economic Development* 77.
Arab Fund for Economic and Social Development, P.O. Box 21923, Kuwait.

Schaeffer-Forrer, Claude Frédéric Armand, M.A.; French archaeologist; b. 6 March 1898; ed. Strasbourg and Paris Univs.
Curator Prehistoric, Roman and Early Medieval Museum, Palais Rohan, Strasbourg 21-32; Curator Coins and Medals Dept. Strasbourg Univ. 26-32; Curator French Nat. Museums 33-54; Dir. of Research at Nat. Centre of Scientific Research, Paris 46-54; Vice-Pres. Comm. des Fouilles, Direction Générale des Relations Culturelles, Ministry of Foreign Affairs; mem. French Inst. 53; Hon. Prof. Collège de France 74; Dir. expedition Ras Shamra, Syria 29- (discovered Canaanite alphabetic cuneiform records); Cyprus 32, 34, 35, 46, 47, 49-, Malatya, Turkey 46, 47, 48, 50; mem. Archaeological Cttee. Ministry of Education; Hon. Fellow St. John's Coll. Oxford; mem. Nat. Society of Antiquaries, France; corresp. mem. Belgian Royal Acad., Danish Royal Acad.; corresp. Fellow of British Acad.; Hon. Fellow Royal Anthropological Inst. of Great Britain and Ireland, etc.; hon. mem. Deutsche Morgenländische Gesellschaft; served as Capt. Corvette with Fighting French Naval Forces 40-45; D.Litt. h.c. (Oxon.), D.C.L. h.c. (Glasgow), Hon. F.S.A.; Gold Medal, Soc. of Antiquaries 58, Scientific and Philological Soc., Famagusta, Cyprus 65, Hon. Citizen of Latakia (Syria), Famagusta (Cyprus).
Publs. *Haches néolithiques* 24, *Tertres funéraires préhistoriques dans la forêt de Haguenau* (2 vols.) 26, 30, *Missions en Chypre* 36, *Ugaritica I* 39, *Cuneiform Texts of Ras Shamra-Ugarit* 39, *Stratigraphie comparée et Chronologie de l'Asie occidentale* 48, *Ugaritica II* 49, *Enkomi-Alasia* 52, *Ugaritica III* 56, *Ugaritica IV* 62, *Ugaritica V* 65, *Ugaritica VI* 69, *Alasia I* 72, *Ugaritica VII* 78.
Le Castel Blanc, 16 rue Turgot, St. Germain-en-Laye; and l'Escale, B.P. 16, La Croix-Valmer (83), France.

Schocken, Gershom; Israeli editor and publisher; b. Sept. 1912; ed. Univ. of Heidelberg and London School of Economics.

Joined staff of *Haaretz* (daily newspaper) 37, publisher and editor 39-; Dir. Schocken Publishing House Ltd.; mem. Knesset (Parl.) 55-59.
Haaretz Building, 21 Salman Schocken Street, P.O. Box 233, Tel-Aviv, Israel.

Scholem, Gershom, PH.D.; Israeli professor; b. 5 Dec. 1897, Berlin, Germany; ed. Berlin, Jena, Berne and Munich Univs.
Lecturer, Hebrew Univ. Jerusalem 25, Prof. of Jewish Mysticism 33-65; Dean, Hebrew Univ. 41-43, now Prof. Emer. Inst. of Jewish Studies; Visiting Prof., Jewish Inst. of Religion, New York 38, 49, Brown Univ., Providence, R.I. 56-57, Hebrew Union Coll., Cincinnati 66; Pres. Israel Acad. of Sciences and Humanities 68-74; mem. The British Acad., Netherlands Acad. of Sciences, American Acad. of Arts and Sciences, American Acad. for Jewish Research, Westfälische Akad. der Wissenschaften; Israel State Prize 55, Rothschild Prize 62, Reuchlin Prize 69, Harvey Prize 74, Lit. Prize, Bavarian Acad. of Arts 74; Dr. h.c. (Univs. of Jerusalem, Zürich, Yale).
Publs. many books on Judaism and Jewish Mysticism (in Hebrew, German and English), *Kabbalah*.
The Israel Academy of Sciences and Humanities, P.O. Boz 4040, Jerusalem; Home: 28 Abarbanel Street, Jerusalem, Israel.

Sela, Michael (Salomonowicz), M.SC., PH.D.; Israeli chemist; b. 6 March 1924, Tomaszow, Poland; ed. Hebrew Univ., Jerusalem and Geneva Univ.
Joined Weizmann Inst. of Science 50; W. Garfield Weston Prof. of Immunology; Head of Dept. of Chem. Immunology 62-75; Dean of Faculty of Biology 70-73; mem. Board of Govs. 70-; Vice-Pres. 70-71, Pres. Weizmann Inst. of Science 75-; Visiting Scientist Nat. Insts. of Health (NIH), U.S.A. 56-57, 60-61, Univ. of Calif., Berkeley 67-68; Fogarty Scholar-in-Residence, Fogarty Int. Centre, U.S.A. 73-74; mem. WHO Expert Advisory Panel on Immunology 62-; mem. Int. Cell Research Org. 65-; mem. Council, Int. Union of Pure and Applied Biophysics 72-; Vice-Pres. Int. Union of Immunological Socs. 74-; Chair. Board of Advisers of Basle Inst. of Immunology 74-, Council of European Molecular Biology Org. 75-; mem. Israel Acad. of Sciences and Humanities 71, Pontifical Acad. of Sciences 75; Hon. mem. American Soc. of Biological Chemists 68, Scandinavian Soc. for Immunology 71, Harvey Soc. 72, American Soc. of Immunologists 73; Foreign mem. Max-Planck Soc., Freiburg 67; Foreign Hon. mem. American Acad. of Arts and Sciences 71; Foreign Assoc. Nat. Acad. of Sciences, U.S.A. 76; serves many editorial boards, incl. *European Journal of Immunology*, *European Journal of Biochemistry*, *Immunogenetics*; Israel Prize in Natural Sciences 59, Otto Warburg Medal of German Soc. of Biological Chem. 68, Rothschild Prize in Chem. 68, Emil von Behring Prize of Phillipps Univ. 73, NIH Lectureship 73.
Publs. over 400 in immunology, biochem. and molecular biology.
Weizmann Institute of Science, Rehovot, Israel.

Senoussi, Ahmad (*see* Snoussi, Ahmed).

Senoussi, Badreddine, LL.M., M.H.; Moroccan politician; b. 30 March 1933, Fez; ed. Univ. of Bordeaux, Chamber of Commerce, Paris.
Adviser, "Haut Tribunal Chérifien", Rabat 56; Civil Service Admin., Ministry of State 57; Sec.-Gen. Nat. Tobacco Co. 58; Head, Royal Cabinet 63; Under-Sec. of State for Commerce and Industry 64, for Admin. Affairs 65; Minister of Post Office and Telecommunications 66, of Youth, Sports and Social Affairs 70-71; Amb. to U.S.A. 71-74, to Iran 75-76, to U.K. 76-; awarded many foreign decorations.
Embassy of the Kingdom of Morocco, 49 Queen's Gate Gardens, London, SW7 5NE, England.

Seter, Mordecai; Israeli composer; b. 1916, Russia.
Studied Paris with Paul Dukas and Nadia Boulanger 32-37; Prof. Israel Acad. of Music, Tel-Aviv; Prix Italia 62; Israel State Prize 65.
Works include: *Sabbath Cantata* 40, *Festivals* 46, *Festive Songs* 51, *Three Motets* 51, *Dithyramb* 66 (choral music); *Elegy* 54, *Ricercar* 56, *Espressivo* 71 (for strings); *Midnight Vigil* (oratorio) 62; *Sinfonietta* 61, *Variations*, *Fantasia* 65, *Judith* 62, *Jephthah's Daughter*, *Yemenite Suite* 65, *Meditation* 67, *Rounds* 68 (orchestral music); *The Legend of Judith* (with Martha Graham) 62, *Part Real, Part Dream* (with Martha Graham) 64 (ballet); *Jerusalem* 66 (symphony for choir and orchestra); *Partita* (violin and piano) 51, *Sonata* for 2 violins 52, for violin solo 53, 32 *Duets* for 2 violins 54, *Monodrama* (clarinet and piano) 70, *Epigrams* 70, *Requiem* 70, *Intimo* 70, *Autumn* 70, *Quartet* 70, *Soliloquio*, *Janus Sine Nomine*, *Intervals*, *Cappricci*, *Fughettas* for piano 73-74, *Trio* 73, *Concertante* 73, *Trio* 74, *Events* 74, *Quintet* 75, *Ensemble* 75, *String Quartet No.* 1 76 (chamber music), *String Quartet No.* 2, *No.* 3 and *No.* 4, *Solo and Tutti* for Clarinet and String Quartet, *Music* for String Quartet 76-77.
The Israel Academy of Music, Tel-Aviv; Home: 1 Kainy Street, Tel-Aviv, Israel.

Shaabi, Qahtan Muhammed as-; Yemeni politician; b. 1920; ed. school in Aden, and studied agricultural engineering, Khartoum Univ.
Director of Agriculture, Lahej State 55-58; joined South Arabian League 58, Public Relations Officer 59-60; Adviser to Ministry of South Yemen Affairs, Govt. of Yemen People's Repub. 63; founder-mem. Nat. Liberation Front (N.L.F.) 63, later Sec.-Gen.; mem. N.L.F. Del. to Geneva talks on independence of S. Arabia Nov. 67; Pres. of People's Repub. of Southern Yemen, also Prime Minister and Supreme Commdr. of Armed Forces Nov. 67, resigned June 69.
c/o National Front, Aden, People's Democratic Republic of Yemen.

Shadli Bin-Jeddid (*see* Chadli, Col. Bendjedid).

Shafei, Col. Hussein; Egyptian army officer and politician; b. 1918; ed. Mil. Coll., Cairo.
Commissioned as 2nd Lieut. 38; took part in Palestine hostilities 48; graduated from Staff Officers' Coll. 53 and apptd. Officer-in-Charge Cavalry Corps; Minister of War and Marine April-Sept. 54, of Social Affairs Sept. 54-58; Minister of Labour and Social Affairs, U.A.R. 58-61; Vice-Pres. and Minister of Social Affairs and Waqfs 61-62; mem. Presidency Council 62-64; Vice-Pres. of U.A.R. (Egypt) 64-67, 70-75; Deputy Prime Minister and Minister of Waqfs 67-71.
Cairo, Egypt.

Shafiq, Mohammad Moussa, LL.M., M.C.L., M.A.; Afghan scholar and politician; b. 30 May 1932, Kabul; ed. Ghazi High School, Al Azhar Univ., Cairo, and Columbia Univ., U.S.A.
Joined Ministry of Justice 57, Dir. Nat. Office for Legislation 57-62; Prof. of Int. Law, Kabul Univ., 57-68; Deputy Minister of Justice 63-64; Adviser, Ministry of Foreign Affairs 66-68; Amb. to Egypt, concurrently to Lebanon, Sudan and Ghana 68-71; Minister of Foreign Affairs 71, Prime Minister 72-73.
Kabul, Afghanistan.

Shah, Idries; professor and author; b. 16 June 1924, Simla, India; ed. private and traditional Middle Eastern schools.
Studied in Middle East, Europe and S. America; Dir. of Studies, Inst. for Cultural Research 66-; Visiting Prof. Univ. of Geneva 72-73, Univ. of Calif. 76, 77, New York Univ. Graduate School, New Jersey Inst. for Advanced Int. Studies; Adviser, Middle Eastern Authorities, Int.

Center for Educ. Advancement (ICEA) 77-; Contributor to VI World Congress of Psychiatry 77; author of numerous works on philosophy; Patron Cambridge Poetry Festival 75; Fellow, Royal Econ. Soc., Royal Soc. of Arts; Life mem. British Asscn., The National Trust; mem. PEN, Club of Rome; Life Gov. Royal Hosp. and Home for Incurables; Gov. Royal Humane Soc.; Prof. h.c. (Univ. of La Plata) 74; Int. Community Service Award 73; six first prizes during UNESCO World Book Year 73; Gold Medal, Services to Poetry 75; Distinguished Contribution to Human Thought Award 75; subject of BBC documentary film 69, of vol. of collected papers in honour of Idries Shah 74.
Publs. *Oriental Magic* 56, *Secret Lore of Magic* 57, *Destination Mecca* 57, *The Sufis* 64, *Special Problems* 66, *Exploits of Nasruddin* 66, *Tales of the Dervishes* 67, *The Pleasantries* 68, *The Way of the Sufi* 68, *Reflections* 68, *Caravan of Dreams* 68, *Wisdom of the Idiots* 69, *The Dermis Probe* 69, *The Book of the Book* 69, *Thinkers of the East* 70, *The Magic Monastery* 72, *The Subtleties of the Inimitable Mulla Nasrudin* 73, *The Elephant in the Dark* 74, *Learning How to Learn* 78, *Beginning to Begin* 78, *Special Illumination* 78, *A Veiled Gazelle* 78, *The Hundred Tales of Wisdom* 78, *A Perfumed Scorpion* 79, *World Tales* 79; Contributor, *Oxford Companion to the Mind*; Advisory Editor, *Human Nature Journal*; articles in specialist journals and reviews in the field of education.
c/o Jonathan Cape Ltd., 30 Bedford Square, London, WC1B 3EL, England.

Shaikhly, Abdul Karim Abdul Sattar al-, M.A., M.D.; Iraqi politician; b. 14 June 1937, Baghdad.
Political emigré in Cairo 60-63; Asst. Attaché Iraqi Embassy, Beirut 63-64; mem. Revolutionary Command Council; Minister of Foreign Affairs 68-71; Perm. Rep. to UN 72-77; Head of del. to UN Gen. Assembly 68-71; Amb. to Fed. Repub. of Germany 77-78; recalled Feb. 78.
c/o Ministry of Foreign Affairs, Baghdad, Karradat Mariam, Iraq.

Shakhbut bin Sultan bin Zaid, H.H. Sheikh; former Ruler of Abu Dhabi; b. 1905.
Succeeded to Sheikdom 28, deposed Aug. 66; sons Zaid b. 30, Sultan b. 36.
Manama, Bahrain.

Shamgar, Meir; Israeli lawyer; b. 1925, Danzig; ed. Govt. law classes, and London Univ.
Settled in Palestine 39; detained by British Admin. for underground activities, deported to East Africa 44-48; Col. in Israeli Army 48-68; Mil. Advocate-Gen. 61-68; Attorney-Gen. 68-75; Justice, Supreme Court of Israel July 75-; Chair. Advisory Council, Inst. of Criminology, Tel-Aviv Univ.; fmr. Law Lecturer, Hebrew Univ., Jerusalem, Tel-Aviv; mem. Israel Bar Council 61-68; mem. of Council, Int. Soc. of Mil. Law and Law of War.
Publs. various legal essays in Israeli and foreign journals.
Supreme Court of Israel, Jerusalem, Israel.

Shamir, Moshe; Israeli writer; b. 15 Sept. 1921; ed. Tel-Aviv Herzliya Gymnasium.
Former mem. Kibbutz Mishmar Haemek; in Haganah underground units 47-48; Capt. in Israel Army 48; Lit. Ed. *Maariv*; mem. Hebrew Acad.; Ussiskin Prize 48, Brenner Prize 53, Bialik Prize 55.
Publs. (novels) *He Walked in the Fields under the Sun*, *With his own Hands*, *King of Flesh and Blood*, *David's Stranger*, *Naked You Are*, *The Border*, *A Dove from an Alien Cote* 73; (plays) *He Walked in the Fields*, *The War of the Sons of Light*, *The Heir*, and others.
15 Misgav Ladach, Old City, Jerusalem, Israel.

Shamloo, Ahmad (A. Bamdad); Iranian poet and writer; b. Dec. 1926, Teheran.
Former Editor *Ketabe hafte*, *Baroo*, *Khooshe* and other publs.
Publs. (poetry) *Fresh Air* 57, *Mirror Garden* 59, *Aida in Mirror* 63, *Aida*, *The Three Daggers and Memory* 66, *Phoenix in the Rain* 67, *Elegies of Earth* 69, *Springing in the Fog* 71, *Abraham in the Fire* 72, and 40 other volumes including translations; *Persian Folklore Encyclopaedia* (50 vols.).
Farhanguestane Zaban, Khiabane Iranshah, Teheran. Iran.

Shankiti, Sheikh Mohammed Amin; Jordanian politician and diplomatist.
Chief Justice, Muslim Religious Courts -59; Minister of Educ. 59-61; fmr. Amb. to Saudi Arabia, also accred. to the Sudan, to the Yemen Arab Repub.; mem. Joint Comm. for Border Disputes 66-.
c/o Ministry of Foreign Affairs, Amman, Jordan.

Sharif, Omar (Michel Shalhoub); Egyptian actor; b. 10 April 1932, Cairo; ed. Victoria Coll., Cairo.
Salesman, lumber-import firm; made first film *The Blazing Sun* 53; starred in 24 Egyptian films and two French co-production films during following five years; commenced int. film career with *Lawrence of Arabia*.
Films include: *Lawrence of Arabia*, *The Fall of the Roman Empire*, *Behold a Pale Horse*, *Ghengis Khan*, *The Yellow Rolls Royce*, *Doctor Zhivago*, *Night of the Generals*, *Mackenna's Gold*, *Funny Girl*, *Cinderella—Italian Style*, *Mayerling*, *The Appointment*, *Che*, *The Last Valley*, *The Horsemen*, *The Burglars*, *The Mysterious Island*, *The Tamarind Seed*, *Juggernaut*, *Funny Lady*, *Ace up My Sleeve*, *Crime and Passion*, *Ashanti*.
Publ. *The Eternal Male* (autobiog.) 78.
c/o William Morris Agency (U.K.) Ltd., 147 Wardour Street, London, W.1, England.

Sharif-Emami, Jaffar, G.C.M.G.; Iranian engineer and politician; b. 8 Sept. 1910, Teheran; ed. Secondary School, Teheran, German Central Railway School and Borås Technical School, Sweden.
Joined Iranian State Railways 31, Technical Deputy Gen. Dir. 42-46, Gen. Dir. 50-51; Chair. and Man. Dir. Independent Irrigation Corpn. 46-50; Under-Sec. of State to Ministry of Roads and Communications, Minister of Roads and Communications 50-51; mem. High Council, Plan Org. 51-52, Man. Dir. and Chair. High Council, Plan Org. 53-54; Senator from Teheran 55-57, 63-79, Pres. of Senate 63-69; Minister of Industry and Mines 57-60; Prime Minister Aug. 60-May 61, Aug.-Nov. 78; Deputy Custodian Pahlavi Foundation 62-79, mem. Board of Trustees 66; Chair. Industrial and Mining Devt. Bank 63-79; Pres. Iranian Asscn. of World Federalists 63-79; Pres. Iranian Engineers Asscn. 66-79; Pres. Third Constituent Assembly 67-79; Pres. of 22nd Int. Conf. of the Red Cross 73; Pres. Int. Bankers Asscn. 75; mem. American Soc. of Civil Engineers 46-, Board of Dirs. Royal Org. of Social Services 62-, Board of Trustees, Pahlavi Univ. 62, Nat. Univ. Teheran 62, Aria Mehr Tech. Univ., Teheran 65, Queen Pahlavi's Foundation; mem. Red Lion and Sun 63, Vice-Pres. 63, Deputy Chair. 66-; mem. of Board of Founders of Soc. for Preservation of Nat. Monuments 66; Iranian decorations: Order of Homayoun, First Grade, Order of Taj, First Class, and nine others; foreign decorations incl. Grosses Kreuz Verdienstorden (Germany), Grand Croix de la Légion d'Honneur (France), Order of Rising Sun, First Class (Japan), Order of St. Michael and St. George (U.K.) and 25 others.
27 Avenue Foch II, Paris 16e, France.

Sharifi, Ahmad-Hushang, PH.D.; Iranian educationist; b. 1925, Teheran; ed. France.
With Iranian Consulate, Paris; mem. Perm. Del. to UNESCO; French Language Translator, Teheran Univ. 57, Finance Teacher 58, Lecturer in Political Science 60, Prof. of Political Science 66; Financial and Admin. Adviser to Ministry of Educ. 64, Under-Sec. of Educ. 64; Principal,

Teachers Training Coll. 68; Chancellor Nat. Univ., Teheran 73, Rector 76-; Minister of Educ. 74-76; fmr. mem. Iran Novin Party.
National University of Iran, Evin, Teheran, Iran.

Sharon, Major-Gen. Ariel; Israeli army officer and politician; b. 1928.
Active in Hagana since early youth; Instructor, Jewish Police units 47; Platoon Commdr. Alexandroni Brigade; Regimental Intelligence Officer 48; Co. Commdr. 49; Commdr. Brigade Reconnaissance Unit 49-50; Intelligence Officer, Cen. Command and Northern Command 50-52; studies at Hebrew Univ. 52-53; in charge of Unit 101, on numerous reprisal operations until 57; studies Staff Coll., Camberley, U.K. 57-58; Training Commdr., Gen. Staff 58; Commdr. Infantry School 58-69; Commdr. Armoured Brigade 62; Head of Staff, Northern Command 64; law studies, Tel-Aviv Univ. 66; Head Brigade Group during Six-Day War 67; resigned from Army July 73; recalled as Commdr. Cen. Section of Sinai Front during Yom Kippur War Oct. 73, forged bridgehead across Suez Canal; with others formed Likud Front Sept. 73; mem. Knesset (Parl.) 73-74, 77-; joined army reserves Dec. 74; Adviser to Prime Minister 75-77; Minister of Agriculture June 77-.
Ministry of Agriculture, 13 Heleni Hamalka, Jerusalem, Israel.

Shazly, Lt.-Gen. Saad Mohamed al Hosseiny el-, M.POL.SC.; Egyptian army officer; b. 1 April 1922, Cairo; ed. Khedive Ismail Secondary School, Cairo, Cairo Univ., Mil. Coll., and in U.S.S.R.
Officer of the Guards 43-48; Platoon Commdr. Arab-Israeli War 48; Commdr. of Parachute School 54-56; Commdr. of Parachute Battalion 56-58; Commdr. United Arab Repub. Contingent, UN, Congo 59-60; Defence Attaché, London 61-63; Brig. Commdr. in Yemen Civil War 65-66; Commdr. Shazly Group, Egyptian-Israeli War 67; Commdr. of Special Forces 67-69; Commdr. Red Sea District 70-71; Chief of Staff of Egyptian Armed Forces 71-73; Amb. to U.K. 74-75, to Portugal Sept. 75-June 78; holder of twenty-two decorations including Order of the Repub., 1st Class, Etoile d'Honneur, Médaille Mil. du Courage, Médaille du Congo, Knight, Syrian Order of Honour.
Publs. *How an Infantry Division Can Cross a Water Barrier* 73, *Fonética Arabe Com Letras Portuguesas* 78, *Kuraanunn Kariim* 78, *Memoires of the 73 War* 79, *The Arab-Israeli Conflicts in the Past and in the Future* (to be published 80).
39 Gamal Eldin Eldessuky, Heliopolis, Cairo, Egypt.

Shebani, Dr. Omar, M.A., PH.D.; Libyan educationist; b. 1930; ed. Cairo, Ain-Shams Univs. and Boston, George Washington Univs., U.S.A.
Assistant Dir. Teachers' Coll., Univ. of Libya (now Univ. of Garyounis) 65, Dir. of Youth Dept. 68, Asst. Prof., Pres. 70-76.
c/o General Administration, University of Garyounis, P.O. Box 1308, Benghazi, Libya.

Shenouda III, Anba, B.A., B.D.; Egyptian ecclesiastic; b. 3 Aug. 1923.
Former Prof. of Theology and Patrology, Coptic Orthodox Theological School, Cairo; Pope of Alexandria and Patriarch of The See of St. Mark in all Africa and the Near East 71-.
St. Mark's Patriarchate, Anba Ruiess Building, Ramses Street, Abbasiya, Cairo, Egypt.

Shiguer, Mohamed Haddou; Moroccan politician; b. 1932; ed. Mohammed V Univ.
Taught for 12 years; mem. Nat. Assembly; Minister of Post and Telecommunications 64-66, of Agriculture 66-67, of the Royal Cabinet 67, of Defence 67-68, of Primary Educ. 68-72, of Nat. Educ. 72-73, of the Interior 73-77, of Co-operation and Professional Training 77-78, of Relations with Parliament 78-.
Ministry of Relations with Parliament, Rabat, Morocco.

Shihata, Ibrahim F. I., L. EN D., S.J.D.; Egyptian lawyer and administrator; b. 19 Aug. 1937; ed. Cairo Univ., Harvard Univ., U.S.A.
Member of the Council of State of Egypt 57-60; Lecturer, Faculty of Law, Ain Shams Univ. 64-66, Assoc. Prof. 70-72; Legal Adviser to Kuwait Fund for Arab Econ. Devt. 66-70, Gen. Counsel 72-76; also adviser and consultant to Arab Govts. and Int. Orgs. 65-; Dir.-Gen. OPEC Special Fund 76-; mem. Exec. Board, Int. Fund for Agricultural Devt. 77-.
Publs. Eleven books and more than fifty essays on different aspects of international law and finance.
OPEC Special Fund, P.O. Box 995, Vienna 1010, Austria.

Shlonsky, Avraham; Israeli poet; b. March 1900; ed. High School and Sorbonne.
Went to Palestine 21; mem. Editorial Board *Davar*; founder and Editor *Groovim, Toopim, Itim, Orlogin;* Literary Editor *Sifriat Hapoalim;* mem. Board, Mosad Bialik; mem. Hebrew Acad.
Publs. *Davai* (poems) 24, *Le-Aba Ima* 25, *Bagalgal* 26, *Be-Ele Hayamim* 29, *Avne Bohu* 34, *Yalkut Shirat Haamim, Al Milet, Shirei Hamapolet Vehapius, Avnei Gvil, Mishivei Haphosdok Haarooch*; trans. several foreign works into Hebrew, including Shakespeare, Pushkin, Gogol, Brecht, Chekhov and Gorki.
50 Gordon Street, Tel-Aviv, Israel.

Shoukry, Mohammed Anwar; Egyptian egyptologist; b. 1905; ed. Cairo Univ. Inst. of Egyptology, Univ. of Göttingen.
Asst. Prof. of Egyptology, Cairo Univ. 48-52, fmr. Prof.; Chief Archæologist Cen. of Documentation of Egyptian Art and Civilization 56-59; Dir.-Gen. Dept. of Egyptian Antiquities 59-66; Asst. Under-Sec. of State, Ministry of Culture and National Guidance 61-70; Resident Archaeologist in Nubia 64.
Publs. *Die Grabstatue im Alten Reich, Egyptian Art from the Beginning till the End of the Ancient Kingdom* (in Arabic).
c/o Ministry of Culture, Cairo, Egypt.

Shragai, Shlomo Zalman; Israeli journalist; b. 31 Dec. 1899; ed. Jeshivoth-Talmudical Colls. in Poland.
Founder of Young Mizrachi Movement in Poland 17; founder of organization for training religious youth or Eretz Israel 19; elected mem. Jewish Nat. Council of Poland 20; Editor religious Zionist-Hebrew newspaper, *Hatechia* 20; migrated to Palestine and employed as builder in Jerusalem 24; elected exec. mem. Hapoel Hamizrachi Party 24-; exec. mem. Va'ad Leumi (Jewish Nat. Council) of Eretz Israel 29, Zionist Actions Cttee. 33; Chair. Broadcasting Services of Palestine 38; elected exec. mem. Jewish Agency, London 46; first Mayor of Jerusalem 50-52; Head of Immigration Dept. of Jewish Agency 53; Contrib. to Israeli daily *Hatzofe* and *Sinai-Monthly for Thora and Jewish History Research.*
Publs. *Vision and Fulfilment* (Hebrew) 25, *Tehumin, Beit Ushbitza, Tahalichey Hageula Vhatmura, Shaa Vanezach, Peame Geula, Zemanim, Besugiot Hador.*
8 Keren Kayemeth Street, Jerusalem, Israel.

Siassi, Ali-Akbar, PH.D.; Iranian psychologist and politician; b. 1896; ed. Persia and France.
Professor Univ. of Teheran 27-; Head Dept. of Advanced Studies of the Ministry of Educ. 32; Chancellor of the Univ. of Teheran 42; Minister of Educ. 43; drafted bill and law for national compulsory free education, and took necessary measures for its enforcement 43; Minister of State without portfolio 45, of Education 48-50, of Foreign Affairs 50; del. III Int. Congress of Persian Art and Archæology 35,

UN Conf. San Francisco 45; Pres. Iranian del. UNESCO Conf. Paris 49, Int. Conf. of Univs. 50, UNESCO Conf. Paris 51, Int. Conf. of Univs., Mexico City 60, Royal Soc. Tricentenary Celebrations, London 60; Perm. mem. Iranian Acad.; Hon. Pres. Univ. of Teheran; Dr. h.c. Univ. of Charles 1st, Prague 47, Univ. of Strasbourg 65, etc.; mem. Int. Cttee. Scientific and Cultural History of Humanity; Pres. Iranian Council of Philosophy and Human Sciences, Iranian Psychological Asscn. of Iran; mem. Royal Cultural Council, etc.; Commdr. Légion d'Honneur; Commdr. Palmes Académiques, etc.
Publs. In French: *L'Education en Perse* 21, *La Perse au Contact de l'Occident* 31, *La Méthode des Tests* 31, *Le Génie et l'Art iraniens aux prises avec l'Islam* 35, *De l'Unesco à la Sorbonne* 53, *L'Iran au XIXe siècle* 55; In Persian: *Psychology* 38, *Educational Psychology for Teachers' Colleges* 41, *Introduction to Philosophy* 47, *Mind and Body* 53, *The Psychology of Avicenna and its similarities with the Modern Psychology* 54, *Logic* 56, *Ethics* 57, *Logic and Philosophy* 58, *Intelligence and Reason* 62, *Criminal Psychology* 64, *Psychology of Personality* 70, *Theories of Personality* 75.
President Roosevelt Avenue, Namdjou Street, Teheran, Iran.

Sidarouss, H.E. Cardinal Stephanos I; Egyptian ecclesiastic; b. 1904; ed. Jesuits' Coll. Cairo, Univ. de Paris, Faculté de Droit, and Ecole Libre des Sciences Politiques. Barrister, Egypt 26-32; Vincentian Priest 39-; Prof Seminaries at Evreux, Dax and Beauvais (France); Rector Coptic Catholic Seminary, Tahta 46, Tanta 47-53, Maadi 53-58; Auxiliary Bishop to the Patriarch of Alexandria 47-58, Patriarch 58-; created Cardinal 65.
34 Ibn Sandar Street, Koubbeh Bridge, Cairo, Egypt.

Sidi-Baba, Dey Ould; Moroccan diplomatist and politician; b. 1921, Atar, Mauritania.
Counsellor, Ministry of Foreign Affairs, Morocco 58, Head of African Div. 59; mem. Moroccan Dels. to UN Gen. Assembly 59-64; Acting Perm. Rep. of Morocco to UN 63-65, Perm. Rep. 65-67; Minister of Royal Cabinet 67-; Amb. to Saudi Arabia 71-72; Dir. Royal Cabinet 72-73; Minister of Educ. 73-74, of Waqfs and Islamic Affairs 74-77; Pres. Chamber of Reps. 77-; mem. Nat. Defence Council March 79-; Commandeur du Trône Alaouite; Niger Grand Order of Merit; Officer of Libyan Order of Independence; Commdr. of Syrian Order of Merit.
Chamber of Representatives, Rabat, Morocco.

Sidky, Aziz, B.ENG., M.A., PH.D.; Egyptian politician; b. 1 July 1920; ed. Cairo Univ., Univ. of Oregon and Harvard Univ.
Minister of Industry 56-63; Deputy Prime Minister for Industry and Mineral Wealth 64-65; Adviser for Production Affairs to Pres. of U.A.R. 66-67; Minister of Industry, Petroleum and Mineral Wealth 68-71; Deputy Prime Minister 71-72, Prime Minister 72-73; Personal Asst. to Pres. Sadat 73-April 75; has attended many int. confs. on industrial affairs.
c/o The Presidency, Cairo, Egypt.

Siilasvuo, Lieut.-Gen. Ensio; Finnish army officer; b. 1 Jan. 1922, Helsinki; ed. Lycée of Oulu, Finnish Mil. Acad., Finnish Command and Staff Coll.
Platoon Commdr., Infantry Co. Commdr. and Chief of Staff, Infantry Regiment 11 41-44; Company Commdr., Infantry Regiment 1 45-50; attended Command and Staff Coll. 51-52; various staff appointments in mil. districts of N. Finland 53-57; Commdr. Finnish Contingent, UN Emergency Force 57; Mil. Observer, UN Observation Group in Lebanon 58; Finnish Defence Attaché in Warsaw 59-61; Staff Officer Third Div. 62-64; Commdr. Finnish Contingent, UN Force in Cyprus 64-65; Instructor, Nat. Defence Coll. 65-67; Chief, Foreign Dept. GHQ 67; Senior Staff Officer, UN Truce Supervision Org. in Palestine 67-70; Chief of Staff, UN Truce Supervision Org. in Palestine 70-73; Commdr. UN Emergency Force 73-75; Chief Co-ordinator of UN Peace-keeping Missions in the Middle East 75-; Grand Cross Order of the Lion of Finland 1st Class; Finnish Cross of Freedom 3rd and 4th Class; Knight of the Order of the White Rose of Finland.
UNCC, P.O. Box 490, Jerusalem, Israel.

Simavi, Haldûn; Turkish journalist; b. 1925; ed. Kabataş Lisesi, Istanbul.
Publisher and Gen. Man. of daily newspapers *Günaydin*, *Saklambac*, weekly mags. *Tarkan*, *Kara Murat*, *Girgir*; *firt*, and monthly publications *Er Dehorasyon*, *Gagdaş Bilim*, *Turkish Treasures*, *Tekshil* and trimestrial *Vizon*, co-owner Istanbul daily newspaper *Hürriyet*.
Veb Ofset, Ileri Matbaacılık A.S. Cağaloğlu, Istanbul, Turkey.

Simon, Akiba Ernst, PH.D., DR. THEOL. (h.c.); Israeli educationist; b. 15 March 1899; ed. Univs. of Berlin and Heidelberg.
Editor (with Martin Buber) *Der Jude* 23-24; Lecturer in Jewish subjects, Frankfurt-am-Main 22-28; taught at various schools in Germany and Palestine 28; Assoc. Dir. of Jewish Adult Education Centre of Germany 33-34; Lecturer Hebrew Univ. of Jerusalem 38-50, Assoc. Prof. of Educ. 50-55, Prof. 55-68, Prof. Emer. 68-; Visiting Prof. of Educ., Jewish Theological Seminary of America, N.Y. 47-48, 62; Visiting Prof. of Educ. at Univ. of Judaism, L.A., Calif. 56-57; mem. Research Board Leo Baeck Inst. of Jews from Germany; mem. Board Ihud Organization for Jewish-Arab Co-operation; mem. Board Religious Youth Village; co-Editor Pedagogical Encyclopaedia, 5 vols. (Hebrew); Israeli State Prize for Educ. 67; Buber-Rosenzweig Medal 69; Prize of the City of Jerusalem.
Publs. *Ranke und Hegel* 29, *Das Werturteil im Geschichtsunterricht* 31, *Bialik* 35, *Educational Meaning of Socratic Irony* (Hebrew) 49, *Pioneers of Social Education—Pestalozzi and Korczak* (Hebrew), *The Teaching of Pestalozzi* 53, 61 (Hebrew), *Jewish Adult Education in Nazi Germany as Spiritual Resistance*, *Franz Rosenzweig's Position in the History of Jewish Education* (Hebrew), *Freud the Jew* (Hebrew, German and English), *Martin Buber and the Faith of Judaism* (Hebrew), *Martin Buber and German Jewry* (English) 58, *Aims of Secondary Education in Israel* (Hebrew) 61, *Brücken* (Collected Essays—German) 65, *M. Buber's Correspondence* (3 vols.) (German, with G. Schaeder), 72-75, *Buber's Political Philosophy and Practice* (Hebrew) 73, Autobiography in *Pedagogics in Autobiographies* (German) 75, *Martin Buber's Lebendige Erbe* (German and Hebrew) 78.
35 Ben Maimon Avenue, Jerusalem, Israel.

Sindi, Sheikh Kamil; Saudi Arabian airline executive; b. 3 Jan. 1932, Mecca.
Joined Saudi Arabian Airlines and Civil Aviation Org. 47; in charge of Operations and Maintenance Dept. 47; Sec. to Dir.-Gen. until 60; Dir.-Gen. of Civil Aviation 61-66; Dir.-Gen. Saudi Arabian Airlines (SAUDIA) 67-; Pres. Arab Air Carriers Organisation (AACO) 71-; mem. Exec. Cttee., IATA 74-; Chevalier de l'Ordre d'Orange Nassau.
SAUDIA, P.O. Box 167, Jeddah, Saudi Arabia.

Slaoui, Driss; Moroccan politician and banker; b. 12 Dec. 1926, Fez; ed. Univs. of Grenoble and Paris, France.
Director-General Sûreté Nationale, Casablanca 56-58; Sec. of State for Interior, then for Commerce and Industry; Minister of Commerce and Industry 59-61; Dir. of Royal Cabinet March 62; Minister of Public Works 62-63, of Finance 63-64, of Nat. Economy and Agriculture Nov. 63-64; Gov. Banque du Maroc (Central Bank) 64-68; Minister of Justice 68-69; Dir.-Gen. Royal Cabinet 69-71; Perm. Rep. to UN 74-76; Counsellor to King Hassan Oct.

77-; Pres. Dir.-Gen. Société Nat. d'Investissement 78-; Rep. to Int. Court of Justice in Western Sahara case June-July 75.
c/o Ministry of Foreign Affairs, Rabat, Morocco.

Slim, Taieb; Tunisian politician and diplomatist; b. 1914; ed. Tunis Lycée and Univ. of Paris.
Member Néo-Destour Party, detained 41-43; Arab Maghreb Bureau, Cairo 46-49; Head, Tunisian Office, Cairo 49, established Tunisian offices, New Delhi, Jakarta, Karachi; Head, Foreign Affairs, Presidency of Council of Ministers 55-56; Ambassador to U.K. 56-62, also accredited to Denmark, Norway and Sweden 60-62; Perm. Rep. to UN 62-67, concurrently Amb. to Canada; Minister, Personal Rep. of the Pres. 67-70; mem. Nat. Assembly 69; Amb. to Morocco 70-71; Minister of State 71-72; Amb., Perm. Rep. to UN, Geneva 73-74; Amb. to Canada 74-76; Minister of State 76-77; mem. Political Bureau Destour Socialist Party 71-.
Office of the Minister of State, Tunis, Tunisia.

Smilanski, Izhar; Israeli writer; b. 1916; ed. Teachers' Seminary and Hebrew Univ.
Former teacher; fmr. mem. Knesset; Brenner Prize for *Midnight Caravan*; Israel Prize 59.
Publs. include: *Midnight Caravan, Hirbeth Hiza'a, The House on the Hill, Days of Ziklag* (2 vols.), *Stories of the Plain.*
14 Moskowitz Street, Rehovot, Israel.

Smith, Wilfred Cantwell, M.A., PH.D., D.D.; Canadian university professor; b. 21 July 1916; ed. Upper Canada Coll., Univ. of Grenoble, Univ. of Madrid, American Univ. Cairo, Univ. of Toronto, Cambridge and Princeton Univs.
Served as rep. among Muslims of the Canadian Overseas Missions Council, chiefly in Lahore 40-49; Lecturer in Indian and Islamic History, Univ. of the Punjab, Lahore 41-45; Prof. of Comparative Religion 49-63, and Dir. Inst. of Islamic Studies, McGill Univ. 51-63; Pres. American Soc. for the Study of Religion 66-69; Prof. of World Religions and Dir. Center for the Study of World Religions, Harvard Univ. 64-73, also Visiting Prof. of History of Religion 74-; McCulloch Prof. of Religion, Dalhousie Univ. 73-78; Prof. of Comparative History of Religion, Chair. The Study of Religion, Harvard Univ. 78-; Pres. Middle East Studies Asscn. of North America 77-78; Fellow, Royal Soc. of Canada (Pres. Humanities and Social Science Section 72-73), American Acad. of Arts and Sciences; Chauveau Medal, Royal Soc. of Canada 74.
Publs. *Modern Islam in India* 43 (revised edns. 47, 65, 78), *Islam in Modern History* 57, 77 (Arabic trans. 75), *Meaning and End of Religion* 63, 78, *Faith of Other Men* 63, *Modernisation of a Traditional Society* 66, *Questions of Religious Truth* 67, *Belief and History* 77, *Faith and Belief* 79.
50 Foster Street, Cambridge, Massachusetts, U.S.A.

Snoussi, Ahmed, LL.D.; Moroccan diplomatist; b. 22 April 1929; ed. Lycées at Meknes and Casablanca, Schools of Law and Political Sciences, Paris.
In Nationalist Movement; cabinet attaché to Minister of State in negotiations with France 56; Head, Press Div. Ministry of External Affairs 56; Sec.-Gen. Conf. on status of Tangiers; Moroccan Del. to UNESCO Conf. and UN; Dir.-Gen. Information; mem. Tech. Co-op. Mission to Congo and King's special envoy to Congo 58-59; UN Conciliation Mission to Congo 61; Sec.-Gen. Ministry of Information, Tourism Handicrafts and Fine Arts 61-65; Ambassador to Nigeria and Cameroon 65-67; Minister of Information 67-71; Amb. to Tunisia 71-73, to Algeria 73-75, to Mauritania July 78-; mem. Moroccan Del. to UN 75-77; Editor numerous magazines, including *Maroc* (Ministry of External Affairs) and *Maroc Documents* (Ministry of Information); Officer Order of the Throne of Morocco, Cross of Courage and Endurance (Mission to Congo), decorations from Jordan and Yugoslavia.
Embassy of the Kingdom of Morocco, Nouakchott, Mauritania.

Solh, Rashid; Lebanese lawyer and politician; b. 1926, Beirut; ed. Coll. des Frères des Ecoles Chrétiennes, Coll. Al Makassed, Faculty of Law, Beirut.
Successively Judge, Pres. of the Labour Arbitration Council, Examining Magistrate, Attorney-Gen. of the Charéi Tribunal; Independent mem. Chamber of Deputies for Beirut 64, 72; Prime Minister Oct. 74-May 75.
Chambre des Députés, Place de l'Etoile, Beirut, Lebanon.

Solh, Takieddine; Lebanese politician and diplomatist; b. 1909; ed. American Univ. of Beirut, and Univ. Saint Joseph, Beirut.
Former Civil Servant; fmr. Counsellor, Embassy to United Arab Repub., and to the Arab League; Prof. of Arabic, Lycée français 35-43; mem. of Parl. 57, 64; Pres. Foreign Affairs Comm. 64-; Minister of the Interior 65; Prime Minister, Minister of Finance 73-74.
rue de Damas, Beirut, Lebanon.

Soliman, Mohammed Sidki; Egyptian army officer and politician; b. 1919; ed. Fuad I Univ., Cairo.
Colonel in U.A.R. Army -62; Minister for the High Dam Sept. 62-Sept. 66; Prime Minister 66-67; Deputy Prime Minister, Minister of Industry and Power 67-70; Pres. Soviet-Egyptian Friendship Soc.; Order of Lenin.
c/o Ministry of Industry, Cairo, Egypt.

Soteriades, Antis; Cypriot lawyer and diplomatist; b. 10 Sept. 1924; ed. London Univ. and Gray's Inn, London.
In legal practice, Nicosia 51-56; detained on suspicion of assisting EOKA 56; escaped and became EOKA leader for Kyrenia district; mem. Exec., Edma Party May 59; High Commr. to U.K. Oct. 60-66; Amb. to United Arab Repub. (now Egypt) 66-, concurrently to Lebanon 67-, to Syria 67-74, to Iraq 73-; Knight of Order of St. Gregory the Great (Vatican) 63.
Embassy of Cyprus, 23A Ismail Mohammed Street, Zamalek, Cairo, Egypt.

Sotoodeh, Fatholah, B.S., M.A.; Iranian engineer and politician; b. 1924; ed. Polytechnical Inst. of Teheran and New York Univ.
Engineer with Vanak Metalworks 45-46; studies in U.S.A., then Senior Engineer and Asst. to Prof. of Industrial Engineering, New York Univ., and consulting engineer 46-58; Consulting Engineer, Plan Org. of Iran 58; Man. Dir. Vanak Metalworks and Rubber Factory 59-64, Iran Fisheries 64-65; Minister of P.T.T. 65-74; Chair. Board of Dirs. Construction Bank, Iranian Nuclear Energy Co.; Prof. of Industrial Management, Teheran Polytechnical Inst.
Publs. research into the use of sunlight in water heaters, water distillators and sun-stoves.
c/o Ministry of Posts, Telegraphs and Telephones, Old Shimran Road, Teheran, Iran.

Soulioti, Stella; Cypriot lawyer and politician; b. 1920; ed. Limassol, Victoria Girls' Coll., Alexandria, St. James' Secretarial Coll., London and Gray's Inn, London.
Worked in Cyprus Govt. Public Information Office; in W.A.A.F. Middle East in Second World War; qualified as barrister after war; joined family practice; Minister of Justice Aug. 60-70, concurrently Minister of Health 64-66; Law Commr. 71-; Co-ordinator for Foreign Aid to Cyprus Refugees Aug. 74-; Chair. Cyprus Overseas Relief Fund 77; Pres. Cyprus Red Cross Soc.; Chair. Scholarship Board; Vice-Pres. Cyprus Anti-Cancer Soc.; Hon. LL.D. (Nottingham Univ.) 72.
P.O. Box 4102, Nicosia, Cyprus.

Sowayel, Ibrahim 'Abd Allah al-; Saudi Arabian diplomatist; b. 31 Aug. 1916; ed. Saudi Inst., Mecca, and Cairo Univ.
Taught Arabic literature for a year in school for Preparation of (Student) Missions Abroad, Mecca; First Sec. Saudi Legation, Cairo 45; later Chargé d'Affaires, Beirut; Counsellor, Ministry of Foreign Affairs, Jeddah 54-56, Minister and Deputy Foreign Minister 56; Amb. to Iraq 57-60; Minister of Foreign Affairs 60-62; Head of Political Branch of Royal Diwan and Special Adviser to King with rank of Minister April-Sept. 62; Minister of Agriculture Oct. 62-Aug. 64; Amb. to U.S.A. 64-75, concurrently to Mexico 65-75.
Ministry of Foreign Affairs, Jeddah, Saudi Arabia.

Spiers, Ronald Ian, B.A., M.A.; American diplomatist; b. 9 July 1925; ed. Dartmouth Coll., Princeton Univ.
Member of U.S. Del. to UN 55-58; Dir. Disarmament Affairs, State Dept., Washington 58-62, NATO Affairs 62-66; Political Counsellor, U.S. Embassy in London 66-69, Minister 74-77; Asst. Sec. of State for Political-Mil. Affairs 69-73; Amb. to the Bahamas 73-74, to Turkey 77-.
American Embassy, Atatürk Bulvari 110, Ankara, Turkey.

Spuler, Bertold, DR. PHIL.; German university professor, b. 5 Dec. 1911; ed. Univs. of Heidelberg, Munich, Hamburg and Breslau.
Collaborator Soc. for Silesian History 34-35; Asst. Dept. of East European History, Univ. of Berlin and Co-editor *Jahrbücher für Geschichte Osteuropas* 35-37; Asst. Dept. of Near Eastern Studies, Univ. of Göttingen 37-38; Dozent, Univ. of Göttingen 38-42; Full Prof. Univ. of Munich 42, Göttingen 45, Hamburg 48-; Ed. *Handbuch der Orientalistik* 49-, *Der Islām* 49-; Hon. Dr. Theol. (Berne); Hon. Dr. ès Lettres (Bordeaux).
Publs. include *Die europäische Diplomatie in Konstantinopel bis 1739* 35, *Die Minderheitenschulen der europäischen Türkei von der Reformzeit bis zum Weltkriege* 36, *Die Mongolen in Iran: Politik, Verwaltung und Kultur der Ilchanzeit 1220-1350* 39, 3rd edn., 68, *Die Goldene Horde, Die Mongolen in Russland, 1223-1302* 43, 2nd edn. 65, *Die Gegenwartslage der Ostkirchen in ihrer staatlichen und volklichen Umwelt* 48, 2nd edn. 69, *Geschichte der islamischen Länder im Überblick I: Chalifenzeit II: Mongolenzeit* 52-53, *Iran in frühislamischer Zeit: Politik, Kultur, Verwaltung und öffentliches Leben 633-1055* 52, *Regenten und Regierungen der Welt* 53, 2nd edn. 62-64 (with additions) 66, 72, *Wissenshaftl. Forschungsbericht: Der Vordere Orient in islamischer Zeit* 54, *The Age of the Caliphs* 60, 2nd edn. 68, *The Age of the Mongols* 60, 2nd edn. 68, *Geschichte der morgenländischen Kirchen* 61, *Les Mongols et l'Europe* (English edn. 71) 61, *Wustenfeld-Mahlersche Vergleichungstabellen der muslimischen, iranischen und orient-christlichen Zeitrechnung*, 3rd edn. 61, *Innerasien seit dem Aufkommen der Türken* 65, *Geschichte des Mongolen nach Zeugnissen des 13 u. 14 Jahrhunderts* (English edn. 71) 68, *Die historische und geographische Literatur Irans* 68, *Der Islam: Saeculum-Weltgeschichte III-VII* 66-72, *Kulturgeschichte des Islams (Östlicher Teil)* 71, *Die Kunst des Islam* (with J. Sourdel-Thomine) 73, *Die Orthodoxen Kirchen* (77 articles in *Int. Kirchl. Zeitschrift*, Bern) 39-78.
Mittelweg 90, Hamburg 13, Federal Republic of Germany.

Stark, Dame Freya Madeline, D.B.E.; British explorer and writer; b. 31 Jan. 1893; ed. School of Oriental Studies and privately.
Travelled in Middle East and Iran 27-39 and in South Arabia 34-35, 37-38; joined Ministry of Information Sept. 39, sent to Aden 39, Cairo 40, Baghdad as attaché to Embassy 41, U.S.A. and Canada 44; Hon. LL.D. (Glasgow Univ.) 52, Hon. D.Litt. (Durham) 70; C.B.E. 53; recipient of the Founders' Medal (Royal Geographical Soc.), of Mungo Park Medal (Royal Scottish Geographical Soc.), Richard Burton Memorial Medal (Royal Asiatic Soc.), and of Sir Percy Sykes Medal (Royal Central Asian Soc.).
Publs. *The Valley of the Assassins* 34, *The Southern Gates of Arabia* 36, *Baghdad Sketches* 37, *Seen in the Hadhramaut* 38, *A Winter in Arabia* 40, *Letters from Syria*, 42, *East is West* 45, *Perseus in the Wind* 48, *Traveller's Prelude* 50, *Beyond Euphrates* 51, *Winter in Arabia* 52, *Ionia* 54, *The Lycian Shore* 56, *Alexander's Path* 58, *Riding to the Tigris* 59, *Dust in the Lion's Paw* 61, *The Journey's Echo* (an anthology) 63, *Rome on the Euphrates* 66, *The Zodiac Arch, Time, Movement and Space in Landscape* 69, *The Minaret of Djam* 70, *Turkey, Sketch of Turkish History* 71, *Selected Letters* Vols. I-V 74, 75, 76, 77, 78, *A Peak in Darien* 76.
Asolo, Treviso, Italy; and c/o John Murray, 50 Albermarle Street, London, W.1, England.

Steel, Sir David Edward Charles, Kt., D.S.O., M.C., B.A.; British company director; b. 29 Nov. 1916; ed. Rugby School and Univ. Coll., Oxford.
Officer, Q.R. Lancers, in France, the Middle East, N. Africa and Italy 40-45; Admitted as solicitor 48, worked for Linklaters and Paines 48-50; Legal Dept., British Petroleum Co. Ltd. 50-56, N.Y. 58, Pres. B.P. (N. America) Ltd. 59-61, Regional Co-ordinator, Western Hemisphere, B.P. Co. Ltd. 61-62; Man. Dir. Kuwait Oil Co. Ltd. 62-65, Dir. 65; Man. Dir. B.P. Co. Ltd. 65-, Deputy Chair. 72-75, Chair. 75-; Dir. Bank of England 78-.
British Petroleum Company Limited, Britannic House, Moor Lane, London, EC2Y 9BU; and 18 Princes Gate, London, S.W.7, England.

Stephani, Christakis, B.COMM., F.C.A.; Cypriot banker; b. 28 Sept. 1926, Cyprus; ed. London School of Econs. and Political Science.
Accountant-General of the Repub. of Cyprus 60-65; Gov. Cen. Bank of Cyprus 65-.
Central Bank of Cyprus, P.O. Box 1087, 36 Metochiou Street, Nicosia, Cyprus.

Stino, Kamal Ramzi; Egyptian international official and former politician.
Minister of Supplies 59, 62-63; Deputy Prime Minister for Supply and Internal Trade 64-66; mem. Gen. Secretariat of Arab Socialist Union 66; now Dir.-Gen. Arab Org. for Agricultural Devt.
Arab Organization for Agricultural Development, 4 el-Gamaa Street, P.O. Box 474, Khartoum, Sudan.

Stirling, Alexander John Dickson, C.M.G.; British diplomatist; b. 10 Oct. 1926, Rawalpindi, India (now Pakistan); ed. Edinburgh Academy and Lincoln Coll., Oxford.
Royal Air Force 45-48; Foreign Office 51; Middle East Centre for Arabic Studies 52; British Embassy, Cairo 52, Foreign Office 56, British Embassy, Baghdad 59, Amman 62, Santiago 65, Foreign Office 67; Political Agent, Bahrain 69, Amb. to Bahrain 71; Counsellor, British Embassy, Beirut 72; Royal Coll. of Defence Studies 76; Amb. to Iraq 77-.
British Embassy, Sharia Salah Ud-Din, Karkh, Baghdad, Iraq; and Foreign and Commonwealth Office, King Charles Street, London, S.W.1, England.

Stylianou, Petros Savva; Cypriot politician; b. 8 June 1933, Kythrea; ed. Pancyprian Gymnasium and Univ. of Athens and Salonika.
Served with Panhellenic Cttee. of the Cyprus Struggle (PEKA) and Nat. Union of Cypriot Univ. Students (EFEK), Pres. EFEK 53-54; Co-founder Dauntless Leaders of the Cypriot Fighters Org. (KARI) joined liberatiog movement 55, detained 55, escaped; leader Nat. Strikinn Group; arrested 56 and sentenced to 15 years imprisonment; transferred to English prison, repatriated 59; mem. Central Cttee. United Democratic Reconstruction Front (EDMA) 59; Deputy Sec.-Gen. Cyprus Labour Confederation (SEK) 59, Sec.-Gen. 60-62; founded Cyprus Demo-

cratic Labour Fed. (DEOK) 62, Sec.-Gen. 62-74, now Hon. Pres.; mem. House of Reps. 60-70, Sec. of House 60-62; Dir. *Ergatika Chronika* (Labour Annals) 60; Man. Editor *Ergatiki Foni* (Voice of the Working Class) 60-62; Man. Editor DEOK Newspaper *Ergatikos* (Workers' Struggle) 62-63; Man. Editor *Allagi* (Change) 63; mem. Co-ordination Cttee. of 28 associated vocational and scientific orgs. 64-66; Gen. Sec. Cypriot Arab Friendship Asscn. 64-66; mem. Cyprus Afro-Asian Solidarity Cttee. 64-66; Vice-Pres. Cyprus-G.D.R. Friendship Asscn. 64-68; Pres. Pancyprian Org. for the Disabled 66-; founder Pancyprian Olive Produce Org. 67; Man. Dir. *Kypriakos Logos* (Scientific Cypriot) 69-; Dir. *Anapericon Vema* magazine (The Step of the Disabled) 70-; founder and Pres. Free Kythrea Asscn. 75; Dir. daily newspaper *Ta Nea* (The News) 70; also founder and Dir. *Oikogenia kai Sholion* (Family and School) magazine 70; Pres. Nicosia Fed. of Parents, Pancyprian Confed. of Parents' Cttees. 69-73; Pres. Council of Cyprus Historical Museum and Archives 74-, Pancyprian Cttee. for Enclaved Greek Population 74-; Cyprus Nat. Sec. of Int. Fed. for Rehabilitation of the Disabled 74-; founder and Pres. Political Cttee. for the Cyprus Struggle (PEKA) 76-; mem. Int. Org. of Archives 76-; mem. Exec. Cttee. of World Org. for the Rehabilitation of the Disabled 76-; Pres. Co-ordination Cttee. for the Cyprus Struggle (SEKA) 76-; silver medal of Cape Andrew's Monastery 73; gold medal of the Pancyprian Cttee. for the Enclaved Greek Population 76; Hon. parchment of the Soc. of Greek Writers (Athens) 78.
Publs. *The Kyrenia Castle* 66, *The Epic of Central Prisons* 67, *Hours of Resurrection* 67, *Problems on Education* 68, *The National, Scientific and Cultural Necessity for the Creation of a National University in Cyprus* 69, *Sean Mac-stiofain, Leader of the IRA and Adorer of Hellenism* 73, *Saint Demetrianos—Bishop of Chytri-Cyprus* 73, *Historical Data relating to the Ethnarchical Role of the Cyprus Church* 73, *Achievements and Targets in the Rehabilitation of the Disabled* 73, *Laographicon Minologion* 73, *Peri to vasilion ton Chytron* 74, *Oi tris ftochoi Agioi tis Kythreas* 75, *To xerizoma* 75, *The Cyprus Revolution of 1606 under the leadership of Petros Avendanios* 75, *Black Book I* 75, *Black Book II, III, IV, V* 76, *Yi mou odinis yi* 76, *Turkish Massacres in Smyrna in* 1922 79, *The Lepers of Cyprus* 79, documents of Cypriot guerrillas detained under British administration.
10 Kimon Street, Engomi, Nicosia, Cyprus.

Sullivan, William Healy; American diplomatist; b. 12 Oct. 1922; ed. Brown Univ. and Fletcher School of Law and Diplomacy.
United States Navy 43-46; Foreign Service 47-, served Bangkok 47-49, Calcutta 49-50, Tokyo 50-52, Rome 52-55, The Hague 55-58; Officer-in-Charge, Burma Affairs, Dept. of State 58-59; Foreign Affairs Officer 59; UN Adviser, Bureau of Far Eastern Affairs 60-63; Special Asst. to Under-Sec. for Political Affairs 63-64; Amb. to Laos 64-69; Deputy Asst. Sec. of State for E. Asia (with special responsibility for Viet-Nam); Amb. to the Philippines 73-77, to Iran 77-79.
c/o Department of State, 2201 C Street, N.W., Washington, D.C. 20520, U.S.A.

Sultan ibn Abdul Aziz, H.R.H. Prince; Saudi Arabian politician; b. 1924; brother of H.M. King Khalid (*q.v.*).
Former Minister of Communications; Minister of Defence and Aviation 62-.
Ministry of Defence, Jeddah, Saudi Arabia.

Sunay, Cevdet; Turkish army officer and politician; b. 10 Feb. 1900; ed. Kuleli Military Lyceum, Istanbul and Military Acad.
With Turkish Army 16-66; served in Palestine 17, later under Atatürk; Capt. 30; Officer Operations Dept. Gen. Staff 33; Teacher Mil. Acad. 42-47; Commdr. Artillery Regt. 47; Chief Operations Dept. Gen. Staff; Gen. 59; Deputy Chief Gen. Staff 58-60; C.-in-C. Land Forces 60, Chief of Staff 60-66; Senator 66; Pres. of Turkey 66-73; Senator 73-; Hon. K.C.B. 67.
Akbaş sok. Botanik Apt. 2/5, Cankaya-Ankara, Turkey.

Sussmann, Joel, LL.B., DR.JUR.; Israeli judge; b. Poland 24 Oct. 1910; ed. Univs. of Frankfurt, Heidelberg, Berlin, and Cambridge.
In private legal practice 38-49; Mil. Prosecutor, Israel Defence Army 49; Judge, Supreme Court of Israel 53-70, Perm. Deputy Pres. 70-76, Pres. Supreme Court 76-; Prof. Hebrew Univ., Jerusalem; Israel Prize 75.
Publs. *Wechsel- und Scheckrecht Palästinas, Bills of Exchange, Dine'i Staroth, Dine'i Borerut, Sidrei Hadin Haesrachi* (Law of Civil Procedure).
41 Harav Berlin Street, Jerusalem; and The Supreme Court, Jerusalem, Israel.

T

Taha, Mohammed Fathi; Egyptian meteorologist; b. 15 Jan. 1914, Cairo; ed. Cairo Univ. and Imperial Coll. of Science and Technology, London.
Under-Secretary of State and Chair. Board of Dirs. Egyptian Meteorological Authority 53-75; Meteorological Counsellor to Ministry of Civil Aviation 76-; Vice-Pres. IAF 65; mem. WMO Exec. Cttee. 55, Second Vice-Pres. 59-63, Pres. 71-79; Pres. Perm. Meteorological Cttee., Arab League 71-77; Chair. Nat. Cttee. on Geodesy and Geophysics 65-75; mem. High Comm. on Outer Space Research for Peaceful Uses, Nat. Comm. for Int. Council of Scientific Unions and many other cttees. dealing with scientific research in Egypt.
Egyptian Meteorological Authority, Koubry El-Quobba P.O., Cairo, Egypt.

Taher, Abdulhady H., PH.D.; Saudi Arabian government official; b. 1930; ed. Ain Shams Univ. Cairo and California Univ.
Entered Saudi Arabian Govt. service 55; Dir.-Gen. Ministry of Petroleum and Mineral Resources 60; Gov.-Gen. Petroleum and Mineral Org. (PETROMIN) 62-; Man. Dir. Saudi Arabian Fertilizers Co. (SAFCO) 66-76, Jeddah Oil Refinery 70-; Chair. Arab Maritime Petroleum Transport Co.; Dir. Coll. of Petroleum and Minerals, Saudi Arabian Railroads, Arabian American Oil Co. (ARAMCO); Hon. mem. American Petroleum Engineers' Asscn.
Publ. *Income Determination in the International Petroleum Industry* 66.
PETROMIN, P.O.B. 757, Riyadh, Saudi Arabia.

Takieddine, Bahiqe Mahmoud; Lebanese politician; b. 1909, Baakline; ed. Université St. Joseph, Beirut.
Barrister 31-47; Deputy for Mont Liban 47; Minister of Agriculture 49; Deputy for Chouf 51, 53, 60, 64; Minister of Social Affairs and Health 53-60; fmr. Pres. Parl. Comm. on the Admin. of Justice; Minister of Economy 64-65; Minister of Information 68-69, of the Interior 73-74, of the Interior and Tourism July 79-.
Ministère de l'Intérieur, Beirut; Home: Rue Verdun, Beirut, Lebanon.

Takla, Philippe; Lebanese politician; b. 1915; ed. Univ. Law School, Beirut.
Law practice, Beirut 35-45; M.P. 45, 47; Minister of Nat. Economy and Communication 45-46, 48-49; Minister of Foreign Affairs 49, 61-64, 64-65; Gov. Bank of Lebanon 64-66, 66-67; Minister of Foreign Affairs and of Justice 66; Perm. Rep. to UN 67-68; Amb. to France 68-71; Minister of Foreign Affairs 74-76, also of Educ. and Planning 75-76; mem. Nat. Dialogue Cttee. Sept. 75.
Rue Maarad, Beirut, Lebanon.

Takriti, Gen. Saddam Husain (*see* Husain, Gen. Saddam).

Tal, Josef; Israeli composer; b. 1910, Poland; ed. Berlin State Acad. of Music.
Went to Israel 34; taught piano and composition at Jerusalem Acad. of Music 37, Dir. 48-52; now Head, Dept. of Musicology, Hebrew Univ., Jerusalem; Dir. Israel Centre for Electronic Music 61-; has appeared with Israel Philharmonic Orchestra and others as pianist and conductor; concert tours of Europe, U.S.A., Far East; UNESCO Scholarship for research in electronic music.
Works include: *Saul at Ein Dor* 57, *Amnon and Tamar* 61, *Ashmedai* 69 (operas), Symphony No. 1 53, No. 2 60, *Concerto for Harpsichord and Electronics* 64, *Double Concerto* (for violin and violoncello) 70, *Masada 1967* 73, other cantatas, quintets, music for ballet and several books on the theory of music.
Department of Musicology, Hebrew University, Jerusalem; Home: 3 Dvora Haneviyah Street, Jerusalem, Israel.

Talal ibn Abdul Aziz, Amir; Saudi Arabian Prince; b. 1930; brother of H.M. King Khalid (*q.v.*); ed. secondary school.
Minister of Communications 53-54; Amb. to France 55-56; Minister of Finance 61.
Cairo, Egypt.

Taleb-Ibrahimi, Ahmed, M.D.; Algerian doctor and politician; b. 5 Jan. 1932; ed. Univ. of Paris.
Son of Sheikh Bachir Ibrahimi, spiritual leader of Islam in Algeria; Dir. Jeune Musulman 52-54, Union Générale des Etudiants Musulmans Algériens 55-56, French Fed. of the FLN 56-57; imprisoned in France 57-62, in Algeria 64-65; Doctor, Hôpital Mustapha, Algiers 62-64; Minister of Nat. Educ. 65-70; mem. UNESCO Exec. Board; Minister of Information and Culture 70-77; Minister and Adviser to the Pres. 77-.
Publs. *Contribution à l'histoire de la médecine arabe au Maghreb* 63, *Lettres de Prison* 66, *De la décolonisation à la révolution culturelle* 73.
Villa Neuve, 14A Chemin de la Madeleine Hydra, Algiers, Algeria.

Taleghani, Khalil, B.SC.; Iranian civil engineer and politician; b. 13 Sept. 1913; ed. American Coll. of Teheran and Univ. of Birmingham.
Junior engineer, England 37-39; Engineer, Persian Army 39-41; Chief Engineer, Technical Dir., Dir. of Ebtekar and other construction companies and Golpayegan Water Co. 41-51; Minister of Agriculture Dec. 51-June 52, July 52-March 53 and 55-56; Minister of State June 56-59; Dir. Taleghani-Tashakori Co. (consulting engineers); Man. Karaj Dam Authority 54-59; Chair. Industrial and Mining Development Bank of Iran 60-62; Dir. Taleghani-Daftari (Consulting Engineers) 60-; Chair. B. F. Goodrich Tyre Manufacturing Co. 60-; Chair. Pars Paper Co. 67-, Iran-California Co. 70-, Manem Consultants 70-; mem. Iranian Asscn. of Consulting Engineers; Fellow A.S.C.E.; Tadj and Homayoun (1st Order) Medals.
Baghe-Bank Street, Golhak, Teheran, Iran.

Talhouni, Bahjat, LL.B.; Jordanian politician; b. 1913, Ma'an; ed. Damascus Univ.
Lawyer 36-38; Judge, Kerak 38-52; Pres. Court of Appeals 52-53; Minister of Interior 53, of Justice 53-54; Chief Royal Cabinet 54-60, 63-64, June-Aug. 69, 73-74; Prime Minister 60-62, 64-65, 67-70, concurrently Minister of Foreign Affairs 67-68, of Defence 68-69, of Interior April-Sept. 68; mem. Senate 62-, Pres. of Senate Dec. 74-; Personal Rep. of H.M. King Hussein 67-69; mem. Consultative Council 67; Pres. Cttee. for Preparation of Civil Law 71; Trustee, Jordan Univ. 62-.
Parliament Buildings, P.O. Box 72, Amman, Jordan.

Talib, Maj.-Gen. Naji; Iraqi soldier and politician; b. 1917; ed. Iraqi Staff Coll. and Sandhurst, England.
Military Attaché, London 54-55; Commdr. Basra Garrison 57-58; Minister of Social Affairs 58-59; lived abroad 59-62; Minister of Industry 63-64; mem. U.A.R.-Iraq Joint Presidency Council 64-65; Minister of Foreign Affairs 64-65; Prime Minister and Minister of Petroleum Affairs 66-May 67.
Baghdad, Iraq.

Talû, Naim; Turkish banker and politician; b. 22 July 1919; ed. Faculty of Economics, Istanbul Univ.
Joined Türkiye Cumhuriyet Merkez Bankası (Central Bank of Repub. of Turkey) 46, Chief 52, Asst. Dir. of Ankara Branch 55-58, Dir. of Exchange Dept. 58-62, Asst. Gen. Dir. 62-66, Acting Pres. and Gen. Dir. 66-67, Pres. and Gen. Dir. 67-70, Gov. 70-71; Chair. Foreign Investment Encouragement Cttee. 67-68; Chair. Banks' Asscn. of Turkey 67-71; Sec.-Gen. Cttee. for Regulation of Bank Credits 67-70; Minister of Commerce 71-73; Prime Minister 73-74; mem. Senate 72-76; Chair. and Man. Dir. Akbank TAŞ 75-76; Chair. Akbank TAŞ, Akçimento Ticaret A.Ş., Olmuk Mukavva San. ve Tic. A.Ş. April 76-; mem. Ankara Educ. Foundation, Soc. for Protection of Children in Turkey.
Akbank TAŞ, Meclisi Mebusan Cad. 65-69, Fındıklı, Istanbul, Turkey.

Tarakki, Nur Muhammed; Afghan politician; b. 1917.
Former journalist; Press attaché, Afghan Embassy, U.S.A. 52-53; Co-founder and Sec.-Gen. People's Democratic Party 65-; arrested 26 April 78, released next day after coup deposed Pres. Daoud; Chair. Revolutionary Council (Head of State) of Democratic Repub. of Afghanistan April 78-; Prime Minister 78-79; Pres. Supreme Defence Council April 79-.
Publ. *Pushtu i De Band Mosafen* 78.
Office of the Chairman, Revolutionary Council, Kabul, Afghanistan.

Tarazi, Salah el Dine, L. EN D., D. EN D.; Syrian diplomatist and judge; b. 1917, Damascus; ed. Coll. des Frères, Damascus and Faculté française de Droit, Beirut.
Lawyer, Damascus 40-47; Ministry of Finance 45-47; lecturer and later Assoc. Prof. of Public Law, Univ. of Damascus 46-49; Ministry of Foreign Affairs 49-50, Sec.-Gen. 56-57; Chargé d'Affaires, Brussels 51-52; Deputy Perm. Rep. to UN 53-56; Amb. of Syria to U.S.S.R. 57-58, of U.A.R. to Czechoslovakia 58-59, to People's Repub. of China 60-61, of Syria to People's Repub. of China 61-62, to UN 62-64, to U.S.S.R. 65-70, to Turkey 70-74; Special Adviser to Minister of Foreign Affairs 74-76; Judge, Int. Court of Justice Feb. 76-.
Publs. *Les Services publics libano-syriens* 46, *The Organization of the Judiciary in the New French Constitution* (in Arabic) 47, *La solution des problèmes de statut personnel dans le droit des pays arabes et africains* 78 and various articles on law in Arabic, French and English.
International Court of Justice, Peace Palace, The Hague 2012, Netherlands.

Tariki, Abdallah; Saudi Arabian oil executive; b. 19 March, 1919; ed. Univs. of Cairo and Texas.
Studied at Univ. of Texas and worked as trainee with Texaco Inc. in W. Texas and California 45-49; Dir. Oil Supervision Office, Eastern Province, Saudi Arabia (under Ministry of Finance) 49-55; Dir.-Gen. of Oil and Mineral Affairs (Saudi Arabia) 55-60; Minister of Oil and Mineral Resources 60; Dir. Arabian American Oil Co. 59-62; Leader Saudi Arabian Del. at Arab Oil Congresses 59, 60; Independent Petroleum Consultant 62-; Pres. Arab Petroleum Consultants; co-founder of OPEC; publisher of monthly petroleum magazine *Naft El-Arab*; adviser to Egyptian, Algerian and Kuwaiti Govts. on oil matters.

KAC Building, Floor 10, Appartment 3, Sharie Hilali, Kuwait; Home: P. O. Box 22699, Kuwait City, Kuwait.

Tartakower, Arie, DR. IUR., D.RER.POL.; Israeli (b. Polish) university professor; b. 24 Sept. 1897; ed. Univ. of Vienna. Co-founder Zionist Labour Movement and Chair. Zionist Labour Party, Poland 22-39; Lecturer, Inst. of Jewish Sciences, Warsaw 32-39; Dir. Dept. of Relief and Rehabilitation of World Jewish Congress (U.S.A.) 39-46; fmr. Prof., Lecturer and Head, Dept. of Sociology of the Jews, Hebrew Univ., Jerusalem; Hon. Vice-Pres. World Jewish Congress; mem. Gen. Council World Zionist Org.; mem. World Secr. Zionist Labour Movement; Co-founder and fmr. Pres. Israel Asscn. for UN; Chair. World Asscn. for Hebrew Language and Culture.
Publs. include: *History of the Jewish Labour Movement, Jewish Emigration and Jewish Policy of Migration, The Jewish Refugee, Jewish Wanderings in the World, The Wandering Man, The Jewish Society, History of Jewish Colonization* (2 vols.), *The Tribes of Israel* (3 vols.), *The Role of Revolution in Jewish History* (vol. I) 74.
1 Ben Yehuda Road, Jerusalem; Home: 45a King George Street, Jerusalem, Israel.

Tawfik Abdel Fattah, Zakaria; Egyptian cotton executive and politician; b. 18 Aug. 1920; ed. Cairo Univ.
With Bank Misr; then Commercial Attaché, Brussels, Madrid 48-57; Dir.-Gen. Exchange Control Office 61; Under-Sec. for Cotton Affairs, Ministry of Econ. 61-65; Chair. Gen. Cotton Org. High Cttee. for Cotton 65-75; Minister of Commerce and Supply 75-78; Chair. Gen. Union of Chambers of Commerce 71-75; Pres. Afro-Asian Org. for Econ. Co-operation (AFRASEC) 72; now Chair. Suez Canal Bank; mem. Econ. Researches Council, Acad. of Scientific Research; awards from Italy, France, Greece, Belgium and Spain.
Suez Canal Bank, 11 Sabry Abu Alam, Cairo, Egypt.

Tawfiq, Mohammad 'Omar; Saudi Arabian politician; b. 1917; ed. Shari'a Coll. of Literature and Islamics, Medina. Former teacher; fmr. clerk, Post and Telegraph Dept. 41-58, rose to Chief Sec. Council of Ministers; retd. 58; business and press activities 58-62; Minister of Communications 62-76, of Pilgrimage and Religious Endowment Affairs 63-70.
c/o Ministry of Communications, Riyadh, Saudi Arabia.

Tekoah, Yosef; Israeli diplomatist; b. 4 March 1925; ed. Université L'Aurore, China, and Harvard Univ.
Instructor in Int. Relations, Harvard Univ. 47-48; Deputy Legal Adviser, Ministry of Foreign Affairs 49-53; Dir. Armistice Affairs, and Head Israel Dels. to Armistice Comms. with Egypt, Jordan, Syria and Lebanon 53-58; Deputy Perm. Rep. to UN 58, Acting Perm. Rep. 59-60; Amb. to Brazil 60-62, to U.S.S.R. 62-65; Asst. Dir.-Gen. Ministry of Foreign Affairs 66-68; Perm. Rep. to UN 68-75; Pres. Ben Gurion Univ. of the Negev, Beersheva 75-.
Publ. *In the Face of Nations: Israel's Struggle for Peace* 76.
Office of the President, Ben Gurion University of the Negev, P.O. Box 2653, Beersheva 84120, Israel.

Thani, Sheikh Abdul-Aziz bin Khalifa al-, B.S.; Qatari politician; b. 12 Dec. 1948, Doha; ed. Indiana North and George Washington Univs., U.S.A.
Deputy Minister of Finance and Petroleum June-Dec. 72; Minister of Finance and Petroleum 72-; Chair. Board of Dirs. Qatar Nat. Bank 72-, Qatar Nat. Petroleum Co. 73-; Chair. Joint Management Cttee., QPC and Shell Qatar 73-; Gov. for Qatar, Int. Monetary Fund and World Bank 72-, also of Islamic Devt. Bank; Chair. State of Qatar Investment Board 72-; Rep. to numerous confs. of OPEC, OAPEC, UN, IMF, IBRD, Islamic Summit, Non-aligned confs., etc.
Ministry of Finance and Petroleum, P.O. Box 83, Doha, Qatar.

Thani, Sheikh Khalifa bin Hamad al-; Amir of Qatar; b. 1932, Doha.
Heir-Apparent 48; served as Chief of Security Forces, Chief of Civil Courts; Deputy Ruler of Qatar 60-72, Minister of Educ. 60-70, of Finance and Petroleum Affairs Sept. 71-Feb. 72; Prime Minister Sept. 71-; Chair. Investment Board for State Reserves 72; deposed his cousin Sheikh Ahmad and took office as Amir of Qatar Feb. 72.
The Royal Palace, Doha, Qatar.

Thesiger, Wilfred, C.B.E., D.S.O., M.A.; British traveller; b. 3 Jan. 1910; ed. Eton and Magdalen Coll., Oxford.
Explored Danakil country of Abyssinia 33-34; Sudan Political Service, Darfur and Upper Nile Provinces 35-39; served in Ethiopia, Syria and Western Desert with Sudan Defence Force and Special Air Service, Second World War; explored the Empty Quarter of Arabia 45-50; lived with the Madan in the Marshes of Southern Iraq 50-58; awarded Back Grant, Royal Geographical Soc. 36, Founders Medal 48; Lawrence of Arabia Medal, Royal Central Asian Soc. 55; David Livingstone Medal, Royal Scottish Geographical Soc. 61, Royal Soc. of Literature Award 64, Burton Memorial Medal, Royal Asiatic Soc. 66; Hon. D.Litt. (Leicester) 68.
Publs. *Arabian Sands* 58, *The Marsh Arabs* 64.
15 Shelley Court, Tite Street, London, S.W.3, England.

Tjeknavorian, Loris-Zare; Iranian composer and conductor; b. 13 Oct. 1937; ed. Vienna Acad. of Music, Salzburg Mozarteum.
Worked in U.S.A. until 70; fmr. Teaching Fellow, Univ. of Michigan; fmr. Composer-in-Residence, Concordia Coll., Minnesota; returned to Iran 70; Composer-in-Residence, Ministry of Culture and Fine Arts; Principal Conductor, Teheran Opera 72-79; Chair. Board of Trustees, Inst. of Armenian Music, London; fmr. mem. Board of Trustees, Shahbanou Farah Foundation, Teheran; Order of Homayoun; several int. tours as a conductor.
Works include: *Requiem for the Massacred* 75, *Simorgh* (ballet music), *Lake Van Suite, Erebouni* for 12 strings 78, a piano concerto, several operas, and documentary film scores.
c/o Basil Douglas Limited, 8 St. George's Terrace, London, NW1 8XJ, England.

Tlass, Maj.-Gen. Mustapha el-; Syrian army officer and politician; b. 11 May 1932, Rastan City, Mouhafazat Homs; ed. Mil. and Law Colls.
Active mem. Baath Arab Socialist Party 47-, Sec. of Rastan Section 51; Sports teacher, Al-Kraya School, Mouhafazat al-Soueda 50-52; attended Mil. Coll. 52-54; deputed to Egyptian army 59-61; Insp. Ministry of Supply 62; mem. Free Officers' Movement 62-63, detained 62-63; Commdr. Tank Bn. and Chief of Cen. Region of Nat. Security Court 63; Chief of Staff, 5th Armoured Brigade 64-66; mem. Regional Command, Regional Congress of Baath Arab Socialist Party 65, 68, 69, 75, of Politbureau 69-, of Nat. Council of Revolution 65-; participated in movement of 23 Feb., promoted to Commdr. of Cen. Region and of 5th Armoured Brigade; rank of Maj.-Gen. Feb. 68-, Chief of Staff of Armed Forces Feb. 68-70, First Deputy Minister of Defence Feb. 68-72; participated in correctional movement installing Pres. Hafez Al-Assad Nov. 70; First Deputy C.-in-C. Armed Forces 70-72, Deputy C.-in-C. 72-; mem. People's Council 71-; Minister of Defence 72-; Deputy Chief of Joint Supreme Mil. Council of Syrian and Egyptian Armed Forces 73; 22 orders and medals.
Publs. *Guerrilla War, Military Studies, An Introduction to Zionist Strategy, The Arab Prophet and Technique of War, The Armoured Brigade as an Advanced Guard, Bitter Memories in the Military Prison of Mezzah, The Fourth War between Arabs and Israel, The Second Chapter of the October Liberation War, Selections of Arab Poetry.*
Ministry of Defence, Damascus, Syria.

Tombazos, George; Cypriot politician; b. 2 Feb. 1919; ed. Pancyprian Gymnasium, Dentists' School of Athens.
Worked as dentist at Morphou 50-66; M.P. for Nicosia 60-66; Minister of Agriculture and Natural Resources 66-70; Head, Central Information Service 70-75; Minister of Communications and Works 75-78, of Agriculture and Natural Resources March 78-.
Ministry of Agriculture, Nicosia, Cyprus.

Tomeh, Georges J., M.A., PH.D.; Syrian university professor and diplomatist; b. 1922; ed. American Univ. of Beirut and Georgetown Univ.
Attaché, London, and Alt. Del. to UNESCO 45-46; Syrian Embassy, Washington 47-52; Alt. Gov. Int. Monetary Fund 50; Dir. UN and Treaties Dept., Ministry of Foreign Affairs, Damascus 53-54; Asst. Prof. of Philosophy and Asst. to Dean of Arts and Sciences, American Univ. of Beirut 54-56; Dir. Research Dept., Ministry of Foreign Affairs, Damascus 56-57; Consul-Gen., New York 57-58, Minister Consul-Gen. of United Arab Republic in New York 58, Minister, New York 61; Consul-Gen. and Deputy Perm. Rep. of Syria to UN 61-63; Minister of Economy, Syrian Arab Repub. 63-64; Prof. of Philosophy, Syrian Univ. 64-65; Perm. Rep. to UN 65-72; Order of Syrian Merit, Commdr. Order of St. Paul and St. Peter.
Publs. (in Arabic) *The Idea of Nationalism* 54, *Philosophy of Leibniz* 54, 65, *Making of the Modern Mind* (2 vols.) (trans. from English) 55-57, 65, *Arab Emigrants to the United States* 65; (in English) *Islam, Year Book of Education and Philosophy* 57, *Neutralism in Syria* 64, *Challenge and Response: A Judgement of History* 69.
c/o Ministry of Foreign Affairs, Damascus, Syria.

Toumazis, Panayotis, M.SC.ENG.; Cypriot civil engineer and company director; b. 1912, Famagusta; ed. Greek secondary school (Gymnasium), Famagusta and Nat. Tech. Univ. (Metsovion), Athens.
Municipal Engineer, Famagusta; private practice as consultant eng.; Founder and Pres. of Pan. and Dion. Toumazis, Consultancy, PANTOUMAZIS Co. Ltd., ATLAS-PANTOU Co. Ltd., ATLAS KATASKEVE Ltd. (building and civil engineering construction firms); Pres. Famagusta Devt. Corpn., Famagusta Fed. of Trade and Industry, Architects' and Civil Eng. Council of Registration; mem. Civil Eng. and Architects' Asscn.; mem. House of Reps. 60-70; Minister of Natural Resources and Agriculture 70-72; Vice-Pres. Cyprus Port Org. 75-.
7 Arnalda Street, Nicosia, Cyprus.

Treadwell, (Charles) James, C.M.G., C.V.O., LL.B.; British diplomatist (retd.); b. 10 Feb. 1920; ed. Wellington Coll., N.Z., Univ. of N.Z.
Military service 39-45; Sudan Political Service and Judiciary 45-55; at Foreign Office 55-57; with High Comm., Lahore 57-60, Embassy, Jeddah 60-62; Deputy High Commr. for Eastern Nigeria 65-66; Head of Joint Inf. Services Dept., FCO 66-68; Political Agent, Abu Dhabi 68-71; Amb. to United Arab Emirates 71-73; High Commr. to Bahamas 73-75; Amb. to Oman 75-79; Adviser to Hill Samuel Group Ltd. on Middle East Affairs 79-.
48 Lindfield Gardens, Guildford, GU1 1TS, England.

Triantafyllides, Michalakis Antoniou; Cypriot judge; b. 12 May 1927, Nicosia; ed. Gray's Inn, London.
Practised as a lawyer in Cyprus 48-60, serving for three years as Sec. of Human Rights Cttee. of Bar; mem. Greek Cypriot del. to Joint Constitutional Comm. which drafted Cyprus Constitution 59-60; Greek Cypriot Judge, Supreme Constitutional Court 60-, now Pres.; mem. European Comm. of Human Rights 63-.
Supreme Constitutional Court of Cyprus, Nicosia, Cyprus.

Tsur, Yaakov; Israeli diplomatist; b. 18 Oct. 1906; ed. Hebrew Coll. Jerusalem, Univ. of Florence and Sorbonne.
Member staff daily newspaper *Haaretz*, Tel-Aviv 29; Dir. French Dept. and later Co-Dir. Propaganda Dept. Jewish Nat. Fund, Jerusalem 30; special Zionist missions, Belgium, Greece, France 34-35, Bulgaria and Greece 40; Dir. Publicity Dept. Jewish Agency Recruiting Council 42; Liaison officer with G.H.Q. British Troops in Egypt 43-45; Head, del. to Greece 45; Pres. Israeli Army Recruiting Cttee. Jerusalem 48; Minister to Argentina 49-53, Uruguay 49-53, Chile 50-53 and Paraguay 50-53; Amb. to France 53-59; Dir.-Gen. Foreign Office 59; Chair. Zionist Gen. Council 61-68; Chair. Jewish Nat. Fund 60-76.
Publs. *Shaharit shel Etmol* (autobiography) 66, French trans.—*Prière du Matin* 67 (English ed. *Sunrise in Zion*), *An Ambassador's Diary in Paris* 68, *La Révolte Juive* (Italian, Spanish and Russian trans.) 70, *Portrait of the Diaspora* 75, *The Saga of Zionism* (in French, English and Spanish) 77.
c/o P.O. Box 283, Jerusalem, Israel.

Tueni, Ghassan, M.A.; Lebanese newspaper editor and politician; b. 1926; ed. Harvard Univ.
Publisher and Editor-in-Chief, *An-Nahar* (daily newspaper) and *An-Nahar Arabe et International* (weekly, published in Paris); Deputy Prime Minister, Minister of Educ. and Information 70-71; fmr. Parl. Deputy; arrested and detained Dec. 73; Minister for Social Affairs and Labour, for Tourism, for Industry and Oil 75-76; Perm. Rep. to UN 77-; mem. Nat. Dialogue Cttee. Sept. 75.
c/o 866 United Nations Plaza, Room 533-535, New York, N.Y. 10017, U.S.A.

Turabi, Hassan A., LL.B., LL.M., D. EN D.; Sudanese lawyer and politician; b. 1 Feb. 1932, Kassala; ed. Univs. of Khartoum, London and Paris.
Lecturer, Faculty of Law, Univ. of Khartoum 57, Dean 64-65; mem. Constituent Assembly 65-68, Advisory Comm. for the Constitution 66-68; Sec.-Gen. Islamic Charter Front 65-69; Constitutional expert, United Arab Emirates 68-69; in political detention for most of 69-77; mem. Politburo and Cen. Cttee., Sudanese Socialist Union, Asst. Sec.-Gen. for Information and External Relations 78-; Order of the Repub. (First Class).
Publs. Articles on constitutional questions 65-69, *Prayer* 71, *Faith in the Life of Man* 74, *The Status of Women* 75 (books in Arabic).
P.O. Box 1515, Khartoum, Sudan.

Turki, Brahim; Tunisian diplomatist; b. 13 Nov. 1930.
Teacher of Arabic until 56; Admin., Secr. of State for Foreign Affairs 56-59, Head Dept. of Econ. Affairs 59; econs. course UN Gen. Secr. 59-60; Counsellor Ministry of Foreign Affairs 60-61; Principal Private Sec. to Sec. of State for Foreign Affairs 61-62; rank of Minister Plenipotentiary 62; Consul-Gen., Paris 62-65; Minister, Tunisian Embassy, Algeria 65-67; Dir. Political Affairs, Ministry of Foreign Affairs 67-70; Amb. to The Netherlands 70-73, to U.K. 74-76; participated in many sessions of UN Gen. Assembly and OAU; Commdr. Order of Repub. of Tunisia; many foreign decorations.
c/o Ministère des Affaires Étrangères, Tunis, Tunisia.

Türkmen, İlter; Turkish diplomatist; b. 1927, Istanbul; ed. Galatasaray Lycée, Istanbul, Faculty of Political Sciences, Ankara.
Director-General of Policy Planning Dept., Ministry of Foreign Affairs 64, Asst. Sec.-Gen. for Political Affairs 67, Amb. to Greece 68, to U.S.S.R. 72; Perm. Rep. to UN 75-78.
c/o Ministry of Foreign Affairs, Dışişleri Bakanlığı, Müdafaa Cad., Bakanlıklar, Ankara, Turkey.

U

Ulfat, Gul Pacha; Afghan poet and writer; b. 1909; ed. private studies.
Staff writer *Anis* (daily) 35-36; Writers' Soc. 36; later mem. staff *Islah* (daily); Editor *Kabul Magazine* 46; Editor *Nangrahar* (weekly) 48; Chief of Tribal Affairs in Nangrahar Province; mem. House of Reps. from Jalalabad (Nangrahar), and Second Deputy to Pres. of House 49, mem. from Karghaie 52; Pres. of Afghan Acad. 56, Afghan-U.S.S.R. Friendship Soc. 59-63, Tribal Affairs (mem. Central Cabinet) 63-65; Rep. in Wolise Jerga (formerly House of Reps.) from Jalalabad 65-69.
Publs. Twenty-five books on literary, social and political subjects, and numerous essays.
Sher Shah Maina, Kabul, Afghanistan.

Umri, Gen. Hassan (*see* Amri, Gen. H.).

Ürgüplü, Suat Hayri; Turkish diplomatist and politician; b. 1903; ed. Galatasaray Lycée and Univ. of Istanbul.
Lawyer; mem. Parl. 39-43; Minister of Customs and Monopolies in Sarajoğlu Govt. 43-46, resigned and left People's Party; re-elected to Grand Nat. Assembly 50 with support of Democratic Party which he subsequently joined; mem. and Vice-Pres. Council of Europe 50-52; Amb. to Fed. Repub. of Germany 52-55, to United Kingdom 55-57, to U.S.A. 57-60, to Spain 60; Independent Senator and Speaker of Senate 61-63; Prime Minister Feb.-Oct. 65; Prime Minister designate April-May 72; Chair. Senate Foreign Affairs Cttee. 66-68, Culture and Art Foundation of Istanbul; Pres. Turkish Section,European League for Econ. Co-operation; Hon. mem. and Kt. of Mark Twain Soc.; Fed. Grand Cross of Merit with Star and Sash; Grand Cross, Order of Merit, Fed. Repub. of Germany.
Yapi ve Kredi Bankasi, Istanbul; Home: Sahil Cad. 19, Yesilyure, Istanbul, Turkey.

Urwick, Alan Bedford, C.M.G., B.A.; British diplomatist; b. 2 May 1930, London; ed. Dragon School, Rugby, New Coll. Oxford.
Joined Foreign Service 52; served in Embassies in Belgium 54-56, U.S.S.R. 58-59, Iraq 60-61, Jordan 65-67, U.S.A. 67-70, Egypt 71-73; seconded to Cabinet Office as Asst. Sec., Cen. Policy Review Staff 73-75; Head of Near East and North Africa Dept., Foreign and Commonwealth Office 75-76; Minister, British Embassy in Madrid 77-79; Amb. to Jordan 79-.
British Embassy, Third Circle, Jebel Amman, P.O. Box 87, Amman, Jordan; c/o Foreign and Commonwealth Office, King Charles Street, London, S.W.1; The Moat House, Slaugham, Sussex, England.

Uzan, Aharon; Israeli agriculturist; b. Tunisia.
Emigrated to Israel 49; co-founder, settler, Moshav Ghilat, in Negev 49, Sec., later Head of supply network; mem. Knesset (Parl.) 65-69; Deputy Minister of Agriculture 66-69; Gen. Sec. Tnuat Hamoshavim 70-74; Minister of Communications March-June 74, of Agriculture 74-June 77, also of Communications 75-77; Labour Party.
Labour Party of Israel, P.O. Box 3263, Tel-Aviv, Israel.

V

Vahidi, Iraj, C.E., D.P.H.E., PH.D.; Iranian politician; b. 1927, Khorramshahr; ed. Univs. of Teheran and Durham.
Engineer, Ministry of Roads; mem. Board of Dirs., Independent Irrigation Inst., subsequently Man. Dir.; Technical Asst. to Ministry of Water and Power; Man. Dir. Khouzestan Water and Power Authority; Minister of Agriculture 71, of Water and Power 71-74, of Energy 74-77.
c/o Ministry of Energy, Teheran, Iran.

Vajda, Georges; French professor; b. 18 Nov. 1908; ed. Séminaire Rabbinique, Budapest, and Paris, Ecole des Langues Orientales and Sorbonne.
Prof., Séminaire Israélite de France 36-; Lecturer, Ecole Pratique des Hautes Etudes, Sorbonne 37, Dir. 54-; Head of Oriental Section, Inst. de Recherche et d'Histoire des Textes 40-; Prof. Univ. de Paris 70-78; Sec. Société des Etudes Juives.
Publs. *Introduction à la Pensée Juive du Moyen Age* 47, *La Théologie ascétique de Bahya ibn Paquda* 47, *Répertoire des Catalogues et Inventaires de Manuscrits Arabes* 49, *Un Recueil de Textes Historiques Judéo-Marocains* 51, *Inventaire des Manuscrits Arabes Musulmans de la Bibliothèque Nationale* 53, *Juda ben Nissim Ibn Malka, philosophe juif marocain* 54, *Les certificats de lecture dans les manuscrits arabes de la Bibliothèque Nationale* 57, *L'amour de Dieu dans la théologie juive du moyen âge* 57, *Isaac Albalag* 60, *Recherches sur les relations entre la Philosophie et la Kabbale* 62, *Le Dictionnaire des Autorités de 'Abd al-Mu'min ad-Dimyati* 62, *Le commentaire d'Ezra de Gérone sur le Cantique* 69, *Deux commentaires Karaïtes sur l'Ecclésiaste* 71, *Revue des Etudes Juives* (Editor).
Institut de Recherche et d'Histoire des Textes, 40 avenue d'Iéna, 75116 Paris; and 51 rue Sainte-Placide, 75006 Paris, France.

van der Meulen, Daniel; Netherlands author and explorer; b. 1894; ed. Arnhem, and Univ. of Leyden.
Dutch East India Civil Service 15-23, 32-41, 45-48; Neths. Consul, Jeddah 26-31; Minister to Saudi Arabia 41-45; Adviser to Lieut. Gov.-Gen. van Mook, Java 45-48; organizer and leader Arabic broadcasts, Neths. World Radio, Hilversum 48-51; exploration of S.W. Arabia 31, 39, 43, 52, 58-59, 62-63, 64, 67, 71, 72, 75; hon. mem. Netherlands Royal Geographical Soc.; Patron's Medal, Royal Geographical Soc., London 47; Officer, Order of Orange Nassau (Netherlands).
Publs. *Hadhramaut, Some of its Mysteries Unveiled* 32, *Aden to The Hadhramaut* in English 47, Swedish and German, *Onbekend Arabië* 51, *Ontwakend Arabië* 53, *The Life Story of King Ibn Saud of Saudi Arabia* (in Indonesian, Dutch and English) 52, revised edn. 57, re-titled *The Wells of Ibn Saud, Faces in Shem* 61, *Ik Stond Erbij* 64, *Verdwijnend Arabië, Mijn Weg Naar Arabië en de Islam, Hoort Gy de donder niet* (autobiog.) 77.
9 Flierderweg, Gorssel, Netherlands.

Veniamin, Christodoulos; Cypriot lawyer and government official; b. 15 Sept. 1922, Kato Moni; ed. Nicosia Samuel School, Middle Temple.
Joined Govt. service 42; joined Admin. Cadre 49; Exec. Officer for resettlement 51-54; Asst. Sec. in Depts. of Local Govt. and Admin., Personnel, Finance, Commerce and Industry, Social Services, Communications and Works, Agriculture and Natural Resources 55-59; Asst. District Commr. Larnaca 59; Head of Admin., Limassol District 60-68; Dir.-Gen. Ministry of Foreign Affairs 68-74; Minister of Interior and Defence 75-; Grand Cross of Honour with Star and Shoulderband (Fed. Repub. of Germany); Grand Officer, Order of Merit (Italy); Order of the Cedar (Lebanon).
Ministry of the Interior, Nicosia, Cyprus.

W

Waely, Faisal el-, PH.D.; Iraqi professor and government official; b. 1922; ed. Teacher Training Coll., Baghdad and Oriental Inst. of Chicago.
Professor, Baghdad Univ. (Coll. of Literature) 53-56; Dir.-Gen. of Technical Affairs, Ministry of Education, Baghdad 58-59; Prof. Cairo Univ. 59-63; Dir.-Gen. of Antiquities,

Baghdad 63-78; Prof., Dept. of Archaeology, Univ. of Kuwait 78-.
Publs. Various articles in journal *Sumer*.
Department of Archaeology, Kuwait University, P.O. Box 5969, Kuwait.

Wahrhaftig, Zorach, D. JUR.; Israeli lawyer and politician; b. Warsaw 2 Feb. 1906; ed. Univ. of Warsaw.
Private law practice, Warsaw 32-39; Vice-Pres. Mizrachi, Poland 26-39; mem. of exec., Keren Hayesod, Hechalutz Hamizrachi, World Jewish Congress; Deputy Dir. Inst. of Jewish Affairs, New York 43-47; Vice-Pres. Hapoel Hamizrachi, U.S.A. 43-47; Dir. Vaad Leumi Law Dept. 47; mem. Provisional Council, Govt. of Israel 49; mem. of Knesset; Deputy Minister for Religious Affairs 56-59, Minister of Religious Affairs 62-74; Chair. Constitution, Law and Justice Cttee., Knesset; mem. Jewish Law Research Inst., Ministry of Justice 48; Lecturer on Talmudic Law, Hebrew Univ.; mem. American Soc. for Int. Law, Board of Trustees, Bar-Ilan Univ.
Publs. *Starvation over Europe* 43, *Relief and Rehabilitation* 44, *Where Shall They Go?* 46, *Uprooted* 46, *Hazaka in Jewish Law* 64, and many publs. in Hebrew on Israel Law and Religion.
7 Narkis Street, Jerusalem, Israel.

Watanyar, Col. Muhammad Aslam; Afghani politician and army officer.
Supporter of coup which overthrew Pres. Daoud April 78; Deputy Prime Minister and Minister of the Interior April 78-March 79; Minister of Defence March 79-; Chief of Staff of the Army March-April 79.
Ministry of Defence, Kabul, Afghanistan.

Weitz, Raanan, PH.D.; Israeli rural development planner; b. 27 July 1913; ed. Hebrew Gymnasia, Jerusalem Hebrew Univ. and Univ. of Florence.
Agricultural Settlement Dept., Jewish Agency 37-, fmr. Village Instructor, now Head of Dept.; service with Intelligence Corps, British 8th Army, Second World War; fmr. mem. Haganah; mem. Exec., Zionist Org. 63-; Chair. Nat. and Univ. Inst. of Agriculture 60-66; Head, Settlement Study Centre 63-; Prof. of Rural Devt. Planning, Univ. of Haifa 73-78, of Rural Devt. Theory, Bar Ilan Univ. 78-.
Publs. *Agriculture and Rural Development in Israel: Projection and Planning* 63, *Rural Planning in Developing Countries* (Editor) 65, *Agricultural Development—Planning and Implementation* 68, *From Peasant to Farmer: A Revolutionary Strategy for Development* 71, *Rural Development in a Changing World* (Editor) 71, *Urbanization and the Developing Countries, Report on the Sixth Rehovot Conference* (Editor) 73, *Employment and Income Generation in New Settlement Projects* 78.
Zionist Organization, P.O. Box 92, Jerusalem; Home: Moshav Ora, Harei-Yehuda, Marei-Yehuda Mobile P.O., Israel.

Weizman, Ezer; Israeli politician and air force officer (retd.); b. 15 June 1924; ed. Hareali School, Haifa and R.A.F. Staff Coll.
Officer, Israel Air Force 48-66 and fmr. Commanding Officer, I.A.F.; Chief General Staff Branch 66-69; Minister of Transport 69-Aug. 70; Chair. Exec. Cttee. Herut Party 71; Minister of Defence June 77-; Likud.
Ministry of Defence, Jerusalem; 28 Hageffen Street, Ramat, Hasheram, Israel.

West, John Carl, A.B., LL.B.; American lawyer, politician and diplomatist; b. 27 Aug. 1922, Camden, South Carolina; ed. The Citadel, Univ. of South Carolina.
Admitted to S. Carolina Bar 48; partner in West, Holland and Firman (law firm) 48-70; mem. S. Carolina Senate 54-66; Lieut.-Gov. of S. Carolina 66-70, Gov. 70-74; partner in West, Cooper, Bowen and Quinn 75-; Amb. to Saudi Arabia June 77-; mem. American Legion, Kershaw County Chamber of Commerce (Pres. 54); Democrat.
American Embassy, Jeddah, Saudi Arabia; (Postal Address) American Embassy to Saudi Arabia, APO New York 09697, U.S.A.

Wilton, Sir (Arthur) John, K.C.M.G., K.C.V.O., M.C., M.A.; British diplomatist; b. 21 Oct. 1921, London; ed. Wanstead High School and St. John's Coll., Oxford.
Open Scholarship, St. John's Coll. 41; Commissioned Royal Ulster Rifles 42, served with Irish Brigade in N. Africa, Italy and Austria 43-46 (mentioned in Despatches 45); H.M. Diplomatic Service 47-; served Lebanon, Egypt, Gulf Sheikhdoms, Romania, Aden, Yugoslavia; Dir. Middle East Centre for Arab Studies 60-65; Amb. to Kuwait 70-74; Asst. Under-Sec., FCO 74-76; Amb. to Saudi Arabia 76-.
British Embassy in Jeddah, c/o Foreign and Commonwealth Office, London, S.W.1, England.

Winder, Richard Bayly, A.M., PH.D.; American university professor; b. 11 Sept. 1920, Greensboro, North Carolina; ed. Haverford Coll., Princeton Univ.
With American Field Service 42-45, mentioned in despatches (U.K.); mem. Staff, American Univ. Beirut (Lebanon) 47-49; Instructor, Princeton Univ., New Jersey 47, later Assoc. Prof., later Asst. Dean of Coll.; Prof. of History and Near Eastern Languages and Literature, New York Univ. 66-, Chair. Dept. of Near Eastern Languages and Literature, Washington Square Coll. 66-68, Acting Dean of Coll. 68-69, Dean 69-71, Dean of Faculty of Arts and Sciences 70-77, Dir. Center for Near Eastern Studies 66-; Chair. Grants Comm., American Research Center in Egypt 71-, mem. Exec. Comm. and Board of Govs.; mem. Board of Dirs. American Friends of the Middle East; Trustee, American Univ. of Cairo; mem. American History Asscn., Royal Asiatic Soc. (U.K.), Middle East Inst., American Oriental Soc., Royal Central Asian Soc., Middle East Studies Asscn., (Dir. 66-71, Pres. 68-69); decorated with Purple Heart.
Publs. *An Introduction to Modern Arabic* (with F. J. Ziadeh) 57, *The World of Islam; Studies in Honour of Philip K. Hitti* (Ed., with J. Kritzeck) 60, *Current Problems in North Africa* (Ed.) 60, *Saudi Arabia in the Nineteenth Century* 65, *Near Eastern Round Table* 1967–68 (Ed.) 69; also some translations.
Department of Near Eastern Languages, New York University, New York, N.Y. 10003, U.S.A.

Wise, George Schneiweis; American university professor; b. 1906, Poland; ed. Columbia Univ.
Associate Dir. Bureau for Applied Social Research, Columbia Univ. 49-52, Lecturer in Sociology 50-52; Visiting Prof., Univ. of Mexico 56; Chair. Board of Govs. Hebrew Univ. 53-62, Jewish Telegraph Agency 51-55; Pres. Tel-Aviv Univ. 63-71, Chancellor (for life) 71-; Trustee Mount Sinai Medical Center, Miami 77-.
Tel-Aviv University, Ramat-Aviv, Tel-Aviv, Israel; Home: 5401 Collins Avenue, Miami Beach, Fla. 33140, U.S.A.

Y

Yaacobi, Gad, M.SC.; Israeli politician; b. 18 Jan. 1935, Moshav Kfar Vitkin; ed. Tel-Aviv Univ., School of Law and Econs.
Member Moshavim Movt. 60-67; Asst. to Minister of Agriculture, Head of Agriculture and Settlement Planning and Devt. Centre 60-66; mem. Cen. Cttee. Histadrut, Labour Union, Rafi Faction 66-; Chair. Econ. Council Rafi Faction 66-67; mem. Cen. Cttee., Secr. Labour Party; Asst. to Sec.

Labour Party 66-70; mem. Parl. (Knesset) 69-, Parl. Finance Cttee. 69-70, Parl. Defence and Foreign Affairs Cttee. 74, Deputy Minister of Transport 70-74, Minister June 74-June 77; Chair. of Cttee. for Econ. Affairs of the Knesset June 77-.
Publs. *The Quality of Power* 71, *The Freedom to Choose* 75 and many articles on economics and politics.
13 Shirtei Israel Street, Ramat Hasharon, Israel.

Yadin (formerly Sukenik), **Lt.-Gen. Yigael,** M.A., PH.D.; Israeli soldier and archaeologist; b. 21 March 1917, Jerusalem; ed. Hebrew Univ., Jerusalem.
Chief of Gen. Staff Branch, Haganah H.Q. 47; Chief of Operations, Gen. Staff, Israel Defence Forces 48; Chief of Gen. Staff Branch 49, Chief of Staff 49-52; Archæological Research Fellow, Hebrew Univ. 53-54, Lecturer in Archaeology 55-59, Assoc. Prof. 59-63, Prof. 63-; Dir. Excavations at Hazor 55-58, 69, Bar Kochba 60-61, Megiddo 60, 66-67, 70-71, Masada 63-65; Leader Democratic Movt. for Change 76-78, Democratic Movt. 78-; Deputy Prime Minister Oct. 77-; mem. Israel Acad. of Sciences and Humanities; corresp. mem. British and French Acads.
Publs. *The Scroll of the War of the Sons of Light against the Sons of Darkness* 55, *The Message of the Scrolls* 57, *Hazor I: The First Season of Excavations, Hazor II: Second Season, Hazor III-IV: Third Season, A Genesis Apocryphon* (with N. Avigad) 56, *Warfare in Biblical Lands* 63, *Finds in a cave in the Judaean Desert* 63, *Masada: First Season of Excavations* 65, *The Ben-Sirah Scroll from Masada* 65, *Masada: Herod's Fort and the Zealots' Last Stand* 66, *Philacteries from Qumran* 69, *Bar-Kochba* 71, *Hazor* Schweich Lectures) 72, *Hazor* 75, *The Temple Scrolls* 77.
47 Ramban Road, Jerusalem, Israel.

Yadlin, Aharon; Israeli politician; b. 17 April 1926; ed. Hebrew Univ.
Co-founder Kibbutz Hatzerim; fmr. mem. Presidium, Israel Scouts Movement; mem. Knesset (Parl.) 59-; Deputy Minister of Educ. and Culture 64-72; Gen. Sec. Israel Labour Party 72-75; Minister of Educ. and Culture 74-June 77; Chair. Educational and Cultural Cttee. of the Knesset, Beit Berl Coll. of Educ., the Labour Party's centre for educ. of leaders.
Publs. *The Aim and the Movement* (*on Socialism*) 69, articles on sociology, education and youth.
Kibbutz Hatzerim, Mobile Post, Hanegev, Israel.

Yafi, Abdullah Aref al-; Lebanese lawyer and politician; b. 1901; ed. Collège des Pères Jésuites, Beirut, and Univ. de Paris a la Sorbonne.
Admitted to Beirut Bar 26; Prime Minister and Minister of Justice 38-39; Lebanese del. to preparatory conf. for founding League of Arab States 44, to San Francisco Conf. 45; Minister of Justice Dec. 46-April 47; Prime Minister 51-52, 53-54, March-Nov. 56, April-Dec. 66, 68-69, concurrently Minister of the Interior 51-52, 53-54, March-Nov. 56, July-Oct. 68, of Defence 53-54, Feb.-Oct. 68, of Information 53-54, April-Dec. 66, 68-69, of Finance March-Sept. 54, April-Dec. 66, Feb.-July 68, 68-69, of Planning June-Nov. 56, of Social Affairs 68-69, of Education 68-69.
rue Fouad Ier, Beirut, Lebanon.

Yahia, General Tahir; Iraqi army officer and politician; b. 1915; ed. primary school, Tikrit, secondary school, Baghdad, Teachers' Training Coll. and Military Coll.
Former teacher, Mamounia School, Baghdad; mem. Nat. Movement 41; Commdr., Armoured Cars' Battalion, Palestine War 48; mem. Military Court, Habaniya 48; mem. Free Officers' Group 58, later Dir.-Gen. of Police; Chief of Staff, Iraqi Army Feb.-Nov. 63; Prime Minister 63-65; Deputy Prime Minister 67; Prime Minister and acting Minister of the Interior 67-68; Al-Khidma Medal, Al-Chaja Medal, Al-Rafidain Medal.
Baghdad, Iraq.

Yahyawi, Muhammad Saleh; Algerian politician; b. 1932, Barika.
Worked as a teacher before start of Algerian war for nat. independence; joined Maquisards 56; promoted Capt., then Commdt. 62-64; elected to Cen. Cttee. of Nat. Liberation Front (FLN) 64, Revolutionary Council July 65; Regional Mil. Commdr. 65; Head Mil. Acad. at Cherchill 69-77; Exec. Sec. of FLN Oct. 77-.
Front de libération nationale, place Emir Abdelkader, Algiers, Algeria.

Yamani, Sheikh Ahmed Zaki; Saudi Arabian politician; b. 1930, Mecca; ed. Cairo Univ., New York Univ. and Harvard Univ.
Saudi Arabian Govt. service; private law practice; Legal Adviser to Council of Ministers 58-60; Minister of State 60-62; mem. Council of Ministers 60-; Minister of Petroleum and Mineral Resources 62-; Dir. Arabian American Oil Co. 62-; Chair. Board of Dirs. Gen. Petroleum and Mineral Org. (PETROMIN) 63-, Coll. of Petroleum and Minerals, Dhahran 63-; Chair., Board of Dirs. Saudi Arabian Fertilizer Co. (SAFCO) 66-; Sec. Gen. Org. of Arab Petroleum Exporting Countries (OAPEC) 68-69, Chair. 74-75; mem. several int. law asscns.
Publ. *Islamic Law and Contemporary Issues.*
Ministry of Petroleum and Mineral Resources, Riyadh, Saudi Arabia.

Yariv, Maj.-Gen. Aharon; Israeli army officer; b. 1920, Latvia; ed. French Staff Coll.
Emigrated to Palestine 35; Capt. British Army 41-46; Haganah 46-47; various posts with Northern Command, Israel Defence Forces 48-50, Operations Div., H.Q. 51; IDF Officers' Staff Coll. 52-56; Mil. Attaché, Washington and Ottawa 57-60; joined Mil. Intelligence 61, Dir. until 72; Special Adviser to the Prime Minister Oct. 72-73; mem. Knesset 74-77; Minister of Transport March-June 74, of Information June 74-Jan. 75; Head, Center of Strategic Studies, Tel-Aviv Univ.
c/o Tel-Aviv University, Tel-Aviv, Israel.

Yasseen, Mustafa Kamil, D. EN D.; Iraqi international lawyer; b. 1920, Iraq; ed. Univs. of Baghdad, Cairo and Paris.
Member, Baghdad Bar 42; Lecturer in Private Int. and Penal Law 50, Asst. Prof. 54; Prof. and Head, Dept. of Int. Law, Univ. of Baghdad 59; Gen. Dir. Political Dept., Ministry of Foreign Affairs 59, Dept. of Int. Orgs. 64; Amb. and Perm. Rep. to Office of UN, Geneva 66; Gen. Dir. Dept. of Int. Orgs., Ministry of Foreign Affairs 71-; mem. Perm. Court of Arbitration; mem. UN Int. Law Comm. 60-70, Pres. 66; Assoc. Inst. of Int. Law 61, mem. 71; mem. Curatorium, Hague Acad. of Int. Law; Corresp. mem. Acad. of Legislation, Toulouse; Iraqi rep. to several int. confs., to Vienna Conf. on the Law of Treaties 68, 69, Chair. of Drafting Cttee., to Council of UNCTAD 66-69, to Gov. Body, ILO 66-69, to UN Gen. Assemblies 58-, to various UN, ILO confs., etc.; Dr. h.c. (Nice) 70; Grand Cross of Civil Merit (Spain); Grand Officer, Nat. Order of Merit (France); Commdr. Order of the Crown (Morocco).
Publs. various books and articles on int. law.
Ministry of Foreign Affairs, Baghdad, Karradat Mariam, Iraq.

Yassin, Aziz Ahmed, PH.D., D.I.C., B.SC.; Egyptian consulting engineer; b. 13 Aug. 1918; ed. Abbassia Secondary School, Cairo Univ., and Imperial Coll., London.
Ministry of Housing and Public Utilities, rising to Under-Sec. of State 39-59; Dir.-Gen., Vice-Chair. Building Research Centre 54-59, Chair., Pres. Tourah Portland Cement Co., Alexandria Portland Cement Co. 59-63; mem. Board of Dirs. Helwan Portland Cement Co., Sudan Portland Cement Co. 59-63; Chair. Egyptian Cement Cos. Marketing Board 59-63; Chair., Pres. Egyptian Gen. Org. for Housing

and Public Building Contracting Cos. 63-65; Minister of Tourism and Antiquities 65-67, of Housing and Construction 66-68; mem. Board of Aswan High Dam Authority 66-68; External Prof. of Soil Mechanics, Cairo Univ. 51-, of Civil Engineering, Ain Shams Univ.; mem. Building Research and Technology Council, Egyptian Acad. of Science and Technology 72-; Sec.-Gen. Federation of Arab Engineers (FAE) 75; mem. several other scientific civil engineering and building orgs.; Order of the Repub. 1st Class, Order of the Banner (Hungary), Commdr.'s Cross with Star of Order of Resurrection of Poland.
Publs. *Model Studies on the Bearing Capacity of Piles* 51, *Bearing Capacity of Deep Foundations in Clay Soils, Testing Sand Dry Samples with the Tri-axial Apparatus* 53, *Bearing Capacity of Piles* 53, *The Industry of Building Materials in Egypt* 57.
4 Waheeb Doas Street, Maadi, Cairo, Egypt.

Yazdi, Dr. Ibrahim; Iranian politician; b. *c.* 1933.
Studied and worked as physician in U.S.A. for sixteen years; close associate of Ayatollah Khomeini (*q.v.*) during exile in Neauphle-le-Château, France Oct. 78-Feb. 79; Deputy Prime Minister with responsibility for Revolutionary Affairs Feb.-April 79; Minister of Foreign Affairs April 79-.
Ministry of Foreign Affairs, Teheran, Iran.

Yazıcı, Bedi, M.SC.; Turkish business executive; b. 1917; ed. Robert Coll., Columbia Univ.
Fire and Marine Man. Nat. Reinsurance Co. 43-48; Prof. of Insurance, Business School of Istanbul 45-50; Man. Dir. The Credit Bank of Turkey 62-63, Porcelain Industries Inc. of Istanbul 62-63; Pres. The Gen. Insurance Co. of Turkey 48-63, Istanbul Chamber of Commerce 60-63; mem. Insurance Board, Ministry of Commerce 44-64; Chair. and Man. Dir. TAM Insurance Co. 64-74; TAM Life Insurance Co. 66-74; Chair. and Man. Dir. AKSIGORTA Insurance Co. 74-; Deputy Chair. and Man. Dir. DOGAN Insurance Co. 76-; Trustee, Robert Coll. 64-70.
Aksu Han, Karakoy, Istanbul, Turkey.

Yazıcı, Bülent, M.S.; Turkish banker; b. 3 Feb. 1911; ed. Robert Coll., Istanbul, and Columbia Univ.
Ministry of Finance 34-38; Insp. 38-45; Financial Counsellor, Turkish Embassy, Washington 45-49; Dep. Gen. Dir. Dept. of the Treasury 49-50; Dep. Gen. Man. Industrial Development Bank of Turkey 50-60; Dir. and Gen. Man. Türkiye İs Bankası A.S. 60-67; Chair. American-Turkish Foreign Trade Bank 64-67, Union of Chambers of Commerce, Industry and Exchanges of Turkey 60-62; Vice-Chair. Asscn. of Banks of Turkey 60-67; Chair. Industrial Devt. Bank of Turkey 60-69, Man. Dir. 69-71; Dir. Tam Hayat Sigorta A.S. 67-; Advisory Dir. Unilever-İş Ticerat ve Sanayi, Sti 68-; Chair. and Man. Dir. Akbank TAŞ 71-75; Chair. Akcimento A.Ş., Cimsa A.Ş., Turkish Management Educ. Foundation; Commodore, Deniz Klubu.
36 Devriye Sok., Moda, Kadiköy, Istanbul, Turkey.

Yeganeh, Mohammed, M.A.; Iranian economist; b. 5 May 1923; ed. Teheran Univ., Columbia Univ., New York.
Economic Affairs Officer, UN Middle East Studies Section 49-58; UNDP Adviser to Govt. of Tunisia 58-59; Head UN Industrial Section 59-64; Deputy Minister for Econ. Affairs 64-69; Minister of Devt. and Housing 69-70; Special Econ. Adviser to Prime Minister 70-71; Alt. Exec. Dir. for Middle East, Int. Bank for Reconstruction and Devt. 71-72; Exec. Dir. Int. Monetary Fund 72-73; Gov. Cen. Bank of Iran 73-76; Minister of State 76-77, in charge of Budget and Plan 77-78; Minister of Econ. Affairs and Finance 77-78; Chair. OPEC Special Fund Vienna; Homayoun Medal 66, First Degree 77, Devt. Medal 67.
Publs. *Suspension of Penalties* 46, *Foreign Trade and Commercial Policies of Iran* 50, *Investments in the Petroleum Industry of the Middle East* 52, *Perspectives décennales des développements économiques en Tunisie* 60, *Economics of the Middle Eastern Oil* (with Charles Issawa, *q.v.*) 62, *Reflections on the Teheran Oil Agreement* 71, *Possibilities for Co-operation among Developing Countries in Development Utilization of Natural Gas* 71.
c/o Ministry of Economic Affairs and Finance, Teheran, Iran.

Yemen, Former King of the (*see* Saif Al-Islam, Mohamed Al-Badr, H.M. The Imam).

Yetkin, Suut Kemal; Turkish scholar; b. 1903; ed. Univs. of Paris and Rennes.
Asst. Prof. of History of Art and Aesthetics, Univ. of Istanbul 33-36; Dir.-Gen. of Fine Arts, Ministry of Education 39-41; Prof. of History of Art and Aesthetics, Ankara Univ. 41-50, of History of Turkish and Islamic Arts 50-59; Rector Ankara Univ. 59-63; Prof. of Turkish Art, Columbia Univ. 63-64; Officier Légion d'Honneur; Republican Party.
Publs. (in Turkish) *Philosophy of Art* 34, *Courses in Aesthetics* 42, *Literary Doctrines* 43, *Speeches on Literature* 44, *The Art of Leonardo da Vinci* 45, *Art Problems* 45, *On Literature* 53, *Famous Painters* 55, *A. Gide: A Selection of his Critical Writings* 55, *History of Islamic Architecture* 59 (3rd edn. 65), *Problems in Art* 62, *Turkish Architecture* 65, *Currents in Literature* 67, *Essays* 72, *Baroque Art* 74, *Art in Islamic Countries* 74; (in French) *L'Architecture turque en Turquie* 62, *Ancienne Peinture Turque* 70.
Kavaklidere Sok., Güney Apartman 23/5, Ankara, Turkey.

Yoseph, Ovadya; Israeli Rabbi; b. Baghdad, Iraq.
Member, Sephardi Rabbinical Court 45; Chief of Rabbinical Court of Appeals and Deputy Chief Rabbi of Egypt (Cairo) 47; mem. regional Rabbinical Court of Petach Tiqva 51, Jerusalem 58; mem. Grand Court of Appeals, Jerusalem 65; Pres. of Great Metivta, Jerusalem; Pres. "Yeshivat Thora Ve-horaa", Tel-Aviv; mem. Management "Yeshivat Porath" Jerusalem; Pres. Cttee. of Building Fund for Yeshivat "Porath Yoseph" in the Old City; Chief Rabbi and Chief of Rabbinical Court of Tel-Aviv May 68-; Sephardi Chief Rabbi of Israel Oct. 72-; Rabbi Kook Prize, Rabbi Uziel Prize.
Publs. *Yobia Omer*, several vols. of Responsa, *Hazon Ovadia*.
Chief Rabbinate, 51 Hamelech David Boulevard, Tel-Aviv, Israel.

Younes, Mahmoud; Egyptian engineer; b. 3 April 1912; ed. Royal Coll. of Engineers, Cairo Univ. and Staff Officers' Coll.
Engineer 37; M.Sc. 42; with Mil. Operations Directorate 43; Lecturer, Staff Officers' Coll. 44 and 47; Dir. Technical Affairs Office, G.H.Q. 52; Man. Dir. and Chair. Gen. Petroleum Authority 54; Counsellor, Ministry of Commerce and Industry for Mineral Wealth; Man. Dir. and Chair. Suez Canal Authority 56; Chair. 57-65; Pres. Engineers' Syndicate 54-65; Dir. and Chair. Cie. Orientale des Pétroles d'Egypte et Soc. Coopérative des Pétroles 58-65; mem. Nat. Assembly 64-; Deputy Prime Minister for Transport and Communications 65-66; for Electric Power, Oil and Mining 66-67, for Petroleum and Transport 67-68; Consultant, ENI GP 68; now in private consulting office in Beirut; Order of Merit (Class I), Order of the Nile (Class III), Military Star, Liberation Medal, Palestine Medal, Grand Cordon of the Order of the Yugoslav Standard, Grand Officer Order of Vasco Núñez de Balboa (Panama), Repub. Medal (Class III), Mil. Service Medal (Class I), Order of the Repub. (Class I).
P.O. Box 7272, Beirut, Lebanon; and 26 July Street 21, Cairo, Egypt.

Younes Gabir, Brig. Abu-Bakr; Libyan army officer; b. Nov. 1942, Zella; ed. locally, Mil. Coll., Tripoli, English Language Centre, Tripoli.

Promoted Lieut. Aug. 67; participated in coup of Sept. 69 which overthrew King Idris (*q.v.*); mem. Revolution Command Council 69-77, Gen. Secretariat of Gen. People's Congress 77-; Commdr.-in-Chief of Armed Forces.
General Headquarters of the Armed Forces, Tripoli, Libya.

Z

Zadok, Haim; Israeli lawyer and politician; b. 2 Oct. 1913, Poland; ed. Rawa Ruska, Poland, Warsaw Univ. and Jerusalem Law School.
Immigrated 35; took up private practice as lawyer 45; with Haganah and Jewish Settlement Police until 48; Major in Reserve I.D.F., War of Independence; Deputy Attorney-Gen. 49-52; in private law practice 52-65, 67-74, 78-; Lecturer, Tel-Aviv Univ. 53-61; mem. Knesset 59-78; mem. Advisory Council, Bank of Israel; Chair. Income Tax Reform Cttee.; Israel Del. to Council of Europe 61-65; Minister of Commerce and Industry May 65-66, concurrently Minister of Devt. May 65-66; Chair. Knesset Foreign Affairs and Defence Cttee. 70-74, mem. Constitutional, Legal and Judicial Cttee. until 74; Minister of Justice 74-June 77, of Religious Affairs June-Nov. 74 and Jan.-June 77; Lecturer, Hebrew Univ. 78-; Chair. Exec. Cttee. Hebrew Univ., Jerusalem 69-74; Labour Party.
31 Hamitnadev Street, Afeka, Tel-Aviv, Israel.

Zahedi, Ardeshir, B.SC.; Iranian diplomatist; b. 17 Oct. 1928; ed. in Teheran, American Univ. of Beirut and State Univ. of Utah (U.S.A.).
Treasurer, Iran-American Comm. 50-52; Civil Adjutant to H.I.M. Shahanshah Aryamehr 54-; Amb. to U.S.A. 60-62, to U.K. 62-66, to Mexico 73-76, to U.S.A. 73-79; Minister of Foreign Affairs 67-71; Hon. LL.D., (Utah State Univ., Chungang Univ., Seoul, East Texas Univ.) 73, (Kent State Univ.) 74, (St. Louis Univ.) 75; numerous decorations from 24 countries including Crown with Grand Cordon, Order of Taj, First Class 75.
c/o Iranian Embassy, 3005 Massachusetts Avenue, N.W., Washington, D.C. 20008, U.S.A.

Zahir, Abdul; Afghan politician; b. 1909, Lagham; ed. Habibia High School, Kabul and Columbia and Johns Hopkins Univs., U.S.A.
Practised medicine in U.S.A. before returning to Kabul 43; Chief Doctor, Municipal Hospital, Kabul 43-50; Deputy Minister of Health 50-55, Minister 55-58; Amb. to Pakistan 58-61; Chair. House of the People 61-64, 65-69; Deputy Prime Minister and Minister of Health 64-65; Amb. to Italy 69-71; Prime Minister 71-72.
Kabul, Afghanistan.

Zayed bin Sultan al-Nahayan, H.H. Sheikh (*see* Nahayan, H.H. Sheikh Zayed bin Sultan al-).

Zayyat, Mohamed Hassan el-, M.A., D.PHIL.; Egyptian diplomatist; b. 14 Feb. 1915; ed. Cairo and Oxford Univs.
Lecturer and Asst. Prof. Alexandria Univ. 42-50; Cultural Attaché, Egyptian Embassy, Washington, D.C. 50-54, First Sec. and Counsellor 54; Counsellor, Egyptian Embassy, Teheran 55-57, Minister 57; Del. of Egypt on UN Advisory Council for Somaliland 57-60, Special Envoy and Ambassador of U.A.R. in Somaliland 60; Head of Dept. of Arab Affairs and Perm. Del. of U.A.R. to Arab League 60-62; Alt. Perm. Rep. of U.A.R. to UN 62-65; Ambassador to India, concurrently accred. to Nepal 64-66; Under-Sec. of State for Foreign Affairs 65-67; Deputy Minister, Chair. U.A.R. State Information Services and Govt. Spokesman 67-69; Perm. Rep. to UN 69-72; Minister of State for Information 72, of Foreign Affairs 72-73; Adviser to the Pres. 73-75; Contributor to several Arabic newspapers; decorations from Egypt, Somalia, Tunisia, Mauritania, Chad, Lebanon, Iran, Thailand, Belgium, Italy, Poland and Senegal.
1 Midan al Nasr, Almaadi, Cairo, Egypt.

Zeayen, Dr. Yusuf; Syrian politician; b. 1931; ed. Damascus Univ. and osteopathy study in the U.K.
Minister of Agrarian Reform Nov. 63-May 64; Ambassador-designate to U.K. Aug. 64; mem. Syrian Presidential Council 64; mem. Nat. Revolutionary Council 65; Prime Minister Sept.-Dec. 65, 66-68; Baath Party.
c/o The Baath Party, Damascus, Syrian Arab Republic.

Zeevy, Maj.-Gen. Rechavam; Israeli officer and government official; b. 20 June 1926, Jerusalem.
Service in Palmach 44-48; Intelligence Officer 48-49; Operations Officer 49; Battalion Commdr. 50-53; Staff Officer G.H.Q. 53-55; Chief of Staff, Southern Command 55-57; Chief of Org. Dept., G.H.Q. 57-59; U.S. Army Command and Gen. Staff Coll. 59-60; Chief of Staff Cen. Command 60-64; Asst. Chief of Operations, G.H.Q. 64-68; G.C.O. Cen. Command 68-73; Asst. Chief of Staff and Chief of Operations 73-74; Intelligence and Special Matters Adviser to the Prime Minister 74-77.
Publs. several articles on the History of the Holy Land.
Home: Ramat-Hasharon, Israel.

Zekia, Mehmed; Cypriot judge; b. 1903; ed. Univ. of Istanbul and Middle Temple, London.
Member, Legislative Council of Cyprus 30; mem. Advisory Council of Cyprus 33; Chair. Cttee. on Turkish Affairs 48; Advocate 31-40; District Judge 40; Pres. District Court 47; Judge, Supreme Court 52; Judge, High Court of Justice 60; Judge, European Court of Human Rights 61-; Chief Justice of Cyprus 64-66.
European Court of Human Rights, Avenue de l'Europe, 67006 Strasbourg, France.

Ziai, Taher, B.SC., PH.D.; Iranian professor and politician; b. 1917; ed. American Coll. of Teheran, Technische Hochschule, Berlin and Univ. of Vienna.
Professor (Geology and Mining) Teheran Univ. 46-; Dir. Nat. Iranian Oil Co. 47; Under-Sec. Ministry of Nat. Econs. 55; Ministry of Industry and Mines 56; Minister of Industry and Mines 60-61, 62-63; mem. of the Senate 67-79; Pres. Iran Chamber of Commerce, Industries and Mines 67-; Order of Homayoun; Grand Cross of Merit (Fed. Repub. of Germany).
Technical Faculty, University of Teheran, Teheran, Iran.

Ziartides, Andreas; Cypriot trade unionist; b. 1919; ed. Pancyprian Gymnasium, Nicosia.
Trade unionist 37-; mem. Pancyprian Trade Union Cttee. 41, Gen. Sec. 43-47; Gen. Sec. Pancyprian Fed. of Labour 47-; mem. Central Cttee. Cyprus Working People's Progressive Party (AKEL); mem. House of Reps. Cyprus 60-; mem. Exec. Cttee. World Fed. of Trade Unions (WFTU).
Pancyprian Federation of Labour, 31-35 Archemou Street, Nicosia, Cyprus.

Ziv-Av, Itzhak; Israeli administrative official; b. 4 June 1907; ed. Inst. of Pedagogy, Smolensk.
Farmer, Magdiel, Sharon Valley, Palestine 26-; Man. Editor *Haboker* 35-48; Dir. Public Relations Div., Ministry of Defence and Gen. H.Q., Israel Defence Forces 48-52; Dir.-Gen. Israel Farmers' Fed. 52-75, Chair. Cen. Cttee. 75-; mem. Exec. Cttee. Int. Fed. of Agricultural Producers (IFAP) 75-; Chair. Exec. Cttee., Co-ordinating Bureau, Israeli Econ. Orgs. 67-; Chair. Land Developing Authority 76-; Editor *Farmers of Israel* (monthly) 62-; mem. Board of Dirs. Jewish Nat. Fund; mem. Council, State Land Authority.
Publs. *The Unknown Land, I seek my Brethren, The Price of Freedom, Forever Ours, From Frontier to Frontier, A*

World to Live In, *Another World*, and poetry for children.
Israel Farmers' Federation, P.O. Box 209, Tel-Aviv; Home: Narkissiun Avenue 20, Ramat-Gan, Israel.

Zukerman, Pinchas; Israeli violinist; b. 16 July 1948, Israeli; ed. Israel Conservatory, Acad. of Music, Tel-Aviv, Juilliard School of Music, New York.
Studied with Ivan Galamian; debut in New York with New York Philharmonic 69, in U.K. at Brighton Festival 69; concert and recital performances throughout U.S.A. and Europe; directs, tours and plays with English Chamber Orchestra; has performed at Spoleto, Pablo Casals and Edinburgh Festivals; Leventritt Award 67.
c/o Harold Holt Ltd., 134 Wigmore Street, London, W1H 0DJ, England.

Zurayk, Constantine Kaysar, M.A., PH.D.; Lebanese educationist; b. 18 April 1909; ed. American Univ. of Beirut, Univ. of Chicago and Princeton Univ.
Assistant Prof. of History, American Univ. of Beirut 30-42, Assoc. Prof. 42-45; First Counsellor, Syrian Legation, Washington 45-46; Syrian Minister to U.S.A. 46-47; Vice-Pres. and Prof. of History, American Univ. of Beirut 47-49; Rector, Syrian Univ. Damascus 49-52; Vice-Pres. American Univ. of Beirut 52-54, Acting Pres. 54-57; Distinguished Prof. of History, American Univ. of Beirut 56-; mem. Syrian Del. to UN Gen. Assembly and Alternate Rep. of Syria on Security Council 46-47; mem. Exec. Board UNESCO 50-54; Pres. Int. Asscn. of Univs. 65-70, Hon. Pres. 70-; mem. Int. Comm. for Scientific and Cultural History of Mankind; Corresp. mem. Iraq Acad., Arab Acad., Damascus; Hon. mem. American Historical Asscn.; Chair. Inst. for Palestine Studies 65-; Order of Merit, Distinguished Class (Syria), Educ. Medal, First Class (Lebanon); Commdr. Order of the Cedar (Lebanon).
Publs. *Al-Wa'y al Qawmi* (National Consciousness); *Ma'na al-Nakbah* (The Meaning of the Disaster); *Ayyu Ghadin* (Whither Tomorrow); *Nahnu wa-al-Tarikh* (Facing History); *Hadha al-'Asr al-Mutafajjir* (This Explosive Age); *Fi Ma'rakat al-Hadarah* (In the Battle for Culture); *Ma'na al-Nakbah Mujaddadan* (The Meaning of the Disaster Again), *More than Conquerors;* Editor, Ismai'l Beg Chol's *Al-Yazidiyyah qadiman wa hadithan* (Yazidis past and present), *Ibn al-Furat's History* Vols. VII-IX (partly with Najla Izzeddin); Editor and translator Miskawayh's *Tahdhib al-Akhlaq* (The Refinement of Character).
American University of Beirut, Beirut, Lebanon.

Calendars, Time Reckoning and Weights and Measures

Muslim Calendar

The Muslim era dates from July 16th, A.D. 622, which was the beginning of the Arab year in which the *Hijra*, Muhammad's flight from Mecca to Medina, took place. The Muslim or Hijra Calendar is lunar, each year having 354 or 355 days, the extra day being intercalated eleven times every thirty years. Accordingly the beginning of the Hijra year occurs earlier in the Gregorian Calendar by a few days each year. The Muslim year 1400 A.H. begins on November 21st, 1979.

The year is divided into the following months:

1. Muharram	30 days	7. Rajab	30 days
2. Safar	29 ,,	8. Shaaban	29 ,,
3. Rabia I	30 ,,	9. Ramadan	30 ,,
4. Rabia II	29 ,,	10. Shawwal	29 ,,
5. Jumada I	30 ,,	11. Dhu'l-Qa'da	30 ,,
6. Jumada II	29 ,,	12. Dhu'l-Hijja	29 or 30 days

The Hijra Calendar is used for religious purposes throughout the Islamic world and is the official calendar in Saudi Arabia and the Yemen. In most Arab countries it is used side by side with the Gregorian Calendar for official purposes, but in Turkey and Egypt the Gregorian Calendar has replaced it.

PRINCIPAL MUSLIM FESTIVALS

New Year: 1st Muharram. The first ten days of the year are regarded as holy, especially the tenth.

Ashoura: 10th Muharram. Celebrates the first meeting of Adam and Eve after leaving Paradise, also the ending of the Flood and the death of Husain, grandson of Muhammad. The feast is celebrated with fairs and processions.

Mouloud (*Birth of Muhammad*): 12th Rabia I.

Leilat al Meiraj (*Ascension of Muhammad*): 27th Rajab.

Ramadan (*Month of Fasting*).

Id ul Fitr or **Id ul Saghir** or **Küçük Bayram** (*The Small Feast*): Three days beginning 1st Shawwal. This celebration follows the constraint of the Ramadan fast.

Id ul Adha or **Id al Kabir** or **Büyük Bayram** (*The Great Feast, Feast of the Sacrifice*): Four days beginning on 10th Dhu'l-Hijja. The principal Muslim festival, commemorating Abraham's sacrifice and coinciding with the pilgrimage to Mecca. Celebrated by the sacrifice of a sheep, by feasting and by donations to the poor.

Hijra Year	1398		1399		1400	
New Year	Dec. 12th,	1977	Dec. 2nd,	1978	Nov. 21st,	1979
Ashoura	Dec. 21st,	,,	Dec. 11th,	,,	Nov. 30th	,,
Mouloud	Feb. 20th,	1978	Feb. 10th,	1979	Jan. 30th,	1980
Leilat al Meiraj	July 3rd,	,,	June 23rd,	,,	June 11th,	,,
Ramadan begins	Aug. 5th,	,,	July 26th,	,,	July 14th,	,,
Id ul Fitr	Sept. 4th,	,,	Aug. 25th,	,,	Aug. 13th,	,,
Id ul Adha	Nov. 11th,	,,	Nov. 1st,	,,	Oct. 20th,	,,

Note: Local determinations may vary by one day from those given here.

Iranian Calendar

The Iranian Calendar, introduced in 1925, was based on the Hijra Calendar, adapted to the solar year. Iranian New Year (*Nowruz*) occurs at the vernal equinox, which usually falls on March 21st Gregorian. In Iran it was decided to base the calendar on the coronation of Cyrus the Great, in place of the Hijra, from 1976, and the year beginning March 21st, 1976, became 2535. During 1978, however, it was decided to revert to the Hijra Calendar, and the year 1358 began on March 21st, 1979.

The Iranian year is divided into the following months:

1. Favardine	31 days	7. Mehr	30 days
2. Ordibehecht	31 ,,	8. Aban	30 ,,
3. Khordad	31 ,,	9. Azar	30 ,,
4. Tir	31 ,,	10. Dey	30 ,,
5. Mordad	31 ,,	11. Bahman	30 ,,
6. Chariver	31 ,,	12. Esfand	29 or 30 days

The Iranian Calendar is used for all purposes in Iran and Afghanistan, except the determining of Islamic religious festivals, for which the lunar Hijra Calendar is used.

Hebrew Calendar

The Hebrew Calendar is solar with respect to the year, but lunar with respect to the months. The normal year has 353–355 days in twelve lunar months, but seven times in each nineteen years an extra month of 30 days (*Adar II*) is intercalated after the normal month of Adar to adjust the calendar to the solar year. New Year (*Rosh Hashanah*) usually falls in September of the Gregorian Calendar, but the day varies considerably. The year 5739 began on October 2nd, 1978, and 5740 starts on September 22nd, 1979.

The months are as follows:

1. Tishri	30 days	7. Nisan	30 days
2. Marcheshvan	29 or 30 days	8. Iyyar	29 ,,
3. Kislev	29 or 30 ,,	9. Sivan	30 ,,
4. Tebeth	29 days	10. Tammuz	29 ,,
5. Shebat	30 ,,	11. Ab	30 ,,
6. Adar	29 ,,	12. Ellul	29 ,,
(Adar II)	30 ,,		

The Hebrew Calendar is used to determine the dates of Jewish religious festivals only.

Standard Time

The table shows zones of standard time, relative to Greenwich Mean Time (G.M.T.). Many of the individual countries adopt daylight saving time at certain times of year.

Traditional Arabic time is still widely used by the local population in Saudi Arabia except in most of the Eastern Province. This system is based upon the local time of sunset when timepieces are all set to 12.

G.M.T.	1 Hour Ahead	2 Hours Ahead	3 Hours Ahead	3½ Hours Ahead	4 Hours Ahead	4½ Hours Ahead
Algeria Morocco Spanish North Africa	Tunisia	Cyprus Egypt Israel Jordan Lebanon Libya Sudan Syria Turkey	Bahrain Iraq Kuwait Yemen, P.D.R.	Iran	Oman Qatar United Arab Emirates	Afghanistan

Note: Saudi Arabia and the Yemen Arab Republic use solar time.

Weights and Measures

Principal weights and units of measurement in common use as alternatives to the Metric and Imperial systems

WEIGHT

Unit	Country	Metric Equivalent	Imperial Equivalent
Charak	Afghanistan	1·764 kilos.	3·89 lb.
Hogga	Iraq	1·27 kilos.	2·8 lb.
Kharwar	Afghanistan	564·528 kilos.	1,246·2 lb.
Khord	Afghanistan	110·28 grammes	3.89 oz.
Maund	Yemen, P.D.R. Saudi Arabia	37·29 kilos.	82·28 lb.
Qintar (Kantar) or Buhar	Cyprus	228·614 kilos.	504 lb.
	Egypt	44·928 kilos.	99·05 lb.
Ratl or Rotl	Saudi Arabia Egypt	0·449 kilo.	0·99 lb.
Seer	Afghanistan	7·058 kilos.	15·58 lb.
Uqqa or Oke	Cyprus	1·27 kilos.	2·8 lb.
	Egypt	1·245 kilos.	2·751 lb.
Yeni Okka	Turkey	1 kilo.	2·205 lb.

LENGTH

Unit	Country	Metric Equivalent	Imperial Equivalent
Busa	Saudi Arabia Sudan	2·54 cm.	1 in.
Dirraa, Dra or Pic	Cyprus	60·96 cm.	2 ft.
Gereh-gaz-sha	Afghanistan	6·6 cm.	2·6 in.
Kadam or Qadam	Sudan	30·48 cm.	1 ft.

CAPACITY

Unit	Country	Metric Equivalent	Imperial Equivalent
Ardabb or Ardeb	Saudi Arabia, Sudan, Egypt	198·024 litres	43·56 gallons
Kadah	Sudan, Egypt	2·063 litres	3·63 pints
Keila	Cyprus	36·368 litres	8 gallons
	Sudan, Egypt	16·502 litres	3·63 gallons
Ratel	Sudan	0·568 litre	1 pint

AREA

Unit	Country	Metric Equivalent	Imperial Equivalent
Donum or Dunum	Cyprus	1,335·8 sq. metres	0·33 acre
	Iraq	2,500 sq. metres	0·62 acre
	Israel, Jordan	1,000 sq. metres	0·2471 acre
	Syria, Turkey	919·04 sq. metres	0·2272 acre
Feddan	Saudi Arabia, Sudan, Egypt	4,201 sq. metres	1·038 acres
Yeni Donum	Turkey	10,000 sq. metres (1 hectare)	2·471 acres

METRIC TO IMPERIAL CONVERSIONS

Metric Units	Imperial Units	To Convert Metric into Imperial Units Multiply by:	To Convert Imperial into Metric Units Multiply by:
Weight			
Gramme	Ounce (Avoirdupois)	0·035274	28·3495
Kilogramme (kg.)	Pound (lb.)	2·204622	0·453592
Metric ton ('000 kg.)	Short ton (2,000 lb.)	1·102311	0·907185
	Long ton (2,240 lb.)	0·984207	1·016047
	(The short ton is in general use in the U.S.A., while the long ton is normally used in Britain and the Commonwealth.)		
Length			
Centimetre	Inch	0·3937008	2·54
Metre	Yard (=3 feet)	1·09361	0·9144
Kilometre	Mile	0·62137	1·609344
Volume			
Cubic metre	Cubic foot	35.315	0.0283
	Cubic yard	1.30795	0.764555
Capacity			
Litre	Gallon (=8 pints)	0·219969	4·54609
	Gallon (U.S.)	0·264172	3·78541
Area			
Square metre	Square yard	1·19599	0·836127
Hectare	Acre	2·47105	0·404686
Square kilometre	Square mile	0·386102	2·589988

SELECT BIBLIOGRAPHIES

BOOKS ON THE MIDDLE EAST

(See also Bibliographies at end of Chapters in Part II)

ABDEL MALEK, A. La Pensée Politique Arab Contemporaine (Editions du Seuil, Paris, 1970).

ABIR, MORDECHAI. Oil, Power and Politics: Conflict in Arabia, The Red Sea and The Gulf (Frank Cass, London, 1974).

ABU JABER, KAMEL S. The Arab Baath Socialist Party (Syracuse University Press, New York, 1966).

ABU-LUGHOD, IBRAHIM (ed.). The Transformation of Palestine: Essays on the Development of the Arab-Israeli Conflict (Northwestern University Press, Evanston, Ill., 1971).

ADAMS, MICHAEL (ed.). The Middle East: A Handbook (Anthony Blond, London, 1971).

ADAMS, MICHAEL and MAYHEW, CHRISTOPHER. Publish it Not . . . the Middle East Cover-up (Longman, London, 1975).

AFIFI, MUHAMMAD. The Arabs and the United Nations (Longmans, London, 1964).

ALDERSON, A. D. The Structure of the Ottoman Dynasty (New York, Oxford University Press, 1956).

ALLEN, RICHARD. Imperialism and Nationalism in the Fertile Crescent: Sources and Prospects of the Arab-Israeli Conflict (Oxford University Press, London, 1975).

ANTONIUS, GEORGE. The Arab Awakening. 4th edition (Beirut, 1961).

ARBERRY, A. J. (ed.). Religion in the Middle East—Volume I Judaism and Christianity, Volume II Islam and General Summary (Cambridge University Press, 1969).

ASHTOR, E. A Social and Economic History of the Near East in the Middle Ages (Collins, London, 1976).

ASKARI, HOSSEIN, and CUMMINGS, JOHN THOMAS. Middle East Economies in the 1970s (Praeger, New York, 1976).

ASTOR, DAVID, AND YORKE, VALERIE. Peace in the Middle East: Superpowers and Security Guarantees (Transworld Publishers—Corgi Books, 1978).

ATIYAH, EDWARD. The Arabs (Baltimore, 1955).

ATLAS OF THE ARAB WORLD AND THE MIDDLE EAST (Macmillan, London, 1960).

BASTER, JAMES. The Introduction of Western Economic Institutions into the Middle East (Royal Inst. of Int. Affairs and O.U.P., 1960).

BAER, GABRIEL. Population and Society in the Arab East (Routledge, London, 1964).

BE'ERI, ELIEZER. Army Officers in Arab Politics and Society (Pall Mall Press, London, 1969).

BELL, J. BOWYER. The Long War, Israel and the Arabs since 1946 (Englewood Cliffs, 1969).

BERQUE, JACQUES and CHARNAY, J.-P. Normes et Valeurs dans l'Islam Contemporaine (Payot, Paris, 1966).

BETHELL, NICHOLAS. The Palestine Triangle (André Deutsch, London, 1979).

BETHMANN, ERICH W. A Selected Basic Bibliography on the Middle East (American Friends of the Middle East, Washington, 1964).

BIDWELL'S GUIDES TO GOVERNMENT MINISTERS, Vol. II, The Arab World 1900-1972. Compiled and edited by Robin Bidwell (Frank Cass, London, 1973).

BINDER, LEONARD. The Ideological Revolution in the Middle East (New York, 1964).

BIROT, P. & DRESCH, J. La Méditerranée et le Moyen Orient, Vol. II (Paris, 1955).

BROCKELMANN, C. History of the Islamic Peoples (New York and London, 1947–48).

BULL, General ODD. War and Peace in the Middle East: the Experience and Views of a UN Observer (London, Leo Cooper, 1976).

BULLARD, Sir R. Britain and the Middle East from the earliest times to 1952 (London, 1952).

BULLOCH, JOHN. The Making of a War: The Middle East from 1967–1973 (Longman, London, 1974).

CARRÉ, OLIVIER. L'Idéologie Palestinienne de Résistance (Armand Colin, Paris, 1972).

CARRÈRE D'ENCAUSSE, HÉLÈNE. La Politique Soviétique au Moyen-Orient, 1955–1975 (Presses de la Fondation Nationale des Sciences Politiques, Paris, 1976).

CATTAN, HENRY. Palestine and International Law: The Legal aspects of the Arab-Israeli Conflict (Longman, London, 1973).

CATTAN, J. Evolution of Oil Concessions in the Middle East and North Africa (Oceana, Dobbs Ferry, New York, 1967).

CHOMSKY, NOAM. Peace in the Middle East?: Reflections on Justice and Nationhood (Collins, 1976).

CLARKE, JOHN I. and FISHER, W. B. (Ed.). Populations of the Middle East and North Africa (University of London Press, 1972).

COOK, M. A. (ed.). Studies in the Economic History of the Middle East (Oxford University Press, 1970).

COOLEY, JOHN K. Green March, Black September: The Story of the Palestinian Arabs (Frank Cass, London, 1973).

COON, C. S. Caravan: the Story of the Middle East (New York, 1951, and London, 1952).
The Impact of the West on Social Institutions (New York, 1952).

COPELAND, MILES. The Game of Nations (Weidenfeld and Nicolson, London, 1969).

COSTELLO, V. F. Urbanisation in the Middle East (Cambridge University Press, 1977).

CRAGG, K. A. Counsels in Contemporary Islam (Edinburgh, 1964).

DANIEL, NORMAN. Islam and the West (Edinburgh University Press, revised edition 1963).
Islam, Europe and Empire (Edinburgh University Press, 1964).

DE VORE, RONALD M. (ed.). The Arab-Israeli Conflict: A Historical, Political, Social and Military Bibliography (Clio Press, Oxford, 1977).

DUPUY, TREVOR N. Elusive Victory: The Arab-Israeli Wars 1947-1974 (MacDonald and Jane's, London, 1979).

EL-GHONEMY, MOHAMMED RIAD (ed.). Land Policy in the Near East (Rome, 1967).

ENCYCLOPAEDIA OF ISLAM, THE. 4 vols. and supplement (Leiden, 1913–38).

EL-ERIAN, TAHANY. References dealing with the Arab World: A selected and annotated list (Org. of Arab Students in the U.S.A. and Canada, New York, 1966).

ETTINGHAUSEN, RICHARD. Books and Periodicals in Western Languages dealing with the Near and Middle East (Washington, Middle East Institute, 1952).

FARIS, N. A. (ed.). The Arab Heritage (Princeton, N.J., Princeton University Press, 1944).

FIELD, HENRY. Bibliography on Southwestern Asia: VII, A Seventh Compilation (University of Miami, 1962).

FIELD, MICHAEL. $100,000,000 a Day—Inside the World of Middle East Money (Sidgwick and Jackson, London, 1975).

FISHER, S. N. Social Forces in the Middle East (Cornell University Press, Ithaca, N.Y., 3rd edition, 1977).
The Middle East: A History (Alfred Knopf, New York, revised edition, 1978).

FISHER, W. B. The Middle East—a Physical, Social and Regional Geography (London, 7th edition, 1978).

FRYE, R. N. (ed.). The Near East and the Great Powers (Harvard University Press, Cambridge, Mass., 1951, and Oxford University Press, London, New York, and Toronto, 1952).

GIBB, H. A. R. Mohammedanism (London, 1949).
Modern Trends in Islam (Chicago, 1947).
Studies on the Civilisation of Islam (London, 1962).

GIBB, H. A. R., and BOWEN, HAROLD. Islamic Society and the West (2 vols., London, 1950, 1957).

GILBERT, MARTIN. The Arab-Israeli Conflict: Its History in Maps (Weidenfeld and Nicolson, London, 1974).

GLUBB, Lt.-Gen. Sir JOHN. A Short History of the Arab Peoples (Hodder and Stoughton, London, 1969).

GOLAN, GALIA. The Soviet Union and the Middle East Crisis (Cambridge University Press, 1977).

GOMAA, AHMED M. The Foundation of the League of Arab States (Longman, London, 1977).

GRANT, D. (ed.). The Islamic Near East (University of Toronto Press, 1960).

GRUNDWALD, K., and RONALL, J. O. Industrialisation in the Middle East (Council for Middle East Affairs, New York, 1960).

GRUNEBAUM, GUSTAVE E. VON (ed.). Unity and Variety in Muslim Civilisation (Chicago, 1955).
Islam: Essays on the Nature and Growth of a Cultural Tradition (London, Routledge and Kegan Paul, 1961).
Modern Islam: the Search for Cultural Identity (London, 1962).

HALPERN, MANFRED. The Politics of Social Change in the Middle East and North Africa (Princeton University Press, N.Y., 1963).

HARTSHORN, J. E. Oil Companies and Governments (Faber, London, 1962).

HATEM, M. ABDEL-KADER. Information and the Arab Cause (Longman, London, 1974).

HAYES, J. R. (Editor). The Genius of Arab Civilisation (London, Phaidon, 1976).

HAZARD. Atlas of Islamic History (Oxford University Press, 1951).

HERSHLAG, Z. Y. Introduction to the Modern Economic History of the Middle East (E. J. Brill, Leiden, 1964).

HERZOG, Maj.-Gen. CHAIM. The War of Atonement (London, Weidenfeld and Nicolson, 1975).

HIGGINS, ROSALYN. United Nations Peacekeeping 1946–67: Documents and Commentary, Volume I The Middle East (Oxford University Press, 1969).

HIRST, DAVID. Oil and Public Opinion in the Middle East (Praeger, New York, 1966).
The Gun and the Olive Branch: the Roots of Violence in the Middle East (Faber, London, 1977).

HIRSZOWICZ, LUKASZ. The Third Reich and the Arab East (Routledge and Kegan Paul, London, 1966).

HITTI, PHILIP K. History of the Arabs (London, 1940, 10th edn., 1970).
A Short History of the Near East (New York, 1966).
Makers of Arab History (Macmillan, London, 1968).
Islam. A Way of Life (Oxford University Press, London, 1971).

HOARE, IAN, and TAYAR, GRAHAM (eds.). The Arabs. A handbook on the politics and economics of the contemporary Arab world (B.B.C. Publications, London, 1971).

HODGKIN, E. C. The Arabs (Modern World Series, Oxford University Press, 1966).

HOLT, P. M. Studies in the History of the Near East (Cass, London, 1973).

HOLT, P. M., LAMBTON, A. K. S., LEWIS, B. (eds.). The Cambridge History of Islam. Vol. I The Central Islamic Lands (Cambridge University Press, 1970); Vol. II The Further Islamic Lands, Islamic Society and Civilization (Cambridge University Press, 1971).

HOURANI, A. H. Minorities in the Arab World (London, 1947).
A Vision of History (Beirut, 1961).
Arabic Thought in the Liberal Age 1798-1939 (Oxford Univ. Press, 1962).

HUDSON, MICHAEL C. Arab Politics: The Search for Legitimacy (Yale University Press, New Haven and London, 1977/78).

HUREWITZ, J. C. Unity and Disunity in the Middle East (New York, Carnegie Endowment for International Peace, 1952).
Middle East Dilemmas (New York, 1953).
Diplomacy in the Near and Middle East (Vol. I, 1535-1914; Vol. II, 1914-56; Van Nostrand, 1956).
Soviet-American Rivalry in the Middle East (ed.) (Pall Mall Press, London, and Praeger, New York, 1969).
Middle East Politics: The Military Dimension (Pall Mall Press, London, 1969).

AL-HUSAY, KHALDUN S. Three Reformers; A Study in Modern Arab Political Thought (Khayats, Beirut, 1966).

HUSSEIN, MAHMOUD. Les Arabes au présent (Seuil, Paris, 1974).

INSIGHT ON THE MIDDLE EAST WAR (André Deutsch, London, 1974) (*Sunday Times* team of writers).

IONIDES, MICHAEL. Divide and Lose: the Arab Revolt 1955-58 (Bles, London, 1960).

INTERNATIONAL INSTITUTE FOR STRATEGIC STUDIES. Sources of Conflict in the Middle East (Adelphi Papers, International Institute for Strategic Studies, London, 1966).

IRWIN, I. J. Islam in the Modern National State (Cambridge University Press, Cambridge, 1965).

ISSAWI, CHARLES (ed.). The Economic History of the Middle East, 1800–1914 (University of Chicago Press, 1966).

Issawi, Charles and Yeganeh, Mohammed. The Economics of Middle Eastern Oil (Faber, London, 1963).

Janin, R. Les Eglises orientales et les Rites orientaux (Paris, 1926).

Jansen, G. H. Non-Alignment and the Afro-Asian States (Praeger, New York, 1966).

Jones, David. The Arab World (Hilary House, New York, 1967).

Karpat, Kemal H. Political and Social Thought in the Contemporary Middle East (Pall Mall Press, London, 1968).

Kedourie, Elie. England and the Middle East (London 1956).
The Chatham House Version and other Middle-Eastern Studies (Weidenfeld and Nicolson, London, 1970).
Arabic Political Memoirs and Other Studies (Frank Cass, London, 1974).
In the Anglo-Arab Labyrinth, 1976.

Kelly, J. B. Eastern Arabian Frontiers (Faber, London, 1963).

Kerr, Malcolm. The Arab Cold War 1958–1964 (Oxford University Press, 1965).

Khadouri, M. Political Trends in the Arab World (Johns Hopkins Press, Baltimore, 1970).

Khadouri, M. & Lievesny, H. J. (ed.). Law in the Middle East, Vol. I (Washington, 1955).

Khalil, Muhammad. The Arab States and the Arab League (historical documents) (Khayat's, Beirut).

Khayat, M. K. and Keatinge, M. C. Food from the Arab World (Beirut, 1959).

Khouri, Fred J. The Arab-Israeli Dilemma (Syracuse/New York, 1968).

Kingsbury, R. C. and Pounds, N. J. G. An Atlas of Middle Eastern Affairs (New York, 1963).

Kirk, George E. The Middle East in the War (London, 1953).
A Short History of the Middle East: from the Rise of Islam to Modern Times (New York, 1955).
Contemporary Arab Politics (Methuen, London, 1961).

Kumar, Ravinder. India and the Persian Gulf Region (London, 1965).

Kurzman, Dan. Genesis 1948: The First Arab/Israeli War (Vallentine, Mitchell, London, 1972).

Lahbabi, Mohamed Aziz. Le Personnalisme Musulmane (Presses Universitaires de France, Paris, 1964).

Lall, Arthur. The UN and the Middle East Crisis (New York/London, 1968).

Landen, R. G. (ed.). The Emergence of the Modern Middle East: Selected Readings (Van Nostrand Reinhold, New York, 1970).

Laqueur, W. Z. Communism and Nationalism in the Middle East (London and New York, 1957).
A History of Zionism (Weidenfeld and Nicolson, London, 1972).
The Struggle for the Middle East: The Soviet Union and the Middle East 1958-68 (Routledge and Kegan Paul, London, 1969).
Confrontation: The Middle-East War and World Politics (Wildwood, London, 1974).
(ed.) The Middle East in Transition (Routledge and Kegan Paul, London, 1958).
(ed.) The Israel-Arab Reader (New York/Toronto/London, 1969).

Lawrence, T. E. The Seven Pillars of Wisdom (London, 1935).

Leiden, Carl (ed.). The conflict of traditionalism and modernism in the Muslim Middle East (Austin, Texas, 1969).

Lenczowski, George. The Middle East in World Affairs (Ithaca, N.Y., Cornell University Press, 1956).
Oil and State in the Middle East (Cornell Univ. Press, 1960).

Lerner, D. The Passing of Traditional Society: Modernising the Middle East (Glencoe, Illinois, 1958).

Lewis, B. The Arabs in History (London, 1950 and 1954).
The Middle East and the West (London, 1964).
Race and Colour in Islam (London, 1971).
Islam in History (London, 1973).
Islam to 1453 (London, 1974).

Lloyd, Selwyn. Suez 1956: A Personal Account (Jonathan Cape, London, 1978).

Longrigg, S. H. Oil in the Middle East (London, 1954, 3rd edn., London, 1968).
The Middle East: a Social Geography (London, 2nd rev. edn., 1970).

Macdonald, Robert W. The League of Arab States (Princeton University Press, Princeton, 1965).

Mannin, Ethel. A Lance for the Arabs (London, 1963).

Mansfield, Peter. The Ottoman Empire and Its Successors (Macmillan, London, 1973).
(ed.). The Middle East: A Political and Economic Survey, 4th edition (Oxford U.P., London, 1972).
The Arabs (London, Allen Lane, 1976).

Mason, Herbert (ed.). Reflections on the Middle East Crisis (Paris/The Hague, 1970).

Michaelis, Alfred. Wirtschaftliche Entwicklungsprobleme des Mittleren Ostens (Kiel, 1960).

Mikdashi, Zuhayr. The Community of Oil Exporting Countries (George Allen and Unwin, London, 1972).

Miquel, André. Islam et sa civilisation (Paris, 1968).

Monroe, Elizabeth. Britain's Moment in the Middle East (Chatto and Windus, London, 1963).

Moore, John Morton. The Arab-Israeli Conflict (3 vols. Readings and Documents, Princeton, 1976).

Mosley, Leonard. Power Play: The Tumultous World of Middle East Oil 1890–1973 (Weidenfeld and Nicolson, London, 1973).

Nasr, Seyyed Hossein. Science and Civilization in Islam (Harvard, 1968).

Nevakivi, Jukka. Britain, France and the Arab Middle East 1914–20 (Athlone Press, University of London, 1969).

Nutting, Anthony. The Arabs (Hollis and Carter, London, 1965).
No End of a Lesson, The Story of Suez (Constable, London, 1967).

O'Ballance, Edgar. The Third Arab-Israeli War (Faber and Faber, London, 1972).

Oxford Regional Economic Atlas. The Middle East and North Africa (Oxford University Press, 1960).

Partner, Peter. The Arab World (Pall Mall, London, 1962).

Pearson, J. D. (ed.). Index Islamicus (Cambridge, 1967).

Pennar, Jaan. The U.S.S.R. and the Arabs: The Ideological Dimension (Hurst, London, 1973).

Playfair, Ian S. O. The Mediterranean and the Middle East (History of the Second World War, H.M.S.O., London, 1966).

POLIAK, A. N. Feudalism in Egypt, Syria, Palestine, and the Lebanon, 1250–1900 (London, Luzac, for the Royal Asiatic Society, 1939).

POLK, W. R. The United States and the Arab World (Harvard University Press, 1965, rev. edn. 1970).
(ed. with CHAMBERS, R. L.) Beginnings of Modernization in the Middle East: the Nineteenth Century (University of Chicago Press, 1969).

PORATH, Y. The Emergence of the Palestinian Arab National Movement 1918–1929 (Frank Cass, London, 1974).

PROCTOR, J. HARRIS (ed.). Islam and International Relations (Pall Mall Press, London, 1965).

QUBAIN, FAHIM I. Education and Science in the Arab World (Johns Hopkins Press, Baltimore, 1967).

RIVLIN, B., and SZYLIOWICZ, J. S. (eds.). The Contemporary Middle East—Tradition and Innovation (Random House, New York, 1965).

RODINSON, MAXIME. Islam and Capitalism (France, 1965, England 1974).

RO'I, YA'ACOV. The Limits of Power: Soviet Policy in the Middle East (Croom Helm, London, 1978).

RONART, STEPHAN and NANDY. Concise Encyclopaedia of Arabic Civilization (Amsterdam, 1966).

RONDOT, PIERRE. The Destiny of the Middle East (Chatto & Windus, London, 1960).
L'Islam (Prismes, Paris, 1965).

ROUHANI, FUAD. A History of OPEC (Pall Mall Press, London, 1972).

SACHAR, HOWARD M. Europe Leaves the Middle East 1936–1954 (Allen Lane, London, 1973).

SAUVAGET, J. Introduction à l'histoire de l'orient musulman (Paris, 1943) (2nd edn. re-cast by C. CAHEN, Univ of Calif. Press, 1965).

SAVORY, R. M. Introduction to Islamic Civilization (Cambridge University Press, 1976).

SAYIGH, YUSIF. The Determinants of Arab Economic Development (Croom Helm, London, 1977).

SEARIGHT, SARAH. The British in the Middle East (Weidenfeld and Nicolson, London, 1969).

SEGESVARY, VICTOR. Le Réalisme Khrouchtchévien: La politique soviétique au Proche-Orient (Editions de la Baconnière, Neuchâtel, Switzerland, 1968).

SHABAN, M. A. The Abbasid Revolution (Cambridge University Press, 1970).
Islamic History A.D. 600–750 (A.H. 132) A New Interpretation (Cambridge University Press, 1971).

SHARABI, H. B. Governments and Politics of the Middle East in the Twentieth Century (Van Nostrand, New York, 1962).
Nationalism and Revolution in the Arab World (Van Nostrand, New York, 1966).
Palestine and Israel: The Lethal Dilemma (Pegasus Press, N.Y., 1969).

SID-AHMED, MUHAMMAD. After the Guns Fell Silent (Croom Helm, London, 1976).

SIMMONS, J. S. & OTHERS. Global Epidemiology, Vol. 3: The Near and Middle East (Philadelphia, 1954).

SIMON, JAN. Men and Medicine in the Middle East (World Health Organization, Alexandria, 1967).

SMITH, W. CANTWELL. Islam and Modern History (Toronto, 1957).

SOUTHERN, R. W. Western Views of Islam in the Middle Ages (Oxford, 1957).

SPECTOR, IVAR. The Soviet Union and the Muslim World (Seattle, University of Washington Press, 1956).

STARK, FREYA. Dust in the Lion's Paw (London and New York, 1961).

STEVENS, GEORGINA G. (ed.). The United States and the Middle East (Prentice Hall, N.J., 1964).

STEWART, DESMOND. The Middle East: Temple of Janus (Hamish Hamilton, London, 1972).

STOCKING, G. W. Middle East Oil. A Study in Political and Economic Controversy (Vanderbilt University Press, Nashville, 1970).

SUMNER, B. H. Tsardom and Imperialism in the Far East and Middle East (London, Oxford University Press, 1940).

THAYER, P. W. (ed.). Tensions in the Middle East (Baltimore, 1958).

THOMAS, D. WINTON (ed.). Archaeology and Old Testament Study (Oxford University Press, 1967).

THOMAS, L. V. and FRYE, R. N The United States and Turkey and Iran (Cambridge, Mass., 1951).

TREVELYAN, HUMPHREY (Lord). The Middle East in Revolution (Macmillan, London, 1970).

TRIMINGHAM, J. SPENCER. The Sufi Orders in Islam (Clarendon Press, Oxford, 1971).

TUGENHADT, C. Oil: The Biggest Business (Eyre and Spottiswoode, London, 1968).

VATIKIOTIS, P. J. Conflict in the Middle East (George Allen and Unwin, London, 1971).

WADSMAN, P., and TEISSEDRE, R.-F. Nos Politiciens face au Conflict Israélo Arabe (Paris, 1969).

WAINES, DAVID. The Unholy War (Medina Press, Wilmette, 1971).

WARRINER, DOREEN. Land and Poverty in the Middle East (London, 1948).
Land Reform and Development in the Middle East: Study of Egypt, Syria and Iraq (London, 1962).

WATT, W. MONTGOMERY. Muhammad at Mecca (Clarendon Press, Oxford, 1953).
Muhammad at Medina (Clarendon Press, Oxford, 1956).
Muhammad, Prophet and Statesman (Oxford University Press, 1961).
Muslim Intellectual—Al Ghazari (Edinburgh University Press, 1962).
Islamic Philosophy and Theology (Edinburgh University Press, 1963).
Islamic Political Thought: The Basic Concepts (Edinburgh University Press, 1968).

WILSON, RODNEY. Trade and Investment in the Middle East (Macmillan Press, 1977).

YALE, WILLIAM. The Near East (University of Michigan Press, Ann Arbor, 1968).

YOUNG, T. C. (ed). Near Eastern Culture and Society (Princeton, N.J., Princeton University Press, 1951)

ZEINE, Z. N. The Struggle for Arab Independence (Beirut, 1960).

BOOKS ON NORTH AFRICA

(See also Bibliographies at end of Chapters in Part III)

ABUN-NASR, JAMIL M. A History of the Maghrib (Cambridge University Press, 1972).

ALLAL EL-FASSI. The Independence Movements in Arab North Africa, trans. H. Z. Nuseibeh (Washington, 1954).

AMIN, SAMIR. L'Economie du Maghreb (2 vols., Editions du Minuit, Paris, 1966).
The Maghreb in the Modern World (Penguin Books, London, 1971).

BARBOUR, NEVILLE, Editor. A Survey of North West Africa (The Maghreb) (Royal Institute of International Affairs, Oxford University Press, 1959).

BERQUE, JAQUES. Le Maghreb entre Deux Guerres (2nd edn., Editions du Seuil, Paris, 1967).

BRACE, R. M. Morocco, Algeria, Tunisia (Prentice-Hall, Englewood Cliffs, N.J., 1964).

BROWN, LEON CARL (ed.). State and Society in Independent North Africa (Middle East Institute, Washington, 1966).

CAPOT-REY, R. Le Sahara Français (Paris, 1953).

CENTRE D'ETUDES DES RELATIONS INTERNATIONALES. Le Maghreb et la Communauté Economique Européenne (Editions F.N.S.P., Paris, 1965).

CENTRE DE RECHERCHES SUR L'AFRIQUE MÉDITERRANÉENNE D'AIX EN PROVENCE. L'Annuaire de l'Afrique du Nord (Centre Nationale de la recherche scientifique, Paris, annually).

CHARBONNEAU, J. Editor. Le Sahara Français (Cahiers Charles de Foucauld, No. 38, Paris, 1955).

DUCLOS, J., LECA, J., and DUVIGNAUD, J. Les Nationalismes Maghrébins (Centre d'Etudes des Relations Internationales, Paris, 1966).

ECONOMIC COMMISSION FOR AFRICA. Main Problems of Economic Co-operation in North Africa (Tangier, 1966).

FURLONGE, Sir GEOFFREY. The Lands of Barbary (Murray, London, 1966).

GALLAGHER, C. F. The U.S. and North Africa (Cambridge, Mass., 1964).

GARDI, RENÉ. Sahara, Monographie einer grossen Wüste (Kummerley and Frey, Berne, 1967).

GAUTIER, E. F. Le Passé de l'Afrique du Nord (Paris, 1937).

GERMIDIS, DIMITRI, with the help of DELAPIERRE, MICHEL. Le Maghreb, la France et l'enjeu technologique (Editions Cujas, Paris, 1976).

GORDON, D. C. North Africa's French Legacy 1954–62 (Harvard, 1962).

HAHN, LORNA. North Africa: from Nationalism to Nationhood (Washington, 1960).

HERMASSI, ELBAKI. Leadership and National Development in North Africa (University of California Press, 1973).

HESELTINE, N. From Libyan Sands to Chad (Leiden, 1960).

JULIEN, CH.-A. Histoire de l'Afrique du Nord (2nd Edition, 2 Vols., Paris 1951-52).
L'Afrique du Nord en Marche (Paris, 1953).
History of North Africa: From the Arab Conquest to 1830. Revised by R. Le Tourneau. Ed. C. C. Stewart (Routledge and Kegan Paul, London, 1970).

KHALDOUN, IBN. History of the Berbers. Translated into French by Slane (4 vols., Algiers, 1852-56).

KNAPP, WILFRID. North West Africa: A Political and Economic Survey (Oxford University Press, 3rd edition 1977).

LE TOURNEAU, ROGER. Evolution Politique de l'Afrique du Nord Musulmane (Paris, 1962).

LEVI-PROVENÇAL, E. Islam d'Occident (Etudes d'Histoire Médiévale, Paris, 1948).

LISKA, G. The Greater Maghreb: From Independence to Unity? (Center of Foreign Policy Research, Washington, 1963).

MARÇAIS, G. La Berberie Musulmane et l'Orient au Moyen Age (Paris, 1946).

MOORE, C. H. Politics in North Africa (Little. Brown, Boston, 1970).

MORTIMER, EDWARD. France and the Africans, 1944–1960 (Faber, London, 1969).

MUZIKÁR, JOSEPH. Les perspectives de l'intégration des pays maghrébins et leur attitude vis-à-vis du Marché Commun (Nancy, 1968).

NICKERSON, JANE S. Short History of North Africa (New York, 1961).

PARRINDER, GEOFFREY. Religion in Africa (Pall Mall Press, London, 1970).

POLK, WILLIAM R. (ed.). Developmental Revolution: North Africa, Middle East, South Asia (Middle East Institute, Washington, 1963).

RAVEN, SUSAN. Rome in Africa (Evans Brothers, London, 1970).

ROBANA, ABDERRAHMA. The Prospects for an Economic Community in North Africa (Pall Mall, London, 1973).

SAHLI, MOHAMED CHERIF. Décoloniser l'Histoire; introduction à l'histoire du Maghreb (Maspero, Paris, 1965)

SCHRAMM, JOSEF. Die Westsahara (Paunonia-Verlag, Freilassing, 1969).

STEEL, R. (ed.). North Africa (Wilson, New York, 1967).

TOYNBEE, Sir ARNOLD. Between Niger and Nile (Oxford University Press, 1965).

TRIMINGHAM, J. S., The Influence of Islam upon Africa (Longmans, London, and Librairie du Liban, Beirut, 1968).

TUTSCH, HANS E. Nordafrika in Gärung (Frankfurt, 1961).
From Ankara to Marrakesh (New York, 1962).

UNESCO. Arid Zone Research, Vol. XIX: Nomades et Nomadisme au Sahara (UNESCO, 1963).

UNIONS, LABOUR AND INDUSTRIAL RELATIONS IN AFRICA; AN ANNOTATED BIBLIOGRAPHY. Cornell Research Papers in International Relations, 4 (Cornell University Press, New York, 1965).

WARREN, CLINE and SANTMYER, C. Agriculture of Northern Africa (U.S. Dept. of Agriculture, Washington, 1965).

ZARTMAN, I. W. Government and Politics in North Africa (New York, 1964).
(ed.) Man, State and Society in the Contemporary Maghrib (Pall Mall, London, 1973).

SELECT BIBLIOGRAPHY (PERIODICALS)

ACTA ORIENTALIA ACADEMIAE SCIENTIARUM HUNGARICAE. H-1363 Budapest, P.O.B. 24, Hungary; 1950; three times a year; text in English, French, German or Russian; Editors K. CZEGLÉDY and F. TÓKEI.

ACTA ORIENTALIA. Publ. Munksgaard, Nørre Søgade 35, DK 1370 Copenhagen K, Denmark, by the Oriental Societies of Denmark, Norway, and Sweden; history, language, archaeology and religions of the Near and Far East; one issue a year; Editor Prof. SØREN EGEROD; Editorial Sec. Mrs. LISE SODE-MOGENSEN, Scandinavian Institute of Asian Studies, Kejsergade 2, DK 1155 Copenhagen K, Denmark.

AFRICA. Dirección General de Promoción de Sahara, Sección de Archivo-Biblioteca y Documentación de Africa, Castellana 5, Madrid 1, Spain. Head of Section ASUNCIÓN DEL VAL.

AFRICA CONTEMPORARY RECORD. Holmes & Meier Publishers Inc., IUB Building, 30 Irving Place, New York, N.Y. 10003, U.S.A.; annual survey and documents.

AFRICA GUIDE. 21 Gold St., Saffron Walden, Essex, CB10 1EJ, England; Editor GRAHAM HANCOCK.

AFRICA QUARTERLY. Indian Centre for Africa, Indian Council for Cultural Relations, Azad Bhavan, Indraprastha Estate, New Delhi, India.

AFRICA RESEARCH BULLETINS. Africa Research Ltd., 18 Lower North St., Exeter, EX4 3EN, Devon, England; f. 1964; monthly bulletins on (*a*) political and (*b*) economic subjects.

L'AFRIQUE ET L'ASIE MODERNES, 13 rue du Four, 75006 Paris, France; f. 1948; political, economic and social review; quarterly.

AGRIBUSINESS IN THE MIDDLE EAST AND NORTH AFRICA. Chase World Information Corporation, One World Trade Center, Suite 4627, New York, N.Y. 10048, U.S.A.; publs. *Saudi Arabia, Iran, Egypt, Sudan.*

AL-ABHATH. Publ. American University of Beirut, Beirut, Lebanon; f. 1948; Editor MAHMUD A. GHUL; quarterly on Arab affairs.

ALAM ATTIJARAT (*The World of Business*). Johnston International Publishing Corpn. (New York), Beirut; Arabic; business; 10 issues a year; Editor NADIM MAKDISI.

AL-TIJARA AL-ARABIYA AL-INKLEEZYA (*Anglo-Arab Trade*). British Industrial Publicity Overseas Ltd., London W.C.2; Arabic; quarterly.

ANATOLIAN STUDIES. c/o British Academy, Burlington House, Piccadilly, London, W1V 0NS, England; f. 1949; annual of the British Inst. of Archaeology at Ankara; Editor Prof. O. R. GURNEY.

ANATOLICA. Netherlands Historical and Archaeological Institute at Istanbul, Istiklâl Caddesi 393, Istanbul-Beyoğlu, Turkey; f. 1967; annual; Editors: HANDAN ALKIM, P. H. E. DONCEEL-VOÛTE, E. J. VAN DONZEL, SEMRA ÖGEL.

ANNALES ARCHÉOLOGIQUES ARABES SYRIENNES. Direction Générale des Antiquités et des Musées, University St., Damascus, Syria; yearly.

ANNUAIRE DE L'AFRIQUE DU NORD. Edited by the Centre de Recherches et d'Etudes sur les Sociétés Mediterranéennes, Faculté de Droit, Avenue Schuman, Aix-en-Provence; published by the Centre National de la Recherche Scientifique, 15 quai Anatole France, 75700 Paris, France; Dir. Prof. FLORY, France; f. 1962; contains special studies, chronologies, chronicles, documentation and bibliographies.

ANNUAL SURVEY OF AFRICAN LAW. Rex Collings Ltd., 69 Marylebone High St., London, W1M 3AQ.

ARAB BUSINESS. 63 Long Acre, London, WC2E 9JH, England; f. 1975; business monthly; Editor FUAD MATTAR.

ARAB BUSINESS REPORT. G. T. Arab Publishing Co. Ltd., 14–18 Heddon St., Regent St., London, W1R 7LJ, England; fortnightly.

THE ARAB ECONOMIST. Centre for Economic, Financial and Social Research and Documentation SAL, Gefinor Tower, Clemenceau Street, Bloc B—P.O.B. 11—6068, Beirut, Lebanon; f. 1969; Chair. Dr. CHAFIC AKHRAS; monthly; circ. 7,300.

ARAB MONTH. 18 Curzon St., London, W1Y 7FA; f. 1978; current affairs, business, arts; Editor LOGAN GOURLEY.

ARAB REPORT. 21 John St., London, WC1N 2BP, England; f. 1966; digest of Arab political economic and social affairs; 2 a month, Editor PETER KILNER.

ARABIA AND THE GULF. International Communications, 63 Long Acre, London, W.C.2; weekly; f. 1977; Editor GRAHAM BENTON.

THE ARABIAN YEAR BOOK. Neville House, Eden Street, Kingston upon Thames, Surry KT1 1BY, England; capital and consumer goods and services; annual.

ARABICA. c/o Département d'Islamologie, Paris IV, Sorbonne, rue Victor-Cousin, Paris 5e, France; Editor G. LECOMTE; 3 a year.

ARAMTEK MIDEAST MONTHLY. Aramtek Corporation, 122 East 42nd St., New York, N.Y. 10017; f. 1975; business news and features; U.S.A. Editor-in-Chief M. HANDAL; Man. Editor B. F. OTTAVIANI.

ARCHIV FÜR ORIENTFORSCHUNG. c/o Institut für Orientalistik der Universität Wien, Universitätsstrasse 7/V, A-1010 Vienna I, Austria; f. 1923; yearly; Editor HANS HIRSCH.

ARMENIAN REVIEW. Hairenik Association, Inc., 212 Stuart St. Boston, Mass. 02116, U.S.A.; Editor JAMES H. TASHJIAN; quarterly.

ASIAN AFFAIRS. Royal Society for Asian Affairs, 42 Devonshire St., London, W.1, England; f. 1901; three times per year.

ASIAN AND AFRICAN STUDIES. Israel Oriental Society, The Hebrew University, Jerusalem, Israel; f. 1965; Editor GABRIEL BAER; 3 a year.

L'ASIE NOUVELLE. 94 rue St. Lazare, Paris 9e, France; weekly and special issues; Dir. ANDRÉ ROUX.

ASIEN-BIBLIOGRAPHIE. Asien Bucherei, D-3590 Bad Wildungen, German Federal Republic; quarterly.

BELLETEN. Türk Tarih Kurumu, Kizilay Sokak no. 1, Ankara, Turkey; f. 1937; history and archaeology; quarterly; Editor ULUĞ IĞDEMIR.

BIBLIOGRAPHY OF THE MIDDLE EAST. P.O.B. 2712, Damascus, Syria; f. 1968; annual.

BIBLIOTHECA ORIENTALIS. Published by Netherlands Institute for the Near East, Noordeindeplein 4A-6A, Leiden, Netherlands; f. 1943; edited by E. VAN DONZEL, M. N. VAN LOON, H. J. A. DE MEULENAERE, M. J. MULDER, C. NIJLAND, M. STOL; bi-monthly.

British Society for Middle Eastern Studies Bulletin. Department of Near Eastern Studies, University of Manchester, Manchester, M13 9PL; published at Middle East Centre, St. Antony's College, 68 Woodstock Rd., Oxford, OX2 6JF; Editor Dr. J. D. Latham; twice a year.

Bulletin of the School of Oriental and African Studies. School of Oriental and African Studies, University of London, London, W.C.1, England; three issues annually.

Bulletin of Sudanese Studies. P.O.B. 321, Khartoum; Arabic; published by Sudan Research Unit, University of Khartoum; f. 1968; bi-annual; Editor Awn al-Sharif Qasim.

Les Cahiers de Tunisie, published by Faculté des Lettres et Sciences Humaines de Tunis, 94 Blvd. de 9 Avril 1938, Tunis; f. 1953; quarterly; Dir. Mohamed Talbi; Editor-in-Chief Béchir Tlili.

Chuto Tsuho (The Middle East News). The Middle East Institute of Japan, Mori Bldg., 8-10 Toranomon 2-chome, Minato-ku, Tokyo, Japan; f. 1958; Editor Y. Nakayama; bi-monthly.

Le Commerce du Levant. Kantari St., SFAH Building, Beirut, Lebanon; two editions (bi-weekly and monthly).

Comunitá Mediterranea. Lungotevere Flaminio 34, Rome; law and political science relating to Mediterranean countries; Pres. E. Bussi.

Cultura Turcica. T. K. Araştirma Enstitüsü, P.K. 14, Çankaya, Ankara, Turkey; f. 1964; articles in English. French and German; semi-annual; Editor Prof. Dr, Şükrü Elçin.

Deutsche Morgenländische Gesellschaft; Zeitschrift. Deutsche Morgenländische Gesellschaft, Seminar für Sprachen und Kulturen Nordafrikas, Otto-Behaghel-Str. 10, D-6300 Lahn-Giessen, Federal Republic of Germany; f. 1847; covers the history, languages and literature of the Orient; bi-annual.

Developing Business in the Middle East and North Africa. Chase World Information Corporation, One World Trade Center, Suite 4627, New York, N.Y. 10048, U.S.A.; publs. *Saudi Arabia, Egypt, Iran, Iraq, Algeria, The Gulf States.*

Developing Economies, The. Institute of Developing Economies, 42 Ichigaya Hommura-cho, Shinjuku-ku, Tokyo 162, Japan; f. 1962; English, quarterly.

L'Economie et les Finances des Pays Arabes. Centre d'Etudes et de Documentation Economiques, Financières et Sociales, S.A.L., B.P. 6068, Beirut, Lebanon; monthly. Pres. Dr. Chafic Akhras, Dir.-Gen. Dr. Sabbah Al Haj.

Egypte Contemporaine. Société Egyptienne d'Economie Politique, de Statistique et de Législation, B.P. 732, Cairo, Egypt; f. 1909; quarterly in Arabic, French and English.

Europe Outremer. 6 rue de Bassano, Paris 16e, France; f. 1923; economic and political material on French-speaking states of Africa; monthly.

Events. 67–71 Southampton Row, London, W.C.1; news magazine on Middle East; fortnightly; Editor-in-Chief Salim al-Lozi.

France-Pays Arabes. Published by L'Association de Solidarité Franco-Arabe, 12-14 rue Augereau, 75007 Paris, France; politics, economics and culture of the Arab world; monthly.

Free Palestine. P.O.B. 492, London, SW19 4PJ; f. 1968; **monthly;** Editor Aziz Yafi; ceased publication 1979.

Gulf Handbook. Trade and Travel Publications, The Mendip Press, Parsonage Lane, Westgate St., Bath, BA1 1EN, England; annual.

Gulf Guide and Diary. 21 Gold St., Saffron Walden, Essex, CB10 1EJ; events in Kuwait, Bahrain, Qatar, Saudi Arabia, the United Arab Emirates, Oman and Yemen; Editor Roger Cooper; annual.

Hamizrah Hehadash. Israel Oriental Society. The **Hebrew University, Jerusalem, Israel; f. 1949; Hebrew with English summary; Middle Eastern, Asian and** African affairs; quarterly; Editor Aharon L. Ayish.

Hesperis-Tamuda. Faculté des Lettres et des Sciences Humaines, Université Mohammed V, 3 rue Ibn Batouta, Rabat, Morocco; f. 1921; history, archaeology, civilization of Maghreb and Western Islam, special reference to bibliography.

Huna London (BBC Arabic Radio Times). BBC Arabic Service, P.O.B. 76, Bush House, Strand, London, WC2B 4PH; f. 1960; circ. throughout the Arab world; monthly; Editor John F. Jones; Advtg. Consultant Leslie Knight, o.b.e.

Ibla. Institut des Belles Lettres Arabes, 12 rue Jamâa el Haoua, Tunis, Tunisia; f. 1937; twice a year.

Indo-Iranian Journal. D. Reidel Publishing Co., P.O.B. 17, Dordrecht, Netherlands; f. 1957; quarterly.

International Crude Oil and Product Prices. P.O.B. 4940, Nicosia, Cyprus; f. 1971; six-monthly review and analysis of crude oil and product price trends in world markets.

International Journal of Middle East Studies. Cambridge University Press, P.O.B. 110, Cambridge CB2 3RL, England; Journal of the Middle East Studies Association of North America and the British Society for Middle Eastern Studies; first issue Jan. 1970; four times per year.

International Petroleum Times. IPC Business Press Ltd., Dorset House, Stamford St., London, SE1 9LU, England; f. 1899; twice-monthly.

Iranistische Mitteilungen. Antigone-Verlag, 3559 Allendorf an der Eder, P.O.B. 1147, Federal Republic of Germany; f. 1967; Editor Helmhart Kanus-Credé.

Iraq. British School of Archaeology in Iraq, 31–34 Gordon Square, London, WC1H 0PY, England; f. 1932; semi-annually.

Der Islam. D2 Hamburg 13, Rothenbaumchaussee 36, Federal Republic of Germany; 2 issues a year.

Islamic Quarterly. The Islamic Cultural Centre, 146 Park Rd., London, N.W.8, England; f. 1954; quarterly; Editor Dr. M. A. Zaki Badawi.

Israel and Palestine. P.O.B. 130-10, Paris Cedex 10, France; f. 1971; monthly; Editor Maxim Ghilan.

Izvestia Akademii Nauk-Otedelenie Literatury i Yazyka. Soviet Academy of Sciences, Moscow, U.S.S.R.; bi-monthly.

Jeune Afrique. Groupe J. A. 51 av. des Ternes, Paris 17e, France; f. 1960; Publisher Bechir ben Yahmed; weekly.

Journal of African Law. School of Oriental and African Studies, University of London, London, WC1E 7HP; two issues annually.

Journal of the American Oriental Society. American Oriental Society, 329 Sterling Memorial Library, New Haven, Conn., U.S.A.; f. 1842; Biblical studies, Ancient Near East, South and Southeast Asia, Islamic Near East, and Far East; quarterly.

Journal Asiatique. Journal de la Société Asiatique, 3 rue Mazarine, Paris 6e, France; f. 1822; Dir. D. Gimaret; covers all phases of Oriental research; quarterly.

Journal of Indian Philosophy. D. Reidel Publishing Co., P.O.B. 17, Dordrecht, Netherlands; f. 1970; quarterly; Editor Bimal K. Matilal.

Journal of Near Eastern Studies. Oriental Institute, University of Chicago, 1155 East 58th St., Chicago, Ill. 60637, U.S.A.; devoted to the Ancient and Medieval Near and Middle East, archaeology, languages, history, Islam.

Journal of Palestine Studies. P.O.B. 11-7164, Beirut, Lebanon; f. 1971; published jointly by Inst. for Palestine Studies and Kuwait Univ.; Palestinian affairs and the Arab-Israeli conflict; Editor Hisham Sharabi; circ. 6,000.

Maghreb-Machrek. Fondation Nationale des Sciences Politiques, La Documentation Française, 29–31 quai Voltaire, 75340 Paris Cedex 07, France; f. 1964; quarterly.

The Maghreb Review. 96 Marchmont St., London, WC1N 1AG; f. 1976; every two months; North African affairs; Editor Mohamed Ben Madani.

Maghreb-Sélection. Ediafric - La Documentation Africaine, 57 ave. d'Iéna, 75783 Paris Cedex 16, France; weekly; French.

M.E.N. **Weekly. Middle East News Agency, 4 Sharia** el Sherifein, Cairo, Egypt; f. 1962; weekly news bulletin.

The Middle East. 63 Long Acre, London, WC2E 9JH, England; f. 1974; political, economic and cultural monthly; Editor Raphael Calis.

Middle East Annual Review. 21 Gold St., Saffron Walden, Essex, CB10 1EJ, England; Editor John Andrews.

Middle East Contemporary Survey. Shiloah Centre for Middle Eastern and African Studies, Tel-Aviv University, P.O.B. 39012, Tel-Aviv, Israel; annual publication describing and analysing events in the Middle East during the year under survey; Editor Colin Legum; Academic Editor Haim Shaked.

Middle East Economic Digest. MEED Ltd., 21 John St., London, WC1N 2BP, England; f. 1957; weekly report on economic developments; Chair. Peter Kilner; Editor Jonathan Wallace.

Middle East Economic Survey. P.O.B. 4940, Nicosia, Cyprus; f. 1957; weekly review of news and views on Middle East/North African oil.

Middle East International. 21 Collingham Rd., London, SW5 0NU; f. 1971; monthly; fortnightly; political and economic developments; Editor Michael Adams.

The Middle East Journal. Middle East Institute, 1761 N St., N.W., Washington, D.C. 20036, U.S.A.; journal in English devoted to the study of the modern Near East; f. 1947; quarterly; Editor William Sands; circ. 4,600.

Middle East Perspective. 850 Seventh Ave., New York, N.Y. 10019, U.S.A.; monthly newsletter; Editor Dr. Alfred Lillienthal.

The Middle East Record. Shiloah Centre for Middle Eastern and African Studies, Tel Aviv University, P.O.B. 39012, Tel Aviv, Israel; annual reference book about Middle East; Editor D. Dishon.

Middle East Studies Association Bulletin. New York University Hagop Kevorkian Center for Near Eastern Studies, 50 Washington Sq. South, New York, N.Y. 10003, U.S.A.; twice yearly.

The Middle East Yearbook. 63 Long Acre, London. WC2E 9JH, England; f. 1976; annual; Editor Richard Synge.

Middle Eastern Studies. Frank Cass & Co. Ltd., Gainsborough House, 11 Gainsborough Rd., London, E11 1RS; England; f. 1964; Editor Elie Kedourie; three times yearly.

Mideast Markets. Bracken House, Cannon St., London, EC4 P4BY; fortnightly newsletter; Editor Patrick Cockburn.

Moyen-Orient Economique. Ediafric - La Documentation Africaine, 57 ave. d'Iéna, 75783 Paris Cedex 16, France; f. 1978; twice monthly; economic information about the Middle East.

The Muslim World. 111 Sherman St., Hartford, Conn. 06105, U.S.A.; f. 1911; Islamic studies in general and Muslim-Christian relations in past and present; quarterly; Editors Willem A. Bijlefeld and Issa J. Boullata.

Narody Asii i Afriki (Istoriya, Ekonomika, Kultura). Akad. Nauk S.S.S.R., ul. Zhdanova, 12, Moscow, U.S.S.R.; f. 1955; bi-monthly.

Near East Report. 444 N. Capitol St., N.W., Washington, D.C. 20001, U.S.A.; f. 1957; analyses U.S. policy in the Near East; circ. 30,000; weekly; Editor Alan M. Tigay.

New Outlook. 8 Karl Netter Street, Tel-Aviv, Israel; f. 1957; Israeli and Middle Eastern Affairs; dedicated to Jewish-Arab rapprochement; monthly; Editor Simha Flapan.

OEL (Zeitschrift für die Mineralölwirtschaft). 2 Hamburg 13, Alsterkamp 20, Federal Republic of Germany; f. 1963; monthly.

Oil and Gas Journal. Petroleum Publishing Co., 1421 S. Sheridan, Tulsa, Oklahoma 74112, U.S.A.; f. 1902; petroleum industry and business weekly; Publisher John Ford; Editor Gene T. Kinney.

Orient. German Orient Institute, 2 Hamburg 13, Mittelweg 150, Federal Republic of Germany; f. 1960; current affairs articles in German, English and French; Documents, Book Reviews and Bibliographies; quarterly; Editors Dr. Udo Steinbach, Dr. Rainer Glagow.

Orient Press International Report. Orient Press S.A.R.L., 27 rue J.-Jacques Rousseau, 75001 Paris, France; weekly; Dir.-Gen. Ali G. Taher.

Oriente Moderno. Istituto per l'Oriente, via A Caroncini 19, 00197 Rome, Italy; f. 1921; chronicle of events, articles, book reviews; monthly.

Palestine Affairs. P.O.B. 1691, Beirut, Lebanon; studies of Palestine problem; f. 1971; monthly in Arabic; Editor Dr. Anis Sayegh.

Persica. Netherlands-Iranian Society; Minnezang 7, B. 3202 Linden, Belgium; f. 1963; annual; Editors Prof. Dr. P. H. L. Eggermont, Drs. K. B. Kremer.

Le Pétrole et Le Gaz Arabes. 7 avenue Ingres, 75781 Paris, France; Arab petroleum and gas; twice monthly.

Petroleum Economist (formerly Petroleum Press Service). 5 Pemberton Row, Fleet St., London, EC4A 3DP, England; f. 1934; monthly, in English, French and Japanese editions; English circ. 6,986; Editor Bryan Cooper.

Revue d'Assyriologie et d'Archeologie Orientale. Presses Universitaires de France, 12 rue Jean-de-Beauvais, 75005 Paris, France; f. 1923; 2 a year; Dirs. André Parrot, Paul Garelli.

La Revue Bibliographique du Moyen Orient. Publisher L. Farès, B.P. 2712, Damascus, Syria.

Revue des Etudes Islamiques. Librairie Orientaliste Paul Geuthner S.A., 12 rue Vavin, 75006 Paris, France; f. 1927; Editors H. Laoust and D. Sourdel.

Rivista Degli Studi Orientali. Scuola Orientale, Facoltà di Lettere, University of Rome, Rome, Italy; quarterly; Publisher Giovanni Bardi.

Rocznik Orientalistyczny. Grójecka 17, Warsaw, Poland; f. 1915; Editor-in-Chief Edward Tryjarski; Sec. Janusz Danecki; semi-annual.

Royal Asiatic Society of Great Britain and Ireland Journal. 56 Queen Anne Street, London, W1M 9LA, England; f. 1823; covers all aspects of Oriental research.

Al-Sina'a (Industry). Iraqi Federation of Industries, P.O.B. 5665, South Gate, Baghdad, Iraq; f. 1977 by merger of *Al-Sinai* and *Alam Al Sina'a*; articles in Arabic and English; bi-monthly.

Studia Islamica, G. P. Maisonneuve et Larose, 15 rue Victor-Cousin, 75005 Paris, France; bi-annual.

Studies in Islam. Indian Institute of Islamic Studies, Panchkuin Rd., New Delhi, India, quarterly.

Sumer. Directorate-General of Antiquities, Baghdad, Iraq; archaeological; bi-annual.

Türk Kültürü. T. K. Araştırma Enstitüsü, P.K. 14, Çankaya, Ankara, Turkey; f. 1962; Turkish language articles on current affairs and history; Editor Dr. Şükrü Elçin; monthly.

Türk Kültürü Araştırmaları. T. K. Araştırma Enstitüsü, P.K. 14, Çankaya, Ankara, Turkey; f. 1964; scholarly articles in Turkish; bi-annual; Editor Dr. Şükrü Elçin.

U.S.S.R. and Third World. Central Asian Research Centre, 8 Wakley St., London, EC1V 7LT, England; surveys development of Soviet and Chinese policies in the Middle East, Asia, Africa, Latin America and the Caribbean; six issues per year.

Die Welt des Islams. Publ. E. J. Brill, Oude Rijn 33a, Leiden, Netherlands; f. 1913; contains articles in German, English and French; Editor Prof. Dr. O. Spies, University of Bonn.

Wiener Zeitschrift für die Kunde des Morgenlandes. **Oriental Institute of the University of Vienna; A-1010 Wien I, Universitätsstrasse 7/V, Austria,** f. 1887; annually.

Research Institutes

Associations and Institutes Studying the Middle East and North Africa.

(*See also* Regional Organizations—Education in Part I)

AFGHANISTAN

Anjumani Tarikh (*Historical Society*): Kabul; f. 1931; to study and promote international knowledge of the history of Afghanistan; Head AHMAD ALI MOTAMEDI; publs. *Aryana* (quarterly, in Pashtu and Dari) and *Afghanistan* (English and French, quarterly).

The Asia Foundation: P.O.B. 257, Kabul.

British Institute of Afghan Studies: P.O.B. 3052, Kabul; f. 1972; supports research relating to history, antiquities, archaeology, languages, literature, art, culture, customs and natural history of Afghanistan; Dir. R. H. PINDER WILSON.

ALGERIA

Institut d'Etudes Arabes: Université d'Alger, 2 rue Didouche Mourad, Algiers.

Institut d'Etudes Orientales: Université d'Alger, 2 rue Didouche Mourad, Algiers; publ. *Annales.*

AUSTRIA

Afro-Asiatisches Institut in Wien: A-1090 Vienna, Türkenstrasse 3; f. 1959; seminars and language courses and other cultural exchange between African and Asian students in Vienna; Gen. Sec. A. GRÜNFELDER; Pres. Bishop Dr. A. WAGNER; publ. *Treffpunkte* (quarterly).

Institut fur Orientalistik der Universität Wien: A-1010 Vienna, Universitätsstrasse 7/V; f. 1886; library of 20,000 vols.; Dirs. Prof. Dr. ARNE A. AMBROS, Prof. Dr. HANS HIRSCH, Prof. Dr. ANDREAS TIETZE; publ. *Wiener Zeitschrift für die Kunde des Morgenlandes* (annual).

BELGIUM

Centre pour l'Etude des Problèmes du Monde Musulman Contemporain: 44 ave. Jeanne, 1050 Brussels; f. 1957; publs. *Correspondance d'Orient-Etudes* (annually) and collections *Correspondance d'Orient* and *Le monde musulman contemporain—Initiations.*

Centrum voor Onderzoek van het Arabisch en de Cultuur van de Arabische Landen (COACAL) (*Center for Research on Arabic and the Culture of the Arab Countries*) (*CRACAC*): 5 St.-Pietersplein, B-9000 Ghent; f. 1975; non-profit organization; Dir. Prof. Dr. M. PLANCKE; Sec. Prof. L. DE MEYER; publ. monographs.

Departement Oriëntalistiek: Faculteit van de Wijsbegeerte en Letteren, Katholieke Universiteit te Leuven, Blijde Inkomststraat 21, B3000 Leuven; f. 1936; Pres. Prof. E. LIPÍNSKI; 25 mems.; publs. *Orientalia Lovaniensia Analecta, Orientalia Lovaniensia Periodica, Bibliothèque du Muséon* (1929-68), *Orientalia et Biblica Lovaniensia* (1957–68).

Fondation Egyptologique Reine Elisabeth: Parc du Cinquantenaire, Brussels B1040; f. 1923 to encourage Egyptian studies; 1,450 mems.; library of 90,000 vols.; Pres. M. E. BONVOISIN; Dir. M. J. BINGEN and H. DE MEULENAERE; publs. *Chronique d'Egypte, Bibliotheca Aegyptiaca, Papyrologica Bruxellensia, Bibliographie Papyrologique sur fiches, Monumenta Aegyptiaca, Rites égyptiens, Papyri Bruxellenses Graecae, Monographies Reine Elisabeth.*

Information Centre on Eastern Arabia: Ave. de l'Exposition 458, Bte. 12, 1090 Brussels; f. 1970; 8,000 documents on Bahrain, Qatar, Oman and the United Arab Emirates; Dir. M. VAN DAELE; publs. monthly list of new acquisitions.

CZECHOSLOVAKIA

Department of Oriental Studies of the Slovak Academy of Sciences: Slovak Academy of Sciences, Klemensova 19, 884 16 Bratislava; f. 1960; 11 mems.; Pres. Dr. I. DOLEZAL; Vice-Dir. Dr. V. KRUPA; publ. *Asian and African Studies* (annual).

Oriental Institute: Prague I, Lázeňská 4; f. 1922; Head of Inst. J. CESAR, D.SC.; publs. *Archiv Orientální* (quarterly), *Nový Orient* (monthly).

DENMARK

Orientalsk Samfund (*Orientalist Association*): Institute of Iranian Studies, Kejsergade 2, 1155 Copenhagen K; f. 1915 to undertake the study and further the understanding of Oriental cultures and civilizations; 50 mems.; Pres. Prof. SØREN EGEROD; Sec. Prof. J. P. ASMUSSEN; publ. *Acta Orientalia* (annually).

EGYPT

Academy of the Arabic Language: 26 Sharia Taha Hussein, Giza; f. 1932; Pres. Dr. IBRAHIM MADKOUR; Sec. Dr. MAHDI ALLAM; publs. *Review* (twice yearly), and books on reviving Arabic heritage and lexicons.

American Research Center in Egypt Inc.: 2 Midan Kasr el Doubara, Cairo, and 40 Witherspoon St., Princeton, N.J. 08540; f. 1948 by American universities to promote research by U.S. and Canadian scholars in all phases of Egyptian civilization, including archaeology, art history, humanities and social sciences; grants and fellowships available; 26 institutional mems. and 600 individual mems.; Pres. MUHSIN MAHDI; Vice-Pres. NICHOLAS B. MILLET; U.S. Dir. LINDA PAPPAS FUNSCH; Cairo Dir. PAUL WALKER; publs. *Journal* (annual), *Newsletter* (quarterly).

Deutsches Archäologisches Institut (*German Institute of Archaeology*): 22 Sharia Gezira al Wusta, Zamalek, Cairo; Dir. Prof. Dr. WERNER KAISER.

Institut Dominicain d'Etudes Orientales: Priory of the Dominican Fathers, 1 Sharia Masna al-Tarabish, Abbasiyah, Cairo; f. 1953; Dir. Père G. C. ANAWATI; publ. *Mélanges* (yearly).

Institut d'Egypte: 13 Sharia Sheikh Rihane, Cairo; f. 1798; studies literary, artistic and scientific questions relating to Egypt and neighbouring countries; Pres. MUHAMMAD REDA MADWAR; Sec.-Gen. P. GHALIOUNGUI; publs. *Bulletin* (annual), *Mémoires* (irregular).

Institut Français d'Archéologie Orientale: 37 Sharia Sheikh Ali Youssef, Cairo; f. 1880; Dir. J. VERCOUTTER; publs. *Bulletin, Annales Islamologiques.*

Netherlands Institute for Archaeology and Arabic Studies: 1 Sharia Dr. Mahmoud Azmi, Zamalek, P.O.B. 1271, Cairo; f. 1971; Dir. Dr. J. J. G. JANSEN; publs. in the field of Arabic Studies.

Société Archéologique d'Alexandrie: 6 Sharia Mahmoud Moukhtar, Alexandria; f. 1893; 150 mems.; Pres. A. M. SADEK; Sec.-Gen. and Editor D. A. DAOUD; Treas. M. F. MANSOUR; publs. *Bulletins, Mémoires, Monuments de l'Egypte Gréco-Romaine, Cahiers, Publications Spéciales*, Archaeological and Historical Studies.

Société Egyptienne d'Economie Politique, de Statistique et de Législation: B.P. 732, Cairo; f. 1909; 1,550 mems.; Pres. Dr. GAMAL EL OTEIFI; Sec.-Gen. Dr. IBRAHIM

Ali Saleh; Tech.-Sec. Dr. Gouda Abdel Khalek; publ. *Revue* (quarterly in Arabic, French and English).

Society for Coptic Archaeology: 222 Avenue Ramses, Cairo; f. 1934; 370 mems.; library of 9,500 vols.; Pres. Mirrit Boutros Ghali; Treas. Dr. Boutros Boutros Ghali; Sec. Dr. Norman Daniel; publs. *Bulletin* (annual), *Fouilles, Bibliothèque d'Art et d'Archéologie, Textes et Documents etc.*

FINLAND

Suomen Itämainen Seura (*Finnish Oriental Society*): Helsinki, Snellmaninkatu 9-11; f. 1917; 200 mems.; Pres. Dr. E. Salonen; Sec. Dr. T. Harviainen; publ. *Studia Orientalia.*

FRANCE

Centre d'Etudes de l'Orient Contemporain: 13 rue du Four, Paris 6e; f. 1943; collaborates with la Documentation française and runs course on contemporary Arab World; Dir. Prof. Cl. Cahen.

Centre de Hautes Etudes sur l'Afrique et l'Asie Modernes: 13 rue du Four, 75006 Paris; f. 1936; Dir. G. R. Malecot; publs. *L'Afrique et L'Asie Modernes* (quarterly), *Cahiers de l'Afrique et l'Asie* (irregular), *Langues et dialectes d'Outre-Mer* (irregular), *Recherches et documents du CHEAM* (irregular), *Cahiers du CHEAM* (irregular).

Centre de Recherches Africaines: 9 rue Malher, 75004 Paris.

Centre de Recherches et d'Etudes sur les Sociétés Méditerranéennes: Faculté de Droit, 3 ave. Robert Schuman, Aix-en-Provence; Dir. M. Flory; publs. *Annuaire de l'Afrique du Nord, Collection du CRESM, Les Cahiers du CRESM.*

Fondation Nationale des Sciences Politiques: 27 rue Saint-Guillaume, Paris 7e; f. 1945; Administrator J. Chapsal; Centre d'Etudes et de Recherches Internationales, Dir. G. Hermet; Arab World section has research team of 9 mems.; publs. include *Maghreb-Machrek* (quarterly).

Institut d'Etudes Arabes et Islamiques: Université de la Sorbonne Nouvelle (Paris III), 13 rue de Santeuil, 75231 Paris Cedex 05; Dir. Prof. Cl. Cahen.

Institut d'Etudes Iraniennes: Université de la Sorbonne Nouvelle, 13 rue de Santeuil, 75231 Paris Cedex 05; f. 1947; Dir. Gilbert Lazard; publs. *Travaux, Studia Iranica* (journal).

Institut d'Etudes Sémitiques: Institut d'Etudes Sémitiques, 11 place Marcelin-Berthelot, 75231 Paris Cedex 05; f. 1930; Pres. A. Dupont-Sommer; publ. *Semitica.*

Institut d'Etudes Turques de l'Université de la Sorbonne Nouvelle—Paris III: 13 rue du Four, 75006 Paris; Dir. Louis Bazin.

Institut National des Langues et Civilisations Orientales: 2 rue de Lille, Paris 7e; attached to Univ. de la Sorbonne Nouvelle Paris III; f. 1795; faculties of languages and civilizations of West Asia and Africa; the Far East, India and Oceania; Eastern Europe; library of 600,000 vols. and 2,000 MSS.; over 8,000 students, 90 teachers, 170 lecturers; Pres. H. de la Bastide; Sec. Mme J. Fiatte; publs. various Oriental studies.

Institut de Papyrologie: Université de Paris-Sorbonne, 1 rue Victor-Cousin, Paris 5e; Dir. Jean Scherer.

Société Asiatique: 3 rue Mazarine, Paris 6e; f. 1822; 700 mems.; library of 80,000 vols.; Pres. Claude Cahen; Vic-Pres. J. Filliozat; Secs. L. Bazin, Y. Hervouet, M. Soymie; publs. *Journal Asiatique* (quarterly), *Cahiers de la Société Asiatique.*

FEDERAL REPUBLIC OF GERMANY

Altorientalisches Seminar der Freien Universität Berlin: D-1000 Berlin 45, Unter den Eichen 78/79; f. 1950.

Arbeitsgemeinschaft Vorderer Orient (AGVO): 2000 Hamburg 13, Mittelweg 150; consists of German research orgs. into politics, science and commerce of the Middle East; 26 mem. insts. (1975); Sec. Dr. Udo Steinbach.

Deutsche Afrika Gesellschaft: Bonn, Markt 10-12; publ. *Afrika Heute* (monthly).

Deutsche Morgenländische Gesellschaft: 1000 Berlin 30, Postfach 1407; Sec. Dr. Dieter George; f. 1845; publs. *Zeitschrift* (semi-annual), *Abhandlungen für die Kunde des Morgenlandes, Bibliotheca Islamica, Wörterbuch der Klassischen Arabischen Sprache, Beiruter Texte und Studien, Verzeichnis der orientalischen Handschriften in Deutschland,* etc.

Das Deutsche Orient-Institut: 2000 Hamburg 13, Mittelweg 150; f. 1960 from the Nah-und Mittelostverein e.V.; since 1965 has been affil. to Deutsches Übersee-Institut; devoted to research in politics, science and commerce of Near and Middle East; Dir. Dr. Udo Steinbach; publ. *Orient* (quarterly).

Internationale Gesellschaft fuer Orientforschung: Mertonstrasse 17-25, Frankfurt/Main; f. 1948; 400 mems.; Pres. Prof. R. Sellheim; publ. *Oriens* (annual).

Nah- und Mittelost Verein e.V. (*German Near and Middle East Association*): D2 Hamburg 13, Mittelweg 151; f. 1934; 600 mems.; Chair. Hans-Otto Thierbach; Gen. Sec. R.-E. Frhr. v. Lüttwitz.

Seminar für Orientalische Sprachen: Adenauerallee 102, 53 Bonn; institute attached to the University of Bonn; Dir. Prof. Dr. R. Trauzettel; Vice-Dir. Prof. Dr. A. Noth, Prof. Dr. J. Kreiner.

HUNGARY

Magyar Tudományos Akadémia, Orientalisztikai Bizottsága (*Oriental Committee of the Hungarian Academy of Sciences*): Budapest V, Roosevelt tér. 9; publ. *Acta Orientalia Hung.* (three times a year).

INDIA

Asiatic Society of Bombay: Town Hall, Bombay 400 023; f. 1804; 1,512 mems.; to investigate and encourage Sciences, Arts and Literature in relation to Asia; maintains Central Library of the State of Maharashtra; Pres. Soli J. Sorabjee; Hon. Sec. Mrs. Bansari K. Sheth; in 1973 the society established the Dr. P. V. Kane Research Inst. to promote, encourage and facilitate research in Oriental studies; publishes critical annotated texts of rare Sanskrit and Pali MSS.

Indian Institute of Islamic Studies: Panchkuin Rd., New Delhi 1 and Tughlaqabad, New Delhi 62; f. 1963; library of 50,000 vols. and 2,400 MSS; Pres. Hakeem Abdul Hameed; Dir. S. A. Ali; publ. *Studies in Islam* (quarterly).

Iran League: Navsari Bldg. (2nd floor), Dr. Dadabhai Navroji Rd., Fort, Bombay 400 001; f. 1922; 500 mems.; Pres. Sir Jamsetjee Jeejeebhoy, Bart.; Sec. D. C. Lelinwalla; publs. *The Iran League Quarterly Newsletter* and translations and commentaries in modern Persian of Avesta texts.

Iran Society: 12 Dr. M. Ishaque Rd., Calcutta 16; f. 1944; 186 mems.; Pres. Rusi B. Gimi; Gen. Sec. M. A. Majid; publs. *Indo-Iranica* (quarterly), etc.

IRAN

The Asia Institute: Pahlavi University, Shiraz; Dir. Dr. Y. M. Nawabi; publs. *Bulletin, Monographs.*

British Institute of Persian Studies: Alvand St. below 1555 Kuroshe Kabir, P.O.B. 2617, Teheran; f. 1961; cultural institute, with emphasis on history and archaeology; 850 individual mems.; Hon. Sec. S. J. WHITWELL, C.M.G., M.C.; Dir. DAVID STRONACH, O.B.E., M.A., F.S.A.; publ. *Iran* (annual).

R.C.D. Cultural Institute: 5 Los Angeles Ave., North of Elizabeth II Blvd., Teheran, branches in Turkey and Pakistan; f. 1966; Dirs. Dr. RASIH GUVEN and N. A. ZAKIR; publs. *Journal* (quarterly), also publications on the history and culture of Iran, Turkey and Pakistan.

IRAQ

American School of Oriental Research: Baghdad; f. 1923; undertakes archaeological surveys and excavations; Dir. (vacant); publ. *Bulletin*, quarterlies and monographs.

British School of Archaeology in Iraq: 31-34 Gordon Sq., London, WC1H 0PY; British Archaeological Expedition to Iraq, Baghdad; Dir. J. N. POSTGATE.

Deutsches Archäologisches Institut: 71B/11 Hurriya Square, Karrada, Baghdad.

Instituto Hispano-Arabe de Cultura: Park Sa'adun, P.O.B. 2256, Baghdad; f. 1958; Dir. JOSEP PUIG.

Iraq Academy: Waziriyah, Baghdad; f. 1947 to maintain the Arabic language to undertake research into Arabic history, Islamic heritage and the history of Iraq, and to encourage research in the modern arts and sciences; Pres. ABDUL RAZZAQ MUHIDDIN; Sec.-Gen. Dr. F. AL-TA'I; publ. *Bulletin of the Iraq Academy* (bi-annual.)

ISRAEL

Academy of the Hebrew Language: P.O.B. 3449, Jerusalem; f. 1953; study of the Hebrew language and compilation of an historical dictionary; Pres. Prof. Z. BEN-HAYYIM; publs. *Zikhronot, Leshonenu, Leshonenu La'am*, monographs and dictionaries.

Albright Institute of Archaeological Research in Jerusalem: 26 Salah ed-Din, P.O.B. 19096, Jerusalem; f. 1900; research in Near Eastern languages, literature and history; archaeological research and sponsors excavations; Pres. ERNEST FRERICHS; Dir. A. GLOCK; publs. *Bulletin, Annual, Biblical Archaeologist, Newsletter.*

The Ben-Zvi Institute: P.O.B. 7504, Jerusalem; f. 1948; sponsors research in the history and culture of Jewish communities in the East; library of MSS. and printed books; Chair. Prof. SHAUL SHAKED; publ. *Sefunot* (annual), monographs and reports.

British School of Archaeology in Jerusalem: P.O.B. 19/283, Jerusalem; f. 1920; archaeological research and excavation; hostel and library; Chair. Rev. Prof. P. R. ACKROYD, M.A., M.TH., PH.D., D.D.; Dir. Rev. J. WILKINSON, M.A., S.T.D.; publ. *Levant.*

Couvent Saint Etienne des Pères Dominicains, Ecole Biblique et Archéologique Française: P.O.B. 19053, Jerusalem; f. 1890; research, Biblical and Oriental studies, exploration and excavation in Palestine; Dir. R. J. TOURNAY; library of 60,000 vols.; publs. *Revue Biblique, Etudes Bibliques, Etudes Palestiniennes et Orientales, Cahiers de la Revue Biblique, Bible de Jérusalem.*

Historical Society of Israel: P.O.B. 4179, Jerusalem; f. 1925 to promote the study of Jewish history and general history; 1,000 mems.; Pres. Prof. H. H. BEN-SASSON; publ. *Zion* (quarterly).

Institute of Asian and African Studies: Hebrew University of Jerusalem, Jerusalem; f. 1926; studies of medieval and modern languages, culture and history of Middle East, Asia and Africa; Chair. Prof. YOHANAN FRIEDMANN; publs. *Max Schloessinger Memorial Series, Jerusalem Studies in Arabic and Islam*, Translation series.

Institute of Holy Land Studies: P.O.B. 1276, Jerusalem; f. 1959; Christian study centre; Pres. Dr. GEORGE GIACUMAKIS.

Israel Exploration Society: 3 Shemuel ha-Nagid St., P.O.B. 7041, Jerusalem; f. 1913; excavations and historical research, congresses and lectures; 4,000 mems.; Chair. Prof. A. BIRAN; Hon. Pres. Prof. B. MAZAR; Hon. Sec. J. AVIRAM; publs. *Eretz Yisrael* (Hebrew annual, with English summaries), *Qadmoniot* (Hebrew quarterly), *Israel Exploration Journal* (English quarterly), various books on archaeology (in Hebrew and English).

Israel Oriental Society: The Hebrew University, Jerusalem; f. 1949; lectures and symposia to study all aspects of contemporary Middle Eastern, Asian and African affairs; Pres. ABBA EBAN; publs. *Hamizrah Hehadash* (Hebrew quarterly), *Oriental Notes and Studies* (irregular), *Asian and African Studies* (three a year).

Orientalisches Institut der Görres-Gesellschaft: P.O.B. 19424, Jerusalem; historical and archaeological studies.

Pontifical Biblical Institute: 3 Paul Emile Botta St., P.O.B. 497, Jerusalem; f. 1927; study of Biblical languages and Biblical archaeology, geography, history, topography, student tours, excavations; Dir. Rev. FRANCIS FURLONG, S.J.; publ. *Biblica, Orientalia.*

Shiloah Center for Middle Eastern and African Studies: Tel-Aviv University, Ramat Aviv, P.O.B. 39012; f. 1959; Head Prof. HAIM SHAKED; publs. *Middle East Record* (annual), *Middle East Contemporary Survey* (annual), also monographs, studies and occasional papers.

Wilfrid Israel House for Oriental Art and Studies: Kibbutz Hazorea, Post Hazorea 30060; f. 1947; opened 1951 in memory of late Wilfrid Israel; a cultural centre for reference, study and art exhbns.; houses Wilfrid Israel collection of Near and Far Eastern art and cultural materials; local archaeological exhibits from neolithic to Byzantine times; science and art library; Dir. Dr. M. MERON; Sec. and Curator for Far and Middle Eastern Art Dr. U. R. BAER; Curator for Archaeology E. MEIRHOF.

ITALY

Istituto Italiano per il Medio ed Estremo Oriente (ISMEO): Palazzo Brancaccio, via Merulana 248, Rome; f. 1933, Pres. Prof. SABATINO MOSCATI; Sec.-Gen. and Cultural Dir. Prof. ANTONIO GARGANO; publs. *East and West* (quarterly), *Rome Oriental Series, Nuovo Ramusio*, Archaeological Reports and Memoirs.

Istituto Italo-Africano: via Ulisse Aldrovandi 16, Rome; Pres. (vacant); Sec.-Gen. Amb. Dott. LUIGI GASBARRI.

Istituto per l'Oriente: via Alberto Caroncini 19, Rome; f. 1921; Pres. Prof. A. BAUSANI; publs. *Oriente Moderno* (monthly), *Rassegna di Studi Etiopici* (annual), *Oriens Antiquus* (quarterly).

Istituto Universitario Orientale: Piazza San Giovanni Maggiore 30, Naples; f. 1888; library of 63,646 vols.; Dir. Prof. A. BOMBACI.

Istituto di Studi del Vicino Oriente: Universita degli Studi, Citta Universitarià, Rome; Dir. Prof. M. LIVERANI.

JAPAN

Ajia Keizai Kenkyusho (*Institute of Developing Economies, formerly Institute of Asian Economic Affairs*): 42 Ichigaya-Hommura-cho, Shinjuku-ku, Tokyo 162; f. 1958; 275 mems.; Chair. YOSHIZANE IWASA; Pres. NOBORU KANOKOGI; library of 143,000 vols.; publs. *Ajia Keizai* (Japanese, monthly), *The Developing Economies* (English, quarterly), occasional papers in English.

Chuto Chosakai (*Middle East Institute of Japan*): 15 Mori Bldg., 8-10 Toranomon 2-chome, Minato-ku, Tokyo; f. 1956; Chair. YOSHIHIRO NAKAYAMA; publs. *Chuto Tsuho* (Middle East News—bi-monthly), *Chuto Nenkan* (Yearbook of Middle East and North Africa), *Chuto Seiji Keizai News* (Political and Economic News of the Middle East) (twice a month).

Nippon Orient Gakkai (*Society for Near Eastern Studies in Japan*): Tokyo Tenrikyokan, 9, 1-chome, Kanda Nishiki-cho, Chiyoda-ku, Tokyo; f. 1954; 693 mems.; Pres. Dr. ATSUUJI ASHIKAGA; publs. *Orient* (Japanese, twice-yearly), *Orient* (European languages annual).

LEBANON

Centre d'Etudes et de Recherches sur le Moyen-Orient Contemporain (CERMOC): Ave. de Damas, B.P. 2691, Beirut; Dir. ANDRÉ BOURGEY.

Centre de Documentation Economique sur le Proche-Orient: Faculté de Sciences Economiques et de gestion des entreprises, Université Saint-Joseph, B.P. 293, Beirut, f. 1971; selection and analysis of documents and publs. on the economy of Middle East Arab countries and oil economy; Dir. Miss KATIA SALAME.

Centre for Economic, Financial and Social Research and Documentation S.A.L.: Gefinor Centre, Bloc B, 500-502 Clemenceau St., P.O.B. 6068, Beirut; f. 1958; Pres. Dr. CHAFIC AKHRAS; Dir.-Gen. Dr. SABBAH AL HAJ.

Institut de Géographie du Proche et Moyen Orient: ave. de Damas, B.P. 2691, Beirut; f. 1946; Dir. M. LE LANNOU.

Institut de Recherches d'Economie Appliquée: Faculté de Sciences Economiques et de gestion des entreprises, Université Saint Joseph, B.P. 293, Beirut; f. 1963; economic studies of the Lebanon and other countries of the Middle East; Dir. Prof. ALEXANDRE CHAIBAN; publ. *Proche-Orient, études économiques* (quarterly).

Institut Français d'Archéologie: rue Omar Daouk, B.P. 11-1424, Beirut; f. 1946; library of 26,000 vols. (Bibliothèque Henri Seyrig); Dir. ERNEST WILL; publs. *Syria, Revue d'Art et d'Archéologie* (annual), *Bibliothèque Archéologique et Historique*.

P.L.O. Research Centre: P.O.B. 1691, Beirut; f. 1964; studies Palestine problem; publs. irregular monographs, books and essays in Arabic, English and French.

MOROCCO

Faculté des Lettres et des Sciences Humaines: Université Mohammed V, Rabat; f. 1959: publs. *Hespéris-Tamuda, Majallat Kulliat al Adab wa-i-Ulum al-insaniya* (in arabic).

THE NETHERLANDS

Assyriologisch Instituut der Rijksuniversiteit: Rijksuniversiteit te Leiden, Noordeindsplein 4A, Leiden; Dir. F. R. KRAUS.

Netherlands Institute for the Middle East (*Midden Oosten Instituut*): 3 Spui, P.O.B. 10, The Hague; f. 1949; publ. *Bulletin* (Press Digest, for members only).

Netherlands Institute for the Near East (*Nederlands Instituut voor het Nabije Oosten*): Noordeindeplein 4A-6A, Leiden; Dir. Dr. E. VAN DONZEL; library of 25,000 vols. and 300 periodicals; Publs. *Bibliotheca Orientalis, Anatolica, Studia Scholten, Scholae de Buck, Publications de l'Institut historique et archéologique néerlandais de Stamboul—Leiden, Tabulae de Liagre Böhl, Studia de Liagre Böhl.*

NORWAY

Indo- Iransk Institutt: Universitetet i Oslo, Niels Treschows Hus, Blindern, Oslo; f. 1920; studies Indian and Iranian languages, culture and history; library of 28,000 vols.; Pres. Amanuensis KNUT KRISTIANSEN.

PAKISTAN

Institute of Islamic Culture: Club Rd., Lahore; f. 1950; Dir. Prof. M. SAEED SHEIKH; Hon. Publication Adviser and Sec. M. ASHRAF DARR; publs. *al-Maarif* (monthly), about 140 publications on Islamic subjects in English and Urdu.

Islamic Research Institute: P.O.B. 1035, Islamabad; f. 1960; Dir. Dr. A. J. HALEPOTA.

R.C.D. Cultural Institute: 366, F6/1, St. 44, Islamabad; Dir. Prof. S. Q. FATIMI.

POLAND

Komitet Nauk Orientalistycznych P.A.N. (*Polish Academy of Sciences Committee for Oriental Studies*): Grójecka 17 pok. 111, 02-021 Warsaw; Pres. Prof. Dr. TADEUSZ LEWICKI; publs. *Rocznik Orientalistyczny, Prace Orientalistyczne.*

Polskie Towarzystwo Orientalistyczne (*Polish Oriental Society*): ul. Sniadeckich 8 IV pietro p. 15, 00-656 Warsaw; f. 1922; mems. 260; Pres. TADEUSZ LEWICKI, STANISŁAW KAŁUZYŃSKI, MIKOŁAJ MELANOWICZ, ALEKSANDER DUBIŃSKI; Sec. MACIEJ POPKO; publ. *Przegląd Orientalistyczny* (quarterly).

Research Centre for Mediterranean Archaeology: Palac Kultury i Nauki, Room 1909, Warsaw; f. 1956; documentation and publication of Polish excavations in the Middle East and antiquities in Polish museums; Dir. Prof. Dr. KAZIMIERZ MICHALOWSKI; publs. *Travaux du Centre d'Archéologie Méditerranéenne, Palmyre, Faras, Etudes et Travaux, Deir el Bahari, Nea Paphos, Alexandrie, Corpus Vasorum Antiquorum, Corpus Signorum Imperii Romani.*

Zaklad Orientalistyki P.A.N. (*Research Centre for Oriental Studies*): Freta 16, Warsaw; f. 1953; Dir. Prof. Dr. ANANIASZ ZAJĄCZKOWSKI.

PORTUGAL

Instituto David Lopes de Lingua Arabe e Cultura Islâmica: Faculdade de Letras, Cidade Universitaria, Lisbon 4; f. 1968; library; 3 teachers; specializes in Arabic and Islamic studies.

Instituto de Linguas Africanas e Orientais: Rua da Junqueira 86, Lisbon 3; f. 1946; library; 4 teachers; specializes in African and Oriental studies.

SPAIN

Asociacion Española de Orientalistas: Juan XXIII 5, Madrid 3; publs. *Boletin* (annual), etc.

Egyptian Institute of Islamic Studies: Francisco de Asis Mendez Casariego 1, Madrid 2; affiliated to Ministry of Higher Education, Cairo; f. 1960; Dir. Dr. ABDEL AZIZ SALEM; publs. *Magazine of the Egyptian Institute* and other educational books.

Instituto "Benito Arias Montano" de Estudios Hebraicos Sefardíes y Oriente Próximo (*Institute of Hebrew, Sephardic and Near East Studies*): Duque de Medinaceli 4, Madrid 14; f. 1940; branch in Barcelona; 18 mems. Dir. JOSÉ LUIS LACAVE RIAÑO; Sec. EMILIA FERNANDEZ TEJERO; publ. *Sefarad* (quarterly) and books.

SWEDEN

Scandinavian Institute of African Studies: P.O.B. 2126, S-75002, Uppsala; information and documentation centre, organizes seminars and publishes wide range of books and pamphlets, also newsletters in Swedish and English; library of 22,000 vols.

Swedish Oriental Society: Stockholm.

SWITZERLAND

Centre d'Etude du Proche-Orient Ancien: Université de Genève, Place de l'Universitaire 3, 1211 Geneva 4; Dir. Mme FRANÇOISE BRUSCHWEILER.

Schweizerische Gesellschaft für Asienkunde: Ostasiatisches Seminar der Universität Zürich, Mühlegasse 21, 8001 Zurich; publ. *Asiatische Studien / Etudes Asiatiques* (bi-annual).

SYRIA

Institut Français d'Etudes Arabes: B.P. 344, Damascus; f. 1922; library of 40,000 vols., 354 periodicals; Dir. THIERRY BIANQUIS; Scient. Sec. JEAN-PAUL PASCUAL; 18 scholars; publs. *Bulletin d'Etudes Orientales* (annually, 29 vols. published), monographs, translations and Arabic texts (103 vols. published).

Near East Foundation: B.P. 427, Damascus.

TUNISIA

Institut des Belles Lettres Arabes: 12 rue Jamâa el Haoua, Tunis; f. 1930; cultural centre; Dir. A. DEMEERSEMAN; publ. *IBLA* (twice yearly) and special studies.

Mission Archéologique Française en Tunisie: 8 rue M'hamed Ali, Tunis; Dir. PIERRE CINTAS; Publications Dir. CL POINSSOT; publ. *Karthago* (quarterly).

TURKEY

British Institute of Archaeology at Ankara: Büklüm Sokak 96, Kavaklidere, Ankara; f. 1948; archaeological research and excavation; Dir. D. H. FRENCH; publs. *Anatolian Studies* (annual), *Occasional Publications*.

Centri di Studi Italiani in Turchia: Dr. Mediha Eldem Sokak 68, Yenışehir, Ankara; Dir. Prof. LUIGI POLACCO; Mesrutiyet Caddesi 161, Istanbul; Dir. Prof. GIOVANNI BATTAGLIA; Ataturk Caddesi, 280, Izmir; Comm. NICOLA DELPINO.

Deutsches Archäologisches Institut: Sira Selvi 123, Taksim, Istanbul; Dir. Prof. Dr.-Ing. W. MÜLLER-WIENER; publs. *Istanbuler Mitteilungen* (annual), *Istanbuler Forschungen, Beihefte zu Istanbuler Mitteilungen.*

Institut Français d'Etudes Anatoliennes: P.K. 280, Istanbul; f. 1930; Dir. HENRI METZGER.

Netherlands Historical and Archaeological Institute: Istiklâl Caddesi 393, Beyoğlu, Istanbul; f. 1958; library of 15,000 vols.; Dir. Dr. J. J. ROODENBERG; publs. *Publications de l'Institut Historique et Archéologique Néerlandais de Stamboul, Anatolica.*

Österreichisches Generalkonsulat Kulturinstitut Istanbul: Belvedere Apt. 101/2, Tesvikiye, Istanbul; Dir. Prof. Dr. J. E. KASPER.

Regional Cultural Institute: University of Istanbul, Faculty of Letters; Dir. Prof. SENCER TONGUÇ.

Türk Dil Kurumu (*Turkish Linguistic Society*): Ankara; f. 1932; 539 mems.; library of 25,000 vols.; Pres. Prof. Dr. SERAFETTIN TURAN; Sec.-Gen. CAHIT KULEBI; publs. *Türk Dili* (monthly), *Türk Dili Arastırmaları-Belleten* (annual).

Türk Kültürünü Araştırma Enstitüsü (*Institute for the Study of Turkish Culture*): P.K. 14, Çankaya, Ankara; f. 1961; scholarly research into all aspects of Turkish culture; Dir. Prof. Dr. AHMET TEMİR; publs. *Türk Kültürü* (monthly), *Cultura Turcica* (semi-annual), *Türk Kültürü Araştırmaları* (semi-annual).

Türk Tarih Kurumu (*Turkish Historical Society*): Ankara; f. 1931; 41 mems.; library of 150,000 vols.; Pres. Ord. Prof. ENVER ZIYA KARAL; Gen. Dir. ULUĞ IĞDEMİR; publs. *Belleten* (quarterly), *Belgeler* (twice a year).

Türkiyat Enstitüsü (*Institute of Turcology*): University of Istanbul, Bayezit, Istanbul; f. 1924; research into Turkish language, literature, history and culture; library of 20,000 vols.; Dir. Dr. M. CAVID BAYSUN.

U.S.S.R.

Commission on Oriental Literature of the Department of Literature and Language, U.S.S.R. Academy of Sciences: Volkhonka 18/2, Moscow; Chair. Acad. N. I. KONRAD.

Institute of Asian Peoples of the Department of History, U.S.S.R. Academy of Sciences: Armyansky per. 2, Moscow, Dir. Acad. B. GAFUROV.

Institute of Oriental Studies of the Academy of Sciences of the Georgian S.S.R.: Tbilisi, Georgian S.S.R.

Institute of Oriental Studies, U.S.S.R. Academy of Sciences: Armyansky per. 2, Moscow; Dir. B. GAFUROV.

Research Institute of Oriental Studies of the Academy of Sciences of the Azerbaijanian S.S.R.: Baku, Azerbaijanian S.S.R.

Section of Oriental Studies of the Academy of Sciences of the Armenian S.S.R.: Erevan, Armenian S.S.R.

Section of Orientology and Calligraphy of the Academy of Sciences of the Tajik S.S.R.: Dushanbe, Tajik S.S.R.

UNITED KINGDOM

Anglo-Arab Association, The: 21 Collingham Rd., London, SW5 0NU; non-political.

Council for the Advancement of Arab-British Understanding (CAABU): The Arab-British Centre, 21 Collingham Rd., London, SW5 0NU; f. 1967; 1,300 mems.

Egypt Exploration Society: 3 Doughty Mews, London, WC1N 2PG; f. 1882; library of 4,500 vols.; Sec. MARY D. ST. B. CRAWFORD; publs. *Excavation Memoirs, Archaeological Survey, Graeco-Roman Memoirs, Journal of Egyptian Archaeology, Texts from Excavations, etc.*

Islamic Cultural Centre (and London Central Mosque): 146 Park Rd., London, N.W.8; f. 1944 to spread Islamic culture in Great Britain; library of 10,000 vols., mostly Arabic; Dr. M. A' ZAKI BADAWI; publ. *Islamic Quarterly.*

Middle East Association: Bury House, 33 Bury St., London, SW1Y 6AX; f. 1961; an asscn. for firms actively promoting U.K. trade with 21 Arab countries, plus Afghanistan, Ethiopia, Iran and Turkey; 450 mems.; Dir.-Gen. H. G. BALFOUR-PAUL, C.M.G.; Sec. C. W. NORTH, M.B.E.

Middle East Centre: Faculty of Oriental Studies, Sidgwick Ave., Cambridge CB3 9DA; Dir. Prof. R. B. SERJEANT, PH.D.; Sec. R. L. BIDWELL, PH.D.; publ. *Arabian Studies* (annual).

Middle East Centre: St. Antony's College, 137 Banbury Rd., Oxford, OX2 7AJ; f. 1958; Dir. ROBERT MABRO; library of 25,000 vols.; Publs. St. Antony's Middle East Monographs.

Palestine Exploration Fund: 2 Hinde Mews, London, W.1. f. 1865; 900 subscribers; Pres. The Archbishop of Canterbury; Hon. Sec. J. M. MATTHERS, M.A.; publ; *Palestine Exploration Quarterly*.

Royal Asiatic Society of Great Britain and Ireland: 56 Queen Anne St., London, W.1; f. 1823 for the study of the history, sociology, institutions, customs, languages and art of Asia; approx. 800 mems.; approx. 500 subscribing libraries; library of 100,000 vols. and 1,500 MSS.; branches in various Asian cities; Pres. Prof. C. F. BECKINGHAM; Sec. Miss E. V. GIBSON; publs. *Journal* and monographs.

Royal Society for Asian Affairs: 42 Devonshire St., London, W.1; f. 1901; 1,500 mems. with past or present knowledge of the Middle East, Central Asia or the Far East; library of about 5,000 vols.; Pres. Lord GREENHILL of HARROW, G.C.M.G., O.B.E.; Chair. Sir ARTHUR DE LA MARE, K.C.M.G., K.C.V.O.; Sec. Miss M. FITZSIMONS; publ. *Journal* (3 times a year).

School of African and Asian Studies: University of Sussex, Falmer, Brighton, Sussex BN1 9QN; Dean IEUAN LL. GRIFFITHS, B.SC.(ECON.), PH.D.

School of Oriental and African Studies, University of London: Malet St., London, WC1E 7HP; f. 1916; library of over 450,000 vols. and 2,000 MSS.; Dir. Prof. C. D. COWAN.

UNITED STATES OF AMERICA

Academy of Asian Studies: 431 Duboce Ave., San Francisco, Calif., 94117; Pres. Dr. EDSZEN N. LANDRUM.

America-Mideast Educational & Training Services, Inc. (AMIDEAST): 1717 Massachusetts Ave., N.W., Washington, D.C. 20036; f. 1951; a private, non-profit organization for furthering communication and understanding between the peoples of the Middle East and N. Africa and the people of the U.S.A. through educational and international programmes; offices in Washington, D.C. and Egypt, Iran, Israel, Jordan, Lebanon, Morocco, Tunisia and Syria.

American Oriental Society: 329 Sterling Memorial Library, Yale Station, New Haven, Conn. 06520; f. 1842; 1,850 mems.; Sec. STANLEY INSLER; publ. *Journal*, monograhp series, essay series and offprint series.

American Schools of Oriental Research: 126 Inman Street, Cambridge, Mass. 02139; f. 1900; approx. 2,000 mems.; support activities of independent archaeological institutions abroad: The Albright Institute of Archaeological Research, Jerusalem, Israel, and the American Center of Oriental Research in Amman, Jordan; Pres. PHILIP J. KING; publs. *Biblical Archaeologist* (quarterly), *Bulletin* (quarterly), *Journal of Cuneiform Studies* (quarterly), *Annual*.

Center for Middle Eastern Studies: University of Chicago, 1130 E. 59th St., Chicago, Ill. 60637; f. 1966; research into medieval and modern cultures of the Middle East from Morocco to Pakistan; Dir. MARVIN ZONIS.

Center for Middle Eastern Studies: Harvard University, 1737 Cambridge St., Cambridge, Mass. 02138; research in social sciences and humanities.

Center for Middle Eastern Studies: The University of Texas at Austin, Tex. 78712; f. 1960; linguistic and social studies of Middle East languages and cultures; Dir. Dr. PAUL W. ENGLISH; publs. two monograph series on 19th and 20th century Middle East.

Center for Near East and North African Studies: University of Michigan, 144 Lane Hall, Ann Arbor, Mich. 48109; f. 1961; research into the ancient, medieval and modern cultures of the Near East and North Africa, Near Eastern languages and literature; Dir. Dr. WILLIAM D. SCHORGER.

The Dropsie University: Broad and York Streets, Philadelphia, Pa. 19132; f. 1907; Pres. L. J. PERELMAN.

Gustave E. von Grunebaum Center for Near Eastern Studies: University of California, Los Angeles, 405 Hilgard Ave., Los Angeles, Calif. 90024; f. 1957; social sciences, culture and language studies of the Near East since the rise of Islam; a growing programme of Ancient Near Eastern Studies; library of over 100,000 vols. and outstanding MSS. collection in Arabic, Armenian, Hebrew, Persian and Turkish; Dir. MALCOLM H. KERR.

Hairenik Association, Inc.: 212 Stuart St., Boston, Mass. 02216; publ. *Armenian Review*.

Hoover Institution on War, Revolution and Peace: Stanford University, Stanford, Calif. 94305; f. 1919; contains important collection of materials on Middle East and North Africa; Dir. W. G. CAMPBELL; publs. about twenty books each year, plus six-volume survey of the Institution's library.

The Iran Foundation, Inc.: Empire State Bldg., New York, N.Y. 10001; project assistance relating to the advancement of health and education in Iran and other culturally related areas.

Institute for Mediterranean Affairs: 1078 Madison Ave., New York, N.Y. 10028; established under charter of the University of the State of New York to evolve a better understanding of the historical background and contemporary political and socio-economic problems of the nations and regions that border on the Mediterranean Sea, with special reference to the Middle East and North Africa; 350 mems.; Pres. Ambassador SEYMOUR M. FINGER; Chair. Prof. N. S. FATEMI; Vice-Chair. Prof. A. P. LERNER; Dir. SAMUEL MERLIN.

Israel Institute: Yeshiva University, Amsterdam Ave. and 185th St., New York, N.Y. 10033; f. 1954; research into modern Israel and her cultural and political problems, Jewish history and culture; publ. *Sura*, *Talpioth*.

Joint Committee on the Near and Middle East: c/o Social Science Research Council, 605 Third Avenue, New York, N.Y. 10016; the Committee is co-sponsored by the American Council of Learned Societies and administers for U.S. and Canadian citizens, a programme of grants for research by individual scholars in the social sciences and humanities, a programme of dissertation research fellowships as well as research conferences and seminars.

Middle East Center: University of Utah, Salt Lake City, Utah 84112; f. 1960; co-ordinates programme in Middle East languages and area studies in 12 academic departments; B.A., M.A. and Ph.D. in Middle East Studies with area of concentration in Arabic, Hebrew, Persian or Turkish, M.A. in Iranian studies; annual summer programme for Utah educators at the AUC in Egypt; student exchange with Univ. of Teheran; research fellowships for pre-doctoral and post-doctoral work in Egypt, Pakistan and several other countries in the region through membership of international study organizations; library of 110,000 vols.; Dir. Dr. KHOSROW MOSTOFI.

Middle East Institute: 1761 N. St., N.W., Washington, D.C. 20036; f. 1946; exists to develop and maintain facilities for research, publication and dissemination of information, with a view to developing in the United States a more thorough understanding of the countries of the Middle East; the Institute holds an annual conference on Middle East affairs; 1,800 mems.; Pres. Hon. L. DEAN BROWN; Sec. MALCOLM C. PECK; Dir. of Publs. WILLIAM SANDS; publs. *Middle East Journal* (quarterly) and occasional books.

Middle East Institute: Columbia University, 1113 International Affairs Bldg., New York, N.Y. 10027; f. 1954; a graduate training programme on the modern Middle East for students seeking professional careers as regional specialists, research into problems of economics, government, law, and international relations of the Middle East countries, and their languages and history; library of more than 125,000 vols. in Middle East vernaculars and equally rich in Western languages; Dir. Prof. J. C. HUREWITZ; publs. *Publications in Near and Middle East studies* (completed), *Modern Middle East Series* (irregular).

Middle East Studies Association: New York University, Washington Square, New York, N.Y. 10003; f. 1967 to promote high standards of scholarship and instruction and to facilitate communication on the area; membership open to all persons of scholarly attainment in the field of Middle Eastern studies; 1,500 mems.; Pres. (1979) Prof. ALAF LUTFI AL-SAYYID MARSOT; Pres. Elect (1980) Prof. FARHAT ZIADEH; Exec. Sec. RICHARD W. BULLIET; publs. *Bulletin* (twice a year), *Newsletter* (four times a year), *International Journal of Middle East Studies* (quarterly), *Directory of Programs and Courses in Middle East Studies in the U.S., Canada and Abroad.*

Middle East Studies Centre: Portland State Univ., Portland, Ore. 97207; language studies in Arabic, Persian, Turkish, Hebrew and Hieroglyphics; area studies in ancient Near East, medieval Islamic civilization and the modern Middle East and North Africa; Dir. Prof. FREDERICK J. COX.

Near East College Association, Inc.: 40 Worth St., New York, N.Y. 10013; and 548 Fifth Ave., New York, N.Y. 10036.

Near East Foundation: 54 East 64th St., New York, N.Y. 10021, U.S.A.; f. 1930. Aims: to conduct educational programmes and agricultural projects in order to improve standards of living in underdeveloped areas of Asia and Africa, primarily the Near East; Hon. Chair. CLEVELAND E. DODGE; Vice-Chair. J. B. SUNDERLAND; Pres. DAVID S. DODGE; Exec. Dir. DELMER J. DOOLEY; publs. *Annual Report*, newspaper (semi-annually).

Near Eastern Languages and Literatures, Department of: Indiana University, Bloomington, Indiana 47401; courses in Arabic, Hebrew and Turkish languages and literature both modern and classical, history, political science and religions of the area are taught through other Departments; Chair. WADIE JWAIDEH.

Oriental Institute: 1155 East 58th St., Chicago, Ill. 60637; f. 1919; principally concerned with cultures and languages of the ancient Near East; extensive museum; affiliated to the University of Chicago; Curator JOHN CARSWELL.

Program in Near Eastern Studies: Princeton University, Jones Hall, Princeton, N.J. 08540; f. 1947; research in all aspects of the modern Near East; library of 300,000 vols.; Dir. JOHN H. MARKS; publs. *Princeton Studies on the Near East* (irregular), *Princeton Near East Papers* (irregular).

Semitic Museum: Harvard University, 6 Divinity Ave., Cambridge, Mass. 02138; f. 1889; sponsors exploration and research in Western Asia; contains collection of exhibits from ancient Near East; Curator Dr. CARNEY E. S. GAVIN.

VATICAN

Pontificium Institutum Orientalium Studiorum (*Pontifical Institute of Oriental Studies*): 7 Piazza Santa Maria Maggiore, 00185-Rome; f. 1917; library of 110,000 vols.; Rector Rev. EDUARD HUBER, S.J.; Sec. Rev. J. ŘEZÁČ, S.J.; publs. *Orientalia Christiana Periodica, Orientalia Christiana Analecta, Concilium Florentinum* (*Documenta et Scriptores*), *Anaphorae Syriacae.*

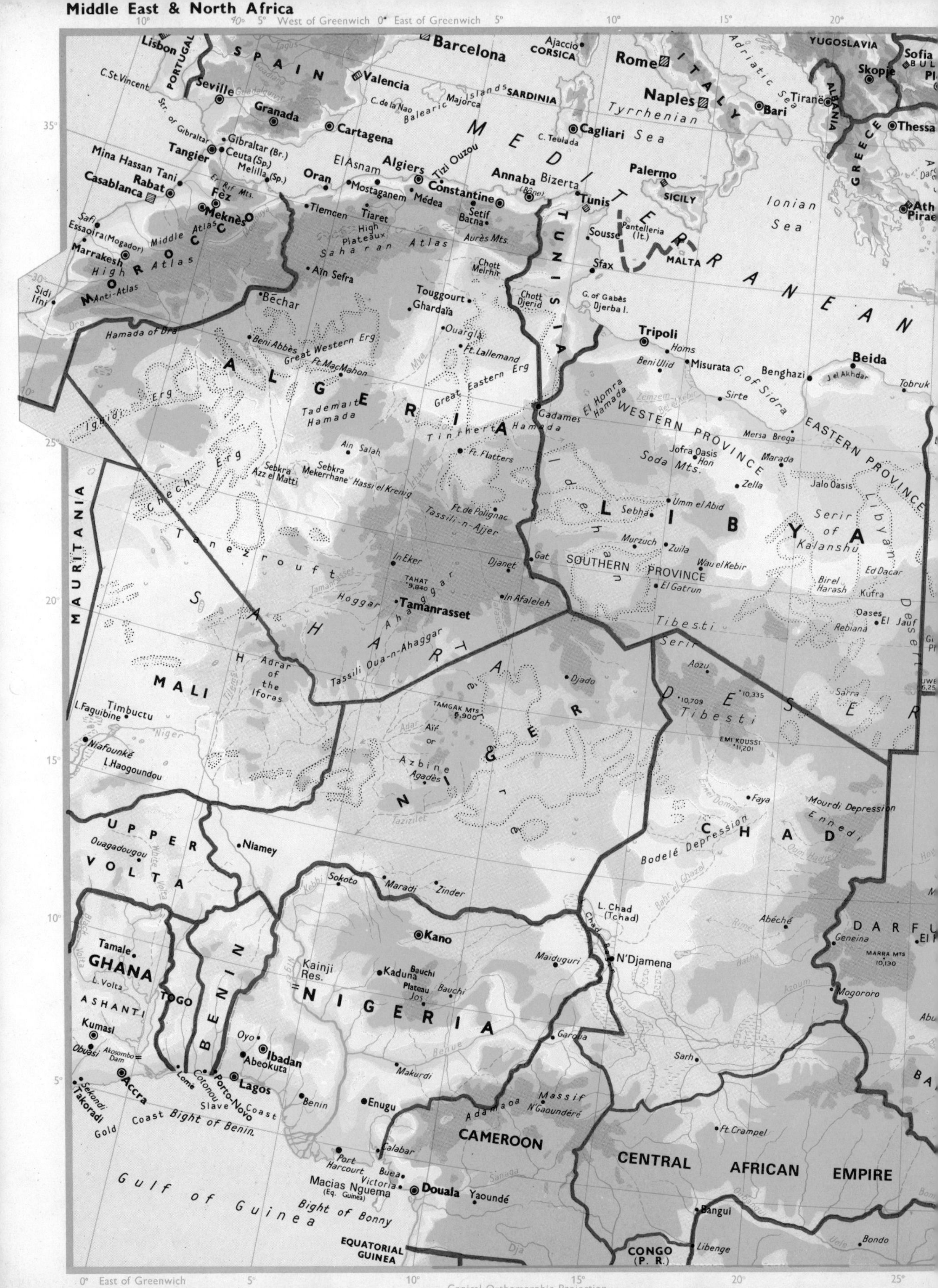
West of Greenwich 0° East of Greenwich
Lisbon
PORTUGAL
SPAIN
Barcelona
Ajaccio
CORSICA
Rome
ITALY
Adriatic Sea
YUGOSLAVIA
Sofia
Skopje
ALBANIA
Tiranë
C. St. Vincent
Seville
Valencia
C. de la Nao
Majorca
Balearic Islands
SARDINIA
Naples
Bari
Granada
Cartagena
Tyrrhenian Sea
GREECE
Thessa
Str. of Gibraltar
Gibraltar (Br.)
Ceuta (Sp.)
Melilla (Sp.)
Tangier
MEDITERRANEAN
C. Teulada
Cagliari
Mina Hassan Tani
Rabat
Casablanca
Fez
Er Rif Mts.
El Asnam
Oran
Algiers
Tizi Ouzou
Mostaganem
Médea
Constantine
Annaba (Bône)
Bizerta
Tunis
Palermo
SICILY
Ionian Sea
Ath
Pirae
Meknès
Tlemcen
Tiaret
Setif
Batna
Safi
Essaoira (Mogador)
MOROCCO
Middle Atlas
High Plateaux
Saharan Atlas
Aurès Mts.
Sousse
Pantelleria (It.)
MALTA
Marrakesh
High Atlas
Aïn Sefra
Chott Melrhir
TUNISIA
Sfax
Sidi Ifni
Anti-Atlas
Béchar
Touggourt
Ghardaïa
Chott Djerid
G. of Gabès
Djerba I.
Hamada of Dra
Beni Abbès
Great Western Erg
Ouargla
Ft. Lallemand
Tripoli
Homs
Beni Ulid
Misurata
G. of Sidra
Benghazi
Beida
J. el Akhdar
Tobruk
ALGERIA
Ft. MacMahon
Great Eastern Erg
Sirte
Igidi Erg
Tademait Hamada
Gadames
El Homra Hamada
WESTERN PROVINCE
EASTERN PROVINCE
Tinrhert Hamada
Mersa Brega
Ain Salah
Ft. Flatters
Jofra Oasis
Hon
Soda Mts.
Marada
Sebkra Azz el Matti
Sebkra Mekerrhane
Hassi el Krenig
Zella
Jalo Oasis
Chech Erg
Umm el Abid
Sebha
LIBYA
Ft. de Polignac
Tassili-n-Ajjer
Serir of Kalanshu
Libyan Desert
MAURITANIA
Tanezrouft
In Eker
Djanet
Gat
Murzuch
Zuila
SOUTHERN PROVINCE
Wau el Kebir
Ed Dacar
TAHAT 9,840
Birel Harash
Kufra
El Gatrun
SAHARA
Hoggar
Ahaggar
Tamanrasset
In Afaleleh
Oases
El Jauf
Rebiana
Tibesti
Serir
Tassili Oua-n-Ahaggar
Adrar of the Iforas
MALI
Djado
Aozu
Timbuctu
L. Faguibine
TAMGAK MTS 5,900
Aïr or Azbine
10,709
10,335
Tibesti
DESERT
Sarra
Niger
Niafounké
L. Haogoundou
NIGER
Agadès
EMI KOUSSI 11,201
Faya
Mourdi Depression
Ennedi
CHAD
Bodelé Depression
UPPER VOLTA
Ouagadougou
Niamey
Sokoto
Maradi
Zinder
L. Chad (Tchad)
DARFU
Abéché
Geneina
MARRA MTS 10,130
Tamale
GHANA
L. Volta
ASHANTI
TOGO
BENIN
Kainji Res.
Kano
Kaduna
Bauchi Plateau
Jos
Bauchi
Maiduguri
N'Djamena
NIGERIA
Mogororo
Kumasi
Obuasi
Akosombo Dam
Oyo
Ibadan
Abeokuta
Garoua
Sarh
Accra
Lomé
Cotonou
Porto-Novo
Lagos
Makurdi
Sekondi
Takoradi
Slave Coast
Benin
Enugu
Adamaoa Massif
N'Gaoundéré
Gold Coast
Bight of Benin
CAMEROON
Ft. Crampel
Port Harcourt
Calabar
Buea
Victoria
Gulf of Guinea
Macias Nguema (Eq. Guinea)
Douala
Yaoundé
CENTRAL AFRICAN EMPIRE
Bight of Bonny
Bangui
EQUATORIAL GUINEA
CONGO (P. R.)
Libenge
Bondo
0° East of Greenwich
Conical Orthomorphic Projection